THE AMERICAN CONSTITUTIONAL ORDER: HISTORY, CASES, AND PHILOSOPHY

SECOND EDITION

by

DOUGLAS W. KMIEC
Professor of Constitutional Law and
Caruso Family Chair in Constitutional Law
Pepperdine University School of Law

STEPHEN B. PRESSER
Raoul Berger Professor of Legal History
Northwestern University School of Law

JOHN C. EASTMAN
Professor of Law and
Director of the Claremont Institute Center for
Constitutional Jurisprudence
Chapman University School of Law

RAYMOND B. MARCIN
Professor of Law
Catholic University of America
Columbus School of Law

LexisNexis™

Library of Congress Cataloging-in-Publication Data

Kmiec, Douglas W.

The American Constitutional Order: History, Cases, and Philosophy
Douglas W. Kmiec
Stephen B. Presser
John C. Eastman
Raymond B. Marcin

ISBN# 1583608001

Editorial Offices
744 Broad Street, Newark, NJ 07102 (973) 820-2000
201 Mission St., San Francisco, CA 94105-1831 (415) 908-3200
701 East Water Street, Charlottesville, VA 22902-7587 (804) 972-7600

(Pub.3502)

DEDICATION

For those who complete us —
Carolyn Keenan Kmiec, Arlynn Leiber Presser, Elizabeth C'de Baca
Eastman, and Mary Julia Regan Marcin.

SUMMARY OF CONTENTS

Chapter One THE PHILOSOPHICAL AND NATURAL
LAW BASIS OF THE AMERICAN
ORDER: REMOTE AND IMMEDIATE
ANCESTORS 1

Chapter Two THE DECLARATION AND ITS
CONSTITUTION — LINKING FIRST
PRINCIPLE TO NECESSARY MEANS 93

Chapter Three A STRUCTURALLY-DIVIDED, BUT WORKABLE, GOVERNMENT

TABLE OF CONTENTS

Chapter Two   THE DECLARATION AND ITS CONSTITUTION — LINKING FIRST PRINCIPLE TO NECESSARY MEANS

Chapter Three A STRUCTURALLY-DIVIDED, BUT WORKABLE, GOVERNMENT

INTRODUCTION TO THE SECOND EDITION

Some American law professors and law students believe that the study of Constitutional law begins and ends solely with the Supreme Court's cases. Our approach in the first edition was to suggest that cases emerge from history and that history, itself, reflects centuries of philosophical understanding. In short, our aim was for a constitutional textbook that puts cases in context.

This remains our aim in this wholly revised second edition. The revisions incorporate many thoughtful comments we received from those who used the first edition in class. In addition, this text is now supplemented by a fulsome teacher's manual as well as the perspectives of two additional collaborators: Professor John Eastman, who came to teaching after completing his doctoral work at Claremont and clerking for the U.S. Supreme Court; and Professor Raymond B. Marcin, who as editor of the *American Journal of Jurisprudence* has spent many years editing and writing scholarship that faithfully addresses the philosophical precepts that still inform the American republic.

Since the text's initial publication, our Nation has been the victim of wanton terrorism and has faced the delicate task of simultaneously securing national security while maintaining civil liberty. This second edition includes the Supreme Court's latest pronouncements on the implications of the war on terror for the separation of powers and individual rights, but it also endeavors to link executive, legislative, and judicial developments to the past practice in war time as well as to note the increasing pressure to understand American constitutional development within a global context.

Like the governmental framework it seeks to elucidate, this text flows from what might be labeled a Burkean pragmatic approach to Constitutional law which stresses that it can only be understood through its history, text, structure and interpretation. We believe that two hundred years of development, rather than any single author's personal perspective is the best guide to constitutional meaning. Those who seek a book favoring a given political outlook or particular academic theory might be better served by a different text. Students using this one will encounter all of the essential doctrinal aspects of constitutional study including, for example, judicial review, separation of powers, federal-state relations, and procedural and substantive due process. Special emphasis is placed, as well, upon the individual liberties of freedom of religion, free speech, and equal protection, but not to the exclusion of equally traditional economic liberties and property rights.

While we doubt that any constitutional textbook will ever merit being described as "lean," we have made a conscientious effort to fashion a *basic* text — that is, one that truly has principal or representative cases, not an agglomeration or cumulative incorporation of everything the Court has ever said on a given subject. Recognizing the on-going nature of constitutional refinement, however, we employ extensive introductions, notes and questions to highlight in plain, understandable language the modern Court's approach. These textual materials permit us to identify areas in ferment and knotty intellectual problems that should inspire spirited classroom discussion and reflection.

We believe that American Constitutional law cannot be understood without some appreciation of legal history and legal philosophy. Yet, standard texts are so crammed with cases and unanswered if not unanswerable questions that the rich historical materials of the founding, whether *Federalist Paper* or Madison's famous *Notes* taken at the Constitutional Convention, are neglected or consigned to fragmentary reference or citation. Consistent with the emerging interests of scholars, and we think Supreme Court Justices as well — whether they be characterized by popular account as liberal, conservative, or in-between — we illustrate a Constitution not cut adrift of its roots, but situated together with the Declaration of Independence as a summation (and on occasion modification) of thought reaching back to Cicero, Aristotle, the medieval scholars, Montesquieu, Locke and others. As teachers who have used these materials as a backdrop for nearly a collective century of constitutional instruction in the classroom, we know that too many students have never seriously encountered these truly great titans of jurisprudence, but when they do, they are captivated and enlightened by them, and understand themselves, as did our Constitution's framers, to be participants in a conversation on government and the good life stretching back more than two millennia.

We have thus tried faithfully to illustrate how our constitutional order was created taking account of many centuries of legal thinking, and, in particular, employing a clear-eyed assessment of natural law and natural rights as they had been developed in a manner that sought to comprehend both the divine destiny, and inherent weakness, of humankind. While the 21st century brought with it the new and uncertain challenges of terror, it also saw a continuation of constitutional discussion about affirmative action, religious freedom, and the balance between personal autonomy and responsibility to the community. Your highly positive response to the first edition confirms that the materials we assembled permit students and teachers to explore for themselves divergent approaches to these difficult issues fully informed by that which has gone before. We believe you will find this even more true of the second edition.

For many years in England and America, an understanding of fundamental law was regarded as an essential part of a liberal education and preparation for good citizenship. The materials here seek to continue this effort — with the initial chapters focused on history, philosophy and structure (Chapters One through Five) revealing the means by which the government honors its commitment to fairness, freedom, equality, and life, itself (Chapters Six through Nine). In this, we are guided by the words of Cicero in *de Re Publica*, "Long before our time," he wrote, "the customs of our ancestors molded admirable men, and in turn those eminent men upheld the ways and institutions of their forebears. Our age, however, inherited the Republic as if it were some beautiful painting of bygone ages, its colors already fading through great antiquity; and not only has our time neglected to freshen the colors of the picture, but we have failed to preserve its form and outlines."

A brief word about case-editing. Within cases, we have omitted without notice as many internal citations as possible to enhance readability and avoid distraction. Where cases are cited, we have avoided unnecessary reporter references. The internal citations that remain largely refer to the principal cases in the text, and therefore, help the student see necessary interconnections or legal evolution. Footnote numbers within cases are the original. We have tried to give a fair, even-handed sampling of majority and dissenting positions, and we have indicated where any opinion has been omitted.

We have greatly benefitted from the comments of those who adopted the first edition, we hope for future editions, and, if there are further materials that you would find useful, or if you have any other suggestions for improvement they will be gratefully received.

Finally, important words of acknowledgment. No one in this life travels alone, and we are immensely grateful for the support and encouragement of our families as well as our colleagues.

Douglas W. Kmiec
Malibu, California
Stephen B. Presser
Chicago, Illinois
John C. Eastman
Orange, California
Raymond B. Marcin
Washington, D.C.

ACKNOWLEDGMENTS

We acknowledge with gratitude the permission of the following copyright holders to quote material contained in the book. Any errors that occurred in editing or reprinting are our responsibility, not that of the copyright holder:

Aristotle, POLITICS 157-60 (1995). Copyright © 1995 by Oxford University Press. Reprinted by permission.

St. Augustine, CITY OF GOD 219-20 (1972) (translation copyright Henry Bettenson). Copyright © 1972 by Penguin Books. Reprinted by permission.

Bracton, ON THE LAWS AND CUSTOMS OF ENGLAND 19-28 (1977) (Samuel E. Thorne ed. and trans.). Copyright © 1977 by Harvard University Press. Reprinted by permission.

Bradley, Gerard V., *Beguiled: Free Exercise Exemptions and the Siren Song of Liberalism*, 20 HOFSTRA L. REV. 245, 259-60 (1991). Copyright © 1991 by the Hofstra Law Review. Reprinted with permission.

Himmelfarb, Dan, *The Constitutional Relevance of the Second Sentence of the Declaration of Independence*, 100 YALE L.J. 169, 170-71, 186-87 (1990) (footnotes omitted). Copyright © 1990 by the Yale Law Journal Co. Reprinted by permission.

Kmiec, Douglas W., THE ATTORNEY GENERAL'S LAWYER 79-86 (1992). Copyright © 1992 by Praeger, an imprint of Greenwood Publishing Group, Inc., Westport, CT. Reprinted by permission.

McConnell, Michael, *The Origins and Historical Understanding of Free Exercise of Religion*, 103 HARV.L. REV. 1409, 1456-58, 1464 (1990). Copyright © 1990 by the Harvard Law Review Association. Reprinted by permission.

O'Sullivan, Richard, *The Natural Law and Common Law*, in 3 NATURAL LAW INSTITUTE PROCEEDINGS 9, 31-43 (1947-51). Copyright © 1947-51 by the Natural Law Institute; University of Notre Dame College of Law. Reprinted by permission.

Scalia, Antonin, *Of Democracy, Morality, and the Majority*, 26 ORIGINS 81, 87-90 (1996). Copyright © 1996 by Origins: Catholic News Service. Reprinted by permission.

Storing, Herbert J., WHAT THE ANTI-FEDERALISTS WERE FOR 22-23 (1981). Copyright © 1981 by the University of Chicago Press. Reprinted by permission.

The Declaration of Independence

In Congress, July 4, 1776

(The Unanimous Declaration of the Thirteen United States of America)

WHEN in the Course of human events, it becomes necessary for one people to dissolve the political bands which have connected them with another, and to assume among the powers of the earth, the separate and equal station to which the Laws of Nature and of Nature's God entitle them, a decent respect to the opinions of mankind requires that they should declare the causes which impel them to the separation.

We hold these truths to be self-evident, that all men are created equal, that they are endowed by their Creator with certain unalienable Rights, that among these are Life, Liberty and the pursuit of Happiness. That to secure these rights, Governments are instituted among Men, deriving their just powers from the consent of the governed, That whenever any Form of Government becomes destructive of these ends, it is the Right of the People to alter or to abolish it, and to institute new Government, laying its foundation on such principles and organizing its powers in such form, as to them shall seem most likely to effect their Safety and Happiness. Prudence, indeed, will dictate that Governments long established should not be changed for light and transient causes; and accordingly all experience hath shown, that mankind are more disposed to suffer, while evils are sufferable, than to right themselves by abolishing the forms to which they are accustomed. But when a long train of abuses and usurpations, pursuing invariably the same Object evinces a design to reduce them under absolute Despotism, it is their right, it is their duty, to throw off such Government, and to provide new Guards for their future security.—Such has been the patient sufferance of these Colonies; and such is now the necessity which constrains them to alter their former Systems of Government. The history of the present King of Great Britain is a history of repeated injuries and usurpations, all having in direct object the establishment of an absolute Tyranny over these States. To prove this, let Facts be submitted to a candid world.

He has refused his Assent to Laws, the most wholesome and necessary for the public good.

He has forbidden his Governors to pass Laws of Immediate and pressing importance, unless suspended in their operation till his Assent should be obtained; and when so suspended, he has utterly neglected to attend to them.

He has refused to pass other Laws for the accommodation of large districts of people, unless those people would relinquish the right of Representation in the Legislature, a right inestimable to them and formidable to tyrants only.

He has called together legislative bodies at places unusual, uncomfortable, and distant from the depository of their Public Records, for the sole purpose of fatiguing them into compliance with his measures.

He has dissolved Representative Houses repeatedly, for opposing with manly firmness his invasions on the rights of the people.

He has refused for a long time, after such dissolutions, to cause others to be elected; whereby the Legislative Powers, incapable of Annihilation, have returned to the People at large for their exercise; the State remaining in the mean time exposed to all the dangers of invasion from without, and convulsions within.

He has endeavoured to prevent the population of these States; for that purpose obstructing the Laws for Naturalization of Foreigners; refusing to pass others to encourage their migration hither, and raising the conditions of new Appropriations of Lands.

He has obstructed the Administration of Justice, by refusing his Assent to Laws for establishing Judiciary Powers.

He has made Judges dependent on his Will alone, for the tenure of their offices, and the amount and payment of their salaries.

He has erected a multitude of New Offices, and sent hither swarms of Officers to harrass our People, and eat out their substance.

He has kept among us, in times of peace, Standing Armies, without the Consent of our legislatures.

He has affected to render the Military independent of and superior to the Civil Power.

He has combined with others to subject us to a jurisdiction foreign to our constitution, and unacknowledged by our laws; giving his Assent to their acts of pretended Legislation:

For quartering large bodies of armed troops among us:

For protecting them, by a mock Trial, from Punishment for any Murders which they should commit on the Inhabitants of these States:

For cutting off our Trade with all parts of the world:

For imposing taxes on us without our Consent:

For depriving us in many cases, of the benefits of Trial by Jury:

For transporting us beyond Seas to be tried for pretended offences:

For abolishing the free System of English Laws in a neighbouring Province, establishing therein an Arbitrary government, and enlarging its Boundaries so as to render it at once an example and fit instrument for introducing the same absolute rule into these Colonies:

For taking away our Charters, abolishing our most valuable Laws, and altering fundamentally the Forms of our Governments:

For suspending our own Legislatures, and declaring themselves invested with Power to legislate for us in all cases whatsoever.

He has abdicated Government here, by declaring us out of his Protection and waging War against us.

He has plundered our seas, ravaged our Coasts, burnt our towns, and destroyed the lives of our people.

He is at this time transporting large Armies of foreign mercenaries to compleat the works of death, desolation and tyranny, already begun with circumstances of Cruelty & perfidy scarcely paralleled in the most barbarous ages, and totally unworthy the Head of a civilized nation.

He has constrained our fellow Citizens taken Captive on the high Seas to bear Arms against their Country, to become the executioners of their friends and Brethren, or to fall themselves by their Hands.

He has excited domestic insurrections amongst us, and has endeavoured to bring on the inhabitants of our frontiers, the merciless Indian Savages, whose known rule of war-fare, is an undistinguished destruction of all ages, sexes and conditions.

In every stage of these Oppressions We have Petitioned for Redress in the most humble terms: Our repeated Petitions have been answered only by repeated injury. A Prince, whose character is thus marked by every act which may define a Tyrant, is unfit to be the ruler of a free people.

Nor have We been wanting in attentions to our Brittish brethren. We have warned them from time to time of attempts by their legislature to extend an unwarrantable jurisdiction over us. We have reminded them of the circumstances of our emigration and settlement here. We have appealed to their native justice and magnanimity, and we have conjured them by the ties of our common kindred to disavow these usurpations, which, would inevitably interrupt our connections and correspondence. They too have been deaf to the voice of justice and of consanguinity. We must, therefore, acquiesce in the necessity, which denounces our Separation, and hold them, as we hold the rest of mankind, Enemies in War, in Peace Friends.

WE, THEREFORE, the REPRESENTATIVES of the UNITED STATES OF AMERICA, in General Congress, Assembled, appealing to the Supreme Judge of the world for the rectitude of our intentions, do, in the Name, and by Authority of the good People of these Colonies, solemnly publish and declare, That these United Colonies are, and of Right ought to be FREE AND INDEPENDENT STATES; that they are Absolved from all Allegiance to the British Crown, and that all political connection between them and the State of Great Britain, is and ought to be totally dissolved; and that as Free and Independent States, they have full Power to levy War, conclude Peace, contract Alliances, establish Commerce, and to do all other Acts and Things which Independent States may of right do. And for the support of this Declaration, with a firm reliance on the protection of Divine Providence, we mutually pledge to each other our Lives, our Fortunes and our sacred Honor.

JOHN HANCOCK

New Hampshire
JOSIAH BARTLETT
WM. WHIPPLE
MATTHEW THORNTON

Massachusetts Bay
SAML. ADAMS
JOHN ADAMS
ROBT. TREAT PAINE
ELBRIDGE GERRY

Rhode Island
STEP. HOPKINS
WILLIAM ELLERY

Connecticut
ROGER SHERMAN
SAM'EL HUNTINGTON
WM. WILLIAMS
OLIVER WOLCOTT

New York
WM. FLOYD
PHIL. LIVINGSTON
FRANS. LEWIS
LEWIS MORRIS

New Jersey
RICHD. STOCKTON
JNO. WITHERSPOON
FRAS. HOPKINSON
JOHN HART
ABRA. CLARK

Pennsylvania
ROBT. MORRIS
BENJAMIN RUSH
BENJA. FRANKLIN
JOHN MORTON
GEO. CLYMER
JAS. SMITH
GEO. TAYLOR
JAMES WILSON
GEO. ROSS

Delaware
CAESAR RODNEY
GEO. READ
THO. M'KEAN

Maryland
SAMUEL CHASE
WM. PACA
THOS. STONE
CHARLES CARROLL of Carrollton.

Virginia
GEORGE WYTHE
RICHARD HENRY LEE
TH. JEFFERSON
BENJA. HARRISON
THS. NELSON, JR.
FRANCIS LIGHTFOOT LEE
CARTER BRAXTON

North Carolina
WM. HOOPER
JOSEPH HEWES
JOHN PENN

South Carolina
EDWARD RUTLEDGE
THOS. HEYWARD, JUNR.
THOMAS LYNCH, JUNR.
ARTHUR MIDDLETON

Georgia
BUTTON GWINNETT
LYMAN HALL
GEO. WALTON

The Constitution of the United States

We the People of the United States, in Order to form a more perfect Union, establish Justice, insure domestic Tranquility, provide for the common defence, promote the general Welfare, and secure the Blessings of Liberty to ourselves and our Posterity, do ordain and establish this Constitution for the United States of America.

Article I.

Section 1. All legislative Powers herein granted shall be vested in a Congress of the United States, which shall consist of a Senate and House of Representatives.

Section 2. The House of Representatives shall be composed of Members chosen every second Year by the People of the several States, and the Electors in each State shall have the Qualifications requisite for Electors of the most numerous Branch of the State Legislature.

No person shall be a Representative who shall not have attained to the Age of twenty five Years, and been seven Years a Citizen of the United States, and who shall not, when elected, be an Inhabitant of that State in which he shall be chosen.

[Representatives and direct Taxes shall be apportioned among the several States which may be included within this Union, according to their respective Numbers, which shall be determined by adding to the whole Number of free Persons, including those bound to Service for a Term of Years, and excluding Indians not taxed, three fifths of all other Persons.] The actual Enumeration shall be made within three Years after the first Meeting of the Congress of the United States, and within every subsequent Term of ten Years, in such Manner as they shall by Law direct. The Number of Representatives shall not exceed one for every thirty Thousand, but each State shall have at Least one Representative; and until such enumeration shall be made, the State of New Hampshire shall be entitled to chuse three, Massachusetts eight, Rhode-Island and Providence Plantations one, Connecticut five, New-York six, New Jersey four, Pennsylvania eight, Delaware one, Maryland six, Virginia ten, North Carolina five, South Carolina five, and Georgia three.

When vacancies happen in the Representation from any State, the Executive Authority thereof shall issue Writs of Election to fill such Vacancies.

The House of Representatives shall chuse their Speaker and other Officers; and shall have the sole Power of Impeachment.

Section 3. The Senate of the United States shall be composed of two Senators from each State, chosen by the Legislature thereof, for six Years; and each Senator shall have one Vote.

Immediately after they shall be assembled in Consequence of the first Election, they shall be divided as equally as may be into three Classes. The Seats of the Senators of the first Class shall be vacated at the Expiration of the second Year, of the second Class at the Expiration of the fourth Year, and of the third Class at the Expiration of the sixth Year, so that one third may be chosen every second Year; and if Vacancies happen by Resignation, or otherwise, during the Recess of the Legislature of any State, the Executive thereof may make temporary Appointments until the next Meeting of the Legislature, which shall then fill such Vacancies.

No Person shall be a Senator who shall not have attained to the Age of thirty Years, and been nine Years a Citizen of the United States, and who shall not, when elected, be an Inhabitant of that State for which he shall be chosen.

The Vice President of the United States shall be President of the Senate, but shall have no Vote, unless they be equally divided.

The Senate shall chuse their other Officers, and also a President pro tempore, in the Absence of the Vice President, or when he shall exercise the Office of President of the United States.

The Senate shall have the sole Power to try all Impeachments. When sitting for that Purpose, they shall be on Oath or Affirmation. When the President of the United States is tried, the Chief Justice shall preside: and no Person shall be convicted without the Concurrence of two thirds of the Members present.

Judgment in Cases of Impeachment shall not extend further than to removal from Office, and disqualification to hold and enjoy any Office of honor, Trust or Profit under the United States: but the Party convicted shall nevertheless be liable and subject to Indictment, Trial, Judgment and Punishment, according to Law.

Section 4. The Times, Places and Manner of holding Elections for Senators and Representatives, shall be prescribed in each State by the Legislature thereof; but the Congress may at any time by Law make or alter such Regulations, except as to the Places of chusing Senators.

The Congress shall assemble at least once in every Year, and such Meeting shall be on the first Monday in December, unless they shall be Law appoint a different Day.

Section 5. Each House shall be the Judge of the Elections, Returns and Qualifications of its own Members, and a Majority of each shall constitute a Quorum to do Business; but a smaller Number may adjourn from day to day, and may be authorized to compel the Attendance of absent Members, in such Manner, and under such Penalties as each House may provide.

Each House may determine the Rules of its Proceedings, punish its Members for disorderly Behaviour, and, with the Concurrence of two thirds, expel a Member.

Each House shall keep a Journal of its Proceedings, and from time to time publish the same, excepting such Parts as may in their Judgment require Secrecy; and the Yeas and Nays of the Members of either House on any question shall, at the Desire of one fifth of those Present, be entered on the Journal.

Neither House, during the Session of Congress, shall, without the consent of the other, adjourn for more than three days, nor to any other Place than that in which the two Houses shall be sitting.

Section 6. The Senators and Representatives shall receive a Compensation for their Services, to be ascertained by Law, and paid out of the Treasury of the United States. They shall in all Cases, except Treason, Felony and Breach of the

Peace, be privileged from Arrest during their Attendance at the Session of their respective Houses, and in going to and returning from the same; and for any Speech or Debate in either House, they shall not be questioned in any other Place.

No Senator or Representative shall, during the Time for which he was elected, be appointed to any civil Office under the Authority of the United States, which shall have been created, or the Emoluments whereof shall have been encreased during such time; and no Person holding any Office under the United States, shall be a Member of either House during his Continuance in Office.

Section 7. All Bills for raising Revenue shall originate in the House of Representatives; but the Senate may propose or concur with Amendments as on other Bills.

Every Bill which shall have passed the House of Representatives and the Senate, shall, before it become a Law, be presented to the President of the United States; If he approve he shall sign it, but if not he shall return it, with his Objections to that House in which it shall have originated, who shall enter the Objections at large on their Journal, and proceed to reconsider it. If after such Reconsideration two thirds of that House shall agree to pass the Bill, it shall be sent, together with the Objections, to the other House, by which it shall likewise be reconsidered, and if approved by two thirds of that House, it shall become a Law. But in all such Cases the Votes of both Houses shall be determined by yeas and Nays, and the Names of the Persons voting for and against the Bill shall be entered on the Journal of each House respectively. If any Bill shall not be returned by the President within ten days (Sundays excepted) after it shall have been presented to him, the Same shall be a Law, in like Manner as if he had signed it, unless the Congress by their Adjournment prevent its Return in which Case it shall not be a Law.

Every Order, Resolution, or Vote to which the Concurrence of the Senate and House of Representatives may be necessary (except on a question of Adjournment) shall be presented to the President of the United States; and before the Same shall take Effect, shall be approved by him, or being disapproved by him, shall be repassed by two thirds of the Senate and House of Representatives, according to the Rules and Limitations prescribed in the Case of a Bill.

Section 8. The Congress shall have Power To lay and collect Taxes, Duties, Imposts and Excises, to pay the Debts and provide for the common Defence and general Welfare of the United States; but all Duties, Imposts and Excises shall be uniform throughout the United States;

To borrow Money on the credit of the United States;

To regulate Commerce with foreign Nations, and among the several States, and with the Indian Tribes;

To establish an uniform Rule of Naturalization, and uniform Laws on the subject of Bankruptcies throughout the United States;

To coin Money, regulate the Value thereof, and of foreign Coin, and fix the Standard of Weights and Measures;

To provide for the Punishment of counterfeiting the Securities and current Coin of the United States;

To establish Post Offices and post Roads;

To promote the Progress of Science and useful Arts, by securing for limited Times to Authors and Inventors the exclusive Right to their respective Writings and Discoveries;

To constitute Tribunals inferior to the supreme Court;

To define and punish Piracies and Felonies committed on the high Seas, and Offences against the Law of Nations;

To declare War, grant Letters of Marque and Reprisal, and make Rules concerning Captures on Land and Water;

To raise and support Armies, but no Appropriation of Money to that Use shall be for a longer Term than two Years;

To provide and maintain a Navy;

To make Rules for the Government and Regulation of the land and naval Forces;

To provide for calling forth the Militia to execute the Laws of the Union, suppress Insurrections and repel Invasions;

To provide for organizing, arming, and disciplining, the Militia, and for governing such Part of them as may be employed in the Service of the United States, reserving to the States respectively, the Appointment of the Officers, and the Authority of training the Militia according to the discipline prescribed by Congress;

To exercise exclusive Legislation in all Cases whatsoever, over such District (not exceeding ten Miles square) as may, by Cession of particular States, and the Acceptance of Congress, become the Seat of the Government of the United States, and to exercise like Authority over all Places purchased by the Consent of the Legislature of the State in which the Same shall be, for the Erection of Forts, Magazines, Arsenals, dock-Yards, and other needful Buildings; -And

To make all Laws which shall be necessary and proper for carrying into Execution the foregoing Powers, and all other Powers vested by this Constitution in the Government of the United States, or in any Department or Officer thereof.

Section 9. The Migration or Importation of such Persons as any of the States now existing shall think proper to admit, shall not be prohibited by the Congress prior to the Year one thousand eight hundred and eight, but a Tax or duty may be imposed on such Importation, not exceeding ten dollars for each Person.

The Privilege of the Writ of Habeas Corpus shall not be suspended, unless when in Cases of Rebellion or Invasion the public Safety may require it.

No Bill of Attainder or ex post facto Law shall be passed.

No Capitation, or other direct, Tax shall be laid, unless in Proportion to the Census or Enumeration herein before directed to be taken.

No Tax or Duty shall be laid on Articles exported from any State.

No Preference shall be given by any Regulation of Commerce or Revenue to the Ports of one State over those of another: nor shall Vessels bound to, or from, one State, be obliged to enter, clear, or pay Duties in another.

No Money shall be drawn from the Treasury, but in Consequence of Appropriations made by Law; and a regular Statement and Account of the Receipts and Expenditures of all public Money shall be published from time to time.

No Title of Nobility shall be granted by the United States: And no Person holding any Office of Profit or Trust under them, shall, without the Consent of the Congress, accept of any present, Emolument, Office, or Title, of any kind whatever, from any King, Prince, or foreign State.

Section 10. No State shall enter into any Treaty, Alliance, or Confederation; grant Letters of Marque and Reprisal; coin Money; emit Bills of Credit; make any Thing but gold and silver Coin a Tender in Payment of Debts; pass any Bill of Attainder, ex post facto Law, or Law impairing the Obligation of Contracts, or grant any Title of Nobility.

No State shall, without the Consent of the Congress, lay any Imposts or Duties on Imports or Exports, except what may be absolutely necessary for executing it's inspection Laws: and the net Produce of all Duties and Imposts, laid by any State on Imports or Exports, shall be for the Use of the Treasury of the United States; and all such Laws shall be subject to the Revision and Controul of the Congress.

No State shall, without the Consent of Congress, lay any Duty of Tonnage, keep Troops, or Ships of War in time of Peace, enter into any Agreement or Compact with another State, or with a foreign Power, or engage in War, unless actually invaded, or in such imminent Danger as will not admit of delay.

Article II

Section 1. The executive Power shall be vested in a President of the United States of America. He shall hold his Office during the Term of four Years, and, together with the Vice President, chosen for the same Term, be elected as follows

Each State shall appoint, in such Manner as the Legislature thereof may direct, a Number of Electors, equal to the whole Number of Senators and Representatives to which the State may be entitled in the Congress: but no Senator or Representative, or Person holding an Office of Trust or Profit under the United States, shall be appointed an Elector.

The Electors shall meet in their respective States, and vote by Ballot for two Persons, of whom one at least shall not be an Inhabitant of the same State with themselves. And they shall make a List of all the Persons voted for, and of the Number of Votes for each; which List they shall sign and certify, and transmit sealed to the Seat of the Government of the United States, directed to the President of the Senate. The President of the Senate shall, in the Presence of the Senate and House of Representatives, open all the Certificates, and the Votes shall then be counted. The Person having the greatest Number of Votes shall be the President, if such Number be a Majority of the whole Number of Electors appointed; and if there be more than one who have such Majority, and have an equal Number of Votes, then the House of Representatives shall immediately chuse by Ballot one of them for President; and if no Person have a Majority, then from the five highest on the List the said House shall in like Manner chuse the President. But in chusing the President, the Votes shall be taken by States, the Representation from each State having one Vote; A quorum for this Purpose shall consist of a Member or Members from two thirds of the States, and a Majority of all the States shall be necessary to a Choice. In every Case, after the Choice of the President, the Person having the greatest Number of Votes of the Electors shall be the Vice President. But if there should remain two or more who have equal Votes, the Senate shall chuse from them by Ballot the Vice President.

The Congress may determine the Time of chusing the Electors, and the Day on which they shall give their Votes; which Day shall be the same throughout the United States.

No Person except a natural born Citizen, or a Citizen of the United States, at the time of the Adoption of this Constitution, shall be eligible to the Office of President; neither shall any Person be eligible to that Office who shall not have attained to the Age of thirty five Years, and been fourteen Years a Resident within the United States.

In Case of the Removal of the President from Office, or of his Death, Resignation, or Inability to discharge the Powers and Duties of the said Office, the Same shall devolve on the Vice president, and the Congress may by Law provide for the Case of Removal, Death, Resignation or Inability, both of the President and Vice President, declaring what Officer shall then act as President, and such Officer shall act accordingly, until the Disability be removed, or a President shall be elected.

The President shall, at stated Times, receive for his Services, a Compensation, which shall neither be encreased nor diminished during the Period for which he shall have been elected, and he shall not receive within that Period any other Emolument from the United States, or any of them.

Before he enter on the Execution of his Office, he shall take the following Oath or Affirmation: -"I do solemnly swear (or affirm) that I will faithfully execute the Office of President of the United States, and will to the best of my Ability, preserve, protect and defend the Constitution of the United States."

Section 2. The president shall be Commander in Chief of the Army and Navy of the United States, and of the Militia of the several States, when called into the actual service of the United States; he may require the Opinion, in writing, of the principal Officer in each of the executive Departments, upon any Subject relating to the Duties of their respective Offices, and he shall have Power to grant Reprieves and Pardons for Offences against the United States, except in Cases of Impeachment.

He shall have Power, by and with the Advice and Consent of the Senate, to make Treaties, provided two thirds of the Senators present concur; and he shall nominate, and by and with the Advice and Consent of the Senate, shall appoint Ambassadors, other public Ministers and Consuls, Judges of the supreme Court, and all other Officers of the United States, whose Appointments are not herein otherwise provided for, and which shall be established by Law but the Congress may by Law vest the Appointment of such inferior Officers, as they think proper, in the President alone, in the Courts of Law, or in the Heads of Departments.

The President shall have Power to fill up all Vacancies that may happen during the Recess of the Senate, by granting Commissions which shall expire at the End of their next Session.

Section 3. He shall from time to time give to the Congress Information of the State of the Union, and recommend to their Consideration such Measures as he shall judge necessary and expedient; he may, on extraordinary Occasions, convene both Houses, or either of them, and in Case of Disagreement between them, with Respect to the Time of Adjournment, he may adjourn them to such Time as he shall think proper; he shall receive Ambassadors and other public Ministers; he shall take Care that the Laws be faithfully executed, and shall Commission all the Officers of the United States.

Section 4. The President, Vice President and all civil Officers of the United States, shall be removed from Office on Impeachment for, and Conviction of, Treason, Bribery, or other high Crimes and Misdemeanors.

Article III

Section 1. The judicial Power of the United States, shall be vested in one supreme Court, and in such inferior Courts as the Congress may from time to time ordain and establish. The Judges, both of the supreme and inferior Courts, shall hold their Offices during good Behaviour, and shall, at stated Times, receive for their Services, a Compensation, which shall not be diminished during their Continuance in Office.

Section 2. The judicial Power shall extend to all Cases, in Law and Equity, arising under this Constitution, the Laws of the United States, and Treaties made, or which shall be made, under their Authority; -to all Cases affecting Ambassadors, other public Ministers and Consuls; -to all Cases of admiralty and maritime Jurisdiction; -to Controversies to which the United States shall be a Party; -to Controversies between two or more States; -between a State and Citizens of another State; -between Citizens of different States,-between Citizens of the same State claiming Lands under Grants of different States, and between a State, or the Citizens thereof, and foreign States, Citizens or Subjects.

In all cases affecting Ambassadors, other public Ministers and Consuls, and those in which a State shall be Party, the supreme Court shall have original Jurisdiction. In all the other Cases before mentioned, the supreme Court shall have appellate Jurisdiction, both as to Law and Fact, with such Exceptions, and under such Regulations as the Congress shall make.

The Trial of all Crimes, except in Cases of Impeachment, shall be by Jury; and such Trial shall be held in the State where the said Crimes shall have been committed; but when not committed within any State, the Trial shall be at such Place or Places as the Congress may by Law have directed.

Section 3. Treason against the United States, shall consist only in levying War against them, or in adhering to their Enemies, giving them Aid and Comfort. No Person shall be convicted of Treason unless on the Testimony of two Witnesses to the same overt Act, or on Confession in open Court.

The Congress shall have Power to declare the Punishment of Treason, but no Attainder of Treason shall work Corruption of Blood, or Forfeiture except during the Life of the Person attainted.

Article IV

Section 1. Full Faith and Credit shall be given in each State to the public Acts, Records, and judicial Proceedings of every other State. And the Congress may by general Laws prescribe the Manner in which such Acts, Records and Proceedings shall be proved, and the Effect thereof.

Section 2. The Citizens of each State shall be entitled to all Privileges and Immunities of Citizens in the several States.

A Person charged in any State with Treason, Felony, or other Crime, who shall flee from Justice, and be found in another State, shall on Demand of the executive Authority of the State from which he fled, be delivered up, to be removed to the State having Jurisdiction of the Crime.

No Person held to Service or Labour in one State, under the Laws thereof, escaping into another, shall, in Consequence of any Law or Regulation therein, be discharged from such Service or Labour, but shall be delivered up on Claim of the Party to whom such Service or Labour may be due.

Section 3. New States may be admitted by the Congress into this Union; but no new State shall be formed or erected within the Jurisdiction of any other State; nor any State be formed by the Junction of two or more States, or Parts of States, without the Consent of the Legislatures of the States concerned as well as of the Congress.

The Congress shall have Power to dispose of and make all needful Rules and Regulations respecting the Territory or other Property belonging to the United States; and nothing in this Constitution shall be so construed as to Prejudice any Claims of the United States, or of any particular State.

Section 4. The United States shall guarantee to every State in this Union a Republican Form of Government, and shall protect each of them against Invasion; and on Application of the Legislature, or of the Executive (when the Legislature cannot be convened) against domestic Violence.

Article V

The Congress, whenever two thirds of both Houses shall deem it necessary, shall propose Amendments to this Constitution, or, on the Application of the Legislatures of two thirds of the several States, shall call a Convention for proposing Amendments, which, in either Case, shall be valid to all Intents and Purposes, as Part of this Constitution, when ratified by the Legislatures of three fourths of the several States, or by Conventions in three fourths thereof, as the one or the other Mode of Ratification may be proposed by the Congress; provided that no Amendment which may be made prior to the Year One thousand eight hundred and eight shall in any Manner affect the first and fourth Clauses in the Ninth Section of the first Article; and that no State, without its Consent, shall be deprived of it's equal Suffrage in the Senate.

Article VI

All Debts contracted and Engagements entered into, before the adoption of this Constitution, shall be as valid against the United States under this Constitution, as under the Confederation.

This Constitution, and the Laws of the United States which shall be made in Pursuance thereof; and all Treaties made, or which shall be made, under the Authority of the United States, shall be the supreme Law of the Land; and the Judges in every State shall be bound thereby, any Thing in the Constitution or Laws of any State to the Contrary notwithstanding.

The Senators and Representatives before mentioned, and the Members of the several State Legislatures, and all executive and judicial Officers, both of the United States and of the several States, shall be bound by Oath or Affirmation, to support this Constitution; but no religious Test shall ever be required as a Qualification to any Office or public Trust under the United States.

Article VII

The Ratification of the Conventions of nine States, shall be sufficient for the Establishment of this Constitution between the States so ratifying the Same.

The Word, "the," being interlined between the seventh and eighth Lines of the first Page, The Word "Thirty" being partly written on an Erazure in the fifteenth Line of the first Page, The Words "is tried" being interlined between the thirty second and thirty third Lines of the first Page and the Word "the" being interlined between the forty third and forty fourth Lines of the second Page.

Attest WILLIAM JACKSON Secretary done in Convention by the Unanimous Consent of the States present the Seventeenth Day of September in the Year of our Lord one thousand seven hundred and Eighty seven and of the Independence of the United States of America the Twelfth In witness whereof We have hereunto subscribed our Names,

Go: WASHINGTON

Presidt. and deputy from Virginia

New Hampshire
JOHN LANGDON
NICHOLAS GILMAN

Massachusetts
NATHANIEL GORHAM
RUFUS KING

Connecticut
WM: SAML. JOHNSON
ROGER SHERMAN

New York
ALEXANDER HAMILTON

New Jersey
WIL: LIVINGSTON
DAVID BREARLEY.
WM: PATERSON.
JONA: DAYTON

Pennsylvania
B FRANKLIN
THOMAS MIFFLIN
ROBT MORRIS
GEO. CLYMER
THOS. FITZSIMONS
JARED INGERSOLL
JAMES WILSON
GOUV MORRIS

Delaware
GEO: READ
GUNNING BEDFORD jun
JOHN DICKINSON
RICHARD BASSETT
JACO: BROOM

Maryland
JAMES McHENRY
DAN OF ST THOS. JENIFER
DANL
Virginia
JOHN BLAIR-
JAMES MADISON Jr.

North Carolina
WM: BLOUNT
RICHD. DOBBS SPAIGHT.
HU WILLIAMSON

South Carolina
J. RUTLEDGE
CHARLES COTESWORTH
  PINCKNEY
CHARLES PINCKNEY
PIERCE BUTLER.

Georgia
WILLIAM FEW
ABR BALDWIN

Amendment I

Congress shall make no law respecting an establishment of religion, or prohibiting the free exercise thereof; or abridging the freedom of speech, or of the press; or the right of the people peaceably to assemble, and to petition the government for a redress of grievances.

Amendment II

A well regulated militia, being necessary to the security of a free state, the right of the people to keep and bear arms, shall not be infringed.

Amendment III

No soldier shall, in time of peace be quartered in any house, without the consent of the owner, nor in time of war, but in a manner to be prescribed by law.

Amendment IV

The right of the people to be secure in their persons, houses, papers, and effects, against unreasonable searches and seizures, shall not be violated, and no warrants shall issue, but upon probable cause, supported by oath or affirmation, and particularly describing the place to be searched, and the persons or things to be seized.

Amendment V

No person shall be held to answer for a capital, or otherwise infamous crime, unless on a presentment or indictment of a grand jury, except in cases arising in the land or naval forces, or in the militia, when in actual service in time of war or public danger; nor shall any person be subject for the same offense to be twice put in jeopardy of life or limb; nor shall be compelled in any criminal case to be a witness against himself, nor be deprived of life, liberty, or property, without due process of law; nor shall private property be taken for public use, without just compensation.

Amendment VI

In all criminal prosecutions, the accused shall enjoy the right to a speedy and public trial, by an impartial jury of the state and district wherein the crime shall have been committed, which district shall have been previously ascertained by law, and to be informed of the nature and cause of the accusation; to be confronted with the witnesses against him; to have compulsory process for obtaining witnesses in his favor, and to have the assistance of counsel for his defense.

Amendment VII

In suits at common law, where the value in controversy shall exceed twenty dollars, the right of trial by jury shall be preserved, and no fact tried by a jury, shall be otherwise reexamined in any court of the United States, than according to the rules of the common law.

Amendment VIII

Excessive bail shall not be required, nor excessive fines imposed, nor cruel and unusual punishments inflicted.

Amendment IX

The enumeration in the Constitution, of certain rights, shall not be construed to deny or disparage others retained by the people.

Amendment X

The powers not delegated to the United States by the Constitution, nor prohibited by it to the states, are reserved to the states respectively, or to the people.

Amendment XI

(1798)

The judicial power of the United States shall not be construed to extend to any suit in law or equity, commenced or prosecuted against one of the United States by citizens of another state, or by citizens or subjects of any foreign state.

Amendment XII

(1804)

The electors shall meet in their respective states and vote by ballot for President and Vice-President, one of whom, at least, shall not be an inhabitant of the same state with themselves; they shall name in their ballots the person voted for as President, and in distinct ballots the person voted for as Vice-President, and they shall make distinct lists of all persons voted for as President, and of all persons voted for as Vice-President, and of the number of votes for each, which lists they shall sign and certify, and transmit sealed to the seat of the government of the United States, directed to the President of the Senate;— The President of the Senate shall, in the presence of the Senate and House of Representatives, open all the certificates and the votes shall then be counted;— the person having the greatest number of votes for President, shall be the President, if such number be a majority of the whole number of electors appointed; and if no person have such majority, then from the persons having the highest numbers not exceeding three on the list of those voted for as President, the House of Representatives shall choose immediately, by ballot, the President. But in choosing the President, the votes shall be taken by states, the representation from each state having one vote; a quorum for this purpose shall consist of a member or members from two-thirds of the states, and a majority of all the states shall be necessary to a choice. And if the House of Representatives shall not choose a President whenever the right of choice shall devolve upon them, before the fourth day of March next following, then the Vice-President shall act as President, as in the case of the death or other constitutional disability of the President. The person having the greatest number of votes as Vice-President, shall be the Vice-President, if such number be a majority of the whole number of electors appointed, and if no person have a majority, then from the two highest numbers on the list, the Senate shall choose the Vice-President; a quorum for the purpose shall consist of two-thirds of the whole number of Senators, and a majority of the whole number shall be necessary to a choice. But no person constitutionally ineligible to the office of President shall be eligible to that of Vice-President of the United States.

Amendment XIII

(1865)

Section 1. Neither slavery nor involuntary servitude, except as a punishment for crime whereof the party shall have been duly convicted, shall exist within the United States, or any place subject to their jurisdiction.

Section 2. Congress shall have power to enforce this article by appropriate legislation.

Amendment XIV

(1868)

Section 1. All persons born or naturalized in the United States, and subject to the jurisdiction thereof, are citizens of the United States and of the state wherein they reside. No state shall make or enforce any law which shall abridge the privileges or immunities of citizens of the United States; nor shall any state deprive any person of life, liberty, or property, without due process of law; nor deny to any person within its jurisdiction the equal protection of the laws.

Section 2. Representatives shall be apportioned among the several states according to their respective numbers, counting the whole number of persons in each state, excluding Indians not taxed. But when the right to vote at any election for the choice of electors for President and Vice President of the United States, Representatives in Congress, the executive and judicial officers of a state, or the members of the legislature thereof, is denied to any of the male inhabitants of such state, being twenty-one years of age, and citizens of the United States, or in any way abridged, except for participation in rebellion, or other crime, the basis of representation therein shall be reduced in the proportion which the number of such male citizens shall bear to the whole number of male citizens twenty-one years of age in such state.

Section 3. No person shall be a Senator or Representative in Congress, or elector of President and Vice President, or hold any office, civil or military, under the United States, or under any state, who, having previously taken an oath, as a member of Congress, or as an officer of the United States, or as a member of any state legislature, or as an executive or judicial officer of any state, to support the Constitution of the United States, shall have engaged in insurrection or rebellion against the same, or given aid or comfort to the enemies thereof. But Congress may by a vote of two-thirds of each House, remove such disability.

Section 4. The validity of the public debt of the United States, authorized by law, including debts incurred for payment of pensions and bounties for services in suppressing insurrection or rebellion, shall not be questioned. But neither the United States nor any state shall assume or pay any debt or obligation incurred in aid of insurrection or rebellion against the United States, or any claim for the loss or emancipation of any slave; but all such debts, obligations and claims shall be held illegal and void.

Section 5. The Congress shall have power to enforce, by appropriate legislation, the provisions of this article.

Amendment XV

(1870)

Section 1. The right of citizens of the United States to vote shall not be denied or abridged by the United States or by any state on account of race, color, or previous condition of servitude.

Section 2. The Congress shall have power to enforce this article by appropriate legislation.

Amendment XVI

(1913)

The Congress shall have power to lay and collect taxes on incomes, from whatever source derived, without apportionment among the several states, and without regard to any census of enumeration.

Amendment XVII

(1913)

The Senate of the United States shall be composed of two Senators from each state, elected by the people thereof, for six years; and each Senator shall have one vote. The electors in each state shall have the qualifications requisite for electors of the most numerous branch of the state legislatures.

When vacancies happen in the representation of any state in the Senate, the executive authority of such state shall issue writs of election to fill such vacancies: Provided, that the legislature of any state may empower the executive thereof to make temporary appointments until the people fill the vacancies by election as the legislature may direct.

This amendment shall not be so construed as to affect the election or term of any Senator chosen before it becomes valid as part of the Constitution.

Amendment XVIII

(1919)

Section 1. After one year from the ratification of this article the manufacture, sale, or transportation of intoxicating liquors within, the importation thereof into, or the exportation thereof from the United States and all territory subject to the jurisdiction thereof for beverage purposes is hereby prohibited.

Section 2. The Congress and the several states shall have concurrent power to enforce this article by appropriate legislation.

Section 3. This article shall be inoperative unless it shall have been ratified as an amendment to the Constitution by the legislatures of the several states, as provided in the Constitution, within seven years from the date of the submission hereof to the states by the Congress.

Amendment XIX

(1920)

The right of citizens of the United States to vote shall not be denied or abridged by the United States or by any state on account of sex.

Congress shall have power to enforce this article by appropriate legislation.

Amendment XX

(1933)

Section 1. The terms of the President and Vice President shall end at noon on the 20th day of January, and the terms of Senators and Representatives at noon on the 3d day of January, of the years in which such terms would have ended if this article had not been ratified; and the terms of their successors shall then begin.

Section 2. The Congress shall assemble at least once in every year, and such meeting shall begin at noon on the 3d day of January, unless they shall by law appoint a different day.

Section 3. If, at the time fixed for the beginning of the term of the President, the President elect shall have died, the Vice President elect shall become President. If a President shall not have been chosen before the time fixed for the beginning of his term, or if the President elect shall have failed to qualify, then the Vice President elect shall act as President until a President shall have qualified; and the Congress may by law provide for the case wherein neither a President elect nor a Vice President elect shall have qualified, declaring who shall then act as President, or the manner in which one who is to act shall be selected, and such person shall act accordingly until a President or Vice President shall have qualified.

Section 4. The Congress may by law provide for the case of the death of any of the persons from whom the House of Representatives may choose a President whenever the right of choice shall have devolved upon them, and for the case of the death of any of the persons from whom the Senate may choose a Vice President whenever the right of choice shall have devolved upon them.

Section 5. Sections 1 and 2 shall take effect on the 15th day of October following the ratification of this article.

Section 6. This article shall be inoperative unless it shall have been ratified as an amendment to the Constitution by the legislatures of three-fourths of the several states within seven years from the date of its submission.

Amendment XXI

(1933)

Section 1. The eighteenth article of amendment to the Constitution of the United States is hereby repealed.

Section 2. The transportation or importation into any state, territory, or possession of the United States for delivery or use therein of intoxicating liquors, in violation of the laws thereof, is hereby prohibited.

Section 3. This article shall be inoperative unless it shall have been ratified as an amendment to the Constitution by conventions in the several states, as provided in the Constitution, within seven years from the date of the submission hereof to the states by the Congress.

Amendment XXII

(1951)

Section 1. No person shall be elected to the office of the President more than twice, and no person who has held the office of President, or acted as President, for more than two years of a term to which some other person was elected President shall be elected to the office of the President more than once. But this article shall not apply to any person holding the office of President when this article was proposed by the Congress, and shall not prevent any person who may be holding the office of President, or acting as President, during the term within which this article becomes operative from holding the office of President or acting as President during the remainder of such term.

Section 2. This article shall be inoperative unless it shall have been ratified as an amendment to the Constitution by the legislatures of three-fourths of the several states within seven years from the date of its submission to the states by the Congress.

Amendment XXIII

(1961)

Section 1. The District constituting the seat of government of the United States shall appoint in such manner as the Congress may direct:

A number of electors of President and Vice President equal to the whole number of Senators and Representatives in Congress to which the District would be entitled if it were a state, but in no event more than the least populous state; they shall be in addition to those appointed by the states, but they shall be considered, for the purposes of the election of President and Vice President, to be electors appointed by a state; and they shall meet in the District and perform such duties as provided by the twelfth article of amendment.

Section 2. The Congress shall have power to enforce this article by appropriate legislation.

Amendment XXIV

(1964)

Section 1. The right of citizens of the United States to vote in any primary or other election for President or Vice President, for electors for President or Vice President, or for Senator or Representative in Congress, shall not be denied or abridged by the United States or any state by reason of failure to pay any poll tax or other tax.

Section 2. The Congress shall have power to enforce this article by appropriate legislation.

Amendment XXV

(1967)

Section 1. In case of the removal of the President from office or of his death or resignation, the Vice President shall become President.

Section 2. Whenever there is a vacancy in the office of the Vice President, the President shall nominate a Vice President who shall take office upon confirmation by a majority vote of both Houses of Congress.

Section 3. Whenever the President transmits to the President pro tempore of the Senate and the Speaker of the House of Representatives his written declaration that he is unable to discharge the powers and duties of his office, and until he transmits to them a written declaration to the contrary, such powers and duties shall be discharged by the Vice President as Acting President.

Section 4. Whenever the Vice President and a majority of either the principal officers of the executive departments or of such other body as Congress may by law provide, transmit to the President pro tempore of the Senate and the Speaker of the House of Representatives their written declaration that the President is unable to discharge the powers and duties of his office, the Vice President shall immediately assume the powers and duties of the office as Acting President.

Thereafter, when the President transmits to the President pro tempore of the Senate and the Speaker of the House of Representatives his written declaration that no inability exists, he shall resume the powers and duties of his office unless the Vice President and a majority of either the principal officers of the executive department or of such other body as Congress may by law provide, transmit within four days to the President pro tempore of the Senate and the Speaker of the House of Representatives their written declaration that the President is unable to discharge the powers and duties of his office.

Thereupon Congress shall decide the issue, assembling within forty-eight hours for that purpose if not in session. If the Congress, within twenty-one days after receipt of the latter written declaration, or, if Congress is not in session, within twenty-one days after Congress is required to assemble, determines by two-thirds vote of both Houses that the President is unable to discharge the powers and duties of his office, the Vice President shall continue to discharge the same as Acting President; otherwise, the President shall resume the powers and duties of his office.

Amendment XXVI

(1971)

Section 1. The right of citizens of the United States, who are 18 years of age or older, to vote, shall not be denied or abridged by the United States or any state on account of age.

Section 2. The Congress shall have the power to enforce this article by appropriate legislation.

Amendment XXVII

(1992)

No law varying the compensation for the services of the Senators and Representatives shall take effect until an election of Representatives shall have intervened.

Supreme Court Justices

Stephen Breyer

Born August 15, 1938, in San Francisco, California. Married, three children. Education. Stanford University, A.B., 1959, Great Distinction; Oxford University, B.A., 1961; Harvard Law School, LL.B., magna cum laude, 1964. Clerk to the Honorable Arthur J. Goldberg, Associate Justice of the United States, 1964-65. Harvard University, Assistant Professor, 1967-70; Professor of Law, 1970-80; Professor, Kennedy School of Government, 1977-80; Lecturer, 1980-present. Visiting Professor, College of Law, Sydney, Australia, 1975; University of Rome, 1993. Nominated by President Jimmy Carter to the United States Court of Appeals for the First Circuit, took oath of office December 10, 1980. Nominated by President Bill Clinton as Associate Justice of the United States; took oath of office August 3, 1994.

Ruth Bader Ginsburg

Born March 15, 1933, in Brooklyn, New York. Married, two children. Education. Cornell University, B.A., 1954, with high honors in Government and distinction in all subjects; attended Harvard Law School (1956-58), Harvard Law Review; Columbia Law School, LL.B. (J.D.) 1959. Clerk to the Honorable Edmund L. Palmieri, United States District Court, Southern District of New York, 1959-61; Columbia Law School Project on International Procedure: Research Associate, 1961-62, Associate Director, 1962-63; Rutgers University School of Law, Professor, 1963-72; Columbia Law School, Professor, 1972-80; General counsel and founder of women's rights project, ACLU, 1973-80. Nominated by President Jimmy Carter to United States Court of Appeals for the District of Columbia Circuit, took oath of office June 30, 1980. Nominated by President Bill Clinton as Associate Justice of the United States, took oath of office August 10, 1993.

Anthony M. Kennedy

Born July 23, 1936 in Sacramento, California. Married, three children. Education. Stanford University, B.A., 1958; Harvard Law School, LL.B., 1961. Private Practice in Sacrament, 1961-75. Professor of constitutional law, McGeorge School of Law, University of the Pacific, 1965-88. Nominated by President Gerald Ford to United States Court of Appeals for the Ninth Circuit, took oath of office May 30, 1975. Nominated by President Ronald Reagan as Associate Justice of the United States, took oath of office February 18, 1988.

Sandra Day O'Connor

Born March 26, 1930 in El Paso, Texas. Married, three children. Education. Stanford University, B.A., 1950, magna cum laude; LL.B., 1952. Deputy County Attorney, San Mateo County, California, 1952-53; Civilian Attorney for Quartermaster Market Center, Frankfurt, Germany, 1954-57. Private practice of law in Maryvale, Arizona, 1958-60. Assistant Attorney General, Arizona, 1965-69; Appointed State Senator in 1969 and subsequently reelected to two two-year terms, serving from 1969-75; elected Senate Majority Leader in 1972; appointed to the Arizona Court of Appeals by Governor Bruce Babbitt and served from 1975-79; nominated by President Ronald Reagan as Associate Justice of the United States, took oath on September 25, 1981.

William Hubbs Rehnquist

Born October 1, 1924, in Milwaukee, Wisconsin. Widowed, three children. Education. Stanford University, B.A., M.A., 1948; Harvard University, M.A., 1950; Stanford University, L.L.B., 1952. Clerk to the Honorable Robert H. Jackson, Justice of the United States, 1952-53. Private practice in Phoenix, Arizona, 1953-69. Assistant Attorney General, Office of Legal Counsel, 1969-71. Distinguished Visiting Professor, Pepperdine University, Summer 1986. Nominated by President Richard Nixon as Associate Justice of the United States, took oath of office on January 7, 1972; nominated by President Ronald Reagan as Chief Justice of the United States on June 17, 1986, took oath of office on September 26, 1986.

Antonin Scalia

Born March 11, 1936 in Trenton, N.J. Married, nine children. Education. Georgetown University, A.B., 1957; Harvard, LL.B., 1960; note editor. General counsel, Office of Telecommunications Policy, Executive Office of the President, 1971-72. Chairman, Administrative Conference of the United States, 1972-74. Assistant Attorney General, Office of Legal Counsel, U.S. Department of Justice, 1974-77. Law Teaching. Professor of Law, University of Virginia, 1967-74 (on leave 1971-74); scholar in residence, American Enterprise Institute, 1977; visiting professor of law, Georgetown University, 1977; professor of law, University of Chicago, 1977-82; visiting professor of law, Stanford University, 1980-81; Straus Distinguished Visiting Professor, Pepperdine University, Summer 1990. Nominated by President Ronald Reagan to United States Court of Appeals for the District of Columbia Circuit, took oath of office August 17, 1982. Nominated by President Reagan as Associate Justice of the United States, took oath of office September 26, 1986.

David Hackett Souter

Born September 17, 1939 in Melrose, Massachusetts. Unmarried. Education. Harvard College, A.B., 1961; Oxford, A.B. in Jurisprudence 1989, M.A., 1989; Harvard Law School, LL.B., 1966. Private practice. 1966-68. Assistant Attorney General of New Hampshire, 1968-71; Deputy Attorney General of New Hampshire, 1971-76; Attorney General of New Hampshire, 1976-78; Associate Justice, New Hampshire Superior Court, 1978-83; Associate Justice, New Hampshire Supreme Court, 1983-90; Judge, United States Court of Appeals for the First Circuit, 1990; Nominated by President George Bush as Associate Justice of the United States, 1990.

John Paul Stevens

Born April 20, 1920 in Chicago, Illinois. Married, four children. Education. University of Chicago, A.B., 1941; Northwestern University, J.D., magna cum laude, 1947. Clerk to the Honorable Wiley Rutledge, Associate Justice of the United States, 1947-48. Private practice in Chicago, 1950-70; Lecturer,

Antitrust Law, Northwestern University School of Law, 1950-54; University of Chicago Law School, 1955-58. Nominated by President Richard Nixon to the United States Court of Appeals for the Seventh Circuit, took oath of office on November 2, 1970. Nominated by President Ford as Associate Justice of the United States on December 1, 1975, took oath of office on December 19, 1975.

Clarence Thomas

Born June 28, 1948 in the Pinpoint community, near Savannah, Georgia. Married, one child. Education. Conception Seminary, 1967-68; Holy Cross College, A.B., cum laude; Yale Law School, J.D., 1974. Assistant Attorney General of Missouri, 1974-77; Attorney, Monsanto Company, 1977-79. Government Service. Legislative assistant to Senator John C. Danforth of Missouri, 1979-81; Assistant Secretary for Civil Rights, U.S. Department of Education, 1981-82; Chairman U.S. Equal Employment Opportunity Commission, 1982-90. Nominated by President George Bush to the United States Court of Appeals for the District of Columbia Circuit, took oath of office, March 12, 1990. Nominated by President George Bush as Associate Justice of the United States, took oath of office October 23, 1991.

Chapter 1

THE PHILOSOPHICAL AND NATURAL LAW BASIS OF THE AMERICAN ORDER: REMOTE AND IMMEDIATE ANCESTORS

A. The Continuing Search for Universal Truths that Advance Human Good: Jerusalem, Athens, Rome, and Bethlehem

Americans have a tendency to believe that their legal and constitutional culture is unique, but the simple fact is that our governing philosophy, our Constitution, and our laws reflect the experience of thousands of years of world civilization. Nevertheless, the manner in which our founders combined elements from Ancient, Medieval, and Modern political theories is arguably distinctive, and it is that distinctive, but multi-faceted tradition which we explore in this Chapter. Consistent with our emphasis on philosophical ideas and the jurisprudential notion that law is more than the command of the temporal sovereign, this Chapter begins our analysis of constitutional law by considering a number of ideas from some early thinkers which have been influential in the forging of the American constitutional order. We begin, in the first part of the Chapter with a sermon of sorts preached by John Winthrop on his way to help found the Massachusetts Bay colony, with regard to the religious nature of the American undertaking, and the correspondence between the founding of America and the ancient Israelites. We continue with readings from Aristotle, perhaps the greatest political philosopher of antiquity, from the great champion of republican Rome, Cicero, and finally from some thinkers ancient and modern, who have tried to understand the manner in which religious faith contributes to civilized society. The second and third parts of the Chapter are devoted to our more "immediate" ancestors, and treat in detail the events of seventeenth and eighteenth century Britain which were crucial to the formation of American ideas about good government. If the materials in this Chapter do their job, you will be struck by how much of what happens in American politics and law today is but a continuation of a conversation among humankind stretching back thousands of years.

1

1. Jerusalem

John Winthrop, *A Model of Christian Charity* (1630)[1] *in* 7 COLLECTIONS OF THE MASSACHUSETTS HISTORICAL SOCIETY 33-34, 44-48 (3d ser. 1838), *reprinted in* 1 A DOCUMENTARY HISTORY OF AMERICAN LIFE 66-69 (Jack P. Greene ed., 1966)

A Modell Herof

GOD ALMIGHTY in his most holy and wise providence, hath soe disposed of the condition of mankind, as in all times some must be rich, some poore, some high and eminent in power and dignite; others mean and in submission.

The Reason Hereof

* * *

3. Reas. Thirdly, that every man might have need of others, and from hence they might be all knitt more nearly together in the Bonds of brotherly affection. From hence it appears plainly that noe man is made more honourable than another or more wealthy &c., out of any particular and singular respect to him-selfe, but for the glory of his creator and the common good of the creature, man
. . . .

. . . When God gives a speciall commission He lookes to have it strictly observed in every article, When He gave Saule a commision to destroy Amaleck, He indented with him upon certain articles, and because He failed in one of the least, and that upon a faire pretense, it lost him the kingdom, which should have been his reward, if he had observed his commission. Thus stands the cause between God and us. We are entered into Covenant with Him for this worke. Wee have taken out a commission. The Lord hath given us leave to drawe our own articles. Wee have professed to enterprise these and those accounts, upon these and those ends. Wee have hereupon besought Him of favour and blessing. Now if the Lord shall please to heare us, and bring us in peace to the place wee desire, than Hathe he ratified this covenant and sealed our Commission, and will expect a strict performance of the articles contained in it; but if wee shall neglect the observation of these articles which are the ends wee have pro-pounded and, dissembling with our God, shall fall to embrace this present world and prosecute our carnall intentions seeking great things for ourselves and our posterity, the Lord will surely breake out in wrathe against us; be revenged of such a [sinful] people and make us knowe the price of the breache of such a Covenant.

Now the only way to avoyde this shipwracke, and to provide for our poster-ity, is to followe the counsell of Micah, *to do justly, to love mercy, to walk humbly with our God*. . . .The Lord will be our God, and delight to dwell among us, as

---

[1] What follows is a sermon originally delivered on the deck of the *Arabella*, on the way to the New World.

His oune poeople, and will command a blessing upon us in all our wayes. Soe that wee shall see much more of His wisdome, power, goodness and truthe, than formerly wee have been acquainted with. Wee shall finde that the God of Israell is among us, when ten of us shall be able to resist a thousand of our enemies; when He shall make us a prayse and glory that men shall say of succeeding plantations, "the Lord make it likely that of *New England*." For wee must consider that wee shall be as a citty upon a hill. The eyes of all people are uppon us. Soe that if wee shall deale falsely with our God in this worke wee have undertaken, and soe cause Him to withdrawe His present help from us, wee shall be made a story and a by-word through the world. Wee shall open the mouthes of enemies to speake evill of the wayes of God, and all professors for God's sake. Wee shall shame the faces of many of God's worthy servants, and cause theire preayers to be turned into curses upon us til wee be consumed out of the good land wither we are a goeing. . . .

> Therefore lett us choose life
> that wee, and our seede
> may live, by obeying His
> voyce and cleaveing to Him, for
> Hee is our life and
> our prosperity.

PROBLEM

Hanging on the courtroom wall behind the bench of Judge Roy Moore, then a circuit court judge for Etowa County, Alabama, were two hand-carved wooden plaques containing the ten commandments. In February of 1997, Judge Charles Price, in response to an ACLU challenge and a visit to Judge Moore's courtroom, ordered Judge Moore to remove the plaques, prompting Alabama Governor Fob James to threaten to employ Alabama's State Police and National Guard to prevent their removal. *See* Rick Bragg, *Judge Allows God's Law to Mix with Alabama's*, N.Y. TIMES, Feb. 13, 1997, at A14. Judge Moore was subsequently elected Chief Justice of Alabama, and in that capacity ordered the installation of a 5,280 lb. granite monument in the center rotunda of the Alabama Supreme Court building. The top of the monument bears a replica of the Ten Commandments; around the base of the monument are several quotations from political statesmen acknowledging God. Another federal judge, Judge Myron Thompson, in response to another suit initiated by the ACLU, ordered Chief Justice Moore to remove the monument. Moore refused, and was ultimately removed from his seat on the Alabama Supreme Court. We will examine the Establishment Clause, the constitutional provision which Judges Price and Thompson believe Judge Moore's displays violate, in detail in Chapter Two. Putting aside Establishment Clause considerations for the moment, on what principles would Winthrop affirm or deny Judge Moore's displays? Should these principles inform modern constitutional analysis?

NOTES AND QUESTIONS

1. Perhaps you have before encountered the notion that America was to be a "City upon a Hill," and now you know where it comes from, although you will have noticed that Winthrop aspires to that goal only for the new colony he is founding in New England.

2. There is no doubt that Winthrop's sermon is an attempt to set forth a deeply religious basis for civilization in Massachusetts Bay, and that he has in mind special burdens to be imposed upon the community. Do these strike you as placing unreasonable demands on the citizenry? What is the modern relevance of Winthrop's specifically Christian approach?

3. Is it fair to state that an early building block of American culture is the Old Testament? Perhaps the greatest of the early American constitutional theoriticians, who was the principal author of the first constitution for the state of Massachusetts in 1776, John Adams (later to serve as the second President), was of this belief. In a letter he wrote to F.A. Vanderkemp, on February 16, 1809 (9 JOHN ADAMS, WORKS 610 (Charles Francis Adams ed., 1854)), Adams observed that at the time America was in a delicate political situation because "The two most powerful, active, and enterprising nations [England and France] that ever existed are now contending with us." Adams went on to say that these were "[t]he two nations, to whom mankind are under more obligations for the progress of science and civilization than to any others, except the Hebrews." Apparently feeling that some explanation was called for, Adams said that he differed with the views of Bolingbroke and Voltaire (two prominant eighteenth century Enlightenment-era thinkers, one English, one French) with regard to their derogation of religion, and specifically that of the ancient Jews. Said Adams to his correspondent,

> I will insist that the Hebrews have done more to civilize men than any other nation. If I were an atheist, and believed in blind eternal fate, I should still believe that fate had ordained the Jews to be the most essential instrument for civilizing the nations. If I were an atheist of the other sect, who believe that all is ordered by chance, I should believe that chance had ordered the Jews to preserve and propagate to all mankind the doctrine of a supreme, intelligent, wise, almighty sovereign of the universe, which I believe to be the great essential principle of all morality, and consequently of all civilization.

Do you agree with Adams? Note that he believes that the idea of an all-powerful benevolent supernatural sovereign of the universe is necessary to morality and civilization, and that he gives full credit for this contribution to the Jews. *Cf.,* John Witte, Jr., *How to Govern a City on a Hill: The Early Puritan Contribution to American Constitutionalism,* 39 EMORY L.J. 41 (1990) (examining the way in which Puritan ideas and theological doctrines formed the basis for much of what are now considered to be fundamental principles of constitutional law) ("all the pregnant ideas and institutions of modern political thought are in essence secularized forms of theological doctrines and institutions").

4. The notion of a divine basis for law in the Old Testament was later independently articulated by the Ancient Greeks, most notably in Plato's *Laws*. Anticipating a famous statement by James Madison at the time of the ratification of the United States Constitution (FEDERALIST NO. 55), that the best form of government for men would be where the actual ruler was a God or a "spirit" sent by a God, Plato suggests (much like the book of Genesis) that this was the way things were in the earliest years of man, but now that this was no longer true, "The lesson is that we should make every effort to imitate the life men are said to have led under Cronus [when a God ruled mankind by sending spirits to govern them]; we should run our public and our private life, our homes and our cities, in obedience to what little spark of immortality lies in us, and dignify this distribution of reason with the name of 'law' [in Greek, *nomos*]." PLATO, THE LAWS 171 (Trevor J. Saunders trans.; 1970). Plato's somewhat complex point was that our powers of reason are divine gifts, and that when we use them properly to make laws we are doing so in accordance with an all-embracing divine plan for the universe — a point not dissimilar to those made by Winthrop or Adams. There was, of course, much more to Greek political philosophy than a divine basis for law, however, and it is to some of these other notions, as expressed by Aristotle, to which we next turn.

2. Athens

ARISTOTLE, POLITICS, bk. IV, ch. 11, at 157-60 (Barker trans., 1995)

We have now to consider what is the best constitution and the best way of life for the majority of cities and the majority of mankind. In doing so, we shall not employ a standard of excellence above the reach of ordinary people, or a standard of education requiring exceptional natural endowments and equipment, or the standard of a constitution which attains an ideal level. We shall be concerned only with the sort of life which most people are able to share and the sort of constitution which is possible for most cities to enjoy. The "aristocracies," so-called . . . either lie at one extreme, beyond the reach of most cities, or they approach so closely to what is called "constitutional government" [polity] that the two can be considered as a single form.

The issues we have just raised can all be decided in the light of one body of fundamental principles. If we were right when, in the *Ethics*, we stated that the truely happy life is one of goodness lived in freedom from impediments and that goodness consists in a mean, it follows that the best way of life is one which consists in a mean, and a mean of the kind attainable by each individual. Further, the same criteria should determine the goodness or badness of the city and that of the constitution; for a constitution is the way in which a city lives. In all cities there are three parts: the very rich, the very poor, and the third class which forms the mean between these two. Now, since it is admitted that moderation and the mean are always best it is clear that in the ownership of all gifts of fortune a middle condition will be the best. Those who are in this condition are the most ready to listen to reason. Those who are over-handsome, over-strong, over-noble, or over-wealthy, and, at the opposite extreme, those who are over-poor, over-weak, or utterly ignoble, find it hard to follow the lead of reason. Those in the first class tend more to arrogance and serious offences: those in the second tend too much to criminality and petty offences; and most wrong-doing arises either from arrogance or criminality. [It is a further characteristic of those in the middle that] they are least prone either to refuse office or to seek it, both of which tendencies are dangerous to cities.

It must also be added that those who enjoy too many advantages — strength, wealth, friends, and so forth — are both unwilling to obey and ignorant how to obey. This [defect] appears in them from the first, during childhood and in home life: nurtured in luxury, they never acquire a habit of obedience, even in school. But those who suffer from a lack of such things are far too mean and poor-spirited. Thus there are those who are ignorant how to rule and only know how to obey, as if they were slaves, and, on the other hand, there are those who are ignorant how to obey any sort of authority and only know how to rule as if they were masters [of slaves]. The result is a city, not of freemen, but only of slaves and masters: a state of envy on the one side and of contempt on the other. Nothing could be further removed from the spirit of friendship or of a political association. An association depends on friendship — after all, people will not even take a journey in common with their enemies. A city aims at being, as far as possible, composed of equals and peers, which is the condition of those in the middle, more than any group. It follows that this kind of city is bound to have the best constitution since it is composed of the elements which, on our view, naturally go to make up a city. The middle classes enjoy a greater security themselves than any other class. They do not, like the poor, desire the goods of others; nor do others desire their possessions, as the poor desire those of the rich, and since they neither plot against others, nor are plotted against themselves, they live free from danger. Phocylides was therefore right when he prayed: "Many things are best for those in the middle; I want to be at the middle of the city."

It is clear from our argument, first, that the best form of political association is one where power is vested in the middle class, and secondly, that good government is attainable in those cities where there is a large middle class — large enough, if possible, to be stronger than both of the other classes, but at any rate large enough to be stronger than either one of them singly; for in that case its addition to either will suffice to turn the scale, and will prevent either of the opposing extremes from becoming dominant. It is therefore the greatest of blessings for a city that its members should possess a moderate and adequate property. Where some have great possessions, and others have nothing at all, the result is either an extreme democracy or an unmixed oligarchy; or it may even be, as a result of the excesses of both sides, a tyranny. Tyranny grows out of the most immature type of democracy, or out of oligarchy, but much less frequently out of constitutions of the middle order, or those which approximate to them. . . .

. . . [I]t is clear that the middle type of constitution is best. It is the one type free from faction. Where the middle class is large, there is less likelihood of faction and dissensions than in any other constitution. Large cities are generally more free from faction just because they have a large middle class. In small cities, on the other hand, it is easy for the whole population to be divided into only two classes; nothing is left in the middle, and all, or almost all, are either poor or rich. Democracies are generally more secure and more permanent than oligarchies because of their middle class. This is more numerous, and has a larger share of [offices and] honors, than it does in oligarchies. Where democracies have no middle class, and the poor are greatly superior in number, trouble ensues, and they are speedily ruined. It must be considered a proof of its value that the best legislators have come from the middle class. Solon was one, as he makes clear in his poems: Lycurgus was another (after all he was not a king): and the same is true of Charondas and most of the other legislators.

What has just been said also serves to explain why most constitutions are either democratic or oligarchical. The middle class in those cities is often small; and the result is that as happens whenever one class — be it the owners of property or the masses — gains the advantage, it oversteps the mean, and draws the constitution in its own direction so that either a democracy or an oligarchy comes into being. In addition, factious disputes and struggles readily arise between the masses and the rich; and the side, whichever it is, that wins the day, instead of establishing a constitution based on the common interest and the principle of equality, exacts as the prize of victory a greater share in the constitution. It then institutes either a democracy or an oligarchy.

NOTES AND QUESTIONS

1. Although Plato and Aristotle are often thought to represent two different philosophical views, the one idealistic, even utopian, the other much more practical and real-world oriented, there are some similarities between the thought of Plato and Aristotle. Plato was, after all, Aristotle's teacher, and Plato's later dialogues, one of which was *The Laws* referred to above, are more practical and less utopian than his *Republic*. There is more than a little in *The Laws* with which Aristotle might have been comfortable. Take, for example, the notion for which *The Laws* has already been cited to you, that there is about human reason and its use something divinely inspired. Thus Aristotle, in his *Ethics* indicates that "the life of the intellect must be divine" compared with other human activities, and that "we ought, so far as in us lies, to put on immortality, and do all that we can to live in conformity with the highest that is in us; for even if it is small in bulk, in power and preciousness it far excels all the rest." ARISTOTLE, ETHICS 330-31 (Thomson trans., 1976). Like Plato, Aristotle seems prepared to concede that there is a "natural" form of "political justice," which "has the same validity everywhere and does not depend upon acceptance." *Id.* at 189. Aristotle also appears to have believed, like the Plato who wrote *The Laws*, that "The rule of law is preferable . . . to that of a single citizen," even where that citizen was an enlightened monarch, and Aristotle did declare in *Politics,* to the precisely same effect as the quote you have read from Plato's *Laws*, that "He who commands that law should rule may thus be regarded as commanding that God and reason alone should rule; he who commands that a man should rule adds the character of the beast." *Politics, supra,* at 127-28. Still, to a much greater extent, perhaps, than did Plato, Aristotle recognizes that some parts of political life are highly contingent on circumstances, and that there exist "Rules of justice established by convention and on the ground of expediency," and further that "laws that are not natural but man-made are not the same everywhere, because forms of government are not the same either," although "everywhere this is only one natural form of government, namely that which is best." *Id.* at 190.

2. We needn't solve these scholastic disputes in order to appreciate the clearer parts of Aristotle, such as the excerpt you have recently read from his *Politics*. In that book, Aristotle tries to lay out workable principles for the formation of constitutions, and principles that must be applied with care to the particular circumstances of a given society. Aristotle believed that man was "by nature a political animal," as explained in Chapter 2 of Book 1 of the *Politics*. To Aristotle, this meant that humankind could only realize its true nature by living together, in friendship, in the *polis*, or city. In order for humans to flourish, Aristotle believed, they had to be engaged in a common and cooperative endeavor to promote justice. Thus Aristotle's thought served as the foundation upon which even the most modern theories of "civic republicanism" have been built. *See generally, e.g.*, Andrew Lockyer, *Aristotle: The Politics, in* THE POLITICAL CLASSICS: A GUIDE TO THE ESSENTIAL TEXTS FROM PLATO TO ROUSSEAU 65-66 (Murray Forsyth & Maruice Keens-Soper eds., 1992). Can you discern anything in Aristotle's thought that is reflected in what you know about American government or society?

3. In particular you may have discerned in the excerpt a main theme to which Aristotle constantly returns, the notion of the "golden mean," that in politics as in life, one ought to avoid extremes and seek some kind of accommodation between competing interests or desires. Thus, in his *Politics*, while he comes close to endorsing the superiority of monarchy and aristocracy as forms of government, ultimately Aristotle appears to conclude that more often than not the best government will combine some features of aristocracy and monarchy with some features of democracy, so that no group in society can totally dominate the others. *See generally* Book III of *Politics*. As you will soon see, this insight about balancing interests in the government will be more fully realized in the United States Constitution, which, following recent advances in continental political theory, seeks to balance not orders in society, but functions within the government. Why should this be so in America? Do you suppose what Aristotle has to say about classes in society gives us a clue? In the excerpt from *Politics* you have just read, Aristotle combines his thoughts on balance in government with the notion of a golden mean of sorts between classes in society. Does what he has to say about the importance of a strong middle class resonate with any of your experience?

4. Are you familiar for example, with Thomas Jefferson's famous notion that an ideal American society ought to be composed of "yeoman farmers," each having an ownership interest in land, with land widely distributed, so that each farmer would have an actual interest in the society to protect and a desire politically to combine to form the best government? Does the following 1787 letter from the young Jefferson contain any echoes of Aristotle? Of Plato?

> Man was destined for society. His morality, therefore was to be formed to this object. He was endowed with a sense of right and wrong, merely relative to this. This sense is as much a part of his nature, as the sense of hearing, seeing, feeling . . . . It may be strengthened by exercise, as may any particular limb of the body.

Letter from Thomas Jefferson to Peter Carr (Aug. 10, 1787).

5. The classical world enriched American law through our founders' study not only of Greek thinkers, but, perhaps to an even greater extent, the writers and orators of republican Rome. We next consider the greatest of these, Cicero.

3. Rome

Marcus Tullius Cicero, De Legibus [Laws] bks. I and II, at 317, 319, 321, 323, 343, 345, 347, 379, 381, 383, 385, 387, 389, 391 (Clinton Walker Keyes trans., 1928)

. . . [N]ow let us investigate the origins of Justice.

Well, then, the most learned men have determined to begin with Law, and it would seem that they are right, if, according to their definition, Law is the higest reason, implanted in Nature, which commands what ought to be done and forbids the opposite. This reason, when firmly fixed and fully developed in the human mind, is Law. And so they believe that Law is intelligence, whose natural function it is to command right conduct and forbid wrongdoing. . . . Now if this is correct, as I think it to be in general, then the origin of Justice is to be found in Law, for Law is a natural force; it is the mind and reason of the intelligent man, the standard by which Justice and Injustice are measured. . . . But in determining what Justice is, let us begin with that supreme Law which had its origin ages before any written law existed or any State had been established.

* * *

. . . I shall seek the root of Justice in Nature, under whose guidance our whole discussion must be conducted.

* * *

. . . [T]hat animal which we call man, endowed with foresight and quick intelligence, complex, keen, possessing memory, full of reason and prudence, has been given a certain distinguished status by the supreme God who created him; for he is the only one among so many different kinds and varieties of living beings who has a share in reason and thought, while all the rest are deprived of it. But what is more divine, I will not say in man only, but in all heaven and earth, than reason? And reason, when it is full grown and perfected, is rightly called wisdom. Therefore, since there is nothing better than reason, and since it exists both in man and God, the first common possession of man and God is reason. But those who have reason in common must also have right reason in common. And since right reason is Law, we must believe that men have Law also in common with the gods. Further, those who share Law must also share Justice; and those who share these are to be regarded as members of the same commonwealth. If indeed they obey the same authorities and powers, this is true in a far greater degree; but as a matter of fact they do obey this celestial system, the divine mind, and the God of transcendent power. Hence we must now conceive of this whole universe as one commonwealth of which both gods and men are members.

* * *

But the most foolish notion of all is the belief that everything is just which is found in the customs or laws of nations. Would that be true, even if these laws had been enacted by tyrants? If the well-known Thirty [the thirty tyrants who ruled in Athens after the democracy] had desired to enact a set of laws at Athens, or if the Athenians without exception were delighted by the tyrants' laws, that would not entitle such laws to be regarded as just, would it? No more, in my opinion, should that law be considered just which a Roman [official] proposed, to the effect that a dictator [a person given plenary power by the Senate and People of Rome] might put to death with impunity any citizen he wished, even without a trial. For Justice is one; it binds all human society, and is based on one Law, which is right reason applied to command and prohibition. Whoever knows not this Law, whether it has been recorded in writing anywhere or not, is without Justice.

But if Justice is conformity to written laws and national customs, and if, as the same persons claim, everything is to be tested by the standard of utility, then anyone who thinks it will be profitable to him will, if he is able, disregard and violate the laws. It follows that Justice does not exist at all, if it does not exist in Nature, and if that form of it which is based on utility can be overthrown by that very utility itself. And if Nature is not to be considered the foundation of Justice, that will mean the destruction [of the virtues on which human society depends]. For where then will there be a place for generosity, or love of country, or loyalty, or the inclination to be of service to others or to show gratitude for favours received? For these virtues originate in our natural inclination to love our fellow-men, and this is the foundation of Justice. . . . But if the principles of

Justice were founded on the decrees of peoples, the edicts of princes, or the decisions of judges, then Justice would sanction robbery and adultery and forgery of wills, in case these acts were approved by the votes or decrees of the populace. . . . But in fact we can perceive the difference between good laws and bad by referring them to no other standard than Nature; indeed, it is not merely Justice and Injustice which are distinguished by Nature, but also and without exception things which are honourable and dishonourable. For since an intelligence common to us all makes things known to us and formulates them in our minds, honourable actions are ascribed by us to virtue, and dishonourable actions to vice; and only a madman would conclude that these judgements are matters of opinion, and not fixed by Nature. . . .

* * *

. . . I find that it has been the opinion of the wisest men that Law is not a product of human thought, nor is it any enactment of peoples, but something eternal which rules the whole universe by its wisdom in command and prohibition. Thus they have been accustomed to say that Law is the primal and ultimate mind of God, whose reason directs all things either by compulsion or restraint. Wherefore that Law which the gods have given to the human race has been justly praised; for it is the reason and mind of a wise lawgiver applied to command and prohibition.

* * *

. . . For the divine mind cannot exist without reason, and divine reason cannot but have this power to establish right and wrong. No written law commanded that a man should take his stand on a bridge alone, against the full force of the enemy, and order the bridge broken down behind him; yet we shall not for that reason suppose that the heroic Cocles was not obeying the law of bravery and following its decrees in doing so noble a deed. Even if there was no written law against rape at Rome in the reign of Lucius Tarquinius, we cannot say on that account that Sextus Tarquinius did not break that eternal Law by violating Lucretia, the daughter of Tricipitinus! For reason did exist, derived from the Nature of the universe, urging men to right conduct and diverting them from wrongdoing, and this reason did not first become Law when it was written down, but when it first came into existence; and it came into existence simultaneously with the divine mind. Wherefore the true and primal Law, applied to command and prohibition, is the right reason of supreme Jupiter [the Roman word for Zeus, the King of the Gods, sometimes also called the Father of Gods and Men].

* * *

Therefore, just as that divine mind is the supreme Law, so when [reason] is perfected in man, [that also is Law; and this perfected reason exists] in the mind of the wise man; but those rules which, in varying forms and for the need of the moment, have been formulated for the guidance of nations, bear the title of laws rather by favour than because they are really such. For every law which really deserves that name is truly praiseworthy, as they prove by approximately the following arguments. It is agreed, of course, that laws were invented for the safety of citizens, the preservation of States, and the tranquillity and happiness of human life, and that those who first put statutes of this kind in force convinced their people that it was their intention to write down and put into effect such rules as, once accepted and adopted, would make possible for them an honourable and happy life; and when such rules were drawn up and put in force, it is clear that men called them "laws." From this point of view it can be readily understood that those who formulated wicked and unjust statutes for nations, thereby breaking their promises and agreements, put into effect anything but "laws." It may thus be clear that in the very definition of the term "law" there inheres the idea and principle of choosing what is just and true. . . .

* * *

. . . What of the many deadly, the many pestilential statutes which nations put in force? These no more deserve to be called laws than the rules a band of robbers might pass in their assembly. For if ignorant and unskillful men have prescribed deadly poisons instead of healing drugs, these cannot possibly be called physicians' prescriptions; neither in a nation can a statute of any sort be called a law, even though the nation, in spite of its being a ruinous regulation has accepted it. Therefore Law is the distinction between things just and unjust, made in agreement with that primal and most ancient of all things, Nature; and in conformity to Nature's standard are framed those human laws which inflict punishment upon the wicked but defend and protect the good.

* * *

So in the very beginning we must persuade our citizens that the gods are the lords and rulers of all things, and that what is done, is done by their will and authority; that they are likewise great benefactors of man, observing the character of every individual, what he does, of what wrong he is guilty, and with what intentions and with what piety he fulfils his religious duties; and that they take note of the pious and impious. For surely minds which are imbued with such ideas will not fail to form true and useful opinions. Indeed, what is more true than that no one ought to be so foolishly proud as to think that, though reason and intellect exist in himself, they do not exist in the heavens and the universe, or that those things which can hardly be understood by the highest reasoning powers of the human intellect are guided by no reason at all? In truth, the man that is not driven to gratitude by the orderly courses of the stars, the regular alternation of day and night, the gentle progress of the seasons, and the produce of the earth brought forth for our sustenance — how can such an one be accounted a man at all? And since all things that possess reason stand above those things which are without reason, and since it would be sacrilege to say that anything stands above universal Nature, we must admit that reason is inherent in Nature. Who will deny that such beliefs are useful when he remembers how often oaths are used to confirm agreements, how important to our well-being is the sanctity of treaties, how many persons are deterred from crime by the fear of divine punishment, and how sacred an association of citizens becomes when the immortal gods are made members of it, either as judges or as witnesses?

NOTES AND QUESTIONS

1. You have been reading excerpts from Cicero's dialogue, *De Legibus*, or "Laws." Cicero, though not born a member of the Roman nobility, still went on to become "the most vividly known personality of the ancient world." Michael Grant, *Introduction* to MARCUS TULLIUS CICERO, ON GOVERNMENT 1 n.2 (Michael Grant trans. & ed., 1993). He was probably the greatest statesman and orator Rome produced. Voltaire said of Cicero that he "taught us how to think." *Id.* at 7 n.3. Did he teach you?

Do these excerpts from Cicero define "law" or "reason" or "nature" in a manner that is familiar or unfamiliar to you? What, for example, does Cicero mean by "right reason"? Is "law" a descriptive or a normative term for Cicero? Does his line of reasoning even make much sense? Why do you suppose we have so much difficulty following Cicero, but his readers or listeners did not?

These excerpts have been concerned with what we often refer to as "natural law." This was a subject of profound importance to Cicero, who wrote about it in many of his works. There is some element of repetition in what you have just read, but perhaps you are still a little perplexed by what Cicero means by "law" or what we mean by "natural law" or "the law of nature." Perhaps your understanding of Cicero might be clarified by one more statement of definition, this time from Cicero's *De Re Publica* or *Republic*, Book III:

> True law is right reason in agreement with nature; it is of universal application, unchanging and everlasting; it summons to duty by its commands, and averts from wrongdoing by its prohibitions. And it does not lay its commands or prohibitions upon good men in vain, though neither have any effect on the wicked. It is a sin to try to alter this law, nor is it allowable to attempt to repeal any part of it, and it is impossible to abolish it entirely. We cannot be freed from its obligations by senate or people, and we need not look outside ourselves for an expounder or interpreter of it. And there will not be different laws at Rome and at Athens, or different laws now and in the future, but one eternal and unchangeable law will be valid for all nations and all times, and there will be one master and ruler, that is, God, over us all, for he is the author of this law, its promulgator, and its enforcing judge. Whoever is disobedient is fleeing from himself and denying his human nature, and by reason of this very fact he will suffer the worst penalties, even if he escapes what is commonly considered punishment. . . .

MARCUS TULLIUS CICERO, DE RE PUBLICA, bk. III, at 211 (Clinton Walker Keyes trans., 1928). You have now read "the most famous and influential passage" in

Cicero's *Republic*. Grant, *supra*, at 183 n.2. If you ever wondered what natural law was, now you know. Do you agree with Cicero?

2. There is more to the excerpts that you have read from Cicero than just his definition of natural law, however, and there is more that the American constitutional tradition took from Cicero than his ideas about natural law. You will have noticed that Cicero hints, in the passages that you have read, of the duties which the law of nature imposes upon individuals. These were another main theme for Cicero, and have been summarized as follows:

> The moral obligation of natural justice [as perceived by Cicero], and hence of the law of nature as it pertains exclusively to humans, can apparently be reduced to four major duties; (1) not to injure others physically without cause; (2) to respect private and common property; (3) to fulfill obligations for which our word has been pledged; and (4) to be kind and generous to others, according to their worth and our means.

NEAL WOOD, CICERO'S SOCIAL AND POLITICAL THOUGHT 76 (1988). Is this Ciceronian code of conduct one with which you are comfortable? Have you ever encountered it before? It might also be said of Cicero's conception of "piety" that it required men not only to treat each other fairly, respectfully, kindly, and generously, but that it imposed duties owed to the gods, to parents and other ancestors, and to one's country. Indeed, Cicero believed that one's duty to any or all of these groups could call upon one to make the ultimate self-sacrifice and, for example, to die for one's country if necessary. Perhaps you will have perceived that this Ciceronian concept of duty was reflected in the British Empire's notion of a "gentlemen," in our founders' notions of patriotism, and even in the old motto that Notre Dame students ought to be devoted to God, to Country and to Notre Dame (presumably in that order). Yale students made a similar pledge, substituting a different institution in the trilogy, of course.

3. Are Cicero's ideas compatible with democratic society, or is there something inherent in them that requires implementation in an aristocracy, or perhaps a monarchy? Cicero himself, following the work of other thinkers of antiquity, most notably the historian Polybius, favored "a constitution blending all the three main reputable forms, monarchy, oligarchy and democracy." Grant, *supra*, at 7. Cicero was the greatest champion of the rule of law in republican Rome, but are his notions about duty and justice compatible with equality among the citizenry, at least in the sense the term is understood today? Who stands to gain the most from Cicero's ideas about law and duty? Who would be expected to be the losers? Are Cicero's ideas appropriate for twenty-first century America? Is there something deeply disturbing or missing from Cicero's conceptions of law, duty, and religion? Consider how some of Cicero's themes are developed in the reading from St. Augustine which follows.

4. Bethlehem

St. Augustine, The City of God, bk. XIX, chs. 23-28, at 889-94

. . . It follows that justice is found where God, the one supreme God, rules an obedient City according to his grace, forbidding sacrifice to any being save himself alone; and where in consequence the soul rules the body in all men who belong to this City and obey God, and the reason faithfully rules the vices in a lawful system of subordination; so that just as the individual righteous man lives on the basis of faith which is active in love, so the association, or people, of righteous men lives on the same basis of faith, active in love, the love with which a man loves God as God ought to be loved, and loves his neighbor as himself. But where this justice does not exist, there is certainly no "association of men united by a common sense of right and by a community of interest." Therefore there is no commonwealth; for where there is no "people," there is no "weal of the people."

24. An alternative definition of "people" and "commonwealth"

If, on the other hand, another definition than this is found for a "people," for example, if one should say, "A people is the association of a multitude of rational beings united by a common agreement on the objects of their love," then it follows that to observe the character of a particular people, we must examine the objects of its love. And yet, whatever those objects, if it is the association of a multitude not of animals but of rational beings, and is united by a common agreement about the objects of its love, then there is no absurdity in applying to it the title of a "people." And, obviously, the better the objects of this agreement, the better the people, the worse the objects of this love, the worse the people. By this definition of ours, the Roman people is a people and its estate is indubitably a commonwealth. But as for the objects of that people's love — both in the earliest times and in subsequent periods — and the morality of that people as it proceeded to bloody strife or parties and then to the social and civil wars, and corrupted and disrupted that very unity which is, as it were, the health of a people — for all this we have the witness of history . . . . For God is not the ruler of the city of the impious, because it disobeys his commandment that sacrifice should be offered to himself alone. The purpose of this law was that in that city the soul should rule over the body and reason over the vicious elements, in righteousness and faith. And because God does not rule there the general characteristics of that city is that it is devoid of true justice.

* * *

27. The peace of God's servants, a perfect tranquillity, not experienced in this life

* * *

. . . In this life, . . .justice in each individual exists when God rules and man obeys, when the mind rules the body and reason governs the vices even when they rebel, either by subduing them or by resisting them, while from God himself favor is sought for good deeds and pardon for offences, and thanks are duly offered to him for benefits received. But in that ultimate peace, to which this justice should be related, and for the attainment of which this justice is to be maintained, our nature will be healed by immortality and incorruption and will have no perverted elements, and nothing at all, in ourselves or any other, will be in conflict with any one of us. And so reason will not need to rule the vices, since there will be no vices, but God will hold sway over man, and the soul over the body, and in this state our delight and facility in obeying will be matched by our felicity in living and reigning. There, for each and every one, this state will be eternal, and its eternity will be assured; and for that reason the peace of this blessedness, or the blessedness of this peace, will be the Supreme Good.

28. The end of the wicked

In contrast with this, however, the wretchedness of those who do not belong to this City of God will be everlasting. This is called also "the second death," because the soul cannot be said to be alive in that state, when it is separated from the life of God, nor can the body, when it is subjected to eternal torments. And this is precisely the reason why this "second death" will be harder to bear, because it cannot come to an end in death. But here a question arises; for just as wretchedness is the opposite of blessedness, and death of life, so war is evidently the opposite of peace. And the question is rightly asked: What war, or what kind of war, can be understood to exist in the final state of the wicked, corresponding, by way of contrast, to that peace which is proclaimed with joyful praises in the final state of the good? Now anyone who puts this question should observe what it is that is harmful and destructive in war; and he will see that it is precisely the mutual opposition and conflict of the forces engaged. What war, then, can be imagined more serious and more bitter than a struggle in which the will is so at odds with the feelings and the feelings with the will, that their hostility cannot be ended by the victory of either — a struggle in which the violence of pain is in such conflict with the nature of the body that neither can yield to the other? For in this life, when such a conflict occurs, either pain wins, and death takes away feeling, or nature conquers, and health removes the pain. But in that other life, pain continues to torment, while nature lasts to feel the pain. Neither ceases to exist, lest the punishment should also cease.

These, then, are the final states of good and evil. The first we should seek to attain, the latter we should strive to escape. . . .

NOTES AND QUESTIONS

1. Aurelius Augustinus (354-430), known to us as St. Augustine, one of the greatest of the early Church fathers, was bishop of Hippo (in Roman North Africa) in 410, and he had a problem. On August 24 of that year, Alaric, the leader of the "barbarian" Goths, had sacked the "eternal city," Rome, thus signaling what looked like the collapse of the Roman Empire. Christianity had become the official religion of Rome by then, and many pagans (who still included among their number powerful senators and intellectuals) blamed Christianity for the empire's end. The pagans agitated for a return to paganism, and Augustine, perhaps the most brilliant intellectual among the Christians, responded with his masterpiece, a one-thousand page treatise, *Concerning the City of God against the Pagans* (usually simply called *The City of God*) from which the above excerpt is taken. The work is commonly accounted to be one of the great classics of political theory, and attains this status because it managed to build on the insights from Jerusalem, Greece, and Rome and integrate them with those of Bethlehem. In other words, Augustine constructed a charter for Christian government, and, in the process, moved the discussion of political and moral philosophy to a new level.

2. Your task at present is simply to seek to understand what the Christian dimension adds or subtracts from the teaching of Jerusalem, Greece, or Rome. Is Augustine's political vision one with which you find yourself in sympathy? Do you understand how Augustine's Christian conception of the imperfections of humankind could lead to the view that the state, while not an end in itself, was nevertheless a necessity, though not something to which one should give his or her complete and exclusive devotion? You will soon see how English and American theorists might use the essentially Christian conceptions both of the transcendent nature of humankind and of the limitations and imperfections of particular men and women in order to construct legal and constitutional traditions.

3. Augustine's view of the nature of the state and its contribution to the spiritual development of its citizens is not necessarily the only Christian approach to political theory, however. As you have seen, with Augustine the state almost seems little more than a necessary evil, a holding action designed to preserve men while they contemplate their real future, in the hereafter. A somewhat more beatific vision of the state is to be found in the work of that other great Christian theoretician, and champion of natural law, St. Thomas Aquinas (1225-74). As one of Aquinas' foremost expositors has explained:

> It is a mistake to think that government exists simply in order to keep the peace and punish evildoers. According to Aquinas, government would be required even if there were no evildoers and even if no one was inclined to break the peace. St. Augustine had been inclined to speak as though the State were a result of the Fall of man and as though political authority existed primarily because fallen human beings stand in need of a coercive power to restrain their evil tendencies and to punish crime. But this was not at all Aquinas's point of view. "Man is by nature a social animal. Hence in a state of innocence (if there had been no Fall) men would have lived in society. But a common social life of many individuals could not exist unless there were someone in control to attend to the common good." [Aquinas, *Summa Theologica* Ia, 96, 4.]

F.C. COPLESTON, AQUINAS 237 (1955). Moreover, for Aquinas, as was true for his mentor Aristotle, "the State possesses a positive function," which is to promote "the moral well-being of the citizens, so far as this can be done by legislation supported by sanctions, and to ensure them a sufficient supply of material necessities," in short to promote "the good life." *Id.* at 238.

It should be stressed, however, that Aquinas was also a firm believer in natural law, the principles which are discoverable by right reason, which are consistent with the moral betterment of humankind, and which come directly from God. The function of human positive law was "primarily to define clearly and support by temporal sanctions the natural law, in all cases at least where this is required by the public good." *Id.* at 239. Moreover, where human positive law ran counter to the natural law, it should be seen as the product of tyrants; it was not entitled to the respect of law, and it should not be obeyed. *See* Aquinas' *Summa Theologica*, Ia, IIae, 95, 2, and 96, 4. Indeed, if tyrants persist in enacting unjust laws they "can legitimately be deposed on the ground that they are guilty of abusing their position and power unless, indeed there is reason for thinking that rebellion would result in as bad a state of affairs as the one which it was designed to remedy." COPELSTON, *supra*, at 240. Compare these views of Aquinas' with what you will shortly read in Locke and the American Declaration of Independence. How much of our political tradition is based in the Christian statecraft of Aquinas and Augustine?

5. Alexis de Tocqueville, the greatest nineteenth-century observer of American social and political life, making an allusion to Augustine in his *Democracy in America*, but perhaps expressing views closer to that of Aquinas, thought that "The spirit of man, left to follow its bent, will regulate political society and the City of God in uniform fashion; it will, if I dare put it so, seek to *harmonize* earth with heaven." ALEXIS DE TOCQUEVILLE, DEMOCRACY IN AMERICA 265 (J.P. Mayer & Max Lerner eds. & George Lawrence trans., Harper & Row 1966) (1835). Tocqueville believed that Christianity in America "Powerfully Contributes to the Maintenance of a Democratic Republic Among the Americans." *Id.* (section heading).

Tocqueville argued that religion had both direct and indirect beneficial effects for America. Directly it prepared Americans to think of themselves as equal to each other because they were all equal in the sight of God, and indirectly it encouraged morality and restraint which facilitated good government. *Id.* at 267-71. In particular, Tocqueville noted that "Up till now [that is, in the 1830s] no one in the United States has dared to profess the maxim that everything is allowed in the interests of society, an impious maxim apparently invented in an age of freedom in order to legitimize every future tyrant." *Id.* at 269. Can you understand what Tocqueville means by an "impious maxim"? Is what he says still true today? If not, is a changed role of religion in American moral and political life responsible?

Tocqueville claimed that "For the Americans the ideas of Christianity and liberty are so completely mingled that it is almost impossible to get them to conceive of the one without the other." *Id.* at 270. Why do you suppose he believed that, and is it in accordance with modern American political thought? On this particular problem, see generally M. STANTON EVANS, THE THEME IS FREEDOM (1994), a modern study of the interconnection between liberty and religion. Tocqueville asked "How could society escape destruction if, when political ties are relaxed [for example, by revolution against a monarch] moral ties are not tightened? And what can be done with a people master of itself if it is not subject to God?" TOCQUEVILLE at 271. What would be your answer to Tocqueville? What would be Saint Augustine's?

6. Even though Tocqueville believed that Christianity and liberty were linked in America, he also thought that Americans were freer because they had no single state church. Indeed, he probably thought that, in America, it was an added strength to both Christianity and liberty that there were a number of "intermediate" associations, such as the family and the local church community, which helped inculcate a spirit of morality and liberty, which in turn helped, in the end, to promote democracy. You can see, then, that the problems addressed by Augustine, Aquinas, and Tocqueville, and in particular, the manner in which government ought to be either subject to or infused with law and morality are perennial ones. Indeed, they go back at least to the time of the New Testament, when St. Paul questioned the ultimate value of adhering to the law, at least as it bound the Hebrews to particular forms of ritual. For him, perhaps as for Augustine, the law was for restraining the unvirtuous, but for the truly worthy faith in God, a belief in salvation through Christ, and a disposition to love one's neighbour as oneself — to do unto others as one would be done by — were much more important than the strictures of the law. *See generally Acts* 13:38, 39; *Romans* 2, 3, 4:28-31; 1 *Corinthians* 6; *Galatians* 2-5; 1 *Timothy* 6-9. Paul's attitude toward the law, however, is very complex and possibily contradictory, so that these statements must be advanced with some trepidation. *See generally* E.P. SANDERS, PAUL 84-100, 131 (1991), and primary and secondary sources there cited.

7. When one is setting up or administering a government, however, one must take some sort of a position with regard to the extent religion or philosophy ought to be involved in the creation, promulgation, teaching, revision, or criticism of the law. We will next turn to one of the most vital test cases for our constitutional tradition, the experience of England in the seventeenth century, and, in particular, the reigns of the Stuart Kings and the English Civil War. Of particular importance to us, as we begin our inquiry, is that much thought was given in England to working out how the ideas of ancient and medieval thinkers ought to be applied in the English legal system. You will soon encounter an attempt by Bracton, the first great systematizer of the English common law, to reconcile the rule of law and the rule of God with contemporary monarchy, but you should understand that there were many attempts by scholars to combine theology with the law. To pick just one important example, Richard Hooker, in his *Of the Laws of Ecclesiastical Polity*, sought to reformulate Thomistic [referring to St. Thomas Aquinas] thought in the Church of England, in order better to understand and enforce the English common law. Hooker sought to demonstrate that we know the "law rational" through our natural reason, and that we use the "law positive" as an inevitable check upon human will, since reliance on morals and scripture alone will be insufficient to create civil society. To put Hooker's insights slightly differently, Hooker's conception of law included a strong Thomistic natural law component — he understood that there did exist an immutable, divinely-inspired law of God which bound humankind — but he also understood that human experience contributed to the building of a man-made legal order, in what we might regard as a progressive nature. With the Thomistic legal theory of Hooker, then, we have the seed of the common law tradition which you are about to explore.

B. The Late Middle Ages

The notion that ours is a government of laws, not men — the concept that is explored in this text — is thoroughly English in development, though not in origin. As we have seen, the antecedents to our form of this notion are to be found, among other places, in the Old and New Testaments, in the thought of the Greeks and Romans, and in the work of St. Augustine. Nevertheless, we need to spend some time considering the developments in the late middle ages, in England, of the ideas we have been observing at work in Jerusalem, Athens, Rome, and Europe. The first important English statement, for our purposes here, is Chapter 29 of the Magna Charta or "Great Charter," a series of promises extracted from a weak English King, John, by strong English nobles in 1215. Freely translated, that clause provided that:

> No freeman shall be arrested or imprisoned or dispossessed or outlawed or banished or in any way molested, nor will [the King proceed against] him, except by the lawful judgment of his peers, or by the law of the land.

This concession from John came almost one hundred and fifty years after the conquest of the unruly English by the Normans. It was part of an internecine struggle among Norman nobles, but the principle it established eventually affected everyone in the realm. Indeed, the idea of "the law of the land" was itself a fairly new one, as England could only be said to have a "common law," a law in use in all the English King's domain, from the reign of Henry II (1154-1189), the grandson of the original Norman conqueror, William I.

Henry II began to lay down the basis for a common law when he transformed many of his royal advisors into a cadre of professional lawyers, appointing several of them as staff members of a central court, known thereafter as the "Court of King's Bench." Henry also sent some of his judges out into the countryside, to bring royal justice to the provinces and to centralize and regularize the content of law. Once in the countryside, the royal justices summoned a group of locals to help them determine the facts involved in the disputes and prosecutions brought before them, and thus the institution which we know as the modern jury began to take form.

The precise content of the law that the King's judges would administer — the "common law," the law of all England purged of local idiosyncrasies — was presumed to be that which was already in use in the realm, and there were a few attempts at writing down what that law was. A cogent summary of the law was needed, however, so that new lawyers and judges could be more easily trained, and so that errant decisions could be avoided.

Before the reign of Henry II, during the so-called anarchy of Stephen, 1135-1154, might rather than right had ruled in England. During that period, there was no powerful central restraining force, so nothing prevented local magnates from oppressing their subjects or waging war against each other. Henry II, his central courts, his common law, and his traveling justices did much to solve that problem, but Henry's son Richard I, while popular, let the needs of the realm take second place to his desire to gain immortality in the Holy War against the Moslems in Jerusalem. When his brother, John, ruling in Richard's absence, tried to impose heavy taxes on his subjects in order to pay for defending the Crown's possessions in France, the country was plunged once again into a civil war, which ended only with the signing of the Magna Charta.

At about this time law began to be recognized as a university specialty at Oxford and Cambridge although, like other university subjects, it was taught as a branch of religious thinking by practitioners who were usually, if not exclusively, churchmen. The university-trained lawyers soon set up the "Inns of Court," communal dining and living arrangements close to the King's court, and these Inns became the focus of an increasingly influential legal profession. The lawyers appear to have sensed that by propagating and practicing a common law they were pursuing a special and noble mission to maintain stability in the realm. They also appear to have recognized that a strong royal authority was essential for this purpose.

The reading from Bracton, which follows, comes from this period and immediately precedes still another short civil war, waged by powerful barons against Henry III, John's son. The end of this war marked the beginnings of the establishment of the English Parliament, assembled by Simon de Montfort, a sort of dictator who ruled briefly before Henry III regained the throne. Edward I, the son of Henry III, extended the royal authority and created additional and even stronger central common law courts.

Bracton's treatise should be read as a statement of how law ought to govern in the hands of a strong monarch. Bracton and the common lawyers he represents did not contemplate an innovative legislature as part of their legal world; they were most concerned with preserving stability and order. It seems that Bracton could sense the troubles of the impending civil war between the King, Henry III, and the barons. It also appears that he hoped his statement of the law might strengthen the rule of the King and avoid some of the turmoil he feared. You will soon see, however, that whatever Bracton's purposes, and whatever limited success he achieved in his own time, his words and his vision of a legal order could be turned to rather different ends than royal ascendence.

1. Bracton

Henry de Bratton (1200?-1268), known by the Latinized version of his name, "Bracton," has been called "the flower and crown of English jurisprudence." Bracton's treatise, from which the following excerpt is taken, *De Legibus et Consuetudinibis Anglia* ("On the Laws and Customs of England"), is the progenitor of the modern Anglo-American legal culture. It is the first systematic exploration of the nature and sources of English law, and the issues it raises are still very much alive today. As indicated earlier, when Bracton wrote this treatise, at about the middle of the thirteenth century (he stopped work on the book in 1256), England was approaching a state of turmoil, and Bracton probably wanted to help alleviate the distress. At that time in English history the Church, which to this day remains an official or "established" Church, the state Church of England, was even more closely involved in secular affairs, and was still tied to Rome. Bracton, though a judge in the Royal Courts, was himself an ordained churchman, his career culminating with his appointment as Chancellor of Exeter Cathedral. Because of these strong ties to the Church, Bracton's jurisprudential efforts could not be completely severed from his religious obligations.

The following excerpt is from the beginning of the treatise, where Bracton seeks to discuss fundamental principles, the basics of the English legal system. As you will probably discern, these fundamentals may have owed as much to the law of Rome as they did to the law of England, and one of Bracton's greatest accomplishments was to buttress the English indigenous legal rules with the system and the authority of classical Roman law principles. As you read the excerpt, you should begin to determine how much of Bracton's jurisprudence is still valid in America today. What have we dropped from Bracton's ideas, and what have we kept?

1 BRACTON, ON THE LAWS AND CUSTOMS OF ENGLAND 19-28 (Samuel E. Thorne, ed. & trans.)

The needs of a king.

To rule well a king requires two things, arms and laws, that by them both times of war and of peace may rightly be ordered. For each stands in need of the other, that the achievement of arms be conserved [by the laws], the laws themselves preserved by the support of arms. . . .

. . . England alone uses unwritten law and custom. There law derives from nothing written [but] from what usage has approved. Nevertheless, it will not be absurd to call English laws *leges* [Latin for "laws," the statutes ostensibly approved by the Roman people], though they are unwritten, since whatever has been rightly decided and approved with the counsel and consent of the magnates and the general agreement of the *res publica* [literally "the public thing," the people acting together, what we will eventually know as "republic"], the authority of the king or prince having first been added thereto, has the force of law. . . .

* * *

Laws command and forbid.

[T]hese English laws and customs, by the authority of kings, sometimes command, sometimes forbid, sometimes castigate and punish offenders. Since they have been approved by the consent of those who use them and confirmed by the oath of kings, they cannot be changed without the common consent of all those by whose counsel and consent they were promulgated. They cannot be nullified without their consent, but may be changed for the better, for to change for the better is not to nullify. . . .

He who judges ought to be wise.

Let no one, unwise and unlearned, presume to ascend the seat of judgment, which is like unto the throne of God, lest for light he bring darkness and for darkness light, and, with unskilful hand, even as a madman, he put the innocent to the sword and set free the guilty, and lest he fall from on high, as from the throne of God, in attempting to fly before he has wings. And though one is fit to judge and to be made a judge, let each one take care for himself lest, by judging perversely and against the laws, because of prayer or price, for the advantage of a temporary and insignificant gain, he dare to bring upon himself sorrow and lamentation everlasting.

What the punishment for evil judging is.

And lest in the day of the wrath of the Lord he feel the vengeance of Him who said, "Vengeance is mine, I will repay," on that day when kings and princes of the earth shall weep and bewail when they behold the Son of Man, because of fear of his torments, where gold and silver will be of no avail to set them free. Who shall not fear that trial, where the Lord shall be the accuser, the advocate and the judge? . . . Who can escape his impending wrath? For the Son of Man shall send His angels and they shall gather out of His kingdom all things that offend and them that do iniquity and bind them bundles to be burnt, and shall cast them into the fiery furnace, where there will be wailing and gnashing of teeth . . . .

* * *

What law is and what custom.

. . . Law is a general command, the decision of judicious men, the restraint of offences knowingly or unwittingly committed, the general agreement of the *res publica*. . . . And though law (*lex*) may in the broadest sense be said to be everything that is read (*legitur*) its special meaning is a just sanction, ordering virtue and prohibiting its opposite. Custom, in truth, in regions where it is approved by the practice of those who use it, is sometimes observed as and takes the place of *lex*. For the authority of custom and long use is not slight.

What justice is.

Since from justice, as from a fountain-head, all rights arise and what justice commands *jus* ["the rights guaranteed by law"] is and whence it is so called and what its precepts are, and what law is and what custom, without which one cannot be just, so [laws and customs exist in order to] do justice and give just judgment between man and man. "Justice is the constant and unfailing will to give to each his right." . . .

* * *

What jurisprudence is.

Jurisprudence is the knowledge of things divine and human, the science of the just and the unjust. . . . Jurisprudence therefore differs in many ways from justice. For jurisprudence discerns, justice awards to each his due. Justice is a virtue, jurisprudence a science. Justice is a certain *summum bonum* ["a good end"], jurisprudence a *medium* ["a way to a good end"].

* * *

What private law is.

Private law is that which pertains primarily to the welfare of individual and secondarily to the *res publica*. Hence we say that it is in the public interest that no one misuse his own. And so conversely, that which is primarily public looks secondarily to the welfare of individuals. Private law has a threefold division: it is deduced partly from the rules of natural law, partly from those of the *jus gentium* ["the law of nations"] and partly from those of the civil law. We have spoken above of public law and private law. Now we must explain what natural law is, what the *jus gentium* is, and what civil law (which may sometimes be called custom) is. . . .

What natural law is.

Natural law is defined in many ways. It may first be said to denote a certain instinctive impulse arising out of animate nature by which individual living things are led to act in certain ways. Hence it is thus defined: Natural law is that which nature, that is, God himself, taught all living things. . . . On the other hand, it may be said that . . . Natural law is that taught all living things by nature, that is by natural instinct. . . . There are some who say that neither will nor impulse may be called *jus, jus naturale,* or *jus gentium,* for they exist in [the realm of] fact; will or impulse are the means by which natural law or justice disclose or manifest their effect, for virtues and *jura* ["rights"] exist in the soul. This perhaps is said more clearly, that natural law is a certain due which nature allows to each man. . . .

What the civil law is.

Civil law, which may be called customary law, has several meanings. It may be taken to mean the statute law of a particular city. Or for that kind of law which is not praetorian; it sometimes detracts from or supplements natural law or the *jus gentium,* for law different from that outside sometimes prevails in cities by force of custom approved by those who use it, since such custom ought to be observed as law. Civil law may also be called all the law used in a state [or the like], whether it is natural law, civil law or the *jus gentium.*

What the jus gentium *is.*

The *jus gentium* is the law which men of all nations use, which falls short of natural law since that is common to all animate things born on the earth, in the sea or in the air. From it comes the union of man and woman, entered into by the mutual consent of both, which is called marriage. . . . From that same law there also comes the procreation and rearing of children. The *jus gentium* is common to men alone, as religion observed toward God, the duty of submission to parents and country, or the right to repel violence and injuria. For it is by virtue of this law that whatever a man does in defence of his own person he is held to do lawfully; since nature makes us all in a sense akin to one another it follows that for one to attack another is forbidden.

. . . It was by virtue of this *jus gentium* that wars were introduced (that is, when declared by the prince for the defence of his country or to repel an attack) and nations separated, kingdoms established and rights of ownership distinguished. . . . By the *jus gentium* boundaries were set to holdings, buildings erected next to one another, from which cities, boroughs and vills were formed. And generally, the *jus gentium* is the source of all contracts and of many other things. . . .

NOTES AND QUESTIONS

1. How can the law be changed, according to Bracton, and who is supposed to do the changing? Is it the job, for example, of the judges to make law? Indeed, is it the job of any human beings to change the law?

2. What prompted Bracton to write his treatise? What does Bracton say will happen to those who render an "evil" judgment? If this is so, do we really need legal treatises? Why do you suppose Bracton feels the need to tell us, in such gripping detail, what the terrors of the Judgment Day and Hell are like? Is this the stuff you would expect to find in a modern legal treatise? Why or why not? Should it be included?

3. What is the purpose of law, according to Bracton? What does Bracton mean when he speaks of the "right" of each person? Is this what you mean when you use the term?

4. Does Bracton believe that there is any difference between public and private law? Does Bracton believe that the law should refrain from enforcing religion, as seems to be the current belief among most American law professors and judges today? Why wouldn't Bracton share this belief? Note that Bracton draws distinctions between natural law, the jus gentium and civil law. Are all of these bodies of law in force in America today? Would you want them to be?

5. Bracton's treatise was very widely circulated among lawyers and judges of Bracton's time, and it remained influential for centuries. The use of the treatise, however, may not always have been in a manner which Bracton would have sanctioned. Consider, for example, its use by Sir Edward Coke, in the excerpt which follows.

2. Sir Edward Coke and James I

The years between publication of Bracton's book and the episode with which the next reading is concerned, the battle over the extent of the Stuart Kings' discretionary powers (the royal prerogative), were some of the most turbulent in all of English history. This was the time of the Black Death, when half the population of England perished from the plague. This was also the period of the "Hundred Years War" against France. Following that foreign adventure were the civil "Wars of the Roses," which decimated the English nobility, as rival clans fought for the throne. Towards the end of this period was the English Reformation, marked by the virtual tyranny of Henry VIII, who broke with the Roman church in order to marry the second of what was eventually to be six wives. Following Henry's Protestant reign, his daughter Mary, known thereafter as "Bloody Mary," married the King of Spain, reinstated Roman Catholicism as the state religion, burned more than 300 Protestants at the stake, and insured a reaction which would make religious discord a pressing political problem for the next century.

When Mary died, the Protestant Elizabeth, Henry VIII's gifted daughter, became Queen and reigned over perhaps the most glorious period yet in English history. During her reign, England won a long war against Spain by defeating the Spanish Armada. English literature flowered with Bacon, Shakespeare, Donne, and a score of others, and a reinvigorated Parliament and the common lawyers helped Elizabeth build a potent administrative machine and lay the foundation for a successful colonial empire. We pick up the story of the law five years after Elizabeth's death, in 1603. Elizabeth, the beloved Virgin Queen, died without a husband or heir, and the English throne passed to Elizabeth's cousin, the Scottish King, James VI, who became James I of England.

James I, the first of the ill-fated English Stuart line, was an effective monarch and brought peace to the realm, but he also sought to govern through an expanded use of the Royal prerogative (governing through his handpicked officials, and without consulting the representatives of the people), and with less reliance on the Parliament. He was aided in his efforts by his Archbishop and his Chancellors, the highest officials of what were called the "prerogative courts." We are concerned with two of these, the courts of Ecclesiastical High Commission (the Church courts), and the Chancery, which was the English analogue to the Roman praetor's court, alluded to by Bracton. In Chancery, as was true of the praetor's court, the strict rules and precedents of the "law" courts (in England these "law" or "common law" courts came to include the Court of King's Bench, the Court of Common Pleas, and the Exchequer) could be ameliorated or, in some cases ignored. The Judges of the King's prerogative courts conceived their task as one of administering "justice," or "equity," whether or not this corresponded strictly with pre-existing legal rules. In many instances, however, the judges of the prerogative courts may have conceived of "equity" or "justice" rather more narrowly, simply as what was necessary to meet the policy needs of the monarch.

The judges of the common law courts, by contrast, and in accordance with the teaching of Bracton and others, saw themselves as bound by the accumulated precedents, which they believed reflected the customs and consent of the English people, as well as the law of nature and nature's God. They too saw themselves as in the business of dispensing "justice," but their conception of "justice" was bottomed on adhering to the rules formerly laid down.

The fact that James and his ministers came to be more and more dependent on the use of the prerogative courts, in order to bypass the common law courts, did not sit well with the common lawyers, particularly Sir Edward Coke, who had formerly been first Elizabeth's and then James' attorney general, and who had become the Chief Justice of the Court of Common Pleas, the common law court concerned principally with matters of property. Believing that the prerogative courts were improperly administering the law and that they were in particular wrongly encroaching on the jurisdiction of his court, Coke took measures to restrain the High Commission, the Chancery, and the other prerogative courts. He did this by issuing "prohibitions" — written orders (issued in the name of the King, but under Coke's authority) — from his court forbidding other courts to hear particular matters.

When Coke issued prohibitions against the Courts of High Commission and Chancery, the King, not unexpectedly, took this to be an affront to the throne and summoned Coke and the common law judges to the Royal presence to explain themselves. The following excerpt is Coke's report on what happened at that meeting:

Prohibitions Del Rey ["Prohibitions of the King"], 12 Co. Rep. 63 (1609)

[U]pon Sunday the 10th of November . . . the King, upon complaint made to him by Bancroft, Archbishop of Canterbury, concerning Prohibitions, the King was informed, that when the Question was made of what Matters the ecclesiastical Judges [of the Court of High Commission] have cognizance, either upon the Expositions of the Statutes concerning Tithes, or any other Thing Ecclesiastical, or upon the Statute I Elizabeth concerning the High Commission, or in any other Case in which there is not express Authority in Law, the King himself may decide it in his Royal person, and that the Judges are but the Delegates of the King, and that the King may take what Causes he shall please to Determine from the Determination of the Judges, and may determine them himself. And the Archbishop said, that this was clear in Divinity, that such Authority belongs to the King by the Word of God in the Scriptures.

To which it was answered by me, in the Presence, and with the clear Consent of all the Justices of England . . . that the King in his own Person cannot adjudge any Case, either criminal, as Treason, Felony, etc. or betwixt party and party, concerning his Inheritance, Chattels, or Goods, etc. but this ought to be determined and adjudged in some Court of Justice, according to the law and Custom of England, and always Judgments are given, *Ideo consideratrum est per Curium*, ["Therefore it has been considered by the court"], so that the Court gives the Judgment: And the King hath his court, viz. in the upper House of Parliament, in which he with his Lords is the Supreme Judge over all other Judges; for if Error be in the Common Pleas, that may be reversed in the King's Bench: And if the court of King's Bench err, that may be reversed in the upper House of Parliament, by the King, with the Assent of the Lords Spiritual and Temporal, without the Commons: And in this respect the King is called the Chief Justice . . . . And the King cannot arrest any Man, . . . for the Party cannot have Remedy against the King, so if the King give any Judgment, what Remedy can the Party have? Vide ["See, for example," the case to be found in one of the reports from the time of Edward III] 39 Ed. 3. 14. One who had a Judgment reversed before the Council of State; it was held utterly void, for that it was not a Place where Judgment may be reversed. Huffey, Chief Justice, who was Attorney to Ed. 4. reports that Sir John Markham, Chief Justice, said to King Ed. 4. that the King cannot arrest a Man for Suspicion of Treason or Felony, as others of his Lieges may; for that if it be a Wrong to the Party grieved, he can have no Remedy.

. . . Man shall be put to answer without Presentment before the Justices, Matter of Record, or by due Process, or by Writ Original, according to the Ancient Law of the Land: And if any Thing be done against it, it shall be void in Law and held for Error. [In the reign of Edward III,] a controversy of Land between parties was heard by the King, and Sentence given, which was repealed, for this, that it did not belong to the Common Law.

Then the King said, that he thought the Law was founded upon Reason, and that he and others had Reason, as well as the Judges: to which it was answered by me, that true it was, that God had endowed his Majesty with excellent Science, and great Endowments of nature; but his majesty was not learned in the Laws of his Realm of England, and Causes which concern the Life, or Inheritance, or Goods, or fortunes of his Subjects, are not to be decided by natural Reason, but by the artificial Reason and Judgment of Law, which Law is an Art which requires long Study and Experience, before that a Man can attain to the Cognizance of it; and that the Law was the Golden met-want and Measure to try the Causes of the Subjects; and which protected his Majesty in Safety and

Peace: With which the King was greatly offended, and said, that then he should be under the Law, which was Treason to affirm, as he said; to which I said that Bracton saith, *Quod rex non debet esse sub homine, sed sub Deo & Lege.* ["The King should not be under any man, but is under God and the Law."]

NOTES AND QUESTIONS

1. There are many things that interest us in Coke's confrontation with James I, but the first must be Coke's use of Magna Charta and Bracton to support his position. You will have seen that Coke's principal assertion is that the King should leave matters of determining the law to his common law judges.

The Archbishop (and several other advisors of the King) had supported James' belief that he could make final legal determinations for himself, that, indeed he was above the law and was therefore not bound by previous legal precedents. This is suggested, for example, by the longstanding English legal rule that "the King can do no wrong," which is invoked to forbid private causes of action, *e.g.,* for illegal arrest, to be brought against the King himself, though such actions could be and occasionally were brought against the King's agents or officers. How would Bracton, acting as a judge, have decided this dispute between Coke and James I over whether final decisions about the law must be made only by judges or could also be made by the King?

You ought to be able to formulate an answer considering what you have read of Bracton so far, but a little more Bracton might be helpful in deciding. The passage from which Coke quotes at the end of his report, is, more or less in its entirety, as follows:

> The king has no equal within his realm nor *a fortiori* ["even more obviously"] a superior, because he would then be subject to those subjected to him. The king must not be under man but under God and under the law, because law makes the king, for there is no *rex* ["king"] where will rules rather than *lex* ["law"]. Since he is the vicar of God, there ought to be no one in his kingdom who surpasses him in the doing of justice, but he ought to be the last, or almost so, to receive it, when he is plaintiff. If it is asked of him, since no writ ["legal cause of action; court proceeding"] runs against him there will [only] be opportunity for a petition ["a request made to the King"], that he correct and amend his act; if he does not, it is punishment enough for him that he await God's vengeance. No one may presume to question his acts, much less contravene them.

2 Thorne's translation of Bracton, *supra,* at 33. Somewhat later in his treatise, Bracton ruminated on whether private persons could question the acts of Kings. This is what he concluded:

> Private persons cannot question the acts of kings, nor ought the justices to discuss the meaning of royal charters: not even if a doubt arises in

them may they resolve it; even as to ambiguities and uncertainties, as where a phrase is open to two meanings, the interpretation and pleasure of the lord king must be awaited, since it is for him who establishes to explain his deed. And even if the document is completely false, because of an erasure or because the seal affixed is a forgery, it is better and safer that the case proceed before the king himself.

2 Thorne's translation of Bracton, *supra*, at 109. Does Coke's use of Bracton, then, seem correct?

2. Coke lost the battle with James I, when the King decided to follow the advice of the Archbishop, and not that of the common lawyers. Soon after, when Coke refused to cease issuing prohibitions against the prerogative courts, he was fired from his job (the King had the power to remove judges at that time), demonstrating that, in the end, the English common law judges could not then restrain the King. Somewhat later, however, Coke mended his fences with the King and became a Privy Councillor to James, one of a group of his most important advisors. James' ideas about the supremacy of Kings were passed on to his son Charles I, however, and Coke soon found himself embroiled in controversy with that monarch, as we will see in the next reading.

The theatre of conflict between the King and those who sought to restrain him, however, had by then shifted from the common law courts to the Halls of Parliament, just beginning to assume its modern role as a maker of new law.

C. The First English Revolution

James I wasn't a very popular King, but the accomplishments of his reign were considerable. In addition to settling the war with Spain, James allowed arts and letters to flourish in his Kingdom. He was a patron of Shakespeare, who produced some of his great tragedies during this period, and James sponsored the preparation of the King James Version of the Bible, perhaps the most magnificent work of English prose ever accomplished.

The ultimate political achievements of James' reign are more problematic. While James eventually made his peace with Coke, he was less successful with Parliament. Elizabeth had "flattered her Commons," as one of Coke's biographers, Catherine Drinker Bowen, wrote, but James viewed Parliaments as "recurrent trials" laid on him, believing, as you have seen (and as Bracton might have suggested), that he possessed a Divine Right to determine policy for the realm.

James believed that it was Parliament's job simply to ratify and to create an environment favorable for the collection of revenue James needed to administer and protect the Kingdom. Unfortunately, the nobility, country gentry, lawyers, and wealthy merchants, who were beginning to comprise Parliament, were not disposed readily to tax themselves for what they perceived as James' benefit. For ten years, from 1611 to 1620, James governed without Parliament, raising his funds principally from duties on imports. When he finally did call another session, Parliament attempted to interfere with James' plans to marry his son, Charles, to a Catholic Spanish princess. Soon thereafter, and as James' reign drew to an end, England entered into another war with Spain, which ended with some devastating losses for England.

After the war, James' son, the new King, Charles I, ascended the throne. Charles was no more adept at dealing with Parliaments than James had been, and although Charles shared his father's adherence to the Stuart principles of the Divine Right of Kings and the King's paramount power to make policy, Charles lacked his father's judgment and shrewd intelligence. Charles received bad advice from incompetent courtiers and embroiled himself in wars waged by incapable commanders against both Spain and France.

Charles, who had Catholic sympathies, persecuted the "Puritans," who sought to liberalize and "purify" the Anglican Church, particularly of its "Popish" features. Parliament had been falling increasingly into the hands of the Puritans, and as that happened, what had begun as a purely political opposition to the King in a struggle for power over taxes turned, for many Parliamentarians, into a divine mission.

Unable to obtain funds from Parliament, Charles embarked on a program of forced loans from the wealthy, interference with local governments, and, through resort to martial law, the imprisonment of those who failed to pay his forced loans, and other acts of persecution. Unfortunately for Charles, even these measures failed to bring in the necessary revenues to redress his military and naval failures, so in 1628 he called another Parliament to request new taxes. Before Parliament would cooperate with him, however, the two Houses of Parliament, pursuant to a compromise worked out by Sir Edward Coke between the upper House, the Lords (the hereditary great nobles of the realm, including members of the Royal family, descendants of the Norman conquerors, and assorted others ennobled by the Kings, as well as the Bishops of the Church) and the lower house, the Commons (the elected representatives of the property-holders of the towns and counties) required Charles to assent to the "Petition of Right," of 1628, which you will soon read.

The House of Commons, further flexing its muscles, proceeded to pass resolutions against Charles' policies, exceeding the formerly limited scope of that House's jurisdiction. Charles responded by imprisoning three of the Commons' leading members. Charles then dissolved Parliament and proceeded to raise revenue for the next eleven years by reviving old import taxes and by selling positions in the English nobility. Charles also condoned the continued persecution of Puritans by his Archbishop, Laud, leading many Puritans to flee to Holland and from thence to America, where they not only founded New England, but planted there a deep fear of absolute Stuart-style rule. Charles' efforts to impose religious orthodoxy on the Scots resulted in a damaging rebellion, and he was once again forced to summon Parliament to help pay the costs of the settlement of that debacle.

A small militant Puritan majority of Parliament, believing that it ought to be their job to make new policy for the realm, passed bills abolishing the offices of the Bishops, the aristocratic leaders of the Church of England, and demanding further reforms in the Church. When the Commons then sought to consider a bill stripping the Command of the nation's armed forces from the King and transferring it to Parliament, the King, believing that the House of Lords would support him, tried to arrest the leaders of the Commons, but they fled to the haven of their supporters in the City of London. Believing that he was now in grave danger, Charles himself fled from his Palace of Westminster to neighboring London, and the first full-scale English civil war began.

Charles' supporters, the "Cavaliers," were the Catholics, the Bishops, most of the members of the Nobility in the House of Lords, and many country gentry. The Parliamentary forces, the "Roundheads," were primarily Puritans, members of the House of Commons, and inhabitants of the great cities, particularly London. The King's forces prevailed for the first two years of the war, but then Parliament allied itself with the Scots, and, with the advantage of easier funding, Parliament's "new model army" under Oliver Cromwell prevailed with the King's surrender in 1645.

The King, who was still allowed to reign, persisted in his attempts to undermine Parliament, eventually persuading the Scots, his family's original subjects, to join him in the Second Civil War against Cromwell and Parliament's Army. Again, however, the King was defeated, and by now Cromwell and the Puritans were firmly in control of the country. They purged the Parliament of the Presbyterians who had sympathized with the King, abolished the House of Lords, put the King on Trail for Treason, and, on January 30, 1649, put him to death.

The readings in this section explore the "constitutional" and legal aspects of the tumultuous political and military events just described. First, you will read a statement by James I, on the nature of the Divine Right of Kings, which his son, Charles I, seems to have adopted in practice. Second you will read the "Five Knights Case," the record of the prosecution of some who resisted Charles' attempt to tax without Parliament's approval. Next, you'll examine the Petition of Right of 1628, the compromise between King and Parliament effected by Coke, and, finally, you'll explore some documents relating to the trial of the King for treason.

Your task while reading these materials is twofold: (1) to determine whether your sympathies lie with Charles I or with the regicides (are you a "Cavalier" or a "Roundhead"?), and (2) to determine the nature of the different models of a constitutional order which Charles and his antagonists used. You should pay particular attention to the role Charles and his antagonists assigned to Parliament. You will remember that the question we closed our last section with was "Who could check an arbitrary King if not his judges?" Could Parliament serve that function?

1. James I on Monarchy

James I, *Speech to Parliament* (Mar. 21, 1610), *in* THE STUART CONSTITUTION 12-14 (Kenyon, ed.)

The state of monarchy is the supremest thing upon earth; for kings are not only God's lieutenants upon earth, and sit upon God's throne, but even by God himself they are called gods. There be three principal similitudes that illustrate the state of monarchy: one taken out of the word of God, and the two other out of the grounds of policy and philosophy. In the Scriptures kings are called gods, and so their powers after a certain relation compared to the divine power. Kings are also compared to fathers of families, for the king is truly *parens patriae* ("parent of the fatherland"), the political father of his people. And lastly, kings are compared to the head of this microcosm of the body of man.

Kings are justly called gods for that they exercise a manner or resemblance of divine power upon earth, for if you will consider the attributes to God you shall see how they agree in the person of a king. God hath power to create or destroy, make or unmake, at his pleasure; to give life or send death, to judge all and to be judged not accountable to none: to raise low things and to make high things low at his pleasure; and to God are both soul and body due. And the like power have kings: they make and unmake their subjects: they have power of raising, and casting down; of life, and of death, judges over all their subjects, and in all causes, and yet accountable to none but God only. They have power to exalt low things, and abase high things, and make of their subjects like men at the chess — a pawn to take a bishop or a knight . . . . And to the king is due both the affection of the soul and the service of the body of his subjects . . . .

* * *

. . . [I]n the first original of kings, whereof some had their beginning by conquest, and some by election of the people, their wills at that time served for law, yet how soon kingdoms began to be settled in civility and policy, then did kings set down their minds by laws, which are properly made by the king only, but at the rogation [request] of the people, the king's grant being obtained thereunto. And so the king came to be *lex loquens* ["the law speaking"], after a sort, binding himself by a double oath to the observation of the fundamental laws of the kingdom: tacitly as by being a king, and so found to protect as well the people as the laws of his kingdom; and expressly, by his oath at his coronation. So, as every just king in a settled kingdom is bound to observe that paction [agreement] made to his people by his laws, in framing his government agreeable thereto, according to that paction with God made with Noah after the deluge, "Hereafter seed time and harvest, cold and heat, summer and winter, and day and night shall not cease, so long as the earth remains;" and therefore a king governing in a settled kingdom leaves to be a king, and degenerates into a tyrant, as soon as he leaves off to rule according to his laws . . . . As for my part, I thank God I have ever given good proof that I never had intention to the contrary, and I am sure to go to my grave with that reputation and comfort, that never king was in all his time more careful to have his laws duly observed, and himself to govern thereafter, than I.

I conclude then this point touching the power of kings with this axiom of Divinity, that as to dispute what God may do is blasphemy, but *quid vult Deus* ["what the will of God is"] that divines [churchmen] may lawfully and do ordinarily dispute and discuss, for to dispute *a posse ad esse* ["that anything that is possible might exist"] is both against logic and divinity; so is it sedition in subjects to dispute what a king may do in the height of his power, but just kings will ever be willing to declare what they will do, if they will not incur the curse of God. I will not be content that my power be disputed upon, but I shall ever be willing to make the reason appear of all my doings, and rule my actions according to my laws.

2. The Five Knights' Case

THE FIVE KNIGHTS' CASE
3 How. S.T. 1 (K.B. 1627), *reprinted in* KENYON,
THE STUART CONSTITUTION 106-109

[Letter from the Privy Council (the King's advisors), November 7, 1627, to the Warden of the Fleet (a jailor), on a writ of habeas corpus from King's Bench. This is a proceeding to establish the lawfulness of the detention of Sir Walter Earl and the other four Knights, his colleagues from the House of Commons.] Whereas Sir Walter Earl, Knight, was heretofore committed to your custody, [this letter is] to will and require you still to detain him, letting you know that both his first commitment and this direction for the continuance of him in prison were and are by his Majesty's special commandment.

[Argument of Sergeant Bramton, November 22, 1627, a lawyer for the defendants, against the King's order of detention, referred to in the November 7 letter.] If this [order from the King] shall be good [found to be lawful], than his imprisonment shall not continue on for a time, but for ever; and the subjects of this kingdom may be restrained of their liberties perpetually, and by law there can be no remedy for the subject: and therefore this [order from the King] cannot stand with the laws of the realm or that of Magna Charta, or with the statute of 28 Edw. 3, c. 3; for if a man be not bailable [that is, able to put up bail money and be released, as the five Knights sought to do in the proceeding] . . . they cannot have the benefit of these two laws, which are the inheritance of the subject . . . . We are not to reflect upon the present time and government, where justice and mercy floweth, but we are to look what may betide us in the time to come, hereafter.

[John Selden, November 22. Another lawyer appearing for the defense to argue against the King's action.] Now, my Lord, I will speak a word or two to the matter [of this letter from the Privy Council, purporting to act on the authority of the King,] that is [I will speak about] . . . the [practice of] imprisonment *per speciale mandatum domini regis* ["by the special mandate of the Lord King"] by the Lords of the Council, without any cause expressed. . . .

The statute of Magna Charta, c. 29, that statute [which] if it were fully executed as it ought to be, every man would enjoy his liberty better than he doth . . . out of the very body of this Act of Parliament, besides the explanation of other statutes, it appears, *nullus liber homo capiatur vel imprisonetur nisi per legem terrae.* ["No man's liberty shall be taken away except by the law of the land"]. My Lords, I know these words, *legem terrae* ["law of the land"] do leave the question where it was, if the interpretation of the statute were not. But I think, under your Lordships' favour, there it must be intended, by "due course of law," to be either by presentiment or by indictment [by formal legal proceedings, charging a specific crime, and not merely by the order of Royal officials without specifying the offense]. My Lords, if the meaning of these words *per legem terre* were but, as we used to say, "according to the law," which leaves the matter very uncertain; and [if] *per speciale mandatum* etc. be within the meaning of these words "according to law," then this Act [of Parliament, that is the statute 28 Edw. 3, c. 3] had done nothing.

* * *

[Lord Chief Justice Hyde, the presiding judge, referred to above as "My Lord," or "Your Lordship" by the advocates, November 28, deciding the case:] . . . I am sure you expect justice from hence, and God forbid we should sit here but to do justice to all men according to our best skill and knowledge, for it is our oaths and duties so to do, and I am sure there is nothing else expected of us. We are sworn to maintain all prerogatives of the King, that is one branch of our oath; and we are likewise sworn to administer justice equally to all people.

. . . That which is now to be judged by us is this: whether one that is committed by the King's authority, and no cause declared of his commitment, according as here it is upon this return, whether we ought to deliver him by bail, or to remand him back again? [Send him back to jail.]

[Lord Chief Justice Hyde then discussed in detail a number of cases in favor of the crown, ending with a declaration by the judges in 1592, upholding similar authority in the King to that which was exercised in the Five Knights' Case.]

. . . You see what hath been the practice in all the Kings' times heretofore, and your own records, and this resolution of the judges teacheth us; and what can we do but walk in the steps of our forefathers? . . . If in justice we ought to deliver you, we would do it. But upon these grounds, and these records, and the precedents and resolutions, we cannot deliver you, but you must be remanded.

NOTES AND QUESTIONS

1. The basic issue in the Five Knights' Case, as you have probably determined, is whether the proceedings of Charles' officials violated the Magna Charta and the statute 28 Edward III, c. 3, a statute similarly worded to Chapter 29 of Magna Charta, which forbids interference with the liberty of a subject except according to the law of the land. Specifically, the question in the case was whether it was permissible for the King to order (through the acts of his officers) someone's imprisonment himself, instead of letting the prosecutors or grand jury initiate proceedings against a wrongdoer that would eventually result in a trial of that person. The Five Knights were several prominent landowners who refused to contribute to the King's forced loan. Charles I felt that their action in refusing to contribute when their sovereign so requested was clearly criminal, and in order to coerce them into cooperation, or to punish them, he ordered their imprisonment. His order of imprisonment, however, specified no reasons why the Five Knights were to be incarcerated. The Knights then sought from the King's Bench what is called a *writ of habeas corpus*, which is an order compelling the prison officials to declare by what legal authority they hold the bodies of their prisoners ["habeas corpus"]. The writ was granted by the Court of King's Bench, which led to the necessity of a "return" to that writ, that is that the jailors (or the King's officials) explain by what authority the prisoners were held. The "return" was the first part of this excerpt, the Letter from the King's Council to the Warden of the Fleet, which gave as a justification for the imprisonment of the Five Knights the simple fact that they were held by order of the King.

2. The next paragraphs, the arguments by Bramston and Seldon, question whether the "return," that is the Letter from the Council, with its sole justification that the prisoners were held by order of the King, is sufficient in law. Attorney General Heath argued that the return was perfectly sufficient and that someone imprisoned by an order of the King is not eligible to post bail and be released.

3. The final part of the excerpt is the opinion of Lord Chief Justice Hyde, settling the arguments. For whom does he rule? Do you find anything in James I's speech to parliament, the excerpt which precedes this one, that supports the ruling of Lord Chief Justice Hyde or the argument of Attorney General Heath? Chief Justice Hyde appears to believe that all the precedents were against the Five Knights, and also that "justice" did not require their release. Would Bracton agree? Do you?

4. Following the King's victory in the Five Knights' Case, the King, as you have read, was forced to agree to the Petitition of Right of 1628, as the price of securing more funding from Parliament. How much, if any, of the Stuart theory of the Divine Right of Kings and of the philosophy of government that led Chief Justice Hyde to rule for the King in the Five Knights' Case can be said to survive the Petition of Right of 1628? Was it a salutary measure?

3. Petition of Right (1628)

The petition exhibited to his Majesty by the Lords Spiritual and Temporal and Commons in this present Parliament assembled, concerning divers rights and liberties of the subjects, with the King's Majesty's Royal answer thereunto in Full Parliament.

To the King's most excellent Majesty:

Humbly show unto our sovereign lord the King, the Lords Spiritual and Temporal and Commons in Parliament assembled, that whereas it is declared and enacted by a statute made in the time of the reign of King Edward the First . . . [that no tax] should be laid or levied by the King or his heirs in this realm without the good will and assent of the archbishops, bishops, earls, barons, knights, burgesses, and other freemen of the commonality of this realm, and by authority of Parliament holden in the five-and-twentieth year of the reign of King Edward the Third, it is declared and enacted that from henceforth no person should be compelled to make any loans to the King against his will because such loans were against reason and the franchise of the land; and . . . [thus by virtue of] the statutes before mentioned and other the good laws and statutes of this realm, your subjects have inherited this freedom that they should not be compelled to contribute to any tax, tallage, aid, or other like charge not set by common consent in Parliament.

Yet nevertheless of late, divers commissions directed to sundry commissioners in several counties with instructions have issued, by means whereof your people have been in divers places assembled and required to lend certain sums of money unto your Majesty; and many of them, upon their refusal so to do, have had an oath administered unto them not warrantable by the laws or statutes of this realm and have been constrained to become bound to make appearance and give attendance before your Privy Council and in other places; and others of them have been therefore imprisoned, confined, and sundry other ways molested and disquieted; and divers other charges have been laid and levied upon your people in several counties by lord lieutenants, deputy lieutenants, commissioners for ministers, justices of peace, and others by command or direction from your Majesty or your Privy Council against the laws and free customs of the realm.

And were also, by the statute called the Great Charter of the Liberties of England [Magna Charta], it is declared and enacted that no freeman may be taken or imprisoned or be disseised of his freehold or liberties or his free customs or be outlawed or exiled or in any manner destroyed, but by the lawful judgment of his peers or by the law of the land.

And in the eight-and-twentieth year of the reign of King Edward the Third, it was declared and enacted by authority of Parliament that no man, of what estate or condition that he be, should be put out of his land or tenements nor taken nor imprisoned nor disinherited nor put to death without being brought to answer by due process of law.

Nevertheless against the tenor of the said statutes and other the good laws and statutes of your realm to that end provided, divers of your subjects have of late been imprisoned without any cause showed; and when for their deliverance they were brought before your justices by your Majesty's writs of habeas corpus, there to undergo and receive as the court should order, and their keepers commanded to certify the cause of their detainer, no cause was certified, by that they were detained by your majesty's special command, signified by the lords of your Privy Council, and yet were returned back to several prisons without being charged with anything to which they might make answer according to the law.

And whereas of late, great companies of soldiers and mariners have been dispersed into divers counties of the realm, and the inhabitants against their wills have been compelled to receive them into their houses, and there to suffer them to sojourn against the laws and customs of this realm and to the great grievance and vexation of the people.

And whereas also by authority of Parliament in the five-and-twentieth year of the reign of King Edward the Third, it is declared and enacted that no man should be forejudged of life or limb against the form of the Great Charter and the law of the land; and by the said Great Charter and other the laws and statutes of this your realm, no man ought to be adjudged to death by the laws established in this your realm, either by the customs of the same realm or by act of Parliament.

And whereas no offender of what kind soever is exempted from the proceedings to be used and punishments to be inflicted by the laws and statutes of this your realm, nevertheless of late time, divers commissions under your Majesty's great seal have issued forth, by which certain persons have been assigned and appointed commissioners with power and authority to proceed within the land according to the justice of martial law against such soldiers or mariners or other dissolute persons joining with them as should commit any murder, robbery, felony, mutiny, or other outrage or misdemeanour whatsoever, and by such summary course and order as is agreeable to martial law and as is used in armies in time of war to proceed to the trial and condemnation of such offenders, and then to cause to be executed and put to death according to the law martial. By pretext whereof some of your Majesty's subjects have been by some of the said commissioners put to death, when and where, if by the laws and statutes of the land they had deserved death, by the same laws and statutes also they might, and by no other ought to have been, judged and executed.

And also sundry grievous offenders, by color thereof claiming an exemption, have escaped the punishments due to them by the laws and statutes of this your realm, by reason that divers of your officers and ministers of justice have unjustly refused or forborne to proceed against such offenders according to the same laws and statutes, upon pretence that the said offenders were punishable only by martial law and by authority of such commissions as aforesaid. Which commissions and all others of like nature are wholly and directly contrary to the said laws and statutes of this your realm.

They do therefore humbly pray your most excellent Majesty, that no man hereafter be compelled to make or yield any gift, loan, benevolence, tax, or such like charge without common consent by act of Parliament; and that none be called to make answer or take such oath or to give attendance or be confined or otherwise molested or disquieted concerning the same or for refusal thereof; and that no freeman, in any such manner as is before mentioned, be imprisoned or detained; and that your Majesty would be pleased to remove the said soldiers and mariners, and that your people may not be so burdened in time to come; and that the aforesaid commissions for proceeding by martial law may be revoked and annulled; and that hereafter no commissions of like nature may issue forth to any person or persons whatsoever to be executed as aforesaid, lest by color of them any of your Majesty's subjects be destroyed or put to death contrary to the laws and franchise of the land.

All which they most humbly pray of your most excellent Majesty as their rights and liberties according to the laws and statutes of his realm, and that your Majesty would also vouchsafe to declare that the awards, doings, and proceedings, to the prejudice of your people in any of the premises shall not be drawn hereafter into consequence or example.

And that your Majesty would be also graciously pleased for the further comfort and safety of your people to declare your royal will and pleasure that in the things aforesaid all your officers and ministers shall serve you according to the laws and statutes of this realm as they tender the honor of your Majesty and the prosperity of this kingdom.

NOTES AND QUESTIONS

1. There was a lot of art used in the compromise that resulted in both the House of Lords and the House of Commons agreeing to place this "Petition" before the King. It was cast in the form not of a statute, but of a petition, such as any private citizen might make for a grievance perceived or a request that the laws be observed. The House of Lords was reluctant to subscribe to a statute setting forth these matters, and, in any event, the King's agreement to a statute would be necessary before it had any force at all. The Petition, however, did represent a formal statement of the wishes of both houses of Parliament. Does the Petition purport to make new law? Is it consistent with the opinion in the Five Knights' Case, or with James I's statement about the Divine Right of Kings?

2. Charles assented to the Petition on June 7, 1628, probably in large part because the Petition purported simply to state the existing law, which he believed he accepted, and over which he simply differed in interpretation. Still, by the Petition he did promise not to impose taxes without Parliament's assent.

During the eleven years from 1629 to 1640, when Parliament did not meet, however, Charles did continue to collect customs duties on wine and wool without the consent of Parliament, and he seems to have paid relatively little attention to other strictures in the Petition. His virtual ignoring of the Petition explains how he could end up tried for treason, following the war between his forces and those of Parliament.

4. The Events Leading up to Civil War and Charles I's Trial

As you have probably guessed from reading the Five Knights' case, the judges interpreted the law in the late 1620s and all through the 1630s in a manner most favourable to the King's prerogative and in a way that would seem consistent with Bracton. It may have had some bearing on the jurisprudence of the judges that they were still removable by the King, but it is also true, as the judges soon discovered, that they could be removed by Parliament. Before Parliament attacked Charles' judges in the 1640s, however, the English judiciary upheld the King's attempts to condemn those who frustrated his efforts to collect taxes and to conduct military operations.

In the meantime, some of the leaders in Parliament became worried that Charles' Archbishop, Laud, was seeking to return the English state church to Roman Catholicism, and thus, in their view, to subject the English state to domination by the Pope. Such critics of Charles were also alarmed by Charles' costly military policies and concerned about his military acumen. Often the best manner to begin an attack on a leader is to first get at his or her advisors. Accordingly, the Parliament "impeached," that is, brought charges of misconduct against, Charles' principal minister, the Earl of Strafford. Strafford was removed and executed by a "Bill of Attainder," a statute directing punishment against a particular individual because such is the wish of the legislature, a process obviously subject to abuse, and which was later forbidden by the American Constitution.

The King was also forced to agree to a number of other reforms, including the abolition of the Court of Star Chamber, one of the prerogative courts, a court where criminals were tried without following some of the niceties of criminal law procedure and where torture had been routinely used in the time of the Tudors. In addition, several of the other prerogative courts, including the Court of Ecclesiastical High Commission, which Coke despised, were abolished. Even before these measures, Charles had agreed to the Triennial Act, which guaranteed that a Parliament would be called and held every three years. Parliament also forced Charles to accede to a provision which took away his power to suspend or adjourn Parliament, thus removing one of the formerly most vital parts of the prerogative. Charles became convinced that Parliament was out to strip him of virtually all power, which he believed that Parliament itself intended to usurp.

Charles' worst nightmares were confirmed some years later by a resolution of the Commons, on January 4, 1649, which provided that:

> The Commons of England, in Parliament assembled, do declare, That the People are, under God, the original of all just power. And do also declare, that the commons of England, in Parliament assembled, being chose by, and representing the people, have the Supreme Power in this nation. And do also declare, That whatsoever is enacted, or declared for law, by the Commons in Parliament assembled, hath the force of a law; and all the people of this nation are concluded thereby, although the consent and concurrence of a king, or house of peers, be not had thereunto.

If Charles believed that the Parliament was out to usurp his powers, his fears were more than matched by the belief of many members of Parliament that the King and the Archbishop were engaged in a "Popish plot," to sell the nation, body and soul, to Rome. This belief was at its height in 1641 when the opposition to the King in Parliament claimed the right to dictate which councillors could and could not serve the King, in effect claiming for Parliament the right completely to control the exercise of executive power in the realm.

In October 1641, while the King was in Edinburgh trying to settle the Scottish War, worry and agitation in Parliament peaked. On Parliament's order, troops were dispersed to guard Westminster, the seat of Parliament, and when the King sought to raise an army to quell a rebellion in Ireland, many members of Parliament asserted that the King was no longer fit to lead the army nor to appoint its general.

The Commons informed the King on 8 November 1641 that if he refused to change his policies and his advisors, they themselves would supervise the quelling of the Irish rebellion. This was a clearly revolutionary proposition that sought, in effect, to end the King's role as commander-in-chief of the military might of the nation. At about this time, London and Westminster were wracked by riots of the unemployed, and rumors abounded that Charles and his officers were planning a military *coup d'etat* to crush Parliament once and for all. The House of Lords, which had until then been looked to by the King as his last bastion of Parliamentary supporters, also seemed to be moving away from the King and toward the views of his critics.

Believing that it was time to strike before the Parliament removed the vestiges of the prerogative that remained, on 4 January 1642, the King and a group of "gentlemen volunteers" burst into the House of Commons in an effort to arrest the Commons' leaders on charges of endeavoring "to subvert the fundamental laws and government of the Kingdom." Do you understand what they meant by these "fundamental laws"? Can you point to comparable "fundamental laws" in our country?

Unfortunately for Charles, the Parliamentary leaders had been warned, and had already fled. Worse yet, Parliament saw Charles' attempt to arrest its leaders as a violation of the historic privilege of its members against arrest while in session and as an attempt to silence its voice by force of arms. This incident was used to turn the population of London against the King, and the King himself was forced to flee from London on 10 January. For about a year, Charles and Parliament jockeyed for support, and Charles refused to give in to Parliament's demand that he surrender control of the army and give up other parts of his prerogative.   Most historians have concluded that the King had the better of what was, essentially, a constitutional debate. Do you agree? Still, the Parliament had command over more resources. In the seven years of armed conflict which followed, both sides believed that only the force of arms could settle the issue of fundamental law involved. In the end Charles *was* beaten militarily, but was he ever defeated constitutionally?

We next consider the legal and political moves that led up to his beheading, and your job is to follow the constitutional arguments involved. England had no written constitution in the sense that we do — that is, one authoritative written document — although the Magna Charta and other documents, such as the 1628 Petition of Right, were thought of as contributing to the "Constitution" or "Fundamental Laws" of the realm. In particular, your job is to determine whether the basic charge against Charles, that he committed treason by waging war against Parliament, is correct. Certainly his troops did engage in battle with those of the House of Commons after the House of Commons had "unconstitutionally" been purged of Charles' supporters by Oliver Cromwell's Puritans, who then controlled the House. How *could* Charles defend himself, then, against the charge of waging war?

In answering this question, consider first the Ordinance for the Trial of the King, passed by the Commons on 2 January 1649, and then the arguments in the House of Lords on that Ordinance from 3 COBBETT'S PARLIAMENTARY HISTORY, at 1253, 1255:

a. Ordinance for the Trial of the King

Whereas it is notorious that Charles Stuart, the now king of England, not content with the many encroachments which his predecessors had made upon the people in their rights and freedom, hath had a wicked design totally to subvert the ancient and fundamental laws and liberties of this nation, and in their place to introduce an arbitrary and tyrannical government; and that, besides all other evil ways and means to bring his design to pass, he hath prosecuted a civil war in the land, against the parliament and Kingdom; whereby this country hath been miserably wasted, the public treasure exhausted, trade decayed, thousands of people murdered, and infinite other mischiefs committed; for all which high and treasonable offences the said Charles Stuart might long since have justly been brought to exemplary and condign punishment; whereas also the parliament, well hoping that the restraint and imprisonment of his person, after it had pleased God to deliver him into their hands, would have quitted the distempers of the kingdom, did forbear to proceed judicially against him; but found, by said experience, that such their remissness served only to encourage him and his accomplices in the continuance of their evil practices and in raising new commotions, rebellions, and invasions;

For prevention therefore of the like or greater inconveniences, and to the end no other chief officer or magistrate whatsoever may hereafter presume, traitorously and maliciously, to imagine or contrive the enslaving or destroying of the English nation, and to expect impunity for so doing; be it enacted and ordained by the [Lords] and commons in Parliament assembled, and it is hereby enacted and ordained by the authority thereof, that the earls of Kent, Nottingham, Pembroke, Denbigh, and Ulgrave; the lord Guy of Warke, lord chief justice Rolle of the king's bench, lord chief justice St. John of the common Pleas, and lord chief baron Wylde [of the Exchequer]; the lord Fairfax, lieut. General Cromwell, &c. [in all about 150] shall be, and hereby appointed and required to be, Commissioners and Judges, for the Hearing, Trying, and Judging of the said Charles Stuart;

And the said Commissioners, or any 20 or more of them, shall be, and are hereby authorized and constituted an High Court of Justice, to meet and sit at such convenient times and place as by the said commissioners, or the major part, or 20 or more of them, under their hands and seals, shall be appointed and notified by public Proclamation in the Great Hall, or Palace yard of Westminster; and to adjourn from time to time, and from place to place, as the said High Court, or the major part thereof, at meeting shall hold fit; and to take order for the charging of him, the said Charles Stuart, with the Crimes and Treasons above-mentioned, and for receiving his personal Answer thereunto, and for examination of witnesses upon oath (which the court hath hereby authority to administer) or otherwise, and taking any other Evidence concerning the same and thereupon, or in default of such Answer, to proceed to final Sentence according to justice and the merit of the cause; and such final Sentence to execute, or cause to be executed, speedily and impartially.

And the said court is hereby authorized and required to chuse and appoint all such officers, attendants, and other circumstances as they, or the major part of them, shall in any sort judge necessary or useful for the orderly and good managing of the premises; and Thomas Lord Fairfax the General, and all officers and soldiers, under his command, and all officers of justice, and other well-affected persons, are hereby authorized and required to be aiding and assisting unto the said court in the due execution of the trust hereby committed unto them; provided that this act, and the authority hereby granted, do continue in force for the space of one month from the date of the making hereof and no longer. . . .

b. Arguments in the House of Lords on the Ordinance for the Trial of the King

Upon this occasion a great debate ensued upon the question, "Whether it be Treason, by the fundamental laws, for the king of England to levy war against the parliament of England?" The earl of Manchester shewed, "that, by the fundamental laws of England, the parliament consists of 3 estates, of which the king is the first: That he, only, hath power to call and dissolve them, and to confirm all their acts, and that without him there can be no parliament; and therefore it was absurd to say, 'The King can be a Traitor against the Parliament.'" His lordship was seconded by the earl of Northumberland, who said, "that the greatest part, even 20 of 1 of the people of England, were not yet satisfied whether the king did levy war against the houses first, or the houses first against him. And besides, if the king did levy war first, they had no law extant, or that could be produced, to make it Treason in him so to do; and for us," said he, "my lords, to declare it Treason by an Ordinance, when the matter of fact is not yet proved, nor any law in being to judge it by, seems to me very unreasonable." The earl of Pembroke swore, "He loved not to meddle with businesses of life and death; and, for his part, he would neither speak against the ordinance [to prosecute the King for treason], nor consent to it." And the earl of Denbeigh declared, that whereas the commons were pleased to put his name into the Ordinance, as one of the commissioners for trying his majesty, he would "chuse to be torn in pieces, rather than have any share in so infamous a business." At length the Question being put, Whether the said Ordinance, now read, should be cast out [rejected]? It was resolved in the affirmative.

The Lords [had thus] voted in the majority against it, and this is how the commons reacted. Sir James Harrington, sir Henry Mildmay, sir Peter Wentworth, Mr. Scott, and some others, so much resented the lords rejecting the Ordinance for Trial of the King, that they insisted upon impeaching such of them as were present upon that Occasion, of High Treason, and favourers of the Grand Delinquent of England, and enemies to the public justice and the liberty of the people: but this was overruled. However, the commons resolved "That the several members of their house and others, appointed by the Orders and Ordinances of parliament to act in any Ordinance wherein the Lords are joined, be empowered and enjoined to sit, act, and execute the said several committees of themselves, notwithstanding the lords will not join with them." After this, a Committee was appointed to draw up another Ordinance for erecting a High Court of Justice for the Trial of the King; in which the names of the six peers [members of the House of Lords] and the three judges [the Chief Justices of the King's Bench, the Court of Common Pleas, and the Exchequer] were left out.

Your final readings on Charles I and his Constitutional beliefs are the beginning of his trial, as taken down in a contemporary report, and a summary of the entire trial from an eighteenth century historian, as printed in the early nineteenth century Parliamentary history.

c. *A Perfect Narrative of the Whole Proceedings of the High Court of Justice, in the Trial of the King, in Westminster-Hall.* **With the Several Speeches of the King, Lord President, and Solicitor General. Published by Authority, to prevent false and impertinent Relations. January 20-27. A.D. 1649. Licensed by Gilbert Mabbot, 4 How. S.T. 993 (1816)**

On Saturday, being the 20th day of January 1649, the Lord President of the High Court of Justice, with near fourscore of the members of the said court, marching before them, came to the place ordered to be prepared for their sitting at the west-end of the great Hall of Westminster; where the Lord President, in a crimson velvet chair, fixed in the midst of the Court, placed himself, having a desk with a crimson-velvet cushion before him; the rest of the members placing themselves on each side of him upon several seats, or benches, prepared and hung with scarlet for that purpose; and the partizans dividing themselves on each side of the court before them.

The Court being thus sat, and Silence made, the great gate of the said Hall was set open, to the end that all persons, without exception, desirous to see or hear, might come into it, Upon which the Hall was presently filled, and silence again ordered.

This done, colonel Thomlinson, who had the charge of the Prisoner [King Charles] was commanded to bring him to the court; who within a quarter of an hour's space brought him, attended with about twenty officers with partizans, marching before him, there being other gentlemen, to whose care and custody he was likewise committed, marching in his rear.

Being thus brought up within the face of the Court, the sergeant at Arms, with his mace receives and conducts him strait to the bar, having a crimson-velvet chair set before him. After a stern looking upon the court, and the people in the Galleries on each side of him, he places himself, not at all moving his hat, or otherwise showing the least respect to the court; but presently rises up again, and turns about, looking downwards upon the guards placed on the left side, and on the multitude of spectators on the right side of the said great Hall. After silence made among the people, the Act of Parliament for the trying of Charles Stuart, king of England, was read over by the Clerk of the court, who sat on one side of a table covered with a rich Turkey-carpet, and placed at the feet of the said Lord-President; upon which table was also laid the sword and mace.

After reading the said Act, the several names of the Commissioners were called over, everyone who was present, being eighty, as aforesaid, rising up, and answering to his call.

Having again placed himself in his Chair, with his face towards the Court, silence being again ordered, the Lord President stood up, and said,

Lord President. Charles Stuart, king of England, the Commons of England assembled in parliament being deeply sensible of the calamities that have been brought upon this nation, which is fixed upon you as the principal author of it, have resolved to make inquisition for blood; and according to that debt and duty they owe to justice, to God, the kingdom, and themselves, they have resolved to bring you to Trial and Judgement; and for that purpose have constituted this High Court of Justice, before which you are brought.

This said, Mr. Cook, Solicitor [lawyer] for the Common-wealth, standing within a bar on the right hand of the Prisoner, offered to speak; but the king having a staff in his hand, held it up and laid it upon the said Mr. Cook's shoulder two or three times, bidding him hold. Nevertheless the Lord President ordering him to go on, he said:

Mr. Cook. My lord, I am commanded to charge Charles Stuart, King of England, in the name of the Commons of England, with Treason and High Misdemeanours; I desire the said Charge may be read.

The said Charge being delivered to the Clerk of the Court, the Lord President ordered it should be read; but the king bid him hold. Nevertheless, being commanded by the Lord President to read it, the Clerk began, and the Prisoner sat down again in his chair, looking sometimes on the High Court, sometimes up to the Galleries; and having risen again, and turned about to behold the guards and spectators, sat down, looking very sternly, and with a countenance not at all moved, till these words, viz. "Charles Stuart to be a Tyrant and Traitor," &c. were read; at which he laughed, as he sat, in the face of the Court.

The Charge being read, the Lord President replied:

Lord President. Sir, You have now heard your Charge, containing such matter as appears in it; you find, that in the close of it, it is prayed to the Court, in the behalf of the Commons of England, that you answer to your Charge. The court expects your Answer.

King. I would know by what power I am called hither; I was not long ago in the Isle of Wight [where he was imprisoned by Parliamentary forces]; how I came there, is a longer story than I think it fit at this present time for me to speak of; but there I entered into a Treaty with both houses of parliament, with as much public faith as it is possible to be had of any people in the world. I treated there with a number of honourable lords and gentlemen, and treated honestly and uprightly;

I cannot say but they did very nobly with me, we were upon the conclusion of the Treaty. Now I would know by what authority, I mean lawful; there are many unlawful authorities in the world, thieves and robbers by the highways; but I would know by what authority I was brought from thence, and carried from place to place, and I know not what; and when I know what lawful authority, I shall answer. Remember I am your king, your lawful king, and what sins you bring upon your head, and the judgement of God upon this land; think well upon it, I say, think well upon it, before you go further from one sin to a greater; therefore let me know by what lawful authority I am seated here, and I shall not be unwilling to answer. In the mean time, I shall not betray my trust; I have a trust committed to me by God, by old and lawful descent; I will not betray it, to answer to a new unlawful authority; therefore resolve me that, and you shall hear more of me.

Lord President. If you had been pleased to have observed what was hinted to you by the Court, at your first coming hither, you would have known by what authority; which authority requires you, in the name of the people of England, of which you are elected king, to answer them.

King. No, Sir, I deny that.

Lord President. If you acknowledge not the authority of the Court, they must proceed.

King. I do tell them so; England was never an elective kingdom, but an hereditary kingdom for near these thousand years; therefore let me know by what authority I am called hither: I do stand more for the Liberty of my people, than any here that come to be my pretended Judges; and therefore let me know by what lawful authority I am seated here, and I will answer it; otherwise I will not answer it.

Ld. President. Sir, how really you have managed your trust, is known; your way of answer is to interrogate the Court, which beseems not you in this condition. You have been told of it twice or thrice.

King. Here is a gentleman, lieutenant Colonel Cobbet; ask him, if he did not bring me from the Isle of Wight by force. I do not come here as submitting to the Court: I will stand as much for the privilege of the house of commons, rightly understood, as any man here whatsoever. I see no house of lords here that may constitute a parliament; and the king too should have been. Is this the bringing of the king to his parliament? Is this the bringing an end to the Treaty in the public faith of the world? Let me see a legal authority warranted by the Word of God, the Scriptures, or warranted by the Constitutions of the kingdom, and I will answer.

Ld. President. Sir; You have propounded a question, and have been answered. Seeing you will not answer, the Court will consider how to proceed: in the mean time, those that brought you hither, are to take charge of you back again. The Court desires to know, whether this be all the Answer you will give, or no.

King. Sir, I desire that you would give me, and all the world satisfaction in this: let me tell you, it is not a slight thing you are about. I am sworn to keep the peace, by that duty I owe to God and my country, and I will do it to the last breath of my body; and therefore you shall do well to satisfy first God, and then the country, by what authority you do it: if you do it by an usurped authority, you cannot answer. There is a God in Heaven, that will call you, and all that give you power, to account. Satisfy me in that, and I will answer; otherwise I betray my Trust, and the Liberties of the people: and therefore think of that, and then I shall be willing. For I do avow, that it is as great a sin to withstand lawful authority, as it is to submit to a tyrannical, or any other ways unlawful authority; and therefore satisfy me that, and you shall receive my answer.

Ld. President. The Court expects you should give them a final Answer; their purpose is to adjourn to Monday next; if you do not satisfy yourself, though we tell you our authority, we are satisfied with our authority, and it is upon God's authority and the Kingdom's; and that peace you speak of will be kept in the doing of justice, and that is our present work.

King. For answer, let me tell you, you have shown no legal authority to satisfy any reasonable man.

Ld. President. That is, in your apprehension; we are satisfied that are your Judges.

King. It is not my apprehension, nor yours neither, that ought to decide it.

Ld. President. The Court hath heard you, and you are to be disposed of as they have commanded.

The Court adjourns to the Painted Chamber, on Monday at ten of the clock in the forenoon, and thence hither.

It is to be observed that as the Charge was reading against the king, the head of his staff fell off, which he wondered at; and seeing none to take it up, he stoops for it himself.

As the King went away, facing the Court, he said, "I do not fear that." (meaning the Sword). The People in the Hall, as he went down the stairs, cried out, some "God save the King," and most for "Justice."

d. The Trial of Charles I, *in* HUME, A HISTORY OF ENGLAND 154-62 *reprinted in* 2 COBBETT'S PARLIAMENTARY HISTORY OF ENGLAND 1260 (1808)

[T]he high court of justice consisted of 113 persons as named by the commons; but there scarcely ever sat above 70: so difficult was it, notwithstanding the blindness of prejudice and the allurements of interest, to engage men of any name or character in that criminal measure. Cromwell, Ireton, Harrison, and the chief officers of the army, most of them of mean birth [that is, not aristocrats], were members, together with some of the lower house; and some citizens of London. The twelve judges [of the common law courts] were at first appointed in the number; but as they had affirmed, that it was contrary to all the ideas of English law to try the king for treason, by whose authority all accusations for treason must necessarily be conducted; their names, as well as those of some peers, were afterwards struck out. Bradshaw, a lawyer, was chosen president

["Lord President" in the prior reading], Coke [not Sir Edward, who died some years before] was appointed solicitor for the people of England. . . .

It is remarkable, that in calling over the court, when the crier pronounced the name of Fairfax, which had been inserted in the number, a voice came from one of the spectators, and cried "he has more wit than to be here." When the charge was read against the king, "in the name of the people of England," the same voice exclaimed, "Not a tenth part of them." Axtel the officer, who guarded the court, giving orders to fire into the box whence these insolent speeches came; it was discovered that lady Fairfax [Lord Fairfax's wife] was there, and that it was she who had the courage to utter them. She was a person of noble extraction, daughter of Horace, Lord Vere of Tilbury; but being seduced by the violence of the times, she had long seconded her husband's zeal against the royal cause, and was now, as well as he, struck with abhorrence at the fatal and unexpected consequences of all his boasted victories.

The pomp, the dignity, the ceremony of this transaction corresponded to the greatest conception that is suggested in the annals of human kind; the delegates of a great people, sitting in judgement upon their supreme magistrate, and trying him for his misgovernment and breach of trust. The solicitor, in the name of the commons, represented that Charles Stuart, being admitted king of England, and entrusted with a limited power; yet nevertheless, from a wicked design to erect an unlimited and tyrannical government, had traitorously and maliciously levied war against the present parliament, and the people whom they represented, and was therefore impeached as a tyrant, traitor, murderer, and a public and implacable enemy to the commonwealth.

After the charge was finished, the president directed to the king, and told him, that the court expected his answer. The king, though long detained a prisoner, and now produced as a criminal, sustained, by his magnanimous courage, the majesty of a monarch. With great temper and dignity, he declined the authority of the court, and refused to submit himself to their jurisdiction.

He represented "That having been engaged in treaty with his two houses of parliament, and having finished almost every article, he had expected to be brought to his capital in another manner, and ere this time, to have been restored to his power, dignity, revenue, as well as to his personal liberty: that he could not now perceive any appearance of the upper house, so essential a member of the constitution; and had learned, that even the commons, whose authority was pretended, were subdued by lawless force, and were bereaved of their liberty; that he himself was their Native Hereditary King: nor was the whole authority of the state, though free and united entitled to try him, who derived his dignity from the Supreme Majesty of Heaven:

[He also stated] that, admitting those extravagant principles which levelled all orders of men, the court could plead no power delegated by the people; unless the consent of every individual, down to the meanest and most ignorant peasant, had been previously asked and obtained; that he acknowledged without scruple, that he had a trust committed to him, and one most sacred and invio-lable; he was entrusted with the liberties of his people, and would not now betray them, by recognizing a power founded on the most atrocious violence and usurpation: that having taken arms, and frequently exposed his life in defence of public liberty, of the constitution, of the fundamental laws of the kingdom, he was willing, in this last and most solemn scene, to seal with his blood those pre-cious rights of which, though in vain, he had so long contended; that those who arrogated a title to sit as his judges, were born his subjects, and born subjects to those laws, which determined, "that the king can do no wrong;" that he was not reduced to the necessity of sheltering himself under this general maxim, which guards every English monarch, even the least deserving; but was able, by the most satisfactory reasons, to justify those measures in which he had been engaged: that, to the whole world, and even to them, his pretended judges, he was desirous, if called upon in another manner, to prove the integrity of his con-duct and assert the justice of those defensive arms, to which, unwillingly and unfortunately, he had had recourse; but that, in order to preserve a uniformity of conduct, he must at present forego the apology of his innocence; lest by rati-fying an authority, no better founded than that of robbers and pirates, to be justly branded as the betrayer, instead of being applauded as the martyr of the constitution."

The president, in order to support the majesty of the people, and maintain the superiority of his court above the prisoner, still [stated], "that he must not decline the authority of his judges; that they over-ruled his objections; that they were delegated by the people, the only source of every lawful power; and that kings themselves acted but in trust from the community, which had invested this high court of justice with its jurisdiction, even according to those principles, which in his present situation he was perhaps obliged to adopt, his behaviour in general will appear not a little harsh and barbarous; but when we consider him as a subject, and one too of no high character, addressing himself to his unfortunate sovereign, his style will be esteemed, to the last degree, audacious and insolent."

Three times was Charles produced before the court, and as often declined their jurisdiction. On the fourth the judges having examined some witnesses, by whom it was proved that the king had appeared in arms against the forces commissioned by the Parliament; they pronounced sentence against him. He seemed very anxious at this time, to be admitted to a conference with the two houses; and it was supposed, that he intended to resign the crown to his son; but the court refused compliance (27th Jan.) and considered that request as noth-ing but a delay of justice.

It is confessed that the King's behaviour, during this last scene of his life, does honor to his memory; and that, in all appearances before his judges, he never forgot his part, either as a prince or as a man. Firm and intrepid, he maintained, in each reply the utmost perspicuity and justness both of thought and expression: mild and equable, he rose into no passion at that unusual authority which was assumed over him.

His soul, without effort or affectation, seemed only to remain in the situation familiar to it, and to look down with contempt on all the efforts of human malice and iniquity. The soldiers, instigated by their superiors, were brought, though with difficulty, to cry aloud for justice: "Poor souls!" said the king to one of his attendants; "for a little money they would do as much against their commanders." Some of them were permitted to go the utmost length of brutal insolence, and to spit in his face as he was conducted along the passage to the court. To excite a sentiment of piety was the only effect which this inhuman insult was able to produce upon him.

The people, though under the rod of lawless, unlimited power, could not forbear, with the most ardent prayers, pouring forth their wishes for his preservation; and, in his present distress, they avowed him, by their generous tears, for their monarch, whom, in their misguided fury, they had before so violently rejected. The king was softened at this moving scene, and expressed his gratitude for their dutiful affection. One soldier too, seized by contagious sympathy, demanded from heaven a blessing on oppressed and fallen majesty: his officer, overhearing the prayer, beat him to the ground in the king's presence. "The punishment, methinks, exceeds the offence": this was the reflection which Charles formed on that occasion.

Three days were allowed the king between his sentence and his execution. This interval he passed with great tranquillity, chiefly in reading and devolution [attending to the disposition of his property among his heirs]. All his family that remained in England were allowed access to him. It consisted only of the princess Elizabeth and the Duke of Gloucester; for the Duke of York had made his escape. Gloucester [the king's third son, after Charles, then Prince of Wales, and later Charles II, and James, then Duke of York and later James II] was little more than an infant; the princess, notwithstanding her tender years, shewed an advanced judgement; and the calamities of her family had made a deep impression upon her.

After many pious consolations and advices, the king gave her in charge to tell the queen, that during the whole course of his life, he had never once, even in thought, failed in his fidelity towards her; and that his conjugal tenderness and his life should have an equal duration. To the young duke too, he could not forbear giving some advice, in order to season his mind with early principles of loyalty and obedience towards his brother [the future Charles II], who was soon to be his sovereign. Holding him on his knee, he said "Now they will cut off thy Father's head." At these words the child looked very steadfastly upon him. "Mark, child! What I say: they will cut off my head! And perhaps make thee a king; but mark what I say, thou must not be a king, as long as thy brothers Charles and James are alive. They will cut off thy brothers' heads, when they can catch them! And thy head too they will cut off at last: therefore I charge thee, do not be made a king by them!"

The duke, sighing, replied, "I will be torn in pieces first!" So determined an answer, from one of such tender years, filled the king's eyes with tears of joy and admiration. Every night, during this interval, the king slept sound as usual; though the noise of workmen, employed in framing the scaffold, and other preparations for his execution, continually resounded in his ears. The morning of the fatal day (30th Jan.) he rose early; and calling Herbert, one of his attendants, he bade him employ more than usual care in dressing him, and preparing him for so great and joyful a solemnity. Bishop Juxon, a man endowed with the same mild and steady virtues by which the king himself was so much distinguished, assisted him in his devotions, and paid the last melancholy duties to his friend and sovereign.

The street before Whitehall was the place destined for the execution: for it was intended by choosing that very place, in sight of his own palace, to display more evidently the triumph of popular justice over royal majesty. When the king came upon the scaffold, he found it so surrounded with soldiers, that he could not expect to be heard by any of the people: he addressed, therefore, his discourse to the few persons who were about him; particularly Colonel Tomlinson, to whose care he had lately been committed, and upon whom, as upon many others, his amiable deportment had wrought an entire conversion.

He justified his own innocence in the late fatal wars, and observed, that he had not taken arms till after the parliament had enlisted forces; nor had he any other object in his warlike operations, than to preserve that authority entire, which his predecessors had transmitted to him. He threw not, however, the blame upon the parliament; but was more inclined to think that ill instruments had interposed and raised in them fears and jealousies with regard to his intentions.

Though innocent towards his people, he acknowledged the equity of his execution in the eyes of his Maker; and observed that an unjust sentence which he had suffered to take effect, was now punished by an unjust sentence upon himself. He forgave all his enemies, even the chief instruments of his death; but exhorted them and the whole nation to return to the ways of peace, by paying obedience to their lawful sovereign, his son and successor.

When he was preparing himself for the block, bishop Juxon called to him: "There is, sir, but one stage more, which though turbulent and troublesome, is yet a very short one. Consider it will soon carry you a great way; it will carry you from earth to heaven; and there you shall find, to your great joy, the prize to which you hasten, a crown of glory." "I go," replied the king, "from a corruptible to an incorruptible crown; where no disturbance can have place."

At one blow was his head severed from his body. A man in a visor performed the office of executioner: another, in a like disguise, held up to the spectators the head streaming with blood, and cried aloud, "This is the head of a traitor."

A fresh instance of hypocrisy was displayed the very day of the king's death. The generous Fairfax, not content with being absent from the trial, had used all the interest which he yet retained, to prevent the execution of the fatal sentence; and had even employed persuasion with his own regiment, though none else would follow him, to rescue the king from his disloyal murderers. Cromwell and Ireton, informed of this intention, endeavoured to convince him, that the Lord had rejected the king; and they exhorted him to seek by prayer some direction from heaven on this important occasion: but they concealed from him that they had already signed the warrant for the execution.

Harrison was the person appointed to join in prayer with the unwary general [Fairfax]. By agreement he prolonged his doleful cant, till intelligence arrived, that the fatal blow was struck. He then rose from his knees, and insisted with Fairfax, that this event was a miraculous and providential answer, which heaven had sent to their devout supplications.

It being remarked, that the king, the moment before he stretched out his neck to the executioner, had said to Juxon, with a very earnest accent, the single word, "Remember" — great mysteries were supposed to be concealed under that expression; and the generals vehemently insisted with the prelate, that he should inform them of the king's meaning. Juxon told them, that the king, having frequently charged him to inculcate on his son the forgiveness of his murderers, had taken this opportunity, in the last moment of his life, when his commands, he supposed, would be regarded as sacred and inviolable, to reiterate that desire; and that his mild spirit thus terminated its present course, by an act of benevolence towards his greatest enemies.

NOTES AND QUESTIONS

1. As you have seen, one of the last acts of the House of Commons before Charles' execution was to declare that it alone had the right to act in the name of and with the power of the English people. Following Charles' execution, the House of Lords, the upper House of Parliament, was abolished altogether. It was restored, along with the monarchy in 1660, but with whom do you agree, those who wanted to abolish or those who wished to maintain the House of Lords? Note that England still maintains this institution today, although virtually all new Peers (members of the House of Lords) are now created as Life Peers, with tenure during their lives, but without the ability to pass membership in the Lords along to their heirs after they have died. Nevertheless, many of the ancient noble families of England still exist, and they are still permitted to pass down their hereditary peerages. Why would anyone want an hereditary House of Lords? Where does this idea of "nobility" come from? Is it healthy? Do you suppose it has anything to do with the principle that "the King can do no wrong"?

2. It is extremely difficult to sort out the political intrigue that led up to the trial and execution of Charles. Following his defeat in the first civil war, and his surrender to the Scots, he apparently reached some sort of a deal with Parliament, which is the "treaty" of which he speaks in his testimony which you have read. Pursuant to this settlement, in 1647, the King was to accept the establishment of Presbyterianism, then the religion of a majority of the House of Commons, also the religion of Scotland (and one which rejected the "Popish" trappings of Laud) as a national religion for a period of three years. The army was to be disbanded, and presumably, some sort of monarchy could continue.

Unfortunately, Parliament soon found itself at odds with the Army, the proposed settlement fell apart, and the Army, as Charles points out in his trial, seized him. Charles proceeded to ask for different terms with the Army, at the same time negotiating with the Scots, in a subtle but dangerous attempt to play his enemies off against each other. With the encouragement of the Scots, in November of 1647, Charles escaped from the Army and fled to the Isle of Wight, where he signed an agreement with the Scots to again impose Presbyterianism on England. This led to the second Civil War, and Charles' decisive defeat by Fairfax's and Cromwell's "New Model Army." Parliament and the Army proceeded, as indicated earlier, to purge those members sympathetic to the King, Cromwell refused to make any further deals, and the machinery for regicide was set in motion.

Cromwell in particular had become convinced that Charles was a "Man of Blood," and Cromwell is reported to have stated even before Charles' trial took place, that "We will cut off the King's head with the crown on it." In light of these events, historians have tended to conclude that, by the end, whatever Charles' previous failings to reign successfully, events had gotten completely out of control, and there was probably nothing Charles could have done to prevent his execution. He found himself faced with a "usurping army," and a "junto parliament." *See, e.g.,* J.P. KENYON, THE STUARTS 94 (1958). Can you now understand the tone of Charles' comments at his trial any better?

3. Notice that Charles speaks with great contempt of his judges' claims that they speak for the people, and notice, in particular, his argument that even if the English monarchy were a creation of the people (which he denies, but which the Lord President more or less asserts), he could not legitimately be ousted, except with the consent of each and every one of the English people. Why doesn't he subscribe to the principle of majority rule in this instance? Should policies be made by a majority or by unanimity? Is there anything in this notion of Charles' that is also to be found in the provisions of the United States Constitution calling for more than a majority to amend it, or even the modern law regarding corporations, which may require the unanimous consent of shareholders before a corporation may act in a manner not expressly authorized by its charter?

4. One other matter that needs clearing up is Charles' serenity as he addressed his children and the extraordinary nobility of his last days that he supposedly displayed to all. These acts have made virtually all historians of the era conclude that those leading up to his execution were Charles' finest hours. You have seen that Charles acknowledged that if he was unjustly executed, it was only fitting, since he had failed to prevent an unjust execution himself. He was here referring to the fact that in a vain attempt to appease the House of

Commons several years before, he had agreed to the impeachment and execution of his extremely unpopular, but very loyal and competent minister and general, Thomas Wentworth, the Earl of Stratford. Note also, before we leave Charles, his poignant comments to his third son, that he must take special care that he (the son) does not allow Parliament to make him a King. Why would Parliament want to do that? Why wouldn't Charles want his son to cooperate? The House of Commons decided against this course of action, however, and within three months after Charles' execution, on 17 March 1649, it passed the following provision:

e. *An Act for the abolishing the kingly office in England and Ireland, and the dominions thereunto belonging, in* KENYON, STUART CONSTITUTION 339-341

Whereas Charles Stuart, late King of England . . ., hath by authority derived from Parliament been, and is hereby declared to be justly condemned, adjudged to die, and put to death, for many treasons, murders and other heinous offences committed by him, by which judgement he stood, and is hereby declared to, be attainted of high treason, whereby his issue and posterity, and all other pretending title under him, are become incapable of the said crowns, or of being king or queen of the said kingdom or dominions, or either or any of them; be it therefore enacted and ordained . . . by this present parliament and by the authority thereof, that all the people of England and Ireland . . ., of what degree or condition soever, are discharged of all fealty, homage and allegiance which is or shall be pretended to be due unto any of the issue and posterity of the said late King, or any claiming under him; and that Charles Stuart, eldest son, and James, called Duke of York, second son, and all other the issue and posterity of him the said late King, and all and every person pretending title from, by or under him, are and be disabled to hold or enjoy the said Crown of England and Ireland . . . .

And whereas it is and hath been found by experience that the office of a king in this nation and Ireland, and to have the power thereof in any single person, is unnecessary, burdensome and dangerous to the liberty, safety and public interest of the people, and that for the most part use hath been made of the regal power and prerogative to oppress and impoverish and enslave the subject, and that usually and naturally any one person in such power makes it in his interest to encroach upon the just freedom and liberty of the people, and to promote the setting up of their own will and power above the laws, that so they might enslave these kingdoms to their own lust, be it therefore enacted and ordained by this present Parliament . . . that the office of a king in this nation shall not henceforth reside in or be exercised by any one single person, and that no one person whatsoever shall or may have or hold the office, style, dignity, power or authority of king of the said kingdoms and dominions, or any of them, or of the Prince of Wales, any law . . . notwithstanding.

And whereas by the abolition of the kingly office provided for in this Act a most happy way is made for this nation (if God see it good) to return to its just and ancient right of being governed by its own Representatives or National Meetings in Council, from time to time chosen and entrusted for that purpose by the people; it is therefore resolved and declared by the Commons assembled in Parliament, that they will put a period to the sitting of this present Parliament, and dissolve the same, so soon as may possibly stand with the safety of the people that hath trusted them, and with what is absolutely necessary for the preserving and upholding the government now settled in the way of a Commonwealth, and that they will carefully provide for the certain choosing, meeting and sitting of the next and future Representatives with such other circumstance of freedom in choice and equality in distribution of Members to be elected thereunto as shall most conduce to the lasting freedom and good of this Commonwealth.

And it is hereby further enacted and declared . . . [that] no person or persons of what condition and quality soever, within the Commonwealth of England and Ireland, Dominion of Wales, . . . shall be discharged from the obedience and subjection which he and they owe to the government of this nation, as it is now declared, but all and every one of them shall in all things render and perform the same, as of right is due unto the Supreme Authority hereby declared to reside in this and the successive Representatives of the people of this nation, and in them only.

D. The Interregnum, the Restoration and the "Glorious Revolution"

1. Milton and Hobbes

So far, we have seen the English response to the King's use of arbitrary power evolve from silent acquiescence and faith in God's commands to the King, to the surveillance of the King's officers by his judges, to Parliament's use of its impeachment powers, leading to the execution of the King himself for treason. After Charles' death, however, it soon became clear that a parliament trifled with could be as arbitrary a force as a King himself. The activities of the Parliament and of the executive during the interregnum [the period between Kings], as well as the conduct of the Stuarts before and after that period, were crucial historical examples of arbitrary rule which sat foremost in the mind of every English and American constitutional lawyer in the late eighteenth century and for many years thereafter. It is for this reason that they are worth so much of our attention.

Turning back to the time of the regicide, you will remember that shortly before the House of Commons executed Charles, and abolished both the monarchy and the House of Lords, Col. Pride, acting in what he believed to be the best interests of the country (or at least the Army), denied 143 members of Parliament their seats. This left about 78 members in the House of Commons, of whom 20, possibily in sympathy with the King or appalled by the actions of "Pride's purge," refused to sit. This truncated or "Rump" Parliament, which was essentially the creature and tool of the army, proceeded to modify the constitution in the ways described in your last readings. Was this legitimate?

In addition to eliminating the monarch and the upper house, the "Rump" set up a Council of State composed of 41 members (three judges, three army officers, five peers, and 30 members of the House of Commons), who were to administer policy for the country. It might be thought that the abolishing of the monarchy and the House of Lords represented a move toward democracy, and, as you have seen, these constitutional changes were justified as being taken in the name of the English people, but Oliver Cromwell, who quickly emerged as the single most effective wielder of power in the country, soon indicated the contrary by the manner in which he treated the Levellers. The Levellers, perhaps the most democratic of political groups in England, were a vocal minority who demanded such reforms as the opening of the franchise even to those without landed property. Cromwell fiercely sought to repress the Levellers. As he informed the Council of State, "you have no other way to deal with these men but to break them in pieces." The Levellers, themselves determined to break Cromwell and his new regime "in pieces," inspired several mutinies of the army in May of 1649, but Cromwell still managed ruthlessly to crush the uprisings, and their instigators.

After successfully quelling the egalitarian movement at home, Cromwell turned his attention to Ireland, where rebellions erupted from 1649 to 1652. When Cromwell's army finally defeated the Irish rebels, Cromwell ordered the Rump Parliament to expropriate 2/3 of Ireland. He then settled that land with his soldiers and with London speculators, which caused a bloody and seething resistance that has not entirely ceased three and a half centuries later. In 1651, Scotland too, had to be pacified by Cromwell's military might.

As these costly military events unfolded abroad, at home the Rump Parliament continued to move further and further away from Cromwell's religious designs. Cromwell soon came to the conviction that Parliament, where passionate Puritanism still reigned, was completely out of touch with the needs of England. Accordingly, on April 21, 1653 Cromwell closed down the Parliament, replacing it in July with a group of 144 men selected by the army and by local church congregations. This group, known as the "Barebones Parliament" after one of its members, the exquisitely-named Puritan, "Praise God Barebones," did not satisfy Cromwell any more than did the Rump, so he dissolved it in December 1653.

At about this time, by a document called the "Instrument of Government," Cromwell had himself created "Lord Protector of the Commonwealth." In addition to this bold declaration, the instrument provided for a new unicameral Parliament and another Council of State, which were set up shortly thereafter. By January of 1655, however, Cromwell decided to dispense with the new Parliament and to rule alone. For the next twenty-two months, Cromwell and his major generals ruled as unchecked by others as any modern military junta.

Because of the firm tradition that taxation required the consent of the people's representatives in Parliament, however, Cromwell and his generals found it almost impossible to collect taxes. Consequently, their martial foreign policy rapidly depleted their funds, and their standing Army of 30,000 virtually bankrupted the realm.

To restore legitimacy and solvency to his government, Cromwell was forced to adopt a set of resolutions that was virtually identical to the "ancient constitution" he and his men had overturned years earlier. At the same time, the military offered him the Crown, but he refused it. Nevertheless, he did allow himself to be addressed thereafter as "His highness," and he also accepted the right to name his successor. In addition, he reinstated a virtual "House of Lords," although it was not given that name. That body was composed of worthies nominated by the Lord Protector (Cromwell) and approved by a new House of Commons, whose numbers were elected by the same possessors of the franchise (substantial owners of landed property) as before the Civil Wars. This final attempt to establish a tolerable Parliament proved as unsatisfactory to Cromwell as had the other attempts, so, in February of 1658, Cromwell dissolved Parliament once again.

Cromwell was an undeniably brilliant general, and his military victories over Ireland, Scotland, Spain and Holland brought England to a martial glory it had never before known. Still, Cromwell ultimately failed in his attempt to rule without the benefit of the tripartite balanced English Constitution — a monarchy, a House of Lords, and an unpurged House of Commons. This failure demonstrates that however pure Cromwell's motives, the historic English belief in a "balanced" Constitution of Crown, Lords, and Commons made it unlikely that England would ever be controlled successfully by a military dictatorship.

Cromwell died on September 3, 1658, and his son Richard took his father's place as "Lord Protector." Richard soon had to reinstate the old "Rump" Parliament, but the Rump refused to cooperate with him, just as it had ultimately refused to cooperate with his father. Religious and democratic agitation among the people surged, and since Richard lacked his father's forcefulness and military talent, the country quickly degenerated into virtual anarchy.

Even some of the Army leaders became convinced that the only possible way to restore order and legitimacy to the realm was to restore the Stuart monarchy to the throne. On February 3, 1660, General Monck, who had been commanding troops in Scotland, marched them to London, and, as one historian, Lacey Baldwin Smith, has put it, began the "process of unpurging Parliament." With 80 of the 143 members whom Pride had purged back in their seats, the Parliament quickly set up a new Council of State, gave it the authority to invite Charles II back to rule, ordered new elections based on the pre-Civil War franchise, and proceeded to dissolve itself. By May 25, 1660, Charles II's exile was over, and the Stuarts were back on the throne.

This period of regicide, theocratic experiment, and virtual anarchy led to two brilliant expressions of political philosophy, one by John Milton and the other by Thomas Hobbes, to which we now turn. Both, as we will see, are progenitors of the American Constitutional order, and the philosophical differences between the two have been replayed many times throughout modern English and American history. With which of these thinkers do you find yourself most in sympathy? Why?

John Milton, *The Tenure of Kings and Magistrates* (1649) *in,* PROSE WRITINGS 191-95, 197-99, 201 (Everyman's Library ed., 1974 reprint)

* * *

No man who knows aught, can be so stupid to deny that all men naturally were born free, being the image and resemblance of God himself, and were, by privilege above all the creatures, born to command and not to obey; and that they lived so, till from the root of Adam's transgression falling among themselves to do wrong and violence, and foreseeing that such courses must needs tend to the destruction of them all, they agreed by common league to bind each other from mutual injury, and jointly to defend themselves against any that gave disturbance or opposition to such agreement. Hence came cities, towns, and commonwealths. And because no faith in all was found sufficiently binding, they saw it needful to ordain some authority that might restrain by force and punishment what was violated against peace and common right.

This authority and power of self-defense and preservation being originally and naturally in every one of them, and unitedly in them all, for ease, for order, and lest each man should be his own partial judge, they communicated and derived either to one whom for the eminence of his wisdom and integrity they chose above the rest, or to more than one whom they thought of equal deserving. The first was called a King, the other, magistrates: not to be their lords and masters . . . but to be their deputies and commissioners, to execute, by virtue of their intrusted power, that justice which else every man by the bond of nature and of covenant must have executed for himself, and for one another. And to him that shall consider well why among free persons one man by civil right should bear authority and jurisdiction over another, no other end or reason can be imaginable. [Can you imagine one? Could the Stuart Kings?]

These for a while governed well and with much equity decided all things at their own arbitrement [by decision after hearing both sides of a dispute], till the temptation of such a power, left absolute in their hands, perverted them at length to injustice and partiality. Then did they who now by trial had found the danger and inconveniences of committing arbitrary power to any invent laws, either framed or consented to by all, that should confine and limit the authority of whom they chose to govern them: that no man, of whose failing they had proof, might no more rule over them, but law and reason, abstracted as much as might be from personal errors and frailties: while as the magistrate was set above the people, so the law was set above the magistrate. When this would not serve, but that the law was either not executed, or misapplied, they were constrained from that time, the only remedy left them, to put conditions and take oaths from all kings and magistrates at their first installment to do impartial justice by law: who, upon those terms and no other, received allegiance from the people, that is to say, bond or covenant to obey them in execution of those laws which they, the people, had themselves made or assented to. And this oft-times with express warning, that if the king or magistrate proved unfaithful to his trust, the people would be disengaged.

* * *

It being thus manifest that the power of kings and magistrates is nothing else but what is only derivative, transferred, and committed to them in trust from the people to the common good of them all, in whom the power yet remains fundamentally and cannot be taken from them without a violation of their natural birthright, and seeing that from hence Aristotle, and the best of political writers, have defined a king, "him who governs to the good and profit of his people, and not for his own ends" . . . .

Secondly, that to say, as is usual, the king hath as good right to his crown and dignity as any man to his inheritance, is to make the subject no better than the king's slave, his chattel, or his possession that may be bought and sold. And doubtless, if hereditary title were sufficiently inquired, the best foundation of it would be found either but in courtesy or convenience. But suppose it to be of right hereditary, what can be more just and legal, if a subject for certain crimes be to forfeit by law from himself and [his] posterity all his inheritance to the king, than that a king, for crimes proportional, should forfeit all his title and inheritance to the people? Unless the people must be thought created all for him he not for them, and they all in one body inferior to him single; which were a kind of treason against the dignity of mankind to affirm.

Thirdly, it follows that the said kings are accountable to none but God, is the overturning of all law and government. For if they may refuse to give account, then all covenants made with them at coronation, all oaths are in vain, and mere mockeries, all laws which they swear to keep, made to no purpose: for if the king fear not God (as how many of them do not?) we hold then our lives and estates by the tenure of his mere grace and mercy, as from a god, not a mortal magistrate — a position that none but court parasites or men besotted would maintain. Aristotle, therefore, whom we commonly allow for one of the best interpreters of nature and morality, writes in the fourth of his Politics, chap. x., that "monarchy unaccountable is the worst sort of tyranny, and least of all to be endured by free-born men."

* * *

It follows, lastly, that since the king or magistrate holds his authority of the people, both originally and naturally for their good in the first place, and not his own, then may the people, as oft as they shall judge it for the best, either choose him or reject him, retain him or depose him, though no tyrant, merely by the liberty and right of freeborn men to be governed as seems to them best. . . .

NOTES AND QUESTIONS

1. John Milton is probably known best to most of you as the second greatest master of the English language (Shakespeare is first, in case you have forgotten), and the author of the masterpiece *Paradise Lost*. That poem, an epic almost as grand as those of Homer or Virgil, was Milton's attempt to "justify the ways of God to man." The excerpt you have just read, however, was more of an attempt to justify "the ways of man to man." Written two weeks after the execution of Charles I by Parliament, it was an attempt to persuade doubters in England and abroad that regicide was, in the circumstances, defensible and just.

2. Is the "law" important to Milton? What does he believe is the source of law, and do you find any similarities in Milton's jurisprudential views and those of any other authors we have so far studied?

3. Our next reading is from another brilliant modern "international" political theorist, indeed from the man usually believed to be the "first," and perhaps the greatest modern political theorist, Thomas Hobbes. As you read Hobbes, ask yourself, whether on the basis of the principles he sets forth, and the manner in which he applies them, he would have been on the same side of the English Civil war as Milton, or whether he would have been a defender of the King.

THOMAS HOBBES, LEVIATHAN (1651)
[selected excerpts, spelling modernized]

[1. Conditions in the State of Nature]

Nature has made men so equal in the faculties of the body and mind as that . . . when all is reckoned together the difference between man and man is not so considerable as that one man can thereupon claim to himself any benefit to which another may not pretend as well as he. . . .

As to the faculties of the mind . . . I find yet a greater equality among men than that of strength. . . .

From this equality of ability arises equality of hope in the attaining of our ends. And therefore if any two men desire the same thing, which nevertheless they cannot both enjoy, they become enemies; and in the way to their end, which is principally their own conservation, and sometimes their delectation only, endeavor to destroy or subdue one another. And from hence it comes to pass that where an invader has no more to fear than another man's single power, if one plant, sow, build, or possess a convenient seat, others may probably be expected to come prepared with forces united to dispossess and deprive him, not only of the fruit of his labor, but also of his life or liberty. And the invader again is in the like danger of another.

And from this diffidence of one another there is no way for any man to secure himself so reasonable as anticipation — that is, by force or wiles to master the persons of all men he can, so long till he see no other power great enough to endanger him . . . . And by consequence, such augmentation of dominion over men being necessary to a man's conservation, it ought to be allowed him.

* * *

Hereby it is manifest that, during the time men live without a common power to keep them all in awe, they are in that condition which is called war, and such a war as is of every man against every man. . . . In such condition there is no place for industry, because the fruit thereof is uncertain: and consequently no culture of the earth; no navigation nor use of the commodities that may be imported by sea; no commodious building; no instruments of moving and removing such things as require much force; no knowledge of the face of the earth; no account of time; no arts; no letters; no society; and, which is worst of all, continual fear and danger of violent death; and the life of man solitary, poor, nasty, brutish, and short.

It may seem strange . . . that nature should thus dissociate and render men apt to invade and destroy one another [but consider that it is true for any man that] . . . when taking a journey he arms himself and seeks to go well accompanied, when going to sleep he locks his doors, when even in his house he locks his chests, and this when he knows there be laws and public officers, armed, to revenge all injuries shall be done him. . . . The desires and other passions of man are in themselves no sin. No more are the actions that proceed from those passions till they know a law that forbids them, which, till laws be made, they cannot know, nor can any law be made till they have agreed upon the person that shall make it.

* * *

[2. The Fundamental Laws of Nature]

[B]ecause the condition of man . . . is a condition of war of every one against every one — in which case everyone is governed by his own reason and there is nothing he can make use of that may not be a help unto him in preserving his life against his enemies — it follows that in such a condition every man has a right to everything, even to one another's body. And therefore, as long as this natural right of every man to everything endures, there can be no security to any man, how strong or wise soever he be, of living out the time which nature ordinarily allows men to live. And consequently it is a precept or general rule of reason that every man ought to endeavor peace, as far as he has hope of obtaining it; and when he cannot obtain it, that he may seek and use all helps and advantages of war. The first branch of which rule contains the first and fundamental law of nature, which is to seek peace and follow it. The second, the sum of the right of nature, which is, by all means we can to defend ourselves.

From this fundamental law of nature, by which men are commanded to endeavor peace, is derived this second law: that a man be willing, when others are so too, as far forth as for peace and defense of himself he shall think it necessary, to lay down this right to all things, and be contented with so much liberty against other men as he would allow other men against himself. For as long as every man holds this right of doing anything he likes, so long are all men in the condition of war. But if other men will not lay down their right as well as he, then there is no reason for anyone to divest himself of his, for that were to expose himself to prey, which no man is bound to, rather than to dispose himself to peace. . . .

From that law of nature by which we are obliged to transfer to another such rights as, being retained, hinder the peace of mankind, there follows a third, which is this: that men perform their covenants made. . . .

And in this law of nature consists the fountain and original of JUSTICE. For where no covenant has preceded there has no right been transferred, and every man has right to every thing; and consequently no action can be unjust. But when a covenant is made, then to break it is unjust; and the definition of INJUSTICE is no other than the not performance of covenant. . . .

* * *

[3. The Formation of Commonwealths]

[Still,] . . . there must be some coercive power to compel men equally to the performance of their covenants by the terror of some punishment greater than the benefit they expect by the breach of their covenant, and to make good that propriety which by mutual contract men acquire in recompense of the universal right they abandon; and such power there is none before the erection of a commonwealth. . . .

* * *

[4. The Nature of the Social Contract and of Sovereignty]

The only way to erect such a common power as may be able to defend them from the invasion of foreigners and the injuries of one another . . . is to confer all their power and strength upon one man, or upon one assembly of men that may reduce all their wills, by plurality of voices, unto one will. . . . This is more than consent or concord; it is a real unity of them all in one and the same person, made by covenant of every man with every man, ... This done, the multitude so united in one person is called a COMMONWEALTH, in Latin CIVITAS. This is the generation of that great LEVIATHAN (or rather to speak more reverently, of that mortal god) to which we owe, under the immortal God, our peace and defense. For by this authority, given him by every particular man in the commonwealth, he has the use of so much power and strength conferred on him that, by terror thereof, he is enabled to form the wills of them all to peace at home and mutual aid against their enemies abroad. And in him consists the essence of the commonwealth, which, to define it, is one person, of whose acts a great multitude, by mutual covenants one with another, have made themselves every one the author, to the end he may use the strength and means of them all as he shall think expedient for their peace and common defense. And he that carries this person is called SOVEREIGN and said to have sovereign power; and everyone besides, his SUBJECT.

* * *

So that it appears plainly, to my understanding, both from reason and Scripture, that the sovereign power, whether placed in one man as in monarchy, or in one assembly of men as in popular and aristocratical commonwealths, is as great as possibly men can be imagined to make it. And though of so unlimited a power men may fancy many evil consequences, yet the consequences of the want of it, which is perpetual war of every man against his neighbor, are much worse. . . .

* * *

[5. Of Civil Laws and Liberty]

[A]s men, for the attaining of peace and conservation of themselves thereby, have made an artificial man, which we call a commonwealth, so also have they made artificial chains, called civil laws, which they themselves, by mutual covenants, have fastened at one end to the lips of that man or assembly to whom they have given the sovereign power, and at the other end to their own ears. These bonds, in their own nature but weak, may nevertheless be made to hold by the danger, though not by the difficulty, of breaking them.

In relation to these bonds only it is that I am to speak now of the liberty of subjects. For seeing there is no commonwealth in the world wherein there be rules enough set down for the regulating of all the actions and words of men, as being a thing impossible, it follows necessarily that in all kinds of actions by the laws pretermitted men have the liberty of doing what their own reasons shall suggest for the most profitable to themselves. For if we take liberty in the proper sense for corporal liberty — that is to say, freedom from chains and prison — it were very absurd for men to clamor as they do for the liberty they so manifestly enjoy. Again, if we take liberty for an exemption from laws, it is no less absurd for men to demand as they do that liberty by which all other men may be masters of their lives. And yet, as absurd as it is, this it is they demand, not knowing that the laws are of no power to protect them without a sword in the hands of a man or men to cause those laws to be put into execution. The liberty of a subject lies, therefore, only in those things which, in regulating their actions, the sovereign has pretermitted: such as the liberty to buy and sell and otherwise contract with one another; to choose their own abode, their own diet, their own trade of life, and institute their children as they themselves think fit; and the like.

Nevertheless we are not to understand that by such liberty the sovereign power of life and death is either abolished or limited. . . .

* * *

To come now to the particulars of the true liberty of a subject — that is to say, what are the things which, though commanded by the sovereign, he may nevertheless without injustice refuse to do — we are to consider what rights we pass away when we make a commonwealth, or which is all one, what liberty we deny ourselves by owning all the actions, without exception, of the man or assembly we make our sovereign. . . .

First, therefore, seeing sovereignty by institution is by covenant of every one to every one, and sovereignty by acquisition by covenants of the vanquished to the victor or child to the parent, it is manifest that every subject has liberty in all those things the right whereof cannot by covenant be transferred. . . . [C]ovenants not to defend a man's own body are void. Therefore, if the sovereign command a man, though justly condemned, to kill, wound, or maim himself, or not to resist those that assault him, or to abstain from the use of good air, medicine, or any other thing without which he cannot live, yet has that man the liberty to disobey.

If a man be interrogated by the sovereign or his authority concerning a crime done by himself, he is not bound, without assurance of pardon, to confess it; because no man . . . can be obliged by covenant to accuse himself.

Again, the consent of a subject to sovereign power is contained in these words: I authorize, or take upon me, all his actions; in which there is no restriction at all of his own former natural liberty, for by allowing him to kill me I am not bound to kill myself when he commands me. . . . It follows therefore, that

No man is bound by the words themselves either to kill himself or any other man, and consequently that the obligation a man may sometimes have, upon the command of the sovereign, to execute any dangerous or dishonorable office depends not on the words of our submission but on the intention, which is to be understood by the end thereof. When, therefore, our refusal to obey frustrates the end for which the sovereignty was ordained, then there is no liberty to refuse; otherwise there is.

Upon this ground, a man that is commanded as a soldier to fight against the enemy, though his sovereign have right enough to punish his refusal with death, may nevertheless in many cases refuse, without injustice — as when he substitutes a sufficient soldier in his place, for in this case he deserts not the service of the commonwealth, and there is allowance to be made for natural timorousness, not only for women, of whom no such dangerous duty is expected, but also to men of feminine courage . . . .

To resist the sword of the commonwealth in defense of another man, guilty or innocent, no man has liberty; because such liberty takes away from the sovereign the means of protecting us, and is therefore destructive of the very essence of government. . . .

As for other liberties, they depend on the silence of the law. In cases where the sovereign has prescribed no rule, there the subject has the liberty to do or forbear according to his own discretion. . . . As, for example, there was a time when in England a man might enter into his own land and dispossess such as wrongfully possessed it by force. But in aftertimes that liberty of forcible entry was taken away by a statute made by the king in parliament. . . .

If a subject have a controversy with his sovereign . . . he has the same liberty to sue for his right as if it were against a subject, and before such judges as are appointed by the sovereign. For seeing the sovereign demands by force of a former law and not by virtue of his power, he declares thereby that he requires no more than shall appear to be due by that law. The suit therefore, is not contrary to the will of the sovereign. . . . But if [the sovereign] demand or take any thing by pretense of his power, there lies in that case no action of law; for all that is done by him in virtue of his power is done by the authority of every subject, and consequently he that brings an action against the sovereign brings it against himself.

* * *

[6. When Sovereignty Ends]

The obligation of subjects to the sovereign is understood to last as long and no longer than the power lasts by which he is able to protect them. . . . The sovereignty is the soul of the commonwealth, which once departed from the body, the members do no more receive their motion from it. The end of obedience is protection which, wheresoever a man sees it, either in his own or in another's sword, nature applies his obedience to it and his endeavor to maintain it. And though sovereignty, in the intention of them that make it, be immortal, yet is it in its own nature not only subject to violent death by foreign war, but also through the ignorance and passions of men, it has in it, from the very institution, many seeds of a natural mortality by [internal] discord.

If a subject be taken prisoner in war, or his person or his means of life be within the guards of the enemy, and has his life and corporal liberty given him on condition to be subject to the victor, he has liberty to accept the condition and, having accepted it, is the subject of him that took him, because he had no other way to preserve himself. . . .

If a monarch shall relinquish the sovereignty, both for himself and his heirs, his subjects return to the absolute liberty of nature . . . .

If the sovereign banish his subject, during the banishment he is not subject. . . .

If a monarch, subdued by war, render himself subject to the victor, his subjects are delivered from their former obligation and become obliged to the victor. But if he be held prisoner, or have not the liberty of his own body, he is not understood to have given away the right of sovereignty; and therefore his subjects are obliged to yield obedience to the magistrates formerly placed, governing not in their own name but in his. . . .

NOTES AND QUESTIONS

1. Thomas Hobbes (1588-1679), though usually regarded as the first great modern political theorist, has certainly had his critics. Are you one of them? In some privately circulated writing in the 1640s, Hobbes advocated the necessity of an absolute monarchy. Having thus offended the Parliamentarians, whose stock in trade had become checking the purportedly arbitrary rule of Charles I, Hobbes fled to France, where he composed his masterpiece, the Leviathan, first published in 1651. Can you imagine what events you have read about in previous sections of this chapter could have prompted Hobbes to write what you have read?

2. Hobbes is probably best known for his description of the "state of nature," that which exists before men and women enter into organized society. Does it sound like a state in which you would like to live? Why is it that Hobbes believed that in a state of nature life is "solitary, poor, nasty, brutish, and short"? Are you comfortable with Hobbes' implicit and explicit views on the nature of humankind?

3. Under Hobbes' political theory, what is the extent of the power of the sovereign? Is this theory consistent with the notions about American law with which you are familiar? Would you define "justice" or "liberty" in the same manner as does Hobbes?

4. But is there, after all, anything which you could say in defense of Hobbes' views on the nature of sovereignty, justice, or liberty? Why is he so well regarded by so many modern political scientists? Could it be said, for instance, that the notions of the rule of law and constitutionalism, twin American ideals of courts adhering to previous decisions by legislatures or people, rest on an Hobbesian foundation?

5. When, according to Hobbes, are subjects justified in rebelling against a monarch? Would Hobbes have found the English Civil Wars justifiable?

6. As you may know, it is not Thomas Hobbes, but John Locke who, for many years, was recognized as the pre-eminent political philosopher of the American revolutionary period, and it is to the events leading up to the statement of Locke's political philosophy, those in England in the late seventeenth century, to which we next turn. As you read about the "Glorious Revolution," the replacement of James II by William and Mary, ask yourself whether Hobbes (or Milton) would have approved.

2. The Glorious Revolution and John Locke

When Charles II, the son of the executed Charles I, was restored to the throne, by and large he made it his policy to forgive and forget. While 13 regicides *were* put to death, and while the exhumed corpses of Oliver Cromwell and General Ireton *were* belatedly given the gallows, still many of Charles II's advisors were men who had committed treason against his father. Charles was the "merry monarch" — he ostentatiously kept beautiful mistresses, and he restored the English theatre and throne — all of which destroyed the puritan austerity which the Interregnum had brought to England. Charles also cooperated in the restoration of much of the confiscated Crown and Church lands. Significantly, however, and to the chagrin of some of the aristocrats who had fought for his father, he did not disturb many of the estates of the Roundheads who had purchased illegally confiscated Cavalier lands. Indeed, Charles II, through his advisor, the astute new Earl of Clarendon, Edward Hyde, made it his policy to protect the possessors of landed property even when it enraged some of his father's loyal supporters.

During his reign, however, Charles II was forced to acknowledge that the ultimate taxing and law-making power of England belonged to the Parliament, which increasingly enacted important legislation for the realm. For the next 170 years, Parliament was dominated by the richest landholders in England, who spent a great deal of their time passing measures to safeguard their own interests. Parliament even went so far as to regulate the restored Anglican church in the interest of the country squires who dominated it.

In theory, the King possessed some checks on Parliament, through the exercise of the royal prerogative. For example, the King could suspend or dissolve the Parliament, forcing new elections, and he could veto acts of legislation. It appears that he also possessed the historic English kingly discretion to suspend or "dispense" with any act of Parliament. Additionally, the King still possessed the power to conduct the nation's foreign policy, including the power to command the armed forces, and could choose his own ministers to help him in his duties. Still, Parliament possessed the power to bring charges against and to remove Charles' ministers for misconduct ("impeachment"). Eventually, Charles found himself locked in a power struggle with his Parliament over the extent to which he could exercise his royal prerogatives.

In 1665, the Parliament was reluctant to grant funds to Charles to fight the Dutch in a war over trade issues, a war which had continued since the days of the Interregnum. Not only did Parliament fail to grant adequate supplies, but it also blamed (perhaps unjustly) Charles' chief minister, Clarendon, for failing to manage the war effort properly. Making matters worse, at almost this time a horrible plague and related fire gutted London. Further, the Anglican orthodoxy held Clarendon responsible for attempts Charles had made to alleviate the burdens of Anglican dominance on English Catholics and Protestant Dissenters (those Protestants who objected to some of the features of the Anglican liturgy or church structure, including, for example, Baptists, Presbyterians, and Quakers). Unable or unwilling to challenge the King himself, the leaders of Parliament, following the humiliating defeat of the English army and navy at the hands of the Dutch, brought articles of impeachment against Clarendon. He fled to France, in order to avoid conviction and possible decapitation.

Charles, after Clarendon's departure, began more astutely to manage his own affairs, occasionally aided by a group of non-Anglican advisors, whose names — Clifford, Arlington, Buckingham, Ashley, and Lauderdale — lent their initials ("CABAL") thereafter to be used to describe any clandestine power-wielding clique. Charles proceeded to set a foreign policy course which favoured France, where he had spent the Interregnum in exile, and he reintroduced measures for religious toleration of Catholics, particularly his "Declaration of Indulgence" of 1672. Through the secret Treaty of Dover of 1670, Charles managed to secure a huge subsidy from his cousin, the "Sun King," Louis XIV of France, in part freeing Charles from the need to turn to Parliament for funds. In return, Charles agreed to protect the Catholics of England and to announce as soon as it was "convenient" his own adherence to Catholicism. Such a "convenient" time never came, however, so while Charles enjoyed the fruits of Louis' funding, he never publicly acknowledged his adherence to Louis' Church, except perhaps on his deathbed. Charles did, however, join Louis in another unpopular war against the Dutch and, through an alliance with France, for a while Charles helped bolster French domination in Europe.

Charles' efforts to carry out his promise to Louis to protect English Catholics continued to create problems with the Anglican dominated and Catholic-fearing Parliament. In return for a badly-needed supplement of funds to fight the Dutch war, his stipend from King Louis apparently proving inadequate, Charles was soon forced to agree to withdraw his Declaration of Indulgence and to give his assent to the Test Act of 1673, which barred all Catholics and Protestant Dissenters from civil and military offices. The Act was particularly aimed at James, Charles' openly Catholic brother, the Duke of York, who was forced to resign his position as leader of the Navy. Eventually, in 1674, Parliament even forced Charles to make peace with Holland and ostensibly to renounce England's French alliance, although Charles still continued to draw from his secret French subsidy.

In the period 1678-1681 religious issues once again embarrassed Charles in the infamous "Popish plots." These disturbances, probably fabricated in part by unscrupulous opportunists such as the Earl of Shaftesbury, Anthony Cooper, were seized upon by anti-Catholic enemies of James and supporters of Parliamentary supremacy, as evidence of designs to suppress the true Church, Anglicanism, and to fasten the slavish yoke of Rome on England. The group around Cooper, called the "Whigs" (an insult taken from the name for Scottish horse thieves), argued for the need to preserve the power of Protestantism and English autonomy. They forced Protestant advisors on the King, inflamed public opinion against Catholics, and sought to pass a Parliamentary Bill excluding

James from the succession. Charles, driven to the wall, repeatedly suspended and dissolved Parliament to prevent that exclusion act from passing.

Charles' sudden illness in the summer of 1679 allowed some respite to the political warfare between James' advocates and his Whig foes, and in order to avoid a virtual civil war between Charles' illegitimate son (the Protestant Duke of Monmouth) and James, the squirearchy began again to support Charles. Charles, who seemed to be turning into an even more subtle politician than Shaftsbury, arrested Shaftsbury for treason. Shaftesbury fled abroad, and soon died, but Charles executed two of Shaftsbury's associates for alleged conspiracy, possibly on trumped-up charges.

After the executions, Charles proceeded to rule (with the aid of the French subsidy) without Parliament. In several masterstrokes, Charles enlisted the aid of the Whigs' opponents, the "Tories," the Anglican county squirearchy and their clergy, and through his visible monetary support to the Anglican church, Charles allowed that church to continue its triumph over Catholics and Dissenters. By doing so, he also managed to avoid another exclusion bill, thus protecting his brother's succession to the throne.

This relatively brief though convoluted account should be enough to suggest the extraordinary degree to which late seventeenth century European politics was dominated by corruption and Byzantine intrigue, arts in which both Charles and Shaftsbury (also incidentally in the pay of the King of France — as were many other Englishmen), were masters. Charles II died in 1685, reportedly accepting the last rites from a Catholic priest and worried about his Catholic brother's ability to hold the throne for the Stuart royal family. Historiographical tradition, dominated by the writings of critics of the prerogative, and sympathizers of Parliament, suggests that Charles' worries were well-founded. Following the views of the pre-eminent Whig historian, the Victorian Lord Macaulay, most historians agree that James II did not possess any of the "saving graces" of his brother Charles II, namely indolence, intelligence, and personal charm. Rather, James has come down to us, in all but a few accounts, as a humourless, blunt and stupid tyrant. Along with Charles I, James has represented the worst in abuses of English royal power.

Our job, in this section of the text, is to try to determine why this characterization of James II is so prevalent among the historians, and why the views of those "Whig" historians have been so widely accepted in America.

When James succeeded to the throne in 1685, he was fifty-three and had two Protestant daughters from his first wife, whom he had married when he was still publicly an Anglican (he announced his conversion to Catholicism in 1672). James had since married a second wife, the Italian Catholic Maria of Modena, but in 1685 she was still childless, so it looked as though the throne would pass to James' daughter, Mary, who was safely married to the Protestant Prince William of Orange, the Stateholder of Holland. Parliament seemed disposed to tolerate a Catholic monarch for a few years, but the country was soon convulsed by a rebellion led by Charles II's illegitimate son, the Duke of Monmouth. Monmouth's rebellion was brutally crushed by James' army and judges, who rapidly convicted 400 of Monmouth's peasant supporters of treason and put them to death, while deporting another 1,200 of them.

Until then it had been rare for simple Protestant peasants to suffer the gallows, and to many Protestants it looked as if the severity of the punishment of the rebels was motivated by the fierce Catholicism of James II and many of his advisors. James had maintained the 13,000 man army that had defeated Monmouth. That army, which remained camped just outside of London, was officered by many Catholics who remained loyal to the Stuart dynasty. To many well-placed Protestants, James' standing army represented the same kind of absolutism as that in France, which was resulting in the withdrawal of political and religious rights from French Protestants.

Nevertheless, in explicit violation of the Test Act (the law which prevented Catholics and Dissenters from holding public office and enjoying many of the rights of Protestants), James continued to appoint many Catholics and Dissenters to public office at court, in the countryside, and in the universities. James' trifling with university offices — he sought to convert the strong bastions of Anglicanism at Oxford to Catholicism — was regarded as particularly offensive because university offices had many of the characteristics of private property, and James seemed to be markedly departing from the policy of his brother Charles II. Equally repellant, to many, was James' trifling with local government, since that had been the preserve of the formerly loyal Tory squirearchy.

Relentlessly, and in an effort to buttress the legitimacy of his actions, James proceeded to seek repeal of the Test Act. Horrified by the "Bloody Assizes," in which the 400 peasant rebels met their death, and worried that James might seek to emulate the rising anti-Protestantism of his cousin Louis XIV, Parliament refused. In response, James suspended Parliament, and, in an attempt to exercise his prerogative and to gain the support for the crown of Catholics and Dissenters, in April of 1687, he issued his first "Declaration of Indulgence," the text of which follows.

James argued that though the Declaration of Indulgence and his appointments of Catholics and Dissenters appeared to violate the Test Act, the King, as the head of the English Church and thus with an explicit mission from God, possessed the power to "suspend" or "dispense" with Acts of Parliament, at least with regard to those touching religious disabilities. You will have noted some similarities in James' claim with that of his grandfather James I, to control the English common law. Which King's claims, James I or II, do you find most obnoxious? As you read the Declaration, ask yourself whether it does indeed seem to be the work of a tyrant, or whether, instead, you would have advised James to proclaim it.

a. The Declaration of Indulgence (1687)

King James the Second his gracious declaration to all his loving subjects for liberty of conscience (4 April 1687).

It having pleased Almighty God not only to bring us to the imperial crown of these kingdoms through the greatest difficulties, but to preserve us by a more than ordinary providence upon the throne of our royal ancestors, there is nothing now that we so earnestly desire as to establish our government on such a foundation as may make our subjects happy, and unite them to us by inclination as well as duty. Which we think can be done by no means so effectually as by granting to them the free exercise of their religion for the time to come, and add that to the perfect enjoyment of their property, which has never been in any case invaded by us since our coming to the crown. Which being the two things men value most, shall ever be preserved in these kingdoms during our reign over them, as the truest methods of their peace and our glory.

We cannot but heartily wish, as it will easily be believed, that all the people of our dominions were members of the Catholic church, yet we humbly thank Almighty God it is and hath of long time been our constant sense and opinion (which upon divers occasions we have declared), that conscience ought not to be constrained, no people forced in matters of mere religion. . . . For after all the frequent and pressing endeavours that were used in each of them to reduce this kingdom to an exact conformity in religion, it is visible the success has not answered the design, and that the difficulty is invincible. We therefore, out of our princely care and affection unto all our loving subjects, that they may live at ease and quiet, and for the increase of trade and encouragement of strangers, have thought fit by virtue of our royal prerogative to issue forth this our Declaration of Indulgence, making no doubt of the concurrence of our two houses of Parliament when we shall think it convenient for them to meet.

In the first place we do declare, that we will protect and maintain our archbishops, bishops and clergy, and all other our subjects of the Church of England in the free exercise of their religion as by law established, and in the quiet and full enjoyment of all their possessions, without any molestation or disturbance whatsoever.

We do likewise declare, that it is our royal will and pleasure that from henceforth the execution of all manner of penal laws in matters ecclesiastical, for not coming to church, or not receiving the sacrament, or for any other nonconformity to the religion established, or for or by reason of the exercise of religion in any manner whatsoever, be immediately suspended; and the further execution of the said penal laws and every one of them is hereby suspended.

* * *

And that all our subjects may enjoy such their religious assemblies with greater assurance and protection, we have thought it requisite, and do hereby command, that no disturbance of any kind be made or given unto them, under pain of our displeasure, and to be further proceeded against with the utmost severity.

And foreasmuch as we are desirous to have the benefit of the service of all our loving subjects, which by the law of nature is inseparably annexed to and inherent in our royal person; and that none of our subjects may for the future be under any discouragement or disability (who are otherwise well inclined and fit to serve us) by reason of some oaths or tests that have been usually administered on such occasions, we do hereby further declare, that it is our royal will and pleasure that the oaths commonly called "the oaths of supremacy and allegiance" and also the several tests and declarations mentioned in the Acts of Parliament made in the 25th and 30th years of the reign of our late royal brother, King Charles II, shall not at any time hereafter be required to be taken, declared or subscribed by any person or persons whatsoever who is or shall be employed in any office or place of trust either civil or military under us, or in our government. And we do further declare it to be our pleasure and intention from time to time hereafter to grant our royal dispensations under our Great Seal to all our loving subjects so to be employed, who shall not take the said oaths, or subscribe or declare the said tests or declarations in the above-mentioned Acts and every one of them.

And to the end that all our loving subjects may receive and enjoy the full benefit and advantage of our gracious indulgence hereby intended, and may be acquitted and discharged from all pains, penalties, forfeitures and disabilities by them or any of them incurred or forfeited, or which they shall or may at any time hereafter be liable to, for or by reason of their nonconformity, or the exercise of their religion, and from all suits, troubles or disturbances for the same, we do hereby give our free and ample pardon unto all nonconformists, recusants and other our loving subjects for all crimes and things by them committed or done contrary to the penal laws formerly made relating to religion and the profession or exercise thereof . . . .

And although the freedom and assurance we have hereby given in relation to religion and property might be sufficient to remove from the minds of our loving subjects all fears and jealousies in relation to either, yet we have thought fit further to declare, that we will maintain them in all their properties and possessions, as well of church and abbey lands as in any other their lands and properties whatsoever.

NOTES AND QUESTIONS

1. Why do you suppose this Declaration was not a popular document? When James reissued it a year later, and required all Anglican clergymen to read it from their pulpits (James, as head of the state church, believed that he had the power to control what was done in the nation's Anglican chapels), he encountered massive resistance. What can you point to in the Declaration which would have led to that massive resistance? Seven of the leading Anglican Bishops protested that to require them to read the Declaration of Indulgence in their churches would be an affront to God, because the Declaration of Indulgence was an "unconstitutional" act on the part of the King. What do you suppose that the Bishops meant by their use of the term "unconstitutional"? How would you have reacted to the Bishops' behavior if you were James?

James' reaction, one of blistering fury, was to arrange for the Bishops to be prosecuted for committing the crime of seditious libel, that is, of engaging in criticism of the crown that threatened the peace of the realm. In a famous trial, however, and in spite of the fact that the Bishops were probably guilty of the offense with which they were charged (since at that time the truth of the criticism against the crown was no defense to a charge for seditious libel), a jury acquitted the Bishops. Why do you suppose that was? Does it have anything in common with the Los Angeles jury's acquittal of O.J. Simpson?

2. Shortly after the acquittal of the Bishops, in an event few had anticipated, James' Catholic Queen gave birth to a son. According to the English laws of inheritance, which favored younger males over older females, James' new Catholic baby became next in line for the throne, and James' Protestant daughters, Mary and Ann, followed him in the line of succession. Also about this time James seemed to be preparing to plunge England into another war on the side of France against the Netherlands.

All of this was just too much for many people in the country and, in particular, for seven influential Protestant aristocrats — six peers and an Anglican Bishop, including in their number both Whigs and Tories. These seven worthies proceeded to invite William of Orange to come with his wife Mary (James' daughter, as you may remember) to England, with the purpose of taking the throne from James, ostensibly in order to save the realm from Catholic oppression and to assure a Protestant succession instead. A few months later, with an Army of 15,000, William of Orange landed in England. Belatedly sensing that the times were against him, James II once again fled to France, and though he was captured once en route, he was allowed, apparently under William's direction, to escape.

3. Virtually all of James' support rapidly melted away, as William received a warm welcome from all Protestant classes. Thus, without any blood being shed, in the so-called "Glorious Revolution" of 1688, William and Mary became King and Queen of England. From one point of view, the "Revolution" of 1688 is regarded as the key event leading to the formation of the eighteenth and early nineteenth century British constitution, and thus the title "Glorious Revolution." From another point of view, of course, the Whig and Tory magnates who deposed James were guilty of treason. With which of these two views do you agree?

4. In any case, the deposing of a legitimate King is never an easy business, and some constitutional justification was badly needed for the acts of the Protestant aristocrats who sacked James. Indeed, for many years, resentment for the betrayal of the Stuarts would smolder, particularly among Catholics and Scotsmen, and there would be several rebellions attempting to put "the Pretender," James II's son, or the "young Pretender," "Bonnie Prince Charlie," the grandson of James II, back on the English throne. All such efforts, of course, failed. Why was it so easy to exclude the Stuarts? Does the "Bill of Rights," passed by Parliament on December 16, 1689, to confirm William and Mary's ascension to the throne, clarify matters? Are you convinced by its assertions? This document, by the way, became the basis for the American Bill of Rights which would be written in the next century.

b. The English Bill of Rights

An Act Declaring the Rights and Liberties of the Subject and Settling the Succession of the Crown, *in* 6 STATUTES OF THE REALM 142-45 (1820)

Whereas the Lords Spiritual and Temporal and Commons assembled at Westminister, lawfully, fully, and freely representing all the states of people of this realm, did upon the thirteenth day of February in the year of our Lord one thousand six hundred eighty-eight present unto their Majesties, then called and known by the names and style of William and Mary, prince and princess of Orange, being present in their proper persons, a certain declaration in writing made by the said Lords and Commons in the words following, viz:

Whereas the late King James the Second, by the assistance of divers evil councilors, judges, and ministers employed by him, did endeavor to subvert and extirpate the Protestant religion and the laws and liberties of the kingdom;

By assuming and exercising a power of dispensing with and suspending of laws and the execution of laws without consent of Parliament;

By committing and prosecuting divers worthy prelates for humbly petitioning to be excused from concurring to the said assumed power;

* * *

By levying money for and to the use of the Crown by pretense of prerogative for other time and in other manner than the same was granted by Parliament;

By raising and keeping a standing army within this kingdom in time of peace without consent of Parliament and quartering soldiers contrary to law;

By causing several good subjects being Protestants to be disarmed at the same time when papists were both armed and employed contrary to law;

By violating the freedom of election of members to serve in Parliament;

By prosecutions in the Court of King's Bench for matters and causes cognizable only in Parliament and by divers other arbitrary and illegal courses;

And whereas of late years, partial corrupt, and unqualified persons have been returned and served on juries in trials, and particularly divers jurors in trials for high treason which were not freeholders;

And excessive bail hath been required of persons committed in criminal cases to elude the benefit of the laws made for the liberty of the subjects;

And excessive fines have been imposed;

And illegal and cruel punishments inflicted;

And several grants and promises made of fines and forfeitures before any conviction or judgment against the persons upon whom the same were to be levied;

All which are utterly and directly contrary to the known laws and statutes and freedom of this realm.

And whereas the said late King James the Second having abdicated the government, and the throne being thereby vacant, his Highness the prince of Orange (whom it hath pleased Almighty God to make the glorious instrument of delivering this kingdom from popery and arbitrary power) did, by the advice of the Lords Spiritual and Temporal and divers principal persons of the Commons, cause letters to be written to the Lords Spiritual and Temporal being Protestants and other letters to the several counties, cities, universities, boroughs, and cinque ports for the choosing of such persons to represent them as were of right to be sent to Parliament, to meet and sit at Westminster upon the two-and-twentieth day of January in this year one thousand six hundred eighty and eight, in order to such an establishment as that their religion, laws, and liberties might not again be in danger of being subverted; upon which letters, elections have accordingly been made.

And thereupon the said Lords Spiritual and Temporal and Commons, pursuant to their respective letters and elections being now assembled in a full and free representative of this nation, taking into their most serious consideration the best means for attaining the ends aforesaid, do in the first place (as their ancestors in like case have usually done) for the vindicating and asserting their ancient rights and liberties, declare

That the pretended power of suspending of laws or the execution of laws by regal authority without consent of Parliament is illegal;

That the pretended power of dispensing with laws or the execution of laws by regal authority, as it hath been assumed and exercised of late, is illegal;

* * *

That levying money for or to the use of the Crown by pretence of prerogative without grant of Parliament, for longer time or in other manner than the same is or shall be granted, is illegal;

That it is the right of the subjects to petition the king, and all commitments and prosecutions for such petitioning are illegal;

That the raising or keeping a standing army within the kingdom in time of peace, unless it be with consent of Parliament, is against law;

That the subjects which are Protestants may have arms for their defense suitable to their conditions and as allowed by law;

That election of members of Parliament ought to be free;

That the freedom of speech and debates or proceedings in Parliament ought not to be impeached or questioned in any court or place out of Parliament;

That excessive bail ought not to be required, nor excessive fines imposed, or cruel and unusual punishments inflicted;

That jurors ought to be duly impaneled and returned, and jurors which pass upon men in trials for high treason ought to be freeholders;

That all grants and promises of fines and forfeitures of particular persons before conviction are illegal and void;

And that, for redress of all grievances and for the amending, strengthening, and preserving of the laws, Parliaments ought to be held frequently.

. . . [T]he said Lords Spiritual and Temporal and Commons assembled at Westminster do resolve that William and Mary, prince and princess of Orange, be and be declared king and queen of England . . . and the dominions thereunto belonging, to hold the Crown and royal dignity of the said kingdom and dominions to them, the said prince and princess, during their lives and the life of the survivor of them; and that the sole and full exercise of the regal power be only in and executed by the said prince of Orange in the names of the said prince and princess during their joint lives, and after their deceases the said Crown and royal dignity of the said kingdoms and dominions to be to the heirs of the body of the said princess, and for default of such issue to the Princess Anne of Denmark [James' other Protestant daughter] and the heirs of her body, and for default of such issue to the heirs of the body of the said prince of Orange . . . .

I, A.B. do sincerely promise and swear that I will be faithful and bear true allegiance to their Majesties King William and Queen Mary. So help me God.

I, A.B. do swear that I do from my heart abhor, detest and abjure as impious and heretical this damnable doctrine and position, that princes excommunicated or deprived by the pope or any authority of the see of Rome may be deposed or murdered by their subjects or any other whatsoever. And I do declare that no foreign prince, person, prelate, state or potentate hath or ought to have any jurisdiction, power, superiority, preeminence, or authority, ecclesiastical or spiritual, within this realm. So help me God.

Upon which their Majesties did accept the Crown and royal dignity . . . according to the resolution and desire of the said Lords and Commons contained in the said declaration. And thereupon their Majesties were pleased that the said Lords Spiritual and Temporal and Commons, being the two Houses of Parliament, should continue to sit and, with their Majesties' royal concurrance, make effectual provision for the settlement of the religion, laws, and liberties of this kingdom, so that the same for the future might not be in danger again of being subverted. To which the said Lords Spiritual and Temporal and Commons did agree and proceed to act accordingly.

* * *

And whereas it hath been found by experience that it is inconsistent with the safety and welfare of this Protestant kingdom to be governed by a popish prince, or by any king or queen marrying a papist, the said Lords Spiritual and Temporal and Commons do further pray that it may be enacted that all and every person and persons that is, are, or shall be reconciled to, or shall hold communion with, the see or church of Rome, or shall profess the popish religion or shall marry a papist, shall be excluded and be forever incapable to inherit, possess, or enjoy the Crown and government of this realm and Ireland and the dominions thereunto belonging or any part of the same . . . .

NOTES AND QUESTIONS

1. The Bill of Rights, as you have seen, linked the accession to the throne of William and Mary with the historic rights of Englishmen, and relied on the "abdication" of James. Do you find the argument of the Bill of Rights convincing on all points? Can you understand what prompted most of the provisions?

2. The justifications contained in the Bill of Rights, and their passage by Parliament and acceptance by William and Mary, went fairly far to justify and legitimate the Glorious Revolution, but a need was felt for a clearer philosophical and political underpinning for the deposing of James. In other words, there was a need for someone to justify the Glorious Revolution in the manner that Milton tried to justify the beheading of Charles I. This philosophical justification came with the work of John Locke, our final, and most important, reading in this section.

3. Locke was perhaps the most important English political theorist for the American Revolution in 1776. As you read the following excerpts from Locke's famous *Second Treatise of Government* (1690), see if you can find any familiar phrases, and see if you can discern what events (particularly acts of James II) might have prompted Locke's comments.

c. John Locke, The Second Treatise of Government 4-10, 15, 48-57, 70-73, 75-81, 112-15, 119-31, 138-39 (Neil H. Alford Jr. et al. eds., Legal Classics 1994)

OF THE STATE OF NATURE

To understand political power right and derive it from its original we must consider what state all men are naturally in, and that is a state of perfect freedom to order their actions and dispose of their possessions and persons as they think fit, within the bounds of the law of nature, without asking leave or depending upon the will of any other man.

A state also of equality, wherein all the power and jurisdiction is reciprocal, no one having more than another; there being nothing more evident than that creatures of the same species and rank, promiscuously born to all the same advantages of nature and the use of the same faculties, should also be equal one amongst another without subordination or subjection; unless the lord and master of them all should, by any manifest declaration of his will, set one above another, and confer on him by an evident and clear appointment an undoubted right to dominion and sovereignty.

* * *

But though this be a state of liberty, yet it is not a state of license; though man in that state has an uncontrollable liberty to dispose of his person or possessions, yet he has not liberty to destroy himself, or so much as any creature in his possession, but where some nobler use than its bare preservation calls for it. The state of nature has a law of nature to govern it, which obliges every one; and reason, which is that law, teaches all mankind who will but consult it that, being all equal and independent, no one ought to harm another in his life, health, liberty, or possessions; for men being all the workmanship of one omnipotent and infinitely wise Maker — all the servants of one sovereign master, sent into the world by his order, and about his business — they are his property whose workmanship they are, made to last during his, not one another's pleasure; and being furnished with like faculties, sharing all in one community of nature, there cannot be supposed any such subordination among us that may authorize us to destroy another, as if we were made for one another's uses as the inferior ranks of creatures are for ours. . . .

And that all men may be restrained from invading others' rights and from doing hurt to one another, and the law of nature be observed, which wills the peace and preservation of all mankind, the execution of the law of nature is, in that state, put into every man's hands, whereby everyone has a right to punish the transgressors of that law to such a degree as may hinder its violation; for the law of nature would, as all other laws that concern men in this world, be in vain if there were nobody that in that state of nature had a power to execute that law and thereby preserve the innocent and restrain offenders. And if anyone in the state of nature may punish another for any evil he has done, everyone may do so; for in that state of perfect equality, where naturally there is no superiority or jurisdiction of one over another, what any may do in prosecution of that law, everyone must needs have a right to do.

And thus in the state of nature one man comes by a power over another; but yet no absolute or arbitrary power to use a criminal, when he has got him in his hands, according to the passionate heats or boundless extravagance of his own will; but only to retribute to him, so far as calm reason and conscience dictate, what is proportionate to his transgression, which is so much as may serve for reparation and restraint; for these two are the only reasons why one man may lawfully do harm to another, which is that we call punishment. In transgressing the law of nature, the offender declares himself to live by another rule than that of reason and common equity, which is that measure God has set to the actions of men for their mutual security; and so he becomes dangerous to mankind, the tie which is to secure them from injury and violence being slighted and broken by him. Which being a trespass against the whole species and the peace and safety of it provided for by the law of nature, every man upon this score, by the right he has to preserve mankind in general, may restrain, or, where it is necessary, destroy things noxious to them, and so may bring such evil on any one who has transgressed that law, as may make him repent the doing of it and thereby deter him, and by his example others, from doing the like mischief. And in this case, and upon this ground, every man has a right to punish the offender and be executioner of the law of nature.

* * *

To this strange doctrine — viz., that in the state of nature every one has the executive power of the law of nature — I doubt not but it will be objected that it is unreasonable for men to be judges in their own cases, that self-love will make men partial to themselves and their friends, and, on the other side, that ill-nature, passion, and revenge will carry them far in punishing others, and hence nothing but confusion and disorder will follow; and that therefore God has certainly appointed government to restrain the partiality and violence of men. I easily grant that civil government is the proper remedy for the inconveniences of the state of nature, which must certainly be great where men may be judges in their own case; since it is easy to be imagined that he who was so unjust as to do his brother an injury will scarce be so just as to condemn himself for it; but I shall desire those who make this objection to remember that absolute monarchs are but men, and if government is to be the remedy of those evils which necessarily follow from men's being judges in their own cases, and the state of nature is therefore not to be endured, I desire to know what kind of government that is, and how much better it is than the state of nature, where one man commanding a multitude has the liberty to be judge in his own case, and may do to all his subjects whatever he pleases, without the least liberty to any one to question or control those who execute his pleasure, and in whatsoever he does, whether led by reason, mistake, or passion, must be submitted to? Much better it is in the state of nature, wherein men are not bound to submit to the unjust will of another; and if he that judges, judges amiss in his own or any other case, he is answerable for it to the rest of mankind.

* * *

OF SLAVERY

The natural liberty of man is to be free from any superior power on earth, and not to be under the will or legislative authority of man, but to have only the law of nature for his rule. The liberty of man in society is to be under no other legislative power but that established by consent in the commonwealth, nor under the dominion of any will or restraint of any law but what that legislative shall enact according to the trust put in it. Freedom then is not . . . "a liberty for everyone to do what he lists, to live as he pleases, and not to be tied by any laws"; but freedom of men under government is to have a standing rule to live by, common to every one of that society and made by the legislative power erected in it, a liberty to follow my own will in all things where the rule prescribes not, and not to be subject to the inconstant, uncertain, unknown, arbitrary will of another man; as freedom of nature is to be under no other restraint but the law of nature.

This freedom from absolute, arbitrary power is so necessary to, and closely joined with, a man's preservation that he cannot part with it but by what forfeits his preservation and life together; for a man not having the power of his own life cannot by compact or his own consent enslave himself to any one, nor put himself under the absolute arbitrary power of another to take away his life when he pleases. Nobody can give more power than he has himself; and he that cannot take away his own life cannot give another power over it. . . .

Man, being born, as has been proved, with a title to perfect freedom and uncontrolled enjoyment of all the rights and privileges of the law of nature equally with any other man or number of men in the world, has by nature a power not only to preserve his property — that is, his life, liberty, and estate — against the injuries and attempts of other men, but to judge of and punish the breaches of that law in others as he is persuaded the offense deserves, even with death itself in crimes where the heinousness of the fact in his opinion requires it. But because no political society can be, nor subsist, without having in itself the power to preserve the property and, in order thereunto, punish the offenses of all those of that society, there and there only is political society where every one of the members has quitted his natural power, resigned it up into the hands of the community in all cases that exclude him not from appealing for protection to the law established by it. And thus all private judgment of every particular member being excluded, the community comes to be umpire by settled standing rules, indifferent and the same to all parties, and by men having authority from the community for the execution of those rules decides all the differences that may happen between any members of that society concerning any matter of right, and punishes those offenses which any member has committed against the society with such penalties as the law has established. . . .

And thus the commonwealth comes by a power to set down what punishment shall belong to the several transgressions which they think worthy of it committed amongst the members of that society — which is the power of making laws — as well as it has the power to punish any injury done unto any of its members by any one that is not of it — which is the power of war and peace — and all this for the preservation of the property of all the members of that society as far as is possible. . . . And herein we have the original of the legislative and executive power of civil society, which is to judge by standing laws how far offenses are to be punished when committed within the commonwealth, and also to determine, by occasional judgments founded on the present circumstances of the fact, how far injuries from without are to be vindicated; and in both these to employ all the force of all the members when there shall be need.

* * *

. . . [A]bsolute monarchy, which by some men is counted the only government in the world, is indeed inconsistent with civil society, and so can be no form of civil government at all . . . .

For he being supposed to have all, both legislative and executive, power in himself alone, there is no judge to be found, no appeal lies open to any one who may fairly and indifferently and with authority decide, and from whose decision relief and redress may be expected of any injury or inconvenience that may be suffered from the prince or by his order; so that such a man, however entitled, "czar," or "grand seignior," or how you please, is as much in the state of nature with all under his dominion as he is with the rest of mankind; for wherever any two men are who have no standing rule and common judge to appeal to on earth for the determination of controversies of right betwixt them, there they are still in the state of nature, and under all the inconveniences of it, with only this woeful difference to the subject, or rather slave, of an absolute prince: that, whereas in the ordinary state of nature he has a liberty to judge of his right and, according to the best of his power to maintain it; now, whenever his property is invaded by the will and order of his monarch, he has not only no appeal as those in society ought to have but, as if he were degraded from the common state of rational creatures, is denied a liberty to judge of or to defend his right; and so is exposed to all the misery and inconveniences that a man can fear from one who, being in the unrestrained state of nature, is yet corrupted with flattery and armed with power.

* * *

OF THE BEGINNING OF POLITICAL SOCIETIES

Men being, as has been said, by nature all free, equal, and independent, no one can be put out of this estate and subjected to the political power of another, without his own consent. The only way whereby any one divests himself of his natural liberty and puts on the bonds of civil society is by agreeing with other men to join and unite into a community for their comfortable, safe, and peaceable living one amongst another, in a secure enjoyment of their properties and a greater security against any that are not of it. This any number of men may do, because it injures not the freedom of the rest; they are left as they were in the liberty of the state of nature. When any number of men have so consented to make one community or government, they are thereby presently incorporated and make one body politic wherein the majority have a right to act and conclude the rest.

For when any number of men have, by the consent of every individual, made a community, they have thereby made that community one body, with a power to act as one body, which is only by the will and determination of the majority; for that which acts any community being only the consent of the individuals of it, and it being necessary to that which is one body to move one way, it is necessary the body should move that way whither the greater force carries it, which is the consent of the majority; or else it is impossible it should act or continue one body, one community, which the consent of every individual that united into it agreed that it should; and so every one is bound by that consent to be concluded by the majority. And therefore we see that in assemblies impowered to act by positive laws, where no number is set by that positive law which impowers them, the act of the majority passes for the act of the whole and, of course, determines, as having by the law of nature and reason the power of the whole.

And thus every man, by consenting with others to make one body politic under one government, puts himself under an obligation to every one of that society to submit to the determination of the majority and to be concluded by it . . . .

For if the consent of the majority shall not in reason be received as the act of the whole and conclude every individual, nothing but the consent of every individual can make anything to be the act of the whole; but such a consent is next to impossible ever to be had if we consider the infirmities of health and avocations of business which in a number, though much less than that of a commonwealth, will necessarily keep many away from the public assembly. To which, if we add the variety of opinions and contrariety of interests which unavoidably happen in all collections of men, the coming into society upon such terms would be [fruitless]. Such a constitution as this would make the mighty leviathan of a shorter duration than the feeblest creatures, and not let it outlast the day it was born in . . . .

*　*　*

OF THE ENDS OF POLITICAL SOCIETY AND GOVERNMENT

If man in the state of nature be so free, as has been said, if he be absolute lord of his own person and possessions, equal to the greatest, and subject to nobody, why will he part with his freedom, why will he give up his empire and subject himself to the dominion and control of any other power? To which it is obvious to answer that though in the state of nature he has such a right, yet the enjoyment of it is very uncertain and constantly exposed to the invasion of others; for all being kings as much as he, every man his equal, and the greater part no strict observers of equity and justice, the enjoyment of the property he has in this state is very unsafe, very insecure. This makes him willing to quit a condition which, however free, is full of fears and continual dangers; and it is not without reason that he seeks out and is willing to join in society with others who are already united, or have a mind to unite, for the mutual preservation of their lives, liberties, and estates, which I call by the general name "property."

The great and chief end, therefore, of men's uniting into commonwealths and putting themselves under government is the preservation of their property. To which in the state of nature there are many things wanting:

First, there wants an established, settled, known law, received and allowed by common consent to be the standard of right and wrong and the common measure to decide all controversies between them; for though the law of nature be plain and intelligible to all rational creatures, yet men, being biased by their interests as well as ignorant for want of studying it, are not apt to allow of it as a law binding to them in the application of their particular cases.

Secondly, in the state of nature there wants a known and indifferent judge with authority to determine all differences according to the established law; for every one in that state being both judge and executioner of the law of nature, men being partial to themselves, passion and revenge is very apt to carry them too far and with too much heat in their own cases, as well as negligence and unconcernedness to make them too remiss in other men's.

Thirdly, in the state of nature there often wants power to back and support the sentence when right, and to give it due execution. They who by any justice offend will seldom fail, where they are able, by force, to make good their injustice; such resistance many times makes the punishment dangerous and frequently destructive to those who attempt it.

* * *

But though men when they enter into society give up the equality, liberty and executive power they had in the state of nature into the hands of the society, to be so far disposed of by the legislative as the good of the society shall require, yet it being only with an intention in every one the better to preserve himself his liberty and property — for no rational creature can be supposed to change his condition with an intention to be worse — the power of the society, or legislative constituted by them, can never be supposed to extend farther than the common good, but is obliged to secure every one's property by providing against those three defects above-mentioned that made the state of nature so unsafe and uneasy. And so whoever has the legislative or supreme power of any commonwealth is bound to govern by established standing laws, promulgated and known to the people, and not by extemporary decrees; by indifferent and upright judges who are to decide controversies by those laws; and to employ the force of the community at home only in the execution of such laws, or abroad to prevent or redress foreign injuries, and secure the community from inroads and invasion.

And all this to be directed to no other end but the peace, safety, and public good of the people.

OF THE EXTENT OF THE LEGISLATIVE POWER

* * *

Though the legislative, whether placed in one or more, whether it be always in being, or only by intervals, though it be the supreme power in every commonwealth; yet:

First, it is not, nor can possibly be, absolutely arbitrary over the lives and fortunes of the people; for it being but the joint power of every member of the society given up to that person or assembly which is legislator, it can be no more than those persons had in a state of nature before they entered into society and gave up to the community; for nobody can transfer to another more power than he has in himself, and nobody has an absolute arbitrary power over himself or over any other, to destroy his own life or take away the life or property of another. A man, as has been proved, cannot subject himself to the arbitrary power of another, and having in the state of nature no arbitrary power over the life, liberty, or possession of another, but only so much as the law of nature gave him for the preservation of himself and the rest of mankind, this is all he does or can give up to the commonwealth, and by it to the legislative power, so that the legislative can have no more than this. Their power, in the utmost bounds of it, is limited to the public good of the society. It is a power that has no other end but preservation, and therefore can never have a right to destroy, enslave, or designedly to impoverish the subjects. The obligations of the law of nature cease not in society but only in many cases are drawn closer and have by human laws known penalties annexed to them to enforce their observation. Thus the law of nature stands as an eternal rule to all men, legislators as well as others. The rules that they make for other men's actions must, as well as their own and other men's actions, be conformable to the law of nature — i.e. to the will of God, of which that is a declaration — and the fundamental law of nature being the preservation of mankind, no human sanction can be good or valid against it.

Secondly, the legislative or supreme authority cannot assume to itself a power to rule by extemporary, arbitrary decrees, but is bound to dispense justice and to decide the rights of the subject by promulgated, standing laws, and known authorized judges. . . .

* * *

Thirdly, the supreme power cannot take away from any man part of his property without his own consent; for the preservation of property being the end of government and that for which men enter into society, it necessarily supposes and requires that the people should have property; without which they must be supposed to lose that, by entering into society, which was the end for which they entered into it — too gross an absurdity for any man to own. Men, therefore, in society having property, they have such right to the goods which by the law of the community are theirs, that nobody has a right to take their substance or any part of it from them without their own consent . . . . Hence it is a mistake to think that the supreme or legislative power of any commonwealth can do what it will and dispose of the estates of the subject arbitrarily, or take any part of them at pleasure. This is not much to be feared in governments where the legislative consists, wholly or in part, in assemblies which are variable, whose members, upon the dissolution of the assembly, are subjects under the common laws of their country, equally without the rest. But in governments where the legislative is one lasting assembly, always in being, or in one man, as in absolute monarchies, there is danger still that they will think themselves to have a distinct interest from the rest of the community, and so will be apt to increase their own riches and power by taking what they think fit from the people . . . .

It is true, governments cannot be supported without great charge, and it is fit every one who enjoys his share of the protection should pay out of his estate his proportion for the maintenance of it. But still it must be with his own consent — i.e., the consent of the majority, giving it either by themselves or their representatives chosen by them. For if any one shall claim a power to lay and levy taxes on the people, by his own authority and without such consent of the people, he thereby invades the fundamental law of property and subverts the end of government; for what property have I in that which another may by right take, when he pleases, to himself?

* * *

OF TYRANNY

As usurpation is the exercise of power which another has a right to, so tyranny is the exercise of power beyond right, which nobody can have a right to. And this is making use of the power any one has in his hands, not for the good of those who are under it, but for his own private separate advantage — when the governor, however entitled, makes not the law, but his will, the rule, and his commands and actions are not directed to the preservation of the properties of his people, but the satisfaction of his own ambition, revenge, covetousness, or any other irregular passion.

* * *

It is a mistake to think this fault is proper only to monarchies; other forms of government are liable to it as well as that. For wherever the power that is put in any hands for the government of the people and the preservation of their properties is applied to other ends, and made use of to impoverish, harass, or subdue them to the arbitrary and irregular commands of those that have it, there it presently becomes tyranny, whether those that thus use it are one or many. . . .

May the commands, then, of a prince be opposed? May he be resisted as often as any one shall find himself aggrieved, and but imagine he has not right done him? This will unhinge and overturn all polities, and, instead of government and order, leave nothing but anarchy and confusion.

To this I answer that force is to be opposed to nothing but to unjust and unlawful force; whoever makes any opposition in any other case draws upon himself a just condemnation both from God and man; and so no such danger or confusion will follow, as is often suggested. . . .

* * *

OF THE DISSOLUTION OF GOVERNMENT

* * *

. . . The constitution of the legislative is the first and fundamental act of society, whereby provision is made for the continuation of their union under the direction of persons and bonds of laws made by persons authorized thereunto by the consent and appointment of the people, without which no one man or number of men amongst them can have authority of making laws that shall be binding to the rest. When any one or more shall take upon them to make laws, whom the people have not appointed so to do, they make laws without authority, which the people are not therefore bound to obey; by which means they come again to be out of subjection and may constitute to themselves a new legislative as they think best, being in full liberty to resist the force of those who without authority would impose anything upon them. . . .

* * *

There is one way more whereby such a government may be dissolved, and that is when he who has the supreme executive power neglects and abandons that charge, so that the laws already made can no longer be put in execution. This is demonstrably to reduce all to anarchy, and so effectually to dissolve the government; for laws not being made for themselves, but to be by their execution the bonds of the society, to keep every part of the body politic in its due place and function, when that totally ceases, the government visibly ceases, and the people become a confused multitude, without order or connection. . . . Where the laws cannot be executed, it is all one as if there were no laws; and a government without laws is, I suppose a mystery in politics, inconceivable to human capacity and inconsistent with human society.

In these and the like cases, when the government is dissolved, the people are at liberty to provide for themselves by erecting a new legislative, differing from the other by the change of persons or form, or both, as they shall find it most for their safety and good; for the society can never by the fault of another lose the native and original right it has to preserve itself, which can only be done by a settled legislative, and a fair and impartial execution of the laws made by it. But the state of mankind is not so miserable that they are not capable of using this remedy till it be too late to look for any. To tell people they may provide for themselves by erecting a new legislative, when by oppression, artifice, or being delivered over to a foreign power, their old one is gone, is only to tell them they may expect relief when it is too late and the evil is past cure. This is in effect no more than to bid them first be slaves, and then to take care of their liberty, and when their chains are on, tell them they may act like freemen. This, if barely so, is rather mockery than relief; and men can never be secure from tyranny if there be no means to escape it till they are perfectly under it; and therefore it is that they have not only a right to get out of it, but to prevent it.

* * *

To this perhaps it will be said that, the people being ignorant and always discontented, to lay the foundation of government in the unsteady opinion and uncertain humor of the people is to expose it to certain ruin; and no government will be able long to subsist if the people may set up a new legislative whenever they take offense at the old one. To this I answer: Quite the contrary. People are not so easily got out of their old forms as some are apt to suggest. They are hardly to be prevailed with to amend the acknowledged faults in the frame they have been accustomed to. And if there be any original defects, or adventitious ones introduced by time or corruption, it is not an easy thing to get them changed, even when all the world sees there is an opportunity for it. This slowness and aversion in the people to quit their old constitutions has in the many revolutions which have been seen in this kingdom, in this and former ages, still kept us to, or after some interval of fruitless attempts still brought us back again to, our old legislative of king, lords, and commons; and whatever provocations have made the crown be taken from some of our princes' heads, they never carried the people so far as to place it in another line.

But it will be said this hypothesis lays a ferment for frequent rebellion. To which I answer:

* * *

Secondly, I answer, such revolutions happen not upon every little mismanagement in public affairs. Great mistakes in the ruling part, many wrong and inconvenient laws, and all the slips of human frailty will be born by the people without mutiny or murmur. But if a long train of abuses, prevarications, and artifices, all tending the same way, make the design visible to the people, and they cannot but feel what they lie under and see whither they are going, it is not to be wondered that they should then rouse themselves and endeavor to put the rule into such hands which may secure to them the ends for which government was at first erected, and without which ancient names and specious forms are so far from being better that they are much worse than the state of nature or pure anarchy . . . .

Thirdly, I answer that this doctrine of a power in the people of providing for their safety anew by a new legislative, when their legislators have acted contrary to their trust by invading their property, is the best fence against rebellion, and the probablest means to hinder it; for rebellion being an opposition, not to persons, but authority which is founded only in the constitutions and laws of the government, those, whoever they be, who by force break through, and by force justify their violation of them, are truly and properly rebels; for when men, by entering into society and civil government, have excluded force and introduced laws for the preservation of property, peace, and unity amongst themselves, those who set up force again in opposition to the laws do *rebellare* — that is, bring back again the state of war — and are properly rebels . . . .

* * *

But if they who say "it lays a foundation for rebellion" mean that it may occasion civil wars or internecine broils, to tell the people they are absolved from obedience when illegal attempts are made upon their liberties or properties, and may oppose the unlawful violence of those who were their magistrates when they invade their properties contrary to the trust put in them, and that therefore this doctrine is not to be allowed, being so destructive to the peace of the world; they may as well say, upon the same ground, that honest men may not oppose robbers or pirates because this may occasion disorder or bloodshed. . . .

* * *

Here, it is likely, the common question will be made: Who shall be the judge whether the prince or legislative act contrary to their trust? This, perhaps, ill-affected and factious men may spread amongst the people, when the prince only makes use of his due prerogative. To this I reply: The people shall be judge; for who shall be judge whether his trustee or deputy acts well and according to the trust reposed in him but he who deputes him and must, by having deputed him, have still a power to discard him when he fails in his trust? If this be reasonable in particular cases of private men, why should it be otherwise in that of the greatest moment when the welfare of millions is concerned, and also where the evil, if not prevented, is greater and the redress very difficult, dear, and dangerous?

But further, this question, Who shall be judge? cannot mean that there is no judge at all; for where there is no judicature on earth to decide controversies amongst men, God in heaven is Judge. He alone, it is true, is Judge of the right. But every man is judge for himself, as in all other cases, so in this, whether another has put himself into a state of war with him, and whether he should appeal to the Supreme Judge . . . .

If a controversy arise betwixt a prince and some of the people in a matter where the law is silent or doubtful, and the thing be of great consequence, I should think the proper umpire in such a case should be the body of the people; for in cases where the prince has a trust reposed in him and is dispensed from the common ordinary rules of the law, there, if any men find themselves aggrieved and think the prince acts contrary to or beyond that trust, who so proper to judge as the body of the people (who, at first, lodged that trust in him) how far they meant it should extend? But if the prince, or whoever they be in the administration, decline that way of determination, the appeal then lies nowhere but to heaven; force between either persons who have no known superior on earth, or which permits no appeal to a judge on earth, being properly a state of war wherein the appeal lies only to heaven; and in that state the injured party must judge for himself when he will think fit to make use of that appeal and put himself upon it.

To conclude, the power that every individual gave the society when he entered into it can never revert to the individuals again as long as the society lasts, but will always remain in the community, because without this there can be no community, no commonwealth, which is contrary to the original agreement; so also when the society has placed the legislative in any assembly of men, to continue in them and their successors with direction and authority for providing such successors, the legislative can never revert to the people while that government lasts, because having provided a legislative with power to continue for ever, they have given up their political power to the legislative and cannot resume it. But if they have set limits to the duration of their legislative and made this supreme power in any person or assembly only temporary, or else when by the miscarriages of those in authority it is forfeited, upon the forfeiture, or at the determination of the time set, it reverts to the society, and the people have a right to act as supreme and continue the legislative in themselves, or erect a new form, or under the old form place it in new hands, as they think good.

NOTES AND QUESTIONS

1. Locke's *Second Treatise of Government* was probably written before the Glorious Revolution, so it is incorrect to view it as being drafted to "legitimate" or "justify" the acts of those who took the throne from James II. Undoubtedly, however, it was written with the historic abuses, or perceived historic abuses, of Stuart absolutism (or even Continental absolutism) in mind. Locke's patron was the fabulous and unscrupulous Whig, the Earl of Shaftesbury. What would you describe as the overriding political principles of Locke's thought, and to which philosophers or politicians we have studied thus far would you say his political ideas are similar?

2. It has been suggested that during most of early American history, there has been a battle between the Hobbesians and the Lockeans. How would you explain the differences between the political philosophies of Hobbes and Locke? Are there similarities? In particular, how, if at all, do they differ on the state of nature and the nature of humankind? How do they differ, if at all, on the right of revolution and the rights of citizens or subjects? Do Hobbes and Locke seek any of the same goals? Do they differ with regard to the sources of the law? Do they differ with regard to the role which the supernatural has in the formation and conduct of governments?

3. For our purposes the most useful part of Locke's analysis may be his suggestion that humans possess certain inalienable rights — rights to life, liberty, and property. What is the precise nature of those inalienable rights, and where do they come from? Why are they "inalienable," and what does that mean? Why is property one of those inalienable rights? Are you comfortable with Locke's treatment of property? Does it carry within it any assumptions about the appropriate nature of society? Note how the "pursuit of happiness" is substituted for "property" in your next reading, and consider why this should be so.

4. Locke provides a justification for revolution, but what is there in Locke's philosophy that guarantees that this "right to revolution" will not be abused? Who is to prevent a dissatisfied majority from imposing its revolutionary will on a weak minority? What, ultimately, was the basis of Locke's political philosophy? George W. Sabine, for instance, in his classic text, A HISTORY OF POLITICAL THEORY, 4th ed., [as revised by Thomas Landon Thorsen] argues at p. 495, that Locke's political philosophy was flawed because Locke never made up his mind what exactly was fundamental and what was derivative. Would you agree with this assessment?

5. From approximately the time of the English Civil Wars, through the Restoration and the Glorious Revolution, on down to the middle of the eighteenth century, England's North American colonies were allowed to flourish in a state often referred to as "benign neglect." From small and tenuous beginnings in Virginia and Massachusetts, the colonies grew to major agricultural and commercial enterprises, so that by the end of the eighteenth century, Philadelphia was the greatest English-speaking metropolis after London.

However, as Britain's commercial activities expanded in the second half of the eighteenth century, and as war loomed with France on the Continent and in North America, England believed it necessary to regulate the colonies more strictly and to collect customs and impose taxation more rigorously, so that the Americans might more closely bear their fair share of the expenses of the British Empire.

The Americans, particularly as a result of the victory of England in the Seven Years War (known in America as the "French and Indian War") which vastly expanded the territory of British North America, derived great benefits from their status as subjects of the Crown. These great benefits, thought the ministry, ought to be enough to make the colonists happy to cooperate by paying their fair share of customs and taxes.

The causes of the American Revolution are exceedingly complex, but can be usefully reduced to the core notion that the Americans felt that the British imposed these financial measures of customs, taxes, and collection machinery, without adequate consultation of the Americans themselves. The measures, including the Sugar Act of 1764, the Stamp Act of 1765, the Tea Tax, and the final blows, the "Intolerable Acts" (closing the port of Boston and modifying some of the procedures for criminal trials), seemed like breaches of what the colonists perceived to be their historic "rights of Englishmen," rights they believed to have been secured by the Bill of Rights of 1689 and the Glorious Revolution itself. In fact, many Americans, although perhaps not the most astute of them, believed that England's policies in the late eighteenth century were characterized by the same kind of corruption, intrigue and irresponsibility as those adopted during the reigns of the Stuarts in seventeenth century England.

With this is mind, compare the text of our Declaration of Independence, reprinted at the front of this volume, with the text of Locke and the sentiments expressed in the English Bill of Rights. You probably do not recall each of the specific causes for the particular clauses in the Declaration, but this short recalling of the context, and what you remember from your training in American history should give you enough of a basis to decide whether you would have been willing to pledge your life, your fortune, and your sacred honor for the cause of separation from England. The English government no longer seemed a sufficient means to preserve pre-existing natural rights. The question remained whether a better one could be fashioned.

Chapter 2

THE DECLARATION AND ITS CONSTITUTION — LINKING FIRST PRINCIPLE TO NECESSARY MEANS

I. The Constitution — Means or End?

Is the Constitution a means to advance particular fundamental ends or principles, or is it a freestanding means to any end, democratically chosen? This is the question taken up in this Chapter. The beginning of an answer is to be found in the English common law tradition. Common law lawyers followed a distinct pattern of legal thinking: the law of God, the law of nature, and the law of the land. Chapter Two addresses all three aspects of the American common law tradition, but concentrates in Part I on the law of nature, or our ability as thinking human beings to reason to good result. Part II of this Chapter turns toward the law of God, at least insofar as it manifests itself in matters of religion. The Declaration of Independence squarely rests the American constitutional order upon both sources, or in its words, "the Laws of Nature and of Nature's God." But from the beginning (see especially, the book of *Genesis*), it has been the nature of human beings to become a law unto themselves through the third source, "the law of the land," or as we know it, positive law. At times, the positive law seemingly has denied not only the relevance of God, but also the very nature of human beings (e.g., slavery). In Part I, we see this turn toward self-centeredness, in the perennial struggle over whether natural law is sufficiently knowable or definite to guide human action, and in particular, constitutional litigation. In Part II, a similar pattern emerges in the struggle to interpret the First Amendment Religion Clauses ("Congress shall make no law respecting an establishment of religion, or prohibiting the free exercise thereof"). At our nation's founding and for a considerable period thereafter, these Clauses preserved, free of an established national church or sect-based favoritism, the individual freedom to choose how best to know and worship God. More recently, however, the Clauses have been transformed into a claim of neutrality between religion and no religion at all. Some say this "neutrality" manifests a hostility to public acknowledgment of the significance of private religious faith.

A. The Common Law and the Natural Law

The common law thought pattern — law of God, law of nature, and law of the land — suffered a major disruption when Henry VIII, in order to secure a divorce contrary to the teaching of the Roman Catholic Church, declared the King of England to be the supreme head of the Church on earth. Thomas More, the King's Lord Chancellor at the time, disagreed, and ultimately for his disagreement, would pay with his life. But as British barrister Richard O'Sullivan reflects below, even as Thomas More died, the idea that the King or Parliament could legislate without limit, or in disregard of some conception of God or our reasoned discovery of human nature, has refused to die.

Richard O'Sullivan, *The Natural Law and Common Law, in* 3 NATURAL LAW INSTITUTE PROCEEDINGS 9, 31-43 (Edward F. Barrett ed., 1950)

In 1468 the Lord Chancellor [Thomas More] told the assembled peers that Justice "was ground, well, and root of all prosperity, peace and public rule of every realm, whereupon all the law of the world had been ground and set, which resteth in three; that is to say, the law of God, the law of nature, and the positive law."

* * *

The Year Books bear witness to the same order or hierarchy of laws. There is in Plowden a report of the well-known case of *Hales vs. Petit* in which the Common Bench declared that suicide (in this case the suicide of one of the King's judges) is an offense against God, against Nature and against the King.

1.) Against God, in that it is a breach of His commandment, "Thou shalt not kill" and to kill oneself, by which act he kills in presumption his own soul, is a greater offense than killing another.

2.) Against Nature; because it is contrary to the rule of self-preservation which is the principle of nature, for every living thing does by instinct of nature defend itself against destruction and then to destroy oneself is contrary to nature and a thing most horrible.

3.) Against the King in that hereby he has lost a subject . . . he being the head has lost one of his mystical members.

At the crisis of English history . . . [a] statute dictated by Thomas Cromwell had declared the King to be the Supreme Head on earth of the Ecclesia Anglicana. It gave the King authority to reform and redress all errors and heresies in the land. A second Statute made it treason for anyone maliciously to wish, will or desire by words or in writing to deprive the King of his dignity, title or name of his royal state.

In the first of the four counts of the Indictment [against Thomas More, the Lord Chancellor,] it was alleged that the prisoner, being asked in the Tower, by the Secretary of State whether he "accepted and reputed the King as the Supreme Head of the Church in England," remained silent and declined to make answer. . . .

To this count in the Indictment, the prisoner took exception: "Touching, I say, this challenge and accusation, I answer that for this my taciturnity and silence neither you nor your law nor any law in the world is able justly and rightly to punish me unless you may beside it lay to my charge either some word or some fact in deed."

The objection was overruled, and the pretended trial proceeded to its close on all four counts in the Indictment. After a verdict of guilty on each count had been returned, Thomas More claimed the right to speak his mind: "seeing that I see ye are determined to condemn me (God knoweth how) I will now in discharge of my conscience speak my mind plainly and freely touching my Indictment and your Statute withal."

He proceeded to argue that the Act under which he had been charged and condemned was contrary to the law of God, the law of reason, and the law of the land.

"And forasmuch as this Indictment is grounded upon an Act of Parliament directly repugnant to the laws of God and His Holy Church . . . it is therefore in law among Christian men insufficient to charge any Christian man."

The Statute was against the law of reason: "For this realm being but one member and a small part of the Church, might not make a particular law, disagreeable with the general law of the Church, no more than the City of London being but one poor member in respect of the whole realm, might make a law against an Act of Parliament to bind the whole realm."

The Statute was against the law of the land. It was "contrary to the law and Statutes of this our land, yet unrepealed, as they might evidently perceive in Magna Carta . . . .["]

In the reign of Henry VIII, says Professor Holdsworth, Vinerian Professor of English Law at the University of Oxford, "It was realized that the Acts of Parliament, whether public or private, were legislative in character and the judges were obligated to admit that these acts however morally unjust must be obeyed . . . . The legislation which had deposed the Pope and made the Church an integral part of the State, had made it clear that the morality of the provisions of a law, or the reasons which induced the legislature to pass it, could not be regarded by the courts."

It was obviously difficult to assign any limits to the power of the Acts of a body which had effected changes so sweeping as those effected by the Reformation Parliament. Lord Burleigh is reported by James I to have said that he knew not what an Act of Parliament could not do in England. When an Act of Parliament had acquired this authority, says Professor Holdsworth, the last remnants of the idea that there might be fundamental laws, which could not be changed by any person or body of persons in the State necessarily disappears.

After the Reformation, the Parliament of England was no longer bound by the laws of nature or the law of God.

* * *

Now, though the theory (or the supposition) of the Omnipotence of Parliament was implicit in the Reformation Statutes, the process of translating this new theory into a practical rule of jurisprudence was not easy or simple. This new theory threatened the whole existence of the Common Law which had its foundation in the natural law . . . .

NOTES AND QUESTIONS

1. Why did the legislation formalizing England's break with the Roman Catholic church also provide, as Professor Holdsworth reports, that henceforth "the morality of the provisions of the law . . . could not be regarded by the courts"? Isn't it the idea of the natural law that truth is knowable and universal regardless of religious denomination? Why would the formation of the Anglican Church threaten the "whole existence of the Common Law"? What is the relationship between natural law and common law?

2. Professor Holdsworth was the Vinerian Professor of English Law at Oxford. This position was first occupied by Sir William Blackstone (1723-1780), whose famous *Commentaries on the Laws of England* was widely regarded by the leading American colonists as the best treatise on the English common law, which became the foundation of American law. The following passage from the *Commentaries* was thus most familiar to the American founders. Note, in particular, how Blackstone coins the terminology "pursuit of happiness," which later finds its way into the Declaration of Independence. Note as well how Blackstone indicates that the natural law, man's reasoned deduction of that impressed by God within the design of human nature, became interwoven with the common law (natural law "is branched in our systems").

1 WILLIAM BLACKSTONE, COMMENTARIES ON THE LAWS OF ENGLAND *38-41 (James Dewitt Andrews ed., Callaghan Co. 4th ed. 1899)

[W]hen the Supreme Being formed the universe, and created matter out of nothing, he impressed certain principles upon that matter, from which it can never depart, and without which it would cease to be . . . .

* * *

This then is the general significance of law, a rule of action dictated by some superior being; and in those creatures that have neither the power to think, nor to will, such laws must be invariably obeyed, so long as the creature itself subsists, for its existence depends on that obedience. But laws, in their more confined sense, and in which it is our present business to consider them, denote the rules, not of action in general, but of *human* action or conduct: that is, the precepts by which man . . . endowed with both reason and free will, is commanded to make use of those faculties in the general regulation of his behaviour.

Man, considered as a creature, must necessarily be subject to the laws of his creator, for he is entirely a dependent being . . . . [A] state of dependence will inevitably oblige the inferior to take the will of him, on whom he depends, as the rule of his conduct . . . in all those points wherein his dependence consists . . . . [C]onsequently, [since] man depends absolutely upon his maker for every thing, it is necessary that he should in all points conform to his maker's will.

This will of his maker is called the law of nature.[a] For as God, when he created matter, and endued it with a principle of mobility, established certain rules for the perpetual direction of that motion; so, when he created man, and endued him with free will to conduct himself in all parts of life, he laid down certain immutable laws of human nature, whereby that free will is in some degree regulated and restrained, and gave him also the faculty of *reason* to discover the purport of those laws . . . .

* * *

. . . [T]he Creator is a being, not only of infinite *power*, and *wisdom*, but also of infinite *goodness*, [therefore,] he has been pleased so to contrive the constitution and frame of humanity, that we should want no other prompter to inquire after and pursue the rule of right, but only our own self love, that universal principle of action. For he has so intimately connected, so inseparably interwoven the laws of eternal justice with the happiness of each individual, that [happiness] cannot be attained but by observing the former; and, if the former be punctually obeyed, it cannot but induce [happiness]. In consequence of which mutual connection of justice and human felicity, [God] has not perplexed the law of nature with a multitude of abstracted rules and precepts . . . but has graciously reduced the rule of obedience to this one paternal precept, *"that man shall pursue his own true and substantial happiness."*[b] This is the foundation of what we call ethics, or natural law. For the several articles into which it is branched in our systems, amount to no more than demonstrating, that this or that action tends to man's real happiness, and therefore very justly concluding that the performance of it is a part of the law of nature; or, on the other hand, that this or that action is destructive of man's real happiness, and therefore that the law of nature forbids it.

NOTES AND QUESTIONS

1. How might Blackstone prove especially useful in the American colonies' dispute with England over representation and related matters, such as trade and taxation? Blackstone described natural law as "binding over all the globe in all countries, and at all times; no human laws are of any validity, if contrary to this; and such of them as are valid derive all of their force, and all of their authority,

---

[a] Emphasis added.

[b] Emphasis added.

mediately or immediately, from this origin." *Id.* at *41. For American colonies looking for persuasive authority to dispute adverse English Parliamentary measures such as the Stamp Act, Blackstone was invaluable. When Blackstone declares the absolute rights of individuals as "the right of personal security, the right of personal liberty, and the right of private property," *id.* at *129, he virtually prescribes the trilogy of unalienable rights in the Declaration of Independence.

2. Blackstone easily saw the natural law as explicated through the application of the common law as binding in theory on all. Thus, returning to the question at issue in this Chapter — whether or not the Constitution must be construed to advance particular fundamental ends — it would thus far appear that Blackstone would be inclined to say that it must. Legislative power no more than the arbitrary prerogatives asserted by the Stuart Kings can contradict the natural law. As Blackstone writes, "acts of Parliament that are impossible to be performed are of no validity; and if there arise out of them . . . any absurd consequences, . . . contradictory to common reason [informed by the natural law, of course — Eds.], they are, with regard to those collateral consequences, void." *Id.* at *91. In other words, *all* of government — even that derived from consent in the legislature — is subject to (or if you will, must advance) particular fundamental (natural law) ends.

3. But there's a problem, *who* was to tell a given government entity that it has acted beyond its authority or in derogation of fundamental principle? As suggested in Chapter 1, this question emerged in England when the Stuart monarchs in the 17th century declared themselves to be superior to the common law and Acts of Parliament. In the words of Lord Chancellor Ellesmere in *Calvin's Case*, "the monarch is the law; the King is the law speaking." 77 Eng. Rep. 377 (K.B. 1608). As we learned, Parliament contested this brazen assertion and would ultimately prevail in the so-called Glorious Revolution of 1688 in which James II fled the country to be replaced by William and Mary, who, in the 1689 English Bill of Rights, acquiesced to legislative supremacy. But what if the legislative body disregards fundamental right? Here, Blackstone posits that "if the parliament will positively enact [an unreasonable thing, there is] no power in the ordinary forms of the constitution, that is vested with authority to control it." 1 BLACKSTONE, *supra*, at *91. Uncomfortably, from the standpoint of principled argumentation, Blackstone appears to stand for the asymmetrical proposition that the King or executive must be under the enacted law, and yes, the legislature is bound by the common (natural) law in the enactment of law, but there is no entity known to man able to correct the legislature when it, itself, exceeds these boundaries. Blackstone explicitly rejects judicial review, arguing "the judges are [not] at liberty to reject it; for that were to set the judicial power above that of the legislature, which would be subversive of all government." *Id.*

4. A recurring question in this book will ask you to evaluate whether there is an inability to constrain legislative action contrary to fundamental natural law in the United States. In the excerpts below, acclaimed Law School Deans Roscoe

Pound of Harvard and Clarence Manion of Notre Dame argue that Blackstone's view did not carry over to America, but as we will see later in this Chapter, today's Supreme Court is ambivalent over the scope of judicial review, and in particular, whether it is to be guided by natural law. Of course, even if Pound, Manion or others convince you to accept judicial review based upon higher or natural law principle, who then is to check the *judiciary* when it goes astray? In this regard, many modern legal historians and commentators perceive the greatest danger to democratic governance and natural law principle to lie with the judiciary. What do you think?

Roscoe Pound, *The Development of Constitutional Guarantees of Liberty*, 20 NOTRE DAME L. REV. 347, 367 (1945)

[T]here are three points of origin of what has been called the American doctrine of the power of the courts with respect to unconstitutional legislation . . . . One is the idea of the law of the land as expounded [by Coke]. A second is Coke's doctrine that statutes contrary to common right and reason and so to fundamental law were void . . . . The third is the practice . . . of appeals to the Privy Council in which statutes enacted by colonial legislatures were held void . . . because in conflict with some provision of the colonial or provincial charter or in contravention of the common law, made by the charter the measure of lawmaking authority. That statutes could be scrutinized to look into the basis of their authority and if in conflict with fundamental law must be disregarded was as much a matter of course to the American lawyer of the era of the Revolution as the doctrine of the absolute binding force of an act of Parliament is to the English lawyer of today. American lawyers were taught to believe in a fundamental law which, after the [American] Revolution, they found declared in written constitutions. After [the English Revolution of] 1688 there was no fundamental law superior to Parliament.

Dean Pound's proposition that America rejected legislative supremacy, and thus, deliberately linked its written Constitution to the fundamental natural law has been repeated by many. The most concise summation of natural law proximate to the founding was the Declaration of Independence. The late Dean Clarence Manion of the University of Notre Dame put it this way:

Clarence E. Manion, *The Natural Law Philosophy of the Founding Fathers, in* 1 NATURAL LAW INSTITUTE PROCEEDINGS 3, 16 (Alfred L. Scanlan ed., 1949)

The fact is that the Declaration is the best possible condensation of the natural law-common law doctrines as they were developed and expounded in England and America for hundreds of years prior to the American Revolution. By pushing and pursuing the principle of parliamentary absolutism it was England and not America who abandoned the ancient traditions of English liberty. In 1776 the British Government was insisting that "the law of the land" and "the immemorial rights of English subjects" were exclusively and precisely what the British Parliament from time to time declared them to be. This claim for parliamentary absolutism was at variance with all the great traditions of the natural law and common law as recorded through the centuries from Bracton to Blackstone. By abandoning their ingrained concepts of the natural law, the colonists undoubtedly could have made a comfortable settlement of their tax and navigation difficulties with England, but they chose the alternatives so well and so logically declared in the Declaration of Independence.

B. The Declaration of Independence — A Summary of American Fundamental Principle

THE DECLARATION OF INDEPENDENCE para. 2 (U.S. 1776) (Preamble)

We hold these truths to be self-evident, that all men are created equal, that they are endowed by their Creator with certain unalienable Rights, that among these are Life, Liberty, and the pursuit of Happiness. That to secure these rights, Governments are instituted among Men, deriving their just powers from the consent of the governed — That whenever any Form of Government becomes destructive of these ends, it is the Right of the People to alter or to abolish it, and to institute new Government, laying its foundation on such principles and organizing its powers in such form, as to them shall seem most likely to effect their Safety and Happiness.

NOTES AND QUESTIONS

1. These relatively few words are viewed by notable political theorists to summarize, as the late political philosopher Russell Kirk revealed in a book by the same name, *The Roots of the American Order*. Chapter One and this Chapter have introduced you to these sources. The Declaration recites that we as a Nation hold at least some *truths to be self-evident*: that is, every proposition isn't equally valid. Some opinions are right; others, wrong. In the phraseology, "the Laws of Nature and of Nature's God," we are further instructed that the measure of the validity of any opinion is to be found in one of two sources — either reasoned reflection upon the intrinsic design of human nature, "the laws of nature," or the "law of Nature's God," that is, the revealed word of God. These are the very same sources of authority relied upon by Thomas More to evaluate the actions of Henry VIII.

Nevertheless, you will shortly learn, if you do not already know from previous study, that referencing God, revelation, or religion generally in terms of constitutional study has been made controversial, in part, as a result of highly contested Supreme Court opinions since about 1940, and especially since 1960. These case developments are explored in Part II.B. of this Chapter. Nevertheless, in 1776 — and indeed throughout much of the history of America — the existence of God (as a "Creator") is an accepted postulate of the American order. Of course, much of God's revealed word, be it located in the Old or New Testaments or informed by other religious instruction, is basic guidance into how to "pursue happiness" — that is, live a good and happy life. The framers recognized as much. In his first inaugural address, for example, George Washington observed that "the propitious smiles of Heaven can never be expected on a nation that disregards the eternal rules of order and right, which Heaven itself has ordained." GEORGE WASHINGTON, FIRST INNAUGURAL ADDRESS (Apr. 30, 1789), *reprinted in* GEORGE WASHINGTON A COLLECTION 460, 462 (W.B. Allen ed., 1988).

Human knowledge being imperfect, we differ in how we come to know God. But arguably, these denominational differences merely reveal the founders' justification for narrowing the role of government by prudently enumerating federal power, and securing religious freedom in the Bill of Rights. More on First Amendment religious freedoms later, but it is enough to observe here that the drafters of the Declaration, and the framers of the Constitution, believed that government authority must necessarily be limited to leave room for individuals to pursue moral instruction within their freely chosen religious community. They anticipated, maybe better than they knew, that where God is banished, the state — as a substitute source of ultimate authority — expands rapidly. This is the totalitarian history of the former Soviet Union, where the exact opposite of the Declaration of Independence was asserted — "man makes religion," claimed Karl Marx arrogantly, "religion does not make man."

The Declaration affirms one further creation-based proposition of some importance: "all men are created equal." This does not mean that all men and women have the very same talents or leanings, but it does mean that no one of us has any better claim to govern than any other. There is no divine kingship in America. We are all equal before God, and therefore, only those persons can lead who are chosen with our consent. Those we consent to be governed by, are bound, as we all are, to observe the "unalienable rights of life, liberty, and the pursuit of happiness." These human rights pre-date all governments, including our own, and entitlement to them stems simply from the intrinsic worth of each created human being.

2. Do these principles embedded within the Declaration have continuing validity, or have they been superseded by events? To give a full answer, one would need not only a responsible approach to constitutional interpretation, but also entire courses in epistemology, theology, philosophy and jurisprudence. A less elaborate, but arguably workable response, is simply to observe that the United States Code includes the Declaration of Independence as one of the Organic Laws upon which all statutory law rests. *See* 1 U.S.C., at xli (1994). In other words, the Declaration has not been repealed. As Lincoln said to Stephen

A. Douglas in debate, "[i]f th[e D]eclaration is not the truth, let us get the statute book, in which we find it, and tear it out!" Abraham Lincoln, Speech in reply to Senator Douglas (July 10, 1858), *in* THE POLITICAL DEBATES BETWEEN ABRAHAM LINCOLN AND STEPHEN A. DOUGLAS 20, 35 (Cleveland, O.S. Hubbel & Co. 1895).

3. But doesn't modern science undermine our founders' belief in a Creator as the ultimate source of unalienable rights? Judging by the consistently high reports of faith belief in the United States (well over 90%), the answer would seem to be no. Scientific developments in evolutionary and genetic theory have not undermined belief in transcendent values or the view that some truth can be known. Perhaps this is so because advances in scientific research and theory neither prove, nor must they depend upon proving, the denial of God. *See* PHILIP E. JOHNSON, REASON IN THE BALANCE (1995); PATRICK GLYNN, GOD — THE EVIDENCE (1997). President Calvin Coolidge once reflected that

> no progress can be made beyond [the propositions of the Declaration]. If anyone wishes to deny their truth or their soundness, the only direction in which he can proceed historically is not forward, but backward toward the time when there was no equality, no rights of the individual, no rule of the people. Those who wish to proceed in this direction cannot claim to progress, they are reactionary.

CALVIN COOLIDGE, FOUNDATIONS OF THE REPUBLIC: SPEECHES & ADDRESSES 451-52 (1928).

4. For a contemporary account of the significance of the natural law by a respected elder statesman of constitutional law, see CHARLES E. RICE, FIFTY QUESTIONS ON THE NATURAL LAW (1993). Modern commentary on a broad range of natural law issues can also be found in the American Journal of Jurisprudence.

1. The Declaration and the Formation of the Constitution

The principal author of the Declaration, Thomas Jefferson, appears to have anticipated a continuing interpretative role for the Declaration. In correspondence, Jefferson first acknowledged that the Declaration was not intended "to invent new ideas," but to re-state well-grounded common or natural law ideas. To the notion that following the successful American Revolution, the Declaration should be set aside "to spare the feeling of our English friends," Jefferson retorted, "it is not to wound them that we wish to keep it in mind; but to cherish the principles of the instrument in the bosoms of our own citizens . . . . I pray God that these principles may be eternal." Letter from Thomas Jefferson to James Madison (Sept. 4, 1823), *in* 15 THE WRITINGS OF THOMAS JEFFERSON 460, 463-64 (Andrew A. Lipscomb & Albert Ellery Bergh eds., 1904). Madison shared this view. In a letter to Jefferson, for example, Madison recommended the Declaration as the first of the "best guides" to the "distinctive principles" of government. Letter from James Madison to Thomas Jefferson (Feb. 8, 1825), *in* 9 THE WRITINGS OF JAMES MADISON 218, 221 (Gaillard Hunt ed., 1910). Similarly, Abraham Lincoln would call the equality principle of the Declaration "the great fundamental principle upon which our free institutions rest." Letter from Abraham Lincoln to James N. Brown (Oct. 18, 1858), *in* 3 THE COLLECTED WORKS OF ABRAHAM LINCOLN 327, 327 (Roy P. Basler ed., 1953). The Reverend Martin Luther King, Jr. called the Declaration the "promissory note to which every American was to fall heir." Martin Luther King, Jr., *I Have a Dream* (Aug. 28, 1963), *in* A TESTAMENT OF HOPE: THE ESSENTIAL WRITINGS OF MARTIN LUTHER KING, JR. 217 (James M. Washington ed., 1986).

The importance of the Declaration is largely assumed in *The Federalist*, a collection of 85 letters written to the general public from October 1787 to August 1788 in an effort to win ratification for the proposed Constitution in New York. Most of these letters, printed under the pseudonym Publius, first appeared in newsprint. They were written chiefly by Alexander Hamilton, who was aided by James Madison, and to a lesser extent, by a distinguished New York lawyer, John Jay. Noted political historian Clinton Rossiter places *The Federalist*:

> third only to the Declaration of Independence and the Constitution itself among all the sacred writings of American political history. It has a quality of legitimacy, of authority and authenticity, that gives it the high status of a public document, one to which, as Thomas Jefferson put it, "appeal is habitually made by all, and rarely declined or denied by any" as to the "genuine meaning" of the Constitution.

Clinton Rossiter, *Introduction* to THE FEDERALIST PAPERS, at vii (Clinton Rositer ed., 1961). The fundamental principles of the Declaration logically preceded *The Federalist* argument because, as the distinguished authors of the papers repeatedly illustrate, the constitutional means there explained depend upon agreement upon governmental ends, such as the "security of liberty," *id*. at Nos. 1, 70 (Hamilton), No. 51 (Madison); guarding the rights of individuals with an independent judiciary, *id*. at No. 78 (Hamilton); and protecting civil and religious rights, *id*. at No. 51 (Madison). The language of the Declaration is directly referenced in THE FEDERALIST NO. 43, where Madison addresses the difficult issue of how a Constitution proposed to be ratified by less than the unanimity required by Article 13 of the Articles of Confederation could be binding and what the relation of any dissenting states would be to the others. Madison's answer to both questions depends, in significant part, on his direct reference to fundamental principles of natural law or the "transcendent law of nature and of nature's God" (the precise language of the Declaration), which delimits the object of all political institutions.

THE FEDERALIST NO. 43 (James Madison)
(Clinton Rossiter ed., 1961)

* * *

9. "The ratification of the conventions of nine States shall be sufficient for the establishment of this Constitution between the States, ratifying the same."

This article speaks for itself. The express authority of the people alone could give due validity to the Constitution. To have required the unanimous ratification of the thirteen States would have subjected the essential interests of the whole to the caprice or corruption of a single member. It would have marked a want of foresight in the convention, which our own experience would have rendered inexcusable.

Two questions of a very delicate nature present themselves on this occasion: 1. On what principle the Confederation, which stands in the solemn form of a compact among the States, can be superseded without the unanimous consent of the parties to it? 2. What relation is to subsist between the nine or more States ratifying the Constitution, and the remaining few who do not become parties to it?

The first question is answered at once by recurring to the absolute necessity of the case; to the great principle of self-preservation; to the transcendent law of nature and of nature's God, which declares that the safety and happiness of society are the objects at which all political institutions aim and to which all such institutions must be sacrificed. *Perhaps*, also, an answer may be found without searching beyond the principles of the compact itself. It has been heretofore noted among the defects of the Confederation that in many of the States it had received no higher sanction than a mere legislative ratification. The principle of reciprocity seems to require that its obligation on the other States should be reduced to the same standard. A compact between independent sovereigns, founded on ordinary acts of legislative authority, can pretend to no higher validity than a league or treaty between the parties. It is an established doctrine on the subject of treaties that all the articles are mutually conditions of each other; that a breach of any one article is a breach of the whole treaty; and that a breach, committed by either of the parties, absolves the others, and authorizes them, if they please, to pronounce the compact violated and void. Should it unhappily be necessary to appeal to these delicate truths for a justification for dispensing with the consent of particular States to a dissolution of the federal pact, will not the complaining parties find it a difficult task to answer the *multiplied* and *important* infractions with which they may be confronted? The time has been when it was incumbent on us all to veil the ideas which this paragraph exhibits. The scene is now changed, and with it the part which the same motives dictate.

The second question is not less delicate; and the flattering prospect of its being merely hypothetical forbids an over-curious discussion of it. It is one of those cases which must be left to provide for itself. In general, it may be observed that although no political relation can subsist between the assenting and dissenting States, yet the moral relations will remain uncanceled. The claims of justice, both on one side and on the other, will be in force, and must be fulfilled; the rights of humanity must in all cases be duly and mutually respected; whilst considerations of a common interest, and, above all, the remembrance of the endearing scenes which are past, and the anticipation of a speedy triumph over the obstacles to reunion, will, it is hoped, not urge in vain *moderation* on one side, and *prudence* on the other.

NOTES AND QUESTIONS

1. The Anti-Federalists who opposed the ratification of the Constitution similarly relied upon the principles of the Declaration. Throughout Anti-Federalist materials there is a reference to how the primary object of any new government must be "to secure . . . natural rights." *Essay by the Impartial Examiner to the Free People of Virginia* (Feb. 20, 1788), *reprinted in* 5 THE COMPLETE ANTI-FEDERALIST 173, 176 (Herbert J. Storing ed., 1981). Indeed, it was with that object in mind that Anti-Federalist opposition was written; the essential complaint being that the proposed union would not guarantee the unalienable natural rights of individuals. Like both the Declaration and *The Federalist* (No. 22), Anti-Federalist leaders assumed that the only legitimate government was one premised upon consent of the governed. In arguing that the proposed constitution did not sufficiently sustain this principle, the Anti-Federalist "Brutus" appears to make direct reference to the language of the Declaration, writing:

> [T]he people of America . . . hold this truth as self evident, that all men are by nature free. No one man, therefore, or any class of men, have a right, by the law of nature, . . . to assume or exercise authority over their fellows. The origin of society then is to be sought . . . in the united consent of those who associate.

Essay of Brutus to the Citizens of New York (Nov. 1, 1787) *reprinted in* 2 THE COMPLETE ANTI-FEDERALIST, *supra*, at 372-73.

2. The significance of the Declaration continues to the present. Dr. Harry Jaffa, whose scholarly career has been substantially devoted to exploring the profound implications of the Declaration for the Constitution, writes:

> *Acts of Congress* admitting new states into the Union are of the highest constitutional standing. Since the Civil War every enabling act has laid down the identical relationship of Constitution and Declaration. For example:

> That the Constitution when formed shall be republican, and not repugnant to the Constitution of the United States and the principles of the Declaration of Independence. [Nebraska, 1864]

> The Constitution of the State of Alaska shall always be republican in form and shall not be repugnant to the Constitution of the United States and the principles of the Declaration of Independence. [1959]

> The Constitution of the State of Hawaii shall always be republican in form and shall not be repugnant to the Constitution of the United States and the principles of the Declaration of Independence. [1959]

Harry V. Jaffa, *Slaying the Dragon of Bad Originalism: Jaffa Answers Cooper*, 1995 Pub. Interest L. Rev. 209, 218 n.20 (emphasis added).

After surveying the founders' reliance upon the Declaration in some depth, Dan Himmelfarb concludes:

> [T]he Declaration of Independence is more than a propaganda instrument or legal brief; that in fact it is fundamental to a proper understanding of the Constitution; and that abundant support for this proposition can be found in the leading writings and debates of the Founding Era. Indeed, it would hardly be an exaggeration to say that the most fundamental pronouncements made in connection with the framing and ratification of the Constitution are restatements of the principles articulated in the second sentence of the Declaration of Independence.

* * *

> On those occasions when the Framers and ratifiers of the Constitution felt it necessary to recur to first principles, they were invariably echoing propositions articulated in the Declaration's second sentence — a sentence that might fairly be said to represent the philosophical infrastructure of the Constitution. What are the implications of this fact?

> A few ideas suggest themselves. First, those whose constitutional theories rest on the premise that the essential feature of American government is popular rule must confront evidence to the contrary in the Declaration and in the Framing and ratifying debates. That evidence suggests that it is the security of rights that is the essential feature of American government; that democracy is merely a means toward that end, one of several forms of government to which a people might consent; that the American regime, in short, is liberal primarily, democratic only secondarily.

* * *

At a minimum, the fact that the principles of the Declaration's second sentence played a central role in the framing and ratification of the Constitution requires us to draw the following conclusion: the prevailing scholarly consensus misconceives the relevance of the Declaration. According to that consensus, the Declaration is a work of propaganda, an instrument of separation, or a lawyer's brief — anything, in short, but a statement of foundational principles designed to serve as a guide for the framers of a constitution of government. This view should not go unchallenged.

Thus, before entering into a discussion of *Marbury v. Madison* (or even of the language of the Constitution itself), it seems entirely appropriate for authors of constitutional law casebooks to direct their readers' attention, and for teachers of constitutional law classes to direct students' attention, to the second sentence of the Declaration of Independence. Rather than being ignored, dismissed, or trivialized, these words should be the starting point for anyone who seeks to understand the meaning and purpose of the Constitution.

Dan Himmelfarb, *The Constitutional Relevance of the Second Sentence of the Declaration of Independence,* 100 YALE L.J. 169, 170-71, 186-87 (1990) (footnotes omitted).

2. The Written Constitution — A Substitute for the Declaration?

The Declaration is a concise summation of natural law principle and, as reflected above, it had continuing significance throughout the founding period. But, notwithstanding the admonitions of Jefferson and Madison, should the Declaration and the vast body of common and natural law tradition it represents have governing significance today? Another way of asking this question is: Did the participants at the federal constitutional convention envision that they were displacing the fundamental principles of the Declaration with a written Constitution?

The short answer is no, or at least, not entirely. The delegates coming into the constitutional convention of 1787 understood a constitution not as a written document, but as the embodiment of long-established laws, traditions, and first principles consistent with natural law. As one writer put it, the "Magna Charta, doth not give the privileges therein mentioned, nor doth our Charters, but must be considered as only declaratory of our rights, and in affirmance of them." Silas Downer, *A Discourse at the Dedication of the Tree of Liberty* (1798), *in* 1 AMERICAN POLITICAL WRITING DURING THE FOUNDING ERA, 1760-1805, at 97, 100 (Charles S. Hyneman & Donald S. Lutz eds., 1983). Judicial cases prior to the constitutional convention similarly make reference to principles of fundamental law without regard to whether the source of the fundamental law was written or not. For example, in the New York case of *Rutgers v. Waddington* (N.Y.

City Mayor's Ct. 1784), *reprinted in* 1 THE LAW PRACTICE OF ALEXANDER HAMIL-TON 392 (Julius Goebel, Jr., ed., 1964), Alexander Hamilton defended a British citizen against a trespass complaint for occupation of property during the Revolutionary War. Hamilton argued not only that the natural law, or "law of nations," justified the defendant's actions in time of war, but also that the New York courts were bound to give effect to such "universal" principles in adjudication. *Id.* at 399-400. The court agreed. New York could enact its trespass statute, but it could not be employed in a manner inconsistent with the unwritten, but nevertheless fundamental, law of nations obligatory upon all. *Id.* at 411. In response to the landowner's argument that "the *customary and voluntary law of nations*" did not bind New York, the court answered, "[b]y our excellent constitution, the common law is declared to be part of the law of the land; and the [law of nations] is a branch of the common law." *Id.* at 402.

Mid-way through the convention in Philadelphia, however, the idea began to take hold that the constitutional document being drafted might itself be fundamental law. As Suzanna Sherry has pointed out in a particularly illuminating article, Alexander Hamilton in a "rambling speech" on June 18 suggested to the convention delegates that the written Constitution could itself be a self-executing source of law — "[a]ll laws of the particular States contrary to the Constitution or laws of the United States [shall] be utterly void." 1 JAMES MADISON, DEBATES IN THE FEDERAL CONVENTION OF 1787, at 119 (Gaillard Hunt & James Brown Scott eds., Promethius Books 1987) (1920). However, Hamilton then obscured the point of self-enforcement by suggesting that the national legislature would be given a negative over state laws. *See* Suzanna Sherry, *The Founders' Unwritten Constitution*, 54 U. CHI. L. REV. 1127, 1147 (1987). In mid-July, Luther Martin introduced what was later to become the Constitution's Supremacy Clause (Article VI, Clause 2), but his proposal made only legislative acts, not the Constitution itself, the supreme law of the land. In late August, however, John Rutledge added the Constitution to this assertion of supremacy, and William Samuel Johnson successfully moved to amend the concept of federal jurisdiction to include cases "arising under the Constitution." *See* Sherry, *supra,* at 1148-50.

Thus, the concept of the Constitution as a written, freestanding, enforceable document of positive law came to life. It got a further boost when the convention discussed how the new Constitution would be ratified. The convention's handiwork well-exceeded "amendments" to the existing Articles of Confederation, even though that is how the draft was disingenuously labeled for reasons of strategy, and there was a practical realization among the delegates that the new Constitution might well go down to defeat if submitted to state legislatures, whose power would be diminished by the new charter. *See id.* at 1150-51. As a cover plan for this practical difficulty, George Mason and later James Madison posited that the product of the convention should not be submitted to state legislatures that were mere creatures of their own state constitutions, but to "the clear [and] undisputed authority of the people." 2 MADISON, *supra,* at 305. Madison elaborated:

He considered the difference between a system founded on the Legislatures only, and one founded on the people, to be the true difference between a *league* or *treaty*, and a *Constitution*. The former in point of *moral obligation* might be as inviolable as the latter . . . . [However, a] law violating a treaty ratified by a pre-existing law, might be respected by the Judges as a law, though an unwise or perfidious one. A law violating a constitution established by the people themselves, would be considered by the Judges as null [and] void.

Id. at 308-9.

Madison's convention speech supporting popular ratification is an obvious foundation for judicial review, but did it mean that the judges should interpret the ratified Constitution as a self-contained positive enactment or as a document to be construed in light of the Declaration and the natural law principles it summarized? Much modern commentary at various points on the political spectrum suggests only the former. In fairly substantial disregard of the historical record just canvassed, former Judge Robert Bork wrote in his book *The Tempting of America*:

[I]f the Founders intended judges to apply natural law, they certainly kept quiet about it. Many historians are not even sure the Founders as a group contemplated any form of judicial review, even review confined to enforcement of the text, much less review according to an unmentioned natural law. No one at the time suggested any such power in the courts, and early courts made no claim that such a power had been delegated to them.

ROBERT H. BORK, THE TEMPTING OF AMERICA 209 (1990). Likewise, Jefferson Powell has written that the framers linked "'the Constitution' with a single normative document instead of a historical tradition, . . . thus . . . creat[ing] the possibility of treating constitutional interpretation as an exercise in the traditional legal activity of construing a written instrument." H. Jefferson Powell, *The Original Understanding of Original Intent*, 98 HARV. L. REV. 885, 902 (1985) (footnote omitted). Both Bork and Powell may seriously understate the accomplishments of the framers: yes, they did establish the written Constitution as a source of authority in itself, but in doing so, there is considerable evidence that they had no intention of displacing the fundamental natural law principles in the Declaration or the common law tradition that preceded its ratification. *See* Eugene V. Rostow, *The Perils of Positivism: A Response to Professor Quigley,* 2 DUKE J. COMP. & INT'L L. 229 (1992) (arguing that positivism is jurisprudentially flawed because it divorces legal rules from their historical and political context). That those who drafted the Constitution thought interpretative reference would continue to be made to the natural law — in giving substance to such clauses as the Privileges and Immunities Clause and the Republican Guarantee Clause of Article IV, for example — can be gleaned from a variety of sources: the convention debates generally, the specific debate in the convention and during ratification over the necessity of an express bill of rights, Madison's comments introducing his draft of the Bill of Rights in the first Congress, the earliest decisions of the Supreme Court, and actions taken by the first Congresses. *See* John C. Eastman, *The Declaration of Independence as Viewed from the States*, *in* SCOTT D. GERBER, ED., THE DECLARATION OF INDEPENDENCE: ORIGINS AND IMPACT 96 (CQ Press 2002). Each of these sources are briefly examined in the materials that follow.

a. Natural Law at the Constitutional Convention

In the convention, several critical discussions reveal the continuing significance of natural law to constitutional interpretation. In Chapter Three, we take up directly the issue of judicial review. Much of what we know about the founders' view of that subject comes from the convention's discussion, and rejection on four separate occasions, of a proposed Council of Revision. As contemplated and promoted by Madison, the Council would consist of members of both the executive and judicial branches, and a primary function would be to review federal legislation before it took effect. The Council would have been empowered to veto or preclude new laws from taking effect, subject to legislative override for laws re-passed by the national legislature. As noted, the Council was rejected and the convention instead gave a qualified veto to the President alone. The rejection of the Council did not mean a rejection of judicial review, though it did signal that the delegates did not see such review including a revisionary power in judges *before* laws took effect. For present purposes, the Council is relevant because the multiple debates surrounding it suggest that judges were expected to make reference to principles of natural justice in assaying constitutionality.

2 JAMES MADISON, DEBATES IN THE FEDERAL CONVENTION OF 1787, at 294-99 (Gaillard Hunt & James Brown Scott eds., Prometheus Books 1987) (1920) (emphasis supplied)

Saturday, July 21, 1787

* * *

MR. WILSON moved as an amendment to Resol[utio]n. 10. that the supreme Nat[iona]l. Judiciary should be associated with the Executive in the Revisionary power. This proposition had been before made and failed: but he was so confirmed by reflection in the opinion of its utility, that he thought it incumbent on him to make another effort: The Judiciary ought to have an opportunity of remonstrating ag[ain]st. projected encroachments on the people as well as on themselves. It had been said that the Judges, as expositors of the Laws would have an opportunity of defending their constitutional rights. There was weight in this observation; *but this power of the Judges did not go far enough. Laws may be unjust, may be unwise, may be dangerous, may be destructive; and yet may not be so unconstitutional as to justify the Judges in refusing to give them effect.* Let them have a share in the Revisionary power, and they will have an opportunity of taking notice of these characters of a law, and of counteracting, by the weight of their opinions the improper views of the Legislature. —

MR. MADISON [seconded] the motion.

MR. GHORUM did not see the advantage of employing the Judges in this way. As Judges they are not to be presumed to possess any peculiar knowledge of the mere policy of public measures . . . .

MR. ELSEWORTH [*sic*] approved heartily of the motion. The aid of the Judges will give more wisdom [and] firmness to the Executive. They will possess a systematic and accurate knowledge of the Laws, which the Executive can not be expected always to possess. *The law of Nations also will frequently come into question. Of this the Judges alone will have competent information.*

MR. MADISON considered the object of the motion as of great importance to the meditated Constitution . . . . It would moreover be useful to the Community at large as an additional *check ag[ain]st. a pursuit of those unwise [and] unjust measures* which constituted so great a portion of our calamities.

* * *

MR. GERRY did not expect to see this point which had undergone full discussion, again revived . . . . *It was making Statesmen of the Judges; and setting them up as the guardians of the Rights of the People.* He relied for his part on the Representatives of the people as the guardians of their Rights [and] interests. It was making the Expositors of the Laws, the Legislators which ought never to be done. . . .

MR. STRONG thought with Mr. Gerry that the *power of making ought to be kept distinct from that of expounding,* the laws. No maxim was better established. The Judges in exercising the function of expositors might be influenced by the part they had taken, in framing the laws.

* * *

MR. L. MARTIN considered the association of the Judges with the Executive as a dangerous innovation; as well as one which could not produce the particular advantage expected from it. A knowledge of Mankind, and of Legislative affairs cannot be presumed to belong in a higher degree to the Judges than to the Legislature. *And as to the Constitutionality of laws, that point will come before the Judges in their proper official character. In this character they have a negative on the laws* . . . .

* * *

COL. MASON observed that the defence of the Executive was not the sole object of the Revisionary power. He expected even greater advantages from it. Notwithstanding the precautions taken in the Constitution of the Legislature, it would still so much resemble that of the individual States, that it must be expected frequently *to pass unjust and pernicious laws.* This restraining power was therefore essentially necessary. It would have the effect not only of hindering the final passage of such laws; but would discourage demagogues from attempting to get them passed. It had been said [by Mr. L. Martin] that if the judges were joined in this check on the laws, they would have a double negative, since in their expository capacity of Judges they would have one negative. He would reply that in this capacity they could impede in one case only, the operation of laws. *They could declare an unconstitutional law void. But with regard to every law however unjust oppressive or pernicious, which did not come plainly under this description, they would be under the necessity as Judges to give it a free course.*

NOTES AND QUESTIONS

1. In the July 21 debate, James Wilson makes plain that the concept of unconstitutionality is not limited to constitutional text. In particular, Wilson relates unconstitutionality to injustice, ill-wisdom, and dangerousness. Ellesworth and Madison second this broader conception of unconstitutionality by making reference to "the law of nations," which as in the *Rutgers* case, *supra*, was merely the natural law differently expressed, and by repeating how a constitutional inquiry is one aimed at avoiding "calamity." Similarly, Mason can logically be read as supporting Wilson, but expressing the worry that not every law may be so plainly "unjust oppressive or pernicious" as to allow judges in the normal exercise of their constitutional review function alone to address such defect. No one in the debates challenges this understanding of constitutional evaluation, and thus the fact that the delegates were simultaneously developing the idea that the constitutional text was a separate source of authoritative, declared, positive law did not mean that they saw this development as repealing the inherent or undeclared natural law. It is true that Mr. Gerry argues against the Council, fearing that it would make "Statesmen of the Judges," but in context, this opposition is directed more at the difficulties of allying judges to the executive and inviting such alliance to perform a lawmaking, rather than interpretative, function — namely, the evaluation of laws before they went into effect and unrelated to actual cases or disputes.

2. Late in the convention, long after the written, declared nature of the new constitutional framework had fully taken shape in the Supremacy Clause, the delegates turned their attention to whether the document should prohibit bills of attainder and ex post facto laws. (A bill of attainder is legislation that singles out individuals for criminal punishment. Ex post facto laws make criminal actions that were lawful when performed.) Professor Sherry reports that bills of attainder were commonplace in the states, so an explicit prohibition was readily thought necessary to alter this practice. *See* Sherry, *supra*, at 1157. However, the delegates did not immediately see the necessity of writing down a prohibition against ex post facto laws. As Wilson relates in the debate, such laws contravene the first principles of legislation, and to include a prohibition of them would make the delegates appear "ignorant." James McHenry, who along with Eldridge Gerry initiated the proposal, recorded the opposition to it this way:

> Gouverneur Morris Wilson Dr. Johnson etc thought the [ex post facto prohibition] an unnecessary guard as the principles of justice law et[c] were a perpetual bar to such. To say that the legislature shall not pass an ex post facto law is the same as to declare they shall not do a thing contrary to common sense — that they shall not cause that to be crime which is no crime.

2 THE RECORDS OF THE FEDERAL CONVENTION OF 1787, at 378-79 (Max Farrand ed., rev. ed. 1966). Here is the full debate on this topic from August 22, 1787, as captured in Madison's notes of Debates in the Federal Convention of 1787:

Wednesday, August 22, 1787

* * *

MR. GERRY & MR. MCHENRY moved to insert after the 2d sec. Art. 7, the Clause following, to wit, "The Legislature shall pass no bill of attainder nor any ex post facto law."

MR. GERRY urged the necessity of this prohibition, which he said was greater in the National than the State Legislature, because the number of members in the former being fewer were on that account the more to be feared.

MR. GOV[ERNOR] MORRIS thought the precaution as to ex post facto laws unnecessary; but essential as to bills of attainder.

MR. ELSEWORTH [sic] contended that there was no lawyer, no civilian who would not say that ex post facto laws were void of themselves. It can not then be necessary to prohibit them.

MR. WILSON was against inserting any thing in the Constitution as to ex post facto laws. It will bring reflections on the Constitution — and proclaim that we are ignorant of the first principles of Legislation, or are constituting a Government which will be so.

The question being divided, The first part of the motion relating to bills of attainder was agreed to nem. contradicente.

On the second part relating to ex post facto laws —

MR. CARROL remarked that experience overruled all other calculations. It had proved that in whatever light they might be viewed by civilians or others, the State Legislatures had passed them, and they had taken effect.

MR. WILSON. If these prohibitions in the State Constitutions have no effect, it will be useless to insert them in this Constitution. Besides, both sides will agree to the principle, [and] will differ as to its application.

MR. WILLIAMSON. Such a prohibitory clause is in the Constitution of N. Carolina, and tho it has been violated, it has done good there [and] may do good here, because the Judges can take hold of it.

D[R]. JOHNSON thought the clause unnecessary, and implying an improper suspicion of the National Legislature.

MR. RUTLIDGE was in favor of the clause.

On the question for inserting the prohibition of ex post facto laws.

N.H. ay. Mas. ay. Cont. no. Pa. no. Del. ay. Md. ay. Virg. ay. N.C. div[ided]. S.C. ay. Geo. ay.

b. Was There a Need For a Declaration or Bill of Rights in the Constitution?

The continuing significance of the natural law to constitutional interpretation is also revealed in the debate which occurred over whether to include within the Constitution an explicit bill or declaration of rights. The word "declaration" is deliberate; the founding generation understood rights to exist prior to government, inherent in human nature, discovered through reason, and thus declared, *not enacted*. Virtually all of the new American states wrote declarations of rights, most patterned directly upon the Declaration of Independence. *See* Eastman, *The Declaration of Independence as Viewed from the States*, *supra*, at 97-102. For example, Pennsylvania wrote in its Declaration of Rights:

> That all men are born equally free and independent, and have certain natural, inherent and inalienable rights, amongst which are, the enjoying and defending life and liberty, acquiring, possessing and protecting property, and pursuing and obtaining happiness and safety.

Pennsylvania Declaration of Rights (1776), *reprinted in* DANIEL A. FARBER & SUZANNA SHERRY, A HISTORY OF THE AMERICAN CONSTITUTION 220 (1990).

Near the end of the convention, delegate Charles Pinckney raised the possibility of including a declaration or bill of rights in the Constitution itself, but the drafting committees did not include any of Pinckney's suggestions, which would have included specific mention of the liberty of the press and the prohibition of religious tests. The issue was raised briefly again in the convention's final week. Again, however, the convention unanimously rejected adding a list of rights.

2 THE RECORDS OF THE FEDERAL CONVENTION OF 1787, at 587-88 (Max Farrand ed., rev. ed. 1966)

MR. WILLIAMSON, observed to the House that no provision was yet made for juries in Civil cases and suggested the necessity of it.

MR. GORHAM. It is not possible to discriminate equity cases from those in which juries are proper. The Representatives of the people may be safely trusted in this matter.

MR. GERRY urged the necessity of Juries to guard ag[ain]st. corrupt Judges. He proposed that the Committee last appointed should be directed to provide a clause for securing the trial by Juries.

COL. MASON perceived the difficulty mentioned by Mr. Gorham. The jury cases cannot be specified. A general principle laid down on this and some other points would be sufficient. He wished the plan had been prefaced with a Bill of Rights, [and] would second a Motion if made for the purpose — it would give great quiet to the people; and with the aid of the State declarations, a bill might be prepared in a few hours.

MR. GERRY concurred in the idea [and] moved for a Committee to prepare a Bill of Rights. Col Mason [seconded] the motion.

MR. SHERMAN was for securing the rights of the people where requisite. The State Declarations of Rights are not repealed by this Constitution; and being in force are sufficient — There are many cases where juries are proper which cannot be discriminated. The Legislature may be safely trusted.

COL. MASON. The Laws of the U.S. are to be paramount to State Bills of Rights. On the question for a Com[mitte]e to prepare a Bill of Rights.

N.H. no. Mas. abst. Ct. no. N.J. no. Pa. no. Del. no. Md. no. Va. no. N.C. no. S.C no. Geo. no. [Ayes — 0; noes — 10; absent — 1]

NOTES AND QUESTIONS

1. George Mason of Virginia, who had a variety of objections to the final document and refused to sign it, saying he would "sooner chop off his right hand than put it to the Constitution as it now stands," *id.* at 479, wrote on blank pages of his copy of the September 12, 1787 draft:

> There is no Declaration of Rights, and the laws of the general government being paramount to the laws and constitution of the several States, the Declaration of Rights in the separate States are no security. Nor are the people secured even in the enjoyment of the benefit of the common law (which stands here upon no other foundation than its having been adopted by the respective acts forming the constitutions of the several States).

George Mason, *Objections to the Constitution of Government formed by the Convention* (1787), *reprinted in* 2 THE COMPLETE ANTI-FEDERALIST, *supra*, at 11.

2. Was Mason right? Take a look at James Iredell's response to Mason below. He argued that express declarations of right were necessary in England because they were responses to usurpations by the Crown in a context where there was no written constitution. In America, there is a written constitution of enumerated power, and thus, a declaration of rights is about as necessary has having a judge enjoin the sheriff to not behead a man who is to be hanged. Iredell later served as an Associate Justice of the Supreme Court, and his response to Mason in this respect seems at first consistent with his later opinion in *Calder v. Bull, infra*, where he admonished Justice Chase that in Supreme Court adjudication, the written Constitution had replaced what he claimed were ill-defined concepts of natural justice. Significantly, however, Iredell also responded to Mason's further complaint that the new Constitution does not secure to the people the benefit of common law by positing that the new Constitution only displaces the common law where there is an enumeration of federal authority. Since we know from Blackstone that the common law is derived from natural law, Iredell thus seems at once to be denying and affirming natural law's continuing constitutional importance. As we shall see, this confusion gets compounded by Justice Iredell's successors on the modern Court.

James Iredell, *Reply to Mr. Mason's Objections* (1788), *reprinted in* 2 LIFE AND CORRESPONDENCE OF JAMES IREDELL 186-88 (photo. reprint 1949) (Griffith J. McRee ed., 1857)

Answers to Mr. Mason's Objections to the New Constitution recommended by the late Convention at Philadelphia. By MARCUS (James Iredell).

I. OBJECTION

"There is no declaration of rights, and the laws of the general government being paramount to the laws and constitutions of the several States, the declarations of rights in the separate States are no security. Nor are the people secured even in the enjoyment of the benefit of the common law, which stands here upon no other foundation than its having been adopted by the respective acts forming the Constitutions of the several States."

ANSWER

1. As to the want of a declaration of rights. The introduction of these in England, from which the idea was originally taken, was in consequence of usurpations of the Crown, contrary, as was conceived, to the principles of their government. But there no original constitution is to be found, and the only meaning of a declaration of rights in that country is, that in certain particulars specified, the Crown had no authority to act. Could this have been necessary had there been a constitution in being by which it could have been clearly discerned whether the Crown had such authority or not? Had the people, by a solemn

instrument, delegated particular powers to the Crown at the formation of their government, surely the Crown, which in that case could claim under that instrument only, could not have contended for more power than was conveyed by it. So it is in regard to the New Constitution here: the future government which may be formed under that authority certainly cannot act beyond the warrant of that authority. As well might they attempt to impose a King upon America, as go one step in any other respect beyond the terms of their institution. The question then only is, whether more power will be vested in the future government than is necessary for the general purposes of the union. This may occasion a ground of dispute — but after expressly defining the powers that are to be exercised, to say that they shall exercise no other powers (either by a general or particular enumeration) would seem to me both nugatory and ridiculous. As well might a Judge when he condemns a man to be hanged, give strong injunctions to the Sheriff that he should not be beheaded.

2. As to the common law, it is difficult to know what is meant by that part of the objection. So far as the people are now entitled to the benefit of the common law, they certainly will have a right to enjoy it under the new Constitution until altered by the general legislature, which even in this point has some cardinal limits assigned to it. What are most acts of Assembly but a deviation in some degree from the principles of the common law? The people are expressly secured (contrary to Mr. Mason's wishes) against *ex post facto* laws; so that the tenure of any property at any time held under the principles of the common law, cannot be altered by any future act of the general legislature. The principles of the common law, as they now apply, must surely always hereafter apply, except in those particulars in which express authority is given by this Constitution; in no other particulars can the Congress have authority to change it, and I believe it cannot be shown that any one power of this kind given is unnecessarily given, or that the power would answer its proper purpose if the legislature was restricted from any innovations on the principles of the common law, which would not in all cases suit the vast variety of incidents that might arise out of it.

c. Natural Law and the Ratification Debate

The debate on the necessity or not of an express declaration of rights thus spilled over to the ratification debates. Again, as mentioned earlier with respect to the Declaration of Independence, Federalists and Anti-Federalists were in agreement over the origin of human rights — these came from God and human nature. The question was how to best protect or secure such rights — with or without written declaration. The Anti-Federalists wanted it in writing.

Essay of Brutus to the Citizens of New York **(Nov. 1, 1787),** *reprinted in* **2 THE COMPLETE ANTI-FEDERALIST 372, 372-74 (Herbert J. Storing ed., 1981)**

If we may collect the sentiments of the people of America, from their own most solemn declarations, they hold this truth as self evident, that all men are by nature free. No one man, therefore, or any class of men, have a right, by the law of nature, or of God, to assume or exercise authority over their fellows. The origin of society then is to be sought, not in any natural right which one man has to exercise authority over another, but in the united consent of those who associate. The mutual wants of men, at first dictated the propriety of forming societies; and when they were established, protection and defence pointed out the necessity of instituting government. In a state of nature every individual pursues his own interest; in this pursuit it frequently happened, that the possessions or enjoyments of one were sacrificed to the views and designs of another; thus the weak were a prey to the strong, the simple and unwary were subject to impositions from those who were more crafty and designing. In this state of things, every individual was insecure; common interest therefore directed, that government should be established, in which the force of the whole community should be collected, and under such directions, as to protect and defend every one who composed it. The common good, therefore, is the end of civil government, and common consent, the foundation on which it is established. To effect this end, it was necessary that a certain portion of natural liberty should be surrendered, in order, that what remained should be preserved: how great a proportion of natural freedom is necessary to be yielded by individuals, when they submit to government, I shall not now enquire. So much, however, must be given up, as will be sufficient to enable those, to whom the administration of the government is committed, to establish laws for the promoting the happiness of the community, and to carry those laws into effect. But it is not necessary, for this purpose, that individuals should relinquish all their natural rights. Some are of such a nature that they cannot be surrendered. Of this kind are the rights of conscience, the right of enjoying and defending life, etc. Others are not necessary to be resigned, in order to attain the end for which government is instituted, these therefore ought not to be given up. To surrender them, would counteract the very end of government, to wit, the common good. From these observations it appears, that in forming a government on its true principles, the foundation should be laid in the manner I before stated, by expressly reserving to the people such of their essential natural rights, as are not necessary to be parted with. The same reasons which at first induced mankind to associate and institute government, will operate to influence them to observe this precaution. If they had been disposed to conform themselves to the rule of immutable righteousness, government would not have been requisite. It was because one part exercised fraud, oppression, and violence on the other, that men came together, and agreed that certain rules should be formed, to regulate the conduct of all, and the power of the whole community lodged in the hands of rulers to enforce an obedience to them. But rulers have the same propensities as other men; they are as likely to use the power with which they are vested for private purposes, and to the injury and oppression of those over whom they are placed, as individuals in a state of nature are to injure and oppress one another. It is therefore as proper that bounds should be set to their authority, as that government should have at first been instituted to restrain private injuries.

This principle, which seems so evidently founded in the reason and nature of things, is confirmed by universal experience. Those who have governed, have been found in all ages ever active to enlarge their powers and abridge the public liberty. This has induced the people in all countries, where any sense of freedom remained, to fix barriers against the encroachments of their rulers. The country from which we have derived our origin, is an eminent example of this. Their magna charta and bill of rights have long been the boast, as well as the security, of that nation. I need say no more, I presume, to an American, than, that this principle is a fundamental one, in all the constitutions of our own states; there is not one of them but what is either founded on a declaration or bill of rights, or has certain express reservation of rights interwoven in the body of them. From this it appears, that at a time when the pulse of liberty beat high and when an appeal was made to the people to form constitutions for the government of themselves, it was their universal sense, that such declarations should make a part of their frames of government. It is therefore the more astonishing, that this grand security, to the rights of the people, is not to be found in this constitution.

The Federalists responded that putting it in writing would be "dangerous" because no enumeration could capture all of the natural rights of man, and those not mentioned would then be argued to be conceded to the government.

THE FEDERALIST No. 84 (Alexander Hamilton) (Clinton Rossiter ed., 1961)

In the course of the foregoing review of the Constitution, I have taken notice of, and endeavoured to answer most of the objections which have appeared against it . . . .

The most considerable of these remaining objections is that the plan of the convention contains no bill of rights . . . .

* * *

It has been several times truly remarked that bills of rights are, in their origin, stipulations between kings and their subjects, abridgements of prerogative in favor of privilege, reservations of rights not surrendered to the prince. Such was MAGNA CHARTA [1215], obtained by the barons, sword in hand, from King John. Such were the subsequent confirmations of that charter by subsequent princes. Such was the *Petition of Right* [1628] assented to by Charles the First in the beginning of his reign. Such, also, was the Declaration of Right presented by the Lords and Commons to the Prince of Orange in 1688, and afterwards thrown into the form of an act of Parliament called the Bill of Rights [1689]. It is evident, therefore, that, according to their primitive signification, they have no application to constitutions, professedly founded upon the power of the people and executed by their immediate representatives and servants. Here, in strictness, the people surrender nothing; and as they retain everything they have no need of particular reservations, "WE, THE PEOPLE of the United States, to secure the blessings of liberty to ourselves and our posterity, do *ordain* and *establish* this Constitution for the United States of America." Here is a better recognition of popular rights than volumes of those aphorisms which make the principal figure in several of our State bills of rights and which would sound much better in a treatise of ethics than in a constitution of government.

. But a minute detail of particular rights is certainly far less applicable to a Constitution like that under consideration, which is merely intended to regulate the general political interests of the nation, than to a constitution which has the regulation of every species of personal and private concerns. If, therefore, the loud clamours against the plan of the convention, on this score, are well founded, no epithets of reprobation will be too strong for the constitution of this State. But the truth is that both of them contain all which, in relation to their objects, is reasonably to be desired.

I go further and affirm that bills of rights, in the sense and to the extent in which they are contended for, are not only unnecessary in the proposed Constitution but would even be dangerous. They would contain various exceptions to powers which are not granted; and, on this very account, would afford a colourable pretext to claim more than were granted. For why declare that things shall not be done which there is no power to do? Why, for instance, should it be said that the liberty of the press shall not be restrained, when no power is given by which restrictions may be imposed? I will not contend that such a provision would confer a regulating power; but it is evident that it would furnish, to men disposed to usurp, a plausible pretence for claiming that power. They might urge with a semblance of reason that the Constitution ought not to be charged with the absurdity of providing against the abuse of an authority which was not given, and that the provision against restraining the liberty of the press afforded a clear implication that a power to prescribe proper regulations concerning it was intended to be vested in the national government. This may serve as a specimen of the numerous handles which would be given to the doctrine of constructive powers, by the indulgence of an injudicious zeal for bills of rights.

* * *

There remains but one other view of this matter to conclude the point. The truth is, after all the declamations we have heard, that the Constitution is itself, in every rational sense, and to every useful purpose, A BILL OF RIGHTS. The several bills of rights in Great Britain form its Constitution, and conversely the constitution of each State is its bill of rights. And the proposed Constitution, if adopted, will be the bill of rights of the union. Is it one object of a bill of rights to declare and specify the political privileges of the citizens in the structure and administration of the government? This is done in the most ample and precise manner in the plan of the convention; comprehending various precautions for the public security which are not to be found in any of the State constitutions. Is another object of a bill of rights to define certain immunities and modes of proceeding, which are relative to personal and private concerns? This we have seen has also been attended to in a variety of cases in the same plan. Adverting therefore to the substantial meaning of a bill of rights, it is absurd to allege that it is not to be found in the work of the convention. It may be said that it does not go far enough though it will not be easy to make this appear; but it can with no propriety be contended that there is no such thing. It certainly must be immaterial what mode is observed as to the order of declaring the rights of the citizens if they are to be found in any part of the instrument which establishes the government. And hence it must be apparent that much of what has been said on this subject rests merely on verbal and nominal distinctions, entirely foreign from the substance of the thing.

3. The Bill of Rights Introduced: Unenumerated Natural Law Rights Preserved

Politically, the competing arguments of whether or not to enumerate rights were eclipsed when Rhode Island and North Carolina refused to ratify the new Constitution, and Virginia and New York threatened and then submitted calls for a new convention. To blunt this possibility, which would have likely meant chaos, Madison promised that if ratification was achieved, he would bring amendments before the House so that a declaration of rights could be added by amendment to the new Constitution. In doing so, Madison did not give up his fear that putting rights down on paper might disparage unenumerated rights. To meet this lingering concern, when Madison rose to get the attention of the House of Representatives on June 8, 1789, to introduce his draft of a bill of rights, he first reiterated the purposes of the new Constitution as those found in the language of the Declaration; second, he listed the specific rights which had been pressed by the ratifying states; finally, and most importantly, he reaffirmed that the origin of these rights are not the written Constitution itself. Instead, he indicated that "[t]he exceptions here or elsewhere in the Constitution, made in favor of particular rights, shall not be so construed as to diminish the just importance of other rights retained by the people." 1 ANNALS OF CONG. 435 (Joseph Gales ed., 1789). What follows is an excerpt of that speech.

1 ANNALS OF CONG. 431-40
(Joseph Gales ed., 1789)

MR. MADISON —

* * *

. . . There have been objections of various kinds made against the Constitution . . . . I believe that the great mass of the people who opposed it, disliked it because it did not contain effectual provisions against the encroachments on particular rights, and those safeguards which they have been long accustomed to have interposed between them and the magistrate who exercises the sovereign power; nor ought we to consider them safe, while a great number of our fellow-citizens think these securities necessary.

It is a fortunate thing that the objection to the Government has been made on the ground I stated; because it will be practicable, on that ground, to obviate the objection, so far as to satisfy the public mind that their liberties will be perpetual, and this without endangering any part of the Constitution, which is considered as essential to the existence of the Government by those who promoted its adoption.

The amendments which have occurred to me, proper to be recommended by Congress to the State Legislatures, are these:

First. That there be prefixed to the Constitution a declaration that all power is originally vested in, and consequently derived from, the people.

That Government is instituted and ought to be exercised for the benefit of the people; which consists in the enjoyment of life and liberty, with the right of acquiring and using property, and generally of pursuing and obtaining happiness and safety.

That the people have an indubitable, unalienable, and indefeasible right to reform or change their Government, whenever it be found adverse or inadequate to the purposes of its institution.

* * *

Fourthly. That in article 1st, section 9, between clauses 3 and 4, be inserted these clauses, to wit: The civil rights of none shall be abridged on account of religious belief or worship, nor shall the full and equal rights of conscience be in any manner, or on any pretext, infringed.

The people shall not be deprived or abridged of their right to speak, to write, or to publish their sentiments; and the freedom of the press, as one of the great bulwarks of liberty, shall be inviolable.

* * *

The right of the people to keep and bear arms shall not be infringed; a well armed and well regulated militia being the best security of a free country: but no person religiously scrupulous of bearing arms shall be compelled to render military service in person.

No soldier shall in time of peace be quartered in any house without the consent of the owner; nor at any time, but in a manner warranted by law.

No person shall be subject, except in cases of impeachment, to more than one punishment or one trial for the same offence; nor shall be compelled to be a witness against himself; nor be deprived of life, liberty, or property, without due process of law; nor be obliged to relinquish his property, where it may be necessary for public use, without a just compensation.

Excessive bail shall not be required, nor excessive fines imposed, nor cruel and unusual punishments inflicted.

The rights of the people to be secured in their persons, their houses, their papers, and their other property, from all unreasonable searches and seizures, shall not be violated by warrants issued without probable cause, supported by oath or affirmation, or not particularly describing the places to be searched, or the persons or things to be seized.

In all criminal prosecutions, the accused shall enjoy the right to a speedy and public trial, to be informed of the cause and nature of the accusation, to be confronted with his accusers, and the witnesses against him; to have a compulsory process for obtaining witnesses in his favor; and to have the assistance of counsel for his defence.

The exceptions here or elsewhere in the Constitution, made in favor of particular rights, shall not be so construed as to diminish the just importance of other rights retained by the people, or as to enlarge the powers delegated by the Constitution; but either as actual limitations of such powers, or as inserted merely for greater caution.

* * *

The first of these amendments relates to what may be called a bill of rights. I will own that I never considered this provision so essential to the Federal Constitution as to make it improper to ratify it, until such an amendment was added; at the same time, I always conceived, that in a certain form, and to a certain extent, such a provision was neither improper nor altogether useless. I am aware that a great number of the most respectable friends to the Government, and champions for republican liberty, have thought such a provision not only unnecessary, but even improper; nay, I believe some have gone so far as to think it even dangerous. Some policy has been made use of, perhaps, by gentlemen on both sides of the question: I acknowledge the ingenuity of those arguments which were drawn against the Constitution, by a comparison with the policy of Great Britain, in establishing a declaration of rights; but there is too great a difference in the case to warrant the comparison: therefore, the arguments drawn from that source were in a great measure inapplicable. In the declaration of rights which that country has established, the truth is, they have gone no farther than to raise a barrier against the power of the Crown; the power of the Legislature is left altogether indefinite. Although I know whenever the great rights, the trial by jury, freedom of the press, or liberty of conscience, come in question in that body, the invasion of them is resisted by able advocates, yet their Magna Charta does not contain any one provision for the security of those rights, respecting which the people of America are most alarmed. The freedom of the press and rights of conscience, those choicest privileges of the people, are unguarded in the British Constitution.

But although the case may be widely different, and it may not be thought necessary to provide limits for the legislative power in that country, yet a different opinion prevails in the United States. The people of many States have thought it necessary to raise barriers against power in all forms and departments of Government, and I am inclined to believe, if once bills of rights are established in all the States as well as the Federal Constitution, we shall find, that, although some of them are rather unimportant, yet, upon the whole, they will have a salutary tendency. It may be said, in some instances, they do no more than state the perfect equality of mankind. This, to be sure, is an absolute truth, yet it is not absolutely necessary to be inserted at the head of a Constitution.

In some instances they assert those rights which are exercised by the people in forming and establishing a plan of Government. In other instances, they specify those rights which are retained when particular powers are given up to be exercised by the Legislature. In other instances, they specify positive rights, which may seem to result from the nature of the compact. Trial by jury cannot be considered as a natural right, but a right resulting from a social compact, which regulates the action of the community, but is as essential to secure the liberty of the people as any one of the pre-existent rights of nature. In other instances, they lay down dogmatic maxims with respect to the construction of the Government; declaring that the Legislative, Executive, and Judicial branches, shall be kept separate and distinct. Perhaps the best way of securing this in practice is, to provide such checks as will prevent the encroachment of the one upon the other.

But, whatever may be the form which the several States have adopted in making declarations in favor of particular rights, the great object in view is to limit and qualify the powers of Government, by excepting out of the grant of power those cases in which the Government ought not to act, or to act only in a particular mode. They point these exceptions sometimes against the abuse of the Executive power, sometimes against the Legislative, and, in some cases, against the community itself; or, in other words, against the majority in favor of the minority.

* * *

It has been said, by way of objection to a bill of rights, by many respectable gentlemen out of doors, and I find opposition on the same principles likely to be made by gentlemen on this floor, that they are unnecessary articles of a Republican Government, upon the presumption that the people have those rights in their own hands, and that is the proper place for them to rest. It would be a sufficient answer to say, that this objection lies against such provisions under the State Governments, as well as under the General Government; and there are, I believe, but few gentlemen who are inclined to push their theory so far as to say that a declaration of rights in those cases is either ineffectual or improper. It has been said, that in the Federal Government they are unnecessary, because the powers are enumerated, and it follows, that all that are not granted by the Constitution are retained; that the Constitution is a bill of powers, the great residuum being the rights of the people; and, therefore, a bill of rights cannot be so necessary as if the residuum was thrown into the hands of the Government. I admit that these arguments are not entirely without foundation; but they are not conclusive to the extent which has been supposed. It is true, the powers of the General Government are circumscribed, they are directed to particular objects; but even if Government keeps within those limits, it has certain discretionary powers with respect to the means, which may admit of abuse to a certain extent, in the same manner as the powers of the State Governments under their constitutions may to an indefinite extent; because in the Constitution of the United States, there is a clause granting to Congress the power to make all laws which shall be necessary and proper for carrying into execution all the powers vested in the Government of the United States, or in any department or officer thereof; this enables them to fulfil every purpose for which the Government was established. Now, may not laws be considered necessary and proper by Congress, (for it is for them to judge of the necessity and propriety to accomplish those special purposes which they may have in contemplation), which laws in themselves are neither necessary nor proper; as well as improper laws could be enacted by the State Legislatures, for fulfilling the more extended objects of those Governments? I will state an instance, which I think in point, and proves that this might be the case. The General Government has a right to pass all laws which shall be necessary to collect its revenue; the means for enforcing the collection are within the direction of the Legislature: may not general warrants be considered necessary for this purpose, as well as for some purposes which it was supposed at the framing of their constitutions the State Governments had in view? If there was reason for restraining the State Governments from exercising this power, there is likely reason for restraining the Federal Government.

It may be said, indeed it has been said, that a bill of rights is not necessary, because the establishment of this Government has not repealed those declarations of rights which are added to the several State constitutions; that those rights of the people which had been established by the most solemn act, could not be annihilated by a subsequent act of that people, who meant and declared at the head of the instrument, that they ordained and established a new system, for the express purpose of securing to themselves and posterity the liberties they had gained by an arduous conflict.

I admit the force of this observation, but I do not look upon it to be conclusive. In the first place, it is too uncertain ground to leave this provision upon, if a provision is at all necessary to secure rights so important as many of those I have mentioned are conceived to be, by the public in general, as well as those in particular who opposed the adoption of this Constitution. Besides, some States have no bills of rights, there are others provided with very defective ones, and there are others whose bills of rights are not only defective, but absolutely improper; instead of securing some in the full extent which republican principles would require, they limit them too much to agree with the common ideas of liberty.

It has been objected also against a bill of rights, that, by enumerating particular exceptions to the grant of power, it would disparage those rights which were not placed in that enumeration; and it might follow by implication, that those rights which were not singled out, were intended to be assigned into the hands of the General Government, and were consequently insecure. This is one of the most plausible arguments I have ever heard urged against the admission of a bill of rights into this system; but, I conceive, that it may be guarded against. I have attempted it, as gentlemen may see by turning to the last clause of the fourth resolution.

It has been said that it is unnecessary to load the Constitution with this provision, because it was not found effectual in the constitution of the particular States. It is true, there are a few particular States in which some of the most valuable articles have not, at one time or other, been violated; but it does not follow but they have, to a certain degree, a salutary effect against the abuse of power. If they are incorporated into the Constitution, independent tribunals of justice will consider themselves in a peculiar manner the guardians of those rights; they will be an impenetrable bulwark against every assumption of power in the Legislative or Executive; they will be naturally led to resist every encroachment upon rights expressly stipulated for in the Constitution by the declaration of rights. Besides this security, there is a great probability that such a declaration in the federal system would be enforced; because the State Legislatures will jealously and closely watch the operations of this Government, and be able to resist with more effect every assumption of power, than any other power on earth can do; and the greatest opponents to a Federal Government admit the State Legislatures to be sure guardians of the people's liberty. I conclude, from this view of the subject, that it will be proper in itself, and highly politic, for the tranquillity of the public mind, and the stability of the Government, that we should offer something, in the form I have proposed, to be incorporated in the system of Government, as a declaration of the rights of the people.

4. Natural Law in the Early Supreme Court

Madison's fourth resolution became the Ninth Amendment, which provides, "[t]he enumeration in the Constitution, of certain rights, shall not be construed to deny or disparage others retained by the people." By this provision, do the vast body of unenumerated common or natural law rights become judicially enforceable against the Congress? This is, of course, just another formulation of the underlying question of this Chapter — whether the Constitution must be construed in accordance with fundamental principle. As will be discussed in Chapter Three, judicial review is an American innovation confirmed in the celebrated case of *Marbury v. Madison*, 5 U.S. (1 Cranch) 137 (1803). At least in part, *Marbury* reflects the American rejection of Blackstonian legislative supremacy, which itself had circumscribed the earlier claims of executive or monarchial prerogative. But by what standards are judges to undertake this review? Do they, in particular, include the standards of natural law as summarized in the Declaration, or are they limited to the text of the Constitution, assuming (and it is a big assumption) that the text always has a uniform and plain meaning? Madison includes natural law, pointing out that "independent tribunals of justice will consider themselves in a peculiar manner the guardians of those [unenumerated but retained] rights; they will be an unpenetrable bulwark against every assumption of power in the Legislative or Executive . . . ."

But not every one agrees that the Ninth Amendment and unenumerated natural rights were to be enforced by the federal judiciary, as Madison plainly seems to prescribe. Judge Bork asserts that:

> Madison, who wrote the amendments, and who wrote with absolute clarity elsewhere, had he meant to put a freehand power concerning rights in the hands of judges, could easily have drafted an amendment that said something like "The courts shall determine what rights, in addition to those enumerated here, are retained by the people," or "The courts shall create new rights as required . . . ."

Robert H. Bork, The Tempting of America 183 (1990). With respect, Judge Bork may misperceive the judicial role envisioned by Madison. Judges were not to create "new rights" under the Ninth Amendment, but they were to be a guardian of pre-existing common law or natural rights. The need for a Ninth Amendment that would be enforceable by federal judges against the federal government in all of its parts also makes sense of Madison's analogy to the equivalent importance of state bills of rights that were enforceable against the states by state judges. As Madison writes, "there are but few gentlemen who are inclined to push their theory so far as to say that a declaration of rights in those [state] cases is either ineffectual or improper."

Whatever the scope of judicial enforcement envisioned by the founders, it is undeniable that natural law was important to early constitutional interpretation. In no decision in the first three decades of its existence, did the early Supreme Court uphold a legislative act contrary to natural law principles. Coincident with the founders' understanding of the Constitution as drawn from multiple sources, written text as well as universal principles of justice, early opinions often relied upon both. Often, the written Constitution would be referenced to answer questions of the allocation of government power, while natural law principles would be employed to weigh claims of individual right. What's more, natural law inquiry was made in a wide variety of disputes, implicating a number of constitutional provisions. For example, in *Corfield v. Coryell*, 6 F. Cas. 546 (C.C.E.D. Pa. 1823) (No. 3,230), Justice Washington, sitting as a circuit justice, employs natural law reasoning to partially identify the fundamental rights of individuals encompassed by the Privileges and Immunities Clause of Article IV, Section 2.

CORFIELD v. CORYELL
6 F. Cas. 546 (C.C.E.D. Pa. 1823) (No. 3,230)

WASHINGTON, Circuit Justice . . . .

* * *

If then the fisheries and oyster beds within the territorial limits of a state are the common property of the citizens of that state, and were not ceded to the United States by the power granted to congress to regulate commerce, it is difficult to perceive how a law of the state regulating the use of this common property, under such penalties and forfeitures as the state legislature may think proper to prescribe, can be said to interfere with the power so granted. The act under consideration forbids the taking of oysters by any persons, whether citizens or not, at unseasonable times, and with destructive instruments; and for breaches of the law, prescribes penalties in some cases, and forfeitures in others. But the free use of the waters of the state for purposes of navigation and commercial intercourse, is interdicted to no person; nor is the slightest restraint imposed upon any to buy and sell, or in any manner to trade within the limits of the state.

It was insisted by the plaintiff's counsel, that, as oysters constituted an article of trade, a law which abridges the right of the citizens of other states to take them, except in particular vessels, amounts to a regulation of the external commerce of the state. But it is a manifest mistake to denominate that a commercial regulation which merely regulates the common property of the citizens of the state, by forbidding it to be taken at improper seasons, or with destructive instruments. The law does not inhibit the buying and selling of oysters after they are lawfully gathered . . . . What are the State inspection laws, but internal restraints upon the buying and selling of certain articles of trade? And yet, the chief judge [Marshall] . . . observes, that "their object is to improve the quality of articles produced by the labour of a country . . . . They act upon the subject before it becomes an article of foreign commerce, . . . and prepare it for that purpose." Is this not precisely the nature of those laws which prescribe the seasons when, and the manner in which, the taking of oysters is permitted?

Paving stones, sand, and many other things, are as clearly articles of trade as oysters; but can it be contended, that the laws of a state, which treat as tort feasors those who shall take them away without the permission of the owner of them, are commercial regulations? We deem it superfluous to pursue this subject further, and close it by stating our opinion to be, that no part of the act under consideration amounts to a regulation of commerce, within the meaning of the eighth section of the first article of the constitution.

[The Court next inquires whether oyster raking is an inherent natural right or privilege of every citizen, whether or not resident of the state where the oysters are found.]

2. The next question is, whether this act infringes that section of the constitution which declares that "the citizens of each state shall be entitled to all the privileges and immunities of citizens in the several states?" The inquiry is, what are the privileges and immunities of citizens in the several states? We feel no hesitation in confining these expressions to those privileges and immunities which are, in their nature, fundamental; which belong, of right, to the citizens of all free governments; and which have, at all times, been enjoyed by the citizens of the several states which compose this Union, from the time of their becoming free, independent, and sovereign. What these fundamental principles are, it would perhaps be more tedious than difficult to enumerate. They may, however, be all comprehended under the following general heads: Protection by the government; the enjoyment of life and liberty, with the right to acquire and possess property of every kind, and to pursue and obtain happiness and safety; subject nevertheless to such restraints as the government may justly prescribe for the general good of the whole. The right of a citizen of one state to pass through, or to reside in any other state, for purposes of trade, agriculture, professional pursuits, or otherwise; to claim the benefit of the writ of habeas corpus; to institute and maintain actions of any kind in the courts of the state; to take, hold and dispose of property, either real or personal; and an exemption from higher taxes or impositions than are paid by the other citizens of the state; may be mentioned as some of the particular privileges and immunities of citizens, which are clearly embraced by the general description of privileges deemed to be fundamental: to which may be added, the elective franchise, as regulated and established by the laws or constitution of the state in which it is to be exercised. These, and many others which might be mentioned, are, strictly speaking, privileges and immunities, and the enjoyment of them by the citizens of each state, in every other state, was manifestly calculated (to use the expressions of the preamble of the corresponding provision in the old articles of confederation) "the better to secure and perpetuate mutual friendship and intercourse among the people of the different states of the Union." But we cannot accede to the proposition which was insisted on by the counsel, that, under this provision of the constitution, the citizens of the several states are permitted to participate in all the rights which belong exclusively to the citizens of any other particular state, merely upon the ground that they are enjoyed by those citizens; much less, that in regulating the use of the common property of the cit-

izens of such state, the legislature is bound to extend to the citizens of all the other states the same advantages as are secured to their own citizens. A several fishery, either as the right to it respects running fish, or such as are stationary, such as oysters, clams, and the like, is as much the property of the individual to whom it belongs, as dry land, or land covered by water; and is equally protected by the laws of the state against the aggressions of others, whether citizens or strangers. Where those private rights do not exist to the exclusion of the common right, that of fishing belongs to all the citizens or subjects of the state. It is the property of all; to be enjoyed by them in subordination to the laws which regulate its use. They may be considered as tenants in common of this property; and they are so exclusively entitled to the use of it, that it cannot be enjoyed by others without the tacit consent, or the express permission of the sovereign who has the power to regulate its use.

This power in the legislature of New Jersey to exclude the citizens of the other states from a participation in the right of taking oysters within the waters of that state, was denied by the plaintiff's counsel, upon principles of public law, independent of the provision of the constitution which we are considering, upon the ground, that they are incapable of being appropriated until they are caught. This argument is unsupported, we think, by authority. Rutherfoth, bk. 1, c. 5, §§ 4, 5, who quotes Grotius as his authority, lays it down, that, although wild beasts, birds, and fishes, which have not been caught, have never in fact been appropriated, so as to separate them from the common stock to which all men are equally entitled, yet where the exclusive right in the water and soil which a person has occasion to use in taking them is vested in others, no other persons can claim the liberty of hunting, fishing, or fowling, on lands, or waters, which are so appropriated. "The sovereign," says Grotius (book 2, c. 2, § 5), "who has dominion over the land, or waters, in which the fish are, may prohibit foreigners (by which expression we understand him to mean others than subjects or citizens of the state) from taking them." That this exclusive right of taking oysters in the waters of New Jersey has never been ceded by that state, in express terms, to the United States, is admitted by the counsel for the plaintiff; and having shown, as we think we have, that this right is a right of property, vested either in certain individuals, or in the state, for the use of the citizens thereof, it would, in our opinion, be going quite too far to construe the grant of privileges and immunities of citizens, as amounting to a grant of a cotenancy in the common property of the state, to the citizens of all the other states. Such a construction would, in many instances, be productive of the most serious public inconvenience and injury, particularly, in regard to those kinds of fish, which, by being exposed to too general use, may be exhausted. The oyster beds belonging to a state may be abundantly sufficient for the use of the citizens of that state, but might be totally exhausted and destroyed if the legislature could not so regulate the use of them as to exclude the citizens of the other states from taking them, except under such limitations and restrictions as the laws may prescribe.

NOTES AND QUESTIONS

1. The raking prohibition is argued to be unconstitutional first as an encroachment upon the federal control over interstate commerce. Why wasn't the state raking prohibition invalid on that basis? The court rejects this argument, distinguishing internal regulation that precedes commerce (*e.g.*, inspection laws and, in this case, laws that regulate the manner of oyster harvesting) from a regulation of subsequent sale or trade; only the latter being within federal power. A later Supreme Court will disregard this distinction, see Chapter Four, but the early court does not. Who's right?

2. Allocation of government power, however, does not answer the question of individual right. Do you see why? In the second part of his opinion, Justice Washington freely consulted common and natural law treatise writers such as Hugo Grotius in an effort to discern whether fishing rights, claimed as inherent natural rights of each citizen, are actually one of the privileges and immunities protected under Article IV. The *Corfield* listing of privileges and immunities is a classic elaboration of the more general principles of the Declaration of Independence. Indeed, we will see that after the Civil War, Congress returns to the *Corfield* list in passing the Fourteenth Amendment, in order to better secure natural rights for freed slaves and all American citizens against encroachments from the state governments. Environmentally-conscious students will also recognize how natural law reasoning is employed to address the so-called "tragedy of the commons," that is, the exhaustion or over-use of commonly held resources.

3. In *Ware v. Hylton*, future Chief Justice John Marshall represented Daniel Hylton and other citizens of Virginia who claim that certain debts owed a British creditor were discharged by a Virginia Act of October 20, 1777, which allowed such debts to be paid to the state instead. The British subjects counter that the Treaty settling the Revolutionary War in September 1783 provided that "creditors on either side, shall meet with no lawful impediment to the recovery of the full value in sterling money, of all bona fide debts heretofore contracted." Marshall lost his case attempting to make an argument contrary to the natural law. Marshall claimed there was no debt for the Treaty to revive because it had been discharged. Justices Chase, Patterson and Wilson observed at some length how the extinguishment of debts would transgress the natural law which is "obligatory" on Virginia and "all the Courts of the United States."

4. In *Fletcher v. Peck*, 10 U.S. (6 Cranch) 87 (1810), Chief Justice Marshall confronted an enormous land swindle. In 1795, members of the Georgia legislature conveyed the better part of what is today Alabama and Mississippi to four corporations (the Yazoo Land companies) for about 1.5 cents per acre. All but one member of the Georgia legislature owned stock in these companies at the time. The public was outraged, and in 1796, a new legislature passed legislation purporting to repeal the earlier grant. There was a problem, however, in that some of the original, though tainted grantees, had conveyed parcels to innocent purchasers. These purchasers argued that the subsequent Georgia legislature could not constitutionally divest their title. Calling into question both individual property rights and federalism (state legislative authority versus that of the federal judiciary), Chief Justice Marshall relies upon both natural law and constitutional text to reach his decision upholding the vested rights of the innocent purchasers. He writes:

> It is, then, the unanimous opinion of the court, that, in this case, the estate having passed into the hands of a purchaser for a valuable consideration, without notice, the state of Georgia was restrained, *either by general principles which are common to our free institutions, or by the particular provisions of the constitution of the United States*, from passing a law whereby the estate of the plaintiff in the premises so purchased could be constitutionally and legally impaired and rendered null and void.

Id. at 139 (emphasis added). We examine *Fletcher* more closely in Chapter Six.

5. The facts giving rise to *Calder v. Bull* — the next case in our brief, early Supreme Court natural law sampler — were simple. Connecticut passed a law allowing Bull to re-open a probate or decedent estate administration judgment after the time for appeal had expired. Calder protested this untimely second bite at the apple unsuccessfully in the Connecticut courts, and came to the Supreme Court arguing that the state legislature passed an unconstitutional, retrospective enactment. Calder lost again, but Justices Chase and Iredell differed significantly as to whether the text of the Constitution alone, or the text in conjunction with natural law, determines the outcome.

CALDER v. BULL
3 U.S. (3 Dall.) 386 (1798)

CHASE, JUSTICE . . . .

The counsel for the plaintiffs in error, contend, that the . . . law of the legislature of Connecticut, granting a *new hearing*, in the above case, is *an ex post facto law*, prohibited by the Constitution of the United States; that any law of the Federal government, or of any of the State governments, contrary to the Constitution of the United States, is *void*; and that this court possess the power to declare *such* law void . . . .

* * *

Whether the legislature of any of the States can revise and correct by law, a decision of any of its Courts of Justice, although not prohibited by the Constitution of the State, is a question of very great importance, and not necessary now to be determined; *because the resolution or law in question does not go so far*. I cannot subscribe to the *omnipotence* of a *state legislature*, or that it is *absolute and without controul*; although its authority should not be *expressly* restrained by the Constitution, or *fundamental law*, of the State. The people of the United

States erected their Constitutions, or forms of government, to establish justice, to promote the general welfare, to secure the blessings of liberty; and to protect their *persons* and *property* from violence. The purposes for which men enter into society will determine the *nature* and *terms* of the *social* compact; and as *they* are the foundation of the *legislative* power, *they* will decide what are the *proper* objects of it: The *nature* and *ends* of *legislative* power will limit the *exercise* of it. This *fundamental* principle flows from the very nature of our free *Republican* governments, that no man should be compelled to do what the laws do *not* require, *nor to refrain from acts which the laws permit*. There are acts which the *Federal*, or *State*, Legislature cannot do, *without exceeding their authority*. There are certain *vital* principles in our *free Republican governments*, which will determine and over-rule an *apparent and flagrant* abuse of *legislative* power; as to authorize *manifest injustice by positive law*; or to take away that security for *personal liberty*, or *private property*, for the protection whereof the government was established. An act of the legislature (for I cannot call it a *law*), contrary to the *great first principles* of the *social compact*, cannot be considered a *rightful exercise* of *legislative* authority. The obligation of a law in governments established on *express compact, and on republican principles*, must be determined by the *nature* of the *power*, on which it is founded. A few instances will suffice to explain what I mean. A law that punished a citizen for an *innocent* action, or, in other words, for an act, which, when done, was in violation of no *existing* law; a law that destroys, or impairs, the *lawful private* contracts of citizens; a law that makes a man *a judge in his own cause*; or a law that takes *property* from A, and gives it to B: It is against all reason and justice, for a people to intrust a Legislature with such powers; and, therefore, it cannot be presumed that they have done it. The *genius*, the *nature*, and the *spirit*, of our State Governments, amount to a prohibition of *such acts of legislation*; and the *general principles of law and reason* forbid them. The legislature may enjoin, permit, forbid, and punish; they may declare *new* crimes; and establish rules of conduct for *all* its citizens in *future* cases; they may *command* what is right, and *prohibit* what is wrong; but they cannot change *innocence* into *guilt*, or punish *innocence* as a *crime*; or violate the right of an *antecedent lawful private contract*; or the *right of private property*. To maintain that our Federal, or State, Legislature possesses *such powers*, if they had not been *expressly* restrained; would, in my opinion, be a *political heresy*, altogether inadmissible in our *free republican governments*.

* * *

I will state *what laws* I consider *ex post facto laws*, within the *words* and the *intent* of the prohibition. 1st. Every law that makes an action done before the passing of the law, and which was *innocent* when done, criminal; and punishes such action. 2d. Every law that *aggravates* a *crime*, or makes it *greater* than it was, when committed. 3d. Every law that *changes the punishment*, and inflicts a *greater punishment*, than the law annexed to the crime, when committed. 4th. Every law that alters the *legal* rules of *evidence*, and receives less, or different, testimony, than the law required at the time of the commission of the offense, *in order to convict the offender*. All these, and similar laws, are manifestly *unjust and oppressive*. In my opinion, the true distinction is between *ex post facto laws*, and *retrospective laws*. Every *ex post facto law* must necessarily be *retrospective*; but every *retrospective law* is not an *ex post facto law*: the former, only, are prohibited. Every law that takes away, or impairs, *rights vested*, agreeably to existing laws, is retrospective, and is generally unjust, and may be oppressive; and it is a good general rule, that a law should have no *retrospect*: but there are cases in which laws may justly, and for the benefit of the community, and also of individuals, relate to a time antecedent to their commencement; as statutes of oblivion, or of *pardon*. They are certainly *retrospective*, and literally both *concerning, and after, the facts committed*. But I do not consider any law *ex post facto*, within the prohibition, that mollifies the rigor of the *criminal* law; but only those that *create*, or *aggravate*, the *crime*; or increase the punishment, or change the rules of evidence, *for the purpose of conviction*. Every law that is to have an operation before the making thereof, as to commence at an antecedent time; or to save time from the statute of limitations; or to excuse acts which were unlawful, and before committed, and the like; is *retrospective*. But such laws may be proper or necessary, as the case may be. There is a great and apparent difference between making an UNLAWFUL act LAWFUL; and the making an *innocent* action *criminal*, and punishing it as a CRIME . . . .

* * *

. . . The restraint against making any *ex post facto laws* was not considered, by the framers of the constitution, as extending to prohibit the depriving a citizen even of a *vested right to property*; or the provision, "that *private* property should not be taken for PUBLIC use, without just compensation," was unnecessary.

It seems to me that the *right of property*, in its origin, could only arise from *compact express*, or *implied*, and I think it the better opinion, that the *right*, as well as the *mode*, or *manner*, of acquiring property, and of alienating or transferring, inheriting, or transmitting it, is conferred by society; is regulated by *civil* institution, and is always subject to the rules prescribed *by positive law*. When I say that a *right* is vested in a citizen, I mean, that he has the *power* to do *certain actions*; or to possess *certain things, according to the law of the land*.

* * *

I am of opinion, that the decree of the Supreme Court of Errors of Connecticut be affirmed, with costs.

* * *

IREDELL, JUSTICE . . . .

* * *

. . . It is true, that some speculative jurists have held, that a legislative act against natural justice must, in itself, be void; but I cannot think that, under

such a government, any Court of Justice would possess a power to declare it so
. . . .

[I]t has been the policy of all the American states, which have, individually,
framed their state constitutions since the revolution, and of the people of the
United States, when they framed the Federal Constitution, to define with precision the objects of the legislative power, and to restrain its exercise within
marked and settled boundaries. If any act of Congress, or of the Legislature of
a state, violates those constitutional provisions, it is unquestionably void;
though, I admit, that as the authority to declare it void is of a delicate and
awful nature, the court will never resort to that authority, but in a clear and
urgent case. If, on the other hand, the Legislature of the Union, or the Legislature of any member of the Union, shall pass a law, within the general scope of
their constitutional power, the Court cannot pronounce it to be void, merely
because it is, in their judgment, contrary to the principles of natural justice. The
ideas of natural justice are regulated by no fixed standard: the ablest and the
purest men have differed upon the subject; and all that the Court could properly
say, in such an event, would be, that the Legislature (possessed of an equal right
of opinion) had passed an act which, in the opinion of the judges, was inconsistent with the abstract principles of natural justice . . . .

Still, however, in the present instance, the act or resolution of the Legislature
of Connecticut, cannot be regarded as an *ex post facto* law; for the true construction of the prohibition extends to criminal, not to civil, cases . . . .

The policy, the reason and humanity, of the prohibition, do not . . . extend to
civil cases, to cases that merely affect the private property of citizens. Some of
the most necessary and important acts of legislation are, on the contrary,
founded upon the principle, that private rights must yield to public exigencies
. . . . Without the possession of this power the operations of Government would
often be obstructed, and society itself would be endangered. It is not sufficient
to urge, that the power may be abused, for, such is the nature of all power, —
such is the tendency of every human institution . . . . We must be content to limit
power where we can, and where we cannot, consistently with its use, we must
be content to repose a salutary confidence. It is our consolation that there never
existed a Government, in ancient or modern times, more free from danger in this
respect, than the Governments of America.

* * *

JUDGMENT AFFIRMED

NOTE AND QUESTION

In 1993, California enacted a new criminal statute of limitations that allowed
prosecution for sex-related child abuse where the prior limitations period had
expired. Marion Stogner was prosecuted under the new statute for abuse he
allegedly committed between 1955 and 1973, for which the three-year statute

of limitations that was applicable at the time of the alleged abuse had long since expired. In *Stogner v. California*, 123 S. Ct. 2446 (2003), the Court held that California's revived statute of limitations violated the Ex Post Facto Clause. Both Justice Breyer for the five-member majority, and Justice Kennedy for the four Justices in dissent relied on *Calder v. Bull* and its English common law precedents and natural rights principles to argue their respective positions. Should judges rely on such common law precedent and natural law principle standing alone, or is their recourse to them limited to gleaning the meaning of express constitutional provisions?

5. The Declaration, Natural Law, and the Modern Court

The Declaration of Independence and its natural law heritage has not been totally without significance in modern Supreme Court jurisprudence, but its overt use has been minimal. Recently, Justice Clarence Thomas has employed the "created equal" language of the Declaration to articulate the view that race ought not be used in the distribution of public benefits and contracts. *See Adarand Constructors, Inc. v. Pena*, 515 U.S. 200 (1995) (discussed in Chapter Eight). Justice Scalia, who often reaches common result with Justice Thomas, is less sanguine about the explicit use of the natural law principles contained in the Declaration. Nevertheless, he, and other Justices, examine common law history and tradition to evaluate claims of fundamental rights that are said to limit legislative action. The following colloquy occurred between Justice Scalia and participants at an international seminar in Italy in May 1996.

Antonin Scalia, *Of Democracy, Morality, and the Majority*, 26 ORIGINS 81, 87-90 (1996)

Q: I would contend that there is a natural law of reason which is separate from theology, separate from any biblical view, separate from the magisterium of the church, which requires and obliges governments and systems to obey certain laws of reason which are derived from man's nature, his substantial nature . . . . I was wondering if you could comment on that.

* * *

Scalia: It just seems to me incompatible with democratic theory that it's good and right for the state to do something that the majority of the people do not want done. Once you adopt democratic theory, it seems to me, you accept that proposition. If the people, for example, want abortion, the state should permit abortion in a democracy. If the people do not want it, the state should be able to prohibit it as well.

It seems to me the crux of the matter for the Christian in a democracy is to use private institutions and his own voice to convert the democratic society, which will then have its effect upon the government . . . .

Moderator: Can I offer an intervention here? I think we have to be a little bit careful about how the term *natural law* is used. It's not equivalent to self-evident to all people at all times. It wouldn't be so hard to use it as a principle of government if it were.

I think, going back to . . . when the justice said the government can't impose virtue, it seems to me you have to make a distinction — and I think the justice did earlier — you have to make a distinction: what you think government can do. And the value of the liberal state was that it avoided civil war better than previous systems, as the losers agreed they would abide by the majority decision even if they were totally opposed to it.

But that's not necessarily identical with the question of virtue. It's a question of what can you ask a political system to do without destroying the system that made a disagreement possible, and agreement, for that matter.

Scalia: Bear in mind that I am not saying, I have never said, I have written my opinions to the contrary, that the government has no business in adopting moral positions such as laws against pornography, but only as a consequence of the desire of the people to have such laws. Not as a consequence of the fact that you are not a just government and a good government unless you have such laws. I have no objection to government acting out of what is ultimately a motivation of morality, but it is a motivation of morality at the level of the individual citizen which then expresses itself in the majority vote that controls what the government does.

But the government, it seems to me, in and of itself is totally neutral on those points. It is the people who must bring out the morality of Christianity or any other morality that is to be reflected through the government. And I think it is inconsistent with democratic theory that the government has an obligation to do that in and of itself.

* * *

Q: [W]hen I was young, being a German, the *Nuremberger gesetze* against the Jews would have been approved by the majority, so it would have been law. And I think there are instances which are beyond constitution and beyond majority. I don't think there are many — but some there are.

Scalia: Well, as I say, we certainly believe that in America, and that's why we have a Bill of Rights. We set them forth in the Bill of Rights. But that is the limit of them, and I do not make up other ones. Because anyone can make up other ones. I mean, you know, to talk about the natural law is not to talk about something we all agree upon. And it seems to me you cannot set yourself if you're going to be a faithful, loyal democrat, if you do not like the Nuremberger laws, your duty is to persuade others.

* * *

Q: I perfectly agree with you that, in speaking about law in a pluralistic society, I don't have to bring in either Christianity or, I would say, natural law.

I feel ill at ease speaking about natural law . . . .

But I would advance only one question: I remember when I was in the United States studying, there was a professor of mine of political philosophy who said, "Well, the Constitution of the United States is not the first document, because the Constitution is changeable. But there is a document which stands behind the Constitution, and it is the Declaration of Independence." If you stand up against the Declaration of Independence you are un-American, out. And the Declaration of Independence strangely enough sets out the ground which has nothing to do with majority, but with self-evidence, when it says, "We hold these truths self-evident." Does that not mean that the Constitution of the United States rests on the self-evidence of something which for Thomas Jefferson, at least, was natural law, . . . ?

Scalia: Well, unfortunately, or to my mind fortunately, the Supreme Court of the United States, no federal court to my knowledge, in 220 years has ever decided a case on the basis of the Declaration of Independence. It is not part of our law. It expresses the underlying sentiment which gave rise to the creation of this Constitution. But it is the Constitution that is the document that governs us.

* * *

Q: You don't like the natural law[?]

Scalia: No, I love the natural law.

Q: But is it possible that some common, fundamental ethics can give something to the positive law?

Scalia: Yes, of course, and it must. But that process is achieved not within the context of government, but outside the context of government, with free men and women persuading one another and then adopting a governmental system that embodies those Christian precepts. I am not saying that the American Constitution did not embody moral values that were central to Christianity. Of course. My court has said that. But once the Constitution was put in place, it is the Constitution that governs my actions. And it is that that must be amended, and it is amended to conform more closely to natural law, if you wish. But do it by persuading me, I'm a worldly judge. I just do what the Constitution tells me to do.

NOTES AND QUESTIONS

1. Justice Scalia repeated his supposition that the natural law was an important, but judicially unenforceable, precept of the American constitutional system in the so-called "grandparents rights" case, *Troxel v. Granville*, 530 U.S. 57, 91-92 (2000) (Scalia, J., dissenting), where he dissented from a ruling finding a

Washington statute to be an overly broad interference in parental decision-making. Wrote Justice Scalia:

> In my view, a right of parents to direct the upbringing of their children is among the "unalienable Rights" with which the Declaration of Independence proclaims "all Men . . . are endowed by their Creator." And in my view that right is also among the "othe[r] [rights] retained by the people" which the Ninth Amendment says the Constitution's enumeration of rights "shall not be construed to deny or disparage." The Declaration of Independence, however, is not a legal prescription conferring powers upon the courts; and the Constitution's refusal to "deny or disparage" other rights is far removed from affirming any one of them, and even farther removed from authorizing judges to identify what they might be, and to enforce the judges' list against laws duly enacted by the people. Consequently, while I would think it entirely compatible with the commitment to representative democracy set forth in the founding documents to argue, in legislative chambers or in electoral campaigns, that the state has no power to interfere with parents' authority over the rearing of their children, I do not believe that the power which the Constitution confers upon me as a judge entitles me to deny legal effect to laws that (in my view) infringe upon what is (in my view) that unenumerated right.

Nevertheless, while Justice Scalia disclaims the use of natural law as a basis for evaluating whether legislative action is in accord with fundamental principle, he does employ a closely related analogue premised upon the common law. For example, in *Michael H. v. Gerald D.*, 491 U.S. 110, 127-28 n.6 (1989), in which the Court rejected the claim of a natural father to have a parental relationship with the child born of an adulterous liaison, Justice Scalia articulated his common law theory for evaluating fundamental right claims this way:

> JUSTICE BRENNAN criticizes our methodology in using historical traditions specifically relating to the rights of an adulterous natural father, rather than inquiring more generally "whether parenthood is an interest that historically has received our attention and protection." There seems to us no basis for the contention that this methodology is "nove[l]." For example, in *Bowers v. Hardwick* (1986), we noted that at the time the Fourteenth Amendment was ratified all but 5 of the 37 States had criminal sodomy laws, that all 50 of the States had such laws prior to 1961, and that 24 States and the District of Columbia continued to have them; and we concluded from that record, regarding that very specific aspect of sexual conduct, that "to claim that a right to engage in such conduct is 'deeply rooted in this Nation's history and tradition' or 'implicit in the concept of ordered liberty' is, at best, facetious." *Id.* at 194. In *Roe v. Wade* (1973), we spent about a fifth of our opinion negating the proposition that there was a longstanding tradition of laws proscribing abortion.

By recognizing rights that are "deeply rooted in this Nation's history and tradition," when that history and tradition is drawn from the natural law views of the founders, does not Justice Scalia effectively embrace the natural law tradition of the founders (perhaps more than he is willing to acknowledge)?

2. In *Michael H.*, Justices O'Connor and Kennedy largely concurred with Justice Scalia's historical methodology, but left the door open to interpret the history more expansively or at a "higher level of generality." Justice O'Connor's concurrence in *Michael H.*, in which Justice Kennedy joined, reads:

> I concur in all but . . . [JUSTICE SCALIA's highly specific] mode of historical analysis to be used when identifying liberty interests protected by the Due Process Clause of the Fourteenth Amendment that may be somewhat inconsistent with our past decisions in this area. *See Griswold v. Connecticut* (1965); *Eisenstadt v. Baird* (1972). On occasion the Court has characterized relevant traditions protecting asserted rights at levels of generality that might not be "the most specific level" available. *See Loving v. Virginia* (1967); *Turner v. Safley* (1987); *cf. United States v. Stanley* (1987); *cf. United States v. Stanley* (1987) (O'CONNOR, J., concurring in part and dissenting in part). I would not foreclose the unanticipated by the prior imposition of a single mode of historical analysis. *Poe v. Ullman* (1961) (HARLAN, J., dissenting).

Michael H., 491 U.S. at 132 (O'Connor, J., concurring). Is it judicial restraint that prompts Justice Scalia to reject the interpretative direction of natural law when it is not explicitly revealed in common law history and adjudication? If so, does this conception of judicial restraint impede the application of human reason (at least by the judiciary) to new experience and understanding?

3. Justice Scalia unsuccessfully sought to employ his historical method to uphold the Commonwealth of Virginia's right to maintain an all-male military academy against an equal protection claim in *United States v. Virginia*, 518 U.S. 515 (1996). He wrote in dissent:

> [I]n my view the function of this Court is to *preserve* our society's values regarding (among other things) equal protection, not to *revise* them; to prevent backsliding from the degree of restriction the Constitution imposed upon democratic government, not to prescribe, on our own authority, progressively higher degrees. For that reason it is my view that, whatever abstract tests we may choose to devise, they cannot supersede — and indeed ought to be crafted *so as to reflect* — those constant and unbroken national traditions that embody the people's understanding of ambiguous constitutional texts. More specifically, it is my view that "when a practice not expressly prohibited by the text of the Bill of Rights bears the endorsement of a long tradition of open, widespread, and unchallenged use that dates back to the beginning of the Republic," we have no proper basis for striking it down.

United States v. Virginia, 518 U.S. at 568 (Scalia, J., dissenting) (quoting *Rutan v. Republican Party of Illinois*, 497 U.S. 62, 95 (1990) (Scalia, J., dissenting)).

5. The modern Court has yet, as a body, to adopt Justice Scalia's historically-anchored, common law method for evaluating all unenumerated fundamental right claims or filling in other constitutional ambiguities as a limit upon legislative action. Should it? Arguably, the view has merit to the extent that it is a conscientious effort to balance deference to democratic outcome with the framer's natural law understanding, and thus, their rejection of the wholesale legislative supremacy accepted by William Blackstone. Curiously, Justice Scalia chose not to use his common law methodology in *Troxel, supra,* attempting to limit its applicability there to *procedural,* as opposed to *substantive,* due process claims, writing "Whether parental rights constitute a 'liberty' interest for purposes of procedural due process is a somewhat different question not implicated here." Why should it be different? If custom and tradition give definition to the words of the Constitution, isn't that historical context relevant to both fair process and the substance of constitutional protections? For an evaluation of Justice Scalia's jurisprudence in this regard by one of your editors, see Douglas W. Kmiec, *Natural Law Originalism — Or Why Justice Scalia Is (Almost) Right,* 21 HARV. J.L. & PUB. POL'Y 1 (1998).

6. To conclude this brief inquiry into how constitutional interpretation is today brought into line with fundamental principle, consider the Court's decision in *Seminole Tribe of Florida v. Florida*, 517 U.S. 44 (1996), in which the Court, per Chief Justice Rehnquist, held that Congress did not have constitutional authority under its commerce power to abrogate a state's Eleventh Amendment immunity from suit in federal court, as interpreted expansively, though not exclusively, in light of common law. The Court's common law conception of state sovereignty caused Justice Souter to react harshly in dissent for himself and Justices Breyer and Ginsburg. Notice how closely Justice Souter parallels Justice Iredell's argument in *Calder* against common or natural law limits on legislative powers:

> [T]oday's decision stands condemned alike by the Framers' abhorrence of any notion that such common-law rules as might be received into the new legal systems would be beyond the legislative power to alter or repeal . . . .

* * *

The imperative of legislative control grew directly out of the Framers' revolutionary idea of popular sovereignty. According to one historian, "[s]hared ideas about the sovereignty of the people and the accountability of government to the people resulted at an early date in a new understanding of the role of legislation in the legal system . . . . Whereas a constitution had been seen in the colonial period as a body of vague and unidentifiable precedents and principles of common law origin that imposed ambiguous restrictions on the power of men to make or change law, after independence it came to be seen as a written charter by which the people delegated powers to various institutions of government and imposed limitations on the exercise of those powers . . . . [T]he power to modify or even entirely to repeal the common law . . . now fell explicitly within the jurisdiction of the legislature."

Virtually every state reception provision, be it constitutional or statutory, explicitly provided that the common law was subject to alteration by statute . . . . Just as the early state governments did not leave reception of the common law to implication, then, neither did they receive it as law immune to legislative alteration.[56]

* * *

. . . The Framers feared judicial power over substantive policy and the ossification of law that would result from transforming common law into constitutional law, and their fears have been borne out every time the Court has ignored Madison's counsel on subjects that we generally group under economic and social policy. It is, in fact, remarkable that as we near the end of this century the Court should choose to open a new constitutional chapter in confining legislative judgments on these matters by resort to textually unwarranted common-law rules, for it was just this practice in the century's early decades that brought this Court to the nadir of competence that we identify with *Lochner v. New York* (1905).

---

[56] It bears emphasis that, in providing for statutory alteration of the common law, the new States were in no way departing from traditional understandings. It is true that the colonial charters had generally rendered colonial legislation void to the extent that it conflicted with English common law, but this principle was simply indicative of the Colonies' legal subjugation to the mother country and, in any event, seldom enforced in practice. See [William B.] Stoebuck, [*Reception of English Common Law in the American Colonies,*]10 WM. & MARY L. REV. [393] at 396-398, 419-420 [1968]. The traditional conception of the common law as it developed in England had always been that it was freely alterable by statute. T. PLUCKNETT, A CONCISE HISTORY OF THE COMMON LAW 336-337 (5th ed. 1956); see also T. PLUCKNETT, STATUTES AND THEIR INTERPRETATION IN THE FIRST HALF OF THE FOURTEENTH CENTURY 26-31 (1922) (finding no historical support for the claim that common law was "fundamental" or otherwise superior to statutes). Coke appears to have attempted at one time to establish a paramount common law, see, e.g., Dr. Bonham's Case, 8 Co. Rep. 107a, 118a, 77 Eng. Rep. 638, 652 (C.P. 1610), but that attempt never took root in England. See PLUCKNETT, CONCISE HISTORY OF THE COMMON LAW, at 337; JONES[, THE COMMON LAW IN THE UNITED STATES] 130 [H. Jones ed., 1976]; J. GOUGH, FUNDAMENTAL LAW IN ENGLISH CONSTITUTIONAL HISTORY 202 (1955) (observing that "by the nineteenth century the overriding authority of statute-law had become the accepted principle in the courts"). And although Coke's dictum was to have a somewhat greater influence in America, that influence took the form of providing an early foundation for the idea that courts might invalidate legislation that they found inconsistent with a *written* constitution. See JONES 130-132; GOUGH, *supra*, at 206-207 (noting that Coke's view of fundamental law came to be transformed and subsumed in American practice by treatment of the written constitution as fundamental law in the exercise of judicial review). As I demonstrate *infra*, the idea that legislation may be struck down based on principles of common law or natural justice not located within the constitutional text has been squarely rejected in this country.

It was the defining characteristic of the *Lochner* era, and its characteristic vice, that the Court treated the common-law background (in those days, common-law property rights and contractual autonomy) as paramount, while regarding congressional legislation to abrogate the common law on these economic matters as constitutionally suspect. *See, e.g., Adkins v. Children's Hospital of D.C.* (1923) (finding abrogation of common-law freedom to contract for any wage an unconstitutional "compulsory exaction"); *see generally* [Cass] Sunstein, Lochner's *Legacy*, 87 COLUM. L. REV. 873 (1987). And yet the superseding lesson that seemed clear after *West Coast Hotel Co. v. Parrish* (1937), that action within the legislative power is not subject to greater scrutiny merely because it trenches upon the case law's ordering of economic and social relationships, seems to have been lost on the Court.

The majority today, indeed, seems to be going *Lochner* one better. When the Court has previously constrained the express Article I powers by resort to common-law or background principles, it has done so at least in an ostensible effort to give content to some other written provision of the Constitution, like the Due Process Clause, the very object of which is to limit the exercise of governmental power. *See, e.g., Adair v. United States* (1908). Some textual argument, at least, could be made that the Court was doing no more than defining one provision that happened to be at odds with another. Today, however, the Court is not struggling to fulfill a responsibility to reconcile two arguably conflicting and Delphic constitutional provisions, nor is it struggling with any Delphic text at all. For even the Court concedes that the Constitution's grant to Congress of plenary power over relations with Indian tribes at the expense of any state claim to the contrary is unmistakably clear, and this case does not even arguably implicate a textual trump to the grant of federal question jurisdiction.

I know of only one other occasion on which the Court has spoken of extending its reach so far as to declare that the plain text of the Constitution is subordinate to judicially discoverable principles untethered to any written provision. Justice Chase once took such a position almost 200 years ago:

> "There are certain vital principles in our free Republican governments, which will determine and overrule an apparent and flagrant abuse of legislative power . . . . An act of the Legislature (for I cannot call it a law) contrary to the great first principles of the social compact, cannot be considered a rightful exercise of legislative authority." *Calder v. Bull* (1798) (emphasis deleted).

This position was no less in conflict with American constitutionalism in 1798 than it is today, being inconsistent with the Framers' view of the Constitution as fundamental law. Justice Iredell understood this, and dissented (again) in an opinion that still answers the position that

"vital" or "background" principles, without more, may be used to confine
a clear constitutional provision:

> "[S]ome speculative jurists have held, that a legislative act
> against natural justice must, in itself, be void; but I cannot
> think that, under such a government, any Court of Justice
> would possess a power to to declare it so . . . .

> ". . . [I]t has been the policy of the American states, . . . and of
> the people of the United States . . . to define with precision the
> objects of the legislative power, and to restrain its exercise
> within marked and settled boundaries. If any act of Congress, or
> of the Legislature of a state, violates those constitutional pro-
> visions, it is unquestionably void . . . . If, on the other hand, the
> Legislature of the Union, or the Legislature of any member of
> the Union, shall pass a law, within the general scope of their
> constitutional power, the Court cannot pronounce it to be void,
> merely because it is, in their judgment, contrary to the princi-
> ples of natural justice. The ideas of natural justice are regu-
> lated by no fixed standard: the ablest and the purest men have
> differed upon the subject; and all that the Court could properly
> say, in such an event, would be, that the Legislature (possessed
> of an equal right of opinion) had passed an act which, in the
> opinion of the judges, was inconsistent with the abstract prin-
> ciples of natural justice." *Id.* (emphasis deleted) (opinion dis-
> senting in part).

Later jurisprudence vindicated Justice Iredell's view, and the idea that
"first principles" or concepts of "natural justice" might take precedence
over the Constitution or other positive law "all but disappeared in American discourse." J. ELY, DEMOCRACY AND DISTRUST 52 (1980).

Seminole Tribe, 517 U.S. 44, 166 (Souter, J., dissenting) (footnotes omitted).

The Chief Justice disputed Justice Souter, calling the dissenting view "a theory cobbled together from law review articles and its own version of historical
events." *Id.* at 68. Who's right?

7. Justice Souter kept up his argument against the natural law in *Alden v.
Maine*, 527 U.S. 706 (1999), where he dissented from the Court's determination
that states generally retain immunity from private lawsuit in their own courts,
even if the cause of action is pursuant to a federal statute within the scope of
Congress' Article I legislative power. Asserting that the Court's conception of sovereign immunity was a postulate not of "common law so much as natural law,
a universally applicable proposition discoverable by reason," *Id.* at 763. Souter
thought the natural law idea shared by only a "doubtful few" of the framers.
Denying any "inherent" nature to state sovereign immunity, Justice Souter
contended that only common law could be its source, "[b]ut if the Court admits
that the source of sovereign immunity is the common law, it must also admit

that the common-law doctrine could be changed by Congress acting under the Commerce Clause." *Id.* at 705.

The Court (per Justice Kennedy) responded to Justice Souter: "In apparent attempt to disparage a conclusion with which it disagrees, the dissent attributes our reasoning to natural law. We seek to discover, however, only what the Framers and those who ratified the Constitution sought to accomplish when they created a federal system. We appeal to no higher authority than the Charter which they wrote and adopted. Theirs was the unique insight that freedom is enhanced by the creation of two governments, not one. We need not attach a label to our dissenting colleagues' insistence that the constitutional structure adopted by the founders must yield to the politics of the moment. Although the Constitution begins with the principle that sovereignty rests with the people, it does not follow that the National Government becomes the ultimate, preferred mechanism for expressing the people's will. The States exist as a refutation of that concept." *Id.* at 758-59.

II. The Special Significance of Preferred Religious Freedom

In Part I, we explored whether the interpretation of the Constitution was to be accomplished in accordance with fundamental ends or principles. We saw how the founders looked to the English common law to define these principles, and how the common law, itself, was often a reflection of the natural law — that is, reasoned deductions about actions that either are, or are not, in accord with human nature. In writing the Declaration of Independence, Jefferson traced the unalienable rights of man to "the Laws of Nature and of Nature's God," and thus, the founding generation anchored fundamental principle in both reason and God's revealed word. Part II of this Chapter, therefore, takes up Jefferson's second source, and with it, the issue of religion. In Part II.A, labeled "The Public Affirmation of God and the Importance of Religion," we first explore how the framers understood that the nation's civic morality and well-being depended upon a corporate or sovereign affirmation of God's existence, while leaving individuals free to worship and to come to understand God in their own uncoerced fashion. In Part II.B, entitled "Public Neutrality Toward God and Religion," we examine Supreme Court opinion as it relates to the interpretation of the Establishment Clause of the First Amendment ("Congress shall make no law respecting an establishment of religion"). Finally, in Part II.C, we study the complementary Free Exercise Clause that prevents Congress from "prohibiting the free exercise thereof" — that is, religious belief and some, but not all, religious practices. We will see that by judicial interpretation both the Establishment and Free Exercise Clauses have been extended to limit the states, as well as Congress, and that the interpretation of the two Clauses in judicial opinion has been both difficult and controversial. Noticeably, modern interpretations of the no establishment limitation have become, contrary to the framers' inclinations, increasingly exclusionary, and perhaps even hostile to religion. Similarly, many perceive the protections under the Free Exercise Clause also to be less protective of religion, either because its application has been diluted to include beliefs that are sincerely held, but not necessarily religious in any formal sense, or because, under recent Court precedent, religious practice is more susceptible to prohibition under generally applicable laws.

A. The Public Affirmation of God and the Importance of Religion

1. Pre-Founding; Colonial America

Colonial America was Christian, largely Protestant Christian. Religious dissension nevertheless arose within Christian denominations. To alleviate this, a measure of religious freedom was conferred by Toleration Acts. The Acts were decidedly intolerant of blasphemy, however, which was punishable, at least according to the letter of the law, "with death and confiscation or forfeiture . . . ." Maryland Toleration Act (1649), *reprinted in* 5 THE FOUNDERS' CONSTITUTION 49 (Philip B. Kurland & Ralph Lerner eds., 1987) (reproduced below). Historians report that the blasphemy provisions were not enforced strictly.

Maryland Toleration Act of 1649

Forasmuch as in a well governed and [Christian] Common Wealth matters concerning Religion and the honor of God ought in the first place to bee taken, into serous considerat[ion] and endeavoured to bee settled. Bee it therefore . . . enacted . . . that whatsoever [per]son or [per]sons within this Province . . . shall from henceforth blaspheme God, . . . or shall deny our Saviour Jesus Christ to bee the sonne of God, or shall deny the holy Trinity the father sonne and holy Ghost, or the Godhead of any of the said Three [per]sons of the trinity or the Unity of the Godhead . . . [shall be] punished with death and confiscat[ion] or forfeiture of all his or her lands . . . . And whereas the inforceing of the conscience in matters of Religion hath frequently fallen out to be of dangerous Consequence in those commonwealthes where it hath been practised, And for the more quiett and peaceable governe[ment] of this Province, and the better to [pre]serve mutuall Love and amity amongst the Inhabitants thereof. Bee it Therefore . . . enacted (except as in this [pre]sent Act is before Declared and sett forth) that noe person or [per]sons whatsoever within this Province, . . . professing to beleive in Jesus Christ, shall from henceforth bee any waies troubled, Molested or discountenanced for or in respect of his or her religion nor in the free exercise thereof within this Province . . . nor any way compelled to the beleife or exercise of any other Religion against his or her consent, soe as they be not unfaithful to the Lord Proprietary, or molest or conspire against the civill Govern[ment] established . . . in this Province under him or his heires.

2. At the Founding

The early state constitutions, framed contemporaneously with the Declaration of Independence, further reflected both belief in God as a sovereign or governmental premise and individual freedom of conscience in matters of denominational choice. These state documents are fully within the natural law tradition, listing rights that pre-exist government as a matter of human nature. Thus, in the Pennsylvania Constitution of 1776, a government is instituted for securing that which already exists; namely "to enable the individuals who compose it to enjoy their natural rights, and other blessings which the Author of existence has bestowed upon man . . . ." Pa. Const. of 1776 para. 1, *reprinted in* 5 FEDERAL AND STATE CONSTITUTIONS, COLONIAL CHARTERS, AND OTHER ORGANIC LAWS 3081, 3082 (Francis W. Thorpe ed., 1909) (reproduced below). Religious freedom consisted not of the denial of God or revelation, but of abolishing specific denominational religious tests or qualifications beyond a general agreement in the Divine.

Constitution of Pennsylvania
(1776)

WHEREAS all government ought to be instituted and supported for the security and protection of the community as such, and to enable the individuals who compose it to enjoy their natural rights, and the other blessings which the Author of existence has bestowed upon man; and whenever these great ends of government are not obtained, the people have a right, by common consent to change it, and take such measures as to them may appear necessary to promote their safety and happiness . . . . We, the representatives of the freemen of Pennsylvania, in general convention met, for the express purpose of framing such a government, confessing the goodness of the great Governor of the universe (who alone knows to what degree of earthly happiness mankind may attain, by perfecting the arts of government) in permitting the people of this State, by common consent, and without violence, deliberately to form for themselves such just rules as they shall think best, for governing their future society . . . .

* * *

SECT. 10. A quorum of the house of representatives shall consist of two-thirds of the whole number of members elected; and having met and chosen their speaker, shall each of them before they proceed to business take and subscribe, as well the oath or affirmation of fidelity and allegiance hereinafter directed, as the following oath or affirmation, viz:

I _____ do swear (or affirm) that as a member of this assembly, I will not propose or assent to any bill, vote, or resolution, which shall appear to me injurious to the people; nor do or consent to any act or thing whatever, that shall have a tendency to lessen or abridge their rights and privileges, as declared in the constitution of this state; but will in all things conduct myself as a faithful honest representative and guardian of the people, according to the best of my judgment and abilities.

And each member, before he takes his seat, shall make and subscribe the following declaration, viz:

I do believe in one God, the creator and governor of the universe, the rewarder of the good and the punisher of the wicked. And I do acknowledge the Scriptures of the Old and New Testament to be given by Divine inspiration.

NOTES AND QUESTIONS

1. Three states (New Hampshire, New York, and Virginia) ratified the Constitution on condition that it be amended to include guarantees of religious freedom. Similarly, Rhode Island and North Carolina would accept the already ratified Constitution only upon acceptance of the proposed guarantee of religious freedom in the Bill of Rights that was then being debated. With the exception of the New Hampshire resolution, which sweepingly called upon Congress to "make no laws touching religion," 1 THE DEBATES IN THE SEVERAL STATE CONVENTIONS ON THE ADOPTION OF THE FEDERAL CONSTITUTION 325, 326 (photo. reprint 1996) (Jonathan Elliot ed., 2d ed. 1891), the others all focused on precluding the federal government from establishing a national church and preventing any federal interference with individual religious exercise. New York's language was typical: "That the people have an equal, natural, and unalienable right freely and peaceably to exercise their religion, according to the dictates of conscience; and that no religious sect or society ought to be favored or established by law in preference to others." *Id.* at 327, 328.

2. Madison brought these ratification concerns to the House of Representatives. On June 8, 1789, Madison submitted a first draft of what would later become the First Amendment Religion Clauses. He wrote: "The civil rights of none shall be abridged on account of religious belief or worship, nor shall any national religion be established, nor shall the full and equal rights of conscience be in any manner, or on any pretext, infringed." 1 ANNALS OF CONG. 434 (Joseph Gales ed., 1789) (reproduced *supra*). After a somewhat meandering debate in the full House, this language, and the other provisions of Madison's suggested bill of rights, went to a drafting committee. What emerged in most cases was language similar, but more concise, than Madison's original. Thus, the committee condensed Madison's religion clauses to: "[N]o religion shall be established by law, nor shall the equal rights of conscience be infringed." *Id.* at 729 (reproduced below). There is nothing in the committee report to suggest that the language change was intended to be substantive. The revised language became the subject of debate in the House on August 15, 1789. As seen in the discussion below, the concern of the House was whether the language failed to convey that its focus was precluding the imposition of a national church, and not to be "hurtful to the cause of religion" or "to patronise those who profess no religion at all." Madison clearly proclaims such not to be his intent, but his efforts to make that more explicit by using the adjective "national," are thwarted by the lingering Federalist/Anti-Federalist debate over the exact nature (and scope of authority) of the newly-created central government.

1 ANNALS OF CONG. 729-31 (Joseph Gales ed., 1789)
August 15, 1789

The fourth proposition being under consideration, as follows:

Article 1. Section 9. Between paragraphs two and three insert "no religion shall be established by law, nor shall the equal rights of conscience be infringed."

Mr. SYLVESTER had some doubts of the propriety of the mode of expression used in this paragraph. He apprehended that it was liable to a construction different from what had been made by the committee. He feared it might be thought to have a tendency to abolish religion altogether.

Mr. VINING suggested the propriety of transposing the two members of the sentence.

Mr. GERRY said it would read better if it was, that no religious doctrine shall be established by law.

Mr. SHERMAN thought the amendment altogether unnecessary, inasmuch as Congress had no authority whatever delegated to them by the Constitution to make religious establishments; he would, therefore, move to have it struck out.

Mr. CARROLL. — As the rights of conscience are, in their nature, of peculiar delicacy, and will little bear the gentlest touch of governmental hand; and as many sects have concurred in opinion that they are not well secured under the present Constitution, he said he was much in favor of adopting the words. He thought it would tend more towards conciliating the minds of the people to the Government than almost any other amendment he had heard proposed. He would not contend with gentlemen about the phraseology, his object was to secure the substance in such a manner as to satisfy the wishes of the honest part of the community.

Mr. MADISON said, he apprehended the meaning of the words to be, that Congress should not establish a religion, and enforce the legal observation of it by law, nor compel men to worship God in any manner contrary to their conscience. Whether the words are necessary or not, he did not mean to say, but they had been required by some of the State Conventions, who seemed to entertain an opinion that under the clause of the Constitution, which gave power to Congress to make all laws necessary and proper to carry into execution the Constitution, and the laws made under it, enabled them to make laws of such a nature as might infringe the rights of conscience, and establish a national religion; to prevent these effects he presumed the amendment was intended, and he thought it as well expressed as the nature of the language would admit.

Mr. HUNTINGTON said that he feared, with the gentleman first up on this subject, that the words might be taken in such latitude as to be extremely hurtful to the cause of religion. He understood the amendment to mean what had been expressed by the gentleman from Virginia; but others might find it convenient to put another construction upon it. The ministers of their congregations to the Eastward were maintained by the contributions of those who belonged to their society; the expense of building meeting-houses was contributed in the same manner. These things were regulated by by-laws. If an action was brought before a Federal Court on any of these cases, the person who had neglected to perform his engagements could not be compelled to do it; for a support of ministers or building of places of worship might be construed into a religious establishment.

By the charter of Rhode Island, no religion could be established by law; he could give a history of the effects of such a regulation; indeed the people were now enjoying the blessed fruits of it. He hoped, therefore, the amendment would be made in such a way as to secure the rights of conscience, and a free exercise of the rights of religion, but not to patronise those who professed no religion at all.

Mr. MADISON thought, if the word "national" was inserted before religion, it would satisfy the minds of honorable gentlemen. He believed that the people feared one sect might obtain a pre-eminence, or two combine together, and establish a religion to which they would compel others to conform. He thought if the word "national" was introduced, it would point the amendment directly to the object it was intended to prevent.

Mr. LIVERMORE was not satisfied with that amendment; but he did not wish them to dwell long on the subject. He thought it would be better if it were altered, and made to read in this manner, that Congress shall make no laws touching religion, or infringing the rights of conscience.

Mr. GERRY did not like the term national, proposed by the gentleman from Virginia, and he hoped it would not be adopted by the House. It brought to his mind some observations that had taken place in the conventions at the time they were considering the present Constitution. It had been insisted upon by those who were called anti-federalists, that this form of Government consolidated the Union; the honorable gentleman's motion shows that he considers it in the same light. Those who were called anti-federalists at that time, complained that they had injustice done them by the title, because they were in favor of a Federal Government, and the others were in favor of a national one; the federalists were for ratifying the Constitution as it stood, and the others not until amendments were made. Their names then ought not to have been distinguished by federalists and anti-federalists, but rats and anti-rats.

Mr. MADISON withdrew his motion, but observed that the words "no national religion shall be established by law," did not imply that the Government was a national one; the question was then taken on Mr. Livermore's motion, and passed in the affirmative, thirty-one for, and twenty against it.

NOTE

While the Anti-Federalists (or opponents of the new Constitution) feared the unstated, and probably unintended, implications of the word "national" in Madison's proposal to make clear that the Religion Clauses were aimed at precluding a national church, the Anti-Federalists clearly recognized the importance of religion generally to the maintenance of civic virtue. They understood that for most people, a good or virtuous life, one directed toward individual happiness and responsible participation in community, was unlikely to result solely from reasoned reflection on the natural law. In part, this reflected the criticism of Justice Iredell and modern positivists like John Hart Ely and Robert Bork, discussed in Part I, that the natural law is too indefinite to be applied. While positivists, liberal or conservative, look to the state to supply answers where reason is unclear, the framers — Federalist and Anti-Federalist — had another source — God's revealed word. Reliance upon religious source was especially important to Anti-Federalists, however, as — given the separation of church and state — the greater the role of religion in the life of the individual citizen, the lesser the role of the new federal government. Religion thus supplied reinforcement for a structurally limited government of enumerated power as well as nourishment for the individual and civic virtue necessary to sustain democratic government. Herbert Storing summarizes the Anti-Federalist position this way:

HERBERT J. STORING, WHAT THE ANTI-FEDERALISTS WERE FOR 22-23 (1981) (endnotes omitted)

[M]any Anti-Federalists were concerned with the maintenance of religious conviction as a support of republican government. "Refiners may weave as fine a web of reason as they please, but the experience of all times," Richard Henry Lee wrote to James Madison in 1784, "shews Religion to be the guardian of morals." The opinions of men need to be formed "in favour of virtue and religion . . . ." Religious support of political institutions is an old idea, and here again the Anti-Federalists tended to be the conservatives. The view was well expressed by an anonymous Massachusetts writer in 1787. He explained that there are but three ways of controlling the "turbulent passions of mankind": by punishment; by reward; and "by prepossessing the people in favour of virtue by affording publick protection to religion." All are necessary, but especially the last. "[I]t is not more difficult to build an elegant house without tools to work with, than it is to establish a durable government without the public protection of religion . . . ." The Anti-Federalists feared that the Americans would follow the example of the Europeans as described by Mercy Warren: "Bent on gratification, at the expense of every moral tie, they have broken down the barriers of religion, and the spirit of infidelity is nourished at the fount; thence the poisonous streams run through every grade that constitutes the mass of nations." Warren insisted that skepticism is not, as some hold, necessarily fostered by republican liberty. Indeed, the history of republics is the history of strict regard to religion.

It is less easy to say what concrete form the Anti-Federalists thought this concern with religion ought to take. They favored religious toleration and sometimes criticized the Constitution for the absence of protection of liberty of conscience; but this was assumed to mean, in practice, toleration of Christian (or only Protestant) sects and was rarely extended even in principle to the protection of professed atheists. They saw no inconsistency between liberty of conscience and the public support of the religious, and generally Protestant, community as the basis of public and private morality.

NOTE

The First Amendment was adopted, and as already mentioned, consists of two clauses — "Congress shall make no law respecting an Establishment of Religion" (the Establishment Clause); "nor prohibiting the free exercise thereof" (the Free Exercise Clause). Later, we will consider the modern Supreme Court's "non-coercion" view of the Establishment Clause, one of several competing contemporary interpretations. This view is arguably the interpretation most consistent with the founders' posture of general religious support and individual denominational freedom. It is also an interpretation that is consistent with Madison's articulations of religious freedom, even as his efforts, along with Jefferson's in Virginia, would later be misidentified in Supreme Court opinion as being wholly separatist or exclusionary of religion. This insight was perceived early by Anti-Federalist Richard Henry Lee, who wrote in 1784 that "[the Virginia] declaration of Rights, it seems to me, rather contends against forcing modes of faith and forms of worship, than against compelling contribution for the support of religion in general." Letter from Richard Henry Lee to James Madison (Nov. 26, 1784), *in* 2 THE LETTERS OF RICHARD HENRY LEE 304 (photo. reprint 1970) (James Curtis Ballagh ed., 1914).

This pattern of denominational tolerance and general support for religion was thus well set at the founding. It became further evident in the original Northwest Ordinance that both pre-dated the Constitution, and was re-enacted several times thereafter, recognizing "[r]eligion, morality, and knowledge, [as] necessary to good government and the happiness of mankind." Northwest Territory Ordinance of 1787, art. III, 1 Stat. 51 n.a, 52 (1789). There was also the funding for legislative chaplains ("There shall be allowed to each chaplain of Congress . . . five hundred dollars per annum during the session of Congress." Act of September 22, 1789, ch. 17, § 4, 1 Stat. 70, 71 (1789). The significance of religion to the well-being of the new republic was also not lost upon George Washington; it is prominent within his farewell guidance to the nation.

George Washington, *Farewell Address* (Sept. 19, 1796), *in* GEORGE WASHINGTON: A COLLECTION 512 (W.B. Allen ed., 1988)

* * *

Of all the dispositions and habits which lead to political prosperity, Religion and morality are indispensable supports. In vain would that man claim the tribute of Patriotism, who should labor to subvert these great Pillars of human happiness, these firmest props of the duties of Men and citizens. The mere Politician, equally with the pious man ought to respect and to cherish them. A volume could not trace all their connections with private and public felicity. Let it simply be asked where is the security for property, for reputation, for life, if the sense of religious obligation *desert* the oaths, which are the instruments of investigation in Courts of Justice? And let us with caution indulge the supposition, that morality can be maintained without religion. Whatever may be conceded to the influence of refined education on minds of peculiar structure, reason and experience both forbid us to expect, that National morality can prevail in exclusion of religious principle.

* * *

. . . Can it be, that Providence has not connected the permanent felicity of a Nation with its virtue? The experiment, at least, is recommended by every sentiment which ennobles human Nature. Alas! is it rendered impossible by its vices?

* * *

Though in reviewing the incidents of my Administration, I am unconscious of intentional error, I am nevertheless too sensible of my defects not to think it probable that I may have committed many errors. Whatever they may be I fervently beseech the Almighty to avert or mitigate the evils to which they may tend. I shall also carry with me the hope that my Country will never cease to view them with indulgence; and that after forty-five years of my life dedicated to its Service, with an upright zeal, the faults of incompetent abilities will be consigned to oblivion, as myself must soon be to the Mansions of rest.

Relying on its kindness in this as in other things, and actuated by that fervent love towards it, which is so natural to a Man, who views it in the native soil of himself and his progenitors for several Generations; I anticipate with pleasing expectation that retreat, in which I promise myself to realize, without alloy, the sweet enjoyment of partaking, in the midst of my fellow Citizens, the benign influence of good laws under a free Government, the ever favorite object of my heart, and the happy reward, as I trust, of our mutual cares, labors and dangers.

Washington was not alone in his recognition of the significance of religion to the well-being of the American republic. In the following excerpt, Alexis de Tocqueville, a French political theorist who came to America in 1831 to study the penal system, and as a result wrote a brilliant, two-part account of the American experiment with democracy entitled *De la dèmocratie en Ameriquè* [*Democracy in America*], grasps the essential fact that separation of church and state was not intended to lessen the civil significance of religion, but to enhance it. A descendant of St. Joan of Arc, Tocqueville was one of the first to clearly perceive that French socialist thought of the 1840s, like modern demands of the social and economic welfare state, inevitably lead to heightened dependence upon the state and a loss of economic and political freedom.

Tocqueville's observations give us a special insight into the attitude of the American population at large to whom the political framers, Madison, Jefferson and the like, were responding in public action. In this, Tocqueville might be considered the equivalent of the framer's polling data, although with considerably more erudition than pollsters supply modernly. As to the special place of religion in America, Tocqueville concludes:

1. the success of a democratic political system depends upon a proper moral formation of its people;

2. there are multiple religious sects in America, but all acknowledge a Creator God;

3. the importance of religion to American political society is not that a particular religion is divinely true [although this is certainly important to the individual], but that it supplies "habits of restraint" or general morality; religion regulates where law cannot effectively; democracy needs this moral or religious infrastructure in ways that more statist or despotic governments do not;

4. to deny faith is to deny man's inherent nature to hope;

5. religion is strengthened by its separation from the state because it is then immune from the state's failings and partisans; religion draws directly on the universal nature of the human person;

6. since religion is beyond the reach of the state, it can bind Americans together when their leaders fail or when the people fail each other;

7. in America, unbelievers hide their disbelief recognizing the utility of religion, and believers openly rely upon their faith; religious difference does not occasion hostility, but thoughtful concern.

ALEXIS DE TOCQUEVILLE, DEMOCRACY IN AMERICA 287-301 (J. P. Mayer ed. & George Lawrence trans., Doubleday 1969) (1835)

I have said earlier that I considered mores to be one of the great general causes responsible for the maintenance of a democratic republic in the United States.

I here mean the term "mores" (*moeurs*) to have its original Latin meaning; I mean it to apply not only to "*moeurs*" in the strict sense, which might be called the habits of the heart, but also to the different notions possessed by men, the various opinions current among them, and the sum of ideas that shape mental habits.

* * *

. . . [Religion's] indirect action seems to me much greater still, and it is just when it is not speaking of freedom at all that it best teaches the Americans the art of being free.

There is an innumerable multitude of sects in the United States. They are all different in the worship they offer to the Creator, but all agree concerning the duties of men to one another. Each sect worships God in its own fashion, but all preach the same morality in the name of God. Though it is very important for man as an individual that his religion should be true, that is not the case for society. Society has nothing to fear or hope from another life; what is most important for it is not that all citizens should profess the true religion but that they should profess religion . . . .

* * *

. . . One cannot therefore say that in the Untied States religion influences the laws or political opinions in detail, but it does direct mores, and by regulating domestic life it helps to regulate the state.

* * *

The imagination of the Americans, therefore, even in its greatest aberrations, is circumspect and hesitant; it is embarrassed from the start and leaves its work unfinished. These habits of restraint are found again in political society and singularly favor the tranquility of the people as well as the durability of the institutions they have adopted. Nature and circumstances have made the inhabitant of the United States a bold man, as is sufficiently attested by the enterprising spirit with which he seeks his fortune. If the spirit of the Americans were free of all impediment, one would soon find among them the boldest innovators and the most implacable logicians in the world. But American revolutionaries are obliged ostensibly to profess a certain respect for Christian morality and equity, and that does not allow them easily to break the laws when those are opposed to the executions of their designs; nor would they find it easy to surmount the scruples of their partisans even if they were able to get over their own. Up to now no one in the United States has dared to profess the maxim that everything is allowed in the interests of society, an impious maxim apparently invented in an age of freedom in order to legitimatize every future tyrant.

Thus, while the law allows the American people to do everything, there are things which religion prevents them from imagining and forbids them to dare.

Religion, which never intervenes directly in the government of American society, should therefore be considered as the first of their political institutions, for although it did not give them the taste for liberty, it singularly facilitates their use thereof.

The inhabitants of the Untied States themselves consider religious beliefs from this angle. I do not know if all Americans have faith in their religion — for who can read the secrets of the heart? — but I am sure that they think it necessary to the maintenance of republican institutions. That is not the view of one class or party among the citizens, but of the whole nation; it is found in all ranks.

In the United States, if a politician attacks a sect, that is no reason why the supporters of that very sect should not support him; but if he attacks all sects together, everyone shuns him, and he remains alone.

While I was in America, a witness called at assizes of the county of Chester (state of New York) declared that he did not believe in the existence of God and the immortality of the soul. The judge refused to allow him to be sworn in, on the ground that the witness had destroyed beforehand all possible confidence in his testimony. Newspapers reported the fact without comment.

* * *

That is what the Americans think, but our [European] pedants find it an obvious mistake; constantly they prove to me that all is fine in America except just that religious spirit which I admire; I am informed that on the other side of the ocean freedom and human happiness lack nothing but Spinoza's belief in the eternity of the world and Cabains' contention that thought is a secretion of the brain. To that I have really no answer to give, except that those who talk like that have never been in America and have never seen either religious peoples or free ones. So I shall wait till they come back from a visit to America.

. . . Despotism may be able to do without faith, but freedom cannot. . . . How could society escape destruction if, when political ties are relaxed, moral ties are not tightened? And what can be done with a people master of itself if it is not subject to God?

* * *

Eighteenth-century philosophers had a very simple explanation for the gradual weakening of beliefs. Religious zeal, they said, was bound to die down as enlightenment and freedom spread. It is tiresome that the facts do not fit this theory at all.

There are sections of the population in Europe where unbelief goes hand in hand with brutishness and ignorance, whereas in America the most free and enlightened people in the world zealously perform all the external duties of religion.

The religious atmosphere of the country was the first thing that struck me on arrival in the United States. The longer I stayed in the country, the more conscious I became of the important political consequences resulting from this novel situation.

* * *

My longing to understand the reason for this phenomenon increased daily.

. . . I found that they all agreed with each other except about details; all thought that the main reason for the quiet sway of religion over their country was the complete separation of church and state. I have no hesitation in stating that throughout my stay in America I met nobody, lay or cleric, who did not agree about that.

* * *

. . . I wondered how it could come about that by diminishing the apparent power of religion one increased its real strength, and I thought it not impossible to discover the reason.

The short space of sixty years can never shut in the whole of man's imagination; the incomplete joys of this world will never satisfy his heart. Alone among all created beings, man shows a natural disgust for existence and an immense longing to exist; he scorns life and fears annihilation. These different instincts constantly drive his soul toward contemplation of the next world, and it is religion that leads him thither. Religion, therefore, is only one particular form of hope, and it is as natural to the human heart as hope itself. It is by a sort of intellectual aberration, and in a way, by doing moral violence to their own nature, that men detach themselves from religious beliefs; an invincible inclination draws them back. Incredulity is an accident; faith is the only permanent state of mankind.

Considering religions from a purely human point of view, one can then say that all religions derive an element of strength which will never fail from man himself, because it is attached to one of the constituent principles of human nature.

I know that, apart from influence proper to itself, religion can at times rely on the artificial strength of laws and the support of the material powers that direct society. There have been religions intimately linked to earthly governments, dominating men's souls both by terror and by faith; but when a religion makes such an alliance, I am not afraid to say that it makes the same mistake as any man might; it sacrifices the future for the present, and by gaining a power to which it has no claim, it risks its legitimate authority.

When a religion seeks to found its sway only on the longing for immortality equally tormenting every human heart, it can aspire to universality; but when it comes to uniting itself with a government, it must adopt maxims which apply only to certain nations. Therefore, by allying itself with any political power, religion increases its strength over some but forfeits the hope of reigning over all.

As long as a religion relies only upon the sentiments which are the consolation of every affliction, it can draw the heart of mankind to itself. When it is mingled with the bitter passions of this world, it is sometimes constrained to defend allies who are such from interest rather than from love; and it has to repulse as adversaries men who still love religion, although they are fighting against religion's allies. Hence religion cannot share the material strength of the rulers without being burdened with some of the animosity roused against them.

* * *

When governments seem so strong and laws so stable, men do not see the danger that religion may run by allying itself with power.

When governments are clearly feeble and laws changeable, the danger is obvious to all, but often then there is no longer time to avoid it. One must therefore learn to perceive it from afar.

When a nation adopts a democratic social state and communities show republican inclinations, it becomes increasingly dangerous for religion to ally itself with authority. For the time is coming when power will pass from hand to hand, political theories follow one another, and men, laws, and even constitutions vanish or alter daily, and that not for a limited time but continually. Agitation and instability are natural elements in democratic republics, just as immobility and somnolence are the rule in absolute monarchies.

If the Americans, who change the head of state every four years, elect new legislators every two years and replace provincial administrators every year, and if the Americans, who have handed over the world of politics to the experiments of innovators, had not placed religion beyond their reach, what could it hold on to in the ebb and flow of human opinions? Amid the struggle of parties, where would the respect due to it be? What would become of its immortality when everything around it was perishing?

* * *

. . . The unbeliever, no longer thinking religion true, still considers it useful. Paying attention to the human side of religious beliefs, he recognizes their sway over mores and their influence over laws. He understands their power to lead men to live in peace and gently to prepare them for death. Therefore he regrets his faith after losing it, and deprived of a blessing whose value he fully appreciates, he fears to take it away from those who still have it.

On the other hand, he who still believes is not afraid openly to avow his faith. He looks on those who do not share his hopes as unfortunate rather than as hostile; he knows he can win their esteem without following their example; hence he is at war with no man; for him society is not an arena where religion has to fight a relentless battle against a thousand enemies, and he loves his contemporaries, while condemning their weaknesses and sorrowing over their mistakes.

With unbelievers hiding their incredulity and believers avowing their faith, a public opinion favorable to religion takes shape; religion is loved, supported, and honored, and only by looking into the depths of men's souls will one see what wounds it has suffered.

* * *

Unbelievers in Europe attack Christians more as political than as religious enemies; they hate the faith as the opinion of a party much more than as a mistaken belief, and they reject the clergy less because they are the representatives of God than because they are the friends of authority.

European Christianity has allowed itself to be intimately united with the powers of this world. Now that these powers are falling, it is as if it were buried under their ruins. A living being has been tied to the dead; cut the bonds holding it and it will arise.

3. Early Establishment Clause Interpretation — America as a "Religious People" Assumed

For the better part of a century, the Supreme Court confronted no Establishment Clause challenges. The few cases that did arise found no violation in providing public support to a religious body to carry out a secular function (*Bradfield v. Roberts*, 175 U.S. 291 (1899)) or to recognize the religious character of the people as a whole (*Zorach v. Clauson*, 343 U.S. 306 (1952)). *Bradfield* and *Zorach* more or less constitute the judicial book-ends for this period, in which an original understanding supportive of the importance of religion was accepted.

BRADFIELD v. ROBERTS
175 U.S. 291 (1899)

This is a suit in equity, brought by the appellant to enjoin the defendant from paying any moneys to the directors of Providence Hospital, in the city of Washington, [for purposes of building and operating a hospital facility]. . . .

* * *

Mr. Justice Peckham . . . delivered the opinion of the court

. . . [T]he contention [of the suit is] that the agreement if carried out would result in an appropriation by Congress of money to a religious society, thereby violating the constitutional provision which forbids Congress from passing any law respecting an establishment of religion. Art. I of the Amendments to Constitution.

* * *

. . . Assuming that the hospital is a private eleemosynary corporation, the fact that its members, according to the belief of the complainant, are members of a monastic order or sisterhood of the Roman Catholic, and the further fact that the hospital is conducted under the auspices of said church, are wholly immaterial. . . . Whether the individuals who compose the corporation under its charter happen to be all Roman Catholics, or all Methodists, or Presbyterians, or Unitarians, or members of any other religious organization, or of no organization at all, is of not the slightest consequence with reference to the law of its incorporation, nor can the individual beliefs upon religious matters of the various incorporators be inquired into. Nor is it material that the hospital may be conducted under the auspices of the Roman Catholic Church. To be conducted under the auspices is to be conducted under the influence or patronage of that church. The meaning of the allegation is that the church exercises great and perhaps controlling influence over the management of the hospital. It must, however, be managed pursuant to the law of its being. That the influence of any particular church may be powerful over the members of a nonsectarian and secular corporation, incorporated for a certain defined purpose and with clearly stated powers, is surely not sufficient to convert such a corporation into a religious or sectarian body. . . .

It is not contended that Congress has no power in the District to appropriate money for the purpose expressed in the appropriation, and it is not doubted that it has power to authorize the commissioners of the District of Columbia to enter into a contract with the trustees of an incorporated hospital for the purposes mentioned in the agreement in this case, and the only objection set up is the alleged "sectarian character of the hospital and the specific and limited object of its creation."

* * *

The act of Congress, however, shows there is nothing sectarian in the corporation, and "the specific and limited object of its creation" is the opening and keeping a hospital in the city of Washington for the care of such sick and invalid persons as may place themselves under the treatment and care of the corporation. To make the agreement was within the discretion of the Commissioners, and was a fair exercise thereof.

* * *

Without adverting to any other objections to the maintenance of this suit, it is plain that complainant wholly fails to set forth a cause of action, and the bill was properly dismissed by the Court of Appeals, and its decree will, therefore, be affirmed.

ZORACH v. CLAUSON
343 U.S. 306 (1952)

MR. JUSTICE DOUGLAS delivered the opinion of the Court.

New York City has a program which permits its public schools to release students during the school day so that they may leave the school buildings and school grounds and go to religious centers for religious instruction or devotional exercises. A student is released on written request of his parents. Those not released stay in the classrooms. The churches make weekly reports to the schools, sending a list of children who have been released from public school but who have not reported for religious instruction.

This "released time" program involves neither religious instruction in public school classrooms nor the expenditure of public funds. All costs, including the application blanks, are paid by the religious organizations. The case is therefore unlike *McCollum v. Board of Education* [(1948)], which involved a "released time" program from Illinois. In that case the classrooms were turned over to religious instructors. We accordingly held that the program violated the First Amendment which (by reason of the Fourteenth Amendment) prohibits the states from establishing religion or prohibiting its free exercise.

Appellants, who are taxpayers and residents of New York City and whose children attend its public schools, challenge the present law, contending it is in essence not different from the one involved in the *McCollum* case. Their argument, stated elaborately in various ways, reduces itself to this: the weight and influence of the school is put behind a program for religious instruction; public school teachers police it, keeping tab on students who are released; the classroom activities come to a halt while the students who are released for religious instruction are on leave; the school is a crutch on which the churches are leaning for support in their religious training; without the cooperation of the schools this "released time" program, like the one in the *McCollum* case, would be futile and ineffective. The New York Court of Appeals sustained the law against this claim of unconstitutionality. The case is here on appeal.

* * *

... There cannot be the slightest doubt that the First Amendment reflects the philosophy that Church and State should be separated. And so far as interference with the "free exercise" of religion and an "establishment" of religion are concerned, the separation must be complete and unequivocal. The First Amendment within the scope of its coverage permits no exception; the prohibition is absolute. The First Amendment, however, does not say that in every and all respects there shall be a separation of Church and State. Rather, it studiously defines the manner, the specific ways, in which there shall be no concert or union or dependency one on the other. That is the common sense of the matter. Otherwise, the state and religion would be aliens to each other — hostile, suspicious, and even unfriendly. Churches could not be required to pay even property taxes. Municipalities would not be permitted to render police or fire protection to religious groups. Policemen who helped parishioners into their places of worship would violate the Constitution. Prayers in our legislative halls; the appeals to the Almighty in the messages of the Chief Executive; the proclamations making Thanksgiving Day a holiday; "so help me God" in our courtroom oaths — these and all other references to the Almighty that run through our laws, our public rituals, our ceremonies would be flouting the First Amendment. A fastidious atheist or agnostic could even object to the supplication with which the Court opens each session: "God save the United States and this Honorable Court."

We would have to press the concept of separation of Church and State to these extremes to condemn the present law on constitutional grounds. The nullification of this law would have wide and profound effects. A Catholic student applies to his teacher for permission to leave the school during hours on a Holy Day of Obligation to attend a mass. A Jewish student asks his teacher for permission to be excused for Yom Kippur. A Protestant wants the afternoon off for a family baptismal ceremony. In each case the teacher requires parental consent in writing. In each case the teacher, in order to make sure the student is not a truant, goes further and requires a report from the priest, the rabbi, or the minister. The teacher in other words cooperates in a religious program to the extent of making it possible for her students to participate in it. Whether she does it occasionally for a few students, regularly for one, or pursuant to a systematized program designed to further the religious needs of all the students does not alter the character of the act.

We are a religious people whose institutions presuppose a Supreme Being. We guarantee the freedom to worship as one chooses. We make room for as wide a variety of beliefs and creeds as the spiritual needs of man deem necessary. We sponsor an attitude on the part of government that shows no partiality to any one group and that lets each flourish according to the zeal of its adherents and the appeal of its dogma. When the state encourages religious instruction or cooperates with religious authorities by adjusting the schedule of public events to sectarian needs, it follows the best of our traditions. For it then respects the religious nature of our people and accommodates the public service to their spiritual needs. To hold that it may not would be to find in the Constitution a requirement that the government show a callous indifference to religious groups. That would be preferring those who believe in no religion over those who do believe. Government may not finance religious groups nor undertake religious instruction nor blend secular and sectarian education nor use secular institutions to force one or some religion on any person. But we find no constitutional requirement which makes it necessary for government to be hostile to religion and to throw its weight against efforts to widen the effective scope of religious influence. The government must be neutral when it comes to competition between sects. It may not thrust any sect on any person. It may not make a religious observance compulsory. It may not coerce anyone to attend church, to observe a religious holiday, or to take religious instruction. But it can close its doors or suspend its operations as to those who want to repair to their religious sanctuary for worship or instruction. No more than that is undertaken here.

* * *

Affirmed.

4. Incorporation of the Religion Clauses Against the States

By their terms, the first nine amendments or Bill of Rights do not apply to the states, a point confirmed by Supreme Court opinion. *Barron v. Mayor of Baltimore*, 32 U.S. (7 Pet.) 243, 247-48 (1833). The Supreme Court specifically held that the Free Exercise Clause did not apply to the states in *Permioli v. First Municipality*, 44 U.S. (3 How.) 589, 610 (1845). Some have argued that the drafters of the Fourteenth Amendment intended to extend all of the provisions of the Bill of Rights to the states. *See Adamson v. California*, 332 U.S. 46, 71-75 (1947) (Black, J., dissenting). Justice Black relied principally upon some persuasive testimony by the sponsors of the Fourteenth Amendment to that effect in the 39th Congress. *See* Hugo Black, *The Bill of Rights*, 35 N.Y.U. L. REV. 865 (1960). Black's view and those like it never gained a majority of the Court, however, and it was also disputed in the law reviews. *See, e.g.*, Stanley Morrison, *Does the Fourteenth Amendment Incorporate the Bill of Rights? The Judicial Interpretation*, 2 STAN. L. REV. 140 (1949); Charles Fairman, *Does the Fourteenth Amendment Incorporate the Bill of Rights? The Original Understanding*, 2 STAN. L. REV. 5 (1949). In the Congress, a few years after the Fourteenth Amendment on December 14, 1875, Representative James G. Blaine introduced the so-called "Blaine Amendment," which was largely an anti-immigrant, anti-Catholic measure to preclude public aid from going to Catholic schools, but it also provided in its first clause that "[n]o State shall make any law respecting an establishment of religion or prohibiting the free exercise thereof . . . ." 4 CONG. REC. 205 (1875). In so providing, it is evident that members of the 44th Congress, which debated the Blaine Amendment, including the holdover members from the 39th Congress that had drafted the Fourteenth Amendment, did not believe that the Fourteenth Amendment had already applied the Bill of Rights, including the Religion Clauses, to the states. *See generally*, Alfred W. Meyer, *The Blaine Amendment and the Bill of Rights*, 64 HARV. L. REV. 939 (1951); F. William O'Brien, *The Blaine Amendment 1875-1876*, 41 U. DET. L.J. 137 (1963). So the Blaine Amendment presumably would have done the job, along with specifically prohibiting the public funding of sectarian schools. But the Blaine Amendment never went to the states for ratification, as it failed to get the requisite two-thirds majority in the Senate. Today, the issue of extending the Religion Clauses to the states is practically moot in light of the Court's practice of selectively incorporating most of the Bill of Rights into the word "liberty" in the Fourteenth Amendment's Due Process Clause with the pseudo-natural law theory that liberty must necessarily include the fundamental freedoms in our concept of civilization. *Palko v. Connecticut*, 302 U.S. 319, 323-25 (1937). By this means, the Court in *Cantwell v. Connecticut*, 310 U.S. 296, 303 (1940), applied the Free Exercise Clause to the states and in *Illinois ex rel. McCollum v. Board of Education*, 333 U.S. 203, 210-11 (1948), applied the Establishment Clause. In neither case did the Supreme Court offer much reasoning to support incorporation of the Establishment Clause to the states. Moreover, as Justice Thomas contends in his concurring opinion in the recent school vouchers case, there is a lingering issue over whether the Establishment Clause applies to the states in the same way that it applies to the federal government:

ZELMAN v. SIMMONS-HARRIS
536 U.S. 639 (2002)

* * *

JUSTICE THOMAS, concurring.

Frederick Douglass once said that "[e]ducation . . . means emancipation. It means light and liberty. It means the uplifting of the soul of man into the glorious light of truth, the light by which men can only be made free." Today many of our inner-city public schools deny emancipation to urban minority students. Despite this Court's observation nearly 50 years ago in *Brown v. Board of Education*, that "it is doubtful that any child may reasonably be expected to succeed in life if he is denied the opportunity of an education," urban children have been forced into a system that continually fails them. These cases present an example of such failures. Besieged by escalating financial problems and declining academic achievement, the Cleveland City School District was in the midst of an academic emergency when Ohio enacted its scholarship program.

The dissents and respondents wish to invoke the Establishment Clause of the First Amendment, as incorporated through the Fourteenth, to constrain a State's neutral efforts to provide greater educational opportunity for underprivileged minority students. Today's decision [considered later in this Chapter — Eds.] properly upholds the program as constitutional, and I join it in full.

I

* * *

I agree with the Court that Ohio's program easily passes muster under our stringent [Establishment Clause] test, but, as a matter of first principles, I question whether this test should be applied to the States.

The Establishment Clause of the First Amendment states that "Congress shall make no law respecting an establishment of religion." On its face, this provision places no limit on the States with regard to religion. The Establishment Clause originally protected States, and by extension their citizens, from the imposition of an established religion by the Federal Government.[2] Whether and how this Clause should constrain state action under the Fourteenth Amendment is a more difficult question.

The Fourteenth Amendment fundamentally restructured the relationship between individuals and the States and ensured that States would not deprive citizens of liberty without due process of law. It guarantees citizenship to all individuals born or naturalized in the United States and provides that "[n]o State shall make or enforce any law which shall abridge the privileges or immunities of citizens of the United States; nor shall any State deprive any person of life, liberty, or property, without due process of law; nor deny to any person within its jurisdiction the equal protection of the laws." As Justice Harlan noted, the Fourteenth Amendment "added greatly to the dignity and glory of American citizenship, and to the security of personal liberty." *Plessy v. Ferguson* (1896) (dissenting opinion). When rights are incorporated against the States through the Fourteenth Amendment they should advance, not constrain, individual liberty.

Consequently, in the context of the Establishment Clause, it may well be that state action should be evaluated on different terms than similar action by the Federal Government. "States, while bound to observe strict neutrality, should be freer to experiment with involvement [in religion] — on a neutral basis — than the Federal Government." *Walz v. Tax Comm'n of City of New York* (1970) (Harlan, J., concurring). Thus, while the Federal Government may "make no law respecting an establishment of religion," the States may pass laws that include or touch on religious matters so long as these laws do not impede free exercise rights or any other individual religious liberty interest. By considering the particular religious liberty right alleged to be invaded by a State, federal courts can strike a proper balance between the demands of the Fourteenth Amendment on the one hand and the federalism prerogatives of States on the other.[3]

---

[2] *See, e.g., School Dist. of Abington Township v. Schempp* (1963) (Stewart, J., dissenting) ("The Establishment Clause was primarily an attempt to insure that Congress not only would be powerless to establish a national church, but would also be unable to interfere with existing state establishments"); *see also Wallace v. Jaffree* (1985) (REHNQUIST, J., dissenting).

[3] Several Justices have suggested that rights incorporated through the Fourteenth Amendment apply in a different manner to the States than they do to the Federal Government. For instance, Justice Jackson stated, "the inappropriateness of a single standard for restricting State and Nation is indicated by the disparity between their functions and duties in relation to those freedoms." *Beauharnais v. Illinois,* 343 U.S. 250, 294 (1952) (dissenting opinion). Justice Harlan noted: "The Constitution differentiates between those areas of human conduct subject to the regulation of the States and those subject to the powers of the Federal Government. The substantive powers of the two governments, in many instances, are distinct. And in every case where we are called upon to balance the interest in free expression against other interests, it seems to me important that we should keep in the forefront the question of whether those other interests are state or federal." *Roth v. United States* (1957) (dissenting opinion). *See also Gitlow v. New York* (1925) (Holmes, J., dissenting).

Whatever the textual and historical merits of incorporating the Establishment Clause, I can accept that the Fourteenth Amendment protects religious liberty rights.[4] But I cannot accept its use to oppose neutral programs of school choice through the incorporation of the Establishment Clause. There would be a tragic irony in converting the Fourteenth Amendment's guarantee of individual liberty into a prohibition on the exercise of educational choice.

II

The wisdom of allowing States greater latitude in dealing with matters of religion and education can be easily appreciated in this context. Respondents advocate using the Fourteenth Amendment to handcuff the State's ability to experiment with education. But without education one can hardly exercise the civic, political, and personal freedoms conferred by the Fourteenth Amendment. Faced with a severe educational crisis, the State of Ohio enacted wide-ranging educational reform that allows voluntary participation of private and religious schools in educating poor urban children otherwise condemned to failing public schools. The program does not force any individual to submit to religious indoctrination or education. It simply gives parents a greater choice as to where and in what manner to educate their children.[5] This is a choice that those with greater means have routinely exercised.

Cleveland parents now have a variety of educational choices. There are traditional public schools, magnet schools, and privately run community schools, in addition to the scholarship program. Currently, 46 of the 56 private schools participating in the scholarship program are church affiliated (35 are Catholic), and 96 percent of students in the program attend religious schools. Thus, were the Court to disallow the inclusion of religious schools, Cleveland children could use their scholarships at only 10 private schools.

In addition to expanding the reach of the scholarship program, the inclusion of religious schools makes sense given Ohio's purpose of increasing educational performance and opportunities. Religious schools, like other private schools, achieve far better educational results than their public counterparts. For example, the students at Cleveland's Catholic schools score significantly higher on Ohio proficiency tests than students at Cleveland public schools. Of Cleveland

---

[4] In particular, these rights inhere in the Free Exercise Clause, which unlike the Establishment Clause protects individual liberties of religious worship. "That the central value embodied in the First Amendment — and, more particularly, in the guarantee of 'liberty' contained in the Fourteenth — is the safeguarding of an individual's right to free exercise of his religion has been consistently recognized." *Schempp, supra* (Stewart, J., dissenting).

[5] This Court has held that parents have the fundamental liberty to choose how and in what manner to educate their children. "The fundamental theory of liberty upon which all governments in this Union repose excludes any general power of the State to standardize its children by forcing them to accept instruction from public teachers only. The child is not the mere creature of the State; those who nurture him and direct his destiny have the right, coupled with the high duty, to recognize and prepare him for additional obligations." *Pierce v. Society of Sisters* (1925). *But see Troxel v. Granville* (2000) (THOMAS, J., concurring in judgment).

eighth graders taking the 1999 Ohio proficiency test, 95 percent in Catholic schools passed the reading test, whereas only 57 percent in public schools passed. And 75 percent of Catholic school students passed the math proficiency test, compared to only 22 percent of public school students. But the success of religious and private schools is in the end beside the point, because the State has a constitutional right to experiment with a variety of different programs to promote educational opportunity. That Ohio's program includes successful schools simply indicates that such reform can in fact provide improved education to underprivileged urban children.

Although one of the purposes of public schools was to promote democracy and a more egalitarian culture, failing urban public schools disproportionately affect minority children most in need of educational opportunity.

* * *

While the romanticized ideal of universal public education resonates with the cognoscenti who oppose vouchers, poor urban families just want the best education for their children, who will certainly need it to function in our high-tech and advanced society. As Thomas Sowell noted 30 years ago: "Most black people have faced too many grim, concrete problems to be romantics. They want and need certain tangible results, which can be achieved only by developing certain specific abilities." The same is true today. An individual's life prospects increase dramatically with each successfully completed phase of education. . . .The failure to provide education to poor urban children perpetuates a vicious cycle of poverty, dependence, criminality, and alienation that continues for the remainder of their lives. If society cannot end racial discrimination, at least it can arm minorities with the education to defend themselves from some of discrimination's effects.

* * *

Ten States have enacted some form of publicly funded private school choice as one means of raising the quality of education provided to underprivileged urban children. These programs address the root of the problem with failing urban public schools that disproportionately affect minority students. Society's other solution to these educational failures is often to provide racial preferences in higher education. Such preferences, however, run afoul of the Fourteenth Amendment's prohibition against distinctions based on race. *See Plessy* (Harlan, J., dissenting). By contrast, school choice programs that involve religious schools appear unconstitutional only to those who would twist the Fourteenth Amendment against itself by expansively incorporating the Establishment Clause. Converting the Fourteenth Amendment from a guarantee of opportunity to an obstacle against education reform distorts our constitutional values and disserves those in the greatest need.

As Frederick Douglass poignantly noted "no greater benefit can be bestowed upon a long benighted people, than giving to them, as we are here earnestly this day endeavoring to do, the means of an education."

Justice Thomas' opinion was not joined by any other member of the Court, but does he raise a challenge to existing Establishment Clause orthodoxy that the Court will one day have to address?

B. Public Neutrality Toward God and Religion

There is ample historical evidence that the word "establishment," as used by the framers of the First Amendment in 1791 meant what it had in Europe — government's "exclusive patronage" of one church. *See generally* LEO PFEFFER, CHURCH, STATE AND FREEDOM 63-70 (1953). The framers were most disturbed by laws that prescribed worship of one favored denomination, provided special subsidies therefore, or imposed disabilities on members of other religious sects, in particular for public office. As discussed in Part A, however, the framers nevertheless understood and encouraged the importance of religious belief generally. This was consistent with the natural law tradition of the Declaration. As Justice Joseph Story wrote: "[t]he real object of the [First] amendment was, not to countenance, much less to advance Mohametanism, or Judaism, or infidelity, by prostrating Christianity; but to exclude all rivalry among Christian sects, and to prevent any national ecclesiastical establishment, which should give to an hierarchy the exclusive patronage of the national government." 3 JOSEPH STORY, COMMENTARIES ON THE CONSTITUTION OF THE UNITED STATES § 1871 (photo. reprint 1991) (Boston, Hilliard, Gray & Co. 1833). From 1791 to 1947, this understanding went unchallenged. In 1947, however, in *Everson v. Board of Education*, 330 U.S. 1 (1947), the Supreme Court took a radical turn. In the guise of neutrality, *Everson* articulated the exclusionary view that government may not aid religion generally — a truly extraordinary proposition for a nation founded upon the "Laws of Nature and of Nature's God." Subsequent to *Everson*, the Establishment Clause case law has taken numerous other twists and turns, and while hardly settled, it has proceeded primarily in an exclusionary progression. By way of overview, the Establishment Clause has been interpreted in the following ways:

1. By the framers, Chief Justice Rehnquist and Justices Scalia and Thomas: as prohibiting the establishment of a national church, the coercion under law of a particular religious belief or practice, or the showing of any favoritism to a particular religious sect (the no coercion view and the equal protection idea — *i.e.*, no coercion, but also no discrimination in expression or government funding against religion);

2. Under *Everson* (the 20th century root of the exclusionary view) and later *Lemon v. Kurtzman*, 403 U.S. 602 (1971), as prohibiting: interpretation (1) above and any public support for (in purpose, effect or entanglement with) religion generally;

3. By Justice O'Connor as prohibiting: interpretation (1) above and any government action that might be perceived by a reasonably informed observer as an endorsement of religion generally (the noncoercion and equal protection view supplemented by concern with improper endorsement);

4. By Justice Souter, and to a lesser extent, Justices Stevens, Ginsburg, and Breyer as prohibiting: interpretations (1), (2), possibly (3) above, and the inclusion of religion in evenhanded governmental programs, providing either subsidies or the provisions of in-kind benefits, like school supplies or bus rides (the exclusionary view plus the rejection of the no coercion and equal protection idea when standing alone).

Simplifying the above progression somewhat, the various interpretations of the Establishment Clause may be grouped under the headings of the exclusionary view, the no coercion view, the no endorsement speculation, and the equal protection idea. The no coercion view and equal protection idea, also known in some case law and academic writing as "nonpreferentialism," are most closely aligned with the original understanding; the exclusionary view and no endorsement speculation are more reflective of a late 20th century embrace of individualism and a corresponding skepticism toward objective normative or moral standards.

1. Modern Judicial Application of the No Establishment Principle

a. The Exclusionary View

EVERSON v. BOARD OF EDUCATION
330 U.S. 1 (1947)

MR. JUSTICE BLACK delivered the opinion of the Court.

A New Jersey statute authorizes its local school districts to make rules and contracts for the transportation of children to and from schools. The appellee, a township board of education, acting pursuant to this statute, authorized reimbursement to parents of money expended by them for the bus transportation of their children on regular busses operated by the public transportation system. Part of this money was for the payment of transportation of some children in the community to Catholic parochial schools. These church schools give their students, in addition to secular education, regular religious instruction conforming to the religious tenets and modes of worship of the Catholic Faith. The superintendent of these schools is a Catholic priest.

The appellant, in his capacity as a district taxpayer, filed suit in a state court challenging the right of the Board to reimburse parents of parochial school students. He contended that the statute and the resolution passed pursuant to it violated both the State and the Federal Constitutions. That court held that the legislature was without power to authorize such payment under the state constitution. The New Jersey Court of Errors and Appeals reversed, holding that neither the statute nor the resolution passed pursuant to it was in conflict with the State constitution or the provisions of the Federal Constitution in issue. The case is here on appeal . . . .

* * *

A large proportion of the early settlers of this country came here from Europe to escape the bondage of laws which compelled them to support and attend government-favored churches . . . .

* * *

The movement toward this end reached its dramatic climax in Virginia in 1785-86 when the Virginia legislative body was about to renew Virginia's tax levy for the support of the established church. Thomas Jefferson and James Madison led the fight against this tax. Madison wrote his great Memorial and Remonstrance against the law. In it, he eloquently argued that a true religion did not need the support of law; that no person, either believer or non-believer, should be taxed to support a religious institution of any kind; that the best interest of a society required that the minds of men always be wholly free; and that cruel persecutions were the inevitable result of government-established religions. Madison's Remonstrance received strong support throughout Virginia, and the Assembly postponed consideration of the proposed tax measure until its next session. When the proposal came up for consideration at that session, it not only died in committee, but the Assembly enacted the famous "Virginia Bill for Religious Liberty" originally written by Thomas Jefferson.

* * *

The meaning and scope of the First Amendment, preventing establishment of religion or prohibiting the free exercise thereof, in the light of its history and the evils it was designed forever to suppress, have been several times elaborated by the decisions of this Court prior to the application of the First Amendment to the states by the Fourteenth . . . .

The "establishment of religion" clause of the First Amendment means at least this: Neither a state nor the Federal Government can set up a church. Neither can pass laws which aid one religion, aid all religions, or prefer one religion over another. Neither can force nor influence a person to go to or to remain away from church against his will or force him to profess a belief or disbelief in any religion. No person can be punished for entertaining or professing religious beliefs or disbeliefs, for church attendance or non-attendance. No tax in any amount, large or small, can be levied to support any religious activities or institutions, whatever they may be called, or whatever form they may adopt to teach or practice religion. Neither a state nor the Federal Government can, openly or secretly, participate in the affairs of any religious organizations or groups and *vice versa*. In the words of Jefferson, the clause against establishment of religion by law was intended to erect "a wall of separation between church and State."

We must consider the New Jersey statute in accordance with the foregoing limitations imposed by the First Amendment. But we must not strike that state statute down if it is within the State's constitutional power even though it approaches the verge of that power . . . .

Measured by these standards, we cannot say that the First Amendment prohibits New Jersey from spending tax-raised funds to pay the bus fares of parochial school pupils as a part of a general program under which it pays the fares of pupils attending public and other schools . . . . Of course, cutting off church schools from these services, so separate and so indisputably marked off from the religious function, would make it far more difficult for the schools to operate. But such is obviously not the purpose of the First Amendment. That Amendment requires the state to be a neutral in its relations with groups of religious believers and non-believers; it does not require the state to be their adversary. State power is no more to be used so as to handicap religions than it is to favor them.

This Court has said that parents may, in the discharge of their duty under state compulsory education laws, send their children to a religious rather than a public school if the school meets the secular educational requirements which the state has power to impose. *See Pierce v. Society of Sisters* [(1925)]. It appears that these parochial schools meet New Jersey's requirements. The State contributes no money to the schools. It does not support them. Its legislation, as applied, does no more than provide a general program to help parents get their children, regardless of their religion, safely and expeditiously to and from accredited schools.

The First Amendment has erected a wall between church and state. That wall must be kept high and impregnable. We could not approve the slightest breach. New Jersey has not breached it here.

Affirmed.

Mr. Justice Jackson, dissenting. [Omitted.]

Mr. Justice Rutledge, with whom Mr. Justice Frankfurter, Mr. Justice Jackson and Mr. Justice Burton agree, dissenting.

* * *

II.

No provision of the Constitution is more closely tied to or given content by its generating history than the religious clause of the First Amendment. It is at once the refined product and the terse summation of that history. The history includes not only Madison's authorship and the proceedings before the First Congress, but also the long and intensive struggle for religious freedom in

America, more especially in Virginia, of which the Amendment was the direct culmination. In the documents of the times, particularly of Madison, who was leader in the Virginia struggle before he became the Amendment's sponsor, but also in the writings of Jefferson and others and in the issues which engendered them is to be found irrefutable confirmation of the Amendment's sweeping content.

* * *

The climax came in the legislative struggle of 1784-1785 over the Assessment Bill. This was nothing more nor less than a taxing measure for the support of religion, designed to revive the payment of tithes suspended since 1777. So long as it singled out a particular sect for preference it incurred the active and general hostility of dissentient groups. It was broadened to include them, with the result that some subsided temporarily in their opposition. As altered, the bill gave to each taxpayer the privilege of designating which church should receive his share of the tax. In default of designation the legislature applied it to pious uses. But what is of the utmost significance here, "in its final form the bill left the taxpayer the option of giving his tax to education."

Madison was unyielding at all times, opposing with all his vigor the general and nondiscriminatory as he had the earlier particular and discriminatory assessments proposed. The modified Assessment Bill passed second reading in December, 1784, and was all but enacted. Madison and his followers, however, maneuvered deferment of final consideration until November, 1785. And before the Assembly reconvened in the fall he issued his historic Memorial and Remonstrance.

This is Madison's complete, though not his only, interpretation of religious liberty. It is a broadside attack upon all forms of "establishment" of religion, both general and particular, nondiscriminatory or selective. Reflecting not only the many legislative conflicts over the Assessment Bill and the Bill for Establishing Religious Freedom but also, for example, the struggles for religious incorporations and the continued maintenance of the glebes, the Remonstrance is at once the most concise and the most accurate statement of the views of the First Amendment's author concerning what is "an establishment of religion . . . ."

The Remonstrance, stirring up a storm of popular protest, killed the Assessment Bill. It collapsed in committee shortly before Christmas, 1785. With this, the way was cleared at last for enactment of Jefferson's Bill for Establishing Religious Freedom. Madison promptly drove it through in January of 1786, seven years from the time it was first introduced. This dual victory substantially ended the fight over establishments, settling the issue against them.

* * *

III

* * *

The funds used here were raised by taxation. The Court does not dispute, nor could it, that their use does in fact give aid and encouragement to religious instruction. It only concludes that this aid is not "support" in law. But Madison and Jefferson were concerned with aid and support in fact, not as a legal conclusion "entangled in precedents." Remonstrance, Par. 3. Here parents pay money to send their children to parochial schools and funds raised by taxation are used to reimburse them. This not only helps the children to get to school and the parents to send them. It aids them in a substantial way to get the very thing which they are sent to the particular school to secure, namely, religious training and teaching.

Believers of all faiths, and others who do not express their feeling toward ultimate issues of existence in any creedal form, pay the New Jersey tax. When the money so raised is used to pay for transportation to religious schools, the Catholic taxpayer to the extent of his proportionate share pays for the transportation of Lutheran, Jewish and otherwise religiously affiliated children to receive their non-Catholic religious instruction. Their parents likewise pay proportionately for the transportation of Catholic children to receive Catholic instruction. Each thus contributes to "the propagation of opinions which he disbelieves" in so far as their religions differ, as do others who accept no creed without regard to those differences. Each thus pays taxes also to support the teaching of his own religion, an exaction equally forbidden since it denies "the comfortable liberty" of giving one's contribution to the particular agency of instruction he approves.

NOTES AND QUESTIONS

1. Is the result in *Everson* inclusionary or exclusionary? At first blush, the opinion in *Everson* may not seem all that exclusionary. In terms of result, the Court upholds governmentally-provided bus service to religious schools. What's more the Court's opinion is phrased in terms of "neutrality," not exclusion. The exclusionary impact of *Everson* will be felt later, however, most notably as the Court struggles with other forms of aid to religious elementary schools. In any event, neutrality between religion and no religion is far different than say, Washington's decidedly non-neutral postulate that "religion and morality" were necessary supports for the political well-being of the republic. *See* John H. Garvey, *Is There a Principle of Religious Liberty?*, 94 MICH. L. REV. 1379 (1996) (discussing theories of religious liberty and arguing that they need not be neutral because nonneutral theories simply explain why society supports the right to do certain things and not others).

2. Revisionist History: The *Everson* opinion is historically questionable. Justice Black makes reference to Jefferson's Statute of Religious Freedom (reprinted below under the noncoercion view), but fails to recognize, as did the Anti-Federalist Richard Henry Lee earlier, that its aim was completing the work of Virginia's disestablishment of the Anglican Church, not mandating that government disavow all support for religion. Not surprisingly, therefore, contemporaneous with the Statute of Religious Freedom, Virginia was continuing in law to support religion generally. For example, fines were imposed for violating the Sabbath, *see* Act of December 26, 1792, ch 141, 1 VA. REV. CODE 554, 555 (1819), and public officials took oaths that ended with the language, "So help me God," or with such other language that was in accord with "the religion in which such person professeth to believe." *See* Act of January 7, 1818, ch. 28, 1 VA. REV. CODE 72, 73 (1819). The Anglican Church in Virginia had received special lands, called glebe lands, as an established church. Such lands were taken away by the Act of January 12, 1802, ch. 32b, 1 VA. REV. CODE 79 (1819). In *Terrett v. Taylor,* 13 U.S. (9 Cranch) 43 (1815), Justice Story held the act unconstitutional at least as applied to lands received by the church prior to the creation of the state of Virginia. In so doing, Story opined on the difference between disestablishment and the continuing importance of even-handed government support for religious corporations:

> It is conceded on all sides that, at the revolution, the Episcopal church no longer retained its character as an exclusive religious establishment. And there can be no doubt that it was competent to the people and to the legislature to deprive it of its superiority over other religious sects, and to withhold from it any support by public taxation. But, although it may be true that "religion can be directed only by reason and conviction, not by force or violence," and that "all men are equally entitled to the free exercise of religion according to the dictates of conscience," as the bill of rights of Virginia declares, yet it is difficult to perceive how it follows as a consequence that the legislature may not enact laws more effectually to enable all sects to accomplish the great objects of religion by giving them corporate rights for the management of their property, and the regulation of their temporal as well as spiritual concerns. Consistent with the constitution of Virginia the legislature could not create or continue a religious establishment which should have exclusive rights and prerogatives, or compel the citizens to worship under a stipulated form or discipline, or to pay taxes to those whose creed they could not conscientiously believe. But the free exercise of religion cannot be justly deemed to be restrained by aiding with equal attention the votaries of every sect to perform their own religious duties, or by establishing funds for the support of ministers, for public charities, for the endowment of churches, or for the sepulture of the dead. And that these purposes could be better secured and cherished by corporate powers, cannot be doubted by any person who has attended to the difficulties which surround all voluntary associations. While, therefore, the legislature might exempt the citizens from a compulsive attendance and payment of taxes in support of any particular sect, it is not perceived that either public or

constitutional principles required the abolition of all religious corporations.

13 U.S. (9 Cranch) at 48-49.

3. The "Wall of Separation" Metaphor: *Everson*'s perspective is far different from *Terrett v. Taylor*'s. It is a judicial attitude less congenial to public reliance upon the work of religion than at any previous time in our nation's history. For example, it is in *Everson* where Jefferson's absolutist phraseology, "a wall of separation between church and state," first appears in Supreme Court Establishment Clause jurisprudence (it first appeared in free exercise case law in *Reynolds v. United States*, 98 U.S. 145, 164 (1878), considered in Part C). As forbidding as the metaphor sounds, even this "wall" was misconstructed in *Everson*. Justice Black does not explain that Jefferson employed the phrase in a letter to the Danbury, Connecticut Baptist Association, not to diminish public support for religion generally, but to decry the establishment of the Congregationalist Church in Connecticut. *See* Thomas Jefferson, Reply to a Committee of the Danbury Baptist Association (Jan. 1, 1802), *in* 16 THE WRITINGS OF THOMAS JEFFERSON 281-82 (Andrew A. Lipscomb & Albert Ellery Bergh eds., 1905).

Despite its historical imperfection, *Everson* has troubled the Court's Establishment Clause jurisprudence ever since, and perhaps the American culture at large. As Washington and Tocqueville implicitly warned, the exclusion of religious influence may be seen in dramatically increased levels of violence, divorce, illegitimacy, and other manifestations of cultural dysfunction. At first, the extreme nature of *Everson*'s exclusionary theory was masked by its expedient, if not inclusionary result, allowing public funds to be used for the bus transportation of all students, including those attending religious schools. Shortly thereafter, however, *Everson* would spawn an ever more mechanically exclusionary formula in *Lemon v. Kurtzman*, 403 U.S. 602 (1971). Under the "*Lemon* test," a law does not violate the Establishment Clause only if it (1) has a secular purpose; (2) neither advances nor inhibits religion as its primary effect; and (3) does not "excessively entangle" the government with religion. *Id*. at 612-13. This multi-prong *Lemon* formula satisfied few of the Justices, and yielded highly inconsistent results over what assistance, if any, the government may render to religious schools, especially at the elementary level.

Outside of the grammar school in other substantive contexts, the ahistorical re-direction of *Everson* has been mitigated somewhat by various Establishment Clause theories that either re-direct the clause to its original purpose of no legal coercion of denominational faith and the equal treatment of religious sects, or less predictably and more subjectively, attempt to measure whether government activity can be perceived as too much "endorsement" of faith.

b. The Noncoercion View

Jefferson justifiably regarded the Virginia Statute of Religious Liberty to be one of his three most memorable contributions, the others being the Declaration of Independence and the founding of the University of Virginia. Jefferson was aided in this pursuit by Madison, as the *Everson* dissenters suggest. But the dissenters overlook that Jefferson and Madison together saw the struggle for religious freedom, not as a limitation of the significance or importance of religion, but as an affirmation of religion's importance to "the natural rights of mankind." That religion has this high place is signaled at the very beginning of Virginia's statute which calls first upon Almighty God. Nothing in this statute is at odds with sovereign acknowledgment of the existence of a Creator God in the Declaration. Indeed, given the common authorship of the two documents, it would be extraordinary for there to be a conflict. The Statute of Religious Liberty is primarily directed at ending the vestiges of Anglicanism (which had been the established church in Virginia) and other similar forms of compelled denominationalism. As you read the Statute, note especially the following testimonials to the importance of faith, freely embraced:

1. God endowed all human persons with free will, aided by a free mind;

2. It is contrary to God's will to coerce religious belief, whether that coercion comes at the hands of the state or the church;

3. Coercion includes not only forced belief, but the compelled financial support of a particular religious opinion or pastor over those religious ministers a person "feels most persuasive to righteousness" [notice the implicit assumption that some pastor or religious body would be freely supported by all moral men — Eds.];

4. Civil rights, including the right to hold public office, do not depend upon holding a particular religious opinion;

5. Religious belief and practice ought to remain free up to the point such "principles break out into overt acts against peace and good order." Thus, note: even religious liberty, as exalted as it is, is not absolute or without limit.

We take up what general laws maintaining "peace and good order" may be applied to religious beliefs and practices in Part C of this Chapter dealing with the interpretation of the Free Exercise Clause.

Virginia Statute of Religious Liberty (Jan. 16, 1786), *reprinted in* THE VIRGINIA STATUTE FOR RELIGIOUS FREEDOM at xvii (Merrill D Peterson & Robert C. Vaughan eds., 1988)

. . . An Act for establishing Religious Freedom.

I. WHEREAS Almighty God hath created the mind free; that all attempts to influence it by temporal punishments or burthens, or by civil incapacitations, tend only to beget habits of hypocrisy and meanness, and are a departure from the plan of the Holy author of our religion, who being Lord both of body and mind, yet chose not to propagate it by coercions either, as was in his Almighty power to do; that the impious presumption of legislators and rulers, civil as well as ecclesiastical, who being themselves but fallible and uninspired men, have assumed dominion over the faith of others, setting up their own opinions and modes of thinking as the only true and infallible, and as such endeavouring to impose them on others, hath established and maintained false religions over the greatest part of the world, and through all time; that to compel a man to furnish contributions of money for the propagation of opinions which he disbelieves, is sinful and tyrannical; that even the forcing him to support this or that teacher of his own religious persuasion, is depriving him of the comfortable liberty of giving his contributions to the particular pastor, whose morals he would make his pattern, and whose powers he feels most persuasive to righteousness, and is withdrawing from the ministry those temporary rewards, which proceeding from an approbation of their personal conduct, are an additional incitement to earnest and unremitting labours for the instruction of mankind; that our civil rights have no dependence on our religious opinions, any more than our opinions in physics or geometry; that therefore the proscribing any citizen as unworthy the public confidence by laying upon him an incapacity of being called to offices of trust and emolument, unless he profess or renounce this or that religious opinion, is depriving him injuriously of those privileges and advantages to which in common with his fellow-citizens he has a natural right; that it tends only to corrupt the principles of that religion it is meant to encourage, by bribing with a monopoly of worldly honours and emoluments, those who will externally profess and conform to it; that though indeed these are criminal who do not withstand such temptation, yet neither are those innocent who lay the bait in their way; that to suffer the civil magistrate to intrude his powers into the field of opinion, and to restrain the profession or propagation of principles on supposition of their ill tendency, is a dangerous fallacy, which at once destroys all religious liberty, because he being of course judge of that tendency will make his opinions the rule of judgment, and approve or condemn the sentiments of others only as they shall square with or differ from his own; that it is time enough for the rightful purposes of civil government, for its officers to interfere when principles break out into overt acts against peace and good order; and finally, that truth is great and will prevail if left to herself, that she is the proper and sufficient antagonist to error, and has nothing to fear from the conflict, unless by human interposition disarmed of her natural weapons, free argument and debate, errors ceasing to be dangerous when it is permitted freely to contradict them:

II. *Be it enacted by the General Assembly*, that no man shall be compelled to frequent or support any religious worship, place, or ministry whatsoever, nor shall be enforced, restrained, molested, or burthened in his body or goods, nor shall otherwise suffer on account of his religious opinions or belief; but that all men shall be free to profess, and by argument to maintain, their opinion in matters of religion, and that the same shall in no way diminish, enlarge, or affect their civil capacities.

III. And though we well know that this assembly elected by the people for the ordinary purposes of legislation only, have no power to restrain the acts of succeeding assemblies, constituted with powers equal to our own, and that therefore to declare this act to be irrevocable would be of no effect in law; yet we are free to declare, and do declare, that the rights hereby asserted are to the natural rights of mankind, and that if any act shall be hereafter passed to repeal the present, or to narrow its operation, such act will be an infringement of natural right.

NOTE

In *Lee v. Weisman*, the issue before the Court was whether a graduation prayer violated the Establishment Clause. In the context of considering this issue, a fairly evenly-divided Court debates whether coercion is a necessary element of an Establishment Clause case. Five members of the Court (Justice Kennedy writing for the majority and the four dissenting justices) believe coercion is necessary. Unlike the dissenters, though, Justice Kennedy extends the concept to include psychological coercion — an analogue, perhaps, of Justice O'Connor's no endorsement speculation considered later in this Chapter.

LEE v. WEISMAN
505 U.S. 577 (1992)

JUSTICE KENNEDY delivered the opinion of the Court.

School principals in the public school system of the city of Providence, Rhode Island, are permitted to invite members of the clergy to offer invocation and benediction prayers as part of the formal graduation ceremonies for middle schools and for high schools. The question before us is whether including clerical members who offer prayers as part of the official school graduation ceremony is consistent with the Religion Clauses of the First Amendment, provisions the Fourteenth Amendment makes applicable with full force to the States and their school districts.

[Robert E. Lee, the principal of Nathan Bishop Middle School, invited Rabbi Leslie Gutterman to deliver prayers at the school's graduation ceremony in

June 1989. Gutterman accepted, and offered both the invocation and benediction. Daniel Weisman, whose 14 year-old daughter graduated in the ceremony, challenged the practice on behalf of himself and his daughter as an unconstitutional establishment of religion.]

I

A

* * *

It has been the custom of Providence school officials to provide invited clergy with a pamphlet entitled "Guidelines for Civic Occasions," prepared by the National Conference of Christians and Jews . . . .

* * *

Rabbi Gutterman's prayers were as follows:

"INVOCATION

"God of the Free, Hope of the Brave:

"For the legacy of America where diversity is celebrated and the rights of minorities are protected, we thank You. May these young men and women grow up to enrich it.

"For the liberty of America, we thank You. May these new graduates grow up to guard it.

"For the political process of America in which all its citizens may participate, for its court system where all may seek justice we thank You. May those we honor this morning always turn to it in trust.

"For the destiny of America we thank You. May the graduates of Nathan Bishop Middle School so live that they might help to share it.

"May our aspirations for our country and for these young people, who are our hope for the future, be richly fulfilled.

AMEN"

"BENEDICTION

"O God, we are grateful to You for having endowed us with the capacity for learning which we have celebrated on this joyous commencement.

"Happy families give thanks for seeing their children achieve an important milestone. Send Your blessings upon the teachers and administrators who helped prepare them.

"The graduates now need strength and guidance for the future, help them to understand that we are not complete with academic knowledge alone. We must each strive to fulfill what You require of us all: To do justly, to love mercy, to walk humbly.

"We give thanks to You, Lord, for keeping us alive, sustaining us and allowing us to reach this special, happy occasion.

AMEN"

* * *

B

* * *

. . . The District Court held that petitioners' practice of including invocations and benedictions in public school graduations violated the Establishment Clause of the First Amendment, and it enjoined petitioners from continuing the practice. The court applied the three-part Establishment Clause test set forth in *Lemon v. Kurtzman* (1971). Under that test as described in our past cases, to satisfy the Establishment Clause a governmental practice must (1) reflect a clearly secular purpose; (2) have a primary effect that neither advances nor inhibits religion; and (3) avoid excessive government entanglement with religion. The District Court held that petitioners' actions violated the second part of the test, and so did not address either the first or the third. The court decided, based on its reading of our precedents, that the effects test of *Lemon* is violated whenever government action "creates an identification of the state with a religion, or with religion in general," or when "the effect of the governmental action is to endorse one religion over another, or to endorse religion in general." The court determined that the practice of including invocations and benedictions, even so-called nonsectarian ones, in public school graduations creates an identification of governmental power with religious practice, endorses religion, and violates the Establishment Clause. In so holding the court expressed the determination not to follow *Stein v. Plainwell Community Schools* (6th Cir. 1987), in which the Court of Appeals for the Sixth Circuit, relying on our decision in *Marsh v. Chambers* (1983), held that benedictions and invocations at public school graduations are not always unconstitutional. In *Marsh* we upheld the constitutionality of the Nebraska State Legislature's practice of opening each of its sessions with a prayer offered by a chaplain paid out of public funds. The District Court in this case disagreed with the Sixth Circuit's reasoning because it believed that *Marsh* was a narrow decision, "limited to the unique situation of legislative prayer," and did not have any relevance to school prayer cases.

On appeal, the United States Court of Appeals for the First Circuit affirmed . . . . We granted certiorari, and now affirm.

II

These dominant facts mark and control the confines of our decision: State officials direct the performance of a formal religious exercise at promotional and graduation ceremonies for secondary schools. Even for those students who object to the religious exercise, their attendance and participation in the state-sponsored religious activity are in a fair and real sense obligatory, though the school district does not require attendance as a condition for receipt of the diploma.

* * *

The principle that government may accommodate the free exercise of religion does not supersede the fundamental limitations imposed by the Establishment Clause. It is beyond dispute that, at a minimum, the Constitution guarantees that government may not coerce anyone to support or participate in religion or its exercise, or otherwise act in a way which "establishes a [state] religion or religious faith, or tends to do so." The State's involvement in the school prayers challenged today violates these central principles.

That involvement is as troubling as it is undenied. A school official, the principal, decided that an invocation and a benediction should be given; this is a choice attributable to the State, and from a constitutional perspective it is as if a state statute decreed that the prayers must occur. The principal chose the religious participant, here a rabbi, and that choice is also attributable to the State. The reason for the choice of a rabbi is not disclosed by the record, but the potential for divisiveness over the choice of a particular member of the clergy to conduct the ceremony is apparent.

Divisiveness, of course, can attend any state decision respecting religions, and neither its existence nor its potential necessarily invalidates the State's attempts to accommodate religion in all cases. The potential for divisiveness is of particular relevance here though, because it centers around an overt religious exercise in a secondary school environment where, as we discuss below, subtle coercive pressures exist and where the student had no real alternative which would have allowed her to avoid the fact or appearance of participation.

* * *

We are asked to recognize the existence of a practice of nonsectarian prayer, prayer within the embrace of what is known as the Judeo-Christian tradition, prayer which is more acceptable than one which, for example, makes explicit references to the God of Israel, or to Jesus Christ, or to a patron saint. There may be some support, as an empirical observation, to the statement of the Court of Appeals for the Sixth Circuit, picked up by Judge Campbell's dissent in the Court of Appeals in this case, that there has emerged in this country a civic religion, one which is tolerated when sectarian exercises are not. If common ground can be defined which permits once conflicting faiths to express the shared conviction that there is an ethic and a morality which transcend human invention, the sense of community and purpose sought by all decent societies might be advanced. But though the First Amendment does not allow the government to stifle prayers which aspire to these ends, neither does it permit the government to undertake that task for itself.

* * *

. . . The undeniable fact is that the school district's supervision and control of a high school graduation ceremony places public pressure, as well as peer pressure, on attending students to stand as a group or, at least, maintain respectful silence during the Invocation and Benediction. This pressure, though subtle and indirect, can be as real as any overt compulsion. Of course, in our culture standing or remaining silent can signify adherence to a view or simple respect for the views of others. And no doubt some persons who have no desire to join a prayer have little objection to standing as a sign of respect for those who do. But for the dissenter of high school age, who has a reasonable perception that she is being forced by the State to pray in a manner her conscience will not allow, the injury is no less real. There can be no doubt that for many, if not most, of the students at the graduation, the act of standing or remaining silent was an expression of participation in the rabbi's prayer. That was the very point of the religious exercise. It is of little comfort to a dissenter, then, to be told that for her the act of standing or remaining in silence signifies mere respect, rather than participation. What matters is that, given our social conventions, a reasonable dissenter in this milieu could believe that the group exercise signified her own participation or approval of it.

Finding no violation under these circumstances would place objectors in the dilemma of participating, with all that implies, or protesting. We do not address whether that choice is acceptable if the affected citizens are mature adults, but we think the State may not, consistent with the Establishment Clause, place primary and secondary school children in this position. Research in psychology supports the common assumption that adolescents are often susceptible to pressure from their peers towards conformity, and that the influence is strongest in matters of social convention. To recognize that the choice imposed by the State constitutes an unacceptable constraint only acknowledges that the government may no more use social pressure to enforce orthodoxy than it may use more direct means.

The injury caused by the government's action, and the reason why Daniel and Deborah Weisman object to it, is that the State, in a school setting, in effect required participation in a religious exercise. It is, we concede, a brief exercise during which the individual can concentrate on joining its message, meditate on her own religion, or let her mind wander. But the embarrassment and the intrusion of the religious exercise cannot be refuted by arguing that these prayers, and similar ones to be said in the future, are of a *de minimis* character. To do so would be an affront to the rabbi who offered them and to all those for whom the prayers were an essential and profound recognition of divine authority . . . .

There was a stipulation in the District Court that attendance at graduation and promotional ceremonies is voluntary. Petitioners and the United States, as *amicus*, made this a center point of the case, arguing that the option of not attending the graduation excuses any inducement or coercion in the ceremony itself. The argument lacks all persuasion. Law reaches past formalism. And to say a teenage student has a real choice not to attend her high school graduation is formalistic in the extreme. True, Deborah could elect not to attend commencement without renouncing her diploma; but we shall not allow the case to turn on this point. Everyone knows that in our society and in our culture high school graduation is one of life's most significant occasions. A school rule which excuses attendance is beside the point . . . .

* * *

Our society would be less than true to its heritage if it lacked abiding concern for the values of its young people, and we acknowledge the profound belief of adherents to many faiths that there must be a place in the student's life for precepts of a morality higher even than the law we today enforce. We express no hostility to those aspirations, nor would our oath permit us to do so. A relentless and all-pervasive attempt to exclude religion from every aspect of public life could itself become inconsistent with the Constitution. We recognize that, at graduation time and throughout the course of the educational process, there will be instances when religious values, religious practices, and religious persons will have some interaction with the public schools and their students. But these matters, often questions of accommodation of religion, are not before us. The sole question presented is whether a religious exercise may be conducted at a graduation ceremony in circumstances where, as we have found, young graduates who object are induced to conform. No holding by this Court suggests that a school can persuade or compel a student to participate in a religious exercise. That is being done here, and it is forbidden by the Establishment Clause of the First Amendment.

For the reasons we have stated, the judgment of the Court of Appeals is

Affirmed.

JUSTICE BLACKMUN, with whom JUSTICE STEVENS and JUSTICE O'CONNOR join, concurring. [Omitted.]

JUSTICE SOUTER, with whom JUSTICE STEVENS and JUSTICE O'CONNOR join, concurring.

I join the whole of the Court's opinion, and fully agree that prayers at public school graduation ceremonies indirectly coerce religious observance. I write separately nonetheless on two issues of Establishment Clause analysis that underlie my independent resolution of this case: whether the Clause applies to governmental practices that do not favor one religion or denomination over others, and whether state coercion of religious conformity, over and above state endorsement of religious exercise or belief, is a necessary element of an Establishment Clause violation.

I

Forty-five years ago, this Court announced a basic principle of constitutional law from which it has not strayed: the Establishment Clause forbids not only state practices that "aid one religion . . . or prefer one religion over another," but also those that "aid all religions." *Everson v. Board of Education of Ewing* (1947). Today we reaffirm that principle, holding that the Establishment Clause forbids state-sponsored prayers in public school settings no matter how nondenominational the prayers may be . . . .

* * *

B

Some have challenged this precedent by reading the Establishment Clause to permit "nonpreferential" state promotion of religion. The challengers argue that, as originally understood by the Framers, "[t]he Establishment Clause did not require government neutrality between religion and irreligion nor did it prohibit the Federal Government from providing nondiscriminatory aid to religion." *Wallace* [*v. Jaffree* (1985)] (REHNQUIST, J., dissenting); see also R. CORD, SEPARATION OF CHURCH AND STATE: HISTORICAL FACT AND CURRENT FICTION (1988). While a case has been made for this position, it is not [] convincing . . . .

* * *

. . . [H]istory neither contradicts nor warrants reconsideration of the settled principle that the Establishment Clause forbids support for religion in general no less than support for one religion or some.[3]

C

While these considerations are, for me, sufficient to reject the nonpreferentialist position, one further concern animates my judgment. In many contexts, including this one, nonpreferentialism requires some distinction between "sectarian" religious practices and those that would be, by some measure, ecumenical enough to pass Establishment Clause muster. Simply by requiring the enquiry, nonpreferentialists invite the courts to engage in comparative theology. I can hardly imagine a subject less amenable to the competence of the federal judiciary, or more deliberately to be avoided where possible.

* * *

---

3 In his dissent in *Wallace v. Jaffree* (1985), THE CHIEF JUSTICE rested his nonpreferentialist interpretation partly on the post-ratification actions of the early National Government. Aside from the willingness of some (but not all) early Presidents to issue ceremonial religious proclamations, which were at worst trivial breaches of the Establishment Clause, he cited such seemingly preferential aid as a treaty provision, signed by Jefferson, authorizing federal subsidization of a Roman Catholic priest and church for the Kaskaskia Indians. But this proves too much, for if the Establishment Clause permits a special appropriation of tax money for the religious activities of a particular sect, it forbids virtually nothing. Although evidence of historical practice can indeed furnish valuable aid in the interpretation of contemporary language, acts like the one in question prove only that public officials, no matter when they serve, can turn a blind eye to constitutional principle.

II

* * *

A

* * *

Our precedents may not always have drawn perfectly straight lines. They simply cannot, however, support the position that a showing of coercion is necessary to a successful Establishment Clause claim.

* * *

III

While the Establishment Clause's concept of neutrality is not self-revealing, our recent cases have invested it with specific content: the state may not favor or endorse either religion generally over nonreligion or one religion over others. . . .

* * *

JUSTICE SCALIA, with whom THE CHIEF JUSTICE, JUSTICE WHITE, and JUSTICE THOMAS join, dissenting.

Three Terms ago, I joined an opinion recognizing that the Establishment Clause must be construed in light of the "[g]overnment policies of accommodation, acknowledgment, and support for religion [that] are an accepted part of our political and cultural heritage." That opinion affirmed that "the meaning of the Clause is to be determined by reference to historical practices and understandings . . . ."

These views of course prevent me from joining today's opinion, which is conspicuously bereft of any reference to history. In holding that the Establishment Clause prohibits invocations and benedictions at public school graduation ceremonies, the Court — with nary a mention that it is doing so — lays waste a tradition that is as old as public school graduation ceremonies themselves, and that is a component of an even more longstanding American tradition of nonsectarian prayer to God at public celebrations generally. As its instrument of destruction, the bulldozer of its social engineering, the Court invents a boundless, and boundlessly manipulable, test of psychological coercion . . . .

* * *

I

* * *

From our Nation's origin, prayer has been a prominent part of governmental ceremonies and proclamations. The Declaration of Independence, the document marking our birth as a separate people, "appeal[ed] to the Supreme Judge of the world for the rectitude of our intentions" and avowed "a firm reliance on the protection of divine Providence." In his first inaugural address, after swearing his oath of office on a Bible, George Washington deliberately made a prayer a part of his first official act as President:

> "it would be peculiarly improper to omit in this first official act my fervent supplications to that Almighty Being who rules over the universe, who presides in the councils of nations, and whose providential aids can supply every human defect, that His benediction may consecrate to the liberties and happiness of the people of the United States a Government instituted by themselves for these essential purposes." INAUGURAL ADDRESSES OF THE PRESIDENTS OF THE UNITED STATES 2 (1989).

Such supplications have been a characteristic feature of inaugural addresses ever since . . . .

* * *

The other two branches of the Federal Government also have a long-established practice of prayer at public events. As we detailed in *Marsh* [*v. Chambers* (1983)], Congressional sessions have opened with a chaplain's prayer ever since the First Congress. And this Court's own sessions have opened with the invocation "God save the United States and this Honorable Court" since the days of Chief Justice Marshall. 1 C. WARREN, THE SUPREME COURT IN UNITED STATES HISTORY 469 (1922).

* * *

II

The Court presumably would separate graduation invocations and benedictions from other instances of public "preservation and transmission of religious beliefs" on the ground that they involve "psychological coercion." I find it a sufficient embarrassment that our Establishment Clause jurisprudence regarding holiday displays, *see Allegheny County v. Greater Pittsburgh ACLU* (1989), has come to "requir[e] scrutiny more commonly associated with interior decorators than with the judiciary." *American Jewish Congress v. Chicago* (7th Cir. 1987) (Easterbrook, J., dissenting). But interior decorating is a rock-hard science compared to psychology practiced by amateurs. A few citations of "research in psychology" that have no particular bearing upon the precise issue here, cannot disguise the fact that the Court has gone beyond the realm where judges know what they are doing. The Court's argument that state officials have "coerced" students to take part in the invocation and benediction at graduation ceremonies is, not to put too fine a point on it, incoherent.

The Court identifies two "dominant facts" that it says dictate its ruling that invocations and benedictions at public-school graduation ceremonies violate the Establishment Clause. Neither of them is in any relevant sense true.

A

The Court declares that students' "attendance and participation in the [invocation and benediction] are in a fair and real sense obligatory." But what exactly is this "fair and real sense"? According to the Court, students at graduation who want "to avoid the fact or appearance of participation," in the invocation and benediction are *psychologically* obligated by "public pressure, as well as peer pressure, . . . to stand as a group or, at least, maintain respectful silence" during those prayers. This assertion — *the very linchpin of the Court's opinion* — is almost as intriguing for what it does not say as for what it says. It does not say, for example, that students are psychologically coerced to bow their heads, place their hands in a Dürer-like prayer position, pay attention to the prayers, utter "Amen," or in fact pray. (Perhaps further intensive psychological research remains to be done on these matters.) It claims only that students are psychologically coerced "to stand . . . *or*, at least, maintain respectful silence." Both halves of this disjunctive (*both* of which must amount to the fact or appearance of participation in prayer if the Court's analysis is to survive on its own terms) merit particular attention.

To begin with the latter: The Court's notion that a student who simply *sits* in "respectful silence" during the invocation and benediction (when all others are standing) has somehow joined — or would somehow be perceived as having joined — in the prayers is nothing short of ludicrous. We indeed live in a vulgar age. But surely "our social conventions," have not coarsened to the point that anyone who does not stand on his chair and shout obscenities can reasonably be deemed to have assented to everything said in his presence. Since the Court does not dispute that students exposed to prayer at graduation ceremonies retain (despite "subtle coercive pressures") the free will to sit, there is absolutely no basis for the Court's decision. It is fanciful enough to say that "a reasonable dissenter," standing head erect in a class of bowed heads, "could believe that the group exercise signified her own participation or approval of it." It is beyond the absurd to say that she could entertain such a belief while pointedly declining to rise.

But let us assume the very worst, that the nonparticipating graduate is "subtly coerced" . . . to stand! Even that half of the disjunctive does not remotely establish a "participation" (or an "appearance of participation") in a religious exercise. The Court acknowledges that "in our culture standing . . . can signify adherence to a view or simple respect for the views of others." (Much more often the latter than the former, I think, except perhaps in the proverbial town meeting, where one votes by standing.) But if it is a permissible inference that one who is standing is doing so simply out of respect for the prayers of others that are in progress, then how can it possibly be said that a "reasonable dissenter . . . could believe that the group exercise signified her own participation or approval"? Quite obviously, it cannot. I may add, moreover, that maintaining respect for the religious observances of others is a fundamental civic virtue that government (including the public schools) can and should cultivate — so that even if it were the case that the displaying of such respect might be mistaken for taking part in the prayer, I would deny that the dissenter's interest in avoiding *even the false appearance of participation* constitutionally trumps the government's interest in fostering respect for religion generally.

The opinion manifests that the Court itself has not given careful consideration to its test of psychological coercion. For if it had, how could it observe, with no hint of concern or disapproval, that students stood for the Pledge of Allegiance, which immediately preceded Rabbi Gutterman's invocation? . . . Moreover, since the Pledge of Allegiance has been revised . . . to include the phrase "under God," recital of the Pledge would appear to raise the same Establishment Clause issue as the invocation and benediction. If students were psychologically coerced to remain standing during the invocation, they must also have been psychologically coerced, moments before, to stand for (and thereby, in the Court's view, take part in or appear to take part in) the Pledge. Must the Pledge therefore be barred from the public schools (both from graduation ceremonies and from the classroom)? . . .

* * *

B

The other "dominant fac[t]" identified by the Court is that "state officials direct the performance of a formal religious exercise" at school graduation ceremonies. "Direct[ing] the performance of a formal religious exercise" has a sound of liturgy to it, summoning up images of the principal directing acolytes where to carry the cross, or showing the rabbi where to unroll the Torah. A Court professing to be engaged in a "delicate and fact-sensitive" line-drawing, would better describe what it means as "prescribing the content of an invocation and benediction." But even that would be false. All the record shows is that principals of the Providence public schools, acting within their delegated authority, have invited clergy to deliver invocations and benedictions at graduations; and that Principal Lee invited Rabbi Gutterman, provided him a two-page pamphlet, prepared by the National Conference of Christians and Jews, giving general advice on inclusive prayer for civic occasions, and advised him that his prayers at graduation should be nonsectarian. How these facts can fairly be transformed into the charges that Principal Lee "directed and controlled the content of [Rabbi Gutterman's] prayer," that school officials "monitor prayer," and attempted to "compose official prayers," and that the "government involvement with religious activity in this case is pervasive," is difficult to fathom. The Court identifies nothing in the record remotely suggesting that school officials have ever drafted, edited, screened, or censored graduation prayers, or that Rabbi Gutterman was a mouthpiece of the school officials.

These distortions of the record are, of course, not harmless error: without them the Court's solemn assertion that the school officials could reasonably be perceived to be "enforc[ing] a religious orthodoxy," would ring as hollow as it ought.

III

The deeper flaw in the Court's opinion does not lie in its wrong answer to the question whether there was state-induced "peer-pressure" coercion; it lies, rather, in the Court's making violation of the Establishment Clause hinge on such a precious question. The coercion that was a hallmark of historical establishments of religion was coercion of religious orthodoxy and of financial support *by force of law and threat of penalty*. Typically, attendance at the state church was required; only clergy of the official church could lawfully perform sacraments; and dissenters, if tolerated, faced an array of civil disabilities. L. LEVY, THE ESTABLISHMENT CLAUSE 4 (1986). Thus, for example, in the colony of Virginia, where the Church of England had been established, ministers were required by law to conform to the doctrine and rites of the Church of England; and all persons were required to attend church and observe the Sabbath, were tithed for the public support of Anglican ministers, and were taxed for the costs of building and repairing churches.

The Establishment Clause was adopted to prohibit such an establishment of religion at the federal level (and to protect state establishments of religion from federal interference). I will further acknowledge for the sake of argument that, as some scholars have argued, by 1790 the term "establishment" had acquired an additional meaning — "financial support of religion generally, by public taxation" — that reflected the development of "general or multiple" establishments, not limited to a single church. But that would still be an establishment coerced *by force of law*. And I will further concede that our constitutional tradition, from the Declaration of Independence and the first inaugural address of Washington, quoted earlier, down to the present day, has, with a few aberrations, *see Holy Trinity Church v. United States* (1892), ruled out of order government-sponsored endorsement of religion — even when no legal coercion is present, and indeed even when no ersatz, "peer-pressure" psycho-coercion is present — where the endorsement is sectarian, in the sense of specifying details upon which men and women who believe in a benevolent, omnipotent Creator and Ruler of the world are known to differ (for example, the divinity of Christ). But there is simply no support for the proposition that the officially sponsored nondenominational invocation and benediction read by Rabbi Gutterman — with no one legally coerced to recite them — violated the Constitution of the United States. To the contrary, they are so characteristically American they could have come from the pen of George Washington or Abraham Lincoln himself.

Thus, while I have no quarrel with the Court's general proposition that the Establishment Clause "guarantees that government may not coerce anyone to support or participate in religion or its exercise," I see no warrant for expanding the concept of coercion beyond acts backed by threat of penalty — a brand of coercion that, happily, is readily discernible to those of us who have made a career of reading the disciples of Blackstone rather than of Freud. The Framers were indeed opposed to coercion of religious worship by the National Government; but, as their own sponsorship of nonsectarian prayer in public events demonstrates, they understood that "[s]peech is not coercive; the listener may do as he likes." *American Jewish Congress v. Chicago* (Easterbrook, J., dissenting).

* * *

The Court relies on our "school prayer" cases, *Engel v. Vitale* (1962), and *Abington School District v. Schempp* (1963). But whatever the merit of those cases, they do not support, much less compel, the Court's psycho-journey. In the first place, *Engel* and *Schempp* do not constitute an exception to the rule, distilled from historical practice, that public ceremonies may include prayer; rather, they simply do not fall within the scope of the rule (for the obvious reason that school instruction is not a public ceremony). Second, we have made clear our understanding that school prayer occurs within a framework in which legal coercion to attend school (i.e., coercion under threat of penalty) provides the ultimate backdrop. In *Schempp*, for example, we emphasized that the prayers were "prescribed as part of the curricular activities of students who are *required by law* to attend school." (emphasis added). *Engel's* suggestion that the school prayer program at issue there — which permitted students "to remain silent or be excused from the room," — involved "indirect coercive pressure," should be understood against this backdrop of legal coercion. . . .

* * *

IV

Our Religion Clause jurisprudence has become bedeviled (so to speak) by reliance on formulaic abstractions that are not derived from, but positively conflict with, our long-accepted constitutional traditions. Foremost among these has been the so-called *Lemon* test, *see Lemon v. Kurtzman* (1971), which has received well-earned criticism from many members of this Court. The Court today demonstrates the irrelevance of *Lemon* by essentially ignoring it, and the interment of that case may be the one happy byproduct of the Court's otherwise lamentable decision. Unfortunately, however, the Court has replaced *Lemon* with its psycho-coercion test, which suffers the double disability of having no roots whatever in our people's historic practice, and being as infinitely expandable as the reasons for psychotherapy itself.

Another happy aspect of the case is that it is only a jurisprudential disaster and not a practical one. Given the odd basis for the Court's decision, invocations and benedictions will be able to be given at public school graduations next June, as they have for the past century and a half, so long as school authorities make clear that anyone who abstains from screaming in protest does not necessarily participate in the prayers. All that is seemingly needed is an announcement, or perhaps a written insertion at the beginning of the graduation Program, to the effect that, while all are asked to rise for the invocation and benediction, none is compelled to join in them, nor will be assumed, by rising, to have done so. That obvious fact recited, the graduates and their parents may proceed to thank God, as Americans have always done, for the blessings He has generously bestowed on them and on their country.

* * *

The reader has been told much in this case about the personal interest of Mr. Weisman and his daughter, and very little about the personal interests on the other side. They are not inconsequential. Church and state would not be such a difficult subject if religion were, as the Court apparently thinks it to be, some purely personal avocation that can be indulged entirely in secret, like pornography, in the privacy of one's room. For most believers it is *not* that, and has never been. Religious men and women of almost all denominations have felt it necessary to acknowledge and beseech the blessing of God as a people, and not just as individuals, because they believe in the "protection of divine Providence," as the Declaration of Independence put it, not just for individuals but for societies; because they believe God to be, as Washington's first Thanksgiving Proclamation put it, the "Great Lord and Ruler of Nations." One can believe in the effectiveness of such public worship, or one can deprecate and deride it. But the longstanding American tradition of prayer at official ceremonies displays with unmistakable clarity that the Establishment Clause does not forbid the government to accommodate it.

The narrow context of the present case involves a community's celebration of one of the milestones in its young citizens' lives, and it is a bold step for this Court to seek to banish from that occasion, and from thousands of similar celebrations throughout this land, the expression of gratitude to God that a majority of the community wishes to make. The issue before us today is not the abstract philosophical question whether the alternative of frustrating this desire of a religious majority is to be preferred over the alternative of imposing "psychological coercion," or a feeling of exclusion, upon nonbelievers. Rather, the question is *whether a mandatory choice in favor of the former has been imposed by the United States Constitution.* As the age-old practices of our people show, the answer to that question is not at all in doubt.

I must add one final observation: The founders of our Republic knew the fearsome potential of sectarian religious belief to generate civil dissension and civil strife. And they also knew that nothing, absolutely nothing, is so inclined to foster among religious believers of various faiths a toleration — no, an affection — for one another than voluntarily joining in prayer together, to the God whom they all worship and seek. Needless to say, no one should be compelled to do that, but it is a shame to deprive our public culture of the opportunity, and indeed the encouragement, for people to do it voluntarily. The Baptist or Catholic who heard and joined in the simple and inspiring prayers of Rabbi Gutterman on this official and patriotic occasion was inoculated from religious bigotry and prejudice in a manner that can not be replicated. To deprive our society of that important unifying mechanism, in order to spare the nonbeliever what seems to me the minimal inconvenience of standing or even sitting in respectful non-participation, is as senseless in policy as it is unsupported in law.

For the foregoing reasons, I dissent.

c. The No Endorsement Speculation

Religious displays in public places are difficult cases only because the Court has made them so. The cases, often dealing with a Christmas nativity scene or Menorah, crystalize the garbled posture of a nation entering the 21st century that historically recognizes the importance of religion, but now putatively must remain neutral toward it because of Supreme Court opinion. In *Lynch v. Donnelly*, 465 U.S. 668 (1984), the Court confronted a display erected by the City of Pawtucket, Rhode Island that featured a Santa Claus house, reindeer, candy-striped poles, carolers, clowns, elephants, a teddy bear, lots of lights, and a creche or nativity scene. *Id.* at 671. The lower courts found an Establishment Clause violation because of the overtly religious nature of the creche, but the Supreme Court, per Chief Justice Burger, reversed. The Chief Justice's analysis, while nominally applying the three-part *Lemon* test (secular purpose, effect that neither advances nor inhibits religion, no entanglement of church and state), largely relied upon the mostly secular, and even commercial, context of the bulk of the display and a conception of Christmas as an historical, rather than a religious tradition. *Id.* at 681-86. *Lynch*'s concern with the make-up of the display probably accounts for Justice Scalia's observation in *Lee* that the outcome of these cases seems to depend more on "interior decorating," than on constitutional analysis. The *Lynch* case is significant, however, because it occasioned some speculation on the part of Justice O'Connor, concurring separately, that many establishment cases can be resolved by examining whether there has been a government endorsement that "sends a message to nonadherents that they are outsiders, not full members of the political community, and an accompanying message to adherents that they are insiders, [or] favored members of the political community." *Id.* at 688 (O'Connor, J., concurring). This is the no endorsement speculation, and since *Lynch*, Justice O'Connor has been proselytizing in its favor. She has won a few converts, but never a clear majority of the Court.

Applying this speculation in *Lynch*, Justice O'Connor found no endorsement, but only a celebration of a public holiday that like the printing of "In God We Trust" on coins serves only to "solemniz[e] public occasions, express[] confidence in the future, and encourag[e] the recognition of what is worthy of appreciation in society." *Id.* at 693 (O'Connor, J., concurring).

In a subsequent case, *Allegheny County v. Greater Pittsburgh ACLU*, 492 U.S. 573 (1989), Justice Blackmun wrote for a highly-divided Court that borrowed from Justice O'Connor's no endorsement speculation. *Allegheny County* involved two displays — another nativity scene, this time set on the main staircase of a county courthouse and one block away, a Jewish Menorah, evergreen tree, and sign saluting liberty in front of the main city-county office building. The local government erected both displays, although the creche had been donated by a Catholic organization, and there was a sign to that effect. The Court allowed the menorah, but not the creche.

Writing partly for a majority, occasionally for a plurality, and sometimes alone, Justice Blackmun found the creche to violate the three-part *Lemon* test, *id*. at 598-602, but found that test satisfied in relation to the menorah, because he asserted the latter display was not exclusively a religious one, in light of the object's history, the sign and evergreen tree, *id*. at 613-21. Justice Blackmun also made reference to Justice O'Connor's no endorsement speculation in *Lynch*, noting that "[i]n recent years, we have paid particularly close attention to whether the challenged governmental practice either has the purpose or effect of 'endorsing' religion." *Id*. at 592. Maybe so, but the entire Court was not prepared to make the no endorsement speculation the "controlling endorsement inquiry," as Justice Blackmun called it. *Id*. at 597. Justice O'Connor agreed with Blackmun's result, though she emphasized that the reason the menorah display was acceptable related to her belief that there was no "message of endorsement of Judaism or of religion in general." *Id*. at 634 (O'Connor, J., concurring).

Justice O'Connor had to defend her no endorsement speculation from a strong challenge from Justice Kennedy, who wrote in dissent in *Allegheny County* for himself, Chief Justice Rehnquist, and Justices White and Scalia. Drawing upon the no coercion view he articulated in *Lee v. Weisman*, Justice Kennedy wrote: "The creche and the menorah are purely passive symbols of religious holidays. Passersby who disagree with the message conveyed by these displays are free to ignore them, or even to turn their backs, just as they are free to do so when they disagree with any other form of government speech." *Id*. at 664 (Kennedy, J., dissenting).

Justice Kennedy saw little future for the no endorsement speculation, as he found it "flawed in its fundamentals and unworkable in practice. The uncritical adoption of this standard is every bit as troubling as the bizarre result it produces in the cases before us." *Id*. at 669 (Kennedy, J., dissenting).

Nevertheless, as the next case illustrates, Justice O'Connor continues to promote this conception of the Establishment Clause. Unlike *Lynch* and *Allegheny County*, *Capitol Square Review and Advisory Board v. Pinette*, 515 U.S. 753 (1995), involved a private display on public property. At least for the plurality, as the opinion by Justice Scalia indicates, if the public property is an open forum where the private expression of views by word or symbol are allowed, there is no meaningful Establishment Clause problem. In this sense, the public forum is merely an extension of the no coercion view — citizens can speak freely and others may agree, disagree, or ignore as they wish. The mere fact that the government facilitates general expression cannot be said to be an establishment of religion. The matter becomes complicated, however, if the no endorsement speculation is indulged. Refining her prior speculations, Justice O'Connor argues that the Establishment Clause "imposes affirmative obligations that may require a State, in some situations, to take steps to avoid being perceived as supporting or endorsing a private religious message." *Id*. at 777 (O'Connor, J., concuring). In other words, according to Justice O'Connor, the government must actively distance itself even from private religious expression if some "hypothetical observer" who is "aware of the history and context of the community" might perceive the private speech or display as a government endorsement of religion. *Id.* at 780 (O'Connor, J., concurring). Justice Scalia rejects the refined concept of "transferred endorsement." *Id.* at 764. In this, Justice Scalia's opinion reminds us that active discrimination against private religious expression is a good distance from Tocqueville's observation of religion as "the first of [America's] political institutions," fostering the proper use of liberty.

CAPITOL SQUARE REVIEW AND ADVISORY BOARD v. PINETTE
515 U.S. 753 (1995)

JUSTICE SCALIA announced the judgment of the Court and delivered the opinion of the Court with respect to Parts I, II, and III, and an opinion with respect to Part IV, in which THE CHIEF JUSTICE, JUSTICE KENNEDY and JUSTICE THOMAS join.

The Establishment Clause of the First Amendment, made binding upon the States through the Fourteenth Amendment, provides that government "shall make no law respecting an establishment of religion." The question in this case is whether a State violates the Establishment Clause when, pursuant to a religiously neutral state policy, it permits a private party to display an unattended religious symbol in a traditional public forum located next to its seat of government.

I

Capitol Square is a 10-acre, state-owned plaza surrounding the Statehouse in Columbus, Ohio. For over a century the square has been used for public speeches, gatherings, and festivals advocating and celebrating a variety of causes, both secular and religious. . . .

It has been the Board's policy "to allow a broad range of speakers and other gatherings of people to conduct events on the Capitol Square . . . ."

In November 1993, after reversing an initial decision to ban unattended holiday displays from the square during December 1993, the Board authorized the State to put up its annual Christmas tree. On November 29, 1993, the Board granted a rabbi's application to erect a menorah. That same day, the Board received an application from respondent Donnie Carr, an officer of the Ohio Ku Klux Klan, to place a cross on the square from December 8, 1993, to December 24, 1993. The Board denied that application on December 3, informing the Klan by letter that the decision to deny "was made upon the advice of counsel, in a good faith attempt to comply with the Ohio and United States Constitutions, as they have been interpreted in relevant decisions by the Federal and State Courts."

Two weeks later, having been unsuccessful in its effort to obtain administrative relief from the Board's decision, the Ohio Klan, through its leader Vincent Pinette, filed the present suit in the United States District Court for the Southern District of Ohio, seeking an injunction requiring the Board to issue the requested permit. The Board defended on the ground that the permit would violate the Establishment Clause. The District Court determined that Capitol Square was a traditional public forum open to all without any policy against freestanding displays; that the Klan's cross was entirely private expression entitled to full First Amendment protection; and that the Board had failed to show that the display of the cross could reasonably be construed as endorsement of Christianity by the State. The District Court issued the injunction and, after the Board's application for an emergency stay was denied, the Board permitted the Klan to erect its cross. The Board then received, and granted, several additional applications to erect crosses on Capitol Square during December 1993 and January 1994.

On appeal by the Board, the United States Court of Appeals for the Sixth Circuit affirmed the District Court's judgment. . . .

II

First, a preliminary matter: Respondents contend that we should treat this as a case in which freedom of speech (the Klan's right to present the message of the cross display) was denied because of the State's disagreement with that message's political content, rather than because of the State's desire to distance itself from sectarian religion. They suggest in their merits brief and in their oral argument that Ohio's genuine reason for disallowing the display was disapproval of the political views of the Ku Klux Klan. Whatever the fact may be, the case was not presented and decided that way. The record facts before us and the opinions below address only the Establishment Clause issue; that is the question upon which we granted certiorari; and that is the sole question before us to decide.

Respondents' religious display in Capitol Square was private expression. Our precedent establishes that private religious speech, far from being a First Amendment orphan, is as fully protected under the Free Speech Clause as secular private expression. *Widmar v. Vincent* (1981) [holding unconstitutional a state university policy preventing student groups from using school facilities for religious worship or religious discussion]. . . . [But the Board] contend[s] that the constitutional protection does not extend to the length of permitting that expression to be made on Capitol Square.

* * *

III

There is no doubt that compliance with the Establishment Clause is a state interest sufficiently compelling to justify content-based restrictions on speech. *See Lamb's Chapel* [*v. Center Moriches Union Free School Dist.* (1993)]; *Widmar*. Whether that interest is implicated here, however, is a different question. And we do not write on a blank slate in answering it. We have twice previously addressed the combination of private religious expression, a forum available for public use, content-based regulation, and a State's interest in complying with the Establishment Clause. Both times, we have struck down the restriction on religious content.

In *Lamb's Chapel*, a school district allowed private groups to use school facilities during off-hours for a variety of civic, social and recreational purposes, excluding, however, religious purposes. We held that even if school property during off-hours was not a public forum, the school district violated an applicant's free-speech rights by denying it use of the facilities solely because of the religious viewpoint of the program it wished to present. We rejected the district's compelling-state-interest Establishment Clause defense (the same made here) because the school property was open to a wide variety of uses, the district was not directly sponsoring the religious group's activity, and "any benefit to religion or to the Church would have been no more than incidental." The *Lamb's Chapel* reasoning applies *a fortiori* here, where the property at issue is not a school but a full-fledged public forum.

Lamb's Chapel followed naturally from our decision in *Widmar*, in which we examined a public university's exclusion of student religious groups from facilities available to other student groups. There also we addressed official discrimination against groups who wished to use a "generally open forum" for religious speech. And there also the State claimed that its compelling interest in complying with the Establishment Clause justified the content-based restriction. We rejected the defense because the forum created by the State was open to a broad spectrum of groups and would provide only incidental benefit to religion. We stated categorically that "an open forum in a public university does not confer any imprimatur of state approval on religious sects or practices."

Quite obviously, the factors that we considered determinative in *Lamb's Chapel* and *Widmar* exist here as well. The State did not sponsor respondents' expression, the expression was made on government property that had been opened to the public for speech, and permission was requested through the same application process and on the same terms required of other private groups.

IV

* * *

We must note, to begin with, that it is not really an "endorsement test" of any sort, much less the "endorsement test" which appears in our more recent Establishment Clause jurisprudence, that petitioners urge upon us. "Endorsement" connotes an expression or demonstration of approval or support. THE NEW SHORTER OXFORD ENGLISH DICTIONARY 818 (1993); WEBSTER'S NEW DICTIONARY 845 (2d ed. 1950). Our cases have accordingly equated "endorsement" with "promotion" or "favoritism." *Allegheny County* [*v. Greater Pittsburgh ACLU* (1989)] (citing cases). We find it peculiar to say that government "promotes" or "favors" a religious display by giving it the same access to a public forum that all other displays enjoy. And as a matter of Establishment Clause jurisprudence, we have consistently held that it is no violation for government to enact neutral policies that happen to benefit religion. Where we have tested for endorsement of religion, the subject of the test was either expression *by the government itself*, *Lynch* [*v. Donnelly* (1984)], or else government action alleged to *discriminate in favor* of private religious expression or activity, *Board of Ed. of Kiryas Joel Village School Dist. v. Grumet* (1994); *Allegheny County, supra.* The test petitioners propose, which would attribute to a neutrally behaving government *private* religious expression, has no antecedent in our jurisprudence, and would better be called a "transferred endorsement" test.

Petitioners rely heavily on *Allegheny County* and *Lynch*, but each is easily distinguished. In *Allegheny County* we held that the display of a privately sponsored creche on the "Grand Staircase" of the Allegheny County Courthouse violated the Establishment Clause. That staircase was not, however, open to all on an equal basis, so the County was *favoring* sectarian religious expression. . . . In *Lynch* we held that a city's display of a creche did not violate the Establishment Clause because, in context, the display did not endorse religion. The opinion does assume, as petitioners contend, that the *government's* use of religious symbols is unconstitutional if it effectively endorses sectarian religious belief. But the case neither holds nor even remotely assumes that the government's neutral treatment of *private* religious expression can be unconstitutional.

Petitioners argue that absence of perceived endorsement was material in *Lamb's Chapel* and *Widmar*. We did state in *Lamb's Chapel* that there was "no realistic danger that the community would think that the District was endorsing religion or any particular creed." But that conclusion was not the result of empirical investigation; it followed directly, we thought, from the fact that the forum was open and the religious activity privately sponsored. It is significant that we referred only to what would be thought by "the community" — not by outsiders or individual members of the community uninformed about the school's practice. Surely some of the latter, hearing of religious ceremonies on school premises, and not knowing of the premises' availability and use for all sorts of other private activities, *might* leap to the erroneous conclusion of state endorsement. But, we in effect said, given an open forum and private sponsorship, erroneous conclusions do not count. So also in *Widmar*. Once we determined that the benefit to religious groups from the public forum was incidental and shared by other groups, we categorically rejected the State's Establishment Clause defense.

What distinguishes *Allegheny County* and the dictum in *Lynch* from *Widmar* and *Lamb's Chapel* is the difference between government speech and private speech. "[T]here is a crucial difference between *government* speech endorsing religion, which the Establishment Clause forbids, and *private* speech endorsing religion, which the Free Speech and Free Exercise Clauses protect." [*Bd. of Educ. of Westside Community Sch. v.*] *Mergens* [(1990)] (O'CONNOR, J., concurring). Petitioners assert, in effect, that that distinction disappears when the private speech is conducted too close to the symbols of government. But that, of course, must be merely a subpart of a more general principle: that the distinction disappears whenever private speech can be mistaken for government speech. That proposition cannot be accepted, at least where, as here, the government has not fostered or encouraged the mistake.

* * *

The contrary view, most strongly espoused by JUSTICE STEVENS, but endorsed by JUSTICE SOUTER and JUSTICE O'CONNOR as well, exiles private religious speech to a realm of less-protected expression heretofore inhabited only by sexually explicit displays and commercial speech. It will be a sad day when this Court casts piety in with pornography, and finds the First Amendment more hospitable to private expletives, than to private prayers. This would be merely bizarre were religious speech simply *as* protected by the Constitution as other forms of private speech; but it is outright perverse when one considers that private religious expression receives *preferential* treatment under the Free Exercise Clause. It is no answer to say that the Establishment Clause tempers religious speech. By its terms that Clause applies only to the words and acts of *government*. It was never meant, and has never been read by this Court, to serve as an impediment to purely *private* religious speech connected to the State only through its occurrence in a public forum.

* * *

The "transferred endorsement" test would also disrupt the settled principle that policies providing incidental benefits to religion do not contravene the Establishment Clause. That principle is the basis for the constitutionality of a broad range of laws, not merely those that implicate free-speech issues, *see, e.g.,* *Witters* [*v. Washington Dep't of Services for the Blind* (1986)]; *Mueller* [*v. Allen* (1983)]. It has radical implications for our public policy to suggest that neutral laws are invalid whenever hypothetical observers may — *even reasonably* — confuse an incidental benefit to religion with state endorsement.

If Ohio is concerned about misperceptions, nothing prevents it from requiring all private displays in the Square to be identified as such. That would be a content-neutral "manner" restriction which is assuredly constitutional. . . .

* * *

Religious expression cannot violate the Establishment Clause where it (1) is purely private and (2) occurs in a traditional or designated public forum, publicly announced and open to all on equal terms. Those conditions are satisfied here, and therefore the State may not bar respondents' cross from Capitol Square.

The judgment of the Court of Appeals is affirmed.

Justice Thomas, concurring. [Omitted.]

Justice O'Connor, with whom Justice Souter and Justice Breyer join, concurring in part and concurring in the judgment.

* * *

While the plurality would limit application of the endorsement test to "expression *by the government itself*, . . . or else government action alleged to *discriminate in favor* of private religious expression or activity," I believe that an impermissible message of endorsement can be sent in a variety of contexts, not all of which involve direct government speech or outright favoritism. . . .

* * *

Our agreement as to the outcome of this case, however, cannot mask the fact that I part company with the plurality on a fundamental point: I disagree that "[i]t has radical implications for our public policy to suggest that neutral laws are invalid whenever hypothetical observers may — *even reasonably* — confuse an incidental benefit to religion with State endorsement." On the contrary, when the reasonable observer would view a government practice as endorsing religion, I believe that it is our *duty* to hold the practice invalid. The plurality today takes an exceedingly narrow view of the Establishment Clause that is out of step both with the Court's prior cases and with well-established notions of what the Constitution requires. The Clause is more than a negative prohibition against certain narrowly defined forms of government favoritism, it also imposes affirmative obligations that may require a State, in some situations, to take steps to avoid being perceived as supporting or endorsing a private religious message. That is, the Establishment Clause forbids a State from hiding behind the application of formally neutral criteria and remaining studiously oblivious to the effects of its actions. Governmental intent cannot control, and not all state policies are permissible under the Religion Clauses simply because they are neutral in form.

* * *

In the end, I would recognize that the Establishment Clause inquiry cannot be distilled into a fixed, *per se* rule. Thus, "[e]very government practice must be judged in its unique circumstances to determine whether it constitutes an endorsement or disapproval of religion." *Lynch* (O'Connor, J., concurring). And this question cannot be answered in the abstract, but instead requires courts to examine the history and administration of a particular practice to determine whether it operates as such an endorsement. I continue to believe that government practices relating to speech on religious topics "must be subjected to careful judicial scrutiny," and that the endorsement test supplies an appropriate standard for that inquiry.

II

* * *

. . . Saying that the endorsement inquiry should be conducted from the perspective of a hypothetical observer who is presumed to possess a certain level of information that all citizens might not share neither chooses the perceptions of the majority over those of a "reasonable non-adherent," *cf.* L. TRIBE, AMERICAN CONSTITUTIONAL LAW 1293 (2d ed. 1988), nor invites disregard for the values the Establishment Clause was intended to protect. It simply recognizes the fundamental difficulty inherent in focusing on actual people: there is always *someone* who, with a particular quantum of knowledge, reasonably might perceive a particular action as an endorsement of religion. A State has not made religion relevant to standing in the political community simply because a particular viewer of a display might feel uncomfortable.

It is for this reason that the reasonable observer in the endorsement inquiry must be deemed aware of the history and context of the community and forum in which the religious display appears. . . . An informed member of the community will know how the public space in question has been used in the past — and it is that fact, not that the space may meet the legal definition of a public forum, which is relevant to the endorsement inquiry.

* * *

JUSTICE SOUTER, with whom JUSTICE O'CONNOR and JUSTICE BREYER join, concurring in part and concurring in the judgment. [Omitted.]

JUSTICE STEVENS, dissenting.

The Establishment Clause should be construed to create a strong presumption against the installation of unattended religious symbols on public property. Although the State of Ohio has allowed Capitol Square, the area around the seat of its government, to be used as a public forum, and although it has occasionally allowed private groups to erect other sectarian displays there, neither fact provides a sufficient basis for rebutting that presumption. On the contrary, the sequence of sectarian displays disclosed by the record in this case illustrates the importance of rebuilding the "wall of separation between church and State" that Jefferson envisioned.

* * *

JUSTICE GINSBURG, dissenting.

* * *

If the aim of the Establishment Clause is genuinely to uncouple government from church, *see Everson v. Board of Ed. of Ewing*, a State may not permit, and a court may not order, a display of this character. *Cf.* Sullivan, *Religion and Lib-*

eral Democracy, 59 U. CHI. L. REV. 195, 197-214 (1992) (negative bar against establishment of religion implies affirmative establishment of secular public order). JUSTICE SOUTER, in the final paragraphs of his opinion, suggests two arrangements that might have distanced the State from "the principal symbol of Christianity around the world": a sufficiently large and clear disclaimer;[1] or an area reserved for unattended displays carrying no endorsement from the State, a space plainly and permanently so marked. Neither arrangement is even arguably present in this case. The District Court's order did not mandate a disclaimer. ("Plaintiffs are entitled to an injunction requiring the defendants to issue a permit to erect a cross on Capitol Square"). And the disclaimer the Klan appended to the foot of the cross was unsturdy: it did not identify the Klan as sponsor; it failed to state unequivocally that Ohio did not endorse the display's message; and it was not shown to be legible from a distance. The relief ordered by the District Court thus violated the Establishment Clause.

Whether a court order allowing display of a cross, but demanding a sturdier disclaimer, could withstand Establishment Clause analysis is a question more difficult than the one this case poses. I would reserve that question for another day and case. . . .

d. The Equal Protection Idea

The equal protection idea is implicit in Justice Scalia's plurality opinion in *Capitol Square*. In several decisions cited by him in Part III of the *Capitol Square* opinion, *e.g.*, *Lamb's Chapel* and *Widmar v. Vincent*, the Court addressed the issue of whether a government school or public university was compelled by the Establishment Clause to exclude religious groups from making use of facilities within educational contexts that were open forums, either in a limited or general sense. These cases were largely resolved on the free speech basis that governmental entities may not draw viewpoint- or content-based distinctions. But along the way, the Court made plain that the Establishment Clause did not excuse such abridgement of speech or denial of equal access to public facilities.

The next case, *Rosenberger v. Rector*, 515 U.S. 819 (1995), is like *Lamb's Chapel* and *Widmar* insofar as it involves equal, religiously neutral access to the

---

[1] *Cf. American Civil Liberties Union v. Wilkinson* (6th Cir. 1990) (approving disclaimer ordered by District Court, which had to be "'prominently displayed immediately in front of'" the religious symbol and "'readable from an automobile passing on the street directly in front of the structure'"; the approved sign read: "'This display was not constructed with public funds and does not constitute an endorsement by the Commonwealth [of Kentucky] of any religion or religious doctrine.'") (quoting District Court); *McCreary v. Stone* (2d Cir. 1984) (disclaimers must meet requirements of size, visibility, and message; disclaimer at issue was too small), Parish, *Private Religious Displays in Public Fora*, 61 U. CHI. L. REV. 253, 285-286 (1994) (disclaimer must not only identify the sponsor, it must say "in no uncertain language" that the government's permit "in no way connotes [government] endorsement of the display's message"; the "disclaimer's adequacy should be measured by its visibility to the average person viewing the religious display").

equivalent of a public forum — this time, not a physical place, but a common fund available for use by student organizations of the University of Virginia. The Court concludes that the Establishment Clause does not mandate that the University scan publications for religious content and exclude those publications from funding, any more than the prior cases established that religious groups could not use university or school meeting rooms for sectarian activities, whether or not accompanied by devotional exercises.

Four dissenting Justices, Souter, Stevens, Ginsburg, and Breyer, reject the equal protection idea, or as they call it, "evenhandedness," as sufficient to meet the requirements of the Establishment Clause. The fact that the student organization publishing the religious magazine acquired its public funds on an evenhanded basis does not, for the dissent, alleviate the fact that the funds were used for a religious purpose. Writes the dissent, "we never held that evenhandedness might be sufficient to render direct aid to religion constitutional." *Id.* at 880 (Souter, J., dissenting).

The dissent's claim, however, is ahistorical, as Justice Thomas' concurring opinion demonstrates. Recognizing the importance the framers assigned to general support for religion, Thomas combs the history yet again to demonstrate that "the Framers saw the Establishment Clause simply as a prohibition on governmental preferences for some religious faiths over others." *Id.* at 855 (Thomas, J., concurring). Moreover, as Thomas points out, even if one rejects the nonpreferential view (which, as students should remember, largely coincides with the no coercion position), there is nothing to warrant the outright hostility that is represented by "the dissent's extreme view that the government must discriminate against religious adherents by excluding them from more generally available financial subsidies." *Id.* at 857 (Thomas, J., concurring).

ROSENBERGER v. RECTOR
515 U.S. 819 (1995)

MR. JUSTICE KENNEDY delivered the opinion of the Court.

The University of Virginia, an instrumentality of the Commonwealth for which it is named and thus bound by the First and Fourteenth Amendments, authorizes the payment of outside contractors for the printing costs of a variety of student publications. It withheld any authorization for payments on behalf of petitioners for the sole reason that their student paper "primarily promotes or manifests a particular belie[f] in or about a deity or an ultimate reality." That the paper did promote or manifest views within the defined exclusion seems plain enough. The challenge is to the University's regulation and its denial of authorization, the case raising issues under the Speech and Establishment Clauses of the First Amendment.

I

The public corporation we refer to as the "University" is denominated by state law as "the Rector and Visitors of the University of Virginia," and it is responsible for governing the school. Founded by Thomas Jefferson in 1819, and ranked by him, together with the authorship of the Declaration of Independence and of the Virginia Act for Religious Freedom, Va. Code Ann. § 57-1, as one of his proudest achievements, the University is among the Nation's oldest and most respected seats of higher learning. It has more than 11,000 undergraduate students, and 6,000 graduate and professional students. An understanding of the case requires a somewhat detailed description of the program the University created to support extracurricular student activities on its campus.

Before a student group is eligible to submit bills from its outside contractors for payment by the fund described below, it must become a "Contracted Independent Organization" (CIO). CIO status is available to any group the majority of whose members are students, whose managing officers are fulltime students, and that complies with certain procedural requirements. . . .

All CIOs may exist and operate at the University, but some are also entitled to apply for funds from the Student Activities Fund (SAF). . . .

Some, but not all, CIOs may submit disbursement requests to the SAF. The Guidelines recognize 11 categories of student groups that may seek payment to third-party contractors because they "are related to the educational purpose of the University of Virginia." The Guidelines also specify, however, that the costs of certain activities of CIOs that are otherwise eligible for funding will not be reimbursed by the SAF. The student activities which are excluded from SAF support are religious activities, philanthropic contributions and activities, political activities, activities that would jeopardize the University's tax exempt status, those which involve payment of honoraria or similar fees, or social entertainment or related expenses. The prohibition on "political activities" is defined so that it is limited to electioneering and lobbying. The Guidelines provide that "[t]hese restrictions on funding political activities are not intended to preclude funding of any otherwise eligible student organization which . . . espouses particular positions or ideological viewpoints, including those that may be unpopular or are not generally accepted." A "religious activity," by contrast, is defined as any activity that "primarily promotes or manifests a particular belie[f] in or about a deity or an ultimate reality."

The Guidelines prescribe these criteria for determining the amounts of third-party disbursements that will be allowed on behalf of each eligible student organization: the size of the group, its financial self-sufficiency, and the University-wide benefit of its activities. If an organization seeks SAF support, it must submit its bills to the Student Council, which pays the organization's creditors upon determining that the expenses are appropriate. No direct payments are made to the student groups. During the 1990-1991 academic year, 343 student groups qualified as CIOs. One hundred thirty-five of them applied for support from the SAF, and 118 received funding. Fifteen of the groups were funded as "student news, information, opinion, entertainment, or academic communications media groups."

Petitioners' organization, Wide Awake Productions (WAP), qualified as a CIO. Formed by petitioner Ronald Rosenberger and other undergraduates in 1990, WAP was established "[t]o publish a magazine of philosophical and religious expression," "[t]o facilitate discussion which fosters an atmosphere of sensitivity to and tolerance of Christian viewpoints," and "[t]o provide a unifying focus for Christians of multicultural backgrounds." . . .

* * *

A few months after being given CIO status, WAP requested the SAF to pay its printer $5,862 for the costs of printing its newspaper. The Appropriations Committee of the Student Council denied WAP's request on the ground that Wide Awake was a "religious activity" within the meaning of the Guidelines, *i.e.*, that the newspaper "promote[d] or manifest[ed] a particular belie[f] in or about a deity or an ultimate reality." It made its determination after examining the first issue. WAP appealed the denial to the full Student Council, contending that WAP met all the applicable Guidelines and that denial of SAF support on the basis of the magazine's religious perspective violated the Constitution. The appeal was denied without further comment, and WAP appealed to the next level, the Student Activities Committee. In a letter signed by the Dean of Students, the committee sustained the denial of funding.

Having no further recourse within the University structure, WAP, Wide Awake, and three of its editors and members filed suit in the United States District Court for the Western District of Virginia, challenging the SAF's action . . . . They alleged that refusal to authorize payment of the printing costs of the publication, [was] solely on the basis of its religious editorial viewpoint . . . .

. . . [T]he District Court ruled for the University, holding that denial of SAF support was not an impermissible content or viewpoint discrimination against petitioners' speech, and that the University's Establishment Clause concern over its "religious activities" was a sufficient justification for denying payment to third-party contractors. . . .

The United States Court of Appeals for the Fourth Circuit, in disagreement with the District Court, held that the Guidelines did discriminate on the basis of content. It ruled that, while the State need not underwrite speech, there was a presumptive violation of the Speech Clause when viewpoint discrimination was invoked to deny third-party payment otherwise available to CIOs. The Court of Appeals affirmed the judgment of the District Court nonetheless, concluding that the discrimination by the University was justified by the "compelling interest in maintaining strict separation of church and state."

II

It is axiomatic that the government may not regulate speech based on its substantive content or the message it conveys. . . .

* * *

The SAF is a forum more in a metaphysical than in a spatial or geographic sense, but the same principles are applicable. . . .

* * *

The University's denial of WAP's request for third-party payments in the present case is based upon viewpoint discrimination not unlike the discrimination the school district relied upon in *Lamb's Chapel* [*v. Center Moriches Union Free School Dist.* (1993)] and that we found invalid. . . .

The University tries to escape the consequences of our holding in *Lamb's Chapel* by urging that this case involves the provision of funds rather than access to facilities. . . .

* * *

It does not follow, . . . that viewpoint-based restrictions are proper when the University does not itself speak or subsidize transmittal of a message it favors but instead expends funds to encourage a diversity of views from private speakers. . . .

* * *

Based on the principles we have discussed, we hold that the regulation invoked to deny SAF support, both in its terms and in its application to these petitioners, is a denial of their right of free speech guaranteed by the First Amendment. It remains to be considered whether the violation following from the University's action is excused by the necessity of complying with the Constitution's prohibition against state establishment of religion. We turn to that question.

III

* * *

A central lesson of our decisions is that a significant factor in upholding governmental programs in the face of Establishment Clause attack is their neutrality towards religion. We have decided a series of cases addressing the receipt of government benefits where religion or religious views are implicated in some degree. The first case in our modern Establishment Clause jurisprudence was *Everson v. Board of Ed. of Ewing* (1947). . . .

* * *

The neutrality of the program distinguishes the student fees from a tax levied for the direct support of a church or group of churches. A tax of that sort, of course, would run contrary to Establishment Clause concerns dating from the earliest days of the Republic. The apprehensions of our predecessors involved the levying of taxes upon the public for the sole and exclusive purpose of establishing and supporting specific sects. The exaction here, by contrast, is a student activity fee designed to reflect the reality that student life in its many dimensions includes the necessity of wide-ranging speech and inquiry and that student expression is an integral part of the University's educational mission. . . .

Government neutrality is apparent in the State's overall scheme in a further meaningful respect. The program respects the critical difference "between *government* speech endorsing religion, which the Establishment Clause forbids, and *private* speech endorsing religion, which the Free Speech and Free Exercise Clauses protect." In this case, "the government has not willfully fostered or encouraged" any mistaken impression that the student newspapers speak for the University. *Capitol Square Review and Advisory Bd. v. Pinette.* The University has taken pains to disassociate itself from the private speech involved in this case. . . .

The Court of Appeals (and the dissent) are correct to extract from our decisions the principle that we have recognized special Establishment Clause dangers where the government makes direct money payments to sectarian institutions. The error is not in identifying the principle but in believing that it controls this case. Even assuming that WAP is no different from a church and that its speech is the same as the religious exercises conducted in *Widmar* [*v. Vincent* (1981)] (two points much in doubt), the Court of Appeals decided a case that was, in essence, not before it, and the dissent would have us do the same. We do not confront a case where, even under a neutral program that includes nonsectarian recipients, the government is making direct money payments to an institution or group that is engaged in religious activity. Neither the Court of Appeals nor the dissent, we believe, takes sufficient cognizance of the undisputed fact that no public funds flow directly to WAP's coffers.

It does not violate the Establishment Clause for a public university to grant access to its facilities on a religion-neutral basis to a wide spectrum of student groups, including groups which use meeting rooms for sectarian activities, accompanied by some devotional exercises. . . . Given our holdings in [*Widmar, Lamb's Chapel*, and *Board of Education v. Mergens* (1990)], it follows that a public university may maintain its own computer facility and give student groups access to that facility, including the use of the printers, on a religion-neutral, say first-come-first-served, basis. If a religious student organization obtained access on that religion-neutral basis and used a computer to compose or a printer or copy machine to print speech with a religious content or viewpoint, the State's action in providing the group with access would no more violate the Establishment Clause than would giving those groups access to an assembly hall. There is no difference in logic or principle, and no difference of constitutional significance, between a school using its funds to operate a facility to which students have access, and a school paying a third-party contractor to operate the facility on its behalf. The latter occurs here. . . .

* * *

Were the dissent's view to become law, it would require the University, in order to avoid a constitutional violation, to scrutinize the content of student speech, lest the expression in question — speech otherwise protected by the Constitution — contain too great a religious content. The dissent, in fact, anticipates such censorship as "crucial" in distinguishing between "works characterized by the evangelism of Wide Awake and writing that merely happens to express views that a given religion might approve." That eventuality raises the specter of governmental censorship, to ensure that all student writings and publications meet some baseline standard of secular orthodoxy. . . .

* * *

To obey the Establishment Clause, it was not necessary for the University to deny eligibility to student publications because of their viewpoint. The neutrality commanded of the State by the separate Clauses of the First Amendment was compromised by the University's course of action. The viewpoint discrimination inherent in the University's regulation required public officials to scan and interpret student publications to discern their underlying philosophic assumptions respecting religious theory and belief. That course of action was a denial of the right of free speech and would risk fostering a pervasive bias or hostility to religion, which could undermine the very neutrality the Establishment Clause requires. There is no Establishment Clause violation in the University's honoring its duties under the Free Speech Clause.

The judgment of the Court of Appeals must be, and is, reversed.

It is so ordered.

JUSTICE O'CONNOR, concurring.

"We have time and again held that the government generally may not treat people differently based on the God or gods they worship, or don't worship." . . . Neutrality, in both form and effect, is one hallmark of the Establishment Clause.

As JUSTICE SOUTER demonstrates, however, there exists another axiom in the history and precedent of the Establishment Clause. "Public funds may not be used to endorse the religious message." Our cases have permitted some government funding of secular functions performed by sectarian organizations. *Bradfield v. Roberts* (1899) (funding of health care for indigent patients). These decisions, however, provide no precedent for the use of public funds to finance religious activities.

This case lies at the intersection of the principle of government neutrality and the prohibition on state funding of religious activities. It is clear that the University has established a generally applicable program to encourage the free exchange of ideas by its students, an expressive marketplace that includes some 15 student publications with predictably divergent viewpoints. It is equally clear that petitioners' viewpoint is religious and that publication of Wide Awake is a religious activity, under both the University's regulation and a fair reading of our precedents. Not to finance Wide Awake, according to petitioners, violates the principle of neutrality by sending a message of hostility toward religion. To finance Wide Awake, argues the University, violates the prohibition on direct state funding of religious activities.

When two bedrock principles so conflict, understandably neither can provide the definitive answer. Reliance on categorical platitudes is unavailing. Resolution instead depends on the hard task of judging — sifting through the details and determining whether the challenged program offends the Establishment Clause. . . .

In *Witters v. Washington Dept. of Services for Blind* (1986), for example, we unanimously held that the State may, through a generally applicable financial aid program, pay a blind student's tuition at a sectarian theological institution. The Court so held, however, only after emphasizing that "vocational assistance provided under the Washington program is paid directly to the student, who transmits it to the educational institution of his or her choice."

* * *

The Court's decision today therefore neither trumpets the supremacy of the neutrality principle nor signals the demise of the funding prohibition in Establishment Clause jurisprudence. As I observed last Term, "[e]xperience proves that the Establishment Clause, like the Free Speech Clause, cannot easily be reduced to a single test." *Kiryas Joel* [*Village Sch. Dist. v. Grumet* (1994)] (O'CONNOR, J., concurring in part and concurring in judgment). When bedrock principles collide, they test the limits of categorical obstinacy and expose the flaws and dangers of a Grand Unified Theory that may turn out to be neither grand nor unified. The Court today does only what courts must do in many Establishment Clause cases — focus on specific features of a particular government action to ensure that it does not violate the Constitution. By withholding from Wide Awake assistance that the University provides generally to all other student publications, the University has discriminated on the basis of the magazine's religious viewpoint in violation of the Free Speech Clause. And particular features of the University's program — such as the explicit disclaimer, the disbursement of funds directly to third-party vendors, the vigorous nature of the forum at issue, and the possibility for objecting students to opt out — convince me that providing such assistance in this case would not carry the danger of impermissible use of public funds to endorse Wide Awake's religious message.

Subject to these comments, I join the opinion of the Court.

JUSTICE THOMAS, concurring.

I agree with the Court's opinion and join it in full, but I write separately to express my disagreement with the historical analysis put forward by the dissent. Although the dissent starts down the right path in consulting the original meaning of the Establishment Clause, its misleading application of history yields a principle that is inconsistent with our Nation's long tradition of allowing religious adherents to participate on equal terms in neutral government programs.

Even assuming that the Virginia debate on the so-called "Assessment Controversy" was indicative of the principles embodied in the Establishment Clause, this incident hardly compels the dissent's conclusion that government must actively discriminate against religion. The dissent's historical discussion glosses over the fundamental characteristic of the Virginia assessment bill that sparked the controversy: The assessment was to be imposed for the support of clergy in the performance of their function of teaching religion. Thus, the "Bill Establishing a Provision for Teachers of the Christian Religion" provided for the collection of a specific tax, the proceeds of which were to be appropriated "by the Vestries, Elders, or Directors of each religious society . . . to a provision for a Minister or Teacher of the Gospel of their denomination, or the providing places of divine worship, and to none other use whatsoever." *See Everson v. Board of Ed. of Ewing* (1947) (appendix to dissent of Rutledge, J.).

James Madison's Memorial and Remonstrance Against Religious Assessments (hereinafter Madison's Remonstrance) must be understood in this context. Contrary to the dissent's suggestion, Madison's objection to the assessment bill did not rest on the premise that religious entities may never participate on equal terms in neutral government programs. Nor did Madison embrace the argument that forms the linchpin of the dissent: that monetary subsidies are constitutionally different from other neutral benefits programs. Instead, Madison's comments are more consistent with the neutrality principle that the dissent inexplicably discards. According to Madison, the Virginia assessment was flawed because it "violate[d] that equality which ought to be the basis of every law." The assessment violated the "equality" principle not because it allowed religious groups to participate in a generally available government program, but because the bill singled out religious entities for special benefits. *See* [*Everson, supra*] (arguing that the assessment violated the equality principle "by subjecting some to peculiar burdens" and "by granting to others peculiar exemptions").

Legal commentators have disagreed about the historical lesson to take from the Assessment Controversy. For some, the experience in Virginia is consistent with the view that the Framers saw the Establishment Clause simply as a prohibition on governmental preferences for some religious faiths over others. Other commentators have rejected this view, concluding that the Establishment Clause forbids not only government preferences for some religious sects over others, but also government preferences for religion over irreligion.

I find much to commend the former view. Madison's focus on the preferential nature of the assessment was not restricted to the fourth paragraph of the Remonstrance discussed above. The funding provided by the Virginia assessment was to be extended only to Christian sects, and the Remonstrance seized on this defect:

> "Who does not see that the same authority which can establish Christianity, in exclusion of all other Religions, may establish with the same ease any particular sect of Christians, in exclusion of all other Sects."

Madison's Remonstrance, reprinted in *Everson*. In addition to the third and fourth paragraphs of the Remonstrance, "Madison's seventh, ninth, eleventh, and twelfth arguments all speak, in some way, to the same intolerance, bigotry, unenlightenment, and persecution that had generally resulted from previous exclusive religious establishments." The conclusion that Madison saw the principle of nonestablishment as barring governmental preferences for *particular* religious faiths seems especially clear in light of statements he made in the more-relevant context of the House debates on the First Amendment. *See Wallace v. Jaffree* (1985) (REHNQUIST, J., dissenting) (Madison's views "as reflected by actions on the floor of the House in 1789, [indicate] that he saw the [First] Amendment as designed to prohibit the establishment of a national religion, and perhaps to prevent discrimination among sects," but not "as requiring neutrality on the part of government between religion and irreligion"). . . .

But resolution of this debate is not necessary to decide this case. Under any understanding of the Assessment Controversy, the history cited by the dissent cannot support the conclusion that the Establishment Clause "categorically condemn[s] state programs directly aiding religious activity" when that aid is part of a neutral program available to a wide array of beneficiaries. Even if Madison believed that the principle of nonestablishment of religion precluded government financial support for religion *per se* (in the sense of government benefits specifically targeting religion), there is no indication that at the time of the framing he took the dissent's extreme view that the government must discriminate against religious adherents by excluding them from more generally available financial subsidies.

In fact, Madison's own early legislative proposals cut against the dissent's suggestion. In 1776, when Virginia's Revolutionary Convention was drafting its Declaration of Rights, Madison prepared an amendment that would have disestablished the Anglican Church. This amendment (which went too far for the Convention and was not adopted) is not nearly as sweeping as the dissent's version of disestablishment; Madison merely wanted the Convention to declare that "no man or class of men ought, on account of religion[,] to be invested with *peculiar* emoluments or privileges . . . ." Madison's Amendments to the Declaration of Rights (May 29-June 12, 1776), *in* 1 PAPERS OF JAMES MADISON 174 (W. Hutchinson & W. Rachal eds., 1962) (emphasis added). Likewise, Madison's Remonstrance stressed that "just government" is "best supported by protecting every citizen in the enjoyment of his Religion with the same equal hand which protects his person and his property; by neither invading the equal rights of any Sect, nor suffering any Sect to invade those of another." Madison's Remonstrance ¶ 8, reprinted in *Everson, supra; cf. Terrett v. Taylor* (1815) (holding that the Virginia constitution did not prevent the government from "aiding the votaries of every sect to . . . perform their own religious duties," or from "establishing funds for the support of ministers, for public charities, for the endowment of churches, or for the sepulture of the dead").

Stripped of its flawed historical premise, the dissent's argument is reduced to the claim that our Establishment Clause jurisprudence permits neutrality in the context of access to government *facilities* but requires discrimination in access to government *funds*. The dissent purports to locate the prohibition against "direct public funding" at the "heart" of the Establishment Clause, but this conclusion fails to confront historical examples of funding that date back to the time of the founding. To take but one famous example, both Houses of the First Congress elected chaplains, and that Congress enacted legislation providing for an annual salary of $500 to be paid out of the Treasury. Madison himself was a member of the committee that recommended the chaplain system in the House. *See* H.R. Jour., at 11-12; 1 Annals of Cong. 891 (1789); [R.] Cord, [Separation of Church and State: Historical Fact and Current Fiction] 25 [(1982)]. This same system of "direct public funding" of congressional chaplains has "continued without interruption ever since that early session of Congress." *Marsh v. Chambers* (1983).[3]

The historical evidence of government support for religious entities through property tax exemptions is also overwhelming. . . . In my view, the dissent's acceptance of this tradition puts to rest the notion that the Establishment Clause bars monetary aid to religious groups even when the aid is equally available to other groups. A tax exemption in many cases is economically and functionally indistinguishable from a direct monetary subsidy. . . .

* * *

Though our Establishment Clause jurisprudence is in hopeless disarray, this case provides an opportunity to reaffirm one basic principle that has enjoyed an uncharacteristic degree of consensus: The Clause does not compel the exclusion

---

[3] A number of other, less familiar examples of what amount to direct funding appear in early Acts of Congress. *See, e.g., Act of Feb. 20, 1833, ch. 42, 4 Stat. 618-619 (authorizing the State of Ohio to sell "all or any part of the lands heretofore reserved and appropriated by Congress for the support of religion within the Ohio Company's . . . purchases . . . and to invest the money arising from the sale thereof, in some productive fund; the proceeds of which shall be for ever annually applied . . . for the support of religion within the several townships for which said lands were originally reserved and set apart, and for no other use or purpose whatsoever"); Act of Mar. 2, 1833, ch. 86, §§ 1, 3, 6 Stat. 538 (granting to Georgetown College — a Jesuit institution — "lots in the city of Washington, to the amount, in value, of twenty-five thousand dollars," and directing the College to sell the lots and invest the proceeds, thereafter using the dividends to establish and endow such professorships as it saw fit); *see also Wallace v. Jaffree* (1985) (Rehnquist, J., dissenting) ("As the United States moved from the 18th into the 19th century, Congress appropriated time and again public moneys in support of sectarian Indian education carried on by religious organizations").

of religious groups from government benefits programs that are generally available to a broad class of participants. . . .

* * *

Our Nation's tradition of allowing religious adherents to participate in even-handed government programs is hardly limited to the class of "essential public benefits" identified by the dissent. . . .

* * *

. . . The dissent identifies no evidence that the Framers intended to disable religious entities from participating on neutral terms in evenhanded government programs. The evidence that does exist points in the opposite direction and provides ample support for today's decision.

JUSTICE SOUTER, with whom JUSTICE STEVENS, JUSTICE GINSBURG and JUSTICE BREYER join, dissenting.

I

* * *

A

The Court, . . . has never before upheld direct state funding of the sort of proselytizing published in Wide Awake and, in fact, has categorically condemned state programs directly aiding religious activity, *School Dist. v. Ball* [(1985)] (striking programs providing secular instruction to nonpublic school students on nonpublic school premises because they are "indistinguishable from the provision of a direct cash subsidy to the religious school that is most clearly prohibited under the Establishment Clause") . . . .

Even when the Court has upheld aid to an institution performing both secular and sectarian functions, it has always made a searching enquiry to ensure that the institution kept the secular activities separate from its sectarian ones, with any direct aid flowing only to the former and never the latter. *Bowen v. Kendrick* (1988) (upholding grant program for services related to premarital adolescent sexual relations on ground that funds cannot be "used by the grantees in such a way as to advance religion"); *Roemer v. Board of Pub. Works of Md.* (1976) (plurality opinion) (upholding general aid program restricting uses of funds to secular activities only); *Hunt v. McNair* (1973) (upholding general revenue bond program excluding from participation facilities used for religious purposes); *Tilton v. Richardson* (1971) (plurality opinion) (upholding general aid program for construction of academic facilities as "[t]here is no evidence that religion seeps into the use of any of these facilities"); *see Board of Ed. of Central School Dist. No. 1 v. Allen* (1968) (upholding textbook loan program limited to secular books requested by individual students for secular educational purposes).

* * *

B

* * *

. . . At the heart of the Establishment Clause stands the prohibition against direct public funding, but that prohibition does not answer the questions that occur at the margins of the Clause's application. Is any government activity that provides any incidental benefit to religion likewise unconstitutional? Would it be wrong to put out fires in burning churches, wrong to pay the bus fares of students on the way to parochial schools, wrong to allow a grantee of special education funds to spend them at a religious college? These are the questions that call for drawing lines, and it is in drawing them that evenhandedness becomes important. However the Court may in the past have phrased its line-drawing test, the question whether such benefits are provided on an evenhanded basis has been relevant, for the question addresses one aspect of the issue whether a law is truly neutral with respect to religion. . . .

Three cases permitting indirect aid to religion, *Mueller v. Allen* (1983), *Witters v. Washington Dept. of Services for Blind* (1986), and *Zobrest v. Catalina Foothills School Dist.* (1993), are among the latest of those to illustrate this relevance of evenhandedness when advancement is not so obvious as to be patently unconstitutional. Each case involved a program in which benefits given to individuals on a religion-neutral basis ultimately were used by the individuals, in one way or another, to support religious institutions. In each, the fact that aid was distributed generally and on a neutral basis was a necessary condition for upholding the program at issue. But the significance of evenhandedness stopped there. We did not, in any of these cases, hold that satisfying the condition was sufficient, or dispositive. Even more importantly, we never held that evenhandedness might be sufficient to render direct aid to religion constitutional. Quite the contrary. Critical to our decisions in these cases was the fact that the aid was indirect; it reached religious institutions "only as a result of the genuinely independent and private choices of aid recipients." In noting and relying on this particular feature of each of the programs at issue, we in fact reaffirmed the core prohibition on direct funding of religious activities. Thus, our holdings in these cases were little more than extensions of the unremarkable proposition that "a State may issue a paycheck to one of its employees, who may then donate all or part of that paycheck to a religious institution, all without constitutional barrier . . . ." Such "attenuated financial benefit[s], ultimately controlled by the private choices of individual[s]," we have found, are simply not within the contemplation of the Establishment Clause's broad prohibition.

Evenhandedness as one element of a permissibly attenuated benefit is, of course, a far cry from evenhandedness as a sufficient condition of constitutionality for direct financial support of religious proselytization, and our cases have unsurprisingly repudiated any such attempt to cut the Establishment Clause down to a mere prohibition against unequal direct aid.

* * *

D

Nothing in the Court's opinion would lead me to end this enquiry into the application of the Establishment Clause any differently from the way I began it. The Court is ordering an instrumentality of the State to support religious evangelism with direct funding. This is a flat violation of the Establishment Clause.

II

Given the dispositive effect of the Establishment Clause's bar to funding the magazine, there should be no need to decide whether in the absence of this bar the University would violate the Free Speech Clause by limiting funding as it has done. *Widmar,* 454 U.S. at 271 (university's compliance with its Establishment Clause obligations can be a compelling interest justifying speech restriction).

QUESTIONS

1. Does the following proposed constitutional amendment pick up some of the themes evident in the majority opinions in *Rosenberger* and *Capitol Square?*

Proposed Constitutional Amendment
for Religious Equality
S.J. Res. 45, 104th Cong., 1st Sess. (1995)

Resolved by the Senate and House of Representatives of the United States of America in Congress assembled (two-thirds of each House concurring therein), That the following article is proposed as an amendment to the Constitution of the United States, which shall be valid to all intents and purposes as part of the Constitution when ratified by the legislatures of three-fourths of the several States within seven years after the date of its submission for ratification:

ARTICLE —

"Neither the United States nor any State shall deny benefits to or otherwise discriminate against any private person or group on account of religious expression, belief, or identity; nor shall the prohibition on laws respecting an establishment of religion be construed to require such discrimination."

2. Should this amendment be approved by Congress and sent to the states? Former law professor and now Tenth Circuit Judge Michael McConnell, a prominent constitutional scholar in matters of religious freedom, argued in its favor because:

1. Tolerance has become a one-way street; a government tolerant of secular views has been intolerant of religious expression;

2. In matters of government funding, the federal government often excludes or discriminates against religious entities, even as the First Amendment (the no Establishment Clause) has been interpreted not to require that discrimination, and the Free Speech Clause often prohibits it; and

3. Even if the federal government did not engage in religious discrimination in funding programs, the First Amendment has, troublingly, not yet been interpreted to preclude state anti-religious discrimination in funding.

See Examining the Status of Religious Liberty in the States and Whether There is a Need for Further Protection: Hearings on S.J. Res. 45 Before the Senate Judiciary Comm., 104th Cong. 79 (testimony of Michael W. McConnell). Do you agree with Professor McConnell? For a concurring view, see Michael S. Paulsen, *Religion, Equality and the Constitution: An Equal Protection Approach to Establishment Clause Adjudication*, 61 NOTRE DAME L. REV. 311 (1986) (discussing the Supreme Court's historical and conceptual errors that resulted in an errant Establishment Clause doctrine and arguing that the religion clauses advance fundamentally similar interests and are best understood in terms of nondiscrimination and equality). The less favorable, but not totally unsympathetic, view of the proposed amendment by Professor Douglas Laycock of the University of Texas posits that religious expression is already well protected under free speech case law — discrimination against private religious speech, he says, is unconstitutional viewpoint discrimination. He further argues that religious speech in public contexts or by public entities is too hard a case to be addressed uniformly by constitutional amendment. Professor Laycock nevertheless agrees with Professor McConnell that religious and secular organizations should be treated equally in funding decisions, but he does not think this extends to cases where the government itself supplies the good. *See Hearings on S.J. 45 Before the Senate Judiciary Committee*, 104 Cong. 68 (1995) (Statement of Professor Laycock). Do you agree with Professor Laycock? Or is government obliged, once it decides to fund education at all, to make education funds it collects from all citizens available for the school of their choice, religious or nonreligious? We take up the issue of school funding next.

3. In the following case, the Court applies the equality principle to the after hours use of a public elementary school.

GOOD NEWS CLUB v. MILFORD CENTRAL SCHOOL
533 U.S. 98 (2001)

JUSTICE THOMAS delivered the opinion of the Court.

This case presents two questions. The first question is whether Milford Central School violated the free speech rights of the Good News Club [a private Christian organization for children ages 6 to 12 that wanted to hold after-school meetings at which children would sing songs, hear Bible stories, and memorize scriptural passages] when it excluded the Club from meeting after hours at the school. The second question is whether any such violation is justified by Milford's concern that permitting the Club's activities would violate the Establishment Clause. We conclude that Milford's restriction violates the Club's free speech rights and that no Establishment Clause concern justifies that violation.

I

In 1992, respondent Milford Central School (Milford) enacted a community use policy adopting purposes for which its building could be used after school. Two of the stated purposes are relevant here. First, district residents may use the school for "instruction in any branch of education, learning or the arts." Second, the school is available for "social, civic and recreational meetings and entertainment events, and other uses pertaining to the welfare of the community, provided that such uses shall be nonexclusive and shall be opened to the general public."

* * *

II

The standards that we apply to determine whether a State has unconstitutionally excluded a private speaker from use of a public forum depend on the nature of the forum.

When the State establishes a limited public forum, the State is not required to and does not allow persons to engage in every type of speech. The State may be justified "in reserving [its forum] for certain groups or for the discussion of certain topics." *Rosenberger v. Rector and Visitors of Univ. of Va.* (1995). The State's power to restrict speech, however, is not without limits. The restriction must not discriminate against speech on the basis of viewpoint, and the restriction must be "reasonable in light of the purpose served by the forum."

III

Applying this test, we first address whether the exclusion constituted viewpoint discrimination. We are guided in our analysis by two of our prior opinions, *Lamb's Chapel* and *Rosenberger*. In *Lamb's Chapel*, we held that a school district violated the Free Speech Clause of the First Amendment when it excluded a private group from presenting films at the school based solely on the films' discussions of family values from a religious perspective. Likewise, in *Rosenberger*, we held that a university's refusal to fund a student publication because the publication addressed issues from a religious perspective violated the Free Speech Clause. Concluding that Milford's exclusion of the Good News Club based on its religious nature is indistinguishable from the exclusions in these cases, we hold that the exclusion constitutes viewpoint discrimination. Because the restriction is viewpoint discriminatory, we need not decide whether it is unreasonable in light of the purposes served by the forum.

Applying *Lamb's Chapel*, we find it quite clear that Milford engaged in viewpoint discrimination when it excluded the Club from the afterschool forum.

* * *

Despite our holdings in *Lamb's Chapel* and *Rosenberger*, the Court of Appeals, like Milford, believed that its characterization of the Club's activities as religious in nature warranted treating the Club's activities as different in kind from the other activities permitted by the school.

We disagree that something that is "quintessentially religious" or "decidedly religious in nature" cannot also be characterized properly as the teaching of morals and character development from a particular viewpoint. ("[W]hen the subject matter is morals and character, it is quixotic to attempt a distinction between religious viewpoints and religious subject matters"). What matters for purposes of the Free Speech Clause is that we can see no logical difference in kind between the invocation of Christianity by the Club and the invocation of teamwork, loyalty, or patriotism by other associations to provide a foundation for their lessons. It is apparent that the unstated principle of the Court of Appeals' reasoning is its conclusion that any time religious instruction and prayer are used to discuss morals and character, the discussion is simply not a "pure" discussion of those issues. According to the Court of Appeals, reliance on Christian principles taints moral and character instruction in a way that other foundations for thought or viewpoints do not. We, however, have never reached such a conclusion. Instead, we reaffirm our holdings in *Lamb's Chapel* and *Rosenberger* that speech discussing otherwise permissible subjects cannot be excluded from a limited public forum on the ground that the subject is discussed from a religious viewpoint. Thus, we conclude that Milford's exclusion of the Club from use of the school, pursuant to its community use policy, constitutes impermissible viewpoint discrimination.

IV

Milford argues that, even if its restriction constitutes viewpoint discrimination, its interest in not violating the Establishment Clause outweighs the Club's interest in gaining equal access to the school's facilities. In other words, according to Milford, its restriction was required to avoid violating the Establishment Clause. We disagree.

* * *

As in *Lamb's Chapel*, the Club's meetings were held after school hours, not sponsored by the school, and open to any student who obtained parental consent, not just to Club members. Thus, Milford's reliance on the Establishment Clause is unavailing.

Milford attempts to distinguish *Lamb's Chapel* by emphasizing that Milford's policy involves elementary school children. According to Milford, children will perceive that the school is endorsing the Club and will feel coercive pressure to participate, because the Club's activities take place on school grounds, even though they occur during nonschool hours. This argument is unpersuasive.

First, we have held that "a significant factor in upholding governmental programs in the face of Establishment Clause attack is their *neutrality* towards religion." *Rosenberger. See also Mitchell v. Helms*, (2000) (plurality opinion) ("In distinguishing between indoctrination that is attributable to the State and indoctrination that is not, [the Court has] consistently turned to the principle of neutrality, upholding aid that is offered to a broad range of groups or persons without regard to their religion" (emphasis added)) (O'CONNOR, J., concurring in judgment) ("[N]eutrality is an important reason for upholding government-aid programs against Establishment Clause challenges"). Milford's implication that granting access to the Club would do damage to the neutrality principle defies logic. For the "guarantee of neutrality is respected, not offended, when the government, following neutral criteria and evenhanded policies, extends benefits to recipients whose ideologies and viewpoints, including religious ones, are broad and diverse." The Good News Club seeks nothing more than to be treated neutrally and given access to speak about the same topics as are other groups. Because allowing the Club to speak on school grounds would ensure neutrality, not threaten it, Milford faces an uphill battle in arguing that the Establishment Clause compels it to exclude the Good News Club.

Second, to the extent we consider whether the community would feel coercive pressure to engage in the Club's activities, *cf. Lee v. Weisman* (1992), the relevant community would be the parents, not the elementary school children. It is the parents who choose whether their children will attend the Good News Club meetings. Because the children cannot attend without their parents' permission, they cannot be coerced into engaging in the Good News Club's religious activities. Milford does not suggest that the parents of elementary school children would be confused about whether the school was endorsing religion. Nor do we believe that such an argument could be reasonably advanced.

Third, whatever significance we may have assigned in the Establishment Clause context to the suggestion that elementary school children are more impressionable than adults, [has] never extended our Establishment Clause jurisprudence to foreclose private religious conduct during nonschool hours merely because it takes place on school premises where elementary school children may be present.

None of the cases discussed by Milford persuades us that our Establishment Clause jurisprudence has gone this far. For example, Milford cites *Lee v. Weisman* for the proposition that "there are heightened concerns with protecting freedom of conscience from subtle coercive pressure in the elementary and secondary public schools. " In *Lee*, however, we concluded that attendance at the graduation exercise was obligatory. *See also Santa Fe Independent School Dist. v. Doe* (2000) (holding the school's policy of permitting prayer at football games unconstitutional where the activity took place during a school-sponsored event and not in a public forum). We did not place independent significance on the fact that the graduation exercise might take place on school premises. Here, where the school facilities are being used for a nonschool function and there is no government sponsorship of the Club's activities, *Lee* is inapposite.

Equally unsupportive is *Edwards v. Aguillard* (1987), in which we held that a Louisiana law that proscribed the teaching of evolution as part of the public school curriculum, unless accompanied by a lesson on creationism, violated the Establishment Clause. In *Edwards*, we mentioned that students are susceptible to pressure in the classroom, particularly given their possible reliance on teachers as role models. But we did not discuss this concern in our application of the law to the facts. Moreover, we did note that mandatory attendance requirements meant that State advancement of religion in a school would be particularly harshly felt by impressionable students. But we did not suggest that, when the school was not actually advancing religion, the impressionability of students would be relevant to the Establishment Clause issue. Even if *Edwards* had articulated the principle Milford believes it did, the facts in *Edwards* are simply too remote from those here to give the principle any weight. *Edwards* involved the content of the curriculum taught by state teachers during the schoolday to children required to attend. Obviously, when individuals who are not schoolteachers are giving lessons after school to children permitted to attend only with parental consent, the concerns expressed in *Edwards* are not present.

* * *

Finally, even if we were to inquire into the minds of schoolchildren in this case, we cannot say the danger that children would misperceive the endorsement of religion is any greater than the danger that they would perceive a hostility toward the religious viewpoint if the Club were excluded from the public forum.

* * *

We cannot operate, as Milford would have us do, under the assumption that any risk that small children would perceive endorsement should counsel in favor of excluding the Club's religious activity. We decline to employ Establishment Clause jurisprudence using a modified heckler's veto, in which a group's religious activity can be proscribed on the basis of what the youngest members of the audience might misperceive. *Cf. Capitol Square Review and Advisory Bd. v. Pinette* (1995) (O'CONNOR, J., concurring in part and concurring in judgment) ("[B]ecause our concern is with the political community writ large, the endorsement inquiry is *not about the perceptions of particular individuals* or saving isolated nonadherents from . . . discomfort . . . . It is for this reason that the reasonable observer in the endorsement inquiry must be deemed aware of the history and context of the community and forum in which the religious [speech takes place]" (emphasis added)). There are countervailing constitutional concerns related to rights of other individuals in the community. In this case, those countervailing concerns are the free speech rights of the Club and its members.

* * *

V

When Milford denied the Good News Club access to the school's limited public forum on the ground that the Club was religious in nature, it discriminated against the Club because of its religious viewpoint in violation of the Free Speech Clause of the First Amendment. Because Milford has not raised a valid Establishment Clause claim, we do not address the question whether such a claim could excuse Milford's viewpoint discrimination.

* * *

The judgment of the Court of Appeals is reversed, and the case is remanded for further proceedings consistent with this opinion.

It is so ordered.

JUSTICE SCALIA, concurring.

I join the Court's opinion but write separately to explain further my views.

I

* * *

II

* * *

As I understand it, the point of disagreement between the Court and the dissenters (and the Court of Appeals) with regard to petitioner's Free Speech Clause claim is not whether the Good News Club must be permitted to present religious viewpoints on morals and character in respondent's forum, which has been opened to secular discussions of that subject. The answer to that is established by our decision in *Lamb's Chapel*. The point of disagreement is not even whether some of the Club's religious speech fell within the protection of *Lamb's Chapel*. It certainly did.

The disagreement, rather, regards the portions of the Club's meetings that are not "purely" "discussions" of morality and character from a religious viewpoint. The Club, for example, urges children "who already believe in the Lord Jesus as their Savior" to "[s]top and ask God for the strength and the 'want' . . . to obey Him." The dissenters and the Second Circuit say that the presence of such additional speech, because it is purely religious, transforms the Club's meetings into something different in kind from other, nonreligious activities that teach moral and character development. *See post* (STEVENS, J., dissenting); *post* (SOUTER, J., dissenting); 202 F.3d, at 509-511. Therefore, the argument goes, excluding the Club is not viewpoint discrimination. I disagree.

The dissenters emphasize that the religious speech used by the Club as the foundation for its views on morals and character is not just any type of religious speech — although they cannot agree exactly what type of religious speech it is. In JUSTICE STEVENS' view, it is speech "aimed principally at proselytizing or inculcating belief in a particular religious faith." This does not, to begin with, distinguish *Rosenberger*, which also involved proselytizing speech, as the above quotations show. But in addition, it does not distinguish the Club's activities from those of the other groups using respondent's forum — which have not, as JUSTICE STEVENS suggests, been restricted to roundtable "discussions" of moral issues. Those groups may seek to inculcate children with their beliefs, and they may furthermore "recruit others to join their respective groups." The Club must therefore have liberty to do the same, even if, as JUSTICE STEVENS fears without support in the record, its actions may prove (shudder!) divisive. *See Lamb's Chapel*, (remarking that worries about "public unrest" caused by "proselytizing" are "difficult to defend as a reason to deny the presentation of a religious point of view").

JUSTICE SOUTER, while agreeing that the Club's religious speech "may be characterized as proselytizing," thinks that it is even more clearly excludable from respondent's forum because it is essentially "an evangelical service of worship." But we have previously rejected the attempt to distinguish worship from other religious speech, saying that "the distinction has [no] intelligible content," and further, no "relevance " to the constitutional issue.[3] Those holdings are surely proved correct today by the dissenters' inability to agree, even between themselves, into which subcategory of religious speech the Club's activities fell. If the distinction did have content, it would be beyond the courts' competence to administer. And if courts (and other government officials) were competent, applying the distinction would require state monitoring of private, religious speech with a degree of pervasiveness that we have previously found unacceptable. I will not endorse an approach that suffers such a wondrous diversity of flaws.

With these words of explanation, I join the opinion of the Court.

JUSTICE BREYER, concurring in part.

I agree with the Court's conclusion and join its opinion to the extent that they are consistent with the following three observations. First, the government's "neutrality" in respect to religion is one, but only one, of the considerations relevant to deciding whether a public school's policy violates the Establishment Clause.

Second, the critical Establishment Clause question here may well prove to be whether a child, participating in the Good News Club's activities, could rea-

---

[3] We *have* drawn a different distinction — between religious speech generally and speech about religion — but only with regard to restrictions the State must place on its own speech, where pervasive state monitoring is unproblematic. *See School Dist. of Abington Township v. Schempp* (1963) (State schools in their official capacity may not teach religion but may teach about religion). . . .

sonably perceive the school's permission for the club to use its facilities as an endorsement of religion. The time of day, the age of the children, the nature of the meetings, and other specific circumstances are relevant in helping to determine whether, in fact, the Club "so dominate[s]" the "forum" that, in the children's minds, "a formal policy of equal access is transformed into a demonstration of approval."

Third, the Court cannot fully answer the Establishment Clause question this case raises, given its procedural posture. The specific legal action that brought this case to the Court of Appeals was the District Court's decision to grant Milford Central School's motion for summary judgment. The Court of Appeals affirmed the grant of summary judgment. We now hold that the school was not entitled to summary judgment, either in respect to the Free Speech or the Establishment Clause issue. Our holding must mean that, viewing the disputed facts (including facts about the children's perceptions) favorably to the Club (the nonmoving party), the school has not shown an Establishment Clause violation.

To deny one party's motion for summary judgment, however, is not to grant summary judgment for the other side. There may be disputed "genuine issue[s]" of "material fact," particularly about how a reasonable child participant would understand the school's role. . . . The Court's invocation of what is missing from the record and its assumptions about what is present in the record only confirm that both parties, if they so desire, should have a fair opportunity to fill the evidentiary gap in light of today's opinion. . . .

JUSTICE STEVENS, dissenting.

The Milford Central School has invited the public to use its facilities for educational and recreational purposes, but not for "religious purposes." Speech for "religious purposes" may reasonably be understood to encompass three different categories. First, there is religious speech that is simply speech about a particular topic from a religious point of view. The film in *Lamb's Chapel v. Center Moriches Union Free School Dist.* Second, there is religious speech that amounts to worship, or its equivalent. Third, there is an intermediate category that is aimed principally at proselytizing or inculcating belief in a particular religious faith.

A public entity may not generally exclude even religious worship from an open public forum. Similarly, a public entity that creates a limited public forum for the discussion of certain specified topics may not exclude a speaker simply because she approaches those topics from a religious point of view.

But, while a public entity may not censor speech about an authorized topic based on the point of view expressed by the speaker, it has broad discretion to "preserve the property under its control for the use to which it is lawfully dedicated." Accordingly, "control over access to a nonpublic forum can be based on subject matter and speaker identity so long as the distinctions drawn are reasonable in light of the purpose served by the forum and are viewpoint neutral."

Cornelius v. NAACP Legal Defense & Ed. Fund, Inc. (1985). The novel question that this case presents concerns the constitutionality of a public school's attempt to limit the scope of a public forum it has created. More specifically, the question is whether a school can, consistently with the First Amendment, create a limited public forum that admits the first type of religious speech without allowing the other two.

Distinguishing speech from a religious viewpoint, on the one hand, from religious proselytizing, on the other, is comparable to distinguishing meetings to discuss political issues from meetings whose principal purpose is to recruit new members to join a political organization. If a school decides to authorize after school discussions of current events in its classrooms, it may not exclude people from expressing their views simply because it dislikes their particular political opinions. But must it therefore allow organized political groups — for example, the Democratic Party, the Libertarian Party, or the Ku Klux Klan — to hold meetings, the principal purpose of which is not to discuss the current-events topic from their own unique point of view but rather to recruit others to join their respective groups? I think not. Such recruiting meetings may introduce divisiveness and tend to separate young children into cliques that undermine the school's educational mission.

School officials may reasonably believe that evangelical meetings designed to convert children to a particular religious faith pose the same risk. And, just as a school may allow meetings to discuss current events from a political perspective without also allowing organized political recruitment, so too can a school allow discussion of topics such as moral development from a religious (or non-religious) perspective without thereby opening its forum to religious proselytizing or worship.

The particular limitation of the forum at issue in this case is one that prohibits the use of the school's facilities for "religious purposes." It is clear that, by "religious purposes," the school district did not intend to exclude all speech from a religious point of view. *See* [the] testimony of the superintendent for Milford schools indicating that the policy would permit people to teach "that man was created by God as described in the Book of Genesis" and that crime was caused by society's "lack of faith in God"). Instead, it sought only to exclude religious speech whose principal goal is to "promote the gospel." In other words, the school sought to allow the first type of religious speech while excluding the second and third types. As long as this is done in an even handed manner, I see no constitutional violation in such an effort. The line between the various categories of religious speech may be difficult to draw, but I think that the distinctions are valid, and that a school, particularly an elementary school, must be permitted to draw them.

This case is undoubtedly close. Nonetheless, regardless of whether the Good News Club's activities amount to "worship," it does seem clear, based on the facts in the record, that the school district correctly classified those activities as falling within the third category of religious speech and therefore beyond the scope of the school's limited public forum. In short, I am persuaded that the school district could (and did) permissibly exclude from its limited public forum proselytizing religious speech that does not rise to the level of actual worship. I would therefore affirm the judgment of the Court of Appeals.

JUSTICE SOUTER, with whom JUSTICE GINSBURG joins, dissenting.

* * *

I

It is beyond question that Good News intends to use the public school premises not for the mere discussion of a subject from a particular, Christian point of view, but for an evangelical service of worship calling children to commit themselves in an act of Christian conversion. The majority avoids this reality only by resorting to the bland and general characterization of Good News's activity as "teaching of morals and character, from a religious standpoint." If the majority's statement ignores reality, as it surely does, then today's holding may be understood only in equally generic terms. Otherwise, indeed, this case would stand for the remarkable proposition that any public school opened for civic meetings must be opened for use as a church, synagogue, or mosque.

II

I also respectfully dissent from the majority's refusal to remand on all other issues, insisting instead on acting as a court of first instance in reviewing Milford's claim that it would violate the Establishment Clause to grant Good News's application. Milford raised this claim to demonstrate a compelling interest for saying no to Good News, even on the erroneous assumption that *Lamb's Chapel*'s public forum analysis would otherwise require Milford to say yes. Whereas the District Court and Court of Appeals resolved this case entirely on the ground that Milford's actions did not offend the First Amendment's Speech Clause, the majority now sees fit to rule on the application of the Establishment Clause, in derogation of this Court's proper role as a court of review.

The Court's usual insistence on resisting temptations to convert itself into a trial court and on remaining a court of review is not any mere procedural nicety, and my objection to turning us into a district court here does not hinge on a preference for immutable procedural rules. Respect for our role as a reviewing court rests, rather, on recognizing that this Court can often learn a good deal from considering how a district court and a court of appeals have worked their way through a difficult issue. It rests on recognizing that an issue as first conceived may come to be seen differently as a case moves through trial and appeal; we are most likely to contribute something of value if we act with the benefit of whatever refinement may come in the course of litigation. And our customary refusal to become a trial court reflects the simple fact that this Court cannot develop a record as well as a trial court can. If I were a trial judge, for example, I would balk at deciding on summary judgment whether an Establishment Clause violation would occur here without having statements of undisputed facts or uncon-

"social and recreational meetings" that, in their view, "pertain to the welfare of the community." The non-preferential, neutrality principle that is the hallmark of the Court's modern-day Establishment Clause doctrine makes it impossible for the Court to make, or allow our schools to make, such distinctions.

John C. Eastman, *Bad News for Good News Clubs?*, LOS ANGELES DAILY JOURNAL (July 2, 2001). Do you agree?

2. The Special Context of the Private, Religious School

Nowhere have disputes over the meaning of the Establishment Clause been more pointed than with regard to the issue of whether private religious schools should have equal access to public education funds. As the materials in this section indicate, it is out of these controversies that the three-part Establishment Clause test inquiring into secular purpose, effect, and entanglement emerges in *Lemon v. Kurtzman*, below. As implemented, *Lemon* precluded most, but somewhat inexplicably on its own terms, not all public funding from being equitably apportioned with private religious schools, even as, time and again, the Court would compliment these schools for their contribution to the educational process. While private religious schools are still excluded from direct public funding, a considerable portion of the constitutional fussiness in this area has subsided with the recognition, first in *Zobrest v. Catalina Foothills School District* and most recently in *Zelman v. Simmons-Harris*, that nothing in the Constitution precludes states from allowing parents to freely choose to spend their pro rata share of public education tax dollars on a private religious school.

a. Direct Funding of Religious Schools

Earlier mention was made of the failed Blaine Amendment that had been proposed in 1876 in part to apply the Religion Clauses to the states. The same proposed amendment provided that "no money raised by taxation in any State for the support of public schools or derived from any public fund therefor, nor any public lands devoted thereto, shall ever be under the control of any religious sect, nor shall any money so raised or lands so devoted be divided between religious sects or denominations." 4 CONG. REC. 205 (1875). This denial of public funding for religiously provided education was a considerable break from precedent.

At the time of the founding until the mid-19th century, elementary schools in America were largely religious schools. As one writer explains: "[t]his plan of elementary education was frankly religious in its aims, and pious books constituted the basic materials of instruction. The religious orientation persisted for at least two centuries, in New England and in other sections . . . ." NELSON R. BURR, A CRITICAL BIBLIOGRAPHY OF RELIGION IN AMERICA 654 (James Ward Smith & Leland Jamison eds., 1961). Many teachers were also ministers, and even in the common or public school, the Bible was the principal textbook. It was the Protestant Bible, however, and problems arose with the substantial emigration of Catholics and persons of other faiths to the United States beginning in the 1840s. The problem was temporarily mitigated, however, by the establishment of private sectarian schools that often were recipients of public funds. The federal government had long given aid to religious schools. 2 ANSON PHELPS STOKES, CHURCH AND STATE 57-58 (1950). For example, land grants were made on the condition that each township set aside two sections for purposes of religion and education. 32 J. CONTINENTAL CONG. 312 (1787). An 1801 New York law directed that public educational funds be given to the Episcopal, Reformed Dutch, Methodist Episcopal, Scotch Presbyterian, Lutheran, Baptist, and Moravian Churches. Thus, there was little evidence before the mid-19th century of a constitutional objection to the direct public funding of religious schools. After that, such objections as arose came not from the Constitution, but from the fact that by 1870 the number of private Protestant schools was rapidly being eclipsed by Catholic schools. It is evident that Representative Blaine did not think the no establishment language of the First Amendment or the parallel language in his proposal banned public assistance for sectarian schools. If it had, the specialized language of Blaine's proposed amendment banning school funding would have been surplusage. As one commentator put it,

> It is of great significance that not a single voice was raised to suggest that the no establishment and/or the "free exercise" clause in the first section of the [Blaine] resolution ruled out the aforesaid use of public funds. It was assumed by all that they did not — an assumption stated explicitly by many Senators, implicitly by others.

F. William O'Brien, *The Blaine Amendment 1875-1876*, 41 U. DET. L.J. 137, 203-04 (1963). Professor O'Brien also notes that detractors of the Blaine proposal asserted that it did nothing to stop *federal* appropriations for religious schools, confirming again the original understanding that the First Amendment did not preclude such direct funding. *Id.* at 204.

That the original understanding did not prohibit, and indeed in practice, was supportive of the funding of religious schools should not be surprising with regard to a Constitution framed in the natural law tradition. Accordingly:

> The natural law principle assumes that there exist some external axioms. Whether they be the beliefs advocated by the Catholic, Jewish, or Lutheran [faith, by way of example,] is not relevant; instead, what is important is that the persons who drafted the Constitution viewed religion as one of the conduits for determining right conduct.

Henry T. Miller, Comment, *Constitutional Fiction: An Analysis of the Supreme Court's Interpretation of the Religion Clauses*, 47 LA. L. REV. 169, 174 (1986). The distance from that tradition to modern Supreme Court jurisprudence can be measured in the following case.

LEMON v. KURTZMAN
403 U.S. 602 (1971)

Mr. Chief Justice Burger delivered the opinion of the Court.

These two appeals raise questions as to Pennsylvania and Rhode Island statutes providing state aid to church-related elementary and secondary schools. Both statutes are challenged as violative of the Establishment and Free Exercise Clauses of the First Amendment and the Due Process Clause of the Fourteenth Amendment.

Pennsylvania has adopted a statutory program that provides financial support to nonpublic elementary and secondary schools by way of reimbursement for the cost of teachers' salaries, textbooks, and instructional materials in specified secular subjects. Rhode Island has adopted a statute under which the State pays directly to teachers in nonpublic elementary schools a supplement of 15% of their annual salary. Under each statute state aid has been given to church-related educational institutions. We hold that both statutes are unconstitutional.

* * *

II

In *Everson v. Board of Education* (1947), this Court upheld a state statute that reimbursed the parents of parochial school children for bus transportation expenses. There Mr. Justice Black, writing for the majority, suggested that the decision carried to "the verge" of forbidden territory under the Religion Clauses. Candor compels acknowledgment, moreover, that we can only dimly perceive the lines of demarcation in this extraordinarily sensitive area of constitutional law.

* * *

... Three [ ] tests may be gleaned from our cases. First, the statute must have a secular legislative purpose; second, its principal or primary effect must be one that neither advances nor inhibits religion, *Board of Education v. Allen* (1968); finally, the statute must not foster "an excessive government entanglement with religion."

Inquiry into the legislative purposes of the Pennsylvania and Rhode Island statutes affords no basis for a conclusion that the legislative intent was to advance religion. On the contrary, the statutes themselves clearly state that they are intended to enhance the quality of the secular education in all schools covered by the compulsory attendance laws. There is no reason to believe the legislatures meant anything else. . . .

* * *

In *Allen*, the Court acknowledged that secular and religious teachings were not necessarily so intertwined that secular textbooks furnished to students by the State were in fact instrumental in the teaching of religion. The legislatures of Rhode Island and Pennsylvania have concluded that secular and religious education are identifiable and separable. In the abstract we have no quarrel with this conclusion.

The two legislatures, however, have also recognized that church-related elementary and secondary schools have a significant religious mission and that a substantial portion of their activities is religiously oriented. They have therefore sought to create statutory restrictions designed to guarantee the separation between secular and religious educational functions and to ensure that State financial aid supports only the former. All these provisions are precautions taken in candid recognition that these programs approached, even if they did not intrude upon, the forbidden areas under the Religion Clauses. We need not decide whether these legislative precautions restrict the principal or primary effect of the programs to the point where they do not offend the Religion Clauses, for we conclude that the cumulative impact of the entire relationship arising under the statutes in each State involves excessive entanglement between government and religion.

* * *

In order to determine whether the government entanglement with religion is excessive, we must examine the character and purposes of the institutions that are benefitted, the nature of the aid that the State provides, and the resulting relationship between the government and the religious authority . . . . Here we find that both statutes foster an impermissible degree of entanglement.

(a) *Rhode Island program*

The District Court made extensive findings on the grave potential for excessive entanglement that inheres in the religious character and purpose of the Roman Catholic elementary schools of Rhode Island, to date the sole beneficiaries of the [statute].

* * *

The substantial religious character of these church-related schools gives rise to entangling church-state relationships of the kind the Religion Clauses sought to avoid. Although the District Court found that concern for religious values did not inevitably or necessarily intrude into the content of secular subjects, the considerable religious activities of these schools led the legislature to provide for careful governmental controls and surveillance by state authorities in order to ensure that state aid supports only secular education.

The dangers and corresponding entanglements are enhanced by the particular form of aid that the Rhode Island Act provides. Our decisions from *Everson* to *Allen* have permitted the States to provide church-related schools with secular, neutral, or nonideological services, facilities, or materials. Bus transportation, school lunches, public health services, and secular textbooks supplied in common to all students were not thought to offend the Establishment Clause. . . .

. . . We cannot, however, refuse here to recognize that teachers have a substantially different ideological character from books. In terms of potential for involving some aspect of faith or morals in secular subjects, a textbook's content is ascertainable, but a teacher's handling of a subject is not. We cannot ignore the danger that a teacher under religious control and discipline poses to the separation of the religious from the purely secular aspects of pre-college education. The conflict of functions inheres in the situation.

* * *

. . . The Rhode Island Legislature has not, and could not, provide state aid on the basis of a mere assumption that secular teachers under religious discipline can avoid conflicts. The State must be certain, given the Religion Clauses, that subsidized teachers do not inculcate religion — indeed the State here has undertaken to do so. To ensure that no trespass occurs, the State has therefore carefully conditioned its aid with pervasive restrictions. An eligible recipient must teach only those courses that are offered in the public schools and use only those texts and materials that are found in the public schools. In addition the teacher must not engage in teaching any course in religion.

A comprehensive, discriminating, and continuing state surveillance will inevitably be required to ensure that these restrictions are obeyed and the First Amendment otherwise respected. Unlike a book, a teacher cannot be inspected once so as to determine the extent and intent of his or her personal beliefs and subjective acceptance of the limitations imposed by the First Amendment. These prophylactic contacts will involve excessive and enduring entanglement between state and church.

There is another area of entanglement in the Rhode Island program that gives concern. The statute excludes teachers employed by nonpublic schools whose average per-pupil expenditures on secular education equal or exceed the comparable figures for public schools. In the event that the total expenditures of an otherwise eligible school exceed this norm, the program requires the government to examine the school's records in order to determine how much of the total expenditures is attributable to secular education and how much to religious activity. This kind of state inspection and evaluation of the religious content of a religious organization is fraught with the sort of entanglement that the Constitution forbids. . . .

(b) *Pennsylvania program*

The Pennsylvania statute also provides state aid to church-related schools for teachers' salaries. The complaint describes an educational system that is very similar to the one existing in Rhode Island. According to the allegations, the church-related elementary and secondary schools are controlled by religious organizations, have the purpose of propagating and promoting a particular religious faith, and conduct their operations to fulfill that purpose. Since this complaint was dismissed for failure to state a claim for relief, we must accept these allegations as true for purposes of our review.

As we noted earlier, the very restrictions and surveillance necessary to ensure that teachers play a strictly nonideological role give rise to entanglements between church and state. The Pennsylvania statute, like that of Rhode Island, fosters this kind of relationship. Reimbursement is not only limited to courses offered in the public schools and materials approved by state officials, but the statute excludes "any subject matter expressing religious teaching, or the morals or forms of worship of any sect." In addition, schools seeking reimbursement must maintain accounting procedures that require the State to establish the cost of the secular as distinguished from the religious instruction.

The Pennsylvania statute, moreover, has the further defect of providing state financial aid directly to the church-related school. This factor distinguishes both *Everson* and *Allen*, for in both those cases the Court was careful to point out that state aid was provided to the student and his parents — not to the church-related school. *Board of Education v. Allen, supra; Everson v. Board of Education, supra.* In *Walz v. Tax Commission* [(1970)], the Court warned of the dangers of direct payments to religious organizations:

> "Obviously a direct money subsidy would be a relationship pregnant with involvement and, as with most governmental grant programs, could encompass sustained and detailed administrative relationships for enforcement of statutory or administrative standards . . . ."

* * *

IV

A broader base of entanglement of yet a different character is presented by the divisive political potential of these state programs. In a community where such a large number of pupils are served by church-related schools, it can be assumed that state assistance will entail considerable political activity. Partisans of parochial schools, understandably concerned with rising costs and sincerely dedicated to both the religious and secular educational missions of their schools, will inevitably champion this cause and promote political action to achieve their goals. Those who oppose state aid, whether for constitutional, religious, or fiscal reasons, will inevitably respond and employ all of the usual political campaign techniques to prevail. Candidates will be forced to declare and voters to choose. It would be unrealistic to ignore the fact that many people confronted with issues of this kind will find their votes aligned with their faith.

* * *

V

* * *

Finally, nothing we have said can be construed to disparage the role of church-related elementary and secondary schools in our national life. Their contribution has been and is enormous. Nor do we ignore their economic plight in a period of rising costs and expanding need. Taxpayers generally have been spared vast sums by the maintenance of these educational institutions by religious organizations, largely by the gifts of faithful adherents.

The merit and benefits of these schools, however, are not the issue before us in these cases. The sole question is whether state aid to these schools can be squared with the dictates of the Religion Clauses. Under our system the choice has been made that government is to be entirely excluded from the area of religious instruction and churches excluded from the affairs of government. The Constitution decrees that religion must be a private matter for the individual, the family, and the institutions of private choice, and that while some involvement and entanglement are inevitable, lines must be drawn.

* * *

MR. JUSTICE MARSHALL took no part in the consideration or decision.

MR. JUSTICE DOUGLAS, whom MR. JUSTICE BLACK joins, concurring [omitted].

MR. JUSTICE BRENNAN [concurring].

* * *

I

In sharp contrast to the "undeviating acceptance given religious tax exemptions from our earliest days as a Nation," subsidy of sectarian educational institutions became embroiled in bitter controversies very soon after the Nation was formed. Public education was, of course, virtually nonexistent when the Constitution was adopted. Colonial Massachusetts in 1647 had directed towns to establish schools, Benjamin Franklin in 1749 proposed a Philadelphia Academy, and Jefferson labored to establish a public school system in Virginia.[2] But these were the exceptions. Education in the Colonies was overwhelmingly a private enterprise, usually carried on as a denominational activity by the dominant Protestant sects. In point of fact, government generally looked to the church to provide education, and often contributed support through donations of land and money. E. CUBBERLEY, PUBLIC EDUCATION IN THE UNITED STATES 171 (1919).

Nor was there substantial change in the years immediately following ratification of the Constitution and the Bill of Rights. Schools continued to be local and, in the main, denominational institutions.[3] But the demand for public education soon emerged. The evolution of the struggle in New York City is illustrative.[4] In 1786, the first New York State Legislature ordered that one section in each township be set aside for the "gospel and schools." With no public schools, various private agencies and churches operated "charity schools" for the

---

[2] E. CUBBERLEY, PUBLIC EDUCATION IN THE UNITED STATES 17 (1919); Abington School District v. Schempp [(1963)], and authorities cited therein (BRENNAN, J., concurring).

[3] C. ANTIEAU, A. DOWNEY, E. ROBERTS, FREEDOM FROM FEDERAL ESTABLISHMENT 174 (1964).

[4] B. CONFREY, SECULARISM IN AMERICAN EDUCATION: ITS HISTORY 127-129 (1931).

poor of New York City and received money from the state common school fund. The forerunner of the city's public schools was organized in 1805 when DeWitt Clinton founded "The Society for Establishment of a Free School in the City of New York for the Education of such poor Children as do not belong to or are not provided for by any Religious Society." The State and city aided the society, and it built many schools. Gradually, however, competition and bickering among the Free School Society and the various church schools developed over the apportionment of state school funds. As a result, in 1825, the legislature transferred to the city council the responsibility for distributing New York City's share of the state funds. The council stopped funding religious societies which operated 16 sectarian schools but continued supporting schools connected with the Protestant Orphan Asylum Society. Thereafter, in 1831, the Catholic Orphan Asylum Society demanded and received public funds to operate its schools but a request of Methodists for funds for the same purpose was denied. Nine years later, the Catholics enlarged their request for public monies to include all parochial schools, contending that the council was subsidizing sectarian books and instruction of the Public School Society, which Clinton's Free School Society had become. The city's Scotch Presbyterian and Jewish communities immediately followed with requests for funds to finance their schools. Although the Public School Society undertook to revise its texts to meet the objections, in 1842, the state legislature closed the bitter controversy by enacting a law that established a City Board of Education to set up free public schools, prohibited the distribution of public funds to sectarian schools, and prohibited the teaching of sectarian doctrine in any public school.

The Nation's rapidly developing religious heterogeneity, the tide of Jacksonian democracy, and growing urbanization soon led to widespread demands throughout the States for secular public education. At the same time strong opposition developed to use of the States' taxing powers to support private sectarian schools.[5] Although the controversy over religious exercises in the public schools continued into this century, the opponents of subsidy to sectarian schools had largely won their fight by 1900. In fact, after 1840, no efforts of sectarian schools to obtain a share of public school funds succeeded. Between 1840 and 1875, 19 States added provisions to their constitutions prohibiting the use of public school funds to aid sectarian schools, and by 1900, 16 more States had added similar provisions. In fact, no State admitted to the Union after 1858, except West Virginia, omitted such provision from its first constitution. Today fewer than a half-dozen States omit such provisions from their constitutions.[6]

---

[5] See generally R. BUTTS, THE AMERICAN TRADITION IN RELIGION AND EDUCATION 111-145 (1950); 2 A. STOKES, CHURCH AND STATE IN THE UNITED STATES 47-72 (1950); CUBBERLEY, supra n.2, at 155-181.

[6] See Ala. Const., Art. XIV, § 263; Alaska Const., Art. VII, § 1; Ariz. Const., Art. II, § 12, Art. XI, §§ 7, 8; Ark. Const., Art. XIV, § 2; Calif. Const., Art. IX, § 8; Colo. Const., Art. IX, § 7; Conn. Const., Art. VIII, § 4; Del. Const., Art. X, § 3; Fla. Const., Decl. of Rights, Art. I, § 3; Ga. Const., Art. VIII, § 12, par. 1; Hawaii Const., Art. IX, § 1; Idaho Const., Art. IX, § 5; Ill. Const., Art. VIII, § 3; Ind.

And in 1897, Congress included in its appropriation act for the District of Columbia a statement declaring it

> "to be the policy of the Government of the United States to make no appropriation of money or property for the purpose of founding, maintaining, or aiding by payment for services, expenses, or otherwise, any church or religious denomination, or any institution or society which is under sectarian or ecclesiastical control."

Thus for more than a century, the consensus, enforced by legislatures and courts with substantial consistency, has been that public subsidy of sectarian schools constitutes an impermissible involvement of secular with religious institutions. . . .

* * *

III

* * *

The common ingredient of the three prongs of the test set forth at the outset of this opinion is whether the statutes involve government in the "essentially religious activities" of religious institutions. My analysis of the operation, purposes, and effects of these statutes leads me inescapably to the conclusion that they do impermissibly involve the States and the Federal Government with the "essentially religious activities" of sectarian educational institutions. More specifically, for the reasons stated, I think each government uses "essentially religious means to serve governmental ends, where secular means would suffice." This Nation long ago committed itself to primary reliance upon publicly supported public education to serve its important goals in secular education. . . .

* * *

MR. JUSTICE WHITE, concurring [for purposes of remand, to determine if the statutes are unconstitutional as applied, but dissenting as to the majority's rationale that the statutes are void on their face].

* * *

Const., Art. 8, § 3; Kan. Const., Art. 6, § 6 (c); Ky. Const., § 189; La. Const., Art. XII, § 13; Mass. Const., Amend. Art. XLVI, § 2; Mich. Const., Art. I, § 4; Minn. Const., Art. VIII, § 2; Miss. Const., Art. 8, § 208; Mo. Const., Art. IX, § 8; Mont. Const., Art. XI, § 8; Neb. Const., Art. VII, § 11; Nev. Const., Art. 11, § 10; N. H. Const., Pt. II, Art. 83; N. J. Const., Art. VIII, § 4, par. 2; N. Mex. Const., Art. XII, § 3; N. Y. Const., Art. XI, § 3; N. Car. Const., Art. IX, §§ 4, 12; N. Dak. Const., Art. VIII, § 152; Ohio Const., Art. VI, § 2; Okla. Const., Art. II, § 5; Ore. Const., Art. VIII, § 2; Penn. Const., Art. 3, § 15; R. I. Const., Art. XII, § 4; S. C. Const., Art. XI, § 9; S. Dak. Const., Art. VIII, § 16; Tenn. Const., Art. XI, § 12; Tex. Const., Art. VII, § 5; Utah Const., Art. X, § 13; Va. Const., Art. IX, § 141; Wash. Const., Art. IX, § 4; W. Va. Const., Art. XII, § 4; Wis. Const., Art. I, § 18, Art. X, § 2; Wyo. Const., Art. 7, § 8.

The overwhelming majority of these constitutional provisions either prohibit expenditures of public funds on sectarian schools, or prohibit the expenditure of public school funds for any purpose other than support of public schools. . . .

The Court thus creates an insoluble paradox for the State and the parochial schools. The State cannot finance secular instruction if it permits religion to be taught in the same classroom; but if it exacts a promise that religion not be so taught — a promise the school and its teachers are quite willing and on this record able to give — and enforces it, it is then entangled in the "no entanglement" aspect of the Court's Establishment Clause jurisprudence.

* * *

. . . There is no specific allegation in the complaint that sectarian teaching does or would invade secular classes supported by state funds. That the schools are operated to promote a particular religion is quite consistent with the view that secular teaching devoid of religious instruction can successfully be maintained . . . . I cannot hold that the First Amendment forbids an agreement between the school and the State that the state funds would be used only to teach secular subjects.

b. School Vouchers or the Equivalent — The Permissible Evenhanded Funding of Students or Parents

In the years following *Lemon*, the courts continued to grapple with drawing the line between permissible and impermissible attempts to provide state aid for educational purposes to parents who choose to send their children to religious schools. In *Zobrest v. Catalina Foothills Sch. Dist.*, 509 U.S. 1 (1993), the Supreme Court held that the Establishment Clause did not prevent the public provision of a sign language interpreter to a deaf child attending a religious high school. With some hedging, it held that so long as educational funds are made available directly to parents or students as part of a government program "that neutrally provide[s] benefits to a broad class of citizens defined without reference to religion" then no Establishment Clause issue arises. *Zobrest*, 509 U.S. at 8. Thus, presumably, a state, if it so chose, could tax all of its citizens (usually through a combination of property and income taxes) to create a general education fund and then return those funds to parents for public or private (including private religious) schooling either in the form of a tax credit or cash payment (voucher).

The hedging in *Zobrest* was removed in *Agostini v. Felton*, 521 U.S. 203 (1997), in which the Supreme Court reopened its previous rulings in *Aguilar v. Felton*, 473 U.S. 402 (1985), and *Grand Rapids Sch. Dist. v. Ball*, 473 U.S. 373 (1985), largely overruling both and holding that "a federally funded program providing supplemental, remedial instruction to disadvantaged children on a neutral basis is not invalid under the Establishment Clause when such instruction is given on the premises of sectarian schools by government employees." *Agostini*, 117 S. Ct. at 234-35. Since *Agostini* lends further strength to the equal protection idea, it is significant that the Court's opinion was written by Justice O'Connor, who explicitly rejected Justice Souter's dissenting analysis that the neutral, generally available educational assistance in reading, English and mathematics created an impermissible "symbolic union" between church and state. *Id.* at 224. Justice O'Connor, of course, has been a consistent advocate of the no endorsement view in other cases. In his dissent, Justice Souter strenuously argued that earlier cases, such as *Zobrest* and *Witters*, involved only individuals receiving isolated services, while the program in *Agostini* assumed the core teaching responsibility of the religious schools. *Id.* at 248-52 (Souter, J., dissenting). The majority refused to engage in what it called the dissent's speculations, and stated that it was also unwilling "to conclude that the constitutionality of an aid program depends on the number of sectarian school students who happen to receive the otherwise neutral aid." *Id.* at 229.

Finally, in *Mitchell v. Helms*, 530 U.S. 793 (2000), the Court in a fractured, 4-2-3 opinion, upheld Louisiana's provision of library books, computers, and video equipment to private religious schools on the same terms as they were provided to public schools. Justice Thomas, writing for the plurality, held that the aid did not run afoul of *Lemon*'s effects prong because the aid was provided to the religious schools "only as a result of the genuinely independent and private choices of individua[l parents]," and because the aid was "allocated on the basis of neutral, secular criteria that neither favor[ed] nor disfavor[ed] religion, and [was] made available to both religious and secular beneficiaries on a nondiscriminatory basis." Justice O'Connor, joined by Justice Breyer, concurred only in the judgment, contending that the plurality opinion treated the neutrality of the aid program as dispositive, when in her view (as well as that of Justice Souter, joned by Justices Stevens and Ginsburg, in dissent) it was a necessary but not a sufficient condition for surviving an Establishment Clause challenge. Justice O'Connor was also troubled by what she described as the plurality's rejection of "the distinction between direct and indirect aid," and its holding "that the actual diversion of secular aid by a religious school to the advancement of its religious mission is permissible." *Agostini* and *Mitchell* were both decided with cases addressing the constitutionality of school voucher programs on the immediate horizon. Can you predict from them the outcome and reasoning of the following case?

ZELMAN v. SIMMONS-HARRIS
536 U.S. 639 (2002)

CHIEF JUSTICE REHNQUIST delivered the opinion of the Court.

The State of Ohio has established a pilot program designed to provide educational choices to families with children who reside in the Cleveland City School District. The question presented is whether this program offends the Establishment Clause of the United States Constitution. We hold that it does not.

* * *

The program provides two basic kinds of assistance to parents of children in a covered district. First, the program provides tuition aid for students in kindergarten through third grade, expanding each year through eighth grade, to attend a participating public or private school of their parent's choosing. Second, the program provides tutorial aid for students who choose to remain enrolled in public school.

The tuition aid portion of the program is designed to provide educational choices to parents who reside in a covered district. Any private school, whether religious or nonreligious, may participate in the program and accept program students so long as the school is located within the boundaries of a covered district and meets statewide educational standards. Participating private schools must agree not to discriminate on the basis of race, religion, or ethnic background, or to "advocate or foster unlawful behavior or teach hatred of any person or group on the basis of race, ethnicity, national origin, or religion." Any public school located in a school district adjacent to the covered district may also participate in the program. Adjacent public schools are eligible to receive a $2,250 tuition grant for each program student accepted in addition to the full amount of per-pupil state funding attributable to each additional student.[1]

Tuition aid is distributed to parents according to financial need. Families with incomes below 200% of the poverty line are given priority and are eligible to receive 90% of private school tuition up to $2,250. . . . If parents choose a private school, checks are made payable to the parents who then endorse the checks over to the chosen school.

* * *

The program has been in operation within the Cleveland City School District since the 1996-1997 school year. In the 1999-2000 school year, 56 private schools participated in the program, 46 (or 82%) of which had a religious affiliation. None of the public schools in districts adjacent to Cleveland have elected to participate. More than 3,700 students participated in the scholarship program, most of whom (96%) enrolled in religiously affiliated schools. . . .

* * *

The Establishment Clause of the First Amendment, applied to the States through the Fourteenth Amendment, prevents a State from enacting laws that have the "purpose" or "effect" of advancing or inhibiting religion. *Agostini v. Felton* ("[W]e continue to ask whether the government acted with the purpose of advancing or inhibiting religion [and] whether the aid has the 'effect' of advancing or inhibiting religion" (citations omitted)). There is no dispute that the program challenged here was enacted for the valid secular purpose of providing

---

[1] Although the parties dispute the precise amount of state funding received by suburban school districts adjacent to the Cleveland City School District, there is no dispute that any suburban district agreeing to participate in the program would receive a $ 2,250 tuition grant *plus* the ordinary allotment of per-pupil state funding for each program student enrolled in a suburban public school.

educational assistance to poor children in a demonstrably failing public school system. Thus, the question presented is whether the Ohio program nonetheless has the forbidden "effect" of advancing or inhibiting religion.

To answer that question, our decisions have drawn a consistent distinction between government programs that provide aid directly to religious schools, . . . and programs of true private choice, in which government aid reaches religious schools only as a result of the genuine and independent choices of private individuals, *Mueller v. Allen* . . . While our jurisprudence with respect to the constitutionality of direct aid programs has "changed significantly" over the past two decades, our jurisprudence with respect to true private choice programs has remained consistent and unbroken. Three times we have confronted Establishment Clause challenges to neutral government programs that provide aid directly to a broad class of individuals, who, in turn, direct the aid to religious schools or institutions of their own choosing. Three times we have rejected such challenges.

In *Mueller,* we rejected an Establishment Clause challenge to a Minnesota program authorizing tax deductions for various educational expenses, including private school tuition costs, even though the great majority of the program's beneficiaries (96%) were parents of children in religious schools. We began by focusing on the class of beneficiaries, finding that because the class included "*all* parents," including parents with "children [who] attend nonsectarian private schools or sectarian private schools," the program was "not readily subject to challenge under the Establishment Clause. Then, viewing the program as a whole, we emphasized the principle of private choice, noting that public funds were made available to religious schools "only as a result of numerous, private choices of individual parents of school-aged children." This, we said, ensured that "'no imprimatur of state approval' can be deemed to have been conferred on any particular religion, or on religion generally." We thus found it irrelevant to the constitutional inquiry that the vast majority of beneficiaries were parents of children in religious schools, saying:

> "We would be loath to adopt a rule grounding the constitutionality of a facially neutral law on annual reports reciting the extent to which various classes of private citizens claimed benefits under the law."

That the program was one of true private choice, with no evidence that the State deliberately skewed incentives toward religious schools, was sufficient for the program to survive scrutiny under the Establishment Clause.

In *Witters,* we used identical reasoning to reject an Establishment Clause challenge to a vocational scholarship program that provided tuition aid to a student studying at a religious institution to become a pastor. Looking at the program as a whole, we observed that "[a]ny aid . . . that ultimately flows to religious institutions does so only as a result of the genuinely independent and private choices of aid recipients." Five Members of the Court, in separate opinions, emphasized the general rule from *Mueller* that the amount of government aid channeled to religious institutions by individual aid recipients was not relevant to the constitutional inquiry. Our holding thus rested not on whether few or many recipients chose to expend government aid at a religious school but, rather, on whether recipients generally were empowered to direct the aid to schools or institutions of their own choosing.

Finally, in *Zobrest,* we applied *Mueller* and *Witters* to reject an Establishment Clause challenge to a federal program that permitted sign-language inter- preters to assist deaf children enrolled in religious schools. Reviewing our ear- lier decisions, we stated that "government programs that neutrally provide benefits to a broad class of citizens defined without reference to religion are not readily subject to an Establishment Clause challenge."

* * *

Mueller, Witters, and *Zobrest* thus make clear that where a government aid program is neutral with respect to religion, and provides assistance directly to a broad class of citizens who, in turn, direct government aid to religious schools wholly as a result of their own genuine and independent private choice, the pro- gram is not readily subject to challenge under the Establishment Clause. A program that shares these features permits government aid to reach religious institutions only by way of the deliberate choices of numerous individual recip- ients. The incidental advancement of a religious mission, or the perceived endorsement of a religious message, is reasonably attributable to the individual recipient, not to the government, whose role ends with the disbursement of benefits. . . . It is precisely for these reasons that we have never found a program of true private choice to offend the Establishment Clause.

We believe that the program challenged here is a program of true private choice, consistent with *Mueller, Witters,* and *Zobrest,* and thus constitutional. As was true in those cases, the Ohio program is neutral in all respects toward religion. It is part of a general and multifaceted undertaking by the State of Ohio to provide educational opportunities to the children of a failed school district. It confers educational assistance directly to a broad class of individuals defined without reference to religion, *i.e.,* any parent of a school-age child who resides in the Cleveland City School District. The program permits the participation of *all* schools within the district, religious or nonreligious. Adjacent public schools also may participate and have a financial incentive to do so. Program benefits are available to participating families on neutral terms, with no reference to reli- gion. The only preference stated anywhere in the program is a preference for low-income families, who receive greater assistance and are given priority for admission at participating schools.

* * *

Respondents suggest that even without a financial incentive for parents to choose a religious school, the program creates a "public perception that the State is endorsing religious practices and beliefs." But we have repeatedly rec- ognized that no reasonable observer would think a neutral program of private choice, where state aid reaches religious schools solely as a result of the numerous independent decisions of private individuals, carries with it the *imprimatur* of government endorsement. . . . Any objective observer familiar with the full history and context of the Ohio program would reasonably view it as one aspect of a broader undertaking to assist poor children in failed schools, not as an endorsement of religious schooling in general. . . .

That 46 of the 56 private schools now participating in the program are religious schools does not condemn it as a violation of the Establishment Clause. The Establishment Clause question is whether Ohio is coercing parents into sending their children to religious schools, and that question must be answered by evaluating *all* options Ohio provides Cleveland schoolchildren, only one of which is to obtain a program scholarship and then choose a religious school.

* * *

Respondents and JUSTICE SOUTER claim that even if we do not focus on the number of participating schools that are religious schools, we should attach constitutional significance to the fact that 96% of scholarship recipients have enrolled in religious schools. They claim that this alone proves parents lack genuine choice, even if no parent has ever said so. We need not consider this argument in detail, since it was flatly rejected in *Mueller,* where we found it irrelevant that 96% of parents taking deductions for tuition expenses paid tuition at religious schools.

* * *

The 96% figure upon which respondents and JUSTICE SOUTER rely discounts entirely (1) the more than 1,900 Cleveland children enrolled in alternative community schools, (2) the more than 13,000 children enrolled in alternative magnet schools, and (3) the more than 1,400 children enrolled in traditional public schools with tutorial assistance. Including some or all of these children in the denominator of children enrolled in nontraditional schools during the 1999-2000 school year drops the percentage enrolled in religious schools from 96% to under 20%.[6]

* * *

In sum, the Ohio program is entirely neutral with respect to religion. It provides benefits directly to a wide spectrum of individuals, defined only by financial need and residence in a particular school district. It permits such individuals

---

[6] JUSTICE SOUTER and JUSTICE STEVENS claim that community schools and magnet schools are separate and distinct from program schools, simply because the program itself does not include community and magnet school options. But none of the dissenting opinions explain how there is any perceptible difference between scholarship schools, community schools, or magnet schools from the perspective of Cleveland parents looking to choose the best educational option for their school-age children. Parents who choose a program school in fact receive from the State precisely what parents who choose a community or magnet school receive — the opportunity to send their children largely at state expense to schools they prefer to their local public school. . . .

to exercise genuine choice among options public and private, secular and religious. The program is therefore a program of true private choice. In keeping with an unbroken line of decisions rejecting challenges to similar programs, we hold that the program does not offend the Establishment Clause.

The judgment of the Court of Appeals is reversed.

It is so ordered.

JUSTICE O'CONNOR, concurring.

While I join the Court's opinion, I write separately for two reasons. First, although the Court takes an important step, I do not believe that today's decision, when considered in light of other longstanding government programs that impact religious organizations and our prior Establishment Clause jurisprudence, marks a dramatic break from the past. Second, given the emphasis the Court places on verifying that parents of voucher students in religious schools have exercised "true private choice," I think it is worth elaborating on the Court's conclusion that this inquiry should consider all reasonable educational alternatives to religious schools that are available to parents. To do otherwise is to ignore how the educational system in Cleveland actually functions.

I

These cases are different from prior indirect aid cases in part because a significant portion of the funds appropriated for the voucher program reach religious schools without restrictions on the use of these funds. The share of public resources that reach religious schools is not, however, as significant as respondents suggest. . . . These statistics do not take into account all of the reasonable educational choices that may be available to students in Cleveland public schools. When one considers the option to attend community schools, the percentage of students enrolled in religious schools falls to 62.1 percent. If magnet schools are included in the mix, this percentage falls to 16.5 percent. . .

* * *

Although $8.2 million is no small sum, it pales in comparison to the amount of funds that federal, state, and local governments already provide religious institutions. Religious organizations may qualify for exemptions from the federal corporate income tax, the corporate income tax in many States, and property taxes in all 50 States.

* * *

These tax exemptions, which have "much the same effect as [cash grants] . . . of the amount of tax [avoided]," are just part of the picture. Federal dollars also reach religiously affiliated organizations through public health programs such as Medicare, and Medicaid, through educational programs such as the Pell Grant program, and the G.I. Bill of Rights, and through child care programs such as the Child Care and Development Block Grant Program (CCDBG).

* * *

A significant portion of the funds appropriated for these programs reach religiously affiliated institutions, typically without restrictions on its subsequent use. . . . Against this background, the support that the Cleveland voucher program provides religious institutions is neither substantial nor atypical of existing government programs. While this observation is not intended to justify the Cleveland voucher program under the Establishment Clause, it places in broader perspective alarmist claims about implications of the Cleveland program and the Court's decision in these cases. . . .

II

Nor does today's decision signal a major departure from this Court's prior Establishment Clause jurisprudence. A central tool in our analysis of cases in this area has been the *Lemon* test. As originally formulated, a statute passed this test only if it had "a secular legislative purpose," if its "principal or primary effect" was one that "neither advance[d] nor inhibit[ed] religion," and if it did "not foster an excessive government entanglement with religion." *Lemon v. Kurtzman* (1971). In *Agostini v. Felton* (1997), we folded the entanglement inquiry into the primary effect inquiry. This made sense because both inquiries rely on the same evidence, and the degree of entanglement has implications for whether a statute advances or inhibits religion. . . .

The Court's opinion in these cases focuses on a narrow question related to the *Lemon* test: how to apply the primary effects prong in indirect aid cases? Specifically, it clarifies the basic inquiry when trying to determine whether a program that distributes aid to beneficiaries, rather than directly to service providers, has the primary effect of advancing or inhibiting religion, *Lemon v. Kurtzman,* or, as I have put it, of "endors[ing] or disapprov[ing] . . . religion," *Lynch v. Donnelly* (concurring opinion); *see also Wallace v. Jaffree* (1985) (O'CONNOR, J., concurring in judgment). Courts are instructed to consider two factors: first, whether the program administers aid in a neutral fashion, without differentiation based on the religious status of beneficiaries or providers of services; second, and more importantly, whether beneficiaries of indirect aid have a genuine choice among religious and nonreligious organizations when determining the organization to which they will direct that aid. If the answer to either query is "no," the program should be struck down under the Establishment Clause.

JUSTICE SOUTER portrays this inquiry as a departure from *Everson*. A fair reading of the holding in that case suggests quite the opposite. Justice Black's opinion for the Court held that the "[First] Amendment requires the state to be a neutral in its relations with groups of religious believers and non-believers; it does not require the state to be their adversary." *Everson, supra.* How else could the Court have upheld a state program to provide students transportation to public and religious schools alike? What the Court clarifies in these cases is that the Establishment Clause also requires that state aid flowing to religious organizations through the hands of beneficiaries must do so only at the direction of those beneficiaries. Such a refinement of the *Lemon* test surely does not betray *Everson*.

III

* * *

Based on the reasoning in the Court's opinion, which is consistent with the realities of the Cleveland educational system, I am persuaded that the Cleveland voucher program affords parents of eligible children genuine nonreligious options and is consistent with the Establishment Clause.

Justice Thomas, concurring. [see *supra*, Part II.A.4]

Justice Stevens, dissenting. [omitted]

Justice Souter, with whom Justice Stevens, Justice Ginsberg, and Justice Breyer, join, dissenting.

* * *

How can a Court consistently leave *Everson* on the books and approve the Ohio vouchers? The answer is that it cannot. It is only by ignoring *Everson* that the majority can claim to rest on traditional law in its invocation of neutral aid provisions and private choice to sanction the Ohio law. It is, moreover, only by ignoring the meaning of neutrality and private choice themselves that the majority can even pretend to rest today's decision on those criteria.

I

The majority's statements of Establishment Clause doctrine cannot be appreciated without some historical perspective on the Court's announced limitations on government aid to religious education, and its repeated repudiation of limits previously set. . . .

Viewed with the necessary generality, the cases can be categorized in three groups. In the period from 1947 to 1968, the basic principle of no aid to religion through school benefits was unquestioned. Thereafter for some 15 years, the Court termed its efforts as attempts to draw a line against aid that would be divertible to support the religious, as distinct from the secular, activity of an institutional beneficiary. Then, starting in 1983, concern with divertibility was gradually lost in favor of approving aid in amounts unlikely to afford substantial benefits to religious schools, when offered evenhandedly without regard to a recipient's religious character, and when channeled to a religious institution only by the genuinely free choice of some private individual. Now, the three stages are succeeded by a fourth, in which the substantial character of government aid is held to have no constitutional significance, and the espoused criteria of neutrality in offering aid, and private choice in directing it, are shown to be nothing but examples of verbal formalism.

A

Everson v. Board of Ed. of Ewing inaugurated the modern development of Establishment Clause doctrine at the behest of a taxpayer challenging state provision of "tax-raised funds to pay the bus fares of parochial school pupils" on regular city buses as part of a general scheme to reimburse the public-transportation costs of children attending both public and private nonprofit schools. Although the Court split, no Justice disagreed with the basic doctrinal principle already quoted, that "[n]o tax in any amount . . . can be levied to support any religious activities or institutions, . . . whatever form they may adopt to teach . . . religion." Nor did any Member of the Court deny the tension between the New Jersey program and the aims of the Establishment Clause. The majority upheld the state law on the strength of rights of religious-school students under the Free Exercise Clause, which was thought to entitle them to free public transportation when offered as a "general government servic[e]" to all school-children. Despite the indirect benefit to religious education, the transportation was simply treated like "ordinary police and fire protection, connections for sewage disposal, public highways and sidewalks," and, most significantly, "state-paid policemen, detailed to protect children going to and from church schools from the very real hazards of traffic." The dissenters, however, found the benefit to religion too pronounced to survive the general principle of no establishment, no aid, and they described it as running counter to every objective served by the establishment ban. . .

The difficulty of drawing a line that preserved the basic principle of no aid was no less obvious some 20 years later in *Board of Ed. of Central School Dist. No. 1 v. Allen* (1968), which upheld a New York law authorizing local school boards to lend textbooks in secular subjects to children attending religious schools, a result not self-evident from *Everson*'s "general government services" rationale. The Court relied instead on the theory that the in-kind aid could only be used for secular educational purposes, and found it relevant that "no funds or books are furnished [directly] to parochial schools, and the financial benefit is to parents and children, not to schools."[4] Justice Black, who wrote *Everson,* led the dissenters.

* * *

B

Allen recognized the reality that "religious schools pursue two goals, religious instruction and secular education," if state aid could be restricted to serve the second, it might be permissible under the Establishment Clause. But in the

---

[4] The Court noted that "the record contains no evidence that any of the private schools . . . previously provided textbooks for their students," and "there is some evidence that at least some of the schools did not." *Allen,* 392 U.S. at 244, n.6. This was a significant distinction: if the parochial schools provided secular textbooks to their students, then the State's provision of the same in their stead might have freed up church resources for allocation to other uses, including, potentially, religious indoctrination.

retrenchment that followed, the Court saw that the two educational functions were so intertwined in religious primary and secondary schools that aid to secular education could not readily be segregated, and the intrusive monitoring required to enforce the line itself raised Establishment Clause concerns about the entanglement of church and state. *See Lemon v. Kurtzman* (1971) (striking down program supplementing salaries for teachers of secular subjects in private schools). To avoid the entanglement, the Court's focus in the post-*Allen* cases was on the principle of divertibility, on discerning when ostensibly secular government aid to religious schools was susceptible to religious uses. The greater the risk of diversion to religion (and the monitoring necessary to avoid it), the less legitimate the aid scheme was under the no-aid principle. On the one hand, the Court tried to be practical, and when the aid recipients were not so "pervasively sectarian" that their secular and religious functions were inextricably intertwined, the Court generally upheld aid earmarked for secular use.

* * *

C

Like all criteria requiring judicial assessment of risk, divertibility is an invitation to argument, but the object of the arguments provoked has always been a realistic assessment of facts aimed at respecting the principle of no aid. In *Mueller v. Allen,* however, that object began to fade, for *Mueller* started down the road from realism to formalism.

* * *

School Dist. of Grand Rapids v. Ball (1985), overruled in part by *Agostini v. Felton* (1997), clarified that the notions of evenhandedness, neutrality, and private choice in *Mueller* did not apply to cases involving direct aid to religious schools, which were still subject to the divertibility test. But in *Agostini,* where the substance of the aid was identical to that in *Ball,* public employees teaching remedial secular classes in private schools, the Court rejected the 30-year-old presumption of divertibility, and instead found it sufficient that the aid "supplement[ed]" but did not "supplant" existing educational services. The Court, contrary to *Ball,* viewed the aid as aid "directly to the eligible students . . . no matter where they choose to attend school."

In the 12 years between *Ball* and *Agostini,* the Court decided two other cases emphasizing the form of neutrality and private choice over the substance of aid to religious uses, but always in circumstances where any aid to religion was isolated and insubstantial. *Zobrest v. Catalina Foothills School Dist.* (1993) involved one student's choice to spend funds from a general public program at a religious school (to pay for a sign-language interpreter). As in *Witters,* the Court reasoned that "[d]isabled children, not sectarian schools, [were] the primary beneficiaries . . .; to the extent sectarian schools benefit at all . . ., they are only incidental beneficiaries."

To be sure, the aid in *Agostini* was systemic and arguably substantial, but, as I have said, the majority there chose to view it as a bare "supplement." And this was how the controlling opinion described the systemic aid in our most recent case, *Mitchell v. Helms* (2000), as aid going merely to a "portion" of the religious schools' budgets. (O'CONNOR, J., concurring in judgment). The plurality in that case did not feel so uncomfortable about jettisoning substance entirely in favor of form, finding it sufficient that the aid was neutral and that there was virtual private choice, since any aid "first passes through the hands (literally or figuratively) of numerous private citizens who are free to direct the aid elsewhere." But that was only the plurality view.

Hence it seems fair to say that it was not until today that substantiality of aid has clearly been rejected as irrelevant by a majority of this Court, just as it has not been until today that a majority, not a plurality, has held purely formal criteria to suffice for scrutinizing aid that ends up in the coffers of religious schools. Today's cases are notable for their stark illustration of the inadequacy of the majority's chosen formal analysis.

II

Although it has taken half a century since *Everson* to reach the majority's twin standards of neutrality and free choice, the facts show that, in the majority's hands, even these criteria cannot convincingly legitimize the Ohio scheme.

A

Consider first the criterion of neutrality. As recently as two Terms ago, a majority of the Court recognized that neutrality conceived of as evenhandedness toward aid recipients had never been treated as alone sufficient to satisfy the Establishment Clause, *Mitchell* (O'CONNOR, J., concurring in judgment); (SOUTER, J., dissenting). But at least in its limited significance, formal neutrality seemed to serve some purpose. Today, however, the majority employs the neutrality criterion in a way that renders it impossible to understand.

* * *

In order to apply the neutrality test, it makes sense to focus on a category of aid that may be directed to religious as well as secular schools, and ask whether the scheme favors a religious direction. Here, one would ask whether the voucher provisions, allowing for as much as $2,250 toward private school tuition (or a grant to a public school in an adjacent district), were written in a way that skewed the scheme toward benefiting religious schools.

This, however, is not what the majority asks. The majority looks not to the provisions for tuition vouchers, but to every provision for educational opportunity: "The program permits the participation of *all* schools within the district [as well as public schools in adjacent districts], religious or nonreligious." The majority then finds confirmation that "participation of *all* schools" satisfies neutrality by noting that the better part of total state educational expenditure goes to public schools, thus showing there is no favor of religion.

The illogic is patent. If regular, public schools (which can get no voucher payments) "participate" in a voucher scheme with schools that can, and public expenditure is still predominantly on public schools, then the majority's reasoning would find neutrality in a scheme of vouchers available for private tuition in districts with no secular private schools at all. "Neutrality" as the majority employs the term is, literally, verbal and nothing more. This, indeed, is the only way the majority can gloss over the very nonneutral feature of the total scheme covering "*all* schools": public tutors may receive from the State no more than $324 per child to support extra tutoring (that is, the State's 90% of a total amount of $360), whereas the tuition voucher schools (which turn out to be mostly religious) can receive up to $2,250.[7]

* * *

B

The majority addresses the issue of choice the same way it addresses neutrality, by asking whether recipients or potential recipients of voucher aid have a choice of public schools among secular alternatives to religious schools. Again, however, the majority asks the wrong question and misapplies the criterion. The majority has confused choice in spending scholarships with choice from the entire menu of possible educational placements, most of them open to anyone willing to attend a public school. I say "confused" because the majority's new use of the choice criterion, which it frames negatively as "whether Ohio is coercing parents into sending their children to religious schools," ignores the reason for having a private choice enquiry in the first place. Cases since *Mueller* have found private choice relevant under a rule that aid to religious schools can be permissible so long as it first passes through the hands of students or parents. The majority's view that all educational choices are comparable for purposes of choice thus ignores the whole point of the choice test: it is a criterion for deciding whether indirect aid to a religious school is legitimate because it passes through private hands that can spend or use the aid in a secular school. The question is whether the private hand is genuinely free to send the money in either a secular direction or a religious one. The majority now has transformed this question about private choice in channeling aid into a question about select-

---

7 The majority's argument that public school students within the program "direct almost twice as much state funding to their chosen school as do program students who receive a scholarship and attend a private school," was decisively rejected in *Committee for Public Ed. & Religious Liberty v. Nyquist,* (1973):

> We do not agree with the suggestion . . . that tuition grants are an analogous endeavor to provide comparable benefits to all parents of schoolchildren whether enrolled in public or nonpublic schools. . . . The grants to parents of private school children are given in addition to the right that they have to send their children to public schools 'totally at state expense.' And in any event, the argument proves too much, for it would also provide a basis for approving through tuition grants the *complete subsidization* of all religious schools on the ground that such action is necessary if the State is fully to equalize the position of parents who elect such schools — a result wholly at variance with the Establishment Clause."

ing from examples of state spending (on education) including direct spending on magnet and community public schools that goes through no private hands and could never reach a religious school under any circumstance. When the choice test is transformed from where to spend the money to where to go to school, it is cut loose from its very purpose.

* * *

Defining choice as choice in spending the money or channeling the aid is, moreover, necessary if the choice criterion is to function as a limiting principle at all. If "choice" is present whenever there is any educational alternative to the religious school to which vouchers can be endorsed, then there will always be a choice and the voucher can always be constitutional, even in a system in which there is not a single private secular school as an alternative to the religious school. And because it is unlikely that any participating private religious school will enroll more pupils than the generally available public system, it will be easy to generate numbers suggesting that aid to religion is not the significant intent or effect of the voucher scheme.

* * *

Confining the relevant choices to spending choices, on the other hand, is not vulnerable to comparable criticism. Although leaving the selection of alternatives for choice wide open, as the majority would, virtually guarantees the availability of a "choice" that will satisfy the criterion, limiting the choices to spending choices will not guarantee a negative result in every case. There may, after all, be cases in which a voucher recipient will have a real choice, with enough secular private school desks in relation to the number of religious ones, and a voucher amount high enough to meet secular private school tuition levels. But, even to the extent that choice-to-spend does tend to limit the number of religious funding options that pass muster, the choice criterion has to be understood this way in order, as I have said, for it to function as a limiting principle. Otherwise there is surely no point in requiring the choice to be a true or real or genuine one.

* * *

III

I do not dissent merely because the majority has misapplied its own law, for even if I assumed *arguendo* that the majority's formal criteria were satisfied on the facts, today's conclusion would be profoundly at odds with the Constitution. Proof of this is clear on two levels. The first is circumstantial, in the now discarded symptom of violation, the substantial dimension of the aid. The second is direct, in the defiance of every objective supposed to be served by the bar against establishment.

A

The scale of the aid to religious schools approved today is unprecedented, both in the number of dollars and in the proportion of systemic school expenditure supported. Each measure has received attention in previous cases.

* * *

On the other hand, the Court has found the gross amount unhelpful for Establishment Clause analysis when the aid afforded a benefit solely to one individual, however substantial as to him, but only an incidental benefit to the religious school at which the individual chose to spend the State's money. When neither the design nor the implementation of an aid scheme channels a series of individual students' subsidies toward religious recipients, the relevant beneficiaries for establishment purposes, the Establishment Clause is unlikely to be implicated. The majority's reliance on the observations of five Members of the Court in *Witters* as to the irrelevance of substantiality of aid in that case, is therefore beside the point in the matter before us, which involves considerable sums of public funds systematically distributed through thousands of students attending religious elementary and middle schools in the city of Cleveland.

* * *

The Cleveland voucher program has cost Ohio taxpayers $33 million since its implementation in 1996 ($28 million in voucher payments, $5 million in administrative costs), and its cost was expected to exceed $8 million in the 2001-2002 school year.

* * *

The gross amounts of public money contributed are symptomatic of the scope of what the taxpayers' money buys for a broad class of religious-school students. In paying for practically the full amount of tuition for thousands of qualifying students, the scholarships purchase everything that tuition purchases, be it instruction in math or indoctrination in faith.

* * *

B

It is virtually superfluous to point out that every objective underlying the prohibition of religious establishment is betrayed by this scheme, but something has to be said about the enormity of the violation. I anticipated these objectives earlier, in discussing *Everson,* which cataloged them, the first being respect for freedom of conscience. Jefferson described it as the idea that no one "shall be compelled to . . . support any religious worship, place, or ministry whatsoever," even a "teacher of his own religious persuasion," and Madison thought it violated by any "'authority which can force a citizen to contribute three pence . . . of his property for the support of any . . . establishment.'"

* * *

As for the second objective, to save religion from its own corruption, Madison wrote of the "'experience . . . that ecclesiastical establishments, instead of maintaining the purity and efficacy of Religion, have had a contrary operation.'" In Madison's time, the manifestations were "pride and indolence in the Clergy; ignorance and servility in the laity[,] in both, superstition, bigotry and persecution," in the 21st century, the risk is one of "corrosive secularism" to religious schools, and the specific threat is to the primacy of the schools' mission to educate the children of the faithful according to the unaltered precepts of their faith. Even "[t]he favored religion may be compromised as political figures reshape the religion's beliefs for their own purposes; it may be reformed as government largesse brings government regulation."

The risk is already being realized. In Ohio, for example, a condition of receiving government money under the program is that participating religious schools may not "discriminate on the basis of . . . religion," which means the school may not give admission preferences to children who are members of the patron faith; children of a parish are generally consigned to the same admission lotteries as non-believers. This indeed was the exact object of a 1999 amendment repealing the portion of a predecessor statute that had allowed an admission preference for "[c]hildren . . . whose parents are affiliated with any organization that provides financial support to the school, at the discretion of the school." Nor is the State's religious antidiscrimination restriction limited to student admission policies: by its terms, a participating religious school may well be forbidden to choose a member of its own clergy to serve as teacher or principal over a layperson of a different religion claiming equal qualification for the job.[23] Indeed, a separate condition that "[t]he school . . . not . . . teach hatred of any person or group on the basis of . . . religion," could be understood (or subsequently broadened) to prohibit religions from teaching traditionally legitimate articles of faith as to the error, sinfulness, or ignorance of others,[24] if they want government money for their schools.

---

[23] And the courts will, of course, be drawn into disputes about whether a religious school's employment practices violated the Ohio statute. In part precisely to avoid this sort of involvement, some Courts of Appeals have held that religious groups enjoy a First Amendment exemption for clergy from state and federal laws prohibiting discrimination on the basis of race or ethnic origin. See, e.g., Rayburn v. General Conference of Seventh-Day Adventists (4th Cir. 1985) ("The application of Title VII to employment decisions of this nature would result in an intolerably close relationship between church and state both on a substantive and procedural level"); EEOC v. Catholic Univ. of America (D.C. Cir. 1996) . . . .

[24] See, e.g., Christian New Testament (2 Corinthians 6:14) (King James Version) ("Be ye not unequally yoked together with unbelievers: for what fellowship hath righteousness with unrighteousness? and what communion hath light with darkness?"); The Book of Mormon (2 Nephi 9:24) ("And if they will not repent and believe in his name, and be baptized in his name, and endure to the end, they must be damned; for the Lord God, the Holy One of Israel, has spoken it"); Pentateuch (Deut. 29:18) (The New Jewish Publication Society Translation) (for one who converts to another faith, "the LORD will never forgive him; rather will the LORD's anger and passion rage against that man, till every sanction recorded in this book comes down upon him, and the LORD blots out his name from under heaven"); The Koran 334 (The Cow Ch. 2:1) (N. Dawood transl. 4th rev. ed. 1974) ("As for the unbelievers, whether you forewarn them or not, they will not have faith. Allah has set a seal upon their hearts and ears; their sight is dimmed and a grievous punishment awaits them").

* * *

When government aid goes up, so does reliance on it; the only thing likely to go down is independence. . . . A day will come when religious schools will learn what political leverage can do, just as Ohio's politicians are now getting a lesson in the leverage exercised by religion.

Increased voucher spending is not, however, the sole portent of growing regulation of religious practice in the school, for state mandates to moderate religious teaching may well be the most obvious response to the third concern behind the ban on establishment, its inextricable link with social conflict. . . .

JUSTICE BREYER has addressed this issue in his own dissenting opinion, which I join, and here it is enough to say that the intensity of the expectable friction can be gauged by realizing that the scramble for money will energize not only contending sectarians, but taxpayers who take their liberty of conscience seriously.

If the divisiveness permitted by today's majority is to be avoided in the short term, it will be avoided only by action of the political branches at the state and national levels. Legislatures not driven to desperation by the problems of public education may be able to see the threat in vouchers negotiable in sectarian schools. Perhaps even cities with problems like Cleveland's will perceive the danger, now that they know a federal court will not save them from it.

My own course as a judge on the Court cannot, however, simply be to hope that the political branches will save us from the consequences of the majority's decision. *Everson*'s statement is still the touchstone of sound law, even though the reality is that in the matter of educational aid the Establishment Clause has largely been read away. True, the majority has not approved vouchers for religious schools alone, or aid earmarked for religious instruction. But no scheme so clumsy will ever get before us, and in the cases that we may see, like these, the Establishment Clause is largely silenced. I do not have the option to leave it silent, and I hope that a future Court will reconsider today's dramatic departure from basic Establishment Clause principle.

JUSTICE BREYER, with whom JUSTICE STEVENS and JUSTICE SOUTER join, dissenting.

I join JUSTICE SOUTER's opinion, and I agree substantially with JUSTICE STEVENS. I write separately, however, to emphasize the risk that publicly financed voucher programs pose in terms of religiously based social conflict. I do so because I believe that the Establishment Clause concern for protecting the Nation's social fabric from religious conflict poses an overriding obstacle to the implementation of this well-intentioned school voucher program.

I

* * *

When it decided these 20th century Establishment Clause cases, the Court did not deny that an earlier American society might have found a less clear-cut church/state separation compatible with social tranquility. Indeed, historians point out that during the early years of the Republic, American schools — including the first public schools — were Protestant in character. Their students recited Protestant prayers, read the King James version of the Bible, and learned Protestant religious ideals. Those practices may have wrongly discriminated against members of minority religions, but given the small number of such individuals, the teaching of Protestant religions in schools did not threaten serious social conflict.

The 20th century Court was fully aware, however, that immigration and growth had changed American society dramatically since its early years. By 1850, 1.6 million Catholics lived in America, and by 1900 that number rose to 12 million. There were similar percentage increases in the Jewish population. Not surprisingly, with this increase in numbers, members of non-Protestant religions, particularly Catholics, began to resist the Protestant domination of the public schools. Scholars report that by the mid-19th century religious conflict over matters such as Bible reading "grew intense," as Catholics resisted and Protestants fought back to preserve their domination. "Dreading Catholic domination," native Protestants "terrorized Catholics." In some States "Catholic students suffered beatings or expulsions for refusing to read from the Protestant Bible, and crowds . . . rioted over whether Catholic children could be released from the classroom during Bible reading."

The 20th century Court was also aware that political efforts to right the wrong of discrimination against religious minorities in primary education had failed; in fact they had exacerbated religious conflict. Catholics sought equal government support for the education of their children in the form of aid for private Catholic schools. But the "Protestant position" on this matter, scholars report, "was that public schools must be 'nonsectarian' (which was usually understood to allow Bible reading and other Protestant observances) and public money must not support 'sectarian' schools (which in practical terms meant Catholic)." . . .

These historical circumstances suggest that the Court, applying the Establishment Clause through the Fourteenth Amendment to 20th century American society, faced an interpretive dilemma that was in part practical. The Court appreciated the religious diversity of contemporary American society. It realized that the status quo favored some religions at the expense of others. And it understood the Establishment Clause to prohibit (among other things) any such favoritism. Yet *how* did the Clause achieve that objective? Did it simply require the government to give each religion an equal chance to introduce religion into the primary schools — a kind of "equal opportunity" approach to the interpretation of the Establishment Clause? Or, did that Clause avoid government favoritism of some religions by insisting upon "separation" — that the government achieve equal treatment by removing itself from the business of providing religious education for children? This interpretive choice arose in respect both to religious activities in public schools and government aid to private education.

In both areas the Court concluded that the Establishment Clause required "separation," in part because an "equal opportunity" approach was not workable. With respect to religious activities in the public schools, how could the Clause require public primary and secondary school teachers, when reading prayers or the Bible, *only* to treat all religions alike? In many places there were too many religions, too diverse a set of religious practices, too many whose spiritual beliefs denied the virtue of formal religious training. This diversity made it difficult, if not impossible, to devise meaningful forms of "equal treatment" by providing an "equal opportunity" for all to introduce their own religious practices into the public schools.

With respect to government aid to private education, did not history show that efforts to obtain equivalent funding for the private education of children whose parents did not hold popular religious beliefs only exacerbated religious strife?
. . .

The upshot is the development of constitutional doctrine that reads the Establishment Clause as avoiding religious strife, *not* by providing every religion with an *equal opportunity* (say, to secure state funding or to pray in the public schools), but by drawing fairly clear lines of *separation* between church and state — at least where the heartland of religious belief, such as primary religious education, is at issue.

II

The principle underlying these cases — avoiding religiously based social conflict — remains of great concern. As religiously diverse as America had become when the Court decided its major 20th century Establishment Clause cases, we are exponentially more diverse today. America boasts more than 55 different religious groups and subgroups with a significant number of members.

* * *

III

I concede that the Establishment Clause currently permits States to channel various forms of assistance to religious schools, for example, transportation costs for students, computers, and secular texts. States now certify the nonsectarian educational content of religious school education. . . .

School voucher programs differ, however, in both *kind* and *degree* from aid programs upheld in the past. They differ in kind because they direct financing to a core function of the church: the teaching of religious truths to young children.

* * *

Vouchers also differ in *degree*. The aid programs recently upheld by the Court involved limited amounts of aid to religion. But the majority's analysis here appears to permit a considerable shift of taxpayer dollars from public secular schools to private religious schools. That fact, combined with the use to which these dollars will be put, exacerbates the conflict problem. State aid that takes the form of peripheral secular items, with prohibitions against diversion of funds to religious teaching, holds significantly less potential for social division. In this respect as well, the secular aid upheld in *Mitchell* differs dramatically from the present case. Although it was conceivable that minor amounts of money could have, contrary to the statute, found their way to the religious activities of the recipients, that case is at worst the camel's nose, while the litigation before us is the camel itself.

IV

I do not believe that the "parental choice" aspect of the voucher program sufficiently offsets the concerns I have mentioned. Parental choice cannot help the taxpayer who does not want to finance the religious education of children. It will not always help the parent who may see little real choice between inadequate nonsectarian public education and adequate education at a school whose religious teachings are contrary to his own. It will not satisfy religious minorities unable to participate because they are too few in number to support the creation of their own private schools. It will not satisfy groups whose religious beliefs preclude them from participating in a government-sponsored program, and who may well feel ignored as government funds primarily support the education of children in the doctrines of the dominant religions. And it does little to ameliorate the entanglement problems or the related problems of social division. Consequently, the fact that the parent may choose which school can cash the government's voucher check does not alleviate the Establishment Clause concerns associated with voucher programs.

V

The Court, in effect, turns the clock back. It adopts, under the name of "neutrality," an interpretation of the Establishment Clause that this Court rejected more than half a century ago. In its view, the parental choice that offers each religious group a kind of equal opportunity to secure government funding overcomes the Establishment Clause concern for social concord. An earlier Court found that "equal opportunity" principle insufficient; it read the Clause as insisting upon greater separation of church and state, at least in respect to primary education. In a society composed of many different religious creeds, I fear that this present departure from the Court's earlier understanding risks creating a form of religiously based conflict potentially harmful to the Nation's social fabric. Because I believe the Establishment Clause was written in part to avoid this kind of conflict, and for reasons set forth by JUSTICE SOUTER and JUSTICE STEVENS, I respectfully dissent.

NOTES AND QUESTIONS

1. *Zelman* has the potential for changing the landscape of American education by its approval of parent-directed vouchers or scholarships. It remains to be seen whether other methods of providing assistance raise different constitutional questions. The Supreme Court indirectly took up this question in *Hibbs v. Winn*, 2004 U.S. LEXIS 4175. *Hibbs* was a federal challenge to an Arizona tax credit for donations to school tuition organizations (STO). State law permitted tax credits up to $625 for joint filers who contributed to an STO. STOs must disburse as scholarship grants at least 90 percent of contributions received, may allow donors to direct scholarships to individual students, may not allow donors to name their own dependents, must designate at least two schools whose students will receive funds, and must not designate schools that "discriminate on the basis of race, color, handicap, familial status or national origin." STOs may designate schools that provide religious instruction or that give admissions preference on the basis of religion or religious affiliation. In essence, the STO gives a taxpayer a choice: to direct tax payments up to the approved amount either to an STO or to the general state treasury.

In a 5-4 opinion by Justice Ginsburg, the Supreme Court refused to block a suit claiming such support violated the Establishment Clause. The suit was sought to be enjoined as contrary to the federal Tax Injunction Act (TIA) which precludes federal court challenges to state tax assessments. The majority reasoned that the TIA applies only in cases where "state taxpayers seek federal-court orders enabling them to avoid paying state taxes." The Court observed further that "the Senate Report commented that the Act had two closely related, state-revenue-protective objectives: (1) to eliminate disparities between taxpayers who could seek injunctive relief in federal court — usually out-of-state corporations asserting diversity jurisdiction — and taxpayers with recourse only to state courts, which generally required taxpayers to pay first and litigate later; and (2) to stop taxpayers, with the aid of a federal injunction, from withholding large sums, thereby disrupting state government finances." These considerations were not implicated in the present matter, said Justice Ginsburg, since the purpose of the suit is a third-party challenge on constitutional grounds which would enlarge, not diminish, state revenues.

The four dissenters lead by Justice Kennedy thought the Court to be disregarding the plain text of the federal statute, and further argued that "the Court shows great skepticism for the state courts' ability to vindicate constitutional wrongs." Thus, this *as applied* challenge to the Arizona credit was permitted to proceed, even as the Arizona Supreme Court had already upheld the *facial* validity of the program. *Kotterman v. Killian*, 193 Ariz. 273 (1999) (en banc) (finding that the tuition tax credit did not prefer one religion over another, or religion over non-religion. Rather, the state high court found it to aid a broad spectrum of citizens by allowing for a wide range of private choices and any perceived state connection to private religious schools was indirect and attenuated).

2. It is now clear that the Establishment Clause does not *require* discrimination in the allocation of public funds for education. *If* a State decides to extend these funds to parents and parents may freely choose among public, private, and religious schools (in the words of Justice O'Connor, exercise "true private choice"), there is neither an impermissible establishment nor endorsement. But what if a state decides not to allow parents to pursue religious educational options? Can it be argued that states not only need not be exclusionary, but also must be inclusionary? Certainly, many would argue that states are entirely free to structure their own educational programs, and given that, are under no obligation to expand educational options beyond the public ones. After all, it is well established that no one can obligate the government to subsidize exercise of constitutional liberty, including religious liberty. However, is it a different question if the reason the government excludes religious participants is animus or bias?

3. Unfortunately, religious discrimination or animus toward 19th century immigrant populations, most notably Catholics and Jews, is the modern day source of many state exclusions of religious schools from the education fund contributed to by all taxpayers. Approximately thirty-seven state constitutions contain provisions commonly known as Blaine Amendments. While the language varies, a reasonably typical formulation forbids "draw[ing money] from the treasury for the benefit of religious societies, or religious or theological seminaries." The term "seminaries" is generally understood to include all religiously affiliated schools. New York's provision reads: "Neither the state nor any subdivision thereof, shall use its property or credit or any public money, or authorize or permit either to be used, *directly or indirectly*, in aid or maintenance, other than for examination or inspection, of any school or institution of learning wholly or in part under the control or direction of any religious denomination, or in which any denominational tenet or doctrine is taught, but the legislature may provide for the transportation of children to and from any school or institution of learning." (Art. 11, Sec. 3, N.Y. Const.; emphasis supplied).

If interpreted literally, provisions like New York's would seemingly prohibit the indirect funding of religious schools, exactly what is permitted under *Zelman*. The notion that the Blaine Amendments may be more restrictive than the Establishment Clause finds support in *Witters v. Washington Department of Services for the Blind*, 112 Wash. 2d 363 (1989), *cert. denied*, 493 U.S. 850 (1989). While the U.S. Supreme Court found no federal Establishment Clause violation for the use of state vocational assistance, as a matter of individual private choice, for religious training, on remand the Washington Supreme Court denied the assistance on state constitutional grounds. The state court rested its holding on the language of the state's Blaine Amendment, which contained language not unlike that of New York noted above. The court concluded that "apply[ing] federal establishment clause analysis . . . would be inappropriate" and also rebuffed Witters' contention that the denial of funding violated the federal Equal Protection Clause. It is not clear that the state court fully grasped the equal protection challenge, but even assuming that it did, the court found a "compelling" interest in maintaining the separation of church and state set forth in the state constitution. Witters petitioned for certiorari, but the United States Supreme Court denied his petition. Would that petition be differently treated in light of *Zelman*? Might such facial religious discrimination now be acknowledged as an equal protection or free exercise violation or considered the censorship of religious thought contrary to First Amendment free speech principles?

4. In a narrowly written, but 7-2, opinion, the Supreme Court rejected the notion that a state was obligated to fund the training of clergy under an otherwise generally available public scholarship program. *Locke v. Davey*, 124 S. Ct. 1307 (2004). Washington had created a scholarship program — the Promise Scholarship — to help academically talented but underprivileged students attend college. Washington excepted devotional theology from qualifying courses of study because its state constitution provides in Article I, section 11 that "No public money or property shall be appropriated for or applied to any religious worship, exercise or instruction, or the support of any religious establishment." To the state this meant that public assistance for tuition to train clergy, even if passed through a private hand through the exercise of private choice, would be a violation of the state constitution.

When Joshua Davey sought to double major in business and devotional theology, he was denied assistance and initially persuaded the Ninth Circuit that this denial was discriminatory and a violation of the *federal* Free Exercise Clause. In an opinion by Chief Justice Rehnquist, the Court reversed. Relying upon the historical exclusion of the public funding for the training of religious clerics and the "play in the joints" between the Establishment and Free Exercise Clauses, Washington was permitted to discriminate in this instance. The Court found that Washington's interest in complying with the terms of its own constitution was substantial and that the burden Davey alleged was minimal since he could study theology more generally (that is, as an academic subject apart from preparation for the ministry) without losing his scholarship. Thus, the Court felt this was not a case akin the imposition of a criminal or civil penalty because of religion or the denial of participation in public assembly because of religious belief, both of which have been held to violate free exercise. Moreover, Davey did not have to choose between his religious belief and the scholarship, since he could receive the state money for use at a wide array of public or religious colleges. Davey simply had to forego "devotional training" with public money. Seeming to write to cabin the holding as much as possible, the Chief Justice opined that "[s]ince the founding of our country, there have been popular uprisings against procuring taxpayer funds to support church leaders, which is one of the hallmarks of an 'established' religion." In this respect, "training someone to lead a congregation is an essentially religious endeavor. Indeed, majoring in devotional theology is akin to a religious calling as well as an academic pursuit."

Justices Scalia and Thomas dissented, criticizing the Court for backing away from earlier precedent where the Court said, that "[a] law burdening religious practice that is not neutral . . . must undergo the most rigorous of scrutiny" and that "the minimum requirement of neutrality is that a law not discriminate on its face." Further, the dissenters argued that "[w]hen the State makes a public benefit generally available, that benefit becomes part of the baseline against which burdens on religion are measured; and when the State withholds that benefit from some individuals solely on the basis of religion, it violates the Free Exercise Clause no less than if it had imposed a special tax." The dissent also questioned the legitimacy of the state's purported interest in the case, asking: "What is the nature of the State's asserted interest here? It can not be protecting the pocketbooks of its citizens; given the tiny fraction of Promise Scholars who would pursue theology degrees . . . . It cannot be preventing mistaken appearance of endorsement [since everyone who qualifies receives the scholarship without regard to course of study]." Rather, Justice Scalia saw the state's interest as "a pure philosophical one: the State's opinion that it would violate taxpayers' freedom of conscience *not* to discrimination against candidates for the ministry."

5. In *Davey,* the Court expressly reserved the question of whether the outcome would be different if the State of Washington had relied on its Blaine Amendment to preclude the scholarship aid. Wrote the Chief Justice in footnote: "Neither Davey nor *amici* have established a credible connection between the Blaine Amendment and Article I, § 11, the relevant constitutional provision," used to deny Joshua Davey assistance for his devotional theology study. "Accordingly," said the Court, "the Blaine Amendment's history [of bigotry] is simply not before us." If the Court does take up a Blaine-inspired case in the future, it may be argued that Blaine Amendment discrimination has dissipated. Passage of time, standing alone, is insufficient to purge the taint of an originally invidious purpose. In *Hunter v. Underwood,* 471 U.S. 222 (1985), the Supreme Court unanimously struck down a provision of the Alabama Constitution that disenfranchised any person convicted of an offense involving moral turpitude. It was not seriously disputed that the provision had been enacted to "establish white supremacy in [Alabama]." The Supreme Court brushed aside Alabama's argument that the provision's original intent was too historically remote to be dispositive because the provision conceivably could serve legitimate, nondiscriminatory state interests:

> Without deciding whether [the provision] would be valid if enacted today without any impermissible motivation, we simply observe that its original enactment was motivated by a desire to discriminate against blacks on account of race and the section continues to this day to have that effect. As such, it violates equal protection . . . .

Hunter thus teaches that the impermissible anti-Catholic motivations that created the Blaine Amendments should not be excused simply because many decades have elapsed since the provisions were enacted.

3. School Prayer

USC law professor Erwin Chemerinsky writes: "[f]ew Supreme Court decisions have been as controversial as those which declared unconstitutional prayers and Bible readings in public schools." ERWIN CHEMERINSKY, CONSTITUTIONAL LAW — PRINCIPLES AND POLICIES 997 (1997). In *Engel v. Vitale*, 370 U.S. 421 (1962), the Court found a non-denominational prayer composed by the New York Board of Regents ("Almighty God, we acknowledge our dependence upon Thee, and we beg Thy blessings upon us, our parents, our teachers and our Country") to violate the Establishment Clause. What would George Washington have thought? In some ways, *Engel* was predictable because it extended the exclusionary foundation laid in *Everson*. Once again, Justice Black argued that the "Establishment Clause, unlike the Free Exercise Clause, does not depend upon any showing of direct governmental compulsion." *Engel*, 370 U.S. at 430. Justice Stewart in dissent maintained the contrary originalist view, with numerous references to prayers by courts, congressmen and presidents, and his argument that the establishment limitation is aimed at faith coerced by law, not the expression of faith generally, whether that expression is by a public or private person.

The year following *Engel*, Black's view would once again prevail in *School District v. Schempp*, 374 U.S. 203 (1963), invalidating a Pennsylvania law that provided that "At least ten verses from the Holy Bible shall be read, without comment, at the opening of each public school on each school day. Any child shall be excused from such Bible reading, or attending such Bible reading, upon the written request of his parent or guardian." *Id*. at 205. Writing for the majority, Justice Clark defined neutrality as a "purpose and a primary effect that neither advances nor inhibits religion." *Id*. at 222. This recital should be familiar. It was to become the second, and most excluding, prong of the Court's establishment standard in *Lemon*. Again Justice Stewart dissented, calling the exclusionary view "doctrinaire" and indicating that it fails to understand the countless ways in which religion and the government interact. *Id*. at 309 (Stewart, J., dissenting). Stewart concluded, "[i]n the absence of coercion upon those who do not wish to participate, . . . such provisions cannot . . . be held to represent the type of support of religion barred by the Establishment Clause." *Id*. at 316 (Stewart, J., dissenting).

Fundamentally, the allowance or disallowance of school prayer raises issues of religious tolerance in a pluralistic society. While popularly it may be thought that any recital of prayer is intolerant of different prayer traditions, Erwin Griswold, a dean of the Harvard Law School and later Solicitor General, had a different perspective:

> When the prayer is recited, if [a] child or his parents feel that he cannot participate, he may stand or sit, in respectful attention, while the other children take part in the ceremony. Or he may leave the room. It is said that this is bad, because it sets him apart from other children. It is

even said that there is an element of compulsion in this . . . . But is this the way it should be looked at? The child of a nonconforming or minority group is, to be sure, different in his beliefs. That is what it means to be a member of a minority. Is it not desirable, and educational, for him to learn and observe this, in the atmosphere of the school — not so much that he is different, as that other children are different from him? And is it not desirable that, at the same time, he experiences and learns the fact that his difference is tolerated and accepted? No compulsion is put upon him. He does not participate. But he, too, has the opportunity to be tolerant. He allows the majority of the group to follow their own tradition, perhaps coming to understand and to respect what they feel is significant to them.

Erwin Griswold, *Absolute Is in the Dark — A Discussion of the Approach of the Supreme Court to Constitutional Questions*, 8 UTAH L. REV. 167, 177 (1963).

In *Wallace v. Jaffree*, 472 U.S. 38 (1985), below, the Court fully disapproves of even the hint of religion in striking down an Alabama law allowing schools to set aside one minute "for meditation or voluntary prayer." *Id.* at 40. Justice Stevens asserts that "the individual freedom of conscience protected by the First Amendment embraces the right to select any religious faith or none at all." *Id.* at 53. Justice Stevens admits that this was not the original meaning of the Constitution, but it is the interpretation that has emerged from the "crucible of litigation." *Id.* at 52. Justice Rehnquist supplies a substantial historical criticism of the Stevens' exclusionary view in his dissent. *Id.* at 91-114 (Rehnquist, J., dissenting).

WALLACE v. JAFFREE
472 U.S. 38 (1985)

JUSTICE STEVENS delivered the opinion of the Court.

At an early stage of this litigation, the constitutionality of three Alabama statutes was questioned: (1) § 16-1-20, enacted in 1978, which authorized a 1-minute period of silence in all public schools "for meditation"; (2) § 16-1-20.1, enacted in 1981, which authorized a period of silence "for meditation or voluntary prayer"; and (3) § 16-1-20.2, enacted in 1982, which authorized teachers to lead "willing students" in a prescribed prayer to "Almighty God . . . the Creator and Supreme Judge of the world."

At the preliminary-injunction stage of this case, the District Court distinguished § 16-1-20 from the other two statutes. It then held that there was "nothing wrong" with § 16-1-20 . . . .

The Court of Appeals agreed with the District Court's initial interpretation of the purpose of both § 16-1-20.1 and § 16-1-20.2, and held them both unconstitutional. We have already affirmed the Court of Appeals' holding with respect to § 16-1-20.2. Moreover, appellees have not questioned the holding that § 16-

1-20 is valid. Thus, the narrow question for decision is whether § 16-1-20.1, which authorizes a period of silence for "meditation or voluntary prayer," is a law respecting the establishment of religion within the meaning of the First Amendment.

I

* * *

. . . With respect to § 16-1-20.1 [meditation or voluntary prayer] and § 16-1-20.2, [which permitted teachers to lead willing students in the prescribed prayer to "Almighty God . . . the Creator and Supreme Judge of the World,"] the Court of Appeals stated that "both statutes advance and encourage religious activities."

* * *

II

Our unanimous affirmance of the Court of Appeals' judgment concerning § 16-1-20.2 makes it unnecessary to comment at length on the District Court's remarkable conclusion that the Federal Constitution imposes no obstacle to Alabama's establishment of a state religion. Before analyzing the precise issue that is presented to us, it is nevertheless appropriate to recall how firmly embedded in our constitutional jurisprudence is the proposition that the several States have no greater power to restrain the individual freedoms protected by the First Amendment than does the Congress of the United States.

As is plain from its text, the First Amendment was adopted to curtail the power of Congress to interfere with the individual's freedom to believe, to worship, and to express himself in accordance with the dictates of his own conscience. Until the Fourteenth Amendment was added to the Constitution, the First Amendment's restraints on the exercise of federal power simply did not apply to the States. But when the Constitution was amended to prohibit any State from depriving any person of liberty without due process of law, that Amendment imposed the same substantive limitations on the States' power to legislate that the First Amendment had always imposed on the Congress' power. This Court has confirmed and endorsed this elementary proposition of law time and time again.

* * *

. . . At one time it was thought that [the Establishment Clause] merely proscribed the preference of one Christian sect over another, but would not require equal respect for the conscience of the infidel, the atheist, or the adherent of a non-Christian faith such as Islam or Judaism. But when the underlying principle has been examined in the crucible of litigation, the Court has unambiguously concluded that the individual freedom of conscience protected by the First Amendment embraces the right to select any religious faith or none at all. This conclusion derives support not only from the interest in respecting the individual's freedom of conscience, but also from the conviction that religious beliefs worthy of respect are the product of free and voluntary choice by the faithful*. . . .

* * *

IV

* * *

The legislative intent to return prayer to the public schools is, of course, quite different from merely protecting every student's right to engage in voluntary prayer during an appropriate moment of silence during the schoolday. The 1978 statute already protected that right, containing nothing that prevented any student from engaging in voluntary prayer during a silent minute of meditation. Appellants have not identified any secular purpose that was not fully served by § 16-1-20 before the enactment of § 16-1-20.1. Thus, only two conclusions are consistent with the text of § 16-1-20.1: (1) the statute was enacted to convey a message of state endorsement and promotion of prayer; or (2) the statute was enacted for no purpose. No one suggests that the statute was nothing but a meaningless or irrational act.

. . . The legislature enacted § 16-1-20.1, despite the existence of § 16-1-20 for the sole purpose of expressing the State's endorsement of prayer activities for one minute at the beginning of each schoolday. The addition of "or voluntary prayer" indicates that the State intended to characterize prayer as a favored practice. Such an endorsement is not consistent with the established principle that the government must pursue a course of complete neutrality toward religion.

* * *

The judgment of the Court of Appeals is affirmed.

It is so ordered.

JUSTICE POWELL, concurring. [Omitted.]

JUSTICE O'CONNOR, concurring in the judgment. [Omitted.]

CHIEF JUSTICE BURGER, dissenting.

Some who trouble to read the opinions in these cases will find it ironic — perhaps even bizarre — that on the very day we heard arguments in the cases, the Court's session opened with an invocation for Divine protection. . . .

* * *

---

* [Justice Stevens overlooks a possibility. As salutary, and wise, as individual choice in matters of conscience may be, might it not be possible to see the framers as *both* allowing individuals the right to select any religious faith or none at all *and* simultaneously endorsing, as a matter of governing philosophy in the Declaration and myriad other legislative actions, the importance of religion for civic virtue? — Eds.]

. . . [A]ll of the opinions fail to mention that the sponsor also testified that one of his purposes in drafting and sponsoring the moment-of-silence bill was to clear up a widespread misunderstanding that a schoolchild is legally *prohibited* from engaging in silent, individual prayer once he steps inside a public school building. . . .

* * *

The several preceding opinions conclude that the principal difference between § 16-1-20.1 and its predecessor statute proves that the sole purpose behind the inclusion of the phrase "or voluntary prayer" in § 16-1-20.1 was to endorse and promote prayer. This reasoning is simply a subtle way of focusing exclusively on the religious component of the statute rather than examining the statute as a whole. Such logic — if it can be called that — would lead the Court to hold, for example, that a state may enact a statute that provides reimbursement for bus transportation to the parents of all schoolchildren, but may not *add* parents of parochial school students to an existing program providing reimbursement for parents of public school students. Congress amended the statutory Pledge of Allegiance 31 years ago to add the words "under God." Do the several opinions in support of the judgment today render the Pledge unconstitutional? That would be the consequence of their method of focusing on the difference between § 16-1-20.1 and its predecessor statute rather than examining § 16-1-20.1 as a whole. Any such holding would of course make a mockery of our decisionmaking in Establishment Clause cases. . . .

* * *

(d) The notion that the Alabama statute is a step toward creating an established church borders on, if it does not trespass into, the ridiculous. The statute does not remotely threaten religious liberty; it affirmatively furthers the values of religious freedom and tolerance that the Establishment Clause was designed to protect. Without pressuring those who do not wish to pray, the statute simply creates an opportunity to think, to plan, or to pray if one wishes — as Congress does by providing chaplains and chapels. It accommodates the purely private, voluntary religious choices of the individual pupils who wish to pray while at the same time creating a time for nonreligious reflection for those who do not choose to pray. . . .

* * *

The mountains have labored and brought forth a mouse.[6]

JUSTICE WHITE, dissenting.

. . . As I read the filed opinions, a majority of the Court would approve statutes that provided for a moment of silence but did not mention prayer. But if a student asked whether he could pray during that moment, it is difficult to believe

---

6 Horace, Epistles, bk. III (Ars Poetica), line 139.

that the teacher could not answer in the affirmative. If that is the case, I would not invalidate a statute that at the outset provided the legislative answer to the question "May I pray?" This is so even if the Alabama statute is infirm, which I do not believe it is, because of its peculiar legislative history.

I appreciate JUSTICE REHNQUIST's explication of the history of the Religion Clauses of the First Amendment. Against that history, it would be quite understandable if we undertook to reassess our cases dealing with these Clauses, particularly those dealing with the Establishment Clause. Of course, I have been out of step with many of the Court's decisions dealing with this subject matter, and it is thus not surprising that I would support a basic reconsideration of our precedents.

JUSTICE REHNQUIST, dissenting.

Thirty-eight years ago this Court, in *Everson v. Board of Education* (1947), summarized its exegesis of Establishment Clause doctrine thus:

> "In the words of Jefferson, the clause against establishment of religion by law was intended to erect 'a wall of separation between church and State.' *Reynolds v. United States* [(1879)]."

This language from *Reynolds*, a case involving the Free Exercise Clause of the First Amendment rather than the Establishment Clause, quoted from Thomas Jefferson's letter to the Danbury Baptist Association the phrase "I contemplate with sovereign reverence that act of the whole American people which declared that their legislature should 'make no law respecting an establishment of religion, or prohibiting the free exercise thereof,' thus building a wall of separation between church and State." 8 WRITINGS OF THOMAS JEFFERSON 113 (H. Washington ed., 1861).

It is impossible to build sound constitutional doctrine upon a mistaken understanding of constitutional history, but unfortunately the Establishment Clause has been expressly freighted with Jefferson's misleading metaphor for nearly 40 years. Thomas Jefferson was of course in France at the time the constitutional Amendments known as the Bill of Rights were passed by Congress and ratified by the States. His letter to the Danbury Baptist Association was a short note of courtesy, written 14 years after the Amendments were passed by Congress. He would seem to any detached observer as a less than ideal source of contemporary history as to the meaning of the Religion Clauses of the First Amendment.

Jefferson's fellow Virginian, James Madison, with whom he was joined in the battle for the enactment of the Virginia Statute of Religious Liberty of 1786, did play as large a part as anyone in the drafting of the Bill of Rights. He had two advantages over Jefferson in this regard: he was present in the United States, and he was a leading Member of the First Congress. But when we turn to the record of the proceedings in the First Congress leading up to the adoption of the Establishment Clause of the Constitution, including Madison's significant contributions thereto, we see a far different picture of its purpose than the highly simplified "wall of separation between church and State."

During the debates in the Thirteen Colonies over ratification of the Constitution, one of the arguments frequently used by opponents of ratification was that without a Bill of Rights guaranteeing individual liberty the new general Government carried with it a potential for tyranny. The typical response to this argument on the part of those who favored ratification was that the general Government established by the Constitution had only delegated powers, and that these delegated powers were so limited that the Government would have no occasion to violate individual liberties. This response satisfied some, but not others, and of the 11 Colonies which ratified the Constitution by early 1789, 5 proposed one or another amendments guaranteeing individual liberty. Three — New Hampshire, New York, and Virginia — included in one form or another a declaration of religious freedom. Rhode Island and North Carolina flatly refused to ratify the Constitution in the absence of amendments in the nature of a Bill of Rights. Virginia and North Carolina proposed identical guarantees of religious freedom:

> "[A]ll men have an equal, natural and unalienable right to the free exercise of religion, according to the dictates of conscience, and . . . no particular religious sect or society ought to be favored or established, by law, in preference to others."

On June 8, 1789, James Madison rose in the House of Representatives and "reminded the House that this was the day that he had heretofore named for bringing forward amendments to the Constitution." 1 ANNALS OF CONG. 424 (Joseph Gales ed., 1789). Madison's subsequent remarks in urging the House to adopt his drafts of the proposed amendments were less those of a dedicated advocate of the wisdom of such measures than those of a prudent statesman seeking the enactment of measures sought by a number of his fellow citizens which could surely do no harm and might do a great deal of good. . . .

The language Madison proposed for what ultimately became the Religion Clauses of the First Amendment was this:

> "The civil rights of none shall be abridged on account of religious belief or worship, nor shall any national religion be established, nor shall the full and equal rights of conscience be in any manner, or on any pretext, infringed."

[Justice Rehnquist then reviewed the debate in Congress and various amendments to Madison's initial proposal, reprinted above at Part I.B.3, which ultimately produced the language of the Religion Clauses of the First Amendment:]

> "Congress shall make no law respecting an establishment of religion, or prohibiting the free exercise thereof."

The House and the Senate both accepted this language on successive days, and the Amendment was proposed in this form.

On the basis of the record of these proceedings in the House of Representatives, James Madison was undoubtedly the most important architect among the Members of the House of the Amendments which became the Bill of Rights . . . . His original language "nor shall any national religion be established" obviously does not conform to the "wall of separation" between church and State idea which latter-day commentators have ascribed to him. His explanation on the floor of the meaning of his language — "that Congress should not establish a religion, and enforce the legal observation of it by law" is of the same ilk. When he replied to Huntington in the debate over the proposal which came from the Select Committee of the House, he urged that the language "no religion shall be established by law" should be amended by inserting the word "national" in front of the word "religion."

It seems indisputable from these glimpses of Madison's thinking, as reflected by actions on the floor of the House in 1789, that he saw the Amendment as designed to prohibit the establishment of a national religion, and perhaps to prevent discrimination among sects. He did not see it as requiring neutrality on the part of government between religion and irreligion. Thus the Court's opinion in *Everson* — while correct in bracketing Madison and Jefferson together in their exertions in their home State leading to the enactment of the Virginia Statute of Religious Liberty — is totally incorrect in suggesting that Madison carried these views onto the floor of the United States House of Representatives when he proposed the language which would ultimately become the Bill of Rights.

The repetition of this error in the Court's opinion in *Illinois ex rel. McCollum v. Board of Education* (1948), and, *inter alia*, *Engel v. Vitale* (1962), does not make it any sounder historically. Finally, in *Abington School District v. Schempp* (1963), the Court made the truly remarkable statement that "the views of Madison and Jefferson, preceded by Roger Williams, came to be incorporated not only in the Federal Constitution but likewise in those of most of our States" (footnote omitted). On the basis of what evidence we have, this statement is demonstrably incorrect as a matter of history. And its repetition in varying forms in succeeding opinions of the Court can give it no more authority than it possesses as a matter of fact; *stare decisis* may bind courts as to matters of law, but it cannot bind them as to matters of history.

None of the other Members of Congress who spoke during the August 15th debate expressed the slightest indication that they thought the language before them from the Select Committee, or the evil to be aimed at, would require that the Government be absolutely neutral as between religion and irreligion. The evil to be aimed at, so far as those who spoke were concerned, appears to have been the establishment of a national church, and perhaps the preference of one religious sect over another; but it was definitely not concerned about whether the Government might aid all religions evenhandedly. If one were to follow the advice of JUSTICE BRENNAN, concurring in *Abington School District v. Schempp*, and construe the Amendment in the light of what particular "practices . . . challenged threaten those consequences which the Framers deeply feared; whether, in short, they tend to promote that type of interdependence between religion and state which the First Amendment was designed to prevent," one would have to say that the First Amendment Establishment Clause should be read no more broadly than to prevent the establishment of a national religion or the governmental preference of one religious sect over another.

The actions of the First Congress, which reenacted the Northwest Ordinance for the governance of the Northwest Territory in 1789, confirm the view that Congress did not mean that the Government should be neutral between religion and irreligion. The House of Representatives took up the Northwest Ordinance on the same day as Madison introduced his proposed amendments which became the Bill of Rights; while at that time the Federal Government was of course not bound by draft amendments to the Constitution which had not yet been proposed by Congress, to say nothing of ratified by the States, it seems highly unlikely that the House of Representatives would simultaneously consider proposed amendments to the Constitution and enact an important piece of territorial legislation which conflicted with the intent of those proposals. The Northwest Ordinance, 1 Stat. 50 (1789), reenacted the Northwest Ordinance of 1787 and provided that "[r]eligion, morality, and knowledge, being necessary to good government and the happiness of mankind, schools and the means of education shall forever be encouraged." Land grants for schools in the Northwest Territory were not limited to public schools. It was not until 1845 that Congress limited land grants in the new States and Territories to nonsectarian schools.

* * *

As the United States moved from the 18th into the 19th century, Congress appropriated time and again public moneys in support of sectarian Indian education carried on by religious organizations. Typical of these was Jefferson's treaty with the Kaskaskia Indians, which provided annual cash support for the Tribe's Roman Catholic priest and church. It was not until 1897, when aid to sectarian education for Indians had reached $500,000 annually, that Congress decided thereafter to cease appropriating money for education in sectarian schools. This history shows the fallacy of the notion found in *Everson* that "no tax in any amount" may be levied for religious activities in any form.

Joseph Story, a Member of this Court from 1811 to 1845, and during much of that time a professor at the Harvard Law School, published by far the most comprehensive treatise on the United States Constitution that had then appeared. Volume 2 of Story's Commentaries on the Constitution of the United States 630-632 (5th ed. 1891) discussed the meaning of the Establishment Clause of the First Amendment this way:

> "Probably at the time of the adoption of the Constitution, and of the amendment to it now under consideration [First Amendment], the general if not the universal sentiment in America was, that Christianity ought to receive encouragement from the State so far as was not incompatible with the private rights of conscience and the freedom of religious

worship. An attempt to level all religions, and to make it a matter of state policy to hold all in utter indifference, would have created universal disapprobation, if not universal indignation."

* * *

Thomas Cooley's eminence as a legal authority rivaled that of Story. Cooley stated in his treatise entitled CONSTITUTIONAL LIMITATIONS that aid to a particular religious sect was prohibited by the United States Constitution, but he went on to say:

"But while thus careful to establish, protect, and defend religious freedom and equality, the American constitutions contain no provisions which prohibit the authorities from such solemn recognition of a superintending Providence in public transactions and exercises as the general religious sentiment of mankind inspires, and as seems meet and proper in finite and dependent beings. Whatever may be the shades of religious belief, all must acknowledge the fitness of recognizing in important human affairs the superintending care and control of the Great Governor of the Universe, and of acknowledging with thanksgiving his boundless favors, or bowing in contrition when visited with the penalties of his broken laws. No principle of constitutional law is violated when thanksgiving or fast days are appointed; when chaplains are designated for the army and navy; when legislative sessions are opened with prayer or the reading of the Scriptures; or when religious teaching is encouraged by a general exemption of the houses of religious worship from taxation for the support of State government. Undoubtedly the spirit of the Constitution will require, in all these cases, that care be taken to avoid discrimination in favor of or against any one religious denomination or sect; but the power to do any of these things does not become unconstitutional simply because of its susceptibility to abuse. . . ."

Cooley added that

"[t]his public recognition of religious worship, however, is not based entirely, perhaps not even mainly, upon a sense of what is due to the Supreme Being himself as the author of all good and of all law; but the same reasons of state policy which induce the government to aid institutions of charity and seminaries of instruction will incline it also to foster religious worship and religious institutions, as conservators of the public morals and valuable, if not indispensable, assistants to the preservation of the public order."

It would seem from this evidence that the Establishment Clause of the First Amendment had acquired a well-accepted meaning: it forbade establishment of a national religion, and forbade preference among religious sects or denominations. Indeed, the first American dictionary defined the word "establishment" as "the act of establishing, founding, ratifying or ordaining," such as in "[t]he episcopal form of religion, so called, in England." The Establishment Clause did not require government neutrality between religion and irreligion nor did it prohibit the Federal Government from providing nondiscriminatory aid to religion. There is simply no historical foundation for the proposition that the Framers intended to build the "wall of separation" that was constitutionalized in *Everson*.

Notwithstanding the absence of a historical basis for this theory of rigid separation, the wall idea might well have served as a useful albeit misguided analytical concept, had it led this Court to unified and principled results in Establishment Clause cases. The opposite, unfortunately, has been true; in the 38 years since *Everson* our Establishment Clause cases have been neither principled nor unified. Our recent opinions, many of them hopelessly divided pluralities, have with embarrassing candor conceded that the "wall of separation" is merely a "blurred, indistinct, and variable barrier," which "is not wholly accurate" and can only be "dimly perceived."

Whether due to its lack of historical support or its practical unworkability, the *Everson* "wall" has proved all but useless as a guide to sound constitutional adjudication. It illustrates only too well the wisdom of Benjamin Cardozo's observation that "[m]etaphors in law are to be narrowly watched, for starting as devices to liberate thought, they end often by enslaving it."

But the greatest injury of the "wall" notion is its mischievous diversion of judges from the actual intentions of the drafters of the Bill of Rights. The "crucible of litigation," is well adapted to adjudicating factual disputes on the basis of testimony presented in court, but no amount of repetition of historical errors in judicial opinions can make the errors true. The "wall of separation between church and State" is a metaphor based on bad history, a metaphor which has proved useless as a guide to judging. It should be frankly and explicitly abandoned.

The Court has more recently attempted to add some mortar to *Everson*'s wall through the three-part test of *Lemon v. Kurtzman*, which served at first to offer a more useful test for purposes of the Establishment Clause than did the "wall" metaphor. Generally stated, the *Lemon* test proscribes state action that has a sectarian purpose or effect, or causes an impermissible governmental entanglement with religion.

Lemon cited *Board of Education v. Allen* (1968), as the source of the "purpose" and "effect" prongs of the three-part test. The *Allen* opinion explains, however, how it inherited the purpose and effect elements from *Schempp* and *Everson*, both of which contain the historical errors described above. Thus the purpose and effect prongs have the same historical deficiencies as the wall concept itself: they are in no way based on either the language or intent of the drafters.

The secular purpose prong has proven mercurial in application because it has never been fully defined, and we have never fully stated how the test is to operate. If the purpose prong is intended to void those aids to sectarian institutions accompanied by a stated legislative purpose to aid religion, the prong will condemn nothing so long as the legislature utters a secular purpose and says nothing about aiding religion. Thus the constitutionality of a statute may depend upon what the legislators put into the legislative history and, more importantly, what they leave out. The purpose prong means little if it only requires the legislature to express any secular purpose and omit all sectarian references, because legislators might do just that. Faced with a valid legislative secular purpose, we could not properly ignore that purpose without a factual basis for doing so.

However, if the purpose prong is aimed to void all statutes enacted with the intent to aid sectarian institutions, whether stated or not, then most statutes providing any aid, such as textbooks or bus rides for sectarian school children, will fail because one of the purposes behind every statute, whether stated or not, is to aid the target of its largesse. In other words, if the purpose prong requires an absence of *any* intent to aid sectarian institutions, whether or not expressed, few state laws in this area could pass the test, and we would be required to void some state aids to religion which we have already upheld.

The entanglement prong of the *Lemon* test came from *Walz v. Tax Comm'n* (1970). *Walz* involved a constitutional challenge to New York's time-honored practice of providing state property tax exemptions to church property used in worship. The *Walz* opinion refused to "undermine the ultimate constitutional objective [of the Establishment Clause] as illuminated by history," and upheld the tax exemption. The Court examined the historical relationship between the State and church when church property was in issue, and determined that the challenged tax exemption did not so entangle New York with the church as to cause an intrusion or interference with religion. Interferences with religion should arguably be dealt with under the Free Exercise Clause, but the entanglement inquiry in *Walz* was consistent with that case's broad survey of the relationship between state taxation and religious property.

We have not always followed *Walz*'s reflective inquiry into entanglement, however. One of the difficulties with the entanglement prong is that, when divorced from the logic of *Walz*, it creates an "insoluable paradox" in school aid cases: we have required aid to parochial schools to be closely watched lest it be put to sectarian use, yet this close supervision itself will create an entanglement. For example, in *Wolman* [*v. Walter* (1977)], the Court in part struck the State's nondiscriminatory provision of buses for parochial school field trips, because the state supervision of sectarian officials in charge of field trips would be too onerous. This type of self-defeating result is certainly not required to ensure that States do not establish religions.

The entanglement test as applied in cases like *Wolman* also ignores the myriad state administrative regulations properly placed upon sectarian institutions such as curriculum, attendance, and certification requirements for sectarian schools, or fire and safety regulations for churches. Avoiding entanglement between church and State may be an important consideration in a case like *Walz*, but if the entanglement prong were applied to all state and church relations in the automatic manner in which it has been applied to school aid cases, the State could hardly require anything of church-related institutions as a condition for receipt of financial assistance.

These difficulties arise because the *Lemon* test has no more grounding in the history of the First Amendment than does the wall theory upon which it rests. The three-part test represents a determined effort to craft a workable rule from a historically faulty doctrine; but the rule can only be as sound as the doctrine it attempts to service. The three-part test has simply not provided adequate standards for deciding Establishment Clause cases, as this Court has slowly come to realize. Even worse, the *Lemon* test has caused this Court to fracture into unworkable plurality opinions, depending upon how each of the three factors applies to a certain state action. The results from our school services cases show the difficulty we have encountered in making the *Lemon* test yield principled results.

For example, a State may lend to parochial school children geography textbooks[7] that contain maps of the United States, but the State may not lend maps of the United States for use in geography class.[8] A State may lend textbooks on American colonial history, but it may not lend a film on George Washington, or a film projector to show it in history class. A State may lend classroom workbooks, but may not lend workbooks in which the parochial school children write, thus rendering them nonreusable.[9] A State may pay for bus transportation to religious schools[10] but may not pay for bus transportation from the parochial school to the public zoo or natural history museum for a field trip.[11] A State may pay for diagnostic services conducted in the parochial school but therapeutic services must be given in a different building; speech and hearing "services" conducted by the State inside the sectarian school are forbidden, *Meek v. Pittenger* (1975), but the State may conduct speech and hearing diagnostic testing inside the sectarian school. *Wolman*. Exceptional parochial school students may receive counseling, but it must take place outside of the parochial school,[12] such as in a trailer parked down the street. A State may give cash to a parochial school to pay for the administration of state-written tests and state-ordered reporting services,[13] but it may not provide funds for teacher-prepared tests on secular subjects.[14] Religious instruction may not be given in public school,[15] but the public school may release students during the day for religion classes elsewhere, and may enforce attendance at those classes with its truancy laws.[16]

---

[7] *Board of Education v. Allen* (1968).

[8] *Meek* [*v. Pittenger* (1975)]. A science book is permissible, a science kit is not.

[9] *See Meek, supra.*

[10] *Everson v. Board of Education* (1947).

[11] *Wolman, supra*

[12] *Wolman, supra; Meek, supra.*

[13] [*Comm. For Pub. Educ. and Religious Liberty v.*] *Regan* [(1980)].

[14] *Levitt* [*v. Comm. For Pub. Educ. and Religious Liberty* (1973)].

[15] *Illinois ex rel. McCollum v. Board of Education* (1948).

[16] *Zorach v. Clauson* (1952).

These results violate the historically sound principle "that the Establishment Clause does not forbid governments . . . to [provide] general welfare under which benefits are distributed to private individuals, even though many of those individuals may elect to use those benefits in ways that 'aid' religious instruction or worship." It is not surprising in the light of this record that our most recent opinions have expressed doubt on the usefulness of the *Lemon* test.

Although the test initially provided helpful assistance, we soon began describing the test as only a "guideline" . . . . We have noted that the *Lemon* test is "not easily applied," and . . . under the *Lemon* test we have "sacrifice[d] clarity and predictability for flexibility." In *Lynch* [*v. Donnelly* (1984),] we reiterated that the *Lemon* test has never been binding on the Court, and we cited two cases where we had declined to apply it.

If a constitutional theory has no basis in the history of the amendment it seeks to interpret, is difficult to apply and yields unprincipled results, I see little use in it. The "crucible of litigation," has produced only consistent unpredictability, and today's effort is just a continuation of "the sisyphean task of trying to patch together the 'blurred, indistinct and variable barrier' described in *Lemon v. Kurtzman*." We have done much straining since 1947, but still we admit that we can only "dimly perceive" the *Everson* wall. Our perception has been clouded not by the Constitution but by the mists of an unnecessary metaphor.

The true meaning of the Establishment Clause can only be seen in its history. As drafters of our Bill of Rights, the Framers inscribed the principles that control today. Any deviation from their intentions frustrates the permanence of that Charter and will only lead to the type of unprincipled decisionmaking that has plagued our Establishment Clause cases since *Everson*.

The Framers intended the Establishment Clause to prohibit the designation of any church as a "national" one. The Clause was also designed to stop the Federal Government from asserting a preference for one religious denomination or sect over others. Given the "incorporation" of the Establishment Clause as against the States via the Fourteenth Amendment in *Everson*, States are prohibited as well from establishing a religion or discriminating between sects. As its history abundantly shows, however, nothing in the Establishment Clause requires government to be strictly neutral between religion and irreligion, nor does that Clause prohibit Congress or the States from pursuing legitimate secular ends through nondiscriminatory sectarian means.

The Court strikes down the Alabama statute because the State wished to "characterize prayer as a favored practice." It would come as much of a shock to those who drafted the Bill of Rights as it will to a large number of thoughtful Americans today to learn that the Constitution, as construed by the majority, prohibits the Alabama Legislature from "endorsing" prayer. George Washington himself, at the request of the very Congress which passed the Bill of Rights, proclaimed a day of "public thanksgiving and prayer, to be observed by acknowledging with grateful hearts the many and signal favors of Almighty God." History must judge whether it was the Father of his Country in 1789, or a majority of the Court today, which has strayed from the meaning of the Establishment Clause.

The State surely has a secular interest in regulating the manner in which public schools are conducted. Nothing in the Establishment Clause of the First Amendment, properly understood, prohibits any such generalized "endorsement" of prayer. I would therefore reverse the judgment of the Court of Appeals.

NOTES AND QUESTIONS

1. Is the Rehnquist view in *Wallace* non-preferentialist? Non-preferentialism is the view that the Establishment Clause prohibits discrimination among religious sects, but that nothing requires government to be strictly neutral between religion and irreligion. Non-preferentialism received its most recent exposition in Justice Thomas' concurrence in *Rosenberger v. Rector*, considered earlier as part of the equal protection idea. However, as seen above, this ground was first broken by then-Justice Rehnquist in *Wallace v. Jaffree*. Both Justice Rehnquist and later Justice Thomas argue that Madison and the Framers intended the Establishment Clause to prohibit a national religion as well as discrimination among denominations. They rely especially upon Madison's *Memorial and Remonstrance Against Religious Assessments*, in which Madison criticized a Virginia plan to assess a tax in order to "support . . . clergy in the performance of their function of teaching religion." *Rosenberger*, 515 U.S. at 853 (Thomas, J., concurring).

2. In response to litigation challenging the constitutionality of the practice at the public high school in Santa Fe, Texas, allowing the "student council chaplain" to deliver a prayer over the public address system before each varsity football game, the Santa Fe Independent School District adopted a series of policies by which it was left entirely to the students to decide, first, if there should be a "message, statement, or invocation" prior to football games and, if so, who should deliver it. The student body dutifully voted In *Santa Fe Independent Sch. Dist. v. Doe*, 530 U.S. 290 (2000), Justice Stevens, writing for the Court, invalidated the policy. Rejecting the school's contention that the pre-game invocation was private speech rather than government prayer because of the election mechanism, Justice Stevens found that the facially neutral majority-rule policy afforded no access to the pre-game invocation slot for minority views, and that the school had not sufficiently distanced itself from the student-led prayer. How well does Justice Stevens reconcile the competing constitutional considerations — preventing government or public schools from coercing religious belief while ensuring that the free speech interests of students, which might voluntarily include prayer, not be censored? In dissent, Chief Justice Rehnquist, joined by Justices Scalia and Thomas, found the tone of Justice Stevens' majority opinion "disturbing" because "it bristles with hostility to all things religious in public life." *Id.* at 318. "Neither the holding nor the tone of the opinion is faithful to the meaning of the Establishment Clause," the Chief Justice continued, "when it is recalled that George Washington himself, at the request of the very Congress which passed the Bill of Rights, proclaimed a day of 'public thanksgiving and prayer, to be observed by acknowledging with grateful hearts the many and signal favors of Almighty God.'" *Id.* (quoting Presidential Proclamation, 1 MESSAGES AND PAPERS OF THE PRESIDENTS, 1789-1897, p. 64 (J. Richardson ed. 1897)).

3. Does the case give adequate guidance to school officials? Before this case, several lower courts had suggested to school principals seeking to navigate the equally important duties of avoiding religious preference and religious censorship that they could successfully do so by letting the students decide by vote. *See, e.g., Jones v. Clear Creek Independent School District*, 977 F.2d 963 (5th Cir. 1992). Is this still possible? According to the *Santa Fe* majority, granting the student body the power to elect a speaker that may choose to pray, "regardless of the students' ultimate use of it, is not acceptable." The reason elections are off-limits is ascribed by the Court to a supposed free speech duty of the government to remain viewpoint neutral. The government, indeed, has this duty, but doesn't it turns matters on its head to say that the government has a duty to insure that private individuals remain viewpoint neutral? The majority does state that it is not its intent to invalidate all student elections. Rather, it says, it is forbidden where a religious message is attributable to the school, not just the student. Because that happened in *Santa Fe* only because of the school's pre-policy behavior, the Court may be less inclined to censor private religious speech in a context where school officials were more circumspect.

4. Is resolving the scope of school prayer important? In a dissent to a lower court decision pre-dating *Santa Fe*, Judge Edith Jones of the Fifth Circuit explains why she thinks it is.

IV. *Why This Case Matters*

. . . The panel's decision [in *Ingebretsen v. Jackson Public School District*, 88 F. 3d 274 (5th Cir. 1996),] is the latest in a long line of cases whose inevitable consequence has been to remake society in a secular image. Two examples suffice: courts have held that the mere existence of a Good Friday holiday "establishes" the Christian religion, and the venerable inscription on a courthouse "The World Needs God" likewise constitutionally offends . . . someone. Only by recognizing the absurdity of holding otherwise have courts allowed us still to pledge that we are "one nation under God, indivisible" and to maintain "In God We Trust" on the currency. When our cultural heritage and tradition, indeed the three-millennial history of the Western world threatens to be erased by three decades of federal court pronouncements, something is amiss. As Prof. Stephen Carter arrestingly concluded, our elite cultural institutions, including federal courts, have imposed on us an historically unprecedented "culture of disbelief."[15]

The elites' tin ear for religious belief and practice has been particularly evident in cases regarding the public schools. Federal courts often seem unable to draw fundamental distinctions between school-sponsored religious "establishment" and benign teaching about religion or, in this case, students' constitutionally protected free exercise of speech and religion. School officials, averse to the emotional and financial costs of litigation, have systematically excised religious references from school curricula and activities in response to the caselaw. This widespread Establishment Clause misconstruction occurs notwithstanding that Supreme Court justices have repeatedly acknowledged the importance of teaching about religion in public schools and that no Supreme Court authority limits students' nondisruptive religious self-expression. Not to belabor the point, I note that Congress passed and the Supreme Court upheld the Equal Access Act, a law guaranteeing students' rights to meet in religious clubs on school property, in order to overturn lower federal court decisions to the contrary. Only last summer, President Clinton spoke of the problem of hostility to religion in public schools and instructed the Departments of Justice and Education to formulate guidelines for the protection of public schools students' religious speech and conduct.[19] Every time a federal court writes an unduly broad Establishment Clause decision concerning public schools, we encourage further misunderstandings, to the detriment of students' constitutional rights and the goal of teaching about religion in public schools.

The courts' broad decisions in this area are not only in my view, uncompelled by precedent, they are also extraordinarily shortsighted. Decisions fostering rigidly secular public education strip school officials of moral tools that lie at the heart of the educational process. As the Reverend Martin Luther King explained:

> "The function of education, therefore, is to teach one to think intensively and to think critically. But education which stops with efficiency may prove the greatest menace to society. The most dangerous criminal may be the man gifted with reason but with no morals.

---

15 STEPHEN L. CARTER, THE CULTURE OF DISBELIEF: HOW AMERICAN LAW AND POLITICS TRIVIALIZE RELIGIOUS DEVOTION (1993).

19 See President's Directive to the Education Dept., and News Release of U.S. Dept. of Education, Aug. 17, 1995. The Directive states that the President "share[s] the concern and frustration that many Americans feel about situations where the protections accorded by the First Amendment are not recognized or understood." President Clinton instructed the Departments of Justice and Education "to provide school officials with guidance [concerning] the extent to which religious expression and activities are permitted in public schools."

"We must remember that intelligence is not enough. Intelligence plus character — that is the goal of true education."

THE WORDS OF MARTIN LUTHER KING, JR. 41 (Coretta Scott King ed., 1993).

Ingebretsen, 88 F.3d at 286–87 (Jones, J., dissenting).

5. Of course, what Judge Jones described as an "absurdity" has come to pass. In *Newdow v. U.S. Congress*, 292 F.3d 597 (9th Cir. 2002), the Ninth Circuit held that the recitation of the Pledge of Allegiance in public schools was an unconstitutional establishment of religion because of the phrase, "under God," in the Pledge. The decision set off a national firestorm — bills were even introduced in Congress prohibiting the Department of Justice from using any of its appropriations to enforce the decision — but the Ninth Circuit held its ground, denying the government's petition for rehearing. (The Supreme Court reversed for lack of standing, see discussion, *supra*.) Is the Ninth Circuit's decision "absurd," or is it the natural outgrowth of the Supreme Court's Establishment Clause precedent since *Everson*?

C. The Free Exercise Clause — Government May Not Prohibit Religious Expression

The First Amendment Religion Clauses have a common goal — advancing religious liberty — even as they accomplish that goal in two different ways. As discussed in Part B, all agree the Establishment Clause at least precludes government from setting up a national or state church or granting special favors to some, but not all, religions. By contrast, the Free Exercise Clause is aimed at advancing religious freedom by preventing the government from prohibiting the holding of religious beliefs or engaging in religious practices.

Today, it is extraordinary for laws to be enacted specifically to disable religious belief or practice. Rather, free exercise disputes arise commonly when a law that is religiously neutral and generally applicable on its face is argued to prevent or burden what someone's religious faith requires, or alternatively, requires someone to undertake an act that faith would preclude. In essence, then, free exercise arguments contemplate religious exemptions from otherwise general laws. As you might guess, this poses a problem for the fair administration of law since manifold faith traditions seemingly necessitate an equal number of exceptions. Relatedly, there is the difficulty of knowing what a given religion requires, and how it is that a court is to inquire into that without getting enmeshed in theological doctrine or commenting upon the sometimes unusual beliefs of someone else's faith. Finally, there is the simple problem of maintaining public order, and evaluating where a religious practice can fairly be said to threaten that order.

1. Distinguishing Between Religious Belief and Religious Practice

Reynolds v. United States, 98 U.S. 145 (1878), addresses the issue of whether a general federal law criminalizing polygamy can be applied to a Mormon whose religion included that practice. Traditionally, matters of marriage and family are state law issues; however, *Reynolds* involved Utah, at the time a federal territory, and hence, Congress was the regulatory body. The federal prohibition of polygamy is justified, according to the Court, because of the importance of monogamous, heterosexual marriage, a practice, says the Court, "[u]pon [which] society may be said to be built," and perhaps even, upon which democratic traditions depend. *Id*. at 165. This important societal interest prevails over the countervailing religious practice by a rather strict, and ultimately unsustainable, distinction between religious belief and practice. This distinction begins to crumble in 1963 with the Court's decision in *Sherbert v. Verner*, 374 U.S. 398 (1963), considered below in Part 4. The difference between belief (fully protected) and conduct (protected if not threatening of public order) is not entirely abandoned, however, as the discussion in the case of *Wisconsin v. Yoder*, 406 U.S. 205 (1972), immediately following *Reynolds,* reveals. The very word, "exercise," in the Free Exercise Clause sustains Chief Justice Burger's conclusion in *Yoder* that "belief and action cannot be neatly confined in logic-tight compartments." *Id*. at 220.

REYNOLDS v. UNITED STATES
98 U.S. 145 (1878)

* * *

This is an indictment found in the District Court for the third judicial district of the Territory of Utah, charging George Reynolds with bigamy, in violation of sect. 5352 of the Revised Statutes, which, omitting its exceptions, is as follows:

> "Every person having a husband or wife living, who marries another, whether married or single, in a Territory, or other place over which the United States have exclusive jurisdiction, is guilty of bigamy, and shall be punished by a fine of not more than $500, and by imprisonment for a term of not more than five years."

* * *

MR. CHIEF JUSTICE WAITE delivered the opinion of the court.

* * *

5. Should the accused have been acquitted if he married the second time, because he believed it to be his religious duty?

* * *

5. As to the defence of religious belief or duty.

On the trial, the plaintiff in error, the accused, proved that at the time of his alleged second marriage he was, and for many years before had been, a member of the Church of Jesus Christ of Latter-Day Saints, commonly called the Mormon Church, and a believer in its doctrines; that it was an accepted doctrine of that church "that it was the duty of male members of said church, circumstances permitting, to practise polygamy; . . . that this duty was enjoined by different books which the members of said church believed to be of divine origin, and among others the Holy Bible, and also that the members of the church believed that the practice of polygamy was directly enjoined upon the male members thereof by the Almighty God, in a revelation to Joseph Smith, the founder and prophet of said church; that the failing or refusing to practise polygamy by such male members of said church, when circumstances would admit, would be punished, and that the penalty for such failure and refusal would be damnation in the life to come." He also proved "that he had received permission from the recognized authorities in said church to enter into polygamous marriage; . . . that Daniel H. Wells, one having authority in said church to perform the marriage ceremony, married the said defendant on or about the time the crime is alleged to have been committed, to some woman by the name of Schofield, and that such marriage ceremony was performed under and pursuant to the doctrines of said church."

* * *

Congress cannot pass a law for the government of the Territories which shall prohibit the free exercise of religion. The first amendment to the Constitution expressly forbids such legislation. Religious freedom is guaranteed everywhere throughout the United States, so far as congressional interference is concerned. The question to be determined is, whether the law now under consideration comes within this prohibition.

The word "religion" is not defined in the Constitution. We must go elsewhere, therefore, to ascertain its meaning, and nowhere more appropriately, we think, than to the history of the times in the midst of which the provision was adopted. The precise point of the inquiry is, what is the religious freedom which has been guaranteed.

Before the adoption of the Constitution, attempts were made in some of the colonies and States to legislate not only in respect to the establishment of religion, but in respect to its doctrines and precepts as well. The people were taxed, against their will, for the support of religion, and sometimes for the support of particular sects to whose tenets they could not and did not subscribe. Punishments were prescribed for a failure to attend upon public worship, and sometimes for entertaining heretical opinions. The controversy upon this general subject was animated in many of the States, but seemed at last to culminate in Virginia. In 1784, the House of Delegates of that State having under consideration "a bill establishing provision for teachers of the Christian religion," postponed it until the next session, and directed that the bill should be published and distributed, and that the people be requested "to signify their opinion respecting the adoption of such a bill at the next session of assembly."

This brought out a determined opposition. Amongst others, Mr. Madison prepared a "Memorial and Remonstrance," which was widely circulated and signed, and in which he demonstrated "that religion, or the duty we owe the Creator," was not within the cognizance of civil government. . . .

. . . Mr. Jefferson was not a member [of the Constitutional Convention], he being then absent as minister to France. As soon as he saw the draft of the Constitution proposed for adoption, he, in a letter to a friend, expressed his disappointment at the absence of an express declaration insuring the freedom of religion, but was willing to accept it as it was, trusting that the good sense and honest intentions of the people would bring about the necessary alterations. . . . Accordingly, at the first session of the first Congress the amendment now under consideration was proposed with others by Mr. Madison. It met the views of the advocates of religious freedom, and was adopted. Mr. Jefferson afterwards, in reply to an address to him by a committee of the Danbury Baptist Association, took occasion to say: "Believing with you that religion is a matter which lies solely between man and his God; that he owes account to none other for his faith or his worship; that the legislative powers of the government reach actions only, and not opinions, — I contemplate with sovereign reverence that act of the whole American people which declared that their legislature should 'make no law respecting an establishment of religion or prohibiting the free exercise thereof' . . . ." Coming as this does from an acknowledged leader of the advocates of the measure, it may be accepted almost as an authoritative declaration of the scope and effect of the amendment thus secured. Congress was deprived of all legislative power over mere opinion, but was left free to reach actions which were in violation of social duties or subversive of good order.

Polygamy has always been odious among the northern and western nations of Europe, and, until the establishment of the Mormon Church, was almost exclusively a feature of the life of Asiatic and of African people. At common law, the second marriage was always void (2 Kent, Com. 79), and from the earliest history of England polygamy has been treated as an offence against society. . . .

By the statute of 1 James I. (c. 11), the offence, if committed in England or Wales, was made punishable in the civil courts, and the penalty was death. As this statute was limited in its operation to England and Wales, it was at a very early period re-enacted, generally with some modifications, in all the colonies. In connection with the case we are now considering, it is a significant fact that on the 8th of December, 1788, after the passage of the act establishing religious freedom, and after the convention of Virginia had recommended as an amendment to the Constitution of the United States the declaration in a bill of rights that "all men have an equal, natural, and unalienable right to the free exercise of religion, according to the dictates of conscience," the legislature of that State substantially enacted the statute of James I., death penalty included, because, as recited in the preamble, "it hath been doubted whether bigamy or poligamy be punishable by the laws of this Commonwealth." 12 Hening's Stat. 691. From that day to this we think it may safely be said there never has been a time in any State of the Union when polygamy has not been an offence against society, cognizable by the civil courts and punishable with more or less severity. In the face of all this evidence, it is impossible to believe that the constitutional guaranty of religious freedom was intended to prohibit legislation in respect to this most important feature of social life. Marriage, while from its very nature a sacred obligation, is nevertheless, in most civilized nations, a civil contract, and usually regulated by law. Upon it society may be said to be built, and out of its fruits spring social relations and social obligations and duties, with which government is necessarily required to deal. In fact, according as monogamous or polygamous marriages are allowed, do we find the principles on which the government of the people, to a greater or less extent, rests. Professor Lieber says, polygamy leads to the patriarchal principle, and which, when applied to large communities, fetters the people in stationary despotism, while that principle cannot long exist in connection with monogamy. . . .

In our opinion, the statute immediately under consideration is within the legislative power of Congress. It is constitutional and valid as prescribing a rule of action for all those residing in the Territories, and in places over which the United States have exclusive control. This being so, the only question which remains is, whether those who make polygamy a part of their religion are excepted from the operation of the statute. If they are, then those who do not make polygamy a part of their religious belief may be found guilty and punished, while those who do, must be acquitted and go free. This would be introducing a new element into criminal law. Laws are made for the government of actions, and while they cannot interfere with mere religious belief and opinions, they may with practices. Suppose one believed that human sacrifices were a necessary part of religious worship, would it be seriously contended that the civil government under which he lived could not interfere to prevent a sacrifice? Or if a wife religiously believed it was her duty to burn herself upon the funeral pile of her dead husband, would it be beyond the power of the civil government to prevent her carrying her belief into practice?

So here, as a law of the organization of society under the exclusive dominion of the United States, it is provided that plural marriages shall not be allowed. Can a man excuse his practices to the contrary because of his religious belief? To permit this would be to make the professed doctrines of religious belief superior to the law of the land, and in effect to permit every citizen to become a law unto himself. Government could exist only in name under such circumstances.

* * *

Upon a careful consideration of the whole case, we are satisfied that no error was committed by the court below.

Judgment affirmed, [except that by later action of the Court, imprisonment was not at hard labor].

MR. JUSTICE FIELD[, concurring]. [Omitted.]

NOTES AND QUESTIONS

1. Does *Reynolds* stand for the proposition that society has a special interest in heterosexual marriage? If so, how would you articulate that interest? What would such special interest mean for homosexual relationships, which, unlike the Mormon interest in polygamy, is usually presented without religious basis? We take up the consideration of homosexuality in Chapter 8 dealing with equality.

2. As you read the next case, *Wisconsin v. Yoder*, 406 U.S. 205 (1972), note not only the already mentioned partial abandonment of the belief/conduct distinction, but also the manner in which the religious claim is weighed against the state interest. The state in *Yoder* was insisting upon compulsory education through the age of 16, and its justification was one largely premised upon ensuring individual competence. The Amish, who as a matter of faith, live as separately from the world as possible, asked for exemption from this state requirement after the 8th grade. In upholding the Amish claim for constitutional exemption, the Court weighs: the centrality of the religious belief (a "life aloof from the world and its values is central to their faith," *id*. at 210); the partial compliance with the state interest, and hence, the reasonableness of the religious claim ("Amish accept compulsory elementary education generally," *id*. at 212); the ability of the state's interest to be accomplished in less religiously-intrusive ways ("the evidence adduced . . . that an additional one or two years of formal high school for Amish children in place of their long-established program of informal vocational education would do little to serve [state] interests . . . ." *id*. at 222); and the fact that more than one constitutional interest was at stake ("when the interests of parenthood are combined with a free exercise claim of the nature revealed by this record, more than merely a 'reasonable relation to some purpose within the competency of the State' is required," *id*. at 233). The last factor, conjoining free exercise with other constitutional interests like parental rights, takes an even greater significance in *Employment Division v. Smith*, 494 U.S. 872 (1990), considered later in this Chapter.

WISCONSIN v. YODER
406 U.S. 205 (1972)

MR. CHIEF JUSTICE BURGER delivered the opinion of the Court.

On petition of the State of Wisconsin, we granted the writ of certiorari in this case to review a decision of the Wisconsin Supreme Court holding that respondents' convictions for violating the State's compulsory school-attendance law were invalid under the Free Exercise Clause of the First Amendment to the

United States Constitution made applicable to the States by the Fourteenth Amendment. For the reasons hereafter stated we affirm the judgment of the Supreme Court of Wisconsin.

Respondents Jonas Yoder and Wallace Miller are members of the Old Order Amish religion . . . . They and their families are residents of Green County, Wisconsin. Wisconsin's compulsory school-attendance law required them to cause their children to attend public or private school until reaching age 16 but the respondents declined to send their children, ages 14 and 15, to public school after they completed the eighth grade. The children were not enrolled in any private school, or within any recognized exception to the compulsory-attendance law, and they are conceded to be subject to the Wisconsin statute.

On complaint of the school district administrator for the public schools, respondents were charged, tried, and convicted of violating the compulsory-attendance law in Green County Court and were fined the sum of $5 each.[3] Respondents defended on the ground that the application of the compulsory-attendance law violated their rights under the First and Fourteenth Amendments. The trial testimony showed that respondents believed, in accordance with the tenets of Old Order Amish communities generally, that their children's attendance at high school, public or private, was contrary to the Amish religion and way of life. They believed that by sending their children to high school, they would not only expose themselves to the danger of the censure of the church community, but, as found by the county court, also endanger their own salvation and that of their children. The State stipulated that respondents' religious beliefs were sincere.

. . . As a result of their common heritage, Old Order Amish communities today are characterized by a fundamental belief that salvation requires life in a church community separate and apart from the world and worldly influence. This concept of life aloof from the world and its values is central to their faith.

A related feature of Old Order Amish communities is their devotion to a life in harmony with nature and the soil, as exemplified by the simple life of the early Christian era that continued in America during much of our early national life. Amish beliefs require members of the community to make their living by farming or closely related activities. Broadly speaking, the Old Order Amish religion pervades and determines the entire mode of life of its adherents. Their con-

---

[3] Prior to trial, the attorney for respondents wrote the State Superintendent of Public Instruction in an effort to explore the possibilities for a compromise settlement. Among other possibilities, he suggested that perhaps the State Superintendent could administratively determine that the Amish could satisfy the compulsory-attendance law by establishing their own vocational training plan similar to one that has been established in Pennsylvania. Under the Pennsylvania plan, Amish children of high school age are required to attend an Amish vocational school for three hours a week, during which time they are taught such subjects as English, mathematics, health, and social studies by an Amish teacher. For the balance of the week, the children perform farm and household duties under parental supervision, and keep a journal of their daily activities. The major portion of the curriculum is home projects in agriculture and homemaking.

duct is regulated in great detail by the *Ordnung*, or rules, of the church community. Adult baptism, which occurs in late adolescence, is the time at which Amish young people voluntarily undertake heavy obligations, not unlike the Bar Mitzvah of the Jews, to abide by the rules of the church community.

Amish objection to formal education beyond the eighth grade is firmly grounded in these central religious concepts. They object to the high school, and higher education generally, because the values they teach are in marked variance with Amish values and the Amish way of life; they view secondary school education as an impermissible exposure of their children to a "worldly" influence in conflict with their beliefs. . . .

* * *

The Amish do not object to elementary education through the first eight grades as a general proposition because they agree that their children must have basic skills in the "three R's" in order to read the Bible, to be good farmers and citizens, and to be able to deal with non-Amish people when necessary in the course of daily affairs. They view such a basic education as acceptable because it does not significantly expose their children to worldly values or interfere with their development in the Amish community during the crucial adolescent period. While Amish accept compulsory elementary education generally, wherever possible they have established their own elementary schools in many respects like the small local schools of the past. In the Amish belief higher learning tends to develop values they reject as influences that alienate man from God.

. . . The testimony of Dr. Donald A. Erickson, an expert witness on education, also showed that the Amish succeed in preparing their high school age children to be productive members of the Amish community. He described their system of learning through doing the skills directly relevant to their adult roles in the Amish community as "ideal" and perhaps superior to ordinary high school education. The evidence also showed that the Amish have an excellent record as law-abiding and generally self-sufficient members of society.

Although the trial court in its careful findings determined that the Wisconsin compulsory school-attendance law "does interfere with the freedom of the Defendants to act in accordance with their sincere religious belief" it also concluded that the requirement of high school attendance until age 16 was a "reasonable and constitutional" exercise of governmental power, and therefore denied the motion to dismiss the charges. The Wisconsin Circuit Court affirmed the convictions. The Wisconsin Supreme Court, however, sustained respondents' claim under the Free Exercise Clause of the First Amendment and reversed the convictions. . . .

I

. . . As [*Pierce v. Society of Sisters* (1925)] suggests, the values of parental direction of the religious upbringing and education of their children in their early and formative years have a high place in our society. Thus, a State's interest in universal education, however highly we rank it, is not totally free from a balancing process when it impinges on fundamental rights and interests, such as those specifically protected by the Free Exercise Clause of the First Amendment, and the traditional interest of parents with respect to the religious upbringing of their children so long as they, in the words of *Pierce*, "prepare [them] for additional obligations."

It follows that in order for Wisconsin to compel school attendance beyond the eighth grade against a claim that such attendance interferes with the practice of a legitimate religious belief, it must appear either that the State does not deny the free exercise of religious belief by its requirement, or that there is a state interest of sufficient magnitude to override the interest claiming protection under the Free Exercise Clause. . . .

* * *

II

. . . In evaluating those claims we must be careful to determine whether the Amish religious faith and their mode of life are, as they claim, inseparable and interdependent. A way of life, however virtuous and admirable, may not be interposed as a barrier to reasonable state regulation of education if it is based on purely secular considerations; to have the protection of the Religion Clauses, the claims must be rooted in religious belief. Although a determination of what is a "religious" belief or practice entitled to constitutional protection may present a most delicate question, the very concept of ordered liberty precludes allowing every person to make his own standards on matters of conduct in which society as a whole has important interests. Thus, if the Amish asserted their claims because of their subjective evaluation and rejection of the contemporary secular values accepted by the majority, much as Thoreau rejected the social values of his time and isolated himself at Walden Pond, their claims would not rest on a religious basis. Thoreau's choice was philosophical and personal rather than religious, and such belief does not rise to the demands of the Religion Clauses.

. . . That the Old Order Amish daily life and religious practice stem from their faith is shown by the fact that it is in response to their literal interpretation of the Biblical injunction from the Epistle of Paul to the Romans, "be not conformed to this world . . . ." This command is fundamental to the Amish faith. Moreover, for the Old Order Amish, religion is not simply a matter of theocratic belief. As the expert witnesses explained, the Old Order Amish religion pervades and determines virtually their entire way of life, regulating it with the detail of the Talmudic diet through the strictly enforced rules of the church community.

* * *

. . . As the record so strongly shows, the values and programs of the modern secondary school are in sharp conflict with the fundamental mode of life mandated by the Amish religion; modern laws requiring compulsory secondary education have accordingly engendered great concern and conflict. . . .

The impact of the compulsory-attendance law on respondents' practice of the Amish religion is not only severe, but inescapable, for the Wisconsin law affirmatively compels them, under threat of criminal sanction, to perform acts undeniably at odds with fundamental tenets of their religious beliefs. Nor is the impact of the compulsory-attendance law confined to grave interference with important Amish religious tenets from a subjective point of view. It carries with it precisely the kind of objective danger to the free exercise of religion that the First Amendment was designed to prevent. As the record shows, compulsory school attendance to age 16 for Amish children carries with it a very real threat of undermining the Amish community and religious practice as they exist today; they must either abandon belief and be assimilated into society at large, or be forced to migrate to some other and more tolerant region.

* * *

III

* * *

Wisconsin concedes that under the Religion Clauses religious beliefs are absolutely free from the State's control, but it argues that "actions," even though religiously grounded, are outside the protection of the First Amendment. But our decisions have rejected the idea that religiously grounded conduct is always outside the protection of the Free Exercise Clause. It is true that activities of individuals, even when religiously based, are often subject to regulation by the States in the exercise of their undoubted power to promote the health, safety, and general welfare, or the Federal Government in the exercise of its delegated powers. But to agree that religiously grounded conduct must often be subject to the broad police power of the State is not to deny that there are areas of conduct protected by the Free Exercise Clause of the First Amendment and thus beyond the power of the State to control, even under regulations of general applicability. This case, therefore, does not become easier because respondents were convicted for their "actions" in refusing to send their children to the public high school; in this context belief and action cannot be neatly confined in logic-tight compartments.

Nor can this case be disposed of on the grounds that Wisconsin's requirement for school attendance to age 16 applies uniformly to all citizens of the State and does not, on its face, discriminate against religions or a particular religion, or that it is motivated by legitimate secular concerns. A regulation neutral on its face may, in its application, nonetheless offend the constitutional requirement for governmental neutrality if it unduly burdens the free exercise of religion.

. . .

We turn, then, to the State's broader contention that its interest in its system of compulsory education is so compelling that even the established religious practices of the Amish must give way. . . .

The State advances two primary arguments in support of its system of compulsory education. It notes, as Thomas Jefferson pointed out early in our history, that some degree of education is necessary to prepare citizens to participate effectively and intelligently in our open political system if we are to preserve freedom and independence. Further, education prepares individuals to be self-reliant and self-sufficient participants in society. We accept these propositions.

However, the evidence adduced by the Amish in this case is persuasively to the effect that an additional one or two years of formal high school for Amish children in place of their long-established program of informal vocational education would do little to serve those interests. . . .

The State attacks respondents' position as one fostering "ignorance" from which the child must be protected by the State. No one can question the State's duty to protect children from ignorance but this argument does not square with the facts disclosed in the record. Whatever their idiosyncrasies as seen by the majority, this record strongly shows that the Amish community has been a highly successful social unit within our society, even if apart from the conventional "mainstream." Its members are productive and very law-abiding members of society; they reject public welfare in any of its usual modern forms. The Congress itself recognized their self-sufficiency by authorizing exemption of such groups as the Amish from the obligation to pay social security taxes.[11]

It is neither fair nor correct to suggests that the Amish are opposed to education beyond the eighth grade level. What this record shows is that they are opposed to conventional formal education of the type provided by a certified high school because it comes at the child's crucial adolescent period of religious development. Dr. Donald Erickson, for example, testified that their system of learning-by-doing was an "ideal system" of education in terms of preparing Amish children for life as adults in the Amish community, and that "I would be inclined to say they do a better job in this than most of the rest of us do." . . .

* * *

---

[11] Title 26 U. S. C. § 1402(h) authorizes the Secretary of Health, Education, and Welfare to exempt members of "a recognized religious sect" existing at all times since December 31, 1950, from the obligation to pay social security taxes if they are, by reason of the tenets of their sect, opposed to receipt of such benefits and agree to waive them, provided the Secretary finds that the sect makes reasonable provision for its dependent members. The history of the exemption shows it was enacted with the situation of the Old Order Amish specifically in view. H.R. Rep. No. 213, 89th Cong., 1st Sess., 101-102 (1965).

The record in this case establishes without contradiction that the Green County Amish had never been known to commit crimes, that none had been known to receive public assistance, and that none were unemployed.

The State, however, supports its interest in providing an additional one or two years of compulsory high school education to Amish children because of the possibility that some such children will choose to leave the Amish community, and that if this occurs they will be ill-equipped for life. . . .

There is nothing in this record to suggest that the Amish qualities of reliability, self-reliance, and dedication to work would fail to find ready markets in today's society. Absent some contrary evidence supporting the State's position, we are unwilling to assume that persons possessing such valuable vocational skills and habits are doomed to become burdens on society should they determine to leave the Amish faith, nor is there any basis in the record to warrant a finding that an additional one or two years of formal school education beyond the eighth grade would serve to eliminate any such problem that might exist.

. . . Indeed, the Amish communities singularly parallel and reflect many of the virtues of Jefferson's ideal of the "sturdy yeoman" who would form the basis of what he considered as the ideal of a democratic society.[14] . . .

* * *

IV

Finally, the State, on authority of *Prince v. Massachusetts*, argues that a decision exempting Amish children from the State's requirement fails to recognize the substantive right of the Amish child to a secondary education, and fails to give due regard to the power of the State as *parens patriae* to extend the benefit of secondary education to children regardless of the wishes of their parents. Taken at its broadest sweep, the Court's language in *Prince* might be read to give support to the State's position. However, the Court was not confronted in *Prince* with a situation comparable to that of the Amish as revealed in this record; this is shown by the Court's severe characterization of the evils that it thought the legislature could legitimately associate with child labor, even when performed in the company of an adult. The Court later took great care to confine *Prince* to a narrow scope in *Sherbert v. Verner*, when it stated:

> "On the other hand, the Court has rejected challenges under the Free Exercise Clause to governmental regulation of certain overt acts prompted by religious beliefs or principles, for 'even when the action is in accord with one's religious convictions, [it] is not totally free from legislative restrictions.' *Braunfeld v. Brown* (1961). The conduct or actions so regulated have invariably posed some substantial threat to public safety, peace or order. *See, e.g., Reynolds v. United States* [(1878)]; *Jacobson v. Massachusetts* [(1905)]; *Prince v. Massachusetts* [(1944)]. . . ."

---

14 While Jefferson recognized that education was essential to the welfare and liberty of the people, he was reluctant to directly force instruction of children "in opposition to the will of the parent." Instead he proposed that state citizenship be conditioned on the ability to "read readily in some tongue, native or acquired." Letter from Thomas Jefferson to Joseph Cabell, Sept. 9, 1817, in 17 WRITINGS OF THOMAS JEFFERSON 417, 423-424 (Mem. ed. 1904). . . .

This case, of course, is not one in which any harm to the physical or mental health of the child or to the public safety, peace, order, or welfare has been demonstrated or may be properly inferred. The record is to the contrary, and any reliance on that theory would find no support in the evidence.

. . . The dissent argues that a child who expresses a desire to attend public high school in conflict with the wishes of his parents should not be prevented from doing so. There is no reason for the Court to consider that point since it is not an issue in the case. The children are not parties to this litigation. . . .

Our holding in no way determines the proper resolution of possible competing interests of parents, children, and the State in an appropriate state court proceeding in which the power of the State is asserted on the theory that Amish parents are preventing their minor children from attending high school despite their expressed desires to the contrary. Recognition of the claim of the State in such a proceeding would, of course, call into question traditional concepts of parental control over the religious upbringing and education of their minor children recognized in this Court's past decisions. It is clear that such an intrusion by a State into family decisions in the area of religious training would give rise to grave questions of religious freedom comparable to those raised here and those presented in *Pierce v. Society of Sisters* (1925). On this record we neither reach nor decide those issues.

* * *

. . . [P]erhaps the most significant statements of the Court in this area are found in *Pierce v. Society of Sisters*, in which the Court observed:

"Under the doctrine of *Meyer v. Nebraska* [(1923)], we think it entirely plain that the Act of 1922 unreasonably interferes with the liberty of parents and guardians to direct the upbringing and education of children under their control. As often heretofore pointed out, rights guaranteed by the Constitution may not be abridged by legislation which has no reasonable relation to some purpose within the competency of the State. The fundamental theory of liberty upon which all governments in this Union repose excludes any general power of the State to standardize its children by forcing them to accept instruction from public teachers only. The child is not the mere creature of the State; those who nurture him and direct his destiny have the right, coupled with the high duty, to recognize and prepare him for additional obligations."

The duty to prepare the child for "additional obligations," referred to by the Court, must be read to include the inculcation of moral standards, religious beliefs, and elements of good citizenship. *Pierce*, of course, recognized that where nothing more than the general interest of the parent in the nurture and education of his children is involved, it is beyond dispute that the State acts "reasonably" and constitutionally in requiring education to age 16 in some public or private school meeting the standards prescribed by the State.

However read, the Court's holding in *Pierce* stands as a charter of the rights of parents to direct the religious upbringing of their children. And, when the interests of parenthood are combined with a free exercise claim of the nature revealed by this record, more than merely a "reasonable relation to some purpose within the competency of the State" is required to sustain the validity of the State's requirement under the First Amendment. . . .

* * *

V

For the reasons stated we hold, with the Supreme Court of Wisconsin, that the First and Fourteenth Amendments prevent the State from compelling respondents to cause their children to attend formal high school to age 16.

* * *

AFFIRMED.

MR. JUSTICE POWELL and MR. JUSTICE REHNQUIST took no part in the consideration or decision of this case.

MR. JUSTICE STEWART, with whom MR. JUSTICE BRENNAN joins, concurring. [Omitted.]

MR. JUSTICE WHITE, with whom MR. JUSTICE BRENNAN and MR. JUSTICE STEWART join, concurring.

* * *

Decision in cases such as this and the administration of an exemption for Old Order Amish from the State's compulsory school-attendance laws will inevitably involve the kind of close and perhaps repeated scrutiny of religious practices, as is exemplified in today's opinion, which the Court has heretofore been anxious to avoid. But such entanglement does not create a forbidden establishment of religion where it is essential to implement free exercise values threatened by an otherwise neutral program instituted to foster some permissible, nonreligious state objective. I join the Court because the sincerity of the Amish religious policy here is uncontested, because the potentially adverse impact of the state requirement is great, and because the State's valid interest in education has already been largely satisfied by the eight years the children have already spent in school.

MR. JUSTICE DOUGLAS, dissenting in part.

I

* * *

. . . It is, of course, beyond question that the parents have standing as defendants in a criminal prosecution to assert the religious interests of their children as a defense. Although the lower courts and a majority of this Court assume an identity of interest between parent and child, it is clear that they have treated the religious interest of the child as a factor in the analysis.

* * *

II

* * *

The views of the two children in question were not canvassed by the Wisconsin courts. The matter should be explicitly reserved so that new hearings can be held on remand of the case.

III

* * *

The Court rightly rejects the notion that actions, even though religiously grounded, are always outside the protection of the Free Exercise Clause of the First Amendment. In so ruling, the Court departs from the teaching of *Reynolds v. United States* (1879) where it was said concerning the reach of the Free Exercise Clause of the First Amendment, "Congress was deprived of all legislative power over mere opinion, but was left free to reach actions which were in violation of social duties or subversive of good order." In that case it was conceded that polygamy was a part of the religion of the Mormons. Yet the Court said, "It matters not that his belief [in polygamy] was a part of his professed religion: it was still belief and belief only."

Action, which the Court deemed to be antisocial, could be punished even though it was grounded on deeply held and sincere religious convictions. What we do today, at least in this respect, opens the way to give organized religion a broader base than it has ever enjoyed; and it even promises that in time *Reynolds* will be overruled.

In another way, however, the Court retreats when in reference to Henry Thoreau it says his "choice was philosophical and personal rather than religious, and such belief does not rise to the demands of the Religion Clauses." That is contrary to what we held in *United States v. Seeger* (1964), where we were concerned with the meaning of the words "religious training and belief" in the Selective Service Act, which were the basis of many conscientious objector claims. We said:

"Within that phrase would come all sincere religious beliefs which are based upon a power or being, or upon a faith, to which all else is subordinate or upon which all else is ultimately dependent. The test might be stated in these words: A sincere and meaningful belief which occupies in the life of its possessor a place parallel to that filled by the God of those admittedly qualifying for the exemption comes within the statutory definition. This construction avoids imputing to Congress an intent to classify different religious beliefs, exempting some and excluding others, and is in accord with the well-established congressional policy of equal treatment for those whose opposition to service is grounded in their religious tenets."

* * *

I adhere to these exalted views of "religion" and see no acceptable alternative to them now that we have become a Nation of many religions and sects, representing all of the diversities of the human race. *United States v. Seeger* (concurring opinion).

NOTES AND QUESTIONS

1. Why do the Mormons lose in *Reynolds*, but the Amish win in *Yoder*? Is it a principled distinction or one that turns on religious preference or the favorable perception of one sect over another? Is public order threatened in one instance, but not the other? All religious belief is protected, but protection is extended only to conduct that does not threaten public order. In his article *The Origins and Historical Understanding of Free Exercise of Religion*, Professor Michael McConnell summarizes the historical understanding of the public order exception as a limitation on the free exercise of religion in the United States:

> [S]tate constitutions provide the most direct evidence of the original understanding [of the Free Exercise Clause], for it is reasonable to infer that those who drafted and adopted the first amendment assumed the term "free exercise of religion" meant what it had meant in their states. The wording of the state provisions thus casts light on the meaning of the first amendment.

New York's 1777 Constitution was typical:

> [T]he free exercise and enjoyment of religious profession and worship, without discrimination or preference, shall forever hereafter be allowed, within this State, to all mankind: Provided, That the liberty of conscience, hereby granted, shall not be so construed as to excuse acts of licentiousness, or justify practices inconsistent with the peace or safety of this State.[239]

Likewise, New Hampshire's provision stated:

> Every individual has a natural and unalienable right to worship GOD according to the dictates of his own conscience, and reason; and no subject shall be hurt, molested, or restrained in his person, liberty or estate for worshipping GOD, in the manner and season most agreeable to the dictates of his own conscience,

---

[239] N.Y. CONST. OF 1777, art. XXXVIII, *reprinted in* 2 FEDERAL AND STATE CONSTITUTIONS, COLONIAL CHARTERS, AND OTHER ORGANIC LAWS OF THE UNITED STATES 1328, 1338 (B. Poore ed., 2d ed. 1878).

. . . provided he doth not disturb the public peace, or disturb others, in their religious worship.[240]

As a final example, Georgia's religious liberty clause read: "All persons whatever shall have the free exercise of their religion; provided it be not repugnant to the peace and safety of the State."[241] . . . In addition to these state provisions, article I of the Northwest Ordinance of 1787, enacted contemporaneously with the drafting of the Constitution and re-enacted by the First Congress, provided: "No person, demeaning himself in a peaceable and orderly manner, shall ever be molested on account of his mode of worship, or religious sentiments, in the said territory."[243]

* * *

The most common feature of the state provisions was the government's right to protect public peace and safety. As Madison expressed it late in life, the free exercise right should prevail "in every case where it does not trespass on private rights or the public peace."[271] This indicates that a believer has no license to invade the private rights of others or to disturb public peace and order, no matter how conscientious the belief or how trivial the private right on the other side.

Michael McConnell, *The Origins and Historical Understanding of Free Exercise of Religion*, 103 HARV. L. REV. 1409, 1456-58, 1464 (1990).

As we saw, the Supreme Court endorsed this historical understanding of the public order exception in *Reynolds v. United States*, 98 U.S. 145 (1878), which held that the Free Exercise Clause did not exempt Reynolds, a Mormon, from a territorial statute making polygamy a criminal offense. The opinion explains the practical basis of the public order exception:

Laws are made for the government of actions, and while they cannot interfere with mere religious belief and opinions, they may with practices. . . .

. . . Can a man excuse his practices to the contrary [of the law] because of his religious belief? To permit this would be to make the professed doctrines of religious belief superior to the law of the land, and in effect to permit every citizen to become a law unto himself.

Id. at 166-67.

---

[240] N.H. CONST. OF 1784, pt. 1, art. V, *reprinted in* 2 FEDERAL AND STATE CONSTITUTIONS, *supra*, at 1280, 1281.

[241] GA. CONST. OF 1777, art. LVI, *reprinted in* 2 FEDERAL AND STATE CONSTITUTIONS, *supra*, at 377, 383.

[243] Northwest Territorial Ordinance of 1787, art. I, *reprinted in* 2 FEDERAL AND STATE CONSTITUTIONS, *supra*, at 429, 431.

[271] Letter from James Madison to Edward Livingston (July 10, 1822), *in* THE WRITINGS OF JAMES MADISON 98, 100 (G. Hunt ed., 1901).

2. In *Cantwell v. Connecticut*, 310 U.S. 296 (1940), the court overturned the convictions of three Jehovah's Witnesses for violations of a state law prohibiting the solicitation of money for religious organizations without prior licensing by a state official. The Court discussed the extent of public order exception:

> The state is . . . free to regulate the time and manner of solicitation generally, in the interest of public safety, peace, comfort or convenience. But to condition the solicitation of aid for the perpetuation of religious views or systems upon a license, the grant of which rests in the exercise of a determination by state authority as to what is a religious cause, is to lay a forbidden burden upon the exercise of liberty protected by the Constitution.

Id. at 306-07. Because Connecticut's regulation went beyond that which was necessary to protect the public order, the Court found that it was an unnecessary, and therefore unconstitutional, burden on the defendants' free exercise of their faith.

The Court expanded on *Cantwell* in *Watchtower Bible and Tract Society of New York, Inc. v. Village of Stratton*, 122 S. Ct. 2080 (June 17, 2002), holding in an 8-1 decision that a city ordinance requiring individuals engaged in religious proselytizing, anonymous political speech, and handbill distribution, among other things, to first register with the mayor and obtain a permit facially violated the First Amendment because the ordinance intruded upon the freedom of speech and the free exercise of religion much more broadly than necessary to serve the government's interest in protecting citizen privacy and preventing fraud.

3. By contrast, in *Prince v. Massachusetts*, 321 U.S. 158 (1943), the Court upheld the conviction of Mrs. Prince, a Jehovah's Witness, under state child labor laws for permitting her nine year old ward, Betty Simmons, to sell religious materials on a public street. Mrs. Prince argued that she and Betty were fulfilling their religious obligation by selling the magazines, and that, therefore, their conduct was constitutionally protected by a combination of the Free Exercise Clause and Mrs. Prince's parental rights. The Court, however, found that neither the Free Exercise Clause nor Mrs. Prince's parental rights limited the state's ability to control Mrs. Prince and Betty's conduct in this matter. "[T]he state has a wide range of power for limiting parental freedom and authority in things affecting the child's welfare; and . . . this includes, to some extent, matters of conscience and religious conviction." *Id.* at 167. The Court's conclusion that the state's interest in Betty's welfare outweighed Mrs. Prince and Betty's interest in the free exercise of their faith is another example of the public order exception to the Free Exercise Clause.

4. Can you discern at what point an individual's interest in the free exercise of conduct motivated by religious faith overcomes the government's interest in preserving the public order? Some commentators believe there is an absence of a substantive principal of limitation for the public order exception. Notre Dame's Gerard V. Bradley writes:

> Defenders of the conduct exemption do not deny that it is a bit fuzzy. Michael McConnell suggests this clarification: "maximum freedom for religious practice consistent with demands of public order."[71] But who disagrees with that? No one rationally can, because it is purely formal, like saying "there shall be no unjustified burdens upon religion." What is formal about it is that all of the substance is suppressed. Most significantly suppressed is: in what does public order consist? That no one has gotten a bloody nose? Does it include legal protection of the aesthetic, or moral, or religious sensibilities of all? Of a majority?
>
> Even so appealing a formulation as Madison's (which McConnell endorses), "that free exercise should be protected in every case where it does not trespass on private rights or the public peace,"[72] is inconclusive. Do the people enjoy a collective right to a decent society? Does the government rightly constrain the religious practices of one or more persons when it makes impossible a cultural order supportive of the conscientious practices of the vast majority?
>
> Does public order extend to a shared religious outlook? To common moral precepts? Does the right of conscience include an immunity from state interference with actions that, while self-regarding, are objectively immoral? Is there, in other words, a free exercise right to do a moral wrong, like ritual self-immolation, or to have adulterous sexual relations? Americans in the founding and antebellum eras thought not. *Both* "licentiousness" *and* "public peace and order" conditioned and limited the religious liberty that they enjoyed. They thought that they enjoyed a nearly perfect freedom of conscience. And they brought blasphemy prosecutions, and compelled ministerial support, as well as sabbath observance. Quite likely, McConnell means "public order" to exclude all perfectionistic state action, in favor of liberal neutrality. Be that as it may, we need to know if that corresponds to the original understanding. Already, the answer appears to be no.

Gerard V. Bradley, *Beguiled: Free Exercise Exemptions and the Siren Song of Liberalism*, 20 HOFSTRA L. REV. 245, 259-60 (1991).

5. The extent of the public order exception is at the core of modern free exercise disagreement. In *Employment Division v. Smith*, 494 U.S. 872 (1990), which we will encounter in Part 5, the Court refused to find drug use in a religious ceremony to merit a free exercise exemption from a generally applicable criminal prohibition. Both Justices O'Connor and Blackmun, however, would

---

[71] Michael W. McConnell, *Free Exercise Revisionism and the* Smith *Decision*, 57 U. CHI. L. REV. 1109, 1111 (1990).

[72] *Id.* at 1128 (quoting a letter from James Madison to Edward Livingston (July 10, 1822).

have provided that exemption, but they differed over the application of the public order exception. In her concurring opinion, Justice O'Connor found that Oregon's criminal prohibition placed a "severe burden on the ability of respondents to freely exercise their religion." *Id.* at 903. However, she concluded that the state's interest in public safety and order was sufficiently compelling to justify the burden placed on claimants:

> [U]niform application of Oregon's criminal prohibition is "essential to accomplish" its overriding interest in preventing the physical harm caused by the use of a Schedule I controlled substance. Oregon's criminal prohibition represents that State's judgment that the possession and use of controlled substances, even by only one person, is inherently harmful and dangerous. Because the health effects caused by the use of controlled substances exist regardless of the motivation of the user, the use of such substances, even for religious purposes, violates the very purpose of the laws that prohibit them. Moreover, in view of the societal interest in preventing trafficking in controlled substances, uniform application of the criminal prohibition at issue is essential to the effectiveness of Oregon's stated interest in preventing any possession of peyote.

Id. at 905 (O'Connor, J., concurring) (citations omitted).

In his dissenting opinion, Justice Blackmun also applied the "compelling interest" test. However, Justice Blackmun differed with Justice O'Connor regarding the nature of the state interest involved. Justice Blackmun defined it as the "State's narrow interest in refusing to make an exception for the religious, ceremonial use of peyote." *Id.* at 910 (Blackmun, J., dissenting). Because the state had provided only a "symbolic" and "speculative" interest in "enforcing its drug laws against religious users of peyote," and "no evidence that the religious use of peyote [had] ever harmed anyone," Justice Blackmun found the state's interest "not sufficiently compelling to outweigh respondent's right to the free exercise of their religion." *Id.* at 910-12, 921.

6. The difference between accommodation and establishment: In Justice White's concurring opinion, he notes: "entanglement does not create a forbidden establishment of religion where it is essential to implement free exercise values threatened by an otherwise neutral program instituted to foster some permissible, nonreligious state objective." *Yoder*, 406 U.S. at 240-41 (White, J., concurring). Justice White's comment suggests that some state efforts could be too accommodating of free exercise values and lead a state to violate the Establishment Clause. Thus, in *Estate of Thornton v. Calder*, 472 U.S. 703 (1984), the Court invalidated a Connecticut statute that gave employees a choice to be absent from work on the sabbath of their choice. Similarly, in *Board of Education v. Grummett*, 512 U.S. 687 (1994), New York's effort to allow Hasidic Jews, who live in a concentrated area, to form their own public school district was seen as favoritism not mandated by free exercise requirements. Notice that in both *Thornton* and *Grummett*, the state was not seeking to exempt religious practice from neutral state laws, but to enact state laws facilitating religious practice.

As we have seen, this facilitation would be inoffensive to our Constitutional framers absent a clear showing of sect-based favoritism, but it does not coincide with the exclusionary posture of establishment case law in the latter third of the 20th century. By contrast, the Court upheld the religious exemption from the otherwise generally applicable employment discrimination provisions of Title VII of the Civil Rights Act of 1964, 42 U.S.C. § 2000e-1(a) (1994), in *Corporation of the Presiding Bishop of the Church of Jesus Christ of Latter Day Saints v. Amos*, 483 U.S. 327 (1984).

2. Judicial Inquiry Into the Sincerity, But Not the Validity, of Religious Belief

Religious belief is often very personal and beyond the standards of proof associated with law or science. By nature, that which is spiritual is not material. Not everyone, of course, holding themselves out as spiritual leaders are completely honest, and *United States v. Ballard* deals with allegations of fraud against certain claimed faith-healers. The appellate court in *Ballard* thought the "truth of religious doctrines" could be submitted to the jury. *See Ballard v. United States*, 138 F.2d 540, 545 (9th Cir. 1943). Here, the Supreme Court reverses, indicating that in evaluating free exercise claims or defenses, an honest, sincere belief is all temporal judges can measure.

UNITED STATES v. BALLARD
322 U.S. 78 (1944)

MR. JUSTICE DOUGLAS delivered the opinion of the Court.

Respondents were indicted and convicted for using, and conspiring to use, the mails to defraud. The indictment was in twelve counts. It charged a scheme to defraud by organizing and promoting the I Am movement through the use of the mails. . . . The false representations charged were eighteen in number. It is sufficient at this point to say that they covered respondents' alleged religious doctrines or beliefs. They were all set forth in the first count. The following are representative:

> . . . that Guy W. Ballard, during his lifetime, and Edna W. Ballard and Donald Ballard had, by reason of supernatural attainments, the power to heal persons of ailments and diseases and to make well persons afflicted with any diseases, injuries, or ailments, and did falsely represent to persons intended to be defrauded that the three designated persons had the ability and power to cure persons of those diseases normally classified as curable and also of diseases which are ordinarily classified by the medical profession as being incurable diseases; and did further represent that the three designated persons had in fact cured

either by the activity of one, either, or all of said persons, hundreds of persons afflicted with diseases and ailments. . . .

Each of the representations enumerated in the indictment was followed by the charge that respondents "well knew" it was false. . . .

. . . [T]he [District C]ourt advised the jury . . . in the following language:

* * *

"[T]he defendants in this case made certain representations of belief in a divinity and in a supernatural power. . . ."

The District Court . . . [also charged to the jury]:

"The question of the defendants' good faith is the cardinal question in this case. You are not to be concerned with the religious belief of the defendants, or any of them. The jury will be called upon to pass on the question of whether or not the defendants honestly and in good faith believed the representations which are set forth in the indictment, and honestly and in good faith believed that the benefits which they represented would flow from their belief to those who embraced and followed their teachings, or whether these representations were mere pretenses without honest belief on the part of the defendants or any of them, and, were the representations made for the purpose of procuring money, and were the mails used for this purpose. . . ."

* * *

. . . [T]he Circuit Court of Appeals held that the question of the truth of the representations concerning respondent's religious doctrines or beliefs should have been submitted to the jury. . . . [W]e do not agree that the truth or verity of respondents' religious doctrines or beliefs should have been submitted to the jury. Whatever this particular indictment might require, the First Amendment precludes such a course, as the United States seems to concede. "The law knows no heresy, and is committed to the support of no dogma, the establishment of no sect." . . . Men may believe what they cannot prove. They may not be put to the proof of their religious doctrines or beliefs. . . . The miracles of the New Testament, the Divinity of Christ, life after death, the power of prayer are deep in the religious convictions of many. If one could be sent to jail because a jury in a hostile environment found those teachings false, little indeed would be left of religious freedom. . . . The religious views espoused by respondents might seem incredible, if not preposterous, to most people. But if those doctrines are subject to trial before a jury charged with finding their truth or falsity, then the same can be done with the religious beliefs of any sect. . . . So we conclude that the District Court ruled properly when it withheld from the jury all questions concerning the truth or falsity of the religious beliefs or doctrines of respondents.

* * *

MR. CHIEF JUSTICE STONE, [and JUSTICES ROBERTS and FRANKFURTER wrote a separate opinion reversing the appellate court and re-instating the trial court conviction].

* * *

. . . With the assent of the prosecution and the defense the trial judge withdrew from the consideration of the jury the question whether the alleged religious experiences had in fact occurred, but submitted to the jury the single issue whether petitioners honestly believed that they had occurred, with the instruction that if the jury did not so find, then it should return a verdict of guilty. . . .

On the issue submitted to the jury in this case it properly rendered a verdict of guilty. . . .

MR. JUSTICE JACKSON, dissenting.

* * *

The Ballard family claimed miraculous communication with the spirit world and supernatural power to heal the sick. They were brought to trial for mail fraud on an indictment which charged that their representations were false and that they "well knew" they were false. The trial judge, obviously troubled, ruled that the court could not try whether the statements were untrue, but could inquire whether the defendants knew them to be untrue; and, if so, they could be convicted.

I find it difficult to reconcile this conclusion with our traditional religious freedoms.

In the first place, as a matter of either practice or philosophy I do not see how we can separate an issue as to what is believed from considerations as to what is believable. The most convincing proof that one believes his statements is to show that they have been true in his experience. Likewise, that one knowingly falsified is best proved by showing that what he said happened never did happen. How can the Government prove these persons knew something to be false which it cannot prove to be false? If we try religious sincerity severed from religious verity, we isolate the dispute from the very considerations which in common experience provide its most reliable answer.

* * *

Prosecutions of this character easily could degenerate into religious persecution. I do not doubt that religious leaders may be convicted of fraud for making false representations on matters other than faith or experience, as for example if one represents that funds are being used to construct a church when in fact they are being used for personal purposes. But that is not this case, which reaches into wholly dangerous ground. When does less than full belief in a professed credo become actionable fraud if one is soliciting gifts or legacies? Such inquiries may discomfort orthodox as well as unconventional religious teachers, for even the most regular of them are sometimes accused of taking their orthodoxy with a grain of salt.

I would dismiss the indictment and have done with this business of judicially examining other people's faiths.

NOTE

Does a free exercise claim depend on others holding similar beliefs? Following *Ballard*, the Court made it clear that sincerity also does not depend upon a religious belief being held or share by others. *Thomas v. Review Bd. of the Ind. Employment Sec. Div.*, 450 U.S. 707, 715-16 (1981). This focus on the individual is consistent with the view of the framers. Madison's *Memorial and Remonstrance* plainly states that it is "the duty of every man to render to the Creator such homage, and such only, as he believes to be acceptable to him." JAMES MADISON, MEMORIAL AND REMONSTRANCE AGAINST RELIGIOUS ASSESSMENTS ¶ 1 (1785), *reprinted in Everson v. Board of Education*, 330 U.S. 1, 64 (1947) (appendix to dissenting opinion of Justice Rutledge). The government can disprove sincerity, however, by showing that the claimant has an ulterior motive, such as greed or immorality, *see, e.g, United States v. Daly*, 756 F.2d 1076, 1081 (5th Cir. 1985) (personal church as tax dodge); or personal drug use, *United States v. Kuch*, 288 F. Supp. 439, 443-45 (D.D.C. 1968).

3. More Than Theism, But How Much More?

The Court has not been entirely clear on what counts as religion for purposes of the Free Exercise Clause. For example, in *Torcaso v. Watkins*, 367 U.S. 488, 495 & n.11 (1961), the Court suggested that Ethical Culture and Secular Humanism were religions, while in *Wisconsin v. Yoder*, it will be recalled that Thoreau's philosophy was said not to count as religious belief. In the next case, the Court takes a particularly liberal view of this definitional question for purposes of construction of a federal statute allowing conscientious objection to military service. While the Court proclaims that religion excludes "essentially political, sociological, or philosophical views," it nevertheless includes "belief that is sincere and meaningful [and that] occupies a place in the life of its possessor parallel to that filled by the orthodox belief in God." *United States v. Seeger*, 380 U.S. 163, 165-66 (1964).

UNITED STATES v. SEEGER
380 U.S. 163 (1964)

MR. JUSTICE CLARK delivered the opinion of the Court.

These cases involve claims of conscientious objectors under § 6(j) of the Universal Military Training and Service Act, 50 U.S.C. App. § 456(j) (1958 ed.), which exempts from combatant training and service in the armed forces of the United States those persons who by reason of their religious training and belief are conscientiously opposed to participation in war in any form. The cases were consolidated for argument and we consider them together although each involves different facts and circumstances. The parties raise the basic question of the constitutionality of the section which defines the term "religious training and belief," as used in the Act, as "an individual's belief in a relation to a Supreme Being involving duties superior to those arising from any human relation, but [not including] essentially political, sociological, or philosophical views or a merely personal moral code." The constitutional attack is launched under the First Amendment's Establishment and Free Exercise Clauses and is twofold: (1) The section does not exempt nonreligious conscientious objectors; and (2) it discriminates between different forms of religious expression in violation of the Due Process Clause of the Fifth Amendment. Jakobson (No. 51) and Peter (No. 29) also claim that their beliefs come within the meaning of the section. Jakobson claims that he meets the standards of § 6(j) because his opposition to war is based on belief in a Supreme Reality and is therefore an obligation superior to one resulting from man's relationship to his fellow man. Peter contends that his opposition to war derives from his acceptance of the existence of a universal power beyond that of man and that this acceptance in fact constitutes belief in a Supreme Being, qualifying him for exemption. We granted certiorari in each of the cases because of their importance in the administration of the Act.

We have concluded that Congress, in using the expression "Supreme Being" rather than the designation "God," was merely clarifying the meaning of religious training and belief so as to embrace all religions and to exclude essentially political, sociological, or philosophical views. We believe that under this construction, the test of belief "in a relation to a Supreme Being" is whether a given belief that is sincere and meaningful occupies a place in the life of its possessor parallel to that filled by the orthodox belief in God of one who clearly qualifies for the exemption. Where such beliefs have parallel positions in the lives of their respective holders we cannot say that one is "in a relation to a Supreme Being" and the other is not. We have concluded that the beliefs of the objectors in these cases meet these criteria . . . .

* * *

Governmental recognition of the moral dilemma posed for persons of certain religious faiths by the call to arms came early in the history of this country. Various methods of ameliorating their difficulty were adopted by the Colonies, and were later perpetuated in state statutes and constitutions. Thus by the time of the Civil War there existed a state pattern of exempting conscientious objectors on religious grounds. . . . With the Federal Conscription Act of 1863, . . . the Federal Government occupied the field entirely, and in the 1864 Draft Act, 13 Stat. 9, it extended exemptions to those conscientious objectors who were members of religious denominations opposed to the bearing of arms and who were prohibited from doing so by the articles of faith of their denominations. . . .

The need for conscription did not again arise until World War I. The Draft Act of 1917, 40 Stat. 76, 78, afforded exemptions to conscientious objectors who were affiliated with a "well-recognized religious sect or organization [then] organized and existing and whose existing creed or principles [forbade] its members to participate in war in any form . . . ." The Act required that all persons be inducted into the armed services, but allowed the conscientious objectors to perform noncombatant service in capacities designated by the President of the United States. . . .

In adopting the 1940 Selective Training and Service Act Congress broadened the exemption afforded in the 1917 Act by making it unnecessary to belong to a pacifist religious sect if the claimant's own opposition to war was based on "religious training and belief." 54 Stat. 889. Those found to be within the exemption were not inducted into the armed services but were assigned to noncombatant service under the supervision of the Selective Service System. . . .

· Between 1940 and 1948 two courts of appeals held that the phrase "religious training and belief" did not include philosophical, social or political policy. Then in 1948 the Congress amended the language of the statute and declared that "religious training and belief" was to be defined as "an individual's belief in a relation to a Supreme Being involving duties superior to those arising from any human relation, but [not including] essentially political, sociological, or philosophical views or a merely personal moral code." The only significant mention of this change in the provision appears in the report of the Senate Armed Services Committee recommending adoption. It said simply this: "This section reenacts substantially the same provisions as were found in subsection 5(g) of the 1940 act. Exemption extends to anyone who, because of religious training and belief in his relation to a Supreme Being, is conscientiously opposed to combatant military service or to both combatant and non-combatant military service."

* * *

2. Few would quarrel, we think, with the proposition that in no field of human endeavor has the tool of language proved so inadequate in the communication of ideas as it has in dealing with the fundamental questions of man's predicament in life, in death or in final judgment and retribution. This fact makes the task of discerning the intent of Congress in using the phrase "Supreme Being" a complex one. Nor is it made the easier by the richness and variety of spiritual life in our country. Over 250 sects inhabit our land. Some believe in a purely personal God, some in a supernatural deity; others think of religion as a way of life envisioning as its ultimate goal the day when all men can live together in perfect understanding and peace. There are those who think of God as the depth of our being; others, such as the Buddhists, strive for a state of lasting rest through self-denial and inner purification; in Hindu philosophy, the Supreme Being is the transcendental reality which is truth, knowledge and bliss. Even those religious groups which have traditionally opposed war in every form have splintered into various denominations: from 1940 to 1947 there were four denominations

using the name "Friends"; the "Church of the Brethren" was the official name of the oldest and largest church body of four denominations composed of those commonly called Brethren; and the "Mennonite Church" was the largest of 17 denominations, including the Amish and Hutterites, grouped as "Mennonite bodies" in the 1936 report on the Census of Religious Bodies. This vast panoply of beliefs reveals the magnitude of the problem which faced the Congress when it set about providing an exemption from armed service. It also emphasizes the care that Congress realized was necessary in the fashioning of an exemption which would be in keeping with its long-established policy of not picking and choosing among religious beliefs.

In spite of the elusive nature of the inquiry, we are not without certain guidelines. In amending the 1940 Act, Congress adopted almost intact the language of Chief Justice Hughes in *United States v. Macintosh* [(1931)]:

> "The essence of religion is belief in a relation to *God* involving duties superior to those arising from any human relation." 283 U.S. at 633-34 (emphasis supplied.)

By comparing the statutory definition with those words, however, it becomes readily apparent that the Congress deliberately broadened them by substituting the phrase "Supreme Being" for the appellation "God." And in so doing it is also significant that Congress did not elaborate on the form or nature of this higher authority which it chose to designate as "Supreme Being." By so refraining it must have had in mind the admonitions of the Chief Justice when he said in the same opinion that even the word "God" had myriad meanings for men of faith:

> "[P]utting aside dogmas with their particular conceptions of deity, freedom of conscience itself implies respect for an innate conviction of paramount duty. The battle for religious liberty has been fought and won with respect to religious beliefs and practices, which are not in conflict with good order, upon the very ground of the supremacy of conscience within its proper field."

* * *

Section 6(j), then, is no more than a clarification of the 1940 provision . . . .

* * *

4. Moreover, we believe this construction embraces the ever-broadening understanding of the modern religious community. The eminent Protestant theologian, Dr. Paul Tillich, whose views the Government concedes would come within the statute, identifies God not as a projection "out there" or beyond the skies but as the ground of our very being.

* * *

Dr. David Saville Muzzey, a leader in the Ethical Culture Movement, states in his book, ETHICS AS A RELIGION (1951), that "[e]verybody except the avowed atheists (and they are comparatively few) believes in some kind of God," and that "The proper question to ask, therefore, is not the futile one, Do you believe in God? but rather, What *kind* of God do you believe in?"

* * *

5. We recognize the difficulties that have always faced the trier of fact in these cases. We hope that the test that we lay down proves less onerous. The examiner is furnished a standard that permits consideration of criteria with which he has had considerable experience. While the applicant's words may differ, the test is simple of application. It is essentially an objective one, namely, does the claimed belief occupy the same place in the life of the objector as an orthodox belief in God holds in the life of one clearly qualified for exemption?

. . . The validity of what he believes cannot be questioned. Some theologians, and indeed some examiners, might be tempted to question the existence of the registrant's "Supreme Being" or the truth of his concepts. But these are inquiries foreclosed to Government. . . .

But we hasten to emphasize that while the "truth" of a belief is not open to question, there remains the significant question whether it is "truly held." This is the threshold question of sincerity which must be resolved in every case. . . .

APPLICATION OF § 6(j) TO THE INSTANT CASES

As we noted earlier, the statutory definition excepts those registrants whose beliefs are based on a "merely personal moral code." The records in these cases, however, show that at no time did any one of the applicants suggest that his objection was based on a "merely personal moral code." Indeed at the outset each of them claimed in his application that his objection was based on a religious belief. We have construed the statutory definition broadly and it follows that any exception to it must be interpreted narrowly. The use by Congress of the words "merely personal" seems to us to restrict the exception to a moral code which is not only personal but which is the sole basis for the registrant's belief and is in no way related to a Supreme Being. . . .

* * *

MR. JUSTICE DOUGLAS, concurring.

* * *

When the present Act was adopted in 1948 we were a nation of Buddhists, Confucianists, and Taoists, as well as Christians. Hawaii, then a Territory, was indeed filled with Buddhists, Buddhism being "probably the major faith, if Protestantism and Roman Catholicism are deemed different faiths." . . .

In the continental United States Buddhism is found "in real strength" in Utah, Arizona, Washington, Oregon, and California. "Most of the Buddhists in the United States are Japanese or Japanese-Americans; however, there are 'English' departments in San Francisco, Los Angeles, and Tacoma." . . .

When the Congress spoke in the vague general terms of a Supreme Being I cannot, therefore, assume that it was so parochial as to use the words in the narrow sense urged on us. I would attribute tolerance and sophistication to the Congress, commensurate with the religious complexion of our communities. In sum, I agree with the Court that any person opposed to war on the basis of a sincere belief, which in his life fills the same place as a belief in God fills in the life of an orthodox religionist, is entitled to exemption under the statute. None comes to us an avowedly irreligious person or as an atheist . . . .

NOTES AND QUESTIONS

Is the *Seeger* opinion too expansive, and therefore, dilutive of the significance of religion? Does a liberalized definition of religion abet the exclusionary Establishment Clause view? Just as religion is removed and deemphasized in terms of public importance under the Court's exclusionary view, formal religion may lose its significance when it becomes indistinguishable from other orientations or motivations for human action. As a Department of Justice Report summarized: "It does not strain credulity to see that [the *Seeger*] approach might ultimately enshrine materialism, narcissism, or even nudism as the ethical or moral motivation for personal action, and hence, 'religion' — a step that seems wholly inconsistent with the intent of the religion clauses." OFFICE OF LEGAL POLICY, U.S. DEP'T. OF JUSTICE, RELIGIOUS LIBERTY UNDER THE FREE EXERCISE CLAUSE 26 (1986). Similarly, a respected American jurisprudence teacher, the late Edward J. Murphy, once wrote:

> In a sense this is a very "religious" society. There are all sorts of gods.
> . . . [T]he question for all of us is not *whether* we will be guided by an ultimate authority, but *who* or *what* that authority will be. Is it to be God? Or is it to be ourselves? Or the State? Or a political party? Or a race? Or an economic class? Or the Stars? Or Satan? Or what? Clearly, each of us will choose, and the choice will be consequential.

Edward J. Murphy, *Conflicting Ultimates: Jurisprudence ss Religious Controversy*, 35 AM. J. JURIS. 129, 129-30 (1990). As a cultural matter, Professor Murphy is undoubtedly correct that who or what we aim our lives toward matters greatly. This again was Washington and Tocqueville's observation about the inumerable connections between religion and morality. It is important, therefore, not to have the Free Exercise Clause patronizing false gods. But which gods are false? In a religiously pluralistic nation, especially one guaranteeing religious freedom, are any and all conceptions of religion entitled to constitutional protection?

4. Prohibitions or Burdens?

The following cases, *Braunfeld v. Brown*, 366 U.S. 398 (1963), and *Sherbert v. Verner*, 374 U.S. 398 (1963), may seem in direct conflict, and perhaps they are.

Both deal with more or less generally applicable laws or regulations — *Braunfeld* with a Sunday closing law that adversely affected orthodox Jews who for religious reasons closed on Saturday, and thus lost an entire weekend's worth of business, and *Sherbert* with a general state law precluding employment compensation for those who refuse to work "without good cause," including by application, a Seventh Day Adventist who, in accord with her faith, would not work on Saturday. Both laws "burdened" the exercise of religious practice, but *Braunfeld* held that it merely made the exercise of faith "more expensive," 366 U.S. at 605, while *Sherbert* reasoned that the Free Exercise Clause precludes forcing a person to "choose between" her religion and government benefits. 374 U.S. at 404. The majority claims *Sherbert* is "wholly dissimilar" from *Braunfeld*, in that the state had a compelling interest in a uniform day of rest in the latter, but not in avoiding fraudulent employment claims in the former. *Id*. at 408. Maybe, but Justice Stewart, concurring only in the result of *Sherbert*, highlights that Mr. Braunfeld's loss of his business far outweighed Mrs. Sherbert's denial of compensation payments. *Id*. at 417-18 (Stewart, J., concurring).

In a subsequent case, *Employment Division v. Smith*, 494 U.S. 872 (1990) (discussed in Part 5), *Sherbert* will be distinguished differently, as a particularized denial of compensation based upon religion — that is, Mrs. Sherbert lost her benefits only after a government administrator concluded that declining work for religious reasons wasn't a "good cause." *Id*. at 884. That distinction at least makes sense; however, there is a lingering problem. Both *Braunfeld* and *Sherbert* assume that government action which indirectly *burdens* a religious practice falls within a constitutional limitation on *prohibiting* religious practice. When the framers wanted to use a word suggesting burden, they knew how to do it, say, in the Free Speech Clause precluding its "abridgment." Thus, it is possible to argue that the words "or prohibiting the free exercise" mean actually forbidding a religious belief or preventing a religious practice — as in *Wisconsin v. Yoder*, above — not merely making it more expensive [*Braunfeld*] or difficult [*Sherbert*]. Nominally, the Court has not been this textualist; after all, Mrs. Sherbert won with only a burden. However, *Employment Division v. Smith* suggests a retrenchment by the Court from protecting religious exercise from religiously neutral, generally applicable statutes. Might this retrenchment not have occurred, had the Court applied the Free Exercise Clause only to prohibitions, thus lessening the occasion for conflict between religious value and government edict?

BRAUNFELD v. BROWN
366 U.S. 599 (1961)

MR. CHIEF JUSTICE WARREN announced the judgment of the Court and an opinion in which MR. JUSTICE BLACK, MR. JUSTICE CLARK, and MR. JUSTICE WHITTAKER concur.

This case concerns the constitutional validity of the application to appellants of the Pennsylvania criminal statute, enacted in 1959, which proscribes the Sunday retail sale of certain enumerated commodities. . . . [T]he only question for consideration is whether the statute interferes with the free exercise of appellants' religion.

Appellants are merchants in Philadelphia who engage in the retail sale of clothing and home furnishings within the proscription of the statute in issue. Each of the appellants is a member of the Orthodox Jewish faith, which requires the closing of their places of business and a total abstention from all manner of work from nightfall each Friday until nightfall each Saturday. They instituted a suit in the court below seeking a permanent injunction against the enforcement of the 1959 statute. Their complaint, as amended, alleged that appellants had previously kept their places of business open on Sunday; that each of appellants had done a substantial amount of business on Sunday, compensating somewhat for their closing on Saturday; that Sunday closing will result in impairing the ability of all appellants to earn a livelihood and will render appellant Braunfeld unable to continue in his business, thereby losing his capital investment; that the statute is unconstitutional for the reasons stated above.

* * *

Certain aspects of religious exercise cannot, in any way, be restricted or burdened by either federal or state legislation. Compulsion by law of the acceptance of any creed or the practice of any form of worship is strictly forbidden. The freedom to hold religious beliefs and opinions is absolute. . . . But this is not the case at bar; the statute before us does not make criminal the holding of any religious belief or opinion, nor does it force anyone to embrace any religious belief or to say or believe anything in conflict with his religious tenets.

However, the freedom to act, even when the action is in accord with one's religious convictions, is not totally free from legislative restrictions. As pointed out in *Reynolds v. United States* [(1878)], legislative power over mere opinion is forbidden but it may reach people's actions when they are found to be in violation of important social duties or subversive of good order, even when the actions are demanded by one's religion. . . .2

Thus, in *Reynolds v. United States*, this Court upheld the polygamy conviction of a member of the Mormon faith despite the fact that an accepted doctrine of his church then imposed upon its male members the *duty* to practice polygamy. And, in *Prince v. Commonwealth of Massachusetts* [(1943)], this Court upheld

---

2 Oliver Ellsworth, a member of the Constitutional Convention and later Chief Justice, wrote:

"But while I assert the rights of religious liberty, I would not deny that the civil power has a right, in some cases, to interfere in matters of religion. It has a right to prohibit and punish gross immoralities and impieties; because the open *practice* of these is of evil example and detriment." (Emphasis added.) Written in the *Connecticut Courant*, Dec. 17, 1787, *as quoted in* 1 STOKES, CHURCH AND STATE IN THE UNITED STATES, 535.

a statute making it a crime for a girl under eighteen years of age to sell any newspapers, periodicals or merchandise in public places despite the fact that a child of the Jehovah's Witnesses faith believed that it was her religious *duty* to perform this work.

It is to be noted that, in the two cases just mentioned, the religious practices themselves conflicted with the public interest. In such cases, to make accommodation between the religious action and an exercise of state authority is a particularly delicate task, because resolution in favor of the State results in the choice to the individual of either abandoning his religious principle or facing criminal prosecution.

But, again, this is not the case before us because the statute at bar does not make unlawful any religious practices of appellants; the Sunday law simply regulates a secular activity and, as applied to appellants, operates so as to make the practice of their religious beliefs more expensive. Furthermore, the law's effect does not inconvenience all members of the Orthodox Jewish faith but only those who believe it necessary to work on Sunday. And even these are not faced with as serious a choice as forsaking their religious practices or subjecting themselves to criminal prosecution. Fully recognizing that the alternatives open to appellants and others similarly situated — retaining their present occupations and incurring economic disadvantage or engaging in some other commercial activity which does not call for either Saturday or Sunday labor — may well result in some financial sacrifice in order to observe their religious beliefs, still the option is wholly different than when the legislation attempts to make a religious practice itself unlawful.

To strike down, without the most critical scrutiny, legislation which imposes only an indirect burden on the exercise of religion, *i.e.*, legislation which does not make unlawful the religious practice itself, would radically restrict the operating latitude of the legislature. Statutes which tax income and limit the amount which may be deducted for religious contributions impose an indirect economic burden on the observance of the religion of the citizen whose religion requires him to donate a greater amount to his church; statutes which require the courts to be closed on Saturday and Sunday impose a similar indirect burden on the observance of the religion of the trial lawyer whose religion requires him to rest on a weekday. The list of legislation of this nature is nearly limitless.

Needless to say, when entering the area of religious freedom, we must be fully cognizant of the particular protection that the Constitution has accorded it. Abhorrence of religious persecution and intolerance is a basic part of our heritage. But we are a cosmopolitan nation made up of people of almost every conceivable religious preference. These denominations number almost three hundred. Consequently, it cannot be expected, much less required, that legislators enact no law regulating conduct that may in some way result in an economic disadvantage to some religious sects and not to others because of the special practices of the various religions. We do not believe that such an effect is an absolute test for determining whether the legislation violates the freedom of religion protected by the First Amendment.

Of course, to hold unassailable all legislation regulating conduct which imposes solely an indirect burden on the observance of religion would be a gross oversimplification. If the purpose or effect of a law is to impede the observance of one or all religions or is to discriminate invidiously between religions, that law is constitutionally invalid even though the burden may be characterized as being only indirect. But if the State regulates conduct by enacting a general law within its power, the purpose and effect of which is to advance the State's secular goals, the statute is valid despite its indirect burden on religious observance unless the State may accomplish its purpose by means which do not impose such a burden.

* * *

MR. JUSTICE BRENNAN, concurring and dissenting.

* * *

Admittedly, these laws do not compel overt affirmation of a repugnant belief, . . . nor do they prohibit outright any of appellants' religious practices, as did the federal law upheld in *Reynolds v. United States* (1878), cited by the Court. That is, the laws do not say that appellants must work on Saturday. But their effect is that appellants may not simultaneously practice their religion and their trade, without being hampered by a substantial competitive disadvantage. Their effect is that no one may at one and the same time be an Orthodox Jew and compete effectively with his Sunday-observing fellow tradesmen. . . .

What, then, is the compelling state interest which impels the Commonwealth of Pennsylvania to impede appellants' freedom of worship? What overbalancing need is so weighty in the constitutional scale that it justifies this substantial, though indirect, limitation of appellants' freedom? It is not the desire to stamp out a practice deeply abhorred by society, such as polygamy, as in *Reynolds*, for the custom of resting one day a week is universally honored, as the Court has amply shown. Nor is it the State's traditional protection of children, as in *Prince v. Commonwealth of Massachusetts* (1944), for appellants are reasoning and fully autonomous adults. It is not even the interest in seeing that everyone rests one day a week, for appellants' religion requires that they take such a rest. It is the mere convenience of having everyone rest on the same day. It is to defend this interest that the Court holds that a State need not follow the alternative route of granting an exemption for those who in good faith observe a day of rest other than Sunday.

* * *

In fine, the Court, in my view, has exalted administrative convenience to a constitutional level high enough to justify making one religion economically disadvantageous. The Court would justify this result on the ground that the effect on religion, though substantial, is indirect. The Court forgets, I think, a warning uttered during the congressional discussion of the First Amendment itself: ". . . the rights of conscience are, in their nature, of peculiar delicacy, and will little bear the gentlest touch of governmental hand . . . ."

I would reverse this judgment and remand for a trial of appellants' allegations, limited to the free-exercise-of-religion issue.

MR. JUSTICE STEWART, dissenting.

I agree with substantially all that MR. JUSTICE BRENNAN has written. Pennsylvania has passed a law which compels an Orthodox Jew to choose between his religious faith and his economic survival. That is a cruel choice. It is a choice which I think no State can constitutionally demand. For me this is not something that can be swept under the rug and forgotten in the interest of enforced Sunday togetherness. I think the impact of this law upon these appellants grossly violates their constitutional right to the free exercise of their religion.

SHERBERT v. VERNER
374 U.S. 398 (1963)

MR. JUSTICE BRENNAN delivered the opinion of the Court.

Appellant, a member of the Seventh-Day Adventist Church, was discharged by her South Carolina employer because she would not work on Saturday, the Sabbath Day of her faith. When she was unable to obtain other employment because from conscientious scruples she would not take Saturday work, she filed a claim for unemployment compensation benefits under the South Carolina Unemployment Compensation Act. That law provides that, to be eligible for benefits, a claimant must be "able to work and . . . available for work"; and, further, that a claimant is ineligible for benefits "[i]f . . . he has failed, without good cause . . . to accept available suitable work when offered him by the employment office or the employer . . . ." The appellee Employment Security Commission, in administrative proceedings under the statute, found that appellant's restriction upon her availability for Saturday work brought her within the provision disqualifying for benefits insured workers who fail, without good cause, to accept "suitable work when offered . . . by the employment office or the employer . . . ." The Commission's finding was sustained by the Court of Common Pleas for Spartanburg County. That court's judgment was in turn affirmed by the South Carolina Supreme Court, which rejected appellant's contention that, as applied to her, the disqualifying provisions of the South Carolina statute abridged her right to the free exercise of her religion secured under the Free Exercise Clause of the First Amendment through the Fourteenth Amendment. The State Supreme Court held specifically that appellant's ineligibility infringed no constitutional liberties because such a construction of the statute "places no restriction upon the appellant's freedom of religion nor does it in any way prevent her in the exercise of her right and freedom to observe her religious beliefs in accordance with the dictates of her conscience." We noted probable jurisdiction of appellant's appeal. We reverse the judgment of the South Carolina Supreme Court and remand for further proceedings not inconsistent with this opinion.

I

The door of the Free Exercise Clause stands tightly closed against any governmental regulation of religious *beliefs* as such, *Cantwell v. Connecticut* [(1940)]. Government may neither compel affirmation of a repugnant belief, *Torcaso v. Watkins* [(1961)]; nor penalize or discriminate against individuals or groups because they hold religious views abhorrent to the authorities, *Fowler v. Rhode Island* [(1953)]; nor employ the taxing power to inhibit the dissemination of particular religious views, *Murdock v. Pennsylvania* [(1943)]; *Follett v. McCormick* [(1944)]; *cf. Grosjean v. American Press Co.* [(1936)]. On the other hand, the Court has rejected challenges under the Free Exercise Clause to governmental regulation of certain overt acts prompted by religious beliefs or principles, for "even when the action is in accord with one's religious convictions, [it] is not totally free from legislative restrictions." *Braunfeld v. Brown* [(1961)]. The conduct or actions so regulated have invariably posed some substantial threat to public safety, peace or order. *See, e.g., Reynolds v. United States* [(1878)]; *Jacobson v. Massachusetts* [(1905)]; *Prince v. Massachusetts* [(1944)]; *Cleveland v. United States* [(1946)].

Plainly enough, appellant's conscientious objection to Saturday work constitutes no conduct prompted by religious principles of a kind within the reach of state legislation. If, therefore, the decision of the South Carolina Supreme Court is to withstand appellant's constitutional challenge, it must be either because her disqualification as a beneficiary represents no infringement by the State of her constitutional rights of free exercise, or because any incidental burden on the free exercise of appellant's religion may be justified by a "compelling state interest in the regulation of a subject within the State's constitutional power to regulate . . . ." *NAACP v. Button* [(1963)].

II

We turn first to the question whether the disqualification for benefits imposes any burden on the free exercise of appellant's religion. We think it is clear that it does. In a sense the consequences of such a disqualification to religious principles and practices may be only an indirect result of welfare legislation within the State's general competence to enact; it is true that no criminal sanctions directly compel appellant to work a six-day week. But this is only the beginning, not the end, of our inquiry. For "[i]f the purpose or effect of a law is to impede the observance of one or all religions or is to discriminate invidiously between religions, that law is constitutionally invalid even though the burden may be characterized as being only indirect." *Braunfeld.* Here not only is it apparent that appellant's declared ineligibility for benefits derives solely from the practice of her religion, but the pressure upon her to forego that practice is unmistakable. The ruling forces her to choose between following the precepts of her religion and forfeiting benefits, on the one hand, and abandoning one of the precepts of her religion in order to accept work, on the other hand. Governmental imposition of such a choice puts the same kind of burden upon the free exercise of religion as would a fine imposed against appellant for her Saturday worship.

Nor may the South Carolina court's construction of the statute be saved from constitutional infirmity on the ground that unemployment compensation benefits are not appellant's "right" but merely a "privilege." It is too late in the day to doubt that the liberties of religion and expression may be infringed by the denial of or placing of conditions upon a benefit or privilege. . . .

Significantly South Carolina expressly saves the Sunday worshipper from having to make the kind of choice which we here hold infringes the Sabbatarian's religious liberty. When in times of "national emergency" the textile plants are authorized by the State Commissioner of Labor to operate on Sunday, "no employee shall be required to work on Sunday . . . who is conscientiously opposed to Sunday work; and if any employee should refuse to work on Sunday on account of conscientious . . . objections he or she shall not jeopardize his or her seniority by such refusal or be discriminated against in any other manner." S.C. Code, § 64-4. No question of the disqualification of a Sunday worshipper for benefits is likely to arise, since we cannot suppose that an employer will discharge him in violation of this statute. The unconstitutionality of the disqualification of the Sabbatarian is thus compounded by the religious discrimination which South Carolina's general statutory scheme necessarily effects.

III

We must next consider whether some compelling state interest enforced in the eligibility provisions of the South Carolina statute justifies the substantial infringement of appellant's First Amendment right. . . . The appellees suggest no more than a possibility that the filing of fraudulent claims by unscrupulous claimants feigning religious objections to Saturday work might not only dilute the unemployment compensation fund but also hinder the scheduling by employers of necessary Saturday work. But that possibility is not apposite here because no such objection appears to have been made before the South Carolina Supreme Court, and we are unwilling to assess the importance of an asserted state interest without the views of the state court. Nor, if the contention had been made below, would the record appear to sustain it; there is no proof whatever to warrant such fears of malingering or deceit as those which the respondents now advance. Even if consideration of such evidence is not foreclosed by the prohibition against judicial inquiry into the truth or falsity of religious beliefs, *United States v. Ballard* [(1944)] — a question as to which we intimate no view since it is not before us — it is highly doubtful whether such evidence would be sufficient to warrant a substantial infringement of religious liberties. For even if the possibility of spurious claims did threaten to dilute the fund and disrupt the scheduling of work, it would plainly be incumbent upon the appellees to demonstrate that no alternative forms of regulation would combat such abuses without infringing First Amendment rights.

In these respects, then, the state interest asserted in the present case is wholly dissimilar to the interests which were found to justify the less direct burden upon religious practices in *Braunfeld v. Brown, supra*. The Court recognized that the Sunday closing law which that decision sustained undoubtedly served "to make the practice of [the Orthodox Jewish merchants'] . . . religious beliefs more expensive." But the statute was nevertheless saved by a countervailing factor which finds no equivalent in the instant case — a strong state interest in providing one uniform day of rest for all workers. That secular objective could be achieved, the Court found, only by declaring Sunday to be that day of rest. Requiring exemptions for Sabbatarians, while theoretically possible, appeared to present an administrative problem of such magnitude, or to afford the exempted class so great a competitive advantage, that such a requirement would have rendered the entire statutory scheme unworkable. . . .

IV

In holding as we do, plainly we are not fostering the "establishment" of the Seventh-Day Adventist religion in South Carolina, for the extension of unemployment benefits to Sabbatarians in common with Sunday worshippers reflects nothing more than the governmental obligation of neutrality in the face of religious differences, and does not represent that involvement of religious with secular institutions which it is the object of the Establishment Clause to forestall.

. . . Our holding today is only that South Carolina may not constitutionally apply the eligibility provisions so as to constrain a worker to abandon his religious convictions respecting the day of rest. This holding but reaffirms a principle that we announced a decade and a half ago, namely that no State may "exclude individual Catholics, Lutherans, Mohammedans, Baptists, Jews, Methodists, Non-believers, Presbyterians, or the members of any other faith, *because of their faith, or lack of it*, from receiving the benefits of public welfare legislation." *Everson v. Board of Education* (1947).

In view of the result we have reached under the First and Fourteenth Amendments' guarantee of free exercise of religion, we have no occasion to consider appellant's claim that the denial of benefits also deprived her of the equal protection of the laws in violation of the Fourteenth Amendment.

The judgment of the South Carolina Supreme Court is reversed and the case is remanded for further proceedings not inconsistent with this opinion.

It is so ordered.

MR. JUSTICE DOUGLAS, concurring.

* * *

This case is resolvable not in terms of what an individual can demand of government, but solely in terms of what government may not do to an individual in violation of his religious scruples. The fact that government cannot exact from me a surrender of one iota of my religious scruples does not, of course, mean that I can demand of government a sum of money, the better to exercise them. For the Free Exercise Clause is written in terms of what the government cannot do to the individual, not in terms of what the individual can exact from the government.

* * *

MR. JUSTICE STEWART, concurring in the result.

Although fully agreeing with the result which the Court reaches in this case, I cannot join the Court's opinion. This case presents a double-barreled dilemma, which in all candor I think the Court's opinion has not succeeded in papering over. The dilemma ought to be resolved.

I

* * *

I am convinced that no liberty is more essential to the continued vitality of the free society which our Constitution guarantees than is the religious liberty protected by the Free Exercise Clause explicit in the First Amendment and imbedded in the Fourteenth. And I regret that on occasion, and specifically in *Braunfeld v. Brown, supra*, the Court has shown what has seemed to me a distressing insensitivity to the appropriate demands of this constitutional guarantee. By contrast I think that the Court's approach to the Establishment Clause has on occasion . . . and specifically in *Engel* [*v. Vitale*, (1962)], [*Sch. Dist. v.*] *Schempp* [(1963)] and *Murray* [*v. Curlett* (companion case to *Schempp*)], been not only insensitive, but positively wooden, and that the Court has accorded to the Establishment Clause a meaning which neither the words, the history, nor the intention of the authors of that specific constitutional provision even remotely suggests.

But my views as to the correctness of the Court's decisions in these cases are beside the point here. The point is that the decisions are on the books. And the result is that there are many situations where legitimate claims under the Free Exercise Clause will run into head-on collision with the Court's insensitive and sterile construction of the Establishment Clause. The controversy now before us is clearly such a case.

Because the appellant refuses to accept available jobs which would require her to work on Saturdays, South Carolina has declined to pay unemployment compensation benefits to her. Her refusal to work on Saturdays is based on the tenets of her religious faith. The Court says that South Carolina cannot under these circumstances declare her to be not "available for work" within the meaning of its statute because to do so would violate her constitutional right to the free exercise of her religion.

Yet what this Court has said about the Establishment Clause must inevitably lead to a diametrically opposite result. If the appellant's refusal to work on

Saturdays were based on indolence, or on a compulsive desire to watch the Saturday television programs, no one would say that South Carolina could not hold that she was not "available for work" within the meaning of its statute. That being so, the Establishment Clause as construed by this Court not only *permits* but affirmatively *requires* South Carolina equally to deny the appellant's claim for unemployment compensation when her refusal to work on Saturdays is based upon her religious creed. For, as said in *Everson v. Board of Education* [(1947)], the Establishment Clause bespeaks "a government . . . stripped of all power . . . to support, or otherwise to assist any or all religions . . .," and no State "can pass laws which aid one religion . . . ." . . .

To require South Carolina to so administer its laws as to pay public money to the appellant under the circumstances of this case is thus clearly to require the State to violate the Establishment Clause as construed by this Court. This poses no problem for me, because I think the Court's mechanistic concept of the Establishment Clause is historically unsound and constitutionally wrong. I think the process of constitutional decision in the area of the relationships between government and religion demands considerably more than the invocation of broad-brushed rhetoric of the kind I have quoted. And I think that the guarantee of religious liberty embodied in the Free Exercise Clause affirmatively requires government to create an atmosphere of hospitality and accommodation to individual belief or disbelief. In short, I think our Constitution commands the positive protection by government of religious freedom — not only for a minority, however small — not only for the majority, however large — but for each of us.

South Carolina would deny unemployment benefits to a mother unavailable for work on Saturdays because she was unable to get a babysitter. Thus, we do not have before us a situation where a State provides unemployment compensation generally, and singles out for disqualification only those persons who are unavailable for work on religious grounds. This is not, in short, a scheme which operates so as to discriminate against religion as such. But the Court nevertheless holds that the State must prefer a religious over a secular ground for being unavailable for work — that state financial support of the appellant's religion is constitutionally required to carry out "the governmental obligation of neutrality in the face of religious differences . . . ."

* * *

II

My second difference with the Court's opinion is that I cannot agree that today's decision can stand consistently with *Braunfeld v. Brown*. The Court says that there was a "less direct burden upon religious practices" in that case than in this. With all respect, I think the Court is mistaken, simply as a matter of fact. The *Braunfeld* case involved a state *criminal* statute. The undisputed effect of that statute, as pointed out by MR. JUSTICE BRENNAN in his dissenting opinion in that case, was that "'Plaintiff, Abraham Braunfeld, will be unable to continue in his business if he may not stay open on Sunday and he will thereby lose his capital investment.' In other words, the issue in this case — and we do not understand either appellees or the Court to contend otherwise — is whether a State may put an individual to a choice between his business and his religion."

The impact upon the appellant's religious freedom in the present case is considerably less onerous. We deal here not with a criminal statute, but with the particularized administration of South Carolina's Unemployment Compensation Act. Even upon the unlikely assumption that the appellant could not find suitable non-Saturday employment, the appellant at the worst would be denied a maximum of 22 weeks of compensation payments. I agree with the Court that the possibility of that denial is enough to infringe upon the appellant's constitutional right to the free exercise of her religion. But it is clear to me that in order to reach this conclusion the court must explicitly reject the reasoning of *Braunfeld v. Brown*. I think the *Braunfeld* case was wrongly decided and should be overruled, and accordingly I concur in the result reached by the Court in the case before us.

Mr. Justice Harlan, whom Mr. Justice White joins, dissenting.

Today's decision is disturbing both in its rejection of existing precedent and in its implications for the future. . . .

* * *

. . . Since virtually all of the mills in the Spartanburg area were operating on a six-day week, the appellant was "unavailable for work," and thus ineligible for benefits, when personal considerations prevented her from accepting employment on a full-time basis in the industry and locality in which she had worked. The fact that these personal considerations sprang from her religious convictions was wholly without relevance to the state court's application of the law. Thus in no proper sense can it be said that the State discriminated against the appellant on the basis of her religious beliefs or that she was denied benefits *because* she was a Seventh-Day Adventist. She was denied benefits just as any other claimant would be denied benefits who was not "available for work" for personal reasons.

With this background, this Court's decision comes into clearer focus. What the Court is holding is that if the State chooses to condition unemployment compensation on the applicant's availability for work, it is constitutionally compelled to *carve out an exception* — and to provide benefits — for those whose unavailability is due to their religious convictions. Such a holding has particular significance in two respects.

First, despite the Court's protestations to the contrary, the decision necessarily overrules *Braunfeld v. Brown*, which held that it did not offend the "Free Exercise" Clause of the Constitution for a State to forbid a Sabbatarian to do business on Sunday. . . .

Second, the implications of the present decision are far more troublesome than its apparently narrow dimensions would indicate at first glance. The meaning of today's holding, as already noted, is that the State must furnish unemployment benefits to one who is unavailable for work if the unavailability stems from the exercise of religious convictions. The State, in other words, must *single out* for financial assistance those whose behavior is religiously motivated, even though it denies such assistance to others whose identical behavior (in this case, inability to work on Saturdays) is not religiously motivated.

It has been suggested that such singling out of religious conduct for special treatment may violate the constitutional limitations on state action. My own view, however, is that at least under the circumstances of this case it would be a permissible accommodation of religion for the State, if it *chose* to do so, to create an exception to its eligibility requirements for persons like the appellant. The constitutional obligation of "neutrality," *see School District of Abington Township v. Schempp* [(1963)], is not so narrow a channel that the slightest deviation from an absolutely straight course leads to condemnation. . . .

For very much the same reasons, however, I cannot subscribe to the conclusion that the State is constitutionally *compelled* to carve out an exception to its general rule of eligibility in the present case. Those situations in which the Constitution may require special treatment on account of religion are, in my view, few and far between, and this view is amply supported by the course of constitutional litigation in this area. Such compulsion in the present case is particularly inappropriate in light of the indirect, remote, and insubstantial effect of the decision below on the exercise of appellant's religion and in light of the direct financial assistance to religion that today's decision requires.

For these reasons I respectfully dissent from the opinion and judgment of the Court.

5. No Religious Exemption from Neutral, Generally Applicable Laws

EMPLOYMENT DIVISION v. SMITH
494 U.S. 872 (1990)

JUSTICE SCALIA delivered the opinion of the Court.

This case requires us to decide whether the Free Exercise Clause of the First Amendment permits the State of Oregon to include religiously inspired peyote use within the reach of its general criminal prohibition on use of that drug, and thus permits the State to deny unemployment benefits to persons dismissed from their jobs because of such religiously inspired use.

I

Oregon law prohibits the knowing or intentional possession of a "controlled substance" unless the substance has been prescribed by a medical practitioner. . . .

Respondents Alfred Smith and Galen Black (hereinafter respondents) were fired from their jobs with a private drug rehabilitation organization because they ingested peyote [a controlled substance] for sacramental purposes at a ceremony of the Native American Church, of which both are members. When respondents applied to petitioner Employment Division (hereinafter petitioner) for unemployment compensation, they were determined to be ineligible for benefits because they had been discharged for work-related "misconduct." . . .

* * *

. . . [T]he Oregon Supreme Court held that respondents' religiously inspired use of peyote fell within the prohibition of the Oregon statute, which "makes no exception for the sacramental use" of the drug. It then considered whether that prohibition was valid under the Free Exercise Clause, and concluded that it was not. The court therefore reaffirmed its previous ruling that the State could not deny unemployment benefits to respondents for having engaged in that practice.

We . . . granted certiorari.

II

* * *

A

* * *

. . . [T]he "exercise of religion" often involves not only belief and profession but the performance of (or abstention from) physical acts: assembling with others for a worship service, participating in sacramental use of bread and wine, proselytizing, abstaining from certain foods or certain modes of transportation. It would be true, we think (though no case of ours has involved the point), that a State would be "prohibiting the free exercise [of religion]" if it sought to ban such acts or abstentions only when they are engaged in for religious reasons, or only because of the religious belief that they display. It would doubtless be unconstitutional, for example, to ban the casting of "statues that are to be used for worship purposes," or to prohibit bowing down before a golden calf.

Respondents in the present case, however, seek to carry the meaning of "prohibiting the free exercise [of religion]" one large step further. They contend that their religious motivation for using peyote places them beyond the reach of a criminal law that is not specifically directed at their religious practice, and that is concededly constitutional as applied to those who use the drug for other reasons. . . .

. . . We have never held that an individual's religious beliefs excuse him from compliance with an otherwise valid law prohibiting conduct that the State is free to regulate. On the contrary, the record of more than a century of our free exercise jurisprudence contradicts that proposition. . . . We first had occasion to assert that principle in *Reynolds v. United States* (1879), where we rejected the claim that criminal laws against polygamy could not be constitutionally applied to those whose religion commanded the practice. "Laws," we said, "are made for the government of actions, and while they cannot interfere with mere religious belief and opinions, they may with practices. . . . Can a man excuse his practices to the contrary because of his religious belief? To permit this would be to make the professed doctrines of religious belief superior to the law of the land, and in effect to permit every citizen to become a law unto himself."

Subsequent decisions have consistently held that the right of free exercise does not relieve an individual of the obligation to comply with a "valid and neutral law of general applicability on the ground that the law proscribes (or prescribes) conduct that his religion prescribes (or proscribes)." In *Prince v. Massachusetts* (1944), we held that a mother could be prosecuted under the child labor laws for using her children to dispense literature in the streets, her religious motivation notwithstanding. We found no constitutional infirmity in "excluding [these children] from doing there what no other children may do." In *Braunfeld v. Brown* (1961) (plurality opinion), we upheld Sunday-closing laws against the claim that they burdened the religious practices of persons whose religions compelled them to refrain from work on other days. . . .

* * *

The only decisions in which we have held that the First Amendment bars application of a neutral, generally applicable law to religiously motivated action have involved not the Free Exercise Clause alone, but the Free Exercise Clause in conjunction with other constitutional protections, such as freedom of speech and of the press, *see Cantwell v. Connecticut* [(1940)] (invalidating a licensing system for religious and charitable solicitations under which the administrator had discretion to deny a license to any cause he deemed nonreligious); *Murdock v. Pennsylvania* (1943) (invalidating a flat tax on solicitation as applied to the dissemination of religious ideas); *Follett v. McCormick* (1944) (same), or the right of parents, acknowledged in *Pierce v. Society of Sisters* (1925), to direct the education of their children, *see Wisconsin v. Yoder* (1972) (invalidating compulsory school-attendance laws as applied to Amish parents who refused on religious grounds to send their children to school). Some of our cases prohibiting compelled expression, decided exclusively upon free speech grounds, have also involved freedom of religion, *cf. Wooley v. Maynard* (1977) (invalidating compelled display of a license plate slogan that offended individual religious beliefs); *West Virginia Bd. of Education v. Barnette* (1943) (invalidating compulsory flag salute statute challenged by religious objectors). . . .

The present case does not present such a hybrid situation, but a free exercise claim unconnected with any communicative activity or parental right. Respondents urge us to hold, quite simply, that when otherwise prohibitable conduct is accompanied by religious convictions, not only the convictions but the conduct itself must be free from governmental regulation. We have never held that, and decline to do so now. There being no contention that Oregon's drug law represents an attempt to regulate religious beliefs, the communication of religious beliefs, or the raising of one's children in those beliefs, the rule to which we have adhered ever since *Reynolds* plainly controls. . . .

B

Respondents argue that even though exemption from generally applicable criminal laws need not automatically be extended to religiously motivated actors, at least the claim for a religious exemption must be evaluated under the balancing test set forth in *Sherbert v. Verner* (1963). Under the *Sherbert* test, governmental actions that substantially burden a religious practice must be justified by a compelling governmental interest. Applying that test we have, on three occasions, invalidated state unemployment compensation rules that conditioned the availability of benefits upon an applicant's willingness to work under conditions forbidden by his religion. We have never invalidated any governmental action on the basis of the *Sherbert* test except the denial of unemployment compensation. Although we have sometimes purported to apply the *Sherbert* test in contexts other than that, we have always found the test satisfied. In recent years we have abstained from applying the *Sherbert* test (outside the unemployment compensation field) at all. In *Bowen v. Roy* (1986), we declined to apply *Sherbert* analysis to a federal statutory scheme that required benefit applicants and recipients to provide their Social Security numbers. The plaintiffs in that case asserted that it would violate their religious beliefs to obtain and provide a Social Security number for their daughter. We held the statute's application to the plaintiffs valid regardless of whether it was necessary to effectuate a compelling interest. In *Lyng v. Northwest Indian Cemetery Protective Assn.* (1988), we declined to apply *Sherbert* analysis to the Government's logging and road construction activities on lands used for religious purposes by several Native American Tribes, even though it was undisputed that the activities "could have devastating effects on traditional Indian religious practices." In *Goldman v. Weinberger* (1986), we rejected application of the *Sherbert* test to military dress regulations that forbade the wearing of yarmulkes. In *O'Lone v. Estate of Shabazz* (1987), we sustained, without mentioning the *Sherbert* test, a prison's refusal to excuse inmates from work requirements to attend worship services.

Even if we were inclined to breathe into *Sherbert* some life beyond the unemployment compensation field, we would not apply it to require exemptions from a generally applicable criminal law. The *Sherbert* test, it must be recalled, was developed in a context that lent itself to individualized governmental assessment of the reasons for the relevant conduct. As a plurality of the Court noted in *Roy*, a distinctive feature of unemployment compensation programs is that their eligibility criteria invite consideration of the particular circumstances behind an applicant's unemployment: "The statutory conditions [in *Sherbert* and *Thomas v. Review Bd. of Indiana Employment Division* (1981)] provided that a person was not eligible for unemployment compensation benefits if, 'without good cause,' he had quit work or refused available work. The 'good cause' standard created a mechanism for individualized exemptions." As the plurality pointed out in *Roy*, our decisions in the unemployment cases stand for the proposition that where the State has in place a system of individual exemptions, it may not refuse to extend that system to cases of "religious hardship" without compelling reason.

Whether or not the decisions are that limited, they at least have nothing to do with an across-the-board criminal prohibition on a particular form of conduct. . . . We conclude today that the sounder approach, and the approach in accord with the vast majority of our precedents, is to hold the [*Sherbert*] test inapplicable to such challenges. The government's ability to enforce generally applicable prohibitions of socially harmful conduct, like its ability to carry out other aspects of public policy, "cannot depend on measuring the effects of a governmental action on a religious objector's spiritual development." To make an individual's obligation to obey such a law contingent upon the law's coincidence with his religious beliefs, except where the State's interest is "compelling" — permitting him, by virtue of his beliefs, "to become a law unto himself," *Reynolds v. United States* — contradicts both constitutional tradition and common sense.

The "compelling government interest" requirement seems benign, because it is familiar from other fields. But using it as the standard that must be met before the government may accord different treatment on the basis of race, or before the government may regulate the content of speech, is not remotely comparable to using it for the purpose asserted here. What it produces in those other fields — equality of treatment and an unrestricted flow of contending speech — are constitutional norms; what it would produce here — a private right to ignore generally applicable laws — is a constitutional anomaly.

Nor is it possible to limit the impact of respondents' proposal by requiring a "compelling state interest" only when the conduct prohibited is "central" to the individual's religion. It is no more appropriate for judges to determine the "centrality" of religious beliefs before applying a "compelling interest" test in the free exercise field, than it would be for them to determine the "importance" of ideas before applying the "compelling interest" test in the free speech field. What principle of law or logic can be brought to bear to contradict a believer's assertion that a particular act is "central" to his personal faith? Judging the centrality of different religious practices is akin to the unacceptable "business of evaluating the relative merits of differing religious claims." . . .

If the "compelling interest" test is to be applied at all, then, it must be applied across the board, to all actions thought to be religiously commanded. Moreover, if "compelling interest" really means what it says (and watering it down here would subvert its rigor in the other fields where it is applied), many laws will not meet the test. Any society adopting such a system would be courting anarchy, but that danger increases in direct proportion to the society's diversity of religious beliefs, and its determination to coerce or suppress none of them. Precisely because "we are a cosmopolitan nation made up of people of almost every conceivable religious preference," and precisely because we value and protect that religious divergence, we cannot afford the luxury of deeming *presumptively invalid*, as applied to the religious objector, every regulation of conduct that does not protect an interest of the highest order. The rule respondents favor would open the prospect of constitutionally required religious exemptions from civic obligations of almost every conceivable kind — ranging from compulsory military service, to the payment of taxes, to health and safety regulation such as manslaughter and child neglect laws, compulsory vaccination laws, drug laws, and traffic laws, to social welfare legislation such as minimum wage laws, child labor laws, animal cruelty laws, *see, e.g., Church of the Lukumi Babalu Aye Inc. v. City of Hialeah* (S.D. Fla. 1989), environmental protection laws, and laws providing for equality of opportunity for the races. The First Amendment's protection of religious liberty does not require this.[5]

Values that are protected against government interference through enshrinement in the Bill of Rights are not thereby banished from the political process. Just as a society that believes in the negative protection accorded to the press by the First Amendment is likely to enact laws that affirmatively foster the dissemination of the printed word, so also a society that believes in the negative protection accorded to religious belief can be expected to be solicitous of that value in its legislation as well. It is therefore not surprising that a number of States have made an exception to their drug laws for sacramental peyote use. But to say that a nondiscriminatory religious-practice exemption is permitted, or even that it is desirable, is not to say that it is constitutionally required, and that the appropriate occasions for its creation can be discerned by the courts. It may fairly be said that leaving accommodation to the political process will place at a relative disadvantage those religious practices that are not widely engaged in; but that unavoidable consequence of democratic government must be preferred to a system in which each conscience is a law unto itself or in which judges weigh the social importance of all laws against the centrality of all religious beliefs.

* * *

Because respondents' ingestion of peyote was prohibited under Oregon law, and because that prohibition is constitutional, Oregon may, consistent with the Free Exercise Clause, deny respondents unemployment compensation when their dismissal results from use of the drug. The decision of the Oregon Supreme Court is accordingly reversed.

---

5 Justice O'Connor contends that the "parade of horribles" in the text only "demonstrates . . . that courts have been quite capable of . . . strik[ing] sensible balances between religious liberty and competing state interests." But the cases we cite have struck "sensible balances" only because they have all applied the general laws, despite the claims for religious exemption. In any event, Justice O'Connor mistakes the purpose of our parade: it is not to suggest that courts would necessarily permit harmful exemptions from these laws (though they might), but to suggest that courts would constantly be in the business of determining whether the "severe impact" of various laws on religious practice (to use Justice Blackmuns terminology), or the "constitutiona[l] significan[ce]" of the "burden on the specific plaintiffs" (to use Justice O'Connor's terminology) suffices to permit us to confer an exemption. It is a parade of horribles because it is horrible to contemplate that federal judges will regularly balance against the importance of general laws the significance of religious practice.

It is so ordered.

JUSTICE O'CONNOR, with whom JUSTICE BRENNAN, JUSTICE MARSHALL, and JUSTICE BLACKMUN join as to Parts I and II, concurring in the judgment. [Although JUSTICE BRENNAN, JUSTICE MARSHALL, and JUSTICE BLACKMUN join Parts I and II of this opinion, they do not concur in the judgment.]

Although I agree with the result the Court reaches in this case, I cannot join its opinion. In my view, today's holding dramatically departs from well-settled First Amendment jurisprudence, appears unnecessary to resolve the question presented, and is incompatible with our Nation's fundamental commitment to individual religious liberty.

I

* * *

Respondents contend that, because the Oregon Supreme Court declined to decide whether the Oregon Constitution prohibits criminal prosecution for the religious use of peyote, any ruling on the federal constitutional question would be premature. Respondents are of course correct that the Oregon Supreme Court may eventually decide that the Oregon Constitution requires the State to provide an exemption from its general criminal prohibition for the religious use of peyote. Such a decision would then reopen the question whether a State may nevertheless deny unemployment compensation benefits to claimants who are discharged for engaging in such conduct. As the case comes to us today, however, the Oregon Supreme Court has plainly ruled that Oregon's prohibition against possession of controlled substances does not contain an exemption for the religious use of peyote. . . . [T]his finding [is] a "necessary predicate to a correct evaluation of respondents' federal claim," [and thus] the question presented and addressed is properly before the Court.

II

The Court today extracts from our long history of free exercise precedents the single categorical rule that "if prohibiting the exercise of religion . . . is . . . merely the incidental effect of a generally applicable and otherwise valid provision, the First Amendment has not been offended." Indeed, the Court holds that where the law is a generally applicable criminal prohibition, our usual free exercise jurisprudence does not even apply. To reach this sweeping result, however, the Court must not only give a strained reading of the First Amendment but must also disregard our consistent application of free exercise doctrine to cases involving generally applicable regulations that burden religious conduct.

* * *

A

* * *

The Court today . . . interprets the Clause to permit the government to prohibit, without justification, conduct mandated by an individual's religious beliefs, so long as that prohibition is generally applicable. But a law that prohibits certain conduct — conduct that happens to be an act of worship for someone — manifestly does prohibit that person's free exercise of his religion. A person who is barred from engaging in religiously motivated conduct is barred from freely exercising his religion. . . .

The Court responds that generally applicable laws are "one large step" removed from laws aimed at specific religious practices. The First Amendment, however, does not distinguish between laws that are generally applicable and laws that target particular religious practices. Indeed, few States would be so naive as to enact a law directly prohibiting or burdening a religious practice as such. Our free exercise cases have all concerned generally applicable laws that had the effect of significantly burdening a religious practice. . . .

To say that a person's right to free exercise has been burdened, of course, does not mean that he has an absolute right to engage in the conduct. Under our established First Amendment jurisprudence, we have recognized that the freedom to act, unlike the freedom to believe, cannot be absolute. Instead, we have respected both the First Amendment's express textual mandate and the governmental interest in regulation of conduct by requiring the government to justify any substantial burden on religiously motivated conduct by a compelling state interest and by means narrowly tailored to achieve that interest. . . .

. . . [I]n [*Wisconsin v.*] *Yoder* [(1972),] we expressly rejected the interpretation the Court now adopts:

"[O]ur decisions have rejected the idea that religiously grounded conduct is always outside the protection of the Free Exercise Clause. It is true that activities of individuals, even when religiously based, are often subject to regulation by the States in the exercise of their undoubted power to promote the health, safety, and general welfare, or the Federal Government in the exercise of its delegated powers. But to agree that religiously grounded conduct must often be subject to the broad police power of the State is not to deny that there are areas of conduct protected by the Free Exercise Clause of the First Amendment and thus beyond the power of the State to control, *even under regulations of general applicability.* . . .

". . . A regulation neutral on its face may, in its application, nonetheless offend the constitutional requirement for government neutrality if it unduly burdens the free exercise of religion." (emphasis added).

The Court endeavors to escape from our decision[] in . . . *Yoder* by labeling [it a] "hybrid" decision[], but there is no denying that [it and others] expressly relied on the Free Exercise Clause. . . .

B

* * *

In my view, however, the essence of a free exercise claim is relief from a burden imposed by government on religious practices or beliefs, whether the burden is imposed directly through laws that prohibit or compel specific religious practices, or indirectly through laws that, in effect, make abandonment of one's own religion or conformity to the religious beliefs of others the price of an equal place in the civil community. . . .

* * *

Legislatures, of course, have always been "left free to reach actions which were in violation of social duties or subversive of good order." . . .

* * *

The Court today gives no convincing reason to depart from settled First Amendment jurisprudence. There is nothing talismanic about neutral laws of general applicability or general criminal prohibitions, for laws neutral toward religion can coerce a person to violate his religious conscience or intrude upon his religious duties just as effectively as laws aimed at religion. Although the Court suggests that the compelling interest test, as applied to generally applicable laws, would result in a "constitutional anomaly," the First Amendment unequivocally makes freedom of religion, like freedom from race discrimination and freedom of speech, a "constitutional nor[m]," not an "anomaly." . . .

Finally, the Court today suggests that the disfavoring of minority religions is an "unavoidable consequence" under our system of government and that accommodation of such religions must be left to the political process. In my view, however, the First Amendment was enacted precisely to protect the rights of those whose religious practices are not shared by the majority and may be viewed with hostility. The history of our free exercise doctrine amply demonstrates the harsh impact majoritarian rule has had on unpopular or emerging religious groups such as the Jehovah's Witnesses and the Amish. . . .

III

The Court's holding today not only misreads settled First Amendment precedent; it appears to be unnecessary to this case. I would reach the same result applying our established free exercise jurisprudence.

A

* * *

There is . . . no dispute that Oregon has a significant interest in enforcing laws that control the possession and use of controlled substances by its citizens. . . .

B

. . . Although the question is close, I would conclude that uniform application of Oregon's criminal prohibition is "essential to accomplish" its overriding interest in preventing the physical harm caused by the use of a Schedule I controlled substance. Oregon's criminal prohibition represents that State's judgment that the possession and use of controlled substances, even by only one person, is inherently harmful and dangerous. . . .

* * *

I would therefore adhere to our established free exercise jurisprudence and hold that the State in this case has a compelling interest in regulating peyote use by its citizens and that accommodating respondents' religiously motivated conduct "will unduly interfere with fulfillment of the governmental interest." Accordingly, I concur in the judgment of the Court.

JUSTICE BLACKMUN, with whom JUSTICE BRENNAN and JUSTICE MARSHALL join, dissenting.

This Court over the years painstakingly has developed a consistent and exacting standard to test the constitutionality of a state statute that burdens the free exercise of religion. Such a statute may stand only if the law in general, and the State's refusal to allow a religious exemption in particular, are justified by a compelling interest that cannot be served by less restrictive means.

* * *

I

In weighing the clear interest of respondents Smith and Black (hereinafter respondents) in the free exercise of their religion against Oregon's asserted interest in enforcing its drug laws, it is important to articulate in precise terms the state interest involved. It is not the State's broad interest in fighting the critical "war on drugs" that must be weighed against respondents' claim, but the State's narrow interest in refusing to make an exception for the religious, ceremonial use of peyote. . . .

The State's interest in enforcing its prohibition, in order to be sufficiently compelling to outweigh a free exercise claim, cannot be merely abstract or symbolic. The State cannot plausibly assert that unbending application of a criminal prohibition is essential to fulfill any compelling interest, if it does not, in fact, attempt to enforce that prohibition. In this case, the State actually has not evinced any concrete interest in enforcing its drug laws against religious users of peyote. Oregon has never sought to prosecute respondents, and does not claim that it has made significant enforcement efforts against other religious users of peyote. The State's asserted interest thus amounts only to the symbolic preservation of an unenforced prohibition. . . .

Similarly, this Court's prior decisions have not allowed a government to rely on mere speculation about potential harms, but have demanded evidentiary support for a refusal to allow a religious exception. . . .

* * *

The fact that peyote is classified as a Schedule I controlled substance does not, by itself, show that any and all uses of peyote, in any circumstance, are inherently harmful and dangerous. The Federal Government, which created the classifications of unlawful drugs from which Oregon's drug laws are derived, apparently does not find peyote so dangerous as to preclude an exemption for religious use. . . .

The carefully circumscribed ritual context in which respondents used peyote is far removed from the irresponsible and unrestricted recreational use of unlawful drugs. . . .

Moreover, just as in *Yoder*, the values and interests of those seeking a religious exemption in this case are congruent, to a great degree, with those the State seeks to promote through its drug laws. Not only does the church's doctrine forbid nonreligious use of peyote; it also generally advocates self-reliance, familial responsibility, and abstinence from alcohol. . . .

The State also seeks to support its refusal to make an exception for religious use of peyote by invoking its interest in abolishing drug trafficking. There is, however, practically no illegal traffic in peyote. . . .

Finally, the State argues that granting an exception for religious peyote use would erode its interest in the uniform, fair, and certain enforcement of its drug laws. The State fears that, if it grants an exemption for religious peyote use, a flood of other claims to religious exemptions will follow. It would then be placed in a dilemma, it says, between allowing a patchwork of exemptions that would hinder its law enforcement efforts, and risking a violation of the Establishment Clause by arbitrarily limiting its religious exemptions. This argument, however, could be made in almost any free exercise case. . . .

The State's apprehension of a flood of other religious claims is purely speculative. Almost half the States, and the Federal Government, have maintained an exemption for religious peyote use for many years, and apparently have not found themselves overwhelmed by claims to other religious exemptions. . . .

II

Finally, although I agree with JUSTICE O'CONNOR that courts should refrain from delving into questions whether, as a matter of religious doctrine, a particular practice is "central" to the religion, I do not think this means that the courts must turn a blind eye to the severe impact of a State's restrictions on the adherents of a minority religion.

Respondents believe, and their sincerity has *never* been at issue, that the peyote plant embodies their deity, and eating it is an act of worship and communion. Without peyote, they could not enact the essential ritual of their religion.

* * *

III

For these reasons, I conclude that Oregon's interest in enforcing its drug laws against religious use of peyote is not sufficiently compelling to outweigh respondents' right to the free exercise of their religion. Since the State could not constitutionally enforce its criminal prohibition against respondents, the interests underlying the State's drug laws cannot justify its denial of unemployment benefits. . . .

I dissent.

NOTE

Do you find *Smith* consistent with the importance of religious faith to the framers? The *Smith* decision stirred considerable controversy, both in and outside Congress. Congress directly reacted with the passage of the Religious Freedom Restoration Act (RFRA) of 1993, Pub. L. No. 103-141, 107 Stat. 1488 (codified at 42 U.S.C. §§ 2000bb to bb-4 (1994)). However, in *City of Boerne v. Flores*, 521 U.S. 507 (1997), the Court found RFRA to be unconstitutional. *Boerne* involved the application of a garden-variety zoning ordinance to a local church that had been placed within an historic zone. The City of Boerne, Texas, had refused to grant the church a demolition or alteration permit in order to expand because of its negative impact on the historic structure, which sat on a hill as a focal point within the community. Archbishop Flores sued on behalf of the church under RFRA.

Writing for seven members of the Court, Justice Kennedy observed that "Congress enacted RFRA in direct response to the Court's decision in [*Smith*]," and the *Smith* Court's declination to apply the balancing test from *Sherbert v. Verner. Id.* at 2160. Justice Kennedy continued:

> The application of the *Sherbert* test, the *Smith* decision explained, would have produced an anomaly in the law, a constitutional right to ignore neutral laws of general applicability. The anomaly would have been accentuated, the Court reasoned, by the difficulty of determining whether a particular practice was central to an individual's religion.

Id. at 2161. Justice Kennedy explained that the Court did not view *Smith* as a substantial break from precedent, since, pre-*Smith*, "[t]he only instances where a neutral, generally applicable law had failed to pass constitutional muster were cases in which other constitutional protections were at stake." *Id.*

This did not satisfy Congress, however, and in passing RFRA Congress announced:

> (1) [T]he framers of the Constitution, recognizing free exercise of religion as an unalienable right, secured its protection in the First Amendment to the Constitution;

> (2) laws "neutral" toward religion may burden religious exercise as surely as laws intended to interfere with religious exercise;

> (3) governments should not substantially burden religious exercise without compelling justification;

> (4) in *Employment Division v. Smith*, 494 U.S. 872 (1990), the Supreme Court virtually eliminated the requirement that the government justify burdens on religious exercise imposed by laws neutral toward religion; and

> (5) the compelling interest test as set forth in prior Federal court rulings is a workable test for striking sensible balances between religious liberty and competing prior governmental interests.

42 U.S.C. § 2000bb(a). Congress further declared the purposes of RFRA as being:

> (1) to restore the compelling interest test as set forth in *Sherbert v. Verner*, 374 U.S. 398 (1963) and *Wisconsin v. Yoder*, 406 U.S. 205 (1972) and to guarantee its application in all cases where free exercise of religion is substantially burdened; and

> (2) to provide a claim or defense to persons whose religious exercise is substantially burdened by government.

Id. § 2000bb(b).

Rather blatantly, RFRA attempted to reverse *Smith* by prohibiting government from "substantially burden[ing] a person's exercise of religion even if the burden results from a rule of general applicability," unless the government could show that the burden "(1) [wa]s in furtherance of a compelling governmental interest; and (2) [wa]s the least restrictive means of furthering that compelling governmental interest." *Id.* § 2000bb-1. RFRA's scope encompassed any "branch, department, agency, instrumentality, and official (or other person acting under color of law) of the United States," as well as any "State, or . . . subdivision of a State." § 2000bb-2(1). RFRA further applied "to all Federal and State law, and the implementation of that law, whether statutory or otherwise, and whether adopted before or after [RFRA's enactment]." *Id.* § 2000bb-3(a). Accordingly, RFRA's broad coverage reached local and municipal ordinances.

The proponents of RFRA argued that RFRA was not a reversal of *Smith*, but a proper exercise of Congress' power under section 5 of the Fourteenth Amendment. This power is discussed more fully in Chapter Four, but briefly it provides that Congress has the power "to enforce" the provisions of section 1 of the amendment, including the provision that no state can deprive anyone of "liberty . . . without due process of law." U.S. CONST. amend. XIV, § 1. The Court agreed that Congress can enact legislation under § 5 enforcing the constitutional right to the free exercise of religion, because the Free Exercise Clause has been "incorporated" against the states through the Fourteenth Amendment's Due Process Clause. *Boerne*, 521 U.S. at 519 (citing *Cantwell v. Connecticut*, 310 U.S. 296, 303 (1940)). However, the Court concluded that RFRA went too far because it was not remedial, but substantive. In the Court's words:

> Legislation which alters the meaning of the Free Exercise Clause cannot be said to be enforcing the Clause. Congress does not enforce a constitutional right by changing what the right is. It has been given the power "to enforce," not the power to determine what constitutes a constitutional violation. Were it not so, what Congress would be enforcing would no longer be, in any meaningful sense, the "provisions of [the Fourteenth Amendment]."

Id. at 519.

In particular, RFRA was not a proper exercise of remedial or preventive power, because it lacked "congruence between the means used and the ends to be achieved." *Id.* at 530. There was no showing in the legislative record that generally applicable laws had been passed out of religious bigotry. Concluded the Court:

> The stringent test RFRA demands of state laws reflects a lack of proportionality or congruence between the means adopted and the legitimate end to be achieved. If an objector can show a substantial burden on his free exercise, the State must demonstrate a compelling governmental interest and show that the law is the least restrictive means of furthering its interest. . . . If "'compelling interest' really means what it says . . . many laws will not meet the test. . . . [The test] would open the prospect of constitutionally required religious exemptions from civic obligations of almost every conceivable kind." Laws valid under *Smith* would fall under RFRA without regard to whether they had the object of stifling or punishing free exercise. We make these observations not to reargue the position of the majority in *Smith* but to illustrate the substantive alteration of its holding attempted by RFRA. Even assuming RFRA would be interpreted in effect to mandate some lesser test, say one equivalent to intermediate scrutiny, the statute nevertheless would require searching judicial scrutiny of state law with the attendant likelihood of invalidation. This is a considerable congressional intrusion into the States' traditional prerogatives and general authority to regulate for the health and welfare of their citizens.

Id. at 533-34 (quoting *Smith*, 494 U.S. at 888).

The Court in *Boerne* did not reargue the merits of *Smith* as a whole, but assumed its continuing validity. Nevertheless, Justice Scalia defended *Smith* in a separate opinion while Justices O'Connor, Breyer, and Souter indicated a desire to have the principle in *Smith* reargued, even as Justice O'Connor fully shared the Court's discussion of the proper scope of Congress' § 5 authority in *Boerne*. Here is part of the colloquy between Justices Scalia and O'Connor:

CITY OF BOERNE v. FLORES
521 U.S. 507 (1997)

[The majority opinion dealing with Congress' § 5 power to define religious freedom is discussed more fully in Chapter Five.]

JUSTICE SCALIA, with whom JUSTICE STEVENS joins, concurring in part.

I write to respond briefly to the claim of JUSTICE O'CONNOR's dissent (hereinafter "the dissent") that historical materials support a result contrary to the one reached in *Employment Div., Dept. of Human Resources of Ore. v. Smith.* . . . The material that the dissent claims is at odds with *Smith* either has little to say about the issue or is in fact more consistent with *Smith* than with the dissent's interpretation of the Free Exercise Clause. . . .

. . . The Free Exercise Clause, the dissent claims, "is best understood as an affirmative guarantee of the right to participate in religious practices and conduct without impermissible governmental interference, even when such conduct conflicts with a neutral, generally applicable law"; thus, even neutral laws of general application may be invalid if they burden religiously motivated conduct. However, the early "free exercise" enactments cited by the dissent protect only against action that is taken "for" or "in respect of" religion . . . . It is eminently arguable that application of neutral, generally applicable laws of the sort the dissent refers to — such as zoning laws — would not constitute action taken "for," "in respect of," or "on account of" one's religion, or "discriminatory" action.

Assuming, however, that the affirmative protection of religion accorded by the early "free exercise" enactments sweeps as broadly as the dissent's theory would require, those enactments do not support the dissent's view, since they contain "provisos" that significantly qualify the affirmative protection they grant. According to the dissent, the "provisos" support its view because they would have been "superfluous" if "the Court was correct in *Smith* that generally applicable laws are enforceable regardless of religious conscience." I disagree. In fact, the most plausible reading of the "free exercise" enactments (if their affirmative provisions are read broadly, as the dissent's view requires) is a virtual restatement of *Smith*: Religious exercise shall be permitted so long as it does not violate general laws governing conduct. The "provisos" in the enactments negate a license to act in a manner "unfaithfull to the Lord Proprietary" (Maryland Act Concerning Religion of 1649), or "behav[e]" in other than a "peaceabl[e] and quie[t]" manner (Rhode Island Charter of 1663), or "disturb the public peace"

(New Hampshire Constitution), or interfere with the "peace [and] safety of th[e] State" (New York, Maryland, and Georgia Constitutions), or "demea[n]" oneself in other than a "peaceable and orderly manner" (Northwest Ordinance of 1787). At the time these provisos were enacted, keeping "peace" and "order" seems to have meant, precisely, obeying the laws. . . . This limitation upon the scope of religious exercise would have been in accord with the background political philosophy of the age (associated most prominently with John Locke), which regarded freedom as the right "to do only what was not lawfully prohibited," Ellis West, *The Case Against a Right to Religion-Based Exemptions*, 4 NOTRE DAME J. L. ETHICS & PUB. POL'Y 591, 624 (1990) . . . .

* * *

The dissent's final source of claimed historical support consists of statements of certain of the Framers in the context of debates about proposed legislative enactments or debates over general principles (not in connection with the drafting of State or Federal Constitutions). Those statements are subject to the same objection as was the evidence about legislative accommodation: There is no reason to think they were meant to describe what was constitutionally required (and judicially enforceable), as opposed to what was thought to be legislatively or even morally desirable. . . .

It seems to me that the most telling point made by the dissent is to be found, not in what it says, but in what it fails to say. Had the understanding in the period surrounding the ratification of the Bill of Rights been that the various forms of accommodation discussed by the dissent were constitutionally required (either by State Constitutions or by the Federal Constitution), it would be surprising not to find a single state or federal case refusing to enforce a generally applicable statute because of its failure to make accommodation. Yet the dissent cites none — and to my knowledge, and to the knowledge of the academic defenders of the dissent's position, none exists. The closest one can come in the period prior to 1850 is the decision of a New York City municipal court in 1813, holding that the New York Constitution of 1777 required acknowledgment of a priest-penitent privilege, to protect a Catholic priest from being compelled to testify as to the contents of a confession. *People v. Philips*, Court of General Sessions, City of New York (June 14, 1813), *excerpted in Privileged Communications to Clergymen*, 1 CATH. LAW. 199 (1955). Even this lone case is weak authority, not only because it comes from a minor court, but also because it did not involve a statute, and the same result might possibly have been achieved (without invoking constitutional entitlement) by the court's simply modifying the common-law rules of evidence to recognize such a privilege. On the other side of the ledger, moreover, there are two cases, from the Supreme Court of Pennsylvania, flatly rejecting the dissent's view. In *Philips v. Gratz* (Pa. 1831), the court held that a litigant was not entitled to a continuance of trial on the ground that appearing on his Sabbath would violate his religious principles. And in *Stansbury v. Marks* (Pa. 1793), decided just two years after the ratification of the Bill of Rights, the court imposed a fine on a witness who "refused to be sworn, because it was his Sabbath."

. . . The issue presented by *Smith* is, quite simply, whether the people, through their elected representatives, or rather this Court, shall control the outcome of concrete cases [like this one]. For example, shall it be the determination of this Court, or rather of the people, whether church construction will be exempt from zoning laws? The historical evidence put forward by the dissent does nothing to undermine the conclusion we reached in *Smith*: It shall be the people.

JUSTICE O'CONNOR, with whom JUSTICE BREYER joins except as to a portion of Part I, dissenting.

I dissent from the Court's disposition of this case. I agree with the Court that the issue before us is whether the Religious Freedom Restoration Act (RFRA) is a proper exercise of Congress' power to enforce § 5 of the Fourteenth Amendment. But as a yardstick for measuring the constitutionality of RFRA, the Court uses its holding in *Employment Div., Dept. of Human Resources of Ore. v. Smith*, the decision that prompted Congress to enact RFRA as a means of more rigorously enforcing the Free Exercise Clause. I remain of the view that *Smith* was wrongly decided, and I would use this case to reexamine the Court's holding there. Therefore, I would direct the parties to brief the question whether *Smith* represents the correct understanding of the Free Exercise Clause and set the case for reargument. If the Court were to correct the misinterpretation of the Free Exercise Clause set forth in *Smith*, it would simultaneously put our First Amendment jurisprudence back on course and allay the legitimate concerns of a majority in Congress who believed that *Smith* improperly restricted religious liberty. We would then be in a position to review RFRA in light of a proper interpretation of the Free Exercise Clause.

I

I agree with much of the reasoning set forth in Part III-A of the Court's opinion. Indeed, if I agreed with the Court's standard in *Smith*, I would join the opinion. As the Court's careful and thorough historical analysis shows, Congress lacks the "power to decree the substance of the Fourteenth Amendment's restrictions on the States." Rather, its power under § 5 of the Fourteenth Amendment extends only to enforcing the Amendment's provisions. In short, Congress lacks the ability independently to define or expand the scope of constitutional rights by statute. Accordingly, whether Congress has exceeded its § 5 powers turns on whether there is a "congruence and proportionality between the injury to be prevented or remedied and the means adopted to that end." This recognition does not, of course, in any way diminish Congress' obligation to draw its own conclusions regarding the Constitution's meaning. Congress, no less than this Court, is called upon to consider the requirements of the Constitution and to act in accordance with its dictates. But when it enacts legislation in furtherance of its delegated powers, Congress must make its judgments consistent with this

Court's exposition of the Constitution and with the limits placed on its legislative authority by provisions such as the Fourteenth Amendment.

. . . [Nevertheless] I continue to believe that *Smith* adopted an improper standard for deciding free exercise claims. . . . Before *Smith*, our free exercise cases were generally in keeping with this idea: where a law substantially burdened religiously motivated conduct — regardless whether it was specifically targeted at religion or applied generally — we required government to justify that law with a compelling state interest and to use means narrowly tailored to achieve that interest.

The Court's rejection of this principle in *Smith* is supported neither by precedent nor . . . by history. . . .

* * *

II

* * *

B

The principle of religious "free exercise" and the notion that religious liberty deserved legal protection were by no means new concepts in 1791, when the Bill of Rights was ratified. To the contrary, these principles were first articulated in this country in the colonies of Maryland, Rhode Island, Pennsylvania, Delaware, and Carolina, in the mid-1600's. These colonies, though established as sanctuaries for particular groups of religious dissenters, extended freedom of religion to groups — although often limited to Christian groups — beyond their own. Thus, they encountered early on the conflicts that may arise in a society made up of a plurality of faiths.

The term "free exercise" appeared in an American legal document as early as 1648, when Lord Baltimore extracted from the new Protestant governor of Maryland and his councilors a promise not to disturb Christians, particularly Roman Catholics, in the "free exercise" of their religion. Soon after, in 1649, the Maryland Assembly enacted the first free exercise clause by passing the Act Concerning Religion: "[N]oe person . . . professing to beleive in Jesus Christ, shall from henceforth bee any waies troubled, Molested or discountenanced for or in respect of his or her religion nor in the free exercise thereof . . . nor any way [be] compelled to the beleife or exercise of any other Religion against his or her consent, soe as they be not unfaithfull to the Lord Proprietary, or molest or conspire against the civill Government." Act Concerning Religion of 1649 . . . .

These documents suggest that, early in our country's history, several colonies acknowledged that freedom to pursue one's chosen religious beliefs was an essential liberty. Moreover, these colonies appeared to recognize that government should interfere in religious matters only when necessary to protect the civil peace or to prevent "licentiousness." In other words, when religious beliefs conflicted with civil law, religion prevailed unless important state interests militated otherwise. Such notions parallel the ideas expressed in our pre-*Smith* cases — that government may not hinder believers from freely exercising their religion, unless necessary to further a significant state interest.

* * *

E

* * *

. . . By its very nature, Madison wrote, the right to free exercise is "unalienable," both because a person's opinion "cannot follow the dictates of other[s]," and because it entails "a duty toward the Creator." Madison continued:

> "This duty [owed the Creator] is precedent both in order of time and degree of obligation, to the claims of Civil Society. . . . [E]very man who becomes a member of any Civil Society, [must] do it with a saving of his allegiance to the Universal Sovereign. We maintain therefore that in matters of Religion, no man's right is abridged by the institution of Civil Society, and that Religion is wholly exempt from its cognizance."

To Madison, then, duties to God were superior to duties to civil authorities — the ultimate loyalty was owed to God above all. Madison did not say that duties to the Creator are precedent only to those laws specifically directed at religion, nor did he strive simply to prevent deliberate acts of persecution or discrimination. The idea that civil obligations are subordinate to religious duty is consonant with the notion that government must accommodate, where possible, those religious practices that conflict with civil law.

* * *

These are but a few examples of various perspectives regarding the proper relationship between church and government that existed during the time the First Amendment was drafted and ratified. Obviously, since these thinkers approached the issue of religious freedom somewhat differently, it is not possible to distill their thoughts into one tidy formula. Nevertheless, a few general principles may be discerned. Foremost, these early leaders accorded religious exercise a special constitutional status. The right to free exercise was a substantive guarantee of individual liberty, no less important than the right to free speech or the right to just compensation for the taking of property. . . .

Second, all agreed that government interference in religious practice was not to be lightly countenanced. Finally, all shared the conviction that "'true religion and good morals are the only solid foundation of public liberty and happiness.'" To give meaning to these ideas — particularly in a society characterized by religious pluralism and pervasive regulation — there will be times when the Constitution requires government to accommodate the needs of those citizens whose religious practices conflict with generally applicable law.

III

The Religion Clauses of the Constitution represent a profound commitment to religious liberty. Our Nation's Founders conceived of a Republic receptive to voluntary religious expression, not of a secular society in which religious expression is tolerated only when it does not conflict with a generally applicable law. As the historical sources discussed above show, the Free Exercise Clause is properly understood as an affirmative guarantee of the right to participate in religious activities without impermissible governmental interference, even where a believer's conduct is in tension with a law of general application. Certainly, it is in no way anomalous to accord heightened protection to a right identified in the text of the First Amendment. For example, it has long been the Court's position that freedom of speech — a right enumerated only a few words after the right to free exercise — has special constitutional status. Given the centrality of freedom of speech and religion to the American concept of personal liberty, it is altogether reasonable to conclude that both should be treated with the highest degree of respect.

Although it may provide a bright line, the rule the Court declared in *Smith* does not faithfully serve the purpose of the Constitution. Accordingly, I believe that it is essential for the Court to reconsider its holding in *Smith* — and to do so in this very case. I would therefore direct the parties to brief this issue and set the case for reargument.

NOTES AND QUESTIONS

1. Should *Smith* be overruled or would that be a misunderstanding of originalism insofar as an individual's free exercise of religious practice was always subject to "public order" limitations? *Compare* Douglas W. Kmiec, *The Original Understanding of the Free Exercise Clause and Religious Diversity*, 59 UMKC L. REV. 591 (1991) (arguing that *Smith* is correct as to laws that burden, but do not prohibit religious exercise, but that as to true prohibitions a compelling governmental purpose of the public order variety must be demonstrated), *with* Edward McGlynn Gaffney, Jr., *The Religion Clause: A Double Guarantee of Religious Liberty,* 1993 B.Y.U. L. REV. 189 (1993) (discussing the adverse impact of Supreme Court jurisprudence, including primarily *Employment Division v. Smith,* on religious freedom and concluding that remedial legislation is needed "to restore the first of civil liberties to the position of honor it deserves in our republic").

2. Some state legislatures, in light of *Boerne*, adopted RFRA-like statutes under state law. Rhode Island, Illinois, Texas, South Carolina, Arizona, Connecticut, Florida, Alabama, Idaho, New Mexico, and Oklahoma all have state enactments requiring a "compelling state interest" to burden religious belief. Other states are discussing the topic, though not without considerable confusion and disagreement. In California, for example, a state RFRA passed the House, but it did not exempt "an act or refusal to act that is substantially motivated by religious belief, whether or not the religious exercise is compulsory or central to a larger system of religious belief" from the state's other anti-discrimination laws, such as those precluding decision making on the basis of marital status. This has led a director of the Christian Legal Society's Center for Laws and Religious Freedom to characterize the measure as "an unmitigated disaster." Press Release, *California Assembly passes religious freedom act,* The Freedom Forum on Line (Jan. 23, 1998) (quoting Steve McFarland). The prohibition of marital status discrimination had been earlier applied by the California Supreme Court to deny a widow the right to refuse on religious grounds to rent part of her property to an unmarried heterosexual couple. *Smith v. FEHC,* 913 P.2d 909 (Cal. 1996).

Chapter 3

A STRUCTURALLY-DIVIDED, BUT WORKABLE, GOVERNMENT

This Chapter deals primarily with the division of federal power into three co-equal branches: legislative, executive, and judicial. Since the scope of legislative power is taken up in a concentrated way in Chapter Four, the examination of legislative authority here is limited to its interplay with executive and judicial interests. In comparison, more time is spent in this Chapter ascertaining the breadth of judicial and executive authority, although, by design of the founders, much of the definition of these powers, too, is drawn out of the dynamic and overlapping relationship among the three great departments.

A. Historical Antecedents

1. Dividing Governmental Power

In fashioning the structure of the American government, the framers were not writing upon a blank slate. By their own admission, they were greatly influenced by the work of Charles de Montesquieu, a French jurist, who visited England in the early 18th century and was particularly fascinated with England's political institutions. Reflecting upon his English visit, Montesquieu wrote *The Spirit of the Laws*, published in Geneva in 1748. The book was unpopular with the French regime, but was widely read throughout England and other parts of Europe. The passage that follows is sufficient to reveal the framers' debt to Montesquieu.

CHARLES DE MONTESQUIEU
THE SPIRIT OF LAWS (1748)
reprinted in 35 GREAT BOOKS OF THE WESTERN WORLD 67-79
(Mortimer J. Adler et al. eds. & Thomas Nugent trans., 2d ed.,
Encyclopaedia Britannica 1990)

In every government there are three sorts of power: the legislative; the executive in respect to things dependent on the law of nations; and the executive in regard to matters that depend on the civil law.

By virtue of the first, the prince or magistrate enacts temporary or perpetual laws, and amends or abrogates those that have been already enacted. By the second, he makes peace or war, sends or receives embassies, establishes the public security, and provides against invasions. By the third, he punishes criminals, or determines the disputes that arise between individuals. The latter we shall call the judiciary power, and the other simply the executive power of the state.

The political liberty of the subject is a tranquility of mind arising from the opinion each person has of his safety. In order to have this liberty, it is requisite the government be so constituted as one man need not be afraid of another.

When the legislative and executive powers are united in the same person, or in the same body of magistrates, there can be no liberty; because apprehensions may arise, lest the same monarch or senate should enact tyrannical laws, to execute them in a tyrannical manner.

Again, there is no liberty, if the judiciary power be not separated from the legislative and executive. Were it joined with the legislative, the life and liberty of the subject would be exposed to arbitrary control; for the judge would be then the legislator. Were it joined to the executive power, the judge might behave with violence and oppression.

There would be an end of everything, were the same man or the same body, whether of the nobles or of the people, to exercise those three powers, that of enacting laws, that of executing the public resolutions, and of trying the causes of individuals.

* * *

Hence it is that many of the princes of Europe, whose aim has been levelled at arbitrary power, have constantly set out with uniting in their own persons all the branches of magistracy, and all the great offices of state.

As in a country of liberty, every man who is supposed a free agent ought to be his own governor; the legislative power should reside in the whole body of the people. But since this is impossible in large states, and in small ones is subject to many inconveniences, it is fit the people should transact by their representatives what they cannot transact by themselves.

The inhabitants of a particular town are much better acquainted with its wants and interests than with those of other places; and are better judges of the capacity of their neighbours than of that of the rest of their countrymen. The members, therefore, of the legislature should not be chosen from the general body of the nation; but it is proper that in every considerable place a representative should be elected by the inhabitants.

* * *

Neither ought the representative body to be chosen for the executive part of government, for which it is not so fit; but for the enacting of laws, or to see whether the laws in being are duly executed, a thing suited to their abilities, and which none indeed but themselves can properly perform.

* * *

Of the three powers above mentioned, the judiciary is in some measure next to nothing: there remain, therefore, only two; and as these have need of a regulating power to moderate them . . . .

The executive power ought to be in the hands of a monarch, because this branch of government, having need of despatch (sic), is better administered by one than by many: on the other hand, whatever depends on the legislative power is oftentimes better regulated by many than by a single person.

But if there were no monarch, and the executive power should be committed to a certain number of persons selected from the legislative body, there would be an end then of liberty; by reason the two powers would be united, as the same persons would sometimes possess, and would be always able to possess, a share in both.

Were the legislative body to be a considerable time without meeting, this would likewise put an end to liberty. For of two things one would naturally follow: either that there would be no longer any legislative resolutions, and then the state would fall into anarchy; or that these resolutions would be taken by the executive power, which would render it absolute.

It would be needless for the legislative body to continue always assembled. This would be troublesome to the representatives, and, moreover, would cut out too much work for the executive power, so as to take off its attention to its office, and oblige it to think only of defending its own prerogatives, and the right it has to execute.

Again, were the legislative body to be always assembled, it might happen to be kept up only by filling the places of the deceased members with new representatives; and in that case, if the legislative body were once corrupted, the evil would be past all remedy. When different legislative bodies succeed one another, the people who have a bad opinion of that which is actually sitting may reasonably entertain some hopes of the next: but were it to be always the same body, the people upon seeing it once corrupted would no longer expect any good from its laws; and of course they would either become desperate or fall into a state of indolence.

* * *

Were the executive power not to have a right of restraining the encroachments of the legislative body, the latter would become despotic; for as it might arrogate to itself what authority it pleased, it would soon destroy all the other powers.

But it is not proper, on the other hand, that the legislative power should have a right to stay the executive. For as the execution has its natural limits, it is useless to confine it; besides, the executive power is generally employed in momentary operations. . . .

But if the legislative power in a free state has no right to stay the executive, it has a right and ought to have the means of examining in what manner its laws have been executed; . . . .

But whatever may be the issue of that examination, the legislative body ought not to have a power of arraigning the person, nor, of course, the conduct, of him who is entrusted with the executive power. His person should be sacred, because as it is necessary for the good of the state to prevent the legislative body from rendering themselves arbitrary, the moment he is accused or tried there is an end of liberty.

In this case the state would be no longer a monarchy, but a kind of republic, though not a free government. But as the person entrusted with the executive power cannot abuse it without bad counsellors, and such as have the laws as ministers, though the laws protect them as subjects, these men may be examined and punished. . . .

Though, in general, the judiciary power ought not to be united with any part of the legislative, yet this is liable to three exceptions, founded on the particular interest of the party accused.

The great are always obnoxious to popular envy; and were they to be judged by the people, they might be in danger from their judges, and would, moreover, be deprived of the privilege which the meanest subject is possessed of in a free state, of being tried by his peers. The nobility, for this reason, ought not to be cited before the ordinary courts of judicature, but before that part of the legislature which is composed of their own body.

* * *

It might also happen that a subject entrusted with the administration of public affairs may infringe the rights of the people, and be guilty of crimes which the ordinary magistrates either could not or would not punish. But, in general, the legislative power cannot try causes: and much less can it try this particular case, where it represents the party aggrieved, which is the people. It can only, therefore, impeach. But before what court shall it bring its impeachment? Must it go and demean itself before the ordinary tribunals, which are its inferiors, and, being composed, moreover, of men who are chosen from the people as well as itself, will naturally be swayed by the authority of so powerful an accuser? No: in order to preserve the dignity of the people, and the security of the subject, the legislative part which represents the people must bring in its charge before the legislative part which represents the nobility, who have neither the same interests nor the same passions.

Here is an advantage which this government has over most of the ancient republics, where this abuse prevailed, that the people were at the same time both judge and accuser.

The executive power, pursuant of what has been already said, ought to have a share in the legislature by the power of rejecting, otherwise it would soon be stripped of its prerogative. But should the legislative power usurp a share of the executive, the latter would be equally undone.

* * *

Here then is the fundamental constitution of the government we are treating of. The legislative body being composed of two parts, they check one another by the mutual privilege of rejecting. They are both restrained by the executive power, as the executive is by the legislative.

These three powers should naturally form a state of repose or inaction. But as there is a necessity for movement in the course of human affairs, they are forced to move, but still in concert.

As the executive power has no other part in the legislative than the privilege of rejecting, it can have no share in the public debates. . . .

Were the executive power to determine the raising of public money, otherwise than by giving its consent, liberty would be at an end; because it would become legislative in the most important point of legislation.

If the legislative power was to settle the subsidies, not from year to year, but for ever, it would run the risk of losing its liberty, because the executive power would be no longer dependent; and when once it was possessed of such a perpetual right, it would be a matter of indifference whether it held it of itself or of another. The same may be said if it should come to a resolution of entrusting, not an annual, but a perpetual command of the fleets and armies to the executive power.

* * *

When once an army is established, it ought not to depend immediately on the legislative, but on the executive, power; and this from the very nature of the thing, its business consisting more in action than in deliberation.

NOTES AND QUESTIONS

Have any of the ideas from the above passage worked their way into the U.S. Constitution? Consider the following:

1. Montesquieu gives a formal definition for each of the powers of government, and Articles I, II, and III of the Constitution draw these same lines of demarcation for the Legislative, Executive, and Judicial branches respectively.

2. The unification of these powers in one hand leads to tyranny — for example, if the same person who writes the law, also enforces or interprets it, there is no check against the abuse of power. This concern figured prominently in *INS v. Chadha*, 462 U.S. 919 (1983), *infra*, where the Supreme Court invalidated the so-called legislative veto, a means by which one or both houses of Congress, and sometimes a single legislative committee, could both pass laws and implement them as well, thereby encroaching on the authority of the executive. Montesquieu was explicit that "the legislative power should have [no] right to stay the executive," but it should have means of "examining in what manner its laws have been executed." In present jargon, the President is subject to congressional or legislative oversight.

3. Direct democracy is an ideal, but it is impractical, therefore, representative democracies are relied upon in their place. The representative features of the Constitution are manifest in the composition of the House and Senate, as well as the electoral college which formally casts votes for President and Vice President (Article II, Section 1).

4. Federalism enhances the effectiveness of representative democracy, because "local inhabitants" are a better judge of their needs and those who should represent them. Federalism is preserved in the Constitution both by the enumeration of federal power in Article I, as well as the express reservation of all remaining power to the states in the Tenth Amendment. Federalism is discussed in Chapter Four.

5. Those who serve in the legislature may not also serve simultaneously in the executive branch. The so-called "Incompatibility Clause" contained in Article I, Section 6, Clause 3 provides similarly that "no Person holding any [executive] Office under the United States, shall be a Member of either House during his Continuance in Office."

6. The judicial power is perceived as "next to nothing" in terms of its potential threat to tyranny; an observation later repeated by Alexander Hamilton in THE FEDERALIST NO. 78. Today, we have a far different impression, but the fact remains that the extent of judicial authority is still highly dependent upon the administrative willingness of the executive to carry out judicial decisions and upon the legislature to both enact laws needful of interpretation and supply funds for the operation of government generally.

7. The executive power should be as unified as possible in order to allow administrative actions to be taken quickly, or with "dispatch," and the legislative power is best regulated by dividing it, facts again apparent in the Constitution's provision of a single President, rather than a committee (an alternative discussed in the Constitutional Convention) and the bicameral, or two-house, nature of the legislative branch.

8. The legislature must meet to prevent it from being overrun by the other branches of government. Article I, Section 4, Clause 2 of the constitution provides that "The Congress shall assemble at least once in every Year." Presently, except for short recesses and a somewhat longer inter-session recess between the first and second year of a single, two-year congressional term, our Congress is generally on duty. This is a departure from Montesquieu's advice, as he thought it would be "needless" and "troublesome" for the legislative body to be always assembled. This, he argued, would produce "too much work for the executive," and require the executive to always be on the defensive. Most modern presidents would likely strongly agree.

9. Montesquieu urges turnover in the legislative assembly so that it does not become corrupted and in order for people to retain hope that a new collection of representatives might be better. Perhaps as a consequence, the Constitution provides for the entire House of Representatives to stand for election every two years. The high likelihood of re-election, perhaps traceable to certain incumbent advantages like name recognition and access to campaign funds, has lessened the practical significance of Montesquieu's prescription. Of course, modern term limit and campaign finance reform movements echo this early sentiment for a periodic exchange of legislators.

10. Montesquieu checked the potential despotism of a legislative body by giving the executive a "right of restraining the encroachments." We know this as the presidential veto contained in Article I, Section 7, Clauses 2 & 3.

11. The executive may abuse power and "be guilty of crimes." As a general matter, Montesquieu cautioned that no "ordinary tribunal" could properly evaluate such abuse against a sitting executive office-holder. Hence, he called for the "legislative part which represents the nobility" to have the power of impeachment. The founders adopted Montesquieu's idea in Article I, Section 3, Clause 6 of the Constitution: "The Senate shall have the sole Power to try all Impeachments."

12. Montesquieu placed the power to raise and appropriate money in the legislature and denied that power to the executive. Our Constitution adopted this idea: "All Bills for raising Revenue shall originate in the House of Representatives" in Article I, Section 7, Clause 1 and Article I, Section 9, Clause 7 that states "No Money shall be drawn from the Treasury, but in Consequence of Appropriations made by Law."

13. The "business" of the military, instructs Montesquieu, is more "in action than in deliberation." An army should be established and it should not in its immediate or short-term deployments depend upon the legislative, but the executive. The Constitution follows this idea in Article II, Section 2, Clause 1 by providing that: "The President shall be Commander in Chief of the Army and Navy of the United States . . . ."

Do you think we owe Montesquieu copyright royalties? Obviously, our framers drew heavily, sometimes directly, from Montesquieu for our plan of government. The significance of his instruction to the founding generation can be seen not only in what ultimately was included in the Constitution, but also in the principal complaints our forebears lodged against King George III in the Declaration of Independence. Look again at the Declaration of Independence reprinted at the beginning of this volume, and especially the portion that begins:

> . . . The history of the present King of Great Britain is a history of repeated injuries and usurpations, all having, in direct object, the estab-

lishment of an absolute tyranny over these states. To prove this, let facts be submitted to a candid world: . . . .

2. Checks and Balances — Public Good From Individual Interest

Power corrupts. Absolute power corrupts absolutely, opined Lord Acton. The framers saw their task as devising a governmental plan that would keep power in bounds, and thereby, preserve liberty. Two theories competed for attention — one optimistic about human nature and the pursuit of virtue; one pessimistic. The optimists emerged from the Opposition or "Country" Party in England. This party was an off-shoot of the Whigs, who had successfully engineered the Glorious Revolution of 1688, removing the tyrannical Stuarts and establishing the supremacy of the Parliament. The Country Party stressed the division or separation of governmental power and the selection of representatives with personal integrity or virtue. Relying upon Montesquieu, Country Party ideologists thought this was the only sure way to prevent corruption, which was then broadly defined, as not just immorality, but as imbalances in governmental power — for example, if the King became overly dependent on Parliament or vice versa.

Running more pessimistically and counter to the ideas of the Country Party were those traceable to England's Court Party. Colonists holding the Court Party's ideology sought to bring virtue out of self-interest, which they perceived as inevitable. Here, they were influenced somewhat by Bernard Mandeville's 1714 satirical work *The Fable of the Bees* which told of how selfish bees yielded a productive beehive: "Millions endeavoring to supply/Each other's lust and vanity . . ./Thus every part was full of vice/Yet the whole a paradise." BERNARD MANDEVILLE, THE FABLE OF THE BEES 30-33 (Douglas Garman ed., 1934). Political philosopher David Hume independently brought the self-interested perspective to government, writing:

> [I]n contriving any system of government, and fixing the several checks and controuls of the constitution, every man ought to be supposed a *Knave*, and to have no other end, in all his actions, than private interest. By this interest we must govern him, and by means of it, make him, notwithstanding his insatiable avarice and ambition, co-operate to public good.

DAVID HUME, ESSAYS, MORALS, POLITICAL AND LITERARY 117-18 (T. H. Green & T.H. Grose eds., 1889). In economic theory, Adam Smith believed that the self-interested "invisible hand" fostered prosperity in the marketplace "by preferring the support of domestic to that of foreign industry, [the individual] intends only his own security; . . . he intends only his own gain, and he is in this, as in many other cases, led by an invisible hand to promote an end which was not part of his intention." ADAM SMITH, THE WEALTH OF NATIONS 423 (Edwin Cannan ed., 1937).

In final form, the Constitution becomes an amalgam of both ideologies — that is, the separated, and hopefully prudent and virtuous, exercise of power that is capable of being checked by the self-interested or overlapping concerns of other branches. Madison explains the thinking of the constitutional convention in THE FEDERALIST Nos. 47 and 51. Note how the former document references Montesquieu, or if you will, the optimist Country Party view, but then shades its meaning to begin the justification for giving each of the powers some "partial agency" in the others. THE FEDERALIST No. 51 reveals more strongly the skeptical influence of the Court Party ideology, recognizing outright that "ambition must be made to counteract ambition." In practical terms, this means dividing the legislative power, feared to be the most subject to abuse, between bicameral houses, and giving the executive a qualified veto over lawmaking.

THE FEDERALIST NO. 47 (James Madison)
(Clinton Rossiter ed., 1961)

One of the principal objections inculcated by the more respectable adversaries to the Constitution, is its supposed violation of the political maxim, that the legislative, executive, and judiciary departments ought to be separate and distinct. . . .

* * *

The oracle who is always consulted and cited on this subject is the celebrated Montesquieu. If he be not the author of this invaluable precept in the science of politics, he has the merit at least of displaying and recommending it most effectually to the attention of mankind. Let us endeavor, in the first place, to ascertain his meaning on this point.

The British Constitution was to Montesquieu what Homer has been to the didactic writers on epic poetry. As the latter have considered the work of the immortal bard as the perfect model from which the principles and rules of the epic art were to be drawn, and by which all similar works were to be judged, so this great political critic appears to have viewed the Constitution of England as the standard, or to use his own expression, as the mirror of political liberty; and to have delivered, in the form of elementary truths, the several characteristic principles of that particular system. That we may be sure, then, not to mistake his meaning in this case, let us recur to the source from which the maxim was drawn.

On the slightest view of the British Constitution, we must perceive that the legislative, executive, and judiciary departments are by no means totally separate and distinct from each other. The executive magistrate forms an integral part of the legislative authority. He alone has the prerogative of making treaties with foreign sovereigns, which, when made, have, under certain limitations, the force of legislative acts. All the members of the judiciary department are appointed by him, can be removed by him on the address of the two Houses of

Parliament, and form, when he pleases to consult them, one of his constitutional councils. One branch of the legislative department forms also a great constitutional council to the executive chief, as, on another hand, it is the sole depositary of judicial power in cases of impeachment, and is invested with the supreme appellate jurisdiction in all other cases. The judges, again, are so far connected with the legislative department as often to attend and participate in its deliberations, though not admitted to a legislative vote.

From these facts, by which Montesquieu was guided, it may clearly be inferred that, in saying "There can be no liberty where the legislative and executive powers are united in the same person, or body of magistrates," or, "if the power of judging be not separated from the legislative and executive powers," he did not mean that these departments ought to have no PARTIAL AGENCY in, or no CONTROL over, the acts of each other. His meaning, as his own words import, and still more conclusively as illustrated by the example in his eye, can amount to no more than this, that where the WHOLE power of one department is exercised by the same hands which possess the WHOLE power of another department, the fundamental principles of a free constitution are subverted. This would have been the case in the constitution examined by him, if the king, who is the sole executive magistrate, had possessed also the complete legislative power, or the supreme administration of justice; or if the entire legislative body had possessed the supreme judiciary, or the supreme executive authority. This, however, is not among the vices of that constitution. The magistrate in whom the whole executive power resides cannot of himself make a law, though he can put a negative on every law; nor administer justice in person, though he has the appointment of those who do administer it. The judges can exercise no executive prerogative, though they are shoots from the executive stock; nor any legislative function, though they may be advised with by the legislative councils. The entire legislature can perform no judiciary act, though by the joint act of two of its branches the judges may be removed from their offices, and though one of its branches is possessed of the judicial power in the last resort. The entire legislature, again, can exercise no executive prerogative, though one of its branches constitutes the supreme executive magistracy, and another, on the impeachment of a third, can try and condemn all the subordinate officers in the executive department.

The reasons on which Montesquieu grounds his maxim are a further demonstration of his meaning. "When the legislative and executive powers are united in the same person or body," says he, "there can be no liberty, because apprehensions may arise lest THE SAME monarch or senate should ENACT tyrannical laws to EXECUTE them in a tyrannical manner." Again: "Were the power of judging joined with the legislative, the life and liberty of the subject would be exposed to arbitrary control, for THE JUDGE would then be THE LEGISLATOR. Were it joined to the executive power, THE JUDGE might behave with all the violence of AN OPPRESSOR." Some of these reasons are more fully explained in other passages; but briefly stated as they are here, they sufficiently establish the meaning which we have put on this celebrated maxim of this celebrated author.

If we look into the constitutions of the several States, we find that, notwithstanding the emphatical and, in some instances, the unqualified terms in which this axiom has been laid down, there is not a single instance in which the several departments of power have been kept absolutely separate and distinct. [Madison then examines the colonial constitutions of several states in some detail.]

The Federalist No. 51 (James Madison) (Clinton Rossiter ed., 1961)

TO WHAT expedient, then, shall we finally resort, for maintaining in practice the necessary partition of power among the several departments, as laid down in the Constitution? By so contriving the interior structure of the government as that its several constituent parts may, by their mutual relations, be the means of keeping each other in their proper places. Without presuming to undertake a full development of this important idea, I will hazard a few general observations. . . .

The great security against a gradual concentration of the several powers in the same department, consists in giving to those who administer each department the necessary constitutional means and personal motives to resist encroachments of the others. The provision for defense must in this, as in all other cases, be made commensurate to the danger of attack. Ambition must be made to counteract ambition. The interest of the man must be connected with the constitutional rights of the place. It may be a reflection on human nature, that such devices should be necessary to control the abuses of government. But what is government itself, but the greatest of all reflections on human nature? If men were angels, no government would be necessary. If angels were to govern men, neither external nor internal controls on government would be necessary. In framing a government which is to be administered by men over men, the great difficulty lies in this: you must first enable the government to control the governed; and in the next place oblige it to control itself. A dependence on the people is, no doubt, the primary control on the government; but experience has taught mankind the necessity of auxiliary precautions.

This policy of supplying, by opposite and rival interests, the defect of better motives, might be traced through the whole system of human affairs, private as well as public. We see it particularly displayed in all the subordinate distributions of power, where the constant aim is to divide and arrange the several offices in such a manner as that each may be a check on the other — that the private interest of every individual may be a sentinel over the public rights. These inventions of prudence cannot be less requisite in the distribution of the supreme powers of the State.

But it is not possible to give to each department an equal power of self-defense. In republican government, the legislative authority necessarily predominates. The remedy for this inconveniency is to divide the legislature into different branches; and to render them, by different modes of election and different principles of action, as little connected with each other as the nature of their common functions and their common dependence on the society will admit. It may even be necessary to guard against dangerous encroachments by still further precautions. As the weight of the legislative authority requires that it should be thus divided, the weakness of the executive may require, on the other hand, that it should be fortified. An absolute negative on the legislature appears, at first view, to be the natural defense with which the executive magistrate should be armed. But perhaps it would be neither altogether safe nor alone sufficient. On ordinary occasions it might not be exerted with the requisite firmness, and on extraordinary occasions it might be perfidiously abused. May not this defect of an absolute negative be supplied by some qualified connection between this weaker department and the weaker branch of the stronger department, by which the latter may be led to support the constitutional rights of the former, without being too much detached from the rights of its own department?

B. The Separation of Powers — In Constitutional Practice

1. The Judicial Power

Because most of the delegates to the 1787 constitutional convention were lawyers, the constitutional provision dealing with the judiciary (Article III) did not engender much controversy. Elaborate colonial courts existed in each of the thirteen colonies. Thus, the issue for the judiciary was how to improve upon inherited English traditions, by addressing particular shortcomings. One problem area in colonial America was that judges were not given life tenure, and therefore, were thought not sufficiently independent to be impartial. In addition, the decisions of all courts were appealable to the King's Privy Council, or more commonly in America, the privy council of a colonial governor — a feature that improperly blended executive and judicial authority.

Following the Declaration of Independence, judicial tenure protections became more common. *See, e.g.*, The Maryland Bill of Rights of 1776, Article XXX (Judges ought to hold commissions during good behavior). However, even after the Declaration, the powers of government were not well-separated, and as Jefferson observed, the legislatures would often vacate or re-decide cases, and "in many instances, decided rights which should have been left to judiciary controversy." THOMAS JEFFERSON, NOTES ON THE STATE OF VIRGINIA, QUERY XIII, *in* THE LIFE AND SELECTED WRITINGS OF THOMAS JEFFERSON 238 (Adrienne Koch & William Peden eds., 1944).

As put forth in the Virginia Plan by Edmund Randolph at the start of the constitutional convention, the members of the national judiciary would hold office during good behavior, be appointed by Congress and not have their compensation diminished or augmented. The subject matter of the national tribunals was limited to matters of admiralty, the collection of national taxes, impeachments, cases between citizens of different states or between a foreigner and a state, and "questions which may involve the national peace and harmony." Cases were to be heard first in an inferior tribunal and then subject to appeal in "one or more supreme tribunals." By mid-July 1787, the idea of never giving a pay raise to judges was abandoned as impractical, though protection against salary diminution was retained, and the number of Supreme Tribunals was limited to one. Two issues triggered significant discussion: who should appoint federal judges and whether any inferior federal courts were needed. Part of the debate in the convention on these topics follows.

RECORDS OF THE FEDERAL CONVENTION OF 1787
(Max Farrand ed., rev. ed. 1966)

DEBATE ON THE APPOINTMENT OF JUDGES

Tuesday, June 5, 1787

MR. MADISON disliked the election of the Judges by the Legislature or any numerous body. Besides the danger of intrigue and partiality, many of the members were not judges of the requisite qualifications. The Legislative talents which were very different from those of a Judge, commonly recommended men to the favor of Legislative Assemblies. It was known too that the accidental circumstances of presence and absence, of being a member or not a member, had a very undue influence on the appointment. On the other hand he was not satisfied with referring the appointment to the Executive. He rather inclined to give it to the Senatorial branch, as numerous eno' to be governed by the motives of the other branch; and as being sufficiently stable and independent to follow their deliberate judgments. He hinted this only and moved that the *appointment by the Legislature* might be struck out, [and] a blank left to be hereafter filled on maturer reflection. Mr. Wilson seconds it. On the question for striking out. Massts. ay. Cont. no. N.Y. ay. N.J. ay. Penn. ay. Del. ay. Md. ay. Va. ay. N.C. ay. S.C. no. Geo. ay.

Saturday, July 21, 1787

The motion made by Mr. Madison July 18. [and] then postponed, "that the Judges sh[oul]d be nominated by the Executive [and] such nominations become appointment unless disagreed to by 2/3 of the [second] branch of the Legislature," was now resumed.

MR. MADISON stated as his reasons for the motion. 1. that it secured the responsibility of the Executive who would in general be more capable [and] likely to select fit characters than the Legislature, or even the [second branch] of it, who might hide their selfish motives under the number concerned in the appointment. 2. that in case of any flagrant partiality of error, in the nomination it might be fairly presumed that 2/3 of the [second] branch would join in putting a negative on it. 3. that as the [second branch] was very differently constituted when the appointment of the Judges was formerly refered to it, and was not to be composed of equal votes from all the States, the principle of compromise which had prevailed in other instances required in this that their sh[oul]d be a concurrence of two authorities, in one of which the people, in the other the States, should be represented. The Executive Magistrate w[oul]d be considered as a national officer, acting for and equally sympathising with every part of the U[nited] States. If the [second] branch alone should have this power, the Judges might be apointed by a minority of the people, tho' by a majority, of the States, which could not be justified on any principle as their proceedings were to relate to the people, rather than to the States: and as it would moreover throw the appointments entirely into the hands of ye Northern States, a perpetual ground of jealousy [and] discontent would be furnished to the Southern States.

MR. PINKNEY was for placing the appointm[en]t in the [second branch] exclusively. The Executive will possess neither the requisite knowledge of characters, nor confidence of the people for so high a trust.

MR. RANDOLPH w[oul]d have preferred the mode of appointm[en]t proposed formerly by Mr. Ghorum, as adopted in the Constitution of Mass[achuset]ts. but thought the motion depending so great an improvement of the clause as it stands, that he anxiously wished it success. He laid great stress on the responsibility of the Executive as a security for fit appointments. Appointments by the Legislatures have generally resulted from cabal, from personal regard, or some other consideration than a title derived from the proper qualifications. The same inconveniences will proportionally prevail, if the appointments be referred to either branch of the Legislature or to any other authority administered by a number of individuals.

MR. ELSEWORTH would prefer a negative in the Executive on a nomination by the [second] branch, the negative to be overruled by a concurrence of 2/3 of the [second branch] to the mode proposed by the motion; but prefered an absolute appointment by the [second] branch to either. The Executive will be regarded by the people with a jealous eye. Every power for augmenting unnecessarily his influence will be disliked. As he will be stationary it was not to be supposed he could have a better knowledge of characters. He will be more open to caresses [and] Intrigues than the Senate. The right to supersede his nomination will be ideal only. A nomination under such circumstances will be equivalent to an appointment.

NOTE

Madison's recommendation, giving the President the power to nominate judges subject to the "consent" or approval of a majority of the Senate, was incorporated in Art. II, Sec. 2 of the final Constitution.

RECORDS OF THE FEDERAL CONVENTION OF 1787
(Max Farrand ed., rev. ed. 1966)

DEBATE ON THE ESTABLISHMENT OF INFERIOR COURTS

Tuesday, June 5, 1787

MR. RUTLIDGE having obtained a rule for reconsideration of the clause for establishing *inferior* tribunals under the national authority, now moved that part of the clause in Propos. 9 should be expunged: arguing that the State Tribunals might and ought to be left in all cases to decide in the first instance the right of appeal to the supreme national rights [and] uniformity of Judgm[en]ts: that it was making an unnecessary encroachment on the jurisdiction of the States and creating unnecessary obstacles to their adoption of the new system. — MR. SHERMAN [secon]ded. the motion.

MR. MADISON observed that unless inferior tribunals were dispersed throughout the Republic with *final* jurisdiction in *many* cases, appeals would be multiplied to a most oppressive degree; that besides, an appeal would not in many cases be a remedy. What was to be done after improper Verdicts in State tribunals obtained under the biased directions of a dependent Judge, or the local prejudices of an undirected jury? To remand the cause for a new trial would answer no purpose. To order a new trial at the Supreme bar would oblige the parties to bring up their witnesses, tho' ever so distant from the seat of the Court. An effective Judiciary establishment commensurate to the legislative authority, was essential. A Government without a proper Executive [and] Judiciary would be the mere trunk of a body, without arms or legs to act or move.

MR. WILSON opposed the motion on like grounds. He said the admiralty jurisdiction ought to be given wholly to the national Government, as it related to cases not within the jurisdiction of particular states, [and] to a scene in which controversies with foreigners would be most likely to happen.

MR. SHERMAN was in favor of the motion. He dwelt chiefly on the supposed expensiveness of having a new set of Courts, when the existing State Courts would answer the same purpose.

MR. DICKINSON contended strongly that if there was to be a National legislature, there ought to be a national Judiciary, and that the former ought to have authority to institute the latter.

On the question for Mr. Rutlidge's motion to strike out "inferior tribunals".

Massts. divided. Cont. ay. N.Y. divd. N.J. ay. Pa. no. Del. no. Md. no. Va. no. N.C. ay. S.C. ay. Geo. ay.

MR. WILSON & MR. MADISON then moved, in pursuance of the idea expressed above by Mr. Dickinson, to add to Resol. 9 the words following "that the National Legislature be empowered to institute inferior tribunals." They observed that there was a distinction between establishing such tribunals absolutely, and giving a discretion to the Legislature to establish or not establish them. They repeated the necessity of some such provision.

MR. BUTLER. The people will not bear such innovations. The States will revolt at such encroachments. Supposing such an establishment to be useful, we must not venture on it. We must follow the example of Solon who gave the Athenians not the best Gov[ernmen]t he could devise; but the best they w[oul]d receive.·

MR. KING remarked as to the comparative expence that the establishment of inferior tribunals w[oul]d cost infinitely less than the appeals that would be prevented by them.

On this question as moved by MR. W. and MR. M.

Mass. ay. Ct. no. N.Y. divd. N.J. ay. Pa. ay. Del. ay. Md. ay. Va. ay. N.C. ay. S.C. no. Geo. ay.

a. Federal Court Jurisdiction and the Justiciable Case

Having constitutionally established one Supreme Court and that federal judges would be appointed by the President with the advice and consent of the Senate and further provided for the optional existence of the lower federal courts, the federal judiciary had pretty much taken shape. Article III thus reads:

> Section 1. The judicial Power of the United States, shall be vested in one supreme Court, and in such inferior Courts as the Congress may from time to time ordain and establish. . . .

> Section 2. The judicial Power shall extend to all Cases, in Law and Equity, arising under this Constitution, [what follows is a description of the types or subject matter of cases suitable for federal courts — Eds.] [or] Controversies . . . .

> [The Constitution then divides the subject matter jurisdiction of the federal courts into the relatively rare original jurisdiction of the Supreme Court, (i.e., those cases that the Supreme Court may choose to hear first), and further that] "In all other Cases . . ., the Supreme Court shall have appellate Jurisdiction, both as to Law and Fact, with such Exceptions, and under such Regulations as the Congress shall make."

In brief, federal courts are limited to hearing "cases or controversies." The Supreme Court may hear a few cases in its original jurisdiction, but mostly it hears appeals, or more precisely exercises its discretion to grant certiorari to review lower court proceedings or cases from state court. Any conflict a federal court hears must be a justiciable one. Justiciability is a judicially created gloss on the words "case or controversy." See generally ERWIN CHEMERINSKY, FEDERAL JURISDICTION 41-166 (2d. ed. 1994). These doctrines, which include standing, ripeness, and mootness, limit the power of the judiciary, conserve judicial resources, improve judicial decision-making, and promote fairness, especially to those who are not litigants before the court.

(1) Standing

Standing determines whether a specific litigant has the requisite personal interest to present a particular matter to a federal court for adjudication. The doctrine serves a number of important constitutional and prudential functions. First, it preserves the separation of powers: by restricting who may sue in federal court, standing requirements prevent courts from using generalized claims to impede the policy decisions of the other elected branches of the government. To relax standing requirements is to expand judicial power over discretion properly reserved to the executive and legislative branches of government. Second, standing serves efficiency and improves judicial decision-making by ensuring that all litigants who come before a court have "such a personal stake in the outcome of the controversy as to assure that concrete adverseness which sharpens the presentation of issues upon which the court so largely depends for illumination." *Baker v. Carr*, 369 U.S. 186, 204 (1962). Standing requirements preclude lawsuits by parties with only an ideological stake in a controversy. Finally, standing requirements promote fairness by ensuring that people generally will assert only their own rights and not the rights of others.

To have standing, a litigant must meet three irreducible constitutional requirements which the Court has derived from Article III, and perhaps other concerns traceable to prudent judicial administration. To satisfy the constitutional requirements, a plaintiff must allege that she has suffered or will imminently suffer an injury, that the injury is fairly traceable to the defendant's conduct, and that a favorable court decision is likely to redress the injury. To meet the prudential requirements, generally a party must: assert only his or her own rights and not the claims of third parties, not sue as a taxpayer who shares a grievance in common with all other taxpayers, nor raise a claim outside the zone of interests protected by the statute at issue.

The injury requirement effectuates many of the aims of the standing doctrine. It assures that there is an actual dispute between adverse litigants and preserves the role of the federal courts as the body which decides particular cases and controversies. A personal stake derived from an injury is also more likely to produce careful presentation of the issues.

Two questions arise when courts implement the injury requirement: what does it mean to require that a litigant must *personally* suffer an injury, and what types of injuries are sufficient for standing? *Sierra Club v. Morton*, 405 U.S. 727 (1972), illustrates the Supreme Court's requirement that a plaintiff "show he personally has suffered some actual or threatened injury." *See also Valley Forge Christian College v. Americans United for Separation of Church and State*, 454 U.S. 464, 472 (1972). In *Sierra Club*, the Supreme Court held that an environmental group lacked standing to challenge the development of a park in California because they failed to allege that any of the Sierra Club's members had ever used the park, "much less that they use it in any way that would be significantly affected by the proposed activities of respondents." *Sierra Club*, 405 U.S. at 735. The decision in *Sierra Club* can be contrasted with *United States v. Students Challenging Regulatory Agency Procedures (SCRAP)*, 412 U.S. 669 (1973). In *SCRAP*, the Supreme Court upheld the standing of a group challenging an Interstate Commerce Commission rate decision. The group alleged that the decision would increase pollution and would lessen *their* enjoyment of the lakes, streams and mountains around Washington, D.C. The Supreme Court held that these aesthetic and environmental injuries were sufficient to confer standing since the group members claimed they would personally suffer the harms.

In general, violations of constitutional rights, statutory rights, and rights recognized at common law are injuries sufficient to confer standing. Beyond this, the Court's outcomes do not always follow a consistent principle. For example, in *SCRAP* the Court held claims of aesthetic and environmental harm sufficient to constitute an injury, while in *Allen v. Wright*, 468 U.S. 737 (1984), the Court rejected the plaintiffs' claim to injury caused by a government policy providing benefits to private schools that discriminated on the basis of race because this policy stigmatized their children. The Court stated that "if the abstract stigmatic injury were cognizable, standing would extend to all members of the particular racial groups against which the Government was alleged to be discriminating." *Id.* at 755-56. In *Roe v. Wade*, 410 U.S. 113 (1973), when dealing with the highly controversial issue of abortion, the Court also rejected the claim that injury to marital happiness could confer standing. The basis for the Court's decision that an aesthetic or environmental injury is cognizable for purposes of standing while stigma or injury to marital happiness is not is less than clear. The only conclusion is that in addition to injuries to common law, constitutional, and statutory rights, a plaintiff has standing if he or she asserts an injury that the Court finds sufficient for standing purposes.

Injury requirements may differ depending upon the remedy sought. For example, a plaintiff seeking injunctive or declaratory relief must show a likelihood that she will be injured in the future. In *City of Los Angeles v. Lyons,* 461 U.S. 95 (1983), Adolph Lyons sued to enjoin as unconstitutional the use of choke holds when the police were not threatened with death or serious bodily injury. The Supreme Court held that Lyons did not have standing to seek injunctive relief. While he could bring a suit seeking damages for his injuries, he lacked standing to request an injunction because he could not demonstrate a substantial likelihood that he would suffer future injury from the use of the choke holds by police officers. *Lyons* establishes that in order for a person to have standing to seek an injunction, the individual must allege a substantial likelihood that he or she will be subjected in the future to the allegedly illegal policy.

The Court relied upon *Lyons* in the later case *Lujan v. Defenders of Wildlife*, 504 U.S. 555 (1992). In *Lujan*, the plaintiffs challenged a federal regulation stating that the Endangered Species Act does not apply to United States Government activities outside the United States. The plaintiffs submitted affidavits describing past trips abroad during which they had viewed endangered animals and indicated that they planned to return "some day." The Court held that the plaintiffs lacked standing to bring the suit because they could not show a sufficient likelihood that they would be injured in the future by a destruction of an endangered species abroad. The Court concluded that a desire to return "some day" was insufficient for standing "without any description of concrete plans or indeed any specification of when the some day will be." *Id.* at 564.

The Court has also refused to find any general standing on the part of Members of Congress. *Raines v. Byrd*, 521 U.S. 811 (1997). In *Raines*, the Court declined to address the merits of the statutory line-item veto, discussed later in this Chapter, because members of Congress could allege no injury to themselves as individuals and any institutional injury that they alleged (vote dilution because the President can ostensibly and selectively change the substance of previously passed legislation by partial veto) was too abstract and widely dispersed. Earlier, the Court had allowed Congressman Adam Clayton Powell to challenge his exclusion from the House on the theory that he had been duly elected and was personally entitled to his seat in the House. *Powell v. McCormack*, 395 U.S. 486, 496, 512-14 (1969). In addition, in *Coleman v. Miller*, 307 U.S. 433 (1939), the Court allowed twenty members of the Kansas legislature to challenge the propriety of a tie-breaking vote by the lieutenant governor with respect to a constitutional amendment because, as a body, the group had the power to defeat or enact specific legislation. In *Raines*, the Court noted that the members bringing suit had not been designated by their chambers to do so, and in fact, both Houses actively opposed their suit. While the United States Court of Appeals for the District of Columbia Circuit has acknowledged some congressional standing, *see, e.g., Kennedy v. Sampson*, 511 F.2d 430, 435-36 (D.C. Cir. 1974); *Barnes v. Kline*, 759 F.2d 21, 28-29 (D.C. Cir. 1985) (Bork, J., dissenting), the Court in *Raines* felt that such litigation "improperly and unnecessarily plunge[s] [the judiciary] into . . . bitter political battle[s] being waged between the President and Congress." *Raines*, 521 U.S. at 827.

Injury alone is not sufficient to confer standing; the Supreme Court has held that causation and redressability are also constitutional prerequisites. In addition to alleging injury, the Supreme Court held in *Allen v. Wright*, 468 U.S. 737, 751 (1984), that a plaintiff must demonstrate that the personal injury is "fairly traceable to the defendant's allegedly unlawful conduct and likely to be redressed by the requested relief." In most cases causation and redressability involve an identical inquiry — if it can be demonstrated that the defendant is the cause of the injury, usually stopping the defendant's conduct remedies the harm — nevertheless, the Court has stated that they are independent requirements.

Allen demonstrates the importance of alleging causation and redressability separately. Here, the plaintiffs claimed two injuries: first, that an IRS policy of providing benefits to private schools that discriminated on the basis of race stigmatized their children, and second, that the IRS policy diminished their children's chances of receiving an integrated education. While the Court recognized that the second claim stated an injury, it denied standing because causation was lacking: the independent action of third parties, not the IRS, had segregated the schools. Although the plaintiffs in *Allen* alleged a serious constitutional violation, they were denied access to the federal courts.

In addition to the constitutional limits on standing — injury, causation, and redressability — the Court has established somewhat less absolute prudential barriers to standing. One of these prudential limitations is the prohibition against third-party standing: A plaintiff may generally only assert injuries that she has suffered; she may not present the claims of third parties.

There are exceptions to the prohibition against third party standing. First, a person may assert the rights of a third party not before the court if there are substantial obstacles to the third party asserting her own rights and if there is reason to believe that the advocate will effectively represent the interests of the third party. *See, e.g., Secretary of State v. Munson Co.*, 467 U.S. 947, 956 (1984).

A second exception to the prohibition against third party standing arises when there is a close relationship between the advocate and the third party. Under this exception a religious school was granted standing to represent the rights of parents, *see Pierce v. Society of Sisters*, 268 U.S. 510 (1925); doctors have been accorded standing to raise the rights of their patients, *see Singleton v. Wulff*, 428 U.S. 106 (1976); and vendors have sometimes been allowed to assert the rights of their customers, *see Craig v. Boren*, 429 U.S. 1012 (1976).

The third and final exception to the ban against third party standing is the "overbreadth doctrine." This doctrine allows a party to challenge a statute on the ground that it violates the First Amendment speech rights of third parties not before the court, even though the law is constitutional as applied to the actual litigant. The Court justified this exception in *Broadrick v. Oklahoma*, 413 U.S. 601, 612 (1973), by explaining that "[l]itigants, therefore, are permitted to challenge a statute not because their own rights of free expression are violated, but because of a judicial prediction or assumption that the statute's very existence may cause others not before the court to refrain from constitutionally protected speech."

Standing may be prudentially denied "when the harm asserted is a *generalized grievance* shared in a substantially equal measure by all or a large class of citizens." *See Warth v. Seldin*, 422 U.S. 490, 499 (1975) (emphasis added). The prohibition against generalized grievances does not prevent a person from claiming someone violated her personal constitutional rights — for example, that she has been denied due process or freedom of speech — even if everyone else in society suffers the same harm. It merely prevents individuals from objecting, as taxpayers or citizens, to allegedly unconstitutional government conduct when a person "suffers in some indefinite way in common with people generally" and her interest is "comparatively minute and indeterminable." *See Frothingham v. Mellon*, 262 U.S. 447, 487-88 (1923). The Supreme Court has recognized only one narrow and somewhat illogical exception to this taxpayer bar: when a plaintiff challenges a government expenditure as violating the Establishment Clause. *See, e.g., Flast v. Cohen*, 392 U.S. 83 (1968).

In *Friends of the Earth v. Laidlaw*, 528 U.S. 167 (2000), the Court leaned in the direction of deference to a Congressional grant of citizen standing in a case that addressed another aspect of the relationship between standing and redressability. Injunctive relief under the citizen suit provisions of the Clean Water Act was not appropriate because Laidlaw, the alleged polluter, had already stopped the improper discharges, but Friends of the Earth (FOE) successfully sought the imposition of a civil penalty as well in the lower court. Laidlaw argued that civil penalties offer no redress to private citizen-plaintiffs because they are paid to the government. Writing for a 7-2 majority, Justice Ginsburg acknowledged "that a plaintiff must demonstrate standing separately for each form of relief sought" but upheld FOE's standing to seek civil penalties that would be paid to the government because of the penalties' "deterrent effect." Justices Scalia and Thomas dissented, contesting both standing and the constitutionality of citizen suit provisions that transfer the enforcement of federal laws from appointed officials to private parties, in violation of the Article II, § 3 requirement that the President "take Care that the Laws be faithfully executed." Justices Scalia and Thomas also expressed concern that the ability of individuals to sue for damages that would be paid into the Federal Treasury (and therefore provide "generalized" relief rather than relief for any particular harm suffered by the individual plaintiff) would lead to abuse:

> By permitting citizens to pursue civil penalties payable to the Federal Treasury, the Act does not provide a mechanism for individual relief in any traditional sense, but turns over to private citizens the function of enforcing the law. A Clean Water Act plaintiff pursuing civil penalties acts as a self-appointed mini-EPA. Where, as is often the case, the plaintiff is a national association, it has significant discretion in choosing enforcement targets. Once the association is aware of a reported violation, it need not look long for an injured member, at least under the theory of injury the Court applies today. And once the target is chosen, the suit goes forward without meaningful public control. The availability of civil penalties vastly disproportionate to the individual injury gives citizen plaintiffs massive bargaining power — which is often used to achieve settlements requiring the defendant to support environmental projects of the plaintiffs' choosing. Thus is a public fine diverted to a private interest.

Previously the Court characterized the prohibition against generalized grievances as "prudential" rather than "constitutional." However, in *Lujan v. Defenders of Wildlife*, 504 U.S. 555 (1992), the Court treated the limitation as constitutional. In the Endangered Species Act, Congress had authorized standing for anyone alleging a violation of the statute. The Supreme Court held that the plaintiffs were asserting a generalized grievance and therefore lacked standing, and that Congress could not authorize standing by statute in such an instance. The Court described the prohibition against citizen standing as deriving from Article III and therefore not subject to statutory override. Whether, after *Lujan*, the Court will bar all generalized grievances on constitutional grounds, or whether taxpayer suits will continue to be barred merely for prudential reasons, remains to be seen.

A final prudential limitation holds that to have standing, the plaintiff must be within the zone of interests protected by the statute in question; plaintiffs suing pursuant to a statutory provision must be part of the group Congress intended to benefit from the law. Recent cases have applied the zone of interests requirement inconsistently. The Court has explained in *Clarke v. Securities Industries Association*, 479 U.S. 388, 394 (1987), that "[i]n cases where the plaintiff is not itself the subject of the contested regulatory action, the test denies a right of review if the plaintiff's interests are so marginally related to or inconsistent with the purposes implicit in the statute that it cannot reasonably be assumed that Congress intended to permit the suit." The Court also observed, however, that the zone of interests test was not meant to be especially demanding and generally should not preclude standing.

(2) Ripeness

While standing determines whether a particular plaintiff is the appropriate person to litigate a particular matter, ripeness relates to *when* review is appropriate. Ripeness seeks to separate matters where the injury is speculative and therefore may never occur, from those which are "ripe," or imminent, and appropriate for present federal court review. Usually a person can challenge the legality of a statute or regulation only when she is prosecuted or otherwise sanctioned for having violated it. To prevent unfairness, Congress passed the Declaratory Judgment Act, 28 U.S.C. § 2201 (1994), which allows for pre-enforcement review of statutes, though only "[i]n a case of actual controversy." Ripeness is the test that determines when an "actual controversy" is present, and therefore, when a federal court can grant pre-enforcement review.

The Supreme Court identified two considerations fundamental to the ripeness inquiry in *Abbott Laboratories v. Gardner*, 387 U.S. 136, 149 (1967): "the hardship to the parties of withholding court consideration" and "the fitness of the issues for judicial decision." The first prong of the ripeness inquiry asks how severe a hardship would result if the Court denied judicial review. The Supreme Court has found hardship justifying pre-enforcement review in three situations. First, the federal courts will find a case ripe if a plaintiff is faced with either foregoing action he or she contends is lawful or risking likely prosecution. In other words, the individual need not violate the law and risk the consequences before being able to challenge the law in court. Second, a court will find substantial hardship and deem a matter ripe although actual proceedings have not yet commenced when the enforcement of a statute or regulation against the plaintiff is certain and imminent. Finally, the Court has found substantial hardship based on collateral injuries. For example, in *Duke Power Co. v. Carolina Environmental Study Group, Inc.*, 438 U.S. 59 (1978), plaintiffs challenged an Act that limited the liability of nuclear power plants in the event of a nuclear accident. While the primary injury — an uncompensated loss from a nuclear accident — was not ripe, the Court concluded that since the Act facilitated the building of the power plant which subjected residents to radiation, pollution, and the fear of a nuclear accident, these collateral injuries were sufficient to render the case ripe and justiciable.

The second prong of the ripeness determination is the fitness of the issues and record for judicial review. Questions that depend heavily on facts (and, consequently, less on issues of law) are less likely to be found ripe. If the factual record does not allow a court a thorough view into the issues of law complained of in the case, the court is often prevented from being able to adjudicate the claim. In these situations, the court will dismiss the case as not yet ripe.

(3) Mootness

The third doctrine of justiciability requires that a particular plaintiff have a personal interest in the litigation from the commencement to the termination of the litigation. If at any point the plaintiff's personal interest disappears, the case should be dismissed as "moot." Many different events may render a case moot. A criminal defendant's appeal is moot if she dies during the appeal process, and a civil suit is moot if the parties settle the matter. If a challenged law is repealed or expires, a challenge to it becomes moot. Any change in the facts that ends a controversy renders a case moot.

While mootness may avoid unnecessary federal court decisions, in some cases dismissing a case for mootness where there is a fully developed record and an opportunity for resolution of an issue will waste judicial resources. These competing policy considerations have given rise to exceptions to the mootness doctrine. The first exception allows a case to continue although the primary injury has been resolved because some secondary or "collateral" injury remains. For example, a defendant who is released from prison still suffers collateral consequences of his conviction, such as loss of voting rights or the possibility that a subsequent conviction will carry a more severe penalty. For these reasons, a criminal defendant's appeal is not considered moot even if he is released from prison because an injury that could be favorably redressed by a court still exists.

The second exception to the mootness doctrine is for wrongs "capable of repetition yet evading review." Some injuries are short-term in nature and therefore will always disappear before they can be redressed by a court. If these injuries are likely to recur, a federal court may continue to exercise jurisdiction over the plaintiff's claim despite the fact that it has become moot. *Roe v. Wade*,

410 U.S. 113 (1973), provides an example of an alleged wrong capable of repetition yet evading review. The plaintiff was pregnant when she filed her complaint and sought an abortion, but by the time her case reached the Supreme Court, she had given birth. Because the duration of pregnancy would likely always be shorter than the time required for federal review of the state prohibition of abortion, the Court concluded that the case was "capable of repetition yet evading review" and that it should not be dismissed as moot.

In *Weinstein v. Bradford*, 423 U.S. 147, 149 (1975), the Court emphasized that there must be a "reasonable expectation that the same complaining party would be subjected to the same action again." Second, the injury must be one of inherently limited duration so that it is likely to always become moot before the completion of federal court review.

A third exception to the mootness doctrine permits federal courts to retain jurisdiction over cases in which the defendant "voluntarily ceases" the allegedly unlawful behavior but is free to resume it at any time. The Supreme Court ruled in *United States v. W.T. Grant Co.*, 345 U.S. 629 (1953), that it would deem cases moot when there is "no reasonable expectation" that the defendant will resume or repeat the allegedly improper behavior. A defendant's mere promise not to resume the offending activity, however, will not satisfy this "heavy" burden. The "voluntary cessation" exception also applies to statutory changes. If a challenged statute is repealed or amended, the case will usually be deemed moot. However, if there is a reasonable possibility that the government would reenact the challenged law if the case were dismissed, the court can retain jurisdiction over the claim.

The fourth and final exception to the mootness doctrine holds that a class action may continue even if the named plaintiff's claims are rendered moot. The Supreme Court reasoned in *Sosna v. Iowa*, 419 U.S. 393, 399 (1975), that unnamed class members acquired a legal status separate from the interest asserted by the named plaintiff, and therefore, a live controversy exists and the case may continue, even after the named plaintiff's case becomes moot.

The requirements of justiciability pose great difficulty for the Court, and students of constitutional law are well-advised to pursue the entirely separate course on federal courts for their learning. Nevertheless, the significance of these justiciability inquiries to maintaining the structural separation of powers cannot be understated.

b. The Subject-Matter of Supreme Court Jurisdiction

As previously mentioned, Article III, Section 2 also fixes the subject-matter jurisdiction of the Supreme Court. According to Section 2, the Supreme Court has subject-matter jurisdiction over cases dealing with:

- A question of Constitutional law or interpretation of a federal statute (so-called "federal question" jurisdiction) **[Appellate Jurisdiction]**

- Controversies between the citizens of different states (so-called "diversity jurisdiction") **[Appellate Jurisdiction]**

- Admiralty, or maritime law (the law of the sea) **[Appellate Jurisdiction]**

- Controversies naming the United States as a party **[Appellate Jurisdiction]**

- Controversies between two or more states **[Original and Exclusive Jurisdiction]**

- Actions in which ambassadors, other public ministers, consuls, or vice consuls of foreign states are parties **[Original and Non-Exclusive Jurisdiction with Lower Federal Courts]**

- Controversies between the United States and a state **[Original and Non-Exclusive Jurisdiction with Lower Federal Courts]**

- Actions by a state against the citizens of another state or against aliens **[Original and Non-Exclusive Jurisdiction with Lower Federal and State Courts]**

(1) Federal Question Jurisdiction

Most cases reaching the Supreme Court come on appeal from lower federal courts involving a federal question under 28 U.S.C. § 1331. To arise under 28 U.S.C. § 1331, the plaintiff's complaint must show a federal question on its face, that is, the complaint must show that the plaintiff has based his cause of action on federal law. A federal question does not arise when the plaintiff claims that his cause of action arises because of the defendant's anticipated affirmative defenses. *See Louisville & Nashville R.R. v. Motley*, 211 U.S. 149 (1908). Thus, absent a federal question in the plaintiff's complaint, an issue of federal law raised in the defendant's answer does not provide the defendant with a basis for removal of a case from state to federal court. Nor may a defendant successfully remove the case based on a related federal issue not claimed by the plaintiff in the complaint.

Federal questions do not necessarily have to be brought in lower federal courts. Under the Supremacy Clause, the Supreme Court has held that "[t]he laws of the United States are laws in the several States, and just as much binding on the citizens and courts thereof as the State laws are." *Claflin v. Houseman*, 93 U.S. 130, 136 (1876). Hence, at least where a state court of general jurisdiction hears claims that are similar to a federal claim in question, the Court has concluded that the state court "may not deny a federal right, when the parties and controversy are properly before it," absent "a neutral state rule regarding the administration of the courts" that precludes state court jurisdiction. *Howlett v. Rose*, 496 U.S. 356, 369, 372 (1990). *See Testa v. Katt*, 330 U.S. 386 (1947); *Mondou v. New York, New Haven, & Hartford R.R. Co.*, 223 U.S. 1

(1912); ERWIN CHEMERINSKY, FEDERAL JURISDICTION 199-200 (2d ed. 1994); Nicole A. Gordon & Douglas Gross, *Justiciability of Federal Claims in State Court*, 59 NOTRE DAME L. REV. 1145, 1156-77 (1984) (arguing that under the Supremacy Clause, state courts must hear all non-exclusive federal claims, even in the absence of similar state law claims); Terrance Sandalow, Henry v. Mississippi *and the Adequate State Ground: Proposals for a Revised Doctrine*, 1965 SUP. CT. REV. 187, 203-07 (discussing the duty of state courts to hear federal claims). Congress may make a particular federal question the exclusive jurisdiction of the federal courts. *See, e.g.*, 28 U.S.C. § 1351 (1994) (denying state courts jurisdiction of cases in which a foreign ambassador is a party). In the absence of such provisions, parties may choose to litigate their federal questions in state courts.

(2) Diversity Jurisdiction

The Supreme Court also has appellate jurisdiction over some cases based upon diversity of citizenship of the parties. 28 U.S.C. § 1332. A case arises in diversity when a civil action between citizens of different states entails an amount in controversy greater than $75,000. In other words, the plaintiff must allege that the plaintiff's harms or defendant's cost of compliance will exceed $75,000 (at least $75,000.01). A court determines diversity at the time the plaintiff files the complaint, and the plaintiff must allege it on the face of the complaint; similarly, a defendant seeking removal from state to federal court must allege diversity at the time of filing a petition for removal. Diversity cases require complete diversity between the parties. Each defendant must be a citizen of a different state than each plaintiff. This doctrine, first articulated by Chief Justice Marshall in *Strawbridge v. Curtis*, 7 U.S. (3 Cranch) 267 (1806), does not prevent co-plaintiffs from being from the same state — it requires only that all plaintiffs come from different states than all defendants. A court decides citizenship of the parties based upon their domicile. While an individual may have multiple residences, he or she has only one domicile — "the one place where he has his true, fixed, and permanent home and principal establishment, and to which he has the intention of returning whenever he is absent therefrom." CHARLES WRIGHT, LAW OF FEDERAL COURTS 146 (4th ed. 1983). A corporation, on the other hand, has at least dual citizenship in the state of incorporation as well as the place where it has its principal place of business.

(3) Original Jurisdiction

Congress may not add to, or subtract from, the Supreme Court's original jurisdiction, a point emphatically affirmed in *Marbury v. Madison*, 5 U.S. (1 Cranch) 137 (1803), which we take up shortly. The Court has written that this original jurisdiction should be exercised "only in appropriate cases." *See Illinois v. City of Milwaukee*, 406 U.S. 91, 93 (1972). The question of what is appropriate concerns the seriousness and dignity of the claim; yet, beyond that, it necessarily involves the availability of another forum where there is jurisdiction over the named parties, where the issues tendered may be litigated, and where appropriate relief may be had. The Court is inclined to a sparing use of its original jurisdiction so that its increasing duties with the appellate docket will not suffer. *Illinois v. City of Milwaukee*, 406 U.S. 91, 93-94 (1972). 28 U.S.C. § 1251 gives original and exclusive jurisdiction to the Supreme Court in all controversies between sovereign states. While rare, these cases most often involve boundaries or water rights. Importantly, the Supreme Court has refused to hear some controversies between states when the case contained no federal interest. *See California v. West Virginia*, 454 U.S. 1027 (1981) (court refused to adjudicate a controversy arising out of an alleged breach of contract covering athletic contests between the state's universities).

(4) Non-Exclusive (and Hence, Concurrent) Jurisdiction

Article III empowers Congress to create inferior courts, and the Supreme Court long ago held that these courts could have concurrent jurisdiction with the Supreme Court. In *Cohens v. Virginia*, 19 U.S. (6 Wheat) 264 (1821), the Court held that it could hear appeals in cases over which it had original jurisdiction. In cases of concurrent jurisdiction, the Court has discretion to refuse to hear a case, requiring instead that the matters come first before a federal or state trial court. The use of concurrent jurisdiction helps the Supreme Court better perform its functions by ensuring that it acts as final arbiter of the law instead of as a high-level trial court, a role which it does not have the resources to play.

Thus, while 28 U.S.C. § 1251 recognizes that the Supreme Court has original jurisdiction over ambassadors and other public ministers, all controversies between the United States and a state, and all actions by a state against citizens of another state, this statute also creates concurrent jurisdiction over these matters in the lower federal courts. The Supreme Court rarely invokes its original jurisdiction in these cases, preferring instead to have a district court proceed in the matter as a finder of fact.

(5) Routes to the Supreme Court: Certiorari, Appeal, or Certification

Today, in almost every situation, cases come before the Supreme Court following the grant of a petition for a writ of certiorari. The Court has complete discretion to grant or deny the petition, and it can hear all issues arising in the case or limit its review to a particular question. 28 U.S.C. § 1254 allows any party to any civil or criminal case to file a petition for a writ of certiorari before or after judgment or decree in a case. In other words, a petition for certiorari could arise out of every case. As a general practice, the Court will not grant certiorari until after a federal court of appeals or state supreme court has rendered its decision. Supreme Court rules provide for prior review, however, upon a showing that the case is of such public importance that the Court should deviate from its normal appellate practice.

(6) Appellate Jurisdiction and Exceptions Thereto

While the Court's little used original jurisdiction is untouchable, *see Marbury v. Madison, infra,* Congress appears to retain sweeping textual authority to "make exceptions" to the Supreme Court's appellate review. Consider, for example, the case below, where one McCardle alleged his unlawful restraint by military force and petitioned for a writ of habeas corpus under an act of February 5, 1867. Congress repealed the 1867 Act after the case was argued, but before the Court decided it. The repeal deprived the Court of subject-matter jurisdiction.

Ex parte MCCARDLE
74 U.S. (7 Wall.) 506 (1868)

THE CHIEF JUSTICE delivered the opinion of the court.

The first question necessarily is that of jurisdiction; for, if the [repealing] act of March, 1868, takes away the jurisdiction defined by the act of February, 1867, it is useless, if not improper, to enter into any discussion of other questions.

It is quite true, as was argued by the counsel for the petitioner, that the appellate jurisdiction of this court is not derived from acts of Congress. It is, strictly speaking, conferred by the Constitution. But it is conferred "with such exceptions and under such regulations as Congress shall make."

It is unnecessary to consider whether, if Congress had made no exceptions and no regulations, this court might not have exercised general appellate jurisdiction under rules prescribed by itself. For among the earliest acts of the first Congress, at its first session, was the act of September 24th, 1789, to establish the judicial courts of the United States. That act provided for the organization of this court, and prescribed regulations for the exercise of its jurisdiction.

The source of that jurisdiction, and the limitations of it by the Constitution and by statute, have been on several occasions subjects of consideration here. . . . [T]he court held, that while "the appellate powers of this court are not given by the judicial act, but are given by the Constitution," they are, nevertheless, "limited and regulated by that act, and by such other acts as have been passed on the subject." The court said, further, that the judicial act was an exercise of the power given by the Constitution to Congress "of making exceptions to the appellate jurisdiction of the Supreme Court." "They have described affirmatively," said the court, "its jurisdiction, and this affirmative description has been understood to imply a negation of the exercise of such appellate power as is not comprehended within it."

The principle that the affirmation of appellate jurisdiction implies the negation of all such jurisdiction not affirmed having been thus established, it was an almost necessary consequence that acts of Congress, providing for the exercise of jurisdiction, should come to be spoken of as acts granting jurisdiction, and not as acts making exceptions to the constitutional grant of it.

The exception to appellate jurisdiction in the case before us, however, is not an inference from the affirmation of other appellate jurisdiction. It is made in terms. The provision of the act of 1867, affirming the appellate jurisdiction of this court in cases of habeas corpus is expressly repealed. It is hardly possible to imagine a plainer instance of positive exception.

We are not at liberty to inquire into the motives of the legislature. We can only examine into its power under the Constitution; and the power to make exceptions to the appellate jurisdiction of this court is given by express words.

What, then, is the effect of the repealing act upon the case before us? We cannot doubt as to this. Without jurisdiction the court cannot proceed at all in any cause. Jurisdiction is power to declare the law, and when it ceases to exist, the only function remaining to the court is that of announcing the fact and dismissing the cause. And this is not less clear upon authority than upon principle.

* * *

It is quite clear, therefore, that this court cannot proceed to pronounce judgment in this case, for it has no longer jurisdiction of the appeal; and judicial duty is not less fitly performed by declining ungranted jurisdiction than in exercising firmly that which the Constitution and the laws confer.

Counsel seem to have supposed, if effect be given to the repealing act in question, that the whole appellate power of the court, in cases of habeas corpus, is denied. But this is an error. The act of 1868 does not except from that jurisdiction any cases but appeals from Circuit Courts under the act of 1867. It does not affect the jurisdiction which was previously exercised.

The appeal of the petitioner in this case must be dismissed for want of jurisdiction.

NOTES AND QUESTIONS

1. Notwithstanding *McCardle*, the withdrawal of appellate jurisdiction has been a rarity. Why do you think that is? Have the people lost the sense of this aspect of the checks and balances? Is the withdrawal of any aspect of court jurisdiction by the legislative branch perceived to be an improper political interference with the rule of law akin to the royal dispensations and prerogatives in English legal history outlined in Chapter One?

2. It should be noted, of course, that until 1875, Congress denied (in the sense that *McCardle* talks about the absence of congressional authorization as a denial) general federal question jurisdiction altogether to the federal courts. More selective withdrawals have been discussed, but not legislatively accomplished. Part of the hesitancy is traceable to the fact that denying appellate jurisdiction over a particular issue, say abortion or school prayer or racial busing — all of which have been proposed — denies the Supreme Court any constitutional role over these important questions. Because of this, Professor Hart argued that Congress cannot "destroy the essential role of the Supreme Court in the constitutional plan." Henry M. Hart, Jr., *The Power of Congress to Limit the Jurisdiction of Federal Courts: An Exercise in Dialectic*, 66 HARV. L. REV. 1362, 1365 (1953). Not every one agrees with Professor Hart's "essential role" limitation. After all, the text suggests that Congress' exception authority is plenary, and thus the only limits may be political judgment. William W. Van Alstyne, *A Critical Guide to* Ex parte McCardle, 15 ARIZ. L. REV. 229 (1973). Relatedly, Professor Wechsler argues that the Court decides cases not as a matter of constitutional entitlement, but only when a case is being litigated that is "within [its] jurisdiction." Herbert Weschler, *The Courts and the Constitution*, 65 COLUM. L. REV. 1001, 1005-06 (1965).

3. One reason to be cautious about selective denials of federal court jurisdiction, especially jurisdiction over state conduct, is implicit in *Martin v. Hunter's Lessee*, 14 U.S. (1 Wheat) 304 (1816). *Martin*, discussed *infra*, deals with Supreme Court review of state court decisions. It is apparent from *Martin* that the absence of Supreme Court review would lead to nonuniform interpretations of constitutional provisions depending merely upon location. As Justice Holmes once observed: "I do not think the United States would come to an end if we lost our power to declare an Act of Congress void. I do think the Union would be impeded if we could not make that declaration as to the laws of the several States." Oliver Wendell Holmes, *Law and the Court, in* THE COLLECTED LEGAL PAPERS OF OLIVER WENDELL HOLMES 295-96 (1920).

4. Does Congress have the power to remove the jurisdiction of the lower federal courts? Technically, the Constitution talks only of exceptions to the Supreme Court's appellate jurisdiction. Yet, insofar as Congress is under no obligation to create inferior federal courts at all, it presumably has the "lesser" authority to deny the lower federal courts jurisdiction over selective subjects. But is this truly a lesser exercise of power? If the intent of Congress in withdrawing particular or selective jurisdiction is to deny vindication of established constitutional rights, arguably Congress' exception power, as broadly stated as it is, would be checked by an independent constitutional bar. For example, Congress couldn't pass a law denying a particular religious denomination the right to participate in voter primaries and then preclude the federal courts from hearing First Amendment free speech and free exercise challenges to such hypothetical statute.

c. The Essence of Judicial Review

THE FEDERALIST NO. 78 (Alexander Hamilton)
(Clinton Rossiter ed., 1961)

WE PROCEED now to an examination of the judiciary department of the proposed government.

* * *

Whoever attentively considers the different departments of power must perceive, that, in a government in which they are separated from each other, the judiciary, from the nature of its functions, will always be the least dangerous to the political rights of the Constitution; because it will be least in a capacity to annoy or injure them. The Executive not only dispenses the honors, but holds the sword of the community. The legislature not only commands the purse, but prescribes the rules by which the duties and rights of every citizen are to be regulated. The judiciary, on the contrary, has no influence over either the sword or the purse; no direction either of the strength or of the wealth of the society; and can take no active resolution whatever. It may truly be said to have neither FORCE nor WILL, but merely judgment; and must ultimately depend upon the aid of the executive arm even for the efficacy of its judgments.

This simple view of the matter suggests several important consequences. It proves incontestably, that the judiciary is beyond comparison the weakest of the three departments of power;[1] that it can never attack with success either of the other two; and that all possible care is requisite to enable it to defend itself against their attacks. It equally proves, that though individual oppression may now and then proceed from the courts of justice, the general liberty of the people can never be endangered from that quarter; I mean so long as the judiciary remains truly distinct from both the legislature and the Executive. For I agree, that "there is no liberty, if the power of judging be not separated from the legislative and executive powers."[2] And it proves, in the last place, that as liberty can have nothing to fear from the judiciary alone, but would have every thing to fear from its union with either of the other departments; that as all the effects of such a union must ensue from a dependence of the former on the latter, notwithstanding a nominal and apparent separation; that as, from the natural feebleness of the judiciary, it is in continual jeopardy of being overpowered, awed, or influenced by its co-ordinate branches; and that as nothing can contribute so much to its firmness and independence as permanency in office, this quality may therefore be justly regarded as an indispensable ingredient in its constitution, and, in a great measure, as the citadel of the public justice and the public security.

---

[1] The celebrated Montesquieu, speaking of them, says: "Of the three powers above mentioned, the judiciary is next to nothing." — "Spirit of Laws." vol. i., page 186.

[2] *Id.* at 181.

The complete independence of the courts of justice is peculiarly essential in a limited Constitution. By a limited Constitution, I understand one which contains certain specified exceptions to the legislative authority; such, for instance, as that it shall pass no bills of attainder, no ex-post-facto laws, and the like. Limitations of this kind can be preserved in practice no other way than through the medium of courts of justice, whose duty it must be to declare all acts contrary to the manifest tenor of the Constitution void. Without this, all the reservations of particular rights or privileges would amount to nothing.

Some perplexity respecting the rights of the courts to pronounce legislative acts void, because contrary to the Constitution, has arisen from an imagination that the doctrine would imply a superiority of the judiciary to the legislative power. It is urged that the authority which can declare the acts of another void, must necessarily be superior to the one whose acts may be declared void. As this doctrine is of great importance in all the American constitutions, a brief discussion of the ground on which it rests cannot be unacceptable.

There is no position which depends on clearer principles, than that every act of a delegated authority, contrary to the tenor of the commission under which it is exercised, is void. No legislative act, therefore, contrary to the Constitution, can be valid. To deny this, would be to affirm, that the deputy is greater than his principal; that the servant is above his master; that the representatives of the people are superior to the people themselves; that men acting by virtue of powers, may do not only what their powers do not authorize, but what they forbid.

If it be said that the legislative body are themselves the constitutional judges of their own powers, and that the construction they put upon them is conclusive upon the other departments, it may be answered, that this cannot be the natural presumption, where it is not to be collected from any particular provisions in the Constitution. It is not otherwise to be supposed, that the Constitution could intend to enable the representatives of the people to substitute their WILL to that of their constituents. It is far more rational to suppose, that the courts were designed to be an intermediate body between the people and the legislature, in order, among other things, to keep the latter within the limits assigned to their authority. The interpretation of the laws is the proper and peculiar province of the courts. A constitution is, in fact, and must be regarded by the judges, as a fundamental law. It therefore belongs to them to ascertain its meaning, as well as the meaning of any particular act proceeding from the legislative body. If there should happen to be an irreconcilable variance between the two, that which has the superior obligation and validity ought, of course, to be preferred; or, in other words, the Constitution ought to be preferred to the statute, the intention of the people to the intention of their agents.

Nor does this conclusion by any means suppose a superiority of the judicial to the legislative power. It only supposes that the power of the people is superior to both; and that where the will of the legislature, declared in its statutes, stands in opposition to that of the people, declared in the Constitution, the judges ought to be governed by the latter rather than the former. They ought to regulate their decisions.

* * *

It can be of no weight to say that the courts, on the pretense of a repugnancy, may substitute their own pleasure to the constitutional intentions of the legislature. This might as well happen in the case of two contradictory statutes; or it might as well happen in every adjudication upon any single statute. The courts must declare the sense of the law; and if they should be disposed to exercise WILL instead of JUDGMENT, the consequence would equally be the substitution of their pleasure to that of the legislative body. The observation, if it prove any thing, would prove that there ought to be no judges distinct from that body.

If, then, the courts of justice are to be considered as the bulwarks of a limited Constitution against legislative encroachments, this consideration will afford a strong argument for the permanent tenure of judicial offices, since nothing will contribute so much as this to that independent spirit in the judges which must be essential to the faithful performance of so arduous a duty.

This independence of the judges is equally requisite to guard the Constitution and the rights of individuals from the effects of those ill humors, which the arts of designing men, or the influence of particular conjunctures, sometimes disseminate among the people themselves, and which, though they speedily give place to better information, and more deliberate reflection, have a tendency, in the meantime, to occasion dangerous innovations in the government, and serious oppressions of the minor party in the community. Though I trust the friends of the proposed Constitution will never concur with its enemies, in questioning that fundamental principle of republican government, which admits the right of the people to alter or abolish the established Constitution, whenever they find it inconsistent with their happiness, yet it is not to be inferred from this principle, that the representatives of the people, whenever a momentary inclination happens to lay hold of a majority of their constituents, incompatible with the provisions in the existing Constitution, would, on that account, be justifiable in a violation of those provisions; or that the courts would be under a greater obligation to connive at infractions in this shape, than when they had proceeded wholly from the cabals of the representative body. Until the people have, by some solemn and authoritative act, annulled or changed the established form, it is binding upon themselves collectively, as well as individually; and no presumption, or even knowledge, of their sentiments, can warrant their representatives in a departure from it, prior to such an act. But it is easy to see, that it would require an uncommon portion of fortitude in the judges to do their duty as faithful guardians of the Constitution, where legislative invasions of it had been instigated by the major voice of the community.

But it is not with a view to infractions of the Constitution only, that the independence of the judges may be an essential safeguard against the effects of occasional ill humors in the society. These sometimes extend no farther than to the injury of the private rights of particular classes of citizens, by unjust and partial laws. Here also the firmness of the judicial magistracy is of vast importance in mitigating the severity and confining the operation of such laws. It not only serves to moderate the immediate mischiefs of those which may have been passed, but it operates as a check upon the legislative body in passing them; who, perceiving that obstacles to the success of iniquitous intention are to be expected from the scruples of the courts, are in a manner compelled, by the very motives of the injustice they meditate, to qualify their attempts. This is a circumstance calculated to have more influence upon the character of our governments, than but few may be aware of. The benefits of the integrity and moderation of the judiciary have already been felt in more States than one; and though they may have displeased those whose sinister expectations they may have disappointed, they must have commanded the esteem and applause of all the virtuous and disinterested. Considerate men, of every description, ought to prize whatever will tend to beget or fortify that temper in the courts: as no man can be sure that he may not be to-morrow the victim of a spirit of injustice, by which he may be a gainer to-day. And every man must now feel, that the inevitable tendency of such a spirit is to sap the foundations of public and private confidence, and to introduce in its stead universal distrust and distress.

NOTES AND QUESTIONS

1. Is judicial review premised upon some unique quality of the judiciary? Hamilton grounds the judiciary's power of judicial review, not upon the supremacy of the judicial branch, but upon the safeguarding of liberty through the separation of powers. Hamilton specifically writes that the legislature is not to be itself "the constitutional judge" of its own powers. Hamilton argues that the interpretation of the Constitution, as this embodiment of the will of the people, is the "proper and peculiar province of the courts." In this, Hamilton is reflecting the thinking of John Locke's *Second Treatise* which we considered in Chapter One. Natural law was sufficient to guide each individual person, said Locke, except that it would be subject to misinterpretation if persons would "be judges in their own cases."

2. The Constitution is referred to by Hamilton as a fundamental law. But what makes it fundamental? A cursory glance of Hamilton's argument suggests that it is so merely because of its adoption by the people. But a more careful reading reveals that the people as well as the judges are bound by the Constitution. Hamilton writes "[u]ntil the people have, by some solemn and authoritative act, annulled or changed the established form, it is binding upon themselves collectively, as well as individually . . . ." It binds even if various momentary majorities want to throw it over. In extolling the virtue of independent judges, Hamilton further reveals that it is not just constitutional "infraction" that judges must safeguard us against, but also "unjust and partial laws." In this sense, the Constitution is revealed as fundamental, not merely because of first majoritarian adoption, but because it is grounded upon moral principles, like those contained in the Declaration of Independence. Hamilton made this view of fundamental law even clearer in an earlier writing when he stated: "The sacred rights of mankind are not to be rummaged for among old parchments or musty records. They are written, as with a sunbeam, in the whole volume of human nature, by the hand of the divinity itself, and can never be erased or obscured by mortal power." Alexander Hamilton, *The Farmer Refuted* (Feb. 23, 1775), *in* 1 THE WORKS OF ALEXANDER HAMILTON (Henry C. Lodge, ed. 1903).

3. The next case moves past theory to application. *Marbury v. Madison* arises out of President John Adams' blatant effort to pack the judiciary with his Federalist supporters before leaving office after being defeated by Thomas Jefferson. Adams nominated one William Marbury for a newly minted judgeship in the District of Columbia. The Senate confirmed the nomination, and Adams signed the commission, but Adams' Secretary of State neglected in the rush of leaving office to deliver the commission. Jefferson took office at midnight of March 4, 1801, and his Secretary of State, James Madison, refused to deliver the commission to Marbury. Marbury sued for a writ of mandamus directly in the U.S. Supreme Court. Marbury claimed his case fell within the Supreme Court's original jurisdiction, because section 13 of the Judiciary Act of 1789 placed it there. As you recall, however, the text of the Constitution limits to specific subject-matter, the types of cases that may be heard by the Court as an original matter. Chief Justice Marshall, like the outgoing Adams, a strong Federalist and opponent of Jefferson, had to decide whether the Act was consistent with the constitutional text. Marshall, a cousin of Thomas Jefferson, was also the neglectful Secretary of State who failed to deliver the commission to Marbury in the first place. For a thorough history see David F. Forte, *Marbury's Travail: Federalist Politics and William Marbury's Appointment as Justice of the Peace*, 45 CATH. U. L. REV. 349 (1996) (describing the life of William Marbury, and the political battle within the Federalist party that resulted in his appointment and the enmity of Jefferson).

MARBURY v. MADISON
5 U.S. (1 Cranch) 137 (1803)

MR. CHIEF JUSTICE MARSHALL delivered the opinion of the court.

At the last term, on the affidavits then read and filed with the clerk, a rule was granted in this case, requiring the secretary of state to show cause why a mandamus should not issue, directing him to deliver to William Marbury his commission as a justice of the peace for the county of Washington, in the district of Columbia.

* * *

The first object of inquiry is,

1. Has the applicant a right to the commission he demands?

[An act of congress passed in February 1801], district of Columbia. . . . It appears from the affidavits, that in compliance with a commission for William Marbury as a justice of peace for the county of Washington was signed by John Adams, then president of the United States; after which the seal of the United States was affixed to it; but the commission has never reached the person for whom it was made out.

* * *

The last act to be done by the president, is the signature of the commission. He has then acted on the advice and consent of the senate to his own nomination. The time for deliberation has then passed. He has decided. His judgment, on the advice and consent of the senate concurring with his nomination, has been made, and the officer is appointed. This appointment is evidenced by an open, unequivocal act; and being the last act required from the person making it, necessarily excludes the idea of its being, so far as it respects the appointment, an inchoate and incomplete transaction.

* * *

The transmission of the commission is a practice directed by convenience, but not by law. It cannot therefore be necessary to constitute the appointment which must precede it, and which is the mere act of the president. . . . A commission is transmitted to a person already appointed; not to a person to be appointed or not, as the letter enclosing the commission should happen to get into the post-office and reach him in safety, or to miscarry.

* * *

Mr. Marbury, then, since his commission was signed by the president and sealed by the secretary of state, was appointed; and as the law creating the office gave the officer a right to hold for five years independent of the executive, the appointment was not revocable; but vested in the officer legal rights which are protected by the laws of his country.

* * *

This brings us to the second inquiry; which is,

2. If he has a right, and that right has been violated, do the laws of his country afford him a remedy?

* * *

The government of the United States has been emphatically termed a government of laws, and not of men. It will certainly cease to deserve this high appellation, if the laws furnish no remedy for the violation of a vested legal right.

* * *

It behooves us then to inquire whether there be in its composition any ingredient which shall exempt from legal investigation, or exclude the injured party from legal redress. . . .

* * *

Is it in the nature of the transaction? Is the act of delivering or withholding a commission to be considered as a mere political act belonging to the executive department alone, for the performance of which entire confidence is placed by our constitution in the supreme executive; and for any misconduct respecting which, the injured individual has no remedy?

* * *

By the constitution of the United States, the president is invested with certain important political powers, in the exercise of which he is to use his own discretion, and is accountable only to his country in his political character, and to his own conscience. To aid him in the performance of these duties, he is authorized to appoint certain officers, who act by his authority and in conformity with his orders.

In such cases, their acts are his acts; and whatever opinion may be entertained of the manner in which executive discretion may be used, still there exists, and can exist, no power to control that discretion. The subjects are political. They respect the nation, not individual rights, and being entrusted to the executive, the decision of the executive is conclusive. The application of this remark will be perceived by adverting to the act of congress for establishing the department of foreign affairs. This officer, as his duties were prescribed by that act, is to conform precisely to the will of the president. He is the mere organ by whom that will is communicated. The acts of such an officer, as an officer, can never be examinable by the courts.

But when the legislature proceeds to impose on that officer other duties; when he is directed peremptorily to perform certain acts; when the rights of individuals are dependent on the performance of those acts; he is so far the officer of the law; is amenable to the laws for his conduct; and cannot at his discretion sport away the vested rights of others.

* * *

If this be the rule, let us inquire how it applies to the case under the consideration of the court.

The power of nominating to the senate, and the power of appointing the person nominated, are political powers, to be exercised by the president according to his own discretion. When he has made an appointment, he has exercised his whole power, and his discretion has been completely applied to the case. If, by law, the officer be removable at the will of the president, then a new appointment may be immediately made, and the rights of the officer are terminated. But as a fact which has existed cannot be made never to have existed, the appointment cannot be annihilated; and consequently if the officer is by law not removable at the will of the president, the rights he has acquired are protected by the law, and are not resumable by the president. They cannot be extinguished by executive authority, and he has the privilege of asserting them in like manner as if they had been derived from any other source.

* * *

It is then the opinion of the court,

1. That by signing the commission of Mr. Marbury, the president of the United States appointed him a justice of peace for the county of Washington in the district of Columbia; and that the seal of the United States, affixed thereto by the secretary of state, is conclusive testimony of the verity of the signature, and of the completion of the appointment; and that the appointment conferred on him a legal right to the office for the space of five years.

2. That, having this legal title to the office, he has a consequent right to the commission; a refusal to deliver which is a plain violation of that right, for which the laws of his country afford him a remedy.

It remains to be inquired whether,

3. He is entitled to the remedy for which he applies. This depends on,

1. The nature of the writ applied for. And,

2. The power of this court.

1. The nature of the writ.

Blackstone, in the third volume of his Commentaries, page 110, defines a mandamus to be, "a command issuing in the king's name from the court of king's bench, and directed to any person, corporation, or inferior court of judicature within the king's dominions, requiring them to do some particular thing therein specified which appertains to their office and duty, and which the court of king's bench has previously determined, or at least supposes, to be consonant to right and justice."

* * *

1. With respect to the officer to whom it would be directed. The intimate political relation, subsisting between the president of the United States and the heads of departments, necessarily renders any legal investigation of the acts of one of those high officers peculiarly irksome, as well as delicate; and excites some hesitation with respect to the propriety of entering into such investigation. Impressions are often received without much reflection or examination; and it is not wonderful that in such a case as this, the assertion, by an individual, of his legal claims in a court of justice, to which claims it is the duty of that court to attend, should at first view be considered by some, as an attempt to intrude into the cabinet, and to intermeddle with the prerogatives of the executive.

* * *

But where he is directed by law to do a certain act affecting the absolute rights of individuals, in the performance of which he is not placed under the particular direction of the president, and the performance of which the president cannot lawfully forbid, and therefore is never presumed to have forbidden; as for example, to record a commission, or a patent for land, which has received all the legal solemnities; or to give a copy of such record; in such cases, it is not perceived on what ground the courts of the country are further excused from the duty of giving judgment, that right to be done to an injured individual, than if the same services were to be performed by a person not the head of a department.

This opinion seems not now for the first time to be taken up in this country.

It must be well recollected that in 1792 an act passed, directing the secretary at war to place on the pension list such disabled officers and soldiers as should be reported to him by the circuit courts, which act, so far as the duty was imposed on the courts, was deemed unconstitutional; but some of the judges, thinking that the law might be executed by them in the character of commissioners, proceeded to act and to report in that character.

This law being deemed unconstitutional at the circuits, was repealed, and a different system was established; but the question whether those persons, who had been reported by the judges, as commissioners, were entitled, in consequence of that report, to be placed on the pension list, was a legal question, properly determinable in the courts, although the act of placing such persons on the list was to be performed by the head of a department.

That this question might be properly settled, congress passed an act in February 1793, making it the duty of the secretary of war, in conjunction with the attorney general, to take such measures as might be necessary to obtain an adjudication of the supreme court of the United States on the validity of any such rights, claimed under the act aforesaid.

After the passage of this act, a mandamus was moved for, to be directed to the secretary at war, commanding him to place on the pension list a person stating himself to be on the report of the judges.

There is, therefore, much reason to believe, that this mode of trying the legal right of the complainant, was deemed by the head of a department, and by the highest law officer of the United States, the most proper which could be selected for the purpose.

When the subject was brought before the court the decision was, not, that a mandamus would not lie to the head of a department, directing him to perform an act, enjoined by law, in the performance of which an individual had a vested interest; but that a mandamus ought not to issue in that case — the decision necessarily to be made if the report of the commissioners did not confer on the applicant a legal right.

The judgment in that case is understood to have decided the merits of all claims of that description; and the persons, on the report of the commissioners, found it necessary to pursue the mode prescribed by the law subsequent to that which had been deemed unconstitutional, in order to place themselves on the pension list.

The doctrine, therefore, now advanced is by no means a novel one.

It is true that the mandamus, now moved for, is not for the performance of an act expressly enjoined by statute.

It is to deliver a commission; on which subjects the acts of congress are silent. This difference is not considered as affecting the case. It has already been stated that the applicant has, to that commission, a vested legal right, of which the executive cannot deprive him. . . .

* * *

This, then, is a plain case of a mandamus, either to deliver the commission, or a copy of it from the record; and it only remains to be inquired,

Whether it can issue from this court.

The act to establish the judicial courts of the United States authorizes the supreme court "to issue writs of mandamus, in cases warranted by the principles and usages of law, to any courts appointed, or persons holding office, under the authority of the United States."

The secretary of state, being a person, holding an office under the authority of the United States, is precisely within the letter of the description; and if this court is not authorized to issue a writ of mandamus to such an officer, it must be because the law is unconstitutional, and therefore absolutely incapable of conferring the authority, and assigning the duties which its words purport to confer and assign.

The constitution vests the whole judicial power of the United States in one supreme court, and such inferior courts as congress shall, from time to time, ordain and establish. This power is expressly extended to all cases arising under the laws of the United States; and consequently, in some form, may be exercised over the present case; because the right claimed is given by a law of the United States.

In the distribution of this power it is declared that "the supreme court shall have original jurisdiction in all cases affecting ambassadors, other public ministers and consuls, and those in which a state shall be a party. In all other cases, the supreme court shall have appellate jurisdiction."

It has been insisted at the bar, that as the original grant of jurisdiction to the supreme and inferior courts is general, and the clause, assigning original jurisdiction to the supreme court, contains no negative or restrictive words; the power remains to the legislature to assign original jurisdiction to that court in other cases than those specified in the article which has been recited; provided those cases belong to the judicial power of the United States.

If it had been intended to leave it in the discretion of the legislature to apportion the judicial power between the supreme and inferior courts according to the will of that body, it would certainly have been useless to have proceeded further than to have defined the judicial power, and the tribunals in which it should be vested. The subsequent part of the section is mere surplusage, is entirely without meaning, if such is to be the construction. If congress remains at liberty to give this court appellate jurisdiction, where the constitution has declared their jurisdiction shall be original; and original jurisdiction where the constitution has declared it shall be appellate; the distribution of jurisdiction made in the constitution, is form without substance.

Affirmative words are often, in their operation, negative of other objects than those affirmed; and in this case, a negative or exclusive sense must be given to them or they have no operation at all.

It cannot be presumed that any clause in the constitution is intended to be without effect; and therefore such construction is inadmissible, unless the words require it.

When an instrument organizing fundamentally a judicial system, divides it into one supreme, and so many inferior courts as the legislature may ordain and establish; then enumerates its powers, and proceeds so far to distribute them, as to define the jurisdiction of the supreme court by declaring the cases in which it shall take original jurisdiction, and that in others it shall take appellate jurisdiction, the plain import of the words seems to be, that in one class of cases its jurisdiction is original, and not appellate; in the other it is appellate, and not original. If any other construction would render the clause inoperative, that is an additional reason for rejecting such other construction, and for adhering to the obvious meaning.

To enable this court then to issue a mandamus, it must be shown to be an exercise of appellate jurisdiction, or to be necessary to enable them to exercise appellate jurisdiction.

* * *

It is the essential criterion of appellate jurisdiction, that it revises and corrects the proceedings in a cause already instituted, and does not create that cause. Although, therefore, a mandamus may be directed to courts, yet to issue such a writ to an officer for the delivery of a paper, is in effect the same as to sustain an original action for that paper, and therefore seems not to belong to appellate, but to original jurisdiction. Neither is it necessary in such a case as this, to enable the court to exercise its appellate jurisdiction.

The authority, therefore, given to the supreme court, by the act establishing the judicial courts of the United States, to issue writs of mandamus to public officers, appears not to be warranted by the constitution; and it becomes necessary to inquire whether a jurisdiction, so conferred, can be exercised.

The question, whether an act, repugnant to the constitution, can become the law of the land, is a question deeply interesting to the United States; but, happily, not of an intricacy proportioned to its interest. It seems only necessary to recognise certain principles, supposed to have been long and well established, to decide it.

* * *

This original and supreme will organizes the government, and assigns to different departments their respective powers. It may either stop here; or establish certain limits not to be transcended by those departments.

The government of the United States is of the latter description. The powers of the legislature are defined and limited; and that those limits may not be mistaken or forgotten, the constitution is written. To what purpose are powers limited, and to what purpose is that limitation committed to writing; if these limits may, at any time, be passed by those intended to be restrained? . . .

Between these alternatives there is no middle ground. The constitution is either a superior, paramount law, unchangeable by ordinary means, or it is on a level with ordinary legislative acts, and like other acts, is alterable when the legislature shall please to alter it.

If the former part of the alternative be true, then a legislative act contrary to the constitution is not law: if the latter part be true, then written constitutions are absurd attempts, on the part of the people, to limit a power in its own nature illimitable.

Certainly all those who have framed written constitutions contemplate them as forming the fundamental and paramount law of the nation, and consequently the theory of every such government must be, that an act of the legislature repugnant to the constitution is void.

This theory is essentially attached to a written constitution, and is consequently to be considered by this court as one of the fundamental principles of our society. It is not therefore to be lost sight of in the further consideration of this subject.

* * *

It is emphatically the province and duty of the judicial department to say what the law is. Those who apply the rule to particular cases, must of necessity expound and interpret that rule. If two laws conflict with each other, the courts must decide on the operation of each.

So if a law be in opposition to the constitution: if both the law and the constitution apply to a particular case, so that the court must either decide that case conformably to the law, disregarding the constitution; or conformably to the constitution, disregarding the law: the court must determine which of these conflicting rules governs the case. This is of the very essence of judicial duty.

* * *

Why does a judge swear to discharge his duties agreeably to the constitution of the United States, if that constitution forms no rule for his government? if it is closed upon him and cannot be inspected by him?

If such be the real state of things, this is worse than solemn mockery. To prescribe, or to take this oath, becomes equally a crime.

It is also not entirely unworthy of observation, that in declaring what shall be the supreme law of the land, the constitution itself is first mentioned; and not the laws of the United States generally, but those only which shall be made in pursuance of the constitution, have that rank.

Thus, the particular phraseology of the constitution of the United States confirms and strengthens the principle, supposed to be essential to all written constitutions, that a law repugnant to the constitution is void, and that courts, as well as other departments, are bound by that instrument.

The rule must be discharged.

NOTES AND QUESTIONS

1. The power of judicial review, and its scope, is much debated. While Chief Justice Marshall is given deserved credit for his exposition of this judicial authority in *Marbury*, the ability to invalidate legislative enactments on constitutional grounds was evident in the convention during the discussion of a proposed, but ultimately rejected, council of revision. The Council was rejected in part because it was viewed as empowering judges to undertake a review that was already inherent in the judicial power, itself. It will be recalled that during the context of this debate, Madison declared that a "law violating a constitution established by the people themselves would be considered by the judges as null and void." *See* Chapter Two.

2. The power to declare legislative enactments unconstitutional was also exercised previously by Justice Patterson, sitting as a Circuit Judge in *Vanhorne's Lessee v. Dorrance*, 2 U.S. (2 Dall.) 304 (1795). *Dorrance* concerned a dispute over a piece of property possessed by John Dorrance and claimed by Vanhorne. Dorrance sought to quiet title under a Pennsylvania statute. Finding the state statute to be unconstitutional, Justice Patterson expansively opined upon how the Constitution limits legislative action in America as compared to England:

It is difficult to say what the constitution of England is; because, not being reduced to written certainty and precision, it lies entirely at the mercy of the Parliament: It bends to every governmental exigency; it varies and is blown about by every breeze of legislative humour or political caprice. Some of the judges in England have had the boldness to assert, that an act of Parliament, made against natural equity, is void; but this opinion contravenes the general position, that the validity of an act of Parliament cannot be drawn into question by the judicial department: It cannot be disputed, and must be obeyed. The power of Parliament is absolute and transcendent; it is omnipotent in the scale of political existence. Besides, in England there is no written constitution, no fundamental law, nothing visible, nothing real, nothing certain, by which a statute can be tested. In America the case is widely different: Every State in the Union has its constitution reduced to written exactitude and precision.

What is a Constitution? It is the form of government, delineated by the mighty hand of the people, in which certain first principles of fundamental laws are established. The Constitution is certain and fixed; it contains the permanent will of the people, and is the supreme law of the land; it is paramount to the power of the Legislature, and can be revoked or altered only by the authority that made it. The life-giving principle and the death-doing stroke must proceed from the same hand. What are Legislatures? Creatures of the Constitution; they owe their existence to the Constitution: they derive their powers from the Constitution: It is their commission; and, therefore, all their acts must be conformable to it, or else they will be void. The Constitution is the work or will of the People themselves, in their original, sovereign, and unlimited capacity. Law is the work or will of the Legislature in their derivative and subordinate capacity. The one is the work of the Creator, and the other of the Creature. The Constitution fixes limits to the exercise of legislative authority, and prescribes the orbit within which it must move. In short, gentlemen, the Constitution is the sun of the political system, around which all Legislative, Executive and Judicial bodies must revolve. Whatever may be the case in other countries, yet in this there can be no doubt, that every act of the Legislature, repugnant to the Constitution, is absolutely void.

3. *Marbury* deals with the use of the Constitution as a check on legislative enactment by Congress. Is the Court to be the sole expositor of the Constitution, or can that role also be played by others, say, the President, the state courts, or a governor?

With regard to the President, Jefferson did not dispute that the Court could pass on the validity of a law, such as the early Alien-Sedition Act which punished criticism of the government. Alien and Sedition Acts of 1798, 1 Stat. 277 (expired), 566 (repealed), 570 (expired), 596 (expired). However, Jefferson did not think that the Court's opinion was binding on the President. Thus, Jefferson stated in 1804: "The judges, believing the [Alien-Sedition] law constitutional, had a right to pass a sentence of fine and imprisonment . . . . But the Executive, believing the law to be unconstitutional, was bound to remit the execution of it, because that power has been confided to him by the Constitution. That instrument meant that its coordinate branches should be checks on each other. But the opinion which gives to the judges the right to decide what laws are constitutional, and what are not, not only for themselves in their own sphere of action, but for the legislative and Executive also in their spheres, would make the Judiciary a despotic branch." Letter from Thomas Jefferson to Abigail Adams (Sept. 11, 1804), *in* 8 THE WRITINGS OF THOMAS JEFFERSON 310 (Paul L. Ford ed., 1897). Jefferson has not been alone in this view, as various presidents — Jackson, Lincoln, Franklin Roosevelt, Nixon and Reagan — have all reserved the right to exercise independent constitutional judgment. This has most often occurred in the exercise of the presidential veto. More controversially, presidents have sometimes refused to enforce particular laws that either encroach directly on Executive authority or, in the President's view, blatantly violate constitutional provision. DOUGLAS W. KMIEC, THE ATTORNEY GENERAL'S LAWYER 53-57 (1992).

With regard to state courts, the issue was settled in *Martin v. Hunter's Lessee*, 14 U.S. (1 Wheat.) 304 (1816), that while the framers contemplated federal constitutional issues being adjudicated in state courts, they also envisaged that the final determination of federal constitutional meaning would be in the Supreme Court. *Martin* was also a title dispute. Virginia had confiscated Martin's land as a British subject and Hunter claimed ownership as a grantee from Virginia. Martin sought to set aside Hunter's claim based on certain anti-forfeiture provisions in treaties between England and the United States. The highest Virginia court held for Hunter, concluding that the state's title had vested prior to the treaty provisions. The Supreme Court reversed, finding that the Virginia title had not vested and the treaty provisions applied, and thus, directed the Virginia courts to enter judgment accordingly pursuant to the federal judiciary act. The Virginia court refused.

Justice Story instructed the state court to comply. Story reasoned that Article VI of the Constitution provides that "this constitution, and the laws of the United States, which shall be made in pursuance thereof, and all treaties made, or which shall be made, under the authority of the United States, shall be the supreme law of the land, and the judges in every state shall be bound thereby, any thing in the constitution or laws of any state to the contrary notwithstanding." This was the Supremacy Clause, but it only partially resolved the controversy, since the Virginia judges could, and did, argue that they were equally capable of interpreting federal law (in this case the federal treaty provisions), and would give federal law supremacy, if in *their* judgment, such was warranted. Story therefore continued: it is not merely that the constitution and federal law is supreme, it is also that Article III judicial power places the ultimate interpretation of federal law in the U.S. Supreme Court, subject only to congressional exception. Story highlighted the Article III words that "'the judicial power (which includes appellate power) shall extend *to all cases*', and 'in all other cases before mentioned the supreme court shall have appellate jurisdiction.'" *Martin*, 14 U.S. (1 Wheat.) at 338. In this way, Story demonstrated that it was the type of *case* (admiralty, federal question, diversity of citizenship, etc.) that gave the Supreme Court appellate review authority, and not the place of origin of the case, as in either state or federal court. If the Supreme Court could not finally determine an issue of federal law that arose in state court, it would be exercising less than *all* of the appellate jurisdiction specified in the constitutional document.

Story made a number of additional arguments, including that the U.S. Supreme Court's ultimate say in matters of federal constitutional interpretation can overcome real or perceived bias that may otherwise arise in state court when a state's own citizen is litigating against a citizen of another state (diversity jurisdiction). In addition, with regard to purely federal questions, confirming U.S. Supreme Court interpretation ensures the "necessity of *uniformity* of decisions throughout the whole United States, upon all subjects within the purview of the constitution." *Id*. at 347 (emphasis added).

With regard to state governors, *Cooper v. Aaron*, 358 U.S. 1 (1958), established that a state governor could not ignore or resist a federal court order to desegregate the Little Rock, Arkansas, schools on the theory that the Court's interpretation of the Fourteenth Amendment equal protection requirement in a case to which Arkansas was not party did not bind the state. After referencing the Supremacy Clause, the Court in *Cooper* unanimously reminded the Arkansas governor that:

> [I]n the notable case of *Marbury v. Madison* "It is emphatically the province and duty of the judicial department to say what the law is." This decision declared the basic principle that the federal judiciary is supreme in the exposition of the law of the Constitution, and that principle has ever since been respected by this Court and the Country as a permanent and indispensable feature of our constitutional system. . . . Every state legislator and executive and judicial officer is solemnly committed by oath taken pursuant to Article VI, cl. 3, "to support this Constitution."

Id. at 1409-10.

Some argue that *Cooper* over-extends *Marbury*, in that the latter was concerned principally with the Constitution as a check upon legislative excess, not with establishing the Court as the sole expositor of constitutional meaning. In truth, *Cooper* has come to mean not that the Court is *sole* interpreter, but that its interpretation establishes a constitutional minimum, from which states can depart upward (but not down) pursuant to state constitutional provisions. So too, members of Congress or the President in carrying out responsibilities assigned to them by the Constitution may on occasion indulge different constitutional assumptions, where those assumptions do not violate the constitutional rights of other citizens or preclude the functioning of a coordinate branch. For example, Congress may refuse to pass legislation it believes unconstitutional, even if prevailing judicial precedent might sustain the proposed law's constitutionality, but Congress cannot pass laws that the Court would clearly hold to be unconstitutional. *See United States v. Eichman*, 496 U.S. 310 (1990) (invalidating the federal Flag Protection Act because, notwithstanding the views of Professor Laurence Tribe of Harvard that such would be constitutional, the Act was contrary to the Court's reasoning used to invalidate a similar Texas statute in *Texas v. Johnson*, 491 U.S. 397 (1989)). Presidents from Jefferson to the present have frequently taken issue with the Court in exercising their veto power, and sometimes even in enforcement decisions, a topic we take up later in the consideration of the Executive power. Indeed, one of your authors has contended that the separation of powers doctrine requires to Court to give serious reconsideration to its position should Congress re-enact legislation after a finding of unconstitutionality by the Court, *see* John C. Eastman, *Judicial Review of Unenumerated Rights: Does* Marbury's *Holding Apply in a Post-Warren Court World?*, presented at the 2003 Annual Meeting of the American Political Science Association, available at http://archive.allacademic.com/publication/search.php?PHPSESSID=54ededdfc068ccd1ff21ce32a04c5e5c.

4. After *Marbury*, there were few occasions for the Court to invalidate congressional legislation. Indeed, it was not until 1857 and the ill-fated *Dred Scott* decision striking the Missouri Compromise and Congress' authority to prohibit slavery in the new territories that the Court saw fit to declare another act of Congress unconstitutional. We take up *Dred Scott* in Chapter Eight, when we turn to the principle of equality. The Court first invalidated a state law in *Fletcher v. Peck*, 10 U.S. (6 Cranch) 87 (1810), a case where the Court applied the Constitution's protection against the impairment of contracts to prevent a state from getting out of a bad land deal. We mentioned *Fletcher* in Chapter Two because of its natural law underpinnings, but it is considered more fully in Chapter Six. Perhaps, the most sweeping use of judicial review occurred in *INS v. Chadha*, 462 U.S. 919 (1983), considered later in this Chapter, where the Court found the legislative veto to be unconstitutional and effectively invalidated portions of over two hundred statutes.

2. The Legislative Power

As noted in the introduction to this Chapter, legislative power is comprehensively examined in Chapter Four. The constitutional definition of legislative power can be found in Article I, including the qualifications for serving in the House and the Senate, as well as a fairly long list of powers in Section 8. Our focus here is the interplay between legislative enactment and executive implementation or execution. The primary case, *INS v. Chadha*, 462 U.S. 919 (1983), addresses whether, after legislating, Congress can direct the application or implementation of statutes. As you will see, the Court answers the question in the negative by referring to Article I, Section 7, which describes the procedure for making law — bicameral passage, approval by both Houses, and presentment to the President for his signature or disapproval by presidential veto. *Chadha* also involves a "veto" — a putative, but as it will turn out, unconstitutional legislative one.

IMMIGRATION AND NATURALIZATION SERVICE v. CHADHA
462 U.S. 919 (1983)

CHIEF JUSTICE BURGER delivered the opinion of the Court.

[This case] presents a challenge to the constitutionality of the provision in § 244(c)(2) of the Immigration and Nationality Act, 8 U.S.C. § 1254(c)(2), authorizing one House of Congress, by resolution, to invalidate the decision of the Executive Branch, pursuant to authority delegated by Congress to the Attorney General of the United States, to allow a particular deportable alien to remain in the United States.

I

[Chadha, an East Indian who was born in Kenya and holds a British passport, was lawfully admitted to the United States in 1966 on a nonimmigrant student visa. His visa expired on June 30, 1972, but Chadha remained in this country illegally, subjecting him to deportation. The Attorney General (after a hearing before the INS) recommended suspension of Chadha's deportation pursuant to authority delegated by the statute[1] and this was duly conveyed to Congress, after which either house of Congress had the power under the Act to veto[2] the Attorney General's determination that Chadha should not be deported. On December 12, 1975, Representative Eilberg, Chairman of the Judiciary Subcommittee on Immigration, Citizenship, and International Law, introduced a resolution opposing "the granting of permanent residence in the United States to [six] aliens," including Chadha. The resolution was passed without debate or recorded vote. Since the House action was pursuant to the Act, the resolution was not treated as an Article I legislative act; it was not submitted to the Senate or presented to the President for his action. After the House veto of the Attorney General's decision to allow Chadha to remain in the United States, the immigration judge reopened the deportation proceedings to implement the House order deporting Chadha.]

. . . [On appeal], the Court of Appeals [for the Ninth Circuit] held that the House was without constitutional authority to order Chadha's deportation; accordingly it directed the Attorney General "to cease and desist from taking any steps to deport this alien based upon the resolution enacted by the House of Representatives." The essence of its holding was that [the legislative veto reserved

---

1 Congress delegated the major responsibilities for enforcement of the Immigration and Nationality Act to the Attorney General. 8 U.S.C. § 1103(a). The Attorney General discharges his responsibilities through the Immigration and Naturalization Service, a division of the Department of Justice.

2 In constitutional terms, "veto" is used to describe the President's power under Art. I, § 7, of the Constitution. It appears, however, that Congressional devices of the type authorized by [this act] have come to be commonly referred to as a "veto."

to either house under the Act] violates the constitutional doctrine of separation of powers.

We granted *certiorari* . . . and we now affirm.

* * *

III

A

* * *

. . . [T]he fact that a given law or procedure is efficient, convenient, and useful in facilitating functions of government, standing alone, will not save it if it is contrary to the Constitution. Convenience and efficiency are not the primary objectives — or the hallmarks — of democratic government and our inquiry is sharpened rather than blunted by the fact that Congressional veto provisions are appearing with increasing frequency in statutes which delegate authority to executive and independent agencies.

JUSTICE WHITE [in dissent] undertakes to make a case for the proposition that the one-House veto is a useful "political invention," and we need not challenge that assertion. We can even concede this utilitarian argument although the long range political wisdom of this "invention" is arguable. . . . But policy arguments supporting even useful "political inventions" are subject to the demands of the Constitution which defines powers and, with respect to this subject, sets out just how those powers are to be exercised. Explicit and unambiguous provisions of the Constitution prescribe and define the respective functions of the Congress and of the Executive in the legislative process. Since the precise terms of those familiar provisions are critical to the resolution of this case, we set them out verbatim. Art. I provides:

"All legislative Powers herein granted shall be vested in a Congress of the United States, which shall consist of a Senate and a House of Representatives." Art. I, § 1.

"Every Bill which shall have passed the House of Representatives and the Senate, shall, before it becomes a Law, be presented to the President of the United States; . . ." Art. I, § 7, cl. 2.

"Every Order, Resolution, or Vote to which the Concurrence of the Senate and House of Representatives may be necessary (except on a question of Adjournment) shall be presented to the President of the United States; and before the Same shall take Effect, shall be approved by him, or being disapproved by him, shall be repassed by two thirds of the Senate and House of Representatives, according to the Rules and Limitations prescribed in the Case of a Bill." Art. I, § 7, cl. 3.

These provisions of Art. I are integral parts of the constitutional design for the separation of powers. We have recently noted that "[t]he principle of separation of powers was not simply an abstract generalization in the minds of the Framers: it was woven into the documents that they drafted in Philadelphia in the summer of 1787."

* * *

B

The Presentment Clauses

The records of the Constitutional Convention reveal that the requirement that all legislation be presented to the President before becoming law was uniformly accepted by the Framers. Presentment to the President and the Presidential veto were considered so imperative that the draftsmen took special pains to assure that these requirements could not be circumvented. During the final debate on Art. I, § 7, cl. 2, James Madison expressed concern that it might easily be evaded by the simple expedient of calling a proposed law a "resolution" or "vote" rather than a "bill." As a consequence, Art. I, § 7, cl. 3, was added.

* * *

The decision to provide the President with a limited and qualified power to nullify proposed legislation by veto was based on the profound conviction of the Framers that the powers conferred on Congress were the powers to be most carefully circumscribed. It is beyond doubt that lawmaking was a power to be shared by both Houses and the President. . . .

The President's role in the lawmaking process also reflects the Framers' careful efforts to check whatever propensity a particular Congress might have to enact oppressive, improvident, or ill-considered measures. . . .

* * *

C

Bicameralism

The bicameral requirement of Art. I, §§ 1, 7 was of scarcely less concern to the Framers than was the Presidential veto and indeed the two concepts are interdependent. By providing that no law could take effect without the concurrence of the prescribed majority of the Members of both Houses, the Framers reemphasized their belief, already remarked upon in connection with the Presentment Clauses, that legislation should not be enacted unless it has been carefully and fully considered by the Nation's elected officials. In the Constitutional Convention debates on the need for a bicameral legislature, James Wilson, later to become a Justice of this Court, commented:

"Despotism comes on mankind in different shapes. Sometimes in an Executive, sometimes in a military, one. Is there danger of a Legislative despotism? Theory & practice both proclaim it. If the Legislative authority be not restrained, there can be neither liberty nor stability; and it can only be restrained by dividing it within itself, into distinct and independent branches. In a single house there is no check, but the inadequate one, of the virtue & good sense of those who compose it."

* * *

We see therefore that the Framers were acutely conscious that the bicameral requirement and the Presentment Clauses would serve essential constitutional functions. The President's participation in the legislative process was to protect the Executive Branch from Congress and to protect the whole people from improvident laws. The division of the Congress into two distinctive bodies assures that the legislative power would be exercised only after opportunity for full study and debate in separate settings. The President's unilateral veto power, in turn, was limited by the power of two thirds of both Houses of Congress to overrule a veto thereby precluding final arbitrary action of one person. It emerges clearly that the prescription for legislative action in Art. I, §§ 1, 7 represents the Framers' decision that the legislative power of the Federal government be exercised in accord with a single, finely wrought and exhaustively considered, procedure.

IV

The Constitution sought to divide the delegated powers of the new federal government into three defined categories, legislative, executive and judicial, to assure, as nearly as possible, that each Branch of government would confine itself to its assigned responsibility. The hydraulic pressure inherent within each of the separate Branches to exceed the outer limits of its power, even to accomplish desirable objectives, must be resisted.

Although not "hermetically" sealed from one another, *Buckley v. Valeo*, the powers delegated to the three Branches are functionally identifiable. When any Branch acts, it is presumptively exercising the power the Constitution has delegated to it. . . .

Beginning with this presumption, we must nevertheless establish that the challenged action is of the kind to which the procedural requirements of Art. I, § 7 apply. Not every action taken by either House is subject to the bicameralism and presentment requirements of Art. I. Whether actions taken by either House are, in law and fact, an exercise of legislative power depends not on their form but upon "whether they contain matter which is properly to be regarded as legislative in its character and effect."

Examination of the action taken here by one House reveals that it was essentially legislative in purpose and effect. In purporting to exercise power defined in Art. I, § 8, cl. 4 to "establish an uniform Rule of Naturalization," the House took action that had the purpose and effect of altering the legal rights, duties and relations of persons, including the Attorney General, Executive Branch officials and Chadha, all outside the legislative branch. This Act purports to authorize one House of Congress to require the Attorney General to deport an individual alien whose deportation otherwise would be canceled under the Act.

The one-House veto operated in this case to overrule the Attorney General and mandate Chadha's deportation; absent the House action, Chadha would remain in the United States. Congress has acted and its action has altered Chadha's status.

The legislative character of the one-House veto in this case is confirmed by the character of the Congressional action it supplants. Neither the House of Representatives nor the Senate contends that, absent the veto provision, either of them, or both of them acting together, could effectively require the Attorney General to deport an alien once the Attorney General, in the exercise of legislatively delegated authority, had determined the alien should remain in the United States. Without the challenged provision, this could have been achieved, if at all, only by legislation requiring deportation. . . .

The nature of the decision implemented by the one-House veto in this case further manifests its legislative character. After long experience with the clumsy, time consuming private bill procedure, Congress made a deliberate choice to delegate to the Executive Branch, and specifically to the Attorney General, the authority to allow deportable aliens to remain in this country in certain specified circumstances. It is not disputed that this choice to delegate authority is precisely the kind of decision that can be implemented only in accordance with the procedures set out in Art. I. Disagreement with the Attorney General's decision on Chadha's deportation — that is, Congress' decision to deport Chadha — no less than Congress' original choice to delegate to the Attorney General the authority to make that decision, involves determinations of policy that Congress can implement in only one way; bicameral passage followed by presentment to the President. Congress must abide by its delegation of authority until that delegation is legislatively altered or revoked.

Finally, we see that when the Framers intended to authorize either House of Congress to act alone and outside of its prescribed bicameral legislative role, they narrowly and precisely defined the procedure for such action. There are but four provisions in the Constitution, explicit and unambiguous, by which one House may act alone with the unreviewable force of law, not subject to the President's veto:

(a) The House of Representatives alone was given the power to initiate impeachments. Art. I, § 2, cl. 6;

(b) The Senate alone was given the power to conduct trials following impeachment on charges initiated by the House and to convict following trial. Art. I, § 3, cl. 5;

(c) The Senate alone was given final unreviewable power to approve or to disapprove presidential appointments. Art. II, § 2, cl. 2;

(d) The Senate alone was given unreviewable power to ratify treaties negotiated by the President. Art. II, § 2, cl. 2.

Clearly, when the Draftsmen sought to confer special powers on one House, independent of the other House, or of the President, they did so in explicit, unambiguous terms. These carefully defined exceptions from presentment and bicameralism underscore the difference between the legislative functions of Congress and other unilateral but important and binding one-House acts provided for in the Constitution. These exceptions are narrow, explicit, and separately justified; none of them authorize the action challenged here. On the contrary, they provide further support for the conclusion that Congressional authority is not to be implied and for the conclusion that the veto provided for is not authorized by the constitutional design of the powers of the Legislative Branch.

Since it is clear that the action by the House under § 244(c)(2) was not within any of the express constitutional exceptions authorizing one House to act alone, and equally clear that it was an exercise of legislative power, that action was subject to the standards prescribed in Article I. The bicameral requirement, the Presentment Clauses, the President's veto, and Congress' power to override a veto were intended to erect enduring checks on each Branch and to protect the people from the improvident exercise of power by mandating certain prescribed steps. To preserve those checks, and maintain the separation of powers, the carefully defined limits on the power of each Branch must not be eroded. To accomplish what has been attempted by one House of Congress in this case requires action in conformity with the express procedures of the Constitution's prescription for legislative action: passage by a majority of both Houses and presentment to the President.

* * *

Affirmed.

JUSTICE WHITE, dissenting.

Today the Court not only invalidates [a section] of the Immigration and Nationality Act, but also sounds the death knell for nearly 200 other statutory provisions in which Congress has reserved a "legislative veto." For this reason, the Court's decision is of surpassing importance. And it is for this reason that the Court would have been well-advised to decide the case, if possible, on the narrower grounds of separation of powers, leaving for full consideration the constitutionality of other congressional review statutes operating on such varied matters as war powers and agency rulemaking, some of which concern the independent regulatory agencies.

The prominence of the legislative veto mechanism in our contemporary political system and its importance to Congress can hardly be overstated. It has become a central means by which Congress secures the accountability of executive and independent agencies. Without the legislative veto, Congress is faced with a Hobson's choice: either to refrain from delegating the necessary authority, leaving itself with a hopeless task of writing laws with the requisite specificity to cover endless special circumstances across the entire policy landscape, or in the alternative, to abdicate its law-making function to the executive branch and independent agencies. To choose the former leaves major national problems unresolved; to opt for the latter risks unaccountable policymaking by those not elected to fill that role. . . .

I

* * *

Even this brief review suffices to demonstrate that the legislative veto is more than "efficient, convenient, and useful." It is an important if not indispensable political invention that allows the President and Congress to resolve major constitutional and policy differences, assures the accountability of independent regulatory agencies, and preserves Congress' control over lawmaking. Perhaps there are other means of accommodation and accountability, but the increasing reliance of Congress upon the legislative veto suggests that the alternatives to which Congress must now turn are not entirely satisfactory.

* * *

II

For all these reasons, the apparent sweep of the Court's decision today is regrettable. The Court's Article I analysis appears to invalidate all legislative vetoes irrespective of form or subject. . . .

* * *

If the legislative veto were as plainly unconstitutional as the Court strives to suggest, its broad ruling today would be more comprehensible. But, the constitutionality of the legislative veto is anything but clear-cut. The issue divides scholars, courts, attorneys general,[14] and the two other branches of the National Government. If the veto devices so flagrantly disregarded the requirements of Article I as the Court today suggests, I find it incomprehensible that Congress, whose members are bound by oath to uphold the Constitution, would have placed these mechanisms in nearly 200 separate laws over a period of 50 years.

* * *

A

The terms of the Presentment Clauses suggest only that bills and their equivalent are subject to the requirements of bicameral passage and presentment to the President. . . .

---

14 *See, e.g.*, 6 Op. Att'y Gen. 680, 683 (1854); Department of Justice, Memorandum re Constitutionality of Provisions in Proposed Reorganization bills Now Pending in Congress, *reprinted in* S. Rep. No. 232, 81st Cong. 1st Sess. 19-20 1949); Robert Jackson, *A Presidential Legal Opinion*, 66 HARV. L. REV. 1353 (1953); 43 Op. Att'y Gen. No. 10, at 2 (1977).

Although the Clause does not specify the actions for which the concurrence of both Houses is "necessary," the proceedings at the Philadelphia Convention suggest its purpose was to prevent Congress from circumventing the presentation requirement in the making of new legislation. . . .

* * *

B

If Congress may delegate lawmaking power to independent and executive agencies, it is most difficult to understand Article I as forbidding Congress from also reserving a check on legislative power for itself. Absent the veto, the agencies receiving delegations of legislative or quasi-legislative power may issue regulations having the force of law without bicameral approval and without the President's signature. It is thus not apparent why the reservation of a veto over the exercise of that legislative power must be subject to a more exacting test. In both cases, it is enough that the initial statutory authorizations comply with the Article I requirements.

* * *

IV

The Court of Appeals struck [the legislative veto] as violative of the constitutional principle of separation of powers. It is true that the purpose of separating the authority of government is to prevent unnecessary and dangerous concentration of power in one branch. For that reason, the Framers saw fit to divide and balance the powers of government so that each branch would be checked by the others. Virtually every part of our constitutional system bears the mark of this judgment.

But the history of the separation of powers doctrine is also a history of accommodation and practicality. Apprehensions of an overly powerful branch have not led to undue prophylactic measures that handicap the effective working of the national government as a whole. The Constitution does not contemplate total separation of the three branches of Government. . . .

Our decisions reflect this judgment. As already noted, the Court, recognizing that modern government must address a formidable agenda of complex policy issues, countenanced the delegation of extensive legislative authority to executive and independent agencies. The separation of powers doctrine has heretofore led to the invalidation of government action only when the challenged action violated some express provision in the Constitution. In *Buckley v. Valeo* (1976) and *Myers v. United States* (1926), congressional action compromised the appointment power of the President. *See also Springer v. Fallopian Islands* (1928). In *United States v. Klein* (1871), an Act of Congress was struck for encroaching upon judicial power, but the Court found that the Act also impinged upon the Executive's exclusive pardon power. Art. II, § 2. Because we must have a workable efficient government, this is as it should be.

This is the teaching of *Nixon v. Administrator of Gen. Servs.* (1977), which, in rejecting a separation of powers objection to a law requiring that the Administrator take custody of certain presidential papers, set forth a framework for evaluating such claims:

> "[I]n determining whether the Act disrupts the proper balance between the coordinate branches, the proper inquiry focuses on the extent to which it prevents the Executive Branch from accomplishing its constitutionally assigned functions. *United States v. Nixon* (1977). Only where the potential for disruption is present must we then determine whether that impact is justified by an overriding need to promote objectives within the constitutional authority of Congress."

The legislative veto provision does not "prevent the Executive Branch from accomplishing its constitutionally assigned functions." First, it is clear that the Executive Branch has no "constitutionally assigned" function of suspending the deportation of aliens. "'Over no conceivable subject is the legislative power of Congress more complete than it is over the admission of aliens." Nor can it be said that the inherent function of the Executive Branch in executing the law is involved. The *Steel Seizure Case* resolved that the Article II mandate for the President to execute the law is a directive to enforce the law which Congress has written. *Youngstown Sheet & Tube Co. v. Sawyer* (1952). "The duty of the President to see that the laws be executed is a duty that does not go beyond the laws or require him to achieve more than Congress sees fit to leave within his power." Here, [the Act] grants the executive only a qualified suspension authority and it is only that authority which the President is constitutionally authorized to execute.

* * *

I do not suggest that all legislative vetoes are necessarily consistent with separation of powers principles. A legislative check on an inherently executive function, for example that of initiating prosecutions, poses an entirely different question. But the legislative veto device here — and in many other settings — is far from an instance of legislative tyranny over the Executive. It is a necessary check on the unavoidably expanding power of the agencies, both executive and independent, as they engage in exercising authority delegated by Congress.

V

I regret that I am in disagreement with my colleagues on the fundamental questions that this case presents. But even more I regret the destructive scope of the Court's holding. It reflects a profoundly different conception of the Constitution than that held by the Courts which sanctioned the modern administrative state. Today's decision strikes down in one fell swoop provisions in more laws enacted by Congress than the Court has cumulatively invalidated in its history. I fear it will now be more difficult "to insure that the fundamental policy decisions in our society will be made not by an appointed official but by the body immediately responsible to the people."

* * *

JUSTICE REHNQUIST, with whom JUSTICE WHITE joins, dissenting.

A severability clause creates a presumption that Congress intended the valid portion of the statute to remain in force when one part is found to be invalid. . . .

* * *

. . . But the history elucidated by the Court shows that Congress was unwilling to give the Executive Branch permission to suspend deportation on its own. Over the years, Congress consistently rejected requests from the Executive for complete discretion in this area. Congress always insisted on retaining ultimate control, whether by concurrent resolution, as in the 1948 Act, or by one-House veto, as in the present Act. Congress has never indicated that it would be willing to permit suspensions of deportation unless it could retain some sort of veto.

It is doubtless true that Congress has the power to provide for suspensions of deportation without a one-House veto. But the Court has failed to identify any evidence that Congress intended to exercise that power. On the contrary, Congress' continued insistence on retaining control of the suspension process indicates that it has never been disposed to give the Executive Branch a free hand. By severing [the legislative veto] the Court has "confounded" Congress' "intention" to permit suspensions of deportation "with their power to carry that intention into effect."

Because I do not believe that [the legislative veto] is severable, I would reverse the judgment of the Court of Appeals.

NOTES AND QUESTIONS

1. Earlier we considered what makes a case "justiciable," that is, capable of being heard by an Article III court, including the Supreme Court. Lack of standing, issues having become moot, or being insufficiently ripe for consideration can each deprive the Court of jurisdiction. The dispute in *Chadha* was also alleged to be nonjusticiable. Why? The answer lies in the so-called political question doctrine. This analytically slippery concept is invoked by the Court when it is unable to discern any non-policy basis for resolving a dispute. In *Chadha*, Congress argued that it had plenary authority to deal with aliens under the Naturalization Clause in Article I, Section 8, Clause 4, and that the Court could not review its determinations.

The Court rejected Congress' argument by referring to the explication of the political question doctrine in *Baker v. Carr*, 369 U.S. 186 (1962). As identified in *Baker*, a political question may arise when there is:

> a textually demonstrable constitutional commitment of the issue to a coordinate political department; or a lack of judicially discoverable and manageable standards for resolving it; or the impossibility of deciding without an initial policy determination of a kind clearly for nonjudicial discretion; or the impossibility of a court's undertaking independent resolution without expressing lack of the respect due coordinate branches of government; or an unusual need for unquestioning adherence to a political decision already made; or the potentiality of embarrassment from multifarious pronouncements by various departments on one question.

Id. at 217.

Applying this standard, the Court reasoned that the mere fact that Congress has been given legislative authority cannot deprive the Court of judicial review. As the Court stated:

> [I]f this turns the question into a political question, virtually every challenge to the constitutionality of a statute would be a political question. . . . No policy underlying the political question doctrine suggests that Congress or the Executive, or both acting in concert and in compliance with Art. I, can decide the constitutionality of a statute; that is a decision for the courts.

Chadha, 462 U.S. at 941-42.

The Court applied the political question principles set out in *Baker*, in *Nixon v. United States*, 506 U.S. 224 (1992). In *Nixon*, the Court found that the issue of whether it was unconstitutional for Senate rules to not allow for an evidentiary hearing before the full Senate in the impeachment of a federal judge was a nonjusticiable political question. Article I, Section 3, Clause 6 provides that the "Senate shall have sole Power to try all Impeachments," and Chief Justice Rehnquist for the Court reasoned that the word "sole" committed the issue of procedure to the Senate, and the word "try" was not a judicially manageable standard by which the Court could second-guess the procedure chosen.

2. Why wasn't the President in *Chadha* estopped from raising an objection to the legislative veto, since he signed the bill, which included this role for Congress, into law? *Marbury v. Madison*, 5 U.S. (1 Cranch) 137 (1803), resolved that question. The assent of the Executive to a bill which contains a provision contrary to the Constitution does not shield it from judicial review. In any event, eleven Presidents, from Wilson through Reagan, who had been presented with this issue went on record at some point to challenge legislative vetoes as unconstitutional. *See* John B. Henry II, *The Legislative Veto: In Search of Constitu-*

tional Limits, 16 Harv. J. Legis. 735, 737-38 n.7 (1979) (collecting citations to presidential statements).

Presidents have had more to do with the legislative veto than just grudgingly accepting them. In fact, President Herbert Hoover first suggested the legislative veto mechanism. Hoover wanted to reorganize the Executive branch, traditionally an act lying within Congress' sound discretion, without seeking legislative approval for each act of the reorganization. Thus, when President Hoover requested authority to reorganize the government in 1929, he asked that the Congress be willing to delegate its authority to the Executive subject to defined principles and legislative review. Hoover proposed that the Executive "should act upon approval of a joint committee of Congress or with the reservation of power of revision by Congress within some limited period adequate for its consideration." Pub. Papers 432 (1929). Congress obliged, and since Hoover, Presidents have submitted 115 reorganization plans, of which Congress has disapproved only 23 pursuant to legislative veto provisions.

3. Even if a President did not object to the presence of a legislative veto, there is often a very practical reason — Congress likely lumped or "bundled" the unacceptable measure in with legislation otherwise thought indispensable. For example, after President Roosevelt signed the Lend-Lease Act of 1941, Attorney General Jackson released a memorandum explaining the President's view that the provision allowing the Act's authorization to be terminated by concurrent resolution (that is, a congressional resolution not presented to the President) was unconstitutional. Robert Jackson, *A Presidential Legal Opinion*, 66 Harv. L. Rev. 1353 (1953).

The "bundling" practices of Congress have come under increasing scrutiny. President Reagan thought they effectively deprived him of his constitutional veto authority in Article I, Section 7, Clause 2. According to that provision, "*every* bill which shall have passed the House of Representatives and the Senate, shall, before, it becomes law, be presented to the President . . . ." (emphasis supplied). The President then has 10 days (Sundays excepted) to either approve or disapprove. If the President disapproves or vetoes, he returns the bill to the House where it originated. Because the framers deliberately chose not to extend the Executive an absolute veto, the measure can become law despite presidential objection if two-thirds of both houses agree. A bill can also become law if the President neglects to act on it within 10 days, though there is an exception. If Congress has adjourned, thereby preventing the bill's return, the President may allow the bill to die, or be "pocket vetoed," by the simple expedient of not signing it. There is some dispute as to how long the congressional adjournment must be, but it is clear that the possibility of a pocket veto exists between the seating of two different Congresses as well as the interim break between the first and second year of a single Congress. *See The Pocket Veto Case*, 279 U.S. 655 (1929). A three-day recess, however, has been held insufficient. *Wright v. United States*, 302 U.S. 583 (1938).

President Reagan speculated that he was being denied his veto authority when bundled measures were presented to him. He asked his legal counsel to determine whether he could "line-item" veto unacceptable parts of bundled legislation on the theory that such presentments were not one bill, but multiple bills that he could properly disaggregate for separate consideration. The question was a close one, but erring on the side of comity with the legislative branch, the President's lawyers advised against asserting an inherent line item veto. *Compare* Douglas W. Kmiec, *OLC's Opinion Writing Function: The Legal Adhesive for a Unitary Executive*, 15 Cardozo L. Rev. 337, 353-59 (1993), *with* Charles J. Cooper, *The President's Veto Power*, 12 Op. Off. Legal Counsel 159 (1988).

President Clinton assumed President Reagan's interest in a line-item veto, especially as it related to budgetary or money bills. Mr. Clinton asserted that absent a line-item veto, money bills were often loaded with "pork," making it impossible to reduce the federal budget deficit. Congress has attempted to meet these concerns with a statutory Line Item Veto Act of 1996, 2 U.S.C. § 681 (1996), effective January 1, 1997.

Proposed statutory item vetoes in the past have not been free from constitutional doubt. Earlier suggestions that would have allowed the President to simply strike out portions of a bill presented to him while signing the remainder were thought to violate the Presentment Clause of Article I, Section 7. In essence, these statutory measures were believed to disregard constitutional symmetry, giving the President a more discretionary role over legislation than members of Congress. If Congressman Smith has to accept a bill with both items A and B or nothing, how, it was asked, can the President be allowed to select either A or B as well as both?

The theory of the new legislation is that the President is not really authorized to disapprove any part of a bill, rather he merely rescinds or refuses to spend some of the money appropriated. Under the 1996 Act, the President must notify Congress of the rescission, and Congress may void it within 30 days by passing new legislation directing the expenditure of funds. However, the President's rescission is effective immediately, and this is a significant change from prior law which allowed a President to propose a rescission, but not act on it unless it was congressionally approved. *See* The Congressional Budget and Impoundment Control Act of 1974, 2 U.S.C. § 681 (1996). Under the new Act the President's legislative will governs unless it is overridden by new legislation. This reversal of burden is argued to be constitutionally flawed, since the President is making new law and sharing in Congress' power of the purse. Assistant Attorney General Walter Dellinger defended the measure with the claim that a President has always had constitutional discretion not to spend authorized funds unless he is specifically required to do so. 141 Cong. Rec. S2679-01, S2708 (daily ed. February 15, 1995) (statement of Assistant Attorney General Dellinger).

Underlying the line item veto issue is the controversial subject of presidential impoundment. While various Presidents from Jefferson onward have refused to spend appropriated sums, *see* Niles Stanton, *History and Practice of*

Executive Impoundment of Appropriated Funds, 53 NEB. L. REV. 1 (1974), this practice has frequently met with legislative objection. Richard Nixon's claimed authority to impound highway funds, for example, triggered the passage of the 1974 Impoundment Control Act referenced above. Beyond the specific issue of the expenditure of funds, the new Line Item Veto Act also raises the question of how precisely the Executive must follow the Legislature's direction in "taking care that the Laws be faithfully executed," Article II, Section 3. In *Kendall v. United States*, 37 U.S. 524, 568 (1838), the Court held that the President could not withhold payment of a contract for the delivery of mail because the obligation was ministerial. However, other cases have allowed the President power to decline to make payments, where the statute allows for the exercise of judgment or discretion. *Decatur v. Pauling*, 39 U.S. 497 (1876).

Against this background, constitutional challenges to the new Line Item Veto Act were almost immediate. In *Raines v. Byrd*, 521 U.S. 811 (1997), six Members of Congress alleged that the 1996 Act violated the Constitution by altering the legal and practical effect of their votes by divesting them of their constitutional role in the repeal of legislation. The President responded that the Members lacked standing, asserting only a generalized grievance, and that in any event, no case was ripe until the President actually utilized the authority of the 1996 Act. The district court disagreed, finding the the Members to have standing because the Act presently dilutes their Article I voting power. Before the Act, a vote gave the President a specific choice; after, it gave him a menu of items to choose from. The trial court also found the case to be ripe since the mere existence of the item veto presently affects legislative considerations and bargaining. For example, when a Member must factor the President's new authority into a decision to oppose him on an appointment, treaty, or general legislation. On the merits, the district court invalidated the Act because it represented not a grant of executive discretion (*e.g.*, spend no more than a certain sum), but "a radical transfer of the legislative power to repeal statutory law." *Byrd v. Raines*, 956 F. Supp. 25, 33 (D.D.C. 1997). In this case, said the district court, Congress has attempted to give the President the unilateral power to effect a partial repeal which is "precisely what the Presentment Clause was designed to prevent." *Id.* at 35.

When the case reached the Supreme Court, the Court found the case to be nonjusticiable for lack of standing. *Raines*, 521 U.S. at 818-28. The Act purported to statutorily confer standing on "any Member of Congress," among others, but the Court reasoned that this was insufficient to satisfy the constitutional standing requirements derived from the separation of powers. The Court distinguished *Powell v. McCormack*, 395 U.S. 486 (1969), where Congressman Powell had been excluded from the Congress because of various ethical improprieties. Powell, reasoned the Court, had been singled out for disfavor and thus was personally injured. By contrast, the injury raised regarding the line item veto (dilution of the effect of Member votes) "runs (in a sense) with the Member's seat." *Raines*, 521 U.S. at 821. The Court also claimed that the one occasion when the Court had recognized congressional standing, in *Coleman v. Miller*,

307 U.S. 433 (1939), was distinguishable. There, it was disputed whether the lieutenant governor could cast a tie-breaking vote for ratification of a constitutional amendment. Said the Court:

> *Coleman* stands . . . for the proposition that legislators whose votes would have been sufficient to defeat (or enact) a specific legislative act have standing to sue if that legislative action goes into effect (or does not go into effect), on the ground that their votes have been completely nullified. . . . There is a vast difference between the level of vote nullification at issue in *Coleman* and the abstract dilution of institutional legislative power that is alleged here.

Raines, 521 U.S. at 823-26. The Court explained that it was wary of granting more liberalized standing because it would plunge the judiciary more quickly into bitter political battles between the President and Congress. Justices Souter and Ginsburg in a separate concurrence agreed that respect for the separation of powers merits waiting for a suit by a private party when the President exercises his disputed statutory authority. Justice Stevens dissented, making the cogent point that a genuine injury existed in the form of "a simple denial of [the Members'] right to vote on the precise text that will ultimately become law," *id.* at 837 (Stevens, J., dissenting), as only the President would have that right. None of the Justices reached the merits of the statutory line-item veto, so its constitutionality remained much in dispute. President Clinton later exercised his statutory item veto authority and, once again, the line-item-veto went before the Court. *City of New York v. Clinton,* 985 F. Supp. 168 (D.D.C. 1998), on appeal by statutory provision. The district court found plaintiffs to have standing as a result of two vetoed provisions. Certain farmer co-ops indirectly lost potential economic opportunities because the agribusiness sellers they were negotiating with lost a capital gains deferral right or tax benefit and the State of New York lost a statutory immunity from having to repay monies it arguably owed under the Medicaid program. By state law, the repayment would be borne by the City. The district court found the Act unconstitutional, reasoning that it allowed the President the unilateral authority to repeal enacted statutes. In *Clinton v. New York*, 521 U.S. 417 (1998), the Supreme Court agreed. An act of Congress cannot authorize the President to create a law whose exact text was not voted on by either House. This would violate Article I, section 7.

4. Today, the federal government is rife with administrative agencies handling important subject matter, from the safety of food and drugs (Food and Drug Administration) to the honesty and practices of the investment industry (Securities and Exchange Commission). Some agencies, like the 14 cabinet departments, the Departments of Justice, State, Health and Human Services, and so on, are said to be executive agencies, while others are described as independent agencies. The primary difference between the two types of agencies is whether the head of the agency is removable at will by the President — executive agency heads are, independent agency heads are not. We take up the issue of presidential appointment and removal below, but introduce it here to ask a further question about the implications of *Chadha*. These agencies of whichever type often undertake administrative rulemaking, which fills in the nuances of broadly worded legislation. These rules, from the standpoint of the general citizen, are often indistinguishable from legislation in tone and effect. Why is it appropriate for Congress to delegate legislative authority or its equivalent to administrative agencies, but not to a subpart of itself? Congress, in seeking to defend the legislative veto in *Chadha*, made a similar argument by asking why the Attorney General could suspend Chadha's deportation.

In responding, the Court admitted that some administrative agency action — rule making, for example — may resemble lawmaking. In this regard, the Administrative Procedure Act, 5 U.S.C. § 551(4), defines an agency's "rule" as "the whole or part of an agency statement of general or particular applicability and future effect designed to implement, interpret, or prescribe law or policy." The Court, itself, has referred to agency activity as being "quasi-legislative" in character. *Humphrey's Executor v. United States*, 295 U.S. 602, 624 (1935). Nevertheless, the Court views these administrative rules differently than legislative enactments. In essence, the Court sees administrative rulemaking as merely part of the President's power to see that "the laws are faithfully executed." Thus, when the Attorney General performed his duties under the immigration laws, as discretionary as they may be, he does not exercise "legislative" power. The bicameral process is not necessary as a check on the Executive's administration of the laws because his administrative activity cannot reach beyond the limits of the statute that created it — a statute duly enacted pursuant to Art. I, §§ 1, 7. The constitutionality of the Attorney General's execution of the authority delegated to him by statute involves only a question of whether the Executive has stayed within delegated authority. The courts, when a case or controversy arises, can always "ascertain whether the will of Congress has been obeyed," *Yakus v. United States*, 321 U.S. 414, 425 (1944), and can enforce adherence to statutory standards. Executive action is always subject to check by the terms of the legislation that authorized it. If that authority is exceeded, it is open to judicial review, as well as the power of Congress to modify or revoke the authority entirely. By contrast, the Court in *Chadha* concluded, a one-House veto is clearly legislative in both character and effect and is not so checked. Therefore, the requirements of bicameral passage and presentment to the President are necessary checks that cannot be avoided merely because Congress may delegate portions of its authority to administrative agencies.

5. As stated just above, something that looks an awful lot like the completion of the legislative process *can* be delegated to administrative agencies. In theory, these delegations must be accomplished with Congress supplying an intelligible standard for the agencies to follow. The necessity for such a standard has come to be known as the non-delegation doctrine. Chief Justice Taft elaborated the standard in *J.W. Hampton & Co. v. United States*, 276 U.S. 394, 409 (1928): "If Congress shall lay down by legislative act an intelligible principle to which the person or body authorized to fix such rates is directed to conform, such legislative action is not a forbidden delegation of legislative power." Theory has not completely matched practice, however. In this regard, restrictions on the scope of the power that could be delegated have diminished and have all but disappeared. The Court has found an unconstitutional delegation in only two instances: *Panama Refining Co. v. Ryan*, 293 U.S. 388 (1935), and *Schechter Poultry Corp. v. United States*, 295 U.S. 495 (1935). As Justice White observes in his dissent in *Chadha*, the "intelligible principle" through which agencies have attained enormous control over the economic affairs of the country was held to include such formulations as "just and reasonable," *see Tagg Bros. & Moorhead v. United States*, 280 U.S. 420 (1930); "public interest," *see New York Central Securities Corp. v. United States*, 287 U.S. 12 (1932); "public convenience, interest, or necessity," *see Federal Radio Comm. v. Nelson Bros. Bond & Mortgage Co.*, 289 U.S. 266, 285 (1933); and "unfair methods of competition," *see FTC v. Gratz*, 253 U.S. 421 (1920).

The wisdom, if not the constitutionality, of these broad delegations is far from settled. There is little question but that the amount of law — the substantive rules that regulate private conduct and direct the operation of government — made by the agencies eclipses the lawmaking engaged in by Congress through the traditional process. What's more, when agencies are authorized to prescribe law through substantive rulemaking, the regulation is not only given deference, it is also accorded "legislative effect." *See, e.g., Schweiker v. Gray Panthers*, 453 U.S. 34, 43-44 (1981). These regulations bind courts and officers of the federal government and may pre-empt state law. Finally, agencies not only issue substantive rules, they also "interpret" the laws enacted by Congress. While substantive agency regulations are clearly exercises of lawmaking authority, a good case can be made that agency interpretations of their statutes are as well. The distinguished law professor and scholar of the administrative process, Henry Monaghan, has observed, "[j]udicial deference to agency 'interpretation' of law is simply one way of recognizing a delegation of lawmaking authority to an agency." Henry Monaghan, Marbury *and the Administrative State*, 83 COLUM. L. REV. 1, 26 (1983).

6. In *Whitman v. American Trucking Association*, 531 U.S. 457 (2001), the Court unanimously rejected an effort to revive a variant of the "non-delegation doctrine" of the *Panama Refining* and *Schecter Poultry* variety. In *Whitman*, the Court was faced with exacting new ozone and particulate matter air quality standards set by the Environmental Protection Agency (EPA). Congress had directed the EPA to devise them "to protect the public health with an adequate margin of safety." Since ozone and particulate matter are both non-threshold pollutants — that is, any amount harms the public health — the D.C. Circuit remanded both new standards to the agency, reasoning that the EPA lacked an "intelligible principle" to identify why it chose the levels it did. To the appellate panel, this lack of explanation raised a severe problem of over-delegation. Since any exposure causes harm, the lower court believed the EPA was left "free to pick any point between zero and a hair below . . . London's Killer fog," a notorious 1952 event in which air pollution is believed to have caused approximately 4000 deaths in little over four days. One member of the panel, Judge

Tatel, dissented from the revival of the non-delegation doctrine, which he posited had been ignored by the Court for the last half-century. The industry argued that the standard could be made intelligible by introducing cost-benefit analysis.

A unanimous Supreme Court, with several opinions, thought the legislative standard intelligible and "well within the outer limits of our non-delegation precedents." What's more, the Court found legislative intent to "unambiguously bar cost considerations." The most interesting aspect of *Whitman* was the appellate court's attempt to revive the non-delegation doctrine in a mutated form that remanded the issue, not to Congress, but to the agency to set its own standard by which to issue rules. This was thought to harmonize the deference judges owe to agency decision-making and Chief Justice Rehnquist's longstanding interest in using the doctrine at least in those cases where the principle of delegation is vague, not by reason of scientific uncertainty, but lack of political will to make hard decisions. But Justice Scalia, writing for the Court, reasoned that "[w]e have never suggested that an agency can cure an unlawful delegation of legislative power by adopting in its discretion a limiting construction of it. . . . The idea that an agency can cure an unconstitutionally standardless delegation of power by declining to exercise some of that power seems to us internally contradictory. The very choice of which portion of the power to exercise — that is to say, the prescription of the standard that Congress had omitted — would itself be an exercise of forbidden legislative authority."

So what then is an improper delegation? A statute, says the Court, that provides literally no guidance for exercise of discretion, or perhaps one empowering an agency to regulate "the whole economy" with the vague aphorism to promote "fair competition." In a separate concurrence, Justice Thomas agreed with the continuation of the loosely formulated intelligible principle standard, but also commented that he believes "that there are cases in which the principle is intelligible and yet the significance of the delegated decision is simply too great for the decision to be called anything other than 'legislation.'"

7. In *Chadha*, Congress conditioned the exercise of authority by the Attorney General on a one-House veto. Since the legislative veto was held to be constitutionally improper, why wasn't the entire grant of authority to stay the deportation also invalid, and not just the veto? Note, that if the Attorney General's authority was invalid, then Chadha would have been deported, and arguably would have lacked standing since the Court would have been unable to redress his alleged injury.

The issue presented by this question is one of severability. As a general matter, the Court holds to the proposition that the invalid portions of a statute are to be severed "'[u]nless it is evident that the Legislature would not have enacted those provisions which are within its power, independently of that which is not.'" *Buckley v. Valeo*, 424 U.S. 1, 108 (1976) (quoting *Champlin Refining Co. v. Corporation Comm'n*, 286 U.S. 210, 234 (1932)). It is unnecessary to search for Congress' intent if they include a severability provision. Congress did in *Chadha*. The provision, § 406 of the Immigration and Nationality Act, 8 U.S.C.

§ 1101, provides: "If any particular provision of this Act, or the application thereof to any person or circumstance, is held invalid, the remainder of the Act and the application of such provision to other persons or circumstances shall not be affected thereby."

Such language is unambiguous and gave rise to a presumption that Congress did not intend the validity of the Act as a whole, or of any part of the Act, to depend upon whether the legislative veto clause was valid. A provision is further presumed severable if what remains after severance "is fully operative as a law." *Champlin Refining Co.*, 286 U.S. at 234. The Court in *Chadha* thought there could be no doubt that the Attorney General's deportation suspension authority was "fully operative" and workable administrative machinery without the veto provision.

8. If Congress cannot exercise a legislative veto, how will Congress check the Executive as to the faithful execution of the laws? More frequent legislative oversight is one way. Every agency of government must justify its budget requests to an oversight committee in Congress, and there is no better time to assess how well the agency has functioned. Of course, legislative hearings are not limited to budget matters, as they can be conducted whenever and wherever Congress has a legislative interest. "[T]he power of inquiry," wrote Justice Van Devanter in *McGrain v. Daughtery*, 273 U.S. 135, 174 (1927), "with process to enforce it — is an essential and appropriate auxiliary to the legislative function." As an example of this power, Congress can compel attendance at an oversight hearing by subpoena.

Another alternative is for Congress to require administrative agencies to report proposed regulations to a committee and wait a reasonable time before putting them into effect, thereby allowing Congress to respond by appropriate legislative means. The result in *Chadha* effectively creates this type of "report and wait" requirement in the immigration area. Without the provision for one-House veto, Congress would presumably retain the power to enact a law, in accordance with the requirements of Article I of the Constitution, mandating a particular alien's deportation, unless, of course, other constitutional principles place substantive limitations on such action. The "report and wait" provision received approval in *Sibbach v. Wilson*, 312 U.S. 1 (1941). The statute examined in *Sibbach* provided that the newly promulgated Federal Rules of Civil Procedure "shall not take effect until they shall have been reported to Congress by the Attorney General at the beginning of a regular session thereof and until after the close of such session." Act of June 19, 1934, ch. 651, § 2, 48 Stat. 1064. This statute gave Congress the opportunity to review the Rules before they became effective and to pass legislation barring their effectiveness if the Rules were found objectionable. This technique was used by Congress when it acted in 1973 to stay, and ultimately to revise, the proposed Federal Rules of Evidence. *Compare* Act of March 30, 1973, Pub. L. No. 93-12, 87 Stat. 9, *with* Act of Jan. 2, 1975, Pub. L. No. 93-595, 88 Stat. 1926.

9. What if Congress sought to delegate an executive function not to itself, as a body or single house, but to a solitary legislative officer? This, too, is unconstitutional, as the Court's subsequent decision in *Bowsher v. Synar*, 478 U.S. 714 (1986), reveals. In *Bowsher*, the Congress passed deficit reduction legislation that instructed the Comptroller General to implement a "sequestration" or holding back of funds in the event that the deficit targets were not met. The President in turn was obligated to issue a "sequestration" order mandating the spending reductions specified by the Comptroller General. In reasoning that parallels *Chadha*, the Court held the legislation violated the separation of powers since the Comptroller General was removable by, and thus subservient to, Congress. The Court explained that the Comptroller General exercises executive functions under the Act. He determines budget cuts and commands even the President to act. While the Court admitted that the overall budget function was assigned by the Constitution to Congress, it stated that:

> [A]s *Chadha* makes clear, once Congress makes its choice in enacting legislation, its participation ends. Congress can thereafter control the execution of its enactment only indirectly — by passing new legislation. By placing the responsibility for execution of the Balanced Budget and Emergency Deficit Control Act in the hands of an officer who is subject to removal only by itself, Congress in effect has retained control over the execution of the Act and has intruded into the executive function. The Constitution does not permit such intrusion.

Bowsher, 478 U.S. at 716.

10. Are bicameralism and presentment required for every legislative action? No. An exception from the Presentment Clauses was indicated in *Hollingsworth v. Virginia*, 3 U.S. (3 Dall.) 378 (1798). There the Court held presidential approval was unnecessary for a proposed constitutional amendment which had passed both Houses of Congress by the requisite two-thirds majority as provided for in Article V of the Constitution. In addition, Article I, Section 7, Clauses 2 and 3, and Section 5, Clause 2 give specific situations where a single House may act alone in determining specified internal matters. However, this exception to bicameralism only empowers Congress to bind itself.

Even where bicameral passage is not required, the structure of the Constitution often reveals other precautions against arbitrary or improvident action. For example, Article II, Section 2 requires that two-thirds of the Senators present concur in the Senate's consent to a treaty, rather than the simple majority required for passage of legislation. *See* THE FEDERALIST NOS. 64, 66, and 75 (Alexander Hamilton). Similarly, the framers adopted an alternative protection, in the place of presidential veto and bicameralism, by requiring the concurrence of two-thirds of the Senators present for a conviction of impeachment. Article I, Section 3. In the case of a constitutional amendment discussed in *Hollingsworth*, a resolution proposing an amendment to the Constitution need not be presented to the President, but it is subject to two alternative protections.

First, a constitutional amendment must command the votes of two-thirds of each House. Second, three-fourths of the states must ratify any amendment.

11. Separation of powers cases often present attractive political expedients to legislative-executive impasse. In an age of political frustration and "gridlock," it can be tempting to pursue these compromises. For example, in *Chadha* a good case could be made that given the vast delegation of legislative authority to the administrative agencies of executive departments, the "spirit" of the separation of powers supported a new, modified check, the legislative veto, upon that vast delegation. The teaching of *Chadha* and *Bowsher*, however, is that one constitutional mutation does not deserve another. The separation of powers is premised upon ancient teaching, carefully designed with many subtle parts to avoid political oppression. In his opinion for the Court in *Bowsher*, 478 U.S. at 721, Chief Justice Burger makes this clear, and his words are a fitting way for us to conclude this brief examination of executive-legislative interaction:

> The declared purpose of separating and dividing the powers of government, of course, was to "diffus[e] power the better to secure liberty." *Youngstown Sheet & Tube Co. v. Sawyer* (1952) (Jackson, J., concurring). Justice Jackson's words echo the famous warning of Montesquieu, quoted by James Madison in THE FEDERALIST NO. 47, that "'there can be no liberty where the legislative and executive powers are united in the same person, or body of magistrates'...." THE FEDERALIST NO. 47, at 325 (J. Cooke ed., 1961).
>
> Even a cursory examination of the Constitution reveals the influence of Montesquieu's thesis that checks and balances were the foundation of a structure of government that would protect liberty. The Framers provided a vigorous Legislative Branch and a separate and wholly independent Executive Branch, with each branch responsible ultimately to the people. The Framers also provided for a Judicial Branch equally independent with "[t]he judicial Power ... extend[ing] to all Cases, in Law and Equity, arising under this Constitution, and the Laws of the United States." Art. III, § 2.
>
> Other, more subtle, examples of separated powers are evident as well. Unlike parliamentary systems such as that of Great Britain, no person who is an officer of the United States may serve as a Member of the Congress. Art. I, § 6. Moreover, unlike parliamentary systems, the President, under Article II, is responsible not to the Congress but to the people, subject only to impeachment proceedings which are exercised by the two Houses as representatives of the people. Art. II, § 4. And even in the impeachment of a President the presiding officer of the ultimate tribunal is not a member of the Legislative Branch, but the Chief Justice of the United States. Art. I, § 3.
>
> That this system of division and separation of powers produces conflicts, confusion, and discordance at times is inherent, but it was delib-

erately so structured to assure full, vigorous, and open debate on the great issues affecting the people and to provide avenues for the operation of checks on the exercise of governmental power.

In the next section, we turn to the role of the President in both domestic and foreign matters. In the initial case, *Youngstown Sheet & Tube Co. v. Sawyer*, 343 U.S. 579 (1952), we see the inverse of *Chadha* and *Bowsher* — a President allegedly assuming legislative authority. The Court has as little tolerance for the executive trespass as it did for the legislative. However, the Court in some contexts has blurred the executive-legislative line, by allowing the Legislature to limit the removal, and thus, the executive supervision of some executive officers. Out of this inability to categorize constitutional function emerges the so-called independent agency, and until recently the roaming independent counsels. See *Myers v. United States*, 272 U.S. 52 (1926), *Humphrey's Executor v. United States*, 295 U.S. 602 (1935), and *Morrison v. Olson*, 487 U.S. 654 (1988), below.

In the area of foreign policy, dueling constitutional provisions — giving some authority to the President as the commander-in-chief and with the power to negotiate treaties, and some to the Congress in the form of raising and supporting an army as well as the power to declare war, seemingly inspires, depending upon one's perspective, either confusion, or a necessary dependency of one branch upon the other in these serious matters. *United States v. Curtiss-Wright*, 299 U.S. 304 (1936), and the notes following it outline some of this foreign affairs indeterminacy, and it is foreshadowed in *Youngstown* where domestic and foreign interests collide.

3. The Executive Power

While the American system of checks and balances is justly praised for its dispersion of power among three co-equal branches of government, problems, as we have already seen, do arise in the practical applications of power. In particular, the often broad mandates of the Constitution give rise to an imprecision in the delineation of each branch's proper authority.

Following the American Revolution, the former colonists were in no mood for a king. Thus, the advocates of the new Constitution and, concomitantly, the executive department took great pains to distinguish the presidency from a monarchical system. In THE FEDERALIST No. 69, Alexander Hamilton expounded upon the Article II grants of and limitations upon executive power, painstakingly documenting the differences between the King of Great Britain and the new President. Hamilton emphasized that, unlike the lifelong, hereditary monarch, the President is elected to a four-year term, "and is to be re-eligible as often as the people of the United States shall think him worthy of their confidence." The President, Hamilton urged, is also subject to removal from office and subsequent prosecution, unlike Britain's monarch whose "person . . . is sacred and inviolable; there is no constitutional court to which he is amenable; no punishment to which he can be subjected without involving the crisis of a national revolution." *Id.* Hamilton concluded, perhaps a bit implausibly, that, "except as to the concurrent authority of the President in the article of treaties, it would be difficult to determine whether that magistrate would, in the aggregate, possess more or less power than the Governor of New York."

Hamilton's persuasive task was difficult. He needed to both allay the fears of monarchy and to convince elements of the populace that the President would possess sufficient authority to govern. Hamilton manages, in *The Federalist* No. 70, to make these seemingly contradictory directions converge. He began by "[t]aking it for granted . . . that all men of sense will agree in the necessity of an energetic Executive." He noted that an energetic President is "essential to the protection of the community against foreign attacks." Defending the logic of a unitary Executive, Hamilton wrote: "Decision, activity, secrecy, and dispatch will generally characterise the proceedings of one man in a much more eminent degree than the proceedings of any greater number." It is this same unitariness, Hamilton contends, that safeguards against king-like abuse. "It is far more safe," he writes, that "there should be a single object for the jealousy and watchfulness of the people; and, in a word, that all multiplication of the Executive is rather dangerous than friendly to liberty." Whatever the merits of a unitary Executive, Hamilton's genius lay in his ability to present the new Presidency as squarely between a monarch on the one hand and an ineffectual figurehead on the other.

Despite Hamilton's assurances and ultimate success in convincing (enough) doubters of the new Executive to ratify the original Constitution, partisans on both sides might today find sufficient evidence in the subsequent history of the Presidency to merit a hearty "I told you so!" For example, Theodore Roosevelt's Presidency might well disturb those fearful of monarchial tendency. In his autobiography, Roosevelt sketched the theory upon which he based his actions in office with little self-doubt. "My view was that every executive officer . . . was a steward of the people bound actively and affirmatively to do all he could for the people, and not to content himself with the negative merit of keeping his talents undamaged in a napkin." While claiming that he "did not usurp power," he acknowledged that he "did greatly broaden the use of executive power." THEODORE ROOSEVELT, AN AUTOBIOGRAPHY 357 (1920).

One such example of this increased "use" of executive power involved the acquisition of Panamanian territory for the building of the Panama Canal. Employing an "odd combination of intrigue and bombast," President Roosevelt orchestrated unilaterally a treaty between the United States and "self-appointed representatives of Panama." *See* PETER COLLIER & DAVID HOROWITZ, THE ROOSEVELTS: AN AMERICAN SAGA 115 (1994). As he later boasted, "If I had followed conventional, conservative methods, I should have submitted a dignified state paper to the Congress and the debate would have been going on yet, but I took the canal zone and let the Congress debate, and while the debate goes on, the canal does also." *Id.* at 116. Roosevelt made an attractive argument for an activist Presidency. "I acted for the public welfare, I acted for the common well-being of all our people, whenever and in whatever manner was necessary, unless prevented by direct constitutional or legislative prohibition." ROOSEVELT, *supra,* at 357.

Many would contrast Roosevelt's broad conception of presidential power with the far more constrained views of his successor, William Howard Taft. Taft succinctly expressed his position: "The true view of the Executive function is, as I conceive it, that the President can exercise no power which cannot be fairly and reasonably traced to some specific grant of power or justly implied and included within such express grant as proper and necessary to exercise." WILLIAM HOWARD TAFT, OUR CHIEF MAGISTRATE AND HIS POWERS 139-140 (1925). Directly contradicting his predecessor's vision, Taft argued that "[t]here is no undefined residuum of power which he can exercise because it seems to him to be in the public interest." *Id.* at 140. He considered Roosevelt's position "an unsafe doctrine and that it might lead under emergencies to results of an arbitrary character, doing irremediable injustice to private right." *Id.* at 144. Rather than actively seek to elevate the Executive over the other branches, Taft specifically endorsed the "cooperation of all branches." *Id.* at 138.

Roosevelt and Taft were debating at opposite poles, but still within the limits of the Article II Executive office. A few Presidents facing grave national emergency, thankfully not many, have had to think beyond those limits and consider before acting when, if ever, is a President justified stepping across constitutional boundary. The influential 18th century philosopher John Locke observed:

> [T]he executor of the laws, having power in his hands, has by the common law of nature a right to make use of it for the good of society, in many cases where the municipal law has given no direction, till the legislature can conveniently be assembled to provide for it.

JOHN LOCKE, THE SECOND TREATISE OF GOVERNMENT 91-92 (Thomas P. Peardon ed., 1952). Yet, Locke went further:

> This power to act according to discretion, for the common good, without the prescription of the law and *sometimes even against it* is that which is called "prerogative," for since in some governments the lawmaking power is not always in being, and is usually too numerous and so too slow for the dispatch requisite to execution, and because also it is impossible to foresee, and so by laws to provide for, all accidents and necessities that may concern the public. . . .

Id. at 92 (emphasis added).

Locke theorized about this issue; Abraham Lincoln faced it. Confronting the onset of civil war, Lincoln took several actions facially violative of federal law, and the Constitution. Most significantly, perhaps, "[h]e suspended the writ of habeas corpus and ordered the arrest and detention of citizens without trial in violation of the Constitution, and he refused to reinstate the writ of habeas corpus when ordered to do so by Chief Justice Roger Taney." THE AMERICAN PRESIDENCY: HISTORICAL AND CONTEMPORARY PERSPECTIVES 31 (Harry A. Bailey, Jr. & Jay M. Shafritz eds., 1988). While Lincoln understood that the Presidency had not "conferred upon me an unrestricted right to act officially" to oppose slavery, he believed the preservation of the union quite another matter. Letter from Abraham Lincoln to A.G. Hodges (April 4, 1864), *in* THE AMERICAN PRESIDENCY, *supra*, at 33. Lincoln asked the question, oft-repeated in later scholarship dealing with this issue: "Was it possible to lose the nation and yet preserve the Constitution?" He answered his own query: "I did understand, however, that my oath to preserve the Constitution to the best of my ability imposed upon me the duty of preserving, by every indispensable means, that government — that nation, of which the Constitution was the organic law." *Id.*

Another President took a similarly elastic view of his authority, this time in the face of economic emergency — the widespread unemployment and dislocation of the Great Depression of the 1930s as well as the necessities of a World War. In his classic work on the Presidency, Clinton Rossiter writes of President Franklin Delano Roosevelt that "[n]ot more than two or three Presidents, it seems safe to say, ever took so broad a view of their powers as did Franklin D. Roosevelt." CLINTON ROSSITER, THE AMERICAN PRESIDENCY (1956). Rossiter averred that, like Lincoln, "[Roosevelt] made himself a 'constitutional dictator' in time of severe national emergency." For example, in 1942, Roosevelt opposed a provision in the Price Control Act of that year. In his message to Congress in opposition to the bill, Roosevelt rendered unmistakable his vision of Presidential authority. "In the event that the Congress should fail to act, and act adequately, I shall assume the responsibility and I will act . . . . The President has the power, under the Constitution and Congressional acts, to take measures necessary to avert a disaster which would interfere with the winning of the war." In Roosevelt's view, "economic chaos" was the looming "disaster" which would merit unilateral executive action. *Id.*

Assuming Roosevelt's position on the Price Control Act to be the correct one in context, his reasoning nonetheless illustrates the inherently dangerous implications of his position. If the President possesses an "emergency" power to transgress constitutional mandates, is it entirely within the discretion of a President to determine when an emergency exists justifying a given action? Lincoln's argument that the preservation of the nation is a necessary prerequisite for the preservation of the Constitution is seductive, but to how many contexts does it extend? Does the "prerogative" of the President, rooted in a conception of the "common law of nature" permit the President to act as a "constitutional dictator"?

a. Source of Domestic Authority

YOUNGSTOWN SHEET & TUBE CO. v. SAWYER
343 U.S. 579 (1952)

MR. JUSTICE BLACK delivered the opinion of the Court.

We are asked to decide whether the President was acting within his constitutional power when he issued an order directing the Secretary of Commerce to take possession of and operate most of the Nation's steel mills. The mill owners argue that the President's order amounts to lawmaking, a legislative function which the Constitution has expressly confided to the Congress and not to the President. The Government's position is that the order was made on findings of the President that his action was necessary to avert a national catastrophe which would inevitably result from a stoppage of steel production, and that in meeting this grave emergency the President was acting within the aggregate of his constitutional powers as the Nation's Chief Executive and the Commander in Chief of the Armed Forces of the United States.

* * *

II.

The President's power, if any, to issue the order must stem either from an act of Congress or from the Constitution itself. There is no statute that expressly authorizes the President to take possession of property as he did here. Nor is there any act of Congress to which our attention has been directed from which such a power can fairly be implied. Indeed, we do not understand the Government to rely on statutory authorization for this seizure. There are two statutes which do authorize the President to take both personal and real property under certain conditions. However, the Government admits that these conditions were not met and that the President's order was not rooted in either of the statutes. The Government refers to the seizure provisions of one of these statutes (§ 201(b) of the Defense Production Act) as "much too cumbersome, involved, and time-consuming for the crisis which was at hand."

Moreover, the use of the seizure technique to solve labor disputes in order to prevent work stoppages was not only unauthorized by any congressional enactment; prior to this controversy, Congress had refused to adopt that method of settling labor disputes. When the Taft-Hartley Act was under consideration in 1947, Congress rejected an amendment which would have authorized such governmental seizures in cases of emergency.

It is clear that if the President had authority to issue the order he did, it must be found in some provisions of the Constitution. And it is not claimed that express constitutional language grants this power to the President. The contention is that presidential power should be implied from the aggregate of his powers under the Constitution. Particular reliance is placed on provisions in

Article II which say that "the executive Power shall be vested in a President . . .";
that "he shall take Care that the Laws be faithfully executed"; and that he
"shall be Commander in Chief of the Army and Navy of the United States."

The order cannot properly be sustained as an exercise of the President's military power as Commander in Chief of the Armed Forces. The Government attempts to do so by citing a number of cases upholding broad powers in military commanders engaged in day-to-day fighting in a theater of war. Such cases need not concern us here. Even though "theater of war" be an expanding concept, we cannot with faithfulness to our constitutional system hold that the Commander in Chief of the Armed Forces has the ultimate power as such to take possession of private property in order to keep labor disputes from stopping production. This is a job for the Nation's lawmakers, not for its military authorities.

Nor can the seizure order be sustained because of the several constitutional provisions that grant executive power to the President. In the framework of our Constitution, the President's power to see that the laws are faithfully executed refutes the idea that he is to be a lawmaker. The Constitution limits his functions in the lawmaking process to the recommending of laws he thinks wise and the vetoing of laws he thinks bad. And the Constitution is neither silent nor equivocal about who shall make laws which the President is to execute. The first section of the first article says that "All legislative Powers herein granted shall be vested in a Congress of the United States . . . ." After granting many powers to the Congress, Article I goes on to provide that Congress may "make all Laws which shall be necessary and proper for carrying into Execution the foregoing Powers and all other Powers vested by this Constitution in the Government of the United States, or in any Department or Officer thereof."

* * *

The Founders of this Nation entrusted the law making power to the Congress alone in both good and bad times. It would do no good to recall the historical events, the fears of power and the hopes for freedom that lay behind their choice. Such a review would but confirm our holding that this seizure order cannot stand.

The judgment of the District Court is affirmed.

Affirmed.

Mr. Justice Jackson, concurring in the judgment and opinion of the court.

. . . The opinions of judges, no less than executives and publicists, often suffer the infirmity of confusing the issue of a power's validity with the cause it is invoked to promote, of confounding the permanent executive office with its temporary occupant. The tendency is strong to emphasize transient results upon policies — such as wages or stabilization — and lose sight of enduring consequences upon the balanced power structure of our Republic.

A judge, like an executive adviser, may be surprised at the poverty of really useful and unambiguous authority applicable to concrete problems of executive power as they actually present themselves. Just what our forefathers did envision, or would have envisioned had they foreseen modern conditions, must be divined from materials almost as enigmatic as the dreams Joseph was called upon to interpret for Pharaoh. A century and a half of partisan debate and scholarly speculation yields no net result but only supplies more or less apt quotations from respected sources on each side of any question. They largely cancel each other.[1] And court decisions are indecisive because of the judicial practice of dealing with the largest questions in the most narrow way.

The actual art of governing under our Constitution does not and cannot conform to judicial definitions of the power of any of its branches based on isolated clauses or even single Articles torn from context. While the Constitution diffuses power the better to secure liberty, it also contemplates that practice will integrate the dispersed powers into a workable government. It enjoins upon its branches separateness but interdependence, autonomy but reciprocity. Presidential powers are not fixed but fluctuate, depending upon their disjunction or conjunction with those of Congress. We may well begin by a somewhat over-simplified grouping of practical situations in which a President may doubt, or others may challenge, his powers, and by distinguishing roughly the legal consequences of this factor of relativity.

1. When the President acts pursuant to an express or implied authorization of Congress, his authority is at its maximum, for it includes all that he possesses in his own right plus all that Congress can delegate.[2] In these circumstances, and in these only, may he be said (for what it may be worth), to personify the federal sovereignty. If his act is held unconstitutional under these circumstances, it usually means that the Federal Government as an undivided whole lacks power. A seizure executed by the President pursuant to an Act of Congress would be supported by the strongest of presumptions and the widest latitude of judicial interpretation, and the burden of persuasion would rest heavily upon any who might attack it.

2. When the President acts in absence of either a congressional grant or denial of authority, he can only rely upon his own independent powers, but there is a zone of twilight in which he and Congress may have concurrent authority, or in which its distribution is uncertain. Therefore, congressional

---

[1] A Hamilton may be matched against a Madison. 7 THE WORKS OF ALEXANDER HAMILTON 76-117; 1 MADISON, LETTERS AND OTHER WRITINGS 611-54. Professor Taft is counterbalanced by Theodore Roosevelt. TAFT, OUR CHIEF MAGISTRATE AND HIS POWERS 139-40; THEODORE ROOSEVELT, AUTOBIOGRAPHY 388-89. It even seems that President Taft cancels out Professor Taft. Compare his "Temporary Petroleum Withdrawal No. 5" of September 27, 1909, *United States v. Midwest Oil Co.*, 236 U.S. 459, 467-68 with his appraisal of executive power in OUR CHIEF MAGISTRATE AND HIS POWER 139-40.

[2] It is in this class of cases that we find the broadest recent statements of presidential power, including those relied on here. *United States v. Curtiss-Wright Export Corp.* involved, not the question of the President's power to act without congressional authority, but the question of his right to act under and in accord with an Act of Congress.

inertia, indifference or quiescence may sometimes, at least as a practical matter, enable, if not invite, measures on independent presidential responsibility. In this area, any actual test of power is likely to depend on the imperatives of events and contemporary imponderables rather than on abstract theories of law.

3. When the President takes measures incompatible with the expressed or implied will of Congress, his power is at its lowest ebb, for then he can rely only upon his own constitutional powers minus any constitutional powers of Congress over the matter. Courts can sustain exclusive Presidential control in such a case only by disabling the Congress from acting upon the subject. Presidential claim to a power at once so conclusive and preclusive must be scrutinized with caution, for what is at stake is the equilibrium established by our constitutional system.

Into which of these classifications does this executive seizure of the steel industry fit? It is eliminated from the first by admission, for it is conceded that no congressional authorization exists for this seizure. . . .

Can it then be defended under flexible tests available to the second category? It seems clearly eliminated from that class because Congress has not left seizure of private property an open field but has covered it by three statutory policies inconsistent with this seizure. In cases where the purpose is to supply needs of the Government itself, two courses are provided: one, seizure of a plant which fails to comply with obligatory orders placed by the Government, another, condemnation of facilities, including temporary use under the power of eminent domain. The third is applicable where it is the general economy of the country that is to be protected rather than exclusive governmental interests. None of these were invoked. In choosing a different and inconsistent way of his own, the President cannot claim that it is necessitated or invited by failure of Congress to legislate upon the occasions, grounds and methods for seizure of industrial properties.

This leaves the current seizure to be justified only by the severe tests under the third grouping, where it can be supported only by any remainder of executive power after subtraction of such powers as Congress may have over the subject. In short, we can sustain the President only by holding that seizure of such strike-bound industries is within his domain and beyond control by Congress. Thus, this Court's first review of such seizures occurs under circumstances which leave Presidential power most vulnerable to attack and in the least favorable of possible constitutional postures.

I did not suppose, and I am not persuaded, that history leaves it open to question, at least in the courts, that the executive branch, like the Federal Government as a whole, possesses only delegated powers. The purpose of the Constitution was not only to grant power, but to keep it from getting out of hand. However, because the President does not enjoy unmentioned powers does not mean that the mentioned ones should be narrowed by a niggardly construction. Some clauses could be made almost unworkable, as well as immutable, by refusal to indulge some latitude of interpretation for changing times. I have heretofore, and do now, give to the enumerated powers the scope and elasticity afforded by what seem to be reasonable practical implications instead of the rigidity dictated by a doctrinaire textualism.

The Solicitor General seeks the power of seizure in three clauses of the Executive Article, the first reading, "The executive Power shall be vested in a President of the United States of America." Lest I be thought to exaggerate, I quote the interpretation which his brief puts upon it: "In our view, this clause constitutes a grant of all the executive powers of which the Government is capable." If that be true, it is difficult to see why the forefathers bothered to add several specific items, including some trifling ones.

The example of such unlimited executive power that must have most impressed the forefathers was the prerogative exercised by George III, and the description of its evils in the Declaration of Independence leads me to doubt that they were creating their new Executive in his image. . . .

The clause on which the Government next relies is that "The President shall be Commander in Chief of the Army and Navy of the United States . . . ." These cryptic words have given rise to some of the most persistent controversies in our constitutional history. Of course, they imply something more than an empty title. But just what authority goes with the name has plagued Presidential advisers who would not waive or narrow it by nonassertion yet cannot say where it begins or ends. It undoubtedly puts the Nation's armed forces under Presidential command. Hence, this loose appellation is sometimes advanced as support for any Presidential action, internal or external, involving use of force, the idea being that it vests power to do anything, anywhere, that can be done with an army or navy.

That seems to be the logic of an argument tendered at our bar — that the President having, on his own responsibility, sent American troops abroad derives from that act "affirmative power" to seize the means of producing a supply of steel for them. To quote, "Perhaps the most forceful illustrations of the scope of Presidential power in this connection is the fact that American troops in Korea, whose safety and effectiveness are so directly involved here, were sent to the field by an exercise of the President's constitutional powers." Thus, it is said he has invested himself with "war powers."

I cannot foresee all that it might entail if the Court should indorse this argument. Nothing in our Constitution is plainer than that declaration of a war is entrusted only to Congress. Of course, a state of war may in fact exist without a formal declaration. But no doctrine that the Court could promulgate would seem to me more sinister and alarming than that a President whose conduct of foreign affairs is so largely uncontrolled, and often even is unknown, can vastly enlarge his mastery over the internal affairs of the country by his own commitment of the Nation's armed forces to some foreign venture. I do not, however, find it necessary or appropriate to consider the legal status of the Korean enterprise to discountenance argument based on it.

* * *

The third clause in which the Solicitor General finds seizure powers is that "he shall take Care that the Laws be faithfully executed." That authority must be matched against words of the Fifth Amendment that "No person shall be . . . deprived of life, liberty, or property, without due process of law . . . ." One gives a governmental authority that reaches so far as there is law, the other gives a private right that authority shall go no farther. These signify about all there is of the principle that ours is a government of laws, not of men, and that we submit ourselves to rulers only if under rules.

The Solicitor General lastly grounds support of the seizure upon nebulous, inherent powers never expressly granted but said to have accrued to the office from the customs and claims of preceding administrations. The plea is for a resulting power to deal with a crisis or an emergency according to the necessities of the case, the unarticulated assumption being that necessity knows no law. Loose and irresponsible use of adjectives colors all non-legal and much legal discussion of presidential powers. "Inherent" powers, "implied" powers, "incidental" powers, "plenary" powers, "war" powers and "emergency" powers are used, often interchangeably and without fixed or ascertainable meanings.

The vagueness and generality of the clauses that set forth presidential powers afford a plausible basis for pressures within and without an administration for presidential action beyond that supported by those whose responsibility it is to defend his actions in court. The claim of inherent and unrestricted presidential powers has long been a persuasive dialectical weapon in political controversy. While it is not surprising that counsel should grasp support from such unadjudicated claims of power, a judge cannot accept self-serving press statements of the attorney for one of the interested parties as authority in answering a constitutional question, even if the advocate was himself. But prudence has counseled that actual reliance on such nebulous claims stop short of provoking a judicial test.

The Solicitor General, acknowledging that Congress has never authorized the seizure here, says practice of prior Presidents has authorized it. He seeks color of legality from claimed executive precedents, chief of which is President Roosevelt's seizure of June 9, 1941, of the California plant of the North American Aviation Company. Its superficial similarities with the present case, upon analysis, yield to distinctions so decisive that it cannot be regarded as even a precedent, much less an authority for the present seizure.[17]

The appeal, however, that we declare the existence of inherent powers *ex necessitate* to meet an emergency asks us to do what many think would be wise,

---

[17] The North American Aviation Company was under direct and binding contracts to supply defense items to the Government. No such contracts are claimed to exist here. Seizure of plants which refused to comply with Government orders had been expressly authorized by Congress in § 9 of the Selective Service Act of 1940, 54 Stat. 885, 892, so that the seizure of the North American plant was entirely consistent with congressional policy. . . .

although it is something the forefathers omitted. They knew what emergencies were, knew the pressures they engender for authoritative action, knew, too, how they afford a ready pretext for usurpation. We may also suspect that they suspected that emergency powers would tend to kindle emergencies. . . .

* * *

This contemporary foreign experience may be inconclusive as to the wisdom of lodging emergency powers somewhere in a modern government. But it suggests that emergency powers are consistent with free government only when their control is lodged elsewhere than in the Executive who exercises them. That is the safeguard that would be nullified by our adoption of the "inherent powers" formula. Nothing in my experience convinces me that such risks are warranted by any real necessity, although such powers would, of course, be an executive convenience.

In the practical working of our Government we already have evolved a technique within the framework of the Constitution by which normal executive powers may be considerably expanded to meet an emergency. Congress may and has granted extraordinary authorities which lie dormant in normal times but may be called into play by the Executive in war or upon proclamation of a national emergency. In 1939, upon congressional request, the Attorney General listed ninety-nine such separate statutory grants by Congress of emergency or war-time executive powers. They were invoked from time to time as need appeared. Under this procedure we retain Government by law — special, temporary law, perhaps, but law nonetheless. The public may know the extent and limitations of the powers that can be asserted, and persons affected may be informed from the statute of their rights and duties.

* * *

But I have no illusion that any decision by this Court can keep power in the hands of Congress if it is not wise and timely in meeting its problems. A crisis that challenges the President equally, or perhaps primarily, challenges Congress. If not good law, there was worldly wisdom in the maxim attributed to Napoleon that "The tools belong to the man who can use them." We may say that power to legislate for emergencies belongs in the hands of Congress, but only Congress itself can prevent power from slipping through its fingers.

* * *

. . . With all its defects, delays and inconveniences, men have discovered no technique for long preserving free government except that the Executive be under the law, and that the law be made by parliamentary deliberations.

Such institutions may be destined to pass away. But it is the duty of the Court to be last, not first, to give them up.[27]

---

[27] We follow the judicial tradition instituted on a memorable Sunday in 1612, when King James took offense at the independence of his judges and, in rage, declared: "Then I am to be under the law 'which it is treason to affirm.'" Chief Justice Coke replied to his King: "Thus wrote Bracton, 'The King

MR. JUSTICE CLARK, concurring in the judgment of the Court.

One of this Court's first pronouncements upon the powers of the President under the Constitution was made by Chief Justice John Marshall some one hundred and fifty years ago. In *Little v. Barreme* (1804), he used this characteristically clear language in discussing the power of the President to instruct the seizure of the "Flying-Fish," a vessel bound from a French port: "It is by no means clear that the President of the United States whose high duty it is to 'take care that the laws be faithfully executed,' and who is commander in chief of the armies and navies of the United States, might not, without any special authority for that purpose, in the then existing state of things, have empowered the officers commanding the armed vessels of the United States, to seize and send into port for adjudication, American vessels which were forfeited by being engaged in this illicit commerce. But when it is observed that (an act of Congress) gives a special authority to seize on the high seas, and limits that authority to the seizure of vessels bound or sailing to a French port, the legislature seems to have prescribed that the manner in which this law shall be carried into execution, was to exclude a seizure of any vessel not bound to a French port." Accordingly, a unanimous Court held that the President's instructions had been issued without authority and that they could not "legalize an act which without those instructions would have been a plain trespass." I know of no subsequent holding of this Court to the contrary.

* * *

I conclude that where Congress has laid down specific procedures to deal with the type of crisis confronting the President, he must follow those procedures in meeting the crisis; but that in the absence of such action by Congress, the President's independent power to act depends upon the gravity of the situation confronting the nation. I cannot sustain the seizure in question because here, as in *Little v. Barreme* (1804), Congress had prescribed methods to be followed by the President in meeting the emergency at hand.

MR. JUSTICE DOUGLAS, concurring.

* * *

The power of the Federal Government to condemn property is well established. *Kohl v. United States* (1875). It can condemn for any public purpose; and I have no doubt but that condemnation of a plant, factory, or industry in order to promote industrial peace would be constitutional. But there is a duty to pay for all property taken by the Government. The command of the Fifth Amendment is that no "private property be taken for public use, without just compensation." That constitutional requirement has an important bearing on the present case.

---

ought not to be under any man, but he is under God and the law.'" 12 Coke 63 (as to its verity, 18 ENG. HIST. REV. 664-75); 1 CAMPBELL, LIVES OF THE CHIEF JUSTICES 272.

The President has no power to raise revenues. That power is in the Congress by Article I, Section 8 of the Constitution. The President might seize and the Congress by subsequent action might ratify the seizure. But until and unless Congress acted, no condemnation would be lawful. The branch of government that has the power to pay compensation for a seizure is the only one able to authorize a seizure or make lawful one that the President had effected. . . .

* * *

The great office of President is not a weak and powerless one. The President represents the people and is their spokesman in domestic and foreign affairs. The office is respected more than any other in the land. It gives a position of leadership that is unique. The power to formulate policies and mold opinion inheres in the Presidency and conditions our national life. The impact of the man and the philosophy he represents may at times be thwarted by the Congress. Stalemates may occur when emergencies mount and the Nation suffers for lack of harmonious, reciprocal action between the White House and Capitol Hill. That is a risk inherent in our system of separation of powers. The tragedy of such stalemates might be avoided by allowing the President the use of some legislative authority. The Framers with memories of the tyrannies produced by a blending of executive and legislative power rejected that political arrangement. Some future generation may, however, deem it so urgent that the President have legislative authority that the Constitution will be amended. We could not sanction the seizures and condemnations of the steel plants in this case without reading Article II as giving the President not only the power to execute the laws but to make some. Such a step would most assuredly alter the pattern of the Constitution.

We pay a price for our system of checks and balances, for the distribution of power among the three branches of government. It is a price that today may seem exorbitant to many. Today a kindly President uses the seizure power to effect a wage increase and to keep the steel furnaces in production. Yet tomorrow another President might use the same power to prevent a wage increase, to curb trade unionists, to regiment labor as oppressively as industry thinks it has been regimented by this seizure.

MR. JUSTICE FRANKFURTER, concurring.

* * *

The issue before us can be met, and therefore should be, without attempting to define the President's powers comprehensively. I shall not attempt to delineate what belongs to him by virtue of his office beyond the power even of Congress to contract; what authority belongs to him until Congress acts; what kind of problems may be dealt with either by the Congress or by the President or by both; what power must be exercised by the Congress and cannot be delegated to the President. It is as unprofitable to lump together in an undiscriminating hotch-potch past presidential actions claimed to be derived from occupancy of the office, as it is to conjure up hypothetical future cases. The judiciary may, as this case proves, have to intervene in determining where authority lies as between the democratic forces in our scheme of government. But in doing so we should be wary and humble. Such is the teaching of this Court's role in the history of the country.

It is in this mood and with this perspective that the issue before the Court must be approached. We must therefore put to one side consideration of what powers the President would have had if there had been no legislation whatever bearing on the authority asserted by the seizure, or if the seizure had been only for a short, explicitly temporary period, to be terminated automatically unless Congressional approval were given. These and other questions, like or unlike, are not now here. I would exceed my authority were I to say anything about them.

The question before the Court comes in this setting. Congress has frequently — at least 16 times since 1916 — specifically provided for executive seizure of production, transportation, communications, or storage facilities. In every case it has qualified this grant of power with limitations and safeguards. . . .

* * *

In adopting the provisions which it did, by the Labor Management Relations Act of 1947, for dealing with a "national emergency" arising out of a breakdown in peaceful industrial relations, Congress was very familiar with Government seizure as a protective measure. On a balance of considerations Congress chose not to lodge this power in the President. . . .

* * *

It cannot be contended that the President would have had power to issue this order had Congress explicitly negated such authority in formal legislation. Congress has expressed its will to withhold this power from the President as though it had said so in so many words. The authoritatively expressed purpose of Congress to disallow such power to the President and to require him, when in his mind the occasion arose for such a seizure, to put the matter to Congress and ask for specific authority from it, could not be more decisive if it had been written into §§ 206-210 of the Labor Management Relations Act of 1947. . . .

* * *

The Defense Production Act affords no ground for the suggestion that the 1947 denial to the President of seizure powers has been impliedly repealed, and its legislative history contradicts such a suggestion. . . .

It is one thing to draw an intention of Congress from general language and to say that Congress would have explicitly written what is inferred, where Congress has not addressed itself to a specific situation. It is quite impossible, however, when Congress did specifically address itself to a problem, as Congress did to that of seizure, to find secreted in the interstices of legislation the very grant of power which Congress consciously withheld. To find authority so explicitly withheld is not merely to disregard in a particular instance the clear will of Congress. It is to disrespect the whole legislative process and the constitutional division of authority between President and Congress.

* * *

MR. CHIEF JUSTICE VINSON, with whom MR. JUSTICE REED and MR. JUSTICE MINTON join, dissenting.

The President of the United States directed the Secretary of Commerce to take temporary possession of the Nation's steel mills during the existing emergency because "a work stoppage would immediately jeopardize and imperil our national defense and the defense of those joined with us in resisting aggression, and would add to the continuing danger of our soldiers, sailors and airmen engaged in combat in the field." The District Court ordered the mills returned to their private owners on the ground that the President's action was beyond his powers under the Constitution.

This Court affirms. Some members of the Court are of the view that the President is without power to act in time of crisis in the absence of express statutory authorization. Other members of the Court affirm on the basis of their reading of certain statutes. Because we cannot agree that affirmance is proper on any ground, and because of the transcending importance of the questions presented not only in this critical litigation but also to the powers the President and of future Presidents to act in time of crisis, we are compelled to register this dissent.

I.

In passing upon the question of Presidential powers in this case, we must first consider the context in which those powers were exercised.

Those who suggest that this is a case involving extraordinary powers should be mindful that these are extraordinary times. A world not yet recovered from the devastation of World War II has been forced to face the threat of another and more terrifying global conflict.

Accepting in full measure its responsibility in the world community, the United States was instrumental in securing adoption of the United Nations Charter, approved by the Senate by a vote of 89 to 2. The first purpose of the United Nations is to "maintain international peace and security, and to that end: to take effective collective measures for the prevention and removal of threats to the peace, and for the suppression of acts of aggression or other breaches of the peace . . . ." In 1950, when the United Nations called upon member nations "to render every assistance" to repel aggression in Korea, the United States furnished its vigorous support. For almost two full years, our armed forces have been fighting in Korea, suffering casualties of over 108,000 men. Hostilities have not abated. The "determination of the United Nations to continue its action in Korea to meet the aggression" has been reaffirmed. Congressional support of the action in Korea has been manifested by provisions for increased military manpower and equipment and for economic stabilization, as hereinafter described.

Further efforts to protect the free world from aggression are found in the congressional enactments of the Truman Plan for assistance to Greece and Turkey and the Marshall Plan for economic aid needed to build up the strength of our friends in Western Europe. In 1949, the Senate approved the North Atlantic Treaty under which each member nation agrees that an armed attack against one is an armed attack against all. Congress immediately implemented the North Atlantic Treaty by authorizing military assistance to nations dedicated to the principles of mutual security under the United Nations Charter. The concept of mutual security recently has been extended by treaty to friends in the Pacific.

* * *

In the Mutual Security Act of 1951, Congress authorized "military, economic, and technical assistance to friendly countries to strengthen the mutual security and individual and collective defenses of the free world . . . ."

* * *

Congress recognized the impact of these defense programs upon the economy. Following the attack in Korea, the President asked for authority to requisition property and to allocate and fix priorities for scarce goods. In the Defense Production Act of 1950, Congress granted the powers requested and, in addition, granted power to stabilize prices and wages and to provide for settlement of labor disputes arising in the defense program. The Defense Production Act was extended in 1951, a Senate Committee noting that in the dislocation caused by the programs for purchase of military equipment "lies the seed of an economic disaster that might well destroy the military might we are straining to build." Significantly, the Committee examined the problem "in terms of just one commodity, steel," and found "a graphic picture of the over-all inflationary danger growing out of reduced civilian supplies and rising incomes." Even before Korea, steel production at levels above theoretical 100% capacity was not capable of supplying civilian needs alone. Since Korea, the tremendous military demand for steel has far exceeded the increases in productive capacity. This Committee emphasized that the shortage of steel, even with the mills operating at full capacity, coupled with increased civilian purchasing power, presented grave danger of disastrous inflation.

The President has the duty to execute the foregoing legislative programs. Their successful execution depends upon continued production of steel and stabilized prices for steel. Accordingly, when the collective bargaining agreements between the Nation's steel producers and their employees, represented by the United Steel Workers, were due to expire on December 31, 1951, and a strike shutting down the entire basic steel industry was threatened, the President acted to avert a complete shutdown of steel production. On December 22, 1951, he certified the dispute to the Wage Stabilization Board, requesting that the

Board investigate the dispute and promptly report its recommendation as to fair and equitable terms of settlement. The Union complied with the President's request and delayed its threatened strike while the dispute was before the Board. After a special Board panel had conducted hearings and submitted a report, the full Wage Stabilization Board submitted its report and recommendations to the President on March 20, 1952.

The Board's report was acceptable to the Union but was rejected by plaintiffs. The Union gave notice of its intention to strike as of 12:01 a.m., April 9, 1952, but bargaining between the parties continued with hope of settlement until the evening of April 8, 1952. After bargaining had failed to avert the threatened shutdown of steel production, the President issued [his] Executive Order.

* * *

The next morning, April 9, 1952, the President addressed the following Message to Congress:

"To the Congress of the United States:

"The Congress is undoubtedly aware of the recent events which have taken place in connection with the management-labor dispute in the steel industry. These events culminated in the action which was taken last night to provide for temporary operation of the steel mills by the Government.

"I took this action with the utmost reluctance. The idea of Government operation of the steel mills is thoroughly distasteful to me and I want to see it ended as soon as possible. However, in the situation which confronted me yesterday, I felt that I could make no other choice. The other alternatives appeared to be even worse — so much worse that I could not accept them.

"One alternative would have been to permit a shut-down in the steel industry. The effects of such a shut-down would have been so immediate and damaging with respect to our efforts to support our Armed Forces and to protect our national security that it made this alternative unthinkable.

"The only way that I know of, other than Government operation, by which a steel shut-down could have been avoided was to grant the demands of the steel industry for a large price increase. I believed and the officials in charge of our stabilization agencies believed that this would have wrecked our stabilization program. I was unwilling to accept the incalculable damage which might be done to our country by following such a course.

"Accordingly, it was my judgment that Government operation of the steel mills for a temporary period was the least undesirable of the courses of action which lay open. In the circumstances, I believed it to be, and now believe it to be, my duty and within my powers as President to follow that course of action.

"It may be that the Congress will deem some other course to be wiser. It may be that the Congress will feel we should give in to the demands of the steel industry for an exorbitant price increase and take the consequences so far as resulting inflation is concerned.

"It may be that the Congress will feel the Government should try to force the steel workers to continue to work for the steel companies for another long period, without a contract, even though the steel workers have already voluntarily remained at work without a contract for 100 days in an effort to reach an orderly settlement of their differences with management.

"It may even be that the Congress will feel that we should permit a shutdown of the steel industry, although that would immediately endanger the safety of our fighting forces abroad and weaken the whole structure of our national security.

"I do not believe the Congress will favor any of these courses of action, but that is a matter for the Congress to determine.

"It may be, on the other hand, that the Congress will wish to pass legislation establishing specific terms and conditions with reference to the operation of the steel mills by the Government. Sound legislation of this character might be very desirable.

"On the basis of the facts that are known to me at this time, I do not believe that immediate congressional action is essential; but I would, of course, be glad to cooperate in developing any legislative proposals which the Congress may wish to consider.

"If the Congress does not deem it necessary to act at this time, I shall continue to do all that is within my power to keep the steel industry operating and at the same time make every effort to bring about a settlement of the dispute so the mills can be returned to their private owners as soon as possible."

Twelve days passed without action by Congress. On April 21, 1952, the President sent a letter to the President of the Senate in which he again described the purpose and need for his action and again stated his position that "The Congress can, if it wishes, reject the course of action I have followed in this matter." Congress has not so acted to this date.

Meanwhile, plaintiffs instituted this action in the District Court to compel defendant to return possession of the steel mills seized under Executive Order 10340. In this litigation for return of plaintiffs' properties, we assume that defendant Charles Sawyer is not immune from judicial restraint and that plaintiffs are entitled to equitable relief if we find that the Executive Order under which defendant acts is unconstitutional. We also assume without deciding that the courts may go behind a President's finding of fact that an emergency exists. But there is not the slightest basis for suggesting that the President's finding in this case can be undermined. Plaintiffs moved for a preliminary injunction before answer or hearing. Defendant opposed the motion, filing uncontroverted affidavits of Government officials describing the facts underlying the President's order.

Secretary of Defense Lovett swore that "a work stoppage in the steel industry will result immediately in serious curtailment of production of essential weapons and munitions of all kinds." He illustrated by showing that 84% of the national production of certain alloy steel is currently used for production of military-end items and that 35% of total production of another form of steel goes into ammunition, 80% of such ammunition now going to Korea. The Secretary of Defense stated that: "We are holding the line [in Korea] with ammunition and not with the lives of our troops."

* * *

One is not here called upon even to consider the possibility of executive seizure of a farm, a corner grocery store or even a single industrial plant. Such considerations arise only when one ignores the central fact of this case — that the Nation's entire basic steel production would have shut down completely if there had been no Government seizure. Even ignoring for the moment whatever confidential information the President may possess as "the Nation's organ for foreign affairs," the uncontroverted affidavits in this record amply support the finding that "a work stoppage would immediately jeopardize and imperil our national defense."

* * *

III.

A review of executive action demonstrates that our Presidents have on many occasions exhibited the leadership contemplated by the Framers when they made the President Commander in Chief, and imposed upon him the trust to "take Care that the Laws be faithfully executed." With or without explicit statutory authorization, Presidents have at such times dealt with national emergencies by acting promptly and resolutely to enforce legislative programs, at least to save those programs until Congress could act. Congress and the courts have responded to such executive initiative with consistent approval.

Our first President displayed at once the leadership contemplated by the Framers. When the national revenue laws were openly flouted in some sections of Pennsylvania, President Washington, without waiting for a call from the state government, summoned the militia and took decisive steps to secure the faithful execution of the laws. When international disputes engendered by the French revolution threatened to involve this country in war, and while congressional policy remained uncertain, Washington issued his Proclamation of

Neutrality. Hamilton, whose defense of the Proclamation has endured the test of time, invoked the argument that the Executive has the duty to do that which will preserve peace until Congress acts and, in addition, pointed to the need for keeping the Nation informed of the requirements of existing laws and treaties as part of the faithful execution of the laws.[31]

* * *

Jefferson's initiative in the Louisiana Purchase, the Monroe Doctrine, and Jackson's removal of Government deposits from the Bank of the United States further serve to demonstrate by deed what the Framers described by word when they vested the whole of the executive power in the President.

Without declaration of war, President Lincoln took energetic action with the outbreak of the War Between the States. He summoned troops and paid them out of the Treasury without appropriation therefor. He proclaimed a naval blockade of the Confederacy and seized ships violating that blockade. Congress, far from denying the validity of these acts, gave them express approval. The most striking action of President Lincoln was the Emancipation Proclamation, issued in aid of the successful prosecution of the War Between the States, but wholly without statutory authority.

In an action furnishing a most apt precedent for this case, President Lincoln without statutory authority directed the seizure of rail and telegraph lines leading to Washington. Many months later, Congress recognized and confirmed the power of the President to seize railroads and telegraph lines and provided criminal penalties for interference with Government operation.

This Act did not confer on the President any additional powers of seizure. Congress plainly rejected the view that the President's acts had been without legal sanction until ratified by the legislature. Sponsors of the bill declared that its purpose was only to confirm the power which the President already possessed. Opponents insisted a statute authorizing seizure was unnecessary and might even be construed as limiting existing Presidential powers.

* * *

Some six months before Pearl Harbor, a dispute at a single aviation plant at Inglewood, California, interrupted a segment of the production of military aircraft. In spite of the comparative insignificance of this work stoppage to total defense production as contrasted with the complete paralysis now threatened by a shutdown of the entire basic steel industry, and even though our armed forces were not then engaged in combat, President Roosevelt ordered the seizure of the plant "pursuant to the powers vested in [him] by the Constitution and laws of the United States, as President of the United States of America and Commander in Chief of the Army and Navy of the United States."[59] The Attorney General [Jackson] . . . stated:

---

[31] 4 THE WORKS OF ALEXANDER HAMILTON 432–44 (Henry Cabot Lodge ed., 1904).

[59] Executive order 8773, 6 Fed. Reg. 2777 (1941).

"The Presidential proclamation rests upon the aggregate of the Presidential powers derived from the Constitution itself and from statutes enacted by the Congress.

"The Constitution lays upon the President the duty 'to take care that the laws be faithfully executed.' Among the laws which he is required to find means to execute are those which direct him to equip an enlarged army, to provide for a strengthened navy, to protect Government property, to protect those who are engaged in carrying out the business of the Government, and to carry out the provisions of the Lend-Lease Act (22 U.S.C.A. § 411 et seq.). For the faithful execution of such laws the President has back of him not only each general law-enforcement power conferred by the various acts of Congress but the aggregate of all such laws plus that wide discretion as to method vested in him by the Constitution for the purpose of executing the laws.

"The Constitution also places on the President the responsibility and vests in him the powers of Commander in Chief of the Army and of the Navy. These weapons for the protection of the continued existence of the Nation are placed in his sole command and the implication is clear that he should not allow them to become paralyzed by failure to obtain supplies for which Congress has appropriated the money and which it has directed the President to obtain."

* * *

This is but a cursory summary of executive leadership. But it amply demonstrates that Presidents have taken prompt action to enforce the laws and protect the country whether or not Congress happened to provide in advance for the particular method of execution. At the minimum, the executive actions reviewed herein sustain the action of the President in this case. And many of the cited examples of Presidential practice go far beyond the extent of power necessary to sustain the President's order to seize the steel mills. The fact that temporary executive seizures of industrial plants to meet an emergency have not been directly tested in this Court furnishes not the slightest suggestion that such actions have been illegal. Rather, the fact that Congress and the courts have consistently recognized and given their support to such executive action indicates that such a power of seizure has been accepted throughout our history.

History bears out the genius of the Founding Fathers, who created a Government subject to law but not left subject to inertia when vigor and initiative are required.

IV.

* * *

Whatever the extent of Presidential power on more tranquil occasions, and whatever the right of the President to execute legislative programs as he sees fit without reporting the mode of execution to Congress, the single Presidential purpose disclosed on this record is to faithfully execute the laws by acting in an emergency to maintain the status quo, thereby preventing collapse of the legislative programs until Congress could act. The President's action served the same purposes as a judicial stay entered to maintain the status quo in order to preserve the jurisdiction of a court. In his Message to Congress immediately following the seizure, the President explained the necessity of his action in executing the military procurement and anti-inflation legislative programs and expressed his desire to cooperate with any legislative proposals approving, regulating or rejecting the seizure of the steel mills. Consequently, there is no evidence whatever of any Presidential purpose to defy Congress or act in any way inconsistent with the legislative will.

* * *

Accordingly, as of December 22, 1951, the President had a choice between alternate procedures for settling the threatened strike in the steel mills: one route created to deal with peacetime disputes; the other route specially created to deal with disputes growing out of the defense and stabilization program. There is no question of by-passing a statutory procedure because both of the routes available to the President in December were based upon statutory authorization. Both routes were available in the steel dispute. The Union, by refusing to abide by the defense and stabilization program, could have forced the President to invoke Taft-Hartley at that time to delay the strike a maximum of 80 days. Instead, the Union agreed to cooperate with the defense program and submit the dispute to the Wage Stabilization Board.

Plaintiffs had no objection whatever at that time to the President's choice of the WSB route. As a result, the strike was postponed, a WSB panel held hearings and reported the position of the parties and the WSB recommended the terms of a settlement which it found were fair and equitable. Moreover, the WSB performed a function which the board of inquiry contemplated by Taft-Hartley could not have accomplished when it checked the recommended wage settlement against its own wage stabilization regulations issued pursuant to its stabilization functions under Title IV of the Defense Production Act. Thereafter, the parties bargained on the basis of the WSB recommendation.

When the President acted on April 8, he had exhausted the procedures for settlement available to him. Taft-Hartley was a route parallel to, not connected with, the WSB procedure. The strike had been delayed 99 days as contrasted with the maximum delay of 80 days under Taft-Hartley. There had been a hearing on the issues in dispute and bargaining which promised settlement up to the very hour before seizure had broken down. Faced with immediate national peril through stoppage in steel production on the one hand and faced with destruction of the wage and price legislative programs on the other, the President took temporary possession of the steel mills as the only course open to him consistent with his duty to take care that the laws be faithfully executed.

Plaintiffs' property was taken and placed in the possession of the Secretary of Commerce to prevent any interruption in steel production. It made no difference whether the stoppage was caused by a union-management dispute over terms and conditions of employment, a union-Government dispute over wage stabilization or a management-Government dispute over price stabilization. The President's action has thus far been effective, not in settling the dispute, but in saving the various legislative programs at stake from destruction until Congress could act in the matter.

VI.

The diversity of views expressed in the six opinions of the majority, the lack of reference to authoritative precedent, the repeated reliance upon prior dissenting opinions, the complete disregard of the uncontroverted facts showing the gravity of the emergency and the temporary nature of the taking all serve to demonstrate how far afield one must go to affirm the order of the District Court.

The broad executive power granted by Article II to an officer on duty 365 days a year cannot, it be said, be invoked to avert disaster. Instead, the President must confine himself to sending a message to Congress recommending action. Under this messenger-boy concept of the Office, the President cannot even act to preserve legislative programs from destruction so that Congress will have something left to act upon. There is no judicial finding that the executive action was unwarranted because there was in fact no basis for the President's finding of the existence of an emergency for, under this view, the gravity of the emergency and the immediacy of the threatened disaster are considered irrelevant as a matter of law.

NOTES AND QUESTIONS

1. President Truman viewed his seizure of the steel mills as necessitated by emergency, not unlike that faced by his predecessor in meeting the needs of World War II. Here are the President's actual words in his Executive Order:

APPENDIX.

Executive Order

Directing the Secretary of Commerce to Take Possession of and Operate the Plants and Facilities of Certain Steel Companies

Whereas on December 16, 1950, I proclaimed the existence of a national emergency which requires that the military, naval, air, and civilian defenses of this country be strengthened as speedily as possible to the end that we may be able to repel any and all threats against our national security and to fulfill our responsibilities in the efforts being made throughout the United Nations and otherwise to bring about a lasting peace; and

Whereas American fighting men and fighting men of other nations of the United Nations are now engaged in deadly combat with the forces of aggression in Korea, and forces of the United States are stationed elsewhere overseas for the purpose of participating in the defense of the Atlantic Community against aggression; and

Whereas the weapons and other materials needed by our armed forces and by those joined with us in the defense of the free world are produced to a great extent in this country, and steel is an indispensable component of substantially all of such weapons and materials; and

* * *

Whereas a controversy has arisen between certain companies in the United States producing and fabricating steel and the elements thereof and certain of their workers represented by the United Steelworkers of America, CIO, regarding terms and conditions of employment; and

Whereas the controversy has not been settled through the processes of collective bargaining or through the efforts of the Government, including those of the Wage Stabilization Board, to which the controversy was referred on December 22, 1951, pursuant to Executive Order No. 10233, and a strike has been called for 12:01 A.M., April 9, 1952; and

Whereas a work stoppage would immediately jeopardize and imperil our national defense and the defense of those joined with us in resisting aggression, and would add to the continuing danger of our soldiers, sailors, and airmen engaged in combat in the field; and

Whereas in order to assure the continued availability of steel and steel products during the existing emergency, it is necessary that the United States take possession of and operate the plants, facilities, and other property of the said companies as hereinafter provided:

Now, therefore, by virtue of the authority vested in me by the Constitution and laws of the United States, and as President of the United States and Commander in Chief of the armed forces of the United States, it is hereby ordered as follows:

1. The Secretary of Commerce is hereby authorized and directed to take possession of all or such of the plants, facilities, and other property of the companies named in the list attached hereto [List of specific Steel Companies and Plants omitted], or any part thereof, as he may deem necessary in the interests of national defense; and to operate or to arrange for the operation thereof and to do all things necessary for, or incidental to, such operation.

* * *

4. Except so far as the Secretary of Commerce shall otherwise provide from time to time, the managements of the plants, facilities, and other

properties possession of which is taken pursuant to this order shall continue their functions, including the collection and disbursement of funds in the usual and ordinary course of business in the names of their respective companies and by means of any instrumentalities used by such companies.

5. Except so far as the Secretary of Commerce may otherwise direct, existing rights and obligations of such companies shall remain in full force and effect, and there may be made, in due course, payments of dividends on stock, and of principal, interest, sinking funds, and all other distributions upon bonds, debentures, and other obligations, and expenditures may be made for other ordinary corporate or business purposes.

6. Whenever in the judgment of the Secretary of Commerce further possession and operation by him of any plant, facility, or other property is no longer necessary or expedient in the interest of national defense, and the Secretary has reason to believe that effective future operation is assured, he shall return the possession and operation of such plant, facility, or other property to the company in possession and control thereof at the time possession was taken under this order.

* * *

Harry S. Truman. The White House, April 8, 1952.

2. Despite the President's assessment of the military emergency, as earlier noted, the times had changed, and the American involvement in Korea was more debatable. Beyond this, however, the President's counsel in the lower court made an overly broad claim of inherent executive authority. The following discussion occurred in the district court between Assistant Attorney General Baldridge, representing the President, and the court:

MR. BALDRIDGE: Section 1, Article II, of the Constitution reposes all of the executive power in the Chief Executive. I think that the distinction that the Constitution itself makes between the powers of the Executive and the powers of the legislative branch of the Government are significant and important. In so far as the Executive is concerned, all executive power is vested in the President. In so far as legislative powers are concerned, the Congress has only those powers that are specifically delegated to it, plus the implied power to carry out the powers specifically enumerated.

THE COURT [JUDGE PINE]: So, when the sovereign people adopted the Constitution, it . . . limited the powers of the Congress and limited the powers of the judiciary, but it did not limit the powers of the Executive. Is that what you say?

MR. BALDRIDGE: That is the way we read Article II of the Constitution.

THE COURT: I see. . . .

ALLAN F. WESTIN, THE ANATOMY OF A CONSTITUTIONAL LAW CASE 64 (1958).

3. Is the President then limited solely to whatever authority he can derive from statute and those few constitutional places where the President's authority is plenary such as the recognition of foreign governments by virtue of his unfettered ability in Article II, Section 3 to "receive Ambassadors and other public ministers"? With various shadings of emphasis, this does seem to be the view of Justice Black and the individual concurrences. Justice Jackson's concurring opinion is realistic enough to recognize, however, that emergencies do arise, but he believes these must be met, however, by emergency powers derived from congressional enactments. Jackson writes: "emergency powers are consistent with free government only when their control is lodged elsewhere than in the Executive who exercises them." Jackson recognizes, however, that while the "power to legislate for emergencies belongs in the hands of Congress," that power will — practically — slip through its fingers unless it is sufficiently alert to meet any new national emergency with adequate legislation.

Was Congress sufficiently responsive to the President? It was President Truman's view, of course, that Congress had defaulted in its responsibility. Chief Justice Vinson shared this view in dissent; indeed, some historical evidence indicates that Vinson was advising President Truman behind the scenes — a matter of some judicial impropriety. ROBERT J. DONOVAN, TUMULTUOUS YEARS, THE PRESIDENCY OF HARRY S. TRUMAN 1949-53, at 386-87 (1982). Vinson apparently saw the President as having authority to act without specific statutory authorization, premised in part upon the broadly stated grants of Executive authority in Article II, and the President's duty to carry out the legislative program as a whole. In the Chief Justice's view, the President had a duty to execute both military and economic (price stabilization) interests that had been, in fact, fashioned or accepted by the Congress.

4. Justice Jackson's concurring opinion containing the three classes of legislative-executive interaction is often cited, but it largely leaves issues to be resolved in context on their facts. Jackson posits that both the President and Congress have exclusive authority in some areas and concurrent authority in others. In the concurrent areas, what Jackson calls a "twilight zone," conflicts are to be resolved by legislative direction. Again, the categories are a good starting place for analysis; however, they leave undecided both the precise definition of the respective areas of authority — for example, what exactly can the President do as "commander in chief" and when does an issue in litigation fall within that or some other Executive power, or vice versa. Jackson, himself, before appointment to the Court, served as Franklin Roosevelt's Attorney General, and in that capacity justified the seizure of the North American Aviation Plant on grounds that the seizure maintained the war effort. Note that Jackson argues in his concurrence that the earlier seizure had only a "superficial similarity" to Truman's action in *Youngstown*.

5. Few cases have recognized any inherent authority in the Executive in domestic matters. The cases that do accept presidential action without legislative authority seem more in the nature of "protective" actions that preserve the status quo in a more limited way than the seizure in *Youngstown*. Professor Henry Monaghan writes of a narrow power "to protect and defend the personnel, property and instrumentalities of the United States from harm." Henry P. Monaghan, *The Protective Power of the Presidency*, 93 COLUM. L. REV. 1, 10-11 (1993). Cases exemplifying this inherent protective authority include *In re Neagle*, 135 U.S. 1 (1890), where the President assigned a guard to protect a Supreme Court Justice without statutory authority, and *United States v. Midwest Oil Co.*, 236 U.S. 459 (1915), where the President placed a moratorium on the private purchase of oil lands that would have jeopardized government interests.

Since the President is therefore largely preoccupied domestically with the implementation of legislative enactments, and these enactments have become voluminous, it is only logical that Presidents would want the unfettered ability to appoint and remove subordinate officials who would complete these tasks consistently with the President's judgment. The extent to which the President can supervise the modern administrative state is taken up next.

b. The Practical Exercise of Executive Authority — The President and the Bureaucracy

(1) Power of Appointment

THE FEDERALIST NO. 77 (Alexander Hamilton) (Clinton Rossiter ed., 1961)

* * *

[In the plan for the proposed government], the power of nomination is unequivocally vested in the Executive. And as there would be a necessity for submitting each nomination to the judgment of an entire branch of the legislature, the circumstances attending an appointment, from the mode of conducting it, would naturally become matters of notoriety; and the public would be at no loss to determine what part had been performed by the different actors. The blame of a bad nomination would fall upon the President singly and absolutely. The censure of rejecting a good one would lie entirely at the door of the Senate; aggravated by the consideration of their having counteracted the good intentions of the Executive. If an ill appointment should be made, the Executive for nominating, and the Senate for approving, would participate, though in different degrees, in the opprobrium and disgrace.

* * *

I could not with propriety conclude my observations on the subject of appointments without taking notice of a scheme for which there have appeared some, though but few advocates; I mean that of uniting the House of Representatives in the power of making them. I shall, however, do little more than mention it, as I cannot imagine that it is likely to gain the countenance of any considerable part of the community. A body so fluctuating and at the same time so numerous, can never be deemed proper for the exercise of that power. Its unfitness will appear manifest to all, when it is recollected that in half a century it may consist of three or four hundred persons. All the advantages of the stability, both of the Executive and of the Senate, would be defeated by this union, and infinite delays and embarrassments would be occasioned. The example of most of the States in their local constitutions encourages us to reprobate the idea.

NOTES AND QUESTIONS

1. From time to time it is argued that the Senate should have some role in the choosing of Executive or judicial nominees by the President. *Compare* David A. Strauss & Cass R. Sunstein, *The Senate, the Constitution, and the Confirmation Process*, 101 YALE L.J. 1491 (1992) (advocating that a more independent role for the Senate in the selection of Supreme Court Justices would produce Justices of greater distinction and more reflective of a diversity of views), *with* John O. McGinnis, *The President, the Senate, the Constitution, and the Confirmation Process: A Reply to Professors Strauss and Sunstein*, 71 TEX. L. REV. 633 (1993) (stating that the President could not properly accept suggestions from Senators to nominate a jurist with constitutional views substantially different than his own). That the Senate is to have no role in the choosing, however, was made plain by Alexander Hamilton:

> In the act of nomination, [the President's] judgment alone would be exercised; and as it would be his sole duty to point out the man who, with the approbation of the Senate, should fill an office, his responsibility would be as complete as if he were to make the final appointment.

THE FEDERALIST NO. 76. (Alexander Hamilton). Hamilton expected that placing the sole responsibility for choosing Executive and judicial officers on the President would "naturally beget a livelier sense of duty and more exact regard to reputation." *Id*. The role of the Senate is to concur, or not. Hamilton makes explicit:

> It will be the office of the President to *nominate*, and, with the advice and consent of the Senate, to *appoint*. There will, of course, be no exertion of *choice* on the part of the Senate. They may defeat one choice of the Executive, and oblige him to make another; but they cannot themselves *choose* — they can only ratify or reject the choice he may have made.

THE FEDERALIST NO. 66 (Alexander Hamilton) (emphasis in the original).

2. The appointment power in the Constitution is found in Article II, Section 2, Clause 2:

> [The President] shall nominate, and by and with the Advice and Consent of the Senate, shall appoint Ambassadors, other public Ministers and Consuls, Judges of the supreme Court, and all other Officers of the United States, whose Appointments are not herein otherwise provided for, and which shall be established by Law: but the Congress may by Law vest the Appointment of such inferior Officers, as they think proper, in the President alone, in the Courts of Law, or in the Heads of Departments.

Note that this provision creates two levels of executive officers — principal and inferior, with different modes of appointment for each. Below, in *Morrison v. Olson*, 487 U.S. 654 (1988), arguments will be made that so-called "independent counsels," who by statute investigate possible wrongdoing by high-level executive officials, must necessarily be principal officers. See if you can determine why the Court rejects this argument.

3. As the Appointments Clause above provides, the appointment of principal officers is subject to confirmation by the advice and consent of the Senate. This role in the appointment of executive officers was not initially provided in the constitutional convention of 1787, which had provided for appointment by the President alone. The Senate's advice and consent function on appointments came about because of the great compromise that settled an unrelated question — the relative political power of populous and non-populous (that is, large and small) states. The jealousies of these interests was calmed by providing for a bicameral legislature, where in the Senate all states would be equally represented regardless of population, and the House where population would determine each state's representation.

Following this compromise, it was also determined that Presidents would be selected by achieving a majority of the electoral college, consisting of a number of individuals chosen by each state equal to the number of that state's Senators and Representatives. This again gave populous states an advantage and to counter that, the Senate, where all states were on equal footing, was given its confirmation role. Today, it is often assumed that the Senate's role was designed solely to check the Executive; indeed, it arose out of a desire to see that *all* state interests — a federalism concern — were equally considered in the appointment of principal federal office holders.

4. Not every person working for the federal government is an "officer." Some are designated as employees, that is "lesser functionaries subordinate to officers of the United States." *Buckley v. Valeo*, 424 U.S. 1, 126 n.162 (1976). In *Buckley*, the Court determined that Federal Election Commissioners exercising significant governmental duties under public law, such as rulemaking and the filing of civil enforcement suits, had to be appointed in accordance with Article II, Section 2, Clause 2. Since some members of the Commission were appointed by members of Congress, the composition of the Commission was held to violate the Constitution. The Court observed that were the Commission's functions solely related to investigation or information gathering, there would have been no constitutional difficulty since information gathering is a congressional function.

5. In recent years, most appointment controversies have concerned the appointment of judges or Justices, not executive officers. The Senate has long operated on the rule of thumb that Presidents deserve greater latitude in the choice of executive officials, who must carry out the President's policies, than in the selection of a constitutionally independent judiciary.

The Senate denied President George W. Bush a number of his nominees, either by defeating them in committee or in an unprecedented use of the filibuster, preventing nominees pending on the Senate floor from being brought to a vote. Effectively, this meant that 60 votes (the number needed to close debate), rather than a simple majority, was now needed for judicial confirmation.

The most notorious judicial confirmation battle in modern time occurred with respect to the nomination of Judge Robert H. Bork by President Ronald Reagan. A well-known conservative and former law professor, Bork was subjected to a nationwide campaign of political opposition, orchestrated by the American Civil Liberties Union and a similar advocacy group known as People for the American Way. Bork's nomination was defeated, but it left many with the uncomfortable feeling that politics had intruded too greatly and correspondingly too shallowly in campaign-like style into the judicial selection process. Nevertheless, for all the ink spilled on the Bork nomination, fundamental questions about the process, *see Symposium, Confirmation Controversy: The Selection of a Supreme Court Justice*, 84 Nw. U. L. REV. 832 (1990), and even more profound questions of substance regarding judicial philosophy were left unresolved, *see* Douglas W. Kmiec, *The Selection of Supreme Court Justices — The Unsettled Relationship between Law and Morality*, 39 CATH. U. L. REV. 1 (1989). *See generally* STEPHEN L. CARTER, THE CONFIRMATION MESS (1994), and for a good summary of the literature on the topic, Michael J. Slinger, et. al., *The Senate Power of Advice and Consent on Judicial Appointments: An Annotated Research Bibliography*, 64 NOTRE DAME L. REV. 106 (1989); HENRY J. ABRAHAM, JUSTICES AND PRESIDENTS: A POLITICAL HISTORY OF APPOINTMENTS TO THE SUPREME COURT (3d ed. 1992) (giving an excellent historical perspective of this topic).

6. The federal bureaucracy: The number of positions requiring presidential appointment and Senate confirmation is relatively small — about 500, with only several thousand additional "middle-management" political appointments. The bulk of the federal work force is quite permanent, governed by the Civil Service Reform Act of 1978, Pub. L. No. 95-454, 92 Stat. 1111 (codified at various points throughout the U.S. Code). The 2.5 to 3 million workers below those presidentially appointed are administratively governed by their immediate agency supervisors and overall by the Office of Personnel Management. About 1.7 million federal positions are obtained by competitive examination; the balance — such as attorneys (roughly 100,000 of them) — are in the so-called "excepted service" for which it is deemed not practicable to give separate examination.

7. The Court has never fully addressed the question of presidential supervision of subordinate officers of the Executive branch once they are properly appointed, preferring instead to come at the question from the side through the issue of presidential removal. The theory: he who fires may also direct. The next case operates on that assumption, and it contains an historically comprehensive defense of unfettered presidential supervision by the only President to later serve on the Supreme Court, William Howard Taft.

MYERS v. UNITED STATES
272 U.S. 52 (1926)

Mr. Chief Justice Taft delivered the opinion of the Court.

This case presents the question whether under the Constitution the President has the exclusive power of removing executive officers of the United States whom he has appointed by and with the advice and consent of the Senate.

Myers, appellant's intestate, was on July 21, 1917, appointed by the President, by and with the advice and consent of the Senate, to be a postmaster of the first class at Portland, Or., for a term of four years. On January 20, 1920, Myers' resignation was demanded. He refused the demand. On February 2, 1920, he was removed from office by order of the Postmaster General, acting by direction of the President. . . . On April 21, 1921, he brought this suit in the Court of Claims for his salary from the date of his removal, which, as claimed by supplemental petition filed after July 21, 1921, the end of his term, amounted to $8,838.71. In August, 1920, the President made a recess appointment of one Jones, who took office September 19, 1920.

The Court of Claims gave judgment against Myers and this is an appeal from that judgment. . . .

By the sixth section of the Act of Congress of July 12, 1876, 19 Stat. 80, 81, under which Myers was appointed with the advice and consent of the Senate as a first-class postmaster, it is provided that:

> "Postmasters of the first, second, and third classes shall be appointed and may be removed by the President by and with the advice and consent of the Senate, and shall hold their offices for four years unless sooner removed or suspended according to law."

The Senate did not consent to the President's removal of Myers during his term. If this statute in its requirement that his term should be four years unless sooner removed by the President by and with the consent of the Senate is valid, the appellant, Myers' administratrix, is entitled to recover his unpaid salary for his full term and the judgment of the Court of Claims must be reversed. The government maintains that the requirement is invalid, for the reason that under article 2 of the Constitution, the President's power of removal of executive officers appointed by him with the advice and consent of the Senate is full and complete without consent of the Senate. If this view is sound, the removal of Myers by the President without the Senate's consent was legal, and the judgment of the Court of Claims against the appellant was correct, and must be affirmed, though for a different reason from that given by that court. We are therefore confronted by the constitutional question and cannot avoid it.

The relevant parts of article 2 of the Constitution are as follows:

"Section 1. The executive Power shall be vested in a President of the United States of America.

* * *

"Section 2. The President . . . shall nominate, and by and with the Advice and Consent of the Senate, shall appoint Ambassadors, other public Ministers and Consuls, Judges of the Supreme Court, and all other Officers of the United States, whose Appointments are not herein otherwise provided for, and which shall be established by Law; but the Congress may by Law vest the Appointment of such inferior Officers, as they think proper, in the President alone, in the Courts of Law, or in the Heads of Departments.

"The President shall have Power to fill up all Vacancies that may happen during the Recess of the Senate, by granting Commissions which shall expire at the End of their next Session."

* * *

The question where the power of removal of executive officers appointed by the President by and with the advice and consent of the Senate was vested, was presented early in the first session of the First Congress. There is no express provision respecting removals in the Constitution, except as section 4 of article 2, above quoted, provides for removal from office by impeachment.

* * *

In the House of Representatives of the First Congress, on Tuesday, May 18, 1789, Mr. Madison moved in the committee of the whole that there should be established three executive departments, one of Foreign Affairs, another of the Treasury, and a third of War, at the head of each of which there should be a Secretary, to be appointed by the President by and with the advice and consent of the Senate, and to be removable by the President.

* * *

The bill was discussed in the House at length and with great ability. The report of it in the Annals of Congress is extended. James Madison was then a leader in the House, as he had been in the convention. His arguments in support of the President's constitutional power of removal independently of congressional provision, and without the consent of the Senate, were masterly, and he carried the House.

It is convenient in the course of our discussion of this case to review the reasons advanced by Mr. Madison and his associates for their conclusion, supplementing them, so far as may be, by additional considerations which lead this court to concur therein.

First. Mr. Madison insisted that article 2 by vesting the executive power in the President was intended to grant to him the power of appointment and removal of executive officers except as thereafter expressly provided in that article. He pointed out that one of the chief purposes of the convention was to separate the legislative from the executive functions. He said:

> "If there is a principle in our Constitution, indeed in any free Constitution more sacred than another, it is that which separates the legislative, executive and judicial powers. If there is any point in which the separation of the legislative and executive powers ought to be maintained with great caution, it is that which relates to officers and offices." 1 ANNALS OF CONG. 581.

Their union under the Confederation had not worked well, as the members of the convention knew. Montesquieu's view that the maintenance of independence, as between the legislative, the executive and the judicial branches, was a security for the people had their full approval. MADISON IN THE CONVENTION, *in* 2 RECORDS OF THE FEDERAL CONVENTION OF 1787, at 56 (Max Farrand ed., rev. ed. 1966); *Kendall v. United States* (1838). Accordingly the Constitution was so framed as to vest in the Congress all legislative powers therein granted, to vest in the President the executive power, and to vest in one Supreme Court and such inferior courts as Congress might establish the judicial power. From this division on principle, the reasonable construction of the Constitution must be that the branches should be kept separate in all cases in which they were not expressly blended, and the Constitution should be expounded to blend them no more than it affirmatively requires. Madison, 1 ANNALS OF CONG 497.

The debates in the Constitutional Convention indicated an intention to create a strong executive, and after a controversial discussion the executive power of the government was vested in one person and many of his important functions were specified so as to avoid the humiliating weakness of the Congress during the Revolution and under the Articles of Confederation. 1 RECORDS OF THE FEDERAL CONVENTION OF 1787, *supra*, at 66-97.

* * *

The vesting of the executive power in the President was essentially a grant of the power to execute the laws. But the President alone and unaided could not execute the laws. He must execute them by the assistance of subordinates. This view has since been repeatedly affirmed by this court. As he is charged specifically to take care that they be faithfully executed, the reasonable implication, even in the absence of express words, was that as part of his executive power he should select those who were to act for him under his direction in the execution of the laws. The further implication must be, in the absence of any express limitation respecting removals, that as his selection of administrative officers is essential to the execution of the laws by him, so must be his power of removing those for whom he cannot continue to be responsible. . . .

* * *

The requirement of the second section of article 2 that the Senate should advise and consent to the presidential appointments, was to be strictly construed. The words of section 2, following the general grant of executive power under section 1, were either an enumeration and emphasis of specific functions of the executive, not all inclusive, or were limitations upon the general grant of the executive power, and as such, being limitations, should not be enlarged beyond the words used. 1 ANNALS OF CONG. 462-64. The executive power was given in general terms strengthened by specific terms where emphasis was regarded as appropriate, and was limited by direct expressions where limitation was needed, and the fact that no express limit was placed on the power of removal by the executive was convincing indication that none was intended. This is the same construction of article 2 as that of Alexander Hamilton quoted *infra*.

The view of Mr. Madison and his associates was that not only did the grant of executive power to the President in the first section of article 2 carry with it the power of removal, but the express recognition of the power of appointment in the second section enforced this view on the well-approved principle of constitutional and statutory construction that the power of removal of executive officers was incident to the power of appointment.

* * *

Under section 2 of article 2, however, the power of appointment by the executive is restricted in its exercise by the provision that the Senate, a part of the legislative branch of the government, may check the action of the executive by rejecting the officers he selects. Does this make the Senate part of the removing power? . . .

The history of the clause by which the Senate was given a check upon the President's power of appointment makes it clear that it was not prompted by any desire to limit removals. As already pointed out, the important purpose of those who brought about the restriction was to lodge in the Senate, where the small states had equal representation with the larger states, power to prevent the President from making too many appointments from the larger states. . . . The formidable opposition to the Senate's veto on the President's power of appointment indicated that in construing its effect, it should not be extended beyond its express application to the matter of appointments. . . .

* * *

The power to prevent the removal of an officer who has served under the President is different from the authority to consent to or reject his appointment. When a nomination is made, it may be presumed that the Senate is, or may become, as well advised as to the fitness of the nominee as the President, but in the nature of things the defects in ability or intelligence or loyalty in the administration of the laws of one who has served as an officer under the President are facts as to which the President, or his trusted subordinates, must be better informed than the Senate, and the power to remove him may therefore be regarded as confined for very sound and practical reasons, to the governmental authority which has administrative control. The power of removal is incident to the power of appointment, not to the power of advising and consenting to appointment, and when the grant of the executive power is enforced by the express mandate to take care that the laws be faithfully executed, it emphasizes the necessity for including within the executive power as conferred the exclusive power of removal.

* * *

Third. Another argument urged against the constitutional power of the President alone to remove executive officers appointed by him with the consent of the Senate is that, in the absence of an express power of removal granted to the President, power to make provision for removal of all such officers is vested in the Congress by section 8 of article 1.

Mr. Madison, mistakenly thinking that an argument like this was advanced by Roger Sherman, took it up and answered it as follows:

> "He seems to think (if I understand him rightly) that the power of displacing from office is subject to legislative discretion, because, it having a right to create, it may limit or modify as it thinks proper. I shall not say but at first view this doctrine may seem to have some plausibility. But when I consider that the Constitution clearly intended to maintain a marked distinction between the legislative, executive and judicial powers of government, and when I consider that, if the Legislature has a power such as is contended for, they may subject and transfer at discretion powers from one department of our government to another, they may, on that principle, exclude the President altogether from exercising any authority in the removal of officers, they may give to the Senate alone, or the President and Senate combined, they may vest it in the whole Congress, or they may reserve it to be exercised by this house. When I consider the consequences of this doctrine, and compare them with the true principles of the Constitution, I own that I cannot subscribe to it. . . ." 1 ANNALS OF CONG. 495-96.

* * *

It is argued that the denial of the legislative power to regulate removals in some way involves the denial of power to prescribe qualifications for office, or reasonable classification for promotion, and yet that has been often exercised.

We see no conflict between the latter power and that of appointment and removal, provided of course that the qualifications do not so limit selection and so trench upon executive choice as to be in effect legislative designation. As Mr. Madison said in the First Congress:

> "The powers relative to offices are partly legislative and partly executive. The Legislature creates the office, defines the powers, limits its duration, and annexes a compensation. This done, the legislative power ceases. They ought to have nothing to do with designating the man to fill the office. That I conceive to be of an executive nature. . . ."

* * *

As Mr. Madison said in the debate in the First Congress:

> "Vest this power in the Senate jointly with the President, and you abolish at once that great principle of unity and responsibility in the executive department, which was intended for the security of liberty and the public good. If the President should possess alone the power of removal from office, those who are employed in the execution of the law will be in their proper situation, and the chain of dependence be preserved; the lowest officers, the middle grade, and the highest will depend, as they ought, on the President, and the President on the community." 1 ANNALS OF CONG. 499.

* * *

Made responsible under the Constitution for the effective enforcement of the law, the President needs as an indispensable aid to meet it the disciplinary influence upon those who act under him of a reserve power of removal. But it is contended that executive officers appointed by the Senate are bound by the statutory law, and are not his servants to do his will, and that his obligation to care for the faithful execution of the laws does not authorize him to treat them as such. The degree of guidance in the discharge of their duties that the President may exercise over executive officers varies with the character of their service as prescribed in the law under which they act. The highest paid and most important duties which his subordinates perform are those in which they act for him. In such cases they are exercising not their own but his discretion. This field is a very large one. It is sometimes described as political. Each head of a department is and must be the President's alter ego in the matters of that department where the president is required by law to exercise authority.

* * *

. . . The ordinary duties of officers prescribed by statute come under the general administrative control of the President by virtue of the general grant to him of the executive power, and he may properly supervise and guide their construction of the statutes under which they act in order to secure that unitary and uniform execution of the laws which article 2 of the Constitution evidently contemplated in vesting general executive power in the President alone. Laws are often passed with specific provision for adoption of regulations by a department or bureau head to make the law workable and effective. The ability and judgment manifested by the official thus empowered, as well as his energy and stimulation of his subordinates, are subjects which the President must consider and supervise in his administrative control. Finding such officers to be negligent and inefficient, the President should have the power to remove them. Of course there may be duties so peculiarly and specifically committed to the discretion of a particular officer as to raise a question whether the President may overrule or revise the officer's interpretation of his statutory duty in a particular instance. Then there may be duties of a quasi judicial character imposed on executive officers and members of executive tribunals whose decisions after hearing affect interests of individuals, the discharge of which the President cannot in a particular case properly influence or control. But even in such a case he may consider the decision after its rendition as a reason for removing the officer, on the ground that the discretion regularly entrusted to that officer by statute has not been on the whole intelligently or wisely exercised. Otherwise he does not discharge his own constitutional duty of seeing that the laws be faithfully executed.

* * *

It is further pressed on us that, even though the legislative decision of 1789 included inferior officers, yet under the legislative power given Congress with respect to such officers it might directly legislate as to the method of their removal without changing their method of appointment by the President with the consent of the Senate. We do not think the language of the Constitution justifies such a contention.

* * *

In *United States v. Perkins*, 116 U. S. 483, a cadet engineer, a graduate of the Naval Academy, brought suit to recover his salary for the period after his removal by the Secretary of the Navy. It was decided that his right was established by Revised Statutes, § 1229 (Comp. St. § 2001), providing that no officer in the military or naval service should in time of peace be dismissed from service, except in pursuance of a sentence of court-martial. The section was claimed to be an infringement upon the constitutional prerogative of the executive. The Court of Claims refused to yield to this argument and said:

> "Whether or not Congress can restrict the power of removal incident to the power of appointment of those officers who are appointed by the President by and with the advice and consent of the Senate under the authority of the Constitution (article 2, section 2), does not arise in this case and need not be considered. We have no doubt that, when Congress by law vests the appointment of inferior officers in the heads of departments it may limit and restrict the power of removal as it deems best for the public interest. The constitutional authority in Congress to thus vest the appointment implies authority to limit, restrict, and regulate

the removal by such laws as Congress may enact in relation to the officers so appointed. The head of a department has no constitutional prerogative of appointment to offices independently of the legislation of Congress, and by such legislation he must be governed, not only in making appointments, but in all that is incident thereto."

This language of the Court of Claims was approved by this court and the judgment was affirmed.

The power to remove inferior executive officers, like that to remove superior executive officers, is an incident of the power to appoint them, and is in its nature an executive power. The authority of Congress given by the excepting clause to vest the appointment of such inferior officers in the heads of departments carries with it authority incidentally to invest the heads of departments with power to remove. It has been the practice of Congress to do so and this court has recognized that power. The court also has recognized in the *Perkins* Case that Congress, in committing the appointment of such inferior officers to the heads of departments, may prescribe incidental regulations controlling and restricting the latter in the exercise of the power of removal. But the court never has held, nor reasonably could hold, although it is argued to the contrary on behalf of the appellant, that the excepting clause enables Congress to draw to itself, or to either branch of it, the power to remove or the right to participate in the exercise of that power. To do this would be to go beyond the words and implications of that clause, and to infringe the constitutional principle of the separation of governmental powers.

Assuming, then, the power of Congress to regulate removals as incidental to the exercise of its constitutional power to vest appointments of inferior officers in the heads of departments, certainly so long as Congress does not exercise that power, the power of removal must remain where the Constitution places it, with the President, as part of the executive power, in accordance with the legislative decision of 1789 which we have been considering.

Whether the action of Congress in removing the necessity for the advice and consent of the Senate and putting the power of appointment in the President alone would make his power of removal in such case any more subject to Congressional legislation than before is a question this court did not decide in the *Perkins* Case. Under the reasoning upon which the legislative decision of 1789 was put, it might be difficult to avoid a negative answer, but it is not before us and we do not decide it.

* * *

We come now to a period in the history of the government when both houses of Congress attempted to reverse this constitutional construction, and to subject the power of removing executive officers appointed by the President and confirmed by the Senate to the control of the Senate, indeed finally to the assumed power in Congress to place the removal of such officers anywhere in the government.

This reversal grew out of the serious political difference between the two houses of Congress and President Johnson. There was a two-thirds majority of the Republican party, in control of each house of Congress, which resented what it feared would be Mr. Johnson's obstructive course in the enforcement of the reconstruction measures in respect to the states whose people had lately been at war against the national government. This led the two houses to enact legislation to curtail the then acknowledged powers of the President. . . .

The chief legislation in support of the reconstruction policy of Congress was the Tenure of Office Act of March 2, 1867, providing that all officers appointed by and with the consent of the Senate should hold their offices until their successors should have in like manner been appointed and qualified; that certain heads of departments, including the Secretary of War, should hold their offices during the term of the President by whom appointed and one month thereafter, subject to removal by consent of the Senate. The Tenure of Office Act was vetoed, but it was passed over the veto. The House of Representatives preferred articles of impeachment against President Johnson for refusal to comply with, and for conspiracy to defeat, the legislation above referred to, but he was acquitted for lack of a two-thirds vote for conviction in the Senate.

* * *

"Mr. Blaine, who was in Congress at the time, in afterwards speaking of this bill, said: 'It was an extreme proposition — a new departure from the long-established usage of the federal government — and for that reason, if for no other, personally degrading to the incumbent of the presidential chair. It could only have grown out of abnormal excitement created by dissensions between the two great departments of the government. . . . The measure was resorted to as one of self-defense against the alleged aggressions and unrestrained power of the Executive Department.'" 2 TWENTY YEARS OF CONGRESS 273-74.

The extreme provisions of all this legislation were a full justification for the considerations, so strongly advanced by Mr. Madison and his associates in the First Congress, for insisting that the power of removal of executive officers by the President alone was essential in the division of powers between the executive and the legislative bodies. It exhibited in a clear degree the paralysis to which a partisan Senate and Congress could subject to executive arm, and destroy the principle of executive responsibility, and separation of the powers sought for by the framers of our government, if the President had no power of removal save by consent of the Senate. It was an attempt to redistribute the powers and minimize those of the President.

After President Johnson's term ended, the injury and invalidity of the Tenure of Office Act in its radical innovation were immediately recognized by the executive and objected to. General Grant, succeeding Mr. Johnson in the presidency, earnestly recommended in his first message the total repeal of the act, saying:

"It may be well to mention here the embarrassment possible to arise from leaving on the statute books the so-called 'Tenure of Office Acts,' and to earnestly recommend their total repeal. It could not have been the intention of the framers of the Constitution, when providing that appointments made by the President should receive the consent of the Senate, that the latter should have the power to retain in office persons placed there by federal appointment against the will of the President. The law is inconsistent with a faithful and efficient administration of the government. What faith can an executive put in officials forced upon him, and those, too, whom he has suspended for reason? How will such officials be likely to serve an administration which they know does not trust them?" 9 MESSAGES AND PAPERS OF THE PRESIDENTS 3992.

While in response to this a bill for repeal of that act passed the House, it failed in the Senate, and, though the law was changed, it still limited the presidential power of removal. The feeling growing out of the controversy with President Johnson retained the act on the statute book until 1887, when it was repealed. . . .

In the same interval, in March, 1886, President Cleveland, in discussing the requests which the Senate had made for his reasons for removing officials, and the assumption that the Senate had the right to pass upon those removals and thus to limit the power of the President, said:

"I believe the power to remove or suspend such officials is vested in the President alone by the Constitution, which in express terms provides that 'the executive power shall be vested in a President of the United States of America,' and that 'he shall take care that the laws be faithfully executed.'

"The Senate belongs to the legislative branch of the government. When the Constitution by express provision superadded to its legislative duties the right to advise and consent to appointments to office and to sit as a court of impeachment, it conferred upon that body all the control and regulation of executive action supposed to be necessary for the safety of the people; and this express and special grant of such extraordinary powers, not in any way related to or growing out of general senatorial duties, and in itself a departure from the general plan of our government, should be held, under a familiar maxim of construction, to exclude every other right of interference with executive functions." 11 MESSAGES AND PAPERS OF THE PRESIDENTS 4964.

The attitude of the Presidents on this subject has been unchanged and uniform to the present day whenever an issue has clearly been raised. . . . President Wilson said:

"It has, I think, always been the accepted construction of the Constitution that the power to appoint officers of this kind carries with it, as an incident, the power to remove. I am convinced that the Congress is without constitutional power to limit the appointing power and its incident, the power of removal, derived from the Constitution." 59 CONG. REC. 8609 (1920).

* * *

Other acts of Congress are referred to which contain provisions said to be inconsistent with the 1789 decision. Since the provision for an Interstate Commerce Commission in 1887, many administrative boards have been created whose members are appointed by the President, by and with the advice and consent of the Senate, and in the statutes creating them have been provisions for the removal of the members for specified causes. Such provisions are claimed to be inconsistent with the independent power of removal by the President. This, however, is shown to be unfounded by the case of *Shurtleff v. United States* (1903). That concerned an act creating a board of general appraisers, and provided for their removal for inefficiency, neglect of duty, or malfeasance in office. The President removed an appraiser without notice or hearing. It was forcibly contended that the affirmative language of the statute implied the negative of the power to remove except for cause and after a hearing. This would have been the usual rule of construction, but the court declined to apply it. Assuming for the purpose of that case only, but without deciding, that Congress might limit the President's power to remove, the court held that, in the absence of constitutional or statutory provision otherwise, the President could by virtue of his general power of appointment remove an officer, though appointed by and with the advice and consent of the Senate, and notwithstanding specific provisions for his removal for cause, on the ground that the power of removal inhered in the power to appoint. This is an indication that many of the statutes cited are to be reconciled to the unrestricted power of the President to remove, if he chooses to exercise his power.

* * *

For the reasons given, we must therefore hold that the provision of the law of 1876 by which the unrestricted power of removal of first-class postmasters is denied to the President is in violation of the Constitution and invalid. This leads to an affirmance of the judgment of the Court of Claims. . . .

Judgment affirmed.

The separate opinion of MR. JUSTICE MCREYNOLDS. [Dissenting.]

* * *

II.

* * *

The long struggle for civil service reform and the legislation designed to insure some security of official tenure ought not to be forgotten. Again and again Congress has enacted statutes prescribing restrictions on removals, and by approving them many Presidents have affirmed its power therein.

The following are some of the officers who have been or may be appointed with consent of the Senate under such restricting statutes:

Members of the Interstate Commerce Commission, Board of General Appraisers, Federal Reserve Board, Federal Trade Commission, Tariff Commission, Shipping Board, Federal Farm Loan Board, Railroad Labor Board; officers of the Army and Navy; Comptroller General; Postmaster General and his assistants; Postmasters of the first, second, and third classes; judge of the United States Court for China; judges of the Court of Claims, established in 1855, the judges to serve "during good behavior"; judges of territorial (statutory) courts; judges of the Supreme Court and Court of Appeals for the District of Columbia (statutory courts), appointed to serve "during good behavior." Also members of the Board of Tax Appeals provided for by the Act of February 26, 1926, to serve for 12 years, who "shall be appointed by the President, by and with the advice and consent of the Senate, solely on the grounds of fitness to perform the duties of the office. Members of the board may be removed by the President, after notice and opportunity for public hearing, for inefficiency, neglect of duty, or malfeasance in office, but for no other cause."

* * *

V.

For the United States it is asserted: Except certain judges, the President may remove all officers whether executive or judicial appointed by him with the Senate's consent, and therein he cannot be limited or restricted by Congress. The argument runs thus: The Constitution gives the President all executive power of the national government, except as this is checked or controlled by some other definite provision; power to remove is executive and unconfined; accordingly, the President may remove at will. Further, the President is required to take care that the laws be faithfully executed; he cannot do this unless he may remove at will all officers whom he appoints; therefore he has such authority.

The argument assumes far too much. Generally, the actual ouster of an officer is executive action; but to prescribe the conditions under which this may be done is legislative. . . .

Judgment should go for the appellant.

MR. JUSTICE BRANDEIS, dissenting [omitted].

* * *

MR. JUSTICE HOLMES, dissenting.

* * *

The arguments drawn from the executive power of the President, and from his duty to appoint officers of the United States (when Congress does not vest the appointment elsewhere), to take care that the laws be faithfully executed, and to commission all officers of the United States, seem to me spiders' webs inadequate to control the dominant facts.

We have to deal with an office that owes its existence to Congress and that Congress may abolish tomorrow. Its duration and the pay attached to it while it lasts depend on Congress alone. Congress alone confers on the President the power to appoint to it and at any time may transfer the power to other hands. With such power over its own creation, I have no more trouble in believing that Congress has power to prescribe a term of life for it free from any interference than I have in accepting the undoubted power of Congress to decree its end. I have equally little trouble in accepting its power to prolong the tenure of an incumbent until Congress or the Senate shall have assented to his removal. The duty of the President to see that the laws be executed is a duty that does not go beyond the laws or require him to achieve more than Congress sees fit to leave within his power.

NOTES AND QUESTIONS

1. Chief Justice Taft, for the Court, views the Decision of 1789 as historically settling the question that the power to remove executive officers appointed by the President with the advice and consent of the Senate is vested in the President alone. Taft points out elsewhere in his opinion that when the issue arose in the House, 8 of the House members present had been members of the 1787 constitutional convention, and of these 8, 6 voted to affirm the President's sole, unfettered removal authority. Some modern commentators have tried to weaken the historical significance of the Decision of 1789, pointing out that shortly thereafter, the same Congress created a Treasury Department with a statutory limit on the removal of the Comptroller. *See* Lawrence Lessig & Cass R. Sunstein, *The President and the Administration*, 94 COLUM. L. REV. 1, 22-32 (1994).

2. May Congress determine the qualifications for executive office? As the opinion in *Myers* reveals, the answer is yes, so long as Congress does not manipulate the qualifications in such a way as to effectively deprive the President of the power of appointment or removal. Congressman Madison affirms Taft's reasoning, writing:

> that if the Legislature determines the powers, the honors, and emoluments of an office, we should be insecure if they were to designate the officer also. The nature of things restrains and confines the legislative and executive authorities in this respect; and hence it is that the Constitution stipulates for the independence of each branch of the government.

1 ANNALS OF CONG. 581-82 (Joseph Gales ed., 1789).

3. As the *Myers* case reveals, one President, Andrew Johnson, was impeached, though not convicted, because he resisted congressional encroachment upon the constitutional power of the Executive to remove presidentially-appointed officers. For a discussion of this unique time in American history, see WILLIAM H. REHNQUIST, GRAND INQUESTS: THE HISTORIC IMPEACHMENTS OF JUSTICE SAMUEL CHASE AND PRESIDENT ANDREW JOHNSON (1992). The impeachment proceedings arose in the politically charged times of Reconstruction. President Johnson, with no previous notice to Congress, removed Edwin Stanton, a Republican holdover from President Lincoln's cabinet, as the Secretary of War. Stanton, who had acted as the eyes and ears of congressional radicals following the death of President Lincoln, refused to leave his office, pursuant to the Tenure of Office Act of 1867 (described as unconstitutional in *Myers*) which denied the President unilateral removal authority. The Senate voted 35-19 for impeachment, one vote short of the two-thirds vote needed to convict and remove the President. *See generally* MILTON LOMASK, ANDREW JOHNSON: PRESIDENT ON TRIAL (1973); MICHAEL L. BENEDICT, THE IMEACHMENT AND TRIAL OF ANDREW JOHNSON (1973). According to Chief Justice Salmon P. Chase, President Johnson avoided impeachment because the President has no duty to execute a statute that "directly attacks and impairs the executive power confided to him by [the Constitution]." R. WARDEN, AN ACCOUNT OF THE PRIVATE LIFE AND PUBLIC SERVICES OF SALMON PORTLAND CHASE 685 (1874).

4. William Jefferson Clinton became the first elected President, and only the second President ever to be impeached (Richard Nixon resigned before facing almost certain impeachment). As in the case of Andrew Johnson, there was no eventual conviction. However, the question was less clear-cut than in the Johnson case, since President Clinton's alleged offenses mixed both private and public misbehavior. Four articles of impeachment were drafted by the House Judiciary Committee, and the full House referred two to the Senate for trial. All of the Articles related to the President's efforts to avoid personal liability in a civil rights cause of action brought against him by Mrs. Paula Jones involving an allegation of sexual harassment while the President was Governor of Arkansas. The civil rights case was initially resolved in favor of the President on a motion for summary judgment in federal district court, 16 F. Supp. 2d 1054 (E.D. Ark. 1998). This ruling in favor of the President was appealed to the Eighth Circuit, but before a decision on appeal was rendered, the case was settled by the President's eventual payment to Mrs. Jones of $800,000. The impeachment inquiry related to whether the President was truthful in his civil deposition in the *Jones* case and then in a subsequent independent counsel investigation under the direction of former Judge Kenneth Starr.

Virtually all of the evidence for the drafted articles came from a referral to the House Judiciary Committee by Independent Counsel Starr. There was considerable debate whether the actions of the President rose to the level necessary to be an impeachable offense within the meaning of Article II, Section 4 that calls for a President's removal upon conviction of "Treason, Bribery or other high Crimes and Misdemeanors." One of your co-authors, Professor Presser, testified before the House Judiciary Committee on the subject:

One very clear indication of what was intended with regard to impeachment is provided in Federalist 64, one of the few numbers written by John Jay, who was to become the first Chief Justice of the United States. . . . Jay makes plain that when a President fails to live up to the requirement of trust, honor, and virtue that is necessary to meet his treaty-making and other executive responsibilities — if, in short, he is not an honorable or virtuous person who will perform his duties in the interest of the people — impeachment is available to remove him. . . .

Professor Presser went on to explain how the Impeachment Clause was at one point limited to treason and bribery, but Virginia delegate George Mason thought that insufficient.

Mason then moved to add after the word "bribery" the words "or maladministration." James Madison, one of the authors of The Federalist, and the man most commonly described at the "Father" of the Constitution, objected on the grounds that "maladministration" was too elusive. "So vague a term," he said, "will be equivalent to a tenure during pleasure of the Senate." To meet Madison's objection, and to make clearer that more than Senatorial whim was required for removal, Mason "withdrew 'maladministration' and substitute[d] 'other high crimes & misdemeanors,'" which was then accepted and became the Constitutional text we now seek to interpret.

The colloquy between Mason and Madison is the only evidence we have from the debates at the 1787 Constitutional convention at Philadelphia, but it appears to suggest that more than mere maladministration, something approaching "great and dangerous offences," or an "[a]ttempt to subvert the Constitution" is required. . . .

On December 19, 1998, President Clinton was impeached by the Full House under two of the four proposed Articles. By a vote of 228 206, the House referred Article I dealing with perjury before the grand jury and by a second vote of 221-212 also referred Article III dealing with obstruction of justice to the Senate for trial.

From early January 1999 to February 12, 1999, the Senate sat as a body listening to designated House members or "managers" presenting the case for conviction and a substantial battery of presidential lawyers arguing the defense of the President. No live witnesses appeared before the Senate, in part, no doubt, because of the embarrassing personal nature of the facts. However, Ms. Lewinsky, Vernon Jordan (a well-connected political ally of the President, who assisted Ms. Lewinsky to get a lucrative job offer at the Revlon Corporation in New York), and Sidney Blumenthal (a presidential assistant) did appear on videotape. The House Managers were reportedly chagrined that their presentation had been so restricted by the Senate, and this was the first time in the history of impeachment were there was no presentation of live witness testimony.

As the Senate trial neared its conclusion, it became apparent that many Senators of both political parties thought the President had engaged in serious wrongdoing, but less than the requisite two-thirds thought that wrongdoing merited the President's removal from office. Great public attention then focused on whether the President could be censured rather than convicted under the two impeachment Articles. Many Senators opposed such a censure as extra-constitutional or perhaps a clearly unconstitutional legislatively imposed criminal penalty or bill of attainder of the type expressly prohibited in Article I, Section 9. A few members of the Senate proposed that the President might be convicted of wrongdoing without being removed. Some interesting historical materials momentarily boosted this possibility. In a *Wall Street Journal* essay, Professor Kmiec noted that: "Article I, section 3 of the Constitution provides that 'Judgment in Cases of Impeachment shall not extend further than to removal . . .,' and thus, by its express terms, appears to allow for a lesser penalty than booting a popular, but flawed, chief executive." Douglas W. Kmiec, *Convict, but Don't Remove, Clinton*, WALL ST. J., p. A14 (January 29, 1999). Professor Kmiec noted that this legal possibility had been somewhat obscured by Article II, Section 4 mandating that "the President . . . be removed . . . on Impeachment for and conviction of Treason, Bribery, or other High Crimes and Misdemeanors." Perhaps the explanation was that the framers contemplated impeachment (but not necessarily removal) in the absence of a "high crime."

Professor Kmiec thus suggested separate votes on conviction and remedy, exactly as was done in the early 1803 impeachment of Judge John Pickering and every impeachment proceeding (mostly of judges) before 1936. By votes of 19-7 and 20-6, for example, Pickering was convicted and then separately sentenced. Pickering's crime — drunkenness — was no high crime, but the Senate chose to remove him anyway. By its terms, the "no further than" language in Article I, Section 3 allows for the imposition of the maximum penalty, though Professor Kmiec speculated it was far more likely in President Clinton's case that if two-thirds of the Senate convicted President Clinton, it would nevertheless allow him to finish his term. While such a result resembled censure, it was unlike it insofar as the formal conviction could not have been later legislatively expunged as was a censure of President Andrew Jackson by a subsequent Congress. In addition, a lesser penalty imposed by the Senate sitting as impeachment tribunal following a two-thirds conviction vote would not be an improper legislatively imposed punishment by simple majority vote, but an intended result of the Senate's "sole" constitutional function to try impeachments.

The Senate choose not to ask Chief Justice Rehnquist, who by constitutional design was presiding over the trial, whether a vote to convict would necessarily lead to removal. Whether for this reason, or in the belief that the impeachment itself was sufficient punishment without conviction, or in the view that the President's private misbehavior did not render him publicly unfit, the Senate, on an evenly divided vote, declined to convict President Clinton on Article II, the obstruction of justice charge, and by a vote of 45-55 also failed to convict on Article I, the perjury count.

President Clinton escaped the punishment of the Senate, but not the court. In April 1999, Judge Susan Webber Wright held the President in contempt and directed that the President reimburse both her court and Mrs. Jones for any additional damages suffered as a result of the President's lies under oath. Judge Wright's order reads in part as follows:

> . . . On two separate occasions, this Court ruled in clear and reasonably specific terms that plaintiff was entitled to information regarding any individuals with whom the President had sexual relations or proposed or sought to have sexual relations and who were during the relevant time frame state or federal employees. . . . Notwithstanding these orders, the record demonstrates by clear and convincing evidence that the President responded by giving false, misleading and evasive answers that were designed to obstruct the judicial process. . . .

> It is difficult to construe the President's sworn statements in this civil lawsuit concerning his relationship with Ms. Lewinsky as anything other than a willful refusal to obey this Court's discovery orders. . . . Simply put, the President's deposition testimony regarding whether he has ever engaged in sexual relations with Ms. Lewinsky was intentionally false and his statements regarding whether he had ever engaged in sexual relations with Ms. Lewinsky likewise were intentionally false, notwithstanding tortured definitions and interpretations of the term "sexual relations."

> . . . [T]he President's contumacious conduct in this case, coming as it did from a member of the bar and the chief law enforcement officer of this Nation, was without justification and undermined the integrity of the judicial system. . . .

> Sanctions must be imposed, not only to redress the misconduct of the President in this case, but to deter others who, having observed the President's televised address to the nation in which his defiance of this court's discovery orders was revealed, might themselves consider emulating the President of the United States by willfully violating discovery orders of this and other courts. . . .

Judge Wright subsequently referred the matter to the Arkansas Bar for disciplinary action. President Clinton signed a disciplinary order on January 19, 2001 (his last full day in office), pursuant to which he surrendered his license to practice law for five years. In November of the same year, the former President resigned from the bar of the Supreme Court rather than face a disbarment proceeding there.

5. The next case qualifies *Myers*. *Humphrey's Executor* was decided during a period when Franklin Roosevelt and the Supreme Court were greatly at odds over the scope of federal power to address the Great Depression of the 1930s. It holds that some presidentially appointed officers may not be removed except for cause. In comparison to the comprehensive analysis of *Myers*, the case is conclusory and anomalous. Justice Scalia has written: "the same mistrust of New Deal executive freewheeling aroused by the truly sweeping [New Deal] proposals . . . colored the companion case [*Humphrey's*] as well." Antonin Scalia, *Historical Anomalies in Administrative Law*, 1985 SUP. CT. HIST. SOC'Y Y.B. 103, 110-11.

(2) Power of Removal

HUMPHREY'S EXECUTOR v. UNITED STATES
295 U.S. 602 (1935)

MR. JUSTICE SUTHERLAND delivered the opinion of the Court.

* * *

William E. Humphrey, the decedent, on December 10, 1931, was nominated by President Hoover to succeed himself as a member of the Federal Trade Commission, and was confirmed by the United States Senate. He was duly commissioned for a term of seven years, expiring September 25, 1938; and, after taking the required oath of office, entered upon his duties. On July 25, 1933, President Roosevelt addressed a letter to the commissioner asking for his resignation, on the ground "that the aims and purposes of the Administration with respect to the work of the Commission can be carried out most effectively with personnel of my own selection," but disclaiming any reflection upon the commissioner personally or upon his services. The commissioner replied, asking time to consult his friends. After some further correspondence upon the subject, the President on August 31, 1933, wrote the commissioner expressing the hope that the resignation would be forthcoming, and saying:

> "You will, I know, realize that I do not feel that your mind and my mind go along together on either the policies or the administering of the Federal Trade Commission, and, frankly, I think it is best for the people of this country that I should have a full confidence."

The commissioner declined to resign; and on October 7, 1933, the President wrote him:

> "Effective as of this date you are hereby removed from the office of Commissioner of the Federal Trade Commission."

Humphrey never acquiesced in this action, but continued thereafter to insist that he was still a member of the commission, entitled to perform its duties and receive the compensation provided by law at the rate of $10,000 per annum. Upon these and other facts set forth in the certificate, which we deem it unnecessary to recite, the following questions are certified:

> "1. Do the provisions of section 1 of the Federal Trade Commission Act, stating that 'any commissioner may be removed by the President for inefficiency, neglect of duty, or malfeasance in office', restrict or limit the

power of the President to remove a commissioner except upon one or more of the causes named?

"If the foregoing question is answered in the affirmative, then —

"2. If the power of the President to remove a commissioner is restricted or limited as shown by the foregoing interrogatory and the answer made thereto, is such a restriction or limitation valid under the Constitution of the United States?"

* * *

. . . The negative contention of the government [in response to the first question] is based principally upon the decision of this court in *Shurtleff v. United States*, 189 U.S. 311. That case involved the power of the President to remove a general appraiser of merchandise appointed under the Act of June 10, 1890, 26 Stat. 131. Section 12 of the act provided for the appointment by the President, by and with the advice and consent of the Senate, of nine general appraisers of merchandise, who "may be removed from office at any time by the President for inefficiency, neglect of duty, or malfeasance in office." The President removed Shurtleff without assigning any cause therefor. The Court of Claims dismissed plaintiff's petition to recover salary, upholding the President's power to remove for causes other than those stated. In this court Shurtleff relied upon the maxim *expressio unius est exclusio alterius*; but this court held that, while the rule expressed in the maxim was a very proper one and founded upon justifiable reasoning in many instances, it "should not be accorded controlling weight when to do so would involve the alteration of the universal practice of the government for over a century, and the consequent curtailment of the powers of the Executive in such an unusual manner." What the court meant by this expression appears from a reading of the opinion. That opinion, after saying that no term of office was fixed by the act and that, with the exception of judicial officers provided for by the Constitution, no civil officer had ever held office by life tenure since the foundation of the government, points out that to construe the statute as contended for by Shurtleff would give the appraiser the right to hold office during his life or until found guilty of some act specified in the statute, the result of which would be a complete revolution in respect of the general tenure of office, effected by implication with regard to that particular office only.

* * *

These circumstances, which led the court to reject the maxim as inapplicable, are exceptional. In the face of the unbroken precedent against life tenure, except in the case of the judiciary, the conclusion that Congress intended that, from among all other civil officers, appraisers alone should be selected to hold office for life was so extreme as to forbid, in the opinion of the court, any ruling which would produce that result if it reasonably could be avoided. The situation here presented is plainly and wholly different. The statute fixes a term of office, in accordance with many precedents. The first commissioners appointed are to continue in office for terms of three, four, five, six, and seven years, respectively; and their successors are to be appointed for terms of seven years — any commissioner being subject to removal by the President for inefficiency, neglect of duty, or malfeasance in office. The words of the act are definite and unambiguous.

. . . The fixing of a definite term subject to removal for cause, unless there be some countervailing provision or circumstance indicating the contrary, which here we are unable to find, is enough to establish the legislative intent that the term is not to be curtailed in the absence of such cause. . . .

The commission is to be nonpartisan; and it must, from the very nature of its duties, act with entire impartiality. It is charged with the enforcement of no policy except the policy of the law. Its duties are neither political nor executive, but predominantly quasi judicial and quasi legislative. Like the Interstate Commerce Commission, its members are called upon to exercise the trained judgment of a body of experts "appointed by law and informed by experience."

* * *

The debates in both houses demonstrate that the prevailing view was that the Commission was not to be "subject to anybody in the government but . . . only to the people of the United States"; free from "political domination or control" or the "probability or possibility of such a thing"; to be "separate and apart from any existing department of the government — not subject to the orders of the President."

* * *

Thus, the language of the act, the legislative reports, and the general purposes of the legislation as reflected by the debates, all combine to demonstrate the congressional intent to create a body of experts who shall gain experience by length of service; a body which shall be independent of executive authority, except in its selection, and free to exercise its judgment without the leave or hindrance of any other official or any department of the government. To the accomplishment of these purposes, it is clear that Congress was of opinion that length and certainty of tenure would vitally contribute. And to hold that, nevertheless, the members of the commission continue in office at the mere will of the President, might be to thwart, in large measure, the very ends which Congress sought to realize by definitely fixing the term of office.

We conclude that the intent of the act is to limit the executive power of removal to the causes enumerated, the existence of none of which is claimed here; and we pass to the second question.

Second. To support its contention that the removal provision of section 1, as we have just construed it, is an unconstitutional interference with the executive power of the President, the government's chief reliance is *Myers v. United States* [(1926)]. That case has been so recently decided, and the prevailing and dissenting opinions so fully review the general subject of the power of executive removal, that further discussion would add little of value to the wealth of material there collected. These opinions examine at length the historical, legislative, and judicial data bearing upon the question, beginning with what is called "the decision of 1789" in the first Congress and coming down almost to the day when the opinions were delivered. They occupy 243 pages of the volume in which they are printed. Nevertheless, the narrow point actually decided was only that the President had power to remove a postmaster of the first class, without the advice and consent of the Senate as required by act of Congress. In the course of the opinion of the court, expressions occur which tend to sustain the government's contention, but these are beyond the point involved and, therefore, do not come within the rule of stare decisis. In so far as they are out of harmony with the views here set forth, these expressions are disapproved. . . .

* * *

The office of a postmaster is so essentially unlike the office now involved that the decision in the *Myers* Case cannot be accepted as controlling our decision here. A postmaster is an executive officer restricted to the performance of executive functions. He is charged with no duty at all related to either the legislative or judicial power. The actual decision in the *Myers* Case finds support in the theory that such an officer is merely one of the units in the executive department and, hence, inherently subject to the exclusive and illimitable power of removal by the Chief Executive, whose subordinate and aide he is. Putting aside dicta, which may be followed if sufficiently persuasive but which are not controlling, the necessary reach of the decision goes far enough to include all purely executive officers. It goes no farther; much less does it include an officer who occupies no place in the executive department and who exercises no part of the executive power vested by the Constitution in the President.

The Federal Trade Commission is an administrative body created by Congress to carry into effect legislative policies embodied in the statute in accordance with the legislative standard therein prescribed, and to perform other specified duties as a legislative or as a judicial aid. Such a body cannot in any proper sense be characterized as an arm or an eye of the executive. Its duties are performed without executive leave and, in the contemplation of the statute, must be free from executive control. In administering the provisions of the statute in respect of "unfair methods of competition," that is to say, in filling in and administering the details embodied by that general standard, the commission acts in part quasi legislatively and in part quasi judicially. In making investigations and reports thereon for the information of Congress under section 6, in aid of the legislative power, it acts as a legislative agency. Under section 7, which authorizes the commission to act as a master in chancery under rules prescribed by the court, it acts as an agency of the judiciary. To the extent that it exercises any executive function, as distinguished from executive power in the constitutional sense, it does so in the discharge and effectuation of its quasi legislative or quasi judicial powers, or as an agency of the legislative or judicial departments of the government.[a]

---

[a] The provision of section 6(d) of the act (15 U.S.C. § 46(d)) which authorizes the President to direct an investigation and report by the commission in relation to alleged violations of the antitrust acts, is so obviously collateral to the main design of the act as not to detract from the force of this general statement as to the character of that body.

If Congress is without authority to prescribe causes for removal of members of the trade commission and limit executive power of removal accordingly, that power at once becomes practically all-inclusive in respect of civil officers with the exception of the judiciary provided for by the Constitution. The Solicitor General, at the bar, apparently recognizing this to be true, with commendable candor, agreed that his view in respect of the removability of members of the Federal Trade Commission necessitated a like view in respect of the Interstate Commerce Commission and the Court of Claims. We are thus confronted with the serious question whether not only the members of these quasi legislative and quasi judicial bodies, but the judges of the legislative Court of Claims, exercising judicial power, continue in office only at the pleasure of the President.

We think it plain under the Constitution that illimitable power of removal is not possessed by the President in respect of officers of the character of those just named. The authority of Congress, in creating quasi legislative or quasi judicial agencies, to require them to act in discharge of their duties independently of executive control cannot well be doubted; and that authority includes, as an appropriate incident, power to fix the period during which they shall continue, and to forbid their removal except for cause in the meantime. For it is quite evident that one who holds his office only during the pleasure of another cannot be depended upon to maintain an attitude of independence against the latter's will.

The fundamental necessity of maintaining each of the three general departments of government entirely free from the control or coercive influence, direct or indirect, of either of the others, has often been stressed and is hardly open to serious question. So much is implied in the very fact of the separation of the powers of these departments by the Constitution; and in the rule which recognizes their essential coequality. The sound application of a principle that makes one master in his own house precludes him from imposing his control in the house of another who is master there. James Wilson, one of the framers of the Constitution and a former justice of this court, said that the independence of each department required that its proceedings "should be free from the remotest influence, direct or indirect, of either of the other two powers." 1 ANDREWS, THE WORKS OF JAMES WILSON 367 (1896). And Mr. Justice Story in the first volume of his work on the Constitution (4th Ed.) § 530, citing No. 48 of THE FEDERALIST, said that neither of the departments in reference to each other "ought to possess, directly or indirectly, an overruling influence in the administration of their respective powers." *And see O'Donoghue v. United States* [(1933)].

The power of removal here claimed for the President falls within this principle, since its coercive influence threatens the independence of a commission, which is not only wholly disconnected from the executive department, but which, as already fully appears, was created by Congress as a means of carrying into operation legislative and judicial powers, and as an agency of the legislative and judicial departments. In the light of the question now under consideration, we have re-examined the precedents referred to in the *Myers*

Case, and find nothing in them to justify a conclusion contrary to that which we have reached. The so-called "decision of 1789" had relation to a bill proposed by Mr. Madison to establish an executive Department of Foreign Affairs. The bill provided that the principal officer was "to be removable from office by the President of the United States." This clause was changed to read "whenever the principal officer shall be removed from office by the President of the United States," certain things should follow, thereby, in connection with the debates, recognizing and confirming, as the court thought in the *Myers* Case, the sole power of the President in the matter. We shall not discuss the subject further, since it is so fully covered by the opinions in the *Myers* Case, except to say that the office under consideration by Congress was not only purely executive, but the officer one who was responsible to the President, and to him alone, in a very definite sense. A reading of the debates shows that the President's illimitable power of removal was not considered in respect of other than executive officers. And it is pertinent to observe that when, at a later time, the tenure of office for the Comptroller of the Treasury was under consideration, Mr. Madison quite evidently thought that, since the duties of that office were not purely of an executive nature but partook of the judiciary quality as well, a different rule in respect of executive removal might well apply. 1 ANNALS OF CONG. 611-612.

* * *

The result of what we now have said is this: Whether the power of the President to remove an officer shall prevail over the authority of Congress to condition the power by fixing a definite term and precluding a removal except for cause will depend upon the character of the office; the *Myers* decision, affirming the power of the President alone to make the removal, is confined to purely executive officers; and as to officers of the kind here under consideration, we hold that no removal can be made during the prescribed term for which the officer is appointed, except for one or more of the causes named in the applicable statute.

To the extent that, between the decision in the *Myers* Case, which sustains the unrestrictable power of the President to remove purely executive officers, and our present decision that such power does not extend to an office such as that here involved, there shall remain a field of doubt, we leave such cases as may fall within it for future consideration and determination as they may arise.

In accordance with the foregoing, the questions submitted are answered:

    Question No. 1, Yes.

    Question No. 2, Yes.

MR. JUSTICE MCREYNOLDS agrees.

NOTES AND QUESTIONS

1. *Humphrey's Executor* is the constitutional birth of the independent agency. How does one distinguish an independent agency from an executive one? The fettering of presidential removal authority is the hallmark of an independent agency, although the extent to which an agency can independently submit a budget to Congress, provide Congress with information, or bring litigation and enforcement proceedings also must be considered to get the complete picture. Naming even a few of the almost twenty independent agencies reveals the importance of the subjects they control: from the stock market (Securities and Exchange Commission) to communications (Federal Communications Commission) to the grocery store and other consumer transactions (Federal Trade Commission) and the money supply (Federal Reserve).

The idea of independent agencies emerged in a more naive time, when it was supposed that regulation was more the product of dispassionate scientific inquiry than interest group lobbying and the press and pull of ordinary politics. In fact, the first independent agency, the Interstate Commerce Commission, emerged in 1887 "[w]ithout too much political theory" at all. JOHN LANDIS, THE ADMINISTRATIVE PROCESS 2 (1938). Its origins are said to be traceable to a Democratic Congress' suspicion of Republican Benjamin Harrison, a former railroad lawyer who was to be inaugurated two days after the ICC's formation. *See* 5 Senate Committee on Governmental Affairs, STUDY ON FEDERAL REGULATION PREPARED PURSUANT TO S. REP. 71, 95TH CONG., 1ST SESS. 28 (1977). Even at the time of their great expansion during Roosevelt's New Deal, however, independent agencies were thought of as something of a "headless fourth branch" of government. In a report to President Roosevelt, the Brownlow Committee stated that independent agencies were "in reality miniature independent governments set up to deal with the railroad problem, the banking problem, or the radio problem. [They constitute] a haphazard deposit of irresponsible agencies and uncoordinated powers." REPORT OF THE PRESIDENT'S COMMITTEE ON ADMINISTRATIVE MANAGEMENT 39-40 (1937).

2. The scope of *Humphrey's Executor* should not be over-stated. On its terms, all the Court held was that Congress could legislatively require that a Commissioner of an independent agency could not be removed without cause. Despite some broad non-binding language, the Court did *not* hold that a President is precluded from supervising the work product of independent agencies. Nevertheless, lawyers for the President have speculated over time that the language might be taken as limiting the extent of the President's constitutional power over independent agencies to the power of appointment. *See* DOUGLAS W. KMIEC, THE ATTORNEY GENERAL'S LAWYER, ch. 3 (1992). This made independent agency compliance with presidential direction a voluntary matter.

The timidity of some presidential lawyers was evident in the case of *Bowsher v. Synar*, 478 U.S. 714 (1986), earlier discussed in conjunction with the legislative veto. It will be recalled that *Bowsher* did not deal with an independent agency, but an independent agent — the Comptroller General, an officer removable only by Congress. Under the Gramm-Rudman Act, the Comptroller General had been charged with making certain executive determinations binding on the President about the budget. The Court squarely rejected this spurious delegation saying: "[t]he structure of the Constitution does not permit Congress to execute the laws; it follows that Congress cannot grant to an officer under its control what it does not possess." *Bowsher*, 478 U.S. at 726. But when asked by Justice O'Connor at oral argument whether the Solicitor General, the highest ranking litigator for the United States, meant to argue the further point that an officer assigned such executive functions must not only be free of Congressional interference but also fully answerable to the President, the Solicitor General declined to make this challenge to the status of independent agencies. It may well be that this limiting concession was necessary to win the case. However, whether motivated by lawyer's caution or litigation strategy, it left independent agencies outside meaningful presidential control.

3. A number of commentators continue to prop up *Humphrey's Executor*, reasoning that the separation of powers can be flexible beneath the first tier division of legislative, executive, and judicial authority in constitutional text. Professor Peter Strauss has written that while the heads of government serve

> distinct functions . . . the same cannot be said of the administrative level of government. . . . These agencies adopt rules having the shape and impact of statutes, mold governmental policy through enforcement decisions and other initiatives, and decide cases in ways that determine the rights of private parties. If in 1787 such a merger of function was unthinkable, in 1987 it is unavoidable. . . .

Peter L. Strauss, *Formal and Functional Approaches to Separation-of-Powers Questions — A Foolish Inconsistency?*, 72 CORNELL L. REV. 488, 492-93 (1986).

Strauss's rationalization of independent agencies has not satisfied everyone. Professor Geoffrey Miller believes that Congress may not constitutionally deny the President the power to remove a policy-making official who refuses to accept lawful presidential direction. Geoffrey Miller, *Independent Agencies*, 1986 SUP. CT. REV. 41, 44-45. Simply on the grounds of accountability, independent agencies pose real difficulty. Treated as outside the direction of the President at least for some purposes, these agencies are nominally responsive to Congress. However, supervision by a multi-member body is haphazard, and a good case can be made that independent agencies are, at best, responsive to external constituencies that may "capture" the agency for their own economic or policy purposes. *See* Douglas W. Kmiec, *Debating Separation of Power*, 53 REV. OF POLITICS 391, 394-95 (1991).

4. The ability of the Executive to resist the balkanization of its authority by the legislature into separate independent agencies was weakened by presidential scandal. Nominally, the next case deals not with the relationship between independent agency and the Executive, but with the inability of a President to obstruct a co-equal branch — namely, the judiciary in the context of a criminal trial, by refusing to comply with a subpoena. *United States v. Nixon* is followed by *Morrison v. Olson*, however, where a weakened Executive's core function — the enforcement of law — is challenged.

(3) Executive Privilege

UNITED STATES v. NIXON
418 U.S. 683 (1974)

MR. CHIEF JUSTICE BURGER delivered the opinion of the Court.

This litigation presents for review the denial of a motion, filed in the District Court on behalf of the President of the United States, . . . to quash a third-party subpoena duces tecum. . . . The subpoena directed the President to produce certain tape recordings and documents relating to his conversations with aides and advisers. The [district] court rejected the President's claims of absolute executive privilege, of lack of jurisdiction, and of failure to satisfy the requirements of Rule 17(c). The President appealed. . . .

On March 1, 1974, a grand jury of the United States District Court for the District of Columbia returned an indictment charging seven named individuals with various offenses, including conspiracy to defraud the United States and to obstruct justice. Although he was not designated as such in the indictment, the grand jury named the President, among others, as an unindicted coconspirator. On April 18, 1974, upon motion of the Special Prosecutor, a subpoena duces tecum was issued pursuant to Rule 17(c) to the President by the United States District Court and made returnable on May 2, 1974. This subpoena required the production, in advance of the September 9 trial date, of certain tapes, memoranda, papers, transcripts or other writings relating to certain precisely identified meetings between the President and others.

* * *

II

JUSTICIABILITY

In the District Court, the President's counsel argued that the court lacked jurisdiction to issue the subpoena because the matter was an intra-branch dispute between a subordinate and superior officer of the Executive Branch and hence not subject to judicial resolution. That argument has been renewed in this Court with emphasis on the contention that the dispute does not present a "case" or "controversy" which can be adjudicated in the federal courts. The President's counsel argues that the federal courts should not intrude into areas committed to the other branches of Government. He views the present dispute as essentially a "jurisdictional" dispute within the Executive Branch which he analogizes to a dispute between two congressional committees. Since the Executive Branch has exclusive authority and absolute discretion to decide whether to prosecute a case . . . .

The mere assertion of a claim of an "intra-branch dispute," without more, has never operated to defeat federal jurisdiction; justiciability does not depend on such a surface inquiry. . . .

Our starting point is the nature of the proceeding for which the evidence is sought — here a pending criminal prosecution. It is a judicial proceeding in a federal court alleging violation of federal laws and is brought in the name of the United States as sovereign. Under the authority of Art. II, § 2, Congress has vested in the Attorney General the power to conduct the criminal litigation of the United States Government. It has also vested in him the power to appoint subordinate officers to assist him in the discharge of his duties. Acting pursuant to those statutes, the Attorney General has delegated the authority to represent the United States in these particular matters to a Special Prosecutor with unique authority and tenure.[8] The regulation gives the Special Prosecutor explicit power to contest the invocation of executive privilege in the process of seeking evidence deemed relevant to the performance of these specially delegated duties.

So long as this regulation is extant it has the force of law. . . .

* * *

In light of the uniqueness of the setting in which the conflict arises, the fact that both parties are officers of the Executive Branch cannot be viewed as a barrier to justiciability. It would be inconsistent with the applicable law and regulation, and the unique facts of this case to conclude other than that the Special

---

[8] The regulation issued by the Attorney General pursuant to his statutory authority, vests in the Special Prosecutor plenary authority to control the course of investigations and litigation related to "all offenses arising out of the 1972 Presidential Election for which the Special Prosecutor deems it necessary and appropriate to assume responsibility, members of the White House staff, or Presidential appointees, and any other matters which he consents to have assigned to him by the Attorney General." In particular, the Special Prosecutor was given full authority, inter alia, "to contest the assertion of 'Executive Privilege' . . . and handle all aspects of any case within his jurisdiction." The regulations then go on to provide:

"In exercising this authority, the Special Prosecutor will have the greatest degree of independence that is consistent with the Attorney General's statutory accountability for all matters falling within the jurisdiction of the Department of Justice. The Attorney General will not countermand or interfere with the Special Prosecutor's decisions or actions. The Special Prosecutor will determine whether and to what extent he will inform or consult with the Attorney General about the conduct of his duties and responsibilities. In accordance with assurances given by the President to the Attorney General that the President will not exercise his Constitutional powers to effect the discharge of the Special Prosecutor or limit the independence that he is hereby given, the Special Prosecutor will not be removed from his duties except for extraordinary improprieties on his part and without the President's first consulting the Majority and Minority Leaders and Chairmen and ranking Minority members of the Judiciary committees of the Senate and House of Representatives and ascertaining that their consensus is in accord with his proposed action."

Prosecutor has standing to bring this action and that a justiciable controversy is presented for decision.

* * *

IV

THE CLAIM OF PRIVILEGE

A

[W]e turn to the claim that the subpoena should be quashed because it demands "confidential conversations between a President and his close advisors that it would be inconsistent with the public interest to produce." The first contention is a broad claim that the separation of powers doctrine precludes judicial review of a President's claim of privilege. The second contention is that if he does not prevail on the claim of absolute privilege, the court should hold as a matter of constitutional law that the privilege prevails over the subpoena duces tecum.

In the performance of assigned constitutional duties each branch of the Government must initially interpret the Constitution, and the interpretation of its powers by any branch is due great respect from the others. The President's counsel, as we have noted, reads the Constitution as providing an absolute privilege of confidentiality for all Presidential communications. Many decisions of this Court, however, have unequivocally reaffirmed the holding of *Marbury v. Madison*, that "[i]t is emphatically the province and duty of the judicial department to say what the law is."

* * *

B

In support of his claim of absolute privilege, the President's counsel urges two grounds, one of which is common to all governments and one of which is peculiar to our system of separation of powers. The first ground is the valid need for protection of communications between high Government officials and those who advise and assist them in the performance of their manifold duties; the importance of this confidentiality is too plain to require further discussion. Human experience teaches that those who expect public dissemination of their remarks may well temper candor with a concern for appearances and for their own interests to the detriment of the decisionmaking process.[15] Whatever the nature of the privilege of confidentiality of Presidential communications in the exercise of Art. II powers, the privilege can be said to derive from the supremacy of each branch within its own assigned area of constitutional duties. Certain

---

[15] There is nothing novel about governmental confidentiality. The meetings of the Constitutional Convention in 1787 were conducted in complete privacy. Moreover, all records of those meetings were sealed for more than 30 years after the Convention. Most of the Framers acknowledge that without secrecy no constitution of the kind that was developed could have been written.

powers and privileges flow from the nature of enumerated powers; the protection of the confidentiality of Presidential communications has similar constitutional underpinnings.

The second ground asserted by the President's counsel in support of the claim of absolute privilege rests on the doctrine of separation of powers. . . .

However, neither the doctrine of separation of powers, nor the need for confidentiality of high-level communications, without more, can sustain an absolute, unqualified Presidential privilege of immunity from judicial process under all circumstances. The President's need for complete candor and objectivity from advisers calls for great deference from the courts. However, when the privilege depends solely on the broad, undifferentiated claim of public interest in the confidentiality of such conversations, a confrontation with other values arises. Absent a claim of need to protect military, diplomatic, or sensitive national security secrets, we find it difficult to accept the argument that even the very important interest in confidentiality of Presidential communications is significantly diminished by production of such material for in camera inspection with all the protection that a district court will be obliged to provide.

The impediment that an absolute, unqualified privilege would place in the way of the primary constitutional duty of the Judicial Branch to do justice in criminal prosecutions would plainly conflict with the function of the courts under Art. III. In designing the structure of our Government and dividing and allocating the sovereign power among three co-equal branches, the Framers of the Constitution sought to provide a comprehensive system, but the separate powers were not intended to operate with absolute independence. . . . "It enjoins upon its branches separateness but interdependence, autonomy but reciprocity." To read the Art. II powers of the President as providing an absolute privilege as against a subpoena essential to enforcement of criminal statutes on no more than a generalized claim of the public interest in confidentiality of nonmilitary and nondiplomatic discussions would upset the constitutional balance of "a workable government" and gravely impair the role of the courts under Art. III.

C

Since we conclude that the legitimate needs of the judicial process may outweigh Presidential privilege, it is necessary to resolve those competing interests in a manner that preserves the essential functions of each branch. The right and indeed the duty to resolve that question does not free the Judiciary from according high respect to the representations made on behalf of the President.

* * *

In this case the President challenges a subpoena served on him as a third party requiring the production of materials for use in a criminal prosecution; he does so on the claim that he has a privilege against disclosure of confidential communications. He does not place his claim of privilege on the ground they are military or diplomatic secrets. As to these areas of Art. II duties the courts

have traditionally shown the utmost deference to Presidential responsibilities.
. . .

The right to the production of all evidence at a criminal trial similarly has constitutional dimensions. The Sixth Amendment explicitly confers upon every defendant in a criminal trial the right "to be confronted with the witnesses against him" and "to have compulsory process for obtaining witnesses in his favor." Moreover, the Fifth Amendment also guarantees that no person shall be deprived of liberty without due process of law. It is the manifest duty of the courts to vindicate those guarantees, and to accomplish that it is essential that all relevant and admissible evidence be produced.

In this case we must weigh the importance of the general privilege of confidentiality of Presidential communications in performance of the President's responsibilities against the inroads of such a privilege on the fair administration of criminal justice. The interest in preserving confidentiality is weighty indeed and entitled to great respect. However, we cannot conclude that advisers will be moved to temper the candor of their remarks by the infrequent occasions of disclosure because of the possibility that such conversations will be called for in the context of a criminal prosecution.

* * *

We conclude that when the ground for asserting privilege as to subpoenaed materials sought for use in a criminal trial is based only on the generalized interest in confidentiality, it cannot prevail over the fundamental demands of due process of law in the fair administration of criminal justice. The generalized assertion of privilege must yield to the demonstrated, specific need for evidence in a pending criminal trial.

* * *

Since this matter came before the Court during the pendency of a criminal prosecution, and on representations that time is of the essence, the mandate shall issue forthwith.

Affirmed.

NOTES AND QUESTIONS

1. In *Nixon*, the Court finds executive privilege to have a constitutional root derived from "the supremacy of each branch within its own assigned area of constitutional duties." When the special prosecutor argued that there was no constitutional text supporting this privilege, the Court asserted that "the silence of the Constitution on this score is not dispositive," and cited the doctrine of implied powers, most often associated with Article I and the Legislative branch, as holding that each branch is entitled to reasonable and appropriate implications of authority that are "relevant to the exercise of a granted power." See

McCulloch v. Maryland, 17 U.S. (4 Wheat) 316 (1819), *infra*, Chapter Four, for a further discussion of implied authority.

2. As suggested in *Nixon*, the strength of a claim of executive privilege often depends on the subject matter, with military secrets and national security matters highly protected and generalized claims of confidentiality for discussions of day-to-day domestic policy matters given less security. Somewhere in between are claims of privilege dealing with the Executive's handling of litigation or other law enforcement.

3. Claims of privilege have not dissipated since the Nixon era. President Reagan issued a memorandum in 1982 which instructed that executive privilege should be "asserted only in the most compelling circumstances, and only after careful review demonstrates that assertion of the privilege is necessary." MEMORANDUM FOR THE HEADS OF EXECUTIVE DEPARTMENTS AND AGENCIES FROM PRESIDENT REAGAN (Nov. 4, 1982), *reprinted in* PETER M. SHANE & HAROLD H. BRUFF, SEPARATION OF POWERS LAW 313 (1996). While successor Presidents have claimed to follow the procedures outlined in the Reagan Memorandum, in fact, the claim can be debated.

Many executive privilege debates concern relations with Congress. Attorney General William French Smith reflected that legislative oversight "can almost always be properly conducted with reference to information concerning decisions which the Executive Branch has already reached." *Id.* Attorney General Smith's view is echoed in case law construing the analogous deliberative process privilege under exemption 5 of the Freedom of Information Act. Thus, as the Office of Legal Counsel has written: "[t]he courts have held [] that 'deliberative process' privilege does *not* protect documents which reflect final opinions, statements of reasons supplying the bases for decisions, or policies actually adopted, or documents that otherwise constitute the 'working law' of the agency." Confidentiality of the Attorney General's Communications in Counseling the President, 6 Op. Off. Legal Counsel 481, 493 (1982).

4. In *Cheney v. United States*, 2004 U.S. LEXIS 4576 (June 24, 2004), however, the Court, 7-2, strongly reaffirmed that the internal deliberations of the executive are not subject to disclosure for insignificant or ill-defined purposes. The Federal Advisory Committee Act (FACA) imposes disclosure requirements upon advisory committees consisting of non-federal officers and employees. It specifically excludes committees "composed wholly of full-time or permanent part-time [federal] officers or employees." Notwithstanding, the D.C. Circuit had earlier judicially crafted the possibility that the disclosure requirements might also be applied where there is regular participation by non-government individuals who were *de facto* members. The Sierra Club and Judicial Watch, two private organizations, alleged that President Bush's energy task force, which was chaired by Vice President Cheney and whose membership was entirely governmental nevertheless broadly consulted with firms and individuals in the energy industry. Pursuing this *de facto* member theory, the district court ordered sweeping discovery to determine whether the task force must meet the statutory disclosure requirements. Of course, complying with discovery would effectively give the plaintiffs everything they wanted to get by disclosure on the merits. When a divided appellate panel affirmed, reasoning that the President could assert executive privilege on a document-by-document basis, the Vice President sought review in the high court.

Writing for the Court, Justice Kennedy took the Vice President's position. The Court reasoned that the lower court had misread *United States v. Nixon* and was insufficiently respectful of a co-equal branch's need for confidentiality in its internal deliberations. *Nixon* was a criminal matter that challenged the Court's own ability to ensure disclosure for a fair trial. *Cheney*, by contrast, was a civil case and unlike the precise document demands in *Nixon*, asked for "everything under the sky." ". . . *Nixon* does not require the Executive Branch to bear the onus of critiquing the unacceptable discovery requests line by line," said Justice Kennedy. Instead, the Court remanded, expressing doubt about the lower court's *de facto* membership theory, and in any event, reminding it to be "mindful of the burdens imposed on the Executive Branch." Justices Ginsburg and Souter dissented, admitting that the discovery order was overbroad, but suggesting that it was the Vice President who failed to ask for it to be narrowed, rather than resisting discovery altogether, and that he still could do so.

5. An undifferentiated deliberative process privilege can have no legitimacy where the issue is abuse of the public trust. This was made clear by Professor, and Watergate Special Prosecutor, Archibald Cox's meticulous review of what were, prior to recent administrations, the historically rare assertions of executive privilege. Archibald Cox, *Executive Privilege*, 122 U. PA. L. REV. 1383 (1974). Professor Cox writes:

> Over a period of a century and a half thirteen Presidents found a total of twenty occasions on which to refuse to turn over information demanded by an arm of Congress. . . .
>
> If one looks at what was done and confines the words to the events, nothing appears which even approaches a solid historical practice of recognizing claims of executive privilege based upon an undifferentiated need for preserving the secrecy of internal communications within the Executive Branch.

Id. at 1404. Similarly, the Supreme Court has insisted upon disclosure and rejected claims of presidential privilege where Congress sought to make materials available from a "desire to restore public confidence in our political processes." *Nixon v. Adm'r of Gen. Services*, 433 U.S. 425, 453 (1977). Justice Powell's concurrence stated that Congress must have "broad authority to investigate, to inform the public, and, ultimately, to legislate against suspected corruption and abuse of power in the Executive Branch." *Id.* at 498 (Powell, J., concurring).

6. While First Lady Hillary Clinton unsuccessfully attempted to assert a governmental attorney-client privilege in response to a federal criminal grand jury subpoena for documents related to meetings between her, White House counsel, and her private counsel regarding the Whitewater land deal and the handling by the White House of the office documents of Vincent W. Foster, Jr., a deputy White House Counsel who is believed to have committed suicide in July 1993. The United States Court of Appeals for the Eighth Circuit ruled that under Rule 501 of the Federal Rules of Evidence privileges are not to be "lightly created" or expanded and that Mrs. Clinton could not assert such privilege. *In re Grand Jury Subpoena Duces Tecum*, 112 F.3d 910 (8th Cir. 1997). While Mrs. Clinton first attempted to assert executive privilege, since she was not President, she abandoned that claim. Because of the presence of her personal attorneys at the White House meetings of interest to the grand jury, she also raised a personal attorney-client privilege. However, for this to apply, the appellate court reasoned, there would have to be a "common interest" between Mrs. Clinton and the White House. The court stated: "Mrs. Clinton's interest in the . . . investigation is, naturally, avoiding prosecution, or else minimizing the consequences if [the United States] decides to pursue charges against her. One searches in vain for any interest of the White House which corresponds to Mrs. Clinton's personal interest." *Id.* at 922. The court was especially disinclined to create a new governmental attorney-client privilege because "executive branch employees, including attorneys, are under a statutory duty to report criminal wrongdoing by other employees to the Attorney General." *Id.* at 920 (citing 28 U.S.C. § 535(b)). Thus, the court reasoned, "[a]n official who fears he or she may have violated the criminal law and wishes to speak with an attorney in confidence should speak with a private attorney, not a government attorney." *Id.* at 921. Mrs. Clinton petitioned the Supreme Court to review the judgment of the appeals court rejecting her claim of privilege, but the Court denied certiorari. *Office of the President v. Office of Indep. Counsel*, 117 S. Ct. 2482 (1997).

President Clinton also raised the issue of attorney-client privilege in the context of his impeachment. The claim was rejected. As the United States Court of Appeals for the D.C. Circuit observed in *In re Lindsey*; "The Office of the President cites no authority for the proposition that communications between White House Counsel and the President would be absolutely privileged in congressional [impeachment] proceedings . . . ." 158 F.3d 1263, 1278 n.12 (D.C. Cir. 1998), *cert. denied sub. nom. Office of the President v. Office of Independent Counsel*, 119 S. Ct. 466 (1998). To the contrary, the duty of White House Counsel "is not to defend clients against criminal charges and it is not to protect wrongdoers from public exposure. The constitutional responsibility of the President, and all members of the Executive Branch [including White House Counsel] is to 'take Care that the Laws be faithfully executed.'"

The courts also rejected President Clinton's claim that the secret service detail assigned to protect his security could not be subpoenaed to appear before a federal grand jury. *Rubin v. United States,* 148 F.3d 1073 (D.C. Cir. 1998), *cert. denied*, 119 S. Ct. 461 (1998). This privilege claim lost at trial, on appeal, and before the Chief Justice of the United States. Perhaps this was unsurprising since the Rules of Evidence articulate a presumption against giving witnesses new ways to avoid telling the truth. Even on its own terms, the privilege didn't make much sense. As argued by the President, the privilege would not apply where the agent thought he was contemporaneously observing the President commit a crime and in any event the privilege was not a specifically presidential one, but one that could only be asserted by the Secretary of the Treasury, the supervisor of the Secret Service, and of course, the President's subordinate. As the appellate court wrote: "we know of no other privilege that works th[is] way . . . and it reinforces our impression that the proposed protective function privilege will provide only a weak incentive for the President to keep his protectors in close proximity." 148 F.3d at 1077. Existing law, then, requires all federal officers who receive information or allegations that another federal officer is engaged in illegal activity to report that immediately to the appropriate investigative authorities.

7. The topic of executive or even governmental attorney-client privilege is not entirely unrelated to the issue of presidential immunity from suit — both have the common purpose of ensuring the President ample freedom to make difficult decisions. In *Nixon v. Fitzgerald*, 457 U.S. 731 (1982), the Court held that the President has absolute immunity from suit for all actions taken within "the outer perimeter" of his official duties. Presidential aides are also entitled to immunity, though of a more qualified nature — that is, they are shielded from suit so long as their official actions do not violate "clearly established" statutory or constitutional rights that should have been reasonably known. *Harlow v. Fitzgerald*, 457 U.S. 800 (1982).

President Clinton unsuccessfully sought to enlarge the scope of presidential immunity. Mr. Clinton argued that because of the responsibilities of the presidential office, he was entitled to a delay for civil claims brought against him for an alleged act of sexual harassment occurring before he was elected President. A unanimous Supreme Court ruled against the President finding that the "reasoning [supporting immunity for official acts] provides no support for an immunity for *unofficial* conduct." *Clinton v. Jones*, 520 U.S. 681, 694 (1997) (emphasis in original). Writing for the Court, Justice Stevens thought the President's strongest argument based on the separation of powers was without merit because "[t]he litigation of questions that relate entirely to the unofficial conduct of the individual who happens to be President poses no perceptible risk of misallocation of either judicial power or executive power." *Id.* at 701. It has long been settled, reasoned the Court, that the separation of powers does not bar every exercise of jurisdiction over the President of the United States, including the determination of whether he has acted within the law and subjecting him to subpoena. *Id.* at 705 (quoting *Nixon v. Fitzgerald*, 457 U.S. at 753-54). While a federal court retains discretion to defer a trial, the President bears the burden of establishing the need for such deferral. *Id.* at 708. The categorical deferral of the trial in this case, however, was an abuse of discretion because it took "no account whatever" of Mrs. Jones' interests, including possible loss of evidence and fading memories which would deny her justice. *Id.*

8. One regrettable effect of the independent counsel law is that it can blur the distinctions between venal personal scandal and political disagreement. Political difference is anticipated, if not encouraged, by the separation of powers. The next case originates out of the latter — that is, an executive privilege dispute. Two congressmen sought enforcement documents from President Reagan's Administrator of the Environmental Protection Agency, Anne Gorsuch Burford. Assistant Attorney General Theodore Olson, who headed the Office of Legal Counsel (and who would later serve as Solicitor General under President George W. Bush), advised the President to release some 50,000 pages of documents, but against releasing certain other law enforcement files. Relying on Olson's advice, the President directed Mrs. Burford not to release "open investigative files, [which] are internal deliberative materials containing enforcement strategy and statements of the Government's position on various legal issues which may be raised in enforcement actions . . . ." PETER SHANE & HAROLD BRUFF, THE LAW OF PRESIDENTIAL POWER 188-89 (1989).

Failing to get every document they wanted, the congressional subcommittee, and ultimately the full House in late December 1982, voted Mrs. Gorsuch in contempt of Congress. After some skirmishing over the enforceability of the contempt in court, the Executive and Legislative branches reached a compromise, with Congress receiving edited copies of the enforcement documents and oral briefings.

Unfortunately, this was not the end of the matter for Mr. Olson. Angered over his defense of the President's privilege, the House Judiciary Committee demanded that Olson testify as to the nature of his legal advice. Olson did, but not to the Committee's satisfaction, and the Democratic members of the Committee asserted that Olson misled them and demanded the appointment of an independent counsel to investigate. In response, Mr. Olson challenged the constitutionality of the independent counsel statute.

(4) The Independent Counsel

MORRISON v. OLSON
487 U.S. 654 (1988)

CHIEF JUSTICE REHNQUIST delivered the opinion of the Court.

This case presents us with a challenge to the independent counsel provisions of the Ethics in Government Act of 1978. We hold today that these provisions of the Act do not violate the Appointments Clause of the Constitution, Art. II, § 2, cl. 2, or the limitations of Article III, nor do they impermissibly interfere with the President's authority under Article II in violation of the constitutional principle of separation of powers.

I

Briefly stated, the Ethics in Government Act allows for the appointment of an "independent counsel" to investigate and, if appropriate, prosecute certain high-ranking Government officials for violations of federal criminal laws.[2] . . .

* * *

The proceedings in this case provide an example of how the Act works in practice. In 1982, two Subcommittees of the House of Representatives issued subpoenas directing the Environmental Protection Agency (EPA) to produce certain documents relating to the efforts of the EPA and the Land and Natural Resources Division of the Justice Department to enforce the "Superfund Law." At that time, appellee Olson was the Assistant Attorney General for the Office of Legal Counsel (OLC). . . . [T]he President ordered the Administrator of EPA to invoke executive privilege to withhold certain of the documents on the ground that they contained "enforcement sensitive information." The Administrator obeyed this order and withheld the documents. In response, the House voted to hold the Administrator in contempt, after which the Administrator and the United States together filed a lawsuit against the House. The conflict abated in March 1983, when the administration agreed to give the House Subcommittees limited access to the documents.

The following year, the House Judiciary Committee began an investigation into the Justice Department's role in the controversy over the EPA documents. During this investigation, appellee Olson testified before a House Subcommittee on March 10, 1983. Both before and after that testimony, the Department complied with several Committee requests that were at first withheld, although these documents were eventually disclosed by the Department after the Committee learned of their existence. In 1985, the majority members of the Judiciary Committee published a lengthy report on the Committee's investigation. The report not only criticized various officials in the Department of Justice for their role in the EPA executive privilege dispute, but it also suggested that appellee Olson had given false and misleading testimony to the Subcommittee on March 10, 1983 . . . . The Chairman of the Judiciary Committee forwarded a copy of the report to the Attorney General with a request, pursuant to 28 U.S.C. § 592(c),

---

2 Under 28 U.S.C. § 591(a) (1982 Supp. V), the statute applies to violations of "any Federal criminal law other than a violation classified as a Class B or C misdemeanor or an infraction." *See also* § 591(c) ("any Federal criminal law other than a violation classified as a Class B or C misdemeanor or an infraction"). Section 591(b) sets forth the individuals who may be the target of an investigation by the Attorney General, including the President and Vice President, Cabinet level officials, certain high-ranking officials in the Executive Office of the President and the Justice Department, the Director and Deputy Director of Central Intelligence, the Commissioner of Internal Revenue, and certain officials involved in the President's national political campaign. Pursuant to § 591(c), the Attorney General may also conduct a preliminary investigation of persons not named in § 591(b) if an investigation by the Attorney General or other Department of Justice official "may result in a personal, financial, or political conflict of interest."

that he seek the appointment of an independent counsel to investigate the allegations against Olson [and two other department officials].

* * *

. . . [Morrison, the independent counsel,] caused a grand jury to issue and serve subpoenas ad testificandum and duces tecum. [Olson] moved to quash the subpoenas, claiming, among other things, that the independent counsel provisions of the Act were unconstitutional and that [Morrison] accordingly had no authority to proceed. . . . [T]he District Court upheld the constitutionality of the Act and denied the motions to quash. . . .

A divided Court of Appeals reversed. The majority ruled first that an independent counsel is not an "inferior Officer" of the United States for purposes of the Appointments Clause. Accordingly, the court found the Act invalid because it does not provide for the independent counsel to be nominated by the President and confirmed by the Senate, as the Clause requires for "principal" officers. The court then went on to consider several alternative grounds for its conclusion that the statute was unconstitutional. In the majority's view, the Act also violates the Appointments Clause insofar as it empowers a court of law to appoint an "inferior" officer who performs core executive functions; the Act's delegation of various powers to the Special Division violates the limitations of Article III; the Act's restrictions on the Attorney General's power to remove an independent counsel violate the separation of powers; and finally, the Act interferes with the Executive Branch's prerogative to "take care that the Laws be faithfully executed," Art. II, § 3. . . . We now reverse.

* * *

III

The Appointments Clause of Article II reads as follows:

"[The President] shall nominate, and by and with the Advice and Consent of the Senate, shall appoint Ambassadors, other public Ministers and Consuls, Judges of the Supreme Court, and all other Officers of the United States, whose Appointments are not herein otherwise provided for, and which shall be established by Law; but the Congress may by Law vest the Appointment of such inferior Officers, as they think proper, in the President alone, in the Courts of Law, or in the Heads of Departments." U.S. Constitution, Article II, Section 2, clause 2.

The parties do not dispute that "[t]he Constitution for purposes of appointment . . . divides all its officers into two classes." "[P]rincipal officers are selected by the President with the advice and consent of the Senate. Inferior officers Congress may allow to be appointed by the President alone, by the heads of departments, or by the Judiciary." The initial question is, accordingly, whether appellant is an "inferior" or a "principal" officer. If she is the latter, as the Court of Appeals concluded, then the Act is in violation of the Appointments Clause.

The line between "inferior" and "principal" officers is one that is far from clear, and the Framers provided little guidance into where it should be drawn. *See, e.g.*, 2 J. STORY, COMMENTARIES ON THE CONSTITUTION § 1536, pp. 397-398 (3d ed. 1858) ("In the practical course of the government there does not seem to have been any exact line drawn, who are and who are not to be deemed inferior officers, in the sense of the constitution, whose appointment does not necessarily require the concurrence of the senate"). We need not attempt here to decide exactly where the line falls between the two types of officers, because in our view appellant clearly falls on the "inferior officer" side of that line. Several factors lead to this conclusion.

First, appellant is subject to removal by a higher Executive Branch official. Although appellant may not be "subordinate" to the Attorney General (and the President) insofar as she possesses a degree of independent discretion to exercise the powers delegated to her under the Act, the fact that she can be removed by the Attorney General indicates that she is to some degree "inferior" in rank and authority. Second, appellant is empowered by the Act to perform only certain, limited duties. An independent counsel's role is restricted primarily to investigation and, if appropriate, prosecution for certain federal crimes. Admittedly, the Act delegates to appellant "full power and independent authority to exercise all investigative and prosecutorial functions and powers of the Department of Justice," but this grant of authority does not include any authority to formulate policy for the Government or the Executive Branch, nor does it give appellant any administrative duties outside of those necessary to operate her office. The Act specifically provides that in policy matters appellant is to comply to the extent possible with the policies of the Department.

Third, appellant's office is limited in jurisdiction [and tenure]. . . .

This does not, however, end our inquiry under the Appointments Clause. Appellees argue that even if appellant is an "inferior" officer, the Clause does not empower Congress to place the power to appoint such an officer outside the Executive Branch. They contend that the Clause does not contemplate congressional authorization of "interbranch appointments," in which an officer of one branch is appointed by officers of another branch. The relevant language of the Appointments Clause is worth repeating. It reads: ". . . but the Congress may by Law vest the Appointment of such inferior Officers, as they think proper, in the President alone, in the courts of Law, or in the Heads of Departments." On its face, the language of this "excepting clause" admits of no limitation on interbranch appointments. Indeed, the inclusion of "as they think proper" seems clearly to give Congress significant discretion to determine whether it is "proper" to vest the appointment of, for example, executive officials in the "courts of Law." We recognized as much in one of our few decisions in this area, *Ex parte Siebold* [(1879)], where we stated:

> "It is no doubt usual and proper to vest the appointment of inferior officers in that department of the government, executive or judicial, or in that particular executive department to which the duties of such officers

appertain. But there is no absolute requirement to this effect in the Constitution. . . ."

* * *

We do not mean to say that Congress' power to provide for interbranch appointments of "inferior officers" is unlimited. In addition to separation-of-powers concerns, which would arise if such provisions for appointment had the potential to impair the constitutional functions assigned to one of the branches, *Siebold* itself suggested that Congress' decision to vest the appointment power in the courts would be improper if there was some "incongruity" between the functions normally performed by the courts and the performance of their duty to appoint. . . . In this case, however, we do not think it impermissible for Congress to vest the power to appoint independent counsel in a specially created federal court. We thus disagree with the Court of Appeals' conclusion that there is an inherent incongruity about a court having the power to appoint prosecutorial officers. . . . Congress, of course, was concerned when it created the office of independent counsel with the conflicts of interest that could arise in situations when the Executive Branch is called upon to investigate its own high-ranking officers. If it were to remove the appointing authority from the Executive Branch, the most logical place to put it was in the Judicial Branch. In the light of the Act's provision making the judges of the Special Division ineligible to participate in any matters relating to an independent counsel they have appointed, we do not think that appointment of the independent counsel by the court runs afoul of the constitutional limitation on "incongruous" interbranch appointments.

* * *

V

We now turn to consider whether the Act is invalid under the constitutional principle of separation of powers. Two related issues must be addressed: The first is whether the provision of the Act restricting the Attorney General's power to remove the independent counsel to only those instances in which he can show "good cause," taken by itself, impermissibly interferes with the President's exercise of his constitutionally appointed functions. The second is whether, taken as a whole, the Act violates the separation of powers by reducing the President's ability to control the prosecutorial powers wielded by the independent counsel.

A

* * *

Unlike both *Bowsher* and *Myers*, this case does not involve an attempt by Congress itself to gain a role in the removal of executive officials other than its established powers of impeachment and conviction. The Act instead puts the removal power squarely in the hands of the Executive Branch; an independent counsel may be removed from office, "only by the personal action of the Attorney General, and only for good cause." There is no requirement of congressional approval of the Attorney General's removal decision, though the decision is subject to judicial review. § 596(a)(3). In our view, the removal provisions of the Act make this case more analogous to *Humphrey's Executor v. United States* than to *Myers* or *Bowsher*.

In *Humphrey's Executor*, the issue was whether a statute restricting the President's power to remove the Commissioners of the Federal Trade Commission (FTC) only for "inefficiency, neglect of duty, or malfeasance in office" was consistent with the Constitution. We stated that whether Congress can "condition the [President's power of removal] by fixing a definite term and precluding a removal except for cause, will depend upon the character of the office." . . . At least in regard to "quasi-legislative" and "quasi-judicial" agencies such as the FTC, "[t]he authority of Congress, in creating [such] agencies, to require them to act in discharge of their duties independently of executive control . . . includes, as an appropriate incident, power to fix the period during which they shall continue in office, and to forbid their removal except for cause in the meantime."

* * *

Appellees contend that *Humphrey's Executor* [is] distinguishable from this case because [it did] not involve officials who performed a "core executive function." They argue that our decision in *Humphrey's Executor* rests on a distinction between "purely executive" officials and officials who exercise "quasi-legislative" and "quasi-judicial" powers. . . .

We undoubtedly did rely on the terms "quasi-legislative" and "quasi-judicial" to distinguish the officials involved in *Humphrey's Executor* and [other cases], but our present considered view is that the determination of whether the Constitution allows Congress to impose a "good cause"-type restriction on the President's power to remove an official cannot be made to turn on whether or not that official is classified as "purely executive." The analysis contained in our removal cases is designed not to define rigid categories of those officials who may or may not be removed at will by the President,[28] but to ensure that Congress

---

[28] The difficulty of defining such categories of "executive" or "quasi-legislative" officials is illustrated by a comparison of our decisions in cases such as *Humphrey's Executor*, *Buckley v. Valeo* (1976), and *Bowsher*. In *Buckley*, we indicated that the functions of the Federal Election Commission are "administrative," and "more legislative and judicial in nature," and are "of kinds usually performed by independent regulatory agencies or by some department in the Executive Branch under the direction of an Act of Congress." In *Bowsher*, we found that the functions of the Comptroller General were "executive" in nature, in that he was required to "exercise judgment concerning facts that affect the application of the Act," and he must "interpret the provisions of the Act to determine precisely what budgetary calculations are required." Compare this with the description of the FTC's powers in *Humphrey's Executor*, which we stated "occupie[d] no place in the executive department": "The [FTC] is an administrative body created by Congress to carry into effect legislative policies embodied in the statute in accordance with the legislative standard therein prescribed, and to perform other specified duties as a legislative or as a judicial aid." 295 U.S. at 628. As JUSTICE WHITE noted in his dissent in *Bowsher*, it is hard to dispute that the powers of the FTC at the time of *Humphrey's Executor* would at the present time be considered "executive," at least to some degree.

does not interfere with the President's exercise of the "executive power" and his constitutionally appointed duty to "take care that the laws be faithfully executed" under Article II. *Myers* was undoubtedly correct in its holding, and in its broader suggestion that there are some "purely executive" officials who must be removable by the President at will if he is to be able to accomplish his constitutional role.[29] But as the Court noted in *Wiener v. United States*:

> "The assumption was short-lived that the *Myers* case recognized the President's inherent constitutional power to remove officials no matter what the relation of the executive to the discharge of their duties and no matter what restrictions Congress may have imposed regarding the nature of their tenure."

At the other end of the spectrum from *Myers*, the characterization of the agencies in *Humphrey's Executor* as "quasi-legislative" or "quasi-judicial" in large part reflected our judgment that it was not essential to the President's proper execution of his Article II powers that these agencies be headed up by individuals who were removable at will. We do not mean to suggest that an analysis of the functions served by the officials at issue is irrelevant. But the real question is whether the removal restrictions are of such a nature that they impede the President's ability to perform his constitutional duty, and the functions of the officials in question must be analyzed in that light.

Considering for the moment the "good cause" removal provision in isolation from the other parts of the Act at issue in this case, we cannot say that the imposition of a "good cause" standard for removal by itself unduly trammels on executive authority. There is no real dispute that the functions performed by the independent counsel are "executive" in the sense that they are law enforcement functions that typically have been undertaken by officials within the Executive Branch. As we noted above, however, the independent counsel is an inferior officer under the Appointments Clause, with limited jurisdiction and tenure and lacking policymaking or significant administrative authority. Although the counsel exercises no small amount of discretion and judgment in deciding how to carry out his or her duties under the Act, we simply do not see how the President's need to control the exercise of that discretion is so central to the functioning of the Executive Branch as to require as a matter of constitutional law that the counsel be terminable at will by the President.

Nor do we think that the "good cause" removal provision at issue here impermissibly burdens the President's power to control or supervise the independent counsel, as an executive official, in the execution of his or her duties under the

---

[29] The dissent says that the language of Article II vesting the executive power of the United States in the President requires that every officer of the United States exercising any part of that power must serve at the pleasure of the President and be removable by him at will. This rigid demarcation — a demarcation incapable of being altered by law in the slightest degree, and applicable to tens of thousands of holders of offices neither known nor foreseen by the Framers — depends upon an extrapolation from general constitutional language which we think is more than the text will bear.

Act. This is not a case in which the power to remove an executive official has been completely stripped from the President, thus providing no means for the President to ensure the "faithful execution" of the laws. Rather, because the independent counsel may be terminated for "good cause," the Executive, through the Attorney General, retains ample authority to assure that the counsel is competently performing his or her statutory responsibilities in a manner that comports with the provisions of the Act. . . . We do not think that this limitation as it presently stands sufficiently deprives the President of control over the independent counsel to interfere impermissibly with his constitutional obligation to ensure the faithful execution of the laws.[33]

B

The final question to be addressed is whether the Act, taken as a whole, violates the principle of separation of powers by unduly interfering with the role of the Executive Branch. Time and again we have reaffirmed the importance in our constitutional scheme of the separation of governmental powers into the three coordinate branches. The system of separated powers and checks and balances established in the Constitution was regarded by the Framers as "a self-executing safeguard against the encroachment or aggrandizement of one branch at the expense of the other." We have not hesitated to invalidate provisions of law which violate this principle. On the other hand, we have never held that the Constitution requires that the three branches of Government "operate with absolute independence." In the often-quoted words of Justice Jackson: "While the Constitution diffuses power the better to secure liberty, it also contemplates that practice will integrate the dispersed powers into a workable government. It enjoins upon its branches separateness but interdependence, autonomy but reciprocity." *Youngstown Sheet & Tube Co. v. Sawyer* (concurring opinion).

We observe first that this case does not involve an attempt by Congress to increase its own powers at the expense of the Executive Branch. Indeed, with the exception of the power of impeachment — which applies to all officers of the United States — Congress retained for itself no powers of control or supervision over an independent counsel. The Act does empower certain Members of Congress to request the Attorney General to apply for the appointment of an independent counsel, but the Attorney General has no duty to comply with the request, although he must respond within a certain time limit. Other than that, Congress' role under the Act is limited to receiving reports or other infor-

---

[33] We see no constitutional problem in the fact that the Act provides for judicial review of the removal decision. § 596(a)(3). The purpose of such review is to ensure that an independent counsel is removed only in accordance with the will of Congress as expressed in the Act. The possibility of judicial review does not inject the Judicial Branch into the removal decision, nor does it, by itself, put any additional burden on the President's exercise of executive authority. Indeed, we note that the legislative history of the most recent amendment to the Act indicates that the scope of review to be exercised by the courts under § 596(a)(3) is to be "the standards established by existing case law on the removal of [other] officials" who are subject to "good cause" removal. H.R.Conf.Rep. No. 100-452, p. 37 (1987).

mation and oversight of the independent counsel's activities, § 595(a), functions that we have recognized generally as being incidental to the legislative function of Congress.

Similarly, we do not think that the Act works any judicial usurpation of properly executive functions. . . .

* * *

Finally, we do not think that the Act "impermissibly undermine[s]" the powers of the Executive Branch, or "disrupts the proper balance between the coordinate branches [by] prevent[ing] the Executive Branch from accomplishing its constitutionally assigned functions." It is undeniable that the Act reduces the amount of control or supervision that the Attorney General and, through him, the President exercises over the investigation and prosecution of a certain class of alleged criminal activity. . . . [Yet] no independent counsel may be appointed without a specific request by the Attorney General, and the Attorney General's decision not to request appointment if he finds "no reasonable grounds to believe that further investigation is warranted" is committed to his unreviewable discretion. The Act thus gives the Executive a degree of control over the power to initiate an investigation by the independent counsel. In addition, the jurisdiction of the independent counsel is defined with reference to the facts submitted by the Attorney General, and once a counsel is appointed, the Act requires that the counsel abide by Justice Department policy unless it is not "possible" to do so. Notwithstanding the fact that the counsel is to some degree "independent" and free from executive supervision to a greater extent than other federal prosecutors, in our view these features of the Act give the Executive Branch sufficient control over the independent counsel to ensure that the President is able to perform his constitutionally assigned duties.

VI

In sum, we conclude today that it does not violate the Appointments Clause for Congress to vest the appointment of independent counsel in the Special Division; that the powers exercised by the Special Division under the Act do not violate Article III; and that the Act does not violate the separation-of-powers principle by impermissibly interfering with the functions of the Executive Branch. The decision of the Court of Appeals is therefore

Reversed.

JUSTICE SCALIA, dissenting.

It is the proud boast of our democracy that we have "a government of laws and not of men." Many Americans are familiar with that phrase; not many know its derivation. It comes from Part the First, Article XXX, of the Massachusetts Constitution of 1780, which reads in full as follows:

"In the government of this Commonwealth, the legislative department shall never exercise the executive and judicial powers, or either of them:

The executive shall never exercise the legislative and judicial powers, or either of them: The judicial shall never exercise the legislative and executive powers, or either of them: to the end it may be a government of laws and not of men."

The Framers of the Federal Constitution similarly viewed the principle of separation of powers as the absolutely central guarantee of a just Government. In No. 47 of THE FEDERALIST, Madison wrote that "[n]o political truth is certainly of greater intrinsic value, or is stamped with the authority of more enlightened patrons of liberty."

The principle of separation of powers is expressed in our Constitution in the first section of each of the first three Articles. Article I, § 1, provides that "[a]ll legislative Powers herein granted shall be vested in a Congress of the United States, which shall consist of a Senate and House of Representatives." Article III, § 1, provides that "[t]he judicial Power of the United States, shall be vested in one supreme Court, and in such inferior Courts as the Congress may from time to time ordain and establish." And the provision at issue here, Art. II, § 1, cl. 1, provides that "[t]he executive Power shall be vested in a President of the United States of America."

But just as the mere words of a Bill of Rights are not self-effectuating, the Framers recognized "[t]he insufficiency of a mere parchment delineation of the boundaries" to achieve the separation of powers. THE FEDERALIST NO. 73, at 442 (Alexander Hamilton) (Clinton Rossiter ed., 1961). "[T]he great security," wrote Madison, "against a gradual concentration of the several powers in the same department consists in giving to those who administer each department the necessary constitutional means and personal motives to resist encroachments of the others. The provision for defense must in this, as in all other cases, be made commensurate to the danger of attack." THE FEDERALIST NO. 51. . . .

The major "fortification" provided, of course, was the veto power. But in addition to providing fortification, the Founders conspicuously and very consciously declined to sap the Executive's strength in the same way they had weakened the Legislature: by dividing the executive power. Proposals to have multiple executives, or a council of advisers with separate authority were rejected. . . .

That is what this suit is about. Power. The allocation of power among Congress, the President, and the courts in such fashion as to preserve the equilibrium the Constitution sought to establish — so that "a gradual concentration of the several powers in the same department," THE FEDERALIST NO. 51, at 321 (James Madison), can effectively be resisted. Frequently an issue of this sort will come before the Court clad, so to speak, in sheep's clothing: the potential of the asserted principle to effect important change in the equilibrium of power is not immediately evident, and must be discerned by a careful and perceptive analysis. But this wolf comes as a wolf.

I

The present case began when the Legislative and Executive Branches became "embroiled in a dispute concerning the scope of the congressional investigatory power." . . . In his decision to assert executive privilege, the President was counseled by appellee Olson, who was then Assistant Attorney General of the Department of Justice for the Office of Legal Counsel, a post that has traditionally had responsibility for providing legal advice to the President (subject to approval of the Attorney General). The House's response was to pass a resolution citing the EPA Administrator, who had possession of the documents, for contempt. . . .

Congress did not, however, leave things there. Certain Members of the House remained angered by the confrontation, particularly by the role played by the Department of Justice. Specifically, the Judiciary Committee remained disturbed by the possibility that the Department had persuaded the President to assert executive privilege despite reservations by the EPA. . . . Accordingly, staff counsel of the House Judiciary Committee were commissioned (apparently without the knowledge of many of the Committee's members) to investigate the Justice Department's role in the controversy. That investigation lasted 2 1/2 years, and produced a 3,000-page report issued by the Committee over the vigorous dissent of all but one of its minority-party members. That report, which among other charges questioned the truthfulness of certain statements made by Assistant Attorney General Olson during testimony in front of the Committee during the early stages of its investigation, was sent to the Attorney General along with a formal request that he appoint an independent counsel to investigate Mr. Olson and others.

As a general matter, the Act before us here requires the Attorney General to apply for the appointment of an independent counsel within 90 days after receiving a request to do so, unless he determines within that period that "there are no reasonable grounds to believe that further investigation or prosecution is warranted." As a practical matter, it would be surprising if the Attorney General had any choice (assuming this statute is constitutional) but to seek appointment of an independent counsel to pursue the charges against the principal object of the congressional request, Mr. Olson. Merely the political consequences (to him and the President) of seeming to break the law by refusing to do so would have been substantial. How could it not be, the public would ask, that a 3,000-page indictment drawn by our representatives over 2 1/2 years does not even establish "reasonable grounds to believe" that further investigation or prosecution is warranted with respect to at least the principal alleged culprit? But the Act establishes more than just practical compulsion. Although the Court's opinion asserts that the Attorney General had "no duty to comply with the [congressional] request," that is not entirely accurate. He had a duty to comply unless he could conclude that there were "no reasonable grounds to believe," not that prosecution was warranted, but merely that "further investigation" was warranted, after a 90-day investigation in which he was prohibited from using such routine investigative techniques as grand juries, plea bargaining, grants of immunity, or even subpoenas, *see* § 592(a)(2). The Court also makes much of the fact that "the courts are specifically prevented from reviewing the Attorney General's decision not to seek appointment, § 592(f)." Yes, but Congress is not prevented from reviewing it. The context of this statute is acrid with the smell of threatened impeachment. Where, as here, a request for appointment of an independent counsel has come from the Judiciary Committee of either House of Congress, the Attorney General must, if he decides not to seek appointment, explain to that Committee why.

Thus, by the application of this statute in the present case, Congress has effectively compelled a criminal investigation of a high-level appointee of the President in connection with his actions arising out of a bitter power dispute between the President and the Legislative Branch. Mr. Olson may or may not be guilty of a crime; we do not know. But we do know that the investigation of him has been commenced, not necessarily because the President or his authorized subordinates believe it is in the interest of the United States, in the sense that it warrants the diversion of resources from other efforts, and is worth the cost in money and in possible damage to other governmental interests; and not even, leaving aside those normally considered factors, because the President or his authorized subordinates necessarily believe that an investigation is likely to unearth a violation worth prosecuting; but only because the Attorney General cannot affirm, as Congress demands, that there are no reasonable grounds to believe that further investigation is warranted. The decisions regarding the scope of that further investigation, its duration, and, finally, whether or not prosecution should ensue, are likewise beyond the control of the President and his subordinates.

II

If to describe this case is not to decide it, the concept of a government of separate and coordinate powers no longer has meaning. The Court devotes most of its attention to such relatively technical details as the Appointments Clause and the removal power, addressing briefly and only at the end of its opinion the separation of powers. As my prologue suggests, I think that has it backwards. Our opinions are full of the recognition that it is the principle of separation of powers, and the inseparable corollary that each department's "defense must . . . be made commensurate to the danger of attack," THE FEDERALIST NO. 51, at 322 (James Madison), which gives comprehensible content to the Appointments Clause, and determines the appropriate scope of the removal power.

* * *

First, however, I think it well to call to mind an important and unusual premise that underlies our deliberations, a premise not expressly contradicted by the Court's opinion, but in my view not faithfully observed. It is rare in a case dealing, as this one does, with the constitutionality of a statute passed by the Congress of the United States, not to find anywhere in the Court's opinion the usual, almost formulary caution that we owe great deference to Congress' view that what it has done is constitutional, and that we will decline to apply the statute only if the presumption of constitutionality can be overcome. That caution is not recited by the Court in the present case because it does not apply. Where a private citizen challenges action of the Government on grounds unrelated to separation of powers, harmonious functioning of the system demands that we ordinarily give some deference, or a presumption of validity, to the actions of the political branches in what is agreed, between themselves at least, to be within their respective spheres. But where the issue pertains to separation of powers, and the political branches are (as here) in disagreement, neither can be presumed correct. The reason is stated concisely by Madison: "The several departments being perfectly co-ordinate by the terms of their common commission, neither of them, it is evident, can pretend to an exclusive or superior right of settling the boundaries between their respective powers . . . ." THE FEDERALIST NO. 49. The playing field for the present case, in other words, is a level one. As one of the interested and coordinate parties to the underlying constitutional dispute, Congress, no more than the President, is entitled to the benefit of the doubt.

To repeat, Article II, § 1, cl. 1, of the Constitution provides:

"The executive Power shall be vested in a President of the United States."

As I described at the outset of this opinion, this does not mean some of the executive power, but all of the executive power. It seems to me, therefore, that the decision of the Court of Appeals invalidating the present statute must be upheld on fundamental separation-of-powers principles if the following two questions are answered affirmatively: (1) Is the conduct of a criminal prosecution (and of an investigation to decide whether to prosecute) the exercise of purely executive power? (2) Does the statute deprive the President of the United States of exclusive control over the exercise of that power? Surprising to say, the Court appears to concede an affirmative answer to both questions, but seeks to avoid the inevitable conclusion that since the statute vests some purely executive power in a person who is not the President of the United States it is void.

The Court concedes that "[t]here is no real dispute that the functions performed by the independent counsel are 'executive'," though it qualifies that concession by adding "in the sense that they are law enforcement functions that typically have been undertaken by officials within the Executive Branch." The qualifier adds nothing but atmosphere. In what other sense can one identify "the executive Power" that is supposed to be vested in the President (unless it includes everything the Executive Branch is given to do) except by reference to what has always and everywhere — if conducted by government at all — been conducted never by the legislature, never by the courts, and always by the executive. There is no possible doubt that the independent counsel's functions fit this description. She is vested with the "full power and independent authority to exercise all investigative and prosecutorial functions and powers of the

Department of Justice [and] the Attorney General." Governmental investigation and prosecution of crimes is a quintessentially executive function.

As for the second question, whether the statute before us deprives the President of exclusive control over that quintessentially executive activity: The Court does not, and could not possibly, assert that it does not. That is indeed the whole object of the statute. Instead, the Court points out that the President, through his Attorney General, has at least some control. That concession is alone enough to invalidate the statute, but I cannot refrain from pointing out that the Court greatly exaggerates the extent of that "some" Presidential control. . . . [I]ndeed, what *Humphrey's Executor* was all about — limiting removal power to "good cause" — is an impediment to, not an effective grant of, Presidential control. We said that limitation was necessary with respect to members of the Federal Trade Commission, which we found to be "an agency of the legislative and judicial departments," and "wholly disconnected from the executive department," because "it is quite evident that one who holds his office only during the pleasure of another, cannot be depended upon to maintain an attitude of independence against the latter's will." What we in *Humphrey's Executor* found to be a means of eliminating Presidential control, the Court today considers the "most importan[t]" means of assuring Presidential control. Congress, of course, operated under no such illusion when it enacted this statute, describing the "good cause" limitation as "protecting the independent counsel's ability to act independently of the President's direct control" since it permits removal only for "misconduct."

* * *

As I have said, however, it is ultimately irrelevant how much the statute reduces Presidential control. The case is over when the Court acknowledges, as it must, that "[i]t is undeniable that the Act reduces the amount of control or supervision that the Attorney General and, through him, the President exercises over the investigation and prosecution of a certain class of alleged criminal activity." It effects a revolution in our constitutional jurisprudence for the Court, once it has determined that (1) purely executive functions are at issue here, and (2) those functions have been given to a person whose actions are not fully within the supervision and control of the President, nonetheless to proceed further to sit in judgment of whether "the President's need to control the exercise of [the independent counsel's] discretion is so central to the functioning of the Executive Branch" as to require complete control, whether the conferral of his powers upon someone else "sufficiently deprives the President of control over the independent counsel to interfere impermissibly with [his] constitutional obligation to ensure the faithful execution of the laws," and whether "the Act give[s] the Executive Branch sufficient control over the independent counsel to ensure that the President is able to perform his constitutionally assigned duties." It is not for us to determine, and we have never presumed to determine, how much of the purely executive powers of government must be within the full control of the President. The Constitution prescribes that they all are.

The utter incompatibility of the Court's approach with our constitutional traditions can be made more clear, perhaps, by applying it to the powers of the other two branches. Is it conceivable that if Congress passed a statute depriving itself of less than full and entire control over some insignificant area of legislation, we would inquire whether the matter was "so central to the functioning of the Legislative Branch" as really to require complete control, or whether the statute gives Congress "sufficient control over the surrogate legislator to ensure that Congress is able to perform its constitutionally assigned duties"? Of course we would have none of that. Once we determined that a purely legislative power was at issue we would require it to be exercised, wholly and entirely, by Congress. Or to bring the point closer to home, consider a statute giving to non-Article III judges just a tiny bit of purely judicial power in a relatively insignificant field, with substantial control, though not total control, in the courts — perhaps "clear error" review, which would be a fair judicial equivalent of the Attorney General's "for cause" removal power here. Is there any doubt that we would not pause to inquire whether the matter was "so central to the functioning of the Judicial Branch" as really to require complete control, or whether we retained "sufficient control over the matters to be decided that we are able to perform our constitutionally assigned duties"? We would say that our "constitutionally assigned duties" include complete control over all exercises of the judicial power — or, as the plurality opinion said in *Northern Pipeline Construction Co. v. Marathon Pipe Line Co.* (1982): "The inexorable command of [Article III] is clear and definite: The judicial power of the United States must be exercised by courts having the attributes prescribed in Art. III." We should say here that the President's constitutionally assigned duties include complete control over investigation and prosecution of violations of the law, and that the inexorable command of Article II is clear and definite: the executive power must be vested in the President of the United States.

Is it unthinkable that the President should have such exclusive power, even when alleged crimes by him or his close associates are at issue? No more so than that Congress should have the exclusive power of legislation, even when what is at issue is its own exemption from the burdens of certain laws. . . . No more so than that this Court should have the exclusive power to pronounce the final decision on justiciable cases and controversies, even those pertaining to the constitutionality of a statute reducing the salaries of the Justices. A system of separate and coordinate powers necessarily involves an acceptance of exclusive power that can theoretically be abused. As we reiterate this very day, "[i]t is a truism that constitutional protections have costs." While the separation of powers may prevent us from righting every wrong, it does so in order to ensure that we do not lose liberty. The checks against any branch's abuse of its exclusive powers are twofold: First, retaliation by one of the other branch's use of its exclusive powers: Congress, for example, can impeach the executive who willfully fails to enforce the laws; the executive can decline to prosecute under unconstitutional statutes; and the courts can dismiss malicious prosecutions. Second, and ultimately, there is the political check that the people will replace those in the political branches (the branches more "dangerous to the political rights of the Constitution," THE FEDERALIST NO. 78, at 465) who are guilty of abuse. Political pressures produced special prosecutors — for Teapot Dome and for Watergate, for example — long before this statute created the independent counsel.

The Court has, nonetheless, replaced the clear constitutional prescription that the executive power belongs to the President with a "balancing test." What are the standards to determine how the balance is to be struck, that is, how much removal of Presidential power is too much? Many countries of the world get along with an executive that is much weaker than ours — in fact, entirely dependent upon the continued support of the legislature. Once we depart from the text of the Constitution, just where short of that do we stop? The most amazing feature of the Court's opinion is that it does not even purport to give an answer. It simply announces, with no analysis, that the ability to control the decision whether to investigate and prosecute the President's closest advisers, and indeed the President himself, is not "so central to the functioning of the Executive Branch" as to be constitutionally required to be within the President's control. Apparently that is so because we say it is so. Having abandoned as the basis for our decision-making the text of Article II that "the executive Power" must be vested in the President, the Court does not even attempt to craft a substitute criterion. . . . Evidently, the governing standard is to be what might be called the unfettered wisdom of a majority of this Court, revealed to an obedient people on a case-by-case basis. This is not only not the government of laws that the Constitution established; it is not a government of laws at all.

In my view, moreover, even as an ad hoc, standardless judgment the Court's conclusion must be wrong. . . . Perhaps the boldness of the President himself will not be affected — though I am not even sure of that. (How much easier it is for Congress, instead of accepting the political damage attendant to the commencement of impeachment proceedings against the President on trivial grounds — or, for that matter, how easy it is for one of the President's political foes outside of Congress — simply to trigger a debilitating criminal investigation of the Chief Executive under this law.) But as for the President's high-level assistants, who typically have no political base of support, it is as utterly unrealistic to think that they will not be intimidated by this prospect, and that their advice to him and their advocacy of his interests before a hostile Congress will not be affected, as it would be to think that the Members of Congress and their staffs would be unaffected by replacing the Speech or Debate Clause with a similar provision. It deeply wounds the President, by substantially reducing the President's ability to protect himself and his staff. That is the whole object of the law, of course, and I cannot imagine why the Court believes it does not succeed.

Besides weakening the Presidency by reducing the zeal of his staff, it must also be obvious that the institution of the independent counsel enfeebles him more directly in his constant confrontations with Congress, by eroding his public support. Nothing is so politically effective as the ability to charge that one's opponent and his associates are not merely wrongheaded, naive, ineffective, but, in all probability, "crooks." And nothing so effectively gives an appearance of validity to such charges as a Justice Department investigation and, even better, prosecution. The present statute provides ample means for that sort of attack, assuring that massive and lengthy investigations will occur, not merely when the Justice Department in the application of its usual standards believes they are called for, but whenever it cannot be said that there are "no reasonable grounds to believe" they are called for. . . .

* * *

The final set of reasons given by the Court for why the independent counsel clearly is an inferior officer emphasizes the limited nature of her jurisdiction and tenure. Taking the latter first, I find nothing unusually limited about the independent counsel's tenure. To the contrary, unlike most high-ranking Executive Branch officials, she continues to serve until she (or the Special Division) decides that her work is substantially completed. This particular independent prosecutor has already served more than two years, which is at least as long as many Cabinet officials. As to the scope of her jurisdiction, there can be no doubt that is small (though far from unimportant). But within it she exercises more than the full power of the Attorney General. The Ambassador to Luxembourg is not anything less than a principal officer, simply because Luxembourg is small. And the federal judge who sits in a small district is not for that reason "inferior in rank and authority." If the mere fragmentation of executive responsibilities into small compartments suffices to render the heads of each of those compartments inferior officers, then Congress could deprive the President of the right to appoint his chief law enforcement officer by dividing up the Attorney General's responsibilities among a number of "lesser" functionaries.

* * *

That "inferior" means "subordinate" is also consistent with what little we know about the evolution of the Appointments Clause. As originally reported to the Committee on Style, the Appointments Clause provided no "exception" from the standard manner of appointment (President with the advice and consent of the Senate) for inferior officers. 2 RECORDS OF THE FEDERAL CONVENTION OF 1787, at 498-99, 599 (Max Farrand ed., rev. ed. 1966). On September 15, 1787, the last day of the Convention before the proposed Constitution was signed, in the midst of a host of minor changes that were being considered, Gouverneur Morris moved to add the exceptions clause. No great debate ensued; the only disagreement was over whether it was necessary at all. Nobody thought that it was a fundamental change, excluding from the President's appointment power and the Senate's confirmation power a category of officers who might function on their own, outside the supervision of those appointed in the more cumbersome fashion. . . . It is perfectly obvious, therefore, both from the relative brevity of the discussion this addition received, and from the content of that discussion, that it was intended merely to make clear that those officers appointed by the President with Senate approval could on their own appoint their subordinates, who would, of course, by chain of command still be under the direct control of the President.

This interpretation is, moreover, consistent with our admittedly sketchy precedent in this area. . . .

* * *

To be sure, it is not a sufficient condition for "inferior" officer status that one be subordinate to a principal officer. Even an officer who is subordinate to a department head can be a principal officer. That is clear from the brief exchange following Gouverneur Morris' suggestion of the addition of the exceptions clause for inferior officers. Madison responded:

> "It does not go far enough if it be necessary at all — *Superior Officers below Heads of Departments* ought in some cases to have the appointment of the lesser offices." 2 RECORDS OF THE FEDERAL CONVENTION OF 1787, at 627 (Max Farrand ed., rev. ed. 1966) (emphasis added).

But it is surely a necessary condition for inferior officer status that the officer be subordinate to another officer.

The independent counsel is not even subordinate to the President. The Court essentially admits as much, noting that "appellant may not be 'subordinate' to the Attorney General (and the President) insofar as she possesses a degree of independent discretion to exercise the powers delegated to her under the Act." In fact, there is no doubt about it. . . .

Because appellant is not subordinate to another officer, she is not an "inferior" officer and her appointment other than by the President with the advice and consent of the Senate is unconstitutional.

IV

* * *

There is, of course, no provision in the Constitution stating who may remove executive officers, except the provisions for removal by impeachment. Before the present decision it was established, however, (1) that the President's power to remove principal officers who exercise purely executive powers could not be restricted, *see Myers v. United States*, and (2) that his power to remove inferior officers who exercise purely executive powers, and whose appointment Congress had removed from the usual procedure of Presidential appointment with Senate consent, could be restricted, at least where the appointment had been made by an officer of the Executive Branch.

The Court could have resolved the removal power issue in this case by simply relying upon its erroneous conclusion that the independent counsel was an inferior officer, and then extending our holding that the removal of inferior officers appointed by the Executive can be restricted, to a new holding that even the removal of inferior officers appointed by the courts can be restricted. That would in my view be a considerable and unjustified extension, giving the Executive full discretion in neither the selection nor the removal of a purely executive officer. The course the Court has chosen, however, is even worse.

* * *

Since our 1935 decision in *Humphrey's Executor v. United States* — which was considered by many at the time the product of an activist, anti-New Deal Court bent on reducing the power of President Franklin Roosevelt — it has been established that the line of permissible restriction upon removal of principal officers lies at the point at which the powers exercised by those officers are no longer purely executive. Thus, removal restrictions have been generally regarded as lawful for so-called "independent regulatory agencies," . . . which engage substantially in what has been called the "quasi-legislative activity" of rulemaking, and for members of Article I courts, such as the Court of Military Appeals, who engage in the "quasi-judicial" function of adjudication. It has often been observed, correctly in my view, that the line between "purely executive" functions and "quasi-legislative" or "quasi- judicial" functions is not a clear one or even a rational one. But at least it permitted the identification of certain officers, and certain agencies, whose functions were entirely within the control of the President. Congress had to be aware of that restriction in its legislation. Today, however, *Humphrey's Executor* is swept into the dustbin of repudiated constitutional principles. "[O]ur present considered view," the Court says, "is that the determination of whether the Constitution allows Congress to impose a 'good cause'-type restriction on the President's power to remove an official cannot be made to turn on whether or not that official is classified as 'purely executive.'" What *Humphrey's Executor* (and presumably *Myers*) really means, we are now told, is not that there are any "rigid categories of those officials who may or may not be removed at will by the President," but simply that Congress cannot "intereference with the President's exercise of the 'executive power' and his constitutionally appointed duty to 'take care that the laws be faithfully executed.'"

One can hardly grieve for the shoddy treatment given today to *Humphrey's Executor*, which, after all, accorded the same indignity (with much less justification) to Chief Justice Taft's opinion 10 years earlier in *Myers v. United States* — gutting, in six quick pages devoid of textual or historical precedent for the novel principle it set forth, a carefully researched and reasoned 70-page opinion. It is in fact comforting to witness the reality that he who lives by the *ipse dixit* dies by the *ipse dixit*. But one must grieve for the Constitution. *Humphrey's Executor* at least had the decency formally to observe the constitutional principle that the President had to be the repository of all executive power, which, as *Myers* carefully explained, necessarily means that he must be able to discharge those who do not perform executive functions according to his liking. By contrast, "our present considered view" is simply that any executive officer's removal can be restricted, so long as the President remains "able to accomplish his constitutional role." There are now no lines. If the removal of a prosecutor, the virtual embodiment of the power to "take care that the laws be faithfully executed," can be restricted, what officer's removal cannot?

* * *

V

The purpose of the separation and equilibration of powers in general, and of the unitary Executive in particular, was not merely to assure effective government but to preserve individual freedom. Those who hold or have held offices covered by the Ethics in Government Act are entitled to that protection as much as the rest of us, and I conclude my discussion by considering the effect of the Act upon the fairness of the process they receive.

Only someone who has worked in the field of law enforcement can fully appreciate the vast power and the immense discretion that are placed in the hands of a prosecutor with respect to the objects of his investigation. Justice Robert Jackson, when he was Attorney General under President Franklin Roosevelt, described it in a memorable speech to United States Attorneys, as follows:

> "There is a most important reason why the prosecutor should have, as nearly as possible, a detached and impartial view of all groups in his community. Law enforcement is not automatic. It isn't blind. One of the greatest difficulties of the position of prosecutor is that he must pick his cases, because no prosecutor can even investigate all of the cases in which he receives complaints. If the Department of Justice were to make even a pretense of reaching every probable violation of federal law, ten times its present staff will be inadequate. We know that no local police force can strictly enforce the traffic laws, or it would arrest half the driving population on any given morning. What every prosecutor is practically required to do is to select the cases for prosecution and to select those in which the offense is the most flagrant, the public harm the greatest, and the proof the most certain.

> "If the prosecutor is obliged to choose his case, it follows that he can choose his defendants. Therein is the most dangerous power of the prosecutor: that he will pick people that he thinks he should get, rather than cases that need to be prosecuted. With the law books filled with a great assortment of crimes, a prosecutor stands a fair chance of finding at least a technical violation of some act on the part of almost anyone. In such a case, it is not a question of discovering the commission of a crime and then looking for the man who has committed it, it is a question of picking the man and then searching the law books, or putting investigators to work, to pin some offense on him. It is in this realm — in which the prosecutor picks some person whom he dislikes or desires to embarrass, or selects some group of unpopular persons and then looks for an offense, that the greatest danger of abuse of prosecuting power lies. It is here that law enforcement becomes personal, and the real crime becomes that of being unpopular with the predominant or

governing group, being attached to the wrong political views, or being personally obnoxious to or in the way of the prosecutor himself." R. Jackson, The Federal Prosecutor, Address Delivered at the Second Annual Conference of United States Attorneys (Apr. 1, 1940).

Under our system of government, the primary check against prosecutorial abuse is a political one. The prosecutors who exercise this awesome discretion are selected and can be removed by a President, whom the people have trusted enough to elect. Moreover, when crimes are not investigated and prosecuted fairly, nonselectively, with a reasonable sense of proportion, the President pays the cost in political damage to his administration. If federal prosecutors "pick people that [they] thin[k] [they] should get, rather than cases that need to be prosecuted," if they amass many more resources against a particular prominent individual, or against a particular class of political protesters, or against members of a particular political party, than the gravity of the alleged offenses or the record of successful prosecutions seems to warrant, the unfairness will come home to roost in the Oval Office. I leave it to the reader to recall the examples of this in recent years. That result, of course, was precisely what the Founders had in mind when they provided that all executive powers would be exercised by a single Chief Executive. As Hamilton put it, "[t]he ingredients which constitute safety in the republican sense are a due dependence on the people, and a due responsibility." THE FEDERALIST NO. 70. The President is directly dependent on the people, and since there is only one President, he is responsible. The people know whom to blame, whereas "one of the weightiest objections to a plurality in the executive . . . is that it tends to conceal faults and destroy responsibility."

That is the system of justice the rest of us are entitled to, but what of that select class consisting of present or former high-level Executive Branch officials? If an allegation is made against them of any violation of any federal criminal law (except Class B or C misdemeanors or infractions) the Attorney General must give it his attention. That in itself is not objectionable. But if, after a 90-day investigation without the benefit of normal investigatory tools, the Attorney General is unable to say that there are "no reasonable grounds to believe" that further investigation is warranted, a process is set in motion that is not in the full control of persons "dependent on the people," and whose flaws cannot be blamed on the President. An independent counsel is selected, and the scope of his or her authority prescribed, by a panel of judges. What if they are politically partisan, as judges have been known to be, and select a prosecutor antagonistic to the administration, or even to the particular individual who has been selected for this special treatment? There is no remedy for that, not even a political one. Judges, after all, have life tenure, and appointing a surefire enthusiastic prosecutor could hardly be considered an impeachable offense. So if there is anything wrong with the selection, there is effectively no one to blame. The independent counsel thus selected proceeds to assemble a staff. As I observed earlier, in the nature of things this has to be done by finding lawyers who are willing to lay aside their current careers for an indeterminate amount of time, to take on a job that has no prospect of permanence and little prospect for promotion. One thing is certain, however: it involves investigating and perhaps prosecuting a particular individual. Can one imagine a less equitable manner of fulfilling the executive responsibility to investigate and prosecute? What would be the reaction if, in an area not covered by this statute, the Justice Department posted a public notice inviting applicants to assist in an investigation and possible prosecution of a certain prominent person? Does this not invite what Justice Jackson described as "picking the man and then searching the law books, or putting investigators to work, to pin some offense on him"? . . .

* * *

The above described possibilities of irresponsible conduct must, as I say, be considered in judging the constitutional acceptability of this process. But they will rarely occur, and in the average case the threat to fairness is quite different. As described in the brief filed on behalf of three ex-Attorneys General from each of the last three administrations:

> "The problem is less spectacular but much more worrisome. It is that the institutional environment of the Independent Counsel — specifically, her isolation from the Executive Branch and the internal checks and balances it supplies — is designed to heighten, not to check, all of the occupational hazards of the dedicated prosecutor; the danger of too narrow a focus, of the loss of perspective, of preoccupation with the pursuit of one alleged suspect to the exclusion of other interests." Brief for Edward H. Levi, Griffin B. Bell, and William French Smith as *Amici Curiae* 11.

It is, in other words, an additional advantage of the unitary Executive that it can achieve a more uniform application of the law. Perhaps that is not always achieved, but the mechanism to achieve it is there. The mini-Executive that is the independent counsel, however, operating in an area where so little is law and so much is discretion, is intentionally cut off from the unifying influence of the Justice Department, and from the perspective that multiple responsibilities provide. What would normally be regarded as a technical violation (there are no rules defining such things), may in his or her small world assume the proportions of an indictable offense. What would normally be regarded as an investigation that has reached the level of pursuing such picayune matters that it should be concluded, may to him or her be an investigation that ought to go on for another year. How frightening it must be to have your own independent counsel and staff appointed, with nothing else to do but to investigate you until investigation is no longer worthwhile — with whether it is worthwhile not depending upon what such judgments usually hinge on, competing responsibilities. And to have that counsel and staff decide, with no basis for comparison, whether what you have done is bad enough, willful enough, and provable enough, to warrant an indictment. How admirable the constitutional system that provides the means to avoid such a distortion. And how unfortunate the judicial decision that has permitted it.

* * *

The notion that every violation of law should be prosecuted, including — indeed, especially — every violation by those in high places, is an attractive one, and it would be risky to argue in an election campaign that is not an absolutely overriding value. *Fiat justitia, ruat coelum.* Let justice be done, though the heavens may fall. The reality is, however, that it is not an absolutely overriding value, and it was with the hope that we would be able to acknowledge and apply such realities that the Constitution spared us, by life tenure, the necessity of election campaigns. I cannot imagine that there are not many thoughtful men and women in Congress who realize that the benefits of this legislation are far outweighed by its harmful effect upon our system of government, and even upon the nature of justice received by those men and women who agree to serve in the Executive Branch. But it is difficult to vote not to enact, and even more difficult to vote to repeal, a statute called, appropriately enough, the Ethics in Government Act. If Congress is controlled by the party other than the one to which the President belongs, it has little incentive to repeal it; if it is controlled by the same party, it dare not. By its shortsighted action today, I fear the Court has permanently encumbered the Republic with an institution that will do it great harm.

Worse than what it has done, however, is the manner in which it has done it. A government of laws means a government of rules. Today's decision on the basic issue of fragmentation of executive power is ungoverned by rule, and hence ungoverned by law.

NOTES AND QUESTIONS

1. Following the decision in *Morrison*, the prosecution against Mr. Olson continued. After several years of litigation and close to two million dollars in legal fees for Mr. Olson, Independent Counsel Morrison found no basis to prosecute and dropped the case. Philip Stenon, *Special Prosecutor Drops E.P.A. Case without Indictment*, N.Y. TIMES, Aug. 27, 1988, § 1, at 1.

2. As mentioned earlier, the case against Mr. Olson suggests that the Independent Counsel Act may at times be an invitation for separation of powers disputes to be transformed into criminal cases. The more this occurs the more the independent counsel law jeopardizes the constitutional structure crafted in Montesquieu's image, and perhaps as well the administration of equal justice under law. Former University of Chicago Law School Dean and U.S. Attorney General Edward Levi was prescient about these risks when the Act was first proposed in 1976. Levi stated: "[i]t would create opportunities for actual or apparent partisan influence in law enforcement; [and] publicize and dignify unfounded, scurrilous allegations against public officials." *Committee on the Judiciary Subcommittee on Administrative Law*, 100th Cong., 1st Sess. 5 (1987) (statement of William French Smith before the House Judiciary Committee 5 (quoting Edward H. Levi)). When the law came up for re-authorization in 1987, former Attorney General William French Smith confirmed that the law had lived up (or more accurately down) to Levi's fears. The act, said Smith, has been used on a continuing basis "for essentially political purposes — in some cases blatantly — by members of Congress and others." *Id.* at 6. Griffin Bell, Attorney General under President Carter, did not originally oppose the legislation because Mr. Carter was one of the law's supporters. However, the gross politicization of law enforcement that resulted, prompted even Bell to testify against the law's continuation. The law from beginning to end, observed Bell, "seems almost to be set up to create publicity." *Independent Counsel Amendments Act of 1987: Hearings on H.R. 1520 and H.R. 2939 Before the Subcomm. on Admin. Law and Gov't Relations of the House Judiciary Comm.*, 100th Cong. 773 (1988) (statement of former Attorney General Griffin B. Bell).

The criticism of the law is thus bipartisan. While Democratic concern with the unfairness of the independent counsel structure was muted during the Republican administrations of Ronald Reagan and George Bush, *see generally*, DOUGLAS W. KMIEC, THE ATTORNEY GENERAL'S LAWYER Chs. 1, 3, and 9 (1992), the extended independent counsel investigation of President Clinton prompted his former White House Counsel, Abner Mikva, to say: "I am very disappointed [in the independent counsel]. He has diminished the institution of the presidency and exacerbated all of the problems of the independent counsel. . . . [The independent counsel] hauled [Mrs. Clinton] before the grand jury to try to please his patrons." Albert R. Hunt, *A Falling Starr,* WALL ST. J., June 19, 1997 at A19.

The independent counsel law was allowed to expire at the end of June 1999. By the time of its expiration, virtually no one — not even present or former independent counsels — appeared to believe that it could or should be salvaged. For example, Judge Starr himself testified against the law's renewal. A day after the law expired, the Attorney General issued rules bringing the investigation of high-ranking officials back within the Department of Justice. The Attorney General claimed that the new rules would "strike the proper balance between accountability and independence." The rules give the Attorney General the sole authority to appoint a prosecutor, to be called a special counsel, if he or she determines the Justice Department would have a conflict of interest in investigating allegations of wrongdoing, and if he or she decides that naming an outside prosecutor would be in the public interest. The Attorney General would then outline the boundaries of the investigation, although a special prosecutor could ask that those boundaries be extended to cover new matters that might later surface. A special counsel would not be subject to day-to-day supervision by the Justice Department, but would be required to comply with its practices and seek guidance from department officials on those policies. Justice Department commentary on the rules said that particular provision would "help to guard against a special counsel becoming too insulated and narrow in his or her view of the matter under investigation." A prosecutor would have to notify the Attorney General before seeking an indictment in a sensitive case, and the Attorney General could veto a planned indictment. The Attorney General also would have veto power over appeals, and in some instances over investigative steps he or she considered unwarranted or inappropriate. If the Attorney General vetoed a proposed action by a prosecutor, the Attorney General would be required to notify Congress at the end of the investigation and explain why the action was not approved. Special counsels could be fired for good cause by the Attorney General. The Justice Department would set a special counsel's budget. Unlike the recently expired law which had the potential of being easily used to tarnish the innocent, an outside prosecutor's final report would be submitted only to the Attorney General, and generally would be kept confidential.

3. Apart from the merits or demerits of independent counsels, *Morrison* subtly raises anew the larger concern with unsupervised, and therefore, uncontrollable independent administrative agencies. Is there anything in the *Morrison* majority opinion that demonstrates sensitivity to this? Perhaps. While not the usual assessment, there is an argument that the Court did advance presidential supervision of independent agencies in *Morrison* even though the Court upheld the constitutionality of the independent counsel statute. In particular, Chief Justice Rehnquist's opinion may reasonably be read as going a fair distance toward limiting the more expansive readings of *Humphrey's Executor* that have been propping up independent agencies generally.

The Court admitted that in its prior cases it had relied on terms like "quasi-legislative" and "quasi-judicial" to explain why Congress could impose a "good cause" limitation on an official exercising such hybrid power. However, in *Morrison*, the Court stated that this missed the essential point, which is:

> not to define rigid categories of those officials who may or may not be removed at will by the President, but to ensure that Congress does not interfere with the President's exercise of "executive power" and his constitutionally appointed duty to "take care that the laws be faithfully executed" under Article II.

Morrison, 487 U.S. at 689-90. In essence, the Court seemed to be saying: worry less about whether an executive officer is removable at will and focus more on whether an officer performing executive duties (in or outside an independent agency) is carrying out the President's instructions. Even in *Morrison*, the Court stressed that its willingness to uphold the removal limitation was contingent on its finding that it would not "impermissibly burden the President's power to control or supervise the independent counsel." *Id.* at 692. Thus, *Morrison* may have refocused the discussion on the control of the substance of independent agency work. In this, *Morrison* was reflecting the modern view that the regulatory work product of all executive agencies, including the independents, should directly reflect presidential policy choices. *Cf. Chevron U.S.A., Inc. v. Natural Resources Defense Council, Inc.*, 467 U.S. 837 (1984).

4. Agencies can reflect presidential policy choices, of course, only if the agency has statutory authority to carry out the President's direction. Statutes are often written broadly (or ambiguously) and so the question arises of how much deference courts should give agencies in the choices they make. President Clinton encouraged the Food and Drug Administration (FDA) to treat tobacco as a drug and to curtail access to tobacco by young people who had not yet become addicted. The FDA had declined to treat tobacco as a drug for over forty years, however, and when it responded to President Clinton's direction in 1996, a 5-4 Court concluded that it was too late, even with the deference judges are to give to agency decision-making. In *Food and Drug Administration v. Brown & Williamson Tobacco Corporation*, 529 U.S. 120 (2000), Justice O'Connor wrote:

> Regardless of how serious the problem an administrative agency seeks to address, however, it may not exercise its authority "in a manner that is inconsistent with the administrative structure that Congress enacted into law." And although agencies are generally entitled to deference in the interpretation of statutes that they administer, a reviewing "court, as well as the agency, must give effect to the unambiguously expressed intent of Congress." *Chevron U.S.A. Inc. v. Natural Resources Defense Council, Inc.* (1984). In this case, we believe that Congress has clearly precluded the FDA from asserting jurisdiction to regulate tobacco products. Such authority is inconsistent with the intent that Congress has expressed in the [Food, Drug and Cosmetics Act (FDCA)], FDCA's overall regulatory scheme and in the tobacco-specific legislation that it has enacted subsequent to the FDCA. In light of this clear intent, the FDA's assertion of jurisdiction is impermissible.
>
> . . . Because this case involves an administrative agency's construction of a statute that it administers, our analysis is governed by *Chevron*. Under *Chevron*, a reviewing court must first ask "whether Congress has directly spoken to the precise question at issue." If Congress has done so, the inquiry is at an end; the court "must give effect to the unambiguously expressed intent of Congress." But if Congress has not specifically addressed the question, a reviewing court must respect the agency's construction of the statute so long as it is permissible. Such deference is justified because "[t]he responsibilities for assessing the wisdom of such policy choices and resolving the struggle between competing views of the public interest are not judicial ones," and because of the agency's greater familiarity with the ever-changing facts and circumstances surrounding the subjects regulated.

Chevron is a key decision in administrative law and well worth special study in a course devoted to that topic. As Justice O'Connor indicated, *Chevron* cautions courts not to substitute their judgment for that of an agency unless the agency has misconstrued the statutory language. Could one really say that is what the FDA did in belatedly regulating tobacco? Justice O'Connor and the majority thought so, explaining:

> . . . These findings logically imply that, if tobacco products were "devices" under the FDCA, the FDA would be required to remove them from the market. Consider, first, the FDCA's provisions concerning the mis-

branding of drugs or devices. The Act prohibits "[t]he introduction or delivery for introduction into interstate commerce of any food, drug, device, or cosmetic that is adultered or misbranded." In light of the FDA's findings, two distinct FDCA provisions would render cigarettes and smokeless tobacco misbranded devices. First, [the Act] deems a drug or device [is] misbranded "[i]f it is dangerous to health when used in the dosage or manner, or with the frequency or duration prescribed, recommended, or suggested in the labeling thereof." The FDA's findings make clear that tobacco products are "dangerous to health" when used in the manner prescribed. Second, a drug or device is misbranded under the Act "[u]nless its labeling bears . . . adequate directions for use . . . in such manner and form, as are necessary for the protection of users," except where such directions are "not necessary for the protection of the public health." Given the FDA's conclusions concerning the health consequences of tobacco use, there are no directions that could adequately protect consumers. That is, there are no directions that could make tobacco products safe for obtaining their intended effects. Thus, were tobacco products within the FDA's jurisdiction, the Act would deem them misbranded devices that could not be introduced into interstate commerce.

But, asserted the majority, the FDA has no authority to remove tobacco from the market because:

Congress, however, has foreclosed the removal of tobacco products from the market. A provision of the United States Code currently in force states that "[t]he marketing of tobacco constitutes one of the greatest basic industries of the United States with ramifying activities which directly affect interstate and foreign commerce at every point, and stable conditions therein are necessary to the general welfare." More importantly, Congress has directly addressed the problem of tobacco and health through legislation on six occasions since 1965. When Congress enacted these statutes, the adverse health consequences of tobacco use were well known, as were nicotine's pharmacological effects. . . . Nonetheless, Congress stopped well short of ordering a ban. Instead, it has generally regulated the labeling and advertisement of tobacco products, expressly providing that it is the policy of Congress that "commerce and the national economy may be . . . protected to the maximum extent consistent with" consumers "be[ing] adequately informed about any adverse health effects." Congress' decisions to regulate labeling and advertising and to adopt the express policy of protecting "commerce and the national economy . . . to the maximum extent" reveal its intent that tobacco products remain on the market. Indeed, the collective premise of these statutes is that cigarettes and smokeless tobacco will continue to be sold in the United States. A ban of tobacco products by the FDA would therefore plainly contradict congressional policy.

Writing for the four person dissent, Justice Breyer, an expert in administrative law and former teacher of the subject at Harvard University, thought the Court had simply substituted its view for that of the agency and the President, and in this, an unelected body's policy prevailed over that of the elected, and more politically accountable officials. Justice Breyer wrote:

> The Food and Drug Administration has the authority to regulate "articles (other than food) intended to affect the structure or any function of the body . . . ." Federal Food, Drug and Cosmetic Act. Unlike the majority, I believe that tobacco products fit within this statutory language.

> In its own interpretation, the majority nowhere denies the following two salient points. First, tobacco products (including cigarettes) fall within the scope of this statutory definition, read literally. Cigarettes achieve their mood-stabilizing effects through the interaction of the chemical nicotine and the cells of the central nervous system. Both cigarette manufacturers and smokers alike know of, and desire, that chemically induced result. Hence, cigarettes are "intended to affect" the body's "structure" and "function," in the literal sense of these words.

> Second, the statute's basic purpose — the protection of public health — supports the inclusion of cigarettes within its scope. Unregulated tobacco use causes "[m]ore than 400,000 people [to] die each year from tobacco-related illnesses, such as cancer, respiratory illnesses, and heart disease." Indeed, tobacco products kill more people in this country every year "than . . . AIDS, car accidents, alcohol, homicides, illegal drugs, suicides, and fires, combined."

Nor did the dissent think that the FDA's broad authority precluded a lesser remedy (regulation of access by the young). Justice Breyer again explained:

> The majority . . . reaches the "inescapable conclusion" that the language and structure of the FDCA as a whole "simply do not fit" the kind of public health problem that tobacco creates. That is because, in the majority's view, the FDCA requires the FDA to ban outright "dangerous" drugs or devices (such as cigarettes); yet, the FDA concedes that an immediate and total cigarette-sale ban is inappropriate.

> This argument is curious because it leads with similarly "inescapable" force to precisely the opposite conclusion, namely, that the FDA does have jurisdiction but that it must ban cigarettes. More importantly, the argument fails to take into account the fact that a statute interpreted as requiring the FDA to pick a more dangerous over a less dangerous remedy [the FDA believed an outright ban would have serious health effects on those addicted and create a black market] would be a perverse statute, causing, rather than preventing, unnecessary harm whenever a total ban is likely the more dangerous response.

As for why the agency previously denied its regulatory authority earlier and should be allowed to follow new presidential direction now, Justice Breyer wrote:

. . . What changed? For one thing, the FDA obtained evidence sufficient to prove the necessary "intent" despite the absence of specific "claims." This evidence, which first became available in the early 1990's, permitted the agency to demonstrate that the tobacco companies knew nicotine achieved appetite-suppressing, mood-stabilizing, and habituating effects through chemical (not psychological) means, even at a time when the companies were publicly denying such knowledge.

Moreover, scientific evidence of adverse health effects mounted, until, in the late 1980's, a consensus on the seriousness of the matter became firm. That is not to say that concern about smoking's adverse health effects is a new phenomenon. It is to say, however, that convincing epidemiological evidence began to appear mid-20th century; that the First Surgeon General's Report documenting the adverse health effects appeared in 1964; and that the Surgeon General's Report establishing nicotine's addictive effects appeared in 1988. At each stage, the health conclusions were the subject of controversy, diminishing somewhat over time, until recently — and only recently — has it become clear that there is a wide consensus about the health problem.

Finally, administration policy changed. Earlier administrations may have hesitated to assert jurisdiction for the reasons prior Commissioners expressed. Commissioners of the current administration simply took a different regulatory attitude.

Nothing in the law prevents the FDA from changing its policy for such reasons.

. . . Insofar as the decision to regulate tobacco reflects the policy of an administration, it is a decision for which that administration, and those politically elected officials who support it, must (and will) take responsibility. And the very importance of the decision taken here, as well as its attendant publicity, means that the public is likely to be aware of it and to hold those officials politically accountable. Presidents, just like Members of Congress, are elected by the public. Indeed, the President and Vice President are the only public officials whom the entire Nation elects. I do not believe that an administrative agency decision of this magnitude — one that is important, conspicuous, and controversial — can escape the kind of public scrutiny that is essential in any democracy. And such a review will take place whether it is the Congress or the Executive Branch that makes the relevant decision.

The majority finds that cigarettes are so dangerous that the FDCA would require them to be banned (a result the majority believes Congress would not have desired); thus, it concludes that the FDA has no tobacco-related authority. I disagree that the statute would require a cigarette ban. But even if I am wrong about the ban, the statute would restrict only the agency's choice of remedies, not its jurisdiction.

5. The Court further trimmed *Chevron* deference in *United States v. Mead Corporation*, 533 U.S. 218 (2001), where in an 8-1 opinion the Court gave reduced deference to informal letter rulings (informal adjudication), rather than formal administrative adjudication or notice and comment rulemaking (sometimes confusingly called informal rulemaking).

Mead imported "day planners," three-ring binders with pages for daily schedules, phone numbers and addresses, a calendar, and suchlike. After classifying the planners as duty-free for several years, Customs Headquarters issued a ruling letter classifying them as bound diaries subject to tariff. Mead filed suit in the Court of International Trade and ultimately prevailed in the Federal Circuit which found that ruling letters should not be treated like Customs regulations, which receive the highest level of deference under *Chevron*, because ruling letters are not preceded by notice and comment as under the Administrative Procedure Act (APA), do not carry the force of law, and are not intended to clarify importers' rights and obligations beyond the specific case. While the Federal Circuit gave no deference at all to the ruling letter at issue, the Supreme Court per Justice Souter found that under *Skidmore v. Swift & Co.*, 323 U.S. 134 (1944), the ruling is eligible to claim respect according to its persuasiveness. The weight accorded to an administrative judgment "will depend upon the thoroughness evident in its consideration, the validity of its reasoning, its consistency with earlier and later pronouncements, and all those factors which give it power to persuade, if lacking power to control." *Skidmore, supra*, at 140.

Justice Scalia vigorously dissented, calling the opinion "one of the most significant opinions ever rendered by the Court dealing with the judicial review of administrative action, and predicting that "[i]ts consequences will be enormous, and almost uniformly bad." (Scalia, J., dissenting). According to Justice Scalia, "[w]hereas previously a reasonable agency application of an ambiguous statutory provision had to be sustained so long as it represented the agency's authoritative interpretation, henceforth such an application can be set aside unless 'it appears that Congress delegated authority to the agency generally to make rules carrying the force of law,' as by giving an agency 'power to engage in adjudication or notice-and-comment rulemaking, or . . . some other [procedure] indicati[ng] comparable congressional intent,' and 'the agency interpretation claiming deference was promulgated in the exercise of that authority.' What was previously a general presumption of authority in agencies to resolve ambiguity in the statutes they have been authorized to enforce has been changed to a presumption of no such authority, which must be overcome by affirmative legislative intent to the contrary. And whereas previously, when agency authority to resolve ambiguity did not exist the court was free to give the statute what it considered the best interpretation, henceforth the court must supposedly give the agency view some indeterminate amount of so-called *Skidmore* deference."

What all that means, says the dissent, is anybody's guess, but at a minimum he predicts that it will result in an "ossification of large portions of statutory law." Why would that be? Well, says Justice Scalia, because where *Chevron* previously applied, statutory ambiguities remain ambiguities subject to the agency's ongoing clarification. "They create a space, so to speak, for the exercise of continuing agency discretion." But "for the indeterminately large number of statutes taken out of *Chevron* by today's decision, however, ambiguity (and hence flexibility) will cease with the first judicial resolution. *Skidmore* deference gives the agency's current position some vague and uncertain amount of respect, but it does not, like *Chevron*, leave the matter within the control of the Executive Branch for the future. Once the court has spoken, it becomes unlawful for the agency to take a contradictory position; the statute now says what the court has prescribed. It will be bad enough when this ossification occurs as a result of judicial determination (under today's new principles) that there is no affirmative indication of congressional intent to 'delegate'; but it will be positively bizarre when it occurs simply because of an agency's failure to act by rulemaking (rather than informal adjudication) before the issue is presented to the courts." Justice Scalia's final words: "We will be sorting out the consequences of the Mead doctrine, which has today replaced the *Chevron* doctrine, for years to come."

c. The President and the World (Herein of Foreign Policy)

UNITED STATES v. CURTISS-WRIGHT EXPORT CORPORATION
299 U.S. 304 (1936)

Mr. Justice Sutherland delivered the opinion of the Court.

On January 27, 1936, an indictment was returned in the court below, the first count of which charges that appellees, beginning with the 29th day of May, 1934, conspired to sell in the United States certain arms of war, namely, fifteen machine guns, to Bolivia, a country then engaged in armed conflict in the Chaco, in violation of the Joint Resolution of Congress approved May 28, 1934, and the provisions of a proclamation issued on the same day by the President of the United States pursuant to authority conferred by section 1 of the resolution. In pursuance of the conspiracy, the commission of certain overt acts was alleged, details of which need not be stated. The Joint Resolution follows:

> "Resolved by the Senate and House of Representatives of the United States of America in Congress assembled, That if the President finds that the prohibition of the sale of arms and munitions of war in the United States to those countries now engaged in armed conflict in the Chaco may contribute to the reestablishment of peace between those

countries, and if after consultation with the governments of other American Republics and with their cooperation, as well as that of such other governments as he may deem necessary, he makes proclamation to that effect, it shall be unlawful to sell . . . ."

The President's proclamation, after reciting the terms of the Joint Resolution, declares:

"Now, Therefore, I, Franklin D. Roosevelt, President of the United States of America, acting under and by virtue of the authority conferred in me by the said joint resolution of Congress, do hereby declare and proclaim that I have found that the prohibition of the sale of arms and munitions of war in the United States to those countries now engaged in armed conflict in the Chaco may contribute to the reestablishment of peace between those countries, . . . and I do hereby admonish all citizens of the United States and every person to abstain from every violation of the provisions of the joint resolution above set forth, hereby made applicable to Bolivia and Paraguay, and I do hereby warn them that all violations of such provisions will be rigorously prosecuted."

On November 14, 1935, this proclamation was revoked . . . .

Appellees severally demurred to the first count of the indictment on the grounds . . . (2) that this count of the indictment charges a conspiracy to violate the Joint Resolution and the Presidential proclamation, both of which had expired according to the terms of the Joint Resolution by reason of the revocation contained in the Presidential proclamation of November 14, 1935, and were not in force at the time when the indictment was found. The points urged in support of the demurrers were, first, that the Joint Resolution effects an invalid delegation of legislative power to the executive . . . .

The court below sustained the demurrers upon the first point . . . .

First. It is contended that by the Joint Resolution the going into effect and continued operation of the resolution was conditioned (a) upon the President's judgment as to its beneficial effect upon the re-establishment of peace between the countries engaged in armed conflict in the Chaco; (b) upon the making of a proclamation, which was left to his unfettered discretion, thus constituting an attempted substitution of the President's will for that of Congress; (c) upon the making of a proclamation putting an end to the operation of the resolution, which again was left to the President's unfettered discretion; and (d) further, that the extent of its operation in particular cases was subject to limitation and exception by the President, controlled by no standard. In each of these particulars, appellees urge that Congress abdicated its essential functions and delegated them to the Executive.

Whether, if the Joint Resolution had related solely to internal affairs, it would be open to the challenge that it constituted an unlawful delegation of legislative power to the Executive, we find it unnecessary to determine. The whole aim of the resolution is to affect a situation entirely external to the United States, and falling within the category of foreign affairs. The determination which we are called to make, therefore, is whether the Joint Resolution, as applied to that situation, is vulnerable to attack under the rule that forbids a delegation of the lawmaking power. In other words, assuming (but not deciding) that the challenged delegation, if it were confined to internal affairs, would be invalid, may it nevertheless be sustained on the ground that its exclusive aim is to afford a remedy for a hurtful condition within foreign territory?

It will contribute to the elucidation of the question if we first consider the differences between the powers of the federal government in respect of foreign or external affairs and those in respect of domestic or internal affairs. That there are differences between them, and that these differences are fundamental, may not be doubted.

The two classes of powers are different, both in respect of their origin and their nature. The broad statement that the federal government can exercise no powers except those specifically enumerated in the Constitution, and such implied powers as are necessary and proper to carry into effect the enumerated powers, is categorically true only in respect of our internal affairs. In that field, the primary purpose of the Constitution was to carve from the general mass of legislative powers then possessed by the states such portions as it was thought desirable to vest in the federal government, leaving those not included in the enumeration still in the states. That this doctrine applies only to powers which the states had is self-evident. And since the states severally never possessed international powers, such powers could not have been carved from the mass of state powers but obviously were transmitted to the United States from some other source. During the Colonial period, those powers were possessed exclusively by and were entirely under the control of the Crown. By the Declaration of Independence, "the Representatives of the United States of America" declared the United (not the several) Colonies to be free and independent states, and as such to have "full Power to levy War, conclude Peace, contract Alliances, establish Commerce and to do all other Acts and Things which Independent States may of right do."

As a result of the separation from Great Britain by the colonies, acting as a unit, the powers of external sovereignty passed from the Crown not to the colonies severally, but to the colonies in their collective and corporate capacity as the United States of America. Even before the Declaration, the colonies were a unit in foreign affairs, acting through a common agency — namely, the Continental Congress, composed of delegates from the thirteen colonies. That agency exercised the powers of war and peace, raised an army, created a navy, and finally adopted the Declaration of Independence. Rulers come and go; governments end and forms of government change; but sovereignty survives. A political society cannot endure without a supreme will somewhere. Sovereignty is never held in suspense. When, therefore, the external sovereignty of Great Britain in respect of the colonies ceased, it immediately passed to the Union.

That fact was given practical application almost at once [by the] treaty of peace, made on September 3, 1783. . . .

The Union existed before the Constitution, which was ordained and established among other things to form "a more perfect Union." Prior to that event, it is clear that the Union, declared by the Articles of Confederation to be "perpetual," was the sole possessor of external sovereignty, and in the Union it remained without change save in so far as the Constitution in express terms qualified its exercise. The Framers' Convention was called and exerted its powers upon the irrefutable postulate that though the states were several their people in respect of foreign affairs were one. In that convention, the entire absence of state power to deal with those affairs was thus forcefully stated by Rufus King:

> "The states were not 'sovereigns' in the sense contended for by some. They did not possess the peculiar features of sovereignty, — they could not make war, nor peace, nor alliances, nor treaties. Considering them as political beings, they were dumb, for they could not speak to any foreign sovereign whatever. They were deaf, for they could not hear any propositions from such sovereign. They had not even the organs or faculties of defence or offence, for they could not of themselves raise troops, or equip vessels, for war."

It results that the investment of the federal government with the powers of external sovereignty did not depend upon the affirmative grants of the Constitution. The powers to declare and wage war, to conclude peace, to make treaties, to maintain diplomatic relations with other sovereignties, if they had never been mentioned in the Constitution, would have vested in the federal government as necessary concomitants of nationality. Neither the Constitution nor the laws passed in pursuance of it have any force in foreign territory unless in respect of our own citizens; and operations of the nation in such territory must be governed by treaties, international understandings and compacts, and the principles of international law. As a member of the family of nations, the right and power of the United States in that field are equal to the right and power of the other members of the international family. Otherwise, the United States is not completely sovereign. The power to acquire territory by discovery and occupation, the power to make such international agreements as do not constitute treaties in the constitutional sense, none of which is expressly affirmed by the Constitution, nevertheless exist as inherently inseparable from the conception of nationality. This the court recognized, and in each of the cases cited [omitted] found the warrant for its conclusions not in the provisions of the Constitution, but in the law of nations.

* * *

Not only, as we have shown, is the federal power over external affairs in origin and essential character different from that over internal affairs, but participation in the exercise of the power is significantly limited. In this vast external realm, with its important, complicated, delicate and manifold problems, the President alone has the power to speak or listen as a representative of the nation. He makes treaties with the advice and consent of the Senate; but he alone negotiates. Into the field of negotiation the Senate cannot intrude; and Congress itself is powerless to invade it. As Marshall said in his great argument of March 7, 1800, in the House of Representatives, "The President is the sole organ of the nation in its external relations, and its sole representative with foreign nations." Annals, 6th Cong., col. 613. The Senate Committee on Foreign Relations at a very early day in our history (February 15, 1816), reported to the Senate, among other things, as follows:

"The President is the constitutional representative of the United States with regard to foreign nations. He manages our concerns with foreign nations and must necessarily be most competent to determine when, how, and upon what subjects negotiation may be urged with the greatest prospect of success. For his conduct he is responsible to the Constitution. The committee considers this responsibility the surest pledge for the faithful discharge of his duty. They think the interference of the Senate in the direction of foreign negotiations calculated to diminish that responsibility and thereby to impair the best security for the national safety. The nature of transactions with foreign nations, moreover, requires caution and unity of design, and their success frequently depends on secrecy and dispatch."

It is important to bear in mind that we are here dealing not alone with an authority vested in the President by an exertion of legislative power, but with such an authority plus the very delicate, plenary and exclusive power of the President as the sole organ of the federal government in the field of international relations — a power which does not require as a basis for its exercise an act of Congress, but which, of course, like every other governmental power, must be exercised in subordination to the applicable provisions of the Constitution. It is quite apparent that if, in the maintenance of our international relations, embarrassment — perhaps serious embarrassment — is to be avoided and success for our aims achieved, congressional legislation which is to be made effective through negotiation and inquiry within the international field must often accord to the President a degree of discretion and freedom from statutory restriction which would not be admissible were domestic affairs alone involved. Moreover, he, not Congress, has the better opportunity of knowing the conditions which prevail in foreign countries, and especially is this true in time of war. He has his confidential sources of information. He has his agents in the form of diplomatic, consular and other officials. Secrecy in respect of information gathered by them may be highly necessary, and the premature disclosure of it productive of harmful results. Indeed, so clearly is this true that the first President refused to accede to a request to lay before the House of Representatives the instructions, correspondence and documents relating to the negotiation of the Jay Treaty — a refusal the wisdom of which was recognized by the House itself and has never since been doubted. In his reply to the request, President Washington said:

"The nature of foreign negotiations requires caution, and their success must often depend on secrecy; and even when brought to a conclusion a full disclosure of all the measures, demands, or eventual concessions which may have been proposed or contemplated would be extremely impolitic; for this might have a pernicious influence on future negotiations, or produce immediate inconveniences, perhaps danger and mischief, in relation to other powers. The necessity of such caution and secrecy was one cogent reason for vesting the power of making treaties in the President, with the advice and consent of the Senate, the principle on which that body was formed confining it to a small number of members. To admit, then, a right in the House of Representatives to demand and to have as a matter of course all the papers respecting a negotiation with a foreign power would be to establish a dangerous precedent."

The marked difference between foreign affairs and domestic affairs in this respect is recognized by both houses of Congress in the very form of their requisitions for information from the executive departments. In the case of every department except the Department of State, the resolution directs the official to furnish the information. In the case of the State Department, dealing with foreign affairs, the President is requested to furnish the information "if not incompatible with the public interest." A statement that to furnish the information is not compatible with the public interest rarely, if ever, is questioned.

When the President is to be authorized by legislation to act in respect of a matter intended to affect a situation in foreign territory, the legislator properly bears in mind the important consideration that the form of the President's action — or, indeed, whether he shall act at all — may well depend, among other things, upon the nature of the confidential information which he has or may thereafter receive, or upon the effect which his action may have upon our foreign relations. This consideration, in connection with what we have already said on the subject discloses the unwisdom of requiring Congress in this field of governmental power to lay down narrowly definite standards by which the President is to be governed. . . .

In the light of the foregoing observations, it is evident that this court should not be in haste to apply a general rule which will have the effect of condemning legislation like that under review as constituting an unlawful delegation of legislative power. The principles which justify such legislation find overwhelming support in the unbroken legislative practice which has prevailed almost from the inception of the national government to the present day.

Let us examine, in chronological order, the acts of legislation which warrant this conclusion:

The Act of June 4, 1794, authorized the President to lay, regulate and revoke embargoes. He was "authorized" "whenever, in his opinion, the public safety shall so require," to lay the embargo upon all ships and vessels in the ports of the United States, including those of foreign nations, "under such regulations as the circumstances of the case may require, and to continue or revoke the same, whenever he shall think proper." [Other examples omitted.]

* * *

Practically every volume of the United States Statutes contains one or more acts or joint resolutions of Congress authorizing action by the President in respect of subjects affecting foreign relations, which either leave the exercise of the power to his unrestricted judgment, or provide a standard far more general than that which has always been considered requisite with regard to domestic affairs.

* * *

We had occasion to review these embargo and kindred acts in connection with an exhaustive discussion of the general subject of delegation of legislative power in a recent case, *Panama Refining Co. v. Ryan* [(1935)], and, in justifying such acts, pointed out that they confided to the President "an authority which was cognate to the conduct by him of the foreign relations of the government."

The result of holding that the joint resolution here under attack is void and unenforceable as constituting an unlawful delegation of legislative power would be to stamp this multitude of comparable acts and resolutions as likewise invalid. And while this court may not, and should not, hesitate to declare acts of Congress, however many times repeated, to be unconstitutional if beyond all rational doubt it finds them to be so, an impressive array of legislation such as we have just set forth, enacted by nearly every Congress from the beginning of our national existence to the present day, must be given unusual weight in the process of reaching a correct determination of the problem. A legislative practice such as we have here, evidenced not by only occasional instances, but marked by the movement of a steady stream for a century and a half of time, goes a long way in the direction of proving the presence of unassailable ground for the constitutionality of the practice, to be found in the origin and history of the power involved, or in its nature, or in both combined.

In *Field v. Clark* [(1892)], this court declared that "the practical construction of the constitution, as given by so many acts of congress, and embracing almost the entire period of our national existence, should not be overruled, unless upon a conviction that such legislation was clearly incompatible with the supreme law of the land." The rule is one which has been stated and applied many times by this court.

. . . We deem it unnecessary to consider, seriatim, the several clauses which are said to evidence the unconstitutionality of the Joint Resolution as involving an unlawful delegation of legislative power. It is enough to summarize by saying that, both upon principle and in accordance with precedent, we conclude there is sufficient warrant for the broad discretion vested in the President to determine whether the enforcement of the statute will have a beneficial effect upon the re-establishment of peace in the affected countries; whether he shall make proclamation to bring the resolution into operation; whether and when the resolution shall cease to operate and to make proclamation accordingly; and to prescribe limitations and exceptions to which the enforcement of the resolution shall be subject.

* * *

It was not within the power of the President to repeal the Joint Resolution; and his second proclamation did not purport to do so. It "revoked" the first proclamation; and the question is, did the revocation of the proclamation have the effect of abrogating the resolution or of precluding its enforcement in so far as that involved the prosecution and punishment of offenses committed during the life of the first proclamation? We are of opinion that it did not.

* * *

The first proclamation of the President was in force from the 28th day of May, 1934, to the 14th day of November, 1935. If the Joint Resolution had in no way depended upon Presidential action, but had provided explicitly that, at any time between May 28, 1934, and November 14, 1935, it should be unlawful to sell arms or munitions of war to the countries engaged in armed conflict in the Chaco, it certainly could not be successfully contended that the law would expire with the passing of the time fixed in respect of offenses committed during the period.

The judgment of the court below must be reversed. . . .

MR. JUSTICE MCREYNOLDS does not agree. He is of opinion that the court below reached the right conclusion and its judgment ought to be affirmed.

MR. JUSTICE STONE took no part in the consideration or decision of this case.

NOTES AND QUESTIONS

1. *Curtiss-Wright* was decided within two years of several cases mentioned earlier, which had invalidated overly broad delegations of legislative authority to the Executive branch. *See Panama Refining*; *Schechter Poultry*, *supra*. It is not clear that these over-delegation precedents retain their vitality in domestic law, but Justice Sutherland makes it clear that the President's vast reservoir of authority in foreign affairs, derived from the sovereign authority of the United States itself, makes these delegation precedents inapplicable in international matters.

2. Presidents, therefore, tend to view *Curtiss-Wright* as establishing the following theorem: Under the Constitution the President is vested with all the authority traditionally available to any head of state in his foreign relations, except insofar as the Constitution limits that authority or places it in Congress. This principle was succinctly stated by Thomas Jefferson: "The transaction of business with foreign nations is Executive altogether. It belongs then to the head of that department *except* as to such portion of it as are specially submitted to the Senate. Arguably, too, exceptions to the theorem are to be construed strictly." Jefferson's Opinion on the Powers of the Senate Respecting Diplomatic Appointments (Apr. 24, 1790), *in* 16 THE PAPERS OF THOMAS JEFFERSON 378-79 (J. Boyd ed., 1961) (emphasis in original). As the Court noted with approval in *Curtiss-Wright*, the Senate Committee on Foreign Relations had acknowledged this principle at an early date in our history:

> *The President is the constitutional representative of the United States with regard to foreign nations.* He manages our concerns with foreign nations and must necessarily be most competent to determine when, how, and upon what subjects negotiation may be urged with the greatest prospect of success. *For his conduct he is responsible to the Constitution.* The committee considers this responsibility the surest pledge for the faithful discharge of his duty. They think the interference of the Senate in the direction of foreign negotiations calculated to diminish that responsibility and thereby to impair the best security for the national safety. The nature of transactions with foreign nations, moreover, requires caution and unity of design, and their success frequently depends on secrecy and dispatch.

Curtiss-Wright, 299 U.S. at 319 (emphasis added) (quoting 8 U.S. SENATE REPORTS, COMMITTEE ON FOREIGN RELATIONS 24 (Feb. 18, 1816)). For a perceptive appraisal of presidential power derived from the Vesting Clause of the Constitution, see Steven G. Calabresi, *The Vesting Clauses as Power Grants*, 88 NW. U. L. REV. 1377 (1994) (arguing that the Vesting Clause of Article II empowers the President to act).

3. Clearly, however, Congress possesses both specific and general powers that may touch on foreign policy. This is evidenced by specific powers such as the Senate's power to approve treaties found in Article II, Section 2, Clause 2; the power to declare war found in Article I, Section 8, Clause 11; and the power to regulate foreign commerce found in Article I, Section 8, Clause 3. Congress also possesses general powers such as the power of the purse found in Article I, Section 8, Clauses 2, 5, 12, and 13 and Article I, Section 7, Clause 1. What happens when Congress exercises its authority in a manner which conflicts with the strongly executive *Curtiss-Wright* theorem? One answer is that Congress may not enact such infringements. As is evident from the text of the Constitution, no power is vested in Congress to preclude or restrict the exercise of diplomacy by the President and such other executive branch officers as he may designate, expressly or impliedly. The exercise of diplomacy includes communication and consultation with foreign governments and foreign nationals in support of the foreign policy objectives of the President, and these diplomatic endeavors may be conducted in secrecy or in public as the President may find necessary.

4. Iran-Contra: The sweep of the *Curtiss-Wright* theorem came into play in a dispute between President Reagan and the Congress over support of certain

Nicaraguan Freedom Fighters, known as Contras, who the President viewed as the equivalent of the patriots of the American revolution. The story begins, however, not in Central America, but in the Middle East.

Apparently, with oral presidential approval, Israel shipped certain armaments it had acquired from the United States to Iran. The President apparently wanted to secure better relations with Iran and perhaps the release of certain American hostages. Legislation required that notice of such shipments be made to Congress "in a timely fashion," and that the President find the shipment "important to the national security." Were these legislative conditions contrary to the *Curtiss-Wright* theorem? Whether or not they were, the President's oral approval and the long-after-the-fact notice to Congress triggered an uproar.

The roar got louder when it was discovered that the President's National Security Advisor, Admiral John Poindexter, and an aide, Marine Corps Lieutenant Colonel Oliver North, directed some of the proceeds from the Iranian arms shipments to the Contras. Between December 1982 and October 1986, Congress enacted 12 different versions of another law, the so-called Boland Amendment, which prohibited the use of funds available to certain named government agencies and those "involved in intelligence activities" from "supporting, directly or indirectly, military or paramilitary operations in Nicaragua by any nation, group, organization, movement or individual." Boland Amendment to Department of Defense Appropriations Act of 1985, Pub. L. No. 98-473, § 8066, 98 Stat. 1838, 1935 (1984). It was far from clear whether the Boland prohibition applied to the National Security Council, which does not gather its own intelligence, the agency for whom Admiral Poindexter and Lieutenant Colonel North worked. However, beyond the technical application of the amendment, would the *Curtiss-Wright* theorem permit such an amendment as a constitutional matter? Some members of Congress thought that the Boland Amendment not only applied, but effectively precluded Poindexter and North from using their government time to help the President solicit funds from other nations or private sources to assist the Contras. To make matters even more interesting, both Poindexter and North viewed the issue as a matter of national security and kept the "covert operation" from Congress.

An independent counsel, Lawrence Walsh, was appointed to prosecute Poindexter and North. After a lengthy and extremely expensive investigation (the investigation took over 6 years and cost the taxpayers close to $40 million), Mr. Walsh obtained perjury and obstruction of justice convictions regarding the presidential aides' congressional testimony. The convictions, however, were overturned because Mr. Walsh took insufficient steps to prevent immunized statements, made by the defendants before Congress, from being used in their criminal trials. *See United States v. North*, 910 F.2d 843 (D.C. Cir.), *modified*, 920 F.2d 940 (D.C. Cir. 1990), *cert. denied*, 506 U.S. 1021 (1992). Iran-Contra thus ended with a whimper and left the contours of executive-legislative authority in foreign policy matters no more discernible than the framers made them. Independent counsel laws could make government officials who take an aggressive interpretation of executive authority in foreign affairs subject to criminal charges, however. *See* DOUGLAS W. KMIEC, THE ATTORNEY GENERAL'S LAWYER ch. 8 (1992).

5. The Supreme Court has expressly recognized the constitutional authority of the President to protect diplomatic and intelligence secrets:

> The President, after all, is the "Commander in Chief of the Army and Navy of the United States." U.S. Const, Article II, Section 2. His authority to . . . control access to information bearing on national security . . . flows primarily from this constitutional investment of power in the President and exists quite apart from any explicit congressional grant. . . . The authority to protect such information falls on the President as head of the Executive Branch and as Commander in Chief.

Department of the Navy v. Egan, 484 U.S. 518, 527 (1988). Similarly, in a concurring opinion in *New York Times Co. v. United States*, 403 U.S. 713, 727-30 (1971) (Stewart, J., concurring), Justice Stewart stated: "[I]t is elementary that the successful conduct of international diplomacy and the maintenance of an effective national defense require both confidentiality and secrecy. . . . In the area of basic national defense the frequent need for absolute secrecy is, of course, self-evident." *See also Chicago & Southern Airlines, Inc. v. Waterman Corp.*, 333 U.S. 103, 111 (1948) ("The President, both as Commander-in-Chief and as the Nation's organ for foreign affairs, has available intelligence services whose reports are not and ought not to be published to the world."); *United States v. Reynolds*, 345 U.S. 1, 10 (1953) (recognizing the executive privilege to protect state secrets); *United States v. Nixon*, 418 U.S. 683, 710 (1974) ("courts have traditionally shown the utmost deference to Presidential responsibilities: to protect military and diplomatic secrets"); *Snepp v. United States*, 444 U.S. 507, 509 n.3 (1980) ("The government has a compelling interest in protecting both the secrecy of information important to our national security and the appearance of confidentiality so essential to the effective operation of our foreign intelligence service."); *Haig v. Agee*, 453 U.S. 280, 307 (1981) ("Protection of the foreign policy of the United States is a governmental interest of great importance, since foreign policy and national security considerations cannot neatly be compartmentalized.").

6. In prosecuting Admiral Poindexter and Lieutenant Colonel North, the President was largely bound by the statute found constitutional in *Morrison*, to defer the conduct of that prosecution to Mr. Walsh. However, President Reagan was not bound to accept the independent counsel's unnuanced conception of the President's foreign affairs authority. One of your co-authors, as Assistant Attorney General to President Reagan, made that clear in a brief filed in the *North* case. Assistant Attorney General Kmiec wrote: "The [independent counsel's] argument throughout his brief fails to acknowledge the President's constitutional right and responsibility to protect diplomatic and intelligence secrets." Brief *Amicus Curiae* by the United States Department of Justice, *United States* *v. North*, 910 F.2d 843 (D.C. Cir.), *modified*, 920 F.2d 940 (D.C. Cir. 1990) (No. 89-3118).

Iran-Contra led to passage of the Intelligence Authorization Act of 1991, Pub. Law No. 102-88, 105 Stat. 429 (1991), which more clearly requires intelligence findings by the President, including those authorizing covert actions, to be in writing and to be furnished to the intelligence committees in Congress, unless the President determines it cannot be so provided, in which case the committees must be notified "in a timely fashion and shall provide a statement of the reasons for not giving prior notice." *Id*. § 503(b)(3). President Bush had vetoed an earlier version of this Act. In approving the revised version, he wrote: "I am pleased that the Act, as revised, omits any suggestion that a 'request' by the United States Government to third parties may constitute 'covert action' as defined by the Act. In addition, I am pleased that the revised provision concerning 'timely' notice to the Congress of covert actions incorporates without substantive change the requirement found in existing law." President Bush's Statement on Signing the Intelligence Authorization Act, 27 WEEKLY COMP. PRES. DOC. (Aug. 14, 1991). Do you think that Admiral Poindexter or Lieutenant Colonel North would be any better advised in light of the new law?

7. The Treaty Power: Presidents do not only speak to other nations by asking for funds as in Iran-Contra, Presidents also communicate through the negotiation of treaties. The Constitution provides that the President shall have the power to make treaties, subject to the approval of two-thirds of the Senate present when the treaty is considered. The treaty process, itself, occurs in a number of steps: negotiation by the President, approval by the Senate, ratification by the President following the Senate's approval, exchange of ratification documents, and proclamation. Because the Senate may modify the treaty negotiated by the President in the approval process, the President has no obligation to ratify the Senate's amended version.

If the President does ratify a treaty, it binds the nation internationally and domestically. International enforcement is beyond the scope of this book; however, without the existence of a comprehensive international court, enforcement is often a matter of diplomacy in peace and military might in war. Domestically, treaties are often described as either self-executing or requiring implementing legislation. For example, any treaty obligating the United States to spend money requires not just the approval of the Senate, but legislation originating in the House of Representatives to comply with Article I, Section 9, Clause 7, which states that "[n]o money shall be drawn from the Treasury, but in consequence of Appropriations made by Law." Other treaties may also call for a signatory sovereign to conform its domestic code to a certain standard, and this too, would be an example of a non-self-executing treaty. Chief Justice Marshall found both the Treaty of 1782 and the Jay Treaty of 1784 (the treaty ending the Revolutionary War), to be self-executing. *See Fairfax's Devisee v. Hunter's Lessee*, 11 U.S. (7 Cranch) 603 (1812).

In terms of its domestic effect, a treaty was recognized long ago by Chief Justice Marshall as the equivalent of an act of Congress. *Foster v. Neilson*, 27 U.S. 253 (1829), *overruled on other grounds, United States v. Percheman*, 32 U.S. 51 (1833). As the equivalent of legislation, treaties can be superseded by subsequent legislation inconsistent with the original treaty. *Whitney v. Robertson*, 124 U.S. 190, 194 (1888). The question has arisen whether the President can end or terminate a treaty unilaterally. In *Goldwater v. Carter*, 617 F.2d 697 (D.C. Cir. 1979), the federal appellate court upheld President Carter's decision to terminate America's mutual defense treaty with Taiwan. The appellate court reasoned that the treaty itself allowed for presidential termination upon the giving of proper notice. The issue remains unsettled, however, because the Supreme Court vacated the appellate decision and four Justices treated the question as a nonjusticiable political question. *Goldwater v. Carter*, 444 U.S. 996 (1979).

8. There is no express constitutional limit on the scope or subject matter of treaties. However, the Supreme Court has held that "it would be manifestly contrary to the . . . Constitution . . . to . . . [allow] the United States to exercise power under an international agreement without observing constitutional prohibitions." *Reid v. Covert*, 354 U.S. 1, 17 (1957) (holding that the civilian wife of a military serviceman could not be subject to court-martial jurisdiction, even if an international agreement may authorize it). However, Congress was permitted by treaty to exceed constitutional limits placed on its legislative power. *See Missouri v. Holland*, 252 U.S. 416 (1920) (upholding a migratory bird treaty between the United States and Canada perceived at the time to encroach upon state authority). The fact that a treaty may become a separate source of domestic federal authority alarms many in the present age when power is sought to be more carefully limited within constitutional boundaries, or devolved to a lower level. Immediately after the decision in *Missouri v. Holland*, Senator Bricker unsuccessfully sought to amend the Constitution to provide, in part, that "[a] treaty shall become effective as internal law in the United States only through legislation which would be valid in the absence of a treaty." Jeffrey L. Friesen, Note, *The Distribution of Treaty-Implementing Powers in Constitutional Federations: Thoughts on the American and Canadian Models*, 94 COLUM. L. REV. 1415, 1424-26 (1994).

9. Executive Agreements: Presidents dating back to President Washington have entered into executive agreements with foreign nations without Senate approval. As a general matter, these agreements are enforceable as the "law of the land" despite the fact that Congress had no part in their making. *United States v. Pink*, 315 U.S. 203, 228-30 (1942); *United States v. Belmont*, 301 U.S. 324, 331 (1937). Moreover, pursuant to his power to conclude executive agreements, the President may settle the claims of American nationals against foreign states. *Dames & Moore v. Regan*, 453 U.S. 654, 679-80 (1981). Executive agreements are often divided into categories: those based on a treaty; those invited by legislation; and those undertaken pursuant to the President's unilateral authority. Treaty-based agreements, like the United Nations Headquarters Agreement, have the same legal status as the treaty itself, so long as it is consistent therewith. Many congressionally authorized agreements relate to matters of international trade. Unilateral presidential agreements, however, run the risk of improperly avoiding the Senate's approval role, unless the agreement is clearly traceable to constitutional power committed to the President, such as agreements necessary to establish diplomatic relations premised on the President's power to receive ambassadors. *See, e.g., United States v. Belmont, supra* (concerning diplomatic relations with the former Soviet Union). Executive agreements that are neither approved by a treaty nor congressionally authorized may not contradict a federal statute. Thus, in *United States v. Guy W. Capps*, 204 F.2d 655 (4th Cir. 1953), *aff'd on other grounds*, 348 U.S. 296 (1955), an appellate court denied effect to an executive agreement relating to the export of food that conflicted with the Agricultural Act of 1948.

Presidents may also make proclamations that have international effect. For example, President Reagan extended the United States' territorial sea from 3 to 12 miles by proclamation in December 1988. This proclamation, considered vital to the modern national security of the United States, was premised, in part, upon the recognition of the *Curtiss-Wright* theorem that the President is the sole organ or representative of the United States in foreign relations. *See* Douglas W. Kmiec, *Legal Issues Raised by the Proposed Presidential Proclamation to Extend the Territorial Sea*, 1 TERRITORIAL SEA J. 1 (1990).

10. War and its Equivalent: A frequent source of controversy between the President and Congress is the appropriateness of military intervention. While we first considered the legal principles that emerged from *Youngstown* as primarily affecting domestic law, you will recall that President Truman's perceived need to take over the steel plants originated with his military decisions in Korea. Presidents, as commander in chief, see a need to act "with dispatch," and hence, often without a formal declaration of war from Congress under Article I, Section 8, Clause 11, in protecting American personnel and property abroad.

Historian Eugene V. Rostow portrays executive power expansively in this context as similar to that of Theodore Roosevelt's view of the presidency generally — that the executive power includes all power which is neither legislative nor judicial. Rostow argues, for example, that declarations of war have not been considered necessary for most military actions. Rather, they have been reserved for only the most protracted of conflicts. "During the last 200 years, the United States has declared war only five times, but Presidents have used the armed forces abroad at least 200 times, usually on their own authority, sometimes with the support of joint resolutions before or after the event." Eugene V. Rostow, *President, Prime Minister or Constitutional Monarch?*, 83 AM. J. INT'L L. 740, 745 (1989). Rostow believes such presidential actions are consistent with the founder's understanding.

Another respected historian, Arthur Schlesinger would beg to differ. Schlesinger claims that the actions of early Presidents were of a different character than modern presidential military activism. The early Presidents, according to Schlesinger, "usurped power and thereby created no constitutional precedent — an action to be distinguished from the claims of legal sanctions for extreme acts characteristic of presidents of the last generation, claims that would set dangerous precedents for the future." While acknowledging the possibility that the President may have some authority to pursue unilateral action in the face of a direct attack upon the nation, Schlesinger argues that all other power to use force resides in the Congress, pursuant to its Article I, Section 8 power to declare war. Arthur M. Schlesinger, *The Legislative-Executive Balance in International Affairs: The Intent of the Framers*, 1 WASH. Q. 99, 104 (1989).

In an effort to address these competing positions, Congress enacted the War Powers Resolution, 50 U.S.C. § 1544(c), authorizing the termination of the use of armed forces in hostilities by concurrent resolution. A concurrent, as opposed to a joint, resolution is one that has passed both Houses of Congress, but is not presented to the President for signature or disapproval. This is a form of the legislative veto, since declared unconstitutional in *Chadha*. Nevertheless, Presidents more or less comply with the War Powers Resolution, often seeking some affirmative congressional support for military engagements, either in the form of appropriations or otherwise. Congress, or its leadership at least, strives to be consulted in advance, and it is seldom fully satisfied with its options when it is not. Presidents have a tendency, sometimes with solid national security or strategic reasons, to ask for approval after troops are underway or international commitments made. Nominally, the War Powers Resolution requires the President to report to Congress within 48 hours of introduction of troops into hostilities, but there is much dispute over what counts as "hostilities." It is not uncommon for Presidents to argue that returning fire in self-defense or remaining in one location without offensive action as a peacekeeping presence is not within the definition. Presidents seek to avoid the hostilities characterization since, if the subsequently informed Congress disapproves, the President is given 60 days to withdraw troops. The timetable, itself, has been cited by Presidents as unconstitutionally interfering with the commander in chief authority.

May Congress use judicial means to prevent the President from introducing troops into hostilities without legislative approval? The decision of one federal district court in *Dellums v. Bush*, 752 F. Supp. 1141 (D.D.C. 1990), suggests the answer is: maybe. *Dellums* arose out of President Bush's response to the Iraqi invasion of Kuwait in August 1990. In early November 1990, the President doubled United States military forces in the Persian Gulf to give the United States and its allies "an adequate offensive military option." In late November 1990, the United Nations authorized the use of force to remove Iraq unless it withdrew on its own by January 15, 1991. Shortly thereafter, 53 members of the House and one Senator filed suit to enjoin the President from launching an offensive operation without congressional approval. President Bush argued that the case was a nonjusticiable political question because the plaintiffs lacked standing and the cause of action was not ripe for adjudication. The court rejected these defenses except for ripeness. Specifically, the court claimed that, in a proper case, it could make factual and legal determination of whether "this nation's military actions constitute war for purposes of [Article I, Section 8, Clause 11]." *Dellums* was not such a proper case, however, since a majority of the members of Congress had not expressed its view or asked for relief. In addition, the court was not convinced that offensive military action was imminent.

Such action became imminent in January, and even as the President felt he did not need authorization, he sought it. On January 12, 1991, the Congress authorized the use of force consistent with the United Nations resolution. The Congress claimed to be following the procedures of the War Powers Resolution. Iraq did not meet the January 15 deadline, and United States forces commenced an offensive on January 17, 1991. The war ended when Iraq surrendered to coalition forces in March 1991. The President stopped short of permitting an offensive that would have removed Saddam Hussein, the Iraqi head of state. Since the United Nations resolution only called for the liberation of Kuwait, and the congressional authorization contained a similar limitation, was the President's military judgment affected by the congressional resolution?

President Clinton introduced United States troops into a number of international conflicts, not always with congressional authorization, but nevertheless "reporting" these actions under the War Powers Resolution. For example, President Clinton introduced 20,000 United States troops into Haiti in September 1994 to restore power to Jean-Bertrand Aristide. The President reported these actions to Congress, but did not ask approval. In October 1994, the Congress passed a resolution that "the President should have sought and welcomed congressional approval before deploying United States armed forces to Haiti." Similarly, on multiple occasions, President Clinton introduced troops into Bosnia. In December 1995, President Clinton facilitated a peace accord among the warring Bosnian factions, the Dayton Peace Agreement, and won grudging congressional approval for a one-year deployment of United States troops into a NATO peacekeeping effort that was to end in late 1996. It did not, and the President, without seeking congressional authorization, reported to the Congress that NATO planned for an 18-month continuation of the mission. In his letter to Congress, President Clinton recited that

> I have directed the participation of United States Armed Forces in these operations pursuant to my constitutional authority to conduct United States foreign relations and as the Commander in Chief and Chief Executive, and in accordance with various statutory authorities. I am providing this report as part of my efforts to keep the Congress fully informed about developments in Bosnia and other states in the region.

Thus, the dance between the President and Congress over foreign affairs continues. Much present concern focuses on whether American personnel should be placed under the command or operational control of foreign or multi-national commanders. Former Senator Robert Dole, who unsuccessfully challenged Mr. Clinton for the Presidency in 1996, proposed legislation that would repeal the War Powers Resolution, thereby allowing freer executive deployment of troops into hostilities, but that would prohibit, except under narrowly drawn conditions and congressional approval, the subordination of American troops to foreign command in international peacekeeping missions.

11. The extent to which the war power provisions of both the Constitution and statute are still ignored is well illustrated by the air war fought in Kosovo (a province within Yugoslavia) between March and June 1999. Together with NATO (the North Atlantic Treaty Organization), President Clinton involved the U.S. military in a massive air war without a declaration of war or even a pretense of a reasonable facsimile. Over a half-million Kosovar Albanians, on whose behalf NATO intervened, were thereafter driven from their homes. Significant numbers of these refugees lost their lives, including many who died as a result of "friendly" or errant fire by NATO forces. Air strikes authorized by President Clinton at times exceeded 500 sorties a day.

Two months before President Clinton launched the air war, Secretary of State Madeline Albright and the Clinton State Department reassured Congress that any U.S. troops assigned to NATO would be sent to Kosovo only if a peace plan with Yugoslav President Milosevic was successfully reached. Said Undersecretary of State Thomas Pickering, "we are not seeking to introduce American ground forces into a situation in which they would have to engage in combat to obtain an objective." In retrospect, was the State Department misleading the Congress? No *ground* troops, after all, were introduced into combat.

In the particular case of Kosovo, it proved difficult to raise constitutional objection to the President's unilateral action because: (a) Slobodan Milosevic allegedly had, as a later indictment by an International War Crimes Tribunal alleges, authorized multiple, gruesome acts of genocide or "ethnic cleansing" against the ethnic Albanians in Kosovo and (b) despite prevailing military wisdom that an air war would fall short of any desired objective, a tenuous peace accord was reached in mid-June 1999, after which the hundreds of thousands of displaced refugees began to return to their now war-shattered homes and villages. Nevertheless, the "victory" was thick with moral ambiguity by virtue of the war's questionable provenance or legality. As a former senior lawyer for the Naval War College pondered, "does our government believe that other nations are required to follow the law but the United States is not?" John McCaslin, *Beyond Law . . .*, WASH. TIMES at A5 (April 13, 1999) (quoting Myron H. Nordquist, a senior international lawyer at the Naval War College and acting general counsel of the Air Force).

Congress was given the opportunity to declare war in Kosovo. It chose not to. Congress was given the opportunity to direct the President to remove American troops from hostilities. It chose not to do this either. Congress even contemplated a resolution endorsing the air campaign. This too was declined. Congress did authorize over $13 billion for the expenses of the military. While eminent scholars, such as Professor John Yoo, of the University of California speculate that control of the purse may be a reasonably effective way for Congress to check misbegotten military missions by a misguided or misinformed executive, John C. Yoo, *The Continuation of Politics by Other Means: The Original Understanding of War Powers*, 84 CALIF. L. REV. 167 (1996), war by unilateral direction still seems to have been far from the minds of the founders. English Kings abused the prerogative of war, and so the framers deliberately transferred the power to declare war to the entire legislative branch (House and Senate), in order to make war's initiation more difficult. The idea was to "clog" the path to war by requiring deliberation by a diverse group before the risks and costs of a military campaign could be imposed. James Madison once observed: "in no part of the constitution is more wisdom to be found than in the clause which confides the question of war or peace to the legislature, and not to the executive department. . . . [T]he trust and the temptation would be too great for any one man." Was Madison mistaken? Why do present conditions lead the Congress to avoid taking direct responsibility?

Does America's agreement to the U.N. Charter authorize the bombing? Few think so. In any event, President Clinton deliberately chose not to take the matter to the Security Council, knowing that the bombing of a foreign sovereign state would be vetoed as a "breach of the peace or act of aggression." At the time of the NATO intervention, there were many international lawyers who argued that the U.N. Charter itself barred intervention in Kosovo without express authorization by the U.N. Security Council, authorization which could not be secured because of veto threats by China and Russia. And even had there been express authorization by the U.N., such action by that international agency alone could not deprive the American people of the full deliberation by both the Executive and the Legislative branches that is constitutionally prescribed. Much less could NATO acting alone trump constitutional procedures, particularly since NATO, as a regional organization provided for in the U.N. Charter, had no authority without Security Council authorization to take "defensive" action outside the territory of its member states, which Yugoslavia was not. Is it possible that a certain looseness that we can now observe in interpretation of the Constitution by the United States Supreme Court now has its counterpart in the interpretation of the U.N. Charter?

12. With respect to the "war on terrorism" begun after the United States was attacked on September 11, 2001, many of the issues regarding presidential power described above have been avoided because Congress, by a nearly unanimous vote, explicitly authorized the use of force shortly after this devastating and unprovoked attack, which took 3000 civilian lives and destroyed major portions of the country's financial and defense facilities. The congressional resolution in response authorized the President "to use all necessary and appropriate force against those nations, organizations, or persons he determines planned, authorized, committed, or aided the terrorist attacks that occurred on September 11, 2001, or harbored such organizations or persons, in order to prevent any future acts of international terrorism against the United States by such nations, organizations or persons." Pub. Law 107-40 (Sept. 18, 2001). Similarly, Congress authorized the use of force against Iraq in October 2002: "The President is authorized to use the Armed Forces of the United States as he determines to be necessary and appropriate in order to — (1) defend the national security of the United States against the continuing threat posed by Iraq; and (2) enforce all relevant United Nations Security Council resolutions regarding Iraq."

A number of war on terror issues have reached the Supreme Court, including: (1) whether the detention at the U.S. military base in Guantanamo Bay, Cuba, of non-citizens (Taliban and al Qaeda combatants captured in Afghanistan) is subject to federal court review by way of the writ of habeas corpus, *see Rasul v. Bush*, 2004 U.S. LEXIS 4760 (holding that such review does exist but leaving the exact contours of that review, for the moment at least, to the district courts); and (2) whether American citizens that have been classified as "enemy combatants" can be detained in military brigs, without charges or access to counsel, compare *Hamdi v. Rumsfeld*, 2004 U.S. LEXIS 4861 (holding that the American-born Hamdi can be detained as an enemy combatant for the length of the on-going combat in Afghanistan, but allowing Hamdi a limited due process right to challenge his detention and to have access to counsel to do so), *with Padilla v. Rumsfeld*, 2004 U.S. LEXIS 4759, finding that Padilla, also an American citizen but captured on American soil and declared to be an "enemy combatant" by the President for allegedly planning with al Qaeda to detonate a "dirty bomb" in the U.S. or blow up apartment buildings, filed his habeas petition in the wrong court, and therefore dismissing his petition subject to refiling).

Lingering in the background of each of the cases are differing views of the President's inherent authority. It was unnecessary, however, for the Court to address that issue fully, given the overwhelming congressional approval of the President's military action. Wrote Justice O'Connor for a plurality of the Court in *Hamdi*: "we conclude that detention of individuals [of enemy combatants] for the duration of the particular conflict in which they are captured, is so funda-mental and accepted an incident to war as to be an exercise of the 'necessary and appropriate force' Congress has authorized the President to use." Only Jus-tices Souter and Ginsburg disagreed, finding Congress' force authorization not to speak to detention. Justices Scalia and Stevens, an unusual pairing, thought detention inappropriate unless the government was prepared to try Hamdi for treason or related offenses. Detention, these Justices reasoned, is the war-time tradition for captured aliens, but "[c]itizens aiding the enemy have been treated as traitors subject to the criminal process." Justice Thomas disagreed strongly, backing the President in war time and finding the due process obligation to be satisfied by the Executive's ability to make "virtually conclusive factual findings" as to who is or is not an enemy combatant without judicial second-guessing. To Justice Thomas, the Court has no business reviewing the President's detention decisions in war any more than the Court could question his tactical military deployments or strategies. "Taking and holding enemy combatants is a quin-tessential aspect of the prosecution of war."

Since the detained American citizens are few in number, and the due process mandated by the Court plurality in *Hamdi* far less than a trial, the conduct of the war by the politically accountable branches (the President and Congress) is not likely impeded by the outcome. The Court's cognizance of its institutional limitations are evident in the fact that the Court permits reliance upon hearsay evidence with a presumption in favor of the Government. The President's lawyers had asked for the Justices to accept a "some evidence" standard. They didn't do that, but the Justices did accept a "credible evidence" standard which is likely not far different. Indeed, the plurality suggested that Article III judges might not be required to be involved at all, as "an appropriately authorized and properly constituted military tribunal" could suffice. On the last point, the plurality rested squarely on past precedent, in particular *Ex Parte Quirin*, 317 U.S. 1 (1942) (upholding the use of military tribunals to try German army saboteurs, including one who was a U.S. citizen, who came ashore on the East Coast out of uniform, in violation of the laws of war).

The decision in *Rasul v. Bush* is more enigmatic and troubling to the exercise of the war power by the Executive and Congress. In *Rasul*, the President relied upon a World War II case, *Johnson v. Eisentrager*, 339 U.S. 763 (1950) (holding that German soldiers, convicted by military tribunal for continuing armed conflict against the United States after Germany's surrender, and who were being held outside the sovereign territory of the United States had no right to writ of habeas corpus to test the legality of their detention). Justice Stevens for six Justices found the cases distinguishable. Unlike the petitioners in *Eisentrager,* the alien detainees in Guantanamo Bay were not nationals of countries at war with the U.S. and were being detained for interrogation without access to any tribunal, even a military one. President Bush has authorized military tribunals for non-citizens captured in the War on Terror, but after two years of detention, no trial had yet to be conducted. Five of the Justices treated *Rasul* as an exercise in statutory interpretation, finding the habeas statute (28 U.S.C. § 2241) to be broad enough to include even aliens held outside the sovereign territory of the U.S. (Guantanamo is occupied by the military under longstanding lease).

The looming and unanswered question is what level of habeas review are alien, enemy combatant war detainees entitled to? The statute allows a detainee to deny the facts being relied upon by the government by "deposition, affidavit, or interrogatories." The prospect of military commanders being hauled into district court for such purposes led Justice Scalia, the Chief Justice, and Justice Thomas to write in dissent: "[t]he consequences of this holding . . . is breathtaking. It permits an alien captured in a foreign theater of active combat to bring a [habeas] petition against the Secretary of Defense. Over the course of the last century, the United States has held millions of alien prisoners abroad. . . . From this point forward, federal courts will entertain petitions from these prisoners, and others like them around the world, challenging actions and events far away, and forcing the courts to oversee one aspect of the Executive's conduct of a foreign war." Quoting *Eisentrager*, which the dissent thinks the majority virtually and erroneously overruled in *Rasul*, these Justices ruefully conclude: "Such trials would hamper the war effort and bring aid and comfort to the enemy."

Chapter 4

A LIMITED GOVERNMENT OF ENUMERATED POWER

A. Limitations on Federal Power

1. Enumerated Powers of the Federal Government

One of the most important political issues in the late twentieth and the beginning of the twenty-first century is likely to be the allocation of governmental responsibility between the state and federal governments. This issue, usually called "Federalism," has been a perennial problem in American history. Until our Civil War in the 1860s, it was nearly universally assumed that the more important governments were those of the states. Indeed, a citizen of the United States (a noun which always was regarded as a plural, rather than the singular it is today) tended to think of himself more as a Virginian, or a New Yorker, for example, rather than as an American. After the Civil War, the power of the national government grew greater for a time, and the end of the nineteenth century saw the establishment of the first important federal regulatory efforts, including the Interstate Commerce Act and the Sherman Antitrust Act. Not until the 1930s, however, in the era of the "New Deal," did the federal government begin to intrude into virtually all aspects of national life. Many Americans appear to feel that this intrusion has gone too far, and even Bill Clinton, in the run-up to the Presidential Campaign of 1996, declared that "the era of big [federal] government is over." Our job in this Chapter is generally to explore the concept of limited government, and, in this section, to try to understand just what power was supposed to be allocated to the federal government.

Our starting point, of course, is the text of the Constitution itself, and for the moment we are concerned with the Constitution's grant of power to Congress, to be found in Article I, Section 8. Review that section, which is reprinted before Chapter One. Does this grant of legislative powers to the federal government seem broad or limited to you? What legislative powers, if any, are not granted to Congress? What is the effect of the last part of this section, known as the "Necessary and Proper Clause"? Consider the explication of that section, and the so-called "Supremacy Clause" of Article VI, by Alexander Hamilton in FEDERALIST No. 33.

THE FEDERALIST NO. 33 (Alexander Hamilton)
(Clinton Rossiter ed., 1961)

* * *

These two clauses have been the source of much virulent invective and petulant declamation against the proposed Constitution. They have been held up to the people in all the exaggerated colours of misrepresentation as the pernicious engines by which their local governments were to be destroyed and their liberties exterminated; . . . and yet, strange as it may appear . . . it may be affirmed with perfect confidence that the constitutional operation of the intended government would be precisely the same, if these clauses were entirely obliterated. . . . They are only declaratory of a truth which would have resulted by necessary and unavoidable implication from the very act of constituting a federal government, and vesting it with certain specified powers. . . .

What is a power, but the ability or faculty of doing a thing? What is the ability to do a thing, but the power of employing the *means* necessary to its execution? What is a LEGISLATIVE power, but a power of making LAWS? What are the *means* to execute a LEGISLATIVE power but LAWS? What is the power of laying and collecting taxes, but a *legislative power*, or a power of *making laws*, to lay and collect taxes? What are the proper means of executing such a power, but *necessary* and *proper* laws?

This simple train of inquiry furnishes us at once with a test by which to judge of the true nature of the clause complained of. It conducts us to this palpable truth, that a power to lay and collect taxes must be a power to pass all laws *necessary* and *proper* for the execution of that power; and what does the unfortunate and calumniated provision in question do more than declare the same truth, to wit, that the national legislature, to whom the power of laying and collecting taxes had been previously given, might, in the execution of that power, pass all laws *necessary* and *proper* to carry it into effect? . . . [T]he same process will lead to the same result, in relation to all other powers declared in the Constitution. And it is *expressly* to execute these powers that the sweeping clause, as it has been affectedly called, authorizes the national legislature to pass all *necessary* and *proper* laws. If there is any thing exceptionable, it must be sought for in the specific powers upon which this general declaration is predicated. . . .

But SUSPICION may ask, Why then was it introduced? The answer is, that it could only have been done for greater caution, and to guard against all cavilling refinements in those who might hereafter feel a disposition to curtail and evade the legitimate authorities of the Union. The Convention probably foresaw, what it has been a principal aim of these papers to inculcate, that the danger which most threatens our political welfare is that the State governments will finally sap the foundations of the Union; and might therefore think it necessary, in so cardinal a point, to leave nothing to construction. . . .

But it may be again asked, Who is to judge of the *necessity* and *propriety* of the laws to be passed for executing the powers of the Union? I answer, first, that this question arises as well and as fully upon the simple grant of those powers as upon the declaratory clause; and I answer, in the second place, that the national government, like every other, must judge, in the first instance, of the proper exercise of its powers, and its constituents in the last. If the federal government should overpass the just bounds of its authority and make a tyrannical use of its powers, the people, whose creature it is, must appeal to the standard they have formed, and take such measures to redress the injury done to the Constitution as the exigency may suggest and prudence justify. . . . Suppose, by some forced constructions of its authority (which, indeed, cannot easily be imagined), the Federal legislature should attempt to vary the law of descent in any State, would it not be evident that, in making such an attempt, it had exceeded its jurisdiction, and infringed upon that of the State? Suppose, again, that upon the pretense of an interference with its revenues, it should undertake to abrogate a land tax imposed by the authority of a State; would it not be equally evident that this was an invasion of that concurrent jurisdiction in respect to this species of tax, which its Constitution plainly supposes to exist in the State governments? . . .

But it is said that the laws of the Union are to be the *supreme law* of the land. But what inference can be drawn from this, or what would they amount to, if they were not to be supreme? It is evident they would amount to nothing. A LAW, by the very meaning of the term, includes supremacy. . . . If individuals enter into a state of society, the laws of that society must be the supreme regulator of their conduct. If a number of political societies enter into a larger political society, the laws which the latter may enact, pursuant to the powers intrusted to it by its constitution, must necessarily be supreme over those societies, and the individuals of whom they are composed. . . . But it will not follow from this doctrine that acts of the larger society which are *not pursuant* to its constitutional powers, but which are invasions of the residuary authorities of the smaller societies, will become the supreme law of the land. These will be merely acts of usurpation, and will deserve to be treated as such. Hence we perceive that the clause which declares the supremacy of the laws of the Union, like the one we have just before considered, only declares a truth, which flows immediately and necessarily from the institution of a federal government. . . .

Though a law, therefore, laying a tax for the use of the United States would be supreme in its nature, and could not legally be opposed or controlled, yet a law for abrogating or preventing the collection of a tax laid by the authority of the State, (unless upon imports and exports), would not be the supreme law of the land, but a usurpation of power not granted by the Constitution. . . . The inference from the whole is, that the individual States would, under the proposed Constitution, retain an independent and uncontrollable authority to raise revenue to any extent of which they may stand in need, by every kind of taxation, except duties on imports and exports. . . . [T]his CONCURRENT JURISDICTION in the article of taxation was the only admissible substitute for an entire subordination, in respect to this branch of power, of the State authority to that of the Union.

NOTES AND QUESTIONS

1. Does Hamilton's exegesis in FEDERALIST NO. 33 reassure you about the purportedly limited nature of the legislative power which Congress was to possess under the new Constitution? As you must have inferred, a principal criticism of the new Constitution, made by those who believed that it too greatly constricted state sovereignty, was that the Necessary and Proper Clause, and the Supremacy Clause, taken together, gave the federal government unlimited power. Does Hamilton effectively meet this criticism?

2. Consider the similar attempt to minimize the importance of the Necessary and Proper Clause made at the Pennsylvania ratifying convention by James Wilson, generally regarded as second in importance only to James Madison as a framer of the Constitution. In response to a critic who had argued that the Clause gave Congress "the power of legislating generally," Wilson fumed:

> Can the words, the congress shall have power to make all laws, which shall be necessary and proper to carry into execution the foregoing powers, be capable of giving them general legislative power? — I hope that it is not meant to give to congress merely an illusive shew of authority, to deceive themselves or constituents any longer. On the contrary, I trust it is meant, that they shall have the power of carrying into effect the laws, which they shall make under the powers vested in them by this constitution.

1 THE DEBATE ON THE CONSTITUTION 826 (Bernard Bailyn ed., 1993). The critics were concerned, among other things, that the Necessary and Proper Clause might authorize the federal government to restrict the freedom of the press, of which more later.

3. Also of significance, perhaps, was the rejection, at the constitutional convention in Philadelphia, of a proposal explicitly to authorize the federal government to establish a National Bank. Supporters of a strong central government saw a National Bank as something which would help further the development of commercial prosperity in the new nation. Opponents of a National Bank, however, feared that such an institution would threaten state banking, and lead to further control over the states by the national government. Accordingly, the Constitution remained silent on the appropriateness of a National Bank.

Just such a National Bank, however, was part of the proposals for commercial development put forward by the first United States Secretary of the Treasury, Alexander Hamilton, and its constitutionality was sharply debated in the Washington administration. Hamilton believed that the Necessary and Proper

Clause authorized such a bank — broadly construing the Clause in precisely the manner critics of the Clause had feared. Thomas Jefferson, Washington's Secretary of State, argued forcefully that the Clause should not be read to authorize the creation of an institution not expressly authorized by other constitutional provisions. Is Jefferson's argument strengthened by the passage of the Tenth Amendment to the Constitution, ratified, along with the rest of the Bill of Rights, on December 15, 1791? The Tenth Amendment provides that "The powers not delegated to the United States by the Constitution, nor prohibited by it to the States, are reserved to the States respectively, or to the people." U.S. CONST., amend. X.

Hamilton won the argument, the National Bank was created, and, eventually, Jefferson resigned as a member of Washington's cabinet. The debate over the National Bank's constitutionality and wisdom raged for some time, however, and was only settled by the opinion of the man most historians believe to be the greatest Chief Justice of the Supreme Court, John Marshall. Given Marshall's nearly-universal reputation for greatness, whose views would you expect him to adopt — those of Jefferson or of Hamilton? See if you guessed correctly by consulting the great case of *McCulloch v. Maryland*, which follows.

2. Implied Powers of the Federal Government

a. The Implied Powers of Congress Through the "Necessary and Proper" and "Supremacy" Clauses

MCCULLOCH v. MARYLAND
17 U.S. (4 Wheat.) 316 (1819)

MR. CHIEF JUSTICE MARSHALL delivered the opinion of the Court.

In the case now to be determined, the defendant, a sovereign State, denies the obligation of a law enacted by the legislature of the Union, and the plaintiff, on his part, contests the validity of an act which has been passed by the legislature of that State. The constitution of our country, in its most interesting and vital parts, is to be considered, the conflicting powers of the government of the Union and of its members, as marked in that constitution, are to be discussed, and an opinion given which may essentially influence the great operations of the Government. . . . On the Supreme Court of the United States has the constitution of our country devolved this important duty.

The first question made in the cause is, has Congress power to incorporate a bank?

It has been truly said that this can scarcely be considered as an open question. . . . The principle now contested was introduced at a very early period of our history, has been recognised by many successive legislatures, and has been acted upon by the judicial department . . . as a law of undoubted obligation.

It will not be denied, that a bold and daring usurpation might be resisted, after an acquiescence still longer and more complete than this. But it is conceived that a doubtful question, . . . in the decision of which the great principles of liberty are not concerned, but the respective powers of those who are equally the representatives of the people, are to be adjusted; if not put at rest by the practice of the government, ought to receive a considerable impression from that practice. An exposition of the constitution, deliberately established by legislative acts, on the faith of which an immense property has been advanced, ought not to be lightly disregarded.

The power now contested was exercised by the first Congress elected under the present constitution. . . . Its principle was completely understood, and was opposed with equal zeal and ability. After being resisted first in the fair and open field of debate, and afterwards in the executive cabinet, with as much persevering talent as any measure has ever experienced, and being supported by arguments which convinced minds as pure and as intelligent as this country can boast, it became a law. The original act was permitted to expire, but a short experience of the embarrassments to which the refusal to revive it exposed the government, convinced those who were most prejudiced against the measure of its necessity, and induced the passage of the present law. It would require no ordinary share of intrepidity to assert that a measure adopted under these circumstances was a bold and plain usurpation, to which the constitution gave no countenance. . . .

In discussing this question, the counsel for the State of Maryland have deemed it of some importance, in the construction of the constitution, to consider that instrument not as emanating from the people, but as the act of sovereign and independent States. The powers of the general government, it has been said, are delegated by the States, who alone are truly sovereign; and must be exercised in subordination to the States, who alone possess supreme dominion.

It would be difficult to sustain this proposition. The convention which framed the constitution was indeed elected by the State legislatures. But the instrument, when it came from their hands, was a mere proposal, without obligation, or pretensions to it. It was reported to the then existing Congress of the United States, with a request that it might "be submitted to a Convention of Delegates, chosen in each State by the people thereof, under the recommendation of its Legislature, for their assent and ratification."

This mode of proceeding was adopted; and by the Convention, by Congress, and by the State Legislatures, the instrument was submitted to the people. They acted upon it in the only manner in which they can act safely, effectively, and wisely, on such a subject, by assembling in Convention. It is true, they assembled in their several States — and where else should they have assembled? . . . Of consequence, when they act, they act in their States. But the measures they adopt do not, on that account, cease to be the measures of the people themselves, or become the measures of the State governments.

From these Conventions the constitution derives its whole authority. The government proceeds directly from the people; is "ordained and established" in the name of the people; and is declared to be ordained, "in order to form a more perfect union, establish justice, insure domestic tranquillity, and secure the blessings of liberty to themselves and to their posterity." The assent of the States, in their sovereign capacity, is implied in calling a Convention, and thus submitting that instrument to the people. But the people were at perfect liberty to accept or reject it; and their act was final. It required not the affirmance, and could not be negatived, by the State governments. The constitution, when thus adopted, was of complete obligation, and bound the State sovereignties.

* * *

This government is acknowledged by all to be one of enumerated powers. . . . But the question respecting the extent of the powers actually granted, is perpetually arising, and will probably continue to arise, so long as our system shall exist. In discussing these questions, the conflicting powers of the general and State governments must be brought into view, and the supremacy of their respective laws, when they are in opposition, must be settled.

If any one proposition could command the universal assent of mankind, we might expect it would be this — that the government of the Union, though limited in its powers, is supreme within its sphere of action. This would seem to result necessarily from its nature. It is the government of all; its powers are delegated by all; it represents all, and acts for all. Though any one State may be willing to control its operations, no State is willing to allow others to control them. The nation, on those subjects on which it can act, must necessarily bind its component parts. But this question is not left to mere reason: the people have, in express terms, decided it, by saying, "this constitution, and the laws of the United States, which shall be made in pursuance thereof," "shall be the supreme law of the land," and by requiring that the members of the State legislatures, and the officers of the executive and judicial departments of the States, shall take the oath of fidelity to it. . . .

Among the enumerated powers, we do not find that of establishing a bank or creating a corporation. But there is no phrase in the instrument which, like the articles of confederation, excludes incidental or implied powers; and which requires that everything granted shall be expressly and minutely described. Even the 10th Amendment, which was framed for the purpose of quieting the excessive jealousies which had been excited, omits the word "expressly," and declares only that the powers "not delegated to the United States, nor prohibited to the States, are reserved to the States or to the people;" thus leaving the question, whether the particular power which may become the subject of contest has been delegated to the one government, or prohibited to the other, to depend on a fair construction of the whole instrument. The men who drew and adopted this amendment had experienced the embarrassments resulting from the insertion of this word in the articles of confederation, and probably omitted it to avoid those embarrassments. A constitution, to contain an accurate detail of all the subdivisions of which its great powers will admit, and of all the means by which they may be carried into execution, would partake of the prolixity of a legal code, and could scarcely be embraced by the human mind. It would probably never be understood by the public. Its nature, therefore, requires, that only its great outlines should be marked, its important objects designated, and the minor ingredients which compose those objects be deduced from the nature of the objects themselves. . . . In considering this question, then, we must never forget that it is *a constitution* we are expounding.

Although, among the enumerated powers of government, we do not find the word "bank" or "incorporation," we find the great powers, to lay and collect taxes; to borrow money; to regulate commerce; to declare and conduct a war; and to raise and support armies and navies. The sword and the purse, all the external relations, and no inconsiderable portion of the industry of the nation, are intrusted to its government. . . . [A] government, intrusted with such ample powers, on the due execution of which the happiness and prosperity of the Nation so vitally depends, must also be intrusted with ample means for their execution. The power being given, it is the interest of the nation to facilitate its execution. It can never be their interest, and cannot be presumed to have been their intention, to clog and embarrass its execution by withholding the most appropriate means. . . . Is that construction of the Constitution to be preferred which would render these operations difficult, hazardous, and expensive? Can we adopt that construction . . . which would impute to the framers of that instrument, when granting these powers for the public good, the intention of impeding their exercise by withholding a choice of means? . . . [T]he constitution . . . does not profess to enumerate the means by which the powers it confers may be executed; nor does it prohibit the creation of a corporation, if the existence of such a being be essential to the beneficial exercise of those powers. It is, then, the subject of fair inquiry, how far such means may be employed.

It is not denied, that the powers given to the Government imply the ordinary means of execution. . . . But it is denied that the government has its choice of means; or that it may employ the most convenient means, if, to employ them, it be necessary to erect a corporation. On what foundation does this argument rest? On this alone: The power of creating a corporation, is one appertaining to sovereignty, and is not expressly conferred on Congress. This is true. But all legislative powers appertain to sovereignty. The original power of giving the law on any subject whatever, is a sovereign power; and if the government of the Union is restrained from creating a corporation, as a means for performing its functions, on the single reason that the creation of a corporation is an act of sovereignty; if the sufficiency of this reason be acknowledged, there would be some difficulty in sustaining the authority of Congress to pass other laws for the accomplishment of the same objects. . . .

The creation of a corporation, it is said, appertains to sovereignty. This is admitted. But to what portion of sovereignty does it appertain? Does it belong to one more than to another? In America, the powers of sovereignty are divided between the government of the Union, and those of the States. They are each sovereign, with respect to the objects committed to it, and neither sovereign with respect to the objects committed to the other. We cannot comprehend that train of reasoning which would maintain, that the extent of power granted by the people is to be ascertained, not by the nature and terms of the grant, but by its date. Some State constitutions were formed *before*, some *since* that of the United States. We cannot believe that their relation to each other is in any degree dependent upon this circumstance. Their respective powers must, we think, be precisely the same as if they had been formed at the same time. Had they been formed at the same time, and had the people conferred on the general government the power contained in the constitution, and on the States the whole residuum of power, would it have been asserted that the government of the Union was not sovereign with respect to those objects which were intrusted to it, in relation to which its laws were declared to be supreme? . . . The power of creating a corporation, though appertaining to sovereignty, is not, like the power of making war, or levying taxes, or of regulating commerce, a great substantive and independent power, which cannot be implied as incidental to other powers, or used as a means of executing them. It is never the end for which other powers are exercised, but a means by which other objects are accomplished. . . . The power of creating a corporation is never used for its own sake, but for the purpose of effecting something else. No sufficient reason is, therefore, perceived, why it may not pass as incidental to those powers which are expressly given, if it be a direct mode of executing them.

But the constitution of the United States has not left the right of Congress to employ the necessary means, for the execution of the powers conferred on the government, to general reasoning. To its enumeration of powers is added that of making "all laws which shall be necessary and proper, for carrying into execution the foregoing powers, and all other powers vested by this constitution, in the government of the United States, or in any department thereof."

The counsel for the State of Maryland have urged various arguments, to prove that this clause, though in terms a grant of power, is not so in effect; but is really restrictive of the general right, which might otherwise be implied, of selecting means for executing the enumerated powers.

In support of this proposition, they have found it necessary to contend, that this clause was inserted for the purpose of conferring on Congress the power of making laws. That, without it, doubts might be entertained, whether Congress could exercise its powers in the form of legislation.

But could this be the object for which it was inserted? A government is created by the people, having legislative, executive, and judicial powers. Its legislative powers are vested in a Congress, which is to consist of a Senate and House of Representatives. Each house may determine the rule of its proceedings; and it is declared that every bill which shall have passed both houses, shall, before it becomes a law, be presented to the President of the United States. The 7th section describes the course of proceedings, by which a bill shall become a law; and, then, the 8th section enumerates the powers of Congress. . . . That a legislature, endowed with legislative powers, can legislate, is a proposition too self-evident to have been questioned.

But the argument on which most reliance is placed, is drawn from that peculiar language of this clause. Congress is not empowered by it to make all laws, which may have relation to the powers conferred on the government, but such only as may be *"necessary and proper"* for carrying them into execution. The word *"necessary,"* is considered as controlling the whole sentence, and as limiting the right to pass laws for the execution of the granted powers, to such as are indispensable, and without which the power would be nugatory. That it excludes the choice of means, and leaves to Congress, in each case, that only which is most direct and simple.

Is it true, that this is the sense in which the word "necessary" is always used? Does it always import an absolute physical necessity, so strong, that one thing, to which another may be termed necessary, cannot exist without that other? We think it does not. If reference be had to its use, in the common affairs of the world, or in approved authors, we find that it frequently imports no more than that one thing is convenient, or useful, or essential to another. . . . Such is the character of human language, that no word conveys to the mind, in all situations, one single definite idea; and nothing is more common than to use words in a figurative sense. Almost all compositions contain words, which, taken in their rigorous sense, would convey a meaning different from that which is obviously intended. It is essential to just construction, that many words which import something excessive, should be understood in a more mitigated sense — in that sense which common usage justifies. The word "necessary" is of this description. It has not a fixed character peculiar to itself. It admits of all degrees of comparison; and is often connected with other words, which increase or diminish the impression the mind receives of the urgency it imports. A thing may be necessary, very necessary, absolutely or indispensably necessary. To no mind would the same idea be conveyed, by these several phrases. The comment on the word is well illustrated, by the passage cited at the bar, from the 10th section of the 1st article of the constitution. It is, we think, impossible to compare the sentence which prohibits a State from laying "imposts, or duties on imports or exports, except what may be *absolutely* necessary for executing its inspection laws," with that which authorizes Congress "to make all laws which shall be necessary and proper for carrying into execution" the powers of the general government, without feeling a conviction that the convention understood itself to change materially the meaning of the word "necessary," by prefixing the word "absolutely." This word, then, like others, is used in various senses; and, in its construction, the subject, the context, the intention of the person using them, are all to be taken into view.

. . . The subject is the execution of those great powers on which the welfare of a nation essentially depends. It must have been the intention of those who gave these powers, to insure, so far as human prudence could insure, their beneficial execution. This could not be done by confiding the choice of means to such narrow limits as not to leave it in the power of Congress to adopt any which might be appropriate, and which were conducive to the end. This provision is made in a constitution intended to endure for ages to come, and, consequently, to be adapted to the various *crises* of human affairs. To have prescribed the means by which government should, in all future time, execute its powers, would have been to change, entirely, the character of the instrument, and give it the properties of a legal code. It would have been an unwise attempt to provide, by immutable rules, for exigencies which, if foreseen at all, must have been seen dimly, and which can be best provided for as they occur. To have declared that the best means shall not be used, but those alone without which the power given would be nugatory, would have been to deprive the legislature of the capacity to avail itself of experience, to exercise its reason, and to accommodate its legislation to circumstances.

* * *

In ascertaining the sense in which the word "necessary" is used in this clause of the constitution, we may derive some aid from that with which it is associated. Congress shall have power "to make all laws which shall be necessary and *proper* to carry into execution" the powers of the government. If the word "necessary" was used in that strict and rigorous sense for which the counsel for the State of Maryland contend, it would be an extraordinary departure from the usual course of the human mind, as exhibited in composition, to add a word, the only possible effect of which is to qualify that strict and rigorous meaning; to present to the mind the idea of some choice of means of legislation not strained and compressed within the narrow limits for which gentlemen contend.

But the argument which most conclusively demonstrates the error of the construction contended for by the counsel for the State of Maryland, is founded on the intention of the Convention, as manifested in the whole clause. To waste time and argument in proving that, without it, Congress might carry its powers into execution, would be not much less idle than to hold a lighted taper to the sun. As little can it be required to prove, that in the absence of this clause, Congress would have some choice of means. That it might employ those which, in its judgment, would most advantageously effect the object to be accomplished. That any means adapted to the end, any means which tended directly to the execution of the constitutional powers of the government, were in themselves constitutional. This clause, as construed by the State of Maryland, would abridge, and almost annihilate, this useful and necessary right of the legislature to select its means. That this could not be intended, is, we should think, had it not been already controverted, too apparent for controversy. We think so for the following reasons:

1st. The clause is placed among the powers of Congress, not among the limitations on those powers.

2nd. Its terms purport to enlarge, not to diminish the powers vested in the government. . . . No reason has been, or can be assigned for thus concealing an intention to narrow the discretion of the national legislature under words which purport to enlarge it. The framers of the constitution wished its adoption, and well knew that it would be endangered by its strength, not by its weakness. Had they been capable of using language which would convey to the eye one idea, and, after deep reflection, impress on the mind another, they would rather have disguised the grant of power, than its limitation. If, then, their intention had been, by this clause, to restrain the free use of means which might otherwise have been implied, that intention would have been inserted in another place, and would have been expressed in terms resembling these. "In carrying into execution the foregoing powers, and all others," &c. "no laws shall be passed but such as are necessary and proper." . . .

The result of the most careful and attentive consideration bestowed upon this clause is, that, if it does not enlarge, it cannot be construed to restrain the powers of Congress, or to impair the right of the legislature to exercise its best judgment in the selection of measures to carry into execution the constitutional powers of the government. If no other motive for its insertion can be suggested, a sufficient one is found in the desire to remove all doubts respecting the right to legislate on that vast mass of incidental powers which must be involved in the constitution, if that instrument be not a splendid bauble.

We admit, as all must admit, that the powers of the government are limited, and that its limits are not to be transcended. But we think the sound construction of the constitution must allow to the national legislature that discretion, with respect to the means by which the powers it confers are to be carried into execution, which will enable that body to perform the high duties assigned to it, in the manner most beneficial to the people. Let the end be legitimate, let it be within the scope of the constitution, and all means which are appropriate, which are plainly adapted to that end, which are not prohibited, but consist with the letter and spirit of the constitution, are constitutional.

. . . If we look to the origin of corporations, to the manner in which they have been framed in that government from which we have derived most of our legal principles and ideas, or to the uses to which they have been applied, we find no reason to suppose that a constitution, omitting, and wisely omitting, to enumerate all the means for carrying into execution the great powers vested in government, ought to have specified this. Had it been intended to grant this power as one which should be distinct and independent, to be exercised in any case whatever, it would have found a place among the enumerated powers of the government. But being considered merely as a means, to be employed only for the purpose of carrying into execution the given powers, there could be no motive for particularly mentioning it.

The propriety of this remark would seem to be generally acknowledged by the universal acquiescence in the construction which has been uniformly put on the 3d section of the 4th article of the constitution. The power to "make all needful rules and regulations respecting the territory or other property belonging to the United States," is not more comprehensive, than the power "to make all laws which shall be necessary and proper for carrying into execution" the powers of the government. Yet all admit the constitutionality of a territorial government, which is a corporate body.

If a corporation may be employed, indiscriminately with other means, to carry into execution the powers of the government, no particular reason can be assigned for excluding the use of a bank, if required for its fiscal operations. To use one, must be within the discretion of Congress, if it be an appropriate mode of executing the powers of government. That it is a convenient, a useful, and essential instrument in the prosecution of its fiscal operations, is not now a subject of controversy. All those who have been concerned in the administration of our finances, have concurred in representing its importance and necessity; and so strongly have they been felt, that statesmen of the first class, whose previous opinions against it had been confirmed by every circumstance which can fix the human judgment, have yielded those opinions to the exigencies of the nation. Under the confederation, Congress, justifying the measure by its necessity, transcended, perhaps, its powers to obtain the advantage of a bank; and our own legislation attests the universal conviction of the utility of this measure. . . .

But, were its necessity less apparent, none can deny its being an appropriate measure; and if it is, the decree of its necessity, as has been very justly observed, is to be discussed in another place. Should Congress, in the execution of its powers, adopt measures which are prohibited by the constitution; or should Congress, under the pretext of executing its powers, pass laws for the accomplishment of objects not entrusted to the government; it would become the painful duty of this tribunal, should a case requiring such a decision come before it, to say that such an act was not the law of the land. But where the law is not prohibited, and is really calculated to effect any of the objects entrusted to the government, to undertake here to inquire into the decree of its necessity, would be to pass the line which circumscribes the judicial department, and to tread on legislative ground. This court disclaims all pretensions to such a power.

After this declaration, it can scarcely be necessary to say, that the existence of State banks can have no possible influence on the question. No trace is to be found in the constitution of an intention to create a dependence of the government of the Union on those of the States, for the execution of the great powers assigned to it. Its means are adequate to its ends; and on those means alone was it expected to rely for the accomplishment of its ends. To impose on it the necessity of resorting to means which it cannot control, which another government may furnish or withhold, would render its course precarious, the result of its measures uncertain, and create a dependence on other governments, which might disappoint its most important designs, and is incompatible with the language of the constitution. But were it otherwise, the choice of means implies a right to choose a national bank in preference to State banks, and Congress alone can make the election.

NOTES AND QUESTIONS

1. Does the opinion in *McCulloch* help you to understand the almost superstitious veneration of John Marshall among modern constitutional scholars? Are you impressed with the number of cases and other legal authorities Marshall cites in support of his position? Is his conclusion, that Congress has the power to incorporate a bank, one that is consistent with the arguments made in Hamilton's FEDERALIST NO. 33? Would you have arrived at this conclusion?

2. Recall some of the extraordinary sweeping language Marshall uses. For example, consider his comments that the Constitution's nature "requires, that only its great outlines should be marked, its important objects designated, and the minor ingredients which compose those objects be deduced from the nature of the objects themselves." 17 U.S. (4 Wheat.) at 407. Is there a slip in his reasoning? How about the notions that "we must never forget, that it is *a constitution* we are expounding," *id.*, or that the Constitution is "intended to endure for ages to come, and, consequently, to be adapted [by the courts, presumably] to the various *crises* in human affairs"? *Id.* at 415. What is the meaning of these two suggestions? If you were concerned about the rule of law or judicial discretion, would you necessarily be comfortable with these sentiments? Would Hamilton have agreed with the idea that the Necessary and Proper Clause was placed in the Constitution because of a "desire to remove all doubts respecting the right to legislate on that vast mass of incidental powers which must be involved in the constitution, if that instrument be not a splendid bauble"? *Id.* at 420-21. What limitations on congressional power are left if one agrees that "[l]et the end be legitimate, let it be within the scope of the constitution, and all means which are appropriate, which are plainly adapted to that end, which are not prohibited, but consist with the letter and spirit of the constitution, are constitutional"? *Id.* at 421. *See* Randy E. Barnett, *Necessary and Proper,* 44 UCLA L. REV. 745 (1997) (discussing the meaning of the term "necessary and proper" and arguing that a strict construction of that standard is needed to protect the rights retained by the people from the ever-encroaching "administrative state"). What, precisely, is the "spirit" of the Constitution? You will encounter these phrases from *McCulloch* in countless federal court opinions that you will read as a lawyer. As you meet them again, consider whether they are invoked to support the kind of measures of which Hamilton, or even Marshall would have approved.

3. For the moment, however, consider only the question of the establishment of a corporation to be operated as a national bank. Do you agree with Marshall's assertion that even if the constitutionality of the bank corporation was dubious (and he does not think it is), the fact that this was the Second National

Bank, that there were profound disagreements about the constitutionality of the First National Bank (established during Washington's administration), that they were apparently resolved in favor of the constitutionality of the bank, and that the First National Bank did operate for many years, powerfully supports the constitutionality of the Second National Bank? This is Marshall's notion that the issue might be settled by "long practice." Is this an appealing argument? You might be interested to learn that Hamilton, making an "implied powers" argument identical to the one that Marshall invokes in *McCulloch*, supported the First National Bank, while Thomas Jefferson and James Madison opposed it. Was Hamilton's support for the bank consistent with his words in FEDERALIST No. 33? Why do you suppose Jefferson and Madison were opposed? Could it have something to do with the idea of state sovereignty to which Marshall refers in *McCulloch*? After the passage of the federal Constitution, just what is left to state sovereignty? We will return to that question at greater length in Chapter 5.

4. Marshall's opinion about the nature of the implied powers of the federal government caused a firestorm of disapproval among several prominent Jeffersonians. Madison himself, who had signed the legislation approving of the bank, was critical of Marshall's opinion, asserting that it left "no practical limits" to be assigned to Congress' power. As the Jacksonians triumphed in 1828, the states' rights arguments invoked in opposition to Marshall's position were dominant in national politics, and the influence of *McCulloch* waned, but as Richard Ellis has argued:

> The Civil War brought an end to Jacksonian hegemony and discredited states' rights. The constitutional revolution that followed took the country in a strong nationalist direction. In the twentieth century *McCulloch v. Maryland* quickly became the virtually undisputed constitutional cornerstone for the federal government's broad involvement in the economy, for the New Deal and the Welfare State, and for various other social, scientific, and educational programs.

Richard E. Ellis, McCulloch v. Maryland, *in* THE OXFORD COMPANION TO THE SUPREME COURT OF THE UNITED STATES 538 (Kermit L. Hall et al. eds., 1992). Marshall's view of congressional power is thus essential for the legitimacy of the modern operation of the federal government.

5. Whether the power exercised by the federal or national government be express or implied, you should understand well even at this early point that the consequence is the displacement or preemption of state authority. This, of course, is the consequence of the Supremacy Clause in Article VI. Preemption may result either where Congress expressly denies state authority or where that is the implication of the exercise of federal power. There are two types of implied preemption: field preemption, "where the scheme of federal regulation is so pervasive as to make reasonable the inference that Congress left no room for the States to supplement it," and conflict preemption, "where compliance with both federal and state regulations is a physical impossibility, or where state law stands as an obstacle to the accomplishment and execution of the full purposes and objectives of Congress." *Gade v. National Solid Waste Management Ass'n*, 505 U.S. 88, 98 (1992) (internal citations and quotations omitted). Many preemption cases are not clear, even when Congress has included an express preemption provision, because the extent of that preemption must still be ascertained. The touchstone is the intent of Congress, though the Court has often stated that such intent must be clearly articulated, since "'[t]he exercise of federal supremacy is not lightly to be presumed.'" *New York State Dep't of Soc. Services v. Dublino*, 413 U.S. 405, 413 (1973) (quoting *Schwartz v. Texas*, 344 U.S. 199, 203 (1952)). The Court has shown some reluctance to find field or implied preemption in the face of an express preemption provision. *Cipolone v. Liggett Group, Inc.*, 505 U.S. 504 (1992) (finding a federal cigarette labelling law to only partially preempt state tort claims of failure to warn and misrepresentation); *see also Medtronic Inc. v. Lohr*, 518 U.S. 470 (1996) (finding that a state cause of action for a failed medical device was not preempted by a federal statute precluding state regulation of the "safety and effectiveness" of medical devices). Field preemption is more likely found where the federal government has substantial interests or expertise. For example, in *Hines v. Davidowitz*, 312 U.S. 52 (1941), the Court found state laws requiring the registration of aliens to be precluded by the extensive federal regulation in the area of immigration. Similarly, in *United States v. Locke*, 529 U.S. 89 (2000), the Court relied upon both field and conflict preemption in the area of maritime commerce, holding that federal regulation must predominate in an area where it had always predominated and where substantial interests were at stake, including national uniformity, the marine environment, and the oil industry.

7. Are the states preempted if Congress employs a "savings clause"? This issue arose in two recent cases in which conflict preemption was found in each. In *Geier v. American Honda Motor Co., Inc*, 529 U.S. 861 (2000), a state negligence action for failure to equip an automobile with an airbag was held to be preempted by a federal safety standard. At issue was the 1984 version of the Federal Motor Vehicle Safety Standard (FMVSS 208) requiring auto manufacturers to equip some, but not all, of their 1987 vehicles with passive restraints (airbags). While driving a 1987 Honda Accord, Geier collided with a tree and was seriously injured. The car was equipped with only manual shoulder and lap belts, which were buckled at the time of the accident. Geier sued Honda and its affiliates under a state common law tort action claiming that Honda had designed its car negligently and defectively because it lacked a driver-side airbag. The Court found no preemption based on the express terms of the statute since the federal law contained a savings clause, which explicitly stated that liability would continue to exist under common law. Nevertheless, the Court thereafter reasoned that the savings clause did not bar conflict preemption, because nothing in the language of the savings clause suggested an intent to save state law tort actions that, in fact, conflicted with federal regulations. The Court located this conflict in the belief that Congress wanted to encourage a range of passive restraint devices to be introduced over time. A single, uniform airbag rule would not advance this goal. Geier's lawsuit was preempted because the suit depended upon the claim that manufacturers had a duty to install an airbag. Such a duty would have presented an obstacle to the variety of devices sought and the gradual phase-in imposed by the federal regulation. Four Justices in dissent would not have preempted, based both on the presumption against preemption applicable to state common law matters, and an unwillingness to find an actual conflict with the words of the statute.

In the second case involving a savings clause, *United States v. Locke*, 529 U.S. 89 (2000), the Court preempted a Washington State law regulating oil tankers and providing for comprehensive remedies in the event of a spill. The appellate court had relied upon a savings clause in the federal Oil Pollution Act of 1990 to sustain the state law. In a unanimous opinion by Justice Kennedy, the Supreme Court disagreed, stating that the "Court of Appeals placed more weight on the saving clauses than those provisions can bear." Although Justice Kennedy recognized that there is a presumption against preemption, *see, e.g., Rice v. Santa Fe Elevator Corp.*, 331 U.S. 218 (1947), he stated that such presumption is only applied if Congress is legislating in a field traditionally occupied by the states. "An assumption of non-preemption is not triggered when the State regulates in an area where there has been a history of significant federal presence." Thus, the Supreme Court drew the line in *Locke*: In areas of traditional federal concern, where national uniformity is of great importance, "it is not always a sufficient answer to a claim of preemption to say that state rules 'supplement, or even mirror, federal requirements.'" Instead, "[t]he appropriate inquiry still remains whether the purposes and objectives of the federal statutes, including the intent to establish a workable, uniform system, are consistent with concurrent state regulation."

8. In *Crosby v. National Foreign Trade Council*, 530 U.S. 363 (2000), the Court found a Massachusetts procurement law to be preempted by federal sanctions against the nation of Myanmar (formerly Burma). With some exceptions, the state law generally barred state entities from buying goods or services from any person (defined to include a business organization) identified as doing business with Burma. Lying geographically between India on the northwest and China and Thailand on the north and southeast, Burma is ruled by a military regime not recognized by the United States. An independent country since 1948, first the socialists and then the military have ignored democratically elected governments. The Burmese military regime has "killed thousands of civilians . . . [and] tortured, raped, imprisoned and forcibly relocated hundreds of thousands of Burmese people." Amnesty International, *Myanmar: 10th Anniversary of Military Repression* (August 7, 1998). The United Nations and the United States have both verified the forced labor of as many as two million people. Forced labor is used on this vast scale not only for basic infrastructure but also to maintain the high profitability of the business enterprises of the regime. Those doing business with Burma have no effective means of discerning the extent to which their investment relies on the product of compulsory labor. To minimize its moral complicity in these international human rights violations, Massachusetts enacted its procurement restriction.

Nonetheless, a unanimous Court, per Justice Souter, found Massachusetts's law to be preempted by a federal statute imposing lesser, conditional sanctions, but also giving the President authority to adjust them as conditions warrant. Massachusetts argued against preemption since it was not express, but Justice Souter wrote:

> . . . [W]e see the state Burma law as an obstacle to the accomplishment of Congress's full objectives under the federal Act. We find that the state law undermines the intended purpose and "natural effect" of at least three provisions of the federal Act, that is, its delegation of effective discretion to the President to control economic sanctions against Burma, its limitation of sanctions solely to United States persons and new investment, and its directive to the President to proceed diplomatically in developing a comprehensive, multilateral strategy towards Burma.

The Court left most of the interesting issues for another day. Specifically, Massachusetts argued, but the Court found unnecessary to address, that there should be a presumption against preemption and that it was not interfering with federal power over foreign commerce or foreign affairs since it was merely exercising its role as a purchaser or "market participant." As will be discussed later in this Chapter, the Court does allow states this latitude insofar as it touches domestic or interstate commerce, but the issue had not been settled with regard to international trade, and it remains open.

Was the Court correct in this instance to find implied preemption? Why not prefer human rights, where Congress has not spoken clearly and expressly? Massachusetts pointed out in argument that if Congress was well aware of the Massachusetts position yet took no express action to preempt, why should the Court? As the state saw it, the absence of an express preemption clause is especially telling in light of the scores of similar laws enacted in the 1980s and Congress's failure to preempt them. *See generally* DOUGLAS W. KMIEC, THE ATTORNEY GENERAL'S LAWYER 138-43 (Praeger 1992) (explaining state activity in protest of apartheid and the Office of Legal Counsel's position finding these state investment boycotts to be constitutionally permissible notwithstanding the federal Comprehensive Anti-Apartheid Act of 1986); *accord Board of Trustees v. Mayor and City Council of Baltimore,* 317 Md. 72 (1989) (no preemption), *cert. denied,* 493 U.S. 1093 (1990). By the way, when Congress wishes to preempt expressly, it knows how to do it. See, *e.g.,* the preemption provision in the Export Administration Act, 50 U.S.C. app. Section 2407(c) (1991).

9. Justice Souter wrote for the Court again in *American Insurance Association v. Garamendi,* 539 U.S. 396 (2003), finding invalid a California law requiring insurers doing business within the state to disclose information about the policies held by Holocaust victims. Unlike *Crosby,* this time the Court was divided 5-4, with the majority concluding that the President's ability to conduct foreign policy was hindered by the state enactment which arguably could foster individual litigation against the companies by the beneficiaries of the policies.

Of note is that the state law was preempted not by conflicting federal statute or treaty, but by executive agreements that preferred voluntary disclosure and claims to be settled not through litigation but against a limited common fund established by the German government. It was conceded that such agreements can preempt state law if preemption is expressly provided, but it had not been in this case. Thus, the issue became whether there was implied field or conflict preemption. The United States, as *amicus*, argued that field preemption would be appropriate given the foreign affairs nature of the dispute, relying upon an older precedent of *Zschernig v. Miller* (1968) (finding preemption of an Oregon law that prohibited inheritance by a foreign national unless the home country of the heir allowed reciprocal rights of inheritance to Oregonians). *Zschernig* had suggested that state action with more than incidental effect on foreign affairs is preempted, even absent any affirmative federal activity in the subject area of the state law, and hence without any showing of conflict. But the Court has never been clear on this point, and a separate opinion by Justice Harlan in *Zchnernig* argued that the states may legislate in areas "of their traditional competence even though their statutes may have an incidental effect on foreign relations."

Justice Souter in *Garamendi* wrote that "it is a fair question whether respect for the executive foreign relations power requires a categorical choice between the contrasting theories of field and conflict preemption evident in the *Zschernig* opinions, but the question requires no answer here," since California was legislating in an area beyond a state's traditional competence and had created a conflict with the federal approach. California was not enacting general consumer protection, the Court reasoned, but inserting itself into a longstanding dispute over the settlement of claims that resulted because of international hostilities. Moreover, "[t]he basic fact is that California seeks to use an iron fist where the President has consistently chosen kid gloves," wrote Justice Souter. Justice Ginsburg, joined by Justices Stevens, Scalia, and Thomas, dissented, arguing that no executive agreement or other formal expression of foreign policy expressly disapproved of state disclosure laws like California's, and therefore, preemption was unwarranted.

10. Omitted from your edited version of *McCulloch* were some statements Marshall made about the power of the Congress to punish offenses committed against the federal government, a power which Marshall claimed exists even if the Constitution does not expressly give Congress the power to legislate regarding particular crimes. If Congress can provide for the punishment of crimes against the federal government, even where the Constitution does not expressly confer this authority, might other bodies of the federal government also be able to combat wrongdoing against the federal government without express authority? What "implied powers," for example, do the federal courts possess?

b. Is There a Federal Common Law as Well?

If the legislature has authority, per *McCulloch*, to deduce necessary and proper implications from its enumerated power in Article I, can the same be said of the federal judiciary? That is, might it ever be said either that Article III defining the Court's subject matter jurisdiction or a federal statute affirming particular aspects of that jurisdiction also contains within it the authority for a judge to *imply* a cause of action? In brief, is there a federal common law?

This has been the subject of much debate. Jeffersonians were strongly critical of any implied federal common law of crimes arguing it to be an encroachment of the reserved power of the states. They further feared that an unwritten federal common law of crimes would open up possibilities for political persecution. Nevertheless, at the founding, some case opinion supported the discovery of federal common law. In *United States v. Worrall*, 28 F. Cas. 774 (C.C.D. Pa. 1798), for example, a lower federal court in Pennsylvania confronted the case of one Worrall, who was indicted for the crime of attempting to bribe the U.S. Commissioner of Revenue. The trouble was that Congress had not yet gotten around to making bribery of the Commissioner of Revenue a federal statutory crime. Thus, Worrall's indictment referred to no federal criminal statute, but merely accused him of "offending . . . against the peace and dignity of the United States." While it was understood that individual states could apply the unwritten common law, as received or selectively imported from England, it was not clear that the courts of the United States could do the same. In *Worrall,* the lower court decided that it could, notwithstanding the concerns of Justice Chase. Chase, sitting as a circuit judge, argued that: "the United States, as a Federal government, has no common law; and consequently, no indictment can be maintained in their Courts, for offenses merely at the common law." Chase didn't doubt the existence of the common law. It was just that it was inherited by the *states* not the national government. And as inherited by the states, it was not uniform. States didn't necessarily accept the whole body of British common law, and the principles that they did accept had undergone some evolution. The prevailing view in *Worrall*, however, was that the power to declare the common law was an aspect of sovereignty, a necessary and inseparable concomitant if the Union was to be able to preserve itself.

In *United States v. Hudson & Goodwin*, 11 U.S. (7 Cranch) 32 (1812), the U.S. Supreme Court repudiated the federal common law of crimes. Hudson & Goodwin were indicted for criminally libeling the President and Congress of secretly voting to give two million dollars to Emperor Napoleon. There was no congressional statute making libel of the President or of Congress a federal crime, and so, Justice Johnson, a Jefferson appointee, stated the issue as "whether the circuit Courts of the United States can exercise a common law jurisdiction in criminal cases?" His answer was, in general, no. He wrote:

> Certain implied powers must necessarily result to our Courts of justice from the nature of their institution. But jurisdiction of crimes against the state is not among these powers. To fine for contempt —

> imprison for contumacy — inforce the observance of order, etc., are powers which cannot be dispensed with in a Court, because they are necessary to the exercise of all others: and so far our Courts no doubt possess powers not immediately derived from statute; but all exercise of criminal jurisdiction in common law cases we are of opinion is not within their implied powers.

Of course, this left the question of whether there was a federal common law in *civil* matters. For a while the Court answered in the affirmative. For example, in *Swift v. Tyson*, 41 U.S. (16 Pet.) 1 (1842), the issue was a highly technical question about negotiable instruments law: whether a particular bill of exchange (an instrument something like the modern check) was negotiable, that is, whether a purchaser of such an instrument could "cash" it without fear that the original maker of the instrument could refuse to honor it because of defects in the original transaction. The decision on whether or not the bill was negotiable turned on whether the court would apply the position taken on the issue by the courts of New York (the place where the bill of exchange was made) or the position taken by most other courts in the nation. No New York statute governed the transaction. The New York common law position would have disfavored negotiability by allowing a myriad of defenses to be raised, while the common law position of other states would not.

Justice Story adopted the non-New York view as the federal view of the matter. Much of the opinion dealt with the so-called Rules of Decision Act — that is, section 34 of the Judiciary Act of 1789 — which required federal courts to treat the "laws of the several states" as rules of decision (*i.e.*, binding) in cases where they apply, assuming of course that there was no applicable federal law. Justice Story, for the majority in *Swift*, held that "laws" in that federal statute merely meant state *statutory* laws, or at most, state common law principles that were inherently *local* in character, like state real property law principles. It didn't mean the state's general common law principles. Story gave a philosophical interpretation to these more general, common law principles. He said:

> In the ordinary use of language it will hardly be contended that the decisions of Courts [he means, of course, the decisions of courts declaring principles of the common law] constitute laws. They are, at most, only evidence of what the laws are; and are not of themselves laws.

Story's view here is very much a natural law understanding of the nature of court decisions pronouncing on the content of the common law. Where do we find common law principles? In court decisions, yes, but really the principles themselves have their source in nature, and the court decisions are really only evidence of what the law of nature is. Story makes this plain by quoting a Latin expression from Cicero:

> *Non erit alia lex Romae, alia Athenis, alia nunc, alia posthac, sed et apud omnes gentes, et omni tempore, una eademque lex obtenebit.*

[There should not be one law of Rome, another of Athens, one now, another later, but one and the same law should hold for all people and for all time.]

All first year law students know that *Swift* was expressly overruled in *Erie R. Co. v. Tompkins*, 304 U.S. 64 (1938), holding that federal courts must look to the general common law principles that a state court in the state in which they are situated would use. Nevertheless, advocates continue to press the U.S. Supreme Court to employ customary international law or the law of nations to build up a new, internationally-based common law.

In *Sosa v. Alvarez-Machain*, 2004 U.S. LEXIS 4763, the Drug Enforcement Administration (DEA) approved using Sosa to abduct Alvarez-Machain, another Mexican national, from Mexico to stand trial in the United States for a DEA agent's torture and murder. After his acquittal, Alvarez-Machain sued the United States for false arrest as a violation of the law of nations under the Alien Tort Statute (ATS), a 1789 law giving district courts "original jurisdiction of any civil action by an alien for a tort only, committed in violation of the law of nations," 28 U.S.C. § 1350. The lower court sustained this claim, but the Supreme Court unanimously reversed. Writing for the majority, Justice Souter opined that the 1789 ATS statute is largely jurisdictional, though it implicitly permitted a handful of common law causes of action related to offenses against ambassadors, impediments to the safe conduct represented by a passport, or the actions of pirates. Did that mean that district courts should not recognize other private causes of action for torts in violation of the law of nations? Yes, said Justice Souter, the federal courts should refrain from doing so. "We have no congressional mandate to seek out and define new and debatable violations of the law of nations, and modern indications of congressional understanding of the judicial role in the field have not affirmatively encouraged greater judicial creativity." Yet, Justice Souter did not totally foreclose the possibility of implying a new cause of action from international law, but to do so, the cause must be founded on an international law norm with no less definite content and acceptance among civilized nations than the handful of actions protecting ambassadors and the like that existed in the 18th century when the ATS was first enacted.

It is not entirely clear how generously the Court will take to this new federal common law implied from international norm. In rejecting Alvarez-Machain's claim for a damages for false arrest, the Court noted several reasons to be very cautious, including that the concept of common law has changed — it is now seen as judicially made in most cases, rather than found; *Erie* disavowed the existence of any federal general common law; a decision to create a private right of action is better left to legislative judgment; and there are foreign relations impacts to recognizing or not recognizing such causes of action and such would impinge on the Legislative and Executive branches.

Three Justices, Scalia, Thomas and the Chief Justice, agreed with much of Justice Souter's opinion for the Court, but thought that his opinion's contemplation of even a limited role for the judicial implication of a cause of action based upon a well-settled international norm was too much discretion to give to a non-lawmaking branch. Wrote Justice Scalia, concurring in the judgment:

> We Americans have a method for making the laws that are over us. We elect representatives to two Houses of Congress, each of which must enact the new law and present it for the approval of a President, whom we also elect. For over two decades now, unelected federal judges have been usurping this lawmaking power by converting what they regard as norms of international law into American law. Today's opinion approves that process in principle, though urging the lower courts to be more restrained.

> This Court seems incapable of admitting that some matters — *any* matters — are none of its business. *See, e.g., Rasul v. Bush* (2004) [finding a habeas corpus right for alien enemy combatants held outside the sovereign territory of the United States — Eds.]. In today's latest victory for its Never Say Never Jurisprudence, the Court ignores its own conclusion that the ATS provides only jurisdiction, wags a finger at the lower courts for going too far, and then — repeating the same formula the ambitious lower courts *themselves* have used — invites them to try again.

> It would be bad enough if there were some assurance that future conversions of perceived international norms into American law would be approved by this Court itself. (Though we know ourselves to be eminently reasonable, self-awareness of eminent reasonableness is not really a substitute for democratic election.) But in this illegitimate lawmaking endeavor, the lower federal courts will be the principal actors; we review but a tiny fraction of their decisions. And no one thinks that all of them are eminently reasonable.

> American law — the law made by the people's democratically elected representatives — does not recognize a category of activity that is so universally disapproved by other nations that it is automatically unlawful here, and automatically gives rise to a private action for money damages in federal court. That simple principle is what today's decision should have announced.

Why is it that judges, unlike Justice Scalia and his dissenting colleagues at least, seem so enamoured with leaving the door open to the federal common law or law of nations? Is it merely that it gives judges more power and discretion or is there something intrinsically important about the particular topics being addressed that begs for uniform treatment by the judiciary? Recall that Justice Story argued strongly for a national commercial law derived from the law of nations in *Swift v. Tyson*. Story cited Cicero, and as pointed out above, Cicero's claim was that the common law based on the law of nations must be philosophically understood to be good in all places and all times. Can it really be true that there is only one correct view of commercial transactions, or is it more likely that there are multiple views and policies worthy of consideration on this topic?

If you think that a law of nations or natural law claim for the definitive position on negotiable instruments would be weak, what about other subjects, such as "torture, genocide, crimes against humanity, and war crimes." Justice Breyer in a separate concurring opinion in *Sosa* suggests that these might be worthy areas for universal jurisdiction. Do you agree? Do you agree even if statutory law has not fully defined these subjects? Justice Breyer writes: "in the 18th century, nations reached a consensus not only on the substantive principle that acts of piracy were universally wrong but also on the jurisdictional principle that any nation that found a pirate could prosecute him." Can we say the same about radical Islamic fundamentalists engaged in terrorism today? Would Justice Breyer?

For more on the nature of the common law and the law of nations in the 18th century, see STEPHEN B. PRESSER & JAMIL S. ZAINALDIN, LAW AND JURISPRUDENCE IN AMERICAN HISTORY: CASES AND MATERIALS 178-200 (3d ed., 1995).

Whatever the contours of the law of nations and any federal common law that may or may not be derived from it, there is a "commerce power" expressly granted to Congress in the Constitution. But from the beginning the Court has played an important interpretative role distinguishing between federal and state interests that may overlap with a commercial subject, determining when a state may act even when the Congress has not, and attempting to ascertain the ultimate scope of the federal power. These questions, among others, will be explored in the section which follows.

3. The Commerce Clause

a. What Is "Commerce"?

GIBBONS v. OGDEN
22 U.S. (9 Wheat.) 1 (1824)

. . . Aaron Ogden filed his bill in the Court of Chancery of [New York], against Thomas Gibbons, setting forth the several acts of the Legislature thereof, enacted for the purpose of securing to Robert R. Livingston and Robert Fulton, the exclusive navigation of all the waters within the jurisdiction of that State, with boats moved by fire or steam, for a term of years which has not yet expired; and authorizing the Chancellor to award an injunction, restraining any person whatever from navigating those waters with boats of that description. The bill stated an assignment from Livingston and Fulton to one John R. Livingston, and from him to the complainant, Ogden, of the right to navigate the waters between Elizabethtown, and other places in New-Jersey, and the city of New-York; and that Gibbons, the defendant below, was in possession of two steam boats, called the Stoudinger and the Bellona, which were actually employed in running between New-York and Elizabethtown, in violation of the exclusive privilege conferred on the complainant, and praying an injunction to restrain the said Gibbons from using the said boats, or any other propelled by fire or steam, in navigating the waters within the territory of New-York. The injunction having been awarded, the answer of Gibbons was filed; in which he stated, that the boats employed by him were duly enrolled and licensed, to be employed in carrying on the coasting trade, under the act of Congress, passed the 18th of February, 1793. . . . And the defendant insisted on his right, in virtue of such licenses, to navigate the waters between Elizabethtown and the city of New-York, the said acts of the Legislature of the State of New-York to the contrary notwithstanding. At the hearing, the Chancellor perpetuated the injunction, being of the opinion, that the said [New York] acts were not repugnant to the constitution and laws of the United States, and were valid. This decree was affirmed in the Court for the Trial of Impeachments and Correction of Errors, which is the highest Court of law and equity in the State . . . and it was thereupon brought to this Court by appeal.

* * *

Mr. Chief Justice Marshall delivered the opinion of the Court . . . :

The appellant contends that this decree is erroneous, because the laws which purport to give the exclusive privilege it sustains, are repugnant to the constitution and laws of the United States.

They are said to be repugnant —

1st. To that clause in the constitution which authorizes Congress to regulate commerce.

2d. To that which authorizes Congress to promote the progress of science and useful arts.

The State of New-York maintains the constitutionality of these laws; and their Legislature, their Council of Revision, and their Judges, have repeatedly concurred in this opinion. . . .

As preliminary to the very able discussions of the constitution, which we have heard from the bar, and as having some influence on its construction, reference has been made to the political situation of these States, anterior to its formation. It has been said, that they were sovereign, were completely independent, and were connected with each other only by a league. This is true. But, when these allied sovereigns converted their league into a government, when they converted their Congress of Ambassadors . . . into a Legislature, empowered to enact laws on the most interesting subjects, the whole character in which the States appear, underwent a change, the extent of which must be determined by a fair consideration of the instrument by which that change was effected.

This instrument contains an enumeration of powers expressly granted by the people to their government. It has been said, that these powers ought to be construed strictly. But why ought they to be so construed? Is there one sentence in the constitution which gives countenance to this rule? In the last of the enumerated powers, that which grants, expressly, the means for carrying all others into execution, Congress is authorized "to make all laws which shall be necessary and proper" for the purpose. But this limitation on the means which may be used, is not extended to the powers which are conferred; nor is there one sentence in the constitution, which has been pointed out by the gentlemen of the bar, or which we have been able to discern, that prescribes this rule. We do not, therefore, think ourselves justified in adopting it. What do gentlemen mean, by a strict construction? If they contend only against that enlarged construction, which would extend words beyond their natural and obvious import, we might question the application of the term, but should not controvert the principle. If they contend for that narrow construction which, in support of some theory not to be found in the constitution, would deny to the government those powers which the words of the grant, as usually understood, import, and which are consistent with the general views and objects of the instrument; for that narrow construction, which would cripple the government, and render it unequal to the object, for which it is declared to be instituted, and to which the powers given, as fairly understood, render it competent; then we cannot perceive the propriety of this strict construction, nor adopt it as the rule by which the constitution is to be expounded. As men, whose intentions require no concealment, generally employ the words which most directly and aptly express the ideas they intend to convey, the enlightened patriots who framed our constitution, and the people who adopted it, must be understood to have employed words in their natural sense, and to have intended what they have said. If, from the imperfection of human language, there should be serious doubts respecting the extent of any given power, it is a well settled rule, that the objects for which it was given, especially when those objects are expressed in the instrument itself, should have great influence in the construction. . . . The grant does not convey power which might be beneficial to the grantor, if retained by himself, or which can enure solely to the benefit of the grantee; but is an investment of power for the general advantage, in the hands of agents selected for that purpose; which power can never be exercised by the people themselves, but must be placed in the hands of agents, or lie dormant. We know of no rule for construing the extent of such powers, other than is given by the language of the instrument which confers them, taken in connexion with the purposes for which they were conferred.

The words are, "Congress shall have power to regulate commerce with foreign nations, and among the several States, and with the Indian tribes."

The subject to be regulated is commerce; and our constitution being, as was aptly said at the bar, one of enumeration, and not of definition, to ascertain the extent of the power, it becomes necessary to settle the meaning of the word. The counsel for the appellee would limit it to traffic, to buying and selling, or the interchange of commodities, and do not admit that it comprehends navigation.

This would restrict a general term, applicable to many objects, to one of its significations. Commerce, undoubtedly, is traffic, but it is something more: it is intercourse. It describes the commercial intercourse between nations, and parts of nations, in all its branches, and is regulated by prescribing rules for carrying on that intercourse. The mind can scarcely conceive a system for regulating commerce between nations, which shall exclude all laws concerning navigation. . . .

If commerce does not include navigation, the government of the Union has no direct power over that subject, and can make no law prescribing what shall constitute American vessels, or requiring that they shall be navigated by American seamen. Yet this power has been exercised from the commencement of the government, has been exercised with the consent of all, and has been understood by all to be a commercial regulation. All America understands, and has uniformly understood, the word "commerce," to comprehend navigation. . . . The power over commerce, including navigation, was one of the primary objects for which the people of America adopted their government, and must have been contemplated in forming it. . . .

If the opinion that "commerce," as the word is used in the constitution, comprehends navigation also, requires any additional confirmation, that additional confirmation is, we think, furnished by the words of the instrument itself.

It is a rule of construction, acknowledged by all, that the exceptions from a power mark its extent. . . . If, then, there are in the constitution plain exceptions from the power over navigation, plain inhibitions to the exercise of that power in a particular way, it is a proof that those who made these exceptions, and prescribed these inhibitions, understood the power to which they applied as being granted.

The 9th section of the 1st article declares, that "no preference shall be given, by any regulation of commerce or revenue, to the ports of one State over those of another." This clause cannot be understood as applicable to those laws only which are passed for the purposes of revenue, because it is expressly applied to commercial regulations; and the most obvious preference which can be given to one port over another, in regulating commerce, relates to navigation. But the subsequent part of the sentence is still more explicit. It is, "nor shall vessels bound to or from one State, be obliged to enter, clear, or pay duties, in another." These words have a direct reference to navigation.

The universally acknowledged power of the government to impose embargoes, must also be considered as showing, that all America is united in that construction which comprehends navigation in the word commerce. Gentlemen have said, in argument, that this is a branch of the war-making power, and that an embargo is an instrument of war, not a regulation of trade.

That it may be, and often is, used as an instrument of war, cannot be denied. An embargo may be imposed for the purpose of facilitating the equipment or manning of a fleet, or for the purpose of concealing the progress of an expedition preparing to sail from a particular port. In these, and in similar cases, it is a military instrument, and partakes of the nature of war. But all embargoes are not of this description. They are sometimes resorted to without a view to war, and with a single view to commerce. In such case, an embargo is no more a war measure, than a merchantman is a ship of war, because both are vessels which navigate the ocean with sails and seamen.

When Congress imposed that embargo which, for a time, engaged the attention of every man in the United States, the avowed object of the law was, the protection of commerce, and the avoiding of war. By its friends and its enemies it was treated as a commercial, not as a war measure. The persevering earnestness and zeal with which it was opposed, in a part of our country which supposed its interests to be vitally affected by the act, cannot be forgotten. . . . Yet they never suspected that navigation was no branch of trade, and was, therefore, not comprehended in the power to regulate commerce. They did, indeed, contest the constitutionality of the act, but, on a principle which admits the construction for which the appellant contends. They denied that the particular law in question was made in pursuance of the constitution, not because the power could not act directly on vessels, but because a perpetual embargo was the annihilation, and not the regulation of commerce. In terms, they admitted the applicability of the words used in the constitution to vessels; and that, in a case which produced a degree and an extent of excitement, calculated to draw forth every principle on which legitimate resistance could be sustained. No example could more strongly illustrate the universal understanding of the American people on this subject.

* * *

To what commerce does this power extend? The constitution informs us, to commerce "with foreign nations, and among the several States, and with the Indian tribes."

It has, we believe, been universally admitted, that these words comprehend every species of commercial intercourse between the United States and foreign nations. . . .

If this be the admitted meaning of the word, in its application to foreign nations, it must carry the same meaning throughout the sentence, and remain a unit, unless there be some plain intelligible cause which alters it.

The subject to which the power is next applied, is to commerce "among the several States." The word "among" means intermingled with. A thing which is among others, is intermingled with them. Commerce among the States, cannot stop at the external boundary line of each State, but may be introduced into the interior.

It is not intended to say that these words comprehend that commerce, which is completely internal, which is carried on between man and man in a State, or between different parts of the same State, and which does not extend to or affect other States. Such a power would be inconvenient, and is certainly unnecessary.

. . . The genius and character of the whole government seem to be, that its action is to be applied to all the external concerns of the nation, and to those internal concerns which affect the States generally; but not to those which are completely within a particular State, which do not affect other States, and with which it is not necessary to interfere, for the purpose of executing some of the general powers of the government. . . .

But, in regulating commerce with foreign nations, the power of Congress does not stop at the jurisdictional lines of the several States. . . . The commerce of the United States with foreign nations, is that of the whole United States. Every district has a right to participate in it. The deep streams which penetrate our country in every direction, pass through the interior of almost every State in the Union, and furnish the means of exercising this right. If Congress has the power to regulate it, that power must be exercised whenever the subject exists. If it exists within the States, if a foreign voyage may commence or terminate at a port within a State, then the power of Congress may be exercised within a State.

This principle is, if possible, still more clear, when applied to commerce "among the several States." They either join each other, in which case they are separated by a mathematical line, or they are remote from each other, in which case other States lie between them. What is commerce "among" them; and how is it to be conducted? Can a trading expedition between two adjoining States, commence and terminate outside of each? And if the trading intercourse be between two States remote from each other, must it not commence in one, terminate in the other, and probably pass through a third? Commerce among the States must, of necessity, be commerce with the States. In the regulation of trade with the Indian tribes, the action of the law, especially when the constitution was made, was chiefly within a State. The power of Congress, then, whatever it may be, must be exercised within the territorial jurisdiction of the several States. . . .

We are now arrived at the inquiry — What is this power?

It is the power to regulate; that is, to prescribe the rule by which commerce is to be governed. This power, like all others vested in Congress, is complete in itself, may be exercised to its utmost extent, and acknowledges no limitations, other than are prescribed in the constitution. These are expressed in plain terms, and do not affect the questions which arise in this case. . . . If, as has always been understood, the sovereignty of Congress, though limited to specified objects, is plenary as to those objects, the power over commerce with foreign nations, and among the several States, is vested in Congress as absolutely as it would be in a single government, having in its constitution the same restrictions on the exercise of the power as are found in the constitution of the United States. The wisdom and the discretion of Congress, their identity with the people, and the influence which their constituents possess at elections, are, in this, as in many other instances, as that, for example, of declaring war, the sole restraints on which they have relied, to secure them from its abuse. . . .

The power of Congress, then, comprehends navigation, within the limits of every State in the Union; so far as that navigation may be, in any manner, connected with "commerce with foreign nations, or among the several States, or with the Indian tribes." It may, of consequence, pass the jurisdictional line of New-York, and act upon the very waters to which the prohibition now under consideration applies.

But it has been urged with great earnestness, that, although the power of Congress to regulate commerce with foreign nations, and among the several States, be co-extensive with the subject itself, and have no other limits than are prescribed in the constitution, yet the States may severally exercise the same power, within their respective jurisdictions. In support of this argument, it is said, that they possessed it as an inseparable attribute of sovereignty, before the formation of the constitution, and still retain it, except so far as they have surrendered it by that instrument; that this principle results from the nature of the government, and is secured by the tenth amendment; that an affirmative grant of power is not exclusive, unless in its own nature it be such that the continued exercise of it by the former possessor is inconsistent with the grant, and that this is not of that description.

The appellant, conceding these postulates, except the last, contends, that full power to regulate a particular subject, implies the whole power, and leaves no residuum; that a grant of the whole is incompatible with the existence of a right in another to any part of it.

* * *

The grant of the power to lay and collect taxes is, like the power to regulate commerce, made in general terms, and has never been understood to interfere with the exercise of the same power by the States; and hence has been drawn an argument which has been applied to the question under consideration. But the two grants are not, it is conceived, similar in their terms or their nature. Although many of the powers formerly exercised by the States, are transferred to the government of the Union, yet the State governments remain, and constitute a most important part of our system. The power of taxation is indispensable to their existence, and is a power which, in its own nature, is capable of residing in, and being exercised by, different authorities at the same time. . . . Taxation is the simple operation of taking small portions from a perpetually accumulating mass, susceptible of almost infinite division; and a power in one to take what is necessary for certain purposes, is not, in its nature, incompatible with a power in another to take what is necessary for other purposes. . . . In imposing taxes for State purposes, [the States] are not doing what Congress is empowered to do. Congress is not empowered to tax for those purposes which are within the exclusive province of the States. When, then, each government exercises the power of taxation, neither is exercising the power of the other. But, when a State proceeds to regulate commerce with foreign nations, or among the several States, it is exercising the very power that is granted to Congress, and is doing the very thing which Congress is authorized to do. . . .

In discussing the question, whether this power is still in the States, in the case under consideration, we may dismiss from it the inquiry, whether it is surrendered by the mere grant to Congress, or is retained until Congress shall exercise the power. We may dismiss that inquiry, because it has been exercised, and the regulations which Congress deemed it proper to make, are now in full operation. The sole question is, can a State regulate commerce with foreign nations and among the States, while Congress is regulating it?

The counsel for the respondent answer this question in the affirmative, and rely very much on the restrictions in the 10th section, as supporting their opinion. They say, very truly, that limitations of a power, furnish a strong argument in favour of the existence of that power, and that the section which prohibits the States from laying duties on imports or exports, proves that this power might have been exercised, had it not been expressly forbidden; and, consequently, that any other commercial regulation, not expressly forbidden, to which the original power of the State was competent, may still be made.

That this restriction shows the opinion of the Convention, that a State might impose duties on exports and imports, if not expressly forbidden, will be conceded; but that it follows as a consequence, from this concession, that a State may regulate commerce with foreign nations and among the States, cannot be admitted.

We must first determine whether the act of laying "duties or imposts on imports or exports," is considered in the constitution as a branch of the taxing power, or of the power to regulate commerce. We think it very clear, that it is considered as a branch of the taxing power. It is so treated in the first clause of the 8th section: "Congress shall have power to lay and collect taxes, duties, imposts, and excises;" and, before commerce is mentioned, the rule by which the exercise of this power must be governed, is declared. It is, that all duties, imposts, and excises, shall be uniform. In a separate clause of the enumeration, the power to regulate commerce is given, as being entirely distinct from the right to levy taxes and imposts, and as being a new power, not before conferred. The constitution, then, considers these powers as substantive, and distinct from each other; and so places them in the enumeration it contains. . . .

. . . The idea that the same measure might, according to circumstances, be arranged with different classes of power, was no novelty to the framers of our constitution. Those illustrious statesmen and patriots had been, many of them, deeply engaged in the discussions which preceded the war of our revolution, and all of them were well read in those discussions. The right to regulate commerce, even by the imposition of duties, was not controverted; but the right to impose a duty for the purpose of revenue, produced a war as important, perhaps, in its consequences to the human race, as any the world has ever witnessed.

These restrictions, then, are on the taxing power, not on that to regulate commerce; and presuppose the existence of that which they restrain, not of that which they do not purport to restrain.

But, the inspection laws are said to be regulations of commerce, and are certainly recognised in the constitution, as being passed in the exercise of a power remaining with the States.

That inspection laws may have a remote and considerable influence on commerce, will not be denied; but that a power to regulate commerce is the source from which the right to pass them is derived, cannot be admitted. The object of inspection laws, is to improve the quality of articles produced by the labour of a country; to fit them for exportation; or, it may be, for domestic use. They act upon the subject before it becomes an article of foreign commerce, or of commerce among the States, and prepare it for that purpose. They form a portion of that immense mass of legislation, which embraces every thing within the territory of a State, not surrendered to the general government: all which can be most advantageously exercised by the States themselves. Inspection laws, quarantine laws, health laws of every description, as well as laws for regulating the internal commerce of a State, and those which respect turnpike roads, ferries, &c., are component parts of this mass.

No direct general power over these objects is granted to Congress; and, consequently, they remain subject to State legislation. . . . It is obvious, that the government of the Union, in the exercise of its express powers, that, for example, of regulating commerce with foreign nations and among the States, may use means that may also be employed by a State, in the exercise of its acknowledged powers; that, for example, of regulating commerce within the State. If Congress license vessels to sail from one port to another, in the same State, the act is supposed to be, necessarily, incidental to the power expressly granted to Congress, and implies no claim of a direct power to regulate the purely internal commerce of a State, or to act directly on its system of police. So, if a State, in passing laws on subjects acknowledged to be within its control, and with a view to those subjects, shall adopt a measure of the same character with one which Congress may adopt, it does not derive its authority from the particular power which has been granted, but from some other, which remains with the State, and may be executed by the same means. . . .

In our complex system, presenting the rare and difficult scheme of one general government, whose action extends over the whole, but which possesses only certain enumerated powers; and of numerous State governments, which retain and exercise all powers not delegated to the Union, contests respecting power must arise. Were it even otherwise, the measures taken by the respective governments to execute their acknowledged powers, would often be of the same description, and might, sometimes, interfere. This, however, does not prove that the one is exercising, or has a right to exercise, the powers of the other.

The acts of Congress, passed in 1796 and 1799, empowering and directing the officers of the general government to conform to, and assist in the execution of the quarantine and health laws of a State, proceed, it is said, upon the idea that these laws are constitutional. It is undoubtedly true, that they do proceed upon that idea; and the constitutionality of such laws has never, so far as we are informed, been denied. But they do not imply an acknowledgment that a State may rightfully regulate commerce with foreign nations, or among the States; for they do not imply that such laws are an exercise of that power, or enacted with a view to it. On the contrary, they are treated as quarantine and health laws, are so denominated in the acts of Congress, and are considered as flowing from the acknowledged power of a State, to provide for the health of its citizens. But, as it was apparent that some of the provisions made for this purpose, and in virtue of this power, might interfere with, and be affected by the laws of the United States, made for the regulation of commerce, Congress, in that spirit of harmony and conciliation, which ought always to characterize the conduct of governments standing in the relation which that of the Union and those of the States bear to each other, has directed its officers to aid in the execution of these laws. . . . But, in making these provisions, the opinion is unequivocally manifested, that Congress may control the State laws, so far as it may be necessary to control them, for the regulation of commerce.

The act passed in 1803, prohibiting the importation of slaves into any State which shall itself prohibit their importation, implies, it is said, an admission that the States possessed the power to exclude or admit them; from which it is inferred, that they possess the same power with respect to other articles.

If this inference were correct; if this power was exercised, not under any particular clause in the constitution, but in virtue of a general right over the subject of commerce, to exist as long as the constitution itself, it might now be exercised. Any State might now import African slaves into its own territory. But it is obvious, that the power of the States over this subject, previous to the year 1808, constitutes an exception to the power of Congress to regulate commerce, and the exception is expressed in such words, as to manifest clearly the intention to continue the pre-existing right of the States to admit or exclude, for a limited period. The words are, "the migration or importation of such persons as any of the States, now existing, *shall* think proper to admit, shall not be prohibited by the Congress prior to the year 1808." The whole object of the exception is, to preserve the power to those States which might be disposed to exercise it. . . . The possession of this particular power, then, during the time limited in the constitution, cannot be admitted to prove the possession of any other similar power.

It has been said, that the act of August 7, 1789, acknowledges a concurrent power in the States to regulate the conduct of pilots, and hence is inferred an admission of their concurrent right with Congress to regulate commerce with foreign nations, and amongst the States. But this inference is not, we think, justified by the fact.

Although Congress cannot enable a State to legislate, Congress may adopt the provisions of a State on any subject. When the government of the Union was brought into existence, it found a system for the regulation of its pilots in full force in every State. The act which has been mentioned, adopts this system, and gives it the same validity as if its provisions had been specially made by Congress. But the act, it may be said, is prospective also, and the adoption of laws to be made in future, presupposes the right in the maker to legislate on the subject.

The act unquestionably manifests an intention to leave this subject entirely to the States, until Congress should think proper to interpose; but the very enactment of such a law indicates an opinion that it was necessary; that the existing system would not be applicable to the new state of things, unless expressly applied to it by Congress. . . . [T]he adoption of the State system being temporary, being only "until further legislative provision shall be made by Congress," shows, conclusively, an opinion that Congress could control the whole subject, and might adopt the system of the States, or provide one of its own.

A State, it is said, or even a private citizen, may construct light houses. But gentlemen must be aware, that if this proves a power in a State to regulate commerce, it proves that the same power is in the citizen. States, or individuals who own lands, may, if not forbidden by law, erect on those lands what buildings they please; but this power is entirely distinct from that of regulating commerce, and may, we presume, be restrained, if exercised so as to produce a public mischief.

These acts were cited at the bar for the purpose of showing an opinion in Congress, that the States possess, concurrently with the Legislature of the Union, the power to regulate commerce with foreign nations and among the States. Upon reviewing them, we think they do not establish the proposition they were intended to prove. They show the opinion, that the States retain powers enabling them to pass the laws to which allusion has been made, not that those laws proceed from the particular power which has been delegated to Congress.

It has been contended by the counsel for the appellant, that, as the word "to regulate" implies in its nature, full power over the thing to be regulated, it excludes, necessarily, the action of all others that would perform the same operation on the same thing. . . . It produces a uniform whole, which is as much disturbed and deranged by changing what the regulating power designs to leave untouched, as that on which it has operated.

There is great force in this argument, and the Court is not satisfied that it has been refuted.

Since, however, in exercising the power of regulating their own purely internal affairs, whether of trading or police, the States may sometimes enact laws, the validity of which depends on their interfering with, and being contrary to, an act of Congress passed in pursuance of the constitution, the Court will enter upon the inquiry, whether the laws of New-York, as expounded by the highest tribunal of that State, have, in their application to this case, come into collision with an act of Congress, and deprived a citizen of a right to which that act entitles him. Should this collision exist, it will be immaterial whether those laws were passed in virtue of a concurrent power "to regulate commerce with foreign nations and among the several States," or, in virtue of a power to regulate their domestic trade and police. . . .

. . . In argument, however, it has been contended, that if a law passed by a State, in the exercise of its acknowledged sovereignty, comes into conflict with a law passed by Congress in pursuance of the constitution, they affect the subject, and each other, like equal opposing powers.

But the framers of our constitution foresaw this state of things, and provided for it, by declaring the supremacy not only of itself, but of the laws made in pursuance of it. The nullity of any act, inconsistent with the constitution, is produced by the declaration, that the constitution is the supreme law. . . .

In pursuing this inquiry at the bar, it has been said, that the constitution does not confer the right of intercourse between State and State. That right derives its source from those laws whose authority is acknowledged by civilized man throughout the world. This is true. The constitution found it an existing right, and gave to Congress the power to regulate it. In the exercise of this power, Congress has passed "an act for enrolling or licensing ships or vessels to be employed in the coasting trade and fisheries, and for regulating the same." The counsel for the respondent contend, that this act does not give the right to sail from port to port, but confines itself to regulating a pre-existing right, so far only as to confer certain privileges on enrolled and licensed vessels in its exercise.

It will at once occur, that, when a Legislature attaches certain privileges and exemptions to the exercise of a right over which its control is absolute, the law must imply a power to exercise the right. The privileges are gone, if the right itself be annihilated. It would be contrary to all reason, and to the course of human affairs, to say that a State is unable to strip a vessel of the particular privileges attendant on the exercise of a right, and yet may annul the right itself; that the State of New-York cannot prevent an enrolled and licensed vessel, proceeding from Elizabethtown, in New-Jersey, to New-York, from enjoying, in her course, and on her entrance into port, all the privileges conferred by the act of Congress; but can shut her up in her own port, and prohibit altogether her entering the waters and ports of another State. To the Court it seems very clear, that the whole act on the subject of the coasting trade, according to those principles which govern the construction of statutes, implies, unequivocally, an authority to licensed vessels to carry on the coasting trade.

* * *

The word "license," means permission, or authority; and a license to do any particular thing, is a permission or authority to do that thing; and if granted by a person having power to grant it, transfers to the grantee the right to do whatever it purports to authorize. It certainly transfers to him all the right which the grantor can transfer, to do what is within the terms of the license.

* * *

The license must be understood to be what it purports to be, a legislative authority to the steamboat Bellona, "to be employed in carrying on the coasting trade, for one year from this date."

It has been denied that these words authorize a voyage from New-Jersey to New-York. It is true, that no ports are specified; but it is equally true, that the words used are perfectly intelligible, and do confer such authority as unquestionably, as if the ports had been mentioned. The coasting trade is a term well understood. The law has defined it; and all know its meaning perfectly. The act describes, with great minuteness, the various operations of a vessel engaged in it; and it cannot, we think, be doubted, that a voyage from New-Jersey to New-York, is one of those operations.

* * *

But, if the license be a permit to carry on the coasting trade, the respondent denies that these boats were engaged in that trade, or that the decree under consideration has restrained them from prosecuting it. The boats of the appellant were, we are told, employed in the transportation of passengers; and this is no part of that commerce which Congress may regulate.

If, as our whole course of legislation on this subject shows, the [commerce] power of Congress has been universally understood in America, to comprehend navigation, it is a very persuasive, if not a conclusive argument, to prove that the construction is correct; and, if it be correct, no clear distinction is perceived between the power to regulate vessels employed in transporting men for hire, and property for hire. The subject is transferred to Congress, and no exception to the grant can be admitted, which is not proved by the words or the nature of the thing. A coasting vessel employed in the transportation of passengers, is as much a portion of the American marine, as one employed in the transportation of a cargo. . . . The argument urged at the bar, rests on the foundation, that the power of Congress does not extend to navigation, as a branch of commerce, and can only be applied to that subject incidentally and occasionally. But if that foundation be removed, we must show some plain, intelligible distinction, supported by the constitution, or by reason, for discriminating between the power of Congress over vessels employed in navigating the same seas. We can perceive no such distinction.

* * *

If the power reside in Congress, as a portion of the general grant to regulate commerce, then acts applying that power to vessels generally, must be construed as comprehending all vessels. . . .

* * *

[The Act of Congress] demonstrates the opinion of Congress, that steam boats may be enrolled and licensed, in common with vessels using sails. They are, of course, entitled to the same privileges, and can no more be restrained from navigating waters, and entering ports which are free to such vessels, than if they were wafted on their voyage by the winds, instead of being propelled by the agency of fire. The one element may be as legitimately used as the other, for every commercial purpose authorized by the laws of the Union; and the act of a State inhibiting the use of either to any vessel having a license under the act of Congress, comes, we think, in direct collision with that act.

As this decides the cause, it is unnecessary to enter in an examination of that part of the constitution which empowers Congress to promote the progress of science and the useful arts.

* * *

Powerful and ingenious minds, taking, as postulates, that the powers expressly granted to the government of the Union, are to be contracted by construction, into the narrowest possible compass, and that the original powers of the States are retained, if any possible construction will retain them, may, by a course of well digested, but refined and metaphysical reasoning, founded on these premises, explain away the constitution of our country, and leave it, a magnificent structure, indeed, to look at, but totally unfit for use. They may so entangle and perplex the understanding, as to obscure principles, which were before thought quite plain, and induce doubts where, if the mind were to pursue its own course, none would be perceived. In such a case, it is peculiarly necessary [as the court has done here] to recur to safe and fundamental principles to sustain those principles, and, when sustained, to make them the tests of the arguments to be examined.

NOTES AND QUESTIONS

1. *Gibbons v. Ogden*, another opinion by the great Chief Justice Marshall, is one of the most-frequently quoted Supreme Court opinions, as is *McCulloch v. Maryland*. Note that this is the first case, thirty five years after the ratification of the Constitution, which explicates the Commerce Clause. Which phrases or principles from *Gibbons* would you expect to be most readily embraced today? Do you find the reasoning which Marshall uses in *Gibbons* to be similar to that he expressed in *McCulloch*? Are there any significant differences? In a part omitted from your edited version of the opinion, Marshall finds it necessary to apologize for the tediousness of his opinion. Why should he have felt the need to do this? What is this opinion all about? Which is more important, the meaning of the Commerce Clause, or the allocation of power between the federal and state governments (federalism)? You have probably assumed that our Civil War was a battle over the legitimacy of slavery, but, at a deeper level, was it about concepts of state sovereignty which are explored in *Gibbons*?

2. Marshall begins by rejecting the notion of "strict construction" of constitutional provisions. Why does Marshall reject it, and why might one want to embrace it?

3. Following the rejection of "strict construction," Marshall next chooses to define "commerce," and to determine whether navigation falls within commerce. He determines that it does, but are you persuaded? How could anyone seriously maintain that navigation is not a part of commerce? Why would one want to limit the federal government's power to regulate commerce?

4. Could the desire to limit the federal power over commerce spring from a particular conception of the sovereignty of states? This must be the case, because Marshall spends most of the rest of his opinion attempting to demarcate the manner in which the states and the federal government might each seek to regulate commerce. Note that he claims that only Congress is permitted to regulate commerce, but that exercises of the states' police powers may, nevertheless, have an affect on commerce. When are the states restricted from the exercise of their police powers because they come in conflict with Congress' power to regulate commerce? Are you persuaded, by the way, that the states' police powers do not come from the same source as Congress' power to regulate commerce? Is the power to tax really that distinct from the power to regulate commerce?

5. There was an interesting political sidelight to *Gibbons v. Ogden*. The New York monopoly had, as indicated, been granted to Livingston, who was an avid Jeffersonian. Still, the granting of monopolies was something which the Jeffersonians, in general, opposed. The crushing of the lucrative exclusive license originally held by the Jeffersonian must have been a particular delight for Marshall, who was cordially despised by his cousin, Thomas Jefferson. You may have also noticed Marshall's subtle use of and the implied criticism of the embargo, which was a measure Jefferson imposed over the objection of New England Federalists, in order to prevent trade with England. How much of this decision is political, and how much is legal?

b. Distinguishing the Commerce and Police Powers

UNITED STATES v. E.C. KNIGHT CO.
156 U.S. 1 (1895)

Appeal from the Circuit Court of Appeals for the Third Circuit.

This was a bill filed by the United States against E.C. Knight Company and others, in the Circuit Court of the United States for the Eastern District of Pennsylvania, charging that the defendants had violated the provisions of an act of Congress approved July 2, 1890, entitled, "An act to protect trade and commerce against unlawful restraints and monopolies," "providing that every contract, combination in the form of trust, or otherwise, or conspiracy in restraint of trade and commerce among the several States is illegal, and that persons who shall monopolize or shall attempt to monopolize, or combine or conspire with other persons to monopolize trade and commerce among the several states, shall be guilty of a misdemeanor." . . .

* * *

Mr. Chief Justice Fuller, after stating the facts in the foregoing language, delivered the opinion of the court.

By the purchase of the stock of the four Philadelphia refineries with shares of its own stock, the American Sugar Refining Company acquired nearly complete control of the manufacture of refined sugar within the United States. The bill charged that the contracts under which these purchases were made constituted combinations in restraint of trade, and that in entering into them the defendants combined and conspired to restrain the trade and commerce in refined sugar among the several states and with foreign nations, contrary to the act of Congress of July 2, 1890.

The relief sought was the cancellation of the agreements under which the stock was transferred; the redelivery of the stock to the parties respectively; and an injunction against the further performance of the agreements and further violations of the act. . . .

* * *

The fundamental question is, whether conceding that the existence of a monopoly in manufacture is established by the evidence, that monopoly can be directly suppressed under the act of Congress in the mode attempted by this bill.

It cannot be denied that the power of a State to protect the lives, health, and property of its citizens, and to preserve good order and the public morals, "the power to govern men and things within the limits of its dominion," is a power originally and always belonging to the States, not surrendered by them to the general government. . . . "Commerce, undoubtedly, is traffic," said Chief Justice Marshall, "but it is something more; it is intercourse. It describes the commercial intercourse between nations and parts of nations in all its branches, and is regulated by prescribing rules for carrying on that intercourse." That which belongs to commerce is within the jurisdiction of the United States, but that which does not belong to commerce is within the jurisdiction of the police power of the State. *Gibbons v. Ogden.*

The argument is that the power to control the manufacture of refined sugar is a monopoly over a necessary of life, to the enjoyment of which by a large part of the population of the United States interstate commerce is indispensable, and that, therefore, the general government in the exercise of the power to regulate commerce may repress such monopoly directly and set aside the instruments which have created it. But this argument cannot be confined to necessaries of life merely, and must include all articles of general consumption. Doubtless the power to control the manufacture of a given thing involves in a certain sense the control of its disposition, but this is a secondary and not the primary sense; and although the exercise of that power may result in bringing the operation of commerce into play, it does not control it, and affects it only incidentally and indirectly. Commerce succeeds to manufacture, and is not a part of it. The power to regulate commerce is the power to prescribe the rule by which commerce shall be governed, and is a power independent of the power to suppress monopoly. But it may operate in repression of monopoly whenever that comes within the rules by which commerce is governed or whenever the transaction is itself a monopoly of commerce.

It is vital that the independence of the commercial power and of the police power, and the delimitation between them, however sometimes perplexing, should always be recognized and observed, for while the one furnishes the strongest bond of union, the other is essential to the preservation of the autonomy of the States as required by our dual form of government; and acknowledged evils, however grave and urgent they may appear to be, had better be borne, than the risk be run, in the effort to suppress them, of more serious consequences by resort to expedients of even doubtful constitutionality.

It will be perceived how far-reaching the proposition is that the power of dealing with a monopoly directly may be exercised by the general government whenever interstate or international commerce may be ultimately affected. The regulation of commerce applies to the subjects of commerce, and not to matters of internal police. Contracts to buy, sell, or exchange goods to be transported among the several States, the transportation and its instrumentalities, and articles bought, sold, or exchanged for the purposes of such transit among the States, or put in the way of transit, may be regulated, but this is because they form part of interstate trade or commerce. The fact that an article is manufactured for export to another State does not of itself make it an article of interstate commerce, and the intent of the manufacturer does not determine the time when the article or product passes from the control of the State and belongs to commerce. . . .

* * *

In *Gibbons v. Ogden*, and other cases often cited, the State laws, which were held inoperative, were instances of direct interference with, or regulations of, interstate or international commerce. . . .

Contracts, combinations, or conspiracies to control domestic enterprise in manufacture, agriculture, mining, production in all its forms, or to raise or lower prices or wages, might unquestionably tend to restrain external as well as domestic trade, but the restraint would be an indirect result, however inevitable and whatever its extent, and such result would not necessarily determine the object of the contract, combination, or conspiracy.

* * *

It was in the light of well-settled principles that the act of July 2, 1890, was framed. . . . [W]hat the law struck at was combinations, contracts, and conspiracies to monopolize trade and commerce among the several States or with foreign nations; but the contracts and acts of the defendants related exclusively to the acquisition of the Philadelphia refineries and the business of sugar refining in Pennsylvania, and bore no direct relation to commerce between the States or with foreign nations. The object was manifestly private gain in the manufacture of the commodity, but not through the control of interstate or foreign commerce. It is true that the bill alleged that the products of these refineries were sold and distributed among the several States, and that all the companies were engaged in trade or commerce with the several States and with foreign nations; but this was no more than to say that trade and commerce served manufacture to fulfill its function. Sugar was refined for sale, and sales were probably made at Philadelphia for consumption, and undoubtedly for resale by the first purchasers throughout Pennsylvania and other States, and refined sugar was also forwarded by the companies to other States for sale. Nevertheless it does not follow that an attempt to monopolize, or the actual monopoly of, the manufacture was an attempt, whether executory or consummated, to monopolize commerce, even though, in order to dispose of the product, the instrumentality of commerce was necessarily invoked. . . .

* * *

Mr. Justice Harlan, dissenting.

* * *

What is commerce among the States? The decisions of this court fully answer the question. "Commerce, undoubtedly, is traffic, but it is something more: it is intercourse.["] It does not embrace the completely interior traffic of the respective States — that which is "carried on between man and man in a State, or between different parts of the same State and which does not extend to or affect other States" — but it does embrace "every species of commercial intercourse" between the United States and foreign nations and among the States, and, therefore, it includes such traffic or trade, buying, selling, and interchange of commodities, as directly affects or necessarily involves the interests of the People of the United States. "Commerce, as the word is used in the Constitution, is a unit," and "cannot stop at the external boundary line of each State, but may be introduced into the interior." "The genius and character of the whole government seem to be, that its action is to be applied to all the external concerns of the nation, *and to those internal concerns which affect the States generally*."

* * *

It may be admitted that an act which did nothing more than forbid, and which had no other object than to forbid, the *mere* refining of sugar in any State, would be in excess of any power granted to Congress. But the act of 1890 is not of that character. It does not strike at the manufacture simply of articles that are legitimate or recognized subjects of commerce, but at *combinations* that unduly restrain, because they monopolize, *the buying and selling of articles which are to go into interstate commerce.* . . .

* * *

While the opinion of the court in this case does not declare the act of 1890 to be unconstitutional, it defeats the main object for which it was passed. For it is, in effect, held that the statute would be unconstitutional if interpreted as embracing such unlawful restraints upon the purchasing of goods in one State to be carried to another State as necessarily arise from the *existence* of combinations formed for the purpose and with the effect, not only of monopolizing the ownership of all such goods in every part of the country, but of controlling the prices for them in all the States. This view of the scope of the act leaves the public, so far as national power is concerned, entirely at the mercy of combinations which arbitrarily control the prices of articles purchased to be transported from one State to another State. I cannot assent to that view. In my judgment, the general government is not placed by the Constitution in such a condition of helplessness that it must fold its arms and remain inactive while capital combines, under the name of a corporation, to destroy competition, not in one State only, but throughout the entire country, in the buying and selling of articles — especially the necessaries of life — that go into commerce among the States. The doctrine of the autonomy of the States cannot properly be invoked to justify a denial of power in the national government to meet such an emergency, involving as it does that freedom of commercial intercourse among the States which the Constitution sought to attain.

* * *

For the reasons stated I dissent from the opinion and judgment of the court.

CHAMPION v. AMES
[THE "LOTTERY CASE"]
188 U.S. 321 (1902)

[This case concerned the constitutionality of the first section of an 1895 federal statute entitled "An act for the suppression of lottery traffic through national and interstate commerce and the postal service subject to the jurisdiction and laws of the United States." The text of that section was:

> That any person who shall cause to be brought within the United States from abroad, for the purpose of disposing of the same, or deposited in or carried by the mails of the United States, or carried from one State to another in the United States, any paper, certificate or instrument purporting to be or represent a ticket, chance, share, or interest in or dependent upon the event of a lottery, . . . offering prizes dependent upon lot or chance, or shall cause any advertisement of such lottery, . . . offering prizes dependent upon lot or chance, to be brought into the United

States, or deposited in or carried by the mails of the United States, or transferred from one State to another in the same, shall be punishable [for] the first offence by imprisonment for not more than two years or by a fine of not more than one thousand dollars, or both, and in the second and after offences by such imprisonment only.]

MR. JUSTICE HARLAN . . . delivered the opinion of the court.

The appellant insists that the carrying of lottery tickets from one State to another State by an express company engaged in carrying freight and packages from State to State . . . does not constitute, and cannot by any act of Congress be legally made to constitute, *commerce* among the States within the meaning of the ["commerce clause"] . . . .

The Government insists that express companies when engaged, for hire, in the business of transportation from one State to another, are instrumentalities of commerce among the States; that the carrying of lottery tickets from one State to another is commerce which Congress may regulate. . . .

* * *

. . . Undoubtedly, the carrying from one State to another by independent carriers of things or commodities that are ordinary subjects of traffic, and which have in themselves a recognized value in money, constitutes interstate commerce. But does not commerce among the several States include something more? Does not the carrying from one State to another, by independent carriers, of lottery tickets that entitle the holder to the payment of a certain amount of money therein specified also constitute commerce among the States?

* * *

The leading case under the commerce clause of the Constitution is *Gibbons v. Ogden*. . . .

* * *

The principles announced in *Gibbons v. Ogden* were reaffirmed in *Brown v. Maryland* (1827). After expressing doubt whether any of the evils proceeding from the feebleness of the Federal Government contributed more to the establishing of the present constitutional system than the deep and general conviction that commerce ought to be regulated by Congress, Chief Justice Marshall, speaking for the court, said: "It is not, therefore, matter of surprise that the grant should be as extensive as the mischief, and should comprehend all foreign commerce, and all commerce among the States." Considering the question as to the just extent of the power to regulate commerce with foreign nations and among the several States, the court reaffirmed the doctrine that the power was "complete in itself, and to acknowledge no limitations other than are prescribed by the Constitution. . . . Commerce is intercourse; one of its most ordinary ingredients is traffic."

* * *

. . . [I]n *Pensacola Tel. Co. v. Western Union Tel. Co.* [(1877)], [the Court held invalid] a statute of Florida, which assumed to confer upon a local telegraph company the exclusive right to establish and maintain lines of electric telegraph in certain counties of Florida. . . . Chief Justice Waite, delivering its judgment, said: "[C]ommercial intercourse is an element of commerce which comes within the regulating power of Congress. Post offices and post roads are established to facilitate the transmission of intelligence. Both commerce and the postal service are placed within the power of Congress, because, being national in their operation, they should be under the protecting care of the National Government. The powers thus granted are not confined to the instrumentalities of commerce, or the postal service known or in use when the Constitution was adopted, but they keep pace with the progress of the country, and adapt themselves to the new developments of time and circumstances. They extend from the horse with its rider to the stage coach, from the sailing vessel to the steamboat, from the coach and the steamboat to the railroad, and from the railroad to the telegraph, as these new agencies are successively brought into use to meet the demands of increasing population and wealth. . . . As [those powers] were entrusted to the General Government for the good of the nation, it is not only the right, but the duty, of Congress to see to it that intercourse among the States and the transmission of intelligence are not obstructed or unnecessarily encumbered by state legislation. The electric telegraph marks an epoch in the progress of time. In a little more than a quarter of a century it has changed the habits of business, and become one of the necessities of commerce. It is indispensable as a means of intercommunication, but especially is it so in commercial transactions." . . .

In *County of Mobile v. Kimball* [(1880)], Mr. Justice Field, delivering the judgment of the court, said: "Commerce with foreign countries and among the States, strictly considered, consists in intercourse and traffic, including in these terms navigation and the transportation and transit of persons and property, as well as the purchase, sale, and exchange of commodities." . . .

Applying the doctrine announced in *Pensacola Tel. Co. v. Western Union Tel. Co.*, it was held in *Telegraph Co. v. Texas* [(1881)], that the law of a State imposing a tax on private telegraph messages sent out of the State was unconstitutional, as being, in effect, a regulation of interstate commerce.

* * *

At the present term of the court we said that "transportation for others, as an independent business, is commerce, irrespective of the purpose to sell or retain the goods which the owner may entertain with regard to them after they shall have been delivered." *Hanley &c. v. Kansas City Southern Railway* [(1903)].

. . . The cases cited . . . sufficiently indicate the grounds upon which this court has proceeded when determining the meaning and scope of the commerce clause. They show that commerce among the States embraces navigation, intercourse, communication, traffic, the transit of persons, and the transmission of messages by telegraph. They also show that . . . in determining the character of the regulations to be adopted Congress has a large discretion which is not to be controlled by the courts, simply because, in their opinion, such regulations may not be the best or most effective that could be employed.

We come then to inquire whether there is any solid foundation upon which to rest the contention that Congress may not regulate the carrying of lottery tickets from one State to another. . . .

* * *

We are of opinion that lottery tickets are subjects of traffic and therefore are subjects of commerce, and the regulation of the carriage of such tickets from State to State, at least by independent carriers, is a regulation of commerce among the several States.

But it is said that the statute in question does not regulate the carrying of lottery tickets from State to State, but by punishing those who cause them to be so carried Congress in effect prohibits such carrying; that in respect of the carrying from one State to another of articles or things that are, in fact, or according to usage in business, the subjects of commerce, the authority given Congress was not to *prohibit*, but only to *regulate*. . . .

It is be remarked that the Constitution does not define what is to be deemed a legitimate regulation of interstate commerce. In *Gibbons v. Ogden* it was said that the power to regulate such commerce is the power to prescribe the rule by which it is to be governed. But this general observation leaves it to be determined, when the question comes before the court, whether Congress in prescribing a particular rule has exceeded its power under the Constitution. While our Government must be acknowledged by all to be one of enumerated powers, . . . the Constitution does not attempt to set forth all the means by which such powers may be carried into execution. It leaves to Congress a large discretion as to the means that may be employed in executing a given power. The sound construction of the Constitution, this court has said, "must allow to the national legislature that discretion, with respect to the means by which the powers it confers are to be carried into execution, which will enable that body to perform the high duties assigned to it, in the manner most beneficial to the people . . . ."

. . . Are we prepared to say that a provision which is, in effect, a *prohibition* of the carriage of [lottery tickets] from State to State is not a fit or appropriate mode for the *regulation* of that particular kind of commerce? If lottery traffic, *carried on through interstate commerce*, is a matter of which Congress may take cognizance and over which its power may be exerted, can it be possible that it must tolerate the traffic, and simply regulate the manner in which it may be carried on? Or may not Congress, for the protection of the people of all the States, and under the power to regulate interstate commerce, devise such means, within the scope of the Constitution, and not prohibited by it, as will drive that traffic out of commerce among the States?

In determining whether regulation may not under some circumstances properly take the form or have the effect of prohibition, the nature of the interstate traffic which it was sought by the act of May 2, 1895, to suppress cannot be overlooked. When enacting that statute Congress no doubt shared the views upon the subject of lotteries heretofore expressed by this court. In *Phalen v. Virginia* [(1850)], after observing that the suppression of nuisances injurious to public health or morality is among the most important duties of Government, this court said: "Experience has shown that the common forms of gambling are comparatively innocuous when placed in contrast with the widespread pestilence of lotteries. The former are confined to a few persons and places, but the latter infests the whole community; it enters every dwelling; it reaches every class; it preys upon the hard earnings of the poor; it plunders the ignorant and simple." In other cases we have adjudged that authority given by legislative enactment to carry on a lottery, although based upon a consideration in money, was not protected by the contract clause of the Constitution; this, for the reason that no State may bargain away its power to protect the public morals, not excuse its failure to perform a public duty by saying that it had agreed, by legislative enactment, not to do so. . . .

If a State, when considering legislation for the suppression of lotteries within its own limits, may properly take into view the evils that inhere in the raising of money, in that mode, why may not Congress, invested with the Power to regulate commerce among the several States, provide that such commerce shall not be polluted by the carrying of lottery tickets from one State to another? In this connection it must not be forgotten that the power of Congress to regulate commerce among the States is plenary, is complete in itself, and is subject to no limitations except such as may be found in the Constitution. What provision in that instrument can be regarded as limiting the exercise of the power granted? What clause can be cited which, in any degree, countenances the suggestion that one may, of right, carry or cause to be carried from one State to another that which will harm the public morals? We cannot think of any clause of that instrument that could possibly be invoked by those who assert their right to send lottery tickets from State to State except the one providing that no person shall be deprived of his liberty without due process of law. We have said that the liberty protected by the Constitution embraces the right to be free in the enjoyment of one's faculties; "to be free to use them in all lawful ways; to live and work where he will; to earn his livelihood by any lawful calling; to pursue any livelihood or avocation, and for that purpose to enter into all contracts that may be proper." . . . But surely it will not be said to be a part of any one's liberty, as recognized by the supreme law of the land, that he shall be allowed to introduce into commerce among the States an element that will be confessedly injurious to the public morals.

If it be said that the act of 1895 is inconsistent with the Tenth Amendment, reserving to the States respectively or to the people the powers not delegated to the United States, the answer is that the power to regulate commerce among the States has been expressly delegated to Congress.

Besides, Congress, by that act, does not assume to interfere with traffic or commerce in lottery tickets carried on exclusively within the limits of any State, but has in view only commerce of that kind among the several States. . . . As a State may, for the purpose of guarding the morals of its own people, forbid all sales of lottery tickets within its limits, so Congress, for the purpose of guarding the people of the United States against the "widespread pestilence of lotteries" and to protect the commerce which concerns all the States, may prohibit the carrying of lottery tickets from one State to another. . . . We should hesitate long before adjudging that an evil of such appalling character, carried on through interstate commerce, cannot be met and crushed by the only power competent to that end. . . . What was said by this court upon a former occasion may well be here repeated: "The Framers of the Constitution never intended that the legislative power of the Nation should find itself incapable of disposing of a subject matter specifically committed to its charge." . . . If the carrying of lottery tickets from one State to another be interstate commerce, and if Congress is of opinion that an effective regulation for the suppression of lotteries, carried on through such commerce, is to make it a criminal offence to cause lottery tickets to be carried from one State to another, we know of no authority in the courts to hold that the means thus devised are not appropriate and necessary to protect the country at large against a species of interstate commerce which, although in general use and somewhat favored in both national and state legislation in the early history of the country, has grown into disrepute and has become offensive to the entire people of the Nation. It is a kind of traffic which no one can be entitled to pursue as of right.

* * *

The judgment is

Affirmed.

MR. CHIEF JUSTICE FULLER, with whom concur MR. JUSTICE BREWER, MR. JUSTICE SHIRAS and MR. JUSTICE PECKHAM, dissenting.

* * *

The power of the State to impose restraints and burdens on persons and property in conservation and promotion of the public health, good order and prosperity is a power originally and always belonging to the States, not surrendered by them to the General Government nor directly restrained by the Constitution of the United States, and essentially exclusive, and the suppression of lotteries as a harmful business falls within this power, commonly called of police. . . .

It is urged, however, that because Congress is empowered to regulate commerce between the several States, it, therefore, may suppress lotteries by prohibiting the carriage of lottery matter. Congress may indeed make all laws necessary and proper for carrying the powers granted to it into execution, and doubtless an act prohibiting the carriage of lottery matter would be necessary and proper to the execution of a power to suppress lotteries; but that power belongs to the States and not to Congress. To hold that Congress has general police power would be to hold that it may accomplish objects not entrusted to the General Government, and to defeat the operation of the Tenth Amendment, declaring that: "The powers not delegated to the United States by the Constitution, nor prohibited by it to the States, are reserved to the States respectively, or to the people."

The ground on which acts forbidding the transmission of lottery matter by the mails was sustained, was that the power vested in Congress to establish post offices and post roads embraced the regulation of the entire postal system of the country, and that under that power Congress might designate what might be carried in the mails and what excluded. . . .

. . . Mr. Justice Field, delivering the unanimous opinion of the court [on this issue], said: "But we do not think that Congress possesses the power to prevent the transportation in other ways, as merchandise, of matter which it excludes from the mails. To give efficiency to its regulations and prevent rival postal systems, it may perhaps prohibit the carriage by others for hire, over postal routes, of articles which legitimately constitute mail matter, in the sense in which those terms were used when the Constitution was adopted, consisting of letters, and of newspapers and pamphlets, when not sent as merchandise; but further than this its power of prohibition cannot extend." . . .

* * *

But apart from the question of *bona fides*, this act cannot be brought within the power to regulate commerce among the several States, unless lottery tickets are articles of commerce, and, therefore, when carried across state lines, of interstate commerce; or unless the power to regulate interstate commerce includes the absolute and exclusive power to prohibit the transportation of anything or anybody from one State to another.

Mr. Justice Catron remarked in the *License Cases* (1847), that "that which does not belong to commerce is within the jurisdiction of the police power of the State; and that which does belong to commerce is within the jurisdiction of the United States;" and the observation has since been repeatedly quoted by this court with approval.

In *United States v. E.C. Knight Company* [(1895)], we said: "It is vital that the independence of the commercial power and of the police power, and the delimitation between them, however sometimes perplexing, should always be recognized and observed, for while the one furnished the strongest bond of union, the other is essential to the preservation of the autonomy of the States as required by our dual form of government; and acknowledged evils, however grave and urgent they may appear to be, had better be borne, than the risk be run, in the effort to suppress them, of more serious consequences by resort to expedients of even doubtful constitutionality. . . .

* * *

If a particular article is not the subject of commerce, the determination of Congress that it is, cannot be so conclusive as to exclude judicial inquiry.

When Chief Justice Marshall said that commerce embraced intercourse, he added, commercial intercourse, and this was necessarily so since, as Chief Justice Taney pointed out, if intercourse were a word of larger meaning than the word commerce, it could not be substituted for the word of more limited meaning contained in the Constitution.

Is the carriage of lottery tickets from one State to another commercial intercourse?

The lottery ticket purports to create contractual relations and to furnish the means of enforcing a contract right.

This is true of insurance policies, and both are contingent in their nature. Yet this court has held that the issuing of fire, marine, and life insurance policies, in one State, and sending them to another, to be there delivered to the insured on payment of premium, is not interstate commerce. . . .

In *Paul v. Virginia* (1869), Mr. Justice Field, in delivering the unanimous opinion of the court, said: "Issuing a policy of insurance is not a transaction of commerce. The policies are simple contracts of indemnity against loss by fire, entered into between the corporations and the assured, for a consideration paid by the latter. These contracts are not articles of commerce in any proper meaning of the word. They are not subjects of trade and barter offered in the market as something having an existence and value independent of the parties to them. They are not commodities to be shipped or forwarded from one State to another, and then put up for sale. They are like other personal contracts between parties which are completed by their signature and the transfer of the consideration. Such contracts are not interstate transactions, though the parties may be domiciled in different States. The policies do not take effect — are not executed contracts — until delivered by the agent in Virginia. They are, then, local transactions, and are governed by the local law. They do not constitute a part of the commerce between the States any more than a contract for the purchase and sale of goods in Virginia by a citizen of New York whilst in Virginia would constitute a portion of such commerce."

This language was quoted with approval in [another case involving insurance contracts] and it was further said: "If the power to regulate interstate commerce applied to all the incidents to which said commerce might give rise and to all contracts which might be made in the course of its transaction, that power would embrace the entire sphere of mercantile activity in any way connected with trade between the States; and would exclude state control over many contracts purely domestic in their nature. The business of insurance is not commerce. The contract of insurance is not an instrumentality of commerce. The making of such a contract is a mere incident of commercial intercourse. . . ."

* * *

Tested by the same reasoning, negotiable instruments are not instruments of commerce; bills of lading are, because they stand for the articles included therein; hence it has been held that a State cannot tax interstate bills of lading because that would be a regulation of interstate commerce. . . .

In *Nathan v. Louisiana* [(1850)], it was held that a broker dealing in foreign bills of exchange was not engaged in commerce, but in supplying an instrumentality of commerce, and that a state tax on all money or exchange brokers was not void as to him as a regulation of commerce.

And in *Williams v. Fears* [(1900)], that the levy of a tax by the State of Georgia on the occupation of a person engaged in hiring laborers to be employed beyond the limits of the State, was not a regulation of interstate commerce, and that the tax fell within the distinction between interstate commerce or an instrumentality thereof, and the mere incidents that might attend the carrying on of such commerce.

In *Cohens v. Virginia* (1821), Congress had empowered the corporation of the city of Washington to "authorize the drawing of lotteries for effecting any improvement in the city, which the ordinary funds or revenue thereof will not accomplish." The corporation had duly provided for such lottery, and this case was a conviction under a statute of Virginia for selling tickets issued by that lottery. That statute forbade the sale within the State of any ticket in a lottery not authorized by the laws of Virginia.

The court held, by Chief Justice Marshall, that the lottery was merely the emanation of a corporate power, and "that the mind of Congress was not directed to any provision for the sale of the tickets beyond the limits of the corporation."

The constitutionality of the act of Congress, as forcing the sale of tickets in Virginia, was therefore not passed on. But if lottery tickets had been deemed articles of commerce, the Virginia statute would have been invalid as a regulation of commerce, and the conviction could hardly have been affirmed, as it was.

* * *

If a State should create a corporation to engage in the business of lotteries, could it enter another State, which prohibited lotteries, on the ground that lottery tickets were the subjects of commerce?

On the other hand, could Congress compel a State to admit lottery matter within it, contrary to its own laws?

In *Alexander v. State*, [the Georgia Supreme Court] held that a state statute prohibiting the business of buying and selling what are commonly known as "futures," was not protected by the commerce clause of the Constitution, as the business was gambling, and that clause protected interstate commerce but did not protect interstate gambling. The same view was expressed [by the Alabama Supreme Court] in *State v. Stripling*, in respect of an act forbidding the sale of pools on horse races conducted without the State.

* * *

If a lottery ticket is not an article of commerce, how can it become so when placed in an envelope or box or other covering, and transported by an express company? To say that the mere carrying of an article which is not an article of commerce in and of itself nevertheless becomes such the moment it is to be transported from one State to another, is to transform a non-commercial article into a commercial one simply because it is transported. I cannot conceive that any such result can properly follow.

It would be to say that everything is an article of commerce the moment it is taken to be transported from place to place, and of interstate commerce if from State to State.

An invitation to dine, or to take a drive, or a note of introduction, all become articles of commerce under the ruling in this case, by being deposited with an express company for transportation. This in effect breaks down all the differences between that which is, and that which is not, an article of commerce, and the necessary consequence is to take from the States all jurisdiction over the subject so far as interstate communication is concerned. It is a long step in the direction of wiping out all traces of state lines, and the creation of a centralized Government.

* * *

It will not do to say — a suggestion which has heretofore been made in this case — that state laws have been found to be ineffective for the suppression of lotteries, and therefore Congress should interfere. The scope of the commerce clause of the Constitution cannot be enlarged because of present views of public interest.

NOTES AND QUESTIONS

1. There was relatively little attention to the scope of the Interstate Commerce Clause at the Constitutional Convention of 1787. On the other hand, there was a great deal of concern with the reach of the powers of the federal government and the need to preserve something of the sovereignties of the individual states. The matter was further complicated by disputes between the representatives of the larger and the smaller states. Edmund Randolph, a delegate from the populous state of Virginia, suggested that there ought to be a bicameral federal legislature, with the lower house elected according to population, and the upper house elected by the lower. This would, of course, have given a greater influence to the more populated states. William Paterson, a delegate from the smaller state of New Jersey offered a different solution, which provided simply for equal representation of the states in Congress. This would have given each state equal influence. The compromise, as you know, often called the "Great Compromise," or the Connecticut compromise, since it was suggested by delegates from that state, Roger Sherman and Oliver Ellsworth, was to create a lower house elected by population, and an upper house in which each state would be equally represented. As part of that compromise, revenue measures were only to originate in the lower house. What light, if any, does this throw on the intended meaning of the Commerce Clause? That Clause, by the way, was approved "without debate," and there was a general understanding that the individual states' interference with interstate commerce through state tariffs under the Articles of Confederation was something to be avoided under the new Constitution. Still, might there be limits that ought to be imposed upon the federal government's "Commerce Clause power"? Does either the *E.C. Knight* or *Champion* case give you a firm sense of those limits?

2. What, exactly, is the "police power" that is supposed to remain a prerogative of the states? In your opinion, does the legislation at issue in *E.C. Knight* or *Champion* trench on the terrain left to the police power of the states? What about the federal law with which you are currently familiar? On the other hand, is the majority's distinction between manufacture and commerce in *E.C. Knight* or the dissent's reading in *Champion* of the Commerce Clause reasonable? For example, under either view could the federal government regulate the interstate trade in the stock of corporations? In your opinion, is it proper for the federal government to undertake to prohibit lotteries or regulate wages and hours? Are these decisions most wisely placed in the hands of the central government or of the local governments? Indeed, what, precisely, is the importance of placing basic matters of the regulation of the morals and the economic behavior of citizens in either the local or national government?

c. What Is "Interstate"?

WICKARD v. FILBURN
317 U.S. 111 (1942)

MR. JUSTICE JACKSON delivered the opinion of the Court.

The appellee . . . sought to enjoin enforcement against himself of the marketing penalty imposed by the . . . [federal] Agricultural Adjustment Act of 1938 upon that part of his 1941 wheat crop which was available for marketing in excess of the marketing quota established [pursuant to the Act] for his farm. He also sought a declaratory judgment that the wheat marketing quota provisions of the Act as amended and applicable to him were unconstitutional because not sustainable under the Commerce Clause. . . .

* * *

The appellee for many years past has owned and operated a small farm in Montgomery County, Ohio, maintaining a herd of dairy cattle, selling milk, raising poultry, and selling poultry and eggs. It has been his practice to raise a small acreage of winter wheat, sown in the Fall and harvested in the following July; to sell a portion of the crop; to feed part to poultry and livestock on the farm, some of which is sold; to use some in making flour for home consumption; and to keep the rest for the following seeding. . . .

In July of 1940, pursuant to the Agricultural Adjustment Act of 1938, as then amended, there were established for the appellee's 1941 crop a wheat acreage allotment of 11.1 acres and a normal yield of 20.1 bushels of wheat an acre. He was given notice of such allotment in July of 1940, before the Fall planting of his 1941 crop of wheat, and again in July of 1941, before it was harvested. He sowed, however, 23 acres, and harvested from his 11.9 acres of excess acreage 239 bushels, which under the terms of the Act as amended on May 26, 1941, constituted farm marketing excess, subject to a penalty of 49 cents a bushel, or $117.11 in all. The appellee has not paid the penalty. . . .

The general scheme of the Agricultural Adjustment Act of 1938 as related to wheat is to control the volume moving in interstate and foreign commerce in order to avoid surpluses and shortages and the consequent abnormally low or high wheat prices and obstructions to commerce. Within prescribed limits and by prescribed standards the Secretary of Agriculture is directed to ascertain and proclaim each year a national acreage allotment for the next crop of wheat, which is then apportioned to the states and their counties, and is eventually broken up into allotments for individual farms. . . .

The Act further provides that whenever it appears that the total supply of wheat as of the beginning of any marketing year, beginning July 1, will exceed a normal year's domestic consumption and export by more than 35 per cent, the Secretary shall so proclaim not later than May 15 prior to the beginning of such marketing year; and that during the marketing year a compulsory national marketing quota shall be in effect with respect to the marketing of wheat. Between the issuance of the proclamation and June 10, the Secretary must, however, conduct a referendum of farmers who will be subject to the quota, to determine whether they favor or oppose it; and, if more than one-third of the farmers voting in the referendum do oppose, the Secretary must, prior to the effective date of the quota, by proclamation suspend its operation.

On May 19, 1941, the Secretary of Agriculture made a radio address to the wheat farmers of the United States in which he advocated approval of the quotas. . . .

Pursuant to the Act, the referendum of wheat growers was held on May 31, 1941. According to the required published statement of the Secretary of Agriculture, 81 per cent of those voting favored the marketing quota, with 19 per cent opposed.

* * *

II

It is urged that under the Commerce Clause of the Constitution, Article I, § 8, clause 3, Congress does not possess the power it has in this instance sought to exercise. The question would merit little consideration since our decision in *United States v. Darby* (1941), sustaining the federal power to regulate production of goods for commerce, except for the fact that this Act extends federal regulation to production not intended in any part for commerce but wholly for consumption on the farm. The Act includes a definition of "market" and its derivatives, so that as related to wheat, in addition to its conventional meaning, it also means to dispose of "by feeding (in any form) to poultry or livestock which, or the products of which, are sold, bartered, or exchanged, or to be so disposed of." Hence, marketing quotas not only embrace all that may be sold without penalty but also what may be consumed on the premises. Wheat produced on excess acreage is designated as "available for marketing" as so defined, and the penalty is imposed thereon. Penalties do not depend upon whether any part of the wheat, either within or without the quota, is sold or intended to be sold. The sum of this is that the Federal Government fixes a quota including all that the farmer may harvest for sale or for his own farm needs, and declares that wheat produced on excess acreage may neither be disposed of nor used except upon payment of the penalty, or except it is stored as required by the Act or delivered to the Secretary of Agriculture.

Appellee says that this is a regulation of production and consumption of wheat. Such activities are, he urges, beyond the reach of Congressional power under the Commerce Clause, since they are local in character, and their effects upon interstate commerce are at most "indirect." In answer the Government argues that the statute regulates neither production nor consumption, but only marketing; and, in the alternative, that if the Act does go beyond the regulation of marketing it is sustainable as a "necessary and proper" implementation of the power of Congress over interstate commerce.

The Government's concern lest the Act be held to be a regulation of production or consumption, rather than of marketing, is attributable to a few dicta and decisions of this Court which might be understood to lay it down that activities such as "production," "manufacturing," and "mining" are strictly "local" and, except in special circumstances which are not present here, cannot be regulated under the commerce power because their effects upon interstate commerce are, as matter of law, only "indirect." Even today, when this power has been held to have great latitude, there is no decision of this Court that such activities may be regulated where no part of the product is intended for interstate commerce or intermingled with the subjects thereof. We believe that a review of the course of decision under the Commerce Clause will make plain, however, that questions of the power of Congress are not to be decided by reference to any formula which would give controlling force to nomenclature such as "production" and "indirect" and foreclose consideration of the actual effects of the activity in question upon interstate commerce.

At the beginning Chief Justice Marshall described the federal commerce power with a breadth never yet exceeded. *Gibbons v. Ogden.* He made emphatic the embracing and penetrating nature of this power by warning that effective restraints on its exercise must proceed from political rather than from judicial processes.

For nearly a century, however, decisions of this Court under the Commerce Clause dealt rarely with questions of what Congress might do in the exercise of its granted power under the Clause, and almost entirely with the permissibility of state activity which it was claimed discriminated against or burdened interstate commerce. During this period there was perhaps little occasion for the affirmative exercise of the commerce power, and the influence of the Clause on American life and law was a negative one, resulting almost wholly from its operation as a restraint upon the powers of the states. . . . Certain activities such as "production," "manufacturing," and "mining" were occasionally said to be within the province of state governments and beyond the power of Congress under the Commerce Clause.

It was not until 1887, with the enactment of the Interstate Commerce Act, that the interstate commerce power began to exert positive influence in American law and life. This first important federal resort to the commerce power was followed in 1890 by the Sherman Anti-Trust Act and, thereafter, mainly after 1903, by many others. These statutes ushered in new phases of adjudication, which required the Court to approach the interpretation of the Commerce Clause in the light of an actual exercise by Congress of its power thereunder.

When it first dealt with this new legislation, the Court adhered to its earlier pronouncements, and allowed but little scope to the power of Congress. *United States v. Knight Co.* (1895). These earlier pronouncements also played an important part in several of the five cases in which this Court later held that Acts of Congress under the Commerce Clause were in excess of its power.

Even while important opinions in this line of restrictive authority were being written, however, other cases called forth broader interpretations of the Commerce Clause destined to supersede the earlier ones, and to bring about a return to the principles first enunciated by Chief Justice Marshall in *Gibbons v. Ogden.*

Not long after the decision of *United States v. Knight Co.*, Mr. Justice Holmes, in sustaining the exercise of national power over intrastate activity, stated for the Court that "commerce among the States is not a technical legal conception, but a practical one, drawn from the course of business." *Swift & Co. v. United States* (1905). It was soon demonstrated that the effects of many kinds of intrastate activity upon interstate commerce were such as to make them a proper subject of federal regulation. In some cases sustaining the exercise of federal power over intrastate matters the term "direct" was used for the purpose of stating, rather than of reaching, a result; in others it was treated as synonymous with "substantial" or "material"; and in others it was not used at all.

Of late its use has been abandoned in cases dealing with questions of federal power under the Commerce Clause.

In the *Shreveport Rate Cases* (1914), the Court held that railroad rates of an admittedly intrastate character and fixed by authority of the state might, nevertheless, be revised by the Federal Government because of the economic effects which they had upon interstate commerce. The opinion of Mr. Justice Hughes found federal intervention constitutionally authorized because of "matters having such a close and substantial relation to interstate traffic that the control is essential or appropriate to the security of that traffic, to the efficiency of the interstate service, and to the maintenance of conditions under which interstate commerce may be conducted upon fair terms and without molestation or hindrance."

The Court's recognition of the relevance of the economic effects in the application of the Commerce Clause, exemplified by this statement, has made the mechanical application of legal formulas no longer feasible. Once an economic measure of the reach of the power granted to Congress in the Commerce Clause is accepted, questions of federal power cannot be decided simply by finding the activity in question to be "production," nor can consideration of its economic effects be foreclosed by calling them "indirect." The present Chief Justice has said in summary of the present state of the law: "The commerce power is not confined in its exercise to the regulation of commerce among the states. It extends to those activities intrastate which so affect interstate commerce, or the exertion of the power of Congress over it, as to make regulation of them appropriate means to the attainment of a legitimate end, the effective execution of the granted power to regulate interstate commerce. . . . The power of Congress over interstate commerce is plenary and complete in itself, may be exercised to its utmost extent, and acknowledges no limitations other than are prescribed in the Constitution. . . . It follows that no form of state activity can constitutionally thwart the regulatory power granted by the commerce clause to Congress. Hence the reach of that power extends to those intrastate activities which in a substantial way interfere with or obstruct the exercise of the granted power."

Whether the subject of the regulation in question was "production," "consumption," or "marketing" is, therefore, not material for purposes of deciding the question of federal power before us. That an activity is of local character may help in a doubtful case to determine whether Congress intended to reach it. The same consideration might help in determining whether in the absence of Congressional action it would be permissible for the state to exert its power on the subject matter, even though in so doing it to some degree affected interstate commerce. But even if appellee's activity be local and though it may not be regarded as commerce, it may still, whatever its nature, be reached by Congress if it exerts a substantial economic effect on interstate commerce, and this irrespective of whether such effect is what might at some earlier time have been defined as "direct" or "indirect."

The parties have stipulated a summary of the economics of the wheat industry. Commerce among the states in wheat is large and important. Although wheat is raised in every state but one, production in most states is not equal to consumption. Sixteen states on average have had a surplus of wheat above their own requirements for feed, seed, and food. Thirty-two states and the District of Columbia, where production has been below consumption, have looked to these surplus-producing states for their supply as well as for wheat for export and carry-over.

The wheat industry has been a problem industry for some years. Largely as a result of increased foreign production and import restrictions, annual exports of wheat and flour from the United States during the ten-year period ending in 1940 averaged less than 10 per cent of total production, while during the 1920's they averaged more than 25 per cent. The decline in the export trade has left a large surplus in production which, in connection with an abnormally large supply of wheat and other grains in recent years, caused congestion in a number of markets; tied up railroad cars; and caused elevators in some instances to turn away grains, and railroads to institute embargoes to prevent further congestion.

Many countries, both importing and exporting, have sought to modify the impact of the world market conditions on their own economy. Importing countries have taken measures to stimulate production and self-sufficiency. The four large exporting countries of Argentina, Australia, Canada, and the United States have all undertaken various programs for the relief of growers. Such measures have been designed, in part at least, to protect the domestic price received by producers. Such plans have generally evolved towards control by the central government.

In the absence of regulation, the price of wheat in the United States would be much affected by world conditions. During 1941, producers who cooperated with the Agricultural Adjustment program received an average price on the farm of about $1.16 a bushel, as compared with the world market price of 40 cents a bushel.

Differences in farming conditions, however, make these benefits mean different things to different wheat growers. There are several large areas of specialization in wheat, and the concentration on this crop reaches 27 per cent of the crop land, and the average harvest runs as high as 155 acres. Except for some use of wheat as stock feed and for seed, the practice is to sell the crop for cash. Wheat from such areas constitutes the bulk of the interstate commerce therein.

On the other hand, in some New England states less than one per cent of the crop land is devoted to wheat, and the average harvest is less than five acres per farm. In 1940 the average percentage of the total wheat production that was sold in each state, as measured by value, ranged from 29 per cent thereof in Wisconsin to 90 per cent in Washington. Except in regions of large-scale production, wheat is usually grown in rotation with other crops; for a nurse crop for grass seeding; and as a cover crop to prevent soil erosion and leaching. Some is sold, some kept for seed, and a percentage of the total production much larger than in areas of specialization is consumed on the farm and grown for such purpose. Such farmers, while growing some wheat, may even find the balance of their interest on the consumer's side.

The effect of consumption of home-grown wheat on interstate commerce is due to the fact that it constitutes the most variable factor in the disappearance of the wheat crop. Consumption on the farm where grown appears to vary in an amount greater than 20 per cent of average production. The total amount of wheat consumed as food varies but relatively little, and use as seed is relatively constant.

The maintenance by government regulation of a price for wheat undoubtedly can be accomplished as effectively by sustaining or increasing the demand as by limiting the supply. The effect of the statute before us is to restrict the amount which may be produced for market and the extent as well to which one may forestall resort to the market by producing to meet his own needs. That appellee's own contribution to the demand for wheat may be trivial by itself is not enough to remove him from the scope of federal regulation where, as here, his contribution, taken together with that of many others similarly situated, is far from trivial.

It is well established by decisions of this Court that the power to regulate commerce includes the power to regulate the prices at which commodities in that commerce are dealt in and practices affecting such prices. One of the primary purposes of the Act in question was to increase the market price of wheat, and to that end to limit the volume thereof that could affect the market. It can hardly be denied that a factor of such volume and variability as home-consumed wheat would have a substantial influence on price and market conditions. This may arise because being in marketable condition such wheat overhangs the market and, if induced by rising prices, tends to flow into the market and check price increases. But if we assume that it is never marketed, it supplies a need of the man who grew it which would otherwise be reflected by purchases in the open market. Home-grown wheat in this sense competes with wheat in commerce. The stimulation of commerce is a use of the regulatory function quite as definitely as prohibitions or restrictions thereon. This record leaves us in no doubt that Congress may properly have considered that wheat consumed on the farm where grown, if wholly outside the scheme of regulation, would have a substantial effect in defeating and obstructing its purpose to stimulate trade therein at increased prices.

It is said, however, that this Act, forcing some farmers into the market to buy what they could provide for themselves, is an unfair promotion of the markets and prices of specializing wheat growers. It is of the essence of regulation that it lays a restraining hand on the self-interest of the regulated and that advantages from the regulation commonly fall to others. The conflicts of economic interest between the regulated and those who advantage by it are wisely left under our system to resolution by the Congress under its more flexible and responsible legislative process. Such conflicts rarely lend themselves to judicial determination. And with the wisdom, workability, or fairness, of the plan of regulation we have nothing to do.

NOTES AND QUESTIONS

1. After reading this case, what do you understand to be the limits of the reach of congressional powers under the Commerce Clause? Note that one prior approach of the Court, as you have seen, was to label some activities "production," or "manufacture," or "consumption" and to distinguish these activities from "marketing" or "commerce." The former activities were said not to be reachable under the Commerce Clause, while the latter activities were. Why did the Court decline to maintain this approach? Note also that one line of reasoning under the Commerce Clause led to distinctions between "direct" and "indirect" effects on interstate commerce, with activities that had "direct" effects being subject to congressional regulation, while those with "indirect" effects were not. Why does the Court reject this line of reasoning?

Of what importance is the Court's review of the regulation of other wheat-producing countries? Is what drives the holding in this case constitutional law, or is something else involved?

2. You may have already realized that this case comes about following some titanic political and judicial struggles related to the Administration of President Franklin D. Roosevelt, and his "New Deal." The New Deal involved unprecedented use by Congress of the commerce power, in an effort to deal with the effects of the Great Depression of 1929, when many Americans were suddenly economically impoverished. At first the Supreme Court rejected many of these New Deal measures to deal with the economy, in part because they sought federally to regulate what had been the province of the states. Thus, in the famous "sick chicken" case, *A.L.A. Schechter Poultry Corp. v. United States*, 295 U.S. 495 (1935), a unanimous Court declared that Congress could not regulate the business practices of a New York poultry slaughterhouse which sold only to New York customers. Slaughtering chickens and selling them intrastate, the court concluded, was *not* interstate commerce. The effects of the conduct of such business on interstate commerce, the Court declared, were at best "indirect" and not "direct."

But just two years later, in *National Labor Relations Board v. Jones & Laughlin Steel Corp.*, 301 U.S. 1 (1937), as part of what has often been described as a "Constitutional Revolution," the Supreme Court voted five to four to sustain federal labor law legislation which regulated management and union activity at manufacturing plants. As indicated, many prior Supreme Court precedents strongly suggested that activities that dealt only with production or manufacturing were not "commerce" subject to congressional regulation, but the Court rejected this authority, and also rejected the "direct/indirect" distinction as a means of determining when Congress could regulate under the Commerce Clause. The new test that emerged, and was applied in *Wickard,* was the "substantial affects" test. You will have already come to some conclusion about just what limits, if any, this test places on the ability of the federal government to regulate activities formerly regarded as strictly local in nature. Why was it that the Court, in the mere space of two years, so fundamentally altered its understanding of what the Constitution permitted the federal government to do?

Many at the time thought that two political developments had an important influence on the Court, and many scholars still adhere to that belief. These two developments were (1) the huge majority by which Franklin Roosevelt was re-elected in 1936, which huge majority apparently endorsed his plan for greater federal activity, and (2) Roosevelt's open attack on the Court pursuant to his "Court-packing" plan. When the Court, in decisions such as *Schechter,* appeared to impose roadblocks in the way of the President's ambitious centralizing regulatory strategy, the President attacked the Court for maintaining a "horse and buggy" definition of interstate commerce, and for refusing to understand that the meaning of the Constitution ought to change with the particular needs of the times. Declaring that he sought to save the Constitution from the Court and the Court from itself, the President asked Congress for legislation to increase the number of Supreme Court Justices, so that he might get a majority more favorable to his views. Following the Court's moves in 1937 this legislation was abandoned, but FDR had made his point, and the "Constitutional Revolution of 1937" also came to be regarded as the "Switch in Time that Saved Nine."

This 1937 "Revolution" also involved a major change in the Court's attitude toward the Due Process Clause, and the permissible latitude for government to regulate the contracts entered into between private parties, a topic which we will treat in Chapter Seven. For the moment, though, we can limit our consideration to the meaning of the "Switch" for the Federal Government's power over the Commerce Clause. Are there now any limits to that power at all? Consider the case which follows.

d. What Are the Limits, If Any, to the Commerce Power?

UNITED STATES v. LOPEZ
514 U.S. 549 (1995)

CHIEF JUSTICE REHNQUIST delivered the opinion of the Court.

In the Gun-Free School Zones Act of 1990, Congress made it a federal offense "for any individual knowingly to possess a firearm at a place that the individual knows, or has reasonable cause to believe, is a school zone." The Act neither regulates a commercial activity nor contains a requirement that the possession be connected in any way to interstate commerce. We hold that the Act exceeds the authority of Congress "[t]o regulate Commerce . . . among the several States . . . ."

On March 10, 1992, respondent, who was then a 12th-grade student, arrived at Edison High School in San Antonio, Texas, carrying a concealed .38 caliber handgun and five bullets. Acting upon an anonymous tip, school authorities confronted respondent, who admitted that he was carrying the weapon. He was arrested and charged under Texas law with firearm possession on school premises. The next day, the state charges were dismissed after federal agents charged respondent by complaint with violating the Gun-Free School Zones Act of 1990.

. . . Respondent moved to dismiss his federal indictment on the ground that [the Gun-Free School Zones Act] "is unconstitutional as it is beyond the power of Congress to legislate control over our public schools." The District Court denied the motion, concluding that [the Act] "is a constitutional exercise of Congress' well-defined power to regulate activities in and affecting commerce, and the 'business' of elementary, middle and high schools . . . affects interstate commerce." Respondent waived his right to a jury trial. The District Court conducted a bench trial, found him guilty of violating [the Act] and sentenced him to six months' imprisonment and two years' supervised release.

On appeal, respondent challenged his conviction based on his claim that [the Gun-Free School Zones Act] exceeded Congress' power to legislate under the Commerce Clause. The Court of Appeals for the Fifth Circuit agreed and reversed respondent's conviction. It held that, in light of what it characterized as insufficient congressional findings and legislative history, "[the Gun-Free School Zones Act] in the full reach of its terms, is invalid as beyond the power of Congress under the Commerce Clause." . . .

We start with first principles. The Constitution creates a Federal Government of enumerated powers. . . . As James Madison wrote, "[t]he powers delegated by the proposed Constitution to the federal government are few and defined. Those which are to remain in the State governments are numerous and indefinite." FEDERALIST NO. 45, at 292-93 (Clinton Rossiter ed., 1961). This constitutionally mandated division of authority "was adopted by the Framers to ensure protection of our fundamental liberties." . . . "Just as the separation and independence of the coordinate branches of the Federal Government serve to prevent the accumulation of excessive power in any one branch, a healthy balance of power between the States and the Federal Government will reduce the risk of tyranny and abuse from either front."

The Constitution delegates to Congress the power "[t]o regulate Commerce with foreign Nations, and among the several States, and with the Indian Tribes." Art. I, § 8, cl. 3. The Court, through Chief Justice Marshall, first defined the nature of Congress' commerce power in *Gibbons v. Ogden* (1824). . . . The *Gibbons* Court, however, acknowledged that limitations on the commerce power are inherent in the very language of the Commerce Clause.

"It is not intended to say that these words comprehend that commerce, which is completely internal, which is carried on between man and man in a State, or between different parts of the same State, and which does not extend to or affect other States. Such a power would be inconvenient, and is certainly unnecessary.

"Comprehensive as the word 'among' is, it may very properly be restricted to that commerce which concerns more States than one. . . . The enumeration presupposes something not enumerated; and that something, if we regard the language or the subject of the sentence, must be the exclusively internal commerce of a State."

For nearly a century thereafter, the Court's Commerce Clause decisions dealt but rarely with the extent of Congress' power, and almost entirely with the Commerce Clause as a limit on state legislation that discriminated against interstate commerce. . . . Under this line of precedent, the Court held that certain categories of activity such as "production," "manufacturing," and "mining" were within the province of state governments, and thus were beyond the power of Congress under the Commerce Clause. . . .

In 1887, Congress enacted the Interstate Commerce Act, and in 1890, Congress enacted the Sherman Antitrust Act. These laws ushered in a new era of federal regulation under the commerce power. When cases involving these laws first reached this Court, we imported from our negative Commerce Clause cases the approach that Congress could not regulate activities such as "production," "manufacturing," and "mining." *See, e.g., United States v. E.C. Knight Co.* (1895) ("Commerce succeeds to manufacture, and is not part of it"). . . . Simultaneously, however, the Court held that, where the interstate and intrastate aspects of commerce were so mingled together that full regulation of interstate commerce required incidental regulation of intrastate commerce, the Commerce Clause authorized such regulation. . . .

In *A.L.A. Schechter Poultry Corp. v. United States* (1935), the Court struck down regulations that fixed the hours and wages of individuals employed by an intrastate business because the activity being regulated related to interstate commerce only indirectly. In doing so, the Court characterized the distinction between direct and indirect effects of intrastate transactions upon interstate commerce as "a fundamental one, essential to the maintenance of our constitutional system." Activities that affected interstate commerce directly were within Congress' power; activities that affected interstate commerce indirectly were beyond Congress' reach. The justification for this formal distinction was rooted in the fear that otherwise "there would be virtually no limit to the federal power and for all practical purposes we should have a completely centralized government."

Two years later, in the watershed case of *NLRB v. Jones & Laughlin Steel Corp.* (1937), the Court upheld the National Labor Relations Act against a Commerce Clause challenge, and in the process, departed from the distinction between "direct" and "indirect" effects on interstate commerce. ("The question [of the scope of Congress' power] is necessarily one of degree"). The Court held that intrastate activities that "have such a close and substantial relation to interstate commerce that their control is essential or appropriate to protect that commerce from burdens and obstructions" are within Congress' power to regulate.

In *United States v. Darby* (1941), the Court upheld the Fair Labor Standards Act, stating:

> "The power of Congress over interstate commerce is not confined to the regulation of commerce among the states. It extends to those activities intrastate which so affect interstate commerce or the exercise of the power of Congress over it as to make regulation of them appropriate means to the attainment of a legitimate end, the exercise of the granted power of Congress to regulate interstate commerce." . . .

In *Wickard v. Filburn*, the Court upheld the application of amendments to the Agricultural Adjustment Act of 1938 to the production and consumption of home-grown wheat. The *Wickard* Court explicitly rejected earlier distinctions between direct and indirect effects on interstate commerce, stating:

> "[E]ven if appellee's activity be local and though it may not be regarded as commerce, it may still, whatever its nature, be reached by Congress if it exerts a substantial economic effect on interstate commerce, and this irrespective of whether such effect is what might at some earlier time have been defined as 'direct' or 'indirect.'"

The *Wickard* Court emphasized that although Filburn's own contribution to the demand for wheat may have been trivial by itself, that was not "enough to remove him from the scope of federal regulation where, as here, his contribution, taken together with that of many others similarly situated, is far from trivial."

Jones & Laughlin Steel, *Darby*, and *Wickard* ushered in an era of Commerce Clause jurisprudence that greatly expanded the previously defined authority of Congress under that Clause. In part, this was a recognition of the great changes that had occurred in the way business was carried on in this country. Enterprises that had once been local or at most regional in nature had become national in scope. But the doctrinal change also reflected a view that earlier Commerce Clause cases artificially had constrained the authority of Congress to regulate interstate commerce.

But even these modern-era precedents which have expanded congressional power under the Commerce Clause confirm that this power is subject to outer limits. In *Jones & Laughlin Steel*, the Court warned that the scope of the interstate commerce power "must be considered in the light of our dual system of government and may not be extended so as to embrace effects upon interstate commerce so indirect and remote that to embrace them, in view of our complex society, would effectually obliterate the distinction between what is national and what is local and create a completely centralized government." Since that time, the Court has heeded that warning and undertaken to decide whether a rational basis existed for concluding that a regulated activity sufficiently affected interstate commerce.

Similarly, in *Maryland v. Wirtz* (1968), the Court reaffirmed that "the power to regulate commerce, though broad indeed, has limits" that "[t]he Court has ample power" to enforce. . . . In response to the dissent's warnings that the Court was powerless to enforce the limitations on Congress' commerce powers because "[a]ll activities affecting commerce, even in the minutest degree, [*Wickard*], may be regulated and controlled by Congress" (Douglas, J., dissenting), the *Wirtz* Court replied that the dissent had misread precedent as "[n]either here nor in *Wickard* has the Court declared that Congress may use a relatively trivial impact on commerce as an excuse for broad general regulation of state or private activities." Rather, "[t]he Court has said only that where *a general regulatory statute bears a substantial relation to commerce*, the *de minimis* character of individual instances arising under that statute is of no consequence." (first emphasis added).

Consistent with this structure, we have identified three broad categories of activity that Congress may regulate under its commerce power. First, Congress may regulate the use of the channels of interstate commerce. Second, Congress is empowered to regulate and protect the instrumentalities of interstate commerce, or persons or things in interstate commerce, even though the threat may come only from intrastate activities. . . . Finally, Congress' commerce authority includes the power to regulate those activities having a substantial relation to interstate commerce, . . . *i.e.*, those activities that substantially affect interstate commerce. . . .

Within this final category, admittedly, our case law has not been clear whether an activity must "affect" or "substantially affect" interstate commerce in order to be within Congress' power to regulate it under the Commerce Clause. . . . We conclude, consistent with the great weight of our case law, that the proper test requires an analysis of whether the regulated activity "substantially affects" interstate commerce.

We now turn to consider the power of Congress, in the light of this framework, to enact [the Gun-Free School Zones Act]. The first two categories of authority may be quickly disposed of: [The Act] is not a regulation of the use of the channels of interstate commerce, nor is it an attempt to prohibit the interstate transportation of a commodity through the channels of commerce; nor can [the Act] be justified as a regulation by which Congress has sought to protect an instrumentality of interstate commerce or a thing in interstate commerce. Thus, if [the Act] is to be sustained, it must be under the third category as a regulation of an activity that substantially affects interstate commerce.

First, we have upheld a wide variety of congressional Acts regulating intrastate economic activity where we have concluded that the activity substantially affected interstate commerce. Examples include the regulation of intrastate coal mining, intrastate extortionate credit transactions, restaurants utilizing substantial interstate supplies, inns and hotels catering to interstate guests, and production and consumption of home-grown wheat. . . . These examples are by no means exhaustive, but the pattern is clear. Where economic activity substantially affects interstate commerce, legislation regulating that activity will be sustained.

Even *Wickard*, which is perhaps the most far reaching example of Commerce Clause authority over intrastate activity, involved economic activity in a way that the possession of a gun in a school zone does not. . . .

[The Gun-Free School Zones Act] is a criminal statute that by its terms has nothing to do with "commerce" or any sort of economic enterprise, however broadly one might define those terms. [The Act] is not an essential part of a larger regulation of economic activity, in which the regulatory scheme could be undercut unless the intrastate activity were regulated. It cannot, therefore, be sustained under our cases upholding regulations of activities that arise out of or are connected with a commercial transaction, which viewed in the aggregate, substantially affects interstate commerce.

Second, [the Gun-Free School Zones Act] contains no jurisdictional element which would ensure, through case-by-case inquiry, that the firearm possession in question affects interstate commerce. For example, in *United States v. Bass* (1971), the Court interpreted former 18 U.S.C. § 1202(a), which made it a crime for a felon to "receiv[e], posses[s], or transpor[t] in commerce or affecting commerce . . . any firearm." The Court interpreted the possession component of § 1202(a) to require an additional nexus to interstate commerce both because the statute was ambiguous and because "unless Congress conveys its purpose clearly, it will not be deemed to have significantly changed the federal-state balance." The *Bass* Court set aside the conviction because although the Government had demonstrated that Bass had possessed a firearm, it had failed "to show the requisite nexus with interstate commerce." The Court thus interpreted the statute to reserve the constitutional question whether Congress could regulate, without more, the "mere possession" of firearms. Unlike the statute in *Bass*, [the Gun-Free School Zones Act] has no express jurisdictional element which might limit its reach to a discrete set of firearm possessions that additionally have an explicit connection with or effect on interstate commerce.

Although as part of our independent evaluation of constitutionality under the Commerce Clause we of course consider legislative findings, and indeed even congressional committee findings, regarding effect on interstate commerce, . . . the Government concedes that "[n]either the statute nor its legislative history contain[s] express congressional findings regarding the effects upon interstate commerce of gun possession in a school zone." We agree with the Government that Congress normally is not required to make formal findings as to the substantial burdens that an activity has on interstate commerce. But to the extent that congressional findings would enable us to evaluate the legislative judgment that the activity in question substantially affected interstate commerce, even though no such substantial effect was visible to the naked eye, they are lacking here.

The Government argues that Congress has accumulated institutional expertise regarding the regulation of firearms through previous enactments. We agree, however, with the Fifth Circuit that importation of previous findings to justify [the Gun-Free School Zones Act] is especially inappropriate here because the "prior federal enactments or Congressional findings [do not] speak to the subject matter of [the Act] or its relationship to interstate commerce. Indeed [the Act] plows thoroughly new ground and represents a sharp break with the long-standing pattern of federal firearms legislation."

The Government's essential contention, *in fine*, is that we may determine here that [the Act] is valid because possession of a firearm in a local school zone does indeed substantially affect interstate commerce. The Government argues that possession of a firearm in a school zone may result in violent crime and that violent crime can be expected to affect the functioning of the national economy in two ways. First, the costs of violent crime are substantial, and, through the mechanism of insurance, those costs are spread throughout the population. Second, violent crime reduces the willingness of individuals to travel to areas within the country that are perceived to be unsafe. The Government also argues that the presence of guns in schools poses a substantial threat to the educational process by threatening the learning environment. A handicapped educational process, in turn, will result in a less productive citizenry. That, in turn, would have an adverse effect on the Nation's economic well-being. As a result, the Government argues that Congress could rationally have concluded that [the Act] substantially affects interstate commerce.

We pause to consider the implications of the Government's arguments. The Government admits, under its "costs of crime" reasoning, that Congress could regulate not only all violent crime, but all activities that might lead to violent crime, regardless of how tenuously they relate to interstate commerce. Similarly, under the Government's "national productivity" reasoning, Congress could regulate any activity that it found was related to the economic productivity of individual citizens: family law (including marriage, divorce, and child custody), for example. Under the theories that the Government presents in support of [the Act], it is difficult to perceive any limitation on federal power, even in areas such as criminal law enforcement or education where States historically have been sovereign. Thus, if we were to accept the Government's arguments, we are hard-pressed to posit any activity by an individual that Congress is without power to regulate.

Although JUSTICE BREYER argues that acceptance of the Government's rationales would not authorize a general federal police power, he is unable to identify any activity that the States may regulate but Congress may not. JUSTICE BREYER posits that there might be some limitations on Congress' commerce power such as family law or certain aspects of education. These suggested limitations, when viewed in light of the dissent's expansive analysis, are devoid of substance.

JUSTICE BREYER focuses, for the most part, on the threat that firearm possession in and near schools poses to the educational process and the potential economic consequences flowing from that threat. Specifically, the dissent reasons that (1) gun-related violence is a serious problem; (2) that problem, in turn, has an adverse effect on classroom learning; and (3) that adverse effect on classroom learning, in turn, represents a substantial threat to trade and commerce. This analysis would be equally applicable, if not more so, to subjects such as family law and direct regulation of education.

For instance, if Congress can, pursuant to its Commerce Clause power, regulate activities that adversely affect the learning environment, then, *a fortiori*, it also can regulate the educational process directly. Congress could determine that a school's curriculum has a "significant" effect on the extent of classroom learning. As a result, Congress could mandate a federal curriculum for local elementary and secondary schools because what is taught in local schools has a significant "effect on classroom learning," and that, in turn, has a substantial effect on interstate commerce.

JUSTICE BREYER rejects our reading of precedent and argues that "Congress . . . could rationally conclude that schools fall on the commercial side of the line." Again, JUSTICE BREYER's rationale lacks any real limits because, depending on the level of generality, any activity can be looked upon as commercial. Under the dissent's rationale, Congress could just as easily look at child rearing as "fall[ing] on the commercial side of the line" because it provides a "valuable service — namely, to equip [children] with the skills they need to survive in life and, more specifically, in the workplace." We do not doubt that Congress has authority under the Commerce Clause to regulate numerous commercial activities that substantially affect interstate commerce and also affect the educational process. That authority, though broad, does not include the authority to regulate each and every aspect of local schools.

Admittedly, a determination whether an intrastate activity is commercial or noncommercial may in some cases result in legal uncertainty. But, so long as Congress' authority is limited to those powers enumerated in the Constitution, and so long as those enumerated powers are interpreted as having judicially enforceable outer limits, congressional legislation under the Commerce Clause always will engender "legal uncertainty." . . . The Constitution mandates this uncertainty by withholding from Congress a plenary police power that would authorize enactment of every type of legislation. . . . Congress has operated within this framework of legal uncertainty ever since this Court determined that it was the judiciary's duty "to say what the law is." . . . Any possible benefit from eliminating this "legal uncertainty" would be at the expense of the Constitution's system of enumerated powers.

In *Jones & Laughlin Steel*, we held that the question of congressional power under the Commerce Clause "is necessarily one of degree." To the same effect is the concurring opinion of Justice Cardozo in *Schechter Poultry*:

> "There is a view of causation that would obliterate the distinction of what is national and what is local in the activities of commerce. Motion at the outer rim is communicated perceptibly, though minutely, to recording instruments at the center. A society such as ours 'is an elastic medium which transmits all tremors throughout its territory; the only question is of their size.'"

These are not precise formulations, and in the nature of things they cannot be. But we think they point the way to a correct decision of this case. The possession of a gun in a local school zone is in no sense an economic activity that might, through repetition elsewhere, substantially affect any sort of interstate commerce. Respondent was a local student at a local school; there is no indication that he had recently moved in interstate commerce, and there is no requirement that his possession of the firearm have any concrete tie to interstate commerce.

To uphold the Government's contentions here, we would have to pile inference upon inference in a manner that would bid fair to convert congressional authority under the Commerce Clause to a general police power of the sort retained by the States. Admittedly, some of our prior cases have taken long steps down that road, giving great deference to congressional action. The broad language in these opinions has suggested the possibility of additional expansion, but we decline here to proceed any further. To do so would require us to conclude that the Constitution's enumeration of powers does not presuppose something not enumerated, *cf. Gibbons v. Ogden*, and that there never will be a distinction between what is truly national and what is truly local, *cf. Jones & Laughlin Steel*. This we are unwilling to do.

For the foregoing reasons the judgment of the Court of Appeals is

Affirmed.

JUSTICE THOMAS, concurring.

. . . Although I join the majority, I write separately to observe that our case law has drifted far from the original understanding of the Commerce Clause. In a future case, we ought to temper our Commerce Clause jurisprudence in a manner that both makes sense of our more recent case law and is more faithful to the original understanding of that Clause.

We have said that Congress may regulate not only "Commerce . . . among the several states," U.S. Const., Art. I, § 8, cl. 3, but also anything that has a "substantial effect" on such commerce. This test, if taken to its logical extreme, would give Congress a "police power" over all aspects of American life. Unfortunately, we have never come to grips with this implication of our substantial effects formula. Although we have supposedly applied the substantial effects test for the past 60 years, we always have rejected readings of the Commerce Clause and the scope of federal power that would permit Congress to exercise a police power; our cases are quite clear that there are real limits to federal power.

* * *

In an appropriate case, I believe that we must further reconsider our "substantial effects" test with an eye toward constructing a standard that reflects the text and history of the Commerce Clause without totally rejecting our more recent Commerce Clause jurisprudence. . . .

I

At the time the original Constitution was ratified, "commerce" consisted of selling, buying, and bartering, as well as transporting for these purposes. *See* 1 S. Johnson, A Dictionary of the English Language 361 (4th ed. 1773). . . .

As one would expect, the term "commerce" was used in contradistinction to productive activities such as manufacturing and agriculture. Alexander Hamilton, for example, repeatedly treated commerce, agriculture, and manufacturing as three separate endeavors. . . .

Moreover, interjecting a modern sense of commerce into the Constitution generates significant textual and structural problems. For example, one cannot replace "commerce" with a different type of enterprise, such as manufacturing. When a manufacturer produces a car, assembly cannot take place "with a foreign nation" or "with the Indian Tribes." Parts may come from different States or other nations and hence may have been in the flow of commerce at one time, but manufacturing takes place at a discrete site. Agriculture and manufacturing involve the production of goods; commerce encompasses traffic in such articles.

* * *

In addition to its powers under the Commerce Clause, Congress has the authority to enact such laws as are "necessary and proper" to carry into execution its power to regulate commerce among the several States. U.S. Const., Art. I, § 8, cl. 18. But on this Court's understanding of congressional power under these two Clauses, many of Congress' other enumerated powers under Art. I, § 8 are wholly superfluous. After all, if Congress may regulate all matters that substantially affect commerce, there is no need for the Constitution to specify that Congress may enact bankruptcy laws, cl. 4, or coin money and fix the standard of weights and measures, cl. 5, or punish counterfeiters of United States coin and securities, cl. 6. Likewise, Congress would not need the separate authority to establish post offices and post roads, cl. 7, or to grant patents and copyrights, cl. 8, or to "punish Piracies and Felonies committed on the high Seas," cl. 10. It might not even need the power to raise and support an Army and Navy, cls. 12 and 13, for fewer people would engage in commercial shipping if they thought that a foreign power could expropriate their property with ease. Indeed, if Congress could regulate matters that substantially affect interstate commerce, there would have been no need to specify that Congress can regulate international trade and commerce with the Indians. As the Framers surely understood, these other branches of trade substantially affect interstate commerce.

Put simply, much if not all of Art. I, § 8 (including portions of the Commerce Clause itself) would be surplusage if Congress had been given authority over matters that substantially affect interstate commerce. An interpretation of cl. 3 that makes the rest of § 8 superfluous simply cannot be correct. Yet this Court's Commerce Clause jurisprudence has endorsed just such an interpretation: the power we have accorded Congress has swallowed Art. I, § 8.

Indeed, if a "substantial effects" test can be appended to the Commerce Clause, why not to every other power of the Federal Government? There is no reason for singling out the Commerce Clause for special treatment. Accordingly, Congress could regulate all matters that "substantially affect" the Army and Navy, bankruptcies, tax collection, expenditures, and so on. In that case, the clauses of § 8 all mutually overlap, something we can assume the Founding Fathers never intended.

Our construction of the scope of congressional authority has the additional problem of coming close to turning the Tenth Amendment on its head. Our case law could be read to reserve to the United States all powers not expressly prohibited by the Constitution. Taken together, these fundamental textual problems should, at the very least, convince us that the "substantial effects" test should be reexamined.

* * *

III

If the principal dissent's understanding of our early case law were correct, there might be some reason to doubt this view of the original understanding of the Constitution. According to that dissent, Chief Justice Marshall's opinion in *Gibbons v. Ogden* established that Congress may control all local activities that "significantly affect interstate commerce." And, "with the exception of one wrong turn subsequently corrected," this has been the "traditiona[l]" method of interpreting the Commerce Clause. . . .

In my view, the dissent is wrong about the holding and reasoning of *Gibbons*. Because this error leads the dissent to characterize the first 150 years of this Court's case law as a "wrong turn," I feel compelled to put the last 50 years in proper perspective.

A

In *Gibbons*, the Court examined whether a federal law that licensed ships to engage in the "coasting trade" preempted a New York law granting a 30-year monopoly to Robert Livingston and Robert Fulton to navigate the State's waterways by steamship. In concluding that it did, the Court noted that Congress could regulate "navigation" because "[a]ll America . . . has uniformly understood, the word 'commerce,' to comprehend navigation. It was so understood, and must have been so understood, when the constitution was framed." The Court also observed that federal power over commerce "among the several States" meant that Congress could regulate commerce conducted partly within a State. Because a portion of interstate commerce and foreign commerce would almost always take place within one or more States, federal power over interstate and foreign commerce necessarily would extend into the States.

At the same time, the Court took great pains to make clear that Congress could not regulate commerce "which is completely internal, which is carried on between man and man in a State, or between different parts of the same State, and which does not extend to or affect other States." Moreover, while suggesting that the Constitution might not permit States to regulate interstate or foreign commerce, the Court observed that "[i]nspection laws, quarantine laws, health laws of every description, as well as laws for regulating the internal commerce of a State" were but a small part "of that immense mass of legislation . . . not surrendered to a general government." From an early moment, the Court rejected the notion that Congress can regulate everything that affects interstate commerce. That the internal commerce of the States and the numerous state inspection, quarantine, and health laws had substantial effects on interstate commerce cannot be doubted. Nevertheless, they were not "surrendered to the general government."

Of course, the principal dissent is not the first to misconstrue *Gibbons*. For instance, the Court has stated that *Gibbons* "described the federal commerce power with a breadth never yet exceeded." *Wickard v. Filburn* (1942). *See also Perez v. United States* (1971) (claiming that with *Darby* and *Wickard*, "the broader view of the Commerce Clause announced by Chief Justice Marshall had been restored"). I believe that this misreading stems from two statements in *Gibbons*.

First, the Court made the uncontroversial claim that federal power does not encompass "commerce" that "does not extend to or affect other States." From this statement, the principal dissent infers that whenever an activity affects interstate commerce, it necessarily follows that Congress can regulate such activities. Of course, Chief Justice Marshall said no such thing and the inference the dissent makes cannot be drawn.

There is a much better interpretation of the "affect[s]" language: because the Court had earlier noted that the commerce power did not extend to wholly intrastate commerce, the Court was acknowledging that although the line between intrastate and interstate/foreign commerce would be difficult to draw, federal authority could not be construed to cover purely intrastate commerce. Commerce that did not affect another State could never be said to be commerce "among the several States."

But even if one were to adopt the dissent's reading, the "affect[s]" language, at most, permits Congress to regulate only intrastate commerce that substantially affects interstate and foreign commerce. There is no reason to believe that Chief Justice Marshall was asserting that Congress could regulate all activities that affect interstate commerce.

The second source of confusion stems from the Court's praise for the Constitution's division of power between the States and the Federal Government:

> "The genius and character of the whole government seem to be, that its action is to be applied to all the external concerns of the nation, and to those internal concerns which affect the States generally; but not to those which are completely within a particular State, which do not affect other States, and with which it is not necessary to interfere, for the purpose of executing some of the general powers of the government."

In this passage, the Court merely was making the well understood point that the Constitution commits matters of "national" concern to Congress and leaves "local" matters to the States. The Court was not saying that whatever Congress believes is a national matter becomes an object of federal control. The matters of national concern are enumerated in the Constitution: war, taxes, patents, and copyrights, uniform rules of naturalization and bankruptcy, types of commerce, and so on. *See generally* U.S. Const., Art. I, § 8. *Gibbons'* emphatic statements that Congress could not regulate many matters that affect commerce confirm that the Court did not read the Commerce Clause as granting Congress control over matters that " affect the States generally." *Gibbons* simply cannot be construed as the principal dissent would have it.

B

I am aware of no cases prior to the New Deal that characterized the power flowing from the Commerce Clause as sweepingly as does our substantial effects test. My review of the case law indicates that the substantial effects test is but an innovation of the 20th century.

* * *

As recently as 1936, the Court continued to insist that the Commerce Clause did not reach the wholly internal business of the States. *See Carter v. Carter Coal Co.* (1936) (Congress may not regulate mine labor because "[t]he relation of employer and employee is a local relation"). . . .

IV

Apart from its recent vintage and its corresponding lack of any grounding in the original understanding of the Constitution, the substantial effects test suffers from the further flaw that it appears to grant Congress a police power over the Nation. When asked at oral argument if there were any limits to the Commerce Clause, the Government was at a loss for words. Likewise, the principal dissent insists that there are limits, but it cannot muster even one example. Indeed, the dissent implicitly concedes that its reading has no limits when it criticizes the Court for "threaten[ing] legal uncertainty in an area of law that . . . seemed reasonably well settled." The one advantage of the dissent's standard is certainty: it is certain that under its analysis everything may be regulated under the guise of the Commerce Clause.

The substantial effects test suffers from this flaw, in part, because of its "aggregation principle." Under so-called "class of activities" statutes, Congress can regulate whole categories of activities that are not themselves either "inter-state" or "commerce." In applying the effects test, we ask whether the class of activities as a whole substantially affects interstate commerce, not whether any specific activity within the class has such effects when considered in isolation. . . .

The aggregation principle is clever, but has no stopping point. . . .

V

This extended discussion of the original understanding and our first century and a half of case law does not necessarily require a wholesale abandonment of our more recent opinions.[8] It simply reveals that our substantial effects test is far removed from both the Constitution and from our early case law and that the Court's opinion should not be viewed as "radical" or another "wrong turn" that must be corrected in the future. The analysis also suggests that we ought to temper our Commerce Clause jurisprudence. . . .

At an appropriate juncture, I think we must modify our Commerce Clause jurisprudence. Today, it is easy enough to say that the Clause certainly does not empower Congress to ban gun possession within 1,000 feet of a school.

JUSTICE BREYER, with whom JUSTICE STEVENS, JUSTICE SOUTER, and JUSTICE GINSBURG join, dissenting.

. . . In my view, the statute falls well within the scope of the commerce power as this Court has understood that power over the last half-century.

I

In reaching this conclusion, I apply three basic principles of Commerce Clause interpretation. First, the power to "regulate Commerce . . . among the several States," U.S. Const. Art. I, § 8, cl. 3, encompasses the power to regulate local activities insofar as they significantly affect interstate commerce. . . . [T]he Court, in describing how much of an effect the Clause requires, sometimes has used the word "substantial" and sometimes has not. . . . And . . . the question of degree (how *much* effect) requires an estimate of the "size" of the effect that no verbal formulation can capture with precision. I use the word "significant" because the word "substantial" implies a somewhat narrower power than recent

---

[8] Although I might be willing to return to the original understanding, I recognize that many believe that it is too late in the day to undertake a fundamental reexamination of the past 60 years. Consideration of stare decisis and reliance interests may convince us that we cannot wipe the slate clean.

precedent suggests. But, to speak of "substantial effect" rather than "significant effect" would make no difference in this case.

Second, in determining whether a local activity will likely have a significant effect upon interstate commerce, a court must consider, not the effect of an individual act (a single instance of gun possession), but rather the cumulative effect of all similar instances (*i.e.*, the effect of all guns possessed in or near schools). *See, e.g., Wickard.* . . .

Third, the Constitution requires us to judge the connection between a regulated activity and interstate commerce, not directly, but at one remove. Courts must give Congress a degree of leeway in determining the existence of a significant factual connection between the regulated activity and interstate commerce — both because the Constitution delegates the commerce power directly to Congress and because the determination requires an empirical judgment of a kind that a legislature is more likely than a court to make with accuracy. The traditional words "rational basis" capture this leeway. Thus, the specific question before us, as the Court recognizes, is not whether the "regulated activity sufficiently affected interstate commerce," but, rather, whether Congress could have had "*a rational basis*" for so concluding. (emphasis added).

* * *

II

Applying these principles to the case at hand, we must ask whether Congress could have had a *rational basis* for finding a significant (or substantial) connection between gun-related school violence and interstate commerce. Or, to put the question in the language of the *explicit* finding that Congress made when it amended this law in 1994: Could Congress rationally have found that "violent crime in school zones," through its effect on the "quality of education," significantly (or substantially) affects "interstate" or "foreign commerce"? As long as one views the commerce connection, not as a "technical legal conception," but as "a practical one," *Swift & Co. v. United States* (1905) (Holmes, J.), the answer to this question must be yes. Numerous reports and studies — generated both inside and outside government — make clear that Congress could reasonably have found the empirical connection that its law, implicitly or explicitly, asserts.

For one thing, reports, hearings, and other readily available literature make clear that the problem of guns in and around schools is widespread and extremely serious. . . . And, they report that this widespread violence in schools throughout the Nation significantly interferes with the quality of education in those schools. Based on reports such as these, Congress obviously could have thought that guns and learning are mutually exclusive. Congress could therefore have found a substantial educational problem — teachers unable to teach, students unable to learn — and concluded that guns near schools contribute substantially to the size and scope of that problem.

Having found that guns in schools significantly undermine the quality of education in our Nation's classrooms, Congress could also have found, given the effect of education upon interstate and foreign commerce, that gun-related violence in and around schools is a commercial, as well as a human, problem. Education, although far more than a matter of economics, has long been inextricably intertwined with the Nation's economy. When this Nation began, most workers received their education in the workplace, typically (like Benjamin Franklin) as apprentices. As late as the 1920's, many workers still received general education directly from their employers — from large corporations, such as General Electric, Ford, and Goodyear, which created schools within their firms to help both the worker and the firm. As public school enrollment grew in the early 20th century, the need for industry to teach basic educational skills diminished. But, the direct economic link between basic education and industrial productivity remained. Scholars estimate that nearly a quarter of America's economic growth in the early years of this century is traceable directly to increased schooling; that investment in "human capital" (through spending on education) exceeded investment in "physical capital" by a ratio of almost two to one; and that the economic returns to this investment in education exceeded the returns to conventional capital investment.

In recent years the link between secondary education and business has strengthened, becoming both more direct and more important. Scholars on the subject report that technological changes and innovations in management techniques have altered the nature of the workplace so that more jobs now demand greater educational skills. . . .

Increasing global competition also has made primary and secondary education economically more important. . . . Indeed, Congress has said, when writing other statutes, that "functionally or technologically illiterate" Americans in the work force "erod[e]" our economic "standing in the international marketplace," and that "[o]ur Nation is . . . paying the price of scientific and technological illiteracy, with our productivity declining, our industrial base ailing, and our global competitiveness dwindling."

Finally, there is evidence that, today more than ever, many firms base their location decisions upon the presence, or absence, of a work force with a basic education. . . . In light of this increased importance of education to individual firms, it is no surprise that half of the Nation's manufacturers have become involved with setting standards and shaping curricula for local schools, that 88 percent think this kind of involvement is important, that more than 20 States have recently passed educational reforms to attract new business, and that business magazines have begun to rank cities according to the quality of their schools.

The economic links I have just sketched seem fairly obvious. Why then is it not equally obvious, in light of those links, that a widespread, serious, and substantial physical threat to teaching and learning *also* substantially threatens the commerce to which that teaching and learning is inextricably tied? . . . The only question, then, is whether the latter threat is (to use the majority's terminology) "substantial." And, the evidence of (1) the *extent* of the gun-related violence problem, (2) the *extent* of the resulting negative effect on classroom learning, and (3) the *extent* of the consequent negative commercial effects, when taken together, indicate a threat to trade and commerce that is "substantial." At the very least, Congress could rationally have concluded that the links are "substantial."

Specifically, Congress could have found that gun-related violence near the classroom poses a serious economic threat (1) to consequently inadequately educated workers who must endure low paying jobs, and (2) to communities and businesses that might (in today's "information society") otherwise gain, from a well-educated work force, an important commercial advantage, of a kind that location near a railhead or harbor provided in the past. Congress might also have found these threats to be no different in kind from other threats that this Court has found within the commerce power, such as the threat that loan sharking poses to the "funds" of "numerous localities," . . . and that unfair labor practices pose to instrumentalities of commerce. . . .

To hold this statute constitutional is not to "obliterate" the "distinction of what is national and what is local"; nor is it to hold that the Commerce Clause permits the Federal Government to "regulate any activity that it found was related to the economic productivity of individual citizens," to regulate "marriage, divorce, and child custody," or to regulate any and all aspects of education. First, this statute is aimed at curbing a particularly acute threat to the educational process — the possession (and use) of life-threatening firearms in, or near, the classroom. The empirical evidence that I have discussed above unmistakably documents the special way in which guns and education are incompatible. This Court has previously recognized the singularly disruptive potential on interstate commerce that acts of violence may have. Second, the immediacy of the connection between education and the national economic well-being is documented by scholars and accepted by society at large in a way and to a degree that may not hold true for other social institutions. It must surely be the rare case, then, that a statute strikes at conduct that (when considered in the abstract) seems so removed from commerce, but which (practically speaking) has so significant an impact upon commerce.

In sum, a holding that the particular statute before us falls within the commerce power would not expand the scope of that Clause. Rather, it simply would apply pre-existing law to changing economic circumstances. It would recognize that, in today's economic world, gun-related violence near the classroom makes a significant difference to our economic, as well as our social, well-being. In accordance with well-accepted precedent, such a holding would permit Congress "to act in terms of economic . . . realities," would interpret the commerce power as "an affirmative power commensurate with the national needs," and would acknowledge that the "commerce clause does not operate so as to render the nation powerless to defend itself against economic forces that Congress decrees inimical or destructive of the national economy." . . .

III

The majority's holding — that [the Gun-Free School Zones Act] falls outside the scope of the Commerce Clause — creates three serious legal problems. First, the majority's holding runs contrary to modern Supreme Court cases that have upheld congressional actions despite connections to interstate or foreign commerce that are less significant than the effect of school violence. In *Perez v. United States,* the Court held that the Commerce Clause authorized a federal statute that makes it a crime to engage in loan sharking ("extortionate credit transactions") at a local level. The Court said that Congress may judge that such transactions, "though purely *intra*state, . . . affect *inter*state commerce." (emphasis added). Presumably, Congress reasoned that threatening or using force, say with a gun on a street corner, to collect a debt occurs sufficiently often so that the activity (by helping organized crime) affects commerce among the States. But, why then cannot Congress also reason that the threat or use of force — the frequent consequence of possessing a gun — in or near a school occurs sufficiently often so that such activity (by inhibiting basic education) affects commerce among the States? The negative impact upon the national economy of an inability to teach basic skills seems no smaller (nor less significant) than that of organized crime.

In *Katzenbach v. McClung* (1964), this Court upheld, as within the commerce power, a statute prohibiting racial discrimination at local restaurants, in part because that discrimination discouraged travel by African Americans and in part because that discrimination affected purchases of food and restaurant supplies from other States. In *Daniel v. Paul* (1969), this Court found an effect on commerce caused by an amusement park located several miles down a country road in the middle of Alabama — because some customers (the Court assumed), some food, 15 paddleboats, and a juke box had come from out of State. In both of these cases, the Court understood that the specific instance of discrimination (at a local place of accommodation) was part of a general practice that, considered as a whole, caused not only the most serious human and social harm, but had nationally significant economic dimensions as well. It is difficult to distinguish the case before us, for the same critical elements are present. Businesses are less likely to locate in communities where violence plagues the classroom. Families will hesitate to move to neighborhoods where students carry guns instead of books. . . . And (to look at the matter in the most narrowly commercial manner), interstate publishers therefore will sell fewer books and other firms will sell fewer school supplies where the threat of violence disrupts learning. Most importantly, like the local racial discrimination at issue in *McClung* and *Daniel*, the local instances here, taken together and considered as a whole, create a problem that causes serious human and social harm, but also has nationally significant economic dimensions.

In *Wickard v. Filburn* (1942), this Court sustained the application of the Agricultural Adjustment Act of 1938 to wheat that Filburn grew and consumed on his own local farm because, considered in its totality, (1) home-grown wheat may be "induced by rising prices" to "flow into the market and check price increases," and (2) even if it never actually enters the market, home-grown wheat nonetheless "supplies a need of the man who grew it which would otherwise be reflected by purchases in the open market" and, in that sense, "competes with wheat in commerce." To find both of these effects on commerce significant in amount, the Court had to give Congress the benefit of the doubt. Why would the Court, to find a significant (or "substantial") effect here, have to give Congress any greater leeway?

The second legal problem the Court creates comes from its apparent belief that it can reconcile its holding with earlier cases by making a critical distinction between "commercial" and noncommercial "transaction[s]." That is to say, the Court believes the Constitution would distinguish between two local activities, each of which has an identical effect upon interstate commerce, if one, but not the other, is "commercial" in nature. As a general matter, this approach fails to heed this Court's earlier warning not to turn "questions of the power of Congress" upon "formulas" that would give

> "controlling force to nomenclature such as 'production' and 'indirect' and foreclose consideration of the actual effects of the activity in question upon interstate commerce." *Wickard, supra.*

. . . Moreover, the majority's test is not consistent with what the Court saw as the point of the cases that the majority now characterizes. Although the majority today attempts to categorize *Perez, McClung,* and *Wickard* as involving intrastate "economic activity," the Courts that decided each of those cases did *not* focus upon the economic nature of the activity regulated. Rather, they focused upon whether that activity *affected* interstate or foreign commerce. In fact, the *Wickard* Court expressly held that Wickard's consumption of home grown wheat, *"though it may not be regarded as commerce,"* could nevertheless be regulated — *"whatever its nature"* — so long as "it exerts a substantial economic effect on interstate commerce." *Wickard, supra* (emphasis added).

More importantly, if a distinction between commercial and noncommercial activities is to be made, this is not the case in which to make it. The majority clearly cannot intend such a distinction to focus narrowly on an act of gun possession standing by itself, for such a reading could not be reconciled with either the civil rights cases (*McClung* and *Daniel*) or *Perez* — in each of those cases the specific transaction (the race-based exclusion, the use of force) was not itself "commercial." And, if the majority instead means to distinguish generally among broad categories of activities, differentiating what is educational from what is commercial, then, as a practical matter, the line becomes almost impossible to draw. Schools that teach reading, writing, mathematics, and related basic skills serve *both* social and commercial purposes, and one cannot easily separate the one from the other. American industry itself has been, and is again, involved in teaching. . . . Even if one were to ignore these practical questions, why should there be a theoretical distinction between education, when it significantly benefits commerce, and environmental pollution, when it causes economic harm? . . .

Regardless, if there is a principled distinction that could work both here and in future cases, Congress (even in the absence of vocational classes, industry involvement, and private management) could rationally conclude that schools fall on the commercial side of the line. In 1990, the year Congress enacted the statute before us, primary and secondary schools spent $230 billion — that is, nearly a quarter of a trillion dollars — which accounts for a significant portion of our $5.5 trillion Gross Domestic Product for that year. The business of schooling requires expenditure of these funds on student transportation, food and custodial services, books, and teachers' salaries. And, these expenditures enable schools to provide a valuable service — namely, to equip students with the skills they need to survive in life and, more specifically, in the workplace. Certainly, Congress has often analyzed school expenditure as if it were a commercial investment, closely analyzing whether schools are efficient, whether they justify the significant resources they spend, and whether they can be restructured to achieve greater returns. . . . Why could Congress, for Commerce Clause purposes, not consider schools as roughly analogous to commercial investments from which the Nation derives the benefit of an educated work force?

The third legal problem created by the Court's holding is that it threatens legal uncertainty in an area of law that, until this case, seemed reasonably well settled. Congress has enacted many statutes (more than 100 sections of the United States Code), including criminal statutes (at least 25 sections), that use the words "affecting commerce" to define their scope, and other statutes that contain no jurisdictional language at all. Do these . . . statutes regulate noncommercial activities? If so, would that alter the meaning of "affecting commerce" in a jurisdictional element? . . . More importantly, in the absence of a jurisdictional element, are the courts nevertheless to take *Wickard* [and later similar cases] as inapplicable, and to judge the effect of a single noncommercial activity on interstate commerce without considering similar instances of the forbidden conduct? However these questions are eventually resolved, the legal uncertainty now created will restrict Congress' ability to enact criminal laws aimed at criminal behavior that, considered problem by problem rather than instance by instance, seriously threatens the economic, as well as social, wellbeing of Americans.

IV

In sum, to find this legislation within the scope of the Commerce Clause would permit "Congress . . . to act in terms of economic . . . realities." . . . It would interpret the Clause as this Court has traditionally interpreted it, with the exception of one wrong turn [involving child labor] subsequently corrected. . . . Upholding this legislation would do no more than simply recognize that Congress had a "rational basis" for finding a significant connection between guns in or near schools and (through their effect on education) the interstate and foreign commerce they threaten.

NOTES AND QUESTIONS

1. After the *Wickard* case you must have been wondering whether there were any limits left to the power of Congress to regulate under the rubric of interstate commerce. Do you understand, after *Lopez*, just what those limits are? How would you formulate the test the majority applies in *Lopez*? When is it appropriate to reject congressional Commerce Clause legislation?

2. There were several other opinions in the case, but the judicial approaches are delineated well simply by considering the majority opinion by Chief Justice Rehnquist (for five justices) and the dissent from Justice Breyer (with whom three other justices joined). Is the majority correct that under Breyer's reasoning there would be no limits to the commerce power? Does he supply any? Justice Breyer, before he assumed the Supreme Court Bench, had served as a Professor at Harvard Law School and as a judge on the United States Court of Appeals for the First Circuit. Is this academic service and this judicial experience reflected in his opinion? Is something more involved in this case than merely objective constitutional application?

3. One of the reasons the expansion of the commerce power has been so resistant to challenge is that it has served as a useful device to secure modern civil rights legislation, especially that prohibiting individual discrimination on the basis of race, from constitutional challenge. As a matter of reason, one might think the civil rights laws would be best accommodated under Congress' power to enforce the equal protection provision of the Fourteenth Amendment. However, the text of the Fourteenth Amendment is limited to constraining state or government action, a subject pursued in Chapter 6 in the discussion of the *Civil Rights Cases*, 109 U.S. 3 (1883), and therefore Congress bootstrapped prohibitions of individual discrimination onto the commerce power. In *Heart of Atlanta Motel, Inc. v. United States*, 379 U.S. 241 (1964), the Court held that "discrimination by hotels and motels impedes interstate travel." *Id.* at 253. This result was extended in *Katzenbach v. McClung*, 379 U.S. 294 (1964), to a local restaurant that purchased nearly 50% of its meat products from out of state. Does anything in Chief Justice Rehnquist's opinion in *Lopez* suggest that either of these opinions are open to challenge? Certainly, preclusion from hotels and inns blocks the "channels" of commercial movement. *Katzenbach*, too, seems to fall into the indefinite third category of economic activity that substantially affects interstate commerce. Of course, as Justice Thomas notes, that third category is highly problematic, and so long as it is accepted, it is not likely that the Court will return to a more narrowly conceived commerce power. Would it be better to re-center civil rights authority on the Thirteenth Amendment — that is, as legislation designed to eliminate "badges" or vestiges of slavery and years of racial discrimination?

4. Immediately after *Lopez,* it was widely speculated that a host of laws would be vulnerable to attack as not being authorized by the Commerce Clause, or otherwise impermissible because they reflected incursions on constitutionally-guaranteed federalism. The endangered list included federal laws protecting access to abortion clinics, enforcing the interstate collection of child support, criminalizing carjacking, and even various federal environmental laws. The lower courts rebuffed hundreds of post-*Lopez* Commerce Clause challenges, however, and the Supreme Court for five years declined to review the cases, leading several legal scholars to conclude that *Lopez* was an anomaly. But in *United States v. Morrison,* 529 U.S. 598 (2000), Chief Justice Rehnquist, writing for a 5-4 majority of the Court, invalidated a key section of the federal Violence Against Women Act (VAWA), as authorized neither by the Commerce Clause nor by section 5 of the Fourteenth Amendment. *Morrison* involved a case brought by Christy Brzonkala, a student at Virginia Tech, who was allegedly raped by a couple of members of the Virginia Tech football team in a college dormitory during a dorm party. Because Morrison, one of the football players, allegedly announced in the dormitory's dining room that he "like[d] to get girls drunk and [have sex with them]," Brzonkala chose to sue in federal court (rather than bringing a sexual assault claim in state court), contending that Morrison's statements demonstrated that the rape was motivated by animosity toward women and thus prohibited by VAWA. The Fourteenth Amendment issue is addressed in Chapter 5, below, but with respect to the Commerce Clause, the Court expounded upon its decision in *Lopez,* holding that even with extensive findings by Congress that gender-based violence had a substantial effect on commerce, the Act was not within Congress' Commerce Clause power. VAWA regulated activity that was not economic in nature; it had no jurisdictional element that would limit it to activities in or substantially affecting interstate commerce, and it intruded upon the core police powers of the states.

In a concurring opinion, Justice Thomas challenged "the very notion of a 'substantial effects' test under the Commerce Clause" as "inconsistent with the original understanding of Congress' powers and with this Court's early Commerce Clause cases." He contended that by "continuing to apply this rootless and malleable standard, . . . the Court has encouraged the Federal Government to persist in its view that the Commerce Clause has virtually no limits," and he urged the Court to replace "its existing Commerce Clause jurisprudence with a standard more consistent with the original understanding" lest it "continue to see Congress appropriating state police powers under the guise of regulating commerce." Justice Souter, in a dissenting opinion joined by Justices Stevens, Ginsburg, and Breyer, contended the majority decision had already rejected the "substantial effects" test by giving only "nominal adherence" to it. He then challenged the view of the Commerce Clause espoused by Chief Justice Rehnquist and Justice Thomas, calling it a throwback not to the founders' understanding (which he thought exemplified by an expansive reading of *Gibbons*) but to the "formalism" of *E.C. Knight* (1895) that was rejected by the New Deal Court in 1937. For Justice Souter, it was "the Founders' considered judgment that politics, not judicial review, should mediate between state and national interests as the strength and legislative jurisdiction of the National Government inevitably increased through the expected growth of the national economy." (citing *Garcia v. San Antonio Municipal Transit Authority*, a case considered in Chapter 5 below). Whose view of the Commerce Clause do you think is more compatible with the founders' views? Does it matter? Justice Breyer, in a separate dissent, pointed out how greatly commerce had changed since 1787. Should changed circumstances have led the Court to give greater deference to Congress' efforts to address national problems?

5. Shortly before *Morrison* was decided, the Court handed down a decision in *Dewey Jones v. United States*, 529 U.S. 848 (2000). Unlike the 5-4 division in *Morrison*, *Dewey Jones* was unanimous, yet, at issue were considerations quite similar to those that animate the majority, pro-federalism side of the *Morrison* case. *Dewey Jones* involved interpretation of the federal arson statute, so the basic question was not whether Congress might reach a particular activity, but whether they actually did. That said, the common sense, almost facile rejection by the entire Court of attenuated "affecting commerce" claims in this statutory context is remarkable, given the profound constitutional differences that remain among the Justices even after *Lopez* and *Morrison*. Consider just a few passages from Justice Ginsburg's opinion for the Court (remembering again the Court's consensus and that Justice Ginsburg, herself, joined the dissent in *Morrison*):

> In support of its argument that § 844(i) reaches the arson of an owner-occupied private residence, the Government relies principally on the breadth of the statutory term "affecting . . . commerce," words that, when unqualified, signal Congress' intent to invoke its full authority under the Commerce Clause. But § 844(i) contains the qualifying words "used in" a commerce-affecting activity. The key word is "used." "Congress did not define the crime described in § 844(i) as the explosion of a building whose damage or destruction might affect interstate commerce . . . ."
>
> The Government urges that the Fort Wayne, Indiana residence into which Jones tossed a Molotov cocktail was constantly "used" in at least three "activit[ies] affecting commerce." First, the homeowner "used" the dwelling as collateral to obtain and secure a mortgage from an Oklahoma lender; the lender, in turn, "used" the property as security for the home loan. Second, the homeowner "used" the residence to obtain a casualty insurance policy from a Wisconsin insurer. That policy, the Government points out, safeguarded the interests of the homeowner and the mortgagee. Third, the homeowner "used" the dwelling to receive natural gas from sources outside Indiana.
>
> * * *
>
> It surely is not the common perception that a private, owner-occupied residence is "used" in the "activity" of receiving natural gas, a mortgage,

or an insurance policy. The Government does not allege that the Indiana residence involved in this case served as a home office or the locus of any commercial undertaking. The home's only "active employment," so far as the record reveals, was for the everyday living of Jones's cousin and his family.

Here, as earlier emphasized, the owner used the property as his home, the center of his family life. He did not use the residence in any trade or business.

Were we to adopt the Government's expansive interpretation of § 844(i), hardly a building in the land would fall outside the federal statute's domain. Practically every building in our cities, towns, and rural areas is constructed with supplies that have moved in interstate commerce, served by utilities that have an interstate connection, financed or insured by enterprises that do business across state lines, or bears some other trace of interstate commerce. If such connections sufficed to trigger § 844(i), the statute's limiting language, "used in" any commerce-affecting activity, would have no office.

Given the concerns brought to the fore in *Lopez*, it is appropriate to avoid the constitutional question that would arise were we to read § 844(i) to render the "traditionally local criminal conduct" in which petitioner Jones engaged "a matter for federal enforcement." Our comprehension of § 844(i) is additionally reinforced by other interpretive guides. We have instructed that "ambiguity concerning the ambit of criminal statutes should be resolved in favor of lenity." We have cautioned, as well, that "unless Congress conveys its purpose clearly, it will not be deemed to have significantly changed the federal-state balance" in the prosecution of crimes. To read § 844(i) as encompassing the arson of an owner-occupied private home would effect such a change, for arson is a paradigmatic common-law state crime.

Justices Stevens and Thomas in concurrence emphasized that there is a "kinship" between our well-established presumption against federal pre-emption of state law, and our reluctance to "believe Congress intended to authorize federal intervention in local law enforcement in a marginal case such as this." The fact that Jones received a sentence of 35 years in prison when the maximum penalty for the comparable state offense was only 10 years illustrated, said these Justices, how a criminal law like this may effectively displace a policy choice made by the state.

Justices Thomas and Scalia in a separate concurrence noted that they were not conceding the constitutionality of the federal arson statute to even all commercial structures.

6. The Court continued to explore the dimensions of the commerce power through statutory interpretation, this time in the environmental context, in *Solid Waste Agency v. U.S. Army Corps of Engineers*, 531 U.S. 159 (2001), where the Court's unanimity disappeared. In *Solid Waste*, the Court was asked to decide if an isolated, intra-state pond (resulting from an abandoned gravel pit) could be regulated under Section 404 of the Clean Water Act because the pond might be visited by migratory birds. 5-4, the answer was "No" in an opinion by Chief Justice Rehnquist that rejected the Corps' so-called migratory birds rule. Opining that the statutory meaning of "navigable waters" could not be stretched that far, the Court felt the proposed interpretation was at the "outer limit" of Congress' power posing a "significant constitutional question" since that would encroach upon the regulation of land use, a function "traditionally performed by local governments." The dissent by Justice Stevens (joined by Justices Souter, Ginsburg and Breyer), argued that the Court had earlier construed the Act to include adjacent wetlands, and Congress had acquiesced in the broader authority claimed here. The dissent also thought the broader statutory interpretation posed no serious constitutional question since the Corps was regulating an intrastate activity (the filling of a pond with landfill waste) that "substantially affects" interstate commerce (the third, catch-all category in *Lopez*). What was the commerce? Well, said the dissent, it might be bird hunting. And wrote Justice Stevens: "the migratory bird rule does not blur the 'distinction between what is truly national and what is truly local.' . . . The destruction of aquatic migratory bird habitat, like so many other environmental problems, is an action in which the benefits (*e.g.,* a new landfill) are disproportionately local, while many of the costs (*e.g.,* fewer migratory birds) are widely dispersed and often borne by citizens living in other States. In such situations, described by economists as involving 'externalities,' federal regulation is both appropriate and necessary. Identifying the Corps' jurisdiction by reference to waters that serve as habitat for birds that migrate over state lines also satisfies this Court's expressed desire for some 'jurisdictional element' that limits federal activity to its proper scope."

This was too much for the majority, which thought the Corps couldn't make up its mind — namely, whether the commerce to be regulated was the landfill operation or the birds. Observed the Chief Justice: "we would have to evaluate the precise object or activity that, in the aggregate, substantially affects interstate commerce. This is not clear, for although the Corps has claimed jurisdiction over petitioner's land because it contains water areas used as habitat by migratory birds, respondents now focus upon the fact that the regulated activity is petitioner's municipal landfill, which is 'plainly of a commercial nature.' But this is a far cry, indeed, from the 'navigable waters' and 'waters of the United States' to which the statute by its terms extends." The way out of the tangle, suggested the Court, requires and understanding that applying the catch-all element demands that the Court "evaluate the precise object or activity that, in the aggregate, substantially affects interstate commerce."

Regulatory protection of migratory birds might be done pursuant to international treaty or as a condition on the receipt of federal money. Additionally, the actual holding of *Solid Waste* does not preclude Congress from seeking to regulate migratory birds under the commerce power as well, if there is some statutory basis to think that Congress had actually made that choice in law and that it would qualify under the Court's Commerce Clause analysis. Nevertheless, to purport to reach the subject via the circuitous route of the "substantial effects" test distorts the commerce power, and correspondingly reduces political accountability. Construction of an intrastate landfill is intrastate land use regulation, and local officials should (and usually do) get an earful from constituents about such matters. Arguably, if Congress is going to displace state and local authority, it should be because there has been an explicit, national debate identifying an overriding national interest or state regulatory incapacity. There may well be a national interest in the protection of migratory birds, but this is not easily discerned from a statute aimed largely, if not entirely, at navigable waters. If the states are incapable of preserving sufficient local habitats to address the interstate demand for the "hunting, trapping, and observing" of birds — which were the interests identified by the Seventh Circuit to sustain a federal role — that case needs to be made, not inferred. *See* Douglas W. Kmiec, *Rediscovering a Principled Commerce Power*, 28 PEPP. L. REV. 547 (2001).

7. A retreat from *Lopez*? *Pierce County, Washington v. Guillen*, 123 S. Ct. 720 (2003), held, per Justice Thomas for a unanimous Court, that Congress had authority to fashion federal and state evidentiary rules precluding discovery or trial use of materials, including accident reports, compiled or collected, by a state to participate in the federal Hazard Elimination Program. 23 U.S.C. § 409, as amended, provides that "reports, etc., compiled or collected for the purpose of identifying, evaluating, or planning the safety enhancement of potential accident sites, hazardous roadway conditions, etc., for the purpose of utilizing Federal-aid highway funds shall not be subject to discovery or admitted into evidence in a Federal or State court proceeding or considered for other purposes in any action for damages arising from any occurrence at a location mentioned or addressed in such reports, surveys, etc." Interpreting the statute, Justice Thomas reasoned that it applied to any document, including accident reports that were either prepared or collected for participation in the federal program. Thus an accident report that stayed in the county sheriff's department could be discovered, but once it went over to public works for federal highway improvement purposes, it was shielded. Recognizing that evidentiary privileges are to be construed narrowly, the Court nevertheless found that Congress had authority under the Commerce Clause to impose the evidentiary limit, since it regulated the use of channels of interstate commerce or protected instrumentalities of interstate commerce "or persons or things in interstate commerce, even though the threat may come only from intrastate activities." (Citing *Lopez*.) In a footnote, Justice Thomas declined to consider a dual sovereignty argument that the federal law "prohibits a State from exercising its sovereign powers to establish discovery and admissibility rules to be used in state court for a state cause of action." Justice Thomas said the argument had not been presented below.

All of this is rather curious. First, Justice Thomas concurred in *Lopez* to express dissatisfaction that even that narrowing of the commerce power was not faithful to original understanding and the powers reserved to the states. His earlier criticism suggested the problem was the "substantially affects" prong of the *Lopez* formulation, but it would appear that the presence of "channels" or "instrumentalities" may be an even more available entry point for federal regulation. As for the point of not making the argument below, the Court had, in fact, granted certiorari on the question "whether private plaintiffs [here the litigant was a widower seeking compensation from the county for a badly designed intersection that arguably contributed to his wife's death] have standing to assert 'state's rights' under the Tenth Amendment where their States' legislative and executive branches expressly approve and accept the benefits of the federal statute in question."

Another case may also suggest backpedaling on the "substantially affects" portion of the *Lopez* standard. In particular, the Court has distanced itself from some speculation in the wake of *Lopez*, *Morrison*, and *Solid Waste Agency* that the combination of the aggregation principle and the substantial effects test of *Wickard v. Filburn* was incompatible with the Court's newly-revived recognition of the outer limits of Commerce Clause authority. In *Citizens Bank v. Alafabco, Inc.*, 539 U.S. 52 (2003) (per curiam), the Court held that the Federal Arbitration Act could apply to a debt restructuring agreement between an Alabama bank and an Alabama construction company, involving loans on Alabama construction projects. The Court rejected the Alabama Supreme Court's more narrow reading of *Lopez* as requiring that the specific contract in question had to involve interstate commerce. "Congress' Commerce Clause power 'may be exercised in individual cases without showing any specific effect upon interstate commerce,'" held the Court, "if in the aggregate the economic activity in question would represent 'a general practice . . . subject to federal control.'"

Citizens Bank, as a per curiam opinion, may or may not have much doctrinal significance. There is something very peculiar about the Court reaching the Commerce Clause issue here. Admittedly, the Alabama Supreme Court forced the issue by deciding this on Commerce Clause grounds, but it is not as if the FAA were applied as a regulatory statute to these entities. The debt restructuring agreement itself incorporated the FAA, which presumably the parties would be free to do even absent Commerce Clause authority for the FAA to apply to them.

4. If Legislative Commerce Power Were Not Enough — Is There Also a Judicial or "Dormant" Commerce Power?

You will remember that the view that the legislative commerce power was exclusive — that is, capable of being exercised only by the national or federal government — was suggested in *Gibbons*, but not actually decided. The following case confirms that states may regulate where the federal government has not, but subject to a judicially grafted limit that such state and local laws not unduly burden interstate commerce. This notion is called the "dormant commerce" power, because there is no textual anchor for it. Instead, as Justice Felix Frankfurter once wrote, "the doctrine [is] that the commerce clause, by its own force and without national legislation, puts it into the power of the Court to place limits upon state authority." FELIX FRANKFURTER, THE COMMERCE CLAUSE UNDER MARSHALL, TANEY & WAITE 18 (1937). While the state law is upheld in *Cooley*, the states will be judicially displaced in many others, as we will see.

COOLEY v. BOARD OF WARDENS
53 U.S. (12 How.) 299 (1851)

MR. JUSTICE CURTIS delivered the opinion of the court.

* * *

[These cases] are actions to recover half-pilotage fees under the 29th section of the act of the Legislature of Pennsylvania, passed on the second day of March, 1803. The plaintiff in error alleges that the highest court of the State has decided against a right claimed by him under the Constitution of the United States. . . .

Like other laws they are framed to meet the most usual cases . . . ; [Pennsylvania's law rests] upon the propriety of securing lives and property exposed to the perils of a dangerous navigation, by taking on board a person peculiarly skilled to encounter or avoid them; upon the policy of discouraging the commanders of vessels from refusing to receive such persons on board at the proper times and places; and upon the expediency, and even intrinsic justice, of not suffering those who have incurred labor, and expense, and danger, to place themselves in a position to render important service generally necessary, to go unrewarded, because the master of a particular vessel either rashly refuses their proffered assistance, or, contrary to the general experience, does not need it.

* * *

It [must be] consider[ed] [whether the State law is] repugnant to the [Commerce Clause].

That the power to regulate commerce includes the regulation of navigation, we consider settled. And when we look to the nature of the service performed by pilots, to the relations which that service and its compensations bear to navigation between the several States, and between the ports of the United States and foreign countries, we are brought to the conclusion, that the regulation of the qualifications of pilots, of the modes and times of offering and rendering their services, of the responsibilities which shall rest upon them, of the powers they shall possess, of the compensation they may demand, and of the penalties by which their rights and duties may be enforced, do constitute regulations of navigation, and consequently of commerce, within the just meaning of this clause of the Constitution.

The power to regulate navigation is the power to prescribe rules in conformity with which navigation must be carried on. It extends to the persons who conduct it, as well as to the instruments used. Accordingly, the first Congress assembled under the Constitution passed laws, requiring the masters of ships and vessels of the United States to be citizens of the United States, and established many rules for the government and regulation of officers and seamen. These have been from time to time added to and changed, and we are not aware that their validity has been questioned.

Now, a pilot, so far as respects the navigation of the vessel in that part of the voyage which is his pilotage-ground, is the temporary master charged with the safety of the vessel and cargo, and of the lives of those on board, and intrusted with the command of the crew. He is not only one of the persons engaged in navigation, but he occupies a most important and responsible place among those thus engaged. And if Congress has power to regulate the seamen who assist the pilot in the management of the vessel, a power never denied, we can perceive no valid reason why the pilot should be beyond the reach of the same power. It is true that, according to the usages of modern commerce on the ocean, the pilot is on board only during a part of the voyage between ports of different States, or between ports of the United States and foreign countries; but if he is on board for such a purpose and during so much of the voyage as to be engaged in navigation, the power to regulate navigation extends to him while thus engaged, as clearly as it would if he were to remain on board throughout the whole passage, from port to port. For it is a power which extends to every part of the voyage, and may regulate those who conduct or assist in conducting navigation in one part of a voyage as much as in another part, or during the whole voyage.

[A 1789 act of Congress] contains a clear legislative exposition of the Constitution by the first Congress, to the effect that the power to regulate pilots was conferred on Congress by the Constitution . . . . The weight to be allowed to this contemporaneous construction, and the practice of Congress under it, has, in another connection, been adverted to. And a majority of the court are of opinion, that a regulation of pilots is a regulation of commerce, within the grant to Congress of the commercial power . . . .

It becomes necessary, therefore, to consider whether this law of Pennsylvania, being a regulation of commerce, is valid.

The act of Congress of the 7th of August, 1789, sect. 4, is as follows:

> "That all pilots in the bays, inlets, rivers, harbors, and ports of the United States shall continue to be regulated in conformity with the existing laws of the States, respectively, wherein such pilots may be, or with such laws as the States may respectively hereafter enact for the purpose, until further legislative provision shall be made by Congress."

If the law of Pennsylvania, now in question, had been in existence at the date of this act of Congress, we might hold it to have been adopted by Congress, and thus made a law of the United States, and so valid. Because this act does, in effect, give the force of an act of Congress, to the then existing State laws on this subject, so long as they should continue unrepealed by the State which enacted them.

But the law on which these actions are founded was not enacted till 1803. What effect then can be attributed to so much of the act of 1789, as declares, that pilots shall continue to be regulated in conformity, "with such laws as the States may respectively hereafter enact for the purpose, until further legislative provision shall be made by Congress"?

If the States were divested of the power to legislate on this subject by the grant of the commercial power to Congress, it is plain this act could not confer upon them power thus to legislate. If the Constitution excluded the States from making any law regulating commerce, certainly Congress cannot regrant, or in any manner reconvey to the States that power. And yet this act of 1789 gives its sanction only to laws enacted by the States. This necessarily implies a constitutional power to legislate; for only a rule created by the sovereign power of a State acting in its legislative capacity, can be deemed a law, enacted by a State; and if the State has so limited its sovereign power that it no longer extends to a particular subject, manifestly it cannot, in any proper sense, be said to enact laws thereon. Entertaining these views we are brought directly and unavoidably to the consideration of the question, whether the grant of the commercial power to Congress, did *per se* deprive the States of all power to regulate pilots. This question has never been decided by this court, nor, in our judgment, has any case depending upon all the considerations which must govern this one, come before this court. The grant of commercial power to Congress does not contain any terms which expressly exclude the States from exercising an authority over its subject-matter. If they are excluded it must be because the nature of the power, thus granted to Congress, requires that a similar authority should not exist in the States. . . .

The diversities of opinion, . . . which have existed on this subject, have arisen from the different views taken of the nature of this power. But when the nature of a power like this is spoken of, when it is said that the nature of the power requires that it should be exercised exclusively by Congress, it must be intended to refer to the subjects of that power, and to say they are of such a nature as to require exclusive legislation by Congress. Now the power to regulate commerce, embraces a vast field, containing not only many, but exceedingly various subjects, quite unlike in their nature; some imperatively demanding a single uniform rule, operating equally on the commerce of the United States in every port; and some, like the subject now in question, as imperatively demanding that diversity, which alone can meet the local necessities of navigation.

. . . Whatever subjects of this power are in their nature national, or admit only of one uniform system, or plan of regulation, may justly be said to be of such a nature as to require exclusive legislation by Congress. That this cannot be affirmed of laws for the regulation of pilots and pilotage is plain. The act of 1789 contains a clear and authoritative declaration by the first Congress, that the nature of this subject is such, that until Congress should find it necessary to exert its power, it should be left to the legislation of the States; that it is local and not national; that it is likely to be the best provided for, not by one system, or plan of regulations, but by as many as the legislative discretion of the several States should deem applicable to the local peculiarities of the ports within their limits.

Viewed in this light, so much of this act of 1789 as declares that pilots shall continue to be regulated "by such laws as the States may respectively hereafter enact for that purpose," instead of being held to be inoperative, as an attempt to confer on the States a power to legislate, of which the Constitution had deprived them, is allowed an appropriate and important signification. It manifests the understanding of Congress, at the outset of the government, that the nature of this subject is not such as to require its exclusive legislation. The practice of the States, and of the national government, has been in conformity with this declaration, from the origin of the national government to this time; and the nature of the subject when examined, is such as to leave no doubt of the superior fitness and propriety, not to say the absolute necessity, of different systems of regulation, drawn from local knowledge and experience, and conformed to local wants. . . . In construing an instrument designed for the formation of a government, and in determining the extent of one of its important grants of power to legislate, we can make no such distinction between the nature of the power and the nature of the subject on which that power was intended practically to operate, nor consider the grant more extensive by affirming of the power, what is not true of its subject now in question.

It is the opinion of a majority of the court that the mere grant to Congress of the power to regulate commerce, did not deprive the States of power to regulate pilots, and that although Congress has legislated on this subject, its legislation manifests an intention, with a single exception, not to regulate this subject, but to leave its regulation to the several States. To these precise questions, which are all we are called on to decide, this opinion must be understood to be confined. It does not extend to the question what other subjects, under the commercial power, are within the exclusive control of Congress, or may be regulated by the States in the absence of all congressional legislation; nor to the general question how far any regulation of a subject by Congress, may be deemed to operate as an exclusion of all legislation by the States upon the same subject. . . .

We have not adverted to the practical consequences of holding that the States possess no power to legislate for the regulation of pilots, though in our apprehension these would be of the most serious importance. For more than sixty years this subject has been acted on by the States, and the systems of some of them created and of others essentially modified during that period. To hold that pilotage fees and penalties demanded and received during that time, have been illegally exacted, under color of void laws, would work an amount of mischief which a clear conviction of constitutional duty, if entertained, must force us to occasion, but which could be viewed by no just mind without deep regret.

Nor would the mischief be limited to the past. If Congress were now to pass a law adopting the existing State laws, if enacted without authority, and in violation of the Constitution, it would seem to us to be a new and questionable mode of legislation.

* * *

Mr. Justice McLean[, concurring in the judgment].

* * *

Why did Congress pass the act of 1789, adopting the pilot-laws of the respective States?

* * *

Congress adopted the pilot-laws of the States, because it was well understood, they could have had no force, as regulations of foreign commerce or of commerce among the States, if not so adopted. By their adoption they were made acts of Congress, and ever since they have been so considered and enforced.

Each State regulates the commerce within its limits; which is not within the range of federal powers. So far, and no farther could effect have been given to the pilot laws of the States, under the Constitution. But those laws were only adopted "until further legislative provisions shall be made by Congress."

This shows that Congress claimed the whole commercial power on this subject, by adopting the pilot laws of the States, making them acts of Congress; and also by declaring that the adoption was only until some further legislative provision could be made by Congress.

Can Congress annul the acts of a State passed within its admitted sovereignty? No one, I suppose, could sustain such a proposition. State sovereignty can neither be enlarged nor diminished by an act of Congress. It is not known that Congress has ever claimed such a power.

If the States had not the power to enact pilot laws, as connected with foreign commerce, in 1789, when did they get it?

* * *

That a State may regulate foreign commerce, or commerce among the States, is a doctrine which has been advanced by individual judges of this court; but never before, I believe, has such a power been sanctioned by the decision of this court. In this case, the power to regulate pilots is admitted to belong to the commercial power of Congress; and yet it is held, that a State, by virtue of its inherent power, may regulate the subject, until such regulation shall be annulled by Congress. This is the principle established by this decision. Its language is guarded, in order to apply the decision only to the case before the court. But such restrictions can never operate, so as to render the principle inapplicable to other cases. And it is in this light that the decision is chiefly to be regretted. The power is recognized in the State, because the subject is more appropriate for State than Federal action; and consequently, it must be presumed the Constitution cannot have intended to inhibit State action. This is not a rule by which the Constitution is to be construed. It can receive but little support from the discussions which took place on the adoption of the Constitution, and none at all from the earlier decisions of this court.

It will be found that the principle in this case, if carried out, will deeply affect the commercial prosperity of the country. If a State has power to regulate foreign commerce, such regulation must be held valid, until Congress shall repeal or annul it. But the present case goes further than this. Congress regulated pilots by the act of 1789, which made the acts of the State, on that subject, the acts of Congress. In 1803, Pennsylvania passed the law in question, which materially modified the act adopted by Congress; and this act of 1803 is held to be constitutional. This, then, asserts the right of a State, not only to regulate foreign commerce, but to modify, and, consequently, to repeal a prior regulation of Congress. Is there a mistake in this statement? There is none, if an adopted act of a State is thereby made an act of Congress, and if the regulation of pilots, in regard to foreign commerce, be a regulation of commerce. The latter position is admitted in the opinion of the court, and no one will controvert the former. I speak of the principle of the opinion, and not of the restricted application given to it by the learned judge who delivered it.

* * *

I think the charge of half-pilotage is correct under the circumstances, and I only object to the power of the State to pass the law. Congress, to whom the subject peculiarly belongs, should have been applied to, and no doubt it would have adopted the act of the State.

Mr. Justice Daniel [concurring in the judgment].

. . . The power and the practice of enacting pilot-laws, which has been exercised by the States from the very origin of their existence, although it is one in some degree connected with commercial intercourse, does not come essentially and regularly within that power of commercial regulation vested by the Constitution in Congress, and which by the Constitution must, when exercised by Congress, be enforced with perfect equality, and without any kind of discrimination, local or otherwise, in its application. The power delegated to Congress by the Constitution relates properly to the terms on which commercial engagements may be prosecuted; the character of the articles which they may embrace; the permission or terms according to which they may be introduced; and do not necessarily nor even naturally extend to the means of precaution and safety adopted within the waters or limits of the States by the authority of the latter for the preservation of vessels and cargoes, and the lives of navigators or passengers. These last subjects are essentially local — they must depend upon local necessities which call them into existence, must differ according to the degrees of that necessity. It is admitted, on all hands, that they cannot be uniform or even general, but must vary so as to meet the purposes to be accomplished. They have no connection with contract, or traffic, or with the permission to trade in any subject, or upon any conditions. They belong to the same conservative power which undertakes to guide the track of the vessel over the rocks or shallows of a coast, or river; which directs her mooring or her position in port, for the safety of life and property, whether in reference to herself or to other vessels, their cargoes and crews, which for security against pestilence subjects vessels to quarantine, and may order the total destruction of the cargoes they contain. This is a power which is deemed indispensable to the safety and existence of every community. . . . I am forced to conclude that this is an original and inherent power in the States, and not one to be merely tolerated, or held subject to the sanction of the federal government.

NOTES AND QUESTIONS

1. Are you surprised at the outcome of the majority's decision in the case? Is *Cooley* the same case as *Gibbons v. Ogden*? How great is the state's concurrent power to regulate interstate commerce? How is it that a state tax on the National Bank was found unconstitutional in *McCulloch v. Maryland*, but a state is permitted to impose particular expenses and/or particular pilots on vessels involved in interstate commerce, thus clearly burdening them? You will have probably discerned that the Pennsylvania statutory scheme at issue in *Cooley* applied to any vessel entering or leaving the port of Philadelphia, and required such a vessel either to pay one-half the usual pilotage fee to Pennsylvania, or to employ a local pilot. The fees were accumulated into a fund for the relief of incapacitated pilots and their widows and orphans. Should this make a difference?

2. According to at least one scholar, "*Cooley* ranks with *Gibbons v. Ogden* (1824) as one of the most important Commerce Clause cases of the nineteenth century." Donald M. Roper, Cooley v. Board of Wardens of the Port of Philadelphia, *in* THE OXFORD COMPANION TO THE SUPREME COURT OF THE UNITED STATES 197 (Kermit L. Hall et al. eds., 1992). Do you understand why this might be so? Do you find in *Cooley* the same kind of decisive logic as employed, for example, in *McCulloch*, or is the reasoning somewhat more elusive? Roper argues that *Cooley*'s "pragmatism has proved enduring." What do you suppose he means by that? The following case, and many like it, suggest that the flexibility seemingly extended to the states in *Cooley* may have been illusory, though the Court is increasingly uncomfortable in its not-so-dormant commerce role.

OREGON WASTE SYSTEMS, INC. v. DEPARTMENT OF ENVIRONMENTAL QUALITY
511 U.S. 93 (1994)

JUSTICE THOMAS delivered the opinion of the Court.

Two Terms ago, in *Chemical Waste Management, Inc. v. Hunt* (1992), we held that the negative Commerce Clause prohibited Alabama from imposing a higher fee on the disposal in Alabama landfills of hazardous waste from other States than on the disposal of identical waste from Alabama. In reaching that conclusion, however, we left open the possibility that such a differential surcharge might be valid if based on the costs of disposing of waste from other States. Today, we must decide whether Oregon's purportedly cost-based surcharge on the in-state disposal of solid waste generated in other States violates the Commerce Clause.

I

Like other States, . . . Oregon levies a wide range of fees on landfill operators. In 1989, the Oregon Legislature imposed an additional fee, called a "surcharge," on "every person who disposes of solid waste generated out-of-state in a disposal site or regional disposal site." The amount of that surcharge[,] . . . "based on the costs to the State of Oregon and its political subdivisions of disposing of solid waste generated out-of-state which are not otherwise paid for" under specified statutes[, was set] at $2.25 per ton [versus $0.85 per ton charged on the disposal of waste generated within Oregon].

. . . Petitioners, Oregon Waste Systems, Inc. (Oregon Waste) and Columbia Resource Company (CRC), joined by Gilliam County, Oregon, sought expedited review of the out-of-state surcharge in the Oregon Court of Appeals. Oregon Waste owns and operates a solid waste landfill in Gilliam County, at which it accepts for final disposal solid waste generated in Oregon and in other States. CRC, pursuant to a 20-year contract with Clark County, in neighboring Washington State, transports solid waste via barge from Clark County to a landfill in Morrow County, Oregon. Petitioners challenged the administrative rule establishing the out-of-state surcharge and its enabling statutes under both state law and the Commerce Clause of the United States Constitution. The Oregon Court of Appeals upheld the statutes and rule.

The State Supreme Court affirmed. As to the Commerce Clause, the court recognized that the Oregon surcharge resembled the Alabama fee invalidated in *Chemical Waste Management, Inc. v. Hunt* (1992), in that both prescribed higher fees for the disposal of waste from other States. Nevertheless, the court viewed the similarity as superficial only. Despite the explicit reference in [the Oregon statute] to out-of-state waste's geographic origin, the court reasoned, the Oregon surcharge is not facially discriminatory "[b]ecause of [its] express nexus to actual costs incurred [by state and local government]." That nexus distinguished *Chemical Waste, supra,* by rendering the surcharge a "compensatory fee," which the court viewed as *"prima facie* reasonable," that is to say, facially constitutional. *Ibid.* The court read our case law as invalidating compensatory fees only if they are "'manifestly disproportionate to the services rendered.'" *Ibid.* . . .

We granted certiorari, because the decision below conflicted with a recent decision of the United States Court of Appeals for the Seventh Circuit. We now reverse.

II

The Commerce Clause provides that "[t]he Congress shall have Power . . . [t]o regulate Commerce . . . among the several States." Art. I, § 8, cl. 3. Though phrased as a grant of regulatory power to Congress, the Clause has long been understood to have a "negative" aspect that denies the States the power unjustifiably to discriminate against or burden the interstate flow of articles of commerce. The Framers granted Congress plenary authority over interstate commerce in "the conviction that in order to succeed, the new Union would have to avoid the tendencies toward economic Balkanization that had plagued relations among the Colonies and later among the States under the Articles of Confederation." See generally FEDERALIST NO. 42 (J. Madison). "This principle that our economic unit is the Nation, which alone has the gamut of powers necessary to control of the economy, . . . has as its corollary that the states are not separable economic units." . . .

Consistent with these principles, we have held that the first step in analyzing any law subject to judicial scrutiny under the negative Commerce Clause is to determine whether it "regulates evenhandedly with only 'incidental' effects on interstate commerce, or discriminates against interstate commerce." As we use the term here, "discrimination" simply means differential treatment of in-state and out-of-state economic interests that benefits the former and burdens the latter. If a restriction on commerce is discriminatory, it is virtually *per se* invalid. By contrast, nondiscriminatory regulations that have only incidental effects on interstate commerce are valid unless "the burden imposed on such commerce is clearly excessive in relation to the putative local benefits." *Pike v. Bruce Church, Inc.* (1970).

* * *

Respondents argue, and the Oregon Supreme Court held, that the statutory nexus between the surcharge and "the [otherwise uncompensated] costs to the State of Oregon and its political subdivisions of disposing of solid waste generated out-of-state," necessarily precludes a finding that the surcharge is discriminatory. We find respondents' narrow focus on Oregon's compensatory aim to be foreclosed by our precedents. As we reiterated in *Chemical Waste*, the purpose of, or justification for, a law has no bearing on whether it is facially discriminatory. Consequently, even if the surcharge merely recoups the costs of disposing of out-of-state waste in Oregon, the fact remains that the differential charge favors shippers of Oregon waste over their counterparts handling waste generated in other States. In making that geographic distinction, the surcharge patently discriminates against interstate commerce.

III

Because the Oregon surcharge is discriminatory, the virtually *per se* rule of invalidity provides the proper legal standard here, not the *Pike* balancing test. As a result, the surcharge must be invalidated unless respondents can "sho[w] that it advances a legitimate local purpose that cannot be adequately served by reasonable nondiscriminatory alternatives." . . . Our cases require that justifications for discriminatory restrictions on commerce pass the "strictest scrutiny." The State's burden of justification is so heavy that "facial discrimination by itself may be a fatal defect."

At the outset, we note two justifications that respondents have *not* presented. No claim has been made that the disposal of waste from other States imposes higher costs on Oregon and its political subdivisions than the disposal of in-state waste. Also, respondents have not offered any safety or health reason unique to nonhazardous waste from other States for discouraging the flow of such waste into Oregon. . . . Consequently, respondents must come forward with other legitimate reasons to subject waste from other States to a higher charge than is levied against waste from Oregon.

Respondents offer two such reasons, each of which we address below.

A

Respondents' principal defense of the higher surcharge on out-of-state waste is that it is a "compensatory tax" necessary to make shippers of such waste pay their "fair share" of the costs imposed on Oregon by the disposal of their waste in the State. In *Chemical Waste* we noted the possibility that such an argument might justify a discriminatory surcharge or tax on out-of-state waste. In making that observation, we implicitly recognized the settled principle that interstate commerce may be made to "'pay its way.'" "It was not the purpose of the commerce clause to relieve those engaged in interstate commerce from their just share of state tax burden[s]." Nevertheless, one of the central purposes of the Clause was to prevent States from "exacting *more* than a just share" from interstate commerce.

At least since our decision in *Hinson v. Lott* (1868), these principles have found expression in the "compensatory" or "complementary" tax doctrine. . . . Under that doctrine, a facially discriminatory tax that imposes on interstate commerce the rough equivalent of an identifiable and "substantially similar" tax on intrastate commerce does not offend the negative Commerce Clause.

To justify a charge on interstate commerce as a compensatory tax, a State must, as a threshold matter, "identif[y] . . . the [intrastate tax] burden for which the State is attempting to compensate." Once that burden has been identified, the tax on interstate commerce must be shown roughly to approximate — but not exceed — the amount of the tax on intrastate commerce. Finally, the events on which the interstate and intrastate taxes are imposed must be "substantially equivalent"; that is, they must be sufficiently similar in substance to serve as mutually exclusive "prox[ies]" for each other. . . .

Although it is often no mean feat to determine whether a challenged tax is a compensatory tax, we have little difficulty concluding that the Oregon surcharge is not such a tax. Oregon does not impose a specific charge of at least $2.25 per ton on shippers of waste generated in Oregon, for which the out-of-state surcharge might be considered compensatory. In fact, the only analogous charge on the disposal of Oregon waste is $0.85 per ton, approximately one-third of the amount imposed on waste from other States. Respondents' failure to identify a specific charge on intrastate commerce equal to or exceeding the surcharge is fatal to their claim.

Respondents argue that, despite the absence of a specific $2.25 per ton charge on in-state waste, intrastate commerce does pay its share of the costs underlying the surcharge through general taxation. Whether or not that is true is difficult to determine, as "[general] tax payments are received for the general purposes of the [government], and are, upon proper receipt, lost in the general revenues." . . . Even assuming, however, that various other means of general taxation, such as income taxes, could serve as an identifiable intrastate burden roughly equivalent to the out-of-state surcharge, respondents' compensatory tax argument fails because the in-state and out-of-state levies are not imposed on substantially equivalent events.

The prototypical example of substantially equivalent taxable events is the sale and use of articles of trade. In fact, use taxes on products purchased out of state are the only taxes we have upheld in recent memory under the compensatory tax doctrine. Typifying our recent reluctance to recognize new categories of compensatory taxes [was the Court's recent holding] that manufacturing and wholesaling are not substantially equivalent events. In our view, earning income and disposing of waste at Oregon landfills are even less equivalent than manufacturing and wholesaling. Indeed, the very fact that in-state shippers of out-of-state waste, such as Oregon Waste, are charged the out-of-state surcharge even though they pay Oregon income taxes refutes respondents' argument that the respective taxable events are substantially equivalent. We conclude that, far from being substantially equivalent, taxes on earning income and utilizing Oregon landfills are "entirely different [k]inds of tax[es]." We are no more inclined here than we were in [an earlier case] to "plunge . . . into the morass of weighing comparative tax burdens" by comparing taxes on dissimilar events.

B

Respondents' final argument is that Oregon has an interest in spreading the costs of the in-state disposal of Oregon waste to all Oregonians. That is, because all citizens of Oregon benefit from the proper in-state disposal of waste from Oregon, respondents claim it is only proper for Oregon to require them to bear more of the costs of disposing of such waste in the State through a higher general tax burden. At the same time, however, Oregon citizens should not be required to bear the costs of disposing of out-of-state waste, respondents claim. The necessary result of that limited cost-shifting is to require shippers of out-of-state waste to bear the full costs of in-state disposal, but to permit shippers of Oregon waste to bear less than the full cost.

We fail to perceive any distinction between respondents' contention and a claim that the State has an interest in reducing the costs of handling in-state waste. Our cases condemn as illegitimate, however, any governmental interest that is not "unrelated to economic protectionism," and regulating interstate commerce in such a way as to give those who handle domestic articles of commerce a cost advantage over their competitors handling similar items produced elsewhere constitutes such protectionism. To give controlling effect to respondents' characterization of Oregon's tax scheme as seemingly benign cost-spreading would require us to overlook the fact that the scheme necessarily incorporates a protectionist objective as well.

Respondents counter that if Oregon is engaged in any form of protectionism, it is "resource protectionism," not economic protectionism. It is true that by discouraging the flow of out-of-state waste into Oregon landfills, the higher surcharge on waste from other States conserves more space in those landfills for waste generated in Oregon. Recharacterizing the surcharge as resource protectionism hardly advances respondents' cause, however. Even assuming that landfill space is a "natural resource," "a State may not accord its own inhabitants a preferred right of access over consumers in other States to natural resources located within its borders." As we held more than a century ago, "if the State, under the guise of exerting its police powers, should [impose a burden] . . . applicable solely to articles [of commerce] . . . produced or manufactured in other States, the courts would find no difficulty in holding such legislation to be in conflict with the Constitution of the United States." . . . Our decision in *Sporhase v. Nebraska ex rel. Douglas* (1982), is not to the contrary. There we held that a State may grant a "limited preference" for its citizens in the utilization of ground water. That holding was premised on several different factors tied to the simple fact of life that "water, unlike other natural resources, is essential for human survival." *Sporhase* therefore provides no support for respondents' position that States may erect a financial barrier to the flow of waste from other States into Oregon landfills. However serious the shortage in landfill space may be, "[n]o State may attempt to isolate itself from a problem common to the several States by raising barriers to the free flow of interstate trade."

IV

We recognize that the States have broad discretion to configure their systems of taxation as they deem appropriate. All we intimate here is that their discretion in this regard, as in all others, is bounded by any relevant limitations of the Federal Constitution, in this case the negative Commerce Clause. Because respondents have offered no legitimate reason to subject waste generated in other States to a discriminatory surcharge approximately three times as high as that imposed on waste generated in Oregon, the surcharge is facially invalid under the negative Commerce Clause. Accordingly, the judgment of the Oregon Supreme Court is reversed, and the cases are remanded for further proceedings not inconsistent with this opinion.

It is so ordered.

CHIEF JUSTICE REHNQUIST, with whom JUSTICE BLACKMUN joins, dissenting.

Landfill space evaporates as solid waste accumulates. State and local governments expend financial and political capital to develop trash control systems that are efficient, lawful, and protective of the environment. The State of Oregon responsibly attempted to address its solid waste disposal problem through enactment of a comprehensive regulatory scheme for the management, disposal, reduction, and recycling of solid waste. For this Oregon should be applauded. The regulatory scheme included a fee charged on out-of-state solid waste. The Oregon Legislature directed the Commission to determine the appropriate surcharge "based on the costs . . . of disposing of solid waste generated out-of-state." The Commission arrived at a surcharge of $2.25 per ton, compared to the $0.85 per ton charged on in-state solid waste. The surcharge works out to an increase of about $0.14 per week for the typical out-of-state solid waste producer. This seems a small price to pay for the right to deposit your "garbage, rubbish, refuse . . .; sewage sludge, septic tank and cesspool pumpings or other sludge; . . . manure, . . . dead animals, [and] infectious waste" on your neighbors.

Nearly 20 years ago, we held that a State cannot ban all out-of-state waste disposal in protecting themselves from hazardous or noxious materials brought across the State's borders. *Philadelphia v. New Jersey* (1978). Two Terms ago in *Chemical Waste Management, Inc. v. Hunt* (1992), in striking down the State of Alabama's $72 per ton fee on the disposal of out-of-state hazardous waste, the Court left open the possibility that such a fee could be valid if based on the costs of disposing of waste from other States. Once again, however, as in *Philadelphia* and *Chemical Waste Management*, the Court further cranks the dormant Commerce Clause ratchet against the States by striking down such cost-based fees, and by so doing ties the hands of the States in addressing the vexing national problem of solid waste disposal. I dissent.

Americans generated nearly 196 million tons of municipal solid waste in 1990, an increase from 128 million tons in 1975. Under current projections, Americans will produce 222 million tons of garbage in the year 2000. Generating solid waste has never been a problem. Finding environmentally safe disposal sites has. By 1991, it was estimated that 45 percent of all solid waste landfills in the Nation had reached capacity. Nevertheless, the Court stubbornly refuses to acknowledge that a clean and healthy environment, unthreatened by the improper disposal of solid waste, is the commodity really at issue in cases such as this.

Notwithstanding the identified shortage of landfill space in the Nation, the Court notes that it has "little difficulty" concluding that the Oregon surcharge does not operate as a compensatory tax, designed to offset the loss of available landfill space in the State caused by the influx of out-of-state waste. The Court reaches this nonchalant conclusion because the State has failed "to identify a specific charge on *intrastate* commerce equal to or exceeding the surcharge." (emphasis added). The Court's myopic focus on "differential fees" ignores the fact that in-state producers of solid waste support the Oregon regulatory program through state income taxes and by paying, indirectly, the numerous fees imposed on landfill operators and the dumping fee on in-state waste.

We confirmed in *Sporhase v. Nebraska ex rel. Douglas* (1982), that a State may enact a comprehensive regulatory system to address an environmental problem or a threat to natural resources within the confines of the Commerce Clause. In the context of threatened ground water depletion, we stated that "[o]bviously, a State that imposes severe withdrawal and use restrictions on its own citizens is not discriminating against interstate commerce when it seeks to prevent the uncontrolled transfer of water out of the State." The same point could be made about a "clean and safe environment" in these cases: where a State imposes restrictions on the ability of its own citizens to dispose of solid waste in an effort to promote a "clean and safe environment," it is not discriminating against interstate commerce by preventing the uncontrolled transfer of out-of-state solid waste into the State.

The availability of safe landfill disposal sites in Oregon did not occur by chance. Through its regulatory scheme, the State of Oregon inspects landfill sites, monitors waste streams, promotes recycling, and imposes an $0.85 per ton disposal fee on in-state waste, all in an effort to curb the threat that its residents will harm the environment and create health and safety problems through excessive and unmonitored solid waste disposal. Depletion of a clean and safe environment will follow if Oregon must accept out-of-state waste at its landfills without a sharing of the disposal costs. The Commerce Clause does not require a State to abide this outcome where the "natural resource has some indicia of a good publicly produced and owned in which a State may favor its own citizens in times of shortage." . . . A shortage of available landfill space is upon us, and with it comes the accompanying health and safety hazards flowing from the improper disposal of solid wastes. We have long acknowledged a distinction between economic protectionism and health and safety regulation promulgated by Oregon.

Far from neutralizing the economic situation for Oregon producers and out-of-state producers, the Court's analysis turns the Commerce Clause on its head. Oregon's neighbors will operate under a competitive advantage against their Oregon counterparts as they can now produce solid waste with reckless abandon and avoid paying concomitant state taxes to develop new landfills and clean up retired landfill sites. While I understand that solid waste is an article of commerce, it is not a commodity sold in the marketplace; rather it is disposed of at a cost to the State. Petitioners do not buy garbage to put in their landfills; solid waste producers pay petitioners to take their waste. Oregon solid waste producers do not compete with out-of-state businesses in the sale of solid waste. Thus, the fees do not alter the price of a product that is competing with other products for common purchasers. If anything, striking down the fees works to the disadvantage of Oregon businesses. They alone will have to pay the "nondisposal" fees associated with solid waste: landfill siting, landfill clean-up, insurance to cover environmental accidents, and transportation improvement costs associated with out-of-state waste being shipped into the State. While we once recognized that "'the collection and disposal of solid wastes should continue to be primarily the function of State, regional, and local agencies,'" the Court today leaves States with only two options: become a dumper and ship as much waste as possible to a less populated State, or become a dumpee, and stoically accept waste from more densely populated States.

The Court asserts that the State has not offered "any safety or health reason[s]" for discouraging the flow of solid waste into Oregon. I disagree. The availability of environmentally sound landfill space and the proper disposal of solid waste strike me as justifiable "safety or health" rationales for the fee. . . .

In exercising its legitimate police powers in regulating solid waste disposal, Oregon is not "needlessly obstructing interstate trade or attempt[ing] to place itself in a position of economic isolation." . . . Quite to the contrary, Oregon accepts out-of-state waste as part of its comprehensive solid waste regulatory program and it "retains broad regulatory authority to protect the health and safety of its citizens and the integrity of its natural resources." *Ibid.* Moreover, Congress also has recognized taxes as an effective method of discouraging consumption of natural resources in other contexts. Nothing should change the analysis when the natural resource — landfill space — was created or regulated by the State in the first place.

* * *

I think that the $2.25 per ton fee that Oregon imposes on out-of-state waste works out to a . . . "fair approximation" of the privilege to use its landfills. Even the Court concedes that our precedents do not demand anything beyond "substantia[l] equivalen[cy]" between the fees charged on in-state and out-of-state waste. The $0.14 per week fee imposed on out-of-state waste producers qualifies as "substantially equivalent" under the reasonableness standard of [our prior cases].

The Court begrudgingly concedes that interstate commerce may be made to "pay its way," yet finds Oregon's nominal surcharge to exact more than a "just share" from interstate commerce. It escapes me how an additional $0.14 per week cost for the average solid waste producer constitutes anything but the type of "incidental effects on interstate commerce" endorsed by the majority. Even-handed regulations imposing such incidental effects on interstate commerce must be upheld unless "the burden imposed on such commerce is clearly excessive in relation to the putative local benefits." If the majority finds $0.14 per week beyond the pale, one is left to wonder what the Court possibly could have contemplated when it stated:

> "'[I]n the absence of conflicting legislation by Congress, there is a residuum of power in the state to make laws governing matters of local concern which nevertheless in some measure affect interstate commerce or even, to some extent, regulate it.'" *Hunt v. Washington State Apple Advertising Comm'n* (1977). . . .

Surely $0.14 per week falls within even the most crabbed definition of "affect" or "regulate." Today the majority has rendered this "residuum of power" a nullity.

The State of Oregon is not prohibiting the export of solid waste from neighboring States; it is only asking that those neighbors pay their fair share for the use of Oregon landfill sites. I see nothing in the Commerce Clause that compels less densely populated States to serve as the low-cost dumping grounds for their neighbors, suffering the attendant risks that solid waste landfills present. The Court, deciding otherwise, further limits the dwindling options available to States as they contend with the environmental, health, safety, and political challenges posed by the problem of solid waste disposal in modern society.

NOTES AND QUESTIONS

1. The majority views the facts in this case as a clear discrimination between in-state and out-of-state waste producers, and believes that the appropriate standard is the "virtually *per se* rule of invalidity . . . not the . . . balancing test." 511 U.S. at 100. Is the dissent seeking to apply a "balancing test," or is the dissent merely suggesting that this is a normal "police power" case and ought not to be viewed as a Commerce Clause problem? Which opinion do you find most convincing? How easy is it to draw the distinction (which we've encountered before) between Commerce Clause matters (which might implicate the negative Commerce Clause and do not permit discrimination between locals and out-of-staters) and police power matters?

In *South Central Bell Telephone Company v. Alabama*, 526 U.S. 160 (1999), the Court reversed an Alabama Supreme Court ruling that had upheld a differential application of a state franchise tax on foreign corporations. Alabama law gave domestic corporations the ability to reduce their franchise tax liability simply by reducing the par value of their stock, but it denied foreign corporations the same ability. Citing *Oregon Waste*, the Court held that the discriminatory practice could not be sustained on the basis that the higher effective tax on foreign corporations was compensatory, off-setting tax burdens uniquely borne by domestic corporations. To be truly compensatory, said the Court, a state must prove that the higher tax on foreign corporations is "roughly approximate" to the special burdens on domestic corporations and that the taxes are similar in substantive character. Alabama invited the Court to reconsider its dormant or negative Commerce Clause jurisprudence in its entirety, but the Court declined since "the State did not make clear it intended to make this argument until it filed its brief on the merits."

Hillside Dairy, Inc. v. Lyons, 539 U.S. 59 (2003), held that a federal statute immunizing from review under the dormant or negative Commerce Clause certain California laws that regulate the composition and labeling of fluid milk products does not immunize California laws that regulate pricing. Said Justice Stevens, "Congress certainly has the power to authorize state regulations that burden or discriminate against interstate commerce, but we will not assume that it has done so unless such an intent is clearly expressed." The Court also reversed a lower court ruling that refused to countenance a privileges and immunities claim under Article IV. There mere fact that the California law does not identify out-of-state citizenship as the basis for disparate treatment does not allow for the rejection of the claim outright. Justice Thomas dissented in part, maintaining his earlier stated view that "the negative Commerce Clause makes little sense, and has proved virtually unworkable in application, and, consequently, cannot serve as a basis for striking down a state statute."

2. A recent attempt to apply the dormant Commerce Clause was in *Camps Newfound/Owatonna, Inc. v. Town of Harrison*, 520 U.S. 564 (1997). In that case an operator of a church camp claimed that a Maine statute which gave special state tax benefits to Maine charitable institutions which served primarily state residents, and denied them to institutions which served primarily out-of-state residents violated the dormant Commerce Clause. How would you have decided the case, based on *Oregon Waste*? In *Camps*, the Court split 5-4, in a decision which found the Maine tax scheme unconstitutional. The majority included Justices Stevens, O'Connor, Kennedy, Souter and Breyer. The dissenters were Scalia, Rehnquist, Thomas, and Ginsburg. Note that Thomas was the author of the majority opinion in *Oregon Waste*. The majority, in essence, applied the *"per se"* test to find measures which facially discriminated against out-of-staters to be violations of the dormant Commerce Clause. Justice Scalia, in the first paragraph of his dissent, explained why, in his view, the case was not concerned with interstate commerce:

> The Court's negative-commerce-clause jurisprudence has drifted far from its moorings. Originally designed to create a national market for commercial activity, it is today invoked to prevent a State from giving a tax break to charities that benefit the State's inhabitants. In my view, Maine's tax exemption, which excuses from taxation only that property used to relieve the State of its burden of caring for its residents, survives even our most demanding commerce-clause scrutiny.

520 U.S. at 595 (Scalia, J., dissenting). In other words, Scalia thought that the matter at issue was how to treat domestic charitable institutions, and not a matter relating to interstate commerce. Justice Thomas, in his dissent, emphasized that the tax at issue was on real estate, and local real estate was at as far

a remove from articles in interstate commerce as possible: "The tax at issue here is a tax on real estate, the quintessential asset that does not move in interstate commerce." *Id.* at 609 (Thomas, J., dissenting). In his dissent, Thomas went even further, and suggested that "[t]he negative Commerce Clause has no basis in the text of the Constitution, makes little sense, and has proved virtually unworkable in application." *Id.* at 610. Do you agree? Justice Thomas is so frustrated by the imprecision, and in his judgment, inappropriateness of the dormant commerce analysis that he suggests that it be abandoned as an example of "failed jurisprudence." *Id.* In an interesting, historically-grounded opinion, Justice Thomas also posits that the entire exercise is unnecessary because the Constitution contains an express check on discriminatory state taxation of interstate commerce — the Import-Export Clause in Article I, Section 10. Under that Clause, no state may impose taxes ("imposts or duties") without the consent of Congress on imports or exports. Justice Thomas argues that, notwithstanding an erroneous Civil War era ruling, that meant both foreign and domestic imports and exports. *See id.* at 621-40. The application of this Clause would have a narrower sweep than the Court's dormant commerce analysis, and in particular, it would not have invalidated the Maine tax at issue in *Camps Newfound*. In other words, outside of the prohibited form of taxation, states could favor their local economies, unless of course, the elected national legislature disagreed. Do you find Justice Thomas' approach appealing?

3. The judicial activism of the dormant commerce cases is blunted somewhat by the ability of states to directly act as a market participant. This factor is considered in the next case.

SOUTH-CENTRAL TIMBER DEVELOPMENT, INC. v. WUNNICKE
467 U.S. 82 (1984)

JUSTICE WHITE announced the judgment of the Court. . . .

We granted certiorari in this case to review a decision of the Court of Appeals for the Ninth Circuit that held that Alaska's requirement that timber taken from state lands be processed within the State prior to export was "implicitly authorized" by Congress and therefore does not violate the Commerce Clause. We hold that it was not authorized and reverse the judgment of the Court of Appeals.

I

In September 1980, the Alaska Department of Natural Resources published a notice that it would sell approximately 49 million board-feet of timber in the area of Icy Cape, Alaska, on October 23, 1980. The notice of sale, the prospectus, and the proposed contract for the sale all provided, pursuant to [an Alaska statute], that "[p]rimary manufacture within the State of Alaska will be required as a special provision of the contract." Under the primary-manufacture requirement, the successful bidder must partially process the timber prior to shipping it outside of the State. The requirement is imposed by contract and does not limit the export of unprocessed timber not owned by the State. The stated purpose of the requirement is to "protect existing industries, provide for the establishment of new industries, derive revenue from all timber resources, and manage the State's forests on a sustained yield basis." When it imposes the requirement, the State charges a significantly lower price for the timber than it otherwise would.

The major method of complying with the primary-manufacture requirement is to convert the logs into *cants*, which are logs slabbed on at least one side. In order to satisfy the Alaska requirement, cants must be either sawed to a maximum thickness of 12 inches or squared on four sides along their entire length.

Petitioner, South-Central Timber Development, Inc., is an Alaska corporation engaged in the business of purchasing standing timber, logging the timber, and shipping the logs into foreign commerce, almost exclusively to Japan. It does not operate a mill in Alaska and customarily sells unprocessed logs. When it learned that the primary-manufacture requirement was to be imposed on the Icy Cape sale, it brought an action in Federal District Court seeking an injunction, arguing that the requirement violated the negative implications of the Commerce Clause. The District Court agreed and issued an injunction. The Court of Appeals for the Ninth Circuit reversed, finding it unnecessary to reach the question whether, standing alone, the requirement would violate the Commerce Clause, because it found implicit congressional authorization in the federal policy of imposing a primary-manufacture requirement on timber taken from federal land in Alaska.

[After finding that Congress had not authorized Alaska's primary-manufacture requirement, the Court considered] two grounds not reached by the Court of Appeals. . . .

* * *

III

. . . The first of these issues is whether Alaska's restrictions on export of unprocessed timber from state-owned lands are exempt from Commerce Clause scrutiny under the "market-participant doctrine."

Our cases make clear that if a State is acting as a market participant, rather than as a market regulator, the dormant Commerce Clause places no limitation on its activities. . . . The precise contours of the market-participant doctrine have yet to be established, however, the doctrine having been applied in only three cases of this Court to date.

The first of the cases, *Hughes v. Alexandria Scrap Corp.* (1976), involved a Maryland program designed to reduce the number of junked automobiles in the State. A "bounty" was established on Maryland-licensed junk cars, and the State imposed more stringent documentation requirements on out-of-state scrap processors than on in-state ones. The Court rejected a Commerce Clause attack on the program, although it noted that under traditional Commerce Clause analysis the program might well be invalid because it had the effect of reducing the flow of goods in interstate commerce. The Court concluded that Maryland's action was not "the kind of action with which the Commerce Clause is concerned," because "[n]othing in the purposes animating the Commerce Clause prohibits a State, in the absence of congressional action, from participating in the market and exercising the right to favor its own citizens over others."

* * *

The State of Alaska contends that its primary-manufacture requirement fits squarely within the market-participant doctrine, arguing that "Alaska's entry into the market may be viewed as precisely the same type of subsidy to local interests that the Court [had earlier] found unobjectionable . . . ." However, when Maryland became involved in the scrap market it was as a purchaser of scrap; Alaska, on the other hand, participates in the timber market, but imposes conditions downstream in the timber-processing market. Alaska is not merely subsidizing local timber processing in an amount "roughly equal to the difference between the price the timber would fetch in the absence of such a requirement and the amount the state actually receives." If the State directly subsidized the timber-processing industry by such an amount, the purchaser would retain the option of taking advantage of the subsidy by processing timber in the State or forgoing the benefits of the subsidy and exporting unprocessed timber. Under the Alaska requirement, however, the choice is made for him: if he buys timber from the State he is not free to take the timber out of state prior to processing.

* * *

The limit of the market-participant doctrine must be that it allows a State to impose burdens on commerce within the market in which it is a participant, but allows it to go no further. The State may not impose conditions, whether by statute, regulation, or contract, that have a substantial regulatory effect outside of that particular market. Unless the "market" is relatively narrowly defined, the doctrine has the potential of swallowing up the rule that States may not impose substantial burdens on interstate commerce even if they act with the permissible state purpose of fostering local industry.

At the heart of the dispute in this case is disagreement over the definition of the market. Alaska contends that it is participating in the processed timber market, although it acknowledges that it participates in no way in the actual processing. South-Central argues, on the other hand, that although the State may be a participant in the timber market, it is using its leverage in that market to exert a regulatory effect in the processing market, in which it is not a participant. We agree with the latter position.

There are sound reasons for distinguishing between a State's preferring its own residents in the initial disposition of goods when it is a market participant and a State's attachment of restrictions on dispositions subsequent to the goods coming to rest in private hands. First, simply as a matter of intuition a state market participant has a greater interest as a "private trader" in the immediate transaction than it has in what its purchaser does with the goods after the State no longer has an interest in them. The common law recognized such a notion in the doctrine of restraints on alienation. Similarly, the antitrust laws place limits on vertical restraints. It is no defense in an action charging vertical trade restraints that the same end could be achieved through vertical integration; if it were, there would be virtually no antitrust scrutiny of vertical arrangements. We reject the contention that a State's action as a market regulator may be upheld against Commerce Clause challenge on the ground that the State could achieve the same end as a market participant. We therefore find it unimportant for present purposes that the State could support its processing industry by selling only to Alaska processors, by vertical integration, or by direct subsidy.

Second, downstream restrictions have a greater regulatory effect than do limitations on the immediate transaction. Instead of merely choosing its own trading partners, the State is attempting to govern the private, separate economic relationships of its trading partners; that is, it restricts the post-purchase activity of the purchaser, rather than merely the purchasing activity. In contrast to the situation in *White* [*v. Massachusetts Council of Construction Employers, Inc.*, 460 U.S. 204 (1983)], this restriction on private economic activity takes place after the completion of the parties' direct commercial obligations, rather than during the course of an ongoing commercial relationship in which the city retained a continuing proprietary interest in the subject of the contract. In sum, the State may not avail itself of the market-participant doctrine to immunize its downstream regulation of the timber-processing market in which it is not a participant.

IV

Finally, the State argues that even if we find that Congress did not authorize the processing restriction, and even if we conclude that its actions do not qualify for the market-participant exception, the restriction does not substantially burden interstate or foreign commerce under ordinary Commerce Clause principles. We need not labor long over that contention.

Viewed as a naked restraint on export of unprocessed logs, there is little question that the processing requirement cannot survive scrutiny under the precedents of the Court. For example, in *Pike v. Bruce Church, Inc.* (1970), we invalidated a requirement of the State of Arizona that all Arizona cantaloupes be packed within the State. The Court noted that the State's purpose was "to protect and enhance the reputation of growers within the State," a purpose we described as "surely legitimate." We observed:

> "[T]he Court has viewed with particular suspicion state statutes requiring business operations to be performed in the home State that could more efficiently be performed elsewhere. Even where the State is pur-

suing a clearly legitimate local interest, this particular burden on commerce has been declared to be virtually *per se* illegal."

We held that if the Commerce Clause forbids a State to require work to be done within the State for the purpose of promoting employment, then, *a fortiori*, it forbids a State to impose such a requirement to enhance the reputation of its producers. Because of the protectionist nature of Alaska's local-processing requirement and the burden on commerce resulting therefrom, we conclude that it falls within the rule of virtual *per se* invalidity of laws that "bloc[k] the flow of interstate commerce at a State's borders." *City of Philadelphia v. New Jersey* (1978).

We are buttressed in our conclusion that the restriction is invalid by the fact that foreign commerce is burdened by the restriction. It is a well-accepted rule that state restrictions burdening foreign commerce are subjected to a more rigorous and searching scrutiny. It is crucial to the efficient execution of the Nation's foreign policy that "the Federal Government . . . speak with one voice when regulating commercial relations with foreign governments." . . . In light of the substantial attention given by Congress to the subject of export restrictions on unprocessed timber, it would be peculiarly inappropriate to permit state regulation of the subject.

The judgment of the Court of Appeals is reversed, and the case is remanded for proceedings consistent with the opinion of this Court.

It is so ordered.

JUSTICE BRENNAN, concurring. [Omitted.]

JUSTICE POWELL, with whom THE CHIEF JUSTICE joins, concurring in part and concurring in the judgment. [Omitted.]

JUSTICE REHNQUIST, with whom JUSTICE O'CONNOR joins, dissenting.

In my view, the line of distinction drawn in the plurality opinion between the State as market participant and the State as market regulator is both artificial and unconvincing. The plurality draws this line "simply as a matter of intuition," but then seeks to bolster its intuition through a series of remarks more appropriate to antitrust law than to the Commerce Clause. For example, the plurality complains that the State is using its "leverage" in the timber market to distort consumer choice in the timber-processing market, a classic example of a tying arrangement. And the plurality cites the common-law doctrine of restraints on alienation and the antitrust limits on vertical restraints in dismissing the State's claim that it could accomplish exactly the same result in other ways.

Perhaps the State's actions do raise antitrust problems. But what the plurality overlooks is that the antitrust laws apply to a State only when it is acting as a market participant. When the State acts as a market regulator, it is immune from antitrust scrutiny. Of course, the line of distinction in cases under the Commerce Clause need not necessarily parallel the line drawn in antitrust law. But the plurality can hardly justify placing Alaska in the market-regulator category, in this Commerce Clause case, by relying on antitrust cases that are relevant only if the State is a market participant.

The contractual term at issue here no more transforms Alaska's sale of timber into "regulation" of the processing industry than the resident-hiring preference imposed by the city of Boston in *White v. Massachusetts Council of Construction Employers, Inc.* (1983), constituted regulation of the construction industry. Alaska is merely paying the buyer of the timber indirectly, by means of a reduced price, to hire Alaska residents to process the timber. Under existing precedent, the State could accomplish that same result in any number of ways. For example, the State could choose to sell its timber only to those companies that maintain active primary-processing plants in Alaska. *Reeves, Inc. v. Stake* (1980). Or the State could directly subsidize the primary-processing industry within the State. *Hughes v. Alexandria Scrap Corp.* (1976). The State could even pay to have the logs processed and then enter the market only to sell processed logs. It seems to me unduly formalistic to conclude that the one path chosen by the State as best suited to promote its concerns is the path forbidden it by the Commerce Clause.

For these reasons, I would affirm the judgment of the Court of Appeals.

NOTES AND QUESTIONS

1. As the contrast between Justice Rehnquist's dissent and the majority opinion makes clear, there is an exception to the negative Commerce Clause which applies when a state is a "market participant" rather than a "market regulator." Which was Alaska here, and does the distinction really make any sense?

2. Did Justice Thomas have a point when he suggested the incoherence of the dormant Commerce Clause decisions?

3. Antitrust law is beyond the scope of this course, but do you understand the antitrust (or, if you like, anticompetitive) issues in the case? Assume, for the moment, that the antitrust laws rather broadly provide that activities which impede competition in the marketplace are impermissible under federal law when the market in question is that involving interstate commerce. Would these laws be an acceptable form of legislation under the congressional power to regulate commerce?

B. State Law and Federal Elections — The Question of Term Limits

States legislate on more than economic subjects. Recently, state laws have attempted to limit the number of terms members of the federal Congress, House or Senate, may serve. You may wonder what business it is of the states to define the criteria for federal election, but if the vast scope of federal commerce power did not reveal it, the next, closely-divided opinion surely illustrates why the states might argue that they have a considerable interest in the composition of who holds federal office. Interest or not, thus far, the states' arguments have not prevailed.

U.S. TERM LIMITS, INC. v. THORNTON
514 U.S. 779 (1995)

JUSTICE STEVENS delivered the opinion of the Court.

The Constitution sets forth qualifications for membership in the Congress of the United States. . . .

Today's cases present a challenge to [Section 3 of Amendment 73] to the Arkansas State Constitution that prohibits the name of an otherwise-eligible candidate for Congress from appearing on the general election ballot if that candidate has already served three terms in the House of Representatives or two terms in the Senate. The Arkansas Supreme Court held that the amendment violates the Federal Constitution. We agree with that holding. Such a state-imposed restriction is contrary to the "fundamental principle of our representative democracy," embodied in the Constitution, that "the people should choose whom they please to govern them." Allowing individual States to adopt their own qualifications for congressional service would be inconsistent with the Framers' vision of a uniform National Legislature representing the people of the United States. If the qualifications set forth in the text of the Constitution are to be changed, that text must be amended.

I

* * *

On November 13, 1992, respondent Bobbie Hill, on behalf of herself, similarly situated Arkansas "citizens, residents, taxpayers and registered voters," and the League of Women Voters of Arkansas, filed a complaint in the Circuit Court for Pulaski County, Arkansas, seeking a declaratory judgment that § 3 of Amendment 73 is "unconstitutional and void." . . .

. . . [T]he Circuit Court held that § 3 of Amendment 73 violated Article I of the Federal Constitution.

With respect to that holding, in a 5-to-2 decision, the Arkansas Supreme Court affirmed. . . .

* * *

II

. . . [T]he constitutionality of Amendment 73 depends critically on the resolution of two distinct issues. The first is whether the Constitution forbids States from adding to or altering the qualifications specifically enumerated in the Constitution. The second is, if the Constitution does so forbid, whether the fact that Amendment 73 is formulated as a ballot access restriction rather than as an outright disqualification is of constitutional significance. Our resolution of these issues draws upon our prior resolution of a related but distinct issue: whether Congress has the power to add to or alter the qualifications of its Members.

Twenty-six years ago, in *Powell v. McCormack* (1969), we reviewed the history and text of the Qualifications Clauses in a case involving an attempted exclusion of a duly elected Member of Congress. The principal issue was whether the power granted to each House in Art. I, § 5, cl. 1, to judge the "Qualifications of its own Members" includes the power to impose qualifications other than those set forth in the text of the Constitution. In an opinion by Chief Justice Warren for eight Members of the Court, we held that it does not. . . .

In November 1966, Adam Clayton Powell, Jr., was elected from a District in New York to serve in the United States House of Representatives for the 90th Congress. Allegations that he had engaged in serious misconduct while serving as a committee chairman during the 89th Congress led to the appointment of a Select Committee to determine his eligibility to take his seat. That Committee found that Powell met the age, citizenship, and residency requirements set forth in Art. I, § 2, cl. 2. The Committee also found, however, that Powell had wrongfully diverted House funds for the use of others and himself and had made false reports on expenditures of foreign currency. Based on those findings, the House after debate adopted House Resolution 278, excluding Powell from membership in the House, and declared his seat vacant.

Powell and several voters of the District from which he had been elected filed suit seeking a declaratory judgment that the House Resolution was invalid because Art. I, § 2, cl. 2, sets forth the exclusive qualifications for House membership. We ultimately accepted that contention, concluding that the House of Representatives has no "authority to *exclude* any person, duly elected by his constituents, who meets all the requirements for membership expressly prescribed in the Constitution." In reaching that conclusion, we undertook a detailed historical review to determine the intent of the Framers. . . . [W]e determined that the "relevant historical materials" reveal that Congress has no power to alter the qualifications in the text of the Constitution.

* * *

We also recognized in *Powell* that the post-Convention ratification debates confirmed that the Framers understood the qualifications in the Constitution to be fixed and unalterable by Congress. For example, we noted that in response to the antifederalist charge that the new Constitution favored the wealthy and well-born, Alexander Hamilton wrote:

"'The truth is that there is no method of securing to the rich the preference apprehended but by prescribing qualifications of property either for those who may elect or be elected. But this forms no part of the power to be conferred upon the national government. . . . *The qualifications of the persons who may choose or be chosen, as has been remarked upon other occasions, are defined and fixed in the Constitution, and are unalterable by the legislature.*'" THE FEDERALIST NO. 60, at 371 (Clinton Rossiter ed., 1961) (emphasis added). . . .

The exercise by Congress of its power to judge the qualifications of its Members further confirmed this understanding. We concluded that, during the first 100 years of its existence, "Congress strictly limited its power to judge the qualifications of its members to those enumerated in the Constitution."

. . . We thus conclude now, as we did in *Powell*, that history shows that, with respect to Congress, the Framers intended the Constitution to establish fixed qualifications.

Powell's Reliance on Democratic Principles

In *Powell*, of course, we did not rely solely on an analysis of the historical evidence, but instead complemented that analysis with "an examination of the basic principles of our democratic system." We noted that allowing Congress to impose additional qualifications would violate that "fundamental principle of our representative democracy . . . 'that the people should choose whom they please to govern them.'"

* * *

III

Our reaffirmation of *Powell* does not necessarily resolve the specific questions presented in these cases. For petitioners argue that whatever the constitutionality of additional qualifications for membership imposed by Congress, the historical and textual materials discussed in *Powell* do not support the conclusion that the Constitution prohibits additional qualifications imposed by States. In the absence of such a constitutional prohibition, petitioners argue, the Tenth Amendment and the principle of reserved powers require that States be allowed to add such qualifications

* * *

Petitioners argue that the Constitution contains no express prohibition against state-added qualifications, and that Amendment 73 is therefore an appropriate exercise of a State's reserved power to place additional restrictions on the choices that its own voters may make. We disagree for two independent reasons. First, we conclude that the power to add qualifications is not within the "original powers" of the States, and thus is not reserved to the States by the Tenth Amendment. Second, even if States possessed some original power in this area, we conclude that the Framers intended the Constitution to be the exclusive source of qualifications for members of Congress, and that the Framers thereby "divested" States of any power to add qualifications.

* * *

Source of the Power

Contrary to petitioners' assertions, the power to add qualifications is not part of the original powers of sovereignty that the Tenth Amendment reserved to the States. Petitioners' Tenth Amendment argument misconceives the nature of the right at issue because that Amendment could only "reserve" that which existed before. As Justice Story recognized, "the states can exercise no powers whatsoever, which exclusively spring out of the existence of the national government, which the constitution does not delegate to them. . . . No state can say, that it has reserved, what it never possessed."

* * *

The Preclusion of State Power

Even if we believed that States possessed as part of their original powers some control over congressional qualifications, the text and structure of the Constitution, the relevant historical materials, and, most importantly, the "basic principles of our democratic system" all demonstrate that the Qualifications Clauses were intended to preclude the States from exercising any such power and to fix as exclusive the qualifications in the Constitution.

* * *

The Convention and Ratification Debates

The available affirmative evidence indicates the Framers' intent that States have no role in the setting of qualifications. In FEDERALIST PAPER No. 52, dealing with the House of Representatives, Madison addressed the "qualifications of the electors and the elected." Madison first noted the difficulty in achieving uniformity in the qualifications for electors [voters — Eds.], which resulted in the Framers' decision to require only that the qualifications for federal electors be the same as those for state electors. Madison argued that such a decision "must be satisfactory to every State, because it is comfortable to the standard already established, or which may be established, by the State itself." Madison then explicitly contrasted the state control over the qualifications of electors with the lack of state control over the qualifications of the elected:

> "The qualifications of the elected, being less carefully and properly defined by the State constitutions, and being at the same time more susceptible of uniformity, have been very properly considered and regulated by the convention. . . . Under these reasonable limitations, the door of this part of the federal government is open to merit of every description, whether native or adoptive, whether young or old, and without regard to poverty or wealth, or to any particular profession of religious faith."
> . . .

The provisions in the Constitution governing federal elections confirm the Framers' intent that States lack power to add qualifications. The Framers feared that the diverse interests of the States would undermine the National Legislature, and thus they adopted provisions intended to minimize the possibility of state interference with federal elections. For example, to prevent discrimination against federal electors, the Framers required in Art. I, § 2, cl. 1, that the qualifications for federal electors be the same as those for state electors. As Madison noted, allowing States to differentiate between the qualifications for state and federal electors "would have rendered too dependent on the State governments that branch of the federal government which ought to be dependent on the people alone." Similarly, in Art. I, § 4, cl. 1, though giving the States the freedom to regulate the "Times, Places and Manner of holding Elections," the Framers created a safeguard against state abuse by giving Congress the power to "by Law make or alter such Regulations." The Convention debates make clear that the Framers' overriding concern was the potential for States' abuse of the power to set the "Times, Places and Manner" of elections. . . . As Hamilton later noted: "Nothing can be more evident than that an exclusive power of regulating elections for the national government, in the hands of the State legislatures, would leave the existence of the Union entirely at their mercy." FEDERALIST NO. 59, at 363.

* * *

We also find compelling the complete absence in the ratification debates of any assertion that States had the power to add qualifications. In those debates, the question whether to require term limits, or "rotation," was a major source of controversy. The draft of the Constitution that was submitted for ratification contained no provision for rotation. In arguments that echo in the preamble to Arkansas' Amendment 73, opponents of ratification condemned the absence of a rotation requirement, noting that "there is no doubt that senators will hold their office perpetually; and in this situation, they must of necessity lose their dependence, and their attachments to the people." . . .

The Federalists' responses to those criticisms and proposals addressed the merits of the issue, arguing that rotation was incompatible with the people's right to choose. As we noted above, Robert Livingston argued:

> "The people are the best judges who ought to represent them. To dictate and control them, to tell them whom they shall not elect, is to abridge their natural rights. This rotation is an absurd species of ostracism."

. . .

Regardless of which side has the better of the debate over rotation, it is most striking that nowhere in the extensive ratification debates have we found any statement by either a proponent or an opponent of rotation that the draft constitution would permit States to require rotation for the representatives of their own citizens. If the participants in the debate had believed that the States retained the authority to impose term limits, it is inconceivable that the Federalists would not have made this obvious response to the arguments of the pro-rotation forces. . . .

* * *

IV

* * *

The judgment is affirmed.

It is so ordered.

JUSTICE KENNEDY, concurring.

* * *

The majority and dissenting opinions demonstrate the intricacy of the question whether or not the Qualifications Clauses are exclusive. In my view, however, it is well settled that the whole people of the United States asserted their political identity and unity of purpose when they created the federal system. The dissent's course of reasoning suggesting otherwise might be construed to disparage the republican character of the National Government, and it seems appropriate to add these few remarks to explain why that course of argumentation runs counter to fundamental principles of federalism.

Federalism was our Nation's own discovery. The Framers split the atom of sovereignty. It was the genius of their idea that our citizens would have two political capacities, one state and one federal, each protected from incursion by the other. The resulting Constitution created a legal system unprecedented in form and design, establishing two orders of government, each with its own direct relationship, its own privity, its own set of mutual rights and obligations to the people who sustain it and are governed by it. It is appropriate to recall these origins, which instruct us as to the nature of the two different governments created and confirmed by the Constitution.

A distinctive character of the National Government, the mark of its legitimacy, is that it owes its existence to the act of the whole people who created it. It must be remembered that the National Government too is republican in essence and in theory. John Jay insisted on this point early in THE FEDERALIST PAPERS, in his comments on the government that preceded the one formed by the Constitution.

> "To all general purposes we have uniformly been one people; each individual citizen everywhere enjoying the same national rights, privileges, and protection. . . .
>
> "A strong sense of the value and blessings of union induced the people, at a very early period, to institute a federal government to preserve and perpetuate it. They formed it almost as soon as they had a political existence. . . ." THE FEDERALIST NO. 2, at 38-39 (Clinton Rossiter ed., 1961).

Once the National Government was formed under our Constitution, the same republican principles continued to guide its operation and practice. As James

Madison explained, the House of Representatives "derives its powers from the people of America," and "the operation of the government on the people in their individual capacities" makes it "a national government," not merely a federal one. *Id.*, No. 39, at 244, 245 (emphasis deleted). . . .

In one sense it is true that "the people of each State retained their separate political identities," for the Constitution takes care both to preserve the States and to make use of their identities and structures at various points in organizing the federal union. It does not at all follow from this that the sole political identity of an American is with the State of his or her residence. It denies the dual character of the Federal Government which is its very foundation to assert that the people of the United States do not have a political identity as well, one independent of, though consistent with, their identity as citizens of the State of their residence. It must be recognized that "'[f]or all the great purposes for which the Federal government was formed, we are one people, with one common country.'"

It might be objected that because the States ratified the Constitution, the people can delegate power only through the States or by acting in their capacities as citizens of particular States. But in *McCulloch v. Maryland*, the Court set forth its authoritative rejection of this idea:

> "The Convention which framed the constitution was indeed elected by the State legislatures. But the instrument . . . was submitted to the people. . . . It is true, they assembled in their several States — and where else should they have assembled? No political dreamer was ever wild enough to think of breaking down the lines which separate the States, and of compounding the American people into one common mass. Of consequence, when they act, they act in their States. But the measures they adopt do not, on that account, cease to be the measures of the people themselves, or become the measures of the State governments."

The political identity of the entire people of the Union is reinforced by the proposition, which I take to be beyond dispute, that, though limited as to its objects, the National Government is and must be controlled by the people without collateral interference by the States. *McCulloch* affirmed this proposition as well, when the Court rejected the suggestion that States could interfere with federal powers. "This was not intended by the American people. They did not design to make their government dependent on the States." The States have no power, reserved or otherwise, over the exercise of federal authority within its proper sphere. That the States may not invade the sphere of federal sovereignty is as incontestable, in my view, as the corollary proposition that the Federal Government must be held within the boundaries of its own power when it intrudes upon matters reserved to the States. *See United States v. Lopez.*

* * *

JUSTICE THOMAS, with whom THE CHIEF JUSTICE, JUSTICE O'CONNOR, and JUS-
TICE SCALIA join, dissenting.

It is ironic that the Court bases today's decision on the right of the people to
"choose whom they please to govern them." Under our Constitution, there is only
one State whose people have the right to "choose whom they please" to represent
Arkansas in Congress. The Court holds, however, that neither the elected legislature of that State nor the people themselves (acting by ballot initiative)
may prescribe any qualifications for those representatives. The majority therefore defends the right of the people of Arkansas to "choose whom they please to
govern them" by invalidating a provision that won nearly 60% of the votes cast
in a direct election and that carried every congressional district in the State.

I dissent. Nothing in the Constitution deprives the people of each State of the
power to prescribe eligibility requirements for the candidates who seek to represent them in Congress. The Constitution is simply silent on this question. And
where the Constitution is silent, it raises no bar to action by the States or the
people.

I

Because the majority fundamentally misunderstands the notion of "reserved"
powers, I start with some first principles. Contrary to the majority's suggestion,
the people of the States need not point to any affirmative grant of power in the
Constitution in order to prescribe qualifications for their representatives in
Congress, or to authorize their elected state legislators to do so.

A

Our system of government rests on one overriding principle: All power stems
from the consent of the people. To phrase the principle in this way, however, is
to be imprecise about something important to the notion of "reserved" powers.
The ultimate source of the Constitution's authority is the consent of the people
of each individual State, not the consent of the undifferentiated people of the
Nation as a whole.

The ratification procedure erected by Article VII makes this point clear. The
Constitution took effect once it had been ratified by the people gathered in convention in nine different States. But the Constitution went into effect only
"between the States so ratifying the same," Art. VII; it did not bind the people
of North Carolina until they had accepted it. In Madison's words, the popular
consent upon which the Constitution's authority rests was "given by the people,
not as individuals composing one entire nation, but as composing the distinct
and independent States to which they respectively belong." FEDERALIST NO. 39,
at 243 (Clinton Rossiter ed., 1961).

When they adopted the Federal Constitution, of course, the people of each
State surrendered some of their authority to the United States (and hence to
entities accountable to the people of other States as well as to themselves).
They affirmatively deprived their States of certain powers, *see, e.g.*, Art. I, § 10,

and they affirmatively conferred certain powers upon the Federal Government, *see, e.g.,* Art. I, § 8. Because the people of the several States are the only true source of power, however, the Federal Government enjoys no authority beyond what the Constitution confers: the Federal Government's powers are limited and enumerated. In the words of Justice Black, "the United States is entirely a creature of the Constitution. Its power and authority have no other source."

In each State, the remainder of the people's powers — "[t]he powers not delegated to the United States by the Constitution, nor prohibited by it to the States," Amdt. 10 — are either delegated to the state government or retained by the people. The Federal Constitution does not specify which of these two possibilities obtains; it is up to the various state constitutions to declare which powers the people of each State have delegated to their state government. As far as the Federal Constitution is concerned, then, the States can exercise all powers that the Constitution does not withhold from them. The Federal Government and the States thus face different default rules: Where the Constitution is silent about the exercise of a particular power — that is, where the Constitution does not speak either expressly or by necessary implication — the Federal Government lacks that power and the States enjoy it.

* * *

. . . Article I begins by providing that the Congress of the United States enjoys "[a]ll legislative Powers herein granted," § 1, and goes on to give a careful enumeration of Congress' powers, § 8. It then concludes by enumerating certain powers that are *prohibited* to the States. The import of this structure is the same as the import of the Tenth Amendment: If we are to invalidate Arkansas' Amendment 73, we must point to something in the Federal Constitution that deprives the people of Arkansas of the power to enact such measures.

B

The majority disagrees that it bears this burden. But its arguments are unpersuasive.

1

* * *

The majority's essential logic is that the state governments could not "reserve" any powers that they did not control at the time the Constitution was drafted. But it was not the state governments that were doing the reserving. The Constitution derives its authority instead from the consent of *the people* of the States. Given the fundamental principle that all governmental powers stem from the people of the States, it would simply be incoherent to assert that the people of the States could not reserve any powers that they had not previously controlled.

* * *

The majority is therefore quite wrong to conclude that the people of the States cannot authorize their state governments to exercise any powers that were unknown to the States when the Federal Constitution was drafted. Indeed, the majority's position frustrates the apparent purpose of the Amendment's final phrase. The Amendment does not pre-empt any limitations on state power found in the state constitutions, as it might have done if it simply had said that the powers not delegated to the Federal Government are reserved to the States. But the Amendment also does not prevent the people of the States from amending their state constitutions to remove limitations that were in effect when the Federal Constitution and the Bill of Rights were ratified.

* * *

2

The majority also sketches out what may be an alternative (and narrower) argument. . . . First, it asserts that because Congress as a whole is an institution of the National Government, the individual Members of Congress "owe primary allegiance not to the people of a State, but to the people of the Nation." Second, it concludes that because each Member of Congress has a nationwide constituency once he takes office, it would be inconsistent with the Framers' scheme to let a single State prescribe qualifications for him.

. . . From the framing to the present, however, the *selection* of the Representatives and Senators from each State has been left entirely to the people of that State or to their state legislature. . . . The very name "congress" suggests a coming together of representatives from distinct entities. In keeping with the complexity of our federal system, once the representatives chosen by the people of each State assemble in Congress, they form a national body and are beyond the control of the individual States until the next election. But the selection of representatives in Congress is indisputably an act of the people of each State, not some abstract people of the Nation as a whole.

* * *

3

In a final effort to deny that the people of the States enjoy "reserved" powers over the selection of their representatives in Congress, the majority suggests that the Constitution expressly delegates to the States certain powers over congressional elections. Such delegations of power, the majority argues, would be superfluous if the people of the States enjoyed reserved powers in this area.

Only one constitutional provision — the Times, Places and Manner Clause of Article I, § 4 — even arguably supports the majority's suggestion. It reads:

"The Times, Places and Manner of holding Elections for Senators and Representatives, shall be prescribed in each State by the Legislature thereof; but the Congress may at any time by Law make or alter such Regulations, except as to the Places of chusing Senators."

Contrary to the majority's assumption, however, this Clause does not delegate any authority to the States. Instead, it simply imposes a duty upon them. The majority gets it exactly right: by specifying that the state legislatures "shall" prescribe the details necessary to hold congressional elections, the Clause "expressly requires action by the States." This command meshes with one of the principal purposes of Congress' "make or alter" power: to ensure that the States hold congressional elections in the first place, so that Congress continues to exist. . . . Constitutional provisions that impose affirmative duties on the States are hardly inconsistent with the notion of reserved powers.

Of course, the second part of the Times, Places and Manner Clause does grant a power rather than impose a duty. As its contrasting uses of the words "shall" and "may" confirm, however, the Clause grants power exclusively to Congress, not to the States. If the Clause did not exist at all, the States would still be able to prescribe the times, places, and manner of holding congressional elections; the deletion of the provision would simply deprive Congress of the power to override these state regulations.

* * *

II

I take it to be established, then, that the people of Arkansas do enjoy "reserved" powers over the selection of their representatives in Congress. Purporting to exercise those reserved powers, they have agreed among themselves that the candidates covered by § 3 of Amendment 73 — those whom they have already elected to three or more terms in the House of Representatives or to two or more terms in the Senate — should not be eligible to appear on the ballot for reelection, but should nonetheless be returned to Congress if enough voters are sufficiently enthusiastic about their candidacy to write in their names. Whatever one might think of the wisdom of this arrangement, we may not override the decision of the people of Arkansas unless something in the Federal Constitution deprives them of the power to enact such measures.

The majority settles on "the Qualifications Clauses" as the constitutional provisions that Amendment 73 violates. Because I do not read those provisions to impose any unstated prohibitions on the States, it is unnecessary for me to decide whether the majority is correct to identify Arkansas' ballot-access restriction with laws fixing true term limits or otherwise prescribing "qualifications" for congressional office. [T]he Qualifications Clauses are merely straightforward recitations of the minimum eligibility requirements that the Framers thought it essential for every Member of Congress to meet. They restrict state power only in that they prevent the States from *abolishing* all eligibility requirements for membership in Congress.

* * *

A

The provisions that are generally known as the Qualifications Clauses read as follows:

> "No Person shall be a Representative who shall not have attained to the age of twenty five Years, and been seven Years a Citizen of the United States, and who shall not, when elected, be an Inhabitant of that State in which he shall be chosen." Art. I, § 2, cl. 2.

> "No Person shall be a Senator who shall not have attained to the Age of thirty Years, and been nine Years a Citizen of the United States, and who shall not, when elected, be an Inhabitant of that State for which he shall be chosen." Art. I, § 3, cl. 3.

Later in Article I, the "Ineligibility Clause" imposes another nationwide disqualification from congressional office: "[N]o Person holding any Office under the United States, shall be a Member of either House during his Continuance in Office." § 6, cl. 2.

. . . [T]hese different formulations — whether negative or affirmative — merely establish *minimum* qualifications. They are quite different from an *exclusive* formulation, such as the following:

> "Every Person who shall have attained to the age of twenty five Years, and been seven Years a Citizen of the United States, and who shall, when elected, be an Inhabitant of that State in which he shall be chosen, shall be eligible to be a Representative."

At least on their face, then, the Qualifications Clauses do nothing to prohibit the people of a State from establishing additional eligibility requirements for their own representatives.

* * *

The majority responds that "a patchwork of state qualifications" would "undermin[e] the uniformity and the national character that the Framers envisioned and sought to ensure." Yet the Framers thought it perfectly consistent with the "national character" of Congress for the Senators and Representatives from each State to be chosen by the legislature or the people of that State. The majority never explains why Congress' fundamental character permits this state-centered system, but nonetheless prohibits the people of the States and their state legislatures from setting any eligibility requirements for the candidates who seek to represent them.

* * *

B

Although the Qualifications Clauses neither state nor imply the prohibition that it finds in them, the majority infers from the Framers' "democratic principles" that the Clauses must have been generally understood to preclude the people of the States and their state legislatures from prescribing any additional qualifications for their representatives in Congress. But the majority's evidence on this point establishes only two more modest propositions: (1) the Framers did not want the Federal Constitution itself to impose a broad set of disqualifications for congressional office, and (2) the Framers did not want the Federal Congress to be able to supplement the few disqualifications that the Constitution does set forth. The logical conclusion is simply that the Framers did not want the people of the States and their state legislatures to be constrained by too many qualifications imposed at the national level. . . .

I agree with the majority that Congress has no power to prescribe qualifications for its own Members. This fact, however, does not show that the Qualifications Clauses contain a hidden exclusivity provision. The reason for Congress' incapacity is not that the Qualifications Clauses deprive Congress of the authority to set qualifications, but rather that nothing in the Constitution grants Congress this power. In the absence of such a grant, Congress may not act. But deciding whether the Constitution denies the qualification-setting power to the States and the people of the States requires a fundamentally different legal analysis.

* * *

The majority appears to believe that restrictions on eligibility for office are inherently undemocratic. But the Qualifications Clauses themselves prove that the Framers did not share this view; eligibility requirements to which the people of the States consent are perfectly consistent with the Framers' scheme. In fact, we have described "the authority of the people of the States to determine the qualifications of their most important government officials" as "an authority that lies at the heart of representative government." When the people of a State themselves decide to restrict the field of candidates whom they are willing to send to Washington as their representatives, they simply have not violated the principle that "the people should choose whom they please to govern them." [quoting Alexander Hamilton]

* * *

In fact, the authority to narrow the field of candidates in this way may be part and parcel of the right to elect Members of Congress. That is, the right to choose may include the right to winnow.

To appreciate this point, it is useful to consider the Constitution as it existed before the Seventeenth Amendment was adopted in 1913. The Framers' scheme called for the legislature of each State to choose the Senators from that State. Art. I, § 3, cl. 1. The majority offers no reason to believe that state legislatures could not adopt prospective rules to guide themselves in carrying out this responsibility; not only is there no express language in the Constitution barring legislatures from passing laws to narrow their choices, but there also is absolutely no basis for inferring such a prohibition. Imagine the worst-case scenario: a state legislature, wishing to punish one of the Senators from its

State for his vote on some bill, enacts a qualifications law that the Senator does not satisfy. The Senator would still be able to serve out his term; the Constitution provides for Senators to be chosen for 6-year terms, Art. I, § 3, cl. 1, and a person who has been seated in Congress can be removed only if two-thirds of the Members of his House vote to expel him, § 5, cl. 2. While the Senator would be disqualified from seeking reappointment, under the Framers' Constitution the state legislature already enjoyed unfettered discretion to deny him reappointment anyway. Instead of passing a qualifications law, the legislature could simply have passed a resolution declaring its intention to appoint someone else the next time around. . . .

While it is easier to coordinate a majority of state legislators than to coordinate a majority of qualified voters, the basic principle should be the same in both contexts. Just as the state legislature enjoyed virtually unfettered discretion over whom to appoint to the Senate under Art. I, § 3, so the qualified voters of the State enjoyed virtually unfettered discretion over whom to elect to the House of Representatives under Art. I, § 2. . . . Now that the people of the States are charged with choosing both Senators and Representatives, it follows that they may adopt eligibility requirements for Senators as well as for Representatives.

* * *

C

In addition to its arguments about democratic principles, the majority asserts that more specific historical evidence supports its view that the Framers did not intend to permit supplementation of the Qualifications Clauses. But when one focuses on the distinction between congressional power to add qualifications for congressional office and the power of the people or their state legislatures to add such qualifications, one realizes that this assertion has little basis.

In particular, the detail with which the majority recites the historical evidence set forth in *Powell v. McCormack* (1969), should not obscure the fact that this evidence has no bearing on the question now before the Court. As the majority ultimately concedes, it does not establish "the Framers' intent that the qualifications in the Constitution be fixed and exclusive"; it shows only that the Framers did not intend Congress to be able to enact qualifications laws. . . .

* * *

3

* * *

It is true that THE FEDERALIST NO. 52 contrasts the Constitution's treatment of the qualifications of voters in elections for the House of Representatives with its treatment of the qualifications of the Representatives themselves. As Madison noted, the Framers did not specify any uniform qualifications for the franchise in the Constitution; instead, they simply incorporated each State's rules about eligibility to vote in elections for the most numerous branch of the state legislature. By contrast, Madison continued, the Framers chose to impose some particular qualifications that all members of the House had to satisfy. But while Madison did say that the qualifications of the elected were "more susceptible of uniformity" than the qualifications of electors, THE FEDERALIST NO. 52, he did not say that the Constitution prescribes anything but uniform minimum qualifications for congressmen. That, after all, is more than it does for congressional electors.

* * *

4

* * *

. . . [S]tate practice immediately after the ratification of the Constitution refutes the majority's suggestion that the Qualifications Clauses were commonly understood as being exclusive. Five States supplemented the constitutional disqualifications in their very first election laws, and the surviving records suggest that the legislatures of these States considered and rejected the interpretation of the Constitution that the majority adopts today.

As the majority concedes, the first Virginia election law erected a property qualification for Virginia's contingent in the Federal House of Representatives. *See* Virginia Election Law (Nov. 20, 1788). What is more, while the Constitution merely requires representatives to be inhabitants of their State, the legislatures of five of the seven States that divided themselves into districts for House elections added that representatives also had to be inhabitants of the district that elected them. Three of these States adopted durational residency requirements too, insisting that representatives have resided within their districts for at least a year (or, in one case, three years) before being elected.

In an attempt to neutralize the significance of the district residency requirements, respondent Hill asserts that "there is no evidence that any state legislature focused, when it created these requirements, on the fact that it was adding to the constitutional qualifications." But this claim is simply false.

In Massachusetts, for instance, the legislature charged a committee with drafting a report on election methods. The fourth article of the resulting report called for the State to be divided into eight districts that would each elect one representative, but did not require that the representatives be residents of the districts that elected them. . . .

* * *

III

It is radical enough for the majority to hold that the Constitution implicitly precludes the people of the States from prescribing any eligibility requirements for the congressional candidates who seek their votes. This holding, after all, does not stop with negating the term limits that many States have seen fit to impose on their Senators and Representatives. Today's decision also means that no State may disqualify congressional candidates whom a court has found to be mentally incompetent, who are currently in prison, or who have past vote-fraud convictions. Likewise, after today's decision, the people of each State must leave open the possibility that they will trust someone with their vote in Congress even though they do not trust him with *a* vote in the election for Congress.

* * *

. . . [T]oday's decision reads the Qualifications Clauses to impose substantial implicit prohibitions on the States and the people of the States. I would not draw such an expansive negative inference from the fact that the Constitution requires Members of Congress to be a certain age, to be inhabitants of the States that they represent, and to have been United States citizens for a specified period. Rather, I would read the Qualifications Clauses to do no more than what they say. I respectfully dissent.

NOTES AND QUESTIONS

1. For Justice Stevens, speaking for the majority, the case of Congressman Adam Clayton Powell, *Powell v. McCormack*, 395 U.S. 486 (1969), is obviously of great importance. Justice Thomas' dissent finds it less persuasive. Is a case regarding what Congress may or may not do with regard to its own membership controlling on what the states may do with regard to their representatives to Congress? Justice Stevens may, however, simply be using *Powell* for the light it threw on the history of the Qualifications Clauses in the Constitution, and, in particular, to support his belief that the qualifications provisions were exclusive. How does Justice Stevens rate as an historian? Why isn't Justice Thomas persuaded? Note, in particular, Justice Stevens' citation, from *Powell*, of Madison's statement that "'A Republic may be converted into an aristocracy or oligarchy as well by limiting the number capable of being elected, as the number authorised to elect.'" 514 U.S. at 790-91 (quoting 2 RECORDS OF THE FEDERAL CONVENTION OF 1787, at 249-50 (Max Farrand ed., 1911)). Do you really suppose that those pushing for term limits in the late twentieth century are motivated by the desire of creating an aristocracy? Indeed, could it be that their efforts are, in fact, aimed at the elimination of an entrenched membership in Congress which, to them at least, represent just the sort of "aristocracy" Madison (and Jefferson) feared? Ronald D. Rotunda & Stephen J. Safranek, *An Essay on Term Limits and a Call for a Constitutional Convention*, 80 MARQ. L. REV. 227 (1996) (considering the utility of various methods of constitutional amendment to provide for federal term limits in light of *Thornton*). Justice Stevens suggests that the decision in *Powell* was grounded upon the proposition "that sovereignty is vested in the people, and that sovereignty confers on the people the right to choose freely their representatives to the National Government." 514 U.S. at 794. Does his opinion rejecting state term limitations on members of Congress further popular sovereignty? Indeed, Justice Stevens even goes so far as to quote Abraham Lincoln's famous statement from the Gettysburg address, that ours is a "government of the people, by the people, for the people." *Id.* at 821. Would Lincoln have approved of the results in *Thornton*? Whose opinion in *Thornton* — that of Justice Stevens or Justice Thomas — strikes you as the more democratic? Does Justice Stevens really come to grips with Justice Thomas' argument that Amendment 73, in attempting to "level the playing field," may well have had a democratic, or, if you like, an anti-aristocratic purpose?

2. Consider Justice Stevens' arguments that the Tenth Amendment does not reserve any powers to the states with regard to setting up additional qualifications for members of Congress, and that even if there were such "reserved powers," prior to the Constitution, they were taken away by the Constitution itself — which Justice Stevens, following Justice Story, believes set up a scheme whereby qualifications for members of the House and Senate are matters for the "people of the United States," and not the states. Does Justice Thomas do an adequate job rebutting these arguments? Does Justice Stevens' position — which he attributes to Justice Story — sufficiently take into account the "Federalism" supposedly inherent in the Constitution? In this regard, see Lynn A. Baker, *"They the People": A Comment on* U.S. Term Limits, Inc. v. Thornton, 38 ARIZ. L. REV. 859 (1996) (pointing to the difficulties involved in the amendment process as a basis for upholding state laws where the Constitution neither prohibits nor permits the state practice and there are no negative externalities on other states), and Robert F. Nagel, *The Term Limits Dissent: What Nerve,* 38 ARIZ. L. REV. 843 (1996) (describing the attraction of the strong nationalism inherent in the *Thornton* majority opinion and arguing that because the Thomas dissent threatens the belief that nationalism is realistic and beneficial, many fear the implications of his thinking).

Note Justice Thomas' quotation of the principal architect of the Constitution, James Madison, that "the popular consent upon which the Constitution's authority rests was 'given by the people, not as individuals composing one entire nation, but as composing the distinct and independent States to which they respectively belong.'" 514 U.S. at 846 (Thomas, J., dissenting) (quoting THE FEDERALIST NO. 39, at 243 (James Madison) (Clinton Rossiter ed., 1961)). Do you understand how Justice Thomas is coming increasingly to be regarded as a champion of federalism?

Justice Kennedy, in his concurring opinion, also invokes the spirit of federalism, which he describes, quite nicely, as "our Nation's own discovery. The Framers split the atom of sovereignty. It was the genius of their idea that our citizens would have two political capacities, one state and one federal, each protected from incursion by the other." 514 U.S. at 838 (Kennedy, J., concurring). Is Justice Kennedy's concurring opinion faithful to the "genius" of the Framers' ideas, and in particular the notion which Justice Thomas attributes to Madison? Note Justice Kennedy's aphorism "[t]hat the States may not invade the sphere of federal sovereignty is as incontestable . . . as the corollary proposition that the Federal Government must be held within the boundaries of its own power when it intrudes upon matters reserved to the States," *id.* at 841, and his supporting citation to *United States v. Lopez,* 514 U.S. 549 (1995), which you have already considered. Is the majority or the dissent in *Thornton* closer in spirit to *Lopez?* When Justice Kennedy makes the assertion that "even though the Constitution uses the qualifications for voters of the most numerous branch of the States' own legislatures to set the qualifications of federal electors, Art. I, § 2, cl. 1, when these electors vote . . . they act in a federal capacity and exercise a federal right," *id.* at 842, does his conclusion follow from his premise? Does either Justice Kennedy or Justice Stevens have an answer to Justice Thomas' claim that "[t]he Federal Government and the States . . . face different default rules," *id.* at 848 (Thomas, J., dissenting), so that if the Constitution is silent on the matter of state imposition of congressional term limitations it should be presumed that the states have that power?

3. Justice Stevens, continuing his argument from history, observes that there was no discussion of possible congressional term limits imposed by the states during the ratification debates, and further, that there are several instances where Congress made clear its belief that the states could not add to either the qualifications of Representatives or Senators. Is this historical evidence persuasive? Why doesn't it persuade Justice Thomas? Could it be his conception of "default rules"? Note that both the majority and the dissent make their ultimate appeals to history. Does this give the lie to those who would argue for a "living constitution"? On the other hand, since Justices Stevens and Thomas have such a divergent reading of the historical evidence, does this suggest anything about the value of the use of history and historical materials in constitutional interpretation? For a thorough discussion of the historical evidence, see John C. Eastman, *Open to Merit of Every Description: An Historical Assessment of the Constitution's Qualifications Clauses,* 73 DENV. U. L. REV. 89 (1995).

4. The provision at issue in *Thornton* did not actually bar anyone from sitting in Congress, but simply barred some candidates from having their names printed on ballots — so that if they were successful in write-in campaigns they could have been returned to Congress even if they had served countless prior terms. This was petitioners' argument "that, even if States may not add qualifications, Amendment 73 is constitutional because it is not such a qualification, and because Amendment 73 is a permissible exercise of state power to regulate the 'Times, Places and Manner of Holding Elections.'" 514 U.S. at 828. Justice Stevens finds this line of argument completely unacceptable. Do you? Do you think Justice Thomas did? What is the extent of the Constitution's grant to the states of "time, place, and manner" discretion in holding elections for Congress? Is Justice Stevens' attribution to the petitioners of a wish to accomplish "indirect[ly] . . . what the Constitution prohibits . . . directly," *id.* at 829, appropriate? Is this an impermissible exploration of the motive of the petitioners? If Amendment 73 would be constitutional as a "time, place, or manner" restriction on the holding of elections for Congress, should it be found unconstitutional because it is indirectly an attempt to alter "qualifications" for Congress?

5. *Thornton* was narrowly decided. Does this tell us anything about the current connection between the exercise of the franchise and federalism? Is there anything in Justice Thomas' opinion, apart from its grounding in federalism, that suggests that the four Justices who signed it might share other aspects of a philosophy of constitutional interpretation? Justice Thomas suggests, for example, that the majority has reached "radical" conclusions. 514 U.S. at 916-17 (Thomas, J., dissenting). What does he mean by that?

6. The *Thornton* case, and, in particular, the opinions written by Justices Kennedy and Thomas have been the subject of considerable commentary. It seems fair to view the case as one of the most important decided by the Court in recent years. As you have probably concluded, the case is best viewed as part of the Court's current struggle to come to grips with Federalism, and its recent tendency to alter its longstanding view that there were few limits on what the federal government could do.

Of great importance in this struggle are the views of Justice Kennedy, who has been described as "the man in the middle" on federalism issues. *See* Richard C. Reuben, *Man in the Middle*, CAL. LAW., Oct. 1992, at 35. One commentator has observed that:

> Kennedy joined with the court's liberal bloc in . . . *Thornton* . . . .
>
> But in two other decisions, Kennedy sided with the court's conservatives to strike down federal laws affecting states' powers. Last year, he voted in . . . *Lopez* . . . to overturn a law making it a federal crime to possess a gun near a school. And earlier this year, he joined in nullifying a law allowing Indian tribes to sue states in federal courts over gambling issues in *Seminole Tribe of Florida v. Florida* . . . .
>
> As one court-watcher observed after the most recent of the rulings, "States' rights, two; federal government, one; and Anthony Kennedy, three."

Kenneth Jost, *Kennedy Comes out Firing in Gun Case*, RECORDER, Dec. 4, 1996, at 1. Should the Supreme Court's attitude toward federalism questions turn so narrowly on the views of one Justice? There are sharply differing conclusions reached by Court-watchers on what the Justices have been up to regarding federalism. Referring to two of the Justices who joined in Thomas's dissent, another commentator, Stuart Taylor, Jr., has noted:

> On the states' rights front, the Rehnquist-Scalia-Thomas bloc has pushed a narrow view of the Commerce Clause and other founts of federal power, and a broad view of state powers and immunities under the 10th and 11th Amendments. They would wipe out decades of precedent allowing the federal government (and courts) to take over traditional state and local functions and to regulate the states themselves.

Stuart Taylor, Jr., *With Clinton or Dole, Supreme Changes Loom*, TEX. LAW, Oct. 28, 1992, at 27. Based on what you have read so far in this course, do you agree? Commenting on the importance of Justice O'Connor's place among the four dissenters in *Thornton*, Taylor observed:

> O'Connor's inclination to go farther than Kennedy down the states' rights road was most evident when she joined Thomas' 88-page dissent in . . . *Thornton*. While the majority struck down all laws limiting the terms of members of Congress, the four dissenters laid down a states' rights manifesto so far-reaching that Linda Greenhouse observed in The New York Times: "[I]t is only a slight exaggeration to say that the dissent brought the court a single vote shy of reinstalling the Articles of Confederation."

Id.

7. In *Cook v. Gralike*, 531 U.S. 510 (2001), the Court confronted an effort to circumvent the ruling in *Thornton*. In response to that decision, the voters of Missouri adopted in 1996 an amendment to Article VIII of their state Constitution designed to lead to the adoption of a specified "Congressional Term Limits Amendment" to the Federal Constitution. Article VIII "instruct[s]" each Member of Missouri's congressional delegation "to use all of his or her delegated powers to pass the Congressional Term Limits Amendment." Failure to do so would be rewarded with a ballot label: "DISREGARDED VOTERS' INSTRUCTION ON TERM LIMITS." Non-incumbents were asked to take a pledge, and failing that, their ballots were emblazoned with "DECLINED TO PLEDGE TO SUPPORT TERM LIMITS." Missouri defended the provision as an exercise of the "right of the people to instruct" their representatives reserved by the Tenth Amendment, and as permissible regulation of the "manner" of electing federal legislators within the authority delegated to the states by the Elections Clause, Art. I, § 4, cl. 1. The Court found no support in the Tenth Amendment since, they said, as Justice Story observed, "the states can exercise no powers whatsoever, which exclusively spring out of the existence of the national government, which the constitution did not delegate to them." Simply put, "[n]o state can say, that it has reserved, what it never possessed."

States do have the power to regulate the "Times, Places and Manner of holding Elections for Senators and Representatives," subject to a grant of authority to Congress to "make or alter such Regulations." Art. I, § 4, cl. 1. Yet, the Court said they had made clear in *Thornton*, that "'the Framers understood the Elections Clause as a grant of authority to issue procedural regulations, and not as a source of power to dictate electoral outcomes, to favor or disfavor a class of candidates, or to evade important constitutional restraints.'" (quoting *Thornton*.) Article VIII was not a procedural regulation, held the Court. "It does not regulate the time of elections; it does not regulate the place of elections; nor, we believe, does it regulate the manner of elections. As to the last point, Article VIII bears no relation to the 'manner' of elections as we understand it, for in our commonsense view that term encompasses matters like 'notices, registration, supervision of voting, protection of voters, prevention of fraud and corrupt practices, counting of votes, duties of inspectors and canvassers, and making and publication of election returns.' . . . Rather, Article VIII is plainly designed to favor candidates who are willing to support the particular form of a term limits amendment set forth in its text and to disfavor those who either oppose term limits entirely or would prefer a different proposal."

Justice Thomas concurred in the judgment, but retained the belief that states have the Tenth Amendment power to impose term limits in federal elections. The point, however, was not relitigated by the parties. Apart from the reserved power issue, why don't the people have the authority to instruct their "agents" in Congress? Justice Kennedy attempted to answer this in a concurring opinion. He admitted that when the Constitution was enacted, *respectful* petitions to legislators were an accepted mode of urging legislative action. This right is preserved to individuals (the people) in the First Amendment. Justice Kennedy continued:

> Even if a State, as an entity, is not itself protected by the Petition Clause, there is no principle prohibiting a state legislature from following a parallel course and by a memorial resolution requesting the Congress of the United States to pay heed to certain state concerns. From the earliest days of our Republic to the present time, States have done so in the context of federal legislation. *See, e.g.,* 22 Annals of Cong. 153-154 (1811) (reprinting a resolution by the General Assembly of the Commonwealth of Pennsylvania requesting that the charter of the Bank of the United States not be renewed); 2000 Ala. Acts 66 (requesting targeted relief for Medicare cuts); 2000 Kan. Sess. Laws ch. 186 (urging Congress to allow state-inspected meat to be shipped in interstate commerce). Indeed, the situation was even more complex in the early days of our Nation, when Senators were appointed by state legislatures rather than directly elected. At that time, it appears that some state legislatures followed a practice of instructing the Senators whom they had appointed to pass legislation, while only requesting that the Representatives, who had been elected by the people, do so. *See* 22 Annals of Cong. 153-154 (1811). I do not believe that the situation should be any different with respect to a proposed constitutional amendment, and indeed history bears this out. *See, e.g.,* 13 Annals of Cong. 95-96 (1803) (reprinting a resolution from the State of Vermont and the Commonwealth of Massachusetts requesting that Congress propose to the legislatures of the States a constitutional amendment akin to the Twelfth Amendment). The fact that the Members of the First Congress decided not to codify a right to instruct legislative representatives does not, in my view, prove that they intended to prohibit nonbinding petitions or memorials by the State as an entity.

> If there are to be cases in which a close question exists regarding whether the State has exceeded its constitutional authority in attempting to influence congressional action, this case is not one of them. In today's case the question is not close. Here the State attempts to intrude

upon the relationship between the people and their congressional delegates by seeking to control or confine the discretion of those delegates, and the interference is not permissible.

Does it make sense that the principal (the people through state initiative) can only *suggest*, but not require, that *their* representatives follow the people's direction? Justice Stevens for the Court, but without the express support of Justice Souter, argues against the historical case for binding direction. At best, says Stevens, "such historical instructions at one point in the early Republic may have had 'de facto binding force' because it might have been 'political suicide' not to follow them. This evidence falls short of demonstrating that either the people or the States had a right to give legally binding, *i.e.*, nonadvisory, instructions to their representatives that the Tenth Amendment reserved, much less that such a right would apply to federal representatives . . . ." Stevens continues:

> Indeed, contrary evidence is provided by the fact that the First Congress rejected a proposal to insert a right of the people "to instruct their representatives" into what would become the First Amendment. The fact that the proposal was made suggests that its proponents thought it necessary, and the fact that it was rejected by a vote of 41 to 10, suggests that we should give weight to the views of those who opposed the proposal. It was their view that binding instructions would undermine an essential attribute of Congress by eviscerating the deliberative nature of that National Assembly. *See* (remarks of Rep. Sherman) ("[W]hen the people have chosen a representative, it is his duty to meet others from the different parts of the Union, and consult, and agree with them to such acts as are for the general benefit of the whole community. If they were to be guided by instructions, there would be no use in deliberation; all that a man would have to do, would be to produce his instructions, and lay them on the table, and let them speak for him"). As a result, James Madison, then a Representative from Virginia, concluded that a right to issue binding instructions would "run the risk of losing the whole system." . . .

Chapter 5

A GOVERNMENT MINDFUL OF DUAL SOVEREIGNTY

A. The Rise and Fall of Traditional State Functions

NATIONAL LEAGUE OF CITIES v. USERY
426 U.S. 833 (1976)

MR. JUSTICE REHNQUIST delivered the opinion of the Court.

Nearly 40 years ago Congress enacted the Fair Labor Standards Act, and required employers covered by the Act to pay their employees a minimum hourly wage and to pay them at one and one-half times their regular rate of pay for hours worked in excess of 40 during a workweek. . . .

* * *

I

In a series of amendments beginning in 1961 Congress began to extend the provisions of the Fair Labor Standards Act to some types of public employees. The 1961 amendments to the Act extended its coverage to persons who were employed in "enterprises" engaged in commerce or in the production of goods for commerce. And in 1966, with the amendment of the definition of employers under the Act, the exemption heretofore extended to the States and their political subdivisions was removed with respect to employees of state hospitals, institutions, and schools. We nevertheless sustained the validity of the combined effect of these two amendments in *Maryland v. Wirtz* (1968).

In 1974, Congress again broadened the coverage of the Act. . . .

By its 1974 amendments, then, Congress has now entirely removed the exemption previously afforded States and their political subdivisions . . . . The Act thus imposes upon almost all public employment the minimum wage and maximum hour requirements previously restricted to employees engaged in interstate commerce. . . .

Challenging these 1974 amendments in the District Court, appellants sought both declaratory and injunctive relief against the amendments' application to them. . . . That court . . . granted appellee Secretary of Labor's motion to dismiss the complaint for failure to state a claim upon which relief might be granted. . . .

We noted probable jurisdiction in order to consider the important questions recognized by the District Court. . . . [W]e have decided that the "far-reaching implications" of *Wirtz* should be overruled, and that the judgment of the District Court must be reversed.

II

It is established beyond peradventure that the Commerce Clause of Art. I of the Constitution is a grant of plenary authority to Congress. . . .

Appellants in no way challenge [the] decisions establishing the breadth of authority granted Congress under the commerce power. Their contention, on the contrary, is that when Congress seeks to regulate directly the activities of States as public employers, it transgresses an affirmative limitation on the exercise of its power akin to other commerce power affirmative limitations contained in the Constitution. Congressional enactments which may be fully within the grant of legislative authority contained in the Commerce Clause may nonetheless be invalid because found to offend against the right to trial by jury contained in the Sixth Amendment . . . or the Due Process Clause of the Fifth Amendment. . . . Appellants' essential contention is that the 1974 amendments to the Act, while undoubtedly within the scope of the Commerce Clause, encounter a similar constitutional barrier because they are to be applied directly to the States and subdivisions of States as employers.

This Court has never doubted that there are limits upon the power of Congress to override state sovereignty, even when exercising its otherwise plenary powers to tax or to regulate commerce which are conferred by Art. I of the Constitution. In *Wirtz*, for example, the Court took care to assure the appellants that it had "ample power to prevent . . . 'the utter destruction of the State as a sovereign political entity,'" which they feared. Appellee Secretary in this case, both in his brief and upon oral argument, has agreed that our federal system of government imposes definite limits upon the authority of Congress to regulate the activities of the States as States by means of the commerce power. . . . [T]he Court [has] recognized that an express declaration of this limitation is found in the Tenth Amendment

> "While the Tenth Amendment has been characterized as a 'truism,' stating merely that 'all is retained which has not been surrendered,' *United States v. Darby*, it is not without significance. The Amendment expressly declares the constitutional policy that Congress may not exercise power in a fashion that impairs the States' integrity or their ability to function effectively in a federal system."

In *New York v. United States* (1946), Mr. Chief Justice Stone, speaking for four Members of an eight-Member Court in rejecting the proposition that Congress could impose taxes on the States so long as it did so in a nondiscriminatory manner, observed:

> "A State may, like a private individual, own real property and receive income. But in view of our former decisions we could hardly say that a general non-discriminatory real estate tax (apportioned), or an income tax laid upon citizens and States alike could be constitutionally applied to the State's capitol, its State-house, its public school houses, public parks, or its revenues from taxes or school lands, even though all real property and all income of the citizen is taxed."[12]

The expressions in these more recent cases trace back to earlier decisions of this Court recognizing the essential role of the States in our federal system of government. Mr. Chief Justice Chase, perhaps because of the particular time at which he occupied that office, had occasion more than once to speak for the Court on this point. In *Texas v. White* (1869), he declared that "[t]he Constitution, in all its provisions, looks to an indestructible Union, composed of indestructible States." In *Lane County v. Oregon* (1869), his opinion for the Court said:

> "Both the States and the United States existed before the Constitution. The people, through that instrument, established a more perfect union by substituting a national government, acting, with ample power, directly upon the citizens, instead of the Confederate government, which acted with powers, greatly restricted, only upon the States. But in many articles of the Constitution the necessary existence of the States, and, within their proper spheres, the independent authority of the States, is distinctly recognized."

In *Metcalf & Eddy v. Mitchell* (1926), the Court likewise observed that "neither government may destroy the other nor curtail in any substantial manner the exercise of its powers."

Appellee Secretary argues that the cases in which this Court has upheld sweeping exercises of authority by Congress, even though those exercises pre-empted state regulation of the private sector, have already curtailed the sovereignty of the States quite as much as the 1974 amendments to the Fair Labor Standards Act. We do not agree. It is one thing to recognize the authority of Congress to enact laws regulating individual businesses necessarily subject to the dual sovereignty of the government of the Nation and of the State in which they reside. It is quite another to uphold a similar exercise of congressional authority directed, not to private citizens, but to the States as States. We have repeat-

---

[12] MR. JUSTICE BRENNAN suggests that "THE CHIEF JUSTICE was addressing not the question of a state sovereignty restraint upon the exercise of the commerce power, but rather the principle of implied immunity of the States and Federal Government from taxation by the other . . . ." The asserted distinction, however, escapes us. Surely the federal power to tax is no less a delegated power than is the commerce power: both find their genesis in Art. I, § 8. Nor can characterizing the limitation recognized upon the federal taxing power as an "implied immunity" obscure the fact that this "immunity" is derived from the sovereignty of the States and the concomitant barriers which such sovereignty presents to otherwise plenary federal authority.

edly recognized that there are attributes of sovereignty attaching to every state government which may not be impaired by Congress, not because Congress may lack an affirmative grant of legislative authority to reach the matter, but because the Constitution prohibits it from exercising the authority in that manner. In *Coyle v. Oklahoma* (1911), the Court gave this example of such an attribute:

> "The power to locate its own seat of government and to determine when and how it shall be changed from one place to another, and to appropriate its own public funds for that purpose, are essentially and peculiarly state powers. That one of the original thirteen States could now be shorn of such powers by an act of Congress would not be for a moment entertained."

One undoubted attribute of state sovereignty is the States' power to determine the wages which shall be paid to those whom they employ in order to carry out their governmental functions, what hours those persons will work, and what compensation will be provided where these employees may be called upon to work overtime. The question we must resolve here, then, is whether these determinations are "'functions essential to separate and independent existence,'" so that Congress may not abrogate the States' otherwise plenary authority to make them.

In their complaint appellants advanced estimates of substantial costs which will be imposed upon them by the 1974 amendments. Since the District Court dismissed their complaint, we take its well-pleaded allegations as true, although it appears from appellee's submissions in the District Court and in this Court that resolution of the factual disputes as to the effect of the amendments is not critical to our disposition of the case.

Judged solely in terms of increased costs in dollars, these allegations show a significant impact on the functioning of the governmental bodies involved. [In some instances there were expenditures of many millions of dollars each year.]
. . .

Increased costs are not, of course, the only adverse effects which compliance with the Act will visit upon state and local governments, and in turn upon the citizens who depend upon those governments. In its complaint in intervention, for example, California asserted that it could not comply with the overtime costs (approximately $750,000 per year) which the Act required to be paid to California Highway Patrol cadets during their academy training program. California reported that it had thus been forced to reduce its academy training program from 2,080 hours to only 960 hours, a compromise undoubtedly of substantial importance to those whose safety and welfare may depend upon the preparedness of the California Highway Patrol.

This type of forced relinquishment of important governmental activities is further reflected in the complaint's allegation that the city of Inglewood, Cal., has been forced to curtail its affirmative action program for providing employment opportunities for men and women interested in a career in law enforcement. . . .

Quite apart from the substantial costs imposed upon the States and their political subdivisions, the Act displaces state policies regarding the manner in which they will structure delivery of those governmental services which their citizens require. The Act, speaking directly to the States *qua* States, requires that they shall pay all but an extremely limited minority of their employees the minimum wage rates currently chosen by Congress. It may well be that as a matter of economic policy it would be desirable that States, just as private employers, comply with these minimum wage requirements. But it cannot be gainsaid that the federal requirement directly supplants the considered policy choices of the States' elected officials and administrators as to how they wish to structure pay scales in state employment. The State might wish to employ persons with little or no training, or those who wish to work on a casual basis, or those who for some other reason do not possess minimum employment requirements, and pay them less than the federally prescribed minimum wage. It may wish to offer part-time or summer employment to teenagers at a figure less than the minimum wage, and if unable to do so may decline to offer such employment at all. But the Act would forbid such choices by the States. The only "discretion" left to them under the Act is either to attempt to increase their revenue to meet the additional financial burden imposed upon them by paying congressionally prescribed wages to their existing complement of employees, or to reduce that complement to a number which can be paid the federal minimum wage without increasing revenue.

This dilemma presented by the minimum wage restrictions may seem not immediately different from that faced by private employers, who have long been covered by the Act and who must find ways to increase their gross income if they are to pay higher wages while maintaining current earnings. The difference, however, is that a State is not merely a factor in the "shifting economic arrangements" of the private sector of the economy, *Kovacs v. Cooper* (1949) (Frankfurter, J., concurring), but is itself a coordinate element in the system established by the Framers for governing our Federal Union

The degree to which the FLSA amendments would interfere with traditional aspects of state sovereignty can be seen even more clearly upon examining the overtime requirements of the Act. The general effect of these provisions is to require the States to pay their employees at premium rates whenever their work exceeds a specified number of hours in a given period. The asserted reason for these provisions is to provide a financial disincentive upon using employees beyond the work period deemed appropriate by Congress. . . . We do not doubt that this may be a salutary result, and that it has a sufficiently rational relationship to commerce to validate the application of the overtime provisions to private employers. But, like the minimum wage provisions, the vice of the Act as sought to be applied here is that it directly penalizes the States for choosing to hire governmental employees on terms different from those which Congress has sought to impose.

This congressionally imposed displacement of state decisions may substantially restructure traditional ways in which the local governments have arranged their affairs. . . . The requirement imposing premium rates upon any employment in excess of what Congress has decided is appropriate for a governmental employee's workweek, for example, appears likely to have the effect of coercing the States to structure work periods in some employment areas, such as police and fire protection, in a manner substantially different from practices which have long been commonly accepted among local governments of this Nation. . . . Another example of congressional choices displacing those of the States in the area of what are without doubt essential governmental decisions may be found in the practice of using volunteer firemen, a source of manpower crucial to many of our smaller towns' existence. Under the regulations proposed by appellee, whether individuals are indeed "volunteers" rather than "employees" subject to the minimum wage provisions of the Act are questions to be decided in the courts. It goes without saying that provisions such as these contemplate a significant reduction of traditional volunteer assistance which has been in the past drawn on to complement the operation of many local governmental functions.

Our examination of the effect of the 1974 amendments, as sought to be extended to the States and their political subdivisions, satisfies us that both the minimum wage and the maximum hour provisions will impermissibly interfere with the integral governmental functions of these bodies. . . . [T]heir application will . . . significantly alter or displace the States' abilities to structure employer-employee relationships in such areas as fire prevention, police protection, sanitation, public health, and parks and recreation. . . . Indeed, it is functions such as these which governments are created to provide, services such as these which the States have traditionally afforded their citizens. If Congress may withdraw from the States the authority to make those fundamental employment decisions upon which their systems for performance of these functions must rest, we think there would be little left of the States' "'separate and independent existence.'" . . . This exercise of congressional authority does not comport with the federal system of government embodied in the Constitution. We hold that insofar as the challenged amendments operate to directly displace the States' freedom to structure integral operations in areas of traditional governmental functions, they are not within the authority granted Congress by Art. I, § 8, cl. 3.

III

One final matter requires our attention. Appellee has vigorously urged that we cannot, consistently with the Court's decisions in *Maryland v. Wirtz* (1968), and *Fry* [*v. U.S.*] (1975), rule against him here. It is important to examine this contention so that it will be clear what we hold today, and what we do not.

With regard to *Fry*, we disagree with appellee. There the Court held that the Economic Stabilization Act of 1970 was constitutional as applied to temporarily freeze the wages of state and local government employees [because it was] "an emergency measure to counter severe inflation that threatened the national economy."

We think our holding today quite consistent with *Fry*. . . . The means selected were carefully drafted so as not to interfere with the States' freedom beyond a very limited, specific period of time. The effect of the across-the-board freeze authorized by that Act, moreover, displaced no state choices as to how governmental operations should be structured, nor did it force the States to remake such choices themselves. Instead, it merely required that the wage scales and employment relationships which the States themselves had chosen be maintained during the period of the emergency. . . .

With respect to the Court's decision in *Wirtz*, we reach a different conclusion. . . . There are undoubtedly factual distinctions between the two situations, but in view of the conclusions expressed earlier in this opinion we do not believe the reasoning in *Wirtz* may any longer be regarded as authoritative.

Wirtz relied heavily on the Court's decision in *United States v. California* (1936). The opinion quotes the following language from that case:

"'[We] look to the activities in which the states have traditionally engaged as marking the boundary of the restriction upon the federal taxing power. But there is no such limitation upon the plenary power to regulate commerce. The state can no more deny the power if its exercise has been authorized by Congress than can an individual.'"

But we have reaffirmed today that the States as States stand on a quite different footing from an individual or a corporation when challenging the exercise of Congress' power to regulate commerce. We think the dicta from *United States v. California* simply wrong. Congress may not exercise that power so as to force directly upon the States its choices as to how essential decisions regarding the conduct of integral governmental functions are to be made. We agree that such assertions of power, if unchecked, would indeed, as Mr. Justice Douglas cautioned in his dissent in *Wirtz*, allow "the National Government [to] devour the essentials of state sovereignty," and would therefore transgress the bounds of the authority granted Congress under the Commerce Clause. While there are obvious differences between the schools and hospitals involved in *Wirtz*, and the fire and police departments affected here, each provides an integral portion of those governmental services which the States and their political subdivisions have traditionally afforded their citizens. We are therefore persuaded that *Wirtz* must be overruled.

* * *

Mr. Justice Blackmun, concurring. [Omitted.]

Mr. Justice Brennan, with whom Mr. Justice White and Mr. Justice Marshall join, dissenting.

* * *

We said in *United States v. California* (1936) . . . : "The sovereign power of the states is necessarily diminished to the extent of the grants of power to the federal government in the Constitution. . . . [T]he power of the state is subordinate to the constitutional exercise of the granted federal power." . . .

"[It] is not a controversy between equals" when the Federal Government "is asserting its sovereign power to regulate commerce. . . . [T]he interests of the nation are more important than those of any State." . . . The commerce power "is an affirmative power commensurate with the national needs." . . . The Constitution reserves to the States "only . . . that authority which is consistent with and not opposed to the grant to Congress. There is no room in our scheme of government for the assertion of state power in hostility to the authorized exercise of Federal power." . . . "The framers of the Constitution never intended that the legislative power of the nation should find itself incapable of disposing of a subject matter specifically committed to its charge." . . .

My Brethren thus have today manufactured an abstraction without substance, founded neither in the words of the Constitution nor on precedent. . . .

* * *

MR. JUSTICE STEVENS, dissenting. [Omitted.]

GARCIA v. SAN ANTONIO METROPOLITAN TRANSIT AUTHORITY
469 U.S. 528 (1985)

JUSTICE BLACKMUN delivered the opinion of the Court.

We revisit in these cases an issue raised in *National League of Cities v. Usery* (1976). . . . Although *National League of Cities* supplied some examples of "traditional governmental functions," it did not offer a general explanation of how a "traditional" function is to be distinguished from a "nontraditional" one. Since then, federal and state courts have struggled with the task . . . .

In the present cases, a Federal District Court concluded that municipal ownership and operation of a mass-transit system is a traditional governmental function and thus, under *National League of Cities*, is exempt from the obligations imposed by the FLSA. Faced with the identical question, three Federal Courts of Appeals and one state appellate court have reached the opposite conclusion.

Our examination of this "function" standard applied in these and other cases over the last eight years now persuades us that the attempt to draw the boundaries of state regulatory immunity in terms of "traditional governmental function" is not only unworkable but is also inconsistent with established principles of federalism and, indeed, with those very federalism principles on which *National League of Cities* purported to rest. That case, accordingly, is overruled.

I

* * *

The present controversy concerns the extent to which SAMTA may be subjected to the minimum-wage and overtime requirements of the FLSA. . . .

The FLSA obligations of public mass-transit systems like SATS were expanded in 1974 when Congress provided for the progressive repeal of the surviving overtime exemption for mass-transit employees. Congress simultaneously brought the States and their subdivisions further within the ambit of the FLSA by extending FLSA coverage to virtually all state and local-government employees. SATS complied with the FLSA's overtime requirements until 1976, when this Court, in *National League of Cities*, overruled *Maryland v. Wirtz*, and held that the FLSA could not be applied constitutionally to the "traditional governmental functions" of state and local governments. Four months after *National League of Cities* was handed down, SATS informed its employees that the decision relieved SATS of its overtime obligations under the FLSA.

Matters rested there until September 17, 1979, when the Wage and Hour Administration of the Department of Labor issued an opinion that SAMTA's operations "are not constitutionally immune from the application of the Fair Labor Standards Act" under *National League of Cities*. On November 21 of that year, SAMTA filed this action against the Secretary of Labor in the United States District Court for the Western District of Texas. It sought a declaratory judgment that . . . *National League of Cities* precluded the application of the FLSA's overtime requirements to SAMTA's operations. . . .

On November 17, 1981, the District Court granted SAMTA's motion for summary judgment. . . . Without further explanation, the District Court ruled that "local public mass transit systems (including [SAMTA]) constitute integral operations in areas of traditional governmental functions" under *National League of Cities*. . . . It recognized that States not always had owned and operated mass-transit systems, but concluded that they had engaged in a longstanding pattern of public regulation, and that this regulatory tradition gave rise to an "inference of sovereignty." . . . Finally, the court compared mass transit to the list of functions identified as constitutionally immune in *National League of Cities* and concluded that it did not differ from those functions in any material respect. The court stated: "If transit is to be distinguished from the exempt [*National League of Cities*] functions it will have to be by identifying a traditional state function in the same way pornography is sometimes identified: someone knows it when they see it, but they can't describe it."

. . . After initial argument, the cases were restored to our calendar for reargument, and the parties were requested to brief and argue the following additional question:

"Whether or not the principles of the Tenth Amendment as set forth in *National League of Cities v. Usery* should be reconsidered?" . . .

II

Appellees have not argued that SAMTA is immune from regulation under the FLSA on the ground that it is a local transit system engaged in intrastate commercial activity. In a practical sense, SAMTA's operations might well be characterized as "local." Nonetheless, it long has been settled that Congress' authority under the Commerce Clause extends to intrastate economic activities that affect interstate commerce. . . . *Wickard v. Filburn* (1942); *United States v. Darby* (1941). Were SAMTA a privately owned and operated enterprise, it could not credibly argue that Congress exceeded the bounds of its Commerce Clause powers in prescribing minimum wages and overtime rates for SAMTA's employees. Any constitutional exemption from the requirements of the FLSA therefore must rest on SAMTA's status as a governmental entity rather than on the "local" nature of its operations.

The prerequisites for governmental immunity under *National League of Cities* [include] four conditions [that] must be satisfied before a state activity may be deemed immune from a particular federal regulation under the Commerce Clause. First, it is said that the federal statute at issue must regulate "the 'States as States.'" Second, the statute must "address matters that are indisputably 'attribute[s] of state sovereignty.'" Third, state compliance with the federal obligation must "directly impair [the States'] ability 'to structure integral operations in areas of traditional governmental functions.'" Finally, the relation of state and federal interests must not be such that "the nature of the federal interest . . . justifies state submission."

The controversy in the present cases has focused on the third . . . requirement — that the challenged federal statute trench on "traditional governmental functions." The District Court voiced a common concern: "Despite the abundance of adjectives, identifying which particular state functions are immune remains difficult." Just how troublesome the task has been is revealed by the results reached in other federal cases. Thus, courts have held that regulating ambulance services, licensing automobile drivers, operating a municipal airport, performing solid waste disposal, and operating a highway authority are functions *protected* under *National League of Cities*. At the same time, courts have held that issuance of industrial development bonds, regulation of intrastate natural gas sales, regulation of traffic on public roads, regulation of air transportation, operation of a telephone system, leasing and sale of natural gas, operation of a mental health facility, and provision of in-house domestic services for the aged and handicapped are *not* entitled to immunity. We find it difficult, if not impossible, to identify an organizing principle that places each of the cases in the first group on one side of a line and each of the cases in the second group on the other side. The constitutional distinction between licensing drivers and regulating traffic, for example, or between operating a highway authority and operating a mental health facility, is elusive at best.

Thus far, this Court itself has made little headway in defining the scope of the governmental functions deemed protected under *National League of Cities*. In that case the Court set forth examples of protected and unprotected functions, but provided no explanation of how those examples were identified. [In] [t]he only other case in which the Court has had occasion to address the problem . . . [we] observed: "The determination of whether a federal law impairs a state's authority with respect to 'areas of traditional [state] functions' may at times be a difficult one." The accuracy of that statement is demonstrated by this Court's own difficulties in [*Transportation Union v.*] *Long Island* [*R. Co.*, 455 U.S. 678 (1982),] in developing a workable standard for "traditional governmental functions." We relied in large part . . . on "the *historical reality* that the operation of railroads is not among the functions *traditionally* performed by state and local governments," but we simultaneously disavowed "a static historical view of state functions generally immune from federal regulation." We held that the inquiry into a particular function's "traditional" nature was merely a means of determining whether the federal statute at issue unduly handicaps "basic state prerogatives," but we did not offer an explanation of what makes one state function a "basic prerogative" and another function not basic. Finally, having disclaimed a rigid reliance on the historical pedigree of state involvement in a particular area, we nonetheless found it appropriate to emphasize the extended historical record of *federal* involvement in the field of rail transportation.

Many constitutional standards involve "undoubte[d] . . . gray areas," . . . and, despite the difficulties that this Court and other courts have encountered so far, it normally might be fair to venture the assumption that case-by-case development would lead to a workable standard for determining whether a particular governmental function should be immune from federal regulation under the Commerce Clause. A further cautionary note is sounded, however, by the Court's experience in the related field of state immunity from federal taxation. [It was 40 years of] uncertainty and instability that led the Court . . . , in *New York v. United States* (1946), unanimously to conclude that the distinction between "governmental" and "proprietary" functions was "untenable" and must be abandoned.

* * *

The distinction the Court discarded as unworkable in the field of tax immunity has proved no more fruitful in the field of regulatory immunity under the Commerce Clause. Neither do any of the alternative standards that might be employed to distinguish between protected and unprotected governmental functions appear manageable. We rejected the possibility of making immunity turn on a purely historical standard of "tradition" . . . and properly so. The most obvious defect of a historical approach to state immunity is that it prevents a court from accommodating changes in the historical functions of States, changes that have resulted in a number of once-private functions like education being assumed by the States and their subdivisions. At the same time, the only apparent virtue of a rigorous historical standard, namely, its promise of a reasonably objective measure for state immunity, is illusory. Reliance on history as an organizing principle results in line-drawing of the most arbitrary sort; the genesis of state governmental functions stretches over a historical continuum from before the Revolution to the present, and courts would have to decide by fiat precisely how longstanding a pattern of state involvement had to be for federal regulatory authority to be defeated.

A nonhistorical standard for selecting immune governmental functions is likely to be just as unworkable as is a historical standard. The goal of identifying "uniquely" governmental functions, for example, has been rejected by the Court in the field of government tort liability in part because the notion of a "uniquely" governmental function is unmanageable. Another possibility would be to confine immunity to "necessary" governmental services, that is, services that would be provided inadequately or not at all unless the government provided them. The set of services that fits into this category, however, may well be negligible. The fact that an unregulated market produces less of some service than a State deems desirable does not mean that the State itself must provide the service; in most if not all cases, the State can "contract out" by hiring private firms to provide the service or simply by providing subsidies to existing suppliers. It also is open to question how well equipped courts are to make this kind of determination about the workings of economic markets.

We believe, however, that there is a more fundamental problem at work here, a problem that explains why the Court was never able to provide a basis for the governmental/proprietary distinction in the intergovernmental tax-immunity cases and why an attempt to draw similar distinctions with respect to federal regulatory authority under *National League of Cities* is unlikely to succeed regardless of how the distinctions are phrased. The problem is that neither the governmental/proprietary distinction nor any other that purports to separate out important governmental functions can be faithful to the role of federalism in a democratic society. The essence of our federal system is that within the realm of authority left open to them under the Constitution, the States must be equally free to engage in any activity that their citizens choose for the common weal, no matter how unorthodox or unnecessary anyone else — including the judiciary — deems state involvement to be. Any rule of state immunity that looks to the "traditional," "integral," or "necessary" nature of governmental functions inevitably invites an unelected federal judiciary to make decisions about which state policies it favors and which ones it dislikes. "The science of government . . . is the science of experiment," . . . and the States cannot serve as laboratories for social and economic experiment, if they must pay an added price when they meet the changing needs of their citizenry by taking up functions that an earlier day and a different society left in private hands. . . .

We therefore now reject, as unsound in principle and unworkable in practice, a rule of state immunity from federal regulation that turns on a judicial appraisal of whether a particular governmental function is "integral" or "traditional." Any such rule leads to inconsistent results at the same time that it disserves principles of democratic self-governance, and it breeds inconsistency precisely because it is divorced from those principles. If there are to be limits on the Federal Government's power to interfere with state functions — as undoubtedly there are — we must look elsewhere to find them. We accordingly return to the underlying issue that confronted this Court in *National League of Cities* — the manner in which the Constitution insulates States from the reach of Congress' power under the Commerce Clause.

* * *

We doubt that courts ultimately can identify principled constitutional limitations on the scope of Congress' Commerce Clause powers over the States merely by relying on *a priori* definitions of state sovereignty. In part, this is because of the elusiveness of objective criteria for "fundamental" elements of state sovereignty, a problem we have witnessed in the search for "traditional governmental functions." There is, however, a more fundamental reason: the sovereignty of the States is limited by the Constitution itself. A variety of sovereign powers, for example, are withdrawn from the States by Article I, § 10. Section 8 of the same Article works an equally sharp contraction of state sovereignty by authorizing Congress to exercise a wide range of legislative powers and (in conjunction with the Supremacy Clause of Article VI) to displace contrary state legislation. By providing for final review of questions of federal law in this Court, Article III curtails the sovereign power of the States' judiciaries to make authoritative determinations of law. . . . Finally, the developed application, through the Fourteenth Amendment, of the greater part of the Bill of Rights to the States limits the sovereign authority that States otherwise would possess to legislate with respect to their citizens and to conduct their own affairs.

The States unquestionably do "retai[n] a significant measure of sovereign authority." . . . They do so, however, only to the extent that the Constitution has not divested them of their original powers and transferred those powers to the Federal Government. In the words of James Madison to the Members of the First Congress: "Interference with the power of the States was no constitutional criterion of the power of Congress. If the power was not given, Congress could not exercise it; if given, they might exercise it, although it should interfere with the laws, or even the Constitution of the States." . . .

As a result, to say that the Constitution assumes the continued role of the States is to say little about the nature of that role. . . . With rare exceptions, like the guarantee, in Article IV, § 3, of state territorial integrity, the Constitution does not carve out express elements of state sovereignty that Congress may not employ its delegated powers to displace. James Wilson reminded the Pennsylvania ratifying convention in 1787: "It is true, indeed, sir, although it presupposes the existence of state governments, yet this Constitution does not suppose them to be the sole power to be respected." . . . The power of the Federal Government is a "power to be respected" as well, and the fact that the States remain sovereign as to all powers not vested in Congress or denied them by the Constitution offers no guidance about where the frontier between state and federal power lies. In short, we have no license to employ freestanding conceptions of state sovereignty when measuring congressional authority under the Commerce Clause.

When we look for the States' "residuary and inviolable sovereignty" . . . in the shape of the constitutional scheme rather than in predetermined notions of sovereign power, a different measure of state sovereignty emerges. Apart from the limitation on federal authority inherent in the delegated nature of Congress' Article I powers, the principal means chosen by the Framers to ensure the role of the States in the federal system lies in the structure of the Federal Government itself. It is no novelty to observe that the composition of the Federal Government was designed in large part to protect the States from overreaching by Congress. The Framers thus gave the States a role in the selection both of the Executive and the Legislative Branches of the Federal Government. The States were vested with indirect influence over the House of Representatives and the Presidency by their control of electoral qualifications and their role in Presidential elections. U.S. CONST., Art. I, § 2, and Art. II, § 1. They were given more direct influence in the Senate, where each State received equal representation and each Senator was to be selected by the legislature of his State. Art. I, § 3. The significance attached to the States' equal representation in the Senate is underscored by the prohibition of any constitutional amendment divesting a State of equal representation without the State's consent. Art. V.

The extent to which the structure of the Federal Government itself was relied on to insulate the interests of the States is evident in the views of the Framers. James Madison explained that the Federal Government "will partake sufficiently of the spirit [of the States], to be disinclined to invade the rights of the individual States, or the prerogatives of their governments." THE FEDERALIST NO. 46, at 332 (B. Wright ed. 1961) (J. Madison). Similarly, James Wilson observed that "it was a favorite object in the Convention" to provide for the security of the States against federal encroachment and that the structure of the Federal Government itself served that end. . . . Madison placed particular reliance on the equal representation of the States in the Senate, which he saw as "at once a constitutional recognition of the portion of sovereignty remaining in the individual States, and an instrument for preserving that residuary sovereignty." THE FEDERALIST NO. 62, at 408 (B. Wright ed. 1961) (J. Madison). . . . In short, the Framers chose to rely on a federal system in which special restraints on federal power over the States inhered principally in the workings of the National Government itself, rather than in discrete limitations on the objects of federal authority. . . .

The effectiveness of the federal political process in preserving the States' interests is apparent even today in the course of federal legislation. On the one hand, the States have been able to direct a substantial proportion of federal revenues into their own treasuries in the form of general and program-specific grants in aid. The federal role in assisting state and local governments is a longstanding one; Congress provided federal land grants to finance state governments from the beginning of the Republic, and direct cash grants were awarded as early as 1887. . . . As a result, federal grants now account for about one-fifth of state and local government expenditures. . . . Moreover, at the same time that the States have exercised their influence to obtain federal support, they have been able to exempt themselves from a wide variety of obligations imposed by Congress under the Commerce Clause. For example, the Federal Power Act, the National Labor Relations Act, the Labor-Management Reporting and Disclosure Act, the Occupational Safety and Health Act, the Employee Retirement Income Security Act, and the Sherman Act all contain express or implied exemptions for States and their subdivisions. The fact that some federal statutes such as the FLSA extend general obligations to the States cannot obscure the extent to which the political position of the States in the federal system has served to minimize the burdens that the States bear under the Commerce Clause.

We realize that changes in the structure of the Federal Government have taken place since 1789, not the least of which has been the substitution of popular election of Senators by the adoption of the Seventeenth Amendment in 1913, and that these changes may work to alter the influence of the States in the federal political process. Nonetheless, against this background, we are convinced that the fundamental limitation that the constitutional scheme imposes on the Commerce Clause to protect the "States as States" is one of process rather than one of result. Any substantive restraint on the exercise of Commerce Clause powers must find its justification in the procedural nature of this basic limitation, and it must be tailored to compensate for possible failings in the national political process rather than to dictate a "sacred province of state autonomy."

* * *

IV

This analysis makes clear that Congress' action in affording SAMTA employees the protections of the wage and hour provisions of the FLSA contravened no affirmative limit on Congress' power under the Commerce Clause. The judgment of the District Court therefore must be reversed.

* * *

We do not lightly overrule recent precedent. We have not hesitated, however, when it has become apparent that a prior decision has departed from a proper understanding of congressional power under the Commerce Clause. Due respect for the reach of congressional power within the federal system mandates that we do so now.

* * *

JUSTICE POWELL, with whom THE CHIEF JUSTICE, JUSTICE REHNQUIST, and JUSTICE O'CONNOR join, dissenting.

* * *

I

There are, of course, numerous examples over the history of this Court in which prior decisions have been reconsidered and overruled. There have been few cases, however, in which the principle of *stare decisis* and the rationale of recent decisions were ignored as abruptly as we now witness. The reasoning of the Court in *National League of Cities*, and the principle applied there, have been reiterated consistently over the past eight years. . . .

* * *

II

* * *

A

Much of the Court's opinion is devoted to arguing that it is difficult to define *a priori* "traditional governmental functions." . . . But nowhere does it mention that *National League of Cities* adopted a familiar type of balancing test for determining whether Commerce Clause enactments transgress constitutional limitations imposed by the federal nature of our system of government. This omission is noteworthy, since the author of today's opinion joined *National League of Cities* and concurred separately to point out that the Court's opinion in that case "adopt[s] a balancing approach [that] does not outlaw federal power in areas . . . where the federal interest is demonstrably greater and where state . . . compliance with imposed federal standards would be essential." . . .

In reading *National League of Cities* to embrace a balancing approach, JUSTICE BLACKMUN quite correctly cited the part of the opinion that reaffirmed *Fry v. United States* (1975). The Court's analysis reaffirming *Fry* explicitly weighed the seriousness of the problem addressed by the federal legislation at issue in that case, against the effects of compliance on state sovereignty. Our subsequent decisions also adopted this approach of weighing the respective interests of the States and Federal Government. In *EEOC v. Wyoming* (1983), for example, the Court stated that "[t]he principle of immunity articulated in *National League of Cities* is a functional doctrine . . . whose ultimate purpose is not to create a sacred province of state autonomy, but to ensure that the unique benefits of a federal system . . . not be lost through undue federal interference in certain core state functions." In overruling *National League of Cities*, the Court incorrectly characterizes the mode of analysis established therein and developed in subsequent cases.

Moreover, the statute at issue in this case, the FLSA, is the identical statute that was at issue in *National League of Cities*. Although JUSTICE BLACKMUN's concurrence noted that he was "not untroubled by certain possible implications of the Court's opinion" in *National League of Cities*, it also stated that "the result with respect to the statute under challenge here [the FLSA] is *necessarily correct*." His opinion for the Court today does not discuss the statute, nor identify any changed circumstances that warrant the conclusion today that *National League of Cities* is *necessarily wrong*.

B

Today's opinion does not explain how the States' role in the electoral process guarantees that particular exercises of the Commerce Clause power will not infringe on residual state sovereignty. Members of Congress are elected from the various States, but once in office they are Members of the Federal Government. Although the States participate in the Electoral College, this is hardly a reason to view the President as a representative of the States' interest against federal encroachment. We noted recently "[t]he hydraulic pressure inherent within each of the separate Branches to exceed the outer limits of its power . . . ." . . . The Court offers no reason to think that this pressure will not operate when Congress seeks to invoke its powers under the Commerce Clause, notwithstanding the electoral role of the States.

The Court apparently thinks that the States' success at obtaining federal funds for various projects and exemptions from the obligations of some federal statutes is indicative of the "effectiveness of the federal political process in preserving the States' interests." But such political success is not relevant to the question whether the political *processes* are the proper means of enforcing constitutional limitations. The fact that Congress generally does not transgress constitutional limits on its power to reach state activities does not make judicial review any less necessary to rectify the cases in which it does do so. The States' role in our system of government is a matter of constitutional law, not of legislative grace. "The powers not delegated to the United States by the Constitution, nor prohibited by it to the States, are reserved to the States, respectively, or to the people." U.S. CONST., Amend. 10.

More troubling than the logical infirmities in the Court's reasoning is the result of its holding, *i.e.*, that federal political officials, invoking the Commerce Clause, are the sole judges of the limits of their own power. This result is inconsistent with the fundamental principles of our constitutional system. *See, e.g.*, THE FEDERALIST NO. 78 (A. Hamilton). At least since *Marbury v. Madison* (1803), it has been the settled province of the federal judiciary "to say what the law is" with respect to the constitutionality of Acts of Congress. In rejecting the role of the judiciary in protecting the States from federal overreaching, the Court's opinion offers no explanation for ignoring the teaching of the most famous case in our history.

III

A

In our federal system, the States have a major role that cannot be pre-empted by the National Government. As contemporaneous writings and the debates at the ratifying conventions make clear, the States' ratification of the Constitution was predicated on this understanding of federalism. Indeed, the Tenth Amendment was adopted specifically to ensure that the important role promised the States by the proponents of the Constitution was realized.

Much of the initial opposition to the Constitution was rooted in the fear that the National Government would be too powerful and eventually would eliminate the States as viable political entities. This concern was voiced repeatedly until proponents of the Constitution made assurances that a Bill of Rights, including a provision explicitly reserving powers in the States, would be among the first business of the new Congress. Samuel Adams argued, for example, that if the several States were to be joined in "one entire Nation, under one Legislature, the Powers of which shall extend to every Subject of Legislation, and its Laws be supreme & controul the whole, the Idea of Sovereignty in these States must be lost." . . . Likewise, George Mason feared that "the general government being paramount to, and in every respect more powerful than the state governments, the latter must give way to the former." . . .

Antifederalists raised these concerns in almost every state ratifying convention. . . . As a result, eight States voted for the Constitution only after proposing amendments to be adopted after ratification. All eight of these included among their recommendations some version of what later became the Tenth Amendment. So strong was the concern that the proposed Constitution was seriously defective without a specific Bill of Rights, including a provision reserving powers to the States, that in order to secure the votes for ratification, the Federalists eventually conceded that such provisions were necessary. . . . It was thus generally agreed that consideration of a Bill of Rights would be among the first business of the new Congress. . . . Accordingly, the 10 Amendments that we know as the Bill of Rights were proposed and adopted early in the first session of the First Congress. . . .

This history, which the Court simply ignores, documents the integral role of the Tenth Amendment in our constitutional theory. It exposes as well, I believe, the fundamental character of the Court's error today. Far from being "unsound in principle," judicial enforcement of the Tenth Amendment is essential to maintaining the federal system so carefully designed by the Framers and adopted in the Constitution.

B

The Framers had definite ideas about the nature of the Constitution's division of authority between the Federal and State Governments. In THE FEDERALIST No. 39, for example, Madison explained this division by drawing a series of contrasts between the attributes of a "national" government and those of the government to be established by the Constitution. While a national form of government would possess an "indefinite supremacy over all persons and things," the form of government contemplated by the Constitution instead consisted of "local or municipal authorities [which] form distinct and independent portions of the supremacy, no more subject within their respective spheres to the general authority, than the general authority is subject to them, within its own sphere." Under the Constitution, the sphere of the proposed government extended to jurisdiction of "certain enumerated objects only, . . . leav[ing] to the several States a residuary and inviolable sovereignty over all other objects."

Madison elaborated on the content of these separate spheres of sovereignty in THE FEDERALIST NO. 45:

> "The powers delegated by the proposed Constitution to the Federal Government, are few and defined. Those which are to remain in the State Governments are numerous and indefinite. The former will be exercised principally on external objects, as war, peace, negociation, and foreign commerce. . . . The powers reserved to the several States will extend to all the objects, which, in the ordinary course of affairs, concern the lives, liberties and properties of the people; and the internal order, improvement, and prosperity of the State."

Madison considered that the operations of the Federal Government would be "most extensive and important in times of war and danger; those of the State Governments in times of peace and security." As a result of this division of powers, the state governments generally would be more important than the Federal Government.

The Framers believed that the separate sphere of sovereignty reserved to the States would ensure that the States would serve as an effective "counterpoise" to the power of the Federal Government. The States would serve this essential role because they would attract and retain the loyalty of their citizens. The roots of such loyalty, the Founders thought, were found in the objects peculiar to state government. For example, Hamilton argued that the States "regulat[e] all those personal interests and familiar concerns to which the sensibility of individuals is more immediately awake . . . ." THE FEDERALIST NO. 17, at 107 (J. Cooke ed. 1961) (A. Hamilton). Thus, he maintained that the people would perceive the States as "the immediate and visible guardian of life and property," a fact which "contributes more than any other circumstance to impressing upon the minds of the people affection, esteem and reverence towards the government." Madison took the same position, explaining that "the people will be more familiarly and minutely conversant" with the business of state governments, and "with the members of these, will a greater proportion of the people have the ties of personal acquaintance and friendship, and of family and party attachments . . . ." THE FEDERALIST NO. 46, at 316 (J. Cooke ed. 1961) (J. Madison). Like Hamilton, Madison saw the States' involvement in the everyday concerns of the people as the source of their citizens' loyalty.

Thus, the harm to the States that results from federal overreaching under the Commerce Clause is not simply a matter of dollars and cents. Nor is it a matter of the wisdom or folly of certain policy choices. Rather, by usurping functions traditionally performed by the States, federal overreaching under the Commerce Clause undermines the constitutionally mandated balance of power between the States and the Federal Government, a balance designed to protect our fundamental liberties.

C

The emasculation of the powers of the States that can result from the Court's decision is predicated on the Commerce Clause as a power "delegated to the United States" by the Constitution. The relevant language states: "Congress shall have power . . . To regulate Commerce with foreign Nations, and among the several States, and with the Indian Tribes." Art. I, § 8, cl. 3. Section 8 identifies a score of powers, listing the authority to lay taxes, borrow money on the credit of the United States, pay its debts, and provide for the common defense and the general welfare *before* its brief reference to "Commerce." It is clear from the debates leading up to the adoption of the Constitution that the commerce to be regulated was that which the States themselves lacked the practical capability to regulate. . . . Indeed, the language of the Clause itself focuses on activities that only a National Government could regulate: commerce with foreign nations and Indian tribes and "*among*" the several States.

To be sure, this Court has construed the Commerce Clause to accommodate unanticipated changes over the past two centuries. As these changes have occurred, the Court has had to decide whether the Federal Government has exceeded its authority by regulating activities beyond the capability of a single State to regulate or beyond legitimate federal interests that outweighed the authority and interests of the States. In so doing, however, the Court properly has been mindful of the essential role of the States in our federal system.

The opinion for the Court in *National League of Cities* was faithful to history in its understanding of federalism. . . .

This Court has recognized repeatedly that state sovereignty is a fundamental component of our system of government. . . . [T]he States are not merely a factor in the "shifting economic arrangements" of our country, . . . but also constitute a "coordinate element in the system established by the Framers for governing our Federal Union."

D

In contrast, the Court today propounds a view of federalism that pays only lipservice to the role of the States. Although it says that the States "unquestionably do 'retai[n] a significant measure of sovereign authority,'" it fails to recognize the broad, yet specific areas of sovereignty that the Framers intended the States to retain. Indeed, the Court barely acknowledges that the Tenth Amendment exists. That Amendment states explicitly that "[t]he powers not delegated to the United States . . . are reserved to the States." The Court recasts this language to say that the States retain their sovereign powers "only to the extent that the Constitution has not divested them of their original powers and transferred those powers to the Federal Government." This rephrasing is not a distinction without a difference; rather, it reflects the Court's unprecedented view that Congress is free under the Commerce Clause to assume a State's traditional sovereign power, and to do so without judicial review of its action. Indeed, the Court's view of federalism appears to relegate the States to precisely the trivial role that opponents of the Constitution feared they would occupy.

* * *

IV

The question presented in these cases is whether the extension of the FLSA to the wages and hours of employees of a city-owned transit system unconstitutionally impinges on fundamental state sovereignty. The Court's sweeping holding does far more than simply answer this question in the negative. In overruling *National League of Cities*, today's opinion apparently authorizes federal control, under the auspices of the Commerce Clause, over the terms and conditions of employment of all state and local employees. Thus, for purposes of federal regulation, the Court rejects the distinction between public and private employers that had been drawn carefully in *National League of Cities*. The Court's action reflects a serious misunderstanding, if not an outright rejection, of the history of our country and the intention of the Framers of the Constitution.

* * *

The Court emphasizes that municipal operation of an intra-city mass transit system is relatively new in the life of our country. It nevertheless is a classic example of the type of service traditionally provided by local government. It is *local* by definition. It is indistinguishable in principle from the traditional services of providing and maintaining streets, public lighting, traffic control, water, and sewerage systems. Services of this kind are precisely those with which citizens are more "familiarly and minutely conversant." THE FEDERALIST NO. 46, at 316 (J. Cooke ed. 1961). State and local officials of course must be intimately familiar with these services and sensitive to their quality as well as cost. Such officials also know that their constituents and the press respond to the adequacy, fair distribution, and cost of these services. It is this kind of state and local control and accountability that the Framers understood would insure the vitality and preservation of the federal system that the Constitution explicitly requires.

V

Although the Court's opinion purports to recognize that the States retain some sovereign power, it does not identify even a single aspect of state authority that would remain when the Commerce Clause is invoked to justify federal regulation. In *Maryland v. Wirtz* (1968), overruled by *National League of Cities* and today reaffirmed, the Court sustained an extension of the FLSA to certain hospitals, institutions, and schools. Although the Court's opinion in *Wirtz* was comparatively narrow, Justice Douglas, in dissent, wrote presciently that the Court's reading of the Commerce Clause would enable "the National Government [to] devour the essentials of state sovereignty, though that sovereignty is attested by the Tenth Amendment." Today's decision makes Justice Douglas' fear once again a realistic one.

* * *

JUSTICE REHNQUIST, dissenting.

I join both Justice Powell's and Justice O'Connor's thoughtful dissents. Justice Powell's reference to the "balancing test" approved in National League of Cities is not identical with the language in that case, which recognized that Congress could not act under its commerce power to infringe on certain fundamental aspects of state sovereignty that are essential to "the States' separate and independent existence." Nor is either test, or Justice O'Connor's suggested approach, precisely congruent with Justice Blackmun's views in 1976, when he spoke of a balancing approach which did not outlaw federal power in areas "where the federal interest is demonstrably greater." But under any one of these approaches the judgment in these cases should be affirmed, and I do not think it incumbent on those of us in dissent to spell out further the fine points of a principle that will, I am confident, in time again command the support of a majority of this Court.

JUSTICE O'CONNOR, with whom JUSTICE POWELL and JUSTICE REHNQUIST join, dissenting. [Omitted.]

NOTES AND QUESTIONS

1. The issues posed by *National League of Cities* and *Garcia*, as the judges well understand, go right to the heart of what the nature of the United States ought to be. They are about what we often refer to as "federalism," our system of "dual sovereignty," shared between the state and federal governments. These are long opinions, even after considerable editing, and even after omitting several concurring and dissenting opinions, there is much to slog through.

Once having done it, however, you have been exposed to some very interesting debate about what federalism ought to mean now and what it meant to the framers, and, in Justice Powell's dissent in *Garcia* at least, to a very elegant mini-treatise on late twentieth century political science.

2. Can you also understand how, when just a few years after *National League of Cities* was decided it was overruled by *Garcia,* many Court observers threw up their hands in despair and wondered whether there was really anything left to constitutional law but the whims of shifting five-person majorities on the Court?

3. How do you preserve the original scheme of dual sovereignty, especially in light of the fact that the power of the state governments has been steadily eroded, not only through things like the explosive growth of the federal bureaucracy in the twentieth century, but also through such "reforms" as the popular election of United States Senators, now codified in the Seventeenth Amendment, and the development of national political parties, which in our era have effectively transformed the nature of American politics? Who has a better grasp on the nature of political reality — the majority in *National League of Cities* or the majority in *Garcia*? And by the way, does natural law have anything to tell us about questions of federalism? Is there, for example, some natural law thinking reflected in Justice Powell's analysis, particularly in his reliance on THE FEDERALIST NOS. 17 and 46?

4. Why do you think the majority in *National League of Cities* and the dissenters in *Garcia* conceded that the FLSA was clearly within the scope of the commerce power (apart from any limits imposed by the Tenth Amendment), even when applied to governmental functions having nothing to do with commerce? Does the *Lopez* case considered in Chapter Four suggest that the current Court has reconsidered that concession?

5. While *Lopez* was not concerned directly with the Tenth Amendment, it still struck a blow in favor of the sort of ideas suggested by Justice Powell's dissent in *Garcia*. What, if anything, is left of the Tenth Amendment? Is the limitation stated in the next case mere formality?

B. No Commandeering Allowed — The States Are Not Sub-Agencies of the Federal Government

PRINTZ v. UNITED STATES
521 U.S. 898 (1997)

JUSTICE SCALIA delivered the opinion of the Court.

The question presented in these cases is whether certain interim provisions of the Brady Handgun Violence Prevention Act, Pub. L. 103-159, 107 Stat. 1536, commanding state and local law enforcement officers to conduct background checks on prospective handgun purchasers and to perform certain related tasks, violate the Constitution.

I

The Gun Control Act of 1968 (GCA) establishes a detailed federal scheme governing the distribution of firearms. It prohibits firearms dealers from transferring handguns to any person under 21, not resident in the dealer's State, or prohibited by state or local law from purchasing or possessing firearms. It also forbids possession of a firearm by, and transfer of a firearm to, convicted felons, fugitives from justice, unlawful users of controlled substances, persons adjudicated as mentally defective or committed to mental institutions, aliens unlawfully present in the United States, persons dishonorably discharged from the Armed Forces, persons who have renounced their citizenship, and persons who have been subjected to certain restraining orders or been convicted of a misdemeanor offense involving domestic violence.

In 1993, Congress amended the GCA by enacting the Brady Act. The Act requires the Attorney General to establish a national instant background check system by November 30, 1998 and immediately puts in place certain interim provisions until that system becomes operative. Under the interim provisions, a firearms dealer who proposes to transfer a handgun must first: (1) receive from the transferee a statement (the Brady Form), containing the name, address and date of birth of the proposed transferee along with a sworn statement that the transferee is not among any of the classes of prohibited purchasers; (2) verify the identity of the transferee by examining an identification document; and (3) provide the "chief law enforcement officer" (CLEO) of the transferee's residence with notice of the contents (and a copy) of the Brady Form. With some exceptions, the dealer must then wait five business days before consummating the sale, unless the CLEO earlier notifies the dealer that he has no reason to believe the transfer would be illegal.

The Brady Act creates two significant alternatives to the foregoing scheme. A dealer may sell a handgun immediately if the purchaser possesses a state handgun permit issued after a background check, or if state law provides for an instant background check. In States that have not rendered one of these alternatives applicable to all gun purchasers, CLEOs are required to perform certain duties. When a CLEO receives the required notice of a proposed transfer from the firearms dealer, the CLEO must "make a reasonable effort to ascertain within 5 business days whether receipt or possession would be in violation of the law, including research in whatever State and local recordkeeping systems are available and in a national system designated by the Attorney General." The Act does not require the CLEO to take any particular action if he determines that a pending transaction would be unlawful; he may notify the firearms dealer to that effect, but is not required to do so. If, however, the CLEO notifies a gun dealer that a prospective purchaser is ineligible to receive a handgun, he must, upon request, provide the would-be purchaser with a written statement of the reasons for that determination. Moreover, if the CLEO does not discover any basis for objecting to the sale, he must destroy any records in his possession relating to the transfer, including his copy of the Brady Form. Under a separate provision of the GCA, any person who "knowingly violates [the section of the GCA amended by the Brady Act] shall be fined under this title, imprisoned for no more than 1 year, or both."

Petitioners Jay Printz and Richard Mack, the CLEOs for Ravalli County, Montana, and Graham County, Arizona, respectively, filed separate actions challenging the constitutionality of the Brady Act's interim provisions. In each case, the District Court held that the provision requiring CLEOs to perform background checks was unconstitutional, but concluded that that provision was severable from the remainder of the Act, effectively leaving a voluntary background-check system in place. A divided panel of the Court of Appeals for the Ninth Circuit reversed, finding none of the Brady Act's interim provisions to be unconstitutional. . . .

II

From the description set forth above, it is apparent that the Brady Act purports to direct state law enforcement officers to participate, albeit only temporarily, in the administration of a federally enacted regulatory scheme. . . .

The petitioners here object to being pressed into federal service, and contend that congressional action compelling state officers to execute federal laws is unconstitutional. Because there is no constitutional text speaking to this precise question, the answer to the CLEOs' challenge must be sought in historical understanding and practice, in the structure of the Constitution, and in the jurisprudence of this Court. . . .

Petitioners contend that compelled enlistment of state executive officers for the administration of federal programs is, until very recent years at least, unprecedented. The Government contends, to the contrary, that "the earliest Congresses enacted statutes that required the participation of state officials in the implementation of federal laws[.]" The Government's contention demands our careful consideration, since early congressional enactments "provid[e] 'contemporaneous and weighty evidence' of the Constitution's meaning" . . . . Indeed, such "contemporaneous legislative exposition of the Constitution . . ., acquiesced in for a long term of years, fixes the construction to be given its provisions." *Myers v. United States* (1926). Conversely if, as petitioners contend, earlier Congresses avoided use of this highly attractive power, we would have reason to believe that the power was thought not to exist.

The Government observes that statutes enacted by the first Congresses required state courts to record applications for citizenship, to transmit abstracts of citizenship applications and other naturalization records to the Secretary of State, and to register aliens seeking naturalization and issue certificates of registry. It may well be, however, that these requirements applied only in States that authorized their courts to conduct naturalization proceedings. . . . Other statutes of that era apparently or at least arguably required state courts to perform functions unrelated to naturalization, such as resolving controversies between a captain and the crew of his ship concerning the seaworthiness of the vessel, hearing the claims of slave owners who had apprehended fugitive slaves and issuing certificates authorizing the slave's forced removal to the State from which he had fled, taking proof of the claims of Canadian refugees who had assisted the United States during the Revolutionary War, and ordering the deportation of alien enemies in times of war.

These early laws establish, at most, that the Constitution was originally understood to permit imposition of an obligation on state *judges* to enforce federal prescriptions, insofar as those prescriptions related to matters appropriate for the judicial power. That assumption was perhaps implicit in one of the provisions of the Constitution, and was explicit in another. In accord with the so-called Madisonian Compromise, Article III, § 1, established only a Supreme Court, and made the creation of lower federal courts optional with the Congress — even though it was obvious that the Supreme Court alone could not hear all federal cases throughout the United States. . . . And the Supremacy Clause, Art. VI, cl. 2, announced that "the Laws of the United States . . . shall be the supreme Law of the Land; and the Judges in every State shall be bound thereby." It is understandable why courts should have been viewed distinctively in this regard; unlike legislatures and executives, they applied the law of other sovereigns all the time. The principle underlying so-called "transitory" causes of action was that laws which operated elsewhere created obligations in justice that courts of the forum state would enforce. The Constitution itself, in the Full Faith and Credit Clause, Art. IV, § 1, generally required such enforcement with respect to obligations arising in other States. . . .

For these reasons, we do not think the early statutes imposing obligations on state courts imply a power of Congress to impress the state executive into its service. Indeed, it can be argued that the numerousness of these statutes, contrasted with the utter lack of statutes imposing obligations on the States' executive (notwithstanding the attractiveness of that course to Congress), suggests an assumed *absence* of such power. The only early federal law the Government has brought to our attention that imposed duties on state executive officers is the Extradition Act of 1793, which required the "executive authority" of a State to cause the arrest and delivery of a fugitive from justice upon the request of the executive authority of the State from which the fugitive had fled. That was in direct implementation, however, of the Extradition Clause of the Constitution itself, *see* Art. IV, § 2.

Not only do the enactments of the early Congresses, as far as we are aware, contain no evidence of an assumption that the Federal Government may command the States' executive power in the absence of a particularized constitutional authorization, they contain some indication of precisely the opposite assumption. On September 23, 1789 — the day before its proposal of the Bill of Rights — the First Congress enacted a law aimed at obtaining state assistance of the most rudimentary and necessary sort for the enforcement of the new Government's laws: the holding of federal prisoners in state jails at federal expense. Significantly, the law issued not a command to the States' executive, but a recommendation to their legislatures. Congress "recommended to the legislatures of the several States to pass laws, making it expressly the duty of the keepers of their gaols, to receive and safe keep therein all prisoners committed under the authority of the United States," and offered to pay 50 cents per month for each prisoner. Moreover, when Georgia refused to comply with the request, Congress's only reaction was a law authorizing the marshal in any State that failed to comply with the Recommendation of September 23, 1789, to rent a temporary jail until provision for a permanent one could be made. . . .

In addition to early legislation, the Government also appeals to other sources we have usually regarded as indicative of the original understanding of the

Constitution. It points to portions of THE FEDERALIST which reply to criticisms that Congress's power to tax will produce two sets of revenue officers — for example, "Brutus's" assertion in his letter to the New York Journal of December 13, 1787, that the Constitution "opens a door to the appointment of a swarm of revenue and excise officers to prey upon the honest and industrious part of the community, eat up their substance, and riot on the spoils of the country." . . . "Publius" responded that Congress will probably "make use of the State officers and State regulations, for collecting" federal taxes, . . . and predicted that "the eventual collection [of internal revenue] under the immediate authority of the Union, will generally be made by the officers, and according to the rules, appointed by the several States," THE FEDERALIST NO. 45 (J. Madison). The Government also invokes the FEDERALIST's more general observations that the Constitution would "enable the [national] government to employ the ordinary magistracy of each [State] in the execution of its laws," THE FEDERALIST NO. 27 (A. Hamilton), and that it was "extremely probable that in other instances, particularly in the organization of the judicial power, the officers of the States will be clothed in the correspondent authority of the Union," THE FEDERALIST NO. 45 (J. Madison). But none of these statements necessarily implies — what is the critical point here — that Congress could impose these responsibilities *without the consent of the States.* They appear to rest on the natural assumption that the States would consent to allowing their officials to assist the Federal Government, an assumption proved correct by the extensive mutual assistance the States and Federal Government voluntarily provided one another in the early days of the Republic, . . . including voluntary *federal implementation of state law.*

Another passage of THE FEDERALIST reads as follows:

> "It merits particular attention . . ., that the laws of the Confederacy as to the *enumerated* and *legitimate* objects of its jurisdiction will become the SUPREME LAW of the land; to the observance of which all officers, legislative, executive, and judicial in each State will be bound by the sanctity of an oath. Thus, the legislatures, courts, and magistrates, of the respective members will be incorporated into the operations of the national government *as far as its just and constitutional authority extends*; and will be rendered auxiliary to the enforcement of its laws." THE FEDERALIST NO. 27 (A. Hamilton) (emphasis in original).

The Government does not rely upon this passage, but JUSTICE SOUTER . . . makes it the very foundation of his position; so we pause to examine it in some detail. JUSTICE SOUTER finds "[t]he natural reading" of the phrases "will be incorporated into the operations of the national government" and "will be rendered auxiliary to the enforcement of its laws" to be that the National Government will have "authority . . ., when exercising an otherwise legitimate power (the commerce power, say), to require state 'auxiliaries' to take appropriate action." There are several obstacles to such an interpretation. First, the consequences in question . . . are said in the quoted passage to flow *automatically* from the officers' oath to observe the "the laws of the Confederacy as to the *enumerated* and *legitimate* objects of its jurisdiction." Thus, if the passage means that state officers must take an active role in the implementation of federal law, it means that they must do so without the necessity for a congressional directive that they implement it. But no one has ever thought, and no one asserts in the present litigation, that that is the law. The second problem with JUSTICE SOUTER's reading is that it makes state *legislatures* subject to federal direction. (The passage in question, after all, does not include legislatures merely incidentally, as by referring to "all state officers"; it refers to legislatures *specifically* and *first of all*.) We have held, however, that state legislatures are not subject to federal direction. *New York v. United States* (1992).

These problems are avoided, of course, if the calculatedly vague consequences the passage recites — "incorporated into the operations of the national government" and "rendered auxiliary to the enforcement of its laws" — are taken to refer to nothing more (or less) than the duty owed to the National Government, on the part of *all* state officials, to enact, enforce, and interpret state law in such fashion as not to obstruct the operation of federal law, and the attendant reality that all state actions constituting such obstruction, even legislative acts, are *ipso facto* invalid. . . .

JUSTICE SOUTER contends that his interpretation of FEDERALIST NO. 27 is "supported by No. 44," written by Madison, wherefore he claims that "Madison and Hamilton" together stand opposed to our view. In fact, FEDERALIST NO. 44 quite clearly contradicts JUSTICE SOUTER's reading. In that Number, Madison justifies the requirement that state officials take an oath to support the Federal Constitution on the ground that they "will have an essential agency in giving effect to the federal Constitution." If the dissent's reading of FEDERALIST NO. 27 were correct (and if Madison agreed with it), one would surely have expected that "essential agency" of state executive officers (if described further) to be described as their responsibility to execute the laws enacted under the Constitution. Instead, however, FEDERALIST NO. 44 continues with the following description:

> "The election of the President and Senate will depend, in all cases, on the legislatures of the several States. And the election of the House of Representatives will equally depend on the same authority in the first instance; and will, probably, forever be *conducted by the officers* and according to the laws *of the States*."

It is most implausible that the person who labored for that example of state executive officers' assisting the Federal Government believed, but neglected to mention, that they had a responsibility to execute federal laws. If it was indeed Hamilton's view that the Federal Government could direct the officers of the States, that view has no clear support in Madison's writings, or as far as we are aware, in text, history, or early commentary elsewhere.

To complete the historical record, we must note that there is not only an absence of executive-commandeering statutes in the early Congresses, but there is an absence of them in our later history as well, at least until very recent years. The Government points to [an 1882 act] which enlisted state officials "to take charge of the local affairs of immigration in the ports within such State, and to provide for the support and relief of such immigrants therein landing as may fall into distress or need of public aid"; to inspect arriving immigrants and exclude any person found to be a "convict, lunatic, idiot," or indigent; and to send convicts back to their country of origin "without compensation." The statute did not, however, *mandate* those duties, but merely empowered the Secretary of the Treasury "to *enter into contracts* with such State . . . officers as *may be designated* for that purpose *by the governor* of any State." (Emphasis added.)

The Government cites the World War I selective draft law that authorized the President "to utilize the service of any or all departments and any or all officers or agents of the United States *and of the several States*, Territories, and the District of Columbia, and subdivisions thereof, in the execution of this Act," and made any person who refused to comply with the President's directions guilty of a misdemeanor. However, it is far from clear that the authorization "to utilize the service" of state officers was an authorization to *compel* the service of state officers; and the misdemeanor provision surely applied only to refusal to comply with the President's *authorized* directions, which might not have included directions to officers of States whose governors had not volunteered their services. It is interesting that in implementing the Act President Wilson did not commandeer the services of state officers, but instead requested the assistance of the States' governors, obtained the consent of each of the governors, and left it to the governors to issue orders to their subordinate state officers. It is impressive that even with respect to a wartime measure the President should have been so solicitous of state independence.

The Government points to a number of federal statutes enacted within the past few decades that require the participation of state or local officials in implementing federal regulatory schemes. Some of these are connected to federal funding measures, and can perhaps be more accurately described as conditions upon the grant of federal funding than as mandates to the States; others, which require only the provision of information to the Federal Government, do not involve the precise issue before us here, which is the forced participation of the States' executive in the actual administration of a federal program. . . . Even assuming they represent assertion of the very same congressional power challenged here, they are of such recent vintage that they are no more probative than the statute before us of a constitutional tradition that lends meaning to the text. Their persuasive force is far outweighed by almost two centuries of apparent congressional avoidance of the practice. . . .

III

The constitutional practice we have examined above tends to negate the existence of the congressional power asserted here, but is not conclusive. We turn next to consideration of the structure of the Constitution, to see if we can discern among its "essential postulate[s]," *Principality of Monaco v. Mississippi* (1934), a principle that controls the present cases.

A

It is incontestible that the Constitution established a system of "dual sovereignty." . . . Although the States surrendered many of their powers to the new Federal Government, they retained "a residuary and inviolable sovereignty," THE FEDERALIST NO. 39 (J. Madison). This is reflected throughout the Constitution's text, including (to mention only a few examples) the prohibition on any involuntary reduction or combination of a State's territory, Art. IV, § 3; the Judicial Power Clause, Art. III, § 2, and the Privileges and Immunities Clause, Art. IV, § 2, which speak of the "Citizens" of the States; the amendment provision, Article V, which requires the votes of three-fourths of the States to amend the Constitution; and the Guarantee Clause, Art. IV, § 4, which "presupposes the continued existence of the states and . . . those means and instrumentalities which are the creation of their sovereign and reserved rights." . . . Residual state sovereignty was also implicit, of course, in the Constitution's conferral upon Congress of not all governmental powers, but only discrete, enumerated ones, Art. I, § 8, which implication was rendered express by the Tenth Amendment's assertion that "[t]he powers not delegated to the United States by the Constitution, nor prohibited by it to the States, are reserved to the States respectively, or to the people."

The Framers' experience under the Articles of Confederation had persuaded them that using the States as the instruments of federal governance was both ineffectual and provocative of federal-state conflict. Preservation of the States as independent political entities being the price of union, and "[t]he practicality of making laws, with coercive sanctions, for the States as political bodies" having been, in Madison's words, "exploded on all hands," . . . the Framers rejected the concept of a central government that would act upon and through the States, and instead designed a system in which the state and federal governments would exercise concurrent authority over the people — who were, in Hamilton's words, "the only proper objects of government," THE FEDERALIST NO. 15 (A. Hamilton). "The Framers explicitly chose a Constitution that confers upon Congress the power to regulate individuals, not States." The great innovation of this design was that "our citizens would have two political capacities, one state and one federal, each protected from incursion by the other" — "a legal system unprecedented in form and design, establishing two orders of government, each with its own direct relationship, its own privity, its own set of mutual rights and obligations to the people who sustain it and are governed by it." . . . The Constitution thus contemplates that a State's government will represent and remain accountable to its own citizens. . . .

This separation of the two spheres is one of the Constitution's structural protections of liberty. "Just as the separation and independence of the coordinate branches of the Federal Government serve to prevent the accumulation of excessive power in any one branch, a healthy balance of power between the States and the Federal Government will reduce the risk of tyranny and abuse from either front." To quote Madison once again:

> "In the compound republic of America, the power surrendered by the people is first divided between two distinct governments, and then the portion allotted to each subdivided among distinct and separate departments. Hence a double security arises to the rights of the people. The different governments will control each other, at the same time that each will be controlled by itself." THE FEDERALIST NO. 51.

. . . The power of the Federal Government would be augmented immeasurably if it were able to impress into its service — and at no cost to itself — the police officers of the 50 States.

B

We have thus far discussed the effect that federal control of state officers would have upon the first element of the "double security" alluded to by Madison: the division of power between State and Federal Governments. It would also have an effect upon the second element: the separation and equilibration of powers between the three branches of the Federal Government itself. The Constitution does not leave to speculation who is to administer the laws enacted by Congress; the President, it says, "shall take Care that the Laws be faithfully executed," Art. II, § 3, personally and through officers whom he appoints . . . Art. II, § 2. The Brady Act effectively transfers this responsibility to thousands of CLEOs in the 50 States, who are left to implement the program without meaningful Presidential control (if indeed meaningful Presidential control is possible without the power to appoint and remove). The insistence of the Framers upon unity in the Federal Executive — to insure both vigor and accountability — is well known. . . . That unity would be shattered, and the power of the President would be subject to reduction, if Congress could act as effectively without the President as with him, by simply requiring state officers to execute its laws. . . .

C

The dissent of course resorts to the last, best hope of those who defend *ultra vires* congressional action, the Necessary and Proper Clause. It reasons that the power to regulate the sale of handguns under the Commerce Clause, coupled with the power to "make all Laws which shall be necessary and proper for carrying into Execution the foregoing Powers," Art. I, § 8, conclusively establishes the Brady Act's constitutional validity, because the Tenth Amendment imposes no limitations on the exercise of *delegated* powers but merely prohibits the exercise of powers "*not* delegated to the United States." What destroys the dissent's Necessary and Proper Clause argument, however, is not the Tenth Amendment but the Necessary and Proper Clause itself. When a "La[w] . . . for carrying into Execution" the Commerce Clause violates the principle of state sovereignty reflected in the various constitutional provisions we mentioned earlier, it is not a "La[w] . . . *proper* for carrying into Execution the Commerce Clause," and is thus, in the words of THE FEDERALIST, "merely [an] ac[t] of usurpation" which "deserve[s] to be treated as such." THE FEDERALIST NO. 33 (A. Hamilton). . . . We in fact answered the dissent's Necessary and Proper Clause argument in *New York*: "[E]ven where Congress has the authority under the Constitution to pass laws requiring or prohibiting certain acts, it lacks the power directly to compel the States to require or prohibit those acts. . . . [T]he Commerce Clause, for example, authorizes Congress to regulate interstate commerce directly; it does not authorize Congress to regulate state governments' regulation of interstate commerce."

The dissent perceives a simple answer in that portion of Article VI which requires that "all executive and judicial Officers, both of the United States and of the several States, shall be bound by Oath or Affirmation, to support this Constitution," arguing that by virtue of the Supremacy Clause this makes "not only the Constitution, but every law enacted by Congress as well," binding on state officers, including laws requiring state-officer enforcement. The Supremacy Clause, however, makes "Law of the Land" only "Laws of the United States which shall be made in Pursuance [of the Constitution]"; so the Supremacy Clause merely brings us back to the question discussed earlier, whether laws conscripting state officers violate state sovereignty and are thus not in accord with the Constitution.

IV

Finally, and most conclusively in the present litigation, we turn to the prior jurisprudence of this Court. Federal commandeering of state governments is such a novel phenomenon that this Court's first experience with it did not occur until the 1970's, when the Environmental Protection Agency promulgated regulations requiring States to prescribe auto emissions testing, monitoring and retrofit programs, and to designate preferential bus and carpool lanes. The Courts of Appeals for the Fourth and Ninth Circuits invalidated the regulations on statutory grounds in order to avoid what they perceived to be grave constitutional issues, . . . and the District of Columbia Circuit invalidated the regulations on both constitutional and statutory grounds. After we granted certiorari to review the statutory and constitutional validity of the regulations, the Government declined even to defend them, and instead rescinded some and conceded the invalidity of those that remained, leading us to vacate the opinions below and remand for consideration of mootness. *EPA v. Brown* (1977).

Although we had no occasion to pass upon the subject in *Brown*, later opinions of ours have made clear that the Federal Government may not compel the States to implement, by legislation or executive action, federal regulatory programs. In *Hodel v. Virginia Surface Mining & Reclamation Assn., Inc.* (1981), and *FERC v. Mississippi* (1982), we sustained statutes against constitutional challenge only after assuring ourselves that they did not require the States to enforce federal law. In *Hodel* we cited the lower court cases [discussing the EPA regulations described above], but concluded that the Surface Mining Control and Reclamation Act did not present the problem they raised because it merely made compliance with federal standards a precondition to continued state regulation in an otherwise pre-empted field. In *FERC*, we construed the most troubling provisions of the Public Utility Regulatory Policies Act of 1978, to contain only the "command" that state agencies "consider" federal standards, and again only as a precondition to continued state regulation of an otherwise pre-empted field. We warned that "this Court never has sanctioned explicitly a federal command to the States to promulgate and enforce laws and regulations[.]"

When we were at last confronted squarely with a federal statute that unambiguously required the States to enact or administer a federal regulatory program, our decision should have come as no surprise. At issue in *New York v. United States* were the so-called "take title" provisions of the Low-Level Radioactive Waste Policy Amendments Act of 1985, which required States either to enact legislation providing for the disposal of radioactive waste generated within their borders, or to take title to, and possession of the waste — effectively requiring the States either to legislate pursuant to Congress's directions, or to implement an administrative solution. We concluded that Congress could constitutionally require the States to do neither. "The Federal Government," we held, "may not compel the States to enact or administer a federal regulatory program."

The Government contends that *New York* is distinguishable on the following ground: unlike the "take title" provisions invalidated there, the background-check provision of the Brady Act does not require state legislative or executive officials to make policy, but instead issues a final directive to state CLEOs. It is permissible, the Government asserts, for Congress to command state or local officials to assist in the implementation of federal law so long as "Congress itself devises a clear legislative solution that regulates private conduct" and requires state or local officers to provide only "limited, non-policymaking help in enforcing that law." "[T]he constitutional line is crossed only when Congress compels the States to make law in their sovereign capacities."

The Government's distinction between "making" law and merely "enforcing" it, between "policymaking" and mere "implementation," is an interesting one. It is perhaps not meant to be the same as, but it is surely reminiscent of, the line that separates proper congressional conferral of Executive power from unconstitutional delegation of legislative authority for federal separation-of-powers purposes. *See A.L.A. Schechter Poultry Corp. v. United States* (1935); *Panama Refining Co. v. Ryan* (1935). This Court has not been notably successful in describing the latter line; indeed, some think we have abandoned the effort to do so. We are doubtful that the new line the Government proposes would be any more distinct. Executive action that has utterly no policymaking component is rare, particularly at an executive level as high as a jurisdiction's chief law-enforcement officer. Is it really true that there is no policymaking involved in deciding, for example, what "reasonable efforts" shall be expended to conduct a background check? It may well satisfy the Act for a CLEO to direct that (a) no background checks will be conducted that divert personnel time from pending felony investigations, and (b) no background check will be permitted to consume more than one-half hour of an officer's time. But nothing in the Act *requires* a CLEO to be so parsimonious; diverting at least *some* felony-investigation time, and permitting at least *some* background checks beyond one-half hour would certainly not be *un*reasonable. Is this decision whether to devote maximum "reasonable efforts" or minimum "reasonable efforts" not preeminently a matter of policy? It is quite impossible, in short, to draw the Government's proposed line at "no policymaking," and we would have to fall back upon a line of "not too much policymaking." How much is too much is not likely to be answered precisely; and an imprecise barrier against federal intrusion upon state authority is not likely to be an effective one.

Even assuming, moreover, that the Brady Act leaves no "policymaking" discretion with the States, we fail to see how that improves rather than worsens the intrusion upon state sovereignty. Preservation of the States as independent and autonomous political entities is arguably less undermined by requiring them to make policy in certain fields than . . . by "reduc[ing] [them] to puppets of a ventriloquist Congress" . . . . It is an essential attribute of the States' retained sovereignty that they remain independent and autonomous within their proper sphere of authority. . . . It is no more compatible with this independence and autonomy that their officers be "dragooned" . . . into administering federal law, than it would be compatible with the independence and autonomy of the United States that its officers be impressed into service for the execution of state laws.

The Government purports to find support for its proffered distinction of *New York* in our decisions in *Testa v. Katt* (1947), and *FERC v. Mississippi*. We find neither case relevant. *Testa* stands for the proposition that state courts cannot refuse to apply federal law — a conclusion mandated by the terms of the Supremacy Clause ("the Judges in every State shall be bound [by federal law]"). . . . [T]hat says nothing about whether state executive officers must administer federal law. . . . As for *FERC*, it stated . . . that "this Court never has sanctioned explicitly a federal command to the States to promulgate and enforce laws and regulations," and upheld the statutory provisions at issue precisely because they did *not* commandeer state government, but merely imposed preconditions to continued state regulation of an otherwise pre-empted field, in accord with *Hodel*, and required state administrative agencies to apply federal law while acting in a judicial capacity, in accord with *Testa*.

The Government also maintains that requiring state officers to perform discrete, ministerial tasks specified by Congress does not violate the principle of *New York* because it does not diminish the accountability of state or federal officials. This argument fails even on its own terms. By forcing state governments to absorb the financial burden of implementing a federal regulatory program, Members of Congress can take credit for "solving" problems without having to ask their constituents to pay for the solutions with higher federal taxes. And even when the States are not forced to absorb the costs of implementing a federal program, they are still put in the position of taking the blame for its burdensomeness and for its defects. Under the present law, for example, it will be the CLEO and not some federal official who stands between the gun purchaser and immediate possession of his gun. And it will likely be the CLEO, not some federal official, who will be blamed for any error . . . that causes a purchaser to be mistakenly rejected.

The dissent makes no attempt to defend the Government's basis for distinguishing *New York*, but instead advances what seems to us an even more implausible theory. The Brady Act, the dissent asserts, is different from the "take title" provisions invalidated in *New York* because the former is addressed to individuals — namely CLEOs — while the latter were directed to the State itself. That is certainly a difference, but it cannot be a constitutionally significant one. While the Brady Act is directed to "individuals," it is directed to them in their official capacities as state officers; it controls their actions, not as private citizens, but as the agents of the State. The distinction between judicial writs and other government action directed against individuals in their personal capacity, on the one hand, and in their official capacity, on the other hand, is an ancient one, principally because it is dictated by common sense. We have observed that "a suit against a state official in his or her official capacity is not a suit against the official but rather is a suit against the official's office. . . . As such, it is no different from a suit against the State itself." . . . And the same must be said of a directive to an official in his or her official capacity. To say that the Federal Government cannot control the State, but can control all of its officers, is to say nothing of significance. . . . By resorting to this, the dissent not so much distinguishes *New York* as disembowels it.

Finally, the Government puts forward a cluster of arguments that can be grouped under the heading: "The Brady Act serves very important purposes, is most efficiently administered by CLEOs during the interim period, and places a minimal and only temporary burden upon state officers." There is considerable disagreement over the extent of the burden, but we need not pause over that detail. Assuming *all* the mentioned factors were true, they might be relevant if we were evaluating whether the incidental application to the States of a federal law of general applicability excessively interfered with the functioning of state governments. But where, as here, it is the whole *object* of the law to direct the functioning of the state executive, and hence to compromise the structural framework of dual sovereignty, such a "balancing" analysis is inappropriate. It is the very *principle* of separate state sovereignty that such a law offends, and no comparative assessment of the various interests can overcome that fundamental defect. We expressly rejected such an approach in *New York*, and what we said bears repeating:

> "Much of the Constitution is concerned with setting forth the form of our government, and the courts have traditionally invalidated measures deviating from that form. The result may appear 'formalistic' in a given case to partisans of the measure at issue, because such measures are

typically the product of the era's perceived necessity. But the Constitution protects us from our own best intentions: It divides power among sovereigns and among branches of government precisely so that we may resist the temptation to concentrate power in one location as an expedient solution to the crisis of the day."

We adhere to that principle today, and conclude categorically, as we concluded categorically in *New York*: "The Federal Government may not compel the States to enact or administer a federal regulatory program." The mandatory obligation imposed on CLEOs to perform background checks on prospective handgun purchasers plainly runs afoul of that rule.

* * *

JUSTICE O'CONNOR, concurring. [Omitted.]

JUSTICE THOMAS, concurring. [Omitted.]

JUSTICE STEVENS, with whom JUSTICE SOUTER, JUSTICE GINSBURG, and JUSTICE BREYER join, dissenting.

When Congress exercises the powers delegated to it by the Constitution, it may impose affirmative obligations on executive and judicial officers of state and local governments as well as ordinary citizens. . . .

* * *

I

The text of the Constitution provides a sufficient basis for a correct disposition of this case.

Article I, § 8, grants the Congress the power to regulate commerce among the States. . . . [T]here can be no question that that provision adequately supports the regulation of commerce in handguns effected by the Brady Act. Moreover, the additional grant of authority in that section of the Constitution "[t]o make all Laws which shall be necessary and proper for carrying into Execution the foregoing Powers" is surely adequate to support the temporary enlistment of local police officers in the process of identifying persons who should not be entrusted with the possession of handguns. . . .

Unlike the First Amendment, which prohibits the enactment of a category of laws that would otherwise be authorized by Article I, the Tenth Amendment imposes no restriction on the exercise of delegated powers. . . . The Amendment confirms the principle that the powers of the Federal Government are limited to those affirmatively granted by the Constitution, but it does not purport to limit the scope or the effectiveness of the exercise of powers that are delegated to Congress. . . . Thus, the Amendment provides no support for a rule that immunizes local officials from obligations that might be imposed on ordinary citizens. Indeed, it would be more reasonable to infer that federal law may impose greater duties on state officials than on private citizens because another provision of the Constitution requires that "all executive and judicial Officers, both of the United States and of the several States, shall be bound by Oath or Affirmation, to support this Constitution." U.S. Const., Art. VI, cl. 3.

It is appropriate for state officials to make an oath or affirmation to support the Federal Constitution because, as explained in The Federalist, they "have an essential agency in giving effect to the federal Constitution." THE FEDERALIST NO. 44 (J. Madison). There can be no conflict between their duties to the State and those owed to the Federal Government because Article VI unambiguously provides that federal law "shall be the supreme Law of the Land," binding in every State. U.S. Const., Art. VI, cl. 2. Thus, not only the Constitution, but every law enacted by Congress as well, establishes policy for the States just as firmly as do laws enacted by state legislatures.

The reasoning in our unanimous opinion explaining why state tribunals with ordinary jurisdiction over tort litigation can be required to hear cases arising under the Federal Employers' Liability Act applies equally to local law enforcement officers whose ordinary duties parallel the modest obligations imposed by the Brady Act:

> "The suggestion that the act of Congress is not in harmony with the policy of the State, and therefore that the courts of the State are free to decline jurisdiction, is quite inadmissible, because it presupposes what in legal contemplation does not exist. When Congress, in the exertion of the power confided to it by the Constitution, adopted that act, it spoke for all the people and all the States, and thereby established a policy for all. That policy is as much the policy of Connecticut as if the act had emanated from its own legislature, and should be respected accordingly in the courts of the State. . . . :
>
>> 'The laws of the United States are laws in the several States, and just as much binding on the citizens and courts thereof as the State laws are. The United States is not a foreign sovereignty as regards the several States, but is a concurrent, and, within its jurisdiction, paramount sovereignty.'" . . .

* * *

There is not a clause, sentence, or paragraph in the entire text of the Constitution of the United States that supports the proposition that a local police officer can ignore a command contained in a statute enacted by Congress pursuant to an express delegation of power enumerated in Article I.

* * *

III

. . . The fact that the Framers intended to preserve the sovereignty of the several States simply does not speak to the question whether individual state employees may be required to perform federal obligations, such as registering young adults for the draft, creating state emergency response commissions designed to manage the release of hazardous substances, collecting and reporting data on underground storage tanks that may pose an environmental hazard, and reporting traffic fatalities and missing children to a federal agency.

As we explained in *Garcia v. San Antonio Metropolitan Transit Authority* (1985): "[T]he principal means chosen by the Framers to ensure the role of the States in the federal system lies in the structure of the Federal Government itself. It is no novelty to observe that the composition of the Federal Government was designed in large part to protect the States from overreaching by Congress." Given the fact that the Members of Congress are elected by the people of the several States, with each State receiving an equivalent number of Senators in order to ensure that even the smallest States have a powerful voice in the legislature, it is quite unrealistic to assume that they will ignore the sovereignty concerns of their constituents. It is far more reasonable to presume that their decisions to impose modest burdens on state officials from time to time reflect a considered judgment that the people in each of the States will benefit therefrom.

Indeed, the presumption of validity that supports all congressional enactments has added force with respect to policy judgments concerning the impact of a federal statute upon the respective States. The majority points to nothing suggesting that the political safeguards of federalism identified in *Garcia* need be supplemented by a rule, grounded in neither constitutional history nor text, flatly prohibiting the National Government from enlisting state and local officials in the implementation of federal law.

Recent developments demonstrate that the political safeguards protecting our Federalism are effective. The majority expresses special concern that were its rule not adopted the Federal Government would be able to avail itself of the services of state government officials "at no cost to itself." But this specific problem of federal actions that have the effect of imposing so-called "unfunded mandates" on the States has been identified and meaningfully addressed by Congress in recent legislation. . . .

[This recent legislation] was designed "to end the imposition, in the absence of full consideration by Congress, of Federal mandates on State . . . governments without adequate Federal funding, in a manner that may displace other essential State . . . governmental priorities." It functions, *inter alia*, by permitting Members of Congress to raise an objection by point of order to a pending bill that contains an "unfunded mandate," as defined by the statute, of over $50 million. The mandate may not then be enacted unless the Members make an explicit decision to proceed anyway. Whatever the ultimate impact of the new legislation, its passage demonstrates that unelected judges are better off leaving the protection of federalism to the political process in all but the most extraordinary circumstances.

Perversely, the majority's rule seems more likely to damage than to preserve the safeguards against tyranny provided by the existence of vital state governments. By limiting the ability of the Federal Government to enlist state officials in the implementation of its programs, the Court creates incentives for the National Government to aggrandize itself. In the name of State's rights, the majority would have the Federal Government create vast national bureaucracies to implement its policies. This is exactly the sort of thing that the early Federalists promised would not occur, in part as a result of the National Government's ability to rely on the magistracy of the states. . . .

With colorful hyperbole, the Court suggests that the unity in the Executive Branch of the Federal Government "would be shattered, and the power of the President would be subject to reduction, if Congress could . . . require . . . state officers to execute its laws." Putting to one side the obvious tension between the majority's claim that impressing state police officers will unduly tip the balance of power in favor of the federal sovereign and this suggestion that it will emasculate the Presidency, the Court's reasoning contradicts *New York v. United States*.

That decision squarely approved of cooperative federalism programs, designed at the national level but implemented principally by state governments. *New York* disapproved of a particular *method* of putting such programs into place, not the existence of federal programs implemented locally. Indeed, nothing in the majority's holding calls into question the three mechanisms for constructing such programs that *New York* expressly approved. Congress may require the States to implement its programs as a condition of federal spending, in order to avoid the threat of unilateral federal action in the area, or as a part of a program that affects States and private parties alike. The majority's suggestion in response to this dissent that Congress' ability to create such programs is limited is belied by the importance and sweep of the federal statutes that meet this description, some of which we described in *New York*.

Nor is there force to the assumption undergirding the Court's entire opinion that if this trivial burden on state sovereignty is permissible, the entire structure of federalism will soon collapse. These cases do not involve any mandate to state legislatures to enact new rules. When legislative action, or even administrative rule-making, is at issue, it may be appropriate for Congress either to preempt the State's lawmaking power and fashion the federal rule itself, or to respect the State's power to fashion its own rules. But this case, unlike any precedent in which the Court has held that Congress exceeded its powers, merely involves the imposition of modest duties on individual officers. The Court seems to accept the fact that Congress could require private persons, such as hospital executives or school administrators, . . . to provide arms merchants with relevant information about a prospective purchaser's fitness to own a weapon; indeed, the Court does not disturb the conclusion that flows directly from our prior holdings that the burden on police officers would be permissible if a similar burden were also imposed on private parties with access to relevant data. . . . A structural problem that vanishes when the statute affects private individuals as well as public officials is not much of a structural problem.

Far more important than the concerns that the Court musters in support of its new rule is the fact that the Framers entrusted Congress with the task of creating a working structure of intergovernmental relationships around the framework that the Constitution authorized. Neither explicitly nor implicitly did the Framers issue any command that forbids Congress from imposing federal duties on private citizens or on local officials. As a general matter, Congress has followed the sound policy of authorizing federal agencies and federal agents to administer federal programs. That general practice, however, does not negate the existence of power to rely on state officials in occasional situations in which such reliance is in the national interest. Rather, the occasional exceptions confirm the wisdom of Justice Holmes' reminder that "the machinery of government would not work if it were not allowed a little play in its joints." . . .

* * *

The provision of the Brady Act that crosses the Court's newly defined constitutional threshold is more comparable to a statute requiring local police officers to report the identity of missing children to the Crime Control Center of the Department of Justice than to an offensive federal command to a sovereign state. If Congress believes that such a statute will benefit the people of the Nation, and serve the interests of cooperative federalism better than an enlarged federal bureaucracy, we should respect both its policy judgment and its appraisal of its constitutional power.

Accordingly, I respectfully dissent.

JUSTICE SOUTER, dissenting. [Omitted.]

JUSTICE BREYER, with whom JUSTICE STEVENS joins, dissenting. [Omitted.]

NOTES AND QUESTIONS

1. There does not appear to be any prominent disagreement over jurisprudential precepts here, such as, for example, the existence of some element of natural law which might circumscribe even the Constitution. The debate is rather purely over the intentions of the Framers and the interpretation of case law with regard to dual sovereignty. Who has the better of the argument?

2. Note that not only is the text of the Constitution of importance in ascertaining the Framers' intent, but so is THE FEDERALIST, the leading contemporary exposition of the meaning of the 1787 Constitution. That document, though it has come to be regarded as America's one outstanding contribution to political theory, was, however, designed as a practical text to get New York's representatives at the ratification convention to accept the new Constitution, and its contemporary political purpose may have shaded its analysis. Do you see any evidence of that here? How authoritative should THE FEDERALIST be? What sort of fears was THE FEDERALIST designed to allay? Are they of concern today? With whom would the Anti-Federalists (those who opposed the adoption of the Constitution on the grounds that it too tightly constricted the sovereignty of the states, and created a federal government which might become tyrannical) be more upset — the majority or the dissent in this case?

3. A unanimous Court found the "no commandeering" principle of *Printz* to be inapplicable in *Reno v. Condon*, 528 U.S. 141 (2000). At issue was the Driver's Privacy Protection Act of 1994 (DPPA), which regulated the disclosure of personal information contained in the records of state motor vehicle departments (DMVs). The DPPA's provisions did not apply solely to states. The Act also regulated the resale and redisclosure of drivers' personal information by private persons who have obtained that information from a state DMV. South Carolina law conflicted with the DPPA's provisions. Under that law, the information contained in the state's DMV records was available to any person or entity filling out a form listing the requester's name and address and stating that the information will not be used for telephone solicitation. . . . First, the sale or release of information in interstate commerce was found to be a proper subject of congressional regulation under *United States v. Lopez* (1995). The motor vehicle information which the states have historically sold is used by insurers, manufacturers, direct marketers, and others engaged in interstate commerce to contact drivers with customized solicitations. The information is also used in the stream of interstate commerce by various public and private entities for matters related to interstate motoring. Because drivers' information is, in this context, an article of commerce, its sale or release into the interstate stream of business is sufficient to support congressional regulation. . . .

But South Carolina further argued that the DPPA violated the Tenth Amendment because like *Printz* it "thrusts upon the States all of the day-to-day responsibility for administering its complex provisions," and thereby makes "state officials the unwilling implementors of federal policy." South Carolina emphasizes that the DPPA requires the state's employees to learn and apply the Act's substantive restrictions, which are summarized above, and notes that these activities will consume the employees' time and thus the state's resources. South Carolina further notes that the DPPA's penalty provisions hang over the states as a potential punishment should they fail to comply with the Act.

The Court disagreed, finding the matter governed not by *Printz*, but the decision in *South Carolina v. Baker* (1988), where the Court upheld a statute that prohibited states from issuing unregistered bonds. The critical distinction between the two circumstances was that in *Baker* and *Reno v. Condon*, the law "regulated state activities," rather than "seeking to control or influence the manner in which states regulate private parties." Like the statute at issue in *Baker*, the DPPA did not require the states in their sovereign capacity to regulate their own citizens. The DPPA regulates the States as the owners of databases. It does not require the South Carolina Legislature to enact any laws or regulations, and it does not require state officials to assist in the enforcement of federal statutes regulating private individuals.

4. After *Garcia*, the Court abandoned the idea of trying to protect dual sovereignty by defining traditional state functions. *Printz*, and its predecessor case, *New York v. United States,* 505 U.S. 144 (1992), look as if they are trying to shore up dual sovereignty by form or procedural doctrine. Do you think the Court's effort successful? Would the Court's commerce decisions, even after *Lopez,* allow Congress simply to prohibit any gun dealer from selling a handgun to anyone unless gun dealers certify that a background check was performed on the purchaser and leave it up to gun dealers to work out (probably with their local governments) how that would get done? Similarly, couldn't the federal government accomplish its purpose in *Printz* merely by conditioning federal subsidies for state law enforcement on the condition that state and local law enforcement officers undertake the desired background check? Consider the next case.

C. In Light of the "Spending" Powers, Does the Restriction on the Commerce Clause Matter?

SOUTH DAKOTA v. DOLE
483 U.S. 203 (1987)

CHIEF JUSTICE REHNQUIST delivered the opinion of the Court.

Petitioner South Dakota permits persons 19 years of age or older to purchase beer containing up to 3.2% alcohol. In 1984 Congress enacted 23 U.S.C. § 158 (1982 ed., Supp. III), which directs the Secretary of Transportation to withhold a percentage of federal highway funds otherwise allocable from States "in which the purchase or public possession . . . of any alcoholic beverage by a person who is less than twenty-one years of age is lawful." The State sued in United States District Court seeking a declaratory judgment that § 158 violates the constitutional limitations on congressional exercise of the spending power and violates the Twenty-first Amendment to the United States Constitution. The District Court rejected the State's claims, and the Court of Appeals for the Eighth Circuit affirmed.

In this Court, the parties direct most of their efforts to defining the proper scope of the Twenty-first Amendment. Relying on our statement . . . that the "Twenty-first Amendment grants the States virtually complete control over whether to permit importation or sale of liquor and how to structure the liquor distribution system," South Dakota asserts that the setting of minimum drinking ages is clearly within the "core powers" reserved to the States under § 2 of the Amendment. Section 158, petitioner claims, usurps that core power. The Secretary in response asserts that the Twenty-first Amendment is simply not implicated by § 158; the plain language of § 2 confirms the States' broad power to impose restrictions on the sale and distribution of alcoholic beverages but does not confer on them any power to permit sales that Congress seeks to *prohibit*. That Amendment, under this reasoning, would not prevent Congress from affirmatively enacting a national minimum drinking age more restrictive than that provided by the various state laws; and it would follow *a fortiori* that the indirect inducement involved here is compatible with the Twenty-first Amendment.

These arguments present questions of the meaning of the Twenty-first Amendment, the bounds of which have escaped precise definition. . . . Despite the extended treatment of the question by the parties, however, we need not decide in this case whether that Amendment would prohibit an attempt by Congress to legislate directly a national minimum drinking age. Here, Congress has acted indirectly under its spending power to encourage uniformity in the States' drinking ages. As we explain below, we find this legislative effort within constitutional bounds even if Congress may not regulate drinking ages directly.

The Constitution empowers Congress to "lay and collect Taxes, Duties, Imposts, and Excises, to pay the Debts and provide for the common Defence and general Welfare of the United States." Art. I, § 8, cl. 1. Incident to this power, Congress may attach conditions on the receipt of federal funds, and has repeatedly employed the power "to further broad policy objectives by conditioning receipt of federal moneys upon compliance by the recipient with federal statutory and administrative directives." . . . The breadth of this power was made clear in *United States v. Butler* (1936), where the Court, resolving a longstanding debate over the scope of the Spending Clause, determined that "the power of Congress to authorize expenditure of public moneys for public purposes is not limited by the direct grants of legislative power found in the Constitution." Thus, objectives not thought to be within Article I's "enumerated legislative fields," may nevertheless be attained through the use of the spending power and the conditional grant of federal funds.

The spending power is of course not unlimited, . . . but is instead subject to several general restrictions articulated in our cases. The first of these limitations is derived from the language of the Constitution itself: the exercise of the spending power must be in pursuit of "the general welfare." . . . In considering whether a particular expenditure is intended to serve general public purposes, courts should defer substantially to the judgment of Congress. . . . Second, we have required that if Congress desires to condition the States' receipt of federal funds, it "must do so unambiguously . . . , enabl[ing] the States to exercise their choice knowingly, cognizant of the consequences of their participation." . . . Third, our cases have suggested (without significant elaboration) that conditions on federal grants might be illegitimate if they are unrelated "to the federal interest in particular national projects or programs." . . . Finally, we have noted that other constitutional provisions may provide an independent bar to the conditional grant of federal funds. . . .

South Dakota does not seriously claim that § 158 is inconsistent with any of the first three restrictions mentioned above. We can readily conclude that the provision is designed to serve the general welfare, especially in light of the fact that "the concept of welfare or the opposite is shaped by Congress . . . ." Congress found that the differing drinking ages in the States created particular incentives for young persons to combine their desire to drink with their ability to drive, and that this interstate problem required a national solution. The means it chose to address this dangerous situation were reasonably calculated to advance the general welfare. The conditions upon which States receive the funds, moreover, could not be more clearly stated by Congress. And the State itself, rather than challenging the germaneness of the condition to federal purposes, admits that it "has never contended that the congressional action was . . . unrelated to a national concern in the absence of the Twenty-first Amendment." Indeed, the condition imposed by Congress is directly related to one of the main purposes for which highway funds are expended — safe interstate travel. This goal of the interstate highway system had been frustrated by varying drinking ages among the States. A Presidential commission appointed to study alcohol-related accidents and fatalities on the Nation's highways concluded that the lack of uniformity in the States' drinking ages created "an incentive to drink and drive" because "young persons commut[e] to border States where the drinking age is lower." . . . By enacting § 158, Congress conditioned the receipt of federal funds in a way reasonably calculated to address this particular impediment to a purpose for which the funds are expended.

The remaining question about the validity of § 158 — and the basic point of disagreement between the parties — is whether the Twenty-first Amendment constitutes an "independent constitutional bar" to the conditional grant of federal funds. . . . Petitioner, relying on its view that the Twenty-first Amendment prohibits direct regulation of drinking ages by Congress, asserts that "Congress may not use the spending power to regulate that which it is prohibited from regulating directly under the Twenty-first Amendment." But our cases show that this "independent constitutional bar" limitation on the spending power is not of the kind petitioner suggests. *United States v. Butler* (1936), for example, established that the constitutional limitations on Congress when exercising its spending power are less exacting than those on its authority to regulate directly.

We have also held that a perceived Tenth Amendment limitation on congressional regulation of state affairs did not concomitantly limit the range of conditions legitimately placed on federal grants. In *Oklahoma v. Civil Service Comm'n*, the Court considered the validity of the Hatch Act insofar as it was applied to political activities of state officials whose employment was financed in whole or in part with federal funds. The State contended that an order under this provision to withhold certain federal funds unless a state official was removed invaded its sovereignty in violation of the Tenth Amendment. Though finding that "the United States is not concerned with, and has no power to regulate, local political activities as such of state officials," the Court nevertheless held that the Federal Government "does have power to fix the terms upon which its money allotments to states shall be disbursed." The Court found no violation of the State's sovereignty because the State could, and did, adopt "the 'simple expedient' of not yielding to what she urges is federal coercion. The offer of benefits to a state by the United States dependent upon cooperation by the state with federal plans, assumedly for the general welfare, is not unusual." . . .

These cases establish that the "independent constitutional bar" limitation on the spending power is not, as petitioner suggests, a prohibition on the indirect achievement of objectives which Congress is not empowered to achieve directly. Instead, we think that the language in our earlier opinions stands for the unexceptionable proposition that the power may not be used to induce the States to engage in activities that would themselves be unconstitutional. Thus, for example, a grant of federal funds conditioned on invidiously discriminatory state action or the infliction of cruel and unusual punishment would be an illegitimate exercise of the Congress' broad spending power. But no such claim can be or is made here. Were South Dakota to succumb to the blandishments offered by Congress and raise its drinking age to 21, the State's action in so doing would not violate the constitutional rights of anyone.

Our decisions have recognized that in some circumstances the financial inducement offered by Congress might be so coercive as to pass the point at which "pressure turns into compulsion." . . . Here, however, Congress has directed only that a State desiring to establish a minimum drinking age lower than 21 lose a relatively small percentage of certain federal highway funds. Petitioner contends that the coercive nature of this program is evident from the degree of success it has achieved. We cannot conclude, however, that a conditional grant of federal money of this sort is unconstitutional simply by reason of its success in achieving the congressional objective.

When we consider, for a moment, that all South Dakota would lose if she adheres to her chosen course as to a suitable minimum drinking age is 5% of the funds otherwise obtainable under specified highway grant programs, the argument as to coercion is shown to be more rhetoric than fact. . . .

Here Congress has offered relatively mild encouragement to the States to enact higher minimum drinking ages than they would otherwise choose. But the enactment of such laws remains the prerogative of the States not merely in theory but in fact. Even if Congress might lack the power to impose a national minimum drinking age directly, we conclude that encouragement to state action found in § 158 is a valid use of the spending power. Accordingly, the judgment of the Court of Appeals is

Affirmed.

JUSTICE BRENNAN, dissenting.

I agree with JUSTICE O'CONNOR that regulation of the minimum age of purchasers of liquor falls squarely within the ambit of those powers reserved to the

States by the Twenty-first Amendment. Since States possess this constitutional power, Congress cannot condition a federal grant in a manner that abridges this right. The Amendment, itself, strikes the proper balance between federal and state authority. I therefore dissent.

JUSTICE O'CONNOR, dissenting.

The Court today upholds the National Minimum Drinking Age Amendment, 23 U.S.C. § 158 (1982 ed., Supp. III), as a valid exercise of the spending power conferred by Article I, § 8. But § 158 is not a condition on spending reasonably related to the expenditure of federal funds and cannot be justified on that ground. Rather, it is an attempt to regulate the sale of liquor, an attempt that lies outside Congress' power to regulate commerce because it falls within the ambit of § 2 of the Twenty-first Amendment.

My disagreement with the Court is relatively narrow on the spending power issue: it is a disagreement about the application of a principle rather than a disagreement on the principle itself. I agree with the Court that Congress may attach conditions on the receipt of federal funds to further "the federal interest in particular national projects or programs." . . . I also subscribe to the established proposition that the reach of the spending power "is not limited by the direct grants of legislative power found in the Constitution." . . . Finally, I agree that there are four separate types of limitations on the spending power. . . . Insofar as two of those limitations are concerned, the Court is clearly correct that § 158 is wholly unobjectionable. Establishment of a national minimum drinking age certainly fits within the broad concept of the general welfare and the statute is entirely unambiguous. I am also willing to assume, *arguendo*, that the Twenty-first Amendment does not constitute an "independent constitutional bar" to a spending condition. . . .

But the Court's application of the requirement that the condition imposed be reasonably related to the purpose for which the funds are expended is cursory and unconvincing. We have repeatedly said that Congress may condition grants under the spending power only in ways reasonably related to the purpose of the federal program. . . . In my view, establishment of a minimum drinking age of 21 is not sufficiently related to interstate highway construction to justify so conditioning funds appropriated for that purpose.

In support of its contrary conclusion, the Court relies on a supposed concession by counsel for South Dakota that the State "has never contended that the congressional action was . . . unrelated to a national concern in the absence of the Twenty-first Amendment." In the absence of the Twenty-first Amendment, however, there is a strong argument that the Congress might regulate the conditions under which liquor is sold under the commerce power, just as it regulates the sale of many other commodities that are in or affect interstate commerce. The fact that the Twenty-first Amendment is crucial to the State's argument does not, therefore, amount to a concession that the condition imposed by § 158 is reasonably related to highway construction. The Court also relies on a portion of the argument transcript in support of its claim that South Dakota conceded the reasonable relationship point. But counsel's statements there are at best ambiguous. Counsel essentially said no more than that he was not prepared to argue the reasonable relationship question. . . .

Aside from these "concessions" by counsel, the Court asserts the reasonableness of the relationship between the supposed purpose of the expenditure — "safe interstate travel" — and the drinking age condition. The Court reasons that Congress wishes that the roads it builds may be used safely, that drunken drivers threaten highway safety, and that young people are more likely to drive while under the influence of alcohol under existing law than would be the case if there were a uniform national drinking age of 21. It hardly needs saying, however, that if the purpose of § 158 is to deter drunken driving, it is far too over- and under-inclusive. It is over-inclusive because it stops teenagers from drinking even when they are not about to drive on interstate highways. It is under-inclusive because teenagers pose only a small part of the drunken driving problem in this Nation. . . .

When Congress appropriates money to build a highway, it is entitled to insist that the highway be a safe one. But it is not entitled to insist as a condition of the use of highway funds that the State impose or change regulations in other areas of the State's social and economic life because of an attenuated or tangential relationship to highway use or safety. Indeed, if the rule were otherwise, the Congress could effectively regulate almost any area of a State's social, political, or economic life on the theory that use of the interstate transportation system is somehow enhanced. If, for example, the United States were to condition highway moneys upon moving the state capital, I suppose it might argue that interstate transportation is facilitated by locating local governments in places easily accessible to interstate highways — or, conversely, that highways might become overburdened if they had to carry traffic to and from the state capital. In my mind, such a relationship is hardly more attenuated than the one which the Court finds supports § 158. . . .

There is a clear place at which the Court can draw the line between permissible and impermissible conditions on federal grants. It is the line identified in the Brief for the National Conference of State Legislatures et al. as *Amici Curiae*:

> "Congress has the power to *spend* for the general welfare, it has the power to *legislate* only for delegated purposes. . . .
>
> "The appropriate inquiry, then, is whether the spending requirement or prohibition is a condition on a grant or whether it is regulation. The difference turns on whether the requirement specifies in some way how the money should be spent, so that Congress' intent in making the grant will be effectuated. Congress has no power under the Spending Clause to impose requirements on a grant that go beyond specifying how the money should be spent. A requirement that is not such a specification is

not a condition, but a regulation, which is valid only if it falls within one of Congress' delegated regulatory powers."

This approach harks back to *United States v. Butler*, the last case in which this Court struck down an Act of Congress as beyond the authority granted by the Spending Clause. There the Court wrote that "[t]here is an obvious difference between a statute stating the conditions upon which moneys shall be expended and one effective only upon assumption of a contractual obligation to submit to a regulation which otherwise could not be enforced." The *Butler* Court saw the Agricultural Adjustment Act for what it was — an exercise of regulatory, not spending, power. The error in *Butler* was not the Court's conclusion that the Act was essentially regulatory, but rather its crabbed view of the extent of Congress' regulatory power under the Commerce Clause. The Agricultural Adjustment Act was regulatory but it was regulation that today would likely be considered within Congress' commerce power. . . .

While *Butler*'s authority is questionable insofar as it assumes that Congress has no regulatory power over farm production, its discussion of the spending power and its description of both the power's breadth and its limitations remain sound. The Court's decision in *Butler* also properly recognizes the gravity of the task of appropriately limiting the spending power. If the spending power is to be limited only by Congress' notion of the general welfare, the reality, given the vast financial resources of the Federal Government, is that the Spending Clause gives "power to the Congress to tear down the barriers, to invade the states' jurisdiction, and to become a parliament of the whole people, subject to no restrictions save such as are self-imposed." . . . This, of course, as *Butler* held, was not the Framers' plan and it is not the meaning of the Spending Clause.

Our later cases are consistent with the notion that, under the spending power, the Congress may only condition grants in ways that can fairly be said to be related to the expenditure of federal funds. For example, in *Oklahoma v. CSC* (1947), the Court upheld application of the Hatch Act to a member of the Oklahoma State Highway Commission who was employed in connection with an activity financed in part by loans and grants from a federal agency. This condition is appropriately viewed as a condition relating to how federal moneys were to be expended. Other conditions that have been upheld by the Court may be viewed as independently justified under some regulatory power of the Congress. Thus, in *Fullilove v. Klutznick* (1980), the Court upheld a condition on federal grants that 10% of the money be "set aside" for contracts with minority business enterprises. But the Court found that the condition could be justified as a valid regulation under the commerce power and § 5 of the Fourteenth Amendment. . . .

This case, however, falls into neither class. As discussed above, a condition that a State will raise its drinking age to 21 cannot fairly be said to be reasonably related to the expenditure of funds for highway construction. The only possible connection, highway safety, has nothing to do with how the funds Congress has appropriated are expended. Rather than a condition determining how federal highway money shall be expended, it is a regulation determining who shall be able to drink liquor. As such it is not justified by the spending power.

Of the other possible sources of congressional authority for regulating the sale of liquor only the commerce power comes to mind. But in my view, the regulation of the age of the purchasers of liquor, just as the regulation of the price at which liquor may be sold, falls squarely within the scope of those powers reserved to the States by the Twenty-first Amendment. . . . As I emphasized in *324 Liquor Corp. v. Duffy* (1987) (dissenting opinion):

> "The history of the Amendment strongly supports Justice Black's view that the Twenty-first Amendment was intended to return absolute control of the liquor trade to the States, and that the Federal Government could not use its Commerce Clause powers to interfere in any manner with the States' exercise of the power conferred by the Amendment."

* * *

The immense size and power of the Government of the United States ought not obscure its fundamental character. It remains a Government of enumerated powers. . . . Because 23 U.S.C. § 158 cannot be justified as an exercise of any power delegated to the Congress, it is not authorized by the Constitution. . . .

NOTES AND QUESTIONS

1. Who gets this one right — Justice Rehnquist, in the majority opinion, or Justice O'Connor, in the dissent? In particular, do you have any trouble with the Congress attempting to impose a national drinking age through coercive withholding of federal highway funds? After *Lopez,* considered in Chapter 4, is it as clear as Justice O'Connor seems to suggest it is that the Federal Government's commerce power would extend to the establishment of a national drinking age? For thoughtful commentary on this topic, see Lynn A. Baker, *Conditional Federal Spending After* Lopez, 95 COLUM. L. REV. 1911, 1916 (1995) ("[T]he *Lopez* majority should reinterpret the Spending Clause to work in tandem, rather than at odds, with its reading of the Commerce Clause").

2. What about Justice Rehnquist's treatment of the first prong of the test he proposes? Does the limitation he described, that the spending be in the "general welfare," amount to any limitation in light of the "substantial deference" he gives to Congress? One of your co-authors has contended that the Clause actually was intended by the framers to impose a strict limitation on federal spending, namely, that it be for national purposes rather than for purely local or regional purposes. *See* John C. Eastman, *Restoring the "General" to the General Welfare Clause,* 4 CHAP. L. REV. 29 (2001); *see also* Robert G. Natelson, *The General Welfare Clause and the Public Trust: An Essay In Original Understanding,* 52 U. KAN. L. REV. 1 (2003). Does Justice Rehnquist disagree with the view that the

Clause is a limitation on federal power, or does he just believe that it is not a judicially-enforceable limitation?

3. In *United States v. Butler*, 297 U.S. 1 (1936), by a vote of 6 to 3, the Supreme Court declared that a federal tax levied on commodities processors, the proceeds of which were to be used to pay subsidies to farmers who reduced their crop acreage, was unconstitutional. The decision struck a harsh blow at an important New Deal measure, the Agricultural Adjustment Act, and along with the Supreme Court's decision in *A.L.A. Schechter Poultry Corp. v. United States*, 295 U.S. 495 (1935), which rejected the similarly important National Industrial Recovery Act, convinced President Roosevelt that he had to save the Constitution from the Court and the Court from itself. The Court in *Butler* conceded that Congress could use its taxing power to promote the general welfare (the analogue to the spending power which was involved in *Dole*), and that the promotion of the general welfare was not limited to the subject matters of specifically enumerated grants of congressional power in the Constitution. Nevertheless, the majority threw out the particular tax as a violation of the Tenth Amendment, because in establishing a national plan to regulate and to control agricultural production by taxing processors and transferring the funds to farmers, Congress had wrongly strayed into an area reserved to the states. As you have seen, the *Butler* opinion's long term impact was relatively slight, since broad congressional regulation of local agriculture under the Commerce Clause was eventually upheld in *Wickard*. The Justices in the majority in *Butler* have been subsequently ridiculed by most legal academics, but can it be said that in rejecting national regulation of agriculture they had a valid point?

4. Can one really reconcile any effort by the Court to limit the scope of the commerce power in *Lopez* or to protect states from being the "commandeered" sub-agents of the federal government with cases such as *Dole*? If Congress were to make educational subsidies, such as the payments that the federal governments makes to local educational authorities where large numbers of federal workers reside, conditional on states passing gun-control laws of a kind rejected in *Lopez* would this pass constitutional muster? What about the great principle of the common law that one may not do indirectly that which is prohibited when done directly?

5. Perhaps the Court is edging toward a new axiom for cabining the spending power — the fact that some conditions could not have been contractually anticipated by the recipient state. In *Barnes v. Gorman*, 536 U.S. 181 (2002), decided by a unanimous court, the Justices held that punitive damages were not within the contractual expectations of a state.

Specifically at issue was whether punitive damages could be awarded in a private cause of action brought under § 202 of the Americans with Disabilities Act of 1990 (ADA), 104 Stat. 337, 42 U.S.C. § 12132 (1994 ed.), and § 504 of the Rehabilitation Act of 1973, 87 Stat. 394, 29 U.S.C. § 794(a). Gorman, a paraplegic, who wore a catheter attached to a urine bag, was arrested for trespass after fighting with a bouncer at a Kansas City, Missouri, nightclub. He was transported for booking to a police station, but because the police van was not equipped to receive his wheelchair, the officers, "over his objection, used a seatbelt and his own belt to strap him to a narrow bench in the rear of the van. During the ride Gorman released his seatbelt, fearing it placed excessive pressure on his urine bag. Eventually, the other belt came loose and [Gorman] fell to the floor, rupturing his urine bag and injuring his shoulder and back. The driver, the only officer in the van, finding it impossible to lift [Gorman], fastened him to a support for the remainder of the trip. Upon arriving at the station, Gorman was booked, processed, and released; later he was convicted of misdemeanor trespass. After these events, [Gorman] suffered serious medical problems including a bladder infection, serious lower back pain, and uncontrollable spasms in his paralyzed areas that left him unable to work full time." Gorman brought suit against members of the Kansas City Board of Police Commissioners, the chief of police, and the officer who drove the van. He claimed they had discriminated against him on the basis of his disability "by failing to maintain appropriate policies for the arrest and transportation of persons with spinal cord injuries." A jury in the District Court ruled for Gorman, and awarded over $1 million in compensatory damages and $1.2 million in punitive damages. The District Court vacated the punitive damages award, holding that punitive damages are unavailable in suits under § 202 of the ADA and § 504 of the Rehabilitation Act. The Court of Appeals for the Eighth Circuit reversed, and reinstated the punitive damages award.

The Court held, per Justice Scalia, that no punitive damages may be pursued against the state. The Court acknowledged that the ADA and the Rehabilitation Act contained a provision indicating that the relief available under them was the same as that available under the civil rights laws. And yes, the Court had previously held that Congress' power under the Spending Clause, U.S. Const., Article I, Section 8, cl. 1, allowed it to place conditions on the grant of federal funds (including the allowance of private causes of action). Nevertheless, punitive damages could not be pursued here since no state would have anticipated this as an implied remedy pursuant to the law of contract, when the federal funds grants were accepted. The Court noted that punitive damages, unlike compensatory damages and injunctions, are generally not available for breach of contract, and that it was highly unlikely states would have agreed to accept federal funds if they knew that by so doing they were subjecting themselves to potentially ruinous punitive damages. Justice Stevens, concurring in the judgment, because of his reliance on a line of cases suggesting that punitive damages should not be permitted unless congressional intent to permit them was clear, suggested that the majority had wrongly fettered the Spending Clause with contractual concepts. It remains to be seen whether this mode of analysis becomes a serious limitation on the power of Congress to impose policy conditions upon the states.

6. The Court was invited to reconsider the breadth of its Spending Clause deference in *Sabri v. United States*, 124 S. Ct. 1941 (2004). In a unanimous opinion by Justice Souter, with some partial concurrences, it declined. Basim Omar

Sabri, a property developer in Minneapolis, Minnesota, was about to begin a large development project. Unsure that he could obtain regulatory approval, he enlisted the illicit help of Brian Herron, a Minneapolis city council member. Sabri allegedly offered Herron three bribes. Sabri was charged with three counts of violating the federal program bribery statute, 18 U.S.C. § 666(a)(2) (Section 666). Section 666 makes it a crime to offer a $5,000 or larger bribe to any agent of a political entity that receives over $10,000 a year in federal funds.

Sabri challenged the constitutionality of the statute, arguing that it was facially unconstitutional because it did not require the government to prove a nexus between the offense conduct and a federal interest. Sabri thus argued that the statute exceeded Congress' power under the Spending Clause in a manner reminiscent of Justice O'Connor's dissent in *Dole*. Justice Souter brushed aside the argument, writing:

> Congress has authority under the Spending Clause to appropriate federal monies to promote the general welfare, and it has corresponding authority under the Necessary and Proper Clause to see to it that taxpayer dollars appropriated under that power are in fact spent for the general welfare, and not frittered away in graft or on projects undermined when funds are siphoned off or corrupt public officers are derelict about demanding value for dollars.

Justice Souter's mention of the Necessary and Proper Clause prompted Justice Thomas to concur only in the judgment. Thomas preferred to base the outcome on the commerce rather than the spending power, as it has been construed, but again noted that he hoped the Court would reconsider its precedents to trim back authority premised on merely "substantial effect" upon commerce. Justice Thomas' main target in *Sabri* was what he called the Court's "greatly and improperly expanded reach of Congress' power under the Necessary and Proper Clause." Justice Thomas said: "[T]he Court appears to hold that the Necessary and Proper Clause authorizes the exercise of any power that is no more than a 'rational means' to effectuate one of Congress' enumerated powers." This, he argued, was an improper reading of *McCulloch v. Maryland* (1819), where Chief Justice Marshall said of the scope of the Necessary and Proper Clause: "Let the end be legitimate, let it be within the scope of the constitution, and all means which are appropriate, which are plainly adapted to that end, which are not prohibited, but consistent with the letter and spirit of the constitution, are constitutional."

Do you think the Court misread *McCulloch*? Does "plainly adapted" mean the same thing as "rational means" in theory or in practice? Given the pervasiveness of federal funding, is there any conduct that Congress can not reach? Most law students receive Stafford student loans. Could Congress make it a crime to assault a recipient of federal aid, on the ground that it is a necessary and proper measure to ensure that debtors remain healthy and thus able to repay their loans? If not, why not?

7. Even as efforts to maintain dual sovereignty in light of federal legislative power may be tentative at best, recent case law suggests that the concept is very much alive when the subject is the jurisdiction of the federal courts.

D. Dual Sovereignty in Court — Herein Eleventh Amendment Sovereign Immunity

SEMINOLE TRIBE v. FLORIDA
517 U.S. 44 (1996)

CHIEF JUSTICE REHNQUIST delivered the opinion of the Court.

The Indian Gaming Regulatory Act [IGRA] provides that an Indian tribe may conduct certain gaming activities only in conformance with a valid compact between the tribe and the State in which the gaming activities are located. The Act, passed by Congress under the Indian Commerce Clause, U.S. Const., Art. I, § 8, cl. 3, imposes upon the States a duty to negotiate in good faith with an Indian tribe toward the formation of a compact, and authorizes a tribe to bring suit in federal court against a State in order to compel performance of that duty. We hold that notwithstanding Congress' clear intent to abrogate the States' sovereign immunity, the Indian Commerce Clause does not grant Congress that power, and therefore [IGRA] cannot grant jurisdiction over a State that does not consent to be sued. We further hold that the doctrine of *Ex parte Young* (1908) may not be used to enforce [IGRA] against a state official.

I

* * *

In September 1991, the Seminole Tribe of Indians, petitioner, sued the State of Florida and its Governor, Lawton Chiles, respondents. . . . [P]etitioner alleged that respondents had "refused to enter into any negotiation for inclusion of [certain gaming activities] in a tribal-state compact," thereby violating the "requirement of good faith negotiation" . . . . Respondents moved to dismiss the complaint, arguing that the suit violated the State's sovereign immunity from suit in federal court. The District Court denied respondents' motion, and the respondents took an interlocutory appeal of that decision.

The Court of Appeals for the Eleventh Circuit reversed the decision of the District Court, holding that the Eleventh Amendment barred petitioner's suit against respondents. . . .

Petitioner sought our review of the Eleventh Circuit's decision and we granted certiorari in order to consider two questions: (1) Does the Eleventh Amendment prevent Congress from authorizing suits by Indian tribes against States for prospective injunctive relief to enforce legislation enacted pursuant to the Indian Commerce Clause?; and (2) Does the doctrine of *Ex parte Young* permit suits against a State's governor for prospective injunctive relief to enforce the good faith bargaining requirement of the Act? . . .

The Eleventh Amendment provides:

> "The Judicial power of the United States shall not be construed to extend to any suit in law or equity, commenced or prosecuted against one of the United States by Citizens of another State, or by Citizens or Subjects of any Foreign State."

Although the text of the Amendment would appear to restrict only the Article III diversity jurisdiction of the federal courts, "we have understood the Eleventh Amendment to stand not so much for what it says, but for the presupposition . . . which it confirms." . . . That presupposition . . . has two parts: first, that each State is a sovereign entity in our federal system; and second, that "'[i]t is inherent in the nature of sovereignty not to be amenable to the suit of an individual without its consent.'" . . .

Here, petitioner has sued the State of Florida and it is undisputed that Florida has not consented to the suit. Petitioner nevertheless contends that its suit is not barred by state sovereign immunity. First, it argues that Congress through the Act abrogated the States' sovereign immunity. Alternatively, petitioner maintains that its suit against the Governor may go forward under *Ex parte Young*. We consider each of those arguments in turn.

II

. . . In order to determine whether Congress has abrogated the States' sovereign immunity, we ask two questions: first, whether Congress has "unequivocally expresse[d] its intent to abrogate the immunity," . . . and second, whether Congress has acted "pursuant to a valid exercise of power."

A

Congress' intent to abrogate the States' immunity from suit must be obvious from "a clear legislative statement." . . . This rule arises from a recognition of the important role played by the Eleventh Amendment and the broader principles that it reflects. *See Atascadero State Hospital v. Scanlon* (1985). . . . In *Atascadero*, we held that "[a] general authorization for suit in federal court is not the kind of unequivocal statutory language sufficient to abrogate the Eleventh Amendment." . . . Rather, as we said in *Dellmuth v. Muth* (1989),

> "To temper Congress' acknowledged powers of abrogation with due concern for the Eleventh Amendment's role as an essential component of our constitutional structure, we have applied a simple but stringent test: 'Congress may abrogate the States' constitutionally secured immunity from suit in federal court only by making its intention unmistakably clear in the language of the statute.'"

Here, we agree with the parties, with the Eleventh Circuit in the decision below, and with virtually every other court that has confronted the question that

Congress has in [IGRA] provided an "unmistakably clear" statement of its intent to abrogate. . . .

B

. . . [W]e turn now to consider whether the Act was passed "pursuant to a valid exercise of power." . . .

Petitioner suggests that one consideration weighing in favor of finding the power to abrogate here is that the Act authorizes only prospective injunctive relief rather than retroactive monetary relief. But we have often made it clear that the relief sought by a plaintiff suing a State is irrelevant to the question whether the suit is barred by the Eleventh Amendment. We think it follows *a fortiori* from this proposition that the type of relief sought is irrelevant to whether Congress has power to abrogate States' immunity. The Eleventh Amendment does not exist solely in order to "preven[t] federal court judgments that must be paid out of a State's treasury," . . . it also serves to avoid "the indignity of subjecting a State to the coercive process of judicial tribunals at the instance of private parties" . . . .

Similarly, petitioner argues that the abrogation power is validly exercised here because the Act grants the States a power that they would not otherwise have, viz., some measure of authority over gaming on Indian lands. It is true enough that the Act extends to the States a power withheld from them by the Constitution. Nevertheless, we do not see how that consideration is relevant to the question whether Congress may abrogate state sovereign immunity. The Eleventh Amendment immunity may not be lifted by Congress unilaterally deciding that it will be replaced by grant of some other authority.

Thus our inquiry into whether Congress has the power to abrogate unilaterally the States' immunity from suit is narrowly focused on one question: Was the Act in question passed pursuant to a constitutional provision granting Congress the power to abrogate? . . . Previously, in conducting that inquiry, we have found authority to abrogate under only two provisions of the Constitution. In *Fitzpatrick v. Bitzer* (1976), we recognized that the Fourteenth Amendment, by expanding federal power at the expense of state autonomy, had fundamentally altered the balance of state and federal power struck by the Constitution. We noted that § 1 of the Fourteenth Amendment contained prohibitions expressly directed at the States and that § 5 of the Amendment expressly provided that "The Congress shall have the power to enforce, by appropriate legislation, the provisions of this article." We held that through the Fourteenth Amendment, federal power extended to intrude upon the province of the Eleventh Amendment and therefore that § 5 of the Fourteenth Amendment allowed Congress to abrogate the immunity from suit guaranteed by that Amendment.

In only one other case has congressional abrogation of the States' Eleventh Amendment immunity been upheld. In *Pennsylvania v. Union Gas Co.* (1989), a plurality of the Court found that the Interstate Commerce Clause, Art. I, § 8, cl. 3, granted Congress the power to abrogate state sovereign immunity, stating that the power to regulate interstate commerce would be "incomplete without the authority to render States liable in damages." . . . Justice White added the fifth vote necessary to the result in that case, but wrote separately in order to express that he "[did] not agree with much of [the plurality's] reasoning." . . .

* * *

Both parties make their arguments from the plurality decision in *Union Gas*, and we, too, begin there. . . .

Following the rationale of the *Union Gas* plurality, our inquiry is limited to determining whether the Indian Commerce Clause, like the Interstate Commerce Clause, is a grant of authority to the Federal Government at the expense of the States. The answer to that question is obvious. If anything, the Indian Commerce Clause accomplishes a greater transfer of power from the States to the Federal Government than does the Interstate Commerce Clause. This is clear enough from the fact that the States still exercise some authority over interstate trade but have been divested of virtually all authority over Indian commerce and Indian tribes. Under the rationale of *Union Gas*, if the States' partial cession of authority over a particular area includes cession of the immunity from suit, then their virtually total cession of authority over a different area must also include cession of the immunity from suit. We agree with the petitioner that the plurality opinion in *Union Gas* allows no principled distinction in favor of the States to be drawn between the Indian Commerce Clause and the Interstate Commerce Clause.

Respondents argue, however, that we need not conclude that the Indian Commerce Clause grants the power to abrogate the States' sovereign immunity. Instead, they contend that if we find the rationale of the *Union Gas* plurality to extend to the Indian Commerce Clause, then "*Union Gas* should be reconsidered and overruled." Generally, the principle of *stare decisis*, and the interests that it serves, viz., "the evenhanded, predictable, and consistent development of legal principles, . . . reliance on judicial decisions, and . . . the actual and perceived integrity of the judicial process," . . . counsel strongly against reconsideration of our precedent. Nevertheless, we always have treated *stare decisis* as a "principle of policy," . . . and not as an "inexorable command" . . . . "[W]hen governing decisions are unworkable or are badly reasoned, 'this Court has never felt constrained to follow precedent.'" . . . Our willingness to reconsider our earlier decisions has been "particularly true in constitutional cases, because in such cases 'correction through legislative action is practically impossible.'" . . .

The Court in *Union Gas* reached a result without an expressed rationale agreed upon by a majority of the Court. We have already seen that Justice Brennan's opinion received the support of only three other Justices. . . . Of the other five, Justice White, who provided the fifth vote for the result, wrote separately in order to indicate his disagreement with the majority's rationale, and four Justices joined together in a dissent that rejected the plurality's rationale.

Since it was issued, *Union Gas* has created confusion among the lower courts that have sought to understand and apply the deeply fractured decision. . . .

The plurality's rationale also deviated sharply from our established federalism jurisprudence. . . . It was well established in 1989 when *Union Gas* was decided that the Eleventh Amendment stood for the constitutional principle that state sovereign immunity limited the federal courts' jurisdiction under Article III. The text of the Amendment itself is clear enough on this point: "The Judicial power of the United States shall not be construed to extend to any suit . . . ." And our decisions . . . had been equally clear that the Eleventh Amendment reflects "the fundamental principle of sovereign immunity [that] limits the grant of judicial authority in Article III" . . . . As the dissent in *Union Gas* recognized, the plurality's conclusion — that Congress could under Article I expand the scope of the federal courts' jurisdiction under Article III — "contradict[ed] our unvarying approach to Article III as setting forth the *exclusive* catalog of permissible federal court jurisdiction."

Never before the decision in *Union Gas* had we suggested that the bounds of Article III could be expanded by Congress operating pursuant to any constitutional provision other than the Fourteenth Amendment. Indeed, it had seemed fundamental that Congress could not expand the jurisdiction of the federal courts beyond the bounds of Article III. *Marbury v. Madison* (1803). The plurality's citation of prior decisions for support was based upon what we believe to be a misreading of precedent. . . . The plurality claimed support for its decision from a case holding the unremarkable, and completely unrelated, proposition that the States may waive their sovereign immunity, . . . and cited as precedent propositions that had been merely assumed for the sake of argument in earlier cases. . . .

The plurality's extended reliance upon our decision in *Fitzpatrick v. Bitzer* that Congress could under the Fourteenth Amendment abrogate the States' sovereign immunity was also, we believe, misplaced. *Fitzpatrick* was based upon a rationale wholly inapplicable to the Interstate Commerce Clause, viz., that the Fourteenth Amendment, adopted well after the adoption of the Eleventh Amendment and the ratification of the Constitution, operated to alter the pre-existing balance between state and federal power achieved by Article III and the Eleventh Amendment. . . .

In the five years since it was decided, *Union Gas* has proven to be a solitary departure from established law. Reconsidering the decision in *Union Gas*, we conclude that none of the policies underlying *stare decisis* require our continuing adherence to its holding. The decision has, since its issuance, been of questionable precedential value, largely because a majority of the Court expressly disagreed with the rationale of the plurality. . . . The case involved the interpretation of the Constitution and therefore may be altered only by constitutional amendment or revision by this Court. Finally, both the result in *Union Gas* and the plurality's rationale depart from our established understanding of the Eleventh Amendment and undermine the accepted function of Article III. We feel bound to conclude that *Union Gas* was wrongly decided and that it should be, and now is, overruled.

The dissent makes no effort to defend the decision in *Union Gas*, but nonetheless would find congressional power to abrogate in this case. Contending that our decision is a novel extension of the Eleventh Amendment, the dissent chides us for "attend[ing]" to dicta. We adhere in this case, however, not to mere *obiter dicta*, but rather to the well-established rationale upon which the Court based the results of its earlier decisions. When an opinion issues for the Court, it is not only the result but also those portions of the opinion necessary to that result by which we are bound. For over a century, we have grounded our decisions in the oft-repeated understanding of state sovereign immunity as an essential part of the Eleventh Amendment.

* * *

The dissent, to the contrary, disregards our case law in favor of a theory cobbled together from law review articles and its own version of historical events. The dissent cites not a single decision since *Hans v. Louisiana* (1890) (other than *Union Gas*) that supports its view of state sovereign immunity, instead relying upon the now-discredited decision in *Chisholm v. Georgia* (1793). Its undocumented and highly speculative extralegal explanation of the decision in *Hans* is a disservice to the Court's traditional method of adjudication.

The dissent mischaracterizes the [1890] *Hans* opinion. That decision found its roots not solely in the common law of England, but in the much more fundamental "'jurisprudence in all civilized nations.'" . . . The dissent's proposition that the common law of England, where adopted by the States, was open to change by the legislature, is wholly unexceptionable and largely beside the point: that common law provided the substantive rules of law rather than jurisdiction. . . . It also is noteworthy that the principle of state sovereign immunity stands distinct from other principles of the common law in that only the former prompted a specific constitutional amendment.

Hans — with a much closer vantage point than the dissent — recognized that the decision in *Chisholm* was contrary to the well-understood meaning of the Constitution. The dissent's conclusion that the decision in *Chisholm* was "reasonable," certainly would have struck the Framers of the Eleventh Amendment as quite odd: that decision created "such a shock of surprise that the Eleventh Amendment was at once proposed and adopted." . . The dissent's lengthy analysis of the text of the Eleventh Amendment is directed at a straw man — we long have recognized that blind reliance upon the text of the Eleventh Amendment is "'to strain the Constitution and the law to a construction never imagined or dreamed of.'" . . . The text dealt in terms only with the problem presented by the decision in *Chisholm*; in light of the fact that the federal courts did not have federal question jurisdiction at the time the Amendment was passed (and would not have it until 1875), it seems unlikely that much thought was given to the prospect of federal question jurisdiction over the States.

* * *

In overruling *Union Gas* today, we reconfirm that the background principle of state sovereign immunity embodied in the Eleventh Amendment is not so ephemeral as to dissipate when the subject of the suit is an area, like the regulation of Indian commerce, that is under the exclusive control of the Federal Government. Even when the Constitution vests in Congress complete law-making authority over a particular area, the Eleventh Amendment prevents congressional authorization of suits by private parties against unconsenting States. The Eleventh Amendment restricts the judicial power under Article III, and Article I cannot be used to circumvent the constitutional limitations placed upon federal jurisdiction. Petitioner's suit against the State of Florida must be dismissed for a lack of jurisdiction.

III

Petitioner argues that we may exercise jurisdiction over its suit to enforce [IGRA] against the Governor notwithstanding the jurisdictional bar of the Eleventh Amendment. Petitioner notes that since our decision in *Ex parte Young* we often have found federal jurisdiction over a suit against a state official when that suit seeks only prospective injunctive relief in order to "end a continuing violation of federal law." . . . The situation presented here, however, is sufficiently different from that giving rise to the traditional *Ex parte Young* action so as to preclude the availability of that doctrine.

Here, the "continuing violation of federal law" alleged by petitioner is the Governor's failure to bring the State into compliance with [IGRA]. But the duty to negotiate imposed upon the State by that statutory provision does not stand alone. Rather, as we have seen, Congress passed [IGRA] in conjunction with the carefully crafted and intricate remedial scheme set forth in [IGRA].

Where Congress has created a remedial scheme for the enforcement of a particular federal right, we have, in suits against federal officers, refused to supplement that scheme with one created by the judiciary. . . . Here, of course, the question is not whether a remedy should be created, but instead is whether the Eleventh Amendment bar should be lifted, as it was in *Ex parte Young*, in order to allow a suit against a state officer. Nevertheless, we think that the same general principle applies: therefore, where Congress has prescribed a detailed remedial scheme for the enforcement against a State of a statutorily created right, a court should hesitate before casting aside those limitations and permitting an action against a state officer based upon *Ex parte Young*.

Here, Congress intended [IGRA] to be enforced against the State in an action brought under [the remedial scheme of that Act]; the intricate procedures set forth in that provision show that Congress intended therein not only to define, but also significantly to limit, the duty imposed by [IGRA]. . . . By contrast with this quite modest set of sanctions, an action brought against a state official under *Ex parte Young* would expose that official to the full remedial powers of a federal court, including, presumably, contempt sanctions. If [IGRA] could be enforced in a suit under *Ex parte Young*, [the remedial scheme of that Act] would have been superfluous; it is difficult to see why an Indian tribe would suffer through the intricate scheme of [IGRA] when more complete and more immediate relief would be available under *Ex parte Young*.

Here, of course, we have found that Congress does not have authority under the Constitution to make the State suable in federal court . . . . Nevertheless, the fact that Congress chose to impose upon the State a liability which is significantly more limited than would be the liability imposed upon the state officer under *Ex parte Young* strongly indicates that Congress had no wish to create the latter under [IGRA]. Nor are we free to rewrite the statutory scheme in order to approximate what we think Congress might have wanted had it known that [the remedial scheme of that Act] was beyond its authority. If that effort is to be made, it should be made by Congress, and not by the federal courts. We hold that *Ex parte Young* is inapplicable to petitioner's suit against the Governor of Florida, and therefore that suit is barred by the Eleventh Amendment and must be dismissed for a lack of jurisdiction.

* * *

JUSTICE STEVENS, dissenting. [Omitted.]

JUSTICE SOUTER, with whom JUSTICE GINSBURG and JUSTICE BREYER join, dissenting.

In holding the State of Florida immune to suit under the Indian Gaming Regulatory Act, the Court today holds for the first time since the founding of the Republic that Congress has no authority to subject a State to the jurisdiction of a federal court at the behest of an individual asserting a federal right. Although the Court invokes the Eleventh Amendment as authority for this proposition, the only sense in which that amendment might be claimed as pertinent here was tolerantly phrased by JUSTICE STEVENS in his concurring opinion in *Pennsylvania v. Union Gas* (1989) (STEVENS, J., concurring). There, he explained how it has come about that we have two Eleventh Amendments, the one ratified in 1795, the other (so-called) invented by the Court nearly a century later in *Hans v. Louisiana* (1890). JUSTICE STEVENS saw in that second Eleventh Amendment no bar to the exercise of congressional authority under the Commerce Clause in providing for suits on a federal question by individuals against a State, and I can only say that after my own canvass of the matter I believe he was entirely correct in that view, for reasons given below. His position, of course, was also the holding in *Union Gas*, which the Court now overrules and repudiates.

* * *

I

It is useful to separate three questions: (1) whether the States enjoyed sovereign immunity if sued in their own courts in the period prior to ratification of the National Constitution; (2) if so, whether after ratification the States were entitled to claim some such immunity when sued in a federal court exercising jurisdiction either because the suit was between a State and a non-state litigant who was not its citizen, or because the issue in the case raised a federal question; and (3) whether any state sovereign immunity recognized in federal court may be abrogated by Congress.

The answer to the first question is not clear, although some of the Framers assumed that States did enjoy immunity in their own courts. The second question was not debated at the time of ratification, except as to citizen-state diversity jurisdiction; there was no unanimity, but in due course the Court in *Chisholm v. Georgia* (1793), answered that a state defendant enjoyed no such immunity. As to federal question jurisdiction, state sovereign immunity seems not to have been debated prior to ratification, the silence probably showing a general understanding at the time that the States would have no immunity in such cases.

The adoption of the Eleventh Amendment soon changed the result in *Chisholm*, not by mentioning sovereign immunity, but by eliminating citizen-state diversity jurisdiction over cases with state defendants. I will explain why the Eleventh Amendment did not affect federal question jurisdiction, a notion that needs to be understood for the light it casts on the soundness of *Hans*'s holding that States did enjoy sovereign immunity in federal question suits. The *Hans* Court erroneously assumed that a State could plead sovereign immunity against a noncitizen suing under federal question jurisdiction, and for that reason held that a State must enjoy the same protection in a suit by one of its citizens. The error of *Hans*'s reasoning is underscored by its clear inconsistency with the Founders' hostility to the implicit reception of common-law doctrine as federal law, and with the Founders' conception of sovereign power as divided between the States and the National Government for the sake of very practical objectives.

The Court's answer today to the third question is likewise at odds with the Founders' view that common law, when it was received into the new American legal systems, was always subject to legislative amendment. In ignoring the reasons for this pervasive understanding at the time of the ratification, and in holding that a nontextual common-law rule limits a clear grant of congressional power under Article I, the Court follows a course that has brought it to grief before in our history, and promises to do so again.

* * *

A

The doctrine of sovereign immunity comprises two distinct rules, which are not always separately recognized. The one rule holds that the King or the Crown, as the font of law, is not bound by the law's provisions; the other provides that the King or Crown, as the font of justice, is not subject to suit in its own courts. . . . The one rule limits the reach of substantive law; the other, the jurisdiction of the courts. We are concerned here only with the latter rule, which took its common-law form in the high middle ages. "At least as early as the thirteenth century, during the reign of Henry III (1216-1272), it was recognized that the king could not be sued in his own courts." . . .

The significance of this doctrine in the nascent American law is less clear, however, than its early development and steady endurance in England might suggest. While some colonial governments may have enjoyed some such immunity, . . . the scope (and even the existence) of this governmental immunity in pre-Revolutionary America remains disputed. *See* Gibbons, *The Eleventh Amendment and State Sovereign Immunity: A Reinterpretation*, 83 COLUM. L. REV. 1889, 1895-1899 (1983).

Whatever the scope of sovereign immunity might have been in the Colonies, however, or during the period of Confederation, the proposal to establish a National Government under the Constitution drafted in 1787 presented a prospect unknown to the common law prior to the American experience: the States would become parts of a system in which sovereignty over even domestic matters would be divided or parceled out between the States and the Nation, the latter to be invested with its own judicial power and the right to prevail against the States whenever their respective substantive laws might be in conflict. With this prospect in mind, the 1787 Constitution might have addressed state sovereign immunity by eliminating whatever sovereign immunity the States previously had, as to any matter subject to federal law or jurisdiction; by recognizing an analogue to the old immunity in the new context of federal jurisdiction, but subject to abrogation as to any matter within that jurisdiction; or by enshrining a doctrine of inviolable state sovereign immunity in the text, thereby giving it constitutional protection in the new federal jurisdiction. . . .

The 1787 draft in fact said nothing on the subject, and it was this very silence that occasioned some, though apparently not widespread, dispute among the Framers and others over whether ratification of the Constitution would preclude a State sued in federal court from asserting sovereign immunity as it could have done on any matter of non-federal law litigated in its own courts. As it has come down to us, the discussion gave no attention to congressional power under the proposed Article I but focused entirely on the limits of the judicial power provided in Article III. And although the jurisdictional bases together constituting the judicial power of the national courts under section 2 of Article III included questions arising under federal law and cases between States and individuals who are not citizens, it was only upon the latter citizen-state diversity provisions that preratification questions about state immunity from suit or liability centered.

* * *

B

The argument among the Framers and their friends about sovereign immunity in federal citizen-state diversity cases, in any event, was short lived and ended when this Court, in *Chisholm v. Georgia*, chose between the constitutional alternatives of abrogation and recognition of the immunity enjoyed at common law. The 4-to-1 majority adopted the reasonable (although not compelled) interpretation that the first of the two Citizen-State Diversity Clauses abrogated for purposes of federal jurisdiction any immunity the States might have enjoyed in their own courts, and Georgia was accordingly held subject to the judicial power in a common-law assumpsit action by a South Carolina citizen suing to collect a debt. The case also settled, by implication, any question there could possibly have been about recognizing state sovereign immunity in actions depending on the federal question (or "arising under") head of jurisdiction as well. The constitutional text on federal question jurisdiction, after all, was just as devoid of immunity language as it was on citizen-state diversity, and at the time of *Chisholm* any influence that general common-law immunity might have had as an interpretive force in construing constitutional language would presumably have been no greater when addressing the federal question language of Article III than its Diversity Clauses.

Although Justice Iredell's dissent in *Chisholm* seems at times to reserve judgment on what I have called the third question, whether Congress could authorize suits against the States, . . . his argument is largely devoted to stating the position taken by several federalists that state sovereign immunity was cognizable under the Citizen-State Diversity Clauses, not that state immunity was somehow invisibly codified as an independent constitutional defense. Justice Iredell's dissent focused on the construction of the Judiciary Act of 1789, not Article III. . . . This would have been an odd focus, had he believed that Congress lacked the constitutional authority to impose liability. Instead, on Justice Iredell's view, States sued in diversity retained the common-law sovereignty "where no special act of Legislation controls it, to be in force in each state, as it existed in England (unaltered by any statute), at the time of the first settlement of the country." While in at least some circumstances States might be held liable to "the authority of the United States," any such liability would depend upon "laws passed under the Constitution and in conformity to it." Finding no congressional action abrogating Georgia's common-law immunity, Justice Iredell concluded that the State should not be liable to suit.

C

The Eleventh Amendment, of course, repudiated *Chisholm* and clearly divested federal courts of some jurisdiction as to cases against state parties:

> "The Judicial power of the United States shall not be construed to extend to any suit in law or equity, commenced or prosecuted against one of the United States by Citizens of another State, or by Citizens or Subjects of any Foreign State."

There are two plausible readings of this provision's text. Under the first, it simply repeals the Citizen-State Diversity Clauses of Article III for all cases in which the State appears as a defendant. Under the second, it strips the federal courts of jurisdiction in any case in which a state defendant is sued by a citizen not its own, even if jurisdiction might otherwise rest on the existence of a federal question in the suit. Neither reading of the Amendment, of course, furnishes authority for the Court's view in today's case, but we need to choose between the competing readings for the light that will be shed on the *Hans* doctrine and the legitimacy of inflating that doctrine to the point of constitutional immutability as the Court has chosen to do.

The history and structure of the Eleventh Amendment convincingly show that it reaches only to suits subject to federal jurisdiction exclusively under the Citizen-State Diversity Clauses.

* * *

. . . Because the plaintiffs in today's case are citizens of the State that they are suing, the Eleventh Amendment simply does not apply to them. We must therefore look elsewhere for the source of that immunity by which the Court says their suit is barred from a federal court. . . .

II

The obvious place to look elsewhere, of course, is *Hans v. Louisiana*, and *Hans* was indeed a leap in the direction of today's holding, even though it does not take the Court all the way. The parties in *Hans* raised, and the Court in that case answered, only what I have called the second question, that is, whether the Constitution, without more, permits a State to plead sovereign immunity to bar the exercise of federal question jurisdiction. Although the Court invoked a principle of sovereign immunity to cure what it took to be the Eleventh Amendment's anomaly of barring only those state suits brought by noncitizen plaintiffs, the *Hans* Court had no occasion to consider whether Congress could abrogate that background immunity by statute. Indeed (except in the special circumstance of Congress's power to enforce the Civil War Amendments), this question never came before our Court until *Union Gas*, and any intimations of an answer in prior cases were mere dicta. In *Union Gas* the Court held that the immunity recognized in *Hans* had no constitutional status and was subject to congressional abrogation. Today the Court overrules *Union Gas* and holds just the opposite. In deciding how to choose between these two positions, the place to begin is with *Hans*'s holding that a principle of sovereign immunity derived from the common law insulates a state from federal question jurisdiction at the suit of its own citizen. A critical examination of that case will show that it was wrongly decided, as virtually every recent commentator has concluded. It follows that the Court's further step today of constitutionalizing *Hans*'s rule against abrogation by Congress compounds and immensely magnifies the century-old mistake of *Hans* itself and takes its place with other historic examples of textually untethered elevations of judicially derived rules to the status of inviolable constitutional law.

A

The Louisiana plaintiff in *Hans* held bonds issued by that State, which, like virtually all of the Southern States, had issued them in substantial amounts during the Reconstruction era to finance public improvements aimed at stimulating industrial development. As Reconstruction governments collapsed, however, the post-Reconstruction regimes sought to repudiate these debts, and the *Hans* litigation arose out of Louisiana's attempt to renege on its bond obligations.

Hans sued the State in federal court, asserting that the State's default amounted to an impairment of the obligation of its contracts in violation of the Contract Clause. This Court affirmed the dismissal of the suit, despite the fact that the case fell within the federal court's "arising under," or federal question, jurisdiction. Justice Bradley's opinion did not purport to hold that the terms either of Article III or of the Eleventh Amendment barred the suit, but that the ancient doctrine of sovereign immunity that had inspired adoption of the Eleventh Amendment applied to cases beyond the Amendment's scope and otherwise within the federal question jurisdiction. Indeed, Bradley explicitly admitted that "[i]t is true, the amendment does so read [as to permit Hans's suit], and if there were no other reason or ground for abating his suit, it might be maintainable." The Court elected, nonetheless, to recognize a broader immunity doctrine, despite the want of any textual manifestation, because of what the Court described as the anomaly that would have resulted otherwise: the Eleventh Amendment (according to the Court) would have barred a federal question suit by a noncitizen, but the State would have been subject to federal jurisdiction at its own citizen's behest. The State was accordingly held to be free to resist suit without its consent, which it might grant or withhold as it pleased.

Hans thus addressed the issue implicated (though not directly raised) in the preratification debate about the Citizen-State Diversity Clauses and implicitly settled by *Chisholm*: whether state sovereign immunity was cognizable by federal courts on the exercise of federal question jurisdiction. According to *Hans*, and contrary to *Chisholm*, it was. But that is all that *Hans* held. Because no federal legislation purporting to pierce state immunity was at issue, it cannot fairly be said that *Hans* held state sovereign immunity to have attained some constitutional status immunizing it from abrogation.

Taking *Hans* only as far as its holding, its vulnerability is apparent. The Court rested its opinion on avoiding the supposed anomaly of recognizing jurisdiction to entertain a citizen's federal question suit, but not one brought by a noncitizen. There was, however, no such anomaly at all. As already explained, federal question cases are not touched by the Eleventh Amendment, which leaves a State open to federal question suits by citizens and noncitizens alike. If *Hans* had been from Massachusetts the Eleventh Amendment would not have barred his action against Louisiana.

Although there was thus no anomaly to be cured by *Hans*, the case certainly created its own anomaly in leaving federal courts entirely without jurisdiction to enforce paramount federal law at the behest of a citizen against a State that broke it. It destroyed the congruence of the judicial power under Article III with the substantive guarantees of the Constitution, and with the provisions of statutes passed by Congress in the exercise of its power under Article I: when a State injured an individual in violation of federal law no federal forum could provide direct relief. Absent an alternative process to vindicate federal law (see Part IV, *infra*) John Marshall saw just what the consequences of this anomaly would be in the early Republic, and he took that consequence as good evidence that the Framers could never have intended such a scheme.

> "Different States may entertain different opinions on the true construction of the constitutional powers of Congress. We know, that at one time, the assumption of the debts contracted by the several States, during the war of our revolution, was deemed unconstitutional by some of them. . . . States may legislate in conformity to their opinions and may enforce those opinions by penalties. It would be hazarding too much to assert, that the judicatures of the States will be exempt from the prejudices by which the legislatures and people are influenced, and will constitute perfectly impartial tribunals. In many States the judges are dependent for office and for salary on the will of the legislature. The constitution of the United States furnishes no security against the universal adoption of this principle. When we observe the importance which that constitution attaches to the independence of judges, we are less inclined to suppose that it can have intended to leave these constitutional questions to tribunals where this independence may not exist."
> *Cohens v. Virginia.*

And yet that is just what *Hans* threatened to do.

How such a result could have been threatened on the basis of a principle not so much as mentioned in the Constitution is difficult to understand. But history provides the explanation. As I have already said, *Hans* was one episode in a long story of debt repudiation by the States of the former Confederacy after the end of Reconstruction. The turning point in the States' favor came with the Compromise of 1877, when the Republican party agreed effectively to end Reconstruction and to withdraw federal troops from the South in return for Southern acquiescence in the decision of the Electoral Commission that awarded the disputed 1876 presidential election to Rutherford B. Hayes. The troop withdrawal, of course, left the federal judiciary "effectively without power to resist the rapidly coalescing repudiation movement." Contract Clause suits like the one brought by Hans thus presented this Court with "a draconian choice between repudiation of some of its most inviolable constitutional doctrines and the humiliation of seeing its political authority compromised as its judgments met the resistance of hostile state governments." Indeed, Louisiana's brief in *Hans* unmistakably bore witness to this Court's inability to enforce a judgment against a recalcitrant State: "The solemn obligation of a government arising on its own acknowledged bond would not be enhanced by a judgment rendered on such bond. If it either could not or would not make provision for paying the bond, it is probable that it could not or would not make provision for satisfying the judgment." Given the likelihood that a judgment against the State could not be enforced, it is not wholly surprising that the *Hans* Court found a way to avoid the certainty of the State's contempt.

So it is that history explains, but does not honor, *Hans*. The ultimate demerit of the case centers, however, not on its politics but on the legal errors on which it rested. Before considering those errors, it is necessary to address the Court's contention that subsequent cases have read into *Hans* what was not there to begin with, that is, a background principle of sovereign immunity that is constitutional in stature and therefore unalterable by Congress.

B

The majority does not dispute the point that *Hans v. Louisiana* had no occasion to decide whether Congress could abrogate a State's immunity from federal question suits. The Court insists, however, that the negative answer to that question that it finds in *Hans* and subsequent opinions is not "mere *obiter dicta*, but rather . . . the well-established rationale upon which the Court based the results of its earlier decisions." The exact rationale to which the majority refers, unfortunately, is not easy to discern. The Court's opinion says, immediately after its discussion of *stare decisis*, that "[f]or over a century, we have grounded our decisions in the oft-repeated understanding of state sovereign immunity as an essential part of the Eleventh Amendment." This cannot be the "rationale," though, because this Court has repeatedly acknowledged that the Eleventh Amendment standing alone cannot bar a federal question suit against a State brought by a state citizen. . . . Indeed, as I have noted, Justice Bradley's opinion in *Hans* conceded that Hans might successfully have pursued his claim "if there were no other reason or ground [other than the Amendment itself] for abating his suit." The *Hans* Court, rather, held the suit barred by a nonconstitutional common-law immunity.

The "rationale" which the majority seeks to invoke is, I think, more nearly stated in its quotation from *Principality of Monaco v. Mississippi* (1934). There, the Court said that "we cannot rest with a mere literal application of the words of § 2 of Article III, or assume that the letter of the Eleventh Amendment exhausts the restrictions upon suits against non-consenting States." This statement certainly is true to *Hans*, which clearly recognized a pre-existing principle of sovereign immunity, broader than the Eleventh Amendment itself, that will ordinarily bar federal question suits against a nonconsenting State. That was the "rationale" which was sufficient to decide *Hans* and all of its progeny prior to *Union Gas*. But leaving aside the indefensibility of that rationale, which I will address further below, that was as far as it went.

The majority, however, would read the "rationale" of *Hans* and its line of subsequent cases as answering the further question whether the "postulate" of sovereign immunity that "limit[s] and control[s]" the exercise of Article III jurisdiction, is constitutional in stature and therefore unalterable by Congress. It is true that there are statements in the cases that point toward just this conclusion. . . . These statements, however, are dicta in the classic sense, that is, sheer speculation about what would happen in cases not before the court. But this is not the only weakness of these statements, which are counterbalanced by many other opinions that have either stated the immunity principle without more . . . or have suggested that the *Hans* immunity is not of constitutional stature. . . . More generally, the proponents of the Court's theory have repeatedly referred to state sovereign immunity as a "background principle," "postulate," or "implicit limitation," and as resting on the "inherent nature of sovereignty," rather than any explicit constitutional provision. But whatever set of quotations one may prefer, taking heed of such jurisprudential creations in assessing the contents of federal common law is a very different thing from reading them into the Founding Document itself.

The most damning evidence for the Court's theory that *Hans* rests on a broad rationale of immunity unalterable by Congress, however, is the Court's proven tendency to disregard the post-*Hans* dicta in cases where that dicta would have mattered. If it is indeed true that "private suits against States [are] not permitted under Article III (by virtue of the understanding represented by the Eleventh Amendment)," then it is hard to see how a State's sovereign immunity may be waived any more than it may be abrogated by Congress. . . . After all, consent of a party is in all other instances wholly insufficient to create subject-matter jurisdiction where it would not otherwise exist. . . . Likewise, the Court's broad theory of immunity runs doubly afoul of the appellate jurisdiction problem that I noted earlier in rejecting an interpretation of the Eleventh Amendment's text that would bar federal question suits. If "the whole sum of the judicial power granted by the Constitution to the United States does not embrace the authority to entertain a suit brought by a citizen against his own State without its consent," and if consent to suit in state court is not sufficient to show consent in federal court, then Article III would hardly permit this Court to exercise appellate jurisdiction over issues of federal law arising in lawsuits brought against the States in their own courts. We have, however, quite rightly ignored any post-*Hans* dicta in that sort of case and exercised the jurisdiction that the plain text of Article III provides.

* * *

III

Three critical errors in *Hans* weigh against constitutionalizing its holding as the majority does today. The first we have already seen: the *Hans* Court misread the Eleventh Amendment. It also misunderstood the conditions under which common-law doctrines were received or rejected at the time of the Founding, and it fundamentally mistook the very nature of sovereignty in the young Republic that was supposed to entail a State's immunity to federal question jurisdiction in a federal court. . . .

A

There is and could be no dispute that the doctrine of sovereign immunity that *Hans* purported to apply had its origins in the "familiar doctrine of the common law," . . . "derived from the laws and practices of our English ancestors" . . . . Although statutes came to affect its importance in the succeeding centuries, the doctrine was never reduced to codification, and Americans took their understanding of immunity doctrine from Blackstone, *see* 3 W. BLACKSTONE, COM-MENTARIES ON THE LAWS OF ENGLAND ch. 17 (1768). Here, as in the mother country, it remained a common-law rule [and was subject to legislative override if it was deemed incompatible with the new conditions and theories of government adopted in the new world].

* * *

B

* * *

1

As I have already noted . . ., the Framers and their contemporaries did not agree about the place of common-law state sovereign immunity even as to federal jurisdiction resting on the Citizen-State Diversity Clauses. Edmund Randolph argued in favor of ratification on the ground that the immunity would not be recognized, leaving the States subject to jurisdiction. Patrick Henry opposed ratification on the basis of exactly the same reading. . . . On the other hand, James Madison, John Marshall, and Alexander Hamilton all appear to have believed that the common-law immunity from suit would survive the ratification of Article III, so as to be at a State's disposal when jurisdiction would depend on diversity. This would have left the States free to enjoy a traditional immunity as defendants without barring the exercise of judicial power over them if they chose to enter the federal courts as diversity plaintiffs or to waive their immunity as diversity defendants. . . . The majority sees in these statements, and chiefly in Hamilton's discussion of sovereign immunity in FEDERALIST NO. 81, an unequivocal mandate "which would preclude all federal jurisdiction over an unconsenting State." But there is no such mandate to be found.

* * *

2

We said in *Blatchford v. Native Village of Noatak* (1991) that "the States entered the federal system with their sovereignty intact," but we surely did not mean that they entered that system with the sovereignty they would have claimed if each State had assumed independent existence in the community of nations. . . . While there is no need here to calculate exactly how close the American States came to sovereignty in the classic sense prior to ratification of the Constitution, it is clear that the act of ratification affected their sovereignty in a way different from any previous political event in America or anywhere else. For the adoption of the Constitution made them members of a novel federal system that sought to balance the States' exercise of some sovereign prerogatives delegated from their own people with the principle of a limited but centralizing federal supremacy.

As a matter of political theory, this federal arrangement of dual delegated sovereign powers truly was a more revolutionary turn than the late war had been.

. . . Before the new federal scheme appeared, 18th-century political theorists had assumed that "there must reside somewhere in every political unit a single, undivided, final power, higher in legal authority than any other power, subject to no law, a law unto itself." . . . The American development of divided sovereign powers, which "shatter[ed] . . . the categories of government that had dominated Western thinking for centuries," . . . was made possible only by a recognition that the ultimate sovereignty rests in the people themselves. . . . The people possessing this plenary bundle of specific powers were free to parcel them out to different governments and different branches of the same government as they saw fit. . . .

Under such a scheme, Alexander Hamilton explained, "[i]t does not follow . . . that each of the portions of powers delegated to [the national or state government] is not sovereign *with regard to its proper objects*." . . . A necessary consequence of this view was that "the Government of the United States has sovereign power as to its declared purposes & trusts." Justice Iredell was to make the same observation in his *Chisholm* dissent, commenting that "[t]he United States are sovereign as to all the powers of government actually surrendered: each State in the Union is sovereign, as to all the powers reserved." And to the same point was Chief Justice Marshall's description of the National and State Governments as "each sovereign, with respect to the objects committed to it, and neither sovereign with respect to the objects committed to the other." *McCulloch v. Maryland* (1819).

Given this metamorphosis of the idea of sovereignty in the years leading up to 1789, the question whether the old immunity doctrine might have been received as something suitable for the new world of federal question jurisdiction is a crucial one. The answer is that sovereign immunity as it would have been known to the Framers before ratification thereafter became inapplicable as a matter of logic in a federal suit raising a federal question. The old doctrine, after all, barred the involuntary subjection of a sovereign to the system of justice and law of which it was itself the font, since to do otherwise would have struck the common-law mind from the Middle Ages onward as both impractical and absurd. But the ratification demonstrated that state governments were subject to a superior regime of law in a judicial system established, not by the State, but by the people through a specific delegation of their sovereign power to a National Government that was paramount within its delegated sphere. When individuals sued States to enforce federal rights, the Government that corresponded to the "sovereign" in the traditional common-law sense was not the State but the National Government, and any state immunity from the jurisdiction of the Nation's courts would have required a grant from the true sovereign, the people, in their Constitution, or from the Congress that the Constitution had empowered. . . . Subjecting States to federal jurisdiction in federal question cases brought by individuals thus reflected nothing more than Professor Amar's apt summary that "[w]here governments are acting within the bounds of their delegated 'sovereign' power, they may partake of sovereign immunity; where not, not." 96 YALE L.J. at 1490-1491 n. 261.

State immunity to federal question jurisdiction would, moreover, have run up against the common understanding of the practical necessity for the new federal relationship. According to Madison, the "multiplicity," "mutability," and "injustice" of then-extant state laws were prime factors requiring the formation of a new government. . . . These factors, Madison wrote to Jefferson, "contributed more to that uneasiness which produced the Convention, and prepared the Public mind for a general reform, than those which accrued to our national character and interest from the inadequacy of the Confederation to its immediate objects." . . . These concerns ultimately found concrete expression in a number of specific limitations on state power, including provisions barring the States from enacting bills of attainder or *ex post facto* laws, coining money or emitting bills of credit, denying the privileges and immunities of out-of-staters, or impairing the obligation of contracts. But the proposed Constitution also dealt with the old problems affirmatively by granting the powers to Congress enumerated in Article I, § 8, and by providing through the Supremacy Clause that Congress could preempt State action in areas of concurrent state and federal authority.

Given the Framers' general concern with curbing abuses by state governments, it would be amazing if the scheme of delegated powers embodied in the Constitution had left the National Government powerless to render the States judicially accountable for violations of federal rights.

This sketch of the logic and objectives of the new federal order is confirmed by what we have previously seen of the preratification debate on state sovereign immunity, which in turn becomes entirely intelligible both in what it addressed and what it ignored. It is understandable that reasonable minds differed on the applicability of the immunity doctrine in suits that made it to federal court only under the original Diversity Clauses, for their features were not wholly novel. While they were, of course, in the courts of the new and, for some purposes, paramount National Government, the law that they implicated was largely the old common law (and in any case was not federal law). It was not foolish, therefore, to ask whether the old law brought the old defenses with it. But it is equally understandable that questions seem not to have been raised about state sovereign immunity in federal question cases. The very idea of a federal question depended on the rejection of the simple concept of sovereignty from which the immunity doctrine had developed; under the English common law, the question of immunity in a system of layered sovereignty simply could not have arisen. The Framers' principal objectives in rejecting English theories of unitary sovereignty, moreover, would have been impeded if a new concept of sovereign immunity had taken its place in federal question cases, and would have been substantially thwarted if that new immunity had been held to be untouchable by any congressional effort to abrogate it.

Today's majority discounts this concern. Without citing a single source to the contrary, the Court dismisses the historical evidence regarding the Framers' vision of the relationship between national and state sovereignty, and reassures us that "the Nation survived for nearly two centuries without the question of the existence of [the abrogation] power ever being presented to this Court." But we are concerned here not with the survival of the Nation but the opportunity of its citizens to enforce federal rights in a way that Congress provides. The absence of any general federal question statute for nearly a century following ratification of Article III (with a brief exception in 1800) hardly counts against the importance of that jurisdiction either in the Framers' conception or in current reality; likewise, the fact that Congress has not often seen fit to use its power of abrogation (outside the Fourteenth Amendment context, at least) does not compel a conclusion that the power is not important to the federal scheme. In the end, is it plausible to contend that the plan of the convention was meant to leave the National Government without any way to render individuals capable of enforcing their federal rights directly against an intransigent state?

C

* * *

1

I have already pointed out how the views of the Framers reflected the caution of state constitutionalists and legislators over reception of common-law rules, a caution that the Framers exalted to the point of vigorous resistance to any idea that English common-law rules might be imported wholesale through the new Constitution. The state politicians also took pains to guarantee that once a common-law rule had been received, it would always be subject to legislative alteration, and again the state experience was reflected in the Framers' thought. Indeed, the Framers' very insistence that no common-law doctrine would be received by virtue of ratification was focused in their fear that elements of the common law might thereby have been placed beyond the power of Congress to alter by legislation.

The imperative of legislative control grew directly out of the Framers' revolutionary idea of popular sovereignty. According to one historian, "[s]hared ideas about the sovereignty of the people and the accountability of government to the people resulted at an early date in a new understanding of the role of legislation in the legal system. . . . Whereas a constitution had been seen in the colonial period as a body of vague and unidentifiable precedents and principles of common law origin that imposed ambiguous restrictions on the power of men to make or change law, after independence it came to be seen as a written charter by which the people delegated powers to various institutions of government and imposed limitations on the exercise of those powers. . . . [T]he power to modify or even entirely to repeal the common law . . . now fell explicitly within the jurisdiction of the legislature." W. NELSON, AMERICANIZATION OF THE COMMON LAW 90 (1975).

Virtually every state reception provision, be it constitutional or statutory, explicitly provided that the common law was subject to alteration by statute. . . . Just as the early state governments did not leave reception of the common law to implication, then, neither did they receive it as law immune to legislative alteration.

I have already indicated that the Framers did not forget the state law examples. When Antifederalists objected that the 1787 draft failed to make an explicit adoption of certain common-law protections of the individual, part of the Federalists' answer was that a general constitutional reception of the common law would bar congressional revision. Madison was particularly concerned with the necessity for legislative control, noting in a letter to George Washington that "every State has made great inroads & with great propriety on this *monarchical* code." . . . Madison went on to insist that "[t]he Common law is nothing more than the unwritten law, and is left by all the Constitutions equally liable to legislative alterations." Indeed, Madison anticipated, and rejected, the Court's approach today when he wrote that if "the common law be admitted as . . . of constitutional obligation, it would confer on the judicial department a discretion little short of a legislative power . . . [which] would be permanent and irremediable by the Legislature." . . . "A discretion of this sort," he insisted, "has always been lamented as incongruous and dangerous . . . ."

2

History confirms the wisdom of Madison's abhorrence of constitutionalizing common-law rules to place them beyond the reach of congressional amendment. The Framers feared judicial power over substantive policy and the ossification of law that would result from transforming common law into constitutional law, and their fears have been borne out every time the Court has ignored Madison's counsel on subjects that we generally group under economic and social policy. It is, in fact, remarkable that as we near the end of this century the Court should choose to open a new constitutional chapter in confining legislative judgments on these matters by resort to textually unwarranted common-law rules, for it was just this practice in the century's early decades that brought this Court to the nadir of competence that we identify with *Lochner v. New York* (1905).

It was the defining characteristic of the *Lochner* era, and its characteristic vice, that the Court treated the common-law background (in those days, common-law property rights and contractual autonomy) as paramount, while regarding congressional legislation to abrogate the common law on these economic matters as constitutionally suspect. *See, e.g., Adkins v. Children's Hospital of D.C.* (1923) (finding abrogation of common-law freedom to contract for any wage an unconstitutional "compulsory exaction"). And yet the superseding lesson that seemed clear after *West Coast Hotel Co. v. Parrish* (1937), that action within the legislative power is not subject to greater scrutiny merely because it trenches upon the case law's ordering of economic and social relationships, seems to have been lost on the Court.

The majority today, indeed, seems to be going *Lochner* one better. When the Court has previously constrained the express Article I powers by resort to common-law or background principles, it has done so at least in an ostensible effort to give content to some other written provision of the Constitution, like the Due Process Clause, the very object of which is to limit the exercise of governmental power. *See, e.g., Adair v. United States* (1908). Some textual argument, at least, could be made that the Court was doing no more than defining one provision that happened to be at odds with another. Today, however, the Court is not struggling to fulfill a responsibility to reconcile two arguably conflicting and Delphic constitutional provisions, nor is it struggling with any Delphic text at all. For even the Court concedes that the Constitution's grant to Congress of plenary power over relations with Indian tribes at the expense of any state claim to the contrary is unmistakably clear, and this case does not even arguably implicate a textual trump to the grant of federal question jurisdiction.

I know of only one other occasion on which the Court has spoken of extending its reach so far as to declare that the plain text of the Constitution is subordinate to judicially discoverable principles untethered to any written provision. Justice Chase once took such a position almost 200 years ago:

> "There are certain vital principles in our free Republican governments, which will determine and overrule an apparent and flagrant abuse of legislative power. . . . An act of the Legislature (for I cannot call it a law) contrary to the great first principles of the social compact, cannot be considered a rightful exercise of legislative authority." *Calder v. Bull* (1798) (emphasis deleted).

This position was no less in conflict with American constitutionalism in 1798 than it is today, being inconsistent with the Framers' view of the Constitution as fundamental law. Justice Iredell understood this, and dissented (again) in an opinion that still answers the position that "vital" or "background" principles, without more, may be used to confine a clear constitutional provision:

> "[S]ome speculative jurists have held, that a legislative act against natural justice must, in itself, be void; but I cannot think that, under such a government, any Court of Justice would possess a power to declare it so. . . .

> ". . . [I]t has been the policy of the American states, . . . and of the people of the United States . . . to define with precision the objects of the legislative power, and to restrain its exercise within marked and settled boundaries. If any act of Congress, or of the Legislature of a state, violates those constitutional provisions, it is unquestionably void. . . . If, on the other hand, the Legislature of the Union, or the Legislature of any member of the Union, shall pass a law, within the general scope of their constitutional power, the Court cannot pronounce it to be void, merely because it is, in their judgment, contrary to the principles of natural justice. The ideas of natural justice are regulated by no fixed standard: the ablest and the purest men have differed upon the subject; and all that the Court could properly say, in such an event, would be, that the Leg-

islature (possessed of an equal right of opinion) had passed an act which, in the opinion of the judges, was inconsistent with the abstract principles of natural justice."

Later jurisprudence vindicated Justice Iredell's view, and the idea that "first principles" or concepts of "natural justice" might take precedence over the Constitution or other positive law "all but disappeared in American discourse." . . . It should take more than references to "background principle[s]," and "implicit limitation[s]," . . . to revive the judicial power to overcome clear text unopposed to any other provision, when that clear text is in harmony with an almost-equally clear intent on the part of the Framers and the constitutionalists of their generation.

IV

The Court's holding that the States' *Hans* immunity may not be abrogated by Congress leads to the final question in this case, whether federal question jurisdiction exists to order prospective relief enforcing IGRA against a state officer, respondent Chiles, who is said to be authorized to take the action required by the federal law. Just as with the issue about authority to order the State as such, this question is entirely jurisdictional. . . . [W]e ask whether the state officer is subject to jurisdiction only on the assumption that action directly against the State is barred. The answer to this question is an easy yes, the officer is subject to suit under the rule in *Ex parte Young* (1908), and the case could, and should, readily be decided on this point alone.

A

In *Ex parte Young*, this Court held that a federal court has jurisdiction in a suit against a state officer to enjoin official actions violating federal law, even though the State itself may be immune. Under *Young*, "a federal court, consistent with the Eleventh Amendment, may enjoin state officials to conform their future conduct to the requirements of federal law." . . .

The fact, without more, that such suits may have a significant impact on state governments does not count under *Young*. . . .

It should be no cause for surprise that *Young* itself appeared when it did in the national law. It followed as a matter of course after the *Hans* Court's broad recognition of immunity in federal question cases, simply because "[r]emedies designed to end a continuing violation of federal law are necessary to vindicate the federal interest in assuring the supremacy of that law." . . . *Young* provided, as it does today, a sensible way to reconcile the Court's expansive view of immunity expressed in *Hans* with the principles embodied in the Supremacy Clause and Article III.

* * *

The decision in *Ex parte Young*, and the historic doctrine it embodies, thus plays a foundational role in American constitutionalism, and while the doctrine is sometimes called a "fiction," the long history of its felt necessity shows it to be something much more estimable. . . .

A rule of such lineage, engendered by such necessity, should not be easily displaced, if indeed it is displaceable at all, for it marks the frontier of the enforceability of federal law against sometimes competing state policies. We have in fact never before inferred a congressional intent to eliminate this time-honored practice of enforcing federal law.

C

There is no question that by its own terms *Young*'s indispensable rule authorizes the exercise of federal jurisdiction over respondent Chiles. . . . Obviously, for jurisdictional purposes it makes no difference in principle whether the injunction orders an official not to act, as in *Young*, or requires the official to take some positive step. . . . Nothing, then, in this case renders *Young* unsuitable as a jurisdictional basis for determining on the merits whether the petitioners are entitled to an order against a state official under general equitable doctrine. The Court does not say otherwise, and yet it refuses to apply *Young*. There is no adequate reason for its refusal.

No clear statement of intent to displace the doctrine of *Ex parte Young* occurs in IGRA, and the Court is instead constrained to rest its effort to skirt *Young* on a series of suggestions thought to be apparent in Congress's provision of "intricate procedures" for enforcing a State's obligation under the Act. . . .

* * *

2

Next, the Court suggests that it may be justified in displacing *Young* because *Young* would allow litigants to ignore the "intricate procedures" of IGRA in favor of a menu of streamlined equity rules from which any litigant could order as he saw fit. But there is no basis in law for this suggestion, and the strongest authority to reject it. *Young* did not establish a new cause of action and it does not impose any particular procedural regime in the suits it permits. It stands, instead, for a jurisdictional rule by which paramount federal law may be enforced in a federal court by substituting a non-immune party (the state officer) for an immune one (the State itself). *Young* does no more and furnishes no authority for the Court's assumption that it somehow pre-empts procedural rules devised by Congress for particular kinds of cases that may depend on *Young* for federal jurisdiction.

* * *

3

* * *

Finally, one must judge the Court's purported inference by stepping back to ask why Congress could possibly have intended to jeopardize the enforcement of the statute by excluding application of *Young*'s traditional jurisdictional rule, when that rule would make the difference between success or failure in the federal court if state sovereign immunity was recognized. Why would Congress have wanted to go for broke on the issue of state immunity in the event the State pleaded immunity as a jurisdictional bar? Why would Congress not have wanted IGRA to be enforced by means of a traditional doctrine giving federal courts jurisdiction over state officers, in an effort to harmonize state sovereign immunity with federal law that is paramount under the Supremacy Clause? There are no plausible answers to these questions.

D

There is, finally, a response to the Court's rejection of *Young* that ought to go without saying. Our long-standing practice is to read ambiguous statutes to avoid constitutional infirmity. . . . This practice alone (without any need for a clear statement to displace *Young*) would be enough to require *Young*'s application. So, too, would the application of another rule, requiring courts to choose any reasonable construction of a statute that would eliminate the need to confront a contested constitutional issue (in this case, the place of state sovereign immunity in federal question cases and the status of *Union Gas*). . . . Construing the statute to harmonize with *Young*, as it readily does, would have saved an act of Congress and rendered a discussion on constitutional grounds wholly unnecessary. This case should be decided on this basis alone.

V

* * *

Because neither text, precedent, nor history supports the majority's abdication of our responsibility to exercise the jurisdiction entrusted to us in Article III, I would reverse the judgment of the Court of Appeals.

NOTES AND QUESTIONS

1. Notice that *Seminole Tribe* does not stand for the proposition that states are immune from suit. The Eleventh Amendment does not preclude any review the U.S. Supreme Court may choose to give a state court judgment by writ of certiorari. So too, the *Ex parte Young* exception discussed by the Court allows a suit to be brought against a state officer in federal court in order to enforce a federal right. The *Ex parte Young* exception was the subject of the Court's attention in *Idaho v. Coeur d'Alene Tribe of Idaho*, 521 U.S. 261 (1997), where the Court held that the exception could not be used to, in essence, settle a title dispute — at least in federal court — between an Indian tribe and the state. *Coeur d'Alene* suggests that there may be disagreement on the Court as to the availability of the *Young* exception, with Chief Justice Rehnquist and Justice Kennedy tendering the view that the exception applies as the result of a balancing test evaluating whether there is an adequate state forum in which to vindicate a claimed federal right, the need for uniform interpretation in federal courts, and the level of intrusion to state sovereignty. Justices O'Connor, Scalia, and Thomas strongly disavowed this balancing notion, stating plainly that the *Ex parte Young* exception applies whenever there is a need to remedy a continuing violation of federal law by a state officer.

2. The majority's decision in *Seminole Tribe* is distinctly non-textual, even as the majority includes some of the strongest advocates for judicial restraint and original understanding. Is this anomalous or reflective of the fact that the Constitution is the embodiment, not the displacement, of common (natural) law principle? Or are governmental immunity doctrines a part of the old English common law that are not grounded in natural law principles?

3. You perhaps noticed the sharpness of the criticism of Justice Souter's opinion by the majority in this case, and you will have also noted the incredible length and complexity of Souter's dissent, even after considerable editing. What prompts such an exchange? Is the issue state sovereignty? Is it common law, as Justice Souter argues? Or is it, as he also suggests, a question of natural law? Recall what you learned about common law crimes and natural law in Chapter One and earlier in this Chapter. How accurate is Justice Souter's reading of history on these questions? Is Chief Justice Rehnquist's suggestion that Souter's reasoning is suspect because of his reliance on "law review articles" a sensible one? Do the law professors who write law review articles properly understand history? For a provocative reading of early American constitutional history which suggests that natural law of a kind that Justice Souter rejects was fundamental to the American experience before and after the American Revolution and before and after the Constitution, see M. SCOTT GERBER, TO SECURE THESE RIGHTS: THE DECLARATION OF INDEPENDENCE AND CONSTITUTIONAL INTERPRETATION (1995). Who does better at reading THE FEDERALIST, Rehnquist or Souter?

4. You will have noted Justice Souter's harsh attack on the "*Lochner* era" as the "nadir of competence" of the Court. *Seminole Tribe*, 517 U.S. at 166 (Souter, J., dissenting). Why does he suggest that? Do you agree? Bear this characterization in mind when you consider *Lochner* again, later in the course. Do you agree with Souter's criticism of Justice Chase? Chase, after all, opposed federal common law crimes, which Souter also castigates. Is he being fair to Chase?

5. Although *Seminole Tribe* involved whether Congress could abrogate the state's immunity from suit in *federal court*, the concept of sovereign immunity embraced by the Court has recently gained even greater importance. In *Alden v. Maine,* 527 U.S. 706 (1999), the Court (Justic Kennedy for the majority) held, over a dissent by Justice Souter, joined by Justices Stevens, Ginsburg and Breyer, that "the powers delegated to the Congress under Article I of the United States do not include the power to subject non-consenting States to private suits for damages in *state courts*." This does not mean that states are above or beyond the federal law, but it does mean that private actions for money damages from a state under federal law are generally not possible. Money damages can be secured on behalf of private individuals by a federal officer suing in federal court, but "[a] general federal power to authorize private suits for money damages would place unwarranted strain on the States' ability to govern in accordance with the will of their citizens."

6. In *Seminole Tribe* and *Alden*, both the majority and dissent argue their respective cases from the perspective of original understanding and historical sources. What does this mean for advocates preparing briefs for the Court? And how can the Court be so divided over what the original understanding is? Might it be that the framers were as divided as the present generation, even over basic questions dealing with federal-state relations?

7. You may remember that Justice Kennedy sided with the federal government on the issue of whether states could impose term limits (an additional qualification for office beyond that listed in Article I, section 2, clause 2), writing that "[t]he political identity of the entire people of the Union is reinforced by the proposition, which I take to be beyond dispute, that, though limited as to its objects, the National Government is and must be controlled by the people without collateral interference by the States." *United States Term Limits, Inc. v. Thornton* (1995) (Kennedy, J., concurring). In *Alden*, Justice Kennedy writes: "[a]lthough the Constitution grants broad powers to Congress, our federalism requires that Congress treat the States in a manner consistent with their status as residuary sovereigns and joint participants in the governance of the Nation." Are these positions consistent? There were no specific textual provisions preventing states from imposing term limits in *U.S. Term Limits*; why didn't state residual sovereignty in the governance of the Nation prevail?

8. Justice Souter in his *Alden* dissent labeled the majority position as one driven by "natural law," for which Justice Souter has obvious disdain. The majority responded that the meaning of state sovereign immunity is derived in part from "common-law tradition, [and] the structure and history of the Constitution," and "not by the principles or limitations derived from natural law." What is going on here? As we discussed earlier, natural law was a significant influence on the founding generation, often embodied in common law application, but deals not with the conventions of government structure, but with natural rights ("self-evident truths" to use the language of the founding Declaration of Independence) that are deduced from reasoned reflection on the human condition, and are expressed in the language of natural rights.

There seems to be some confusion for both the majority and dissent about where "natural law," as the Court uses that term, leaves off, and "common law" begins. Of what significance is the fact that for Blackstone and for the late eighteenth century framers the "common law" reflected, was grounded in, and incorporated "natural law." Of what significance is the fact that for the founding generation it was very difficult to draw fine distinctions between "the common law," "natural law," and the *jus gentium* or law of nations. On these points see generally Chapter I of MORTON HORWITZ, THE TRANSFORMATION OF AMERICAN LAW 1780-1860 (1977), and Chapter VI of STEPHEN B. PRESSER, THE ORIGINAL

MISUNDERSTANDING: THE ENGLISH, THE AMERICANS, AND THE DIALECTIC OF FED-
ERALIST JURISPRUDENCE (1991).

9. States can be sued with their explicit consent, but not with mere implied
consent. Congress may authorize a private cause of action pursuant to its
enforcement authority under section 5 of the Fourteenth Amendment, but only
when it is enforcing, not redefining, a constitutional right of privilege or immunity, equal protection, or due process protected by section 1 of the Fourteenth
Amendment, and its enforcement efforts are bounded by the considerations of
"proportionality" and "congruence" first outlined in *City of Boerne v. Flores*
(1997). In *Kimel v. Florida Board of Regents*, 528 U.S. 62 (2000), for example,
Justice O'Connor, writing for a 5-member majority of the Court, held that the
Age Discrimination in Employment Act was not a valid exercise of Congress'
remedial power under § 5 of the Fourteenth Amendment because it was not a
"congruent and proportional" remedy for any pattern of state violation of rights
protected by the Fourteenth Amendment. As a result, Congress' abrogation of
state sovereign immunity was invalid. Similarly, in *Florida Prepaid Postsecondary Education Expense Board v. College Savings Bank*, 527 U.S. 627 (1999),
Chief Justice Rehnquist, again for a 5-4 majority, rejected Congress' attempt to
abrogate state sovereign immunity in the Patent and Plant Variety Protection
Remedy Clarification Act. The Act failed to meet the Court's "congruence and
proportionality test" because "Congress identified no pattern of patent infringement by the States, let alone a pattern of constitutional violations." As a result,
the Act was not an appropriate exercise of § 5 power, and its validity under the
Commerce Clause could not support abrogation of sovereign immunity.

In *Board of Trustees v. Garrett*, 531 U.S. 356 (2001), writing for the usual 5-
4 line-up, the Chief Justice determined that disability was not a suspect or
quasi-suspect classification, and thus, states could draw rational distinctions
based upon this trait. Title I of the Americans with Disabilities Act (ADA),
however, required more, and while state employers could be exempt upon showing an undue hardship in making accommodation, even that exceeded the constitutional requirement and could not be imposed on the states without their
consent. In any event, the majority saw little evidence of state discrimination,
and hence, the requirement that federal monetary remedies against State sovereigns be congruent and proportional to demonstrated discrimination was not
shown. Justice Breyer dissented, joined by Justices Stevens, Souter and Ginsburg. Justice Breyer attached to his opinion an Appendix of state discriminatory
treatment of the disabled which he reasoned more than justified the ADA liability provision. Justice Breyer was particularly disturbed by the fact that the
majority placed the burden on Congress to demonstrate that state actions were
not presumptively rational and constitutional. This burden of restraint, argued
Breyer, applies to judges, not the Congress. Congress under § 5 has the institutional capacity to find facts that the Court does not. The majority wasn't
swayed, and it invited the dissent to compare the careful assessment and identification of serious constitutional violations that accompanied the Voting Rights

Act of 1965, which remedied improper use of literacy tests and other voting qualifications by the states.

There are a few related contexts where state liability may attach as a result of the exercise of Article I power by the Congress. First, liability may result by virtue of state participation in an interstate compact. *Petty v. Tennessee-Missouri Bridge Comm'n* (1959), holding that a bi-state commission which had been created pursuant to an interstate compact (and which the Court assumed partook of state sovereign immunity) had consented to suit by reason of a suability provision attached to the congressional approval of the compact. So too, liability may result as a condition of federal spending. *See South Dakota v. Dole* (1987), discussed earlier in this Chapter. Congress may, in the exercise of its spending power, condition its grant of funds to the states upon their taking certain actions that Congress could not require them to take. Under the Compact Clause, Art. I, § 10, cl. 3, states cannot form an interstate compact without first obtaining the express consent of Congress; the granting of such consent is a gratuity. So also, Congress has no obligation to use its Spending Clause power to disburse funds to the states; such funds are "gifts," according to the Court — though citizens being "gifted" with a return of their own money may dispute this characterization. The Court does note that some spending conditions may be off-limits — namely, those where "the financial inducement offered by Congress might be so coercive as to pass the point at which 'pressure turns into compulsion.'"

10. As the Court's cases reveal, Eleventh Amendment immunity has less and less to do with the text of the Eleventh Amendment, and far more to do with the background principles of state sovereignty as mediated by the Court itself. The Eleventh Amendment is phrased as a construction and limitation upon judicial power. After *Federal Maritime Commission v. South Carolina State Ports Authority*, 535 U.S. 1111 (2002), it is a limitation upon the executive branch as well.

South Carolina Maritime Services, Inc. (Maritime Services) filed a complaint with the Federal Maritime Commission (FMC), contending that respondent South Carolina State Ports Authority (the state authority) violated the Shipping Act of 1984 when it denied Maritime Services permission to berth a cruise ship at the state authority's port facilities in Charleston, South Carolina. Maritime Services asked the executive agency to direct the state authority to pay reparations to Maritime Services, order the state authority to cease and desist from violating the Shipping Act, and ask the United States District Court for the District of South Carolina to enjoin the state authority from refusing berthing space and passenger services to Maritime Services. The complaint was referred to an Administrative Law Judge (ALJ), who found that the state authority, as an arm of the State of South Carolina, was entitled to sovereign immunity and thus dismissed the complaint. Reversing on its own motion, the executive commission, the FMC, concluded that state sovereign immunity covers proceedings before judicial tribunals, not Executive Branch agencies. The Fourth Circuit reversed, and in a 5-4 opinion, the Supreme Court affirmed. *Held:* State sovereign immunity bars an executive agency, the FMC, from adjudicating a private party's complaint against a nonconsenting state. Justice Thomas wrote for the five person majority (including Rehnquist, Scalia, O'Connor and Kennedy). Thomas observed that "formalized administrative adjudications" were not known in the 18th and early 19th century, but because of the reluctance to subject states to onerous proceedings at the time of formation of the Constitution, it was sensible to apply the general reasoning about sovereign immunity to extend to such administrative proceedings. The Court subscribed to "the Fourth Circuit's characterization that such a proceeding walks, talks, and squawks like a lawsuit" and that the policies that would suggest sovereign immunity for lawsuits also applied to administrative proceedings before administrative law judges. Justice Stevens, in his dissenting opinion (which he filed on his own), indicated his disagreement with the majority's conclusion, drawn from history, about the Constitution's structure and the need to protect the "dignity of the individual states." Justice Breyer, in a dissent joined by Justices Stevens, Souter, and Ginsburg, argued that there was no "text, tradition, or relevant purpose" which would support the majority's application of the doctrine of sovereign immunity to an administrative law proceeding.

11. Below, Chief Justice Rehnquist and Justice O'Connor joined with the *Seminole Tribe, Alden, Kimel,* and *Florida Prepaid* dissenters to uphold Congress' abrogation of state sovereign immunity under the Family and Medical Leave Act of 1993. See if you can ascertain the grounds on which Chief Justice Rehnquist distinguished *Kimel* and *Florida Prepaid*. Are you persuaded, or have Chief Justice Rehnquist and Justice O'Connor changed their minds about the Court's recent Eleventh Amendment sovereign immunity cases?

NEVADA DEPARTMENT OF HUMAN RESOURCES v. HIBBS
538 U.S. 721 (2003)

CHIEF JUSTICE REHNQUIST delivered the opinion of the Court.

The Family and Medical Leave Act of 1993 (FMLA or Act) entitles eligible employees to take up to 12 work weeks of unpaid leave annually for any of several reasons, including the onset of a "serious health condition" in an employee's spouse, child, or parent. . . . The Act creates a private right of action to seek both equitable relief and money damages "against any employer (including a public agency) in any Federal or State court of competent jurisdiction," . . . should that employer "interfere with, restrain, or deny the exercise of" FMLA rights . . . . We hold that employees of the State of Nevada may recover money damages in the event of the State's failure to comply with the family-care provision of the Act.

Petitioners include the Nevada Department of Human Resources (Department) and two of its officers. Respondent William Hibbs (hereinafter respondent) worked for the Department's Welfare Division. In April and May 1997, he sought leave under the FMLA to care for his ailing wife, who was recovering from a car accident and neck surgery. The Department granted his request for the full 12 weeks of FMLA leave and authorized him to use the leave intermittently as needed between May and December 1997. Respondent did so until August 5, 1997, after which he did not return to work. In October 1997, the Department informed respondent that he had exhausted his FMLA leave, that no further leave would be granted, and that he must report to work by November 12, 1997. Respondent failed to do so and was terminated.

* * *

The district court found the FMLA barred by the eleventh amendment. The Ninth Circuit reversed.

For over a century now, we have made clear that the Constitution does not provide for federal jurisdiction over suits against nonconsenting States.

Congress may, however, abrogate such immunity in federal court if it makes its intention to abrogate unmistakably clear in the language of the statute and acts pursuant to a valid exercise of its power under § 5 of the Fourteenth Amendment. The clarity of Congress' intent here is not fairly debatable.

In enacting the FMLA, Congress relied on two of the powers vested in it by the Constitution: Its Article I commerce power and its power under § 5 of the Fourteenth Amendment to enforce that Amendment's guarantees. Congress may not abrogate the States' sovereign immunity pursuant to its Article I power over commerce. *Seminole Tribe.* Congress may, however, abrogate States' sovereign immunity through a valid exercise of its § 5 power, for "the Eleventh Amendment, and the principle of state sovereignty which it embodies, are necessarily limited by the enforcement provisions of § 5 of the Fourteenth Amendment."

* * *

Two provisions of the Fourteenth Amendment are relevant here: Section 5 grants Congress the power "to enforce" the substantive guarantees of § 1 — among them, equal protection of the laws — by enacting "appropriate legislation." Congress may, in the exercise of its § 5 power, do more than simply proscribe conduct that we have held unconstitutional. "'Congress' power "to enforce" the Amendment includes the authority both to remedy and to deter violation of rights guaranteed thereunder by prohibiting a somewhat broader swath of conduct, including that which is not itself forbidden by the Amendment's text.' . . . In other words, Congress may enact so-called prophylactic legislation that proscribes facially constitutional conduct, in order to prevent and deter unconstitutional conduct.

City of Boerne also confirmed, however, that it falls to this Court, not Congress, to define the substance of constitutional guarantees. Valid § 5 legislation must exhibit "congruence and proportionality between the injury to be prevented or remedied and the means adopted to that end."

The FMLA aims to protect the right to be free from gender-based discrimination in the workplace. We have held that statutory classifications that distinguish between males and females are subject to heightened scrutiny. For a gender-based classification to withstand such scrutiny, it must "serv[e] important governmental objectives," and "the discriminatory means employed [must be] substantially related to the achievement of those objectives." We now inquire whether Congress had evidence of a pattern of constitutional violations on the part of the States in this area.

The history of the many state laws limiting women's employment opportunities is chronicled in — and, until relatively recently, was sanctioned by — this Court's own opinions. The Court upheld state laws prohibiting women from practicing law and tending bar. State laws frequently subjected women to distinctive restrictions, terms, conditions, and benefits for those jobs they could take. In *Muller v. Oregon* (1908), for example, this Court approved a state law limiting the hours that women could work for wages, and observed that 19 States had such laws at the time. Such laws were based on the related beliefs that (1) woman is, and should remain, "the center of home and family life" and (2) "a proper discharge of [a woman's] maternal functions — having in view not merely her own health, but the well-being of the race — justif[ies] legislation to protect her from the greed as well as the passion of man." Until our decision in *Reed v. Reed* (1971), "it remained the prevailing doctrine that government, both federal and state, could withhold from women opportunities accorded men so long as any 'basis in reason'" — such as the above beliefs — "could be conceived for the discrimination."

Congress responded to this history of discrimination by abrogating States' sovereign immunity in Title VII of the Civil Rights Act of 1964, and we sustained this abrogation. But state gender discrimination did not cease. According to evidence that was before Congress when it enacted the FMLA, States continue to rely on invalid gender stereotypes in the employment context, specifically in the administration of leave benefits. Reliance on such stereotypes cannot justify the States' gender discrimination in this area. The long and extensive history of sex discrimination prompted us to hold that measures that differentiate on the basis of gender warrant heightened scrutiny; here, as in *Fitzpatrick* [*v. Bitzer* (1976)], the persistence of such unconstitutional discrimination by the States justifies Congress' passage of prophylactic § 5 legislation.

As the FMLA's legislative record reflects, a 1990 Bureau of Labor Statistics (BLS) survey stated that 37 percent of surveyed private-sector employees were covered by maternity leave policies, while only 18 percent were covered by paternity leave policies. Stereotype-based beliefs about the allocation of family duties remained firmly rooted, and employers' reliance on them in establishing discriminatory leave policies remained widespread.[1]

---

1 While this and other material described leave policies in the private sector, a 50-state survey also before Congress demonstrated that "[t]he proportion and construction of leave policies available to public sector employees differs little from those offered private sector employees."

Congress also heard testimony that "[p]arental leave for fathers . . . is rare. Even . . . [w]here child-care leave policies do exist, men, both in the public and private sectors, receive notoriously discriminatory treatment in their requests for such leave." Many States offered women extended "maternity" leave that far exceeded the typical 4- to 8-week period of physical disability due to pregnancy and childbirth, but very few States granted men a parallel benefit: Fifteen States provided women up to one year of extended maternity leave, while only four provided men with the same. This and other differential leave policies were not attributable to any differential physical needs of men and women, but rather to the pervasive sex-role stereotype that caring for family members is women's work.

* * *

Finally, Congress had evidence that, even where state laws and policies were not facially discriminatory, they were applied in discriminatory ways. It was aware of the "serious problems with the discretionary nature of family leave," because when "the authority to grant leave and to arrange the length of that leave rests with individual supervisors," it leaves "employees open to discretionary and possibly unequal treatment."

In spite of all of the above evidence, JUSTICE KENNEDY argues in dissent that Congress' passage of the FMLA was unnecessary because "the States appear to have been ahead of Congress in providing gender-neutral family leave benefits," . . . and points to Nevada's leave policies in particular.

The dissent's statement that some States "had adopted some form of family-care leave" before the FMLA's enactment, glosses over important shortcomings of some state policies. First, seven States had childcare leave provisions that applied to women only. Indeed, Massachusetts required that notice of its leave provisions be posted only in "establishment[s] in which females are employed." These laws reinforced the very stereotypes that Congress sought to remedy through the FMLA. Second, 12 States provided their employees no family leave, beyond an initial childbirth or adoption, to care for a seriously ill child or family member. Third, many States provided no statutorily guaranteed right to family leave, offering instead only voluntary or discretionary leave programs. Three States left the amount of leave time primarily in employers' hands. Congress could reasonably conclude that such discretionary family-leave programs would do little to combat the stereotypes about the roles of male and female employees that Congress sought to eliminate. Finally, four States provided leave only through administrative regulations or personnel policies, which Congress could reasonably conclude offered significantly less firm protection than a federal law. Against the above backdrop of limited state leave policies, no matter how generous petitioner's own may have been Congress was justified in enacting the FMLA as remedial legislation.

* * *

In sum, the States' record of unconstitutional participation in, and fostering of, gender-based discrimination in the administration of leave benefits is weighty enough to justify the enactment of prophylactic § 5 legislation.

We reached the opposite conclusion in *Garrett* and *Kimel*. In those cases, the § 5 legislation under review responded to a purported tendency of state officials to make age- or disability-based distinctions. Under our equal protection case law, discrimination on the basis of such characteristics is not judged under a heightened review standard, and passes muster if there is "a rational basis for doing so at a class-based level, even if it 'is probably not true' that those reasons are valid in the majority of cases." Thus, in order to impugn the constitutionality of state discrimination against the disabled or the elderly, Congress must identify, not just the existence of age- or disability-based state decisions, but a "widespread pattern" of irrational reliance on such criteria. We found no such showing with respect to the ADEA and Title I of the Americans with Disabilities Act of 1990 (ADA).

Because the standard for demonstrating the constitutionality of a gender-based classification is more difficult to meet than our rational-basis test — it must "serv[e] important governmental objectives" and be "substantially related to the achievement of those objectives" — it was easier for Congress to show a pattern of state constitutional violations. Congress was similarly successful in *South Carolina v. Katzenbach* (1966), where we upheld the Voting Rights Act of 1965: Because racial classifications are presumptively invalid, most of the States' acts of race discrimination violated the Fourteenth Amendment.

The impact of the discrimination targeted by the FMLA is significant. Congress determined:

> "Historically, denial or curtailment of women's employment opportunities has been traceable directly to the pervasive presumption that women are mothers first, and workers second. This prevailing ideology about women's roles has in turn justified discrimination against women when they are mothers or mothers-to-be."

We believe that Congress' chosen remedy, the family-care leave provision of the FMLA, is "congruent and proportional to the targeted violation." Congress had already tried unsuccessfully to address this problem through Title VII and the amendment of Title VII by the Pregnancy Discrimination Act.

In the dissent's view, in the face of evidence of gender-based discrimination by the States in the provision of leave benefits, Congress could do no more in exercising its § 5 power than simply proscribe such discrimination. But this position cannot be squared with our recognition that Congress "is not confined to the enactment of legislation that merely parrots the precise wording of the Fourteenth Amendment," but may prohibit "a somewhat broader swath of conduct, including that which is not itself forbidden by the Amendment's text."

* * *

substantive entitlement program of its own. If Congress had been concerned about different treatment of men and women with respect to family leave, a congruent remedy would have sought to ensure the benefits of any leave program enacted by a State are available to men and women on an equal basis.

Well before the federal enactment, Nevada not only provided its employees, on a gender-neutral basis, with an option of requesting up to one year of unpaid leave. Nevada state employees were also entitled to use up to 10 days of their accumulated paid sick leave to care for an ill relative. Nevada, in addition, had a program of special "catastrophic leave." State employees could donate their accrued sick leave to a general fund to aid employees who needed additional leave to care for a relative with a serious illness.

Were more proof needed to show that this is an entitlement program, not a remedial statute, it should suffice to note that the Act does not even purport to bar discrimination in some leave programs the States do enact and administer. Under the Act, a State is allowed to provide women with, say, 24 weeks of family leave per year but provide only 12 weeks of leave to men. As the counsel for the United States conceded during the argument, a law of this kind might run afoul of the Equal Protection Clause or Title VII, but it would not constitute a violation of the Act. The Act on its face is not drawn as a remedy to gender-based discrimination in family leave.

The Court's precedents upholding the Voting Rights Act of 1965 as a proper exercise of Congress' remedial power are instructive. In *South Carolina v. Katzenbach* (1966), the Court concluded that the Voting Rights Act's prohibition on state literacy tests was an appropriate method of enforcing the constitutional protection against racial discrimination in voting. This measure was justified because "Congress documented a marked pattern of unconstitutional action by the States." This scheme was both congruent, because it "aimed at areas where voting discrimination has been most flagrant," and proportional, because it was necessary to "banish the blight of racial discrimination in voting, which has infected the electoral process in parts of our country for nearly a century." The Court acknowledged Congress' power to devise "strong remedial and preventive measures" to safeguard voting rights on subsequent occasions, but always explained that these measures were legitimate because they were responding to a pattern of "the widespread and persisting deprivation of constitutional rights resulting from this country's history of racial discrimination."

This principle of our § 5 jurisprudence is well illustrated not only by the Court's opinions in these cases but also by the late Justice Harlan's dissent in *Katzenbach v. Morgan*. There, Justice Harlan contrasted his vote to invalidate a federal ban on New York state literacy tests from his earlier decision, in *South Carolina v. Katzenbach*, to uphold stronger remedial measures against the State of South Carolina, such as suspension of literacy tests, imposition of preclearance requirements for any changes in state voting laws, and appointment of federal voting examiners. Justice Harlan explained that in the case of South Carolina there was "'voluminous legislative history' as well as judicial precedents supporting the basic congressional findings that the clear commands of the Fifteenth Amendment had been infringed by various state subterfuges . . . . Given the existence of the evil, we held the remedial steps taken by the legislature under the Enforcement Clause of the Fifteenth Amendment to be a justifiable exercise of congressional initiative." By contrast, the New York case, in his view, lacked a showing that "there has in fact been an infringement of that constitutional command, that is, whether a particular state practice . . . offend[ed] the command of the Equal Protection Clause of the Fourteenth Amendment." In the absence of evidence that a State has engaged in unconstitutional conduct, Justice Harlan would have concluded that the literacy test ban Congress sought to impose was not an "appropriate remedial measur[e] to redress and prevent the wrongs," but an impermissible attempt "to define the *substantive* scope of the Amendment."

It bears emphasis that, even were the Court to bar unconsented federal suits by private individuals for money damages from a State, individuals whose rights under the Act were violated would not be without recourse. The Act is likely a valid exercise of Congress' power under the Commerce Clause, Art. I, § 8, cl. 3, and so the standards it prescribes will be binding upon the States. The United States may enforce these standards in actions for money damages; and private individuals may bring actions against state officials for injunctive relief under *Ex parte Young* (1908). What is at issue is only whether the States can be subjected, without consent, to suits brought by private persons seeking to collect moneys from the state treasury. Their immunity cannot be abrogated without documentation of a pattern of unconstitutional acts by the States, and only then by a congruent and proportional remedy. There has been a complete failure by respondents to carry their burden to establish each of these necessary propositions. I would hold that the Act is not a valid abrogation of state sovereign immunity and dissent with respect from the Court's conclusion to the contrary.

NOTES AND QUESTIONS

1. The development in *Hibbs*, allowing the federal government greater latitude to overcome state sovereign immunity where a matter of heightened interest was at stake, whether a quasi-suspect class or fundamental right, continued in *Tennessee v. Lane*, 124 S. Ct. 1978 (2004). George Lane, a paraplegic, went to his county courthouse to answer misdemeanor criminal charges. The trial courtroom where he was scheduled to appear was on the second floor. To make his initial appearance, Lane crawled up two flights of stairs. At his next appearance he refused to crawl up the stairs. He also refused the help of deputies who offered to carry him upstairs. Consequently, he was charged with and jailed for failure to appear in court. He then brought suit against the state alleging violations of his right to public access of the courts protected under Title II of the Americans With Disabilities Act.

The question before the Court was whether Congress had acted properly when it abrogated state sovereign immunity under Title II of the ADA. You'll remember that the Court had previously found no abrogation with respect to Title I of the ADA dealing with employment discrimination against the disabled in *Board of Trustees v. Garrett*, 531 U.S. 356 (2001). In *Lane*, the Court reached a different result because of the fundamental due process interest in access to a court.

Per Justice Stevens, the Court said:

Title II's requirement of program accessibility, is congruent and proportional to its object of enforcing the right of access to the courts. The unequal treatment of disabled persons in the administration of judicial services has a long history, and has persisted despite several legislative efforts to remedy the problem of disability discrimination. Faced with considerable evidence of the shortcomings of previous legislative responses, Congress was justified in concluding that this "difficult and intractable proble[m]" warranted "added prophylactic measures in response."

The remedy Congress chose is nevertheless a limited one. Recognizing that failure to accommodate persons with disabilities will often have the same practical effect as outright exclusion, Congress required the States to take reasonable measures to remove architectural and other barriers to accessibility. But Title II does not require States to employ any and all means to make judicial services accessible to persons with disabilities, and it does not require States to compromise their essential eligibility criteria for public programs. It requires only "reasonable modifications" that would not fundamentally alter the nature of the service provided, and only when the individual seeking modification is otherwise eligible for the service. As Title II's implementing regulations make clear, the reasonable modification requirement can be satisfied in a number of ways. In the case of facilities built or altered after 1992, the regulations require compliance with specific architectural accessibility standards. But in the case of older facilities, for which structural change is likely to be more difficult, a public entity may comply with Title II by adopting a variety of less costly measures, including relocating services to alternative, accessible sites and assigning aides to assist persons with disabilities in accessing services. Only if these measures are ineffective in achieving accessibility is the public entity required to make reasonable structural changes. And in no event is the entity required to undertake measures that would impose an undue financial or administrative burden, threaten historic preservation interests, or effect a fundamental alteration in the nature of the service.

This duty to accommodate is perfectly consistent with the well-established due process principle that, "within the limits of practicability, a State must afford to all individuals a meaningful opportunity to be heard" in its courts. Our cases have recognized a number of affirmative obligations that flow from this principle: the duty to waive filing fees in certain family-law and criminal cases, the duty to provide transcripts to criminal defendants seeking review of their convictions, and the duty to provide counsel to certain criminal defendants. Each of these cases makes clear that ordinary considerations of cost and convenience alone cannot justify a State's failure to provide individuals with a meaningful right of access to the courts. Judged against this backdrop, Title II's affirmative obligation to accommodate persons with disabilities in the administration of justice cannot be said to be "so out of proportion to a supposed remedial or preventive object that it cannot be understood as responsive to, or designed to prevent, unconstitutional behavior." It is, rather, a reasonable prophylactic measure, reasonably targeted to a legitimate end.

Slip opinion at 20-21. (footnotes and citations omitted).

To three of the four dissenters (Chief Justice Rehnquist and Justices Kennedy and Thomas), *Garrett* should have governed. The dissent observed:

> With respect to the due process "access to the courts" rights on which the Court ultimately relies, Congress' failure to identify a pattern of actual constitutional violations by the States is even more striking. Indeed, there is *nothing* in the legislative record or statutory findings to indicate that disabled persons were systematically denied the right to be present at criminal trials, denied the meaningful opportunity to be heard in civil cases, unconstitutionally excluded from jury service, or denied the right to attend criminal trials.

Justice Scalia wrote a separate dissent where he disavowed the majority's and Chief Justice Rehnquist's reliance on the "congruence and proportionality" test. Since this deals with the scope of Congress' section 5 enforcement authority under the Fourteenth Amendment, rather than the appropriateness of abrogation, we defer Justice Scalia's observations on this until after the *Boerne* case, *infra*.

What new evidence did the Court point to that permitted it to distinguish *Garret*? Was there any?

E. Individual Rights Limitations on the Powers of the States

Seminole Tribe is a clearly stated reaffirmation of state (or dual) sovereignty as a background principle of constitutional adjudication. Yet, the history of the formation of the Constitution reveals that there were several important reasons for those who met at the Philadelphia Convention in 1787 to limit state sovereignty. Under the Articles of Confederation, the states were clearly still the only relevant sovereign powers, and it often took unanimous concurrence before any major national initiatives could be taken. Worse, the states often neglected their obligations to the national government, such as making contributions to the costs of the Revolutionary War. Finally, and in some ways most importantly, the sovereign states had a tendency to pass measures which interfered with the vested rights of individuals, such as negating existing contracts or suspending payment of debts or requiring that increasingly-worthless state paper currency be accepted as legal tender in payment of pre-existing debts. In order to avoid the evils of such state legislation, James Madison and others believed that the new Constitution should give the national government some sort of veto of state legislation. Madison and his allies were unsuccessful in their efforts to implement such a national veto of state legislation, probably because such a measure would have jeopardized the ratification of the proposed Constitution on the grounds that it had a tendency to obliterate the sovereignty of the states. The cases in this section explore the means the judiciary has employed to constrain state sovereignty as it relates to individual rights.

BARRON v. MAYOR OF BALTIMORE
32 U.S. (7 Pet.) 243 (1833)

MR. CHIEF JUSTICE MARSHALL delivered the opinion of the Court.

* * *

The plaintiff in error contends that [the] clause in the fifth amendment to the constitution, which inhibits the taking of private property for public use, without just compensation . . . , being in favour of the liberty of the citizen, ought to be so construed as to restrain the legislative power of a state, as well as that of the United States. . . .

The question thus presented is, we think, of great importance, but not of much difficulty.

The constitution was ordained and established by the people of the United States for themselves, for their own government, and not for the government of the individual states. Each state established a constitution for itself, and, in that constitution, provided such limitations and restrictions on the powers of its particular government as its judgment dictated. The people of the United States framed such a government for the United States as they supposed best adapted to their situation, and best calculated to promote their interests. The powers they conferred on this government were to be exercised by itself; and the limitations on power, if expressed in general terms, are naturally, and, we think, necessarily applicable to the government created by the instrument. They are limitations of power granted in the instrument itself; not of distinct governments, framed by different persons and for different purposes.

If these propositions be correct, the fifth amendment must be understood as restraining the power of the general government, not as applicable to the states. In their several constitutions they have imposed such restrictions on their respective governments as their own wisdom suggested; such as they deemed most proper for themselves. It is a subject on which they judge exclusively, and with which others interfere no farther than they are supposed to have a common interest.

The counsel for the plaintiff in error insists that the constitution was intended to secure the people of the several states against the undue exercise of power by their respective state governments; as well as against that which might be attempted by their general government. In support of this argument he relies on the inhibitions contained in the tenth section of the first article.

We think that section affords a strong if not a conclusive argument in support of the opinion already indicated by the court.

The preceding section contains restrictions which are obviously intended for the exclusive purpose of restraining the exercise of power by the departments of the general government. Some of them use language applicable only to congress: others are expressed in general terms. The third clause, for example, declares that "no bill of attainder or ex post facto law shall be passed." No language can be more general; yet the demonstration is complete that it applies solely to the government of the United States. In addition to the general arguments furnished by the instrument itself, some of which have been already suggested, the succeeding section, the avowed purpose of which is to restrain state legislation, contains in terms the very prohibition. It declares that "no state shall pass any bill of attainder or ex post facto law." This provision, then, of the ninth section, however comprehensive its language, contains no restriction on state legislation.

The ninth section having enumerated, in the nature of a bill of rights, the limitations intended to be imposed on the powers of the general government, the tenth proceeds to enumerate those which were to operate on the state legislatures. These restrictions are brought together in the same section, and are by express words applied to the states. "No state shall enter into any treaty," &c. Perceiving that in a constitution framed by the people of the United States for the government of all, no limitation of the action of government on the people would apply to the state government, unless expressed in terms; the restrictions contained in the tenth section are in direct words so applied to the states.

It is worthy of remark, too, that these inhibitions generally restrain state legislation on subjects entrusted to the general government, or in which the people of all the states feel an interest.

A state is forbidden to enter into any treaty, alliance or confederation. If these compacts are with foreign nations, they interfere with the treaty making power which is conferred entirely on the general government; if with each other, for political purposes, they can scarcely fail to interfere with the general purpose and intent of the constitution. To grant letters of marque and reprisal, would lead directly to war; the power of declaring which is expressly given to congress. To coin money is also the exercise of a power conferred on congress. It would be tedious to recapitulate the several limitations on the powers of the states which are contained in this section. They will be found, generally, to restrain state legislation on subjects entrusted to the government of the union, in which the citizens of all the states are interested. In these alone were the whole people concerned. The question of their application to states is not left to construction. It is averred in positive words.

If the original constitution, in the ninth and tenth sections of the first article, draws this plain and marked line of discrimination between the limitations it imposes on the powers of the general government, and on those of the states; if in every inhibition intended to act on state power, words are employed which directly express that intent; some strong reason must be assigned for departing from this safe and judicious course in framing the amendments, before that departure can be assumed.

We search in vain for that reason.

Had the people of the several states, or any of them, required changes in their constitutions; had they required additional safeguards to liberty from the apprehended encroachments of their particular governments: the remedy was in their own hands, and would have been applied by themselves. A convention would have been assembled by the discontented state, and the required improvements would have been made by itself. The unwieldy and cumbrous machinery of procuring a recommendation from two-thirds of congress, and the assent of three-fourths of their sister states, could never have occurred to any human being as a mode of doing that which might be effected by the state itself. Had the framers of these amendments intended them to be limitations on the powers of the state governments, they would have imitated the framers of the original constitution, and have expressed that intention. Had congress engaged in the extraordinary occupation of improving the constitutions of the several states by affording the people additional protection from the exercise of power by their own governments in matters which concerned themselves alone, they would have declared this purpose in plain and intelligible language.

But it is universally understood, it is a part of the history of the day, that the great revolution which established the constitution of the United States, was not effected without immense opposition. Serious fears were extensively entertained that those powers which the patriot statesmen, who then watched over the interests of our country, deemed essential to union, and to the attainment of those invaluable objects for which union was sought, might be exercised in a manner dangerous to liberty. In almost every convention by which the constitution was adopted, amendments to guard against the abuse of power were recommended. These amendments demanded security against the apprehended encroachments of the general government — not against those of the local governments.

In compliance with a sentiment thus generally expressed, to quiet fears thus extensively entertained, amendments were proposed by the required majority in congress, and adopted by the states. These amendments contain no expression indicating an intention to apply them to the state governments. This court cannot so apply them.

We are of opinion that the provision in the fifth amendment to the constitution, declaring that private property shall not be taken for public use without just compensation, is intended solely as a limitation on the exercise of power by the government of the United States, and is not applicable to the legislation of the states.

NOTES AND QUESTIONS

1. Does this case surprise you? Were you of the opinion that the great provisions of the Bill of Rights — such as the protections of the freedom of speech, press, and religion and the prohibition on establishing churches applied against the state governments? What gave you that idea? Why, in the opinion of the Supreme Court, were such provisions *not* intended to apply against the states? There can be little doubt, by the way, that the Court is correct on this point, as a glance at any of the better histories of the period will confirm. Better still, a review of the materials involved in the debate over the Constitution renders inescapable the conclusion that the Bill of Rights was offered as a means of pacifying those who were worried that the Federal Government might be too powerful and unrestrained, and who were intent on preserving a maximum of state sovereignty. *See generally*, JACK N. RAKOVE, ORIGINAL MEANINGS: POLITICS AND IDEAS IN THE MAKING OF THE CONSTITUTION (1996) (for a recent historical treatment); THE DEBATE ON THE CONSTITUTION (Bernard Bailyn ed., 2 vols. 1993) (for the primary sources).

2. Nevertheless, there are some provisions in the Constitution which clearly do restrict state sovereignty, such as, for example the Contracts Clause, and the other clauses referred to in the opinion in *Barron*, such as those which restrict the states' ability to issue paper money or to engage in taxing measures reserved to the federal government. Moreover, there is also the provision in Article IV, Section 2 of the Constitution, which provides that "[t]he Citizens of each State shall be entitled to all Privileges and Immunities of Citizens in the several states." These "privileges and immunities" are not defined in the Constitution, but there is some historical evidence that they were intended to yield a number of protections against state and local governments for individuals. We take this up more directly in Chapter Six.

The Fourteenth Amendment offered a new lease on life to the Privileges or Immunities Clause by indicating that "[n]o State shall make or enforce any law which shall abridge the privileges or immunities of citizens of the United States," Amend. XIV, § 1, but again no definition was provided. Following a reading of the Fourteenth Amendment's Privileges or Immunities Clause by the majority in the *Slaughterhouse Cases*, 83 U.S. (16 Wall.) 36 (1873), which virtually eviscerated it of any meaning, that Clause has not loomed large in constitutional jurisprudence. There are an increasing number of scholars, and a few jurists (some on the Supreme Court) who maintain, however, that the majority in the *Slaughterhouse Cases* was in error. Again, more on this later.

3. Your notion that the Bill of Rights has been applied against the states was not in error, however, though the Privileges or Immunities Clause was not the vehicle through which this was done. Consider the following case, which laid out the rationale for selective *judicial* "incorporation" of the Bill of Rights through the Due Process Clause of the Fourteenth Amendment.

PALKO v. CONNECTICUT
302 U.S. 319 (1937)

MR. JUSTICE CARDOZO delivered the opinion of the Court.

A statute of Connecticut permitting appeals in criminal cases to be taken by the state is challenged by appellant as an infringement of the Fourteenth Amendment of the Constitution of the United States. Whether the challenge should be upheld is now to be determined.

Appellant was indicted in Fairfield County, Connecticut, for the crime of murder in the first degree. A jury found him guilty of murder in the second degree, and he was sentenced to confinement in the state prison for life. Thereafter the State of Connecticut, with the permission of the judge presiding at the trial, gave notice of appeal to the [Connecticut] Supreme Court of Errors. . . . Upon such appeal, the Supreme Court of Errors reversed the judgment and ordered a new trial. It found that there had been error of law to the prejudice of the state (1) in excluding testimony as to a confession by defendant; (2) in excluding testimony upon cross-examination of defendant to impeach his credibility; and (3) in the instructions to the jury as to the difference between first and second degree murder.

Pursuant to the mandate of the Supreme Court of Errors, defendant was brought to trial again. Before a jury was impaneled and also at later stages of the case he made the objection that the effect of the new trial was to place him twice in jeopardy for the same offense, and in so doing to violate the Fourteenth Amendment of the Constitution of the United States. Upon the overruling of the objection the trial proceeded. The jury returned a verdict of murder in the first degree, and the court sentenced the defendant to the punishment of death. The Supreme Court of Errors affirmed the judgment of conviction. . . . The case is here upon appeal. . . .

1. The execution of the sentence will not deprive appellant of his life without the [due] process of law assured to him by the Fourteenth Amendment of the Federal Constitution.

The argument for appellant is that whatever is forbidden by the Fifth Amendment is forbidden by the Fourteenth also. The Fifth Amendment, which is not directed to the states, but solely to the federal government, creates immunity from double jeopardy. No person shall be "subject for the same offense to be twice put in jeopardy of life or limb." The Fourteenth Amendment ordains, "nor shall any State deprive any person of life, liberty, or property, without due process of law." To retry a defendant, though under one indictment and only one, subjects him, it is said, to double jeopardy in violation of the Fifth Amendment, if the prosecution is one on behalf of the United States. From this the consequence is said to follow that there is a denial of life or liberty without due process of law, if the prosecution is one on behalf of the People of a State. . . .

* * *

We have said that in appellant's view the Fourteenth Amendment is to be taken as embodying the prohibitions of the Fifth. His thesis is even broader. Whatever would be a violation of the original bill of rights (Amendments I to VIII) if done by the federal government is now equally unlawful by force of the Fourteenth Amendment if done by a state. There is no such general rule.

The Fifth Amendment provides, among other things, that no person shall be held to answer for a capital or otherwise infamous crime unless on presentment or indictment of a grand jury. This court has held that, in prosecutions by a state, presentment or indictment by a grand jury may give way to informations at the instance of a public officer. The Fifth Amendment provides also that no person shall be compelled in any criminal case to be a witness against himself. This court has said that, in prosecutions by a state, the exemption will fail if the state elects to end it. The Sixth Amendment calls for a jury trial in criminal cases and the Seventh for a jury trial in civil cases at common law where the value in controversy shall exceed twenty dollars. This court has ruled that consistently with those amendments trial by jury may be modified by a state or abolished altogether. . . .

On the other hand, the due process clause of the Fourteenth Amendment may make it unlawful for a state to abridge by its statutes the freedom of speech which the First Amendment safeguards against encroachment by the Congress; or the like freedom of the press, *Near v. Minnesota ex rel. Olson* [(1931)]; or the free exercise of religion, *Pierce v. Society of Sisters* [(1925)]; or the right of peaceable assembly, without which speech would be unduly trammeled; or the right of one accused of crime to the benefit of counsel. In these and other situations immunities that are valid as against the federal government by force of the specific pledges of particular amendments have been found to be implicit in the concept of ordered liberty, and thus, through the Fourteenth Amendment, become valid as against the states.

The line of division may seem to be wavering and broken if there is a hasty catalogue of the cases on the one side and the other. Reflection and analysis will induce a different view. There emerges the perception of a rationalizing principle which gives to discrete instances a proper order and coherence. The right to trial by jury and the immunity from prosecution except as the result of an indictment may have value and importance. Even so, they are not of the very essence of a scheme of ordered liberty. To abolish them is not to violate a "principle of justice so rooted in the traditions and conscience of our people as to be ranked as fundamental." Few would be so narrow or provincial as to maintain that a fair and enlightened system of justice would be impossible without them. What is true of jury trials and indictments is true also, as the cases show, of the immunity from compulsory self-incrimination. This too might be lost, and justice still be done. Indeed, today as in the past there are students of our penal system who look upon the immunity as a mischief rather than a benefit, and who would limit its scope, or destroy it altogether. No doubt there would remain the need to give protection against torture, physical or mental. Justice, however, would not perish if the accused were subject to a duty to respond to orderly inquiry. The exclusion of these immunities and privileges from the privileges and immunities protected against the action of the states has not been arbitrary or casual. It has been dictated by a study and appreciation of the meaning, the essential implications, of liberty itself.

We reach a different plane of social and moral values when we pass to the privileges and immunities that have been taken over from the earlier articles of the federal bill of rights and brought within the Fourteenth Amendment by a process of absorption. These in their origin were effective against the federal government alone. If the Fourteenth Amendment has absorbed them, the process of absorption has had its source in the belief that neither liberty nor justice would exist if they were sacrificed. . . . This is true, for illustration, of freedom of thought, and speech. Of that freedom one may say that it is the matrix, the indispensable condition, of nearly every other form of freedom. With rare aberrations a pervasive recognition of that truth can be traced in our history, political and legal. So it has come about that the domain of liberty, withdrawn by the Fourteenth Amendment from encroachment by the states, has been enlarged by latter-day judgments to include liberty of the mind as well as liberty of action. The extension became, indeed, a logical imperative when once it was recognized, as long ago it was, that liberty is something more than exemption from physical restraint, and that even in the field of substantive rights and duties the legislative judgment, if oppressive and arbitrary, may be overridden by the courts. *Cf. Near v. Minnesota ex rel. Olson* (1931). . . . Fundamental too in the concept of due process, and so in that of liberty, is the thought that condemnation shall be rendered only after trial. The hearing, moreover, must be a real one, not a sham or a pretense. For that reason, ignorant defendants in a capital case were held to have been condemned unlawfully when in truth, though not in form, they were refused the aid of counsel. The decision did not turn upon the fact that the benefit of counsel would have been guaranteed to the defendants by the provisions of the Sixth Amendment if they had been prosecuted in a federal court. The decision turned upon the fact that in the particular situation laid before us in the evidence the benefit of counsel was essential to the substance of a hearing.

Our survey of the cases serves, we think, to justify the statement that the dividing line between them, if not unfaltering throughout its course, has been true for the most part to a unifying principle. On which side of the line the case made out by the appellant has appropriate location must be the next inquiry and the final one. Is that kind of double jeopardy to which the statute has subjected him a hardship so acute and shocking that our polity will not endure it? Does it violate those "fundamental principles of liberty and justice which lie at the base of all our civil and political institutions"? The answer surely must be "no." What the answer would have to be if the state were permitted after a trial free from error to try the accused over again or to bring another case against him, we have no occasion to consider. We deal with the statute before us and no other. The state is not attempting to wear the accused out by a multitude of cases with accumulated trials. It asks no more than this, that the case against him shall go on until there shall be a trial free from the corrosion of substantial legal error. This is not cruelty at all, nor even vexation in any immoderate degree. If the trial had been infected with error adverse to the accused, there might have been review at his instance, and as often as necessary to purge the vicious taint. A reciprocal privilege, subject at all times to the discretion of the presiding judge, has now been granted to the state. There is here no seismic innovation. The edifice of justice stands, its symmetry, to many, greater than before.

* * *

The judgment is

Affirmed.

MR. JUSTICE BUTLER dissents [but filed no dissenting opinion].

NOTE

Justice Cardozo in this opinion is most focused on the Due Process Clause of the Fourteenth Amendment, and the judicially-fashioned proposition in favor of the "selective incorporation" doctrine, by which selected parts of the Bill of Rights are read, through the Fourteenth Amendment, to circumscribe activities of the state and local governments. Setting aside, for a moment, the constitutional validity of such "incorporation," are you able to discern just which parts of the Bill of Rights are to be "incorporated," and which are not? Cardozo explains that the relevant provisions are those which "have been found to be implicit in the concept of ordered liberty." 302 U.S. at 325. Does that make it any more lucid? How about the suggestion that the matters in question are "principle[s] of justice so rooted in the traditions and conscience of our people as to be ranked as fundamental." *Id.* (quoting *Snyder v. Massachusetts*, 291 U.S. 97,

105 (1934)). Does that clarify matters? Is judicial incorporation a modern-day statement of natural law?

ADAMSON v. CALIFORNIA
332 U.S. 46 (1947)

MR. JUSTICE REED delivered the opinion of the Court.

The appellant, Adamson, a citizen of the United States, was convicted, without recommendation for mercy, by a jury in a Superior Court of the State of California of murder in the first degree. After considering the same objections to the conviction that are pressed here, the sentence of death was affirmed by the Supreme Court of the state. Review of that judgment by this Court was sought and allowed. . . . The provisions of California law which were challenged in the state proceedings as invalid under the Fourteenth Amendment . . . permit the failure of a defendant to explain or to deny evidence against him to be commented upon by court and by counsel and to be considered by court and jury. The defendant did not testify. As the trial court gave its instructions and the District Attorney argued the case in accordance with the constitutional and statutory provisions just referred to, we have for decision the question of their constitutionality. . . .

The appellant was charged in the information with former convictions for burglary, larceny and robbery and pursuant to § 1025, California Penal Code, answered that he had suffered the previous convictions. This answer barred allusion to these charges of convictions on the trial. Under California's interpretation of § 1025 of the Penal Code and § 2051 of the Code of Civil Procedure, however, if the defendant, after answering affirmatively charges alleging prior convictions, takes the witness stand to deny or explain away other evidence that has been introduced "the commission of these crimes could have been revealed to the jury on cross-examination to impeach his testimony." This forces an accused who is a repeat offender to choose between the risk of having his prior offenses disclosed to the jury or of having it draw harmful inferences from uncontradicted evidence that can only be denied or explained by the defendant.

In the first place, appellant urges that the provision of the Fifth Amendment that no person "shall be compelled in any criminal case to be a witness against himself" is a fundamental national privilege or immunity protected against state abridgment by the Fourteenth Amendment or a privilege or immunity secured, through the Fourteenth Amendment, against deprivation by state action because it is a personal right, enumerated in the federal Bill of Rights.

Secondly, appellant relies upon the due process of law clause of the Fourteenth Amendment to invalidate the provisions of the California law . . . (a) because comment on failure to testify is permitted, (b) because appellant was forced to forego testimony in person because of danger of disclosure of his past convictions through cross-examination, and (c) because the presumption of innocence was infringed by the shifting of the burden of proof to appellant in permitting comment on his failure to testify.

We shall assume, but without any intention thereby of ruling upon the issue, that permission by law to the court, counsel and jury to comment upon and consider the failure of defendant "to explain or to deny by his testimony any evidence or facts in the case against him" would infringe defendant's privilege against self-incrimination under the Fifth Amendment if this were a trial in a court of the United States under a similar law. Such an assumption does not determine appellant's rights under the Fourteenth Amendment. It is settled law that the clause of the Fifth Amendment, protecting a person against being compelled to be a witness against himself, is not made effective by the Fourteenth Amendment as a protection against state action on the ground that freedom from testimonial compulsion is a right of national citizenship, or because it is a personal privilege or immunity secured by the Federal Constitution as one of the rights of man that are listed in the Bill of Rights.

The reasoning that leads to those conclusions starts with the unquestioned premise that the Bill of Rights, when adopted, was for the protection of the individual against the federal government and its provisions were inapplicable to similar actions done by the states. *Barron v. Baltimore* [(1833)]. With the adoption of the Fourteenth Amendment, it was suggested that the dual citizenship recognized by its first sentence secured for citizens federal protection for their elemental privileges and immunities of state citizenship. The *Slaughter-House Cases* [(1872)] decided, contrary to the suggestion, that these rights, as privileges and immunities of state citizenship, remained under the sole protection of the state governments. . . . The power to free defendants in state trials from self-incrimination was specifically determined to be beyond the scope of the privileges and immunities clause of the Fourteenth Amendment in *Twining v. New Jersey* [(1908)]. . . . The *Twining* case likewise disposed of the contention that freedom from testimonial compulsion, being specifically granted by the Bill of Rights, is a federal privilege or immunity that is protected by the Fourteenth Amendment against state invasion. This Court held that the inclusion in the Bill of Rights of this protection against the power of the national government did not make the privilege a federal privilege or immunity secured to citizens by the Constitution against state action. *Twining v. New Jersey*; *Palko v. Connecticut* [(1937)]. After declaring that state and national citizenship coexist in the same person, the Fourteenth Amendment forbids a state from abridging the privileges and immunities of citizens of the United States. As a matter of words, this leaves a state free to abridge, within the limits of the due process clause, the privileges and immunities flowing from state citizenship. This reading of the Federal Constitution has heretofore found favor with the majority of this Court as a natural and logical interpretation. It accords with the constitutional doctrine of federalism by leaving to the states the responsibility of dealing with the privileges and immunities of their citizens except those inherent in national citizenship. . . .

Appellant secondly contends that if the privilege against self-incrimination is not a right protected by the privileges and immunities clause of the Fourteenth Amendment against state action, this privilege, to its full scope under the Fifth Amendment, inheres in the right to a fair trial. A right to a fair trial is a right admittedly protected by the due process clause of the Fourteenth Amendment. Therefore, appellant argues, the due process clause of the Fourteenth Amendment protects his privilege against self-incrimination. The due process clause of the Fourteenth Amendment, however, does not draw all the rights of the federal Bill of Rights under its protection. That contention was made and rejected in *Palko v. Connecticut.* . . . Nothing has been called to our attention that either the framers of the Fourteenth Amendment or the states that adopted intended its due process clause to draw within its scope the earlier amendments to the Constitution. *Palko* held that such provisions of the Bill of Rights as were "implicit in the concept of ordered liberty," became secure from state interference by the clause. But it held nothing more.

Specifically, the due process clause does not protect, by virtue of its mere existence, the accused's freedom from giving testimony by compulsion in state trials that is secured to him against federal interference by the Fifth Amendment. For a state to require testimony from an accused is not necessarily a breach of a state's obligation to give a fair trial. Therefore, we must examine the effect of the California law applied in this trial to see whether the comment on failure to testify violates the protection against state action that the due process clause does grant to an accused. The due process clause forbids compulsion to testify by fear of hurt, torture or exhaustion. . . . California follows Anglo-American legal tradition in excusing defendants in criminal prosecutions from compulsory testimony. That is a matter of legal policy and not because of the requirements of due process under the Fourteenth Amendment. So our inquiry is directed, not at the broad question of the constitutionality of compulsory testimony from the accused under the due process clause, but to the constitutionality of the provision of the California law that permits comment upon his failure to testify. It is, of course, logically possible that while an accused might be required, under appropriate penalties, to submit himself as a witness without a violation of due process, comment by judge or jury on inferences to be drawn from his failure to testify, in jurisdictions where an accused's privilege against self-incrimination is protected, might deny due process. For example, a statute might declare that a permitted refusal to testify would compel an acceptance of the truth of the prosecution's evidence.

Generally, comment on the failure of an accused to testify is forbidden in American jurisdictions. This arises from state constitutional or statutory provisions similar in character to the federal provisions. California, however, is one of a few states that permit limited comment upon a defendant's failure to testify. That permission is narrow. The California law . . . authorizes comment by court and counsel upon the "failure of the defendant to explain or to deny by his testimony any evidence or facts in the case against him." This does not involve any presumption, rebuttable or irrebuttable, either of guilt or of the truth of any fact, that is offered in evidence. It allows inferences to be drawn from proven facts. Because of this clause, the court can direct the jury's attention to whatever evidence there may be that a defendant could deny and the prosecution can argue as to inferences that may be drawn from the accused's failure to testify. There is here no lack of power in the trial court to adjudge and no denial of a hearing. California has prescribed a method for advising the jury in the search for truth. However sound may be the legislative conclusion that an accused should not be compelled in any criminal case to be a witness against himself, we see no reason why comment should not be made upon his silence. It seems quite natural that when a defendant has opportunity to deny or explain facts and determines not to do so, the prosecution should bring out the strength of the evidence by commenting upon defendant's failure to explain or deny it. The prosecution evidence may be of facts that may be beyond the knowledge of the accused. If so, his failure to testify would have little if any weight. But the facts may be such as are necessarily in the knowledge of the accused. In that case a failure to explain would point to an inability to explain.

Appellant sets out the circumstances of this case, however, to show coercion and unfairness in permitting comment. The guilty person was not seen at the place and time of the crime. There was evidence, however, that entrance to the place or room where the crime was committed might have been obtained through a small door. It was freshly broken. Evidence showed that six fingerprints on the door were petitioner's. Certain diamond rings were missing from the deceased's possession. There was evidence that appellant, sometime after the crime, asked an unidentified person whether the latter would be interested in purchasing a diamond ring. As has been stated, the information charged other crimes to appellant and he admitted them. His argument here is that he could not take the stand to deny the evidence against him because he would be subjected to a cross-examination as to former crimes to impeach his veracity and the evidence so produced might well bring about his conviction. Such cross-examination is allowable in California. Therefore, appellant contends the California statute permitting comment denies him due process.

It is true that if comment were forbidden, an accused in this situation could remain silent and avoid evidence of former crimes and comment upon his failure to testify. We are of the view, however, that a state may control such a situation in accordance with its own ideas of the most efficient administration of criminal justice. The purpose of due process is not to protect an accused against a proper conviction but against an unfair conviction. When evidence is before a jury that threatens conviction, it does not seem unfair to require him to choose between leaving the adverse evidence unexplained and subjecting himself to impeachment through disclosure of former crimes. Indeed, this is a dilemma with which any defendant may be faced. If facts, adverse to the defendant, are proven by the prosecution, there may be no way to explain them favorably to the accused except by a witness who may be vulnerable to impeachment on cross-examination. The defendant must then decide whether or not to use such a witness. The fact that the witness may also be the defendant makes the choice more difficult but a denial of due process does not emerge from the circumstances.

There is no basis in the California law for appellant's objection on due process or other grounds that the statutory authorization to comment on the failure to explain or deny adverse testimony shifts the burden of proof or the duty to go forward with the evidence. Failure of the accused to testify is not an admission of the truth of the adverse evidence. Instructions told the jury that the burden of proof remained upon the state and the presumption of innocence with the accused. Comment on failure to deny proven facts does not in California tend to supply any missing element of proof of guilt. It only directs attention to the strength of the evidence for the prosecution or to the weakness of that for the defense. . . .

* * *

Affirmed.

MR. JUSTICE FRANKFURTER, concurring:

* * *

For historical reasons a limited immunity from the common duty to testify was written into the Federal Bill of Rights, and I am prepared to agree that, as part of that immunity, comment on the failure of an accused to take the witness stand is forbidden in federal prosecutions. It is so, of course, by explicit act of Congress. . . . But to suggest that such a limitation can be drawn out of "due process" in its protection of ultimate decency in a civilized society is to suggest that the Due Process Clause fastened fetters of unreason upon the States. . . .

* * *

The short answer to the suggestion that the provision of the Fourteenth Amendment, which ordains "nor shall any State deprive any person of life, liberty, or property, without due process of law," was a way of saying that every State must thereafter initiate prosecutions through indictment by a grand jury, must have a trial by a jury of twelve in criminal cases, and must have trial by such a jury in common law suits where the amount in controversy exceeds twenty dollars, is that it is a strange way of saying it. It would be extraordinarily strange for a Constitution to convey such specific commands in such a roundabout and inexplicit way. After all, an amendment to the Constitution should be read in a "'sense most obvious to the common understanding at the time of its adoption.' . . . For it was for public adoption that it was proposed." . . . Those reading the English language with the meaning which it ordinarily conveys, those conversant with the political and legal history of the concept of due process, those sensitive to the relations of the States to the central government as well as the relation of some of the provisions of the Bill of Rights to the process of justice, would hardly recognize the Fourteenth Amendment as a cover for the various explicit provisions of the first eight Amendments. Some of these are enduring reflections of experience with human nature, while some express the restricted views of Eighteenth-Century England regarding the best methods for the ascertainment of facts. The notion that the Fourteenth Amendment was a covert way of imposing upon the States all the rules which it seemed important to Eighteenth Century statesmen to write into the Federal Amendments, was rejected by judges who were themselves witnesses of the process by which the Fourteenth Amendment became part of the Constitution. . . .

* * *

. . . There is suggested merely a selective incorporation of the first eight Amendments into the Fourteenth Amendment. Some are in and some are out, but we are left in the dark as to which are in and which are out. Nor are we given the calculus for determining which go in and which stay out. If the basis of selection is merely that those provisions of the first eight Amendments are incorporated which commend themselves to individual justices as indispensable to the dignity and happiness of a free man, we are thrown back to a merely subjective test. The protection against unreasonable search and seizure might have primacy for one judge, while trial by a jury of twelve for every claim above twenty dollars might appear to another as an ultimate need in a free society. In the history of thought "natural law" has a much longer and much better founded meaning and justification than such subjective selection of the first eight Amendments for incorporation into the Fourteenth. If all that is meant is that due process contains within itself certain minimal standards which are "of the very essence of a scheme of ordered liberty," *Palko v. Connecticut*, putting upon this Court the duty of applying these standards from time to time, then we have merely arrived at the insight which our predecessors long ago expressed. We are called upon to apply to the difficult issues of our own day the wisdom afforded by the great opinions in this field, such as those in . . . *Twining v. New Jersey* [(1908)], and *Palko v. Connecticut*. This guidance bids us to be duly mindful of the heritage of the past, with its great lessons of how liberties are won and how they are lost. As judges charged with the delicate task of subjecting the government of a continent to the Rule of Law we must be particularly mindful that it is "a *constitution* we are expounding," so that it should not be imprisoned in what are merely legal forms even though they have the sanction of the Eighteenth Century.

* * *

A construction which gives to due process no independent function but turns it into a summary of the specific provisions of the Bill of Rights would, as has been noted, tear up by the roots much of the fabric of law in the several States, and would deprive the States of opportunity for reforms in legal process designed for extending the area of freedom. It would assume that no other abuses would reveal themselves in the course of time than those which had become manifest in 1791. Such a view not only disregards the historic meaning of "due process." It leads inevitably to a warped construction of specific provisions of the Bill of Rights to bring within their scope conduct clearly condemned by due process but not easily fitting into the pigeon-holes of the specific provisions. . . .

And so, when, as in a case like the present, a conviction in a State court is here for review under a claim that a right protected by the Due Process Clause of the Fourteenth Amendment has been denied, the issue is not whether an infraction of one of the specific provisions of the first eight Amendments is disclosed by the record. The relevant question is whether the criminal proceedings which resulted in conviction deprived the accused of the due process of law to which the United States Constitution entitled him. Judicial review of that guaranty of the Fourteenth Amendment inescapably imposes upon this Court an exercise of judgment upon the whole course of the proceedings in order to ascertain whether they offend those canons of decency and fairness which express the notions of justice of English-speaking peoples even toward those charged with the most heinous offenses. These standards of justice are not authoritatively formulated anywhere as though they were prescriptions in a pharmacopoeia. But neither does the application of the Due Process Clause imply that judges are wholly at large. The judicial judgment in applying the Due Process Clause must move within the limits of accepted notions of justice and is not to be based upon the idiosyncrasies of a merely personal judgment. . . . An important safeguard against such merely individual judgment is an alert deference to the judgment of the State court under review.

MR. JUSTICE BLACK, dissenting.

* * *

This decision [by the majority] reasserts a constitutional theory spelled out in *Twining v. New Jersey* [(1908)], that this Court is endowed by the Constitution with boundless power under "natural law" periodically to expand and contract constitutional standards to conform to the Court's conception of what at a particular time constitutes "civilized decency" and "fundamental liberty and justice." Invoking this *Twining* rule, the Court concludes that although comment upon testimony in a federal court would violate the Fifth Amendment, identical comment in a state court does not violate today's fashion in civilized decency and fundamentals and is therefore not prohibited by the Federal Constitution as amended.

The *Twining* case was the first, as it is the only, decision of this Court which has squarely held that states were free, notwithstanding the Fifth and Fourteenth Amendments, to extort evidence from one accused of crime. I agree that if *Twining* be reaffirmed, the result reached might appropriately follow. But I would not reaffirm the *Twining* decision. I think that decision and the "natural law" theory of the Constitution upon which it relies degrade the constitutional safeguards of the Bill of Rights and simultaneously appropriate for this Court a broad power which we are not authorized by the Constitution to exercise. . . .

The first ten amendments were proposed and adopted largely because of fear that Government might unduly interfere with prized individual liberties. The people wanted and demanded a Bill of Rights written into their Constitution. The amendments embodying the Bill of Rights were intended to curb all branches of the Federal Government in the fields touched by the amendments — Legislative, Executive, and Judicial. The Fifth, Sixth, and Eighth Amendments were pointedly aimed at confining exercise of power by courts and judges within precise boundaries, particularly in the procedure used for the trial of criminal cases. Past history provided strong reasons for the apprehensions which brought these procedural amendments into being and attest the wisdom of their adoption. . . .

But these limitations were not expressly imposed upon state court action. In 1833, *Barron v. Baltimore* [(1833)] was decided by this Court. It specifically held inapplicable to the states that provision of the Fifth Amendment which declares: "nor shall private property be taken for public use, without just compensation." In deciding the particular point raised, the Court there said that it could not hold that the first eight amendments applied to the states. This was the controlling constitutional rule when the Fourteenth Amendment was proposed in 1866.

My study of the historical events that culminated in the Fourteenth Amendment, and the expressions of those who sponsored and favored, as well as those who opposed its submission and passage, persuades me that one of the chief objects that the provisions of the Amendment's first section, separately, and as a whole, were intended to accomplish was to make the Bill of Rights, applicable to the states. With full knowledge of the import of the *Barron* decision, the framers and backers of the Fourteenth Amendment proclaimed its purpose to be to overturn the constitutional rule that case had announced. . . .

* * *

. . . In the *Twining* opinion, the Court explicitly declined to give weight to the historical demonstration that the first section of the Amendment was intended to apply to the states the several protections of the Bill of Rights. It held that that question was "no longer open" because of previous decisions of this Court which, however, had not appraised the historical evidence on that subject. The Court admitted that its action had resulted in giving "much less effect to the Fourteenth Amendment than some of the public men active in framing it" had intended it to have. . . .

For this reason, I am attaching to this dissent an appendix which contains a resume, by no means complete, of the Amendment's history. In my judgment that history conclusively demonstrates that the language of the first section of the Fourteenth Amendment, taken as a whole, was thought by those responsible for its submission to the people, and by those who opposed its submission, sufficiently explicit to guarantee that thereafter no state could deprive its citizens of the privileges and protections of the Bill of Rights. . . . And I further contend that the "natural law" formula which the Court uses to reach its conclusion in this case should be abandoned as an incongruous excrescence on our Constitution. I believe that formula to be itself a violation of our Constitution, in that it subtly conveys to courts, at the expense of legislatures, ultimate power over public policies in fields where no specific provision of the Constitution limits legislative power. . . .

* * *

In *Palko v. Connecticut*, a case which involved former jeopardy only, this Court re-examined the path it had traveled in interpreting the Fourteenth Amendment since the *Twining* opinion was written. In *Twining* the Court had declared that none of the rights enumerated in the first eight amendments were protected against state invasion because they were incorporated in the Bill of Rights. But the Court in *Palko* answered a contention that all eight applied with the more guarded statement . . . that "there is no such general rule." Implicit in this statement, and in the cases decided in the interim between *Twining* and *Palko* and since, is the understanding that some of the eight amendments do apply by their very terms. . . . In the *Twining* case fundamental liberties were things apart from the Bill of Rights. Now it appears that at least some of the provisions of the Bill of Rights in their very terms satisfy the Court as sound and meaningful expressions of fundamental liberty. If the Fifth Amendment's protection against self-incrimination be such an expression of fundamental liberty, I ask, and have not found a satisfactory answer, why the Court today should consider that it should be "absorbed" in part but not in full? . . . Nothing in the *Palko* opinion requires that when the Court decides that a Bill of Rights' provision is to be applied to the States, it is to be applied piecemeal. Nothing in the *Palko* opinion recommends that the Court apply part of an amendment's established meaning and discard that part which does not suit the current style of fundamentals.

* * *

I cannot consider the Bill of Rights to be an outworn 18th Century "strait jacket" as the *Twining* opinion did. Its provisions may be thought outdated abstractions by some. And it is true that they were designed to meet ancient evils. But they are the same kind of human evils that have emerged from century to century wherever excessive power is sought by the few at the expense of the many. . . . I fear to see the consequences of the Court's practice of substituting its own concepts of decency and fundamental justice for the language of the Bill of Rights as its point of departure in interpreting and enforcing that Bill of Rights. . . . I would follow what I believe was the original purpose of the Fourteenth Amendment — to extend to all the people of the nation the complete protection of the Bill of Rights. To hold that this Court can determine what, if any, provisions of the Bill of Rights will be enforced, and if so to what degree, is to frustrate the great design of a written Constitution.

Conceding the possibility that this Court is now wise enough to improve on the Bill of Rights by substituting natural law concepts for the Bill of Rights, I think the possibility is entirely too speculative to agree to take that course. I would therefore hold in this case that the full protection of the Fifth Amendment's proscription against compelled testimony must be afforded by California.

This I would do because of reliance upon the original purpose of the Fourteenth Amendment.

It is an illusory apprehension that literal application of some or all of the provisions of the Bill of Rights to the States would unwisely increase the sum total of the powers of this Court to invalidate state legislation. The Federal Government has not been harmfully burdened by the requirement that enforcement of federal laws affecting civil liberty conform literally to the Bill of Rights. Who would advocate its repeal? It must be conceded, of course, that the natural-law-due-process formula, which the Court today reaffirms, has been interpreted to limit substantially this Court's power to prevent state violations of the individual civil liberties guaranteed by the Bill of Rights. But this formula also has been used in the past, and can be used in the future, to license this Court, in considering regulatory legislation, to roam at large in the broad expanses of policy and morals and to trespass, all too freely, on the legislative domain of the States as well as the Federal Government

Since *Marbury v. Madison* [(1803)] was decided, the practice has been firmly established, for better or worse, that courts can strike down legislative enactments which violate the Constitution. This process, of course, involves interpretation, and since words can have many meanings, interpretation obviously may result in contraction or extension of the original purpose of a constitutional provision, thereby affecting policy. But to pass upon the constitutionality of statutes by looking to the particular standards enumerated in the Bill of Rights and other parts of the Constitution is one thing; to invalidate statutes because of application of "natural law" deemed to be above and undefined by the Constitution is another. . . .

MR. JUSTICE DOUGLAS joins in this opinion.

APPENDIX.

I.

The legislative origin of the first section of the Fourteenth Amendment seems to have been in the Joint Committee on Reconstruction. . . . On January 27, 1866, Mr. Bingham on behalf of [a] select committee [composed of three members], presented this recommended amendment to the full committee:

> "Congress shall have power to make all laws which shall be necessary and proper to secure all persons in every State full protection in the enjoyment of life, liberty, and property; and to all citizens of the United States, in any State, the same immunities and also equal political rights and privileges."

This was not accepted. But on February 3, 1866, Mr. Bingham submitted an amended version:

> "The Congress shall have power to make all laws which shall be necessary and proper to secure to the citizens of each State all privileges

and immunities of citizens in the several States (Art. 4, sec. 2); and to all persons in the several States equal protection in the rights of life, liberty, and property (5th amendment)."

This won committee approval, and was presented by Mr. Bingham to the House on behalf of the Committee on February 13, 1866.

II.

When, on February 26, the proposed amendment came up for debate, Mr. Bingham stated that "by order . . . of the committee . . . I propose the adoption of this amendment." In support of it he said:

"... the amendment proposed stands in the very words of the Constitution of the United States as it came to us from the hands of its illustrious framers. Every word of the proposed amendment is to-day in the Constitution of our country, save the words conferring the express grant of power upon the Congress of the United States. The residue of the resolution, as the House will see by a reference to the Constitution, is the language of the second section of the fourth article, and of a portion of the fifth amendment adopted by the First Congress in 1789, and made part of the Constitution of the country. . . .

"Sir, it has been the want of the Republic that there was not an express grant of power in the Constitution to enable the whole people of every State, by congressional enactment, to enforce obedience to these requirements of the Constitution. Nothing can be plainer to thoughtful men than that if the grant of power had been originally conferred upon the Congress of the nation, and legislation had been upon your statute-books to enforce these requirements of the Constitution in every State, that rebellion, which has scarred and blasted the land, would have been an impossibility. . . .

* * *

"And, sir, it is equally clear by every construction of the Constitution, its contemporaneous construction, its continued construction, legislative, executive, and judicial, that these great provisions of the Constitution, this immortal bill of rights embodied in the Constitution, rested for its execution and enforcement hitherto upon the fidelity of the States. . . ."

Opposition speakers emphasized that the Amendment would destroy state's rights and empower Congress to legislate on matters of purely local concern. Some took the position that the Amendment was unnecessary because the Bill of Rights were already secured against state violation. Mr. Bingham joined issue on this contention:

"The gentleman seemed to think that all persons could have remedies for all violations of their rights of 'life, liberty, and property' in the Federal courts.

"I ventured to ask him yesterday when any action of that sort was ever maintained in any of the Federal courts of the United States to redress the great wrong which has been practiced, and which is being practiced now in more States than one of the Union under the authority of State laws, denying to citizens therein equal protection or any protection in the rights of life, liberty, and property.

* * *

". . . A gentleman on the other side interrupted me and wanted to know if I could cite a decision showing that the power of the Federal Government to enforce in the United States courts the bill of rights under the articles of amendment to the Constitution had been denied. I answered that I was prepared to introduce such decisions; and that is exactly what makes plain the necessity of adopting this amendment.

"Mr. Speaker, on this subject I refer the House and the country to a decision of the Supreme Court, to be found in 7 Peters, 247, in the case of Barron *vs.* The Mayor and City Council of Baltimore, involving the question whether the provisions of the fifth article of the amendments to the Constitution are binding upon the State of Maryland and to be enforced in the Federal courts. The Chief Justice says:

"'The people of the United States framed such a Government for the United States as they supposed best adapted to their situation and best calculated to promote their interests. The powers they conferred on this Government were to be exercised by itself; and the limitations of power, if expressed in general terms, are naturally, and we think necessarily, applicable to the Government created by the instrument. They are limitations of power granted in the instrument itself, not of distinct governments, framed by different persons and for different purposes.

"'If these propositions be correct, the fifth amendment must be understood as restraining the power of the General Government, not as applicable to the States.'

* * *

"The question is, simply, whether you will give by this amendment to the people of the United States the power, by legislative enactment, to punish officials of States for violation of the oaths enjoined upon them by their Constitution? . . . Is the bill of rights to stand in our Constitution hereafter, as in the past five years within eleven States, a mere dead letter? It is absolutely essential to the safety of the people that it should be enforced."

* * *

. . . A reading of the debates indicates that no member except Mr. Hale had contradicted Mr. Bingham's argument that without this Amendment the states had power to deprive persons of the rights guaranteed by the first eight amendments. Mr. Hale had conceded that he did not "know of a case where it has ever been decided that the United States Constitution is sufficient for the protection of the liberties of the citizen." But he was apparently unaware of the decision of this Court in *Barron v. Baltimore, supra*. . . . He further objected, as had most of the other opponents to the proposal, that the Amendment authorized the Congress to "arrogate" to itself vast powers over all kinds of affairs which should properly be left to the States.

When Mr. Hotchkiss suggested that the amendment should be couched in terms of a prohibition against the States in addition to authorizing Congress to legislate against state deprivations of privileges and immunities, debate on the amendment was postponed until the second Tuesday of April, 1866.

III.

Important events which apparently affected the evolution of the Fourteenth Amendment transpired during the period during which discussion of it was postponed. The Freedman's Bureau Bill which made deprivation of certain civil rights of negroes an offense punishable by military tribunals had been passed. It applied, not to the entire country, but only to the South. On February 19, 1866, President Johnson had vetoed the bill principally on the ground that it was unconstitutional. Forthwith, a companion proposal known as the Civil Rights Bill empowering federal courts to punish those who deprived any person anywhere in the country of certain defined civil rights was pressed to passage. Senator Trumbull, Chairman of the Senate Judiciary Committee, who offered the bill in the Senate on behalf of that Committee, had stated that "the late slaveholding States" had enacted laws ". . . depriving persons of African descent of privileges which are essential to freemen . . . . [S]tatutes of Mississippi . . . provide that . . . if any person of African descent residing in that State travels from one county to another without having a pass or a certificate of his freedom, he is liable to be committed to jail and to be dealt with as a person who is in the State without authority. Other provisions of the statute prohibit any negro or mulatto from having fire-arms; and one provision of the statute declares that for 'exercising the functions of a minister of the Gospel free negroes . . . on conviction, may be punished by . . . lashes . . . .' Other provisions . . . prohibit a free negro . . . from keeping a house of entertainment, and subject him to trial before two justices of the peace and five slaveholders for violating . . . this law. The statutes of South Carolina make it a highly penal offense for any person, white or colored, to teach slaves; and similar provisions are to be found running through all the statutes of the late slaveholding States. . . . The purpose of the bill . . . is to destroy all these discriminations . . . ."

In the House, after Mr. Bingham's original proposal for a constitutional amendment had been rejected, the suggestion was also advanced that the bill secured for all "the right of speech, . . . transit, . . . domicil, . . . the right to sue, the writ of *habeas corpus*, and the right of petition." And an opponent of the measure, Mr. Raymond, conceded that it would guarantee to the negro "the right of free passage . . . . He has a defined *status* . . . a right to defend himself . . . to bear arms . . . to testify in the Federal courts . . . ." But opponents took the position that without a constitutional amendment such as that proposed by Mr. Bingham, the Civil Rights Bill would be unconstitutional.

Mr. Bingham himself vigorously opposed and voted against the Bill. His objection was twofold: First, insofar as it extended the protections of the Bill of Rights as against state invasion, he believed the measure to be unconstitutional because of the Supreme Court's holding in *Barron v. Baltimore, supra.* While favoring the extension of the Bill of Rights guarantees as against state invasion, he thought this could be done only by passage of his amendment. His second objection to the Bill was that, in his view, it would go beyond his objective of making the states observe the Bill of Rights and would actually strip the states of power to govern, centralizing all power in the Federal Government.

* * *

In vetoing the Civil Rights Bill, President Johnson said among other things that the bill was unconstitutional for many of the same reasons advanced by Mr. Bingham. . . .

The bill, however, was passed over President Johnson's veto and in spite of the constitutional objections of Bingham and others.

IV.

Thereafter the scene changed back to the Committee on Reconstruction. There Mr. Stevens had proposed an amendment, § 1 of which provided "No discrimination shall be made by any State, nor by the United States, as to the civil rights of persons because of race, color, or previous condition of servitude." Mr. Bingham proposed an additional section providing that "No State shall make or enforce any law which shall abridge the privileges or immunities of citizens of the United States; nor shall any State deprive any person of life, liberty or property without due process of law, nor deny to any person within its jurisdiction the equal protection of the laws." After the committee had twice declined to recommend Mr. Bingham's proposal, on April 28 it was accepted by the Committee, substantially in the form he had proposed it, as § 1 of the recommended Amendment.

V.

In introducing the proposed Amendment to the House on May 8, 1866, Mr. Stevens speaking for the Committee said:

"The first section [of the proposed amendment] prohibits the States from abridging the privileges and immunities of citizens of the United States, or unlawfully depriving them of life, liberty, or property, or of denying to any person within their jurisdiction the 'equal' protection of the laws.

"I can hardly believe that any person can be found who will not admit that every one of these provisions is just. They are all asserted, in some form or other, in our DECLARATION or organic law. But the Constitution limits only the action of Congress, and is not a limitation on the States. This amendment supplies that defect, and allows Congress to correct the unjust legislation of the States, so far that the law which operates upon one man shall operate *equally* upon all."

On May 23, 1866, Senator Howard introduced the proposed amendment to the Senate. . . . Senator Howard prefaced his remarks by stating:

"I . . . present to the Senate . . . the views and the motives [of the Reconstruction Committee]. . . . One result of their investigations has been the joint resolution for the amendment of the Constitution of the United States now under consideration. . . .

* * *

"It would be a curious question to solve what are the privileges and immunities of citizens of each of the States in the several States. . . . I am not aware that the Supreme Court have ever undertaken to define either the nature or extent of the privileges and immunities thus guarantied.

* * *

". . . To these privileges and immunities, whatever they may be — for they are not and cannot be fully defined in their entire extent and precise nature — to these should be added the personal rights guarantied and secured by the first eight amendments of the Constitution; such as the freedom of speech and of the press; the right of the people peaceably to assemble and petition the Government for a redress of grievances, a right appertaining to each and all the people; the right to keep and to bear arms; the right to be exempted from the quartering of soldiers in a house without the consent of the owner; the right to be exempt from unreasonable searches and seizures, and from any search or seizure except by virtue of a warrant issued upon a formal oath or affidavit; the right of an accused person to be informed of the nature of the accusation against him, and his right to be tried by an impartial jury of the vicinage; and also the right to be secure against excessive bail and against cruel and unusual punishments.

"Now, sir, here is a mass of privileges, immunities, and rights, some of them secured by the second section of the fourth article of the Constitution, which I have recited, some by the first eight amendments of the Constitution; and it is a fact well worthy of attention that the course of decision of our courts and the present settled doctrine is, that all these immunities, privileges, rights, thus guarantied by the Constitution or recognized by it, are secured to the citizens solely as a citizen of the United States and as a party in their courts. They do not operate in the slightest degree as a restraint or prohibition upon State legislation. States are not affected by them, and it has been repeatedly held that the restriction contained in the Constitution against the taking of private property for public use without just compensation is not a restriction upon State legislation, but applies only to the legislation of Congress.

"Now, sir, there is no power given in the Constitution to enforce and to carry out any of these guarantees. They are not powers granted by the Constitution to Congress, and of course do not come within the sweeping clause of the Constitution authorizing Congress to pass all laws necessary and proper for carrying out the foregoing or granted powers, but they stand simply as a bill of rights in the Constitution, without power on the part of Congress to give them full effect; while at the same time the States are not restrained from violating the principles embraced in them except by their own local constitutions, which may be altered from year to year. The great object of the first section of this amendment is, therefore, to restrain the power of the States and compel them at all times to respect these great fundamental guarantees."

* * *

Both proponents and opponents of § 1 of the amendment spoke of its relation to the Civil Rights Bill which had been previously passed over the President's veto. Some considered that the amendment settled any doubts there might be as to the constitutionality of the Civil Rights Bill. Others maintained that the Civil Rights Bill would be unconstitutional unless and until the amendment was adopted. Some thought that amendment was nothing but the Civil Rights Bill "in another shape." One attitude of the opponents was epitomized by a statement by Mr. Shanklin that the amendment strikes "down the reserved rights of the States, . . . declared by the framers of the Constitution to belong to the States exclusively and necessary for the protection of the property and liberty of the people. The first section of this proposed amendment . . . is to strike down those State rights and invest all power in the General Government."

Except for the addition of the first sentence of § 1 which defined citizenship, the amendment weathered the Senate debate without substantial change. It is significant that several references were made in the Senate debate to Mr. Bingham's great responsibility for § 1 of the amendment as passed by the House.

VI.

Also just prior to the final votes in both Houses passing the resolution of adoption, the Report of the Joint Committee on Reconstruction was submitted. This report was apparently not distributed in time to influence the debates in Congress. But a student of the period reports that 150,000 copies of the Report and the testimony which it contained were printed in order that senators and representatives might distribute them among their constituents. Apparently the Report was widely reprinted in the press and used as a campaign document in the election of 1866.

The Report of the Committee had said with reference to the necessity of amending the Constitution:

> ". . . [T]he so-called Confederate States are not, at present, entitled to representation in the Congress of the United States; that, before allowing such representation, adequate security for future peace and safety should be required; that this can only be found in such changes of the organic law as shall determine the civil rights and privileges of all citizens in all parts of the republic. . . ."

Among the examples recited by the testimony were discrimination against negro churches and preachers by local officials and criminal punishment of those who attended objectionable church services. Testimony also cited recently enacted Louisiana laws which made it "a highly penal offence for anyone to do anything that might be construed into encouraging the blacks to leave the persons with whom they had made contracts for labor . . . ."

[One author], who canvassed newspaper coverage and speeches concerning the popular discussion of the adoption of the Fourteenth Amendment, indicates that Senator Howard's speech stating that one of the purposes of the first section was to give Congress power to enforce the Bill of Rights, as well as extracts and digests of other speeches were published widely in the press. [He] summarizes his observation that

> "The declarations and statements of newspapers, writers and speakers, . . . show very clearly, . . . the general opinion held in the North. That opinion, briefly stated, was that the Amendment embodied the Civil Rights Bill and gave Congress the power to define and secure the privileges of citizens of the United States. There does not seem to have been any statement at all as to whether the first eight Amendments were to be made applicable to the States or not, whether the privileges guaranteed by those Amendments were to be considered as privileges secured by the Amendment, but it may be inferred that this was recognized to be the logical result by those who thought that the freedom of speech and of the press as well as due process of law, including a jury trial, were secured by it." . . .

VII.

Formal statements subsequent to adoption of the Amendment by the congressional leaders who participated in the drafting and enactment of it are significant. In 1871, a bill was before the House which contemplated enforcement of the Fourteenth Amendment. Mr. Garfield, who had participated in the debates on the Fourteenth Amendment in 1866, said:

* * *

"The . . . clause of the section under debate declares: 'Nor shall any State deprive any person of life, liberty, or property, without due process of law.'

"This is copied from the fifth article of amendments, with this difference: as it stood in the fifth article it operated only as a restraint upon Congress, while here it is a direct restraint upon the governments of the States. The addition is very valuable. It realizes the full force and effect of the clause in Magna Charta, from which it was borrowed; and there is now no power in either the State or the national Government to deprive any person of those great fundamental rights on which all true freedom rests, the rights of life, liberty, and property, except by due process of law; that is, by an impartial trial according to the laws of the land. . . ."

A few days earlier, in a debate on this same bill to enforce the Fourteenth Amendment, Mr. Bingham, still a member of Congress, had stated at length his understanding of the purpose of the Fourteenth Amendment as he had originally conceived it:

"Mr. Speaker, the honorable gentleman from Illinois [Mr. FARNSWORTH] did me unwittingly, great service, when he ventured to ask me why I changed the form of the first section of the fourteenth article of amendment from the form in which I reported it to the House in February, 1866, from the Committee on Reconstruction. . . .

＊ ＊ ＊

"I answer the gentleman, how I came to change the form of February to the words now in the first section of the fourteenth article of amendment, as they stand, and I trust will forever stand, in the Constitution of my country. I had read — and that is what induced me to attempt to impose by constitutional amendments new limitations upon the power of the States — the great decision of Marshall in Barron *vs.* the Mayor and City Council of Baltimore, wherein the Chief Justice said, in obedience to his official oath and the Constitution as it then was: 'The amendments [to the Constitution] contain no expression indicating an intention to apply them to the State governments. This court cannot so apply them.'

"In this case the city had taken private property for public use, without compensation as alleged, and there was no redress for the wrong in the Supreme Court of the United States; and only for this reason, the first eight amendments were not limitations on the power of the States.

". . . Jefferson well said of the first eight articles of amendments to the Constitution of the United States, they constitute the American Bill of Rights. . . .

"In reexamining that case of Barron, Mr. Speaker, after my struggle in the House in February, 1866, to which the gentleman has alluded, I noted and apprehended as I never did before, certain words in that opinion of Marshall. Referring to the first eight articles of amendments to the Constitution of the United States, the Chief Justice said: 'Had the framers of these amendments intended them to be limitations on the powers of the State governments they would have imitated the framers of the original Constitution, and have expressed that intention.'

"Acting upon this suggestion I did imitate the framers of the original Constitution. As they had said 'no State shall emit bills of credit, pass any bill of attainder, *ex post facto* law, or law impairing the obligations of contracts;' imitating their example and imitating it to the letter, I prepared the provision of the first section of the fourteenth amendment as it stands in the Constitution, as follows: 'No State shall make or enforce any law which shall abridge the privileges or immunities of the citizens of the United States, nor shall any State deprive any person of life, liberty, or property without due process of law, nor deny to any person within its jurisdiction the equal protection of the laws.'

"I hope the gentleman now knows why I changed the form of the amendment of February, 1866.

"Mr. Speaker, that the scope and meaning of the limitations imposed by the first section, fourteenth amendment of the Constitution may be more fully understood, permit me to say that the privileges and immunities of citizens of the United States, as contradistinguished from citizens of a State, are chiefly defined in the first eight amendments to the Constitution of the United States. . . ."

* * *

Mr. Justice Murphy, dissenting. [Omitted.]

NOTES AND QUESTIONS

1. It may be that requiring you to read even these substantially edited versions of the long opinions in the *Adamson* case and, in particular, the appendix to Justice Black's opinion, violates the Eighth Amendment, which Justice Black would assure us was incorporated into the Fourteenth against the states. Still, these opinions encapsulate a debate, usually based on the history as outlined by Justice Black's appendix, which remains ongoing, and which seeks to determine the essential attributes of federalism and liberty under the Constitution. They also loudly sound our favorite theme of natural law and the Constitution. They will repay careful study by you, and they will illuminate several other areas which we will be examining in the course, particularly those concerned with governmental regulation of the dealings of private parties.

2. What do you make of the arguments for and against incorporation of the Bill of Rights into the Fourteenth Amendment? Justice Frankfurter, following *Palko,* mounts a defense of the "selective incorporation" view, which is still good law today. Frankfurter claims that he is being faithful to the history of the Fourteenth Amendment, but is he? Obviously Justice Black doesn't agree, but you have now had the chance to consider the materials on which Justice Black relies, and you should be able to reach your own conclusions. To pick up just one point made by Justice Frankfurter, if it had been the understanding of those who framed and ratified the Fourteenth Amendment that it was to incorporate the Bill of Rights, might clearer language have been used to indicate this fact? How would you have drafted the Fourteenth Amendment if you had wanted to incorporate the Bill of Rights?

3. Justice Black argues forcefully, however, that the principal drafter of the First Section of the Fourteenth Amendment, Congressman Bingham, believed that he was incorporating the Bill of Rights (for him the first eight amendments) into the Fourteenth. As you have also seen this was the belief of some other Congressmen, most notably Senator Howard, another framer of the Amendment. Is the belief of the framers enough to determine the construction of the Amendment? How about what they said on the floor of Congress, to which Black's appendix devotes considerable attention? The current school of thought seems to be that one should derive the original understanding of a constitutional provision not from the intentions of its drafters, or even from the statements made in debate over the initial drafting of the provision, but rather from the tenor of the times and the plain meaning of the language used, as it would have been understood by those who ratified the provision of the Constitution or amendment. How far does Black's appendix go in clarifying this issue? How would the ratifiers of the Fourteenth Amendment have understood the measure?

4. And this brings us to one of the thorniest difficulties, albeit one rarely discussed, that ratification of the Fourteenth Amendment was a condition of readmission to the Union for the Southern states, imposed by the victorious North following the Civil War. Where in the Constitution is such a power to impose conditions to readmission to the Union? Some scholars have argued, if one of the reasons for fighting the Civil War was to make the point that individual states were not free to secede from the Union, that is, that the Constitution did not permit a state to nullify the Constitution by withdrawing, might it not be said that the Southern states had not actually been constitutionally separated from the Union at all? Wasn't the Reconstruction Congress acting with hypocrisy, if not blatant illegality, in denying readmission unless particular conditions were met? Since it was clear that the Southern states were likely to continue to suffer military occupation and be deprived of self government until they were "readmitted" to the Union, they paid the price and ratified the Fourteenth Amendment. This has led some historians to argue, however, that the Reconstruction Amendments (as the Thirteenth, Fourteenth, and Fifteenth are sometimes called) were ratified at "gunpoint." Should this have any effect on their interpretation? You can examine the evidence for the "gunpoint" theory in the extraordinary book by Chief Justice William Rehnquist, GRAND INQUESTS: THE HISTORIC IMPEACHMENTS OF JUSTICE SAMUEL CHASE AND PRESIDENT ANDREW JOHNSON (1992). What's extraordinary about the book, by the way, is the sweep and scope and the historical understanding of the work, made doubly impressive by the fact that it was written while its author was performing his judicial duties.

5. Whether it is from the unsavory history of the ratification of the Fourteenth Amendment, or from the weaknesses of the incorporation doctrine as exposed in *Adamson* and many other cases, there has been a tendency among some bolder constitutional theorists to suggest that we should simply scrap the incorporation doctrine altogether, and take the position that all the Fourteenth Amendment was meant to do was to furnish a constitutional basis for the 1866 Civil Rights Act. This is argued, for example, in RAOUL BERGER, GOVERNMENT BY JUDICIARY 115-19 (1977), and in M.E. BRADFORD, ORIGINAL INTENTIONS: ON THE MAKING AND RATIFICATION OF THE UNITED STATES CONSTITUTION 103-31 (1993). *See also* STEPHEN B. PRESSER, RECAPTURING THE CONSTITUTION: RACE, RELIGION AND ABORTION RECONSIDERED 160-70 & 331 nn.488-89 (1994) (for a summary of the arguments of scholars against "selective incorporation"), and sources there cited.

In the 1980s, during the administration of Ronald Reagan, his Attorney General, former law professor Edwin Meese III, publicly questioned the selective incorporation doctrine through the Due Process Clause. The wrath of the legal academy and constitutional scholars unleashed against this proposal caused it to wither on the vine. But was it such a bad idea? On the other hand, if one believes in "natural law," should one be committed to "selective incorporation"?

Whether or not selective incorporation is open to historical question, it is reasonably clear that the drafters of the Fourteenth Amendment expected that a citizen's fundamental rights were to be protected by the Amendment's protection of privileges and immunities. The drafters gave substantive meaning to this language by their explicit reference to the Bill of Rights and the larger natural law rights reflected in *Corfield v. Coryell*, 6 F. Cas. 546 (C.C.E.D. Pa. 1823) (No. 3,230). For a modern expression of a similar view, see Akhil Reed Amar, *The Bill of Rights and the Fourteenth Amendment,* 101 YALE L.J. 1193 (1992) (proposing a new approach to the Fourteenth Amendment's incorporation problem that would require a clause analysis and would ask whether the provision really "guarantees a privilege or immunity of individual citizens rather than a right of states or the public at large"). The Court, however, would disregard the intent of the drafters of the Fourteenth Amendment and render the concept of privileges and immunities without important content in *The Slaughterhouse Cases*, 83 U.S. (16 Wall.) (1873), discussed in Chapter Seven.

6. The next case also deals with the content of the Fourteenth Amendment, though from a slightly different angle. Assuming that the Bill of Rights are largely incorporated against the states, whose interpretation of those rights governs — that of the Supreme Court or Congress? Congress' claim to have some definitional authority is said to derive from Section 5 of the Fourteenth

Amendment, which gives power to Congress to enforce the Amendment "by appropriate legislation." The question in *Boerne* is whether appropriate legislation includes defining the rights in issue in an entirely different manner than the Supreme Court.

CITY OF BOERNE v. FLORES
521 U.S. 507 (1997)

JUSTICE KENNEDY delivered the opinion of the Court.

A decision by local zoning authorities to deny a church a building permit was challenged under the Religious Freedom Restoration Act of 1993 (RFRA). The case calls into question the authority of Congress to enact RFRA. We conclude the statute exceeds Congress' power.

I

Situated on a hill in the city of Boerne, Texas, some 28 miles northwest of San Antonio, is St. Peter Catholic Church. [Located in an historic preservation zone,] . . . [t]he church seats about 230 worshipers, a number too small for its growing parish. [The Archbishop wishes to alter or demolish the existing church structure in order to increase capacity.] . . .

* * *

. . . City authorities, relying on the ordinance and the designation of a historic district (which, they argued, included the church), denied the application. . . .

* * *

II

Congress enacted RFRA in direct response to the Court's decision in *Employment Div., Dept. of Human Resources of Ore. v. Smith* (1990). . . . In evaluating the [*Smith*] claim, we declined to apply the balancing test set forth in *Sherbert v. Verner* (1963) [which would have required application of the "compelling" justification standard]. . . . The application of the *Sherbert* test, the *Smith* decision explained, would have produced an anomaly in the law, a constitutional right to ignore neutral laws of general applicability. The anomaly would have been accentuated, the Court reasoned, by the difficulty of determining whether a particular practice was central to an individual's religion. . . .

The only instances where a neutral, generally applicable law had failed to pass constitutional muster, the *Smith* Court noted, were cases in which other constitutional protections were at stake. In *Wisconsin v. Yoder* (1972), for example, we invalidated Wisconsin's mandatory school-attendance law as applied to Amish parents who refused on religious grounds to send their children to school. That case implicated not only the right to the free exercise of religion but also the right of parents to control their children's education.

* * *

These points of constitutional interpretation [in *Smith*] were debated by Members of Congress in hearings and floor debates. Many criticized the Court's reasoning, and this disagreement resulted in the passage of RFRA. Congress announced:

> "(1) [T]he framers of the Constitution, recognizing free exercise of religion as an unalienable right, secured its protection in the First Amendment to the Constitution;

> "(2) laws 'neutral' toward religion may burden religious exercise as surely as laws intended to interfere with religious exercise;

> "(3) governments should not substantially burden religious exercise without compelling justification;

> "(4) in *Employment Division v. Smith* (1990), the Supreme Court virtually eliminated the requirement that the government justify burdens on religious exercise imposed by laws neutral toward religion; and

> "(5) the compelling interest test as set forth in prior Federal court rulings is a workable test for striking sensible balances between religious liberty and competing prior governmental interests." 42 U.S.C. § 2000bb(a).

The Act's stated purposes are:

> "(1) to restore the compelling interest test as set forth in *Sherbert v. Verner* (1963) and *Wisconsin v. Yoder* (1972) and to guarantee its application in all cases where free exercise of religion is substantially burdened; and

> "(2) to provide a claim or defense to persons whose religious exercise is substantially burdened by government." § 2000bb(b).

RFRA prohibits "[g]overnment" from "substantially burden[ing]" a person's exercise of religion even if the burden results from a rule of general applicability unless the government can demonstrate the burden "(1) is in furtherance of a compelling governmental interest; and (2) is the least restrictive means of furthering that compelling governmental interest." The Act's mandate applies to any "branch, department, agency, instrumentality, and official (or other person acting under color of law) of the United States," as well as to any "State, or . . . subdivision of a State." The Act's universal coverage is confirmed in § 2000bb-3(a), under which RFRA "applies to all Federal and State law, and the implementation of that law, whether statutory or otherwise, and whether adopted before or after [RFRA's enactment]." In accordance with RFRA's usage of the term, we shall use "state law" to include local and municipal ordinances.

III

A

Under our Constitution, the Federal Government is one of enumerated powers. The judicial authority to determine the constitutionality of laws, in cases and controversies, is based on the premise that the "powers of the legislature are defined and limited; and that those limits may not be mistaken, or forgotten, the constitution is written." *Marbury v. Madison* (1803).

Congress relied on its Fourteenth Amendment enforcement power in enacting the most far reaching and substantial of RFRA's provisions, those which impose its requirements on the States. The Fourteenth Amendment provides, in relevant part:

> "Section 1. . . . No State shall make or enforce any law which shall abridge the privileges or immunities of citizens of the United States; nor shall any State deprive any person of life, liberty, or property, without due process of law; nor deny to any person within its jurisdiction the equal protection of the laws.

* * *

> "Section 5. The Congress shall have power to enforce, by appropriate legislation, the provisions of this article."

The parties disagree over whether RFRA is a proper exercise of Congress' § 5 power "to enforce" by "appropriate legislation" the constitutional guarantee that no State shall deprive any person of "life, liberty, or property, without due process of law" nor deny any person "equal protection of the laws."

In defense of the Act respondent contends, with support from the United States as *amicus*, that RFRA is permissible enforcement legislation. Congress, it is said, is only protecting by legislation one of the liberties guaranteed by the Fourteenth Amendment's Due Process Clause, the free exercise of religion, beyond what is necessary under *Smith*. It is said the congressional decision to dispense with proof of deliberate or overt discrimination and instead concentrate on a law's effects accords with the settled understanding that § 5 includes the power to enact legislation designed to prevent as well as remedy constitutional violations. It is further contended that Congress' § 5 power is not limited to remedial or preventive legislation.

All must acknowledge that § 5 is "a positive grant of legislative power" to Congress, *Katzenbach v. Morgan* (1966). In *Ex parte Virginia* (1880), we explained the scope of Congress' § 5 power in the following broad terms:

> "Whatever legislation is appropriate, that is, adapted to carry out the objects the amendments have in view, whatever tends to enforce submission to the prohibitions they contain, and to secure to all persons the enjoyment of perfect equality of civil rights and the equal protection of

the laws against State denial or invasion, if not prohibited, is brought within the domain of congressional power."

Legislation which deters or remedies constitutional violations can fall within the sweep of Congress' enforcement power even if in the process it prohibits conduct which is not itself unconstitutional and intrudes into "legislative spheres of autonomy previously reserved to the States." *Fitzpatrick v. Bitzer* (1976). . . .

It is also true, however, that "[a]s broad as the congressional enforcement power is, it is not unlimited." . . . In assessing the breadth of § 5's enforcement power, we begin with its text. Congress has been given the power "to enforce" the "provisions of this article." We agree with respondent, of course, that Congress can enact legislation under § 5 enforcing the constitutional right to the free exercise of religion. The "provisions of this article," to which § 5 refers, include the Due Process Clause of the Fourteenth Amendment. Congress' power to enforce the Free Exercise Clause follows from our holding in *Cantwell v. Connecticut* (1940), that the "fundamental concept of liberty embodied in [the Fourteenth Amendment's Due Process Clause] embraces the liberties guaranteed by the First Amendment."

Congress' power under § 5, however, extends only to "enforc[ing]" the provisions of the Fourteenth Amendment. The Court has described this power as "remedial" . . . . The design of the Amendment and the text of § 5 are inconsistent with the suggestion that Congress has the power to decree the substance of the Fourteenth Amendment's restrictions on the States. Legislation which alters the meaning of the Free Exercise Clause cannot be said to be enforcing the Clause. Congress does not enforce a constitutional right by changing what the right is. It has been given the power "to enforce," not the power to determine what constitutes a constitutional violation. Were it not so, what Congress would be enforcing would no longer be, in any meaningful sense, the "provisions of [the Fourteenth Amendment]."

While the line between measures that remedy or prevent unconstitutional actions and measures that make a substantive change in the governing law is not easy to discern, and Congress must have wide latitude in determining where it lies, the distinction exists and must be observed. There must be a congruence and proportionality between the injury to be prevented or remedied and the means adopted to that end. . . .

1

The Fourteenth Amendment's history confirms the remedial, rather than substantive, nature of the Enforcement Clause. The Joint Committee on Reconstruction of the 39th Congress began drafting what would become the Fourteenth Amendment in January 1866. The objections to the Committee's first draft of the Amendment, and the rejection of the draft, have a direct bearing on the central issue of defining Congress' enforcement power. In February, Republican Representative John Bingham of Ohio reported the following draft amendment to the House of Representatives on behalf of the Joint Committee:

"The Congress shall have power to make all laws which shall be necessary and proper to secure to the citizens of each State all privileges and immunities of citizens in the several States, and to all persons in the several States equal protection in the rights of life, liberty, and property."

The proposal encountered immediate opposition, which continued through three days of debate. Members of Congress from across the political spectrum criticized the Amendment, and the criticisms had a common theme: The proposed Amendment gave Congress too much legislative power at the expense of the existing constitutional structure. Democrats and conservative Republicans argued that the proposed Amendment would give Congress a power to intrude into traditional areas of state responsibility, a power inconsistent with the federal design central to the Constitution. . . . Senator William Stewart of Nevada likewise stated the Amendment would permit "Congress to legislate fully upon all subjects affecting life, liberty, and property," such that "there would not be much left for the State Legislatures," and would thereby "work an entire change in our form of government." . . .

As a result of these objections having been expressed from so many different quarters, the House voted to table the proposal until April. . . . The Amendment in its early form was not again considered. Instead, the Joint Committee began drafting a new article of Amendment, which it reported to Congress on April 30, 1866.

Section 1 of the new draft Amendment imposed self-executing limits on the States. Section 5 prescribed that "[t]he Congress shall have power to enforce, by appropriate legislation, the provisions of this article." Under the revised Amendment, Congress' power was no longer plenary but remedial. Congress was granted the power to make the substantive constitutional prohibitions against the States effective. Representative Bingham said the new draft would give Congress "the power . . . to protect by national law the privileges and immunities of all the citizens of the Republic . . . whenever the same shall be abridged or denied by the unconstitutional acts of any State." . . . After revisions not relevant here, the new measure passed both Houses and was ratified in July 1868 as the Fourteenth Amendment.

* * *

The design of the Fourteenth Amendment has proved significant also in maintaining the traditional separation of powers between Congress and the Judiciary. The first eight Amendments to the Constitution set forth self-executing prohibitions on governmental action, and this Court has had primary authority to interpret those prohibitions. The Bingham draft, some thought, departed from that tradition by vesting in Congress primary power to interpret and elaborate on the meaning of the new Amendment through legislation. Under it, "Congress, and not the courts, was to judge whether or not any of the privileges or immunities were not secured to citizens in the several States." While this separation of powers aspect did not occasion the widespread resistance which was caused by the proposal's threat to the federal balance, it nonetheless attracted the attention of various Members. . . .

2

The remedial and preventive nature of Congress' enforcement power, and the limitation inherent in the power, were confirmed in our earliest cases on the Fourteenth Amendment. In the *Civil Rights Cases* (1883), the Court invalidated sections of the Civil Rights Act of 1875 which prescribed criminal penalties for denying to any person "the full enjoyment of" public accommodations and conveyances, on the grounds that it exceeded Congress' power by seeking to regulate private conduct. The Enforcement Clause, the Court said, did not authorize Congress to pass "general legislation upon the rights of the citizen, but corrective legislation; that is, such as may be necessary and proper for counteracting such laws as the States may adopt or enforce, and which, by the amendment, they are prohibited from making or enforcing . . . ." The power to "legislate generally upon" life, liberty, and property, as opposed to the "power to provide modes of redress" against offensive state action, was "repugnant" to the Constitution. . . .

* * *

3

Any suggestion that Congress has a substantive, non-remedial power under the Fourteenth Amendment is not supported by our case law. In *Oregon v. Mitchell*, a majority of the Court concluded Congress had exceeded its enforcement powers by enacting legislation lowering the minimum age of voters from 21 to 18 in state and local elections. The five Members of the Court who reached this conclusion explained that the legislation intruded into an area reserved by the Constitution to the States. . . . Four of these five were explicit in rejecting the position that § 5 endowed Congress with the power to establish the meaning of constitutional provisions. Justice Black's rejection of this position might be inferred from his disagreement with Congress' interpretation of the Equal Protection Clause.

There is language in our opinion in *Katzenbach v. Morgan* (1966), which could be interpreted as acknowledging a power in Congress to enact legislation that expands the rights contained in § 1 of the Fourteenth Amendment. This is not a necessary interpretation, however, or even the best one. . . .

If Congress could define its own powers by altering the Fourteenth Amendment's meaning, no longer would the Constitution be "superior paramount law, unchangeable by ordinary means." It would be "on a level with ordinary legislative acts, and, like other acts, . . . alterable when the legislature shall please to alter it." *Marbury v. Madison.* . . . Shifting legislative majorities could change the Constitution and effectively circumvent the difficult and detailed amendment process contained in Article V.

We now turn to consider whether RFRA can be considered enforcement legislation under § 5 of the Fourteenth Amendment.

B

Respondent contends that RFRA is a proper exercise of Congress' remedial or preventive power. The Act, it is said, is a reasonable means of protecting the free exercise of religion as defined by *Smith*. It prevents and remedies laws which are enacted with the unconstitutional object of targeting religious beliefs and practices. To avoid the difficulty of proving such violations, it is said, Congress can simply invalidate any law which imposes a substantial burden on a religious practice unless it is justified by a compelling interest and is the least restrictive means of accomplishing that interest. If Congress can prohibit laws with discriminatory effects in order to prevent racial discrimination in violation of the Equal Protection Clause . . . then it can do the same, respondent argues, to promote religious liberty.

While preventive rules are sometimes appropriate remedial measures, there must be a congruence between the means used and the ends to be achieved. The appropriateness of remedial measures must be considered in light of the evil presented. Strong measures appropriate to address one harm may be an unwarranted response to another, lesser one.

A comparison between RFRA and the Voting Rights Act is instructive. In contrast to the record which confronted Congress and the judiciary in the voting rights cases, RFRA's legislative record lacks examples of modern instances of generally applicable laws passed because of religious bigotry. The history of persecution in this country detailed in the hearings mentions no episodes occurring in the past 40 years. . . .

Regardless of the state of the legislative record, RFRA cannot be considered remedial, preventive legislation, if those terms are to have any meaning. RFRA is so out of proportion to a supposed remedial or preventive object that it cannot be understood as responsive to, or designed to prevent, unconstitutional behavior. It appears, instead, to attempt a substantive change in constitutional protections. Preventive measures prohibiting certain types of laws may be appropriate when there is reason to believe that many of the laws affected by the congressional enactment have a significant likelihood of being unconstitutional. . . . Remedial legislation under § 5 "should be adapted to the mischief and wrong which the [Fourteenth] [A]mendment was intended to provide against." *Civil Rights Cases*.

RFRA is not so confined. Sweeping coverage ensures its intrusion at every level of government, displacing laws and prohibiting official actions of almost every description and regardless of subject matter. RFRA's restrictions apply to every agency and official of the Federal, State, and local Governments. RFRA applies to all federal and state law, statutory or otherwise, whether adopted before or after its enactment. RFRA has no termination date or termination mechanism. Any law is subject to challenge at any time by any individual who alleges a substantial burden on his or her free exercise of religion.

The reach and scope of RFRA distinguish it from other measures passed under Congress' enforcement power, even in the area of voting rights. . . .

The stringent test RFRA demands of state laws reflects a lack of proportionality or congruence between the means adopted and the legitimate end to be achieved. If an objector can show a substantial burden on his free exercise, the State must demonstrate a compelling governmental interest and show that the law is the least restrictive means of furthering its interest. . . . If "'compelling interest' really means what it says . . . many laws will not meet the test. . . . [The test] would open the prospect of constitutionally required religious exemptions from civic obligations of almost every conceivable kind." Laws valid under *Smith* would fall under RFRA without regard to whether they had the object of stifling or punishing free exercise. We make these observations not to reargue the position of the majority in *Smith* but to illustrate the substantive alteration of its holding attempted by RFRA. Even assuming RFRA would be interpreted in effect to mandate some lesser test, say one equivalent to intermediate scrutiny, the statute nevertheless would require searching judicial scrutiny of state law with the attendant likelihood of invalidation. This is a considerable congressional intrusion into the States' traditional prerogatives and general authority to regulate for the health and welfare of their citizens.

. . . In most cases, the state laws to which RFRA applies are not ones which will have been motivated by religious bigotry. If a state law disproportionately burdened a particular class of religious observers, this circumstance might be evidence of an impermissible legislative motive. RFRA's substantial burden test, however, is not even a discriminatory effects or disparate impact test. It is a reality of the modern regulatory state that numerous state laws, such as the zoning regulations at issue here, impose a substantial burden on a large class of individuals. When the exercise of religion has been burdened in an incidental way by a law of general application, it does not follow that the persons affected have been burdened any more than other citizens, let alone burdened because of their religious beliefs. In addition, the Act imposes in every case a least restrictive means requirement — a requirement that was not used in the pre-*Smith* jurisprudence RFRA purported to codify — which also indicates that the legislation is broader than is appropriate if the goal is to prevent and remedy constitutional violations.

When Congress acts within its sphere of power and responsibilities, it has not just the right but the duty to make its own informed judgment on the meaning and force of the Constitution. This has been clear from the early days of the Republic. In 1789, when a Member of the House of Representatives objected to a debate on the constitutionality of legislation based on the theory that "it would be officious" to consider the constitutionality of a measure that did not affect the House, James Madison explained that "it is incontrovertibly of as much importance to this branch of the Government as to any other, that the constitution should be preserved entire. It is our duty." Were it otherwise, we would not afford Congress the presumption of validity its enactments now enjoy.

Our national experience teaches that the Constitution is preserved best when each part of the government respects both the Constitution and the proper actions and determinations of the other branches. When the Court has interpreted the Constitution, it has acted within the province of the Judicial Branch, which embraces the duty to say what the law is. *Marbury v. Madison*. When the political branches of the Government act against the background of a judicial interpretation of the Constitution already issued, it must be understood that in later cases and controversies the Court will treat its precedents with the respect due them under settled principles, including *stare decisis*, and contrary expectations must be disappointed. RFRA was designed to control cases and controversies, such as the one before us; but as the provisions of the federal statute here invoked are beyond congressional authority, it is this Court's precedent, not RFRA, which must control.

* * *

. . . The judgment of the Court of Appeals sustaining the Act's constitutionality is reversed.

It is so ordered.

JUSTICE STEVENS, concurring. [Omitted.]

JUSTICE SCALIA, with whom JUSTICE STEVENS joins, concurring in part. [Omitted.]

JUSTICE O'CONNOR, with whom JUSTICE BREYER joins except as to a portion of Part I, dissenting.

* * *

I

I agree with much of the reasoning set forth in Part III-A of the Court's opinion. Indeed, if I agreed with the Court's standard in *Smith*, I would join the opinion. As the Court's careful and thorough historical analysis shows, Congress lacks the "power to decree the substance of the Fourteenth Amendment's restrictions on the States." Rather, its power under § 5 of the Fourteenth Amendment extends only to *enforcing* the Amendment's provisions.

. . . [Nevertheless] I continue to believe that *Smith* adopted an improper standard for deciding free exercise claims. . . . Before *Smith*, our free exercise cases were generally in keeping with this idea: where a law substantially burdened religiously motivated conduct — regardless whether it was specifically targeted at religion or applied generally — we required government to justify that law with a compelling state interest and to use means narrowly tailored to achieve that interest.

The Court's rejection of this principle in *Smith* is supported neither by precedent nor by history. . . .

* * *

JUSTICE SOUTER, dissenting. [Omitted.]

JUSTICE BREYER, dissenting.

I agree with JUSTICE O'CONNOR that the Court should direct the parties to brief the question whether *Employment Div., Dept. of Human Resources of Ore. v. Smith* (1990) was correctly decided, and set this case for reargument. I do not, however, find it necessary to consider the question whether, assuming *Smith* is correct, § 5 of the Fourteenth Amendment would authorize Congress to enact the legislation before us.

NOTES AND QUESTIONS

1. The *Boerne* case brings in many interesting issues for our consideration, perhaps most importantly the meaning of Section 5 of the Fourteenth Amendment. That section gave Congress power to implement the other provisions of the Fourteenth Amendment. Why isn't RFRA such an attempt, in the view of the majority? Given the majority's holding, is there really much scope left for Section 5 to operate? Does it matter, for example, what the precise nature of the Fourteenth Amendment rights in question are? This might mean, as the Court seems to imply, that there is a greater congressional role to be played in legislating with regard to matters of race than there is with regard to matters involving religion. Why should this be the case?

2. The meaning of Congress' Section 5 enforcement authority has been anything but settled. An earlier decision, *Katzenbach v. Morgan*, 384 U.S. 641 (1966), is the source of much of this confusion. In *Katzenbach,* the Court allowed Congress to prohibit certain voter literacy requirements without regard to whether the Court would have found those requirements in individual cases to be violative of Section 1 of the Fourteenth Amendment. Over time, *Katzenbach* has been given two competing interpretations that go to the heart of this case. One interpretation is that Section 5 authority is remedial; that is, Congress — based in part upon its superior fact-finding ability — can enact so-called prophylactic or preventive rules that address, without case-by-case adjudication, conduct that the Court has already determined to be a violation of the Fourteenth Amendment, or those rights judicially incorporated into it. A competing and far more sweeping claim is that Section 5 is a grant of substantive authority, allowing Congress to determine for itself the meaning of the relevant constitutional rights. A view of Section 5 authority inclined toward the substantive was needed to sustain RFRA, and as indicated, the Court refused to grant it.

3. *Katzenbach* had been limited before *Boerne*, but in divided opinions. For example, in *Oregon v. Mitchell*, 400 U.S. 112 (1970), decided a few years after

Katzenbach, the Court seemed to confirm the absence of substantive authority in Congress to redefine constitutional provisions. *Mitchell* invalidated a putative Section 5 statutory extension of voting rights to 18 year olds in state elections. It took the Twenty-Sixth Amendment to accomplish this. The late Chief Justice Warren Burger observed, "I have always read *Oregon v. Mitchell* as finally imposing a limitation on the extent to which Congress may substitute its own judgment for that of the states and assume this Court's 'role of final arbiter.'" *EEOC v. Wyoming*, 460 U.S. 226, 262 (1983) (Burger, C.J., dissenting) (quoting *Mitchell*, 460 U.S. at 205 (Harlan, J., dissenting)). Nevertheless, the substantive version was championed by the late Justice William Brennan who argued that Congress should have the power to expand constitutional rights beyond the interpretations of the Court — the so-called "one-way ratchet" theory traceable to a footnote in Justice Brennan's opinion in *Katzenbach*. 384 U.S. at 651 n.10. The problem, of course, is that one person's expanded constitutional right may well be the restriction of another's.

4. Certainly, a substantive power of this nature would affect the federal-state balance, or what we have referred to in this Chapter as dual federalism. Representative John Bingham's first draft of the Fourteenth Amendment in 1866 would have radically altered the federal-state relationship by empowering Congress to make uniform laws guaranteeing, among other things, equal protection. Bingham's draft in light of the subsequent judicial incorporation of the bill of rights would clearly have sustained RFRA. But Bingham's draft was immediately objected to and rejected as "the embodiment of centralization and the disenfranchisement of the States." CONG. GLOBE, 39th Cong., 1st Sess. app. 133, 134 (1866). The redrafted proposal of Thaddeus Stevens became the Fourteenth Amendment. Unlike Bingham's extensive grant of federal legislative power, Stevens' version and the ratified Fourteenth Amendment created a constitutional standard accompanied by supplementary enforcement authority.

The Court reiterated this point in *United States v. Morrison*, 529 U.S. 598 (2000), invalidating a key section (§ 13891) of the Violence Against Women's Act under both the commerce power and § 5 of the Fourteenth Amendment. *City of Boerne*, the Court stated that the principles governing an analysis of congressional legislation under § 5 are well settled. The proponents of the Act had argued that states were not fully prosecuting gender crime, and therefore, a private cause of action for such violence under federal law was justified. The Court disagreed, noting that foremost among the limitations on Congress' power is the time-honored principle that the Fourteenth Amendment, by its very terms, prohibits only state action. The Court majority noted:

> Shortly after the Fourteenth Amendment was adopted, we decided two cases interpreting the Amendment's provisions, *United States v. Harris* (1883) and the *Civil Rights Cases* (1883). In *Harris*, the Court considered a challenge to § 2 of the Civil Rights Act of 1871. That section sought to punish "private persons" for "conspiring to deprive any one of the equal protection of the laws enacted by the State." We con-

cluded that this law exceeded Congress' § 5 power because the law was "directed exclusively against the action of private persons, without reference to the laws of the State, or their administration by her officers."

We reached a similar conclusion in the *Civil Rights Cases.*

* * *

[Nothing can] save § 13981's civil remedy. For the remedy is simply not "corrective in its character, adapted to counteract and redress the operation of such prohibited [s]tate laws or proceedings of [s]tate officers." Or, as we have phrased it in more recent cases, prophylactic legislation under § 5 must have a "congruence and proportionality between the injury to be prevented or remedied and the means adopted to that end." *Florida Prepaid Postsecondary Ed. Expense Bd. v. College Savings Bank* (1999). Section 13981 is not aimed at proscribing discrimination by officials which the Fourteenth Amendment might not itself proscribe; it is directed not at any State or state actor, but at individuals who have committed criminal acts motivated by gender bias.

In the present cases, for example, § 13981 visits no consequence whatever on any Virginia public official involved in investigating or prosecuting Brzonkala's assault. The section is, therefore, unlike any of the § 5 remedies that we have previously upheld. For example, in *Katzenbach v. Morgan* (1966), Congress prohibited New York from imposing literacy tests as a prerequisite for voting because it found that such a requirement disenfranchised thousands of Puerto Rican immigrants who had been educated in the Spanish language of their home territory. That law, which we upheld, was directed at New York officials who administered the State's election law and prohibited them from using a provision of that law. In *South Carolina v. Katzenbach* (1966), Congress imposed voting rights requirements on States that, Congress found, had a history of discriminating against blacks in voting. The remedy was also directed at state officials in those States. Similarly, in *Ex parte Virginia* (1879), Congress criminally punished state officials who intentionally discriminated in jury selection; again, the remedy was directed to the culpable state official.

Section 13981 is also different from these previously upheld remedies in that it applies uniformly throughout the Nation. Congress' findings indicate that the problem of discrimination against the victims of gender-motivated crimes does not exist in all States, or even most States. By contrast, the § 5 remedy upheld in *Katzenbach v. Morgan, supra*, was directed only to the State where the evil found by Congress existed, and in *South Carolina v. Katzenbach, supra*, the remedy was directed only to those States in which Congress found that there had been discrimination.

For these reasons, we conclude that Congress' power under § 5 does not extend to the enactment of § 13981.

5. In *Tennessee v. Lane*, 124 S. Ct. 1978 (2004), Justice Scalia dissented, suggesting that he would no longer use the inquiry of congruence and proportionality to measure the constitutionality of an exercise of section 5 authority. He wrote:

> The "congruence and proportionality" standard, like all such flabby tests, is a standing invitation to judicial arbitrariness and policy-driven decisionmaking. Worse still, it casts this Court in the role of Congress's taskmaster. Under it, the courts (and ultimately this Court) must regularly check Congress's homework to make sure that it has identified sufficient constitutional violations to make its remedy congruent and proportional. As a general matter, we are ill advised to adopt or adhere to constitutional rules that bring us into constant conflict with a coequal branch of Government. And when conflict is unavoidable, we should not come to do battle with the United States Congress armed only with a test ("congruence and proportionality") that has no demonstrable basis in the text of the Constitution and cannot objectively be shown to have been met or failed. As I wrote for the Court in an earlier case, "low walls and vague distinctions will not be judicially defensible in the heat of interbranch conflict."

Justice Scalia suggests that the better approach is to give little deference to prophylactic legislation outside of the race context, one of the core purposes of the Fourteenth Amendment. In this regard, Justice Scalia indicates that the words "to enforce" in that Amendment does not authorize Congress to go beyond the prohibitions of the Amendment itself. "So-called 'prophylactic legislation,' [which is what he thought Title II of the Americans with Disabilities Act to be] is reinforcement rather than enforcement" and therefore, ultra vires. Do you think his distrust of this test stems from a disdain for judicial activism, or because this test has led to abrogation twice in as many terms? Is the only "correct" test one that will never lead to abrogation of state sovereign immunity except in racial discrimination cases?

Chapter 6

A FAIR GOVERNMENT

I. The Substantive Protection of Vested Rights

Law is perceived as substantively unfair when it disappoints well-settled and reasonable expectations — that is, when it undermines vested rights. In his influential *Second Treatise on Civil Government*, John Locke reflects that no person would yield liberty to a civil society, if government thereafter could apply laws retrospectively to conduct that conformed to the law at the time it was undertaken. The Constitution reflects this precept in favor of a rule of law (general enactments, prospectively applied) through a number of provisions: In Article I, Sections 9 and 10, the Constitution prohibits ex post facto laws, laws punishing individuals for conduct that was legal at the time they committed it, as well as bills of attainder, laws where the legislature singles out an individual or discrete group for punishment; the Fifth Amendment protects against the taking of property without just compensation; and the Contract Clause in Article I, Section 10, Clause 1 states that "no state shall . . . pass any . . . Law impairing the Obligation of Contracts." Matters of ex post facto legislation and bills of attainder are normally taken up with the study of criminal law. Here, we turn first to the protection of contract and then property.

A. The Protection of Contract Against State Impairment

1. The Precipitating Hardship

Harvard historian Benjamin Wright concludes after exhaustive study that "[d]uring the nineteenth century no constitutional clause was so frequently the basis of decisions by the Supreme Court of the United States as that forbidding the states to pass laws impairing the obligation of contracts." BENJAMIN WRIGHT, THE CONTRACT CLAUSE OF THE CONSTITUTION at xiii (1938). The immediate need for the Clause originated out of the economic depression following the Revolutionary War. These sour economic times were especially difficult for small farmers, who in great numbers were losing their lands to foreclosure. A number of states sought to rectify the plight of the farmers by enacting debtor relief or "stay" laws that deferred foreclosure. Some states allowed debts to be paid with paper currency of little or no value that effectively canceled underlying debt. Farmers in Massachusetts petitioned the legislature for such economic relief, but to no avail. In September 1786, farmer and former army captain Daniel Shays organized a small force to capture an arsenal to provide farmers with military protection from their creditors. "Shay's Rebellion," as it was called, lasted for three weeks. Pointing to this insurrection, creditors and property owners

791

advanced the need to rework the Articles of Confederation to prevent states from pursuing policies that undermined commerce and vested economic rights. Congress responded by passing a resolution calling for the constitutional convention.

Wright reports that the delegates to the constitutional convention were indeed greatly distressed by the "evils" of debtor relief laws and the like, as Madison called them. *See* WRIGHT, *supra*, at 3-6. However, it should not be assumed that our founders were unsympathetic to their less well-off countrymen. The constitutional delegates recognized that farmers faced difficult economic times, but prudently supposed that these could not be overcome with counterfeit accounting. Such would merely jeopardize the commercial reputation of the young republic and curtail lines of credit. The sounder course, the delegates reasoned, would be to address the underlying cause: the unstructured state sovereignty of the Articles of Confederation which yielded an inadequate supply of money of fixed value. Fairly early in the convention, the drafters directly addressed this problem by forbidding the states from issuing bills of credit or coining money. It was the national government that would do that and regulate its value.

Having addressed the issue of the supply and value of money, the framers did not at first perceive any additional need to secure the vested rights of contract. However, six weeks into the convention on July 13, 1787, the Congress under the Articles sitting in New York passed the Northwest Ordinance regulating territories that eventually became several midwestern states. Among other provisions, that Ordinance provided that "in the just preservation of rights and property, it is understood and declared, that no law ought ever to be made or have force in the said territory, that shall, in any manner whatever, interfere with or affect private contracts . . . previously formed." Northwest Territory Ordinance of 1787, art. II, 1 Stat. 51, 52 (1789). Richard Henry Lee sent a copy of the Ordinance to George Washington urging that such a clause was necessary to secure vested rights against "licentious" settlers who might use legislative power to divest them. Shortly thereafter, a similar provision was brought before the convention.

2. Debate in Convention

2 THE RECORDS OF THE FEDERAL CONVENTION 434, 439-40 (Max Farrand ed., 1911)

Tuesday, August 28, 1787

* * *

MR. KING moved to add . . . a prohibition on the States to interfere in private contracts.

MR. GOVR. MORRIS. This would be going too far. There are a thousand laws relating to bringing actions — limitations of actions [and] which affect contracts — The Judicial power of the [United States] will be a protection in cases within their jurisdiction; and within the State itself a majority must rule, whatever may be the mischief done among themselves.

MR. SHERMAN. Why then prohibit bills of credit?

MR. WILSON was in favor of Mr. King's motion.

MR. MADISON admitted that inconveniences might arise from such a prohibition but thought on the whole it would be overbalanced by the utility of it. He conceived however that a negative on the State laws could alone secure the effect. Evasions might and would be devised by the ingenuity of the Legislatures —

COL. MASON. This is carrying the restraint too far. Cases will happen that can not be foreseen, where some kind of interference will be proper, [and] essential — He mentioned the case of limiting the period for bringing actions on open account — that of bonds after a certain (lapse of time,) — asking whether it was proper to tie the hands of the States from making provisions in such cases?

MR. WILSON. The answer to these objections is that *retrospective* interferences only are to be prohibited.

MR. MADISON. Is not that already done by the prohibition of ex post facto laws, which will oblige the Judges to declare such interferences null [and] void?

MR. RUTLIDGE moved instead of Mr. King's Motion to insert — "nor pass bills of attainder nor retrospective laws" . . . .

* * *

Wednesday, August 29, 1787

* * *

MR. DICKENSON mentioned to the House that on examining Blackstone's Commentaries, he found that the terms "ex post facto" related to criminal cases only; that they would not consequently restrain the States from retrospective laws in civil cases, and that some further provision for this purpose would be requisite.

* * *

Friday, September 14, 1787

* * *

MR. GERRY entered into observations inculcating the importance of public faith, and the propriety of the restraint put on the States from impairing the obligation of contracts — Alledging that Congress ought to be laid under the like prohibitions.

3. Post-Convention Justification

THE FEDERALIST NO. 7 (Alexander Hamilton)

* * *

Laws in violation of private contracts as they amount to aggressions on the rights of those States, whose citizens are injured by them, may be considered as another probable source of hostility. We are not authorized to expect, that a more liberal or more equitable spirit would preside over the legislations of the individual States hereafter, if unrestrained by any additional checks, than we have heretofore seen, in too many instances, disgracing their several codes. We have observed the disposition to retaliation excited in Connecticut, in consequence of the enormities perpetrated by the legislature of Rhode Island; and we may reasonably infer, that in similar cases, under other circumstances, a war not of *parchment* but of the sword would chastise such atrocious breaches of moral obligation and social justice.

THE FEDERALIST NO. 44 (James Madison)

A *fifth* class of provisions in favor of the federal authority, consists of the following restrictions on the authority of the several States:

1. "No State shall enter into any treaty, alliance, or confederation, grant letters of marque and reprisal, coin money, emit bills of credit, make any thing but gold and silver a legal tender in payment of debts; pass any bill of attainder, ex post facto law, or law impairing the obligation of contracts, or grant any title of nobility."

* * *

Bills of attainder, ex post facto laws, and laws impairing the obligation of contracts, are contrary to the first principles of the social compact, and to every principle of sound legislation. The two former are expressly prohibited by the declarations prefixed to some of the State Constitutions, and all of them are prohibited by the spirit and scope of these fundamental charters. Our own experience has taught us nevertheless, that additional fences against these dangers ought not to be omitted. Very properly therefore have the Convention added this constitutional bulwark in favor of personal security and private rights; and I am much deceived if they have not in so doing as faithfully consulted the genuine sentiments, as the undoubted interests of their constituents. The sober people of America are weary of the fluctuating policy which has directed the public councils. They have seen with regret and with indignation, that sudden changes and legislative interferences in cases affecting personal rights, become jobs in the hands of enterprising and influential speculators; and snares to the more industrious and less informed part of the community. They have seen, too, that legislative interference, is but the first link of a long chain of repetitions; every subsequent interference being naturally produced by the effects of the preceding. They very rightly infer, therefore, that some thorough reform is wanting which will banish speculations on public measures, inspire a general prudence and industry, and give a regular course to the business of society.

NOTE

The objectives of the founders in adding the Contract Clause are ably summarized by Joseph Story. Appointed as an Associate Justice of the Supreme Court by Madison in 1811, Story was named to the Court at the age of 32 and served until his death in 1845. A serious student of the law, his *Commentaries* are accepted by many as a classic exposition of original meaning. *See* GERARD DUNNE, JUSTICE JOSEPH STORY AND THE RISE OF THE SUPREME COURT (1970). As Story reflects in the excerpt below and in a number that will be referred to throughout this Chapter, contract was a mixed natural law/positive law concept. Society through the positive law gives application, says Story, to contractual obligations that arise by promise — conferring moral right under natural or universal law. Law, then, does not create the obligation, it merely supplies a means of enforcement so long as the agreement, itself, does not transgress the public policy.

3 JOSEPH STORY, COMMENTARIES ON THE CONSTITUTION (1833)

§ 1372. [W]hat is the obligation of a contract? It would seem difficult to substitute words more intelligible, or less liable to misconstruction, than these. And yet they have given rise to much acute disquisition, as to their real meaning in the constitution. It has been said, that right and obligation are correlative terms. Whatever I, by my contract, give another a right to require of me, I, by that act, lay myself under an obligation to yield or bestow. The obligation of every contract, then, will consist of that right, or power over my will or actions, which I, by my contract, confer on another. And that right and power will be found to be measured, neither by moral law alone, nor by universal law alone, nor by the laws of society alone; but by a combination of the three; an operation, in which the moral law is explained, and applied by the law of nature, and both modified and adapted to the exigencies of society by positive law.

* * *

§ 1379. In the next place, what may properly be deemed impairing the obligation of contracts in the sense of the constitution? It is perfectly clear, that any law, which enlarges, abridges, or in any manner changes the intention of the parties, resulting from the stipulations in the contract, necessarily impairs it. The manner or degree, in which this change is effected, can in no respect influence the conclusion; for whether the law affect the validity, the construction, the duration, the discharge, or the evidence of the contract, it impairs its obligation, though it may not do so to the same extent in all the supposed cases. Any deviation from its terms by postponing, or accelerating the period of performance, which it prescribes; imposing conditions not expressed in the contract; or dispensing with the performance of those, which are a part of the contract; however minute or apparently immaterial in their effect upon it, impair its obligation. *A fortiori*, a law, which makes the contract wholly invalid, or extinguishes, or releases it, is a law impairing it. Nor is this all. Although there is a distinction between the obligation of a contract, and a remedy upon it; yet if there are certain remedies existing at the time, when it is made, all of which are afterwards wholly extinguished by new laws, so that there remain no means of enforcing its obligation, and no redress; such an abolition of all remedies, operating *in presenti*, is also an impairing of the obligation of such contract.

* * *

§ 1392. Before quitting this subject it may be proper to remark, that as the prohibition, respecting *ex post facto* laws, applies only to criminal cases; and the other is confined to impairing the obligation of contracts; there are many laws of a retrospective character, which may yet be constitutionally passed by the state legislatures, however unjust, oppressive, or impolitic they may be. Retrospective laws are, indeed, generally unjust; and, as has been forcibly said, neither accord with sound legislation, nor with the fundamental principles of the social compact. Still they are, with the exceptions above stated, left open to the states, according to their own constitutions of government; and become obligatory, if not prohibited by the latter. Thus, for instance, where the legislature of Connecticut, in 1795, passed a resolve, setting aside a decree of a court of probate disapproving of a will, and granted a new hearing; it was held, that the resolve, not being against any constitutional principle in that state, was valid; and that the will, which was approved upon the new hearing, was conclusive, as to the rights obtained under it [Eds. — *See Calder v. Bull*, 3 U.S. (3 Dall.) 386 (1798), discussed *supra* in Chapter 2]. There is nothing in the constitution of the United States, which forbids a state legislature from exercising judicial functions; nor from divesting rights, vested by law in an individual; provided its effect be not to impair the obligation of a contract. If such a law be void, it is upon principles derived from the general nature of free governments, and the necessary limitations created thereby, or from the state restrictions upon the legislative authority, and not from the prohibitions of the constitution of the United States.

§ 1393. Whether, indeed, independently of the constitution of the United States, the nature of republican and free governments does not necessarily impose some restraints upon the legislative power, has been much discussed. It seems to be the general opinion, fortified by a strong current of judicial opinion, that since the American revolution no state government can be presumed to possess the transcendental sovereignty, to take away vested rights of property; to take the property of A and transfer it to B by a mere legislative act. That government can scarcely be deemed to be free, where the rights of property are left solely dependent upon a legislative body, without any restraint. The fundamental maxims of a free government seem to require, that the rights of personal liberty, and private property, should be held sacred. At least, no court of justice, in this country, would be warranted in assuming, that any state legislature possessed a power to violate and disregard them; or that such a power, so repugnant to the common principles of justice and civil liberty, lurked under any general grant of legislative authority, or ought to be implied from any general expression of the will of the people, in the usual forms of the constitutional delegation of power. The people ought not to be presumed to part with rights, so vital to their security and well-being, without very strong, and positive declarations to that effect.

4. Judicial Application

a. Prohibiting Retrospective Debtor Relief

STURGES v. CROWNINSHIELD
17 U.S. (4 Wheat.) 122 (1819)

MARSHALL, CH. J., delivered the opinion of the court.

This case is adjourned from the court of the United States for the first circuit and the district of Massachusetts, on several points on which the judges of that court were divided, which are stated in the record for the opinion of this court.

* * *

We proceed to the great question on which the cause must depend. Does the law of New York, which is pleaded in this case, impair the obligation of contracts, within the meaning of the constitution of the United States? This act liberates the person of the debtor, and discharges him from all liability for any debt previously contracted, on his surrendering his property in the manner it prescribes.

In discussing the question, whether a state is prohibited from passing such a law as this, our first inquiry is, into the meaning of words in common use — what is the obligation of a contract? and what will impair it? It would seem difficult to substitute words which are more intelligible, or less liable to misconstruction, than those who are to be explained. A contract is an agreement, in which a party undertakes to do, or not to do, a particular thing. The law binds him to perform his undertaking, and this is, of course, the obligation of his contract. In the case at bar, the defendant has given his promissory note to pay the plaintiff a sum of money, on or before a certain day. The contract binds him to pay that money, on that day; and this is its obligation. Any law which releases a part of this obligation, must, in the literal sense of the word, impair it. Much more must a law impair it, which makes it totally invalid, and entirely discharges it.

The words of the constitution, then, are express, and incapable of being misunderstood. They admit of no variety of construction, and are acknowledged to apply to that species of contract, an engagement between man and man for the payment of money, which has been entered into by these parties. Yet, the opinion, that this law is not within the prohibition of the constitution has been entertained by those who are entitled to great respect, and has been supported by arguments which deserve to be seriously considered. It has been contended, that as a contract can only bind a man to pay to the full extent of his property, it is an implied condition that he may be discharged on surrendering the whole of it. But it is not true, that the parties have in view only the property in possession when the contract is formed, or that its obligation does not extend to future acquisitions. Industry, talents and integrity constitute a fund which is as confidently trusted as property itself. Future acquisitions are, therefore, liable for contracts; and to release them from this liability impairs their obligation.

* * *

. . . It is said, the colonial and state legislatures have been in the habit of passing laws of this description for more than a century; that they have never been the subject of complaint, and, consequently, could not be within the view of the general convention. The fact is too broadly stated. The insolvent laws of many, indeed, of by far the greater number of the states, do not contain this principle. They discharge the person of the debtor, but leave his obligation to pay in full force. To this the constitution is not opposed.

* * *

. . . [T]his court is of opinion, that, since the adoption of the constitution of the United States, a state has authority to pass a bankrupt law, provided such law does not impair the obligation of contracts, within the meaning of the constitution, and provided there be no act of congress in force to establish a uniform system of bankruptcy, conflicting with such law. This court is further of opinion, that the act of New York, which is pleaded in this case, so far as it attempts to discharge the contract on which this suit was instituted, is a law impairing the obligation of contracts within the meaning of the constitution of the United States, and that the plea of the defendant is not a good and sufficient bar of the plaintiff's action. All which is directed to be certified to the said circuit court.

NOTES AND QUESTIONS

1. Following *Sturges*, the issue arose whether a bankruptcy act that *preceded* a contract was valid. In *Ogden v. Saunders*, 25 U.S. (12 Wheat.) 213 (1827), the Court held that such an act did not offend the Contract Clause. For the only time in his thirty-four years as Chief Justice, John Marshall was in dissent. In separate opinions, the majority in *Ogden* reasoned that a statute, including a bankruptcy statute, in effect at the time a contract is formed becomes "the law of the contract" and is in fact a "part of the contract." Justice Johnson wrote that the Contract Clause was intended solely as "a general provision against arbitrary and tyrannical legislation over existing rights, whether of person or property." *Id.* at 286. The majority's argument seems reasonable enough in context and generally in terms of notice to contracting parties. However, if carried to an extreme, the majority position incorporating the law of the place into all subsequent contracts can be problematic. As will be seen below in the discussion of the reserved police power, the majority's principle is too unrefined. Theoretically, it would allow a state to have general laws in place prohibiting all private contracting regardless of police power interest or public harm.

For this and other reasons, Marshall strongly disagreed with the majority. The interpretation of the majority, he wrote, "convert[ed] an inhibition to pass laws impairing the obligation of contracts, into an inhibition to pass retrospective laws." *Id.* at 355-56 (Marshall, C.J., dissenting). Marshall argued that the Contract Clause was intended as a far more substantial limitation on state authority, one that would preclude all legislation impairing contractual obligations, whether prospective or retrospective. Marshall's dissenting position avoids the risk of unlimited police power seemingly invited by the majority with the opposite extreme. In other words, it is, itself, an unrefined limitation upon state legislative power to address economic subject matter.

The constitutional convention provides little, if any, support for the extreme positions put forward by either the majority or Marshall. *See* Douglas W. Kmiec & John O. McGinnis, *The Contract Clause: A Return to the Original Understanding*, 14 HASTINGS CONST. L.Q. 525, 538 (1987). Similarly, the natural law tradition of the founding fathers only partially supports Marshall, even as, in his *Ogden* dissent, Marshall expressly relies upon natural law to bolster his case for broader economic freedom. Wrote Marshall, "individuals do not derive from government their right to contract, but bring that right with them into society." *Ogden*, 25 U.S. (12 Wheat.) at 346 (Marshall, C.J., dissenting). Professor Wright at Harvard speculated that "[h]ad this case come to the Court a few years earlier [Marshall] might have had his way and made the obligation of contract as inclusive as the later interpretation of liberty of contract under the due process clause." BENJAMIN WRIGHT, THE CONTRACT CLAUSE OF THE CONSTITUTION 52 (1938). If Professor Wright is correct, it would have been interesting to learn whether Marshall's conception of economic freedom premised upon natural law would have had a more discernible or principled foundation than the later suspect judicial activism of substantive economic due process of the industrial age, whereby judges second-guessed state legislatures at will.

In theory, natural law might have been more capable of balancing individual economic freedom with needful economic regulation than personal judicial bias. For example, the natural law might have been looked to for limits upon legislative acts that contradict fundamental aspects of human nature — say, those that promote public monopoly or totally foreclose entry to legitimate occupation. However, this high moral principle could not be relied upon to determine the advisability of the day-to-day economic decisions modernly considered by legislatures, such as whether or not to raise the minimum wage. The founders did not understand the natural law to be a detailed codebook, but a set of principles derived from human reason that could then be freely applied in often innumerable, and from the standpoint of philosophical principle, indifferent ways.

Apart from the text or foundational principles of the Contract Clause, Professor Richard Epstein makes an economic case that the inability to limit prospective legislative impediments to contract invites the misuse of power for covert wealth redistribution and other forms of "rent-seeking" behavior. *See* Richard A. Epstein, *Toward a Revitalization of the Contract Clause*, 51 U. CHI. L. REV. 703, 723-30 (1984). Epstein's argument in favor of having the Contract Clause apply to both retrospective and prospective impairment might be seen as partially derived from James Madison's concern that factions would capture local legislatures to disadvantage particular commercial actors. In THE FEDERALIST NO. 10 (James Madison), Madison speculates that oppression is less likely in a large body like that governing the entire republic because no one faction, or special interest, will easily come to dominate. However, in correspondence with Jefferson, he opined that the Contract Clause is necessary to prevent oppression by states or smaller republics.

This observation remains valid, but the problem of oppression that Madison feared, or rent-seeking in Professor Epstein's words, is greater with legislation interfering with pre-existing, rather than future, contracts. This is so, since with new laws applied to existing contracts, a faction capturing the legislature can clearly impose losses on the identifiable group who has earlier invested. Sensible political action is more likely in the prospective context, because any losses associated with the public policy are less concentrated or identified, and thus, the chance of passing self-serving, faction-dominated laws is also less.

2. An argument was made in *Sturges* that the language of the Contract Clause should be applied only to the specific type of state legislative enactments of concern to the framers. Chief Justice Marshall soundly rejected this narrowing of general principle, writing: "[t]his question will scarcely admit of discussion. If this was the only remaining mischief against which the constitution intended to provide, it would undoubtedly have been, like paper money and tender laws, expressly forbidden. At any rate, terms more directly applicable to the subject, more appropriately expressing the intention of the convention, would have been used." *Sturges*, 17 U.S. (4 Wheat.) at 205.

Similarly, Justice Story writes in his COMMENTARIES, *supra*, at § 1389:

It is probable, that the other great evils, already alluded to, constituted the main inducement to insert [the Contract Clause], where the temptations were more strong, and the interest more immediate and striking, to induce a violation of contracts. But though the motive may thus have been to reach other more pressing mischiefs, the prohibition itself is made general. It is applicable to all contracts, and not confined to the forms then most known, and most divided. Although a rare or particular case may not of itself be of sufficient magnitude to induce the establishment of a constitutional rule; yet it must be governed by that rule, when established, unless some plain and strong reason for excluding it can be given. It is not sufficient to show, that it may not have been foreseen, or intentionally provided for. To exclude it, it is necessary to go farther, and show, that if the case had been suggested, the language of the convention would have been varied so, as to exclude and except it. Where a case falls within the words of a rule or prohibition, it must be held within its operation, unless there is something obviously absurd, or mischievous, or repugnant to the general spirit of the instrument, arising from such a construction.

3. *Sturges* is a rich opinion, not just for the meaning of the Contract Clause, but also for an understanding of constitutional structure and interpretation. As to structure, Marshall rejected in *Sturges* a type of constitutional preemption argument that since Congress was authorized to pass uniform laws regarding bankruptcy, that the states had no residual authority. Marshall noted that Article I, Section 8 does provide that "The congress shall have power . . . to establish a uniform rule of naturalization, and uniform laws on the subject of bankruptcies, throughout the United States." *Sturges*, 17 U.S. (4 Wheat.) at 192. Nevertheless, a constitutional grant of federal authority, said Marshall, was not a denial of state power. Marshall reasoned that:

> When the American people created a national legislature, with certain enumerated powers, it was neither necessary nor proper to define the powers retained by the states. These powers proceed, not from the people of America, but from the people of the several states; and remain, after the adoption of the constitution, what they were before, except so far as they may be abridged by that instrument. In some instances, as in making treaties, we find an express prohibition; and this shows the sense of the convention to have been, that the mere grant of a power to congress, did not imply a prohibition on the states to exercise the same power. But it has never been supposed, that this concurrent power of legislation extended to every possible case in which its exercise by the states has not been expressly prohibited.

* * *

> . . . But be this as it may, the power granted to congress may be exercised or declined, as the wisdom of that body shall decide. If, in the opinion of congress, uniform laws concerning bankruptcies ought not to be established, it does not follow, that partial laws may not exist, or that state legislation on the subject must cease. It is not the mere existence of the power, but its exercise, which is incompatible with the exercise of

the same power by the states. It is not the right to establish these uniform laws, but their actual establishment, which is inconsistent with the partial acts of the states.

Sturges, 17 U.S. (4 Wheat) at 193-96.

4. *Sturges* also gave future constitutional litigants advice on how best to interpret the Constitution. Chief Justice Marshall instructs:

> [A]lthough the spirit of an instrument, especially of a constitution, is to be respected not less than its letter, yet the spirit is to be collected chiefly from its words. It would be dangerous in the extreme, to infer from extrinsic circumstances, that a case for which the words of an instrument expressly provide, shall be exempted from its operation. Where words conflict with each other, where the different clauses of an instrument bear upon each other, and would be inconsistent, unless the natural and common import of words be varied, construction becomes necessary, and a departure from the obvious meaning of words, is justifiable. But if, in any case, the plain meaning of a provision, not contradicted by any other provision in the same instrument, is to be disregarded, because we believe the framers of that instrument could not intend what they say, it must be one in which the absurdity and injustice of applying the provision to the case would be so monstrous, that all mankind would, without hesitation, unite in rejecting the application.

Sturges, 17 U.S. (4 Wheat) at 202-03. Chief Justice Marshall's view comports most closely with that of Justice Antonin Scalia as described in his book A MATTER OF INTERPRETATION: FEDERAL COURTS AND THE LAW (1997).

b. Extension to Public Contracts

The next case, *Fletcher v. Peck*, 10 U.S. (6 Cranch) 87 (1810), is one we mentioned briefly in Chapter Two to illustrate natural law reasoning in the early Supreme Court. We return to the case now to learn whether the Contract Clause applies to property conveyances. The Court decides that it does, and in so doing expands the Clause to contracts with the government. There is nothing in the framing of the Clause at the convention to suggest that this was intended. On the contrary, it is state interference with private contract that prompted the Clause. Marshall cites no authority for the expansion, but relies merely upon the proposition that the words of the Constitution "are general and are applicable to contracts of every description." *Id.* at 137. Perhaps Marshall felt no hesitancy in giving the Clause this sweep because doing so coincided with natural law principle, or as Marshall puts it, "by general principles which are common to our free institutions." *Id.* at 139.

FLETCHER v. PECK
10 U.S. (6 Cranch) 87 (1810)

MARSHALL, CH. J. delivered the opinion of the court as follows:

* * *

The suit was instituted on several covenants contained in a deed made by John Peck . . . conveying to Robert Fletcher . . . certain lands which were part of a large purchase made by James Gunn and others, in the year 1795, from the state of Georgia, the contract for which was made in the form of a bill passed by the legislature of that state.

* * *

. . . [Because the initial conveyance from the state was corrupted by the participating financial interest of all but one member of the state legislature] a subsequent legislature passed an act annulling and rescinding the law under which the conveyance to the original grantees was made, declaring that conveyance void, and asserting the title of the state to the lands it contained.

* * *

. . . The constitution of the United States declares that no state shall pass any bill of attainder, *ex post facto* law, or law impairing the obligation of contracts.

Does the case now under consideration come within this prohibitory section of the constitution?

In considering this very interesting question, we immediately ask ourselves what is a contract? Is a grant [or conveyance] a contract?

A contract is a compact between two or more parties, and is either executory or executed. An executory contract is one in which a party binds himself to do, or not to do, a particular thing; such was the law under which the conveyance was made by the governor. A contract executed is one in which the object of contract is performed; and this, says Blackstone, differs in nothing from a grant. The contract between Georgia and the purchasers was executed by the grant. A contract executed, as well as one which is executory, contains obligations binding on the parties. A grant, in its own nature, amounts to an extinguishment of the right of the grantor, and implies a contract not to reassert that right. A party is, therefore, always estopped by his own grant.

Since, then, in fact, a grant is a contract executed, the obligation of which still continues, and since the constitution uses the general term contract, without distinguishing between those which are executory and those which are executed, it must be construed to comprehend the latter as well as the former. A law annulling conveyances between individuals, and declaring that the grantors should stand seised of their former estates, notwithstanding those grants, would be as repugnant to the constitution as a law discharging the vendors of property from the obligation of executing their contracts by conveyances. It would be strange if a contract to convey was secured by the constitution, while an absolute conveyance remained unprotected.

If, under a fair construction of the constitution, grants are comprehended under the term contracts, is a grant from the state excluded from the operation of the provision? Is the clause to be considered as inhibiting the state from impairing the obligation of contracts between two individuals, but as excluding from that inhibition contracts made with itself?

The words themselves contain no such distinction. They are general, and are applicable to contracts of every description. If contracts made with the state are to be exempted from their operation, the exception must arise from the character of the contracting party, not from the words which are employed.

* * *

In this form the power of the legislature over the lives and fortunes of individuals is expressly restrained. What motive, then, for implying, in words which import a general prohibition to impair the obligation of contracts, an exception in favour of the right to impair the obligation of those contracts into which the state may enter?

The state legislatures can pass no *ex post facto* law. An *ex post facto* law is one which renders an act punishable in a manner in which it was not punishable when it was committed. Such a law may inflict penalties on the person, or may inflict pecuniary penalties which swell the public treasury. The legislature is then prohibited from passing a law by which a man's estate, or any part of it, shall be seized for a crime which was not declared, by some previous law, to render him liable to that punishment. Why, then, should violence be done to the natural meaning of words for the purpose of leaving to the legislature the power of seizing, for public use, the estate of an individual in the form of a law annulling the title by which he holds that estate? The court can perceive no sufficient grounds for making this distinction. This rescinding act would have the effect of an *ex post facto* law. It forfeits the estate of Fletcher for a crime not committed by himself, but by those from whom he purchased. This cannot be effected in the form of an *ex post facto* law, or bill of attainder; why, then, is it allowable in the form of a law annulling the original grant?

The argument in favour of presuming an intention to except a case, not excepted by the words of the constitution, is susceptible of some illustration from a principle originally ingrafted in that instrument, though no longer a part of it. The constitution, as passed, gave the courts of the United States jurisdiction in suits brought against individual states. A state, then, which violated its own contract was suable in the courts of the United States for that violation. Would it have been a defence in such a suit to say that the state had passed a law absolving itself from the contract? It is scarcely to be conceived that such a defence could be set up. And yet, if a state is neither restrained by the general principles of our political institutions, nor by the words of the constitution, from impairing the obligation of its own contracts, such a defence would be a valid one. This feature is no longer found in the constitution; but it aids in the construction of those clauses with which it was originally associated.

It is, then, the unanimous opinion of the court, that, in this case, the estate having passed into the hands of a purchaser for a valuable consideration, without notice, the state of Georgia was restrained, either by general principles which are common to our free institutions, or by the particular provisions of the constitution of the United States, from passing a law whereby the estate of the plaintiff in the premises so purchased could be constitutionally and legally impaired and rendered null and void.

* * *

Judgment affirmed with costs.

JOHNSON, J.

In this case I entertain [a concurring] opinion different from that which has been delivered by the court.

I do not hesitate to declare that a state does not possess the power of revoking its own grants. But I do it on a general principle, on the reason and nature of things: a principle which will impose laws even on the deity.

* * *

I enter with great hesitation upon this question, because it involves a subject of the greatest delicacy and much difficulty. The states and the United States are continually legislating on the subject of contracts, prescribing the mode of authentication, the time within which suits shall be prosecuted for them, in many cases affecting existing contracts by the laws which they pass, and declaring them to cease or lose their effect for want of compliance, in the parties, with such statutory provisions. All these acts appear to be within the most correct limits of legislative powers, and most beneficially exercised, and certainly could not have been intended to be affected by this constitutional provision; yet where to draw the line, or how to define or limit the words, "obligation of contracts," will be found a subject of extreme difficulty.

To give it the general effect of a restriction of the state powers in favour of private rights, is certainly going very far beyond the obvious and necessary import of the words, and would operate to restrict the states in the exercise of that right which every community must exercise, of possessing itself of the property of the individual, when necessary for public uses; a right which a magnanimous and just government will never exercise without amply indemnifying the individual, and which perhaps amounts to nothing more than a power to oblige him to sell and convey, when the public necessities require it.

NOTES AND QUESTIONS

1. Note that the lawsuit in *Fletcher* was not brought directly against the state of Georgia in federal court, a proceeding precluded after the passage of the Eleventh Amendment in 1791.

2. The lawsuit, as it was, existed between grantor, John Peck, and grantee, Robert Fletcher. Since both stood to gain by upholding title (Fletcher would have title and Peck consideration), where was the case or controversy? In a portion of his concurring opinion not reprinted, Justice Johnson indicates that he was reluctant "to proceed . . . at all" since the proceeding appeared to be "a mere feigned case." *Fletcher*, 10 U.S. (6 Cranch) at 147 (Johnson, J., concurring). Johnson said he concurred since he had confidence that "the respectable gentlemen who have been engaged for the parties . . . would never consent to impose a mere feigned case upon this court." *Id.* at 147-48.

3. In his concurrence, Justice Johnson declines to rely upon the Contract Clause, preferring instead to rely upon "the reason and nature of things." This natural law ground was preferable to Johnson because he anticipated that bringing a public contract within the phraseology of the Contract Clause would cause "much difficulty." "[W]here to draw the line, or how to define or limit the words, 'obligation of contracts,' will be found a subject of extreme difficulty." As you read the balance of cases dealing with the Contract Clause, ask yourself whether or not Johnson has been proven correct. If Johnson was right, does that account for, or justify, the modern reluctance to judicially enforce the Clause?

4. Marshall confirmed and enlarged his extension of the Contract Clause to public contracts in *Dartmouth College v. Woodward*, 17 U.S. (4 Wheat) 518 (1819). *Dartmouth* involved a charter granted originally in 1769 by Governor Wentworth of New Hampshire on behalf of George III. In 1815, a dispute arose between the existing board of trustees and the school's president. The legislature sided with the president and, to bolster his position, altered the charter of the school by, among other things, increasing the number of trustees and providing for a Board of Overseers that could veto acts by the trustees. The New Hampshire court of appeals approved the modification, reasoning that the charter of the college was a civil institution, not a private contract, in the nature of a public trust. Marshall disagreed and applied the Contract Clause to disallow the changes in the charter, even as he admitted that a public charter was not likely in the minds of the framers in the drafting of the Contract Clause. Marshall writes:

> It is not enough to say, that this particular case was not in the mind of the convention, when the article was framed, nor of the American people, when it was adopted. It is necessary to go further, and to say that, had this particular case been suggested, the language would have been so varied, as to exclude it, or it would have been made a special exception. The case being within the words of the rule, must be within its operation likewise, unless there be something in the literal construction,

so obviously absurd or mischievous, or repugnant to the general spirit of the instrument, as to justify those who expound the constitution in making it an exception.

On what safe and intelligible ground, can this exception stand? There is no expression in the constitution, no sentiment delivered by its contemporaneous expounders, which would justify us in making it. In the absence of all authority of this kind, is there, in the nature and reason of the case itself, that which would sustain a construction of the constitution, not warranted by its words? Are contracts of this description of a character to excite so little interest, that we must exclude them from the provisions of the constitution, as being unworthy of the attention of those who framed the instrument? Or does public policy so imperiously demand their remaining exposed to legislative alteration, as to compel us, or rather permit us, to say, that these words, which were introduced to give stability to contracts, and which in their plain import comprehend this contract, must yet be so construed as to exclude it?

17 U.S. (4 Wheat.) at 644-45. This method of reasoning seems far removed from the textualist prescription proposed by Marshall in *Sturges* and is well-nigh akin to what would modernly be viewed as a judicially active posture. The consequence of this aggressive position was to make it more difficult to reconcile the competing interests of private right and public need. In particular, it confused the state's prerogative to establish its own civil institutions, whether they be colleges or local governments, with a contract made by a civil institution with a private party. The latter is clearly within the terms of the Clause as a result of *Fletcher*, but the former seems very much at odds with the reserved police power of the state (discussed in the next section of this Chapter). Marshall argued, and concluded, however, that the charter was not a revocable public privilege, because private monies were contributed in reliance upon the grant of the charter.

5. The impact of *Dartmouth College* was muted somewhat by the later opinion in *Charles River Bridge v. Warren Bridge*, 36 U.S. (11 Pet.) 420 (1837), which held that the grant of a charter to one private company to operate a toll bridge did not prevent the state from authorizing the construction of a competing free bridge. In an opinion by Chief Justice Roger Taney, Marshall's successor, the Court held that "ambiguity in the terms of the contract, must operate against the adventurers, and in favour of the public." *Id*. at 544.

6. Modernly, the protection of public contracts under the Clause has continued, invertedly, to the effect that government now needs greater justification for such interference than it does with regard to private contracts. In *United States Trust Co. v. New Jersey*, 431 U.S. 1 (1977), the Court found New York and New Jersey's attempt to welsh on a bond covenant to violate the Contract Clause. Writing for the Court, Justice Blackmun opined that a state impairment of its own contract must be shown to be "reasonable and necessary to serve an important public purpose." *Id*. at 25. While this is the same standard modernly applied to private contracts, Justice Blackmun held that the state would be given less deference when it was self-interested. In dissent, Justice Brennan argued that the Court stood the Clause "completely on its head," *id.* at 53 (Brennan, J., dissenting), but arguably, Justice Brennan's complaint should have been directed not at his brother Blackmun, but toward the legacy of Chief Justice Marshall and the extension of the Clause to public contracts.

c. The Reserved Police Power

While states are precluded from impairing the obligation of contract, public or private, the Court has held that a state may not contract away its police power, or its ability to deal with fundamental issues of health and safety. In the next case, Mississippi passed an act in 1867 authorizing a lottery. In December 1869, the state constitution was amended providing that "the legislature shall never authorize any lottery; . . . nor shall any lottery heretofore authorized be permitted to be drawn, or tickets therein to be sold."

STONE v. MISSISSIPPI
101 U.S. 814 (1879)

MR. CHIEF JUSTICE WAITE delivered the opinion of the court.

It is now too late to contend that any contract which a State actually enters into when granting a charter to a private corporation is not within the protection of the clause in the Constitution of the United States that prohibits States from passing laws impairing the obligation of contracts. Art. 1, sect. 10. The doctrines of *Trustees of Dartmouth College v. Woodward* 17 U.S. (4 Wheat) 518, announced by this court more than sixty years ago, have become so imbedded in the jurisprudence of the United States as to make them to all intents and purposes a part of the Constitution itself. In this connection, however, it is to be kept in mind that it is not the charter which is protected, but only any contract the charter may contain. If there is no contract, there is nothing in the grant on which the Constitution can act. Consequently, the first inquiry in this class of cases always is, whether a contract has in fact been entered into, and if so, what its obligations are.

* * *

All agree that the legislature cannot bargain away the police power of a State. "Irrevocable grants of property and franchises may be made if they do not impair the supreme authority to make laws for the right government of the State; but no legislature can curtail the power of its successors to make such laws as they may deem proper in matters of police." Many attempts have been made in this court and elsewhere to define the police power, but never with entire success. It is always easier to determine whether a particular case comes within the general scope of the power, than to give an abstract definition of the power itself which will be in all respects accurate. No one denies, however, that it extends to all matters affecting the public health or the public morals. . . . Neither can it be denied that lotteries are proper subjects for the exercise of this power. We are aware that formerly, when the sources of public revenue were fewer than now, they were used in some or all of the States, and even in the District of Columbia, to raise money for the erection of public buildings, making public improvements, and not unfrequently for educational and religious purposes; but this court said, more than thirty years ago, speaking through Mr. Justice Grier, in *Phalen v. Virginia,* 49 U.S. (8 How) 163, 168, that "experience has shown that the common forms of gambling are comparatively innocuous when placed in contrast with the wide-spread pestilence of lotteries. The former are confined to a few persons and places, but the latter infests the whole community; it enters every dwelling; it reaches every class; it preys upon the hard earnings of the poor; and it plunders the ignorant and simple." Happily, under the influence of restrictive legislation, the evils are not so apparent now; but we very much fear that with the same opportunities of indulgence the same results would be manifested.

If lotteries are to be tolerated at all, it is no doubt better that they should be regulated by law, so that the people may be protected as far as possible against the inherent vices of the system; but that they are demoralizing in their effects, no matter how carefully regulated, cannot admit of a doubt. When the government is untrammelled by any claim of vested rights or chartered privileges, no one has ever supposed that lotteries could not lawfully be suppressed, and those who manage them punished severely as violators of the rules of social morality. From 1822 to 1867, without any constitutional requirement, they were prohibited by law in Mississippi, and those who conducted them punished as a kind of gamblers. During the provisional government of that State, in 1867, at the close of the late civil war, the present act of incorporation, with more of like character, was passed. The next year, 1868, the people, in adopting a new constitution with a view to the resumption of their political rights as one of the United States, provided that "the legislature shall never authorize any lottery . . . ."

The question is therefore directly presented, whether, in view of these facts, the legislature of a State can, by the charter of a lottery company, defeat the will of the people, authoritatively expressed, in relation to the further continuance of such business in their midst. We think it cannot. No legislature can bargain away the public health or the public morals. The people themselves cannot do it, much less their servants. The supervision of both these subjects of governmental power is continuing in its nature, and they are to be dealt with as the special exigencies of the moment may require. Government is organized with a view to their preservation, and cannot divest itself of the power to provide for them. For this purpose the largest legislative discretion is allowed, and the discretion cannot be parted with any more than the power itself.

In *Trustees of Dartmouth College v. Woodward* 17 U.S. (4 Wheat) 518, it was argued that the contract clause of the Constitution, if given the effect contended for in respect to corporate franchises, "would be an unprofitable and vexatious interference with the internal concerns of a State, would unnecessarily and unwisely embarrass its legislation, and render immutable those civil institutions which are established for the purpose of internal government, and which, to subserve those purposes, ought to vary with varying circumstances" (p. 628); but Mr. Chief Justice Marshall, when he announced the opinion of the court, was careful to say (p. 629), "that the framers of the Constitution did not intend to restrain States in the regulation of their civil institutions, adopted for internal government, and that the instrument they have given us is not to be so construed." The present case, we think, comes within this limitation.

* * *

The contracts which the Constitution protects are those that relate to property rights, not governmental. It is not always easy to tell on which side of the line which separates governmental from property rights a particular case is to be put; but in respect to lotteries there can be no difficulty. They are not, in the legal acceptation of the term, *mala in se*, but, as we have just seen, may properly be made *mala prohibita*. They are a species of gambling, and wrong in their influences. They disturb the checks and balances of a well-ordered community. Society built on such a foundation would almost of necessity bring forth a population of speculators and gamblers, living on the expectation of what, "by the casting of lots, or by lot, chance, or otherwise," might be "awarded" to them from the accumulations of others. Certainly the right to suppress them is governmental, to be exercised at all times by those in power, at their discretion. Any one, therefore, who accepts a lottery charter does so with the implied understanding that the people, in their sovereign capacity, and through their properly constituted agencies, may resume it at any time when the public good shall require, whether it be paid for or not. All that one can get by such a charter is a suspension of certain governmental rights in his favor, subject to withdrawal at will. He has in legal effect nothing more than a license to enjoy the privilege on the terms named for the specified time, unless it be sooner abrogated by the sovereign power of the State. It is a permit, good as against existing laws, but subject to future legislative and constitutional control or withdrawal.

On the whole, we find no error in the record.

Judgment affirmed.

NOTES AND QUESTIONS

1. The issue with respect to the reserved police power is how much deference the judiciary should accord putative exercises of that power which clearly impair a contract. Prior to *Stone*, the Court had established in *Fertilizing Co. v. Hyde Park*, 97 U.S. 659 (1878), that a private contract or charter could not be used to shield a nuisance. In *Hyde Park*, the Illinois General Assembly granted to a fertilizer company a corporate charter to run for 50 years. The corporation thereafter invested in a factory and shipment depot. Five years later, the village authorities of Hyde Park adopted an ordinance that rendered the company's charter valueless by forbidding the operation of a fertilizer factory within the village confines. The Court nonetheless rejected the contention that the new ordinance offended the Contract Clause, writing: "We cannot doubt that the police power of the State was applicable and adequate to give an effectual remedy [to the nuisance]. That power belonged to the States when the Federal Constitution was adopted. They did not surrender it, and they all have it now." *Id.* at 667.

2. At first, the Court was reasonably careful to ensure that contracts were only subject to legislative activity truly implicating health and safety issues. For example, in *Grand Trunk Western Railway Company v. City of South Bend*, 227 U.S. 544 (1912), the Court refused to allow the City of South Bend, Indiana, to repeal an easement previously granted for the laying of track. Said the Court: "the inconvenience consequent upon the running of a railroad through a city, under state authority, is not a nuisance in law, but is insuperably connected with the exercise of the franchise granted by the state." *Id.* at 554. Other examples of the regulation of railways or their use of city streets "are examples of the persistence of the power to regulate, and do not sustain the validity of the repealing ordinance . . ., since it is not regulative of the use, but destructive of the franchise." *Id.* at 553. Gradually, however, the Court gave ever greater deference to state and local legislative judgment in the exercise of the police power. Thus, in *Atlantic Coast Line R.R. Co. v. City of Goldsboro*, 232 U.S. 548 (1914), the state of North Carolina chartered and contracted with the plaintiff railway company to operate rail lines within the state. Pursuant to this contract, the railroad acquired in fee land for use as rights-of-way and similar transportation activities. The Court recognized that the charter was a binding contract, and that the company, in reliance on the agreement, had acquired land which it enjoys as "complete and unqualified" owner. *Id.* at 557-58. Yet, the Court declined to sustain a constitutional challenge to subsequent ordinances that greatly circumscribed the railroad's activities on its own land stating: "For it is settled that neither the 'contract' clause nor the 'due process' clause has the effect of overriding the power of the state to establish all regulations that are reasonably necessary to secure the health, safety, good order, comfort, or general welfare of the community; that this power can neither be abdicated nor bargained away, and is inalienable even by express grant; and that all contract and property rights are held subject to its fair exercise." *Id.* at 558 (citations omitted).

3. In a portion of the opinion not reprinted, *Stone* did recognize that it was possible for the government to bargain away its taxation authority — at least in part. In other words, a state government that grants a corporation tax-exempt status can be held to the bargain. The Court reasoned that while taxation is in general necessary for the support of government, it is not part of the government itself. Taxation is an incident to the exercise of the legitimate functions of government, said the Court, "but nothing more." *Stone*, 101 U.S. at 820.

d. Modern Ambiguity

HOME BUILDING & LOAN ASS'N v. BLAISDELL
290 U.S. 398 (1933)

MR. CHIEF JUSTICE HUGHES delivered the opinion of the Court.

Appellant contests the validity of . . . the Minnesota Mortgage Moratorium Law, as being repugnant to the contract clause (Article 1, Section 10) . . . of the Federal Constitution. . . .

The Act provides that, during the emergency declared to exist, relief may be had through authorized judicial proceedings with respect to foreclosures of mortgages, and execution sales, of real estate; that sales may be postponed and periods of redemption may be extended. The Act does not apply to mortgages subsequently made nor to those made previously which shall be extended for a period ending more than a year after the passage of the Act. . . . The act is to remain in effect "only during the continuance of the emergency and in no event beyond May 1, 1935." No extension of the period for redemption and no postponement of sale is to be allowed which would have the effect of extending the period of redemption beyond that date. Part 2, Section 8.

The Act declares that the various provisions for relief are severable; that each is to stand on its own footing with respect to validity. Part 1, Section 9. We are here concerned with the provisions of Part 1, Section 4, authorizing the District Court of the county to extend the period of redemption from foreclosure sales "for such additional time as the court may deem just and equitable," subject to the above-described limitation. The extension is to be made upon application to the court, on notice, for an order determining the reasonable value of the income on the property involved in the sale, or, if it has no income, then the reasonable rental value of the property, and directing the mortgagor "to pay all or a reasonable part of such income or rental value, in or toward the payment of taxes, insurance, interest, mortgage . . . indebtedness at such times and in such manner" as shall be determined by the court. The section also provides that the time for redemption from foreclosure sales theretofore made, which otherwise would expire less than thirty days after the approval of the Act, shall be extended to a date thirty days after its approval, and application may be made to the court within that time for a further extension as provided in the section. By another provision of the Act, no action, prior to May 1, 1935, may be maintained for a deficiency judgment until the period of redemption as allowed by existing law or as extended under the provisions of the Act has expired. . . .

Invoking the relevant provision of the statute, appellees applied to the District Court of Hennepin County for an order extending the period of redemption from a foreclosure sale. Their petition stated that they owned a lot in Minneapolis which they had mortgaged to appellant; that the mortgage contained a valid power of sale by advertisement, and that by reason of their default the mortgage had been foreclosed and sold to appellant on May 2, 1932, for $3,700.98; that appellant was the holder of the sheriff's certificate of sale; that, because of the economic depression, appellees had been unable to obtain a new loan or to redeem, and that, unless the period of redemption were extended, the property would be irretrievably lost; and that the reasonable value of the property greatly exceeded the amount due on the mortgage, including all liens, costs, and expenses.

* * *

Justice Olsen of the state court, in a concurring opinion, stated:

"The present nation wide and world wide business and financial crisis has the same results as if it were caused by flood, earthquake, or disturbance in nature. It has deprived millions of persons in this nation of their employment and means of earning a living for themselves and their families; it has destroyed the value of and the income from all property on which thousands of people depended for a living; it actually has resulted in the loss of their homes by a number of our people, and threatens to result in the loss of their homes by many other people, in this state; it has resulted in such widespread want and suffering among our people that private, state, and municipal agencies are unable to adequately relieve the want and suffering, and Congress has found it necessary to step in and attempt to remedy the situation by federal aid. Millions of the people's money were and are yet tied up in closed banks and in business enterprises."

* * *

. . . The statute does not impair the integrity of the mortgage indebtedness. The obligation for interest remains. The statute does not affect the validity of the sale or the right of a mortgagee-purchaser to title in fee, or his right to obtain a deficiency judgment, if the mortgagor fails to redeem within the prescribed period. Aside from the extension of time, the other conditions of redemption are unaltered. While the mortgagor remains in possession he must pay the rental value as that value has been determined, upon notice and hearing, by the court. The rental value so paid is devoted to the carrying of the property by the application of the required payments to taxes, insurance, and interest on the mortgage indebtedness. While the mortgagee-purchaser is debarred from actual possession, he has, so far as rental value is concerned, the equivalent of possession during the extended period.

In determining whether the provision for this temporary and conditional relief exceeds the power of the State by reason of the clause in the Federal Constitution prohibiting impairment of the obligations of contracts, we must consider the relation of emergency to constitutional power, the historical setting of the contract clause, the development of the jurisprudence of this Court in the construction of that clause, and the principles of construction which we may consider to be established.

* * *

While emergency does not create power, emergency may furnish the occasion for the exercise of power. "Although an emergency may not call into life a power which has never lived, nevertheless emergency may afford a reason for the exertion of a living power already enjoyed." . . . When the provisions of the Constitution, in grant or restriction, are specific, so particularized as not to admit of construction, no question is presented. Thus, emergency would not permit a State to have more than two Senators in the Congress, or permit the election of President by a general popular vote without regard to the number of electors to which the States are respectively entitled, or permit the States to "coin money" or to "make anything but gold and silver coin a tender in payment of debts." But, where constitutional grants and limitations of power are set forth in general clauses, which afford a broad outline, the process of construction is essential to fill in the details. That is true of the contract clause. . . .

. . . The occasion and general purpose of the contract clause are summed up in the terse statement of Chief Justice Marshall in *Ogden v. Saunders* [(1827)]:

> "The power of changing the relative situation of debtor and creditor, of interfering with contracts, a power which comes home to every man, touches the interest of all, and controls the conduct of every individual in those things which he supposes to be proper for his own exclusive management, had been used to such an excess by the state legislatures, as to break in upon the ordinary intercourse of society, and destroy all confidence between man and man. This mischief had become so great, so alarming, as not only to impair commercial intercourse, and threaten the existence of credit, but to sap the morals of the people, and destroy the sanctity of private faith. To guard against the continuance of the evil was an object of deep interest with all the truly wise, as well as the virtuous, of this great community, and was one of the important benefits expected from a reform of the government."

But full recognition of the occasion and general purpose of the clause does not suffice to fix its precise scope. Nor does an examination of the details of prior legislation in the States yield criteria which can be considered controlling. To ascertain the scope of the constitutional prohibition, we examine the course of judicial decisions in its application. These put it beyond question that the prohibition is not an absolute one and is not to be read with literal exactness like a mathematical formula. . . .

The inescapable problems of construction have been: What is a contract?[8] What are the obligations of contracts? What constitutes impairment of these

---

[8] Contracts, within the meaning of the clause, have been held to embrace those that are executed, that is, grants, as well as those that are executory. They embrace the charters of private corpora-

obligations? What residuum of power is there still in the States in relation to the operation of contracts, to protect the vital interests of the community? Questions of this character, "of no small nicety and intricacy, have vexed the legislative halls, as well as the judicial tribunals, with an uncounted variety and frequency of litigation and speculation." STORY ON THE CONSTITUTION, § 13[69].

The obligation of a contract is the "law which binds the parties to perform their agreement." *Sturges v. Crowninshield* [(1819)]. This Court has said that "the laws which subsist at the time and place of the making of a contract, and where it is to be performed, enter into and form a part of it, as if they were expressly referred to or incorporated in its terms. This principle embraces alike those which affect its validity, construction, discharge, and enforcement. . . . Nothing can be more material to the obligation than the means of enforcement. . . ." [However,] the general statement above quoted was limited by the further observation that "It is competent for the States to change the form of the remedy, or to modify it otherwise, as they may see fit, provided no substantial right secured by the contract is thereby impaired. No attempt has been made to fix definitely the line between alterations of the remedy, which are to be deemed legitimate, and those which, under the form of modifying the remedy, impair substantial rights. Every case must be determined upon its own circumstances." . . .

The obligations of a contract are impaired by a law which renders them invalid, or releases or extinguishes them and impairment, as above noted, has been predicated of laws which without destroying contracts derogate from substantial contractual rights. . . .

* * *

Not only is the constitutional provision qualified by the measure of control which the State retains over remedial processes, but the State also continues to possess authority to safeguard the vital interests of its people. It does not matter that legislation appropriate to that end "has the result of modifying or abrogating contracts already in effect." *Stephenson v. Binford* [(1932)]. Not only are existing laws read into contracts in order to fix obligations as between the parties, but the reservation of essential attributes of sovereign power is also read into contracts as a postulate of the legal order. The policy of protecting contracts against impairment presupposes the maintenance of a government by virtue of which contractual relations are worth while, — a government which retains adequate authority to secure the peace and good order of society. This principle of harmonizing the constitutional prohibition with the necessary residuum of state power has had progressive recognition in the decisions of this Court.

* * *

---

tions. But not the marriage contract, so as to limit the general right to legislate on the subject of divorce. Nor are judgments, though rendered upon contracts, deemed to be within the provision. Nor does a general law, giving the consent of a State to be sued, constitute a contract.

. . . [S]peaking through Mr. Justice Brewer, . . . in *Long Island Water Supply Co. v. Brooklyn* [(1897)], [this Court stated]:

> "But into all contracts, whether made between States and individuals, or between individuals only, there enter conditions which arise, not out of the literal terms of the contract itself, they are superinduced by the pre-existing and higher authority of the laws of nature, of nations, or of the community to which the parties belong. They are always presumed, and must be presumed, to be known and recognized by all, are binding upon all, and need never, therefore, be carried into express stipulation, for this could add nothing to their force. Every contract is made in subordination to them, and must yield to their control, as conditions inherent and paramount, wherever a necessity for their execution shall occur."

The Legislature cannot "bargain away the public health or the public morals." Thus, the constitutional provision against the impairment of contracts was held not to be violated by an amendment of the state constitution which put an end to a lottery theretofore authorized by the Legislature. *Stone v. Mississippi* [(1879)]. The lottery was a valid enterprise when established under express state authority, but the legislature in the public interest could put a stop to it. A similar rule has been applied to the control by the state of the sale of intoxicating liquors. *Beer Company v. Massachusetts* [(1877)]. *See Mugler v. Kansas* [(1887)]. The states retain adequate power to protect the public health against the maintenance of nuisances despite insistence upon existing contracts. *Fertilizing Compan. v. Hyde Park* [(1878)]. . . .

* * *

The argument is pressed that in the cases we have cited the obligation of contracts was affected only incidentally. This argument proceeds upon a misconception. The question is not whether the legislative action affects contracts incidentally, or directly or indirectly, but whether the legislation is addressed to a legitimate end and the measures taken are reasonable and appropriate to that end. Another argument, which comes more closely to the point, is that the state power may be addressed directly to the prevention of the enforcement of contracts only when these are of a sort which the legislature in its discretion may denounce as being in themselves hostile to public morals, or public health, safety, or welfare, or where the prohibition is merely of injurious practices; that interference with the enforcement of other and valid contracts according to appropriate legal procedure, although the interference is temporary and for a public purpose, is not permissible. This is but to contend that in the latter case the end is not legitimate in the view that it cannot be reconciled with a fair interpretation of the constitutional provision.

Undoubtedly, whatever is reserved of state power must be consistent with the fair intent of the constitutional limitation of that power. The reserved power cannot be construed so as to destroy the limitation, nor is the limitation to be construed to destroy the reserved power in its essential aspects. They must be construed in harmony with each other. This principle precludes a construction which would permit the state to adopt as its policy the repudiation of debts or the destruction of contracts or the denial of means to enforce them. But it does not follow that conditions may not arise in which a temporary restraint of enforcement may be consistent with the spirit and purpose of the constitutional provision and thus be found to be within the range of the reserved power of the state to protect the vital interests of the community. It cannot be maintained that the constitutional prohibition should be so construed as to prevent limited and temporary interpositions with respect to the enforcement of contracts if made necessary by a great public calamity such as fire, flood, or earthquake. The reservation of state power appropriate to such extraordinary conditions may be deemed to be as much a part of all contracts, as is the reservation of state power to protect the public interest in the other situations to which we have referred. And, if state power exists to give temporary relief from the enforcement of contracts in the presence of disasters due to physical causes such as fire, flood, or earthquake, that power cannot be said to be non-existent when the urgent public need demanding such relief is produced by other and economic causes.

Whatever doubt there may have been that the protective power of the state, its police power, may be exercised — without violating the true intent of the provision of the Federal Constitution — in directly preventing the immediate and literal enforcement of contractual obligations, by a temporary and conditional restraint, where vital public interests would otherwise suffer, was removed by our decisions relating to the enforcement of provisions of leases during a period of scarcity of housing. . . .

* * *

Applying the criteria established by our decisions, we conclude:

1. An emergency existed in Minnesota which furnished a proper occasion for the exercise of the reserved power of the state to protect the vital interests of the community. . . .

2. The legislation was addressed to a legitimate end; that is, the legislation was not for the mere advantage of particular individuals but for the protection of a basic interest of society.

3. In view of the nature of the contracts in question — mortgages of unquestionable validity — the relief afforded and justified by the emergency, in order not to contravene the constitutional provision, could only be of a character appropriate to that emergency, and could be granted only upon reasonable conditions.

4. The conditions upon which the period of redemption is extended do not appear to be unreasonable. The initial extension of the time of redemption for thirty days from the approval of the Act was obviously to give a reasonable

opportunity for the authorized application to the court. As already noted, the integrity of the mortgage indebtedness is not impaired; interest continues to run; the validity of the sale and the right of a mortgagee-purchaser to title or to obtain a deficiency judgment, if the mortgagor fails to redeem within the extended period, are maintained; and the conditions of redemption, if redemption there be, stand as they were under the prior law. The mortgagor during the extended period is not ousted from possession, but he must pay the rental value of the premises as ascertained in judicial proceedings and this amount is applied to the carrying of the property and to interest upon the indebtedness. . . .

5. The legislation is temporary in operation. It is limited to the exigency which called it forth. While the postponement of the period of redemption from the foreclosure sale is to May 1, 1935, that period may be reduced by the order of the court under the statute, in case of a change in circumstances, and the operation of the statute itself could not validly outlast the emergency or be so extended as virtually to destroy the contracts.

We are of the opinion that the Minnesota statute as here applied does not violate the contract clause of the Federal Constitution. Whether the legislation is wise or unwise as a matter of policy is a question with which we are not concerned.

* * *

Judgment affirmed.

MR. JUSTICE SUTHERLAND, dissenting.

Few questions of greater moment than that just decided have been submitted for judicial inquiry during this generation. He simply closes his eyes to the necessary implications of the decision who fails to see in it the potentiality of future gradual but ever-advancing encroachments upon the sanctity of private and public contracts. . . .

* * *

It is quite true that an emergency may supply the occasion for the exercise of power, dependent upon the nature of the power and the intent of the Constitution with respect thereto. The emergency of war furnishes an occasion for the exercise of certain of the war powers. This the Constitution contemplates, since they cannot be exercised upon any other occasion. The existence of another kind of emergency authorizes the United States to protect each of the states of the Union against domestic violence. Const. Article 4, Section 4. But we are here dealing, not with a power granted by the Federal Constitution, but with the state police power, which exists in its own right. Hence the question is, not whether an emergency furnishes the occasion for the exercise of that state power, but whether an emergency furnishes an occasion for the relaxation of the restrictions upon the power imposed by the contract impairment clause; and the difficulty is that the contract impairment clause forbids state action under any circumstances, if it have the effect of impairing the obligation of contracts. That clause restricts every state power in the particular specified, no matter what may be the occasion. It does not contemplate that an emergency shall furnish an occasion for softening the restriction or making it any the less a restriction upon state action in that contingency than it is under strictly normal conditions.

* * *

I am authorized to say that MR. JUSTICE VAN DEVANTER, MR. JUSTICE McREYNOLDS, and MR. JUSTICE BUTLER concur in this opinion.

NOTES AND QUESTIONS

1. While the original mortgage contract is not fully protected in *Blaisdell*, note that, notwithstanding the profound economic emergency that the Great Depression of the 1930s represented, the Court did not merely assume that the contract could be set aside under a broad, undifferentiated claim of reserved police power. Rather, the Court carefully circumscribed its opinion in its own five-point summary to fit the emergency circumstance. Likewise, the cases the *Blaisdell* Court relied upon are similarly limited in language. For example, in *Block v. Hirsh*, 256 U.S. 135 (1921), the Court upheld a law that suspended the removal of tenants after the expiration of leases in light of a well-documented housing shortage. The *Blaisdell* Court correctly noted that the relief afforded was temporary and conditional. It was sustained because of the emergency due to scarcity of housing, and because the statute made provision for reasonable compensation to the landlord during the period he was prevented from regaining possession.

Even this temporary explanation did not satisfy four members of the Court. Justice Sutherland wrote in dissent:

> The rent cases — *Block v. Hirsh* [(1921)]; *Marcus Brown Holding Co. v. Feldman* [(1921)]; *Edgar A. Levy Leasing Co. v. Siegel* [(1922)] — which are here relied upon, dealt with an exigent situation due to a period of scarcity of housing caused by the war. I do not stop to consider the distinctions between them and the present case or to do more than point out that the question of contract impairment received little, if any, more than casual consideration. The writer of the opinions in the first two cases [Justice Oliver Wendell Holmes], speaking for this Court in a later case, *Pennsylvania Coal Co. v. Mahon* [(1922)], characterized all of them as having gone "to the verge of the law." It, therefore, seems pertinent to say that decisions which confessedly escape the limbo of unconstitutionality by the exceedingly narrow margin suggested by this characterization should be applied toward the solution of a doubtful question arising in a different field with a very high degree of caution. Reasonably considered, they do not foreclose the question here involved, and it should be determined upon its merits without regard to those cases.

Blaisdell, 290 U.S. at 478-79 (Sutherland, J., dissenting).

2. One of the limiting features the Court highlights is the difference between modification of remedy and impairment of obligation of contract. This distinction was made quite early by Justice Joseph Story who wrote:

> [E]very change and modification of the remedy does not involve such a consequence. No one will doubt, that the legislature may vary the nature and extent of remedies, so always, that some substantive remedy be in fact left. Nor can it be doubted, that the legislature may prescribe the times and modes, in which remedies may be pursued; and bar suits not brought within such periods, and not pursued in such modes. Statutes of limitations are of this nature; and have never been supposed to destroy the obligation of contracts, but to prescribe the times, within which that obligation shall be enforced by a suit; and in default to deem it either satisfied, or abandoned. The obligation to perform a contract is coequal with the undertaking to perform it. It originates with the contract itself, and operates anterior to the time of performance. The remedy acts upon the broken contract, and enforces a pre-existing obligation.

JOSEPH STORY, COMMENTARIES ON THE CONSTITUTION OF THE UNITED STATES § 1379 (1833).

3. Beyond emergency and the difference between obligation and remedy, Chief Justice Hughes further suggests another important way for distinguishing between unconstitutional impairments and valid modifications pursuant to the police power. Hughes emphasizes that the legislation "was not for the mere advantage of particular individuals." *Blaisdell*, 290 U.S. at 4445. Recall that Madison was greatly concerned with factions using legislative power to secure self-interested advantages for themselves. *See* THE FEDERALIST NOS. 10 & 44 (James Madison). While such factions will always attempt to dress their self-interest in public terms, where the effect of a law is to do little other than to redistribute the benefit of a contractual right from one private party to another, Chief Justice Hughes — like Madison — properly instructs that such law should be invalidated.

4. Obviously, all of the qualifications that attend *Blaisdell* help define what the scope of the reserved police power is with respect to the Contract Clause. In dissent, Justice Sutherland sought to add another qualification in the difference between a total prohibition of a contractual activity and a selective interference. For Sutherland, the essential attributes of reserved sovereign power that are read into contracts includes the former, but not the latter. He gives an example:

> [L]et us revert to the example already given with respect to an agreement for the manufacture and sale of intoxicating liquor. And let us suppose that the state, instead of passing legislation prohibiting the manufacture and sale of the commodity, in which event the doctrine of implied conditions would be pertinent, continues to recognize the gen-

eral lawfulness of the business, but, because of what it conceives to be a justifying emergency, provides that the time for the performance of existing contracts for future manufacture and sale shall be extended for a specified period of time. It is perfectly admissible, in view of the state power to prohibit the business, to read into the contract an implied proviso to the effect that the business of manufacturing and selling intoxicating liquors shall not, prior to the date when performance is due, become unlawful; but in the case last put, to read into the contract a pertinent provisional exception in the event of intermeddling state action would be more than unreasonable, it would be absurd, since we must assume that the contract was made on the footing that, so long as the obligation remained lawful, the impairment clause would effectively preclude a law altering or nullifying it however exigent the occasion might be.

Blaisdell, 290 U.S. at 477-78 (Sutherland, J., dissenting).

5. *Blaisdell* did not signify the end of modern Contract Clause enforcement. Indeed, immediately thereafter, the Clause was applied in a manner which made it clear that *Blaisdell* was largely confined to its emergency context. For example, in *W.B. Worthen Co. v. Thomas*, 292 U.S. 426 (1934), the Court dealt with an Arkansas law that exempted the proceeds of a life insurance policy from collection by the beneficiary's judgment creditors. Stressing the retroactive effect of the state law, the Court held that it was invalid under the Contract Clause, since it was not precisely and reasonably designed to meet a grave temporary emergency in the interest of the general welfare. In *W.B. Worthen Co. v. Kavanaugh*, 295 U.S. 56 (1935), the Court was confronted with another Arkansas law that diluted the rights and remedies of mortgage bondholders. The Court held the law invalid under the Contract Clause. "Even when the public welfare is invoked as an excuse," Mr. Justice Cardozo wrote for the Court, the security of a mortgage cannot be cut down "without moderation or reason or in a spirit of oppression." *Id.* at 60. And finally, in *Treigle v. Acme Homestead Assn.*, 297 U.S. 189 (1936), the Court held invalid under the Contract Clause a Louisiana law that modified the existing withdrawal rights of the members of a building and loan association. "Such an interference with the right of contract," said the Court, "cannot be justified by saying that in the public interest the operations of building associations may be controlled and regulated, or that in the same interest their charters may be amended." *Id.* at 196.

In the late 1960s, however, the Warren Court appeared to depart from precedent in upholding a Texas statute that limited statutory rights to reclaim title to land that had been forfeited because of certain delinquent interest payments. *City of El Paso v. Simmons*, 379 U.S. 497 (1965). In the early 20th century, desirous to have its territory settled, Texas made unusually generous credit sales of public lands into private hands. These sales required little upfront capital and often only interest payment. Further, if interest went unpaid, the purchaser could redeem at any time until third party interests intervened. With oil discoveries, these lands became more valuable, and Texas limited the right of redemption to five years. Texas sought to justify the limitation as a mere change in remedy, not obligation. Breaking from earlier case law, the Court held that it was unnecessary to make that distinction since even if the state was impairing its obligation, such impairment was not "substantial." In the majority's judgment, the right of reinstatement was not an essential element of the bargain Texas made, and hence, in light of the changed land values and need to eliminate title uncertainty, the reinstatement right could be limited. *Id.* at 513-16.

This introduction of a balancing test into Contract Clause application outraged Justice Black. Dissenting, Black wrote:

> At most the Court's reasons boil down to the fact that Texas' contracts, perhaps very wisely made a long time ago, turned out when land soared in value, and particularly after oil was discovered, to be costly to the State. As the Court euphemistically puts it, the contracts were "not wholly effectual to serve the objectives of the State's land program many decades later. Settlement was no longer the objective, but revenues . . ." among other things were. In plainer language, the State decided it had made a bad deal and wanted out. There is nothing unusual in this. It is a commonplace that land values steadily rise when population increases and rise sharply when valuable minerals are discovered, and that many sellers would be much richer and happier if when lands go up in value they were able to welch on their sales. No plethora of words about state school funds can conceal the fact that to get money easily without having to tax the whole public Texas took the easy way out and violated the Contract Clause of the Constitution as written and as applied up to now. . . .
>
> . . . As the Court's opinion demonstrates, constitutional adjudication under the balancing method becomes simply a matter of this Court's deciding for itself which result in a particular case seems in the circumstances the more acceptable governmental policy and then stating the facts in such a way that the considerations in the balance lead to the result. Even if I believed that we as Justices of this Court had the authority to rely on our judgment of what is best for the country instead of trying to interpret the language and purpose of our written Constitution, I would not agree that Texas should be permitted to do what it has done here. But more importantly, I most certainly cannot agree that constitutional law is simply a matter of what the Justices of this Court decide is not harmful for the country, and therefore is "reasonable."

Id. at 532-33 (Black, J., dissenting). Despite the unfortunate qualification of the Contract Clause with indeterminate judicial balancing, it remains available as the next case indicates.

ALLIED STRUCTURAL STEEL COMPANY v. SPANNAUS
438 U.S. 234 (1978)

MR. JUSTICE STEWART delivered the opinion of the Court.

The issue in this case is whether the application of Minnesota's Private Pension Benefits Protection Act[1] to the appellant violates the Contract Clause of the United States Constitution.

I

In 1974 appellant Allied Structural Steel Co. (company), a corporation with its principal place of business in Illinois, maintained an office in Minnesota with 30 employees. . . .

* * *

[Under the company's general pension plan] an employee who did not die, did not quit, and was not discharged before meeting one of the [several]* requirements of the plan would receive a fixed pension at age 65 if the company remained in business and elected to continue the pension plan in essentially its existing form.

On April 9, 1974, Minnesota enacted the law here in question, the Private Pension Benefits Protection Act. Under the Act, a private employer of 100 employees or more — at least one of whom was a Minnesota resident — who provided pension benefits . . . was subject to a "pension funding charge" if he either terminated the plan or closed a Minnesota office. The charge was assessed if the pension funds were not sufficient to cover full pensions for all employees who had worked at least 10 years. The Act required the employer to satisfy the deficiency by purchasing deferred annuities, payable to the employees at their normal retirement age. A separate provision specified that periods of employment prior to the effective date of the Act were to be included in the 10-year employment criterion.

During the summer of 1974 the company began closing its Minnesota office. On July 31, it discharged 11 of its 30 Minnesota employees, and the following month it notified the Minnesota Commissioner of Labor and Industry, as required by the Act, that it was terminating an office in the State. At least nine of the discharged employees did not have any vested pension rights under the company's plan, but had worked for the company for 10 years or more and thus qualified as pension obligees of the company under the law that Minnesota

---

[1] Minn. Stat. § 181B.01 *et seq.* (1974). This is the same Act that was considered in *Malone v. White Motor Corp.* [(1978)], a case presenting a quite different legal issue.

* "(1) he had worked 15 years for the company and reached the age of 60; or (2) he was at least 55 years old and the sum of his age and his years of service with the company was at least 75; or (3) he was less than 55 years old but the sum of his age and his years of service with the company was at least 80." 438 U.S. at 237.

had enacted a few months earlier. On August 18, the State notified the company that it owed a pension funding charge of approximately $185,000 under the provisions of the Private Pension Benefits Protection Act.

* * *

II

A

There can be no question of the impact of the Minnesota Private Pension Benefits Protection Act upon the company's contractual relationships with its employees. The Act substantially altered those relationships by superimposing pension obligations upon the company conspicuously beyond those that it had voluntarily agreed to undertake. But it does not inexorably follow that the Act, as applied to the company, violates the Contract Clause of the Constitution.

* * *

B

* * *

In *Home Building & Loan Assn. v. Blaisdell* [(1933)], the Court upheld against a Contract Clause attack a mortgage moratorium law that Minnesota had enacted to provide relief for homeowners threatened with foreclosure. . . . In upholding the state mortgage moratorium law, the Court found five factors significant. First, the state legislature had declared in the Act itself that an emergency need for the protection of homeowners existed. Second, the state law was enacted to protect a basic societal interest, not a favored group. Third, the relief was appropriately tailored to the emergency that it was designed to meet. Fourth, the imposed conditions were reasonable. And, finally, the legislation was limited to the duration of the emergency.

The *Blaisdell* opinion thus clearly implied that if the Minnesota moratorium legislation had not possessed the characteristics attributed to it by the Court, it would have been invalid under the Contract Clause of the Constitution.[13] These implications were given concrete force in three cases that followed closely in *Blaisdell*'s wake.

The most recent Contract Clause case in this Court was *United States Trust Co. v. New Jersey* [(1977)]. In that case the Court again recognized that although the absolute language of the Clause must leave room for "the 'essential attributes of sovereign power,' . . . necessarily reserved by the States to safeguard the welfare of their citizens," *id.* at 21, that power has limits when its exercise effects substantial modifications of private contracts. . . .

---

13 In *Veix v. Sixth Ward Building & Loan Assn.* [(1940)], the Court took into account still another consideration in upholding a state law against a Contract Clause attack: the petitioner had "purchased into an enterprise already regulated in the particular to which he now objects."

III

In applying these principles to the present case, the first inquiry must be whether the state law has, in fact, operated as a substantial impairment of a contractual relationship. The severity of the impairment measures the height of the hurdle the state legislation must clear. . . .

The severity of an impairment of contractual obligations can be measured by the factors that reflect the high value the Framers placed on the protection of private contracts. Contracts enable individuals to order their personal and business affairs according to their particular needs and interests. Once arranged, those rights and obligations are binding under the law, and the parties are entitled to rely on them.

* * *

The effect of Minnesota's Private Pension Benefits Protection Act on this contractual obligation was severe. . . .

Not only did the state law thus retroactively modify the compensation that the company had agreed to pay its employees from 1963 to 1974, but also it did so by changing the company's obligations in an area where the element of reliance was vital — the funding of a pension plan. . . .

Moreover, the retroactive state-imposed vesting requirement was applied only to those employers who terminated their pension plans or who, like the company, closed their Minnesota offices. The company was thus forced to make all the retroactive changes in its contractual obligations at one time. By simply proceeding to close its office in Minnesota, a move that had been planned before the passage of the Act, the company was assessed an immediate pension funding charge of approximately $185,000.

Thus, the statute in question here nullifies express terms of the company's contractual obligations and imposes a completely unexpected liability in potentially disabling amounts. There is not even any provision for gradual applicability or grace periods. . . .

* * *

But whether or not the legislation was aimed largely at a single employer, it clearly has an extremely narrow focus. . . . Thus, this law can hardly be characterized, like the law at issue in the *Blaisdell* case, as one enacted to protect a broad societal interest rather than a narrow class.

Moreover, in at least one other important respect the Act does not resemble the mortgage moratorium legislation whose constitutionality was upheld in the *Blaisdell* case. This legislation, imposing a sudden, totally unanticipated, and substantial retroactive obligation upon the company to its employees, was not enacted to deal with a situation remotely approaching the broad and desperate emergency economic conditions of the early 1930's — conditions of which the Court in *Blaisdell* took judicial notice.

* * *

This Minnesota law simply does not possess the attributes of those state laws that in the past have survived challenge under the Contract Clause of the Constitution. The law was not even purportedly enacted to deal with a broad, generalized economic or social problem. It did not operate in an area already subject to state regulation at the time the company's contractual obligations were originally undertaken, but invaded an area never before subject to regulation by the State. It did not effect simply a temporary alteration of the contractual relationships of those within its coverage, but worked a severe, permanent, and immediate change in those relationships — irrevocably and retroactively. And its narrow aim was leveled, not at every Minnesota employer, not even at every Minnesota employer who left the State, but only at those who had in the past been sufficiently enlightened as voluntarily to agree to establish pension plans for their employees.

* * *

The judgment of the District Court is reversed.

It is so ordered.

MR. JUSTICE BLACKMUN took no part in the consideration or decision of this case.

MR. JUSTICE BRENNAN, with whom MR. JUSTICE WHITE and MR. JUSTICE MARSHALL join, dissenting.

* * *

Today's conversion of the Contract Clause into a limitation on the power of States to enact laws that impose duties additional to obligations assumed under private contracts must inevitably produce results difficult to square with any rational conception of a constitutional order. Under the Court's opinion, any law that may be characterized as "superimposing" new obligations on those provided for by contract is to be regarded as creating "sudden, substantial, and unanticipated burdens" and then to be subjected to the most exacting scrutiny. The validity of such a law will turn upon whether judges see it as a law that deals with a generalized social problem, whether it is temporary (as few will be) or permanent, whether it operates in an area previously subject to regulation, and, finally, whether its duties apply to a broad class of persons. The necessary consequence of the extreme malleability of these rather vague criteria is to vest judges with broad subjective discretion to protect property interests that happen to appeal to them.

NOTES AND QUESTIONS

1. Unlike *Blaisdell*, this Minnesota Act had a narrow, targeted focus. This made it more vulnerable to Contract Clause attack since the character of the legislation looked wholly redistributive among particular contracting parties. Nor could the state easily argue that the Act was necessary to meet a widespread economic problem. This was especially so since, as the state knew, the federal government was about to legislate to protect the pension rights of employees. As the *Allied* Court noted:

> Not only did the Act have an extremely narrow aim, but also its effective life was extremely short. The United States House of Representatives had passed a version of the Employee Retirement Income Security Act of 1974 [ERISA], 29 U.S.C. § 1001 *et seq.* (1976 ed.), on February 28, 1974, 120 Cong. Rec. 4781-4782 (1974), and the Senate on March 4, 1974, *id.* at 5011. Both versions expressly pre-empted state laws. That the Minnesota Legislature was aware of the impending federal legislation is reflected in the explicit provision of the Act that it will "become null and void upon the institution of a mandatory plan of termination insurance guaranteeing the payment of a substantial portion of an employee's vested pension benefits pursuant to any law of the United States." Minn. Stat. § 181B.17. ERISA itself, effective January 1, 1975, expressly pre-empts all state laws regulating covered plans. 29 U.S.C. § 1144(a) (1976 ed.). Thus, the Minnesota Act was in force less than nine months, from April 10, 1974, until January 1, 1975.

Allied Structural Steel Co., 438 U.S. at 248 n.21.

2. In footnote 13, the Court in *Allied* notes an addition to the list of qualifications to the Contract Clause, namely, whether the contract was made in "an enterprise already regulated." 438 U.S. at 292 n.13 (quoting *Veix v. Sixth Ward Building & Loan Ass'n,* 310 U.S. 32, 38 (1940)). In several cases subsequent to *Allied,* this factor proved to be important or dispositive. For example, in *Energy Reserves Group v. Kansas Power and Light Co.,* 459 U.S. 400 (1982), the Court upheld a Kansas statute that precluded certain gas price increases by suppliers of natural gas. The statute's provision contradicted existing contractual provisions between the Energy Reserves Group, a natural gas provider, and the Kansas Power and Light Company, a public utility, that authorized periodic price increases. Justice Blackmun, writing for the Court, wrote that "[s]ignificant here is the fact that the parties are operating in a heavily regulated industry." *Energy Reserves Group,* 459 U.S. at 413. Moreover, said the Court, "the contracts expressly recognize the existence of extensive regulation by providing that any contractual terms are subject to relevant present and future state and federal law. This latter provision could be interpreted to incorporate all future state regulation, and thus dispose of the Contract Clause claim." *Id.* at 416.

Another decision, *Exxon Corp v. Eagerton,* 462 U.S. 176 (1983), was resolved in a similar way. In *Exxon,* the Court upheld an Alabama statute that increased an oil severance tax and precluded passing on the increase to purchasers. Provisions of existing contracts would have allowed the increased taxes to be passed on, but the Court analogized the position of the oil producer to that of a highly-regulated common carrier limited by rate regulation. *Id.* at 193-94. The Court somewhat gratuitously added that the denial of the pass through was a generally applicable law not targeted at a particular contract obligation, *id.* at 191-92, but this feature of the state law does not explain the case. While Marshall was surely correct that the police power allows the states to eliminate some types of contract opportunities altogether (*see, e.g., Stone v. Mississippi, supra,* and the elimination of the state lottery), such police power exercises, concerned as they are with the health, safety and welfare, are qualitatively different than the redistribution of a tax increase. Nevertheless, since Justice Thurgood Marshall saw no difference between the cases, *Exxon* muddies the water of modern Contract Clause interpretation.

3. In *General Motors Corp. v. Romein,* 503 U.S. 181 (1992), the Court rejected a Contract Clause challenge to a 1987 Michigan law that effectively repealed the "coordination of benefits" that employers were permitted to do under a prior 1981 Michigan law. Under the 1981 law, employers were coordinating, or reducing, the benefits of disabled or injured workers who had multiple compensation sources. The Court held there was no contractual agreement with regard to the coordination of benefits, and therefore, there was nothing impaired by the 1987 law. *Id.* at 186-87. To the employers' argument that the 1981 law had been impliedly incorporated into private contracts, the Court stated "we have not held that all state regulations are implied terms of every contract entered into while they are effective, especially when the regulations themselves cannot be fairly interpreted to require such incorporation." *Id.* at 189. Justice O'Connor went on to say that state laws are implied into private contract regardless of the assent of the parties only when that law affects "the validity, construction, and enforcement of contracts." *Id.* The 1987 repeal in *General Motors* did not affect the legal validity of the underlying employment contracts.

4. As noted throughout, by its express terms, the Contract Clause applies only to the states, and not to the federal government. However, some early case law employs the Due Process Clause to limit federal interferences with contract. *Lynch v. United States*, 292 U.S. 571 (1934) (invalidating federal cancellation of life insurance policies). However, other more recent cases indicate that the Due Process Clause standards are less searching than those applied under the Contract Clause. *Pension Benefit Guaranty Corp. v. R.A. Gray & Co.*, 467 U.S. 717, 733 (1984) (upholding retroactive "withdrawal liability" imposed by federal law upon private companies leaving a multi-employer pension plan). *See also Usery v. Turner Elkhorn Mining Co.*, 428 U.S. 1, 14-20 (1976) (validating a federal statute that required the operators of coal mines to compensate employees who had contracted pneumoconiosis even though the employees had terminated their work in the coal-mining industry before the Act was passed. This federal statute imposed this new duty on operators based on past acts and applied even though the coal mine operators might not have known of the danger that their employees would contract pneumoconiosis at the time of a particular employee's service).

United States v. Winstar, 518 U.S. 839 (1996), applied a type of Contract Clause analysis to a breach of contract by the federal government itself. The case arose out of the savings and loan crisis of the late 1980s. Because the Federal Savings and Loan Insurance Corporation (FSLIC) was insufficiently funded to liquidate all of the failing thrifts, the Federal Home Loan Bank Board induced healthy thrifts and outside investors to purchase the failing thrifts by permitting the acquiring entities to treat the amount that the purchase price of the thrifts exceeded their fair market value as "supervisory goodwill." The purchasers were further permitted to treat the goodwill and other capital credits as "capital reserves," in satisfaction of their capital reserve requirements established by federal regulations. Subsequently, Congress passed the Financial Institutions Reform, Recovery, and Enforcement Act of 1989 (FIRREA). FIRREA prevented thrifts from treating goodwill and capital credits as capital reserves. Three thrifts created by way of supervisory mergers, two of which later failed because of the government change of regulation, and one which survived only with a great infusion of private capital, brought suit against the United States seeking damages for breach of contract.

In a plurality opinion for the Court, Justice Souter rejected several variants of the reserved power doctrine — that is, to allow recovery for the breach would impede valid regulatory authority — with the proposition that the government is free to regulate, but it must bear the cost of any regulatory changes that result in a breach of its existing contracts. *Id.* at 871-91. Interestingly, Justice Souter, who has been hostile to natural law reasoning in other opinions, relied in his opinion upon several distinctly natural law sources — for example, Chief Justice John Marshall's opinion in *Fletcher v. Peck*. Justice Souter wrote:

> In England, of course, Parliament was historically supreme in the sense that no "higher law" limited the scope of legislative action or provided mechanisms for placing legally enforceable limits upon it in specific instances; the power of American legislative bodies, by contrast, is subject to the overriding dictates of the Constitution and the obligations that it authorizes. Hence, although we have recognized that "a general law . . . may be repealed, amended or disregarded by the legislature which enacted it," and "is not binding upon any subsequent legislature," on this side of the Atlantic, the principle has always lived in some tension with the constitutionally created potential for a legislature, under certain circumstances, to place effective limits on its successors, or to authorize executive action resulting in such a limitation.

> The development of this latter, American doctrine in federal litigation began in cases applying limits on state sovereignty imposed by the National Constitution. Thus Chief Justice Marshall's exposition in *Fletcher v. Peck*, where the Court held that the Contract Clause, U.S. Const., Art. I, § 10, cl. 1, barred the State of Georgia's effort to rescind land grants made by a prior state legislature.

Id. at 871-73.

With regard to the reserved power doctrine, Justice Souter concluded that it was not implicated because the government did not contract away its sovereign authority, it merely (to the tune of $140 billion dollars or so) agreed to indemnify the private thrifts for losses sustained by later regulatory change which limited use of supervisory goodwill as an asset. In Justice Souter's words:

> The [argument] rests on the reserved powers doctrine, developed in the course of litigating claims that States had violated the Contract Clause. It holds that a state government may not contract away "an essential attribute of its sovereignty," *United States Trust*, 431 U.S. at 23, with the classic example of its limitation on the scope of the Contract Clause being found in *Stone v. Mississippi*, 101 U.S. 814 (1880). There a corporation bargained for and received a state legislative charter to conduct lotteries, only to have them outlawed by statute a year later. This Court rejected the argument that the charter immunized the corporation from the operation of the statute, holding that "the legislature cannot bargain away the police power of a State." *Id*. at 817. The Government says that "[t]he logic of the doctrine . . . applies equally to contracts alleged to have been made by the federal government." This may be so but is also beside the point, for the reason that the Government's ability to set capital requirements is not limited by the Bank Board's and FSLIC's promises to make good any losses arising from subsequent regulatory changes. The answer to the Government's contention that the State cannot barter away certain elements of its sovereign power is that a contract to adjust the risk of subsequent legislative change does not strip the Government of its legislative sovereignty.

Id. at 888–89.

5. The Contract Clause is not the only substantive constitutional protection of vested rights. The Fifth Amendment also precludes the taking of private property for public use without the payment of just compensation. Since contract is a species of property, cases brought under the Contract Clause frequently implicate the so-called "Takings Clause" as well. For example, in his *El Paso* dissent, *supra*, Justice Black observed:

> In spite of all the Court's discussion of clouds on land titles and need for "efficient utilization" of land, the real issue in this case is not whether Texas has constitutional power to pass legislation to correct these problems, by limiting reinstatements to five years following forfeiture. I think that there was and is a constitutional way for Texas to do this. But I think the Fifth Amendment forbids Texas to do so without compensating the holders of contractual rights for the interests it wants to destroy. Contractual rights, this Court has held, are property, and the Fifth Amendment requires that property shall not be taken for public use without just compensation. [Citations omitted.] This constitutional requirement is made applicable to the States by the Fourteenth Amendment. The need to clear titles and stabilize the market in land would cer-

tainly be a valid public purpose to sustain exercise of the State's power of eminent domain, and while the Contract Clause protects the value of the property right in contracts, it does not stand in the way of a State's taking those property rights as it would any other property, provided it is willing to pay for what it has taken. . . .

The Court seems to say that because it was "necessary" to raise money and clear titles, Texas was not obligated to pay for rights which it took. I suppose that if Texas were building a highway and a man's house stood in the way, it would be "necessary" to tear it down. Until today I had thought there could be no doubt that he would be entitled to just compensation. Yet the Fifth and Fourteenth Amendments protect his rights no more nor less than they do those of people to whom Texas was contractually obligated. Texas' "necessity" as seen by this Court is the mother of a regrettable judicial invention which I think has no place in our constitutional law. Our Constitution provides that property needed for public use, whether for schools or highways or any other public purpose, shall be paid for out of tax-raised funds fairly contributed by all the taxpayers, not just by a few purchasers of land who trusted the State not wisely but too well. It is not the happiest of days for me when one of our wealthiest States is permitted to enforce a law that breaks faith with those who contracted with it.

379 U.S. at 533-35 (Black, J., dissenting). We now take a closer look at why the framers assigned high importance to the protection of property, and the Court's application of the Takings Clause.

B. The Protection of Property

1. Historical and Philosophical Justification

The founders understood the importance of property both from their grounding in natural law (see the excerpt from Locke, *infra*) and practical experience, reflected below in William Bradford's reflection on the relationship between private property and industriousness in the Plymouth colony. In Madison's words, "[g]overnment is instituted to protect property of every sort. . . . This being the end of government, that alone is a *just* government, which *impartially* secures to every man, whatever is his *own*." JAMES MADISON, *Property, in* 14 THE PAPERS OF JAMES MADISON 266 (William T. Hutchinson ed., 1977) (emphasis in the original). The protection of vested rights, especially private property and contract, advanced liberty and invited greater participation in the political life of the community, upon which the new republic would depend.

WILLIAM BRADFORD, OF PLYMOUTH PLANTATION 120-21
(Samuel Eliot Morison ed., 1952)

. . . So they began to think how they might raise as much corn as they could, and obtain a better crop than they had done, that they might not still thus languish in misery. At length, after much debate of things, the Governor (with the advice of the chiefest amongst them) gave way that they should set corn every man for his own particular, and in that regard trust to themselves; in all other things to go on in the general way as before. And so assigned to every family a parcel of land, according to the proportion of their number, for that end, only for present use (but made no division for inheritance) and ranged all boys and youth under some family. This had very good success, for it made all hands very industrious, so as much more corn was planted than otherwise would have been by any means the Governor or any other could use, and saved him a great deal of trouble, and gave far better content. The women now went willingly into the field, and took their little ones with them to set corn; which before would allege weakness and inability; whom to have compelled would have been thought great tyranny and oppression.

The experience that was had in this common course and condition, tried sundry years and that amongst godly and sober men, may well evince the vanity of that conceit of Plato's and other ancients applauded by some of later times; that the taking away of property and bringing in community into a commonwealth would make them happy and flourishing; as if they were wiser than God. For this community (so far as it was) was found to breed much confusion and discontent and retard much employment that would have been to their benefit and comfort.

NOTES AND QUESTIONS

1. Governor Bradford chastises ancient philosophers for suggesting that commonly-held property, rather than private, individually-vested allocations would allow a people to flourish. The hard experience of the Plymouth Plantation conclusively demonstrated to Bradford the contrary and that these ancients were wrong to presume themselves "wiser than God." But didn't God bestow the entire earth as a gift in common? Or is the commandment "not to steal," as illustrated in Judeo-Christian Scriptures, sufficient to indicate God's support for the division of the common into separately owned shares? Much of the Judeo-Christian tradition familiar to the framers supported private property as a means to secure the lives of men and women from both poverty and violence. Nevertheless, recognizing property's common, Divine origin, the private allocations were owned subject to an accompanying stewardship obligation. Stewardship entailed both using property in its highest and best use ("making it fruitful") as well as reserving and sharing any surplus with those less well off. The latter obligation was reinforced by additional religious teaching that promoted the virtue of temperance, including having only a moderate attachment to earthly goods.

2. In the next excerpt, philosopher John Locke explains how man comes to have a justifiable vested right to particular property, apart from the positive laws of any government. In this, Locke states the natural law justification for property that the framers brought with them into the constitutional convention.

JOHN LOCKE, SECOND TREATISE OF GOVERNMENT
§§ 25-51, 123-26
(C.B. Macpherson ed., Hackett Publ'g Co. 1980) (1690)

§ 25. Whether we consider natural *reason*, which tells us, that men, being once born, have a right to their preservation, and consequently to meat and drink, and such other things as nature affords for their subsistence: or *revelation*, which gives us an account of those grants God made of the world to *Adam*, and to *Noah*, and his sons, it is very clear, that God, as King *David* says, *Psal.* cxv. 16. *has given the earth to the children of men*; given it to mankind in common. But this being supposed, it seems to some a very great difficulty, how any one should ever come to have a *property* in any thing: I will not content myself to answer, that if it be difficult to make out *property*, upon a supposition that God gave the world to *Adam*, and his posterity in common, it is impossible that any man, but one universal monarch, should have any *property* upon a supposition, that God gave the world to *Adam*, and his heirs in succession, exclusive of all the rest of his posterity. But I shall endeavour to shew, how men might come to have a *property* in several parts of that which God gave to mankind in common, and that without any express compact of all the commoners.

§ 26. God, who hath given the world to men in common, hath also given them reason to make use of it to the best advantage of life, and convenience. The earth, and all that is therein, is given to men for the support and comfort of their being. And tho' all the fruits it naturally produces, and beasts it feeds, belong to mankind in common, as they are produced by the spontaneous hand of nature; and no body has originally a private dominion, exclusive of the rest of mankind, in any of them, as they are thus in their natural state: yet being given for the use of men, there must of necessity be *a means to appropriate* them some way or other, before they can be of any use, or at all beneficial to any particular man. The fruit, or venison, which nourishes the wild *Indian*, who knows no inclosure, and is still a tenant in common, must be his, and so his, *i.e.* a part of him, that another can no longer have any right to it, before it can do him any good for the support of his life.

§ 27. Though the earth, and all inferior creatures be common to all men, yet every man has a *property* in his own *person*: this no body has any right to but himself. The *labour* of his body, and the *work* of his hands, we may say, are properly his. Whatsoever then he removes out of the state that nature hath provided, and left it in, he hath mixed his *labour* with, and joined to it something that is his own, and thereby makes it his *property*. It being by him removed from the common state nature hath placed it in, it hath by this *labour* something annexed to it, that excludes the common right of other men: for this *labour* being the unquestionable property of the labourer, no man but he can have a right to what that is once joined to, at least where there is enough, and as good, left in common for others.

§ 28. He that is nourished by the acorns he picked up under an oak, or the apples he gathered from the trees in the wood, has certainly appropriated them to himself. No body can deny but the nourishment is his. I ask then, when did they begin to be his? when he digested? or when he eat? or when he boiled? or when he brought them home? or when he picked them up? and it is plain, if the first gathering made them not his, nothing else could. That *labour* put a distinction between them and common: that added something to them more than nature, the common mother of all, had done; and so they became his private right. And will any one say, he had no right to those acorns or apples he thus appropriated, because he had not the consent of all mankind to make them his? Was it a robbery thus to assume to himself what belonged to all in common? If such a consent as that was necessary, man had starved, notwithstanding the plenty God had given him. We see in *commons*, which remain so by compact, that it is the taking any part of what is common, and removing it out of the state nature leaves it in, which *begins the property*; without which the common is of no use. And the taking of this or that part, does not depend on the express consent of all the commoners. Thus the grass my horse has bit; the turfs my servant has cut; and the ore I have digged in any place, where I have a right to them in common with others, become my *property*, without the assignation or consent of any body. The *labour* that was mine, removing them out of that common state they were in, hath *fixed* my *property* in them.

§ 29. By making an explicit consent of every commoner, necessary to any one's appropriating to himself any part of what is given in common, children or servants could not cut the meat which their father or master had provided for them in common, without assigning to every one his peculiar part. Though the water running in the fountain be every one's, yet who can doubt, but that in the pitcher is his only who drew it out? His *labour* hath taken it out of the hands of nature, where it was common, and belonged equally to all her children, and *hath* thereby *appropriated* it to himself.

§ 30. Thus this law of reason makes the deer that *Indian's* who hath killed it; it is allowed to be his goods, who hath bestowed his labour upon it, though before it was the common right of every one. And amongst those who are counted the civilized part of mankind, who have made and multiplied positive laws to determine *property*, this original law of nature, for the *beginning of property*, in what was before common, still takes place . . . .

§ 31. It will perhaps be objected to this, that if gathering the acorns, or other fruits of the earth, &c. makes a right to them, then any one may *ingross* as much as he will. To which I answer, Not so. The same law of nature, that does by this means give us property, does also *bound* that *property* too. *God has given us all things richly*, 1 *Tim.* vi. 12. is the voice of reason confirmed by inspiration. But how far has he given it us? *To enjoy.* As much as any one can make use of to any advantage of life before it spoils, so much he may by his labour fix a property in: whatever is beyond this, is more than his share, and belongs to others. Nothing was made by God for man to spoil or destroy. And thus, considering the plenty of natural provisions there was a long time in the world, and the few spenders; and to how small a part of that provision the industry of one man could extend itself, and ingross it to the prejudice of others; especially keeping within the *bounds*, set by reason, of what might serve for his *use*; there could be then little room for quarrels or contentions about property so established.

§ 32. But the *chief matter of property* being now not the fruits of the earth, and the beasts that subsist on it, but *the earth itself*; as that which takes in and carries with it all the rest; I think it is plain, that *property* in that too is acquired as the former. *As much land* as a man tills, plants, improves, cultivates, and can use the product of, so much is his *property*. He by his labour does, as it were, inclose it from the common. Nor will it invalidate his right, to say every body else has an equal title to it; and therefore he cannot appropriate, he cannot inclose, without the consent of all his fellow-commoners, all mankind. God, when he gave the world in common to all mankind, commanded man also to labour, and the penury of his condition required it of him. God and his reason commanded him to subdue the earth, *i.e.* improve it for the benefit of life, and therein lay out something upon it that was his own, his labour. He that in obedience to this command of God, subdued, tilled and sowed any part of it, thereby annexed to it something that was his *property*, which another had no title to, nor could without injury take from him.

§ 33. Nor was this *appropriation* of any parcel of *land*, by improving it, any prejudice to any other man, since there was still enough, and as good left; and more than the yet unprovided could use. So that, in effect, there was never the less left for others because of his inclosure for himself: for he that leaves as much as another can make use of, does as good as take nothing at all. No body could think himself injured by the drinking of another man, though he took a good draught, who had a whole river of the same water left him to quench his thirst: and the case of land and water, where there is enough of both, is perfectly the same.

* * *

§ 36. . . . [T]hat the same *rule of property, (viz.)* that every man should have as much as he could make use of, would hold still in the world, without straitening any body; since there is land enough in the world to suffice double the inhabitants, had not the *invention of money*, and the tacit agreement of men to put a value on it, introduced (by consent) larger possessions, and a right to them; which, how it has done, I shall by and by shew more at large.

* * *

§ 47. And thus *came in the use of money*, some lasting thing that men might keep without spoiling, and that by mutual consent men would take in exchange for the truly useful, but perishable supports of life.

§ 48. And as different degrees of industry were apt to give men possessions in different proportions, so this *invention of money* gave them the opportunity to continue and enlarge them . . .: Where there is not some thing, both lasting and scarce, and so valuable to be hoarded up, there men will not be apt to enlarge their *possessions of land*, were it never so rich, never so free for them to take: for I ask, what would a man value ten thousand, or an hundred thousand acres of excellent *land*, ready cultivated, and well stocked too with cattle, in the middle of the inland parts of *America*, where he had no hopes of commerce with other parts of the world, to draw *money* to him by the sale of the product? It would not be worth the inclosing, and we should see him give up again to the wild common of nature, whatever was more than would supply the conveniencies of life to be had there for him and his family.

§ 49. Thus in the beginning all the world was *America*, and more so than that is now; for no such thing as *money* was any where known. Find out something that hath the *use and value of money* amongst his neighbours, you shall see the same man will begin presently to enlarge his possessions.

§ 50. But since gold and silver, being little useful to the life of man in proportion to food, raiment, and carriage, has its *value* only from the consent of men, whereof *labour* yet *makes*, in great part, *the measure*, it is plain, that men have agreed to disproportionate and unequal *possession of the earth*, they having, by a tacit and voluntary consent, found out a way how a man may fairly possess more land than he himself can use the product of, by receiving in exchange for the overplus gold and silver, which may be hoarded up without injury to any one; these metals not spoiling or decaying in the hands of the possessor. . . .

§ 51. And thus, I think, it is very easy to conceive, without any difficulty, *how labour could at first begin a title of property* in the common things of nature, and how the spending it upon our uses bounded it. So that there could then be no reason of quarrelling about title, nor any doubt about the largeness of possession it gave. Right and conveniency went together; for as a man had a right to all he could employ his labour upon, so he had no temptation to labour for more than he could make use of. This left no room for controversy about the title, nor for incroachment on the right of others; what portion a man carved to himself, was easily seen; and it was useless, as well as dishonest, to carve himself too much, or take more than he needed.

* * *

Chap. IX. Of the Ends of Political Society and Government

§ 123. If man in the state of nature be so free, as has been said; if he be absolute lord of his own person and possessions, equal to the greatest, and subject to no body, why will he part with his freedom? why will he give up this empire, and subject himself to the dominion and controul of any other power? To which it is obvious to answer, that though in the state of nature he hath such a right, yet the enjoyment of it is very uncertain, and constantly exposed to the invasion of others: for all being kings as much as he, every man his equal, and the greater part no strict observers of equity and justice, the enjoyment of the property he has in this state is very unsafe, very unsecure. This makes him willing to quit a condition, which, however free, is full of fears and continual dangers: and it is not without reason, that he seeks out, and is willing to join in society with others, who are already united, or have a mind to unite, for the mutual *preservation* of their lives, liberties and estates, which I call by the general name, *property*.

§ 124. The great and *chief end,* therefore, of men's uniting into common-wealths, and putting themselves under government, *is the preservation of their property*. To which in the state of nature there are many things wanting.

First, There wants an *establshed*, settled, known *law*, received and allowed by common consent to be the standard of right and wrong, and the common measure to decide all controversies between them: for though the law of nature be plain and intelligible to all rational creatures; yet men being biassed by their interest, as well as ignorant for want of study of it, are not apt to allow of it as a law binding to them in the application of it to their particular cases.

§ 125. *Secondly*, In the state of nature there wants *a known and indifferent judge*, with authority to determine all differences according to the established law: for every one in that state being both judge and executioner of the law of nature, men being partial to themselves, passion and revenge is very apt to carry them too far, and with too much heat, in their own cases; as well as negligence, and unconcernedness, to make them too remiss in other men's.

§ 126. *Thirdly*, In the state of nature there often wants *power* to back and support the sentence when right, and to *give* it due *execution*. They who by any injustice offended, will seldom fail, where they are able, by force to make good their injustice; such resistance many times makes the punishment dangerous, and frequently destructive, to those who attempt it.

NOTES AND QUESTIONS

1. Locke premises individual ownership on the claim that "every man has a *property* in his own *person*: this no body has any right to but himself." LOCKE, *supra*, at § 27. This proposition is often viewed as self-evident, yet, is it contrary to St. Paul's admonition that no person owns himself or herself? 1 *Corinthians*

6:19? In scripture, it is made plain that man is God's creature, not an independent contractor. *See, e.g., Psalm* 100:3, 139:13-16. Did Locke fail to reaffirm this religious point, thereby steering private property in America onto an overly individualistic or self-centered course? Was this less of a problem at the time of the founding since both the nature of earth and individual life as gift, rather than entitlement, was then manifest in the duties individuals were impliedly expected to fulfill toward their community? In fact, Locke himself rejected the idea that inherent in the human person is right divorced from obligation, although the framers were likely unaware of any such proclamation from Locke's pen. In a manuscript that remarkably remained unpublished until 1954, Locke writes:

> [S]ince it is necessary to conclude . . . that there exists some creator of all these things, . . . it follows from this that he has not made this world at random and to no end before it. Nor, indeed, since he perceives that he possesses a mind which is quick, receptive, ready for everything, and versatile, adorned with reason and knowledge, and a body too which is agile and can move to one place or another as the mind commands, can man believe that all of these things have been given to him by a most wise creator, ready for use, so that he can do nothing; that he is provided with all of these faculties so that with all the more brilliance he can remain idle and languish? From this is perfectly clear that God wills him to do something. . . . It seems that the function of man is what he is naturally equipped to do; that is, since he discovers in himself sense and reason, and perceives himself inclined and ready to perform the works of God, as he ought, . . . [t]hen, [he perceives that he is] impelled to form and preserve a union of his life with other men, not only by the needs and necessities of life, but [he perceives also that] he is driven by a certain natural propensity to enter society and is fitted to preserve it by the gift of speech and the commerce of language.

JOHN LOCKE, QUESTIONS CONCERNING THE LAW OF NATURE 167, 169 (Robert Horwitz et al. trans., Cornell Univ. Press 1990) (1954).

   2. Under Locke's natural law theory, prior to the invention of money, there is a natural limit on acquisition which helps to reinforce the virtue of moderation and to leave sufficient property ownership opportunities for others. The limit, of course, is how much property an individual person can "enjoy" without waste or spoilage. Money, however, allows men and women to enlarge their possessions beyond that which they can enjoy presently. Does Locke suggest any limit on the inequality of possessions resulting from the invention of money? Note Locke's argument that "putting a value on gold and silver, and tacitly agreeing in the use of money" arose without benefit of law "out of the bounds of society." LOCKE, SECOND TREATISE OF GOVERNMENT, *supra*, at § 50. Modernly, does this remain true given the role played by such institutions as the Federal Reserve, which controls the domestic money supply, and the International Monetary Fund, influencing the same internationally?

3. Finally, with regard to Locke, note that he squarely identifies the purpose of government as the preservation of property. LOCKE, *supra*, at § 124. While human reason would know the "right and wrong" in property dealings in the state of nature, controversies are better settled in society where the contesting claimants are not also the judge. Nevertheless, even when the function of protecting vested rights or property is given over to society, the impartial judge is to decide matters in accordance with "the law of nature [that is] plain and intelligible to all rational creatures." *Id.* at §§ 124-25.

4. The Constitution mentions the word property four times. Article IV, Section 2, grants Congress plenary authority to regulate and dispose of property belonging to the United States. Of greater interest to us in this Chapter, though, is how the Fifth and Fourteenth Amendments expressly protect privately held property from some government interference. In Part II of this Chapter, our focus will be upon the Due Process Clauses of the Fifth and Fourteenth Amendments, which prohibit both the federal government and the states from depriving any person of property without constitutionally adequate procedures. Our immediate attention, however, is the Fifth Amendment Takings Clause, which precludes the taking of private property for public use without the payment of just compensation. This provision is relatively unproblematic when government physically assumes or desires possession of private property. Compensation in such case must be paid for the title taken or the physical occupancy. This is studied in courses on property, under the law of eminent domain, or condemnation. The most important issue in physical takings is an understanding of the qualifier, "public use." While some states by constitution, and many states by statute, require an actual use by the public or a distinctly public purpose, say, a road or government building, the Supreme Court has virtually read the public use limitation out of the Federal Constitution. *See Hawaii Housing Authority v. Midkiff*, 467 U.S. 229 (1984) (sustaining a Hawaiian law that allowed tenants to use public condemnation to force owners of large estates to sell them the property the tenants occupied). In *Midkiff*, the Court described its review of what constitutes a public use as "'extremely narrow.'" *Id.* at 240 (quoting *Berman v. Parker*, 348 U.S. 26, 32 (1954)). Further, the Court wrote that "[t]he mere fact that property taken outright by eminent domain is transferred in the first instance to private beneficiaries does not condemn that taking as having only a private purpose. The Court long ago rejected any literal requirement that condemned property be put into use for the general public." *Id.* at 243-44. There are strong reasons to believe that *Midkiff* is a substantial departure from the natural law tradition as explicated by Locke and followed in early Supreme Court cases. In *Vanhorne's Lessee v. Dorrance*, 2 U.S. (2 Dall.) 304 (1795), for example, Justice Paterson wrote that that the Legislature had no "authority to make an act, divesting one citizen of his freehold and vesting it in another, even with compensation." And in *Calder v. Bull*, 3 U.S. (3 Dall.) 386 (1798), the Court noted that a "law that takes property from A and gives it to B" would be "against all reason and justice." Professor Richard Epstein makes this point elegantly and comprehensively in his book, TAKINGS — PRIVATE PROPERTY AND THE POWER OF

EMINENT DOMAIN 161 (1985). Professor Epstein carefully explains how the public use limitation was intended as a strict limitation upon the power of government, even when accompanied by compensation. In addition, writing in the law and economics tradition, he argues that the public use limitation ought to be informed by the economic concept of public good — that is, those goods which are nonexclusive and in which one person's consumption does not significantly reduce or preclude enjoyment by another. National defense needs are the stock example, but public highways and parks generally fit this description as well.

Recently, the lower courts have begun to put some teeth back in the "public use" limitation on the eminent domain power. In *99 Cents Only Stores v. Lancaster Redevelopment Agency*, 237 F. Supp. 2d 1123 (C.D. Cal. 2001), for example, the court held that condemnation could not be used to transfer a lease from one privately-owned store to another because such was for private gain and not a public use. In *Wayne County v. Hathcock*, the Michigan Supreme Court is considering whether to overturn the landmark case, *Poletown Neighborhood Council v. City of Detroit*, 410 Mich. 616 (1981), that allowed Detroit to condemn a low-income neighborhood known as Poletown and sell the land at a discount to General Motors Corporation in 1981. And in *Southwestern Illinois Development Authority v. National City Environmental, LLC*, 768 N.E.2d 1 (Ill. 2002), the Illinois Supreme Court rejected an Illinois redevelopment agency's condemnation of private property to make way for a parking lot for a privately-owned speedway as not a permissible public use.

5. The application of the Takings Clause becomes even more difficult when it is sought to be applied to government regulation. As a structural matter, you will recall that the Takings Clause initially applied only to the federal government. *Barron v. Mayor of Baltimore*, 32 U.S. (7 Pet.) 243 (1833). Subsequently, either the Takings Clause directly or its substantive meaning was incorporated into the Fourteenth Amendment Due Process Clause and applied to the states. *Chicago, Burlington & Quincy R.R. Co. v. City of Chicago*, 166 U.S. 226 (1897). As Chief Justice Rehnquist writes in *Dolan v. City of Tigard*, 512 U.S. 374, 384 n.5 (1994), considered below, "there is no doubt that later cases have held that the Fourteenth Amendment does make the Takings Clause . . . applicable to the States." For related commentary on these developments, see Jan. G. Laitos, *The Public Use Paradox and the Takings Clause,* 13 J. ENERGY NAT. RESOURCES & ENVTL. L. 9 (1993) (analyzing the police power takings test and concluding that to require "just compensation" only when a taking is *not* for public use is to ignore the language of the Fifth Amendment and that doing so removes an effective check on the police power).

As a matter of definition, the Constitution is silent about what constitutes property. Sir William Blackstone in the 18th Century, however, described property as being both an absolute, pre-societal natural right and a relative right dependent upon positive law. 1 WILLIAM BLACKSTONE, COMMENTARIES *138 ("The third absolute right, inherent in every Englishman, is that of property[; but its] free use, enjoyment, and disposal [is subject to] the laws of the land."). *See gen-*

erally Douglas W. Kmiec, *The Coherence of the Natural Law of Property*, 26 VAL. U. L. REV. 367 (1991). That property has elements of both characteristics goes a good distance toward explaining the constitutional difficulty. A member of the constitutional convention, James Wilson, sought to reconcile the seeming contradiction, writing: "[o]ur law recognizes no such thing as absolute power or absolute rights, but does recognize the distinction between the abstract right to acquire property as one of the civil rights of persons and the right of property as applied to things." 2 THE WORKS OF JAMES WILSON 309 n.1 (James DeWitt Andrews ed., 1896). Knowing where the natural right to acquire and own ends, and where the relative right of specific ownership activities begins is the modern story of the conflict between private property and its limitation by governmental police or regulatory power. The following decision by Justice Oliver Wendell Holmes, dealing with the regulation of subsidence from the extraction of coal, begins the tale of the Constitution and regulatory takings.

2. Regulatory Takings and the Supreme Court

PENNSYLVANIA COAL CO. v. MAHON
260 U.S. 393 (1922)

MR. JUSTICE HOLMES delivered the opinion of the Court.

[T]he Pennsylvania Coal Company [sold property to the Mahons]. . . . The deed conveys the surface, but in express terms reserves the right to remove all the coal under the same, and the [Mahons] take[] the premises with the risk, and waive[] all claim for damages that may arise from mining out the coal. But the [Mahons] say that whatever may have been the Coal Company's rights, they were taken away by an Act of Pennsylvania. . . . On appeal the Supreme Court of the State agreed that the [Coal Company] had contract and property rights protected by the Constitution of the United States, but held that the statute was a legitimate exercise of the police power. . . .

The statute forbids the mining of anthracite coal in such way as to cause the subsidence of, among other things, any structure used as a human habitation, with certain exceptions, including among them land where the surface is owned by the owner of the underlying coal and is distant more than one hundred and fifty feet from any improved property belonging to any other person. As applied to this case the statute is admitted to destroy previously existing rights of property and contract. The question is whether the police power can be stretched so far.

Government hardly could go on if to some extent values incident to property could not be diminished without paying for every such change in the general law. As long recognized, some values are enjoyed under an implied limitation and must yield to the police power. But obviously the implied limitation must have its limits, or the contract and due process clauses are gone. One fact for consideration in determining such limits is the extent of the diminution. When it reaches a certain magnitude, in most if not in all cases there must be an exercise of eminent domain and compensation to sustain the act. So the question depends upon the particular facts. The greatest weight is given to the judgment of the legislature, but it always is open to interested parties to contend that the legislature has gone beyond its constitutional power.

This is the case of a single private house. . . . The extent of the public interest is shown by the statute to be limited, since the statute ordinarily does not apply to land when the surface is owned by the owner of the coal. Furthermore, it is not justified as a protection of personal safety. That could be provided for by notice. . . . On the other hand the extent of the taking is great. It purports to abolish what is recognized in Pennsylvania as an estate in land — a very valuable estate — and what is declared by the Court below to be a contract hitherto binding the [Mahons]. If we were called upon to deal with the [Mahons'] position alone, we should think it clear that the statute does not disclose a public interest sufficient to warrant so extensive a destruction of the [Coal Company's] constitutionally protected rights.

But the case has been treated as one in which the general validity of the act should be discussed. . . .

To make it commercially impracticable to mine certain coal has very nearly the same effect for constitutional purposes as appropriating or destroying it. This we think that we are warranted in assuming that the statute does.

It is true that in *Plymouth Coal Co. v. Pennsylvania* [(1914)], it was held competent for the legislature to require a pillar of coal to be left along the line of adjoining property, that, with the pillar on the other side of the line, would be a barrier sufficient for the safety of the employees of either mine in case the other should be abandoned and allowed to fill with water. But that was a requirement for the safety of employees invited into the mine, and secured an average reciprocity of advantage that has been recognized as a justification of various laws.

The rights of the public in a street purchased or laid out by eminent domain are those that it has paid for. If in any case its representatives have been so short sighted as to acquire only surface rights without the right of support, we see no more authority for supplying the latter without compensation than there was for taking the right of way in the first place and refusing to pay for it because the public wanted it very much. The protection of private property in the Fifth Amendment presupposes that it is wanted for public use, but provides that it shall not be taken for such use without compensation. A similar assumption is made in the decisions upon the Fourteenth Amendment. When this seemingly absolute protection is found to be qualified by the police power, the natural tendency of human nature is to extend the qualification more and more until at last private property disappears. But that cannot be accomplished in this way under the Constitution of the United States.

The general rule at least is, that while property may be regulated to a certain extent, if regulation goes too far it will be recognized as a taking. . . . We are in danger of forgetting that a strong public desire to improve the public condition is not enough to warrant achieving the desire by a shorter cut than the constitutional way of paying for the change. . . .

We assume, of course, that the statute was passed upon the conviction that an exigency existed that would warrant it, and we assume that an exigency exists that would warrant the exercise of eminent domain. But the question at bottom is upon whom the loss of the changes desired should fall. So far as private persons or communities have seen fit to take the risk of acquiring only surface rights, we cannot see that the fact that their risk has become a danger warrants the giving to them greater rights than they bought.

Decree reversed.

MR. JUSTICE BRANDEIS dissenting.

* * *

Every restriction upon the use of property imposed in the exercise of the police power deprives the owner of some right theretofore enjoyed, and is, in that sense, an abridgment by the state of rights in property without making compensation. But restriction imposed to protect the public health, safety or morals from dangers threatened is not a taking. The restriction here in question is merely the prohibition of a noxious use. The property so restricted remains in the possession of its owner. The state does not appropriate it or make any use of it. The state merely prevents the owner from making a use which interferes with paramount rights of the public. Whenever the use prohibited ceases to be noxious — as it may because of further change in local or social conditions — the restriction will have to be removed and the owner will again be free to enjoy his property as heretofore.

The restriction upon the use of this property cannot, of course, be lawfully imposed, unless its purpose is to protect the public. But the purpose of a restriction does not cease to be public, because incidentally some private persons may thereby receive gratuitously valuable special benefits. . . . Nor is a restriction imposed through exercise of the police power inappropriate as a means, merely because the same end might be effected through exercise of the power of eminent domain, or otherwise at public expense. Every restriction upon the height of buildings might be secured through acquiring by eminent domain the right of each owner to build above the limiting height; but it is settled that the state need not resort to that power. If by mining anthracite coal the owner would necessarily unloose poisonous gases, I suppose no one would doubt the power of the state to prevent the mining, without buying his coal fields. And why may not the state, likewise, without paying compensation, prohibit one from digging so deep or excavating so near the surface, as to expose the community to like dangers? In the latter case, as in the former, carrying on the business would be a public nuisance.

It is said that one fact for consideration in determining whether the limits of the police power have been exceeded is the extent of the resulting diminution in value; and that here the restriction destroys existing rights of property and contract. But values are relative. If we are to consider the value of the coal kept in place by the restriction, we should compare it with the value of all other parts of the land. That is, with the value not of the coal alone, but with the value of the whole property.

NOTES AND QUESTIONS

1. *Pennsylvania Coal* is sometimes characterized as the first time the Takings or Just Compensation Clause was extended as a limit upon police power regulation. *See* William M. Treanor, *The Original Understanding of the Takings Clause and the Political Process*, 95 COLUM. L. REV. 782 (1995). In fact, Justice Holmes' reasoning reflects the high importance assigned to the protection of property by the framers. *See* Douglas W. Kmiec, *The Coherence of the Natural Law of Property*, 26 VAL. U. L. REV. 367 (1991). As a common law right that is part natural law (all entering society have a right by human nature to acquire, possess, and use property) and part positive law (the particular features of ownership and use are elaborated and specified by state common and statutory law), the right of property has never been assumed to include the right to harm others with that property. The question is how to define what constitutes a "harm." Both Holmes for the majority and Brandeis for the dissent largely premise that definition upon the common law concept of nuisance. Defined at the state level incrementally through the adjudication of particular cases, nuisance seemingly allows each local community to keep the rights of property and the limitations on those rights in reasonable balance. Moreover, from the standpoint of federalism, that balance can be differently defined in different locations, and of course, differently over time as the perception of harm changes. Holmes and Brandeis fundamentally disagree over whether preventing subsidence should be viewed as a nuisance. Unfortunately, neither makes particular reference to Pennsylvania nuisance law to decide the issue, relying instead upon prior federal treatments of the issue. That was likely a misstep in light of both the interests in federalism and the protection of property, though in context probably a small one given the similarity between Holmes' conclusions and the common law at the time.

2. Holmes sees no need to distinguish regulatory from physical takings. He writes: "[t]o make it commercially impracticable to mine certain coal has very nearly the same effect for constitutional purposes as appropriating or destroying it." 260 U.S. at 414. Brandeis does not disagree, other than to say that "merely because the same end might be effected through the exercise of the power of eminent domain" does not mean that the state must resort to that power. *Id.* at 418 (Brandeis, J., dissenting). Holmes says, however, that the state must exercise eminent domain when the regulation renders the intended use "commercially impracticable" or when the regulation goes "too far." *Id.* at

414-15. This raises the diminution in value issue; one that will haunt regulatory taking cases thereafter. Note first that the Court and the dissent differ over how to calculate the loss. The Court views only the mining right affected by the regulation. The dissent views the property as a whole. Perhaps this focus on loss calculation was a surrogate for judicial restraint, with the dissent suggesting that only substantial losses calculated with reference to the entire property ought to be a federal case. In truth, however, the focus on the value impact of regulation seems off-point, or at least secondary. Isn't the heart of the issue whether or not the regulatory exercise could be said to fall within the harm-prevention purposes of the police power? And aren't those harm-prevention purposes defined in relation to state nuisance law? The Court left these questions unanswered for many years, and when they returned to it in the next case, by their own admission, they gave an "ad hoc" answer.

PENN CENTRAL TRANSPORTATION COMPANY v. CITY OF NEW YORK
438 U.S. 104 (1978)

[Following refusal of New York City's Landmarks Preservation Commission to approve plans for construction of a 50-story office building over Grand Central Terminal, which had been designated a "landmark," the terminal owner filed suit charging that the application of the Landmarks Preservation Law constituted a "taking" of the property without just compensation and arbitrarily deprived owners of their property without due process.]

MR. JUSTICE BRENNAN delivered the opinion of the Court.

* * *

The New York Court of Appeals . . . summarily rejected any claim that the Landmarks Law had "taken" property without "just compensation," indicating that there could be no "taking" since the law had not transferred control of the property to the city, but only restricted appellants' exploitation of it. . . .

* * *

II

The issues presented by appellants are (1) whether the restrictions imposed by New York City's law upon appellants' exploitation of the Terminal site effect a "taking" of appellants' property for a public use within the meaning of the Fifth Amendment, which of course is made applicable to the States through the Fourteenth Amendment, *see Chicago, B. & Q. R. Co. v. Chicago* (1897), and, (2), if so, whether the transferable development rights afforded appellants constitute "just compensation" within the meaning of the Fifth Amendment. We need only address the question whether a "taking" has occurred.[25]

---

[25] As is implicit in our opinion, we do not embrace the proposition that a "taking" can never occur unless government has transferred physical control over a portion of a parcel.

A

Before considering appellants' specific contentions, it will be useful to review the factors that have shaped the jurisprudence of the Fifth Amendment injunction "nor shall private property be taken for public use, without just compensation." The question of what constitutes a "taking" for purposes of the Fifth Amendment has proved to be a problem of considerable difficulty. While this Court has recognized that the "Fifth Amendment's guarantee . . . [is] designed to bar Government from forcing some people alone to bear public burdens which, in all fairness and justice, should be borne by the public as a whole," this Court, quite simply, has been unable to develop any "set formula" for determining when "justice and fairness" require that economic injuries caused by public action be compensated by the government, rather than remain disproportionately concentrated on a few persons. Indeed, we have frequently observed that whether a particular restriction will be rendered invalid by the government's failure to pay for any losses proximately caused by it depends largely "upon the particular circumstances [in that] case."

In engaging in these essentially ad hoc, factual inquiries, the Court's decisions have identified several factors that have particular significance. The economic impact of the regulation on the claimant and, particularly, the extent to which the regulation has interfered with distinct investment-backed expectations are, of course, relevant considerations. So, too, is the character of the governmental action. A "taking" may more readily be found when the interference with property can be characterized as a physical invasion by government, than when interference arises from some public program adjusting the benefits and burdens of economic life to promote the common good. . . .

B

. . . Because this Court has recognized, in a number of settings, that States and cities may enact land-use restrictions or controls to enhance the quality of life by preserving the character and desirable aesthetic features of a city, appellants do not contest that New York City's objective of preserving structures and areas with special historic, architectural, or cultural significance is an entirely permissible governmental goal. They also do not dispute that the restrictions imposed on its parcel are appropriate means of securing the purposes of the New York City law. Finally, appellants do not challenge any of the specific factual premises of the decision below. They accept for present purposes both that the parcel of land occupied by Grand Central Terminal must, in its present state, be regarded as capable of earning a reasonable return, and that the transferable development rights afforded appellants by virtue of the Terminal's designation as a landmark are valuable, even if not as valuable as the rights to construct above the Terminal. . . .

[Appellants] first observe that the airspace above the Terminal is a valuable property interest. They urge that the Landmarks Law has deprived them of any gainful use of their "air rights" above the Terminal and that, irrespective of the value of the remainder of their parcel, the city has "taken" their right to this superadjacent airspace, thus entitling them to "just compensation" measured by the fair market value of these air rights.

. . . "Taking" jurisprudence does not divide a single parcel into discrete segments and attempt to determine whether rights in a particular segment have been entirely abrogated. In deciding whether a particular governmental action has effected a taking, this Court focuses rather both on the character of the action and on the nature and extent of the interference with rights in the parcel as a whole — here, the city tax block designated as the "landmark site."

. . . Appellants concede that the decisions sustaining other land-use regulations, which, like the New York City law, are reasonably related to the promotion of the general welfare, uniformly reject the proposition that diminution in property value, standing alone, can establish a "taking," see *Euclid v. Ambler Realty Co.* (1926) (75% diminution in value caused by zoning law); *Hadacheck v. Sebastian* (1915) (87% diminution in value). . . .

* * *

Next, appellants observe that New York City's law differs from zoning laws and historic-district ordinances in that the Landmarks Law does not impose identical or similar restrictions on all structures located in particular physical communities. It follows, they argue, that New York City's law is inherently incapable of producing the fair and equitable distribution of benefits and burdens of governmental action which is characteristic of zoning laws and historic-district legislation and which they maintain is a constitutional requirement if "just compensation" is not to be afforded. It is, of course, true that the Landmarks Law has a more severe impact on some landowners than on others, but that in itself does not mean that the law effects a "taking." Legislation designed to promote the general welfare commonly burdens some more than others. The owners of the brickyard in *Hadacheck*, of the cedar trees in *Miller v. Schoene* [(1928)], and of the gravel and sand mine in *Goldblatt v. Hempstead* [(1962)], were uniquely burdened by the legislation sustained in those cases.[30]

* * *

---

[30] Appellants attempt to distinguish these cases on the ground that, in each, government was prohibiting a "noxious" use of land and that in the present case, in contrast, appellants' proposed construction above the Terminal would be beneficial. We observe that the uses in issue [earlier cases] were perfectly lawful in themselves. They involved no "blameworthiness, . . . moral wrongdoing or conscious act of dangerous risk-taking which induce[d society] to shift the cost to a pa[rt]icular individual." [quoting Joseph L. Sax, *Takings and the Police Power*, 74 YALE L.J. 36, 50 (1964).] These cases are better understood as resting not on any supposed "noxious" quality of the prohibited uses but rather on the ground that the restrictions were reasonably related to the implementation of a policy — not unlike historic preservation — expected to produce a widespread public benefit and applicable to all similarly situated property.

* * *

C

* * *

Unlike the governmental acts in [other cases], the New York City law does not interfere in any way with the present uses of the Terminal. Its designation as a landmark not only permits but contemplates that appellants may continue to use the property precisely as it has been used for the past 65 years: as a railroad terminal containing office space and concessions. So the law does not interfere with what must be regarded as Penn Central's primary expectation concerning the use of the parcel. More importantly, on this record, we must regard the New York City law as permitting Penn Central not only to profit from the Terminal but also to obtain a "reasonable return" on its investment.

* * *

Second, to the extent appellants have been denied the right to build above the Terminal, it is not literally accurate to say that they have been denied all use of even those pre-existing air rights. Their ability to use these rights has not been abrogated; they are made transferable to at least eight parcels in the vicinity of the Terminal, one or two of which have been found suitable for the construction of new office buildings. Although appellants and others have argued that New York City's transferable development-rights program is far from ideal, the New York courts here supportably found that, at least in the case of the Terminal, the rights afforded are valuable. While these rights may well not have constituted "just compensation" if a "taking" had occurred, the rights nevertheless undoubtedly mitigate whatever financial burdens the law has imposed on appellants and, for that reason, are to be taken into account in considering the impact of regulation.

* * *

Affirmed.

Mr. Justice Rehnquist, with whom The Chief Justice and Mr. Justice Stevens join, dissenting.

. . . The question in this case is whether the cost associated with the city of New York's desire to preserve a limited number of "landmarks" within its borders must be borne by all of its taxpayers or whether it can instead be imposed entirely on the owners of the individual properties.

* * *

I

The Fifth Amendment provides in part: "nor shall private property be taken for public use, without just compensation." In a very literal sense, the actions of appellees violated this constitutional prohibition. Before the city of New York declared Grand Central Terminal to be a landmark, Penn Central could have used its "air rights" over the Terminal to build a multistory office building, at an apparent value of several million dollars per year. Today, the Terminal cannot be modified in *any* form, including the erection of additional stories, without the permission of the Landmark Preservation Commission, a permission which appellants, despite good-faith attempts, have so far been unable to obtain. . . .

* * *

B

Appellees have thus destroyed — in a literal sense, "taken" — substantial property rights of Penn Central. While the term "taken" might have been narrowly interpreted to include only physical seizures of property rights, "the construction of the phrase has not been so narrow. The courts have held that the deprivation of the former owner rather than the accretion of a right or interest to the sovereign constitutes the taking." *See also United States v. Lynah* (1903);[7] *Dugan v. Rank* (1963). Because "not every destruction or injury to property by governmental action has been held to be a 'taking' in the constitutional sense," however, this does not end our inquiry. But an examination of the two exceptions where the destruction of property does *not* constitute a taking demonstrates that a compensable taking has occurred here.

1

As early as 1887, the Court recognized that the government can prevent a property owner from using his property to injure others without having to compensate the owner for the value of the forbidden use.

> "A prohibition simply upon the use of property for purposes that are declared, by valid legislation, to be *injurious to the health, morals, or safety of the community*, cannot, in any just sense, be deemed a taking or an appropriation of property for the public benefit. Such legislation does not disturb the owner in the control or use of his property for lawful purposes, nor restrict his right to dispose of it, but is only a declaration by the State that its use by any one, for certain forbidden purposes, is prejudicial to the public interests. . . . The power which the States have of prohibiting such use by individuals of their property as will be prejudicial to the health, the morals, or the safety of the public, is not — and, consistently with the existence and safety of organized society, cannot be — burdened with the condition that the State must compensate such individual owners for pecuniary losses they may sustain, *by reason of their not being permitted, by a noxious use of their property, to inflict injury upon the community*." *Mugler v. Kansas* [(1887)]. . . .

---

[7] "Such a construction would pervert the constitutional provision into a restriction upon the rights of the citizen, as those rights stood at the common law, instead of the government, and make it an authority for invasion of private right under the pretext of the public good, which had no warrant in the laws or practices of our ancestors." 188 U.S. at 470.

. . . The prohibition in question, however, was "not a prevention of a misuse or illegal use but the prevention of a legal and essential use, an attribute of its ownership."

Appellees are not prohibiting a nuisance. The record is clear that the proposed addition to the Grand Central Terminal would be in full compliance with zoning, height limitations, and other health and safety requirements. Instead, appellees are seeking to preserve what they believe to be an outstanding example of beaux arts architecture. Penn Central is prevented from further developing its property basically because *too good* a job was done in designing and building it. The city of New York, because of its unadorned admiration for the design, has decided that the owners of the building must preserve it unchanged for the benefit of sightseeing New Yorkers and tourists.

Unlike land-use regulations, appellees' actions do not merely *prohibit* Penn Central from using its property in a narrow set of noxious ways. Instead, appellees have placed an *affirmative* duty on Penn Central to maintain the Terminal in its present state and in "good repair." . . .

2

Even where the government prohibits a noninjurious use, the Court has ruled that a taking does not take place if the prohibition applies over a broad cross section of land and thereby "secure[s] an average reciprocity of advantage." *Pennsylvania Coal Co. v. Mahon*. It is for this reason that zoning does not constitute a "taking." While zoning at times reduces *individual* property values, the burden is shared relatively evenly and it is reasonable to conclude that on the whole an individual who is harmed by one aspect of the zoning will be benefited by another.

Here, however, a multimillion dollar loss has been imposed on appellants; it is uniquely felt and is not offset by any benefits flowing from the preservation of some 400 other "landmarks" in New York City. Appellees have imposed a substantial cost on less than one one-tenth of one percent of the buildings in New York City for the general benefit of all its people. It is exactly this imposition of general costs on a few individuals at which the "taking" protection is directed. The Fifth Amendment:

> "prevents the public from loading upon one individual more than his just share of the burdens of government, and says that when he surrenders to the public something more and different from that which is exacted from other members of the public, a full and just equivalent shall be returned to him."

Monongahela Navigation Co. v. United States (1893).

Less than 20 years ago, this Court reiterated that the:

> "Fifth Amendment's guarantee that private property shall not be taken for a public use without just compensation was designed to bar Gov-

ernment from forcing some people alone to bear public burdens which, in all fairness and justice, should be borne by the public as a whole."

Armstrong v. United States [(1960)]. *Cf. Nashville, C. & St. L. R. Co. v. Walters* (1935).11

As Mr. Justice Holmes pointed out in *Pennsylvania Coal Co. v. Mahon*, "the question at bottom" in an eminent domain case "is upon whom the loss of the changes desired should fall." The benefits that appellees believe will flow from preservation of the Grand Central Terminal will accrue to all the citizens of New York City. There is no reason to believe that appellants will enjoy a substantially greater share of these benefits. If the cost of preserving Grand Central Terminal were spread evenly across the entire population of the city of New York, the burden per person would be in cents per year — a minor cost appellees would surely concede for the benefit accrued. Instead, however, appellees would impose the entire cost of several million dollars per year on Penn Central. But it is precisely this sort of discrimination that the Fifth Amendment prohibits.

Appellees in response would argue that a taking only occurs where a property owner is denied *all* reasonable value of his property.13 The Court has frequently held that, even where a destruction of property rights would not *otherwise* constitute a taking, the inability of the owner to make a reasonable return on his property requires compensation under the Fifth Amendment. But the converse is not true. A taking does not become a noncompensable exercise of police power simply because the government in its grace allows the owner to make some "reasonable" use of his property. "[I]t is the character of the invasion, not the amount of damage resulting from it, so long as the damage is substantial, that determines the question whether it is a taking."

---

11 "It is true that the police power embraces regulations designed to promote public convenience or the general welfare, and not merely those in the interest of public health, safety and morals. . . . But when particular individuals are singled out to bear the cost of advancing the public convenience, that imposition must bear some reasonable relation to the evils to be eradicated or the advantages to be secured. . . . While moneys raised by general taxation may constitutionally be applied to purposes from which the individual taxed may receive no benefit, and indeed, suffer serious detriment, . . . so-called assessments for public improvements laid upon particular property owners are ordinarily constitutional only if based on benefits received by them."

13 Difficult conceptual and legal problems are posed by a rule that a taking only occurs where the property owner is denied all reasonable return on his property. Not only must the Court define "reasonable return" for a variety of types of property (farmlands, residential properties, commercial and industrial areas), but the Court must define the particular property unit that should be examined. For example, in this case, if appellees are viewed as having restricted Penn Central's use of its "air rights," *all* return has been denied. *See Pennsylvania Coal Co. v. Mahon* (1922). The Court does little to resolve these questions in its opinion. Thus, at one point, the Court implies that the question is whether the restrictions have "an unduly harsh impact upon the owner's use of the property"; at another point, the question is phrased as whether Penn Central can obtain "a 'reasonable return' on its investment"; and, at yet another point, the question becomes whether the landmark is "economically viable."

C

Appellees, apparently recognizing that the constraints imposed on a landmark site constitute a taking for Fifth Amendment purposes, do not leave the property owner empty-handed. As the Court notes, the property owner may theoretically "transfer" his previous right to develop the landmark property to adjacent properties if they are under his control. Appellees have coined this system "Transfer Development Rights," or TDR's.

Of all the terms used in the Taking Clause, "just compensation" has the strictest meaning. The Fifth Amendment does not allow simply an approximate compensation but requires "a full and perfect equivalent for the property taken." . . .

. . . Because the record on appeal is relatively slim, I would remand to the Court of Appeals for a determination of whether TDR's constitute a "full and perfect equivalent for the property taken."

II

Over 50 years ago, Mr. Justice Holmes, speaking for the Court, warned that the courts were "in danger of forgetting that a strong public desire to improve the public condition is not enough to warrant achieving the desire by a shorter cut than the constitutional way of paying for the change." *Pennsylvania Coal Co. v. Mahon*. The Court's opinion in this case demonstrates that the danger thus foreseen has not abated. The city of New York is in a precarious financial state, and some may believe that the costs of landmark preservation will be more easily borne by corporations such as Penn Central than the overburdened individual taxpayers of New York. But these concerns do not allow us to ignore past precedents construing the Eminent Domain Clause to the end that the desire to improve the public condition is, indeed, achieved by a shorter cut than the constitutional way of paying for the change.

NOTES AND QUESTIONS

1. The Zeitgeist was at work in Justice Brennan's majority opinion in *Penn Central*. Without comment, Brennan adopts Justice Brandeis' dissenting opinion in *Pennsylvania Coal* with respect to the calculation of loss. Unlike the holding in *Pennsylvania Coal*, losses associated with regulatory takings are to be calculated in reference to the whole property, not merely the regulated portion. As Justice Rehnquist reflected in footnote 13 of his dissent, this disregard of prior precedent poses "difficult conceptual and legal problems" regarding the definition of the property interest for purposes of regulatory taking assessment which the majority chooses to ignore or state inconsistently. As we will see, the Court will return to this difficulty in *Lucas v. South Carolina Coastal Council* considered later in this Chapter.

2. The entire difficulty of calculating loss is, as mentioned in earlier notes, traceable to the unfortunate reliance by Justice Holmes upon this factor as a measure of a regulatory taking. The more apt inquiry is whether property is being regulated for a genuine police power purpose — that is, the prevention of something equivalent to a common law nuisance. On this issue, Justice Brennan revises both the majority and dissenting opinions of *Pennsylvania Coal*; both Holmes and Brandeis linked the police power with the avoidance of nuisance-like harms. As Justice Rehnquist relates, this is not the purpose of the New York landmark preservation ordinance. He writes: "Appellees are not prohibiting a nuisance. . . . Instead, appellees have placed an *affirmative* duty on Penn Central to maintain the Terminal in its present state and in 'good repair.'" 438 U.S. at 146 (Rehnquist, J., dissenting).

3. Does this mean the police power is confined to the prevention of harm? A case can be made for this. *See* Douglas W. Kmiec, *Inserting the Last Remaining Pieces into the Takings Puzzle*, 38 WM. & MARY L. REV. 995 (1997). Justice Rehnquist is somewhat more deferential to broader exercises of the police power, writing that in addition to the prevention of harm, the police power can be used to impose a broadly applicable regulation that secures an "average reciprocity of advantage" and de minimis losses in value. 438 U.S. at 147 (Rehnquist, J., dissenting). By virtue of this statement, Justice Rehnquist would allow garden-variety zoning ordinances that are generally applied and do not involve substantial, individualized losses. By contrast, it is not immediately clear whether any regulation falls outside the undifferentiated conception of the police power nursed along by Justice Brennan. Justice Brennan writes in footnote 30 that there is no difference in his mind between the prohibition of noxious uses and regulation designed to produce a widespread public benefit. Note that the only authority Justice Brennan cites for this assertion is a law review article. In footnote 7 of the dissent, Justice Rehnquist answers that Justice Brennan's novel construction makes the police power "'an authority for invasion of private right under the pretext of public good, which had no warrant in the laws or practices of our ancestors.'" *Id.* at 144 n.7 (Rehnquist, J., dissenting) (quoting *United States v. Lynah*, 188 U.S. 445, 470 (1903)).

4. How far can a regulation go before it will be considered a "taking"? If a regulation deprives private property of all beneficial use, does it matter whether the regulation is designed to prevent harm? Is it even possible to distinguish between regulations that prevent harm and those that confer benefits on the general public? Justice Scalia takes up these thorny issues in the next case.

LUCAS v. SOUTH CAROLINA COASTAL COUNCIL
505 U.S. 1003 (1992)

JUSTICE SCALIA delivered the opinion of the Court.

In 1986, petitioner David H. Lucas paid $975,000 for two residential lots on the Isle of Palms in Charleston County, South Carolina, on which he intended to build single-family homes. In 1988, however, the South Carolina Legislature enacted the Beachfront Management Act, which had the direct effect of barring petitioner from erecting any permanent habitable structures on his two parcels. A state trial court found that this prohibition rendered Lucas's parcels "valueless." This case requires us to decide whether the Act's dramatic effect on the economic value of Lucas's lots accomplished a taking of private property under the Fifth and Fourteenth Amendments requiring the payment of "just compensation." U.S. CONST., Amdt. 5.

* * *

III

A

* * *

[O]ur decision in [*Pennsylvania Coal v.*] *Mahon* offered little insight into when, and under what circumstances, a given regulation would be seen as going "too far" for purposes of the Fifth Amendment. In 70-odd years of succeeding "regulatory takings" jurisprudence, we have generally eschewed any "'set formula'" for determining how far is too far, preferring to "[e]ngage in . . . essentially ad hoc, factual inquiries." *Penn Central Transportation Co. v. New York City* (1978). We have, however, described at least two discrete categories of regulatory action as compensable without case-specific inquiry into the public interest advanced in support of the restraint. The first encompasses regulations that compel the property owner to suffer a physical "invasion" of his property. In general (at least with regard to permanent invasions), no matter how minute the intrusion, and no matter how weighty the public purpose behind it, we have required compensation. For example, in *Loretto v. Teleprompter Manhattan CATV Corp.* (1982), we determined that New York's law requiring landlords to allow television cable companies to emplace cable facilities in their apartment buildings constituted a taking. . . .

The second situation in which we have found categorical treatment appropriate is where regulation denies all economically beneficial or productive use of land. . . .[7]

---

[7] Regrettably, the rhetorical force of our "deprivation of all economically feasible use" rule is greater than its precision, since the rule does not make clear the "property interest" against which the loss of value is to be measured. When, for example, a regulation requires a developer to leave 90% of a rural tract in its natural state, it is unclear whether we would analyze the situation as one in which the owner has been deprived of all economically beneficial use of the burdened portion of the tract, or as one in which the owner has suffered a mere diminution in value of the tract as a whole. (For an extreme — and, we think, unsupportable — view of the relevant calculus, *see Penn Central Transportation Co. v. New York City* (N.Y. 1977), *aff'd* (1978), where the state court examined the diminution in a particular parcel's value produced by a municipal ordinance in light of total value of the takings claimant's other holdings in the vicinity.) Unsurprisingly, this uncertainty regarding the composition of the denominator in our "deprivation" fraction has produced inconsis-

We have never set forth the justification for this rule. Perhaps it is simply, as Justice Brennan suggested, that total deprivation of beneficial use is, from the landowner's point of view, the equivalent of a physical appropriation. . . .

On the other side of the balance, affirmatively supporting a compensation requirement, is the fact that regulations that leave the owner of land without economically beneficial or productive options for its use — typically, as here, by requiring land to be left substantially in its natural state — carry with them a heightened risk that private property is being pressed into some form of public service under the guise of mitigating serious public harm. . . .

* * *

B

The trial court found Lucas's two beachfront lots to have been rendered valueless by respondent's enforcement of the coastal-zone construction ban. Under Lucas's theory of the case, which rested upon our "no economically viable use" statements, that finding entitled him to compensation. Lucas believed it unnecessary to take issue with either the purposes behind the Beachfront Management Act, or the means chosen by the South Carolina Legislature to effectuate those purposes. The South Carolina Supreme Court, however, thought otherwise. In its view, the Beachfront Management Act was no ordinary enactment, but involved an exercise of South Carolina's "police powers" to mitigate the harm to the public interest that petitioner's use of his land might occasion. By neglecting to dispute the findings enumerated in the Act or otherwise to challenge the legislature's purposes, petitioner "concede[d] that the beach/dune area of South Carolina's shores is an extremely valuable public resource; that the erection of new construction, *inter alia*, contributes to the erosion and destruction of this public resource; and that discouraging new construction in close proximity to the beach/dune area is necessary to prevent a great public harm." In the court's view, these concessions brought petitioner's challenge within a long line of this Court's cases sustaining against Due Process and Takings Clause challenges the State's use of its "police powers" to enjoin a property owner from activities akin to public nuisances. . . .

It is correct that many of our prior opinions have suggested that "harmful or noxious uses" of property may be proscribed by government regulation without

---

tent pronouncements by the Court. Compare *Pennsylvania Coal Co. v. Mahon* (1922) (law restricting subsurface extraction of coal held to effect a taking), with *Keystone Bituminous Coal Assn. v. DeBenedictis* (1987) (nearly identical law held not to effect a taking). The answer to this difficult question may lie in how the owner's reasonable expectations have been shaped by the State's law of property — *i.e.*, whether and to what degree the State's law has accorded legal recognition and protection to the particular interest in land with respect to which the takings claimant alleges a diminution in (or elimination of) value. In any event, we avoid this difficulty in the present case, since the "interest in land" that Lucas has pleaded (a fee simple interest) is an estate with a rich tradition of protection at common law, and since the South Carolina Court of Common Pleas found that the Beachfront Management Act left each of Lucas's beachfront lots without economic value.

the requirement of compensation. For a number of reasons, however, we think the South Carolina Supreme Court was too quick to conclude that that principle decides the present case. The "harmful or noxious uses" principle was the Court's early attempt to describe in theoretical terms why government may, consistent with the Takings Clause, affect property values by regulation without incurring an obligation to compensate — a reality we nowadays acknowledge explicitly with respect to the full scope of the State's police power. . . .

The transition from our early focus on control of "noxious" uses to our contemporary understanding of the broad realm within which government may regulate without compensation was an easy one, since the distinction between "harm-preventing" and "benefit-conferring" regulation is often in the eye of the beholder. It is quite possible, for example, to describe in *either* fashion the ecological, economic, and esthetic concerns that inspired the South Carolina Legislature in the present case. One could say that imposing a servitude on Lucas's land is necessary in order to prevent his use of it from "harming" South Carolina's ecological resources; or, instead, in order to achieve the "benefits" of an ecological preserve. . . .

When it is understood that "prevention of harmful use" was merely our early formulation of the police power justification necessary to sustain (without compensation) *any* regulatory diminution in value; and that the distinction between regulation that "prevents harmful use" and that which "confers benefits" is difficult, if not impossible, to discern on an objective, value-free basis; it becomes self-evident that noxious-use logic cannot serve as a touchstone to distinguish regulatory "takings" — which require compensation — from regulatory deprivations that do not require compensation. *A fortiori* the legislature's recitation of a noxious-use justification cannot be the basis for departing from our categorical rule that total regulatory takings must be compensated. . . .

Where the State seeks to sustain regulation that deprives land of all economically beneficial use, we think it may resist compensation only if the logically antecedent inquiry into the nature of the owner's estate shows that the proscribed use interests were not part of his title to begin with. This accords, we think, with our "takings" jurisprudence, which has traditionally been guided by the understandings of our citizens regarding the content of, and the State's power over, the "bundle of rights" that they acquire when they obtain title to property. It seems to us that the property owner necessarily expects the uses of his property to be restricted, from time to time, by various measures newly enacted by the State in legitimate exercise of its police powers; "[a]s long recognized, some values are enjoyed under an implied limitation and must yield to the police power." *Pennsylvania Coal Co. v. Mahon.* And in the case of personal property, by reason of the State's traditionally high degree of control over commercial dealings, he ought to be aware of the possibility that new regulation might even render his property economically worthless (at least if the property's only economically productive use is sale or manufacture for sale). In the case of land, however, we think the notion pressed by the Council that title is somehow held subject to the "implied limitation" that the State may subsequently eliminate all economically valuable use is inconsistent with the historical compact recorded in the Takings Clause that has become part of our constitutional culture.

Where "permanent physical occupation" of land is concerned, we have refused to allow the government to decree it anew (without compensation), no matter how weighty the asserted "public interests" involved. . . . Any limitation so severe cannot be newly legislated or decreed (without compensation), but must inhere in the title itself, in the restrictions that background principles of the State's law of property and nuisance already place upon land ownership. A law or decree with such an effect must, in other words, do no more than duplicate the result that could have been achieved in the courts — by adjacent landowners (or other uniquely affected persons) under the State's law of private nuisance, or by the State under its complementary power to abate nuisances that affect the public generally, or otherwise.

On this analysis, the owner of a lake-bed, for example, would not be entitled to compensation when he is denied the requisite permit to engage in a landfilling operation that would have the effect of flooding others' land. Nor the corporate owner of a nuclear generating plant, when it is directed to remove all improvements from its land upon discovery that the plant sits astride an earthquake fault. Such regulatory action may well have the effect of eliminating the land's only economically productive use, but it does not proscribe a productive use that was previously permissible under relevant property and nuisance principles. The use of these properties for what are now expressly prohibited purposes was *always* unlawful, and (subject to other constitutional limitations) it was open to the State at any point to make the implication of those background principles of nuisance and property law explicit. In light of our traditional resort to "existing rules or understandings that stem from an independent source such as state law" to define the range of interests that qualify for protection as "property" under the Fifth and Fourteenth Amendments, this recognition that the Takings Clause does not require compensation when an owner is barred from putting land to a use that is proscribed by those "existing rules or understandings" is surely unexceptional. When, however, a regulation that declares "off-limits" all economically productive or beneficial uses of land goes beyond what the relevant background principles would dictate, compensation must be paid to sustain it.[17]

The "total taking" inquiry we require today will ordinarily entail (as the application of state nuisance law ordinarily entails) analysis of, among other things, the degree of harm to public lands and resources, or adjacent private

---

[17] Of course, the State may elect to rescind its regulation and thereby avoid having to pay compensation for a permanent deprivation. See *First English Evangelical Lutheran Church [of Glendale v. County of Los Angeles* (1987)]. But "where the [regulation has] already worked a taking of all use of property, no subsequent action by the government can relieve it of the duty to provide compensation for the period during which the taking was effective." *Ibid.*

property, posed by the claimant's proposed activities, *see, e.g., Restatement (Second) of Torts* §§ 826, 827, the social value of the claimant's activities and their suitability to the locality in question, *see, e.g., id.,* §§ 828(a) and (b), 831, and the relative ease with which the alleged harm can be avoided through measures taken by the claimant and the government (or adjacent private landowners) alike, *see, e.g., id.,* §§ 827(e), 828(c), 830. The fact that a particular use has long been engaged in by similarly situated owners ordinarily imports a lack of any common-law prohibition (though changed circumstances or new knowledge may make what was previously permissible no longer so, *see id.,* § 827, Comment *g*). So also does the fact that other landowners, similarly situated, are permitted to continue the use denied to the claimant.

It seems unlikely that common-law principles would have prevented the erection of any habitable or productive improvements on petitioner's land; they rarely support prohibition of the "essential use" of land. The question, however, is one of state law to be dealt with on remand. We emphasize that to win its case South Carolina must do more than proffer the legislature's declaration that the uses Lucas desires are inconsistent with the public interest, or the conclusory assertion that they violate a common-law maxim such as *sic utere tuo ut alienum non laedas.* As we have said, a "State, by *ipse dixit,* may not transform private property into public property without compensation . . . ." Instead, as it would be required to do if it sought to restrain Lucas in a common-law action for public nuisance, South Carolina must identify background principles of nuisance and property law that prohibit the uses he now intends in the circumstances in which the property is presently found. Only on this showing can the State fairly claim that, in proscribing all such beneficial uses, the Beachfront Management Act is taking nothing.

* * *

The judgment is reversed, and the case is remanded for proceedings not inconsistent with this opinion.

So ordered.

JUSTICE KENNEDY, concurring in the judgment.

The case comes to the Court in an unusual posture, as all my colleagues observe. After the suit was initiated but before it reached us, South Carolina amended its Beachfront Management Act to authorize the issuance of special permits at variance with the Act's general limitations. Petitioner has not applied for a special permit but may still do so. The availability of this alternative, if it can be invoked, may dispose of petitioner's claim of a permanent taking. As I read the Court's opinion, it does not decide the permanent taking claim, but neither does it foreclose the Supreme Court of South Carolina from considering the claim or requiring petitioner to pursue an administrative alternative not previously available.

The potential for future relief does not control our disposition, because whatever may occur in the future cannot undo what has occurred in the past. The Beachfront Management Act was enacted in 1988. It may have deprived petitioner of the use of his land in an interim period. If this deprivation amounts to a taking, its limited duration will not bar constitutional relief. It is well established that temporary takings are as protected by the Constitution as are permanent ones. *First English Evangelical Lutheran Church of Glendale v. County of Los Angeles* (1987).

The issues presented in the case are ready for our decision. The Supreme Court of South Carolina decided the case on constitutional grounds, and its rulings are now before us. There exists no jurisdictional bar to our disposition, and prudential considerations ought not to militate against it. The State cannot complain of the manner in which the issues arose. . . .

* * *

The finding of no value must be considered under the Takings Clause by reference to the owner's reasonable, investment-backed expectations. The Takings Clause, while conferring substantial protection on property owners, does not eliminate the police power of the State to enact limitations on the use of their property. The rights conferred by the Takings Clause and the police power of the State may coexist without conflict. Property is bought and sold, investments are made, subject to the State's power to regulate. Where a taking is alleged from regulations which deprive the property of all value, the test must be whether the deprivation is contrary to reasonable, investment-backed expectations.

There is an inherent tendency towards circularity in this synthesis, of course; for if the owner's reasonable expectations are shaped by what courts allow as a proper exercise of governmental authority, property tends to become what courts say it is. Some circularity must be tolerated in these matters, however, as it is in other spheres. The definition, moreover, is not circular in its entirety. The expectations protected by the Constitution are based on objective rules and customs that can be understood as reasonable by all parties involved.

In my view, reasonable expectations must be understood in light of the whole of our legal tradition. The common law of nuisance is too narrow a confine for the exercise of regulatory power in a complex and interdependent society. The State should not be prevented from enacting new regulatory initiatives in response to changing conditions, and courts must consider all reasonable expectations whatever their source. The Takings Clause does not require a static body of state property law; it protects private expectations to ensure private investment. I agree with the Court that nuisance prevention accords with the most common expectations of property owners who face regulation, but I do not believe this can be the sole source of state authority to impose severe restrictions. Coastal property may present such unique concerns for a fragile land system that the State can go further in regulating its development and use than the common law of nuisance might otherwise permit.

The Supreme Court of South Carolina erred, in my view, by reciting the general purposes for which the state regulations were enacted without a determination that they were in accord with the owner's reasonable expectations and therefore sufficient to support a severe restriction on specific parcels of property. The promotion of tourism, for instance, ought not to suffice to deprive specific property of all value without a corresponding duty to compensate. Furthermore, the means, as well as the ends, of regulation must accord with the owner's reasonable expectations. Here, the State did not act until after the property had been zoned for individual lot development and most other parcels had been improved, throwing the whole burden of the regulation on the remaining lots. This too must be measured in the balance.

With these observations, I concur in the judgment of the Court.

JUSTICE BLACKMUN, dissenting.

Today the Court launches a missile to kill a mouse.

* * *

II

* * *

. . . The Court creates its new takings jurisprudence based on the trial court's finding that the property had lost all economic value. This finding is almost certainly erroneous. Petitioner still can enjoy other attributes of ownership, such as the right to exclude others, "one of the most essential sticks in the bundle of rights that are commonly characterized as property." Petitioner can picnic, swim, camp in a tent, or live on the property in a movable trailer. State courts frequently have recognized that land has economic value where the only residual economic uses are recreation or camping. Petitioner also retains the right to alienate the land, which would have value for neighbors and for those prepared to enjoy proximity to the ocean without a house.

* * *

V

The Court makes sweeping and, in my view, misguided and unsupported changes in our takings doctrine. While it limits these changes to the most narrow subset of government regulation — those that eliminate all economic value from land — these changes go far beyond what is necessary to secure petitioner Lucas' private benefit. One hopes they do not go beyond the narrow confines the Court assigns them to today.

I dissent.

JUSTICE STEVENS, dissenting.

* * *

II

* * *

In addition to lacking support in past decisions, the Court's new rule is wholly arbitrary. A landowner whose property is diminished in value 95% recovers nothing, while an owner whose property is diminished 100% recovers the land's full value. . . .

Moreover, because of the elastic nature of property rights, the Court's new rule will also prove unsound in practice. In response to the rule, courts may define "property" broadly and only rarely find regulations to effect total takings. . . .

On the other hand, developers and investors may market specialized estates to take advantage of the Court's new rule. The smaller the estate, the more likely that a regulatory change will effect a total taking. Thus, an investor may, for example, purchase the right to build a multifamily home on a specific lot, with the result that a zoning regulation that allows only single-family homes would render the investor's property interest "valueless." In short, the categorical rule will likely have one of two effects: Either courts will alter the definition of the "denominator" in the takings "fraction," rendering the Court's categorical rule meaningless, or investors will manipulate the relevant property interests, giving the Court's rule sweeping effect. To my mind, neither of these results is desirable or appropriate, and both are distortions of our takings jurisprudence.

* * *

[T]he Court suggests that "regulations that leave the owner . . . without economically beneficial . . . use . . . carry with them a heightened risk that private property is being pressed into some form of public service . . . ." I agree that the risks of such singling out are of central concern in takings law. However, such risks do not justify a *per se* rule for total regulatory takings. There is no necessary correlation between "singling out" and total takings: A regulation may single out a property owner without depriving him of all of his property, *see, e.g., Nollan v. California Coastal Comm'n* (1987). . . . What matters in such cases is not the degree of diminution of value, but rather the specificity of the expropriating act. . . .

* * *

The Court's holding today effectively freezes the State's common law, denying the legislature much of its traditional power to revise the law governing the rights and uses of property. Until today, I had thought that we had long abandoned this approach to constitutional law. More than a century ago we recognized that "the great office of statutes is to remedy defects in the common law as they are developed, and to adapt it to the changes of time and circumstances. . . ."

Arresting the development of the common law is not only a departure from our prior decisions; it is also profoundly unwise. The human condition is one of constant learning and evolution — both moral and practical. Legislatures implement that new learning; in doing so they must often revise the definition of property and the rights of property owners. Thus, when the Nation came to understand that slavery was morally wrong and mandated the emancipation of all slaves, it, in effect, redefined "property." On a lesser scale, our ongoing self-education produces similar changes in the rights of property owners: New appreciation of the significance of endangered species; the importance of wetlands; and the vulnerability of coastal lands, shapes our evolving understandings of property rights.

Of course, some legislative redefinitions of property will effect a taking and must be compensated — but it certainly cannot be the case that every movement away from common law does so. There is no reason, and less sense, in such an absolute rule. We live in a world in which changes in the economy and the environment occur with increasing frequency and importance. . . .

The Court's categorical approach rule will, I fear, greatly hamper the efforts of local officials and planners who must deal with increasingly complex problems in land-use and environmental regulation. . . .

* * *

III

* * *

The Just Compensation Clause "was designed to bar Government from forcing some people alone to bear public burdens which, in all fairness and justice, should be borne by the public as a whole." Accordingly, one of the central concerns of our takings jurisprudence is "prevent[ing] the public from loading upon one individual more than his just share of the burdens of government . . . ." We have, therefore, in our takings law frequently looked to the *generality* of a regulation of property.

. . . Similarly, in distinguishing between the Kohler Act (at issue in *Mahon*) and the Subsidence Act (at issue in *Keystone*), we found significant that the regulatory function of the latter was substantially broader. Unlike the Kohler Act, which simply transferred back to the surface owners certain rights that they had earlier sold to the coal companies, the Subsidence Act affected all surface owners — including the coal companies — equally. Perhaps the most familiar application of this principle of generality arises in zoning cases. A diminution in value caused by a zoning regulation is far less likely to constitute a taking if it is part of a general and comprehensive land-use plan; conversely, "spot zoning" is far more likely to constitute a taking.

* * *

Accordingly, I respectfully dissent.

Statement of JUSTICE SOUTER.

I would dismiss the writ of certiorari in this case as having been granted improvidently.

NOTES AND QUESTIONS

1. The linchpin of *Lucas* is its establishment of a relationship between the application of the Takings Clause and the meaning of property under state law. This "solved" the takings puzzle by effectively letting the Court check legislative and regulatory abuse under the text of the Fifth Amendment without seeming to usurp legislative function. The reasons why the *Lucas* antecedent inquiry solves the takings puzzle is a long story, but its essence is this: reliance upon an objective, third party source or definition for property and corresponding police power limits thereon (primarily state judges in common law proceedings) precludes the Justices from substituting their own will a la *Lochner*, and avoids the abdication of judicial enforcement of the Takings Clause that is entailed when the Court deferentially allows the legislature to redefine private property as it sees fit, even post-investment. *See* Douglas W. Kmiec, *At Last, The Supreme Court Solves the Takings Puzzle*, 19 HARV. J. L. & PUB. POL'Y 147, 151-54 (1995); Douglas W. Kmiec, *Inserting the Last Remaining Pieces into the Takings Puzzle*, 38 WM. & MARY L. REV. 995, 1009-10 (1997).

2. What should happen if, after the decision in *Lucas*, the South Carolina legislature chose to repeal the Beachfront Management Act rather than pay Lucas a "just compensation"? The Supreme Court considered the remedy issue in *First English Evangelical Lutheran Church v. County of Los Angeles*, 482 U.S. 304 (1987). After a flood destroyed First English's summer camp facilities, Los Angeles County enacted an ordinance barring their reconstruction, and the Church promptly filed suit claiming that the ordinance effected an inverse condemnation of its property for which it was entitled to just compensation. Six years later, the California Supreme Court had still not ruled on the merits of the Church's claim, but held that the Church was not entitled to damages for the interim loss of use of its property even if the ordinance was a taking. Comparing the Church's temporary loss to World War II-era cases holding that the Takings Clause required payment of just compensation for temporary physical takings, the Supreme Court noted that

> "temporary" takings which, as here, deny a landowner all use of his property, are not different in kind from permanent takings, for which the Constitution clearly requires compensation. It is axiomatic that the Fifth Amendment's just compensation provision is "designed to bar Government from forcing some people alone to bear public burdens which,

in all fairness and justice, should be borne by the public as a whole." In the present case the interim ordinance was adopted by the County of Los Angeles in January 1979, and became effective immediately. Appellant filed suit within a month after the effective date of the ordinance and yet when the California Supreme Court denied a hearing in the case on October 17, 1985, the merits of appellant's claim had yet to be determined. The United States has been required to pay compensation for leasehold interests of shorter duration than this. The value of a leasehold interest in property for a period of years may be substantial, and the burden on the property owner in extinguishing such an interest for a period of years may be great indeed. Where this burden results from governmental action that amounted to a taking, the Just Compensation Clause of the Fifth Amendment requires that the government pay the landowner for the value of the use of the land during this period. *Cf. United States v. Causby* ("It is the owner's loss, not the taker's gain, which is the measure of the value of the property taken"). Invalidation of the ordinance or its successor ordinance after this period of time, though converting the taking into a "temporary" one, is not a sufficient remedy to meet the demands of the Just Compensation Clause.

Justice Stevens, in dissent, contended that there was a distinction between temporary physical occupations and temporary regulatory imposition, and that with respect to the latter, the courts should assess both the scope of the regulation and its duration before determining that it has caused such a diminution in the property's value as to amount to a taking. While he acknowledged that even temporary restrictions on the use of property would amount to a compensable taking if the were both substantial and remained in effect for a significant percentage of the property's useful life, the few years for which First English was restricted in the use of its property was not a taking, in his view.

3. In *Tahoe-Sierra Preservation Council, Inc. v. Tahoe Regional Planning Agency*, 122 S. Ct. 1465 (2002), the Supreme Court severely limited the reach of *First English* and of *Lucas*, holding that a temporary development moratoria did not constitute a per se taking under *Lucas* but rather should be assessed under the balancing test applied in *Penn Central*. Justice Stevens, writing for six members of the Court, held that the "denominator" question addressed in *Penn Central* applied as much to the "temporal" dimension of property as to the geographic dimension; because only regulations that deprive a property owner of all economically viable use of the entire parcel are considered categorical takings under *Lucas*, a temporary regulation that restricts a property's use only during a discreet temporal segment rather than the entire life of the parcel is not a categorical taking. In separate dissents, Chief Justice Rehnquist and Justice Thomas, joined by Justice Scalia, contended that *First English* required treating as a taking the temporary deprivation of all economic use beyond the normal delays in the development permit process. "I had thought that *First English* put to rest the notion that the 'relevant denominator' is land's infinite life," noted Justice Thomas.

4. As the Court noted in *Lucas*, even minor physical occupations are takings for which just compensation must be paid. *See Loretto v. Teleprompter Manhattan CATV Corp.*, 458 U.S. 419 (1982) (invalidating a New York ordinance which authorized the coercive installation of cable television. Such regulations are invalid without regard to assessment of public purpose or economic impact). But what of physical occupations made pursuant to a regulatory policy, exacted as a condition on a governmental permit? Are they to be treated as regulatory takings or as physical takings? In *Nollan v. California Coastal Commission*, 483 U.S. 825 (1987), the Court considered whether the California Coastal Commission could require an ocean-front property owner to convey a public-access easement as a condition on obtaining a building permit. The Commission contended that because it had a legitimate governmental interest in protecting the public's view of the ocean, which it could further by denying Nollan's building permit altogether, the easement was a permissible permit condition. Justice Scalia, writing for a 5-4 majority of the Court, held that the exaction was a compensable taking. "[U]nless the permit condition serves the same governmental purpose as the development ban," he noted, "the building restriction is not a valid regulation of land use but 'an out-and-out plan of extortion.'"

5. Even when a permit condition has a nexus to a legitimate governmental interest, the exaction must bear a "roughly proportionality" to the impact to the public posed by the permitted use. *Dolan v. City of Tigard*, 512 U.S. 374 (1994), involved whether the City of Tigard, Oregon, could require Dolan to convey a 15-foot strip of land — about 10% of his property — as a condition on granting Dolan a permit to expand his plumbing and electric supply store. The City wanted the land for flood control purposes (to help mitigate the additional run-off that would be caused by Dolan's additional paving on his property) and also for a bike path (to help mitigate the increased traffic that would result from the expanded business use of the property). The Court held that both conditions had a sufficient nexus to the proposed expansion, but that they were invalid because not "roughly proportional" to the impact posed by the development. An open space requirement would have sufficed to address the City's flood control concerns, noted the Court, "[b]ut the city demanded more — it not only wanted petitioner not to build in the floodplain, but it also wanted petitioner's property along Fanno Creek for its greenway system. The city has never said why a public greenway, as opposed to a private one, was required in the interest of flood control." As for the bike path, the Court held that the City had "not met its burden of demonstrating that the additional number of vehicle and bicycle trips generated by the development" was reasonably related to the requirement that Dolan dedicate a bike path easement. For more on the issues addressed in *Nollan* and *Dolan, see* Douglas W. Kmiec, *The Original Understanding of the Taking Clause is Neither Weak Nor Obtuse*, 88 COLUM. L. REV. 1630, 1650-52 (1988).

6. A fair government is assured not only by the protection of vested contract and property rights, but also by the observance of fair procedures. This idea is embodied in the Due Process Clauses of the Fifth and Fourteenth Amendments, a topic to which we now turn. Our initial inquiry is into a concept called "state action," reflecting the fact that the obligation of fair process is one that applies to governmental entities, not individuals. The natural law obligations of individuals to do justice are not capable of enforcement under law since, as the great natural law thinker Thomas Aquinas observed, the law is not to enact every virtue or prohibit every vice. It is instead to legislate against the "more grievous vices . . . chiefly those that are to the hurt of others, without the prohibition of which human society could not be maintained: thus human law prohibits murder, theft, and suchlike." II THOMAS AQUINAS, SUMMA THEOLOGICA, Q. 96, art. 2 (Fathers of the English Dominican Province trans., Benzinger Brothers 1947). Consider as you read the due process materials whether the Constitution has been interpreted to prohibit more or less of the grievous vices.

II. Procedural Due Process

A. What Constitutes State Action?

THE CIVIL RIGHTS CASES
109 U.S. 3 (1883)

These cases were all founded on the first and second sections of the Act of Congress, known as the Civil Rights Act, passed March 1st, 1875, entitled "An Act to protect all citizens in their civil and legal rights." . . . Two of the cases, those against Stanley and Nichols, were indictments for denying to persons of color the accommodations and privileges of an inn or hotel; two of them, those against Ryan and Singleton, were . . . for denying to individuals the privileges and accommodations of a theatre, . . . "said denial not being made for any reasons by law applicable to citizens of every race and color, and regardless of any previous condition of servitude." The case of Robinson and wife against the Memphis & Charleston R.R. Company was an action brought . . . to recover the penalty of five hundred dollars given by the second section of the act; and the gravamen was the refusal by the conductor of the railroad company to allow the wife to ride in the ladies' car, for the reason, as stated in one of the counts, that she was a person of African descent. The jury rendered a verdict for the defendants in this case upon the merits, under a charge of the court to which a bill of exceptions was taken by the plaintiffs. The case was tried on the assumption by both parties of the validity of the act of Congress. . . .

* * *

MR. JUSTICE BRADLEY delivered the opinion of the court. . . .

It is obvious that the primary and important question in all the cases is the constitutionality of the law: for if the law is unconstitutional none of the prosecutions can stand.

The sections of the law referred to provide as follows:

"Sec. 1. That all persons within the jurisdiction of the United States shall be entitled to the full and equal enjoyment of the accommodations, advantages, facilities, and privileges of inns, public conveyances on land or water, theatres, and other places of public amusement; subject only to the conditions and limitations established by law, and applicable alike to citizens of every race and color, regardless of any previous condition of servitude.

"Sec. 2. That any person who shall violate the foregoing section by denying to any citizen, except for reasons by law applicable to citizens of every race and color, and regardless of any previous condition of servitude, the full enjoyment of any of the accommodations, advantages, facilities, or privileges in said section enumerated, or by aiding or inciting such denial, shall for every such offence forfeit and pay the sum of five hundred dollars to the person aggrieved thereby, to be recovered in an action of debt, with full costs; and shall also, for every such offence, be deemed guilty of a misdemeanor, and, upon conviction thereof, shall be fined not less than five hundred nor more than one thousand dollars, or shall be imprisoned not less than thirty days nor more than one year. . . ."

* * *

Has Congress constitutional power to make such a law? Of course, no one will contend that the power to pass it was contained in the Constitution before the adoption of the last three amendments. The power is sought, first, in the Fourteenth Amendment, and the views and arguments of distinguished Senators, advanced whilst the law was under consideration, claiming authority to pass it by virtue of that amendment, are the principal arguments adduced in favor of the power. . . .

The first section of the Fourteenth Amendment . . . declares that:

"No State shall make or enforce any law which shall abridge the privileges or immunities of citizens of the United States; nor shall any State deprive any person of life, liberty, or property without due process of law; nor deny to any person within its jurisdiction the equal protection of the laws."

It is State action of a particular character that is prohibited. Individual invasion of individual rights is not the subject-matter of the amendment. It has a deeper and broader scope. It nullifies and makes void all State legislation, and State action of every kind, which impairs the privileges and immunities of citizens of the United States, or which injures them in life, liberty or property without due process of law, or which denies to any of them the equal protection of the laws. It not only does this, but, in order that the national will, thus declared, may not be a mere *brutum fulmen*, the last section of the amendment invests Congress with power to enforce it by appropriate legislation. To enforce what? To enforce the prohibition. To adopt appropriate legislation for correcting the effects of such prohibited State laws and State acts, and thus to render them effectually null, void, and innocuous. This is the legislative power conferred upon Congress, and this is the whole of it. It does not invest Congress with power to legislate upon subjects which are within the domain of State legislation; but to provide modes of relief against State legislation, or State action, of the kind referred to. It does not authorize Congress to create a code of municipal law for the regulation of private rights; but to provide modes of redress against the operation of State laws, and the action of State officers executive or judicial, when these are subversive of the fundamental rights specified in the amendment. . . .

An apt illustration of this distinction may be found in some of the provisions of the original Constitution. Take the subject of contracts, for example. The Constitution prohibited the States from passing any law impairing the obligation of contracts. This did not give to Congress power to provide laws for the general enforcement of contracts; nor power to invest the courts of the United States with jurisdiction over contracts, so as to enable parties to sue upon them in those courts. . . .

And so in the present case, until some State law has been passed, or some State action through its officers or agents has been taken, adverse to the rights of citizens sought to be protected by the Fourteenth Amendment, no legislation of the United States under said amendment, nor any proceeding under such legislation, can be called into activity: for the prohibitions of the amendment are against State laws and acts done under State authority. . . .

An inspection of the law shows that it makes no reference whatever to any supposed or apprehended violation of the Fourteenth Amendment on the part of the States. . . .

If this legislation is appropriate for enforcing the prohibitions of the amendment, it is difficult to see where it is to stop. Why may not Congress with equal show of authority enact a code of laws for the enforcement and vindication of all rights of life, liberty, and property? If it is supposable that the States may deprive persons of life, liberty, and property without due process of law (and the amendment itself does suppose this), why should not Congress proceed at once to prescribe due process of law for the protection of every one of these fundamental rights, in every possible case, as well as to prescribe equal privileges in inns, public conveyances, and theatres? The truth is, that the implication of a power to legislate in this manner is based upon the assumption that if the States are forbidden to legislate or act in a particular way on a particular subject, and power is conferred upon Congress to enforce the prohibition, this gives Congress power to legislate generally upon that subject, and not merely power to provide modes of redress against such State legislation or action. The assumption is certainly unsound. It is repugnant to the Tenth Amendment of the Constitution, which declares that powers not delegated to the United States by the Constitution, nor prohibited by it to the States, are reserved to the States respectively or to the people.

* * *

In this connection it is proper to state that civil rights, such as are guaranteed by the Constitution against State aggression, cannot be impaired by the wrongful acts of individuals, unsupported by State authority in the shape of laws, customs, or judicial or executive proceedings. The wrongful act of an individual, unsupported by any such authority, is simply a private wrong, or a crime of that individual . . . .

Of course, these remarks do not apply to those cases in which Congress is clothed with direct and plenary powers of legislation over the whole subject, accompanied with an express or implied denial of such power to the States, as in the regulation of commerce with foreign nations, among the several States, and with the Indian tribes, the coining of money, the establishment of post offices and post roads, the declaring of war, etc. In these cases Congress has power to pass laws for regulating the subjects specified in every detail, and the conduct and transactions of individuals in respect thereof. But where a subject is not submitted to the general legislative power of Congress, but is only submitted thereto for the purpose of rendering effective some prohibition against particular State legislation or State action in reference to that subject, the power given is limited by its object, and any legislation by Congress in the matter must necessarily be corrective in its character, adapted to counteract and redress the operation of such prohibited State laws or proceedings of State officers.

. . . This is not corrective legislation; it is primary and direct; it takes immediate and absolute possession of the subject of the right of admission to inns, public conveyances, and places of amusement. It supersedes and displaces State legislation on the same subject, or only allows it permissive force. . . .

* * *

But the power of Congress to adopt direct and primary, as distinguished from corrective legislation, on the subject in hand, is sought, in the second place, from the Thirteenth Amendment, which abolishes slavery. This amendment declares "that neither slavery, nor involuntary servitude, except as a punishment for crime, whereof the party shall have been duly convicted, shall exist within the United States, or any place subject to their jurisdiction;" and it gives Congress power to enforce the amendment by appropriate legislation.

This amendment, as well as the Fourteenth, is undoubtedly self-executing without any ancillary legislation, so far as its terms are applicable to any existing state of circumstances. By its own unaided force and effect it abolished slavery, and established universal freedom. Still, legislation may be necessary and proper to meet all the various cases and circumstances to be affected by it, and to prescribe proper modes of redress for its violation in letter or spirit. And such legislation may be primary and direct in its character; for the amendment is not a mere prohibition of State laws establishing or upholding slavery, but an absolute declaration that slavery or involuntary servitude shall not exist in any part of the United States.

It is true, that slavery cannot exist without law, any more than property in lands and goods can exist without law: and, therefore, the Thirteenth Amendment may be regarded as nullifying all State laws which establish or uphold slavery. But it has a reflex character also, establishing and decreeing universal civil and political freedom throughout the United States; and it is assumed, that the power vested in Congress to enforce the article by appropriate legislation, clothes Congress with power to pass all laws necessary and proper for abolishing all badges and incidents of slavery in the United States: and upon this assumption it is claimed, that this is sufficient authority for declaring by law that all persons shall have equal accommodations and privileges in all inns, public conveyances, and places of amusement; the argument being, that the denial of such equal accommodations and privileges is, in itself, a subjection to a species of servitude within the meaning of the amendment. Conceding the major proposition to be true, that Congress has a right to enact all necessary and proper laws for the obliteration and prevention of slavery with all its badges and incidents, is the minor proposition also true, that the denial to any person of admission to the accommodations and privileges of an inn, a public conveyance, or a theatre, does subject that person to any form of servitude, or tend to fasten upon him any badge of slavery? . . .

In a very able and learned presentation of the cognate question as to the extent of the rights, privileges and immunities of citizens which cannot rightfully be abridged by state laws under the Fourteenth Amendment, made in a former case, a long list of burdens and disabilities of a servile character, incident to feudal vassalage in France, and which were abolished by the decrees of the National Assembly, was presented for the purpose of showing that all inequalities and observances exacted by one man from another were servitudes, or badges of slavery, which a great nation, in its effort to establish universal liberty, made haste to wipe out and destroy. But these were servitudes imposed by the old law, or by long custom, which had the force of law, and exacted by one man from another without the latter's consent. Should any such servitudes be imposed by a state law, there can be no doubt that the law would be repugnant to the Fourteenth, no less than to the Thirteenth Amendment; nor any greater doubt that Congress has adequate power to forbid any such servitude from being exacted.

But is there any similarity between such servitudes and a denial by the owner of an inn, a public conveyance, or a theatre, of its accommodations and privileges to an individual, even though the denial be founded on the race or color of that individual? Where does any slavery or servitude, or badge of either, arise from such an act of denial? Whether it might not be a denial of a right which, if sanctioned by the state law, would be obnoxious to the prohibitions of the Fourteenth Amendment, is another question. But what has it to do with the question of slavery?

It may be that by the Black Code (as it was called), in the times when slavery prevailed, the proprietors of inns and public conveyances were forbidden to receive persons of the African race, because it might assist slaves to escape from the control of their masters. This was merely a means of preventing such escapes, and was no part of the servitude itself. A law of that kind could not have any such object now, however justly it might be deemed an invasion of the party's legal right as a citizen, and amenable to the prohibitions of the Fourteenth Amendment.

The long existence of African slavery in this country gave us very distinct notions of what it was, and what were its necessary incidents. Compulsory service of the slave for the benefit of the master, restraint of his movements except by the master's will, disability to hold property, to make contracts, to have a standing in court, to be a witness against a white person, and such like burdens and incapacities, were the inseparable incidents of the institution. Severer punishments for crimes were imposed on the slave than on free persons guilty of the same offences. Congress, as we have seen, by the Civil Rights Bill of 1866, passed in view of the Thirteenth Amendment, before the Fourteenth was adopted, undertook to wipe out these burdens and disabilities, the necessary incidents of slavery, constituting its substance and visible form; and to secure to all citizens of every race and color, and without regard to previous servitude, those fundamental rights which are the essence of civil freedom, namely, the same right to make and enforce contracts, to sue, be parties, give evidence, and to inherit, purchase, lease, sell and convey property, as is enjoyed by white citizens. Whether this legislation was fully authorized by the Thirteenth Amendment alone, without the support which it afterward received from the Fourteenth Amendment, after the adoption of which it was re-enacted with some additions, it is not necessary to inquire. It is referred to for the purpose of showing that at that time (in 1866) Congress did not assume, under the authority given by the Thirteenth Amendment, to adjust what may be called the social rights of men and races in the community; but only to declare and vindicate those fundamental rights which appertain to the essence of citizenship, and the enjoyment or deprivation of which constitutes the essential distinction between freedom and slavery.

* * *

The only question under the present head, therefore, is, whether the refusal to any persons of the accommodations of an inn, or a public conveyance, or a place of public amusement, by an individual, and without any sanction or support from any State law or regulation, does inflict upon such persons any manner of servitude, or form of slavery, as those terms are understood in this country? Many wrongs may be obnoxious to the prohibitions of the Fourteenth Amendment which are not, in any just sense, incidents or elements of slavery. . . . The Thirteenth Amendment has respect, not to distinctions of race, or class, or color, but to slavery. The Fourteenth Amendment extends its protection to races and classes, and prohibits any State legislation which has the effect of denying to any race or class, or to any individual, the equal protection of the laws.

Now, conceding, for the sake of the argument, that the admission to an inn, a public conveyance, or a place of public amusement, on equal terms with all other citizens, is the right of every man and all classes of men, is it any more than one of those rights which the states by the Fourteenth Amendment are forbidden to deny to any person? And is the Constitution violated until the denial of the right has some State sanction or authority? Can the act of a mere individual, the owner of the inn, the public conveyance or place of amusement, refusing the accommodation, be justly regarded as imposing any badge of slavery or servitude upon the applicant, or only as inflicting an ordinary civil injury, properly cognizable by the laws of the State, and presumably subject to redress by those laws until the contrary appears?

. . . It would be running the slavery argument into the ground to make it apply to every act of discrimination which a person may see fit to make as to the guests he will entertain, or as to the people he will take into his coach or cab or car, or admit to his concert or theatre, or deal with in other matters of intercourse or business. Innkeepers and public carriers, by the laws of all the States, so far as we are aware, are bound, to the extent of their facilities, to furnish proper accommodation to all unobjectionable persons who in good faith apply for them. If the laws themselves make any unjust discrimination, amenable to the prohibitions of the Fourteenth Amendment, Congress has full power to afford a remedy under that amendment and in accordance with it.

When a man has emerged from slavery, and by the aid of beneficent legislation has shaken off the inseparable concomitants of that state, there must be some stage in the progress of his elevation when he takes the rank of a mere citizen, and ceases to be the special favorite of the laws, and when his rights as a citizen, or a man, are to be protected in the ordinary modes by which other men's rights are protected. There were thousands of free colored people in this country before the abolition of slavery, enjoying all the essential rights of life, liberty and property the same as white citizens; yet no one, at that time, thought that it was any invasion of his personal status as a freeman because he was not admitted to all the privileges enjoyed by white citizens, or because he was subjected to discriminations in the enjoyment of accommodations in inns, public conveyances and places of amusement. Mere discriminations on account of race or color were not regarded as badges of slavery. . . .

On the whole we are of opinion, that no countenance of authority for the passage of the law in question can be found in either the Thirteenth or Fourteenth Amendment of the Constitution; and no other ground of authority for its passage being suggested, it must necessarily be declared void, at least so far as its operation in the several States is concerned.

* * *

MR. JUSTICE HARLAN dissenting.

The opinion in these cases proceeds, it seems to me, upon grounds entirely too narrow and artificial. I cannot resist the conclusion that the substance and spirit of the recent amendments of the Constitution have been sacrificed by a subtle and ingenious verbal criticism. "It is not the words of the law but the internal sense of it that makes the law: the letter of the law is the body; the sense and reason of the law is the soul." Constitutional provisions, adopted in the interest of liberty, and for the purpose of securing, through national legislation, if need be, rights inhering in a state of freedom, and belonging to American citizenship, have been so construed as to defeat the ends the people desired to accomplish, which they attempted to accomplish, and which they supposed they had accomplished by changes in their fundamental law. By this I do not mean that the determination of these cases should have been materially controlled by considerations of mere expediency or policy. I mean only, in this form, to express an earnest conviction that the court has departed from the familiar rule requiring, in the interpretation of constitutional provisions, that full effect be given to the intent with which they were adopted.

* * *

There seems to be no substantial difference between my brethren and myself as to the purpose of Congress. . . .

The court adjudges, I think erroneously, that Congress is without power, under either the Thirteenth or Fourteenth Amendment, to establish such regulations, and that the first and second sections of the statute are, in all their parts, unconstitutional and void.

* * *

The first section of the Thirteenth Amendment provides that "neither slavery nor involuntary servitude, except as a punishment for crime, whereof the party shall have been duly convicted, shall exist within the United States, or any place subject to their jurisdiction." Its second section declares that "Congress shall have power to enforce this article by appropriate legislation." . . .

The terms of the Thirteenth Amendment are absolute and universal. They embrace every race which then was, or might thereafter be, within the United States. No race, as such, can be excluded from the benefits or rights thereby conferred. Yet, it is historically true that that amendment was suggested by the condition, in this country, of that race which had been declared, by this court, to have had — according to the opinion entertained by the most civilized portion of the white race, at the time of the adoption of the Constitution — "no rights which the white man was bound to respect," none of the privileges or immunities secured by that instrument to citizens of the United States. It had reference, in a peculiar sense, to a people which (although the larger part of them were in slavery) had been invited by an act of Congress to aid in saving from overthrow a government which, theretofore, by all of its departments, had treated them as an inferior race, with no legal rights or privileges except such as the white race might choose to grant them.

* * *

The Thirteenth Amendment, it is conceded, did something more than to prohibit slavery as an *institution*, resting upon distinctions of race, and upheld by positive law. My brethren admit that it established and decreed universal *civil freedom* throughout the United States. But did the freedom thus established involve nothing more than exemption from actual slavery? Was nothing more intended than to forbid one man from owning another as property? Was it the purpose of the nation simply to destroy the institution, and then remit the race, theretofore held in bondage, to the several States for such protection, in their civil rights, necessarily growing out of freedom, as those States, in their discretion, might choose to provide? . . . Had the Thirteenth Amendment stopped with the sweeping declaration, in its first section, against the existence of slavery and involuntary servitude, except for crime, Congress would have had the power, by implication, according to the doctrines of *Prigg v. Commonwealth of Pennsylvania* . . . to protect the freedom established, and consequently, to secure the enjoyment of such civil rights as were fundamental in freedom. That it can exert its authority to that extent is made clear, and was intended to be made clear, by the express grant of power contained in the second section of the Amendment.

That there are burdens and disabilities which constitute badges of slavery and servitude, and that the power to enforce by appropriate legislation the Thirteenth Amendment may be exerted by legislation of a direct and primary character, for the eradication, not simply of the institution, but of its badges and incidents, are propositions which ought to be deemed indisputable. . . . These propositions being conceded, it is impossible, as it seems to me, to question the constitutional validity of the Civil Rights Act of 1866. I do not contend that the Thirteenth Amendment invests Congress with authority, by legislation, to define and regulate the entire body of the civil rights which citizens enjoy, or may enjoy, in the several States. But I hold that since slavery, as the court has repeatedly declared, . . . was the moving or principal cause of the adoption of that amendment, and since that institution rested wholly upon the inferiority, as a race, of those held in bondage, their freedom necessarily involved immunity from, and protection against, all discrimination against them, because of their race, in respect of such civil rights as belong to freemen of other races. Congress, therefore, under its express power to enforce that amendment, by appropriate legislation, may enact laws to protect that people against the deprivation, *because of their race*, of any civil rights granted to other freemen in the same State; and such legislation may be of a direct and primary character, operating upon States, their officers and agents, and, also, upon, at least, such individuals and corporations as exercise public functions and wield power and authority under the State.

To test the correctness of this position, let us suppose that, prior to the adoption of the Fourteenth Amendment, a State had passed a statute denying to freemen of African descent, resident within its limits, the same right which was accorded to white persons, of making and enforcing contracts, and of inheriting, purchasing, leasing, selling and conveying property; or a statute subjecting colored people to severer punishment for particular offences than was prescribed for white persons, or excluding that race from the benefit of the laws exempting homesteads from execution. . . . Can there be any doubt that all such enactments might have been reached by direct legislation upon the part of Congress under its express power to enforce the Thirteenth Amendment? Would any court have hesitated to declare that such legislation imposed badges of servitude in conflict with the civil freedom ordained by that amendment? That it would have been also in conflict with the Fourteenth Amendment, because inconsistent with the fundamental rights of American citizenship, does not prove that it would have been consistent with the Thirteenth Amendment.

What has been said is sufficient to show that the power of Congress under the Thirteenth Amendment is not necessarily restricted to legislation against slavery as an institution upheld by positive law, but may be exerted to the extent, at least, of protecting the liberated race against discrimination, in respect of legal rights belonging to freemen, where such discrimination is based upon race.

It remains now to inquire what are the legal rights of colored persons in respect of the accommodations, privileges and facilities of public conveyances, inns and places of public amusement?

* * *

Such being the relations these corporations hold to the public, it would seem that the right of a colored person to use an improved public highway, upon the terms accorded to freemen of other races, is as fundamental, in the state of freedom established in this country, as are any of the rights which my brethren concede to be so far fundamental as to be deemed the essence of civil freedom. "Personal liberty consists," says Blackstone, "in the power of locomotion, of changing situation, or removing one's person to whatever places one's own inclination may direct, without restraint, unless by due course of law." But of what value is this right of locomotion, if it may be clogged by such burdens as Congress intended by the act of 1875 to remove? . . .

Second, as to inns. The same general observations which have been made as to railroads are applicable to inns. The word "inn" has a technical legal signification. It means, in the act of 1875, just what it meant at common law. A mere private boarding-house is not an inn, nor is its keeper subject to the responsibilities, or entitled to the privileges of a common innkeeper. . . .

* * *

These authorities are sufficient to show that a keeper of an inn is in the exercise of a quasi public employment. The law gives him special privileges and he is charged with certain duties and responsibilities to the public. The public nature of his employment forbids him from discriminating against any person asking admission as a guest on account of the race or color of that person.

Third. As to places of public amusement. It may be argued that the managers of such places have no duties to perform with which the public are, in any legal sense, concerned, or with which the public have any right to interfere; and, that the exclusion of a black man from a place of public amusement, on account of his race, or the denial to him, on that ground, of equal accommodations at such places, violates no legal right for the vindication of which he may invoke the aid of the courts. My answer is, that places of public amusement, within the meaning of the act of 1875, are such as are established and maintained under direct license of the law. The authority to establish and maintain them comes from the public. The colored race is a part of that public. The local government granting the license represents them as well as all other races within its jurisdiction. A license from the public to establish a place of public amusement, imports, in law, equality of right, at such places, among all the members of that public. This must be so, unless it be — which I deny — that the common municipal government of all the people may, in the exertion of its powers, conferred for the benefit of all, discriminate or authorize discrimination against a particular race, solely because of its former condition of servitude.

* * *

Congress has not, in these matters, entered the domain of State control and supervision. It does not, as I have said, assume to prescribe the general conditions and limitations under which inns, public conveyances, and places of public amusement, shall be conducted or managed. It simply declares, in effect, that since the nation has established universal freedom in this country, for all time, there shall be no discrimination, based merely upon race or color, in respect of the accommodations and advantages of public conveyances, inns, and places of public amusement.

I am of the opinion that such discrimination practised by corporations and individuals in the exercise of their public or quasi-public functions is a badge of servitude the imposition of which Congress may prevent under its power, by appropriate legislation, to enforce the Thirteenth Amendment. . . .

It remains now to consider these cases with reference to the power Congress has possessed since the adoption of the Fourteenth Amendment. . . .

* * *

Remembering that this court, in the *Slaughter-House Cases*, declared that the one pervading purpose found in all the recent amendments, lying at the foundation of each, and without which none of them would have been suggested — was "the freedom of the slave race, the security and firm establishment of that freedom, and the protection of the newly-made freeman and citizen from the oppression of those who had formerly exercised unlimited dominion over him" — that each amendment was addressed primarily to the grievances of that race — let us proceed to consider the language of the Fourteenth Amendment.

Its first and fifth sections are in these words:

"SEC. 1. All persons born or naturalized in the United States, and subject to the jurisdiction thereof, are citizens of the United States and of the State wherein they reside. No State shall make or enforce any law which shall abridge the privileges or immunities of citizens of the United States; nor shall any State deprive any person of life, liberty, or property, without due process of law; nor deny to any person within its jurisdiction the equal protection of the laws.

* * *

"SEC. 5. That Congress shall have power to enforce, by appropriate legislation, the provisions of this article."

* * *

But when, under what circumstances, and to what extent, may Congress, by means of legislation, exert its power to enforce the provisions of this amendment? The theory of the opinion of the majority of the court . . . is, that the general government cannot, in advance of hostile State laws or hostile State proceedings, actively interfere for the protection of any of the rights, privileges, and immunities secured by the Fourteenth Amendment. . . .

* * *

The assumption that this amendment consists wholly of prohibitions upon State laws and State proceedings in hostility to its provisions, is unauthorized by its language. The first clause of the first section — "All persons born or naturalized in the United States, and subject to the jurisdiction thereof, are citizens of the United States, and of the State wherein they reside" — is of a distinctly affirmative character. In its application to the colored race, previously liberated, it created and granted, as well citizenship of the United States, as citizenship of the State in which they respectively resided. It introduced all of that race, whose ancestors had been imported and sold as slaves, at once, into the political community known as the "People of the United States." They became, instantly, citizens of the United States, *and* of their respective States. . . .

The citizenship thus acquired, by that race, in virtue of an affirmative grant from the nation, may be protected, not alone by the judicial branch of the government, but by congressional legislation of a primary direct character; this, because the power of Congress is not restricted to the enforcement of prohibitions upon State laws or State action. It is, in terms distinct and positive, to enforce "the *provisions of this article*" of amendment; not simply those of a prohibitive character, but the provisions — *all* of the provisions — affirmative and prohibitive, of the amendment. . . . If any right was created by that amendment, the grant of power, through appropriate legislation, to enforce its provisions, authorizes Congress, by means of legislation, operating throughout the entire Union, to guard, secure, and protect that right.

It is, therefore, an essential inquiry what, if any, right, privilege or immunity was given, by the nation, to colored persons, when they were made citizens of the State in which they reside? Did the constitutional grant of State citizenship to that race, of its own force, invest them with any rights, privileges and immunities whatever? . . . What are the privileges and immunities to which, by that clause of the Constitution, they became entitled? To this it may be answered, generally, upon the authority of the adjudged cases, that they are those which are fundamental in citizenship in a free republican government, such as are "common to the citizens in the latter States under their constitutions and laws by virtue of their being citizens." . . .

* * *

But what was secured to colored citizens of the United States — as between them and their respective States — by the national grant to them of State citizenship? With what rights, privileges, or immunities did this grant invest them? There is one, if there be no other — exemption from race discrimination in respect of any civil right belonging to citizens of the white race in the same State. . . . And such must be their constitutional right, in their own State, unless the recent amendments be splendid baubles, thrown out to delude those who deserved fair and generous treatment at the hands of the nation. Citizenship in this country necessarily imports at least equality of civil rights among citizens of every race in the same State. . . .

* * *

Here, in language at once clear and forcible, is stated the principle for which I contend. It can scarcely be claimed that exemption from race discrimination, in respect of civil rights, against those to whom State citizenship was granted by the nation, is any less, for the colored race, a new constitutional right, derived from and secured by the national Constitution, than is exemption from such discrimination in the exercise of the elective franchise. It cannot be that the latter is an attribute of national citizenship, while the other is not essential in national citizenship, or fundamental in State citizenship.

If, then, exemption from discrimination, in respect of civil rights, is a new constitutional right, secured by the grant of State citizenship to colored citizens of the United States . . . why may not the nation, by means of its own legislation of a primary direct character, guard, protect and enforce that right? It is a right and privilege which the nation conferred. It did not come from the States in which those colored citizens reside. It has been the established doctrine of this court during all its history, accepted as essential to the national supremacy, that Congress, in the absence of a positive delegation of power to the State legislatures, may, by its own legislation, enforce and protect any right derived from or created by the national Constitution. . . . How then can it be claimed in view of the declarations of this court in former cases, that exemption of colored citizens, within their States, from race discrimination, in respect of the civil rights of citizens, is not an immunity created or derived from the national Constitution?

* * *

. . . If the grant to colored citizens of the United States of citizenship in their respective States, imports exemption from race discrimination, in their States, in respect of such civil rights as belong to citizenship, then, to hold that the amendment remits that right to the States for their protection, primarily, and stays the hands of the nation, until it is assailed by State laws or State proceedings, is to adjudge that the amendment, so far from enlarging the powers of Congress — as we have heretofore said it did — not only curtails them, but reverses the policy which the general government has pursued from its very organization. Such an interpretation of the amendment is a denial to Congress of the power, by appropriate legislation, to enforce one of its provisions. In view of the circumstances under which the recent amendments were incorporated into the Constitution, and especially in view of the peculiar character of the new rights they created and secured, it ought not to be presumed that the general government has abdicated its authority, by national legislation, direct and primary in its character, to guard and protect privileges and immunities secured by that instrument. Such an interpretation of the Constitution ought not to be accepted if it be possible to avoid it. Its acceptance would lead to this anomalous result: that whereas, prior to the amendments, Congress, with the sanction of this court, passed the most stringent laws — operating directly and primarily upon States and their officers and agents, as well as upon individuals — in vindication of slavery and the right of the master, it may not now, by legislation of a like primary and direct character, guard, protect, and secure the freedom established, and the most essential right of the citizenship granted, by the constitutional amendments. . . .

It does not seem to me that the fact that, by the second clause of the first section of the Fourteenth Amendment, the States are expressly prohibited from making or enforcing laws abridging the privileges and immunities of citizens of the United States, furnishes any sufficient reason for holding or maintaining that the amendment was intended to deny Congress the power, by general, primary, and direct legislation, of protecting citizens of the several States, being also citizens of the United States, against all discrimination, in respect of their rights as citizens, which is founded on race, color, or previous condition of servitude.

* * *

This construction does not in any degree intrench upon the just rights of the States in the control of their domestic affairs. It simply recognizes the enlarged powers conferred by the recent amendments upon the general government. In the view which I take of those amendments, the States possess the same authority which they have always had to define and regulate the civil rights which their own people, in virtue of State citizenship, may enjoy within their respective limits; except that its exercise is now subject to the expressly granted power of Congress, by legislation, to enforce the provisions of such amendments — a power which necessarily carries with it authority, by national legislation, to protect and secure the privileges and immunities which are created by or are derived from those amendments. That exemption of citizens from discrimination based on race or color, in respect of civil rights, is one of those privileges or immunities, can no longer be deemed an open question in this court.

* * *

In every material sense applicable to the practical enforcement of the Fourteenth Amendment, railroad corporations, keepers of inns, and managers of places of public amusement are agents or instrumentalities of the State, because they are charged with duties to the public, and are amenable, in respect of their duties and functions, to governmental regulation. It seems to me that . . . a denial, by these instrumentalities of the State, to the citizen, because of his race, of that equality of civil rights secured to him by law, is a denial by the State, within the meaning of the Fourteenth Amendment. If it be not, then that race is left, in respect of the civil rights in question, practically at the mercy of corporations and individuals wielding power under the States.

* * *

The court, in its opinion, reserves the question whether Congress, in the exercise of its power to regulate commerce amongst the several States, might or might not pass a law regulating rights in public conveyances passing from one State to another. I beg to suggest that that precise question was substantially presented here in the only one of these cases relating to railroads — *Robinson and Wife v. Memphis & Charleston Railroad Company*. In that case it appears that Mrs. Robinson, a citizen of Mississippi, purchased a railroad ticket entitling her to be carried from Grand Junction, Tennessee, to Lynchburg, Virginia. Might not the act of 1875 be maintained in that case, as applicable at least to commerce between the States, notwithstanding it does not, upon its face, profess to have been passed in pursuance of the power of Congress to regulate commerce? . . .

My brethren say, that when a man has emerged from slavery, and by the aid of beneficent legislation has shaken off the inseparable concomitants of that state, there must be some stage in the progress of his elevation when he takes the rank of a mere citizen, and ceases to be the special favorite of the laws, and when his rights as a citizen, or a man, are to be protected in the ordinary modes by which other men's rights are protected. It is, I submit, scarcely just to say that the colored race has been the special favorite of the laws. The statute of 1875, now adjudged to be unconstitutional, is for the benefit of citizens of every race and color. What the nation through Congress, has sought to accomplish in reference to that race, is — what had already been done in every State of the Union for the white race — to secure and protect rights belonging to them as freemen and citizens; nothing more. It was not deemed enough "to help the feeble up, but to support him after." The one underlying purpose of congressional legislation has been to enable the black race to take the rank of mere citizens. The difficulty has been to compel a recognition of the legal right of the black race to take the rank of citizens, and to secure the enjoyment of privileges belonging, under the law, to them as a component part of the people for whose welfare and happiness government is ordained. . . . To-day, it is the colored race which is denied, by corporations and individuals wielding public authority, rights fundamental in their freedom and citizenship. At some future time, it may be that some other race will fall under the ban of race discrimination. If the constitutional amendments be enforced, according to the intent with which, as I conceive, they were adopted, there cannot be, in this republic, any class of human beings in practical subjection to another class, with power in the latter to dole out to the former just such privileges as they may choose to grant. . . .

NOTES AND QUESTIONS

1. The essence of the majority's reasoning is captured by its language that "it is proper to state that civil rights, such as are guaranteed by the Constitution against State aggression, cannot be impaired by the wrongful acts of individuals, unsupported by State authority in the shape of laws, customs, or judicial or executive proceedings." 109 U.S. at 17. This leads the majority to conclude that acts of racial discrimination against the plaintiffs in the cases (who were clearly the victims of such discrimination) cannot be prohibited pursuant to Congress' legislative authority under the Fourteenth Amendment. Why the narrow reading of the "state action" requirement of the Fourteenth Amendment? Is it one with which you agree? Does the Court, or Justice Harlan, suggest any other possibilities which might constitutionally permit the federal government to prohibit racial discrimination? Is there now such federal legislation? What is the authority on which it is based?

2. In light of the reasons for which the Fourteenth Amendment was passed, why isn't the majority persuaded to give the Amendment the broadened reading that Justice Harlan does? What constitutional values is the majority seeking to protect, and why does Harlan not find them as important? Why does the majority reject the Thirteenth Amendment (the one that abolished slavery) as an insufficient ground for supporting the legislation at hand?

3. Note that Justice Harlan relies for support of his conclusion that the Fourteenth Amendment permits Congress to prohibit individuals' acts of discrimination in large part on congressional actions in support of the Constitution's Fugitive Slave Clause, and also — remarkably — on the Court's opinion in the infamous *Dred Scott* case. What bearing does this have on the interpretation of the Fourteenth Amendment?

4. Justice Harlan would also have sustained the legislation based on Congress's authority given by the Thirteenth Amendment, but for our purposes at this point, his interpretation of "state action" under the Fourteenth Amendment is more important. Do you agree with the core passage on this matter:

In every material sense applicable to the practical enforcement of the Fourteenth Amendment, railroad corporations, keepers of inns, and managers of places of public amusement are agents or instrumentalities of the State, because they are charged with duties to the public, and are amenable, in respect of their duties and functions, to governmental regulation. It seems to me that . . . a denial, by these instrumentalities of the State, to the citizen, because of his race, of that equality of civil rights secured to him by law, is a denial by the State, within the meaning of the Fourteenth Amendment.

109 U.S. at 58-59 (Harlan, J., dissenting). Is there a slip in Justice Harlan's reasoning, or is his implicit point — the difficulty of drawing a distinction between strictly private and public action — a valid one? As you may have guessed, Harlan's dissenting opinion on this point was, in our own time, to become the view of a majority of the members of the court, as indicated in the case which follows.

SHELLEY v. KRAEMER
334 U.S. 1 (1948)

MR. CHIEF JUSTICE VINSON delivered the opinion of the Court.

These cases present for our consideration questions relating to the validity of court enforcement of private agreements, generally described as restrictive covenants, which have as their purpose the exclusion of persons of designated race or color from the ownership or occupancy of real property. . . .

The first of these cases comes to this Court on certiorari to the Supreme Court of Missouri. On February 16, 1911, thirty out of a total of thirty-nine owners of property fronting both sides of Labadie Avenue between Taylor Avenue and Cora Avenue in the city of St. Louis, signed an agreement, which was subsequently recorded, providing in part:

". . . the said property is hereby restricted to the use and occupancy for the term of Fifty (50) years from this date, so that it shall be a condition all the time and whether recited and referred to as [sic] not in subsequent conveyances and shall attach to the land as a condition precedent to the sale of the same, that hereafter no part of said property or any portion thereof shall be, for said term of Fifty-years, occupied by any person not of the Caucasian race, it being intended hereby to restrict the use of said property for said period of time against the occupancy as owners or tenants of any portion of said property for resident or other purpose by people of the Negro or Mongolian Race."

* * *

The Supreme Court of Missouri . . . held the agreement effective and concluded that enforcement of its provisions violated no rights guaranteed to petitioners by the Federal Constitution. . . .

The second of the cases under consideration comes to this Court from the Supreme Court of Michigan. The circumstances presented do not differ materially from the Missouri case. . . .

* * *

Petitioners have placed primary reliance on their contentions, first raised in the state courts, that judicial enforcement of the restrictive agreements in these cases has violated rights guaranteed to petitioners by the Fourteenth Amendment of the Federal Constitution and Acts of Congress passed pursuant to that Amendment. Specifically, petitioners urge that they have been denied the equal protection of the laws. . . .

I.

Whether the equal protection clause of the Fourteenth Amendment inhibits judicial enforcement by state courts of restrictive covenants based on race or color is a question which this Court has not heretofore been called upon to consider. . . .

* * *

It should be observed that these covenants do not seek to proscribe any particular use of the affected properties. Use of the properties for residential occupancy, as such, is not forbidden. The restrictions of these agreements, rather, are directed toward a designated class of persons and seek to determine who may and who may not own or make use of the properties for residential purposes. . . .

It cannot be doubted that among the civil rights intended to be protected from discriminatory state action by the Fourteenth Amendment are the rights to acquire, enjoy, own and dispose of property. Equality in the enjoyment of property rights was regarded by the framers of that Amendment as an essential pre-condition to the realization of other basic civil rights and liberties which the Amendment was intended to guarantee. Thus, § 1978 of the Revised Statutes, derived from § 1 of the Civil Rights Act of 1866 which was enacted by Congress while the Fourteenth Amendment was also under consideration, provides:

> "All citizens of the United States shall have the same right, in every State and Territory, as is enjoyed by white citizens thereof to inherit, purchase, lease, sell, hold, and convey real and personal property." . . .

It is likewise clear that restrictions on the right of occupancy of the sort sought to be created by the private agreements in these cases could not be squared with the requirements of the Fourteenth Amendment if imposed by state statute or local ordinance. . . . In the case of *Buchanan v. Warley* [(1917)], a unanimous Court declared unconstitutional the provisions of a city ordinance which denied to colored persons the right to occupy houses in blocks in which the greater number of houses were occupied by white persons, and imposed similar restrictions on white persons with respect to blocks in which the greater number of houses were occupied by colored persons. During the course of the opinion in that case, this Court stated: "The Fourteenth Amendment and these statutes enacted in furtherance of its purpose operate to qualify and entitle a colored man to acquire property without state legislation discriminating against him solely because of color."

In *Harmon v. Tyler* (1927), a unanimous court, on the authority of *Buchanan v. Warley*, *supra*, declared invalid an ordinance which forbade any Negro to establish a home on any property in a white community or any white person to establish a home in a Negro community, "except on the written consent of a majority of the persons of the opposite race inhabiting such community or portion of the City to be affected."

* * *

But the present cases, unlike those just discussed, do not involve action by state legislatures or city councils. Here the particular patterns of discrimination and the areas in which the restrictions are to operate, are determined, in the first instance, by the terms of agreements among private individuals. Participation of the State consists in the enforcement of the restrictions so defined. The crucial issue with which we are here confronted is whether this distinction removes these cases from the operation of the prohibitory provisions of the Fourteenth Amendment.

Since the decision of this Court in the *Civil Rights Cases* (1883), the principle has become firmly embedded in our constitutional law that the action inhibited by the first section of the Fourteenth Amendment is only such action as may fairly be said to be that of the States. That Amendment erects no shield against merely private conduct, however discriminatory or wrongful.

We conclude, therefore, that the restrictive agreements standing alone cannot be regarded as violative of any rights guaranteed to petitioners by the Fourteenth Amendment. So long as the purposes of those agreements are effectuated by voluntary adherence to their terms, it would appear clear that there has been no action by the State and the provisions of the Amendment have not been violated.

But here there was more. These are cases in which the purposes of the agreements were secured only by judicial enforcement by state courts of the restrictive terms of the agreements. The respondents urge that judicial enforcement of private agreements does not amount to state action; or, in any event, the participation of the State is so attenuated in character as not to amount to state action within the meaning of the Fourteenth Amendment. Finally, it is suggested, even if the States in these cases may be deemed to have acted in the constitutional sense, their action did not deprive petitioners of rights guaranteed by the Fourteenth Amendment. We move to a consideration of these matters.

II.

That the action of state courts and judicial officers in their official capacities is to be regarded as action of the State within the meaning of the Fourteenth Amendment, is a proposition which has long been established by decisions of this Court. That principle was given expression in the earliest cases involving the construction of the terms of the Fourteenth Amendment. Thus, in *Virginia v. Rives* (1880), this Court stated: "It is doubtless true that a State may act through different agencies, — either by its legislative, its executive, or its judicial authorities; and the prohibitions of the amendment extend to all action of the State denying equal protection of the laws, whether it be action by one of these agencies or by another." In *Ex parte Virginia* (1880), the Court observed: "A State acts by its legislative, its executive, or its judicial authorities. It can act in no other way." In the *Civil Rights Cases* (1883), this Court pointed out that the Amendment makes void "State action of every kind" which is inconsistent with the guaranties therein contained, and extends to manifestations of "State authority in the shape of laws, customs, or judicial or executive proceedings." . . .

Similar expressions, giving specific recognition to the fact that judicial action is to be regarded as action of the State for the purposes of the Fourteenth Amendment, are to be found in numerous cases which have been more recently decided. In *Twining v. New Jersey* (1908), the Court said: "The judicial act of the highest court of the State, in authoritatively construing and enforcing its laws, is the act of the State." In *Brinkerhoff-Faris Trust & Savings Co. v. Hill* (1930), the Court, through Mr. Justice Brandeis, stated: "The federal guaranty of due process extends to state action through its judicial as well as through its legislative, executive or administrative branch of government." . . .

One of the earliest applications of the prohibitions contained in the Fourteenth Amendment to action of state judicial officials occurred in cases in which Negroes had been excluded from jury service in criminal prosecutions by reason of their race or color. These cases demonstrate, also, the early recognition by this Court that state action in violation of the Amendment's provisions is equally repugnant to the constitutional commands whether directed by state statute or taken by a judicial official in the absence of statute. Thus, in *Strauder v. West Virginia* (1880), this Court declared invalid a state statute restricting jury service to white persons as amounting to a denial of the equal protection of the laws to the colored defendant in that case. In the same volume of the reports, the Court in *Ex parte Virginia*, *supra*, held that a similar discrimination imposed by the action of a state judge denied rights protected by the Amendment, despite the fact that the language of the state statute relating to jury service contained no such restrictions.

The action of state courts in imposing penalties or depriving parties of other substantive rights without providing adequate notice and opportunity to defend, has, of course, long been regarded as a denial of the due process of law guaranteed by the Fourteenth Amendment.

* * *

But the examples of state judicial action which have been held by this Court to violate the Amendment's commands are not restricted to situations in which the judicial proceedings were found in some manner to be procedurally unfair. It has been recognized that the action of state courts in enforcing a substantive common-law rule formulated by those courts, may result in the denial of rights guaranteed by the Fourteenth Amendment, even though the judicial proceedings in such cases may have been in complete accord with the most rigorous conceptions of procedural due process. Thus, in *American Federation of Labor v. Swing* (1941), enforcement by state courts of the common-law policy of the State, which resulted in the restraining of peaceful picketing, was held to be state action of the sort prohibited by the Amendment's guaranties of freedom of discussion. In *Cantwell v. Connecticut* (1940), a conviction in a state court of the common-law crime of breach of the peace was, under the circumstances of the case, found to be a violation of the Amendment's commands relating to freedom of religion. In *Bridges v. California* (1941), enforcement of the state's common-law rule relating to contempts by publication was held to be state action inconsistent with the prohibitions of the Fourteenth Amendment.

The short of the matter is that from the time of the adoption of the Fourteenth Amendment until the present, it has been the consistent ruling of this Court that the action of the States to which the Amendment has reference includes action of state courts and state judicial officials. . . .

III.

* * *

We have no doubt that there has been state action in these cases in the full and complete sense of the phrase. The undisputed facts disclose that petitioners were willing purchasers of properties upon which they desired to establish homes. The owners of the properties were willing sellers; and contracts of sale were accordingly consummated. It is clear that but for the active intervention of the state courts, supported by the full panoply of state power, petitioners would have been free to occupy the properties in question without restraint.

These are not cases, as has been suggested, in which the States have merely abstained from action, leaving private individuals free to impose such discriminations as they see fit. Rather, these are cases in which the States have made available to such individuals the full coercive power of government to deny to petitioners, on the grounds of race or color, the enjoyment of property rights in premises which petitioners are willing and financially able to acquire and which the grantors are willing to sell. The difference between judicial enforcement and non-enforcement of the restrictive covenants is the difference to petitioners between being denied rights of property available to other members of the community and being accorded full enjoyment of those rights on an equal footing.

* * *

We hold that in granting judicial enforcement of the restrictive agreements in these cases, the States have denied petitioners the equal protection of the laws and that, therefore, the action of the state courts cannot stand. We have noted that freedom from discrimination by the States in the enjoyment of property rights was among the basic objectives sought to be effectuated by the framers of the Fourteenth Amendment. That such discrimination has occurred in these cases is clear. Because of the race or color of these petitioners they have been denied rights of ownership or occupancy enjoyed as a matter of course by other citizens of different race or color. The Fourteenth Amendment declares "that all persons, whether colored or white, shall stand equal before the laws of the States, and, in regard to the colored race, for whose protection the amendment was primarily designed, that no discrimination shall be made against them by law because of their color." . . . Nor may the discriminations imposed by the state courts in these cases be justified as proper exertions of state police power.

Respondents urge, however, that since the state courts stand ready to enforce restrictive covenants excluding white persons from the ownership or occupancy of property covered by such agreements, enforcement of covenants excluding colored persons may not be deemed a denial of equal protection of the laws to the colored persons who are thereby affected. This contention does not bear scrutiny. The parties have directed our attention to no case in which a court, state or federal, has been called upon to enforce a covenant excluding members of the white majority from ownership or occupancy of real property on grounds of race or color. But there are more fundamental considerations. The rights created by the first section of the Fourteenth Amendment are, by its terms, guaranteed to the individual. The rights established are personal rights. It is, therefore, no answer to these petitioners to say that the courts may also be induced to deny white persons rights of ownership and occupancy on grounds of race or color. Equal protection of the laws is not achieved through indiscriminate imposition of inequalities.

Nor do we find merit in the suggestion that property owners who are parties to these agreements are denied equal protection of the laws if denied access to the courts to enforce the terms of restrictive covenants and to assert property rights which the state courts have held to be created by such agreements. The Constitution confers upon no individual the right to demand action by the State which results in the denial of equal protection of the laws to other individuals. And it would appear beyond question that the power of the State to create and enforce property interests must be exercised within the boundaries defined by the Fourteenth Amendment.

* * *

The historical context in which the Fourteenth Amendment became a part of the Constitution should not be forgotten. Whatever else the framers sought to achieve, it is clear that the matter of primary concern was the establishment of equality in the enjoyment of basic civil and political rights and the preservation of those rights from discriminatory action on the part of the States based on considerations of race or color. Seventy-five years ago this Court announced that the provisions of the Amendment are to be construed with this fundamental purpose in mind. Upon full consideration, we have concluded that in these cases the States have acted to deny petitioners the equal protection of the laws guaranteed by the Fourteenth Amendment. . . .

* * *

MR. JUSTICE REED, MR. JUSTICE JACKSON, and MR. JUSTICE RUTLEDGE took no part in the consideration or decision of these cases.

NOTES AND QUESTIONS

1. Do you understand why enforcement by the state courts of racially-restrictive covenants is "state action" within the meaning of the Fourteenth Amendment? Is this what you suppose the framers of the Fourteenth Amendment had in mind? There is no denying that when the courts are used to enforce racially-restrictive covenants, they have been used as instruments for employing "the full coercive power of government to deny to petitioners, on the grounds of race or color, the enjoyment of property rights in premises which petitioners are willing and financially able to acquire and which the grantors are willing to sell." 334 U.S. at 19. There is also no denying that at the time the Fourteenth Amendment was passed, "the matter of primary concern was the establishment of equality in the enjoyment of basic civil and political rights and the preservation of those rights from discriminatory action on the part of the States based on considerations of race or color." *Id.* at 23. Does it necessarily follow, however, that the Fourteenth Amendment prohibits the use of the courts by individuals who seek racially to discriminate? Would it have been clearer if the Amendment had stated "No *person* . . . shall deny to any person . . . the equal protection of the laws"? Is there force in the claim that so long as whites may be discriminated against as well by racially-restrictive covenants, there is no equal protection problem?

2. The court concludes that there is no violation of the Fourteenth Amendment when parties agree to racially restrictive covenants, but only when they seek to use the courts to enforce such agreements. But if such agreements are not unconstitutional when made, why do they violate the Constitution when they are enforced? Indeed, if they cannot be enforced in the courts, can they really be regarded as binding contracts? Could the meaning of the Fourteenth Amendment be that individuals are free to discriminate and can use the courts to effect that discrimination, though legislators may not pass discriminatory legislation? This was the conclusion apparently reached in a famous critique of *Shelley v. Kraemer*, Herbert Wechsler, *Toward Neutral Principles of Constitutional Law*, 73 HARV. L. REV. 1 (1959). Professor Wechsler asked, "[a]ssuming that the Constitution speaks to state discrimination on the ground of race but not to such discrimination by an individual . . . , why is the enforcement of the private covenant a state discrimination rather than a legal recognition of the freedom of the individual?" *Id.* at 29. Can you answer Wechsler's question?

3. One analyst of the opinion, apparently conceding Wechsler's point, stated that "[t]he facts surrounding the covenant cases, however, suggest that in enforcing the racial covenants the states did more than provide neutral enforcement of private contracts, but had, in fact, adopted policies of racial residential segregation in the supposed interests of protecting property values, suppressing crime, and promoting racial purity." Francis A. Allen, Shelley v. Kramer, *in* THE OXFORD COMPANION TO THE SUPREME COURT OF THE UNITED STATES 781 (Kermit L. Hall et al. eds., 1992). Should this make a difference in your view of the case? Allen further notes that "[u]nfortunately these matters were not fully canvassed in the Court's opinion, nor were adequate indicia suggested to determine the point at which enforcement of private agreements becomes transmuted into state action to advance public policies." *Id.* You may have noticed that these matters were not "canvassed" at all in the Court's opinion that you have read, but do you agree with Allen's observation that "adequate indicia" of the public/private distinction were not provided? Allen still concludes that the opinion was "an important event in modern constitutional history." *Id.* at 782. Why do you suppose that was, and do you agree?

4. *Shelley* is not the only case to find state action on the basis of entanglement. All of these cases are premised on the fact that the government is somehow authorizing, encouraging, or facilitating private conduct that, if performed directly by government, would violate the Constitution. Other judicial activities beyond the peremptory and covenant contexts already studied include use of judicial process in the context of pre-judgment attachment. *Lugar v. Edmonson Oil Co.*, 457 U.S. 922 (1982) (due process required to be observed where state law creates attachment privilege and sheriff enforces it on behalf of private party). It is less clear whether government licensing is sufficient entanglement. In an early case, *Burton v. Wilmington Parking Authority*, 365 U.S. 715 (1961), the Court found a "symbiotic realtionship" between a private discriminating restaurant in a public building. The government was partially dependent upon the revenue of the restaurant. However, in *Moose Lodge Number 107 v. Irvis*, 407 U.S. 163 (1972), the Court found the mere grant of liquor license to a discriminating private club did not make the club a state actor. Similarly, licensed television stations can refuse to accept advertisements on the basis of content without violating the First Amendment. *Columbia Broad. Sys. v. Democratic Nat'l Comm.*, 412 U.S. 94 (1972). And private utilities operating with a state charter can terminate service for nonpayment without the provision of notice and hearing. *Jackson v. Metropolitan Edison Co.*, 419 U.S. 345 (1974).

State law, however, cannot encourage private discriminatory behavior. In *Reitman v. Mulkey*, 387 U.S. 369 (1967), the Court invalidated a California initiative that authorized total private discretion in the sale or lease of real property. This, reasoned the Court, would too greatly implicate the courts in private racial discrimination. However, another California initiative prohibiting school busing unless needed to remedy a Fourteenth Amendment violation was upheld because it did not impede remedies required by the Constitution. *Crawford v. Board of Education*, 458 U.S. 527 (1982).

5. In *Edmonson v. Leesville Concrete Co., Inc.*, 500 U.S. 614 (1991), Justice Kennedy, for a 6-3 Court, held that private attorneys in civil litigation between private parties could not use their peremptory challenges to strike prospective jurors based on race. The Court had previously held race-based peremptory challenges by a government prosecutor to violate the Equal Protection rights of jurors, *see Batson v. Kentucky*, 476 U.S. 79 (1986), but Justice Kennedy rightly pointed out that whether "an act violates the Constitution when committed by a government official . . . does not answer the question whether the same act offends constitutional guarantees if committed by a private litigant or his attorney." Is there a difference between the use of peremptory challenges by the government prosecutor — clearly a state actor — and a private attorney representing private clients? Here is the test the Court applied to determine whether action by a private actor should be deemed state action for purposes of the Fourteenth Amendment:

> Our precedents establish that, in determining whether a particular action or course of conduct is governmental in character, it is relevant to examine the following: the extent to which the actor relies on governmental assistance and benefits; whether the actor is performing a traditional governmental function; and whether the injury caused is aggravated in a unique way by the incidents of governmental authority.
>
> . . .

Justice Kennedy thought the involvement of the court in the jury selection process, and of the legislature in authorizing peremptory challenges in the first place, to be enough to bring the private attorney's actions under the state action umbrella, and that the race-based peremptories violated the equal protection rights of jurors.

Justice O'Connor, joined by Chief Justice Rehnquist and Justice Scalia, dissented:

> Not everything that happens in a courtroom is state action. A trial, particularly a civil trial is by design largely a stage on which private parties may act; it is a forum through which they can resolve their disputes in a peaceful and ordered manner. The government erects the platform; it does not thereby become responsible for all that occurs upon it. As much as we would like to eliminate completely from the courtroom the specter of racial discrimination, the Constitution does not sweep that broadly. Because I believe that a peremptory strike by a private litigant is fundamentally a matter of private choice and not state action, I dissent.

Justice Scalia also noted in a separate dissenting opinion that the Court's new rule "will not necessarily be a net help rather than hindrance to minority litigants in obtaining racially diverse juries. In criminal cases, *Batson v. Kentucky* (1986), already prevents the *prosecution* from using race-based strikes. The effect of today's decision (which logically must apply to criminal prosecutions) will be to prevent the *defendant* from doing so — so that the minority defendant can no longer seek to prevent an all-white jury, or to seat as many jurors of his own race as possible."

6. Why is the use of race-based peremptory challenges "state action" as that term is understood in the Fourteenth Amendment? Would Justice Harlan have agreed? How, if at all, does this affect the holding in the *Civil Rights Cases*? Are race-based peremptories closer to state action than the conduct rejected as state action in the *Civil Rights Cases*? Undeniably there is some government action involved here, as the majority points out. Is it as *de minimus* as Justice O'Connor suggests in her dissent?

7. What do you make of the institution of peremptory challenges itself? Is it something that should be encouraged? Do you understand the argument that peremptory challenges contribute to the perceived "fairness" of a trial? Are there different implications with regard to barring race-based peremptories in criminal trials as opposed to civil trials? In which are they the more odious? Clarence Thomas, currently the only black Justice on the Supreme Court, and a one-time champion of natural law, has spoken out strongly against the holdings rejecting race-based peremptories, *especially* in criminal trials. Why do you suppose that is?

8. The majority was striving, through its rejection of race-based peremptories, to build a color-blind society, or at least to lessen the amount of state-sanctioned racial discrimination. This is obviously a worthy goal. Is it furthered by the majority's decision? Justice O'Connor has been a strong foe of racial classifications drawn by governmental bodies (even those which favor racial minorities). Why might even she oppose barring race-based peremptories? Is Justice Scalia correct that the costs of banning race-based peremptories far outweighs the benefits? Is this an area that ought to be subject to cost-benefit analysis?

9. By now, you realize that the Constitution's protection of equal protection — like other provisions of the Fourteenth Amendment — textually only limits the government. However, over time, as the *Edmonson* case reflects, the Court has developed a number of doctrines treating private individuals as if they were state actors. If a private entity has been given a public function or it has become too entangled with government activity, it may be treated as a state actor. *Edmonson* is built on both of these foundations. The public function doctrine is premised on the belief that the government ought not to avoid the strictures of the Constitution merely by contracting its duty to the private sector. The public function exception originated with *Marsh v. Alabama*, 326 U.S. 501 (1946), where a private company town performing virtually all municipal duties was precluded from excluding religious leafletters exercising their First Amendment rights. In addition, the Court invalidated several attempts to allow private political bodies to discriminate on the basis of race. *Smith v. Allwright*, 321 U.S. 649 (1944) (the Democratic party of Texas, a private entity, could not conduct discriminatory primary elections). *See also Terry v. Adams*, 345 U.S. 461 (1953) (holding that the rule stated in *Allwright* could not be avoided by conducting a pre-primary through a private group called the Jaybirds).

To be a public function, it must be the type of activity that is *exclusively* run by the government. Thus, in *Rendell-Baker v. Kohn*, 457 U.S. 830 (1982), the Court refused to find a private school to be a state actor, in part, because schooling has never been an exclusive government function; indeed, just the opposite, public schools were the Johnny-come-latelys. The *Kohn* case also involved the question of whether the receipt of government funding makes a private entity into a state actor. *Kohn* held that it did not, however, the case is in tension with *Norwood v. Harrison*, 413 U.S. 455 (1973), finding it unconstitutional for a state to provide textbooks to a discriminatory private school. Effectively, *Norwood* meant the school, a private entity, had to stop discriminating if it wanted the state textbooks, and in this sense, the equal protection requirement was extended to the private sector. Of course, the restriction on the private school is derivative of the prohibition of the state. In *Kohn* there was no state activity to directly restrict, since the issue was whether a private school could fire a teacher on speech grounds.

10. In *Brentwood Academy v. Tennessee,* 531 U.S. 288 (2001), the Court addressed the issue of whether a statewide association incorporated to regulate interscholastic athletic competition among public and private secondary schools may be regarded as engaging in state action when it enforces a rule against a member school. 5-4, the Court, per Justice Souter, held that since the association in question here includes most public schools located within the state, acts through their representatives, draws it officers from them, is largely funded by their dues and income received in their stead, and has historically been seen to regulate in lieu of the State Board of Education's exercise of its own authority, the association's regulatory activity may and should be treated as state action. Justice Souter summarized these factors as "pervasive entwinement of state school officials in the structure of the association." Justice Souter described the Court's obligation as directed at not only to "'preserv[e] an area of individual freedom by limiting the reach of federal law' and avoi[d] the imposition of responsibility on a State for conduct it could not control," but also to assure that constitutional standards are invoked "when it can be said that the State is *responsible* for the specific conduct of which the plaintiff complains."

The Court opined that what is fairly attributable to the state is a matter of normative judgment, and the criteria lack rigid simplicity. And by now, you certainly appreciate the fluidity of the Court's state action inquiries. According to the Justices, they have treated a nominally private entity as a state actor when it is controlled by an "agency of the State," when it has been delegated a public function by the state, *cf.*, *Edmonson v Leesville Concrete Co.* (1991), when

Based on the recommendation of the Child Protection Team, the juvenile court dismissed the child protection case and returned Joshua to the custody of his father. A month later, emergency room personnel called the DSS caseworker handling Joshua's case to report that he had once again been treated for suspicious injuries. The caseworker concluded that there was no basis for action. For the next six months, the caseworker made monthly visits to the DeShaney home, during which she observed a number of suspicious injuries on Joshua's head; she also noticed that he had not been enrolled in school, and that the girlfriend had not moved out. The caseworker dutifully recorded these incidents in her files, along with her continuing suspicions that someone in the DeShaney household was physically abusing Joshua, but she did nothing more. In November 1983, the emergency room notified DSS that Joshua had been treated once again for injuries that they believed to be caused by child abuse. On the caseworker's next two visits to the DeShaney home, she was told that Joshua was too ill to see her. Still DSS took no action.

In March 1984, Randy DeShaney beat 4-year-old Joshua so severely that he fell into a life-threatening coma. Emergency brain surgery revealed a series of hemorrhages caused by traumatic injuries to the head inflicted over a long period of time. Joshua did not die, but he suffered brain damage so severe that he is expected to spend the rest of his life confined to an institution for the profoundly retarded. Randy DeShaney was subsequently tried and convicted of child abuse.

Joshua and his mother brought this action under 42 U.S.C. § 1983 in the United States District Court for the Eastern District of Wisconsin against respondents Winnebago County, DSS, and various individual employees of DSS. The complaint alleged that respondents had deprived Joshua of his liberty without due process of law, in violation of his rights under the Fourteenth Amendment, by failing to intervene to protect him against a risk of violence at his father's hands of which they knew or should have known. The District Court granted summary judgment for respondents.

The Court of Appeals for the Seventh Circuit affirmed. . . .

* * *

II

The Due Process Clause of the Fourteenth Amendment provides that "[n]o State shall . . . deprive any person of life, liberty, or property, without due process of law." Petitioners contend that the State deprived Joshua of his liberty interest in "free[dom] from . . . unjustified intrusions on personal security," by failing to provide him with adequate protection against his father's violence. The claim is one invoking the substantive rather than the procedural component of the Due Process Clause; petitioners do not claim that the State denied Joshua protection without according him appropriate procedural safeguards, but that it was categorically obligated to protect him in these circumstances.

But nothing in the language of the Due Process Clause itself requires the State to protect the life, liberty, and property of its citizens against invasion by private actors. The Clause is phrased as a limitation on the State's power to act, not as a guarantee of certain minimal levels of safety and security. It forbids the State itself to deprive individuals of life, liberty, or property without "due process of law," but its language cannot fairly be extended to impose an affirmative obligation on the State to ensure that those interests do not come to harm through other means. Nor does history support such an expansive reading of the constitutional text. Like its counterpart in the Fifth Amendment, the Due Process Clause of the Fourteenth Amendment was intended to prevent government "from abusing [its] power, or employing it as an instrument of oppression." Its purpose was to protect the people from the State, not to ensure that the State protected them from each other. The Framers were content to leave the extent of governmental obligation in the latter area to the democratic political processes.

Consistent with these principles, our cases have recognized that the Due Process Clauses generally confer no affirmative right to governmental aid, even where such aid may be necessary to secure life, liberty, or property interests of which the government itself may not deprive the individual. *See, e.g., Harris v. McRae* (1980) (no obligation to fund abortions or other medical services) . . .; *Lindsey v. Normet* (1972) (no obligation to provide adequate housing). . . . As we said in *Harris v. McRae*: "Although the liberty protected by the Due Process Clause affords protection against unwarranted *government* interference . . ., it does not confer an entitlement to such [governmental aid] as may be necessary to realize all the advantages of that freedom." (emphasis added). If the Due Process Clause does not require the State to provide its citizens with particular protective services, it follows that the State cannot be held liable under the Clause for injuries that could have been averted had it chosen to provide them. As a general matter, then, we conclude that a State's failure to protect an individual against private violence simply does not constitute a violation of the Due Process Clause.

Petitioners contend, however, that even if the Due Process Clause imposes no affirmative obligation on the State to provide the general public with adequate protective services, such a duty may arise out of certain "special relationships" created or assumed by the State with respect to particular individuals. Petitioners argue that such a "special relationship" existed here because the State knew that Joshua faced a special danger of abuse at his father's hands, and specifically proclaimed, by word and by deed, its intention to protect him against that danger. Having actually undertaken to protect Joshua from this danger — which petitioners concede the State played no part in creating — the State acquired an affirmative "duty," enforceable through the Due Process Clause, to do so in a reasonably competent fashion. Its failure to discharge that duty, so the argument goes, was an abuse of governmental power that so "shocks the conscience," *Rochin v. California* (1952), as to constitute a substantive due process violation.

We reject this argument. It is true that in certain limited circumstances the Constitution imposes upon the State affirmative duties of care and protection with respect to particular individuals. In *Estelle v. Gamble* (1976), we recognized that the Eighth Amendment's prohibition against cruel and unusual punishment, made applicable to the States through the Fourteenth Amendment's Due Process Clause, *Robinson v. California* (1962), requires the State to provide adequate medical care to incarcerated prisoners. We reasoned that because the prisoner is unable "'by reason of the deprivation of his liberty [to] care for himself,'" it is only "'just'" that the State be required to care for him.

In *Youngberg v. Romeo* (1982), we extended this analysis beyond the Eighth Amendment setting, holding that the substantive component of the Fourteenth Amendment's Due Process Clause requires the State to provide involuntarily committed mental patients with such services as are necessary to ensure their "reasonable safety" from themselves and others. As we explained: "If it is cruel and unusual punishment to hold convicted criminals in unsafe conditions, it must be unconstitutional [under the Due Process Clause] to confine the involuntarily committed — who may not be punished at all — in unsafe conditions."

But these cases afford petitioners no help. Taken together, they stand only for the proposition that when the State takes a person into its custody and holds him there against his will, the Constitution imposes upon it a corresponding duty to assume some responsibility for his safety and general well-being. The rationale for this principle is simple enough: when the State by the affirmative exercise of its power so restrains an individual's liberty that it renders him unable to care for himself, and at the same time fails to provide for his basic human needs — *e.g.*, food, clothing, shelter, medical care, and reasonable safety — it transgresses the substantive limits on state action set by the Eighth Amendment and the Due Process Clause. The affirmative duty to protect arises not from the State's knowledge of the individual's predicament or from its expressions of intent to help him, but from the limitation which it has imposed on his freedom to act on his own behalf. In the substantive due process analysis, it is the State's affirmative act of restraining the individual's freedom to act on his own behalf — through incarceration, institutionalization, or other similar restraint of personal liberty — which is the "deprivation of liberty" triggering the protections of the Due Process Clause, not its failure to act to protect his liberty interests against harms inflicted by other means.

The *Estelle-Youngberg* analysis simply has no applicability in the present case. . . .

It may well be that, by voluntarily undertaking to protect Joshua against a danger it concededly played no part in creating, the State acquired a duty under state tort law to provide him with adequate protection against that danger. *See* RESTATEMENT (SECOND) OF TORTS § 323 (1965) (one who undertakes to render services to another may in some circumstances be held liable for doing so in a negligent fashion). . . . But the claim here is based on the Due Process Clause of the Fourteenth Amendment, which, as we have said many times, does not

transform every tort committed by a state actor into a constitutional violation.
. . .

* * *

The people of Wisconsin may well prefer a system of liability which would place upon the State and its officials the responsibility for failure to act in situations such as the present one. They may create such a system, if they do not have it already, by changing the tort law of the State in accordance with the regular lawmaking process. But they should not have it thrust upon them by this Court's expansion of the Due Process Clause of the Fourteenth Amendment.

Affirmed.

Justice Brennan, with whom Justice Marshall and Justice Blackmun join, dissenting.

"The most that can be said of the state functionaries in this case," the Court today concludes, "is that they stood by and did nothing when suspicious circumstances dictated a more active role for them." Because I believe that this description of respondents' conduct tells only part of the story and that, accordingly, the Constitution itself "dictated a more active role" for respondents in the circumstances presented here, I cannot agree that respondents had no constitutional duty to help Joshua DeShaney.

It may well be, as the Court decides, that the Due Process Clause as construed by our prior cases creates no general right to basic governmental services. That however, is not the question presented here. . . . No one . . . has asked the Court to proclaim that, as a general matter, the Constitution safeguards positive as well as negative liberties.

* * *

The Court's baseline is the absence of positive rights in the Constitution and a concomitant suspicion of any claim that seems to depend on such rights. From this perspective, the DeShaneys' claim is first and foremost about inaction (the failure, here, of respondents to take steps to protect Joshua), and only tangentially about action (the establishment of a state program specifically designed to help children like Joshua). And from this perspective, holding these Wisconsin officials liable — where the only difference between this case and one involving a general claim to protective services is Wisconsin's establishment and operation of a program to protect children — would seem to punish an effort that we should seek to promote.

I would begin from the opposite direction. I would focus first on the action that Wisconsin *has* taken with respect to Joshua and children like him, rather than on the actions that the State failed to take. Such a method is not new to this Court. Both *Estelle v. Gamble* (1976), and *Youngberg v. Romeo* (1982), began by emphasizing that the States [had confined J.W. Gamble to prison and Nicholas Romeo to a psychiatric hospital]. This initial action rendered these people helpless to help themselves or to seek help from persons unconnected to the government. Cases from the lower courts also recognize that a State's actions can be decisive in assessing the constitutional significance of subsequent inaction. For these purposes, moreover, actual physical restraint is not the only state action that has been considered relevant. *See, e.g., White v. Rochford* (7th Cir. 1979) (police officers violated due process when, after arresting the guardian of three young children, they abandoned the children on a busy stretch of highway at night).

Because of the Court's initial fixation on the general principle that the Constitution does not establish positive rights, it is unable to appreciate our recognition in *Estelle* and *Youngberg* that this principle does not hold true in all circumstances. Thus, in the Court's view, *Youngberg* can be explained (and dismissed) in the following way: "In the substantive due process analysis, it is the State's affirmative act of restraining the individual's freedom to act on his own behalf — through incarceration, institutionalization, or other similar restraint of personal liberty — which is the 'deprivation of liberty' triggering the protections of the Due Process Clause, not its failure to act to protect his liberty interests against harms inflicted by other means." This restatement of *Youngberg*'s holding should come as a surprise when one recalls our explicit observation in that case that Romeo did not challenge his commitment to the hospital, but instead "argue[d] that he ha[d] a constitutionally protected liberty interest in safety, freedom of movement, and training within the institution; and that petitioners infringed these rights *by failing to provide* constitutionally required conditions of confinement." (emphasis added). I do not mean to suggest that "the State's affirmative act of restraining the individual's freedom to act on his own behalf," was irrelevant in *Youngberg*; rather, I emphasize that this conduct would have led to no injury, and consequently no cause of action under § 1983, unless the State then had failed to take steps to protect Romeo from himself and from others. In addition, the Court's exclusive attention to state-imposed restraints of "the individual's freedom to act on his own behalf," suggests that it was the State that rendered Romeo unable to care for himself, whereas in fact — with an I.Q. of between 8 and 10, and the mental capacity of an 18-month-old child — he had been quite incapable of taking care of himself long before the State stepped into his life. Thus, the fact of hospitalization was critical in *Youngberg* not because it rendered Romeo helpless to help himself, but because it separated him from other sources of aid that, we held, the State was obligated to replace. Unlike the Court, therefore, I am unable to see in *Youngberg* a neat and decisive divide between action and inaction.

Moreover, to the Court, the only fact that seems to count as an "affirmative act of restraining the individual's freedom to act on his own behalf" is direct physical control. I would not, however, give *Youngberg* and *Estelle* such a stingy scope. I would recognize, as the Court apparently cannot, that "the State's knowledge of [an] individual's predicament [and] its expressions of intent to help him" can amount to a "limitation . . . on his freedom to act on his own behalf" or to obtain help from others. Thus, I would read *Youngberg* and *Estelle* to stand for the much more generous proposition that, if a State cuts off private sources of aid and then refuses aid itself, it cannot wash its hands of the harm that results from its inaction.

Youngberg and *Estelle* are not alone in sounding this theme. In striking down a filing fee as applied to divorce cases brought by indigents, *see Boddie v. Connecticut* (1971), and in deciding that a local government could not entirely foreclose the opportunity to speak in a public forum, *see, e.g., Schneider v. State* (1939); *Hague v. Committee for Industrial Organization* (1939); *United States v. Grace* (1983), we have acknowledged that a State's actions — such as the monopolization of a particular path of relief — may impose upon the State certain positive duties. Similarly, *Shelley v. Kraemer* (1948), and *Burton v. Wilmington Parking Authority* (1961) [racial discrimination by private lessee of restaurant space in state-owned parking garage constituted "state action" because the state's ownership of the building carried with it a responsibility to prevent such discrimination], suggest that a State may be found complicit in an injury even if it did not create the situation that caused the harm.

Arising as they do from constitutional contexts different from the one involved here, cases like *Boddie* and *Burton* are instructive rather than decisive in the case before us. But they set a tone equally well established in precedent as, and contradictory to, the one the Court sets by situating the DeShaneys' complaint within the class of cases epitomized by the Court's decision in *Harris v. McRae* (1980). The cases that I have cited tell us that *Goldberg v. Kelly* (1970) (recognizing entitlement to welfare under state law), can stand side by side with *Dandridge v. Williams* (1970) (implicitly rejecting idea that welfare is a fundamental right), and that *Goss v. Lopez* (1975) (entitlement to public education under state law), is perfectly consistent with *San Antonio Independent School Dist. v. Rodriguez* (1973) (no fundamental right to education). To put the point more directly, these cases signal that a State's prior actions may be decisive in analyzing the constitutional significance of its inaction. I thus would locate the DeShaneys' claims within the framework of cases like *Youngberg* and *Estelle*, and more generally, *Boddie* and *Schneider*, by considering the actions that Wisconsin took with respect to Joshua.

Wisconsin has established a child-welfare system specifically designed to help children like Joshua. Wisconsin law places upon the local departments of social services such as respondent (DSS or Department) a duty to investigate reported instances of child abuse. While other governmental bodies and private persons are largely responsible for the reporting of possible cases of child abuse, Wisconsin law channels all such reports to the local departments of social services for evaluation and, if necessary, further action. Even when it is the sheriff's office or police department that receives a report of suspected child abuse, that report is referred to local social services departments for action; the only exception to this occurs when the reporter fears for the child's *immediate* safety. In this way, Wisconsin law invites — indeed, directs — citizens and other governmental entities to depend on local departments of social services such as respondent to protect children from abuse.

* * *

In these circumstances, a private citizen, or even a person working in a government agency other than DSS, would doubtless feel that her job was done as soon as she had reported her suspicions of child abuse to DSS. Through its child-welfare program, in other words, the State of Wisconsin has relieved ordinary citizens and governmental bodies other than the Department of any sense of obligation to do anything more than report their suspicions of child abuse to DSS. If DSS ignores or dismisses these suspicions, no one will step in to fill the gap. Wisconsin's child-protection program thus effectively confined Joshua DeShaney within the walls of Randy DeShaney's violent home until such time as DSS took action to remove him. Conceivably, then, children like Joshua are made worse off by the existence of this program when the persons and entities charged with carrying it out fail to do their jobs.

It simply belies reality, therefore, to contend that the State "stood by and did nothing" with respect to Joshua. Through its child-protection program, the State actively intervened in Joshua's life and, by virtue of this intervention, acquired ever more certain knowledge that Joshua was in grave danger. These circumstances, in my view, plant this case solidly within the tradition of cases like *Youngberg* and *Estelle*.

It will be meager comfort to Joshua and his mother to know that, if the State had "selectively den[ied] its protective services" to them because they were "disfavored minorities," their § 1983 suit might have stood on sturdier ground. Because of the posture of this case, we do not know why respondents did not take steps to protect Joshua; the Court, however, tells us that their reason is irrelevant so long as their inaction was not the product of invidious discrimination. Presumably, then, if respondents decided not to help Joshua because his name began with a "J," or because he was born in the spring, or because they did not care enough about him even to formulate an intent to discriminate against him based on an arbitrary reason, respondents would not be liable to the DeShaneys because they were not the ones who dealt the blows that destroyed Joshua's life.

* * *

As the Court today reminds us, "the Due Process Clause of the Fourteenth Amendment was intended to prevent government 'from abusing [its] power, or employing it as an instrument of oppression.'" My disagreement with the Court arises from its failure to see that inaction can be every bit as abusive of power as action, that oppression can result when a State undertakes a vital duty and then ignores it. Today's opinion construes the Due Process Clause to permit a State to displace private sources of protection and then, at the critical moment, to shrug its shoulders and turn away from the harm that it has promised to try to prevent. Because I cannot agree that our Constitution is indifferent to such indifference, I respectfully dissent.

JUSTICE BLACKMUN, dissenting [omitted].

NOTES AND QUESTIONS

1. Our concern is still what constitutes "state action" of a sort the Fourteenth Amendment is designed to guard against. "Poor Joshua!" said the dissenters in this case, believing that the state of Wisconsin child welfare authorities had horribly failed him. And so, even Justice Rehnquist in his recitation of the excruciating facts of the case, makes clear. Why then, if the state social worker was clearly at fault for failing to do her job, was the relief sought in the case denied? "The complaint alleged that respondents had deprived Joshua of his liberty without due process of law, in violation of his rights under the Fourteenth Amendment, by failing to intervene to protect him against a risk of violence at his father's hands of which they knew or should have known." 489 U.S. at 193. The statute under which relief was sought provides a remedy for a state's depriving one of one's civil rights under color of law, and was passed pursuant to the authority of the Fourteenth Amendment. Why, if the state officials, in effect, could have prevented the harm that took place, are they not liable? Why, in short, was this not "state action"?

2. Note that the majority explains that we are dealing with the "substantive" component of "due process." There is no doubt, really, that state action, or perhaps state "inaction" is involved, but the question the Court is addressing is whether a failure to prevent someone else from doing harm is a deprivation of the "life, liberty, or property" interest protected by the Due Process Clause. What would be your answer? For a view highly critical of the Chief Justice in this case and others, see Alan R. Madry, *State Action and the Obligation of the States to Prevent Private Harm: The Rehnquist Transformation and the Betrayal of Fundamental Commitments*, 65 So. Cal. L. Rev. 781 (1992) ("If there is at least one right [the right to private property] that the states must protect against invasion by private agents, then one cannot claim that the Fourteenth Amendment as a general matter imposes no responsibility on the states to provide such protection. The burden would then shift to the proponents of state discretion to show how and why rights or interests other than property are not protected by the Amendment"). Would Joshua's claim have been more successful had he asserted that Wisconsin failed to afford him the equal *protection* of the law?

3. The majority is willing to concede that "[i]t is true that in certain limited circumstances the Constitution imposes upon the state affirmative duties of care and protection with respect to particular individuals." 489 U.S. at 198. Why isn't "poor Joshua" one of those individuals?

4. You may have been struck by the fact that the dissent cites *Shelley v. Kramer* in support of its position. Do you see the connection? How might Justice Harlan have voted in this case? The majority makes much of the historical reasons for the passage of the Fourteenth Amendment. Are they relevant here?

5. The critics of the *DeShaney* decision (and there are many) have sought to portray the majority as insufficiently sensitive to the plight of children such as

Joshua. Are such children left, however, with no legal remedy after the majority's opinion? What policies are served by leaving Joshua's family only to the state tort system for redress? Why would anyone want to regard the father's conduct as implicating federally-protected rights? Does the dissenters' focus on cases involving the welfare system and indigents give you any clues? In the dissenters' view, should the Fourteenth Amendment be used only as a means of improving the lot of African Americans, as the Amendment's framers had most prominent in their minds, or does it express a different vision of American society? In order to understand just what vision of American society is inherent in the Fourteenth Amendment, it is useful to spend some time trying to outline with more precision the meaning of the protected sphere of "life, liberty, and property." This is the subject of the next case.

B. What Constitutes "Life, Liberty, or Property"?

BOARD OF REGENTS v. ROTH
408 U.S. 564 (1972)

MR. JUSTICE STEWART delivered the opinion of the Court.

In 1968 the respondent, David Roth, was hired for his first teaching job as assistant professor of political science at Wisconsin State University-Oshkosh. He was hired for a fixed term of one academic year. . . . The respondent completed that term. But he was informed that he would not be rehired for the next academic year.

The respondent had no tenure rights to continued employment. Under Wisconsin statutory law a state university teacher can acquire tenure as a "permanent" employee only after four years of year-to-year employment. Having acquired tenure, a teacher is entitled to continued employment "during efficiency and good behavior." A relatively new teacher without tenure, however, is under Wisconsin law entitled to nothing beyond his one-year appointment. There are no statutory or administrative standards defining eligibility for re-employment. State law thus clearly leaves the decision whether to rehire a nontenured teacher for another year to the unfettered discretion of university officials.

The procedural protection afforded a Wisconsin State University teacher before he is separated from the University corresponds to his job security. As a matter of statutory law, a tenured teacher cannot be "discharged except for cause upon written charges" and pursuant to certain procedures. A nontenured teacher, similarly, is protected to some extent *during* his one-year term. Rules promulgated by the Board of Regents provide that a nontenured teacher "dismissed" before the end of the year may have some opportunity for review of the "dismissal." But the Rules provide no real protection for a nontenured teacher who simply is not re-employed for the next year. He must be informed by February 1 "concerning retention or nonretention for the ensuing year." But "no reason for non-retention need be given. No review or appeal is provided in such case."

In conformance with these Rules, the President of Wisconsin State University-Oshkosh informed the respondent before February 1, 1969, that he would not be rehired for the 1969-1970 academic year. He gave the respondent no reason for the decision and no opportunity to challenge it at any sort of hearing.

The respondent then brought this action in Federal District Court alleging that the decision not to rehire him for the next year infringed his Fourteenth Amendment rights. He attacked the decision both in substance and procedure. First, he alleged that the true reason for the decision was to punish him for certain statements critical of the University administration, and that it therefore violated his right to freedom of speech. Second, he alleged that the failure of University officials to give him notice of any reason for nonretention and an opportunity for a hearing violated his right to procedural due process of law.

The District Court granted summary judgment for the respondent on the procedural issue, ordering the University officials to provide him with reasons and a hearing. The Court of Appeals, with one judge dissenting, affirmed this partial summary judgment. We granted certiorari. The only question presented to us at this stage in the case is whether the respondent had a constitutional right to a statement of reasons and a hearing on the University's decision not to rehire him for another year. We hold that he did not.

I

The requirements of procedural due process apply only to the deprivation of interests encompassed by the Fourteenth Amendment's protection of liberty and property. When protected interests are implicated, the right to some kind of prior hearing is paramount. But the range of interests protected by procedural due process is not infinite.

The District Court decided that procedural due process guarantees apply in this case by assessing and balancing the weights of the particular interests involved. It concluded that the respondent's interest in re-employment at Wisconsin State University-Oshkosh outweighed the University's interest in denying him re-employment summarily. Undeniably, the respondent's re-employment prospects were of major concern to him — concern that we surely cannot say was insignificant. And a weighing process has long been a part of any determination of the *form* of hearing required in particular situations by procedural due process. But, to determine whether due process requirements apply in the first place, we must look not to the "weight" but to the nature of the interest at stake. We must look to see if the interest is within the Fourteenth Amendment's protection of liberty and property.

"Liberty" and "property" are broad and majestic terms. They are among the "[g]reat [constitutional] concepts . . . purposely left to gather meaning from experience. . . . [T]hey relate to the whole domain of social and economic fact, and the statesmen who founded this Nation knew too well that only a stagnant society remains unchanged." For that reason, the Court has fully and finally rejected the wooden distinction between "rights" and "privileges" that once seemed to govern the applicability of procedural due process rights. The Court has also made clear that the property interests protected by procedural due process extend well beyond actual ownership of real estate, chattels, or money. By the same token, the Court has required due process protection for deprivations of liberty beyond the sort of formal constraints imposed by the criminal process.

Yet, while the Court has eschewed rigid or formalistic limitations on the protection of procedural due process, it has at the same time observed certain boundaries. . . .

II

"While this Court has not attempted to define with exactness the liberty . . . guaranteed [by the Fourteenth Amendment], the term has received much consideration and some of the included things have been definitely stated. Without doubt, it denotes not merely freedom from bodily restraint but also the right of the individual to contract, to engage in any of the common occupations of life, to acquire useful knowledge, to marry, establish a home and bring up children, to worship God according to the dictates of his own conscience, and generally to enjoy those privileges long recognized . . . as essential to the orderly pursuit of happiness by free men." *Meyer v. Nebraska* (1923). In a Constitution for a free people, there can be no doubt that the meaning of "liberty" must be broad indeed.

There might be cases in which a State refused to reemploy a person under such circumstances that interests in liberty would be implicated. But this is not such a case.

The State, in declining to rehire the respondent, did not make any charge against him that might seriously damage his standing and associations in his community. It did not base the nonrenewal of his contract on a charge, for example, that he had been guilty of dishonesty, or immorality. Had it done so, this would be a different case. For "[w]here a person's good name, reputation, honor, or integrity is at stake because of what the government is doing to him, notice and an opportunity to be heard are essential." In such a case, due process would accord an opportunity to refute the charge before University officials. In the present case, however, there is no suggestion whatever that the respondent's "good name, reputation, honor, or integrity" is at stake.

Similarly, there is no suggestion that the State, in declining to re-employ the respondent, imposed on him a stigma or other disability that foreclosed his freedom to take advantage of other employment opportunities. The State, for example, did not invoke any regulations to bar the respondent from all other public employment in state universities. . . .

To be sure, the respondent has alleged that the nonrenewal of his contract was based on his exercise of his right to freedom of speech. But this allegation is not now before us. The District Court stayed proceedings on this issue, and the respondent has yet to prove that the decision not to rehire him was, in fact, based on his free speech activities.

Hence, on the record before us, all that clearly appears is that the respondent was not rehired for one year at one university. It stretches the concept too far to suggest that a person is deprived of "liberty" when he simply is not rehired in one job but remains as free as before to seek another.

III

The Fourteenth Amendment's procedural protection of property is a safeguard of the security of interests that a person has already acquired in specific benefits. These interests — property interests — may take many forms.

Thus, the Court has held that a person receiving welfare benefits under statutory and administrative standards defining eligibility for them has an interest in continued receipt of those benefits that is safeguarded by procedural due process. *Goldberg v. Kelly* (1970). Similarly, in the area of public employment, the Court has held that a public college professor dismissed from an office held under tenure provisions, and college professors and staff members dismissed during the terms of their contracts, have interests in continued employment that are safeguarded by due process. Only last year, the Court held that this principle "proscribing summary dismissal from public employment without hearing or inquiry required by due process" also applied to a teacher recently hired without tenure or a formal contract, but nonetheless with a clearly implied promise of continued employment.

Certain attributes of "property" interests protected by procedural due process emerge from these decisions. To have a property interest in a benefit, a person clearly must have more than an abstract need or desire for it. He must have more than a unilateral expectation of it. He must, instead, have a legitimate claim of entitlement to it. It is a purpose of the ancient institution of property to protect those claims upon which people rely in their daily lives, reliance that must not be arbitrarily undermined. It is a purpose of the constitutional right to a hearing to provide an opportunity for a person to vindicate those claims.

Property interests, of course, are not created by the Constitution. Rather, they are created and their dimensions are defined by existing rules or understandings that stem from an independent source such as state law — rules or understandings that secure certain benefits and that support claims of entitlement to those benefits. Thus, the welfare recipients in *Goldberg v. Kelly, supra,* had a claim of entitlement to welfare payments that was grounded in the statute defining eligibility for them. The recipients had not yet shown that they were, in fact, within the statutory terms of eligibility. But we held that they had a right to a hearing at which they might attempt to do so.

Just as the welfare recipients' "property" interest in welfare payments was created and defined by statutory terms, so the respondent's "property" interest in employment at Wisconsin State University-Oshkosh was created and defined by the terms of his appointment. Those terms secured his interest in employment up to June 30, 1969. But the important fact in this case is that they specifically provided that the respondent's employment was to terminate on June 30. They did not provide for contract renewal absent "sufficient cause." Indeed, they made no provision for renewal whatsoever.

Thus, the terms of the respondent's appointment secured absolutely no interest in re-employment for the next year. They supported absolutely no possible claim of entitlement to re-employment. Nor, significantly, was there any state statute or University rule or policy that secured his interest in re-employment or that created any legitimate claim to it. In these circumstances, the respondent surely had an abstract concern in being rehired, but he did not have a *property* interest sufficient to require the University authorities to give him a hearing when they declined to renew his contract of employment.

IV

Our analysis of the respondent's constitutional rights in this case in no way indicates a view that an opportunity for a hearing or a statement of reasons for nonretention would, or would not, be appropriate or wise in public colleges and universities. For it is a written Constitution that we apply. Our role is confined to interpretation of that Constitution.

* * *

Mr. Justice Douglas, dissenting.

. . . Though Roth was rated by the faculty as an excellent teacher, he had publicly criticized the administration for suspending an entire group of 94 black students without determining individual guilt. He also criticized the university's regime as being authoritarian and autocratic. He used his classroom to discuss what was being done about the black episode; and one day, instead of meeting his class, he went to the meeting of the Board of Regents.

In this case . . . an action was started in Federal District Court under 42 U.S.C. § 1983[18] claiming in part that the decision of the school authorities not to rehire was in retaliation for his expression of opinion. . . .

---

[18] Section 1983 reads as follows:

"Every person who, under color of any statute, ordinance, regulation, custom, or usage, of any State or Territory, subjects, or causes to be subjected, any citizen of the United States or other person within the jurisdiction thereof to the deprivation of any rights, privileges, or immunities secured by the Constitution and laws, shall be liable to the party injured in an action at law, suit in equity, or other proper proceeding for redress."

Professor Will Herberg, of Drew University, in writing of "academic freedom" recently said:

"[I]t is sometimes conceived as a basic constitutional right guaranteed and protected under the First Amendment.

"But, of course, this is not the case. Whereas a man's right to speak out on this or that may be guaranteed and protected, he can have no imaginable human or constitutional right to remain a member of a university faculty. Clearly, the right to academic freedom is an acquired one, yet an acquired right of such value to society that in the minds of many it has verged upon the constitutional."

There may not be a constitutional right to continued employment if private schools and colleges are involved. But Prof. Herberg's view is not correct when public schools move against faculty members. For the First Amendment, applicable to the States by reason of the Fourteenth Amendment, protects the individual against state action when it comes to freedom of speech and of press and the related freedoms guaranteed by the First Amendment; and the Fourteenth protects "liberty" and "property" . . . .

No more direct assault on academic freedom can be imagined than for the school authorities to be allowed to discharge a teacher because of his or her philosophical, political, or ideological beliefs. The same may well be true of private schools, if through the device of financing or other umbilical cords they become instrumentalities of the State. . . .

* * *

When a violation of First Amendment rights is alleged, the reasons for dismissal or for nonrenewal of an employment contract must be examined to see if the reasons given are only a cloak for activity or attitudes protected by the Constitution. A statutory analogy is present under the National Labor Relations Act. While discharges of employees for "cause" are permissible, discharges because of an employee's union activities are banned. So the search is to ascertain whether the stated ground was the real one or only a pretext.

In the case of teachers whose contracts are not renewed, tenure is not the critical issue. . . . [C]onditioning renewal of a teacher's contract upon surrender of First Amendment rights is beyond the power of a State.

There is sometimes a conflict between a claim for First Amendment protection and the need for orderly administration of the school system. . . . That is one reason why summary judgments in this class of cases are seldom appropriate. Another reason is that careful factfinding is often necessary to know whether the given reason for nonrenewal of a teacher's contract is the real reason or a feigned one.

It is said that since teaching in a public school is a privilege, the State can grant it or withhold it on conditions. We have, however, rejected that thesis in numerous cases . . . .

. . . [W]hen a State proposes to deny a privilege to one who it alleges has engaged in unprotected speech, Due Process requires that the State bear the burden of proving that the speech was not protected. "[T]he 'protection of the individual against arbitrary action' . . . [is] the very essence of due process," but where the State is allowed to act secretly behind closed doors and without any notice to those who are affected by its actions, there is no check against the possibility of such "arbitrary action."

Moreover, where "important interests" of the citizen are implicated they are not to be denied or taken away without due process. [One such case] involved a driver's license. But also included are disqualification for unemployment compensation, discharge from public employment, denial of tax exemption, and withdrawal of welfare benefits (*Goldberg v. Kelly* (1970)). We should now add that nonrenewal of a teacher's contract, whether or not he has tenure, is an entitlement of the same importance and dignity.

. . . Nonrenewal of a teacher's contract is tantamount in effect to a dismissal and the consequences may be enormous. Nonrenewal can be a blemish that turns into a permanent scar and effectively limits any chance the teacher has of being rehired as a teacher, at least in his State.

If this nonrenewal implicated the First Amendment, then Roth was deprived of constitutional rights because his employment was conditioned on a surrender of First Amendment rights; and, apart from the First Amendment, he was denied due process when he received no notice and hearing of the adverse action contemplated against him. Without a statement of the reasons for the discharge and an opportunity to rebut those reasons — both of which were refused by petitioners — there is no means short of a lawsuit to safeguard the right not to be discharged for the exercise of First Amendment guarantees.

* * *

MR. JUSTICE MARSHALL, dissenting.

* * *

While I agree with Part I of the Court's opinion, setting forth the proper framework for consideration of the issue presented, and also with those portions of Parts II and III of the Court's opinion that assert that a public employee is entitled to procedural due process whenever a State stigmatizes him by denying employment, or injures his future employment prospects severely, or whenever the State deprives him of a property interest, I would go further than the Court does in defining the terms "liberty" and "property."

The prior decisions of this Court . . . establish a principle that is as obvious as it is compelling — *i.e.*, federal and state governments and governmental agencies are restrained by the Constitution from acting arbitrarily with respect to employment opportunities that they either offer or control. Hence, it is now firmly established that whether or not a private employer is free to act capriciously or unreasonably with respect to employment practices, at least absent statutory or contractual controls, a government employer is different. The government may only act fairly and reasonably.

This Court has long maintained that "the right to work for a living in the common occupations of the community is of the very essence of the personal freedom and opportunity that it was the purpose of the [Fourteenth] Amendment to secure." It has also established that the fact that an employee has no contract guaranteeing work for a specific future period does not mean that as the result of action by the government he may be "discharged at any time for any reason or for no reason."

In my view, every citizen who applies for a government job is entitled to it unless the government can establish some reason for denying the employment. This is the "property" right that I believe is protected by the Fourteenth Amendment and that cannot be denied "without due process of law." And it is also liberty — liberty to work — which is the "very essence of the personal freedom and opportunity" secured by the Fourteenth Amendment.

This Court has often had occasion to note that the denial of public employment is a serious blow to any citizen. Thus, when an application for public employment is denied or the contract of a government employee is not renewed, the government must say why, for it is only when the reasons underlying government action are known that citizens feel secure and protected against arbitrary government action.

Employment is one of the greatest, if not the greatest, benefits that governments offer in modern-day life. When something as valuable as the opportunity to work is at stake, the government may not reward some citizens and not others without demonstrating that its actions are fair and equitable. And it is procedural due process that is our fundamental guarantee of fairness, our protection against arbitrary, capricious, and unreasonable government action.

Mr. Justice Douglas has written that:

> "It is not without significance that most of the provisions of the Bill of Rights are procedural. It is procedure that spells much of the difference between rule by law and rule by whim or caprice. Steadfast adherence to strict procedural safeguards is our main assurance that there will be equal justice under law."

And Mr. Justice Frankfurter has said that "[t]he history of American freedom is, in no small measure, the history of procedure." With respect to occupations controlled by the government, one lower court has said that "[t]he public has the right to expect its officers . . . to make adjudications on the basis of merit." The first step toward insuring that these expectations are realized is to require adherence to the standards of due process; absolute and uncontrolled discretion invites abuse.

We have often noted that procedural due process means many different things in the numerous contexts in which it applies. Prior decisions have held that an applicant for admission to practice as an attorney before the United States Board of Tax Appeals may not be rejected without a statement of reasons and a chance for a hearing on disputed issues of fact; that a tenured teacher could not be summarily dismissed without notice of the reasons and a hearing; that an applicant for admission to a state bar could not be denied the opportunity to practice law without notice of the reasons for the rejection of his application and a hearing; and even that a substitute teacher who had been employed only two months could not be dismissed merely because she refused to take a loyalty oath without an inquiry into the specific facts of her case and a hearing on those in dispute. I would follow these cases and hold that respondent was denied due process when his contract was not renewed and he was not informed of the reasons and given an opportunity to respond.

NOTES AND QUESTIONS

1. The subject of this case, as indicated, is what sort of "rights" are protected by the terms "liberty and property" under the Fourteenth Amendment. Note that even the majority (which denies the relief sought) is careful to suggest that there is no easy answer to this question, and that it is not a matter of "rigid or formalistic" categorization — the sort of thinking which might say, for example, that "rights" are protected but "privileges" are not. Is "rigid or formalistic" thinking inconsistent with the interpretation of the Constitution? Has this always been the case?

2. Quoting from a famous case on the point, the majority observes that the Fourteenth Amendment term, "liberty,"

> denotes not merely freedom from bodily restraint but also the right of the individual to contract, to engage in any of the common occupations of life, to acquire useful knowledge, to marry, establish a home and bring up children, to worship God according to the dictates of his own conscience, and generally to enjoy those privileges long recognized . . . as essential to the orderly pursuit of happiness by free men.

408 U.S. at 572 (quoting *Meyer v. Nebraska*, 262 U.S. 390, 399 (1923)). This is very much a definition informed by the natural law rights of individuals. Modernly, why isn't job security in a nontenured academic position such a protected "right," or is it? Is it the object in controversy — the teacher's job — or the manner in which he lost it that is important?

3. The majority finally appears to zero in on the concept of protected "property" interests under the Fourteenth Amendment, and then describes those interests as follows:

> Property interests, of course, are not created by the Constitution. Rather, they are created and their dimensions are defined by existing rules or understandings that stem from an independent source such as state law — rules or understandings that secure certain benefits and that support claims of entitlement to those benefits.

408 U.S. at 577. Note, then, that this means that one cannot fully understand the law of the federal Constitution, at least insofar as one studies the Fourteenth Amendment, without having an appreciation of state law as well. Note further, that the meaning of this passage is that what is protected under the Fourteenth Amendment may vary from state to state. Is this appropriate? Is the dissent in agreement with the majority on this point? Are you? What is it that leads to dissents in the case? Is it the point about what constitutes protected "property" interests, is it about the supposed "First Amendment" implications (not addressed by the majority), or is it, as seems to be implicit in Justice Marshall's dissent, the notion that "public employment" of any kind cannot be terminated without due process?

4. Thus far, we have seen that due process protection requires both a finding of state action and a protectible life, liberty or property interest. It should be kept in mind that due process arises only when the subject is the application of an already enacted law to a particular person or group. Long ago, the Court made it clear that due process cannot be raised against general legislative activity. *Bi-Metallic Investment Co. v. State Board of Equalization*, 239 U.S. 441 (1915) (increasing the valuation of all property in Denver by 40 percent without notice or hearing; the remedy, said the Court, is to throw the bums out). We turn next to the issue of just what constitutes "due process" if one is entitled to it. The dissenters in *Roth* suggest that some notification of charges for dismissal, at the very least, ought to be required. What else constitutes "due process," and does it vary depending on the type of interest protected? This is the subject of the next section.

C. What Process is Due?

GOLDBERG v. KELLY
397 U.S. 254 (1970)

MR. JUSTICE BRENNAN delivered the opinion of the Court.

* * *

I

The constitutional issue to be decided . . . is . . . whether the Due Process Clause requires that [a welfare] recipient be afforded an evidentiary hearing *before* the termination of benefits. The District Court held that only a pre-termination evidentiary hearing would satisfy the constitutional command, and rejected the argument of the state and city officials that the combination of the post-termination "fair hearing" with the informal pre-termination review disposed of all due process claims. The court said: "While post-termination review is relevant, there is one overpowering fact which controls here. By hypothesis, a welfare recipient is destitute, without funds or assets. . . . Suffice it to say that to cut off a welfare recipient in the face of . . . 'brutal need' without a prior hearing of some sort is unconscionable, unless overwhelming considerations justify it." The court rejected the argument that the need to protect the public's tax revenues supplied the requisite "overwhelming consideration." "Against the justified desire to protect public funds must be weighed the individual's overpowering need in this unique situation not to be wrongfully deprived of assistance. . . . While the problem of additional expense must be kept in mind, it does not justify denying a hearing meeting the ordinary standards of due process. . . ."

Appellant does not contend that procedural due process is not applicable to the termination of welfare benefits. Such benefits are a matter of statutory entitlement for persons qualified to receive them. Their termination involves state action that adjudicates important rights. The constitutional challenge cannot be answered by an argument that public assistance benefits are "a 'privilege' and not a 'right.'" Relevant constitutional restraints apply as much to the withdrawal of public assistance benefits as to disqualification for unemployment compensation, or to denial of a tax exemption, or to discharge from public employment. The extent to which procedural due process must be afforded the recipient is influenced by the extent to which he may be "condemned to suffer grievous loss," and depends upon whether the recipient's interest in avoiding that loss outweighs the governmental interest in summary adjudication. Accordingly, . . . "consideration of what procedures due process may require under any given set of circumstances must begin with a determination of the precise nature of the government function involved as well as of the private interest that has been affected by governmental action."

It is true, of course, that some governmental benefits may be administratively terminated without affording the recipient a pre-termination evidentiary hearing. But we agree with the District Court that when welfare is discontinued, only a pre-termination evidentiary hearing provides the recipient with procedural due process. For qualified recipients, welfare provides the means to obtain essential food, clothing, housing, and medical care. Thus the crucial factor in this context — a factor not present in the case of the blacklisted government contractor, the discharged government employee, the taxpayer denied a tax exemption, or virtually anyone else whose governmental entitlements are ended — is that termination of aid pending resolution of a controversy over eligibility may deprive an eligible recipient of the very means by which to live while he waits. Since he lacks independent resources, his situation becomes immediately desperate. His need to concentrate upon finding the means for daily subsistence, in turn, adversely affects his ability to seek redress from the welfare bureaucracy.

* * *

Appellant does not challenge the force of these considerations but argues that they are outweighed by countervailing governmental interests in conserving fiscal and administrative resources. These interests, the argument goes, justify the delay of any evidentiary hearing until after discontinuance of the grants. Summary adjudication protects the public fisc by stopping payments promptly upon discovery of reason to believe that a recipient is no longer eligible. Since most terminations are accepted without challenge, summary adjudication also conserves both the fisc and administrative time and energy by reducing the number of evidentiary hearings actually held.

We agree with the District Court, however, that these governmental interests are not overriding in the welfare context. The requirement of a prior hearing doubtless involves some greater expense, and the benefits paid to ineligible recipients pending decision at the hearing probably cannot be recouped, since these recipients are likely to be judgment-proof. But the State is not without weapons to minimize these increased costs. . . . Thus, the interest of the eligible recipient in uninterrupted receipt of public assistance, coupled with the State's interest that his payments not be erroneously terminated, clearly outweighs the State's competing concern to prevent any increase in its fiscal and administrative burdens. . . .

II

We also agree with the District Court, however, that the pre-termination hearing need not take the form of a judicial or quasi-judicial trial. We bear in mind that the statutory "fair hearing" will provide the recipient with a full administrative review. Accordingly, the pre-termination hearing has one function only: to produce an initial determination of the validity of the welfare department's grounds for discontinuance of payments in order to protect a recipient against an erroneous termination of his benefits. Thus, a complete record and a comprehensive opinion, which would serve primarily to facilitate judicial review and to guide future decisions, need not be provided at the pre-termination stage. . . . We wish to add that we, no less than the dissenters, recognize the importance of not imposing upon the States or the Federal Government in this developing field of law any procedural requirements beyond those demanded by rudimentary due process.

"The fundamental requisite of due process of law is the opportunity to be heard." . . . The hearing must be "at a meaningful time and in a meaningful manner." . . . In the present context these principles require that a recipient have timely and adequate notice detailing the reasons for a proposed termination, and an effective opportunity to defend by confronting any adverse witnesses and by presenting his own arguments and evidence orally. . . .

* * *

The city's procedures presently do not permit recipients to appear personally with or without counsel before the official who finally determines continued eligibility. Thus a recipient is not permitted to present evidence to that official orally, or to confront or cross-examine adverse witnesses. These omissions are fatal to the constitutional adequacy of the procedures.

The opportunity to be heard must be tailored to the capacities and circumstances of those who are to be heard. It is not enough that a welfare recipient may present his position to the decision maker in writing or secondhand through his caseworker. Written submissions are an unrealistic option for most recipients, who lack the educational attainment necessary to write effectively and who cannot obtain professional assistance. Moreover, written submissions do not afford the flexibility of oral presentations; they do not permit the recipient to mold his argument to the issues the decision maker appears to regard as important. Particularly where credibility and veracity are at issue, as they must be in many termination proceedings, written submissions are a wholly unsatisfactory basis for decision. . . . Therefore a recipient must be allowed to state his position orally. Informal procedures will suffice; in this context due process does not require a particular order of proof or mode of offering evidence.

In almost every setting where important decisions turn on questions of fact, due process requires an opportunity to confront and cross-examine adverse witnesses. . . .

"The right to be heard would be, in many cases, of little avail if it did not comprehend the right to be heard by counsel." We do not say that counsel must be provided at the pre-termination hearing, but only that the recipient must be allowed to retain an attorney if he so desires. . . .

Finally, the decisionmaker's conclusion as to a recipient's eligibility must rest solely on the legal rules and evidence adduced at the hearing. To demonstrate compliance with this elementary requirement, the decision maker should state the reasons for his determination and indicate the evidence he relied on, though his statement need not amount to a full opinion or even formal findings of fact and conclusions of law. And, of course, an impartial decision maker is essential. We agree with the District Court that prior involvement in some aspects of a case will not necessarily bar a welfare official from acting as a decision maker. He should not, however, have participated in making the determination under review.

* * *

MR. JUSTICE BLACK, dissenting.

In the last half century the United States, along with many, perhaps most, other nations of the world, has moved far toward becoming a welfare state, that is, a nation that for one reason or another taxes its most affluent people to help support, feed, clothe, and shelter its less fortunate citizens. The result is that today more than nine million men, women, and children in the United States receive some kind of state or federally financed public assistance in the form of allowances or gratuities, generally paid them periodically, usually by the week, month, or quarter. Since these gratuities are paid on the basis of need, the list of recipients is not static, and some people go off the lists and others are added from time to time. These ever-changing lists put a constant administrative burden on government and it certainly could not have reasonably anticipated that this burden would include the additional procedural expense imposed by the Court today.

The dilemma of the ever-increasing poor in the midst of constantly growing affluence presses upon us and must inevitably be met within the framework of our democratic constitutional government, if our system is to survive as such. It was largely to escape just such pressing economic problems and attendant government repression that people from Europe, Asia, and other areas settled this country and formed our Nation. Many of those settlers had personally suffered from persecutions of various kinds and wanted to get away from governments that had unrestrained powers to make life miserable for their citizens. It was for this reason, or so I believe, that on reaching these new lands the early settlers undertook to curb their governments by confining their powers within written boundaries, which eventually became written constitutions. They wrote their basic charters as nearly as men's collective wisdom could do so as to proclaim to their people and their officials an emphatic command that: "Thus far and no farther shall you go; and where we neither delegate powers to you, nor prohibit your exercise of them, we the people are left free."

Representatives of the people of the Thirteen Original Colonies spent long, hot months in the summer of 1787 in Philadelphia, Pennsylvania, creating a government of limited powers. They divided it into three departments — Legislative, Judicial, and Executive. The Judicial Department was to have no part whatever in making any laws. In fact proposals looking to vesting some power in the Judiciary to take part in the legislative process and veto laws were offered, considered, and rejected by the Constitutional Convention. In my judgment there is not one word, phrase, or sentence from the beginning to the end of the Constitution from which it can be inferred that judges were granted any such legislative power. True, *Marbury v. Madison* (1803), held, and properly, I think, that courts must be the final interpreters of the Constitution, and I recognize that the holding can provide an opportunity to slide imperceptibly into constitutional amendment and law making. But when federal judges use this judicial power for legislative purposes, I think they wander out of their field of vested powers and transgress into the area constitutionally assigned to the Congress and the people. That is precisely what I believe the Court is doing in this case. Hence my dissent.

The more than a million names on the relief rolls in New York, and the more than nine million names on the rolls of all the 50 States were not put there at random. The names are there because state welfare officials believed that those people were eligible for assistance. Probably in the officials' haste to make out the lists many names were put there erroneously in order to alleviate immediate suffering, and undoubtedly some people are drawing relief who are not entitled under the law to do so. Doubtless some draw relief checks from time to time who know they are not eligible, either because they are not actually in need or for some other reason. Many of those who thus draw undeserved gratuities are without sufficient property to enable the government to collect back from them any money they wrongfully receive. But the Court today holds that it would violate the Due Process Clause of the Fourteenth Amendment to stop paying those people weekly or monthly allowances unless the government first affords them a full "evidentiary hearing" even though welfare officials are persuaded that the recipients are not rightfully entitled to receive a penny under the law. In other words, although some recipients might be on the lists for payment wholly because of deliberate fraud on their part, the Court holds that the government is helpless and must continue, until after an evidentiary hearing, to pay money that it does not owe, never has owed, and never could owe. I do not believe there is any provision in our Constitution that should thus paralyze the government's efforts to protect itself against making payments to people who are not entitled to them.

Particularly do I not think that the Fourteenth Amendment should be given such an unnecessarily broad construction. That Amendment came into being primarily to protect Negroes from discrimination, and while some of its language can and does protect others, all know that the chief purpose behind it was to protect ex-slaves. The Court, however, relies upon the Fourteenth Amendment and in effect says that failure of the government to pay a promised charitable instalment to an individual deprives that individual *of his own property*, in violation of the Due Process Clause of the Fourteenth Amendment. It somewhat strains credulity to say that the government's promise of charity to an individual is property belonging to that individual when the government denies that the individual is honestly entitled to receive such a payment.

I would have little, if any, objection to the majority's decision in this case if it were written as the report of the House Committee on Education and Labor, but as an opinion ostensibly resting on the language of the Constitution I find it woefully deficient. Once the verbiage is pared away it is obvious that this Court today adopts the views of the District Court "that to cut off a welfare recipient in the face of . . . 'brutal need' without a prior hearing of some sort is unconscionable," and therefore, says the Court, unconstitutional. The majority reaches this result by a process of weighing "the recipient's interest in avoiding" the termination of welfare benefits against "the governmental interest in summary adjudication." Today's balancing act requires a "pre-termination evidentiary hearing," yet there is nothing that indicates what tomorrow's balance will be. . . . [I]t is obvious that today's result does not depend on the language of the Constitution itself or the principles of other decisions, but solely on the collective judgment of the majority as to what would be a fair and humane procedure in this case.

This decision is thus only another variant of the view often expressed by some members of this Court that the Due Process Clause forbids any conduct that a majority of the Court believes "unfair," "indecent," or "shocking to their consciences." Neither these words nor any like them appear anywhere in the Due Process Clause. If they did, they would leave the majority of Justices free to hold any conduct unconstitutional that they should conclude on their own to be unfair or shocking to them. Had the drafters of the Due Process Clause meant to leave judges such ambulatory power to declare laws unconstitutional, the chief value of a written constitution, as the Founders saw it, would have been lost. In fact, if that view of due process is correct, the Due Process Clause could easily swallow up all other parts of the Constitution. And truly the Constitution would always be "what the judges say it is" at a given moment, not what the Founders wrote into the document. A written constitution, designed to guarantee protection against governmental abuses, including those of judges, must have written standards that mean something definite and have an explicit content. I regret very much to be compelled to say that the Court today makes a drastic and dangerous departure from a Constitution written to control and limit the government and the judges and moves toward a constitution designed to be no more and no less than what the judges of a particular social and economic philosophy declare on the one hand to be fair or on the other hand to be shocking and unconscionable.

The procedure required today as a matter of constitutional law finds no precedent in our legal system. Reduced to its simplest terms, the problem in this case is similar to that frequently encountered when two parties have an ongoing legal relationship that requires one party to make periodic payments to the other. Often the situation arises where the party "owing" the money stops paying it and justifies his conduct by arguing that the recipient is not legally entitled to payment. The recipient can, of course, disagree and go to court to compel payment. But I know of no situation in our legal system in which the person alleged to owe money to another is required by law to continue making payments to a judgment-proof claimant without the benefit of any security or bond to insure that these payments can be recovered if he wins his legal argument. Yet today's decision in no way obligates the welfare recipient to pay back any benefits wrongfully received during the pre-termination evidentiary hearings or post any bond, and in all "fairness" it could not do so. These recipients are by definition too poor to post a bond or to repay the benefits that, as the majority assumes, must be spent as received to insure survival.

The Court apparently feels that this decision will benefit the poor and needy. In my judgment the eventual result will be just the opposite. While today's decision requires only an administrative, evidentiary hearing, the inevitable logic of the approach taken will lead to constitutionally imposed, time-consuming delays of a full adversary process of administrative and judicial review. In the next case the welfare recipients are bound to argue that cutting off benefits before judicial review of the agency's decision is also a denial of due process. Since, by hypothesis, termination of aid at that point may still "deprive an *eligible* recipient of the very means by which to live while he waits," I would be surprised if the weighing process did not compel the conclusion that termination without full judicial review would be unconscionable. After all, at each step, as the majority seems to feel, the issue is only one of weighing the government's pocketbook against the actual survival of the recipient, and surely that balance must always tip in favor of the individual. Similarly today's decision requires only the opportunity to have the benefit of counsel at the administrative hearing, but it is difficult to believe that the same reasoning process would not require the appointment of counsel, for otherwise the right to counsel is a meaningless one since these people are too poor to hire their own advocates. Thus the end result of today's decision may well be that the government, once it decides to give welfare benefits, cannot reverse that decision until the recipient has had the benefits of full administrative and judicial review, including, of course, the opportunity to present his case to this Court. Since this process will usually entail a delay of several years, the inevitable result of such a constitutionally imposed burden will be that the government will not put a claimant on the rolls initially until it has made an exhaustive investigation to determine his eligibility. While this Court will perhaps have insured that no needy person will be taken off the rolls without a full "due process" proceeding, it will also have insured that many will never get on the rolls, or at least that they will remain destitute during the lengthy proceedings followed to determine initial eligibility.

. . . The operation of a welfare state is a new experiment for our Nation. For this reason, among others, I feel that new experiments in carrying out a welfare program should not be frozen into our constitutional structure. They should be left, as are other legislative determinations, to the Congress and the legislatures that the people elect to make our laws.

NOTES AND QUESTIONS

1. *Goldberg v. Kelly* is one of the most frequently-cited of the "procedural due process" cases. Note, first of all, that the Justice Black disagrees even with the majority's assumption that the receipt of welfare is a protected property interest under the Fourteenth Amendment, claiming that it "strains credulity" to treat the government's promise of charitable payments as "property" even though the government has determined that the claimant is ineligible. What view of "property" is the majority putting forward, and is it consistent with Locke's? *See* Richard A. Epstein, *No New Property*, 56 BROOK. L. REV. 747 (1990) (discussing the efforts of Justice Brennan to create and defend the concept of "new property" and arguing that the term is meaningless because property rights are the result of the activity of individuals, not governmental dictates). More important, perhaps, why should the requirements of procedural due process include a hearing prior to termination of benefits? Of what relevance are Justice Brennan's assertions that "[f]rom its founding the Nation's basic commitment has been to foster the dignity and well-being of all persons within its borders. We have come to recognize that forces not within the control of the poor contribute to their poverty"? 397 U.S. at 264-65 (Brennan, J., dissenting). Are those two sentences correct, by the way? Is the nation's basic commitment to "dignity and well-being of all persons within its borders"? The pledge of allegiance speaks of "one nation, indivisible, with liberty and justice for all." Is this the same thing? Would all agree on the proposition that "forces not within the control of the poor contribute to their poverty"? Is it a helpful statement with regard to decisions to be made concerning procedural due process? Is Justice Brennan advocating that there should be a different constitutional law for the poor and the rich? Would you? The French satirist, Anatole France, praised the majesty of his country's law, which forbids, with equal force, the rich or the poor from sleeping under bridges. Is Brennan reflecting similar insight? Should the law?

2. Note that Justice Brennan also justifies the welfare system on the grounds that it tends to "promote the general Welfare, and secure the Blessings of Liberty to ourselves and our Posterity." 397 U.S. at 265. How exactly does providing aid to the poorest in society do this? Is this persuasive? Is this constitutional law? Suppose there were more effective means of improving the economic conditions of the poor than state-supplied welfare payments. Would that have any bearing on procedural due process?

3. Why does Justice Black dissent? Surely he cannot object to the notion that the Due Process Clause requires that particular procedures be followed. What is one to make of his quite emphatic suggestions that:

> The Judicial Department was to have no part whatever in making any laws. In fact proposals looking to vesting some power in the Judiciary to take part in the legislative process and veto laws were offered, considered, and rejected by the Constitutional Convention. In my judgment there is not one word, phrase, or sentence from the beginning to the end of the Constitution from which it can be inferred that judges were granted any such legislative power.

397 U.S. at 273-74 (Black, J., dissenting). What does that have to do with "procedural due process" as applied in the case at hand? Could it be that "procedural due process" also has substantive aspects? How does Justice Brennan know, for example, that the kind of hearing required before welfare benefits can be suspended is not the same as the kind to be seen in courtrooms or formal proceedings of administrative agencies? The late Justice Brennan was regarded by liberals and conservatives alike as the foremost champion of the view that the meaning of the Constitution changed with the times. Do you see that view in evidence here? What do you suppose the essential elements of Justice Black's jurisprudence were? With whose perspective are you the most comfortable?

4. Note, in particular, Justice Black's charge that the "balancing act" in which the majority engages — balancing the needs of the state government to conserve the funds available for welfare, and to pay them only to deserving recipients, with the needs of the individual recipients — is an improper means of deciding constitutional law questions. Why is that, and do you agree? Justice Black's criticism of the majority minces no words. Is his tone justified?

MATHEWS v. ELDRIDGE
424 U.S. 319 (1976)

MR. JUSTICE POWELL delivered the opinion of the Court.

The issue in this case is whether the Due Process Clause of the Fifth Amendment requires that prior to the termination of Social Security disability benefit payments the recipient be afforded an opportunity for an evidentiary hearing.

I

Cash benefits are provided to workers during periods in which they are completely disabled under the disability insurance benefits program created by the 1956 amendments to Title II of the Social Security Act., 42 U.S.C. § 423. Respondent Eldridge was first awarded benefits in June 1968 [but they were terminated in July 1972 after extensive review of Eldridge's medical records by the Social Security Administration]. . . . [Eldridge was advised] of his right to seek reconsideration by the state agency of this initial determination within six months.

Instead of requesting reconsideration Eldridge commenced this action challenging the constitutional validity of the administrative procedures established by the Secretary of Health, Education, and Welfare for assessing whether there exists a continuing disability. He sought an immediate reinstatement of benefits pending a hearing on the issue of his disability.[3] . . . In support of his contention that due process requires a pretermination hearing, Eldridge relied

---

[3] The District Court ordered reinstatement of Eldridge's benefits pending its final disposition on the merits.

exclusively upon this Court's decision in *Goldberg v. Kelly* (1970), which established a right to an "evidentiary hearing" prior to termination of welfare benefits. The Secretary contended that *Goldberg* was not controlling since eligibility for disability benefits, unlike eligibility for welfare benefits, is not based on financial need and since issues of credibility and veracity do not play a significant role in the disability entitlement decision, which turns primarily on medical evidence.

. . . Reasoning that disability determinations may involve subjective judgments based on conflicting medical and nonmedical evidence, the District Court held that prior to termination of benefits Eldridge had to be afforded an evidentiary hearing of the type required for welfare beneficiaries under Title IV of the Social Security Act. . . . We reverse.

* * *

III

A

* * *

. . . "'[D]ue process,' unlike some legal rules, is not a technical conception with a fixed content unrelated to time, place and circumstances." "[D]ue process is flexible and calls for such procedural protections as the particular situation demands." Accordingly, resolution of the issue whether the administrative procedures provided here are constitutionally sufficient requires analysis of the governmental and private interests that are affected. . . .

* * *

B

* * *

The principal reasons for benefits terminations are that the worker is no longer disabled or has returned to work. As Eldridge's benefits were terminated because he was determined to be no longer disabled, we consider only the sufficiency of the procedures involved in such cases.

The continuing-eligibility investigation is made by a state agency acting through a "team" consisting of a physician and a nonmedical person trained in disability evaluation. The agency periodically communicates with the disabled worker, usually by mail — in which case he is sent a detailed questionnaire — or by telephone, and requests information concerning his present condition, including current medical restrictions and sources of treatment, and any additional information that he considers relevant to his continued entitlement to benefits.

Information regarding the recipient's current condition is also obtained from his sources of medical treatment. If there is a conflict between the information provided by the beneficiary and that obtained from medical sources such as his physician, or between two sources of treatment, the agency may arrange for an examination by an independent consulting physician. Whenever the agency's tentative assessment of the beneficiary's condition differs from his own assessment, the beneficiary is informed that benefits may be terminated, provided a summary of the evidence upon which the proposed determination to terminate is based, and afforded an opportunity to review the medical reports and other evidence in his case file. He also may respond in writing and submit additional evidence.

The state agency then makes its final determination, which is reviewed by an examiner in the SSA Bureau of Disability Insurance. If, as is usually the case, the SSA accepts the agency determination it notifies the recipient in writing, informing him of the reasons for the decision, and of his right to seek *de novo* reconsideration by the state agency. Upon acceptance by the SSA, benefits are terminated effective two months after the month in which medical recovery is found to have occurred.

If the recipient seeks reconsideration by the state agency and the determination is adverse, the SSA reviews the reconsideration determination and notifies the recipient of the decision. He then has a right to an evidentiary hearing before an SSA administrative law judge. The hearing is nonadversary, and the SSA is not represented by counsel. As at all prior and subsequent stages of the administrative process, however, the claimant may be represented by counsel or other spokesmen. If this hearing results in an adverse decision, the claimant is entitled to request discretionary review by the SSA Appeals Council, and finally may obtain judicial review.

Should it be determined at any point after termination of benefits, that the claimant's disability extended beyond the date of cessation initially established, the worker is entitled to retroactive payments. If, on the other hand, a beneficiary receives any payments to which he is later determined not to be entitled, the statute authorizes the Secretary to attempt to recoup these funds in specified circumstances.

C

Despite the elaborate character of the administrative procedures provided by the Secretary, the courts below held them to be constitutionally inadequate, concluding that due process requires an evidentiary hearing prior to termination. In light of the private and governmental interests at stake here and the nature of the existing procedures, we think this was error.

Since a recipient whose benefits are terminated is awarded full retroactive relief if he ultimately prevails, his sole interest is in the uninterrupted receipt of this source of income pending final administrative decision on his claim. . . .

Only in *Goldberg* has the Court held that due process requires an evidentiary hearing prior to a temporary deprivation. It was emphasized there that welfare assistance is given to persons on the very margin of subsistence. . . . Eligibility for disability benefits, in contrast, is not based upon financial need. Indeed, it is wholly unrelated to the worker's income or support from many other sources. . . .

* * *

In view of the torpidity of this administrative review process, and the typically modest resources of the family unit of the physically disabled worker, the hardship imposed upon the erroneously terminated disability recipient may be significant. Still, the disabled worker's need is likely to be less than that of a welfare recipient. In addition to the possibility of access to private resources, other forms of government assistance will become available where the termination of disability benefits places a worker or his family below the subsistence level. In view of these potential sources of temporary income, there is less reason here than in *Goldberg* to depart from the ordinary principle, established by our decisions, that something less than an evidentiary hearing is sufficient prior to adverse administrative action.

D

An additional factor to be considered here is the fairness and reliability of the existing pretermination procedures, and the probable value, if any, of additional procedural safeguards. Central to the evaluation of any administrative process is the nature of the relevant inquiry. In order to remain eligible for benefits the disabled worker must demonstrate by means of "medically acceptable clinical and laboratory diagnostic techniques," that he is unable "to engage in any substantial gainful activity by reason of any *medically determinable physical or mental impairment* . . . ." In short, a medical assessment of the worker's physical or mental condition is required. This is a more sharply focused and easily documented decision than the typical determination of welfare entitlement. In the latter case, a wide variety of information may be deemed relevant, and issues of witness credibility and veracity often are critical to the decisionmaking process. *Goldberg* noted that in such circumstances "written submissions are a wholly unsatisfactory basis for decision."

By contrast, the decision whether to discontinue disability benefits will turn, in most cases, upon "routine, standard, and unbiased medical reports by physician specialists," concerning a subject whom they have personally examined. In [an earlier case we] recognized the "reliability and probative worth of written medical reports," emphasizing that while there may be "professional disagreement with the medical conclusions" the "specter of questionable credibility and veracity is not present." To be sure, credibility and veracity may be a factor in the ultimate disability assessment in some cases. But procedural due process rules are shaped by the risk of error inherent in the truthfinding process as applied to the generality of cases, not the rare exceptions. The potential value of an evidentiary hearing, or even oral presentation to the decisionmaker, is substantially less in this context than in *Goldberg*.

* * *

minimum procedures required are said to be a constitutional question to be answered by the judiciary, not a statutory question for the legislature. *Cleveland Bd. of Educ. v. Loudermill*, 470 U.S. 532 (1985). You may have noticed that *Mathews* supplies a balancing test for determining what process is due. The factors listed as being balanced are:

> First, the private interest that will be affected by the official action; second, the risk of an erroneous deprivation of such interest through the procedures used, and the probable value, if any, of additional or substitute procedural safeguards; and finally, the Government's interest, including the function involved and the fiscal and administrative burdens that the additional or substitute procedural requirements would entail.

470 U.S. at 535. Are you convinced that the *Mathews* balancing formulation provides a genuine standard? Justice Rehnquist has remarked that under *Mathews* "[t]he balance is simply an ad hoc weighing which depends to a great extent upon how the Court subjectively views the underlying interests at stake." *Cleveland Bd. of Educ. v. Loudermill*, 470 U.S. 532, 562 (1985) (Rehnquist, J., dissenting).

3. You may be getting the sense that the rules regarding procedural due process are amorphous indeed. So far you have seen two cases where plaintiffs sought to recover government benefits, but the language of procedural due process is ambiguous enough so that other victims of "undue process" might logically seek the aid of the courts. This has been especially true with regard to process that has resulted in large punitive damage awards. In *Browning-Ferris Industries of Vermont v. Kelco Disposal, Inc.*, 492 U.S. 257 (1989), the Court both rejected a challenge to punitive damages under the Eighth Amendment's Excessive Fines Clause and declined to address any due process implications. However, Justice Brennan in a separate concurrence said the Court was leaving "the door open for a holding that the Due Process Clause constrains the imposition of punitive damages." That was especially true, said Brennan, if those damages could be said to be "grossly excessive" or "so severe and oppressive as to be wholly disproportioned to the offense and obviously unreasonable."

4. The Court started to develop this due process limitation on punitive damages in *Pacific Mutual Life Ins. Co v. Haslip*, 499 U.S. 1 (1990). In *Haslip*, plaintiffs alleged an insurance agent fraudulently misappropriated insurance premiums. An Alabama jury awarded $200,000 in compensatory damages and made an $840,000 punitive award. While the Court again hinted that "unlimited jury discretion" fixing a punitive award might cross the constitutional line, the Justices refused to "draw a mathematical bright line between the constitutionally acceptable and the constitutionally unacceptable that would fit every case." The Court did note, however, that the jury had been properly instructed to award punitive damages only to serve the state's policies of retribution and deterrence. Moreover, Alabama had appropriate procedures for post-trial review of the award, ensuring "that punitive damages awards are not grossly out of proportion to the severity of the offense and have some understandable relationship to compensatory damages." As a consequence, the Court upheld a punitive award that was four times compensatory damages, and 200 times plaintiff's out-of-pocket expenses. The Court repeated these sentiments in *TXO Production Corp. v. Alliance Resources Corp.*, 509 U.S. 443 (1993), sustaining a $10 million punitive damage award that was 526 times greater than the $19,000 in compensatory damages.

The line was crossed, however, in *BMW of North America, Inc. v. Gore*, 517 U.S. 559 (1996). Gore bought a new Beemer, but BMW failed to disclose that it had been damaged and re-painted before sale. An Alabama jury awarded $4,000 in compensatory damages and $4 million in punitives. The Alabama Supreme Court reduced the punitive award to $2 million. But the Supreme Court found even this reduced award — 500 times the compensatory award — so "grossly excessive" as to violate the Due Process Clause. Writing for the majority, Justice Stevens set forth three "guideposts" to evaluate the award: (1) the "degree of reprehensibility" of the defendant's conduct; (2) the "disparity" between the punitive damages and the actual or potential harm to the plaintiff; and (3) the difference between the punitive damages and any civil penalties authorized or imposed for comparable misconduct. The Court did not think any of these factors were met: it was mere economic harm involving no issue of performance or safety; the 500 to 1 ratio was "breathtaking"; and the available civil penalty was no more than $2000.

The notion of using the Due Process Clause as a *substantive* limit on punitive damages has been roundly criticized by Justice Scalia. He explained his view in a separate opinion in *Haslip*. He wrote, in part:

> [T]he due process point has been thoroughly briefed and argued, but the Court chooses to decide only that the jury discretion in the present case was not undue. It says that Alabama's particular procedures (at least as applied here) are not so "unreasonable" as to "cross the line into the area of constitutional impropriety." This jury-like verdict provides no guidance as to whether any other procedures are sufficiently "reasonable," and thus perpetuates the uncertainty that our grant of *certiorari* in this case was intended to resolve. Since it has been the traditional practice of American courts to leave punitive damages (where the evidence satisfies the legal requirements for imposing them) to the discretion of the jury; and since in my view a process that accords with such a tradition and does not violate the Bill of Rights necessarily constitutes "due" process; I would approve the procedure challenged here without further inquiry into its "fairness" or "reasonableness." I therefore concur only in the judgment of the Court.

I

As the Court notes, punitive or "exemplary" damages have long been a part of Anglo-American law. They have always been controversial. As recently as the mid-19th century, treatise writers sparred over whether they even existed. One respected commentator, Professor Simon Greenleaf, argued that no doctrine of authentically "punitive" damages could be found in the cases; he attempted to explain judgments that ostensibly included punitive damages as in reality no more than full compensation. This view was not widely shared. In his influential treatise on the law of damages, Theodore Sedgwick stated that "the rule" with respect to the "salutary doctrine" of exemplary damages is that "where gross fraud, malice, or oppression appears, the jury are not bound to adhere to the strict line of compensation, but may, by a severer verdict, at once impose a punishment on the defendant and hold up an example to the community." MEASURE OF DAMAGES 522 (4th ed. 1868). The doctrine, Sedgwick noted, "seems settled in England, and in the general jurisprudence of this country." . . .

Even fierce opponents of the doctrine acknowledged that it was a firmly established feature of American law. Justice Foster of the New Hampshire Supreme Court, in a lengthy decision disallowing punitive damages, called them "a perversion of language and ideas so ancient and so common as seldom to attract attention," *Fay v. Parker* (1873). . . .

In 1868, therefore, when the Fourteenth Amendment was adopted, punitive damages were undoubtedly an established part of the American common law of torts. It is just as clear that no particular procedures were deemed necessary to circumscribe a jury's discretion regarding the award of such damages, or their amount. As this Court noted in *Barry v. Edmunds* (1886), "nothing is better settled than that, in cases such as the present, and other actions for torts where no precise rule of law fixes the recoverable damages, it is the peculiar function of the jury to determine the amount by their verdict." . . .

Although both the majority and the dissenting opinions today concede that the common-law system for awarding punitive damages is firmly rooted in our history, both reject the proposition that this is dispositive for due process purposes. I disagree. In my view, it is not for the Members of this Court to decide from time to time whether a process approved by the legal traditions of our people is "due" process, nor do I believe such a rootless analysis to be dictated by our precedents.

II

Determining whether common-law procedures for awarding punitive damages can deny "due process of law" requires some inquiry into the meaning of that majestic phrase. Its first prominent use appears to have been in an English statute of 1354: "[N]o man of what estate or condition that he be, shall be put out of land or tenement, nor taken nor imprisoned, nor disinherited, nor put to death, without being brought in answer by due process of the law." 28 Edw. III, ch. 3. Although historical evidence suggests that the word "process" in this provision referred to specific writs employed in the English courts (a usage retained in the phrase "service of process") Sir Edward Coke had a different view. In the second part of his Institutes, *see* 2 INSTITUTES 50 (5th ed. 1797), Coke equated the phrase "due process of the law" in the 1354 statute with the phrase "Law of the Land" in Chapter 29 of Magna Charta (Chapter 39 of the original Magna Charta signed by King John at Runnymede in 1215), which provides: "No Freeman shall be taken, or imprisoned, or be disseised of his Freehold, or Liberties, or free Customs, or be outlawed, or exiled, or any otherwise destroyed; nor will we not pass upon him, nor condemn him, but by lawful Judgment of his Peers, or by the Law of the Land." 9 Hen. III, ch. 29 (1225). In Coke's view, the phrase "due process of law" referred to the customary procedures to which freemen were entitled by "the old law of England."

* * *

Hurtado [*v. California* (1884)] . . . clarified the proper role of history in a due process analysis: If the government chooses to *follow* a historically approved procedure, it necessarily *provides* due process, but if it chooses to *depart* from historical practice, it does not necessarily *deny* due process. The remaining business, of course, was to develop a test for determining *when* a departure from historical practice denies due process. *Hurtado* provided scant guidance. It merely suggested that due process could be assessed in such cases by reference to "those *fundamental principles of liberty and justice* which lie at the base of all our civil and political institutions."

The concept of "fundamental justice" thus entered the due process lexicon not as a description of what due process entails in general, but as a description of what it entails when traditional procedures are dispensed with. . . .

* * *

By the time the Court decided *Snyder v. Massachusetts* (1934), its understanding of due process had shifted in a subtle but significant way. That case rejected a criminal defendant's claim that he had been denied due process by being prevented from accompanying his jury on a visit to the scene of the crime. Writing for the Court, Justice Cardozo assumed that due process required "fundamental justice" or "fairness" in *all* cases, and not merely when evaluating nontraditional procedures. The opinion's analysis began from the premise that "Massachusetts is free to regulate the procedure of its courts in accordance with its own conception of policy and fairness *unless in so doing it offends some principle of justice so rooted in the traditions and conscience of our people to be ranked as fundamental*." Even so, however, only the mode of analysis and not the content of the Due Process Clause had changed, since in assessing whether some principle of "fundamental justice" had been violated, the Court was willing to accord historical practice dispositive weight. Justice Cardozo noted that the practice of showing evidence to the jury outside the presence of the defendant could be traced back to 18th-century England, and had been widely adopted in the States. "The Fourteenth Amendment," he wrote, "has not displaced the procedure of the ages."

In the ensuing decades, however, the concept of "fundamental fairness" under the Fourteenth Amendment became increasingly decoupled from the traditional historical approach. The principal mechanism for that development was the incorporation within the Fourteenth Amendment of the Bill of Rights guarantees. Although the Court resisted for some time the idea that "fundamental fairness" necessarily included the protections of the Bill of Rights, it ultimately incorporated virtually all of them. Of course, most of the procedural protections of the federal Bill of Rights simply codified traditional common-law privileges and had been widely adopted by the States. However, in the days when they were deemed to apply only to the Federal Government and not to impose uniformity upon the States, the Court had interpreted several provisions of the Bill of Rights in a way that departed from their strict common-law meaning. Thus, by the mid-20th century there had come to be some considerable divergence between historical practice followed by the States and the guarantees of the Bill of Rights. [For example, *Gideon v. Wainright*] established that no matter how strong its historical pedigree, a procedure prohibited by the Sixth Amendment (failure to appoint counsel in certain criminal cases) violates "fundamental fairness" and must be abandoned by the States.

To say that unbroken historical usage cannot save a procedure that violates one of the explicit procedural guarantees of the Bill of Rights (applicable through the Fourteenth Amendment) is not necessarily to say that such usage cannot demonstrate the procedure's compliance with the more general guarantee of "due process." In principle, what is important enough to have been included within the Bill of Rights has good claim to being an element of "fundamental fairness," whatever history might say; and as a practical matter, the invalidation of traditional state practices achievable through the Bill of Rights is at least limited to enumerated subjects. But disregard of "the procedure of the ages" for incorporation purposes has led to its disregard more generally. There is irony in this, since some of those who most ardently supported the incorporation doctrine did so in the belief that it was a means of avoiding, rather than producing, a subjective due-process jurisprudence. See, for example, the dissent of Justice Black, author of *Gideon*, from the Court's refusal to replace "fundamental fairness" with the Bill of Rights as the *sole* test of due process:

"[T]he 'natural law' formula which the Court uses to reach its conclusion in this case should be abandoned as an incongruous excrescence on our Constitution. I believe that formula to be itself a violation of our Constitution, in that it subtly conveys to courts, at the expense of legislatures, ultimate power over public policies in fields where no specific provision of the Constitution limits its legislative power." (Black, J., dissenting).

In any case, our due process opinions in recent decades have indiscriminately applied balancing analysis to determine "fundamental fairness," without regard to whether the procedure under challenge was (1) a traditional one and, if so, (2) prohibited by the Bill of Rights. . . . Even so, however, very few cases have used the Due Process Clause, without the benefit of an accompanying Bill of Rights guarantee, to strike down a procedure concededly approved by traditional and continuing American practice. Most notably, in *Sniadach v. Family Finance Corp. of Bay View* (1969), over the strenuous dissent of Justice Black, the Court declared unconstitutional the garnishment of wages, saying that "[t]he fact that a procedure would pass muster under a feudal regime does not mean it gives necessary protection to all property in its modern forms." And in *Shaffer v. Heitner* (1977), the Court invalidated general *quasi in rem* jurisdiction, saying that "'traditional notions of fair play and substantial justice' can be as readily offended by the perpetuation of ancient forms that are no longer justified as by the adoption of new procedures that are inconsistent with the basic values of our constitutional heritage." Such cases, at least in their broad pronouncements if not with respect to the particular provisions at issue, were in my view wrongly decided.

I might, for reasons of *stare decisis*, adhere to the principle that these cases announce, except for the fact that our later cases give it nothing but lipservice, and by their holdings reaffirm the view that traditional practice (unless contrary to the Bill of Rights) is conclusive of "fundamental fairness." As I wrote last Term in *Burnham v. Superior Court of Cal., County of Marin* (1990), nothing but the conclusiveness of history can explain why jurisdiction based upon mere service of process within a State — either generally or on the precise facts of that case — is "fundamentally fair." Nor to my mind can anything else explain today's decision that a punishment whose assessment and extent are committed entirely to the discretion of the jury is "fundamentally fair." . . .

When the rationale of earlier cases is contradicted by later holdings — and particularly when that rationale has no basis in constitutional text and itself contradicts opinions never explicitly overruled — I think it has no valid *stare decisis* claim upon me. Our holdings remain in conflict, no matter which course I take. I choose, then, to take the course that accords with the language of the Constitution and with our interpretation of it through the first half of this century. I reject the principle, aptly described and faithfully followed in JUSTICE O'CONNOR's dissent, that a traditional procedure of our society becomes unconstitutional whenever the Members of this Court "lose . . . confidence" in it. And like Justice Cardozo in *Snyder*, I affirm that no procedure firmly rooted in the practices of our people can be so "fundamentally unfair" as to deny due process of law.

* * *

A harsh or unwise procedure is not necessarily unconstitutional, just as the most sensible of procedures may well violate the Constitution. State legislatures and courts have the power to restrict or abolish the common-law practice of punitive damages, and in recent years have increasingly done so. It is through those means — State by State, and, at the federal level, by Congress — that the legal procedures affecting our citizens are improved. Perhaps, when the operation of that process has purged a historically approved practice from our national life, the Due Process Clause would permit this Court to announce that it is no longer in accord with the law of the land. But punitive damages assessed under common-law procedures are far from a fossil, or even an endangered species. They are (regrettably to many) vigorously alive. To effect their elimination may well be wise, but is not the role of the Due Process Clause. "Its function is negative, not affirmative, and it carries no mandate for particular measures of reform."

Notwithstanding Justice Scalia's misgivings, *BMW* introduces the notion that due process, as construed by the Court, has both a procedural and substantive component. This is controversial from the standpoint of modern constitutional interpretation. Some will argue that only the substantive protections of vested rights we first discussed in this Chapter (*e.g.*, the protection of contract from impairment or property from unauthorized taking) exist under the Constitution. Nevertheless, as we will see in the next Chapter, at one time, substantive due process broadly protected economic liberty, and later in Chapter Nine, we will see it used again to create highly speculative and controversial rights of privacy and autonomy.

Opponents of punitive damages won a substantial victory in *Cooper Industries, Inc. v. Leatherman Tool Group, Inc.*, 532 U.S. 424 (2001), where Justice Stevens wrote for eight members of the Court that appellate judges reviewing punitive awards for excessiveness must apply *de novo* review, rather than the more lenient abuse of discretion standard. Punitive awards, reasoned the Court, were more legal, than factual, in nature, and therefore, they raised both due process and Eighth Amendment "excessive fines" issues suitable for searching review by appellate judges. Justices Thomas and Scalia in separate opinions separately concurred, re-stating their view that the Due Process Clause does not place a substantive limit on punitive damages, but insofar as the Court has held otherwise and in light of past precedent, concurring in the application of *de novo* appellate review. Justice Ginsburg dissented, finding the distinction between compensatory and punitive damages to be artificial.

In *State Farm v. Campbell* (2003), the Court elaborated on the guideposts it had set out in *BMW v. Gore*, and found that a $145 million punitive damages award against an automobile insurance company violated due process.

STATE FARM v. CAMPBELL
538 U.S. 408 (2003)

JUSTICE KENNEDY delivered the opinion of the Court.

I.

In 1981, Curtis Campbell (Campbell) was driving with his wife, Inez Preece Campbell, in Cache County, Utah. He decided to pass six vans traveling ahead of them on a two-lane highway. Todd Ospital was driving a small car approaching from the opposite direction. To avoid a head-on collision with Campbell, who by then was driving on the wrong side of the highway and toward oncoming traffic, Ospital swerved onto the shoulder, lost control of his automobile, and collided with a vehicle driven by Robert G. Slusher. Ospital was killed, and Slusher was rendered permanently disabled. The Campbells escaped unscathed.

In the ensuing wrongful death and tort action, Campbell insisted he was not at fault. Early investigations did support differing conclusions as to who caused the accident, but "a consensus was reached early on by the investigators and witnesses that Mr. Campbell's unsafe pass had indeed caused the crash." . . . Campbell's insurance company, petitioner State Farm Mutual Automobile Insurance Company (State Farm), nonetheless decided to contest liability and declined offers by Slusher and Ospital's estate (Ospital) to settle the claims for the policy limit of $50,000 ($25,000 per claimant). State Farm also ignored the advice of one of its own investigators and took the case to trial, assuring the Campbells that "their assets were safe, that they had no liability for the accident, that [State Farm] would represent their interests, and that they did not need to procure separate counsel." . . . To the contrary, a jury determined that Campbell was 100 percent at fault, and a judgment was returned for $185,849, far more than the amount offered in settlement.

At first State Farm refused to cover the $135,849 in excess liability. Its counsel made this clear to the Campbells: "'You may want to put for sale signs on your property to get things moving.'" . . . Campbell obtained his own counsel to appeal the verdict. During the pendency of the appeal, in late 1984, Slusher, Ospital, and the Campbells reached an agreement whereby Slusher and Ospital agreed not to seek satisfaction of their claims against the Campbells. In exchange the Campbells agreed to pursue a bad faith action against State Farm and to be represented by Slusher's and Ospital's attorneys. The Campbells also agreed that Slusher and Ospital would have a right to play a part in all major decisions concerning the bad faith action. No settlement could be concluded without Slusher's and Ospital's approval, and Slusher and Ospital would receive 90 percent of any verdict against State Farm.

In 1989, the Utah Supreme Court denied Campbell's appeal in the wrongful death and tort actions. . . . State Farm then paid the entire judgment, including the amounts in excess of the policy limits. The Campbells nonetheless filed a complaint against State Farm alleging bad faith, fraud, and intentional infliction of emotional distress. The trial court initially granted State Farm's motion for summary judgment because State Farm had paid the excess verdict, but that ruling was reversed on appeal. . . . On remand State Farm moved . . . to exclude evidence of alleged conduct that occurred in unrelated cases outside of Utah, but the trial court denied the motion. At State Farm's request the trial court bifurcated the trial into two phases conducted before different juries. In the first phase the jury determined that State Farm's decision not to settle was unreasonable because there was a substantial likelihood of an excess verdict.

Before the second phase of the action against State Farm we decided *BMW of North America, Inc. v. Gore* (1996), and refused to sustain a $2 million punitive damages award which accompanied a verdict of only $4,000 in compensatory damages. Based on that decision, State Farm again moved for the exclusion of evidence of dissimilar out-of-state conduct. . . . The trial court denied State Farm's motion. . . .

The second phase addressed State Farm's liability for fraud and intentional infliction of emotional distress, as well as compensatory and punitive damages. The Utah Supreme Court aptly characterized this phase of the trial:

> "State Farm argued during phase II that its decision to take the case to trial was an 'honest mistake' that did not warrant punitive damages. In contrast, the Campbells introduced evidence that State Farm's decision to take the case to trial was a result of a national scheme to meet corporate fiscal goals by capping payouts on claims company wide. This scheme was referred to as State Farm's 'Performance, Planning and Review,' or PP & R, policy. To prove the existence of this scheme, the trial court allowed the Campbells to introduce extensive expert testimony regarding fraudulent practices by State Farm in its nation-wide operations. Although State Farm moved prior to phase II of the trial for the exclusion of such evidence and continued to object to it at trial, the trial court ruled that such evidence was admissible to determine whether State Farm's conduct in the Campbell case was indeed intentional and sufficiently egregious to warrant punitive damages." . . .

Evidence pertaining to the PP&R policy concerned State Farm's business practices for over 20 years in numerous States. Most of these practices bore no relation to third-party automobile insurance claims, the type of claim underlying the Campbells' complaint against the company. The jury awarded the Campbells $2.6 million in compensatory damages and $145 million in punitive damages, which the trial court reduced to $1 million and $25 million respectively. Both parties appealed.

The Utah Supreme Court sought to apply the three guideposts we identified in *Gore, supra* . . . and it reinstated the $145 million punitive damages award. Relying in large part on the extensive evidence concerning the PP&R policy, the court concluded State Farm's conduct was reprehensible. The court also relied upon State Farm's "massive wealth" and on testimony indicating that "State Farm's actions, because of their clandestine nature, will be punished at most in one out of every 50,000 cases as a matter of statistical probability," . . . and concluded that the ratio between punitive and compensatory damages was not unwarranted. Finally, the court noted that the punitive damages award was not excessive when compared to various civil and criminal penalties State Farm could have faced, including $10,000 for each act of fraud, the suspension of its license to conduct business in Utah, the disgorgement of profits, and imprisonment. . . . We granted certiorari. . . .

II

We recognized in *Cooper Industries, Inc. v. Leatherman Tool Group, Inc.* (2001), that in our judicial system compensatory and punitive damages, although usually awarded at the same time by the same decisionmaker, serve different purposes. . . . Compensatory damages "are intended to redress the concrete loss that the plaintiff has suffered by reason of the defendant's wrongful conduct." . . . By contrast, punitive damages serve a broader function; they are aimed at deterrence and retribution . . . ; *see also Gore* ("Punitive damages may properly be imposed to further a State's legitimate interests in punishing unlawful conduct and deterring its repetition"); *Pacific Mut. Life Ins. Co. v. Haslip* (1991) ("Punitive damages are imposed for purposes of retribution and deterrence").

While States possess discretion over the imposition of punitive damages, it is well established that there are procedural and substantive constitutional limitations on these awards. . . . The Due Process Clause of the Fourteenth Amendment prohibits the imposition of grossly excessive or arbitrary punishments on a tortfeasor. *Gore; see also id.* (BREYER, J., concurring) ("This constitutional concern, itself harkening back to the Magna Carta, arises out of the basic unfairness of depriving citizens of life, liberty, or property, through the application, not of law and legal processes, but of arbitrary coercion"). The reason is that "elementary notions of fairness enshrined in our constitutional jurisprudence dictate that a person receive fair notice not only of the conduct that will subject him to punishment, but also of the severity of the penalty that a State may impose." . . . ; *Cooper Industries, supra* ("Despite the broad discretion that States possess with respect to the imposition of criminal penalties and punitive damages, the Due Process Clause of the Fourteenth Amendment to the Federal Constitution imposes substantive limits on that discretion"). To the extent an award is grossly excessive, it furthers no legitimate purpose and constitutes an arbitrary deprivation of property. *Haslip, supra* (O'CONNOR, J., dissenting)

("Punitive damages are a powerful weapon. Imposed wisely and with restraint, they have the potential to advance legitimate state interests. Imposed indiscriminately, however, they have a devastating potential for harm. Regrettably, common-law procedures for awarding punitive damages fall into the latter category").

Although these awards serve the same purposes as criminal penalties, defendants subjected to punitive damages in civil cases have not been accorded the protections applicable in a criminal proceeding. This increases our concerns over the imprecise manner in which punitive damages systems are administered. We have admonished that "punitive damages pose an acute danger of arbitrary deprivation of property. Jury instructions typically leave the jury with wide discretion in choosing amounts, and the presentation of evidence of a defendant's net worth creates the potential that juries will use their verdicts to express biases against big businesses, particularly those without strong local presences." *Honda Motor* [*Corp. v. Oberg* (1994)]; *see also Haslip, supra* (O'CONNOR, J., dissenting) ("The Due Process Clause does not permit a State to classify arbitrariness as a virtue. Indeed, the point of due process — of the law in general — is to allow citizens to order their behavior. A State can have no legitimate interest in deliberately making the law so arbitrary that citizens will be unable to avoid punishment based solely upon bias or whim"). Our concerns are heightened when the decisionmaker is presented, as we shall discuss, with evidence that has little bearing as to the amount of punitive damages that should be awarded. Vague instructions, or those that merely inform the jury to avoid "passion or prejudice," do little to aid the decisionmaker in its task of assigning appropriate weight to evidence that is relevant and evidence that is tangential or only inflammatory.

In light of these concerns, in *Gore, supra*, we instructed courts reviewing punitive damages to consider three guideposts: (1) the degree of reprehensibility of the defendant's misconduct; (2) the disparity between the actual or potential harm suffered by the plaintiff and the punitive damages award; and (3) the difference between the punitive damages awarded by the jury and the civil penalties authorized or imposed in comparable cases. We reiterated the importance of these three guideposts in *Cooper Industries* and mandated appellate courts to conduct *de novo* review of a trial court's application of them to the jury's award. Exacting appellate review ensures that an award of punitive damages is based upon an "'application of law, rather than a decisionmaker's caprice.'" (quoting *Gore, supra* (BREYER, J., concurring)).

III

Under the principles outlined in *BMW of North America, Inc. v. Gore*, this case is neither close nor difficult. It was error to reinstate the jury's $145 million punitive damages award. We address each guidepost of *Gore* in some detail.

A

"The most important indicium of the reasonableness of a punitive damages award is the degree of reprehensibility of the defendant's conduct." *Gore, supra.* . . . We have instructed courts to determine the reprehensibility of a defendant by considering whether: the harm caused was physical as opposed to economic; the tortious conduct evinced an indifference to or a reckless disregard of the health or safety of others; the target of the conduct had financial vulnerability; the conduct involved repeated actions or was an isolated incident; and the harm was the result of intentional malice, trickery, or deceit, or mere accident. . . . The existence of any one of these factors weighing in favor of a plaintiff may not be sufficient to sustain a punitive damages award; and the absence of all of them renders any award suspect. It should be presumed a plaintiff has been made whole for his injuries by compensatory damages, so punitive damages should only be awarded if the defendant's culpability, after having paid compensatory damages, is so reprehensible as to warrant the imposition of further sanctions to achieve punishment or deterrence. . . .

Applying these factors in the instant case, we must acknowledge that State Farm's handling of the claims against the Campbells merits no praise. The trial court found that State Farm's employees altered the company's records to make Campbell appear less culpable. State Farm disregarded the overwhelming likelihood of liability and the near-certain probability that, by taking the case to trial, a judgment in excess of the policy limits would be awarded. State Farm amplified the harm by at first assuring the Campbells their assets would be safe from any verdict and by later telling them, postjudgment, to put a for-sale sign on their house. While we do not suggest there was error in awarding punitive damages based upon State Farm's conduct toward the Campbells, a more modest punishment for this reprehensible conduct could have satisfied the State's legitimate objectives, and the Utah courts should have gone no further.

This case, instead, was used as a platform to expose, and punish, the perceived deficiencies of State Farm's operations throughout the country. The Utah Supreme Court's opinion makes explicit that State Farm was being condemned for its nationwide policies rather than for the conduct direct toward the Campbells. ("The Campbells introduced evidence that State Farm's decision to take the case to trial was a result of a national scheme to meet corporate fiscal goals by capping payouts on claims company wide"). This was, as well, an explicit rationale of the trial court's decision in approving the award, though reduced from $145 million to $25 million. ("The Campbells demonstrated, through the testimony of State Farm employees who had worked outside of Utah, and through expert testimony, that this pattern of claims adjustment under the PP&R program was not a local anomaly, but was a consistent, nationwide feature of State Farm's business operations, orchestrated from the highest levels of corporate management").

* * *

A State cannot punish a defendant for conduct that may have been lawful where it occurred. . . . Nor, as a general rule, does a State have a legitimate concern in imposing punitive damages to punish a defendant for unlawful acts committed outside of the State's jurisdiction. Any proper adjudication of conduct that occurred outside Utah to other persons would require their inclusion, and, to those parties, the Utah courts, in the usual case, would need to apply the laws of their relevant jurisdiction. . . .

Here, the Campbells do not dispute that much of the out-of-state conduct was lawful where it occurred. They argue, however, that such evidence was not the primary basis for the punitive damages award and was relevant to the extent it demonstrated, in a general sense, State Farm's motive against its insured. . . . This argument misses the mark. Lawful out-of-state conduct may be probative when it demonstrates the deliberateness and culpability of the defendant's action in the State where it is tortious, but that conduct must have a nexus to the specific harm suffered by the plaintiff. A jury must be instructed, furthermore, that it may not use evidence of out-of-state conduct to punish a defendant for action that was lawful in the jurisdiction where it occurred. . . . A basic principle of federalism is that each State may make its own reasoned judgment about what conduct is permitted or proscribed within its borders, and each State alone can determine what measure of punishment, if any, to impose on a defendant who acts within its jurisdiction. . . .

For a more fundamental reason, however, the Utah courts erred in relying upon this and other evidence: The courts awarded punitive damages to punish and deter conduct that bore no relation to the Campbells' harm. A defendant's dissimilar acts, independent from the acts upon which liability was premised, may not serve as the basis for punitive damages. A defendant should be punished for the conduct that harmed the plaintiff, not for being an unsavory individual or business. Due process does not permit courts, in the calculation of punitive damages, to adjudicate the merits of other parties' hypothetical claims against a defendant under the guise of the reprehensibility analysis, but we have no doubt the Utah Supreme Court did that here. . . .

* * *

. . . The reprehensibility guidepost does not permit courts to expand the scope of the case so that a defendant may be punished for any malfeasance, which in this case extended for a 20-year period. In this case, because the Campbells have shown no conduct by State Farm similar to that which harmed them, the conduct that harmed them is the only conduct relevant to the reprehensibility analysis.

B

Turning to the second *Gore* guidepost, we have been reluctant to identify concrete constitutional limits on the ratio between harm, or potential harm, to the plaintiff and the punitive damages award. *Gore* ("We have consistently rejected the notion that the constitutional line is marked by a simple mathematical formula, even one that compares actual *and potential* damages to the punitive award"). . . . We decline again to impose a bright-line ratio which a punitive damages award cannot exceed. Our jurisprudence and the principles it has now established demonstrate, however, that, in practice, few awards exceeding a single-digit ratio between punitive and compensatory damages, to a significant degree, will satisfy due process. In *Haslip*, in upholding a punitive damages award, we concluded that an award of more than four times the amount of compensatory damages might be close to the line of constitutional impropriety. . . . We cited that 4-to-1 ratio again in *Gore* . . . . The Court further referenced a long legislative history, dating back over 700 years and going forward to today, providing for sanctions of double, treble, or quadruple damages to deter and punish. . . . While these ratios are not binding, they are instructive. They demonstrate what should be obvious: Single-digit multipliers are more likely to comport with due process, while still achieving the State's goals of deterrence and retribution, than awards with ratios in range of 500 to 1 . . . , or, in this case, of 145 to 1.

Nonetheless, because there are no rigid benchmarks that a punitive damages award may not surpass, ratios greater than those we have previously upheld may comport with due process where "a particularly egregious act has resulted in only a small amount of economic damages." . . . *see also ibid.* (positing that a higher ratio *might* be necessary where "the injury is hard to detect or the monetary value of noneconomic harm might have been difficult to determine"). The converse is also true, however. When compensatory damages are substantial, then a lesser ratio, perhaps only equal to compensatory damages, can reach the outermost limit of the due process guarantee. The precise award in any case, of course, must be based upon the facts and circumstances of the defendant's conduct and the harm to the plaintiff.

In sum, courts must ensure that the measure of punishment is both reasonable and proportionate to the amount of harm to the plaintiff and to the general damages recovered. In the context of this case, we have no doubt that there is a presumption against an award that has a 145-to-1 ratio. The compensatory award in this case was substantial; the Campbells were awarded $1 million for a year and a half of emotional distress. This was complete compensation. . . .

The Utah Supreme Court sought to justify the massive award by pointing to . . . the fact that State Farm will only be punished in one out of every 50,000 cases as a matter of statistical probability; and State Farm's enormous wealth. . . .

. . . [T]he argument that State Farm will be punished in only the rare case, coupled with reference to its assets (which, of course, are what other insured parties in Utah and other States must rely upon for payment of claims) had little to do with the actual harm sustained by the Campbells. The wealth of a defendant cannot justify an otherwise unconstitutional punitive damages award. . . .

C

The third guidepost in *Gore* is the disparity between the punitive damages award and the "civil penalties authorized or imposed in comparable cases." . . . We note that, in the past, we have also looked to criminal penalties that could be imposed. . . . The existence of a criminal penalty does have bearing on the seriousness with which a State views the wrongful action. When used to determine the dollar amount of the award, however, the criminal penalty has less utility. Great care must be taken to avoid use of the civil process to assess criminal penalties that can be imposed only after the heightened protections of a criminal trial have been observed, including, of course, its higher standards of proof. Punitive damages are not a substitute for the criminal process, and the remote possibility of a criminal sanction does not automatically sustain a punitive damages award.

Here, we need not dwell long on this guidepost. The most relevant civil sanction under Utah state law for the wrong done to the Campbells appears to be a $10,000 fine for an act of fraud, . . . an amount dwarfed by the $145 million punitive damages award. The Supreme Court of Utah speculated about the loss of State Farm's business license, the disgorgement of profits, and possible imprisonment, but here again its references were to the broad fraudulent scheme drawn from evidence of out-of-state and dissimilar conduct. This analysis was insufficient to justify the award.

IV

An application of the *Gore* guideposts to the facts of this case, especially in light of the substantial compensatory damages awarded (a portion of which contained a punitive element), likely would justify a punitive damages award at or near the amount of compensatory damages. The punitive award of $145 million, therefore, was neither reasonable nor proportionate to the wrong committed, and it was an irrational and arbitrary deprivation of the property of the defendant. . . .

The judgment of the Utah Supreme Court is reversed, and the case is remanded for proceedings not inconsistent with this opinion.

It is so ordered.

JUSTICE SCALIA, dissenting.

I adhere to the view expressed in my dissenting opinion in *BMW of North America, Inc. v. Gore* . . . that the Due Process Clause provides no substantive protections against "excessive" or "'unreasonable'" awards of punitive damages. I am also of the view that the punitive damages jurisprudence which has sprung forth from *BMW v. Gore* is insusceptible of principled application; accordingly, I do not feel justified in giving the case *stare decisis* effect. . . . I would affirm the judgment of the Utah Supreme Court.

JUSTICE THOMAS, dissenting.

I would affirm the judgment below because "I continue to believe that the Constitution does not constrain the size of punitive damages awards."

JUSTICE GINSBURG, dissenting.

Not long ago, this Court was hesitant to impose a federal check on state-court judgments awarding punitive damages.

It was not until 1996, in *BMW of North America, Inc. v. Gore* that the Court, for the first time, invalidated a state-court punitive damages assessment as unreasonably large. . . .

In *Gore*, I stated why I resisted the Court's foray into punitive damages "territory traditionally within the States' domain." (dissenting opinion). I adhere to those views, and note again that, unlike federal habeas corpus review of state-court convictions under 28 U.S.C. § 2254, the Court "works at this business [of checking state courts] alone," unaided by the participation of federal district courts and courts of appeals. . . . It was once recognized that "the laws of the particular State must suffice [to superintend punitive damages awards] until judges or legislators authorized to do so initiate system-wide change." *Haslip* (Kennedy, J., concurring in judgment). I would adhere to that traditional view.

I

The large size of the award upheld by the Utah Supreme Court in this case indicates why damage-capping legislation may be altogether fitting and proper. Neither the amount of the award nor the trial record, however, justifies this Court's substitution of its judgment for that of Utah's competent decisionmakers. In this regard, I count it significant that, on the key criterion "reprehensibility," there is a good deal more to the story than the Court's abbreviated account tells.

* * *

State Farm's "wrongful profit and evasion schemes," the trial court underscored, were directly relevant to the Campbells' case . . . :

> "The record fully supports the conclusion that the bad-faith claim handling that exposed the Campbells to an excess verdict in 1983, and resulted in severe damages to them, was a product of the unlawful profit scheme that had been put in place by top management at State Farm years earlier. The Campbells presented substantial evidence showing how State Farm's improper insistence on claims-handling employees' reducing their claim payouts . . . regardless of the merits of each claim, manifested itself . . . in the Utah claims operations during the period when the decisions were made not to offer to settle the Campbell case for the $50,000 policy limits — indeed, not to make any offer to settle at a lower amount. This evidence established that high-level manager Bill Brown was under heavy pressure from the PP&R scheme

to control indemnity payouts during the time period in question. In particular, when Brown declined to pay the excess verdict against Curtis Campbell, or even post a bond, he had a special need to keep his year-end numbers down, since the State Farm incentive scheme meant that keeping those numbers down was important to helping Brown get a much-desired transfer to Colorado . . . . There was ample evidence that the concepts taught in the Excess Liability Handbook, including the dishonest alteration and manipulation of claim files . . . were dutifully carried out in this case . . . . There was ample basis for the jury to find that everything that had happened to the Campbells — when State Farm repeatedly refused in bad-faith to settle for the $50,000 policy limits and went to trial, and then failed to pay the 'excess' verdict, or at least post a bond, after trial — was a direct application of State Farm's overall profit scheme, operating through Brown and others." . . .

State Farm's "policies and practices," the trial evidence thus bore out, were "responsible for the injuries suffered by the Campbells," and the means used to implement those policies could be found "callous, clandestine, fraudulent, and dishonest." . . . ([There was] "ample evidence" that State Farm's reprehensible corporate policies were responsible for injuring "many other Utah consumers during the past two decades"). The Utah Supreme Court, relying on the trial court's record-based recitations, understandably characterized State Farm's behavior as "egregious and malicious." . . .

II

The Court dismisses the evidence describing and documenting State Farm's PP&R policy and practices as essentially irrelevant, bearing "no relation to the Campbells' harm." . . . It is hardly apparent why that should be so. What is infirm about the Campbells' theory that their experience with State Farm exemplifies and reflects an overarching underpayment scheme, one that caused "repeated misconduct of the sort that injured them," . . . ? The Court's silence on that score is revealing: Once one recognizes that the Campbells did show "conduct by State Farm similar to that which harmed them," . . . it becomes impossible to shrink the reprehensibility analysis to this sole case, or to maintain, at odds with the determination of the trial court, . . . that "the adverse effect on the State's general population was in fact minor[.]" . . .

Evidence of out-of-state conduct, the Court acknowledges, may be "probative [even if the conduct is lawful in the state where it occurred] when it demonstrates the deliberateness and culpability of the defendant's action in the State where it is tortious . . . ." "Other acts" evidence concerning practices both in and out of State was introduced in this case to show just such "deliberateness" and "culpability." The evidence was admissible, the trial court ruled: (1) to document State Farm's "reprehensible" PP&R program; and (2) to "rebut [State Farm's] assertion that [its] actions toward the Campbells were inadvertent errors or mistakes in judgment." . . . Viewed in this light, there surely was "a nexus" between much of the "other acts" evidence and "the specific harm suffered by [the Campbells]." . . .

III

When the Court first ventured to override state-court punitive damages awards, it did so moderately. The Court recalled that "in our federal system, States necessarily have considerable flexibility in determining the level of punitive damages that they will allow in different classes of cases and in any particular case." *Gore*. Today's decision exhibits no such respect and restraint. No longer content to accord state-court judgments "a strong presumption of validity," the Court announces that "few awards exceeding a single-digit ratio between punitive and compensatory damages, to a significant degree, will satisfy due process." Moreover, the Court adds, when compensatory damages are substantial, doubling those damages "can reach the outermost limit of the due process guarantee." In a legislative scheme or a state high court's design to cap punitive damages, the handiwork in setting single-digit and 1-to-1 benchmarks could hardly be questioned; in a judicial decree imposed on the States by this Court under the banner of substantive due process, the numerical controls today's decision installs seem to me boldly out of order.

. . . I remain of the view that this Court has no warrant to reform state law governing awards of punitive damages. *Gore* (GINSBURG, J., dissenting). Even if I were prepared to accept the flexible guides prescribed in *Gore*, I would not join the Court's swift conversion of those guides into instructions that begin to resemble marching orders. For the reasons stated, I would leave the judgment of the Utah Supreme Court undisturbed.

NOTES AND QUESTIONS

1. *State Farm* continues the development of the jurisprudence in *BMW v. Gore*, and, in particular, the notion that the Due Process Clause includes a substantive limit on punitive damages. Can you determine precisely what that substantive limit is? Note that three Justices of the Supreme Court (Scalia, Thomas, and Ginsburg) remain unconvinced that the Supreme Court ought to be operating in this area. Scalia and Thomas have generally resisted the Supreme Court's supervision over areas that have traditionally been regarded as the province of the state courts or legislatures, and while some of this may also have to do with Justice Ginsburg's dissent, do you find anything else that may explain her (relatively lengthy — at least compared to that of Scalia and Thomas) dissenting opinion? Do the majority and Justice Ginsburg agree on the seriousness of the kind of misconduct in which State Farm was apparently engaged?

In *State Farm*, a Utah jury had imposed the punitive figure after awarding $1 million in compensatory damages for intentional infliction of emotional distress based on State Farm's bad faith refusal to settle a fatal automobile accident claim within policy limits. At trial, the court allowed evidence of State Farm's national claims handling practices. As the Court notes, this permitted the jury to sanction State Farm for its conduct in other jurisdictions, even though the conduct may have been lawful in those jurisdictions. The Court believes that the jury should have focused on "that conduct [having] a nexus to the specific harm suffered by the plaintiff." Note that the Court once again refused to apply a "bright line" ratio to evaluate the relationship between the punitive and compensatory awards, but it came close in observing that "few awards exceeding a single-digit ratio between punitive and compensatory damages, to a significant degree, will satisfy due process." Moreover, the Court maintained its earlier dictum that " an award of more than four times the amount of compensatory damages might be close to the line of constitutional propriety."

The Court also noted that, "[w]hen compensatory damages are substantial, then a lesser ratio, perhaps only equal to compensatory damages, can reach the outermost limit of the due process guarantee." However, "the wealth of a defendant cannot justify an otherwise unconstitutional punitive damages award."

2. While the *BMW v. Gore* line of cases may be thought to involve substantive due process, it is also important to understand the majority's view that procedural differences between civil and criminal actions dictate caution when punitive damages are assessed. Thus, in a criminal trial (even if only fines and not imprisonments are involved), among other procedural protections the state has the burden of proving the relevant facts beyond a reasonable doubt, and one cannot be tried twice for the same crime. Do the dissenters adequately take this into account?

3. As explored in other parts of this volume, the same term in which the Supreme Court issues its decision in *State Farm*, it also published landmark holdings finding unconstitutional the Texas sodomy statute and upholding some aspects of the University of Michigan's affirmative action plan. The latter two cases received much more attention in the general press, but *State Farm* was regarded by some analysts as equally important, given the current explosion in multi-million, and, in some cases, multi-billion dollar judgments in American courts. It may also be significant that the *BMW* case was decided by a 5 to 4 majority, while *State Farm* was 6-3 (Justice Rehnquist was with the dissenters in the former, but with the majority in the latter).

If *State Farm* was an important victory for those seeking civil justice reform, however, the Court's decision from the same term in *Norfolk & Western Railway Co. v. Ayers*, would perhaps be seen as a defeat. The Court ruled 5 to 4 that some workers who have developed asbestos-related but noncancerous disease can still recover damages based on their "genuine and serious" fear of eventually developing cancer. As the New York Times's esteemed court-watcher Linda Greenhouse wrote, the decision "was a disappointment to a broad swath of businesses that had expected to enlist the court in addressing the asbestos liability issue. In an unusual alignment, Justice Ginsburg wrote the majority opinion, joined by Justices Stevens, Scalia, Souter, and Thomas. Justice Kennedy dissented, joined by Justices O'Connor and Breyer and by Chief Justice Rehnquist." Linda Greenhouse, *In a Momentous Term Justices Remake the Law, and the Court,* N.Y. Times, July 1, 2002, Section A, p. 1. Given your reading of the opinions in *State Farm,* would you agree with Greenhouse that the line-up in the asbestos case was "unusual"?

4. In Justice Kennedy's majority opinion in the Texas sodomy case, he referred to a developing consensus in other Western countries that punishing sexual acts between consenting adults was improper given emerging ideas about rights to privacy in such matters. Justice Scalia, in dissent in that case, criticized Justice Kennedy's reliance on events in other countries for interpretation of the United States Constitution. It has become evident in recent years that the cost of accommodating a torts jurisprudence that imposes, in effect, a tax of many billions of dollars each year on American industry may place American firms (or American consumers) at a disadvantage when competing with firms whose nations do not permit punitive damages, contingency fees, excessive discovery, and, in some cases, jury trials in the case of private controversies. *See generally* Stephen B. Presser, *How Should the Law of Products Liability Be Harmonized? What Americans Can Learn From Europeans,* MANHATTAN INSTITUTE CENTER FOR LEGAL POLICY: GLOBAL LIABILITY ISSUES, vol 2, February 2002 (available on the web, at http://www.manhattan-institute.org/html/gli_2.htm). Could the majority in *State Farm* (Justice Kennedy is the author, again) have the same sort of international focus? When international business matters are involved, should the nature of constitutional "due process" be altered? Justice Ginsburg was with the majority in the Texas sodomy case, but, as you have seen, dissented in *State Farm.* Are the international cultural aspects of the two cases similar or different?

Chapter 7

A GOVERNMENT COMMITMENT TO FREEDOM

A. First Amendment Speech

1. Prior Restraint and Criticism of the Government

NEW YORK TIMES CO. v. UNITED STATES
403 U.S. 713 (1971)

PER CURIAM.

We granted certiorari in these cases in which the United States seeks to enjoin the New York Times and the Washington Post from publishing the contents of a classified study entitled "History of U.S. Decision-Making Process on Viet Nam Policy."

"Any system of prior restraints of expression comes to this Court bearing a heavy presumption against its constitutional validity." The Government "thus carries a heavy burden of showing justification for the imposition of such a restraint." The District Court for the Southern District of New York in the *New York Times* case and the District Court for the District of Columbia and the Court of Appeals for the District of Columbia Circuit in the *Washington Post* case held that the Government had not met that burden. We agree.

* * *

MR. JUSTICE BLACK, with whom MR. JUSTICE DOUGLAS joins, concurring.

. . . I believe that every moment's continuance of the injunctions against these newspapers amounts to a flagrant, indefensible, and continuing violation of the First Amendment. . . . In my view it is unfortunate that some of my Brethren are apparently willing to hold that the publication of news may sometimes be enjoined. Such a holding would make a shambles of the First Amendment.

Our Government was launched in 1789 with the adoption of the Constitution. The Bill of Rights, including the First Amendment, followed in 1791. Now, for the first time in the 182 years since the founding of the Republic, the federal courts are asked to hold that the First Amendment does not mean what it says, but rather means that the Government can halt the publication of current news of vital importance to the people of this country.

In seeking injunctions against these newspapers and in its presentation to the Court, the Executive Branch seems to have forgotten the essential purpose and history of the First Amendment. When the Constitution was adopted, many people strongly opposed it because the document contained no Bill of Rights to safeguard certain basic freedoms. They especially feared that the new powers granted to a central government might be interpreted to permit the government to curtail freedom of religion, press, assembly, and speech. In response to an overwhelming public clamor, James Madison offered a series of amendments to satisfy citizens that these great liberties would remain safe and beyond the power of government to abridge. Madison proposed what later became the First Amendment in three parts, . . . one of which proclaimed: "The people shall not be deprived or abridged of their right to speak, to write, or to publish their sentiments; *and the freedom of the press, as one of the great bulwarks of liberty, shall be inviolable.*" (Emphasis added.) The amendments were offered to *curtail* and *restrict* the general powers granted to the Executive, Legislative, and Judicial Branches two years before in the original Constitution. The Bill of Rights changed the original Constitution into a new charter under which no branch of government could abridge the people's freedoms of press, speech, religion, and assembly. Yet the Solicitor General argues and some members of the Court appear to agree that the general powers of the Government adopted in the original Constitution should be interpreted to limit and restrict the specific and emphatic guarantees of the Bill of Rights adopted later. I can imagine no greater perversion of history. Madison and the other Framers of the First Amendment, able men that they were, wrote in language they earnestly believed could never be misunderstood: "Congress shall make no law . . . abridging the freedom . . . of the press. . . ." Both the history and language of the First Amendment support the view that the press must be left free to publish news, whatever the source, without censorship, injunctions, or prior restraints.

In the First Amendment the Founding Fathers gave the free press the protection it must have to fulfill its essential role in our democracy. The press was to serve the governed, not the governors. The Government's power to censor the press was abolished so that the press would remain forever free to censure the Government. . . . And paramount among the responsibilities of a free press is the duty to prevent any part of the government from deceiving the people and sending them off to distant lands to die of foreign fevers and foreign shot and shell. In my view, far from deserving condemnation for their courageous reporting, the New York Times, the Washington Post, and other newspapers should be commended for serving the purpose that the Founding Fathers saw so clearly. In revealing the workings of government that led to the Vietnam war, the newspapers nobly did precisely that which the Founders hoped and trusted they would do.

The Government's case here is based on premises entirely different from those that guided the Framers of the First Amendment. The Solicitor General has carefully and emphatically stated:

"Now, MR. JUSTICE [BLACK], your construction of . . . [the First Amendment] is well known, and I certainly respect it. You say that no law means no law, and that should be obvious. I can only say, Mr. Justice, that to me it is equally obvious that 'no law' does not mean 'no law', and I would seek to persuade the Court that that is true. . . . [T]here are other parts of the Constitution that grant powers and responsibilities to the Executive, and . . . the First Amendment was not intended to make it impossible for the Executive to function or to protect the security of the United States."

And the Government argues in its brief that in spite of the First Amendment, "[t]he authority of the Executive Department to protect the nation against publication of information whose disclosure would endanger the national security stems from two interrelated sources: the constitutional power of the President over the conduct of foreign affairs and his authority as Commander-in-Chief."

In other words, we are asked to hold that despite the First Amendment's emphatic command, the Executive Branch, the Congress, and the Judiciary can make laws enjoining publication of current news and abridging freedom of the press in the name of "national security." The Government does not even attempt to rely on any act of Congress. Instead it makes the bold and dangerously far-reaching contention that the courts should take it upon themselves to "make" a law abridging freedom of the press in the name of equity, presidential power and national security, even when the representatives of the people in Congress have adhered to the command of the First Amendment and refused to make such a law. To find that the President has "inherent power" to halt the publication of news by resort to the courts would wipe out the First Amendment and destroy the fundamental liberty and security of the very people the Government hopes to make "secure." No one can read the history of the adoption of the First Amendment without being convinced beyond any doubt that it was injunctions like those sought here that Madison and his collaborators intended to outlaw in this Nation for all time.

The word "security" is a broad, vague generality whose contours should not be invoked to abrogate the fundamental law embodied in the First Amendment. The guarding of military and diplomatic secrets at the expense of informed representative government provides no real security for our Republic. The Framers of the First Amendment, fully aware of both the need to defend a new nation and the abuses of the English and Colonial governments, sought to give this new society strength and security by providing that freedom of speech, press, religion, and assembly should not be abridged. . . .

MR. JUSTICE DOUGLAS, with whom MR. JUSTICE BLACK joins, concurring.

* * *

It should be noted at the outset that the First Amendment provides that "Congress shall make no law . . . abridging the freedom of speech, or of the press." That leaves, in my view, no room for governmental restraint on the press.

There is, moreover, no statute barring the publication by the press of the material which the Times and the Post seek to use. Title 18 U.S.C. § 793(e) provides that "[w]hoever having unauthorized possession of, access to, or control over any document, writing . . . or information relating to the national defense which information the possessor has reason to believe could be used to the injury of the United States or to the advantage of any foreign nation, willfully communicates . . . the same to any person not entitled to receive it . . . [s]hall be fined not more than $10,000 or imprisoned not more than ten years, or both."

The Government suggests that the word "communicates" is broad enough to encompass publication.

There are eight sections in the chapter on espionage and censorship, §§ 792-799. In three of those eight "publish" is specifically mentioned: § 794(b) applies to "Whoever, in time of war, with intent that the same shall be communicated to the enemy, collects, records, *publishes*, or communicates . . . [the disposition of armed forces]."

Section 797 applies to whoever "reproduces, *publishes*, sells, or gives away" photographs of defense installations.

Section 798 relating to cryptography applies to whoever: "communicates, furnishes, transmits, or otherwise makes available . . . *or publishes*" the described material. (Emphasis added.)

Thus it is apparent that Congress was capable of and did distinguish between publishing and communication in the various sections of the Espionage Act.

The other evidence that § 793 does not apply to the press is a rejected version of § 793. That version read: "During any national emergency resulting from a war to which the United States is a party, or from threat of such a war, the President may, by proclamation, declare the existence of such emergency and, by proclamation, prohibit the publishing or communicating of, or the attempting to publish or communicate any information relating to the national defense which, in his judgment, is of such character that it is or might be useful to the enemy." 55 Cong. Rec. 1763. During the debates in the Senate the First Amendment was specifically cited and that provision was defeated. 55 Cong. Rec. 2167.

Judge Gurfein's holding in the *Times* case that this Act does not apply to this case was therefore preeminently sound. . . .

So any power that the Government possesses must come from its "inherent power."

The power to wage war is "the power to wage war successfully." But the war power stems from a declaration of war. The Constitution by Art. I, § 8, gives Congress, not the President, power "[t]o declare War." Nowhere are presidential wars authorized. We need not decide therefore what leveling effect the war power of Congress might have.

These disclosures may have a serious impact. But that is no basis for sanctioning a previous restraint on the press. . . .

* * *

The Government says that it has inherent powers to go into court and obtain an injunction to protect the national interest, which in this case is alleged to be national security.

* * *

The dominant purpose of the First Amendment was to prohibit the widespread practice of governmental suppression of embarrassing information. It is common knowledge that the First Amendment was adopted against the widespread use of the common law of seditious libel to punish the dissemination of material that is embarrassing to the powers-that-be. The present cases will, I think, go down in history as the most dramatic illustration of that principle. A debate of large proportions goes on in the Nation over our posture in Vietnam. That debate antedated the disclosure of the contents of the present documents. The latter are highly relevant to the debate in progress.

Secrecy in government is fundamentally anti-democratic, perpetuating bureaucratic errors. Open debate and discussion of public issues are vital to our national health. On public questions there should be "uninhibited, robust, and wide-open" debate. . . .

* * *

Mr. Justice Brennan, concurring.

I

I write separately in these cases only to emphasize what should be apparent: that our judgments in the present cases may not be taken to indicate the propriety, in the future, of issuing temporary stays and restraining orders to block the publication of material sought to be suppressed by the Government. So far as I can determine, never before has the United States sought to enjoin a newspaper from publishing information in its possession. The relative novelty of the questions presented, the necessary haste with which decisions were reached, the magnitude of the interests asserted, and the fact that all the parties have concentrated their arguments upon the question whether permanent restraints were proper may have justified at least some of the restraints heretofore imposed in these cases. . . . But even if it be assumed that some of the interim restraints were proper in the two cases before us, that assumption has no bearing upon the propriety of similar judicial action in the future. To begin with, there has now been ample time for reflection and judgment; whatever values there may be in the preservation of novel questions for appellate review may not support any restraints in the future. More important, the First Amendment stands as an absolute bar to the imposition of judicial restraints in circumstances of the kind presented by these cases.

* * *

MR. JUSTICE STEWART, with whom MR. JUSTICE WHITE joins, concurring. [Omitted.]

MR. JUSTICE WHITE, with whom MR. JUSTICE STEWART joins, concurring.

I concur in today's judgments, but only because of the concededly extraordinary protection against prior restraints enjoyed by the press under our constitutional system. I do not say that in no circumstances would the First Amendment permit an injunction against publishing information about government plans or operations. Nor, after examining the materials the Government characterizes as the most sensitive and destructive, can I deny that revelation of these documents will do substantial damage to public interests. Indeed, I am confident that their disclosure will have that result. But I nevertheless agree that the United States has not satisfied the very heavy burden that it must meet to warrant an injunction against publication in these cases, at least in the absence of express and appropriately limited congressional authorization for prior restraints in circumstances such as these.

The Government's position is simply stated: The responsibility of the Executive for the conduct of the foreign affairs and for the security of the Nation is so basic that the President is entitled to an injunction against publication of a newspaper story whenever he can convince a court that the information to be revealed threatens "grave and irreparable" injury to the public interest; and the injunction should issue whether or not the material to be published is classified, whether or not publication would be lawful under relevant criminal statutes enacted by Congress, and regardless of the circumstances by which the newspaper came into possession of the information.

At least in the absence of legislation by Congress, based on its own investigations and findings, I am quite unable to agree that the inherent powers of the Executive and the courts reach so far as to authorize remedies having such sweeping potential for inhibiting publications by the press. Much of the difficulty inheres in the "grave and irreparable danger" standard suggested by the United States. If the United States were to have judgment under such a standard in these cases, our decision would be of little guidance to other courts in other cases, for the material at issue here would not be available from the Court's opinion or from public records, nor would it be published by the press. Indeed, even today where we hold that the United States has not met its burden, the material remains sealed in court records and it is properly not discussed in today's opinions. Moreover, because the material poses substantial dangers to national interests and because of the hazards of criminal sanctions, a responsible press may choose never to publish the more sensitive materials. To sustain the Government in these cases would start the courts down a long and hazardous road that I am not willing to travel, at least without congressional guidance and direction.

* * *

MR. JUSTICE MARSHALL, concurring.

The Government contends that the only issue in these cases is whether in a suit by the United States, "the First Amendment bars a court from prohibiting a newspaper from publishing material whose disclosure would pose a 'grave and immediate danger to the security of the United States.'" With all due respect, I believe the ultimate issue in these cases is even more basic than the one posed by the Solicitor General. The issue is whether this Court or the Congress has the power to make law.

In these cases there is no problem concerning the President's power to classify information as "secret" or "top secret." Congress has specifically recognized Presidential authority, which has been formally exercised in Exec. Order 10501 (1953), to classify documents and information. Nor is there any issue here regarding the President's power as Chief Executive and Commander in Chief to protect national security by disciplining employees who disclose information and by taking precautions to prevent leaks.

The problem here is whether in these particular cases the Executive Branch has authority to invoke the equity jurisdiction of the courts to protect what it believes to be the national interest. The Government argues that in addition to the inherent power of any government to protect itself, the President's power to conduct foreign affairs and his position as Commander in Chief give him authority to impose censorship on the press to protect his ability to deal effectively with foreign nations and to conduct the military affairs of the country. . . .

It would, however, be utterly inconsistent with the concept of separation of powers for this Court to use its power of contempt to prevent behavior that Congress has specifically declined to prohibit. . . .

* * *

MR. CHIEF JUSTICE BURGER, dissenting.

So clear are the constitutional limitations on prior restraint against expression, that from the time of *Near v. Minnesota* (1931), until recently in *Organization for a Better Austin v. Keefe* (1971), we have had little occasion to be concerned with cases involving prior restraints against news reporting on matters of public interest. There is, therefore, little variation among the members of the Court in terms of resistance to prior restraints against publication. Adherence to this basic constitutional principle, however, does not make these cases simple. In these cases, the imperative of a free and unfettered press comes into collision with another imperative, the effective functioning of a complex modern government and specifically the effective exercise of certain constitutional powers of the Executive. Only those who view the First Amendment as an absolute in all circumstances — a view I respect, but reject — can find such cases as these to be simple or easy.

These cases are not simple for another and more immediate reason. We do not know the facts of the cases. No District Judge knew all the facts. No Court of Appeals judge knew all the facts. No member of this Court knows all the facts.

Why are we in this posture, in which only those judges to whom the First Amendment is absolute and permits of no restraint in any circumstances or for any reason, are really in a position to act?

I suggest we are in this posture because these cases have been conducted in unseemly haste. Mr. Justice Harlan covers the chronology of events demonstrating the hectic pressures under which these cases have been processed [omitted] and I need not restate them. The prompt setting of these cases reflects our universal abhorrence of prior restraint. But prompt judicial action does not mean unjudicial haste.

Here, moreover, the frenetic haste is due in large part to the manner in which the Times proceeded from the date it obtained the purloined documents. It seems reasonably clear now that the haste precluded reasonable and deliberate judicial treatment of these cases and was not warranted. The precipitate action of this Court aborting trials not yet completed is not the kind of judicial conduct that ought to attend the disposition of a great issue.

The newspapers make a derivative claim under the First Amendment; they denominate this right as the public "right to know"; by implication, the Times asserts a sole trusteeship of that right by virtue of its journalistic "scoop." The right is asserted as an absolute. Of course, the First Amendment right itself is not an absolute, as Justice Holmes so long ago pointed out in his aphorism concerning the right to shout "fire" in a crowded theater if there was no fire. There are other exceptions. . . . Conceivably such exceptions may be lurking in these cases and would have been flushed had they been properly considered in the trial courts, free from unwarranted deadlines and frenetic pressures. An issue of this importance should be tried and heard in a judicial atmosphere conducive to thoughtful, reflective deliberation, especially when haste, in terms of hours, is unwarranted in light of the long period the Times, by its own choice, deferred publication.

It is not disputed that the Times has had unauthorized possession of the documents for three to four months, during which it has had its expert analysts studying them, presumably digesting them and preparing the material for publication. During all of this time, the Times, presumably in its capacity as trustee of the public's "right to know," has held up publication for purposes it considered proper and thus public knowledge was delayed. No doubt this was for a good reason; the analysis of 7,000 pages of complex material drawn from a vastly greater volume of material would inevitably take time and the writing of good news stories takes time. But why should the United States Government, from whom this information was illegally acquired by someone, along with all the counsel, trial judges, and appellate judges be placed under needless pressure? After these months of deferral, the alleged "right to know" has somehow and suddenly become a right that must be vindicated instanter.

Would it have been unreasonable, since the newspaper could anticipate the Government's objections to release of secret material, to give the Government an opportunity to review the entire collection and determine whether agreement could be reached on publication? Stolen or not, if security was not in fact jeopardized, much of the material could no doubt have been declassified, since it spans a period ending in 1968. With such an approach — one that great newspapers have in the past practiced and stated editorially to be the duty of an honorable press — the newspapers and Government might well have narrowed the area of disagreement as to what was and was not publishable, leaving the remainder to be resolved in orderly litigation, if necessary. To me it is hardly believable that a newspaper long regarded as a great institution in American life would fail to perform one of the basic and simple duties of every citizen with respect to the discovery or possession of stolen property or secret government documents. That duty, I had thought — perhaps naively — was to report forthwith, to responsible public officers. This duty rests on taxi drivers, Justices, and the New York Times. The course followed by the Times, whether so calculated or not, removed any possibility of orderly litigation of the issues. . . .

Our grant of the writ of certiorari before final judgment in the *Times* case aborted the trial in the District Court before it had made a complete record pursuant to the mandate of the Court of Appeals for the Second Circuit.

The consequence of all this melancholy series of events is that we literally do not know what we are acting on. As I see it, we have been forced to deal with litigation concerning rights of great magnitude without an adequate record, and surely without time for adequate treatment either in the prior proceedings or in this Court. It is interesting to note that counsel on both sides, in oral argument before this Court, were frequently unable to respond to questions on factual points. Not surprisingly they pointed out that they had been working literally "around the clock" and simply were unable to review the documents that give rise to these cases and were not familiar with them. This Court is in no better posture. . . . I am not prepared to reach the merits.

I would affirm the Court of Appeals for the Second Circuit and allow the District Court to complete the trial aborted by our grant of certiorari, meanwhile preserving the status quo in the *Post* case. I would direct that the District Court on remand give priority to the *Times* case to the exclusion of all other business of that court but I would not set arbitrary deadlines.

* * *

We all crave speedier judicial processes but when judges are pressured as in these cases the result is a parody of the judicial function.

MR. JUSTICE HARLAN, with whom THE CHIEF JUSTICE and MR. JUSTICE BLACKMUN join, dissenting.

These cases forcefully call to mind the wise admonition of Mr. Justice Holmes, dissenting in *Northern Securities Co. v. United States* (1904):

"Great cases like hard cases make bad law. For great cases are called great, not by reason of their real importance in shaping the law of the future, but because of some accident of immediate overwhelming interest which appeals to the feelings and distorts the judgment. These immediate interests exercise a kind of hydraulic pressure which makes what previously was clear seem doubtful, and before which even well settled principles of law will bend."

With all respect, I consider that the Court has been almost irresponsibly feverish in dealing with these cases.

Both the Court of Appeals for the Second Circuit and the Court of Appeals for the District of Columbia Circuit rendered judgment on June 23. The New York Times' petition for certiorari, its motion for accelerated consideration thereof, and its application for interim relief were filed in this Court on June 24 at about 11 a.m. The application of the United States for interim relief in the *Post* case was also filed here on June 24 at about 7:15 p.m. This Court's order setting a hearing before us on June 26 at 11 a.m., a course which I joined only to avoid the possibility of even more peremptory action by the Court, was issued less than 24 hours before. The record in the *Post* case was filed with the Clerk shortly before 1 p.m. on June 25; the record in the *Times* case did not arrive until 7 or 8 o'clock that same night. The briefs of the parties were received less than two hours before argument on June 26.

This frenzied train of events took place in the name of the presumption against prior restraints created by the First Amendment. Due regard for the extraordinarily important and difficult questions involved in these litigations should have led the Court to shun such a precipitate timetable. In order to decide the merits of these cases properly, some or all of the following questions should have been faced:

1. Whether the Attorney General is authorized to bring these suits in the name of the United States. This question involves as well the construction and validity of a singularly opaque statute — the Espionage Act, 18 U.S.C. § 793(e).

2. Whether the First Amendment permits the federal courts to enjoin publication of stories which would present a serious threat to national security.

3. Whether the threat to publish highly secret documents is of itself a sufficient implication of national security to justify an injunction on the theory that regardless of the contents of the documents harm enough results simply from the demonstration of such a breach of secrecy.

4. Whether the unauthorized disclosure of any of these particular documents would seriously impair the national security.

5. What weight should be given to the opinion of high officers in the Executive Branch of the Government with respect to questions 3 and 4.

6. Whether the newspapers are entitled to retain and use the documents notwithstanding the seemingly uncontested facts that the documents, or the originals of which they are duplicates, were purloined from the Government's possession and that the newspapers received them with knowledge that they had been feloniously acquired.

7. Whether the threatened harm to the national security or the Government's possessory interest in the documents justifies the issuance of an injunction against publication in light of —

      a. The strong First Amendment policy against prior restraints on publication;

      b. The doctrine against enjoining conduct in violation of criminal statutes; and

      c. The extent to which the materials at issue have apparently already been otherwise disseminated.

These are difficult questions of fact, of law, and of judgment; the potential consequences of erroneous decision are enormous. The time which has been available to us, to the lower courts, and to the parties has been wholly inadequate for giving these cases the kind of consideration they deserve. . . .

* * *

Accordingly, I would vacate the judgment of the Court of Appeals for the District of Columbia Circuit on this ground and remand the case for further proceedings in the District Court. Before the commencement of such further proceedings, due opportunity should be afforded the Government for procuring from the Secretary of State or the Secretary of Defense or both an expression of their views on the issue of national security. The ensuing review by the District Court should be in accordance with the views expressed in this opinion. And for the reasons stated above I would affirm the judgment of the Court of Appeals for the Second Circuit.

Pending further hearings in each case conducted under the appropriate ground rules, I would continue the restraints on publication. I cannot believe that the doctrine prohibiting prior restraints reaches to the point of preventing courts from maintaining the *status quo* long enough to act responsibly in matters of such national importance as those involved here.

MR. JUSTICE BLACKMUN, dissenting.

* * *

The New York Times clandestinely devoted a period of three months to examining the 47 volumes that came into its unauthorized possession. Once it had begun publication of material from those volumes, the New York case now before us emerged. It immediately assumed, and ever since has maintained, a frenetic pace and character. Seemingly, once publication started, the material could not be made public fast enough. Seemingly, from then on, every deferral or delay, by restraint or otherwise, was abhorrent and was to be deemed violative of the First Amendment and of the public's "right immediately to know." Yet that newspaper stood before us at oral argument and professed criticism of the Government for not lodging its protest earlier than by a Monday telegram following the initial Sunday publication.

The District of Columbia case is much the same.

* * *

With such respect as may be due to the contrary view, this, in my opinion, is not the way to try a lawsuit of this magnitude and asserted importance. It is not the way for federal courts to adjudicate, and to be required to adjudicate, issues that allegedly concern the Nation's vital welfare. The country would be none the worse off were the cases tried quickly, to be sure, but in the customary and properly deliberative manner. The most recent of the material, it is said, dates no later than 1968, already about three years ago, and the Times itself took three months to formulate its plan of procedure and, thus, deprived its public for that period.

The First Amendment, after all, is only one part of an entire Constitution. Article II of the great document vests in the Executive Branch primary power over the conduct of foreign affairs and places in that branch the responsibility for the Nation's safety. Each provision of the Constitution is important, and I cannot subscribe to a doctrine of unlimited absolutism for the First Amendment at the cost of downgrading other provisions. First Amendment absolutism has never commanded a majority of this Court. What is needed here is a weighing, upon properly developed standards, of the broad right of the press to print and of the very narrow right of the Government to prevent. Such standards are not yet developed. The parties here are in disagreement as to what those standards should be. But even the newspapers concede that there are situations where restraint is in order and is constitutional. Mr. Justice Holmes gave us a suggestion when he said in *Schenck* [*v. United States* (1919)],

> "It is a question of proximity and degree. When a nation is at war many things that might be said in time of peace are such a hindrance to its effort that their utterance will not be endured so long as men fight and that no Court could regard them as protected by any constitutional right."

I therefore would remand these cases to be developed expeditiously, of course, but on a schedule permitting the orderly presentation of evidence from both sides, with the use of discovery, if necessary, as authorized by the rules, and with the preparation of briefs, oral argument, and court opinions of a quality better than has been seen to this point. . . .

It may well be that if these cases were allowed to develop as they should be developed, and to be tried as lawyers should try them and as courts should hear them, free of pressure and panic and sensationalism, other light would be shed on the situation and contrary considerations, for me, might prevail. But that is not the present posture of the litigation.

The Court, however, decides the cases today the other way. I therefore add one final comment.

I strongly urge, and sincerely hope, that these two newspapers will be fully aware of their ultimate responsibilities to the United States of America. Judge Wilkey, dissenting in the District of Columbia case, after a review of only the affidavits before his court (the basic papers had not then been made available by either party), concluded that there were a number of examples of documents that, if in the possession of the Post, and if published, "could clearly result in great harm to the nation," and he defined "harm" to mean "the death of soldiers, the destruction of alliances, the greatly increased difficulty of negotiation with our enemies, the inability of our diplomats to negotiate . . . ." I, for one, have now been able to give at least some cursory study not only to the affidavits, but to the material itself. I regret to say that from this examination I fear that Judge Wilkey's statements have possible foundation. I therefore share his concern. I hope that damage has not already been done. If, however, damage has been done, and if, with the Court's action today, these newspapers proceed to publish the critical documents and there results therefrom "the death of soldiers, the destruction of alliances, the greatly increased difficulty of negotiation with our enemies, the inability of our diplomats to negotiate," to which list I might add the factors of prolongation of the war and of further delay in the freeing of United States prisoners, then the Nation's people will know where the responsibility for these sad consequences rests.

NOTES AND QUESTIONS

1. You have just read the infamous "Pentagon Papers" case. Do you understand why the government was not permitted to suppress the information contained within the Pentagon Papers? Why should citizens be able to publish material critical of the government? Suppose that even true information critical of the government, if published, will fundamentally impair the ability of the government to preserve order and carry out its duties to the people — should that information be allowed to be published? In England, until the late eighteenth century, even truthful criticism of the government was not permitted, pursuant to the doctrine of seditious libel. Under traditional English common law seditious libel doctrine, one could be criminally punished for the publication of any information, true or false, which tended to turn the sentiments of the people against the government. Did that doctrine make any sense? In colonial America the doctrine of seditious libel early came under fire, most notably in the trial of John Peter Zenger, a New York printer, who was prosecuted for seditious libel in the 1730s for comments critical of the New York Governor (then a Crown appointee). There was no doubt that Zenger had published the critical articles in question, nor was there any doubt that under the English common law of seditious libel Zenger was guilty of the crime whether what he published was true or not. "The greater the truth, the greater the libel," was the English common law maxim. Did it make any sense? What sort of a view of government did the English common law of seditious libel reveal?

Zenger's lawyer, a hoary barrister from Philadelphia, one Andrew Hamilton, argued to the jury that whatever the law was in England, in America citizens needed more freedom to criticize their governors, who were not, after all, members of the royal family, but just their representatives in the colonies. Hamilton was not permitted to prove the truth of Zenger's allegations, since the common law rule was that truth was no defense to a charge of seditious libel. In a famous and elegant move, Hamilton then argued to the jury that they should take the fact that he was not permitted to prove truth as a strong argument for the truth of what Zenger published. Remarkably, Hamilton was not censured by the court. What Hamilton argued — that truth ought to be a defense — was clearly not then the law, but he did manage to get the jury to acquit Zenger, even though, under the law as it then was, he should have been convicted. Can you understand what is meant by the term "Philadelphia lawyer"? From that time to this the Zenger trial has been taken to stand for the proposition that freedom of the press is one of the most important features of American law.

2. Just what was meant by "freedom of the press," as that term was used in the First Amendment, is far from clear, however. By 1798 several American theorists, most notably Jefferson and Madison, had begun to argue that the First Amendment forbade any American law of seditious libel. Nevertheless, in 1798 in the famous Alien and Sedition Laws, the United States Congress, controlled by the partisans of John Adams and Alexander Hamilton, fearing subversive activities on the part of a press hostile to the administration and friendly to France, with whom we were engaged in an undeclared naval war, passed a federal statute making it a crime to publish criticism of the government which tended to excite the people of the United States against the government. Alien and Sedition Laws, ch. 74, § 2, 1 Stat. 596, 596-97 (1798) (expired 1801). The 1798 statute departed from the English common law, and made truth a defense to the crime, but approximately 15 editors and publishers critical of the Adams administration were convicted under the statute and served several months in jail and had fines of up to two thousand dollars levied against them. Jefferson argued that the federal seditious libel law was unconstitutional (under the First Amendment), and succeeded in winning the Presidency in 1800 in part because of his campaign against the act. Once in office, he swiftly pardoned all who had been convicted under the act, although there is evidence that he began state prosecutions for seditious libel against some of *his* critics. Jefferson's and Madison's views — that the First Amendment forbade seditious libel prosecutions — were very much in the minority in the late eighteenth century. What then, did the First Amendment's preservation of "freedom of the press" mean? Most likely it simply meant freedom from what the English called "prior restraint." As Blackstone, the great exponent of the English common law, made clear, for a long time in England there had been a requirement that anyone seeking to publish anything first receive permission from the government. 4 WILLIAM BLACKSTONE, COMMENTARIES *152. This was the so-called law of prior restraint. Under that law, no one could publish anything without the Crown's permission. The late eighteenth-century freedom of the press, achieved at roughly the same time in America and England, was simply freedom from licensing, from prior restraint. In both England and America at that time, the ideal notion was that one should be free to publish anything one wanted, but that one's publications might nevertheless — after publication — subject one to liability for criminal or civil libel. Criminal libel resulted when one published pieces critical of the government, civil libel when one criticized one's fellow subject or citizen. Criminal libel could result in fine and/or imprisonment, civil libel could result in the payment of damages to the person wronged. Another common development — in both England and America in the 1790s — was to establish truth as a defense to seditious libel, and as a matter that was for the determination of the jury. Seditious libel, as late as 1800, however, was alive (if not completely well) in both places.

The Pentagon Papers case reveals how far American society had come on the issue of freedom of the press by the middle of the twentieth century. Should there have been a prior restraint on the publication of the Pentagon Papers?

3. Do you understand from the Pentagon Papers case whether prior restraint is ever permissible? Would it be permissible to publish information regarding our troop movements during time of war? Why was it permissible to publish information critical of the war effort in Vietnam while that war still raged? How does 9-11 and the War on Terror figure into this.

For a re-consideration of the Pentagon Papers case in light of the subsequently disclosed "secret brief" filed by Solicitor General Erwin Griswold in the matter, see Douglas W. Kmiec, *The Supreme Court in Times of Hot and Cold War*, 28 J. SUP. CT. HISTORY 270, 290-92 (2003). Professor Kmiec observes:

> While it would later be learned that the negotiating volumes had not, in fact, been leaked to the news organizations, there was ample other classified information of potentially great value to our enemies that had. For example, the stolen materials sought to be enjoined contained: the names of CIA and National Security Agency operatives still active in Southeast Asia; military plans for dealing with armed aggression in Laos; a discussion of our intelligence methods not then known to the Soviet Union; a Joint Chiefs memorandum recommending "a nuclear response" in the event of a Chinese attack on Thailand; and a fulsome discussion of the extent to which the National Security Agency had been able to break the codes of other nations. With respect to the last item, the Solicitor General pointed out the obvious: disclosure of our code-breaking abilities would permit an enemy nation "'to minimize

our chance of successful interception' with adverse consequences for current U.S. military operations."

Why wasn't this enough to warrant injunctive relief? Largely for reasons that had developed separately in the First Amendment cases during cold war periods — specifically, the need to show that advocacy (or publication) would result in *immediate* or *imminent* harm. Not fully realizing how this nuance of speech jurisprudence might trump inherent executive power over foreign affairs, Griswold lost his case at oral argument when he conceded:

> the materials specified in my closed brief . . . materially affect the security of the United States. It will affect lives. It will affect the process of termination of the war. It will affect the process of recovering prisoners of war. However, I cannot say that the termination of the war, or recovering prisoners of war, is something which has an "immediate" effect on the security of the United States. Nevertheless, I say that it has such an effect on the security of the United States that it ought to be the basis of an injunction in this case.

Why did Griswold not see this as a fatal concession? Perhaps it was because the need for immediacy or imminent lawless action to punish speech or publication is a later judicial graft on the First Amendment. Proximate to the founding, Joseph Story writes: "the language of [the First Amendment] imports no more, than that every man shall have a right to speak, write, and print his opinions upon any subject whatsoever, without any prior restraint . . . ." But Story also observes that the speech right exists *only if* the speaker "does not injure any other person in his rights, person, property, or reputation; and so always that he does not thereby disturb the public peace, or attempt to subvert the government. That this amendment was intended to secure to every citizen an absolute right to speak, or write, or print, whatever he might please, without any responsibility, public or private, therefor, is a supposition too wild to be indulged by any rational man." In Griswold's day, the accepted reading of this passage condemned prior restraints, but it did not necessarily make them all unconstitutional. Griswold might well have understood the Story passage as confirming a right to speak without restraint only if there is no disturbance of public peace or no subversion of the government. After *New York Times*, by contrast, speech or publication can be punished only after the fact, and only when harm is immediately upon us. This is now standard doctrine, but is it completely faithful to the original understanding and sustainable in the national security context? Erwin Griswold, I believe, was suggesting otherwise in a time of cold war. . . .

Does the terrorist threat now undermine the standard academic commentary that reflexively immunizes all speech activity short of imminent harm from illegal action? What would Solicitor General Griswold tell us? My supposition is that it was startling to Solicitor General Griswold that a lack of immediate or imminent damage to national security would preclude the injunctive relief he sought in *New York Times*. Griswold argued that an imminence standard was overly narrow and that it would be better phrased as "great and irreparable harm to the security of the United States." Griswold did not know the diabolical nature of the present al-Qaida threat, of course, but with extraordinary prescience, he further stated, "In the whole diplomatic area the things don't happen at 8:15 tomorrow morning. It may be weeks or months." Indeed, al-Qaida would bring it to New York at 8:48 a.m. one unexceptional September morning, and an anxious nation is still uncertain what dangers lie ahead.

4. Note the arguments of the dissenters. Why do they object to the speed with which this issue found its way to the court and resulted in a decision? Do they also disagree with the substantive law as the majority lays it down? What, if anything, is left of the doctrine of prior restraint? What, precisely, is the public's right to know with regard to the war effort in Vietnam?

You will have noticed the government's argument that the publication of the Pentagon Papers would endanger the lives of United States soldiers in Vietnam, jeopardize the release of prisoners of war, and put in peril the peace process then underway. Why wasn't this persuasive to the court?

5. A noted First Amendment scholar, Thomas Emerson, wrote:

> A system of prior restraint is in many ways more inhibiting than a system of subsequent punishment: It is likely to bring under government scrutiny a far wider range of expression; it shuts off communication before it takes place; suppression by a stroke of the pen is more likely to be applied than suppression through a criminal process; the procedures do not require attention to the safeguards of the criminal process; the system allows less opportunity for public appraisal and criticism; the dynamics of the system drive toward excesses, as the history of all censorship shows.

THOMAS EMERSON, THE SYSTEM OF FREEDOM OF EXPRESSION 506 (1970).

6. One reason prior restraints are viewed with distaste is that they are frequently incapable of being challenged even if unconstitutional. In other words, a person violating an unconstitutional prior restraint, especially if issued by a court, may be punished, and precluded from raising the "collateral" issue of unconstitutionality as a defense to contempt of court charges. Thus, in *Walker v. City of Birmingham*, 388 U.S. 307 (1967), Dr. Martin Luther King, Jr. and several other civil rights protestors were not permitted to challenge the punishment meted out for violating a court order that arguably violated the Constitution by preventing them from undertaking a demonstration on a city street without a permit. Why? Because, reasoned the Court, "petitioners were not free to ignore all procedures of the law and carry their battle to the streets. . . . [R]espect for judicial process is a small price to pay for the civilizing hand of law, which alone can give abiding meaning to constitutional freedom." *Id.* at 321.

7. Technically, a prior restraint is any administrative requirement (e.g., a license or permit) or judicial order directed at suppressing speech before it is undertaken. However, the Court has allowed such restraints in the context of abortion protests. *See Schenck v. Pro-Choice Network*, 519 U.S. 357 (1997) (upholding an injunction against sidewalk counseling where a request is made to cease and desist), and *Madsen v. Women's Health Center*, 512 U.S. 753 (1994) (upholding a 36-foot buffer zone around an abortion clinic). In both cases, the Court asserted that the judicial orders suppressing the demonstrations or counseling was not aimed at that expression, but at prior unlawful conduct that had impeded the free access of patients and staff to the abortion facility.

8. The guarantee of a fair trial may also implicate the prior restraint issue. Courts have fairly frequently directed attorneys and other trial participants not to talk with the media. While the Supreme Court has not passed on the constitutionality of this, the logic of such action is bolstered not only by the defendant's rights, but also by the control courts have over attorneys as "officer[s] of the court." By contrast, the Supreme Court has all but eliminated the enforceability of orders regarding pretrial publicity directed at the media, itself. In *Nebraska Press Association v. Stuart*, 427 U.S. 539 (1976), the Court held there is a strong presumption against such orders, absent a showing that the publicity will jeopardize the fairness of the trial, that alternative measures, such as changing location, postponement or juror screening are unavailing, and that such order would in fact be observed and workable.

2. What Constitutes a "Public Forum"?

INTERNATIONAL SOCIETY FOR KRISHNA CONSCIOUSNESS, INC. v. LEE
505 U.S. 672 (1992)

CHIEF JUSTICE REHNQUIST delivered the opinion of the Court.

In this case we consider whether an airport terminal operated by a public authority is a public forum and whether a regulation prohibiting solicitation in the interior of an airport terminal violates the First Amendment.

The relevant facts in this case are not in dispute. Petitioner International Society for Krishna Consciousness, Inc. (ISKCON), is a not-for-profit religious corporation whose members perform a ritual known as *sankirtan*. The ritual consists of "'going into public places, disseminating religious literature and soliciting funds to support the religion.'" The primary purpose of this ritual is raising funds for the movement.

Respondent Walter Lee, now deceased, was the police superintendent of the Port Authority of New York and New Jersey and was charged with enforcing the regulation at issue. The Port Authority owns and operates three major airports in the greater New York City area. . . .

The airports are funded by user fees and operated to make a regulated profit. Most space at the three airports is leased to commercial airlines, which bear primary responsibility for the leasehold. The Port Authority retains control over unleased portions . . . (we refer to these areas collectively as the "terminals"). The terminals are generally accessible to the general public and contain various commercial establishments such as restaurants, snack stands, bars, newsstands, and stores of various types. Virtually all who visit the terminals do so for purposes related to air travel. . . .

The Port Authority has adopted a regulation forbidding within the terminals the repetitive solicitation of money or distribution of literature. . . .

The regulation governs only the terminals; the Port Authority permits solicitation and distribution on the sidewalks outside the terminal buildings. The regulation effectively prohibits ISKCON from performing *sankirtan* in the terminals. As a result, ISKCON brought suit seeking declaratory and injunctive relief under 42 U.S.C. § 1983, alleging that the regulation worked to deprive its members of rights guaranteed under the First Amendment. The District Court analyzed the claim under the "traditional public forum" doctrine. It concluded that the terminals were akin to public streets, the quintessential traditional public fora. This conclusion in turn meant that the Port Authority's terminal regulation could be sustained only if it was narrowly tailored to support a compelling state interest. In the absence of any argument that the blanket prohibition constituted such narrow tailoring, the District Court granted ISKCON summary judgment.

The Court of Appeals affirmed in part and reversed in part. Relying on our recent decision in *United States v. Kokinda* (1990), a divided panel concluded that the terminals are not public fora. As a result, the restrictions were required only to satisfy a standard of reasonableness. The Court of Appeals then concluded that, presented with the issue, this Court would find that the ban on solicitation was reasonable, but the ban on distribution was not. ISKCON and one of its members, also a petitioner here, sought certiorari respecting the Court of Appeals' decision that the terminals are not public fora and upholding the solicitation ban. Respondent cross-petitioned respecting the court's holding striking down the distribution ban. We granted both petitions, to resolve whether airport terminals are public fora, a question on which the Circuits have split. . . .

It is uncontested that the solicitation at issue in this case is a form of speech protected under the First Amendment. But it is also well settled that the government need not permit all forms of speech on property that it owns and controls. Where the government is acting as a proprietor, managing its internal operations, rather than acting as lawmaker with the power to regulate or license, its action will not be subjected to the heightened review to which its actions as a lawmaker may be subject. Thus, we have upheld a ban on political advertisements in city-operated transit vehicles, even though the city permitted other types of advertising on those vehicles. Similarly, we have permitted a school district to limit access to an internal mail system used to communicate with teachers employed by the district.

These cases reflect, either implicitly or explicitly, a "forum based" approach for assessing restrictions that the government seeks to place on the use of its property. Under this approach, regulation of speech on government property that has traditionally been available for public expression is subject to the highest scrutiny. Such regulations survive only if they are narrowly drawn to achieve a compelling state interest. The second category of public property is the designated public forum, whether of a limited or unlimited character — property that the State has opened for expressive activity by part or all of the public. Regulation of such property is subject to the same limitations as that governing a traditional public forum. Finally, there is all remaining public property. Limitations on expressive activity conducted on this last category of property must survive only a much more limited review. The challenged regulation need only be reasonable, as long as the regulation is not an effort to suppress the speaker's activity due to disagreement with the speaker's view.

The parties do not disagree that this is the proper framework. Rather, they disagree whether the airport terminals are public fora or nonpublic fora. They also disagree whether the regulation survives the "reasonableness" review governing nonpublic fora, should that prove the appropriate category. Like the Court of Appeals, we conclude that the terminals are nonpublic fora and that the regulation reasonably limits solicitation.

The suggestion that the government has a high burden in justifying speech restrictions relating to traditional public fora made its first appearance in *Hague v. Committee for Industrial Organization* (1939). Justice Roberts, concluding that individuals have a right to use "streets and parks for communication of views," reasoned that such a right flowed from the fact that "streets and parks . . . have immemorially been held in trust for the use of the public and, time out of mind, have been used for purposes of assembly, communicating thoughts between citizens, and discussing public questions." We confirmed this observation in *Frisby v. Schultz* (1988), where we held that a residential street was a public forum.

Our recent cases provide additional guidance on the characteristics of a public forum. In *Cornelius* [*v. NAACP Legal Defense & Ed. Fund, Inc.* (1985),] we noted that a traditional public forum is property that has as "a principal purpose . . . the free exchange of ideas." Moreover, consistent with the notion that the government — like other property owners — "has power to preserve the property under its control for the use to which it is lawfully dedicated," the government does not create a public forum by inaction. Nor is a public forum created "whenever members of the public are permitted freely to visit a place owned or operated by the Government." The decision to create a public forum must instead be made "by intentionally opening a nontraditional forum for public discourse." Finally, we have recognized that the location of property also has bearing because separation from acknowledged public areas may serve to indicate that the separated property is a special enclave, subject to greater restriction.

These precedents foreclose the conclusion that airport terminals are public fora. Reflecting the general growth of the air travel industry, airport terminals have only recently achieved their contemporary size and character. But given the lateness with which the modern air terminal has made its appearance, it hardly qualifies for the description of having "immemorially . . . time out of mind" been held in the public trust and used for purposes of expressive activity. Moreover, even within the rather short history of air transport, it is only "[i]n recent years [that] it has become a common practice for various religious and nonprofit organizations to use commercial airports as a forum for the distribution of literature, the solicitation of funds, the proselytizing of new members, and other similar activities." Thus, the tradition of airport activity does not demonstrate that airports have historically been made available for speech activity. Nor can we say that these particular terminals, or airport terminals generally, have been intentionally opened by their operators to such activity; the frequent and continuing litigation evidencing the operators' objections belies any such claim. In short, there can be no argument that society's time-tested judgment, expressed through acquiescence in a continuing practice, has resolved the issue in petitioners' favor.

Petitioners attempt to circumvent the history and practice governing airport activity by pointing our attention to the variety of speech activity that they claim historically occurred at various "transportation nodes" such as rail stations, bus stations, wharves, and Ellis Island. Even if we were inclined to accept petitioners' historical account describing speech activity at these locations, an account respondent contests, we think that such evidence is of little import for two reasons. First, much of the evidence is irrelevant to *public* fora analysis, because sites such as bus and rail terminals traditionally have had *private* ownership. The development of privately owned parks that ban speech activity would not change the public fora status of publicly held parks. But the reverse is also true. The practices of privately held transportation centers do not bear on the government's regulatory authority over a publicly owned airport.

Second, the relevant unit for our inquiry is an airport, not "transportation nodes" generally. When new methods of transportation develop, new methods for accommodating that transportation are also likely to be needed. And with each new step, it therefore will be a new inquiry whether the transportation necessities are compatible with various kinds of expressive activity. To make a category of "transportation nodes," therefore, would unjustifiably elide what may prove to be critical differences of which we should rightfully take account. The "security magnet," for example, is an airport commonplace that lacks a counterpart in bus terminals and train stations. And public access to air terminals is also not infrequently restricted — just last year the Federal Aviation Administration required airports for a 4-month period to limit access to areas normally publicly accessible. To blithely equate airports with other transportation centers, therefore, would be a mistake.

The differences among such facilities are unsurprising since, as the Court of Appeals noted, airports are commercial establishments funded by users fees and designed to make a regulated profit, and where nearly all who visit do so for some travel related purpose. As commercial enterprises, airports must provide services attractive to the marketplace. In light of this, it cannot fairly be said that an airport terminal has as a principal purpose promoting "the free exchange of ideas." To the contrary, the record demonstrates that Port Authority management considers the purpose of the terminals to be the facilitation of passenger air travel, not the promotion of expression. Even if we look beyond the intent of the Port Authority to the manner in which the terminals have been operated, the terminals have never been dedicated (except under the threat of court order) to expression in the form sought to be exercised here: *i.e.*, the solicitation of contributions and the distribution of literature.

The terminals here are far from atypical. Airport builders and managers focus their efforts on providing terminals that will contribute to efficient air travel. The Federal Government is in accord; the Secretary of Transportation has been directed to publish a plan for airport development necessary "to anticipate and meet the needs *of civil aeronautics*, to meet requirements in support of the national defense . . . and to meet identified needs of the Postal Service." (emphasis added). Although many airports have expanded their function beyond merely contributing to efficient air travel, few have included among their purposes the designation of a forum for solicitation and distribution activities. Thus, we think that neither by tradition nor purpose can the terminals be described as satisfying the standards we have previously set out for identifying a public forum.

The restrictions here challenged, therefore, need only satisfy a requirement of reasonableness. . . . The restriction "'need only be *reasonable*; it need not be the most reasonable or the only reasonable limitation.'" We have no doubt that under this standard the prohibition on solicitation passes muster.

We have on many prior occasions noted the disruptive effect that solicitation may have on business. "Solicitation requires action by those who would respond: The individual solicited must decide whether or not to contribute (which itself might involve reading the solicitor's literature or hearing his pitch), and then, having decided to do so, reach for a wallet, search it for money, write a check, or produce a credit card." Passengers who wish to avoid the solicitor may have to alter their paths, slowing both themselves and those around them. The result is that the normal flow of traffic is impeded. This is especially so in an airport, where "[a]ir travelers, who are often weighted down by cumbersome baggage . . . may be hurrying to catch a plane or to arrange ground transportation." Delays may be particularly costly in this setting, as a flight missed by only a few minutes can result in hours worth of subsequent inconvenience.

In addition, face-to-face solicitation presents risks of duress that are an appropriate target of regulation. The skillful, and unprincipled, solicitor can target the most vulnerable, including those accompanying children or those suffering physical impairment and who cannot easily avoid the solicitation. The unsavory solicitor can also commit fraud through concealment of his affiliation or through deliberate efforts to shortchange those who agree to purchase. Compounding this problem is the fact that, in an airport, the targets of such activity frequently are on tight schedules. This in turn makes such visitors unlikely to stop and formally complain to airport authorities. As a result, the airport faces considerable difficulty in achieving its legitimate interest in monitoring solicitation activity to assure that travelers are not interfered with unduly.

The Port Authority has concluded that its interest in monitoring the activities can best be accomplished by limiting solicitation and distribution to the sidewalk areas outside the terminals. This sidewalk area is frequented by an overwhelming percentage of airport users. Thus the resulting access of those who would solicit the general public is quite complete. In turn we think it would be odd to conclude that the Port Authority's terminal regulation is unreasonable despite the Port Authority having otherwise assured access to an area universally traveled.

The inconveniences to passengers and the burdens on Port Authority officials flowing from solicitation activity may seem small, but viewed against the fact that "pedestrian congestion is one of the greatest problems facing the three terminals," the Port Authority could reasonably worry that even such incremental effects would prove quite disruptive. Moreover, "[t]he justification for the Rule should not be measured by the disorder that would result from granting an exemption solely to ISKCON." For if ISKCON is given access, so too must other groups. "Obviously, there would be a much larger threat to the State's interest in crowd control if all other religious, nonreligious, and noncommercial organizations could likewise move freely." As a result, we conclude that the solicitation ban is reasonable.

* * *

JUSTICE SOUTER, with whom JUSTICE BLACKMUN and JUSTICE STEVENS join, . . . dissenting. . . .

* * *

II

From the Court's conclusion . . . sustaining the total ban on solicitation of money for immediate payment, I respectfully dissent. "We have held the solicitation of money by charities to be fully protected as the dissemination of ideas. It is axiomatic that, although fraudulent misrepresentation of facts can be regulated, the dissemination of ideas cannot be regulated to prevent it from being unfair or unreasonable."

Even if I assume, *arguendo*, that the ban on the petitioners' activity at issue here is both content neutral and merely a restriction on the manner of communication, the regulation must be struck down for its failure to satisfy the requirements of narrow tailoring to further a significant state interest, and availability of "ample alternative channels for communication."

. . . [R]espondent comes closest to justifying the restriction as one furthering the government's interest in preventing coercion and fraud. The claim to be preventing coercion is weak to start with. While a solicitor can be insistent, a pedestrian on the street or airport concourse can simply walk away or walk on. In any event, we have held in a far more coercive context than this one, that of a black boycott of white stores in Claiborne County, Mississippi, that "[s]peech does not lose its protected character . . . simply because it may embarrass others or coerce them into action." Since there is here no evidence of any type of coercive conduct, over and above the merely importunate character of the open and public solicitation, that might justify a ban, the regulation cannot be sustained to avoid coercion.

As for fraud, our cases do not provide government with plenary authority to ban solicitation just because it could be fraudulent. "Broad prophylactic rules in the area of free expression are suspect," and more than a laudable intent to prevent fraud is required to sustain the present ban. The evidence of fraudulent conduct here is virtually nonexistent. It consists of one affidavit describing eight complaints, none of them substantiated, "involving some form of fraud, deception, or larceny" over an entire 11-year period between 1975 and 1986, during which the regulation at issue here was, by agreement, not enforced. Petitioners claim, and respondent does not dispute, that by the Port Authority's own calculation, there has not been a single claim of fraud or misrepresentation since 1981. As against these facts, respondent's brief is ominous in adding that "[t]he Port Authority is also aware that members of [International Society for Krishna Consciousness] have engaged in misconduct elsewhere." This is precisely the type of vague and unsubstantiated allegation that could never support a restriction on speech. Finally, the fact that other governmental bodies have also enacted restrictions on solicitation in other places, is not evidence of fraudulent conduct.

Even assuming a governmental interest adequate to justify some regulation, the present ban would fall when subjected to the requirement of narrow tailoring. "Precision of regulation must be the touchstone . . . ." Thus, . . . we [have] said:

> "The Village's legitimate interest in preventing fraud can be better served by measures less intrusive than a direct prohibition on solicitation. Fraudulent misrepresentations can be prohibited and the penal laws used to punish such conduct directly. Efforts to promote disclosure

of the finances of charitable organizations also may assist in preventing fraud by informing the public of the ways in which their contributions will be employed. Such measures may help make contribution decisions more informed, while leaving to individual choice the decision whether to contribute. . . ."

Similarly, in [another case] we required the State to cure its perceived fraud problem by more narrowly tailored means than compelling disclosure by professional fundraisers of the amount of collected funds that were actually turned over to charity during the previous year:

"In contrast to the prophylactic, imprecise, and unduly burdensome rule the State has adopted to reduce its alleged donor misperception, more benign and narrowly tailored options are available. For example, as a general rule, the State may itself publish the detailed financial disclosure forms it requires professional fund-raisers to file. This procedure would communicate the desired information to the public without burdening a speaker with unwanted speech during the course of a solicitation. Alternatively, the State may vigorously enforce its antifraud laws to prohibit professional fund-raisers from obtaining money on false pretenses or by making false statements."

Finally, I do not think the Port Authority's solicitation ban leaves open the "ample" channels of communication required of a valid content-neutral time, place, and manner restriction. A distribution of preaddressed envelopes is unlikely to be much of an alternative. The practical reality of the regulation, which this Court can never ignore, is that it shuts off a uniquely powerful avenue of communication for organizations like the International Society for Krishna Consciousness, and may, in effect, completely prohibit unpopular and poorly funded groups from receiving funds in response to protected solicitation.

Accordingly, I would . . . strike down the ban on solicitation.

NOTES AND QUESTIONS

1. Why did the parties in the case who sought to raise funds in airports to support their religious faith believe that they were entitled so to do because of the First Amendment? What has the First Amendment got to do with airports? Do you find the reasoning of the majority — that the airport can bar solicitations by the Krishna group if it has a "reasonable basis" for doing so — persuasive? Why don't the dissenters?

2. Does this case present an issue in freedom of speech, in freedom of religion, or a hybrid of both? What does it mean to suggest that time, place, and manner restrictions of the exercise of freedom of speech (in an airport) are permissible, so long as they are "content neutral"? Will such restrictions really ever be "content neutral"?

3. As an abstract matter, government can control, and decide the use of, its property. However, long ago, the Court decided that some public property must remain open for public assembly. Thus, in *Hague v. CIO*, 307 U.S. 496 (1939), the Court invalidated an ordinance which sought to limit the availability of public streets and sidewalks without a permit. Modernly, the extent of the government's control over public property often depends on whether the property is a public forum, a designated or limited public forum, or a non-public forum. The distinctions were articulated in *Perry Education Association v. Perry Local Educators' Association,* 460 U.S. 37 (1983), where the Court upheld limiting access to an inter-school mail system. There, the Court defined a public forum as a place, where by long tradition, assembly and debate have been permitted, such as streets, sidewalks, and parks. In a public forum, any government regulation must be content-neutral. This means neutral as to subject matter and viewpoint. Any content-based regulation would need to have a compelling governmental justification. In only one modern case, has a content restriction of this type survived strict scrutiny. In *Burson v. Freeman*, 504 U.S. 191 (1992), the Court upheld a prohibition of the distribution of campaign literature within 100 feet of the entrance of a polling place. Also allowed in a public forum are time, place and manner restrictions. These, too, must be content-neutral, though they must merely serve a significant governmental interest and leave open ample channels of communication. Thus, in *Grayned v. Rockford*, 408 U.S. 104 (1972), the Court sustained a noise control ordinance in a school zone. However, a government regulating a public forum need not employ the least restrictive means. The question is whether the regulation is not substantially broader than necessary to achieve the government's interest. The issue is not whether the Court could envision a less restrictive alternative. *Ward v. Rock Against Racism*, 491 U.S. 781 (1989) (upholding the requirement that those using a public park use the public sound system and engineers).

A designated public forum is an area voluntarily opened by the government as a place for expressive activity. The government need not retain it indefinitely in that status, though as long as it does so, it will be treated by the same rules that govern a public forum. Thus, in *Lamb's Chapel v. Center Moriches Union Free School Dist.*, 508 U.S. 384 (1993), school facilities that were made generally available after hours could not exclude certain viewpoints. "[A]bove all else, the First Amendment means that government has no power to restrict expression because of its message, its ideas, its subject matter or its content." *Police Department of Chicago v. Mosley*, 408 U.S. 92, 95-96 (1972). Thus, content restrictions are presumptively invalid and can be justified only by meeting the strict scrutiny with a compelling governmental interest. When it is said that a government regulation must be content-neutral, it means both neutrality as to viewpoint and subject matter. Viewpoint restrictions regulate on the ideology of the message. For example, in *Boos v. Berry*, 485 U.S. 312 (1988), the Court invalidated a District of Columbia ordinance that prohibited signs critical of a foreign government within 500 feet of an embassy. By comparison, in *Carey v. Brown*, 447 U.S. 455 (1980), the Court invalidated a ban on all picketing in residential areas other than that related to the subject of labor or employment. Unlike viewpoint and subject matter restrictions that result in strict scrutiny, a regulation that affects speech but is not aimed at content or viewpoint is subject to an intermediate level of scrutiny or review.

The government may also designate a public forum limited to particular purposes. In a sense, it can limit the subject matter, or content, of the forum, but even here it cannot discriminate on the basis of viewpoint, a point we address in the next section.

By contrast to either public fora (traditional or designated) or limited public fora, a non-public forum can be closed to speech activity, pursuant to any reasonable regulation that is viewpoint neutral. Thus, in *Members of the City Council of the City of Los Angeles v. Taxpayers for Vincent*, 466 U.S. 789 (1984), the Court upheld the prohibition of the posting of signs on public property. Within a non-public forum, the government may also draw distinctions on the basis of subject-matter or speaker identity, but not viewpoint. In *Cornelius v. NAACP Legal Defense and Education Fund, Inc.*, 473 U.S. 788 (1985), the Court allowed the federal government to exclude from its charitable fund raising campaign, legal defense and political organizations. Of course, as the principal case reveals, not every regulation in a non-public forum will be held reasonable. Thus, notwithstanding *Krishna*'s conclusion that the airport was a non-public forum, Justice O'Connor, who provided the pivotal vote, was unable to find the literature distribution ban, as opposed to the solicitation ban, to be reasonable.

4. What then determines the status of a forum? This somewhat divides the Court in *Krishna*, with some members of the Court holding onto tradition as the primary, if not dispositive, criterion, and others seeking to evaluate more contextually whether speech activities would be compatible with the general functioning of the enterprise.

5. Even though the Court in *Krishna* found the airport to be a non-public forum, that did not mean that all regulation of this public space would be deemed "reasonable." In a portion of the opinion not reprinted, the Court held a similar ban on mere distribution of literature as invalid under the First Amendment. Justice O'Connor had supported the characterization of the airport as non-public and the ban on solicitation, but she switched sides when the issue was prohibiting the distribution of literature. "Leafletting does not entail the same kinds of problems presented by face-to-face solicitation," wrote Justice O'Connor, who was supported in this view by Justices Kennedy, Souter, Blackmun, and Stevens, the last three of which, were in dissent on the earlier solicitation ban. Chief Justice Rehnquist who wrote the majority opinion for the solicitation aspects of the regulation dissented along with Justices White, Scalia, and Thomas, fearing that the split result would be overly burdensome on the Port Authority.

6. The next section considers time, place, and manner restrictions on speech that are permitted even in public fora, as long as they do not distriminate on the basis of either content or viewpoint.

3. The Impermissibility of Content and Viewpoint Discrimination by the Government

HILL v. COLORADO
530 U.S. 703 (2000)

JUSTICE STEVENS delivered the opinion of the Court.

At issue is the constitutionality of a 1993 Colorado statute that regulates speech-related conduct within 100 feet of the entrance to any health care facility. The specific section of the statute that is challenged, . . . makes it unlawful within the regulated areas for any person to "knowingly approach" within eight feet of another person, without that person's consent, "for the purpose of passing a leaflet or handbill to, displaying a sign to, or engaging in oral protest, education, or counseling with such other person . . . ."[1] . . . [The Statute] makes it

---

[1] § 18-9-122 reads [in part] as follows:

"(1) The general assembly recognizes that access to health care facilities for the purpose of obtaining medical counseling and treatment is imperative for the citizens of this state; that the exercise of a person's right to protest or counsel against certain medical procedures must be balanced against another person's right to obtain medical counseling and treatment in an unobstructed manner; and that preventing the willful obstruction of a person's access to medical counseling and treatment at a health care facility is a matter of statewide concern. The general assembly therefore declares that it is appropriate to enact legislation that prohibits a person from knowingly obstructing another person's entry to or exit from a health care facility.

"(2) A person commits a class 3 misdemeanor if such person knowingly obstructs, detains, hinders, impedes, or blocks another person's entry to or exit from a health care facility.

"(3) No person shall knowingly approach another person within eight feet of such person, unless such other person consents, for the purpose of passing a leaflet or handbill to, displaying a sign to, or engaging in oral protest, education, or counseling with such other person in the public way or sidewalk area within a radius of one hundred feet from any entrance door to a health care facility. Any person who violates this subsection (3) commits a class 3 misdemeanor.

* * *

"(6) In addition to, and not in lieu of, the penalties set forth in this section, a person who violates the provisions of this section shall be subject to civil liability, as provided in section 13-21-106.7, C.R.S."

more difficult to give unwanted advice, particularly in the form of a handbill or leaflet, to persons entering or leaving medical facilities.

The question is whether the First Amendment rights of the speaker are abridged by the protection the statute provides for the unwilling listener.

I

Five months after the statute was enacted, petitioners filed a complaint in the District Court for Jefferson County, Colorado, praying for a declaration that [it] was facially invalid and seeking an injunction against its enforcement. They stated that prior to the enactment of the statute, they had engaged in "sidewalk counseling" on the public ways and sidewalks within 100 feet of the entrances to facilities where human abortion is practiced or where medical personnel refer women to other facilities for abortions. "Sidewalk counseling" consists of efforts "to educate, counsel, persuade, or inform passersby about abortion and abortion alternatives by means of verbal or written speech, including conversation and/or display of signs and/or distribution of literature." They further alleged that such activities frequently entail being within eight feet of other persons and that their fear of prosecution under the new statute caused them "to be chilled in the exercise of fundamental constitutional rights."

. . . [Petitioners contended the law] was content based for two reasons: The content of the speech must be examined to determine whether it "constitutes oral protest, counseling and education"; and that it is "viewpoint-based" because the statute "makes it likely that prosecution will occur based on displeasure with the position taken by the speaker."

. . . There was no evidence that the "sidewalk counseling" conducted by petitioners in this case was ever abusive or confrontational.

* * *

In 1996, the Supreme Court of Colorado denied review, and petitioners sought a writ of certiorari from our Court. While their petition was pending, we decided *Schenck v. Pro-Choice Network of Western N.Y.* (1997). Because we held in that case that an injunctive provision creating a speech-free "floating buffer zone" with a 15-foot radius violates the First Amendment, we granted certiorari, vacated the judgment of the Colorado Court of Appeals, and remanded the case to that court for further consideration in light of *Schenck*.

On remand the Court of Appeals reinstated its judgment upholding the statute. It noted that in *Schenck* we had "expressly declined to hold that a valid governmental interest in ensuring ingress and egress to a medical clinic may never be sufficient to justify a zone of separation between individuals entering and leaving the premises and protesters" and that our opinion in *Ward* [*v. Rock Against Racism* (1989)] provided the standard for assessing the validity of a content-neutral, generally applicable statute. Under that standard, even though a 15-foot floating buffer might preclude protesters from expressing their views from a normal conversational distance, a lesser distance of eight feet was sufficient to protect such speech on a public sidewalk.

The Colorado Supreme Court granted certiorari and affirmed the judgment of the Court of Appeals. . . . It noted that both the trial court and the Court of Appeals had concluded that the statute was content neutral, that petitioners no longer contended otherwise, and that they agreed that the question for decision was whether the statute was a valid time, place, and manner restriction under the test announced in *Ward*.

The court identified two important distinctions between this case and *Schenck*. First, *Schenck* involved a judicial decree and therefore, as explained in *Madsen*, posed "greater risks of censorship and discriminatory application than do general ordinances." Second, unlike the floating buffer zone in *Schenck*, which would require a protester either to stop talking or to get off the sidewalk whenever a patient came within 15 feet, the "knowingly approaches" requirement in the Colorado statute allows a protester to stand still while a person moving towards or away from a health care facility walks past her. Applying the test in *Ward*, the court concluded that the statute was narrowly drawn to further a significant government interest. It rejected petitioners' contention that it was not narrow enough because it applied to all health care facilities in the State. In the court's view, the comprehensive coverage of the statute was a factor that supported its content neutrality. Moreover, the fact that the statute was enacted, in part, because the General Assembly "was concerned with the safety of individuals seeking wide-ranging health care services, not merely abortion counseling and procedures," added to the substantiality of the government interest that it served. Finally, it concluded that ample alternative channels remain open because petitioners. . . . We now affirm.

II

Before confronting the question whether the Colorado statute reflects an acceptable balance between the constitutionally protected rights of law-abiding speakers and the interests of unwilling listeners, it is appropriate to examine the competing interests at stake. A brief review of both sides of the dispute reveals that each has legitimate and important concerns.

The First Amendment interests of petitioners are clear and undisputed. . . . There is no disagreement on this point, even though the legislative history makes it clear that its enactment was primarily motivated by activities in the vicinity of abortion clinics. Second, they correctly state that their leafletting, sign displays, and oral communications are protected by the First Amendment. The fact that the messages conveyed by those communications may be offensive to their recipients does not deprive them of constitutional protection. Third, the public sidewalks, streets, and ways affected by the statute are "quintessential" public forums for free speech. Finally, although there is debate about the magnitude of the statutory impediment to their ability to communicate effectively with persons in the regulated zones, that ability, particularly the ability to distribute leaflets, is unquestionably lessened by this statute.

On the other hand, petitioners do not challenge the legitimacy of the state interests that the statute is intended to serve. It is a traditional exercise of the States' "police powers to protect the health and safety of their citizens." That interest may justify a special focus on unimpeded access to health care facilities and the avoidance of potential trauma to patients associated with confrontational protests. *See Madsen v. Women's Health Center, Inc.* . . .

The right to free speech, of course, includes the right to attempt to persuade others to change their views, and may not be curtailed simply because the speaker's message may be offensive to his audience. But the protection afforded to offensive messages does not always embrace offensive speech that is so intrusive that the unwilling audience cannot avoid it. *Frisby v. Schultz* (1988).

* * *

The unwilling listener's interest in avoiding unwanted communication has been repeatedly identified in our cases. It is an aspect of the broader "right to be let alone" that one of our wisest Justices characterized as "the most comprehensive of rights and the right most valued by civilized men." The right to avoid unwelcome speech has special force in the privacy of the home, *Rowan v. United States Post Office Dept.* (1970), and its immediate surroundings, *Frisby v. Schultz*, but can also be protected in confrontational settings.

We have since recognized that the "right to persuade" discussed in that case is protected by the First Amendment, *Thornhill v. Alabama* (1940), as well as by federal statutes. Yet we have continued to maintain that "no one has a right to press even 'good' ideas on an unwilling recipient." None of our decisions has minimized the enduring importance of "the right to be free" from persistent "importunity, following and dogging" after an offer to communicate has been declined.

* * *

III

All four of the state court opinions upholding the validity of this statute concluded that it is a content-neutral time, place, and manner regulation. Moreover, they all found support for their analysis in *Ward v. Rock Against Racism* (1989). It is therefore appropriate to comment on the "content neutrality" of the statute. As we explained in *Ward*:

> "The principal inquiry in determining content neutrality, in speech cases generally and in time, place, or manner cases in particular, is whether the government has adopted a regulation of speech because of disagreement with the message it conveys."

The Colorado statute passes that test for three independent reasons. First, it is not a "regulation of speech." Rather, it is a regulation of the places where some speech may occur. Second, it was not adopted "because of disagreement with the message it conveys." This conclusion is supported not just by the Colorado courts' interpretation of legislative history, but more importantly by the State Supreme Court's unequivocal holding that the statute's "restrictions apply equally to all demonstrators, regardless of viewpoint, and the statutory language makes no reference to the content of the speech." Third, the State's interests in protecting access and privacy, and providing the police with clear guidelines, are unrelated to the content of the demonstrators' speech. As we have repeatedly explained, government regulation of expressive activity is "content neutral" if it is justified without reference to the content of regulated speech. . . .

. . . Petitioners contend that an individual near a health care facility who knowingly approaches a pedestrian to say "good morning" or to randomly recite lines from a novel would not be subject to the statute's restrictions. Because the content of the oral statements made by an approaching speaker must sometimes be examined to determine whether the knowing approach is covered by the statute, petitioners argue that the law is "content-based."

* * *

It is common in the law to examine the content of a communication to determine the speaker's purpose. Whether a particular statement constitutes a threat, blackmail, an agreement to fix prices, a copyright violation, a public offering of securities, or an offer to sell goods often depends on the precise content of the statement. We have never held, or suggested, that it is improper to look at the content of an oral or written statement in order to determine whether a rule of law applies to a course of conduct. With respect to the conduct that is the focus of the Colorado statute, it is unlikely that there would often be any need to know exactly what words were spoken in order to determine whether "sidewalk counselors" are engaging in "oral protest, education, or counseling" rather than pure social or random conversation.

Theoretically, of course, cases may arise in which it is necessary to review the content of the statements made by a person approaching within eight feet of an unwilling listener to determine whether the approach is covered by the statute. But that review need be no more extensive than a determination of whether a general prohibition of "picketing" or "demonstrating" applies to innocuous speech. The regulation of such expressive activities, by definition, does not cover social, random, or other everyday communications. . . . Nevertheless, we have never suggested that the kind of cursory examination that might be required to exclude casual conversation from the coverage of a regulation of picketing would be problematic.

In *Carey v. Brown* we examined a general prohibition of peaceful picketing that contained an exemption for picketing of a place of employment involved in a labor dispute. We concluded that this statute violated the Equal Protection Clause of the Fourteenth Amendment, because it discriminated between lawful and unlawful conduct based on the content of the picketers' messages. That discrimination was impermissible because it accorded preferential treatment to expression concerning one particular subject matter — labor disputes — while prohibiting discussion of all other issues. Although our opinion stressed that "it is the content of the speech that determines whether it is within or without the statute's blunt prohibition," we appended a footnote to that sentence explaining that it was the fact that the statute placed a prohibition on discussion of particular topics, while others were allowed, that was constitutionally repugnant. Regulation of the subject matter of messages, though not as obnoxious as viewpoint-based regulation, is also an objectionable form of content-based regulation.

The Colorado statute's regulation of the location of protests, education, and counseling is easily distinguishable from *Carey*. It places no restrictions on — and clearly does not prohibit — either a particular viewpoint or any subject matter that may be discussed by a speaker. Rather, it simply establishes a minor place restriction on an extremely broad category of communications with unwilling listeners. Instead of drawing distinctions based on the subject that the approaching speaker may wish to address, the statute applies equally to used car salesmen, animal rights activists, fundraisers, environmentalists, and missionaries. Each can attempt to educate unwilling listeners on any subject, but without consent may not approach within eight feet to do so.

* * *

IV

We also agree with the state courts' conclusion that [the law] is a valid time, place, and manner regulation under the test applied in *Ward* because it is "narrowly tailored." We already have noted that the statute serves governmental interests that are significant and legitimate and that the restrictions are content neutral. We are likewise persuaded that the statute is "narrowly tailored" to serve those interests and that it leaves open ample alternative channels for communication. As we have emphasized on more than one occasion, when a content-neutral regulation does not entirely foreclose any means of communication, it may satisfy the tailoring requirement even though it is not the least restrictive or least intrusive means of serving the statutory goal.

The three types of communication regulated are the display of signs, leafletting, and oral speech. The 8-foot separation between the speaker and the audience should not have any adverse impact on the readers' ability to read signs displayed by demonstrators. In fact, the separation might actually aid the pedestrians' ability to see the signs by preventing others from surrounding them and impeding their view. Furthermore, the statute places no limitations on the number, size, text, or images of the placards. And, as with all of the restrictions, the 8-foot zone does not affect demonstrators with signs who remain in place.

. . . Unlike the 15-foot zone in *Schenck*, this 8-foot zone allows the speaker to communicate at a "normal conversational distance." Additionally, the statute allows the speaker to remain in one place, and other individuals can pass within eight feet of the protester without causing the protester to violate the statute. Finally, here there is a "knowing" requirement that protects speakers "who thought they were keeping pace with the targeted individual" at the proscribed distance from inadvertently violating the statute.

* * *

The burden on the ability to distribute handbills is more serious because it seems possible that an 8-foot interval could hinder the ability of a leafletter to deliver handbills to some unwilling recipients. The statute does not, however, prevent a leafletter from simply standing near the path of oncoming pedestrians and proffering his or her material, which the pedestrians can easily accept. And, as in all leafletting situations, pedestrians continue to be free to decline the tender. In *Heffron v. International Soc. for Krishna Consciousness, Inc.* (1981), we upheld a state fair regulation that required a religious organization desiring to distribute literature to conduct that activity only at an assigned location — in that case booths. As in this case, the regulation primarily burdened the distributors' ability to communicate with unwilling readers. We concluded our opinion by emphasizing that the First Amendment protects the right of every citizen to "reach the minds of willing listeners and to do so there must be opportunity to win their attention." The Colorado statute adequately protects those rights.

Finally, in determining whether a statute is narrowly tailored, we have noted that "[w]e must, of course, take account of the place to which the regulations apply in determining whether these restrictions burden more speech than necessary." States and municipalities plainly have a substantial interest in controlling the activity around certain public and private places. For example, we have recognized the special governmental interests surrounding schools, courthouses, polling places, and private homes. Additionally, we previously have noted the unique concerns that surround health care facilities.

* * *

The statute takes a prophylactic approach; it forbids all unwelcome demonstrators to come closer than eight feet. We recognize that by doing so, it will sometimes inhibit a demonstrator whose approach in fact would have proved harmless. But the statute's prophylactic aspect is justified by the great difficulty of protecting, say, a pregnant woman from physical harassment with legal rules that focus exclusively on the individual impact of each instance of behavior, demanding in each case an accurate characterization (as harassing or not harassing) of each individual movement within the 8-foot boundary. Such individualized characterization of each individual movement is often difficult to make accurately. A bright-line prophylactic rule may be the best way to provide protection, and, at the same time, by offering clear guidance and avoiding subjectivity, to protect speech itself.

* * *

V

[Petitioners also contend that the law] is invalid because it is "overbroad." There are two parts to petitioners' "overbreadth" argument. On the one hand, they argue that the statute is too broad because it protects too many people in too many places, rather than just the patients at the facilities where confrontational speech had occurred. Similarly, it burdens all speakers, rather than just persons with a history of bad conduct. On the other hand, petitioners also contend that the statute is overbroad because it "bans virtually the universe of protected expression, including displays of signs, distribution of literature, and mere verbal statements."

The first part of the argument does not identify a constitutional defect. . . . In this case, it is not disputed that the regulation affects protected speech activity, the question is thus whether it is a "reasonable restrictio[n] on the time, place, or manner of protected speech."

. . . The second part of the argument is based on a misreading of the statute and an incorrect understanding of the overbreadth doctrine. As we have already noted, [the law] simply does not "ban" any messages, and likewise it does not "ban" any signs, literature, or oral statements. It merely regulates the places where communications may occur. As we explained in *Broadrick v. Oklahoma* (1973), the overbreadth doctrine enables litigants "to challenge a statute, not because their own rights of free expression are violated, but because of a judicial prediction or assumption that the statute's very existence may cause others not before the court to refrain from constitutionally protected speech or expression." Moreover, "particularly where conduct and not merely speech is involved, we believe that the overbreadth of a statute must not only be real, but substantial as well, judged in relation to the statute's plainly legitimate sweep." Petitioners have not persuaded us that the impact of the statute on the conduct of other speakers will differ from its impact on their own sidewalk counseling. Like petitioners' own activities, the conduct of other protesters and counselors at all health care facilities are encompassed within the statute's "legitimate sweep." Therefore, the statute is not overly broad.

VI

Petitioners also claim that [the law] is unconstitutionally vague. They find a lack of clarity in three parts of the section: the meaning of "protest, education, or counseling"; the "consent" requirement; and the determination of whether one is "approaching" within eight feet of another.

A statute can be impermissibly vague for either of two independent reasons. First, if it fails to provide people of ordinary intelligence a reasonable opportunity to understand what conduct it prohibits. Second, if it authorizes or even encourages arbitrary and discriminatory enforcement. *Chicago v. Morales* (1999).

In this case, the first concern is ameliorated by the fact that [the law] contains a scienter requirement. The statute only applies to a person who "knowingly" approaches within eight feet of another, without that person's consent, for the purpose of engaging in oral protest, education, or counseling. The likelihood that anyone would not understand any of those common words seems quite remote.

* * *

For the same reason, we are similarly unpersuaded by the suggestion that [the law] fails to give adequate guidance to law enforcement authorities. Indeed, it seems to us that one of the section's virtues is the specificity of the definitions of the zones described in the statute. "As always, enforcement requires the exercise of some degree of police judgment," and the degree of judgment involved here is acceptable.

VII

Finally, petitioners argue that [the law's] consent requirement is invalid because it imposes an unconstitutional "prior restraint" on speech. We rejected this argument previously in *Schenck*, and *Madsen*. Moreover, the restrictions in this case raise an even lesser prior restraint concern than those at issue in *Schenck* and *Madsen* where particular speakers were at times completely banned within certain zones. Under this statute, absolutely no channel of communication is foreclosed. No speaker is silenced. And no message is prohibited. Petitioners are simply wrong when they assert that "[t]he statute compels speakers to obtain consent to speak and it authorizes private citizens to deny petitioners' requests to engage in expressive activities." To the contrary, this statute does not provide for a "heckler's veto" but rather allows every speaker to engage freely in any expressive activity communicating all messages and viewpoints subject only to the narrow place requirement imbedded within the "approach" restriction.

Furthermore, our concerns about "prior restraints" relate to restrictions imposed by official censorship. The regulations in this case, however, only apply if the pedestrian does not consent to the approach. Private citizens have always retained the power to decide for themselves what they wish to read, and within limits, what oral messages they want to consider. This statute simply empowers private citizens entering a health care facility with the ability to prevent a speaker, who is within eight feet and advancing, from communicating a message they do not wish to hear. Further, the statute does not authorize the pedestrian to affect any other activity at any other location or relating to any other person. These restrictions thus do not constitute an unlawful prior restraint.

* * *

The judgment of the Colorado Supreme Court is affirmed.

It is so ordered.

JUSTICE SOUTER, with whom JUSTICE O'CONNOR, JUSTICE GINSBURG, and JUSTICE BREYER join, concurring.

I join the opinion of the Court and add this further word. The key to determining whether [the law], makes a content-based distinction between varieties of speech lies in understanding that content-based discriminations are subject to strict scrutiny because they place the weight of government behind the disparagement or suppression of some messages, whether or not with the effect of approving or promoting others. . . .

Concern about employing the power of the State to suppress discussion of a subject or a point of view is not, however, raised in the same way when a law addresses not the content of speech but the circumstances of its delivery. The right to express unpopular views does not necessarily immunize a speaker from liability for resorting to otherwise impermissible behavior meant to shock members of the speaker's audience, *see United States v. O'Brien* (1968) (burning draft card), or to guarantee their attention, *see Kovacs v. Cooper* (1949) (sound trucks); *Frisby v. Schultz* (1988) (residential picketing); *Heffron v. International Soc. for Krishna Consciousness, Inc.* (1981) (soliciting). Unless regulation limited to the details of a speaker's delivery results in removing a subject or viewpoint from effective discourse (or otherwise fails to advance a significant public interest in a way narrowly fitted to that objective), a reasonable restriction intended to affect only the time, place, or manner of speaking is perfectly valid. *See Ward v. Rock Against Racism*, (1989).

* * *

JUSTICE SCALIA, with whom JUSTICE THOMAS joins, dissenting.

The Court today concludes that a regulation requiring speakers on the public thoroughfares bordering medical facilities to speak from a distance of eight feet is "not a 'regulation of speech,'" but "a regulation of the places where some speech may occur," and that a regulation directed to only certain categories of speech (protest, education, and counseling) is not "content-based." For these reasons, it says, the regulation is immune from the exacting scrutiny we apply to content-based suppression of speech in the public forum. The Court then determines that the regulation survives the less rigorous scrutiny afforded content-neutral time, place, and manner restrictions because it is narrowly tailored to serve a government interest — protection of citizens' "right to be let alone" — that has explicitly been disclaimed by the State, probably for the reason that, as a basis for suppressing peaceful private expression, it is patently incompatible with the guarantees of the First Amendment.

None of these remarkable conclusions should come as a surprise. What is before us, after all, is a speech regulation directed against the opponents of abortion, and it therefore enjoys the benefit of the "ad hoc nullification machine" that the Court has set in motion to push aside whatever doctrines of constitutional law stand in the way of that highly favored practice. . . . Having deprived abortion opponents of the political right to persuade the electorate that abortion should be restricted by law, the Court today continues and expands its assault upon their individual right to persuade women contemplating abortion that what they are doing is wrong. Because, like the rest of our abortion jurisprudence, today's decision is in stark contradiction of the constitutional principles we apply in all other contexts, I dissent.

I

. . . Whatever may be said about the restrictions on the other types of expressive activity, the regulation as it applies to oral communications is obviously and undeniably content-based. A speaker wishing to approach another for the purpose of communicating any message except one of protest, education, or counseling may do so without first securing the other's consent. Whether a speaker must obtain permission before approaching within eight feet — and whether he will be sent to prison for failing to do so — depends entirely on what he intends to say when he gets there. I have no doubt that this regulation would be deemed content-based in an instant if the case before us involved antiwar protesters, or union members seeking to "educate" the public about the reasons for their strike. . . . But the jurisprudence of this Court has a way of changing when abortion is involved.

The Court asserts that this statute is not content-based for purposes of our First Amendment analysis because it neither (1) discriminates among viewpoints nor (2) places restrictions on "any subject matter that may be discussed by a speaker." But we have never held that the universe of content-based regulations is limited to those two categories, and such a holding would be absurd. Imagine, for instance, special place-and-manner restrictions on all speech except that which "conveys a sense of contentment or happiness." This "happy speech" limitation would not be "viewpoint-based" — citizens would be able to express their joy in equal measure at either the rise or fall of the NASDAQ, at either the success or the failure of the Republican Party — and would not discriminate on the basis of subject matter, since gratification could be expressed about anything at all. Or consider a law restricting the writing or recitation of poetry — neither viewpoint-based nor limited to any particular subject matter. Surely this Court would consider such regulations to be "content-based" and deserving of the most exacting scrutiny.

"The vice of content-based legislation — what renders it deserving of the high standard of strict scrutiny — is not that it is always used for invidious, thought-control purposes, but that it lends itself to use for those purposes." A restriction that operates only on speech that communicates a message of protest, education, or counseling presents exactly this risk. When applied, as it is here, at the entrance to medical facilities, it is a means of impeding speech against abortion. The Court's confident assurance that the statute poses no special threat to First Amendment freedoms because it applies alike to "used car salesmen, animal rights activists, fundraisers, environmentalists, and missionaries," is a wonderful replication (except for its lack of sarcasm) of Anatole France's observation that "[t]he law, in its majestic equality, forbids the rich as well as the poor to sleep under bridges . . . ." *see* J. BARTLETT, FAMILIAR QUOTATIONS 550 (16th ed.1992). This Colorado law is no more targeted at used car salesmen, animal rights activists, fund raisers, environmentalists, and missionaries than French vagrancy law was targeted at the rich. We know what the Colorado legislators, by their careful selection of content ("protest, education, and counseling"), were taking aim at, for they set it forth in the statute itself: the "right to protest or counsel *against* certain medical procedures" on the sidewalks and streets surrounding health care facilities. Col.Rev.Stat. § 18-9-122(1) (1999) (emphasis added).

The Court is unpersuasive in its attempt to equate the present restriction with content-neutral regulation of demonstrations and picketing. . . . When the government regulates "picketing," or "demonstrating," it restricts a particular manner of expression that is, as the author of today's opinion has several times explained, "a mixture of conduct and communication." . . .

. . . Today, of course, JUSTICE STEVENS gives us an opinion restricting not only handbilling but even one-on-one conversation of a particular content. There comes a point — and the Court's opinion today passes it — at which the regulation of action intimately and unavoidably connected with traditional speech is a regulation of speech itself. The strictures of the First Amendment cannot be avoided by regulating the act of moving one's lips; and they cannot be avoided by regulating the act of extending one's arm to deliver a handbill, or peacefully approaching in order to speak. All of these acts can be regulated, to be sure; but not, on the basis of content, without satisfying the requirements of our strict-scrutiny First Amendment jurisprudence.

* * *

If one accepts the Court's description of the interest served by this regulation, it is clear that the regulation is both based on content and justified by reference to content. Constitutionally proscribable "secondary effects" of speech are directly addressed in subsection (2) of the statute, which makes it unlawful to obstruct, hinder, impede, or block access to a health care facility — a prohibition broad enough to include all physical threats and all physically threatening approaches. The purpose of subsection (3), however (according to the Court), is to protect "[t]he unwilling listener's interest in avoiding unwanted communication." On this analysis, Colorado has restricted certain categories of speech — protest, counseling, and education — out of an apparent belief that only speech with this content is sufficiently likely to be annoying or upsetting as to require consent before it may be engaged in at close range. It is reasonable enough to conclude that even the most gentle and peaceful close approach by a so-called "sidewalk counselor" — who wishes to "educate" the woman entering an abortion clinic about the nature of the procedure, to "counsel" against it and in favor of other alternatives, and perhaps even (though less likely if the approach is to be successful) to "protest" her taking of a human life — will often, indeed usually, have what might be termed the "secondary effect" of annoying or deeply upsetting the woman who is planning the abortion. But that is not an effect which occurs "without reference to the content" of the speech. This singling out of presumptively "unwelcome" communications fits precisely the description of prohibited regulation set forth in *Boos v. Barry* (1988): It "targets the direct impact of a particular category of speech, not a secondary feature that happens to be associated with that type of speech."

In sum, it blinks reality to regard this statute, in its application to oral communications, as anything other than a content-based restriction upon speech in the public forum. As such, it must survive that stringent mode of constitutional analysis our cases refer to as "strict scrutiny," which requires that the restriction be narrowly tailored to serve a compelling state interest. . . . Since the Court does not even attempt to support the regulation under this standard, I shall discuss it only briefly. Suffice it to say that if protecting people from unwelcome communications (the governmental interest the Court posits) is a compelling state interest, the First Amendment is a dead letter. And if forbidding peaceful, nonthreatening, but uninvited speech from a distance closer than eight feet is a "narrowly tailored" means of preventing the obstruction of entrance to medical facilities (the governmental interest the State asserts) narrow tailoring must refer not to the standards of Versace, but to those of Omar the tentmaker. In the last analysis all of this does not matter, however, since as I proceed to discuss neither the restrictions upon oral communications nor those upon handbilling can withstand a proper application of even the less demanding scrutiny we apply to truly content-neutral regulations of speech in a traditional public forum.

II

As the Court explains, under our precedents even a content-neutral, time, place, and manner restriction must be narrowly tailored to advance a significant state interest, and must leave open ample alternative means of communication. . . . It cannot be sustained if it "burden[s] substantially more speech than is necessary to further the government's legitimate interests."

This requires us to determine, first, what is the significant interest the State seeks to advance? Here there appears to be a bit of a disagreement between the State of Colorado (which should know) and the Court (which is eager to speculate). Colorado has identified in the text of the statute itself the interest it sought to advance: to ensure that the State's citizens may "obtain medical counseling and treatment in an unobstructed manner" by "preventing the willful obstruction of a person's access to medical counseling and treatment at a health care facility." . . . The Court nevertheless concludes that the Colorado provision is narrowly tailored to serve . . . the State's interest in protecting its citizens' rights to be let alone from unwanted speech.

Indeed, the situation is even more bizarre than that. The interest that the Court makes the linchpin of its analysis was not only unasserted by the State; it is not only completely different from the interest that the statute specifically

sets forth; it was explicitly disclaimed by the State in its brief before this Court.
. . .

I shall discuss below the obvious invalidity of this statute assuming, first (in Part A), the fictitious state interest that the Court has invented, and then (in Part B), the interest actually recited in the statute and asserted by counsel for Colorado.

A

It is not without reason that Colorado claimed that, in attributing to this statute the false purpose of protecting citizens' right to be let alone, petitioners were seeking to discredit it. Just three Terms ago, in upholding an injunction against antiabortion activities, the Court refused to rely on any supposed "'right of the people approaching and entering the facilities to be left alone.'" *Schenck v. Pro-Choice Network of Western N.Y.* (1997). It expressed "doubt" that this "right . . . accurately reflects our First Amendment jurisprudence." . . .

To support the legitimacy of its self-invented state interest, the Court relies upon a bon mot in a 1928 dissent (which we evidently overlooked in *Schenck*). It characterizes the "unwilling listener's interest in avoiding unwanted communication" as an "aspect of the broader 'right to be let alone.'" Justice Brandeis coined in [a] dissent. The amusing feature is that even this slim reed contradicts rather than supports the Court's position. The right to be let alone that Justice Brandeis identified was a right the Constitution "conferred, as against the government"; it was that right, not some generalized "common-law right" or "interest" to be free from hearing the unwanted opinions of one's fellow citizens, which he called the "most comprehensive" and "most valued by civilized men." . . . To the extent that there can be gleaned from our cases a "right to be let alone" in the sense that Justice Brandeis intended, it is the right of the speaker in the public forum to be free from government interference of the sort Colorado has imposed here.

* * *

B

I turn now to the real state interest at issue here — the one set forth in the statute and asserted in Colorado's brief: the preservation of unimpeded access to health care facilities. We need look no further than subsection (2) of the statute to see what a provision would look like that is narrowly tailored to serve that interest. Under the terms of that subsection, any person who "knowingly obstructs, detains, hinders, impedes, or blocks another person's entry to or exit from a health care facility" is subject to criminal and civil liability. It is possible, I suppose, that subsection (2) of the Colorado statute will leave unrestricted some expressive activity that, if engaged in from within eight feet, may be sufficiently harassing as to have the effect of impeding access to health care facilities. In subsection (3), however, the State of Colorado has prohibited a vast amount of speech that cannot possibly be thought to correspond to that evil.

. . . The Court makes no attempt to justify on the facts this blatant violation of the narrow-tailoring principle. Instead, it flirts with the creation of yet a new constitutional "first" designed for abortion cases: "[W]hen," it says, "a content-neutral regulation does not entirely foreclose any means of communication, it may satisfy the tailoring requirement even though it is not the least restrictive or least intrusive means of serving the statutory goal." The implication is that the availability of alternative means of communication permits the imposition of the speech restriction upon more individuals, or more types of communication, than narrow tailoring would otherwise demand. The Court assures us that "we have emphasized" this proposition "on more than one occasion." The only citation the Court provides, however, says no such thing. *Ward v. Rock Against Racism*, says only that narrow tailoring is not synonymous with "least restrictive alternative." It does not at all suggest — and to my knowledge no other case does either — that narrow tailoring can be relaxed when there are other speech alternatives.

* * *

The Court seems prepared, if only for a moment, to take seriously the magnitude of the burden the statute imposes on simple handbilling and leafletting. That concern is fleeting, however, since it is promptly assuaged by the realization that a leafletter may, without violating the statute, stand "near the path" of oncoming pedestrians and make his "proffe[r] . . ., which the pedestrians can easily accept." It does not take a veteran labor organizer to recognize — although surely any would, *see* Brief for American Federation of Labor and Congress of Industrial Organization as *Amicus Curiae* — that leafletting will be rendered utterly ineffectual by a requirement that the leafletter obtain from each subject permission to approach, or else man a stationary post (one that does not obstruct access to the facility, lest he violate subsection (2) of statute) and wait for passersby voluntarily to approach an outstretched hand. That simply is not how it is done, and the Court knows it — or should. A leafletter, whether he is working on behalf of Operation Rescue, Local 109, or Bubba's Bar-B-Que, stakes out the best piece of real estate he can, and then walks a few steps toward individuals passing in his vicinity, extending his arm and making it as easy as possible for the passerby, whose natural inclination is generally not to seek out such distributions, to simply accept the offering. Few pedestrians are likely to give their "consent" to the approach of a handbiller (indeed, by the time he requested it they would likely have passed by), and even fewer are likely to walk over in order to pick up a leaflet. In the abortion context, therefore, ordinary handbilling, which we have in other contexts recognized to be a "classic for[m] of speech that lie[s] at the heart of the First Amendment," *Schenck*, will in its most effective locations be rendered futile, the Court's implausible assertions to the contrary notwithstanding.

The Colorado provision differs in one fundamental respect from the "content-neutral" time, place, and manner restrictions the Court has previously upheld. Each of them rested upon a necessary connection between the regulated expression and the evil the challenged regulation sought to eliminate. So, for instance, in *Ward v. Rock Against Racism*, the Court approved the city's control over sound amplification because every occasion of amplified sound presented the evil of excessive noise and distortion disturbing the areas surrounding the public forum. The regulation we upheld in *Ward*, rather than "bann[ing] all concerts, or even all rock concerts, . . . instead focus[ed] on the source of the evils the city seeks to eliminate . . . and eliminates them without at the same time banning or significantly restricting a substantial quantity of speech that does not create the same evils." . . .

In contrast to the laws approved in those cases, the law before us here enacts a broad prophylactic restriction which does not "respon[d] precisely to the substantive problem which legitimately concern[ed]" the State, namely (the only problem asserted by Colorado), the obstruction of access to health facilities. Such prophylactic restrictions in the First Amendment context — even when they are content-neutral — are not permissible. "Broad prophylactic rules in the area of free expression are suspect. . . . Precision of regulation must be the touchstone in an area so closely touching our most precious freedoms." In *United States v. Grace* (1983), we declined to uphold a ban on certain expressive activity on the sidewalks surrounding the Supreme Court. The purpose of the restriction was the perfectly valid interest in security, just as the purpose of the restriction here is the perfectly valid interest in unobstructed access; and there, as here, the restriction furthered that interest — but it furthered it with insufficient precision and hence at excessive cost to the freedom of speech. There was, we said, "an insufficient nexus" between security and all the expressive activity that was banned, just as here there is an insufficient nexus between the assurance of access and forbidding unconsented communications within eight feet.

* * *

. . . It is one thing to assume, as in *Schenck*, that a prophylactic injunction is necessary when the specific targets of that measure have demonstrated an inability or unwillingness to engage in protected speech activity without also engaging in conduct that the Constitution clearly does not protect. It is something else to assume that all those who wish to speak outside health care facilities across the State will similarly abuse their rights if permitted to exercise them. The First Amendment stands as a bar to exactly this type of prophylactic legislation. I cannot improve upon the Court's conclusion in *Madsen* that "it is difficult, indeed, to justify a prohibition on all uninvited approaches of persons seeking the services of the clinic, regardless of how peaceful the contact may be, without burdening more speech than necessary to prevent intimidation and to ensure access to the clinic. Absent evidence that the protestors' speech is independently proscribable (i.e., 'fighting words' or threats), or is so infused with violence as to be indistinguishable from a threat of physical harm, this provision cannot stand."

* * *

It is interesting to compare the present decision, which upholds an utterly bizarre proabortion "request to approach" provision of Colorado law, with [*Carhart v. Stenberg*], . . . also announced today, which strikes down a live-birth abortion prohibition adopted by 30 States and twice passed by both Houses of Congress (though vetoed both times by the President). The present case disregards the State's own assertion of the purpose of its proabortion law, and posits instead a purpose that the Court believes will be more likely to render the law constitutional. *Stenberg* rejects the State's assertion of the very meaning of its antiabortion law, and declares instead a meaning that will render the law unconstitutional. The present case rejects overbreadth challenges to a proabortion law that regulates speech, on grounds that have no support in our prior jurisprudence and that instead amount to a total repudiation of the doctrine of overbreadth. *Stenberg* applies overbreadth analysis to an antiabortion law that has nothing to do with speech, even though until eight years ago overbreadth was unquestionably the exclusive preserve of the First Amendment. . . .

Does the deck seem stacked? You bet. As I have suggested throughout this opinion, today's decision is not an isolated distortion of our traditional constitutional principles, but is one of many aggressively proabortion novelties announced by the Court in recent years. . . .

I dissent.

JUSTICE KENNEDY, dissenting.

The Court's holding contradicts more than a half century of well-established First Amendment principles. For the first time, the Court approves a law which bars a private citizen from passing a message, in a peaceful manner and on a profound moral issue, to a fellow citizen on a public sidewalk. If from this time forward the Court repeats its grave errors of analysis, we shall have no longer the proud tradition of free and open discourse in a public forum. In my view, JUSTICE SCALIA's First Amendment analysis is correct and mandates outright reversal. In addition to undermining established First Amendment principles, the Court's decision conflicts with the essence of the joint opinion in *Planned Parenthood of Southeastern Pa. v. Casey* (1992).

I

* * *

The statute is content based for an additional reason: It restricts speech on particular topics. Of course, the enactment restricts "oral protest, education, or counseling" on any subject; but a statute of broad application is not content neutral if its terms control the substance of a speaker's message. If oral protest, education, or counseling on every subject within an 8-foot zone present a danger to the public, the statute should apply to every building entrance in the State. It does not. It applies only to a special class of locations: entrances to buildings with health care facilities. We would close our eyes to reality were we to deny that "oral protest, education, or counseling" outside the entrances to medical facilities concern a narrow range of topics — indeed, one topic in particular. By confining the law's application to the specific locations where the prohibited discourse occurs, the State has made a content-based determination. The Court ought to so acknowledge. Clever content-based restrictions are no less offensive than censoring on the basis of content. *See, e.g., United States v. Eichman* (1990). If, just a few decades ago, a State with a history of enforcing racial discrimination had enacted a statute like this one, regulating "oral protest, education, or counseling" within 100 feet of the entrance to any lunch counter, our predecessors would not have hesitated to hold it was content based or viewpoint based. It should be a profound disappointment to defenders of the First Amendment that the Court today refuses to apply the same structural analysis when the speech involved is less palatable to it.

* * *

After the Court errs in finding the statute content neutral, it compounds the mistake by finding the law viewpoint neutral. Viewpoint-based rules are invidious speech restrictions, yet the Court approves this one. The purpose and design of the statute — as everyone ought to know and as its own defenders urge in attempted justification — are to restrict speakers on one side of the debate: those who protest abortions. The statute applies only to medical facilities, a convenient yet obvious mask for the legislature's true purpose and for the prohibition's true effect. One need read no further than the statute's preamble to remove any doubt about the question. The Colorado Legislature sought to restrict "a person's right to protest or counsel against certain medical procedures." The word "against" reveals the legislature's desire to restrict discourse on one side of the issue regarding "certain medical procedures." The testimony to the Colorado Legislature consisted, almost in its entirety, of debates and controversies with respect to abortion, a point the majority acknowledges. The legislature's purpose to restrict unpopular speech should be beyond dispute.

* * *

II

The Colorado statute offends settled First Amendment principles in another fundamental respect. It violates the constitutional prohibitions against vague or overly broad criminal statutes regulating speech. The enactment's fatal ambiguities are multiple and interact to create further imprecisions. The result is a law more vague and overly broad than any criminal statute the Court has sustained as a permissible regulation of speech. The statute's imprecisions are so evident that this, too, ought to have ended the case without further discussion.

* * *

The 8-foot no-approach zone is so unworkable it will chill speech. Assume persons are about to enter a building from different points and a protestor is walking back and forth with a sign or attempting to hand out leaflets. If she stops to create the 8-foot zone for one pedestrian, she cannot reach other persons with her message; yet if she moves to maintain the 8-foot zone while trying to talk to one patron she may move knowingly closer to a patron attempting to enter the facility from a different direction. In addition, the statute requires a citizen to give affirmative consent before the exhibitor of a sign or the bearer of a leaflet can approach. . . . The only sure way to avoid violating the law is to refrain from picketing, leafleting, or oral advocacy altogether. Scienter cannot save so vague a statute as this.

A statute is vague when the conduct it forbids is not ascertainable. *See Chicago v. Morales* (1999).

* * *

III

Even aside from the erroneous, most disturbing assumptions that the statute is content neutral, viewpoint neutral, and neither vague nor overbroad, the Court falls into further serious error when it turns to the time, place, and manner rules set forth in *Ward*.

* * *

Colorado's excuse, and the Court's excuse, for the serious burden imposed upon the right to leaflet or to discuss is that it occurs at the wrong place. Again, Colorado and the Court have it just backwards. For these protestors the 100-foot zone in which young women enter a building is not just the last place where the message can be communicated. It likely is the only place. It is the location where the Court should expend its utmost effort to vindicate free speech, not to burden or suppress it.

Perhaps the leaflet will contain a picture of an unborn child, a picture the speaker thinks vital to the message. One of the arguments by the proponents of abortion, I had thought, was that a young woman might have been so uninformed that she did not know how to avoid pregnancy. The speakers in this case seek to ask the same uninformed woman, or indeed any woman who is considering an abortion, to understand and to contemplate the nature of the life she carries within her. To restrict the right of the speaker to hand her a leaflet, to hold a sign, or to speak quietly is for the Court to deny the neutrality that must be the first principle of the First Amendment. In this respect I am in full agreement with JUSTICE SCALIA's explanation of the insult the Court gives when it tells us these grave moral matters can be discussed just as well through a bullhorn. It would be remiss, moreover, not to observe the profound difference a leaflet can have in a woman's decisionmaking process. Consider the account of one young woman who testified before the Colorado Senate:

> "Abortion is a major decision. Unfortunately, most women have to make this decision alone. I did and I know that I am not the only one. As soon as I said the word 'pregnant,' he was history, never to be heard of, from again. I was scared and all alone. I was too embarrassed to ask for help. If this law had been in effect then, I would not have got any infor-

mation at all and gone through with my abortion because the only people that were on my side were the people at the abortion clinic. They knew exactly how I was feeling and what to say to make it all better. In my heart, I knew abortion was wrong, but it didn't matter. I had never taken responsibility for my actions so why start then. One of the major reasons I did not go through with my scheduled abortion was the picture I was given while I was pregnant. This was the first time I had ever seen the other side of the story. I think I speak for a lot of women, myself included, when I say abortion is the only way out because of [sic] it's all I knew. In Sex Education, I was not taught about adoption or the fetus or anything like that. All I learned about was venereal diseases and abortion. The people supplying the pamphlet helped me make my choice. I got an informed decision, I got information from both sides, and I made an informed decision that my son and I could both live with. Because of this picture I was given, right there, this little boy got a chance at life that he would never have had."

There are, no doubt, women who would testify that abortion was necessary and unregretted. The point here is simply that speech makes a difference, as it must when acts of lasting significance and profound moral consequence are being contemplated. The majority reaches a contrary conclusion only by disregarding settled free speech principles. In doing so it delivers a grave wound to the First Amendment as well as to the essential reasoning in the joint opinion in Casey, a concern to which I now turn.

IV

In *Planned Parenthood of Southeastern Pa. v. Casey*, the Court reaffirmed its prior holding that the Constitution protects a woman's right to terminate her pregnancy in its early stages. The joint opinion in Casey considered the woman's liberty interest and principles of stare decisis, but took care to recognize the gravity of the personal decision: "[Abortion] is an act fraught with consequences for others: for the woman who must live with the implications of her decision; for the persons who perform and assist in the procedure; for the spouse, family, and society which must confront the knowledge that these procedures exist, procedures some deem nothing short of an act of violence against innocent human life; and, depending on one's beliefs, for the life or potential life that is aborted."

The Court now strikes at the heart of the reasoned, careful balance I had believed was the basis for the joint opinion in *Casey*. The vital principle of the opinion was that in defined instances the woman's decision whether to abort her child was in its essence a moral one, a choice the State could not dictate. Foreclosed from using the machinery of government to ban abortions in early term, those who oppose it are remitted to debate the issue in its moral dimensions. In a cruel way, the Court today turns its back on that balance. It in effect tells us the moral debate is not so important after all and can be conducted just as well through a bullhorn from an 8-foot distance as it can through a peaceful, face-to-face exchange of a leaflet. The lack of care with which the Court sustains the

Colorado statute reflects a most troubling abdication of our responsibility to enforce the First Amendment.

There runs through our First Amendment theory a concept of immediacy, the idea that thoughts and pleas and petitions must not be lost with the passage of time. . . . So committed is the Court to its course that it denies these protesters, in the face of what they consider to be one of life's gravest moral crises, even the opportunity to try to offer a fellow citizen a little pamphlet, a handheld paper seeking to reach a higher law.

I dissent.

NOTES AND QUESTIONS

1. The majority sees this case as an unexceptional extension of *Madsen* and *Schenck*, while the dissent perceives it as a troubling disregard of longstanding free speech precedent. Which is it? Are you bothered by the fact that the activity suppressed here was stipulated to be entirely peaceful (educational counseling), and not aimed at prior unlawful conduct as was the limited injunctive relief in prior cases?

2. Was the Colorado statute content-based? The dissent argues that it is because before it can be applied, the content (counseling, education, protest) must be determined. But aren't these categories simply broad descriptions of the prohibited conduct? Or is the real problem the fact that the statute is limited to protest *against* certain medical procedures? Is the generality of that phrasing merely a disguise designed to preserve a prior restraint of not only a disfavored content (abortion counseling), but also a disfavored viewpoint (counseling *against* obtaining the procedure)? Certainly, the dissent is right that if in the midst of the civil rights movement of the 1950s and 1960s, Alabama passed a statute outlawing protests in front of lunch counters, everyone would have known its purpose was not to regulate café accessibility, but to maintain racial segregation. Can these examples be distinguished?

3. Do you understand the limits of the majority's proposition that the government can protect people from unwelcome communication? Later in this Chapter we will see the Court find that even the "unwelcome-ness" of flag-burning must be tolerated in a free republic. Why is the abortion protest different? Isn't the wounded military veteran or the mother of soldier killed in action to be as deeply troubled by flag destruction as a woman contemplating terminating a pregnancy by counseling? The dissent writes that: "[t]oday's decision is an unprecedented departure from this Court's teachings respecting unpopular speech in public fora." Do you agree?

4. In *Rosenberger v. Rector*, 515 U.S. 819 (1995), which you read in Chapter 2, the Court invalidated the University of Virginia's restriction that student activity fees could not be used by a student group to publish a newsletter that "primarily promotes or manifests a particular belie[f] in or about a deity or an ultimate reality," though student newsletters expressing other viewpoints were readily permitted:

> It is axiomatic that the government may not regulate speech based on its substantive content or the message it conveys. *Police Dept. of Chicago v. Mosley* (1972). Other principles follow from this precept. In the realm of private speech or expression, government regulation may not favor one speaker over another. *Members of City Council of Los Angeles v. Taxpayers for Vincent* (1984). Discrimination against speech because of its message is presumed to be unconstitutional. *See Turner Broadcasting System, Inc. v. FCC* (1994). These rules informed our determination that the government offends the First Amendment when it imposes financial burdens on certain speakers based on the content of their expression. *Simon & Schuster, Inc. v. Members of N.Y. State Crime Victims Bd.* (1991). When the government targets not subject matter, but particular views taken by speakers on a subject, the violation of the First Amendment is all the more blatant. *See R.A.V. v. St. Paul* (1992). Viewpoint discrimination is thus an egregious form of content discrimination. The government must abstain from regulating speech when the specific motivating ideology or the opinion or perspective of the speaker is the rationale for the restriction. *See Perry Ed. Assn. v. Perry Local Educators' Assn.* (1983).

Rosenberger, 515 U.S. at 828-29. The Court treated the University's student activities fee fund as a "limited public forum," which, as noted above, differs from a traditional public forum in that the government may impose restrictions on subject matter in order to further the purpose of the limited forum it has created. The University's restrictions were unconstitutional, though, because they were not just content-based restrictions, but viewpoint-based restrictions, which are unconstitutional even in the more confined limited public forum:

> The necessities of confining a forum to the limited and legitimate purposes for which it was created may justify the State in reserving it for certain groups or for the discussion of certain topics. *See, e.g., Cornelius v. NAACP Legal Defense & Ed. Fund, Inc.* (1985). Once it has opened a limited forum, however, the State must respect the lawful boundaries it has itself set. The State may not exclude speech where its distinction is not "reasonable in light of the purpose served by the forum," nor may it discriminate against speech on the basis of its viewpoint. . . . Thus, in determining whether the State is acting to preserve the limits of the forum it has created so that the exclusion of a class of speech is legitimate, we have observed a distinction between, on the one hand, content discrimination, which may be permissible if it preserves the purposes of that limited forum, and, on the other hand, viewpoint discrimination, which is presumed impermissible when directed against speech otherwise within the forum's limitations.

. . . By the very terms of the [student activity fund] prohibition, the University does not exclude religion as a subject matter but selects for disfavored treatment those student journalistic efforts with religious editorial viewpoints. Religion may be a vast area of inquiry, but it also provides, as it did here, a specific premise, a perspective, a standpoint from which a variety of subjects may be discussed and considered. The prohibited perspective, not the general subject matter, resulted in the refusal to make third-party payments, for the subjects discussed were otherwise within the approved category of publications.

Does *Rosenberger*'s holding of unconstitutional viewpoint discrimination in a limited public forum context bolster Justice Scalia's dissenting position that the Court has crafted a First Amendment exception for speech *against* abortion in *Hill v. Colorado*? After all, *Hill* involved the more protected, traditional public forum of public sidewalks, where even content restrictions are subject to strict scrutiny and are presumptively invalid unless narrowly tailored to further a compelling governmental interest. When it is said that a government regulation must be content-neutral, it means both neutrality as to viewpoint and subject matter. Viewpoint restrictions regulate on the ideology of the message. For example, in *Boos v. Berry*, 485 U.S. 312 (1988), the Court invalidated a District of Columbia ordinance that prohibited signs critical of a foreign government within 500 feet of an embassy. By comparison, in *Carey v. Brown*, 447 U.S. 455 (1980), the Court invalidated a ban on all picketing in residential areas other than that related to the subject of labor or employment. Unlike viewpoint and subject matter restrictions that result in strict scrutiny, a regulation that affects speech but is not aimed at content or viewpoint is subject to an intermediate level of scrutiny or review.

5. As we will discuss later in this Chapter, government may favor some content over others when it is either speaking itself or subsidizing private speakers to transmit its information. *Rust v. Sullivan*, 500 U.S. 173 (1991) (upholding a limitation on abortion counseling with federal money). Why then, couldn't the University of Virginia refuse to fund religious speech in *Rosenberger*? Is it because the University was not seeking to speak itself, or articulate a particular point of view, but to facilitate a diversity of views? Does that distinction support or undermine the Court's holding in *Hill*?

6. Does the funding of partisan political speech through the use of mandatory student fees amount to unconstitutional viewpoint discrimination? In *Board of Regents of the University of Wisconsin v. Southworth*, 529 U.S. 217 (2000), the Court upheld the University of Wisconsin's mandatory student fee program against a challenge that it compelled students to support speech with which they disagreed. The parties had stipulated in the lower courts that the primary means of allocating the fees to student groups were viewpoint neutral, so the Court did not consider the students' contention that the program lacked viewpoint neutrality by funding partisan political speech. Nevertheless, the Court remanded for consideration whether one aspect of the program — a mechanism for funding some viewpoints pursuant to student referendum — did amount to unconstitutional viewpoint discrimination.

7. *Southworth* signifies that the university is a special forum unlike a bar association or labor union. Other special contexts or distinctions are drawn in the First Amendment area among different types of media, most notably between print and over-the-air broadcasting. In *Red Lion Broadcasting Co. v. FCC*, 395 U.S. 367 (1969), the Court upheld the so-called fairness doctrine requiring commercial over-the-air broadcast stations to present an even-handed discussion of public issues. This content-limitation is clearly inappropriate outside this context, but the Court asserted that broadcasting was different because of the inherent scarcity of broadcast frequencies. By contrast, the Court invalidated in *Miami Herald v. Tornillo*, 418 U.S. 241 (1974), a right of reply statute that required newspapers to print a reply from a political candidate whose character or official record had been attacked in its pages. This requirement would chill editors and writers, reasoned the Court. Why isn't the same true in broadcasting? And, for that matter, are broadcast opportunities really more scarce than those in the print media? In 1987, the FCC repealed the fairness doctrine because of the vast explosion of cable and satellite television operations. If the print and broadcast media are equivalent, doesn't the First Amendment preclude content limitation in either context? Cable television, by the way, is treated somewhat more generously — in theory — than broadcast television. In *Turner Broadcasting System Inc. v. Federal Communication Commission*, 512 U.S. 622 (1994), Justice Kennedy for the Court stated: "[t]he rationale for applying a less rigorous standard of First Amendment scrutiny to broadcast regulation does not apply in the context of cable regulation. . . . The broadcast cases are inapposite in the present context because cable television does not suffer from the inherent limitations that characterize the broadcast medium." *Id.* at 638-39. However, the more rigorous protection was not sufficient to immunize the cable industry from Congress's requirement that cable operators set aside one-third of their channel capacity for use by over-the-air-broadcasters. *Turner Broadcasting System, Inc. v. Federal Communications Commission*, 520 U.S. 180 (1997). The cable industry argued that this was effectively a content regulation, since commercial broadcasts were subject to greater government scrutiny and licensing. The Court disagreed finding the "must-carry" law to be justified by an important government purpose — preserving the broadcast industry and promoting fair competition — by a means that was no broader than necessary (the usual intermediate standard of review). Regulation of the Internet has been held by the Court to merit First Amendment protection equivalent to the print media. *Reno v. ACLU*, 521 U.S. 844 (1997). Said Justice Stevens for the Court: "unlike the conditions that prevailed when Congress first authorized regulation of the broadcast spectrum, the Internet can hardly be considered a 'scarce' expressive commodity. It provides relatively unlimited, low-cost capacity for communication of all kinds. . . . We agree . . . that our cases provide no basis for qualifying the level of First Amendment scrutiny that should be applied to this medium." *Id.* at 897 For a thoughtful appraisal of old law applied to new technology, see Marie A. Failinger, *New Wine, New Bottles: Private Property*

Metaphors and Public Forum Speech, 71 St. John's L. Rev. 217 (1997) (suggesting that the "public forum" metaphor in free speech analysis is not suited for new communication methods like the Internet).

4. Qualified Speech Protection

a. Libel and the "Actual Malice" Standard

NEW YORK TIMES CO. v. SULLIVAN
376 U.S. 254 (1964)

Mr. Justice Brennan delivered the opinion of the Court.

* * *

Respondent L. B. Sullivan is one of the three elected Commissioners of the City of Montgomery, Alabama. He testified that he was "Commissioner of Public Affairs and the duties are supervision of the Police Department, Fire Department, Department of Cemetery and Department of Scales." He brought this civil libel action against the four individual petitioners, who are Negroes and Alabama clergymen, and against petitioner the New York Times Company. . . . A jury in the Circuit Court of Montgomery County awarded him damages of $500,000, the full amount claimed, against all the petitioners, and the Supreme Court of Alabama affirmed.

Respondent's complaint alleged that he had been libeled by statements in a full-page advertisement that was carried in the New York Times on March 29, 1960. Entitled "Heed Their Rising Voices," the advertisement began by stating that "As the whole world knows by now, thousands of Southern Negro students are engaged in widespread non-violent demonstrations in positive affirmation of the right to live in human dignity as guaranteed by the U.S. Constitution and the Bill of Rights." It went on to charge that "in their efforts to uphold these guarantees, they are being met by an unprecedented wave of terror by those who would deny and negate that document which the whole world looks upon as setting the pattern for modern freedom . . . ." Succeeding paragraphs purported to illustrate the "wave of terror" by describing certain alleged events. The text concluded with an appeal for funds for three purposes: support of the student movement, "the struggle for the right-to-vote," and the legal defense of Dr. Martin Luther King, Jr., leader of the movement, against a perjury indictment then pending in Montgomery.

* * *

Of the 10 paragraphs of text in the advertisement, the third and a portion of the sixth were the basis of respondent's claim of libel. They read as follows:

Third paragraph:

> "In Montgomery, Alabama, after students sang 'My Country, 'Tis of Thee' on the State Capitol steps, their leaders were expelled from school, and truckloads of police armed with shotguns and tear-gas ringed the Alabama State College Campus. When the entire student body protested to state authorities by refusing to re-register, their dining hall was padlocked in an attempt to starve them into submission."

Sixth paragraph:

> "Again and again the Southern violators have answered Dr. King's peaceful protests with intimidation and violence. They have bombed his home almost killing his wife and child. They have assaulted his person. They have arrested him seven times — for 'speeding,' 'loitering' and similar 'offenses.' And now they have charged him with 'perjury' — a *felony* under which they could imprison him for *ten years*. . . ."

Although neither of these statements mentions respondent by name, he contended that the word "police" in the third paragraph referred to him as the Montgomery Commissioner who supervised the Police Department, so that he was being accused of "ringing" the campus with police. He further claimed that the paragraph would be read as imputing to the police, and hence to him, the padlocking of the dining hall in order to starve the students into submission. As to the sixth paragraph, he contended that since arrests are ordinarily made by the police, the statement "They have arrested [Dr. King] seven times" would be read as referring to him; he further contended that the "They" who did the arresting would be equated with the "They" who committed the other described acts and with the "Southern violators." Thus, he argued, the paragraph would be read as accusing the Montgomery police, and hence him, of answering Dr. King's protests with "intimidation and violence," bombing his home, assaulting his person, and charging him with perjury. Respondent and six other Montgomery residents testified that they read some or all of the statements as referring to him in his capacity as Commissioner.

It is uncontroverted that some of the statements contained in the two paragraphs were not accurate descriptions of events which occurred in Montgomery. Although Negro students staged a demonstration on the State Capitol steps, they sang the National Anthem and not "My Country, 'Tis of Thee." Although nine students were expelled by the State Board of Education, this was not for leading the demonstration at the Capitol, but for demanding service at a lunch counter in the Montgomery County Courthouse on another day. Not the entire student body, but most of it, had protested the expulsion, not by refusing to register, but by boycotting classes on a single day; virtually all the students did register for the ensuing semester. The campus dining hall was not padlocked on any occasion, and the only students who may have been barred from eating there were the few who had neither signed a preregistration application nor requested temporary meal tickets. Although the police were deployed near the campus in large numbers on three occasions, they did not at any time "ring" the campus, and they were not called to the campus in connection with the demonstration on the State Capitol steps, as the third paragraph implied. Dr. King had not been arrested seven times, but only four; and although he claimed to have been assaulted some years earlier in connection with his arrest for loitering outside a courtroom, one of the officers who made the arrest denied that there was such an assault.

On the premise that the charges in the sixth paragraph could be read as referring to him, respondent was allowed to prove that he had not participated in the events described. Although Dr. King's home had in fact been bombed twice when his wife and child were there, both of these occasions antedated respondent's tenure as Commissioner, and the police were not only not implicated in the bombings, but had made every effort to apprehend those who were. Three of Dr. King's four arrests took place before respondent became Commissioner. Although Dr. King had in fact been indicted (he was subsequently acquitted) on two counts of perjury, each of which carried a possible five-year sentence, respondent had nothing to do with procuring the indictment.

Respondent made no effort to prove that he suffered actual pecuniary loss as a result of the alleged libel. One of his witnesses, a former employer, testified that if he had believed the statements, he doubted whether he "would want to be associated with anybody who would be a party to such things that are stated in that ad," and that he would not re-employ respondent if he believed "that he allowed the Police Department to do the things that the paper say he did." But neither this witness nor any of the others testified that he had actually believed the statements in their supposed reference to respondent.

The cost of the advertisement was approximately $4800, and it was published by the Times upon an order from a New York advertising agency. . . . The agency submitted the advertisement with a letter from A. Philip Randolph . . . certifying that the persons whose names appeared on the advertisement had given their permission. Mr. Randolph was known to the Times' Advertising Acceptability Department as a responsible person, and in accepting the letter as sufficient proof of authorization it followed its established practice. . . . The manager of the Advertising Acceptability Department testified that he had approved the advertisement for publication because he knew nothing to cause him to believe that anything in it was false, and because it bore the endorsement of "a number of people who are well known and whose reputation" he "had no reason to question." Neither he nor anyone else at the Times made an effort to confirm the accuracy of the advertisement. . . .

Alabama law denies a public officer recovery of punitive damages in a libel action brought on account of a publication concerning his official conduct unless he first makes a written demand for a public retraction and the defendant fails or refuses to comply. Respondent served such a demand upon each of the petitioners. . . . The Times did not publish a retraction in response to the demand, but wrote respondent a letter stating, among other things, that "we . . . are somewhat puzzled as to how you think the statements in any way reflect on you," and "you might, if you desire, let us know in what respect you claim that the statements in the advertisement reflect on you." Respondent filed this suit a few days later without answering the letter. The Times did, however, subsequently publish a retraction of the advertisement upon the demand of Governor John Patterson of Alabama, who asserted that the publication charged him with "grave misconduct and . . . improper actions and omissions as Governor of Alabama and Ex-Officio Chairman of the State Board of Education of Alabama." When asked to explain why there had been a retraction for the Governor but not for respondent, the Secretary of the Times testified: "We did that because we didn't want anything that was published by The Times to be a reflection on the State of Alabama and the Governor was, as far as we could see, the embodiment of the State of Alabama and the proper representative of the State and, furthermore, we had by that time learned more of the actual facts which the ad purported to recite and, finally, the ad did refer to the action of the State authorities and the Board of Education presumably of which the Governor is the ex-officio chairman. . . ." On the other hand, he testified that he did not think that "any of the language in there referred to Mr. Sullivan."

The trial judge submitted the case to the jury under instructions that the statements in the advertisement were "libelous per se" and were not privileged, so that petitioners might be held liable if the jury found that they had published the advertisement and that the statements were made "of and concerning" respondent. The jury was instructed that, because the statements were libelous per se, "the law . . . implies legal injury from the bare fact of publication itself," "falsity and malice are presumed," "general damages need not be alleged or proved but are presumed," and "punitive damages may be awarded by the jury even though the amount of actual damages is neither found nor shown." An award of punitive damages — as distinguished from "general" damages, which are compensatory in nature — apparently requires proof of actual malice under Alabama law, and the judge charged that "mere negligence or carelessness is not evidence of actual malice or malice in fact, and does not justify an award of exemplary or punitive damages." He refused to charge, however, that the jury must be "convinced" of malice, in the sense of "actual intent" to harm or "gross negligence and recklessness," to make such an award, and he also refused to require that a verdict for respondent differentiate between compensatory and punitive damages. The judge rejected petitioners' contention that his rulings abridged the freedoms of speech and of the press that are guaranteed by the First and Fourteenth Amendments.

In affirming the judgment, the Supreme Court of Alabama sustained the trial judge's rulings and instructions in all respects. . . .

* * *

Because of the importance of the constitutional issues involved, we granted the separate petitions for certiorari of the individual petitioners and of the Times. We reverse the judgment. We hold that the rule of law applied by the

Alabama courts is constitutionally deficient for failure to provide the safeguards for freedom of speech and of the press that are required by the First and Fourteenth Amendments in a libel action brought by a public official against critics of his official conduct. We further hold that under the proper safeguards the evidence presented in this case is constitutionally insufficient to support the judgment for respondent.

I.

We may dispose at the outset of two grounds asserted to insulate the judgment of the Alabama courts from constitutional scrutiny. The first is the proposition relied on by the State Supreme Court — that "The Fourteenth Amendment is directed against State action and not private action." That proposition has no application to this case. Although this is a civil lawsuit between private parties, the Alabama courts have applied a state rule of law which petitioners claim to impose invalid restrictions on their constitutional freedoms of speech and press. It matters not that that law has been applied in a civil action and that it is common law only, though supplemented by statute. The test is not the form in which state power has been applied but, whatever the form, whether such power has in fact been exercised.

The second contention is that the constitutional guarantees of freedom of speech and of the press are inapplicable here, at least so far as the Times is concerned, because the allegedly libelous statements were published as part of a paid, "commercial" advertisement. . . .

The publication here was not a [purely] "commercial" advertisement. . . . It communicated information, expressed opinion, recited grievances, protested claimed abuses, and sought financial support on behalf of a movement whose existence and objectives are matters of the highest public interest and concern. That the Times was paid for publishing the advertisement is as immaterial in this connection as is the fact that newspapers and books are sold. Any other conclusion would discourage newspapers from carrying "editorial advertisements" of this type, and so might shut off an important outlet for the promulgation of information and ideas by persons who do not themselves have access to publishing facilities — who wish to exercise their freedom of speech even though they are not members of the press. The effect would be to shackle the First Amendment in its attempt to secure "the widest possible dissemination of information from diverse and antagonistic sources." To avoid placing such a handicap upon the freedoms of expression, we hold that if the allegedly libelous statements would otherwise be constitutionally protected from the present judgment, they do not forfeit that protection because they were published in the form of a paid advertisement.

II.

Under Alabama law as applied in this case, a publication is "libelous per se" if the words "tend to injure a person . . . in his reputation" or to "bring [him] into public contempt"; the trial court stated that the standard was met if the words are such as to "injure him in his public office, or impute misconduct to him in his office, or want of official integrity, or want of fidelity to a public trust . . . ." The jury must find that the words were published "of and concerning" the plaintiff, but where the plaintiff is a public official his place in the governmental hierarchy is sufficient evidence to support a finding that his reputation has been affected by statements that reflect upon the agency of which he is in charge. Once "libel per se" has been established, the defendant has no defense as to stated facts unless he can persuade the jury that they were true in all their particulars. . . . Unless he can discharge the burden of proving truth, general damages are presumed, and may be awarded without proof of pecuniary injury. A showing of actual malice is apparently a prerequisite to recovery of punitive damages, and the defendant may in any event forestall a punitive award by a retraction meeting the statutory requirements. Good motives and belief in truth do not negate an inference of malice, but are relevant only in mitigation of punitive damages if the jury chooses to accord them weight.

The question before us is whether this rule of liability, as applied to an action brought by a public official against critics of his official conduct, abridges the freedom of speech and of the press that is guaranteed by the First and Fourteenth Amendments.

Respondent relies heavily, as did the Alabama courts, on statements of this Court to the effect that the Constitution does not protect libelous publications. Those statements do not foreclose our inquiry here. . . .

* * *

. . . [W]e consider this case against the background of a profound national commitment to the principle that debate on public issues should be uninhibited, robust, and wide-open, and that it may well include vehement, caustic, and sometimes unpleasantly sharp attacks on government and public officials. The present advertisement, as an expression of grievance and protest on one of the major public issues of our time, would seem clearly to qualify for the constitutional protection. The question is whether it forfeits that protection by the falsity of some of its factual statements and by its alleged defamation of respondent.

Authoritative interpretations of the First Amendment guarantees have consistently refused to recognize an exception for any test of truth — whether administered by judges, juries, or administrative officials — and especially one that puts the burden of proving truth on the speaker. The constitutional protection does not turn upon "the truth, popularity, or social utility of the ideas and beliefs which are offered." *N.A.A.C.P. v. Button*, 371 U.S. 415, 445. As Madison said, "Some degree of abuse is inseparable from the proper use of every thing; and in no instance is this more true than in that of the press." 4 ELLIOT'S DEBATES ON THE FEDERAL CONSTITUTION 571 (1876). . . . That erroneous statement is inevitable in free debate, and that it must be protected if the freedoms of expression are to have the "breathing space" that they "need . . . to survive," *N.A.A.C.P. v. Button,* was also recognized by the Court of Appeals for the District of Columbia Circuit in *Sweeney v. Patterson* (D.C. Cir. 1942). Judge Edgerton spoke for a unanimous court which affirmed the dismissal of a Congressman's libel suit based upon a newspaper article charging him with anti-Semitism in opposing a judicial appointment. He said:

> "Cases which impose liability for erroneous reports of the political conduct of officials reflect the obsolete doctrine that the governed must not criticize their governors. . . . The interest of the public here outweighs the interest of appellant or any other individual. The protection of the public requires not merely discussion, but information. Political conduct and views which some respectable people approve, and others condemn, are constantly imputed to Congressmen. Errors of fact, particularly in regard to a man's mental states and processes, are inevitable. . . . Whatever is added to the field of libel is taken from the field of free debate."

Injury to official reputation affords no more warrant for repressing speech that would otherwise be free than does factual error. Where judicial officers are involved, this Court has held that concern for the dignity and reputation of the courts does not justify the punishment as criminal contempt of criticism of the judge or his decision. This is true even though the utterance contains "half-truths" and "misinformation." Such repression can be justified, if at all, only by a clear and present danger of the obstruction of justice. If judges are to be treated as "men of fortitude, able to thrive in a hardy climate," surely the same must be true of other government officials, such as elected city commissioners. Criticism of their official conduct does not lose its constitutional protection merely because it is effective criticism and hence diminishes their official reputations.

If neither factual error nor defamatory content suffices to remove the constitutional shield from criticism of official conduct, the combination of the two elements is no less inadequate. This is the lesson to be drawn from the great controversy over the Sedition Act of 1798, 1 Stat. 596, which first crystallized a national awareness of the central meaning of the First Amendment. That statute made it a crime, punishable by a $5,000 fine and five years in prison, "if any person shall write, print, utter or publish . . . any false, scandalous and malicious writing or writings against the government of the United States, or either house of the Congress . . . , or the President . . . , with intent to defame . . . or to bring them, or either of them, into contempt or disrepute; or to excite against them, or either or any of them, the hatred of the good people of the United States." The Act allowed the defendant the defense of truth, and provided that the jury were to be judges both of the law and the facts. Despite these qualifications, the Act was vigorously condemned as unconstitutional in an attack joined in by Jefferson and Madison. In the famous Virginia Resolutions of 1798, the General Assembly of Virginia resolved that it

> "doth particularly protest against the palpable and alarming infractions of the Constitution, in the two late cases of the 'Alien and Sedition Acts,' passed at the last session of Congress. . . . [The Sedition Act]

exercises . . . a power not delegated by the Constitution, but, on the contrary, expressly and positively forbidden by one of the amendments thereto — a power which, more than any other, ought to produce universal alarm, because it is levelled against the right of freely examining public characters and measures, and of free communication among the people thereon, which has ever been justly deemed the only effectual guardian of every other right."

Madison prepared the Report in support of the protest. His premise was that the Constitution created a form of government under which "The people, not the government, possess the absolute sovereignty." The structure of the government dispersed power in reflection of the people's distrust of concentrated power, and of power itself at all levels. This form of government was "altogether different" from the British form, under which the Crown was sovereign and the people were subjects. "Is it not natural and necessary, under such different circumstances," he asked, "that a different degree of freedom in the use of the press should be contemplated?" Earlier, in a debate in the House of Representatives, Madison had said: "If we advert to the nature of Republican Government, we shall find that the censorial power is in the people over the Government, and not in the Government over the people." Of the exercise of that power by the press, his Report said: "In every state, probably, in the Union, the press has exerted a freedom in canvassing the merits and measures of public men, of every description, which has not been confined to the strict limits of the common law. On this footing the freedom of the press has stood; on this foundation it yet stands. . . ." The right of free public discussion of the stewardship of public officials was thus, in Madison's view, a fundamental principle of the American form of government.

Although the Sedition Act was never tested in this Court, the attack upon its validity has carried the day in the court of history. Fines levied in its prosecution were repaid by Act of Congress on the ground that it was unconstitutional. Calhoun, reporting to the Senate on February 4, 1836, assumed that its invalidity was a matter "which no one now doubts." . . . Jefferson, as President, pardoned those who had been convicted and sentenced under the Act and remitted their fines, stating: "I discharged every person under punishment or prosecution under the sedition law, because I considered, and now consider, that law to be a nullity, as absolute and as palpable as if Congress had ordered us to fall down and worship a golden image." . . . The invalidity of the Act has also been assumed by Justices of this Court. . . . These views reflect a broad consensus that the Act, because of the restraint it imposed upon criticism of government and public officials, was inconsistent with the First Amendment.

There is no force in respondent's argument that the constitutional limitations implicit in the history of the Sedition Act apply only to Congress and not to the States. It is true that the First Amendment was originally addressed only to action by the Federal Government, and that Jefferson, for one, while denying the power of Congress "to controul the freedom of the press," recognized such a power in the States. But this distinction was eliminated with the adoption of the Fourteenth Amendment and the application to the States of the First Amendment's restrictions.

What a State may not constitutionally bring about by means of a criminal statute is likewise beyond the reach of its civil law of libel. The fear of damage awards under a rule such as that invoked by the Alabama courts here may be markedly more inhibiting than the fear of prosecution under a criminal statute. . . .

The state rule of law is not saved by its allowance of the defense of truth. . . . A rule compelling the critic of official conduct to guarantee the truth of all his factual assertions — and to do so on pain of libel judgments virtually unlimited in amount — leads to a comparable "self-censorship." Allowance of the defense of truth, with the burden of proving it on the defendant, does not mean that only false speech will be deterred. Even courts accepting this defense as an adequate safeguard have recognized the difficulties of adducing legal proofs that the alleged libel was true in all its factual particulars. Under such a rule, would-be critics of official conduct may be deterred from voicing their criticism, even though it is believed to be true and even though it is in fact true, because of doubt whether it can be proved in court or fear of the expense of having to do so. . . . The rule thus dampens the vigor and limits the variety of public debate. It is inconsistent with the First and Fourteenth Amendments.

The constitutional guarantees require, we think, a federal rule that prohibits a public official from recovering damages for a defamatory falsehood relating to his official conduct unless he proves that the statement was made with "actual malice" — that is, with knowledge that it was false or with reckless disregard of whether it was false or not. An oft-cited statement of a like rule, which has been adopted by a number of state courts, is found in the Kansas case of *Coleman v. MacLennan* (Kan. 1908). The State Attorney General, a candidate for re-election and a member of the commission charged with the management and control of the state school fund, sued a newspaper publisher for alleged libel in an article purporting to state facts relating to his official conduct in connection with a school-fund transaction. The defendant pleaded privilege and the trial judge, over the plaintiff's objection, instructed the jury that

> "where an article is published and circulated among voters for the sole purpose of giving what the defendant believes to be truthful information concerning a candidate for public office and for the purpose of enabling such voters to cast their ballot more intelligently, and the whole thing is done in good faith and without malice, the article is privileged, although the principal matters contained in the article may be untrue in fact and derogatory to the character of the plaintiff; and in such a case the burden is on the plaintiff to show actual malice in the publication of the article."

In answer to a special question, the jury found that the plaintiff had not proved actual malice, and a general verdict was returned for the defendant. On appeal the Supreme Court of Kansas, in an opinion by Justice Burch, reasoned as follows:

> "It is of the utmost consequence that the people should discuss the character and qualifications of candidates for their suffrages. The importance to the state and to society of such discussions is so vast, and the advantages derived are so great, that they more than counterbalance the inconvenience of private persons whose conduct may be involved, and occasional injury to the reputations of individuals must yield to the public welfare, although at times such injury may be great. The public benefit from publicity is so great, and the chance of injury to private character so small, that such discussion must be privileged."

* * *

Such a privilege for criticism of official conduct is appropriately analogous to the protection accorded a public official when *he* is sued for libel by a private citizen. In *Barr v. Matteo* (1959), this Court held the utterance of a federal official to be absolutely privileged if made "within the outer perimeter" of his duties. The States accord the same immunity to statements of their highest officers, although some differentiate their lesser officials and qualify the privilege they enjoy. But all hold that all officials are protected unless actual malice can be proved. The reason for the official privilege is said to be that the threat of damage suits would otherwise "inhibit the fearless, vigorous, and effective administration of policies of government" and "dampen the ardor of all but the most resolute, or the most irresponsible, in the unflinching discharge of their duties." Analogous considerations support the privilege for the citizen-critic of government. It is as much his duty to criticize as it is the official's duty to administer. . . . It would give public servants an unjustified preference over the public they serve, if critics of official conduct did not have a fair equivalent of the immunity granted to the officials themselves.

We conclude that such a privilege is required by the First and Fourteenth Amendments.

III.

We hold today that the Constitution delimits a State's power to award damages for libel in actions brought by public officials against critics of their official conduct. Since this is such an action, the rule requiring proof of actual malice is applicable. While Alabama law apparently requires proof of actual malice for an award of punitive damages, where general damages are concerned malice is "presumed." Such a presumption is inconsistent with the federal rule. "The power to create presumptions is not a means of escape from constitutional restrictions"; "the showing of malice required for the forfeiture of the privilege is not presumed but is a matter for proof by the plaintiff . . . ." Since the trial judge did not instruct the jury to differentiate between general and punitive damages, it may be that the verdict was wholly an award of one or the other. But it is impossible to know, in view of the general verdict returned. Because of this uncertainty, the judgment must be reversed and the case remanded.

Since respondent may seek a new trial, we deem that considerations of effective judicial administration require us to review the evidence in the present record to determine whether it could constitutionally support a judgment for respondent. This Court's duty is not limited to the elaboration of constitutional principles; we must also in proper cases review the evidence to make certain that those principles have been constitutionally applied. . . .

Applying these standards, we consider that the proof presented to show actual malice lacks the convincing clarity which the constitutional standard demands, and hence that it would not constitutionally sustain the judgment for respondent under the proper rule of law. . . .

As to the Times, we . . . conclude that the facts do not support a finding of actual malice. The statement by the Times' Secretary that, apart from the padlocking allegation, he thought the advertisement was "substantially correct," affords no constitutional warrant for the Alabama Supreme Court's conclusion that it was a "cavalier ignoring of the falsity of the advertisement [from which] the jury could not have but been impressed with the bad faith of The Times, and its maliciousness inferable therefrom." The statement does not indicate malice at the time of the publication; even if the advertisement was not "substantially correct" — although respondent's own proofs tend to show that it was — that opinion was at least a reasonable one, and there was no evidence to impeach the witness' good faith in holding it. The Times' failure to retract upon respondent's demand, although it later retracted upon the demand of Governor Patterson, is likewise not adequate evidence of malice for constitutional purposes. Whether or not a failure to retract may ever constitute such evidence, there are two reasons why it does not here. *First*, the letter written by the Times reflected a reasonable doubt on its part as to whether the advertisement could reasonably be taken to refer to respondent at all. *Second*, it was not a final refusal, since it asked for an explanation on this point — a request that respondent chose to ignore. Nor does the retraction upon the demand of the Governor supply the necessary proof. It may be doubted that a failure to retract which is not itself evidence of malice can retroactively become such by virtue of a retraction subsequently made to another party. But in any event that did not happen here, since the explanation given by the Times' Secretary for the distinction drawn between respondent and the Governor was a reasonable one, the good faith of which was not impeached.

Finally, there is evidence that the Times published the advertisement without checking its accuracy against the news stories in the Times' own files. The mere presence of the stories in the files does not, of course, establish that the Times "knew" the advertisement was false, since the state of mind required for actual malice would have to be brought home to the persons in the Times' organization having responsibility for the publication of the advertisement. With respect to the failure of those persons to make the check, the record shows that they relied upon their knowledge of the good reputation of many of those whose names were listed as sponsors of the advertisement, and upon the letter from A. Philip Randolph, known to them as a responsible individual, certifying that the use of the names was authorized. There was testimony that the persons handling the advertisement saw nothing in it that would render it unacceptable under the Times' policy of rejecting advertisements containing "attacks of a personal character"; their failure to reject it on this ground was not unreasonable. We think the evidence against the Times supports at most a finding of negligence in failing to discover the misstatements, and is constitutionally insufficient to show the recklessness that is required for a finding of actual malice.

We also think the evidence was constitutionally defective in another respect: it was incapable of supporting the jury's finding that the allegedly libelous statements were made "of and concerning" respondent. Respondent relies on the words of the advertisement and the testimony of six witnesses to establish a connection between it and himself . . . . There was no reference to respondent in the advertisement, either by name or official position. . . . [The Supreme Court of Alabama], in holding that the trial court "did not err in overruling the demurrer [of the Times] in the aspect that the libelous matter was not of and concerning the [plaintiff,]" based its ruling on the proposition that:

> "We think it common knowledge that the average person knows that municipal agents, such as police and firemen, and others, are under the control and direction of the city governing body, and more particularly under the direction and control of a single commissioner. In measuring the performance or deficiencies of such groups, praise or criticism is usually attached to the official in complete control of the body."

This proposition has disquieting implications for criticism of governmental conduct. For good reason, "no court of last resort in this country has ever held, or even suggested, that prosecutions for libel on government have any place in the American system of jurisprudence." . . . The present proposition would side-step this obstacle by transmuting criticism of government, however impersonal it may seem on its face, into personal criticism, and hence potential libel, of the officials of whom the government is composed. There is no legal alchemy by which a State may thus create the cause of action that would otherwise be denied for a publication which, as respondent himself said of the advertisement, "reflects not only on me but on the other Commissioners and the community." Raising as it does the possibility that a good-faith critic of government will be penalized for his criticism, the proposition relied on by the Alabama courts strikes at the very center of the constitutionally protected area of free expression. We hold that such a proposition may not constitutionally be utilized to establish that an otherwise impersonal attack on governmental operations was a libel of an official responsible for those operations. Since it was relied on exclusively here, and there was no other evidence to connect the statements with respondent, the evidence was constitutionally insufficient to support a finding that the statements referred to respondent.

* * *

Mr. Justice Black, with whom Mr. Justice Douglas joins, concurring.

. . . I base my vote to reverse on the belief that the First and Fourteenth Amendments not merely "delimit" a State's power to award damages to "public officials against critics of their official conduct" but completely prohibit a State from exercising such a power. The Court goes on to hold that a State can subject such critics to damages if "actual malice" can be proved against them. "Malice," even as defined by the Court, is an elusive, abstract concept, hard to prove and hard to disprove. The requirement that malice be proved provides at best an evanescent protection for the right critically to discuss public affairs and certainly does not measure up to the sturdy safeguard embodied in the First Amendment. Unlike the Court, therefore, I vote to reverse exclusively on the ground that the Times and the individual defendants had an absolute, unconditional constitutional right to publish in the Times advertisement their criticisms of the Montgomery agencies and officials. . . .

* * *

Mr. Justice Goldberg, with whom Mr. Justice Douglas joins, concurring in the result.

The Court today announces a constitutional standard which prohibits "a public official from recovering damages for a defamatory falsehood relating to his official conduct unless he proves that the statement was made with 'actual malice' — that is, with knowledge that it was false or with reckless disregard of whether it was false or not." The Court thus rules that the Constitution gives citizens and newspapers a "conditional privilege" immunizing nonmalicious misstatements of fact regarding the official conduct of a government officer. The impressive array of history and precedent marshaled by the Court, however, confirms my belief that the Constitution affords greater protection than that provided by the Court's standard to citizen and press in exercising the right of public criticism.

In my view, the First and Fourteenth Amendments to the Constitution afford to the citizen and to the press an absolute, unconditional privilege to criticize official conduct despite the harm which may flow from excesses and abuses. . . . Such criticism cannot, in my opinion, be muzzled or deterred by the courts at the instance of public officials under the label of libel.

NOTES AND QUESTIONS

1. *New York Times v. Sullivan* is surely one of the most important First Amendment decisions ever rendered by the Supreme Court. It is both a product of the times, and deeply anchored in a particular view of American history. You have had a very small bit of historical introduction to the time of the framing of the First Amendment. Putting to the side the highly problematical nature of applying the First Amendment against the states in the first place (the problem of "incorporation," which we have dealt with elsewhere), do you think the framers of the First Amendment would have believed that they were declaring a qualified immunity for newspapers engaging in the criticism of public figures? Do you agree with the Court's reading of the relevant history? Recall that at the time of the First Amendment's passage it was believed by all but a few (though among that few were counted Jefferson and Madison) that the English doctrine of seditious libel was not obliterated by the First Amendment, which, with regard to the press, was only supposed to have prohibited prior restraint. How does the majority deal with this?

We have here, of course, a private libel case, but if what the New York Times published would have been seditious libel in the late eighteenth century (would it have?), isn't it pretty clear that it also would have been a violation of private libel law? Private libel law, simply stated, allows private persons who have been damaged in reputation by a publication to recover from the publisher for such damage. Truth is a defense for the publisher, but note that truth is unavailable as a defense in *New York Times v. Sullivan*, because of the inaccuracy of the items published. Where does the Court come up with its notion that there is no liability for civil libel in the case of a public official such as Sullivan, even if the publication falsely criticizes him, so long as the publication was not done with actual malice? If you were making up the rules of libel, would this be your solution? How do you account for the fact that the Court's decision, at least in terms of the result, is unanimous?

2. Before *New York Times v. Sullivan*, it was generally believed that libel (of a kind that the New York Times had clearly been guilty of) was unprotected speech, just as obscenity, or child pornography, or, for most of our history, commercial advertising was. If libel were not to be thought to be something that came under the protection of the First Amendment, of course, the Times or any other newspaper would have been subject to litigation whenever a public official was falsely criticized. Would this have been such a bad thing?

3. By its facts, *New York Times v. Sullivan* is limited to the case of governmental officials, but should it be so limited? Within a few years, the logic of *New York Times v. Sullivan* was extended to grant the press freedom from libel suits (save when malice could be shown) in the case not just of public officials, but also of "public figures" generally, including all sorts of celebrities — TV and motion picture stars, sports figures, and even ordinary citizens whom catastrophic or serendipitous events had placed in the public eye. *See Curtis Publ'g Co. v. Butts*, 388 U.S. 130, 162-65 (1967) (Warren, C.J., concurring in result). Was this a felicitous development?

4. Do you believe that decisions such as *New York Times v. Sullivan* have led to a situation in which the press, with impunity, can destroy the reputations or even the privacy of too many American citizens? On the other hand, do you suppose potential press irresponsibility really entered into the calculation of the Court which decided the case? What other features of the case, and of the time in which it was decided explain the outcome? Does it have anything to do with the contemporary challenge to racial segregation in the South?

5. Summarizing then, understand that there is an enormous difference between a libel action brought by a public figure or official and an action initiated by a private party. Under *New York Times*, a case brought by a public official or figure must prove with clear and convincing evidence that the statement was false and that the defendant knew it was false or at least acted with reckless disregard of the truth — that is, with actual malice. By contrast, a private citizen bringing a defamation action must prove merely negligence on the part of the defendant and that the statement was false. One qualification: if a private citizen is suing for punitive damages, in addition to compensatory damages, and the matter involved is an issue of public concern, then those punitive damages cannot be awarded without proof of actual malice. *Gertz v. Welch*, 418 U.S. 323, 349 (1974).

Many other issues complicate this area. On the question of falsity, for example, the question arises whether labeling a statement "opinion" is enough to insulate from libel liability. In *Milkovich v. Lorain Journal Co.*, 497 U.S. 1 (1990), the Court held that the label was not dispositive. Nevertheless, in order for opinion to be the basis of a defamation action, it must contain within it a false statement of fact.

However, even the partial fabrication of quotations may not be sufficient to demonstrate falsity. In *Masson v. New Yorker*, 501 U.S. 496 (1991), the Court indicated that quotation marks do not signify that the material therein is a verbatim transcription of the words. Rather, quotation marks signify substantial accuracy. There is also some difficulty in ascertaining whether a person is or is not a public figure. Generally, such persons enjoy particularly good access to channels of communication and have involved themselves significantly in matters of public debate. In addition, if the subject is not a matter of public concern, then punitive damages may be awarded without a showing of actual malice. *Dunn & Bradstreet v. Greenmoss Builders*, 472 U.S. 749 (1985) (false credit report indicating inaccurately that a company had filed bankruptcy; the Court found the matter to be one of private concern since it was distributed narrowly and of interest only to a narrow business audience).

6. The Supreme Court dealt with another media issue: the presence of media as "ride alongs" in the serving of an arrest warrant. In *Wilson v. Layne*, 526 U.S. 603 (1999), the Court held that it violates the privacy protected by the Fourth Amendment for the police to bring members of the media or other third parties into arrestees' homes during the execution of the warrant. "[T]he presence of reporters inside the home was not related to the objectives of the authorized intrusion." This was true since the reporters were not in any way assisting in the warrant's execution. The argument that the media would facilitate efforts to combat crime or the accurate reporting of law enforcement activities was not enough to overcome the residential privacy protected by the Fourth Amendment.

b. Commercial Speech

CENTRAL HUDSON GAS & ELECTRIC CORP. v. PUBLIC SERVICECOMMISSION OF NEW YORK
447 U.S. 557 (1980)

MR. JUSTICE POWELL delivered the opinion of the Court.

This case presents the question whether a regulation of the Public Service Commission of the State of New York violates the First and Fourteenth Amendments because it completely bans promotional advertising by an electrical utility.

I

In December 1973, the Commission . . . ordered electric utilities in New York State to cease all advertising that "promot[es] the use of electricity." The order was based on the Commission's finding that "the interconnected utility system in New York State does not have sufficient fuel stocks or sources of supply to continue furnishing all customer demands for the 1973-1974 winter."

Three years later, when the fuel shortage had eased, the Commission requested comments from the public on its proposal to continue the ban on promotional advertising. Central Hudson Gas & Electric Corp. . . . opposed the ban on First Amendment grounds. After reviewing the public comments, the Commission extended the prohibition. . . .

* * *

Appellant challenged the order in state court, arguing that the Commission had restrained commercial speech in violation of the First and Fourteenth Amendments. The Commission's order was upheld by the trial court and at the intermediate appellate level. The New York Court of Appeals affirmed. It found little value to advertising in "the noncompetitive market in which electric corporations operate." Since consumers "have no choice regarding the source of their electric power," the court denied that "promotional advertising of electricity might contribute to society's interest in 'informed and reliable' economic decisionmaking." The court also observed that by encouraging consumption, promotional advertising would only exacerbate the current energy situation. The court concluded that the governmental interest in the prohibition outweighed the limited constitutional value of the commercial speech at issue. We . . . now reverse.

II

The Commission's order restricts only commercial speech, that is, expression related solely to the economic interests of the speaker and its audience. The

First Amendment, as applied to the States through the Fourteenth Amendment, protects commercial speech from unwarranted governmental regulation. Commercial expression not only serves the economic interest of the speaker, but also assists consumers and furthers the societal interest in the fullest possible dissemination of information. In applying the First Amendment to this area, we have rejected the "highly paternalistic" view that government has complete power to suppress or regulate commercial speech. "[P]eople will perceive their own best interests if only they are well enough informed, and . . . the best means to that end is to open the channels of communication, rather than to close them . . . ." Even when advertising communicates only an incomplete version of the relevant facts, the First Amendment presumes that some accurate information is better than no information at all.

Nevertheless, our decisions have recognized "the 'commonsense' distinction between speech proposing a commercial transaction, which occurs in an area traditionally subject to government regulation, and other varieties of speech." The Constitution therefore accords a lesser protection to commercial speech than to other constitutionally guaranteed expression. The protection available for particular commercial expression turns on the nature both of the expression and of the governmental interests served by its regulation.

The First Amendment's concern for commercial speech is based on the informational function of advertising. Consequently, there can be no constitutional objection to the suppression of commercial messages that do not accurately inform the public about lawful activity. The government may ban forms of communication more likely to deceive the public than to inform it, or commercial speech related to illegal activity.

If the communication is neither misleading nor related to unlawful activity, the government's power is more circumscribed. The State must assert a substantial interest to be achieved by restrictions on commercial speech. Moreover, the regulatory technique must be in proportion to that interest. The limitation on expression must be designed carefully to achieve the State's goal. Compliance with this requirement may be measured by two criteria. First, the restriction must directly advance the state interest involved; the regulation may not be sustained if it provides only ineffective or remote support for the government's purpose. Second, if the governmental interest could be served as well by a more limited restriction on commercial speech, the excessive restrictions cannot survive.

Under the first criterion, the Court has declined to uphold regulations that only indirectly advance the state interest involved. In [two cases], the Court concluded that an advertising ban could not be imposed to protect the ethical or performance standards of a profession. The Court noted in [one case] that "[t]he advertising ban does not directly affect professional standards one way or the other." In [the other,] the Court overturned an advertising prohibition that was designed to protect the "quality" of a lawyer's work. "Restraints on advertising . . . are an ineffective way of deterring shoddy work."

The second criterion recognizes that the First Amendment mandates that speech restrictions be "narrowly drawn." The regulatory technique may extend only as far as the interest it serves. The State cannot regulate speech that poses no danger to the asserted state interest, nor can it completely suppress information when narrower restrictions on expression would serve its interest as well. . . .

In commercial speech cases, then, a four-part analysis has developed. At the outset, we must determine whether the expression is protected by the First Amendment. For commercial speech to come within that provision, it at least must concern lawful activity and not be misleading. Next, we ask whether the asserted governmental interest is substantial. If both inquiries yield positive answers, we must determine whether the regulation directly advances the governmental interest asserted, and whether it is not more extensive than is necessary to serve that interest.

III

We now apply this four-step analysis for commercial speech to the Commission's arguments in support of its ban on promotional advertising.

A

The Commission does not claim that the expression at issue either is inaccurate or relates to unlawful activity. . . .

* * *

Even in monopoly markets, the suppression of advertising reduces the information available for consumer decisions and thereby defeats the purpose of the First Amendment. . . .

B

The Commission offers two state interests as justifications for the ban on promotional advertising. The first concerns energy conservation. Any increase in demand for electricity — during peak or off-peak periods — means greater consumption of energy. The Commission argues, and the New York court agreed, that the State's interest in conserving energy is sufficient to support suppression of advertising designed to increase consumption of electricity. In view of our country's dependence on energy resources beyond our control, no one can doubt the importance of energy conservation. Plainly, therefore, the state interest asserted is substantial.

The Commission also argues that promotional advertising will aggravate inequities caused by the failure to base the utilities' rates on marginal cost. The utilities argued to the Commission that if they could promote the use of electricity in periods of low demand, they would improve their utilization of generating capacity. The Commission responded that promotion of off-peak consumption also would increase consumption during peak periods. . . .

C

Next, we focus on the relationship between the State's interests and the advertising ban. Under this criterion, the Commission's laudable concern over the equity and efficiency of appellant's rates does not provide a constitutionally adequate reason for restricting protected speech. The link between the advertising prohibition and appellant's rate structure is, at most, tenuous. The impact of promotional advertising on the equity of appellant's rates is highly speculative. Advertising to increase off-peak usage would have to increase peak usage, while other factors that directly affect the fairness and efficiency of appellant's rates remained constant. Such conditional and remote eventualities simply cannot justify silencing appellant's promotional advertising.

In contrast, the State's interest in energy conservation is directly advanced by the Commission order at issue here. There is an immediate connection between advertising and demand for electricity. Central Hudson would not contest the advertising ban unless it believed that promotion would increase its sales. Thus, we find a direct link between the state interest in conservation and the Commission's order.

D

We come finally to the critical inquiry in this case: whether the Commission's complete suppression of speech ordinarily protected by the First Amendment is no more extensive than necessary to further the State's interest in energy conservation. The Commission's order reaches all promotional advertising, regardless of the impact of the touted service on overall energy use. But the energy conservation rationale, as important as it is, cannot justify suppressing information about electric devices or services that would cause no net increase in total energy use. In addition, no showing has been made that a more limited restriction on the content of promotional advertising would not serve adequately the State's interests.

Appellant insists that but for the ban, it would advertise products and services that use energy efficiently. These include the "heat pump," which both parties acknowledge to be a major improvement in electric heating, and the use of electric heat as a "backup" to solar and other heat sources. Although the Commission has questioned the efficiency of electric heating before this Court, neither the Commission's Policy Statement nor its order denying rehearing made findings on this issue. In the absence of authoritative findings to the contrary, we must credit as within the realm of possibility the claim that electric heat can be an efficient alternative in some circumstances.

The Commission's order prevents appellant from promoting electric services that would reduce energy use by diverting demand from less efficient sources, or that would consume roughly the same amount of energy as do alternative sources. In neither situation would the utility's advertising endanger conservation or mislead the public. To the extent that the Commission's order suppresses speech that in no way impairs the State's interest in energy conservation, the Commission's order violates the First and Fourteenth Amendments and must be invalidated.

The Commission also has not demonstrated that its interest in conservation cannot be protected adequately by more limited regulation of appellant's commercial expression. To further its policy of conservation, the Commission could attempt to restrict the format and content of Central Hudson's advertising. It might, for example, require that the advertisements include information about the relative efficiency and expense of the offered service, both under current conditions and for the foreseeable future. In the absence of a showing that more limited speech regulation would be ineffective, we cannot approve the complete suppression of Central Hudson's advertising.

* * *

MR. JUSTICE BRENNAN, concurring in the judgment [omitted].

MR. JUSTICE BLACKMUN, with whom MR. JUSTICE BRENNAN joins, concurring in the judgment.

I agree with the Court that the Public Service Commission's ban on promotional advertising of electricity by public utilities is inconsistent with the First and Fourteenth Amendments. I concur only in the Court's judgment, however, because I believe the test now evolved and applied by the Court is not consistent with our prior cases and does not provide adequate protection for truthful, non-misleading, noncoercive commercial speech.

The Court asserts, that "a four-part analysis has developed" from our decisions concerning commercial speech. Under this four-part test a restraint on commercial "communication [that] is neither misleading nor related to unlawful activity" is subject to an intermediate level of scrutiny, and suppression is permitted whenever it "directly advances" a "substantial" governmental interest and is "not more extensive than is necessary to serve that interest." I agree with the Court that this level of intermediate scrutiny is appropriate for a restraint on commercial speech designed to protect consumers from misleading or coercive speech, or a regulation related to the time, place, or manner of commercial speech. I do not agree, however, that the Court's four-part test is the proper one to be applied when a State seeks to suppress information about a product in order to manipulate a private economic decision that the State cannot or has not regulated or outlawed directly.

* * *

If the First Amendment guarantee means anything, it means that, absent clear and present danger, government has no power to restrict expression because of the effect its message is likely to have on the public. Our cases indicate that this guarantee applies even to commercial speech. In *Virginia Phar-*

macy Board v. Virginia Consumer Council (1976), we held that Virginia could not pursue its goal of encouraging the public to patronize the "professional pharmacist" (one who provided individual attention and a stable pharmacist-customer relationship) by "keeping the public in ignorance of the entirely lawful terms that competing pharmacists are offering." We noted that our decision left the State free to pursue its goal of maintaining high standards among its pharmacists by "requir[ing] whatever professional standards it wishes of its pharmacists."

We went on in *Virginia Pharmacy Board* to discuss the types of regulation of commercial speech that, due to the "commonsense differences" between this form of speech and other forms, are or may be constitutionally permissible. We indicated that government may impose reasonable "time, place, and manner" restrictions, and that it can deal with false, deceptive, and misleading commercial speech. . . .

Concluding with a restatement of the type of restraint that is not permitted, we said: "What is at issue is whether a State may completely suppress the dissemination of concededly truthful information about entirely lawful activity, fearful of that information's effect upon its disseminators and its recipients. . . . [W]e conclude that the answer to this [question] is in the negative."

* * *

Carey v. Population Services International (1977), also applied to content-based restraints on commercial speech the same standard of review we have applied to other varieties of speech. There the Court held that a ban on advertising of contraceptives could not be justified by the State's interest in avoiding "'legitimation' of illicit sexual behavior" because the advertisements could not be characterized as "'directed to inciting or producing imminent lawless action and . . . likely to incite or produce such action.'"

Our prior references to the "'commonsense differences'" between commercial speech and other speech "'suggest that a different degree of protection is necessary to insure that the flow of truthful and legitimate commercial information is unimpaired.'" We have not suggested that the "commonsense differences" between commercial speech and other speech justify relaxed scrutiny of restraints that suppress truthful, nondeceptive, noncoercive commercial speech. The differences articulated by the Court justify a more permissive approach to regulation of the manner of commercial speech for the purpose of protecting consumers from deception or coercion, and these differences explain why doctrines designed to prevent "chilling" of protected speech are inapplicable to commercial speech. No differences between commercial speech and other protected speech justify suppression of commercial speech in order to influence public conduct through manipulation of the availability of information. . . .

It appears that the Court would permit the State to ban all direct advertising of air conditioning, assuming that a more limited restriction on such advertising would not effectively deter the public from cooling its homes. In my view, our cases do not support this type of suppression. If a governmental unit believes that use or overuse of air conditioning is a serious problem, it must attack that problem directly, by prohibiting air conditioning or regulating thermostat levels. Just as the Commonwealth of Virginia may promote professionalism of pharmacists directly, so too New York may *not* promote energy conservation "by keeping the public in ignorance."

MR. JUSTICE STEVENS, with whom MR. JUSTICE BRENNAN joins, concurring in the judgment.

Because "commercial speech" is afforded less constitutional protection than other forms of speech, it is important that the commercial speech concept not be defined too broadly lest speech deserving of greater constitutional protection be inadvertently suppressed. . . .

In my judgment one of the two definitions the Court uses in addressing that issue is too broad and the other may be somewhat too narrow. The Court first describes commercial speech as "expression related solely to the economic interests of the speaker and its audience." Although it is not entirely clear whether this definition uses the subject matter of the speech or the motivation of the speaker as the limiting factor, it seems clear to me that it encompasses speech that is entitled to the maximum protection afforded by the First Amendment. Neither a labor leader's exhortation to strike, nor an economist's dissertation on the money supply, should receive any lesser protection because the subject matter concerns only the economic interests of the audience. Nor should the economic motivation of a speaker qualify his constitutional protection; even Shakespeare may have been motivated by the prospect of pecuniary reward. Thus, the Court's first definition of commercial speech is unquestionably too broad.

The Court's second definition refers to "'speech proposing a commercial transaction.'" A saleman's solicitation, a broker's offer, and a manufacturer's publication of a price list or the terms of his standard warranty would unquestionably fit within this concept. Presumably, the definition is intended to encompass advertising that advises possible buyers of the availability of specific products at specific prices and describes the advantages of purchasing such items. Perhaps it also extends to other communications that do little more than make the name of a product or a service more familiar to the general public. Whatever the precise contours of the concept, and perhaps it is too early to enunciate an exact formulation, I am persuaded that it should not include the entire range of communication that is embraced within the term "promotional advertising."

This case involves a governmental regulation that completely bans promotional advertising by an electric utility. This ban encompasses a great deal more than mere proposals to engage in certain kinds of commercial transactions. It prohibits all advocacy of the immediate or future use of electricity. It curtails expression by an informed and interested group of persons of their point of view on questions relating to the production and consumption of electrical energy — questions frequently discussed and debated by our political leaders. For example, an electric company's advocacy of the use of electric heat for environmental reasons, as opposed to wood-burning stoves, would seem to fall squarely within New York's promotional advertising ban and also within the bounds of maximum First Amendment protection. . . .

The justification for the regulation is nothing more than the expressed fear that the audience may find the utility's message persuasive. Without the aid of any coercion, deception, or misinformation, truthful communication may persuade some citizens to consume more electricity than they otherwise would. I assume that such a consequence would be undesirable and that government may therefore prohibit and punish the unnecessary or excessive use of electricity. But if the perceived harm associated with greater electrical usage is not sufficiently serious to justify direct regulation, surely it does not constitute the kind of clear and present danger that can justify the suppression of speech.

* * *

In sum, I concur in the result because I do not consider this to be a "commercial speech" case. Accordingly, I see no need to decide whether the Court's four-part analysis adequately protects commercial speech — as properly defined — in the face of a blanket ban of the sort involved in this case.

Mr. Justice Rehnquist, dissenting.

The Court today invalidates an order issued by the New York Public Service Commission designed to promote a policy that has been declared to be of critical national concern. The order was issued by the Commission in 1973 in response to the Mideastern oil embargo crisis. It prohibits electric corporations "from *promoting* the use of electricity through the use of advertising, subsidy payments . . . , or employee incentives." (emphasis added). Although the immediate crisis created by the oil embargo has subsided, the ban on promotional advertising remains in effect. The regulation was re-examined by the New York Public Service Commission in 1977. Its constitutionality was subsequently upheld by the New York Court of Appeals, which concluded that the paramount national interest in energy conservation justified its retention.

The Court's asserted justification for invalidating the New York law is the public interest discerned by the Court to underlie the First Amendment in the free flow of commercial information. Prior to this Court's recent decision in *Virginia Pharmacy Board v. Virginia Citizens Consumer Council* (1976), however, commercial speech was afforded no protection under the First Amendment whatsoever. Given what seems to me full recognition of the holding of *Virginia Pharmacy Board* that commercial speech is entitled to some degree of First Amendment protection, I think the Court is nonetheless incorrect in invalidating the carefully considered state ban on promotional advertising in light of pressing national and state energy needs.

* * *

II

This Court has previously recognized that although commercial speech may be entitled to First Amendment protection, that protection is not as extensive as that accorded to the advocacy of ideas. Thus, we stated in *Ohralik v. Ohio State Bar Assn.* (1978):

> "Expression concerning purely commercial transactions has come within the ambit of the Amendment's protection only recently. In rejecting the notion that such speech 'is wholly outside the protection of the First Amendment,' we were careful not to hold 'that it is wholly undifferentiable from other forms' of speech. We have not discarded the 'commonsense' distinction between speech proposing a commercial transaction, which occurs in an area traditionally subject to government regulation, and other varieties of speech. To require a parity of constitutional protection for commercial and noncommercial speech alike could invite dilution, simply by a leveling process, of the force of the Amendment's guarantee with respect to the latter kind of speech. Rather than subject the First Amendment to such a devitalization, we instead have afforded commercial speech a limited measure of protection, commensurate with its subordinate position in the scale of First Amendment values, while allowing modes of regulation that might be impermissible in the realm of noncommercial expression."

* * *

I remain of the view that the Court unlocked a Pandora's Box when it "elevated" commercial speech to the level of traditional political speech by according it First Amendment protection in *Virginia Pharmacy Board*. The line between "commercial speech," and the kind of speech that those who drafted the First Amendment had in mind, may not be a technically or intellectually easy one to draw, but it surely produced far fewer problems than has the development of judicial doctrine in this area since *Virginia Pharmacy Board*. For in the world of political advocacy and *its* marketplace of ideas, there is no such thing as a "fraudulent" idea: there may be useless proposals, totally unworkable schemes, as well as very sound proposals that will receive the imprimatur of the "marketplace of ideas" through our majoritarian system of election and representative government. The free flow of information is important in this context not because it will lead to the discovery of any objective "truth," but because it is essential to our system of self-government.

The notion that more speech is the remedy to expose falsehood and fallacies is wholly out of place in the commercial bazaar, where if applied logically the remedy of one who was defrauded would be merely a statement, available upon request, reciting the Latin maxim *"caveat emptor."* But since "fraudulent speech" in this area is to be remediable under *Virginia Pharmacy Board, supra,* the remedy of one defrauded is a lawsuit or an agency proceeding based on common-law notions of fraud that are separated by a world of difference from the realm of politics and government. What time, legal decisions, and common sense have so widely severed, I declined to join in *Virginia Pharmacy Board*, and regret now to see the Court reaping the seeds that it there sowed. For in a democracy, the economic is subordinate to the political, a lesson that our ancestors learned long ago, and that our descendants will undoubtedly have to relearn many years hence.

III

* * *

It is in my view inappropriate for the Court to invalidate the State's ban on commercial advertising here, based on its speculation that in some cases the advertising may result in a net savings in electrical energy use, and in the cases in which it is clear a net energy savings would result from utility advertising, the Public Service Commission would apply its ban so as to proscribe such advertising. Even assuming that the Court's speculation is correct, I do not think it follows that facial invalidation of the ban is the appropriate course. As stated in *Parker v. Levy* (1974), "even if there are marginal applications in which a statute would infringe on First Amendment values, facial invalidation is inappropriate if the 'remainder of the statute . . . covers a whole range of easily identifiable and constitutionally proscribable . . . conduct . . . .'" This is clearly the case here.

NOTES AND QUESTIONS

1. Note that we do not here have the same kind of unanimity we found in cases like *New York Times v. Sullivan*, or even the nearly-unanimous attitude in cases like *New York Times v. United States*. Still, can you discern a doctrinal movement, at least in the opinion of the majority, that is close in spirit to those other cases?

2. Before the 1970s, as you may have been able to discern, commercial speech was simply unprotected under the First Amendment. Are all types of commercial speech equally subject to First Amendment protection once the decision is made to remove commercial speech from the unprotected category? If only some kinds of commercial speech are to be protected, which are deserving, and why? Is it the interests of the speaker that are accorded protection, or those of the audience? Which is the traditionally First Amendment-protected interest?

Only in one case has the Court attempted a definition of commercial speech. In *Bolger v. Young Drug Products Corp.*, 463 U.S. 60 (1983), the Court opined that commercial speech must have three elements: that of advertisement; referring to specific product; where the speaker is economically motivated. If a tobacco company decided to undertake advertisements discussing the reliability of various scientific studies of the tobacco-cancer risk, would such advertisements be commercial speech?

3. You will have noted that the doctrine of protecting commercial speech results in, for example, forbidding the states from banning the advertisement of prescription drug prices, or from banning advertising by lawyers. Are these conclusions unequivocal goods for society? Who should be balancing the harm and benefits of such regulatory moves? The court or the legislature? What does the dissent in this case suggest on this question? Does the fact that the majority has formulated an involved four-part test for determining when commercial speech is to be protected make you more or less sanguine about having courts rather than legislatures make the ultimate determinations here?

4. The Court has not consistently applied the elements of the *Central Hudson* test. In *Board of Trustees of the State of New York v. Fox,* 492 U.S. 469 (1989), the Court suggested that the fourth element did not require the least restrictive regulatory means. Rather, the government must merely choose a means that is narrowly tailored to achieve the desired objective. In contrast, in *Rubin v. Coors Brewing Co.*, 514 U.S. 476 (1995), dealing with a federal regulation that prevented labels with a listing of alcohol content, the Court said the regulation must advance the government's interest in a "direct and material" way, that the harms addressed by the regulation be real, and the restriction will alleviate them in a material fashion. *Id.* at 1592. The Court invalidated the regulation since it could conceive of more effective alternatives to the labeling restriction. Similarly, in *44 Liquormart Inc. v. Rhode Island*, 517 U.S. 484 (1996), a Court plurality found a prohibition on liquor prices not to be the best alternative for promoting temperance. *Fox* seems to have been overruled in everything but name.

5. In *Greater New Orleans Broadcasting Ass'n, Inc. v. United States*, 527 U.S. 173 (1999), the Court continues its close examination of the third and fourth elements of *Central Hudson* — namely, whether regulation directly advances a substantial governmental interest and whether the restriction is no more extensive than necessary. The Court found that a prohibition of private casino gambling advertising in states where such gaming is lawful is unconstitutional. While admitting that casino gambling has enormous social costs, the Court was unwilling to accept limits on speech as the way to address them, especially where the government has been ambivalent, exempting advertising about state-run casinos and lotteries, certain occasional commercial gambling, and tribal casino gambling even when the broadcaster is located in a strict anti-gambling locale. Distinguishing on the basis of the identity of a casino's owner, reasoned the Court, is no way to directly advance the government's interests in avoiding the manifold harms gambling produces, including corruption and organized crime, bribery, narcotics trafficking, diversion of the least affluent families' scarce resources, and the serious abetting of pathological or compulsive gambling by close to three million Americans. Justice Thomas, concurring in the judgment, would find any suppression of speech about a lawful subject — commercial or noncommercial — to be incapable of justification, even under *Central Hudson*. Does the logic of the Court's opinion suggest that the only way the gambling epidemic in the United States can be addressed is by banning or limiting gaming directly?

6. The Court confronted commercial speech again in *Lorillard Tobacco Co. v. Reilly,* 533 U.S. 525 (2001), invalidating a Massachusetts law limiting various tobacco advertising on preemption and free speech grounds, but sustaining sale regulations. The Attorney General of Massachusetts (Attorney General) promulgated comprehensive regulations governing the advertising and sale of cigarettes, smokeless tobacco, and cigars, all of which were challenged by tobacco manufacturers and retailers. The cigarette advertising restrictions were preempted by the Federal Cigarette Labeling and Advertising Act of 1969 (FCLAA), said the Court, which prescribes mandatory health warnings for cigarette packaging and advertising, and precludes similar state regulations. Massachusetts had argued that the FCLAA only pre-empted regulations of the content of cigarette advertising and that its exclusion of cigarette billboards from school zones and the like was a form of zoning, a traditional area of state power, and thus, the presumption against preemption should apply. The Court rejected that view. In addition, while Massachusetts' outdoor and point-of-sale advertising regulations relating to smokeless tobacco and cigars were not preempted, those were found to violate the First Amendment.

No one contested the importance of the state's interest in preventing the use of tobacco by minors, and the Court found that interest directly advanced by the regulations in issue. The problem was the fourth — or "reasonable fit" — step of *Central Hudson.* Because the record indicated that the regulations prohibit advertising in a substantial portion of Massachusetts' major metropolitan areas, and that "outdoor" advertising included not only advertising located outside an establishment, but also advertising inside a store if visible from outside, the regulations were insufficiently tailored. Said Justice O'Connor for the Court: "The State's interest in preventing underage tobacco use is substantial, and even compelling, but it is no less true that the sale and use of tobacco products by adults is a legal activity. We must consider that tobacco retailers and manufacturers have an interest in conveying truthful information about their products to adults, and adults have a corresponding interest in receiving truthful information about tobacco products." In other words, since adults would have a harder time finding tobacco products, the compelling interest of lessening underage tobacco addiction is outweighed. This is a curiously myopic, if not self-centered, calculus in light of the unhealthy, life-threatening qualities of the (nevertheless still lawful) product, but here are the Court's own words, "[a] careful calculation of the costs of a speech regulation does not mean that a State must demonstrate that there is no incursion on legitimate speech interests, but a speech regulation cannot unduly impinge on the speaker's ability to propose a commercial transaction and the adult listener's opportunity to obtain information about products. After reviewing the outdoor advertising regulations, we find the calculation in this case insufficient for purposes of the First Amendment."

The Court also invalidated on free speech grounds a restriction requiring point of sale advertising to be placed above five feet. Some kids are taller or would look up, reasoned the Justices, so the Court thought neither the third (directly advance) or fourth (reasonable fit) aspects of *Central Hudson* were met. By contrast, Massachusetts' sales provisions regulating the placement of the products within the store were sustained. While such conduct may have a communicative component, Massachusetts sought only to regulate the placement of tobacco products for reasons unrelated to the communication of ideas. Under the *O'Brien* expressive conduct standard, the Court concluded that the state had demonstrated a substantial interest in preventing access to tobacco products by minors and had adopted an appropriately narrow means of advancing that interest. "Unattended displays of tobacco products present an opportunity for access without the proper age verification required by law. Thus, the State prohibits self-service and other displays that would allow an individual to obtain tobacco products without direct contact with a salesperson. It was clear that the regulations leave open ample channels of communication. The regulations do not significantly impede adult access to tobacco products."

Concurring, Justice Thomas noted that he continues to believe that when the government seeks to restrict truthful speech in order to suppress the ideas it conveys, strict scrutiny is appropriate, whether or not the speech in question may be characterized as "commercial." He would subject all of the advertising restrictions to strict scrutiny and would hold that they violate the First Amendment. Justices Kennedy and Scalia in a separate concurrence implied agreement. Assuming the Thomas view were the Court's position, is it as clear to you (as apparently it is to Justice Thomas) that strict scrutiny could not be fulfilled given the "compelling" interest in preventing underage addiction to tobacco? Justice Stevens wrote one of the several dissenting opinions from the preemption ruling, but the dissenters (perhaps subject to further fact-finding) largely accepted the First Amendment analysis because the regulations "unduly restrict[ed] the ability of cigarette manufacturers to convey lawful information to adult consumers."

5. Do Actions Speak as Loud as Words? Expressive Conduct and the First Amendment

a. Draft Card Burning

UNITED STATES v. O'BRIEN
391 U.S. 367 (1968)

MR. CHIEF JUSTICE WARREN delivered the opinion of the Court.

On the morning of March 31, 1966, David Paul O'Brien and three companions burned their Selective Service registration certificates on the steps of the South

Boston Courthouse. A sizable crowd, including several agents of the Federal Bureau of Investigation, witnessed the event. Immediately after the burning, members of the crowd began attacking O'Brien and his companions. An FBI agent ushered O'Brien to safety inside the courthouse. After he was advised of his right to counsel and to silence, O'Brien stated to FBI agents that he had burned his registration certificate because of his beliefs, knowing that he was violating federal law. He produced the charred remains of the certificate, which, with his consent, were photographed.

For this act, O'Brien was indicted, tried, convicted, and sentenced in the United States District Court for the District of Massachusetts. He did not contest the fact that he had burned the certificate. He stated in argument to the jury that he burned the certificate publicly to influence others to adopt his antiwar beliefs, as he put it, "so that other people would reevaluate their positions with Selective Service, with the armed forces, and reevaluate their place in the culture of today, to hopefully [sic] consider my position."

The indictment upon which he was tried charged that he "willfully and knowingly did mutilate, destroy, and change by burning . . . [his] Registration Certificate . . . in violation of Title 50, App., United States Code, Section 462(b)." Section 462(b) is part of the Universal Military Training and Service Act of 1948. Section 462(b)(3), one of six numbered subdivisions of § 462(b), was amended by Congress in 1965, so that at the time O'Brien burned his certificate an offense was committed by any person,

> "who forges, alters, *knowingly destroys*, *knowingly mutilates*, or in any manner changes any such certificate . . . ." (Italics supplied.)

In the District Court, O'Brien argued that the 1965 Amendment prohibiting the knowing destruction or mutilation of certificates was unconstitutional because it was enacted to abridge free speech, and because it served no legitimate legislative purpose. The District Court rejected these arguments, holding that the statute on its face did not abridge First Amendment rights, that the court was not competent to inquire into the motives of Congress in enacting the 1965 Amendment, and that the Amendment was a reasonable exercise of the power of Congress to raise armies.

On appeal, the Court of Appeals for the First Circuit held the 1965 Amendment unconstitutional as a law abridging freedom of speech. . . . The court ruled, however, that O'Brien's conviction should be affirmed under the statutory provision, 50 U.S.C. App. § 462(b)(6), which in its view made violation of the non-possession regulation a crime, because it regarded such violation to be a lesser included offense of the crime defined by the 1965 Amendment.

* * *

I.

When a male reaches the age of 18, he is required by the Universal Military Training and Service Act to register with a local draft board. He is assigned a

Selective Service number, and within five days he is issued a registration certificate. . . . Subsequently, and based on a questionnaire completed by the registrant, he is assigned a classification denoting his eligibility for induction, and "[a]s soon as practicable" thereafter he is issued a Notice of Classification. . . .

Both the registration and classification certificates are small white cards, approximately 2 by 3 inches. The registration certificate specifies the name of the registrant, the date of registration, and the number and address of the local board with which he is registered. Also inscribed upon it are the date and place of the registrant's birth, his residence at registration, his physical description, his signature, and his Selective Service number. The Selective Service number itself indicates his State of registration, his local board, his year of birth, and his chronological position in the local board's classification record.

The classification certificate shows the registrant's name, Selective Service number, signature, and eligibility classification. It specifies whether he was so classified by his local board, an appeal board, or the President. It contains the address of his local board and the date the certificate was mailed.

Both the registration and classification certificates bear notices that the registrant must notify his local board in writing of every change in address, physical condition, and occupational, marital, family, dependency, and military status, and of any other fact which might change his classification. Both also contain a notice that the registrant's Selective Service number should appear on all communications to his local board.

Congress demonstrated its concern that certificates issued by the Selective Service System might be abused well before the 1965 Amendment here challenged. The 1948 Act, 62 Stat. 604, itself prohibited many different abuses involving "any registration certificate, . . . or any other certificate issued pursuant to or prescribed by the provisions of this title, or rules or regulations promulgated hereunder . . . ." Under §§ 12(b)(1)-(5) of the 1948 Act, it was unlawful (1) to transfer a certificate to aid a person in making false identification; (2) to possess a certificate not duly issued with the intent of using it for false identification; (3) to forge, alter, "or in any manner" change a certificate or any notation validly inscribed thereon; (4) to photograph or make an imitation of a certificate for the purpose of false identification; and (5) to possess a counterfeited or altered certificate. In addition, as previously mentioned, regulations of the Selective Service System required registrants to keep both their registration and classification certificates in their personal possession at all times. . . .

By the 1965 Amendment, Congress added to § 12(b)(3) of the 1948 Act the provision here at issue, subjecting to criminal liability not only one who "forges, alters, or in any manner changes" but also one who "knowingly destroys, [or] knowingly mutilates" a certificate. We note at the outset that the 1965 Amendment plainly does not abridge free speech on its face, and we do not understand O'Brien to argue otherwise. Amended § 12(b)(3) on its face deals with conduct having no connection with speech. It prohibits the knowing destruction of certificates issued by the Selective Service System, and there is nothing necessarily expressive about such conduct. The Amendment does not distinguish between public and private destruction, and it does not punish only destruction engaged in for the purpose of expressing views. A law prohibiting destruction of Selective Service certificates no more abridges free speech on its face than a motor vehicle law prohibiting the destruction of drivers' licenses, or a tax law prohibiting the destruction of books and records.

O'Brien nonetheless argues that the 1965 Amendment is unconstitutional in its application to him, and is unconstitutional as enacted because what he calls the "purpose" of Congress was "to suppress freedom of speech." We consider these arguments separately.

II.

O'Brien first argues that the 1965 Amendment is unconstitutional as applied to him because his act of burning his registration certificate was protected "symbolic speech" within the First Amendment. His argument is that the freedom of expression which the First Amendment guarantees includes all modes of "communication of ideas by conduct," and that his conduct is within this definition because he did it in "demonstration against the war and against the draft."

We cannot accept the view that an apparently limitless variety of conduct can be labeled "speech" whenever the person engaging in the conduct intends thereby to express an idea. However, even on the assumption that the alleged communicative element in O'Brien's conduct is sufficient to bring into play the First Amendment, it does not necessarily follow that the destruction of a registration certificate is constitutionally protected activity. This Court has held that when "speech" and "nonspeech" elements are combined in the same course of conduct, a sufficiently important governmental interest in regulating the nonspeech element can justify incidental limitations on First Amendment freedoms. To characterize the quality of the governmental interest which must appear, the Court has employed a variety of descriptive terms: compelling; substantial; subordinating; paramount; cogent; strong. Whatever imprecision inheres in these terms, we think it clear that a government regulation is sufficiently justified if it is within the constitutional power of the Government; if it furthers an important or substantial governmental interest; if the governmental interest is unrelated to the suppression of free expression; and if the incidental restriction on alleged First Amendment freedoms is no greater than is essential to the furtherance of that interest. We find that the 1965 Amendment to § 12(b)(3) of the Universal Military Training and Service Act meets all of these requirements, and consequently that O'Brien can be constitutionally convicted for violating it.

The constitutional power of Congress to raise and support armies and to make all laws necessary and proper to that end is broad and sweeping. . . .

* * *

2. The information supplied on the certificates facilitates communication between registrants and local boards, simplifying the system and benefiting all concerned. To begin with, each certificate bears the address of the registrant's local board, an item unlikely to be committed to memory. Further, each card bears the registrant's Selective Service number, and a registrant who has his number readily available so that he can communicate it to his local board when he supplies or requests information can make simpler the board's task in locating his file. Finally, a registrant's inquiry, particularly through a local board other than his own, concerning his eligibility status is frequently answerable simply on the basis of his classification certificate. . . .

3. Both certificates carry continual reminders that the registrant must notify his local board of any change of address, and other specified changes in his status. The smooth functioning of the system requires that local boards be continually aware of the status and whereabouts of registrants, and the destruction of certificates deprives the system of a potentially useful notice device.

4. The regulatory scheme involving Selective Service certificates includes clearly valid prohibitions against the alteration, forgery, or similar deceptive misuse of certificates. The destruction or mutilation of certificates obviously increases the difficulty of detecting and tracing abuses such as these. Further, a mutilated certificate might itself be used for deceptive purposes.

The many functions performed by Selective Service certificates establish beyond doubt that Congress has a legitimate and substantial interest in preventing their wanton and unrestrained destruction and assuring their continuing availability by punishing people who knowingly and wilfully destroy or mutilate them. . . .

* * *

We think it apparent that the continuing availability to each registrant of his Selective Service certificates substantially furthers the smooth and proper functioning of the system that Congress has established to raise armies. We think it also apparent that the Nation has a vital interest in having a system for raising armies that functions with maximum efficiency and is capable of easily and quickly responding to continually changing circumstances. For these reasons, the Government has a substantial interest in assuring the continuing availability of issued Selective Service certificates.

It is equally clear that the 1965 Amendment specifically protects this substantial governmental interest. We perceive no alternative means that would more precisely and narrowly assure the continuing availability of issued Selective Service certificates than a law which prohibits their wilful mutilation or destruction. The 1965 Amendment prohibits such conduct and does nothing more. In other words, both the governmental interest and the operation of the

1965 Amendment are limited to the noncommunicative aspect of O'Brien's conduct. . . .

The case at bar is therefore unlike one where the alleged governmental interest in regulating conduct arises in some measure because the communication allegedly integral to the conduct is itself thought to be harmful. In *Stromberg v. California* (1931), for example, this Court struck down a statutory phrase which punished people who expressed their "opposition to organized government" by displaying "any flag, badge, banner, or device." Since the statute there was aimed at suppressing communication it could not be sustained as a regulation of noncommunicative conduct.

In conclusion, we find that because of the Government's substantial interest in assuring the continuing availability of issued Selective Service certificates, because amended § 462(b) is an appropriately narrow means of protecting this interest and condemns only the independent noncommunicative impact of conduct within its reach, and because the noncommunicative impact of O'Brien's act of burning his registration certificate frustrated the Government's interest, a sufficient governmental interest has been shown to justify O'Brien's conviction.

III.

O'Brien finally argues that the 1965 Amendment is unconstitutional as enacted because what he calls the "purpose" of Congress was "to suppress freedom of speech." We reject this argument because under settled principles the purpose of Congress, as O'Brien uses that term, is not a basis for declaring this legislation unconstitutional.

It is a familiar principle of constitutional law that this Court will not strike down an otherwise constitutional statute on the basis of an alleged illicit legislative motive. As the Court long ago stated:

> "The decisions of this court from the beginning lend no support whatever to the assumption that the judiciary may restrain the exercise of lawful power on the assumption that a wrongful purpose or motive has caused the power to be exerted." . . .

Inquiries into congressional motives or purposes are a hazardous matter. When the issue is simply the interpretation of legislation, the Court will look to statements by legislators for guidance as to the purpose of the legislature, because the benefit to sound decision-making in this circumstance is thought sufficient to risk the possibility of misreading Congress' purpose. It is entirely a different matter when we are asked to void a statute that is, under well-settled criteria, constitutional on its face, on the basis of what fewer than a handful of Congressmen said about it. What motivates one legislator to make a speech about a statute is not necessarily what motivates scores of others to enact it, and the stakes are sufficiently high for us to eschew guesswork. We decline to void essentially on the ground that it is unwise legislation which

Congress had the undoubted power to enact and which could be reenacted in its exact form if the same or another legislator made a "wiser" speech about it.

* * *

We think it not amiss, in passing, to comment upon O'Brien's legislative-purpose argument. There was little floor debate on this legislation in either House. [In the Senate debate only one Senator, Thurmond, spoke.] In the House debate only two Congressmen addressed themselves to the Amendment — Congressmen Rivers and Bray. The bill was passed after their statements without any further debate by a vote of 393 to 1. It is principally on the basis of the statements by these three Congressmen that O'Brien makes his congressional-"purpose" argument. We note that if we were to examine legislative purpose in the instant case, we would be obliged to consider not only these statements but also the more authoritative reports of the Senate and House Armed Services Committees. . . . While both reports make clear a concern with the "defiant" destruction of so-called "draft cards" and with "open" encouragement to others to destroy their cards, both reports also indicate that this concern stemmed from an apprehension that unrestrained destruction of cards would disrupt the smooth functioning of the Selective Service System.

* * *

Mr. Justice Marshall took no part in the consideration or decision of these cases.

Mr. Justice Harlan, concurring.

The crux of the Court's opinion, which I join, is of course its general statement, that:

> "a government regulation is sufficiently justified if it is within the constitutional power of the Government; if it furthers an important or substantial governmental interest; if the governmental interest is unrelated to the suppression of free expression; and if the incidental restriction on alleged First Amendment freedoms is no greater than is essential to the furtherance of that interest."

I wish to make explicit my understanding that this passage does not foreclose consideration of First Amendment claims in those rare instances when an "incidental" restriction upon expression, imposed by a regulation which furthers an "important or substantial" governmental interest and satisfies the Court's other criteria, in practice has the effect of entirely preventing a "speaker" from reaching a significant audience with whom he could not otherwise lawfully communicate. This is not such a case, since O'Brien manifestly could have conveyed his message in many ways other than by burning his draft card.

Mr. Justice Douglas, dissenting.

The Court states that the constitutional power of Congress to raise and support armies is "broad and sweeping" and that Congress' power "to classify and conscript manpower for military service is 'beyond question.'" This is undoubt-edly true in times when, by declaration of Congress, the Nation is in a state of war. The underlying and basic problem in this case, however, is whether con-scription is permissible in the absence of a declaration of war. That question has not been briefed nor was it presented in oral argument; but it is, I submit, a question upon which the litigants and the country are entitled to a ruling. I have discussed in *Holmes v. United States* the nature of the legal issue and it will be seen from my dissenting opinion in that case that this Court has never ruled on the question. . . .

The rule that this Court will not consider issues not raised by the parties is not inflexible and yields in "exceptional cases" to the need correctly to decide the case before the court.

In such a case it is not unusual to ask for reargument even on a constitutional question not raised by the parties [citing four cases]. . . .

These precedents demonstrate the appropriateness of restoring the instant case to the calendar for reargument on the question of the constitutionality of a peacetime draft.

NOTES AND QUESTIONS

1. Why wasn't Mr. O'Brien successful in his claim that burning his draft card was speech protected by the First Amendment? Was there any doubt that he intended to communicate a political message by his actions? When the govern-ment forbids him to communicate this message by his chosen method why isn't the First Amendment infringed? Why did Justice Douglas dissent?

2. To what extent can the government abridge Mr. O'Brien's First Amendment rights? Suppose the congressional purpose in passing the legislation in question was to suppress dissent? We will next examine the Supreme Court's 1989 deci-sion that announced that flag burning was speech protected by the First Amend-ment. Would you have anticipated this result after reading *O'Brien*? Using only what you have learned from the *O'Brien* case, would a statute which punished those who burned the flag intentionally seeking to outrage onlookers, but not those who burned aged and soiled flags ceremoniously to dispose of them, pass constitutional muster?

3. It is possible to find some communicative content in virtually every activ-ity. That said, the Court does not treat all conduct as expressive. Only that conduct which is intended to convey a message and which has a substantial like-lihood of having that message understood falls within the expressive category. A good example of communicative conduct is *Tinker v. Des Moines Independent Community School District*, 393 U.S. 503 (1969), where the Court held that wearing a black armband to school as an anti-war protest was protected speech.

4. However, as O'Brien indicates, the mere fact that conduct is communicative does not mean that it is beyond all regulation. O'Brien allows regulation of communicative conduct if the purpose of the regulation is other than suppression of speech and if the impact of the regulation is no greater than necessary to achieve the government's purpose. Many constitutional scholars conclude that the standard is basically one of intermediate scrutiny.

b. Flag Burning

TEXAS v. JOHNSON
491 U.S. 397 (1989)

JUSTICE BRENNAN delivered the opinion of the Court.

* * *

I

While the Republican National Convention was taking place in Dallas in 1984, respondent Johnson participated in a political demonstration dubbed the "Republican War Chest Tour." . . .

The demonstration ended in front of Dallas City Hall, where Johnson unfurled the American flag, doused it with kerosene, and set it on fire. While the flag burned, the protestors chanted: "America, the red, white, and blue, we spit on you." After the demonstrators dispersed, a witness to the flag burning collected the flag's remains and buried them in his backyard. No one was physically injured or threatened with injury, though several witnesses testified that they had been seriously offended by the flag burning.

Of the approximately 100 demonstrators, Johnson alone was charged with a crime. The only criminal offense with which he was charged was the desecration of a venerated object in violation of Tex. Penal Code Ann. § 42.09(a)(3) (1989).[1] After a trial, he was convicted, sentenced to one year in prison, and fined $2,000. . . .

---

[1] Texas Penal Code Ann. § 42.09 (1989) provides in full:

    "§ 42.09. Desecration of Venerated Object.

    "(a) A person commits an offense if he intentionally or knowingly desecrates:

    "(1) a public monument;

    "(2) a place of worship or burial; or

    "(3) a state or national flag.

    "(b) For purposes of this section, 'desecrate' means deface, damage, or otherwise physically mistreat in a way that the actor knows will seriously offend one or more persons likely to observe or discover his action."

* * *

* * *

II

Johnson was convicted of flag desecration for burning the flag rather than for uttering insulting words. This fact somewhat complicates our consideration of his conviction under the First Amendment. We must first determine whether Johnson's burning of the flag constituted expressive conduct, permitting him to invoke the First Amendment in challenging his conviction. If his conduct was expressive, we next decide whether the State's regulation is related to the suppression of free expression. *See, e.g., United States v. O'Brien* (1968). If the State's regulation is not related to expression, then the less stringent standard we announced in *United States v. O'Brien* for regulations of noncommunicative conduct controls. If it is, then we are outside of *O'Brien*'s test, and we must ask whether this interest justifies Johnson's conviction under a more demanding standard. A third possibility is that the State's asserted interest is simply not implicated on these facts, and in that event the interest drops out of the picture.

The First Amendment literally forbids the abridgment only of "speech," but we have long recognized that its protection does not end at the spoken or written word. While we have rejected "the view that an apparently limitless variety of conduct can be labeled 'speech' whenever the person engaging in the conduct intends thereby to express an idea," we have acknowledged that conduct may be "sufficiently imbued with elements of communication to fall within the scope of the First and Fourteenth Amendments."

In deciding whether particular conduct possesses sufficient communicative elements to bring the First Amendment into play, we have asked whether "[a]n intent to convey a particularized message was present, and [whether] the likelihood was great that the message would be understood by those who viewed it." Hence, we have recognized the expressive nature of students' wearing of black armbands to protest American military involvement in Vietnam; of a sit-in by blacks in a "whites only" area to protest segregation; of the wearing of American military uniforms in a dramatic presentation criticizing American involvement in Vietnam; and of picketing about a wide variety of causes.

Especially pertinent to this case are our decisions recognizing the communicative nature of conduct relating to flags. Attaching a peace sign to the flag; refusing to salute the flag; and displaying a red flag, we have held, all may find shelter under the First Amendment. That we have had little difficulty identifying an expressive element in conduct relating to flags should not be surprising. . . . Pregnant with expressive content, the flag as readily signifies this Nation as does the combination of letters found in "America."

We have not automatically concluded, however, that any action taken with respect to our flag is expressive. Instead, in characterizing such action for First Amendment purposes, we have considered the context in which it occurred. In *Spence* [*v. Washington* (1974)], for example, we emphasized that Spence's taping of a peace sign to his flag was "roughly simultaneous with and concededly triggered by the Cambodian incursion and the Kent State tragedy." The State of Washington had conceded, in fact, that Spence's conduct was a form of communication, and we stated that "the State's concession is inevitable on this record."

The State of Texas conceded for purposes of its oral argument in this case that Johnson's conduct was expressive conduct, and this concession seems to us as prudent as was Washington's in *Spence*. Johnson burned an American flag as part — indeed, as the culmination — of a political demonstration that coincided with the convening of the Republican Party and its renomination of Ronald Reagan for President. The expressive, overtly political nature of this conduct was both intentional and overwhelmingly apparent. At his trial, Johnson explained his reasons for burning the flag as follows: "The American Flag was burned as Ronald Reagan was being renominated as President. And a more powerful statement of symbolic speech, whether you agree with it or not, couldn't have been made at that time. It's quite a just position [juxtaposition]. We had new patriotism and no patriotism." In these circumstances, Johnson's burning of the flag was conduct "sufficiently imbued with elements of communication," to implicate the First Amendment.

III

The government generally has a freer hand in restricting expressive conduct than it has in restricting the written or spoken word. It may not, however, proscribe particular conduct *because* it has expressive elements. "[W]hat might be termed the more generalized guarantee of freedom of expression makes the communicative nature of conduct an inadequate *basis* for singling out that conduct for proscription. A law *directed* at the communicative nature of conduct must, like a law directed at speech itself, be justified by the substantial showing of need that the First Amendment requires." It is, in short, not simply the verbal or nonverbal nature of the expression, but the governmental interest at stake, that helps to determine whether a restriction on that expression is valid.

Thus, although we have recognized that where "'speech' and 'nonspeech' elements are combined in the same course of conduct, a sufficiently important governmental interest in regulating the nonspeech element can justify incidental limitations on First Amendment freedoms," *O'Brien*, we have limited the applicability of *O'Brien*'s relatively lenient standard to those cases in which "the governmental interest is unrelated to the suppression of free expression." In stating, moreover, that *O'Brien*'s test "in the last analysis is little, if any, different from the standard applied to time, place, or manner restrictions," we have highlighted the requirement that the governmental interest in question be unconnected to expression in order to come under *O'Brien*'s less demanding rule.

In order to decide whether *O'Brien*'s test applies here, therefore, we must decide whether Texas has asserted an interest in support of Johnson's conviction that is unrelated to the suppression of expression. . . . The State offers two separate interests to justify this conviction: preventing breaches of the peace and preserving the flag as a symbol of nationhood and national unity. We hold that the first interest is not implicated on this record and that the second is related to the suppression of expression.

A

Texas claims that its interest in preventing breaches of the peace justifies Johnson's conviction for flag desecration. However, no disturbance of the peace actually occurred or threatened to occur because of Johnson's burning of the flag. Although the State stresses the disruptive behavior of the protestors during their march toward City Hall, it admits that "no actual breach of the peace occurred at the time of the flagburning or in response to the flagburning." . . .

The State's position, therefore, amounts to a claim that an audience that takes serious offense at particular expression is necessarily likely to disturb the peace and that the expression may be prohibited on this basis. Our precedents do not countenance such a presumption. On the contrary, they recognize that a principal "function of free speech under our system of government is to invite dispute. It may indeed best serve its high purpose when it induces a condition of unrest, creates dissatisfaction with conditions as they are, or even stirs people to anger." It would be odd indeed to conclude *both* that "if it is the speaker's opinion that gives offense, that consequence is a reason for according it constitutional protection," *and* that the government may ban the expression of certain disagreeable ideas on the unsupported presumption that their very disagreeableness will provoke violence.

Thus, we have not permitted the government to assume that every expression of a provocative idea will incite a riot, but have instead required careful consideration of the actual circumstances surrounding such expression, asking whether the expression "is directed to inciting or producing imminent lawless action and is likely to incite or produce such action." *Brandenburg v. Ohio* (1969) (reviewing circumstances surrounding rally and speeches by Ku Klux Klan). To accept Texas' arguments that it need only demonstrate "the potential for a breach of the peace," and that every flag burning necessarily possesses that potential, would be to eviscerate our holding in *Brandenburg*. This we decline to do.

Nor does Johnson's expressive conduct fall within that small class of "fighting words" that are "likely to provoke the average person to retaliation, and thereby cause a breach of the peace." *Chaplinsky v. New Hampshire* (1942). No reasonable onlooker would have regarded Johnson's generalized expression of dissatisfaction with the policies of the Federal Government as a direct personal insult or an invitation to exchange fisticuffs.

We thus conclude that the State's interest in maintaining order is not implicated on these facts. The State need not worry that our holding will disable it from preserving the peace. We do not suggest that the First Amendment forbids a State to prevent "imminent lawless action." *Brandenburg*. And, in fact, Texas already has a statute specifically prohibiting breaches of the peace, which tends to confirm that Texas need not punish this flag desecration in order to keep the peace.

B

The State also asserts an interest in preserving the flag as a symbol of nationhood and national unity. In *Spence*, we acknowledged that the government's interest in preserving the flag's special symbolic value "is directly related to expression in the context of activity" such as affixing a peace symbol to a flag. We are equally persuaded that this interest is related to expression in the case of Johnson's burning of the flag. The State, apparently, is concerned that such conduct will lead people to believe either that the flag does not stand for nationhood and national unity, but instead reflects other, less positive concepts, or that the concepts reflected in the flag do not in fact exist, that is, that we do not enjoy unity as a Nation. These concerns blossom only when a person's treatment of the flag communicates some message, and thus are related "to the suppression of free expression" within the meaning of *O'Brien*. We are thus outside of *O'Brien*'s test altogether.

IV

It remains to consider whether the State's interest in preserving the flag as a symbol of nationhood and national unity justifies Johnson's conviction.

As in *Spence*, "[w]e are confronted with a case of prosecution for the expression of an idea through activity," and "[a]ccordingly, we must examine with particular care the interests advanced by [petitioner] to support its prosecution." Johnson was not, we add, prosecuted for the expression of just any idea; he was prosecuted for his expression of dissatisfaction with the policies of this country, expression situated at the core of our First Amendment values.

Moreover, Johnson was prosecuted because he knew that his politically charged expression would cause "serious offense." If he had burned the flag as a means of disposing of it because it was dirty or torn, he would not have been convicted of flag desecration under this Texas law: federal law designates burning as the preferred means of disposing of a flag "when it is in such condition that it is no longer a fitting emblem for display," and Texas has no quarrel with this means of disposal. The Texas law is thus not aimed at protecting the physical integrity of the flag in all circumstances, but is designed instead to protect it only against impairments that would cause serious offense to others. Texas concedes as much: "Section 42.09(b) reaches only those severe acts of physical abuse of the flag carried out in a way likely to be offensive . . . ."

Whether Johnson's treatment of the flag violated Texas law thus depended on the likely communicative impact of his expressive conduct. Our decision in *Boos v. Barry* [(1988)] tells us that this restriction on Johnson's expression is content based. In *Boos*, we considered the constitutionality of a law prohibiting "the display of any sign within 500 feet of a foreign embassy if that sign tends to bring that foreign government into 'public odium' or 'public disrepute.'" Rejecting the argument that the law was content neutral because it was justified by "our international law obligation to shield diplomats from speech that offends their dignity," we held that "[t]he emotive impact of speech on its audience is not a 'secondary effect'" unrelated to the content of the expression itself.

According to the principles announced in *Boos*, Johnson's political expression was restricted because of the content of the message he conveyed. We must therefore subject the State's asserted interest in preserving the special symbolic character of the flag to "the most exacting scrutiny."

Texas argues that its interest in preserving the flag as a symbol of nationhood and national unity survives this close analysis. Quoting extensively from the writings of this Court chronicling the flag's historic and symbolic role in our society, the State emphasizes the "'special place'" reserved for the flag in our Nation. The State's argument is not that it has an interest simply in maintaining the flag as a symbol of *something*, no matter what it symbolizes; indeed, if that were the State's position, it would be difficult to see how that interest is endangered by highly symbolic conduct such as Johnson's. Rather, the State's claim is that it has an interest in preserving the flag as a symbol of *nationhood* and *national unity*, a symbol with a determinate range of meanings. According to Texas, if one physically treats the flag in a way that would tend to cast doubt on either the idea that nationhood and national unity are the flag's referents or that national unity actually exists, the message conveyed thereby is a harmful one and therefore may be prohibited.

If there is a bedrock principle underlying the First Amendment, it is that the government may not prohibit the expression of an idea simply because society finds the idea itself offensive or disagreeable.

We have not recognized an exception to this principle even where our flag has been involved. In *Street v. New York* (1969), we held that a State may not criminally punish a person for uttering words critical of the flag. Rejecting the argument that the conviction could be sustained on the ground that Street had "failed to show the respect for our national symbol which may properly be demanded of every citizen," we concluded that "the constitutionally guaranteed 'freedom to be intellectually . . . diverse or even contrary,' and the 'right to differ as to things that touch the heart of the existing order,' encompass the freedom to express publicly one's opinions about our flag, including those opinions which are defiant or contemptuous." Nor may the government, we have held, compel conduct that would evince respect for the flag. "To sustain the compulsory flag salute we are required to say that a Bill of Rights which guards the individual's right to speak his own mind, left it open to public authorities to compel him to utter what is not in his mind."

In holding . . . that the Constitution did not leave this course open to the government, Justice Jackson described one of our society's defining principles in words deserving of their frequent repetition: "If there is any fixed star in our constitutional constellation, it is that no official, high or petty, can prescribe what shall be orthodox in politics, nationalism, religion, or other matters of opinion or force citizens to confess by word or act their faith therein." In *Spence*, we held that the same interest asserted by Texas here was insufficient to support a criminal conviction under a flag-misuse statute for the taping of a peace sign to an American flag. "Given the protected character of [Spence's] expression and in light of the fact that no interest the State may have in preserving the physical integrity of a privately owned flag was significantly impaired on these facts," we held, "the conviction must be invalidated."

In short, nothing in our precedents suggests that a State may foster its own view of the flag by prohibiting expressive conduct relating to it. To bring its argument outside our precedents, Texas attempts to convince us that even if its interest in preserving the flag's symbolic role does not allow it to prohibit words or some expressive conduct critical of the flag, it does permit it to forbid the outright destruction of the flag. The State's argument cannot depend here on the distinction between written or spoken words and nonverbal conduct. That distinction, we have shown, is of no moment where the nonverbal conduct is expressive, as it is here, and where the regulation of that conduct is related to expression, as it is here. . . .

* * *

We never before have held that the Government may ensure that a symbol be used to express only one view of that symbol or its referents. Indeed, in *Schacht v. United States*, we invalidated a federal statute permitting an actor portraying a member of one of our Armed Forces to "'wear the uniform of that armed force if the portrayal does not tend to discredit that armed force.'" This proviso, we held, "which leaves Americans free to praise the war in Vietnam but can send persons like Schacht to prison for opposing it, cannot survive in a country which has the First Amendment."

We perceive no basis on which to hold that the principle underlying our decision in *Schacht* does not apply to this case. To conclude that the government may permit designated symbols to be used to communicate only a limited set of messages would be to enter territory having no discernible or defensible boundaries. Could the government, on this theory, prohibit the burning of state flags? Of copies of the Presidential seal? Of the Constitution? In evaluating these choices under the First Amendment, how would we decide which symbols were sufficiently special to warrant this unique status? To do so, we would be forced to consult our own political preferences, and impose them on the citizenry, in the very way that the First Amendment forbids us to do.

There is, moreover, no indication — either in the text of the Constitution or in our cases interpreting it — that a separate juridical category exists for the American flag alone. Indeed, we would not be surprised to learn that the persons who framed our Constitution and wrote the Amendment that we now construe were not known for their reverence for the Union Jack. The First

Amendment does not guarantee that other concepts virtually sacred to our Nation as a whole — such as the principle that discrimination on the basis of race is odious and destructive — will go unquestioned in the market-place of ideas. *See Brandenburg v. Ohio* (1969). We decline, therefore, to create for the flag an exception to the joust of principles protected by the First Amendment. . . .

* * *

We are tempted to say, in fact, that the flag's deservedly cherished place in our community will be strengthened, not weakened, by our holding today. Our decision is a reaffirmation of the principles of freedom and inclusiveness that the flag best reflects, and of the conviction that our toleration of criticism such as Johnson's is a sign and source of our strength. Indeed, one of the proudest images of our flag, the one immortalized in our own national anthem, is of the bombardment it survived at Fort McHenry. It is the Nation's resilience, not its rigidity, that Texas sees reflected in the flag — and it is that resilience that we reassert today.

The way to preserve the flag's special role is not to punish those who feel differently about these matters. It is to persuade them that they are wrong. "To courageous, self-reliant men, with confidence in the power of free and fearless reasoning applied through the processes of popular government, no danger flowing from speech can be deemed clear and present, unless the incidence of the evil apprehended is so imminent that it may befall before there is opportunity for full discussion. If there be time to expose through discussion the falsehood and fallacies, to avert the evil by the processes of education, the remedy to be applied is more speech, not enforced silence." And, precisely because it is our flag that is involved, one's response to the flag burner may exploit the uniquely persuasive power of the flag itself. We can imagine no more appropriate response to burning a flag than waving one's own, no better way to counter a flag burner's message than by saluting the flag that burns, no surer means of preserving the dignity even of the flag that burned than by — as one witness here did — according its remains a respectful burial. We do not consecrate the flag by punishing its desecration, for in doing so we dilute the freedom that this cherished emblem represents.

* * *

JUSTICE KENNEDY, concurring. [Omitted.]

CHIEF JUSTICE REHNQUIST, with whom JUSTICE WHITE and JUSTICE O'CONNOR join, dissenting.

In holding this Texas statute unconstitutional, the Court ignores Justice Holmes' familiar aphorism that "a page of history is worth a volume of logic." For more than 200 years, the American flag has occupied a unique position as the symbol of our Nation, a uniqueness that justifies a governmental prohibition against flag burning in the way respondent Johnson did here.

At the time of the American Revolution, the flag served to unify the Thirteen Colonies at home, while obtaining recognition of national sovereignty abroad. Ralph Waldo Emerson's "Concord Hymn" describes the first skirmishes of the Revolutionary War in these lines:

"By the rude bridge that arched the flood
Their flag to April's breeze unfurled,
Here once the embattled farmers stood
And fired the shot heard round the world."

During that time, there were many colonial and regimental flags, adorned with such symbols as pine trees, beavers, anchors, and rattlesnakes, bearing slogans such as "Liberty or Death," "Hope," "An Appeal to Heaven," and "Don't Tread on Me." The first distinctive flag of the Colonies was the "Grand Union Flag" — with 13 stripes and a British flag in the left corner — which was flown for the first time on January 2, 1776, by troops of the Continental Army around Boston. By June 14, 1777, after we declared our independence from England, the Continental Congress resolved: "That the flag of the thirteen United States be thirteen stripes, alternate red and white: that the union be thirteen stars, white in a blue field, representing a new constellation." One immediate result of the flag's adoption was that American vessels harassing British shipping sailed under an authorized national flag. Without such a flag, the British could treat captured seamen as pirates and hang them summarily; with a national flag, such seamen were treated as prisoners of war.

During the War of 1812, British naval forces sailed up Chesapeake Bay and marched overland to sack and burn the city of Washington. They then sailed up the Patapsco River to invest the city of Baltimore, but to do so it was first necessary to reduce Fort McHenry in Baltimore Harbor. Francis Scott Key, a Washington lawyer, had been granted permission by the British to board one of their warships to negotiate the release of an American who had been taken prisoner. That night, waiting anxiously on the British ship, Key watched the British fleet firing on Fort McHenry. Finally, at daybreak, he saw the fort's American flag still flying; the British attack had failed. Intensely moved, he began to scribble on the back of an envelope the poem that became our national anthem:

"O say can you see by the dawn's early light
What so proudly we hail'd at the twilight's last gleaming,
Whose broad stripes & bright stars through the perilous fight
O'er the ramparts we watch'd, were so gallantly streaming?
And the rocket's red glare, the bomb bursting in air,
Gave proof through the night that our flag was still there,
O say does that star-spangled banner yet wave
O'er the land of the free & the home of the brave?"

The American flag played a central role in our Nation's most tragic conflict, when the North fought against the South. The lowering of the American flag at Fort Sumter was viewed as the start of the war. The Southern States, to formalize their separation from the Union, adopted the "Stars and Bars" of the Confederacy. The Union troops marched to the sound of "Yes We'll Rally Round The Flag Boys, We'll Rally Once Again." President Abraham Lincoln refused proposals to remove from the American flag the stars representing the rebel States, because he considered the conflict not a war between two nations but an attack by 11 States against the National Government. By war's end, the American flag again flew over "an indestructible union, composed of indestructible states."

* * *

In the First and Second World Wars, thousands of our countrymen died on foreign soil fighting for the American cause. At Iwo Jima in the Second World War, United States Marines fought hand to hand against thousands of Japanese. By the time the Marines reached the top of Mount Suribachi, they raised a piece of pipe upright and from one end fluttered a flag. That ascent had cost nearly 6,000 American lives. The Iwo Jima Memorial in Arlington National Cemetery memorializes that event. President Franklin Roosevelt authorized the use of the flag on labels, packages, cartons, and containers intended for export as lend-lease aid, in order to inform people in other countries of the United States' assistance.

During the Korean war, the successful amphibious landing of American troops at Inchon was marked by the raising of an American flag within an hour of the event. Impetus for the enactment of the Federal Flag Desecration Statute in 1967 came from the impact of flag burnings in the United States on troop morale in Vietnam. . . .

The flag symbolizes the Nation in peace as well as in war. It signifies our national presence on battleships, airplanes, military installations, and public buildings from the United States Capitol to the thousands of county courthouses and city halls throughout the country. . . .

No other American symbol has been as universally honored as the flag. In 1931, Congress declared "The Star-Spangled Banner" to be our national anthem. In 1949, Congress declared June 14th to be Flag Day. In 1987, John Philip Sousa's "The Stars and Stripes Forever" was designated as the national march. Congress has also established "The Pledge of Allegiance to the Flag" and the manner of its deliverance. The flag has appeared as the principal symbol on approximately 33 United States postal stamps and in the design of at least 43 more, more times than any other symbol.

Both Congress and the States have enacted numerous laws regulating misuse of the American flag. Until 1967, Congress left the regulation of misuse of the flag up to the States. Now, however, 18 U.S.C. § 700(a) provides that:

> "Whoever knowingly casts contempt upon any flag of the United States by publicly mutilating, defacing, defiling, burning, or trampling upon it shall be fined not more than $1,000 or imprisoned for not more than one year, or both."

Congress has also prescribed, *inter alia*, detailed rules for the design of the flag, the time and occasion of flag's display, the position and manner of its display, respect for the flag, and conduct during hoisting, lowering, and passing of the flag. With the exception of Alaska and Wyoming, all of the States now have statutes prohibiting the burning of the flag. . . .

The American flag, then, throughout more than 200 years of our history, has come to be the visible symbol embodying our Nation. It does not represent the views of any particular political party, and it does not represent any particular political philosophy. The flag is not simply another "idea" or "point of view" competing for recognition in the marketplace of ideas. Millions and millions of Americans regard it with an almost mystical reverence regardless of what sort of social, political, or philosophical beliefs they may have. I cannot agree that the First Amendment invalidates the Act of Congress, and the laws of 48 of the 50 States, which make criminal the public burning of the flag.

More than 80 years ago in *Halter v. Nebraska* (1907), this Court upheld the constitutionality of a Nebraska statute that forbade the use of representations of the American flag for advertising purposes upon articles of merchandise. The Court there said:

> "For that flag every true American has not simply an appreciation but a deep affection. . . . Hence, it has often occurred that insults to a flag have been the cause of war, and indignities put upon it, in the presence of those who revere it, have often been resented and sometimes punished on the spot."

Only two Terms ago, in *San Francisco Arts & Athletics, Inc. v. United States Olympic Committee* (1987), the Court held that Congress could grant exclusive use of the word "Olympic" to the United States Olympic Committee. The Court thought that this "restrictio[n] on expressive speech properly [was] characterized as incidental to the primary congressional purpose of encouraging and rewarding the USOC's activities." As the Court stated, "when a word [or symbol] acquires value 'as the result of organization and the expenditure of labor, skill, and money' by an entity, that entity constitutionally may obtain a limited property right in the word [or symbol]." Surely Congress or the States may recognize a similar interest in the flag.

But the Court insists that the Texas statute prohibiting the public burning of the American flag infringes on respondent Johnson's freedom of expression. Such freedom, of course, is not absolute. In *Chaplinsky v. New Hampshire* (1942), a unanimous Court said:

> "Allowing the broadest scope to the language and purpose of the Fourteenth Amendment, it is well understood that the right of free speech is not absolute at all times and under all circumstances. There are certain well-defined and narrowly limited classes of speech, the prevention and punishment of which have never been thought to raise any Constitutional problem. These include the lewd and obscene, the profane, the

libelous, and the insulting or 'fighting' words — those which by their very utterance inflict injury or tend to incite an immediate breach of the peace. It has been well observed that such utterances are no essential part of any exposition of ideas, and are of such slight social value as a step to truth that any benefit that may be derived from them is clearly outweighed by the social interest in order and morality."

The Court upheld Chaplinsky's conviction under a state statute that made it unlawful to "address any offensive, derisive or annoying word to any person who is lawfully in any street or other public place." Chaplinsky had told a local marshal, "You are a God damned racketeer" and a "damned Fascist and the whole government of Rochester are Fascists or agents of Fascists."

Here it may equally well be said that the public burning of the American flag by Johnson was no essential part of any exposition of ideas, and at the same time it had a tendency to incite a breach of the peace. Johnson was free to make any verbal denunciation of the flag that he wished; indeed, he was free to burn the flag in private. He could publicly burn other symbols of the Government or effigies of political leaders. He did lead a march through the streets of Dallas, and conducted a rally in front of the Dallas City Hall. He engaged in a "die-in" to protest nuclear weapons. He shouted out various slogans during the march, including: "Reagan, Mondale which will it be? Either one means World War III"; "Ronald Reagan, killer of the hour, Perfect example of U.S. power"; and "red, white and blue, we spit on you, you stand for plunder, you will go under." For none of these acts was he arrested or prosecuted; it was only when he proceeded to burn publicly an American flag stolen from its rightful owner that he violated the Texas statute.

The Court could not, and did not, say that Chaplinsky's utterances were not expressive phrases — they clearly and succinctly conveyed an extremely low opinion of the addressee. The same may be said of Johnson's public burning of the flag in this case; it obviously did convey Johnson's bitter dislike of his country. But his act, like Chaplinsky's provocative words, conveyed nothing that could not have been conveyed and was not conveyed just as forcefully in a dozen different ways. As with "fighting words," so with flag burning, for purposes of the First Amendment: It is "no essential part of any exposition of ideas, and [is] of such slight social value as a step to truth that any benefit that may be derived from [it] is clearly outweighed" by the public interest in avoiding a probable breach of the peace. The highest courts of several States have upheld state statutes prohibiting the public burning of the flag on the grounds that it is so inherently inflammatory that it may cause a breach of public order.

The result of the Texas statute is obviously to deny one in Johnson's frame of mind one of many means of "symbolic speech." Far from being a case of "one picture being worth a thousand words," flag burning is the equivalent of an inarticulate grunt or roar that, it seems fair to say, is most likely to be indulged in not to express any particular idea, but to antagonize others. Only five years ago we said in *City Council of Los Angeles v. Taxpayers for Vincent* (1984), that "the

First Amendment does not guarantee the right to employ every conceivable method of communication at all times and in all places." The Texas statute deprived Johnson of only one rather inarticulate symbolic form of protest — a form of protest that was profoundly offensive to many — and left him with a full panoply of other symbols and every conceivable form of verbal expression to express his deep disapproval of national policy. Thus, in no way can it be said that Texas is punishing him because his hearers — or any other group of people — were profoundly opposed to the message that he sought to convey. Such opposition is no proper basis for restricting speech or expression under the First Amendment. It was Johnson's use of this particular symbol, and not the idea that he sought to convey by it or by his many other expressions, for which he was punished.

Our prior cases dealing with flag desecration statutes have left open the question that the Court resolves today. In *Street v. New York* (1969), the defendant burned a flag in the street, shouting "We don't need no damned flag" and "[i]f they let that happen to Meredith we don't need an American flag." The Court ruled that since the defendant might have been convicted solely on the basis of his words, the conviction could not stand, but it expressly reserved the question whether a defendant could constitutionally be convicted for burning the flag.

Chief Justice Warren, in dissent, stated: "I believe that the States and Federal Government do have the power to protect the flag from acts of desecration and disgrace. . . . [I]t is difficult for me to imagine that, had the Court faced this issue, it would have concluded otherwise." Justices Black and Fortas also expressed their personal view that a prohibition on flag burning did not violate the Constitution. ([Said Justice Black in dissent,] "It passes my belief that anything in the Federal Constitution bars a State from making the deliberate burning of the American Flag an offense"); ([Said Justice Fortas in his dissent,] "[T]he States and the Federal Government have the power to protect the flag from acts of desecration committed in public. . . . [T]he flag is a special kind of personality. Its use is traditionally and universally subject to special rules and regulation. . . . A person may 'own' a flag, but ownership is subject to special burdens and responsibilities. A flag may be property, in a sense; but it is property burdened with peculiar obligations and restrictions. Certainly . . . these special conditions are not *per se* arbitrary or beyond governmental power under our Constitution").

In *Spence v. Washington* (1974), the Court reversed the conviction of a college student who displayed the flag with a peace symbol affixed to it by means of removable black tape from the window of his apartment. Unlike the instant case, there was no risk of a breach of the peace, no one other than the arresting officers saw the flag, and the defendant owned the flag in question. The Court concluded that the student's conduct was protected under the First Amendment, because "no interest the State may have in preserving the physical integrity of a privately owned flag was significantly impaired on these facts."

The Court was careful to note, however, that the defendant "was not charged under the desecration statute, nor did he permanently disfigure the flag or destroy it."

In another related case, *Smith v. Goguen* (1974), the appellee, who wore a small flag on the seat of his trousers, was convicted under a Massachusetts flag-misuse statute that subjected to criminal liability anyone who "publicly . . . treats contemptuously the flag of the United States." The Court affirmed the lower court's reversal of appellee's conviction, because the phrase "treats contemptuously" was unconstitutionally broad and vague. The Court was again careful to point out that "[c]ertainly nothing prevents a legislature from defining with substantial specificity what constitutes forbidden treatment of United States flags." ([Justice White said, in his concurring opinion,] "The flag is a national property, and the Nation may regulate those who would make, imitate, sell, possess, or use it. I would not question those statutes which proscribe mutilation, defacement, or burning of the flag or which otherwise protect its physical integrity, without regard to whether such conduct might provoke violence. . . . There would seem to be little question about the power of Congress to forbid the mutilation of the Lincoln Memorial. . . . The flag is itself a monument, subject to similar protection"); ([Justice Blackmun, dissenting, said,] "Goguen's punishment was constitutionally permissible for harming the physical integrity of the flag by wearing it affixed to the seat of his pants").

But the Court today will have none of this. The uniquely deep awe and respect for our flag felt by virtually all of us are bundled off under the rubric of "designated symbols," that the First Amendment prohibits the government from "establishing." But the government has not "established" this feeling; 200 years of history have done that. . . .

The Court concludes its opinion with a regrettably patronizing civics lecture, presumably addressed to the Members of both Houses of Congress, the members of the 48 state legislatures that enacted prohibitions against flag burning, and the troops fighting under that flag in Vietnam who objected to its being burned: "The way to preserve the flag's special role is not to punish those who feel differently about these matters. It is to persuade them that they are wrong." The Court's role as the final expositor of the Constitution is well established, but its role as a Platonic guardian admonishing those responsible to public opinion as if they were truant schoolchildren has no similar place in our system of government. The cry of "no taxation without representation" animated those who revolted against the English Crown to found our Nation — the idea that those who submitted to government should have some say as to what kind of laws would be passed. Surely one of the high purposes of a democratic society is to legislate against conduct that is regarded as evil and profoundly offensive to the majority of people — whether it be murder, embezzlement, pollution, or flag burning.

Our Constitution wisely places limits on powers of legislative majorities to act, but the declaration of such limits by this Court "is, at all times, a question of much delicacy, which ought seldom, if ever, to be decided in the affirmative, in a doubtful case." *Fletcher v. Peck* (1810) (Marshall, C.J.). Uncritical extension of constitutional protection to the burning of the flag risks the frustration of the very purpose for which organized governments are instituted. The Court decides that the American flag is just another symbol, about which not only must opinions pro and con be tolerated, but for which the most minimal public respect may not be enjoined. The government may conscript men into the Armed Forces where they must fight and perhaps die for the flag, but the government may not prohibit the public burning of the banner under which they fight. I would uphold the Texas statute as applied in this case.

JUSTICE STEVENS, dissenting.

As the Court analyzes this case, it presents the question whether the State of Texas, or indeed the Federal Government, has the power to prohibit the public desecration of the American flag. The question is unique. In my judgment rules that apply to a host of other symbols, such as state flags, armbands, or various privately promoted emblems of political or commercial identity, are not necessarily controlling. Even if flag burning could be considered just another species of symbolic speech under the logical application of the rules that the Court has developed in its interpretation of the First Amendment in other contexts, this case has an intangible dimension that makes those rules inapplicable.

A country's flag is a symbol of more than "nationhood and national unity." It also signifies the ideas that characterize the society that has chosen that emblem as well as the special history that has animated the growth and power of those ideas. The fleurs-de-lis and the tricolor both symbolized "nationhood and national unity," but they had vastly different meanings. The message conveyed by some flags — the swastika, for example — may survive long after it has outlived its usefulness as a symbol of regimented unity in a particular nation.

So it is with the American flag. It is more than a proud symbol of the courage, the determination, and the gifts of nature that transformed 13 fledgling Colonies into a world power. It is a symbol of freedom, of equal opportunity, of religious tolerance, and of good will for other peoples who share our aspirations. The symbol carries its message to dissidents both at home and abroad who may have no interest at all in our national unity or survival.

The value of the flag as a symbol cannot be measured. Even so, I have no doubt that the interest in preserving that value for the future is both significant and legitimate. Conceivably that value will be enhanced by the Court's conclusion that our national commitment to free expression is so strong that even the United States as ultimate guarantor of that freedom is without power to prohibit the desecration of its unique symbol. But I am unpersuaded. The creation of a federal right to post bulletin boards and graffiti on the Washington Monument might enlarge the market for free expression, but at a cost I would not pay. Similarly, in my considered judgment, sanctioning the public desecration of the flag will tarnish its value — both for those who cherish the ideas for which it waves and for those who desire to don the robes of martyrdom by burning it. That tarnish is not justified by the trivial burden on free expression occasioned by requiring that an available, alternative mode of expression — including uttering words critical of the flag — be employed.

* * *

The Court is . . . quite wrong in blandly asserting that respondent "was prosecuted for his expression of dissatisfaction with the policies of this country, expression situated at the core of our First Amendment values." Respondent was prosecuted because of the method he chose to express his dissatisfaction with those policies. Had he chosen to spray-paint — or perhaps convey with a motion picture projector — his message of dissatisfaction on the facade of the Lincoln Memorial, there would be no question about the power of the Government to prohibit his means of expression. The prohibition would be supported by the legitimate interest in preserving the quality of an important national asset. Though the asset at stake in this case is intangible, given its unique value, the same interest supports a prohibition on the desecration of the American flag.

NOTES AND QUESTIONS

1. The result in *Texas v. Johnson*, that for the first time the Supreme Court rejected as unconstitutional flag protection or flag "desecration" statutes, was met with a political firestorm. The first President Bush called for a Constitutional Amendment to protect the flag, as did several veterans' groups. Congress held hearings on the Amendment, but instead decided to pass the Flag Protection Act of 1989, Pub. L. No. 101-131, 103 Stat. 777, which, in carefully crafted language avoiding the term "desecration," sought to be a measure which would not be content discrimination of speech, but would prohibit the knowing "mutilat[ion], deface[ment], physical[] defile[ment], burn[ing of], or trampl[ing] upon" any American flag. *Id.* Several law professors and legal scholars had assured Congress that such a statute could pass constitutional muster. Others, including former Judge Robert Bork and one of the authors of your casebook, told Congress that any such statute would be declared unconstitutional by the Supreme Court. *See Statutory and Constitutional Responses to the Supreme Court Decision in* Texas v. Johnson: *Hearings Before the Subcomm. on Civil and Constitutional Rights of the House Comm. on the Judiciary*, 101st Cong. (1989); *Hearings on Measures to Protect the Physical Integrity of the American Flag: Hearings Before the Senate Comm. on the Judiciary*, 101st Cong. (1989). Roughly one year after *Johnson*, in *United States v. Eichman*, 496 U.S. 310 (1990), the Supreme Court, by the same 5 to 4 votes in *Johnson*, held that the new federal statute was as invalid as was the Texas measure rejected in *Johnson*. A proposed Amendment to the Constitution, the Flag Protection Amendment, was then introduced into both Houses of Congress. The Amendment would have given both Congress and the state legislatures "the power to prohibit the physical desecration of the Flag of the United States." *See* H.R.J. Res. 350,

101st Cong. (1990); S.J. Res. 332, 101st Cong. (1990). After that proposed Amendment failed to win the required two-thirds majority in either House of Congress, proponents went to the state legislatures, and over the course of the next five years secured resolutions from forty-nine of the state legislatures asking Congress to pass the Flag Protection Amendment. Then, following the election of Republican majorities to both Houses of Congress in 1994, the proponents of the Amendment returned to Congress. The new Amendment had been slightly revised to focus only on federal power, and its text then was, "Congress shall have power to prohibit the physical desecration of the flag of the United States." S.J. Res. 31, 104th Cong. (1995). The Amendment easily garnered the required two-thirds majority in the House of Representatives, but failed by three votes in the Senate. *See* Helen Dewar, *Senate Falls Short on Flag Amendment*, WASH. POST, Dec. 13, 1995, at A1. Proponents of the Amendment, which has the support of approximately 80% of the American people (and approximately 1% of the press and the legal academy), argue that the Amendment would simply correct an erroneous Supreme Court decision that wrongly regarded an inarticulate act as protected speech. They also stress, as did the dissenting Justices in *Johnson*, that the Amendment would reaffirm a traditional American commitment to the exercise of rights tempered by responsibilities, and the traditional American high regard in which the flag is held as a symbol of the sacrifice of members of the American armed forces. However, only one national newspaper, the Wall Street Journal, endorsed the Amendment, and that was more on the theory that something ought to be done to indicate to the Supreme Court that the people — and not it — still rule than it was in support of the principles behind the Amendment itself. *See Sending Judges a Message*, WALL ST. J., Nov. 18, 1996, at A12.

2. Some of the Court's greatest champions of First Amendment liberty, including Earl Warren and Hugo Black, saw no constitutional problem with flag desecration statutes. One of your co-authors agrees and has suggested a government speech or property-based theory (the government of the United States owns the design of the flag) as a basis for protecting the standard without constitutional amendment. *See* Douglas W. Kmiec, *In the Aftermath of* Johnson *and* Eichman: *The Constitution Need Not Be Mutilated to Preserve the Government's Speech and Property Interests in the Flag*, 1990 B.Y.U. L. REV. 577.

3. Returning to the strictly legal issues for a moment, you will have observed that the majority distinguishes *Johnson* from *O'Brien* on the basis that the criminal provision at issue in the latter was not targeted at the suppression of speech, while that in the former was. Note that the dissenters do not agree with the assumption that flag desecration statutes regulate "speech," but rather, in Justice Rehnquist's memorable words, seek to regulate an act that is more like "an inarticulate grunt." Still, if the majority was correct, instead of applying the lesser *O'Brien* standard, which upheld a criminal provision not aimed at speech, but which incidentally affected speech, if there was a "valid and important" state interest at stake, a different standard would have to be applied. That different standard was the "compelling interest" standard. The "compelling interest" standard recognizes that First Amendment rights are not absolute, but are so important that any measure seeking to restrict their exercise has to be justified by a "compelling" government interest. You may have sensed by now that a frequent tactic to defeat a piece of legislation is to raise the "compelling interest" standard to defeat it, since almost no legislation can ever survive this "strict scrutiny test." Even so, why isn't the interest of the state or federal government in reinforcing the nation's symbolic commitment (which the flag represents) to the sacrifice of its men and women in arms, a "compelling interest"? Why isn't the state or federal government's interest in promoting the idea that with liberty comes responsibility a "compelling interest"? Or, most simply, why isn't the state's interest in preventing breaches of the peace, the ostensible justification for the Texas legislation at issue, a "compelling interest"?

4. In one of the most interesting and curious side arguments related to this issue, a student note in the Yale Law Journal, written by an individual who would soon become the New Republic's principal writer on Constitutional issues and a law professor, argued that if the Flag Protection Amendment passed it should be declared unconstitutional by the Supreme Court, since it was a violation of natural law. This would have been the nation's first case, the author argued, of an unconstitutional amendment. *See* Jeffrey Rosen, Note, *Was the Flag Burning Amendment Unconstitutional?*, 100 YALE L.J. 1073 (1991). Does that concept make any sense? Does the natural law invoked against the Flag Amendment seem like the natural law we have seen at work in any other cases?

c. Adult Entertainment

BARNES v. GLEN THEATRE, INC.
501 U.S. 560 (1991)

CHIEF JUSTICE REHNQUIST announced the judgment of the Court, and delivered an opinion, in which JUSTICE O'CONNOR and JUSTICE KENNEDY join.

Respondents are two establishments in South Bend, Indiana, that wish to provide totally nude dancing as entertainment, and individual dancers who are employed at these establishments. They claim that the First Amendment's guarantee of freedom of expression prevents the State of Indiana from enforcing its public indecency law to prevent this form of dancing. We reject their claim.

. . . The Kitty Kat Lounge, Inc. (Kitty Kat), is located in the city of South Bend. It sells alcoholic beverages and presents "go-go dancing." Its proprietor desires to present "totally nude dancing," but an applicable Indiana statute regulating public nudity requires that the dancers wear "pasties" and "G-strings" when they dance. The dancers are not paid an hourly wage, but work on commission. They receive a 100 percent commission on the first $60 in drink sales during their performances. Darlene Miller, one of the respondents in the action, had worked at the Kitty Kat for about two years at the time this action was brought. Miller wishes to dance nude because she believes she would make more money doing so.

Respondent Glen Theatre, Inc., is an Indiana corporation with a place of business in South Bend. Its primary business is supplying so-called adult entertainment through written and printed materials, movie showings, and live entertainment at an enclosed "bookstore." The live entertainment at the "bookstore" consists of nude and seminude performances and showings of the female body through glass panels. Customers sit in a booth and insert coins into a timing mechanism that permits them to observe the live nude and seminude dancers for a period of time. One of Glen Theatre's dancers, Gayle Ann Marie Sutro, has danced, modeled, and acted professionally for more than 15 years, and in addition to her performances at the Glen Theatre, can be seen in a pornographic movie at a nearby theater.

Respondents sued in the United States District Court for the Northern District of Indiana to enjoin the enforcement of the Indiana public indecency statute, asserting that its prohibition against complete nudity in public places violated the First Amendment. . . . [T]he District Court concluded that "the type of dancing these plaintiffs wish to perform is not expressive activity protected by the Constitution of the United States," and rendered judgment in favor of the defendants. The case was . . . appealed to the Seventh Circuit, and a panel of that court reversed the District Court, holding that the nude dancing involved here was expressive conduct protected by the First Amendment. The Court of Appeals then heard the case en banc, and the court rendered a series of comprehensive and thoughtful opinions. The majority concluded that nonobscene nude dancing performed for entertainment is expression protected by the First Amendment, and that the public indecency statute was an improper infringement of that expressive activity because its purpose was to prevent the message of eroticism and sexuality conveyed by the dancers. . . .

Several of our cases contain language suggesting that nude dancing of the kind involved here is expressive conduct protected by the First Amendment. . . . This, of course, does not end our inquiry. We must determine the level of protection to be afforded to the expressive conduct at issue, and must determine whether the Indiana statute is an impermissible infringement of that protected activity.

Indiana, of course, has not banned nude dancing as such, but has proscribed public nudity across the board. The Supreme Court of Indiana has construed the Indiana statute to preclude nudity in what are essentially places of public accommodation such as the Glen Theatre and the Kitty Kat Lounge. In such places, respondents point out, minors are excluded and there are no nonconsenting viewers. Respondents contend that while the State may license establishments such as the ones involved here, and limit the geographical area in which they do business, it may not in any way limit the performance of the dances within them without violating the First Amendment. The petitioners contend, on the other hand, that Indiana's restriction on nude dancing is a valid "time, place, or manner" restriction. . . .

The "time, place, or manner" test was developed for evaluating restrictions on expression taking place on public property which had been dedicated as a "public forum," although we have on at least one occasion applied it to conduct occurring on private property. . . . [T]his test has been interpreted to embody much the same standards as those set forth in *United States v. O'Brien* (1968), and we turn, therefore, to the rule enunciated in *O'Brien*.

O'Brien . . . claimed that his conviction was contrary to the First Amendment because his act was "symbolic speech" — expressive conduct. The Court rejected his contention that symbolic speech is entitled to full First Amendment protection. . . .

Applying the four-part *O'Brien* test . . . we find that Indiana's public indecency statute is justified despite its incidental limitations on some expressive activity. [1] The public indecency statute is clearly within the constitutional power of the State and [2] furthers substantial governmental interests. It is impossible to discern, other than from the text of the statute, exactly what governmental interest the Indiana legislators had in mind when they enacted this statute, for Indiana does not record legislative history, and the State's highest court has not shed additional light on the statute's purpose. Nonetheless, the statute's purpose of protecting societal order and morality is clear from its text and history. Public indecency statutes of this sort are of ancient origin and presently exist in at least 47 States. Public indecency, including nudity, was a criminal offense at common law, and this Court recognized the common-law roots of the offense of "gross and open indecency" in *Winters v. New York* (1948). Public nudity was considered an act *malum in se. Le Roy v. Sidley* (K.B. 1664). Public indecency statutes such as the one before us reflect moral disapproval of people appearing in the nude among strangers in public places.

This public indecency statute follows a long line of earlier Indiana statutes banning all public nudity. The history of Indiana's public indecency statute shows that it predates bar-room nude dancing and was enacted as a general prohibition. At least as early as 1831, Indiana had a statute punishing "open and notorious lewdness, or . . . any grossly scandalous and public indecency." A gap during which no statute was in effect was filled by the Indiana Supreme Court in *Ardery v. State* (1877), which held that the court could sustain a conviction for exhibition of "privates" in the presence of others. The court traced the offense to the Bible story of Adam and Eve. In 1881, a statute was enacted that would remain essentially unchanged for nearly a century:

> "Whoever, being over fourteen years of age, makes an indecent exposure of his person in a public place, or in any place where there are other persons to be offended or annoyed thereby, . . . is guilty of public indecency
> . . . ."

The language quoted above remained unchanged until it was simultaneously repealed and replaced with the present statute in 1976.

This and other public indecency statutes were designed to protect morals and public order. The traditional police power of the States is defined as the authority to provide for the public health, safety, and morals, and we have upheld such a basis for legislation. In *Paris Adult Theatre I v. Slaton* (1973), we said:

> "In deciding *Roth* [*v. United States* (1957)], this Court implicitly accepted that a legislature could legitimately act on such a conclusion to protect 'the social interest in order and morality.'"

And in *Bowers v. Hardwick* (1986), we said:

> "The law, however, is constantly based on notions of morality, and if all laws representing essentially moral choices are to be invalidated under the Due Process Clause, the courts will be very busy indeed."

Thus, the public indecency statute furthers a substantial government interest in protecting order and morality.

This interest is unrelated to the suppression of free expression. Some may view restricting nudity on moral grounds as necessarily related to expression. We disagree. It can be argued, of course, that almost limitless types of conduct — including appearing in the nude in public — are "expressive," and in one sense of the word this is true. People who go about in the nude in public may be expressing something about themselves by so doing. But the court rejected this expansive notion of "expressive conduct" in *O'Brien*, saying: "We cannot accept the view that an apparently limitless variety of conduct can be labeled 'speech' whenever the person engaging in the conduct intends thereby to express an idea."

* * *

Respondents contend that even though prohibiting nudity in public generally may not be related to suppressing expression, prohibiting the performance of nude dancing is related to expression because the State seeks to prevent its erotic message. Therefore, they reason that the application of the Indiana statute to the nude dancing in this case violates the First Amendment, because it fails the third part of the *O'Brien test*, viz: the governmental interest must be unrelated to the suppression of free expression.

But we do not think that when Indiana applies its statute to the nude dancing in these nightclubs it is proscribing nudity because of the erotic message conveyed by the dancers. Presumably numerous other erotic performances are presented at these establishments and similar clubs without any interference from the State, so long as the performers wear a scant amount of clothing. Likewise, the requirement that the dancers don pasties and G-strings does not deprive the dance of whatever erotic message it conveys; it simply makes the message slightly less graphic. The perceived evil that Indiana seeks to address is not erotic dancing, but public nudity. The appearance of people of all shapes, sizes and ages in the nude at a beach, for example, would convey little if any erotic message, yet the State still seeks to prevent it. Public nudity is the evil the State seeks to prevent, whether or not it is combined with expressive activity.

This conclusion is buttressed by a reference to the facts of *O'Brien*. An Act of Congress provided that anyone who knowingly destroyed a Selective Service registration certificate committed an offense. O'Brien burned his certificate on the steps of the South Boston Courthouse to influence others to adopt his antiwar beliefs. This Court upheld his conviction, reasoning that the continued availability of issued certificates served a legitimate and substantial purpose in the administration of the Selective Service system. O'Brien's deliberate destruction of his certificate frustrated this purpose and "[f]or this noncommunicative impact of his conduct, and for nothing else, he was convicted." . . .

The fourth part of the *O'Brien* test requires that the incidental restriction on First Amendment freedom be no greater than is essential to the furtherance of the governmental interest. As indicated in the discussion above, the governmental interest served by the text of the prohibition is societal disapproval of nudity in public places and among strangers. The statutory prohibition is not a means to some greater end, but an end in itself. It is without cavil that the public indecency statute is "narrowly tailored"; Indiana's requirement that the dancers wear at least pasties and G-strings is modest, and the bare minimum necessary to achieve the State's purpose.

* * *

JUSTICE SCALIA, concurring in the judgment.

. . . In my view, . . . the challenged regulation must be upheld, not because it survives some lower level of First Amendment scrutiny, but because, as a general law regulating conduct and not specifically directed at expression, it is not subject to First Amendment scrutiny at all.

I

Indiana's public indecency statute provides:

"(a) A person who knowingly or intentionally, in a public place:

"(1) engages in sexual intercourse;

"(2) engages in deviate sexual conduct;

"(3) appears in a state of nudity; or

"(4) fondles the genitals of himself or another person; commits public indecency, a Class A misdemeanor.

"(b) 'Nudity' means the showing of the human male or female genitals, pubic area, or buttocks with less than a fully opaque covering, the showing of the female breast with less than a fully opaque covering of any part of the nipple, or the showing of covered male genitals in a discernibly turgid state."

On its face, this law is not directed at expression in particular. As Judge Easterbrook put it in his dissent below: "Indiana does not regulate dancing. It regulates public nudity. . . . Almost the entire domain of Indiana's statute is unrelated to expression, unless we view nude beaches and topless hot dog vendors as speech." The intent to convey a "message of eroticism" (or any other message) is not a necessary element of the statutory offense of public indecency; nor does one commit that statutory offense by conveying the most explicit "message of eroticism," so long as he does not commit any of the four specified acts in the process.

Indiana's statute is in the line of a long tradition of laws against public nudity, which have never been thought to run afoul of traditional understanding of "the freedom of speech." Public indecency — including public nudity — has long been an offense at common law. Indiana's first public nudity statute (1831), predated by many years the appearance of nude barroom dancing. It was general in scope, directed at all public nudity, and not just at public nude expression; and all succeeding statutes, down to the present one, have been the same. Were it the case that Indiana *in practice* targeted only expressive nudity, while turning a blind eye to nude beaches and unclothed purveyors of hot dogs and machine tools, it might be said that what posed as a regulation of conduct in general was in reality a regulation of only communicative conduct. Respondents have adduced no evidence of that. Indiana officials have brought many public indecency prosecutions for activities having no communicative element.

The dissent confidently asserts that the purpose of restricting nudity in public places in general is to protect nonconsenting parties from offense; and argues that since only consenting, admission-paying patrons see respondents dance, that purpose cannot apply and the only remaining purpose must relate to the communicative elements of the performance. Perhaps the dissenters believe that "offense to others" *ought* to be the only reason for restricting nudity in public places generally, but there is no basis for thinking that our society has ever shared that Thoreauvian "you-may-do-what-you-like-so-long-as-it-does-not-injure-someone-else" beau ideal — much less for thinking that it was written into the Constitution. The purpose of Indiana's nudity law would be violated, I think, if 60,000 fully consenting adults crowded into the Hoosier Dome to display their genitals to one another, even if there were not an offended innocent in the crowd. Our society prohibits, and all human societies have prohibited, certain activities not because they harm others but because they are considered, in the traditional phrase, "*contra bonos mores*," *i.e.*, immoral. In American society, such prohibitions have included, for example, sadomasochism, cockfighting, bestiality, suicide, drug use, prostitution, and sodomy. While there may be great diversity of view on whether various of these prohibitions should exist (though I have found few ready to abandon, in principle, all of them), there is no doubt that, absent specific constitutional protection for the conduct involved, the Constitution does not prohibit them simply because they regulate "morality." *See Bowers v. Hardwick* (1986) (upholding prohibition of private homosexual sodomy enacted solely on "the presumed belief of a majority of the electorate in [the jurisdiction] that homosexual sodomy is immoral and unacceptable"). The purpose of the Indiana statute, as both its text and the manner of its enforcement demonstrate, is to enforce the traditional moral belief that people should not expose their private parts indiscriminately, regardless of whether those who see them are disedified. Since that is so, the dissent has no basis for positing that, where only thoroughly edified adults are present, the purpose must be repression of communication.

II

Since the Indiana regulation is a general law not specifically targeted at expressive conduct, its application to such conduct does not in my view implicate the First Amendment.

* * *

All our holdings . . . support the conclusion that "the only First Amendment analysis applicable to laws that do not directly or indirectly impede speech is the threshold inquiry of whether the purpose of the law is to suppress communication. If not, that is the end of the matter so far as First Amendment guarantees are concerned; if so, the court then proceeds to determine whether there is substantial justification for the proscription." Such a regime ensures that the government does not act to suppress communication, without requiring that all conduct-restricting regulation . . . survive an enhanced level of scrutiny.

We have explicitly adopted such a regime in another First Amendment context: that of free exercise. In *Employment Div., Dept. of Human Resources of Ore. v. Smith* (1990), we held that general laws not specifically targeted at religious practices did not require heightened First Amendment scrutiny even though they diminished some people's ability to practice their religion. "The government's ability to enforce generally applicable prohibitions of socially harmful conduct, like its ability to carry out other aspects of public policy, 'cannot depend on measuring the effects of a governmental action on a religious objector's spiritual development.'" *See also Minersville School District v. Gobitis* (1940) (Frankfurter, J.) ("Conscientious scruples have not, in the course of the long struggle for religious toleration, relieved the individual from obedience to a general law not aimed at the promotion or restriction of religious beliefs"). There is even greater reason to apply this approach to the regulation of expressive conduct. Relatively few can plausibly assert that their illegal conduct is being engaged in for religious reasons; but almost anyone can violate almost any law as a means of expression. In the one case, as in the other, if the law is not directed against the protected value (religion or expression) the law must be obeyed.

III

While I do not think the plurality's conclusions differ greatly from my own, I cannot entirely endorse its reasoning. The plurality purports to apply to this general law, insofar as it regulates this allegedly expressive conduct, an intermediate level of First Amendment scrutiny: The government interest in the regulation must be "'important or substantial.'" As I have indicated, I do not believe such a heightened standard exists. I think we should avoid wherever possible, moreover, a method of analysis that requires judicial assessment of the "importance" of government interests — and especially of government interests in various aspects of morality.

Neither of the cases that the plurality cites to support the "importance" of the State's interest here is in point. *Paris Adult Theatre I v. Slaton* and *Bowers v. Hardwick* did uphold laws prohibiting private conduct based on concerns of decency and morality; but neither opinion held that those concerns were particularly "important" or "substantial," or amounted to anything more than a *rational basis* for regulation. *Slaton* involved an exhibition which, since it was obscene and at least to some extent public, was unprotected by the First Amendment; the State's prohibition could therefore be invalidated only if it had no rational basis. We found that the State's "right . . . to maintain a decent society" provided a "legitimate" basis for regulation — even as to obscene material viewed by consenting adults. In *Bowers*, we held that since homosexual behavior is not a fundamental right, a Georgia law prohibiting private homosexual intercourse needed only a rational basis in order to comply with the Due Process Clause. Moral opposition to homosexuality, we said, provided that rational basis. I would uphold the Indiana statute on precisely the same ground: Moral opposition to nudity supplies a rational basis for its prohibition, and since the First Amendment has no application to this case no more than that is needed.

* * *

Indiana may constitutionally enforce its prohibition of public nudity even against those who choose to use public nudity as a means of communication. The State is regulating conduct, not expression, and those who choose to employ conduct as a means of expression must make sure that the conduct they select is not generally forbidden. For these reasons, I agree that the judgment should be reversed.

JUSTICE SOUTER, concurring in the judgment.

* * *

I . . . agree with the plurality that the appropriate analysis to determine the actual protection required by the First Amendment is the four-part enquiry described in *United States v. O'Brien*. . . . I nonetheless write separately to rest my concurrence in the judgment, not on the possible sufficiency of society's moral views to justify the limitations at issue, but on the State's substantial interest in combating the secondary effects of adult entertainment establishments of the sort typified by respondents' establishments.

* * *

In *Renton v. Playtime Theatres, Inc.* (1986), we upheld a city's zoning ordinance designed to prevent the occurrence of harmful secondary effects, including the crime associated with adult entertainment, by protecting approximately 95% of the city's area from the placement of motion picture theaters emphasizing "'matter depicting, describing or relating to "specified sexual activities" or "specified anatomical areas" . . . for observation by patrons therein.'" Of particular importance to the present enquiry, we held that the city of Renton was not compelled to justify its restrictions by studies specifically relating to the problems that would be caused by adult theaters in that city. Rather, "Renton was entitled to rely on the experiences of Seattle and other cities," which demonstrated the harmful secondary effects correlated with the presence "of even one [adult] theater in a given neighborhood."

The type of entertainment respondents seek to provide is plainly of the same character as that at issue in *Renton*. . . . It therefore is no leap to say that live nude dancing of the sort at issue here is likely to produce the same pernicious secondary effects as the adult films displaying "specified anatomical areas" at issue in *Renton*. Other reported cases from the Circuit in which this litigation arose confirm the conclusion. In light of *Renton*'s recognition that legislation seeking to combat the secondary effects of adult entertainment need not await localized proof of those effects, the State of Indiana could reasonably conclude that forbidding nude entertainment of the type offered at the Kitty Kat Lounge and the Glen Theatre's "bookstore" furthers its interest in preventing prostitution, sexual assault, and associated crimes. Given our recognition that "society's interest in protecting this type of expression is of a wholly different, and lesser, magnitude than the interest in untrammeled political debate," I do not believe that a State is required affirmatively to undertake to litigate this issue repeatedly in every case. . . .

* * *

JUSTICE WHITE, with whom JUSTICE MARSHALL, JUSTICE BLACKMUN, and JUSTICE STEVENS join, dissenting.

* * *

We are told by the attorney general of Indiana that, in *State v. Baysinger* (1979), the Indiana Supreme Court held that the statute at issue here cannot and does not prohibit nudity as a part of some larger form of expression meriting protection when the communication of ideas is involved. Petitioners also state that the evils sought to be avoided by applying the statute in this case would not obtain in the case of theatrical productions, such as "Salome" or "Hair." Neither is there any evidence that the State has attempted to apply the statute to nudity in performances such as plays, ballets, or operas. "No arrests have ever been made for nudity as part of a play or ballet."

Thus, the Indiana statute is not a *general* prohibition of the type we have upheld in prior cases. As a result, the plurality and JUSTICE SCALIA's simple references to the State's general interest in promoting societal order and morality is not sufficient justification for a statute which concededly reaches a significant amount of protected expressive activity. Instead, in applying the *O'Brien* test, we are obligated to carefully examine the reasons the State has chosen to regulate this expressive conduct in a less than general statute. In other words, when the State enacts a law which draws a line between expressive conduct which is regulated and nonexpressive conduct of the same type which is not regulated, *O'Brien* places the burden on the State to justify the distinctions it has made. Closer inquiry as to the purpose of the statute is surely appropriate.

Legislators do not just randomly select certain conduct for proscription; they have reasons for doing so and those reasons illuminate the purpose of the law that is passed. Indeed, a law may have multiple purposes. The purpose of forbidding people from appearing nude in parks, beaches, hot dog stands, and like public places is to protect others from offense. But that could not possibly be the purpose of preventing nude dancing in theaters and barrooms since the viewers are exclusively consenting adults who pay money to see these dances. The purpose of the proscription in these contexts is to protect the viewers from what the State believes is the harmful message that nude dancing communicates. This is why *Clark v. Community for Creative Non-Violence* (1984), is of no help to the State: "In *Clark* . . . the damage to the parks was the same whether the sleepers were camping out for fun, were in fact homeless, or wished by sleeping in the park to make a symbolic statement on behalf of the homeless." (Posner, J., concurring). That cannot be said in this case: The perceived damage to the public interest caused by appearing nude on the streets or in the parks, as I have said, is not what the State seeks to avoid in preventing nude dancing in theaters and taverns. There the perceived harm is the communicative aspect of the erotic dance. As the State now tells us, and as JUSTICE SOUTER agrees, the State's goal in applying what it describes as its "content neutral" statute to the nude dancing in this case is "deterrence of prostitution, sexual assaults, criminal activity, degradation of women, and other activities which break down family structure." The attainment of these goals, however, depends on preventing an expressive activity.

* * *

That the performances in the Kitty Kat Lounge may not be high art, to say the least, and may not appeal to the Court, is hardly an excuse for distorting and ignoring settled doctrine. The Court's assessment of the artistic merits of nude dancing performances should not be the determining factor in deciding this case. In the words of Justice Harlan: "[I]t is largely because governmental officials cannot make principled decisions in this area that the Constitution leaves matters of taste and style so largely to the individual." "[W]hile the entertainment afforded by a nude ballet at Lincoln Center to those who can pay the price may differ vastly in content (as viewed by judges) or in quality (as viewed by critics), it may not differ in substance from the dance viewed by the person who . . . wants some 'entertainment' with his beer or shot of rye."

The plurality and JUSTICE SOUTER do not go beyond saying that the state interests asserted here are important and substantial. But even if there were compelling interests, the Indiana statute is not narrowly drawn. If the State is genuinely concerned with prostitution and associated evils, as JUSTICE SOUTER seems to think, . . . it can adopt restrictions that do not interfere with the expressiveness of nonobscene nude dancing performances. For instance, the State could perhaps require that, while performing, nude performers remain at all times a certain minimum distance from spectators, that nude entertainment be limited to certain hours, or even that establishments providing such entertainment be dispersed throughout the city. Likewise, the State clearly has the authority to criminalize prostitution and obscene behavior. Banning an entire category of expressive activity, however, generally does not satisfy the narrow tailoring requirement of strict First Amendment scrutiny. Furthermore, if nude dancing in barrooms, as compared with other establishments, is the most worrisome problem, the State could invoke its Twenty-first Amendment powers and impose appropriate regulation.

* * *

JUSTICE SCALIA's views are similar to those of the plurality and suffer from the same defects. The Justice asserts that a general law barring specified conduct does not implicate the First Amendment unless the purpose of the law is to suppress the expressive quality of the forbidden conduct, and that, absent such purpose, First Amendment protections are not triggered simply because the incidental effect of the law is to proscribe conduct that is unquestionably expressive. The application of the Justice's proposition to this case is simple to state: The statute at issue is a general law banning nude appearances in public places, including barrooms and theaters. There is no showing that the purpose of this general law was to regulate expressive conduct; hence, the First Amendment is irrelevant and nude dancing in theaters and barrooms may be forbidden, irrespective of the expressiveness of the dancing.

As I have pointed out, however, the premise for the Justice's position — that the statute is a *general* law of the type our cases contemplate — is nonexistent in this case. Reference to JUSTICE SCALIA's own hypothetical makes this clear. We agree with JUSTICE SCALIA that the Indiana statute would not permit 60,000 consenting Hoosiers to expose themselves to each other in the Hoosier Dome. No one can doubt, however, that those same 60,000 Hoosiers would be perfectly free to drive to their respective homes all across Indiana and, once there, to parade around, cavort, and revel in the nude for hours in front of relatives and friends. It is difficult to see why the State's interest in morality is any less in that situation, especially if, as JUSTICE SCALIA seems to suggest, nudity is inherently evil, but clearly the statute does not reach such activity. As we pointed out earlier, the

State's failure to enact a truly general proscription requires closer scrutiny of the reasons for the distinctions the State has drawn.

As explained previously, the purpose of applying the law to the nude dancing performances in respondents' establishments is to prevent their customers from being exposed to the distinctive communicative aspects of nude dancing. That being the case, JUSTICE SCALIA's observation is fully applicable here: "Where the government prohibits conduct *precisely because of its communicative attributes*, we hold the regulation unconstitutional."

The *O'Brien* decision does not help JUSTICE SCALIA. Indeed, his position, like the Court's, would eviscerate the *O'Brien* test. *Employment Div., Dept. of Human Resources of Ore. v. Smith* (1990), is likewise not on point. The Indiana law, as applied to nude dancing, targets the expressive activity itself; in Indiana nudity in a dancing performance is a crime because of the message such dancing communicates. In *Smith*, the use of drugs was not criminal because the use was part of or occurred within the course of an otherwise protected religious ceremony, but because a general law made it so and was supported by the same interests in the religious context as in others.

Accordingly, I would affirm the judgment of the Court of Appeals, and dissent from this Court's judgment.

NOTES AND QUESTIONS

1. We learned in the *O'Brien* case that if there is a valid governmental purpose in legislation which regulates communicative acts in the interests of some other non-speech related goal, that legislation will not infringe the First Amendment if it is narrowly tailored to accomplish its goal and minimally restricts the speech protected by the First Amendment. Is nude dancing speech protected by the First Amendment? Is the legislation in question narrowly tailored? Prior to this case, as you will soon see, Justice Scalia joined with the majority in *Texas v. Johnson* (1989) to hold that flag-burning was speech protected by the First Amendment. Why doesn't he hold that nude dancing is similarly-protected speech? Is he discriminating on the basis of content?

2. Chief Justice Rehnquist apparently believed that the *O'Brien* test dictated that the statute be upheld. Why didn't Justice White agree? *O'Brien*, you will remember, indicated that under certain circumstances legislation which had the effect of curtailing speech could be upheld, particularly if the legislation was not actually targeted at the suppression of free expression. Why does Justice White believe that an act which generally prohibits public nudity "cannot be said [to be] unrelated to expressive conduct"? Is *Barnes* a case in which First Amendment doctrine is neutrally applied, or does it result from particular prejudices on the part of the majority?

3. In *Pap's A.M. v. City of Erie*, 719 A.2d 273 (Pa. 1998), *rev'd.*, 529 U.S. 277 (2000), the Pennsylvania Supreme Court struck down a public indecency ordinance as constitutionally overbroad. Although the Pennsylvania court agreed that Justice Souter's opinion in *Barnes* stood for the "narrowest grounds," that opinion, argued the state court, did not command the majority of the Court. Therefore, the Pennsylvania court found that *Barnes* offered no precedential effect aside from the agreement that nude dancing is entitled to some First Amendment protection. The court then independently determined that the public indecency ordinance acted to suppress constitutionally protected freedom of expression as there were other more narrowly tailored means to curb adverse secondary effects while not infringing on what the state judges to be freedom of expression protected by the First Amendment.

In reversing, the Supreme Court reaffirmed *Barnes*, but again without a clear majority favoring a single rationale. A majority did accept, however, that Erie's ordinance was a content-neutral regulation that satisfies the four-part test of *United States v. O'Brien*, (1968). Explained Justice O'Connor:

> The ordinance here, like the statute in *Barnes*, is on its face a general prohibition on public nudity. By its terms, the ordinance regulates conduct alone. It does not target nudity that contains an erotic message; rather, it bans all public nudity, regardless of whether that nudity is accompanied by expressive activity. And like the statute in *Barnes*, the Erie ordinance replaces and updates provisions of an "Indecency and Immorality" ordinance that has been on the books since 1866, predating the prevalence of nude dancing establishments such as Kandyland.

* * *

> . . . The ordinance prohibiting public nudity is aimed at combating crime and other negative secondary effects caused by the presence of adult entertainment establishments like Kandyland and not at suppressing the erotic message conveyed by this type of nude dancing. Put another way, the ordinance does not attempt to regulate the primary effects of the expression, i.e., the effect on the audience of watching nude erotic dancing, but rather the secondary effects, such as the impacts on public health, safety, and welfare, which we have previously recognized are "caused by the presence of even one such" establishment.

In meeting the *O'Brien* standard, Justice O'Connor indicated that the city need not "conduct new studies or produce evidence independent of that already generated by other cities" to demonstrate the problem of secondary effects, "so long as whatever evidence the city relies upon is reasonably believed to be relevant to the problem that the city addresses." Because the nude dancing at Kandyland is of the same character as the adult entertainment at issue in *Renton, Young v. American Mini Theatres, Inc.* (1976) (see Note 4 below), it was reasonable for Erie to conclude that such nude dancing was likely to produce the same secondary effects. And Erie could reasonably rely on the evidentiary foundation set forth in *Renton* and *American Mini Theatres* to the effect that secondary effects are caused by the presence of even one adult entertainment establishment in a given neighborhood.

The Pennsylvania Supreme Court did correctly perceive Justice Souter to be ambivalent in *Barnes*, but his ambivalence made no difference to the outcome. In *Pap's*, Justice Souter attempted to disavow his opinion in *Barnes* at least to the extent of requiring greater empirical evidence of secondary effect. The Court disagreed saying bluntly: the evidentiary standard described in *Renton* controls here, and Erie meets that standard.

Justice Scalia repeated his view from *Barnes* (but now shared by Justice Thomas) that when conduct other than speech itself is regulated, the First Amendment is violated only "[w]here the government prohibits conduct precisely because of its communicative attributes." Here, said Justice Scalia, even if one hypothesizes that the city's object was to suppress only nude dancing, that would not establish an intent to suppress what (if anything) nude dancing communicates. Under the Scalia and Thomas view, the city would not be obligated to identify some "secondary effects" associated with nude dancing that the city could properly seek to eliminate since the traditional power of government to foster good morals has not been repealed by the First Amendment. *Bonos mores,* and the acceptability of the traditional judgment (if Erie wishes to endorse it) that nude public dancing itself is immoral, have not been repealed by the First Amendment.

Justices Stevens and Ginsburg dissented. They would have confined the secondary effects rationale to the regulation of the location of adult establishments. Moreover, claim the dissenters, "Nude dancing fits well within a broad, cultural tradition recognized as expressive in nature and entitled to First Amendment protection. The nudity of the dancer is both a component of the protected expression and the specific target of the ordinance. It is pure sophistry to reason from the premise that the regulation of the nudity component of nude dancing is unrelated to the message conveyed by nude dancers . . . ."

4. Apart from a community's ability to preclude public nudity, as *Barnes* allows, laws may also prohibit obscenity. Obscenity has been declared by the Court to be a category of speech that is unprotected by the First Amendment. *Roth v. United States*, 354 U.S. 476 (1957). As a general matter, obscenity laws reflect the obvious desire of a community to set minimum standards of civil behavior. In addition, there is some evidence that exposure to obscene or violent pornographic material increases a willingness to undertake such dysfunctional conduct. *See generally* Report of the Attorney General's Commission on Pornography (1986). As Professor Catherine MacKinnon has argued, "[r]ecent experimental research on pornography shows that . . . exposure to [it] increases normal men's immediately subsequent willingness to aggress against women under laboratory conditions. . . . It also significantly increases attitudinal measures known to correlate with rape." Catherine R. MacKinnon, *Pornography,*

Civil Rights, and Speech, 20 HARV. C.R.-C.L. L. REV. 1, 52, 54 (1985). Professor Fred Schauer argues that pornographic material is less speech (a mental exercise), than a rather blatant physical stimulus. Frederick Schauer, *Speech and "Speech" — Obscenity and "Obscenity": An Exercise in the Interpretation of Constitutional Language,* 67 GEO. L.J. 899, 922 (1979).

In *Miller v. California,* 413 U.S. 15 (1973), the Court defined obscenity as material that (1) the average person would find "taken as a whole, appeals to the prurient interest"; (2) describes or depicts, "in a patently offensive way, sexual conduct specifically defined by state law"; and (3) "as a whole, lacks serious literary, artistic, political or scientific value." *Id.* at 24. The first two issues of fact are determined in relation to local community standards, allowing the religious and moral standards of different communities to be reflected in a healthy federalist sense. The third issue is determined by a national standard — that is, how a given work would be evaluated as a literary document, etc. across the entire country. *Pope v. Illinois,* 481 U.S. 497 (1987). Something that is "prurient" is said to be that which reflects a shameful or morbid, rather than a normal, interest in sex. Patently offensive representations can be differently defined from state to state, but the Court in *Miller* suggested by way of example normal or perverted sexual acts whether real or simulated and masturbation, excretory functions and lewd exhibition of the genitals.

This description of obscenity may well not include a variety of other sexually explicit materials. For this reason, some commentators argue that a broader class of pornography simply be recognized as demeaning and discriminatory toward women. Professor MacKinnon proposes an ordinance, for example, that would outlaw portraying women as "sexual objects." A federal court of appeals rejected this approach, *American Booksellers Assn., Inc. v. Hudnut,* 771 F.2d 323 (7th Cir. 1985) (describing the MacKinnon ordinance in more detail), but one can certainly appreciate how pornography generally diminishes the human person in the natural law sense and thus would historically be well outside the First Amendment as envisioned by the founders. For a different view see Nadine Strossen, *Hate Speech and Pornography: Do We Have to Choose Between Freedom of Speech and Equality?,* 46 CASE W. RES. L. REV. 449 (1996) (outlining the traditional approach to hate speech and pornography and arguing that the censorship of these forms of speech would not foster equality for targeted groups, but could actually undermine it).

The Court does allow non-obscene pornographic material to be addressed in another way. In particular, local governments may use land use controls such as zoning to regulate the location of adult theaters and bookstores. *Young v. American Mini-Theaters, Inc.,* 427 U.S. 50 (1976) (keeping these uses away from residential areas). The Court posits that such regulation is not directed at content, but the secondary effects of such uses in terms of crime and urban blight. *City of Renton v. Playtime Theaters, Inc.,* 475 U.S. 41 (1986) (upholding the exclusion of pornographic uses from roughly 95 percent of the land area of the city); *City of Los Angeles v. Alameda Books, Inc.*, 535 U.S. 425 (2002) (upholding ordinance banning multiple adult uses in a single building).

Efforts to zone out pornographic speech from the internet have been less successful, and presently the information superhighway is littered with what many would find to be denigrating depictions and descriptions of both men and women. *Reno v. American Civil Liberties Union*, 521 U.S. 844 (1997) (invalidating provisions of the federal Communications Decency Act that punished knowingly making an indecent communication to a person under the age of 18). The Court had previously upheld laws that criminalized the sale of pornographic materials, like *Playboy*, to children, *Ginsberg v. New York*, 390 U.S. 629 (1968), and in *FCC v. Pacifica Foundation*, 438 U.S. 736 (1978), sustained a ban on indecent speech over the airwaves except late at night when children would normally be expected to be asleep. The Court reasoned that the internet was less invasive than broadcasting, and theoretically, more controllable by parents and others. The Court also found that the use of the terms "patently offensive" or "indecent" was too vague. Fundamentally, however, there was no practicable way for the supplier of information to the internet to know in many circumstances if the recipient of that information was a minor. Thus, the law was also held to be overbroad, suppressing speech that adults are entitled to receive, whether it is harmful to them or not.

Congress attempted to address the Court's concerns with the Child Online Protection Act. Unlike the Communications Decency Act invalidated in *Reno*, COPA applies only to material displayed on the World Wide Web, covers only communications made for commercial purposes, and restricts only "material that is harmful to minors," defined by drawing on the three-part obscenity test in *Miller*. The Third Circuit held that COPA's use of the *Miller* "contemporary community standard" test was unconstitutionally overbroad in the context of the internet, but the Supreme Court disagreed, holding in a split decision in *Ashcroft v. American Civil Liberties Union*, 535 U.S. 564 (2002), that COPA's reliance on contemporary community standards — which by definition vary from community to community — did not itself render the statute substantially overbroad. The Court remanded for further consideration by the lower courts, which again enjoined the statute on the supposition that COPA was not the least restrictive means to protect minors from this material. In *Ashcroft v. American Civil Liberties Union (II)*, 2004 U.S. LEXIS 4762, the Court, 5-4, affirmed. Admitting that the constitutional question was a close one, the majority opinion per Justice Kennedy held that it was not an abuse of discretion for the lower court to preliminarily enjoin the statute. In the context of a content-based restriction, the government must prove that proposed alternatives are not as effective as the challenged statute. The Court believed that filtering devices available to parents were likely better alternatives, since they would block all pornography, not just the estimated sixty percent or so originating from the United States. Nominally, the case will now go to trial on whether filtering is in fact as effective as believed. A strongly worded dissent written by Justice Breyer, and joined by the Chief Justice and Justice O'Connor, and supported by Justice Scalia who separately dissented, pointed out that filtering had worse problems — over- and under-blocking sites, cost, and in terms of the overall government interest of protecting minors, was far less effective, since children could access the Internet from multiple, unfiltered locations. Pointing out that COPA regulates the obscene or near obscene and that COPA does not censor the material but only requires it to be placed behind age verification screens, the dissent found the statute to achieve the compelling congressional goal with a modest burden on protected speech. "After eight years of legislative effort, two statutes, and three Supreme Court cases, the Court sent the case back to the District Court for further proceedings. What proceedings? . . . What remains to be litigated."

Finally, the Court has allowed the prohibition, sale, or distribution of child pornography even if it does not meet the *Miller* test for obscenity. *New York v. Ferber*, 458 U.S. 747 (1982). The Court had little difficulty recognizing that the use of children "as subjects of pornographic materials is harmful to the physiological, emotional, and mental health of the child." *Id.* at 757-58. It is, said the Court, while nigh equivalent to child abuse. But the Court drew the line at "virtual" child pornography — pornography that uses computer-generated images of children or youthful-looking adults rather than actual children. Justice Kennedy, writing for five members of the Court in *Ashcroft v. Free Speech Coalition,* claimed that, as written, the "virtual porn" provisions of the Child Pornography Prevention Act of 1996 prohibited a substantial amount of lawful speech (including, according to Justice Kennedy, Shakespeare's Romeo and Juliet, and the recent Academy Award-winning films Traffic and American Beauty) and were thus unconstitutionally overbroad. Justice Thomas concurred in the judgment, leaving open the possibility that advances in technology might well require government to ban virtual child pornography in order to enforce laws against actual child pornography effectively. Justice O'Connor, dissenting in part, would have upheld the ban on computer-generated child pornography but not the ban on youthful-looking adult pornography. Chief Justice Rehnquist, joined by Justice Scalia, also dissented, contending that the statute was constitutional with a reasonable narrowing construction.

5. In *United States v. Playboy Entertainment Group, Inc.*, 529 U.S. 803 (2000), Justice Kennedy writing for the Court invalidated § 505 of the Telecommunications Act of 1996, which required cable television operators who provide channels "primarily dedicated to sexually-oriented programming" either to "fully scramble or otherwise fully block" those channels or to limit their transmission to hours when children are unlikely to be viewing, set by administrative regulation as the time between 10 p.m. and 6 a.m. The purpose of § 505 was to shield children from hearing or seeing images resulting from signal bleed. All parties to the case assumed Playboy's programming not to be obscene. However, since § 505 is a content-based speech restriction, it could stand only if it satisfied strict scrutiny. *Sable Communications of Cal., Inc. v. FCC* (1989). If a statute regulates speech based on its content, it must be narrowly tailored to promote a compelling Government interest. If a less restrictive alternative would serve the Government's purpose, the legislature must use that alternative.

Justice Kennedy found that less restrictive alternative in § 504, which requires cable operators to block undesired channels at individual households upon request. It was the government's obligation to prove that this was ineffective, and it failed to meet that burden to the majority's satisfaction. The Government failed to establish a pervasive, nationwide problem justifying its nationwide daytime speech ban, concluded the majority.

Justice Breyer wrote in dissent for himself and the Chief Justice and Justices O'Connor and Scalia. He started out by noting that the Court has recognized that material the First Amendment guarantees adults the right to see may not be suitable for children. And it has consequently held that legislatures maintain a limited power to protect children by restricting access to, but not banning, adult material. *Compare Ginsberg v. New York* (1968) (upholding ban on sale of pornographic magazines to minors), *with Butler v. Michigan* (1957) (invalidating ban on all books unfit for minors). Moreover, the case concerned only the regulation of commercial actors who broadcast "virtually 100% sexually explicit" material. The channels do not broadcast more than trivial amounts of more serious material such as birth control information, artistic images, or the visual equivalents of classical or serious literature. This case therefore does not present the kind of narrow tailoring concerns seen in other cases. *See, e.g., Reno* [and the consideration of an Indecency limitation applied to the Internet] ("The breadth of the [statute's] coverage is wholly unprecedented . . . . [It] covers] large amounts of non-pornographic material with serious educational or other value").

The dissent thought the majority "flat-out wrong" on the facts. 29 million children are potentially exposed to audio and video bleed from adult programming. Unlike the majority, the dissent thought that § 504's opt-out was not a similarly effective alternative. The opt-out mechanism is less effective because it fails to inhibit the transmission of adult cable channels to children whose parents may be unaware of what they are watching, whose parents cannot easily supervise television viewing habits, whose parents do not know of their § 504 "opt-out" rights, or whose parents are simply unavailable at critical times. In this respect, § 505 serves the same interests as the laws that deny children access to adult cabarets or X-rated movies. These laws, and § 505, all act in the absence of direct parental supervision. Wrote Justice Breyer:

> This legislative objective is perfectly legitimate. Where over 28 million school age children have both parents or their only parent in the work force, where at least 5 million children are left alone at home without supervision each week, and where children may spend afternoons and evenings watching television outside of the home with friends, § 505 offers independent protection for a large number of families. I could not disagree more when the majority implies that the Government's independent interest in offering such protection — preventing, say, an 8-year-old child from watching virulent pornography without parental consent — might not be "compelling." No previous case in which the protection of children was at issue has suggested any such thing. They

make clear that Government has a compelling interest in helping parents by preventing minors from accessing sexually explicit materials in the absence of parental supervision. *See Ginsberg, supra.*

Justice Thomas concurred in the judgment, but reminded the government that it might well pursue blocking this material as obscene in the future. Though perhaps not all of the programming at issue in the case is obscene as this Court defined the term in *Miller v. California* (1973), one could fairly conclude that, under the standards applicable in many communities, some of the programming meets the *Miller* test, he said.

As part of the dissent, Justice Scalia took a different tack. He agreed with Justice Breyer and the principal dissent, but would have sustained § 505 simply as a regulation of the business of obscenity. Even if not all of the material is obscene under *Miller*, Justice Scalia pointed out that the Court had previously recognized that commercial entities which engage in "the sordid business of pandering" by "deliberately emphasi[zing] the sexually provocative aspects of [their nonobscene products], in order to catch the salaciously disposed," engage in constitutionally unprotected behavior. *Ginzburg v. United States* (1966). "We are more permissive of government regulation in these circumstances because it is clear from the context in which exchanges between such businesses and their customers occur that neither the merchant nor the buyer is interested in the work's literary, artistic, political, or scientific value. . . . The deliberate representation of petitioner's publications as erotically arousing . . . stimulate[s] the reader to accept them as prurient; he looks for titillation, not for saving intellectual content." Section 505 was just this sort of business.

Playboy's advertisements reveal its status as commercial pornographer, said Justice Scalia, calling on viewers to "Enjoy the sexiest, hottest adult movies in the privacy of your own home." "Thus, while I agree with Justice BREYER's child-protection analysis, it leaves me with the same feeling of true-but-inadequate as the conclusion that Al Capone did not accurately report his income. It is not only children who can be protected from occasional uninvited exposure to what appellee calls 'adult-oriented programming'; we can all be."

Justice Scalia concluded that since the Government is entirely free to block these transmissions, it may certainly take the less drastic step of dictating how, and during what times, they may occur. Justice Stevens, in a separate concurrence, disagreed, reasoning that what Justice Scalia was proposing was a regulation of commercial speech based on *Ginzburg*, which pre-dated the Court opinions extending greater protection to commercial speech.

6. Regardless of whether one sides with Justice Kennedy or Breyer in the disposition of the *Playboy* case, Justice Kennedy's majority opinion contained the following interesting observation for students of free speech doctrine:

> When a student first encounters our free speech jurisprudence, he or she might think it is influenced by the philosophy that one idea is as good as any other, and that in art and literature objective standards of style,

taste, decorum, beauty, and esthetics are deemed by the Constitution to be inappropriate, indeed unattainable. Quite the opposite is true. The Constitution no more enforces a relativistic philosophy or moral nihilism than it does any other point of view. The Constitution exists precisely so that opinions and judgments, including esthetic and moral judgments about art and literature, can be formed, tested, and expressed. What the Constitution says is that these judgments are for the individual to make, not for the Government to decree, even with the mandate or approval of a majority. Technology expands the capacity to choose; and it denies the potential of this revolution if we assume the Government is best positioned to make these choices for us.

Does this sentiment suggest that there are objective standards, perhaps even standards anchored in the natural law, by which artistic expression can be measured? Do you believe that one can fairly call pornographic material demeaning to the human body and spirit? If you do, should there be a role for the government where young children are likely to be unsupervised and exposed to material that may be psychologically harmful or denigrating, especially in its portrayal of women? Or is freedom so important that no government role can be trusted to stay benign and free from the inclination toward censorship? Is freedom a good in itself, or is what we value the freedom to do good?

d. Expressions of Hate

WISCONSIN v. MITCHELL
508 U.S. 476 (1993)

CHIEF JUSTICE REHNQUIST delivered the opinion of the Court.

Respondent Todd Mitchell's sentence for aggravated battery was enhanced because he intentionally selected his victim on account of the victim's race. The question presented in this case is whether this penalty enhancement is prohibited by the First and Fourteenth Amendments. We hold that it is not.

On the evening of October 7, 1989, a group of young black men and boys, including Mitchell, gathered at an apartment complex in Kenosha, Wisconsin. Several members of the group discussed a scene from the motion picture "Mississippi Burning," in which a white man beat a young black boy who was praying. The group moved outside and Mitchell asked them: "'Do you all feel hyped up to move on some white people?'" Shortly thereafter, a young white boy approached the group on the opposite side of the street where they were standing. As the boy walked by, Mitchell said: "'You all want to fuck somebody up? There goes a white boy; go get him.'" Mitchell counted to three and pointed in the boy's direction. The group ran toward the boy, beat him severely, and stole his tennis shoes. The boy was rendered unconscious and remained in a coma for four days.

After a jury trial in the Circuit Court for Kenosha County, Mitchell was convicted of aggravated battery. That offense ordinarily carries a maximum sentence of two years' imprisonment. But because the jury found that Mitchell had intentionally selected his victim because of the boy's race, the maximum sentence for Mitchell's offense was increased to seven years. . . . That provision [of Wisconsin's criminal statutes] enhances the maximum penalty for an offense whenever the defendant "[i]ntentionally selects the person against whom the crime . . . is committed . . . because of the race, religion, color, disability, sexual orientation, national origin or ancestry of that person . . . ." The Circuit Court sentenced Mitchell to four years' imprisonment for the aggravated battery.

Mitchell . . . appealed his conviction and sentence, challenging the constitutionality of Wisconsin's penalty-enhancement provision on First Amendment grounds. The Wisconsin Court of Appeals rejected Mitchell's challenge, but the Wisconsin Supreme Court reversed. The Supreme Court held that the statute "violates the First Amendment directly by punishing what the legislature has deemed to be offensive thought." It rejected the State's contention "that the statute punishes only the 'conduct' of intentional selection of a victim." According to the court, "[t]he statute punishes the 'because of' aspect of the defendant's selection, the *reason* the defendant selected the victim, the *motive* behind the selection." And under *R.A.V. v. St. Paul* (1992), "the Wisconsin legislature cannot criminalize bigoted thought with which it disagrees."

The Supreme Court also held that the penalty-enhancement statute was unconstitutionally overbroad. It reasoned that, in order to prove that a defendant intentionally selected his victim because of the victim's protected status, the State would often have to introduce evidence of the defendant's prior speech, such as racial epithets he may have uttered before the commission of the offense. This evidentiary use of protected speech, the court thought, would have a "chilling effect" on those who feared the possibility of prosecution for offenses subject to penalty enhancement. Finally, the court distinguished antidiscrimination laws, which have long been held constitutional, on the ground that the Wisconsin statute punishes the "subjective mental process" of selecting a victim because of his protected status, whereas antidiscrimination laws prohibit "objective acts of discrimination."

* * *

Mitchell argues that we are bound by the Wisconsin Supreme Court's conclusion that the statute punishes bigoted thought and not conduct. There is no doubt that we are bound by a state court's construction of a state statute. . . . But here the Wisconsin Supreme Court did not, strictly speaking, construe the Wisconsin statute in the sense of defining the meaning of a particular statutory word or phrase. Rather, it merely characterized the "practical effect" of the statute for First Amendment purposes. This assessment does not bind us. Once any ambiguities as to the meaning of the statute are resolved, we may form our own judgment as to its operative effect.

The State argues that the statute does not punish bigoted thought, as the Supreme Court of Wisconsin said, but instead punishes only conduct. While this argument is literally correct, it does not dispose of Mitchell's First Amendment challenge. To be sure, our cases reject the "view that an apparently limitless variety of conduct can be labeled 'speech' whenever the person engaging in the conduct intends thereby to express an idea." *United States v. O'Brien*. Thus, a physical assault is not by any stretch of the imagination expressive conduct protected by the First Amendment.

But the fact remains that under the Wisconsin statute the same criminal conduct may be more heavily punished if the victim is selected because of his race or other protected status than if no such motive obtained. Thus, although the statute punishes criminal conduct, it enhances the maximum penalty for conduct motivated by a discriminatory point of view more severely than the same conduct engaged in for some other reason or for no reason at all. Because the only reason for the enhancement is the defendant's discriminatory motive for selecting his victim, Mitchell argues (and the Wisconsin Supreme Court held) that the statute violates the First Amendment by punishing offenders' bigoted beliefs.

Traditionally, sentencing judges have considered a wide variety of factors in addition to evidence bearing on guilt in determining what sentence to impose on a convicted defendant. The defendant's motive for committing the offense is one important factor. . . . Thus, in many States the commission of a murder, or other capital offense, for pecuniary gain is a separate aggravating circumstance under the capital sentencing statute.

But it is equally true that a defendant's abstract beliefs, however obnoxious to most people, may not be taken into consideration by a sentencing judge. *Dawson v. Delaware* (1992). In *Dawson*, the State introduced evidence at a capital sentencing hearing that the defendant was a member of a white supremacist prison gang. Because "the evidence proved nothing more than [the defendant's] abstract beliefs," we held that its admission violated the defendant's First Amendment rights. In so holding, however, we emphasized that "the Constitution does not erect a *per se* barrier to the admission of evidence concerning one's beliefs and associations at sentencing simply because those beliefs and associations are protected by the First Amendment." Thus, in *Barclay v. Florida* (1983) (plurality opinion), we allowed the sentencing judge to take into account the defendant's racial animus towards his victim. The evidence in that case showed that the defendant's membership in the Black Liberation Army and desire to provoke a "race war" were related to the murder of a white man for which he was convicted. Because "the elements of racial hatred in [the] murder" were relevant to several aggravating factors, we held that the trial judge permissibly took this evidence into account in sentencing the defendant to death.

Mitchell suggests that *Dawson* and *Barclay* are inapposite because they did not involve application of a penalty-enhancement provision. But in *Barclay* we held that it was permissible for the sentencing court to consider the defendant's racial animus in determining whether he should be sentenced to death, surely the most severe "enhancement" of all. And the fact that the Wisconsin Legislature has decided, as a general matter, that bias-motivated offenses warrant greater maximum penalties across the board does not alter the result here. For the primary responsibility for fixing criminal penalties lies with the legislature.

Mitchell argues that the Wisconsin penalty-enhancement statute is invalid because it punishes the defendant's discriminatory motive, or reason, for acting. But motive plays the same role under the Wisconsin statute as it does under federal and state antidiscrimination laws, which we have previously upheld against constitutional challenge. Title VII of the Civil Rights Act of 1964, for example, makes it unlawful for an employer to discriminate against an employee "*because of* such individual's race, color, religion, sex, or national origin." (emphasis added). . . . [W]e [have previously] rejected the argument that Title VII infringed employers' First Amendment rights. And more recently, in *R.A.V. v. St. Paul* we cited Title VII . . . as an example of a permissible content-neutral regulation of conduct.

Nothing in our decision last Term in *R.A.V.* compels a different result here. That case involved a First Amendment challenge to a municipal ordinance prohibiting the use of "'fighting words' that insult, or provoke violence, 'on the basis of race, color, creed, religion or gender.'" Because the ordinance only proscribed a class of "fighting words" deemed particularly offensive by the city — *i.e.*, those "that contain . . . messages of 'bias-motivated' hatred" — we held that it violated the rule against content-based discrimination. But whereas the ordinance struck down in *R.A.V.* was explicitly directed at expression (*i.e.*, "speech" or "messages"), the statute in this case is aimed at conduct unprotected by the First Amendment.

Moreover, the Wisconsin statute singles out for enhancement bias-inspired conduct because this conduct is thought to inflict greater individual and societal harm. For example, according to the State and its *amici*, bias-motivated crimes are more likely to provoke retaliatory crimes, inflict distinct emotional harms on their victims, and incite community unrest. The State's desire to redress these perceived harms provides an adequate explanation for its penalty-enhancement provision over and above mere disagreement with offenders' beliefs or biases. As Blackstone said long ago, "it is but reasonable that among crimes of different natures those should be most severely punished, which are the most destructive of the public safety and happiness." 4 W. BLACKSTONE, COMMENTARIES *16.

Finally, there remains to be considered Mitchell's argument that the Wisconsin statute is unconstitutionally overbroad because of its "chilling effect" on free speech. Mitchell argues (and the Wisconsin Supreme Court agreed) that the statute is "overbroad" because evidence of the defendant's prior speech or associations may be used to prove that the defendant intentionally selected his victim on account of the victim's protected status. Consequently, the argument goes, the statute impermissibly chills free expression with respect to such matters by those concerned about the possibility of enhanced sentences if they should in the future commit a criminal offense covered by the statute. We find no merit in this contention.

The sort of chill envisioned here is far more attenuated and unlikely than that contemplated in traditional "over-breadth" cases. We must conjure up a vision of a Wisconsin citizen suppressing his unpopular bigoted opinions for fear that if he later commits an offense covered by the statute, these opinions will be offered at trial to establish that he selected his victim on account of the victim's protected status, thus qualifying him for penalty enhancement. To stay within the realm of rationality, we must surely put to one side minor misdemeanor offenses covered by the statute, such as negligent operation of a motor vehicle; for it is difficult, if not impossible, to conceive of a situation where such offenses would be racially motivated. We are left, then, with the prospect of a citizen suppressing his bigoted beliefs for fear that evidence of such beliefs will be introduced against him at trial if he commits a more serious offense against person or property. This is simply too speculative a hypothesis to support Mitchell's overbreadth claim.

The First Amendment, moreover, does not prohibit the evidentiary use of speech to establish the elements of a crime or to prove motive or intent. Evidence of a defendant's previous declarations or statements is commonly admitted in criminal trials subject to evidentiary rules dealing with relevancy, reliability, and the like. Nearly half a century ago, in *Haupt v. United States* (1947), we rejected a contention similar to that advanced by Mitchell here. Haupt was tried for the offense of treason, which, as defined by the Constitution (Art. III, § 3), may depend very much on proof of motive. To prove that the acts in question were committed out of "adherence to the enemy" rather than "parental solicitude," the Government introduced evidence of conversations that had taken place long prior to the indictment, some of which consisted of statements showing Haupt's sympathy with Germany and Hitler and hostility towards the United States. We rejected Haupt's argument that this evidence was improperly admitted. While "[s]uch testimony is to be scrutinized with care to be certain the statements are not expressions of mere lawful and permissible difference of opinion with our own government or quite proper appreciation of the land of birth," we held that "these statements . . . clearly were admissible on the question of intent and adherence to the enemy."

For the foregoing reasons, we hold that Mitchell's First Amendment rights were not violated by the application of the Wisconsin penalty-enhancement provision in sentencing him. The judgment of the Supreme Court of Wisconsin is therefore reversed, and the case is remanded for further proceedings not inconsistent with this opinion.

NOTES AND QUESTIONS

1. We know that there is no proposition more central to the Court's First Amendment thinking than that the government may not favor certain types of speech over others based on the content of the message they advance. For example, the government clearly would not be permitted to outlaw one particular view about racial issues confronting American society. This attitude on the part of the courts not only led to the *R.A.V.* decision discussed in Chief Justice Rehnquist's opinion, but also has led to the declaring unconstitutional so-called "campus speech codes," which penalize racially derogatory or sexually suggestive remarks. This is done pursuant to classic First Amendment theory, especially that put forward by Brandeis and Holmes, that the best remedy for speech you dislike is more speech, *see Whitney v. California*, 274 U.S. 357, 377 (1927) (Brandeis, J., concurring); or the equally classic notion that freedom of speech, in order to be effective, must include freedom for the ideas you hate as well as those you love. Why then, is Wisconsin permitted to punish crimes more severely when they are motivated by beliefs the expression of which would be protected under the First Amendment? Why is this not content discrimination of a kind that is unconstitutional?

2. Why were there no dissenters in the case? Could the reason have something to do with the particular species of hate crime of which the defendant was guilty? *New York Times v. Sullivan* may have been influenced by contemporary civil rights struggles, particularly of Blacks in the South. Is something similar (or different) at work in *Wisconsin v. Mitchell*?

3. There are a number of categories of speech that are described as unprotected — the advocacy of illegal activity, fighting words, and obscenity. Obscenity is discussed in the note following the *Barnes v. Glen Theatre* case elsewhere in this Chapter. We take up illegal activity and fighting words here. The categories of unprotected speech reflect the view of the Court that these forms of speech add very little, if anything, to a correct understanding of human nature or political discussion. *See generally*, Robert Bork, *Neutral Principles and Some First Amendment Problems*, 47 IND. L.J. 1, 31 (1971). Much of the law of illegal activity is traceable to war time or times of social unrest. During World War I, Congress passed the Espionage Act of 1917, which made it a crime to promote the success of the enemies of the United States. The Sedition Act of 1918 prohibited individuals from saying or writing anything that was intended to cause contempt for the government of the United States. The Court upheld both acts. For example, in *Schenck v. United States*, 249 U.S. 17 (1919), the Court sustained the convictions of those who had circulated a leaflet against the draft. Writing for the Court, Justice Holmes articulated the view that the place and the times have much to do with the successful prosecution. Said Holmes:

> [T]he character of every act depends upon the circumstance in which it is done. The most stringent protection of free speech would not protect a man in falsely shouting fire in a theatre, and causing a panic. . . . The

question in every case is whether the words used are used in such circumstances and are of such a nature as to create a clear and present danger that they will bring about the substantive evils that Congress has a right to prevent.

Id. at 52.

The clear and present danger test for illegal advocacy has not always been consistently applied. In the 1950s during the so-called "red scare," when there were efforts to identify and remove any communist influence in government, the Court sustained the Smith Act in *Dennis v. United States*, 341 U.S. 494 (1951). The Smith Act made it a crime to knowingly or willfully advocate the necessity or desirability "of overthrowing or destroying any government in the United States by force or violence, or by the assassination of any officer of any such government." Act of June 28, 1940, 54 Stat. 670, 671. Writing for a Court plurality, Chief Justice Vinson said that the clear and present danger test was to be understood in light of a formula articulated by a well-regarded lower court judge, Learned Hand, namely, that "[i]n each case [courts] must ask whether the gravity of the 'evil,' discounted by its improbability, justifies such invasion of free speech as is necessary to avoid the danger." 341 U.S. at 570. Obviously under that formulation, the supposed danger need not be "clear and present" if it is great enough. Somewhat later in this period, the clear and present danger test was again refined to draw a distinction between "advocacy of abstract doctrine and advocacy directed at promoting unlawful action." *Yates v. United States*, 354 U.S. 298, 318 (1957) (overturning convictions under the Smith Act, and distinguishing *Dennis*). In order for advocacy to be punished, said the Court, there must be an urging to "*do* something, now or in the future, rather than merely to *believe* in something." *Id.* at 324-25 (emphasis in the original).

The view in *Yates* ultimately crystallized in *Brandenburg v. Ohio*, 395 U.S. 444 (1966), where the Court was of the view that only where advocacy is directed and intended toward "inciting or producing imminent lawless action and is likely to incite or produce such action," may it be punished. *Id.* at 447. *Brandenburg* remains the key test in the illegal advocacy area, though it does not make clear whether risk is to be measured in relation to the gravity of the harm. *Brandenburg* was applied in *Hess v. Indiana*, 414 U.S. 105 (1973), where the Court overturned the conviction of an anti-war protestor for declaring "We'll take the f------g street later." Under *Brandenburg*, the Court found no evidence that there was a likelihood of imminent disruption of the peace. Similarly, in *NAACP v. Claiborne Hardware Co.*, 458 U.S. 886 (1982), the Court reversed a judgment against an NAACP official (Charles Evers) who had threatened violence against anyone not observing a boycott against white businesses. This was mere advocacy of violence, not proof of the likelihood of imminent illegal conduct and intent to cause such conduct.

4. Fighting words is defined under the few Court decisions to consider it as speech that is directed at another that is likely to provoke a violent response. The notion originated with *Chaplinsky v. New Hampshire*, 315 U.S. 568, 569

(1942) (upholding the conviction of a speaker for speech that does not seem to meet the Court's own definition — *e.g.*, "You are a God damned racketeer" and a "damned Facist and the whole government of Rochester are Fascists or agents of Fascists.") They would have to be awfully thin-skinned Fascists for that feeble statement to provoke a fight. Nevertheless, whether *Chaplinsky's* facts fit its test or not, the test is reasonably plain — speech directed at another, calculated to cause a violent response, and whose "very utterance inflict[s] injury or tend[s] to incite an immediate breach of the peace." *Id.* at 571-72. The importance that the fighting words being directed at a specific person was made plain in *Cohen v. California*, 403 U.S. 15 (1971), where a disturbing the peace conviction was overturned for the wearing of a jacket with the words "F—k the Draft" on its back. Obviously, the uncivil language was not directed at anyone in particular.

The *Chaplinsky* "fighting words" doctrine has been examined closely in recent years to see if it can sustain codes against hate speech. In *R.A.V. v. City of St. Paul*, 505 U.S. 377 (1992), the Court invalidated a criminal prohibition for placing, among other things, a burning cross or Nazi swastika, where the person doing so could reasonably know it would arouse "anger, alarm or resentment in others on the basis of race, color, creed, religion or gender." *Id.* at 380. The Court held that to describe a category of speech as unprotected means that it is subject to regulation because of its constitutionally proscribable content, but not that it is "entirely invisible to the First Amendment so that [it] may be made the vehicl[e] for content discrimination unrelated to [its] distinctly proscribable content. Thus, the government may proscribe libel; but it may not make the further content discrimination of proscribing only libel critical of the government." *Id.* at 383-84.

The *R.A.V.* case makes it difficult, if not impossible, for public colleges and universities to promulgate campus codes against hate speech. It also raises questions about "hostile work environment" claims. *See* Eugene Volokh, *What Speech Does "Hostile Work Environment" Harassment Law Restrict?*, 85 GEO. L.J. 627 (1997) (arguing that "hostile work environment" harassment law is overly suppressive of speech because it draws no distinction among differing forms of speech and defines itself with vague terms that have been interpreted broadly); Jules B. Gerard, *The First Amendment in a Hostile Environment: A Primer on Free Speech and Sexual Harassment*, 68 NOTRE DAME L. REV. 1003 (1993) (suggesting that federal regulations under Title VII's sexual discrimination prohibitions are overly broad and are misapplied to situations where constitutionally protected speech is the sole basis for establishing a sexually hostile environment). Generally, campus codes and anti-harrassment rules may only prohibit certain categories of speech, and thus, under *R.A.V.*, present an impermissible content line. When the categories are broadened to include more generalized expressions of hate, a challenge can be brought on vagueness or overbreadth grounds.

In *Virginia v. Black*, 538 U.S. 343 (2003), the Court held, per Justice O'Connor, that a state may, consistent with the First Amendment, ban cross burning carried out with the intent to intimidate. A plurality of the Court found the aspect of the statute that characterized the burning, itself, as evidence of intimidation to be unconstitutional. Virginia's cross-burning statute made it a felony offense for any person or persons, with the intent of intimidating any person or group of persons, to burn a cross on the property of another, a highway, or another public place.

The majority noted that "[c]ross burning in the United States is inextricably intertwined with the history of the Ku Klux Klan." The Klan was responsible for "'a veritable reign of terror' throughout the South." It frequently employed tactics ranging from whipping to murder and it burned a cross to threaten such violence. Categorically, cross burning, said the Court, is a "symbol of hate." First Amendment protections, reasoned the Justices, are not absolute, and the states are permitted to prohibit "fighting words," "true threats," and speech directed at inciting imminent lawless action. "The First Amendment permits Virginia to outlaw cross burnings done with the intent to intimidate because burning a cross is a particularly virulent form of intimidation," Justice O'Connor wrote, in distinguishing the Court's previous decision in *R.A.V. v. St. Paul* (1992), which banned cross burning done with knowledge that such action would arouse alarm in others on the basis of race, color, creed, religion, or gender. Unlike the St. Paul ordinance that specified particular content for disfavor, the Virginia statute "does not single out for opprobrium only that speech directed toward 'one of the specified disfavored topics.'" Virginia can prohibit all forms of intimidation or a subset thereof. "[J]ust as a State may regulate only that obscenity which is the most obscene due to its prurient content, so too may a State choose to prohibit only those forms of intimidation that are most likely to inspire fear of bodily harm," the majority concluded. However, Virginia cannot presume intimidation from the burning, itself. It must be separately proven beyond a reasonable doubt. To allow the presumption, said the plurality, would "strip away the very reason why a State may ban cross burning with the intent to intimidate," Justice O'Connor stated. The provision makes no attempt to distinguish among the different motivations for cross burnings. By permitting the state to arrest, prosecute, and convict a person based solely on the fact of cross burning itself, the provision would create an unacceptable risk of the suppression of ideas, given the possibility that a state would prosecute and convict somebody engaging only in lawful political speech at the core of what the First Amendment is designed to protect, Justice O'Connor wrote. Justice Stevens filed a brief concurring opinion. Justice Scalia, joined in part by Justice Thomas, believed that there was no justification for the plurality's apparent decision to invalidate the statute's prima facie evidence provision on its face, but agreed that the Court should vacate and remand the Virginia Supreme Court's judgment so that the state court could have an opportunity authoritatively to construe its own law.

Three Justices, Souter, Kennedy and Ginsburg, would have invalidated the law in its entirety. The dissenters agreed hypothetically with the majority that the Virginia statute makes a content-based distinction within the category of punishable intimidating or threatening expression, "the very type of distinction

. . . considered [appropriate in *dicta*] in *R.A.V.*," but disagreed that this statute could be saved. The dissent thought the so-called virulence exception ill-fitting, since "the statute fits poorly with the illustrative examples given in *R.A.V.*, none of which involves communication generally associated with a particular message, and [thus] the majority's discussion of a special virulence exception here moves that exception toward a more flexible conception than the version" contemplated in the earlier case.

For example, wrote Justice Souter, *R.A.V.* had explained the special virulence exception to the rule barring content-based subclasses of categorically proscribable expression this way: prohibition by subcategory is nonetheless constitutional if it is made "entirely" on the "basis" of "the very reason" that "the entire class of speech at issue is proscribable" at all. This is okay since where the subcategory is confined to the most obviously proscribable instances, "no significant danger of idea or viewpoint discrimination exists."

Comparing examples from *R.A.V.*, Justice Souter noted that one permissible distinction is for a prohibition of particularly virulent obscenity, such as the difference between obscene depictions of actual people and simulations. Such a prohibition does not suggest a desire to suppress any particular message. Here, however, "the cross may have been selected because of its special power to threaten, but it may also have been singled out because of disapproval of its message of white supremacy, either because a legislature thought white supremacy was a pernicious doctrine or because it found that dramatic, public espousal of it was a civic embarrassment."

Justice Thomas, in a partial dissent, would not have applied the First Amendment at all to what he considered pure intimidation, rather than expressive conduct. He also thought that it was permissible to construe the presumption as merely permitting the jury to draw an inference of intent to intimidate from the cross burning itself.

5. In *Wisconsin v. Mitchell*, the Court considered and rejected the claim that the statute was unconstitutionally overbroad. Vagueness and overbreadth challenges are frequently brought together, though they need not be. A law is vague if it cannot be understood by a person of ordinary intelligence. The idea is to ensure that laws give adequate notice of what is expected and also to avoid selective prosecution. This is a special concern for the Court in the area of free speech. Thus, the Court invalidated a law that made it a crime to treat a flag "contemptuously," since the law failed to convey what type of behavior that terminology covered. *Smith v. Goguen*, 415 U.S. 566, 569 (1974). By comparison, overbreadth deals with a law that regulates *substantially* more speech than is allowed. An overbreadth challenge may be brought even by a person to whom the statute may be constitutionally applied. This is characterized by the Court as an exception to the usual standing principle that one may only raise one's own claims and not those of third parties. In *Schad v. Borough of Mt. Ephraim*, 452 U.S. 61 (1981), the Court invalidated a city ordinance that prohibited all live entertainment. The challenge was brought by an adult bookstore that had live nude dancers. In the *Barnes* case below, the Court finds nude dancing to be outside the protection of the First Amendment; nevertheless, in *Schad* the bookstore was allowed to raise the interests of a wide range of others who would be affected by the overbroad law, such as those seeking to run live sporting or theater events. A finding that a statute is vague or overbroad will render it void in all applications, and thus, a finding of either vagueness or overbreadth is viewed by the Court as "strong medicine." *Broadrick v. Oklahoma,* 413 U.S. 601, 613 (1973) (upholding an Oklahoma law that prohibited political activities by government employees). To avoid taking this medicine, the Court requires *substantial* overbreadth and will often try to construe a statute narrowly.

6. In *Los Angeles Police Department v. United Reporting Publishing Company,* 528 U.S. 32 (1999), the Court per Chief Justice Rehnquist refused to apply the overbreadth doctrine in a facial challenge to California Government Code § 6254(f)(3), which places two conditions on public access to arrestees' addresses — that the person requesting an address declare that the request is being made for one of five prescribed purposes, and that the requestor also declare that the address will not be used directly or indirectly to sell a product or service. United Reporting Publishing Corporation is a private publishing service that provides the names and addresses of recently arrested individuals to its customers, who include attorneys, insurance companies, drug and alcohol counselors, and driving schools. The Ninth Circuit had concluded that the statute restricted commercial speech, and while the government interest in privacy was substantial, the numerous exceptions to § 6254(f)(3) for journalistic, scholarly, political, governmental, and investigative purposes rendered the statute unconstitutional under the First Amendment.

The Court refused to apply the overbreadth doctrine because the traditional rule is that "a person to whom a statute may constitutionally be applied may not challenge that statute on the ground that it may conceivably be applied unconstitutionally to others in situations not before the Court." This traditional rule, said the Court, should only be set aside under the overbreadth doctrine "as a last resort." That was not true in *LAPD*, because the government was not prohibiting a speaker from conveying information that the speaker already possesses. *See Rubin v. Coors Brewing Co.* (1995). The California statute in question merely requires that if respondent wished to obtain the addresses of arrestees it must qualify under the statute to do so. Respondent did not attempt to qualify and was therefore denied access to the addresses. For purposes of assessing the propriety of a facial invalidation, the Court thus saw the case as little more than a governmental denial of access to information in its possession. California could decide not to give out arrestee information at all without violating the First Amendment. Concurring, Justice Ginsburg pointed out that California could not release address information only to those whose political views were in line with the party in power. But absent an illegitimate criterion such as viewpoint, California is free to support some speech without supporting other speech.

6. Special Contexts

a. Government Speech

RUST v. SULLIVAN
500 U.S. 173 (1991)

CHIEF JUSTICE REHNQUIST delivered the opinion of the Court.

* * *

I

A

In 1970, Congress enacted Title X of the Public Health Service Act (Act), which provides federal funding for family-planning services. The Act authorizes the Secretary to "make grants to and enter into contracts with public or non-profit private entities to assist in the establishment and operation of voluntary family planning projects which shall offer a broad range of acceptable and effective family planning methods and services." Grants and contracts under Title X must "be made in accordance with such regulations as the Secretary may promulgate." Section 1008 of the Act, however, provides that "[n]one of the funds appropriated under this subchapter shall be used in programs where abortion is a method of family planning." That restriction was intended to ensure that Title X funds would "be used only to support preventive family planning services, population research, infertility services, and other related medical, informational, and educational activities."

In 1988, the Secretary promulgated new regulations designed to provide "'clear and operational guidance' to grantees about how to preserve the distinction between Title X programs and abortion as a method of family planning." The regulations clarify, through the definition of the term "family planning," that Congress intended Title X funds "to be used only to support *preventive* family planning services." Accordingly, Title X services are limited to "preconceptional counseling, education, and general reproductive health care," and expressly exclude "pregnancy care (including obstetric or prenatal care)." The regulations "focus the emphasis of the Title X program on its traditional mission: The provision of preventive family planning services specifically designed to enable individuals to determine the number and spacing of their children, while clarifying that pregnant women must be referred to appropriate prenatal care services."

The regulations attach three principal conditions on the grant of federal funds for Title X projects. First, the regulations specify that a "Title X project may not provide counseling concerning the use of abortion as a method of family planning or provide referral for abortion as a method of family planning." Because Title X is limited to preconceptional services, the program does not furnish services related to childbirth. Only in the context of a referral out of the

Title X program is a pregnant woman given transitional information. Title X projects must refer every pregnant client "for appropriate prenatal and/or social services by furnishing a list of available providers that promote the welfare of mother and unborn child." The list may not be used indirectly to encourage or promote abortion, "such as by weighing the list of referrals in favor of health care providers which perform abortions, by including on the list of referral providers health care providers whose principal business is the provision of abortions, by excluding available providers who do not provide abortions, or by 'steering' clients to providers who offer abortion as a method of family planning." The Title X project is expressly prohibited from referring a pregnant woman to an abortion provider, even upon specific request. One permissible response to such an inquiry is that "the project does not consider abortion an appropriate method of family planning and therefore does not counsel or refer for abortion."

Second, the regulations broadly prohibit a Title X project from engaging in activities that "encourage, promote or advocate abortion as a method of family planning." Forbidden activities include lobbying for legislation that would increase the availability of abortion as a method of family planning, developing or disseminating materials advocating abortion as a method of family planning, providing speakers to promote abortion as a method of family planning, using legal action to make abortion available in any way as a method of family planning, and paying dues to any group that advocates abortion as a method of family planning as a substantial part of its activities.

Third, the regulations require that Title X projects be organized so that they are "physically and financially separate" from prohibited abortion activities. To be deemed physically and financially separate, "a Title X project must have an objective integrity and independence from prohibited activities. Mere bookkeeping separation of Title X funds from other monies is not sufficient." The regulations provide a list of nonexclusive factors for the Secretary to consider in conducting a case-by-case determination of objective integrity and independence, such as the existence of separate accounting records and separate personnel, and the degree of physical separation of the project from facilities for prohibited activities.

B

Petitioners are Title X grantees and doctors who supervise Title X funds suing on behalf of themselves and their patients. Respondent is the Secretary of HHS. After the regulations had been promulgated, but before they had been applied, petitioners filed two separate actions, later consolidated, challenging the facial validity of the regulations and seeking declaratory and injunctive relief to prevent implementation of the regulations. Petitioners challenged the regulations on the grounds that they were not authorized by Title X and that they violate the First and Fifth Amendment rights of Title X clients and the First Amendment rights of Title X health providers. . . .

* * *

II

We begin by pointing out the posture of the cases before us. Petitioners are challenging the *facial* validity of the regulations. Thus, we are concerned only with the question whether, on their face, the regulations are both authorized by the Act and can be construed in such a manner that they can be applied to a set of individuals without infringing upon constitutionally protected rights. Petitioners face a heavy burden in seeking to have the regulations invalidated as facially unconstitutional. "A facial challenge to a legislative Act is, of course, the most difficult challenge to mount successfully, since the challenger must establish that no set of circumstances exists under which the Act would be valid . . . ."

We turn first to petitioners' contention that the regulations exceed the Secretary's authority under Title X and are arbitrary and capricious. We begin with an examination of the regulations concerning abortion counseling, referral, and advocacy, which every Court of Appeals has found to be authorized by the statute, and then turn to the "program integrity requirement," with respect to which the courts below have adopted conflicting positions. We then address petitioners' claim that the regulations must be struck down because they raise a substantial constitutional question.

A

We need not dwell on the plain language of the statute because we agree with every court to have addressed the issue that the language is ambiguous. The language of § 1008 — that "[n]one of the funds appropriated under this subchapter shall be used in programs where abortion is a method of family planning" — does not speak directly to the issues of counseling, referral, advocacy, or program integrity. If a statute is "silent or ambiguous with respect to the specific issue, the question for the court is whether the agency's answer is based on a permissible construction of the statute."

The Secretary's construction of Title X may not be disturbed as an abuse of discretion if it reflects a plausible construction of the plain language of the statute and does not otherwise conflict with Congress' expressed intent. In determining whether a construction is permissible, "[t]he court need not conclude that the agency construction was the only one it permissibly could have adopted . . . or even the reading the court would have reached if the question initially had arisen in a judicial proceeding." Rather, substantial deference is accorded to the interpretation of the authorizing statute by the agency authorized with administering it.

The broad language of Title X plainly allows the Secretary's construction of the statute. By its own terms, § 1008 prohibits the use of Title X funds "in programs where abortion is a method of family planning." Title X does not define the term "method of family planning," nor does it enumerate what types of medical and counseling services are entitled to Title X funding. Based on the broad directives provided by Congress in Title X in general and § 1008 in particular, we are unable to say that the Secretary's construction of the prohibition in § 1008 to require a ban on counseling, referral, and advocacy within the Title X project is impermissible.

The District Courts and Courts of Appeals that have examined the legislative history have all found, at least with regard to the Act's counseling, referral, and advocacy provisions, that the legislative history is ambiguous with respect to Congress' intent in enacting Title X and the prohibition of § 1008. We join these courts in holding that the legislative history is ambiguous and fails to shed light on relevant congressional intent. At no time did Congress directly address the issues of abortion counseling, referral, or advocacy. . . .

When we find, as we do here, that the legislative history is ambiguous and unenlightening on the matters with respect to which the regulations deal, we customarily defer to the expertise of the agency. Petitioners argue, however, that the regulations are entitled to little or no deference because they "reverse a long-standing agency policy that permitted nondirective counseling and referral for abortion," and thus represent a sharp break from the Secretary's prior construction of the statute. Petitioners argue that the agency's prior consistent interpretation of § 1008 to permit nondirective counseling and to encourage coordination with local and state family planning services is entitled to substantial weight.

This Court has rejected the argument that an agency's interpretation "is not entitled to deference because it represents a sharp break with prior interpretations" of the statute in question. . . . [W]e [have] held that a revised interpretation deserves deference because "[a]n initial agency interpretation is not instantly carved in stone" and "the agency, to engage in informed rulemaking, must consider varying interpretations and the wisdom of its policy on a continuing basis." An agency is not required to "'establish rules of conduct to last forever,'" but rather "must be given ample latitude to 'adapt [its] rules and policies to the demands of changing circumstances.'"

We find that the Secretary amply justified his change of interpretation with a "reasoned analysis." The Secretary explained that the regulations are a result of his determination, in the wake of the critical reports of the General Accounting Office (GAO) and the Office of the Inspector General (OIG), that prior policy failed to implement properly the statute and that it was necessary to provide "'clear and operational guidance' to grantees about how to preserve the distinction between Title X programs and abortion as a method of family planning." He also determined that the new regulations are more in keeping with the original intent of the statute, are justified by client experience under the prior policy, and are supported by a shift in attitude against the "elimination of unborn children by abortion." We believe that these justifications are sufficient to support the Secretary's revised approach. Having concluded that the plain language and legislative history are ambiguous as to Congress' intent in enacting Title X, we must defer to the Secretary's permissible construction of the statute.

B

We turn next to the "program integrity" requirements embodied at § 59.9 of the regulations, mandating separate facilities, personnel, and records. These requirements are not inconsistent with the plain language of Title X. Petitioners contend, however, that they are based on an impermissible construction of the statute because they frustrate the clearly expressed intent of Congress that Title X programs be an integral part of a broader, comprehensive, health-care system. They argue that this integration is impermissibly burdened because the efficient use of non-Title X funds by Title X grantees will be adversely affected by the regulations.

The Secretary defends the separation requirements of § 59.9 on the grounds that they are necessary to assure that Title X grantees apply federal funds only to federally authorized purposes and that grantees avoid creating the appearance that the Government is supporting abortion-related activities. The program integrity regulations were promulgated in direct response to the observations in the GAO and OIG reports that "[b]ecause the distinction between the recipients' title X and other activities may not be easily recognized, the public can get the impression that Federal funds are being improperly used for abortion activities." . . .

The Secretary further argues that the separation requirements do not represent a deviation from past policy because the agency has consistently taken the position that § 1008 requires some degree of physical and financial separation between Title X projects and abortion-related activities.

We agree that the program integrity requirements are based on a permissible construction of the statute and are not inconsistent with congressional intent. As noted, the legislative history is clear about very little, and program integrity is no exception. The statements relied upon by petitioners to infer such an intent are highly generalized and do not directly address the scope of § 1008.

For example, the cornerstone of the conclusion that in Title X Congress intended a comprehensive, integrated system of family planning services is the statement in the statute requiring state health authorities applying for Title X funds to submit "a State plan for a coordinated and comprehensive program of family planning services." § 1002. This statement is, on its face, ambiguous as to Congress' intent in enacting Title X and the prohibition of § 1008. Placed in context, the statement merely requires that a state health authority submit a plan for a "coordinated and comprehensive program of family planning services" in order to be eligible for Title X funds. By its own terms, the language evinces Congress' intent to place a duty on state entities seeking federal funds; it does not speak either to an overall view of family planning services or to the Secretary's responsibility for implementing the statute. Likewise, the statement in the original House Report on Title X that the Act was "not intended to interfere with or limit programs conducted in accordance with State or local laws" and supported through non-Title X funds is equally unclear. This language directly follows the statement that it is the "intent of both Houses that the funds authorized under this legislation be used only to support preventive family planning services. . . . The conferees have adopted the language contained in section 1008, which prohibits the use of such funds for abortion, in order to make this intent clear." When placed in context and read in light of the express prohibition of § 1008, the statements fall short of evidencing a congressional intent that would render the Secretary's interpretation of the statute impermissible.

While petitioners' interpretation of the legislative history may be a permissible one, it is by no means the only one, and it is certainly not the one found by the Secretary. It is well established that legislative history which does not demonstrate a clear and certain congressional intent cannot form the basis for enjoining regulations. The Secretary based the need for the separation requirements "squarely on the congressional intent that abortion not be a part of a Title X funded program." Indeed, if one thing is clear from the legislative history, it is that Congress intended that Title X funds be kept separate and distinct from abortion-related activities. . . .

Petitioners also contend that the regulations must be invalidated because they raise serious questions of constitutional law. They rely on [decisions] which hold that "an Act of Congress ought not be construed to violate the Constitution if any other possible construction remains available." Under this canon of statutory construction, "'[t]he elementary rule is that every reasonable construction must be resorted to, in order to *save* a *statute* from unconstitutionality.'" (emphasis added).

* * *

Here Congress forbade the use of appropriated funds in programs where abortion is a method of family planning. It authorized the Secretary to promulgate regulations implementing this provision. The extensive litigation regarding governmental restrictions on abortion since our decision in *Roe v. Wade* (1973), suggests that it was likely that any set of regulations promulgated by the Secretary — other than the ones in force prior to 1988 and found by him to be relatively toothless and ineffectual — would be challenged on constitutional grounds. While we do not think that the constitutional arguments made by petitioners in these cases are without some force, in Part III, *infra*, we hold that they do not carry the day. Applying the canon of construction under discussion as best we can, we hold that the regulations promulgated by the Secretary do not raise the sort of "grave and doubtful constitutional questions," that would lead us to assume Congress did not intend to authorize their issuance. Therefore, we need not invalidate the regulations in order to save the statute from unconstitutionality.

III

Petitioners contend that the regulations violate the First Amendment by impermissibly discriminating based on viewpoint because they prohibit "all discussion about abortion as a lawful option — including counseling, referral, and the provision of neutral and accurate information about ending a pregnancy — while compelling the clinic or counselor to provide information that promotes continuing a pregnancy to term." They assert that the regulations violate the "free speech rights of private health care organizations that receive Title X funds, of their staff, and of their patients" by impermissibly imposing "viewpoint-discriminatory conditions on government subsidies" and thus "penaliz[e] speech funded with non-Title X monies." Because "Title X continues to fund speech ancillary to pregnancy testing in a manner that is not evenhanded with respect to views and information about abortion, it invidiously discriminates on the basis of viewpoint." . . . [P]etitioners also assert that while the Government may place certain conditions on the receipt of federal subsidies, it may not "discriminate invidiously in its subsidies in such a way as to 'ai[m] at the suppression of dangerous ideas.'"

There is no question but that the statutory prohibition contained in § 1008 is constitutional. In *Maher v. Roe* (1977), we upheld a state welfare regulation under which Medicaid recipients received payments for services related to childbirth, but not for nontherapeutic abortions. The Court rejected the claim that this unequal subsidization worked a violation of the Constitution. We held that the government may "make a value judgment favoring childbirth over abortion, and . . . implement that judgment by the allocation of public funds." Here the Government is exercising the authority it possesses . . . to subsidize family planning services which will lead to conception and childbirth, and declining to "promote or encourage abortion." The Government can, without violating the Constitution, selectively fund a program to encourage certain activities it believes to be in the public interest, without at the same time funding an alternative program which seeks to deal with the problem in another way. In so doing, the Government has not discriminated on the basis of viewpoint; it has merely chosen to fund one activity to the exclusion of the other. "[A] legislature's decision not to subsidize the exercise of a fundamental right does not infringe the right." "A refusal to fund protected activity, without more, cannot be equated with the imposition of a 'penalty' on that activity." "There is a basic difference between direct state interference with a protected activity and state encouragement of an alternative activity consonant with legislative policy."

The challenged regulations implement the statutory prohibition by prohibiting counseling, referral, and the provision of information regarding abortion as a method of family planning. They are designed to ensure that the limits of the federal program are observed. The Title X program is designed not for prenatal care, but to encourage family planning. A doctor who wished to offer prenatal care to a project patient who became pregnant could properly be prohibited from doing so because such service is outside the scope of the federally funded program. The regulations prohibiting abortion counseling and referral are of the same ilk; "no funds appropriated for the project may be used in programs where abortion is a method of family planning," and a doctor employed by the project may be prohibited in the course of his project duties from counseling abortion or referring for abortion. This is not a case of the Government "suppressing a dangerous idea," but of a prohibition on a project grantee or its employees from engaging in activities outside of the project's scope.

To hold that the Government unconstitutionally discriminates on the basis of viewpoint when it chooses to fund a program dedicated to advance certain permissible goals, because the program in advancing those goals necessarily discourages alternative goals, would render numerous Government programs constitutionally suspect. When Congress established a National Endowment for Democracy to encourage other countries to adopt democratic principles, it was not constitutionally required to fund a program to encourage competing lines of political philosophy such as communism and fascism. Petitioners' assertions ultimately boil down to the position that if the Government chooses to subsidize one protected right, it must subsidize analogous counterpart rights. But the Court has soundly rejected that proposition. . . .

We believe that petitioners' reliance upon our decision in *Arkansas Writers' Project*[, *Inc. v. Ragland* (1987)], is misplaced. That case involved a state sales tax which discriminated between magazines on the basis of their content. Relying on this fact, and on the fact that the tax "targets a small group within the press," . . . the Court held the tax invalid. But we have here not the case of a general law singling out a disfavored group on the basis of speech content, but a case of the Government refusing to fund activities, including speech, which are specifically excluded from the scope of the project funded.

Petitioners rely heavily on their claim that the regulations would not, in the circumstance of a medical emergency, permit a Title X project to refer a woman whose pregnancy places her life in imminent peril to a provider of abortions or abortion-related services. These cases, of course, involve only a facial challenge to the regulations, and we do not have before us any application by the Secretary to a specific fact situation. On their face, we do not read the regulations to bar abortion referral or counseling in such circumstances. Abortion counseling as a "method of family planning" is prohibited, and it does not seem that a medically necessitated abortion in such circumstances would be the equivalent of its use as a "method of family planning." Neither § 1008 nor the specific restrictions of the regulations would apply. Moreover, the regulations themselves contemplate that a Title X project would be permitted to engage in otherwise-prohibited, abortion-related activity in such circumstances. Section 59.8(a)(2) provides a specific exemption for emergency care and requires Title X recipients "to refer the client immediately to an appropriate provider of emergency medical services." Section 59.5(b)(1) also requires Title X projects to provide "necessary referral to other medical facilities when medically indicated."

Petitioners also contend that the restrictions on the subsidization of abortion-related speech contained in the regulations are impermissible because they condition the receipt of a benefit, in these cases Title X funding, on the relinquishment of a constitutional right, the right to engage in abortion advocacy and counseling. . . .

[Nevertheless,] . . . here the Government is not denying a benefit to anyone, but is instead simply insisting that public funds be spent for the purposes for which they were authorized. The Secretary's regulations do not force the Title X grantee to give up abortion-related speech; they merely require that the grantee keep such activities separate and distinct from Title X activities. Title X expressly distinguishes between a Title X *grantee* and a Title X *project*. The grantee, which normally is a health-care organization, may receive funds from a variety of sources for a variety of purposes. The grantee receives Title X funds, however, for the specific and limited purpose of establishing and operating a Title X project. The regulations govern the scope of the Title X *project's* activities, and leave the grantee unfettered in its other activities. The Title X *grantee* can continue to perform abortions, provide abortion-related services, and engage in abortion advocacy; it simply is required to conduct those activities through programs that are separate and independent from the project that receives Title X funds.

In contrast, our "unconstitutional conditions" cases involve situations in which the Government has placed a condition on the *recipient* of the subsidy rather than on a particular program or service, thus effectively prohibiting the recipient from engaging in the protected conduct outside the scope of the federally funded program. In *FCC v. League of Women Voters of Cal.* [(1984)], we invalidated a federal law providing that noncommercial television and radio stations that receive federal grants may not "engage in editorializing." Under that law, a recipient of federal funds was "barred absolutely from all editorializing" because it "is not able to segregate its activities according to the source of its funding" and thus "has no way of limiting the use of its federal funds to all noneditorializing activities." The effect of the law was that "a noncommercial educational station that receives only 1% of its overall income from [federal] grants is barred absolutely from all editorializing" and "barred from using even wholly private funds to finance its editorial activity." We expressly recognized, however, that were Congress to permit the recipient stations to "establish 'affiliate' organizations which could then use the station's facilities to editorialize with nonfederal funds, such a statutory mechanism would plainly be valid." Such a scheme would permit the station "to make known its views on matters of public importance through its nonfederally funded, editorializing affiliate without losing federal grants for its noneditorializing broadcast activities."

Similarly, . . . we [have] held that Congress could, in the exercise of its spending power, reasonably refuse to subsidize the lobbying activities of tax-exempt charitable organizations by prohibiting such organizations from using tax-deductible contributions to support their lobbying efforts. In so holding, we explained that such organizations remained free "to receive deductible contributions to support . . . nonlobbying activit[ies]." Thus, a charitable organization could create, under § 501(c)(3) of the Internal Revenue Code of 1954, 26 U.S.C. § 501(c)(3), an affiliate to conduct its nonlobbying activities using tax-deductible contributions, and at the same time establish, under § 501(c)(4), a separate affiliate to pursue its lobbying efforts without such contributions. Given that alternative, the Court concluded that "Congress has not infringed any First Amendment rights or regulated any First Amendment activity[; it] has simply chosen not to pay for [appellee's] lobbying." . . .

By requiring that the Title X grantee engage in abortion-related activity separately from activity receiving federal funding, Congress has, consistent with our teachings in [prior cases], not denied it the right to engage in abortion-related activities. Congress has merely refused to fund such activities out of the public fisc, and the Secretary has simply required a certain degree of separation from the Title X project in order to ensure the integrity of the federally funded program.

The same principles apply to petitioners' claim that the regulations abridge the free speech rights of the grantee's staff. Individuals who are voluntarily employed for a Title X project must perform their duties in accordance with the regulation's restrictions on abortion counseling and referral. The employees remain free, however, to pursue abortion-related activities when they are not acting under the auspices of the Title X project. . . .

* * *

IV

We turn now to petitioners' argument that the regulations violate a woman's Fifth Amendment right to choose whether to terminate her pregnancy. We recently reaffirmed the long-recognized principle that "'the Due Process Clauses generally confer no affirmative right to governmental aid, even where such aid may be necessary to secure life, liberty, or property interests of which the government itself may not deprive the individual.'" The Government has no constitutional duty to subsidize an activity merely because the activity is constitutionally protected and may validly choose to fund childbirth over abortion and "'implement that judgment by the allocation of public funds'" for medical services relating to childbirth but not to those relating to abortion. The Government has no affirmative duty to "commit any resources to facilitating abortions," and its decision to fund childbirth but not abortion "places no governmental obstacle in the path of a woman who chooses to terminate her pregnancy, but rather, by means of unequal subsidization of abortion and other medical services, encourages alternative activity deemed in the public interest."

That the regulations do not impermissibly burden a woman's Fifth Amendment rights is evident from the line of cases beginning with *Maher* [*v. Roe* (1977)] and [*Harris v.*] *McRae* [(1980),] and culminating in our most recent decision in *Webster* [*v. Reproductive Health Services* (1989)]. Just as Congress' refusal to fund abortions in *McRae* left "an indigent woman with at least the same range of choice in deciding whether to obtain a medically necessary abortion as she would have had if Congress had chosen to subsidize no health care costs at all," and "Missouri's refusal to allow public employees to perform abortions in public hospitals leaves a pregnant woman with the same choices as if the State had chosen not to operate any public hospitals," *Webster*, Congress' refusal to fund abortion counseling and advocacy leaves a pregnant woman with the same choices as if the Government had chosen not to fund family-planning services at all. The difficulty that a woman encounters when a Title X project does not provide abortion counseling or referral leaves her in no different position than she would have been if the Government had not enacted Title X.

In *Webster*, we stated that "[h]aving held that the State's refusal [in *Maher*] to fund abortions does not violate *Roe v. Wade*, it strains logic to reach a contrary result for the use of public facilities and employees." It similarly would strain logic, in light of the more extreme restrictions in those cases, to find that the mere decision to exclude abortion-related services from a federally funded *preconceptional* family planning program is unconstitutional.

Petitioners also argue that by impermissibly infringing on the doctor-patient relationship and depriving a Title X client of information concerning abortion as a method of family planning, the regulations violate a woman's Fifth Amendment right to medical self-determination and to make informed medical decisions free of government-imposed harm. . . .

In [a prior case], we invalidated a city ordinance requiring *all* physicians to make specified statements to the patient prior to performing an abortion in order to ensure that the woman's consent was "truly informed." Similarly, in [another], we struck down a state statute mandating that a list of agencies offering alternatives to abortion and a description of fetal development be provided to *every* woman considering terminating her pregnancy through an abortion. Critical to [these] decisions . . . to invalidate a governmental intrusion into the patient-doctor dialogue was the fact that the laws in both cases required *all* doctors within their respective jurisdictions to provide *all* pregnant patients contemplating an abortion a litany of information, regardless of whether the patient sought the information or whether the doctor thought the information necessary to the patient's decision. Under the Secretary's regulations, however, a doctor's ability to provide, and a woman's right to receive, information concerning abortion and abortion-related services outside the context of the Title X project remains unfettered. . . .

Petitioners contend, however, that most Title X clients are effectively precluded by indigency and poverty from seeing a health-care provider who will provide abortion-related services. But once again, even these Title X clients are in no worse position than if Congress had never enacted Title X. "The financial constraints that restrict an indigent woman's ability to enjoy the full range of constitutionally protected freedom of choice are the product not of governmental restrictions on access to abortion, but rather of her indigency."

* * *

JUSTICE BLACKMUN, with whom JUSTICE MARSHALL joins, with whom JUSTICE STEVENS joins as to Parts II and III, and with whom JUSTICE O'CONNOR joins as to Part I, dissenting.

* * *

II

* * *

A

* * *

Remarkably, the majority concludes that "the Government has not discriminated on the basis of viewpoint; it has merely chosen to fund one activity to the exclusion of the other." But the majority's claim that the regulations merely limit a Title X project's speech to preventive or preconceptional services, rings hollow in light of the broad range of nonpreventive services that the regulations authorize Title X projects to provide. By refusing to fund those family-planning projects that advocate abortion *because* they advocate abortion, the Government plainly has targeted a particular viewpoint. The majority's reliance on the fact that the regulations pertain solely to funding decisions simply begs the question. Clearly, there are some bases upon which government may not rest its decision to fund or not to fund. For example, the Members of the majority surely would agree that government may not base its decision to support an activity upon considerations of race. As demonstrated above, our cases make clear that ideological viewpoint is a similarly repugnant ground upon which to base funding decisions.

* * *

B

The Court concludes that the challenged regulations do not violate the First Amendment rights of Title X staff members because any limitation of the employees' freedom of expression is simply a consequence of their decision to accept employment at a federally funded project. But it has never been sufficient to justify an otherwise unconstitutional condition upon public employment that the employee may escape the condition by relinquishing his or her job. It is beyond question "that a government may not require an individual to relinquish rights guaranteed him by the First Amendment as a condition of public employment." . . .

The majority attempts to circumvent this principle by emphasizing that Title X physicians and counselors "remain free . . . to pursue abortion-related activities when they are not acting under the auspices of the Title X project." "The regulations," the majority explains, "do not in any way restrict the activities of those persons acting as private individuals." Under the majority's reasoning, the First Amendment could be read to tolerate *any* governmental restriction upon an employee's speech so long as that restriction is limited to the funded workplace. This is a dangerous proposition, and one the Court has rightly rejected in the past.

In [an earlier case], it was no answer to the petitioners' claim of compelled speech as a condition upon public employment that their speech outside the workplace remained unregulated by the State. Nor was the public employee's First Amendment claim in [another case] derogated because the communication that her employer sought to punish occurred during business hours. At the least, such conditions require courts to balance the speaker's interest in the message against those of government in preventing its dissemination.

In the cases at bar, the speaker's interest in the communication is both clear and vital. In addressing the family-planning needs of their clients, the physicians and counselors who staff Title X projects seek to provide them with the full range of information and options regarding their health and reproductive freedom. Indeed, the legitimate expectations of the patient and the ethical responsibilities of the medical profession demand no less. "The patient's right of self-decision can be effectively exercised only if the patient possesses enough information to enable an intelligent choice. . . . The physician has an ethical obligation to help the patient make choices from among the therapeutic alternatives consistent with good medical practice." When a client becomes pregnant, the full range of therapeutic alternatives includes the abortion option, and Title X counselors' interest in providing this information is compelling.

The Government's articulated interest in distorting the doctor-patient dialogue — ensuring that federal funds are not spent for a purpose outside the scope of the program — falls far short of that necessary to justify the suppression of truthful information and professional medical opinion regarding constitutionally protected conduct. Moreover, the offending regulation is not narrowly tailored to serve this interest. For example, the governmental interest at stake could be served by imposing rigorous bookkeeping standards to ensure financial separation or adopting content-neutral rules for the balanced dissemination of family-planning and health information. By failing to balance or even to consider the free speech interests claimed by Title X physicians against the Government's asserted interest in suppressing the speech, the Court falters in its duty to implement the protection that the First Amendment clearly provides for this important message.

C

Finally, it is of no small significance that the speech the Secretary would suppress is truthful information regarding constitutionally protected conduct of vital importance to the listener. One can imagine no legitimate governmental interest that might be served by suppressing such information. Concededly, the abortion debate is among the most divisive and contentious issues that our Nation has faced in recent years. "But freedom to differ is not limited to things that do not matter much. That would be a mere shadow of freedom. The test of its substance is the right to differ as to things that touch the heart of the existing order."

III

By far the most disturbing aspect of today's ruling is the effect it will have on the Fifth Amendment rights of the women who, supposedly, are beneficiaries of Title X programs. The majority rejects petitioners' Fifth Amendment claims summarily. . . .

Until today, the Court has allowed to stand only those restrictions upon reproductive freedom that, while limiting the availability of abortion, have left intact a woman's ability to decide without coercion whether she will continue her pregnancy to term. . . . Today's decision abandons that principle, and with disastrous results.

Contrary to the majority's characterization, this is not a situation in which individuals seek Government aid in exercising their fundamental rights. The Fifth Amendment right asserted by petitioners is the right of a pregnant woman to be free from affirmative governmental *interference* in her decision. *Roe v. Wade* (1973), and its progeny are not so much about a medical procedure as they are about a woman's fundamental right to self-determination. Those cases serve to vindicate the idea that "liberty," if it means anything, must entail freedom from governmental domination in making the most intimate and personal of decisions. By suppressing medically pertinent information and injecting a restrictive ideological message unrelated to considerations of maternal health, the Government places formidable obstacles in the path of Title X clients' freedom of choice and thereby violates their Fifth Amendment rights.

It is crystal clear that the aim of the challenged provisions — an aim the majority cannot escape noticing — is not simply to ensure that federal funds are not used to perform abortions, but to "reduce the incidence of abortion." As recounted above, the regulations require Title X physicians and counselors to provide information pertaining only to childbirth, to refer a pregnant woman for prenatal care irrespective of her medical situation, and, upon direct inquiry, to respond that abortion is not an "appropriate method" of family planning.

The undeniable message conveyed by this forced speech, and the one that the Title X client will draw from it, is that abortion nearly always is an improper medical option. Although her physician's words, in fact, are strictly controlled by the Government and wholly unrelated to her particular medical situation, the Title X client will reasonably construe them as professional advice to forgo her right to obtain an abortion. As would most rational patients, many of these women will follow that perceived advice and carry their pregnancy to term, despite their needs to the contrary and despite the safety of the abortion procedure for the vast majority of them. Others, delayed by the regulations' mandatory prenatal referral, will be prevented from acquiring abortions during the period in which the process is medically sound and constitutionally protected.

In view of the inevitable effect of the regulations, the majority's conclusion that "[t]he difficulty that a woman encounters when a Title X project does not provide abortion counseling or referral leaves her in no different position than she would have been if the Government had not enacted Title X," is insensitive and contrary to common human experience. Both the purpose and result of the challenged regulations are to deny women the ability voluntarily to decide their procreative destiny. For these women, the Government will have obliterated the freedom to choose as surely as if it had banned abortions outright. The denial of this freedom is not a consequence of poverty but of the Government's ill-intentioned distortion of information it has chosen to provide.

* * *

JUSTICE STEVENS, dissenting.

In my opinion, the Court has not paid sufficient attention to the language of the controlling statute or to the consistent interpretation accorded the statute by the responsible cabinet officers during four different Presidencies and 18 years.

* * *

The entirely new approach adopted by the Secretary in 1988 was not, in my view, authorized by the statute. The new regulations did not merely reflect a change in a policy determination that the Secretary had been authorized by Congress to make. Rather, they represented an assumption of policymaking responsibility that Congress had not delegated to the Secretary. In a society that abhors censorship and in which policymakers have traditionally placed the highest value on the freedom to communicate, it is unrealistic to conclude that statutory authority to regulate conduct implicitly authorized the Executive to regulate speech.

Because I am convinced that the 1970 Act did not authorize the Secretary to censor the speech of grant recipients or their employees, I would hold the challenged regulations invalid. . . .

* * *

JUSTICE O'CONNOR, dissenting.

* * *

This Court acts at the limits of its power when it invalidates a law on constitutional grounds. In recognition of our place in the constitutional scheme, we must act with "great gravity and delicacy" when telling a coordinate branch that its actions are absolutely prohibited absent constitutional amendment. In these cases, we need only tell the Secretary that his regulations are not a reasonable interpretation of the statute; we need not tell Congress that it cannot pass such legislation. If we rule solely on statutory grounds, Congress retains the power to force the constitutional question by legislating more explicitly. It may instead choose to do nothing. That decision should be left to Congress; we should not tell Congress what it cannot do before it has chosen to do it. It is enough in this litigation to conclude that neither the language nor the history of § 1008 compels the Secretary's interpretation, and that the interpretation raises serious First

Amendment concerns. On this basis alone, I would . . . invalidate the challenged regulations.

NOTES AND QUESTIONS

1. With the possible exception of matters involving race, there is no more important social issue which divides Americans than does the question of abortion. How could the government silence anyone, even government employees, from expressing their point of view on this fundamentally important political question? Why is it that government grantees, under these circumstances, had, in effect, to surrender some of their First Amendment rights? The dissenters believe this was unconstitutional — why doesn't the majority? Suppose you were a publisher hired to print the Federal Register (the official compendium of agency regulations). Could you claim that you had a First Amendment right to supply your own editorial commentary on some of the agency regulations? Is *Rust v. Sullivan* the same case?

2. Is it constitutionally permissible to require "family planning" clinics who accept federal funds to inform women who come to them seeking help obtaining an abortion that "We do not consider abortion an appropriate method of family planning"? This was one of the requirements which Congress, through the regulations issued from HHS, sought to impose on the acceptance of federal funds. Do you agree or disagree with the proposition that this raises First Amendment problems? Is it the furtherance of government policy or a troubling interference with a protected constitutional right? Do you suppose that the federal officials who imposed the regulation referred to in the case were committed to the enforcement of a constitutionally-protected freedom to secure an abortion? Should this make a difference in the Court's treatment of the rule?

3. One of the first acts of the Clinton administration was to lift the "gag rule" at issue in this case by directing that his Department of Health and Human Services simply not comply with the existing regulations. Was this lawful?

4. Did *Rust* involve an unconstitutional condition? This doctrine posits that it is wrong for government to condition a benefit or a subsidy on the condition that a person forego a constitutional right. Were the recipients of the Title X funds being told to give up their right to promote abortion on their own time and with their own resources or were they merely being told that they couldn't promote abortion as a method of family planning with the government's money? Despite President Clinton's political reservations, if *Rust* was merely defining how the federal money was to be spent (and that seems to be the Court's assumption) then the *Rust* opinion was well-anchored in the Court's prior case law, including *Regan v. Taxation With Representation,* 461 U.S. 540 (1983) (upholding the denial of a tax subsidy for lobbying), and government limitations on public expenditures for abortion, *Harris v. McRae,* 448 U.S. 297 (1980), and *Maher v. Roe,* 432 U.S. 464 (1977). The issue has re-surfaced in the implementation of a statutory provision requiring the National Endowment for the Arts (NEA) which instructs the NEA Chairperson to ensure that "artistic excellence and artistic merit are the criteria by which applications are judged, taking into consideration general standards of decency and respect for the diverse beliefs and values of the American public." 20 U.S.C. § 954(d). Is this constitutional? The issue came before the Court again in *NEA v. Finley*, decided in 1998. In defending this statute, the government argued that the Court's decisions precluding content and viewpoint discrimination are largely inapposite to a funding program that selectively subsidizes expressive conduct. For this proposition, President Clinton's Solicitor General relied heavily on the Court's decision in *Rust*. The Solicitor General expansively quotes *Rust* for the proposition that "[t]he Government can, without violating the Constitution, selectively fund a program to encourage certain activities it believes to be in the public interest, without at the same time funding an alternative program. . . . In doing so, the Government has not discriminated on the basis of viewpoint; it has merely chosen to fund one activity to the exclusion of the other." 500 U.S. at 193. The Court held that the government has this funding latitude. There is a fundamental difference between government as patron and government as sovereign.

5. In *Legal Services Corp. v. Velazquez*, 531 U.S. 533 (2001), the Court struck down a provision of the Legal Services Corporation Act that prevented LSC attorneys from using government funds for representations that involve efforts to amend or challenge the constitutionality of existing welfare law. Distinguishing *Rust*, the Court thought the program more like the limited public forum established by the University of Virginia, restrictions on which were struck down in *Rosenberger*: "Although the LSC program differs from the program at issue in *Rosenberger* in that its purpose is not to 'encourage a diversity of views,' the salient point is that, like the program in *Rosenberger,* the LSC program was designed to facilitate private speech, not to promote a governmental message." Could not the same have been said of the program in *Rust*? Indeed, unlike in *Rust*, the prohibition in *Velazquez* was designed to prevent taxpayer funds from being used to effect political change via the courts. Justice Scalia, joined in dissent by Chief Justice Rehnquist and Justices O'Connor and Thomas, found the majority's attempt to distinguish *Rust* entirely unpersuasive.

> The LSC Act, like the scheme in *Rust,* does not create a public forum. Far from encouraging a diversity of views, it has always, as the Court accurately states, "placed restrictions on its use of funds." Nor does [the Act] discriminate on the basis of viewpoint, since it funds neither challenges to nor defenses of existing welfare law. The provision simply declines to subsidize a certain class of litigation, and under *Rust* that decision "does not infringe the right" to bring such litigation. . . . No litigant who, in the absence of LSC funding, would bring a suit challenging existing welfare law is deterred from doing so. *Rust* thus controls these cases and compels the conclusion that [it] is constitutional.

The Court contends that *Rust* is different because the program at issue subsidized government speech, while the LSC funds private speech. This is so unpersuasive it hardly needs response. If the private doctors' confidential advice to their patients at issue in *Rust* constituted "government speech," it is hard to imagine what subsidized speech would *not* be government speech. Moreover, the majority's contention that the subsidized speech in these cases is not government speech because the lawyers have a professional obligation to represent the interests of their clients founders on the reality that the doctors in *Rust* had a professional obligation to serve the interests of their patients. . . .

Who has the better argument here? Has the Court just created a special privilege for lawyers?

6. In *United States and Department of Agriculture v. United Foods, Inc.*, 533 U.S. 405 (2001), the Court may have fashioned another indirect limitation on government speech — or at least that aspect of government speech sought to be financed out of compelled assessments. In *United Foods*, the Court struck down a federal assessment for generic mushroom advertising. The Court divided over whether the issue should be analyzed under free speech doctrine, as a commercial speech question, or as garden-variety economic regulation. 6-3 the Court found the assessment to be contrary to First Amendment free speech protection that prevents government from compelling individuals to pay subsidies for speech to which they object. The respondents wanted to convey the message that branded mushrooms were superior to those grown by others and they objected to the generic advertising which contained the contrary message.

Just as the First Amendment may prevent the government from prohibiting speech, the Amendment may prevent the government from compelling individuals to express certain views, *see Wooley v. Maynard* (1977); *West Virginia Bd. of Ed. v. Barnette* (1943), or from compelling certain individuals to pay subsidies for speech to which they object. *See Abood v. Detroit Bd. of Ed.* (1977); *Keller v. State Bar of Cal.* (1990). A precedential problem for the Court, however, was that just a few years earlier, the Justices had sustained a compelled advertising initiative as part of a "marketing order" scheme in *Glickman v. Wileman Brothers & Elliott, Inc.* (1997) relating to California fruit trees. The Court attempted to differentiate *Glickman* by arguing that the mandated assessments there were ancillary to a more comprehensive regulatory program, which displaced competition to such an extent that marketing practices in the industry were exempt from the antitrust laws. By contrast, beyond the collection and disbursement of advertising funds in *United Foods*, there were no marketing orders that regulate how mushrooms may be produced and sold, no exemption from the antitrust laws, and nothing preventing individual producers from making their own marketing decisions. Justice Kennedy for the majority recognized that the law sometimes does permit compelled association (e.g., labor unions, bar associations), but such compelled association to advance legitimate purposes does not support compelled speech where there is a conflict of belief. Hence, we may have to be members of the state bar, but we do not have to contribute to the political activities of the bar that are not germane to its professional mission. *Keller v. State Bar of Cal.* (1990). So too, said the Court, a compelled subsidy for speech cannot be allowed where the context or bulk of the program is the speech, itself. The majority noted that the government did not fully argue whether its regulation could be sustained either under *Central Hudson*, as a commercial speech regulation substantially advancing a particular governmental interest, or as government speech, *see Rust*, so the Court did not address either.

Justices Breyer, Ginsburg and O'Connor dissented, arguing that speech was not implicated in this matter of economic regulation because first, money isn't speech, and only money is required to be paid; second, the speech promoted advances the truthfulness of commercial transaction and hence is consistent with *Central Hudson*; and third, there is no special threat to freedom of belief or expression. Lamented the dissent: "The Court, in applying stricter First Amendment standards and finding them violated, sets an unfortunate precedent. That precedent suggests, perhaps requires, striking down any similar program that, for example, would require tobacco companies to contribute to an industry fund for advertising the harms of smoking or would use a portion of museum entry charges for a citywide campaign to promote the value of art." Are the dissenters correct? What's so bad about construing the First Amendment to prevent coerced assessments to finance government speech against the interests of those required to pay the assessments? Does the majority's rationale threaten to undermine the whole idea of government speech, itself, insofar as someone is always compelled to pay for it unwillingly?

7. In *United States v. American Library Association*, 539 U.S. 194 (2003), the Court considered the Children's Internet Protection Act (CIPA), which forbade public libraries from receiving federal assistance for Internet access unless they installed software "to block obscene or pornographic images and to prevent minors from accessing material harmful to them."* Such federal assistance has been important in providing Internet access for many libraries, and, arguing that the CIPA violated the First Amendment, "a group of libraries, patrons, Web site publishers, and related parties" challenged the legislation. A District Court held that "Congress had exceeded its authority under the Spending Clause because any public library that complies with CIPA's conditions will necessarily violate the First Amendment; that the CIPA filtering software constitutes a content-based restriction on access to a public forum that is subject to strict scrutiny; and that, although the Government has a compelling interest in preventing the dissemination of obscenity, child pornography, or material harmful to minors, the use of software filters is not narrowly tailored to further that interest." By a 6-3 vote, the United States Supreme Court reversed the District Court, essentially rejecting its application of the "public forum" doctrine, and its concomitant use of the "strict scrutiny" test.

---

* Quotations are from the official syllabus of the case.

In a plurality opinion by Chief Justice Rehnquist (joined by O'Connor, Scalia, and Thomas), he concluded that "public libraries' use of Internet filtering software does not violate their patrons' First Amendment rights . . . and is a valid exercise of Congress' spending power. Congress has wide latitude to attach conditions to the receipt of federal assistance to further its policy objectives, *South Dakota v. Dole*, 483 U.S. 203, 206 . . . ." Rehnquist concluded that "[t]o fulfill their traditional missions of facilitating learning and cultural enrichment, public libraries must have broad discretion to decide what material to provide to their patrons." Just as the Court had held in *Arkansas Ed. Television Comm'n v. Forbes*, 523 U.S. 666, 672-674 (1998), and *National Endowment for Arts v. Finley*, 524 U.S. 569, 585-586 (1998), that governmental agencies had broad discretion in deciding what content to provide, so when libraries provide information they should not be thought of as "public forums," and should not be subject to "strict scrutiny" analysis for "content-based decisions." It was thus appropriate for Congress to condition aid on blocking web-based pornography to minors, just as most libraries make decisions "to exclude pornography from their print collections," and these decisions "are not subjected to heightened scrutiny." Rehnquist also observed that concerns about access to materials for adults "are dispelled by the ease with which patrons may have the filtering software disabled." Further, "[w]hen the Government appropriates public funds to establish a program, it is entitled to broadly define that program's limits. *Rust v. Sullivan*, 500 U.S. 173, 194. As in *Rust*, the Government here is not denying a benefit to anyone, but is instead simply insisting that public funds be spent for the purpose for which they are authorized: helping public libraries fulfill their traditional role of obtaining material of requisite and appropriate quality for educational and informational purposes."

In his concurring opinion "Justice Kennedy concluded that if, as the Government represents, a librarian will unblock filtered material or disable the Internet software filter without significant delay on an adult user's request, there is little to this case." He observed that "The interest in protecting young library users from material inappropriate for minors is legitimate, and even compelling . . . . Given this interest, and the failure to show that adult library users' access to the material is burdened in any significant degree, the statute is not unconstitutional on its face."

Justice Breyer concurred in the result, but would have required something less than "strict scrutiny," but something more than the Rehnquist opinion's "rational basis" to justify government regulation in this context that raises First Amendment concerns. The "heightened scrutiny" test he applied was met in the case at hand, because CIPA's "objectives — of restricting access to obscenity, child pornography, and material that is comparably harmful to minors — are 'legitimate,' and indeed often 'compelling.' No clearly superior or better fitting alternative to Internet software filters has been presented. Moreover, the statute contains an important exception that limits the speech-related harm: It allows libraries to permit any adult patron access to an 'overblocked' Web site or to disable the software filter entirely upon request. Given the comparatively small burden imposed upon library patrons seeking legitimate Internet materials, it cannot be said that any speech-related harm that the statute may cause is disproportionate when considered in relation to the statute's legitimate objectives."

Justice Stevens dissented on the grounds that the blocking software was overbroad, and thus, presumably, did not meet the "narrow tailoring" the First Amendment required in such a situation. Justice Souter, joined by Justice Ginsburg in dissent, "agree[d] in the main" with Justice Stevens, but wrote to make clear his belief that the CIPA was not a valid exercise of the spending power because it "mandates action by recipient libraries that would violate the First Amendment's guarantee of free speech if the libraries took that action entirely on their own." Justice Souter believed that "strict scrutiny" analysis was appropriate, and his principal concern was that it would be too difficult for adults to "unblock" access to whatever they might desire to see on the web. He noted that "the District Court expressly found that 'unblocking may take days, and may be unavailable, especially in branch libraries, which are often less well staffed than main libraries.'" "In any event," he observed, "we are here to review a statute, and the unblocking provisions simply cannot be construed, even for constitutional avoidance purposes, to say that a library must unblock upon adult request, no conditions imposed and no questions asked. . . . [T]he statute says only that a library 'may' unblock, not that it must."

Note that the dissenters' disagreement with the majority was probably as much over the technical nature of the blocking software as it was over the correct first Amendment scrutiny standard to apply. Justice Kennedy appears to be relying on the ease of "unblocking" which Stevens rejects. Both Stevens and Souter believe that the majority is in error in relying on cases such as *Rust* to sustain CIPA. Who gets that issue right? Are you comfortable with the notion of First Amendment jurisprudence proposed by Justice Breyer that might bounce back and forth among three different levels of mandated scrutiny?

8. In the next cases, you are introduced to limitations that apply in two other special contexts. As you read them, pay special attention to the importance of the factor that the speech raises a matter of public concern. In the first case, *Waters v. Churchill*, this factor is eclipsed by the government's interest in running an orderly workplace, but in the case discussed in the Notes following *Waters*, *Bartnicki v. Vopper*, even substantial privacy interests do not outweigh that factor.

b. Termination of Public Employees as a Result of Speech

WATERS v. CHURCHILL
511 U.S. 661 (1994)

JUSTICE O'CONNOR announced the judgment of the Court and delivered an opinion, in which THE CHIEF JUSTICE, JUSTICE SOUTER, and JUSTICE GINSBURG join.

* * *

I

This case arises out of a conversation that respondent Cheryl Churchill had on January 16, 1987, with Melanie Perkins-Graham. Both Churchill and Perkins-Graham were nurses working at McDonough District Hospital; Churchill was in the obstetrics department, and Perkins-Graham was considering transferring to that department. The conversation took place at work during a dinner break. Petitioners heard about it, and fired Churchill, allegedly because of it. There is, however, a dispute about what Churchill actually said, and therefore about whether petitioners were constitutionally permitted to fire Churchill for her statements.

The conversation was overheard in part by two other nurses, Mary Lou Ballew and Jean Welty, and by Dr. Thomas Koch, the clinical head of obstetrics. A few days later, Ballew told Cynthia Waters, Churchill's supervisor, about the incident. According to Ballew, Churchill took "'the cross trainee into the kitchen for . . . at least 20 minutes to talk about [Waters] and how bad things are in [obstetrics] in general.'" Ballew said that Churchill's statements led Perkins-Graham to no longer be interested in switching to the department.

Shortly after this, Waters met with Ballew a second time for confirmation of Ballew's initial report. Ballew said that Churchill "was knocking the department" and that "in general [Churchill] was saying what a bad place [obstetrics] is to work." Ballew said she heard Churchill say Waters "was trying to find reasons to fire her." Ballew also said Churchill described a patient complaint for which Waters had supposedly wrongly blamed Churchill.

Waters, together with petitioner Kathleen Davis, the hospital's vice president of nursing, also met with Perkins-Graham, who told them that Churchill "had indeed said unkind and inappropriate negative things about [Waters]." Also, according to Perkins-Graham, Churchill mentioned a negative evaluation that Waters had given Churchill, which arose out of an incident in which Waters had cited Churchill for an insubordinate remark. The evaluation stated that Churchill "'promotes an unpleasant atmosphere and hinders constructive communication and cooperation,'" and "'exhibits negative behavior towards [Waters] and [Waters'] leadership through her actions and body language'"; the evaluation said Churchill's work was otherwise satisfactory. Churchill allegedly told Perkins-Graham that she and Waters had discussed the evaluation, and that Waters "wanted to wipe the slate clean . . . but [Churchill thought] this wasn't possible." Churchill also allegedly told Perkins-Graham "that just in general things were not good in OB and hospital administration was responsible." Churchill specifically mentioned Davis, saying Davis "was ruining MDH." Perkins-Graham told Waters that she knew Waters and Davis "could not tolerate that kind of negativism."

Churchill's version of the conversation is different. For several months, Churchill had been concerned about the hospital's "cross-training" policy, under which nurses from one department could work in another when their usual location was overstaffed. Churchill believed this policy threatened patient care because it was designed not to train nurses but to cover staff shortages, and she had complained about this to Davis and Waters. According to Churchill, the conversation with Perkins-Graham primarily concerned the cross-training policy. Churchill denies that she said some of what Ballew and Perkins-Graham allege she said. She does admit she criticized Kathy Davis, saying her staffing policies threatened to "ruin" the hospital because they "'seemed to be impeding nursing care.'" She claims she actually defended Waters and encouraged Perkins-Graham to transfer to obstetrics.

Koch's and Welty's recollections of the conversation match Churchill's. Davis and Waters, however, never talked to Koch or Welty about this, and they did not talk to Churchill until the time they told her she was fired. Moreover, Churchill claims, Ballew was biased against Churchill because of an incident in which Ballew apparently made an error and Churchill had to cover for her.

After she was discharged, Churchill filed an internal grievance. The president of the hospital, petitioner Stephen Hopper, met with Churchill in regard to this and heard her side of the story. He then reviewed Waters' and Davis' written reports of their conversations with Ballew and Perkins-Graham, and had Bernice Magin, the hospital's vice president of human resources, interview Ballew one more time. After considering all this, Hopper rejected Churchill's grievance.

Churchill then sued under 42 U.S.C. § 1983, claiming that the firing violated her First Amendment rights because her speech was protected under *Connick v. Myers* (1983). . . .

* * *

II

A

There is no dispute in this case about when speech by a government employee is protected by the First Amendment: To be protected, the speech must be on a matter of public concern, and the employee's interest in expressing herself on this matter must not be outweighed by any injury the speech could cause to "'the interest of the State, as an employer, in promoting the efficiency of the public services it performs through its employees.'" *Connick, supra*. It is also agreed that it is the court's task to apply the *Connick* test to the facts.

The dispute is over how the factual basis for applying the test — what the speech was, in what tone it was delivered, what the listener's reactions were — is to be determined. Should the court apply the *Connick* test to the speech as the government employer found it to be, or should it ask the jury to determine the facts for itself? The Court of Appeals held that the employer's factual conclusions were irrelevant, and that the jury should engage in its own factfinding. Petitioners argue that the employer's factual conclusions should be dispositive. Respondents take a middle course: They suggest that the court should accept the employer's factual conclusions, but only if those conclusions were arrived at reasonably, something they say did not happen here.

We agree that it is important to ensure not only that the substantive First Amendment standards are sound, but also that they are applied through reliable procedures. This is why we have often held some procedures — a particular allocation of the burden of proof, a particular quantum of proof, a particular type of appellate review, and so on — to be constitutionally required in proceedings that may penalize protected speech.

[Our] cases [on these points] establish a basic First Amendment principle: Government action based on protected speech may under some circumstances violate the First Amendment even if the government actor honestly believes the speech is unprotected. And though JUSTICE SCALIA suggests that this principle be limited to licensing schemes and to "deprivation[s] of the freedom of speech specifically *through the judicial process*," we do not think the logic of the cases supports such a limitation. Speech can be chilled and punished by administrative action as much as by judicial processes; in no case have we asserted or even implied the contrary. In fact, in *Speiser v. Randall* [(1958)], we struck down procedures, on the grounds that they were insufficiently protective of free speech, which involved both administrative and judicial components. *Speiser*, like this case, dealt with a government decision to deny a speaker certain benefits — in *Speiser* a tax exemption, in this case a government job — based on what the speaker said. Our holding there did not depend on the deprivation taking place "specifically through the judicial process," and we cannot see how the result could have been any different had the process been entirely administrative, with no judicial review. . . .

Nonetheless, not every procedure that may safeguard protected speech is constitutionally mandated. True, the procedure adopted by the Court of Appeals may lower the chance of protected speech being erroneously punished. A speaker is more protected if she has two opportunities to be vindicated — first by the employer's investigation and then by the jury — than just one. But each procedure involves a different mix of administrative burden, risk of erroneous punishment of protected speech, and risk of erroneous exculpation of unprotected speech. Though the First Amendment creates a strong presumption against punishing protected speech even inadvertently, the balance need not always be struck in that direction. We have never, for instance, required proof beyond a reasonable doubt in civil cases where First Amendment interests are at stake, though such a requirement would protect speech more than the alternative standards would. Likewise, the possibility that defamation liability would chill even true speech has not led us to require an actual malice standard in all libel cases. Nor has the possibility that overbroad regulations may chill commercial speech convinced us to extend the overbreadth doctrine into the commercial speech area.

We have never set forth a general test to determine when a procedural safeguard is required by the First Amendment — just as we have never set forth a general test to determine what constitutes a compelling state interest, or what categories of speech are so lacking in value that they fall outside the protection of the First Amendment, or many other matters — and we do not purport to do so now. . . . None of us have discovered a general principle to determine where the line is to be drawn. We must therefore reconcile ourselves to answering the question on a case-by-case basis, at least until some workable general rule emerges.

Accordingly, all we say today is that the propriety of a proposed procedure must turn on the particular context in which the question arises — on the cost of the procedure and the relative magnitude and constitutional significance of the risks it would decrease and increase. And to evaluate these factors here we have to return to the issue we dealt with in *Connick* and in the cases that came before it: What is it about the government's role as employer that gives it a freer hand in regulating the speech of its employees than it has in regulating the speech of the public at large?

B

We have never explicitly answered this question, though we have always assumed that its premise is correct — that the government as employer indeed has far broader powers than does the government as sovereign. This assumption is amply borne out by considering the practical realities of government employment, and the many situations in which, we believe, most observers would agree that the government must be able to restrict its employees' speech.

To begin with, even many of the most fundamental maxims of our First Amendment jurisprudence cannot reasonably be applied to speech by government employees. The First Amendment demands a tolerance of "verbal tumult, discord, and even offensive utterance," as "necessary side effects of . . . the process of open debate." But we have never expressed doubt that a government employer may bar its employees from using [an] offensive utterance to members of the public, or to the people with whom they work. "Under the First Amendment there is no such thing as a false idea"; the "fitting remedy for evil counsels is good ones." But when an employee counsels her coworkers to do their job in a way with which the public employer disagrees, her managers may tell her to stop, rather than relying on counter-speech. The First Amendment reflects the "profound national commitment to the principle that debate on public issues should be uninhibited, robust, and wide-open." But though a private person is perfectly free to uninhibitedly and robustly criticize a state governor's legislative program, we have never suggested that the Constitution bars the governor from firing a high-ranking deputy for doing the same thing. Even something as close to the core of the First Amendment as participation in political campaigns may be prohibited to government employees.

Government employee speech must be treated differently with regard to procedural requirements as well. For example, speech restrictions must generally precisely define the speech they target. Yet surely a public employer may, consistently with the First Amendment, prohibit its employees from being "rude to customers," a standard almost certainly too vague when applied to the public at large.

Likewise, we have consistently given greater deference to government predictions of harm used to justify restriction of employee speech than to predictions of harm used to justify restrictions on the speech of the public at large. Few of the examples we have discussed involve tangible, present interference with the agency's operation. The danger in them is mostly speculative. One could make a respectable argument that political activity by government employees is generally not harmful; or that high officials should allow more public dissent by their subordinates; or that even in a government workplace the free market of ideas is superior to a command economy. But we have given substantial weight to government employers' reasonable predictions of disruption, even when the speech involved is on a matter of public concern, and even though when the government is acting as sovereign our review of legislative predictions of harm is considerably less deferential. Similarly, we have refrained from intervening in government employer decisions that are based on speech that is of entirely private concern. Doubtless some such speech is sometimes nondisruptive; doubtless it is sometimes of value to the speakers and the listeners. But we have declined to question government employers' decisions on such matters.

This does not, of course, show that the First Amendment should play no role in government employment decisions. Government employees are often in the best position to know what ails the agencies for which they work; public debate may gain much from their informed opinions. And a government employee, like any citizen, may have a strong, legitimate interest in speaking out on public matters. In many such situations the government may have to make a substantial showing that the speech is, in fact, likely to be disruptive before it may be punished. Moreover, the government may certainly choose to give additional protections to its employees beyond what is mandated by the First Amendment, out of respect for the values underlying the First Amendment, values central to our social order as well as our legal system.

But the above examples do show that constitutional review of government employment decisions must rest on different principles than review of speech restraints imposed by the government as sovereign. . . .

. . . Government agencies are charged by law with doing particular tasks. Agencies hire employees to help do those tasks as effectively and efficiently as possible. When someone who is paid a salary so that she will contribute to an agency's effective operation begins to do or say things that detract from the agency's effective operation, the government employer must have some power to restrain her. The reason the governor may, in the example given above, fire the deputy is not that this dismissal would somehow be narrowly tailored to a compelling government interest. It is that the governor and the governor's staff have a job to do, and the governor justifiably feels that a quieter subordinate would allow them to do this job more effectively.

The key to First Amendment analysis of government employment decisions, then, is this: The government's interest in achieving its goals as effectively and efficiently as possible is elevated from a relatively subordinate interest when it acts as sovereign to a significant one when it acts as employer. . . .

C

1

The Court of Appeals' decision, we believe, gives insufficient weight to the government's interest in efficient employment decisionmaking. In other First Amendment contexts the need to safeguard possibly protected speech may indeed outweigh the government's efficiency interests. But where the government is acting as employer, its efficiency concerns should . . . be assigned a greater value.

The problem with the Court of Appeals' approach — under which the facts to which the *Connick* test is applied are determined by the judicial factfinder — is that it would force the government employer to come to its factual conclusions through procedures that substantially mirror the evidentiary rules used in court. The government manager would have to ask not what conclusions she, as an experienced professional, can draw from the circumstances, but rather what conclusions a jury would later draw. If she relies on hearsay, or on what she knows about the accused employee's character, she must be aware that this evidence might not be usable in court. If she knows one party is, in her personal experience, more credible than another, she must realize that the jury will not share that personal experience. If she thinks the alleged offense is so egregious that it is proper to discipline the accused employee even though the evidence is ambiguous, she must consider that a jury might decide the other way.

But employers, public and private, often do rely on hearsay, on past similar conduct, on their personal knowledge of people's credibility, and on other factors that the judicial process ignores. Such reliance may sometimes be the most effective way for the employer to avoid future recurrences of improper and disruptive conduct. What works best in a judicial proceeding may not be appropriate in the employment context. If one employee accuses another of misconduct, it is reasonable for a government manager to credit the allegation more if it is consistent with what the manager knows of the character of the accused. Likewise, a manager may legitimately want to discipline an employee based on complaints by patrons that the employee has been rude, even though these complaints are hearsay.

It is true that these practices involve some risk of erroneously punishing protected speech. The government may certainly choose to adopt other practices, by law or by contract. But we do not believe that the First Amendment requires it to do so. . . .

2

On the other hand, we do not believe that the court must apply the *Connick* test only to the facts as the employer thought them to be, without considering the reasonableness of the employer's conclusions. Even in situations where courts have recognized the special expertise and special needs of certain decisionmakers, the deference to their conclusions has never been complete. It is necessary that the decisionmaker reach its conclusion about what was said in good faith, rather than as a pretext; but it does not follow that good faith is sufficient. . . .

We think employer decisionmaking will not be unduly burdened by having courts look to the facts as the employer *reasonably* found them to be. It may be unreasonable, for example, for the employer to come to a conclusion based on no evidence at all. Likewise, it may be unreasonable for an employer to act based on extremely weak evidence when strong evidence is clearly available — if, for instance, an employee is accused of writing an improper letter to the editor, and instead of just reading the letter, the employer decides what it said based on unreliable hearsay.

If an employment action is based on what an employee supposedly said, and a reasonable supervisor would recognize that there is a substantial likelihood that what was actually said was protected, the manager must tread with a certain amount of care. This need not be the care with which trials, with their rules of evidence and procedure, are conducted. It should, however, be the care that a reasonable manager would use before making an employment decision — discharge, suspension, reprimand, or whatever else — of the sort involved in the particular case. . . .

Of course, there will often be situations in which reasonable employers would disagree about who is to be believed, or how much investigation needs to be done, or how much evidence is needed to come to a particular conclusion. In those situations, many different courses of action will necessarily be reasonable. . . .

* * *

3

We disagree with JUSTICE STEVENS' contention that the test we adopt "provides less protection for a fundamental constitutional right than the law ordinarily provides for less important rights." We have never held that it is a violation of the Constitution for a government employer to discharge an employee based on substantively incorrect information. Where an employee has a property interest in her job, the only protection we have found the Constitution gives her is a right to adequate procedure. And an at-will government employee — such as Churchill apparently was — generally has no claim based on the Constitution at all.

Of course, an employee may be able to challenge the substantive accuracy of the employer's factual conclusions under state contract law, or under some state statute or common-law cause of action. In some situations, the employee may even have a federal statutory claim. Likewise, the State or Federal Governments may, if they choose, provide similar protection to people fired because of their speech. But this protection is not mandated by the Constitution.

* * *

III

Applying the foregoing to this case, it is clear that if petitioners really did believe Perkins-Graham's and Ballew's story, and fired Churchill because of it, they must win. Their belief, based on the investigation they conducted, would have been entirely reasonable. After getting the initial report from Ballew, who overheard the conversation, Waters and Davis approached and interviewed Perkins-Graham, and then interviewed Ballew again for confirmation. In response to Churchill's grievance, Hopper met directly with Churchill to hear her side of the story, and instructed Magin to interview Ballew one more time. Management can spend only so much of their time on any one employment decision. By the end of the termination process, Hopper, who made the final decision, had the word of two trusted employees, the endorsement of those employees' reliability by three hospital managers, and the benefit of a face-to-face meeting with the employee he fired. With that in hand, a reasonable manager could have concluded that no further time needed to be taken. . . .

And under the *Connick* test, Churchill's speech as reported by Perkins-Graham and Ballew was unprotected. Even if Churchill's criticism of cross-training reported by Perkins-Graham and Ballew was speech on a matter of public concern — something we need not decide — the potential disruptiveness of the speech as reported was enough to outweigh whatever First Amendment value it might have had. According to Ballew, Churchill's speech may have substantially dampened Perkins-Graham's interest in working in obstetrics. Discouraging people from coming to work for a department certainly qualifies as disruption. Moreover, Perkins-Graham perceived Churchill's statements about Waters to be "unkind and inappropriate," and told management that she knew they could not continue to "tolerate that kind of negativism" from Churchill. This is strong evidence that Churchill's complaining, if not dealt with, threatened to undermine management's authority in Perkins-Graham's eyes. And finally, Churchill's statement, as reported by Perkins-Graham, that it "wasn't possible" to "wipe the slate clean" between her and Waters could certainly make management doubt Churchill's future effectiveness. As a matter of law, this potential disruptiveness was enough to outweigh whatever First Amendment value the speech might have had.

* * *

Nonetheless, we agree with the Court of Appeals that the District Court erred in granting summary judgment in petitioners' favor. Though Davis and Waters would have been justified in firing Churchill for the statements outlined above, there remains the question whether Churchill was actually fired because of those statements, or because of something else.

Churchill has produced enough evidence to create a material issue of disputed fact about petitioners' actual motivation. Churchill had criticized the cross-training policy in the past; management had exhibited some sensitivity about the criticisms; Churchill pointed to some other conduct by hospital management that, if viewed in the light most favorable to her, would show that they were hostile to her because of her criticisms. A reasonable factfinder might therefore, on this record, conclude that petitioners actually fired Churchill not because of the disruptive things she said to Perkins-Graham, but because of nondisruptive statements about cross-training that they thought she may have made in the same conversation, or because of other statements she may have made earlier. If this is so, then the court will have to determine whether those statements were protected speech, a different matter than the one before us now.

. . . [W]e vacate the judgment of the Court of Appeals and remand the case for further proceedings consistent with this opinion.

* * *

JUSTICE SCALIA, with whom JUSTICE KENNEDY and JUSTICE THOMAS join, concurring in the judgment.

The central issue in this case is whether we shall adhere to our previously stated rule that a public employer's disciplining of an employee violates the Speech and Press Clause of the First Amendment only if it is in retaliation for the employee's speech on a matter of public concern. JUSTICE O'CONNOR would add to this prohibition a requirement that the employer conduct an investigation before taking disciplinary action in certain circumstances. This recognition of a broad new First Amendment procedural right is in my view unprecedented, superfluous to the decision in the present case, unnecessary for protection of public-employee speech on matters of public concern, and unpredictable in its application and consequences.

I

* * *

The proposed right to an investigation before dismissal for speech not only expands the concept of "First Amendment procedure" into brand new areas, but brings it into disharmony with our cases involving government employment decided under the Due Process Clause. As JUSTICE O'CONNOR acknowledges, those cases hold that public employees who, like Churchill, lack a protected property interest in their jobs, are not entitled to any sort of a hearing before dismissal. *See, e.g., Board of Regents of State Colleges v. Roth* (1972). Such employees can be dismissed with impunity (insofar as federal constitutional protections are concerned) for the reason, *accurate or not*, that they are incompetent, that they have been guilty of unexcused absences, that they have stolen money from the faculty honor bar — or indeed *for no reason at all*. But under JUSTICE O'CONNOR's opinion, if a reason happens to be given, and if the reason relates to speech and "there is a substantial likelihood that what was actually said was protected" (whatever that means), an investigation to assure that the speech was not the sort protected by the First Amendment must be conducted — after which, presumably, the dismissal can still proceed even if the speech was not what the employer had thought it was, so long as it was not speech on an issue of public importance. In the present case, for example, if the requisite "First Amendment investigation" disclosed that Nurse Churchill had not been demeaning her superiors, but had been complaining about the perennial end-of-season slump of the Chicago Cubs, her dismissal, erroneous as it was, would have been perfectly OK.

This is a strange jurisprudence indeed. And the reason it is strange is that JUSTICE O'CONNOR has in effect converted the government employer's First Amendment liability with respect to "public concern" speech from liability for intentional wrong to liability for mere negligence. What she proposes is, at bottom, not new procedural protections for established First Amendment rights, but rather new First Amendment rights. *Pickering v. Board of Ed. of Township High School Dist. 205, Will Cty.* (1968), did not require government-employer "protection" of "public concern" speech, but merely forbade government-employer hostility to such speech. "[I]t is essential," *Pickering* said, "that [public employees] be able to speak out freely on such questions without fear of *retaliatory* dismissal." (emphasis added). *See also Connick v. Myers* (1983) (same). The critical inquiry for the factfinder in these cases is whether the employment decision was, "in fact, made in retaliation for [the] exercise of the constitutional right of free speech." A category of employee speech is certainly not being "retaliated against" if it is no more and no less subject to being mistaken for a disciplinable infraction than is any other category of speech or conduct.

II

The creation of procedural First Amendment rights in this case is all the more remarkable because it is unnecessary to the disposition of the matter. After imposing the new duty upon government employers, JUSTICE O'CONNOR's opinion concludes that it was satisfied anyway — *i.e.*, that the investigation conducted by the hospital was "entirely reasonable." And then, to make the creation of the new duty doubly irrelevant, it finds that the case must be remanded anyway for a pretext inquiry: whether "petitioners actually fired Churchill not because of the disruptive things she said to Perkins-Graham, but because of nondisruptive statements about cross-training that they thought she may have made in the same conversation, or because of other statements she may have made earlier." Surely this offends the doctrine that constitutional questions that need not be addressed should be avoided.

The requirement of a pretext inquiry, I think, renders creation of the new First Amendment right of investigation not only superfluous to the disposition of the present case, but superfluous to the protection of previously established speech rights. JUSTICE O'CONNOR makes no attempt to justify the right of investigation on historical grounds (it is quite unheard of). The entire asserted basis for it is pragmatic and functional: without it the government employee's right not to be fired for his speech cannot be protected. The availability of a pretext inquiry disproves that argument. Judicial inquiry into the genuineness of a public employer's asserted permissible justification for an employment decision — be it unprotected speech, general insubordination, or laziness — is all that is necessary to avoid the targeting of "public interest" speech condemned in *Pickering*.

Our cases have hitherto considered this sort of inquiry all the protection needed. *Mt. Healthy City Bd. of Ed. v. Doyle* (1977) involved an arguably weaker case for the public employer than the present one, in that there was a "mixed motive" for the disciplinary action — that is, the employer admitted that the "public concern" speech was part of the reason for the discharge, but asserted that other valid reasons were in any event sufficient. In deciding that case, we found no need to invent procedural requirements, but simply directed the District Court "to determine whether the Board had shown by a preponderance of the evidence that it would have reached the same decision as to respondent's [e]mployment even in the absence of the protected conduct." The objective, we said, was to "protec[t] against the invasion of constitutional rights without commanding undesirable consequences not necessary to the assurance of those rights."

The Court considers "pretext" analysis sufficient in many other areas. And it considers "pretext" analysis sufficient in other First Amendment contexts. For example, in *Renton v. Playtime Theatres, Inc.* (1986), after holding that zoning laws restricting the location of movie theaters do not violate the First Amendment unless they are a pretext for preventing free speech, we did not think it necessary to prescribe "reasonable" procedures for zoning commissions across the Nation; we left it to factfinders to determine whether zoning regulations are prompted by legitimate or improper factors. . . .

JUSTICE STEVENS believes that "pretext" review is inadequate, since "it provides less protection for a fundamental constitutional right than the law ordinarily provides for less exalted rights"; and "[o]rdinarily," he contends, "when someone acts to another person's detriment based upon a factual judgment, the actor assumes the risk that an impartial adjudicator may come to a different conclusion." But that is true in contractual realms only to the extent that the contract provides a "right" whose elimination constitutes a legal "detriment." An employee dismissable at will *can* be fired on the basis of an erroneous factual judgment, with no legal recourse — which is what happened here. Churchill also had a *non*contractual right: the right not to be dismissed (even from an at-will government job) in retaliation for her expression of views on a matter of public concern. That right was not violated, since she was dismissed for another reason, erroneous though it may have been. The issue before us has nothing to do with according the deprivation of a right the ordinary degree of protection; it has to do with expanding the protection accorded a government employee's public-interest speech from (1) protection against retaliation, to (2) protection against retaliation and mistake.

* * *

JUSTICE STEVENS, with whom JUSTICE BLACKMUN joins, dissenting.

* * *

The plurality correctly points out that we have never decided whether the governing version of the facts in public employment free speech cases is "what the government employer thought was said, or . . . what the trier of fact ultimately determines to have been said." To me it is clear that the latter must be controlling. The First Amendment assures public employees that they may express their views on issues of public concern without fear of discipline or termination as long as they do so in an appropriate manner and at an appropriate time and place. A violation occurs when a public employee is fired for uttering speech on a matter of public concern that is not unduly disruptive of the operations of the relevant agency. The violation does not vanish merely because the firing was based upon a reasonable mistake about what the employee said. A First Amendment claimant need not allege bad faith; the controlling question is not the regularity of the agency's investigative procedures, or the purity of its motives, but whether the employee's freedom of speech has been "abridged."

* * *

NOTES AND QUESTIONS

1. Consider the plurality's statement of the basic constitutional doctrine which governs whether public employees may be terminated on the basis of the exercise of their First Amendment rights:

> To be protected, the speech must be on a matter of public concern, and the employee's interest in expressing herself on this matter must not be outweighed by any injury the speech could cause to "'the interest of the State, as an employer, in promoting the efficiency of the public services it performs through its employees.'"

511 U.S. at 668 (quoting *Connick v. Myers*, 461 U.S. 138, 142 (1983) (quoting *Pickering v. Bd. of Educ.*, 391 U.S. 563, 568 (1968))). Do the Justices all agree that this is the standard? Do you see that the standard has three elements, with the employee first proving an adverse employment action premised upon the employee's speech; second, that the speech was of public concern; and third, that the exercise of the speech right outweighs the government employer's interest in the efficient functioning of the office? Why did Justice Scalia file a separate concurring opinion? Does this decision advance or retard the protection of First Amendment interests? Does it advance or retard any other governmental interests?

2. Beyond restricting an employee's speech, the First Amendment may be implicated if the government seeks to fire or refuse to promote an individual because of their political party affiliation. In *Elrod v. Burns*, 427 U.S. 347 (1976), a Court plurality under the late Justice Brennan found that party affiliation could not be used at least with respect to nonpolicymaking employees. In *Branti v. Finkel*, 445 U.S. 507 (1980), the Court extended the ruling when a Democratic administration sought to discharge two Republican public defenders. The Court disavowed the policymaking distinction and indicated that the essential inquiry was whether the government hiring authority could demonstrate that party affiliation is an appropriate requirement for the effective performance of the public office involved. The Court's decision in *Rutan v. Republican Party of Illinois*, 497 U.S. 62 (1990), extended the same principle to promotions, transfers and recalls after layoffs. Finally, in *O'Hare Truck Service Inc. v. Northlake, Ill.*, 518 U.S. 712 (1996), the Court applied the principle even to an independent contractor who lost his service contract for refusing to support the local political party. Justice Scalia has consistently dissented in this line of cases premised on the long history of political patronage, noting in particular, that even Supreme Court Justices owe their initial appointment to their political loyalties.

3. An older line of cases allows government to prohibit its employees from engaging in partisan political activities, whether on the job or off. For example, the federal Hatch Act precludes government job holders from taking "an active part in political management or political campaigns." 5 U.S.C. § 7324 (1994). The Court accepted the limitation reasoning that public officials would be more even-handed if not involved politically. *United Public Workers v. Mitchell*, 330 U.S. 75 (1947). *Accord, United States Civil Service Commission v. National Association of Letter Carriers, AFL-CIO*, 413 U.S. 548 (1973). While Justice Douglas strongly dissented arguing that "it was of no concern of Government what an employee does in his spare time, whether religion, recreation, social work, or politics is his hobby — unless what he does impairs efficiency or other facets of the merits of his job." *Id.* at 597 (Douglas, J., dissenting). What do you think? Would you be comfortable pursuing an important licensing matter for your business if the administrator was wearing the opposite political button from the one you were sporting?

4. There have been many other cases which have involved governmental actions attempting to curtail speech in a variety of government-run settings, for example in schools and libraries. During the Vietnam war era, one Supreme Court decision mentioned briefly earlier, *Tinker v. Des Moines Independent Community School District*, 393 U.S. 503 (1969), held that students might engage in expressive activities at school so long as their actions did not cause "substantial disruption" of school activities. *Id.* at 514. Does this effectively balance the students' need to exercise their First Amendment rights with the school authorities' needs to maintain order to carry out their educational tasks? This is one of the murkier areas of the Supreme Court's First Amendment jurisprudence. Subsequent decisions have ruled that "vulgar or offensive" speech is not entitled to the same protection as that in *Tinker* (*Bethel School District v. Fraser*, 478 U.S. 675 (1986)), and that the rule in *Tinker* does not apply when a school administrator restricts the content of articles published in a school news-paper, which is a part of the curriculum. *Hazelwood Sch. Dist. v. Kuhlmeier*, 484 U.S. 260 (1988). Finally, the Court has ruled that administrators may remove books from the school libraries which are thought to be "vulgar or obscene," but may not remove books if their purpose is to impose an official political orthodoxy or ideology. *Board of Education v. Pico*, 457 U.S. 853 (1982).

5. Would you have predicted the result in each of the holdings described in the previous Note? Do you understand why several of these cases raised anew the question of whether or not it was appropriate for the Supreme Court to have extended the First Amendment's prohibitions on Congress to the state and local authorities? Should education be something that ought exclusively to be in the hands of state and local authorities, or should the federal courts be involved in the manner they have been in recent years? In *Bartnicki v. Vopper*, 532 U.S. 514 (2001), a conversation in which union leaders made threats against the public school officials opposing them in a labor dispute was illegally intercepted and then provided to a radio station, which broadcast it. The Court, per Justice Stevens, held that the First Amendment protected the broadcast from criminal prosecution, trumping countervailing privacy and statutory limits:

> In this case, the basic purpose of the statute at issue is to "protec[t] the privacy of wire[, electronic,] and oral communications." The statute does not distinguish based on the content of the intercepted conversa-tions, nor is it justified by reference to the content of those conversa-tions. Rather, the communications at issue are singled out by virtue of the fact that they were illegally intercepted — by virtue of the source, rather than the subject matter.

> On the other hand, the naked prohibition against disclosures is fairly characterized as a regulation of pure speech [and] is not a regulation of conduct. . . .

> As a general matter, "state action to punish the publication of truth-ful information seldom can satisfy constitutional standards." *Smith v. Daily Mail Publishing Co.* (1979). More specifically, this Court has

repeatedly held that "if a newspaper lawfully obtains truthful information about a matter of public significance then state officials may not constitutionally punish publication of the information, absent a need . . . of the highest order."

* * *

. . . Privacy of communication is an important interest, and Title III's restrictions are intended to protect that interest, thereby "encouraging the uninhibited exchange of ideas and information among private parties . . . ." Moreover, the fear of public disclosure of private conversations might well have a chilling effect on private speech.

* * *

Accordingly, it seems to us that there are important interests to be considered on *both* sides of the constitutional calculus. In considering that balance, we acknowledge that some intrusions on privacy are more offensive than others, and that the disclosure of the contents of a private conversation can be an even greater intrusion on privacy than the interception itself. As a result, there is a valid independent justification for prohibiting such disclosures by persons who lawfully obtained access to the contents of an illegally intercepted message, even if that prohibition does not play a significant role in preventing such interceptions from occurring in the first place.

* * *

In this case, privacy concerns give way when balanced against the interest in publishing matters of public importance. As Warren and Brandeis stated in their classic law review article: "The right of privacy does not prohibit any publication of matter which is of public or general interest." *The Right to Privacy*, 4 HARV. L.REV. 193, 214 (1890). One of the costs associated with participation in public affairs is an attendant loss of privacy.

* * *

We think it clear that parallel reasoning requires the conclusion that a stranger's illegal conduct does not suffice to remove the First Amendment shield from speech about a matter of public concern. The months of negotiations over the proper level of compensation for teachers at the Wyoming Valley West High School were unquestionably a matter of public concern, and respondents were clearly engaged in debate about that concern.

6. What about speech by judges or those seeking election as judges? May a state choose to have judges elected by the voters (rather than appointed, as is the case for federal judges) and then limit what judges can say during their election campaigns? In *Republican Party of Minnesota v. White*, 536 U.S. 765 (2002), the Court considered a Minnesota restriction barring candidates for judicial office from "announc[ing] his or her views on disputed legal or political issues." The Court held that the so-called "announce clause" violated the First Amendment:

> There is an obvious tension between the article of Minnesota's popularly approved Constitution which provides that judges shall be elected, and the Minnesota Supreme Court's announce clause which places most subjects of interest to the voters off limits. The candidate-speech restrictions of all the other States that have them are also the product of judicial fiat. The disparity is perhaps unsurprising, since the ABA, which originated the announce clause, has long been an opponent of judicial elections. . . . That opposition may be well taken (it certainly had the support of the Founders of the Federal Government), but the First Amendment does not permit it to achieve its goal by leaving the principle of elections in place while preventing candidates from discussing what the elections are about. "[T]he greater power to dispense with elections altogether does not include the lesser power to conduct elections under conditions of state-imposed voter ignorance. If the State chooses to tap the energy and the legitimizing power of the democratic process, it must accord the participants in that process . . . the First Amendment rights that attach to their roles." . . .

Justice Ginsburg, joined by Justices Stevens, Souter, and Breyer, dissented. For them, Minnesota's announce clause was a legimate method of insuring judicial independence and furthering due process:

> Prohibiting a judicial candidate from pledging or promising certain results if elected directly promotes the State's interest in preserving public faith in the bench. When a candidate makes such a promise during a campaign, the public will no doubt perceive that she is doing so in the hope of garnering votes. And the public will in turn likely conclude that when the candidate decides an issue in accord with that promise, she does so at least in part to discharge her undertaking to the voters in the previous election and to prevent voter abandonment in the next. The perception of that unseemly *quid pro quo* — a judicial candidate's promises on issues in return for the electorate's votes at the polls — inevitably diminishes the public's faith in the ability of judges to administer the law without regard to personal or political self-interest.

Is the real problem judicial elections themselves? Justice Kennedy noted in concurrence that "By abridging speech based on its content, Minnesota impeaches its own system of free and open elections. . . . The State cannot opt for an elected judiciary and then assert that its democracy, in order to work as desired, compels the abridgement of speech." Kennedy cautioned the court to avoid criticizing the State's choice to use open elections as to do so would "implicitly condemn countless elected state judges without warrant." Interestingly, Justice O'Connor — the only Justice who has ever stood for election as a state court judge — argued strongly in a separate concurrence against the practice of electing judges. Apart from the announce clause, which she agreed could not withstand constitutional scrutiny, Justice O'Connor stated that she was "concerned that, even aside from what judicial candidates may say while campaigning, the very practice of electing judges undermines" the interest of fairness and impartiality. Elected judges, she argued, were aware that their decisions in cases affect election prospects, and even if judges resisted such pressure, the public would doubt the impartiality of elected judges. Beyond this, contested judicial elections often require substantial funds. *See* Schotland, *Financing Judicial Elections, 2000: Change and Challenge*, 2001 L. REV. MICH. STATE U. DETROIT COLLEGE OF LAW 849, 866 (reporting that in 2000, the 13 candidates in a partisan election for 5 seats on the Alabama Supreme Court spent an average of $1,092,076 on their campaigns); American Bar Association, Report and Recommendations of the Task Force on Lawyers' Political Contributions, pt.2 (July 1998) (reporting that in 1995, one candidate for the Pennsylvania Supreme Court raised $1,848,142 in campaign funds, and that in 1986, $2,700,000 was spent on the race for Chief Justice of the Ohio Supreme Court). Wrote Justice O'Connor: "unless the pool of judicial candidates is limited to those wealthy enough to independently fund their campaigns, a limitation unrelated to judicial skill, the cost of campaigning requires judicial candidates to engage in fundraising. Yet relying on campaign donations may leave judges feeling indebted to certain parties or interest groups." Again, the public's confidence in judicial actors would lessen as they engaged in ever greater fundraising.

What is the counterpoint in support of judicial elections? Is it a sufficient justification for judicial elections at the state level that state court judges possess the power to make common law, and sometimes, shape state constitutions as well?

c. Speech Within Private Associations

ROBERTS v. UNITED STATES JAYCEES
468 U.S. 609 (1984)

JUSTICE BRENNAN delivered the opinion of the Court.

This case requires us to address a conflict between a State's efforts to eliminate gender-based discrimination against its citizens and the constitutional freedom of association asserted by members of a private organization. In the decision under review, the Court of Appeals for the Eighth Circuit concluded that, by requiring the United States Jaycees to admit women as full voting members, the Minnesota Human Rights Act violates the First and Fourteenth Amendment rights of the organization's members. We . . . now reverse.

A

The United States Jaycees (Jaycees), founded in 1920 as the Junior Chamber of Commerce, is a nonprofit membership corporation, incorporated in Missouri with national headquarters in Tulsa, Okla. The objective of the Jaycees, as set out in its bylaws, is to pursue

> "such educational and charitable purposes as will promote and foster the growth and development of young men's civic organizations in the United States, designed to inculcate in the individual membership of such organization a spirit of genuine Americanism and civic interest, and as a supplementary education institution to provide them with opportunity for personal development and achievement and an avenue for intelligent participation by young men in the affairs of their community, state and nation, and to develop true friendship and understanding among young men of all nations."

The organization's bylaws establish seven classes of membership, including individual or regular members, associate individual members, and local chapters. Regular membership is limited to young men between the ages of 18 and 35, while associate membership is available to individuals or groups ineligible for regular membership, principally women and older men. An associate member, whose dues are somewhat lower than those charged regular members, may not vote, hold local or national office, or participate in certain leadership training and awards programs. The bylaws define a local chapter as "[a]ny young men's organization of good repute existing in any community within the United States, organized for purposes similar to and consistent with those" of the national organization. The ultimate policymaking authority of the Jaycees rests with an annual national convention, consisting of delegates from each local chapter, with a national president and board of directors. At the time of trial in August 1981, the Jaycees had approximately 295,000 members in 7,400 local chapters affiliated with 51 state organizations. There were at that time about 11,915 associate members. The national organization's executive vice president estimated at trial that women associate members make up about two percent of the Jaycees' total membership.

New members are recruited to the Jaycees through the local chapters, although the state and national organizations are also actively involved in recruitment through a variety of promotional activities. A new regular member pays an initial fee followed by annual dues; in exchange, he is entitled to participate in all of the activities of the local, state, and national organizations. The national headquarters employs a staff to develop "program kits" for use by local chapters that are designed to enhance individual development, community development, and members' management skills. These materials include courses in public speaking and personal finances as well as community programs related to charity, sports, and public health. The national office also makes available to members a range of personal products, including travel accessories, casual wear, pins, awards, and other gifts. The programs, products, and other activities of the organization are all regularly featured in publications made available to the membership, including a magazine entitled "Future."

B

In 1974 and 1975, respectively, the Minneapolis and St. Paul chapters of the Jaycees began admitting women as regular members. Currently, the memberships and boards of directors of both chapters include a substantial proportion of women. As a result, the two chapters have been in violation of the national organization's bylaws for about 10 years. The national organization has imposed a number of sanctions on the Minneapolis and St. Paul chapters for violating the bylaws, including denying their members eligibility for state or national office or awards programs, and refusing to count their membership in computing votes at national conventions.

In December 1978, the president of the national organization advised both chapters that a motion to revoke their charters would be considered at a forthcoming meeting of the national board of directors in Tulsa. Shortly after receiving this notification, members of both chapters filed charges of discrimination with the Minnesota Department of Human Rights. The complaints alleged that the exclusion of women from full membership required by the national organization's bylaws violated the Minnesota Human Rights Act (Act), which provides in part:

> "It is an unfair discriminatory practice:

> "To deny any person the full and equal enjoyment of the goods, services, facilities, privileges, advantages, and accommodations of a place of public accommodation because of race, color, creed, religion, disability, national origin or sex."

The term "place of public accommodation" is defined in the Act as "a business, accommodation, refreshment, entertainment, recreation, or transportation facility of any kind, whether licensed or not, whose goods, services, facilities, privileges, advantages or accommodations are extended, offered, sold, or otherwise made available to the public."

After an investigation, the Commissioner of the Minnesota Department of Human Rights found probable cause to believe that the sanctions imposed on the local chapters by the national organization violated the statute and ordered that an evidentiary hearing be held before a state hearing examiner. Before that hearing took place, however, the national organization brought suit against various state officials, appellants here, in the United States District Court for the District of Minnesota, seeking declaratory and injunctive relief to prevent enforcement of the Act. The complaint alleged that, by requiring the organization to accept women as regular members, application of the Act would violate the male members' constitutional rights of free speech and association. With the agreement of the parties, the District Court dismissed the suit without prejudice, stating that it could be renewed in the event the state administrative proceeding resulted in a ruling adverse to the Jaycees.

The proceeding before the Minnesota Human Rights Department hearing examiner then went forward and, upon its completion, the examiner filed findings of fact and conclusions of law. The examiner concluded that the Jaycees organization is a "place of public accommodation" within the Act and that it had engaged in an unfair discriminatory practice by excluding women from regular membership. He ordered the national organization to cease and desist from discriminating against any member or applicant for membership on the basis of sex and from imposing sanctions on any Minnesota affiliate for admitting women. The Jaycees then filed a renewed complaint in the District Court, which in turn certified to the Minnesota Supreme Court the question whether the Jaycees organization is a "place of public accommodation" within the meaning of the State's Human Rights Act.

With the record of the administrative hearing before it, the Minnesota Supreme Court answered that question in the affirmative. Based on the Act's legislative history, the court determined that the statute is applicable to any "public business facility." It then concluded that the Jaycees organization (a) is a "business" in that it sells goods and extends privileges in exchange for annual membership dues; (b) is a "public" business in that it solicits and recruits dues-paying members based on unselective criteria; and (c) is a public business "facility" in that it conducts its activities at fixed and mobile sites within the State of Minnesota.

Subsequently, the Jaycees amended its complaint in the District Court to add a claim that the Minnesota Supreme Court's interpretation of the Act rendered it unconstitutionally vague and overbroad. The federal suit then proceeded to trial, after which the District Court entered judgment in favor of the state officials. On appeal, a divided Court of Appeals for the Eighth Circuit reversed. The Court of Appeals determined that, because "the advocacy of political and public causes, selected by the membership, is a not insubstantial part of what [the Jaycees] does," the organization's right to select its members is protected by the freedom of association guaranteed by the First Amendment. It further decided that application of the Minnesota statute to the Jaycees' membership policies would produce a "direct and substantial" interference with that freedom, because it would necessarily result in "some change in the Jaycees' philosophical cast," and would attach penal sanctions to those responsible for maintaining the policy. The court concluded that the State's interest in eradicating discrimination is not sufficiently compelling to outweigh this interference with the Jaycees' constitutional rights, because the organization is not wholly "public," the state interest had been asserted selectively, and the antidiscrimination policy could be served in a number of ways less intrusive of First Amendment freedoms.

Finally, the court held, in the alternative, that the Minnesota statute is vague as construed and applied and therefore unconstitutional under the Due Process

Clause of the Fourteenth Amendment. In support of this conclusion, the court relied on a statement in the opinion of the Minnesota Supreme Court suggesting that, unlike the Jaycees, the Kiwanis Club is "private" and therefore not subject to the Act. By failing to provide any criteria that distinguish such "private" organizations from the "public accommodations" covered by the statute, the Court of Appeals reasoned, the Minnesota Supreme Court's interpretation rendered the Act unconstitutionally vague.

II

Our decisions have referred to constitutionally protected "freedom of association" in two distinct senses. In one line of decisions, the Court has concluded that choices to enter into and maintain certain intimate human relationships must be secured against undue intrusion by the State because of the role of such relationships in safeguarding the individual freedom that is central to our constitutional scheme. In this respect, freedom of association receives protection as a fundamental element of personal liberty. In another set of decisions, the Court has recognized a right to associate for the purpose of engaging in those activities protected by the First Amendment — speech, assembly, petition for the redress of grievances, and the exercise of religion. The Constitution guarantees freedom of association of this kind as an indispensable means of preserving other individual liberties.

The intrinsic and instrumental features of constitutionally protected association may, of course, coincide. In particular, when the State interferes with individuals' selection of those with whom they wish to join in a common endeavor, freedom of association in both of its forms may be implicated. The Jaycees contend that this is such a case. Still, the nature and degree of constitutional protection afforded freedom of association may vary depending on the extent to which one or the other aspect of the constitutionally protected liberty is at stake in a given case. We therefore find it useful to consider separately the effect of applying the Minnesota statute to the Jaycees on what could be called its members' freedom of intimate association and their freedom of expressive association.

A

The Court has long recognized that, because the Bill of Rights is designed to secure individual liberty, it must afford the formation and preservation of certain kinds of highly personal relationships a substantial measure of sanctuary from unjustified interference by the State. Without precisely identifying every consideration that may underlie this type of constitutional protection, we have noted that certain kinds of personal bonds have played a critical role in the culture and traditions of the Nation by cultivating and transmitting shared ideals and beliefs; they thereby foster diversity and act as critical buffers between the individual and the power of the State. Moreover, the constitutional shelter afforded such relationships reflects the realization that individuals draw much of their emotional enrichment from close ties with others. Protecting these relationships from unwarranted state interference therefore safeguards the ability independently to define one's identity that is central to any concept of liberty.

The personal affiliations that exemplify these considerations, and that therefore suggest some relevant limitations on the relationships that might be entitled to this sort of constitutional protection, are those that attend the creation and sustenance of a family — marriage, childbirth, the raising and education of children, and cohabitation with one's relatives. Family relationships, by their nature, involve deep attachments and commitments to the necessarily few other individuals with whom one shares not only a special community of thoughts, experiences, and beliefs but also distinctively personal aspects of one's life. Among other things, therefore, they are distinguished by such attributes as relative smallness, a high degree of selectivity in decisions to begin and maintain the affiliation, and seclusion from others in critical aspects of the relationship. As a general matter, only relationships with these sorts of qualities are likely to reflect the considerations that have led to an understanding of freedom of association as an intrinsic element of personal liberty. Conversely, an association lacking these qualities — such as a large business enterprise — seems remote from the concerns giving rise to this constitutional protection. Accordingly, the Constitution undoubtedly imposes constraints on the State's power to control the selection of one's spouse that would not apply to regulations affecting the choice of one's fellow employees.

Between these poles, of course, lies a broad range of human relationships that may make greater or lesser claims to constitutional protection from particular incursions by the State. Determining the limits of state authority over an individual's freedom to enter into a particular association therefore unavoidably entails a careful assessment of where that relationship's objective characteristics locate it on a spectrum from the most intimate to the most attenuated of personal attachments. We need not mark the potentially significant points on this terrain with any precision. We note only that factors that may be relevant include size, purpose, policies, selectivity, congeniality, and other characteristics that in a particular case may be pertinent. In this case, however, several features of the Jaycees clearly place the organization outside of the category of relationships worthy of this kind of constitutional protection.

The undisputed facts reveal that the local chapters of the Jaycees are large and basically unselective groups. At the time of the state administrative hearing, the Minneapolis chapter had approximately 430 members, while the St. Paul chapter had about 400. Apart from age and sex, neither the national organization nor the local chapters employ any criteria for judging applicants for membership, and new members are routinely recruited and admitted with no inquiry into their backgrounds. In fact, a local officer testified that he could recall no instance in which an applicant had been denied membership on any basis other than age or sex. Furthermore, despite their inability to vote, hold office, or receive certain awards, women affiliated with the Jaycees attend various meetings, participate in selected projects, and engage in many of the organization's social functions. Indeed, numerous nonmembers of both genders regularly participate in a substantial portion of activities central to the decision of many members to associate with one another, including many of the organization's various community programs, awards ceremonies, and recruitment meetings.

In short, the local chapters of the Jaycees are neither small nor selective. Moreover, much of the activity central to the formation and maintenance of the association involves the participation of strangers to that relationship. Accordingly, we conclude that the Jaycees chapters lack the distinctive characteristics that might afford constitutional protection to the decision of its members to exclude women. We turn therefore to consider the extent to which application of the Minnesota statute to compel the Jaycees to accept women infringes the group's freedom of expressive association.

B

An individual's freedom to speak, to worship, and to petition the government for the redress of grievances could not be vigorously protected from interference by the State unless a correlative freedom to engage in group effort toward those ends were not also guaranteed. According protection to collective effort on behalf of shared goals is especially important in preserving political and cultural diversity and in shielding dissident expression from suppression by the majority. Consequently, we have long understood as implicit in the right to engage in activities protected by the First Amendment a corresponding right to associate with others in pursuit of a wide variety of political, social, economic, educational, religious, and cultural ends. In view of the various protected activities in which the Jaycees engages, that right is plainly implicated in this case.

Government actions that may unconstitutionally infringe upon this freedom can take a number of forms. Among other things, government may seek to impose penalties or withhold benefits from individuals because of their membership in a disfavored group; it may attempt to require disclosure of the fact of membership in a group seeking anonymity; and it may try to interfere with the internal organization or affairs of the group. By requiring the Jaycees to admit women as full voting members, the Minnesota Act works an infringement of the last type. There can be no clearer example of an intrusion into the internal structure or affairs of an association than a regulation that forces the group to accept members it does not desire. Such a regulation may impair the ability of the original members to express only those views that brought them together. Freedom of association therefore plainly presupposes a freedom not to associate.

The right to associate for expressive purposes is not, however, absolute: Infringements on that right may be justified by regulations adopted to serve compelling state interests, unrelated to the suppression of ideas, that cannot be achieved through means significantly less restrictive of associational freedoms. We are persuaded that Minnesota's compelling interest in eradicating discrimination against its female citizens justifies the impact that application of the statute to the Jaycees may have on the male members' associational freedoms.

On its face, the Minnesota Act does not aim at the suppression of speech, does not distinguish between prohibited and permitted activity on the basis of viewpoint, and does not license enforcement authorities to administer the statute on the basis of such constitutionally impermissible criteria. Nor does the Jaycees contend that the Act has been applied in this case for the purpose of hampering the organization's ability to express its views. Instead, as the Minnesota Supreme Court explained, the Act reflects the State's strong historical commitment to eliminating discrimination and assuring its citizens equal access to publicly available goods and services. That goal, which is unrelated to the suppression of expression, plainly serves compelling state interests of the highest order.

* * *

. . . [T]he Jaycees has failed to demonstrate that the Act imposes any serious burdens on the male members' freedom of expressive association. *See Hishon v. King & Spalding* (1984) (law firm "has not shown how its ability to fulfill [protected] function[s] would be inhibited by a requirement that it consider [a woman lawyer] for partnership on her merits"). To be sure, as the Court of Appeals noted, a "not insubstantial part" of the Jaycees' activities constitutes protected expression on political, economic, cultural, and social affairs. Over the years, the national and local levels of the organization have taken public positions on a number of diverse issues, and members of the Jaycees regularly engage in a variety of civic, charitable, lobbying, fundraising, and other activities worthy of constitutional protection under the First Amendment. There is, however, no basis in the record for concluding that admission of women as full voting members will impede the organization's ability to engage in these protected activities or to disseminate its preferred views. The Act requires no change in the Jaycees' creed of promoting the interests of young men, and it imposes no restrictions on the organization's ability to exclude individuals with ideologies or philosophies different from those of its existing members. *Cf. Democratic Party of United States v. Wisconsin* [(1981)] (recognizing the right of political parties to "protect themselves 'from intrusion by those with adverse political principles'"). Moreover, the Jaycees already invites women to share the group's views and philosophy and to participate in much of its training and community activities. Accordingly, any claim that admission of women as full voting members will impair a symbolic message conveyed by the very fact that women are not permitted to vote is attenuated at best.

While acknowledging that "the specific content of most of the resolutions adopted over the years by the Jaycees has nothing to do with sex," the Court of Appeals nonetheless entertained the hypothesis that women members might have a different view or agenda with respect to these matters so that, if they are allowed to vote, "some change in the Jaycees' philosophical cast can reasonably be expected." It is similarly arguable that, insofar as the Jaycees is organized to promote the views of young men whatever those views happen to be, admission of women as voting members will change the message communicated by the group's speech because of the gender-based assumptions of the audience. Neither supposition, however, is supported by the record. In claiming that women might have a different attitude about such issues as the federal budget, school prayer, voting rights, and foreign relations, or that the organization's public positions would have a different effect if the group were not "a purely young men's association," the Jaycees relies solely on unsupported generalizations about the relative interests and perspectives of men and women. Although such generalizations may or may not have a statistical basis in fact with respect to particular positions adopted by the Jaycees, we have repeatedly condemned legal decisionmaking that relies uncritically on such assumptions. In the absence of a showing far more substantial than that attempted by the Jaycees, we decline to indulge in the sexual stereotyping that underlies appellee's contention that, by allowing women to vote, application of the Minnesota Act will change the content or impact of the organization's speech.

In any event, even if enforcement of the Act causes some incidental abridgment of the Jaycees' protected speech, that effect is no greater than is necessary to accomplish the State's legitimate purposes. . . .

III

We turn finally to appellee's contentions that the Minnesota Act, as interpreted by the State's highest court, is unconstitutionally vague and overbroad. The void-for-vagueness doctrine reflects the principle that "a statute which either forbids or requires the doing of an act in terms so vague that [persons] of common intelligence must necessarily guess at its meaning and differ as to its application, violates the first essential of due process of law." The requirement that government articulate its aims with a reasonable degree of clarity ensures that state power will be exercised only on behalf of policies reflecting an authoritative choice among competing social values, reduces the danger of caprice and discrimination in the administration of the laws, enables individuals to conform their conduct to the requirements of law, and permits meaningful judicial review.

We have little trouble concluding that these concerns are not seriously implicated by the Minnesota Act, either on its face or as construed in this case. In deciding that the Act reaches the Jaycees, the Minnesota Supreme Court used a number of specific and objective criteria — regarding the organization's size, selectivity, commercial nature, and use of public facilities — typically employed in determining the applicability of state and federal antidiscrimination statutes to the membership policies of assertedly private clubs. The Court of Appeals seemingly acknowledged that the Minnesota court's construction of the Act by use of these familiar standards ensures that the reach of the statute is readily ascertainable. It nevertheless concluded that the Minnesota court introduced a constitutionally fatal element of uncertainty into the statute by suggesting that the Kiwanis Club might be sufficiently "private" to be outside the scope of the Act. Like the dissenting judge in the Court of Appeals, however, we read the illustrative reference to the Kiwanis Club, which the record indicates has a formal procedure for choosing members on the basis of specific and selective criteria, as simply providing a further refinement of the standards used to determine whether an organization is "public" or "private." By offering this counter-example, the Minnesota Supreme Court's opinion provided the statute with more, rather than less, definite content.

The contrast between the Jaycees and the Kiwanis Club drawn by the Minnesota court also disposes of appellee's contention that the Act is unconstitutionally overbroad. The Jaycees argues that the statute is "susceptible of sweeping and improper application," because it could be used to restrict the membership decisions of wholly private groups organized for a wide variety of political, religious, cultural, or social purposes. Without considering the extent to which such groups may be entitled to constitutional protection from the operation of the Minnesota Act, we need only note that the Minnesota Supreme Court expressly rejected the contention that the Jaycees should "be viewed analogously to private organizations such as the Kiwanis International Organization." The state court's articulated willingness to adopt limiting constructions that would exclude private groups from the statute's reach, together with the commonly used and sufficiently precise standards it employed to determine that the Jaycees is not such a group, establish that the Act, as currently construed, does not create an unacceptable risk of application to a substantial amount of protected conduct.

* * *

JUSTICE O'CONNOR, concurring in part and concurring in the judgment.

* * *

I

The Court analyzes Minnesota's attempt to regulate the Jaycees' membership using a test that I find both overprotective of activities undeserving of constitutional shelter and underprotective of important First Amendment concerns. The Court declares that the Jaycees' right of association depends on the organization's making a "substantial" showing that the admission of unwelcome members "will change the message communicated by the group's speech." I am not sure what showing the Court thinks would satisfy its requirement of proof of a membership-message connection, but whatever it means, the focus on such a connection is objectionable.

. . . Whether an association is or is not constitutionally protected in the selection of its membership should not depend on what the association says or why its members say it.

* * *

. . . [T]his Court's case law recognizes radically different constitutional protections for expressive and nonexpressive associations. The First Amendment is offended by direct state control of the membership of a private organization engaged exclusively in protected expressive activity, but no First Amendment interest stands in the way of a State's rational regulation of economic transactions by or within a commercial association. The proper approach to analysis of First Amendment claims of associational freedom is, therefore, to distinguish nonexpressive from expressive associations and to recognize that the former lack the full constitutional protections possessed by the latter.

II

Minnesota's attempt to regulate the membership of the Jaycees chapters operating in that State presents a relatively easy case for application of the expressive-commercial dichotomy. Both the Minnesota Supreme Court and the United States District Court, which expressly adopted the state court's findings, made findings of fact concerning the commercial nature of the Jaycees' activities. The Court of Appeals, which disagreed with the District Court over the legal conclusions to be drawn from the facts, did not dispute any of those findings. "The Jaycees is not a political party, or even primarily a political pressure group, but the advocacy of political and public causes, selected by the membership, is a not insubstantial part of what it does. . . . [A] good deal of what the [Jaycees] does indisputably comes within the right of association . . . in pursuance of the specific ends of speech, writing, belief, and assembly for redress of grievances."

There is no reason to question the accuracy of this characterization. Notwithstanding its protected expressive activities, the Jaycees — otherwise known as the Junior Chamber of Commerce — is, first and foremost, an organization that, at both the national and local levels, promotes and practices the art of solicitation and management. The organization claims that the training it offers its members gives them an advantage in business, and business firms do indeed sometimes pay the dues of individual memberships for their employees. Jaycees members hone their solicitation and management skills, under the direction and supervision of the organization, primarily through their active recruitment of new members. "One of the major activities of the Jaycees is the sale of memberships in the organization. It encourages continuous recruitment of members with the expressed goal of increasing membership. . . . The Jaycees itself refers to its members as customers and membership as a product it is selling. More than 80 percent of the national officers' time is dedicated to recruitment, and more than half of the available achievement awards are in part conditioned on achievement in recruitment." The organization encourages record-breaking performance in selling memberships: the current records are 348 for most memberships sold in a year by one person, 134 for most sold in a month, and 1,586 for most sold in a lifetime.

Recruitment and selling are commercial activities, even when conducted for training rather than for profit. The "not insubstantial" volume of protected Jaycees activity found by the Court of Appeals is simply not enough to preclude state regulation of the Jaycees' commercial activities. The State of Minnesota has a legitimate interest in ensuring nondiscriminatory access to the commercial opportunity presented by membership in the Jaycees. The members of the Jaycees may not claim constitutional immunity from Minnesota's antidiscrimination law by seeking to exercise their First Amendment rights through this commercial organization.

NOTES AND QUESTIONS

1. Does the result in this case surprise you? Why can't the Jaycees discriminate on the basis of sex? Why doesn't the First Amendment, as incorporated through the Fourteenth, protect their right to associate with whom they choose? All seven of the Justices who participated in this case concurred in the outcome (Justices Burger and Blackmun did not participate — could the fact that they were both Minnesotans have anything to do with this?). Would you have predicted the unanimity?

2. Justice Brennan appears to have ruled that some freedom of association, most notably that involving marriage, procreation, contraception, and family and children, is entitled to more protection than the associational freedom of the Jaycees. Why should this be the case? Justice Brennan did appear to be willing to concede that the Jaycees did have some freedom of association related to their expression of collective views and interests, but he claimed that the state's aim in reducing discrimination on the basis of gender trumped this associational freedom on the part of the Jaycees. Why should this be the case?

3. Notice that Justice O'Connor (the court's only woman at the time) went so far as to suggest that the Jaycees were not really an expressive organization at all, but had as their purpose commercial rather than speech aims. Is there really a difference? Is O'Connor persuasive on this point? Imagine a Minnesota organization formed by lesbians to promote the success of lesbian-owned businesses in Minnesota. Suppose a heterosexual male or female (or alternatively, a gay male) seeks to become a member of the organization and is refused membership. Would this refusal be impermissible under Minnesota law? Would the Minnesota law, as applied to our hypothetical lesbian organization, violate the federal Constitution? Would you need more facts regarding the operation of our hypothetical organization before you could answer the question?

4. The Court has suggested that an intimate association might be allowed greater latitude to discriminate. *See generally* Kenneth Karst, *The Freedom of Intimate Association*, 89 YALE L.J. 624 (1980). Relatedly, perhaps, in *Hurley v. Irish-American Gay, Lesbian, and Bisexual Group of Boston*, 515 U.S. 557 (1995), the Court allowed the private groups organizing the St. Patrick's Day Parade to exclude gays. A unanimous Court found the parade to be an expressive activity, with those organizing it having the right to exclude messages that were antagonistic to that expression.

BOY SCOUTS OF AMERICA v. DALE
530 U.S. 640 (2000)

REHNQUIST, C.J., delivered the opinion of the Court.

* * *

Petitioners are the Boy Scouts of America and the Monmouth Council, a division of the Boy Scouts of America (collectively, Boy Scouts). The Boy Scouts is a private, not-for-profit organization engaged in instilling its system of values in young people. The Boy Scouts asserts that homosexual conduct is inconsistent with the values it seeks to instill. Respondent is James Dale, a former Eagle Scout whose adult membership in the Boy Scouts was revoked when the Boy Scouts learned that he is an avowed homosexual and gay rights activist. The New Jersey Supreme Court held that New Jersey's public accommodations law requires that the Boy Scouts admit Dale. This case presents the question whether applying New Jersey's public accommodations law in this way violates the Boy Scouts' First Amendment right of expressive association. We hold that it does.

* * *

II

In *Roberts v. United States Jaycees* (1984), we observed that "implicit in the right to engage in activities protected by the First Amendment" is "a corresponding right to associate with others in pursuit of a wide variety of political, social, economic, educational, religious, and cultural ends." This right is crucial in preventing the majority from imposing its views on groups that would rather express other, perhaps unpopular, ideas (stating that protection of the right to expressive association is "especially important in preserving political and cultural diversity and in shielding dissident expression from suppression by the majority"). Government actions that may unconstitutionally burden this freedom may take many forms, one of which is "intrusion into the internal structure or affairs of an association" like a "regulation that forces the group to accept members it does not desire." Forcing a group to accept certain members may impair the ability of the group to express those views, and only those views, that it intends to express. Thus, "[f]reedom of association . . . plainly presupposes a freedom not to associate."

The forced inclusion of an unwanted person in a group infringes the group's freedom of expressive association if the presence of that person affects in a significant way the group's ability to advocate public or private viewpoints. *New York State Club Assn., Inc. v. City of New York* (1988). But the freedom of expressive association, like many freedoms, is not absolute. We have held that the freedom could be overridden "by regulations adopted to serve compelling state interests, unrelated to the suppression of ideas, that cannot be achieved through means significantly less restrictive of associational freedoms."

To determine whether a group is protected by the First Amendment's expressive associational right, we must determine whether the group engages in "expressive association." The First Amendment's protection of expressive association is not reserved for advocacy groups. But to come within its ambit, a group must engage in some form of expression, whether it be public or private.

Because this is a First Amendment case where the ultimate conclusions of law are virtually inseparable from findings of fact, we are obligated to independently review the factual record to ensure that the state court's judgment does not unlawfully intrude on free expression. The record reveals the following. The Boy Scouts is a private, nonprofit organization. According to its mission statement:

"It is the mission of the Boy Scouts of America to serve others by helping to instill values in young people and, in other ways, to prepare them to make ethical choices over their lifetime in achieving their full potential.

"The values we strive to instill are based on those found in the Scout Oath and Law:

"Scout Oath

"On my honor I will do my best
"To do my duty to God and my country
"and to obey the Scout Law;
"To help other people at all times;
"To keep myself physically strong,
"mentally awake, and morally straight.

"Scout Law

"A Scout is:
"Trustworthy Obedient
"Loyal Cheerful
"Helpful Thrifty
"Friendly Brave
"Courteous Clean
"Kind Reverent."

Thus, the general mission of the Boy Scouts is clear: "[T]o instill values in young people." The Boy Scouts seeks to instill these values by having its adult leaders spend time with the youth members, instructing and engaging them in activities like camping, archery, and fishing. During the time spent with the youth members, the scoutmasters and assistant scoutmasters inculcate them with the Boy Scouts' values — both expressly and by example. . . .

Given that the Boy Scouts engages in expressive activity, we must determine whether the forced inclusion of Dale as an assistant scoutmaster would significantly affect the Boy Scouts' ability to advocate public or private viewpoints.

This inquiry necessarily requires us first to explore, to a limited extent, the nature of the Boy Scouts' view of homosexuality.

* * *

Obviously, the Scout Oath and Law do not expressly mention sexuality or sexual orientation. And the terms "morally straight" and "clean" are by no means self-defining. . . .

* * *

The Boy Scouts asserts that it "teach[es] that homosexual conduct is not morally straight," and that it does "not want to promote homosexual conduct as a legitimate form of behavior." We accept the Boy Scouts' assertion. We need not inquire further to determine the nature of the Boy Scouts' expression with respect to homosexuality. But because the record before us contains written evidence of the Boy Scouts' viewpoint, we look to it as instructive, if only on the question of the sincerity of the professed beliefs.

A 1978 position statement to the Boy Scouts' Executive Committee, signed by Downing B. Jenks, the President of the Boy Scouts, and Harvey L. Price, the Chief Scout Executive, expresses the Boy Scouts' "official position" with regard to "homosexuality and Scouting":

> "Q. May an individual who openly declares himself to be a homosexual be a volunteer Scout leader?
>
> "A. No. The Boy Scouts of America is a private, membership organization and leadership therein is a privilege and not a right. We do not believe that homosexuality and leadership in Scouting are appropriate. We will continue to select only those who in our judgment meet our standards and qualifications for leadership."

Thus, at least as of 1978 — the year James Dale entered Scouting — the official position of the Boy Scouts was that avowed homosexuals were not to be Scout leaders.

A position statement promulgated by the Boy Scouts in 1991 (after Dale's membership was revoked but before this litigation was filed) also supports its current view.

* * *

We must then determine whether Dale's presence as an assistant scoutmaster would significantly burden the Boy Scouts' desire to not "promote homosexual conduct as a legitimate form of behavior." As we give deference to an association's assertions regarding the nature of its expression, we must also give deference to an association's view of what would impair its expression. . . . That is not to say that an expressive association can erect a shield against antidiscrimination laws simply by asserting that mere acceptance of a member from a particular group would impair its message. But here Dale, by his own admission, is one of a group of gay Scouts who have "become leaders in their community and are open and honest about their sexual orientation." Dale was the copresident of a gay and lesbian organization at college and remains a gay rights activist. Dale's presence in the Boy Scouts would, at the very least, force the organization to send a message, both to the youth members and the world, that the Boy Scouts accepts homosexual conduct as a legitimate form of behavior.

Hurley [*v. Irish-American Gay, Lesbian, and Bisexual Group of Boston* (1995)] is illustrative on this point. There we considered whether the application of Massachusetts' public accommodations law to require the organizers of a private St. Patrick's Day parade to include among the marchers an Irish-American gay, lesbian, and bisexual group, GLIB, violated the parade organizers' First Amendment rights. We noted that the parade organizers did not wish to exclude the GLIB members because of their sexual orientations, but because they wanted to march behind a GLIB banner.

* * *

The New Jersey Supreme Court determined that the Boy Scouts' ability to disseminate its message was not significantly affected by the forced inclusion of Dale as an assistant scoutmaster.

We disagree. . . .

First, associations do not have to associate for the "purpose" of disseminating a certain message in order to be entitled to the protections of the First Amendment. An association must merely engage in expressive activity that could be impaired in order to be entitled to protection. For example, the purpose of the St. Patrick's Day parade in *Hurley* was not to espouse any views about sexual orientation, but we held that the parade organizers had a right to exclude certain participants nonetheless.

Second, even if the Boy Scouts discourages Scout leaders from disseminating views on sexual issues — a fact that the Boy Scouts disputes with contrary evidence — the First Amendment protects the Boy Scouts' method of expression. If the Boy Scouts wishes Scout leaders to avoid questions of sexuality and teach only by example, this fact does not negate the sincerity of its belief discussed above.

Third, the First Amendment simply does not require that every member of a group agree on every issue in order for the group's policy to be "expressive association." The Boy Scouts takes an official position with respect to homosexual conduct, and that is sufficient for First Amendment purposes. . . .

* * *

Having determined that the Boy Scouts is an expressive association and that the forced inclusion of Dale would significantly affect its expression, we inquire whether the application of New Jersey's public accommodations law to require that the Boy Scouts accept Dale as an assistant scoutmaster runs afoul of the Scouts' freedom of expressive association. We conclude that it does.

State public accommodations laws were originally enacted to prevent discrimination in traditional places of public accommodation — like inns and trains. Over time, the public accommodations laws have expanded to cover more places. New Jersey's statutory definition of "'[a] place of public accommodation'" is extremely broad. . . . As the definition of "public accommodation" has expanded from clearly commercial entities, such as restaurants, bars, and hotels, to membership organizations such as the Boy Scouts, the potential for conflict between state public accommodations laws and the First Amendment rights of organizations has increased.

* * *

We recognized in cases such as *Roberts* and [*Board of Directors of Rotary Int'l v. Rotary Club of*] *Duarte* [(1987)] that States have a compelling interest in eliminating discrimination against women in public accommodations. But in each of these cases we went on to conclude that the enforcement of these statutes would not materially interfere with the ideas that the organization sought to express.

* * *

In *Hurley*, we said that public accommodations laws "are well within the State's usual power to enact when a legislature has reason to believe that a given group is the target of discrimination, and they do not, as a general matter, violate the First or Fourteenth Amendments." But we went on to note that in that case "the Massachusetts [public accommodations] law has been applied in a peculiar way" because "any contingent of protected individuals with a message would have the right to participate in petitioners' speech, so that the communication produced by the private organizers would be shaped by all those protected by the law who wish to join in with some expressive demonstration of their own." And in the associational freedom cases such as *Roberts*, *Duarte*, and *New York State Club Assn.*, after finding a compelling state interest, the Court went on to examine whether or not the application of the state law would impose any "serious burden" on the organization's rights of expressive association. So in these cases, the associational interest in freedom of expression has been set on one side of the scale, and the State's interest on the other.

Dale contends that we should apply the intermediate standard of review enunciated in *United States v. O'Brien* (1968), to evaluate the competing interests. There the Court enunciated a four-part test for review of a governmental regulation that has only an incidental effect on protected speech — in that case the symbolic burning of a draft card. A law prohibiting the destruction of draft cards only incidentally affects the free speech rights of those who happen to use a violation of that law as a symbol of protest. But New Jersey's public accommodations law directly and immediately affects associational rights, in this case associational rights that enjoy First Amendment protection. Thus, *O'Brien* is inapplicable.

In *Hurley*, we applied traditional First Amendment analysis to hold that the application of the Massachusetts public accommodations law to a parade violated the First Amendment rights of the parade organizers. Although we did not explicitly deem the parade in *Hurley* an expressive association, the analysis we applied there is similar to the analysis we apply here. We have already concluded that a state requirement that the Boy Scouts retain Dale as an assistant scoutmaster would significantly burden the organization's right to oppose or disfavor homosexual conduct. The state interests embodied in New Jersey's public accommodations law do not justify such a severe intrusion on the Boy Scouts' rights to freedom of expressive association. That being the case, we hold that the First Amendment prohibits the State from imposing such a requirement through the application of its public accommodations law.

* * *

JUSTICE STEVENS' dissent makes much of its observation that the public perception of homosexuality in this country has changed. Indeed, it appears that homosexuality has gained greater societal acceptance. But this is scarcely an argument for denying First Amendment protection to those who refuse to accept these views. The First Amendment protects expression, be it of the popular variety or not. *See, e.g., Texas v. Johnson* (1989). . . . And the fact that an idea may be embraced and advocated by increasing numbers of people is all the more reason to protect the First Amendment rights of those who wish to voice a different view.

* * *

We are not, as we must not be, guided by our views of whether the Boy Scouts' teachings with respect to homosexual conduct are right or wrong; public or judicial disapproval of a tenet of an organization's expression does not justify the State's effort to compel the organization to accept members where such acceptance would derogate from the organization's expressive message. "While the law is free to promote all sorts of conduct in place of harmful behavior, it is not free to interfere with speech for no better reason than promoting an approved message or discouraging a disfavored one, however enlightened either purpose may strike the government."

The judgment of the New Jersey Supreme Court is reversed, and the cause remanded for further proceedings not inconsistent with this opinion.

It is so ordered.

JUSTICE STEVENS, with whom JUSTICE SOUTER, JUSTICE GINSBURG and JUSTICE BREYER join, dissenting.

* * *

The majority holds that New Jersey's law violates BSA's right to associate and its right to free speech. But that law does not "impos[e] any serious burdens" on BSA's "collective effort on behalf of [its] shared goals," *Roberts v. United States Jaycees* (1984), nor does it force BSA to communicate any message that it does not wish to endorse. New Jersey's law, therefore, abridges no constitutional right of the Boy Scouts.

* * *

BSA's published guidance on that topic underscores this point. Scouts, for example, are directed to receive their sex education at home or in school, but not from the organization: "Your parents or guardian or a sex education teacher should give you the facts about sex that you must know." Boy Scout Handbook (1992). . . .

* * *

. . . Insofar as religious matters are concerned, BSA's bylaws state that it is "absolutely nonsectarian in its attitude toward . . . religious training." "The BSA does not define what constitutes duty to God or the practice of religion. This is the responsibility of parents and religious leaders." In fact, many diverse religious organizations sponsor local Boy Scout troops. Because a number of religious groups do not view homosexuality as immoral or wrong and reject discrimination against homosexuals,[3] it is exceedingly difficult to believe that BSA nonetheless adopts a single particular religious or moral philosophy when it comes to sexual orientation. . . . BSA surely is aware that some religions do not teach that homosexuality is wrong.

* * *

II

* * *

At most the 1991 and 1992 statements declare only that BSA believed "homosexual conduct is inconsistent with the requirement in the Scout Oath that a

---

[3] *See, e.g.*, Brief for Deans of Divinity Schools and Rabbinical Institutions as *Amicus Curiae* 8 ("The diverse religi[ous] traditions of this country present no coherent moral message that excludes gays and lesbians from participating as full and equal members of those institutions. Indeed, the movement among a number of the nation's major religious institutions for many decades has been toward public recognition of gays and lesbians as full members of moral communities, and acceptance of gays and lesbians as religious leaders, elders and clergy"); Brief for General Board of Church and Society of the United Methodist Church et al. as *Amicus Curiae* 3 (describing views of The United Methodist Church, the Episcopal Church, the Religious Action Center of Reform Judaism, the United Church Board of Homeland Ministries, and the Unitarian Universalist Association, all of whom reject discrimination on the basis of sexual orientation).

Scout be morally straight and in the Scout Law that a Scout be clean in word and deed." But New Jersey's law prohibits discrimination on the basis of sexual orientation. And when Dale was expelled from the Boy Scouts, BSA said it did so because of his sexual orientation, not because of his sexual conduct.[8]

* * *

Several principles are made perfectly clear by *Jaycees* and *Rotary Club*. First, to prevail on a claim of expressive association in the face of a State's antidiscrimination law, it is not enough simply to engage in some kind of expressive activity. Both the Jaycees and the Rotary Club engaged in expressive activity protected by the First Amendment, yet that fact was not dispositive. Second, it is not enough to adopt an openly avowed exclusionary membership policy. Both the Jaycees and the Rotary Club did that as well. Third, it is not sufficient merely to articulate some connection between the group's expressive activities and its exclusionary policy. The Rotary Club, for example, justified its male-only membership policy by pointing to the "'aspect of fellowship . . . that is enjoyed by the [exclusively] male membership'" and by claiming that only with an exclusively male membership could it "operate effectively" in foreign countries.

Rather, in *Jaycees*, we asked whether Minnesota's Human Rights Law requiring the admission of women "impose[d] any serious burdens" on the group's "collective effort on behalf of [its] shared goals." . . .

The evidence before this Court makes it exceptionally clear that BSA has, at most, simply adopted an exclusionary membership policy and has no shared goal of disapproving of homosexuality. . . .

* * *

. . . A State's antidiscrimination law does not impose a "serious burden" or a "substantial restraint" upon the group's "shared goals" if the group itself is unable to identify its own stance with any clarity.

IV

The majority pretermits this entire analysis. It finds that BSA in fact "'teach[es] that homosexual conduct is not morally straight.'" This conclusion, remarkably, rests entirely on statements in BSA's briefs. . . .

This is an astounding view of the law. I am unaware of any previous instance in which our analysis of the scope of a constitutional right was determined by looking at what a litigant asserts in his or her brief and inquiring no further. It is even more astonishing in the First Amendment area, because, as the major-

---

[8] At oral argument, BSA's counsel was asked: "[W]hat if someone is homosexual in the sense of having a sexual orientation in that direction but does not engage in any homosexual conduct?" Counsel answered: "[I]f that person also were to take the view that the reason they didn't engage in that conduct [was because] it would be morally wrong . . . that person would not be excluded."

ity itself acknowledges, "we are obligated to independently review the factual record." . . .

. . . More critically, that inquiry requires our independent analysis, rather than deference to a group's litigating posture. Reflection on the subject dictates that such an inquiry is required.

Surely there are instances in which an organization that truly aims to foster a belief at odds with the purposes of a State's antidiscrimination laws will have a First Amendment right to association that precludes forced compliance with those laws. But that right is not a freedom to discriminate at will, nor is it a right to maintain an exclusionary membership policy simply out of fear of what the public reaction would be if the group's membership were opened up. . . .

* * *

There is, of course, a valid concern that a court's independent review may run the risk of paying too little heed to an organization's sincerely held views. But unless one is prepared to turn the right to associate into a free pass out of antidiscrimination laws, an independent inquiry is a necessity. Though the group must show that its expressive activities will be substantially burdened by the State's law, if that law truly has a significant effect on a group's speech, even the subtle speaker will be able to identify that impact.

In this case, no such concern is warranted. It is entirely clear that BSA in fact expresses no clear, unequivocal message burdened by New Jersey's law.

V

Even if BSA's right to associate argument fails, it nonetheless might have a First Amendment right to refrain from including debate and dialogue about homosexuality as part of its mission to instill values in Scouts. It can, for example, advise Scouts who are entering adulthood and have questions about sex to talk "with your parents, religious leaders, teachers, or Scoutmaster," and, in turn, it can direct Scoutmasters who are asked such questions "not undertake to instruct Scouts, in any formalized manner, in the subject of sex and family life" because "it is not construed to be Scouting's proper area." Dale's right to advocate certain beliefs in a public forum or in a private debate does not include a right to advocate these ideas when he is working as a Scoutmaster. And BSA cannot be compelled to include a message about homosexuality among the values it actually chooses to teach its Scouts, if it would prefer to remain silent on that subject.

* * *

[A newspaper] article did say that Dale was co-president of the Lesbian/Gay Alliance at Rutgers University, and that group presumably engages in advocacy regarding homosexual issues. But surely many members of BSA engage in expressive activities outside of their troop, and surely BSA does not want all of that expression to be carried on inside the troop. For example, a Scoutmaster may be a member of a religious group that encourages its followers to convert others to its faith. Or a Scoutmaster may belong to a political party that encourages its members to advance its views among family and friends. Yet BSA does not think it is appropriate for Scoutmasters to proselytize a particular faith to unwilling Scouts or to attempt to convert them from one religion to another. Nor does BSA think it appropriate for Scouts or Scoutmasters to bring politics into the troop. From all accounts, then, BSA does not discourage or forbid outside expressive activity, but relies on compliance with its policies and trusts Scouts and Scoutmasters alike not to bring unwanted views into the organization. Of course, a disobedient member who flouts BSA's policy may be expelled. But there is no basis for BSA to presume that a homosexual will be unable to comply with BSA's policy not to discuss sexual matters any more than it would presume that politically or religiously active members could not resist the urge to proselytize or politicize during troop meetings. As BSA itself puts it, its rights are "not implicated unless a prospective leader presents himself as a role model inconsistent with Boy Scouting's understanding of the Scout Oath and Law."

* * *

The majority, though, does not rest its conclusion on the claim that Dale will use his position as a bully pulpit. Rather, it contends that Dale's mere presence among the Boy Scouts will itself force the group to convey a message about homosexuality — even if Dale has no intention of doing so. The majority holds that "[t]he presence of an avowed homosexual and gay rights activist in an assistant scoutmaster's uniform sends a distinc[t] . . . message," and, accordingly, BSA is entitled to exclude that message. . . .

The majority's argument relies exclusively on *Hurley v. Irish-American Gay, Lesbian and Bisexual Group of Boston, Inc.* (1995). In that case, petitioners John Hurley and the South Boston Allied War Veterans Council ran a privately operated St. Patrick's Day parade. Respondent, an organization known as "GLIB," represented a contingent of gays, lesbians, and bisexuals who sought to march in the petitioners' parade "as a way to express pride in their Irish heritage as openly gay, lesbian, and bisexual individuals." . . .

First, it was critical to our analysis that GLIB was actually conveying a message by participating in the parade — otherwise, the parade organizers could hardly claim that they were being forced to include any unwanted message at all. Our conclusion that GLIB was conveying a message was inextricably tied to the fact that GLIB wanted to march in a parade, as well as the manner in which it intended to march. We noted the "inherent expressiveness of marching [in a parade] to make a point," and in particular that GLIB was formed for the purpose of making a particular point about gay pride. . . .

Second, we found it relevant that GLIB's message "would likely be perceived" as the parade organizers' own speech. That was so because "[p]arades and demonstrations . . . are not understood to be so neutrally presented or selectively viewed" as, say, a broadcast by a cable operator, who is usually considered to be "merely 'a conduit' for the speech" produced by others. Rather, parade organizers are usually understood to make the "customary determination about a unit admitted to the parade."

Dale's inclusion in the Boy Scouts is nothing like the case in *Hurley*. His participation sends no cognizable message to the Scouts or to the world. Unlike GLIB, Dale did not carry a banner or a sign; he did not distribute any fact sheet; and he expressed no intent to send any message. If there is any kind of message being sent, then, it is by the mere act of joining the Boy Scouts. Such an act does not constitute an instance of symbolic speech under the First Amendment.

* * *

Furthermore, it is not likely that BSA would be understood to send any message, either to Scouts or to the world, simply by admitting someone as a member. Over the years, BSA has generously welcomed over 87 million young Americans into its ranks. In 1992 over one million adults were active BSA members. The notion that an organization of that size and enormous prestige implicitly endorses the views that each of those adults may express in a non-Scouting context is simply mind boggling. Indeed, in this case there is no evidence that the young Scouts in Dale's troop, or members of their families, were even aware of his sexual orientation, either before or after his public statements at Rutgers University. It is equally farfetched to assert that Dale's open declaration of his homosexuality, reported in a local newspaper, will effectively force BSA to send a message to anyone simply because it allows Dale to be an Assistant Scoutmaster. For an Olympic gold medal winner or a Wimbledon tennis champion, being "openly gay" perhaps communicates a message — for example, that openness about one's sexual orientation is more virtuous than concealment; that a homosexual person can be a capable and virtuous person who should be judged like anyone else; and that homosexuality is not immoral — but it certainly does not follow that they necessarily send a message on behalf of the organizations that sponsor the activities in which they excel. The fact that such persons participate in these organizations is not usually construed to convey a message on behalf of those organizations any more than does the inclusion of women, African-Americans, religious minorities, or any other discrete group. Surely the organizations are not forced by antidiscrimination laws to take any position on the legitimacy of any individual's private beliefs or private conduct.

* * *

I respectfully dissent.

JUSTICE SOUTER, with whom JUSTICE GINSBURG and JUSTICE BREYER join, dissenting.

* * *

. . . I conclude that BSA has not made out an expressive association claim, therefore, not because of what BSA may espouse, but because of its failure to make sexual orientation the subject of my unequivocal advocacy, using the channels it customarily employs to state its message.

* * *

If, on the other hand, an expressive association claim has met the conditions JUSTICE STEVENS describes as necessary, there may well be circumstances in which the antidiscrimination law must yield, as he says. It is certainly possible for an individual to become so identified with a position as to epitomize it publicly. When that position is at odds with a group's advocated position, applying an antidiscrimination statute to require the group's acceptance of the individual in a position of group leadership could so modify or muddle or frustrate the group's advocacy as to violate the expressive associational right. While it is not our business here to rule on any such hypothetical, it is at least clear that our estimate of the progressive character of the group's position will be irrelevant to the First Amendment analysis if such a case comes to us for decision.

NOTES AND QUESTIONS

1. Does the ruling in *Dale* extend to homosexual membership, as well as leadership?

2. Why was the Court so deferential to the Boy Scouts on the issue of whether they associate for the purpose of engaging in expressive activity and whether that expression would be unconstitutionally burdened by the forced inclusion of an unwanted leader? Is it because of the sensitivities of any First Amendment speech claim and that the Court (as an arm of government) should not sit in judgment of the worth of private expression? The Court's deference was criticized by the dissent, but would the dissent have been comfortable with forcing a national civil rights organization to accept a proclaimed Neo-Nazi as one of its leaders?

3. Lingering in the background of this case is whether status discrimination is ever appropriate. The military has attempted to avoid this dilemma with a "don't ask, don't tell" policy — basically, if a member of the service neither volunteers the fact of homosexual status or engages in homosexual practice, there is no basis to exclude such service member from the military. Would this have been a better course for the Boy Scouts? Or are there some sensitive positions (teachers, athletic coaches, etc.) where orientation raises its own moral dilemmas? The dissent notes that some churches caution, as a matter of morality, against any differentiation on the basis of homosexual orientation, but this is not true of all, as some mainline denominations view the orientation, itself, as inclined toward an immoral practice. *See generally,* Vatican Congregation for the Doctrine of Faith, *Responding to Legislative Proposals on Discrimination Against Homosexuals,* 22 ORIGINS 174, 176 (August 6, 1992) ("There are areas in which it is not unjust discrimination to take sexual orientation into account, for example, in the placement of children for adoption or foster care, in employment of teachers or athletic coaches, and in military recruitment.")

4. The dissent claims that the Boy Scouts were merely interested in the public's reaction. But what is wrong with that? Isn't public reaction merely the consequence of expression?

5. Associations may be protected from government regulation that requires disclosure of membership. Such disclosure may chill participation and thus it requires a compelling state interest. *NAACP v. Alabama ex rel. Patterson*, 357 U.S. 449 (1958). However, in *Buckley v. Valeo*, 424 U.S. 1 (1976), the Court upheld a statute requiring every political candidate and committee to keep records of their contributors and to make these records available to the public. Because the Court felt that the disclosure requirements would curtail corruption in campaign finance, there was a significant governmental interest shown.

6. In 1996, nearly 60% of the voters of California by Proposition 198 changed California's closed partisan primary system, used to determine the nominees of political parties, to a blanket primary. Under this new system, all registered voters in a primary could vote for any candidate, regardless of the voter's prior political affiliation. Four political parties, including California's Republicans and Democrats, sought to enforce their respective rules prohibiting non-party members from voting in their primaries, alleging that California's blanket primary violated the First Amendment right of association. In a 7-2 decision, *California Democratic Party v. Jones*, 530 U.S. 567 (2000), the Court invalidated the blanket primary. Justice Scalia's opinion for the Court acknowledges the role states play in the regulation of elections. For example, states can require parties to use the primary format for selecting nominees, mandate a showing of some level of support before allowing candidates ballot space, or require party registration for a reasonable period of time before a primary election. States may not, however, "regulate freely" the processes by which political parties select their nominees. In making the point that the "corollary of the right to associate is the right to not associate," the majority reiterated the notion that political parties may limit control over their decisions to those who share their "interests and persuasions." And perhaps no decision is more important for a political party than nominee selection, which is, in the Court's view, "the crucial juncture at which the appeal to common principles may be translated into . . . political power." Thus, Proposition 198, in order to be held constitutional, needed to be narrowly tailored to serve a compelling state interest, and the Court rejected each of the seven interests proffered by the state as either not sufficiently compelling or as not narrowly tailored to the open-primary requirement

7. In *McConnell v. Federal Elections Committee*, 124 S. Ct. 619 (2003), the Supreme Court, 5-4, considered and upheld most of the Bipartisan Campaign Reform Act of 2002 (BCRA). BCRA primarily amended the Federal Election Campaign Act of 1971 (FECA). FECA regulated the amounts contributed to or expended by candidates. In *Buckley v. Valeo*, 425 U.S. 1 (1976), the Court considered contributions and expenditures to both be forms of speech, with the former more susceptible to limitation. Spending limits go directly to speech, and the Court was unwilling to accept the notion that some speakers are less able than others to spend. In other words, as a matter of constitutional judgment, the Court does not share any public misgiving generally about the expensive nature of campaigns or how such expense may essentially limit public office to the wealthy or their friends.

By contrast, campaign contribution limits are subject to lesser, albeit "closely drawn" scrutiny, the Court reasoned, because campaign contribution (unlike expenditure) limits "entail only a marginal restriction upon the contributor's ability to engage in free communication." Contribution limits are grounded in the important government interest in preventing "both the actual corruption threatened by large financial contributions and the eroding of public confidence in the electoral process through the appearance of corruption."

BCRA continued this theme, bringing into congressional purview so-called "soft money" and issue ads. Soft money was defined very generally as "money as yet unregulated under FECA." FECA had previously only regulated "hard money," or money contributed to a candidate or his or her campaign committee for the purpose of influencing a federal election. Soft money was used to fund activities intended to influence state and local elections, mixed federal and state uses such as get out the vote drives, and to advertise the party in general, even if it mentioned a federal candidate.

Moreover, since FECA's disclosure and reporting requirements applied only to funds designed to explicitly advocate the election or defeat of a particular candidate for federal office, issue ads escaped regulation because they did not directly say, "Vote for Smith." Rather, an issue ad would highlight a politician's voting record on a specific topic, such as gun control, crime, or the protection of unborn life. And so, instead of saying "Vote for Jim Smith," an issue ad would say, "Here is Jim Smith's voting record on gun-control."

BCRA banned the use of soft money by political parties and candidates for a federal election activity. State and local political associations could no longer use soft money in association with federal political parties to coordinate efforts to elect a federal candidate or to donate party money to tax exempt organizations making expenditures in connection with a federal election. Soft money could no longer be used to pay for issue ads that clearly identified a federal candidate. Corporations and labor unions could no longer use general treasury funds to pay for any electioneering communication (issue ads aired to a wide audience within 60 days of a general election or 30 days before a primary). Also, disclosure of anyone who donates $10,000 or more to air an issue ad was required and in certain instances, disclosure was required of any individual who donated $1,000 or more for the ad.

Groups across the political spectrum brought free speech challenges against BCRA. The named plaintiff was Senator Mitch McConnell, a top-ranking Republican Senator, but other plaintiffs included the ACLU, NOW, NRA, and National

Right to Life. The challenge narrowly failed. As an initial matter, the Court reiterated the distinction that first emerged in the seminal decision of *Buckley v. Valeo* between campaign contributions and spending limits. Subject to the lesser level of review applicable to contributions, BCRA passed muster as it was closely tailored to address the compelling government interest of avoiding actual or apparent corruption in politics. Opponents argued that the law was overbroad because the record suggested that the "appearance of corruption" was no more than the usual give and take of politics or attention to constituents. Moreover, said the challengers, there were other narrower ways to address real corruption in politics, namely the federal bribery statutes.

The Court rejected these arguments because anti-bribery laws reach only the most egregious uses of money to obtain influence. Thus, "[i]n speaking of 'improper influence' and 'opportunities for abuse' in addition to 'quid pro quo arrangements,' we [have] recognized a concern not confined to bribery of public officials, but extending to the broader threat from politicians too compliant with the wishes of large contributors." The Court also relied heavily upon stare decisis. "We are also mindful of the fact that in its lengthy deliberations leading to the enactment of BCRA, Congress properly relied on the recognition of its authority contained in *Buckley* and its progeny."

Justice Scalia's dissent lamented that *McConnell* was

> a sad day for freedom of speech. Who could have imagined that the same Court which, within the past four years, has sternly disapproved of restrictions upon such inconsequential forms of expression as virtual child pornography, tobacco advertising, dissemination of illegally intercepted communications, and sexually explicit cable programming, would smile with favor upon a law that cuts to the heart of what the First Amendment is meant to protect: the right to criticize the government.

Given BCRA's complex regulatory scheme and attendant criminal penalties, a person running for a federal office is well in need of an attorney specializing in election and campaign finance law. Thus, yet another impediment has been erected to service by Americans of moderate wealth. Moreover, BCRA is widely perceived as benefitting incumbents over challengers generally. In his dissent, Justice Scalia mentioned that incumbents raise approximately three times more hard money than soft money and that donations from lobbyists to these same incumbents is substantially (approximately 92%) hard money. Is it a coincidence that incumbent members of Congress chose only to regulate soft money in BCRA?

Beyond access to public office, BCRA is said to favor some voices over others, even as the Court majority held that "contribution limits, like other measures aimed at protecting the integrity of the [political] process, tangibly benefit public participation in public debate." But the dissent and other critics of BCRA asked: is it fair that the New York Times (a multibillion dollar media corporation) can produce editorials advocating the election of a given candidate unrestrained by BRCA while the NRA or the ACLU can not? Keep in mind that the NRA and the ACLU are funded by contributions or modest annual membership fees (approximately $35 and $20 a year, respectively).

8. We leave First Amendment free speech and related liberties now to turn to economic liberty. Part of this topic was covered in Chapter Six when we explored the express textual protections of vested contract and property rights. Most, if not all, standard texts on constitutional law fail to consider the relationship between personal and economic liberties in any depth, reflecting an odd modern dichotomy between the two. Should they be treated differently? In a classic article, Robert McCloskey argues that the primary reason personal liberties have been protected more than economic ones is that the former are of great importance to intellectuals, such as lawyers and law professors who populate the Court. Robert McCloskey, *Economic Due Process and the Supreme Court: An Exhumation and Reburial*, 1962 SUP. CT. REV. 34. It's McCloskey's view that economic liberty need not be effaced from constitutional protection, and that the "extreme of the past [*Lochner* era] ha[s] generated the extreme of the present." *Id.* at 43. Along the same lines, Justice Potter Stewart once observed that:

> [T]he dichotomy between personal liberties and property rights is a false one. Property does not have rights. People have rights. The right to enjoy property without unlawful deprivation, no less than the right to speak or the right to travel, is in truth, a "personal" right, whether the "property" in question be a welfare check, a home, or a savings account.

Lynch v. Household Fin. Corp., 405 U.S. 538, 552 (1972). Or might one add the right to pursue a lawful calling? For an excellent, scholarly appraisal of this topic, see BERNARD H. SIEGAN, ECONOMIC LIBERTIES AND THE CONSTITUTION (University of Chicago 1980). Before turning to the controversial subject of substantive economic due process, we examine the guarantees of privileges and immunities in Article IV and a related, similarly worded provision in the Fourteenth Amendment.

B. Economic Liberty

1. Privileges *and* Immunities

The Privileges and Immunities Clause in Article IV, Section 2, reads "The Citizens of each State shall be entitled to all Privileges and Immunities of Citizens in the several states." Under this Clause, there can be no discrimination against out-of-state residents with regard either to express constitutional rights or those economic liberties that relate to livelihood. Thus, the primary focus of Article IV, as it has been interpreted, is the avoidance of interstate discrimination, not the promotion or safeguarding of economic liberty, per se. At various points in history, however, the clause has been argued to have a larger purpose. The Republican abolitionists, for example, in the 19th century posited that it was the intent of Article IV, Section 2 to establish an unbreakable connection between United States citizenship and certain fundamental rights. When this proposition was doubted, the post-Civil War Congress approved the Fourteenth Amendment's Privileges or Immunities Clause to protect certain fundamental rights, including life and liberty, acquiring and possessing property, pursuing one's trade or calling, and in general, happiness. We first take up the non-discrimination interpretation of Article IV, and then turn our attention to the Fourteenth Amendment and, in particular, efforts to secure economic liberty under the Privileges or Immunities Clause and the Due Process Clause of Section 1 of that Amendment.

a. Historical Origins

Article IV, Section 2 is traced by one writer to the concept of "alien friends" in the Magna Carta. R. HOWELL, THE PRIVILEGES AND IMMUNITIES OF STATE CITIZENSHIP 9-13 (1918). More proximately, Article IV repeats a provision of the Articles of Confederation:

> ARTICLE IV. The better to secure and perpetuate mutual friendship and intercourse among the people of the different States in this Union, the free inhabitants of each of these States, paupers, vagabonds and fugitives from justice excepted, shall be entitled to all privileges and immunities of free citizens in the several states; and the people of each State shall have free ingress and regress to and from any other State, and shall enjoy therein all the privileges of trade and commerce, subject to the same duties, impositions and restrictions as the inhabitants thereof respectively, provided that such restriction shall not extend so far as to prevent the removal of property imported into any State, to any other State of which the owner is an inhabitant; provided also that no imposition, duties or restriction shall be laid by any State, on the property of the United States, or either of them.

ARTICLES OF CONFEDERATION art. IV (1781), *reprinted in* 1 U.S.C. at xlv (1994).

Joseph Story explains that this provision in the Articles of Confederation gave rise to confusion:

> It was remarked by the Federalist, that there is a strange confusion in this language. Why the terms, *free inhabitants*, are used in one part of the article, *free citizens* in another, and *people* in another; or what is meant by superadding to "all privileges and immunities of free citizens," "all the privileges of trade and commerce," cannot easily be determined.

3 JOSEPH STORY, COMMENTARIES ON THE CONSTITUTION OF THE UNITED STATES § 1799, at 673 (photo. reprint 1991) (Boston, Hilliard, Gray & Co. 1833). Story then writes:

The provision in the constitution [Article IV, Section 2] avoids all this ambiguity. It is plain and simple in its language; and its object is not easily to be mistaken. Connected with the exclusive power of naturalization in the national government, it puts at rest many of the difficulties, which affected the construction of the article of the confederation. It is obvious, that, if the citizens of each state were to be deemed aliens to each other, they could not take, or hold real estate, or other privileges, except as other aliens. The intention of this clause was to confer on them, if one may so say, a general citizenship; and to communicate all the privileges and immunities, which the citizens of the same state would be entitled to under the like circumstances.

Id. § 1800, at 674-75 (footnotes omitted).

If the purpose of Article IV is the conferral of "general citizenship," it might be thought that this idea would have been more easily and directly achieved with a national, rather than a federalist, government. As discussed in Chapter Four, however, this was not the American objective. The several states were to remain sovereign political communities, possessing large amounts of reserved lawmaking authority. Such lawmaking authority allows for experimentation and different public policy decisions respecting what goods and services are to be provided publicly, and what privately. Thus, the American attachment to federalism mandated that state governments retain some authority to draw distinctions between residents and nonresidents. Politically, nonresidents are denied the vote. Socially, group benefits logically are limited to contributing members of the group. While it is true that there is not a perfect correlation between residency and those who contribute state tax resources (states do tax nonresidents engaged in business within the state and impose sales taxes on nonresidents, for example), residents are perceived as contributing more to state revenue. This perception thus allows states to restrict some state-provided goods to residents, or to favor residents in some way, such as with reduced tuition costs at the state university. *Vlandis v. Kline*, 412 U.S. 441 (1973).

Nevertheless, Article IV does create a general citizenship, and that citizenship entails certain fundamental rights because states cannot draw resident/nonresident distinctions with respect to at least some fundamental or basic rights. The importance of this general citizenship was explained by James Wilson:

James Wilson, *Of Man, as a Member of a Confederation — A History of Confederacies*, in
1 THE WORKS OF JAMES WILSON 313-14
(James DeWitt Andrews ed., Chicago, Callaghan & Co. 1896)
(1791)

When we say, that the government of those states, which unite in the same confederacy, ought to be of the same nature; it is not to be understood, that there should be a precise and exact uniformity in all their particular establishments and laws. It is sufficient that the fundamental principles of their laws and constitutions be consistent and congenial; and that some general rights and privileges should be diffused indiscriminately among them. Among these, the rights and privileges of naturalization hold an important place. Of such consequence was the intercommunication of these rights and privileges in the opinion of my Lord Bacon, that he considered them as the strongest of all bonds to cement and to preserve the union of states. "Let us take a view," says he, "and we shall find, that wheresoever kingdoms and states have been united, and that union incorporated by a bond of mutual naturalization, you shall never observe them afterwards, upon any occasion of trouble or otherwise, to break and sever again." Machiavel, when he inquires concerning the causes, to which Rome was indebted for her splendour and greatness, assigns none of stronger or more extensive operation than this — she easily compounded and incorporated with strangers. This important subject has received a proportioned degree of attention in forming the constitution of the United States. "The citizens of each state shall be entitled to all privileges and immunities of citizens in the several states." In addition to this, the congress have power to "establish a uniform rule of naturalization throughout the United States."

Though a union of laws is, by no means, necessary to a union of states; yet a similarity in their code of *publick* laws is a most desirable object. The publick law is the great sinew of government. The sinews of the different governments, composing the union, should, as far as it can be effected, be equally strong. "In this point," says my Lord Bacon, "the rule holdeth, which was pronounced by an ancient father, touching the diversity of rites in the church; for finding the vesture of the queen in the psalm (who prefigured the church) was of divers colours; and finding again that Christ's coat was without a seam, concludeth well, in veste varietas sit, scissura non sit."

b. Giving Definition

Corfield v. Coryell was the first attempt to give greater definition to what constitutes these basic privileges and immunities of citizenship. We previously saw *Corfield* in Chapter Two, when we discussed the importance of natural law for the interpretation of the Constitution. It will be recalled that *Corfield* was a trespass action for seizing a certain boat, called the Hiram, that had been captured after it was found oyster raking in a cove contrary to local ordinance. The local ordinance provided that those raking oysters in the seabed belonging to the state had either to be state inhabitants or on-board a vessel "owned by some person, inhabitant of, and actually residing in this state." The ordinance was argued to violate the Privileges and Immunities Clause in Article IV. The court disagrees, finding oyster raking not to be one of those fundamental privileges, in part because the court understands the oyster beds to be under the unique and preservative influence of the particular state. As interesting as the ownership of oysters may be, our interest is in the court's description of the fundamental privileges and immunities of citizens.

CORFIELD v. CORYELL
6 F. Cas. 546 (C.C.E.D. Pa. 1823) (No. 3,230)

WASHINGTON, CIRCUIT JUSTICE

[The court inquires whether oyster raking is an inherent natural right or privilege of every citizen, whether or not resident of the state where the oysters are found.]

* * *

The next question is, whether this act infringes that section of the constitution which declares that "the citizens of each state shall be entitled to all the privileges and immunities of citizens in the several states"? The inquiry is, what are the privileges and immunities of citizens in the several states? We feel no hesitation in confining these expressions to those privileges and immunities which are, in their nature, fundamental; which belong, of right, to the citizens of all free governments; and which have, at all times, been enjoyed by the citizens of the several states which compose this Union, from the time of their becoming free, independent, and sovereign. What these fundamental principles are, it would perhaps be more tedious than difficult to enumerate. They may, however, be all comprehended under the following general heads: Protection by the government; the enjoyment of life and liberty, with the right to acquire and possess property of every kind, and to pursue and obtain happiness and safety; subject nevertheless to such restraints as the government may justly prescribe for the general good of the whole. The right of a citizen of one state to pass through, or to reside in any other state, for purposes of trade, agriculture, professional pursuits, or otherwise; to claim the benefit of the writ of habeas corpus; to institute and maintain actions of any kind in the courts of the state; to take, hold and dispose of property, either real or personal; and an exemption from higher taxes or impositions than are paid by the other citizens of the state; may be mentioned as some of the particular privileges and immunities of citizens, which are clearly embraced by the general description of privileges deemed to be fundamental: to which may be added, the elective franchise, as regulated and established by the laws or constitution of the state in which it is to be exercised. These, and many others which might be mentioned, are, strictly speaking, privileges and immunities, and the enjoyment of them by the citizens of each state, in every other state, was manifestly calculated (to use the expressions of the preamble of the corresponding provision in the old articles of confederation) "the better to secure and perpetuate mutual friendship and intercourse among the people of the different states of the Union." But we cannot accede to the proposition which was insisted on by the counsel, that, under this provision of the constitution, the citizens of the several states are permitted to participate in all the rights which belong exclusively to the citizens of any other particular state, merely upon the ground that they are enjoyed by those citizens; much less, that in regulating the use of the common property of the citizens of such state, the legislature is bound to extend to the citizens of all the other states the same advantages as are secured to their own citizens. A several fishery, either as the right to it respects running fish, or such as are stationary, such as oysters, clams, and the like, is as much the property of the individual to whom it belongs, as dry land, or land covered by water; and is equally protected by the laws of the state against the aggressions of others, whether citizens or strangers. Where those private rights do not exist to the exclusion of the common right, that of fishing belongs to all the citizens or subjects of the state. It is the property of all; to be enjoyed by them in subordination to the laws which regulate its use. They may be considered as tenants in common of this property; and they are so exclusively entitled to the use of it, that it cannot be enjoyed by others without the tacit consent, or the express permission of the sovereign who has the power to regulate its use.

This power in the legislature of New Jersey to exclude the citizens of the other states from a participation in the right of taking oysters within the waters of that state, was denied by the plaintiff's counsel, upon principles of public law, independent of the provision of the constitution which we are considering, upon the ground, that they are incapable of being appropriated until they are caught. This argument is unsupported, we think, by authority. Rutherfoth, bk. 1, ch. 5, §§ 4, 5, who quotes Grotius as his authority, lays it down, that, although wild beasts, birds, and fishes, which have not been caught, have never in fact been appropriated, so as to separate them from the common stock to which all men are equally entitled, yet where the exclusive right in the water and soil which a person has occasion to use in taking them is vested in others, no other persons can claim the liberty of hunting, fishing, or fowling, on lands, or waters, which are so appropriated. "The sovereign," says Grotius (bk. 2, ch. 2, § 5), "who has dominion over the land, or waters, in which the fish are, may prohibit foreigners (by which expression we understand him to mean others than subjects or citizens of the state) from taking them." That this exclusive right of taking oysters in the waters of New Jersey has never been ceded by that state, in express terms, to the United States, is admitted by the counsel for the plaintiff; and having shown, as we think we have, that this right is a right of property, vested either in certain individuals, or in the state, for the use of the citizens thereof, it would, in our opinion, be going quite too far to construe the grant of privileges and immunities of citizens, as amounting to a grant of a cotenancy in the common property of the state, to the citizens of all the other states. Such a construction would, in many instances, be productive of the most serious public inconvenience and injury, particularly, in regard to those kinds of fish, which, by being exposed to too general use, may be exhausted. The oyster beds belonging to a state may be abundantly sufficient for the use of the citizens of that state, but might be totally exhausted and destroyed if the legislature could not so regulate the use of them as to exclude the citizens of the other states from taking them, except under such limitations and restrictions as the laws may prescribe.

NOTES AND QUESTIONS

1. Citizenship for Article IV purposes does not include corporations. *Paul v. Virginia*, 75 U.S. (8 Wall.) 168 (1868) (out of state insurance firm was not a citizen within the scope of Article IV, even as it may be a citizen of the place of incorporation for purposes of diversity jurisdiction). As for human persons, citizenship is treated as the equivalent of residence. *Hicklin v. Orbeck*, 437 U.S. 518, 524 n.8 (1978) (citizenship and residence are "essentially interchangeable"). *See also United Bldg. and Constr. Trades Council v. Mayor of Camden*, 465 U.S. 208, 216 (1984).

2. As indicated in *Corfield*, the court found the Privileges and Immunities Clause not to be implicated where the question was distribution of public resources "owned" by the state in question. Professor Jonathan Varat writes: "[s]ome, but not all, public benefits can be reserved for the exclusive or preferential use of the state's inhabitants. The task of separating which can and cannot be reserved poses impressive obstacles." Jonathan D. Varat, *State "Citizenship" and Interstate Equality*, 48 U. CHI. L. REV. 487, 492 (1981). While dispositive in *Corfield*, and some later cases, *see, e.g., McCready v. Virginia*, 94 U.S. 391 (1877) (state power to forbid planting of oysters in state tideland upheld), in *Hicklin v. Orbeck*, 437 U.S. 518 (1978), the Court refused to let Alaska condition contracts for the extraction of oil and gas on an employment preference for state residents. In *Hicklin*, state ownership of the resource was described as "a factor — although often the crucial factor — to be considered in evaluating whether the statute's discrimination against noncitizens violates the Clause." 437 U.S. at 529. In *Hicklin*, the Court reasoned that Alaska's ownership interest in oil and gas was too "attenuated" to allow discrimination against nonresidents. *Id.*

3. Overlap with the dormant Commerce Clause. The Privileges and Immunities Clause and the dormant Commerce Clause are mutually reinforcing, but not entirely coincident. *Hicklin*, 437 U.S. at 531-32. As earlier discussed in Chapter Four, the focus of the dormant Commerce Clause is the avoidance of burdens on interstate commerce; whereas, the Privileges and Immunities Clause is intended to preclude states from discriminating against citizens of other states in favor of its own. *Hague v. CIO*, 307 U.S. 496, 511 (1939). How do the clauses differ otherwise? For starters, corporations may sue under the dormant Commerce Clause. In addition, there are several exceptions to the dormant Commerce Clause which don't carry over to privileges and immunities analysis. First, Congress may expressly remove a dormant Commerce Clause limitation by legislative approval. Second, when a state or local government is acting as a market participant, there is no application of the dormant Commerce Clause. Thus, in *White v. Massachusetts Council of Construction Employers, Inc.*, 460 U.S. 204 (1983), a city requirement that 50 percent of those hired for city construction be city residents did not violate the dormant Commerce Clause, but a similar restriction was held to transgress privileges and immunities. *United Bldg. and Constr. Trades Council v. Mayor of Camden*, 465 U.S. 208 (1984).

4. Defining Privileges and Immunities. *Corfield* is the basic exposition. Many of these rights are expressly protected by the Bill of Rights, and hence, when they are violated, there is little need to state a separate cause of action under the Privileges and Immunities Clause. *Duncan v. Louisiana*, 391 U.S. 145, 166 (1968) (Black, J. concurring) ("What more precious 'privilege' of American citizenship could there be than that privilege to claim the protections of our great Bill of Rights?"). But occasionally a case arises separately, *e.g.*, *Blake v. McClung*, 172 U.S. 239 (1898) (in-state creditor could not be favored over out-of-state creditor with regard to disposition of insolvent's property; to provide such favoritism is to disregard the privilege of owning and disposing of property).

SUPREME COURT OF NEW HAMPSHIRE v. PIPER
470 U.S. 274 (1985)

JUSTICE POWELL delivered the opinion of the Court.

The Rules of the Supreme Court of New Hampshire limit bar admission to state residents. We here consider whether this restriction violates the Privileges and Immunities Clause of the United States Constitution, Art. IV, § 2.

I

A

Kathryn Piper lives in Lower Waterford, Vermont, about 400 yards from the New Hampshire border. In 1979, she applied to take the February 1980 New Hampshire bar examination. Piper submitted with her application a statement of intent to become a New Hampshire resident. Following an investigation, the Board of Bar Examiners found that Piper was of good moral character and met the other requirements for admission. She was allowed to take, and passed, the examination. Piper was informed by the Board that she would have to establish a home address in New Hampshire prior to being sworn in.

On May 7, 1980, Piper requested from the Clerk of the New Hampshire Supreme Court a dispensation from the residency requirement. Although she had a "possible job" with a lawyer in Littleton, New Hampshire, Piper stated that becoming a resident of New Hampshire would be inconvenient. Her house in Vermont was secured by a mortgage with a favorable interest rate, and she and her husband recently had become parents. According to Piper, these "problems peculiar to [her] situation . . . warrant[ed] that an exception be made." [Her request was denied and the lower federal courts decided in her favor]

* * *

B

* * *

The Supreme Court of New Hampshire filed a timely notice of appeal, and we noted probable jurisdiction. We now affirm the judgment of the court below.

II

A

Article IV, § 2, of the Constitution provides that the "Citizens of each State shall be entitled to all Privileges and Immunities of Citizens in the several States." This Clause was intended to "fuse into one Nation a collection of independent, sovereign States." *Toomer v. Witsell*, 334 U.S. 385, 395 (1948). Recognizing this purpose, we have held that it is "[o]nly with respect to those 'privileges' and 'immunities' bearing on the vitality of the Nation as a single entity" that a State must accord residents and nonresidents equal treatment.

* * *

There is nothing in [prior cases] suggesting that the practice of law should not be viewed as a "privilege" under Art. IV, § 2. Like the occupations considered in our earlier cases, the practice of law is important to the national economy. . . .

The lawyer's role in the national economy is not the only reason that the opportunity to practice law should be considered a "fundamental right." We believe that the legal profession has a noncommercial role and duty that reinforce the view that the practice of law falls within the ambit of the Privileges and Immunities Clause. Out-of-state lawyers may — and often do — represent persons who raise unpopular federal claims. In some cases, representation by nonresident counsel may be the only means available for the vindication of federal rights. The lawyer who champions unpopular causes surely is as important to the "maintenance or well-being of the Union" . . . .

B

[New Hampshire] asserts that the Privileges and Immunities Clause should be held inapplicable to the practice of law because a lawyer's activities are "bound up with the exercise of judicial power and the administration of justice." Its contention is based on the premise that the lawyer is an "officer of the court," who "exercises state power on a daily basis." . . .

. . . [A] lawyer is not an "officer" within the ordinary meaning of that word. He "'makes his own decisions, follows his own best judgment, collects his own fees and runs his own business.'" Moreover, we held that the state powers entrusted to lawyers do not "involve matters of state policy or acts of such unique responsibility as to entrust them only to citizens."

Because . . . a lawyer is not an "officer" of the State in any political sense, there is no reason for New Hampshire to exclude from its bar nonresidents. We therefore conclude that the right to practice law is protected by the Privileges and Immunities Clause.[16]

---

[16] . . . Our holding in this case does not interfere with the ability of the States to regulate their bars. The nonresident who seeks to join a bar, unlike the *pro hac* vice applicant, must have the same professional and personal qualifications required of resident lawyers. Furthermore, the nonresident member of the bar is subject to the full force of New Hampshire's disciplinary rules.

III

The conclusion that Rule 42 [of the New Hampshire Supreme Court, excluding nonresidents from the bar,] deprives nonresidents of a protected privilege does not end our inquiry. The Court has stated that "[l]ike many other constitutional provisions, the privileges and immunities clause is not an absolute." The Clause does not preclude discrimination against nonresidents where (i) there is a substantial reason for the difference in treatment; and (ii) the discrimination practiced against nonresidents bears a substantial relationship to the State's objective. In deciding whether the discrimination bears a close or substantial relationship to the State's objective, the Court has considered the availability of less restrictive means.

The Supreme Court of New Hampshire offers several justifications for its refusal to admit nonresidents to the bar. It asserts that nonresident members would be less likely (i) to become, and remain, familiar with local rules and procedures; (ii) to behave ethically; (iii) to be available for court proceedings; and (iv) to do *pro bono* and other volunteer work in the State. We find that none of these reasons meets the test of "substantiality," and that the means chosen do not bear the necessary relationship to the State's objectives.

There is no evidence to support [the New Hampshire Court's] claim that nonresidents might be less likely to keep abreast of local rules and procedures. Nor may we assume that a nonresident lawyer — any more than a resident — would disserve his clients by failing to familiarize himself with the rules. As a practical matter, we think that unless a lawyer has, or anticipates, a considerable practice in the New Hampshire courts, he would be unlikely to take the bar examination and pay the annual dues of $125.

We also find the . . . second justification to be without merit, for there is no reason to believe that a nonresident lawyer will conduct his practice in a dishonest manner. The nonresident lawyer's professional duty and interest in his reputation should provide the same incentive to maintain high ethical standards as they do for resident lawyers. A lawyer will be concerned with his reputation in any community where he practices, regardless of where he may live. Furthermore, a nonresident lawyer may be disciplined for unethical conduct. The Supreme Court of New Hampshire has the authority to discipline all members of the bar, regardless of where they reside.

There is more merit to the . . . assertion that a nonresident member of the bar at times would be unavailable for court proceedings. In the course of litigation, pretrial hearings on various matters often are held on short notice. At times a court will need to confer immediately with counsel. Even the most conscientious lawyer residing in a distant State may find himself unable to appear in court for an unscheduled hearing or proceeding. Nevertheless, we do not believe that this type of problem justifies the exclusion of nonresidents from the state bar. One may assume that a high percentage of nonresident lawyers willing to take the state bar examination and pay the annual dues will reside in places reasonably convenient to New Hampshire. Furthermore, in those cases where the nonresident counsel will be unavailable on short notice, the State can protect its interests through less restrictive means. The trial court, by rule or as an exercise of discretion, may require any lawyer who resides at a great distance to retain a local attorney who will be available for unscheduled meetings and hearings.

The final reason advanced by appellant is that nonresident members of the state bar would be disinclined to do their share of *pro bono* and volunteer work. Perhaps this is true to a limited extent, particularly where the member resides in a distant location. We think it is reasonable to believe, however, that most lawyers who become members of a state bar will endeavor to perform their share of these services. This sort of participation, of course, would serve the professional interest of a lawyer who practices in the State. Furthermore, a nonresident bar member, like the resident member, could be required to represent indigents and perhaps to participate in formal legal-aid work.

* * *

IV

We conclude that New Hampshire's bar residency requirement violates the Privileges and Immunities Clause of Art. IV, § 2, of the United States Constitution. The nonresident's interest in practicing law is a "privilege" protected by the Clause. . . .

JUSTICE WHITE, concurring in the result. [Omitted.]

JUSTICE REHNQUIST, dissenting.

Today the Court holds that New Hampshire cannot decide that a New Hampshire lawyer should live in New Hampshire. This may not be surprising to those who view law as just another form of business frequently practiced across state lines by interchangeable actors; the Privileges and Immunities Clause of Art. IV, § 2, has long been held to apply to States' attempts to discriminate against nonresidents who seek to ply their trade interstate. The decision will be surprising to many, however, because it so clearly disregards the fact that the practice of law is — almost by definition — fundamentally different from those other occupations that are practiced across state lines without significant deviation from State to State. The fact that each State is free, in a large number of areas, to establish *independently* of the other States its own laws for the governance of its citizens, is a fundamental precept of our Constitution that, I submit, is of equal stature with the need for the States to form a cohesive union. What is at issue here is New Hampshire's right to decide that those people who in many ways will intimately deal with New Hampshire's self-governance should reside within that State.

* * *

The Framers of our Constitution undoubtedly wished to ensure that the newly created Union did not revert to its component parts because of inter-state jealousies and insular tendencies, and it seems clear that the Art. IV Privileges and Immunities Clause was one result of these concerns. But the Framers also created a system of federalism that deliberately allowed for the independent operation of many sovereign States, each with their own laws created by their own legislators and judges. The assumption from the beginning was that the various States' laws need not, and would not, be the same; the lawmakers of each State might endorse different philosophies and would have to respond to differing interests of their constituents, based on various factors that were of inherently local character. Any student of our Nation's history is well aware of the differing interests of the various States that were represented at Philadelphia; despite the tremendous improvements in transportation and communication that have served to create a more homogeneous country the differences among the various States have hardly disappeared.

It is but a small step from these facts to the recognition that a State has a very strong interest in seeing that its legislators and its judges come from among the constituency of state residents, so that they better understand the local interests to which they will have to respond. The Court does not contest this point; it recognizes that a State may require its lawmakers to be residents without running afoul of the Privileges and Immunities Clause of Art. IV, § 2.

Unlike the Court, I would take the next step, and recognize that the State also has a very "substantial" interest in seeing that its lawyers also are members of that constituency. . . . My belief that the practice of law differs from other trades and businesses for Art. IV, § 2, purposes is not based on some notion that law is for some reason a superior profession. The reason that the practice of law should be treated differently is that law is one occupation that does not readily translate across state lines. Certain aspects of legal practice are distinctly and intentionally *nonnational*; in this regard one might view this country's legal system as the antithesis of the norms embodied in the Art. IV Privileges and Immunities Clause. . . .

* * *

In any event, I find the less-restrictive-means analysis, which is borrowed from our First Amendment jurisprudence, to be out of place in the context of the Art. IV Privileges and Immunities Clause. . . . This approach perhaps has a place: to the extent that an obvious way to accomplish the State's proffered goal is apparent, the fact that the State did not follow that path may indicate that the State had another, less legitimate goal in mind. But I believe the challenge of a "less restrictive means" should be overcome if merely a legitimate reason exists for not pursuing that path. And in any event courts should not play the game that the Court has played here — independently scrutinizing each asserted state interest to see if it could devise a better way than the State to accomplish that goal.

* * *

NOTES AND QUESTIONS

1. What if the form of the discrimination was not exclusion, but merely differential licensing? In *Ward v. Maryland*, 79 U.S. (12 Wall.) 418 (1870), the Court invalidated a higher licensing fee for non-residential traders of goods, and in *Toomer v. Witsell*, 334 U.S. 385 (1948), the Court struck down a $2,500 license fee for nonresident commercial shrimp fisherman, when residents paid only $25. The Court stated: "one of the privileges which the clause guarantees to citizens of State A is that of doing business in State B on terms of substantial equality with citizens of that State." 334 U.S. at 396.

2. However, discrimination is allowed when the activity is not economic livelihood or a fundamental constitutional right. Thus, in *Baldwin v. Fish and Game Commission*, 436 U.S. 371 (1978), the Court allowed substantially higher elk-hunting license fees for out of state residents, writing, "[the sport] is not a means to the nonresident's livelihood. . . . Equality in access to Montana elk is not basic to the maintenance or well-being of the union." *Id.* at 388. The Court explained in *Baldwin* that the underlying purpose of the Privileges and Immunities Clause in Article IV was to promote a level of interstate harmony, or at least not to allow practices that "frustrate the purposes of the formation of the Union." *Id.* at 387. State discrimination with respect to nonessential activities does not pose the risk of such frustration.

3. Theoretically, as suggested in *Piper*, a state or locality may continue discrimination if it has a substantial reason for doing so and the discrimination itself bears a substantial relationship to the advancement of that reason. In evaluating the substantiality of the relationship between the discrimination and the state's objective, the Court asks if the state could employ less restrictive means. *Piper*, 470 U.S. at 284. The Court has not yet supplied a case that adequately meets this justification. In *Toomer v. Witsell*, 334 U.S. 385 (1948), for example, the Court noted that the state could eliminate the danger of excessive trawling through less restrictive means than discrimination against nonresidents: restricting the type of equipment used in its fisheries, graduating license fees according to the size of the boats, or charging nonresidents a differential to compensate for the added enforcement burden they imposed. *Id.* at 398-99. Chief Justice Rehnquist thought the least restrictive means inquiry too judicially intrusive. *Piper*, 470 U.S. at 294-95 (Renquist, J., dissenting).

4. Note that the Court decides in favor of Ms. Piper because of the discrimination with respect to a fundamental interest, and not merely because of interference with a fundamental interest — namely, the pursuit of a calling or trade. In the *Slaughter-House Cases* considered in the next section, the pursuit of one's lawful occupation is argued to be a protected privilege of all citizens in the fashion of Justice Washington in *Corfield*. In *Piper*, the Court lamely characterizes *Corfield* as representing a theory of "natural rights . . . discarded long ago," 470 U.S. at 281 n.10. The Court cites for this cavalier disregard of natural law originalism, a 1939 opinion dealing with labor picketing and the First

Amendment. Examining that opinion, one does not see any reasoned basis for the disregard of natural law. Indeed, all the Court observes in the earlier cited case is that:

> At one time it was thought that [the privileges and immunities of Article IV] recognized a group of rights which, according to the jurisprudence of the day, were classed as "natural rights"; and that the purpose of the section was to create rights of citizens of the United States by guaranteeing the citizens of every State the recognition of this group of rights by every other State. Such was the view of Justice Washington.

Hague v. CIO, 307 U.S. 496, 511 (1939) (citing *Corfield*).

5. Even though the Court has limited Article IV privileges and immunities to ferreting out improper discrimination between resident and nonresident, it recognizes that licensing laws and grants of exclusive franchises may result from less than pure motive. For example, the Court in a footnote in *Piper* mentions that "[a] former president of the American Bar Association has suggested another possible reason for the rule [excluding nonresident lawyers]: 'Many of the states that have erected fences against out-of-state lawyers have done so primarily to protect their own lawyers from professional competition.' This reason is not 'substantial.'" 470 U.S. at 285 n.18 (quoting Chesterfield Smith, *Time for a National Practice of Law Act*, 64 A.B.A. J. 557, 557 (1978)). The Court went on to observe that "[t]he Privileges and Immunities Clause was designed primarily to prevent such economic protectionism." *Id.* True enough, but the fact that Article IV privilege and immunity analysis is confined to discrimination and separated from its natural rights origin makes it more difficult for the Court to protect all citizens from such illicit, protectionist use of public power. Many thought the Fourteenth Amendment Privileges or Immunities Clause would rectify this difficulty.

2. Privileges *or* Immunities

The Fourteenth Amendment adopted after the Civil War provides, in part: "No State shall make or enforce any law which shall abridge the privileges or immunities of the citizens of the United States." In Chapters Two and Four, we briefly raised the issue of whether this provision was intended to apply (or "incorporate") the Bill of Rights to the states. Justice Hugo Black thought so, writing that these words "seem to me an eminently reasonable way of expressing the idea that henceforth the Bill of Rights shall apply to the States." *Duncan v. Louisiana*, 391 U.S. 145, 166 (Black, J., concurring). There is much historical dispute here, however. In an extensive article, Professor Charles Fairman argues that "Congress would not have attempted [incorporation by this means], the country would not have stood for it, the legislatures would not have ratified." Charles Fairman, *Does the Fourteenth Amendment Incorporate the Bill of Rights? The Original Understanding*, 2 STAN. L. REV. 5, 137 (1949). The most prominent framers of the Fourteenth Amendment spoke differently. Senator

Howard, for example, referenced Justice Washington's earlier articulation of privileges and immunities in *Corfield*, indicating that "[s]uch is the character of the privileges and immunities spoken of in the second section of the fourth article of the Constitution. [And t]o these privileges and immunities . . . should be added the personal rights guarantied and secured by the first eight amendments of the Constitution." Cong. Globe, 39th Cong., 1st Sess. 2765 (1866).

Whatever the intent of the 39th Congress that drafted the Fourteenth Amendment Privileges or Immunities Clause, the claim that this provision places limits upon the states either with natural law rights like those articulated in *Corfield* or the express Bill of Rights was narrowly defeated in the *Slaughter-House Cases*, 83 U.S. (16 Wall.) 36 (1873). *Slaughter-House* involved a state-granted monopoly to the Crescent City Live-Stock and Slaughter-House Company, which greatly diminished the economic liberties of competing houses and the suppliers of meat products. Writing for the Court, Justice Miller nevertheless sustained the government-imposed monopoly on the dubious ground that the Fourteenth Amendment merely had the purpose of establishing or affirming the freedom of slaves, and little else. Justice Miller explicitly refused to apply the Bill of Rights to the states pursuant to the Privileges or Immunities Clause, as Senator Howard had described, because he said:

> [S]uch a construction . . . would constitute this court a perpetual censor upon all legislation of the States, on the civil rights of their own citizens, with authority to nullify such as it did not approve as consistent with those rights, as they existed at the time of the adoption of the amendment.

Id. at 78. Instead, Justice Miller's conception of the protected privileges or immunities of federal citizenship were so abstract and inconsequential that it prompted the dissenters to write that if such is all the amendment means, "it was a vain and idle enactment, which accomplished nothing, and most unnecessarily excited Congress and the people on its passage." *Id.* at 96 (Field, J., dissenting).

SLAUGHTER-HOUSE CASES
83 U.S. (16 Wall.) 36 (1873)

Mr. Justice Miller . . . delivered the opinion of the court.

* * *

The records show that the [Butchers' Association] relied upon, and asserted throughout the entire course of the litigation in the [Louisiana] courts, that the grant of privileges in the charter of defendant, which they were contesting, was a violation of the most important provisions of the thirteenth and fourteenth articles of amendment of the Constitution of the United States. The jurisdiction and the duty of this court to review the judgment of the State court on those questions is clear and is imperative.

The statute . . . assailed as unconstitutional was passed March 8th, 1869, and is entitled "An act to protect the health of the city of New Orleans, to locate the stock-landings and slaughter-houses, and to incorporate the Crescent City Live-Stock Landing and Slaughter-House Company."

* * *

It declares that the company . . . shall have the sole and exclusive privilege of conducting and carrying on the live-stock landing and slaughter-house business within the limits and privilege granted by the act, and that all such animals shall be landed at the stock-landings and slaughtered at the slaughter-houses of the company, and nowhere else. Penalties are enacted for infractions of this provision, and prices fixed for the maximum charges of the company for each steamboat and for each animal landed.

Section five orders the closing up of all other stock-landings and slaughter-houses after the first day of June, in the parishes of Orleans, Jefferson, and St. Bernard, and makes it the duty of the company to permit any person to slaughter animals in their slaughter-houses under a heavy penalty for each refusal. Another section fixes a limit to the charges to be made by the company for each animal so slaughtered in their building, and another provides for an inspection of all animals intended to be so slaughtered, by an officer appointed by the governor of the State for that purpose.

These are the principal features of the statute, and are all that have any bearing upon the questions to be decided by us.

This statute is denounced not only as creating a monopoly and conferring odious and exclusive privileges upon a small number of persons at the expense of the great body of the community of New Orleans, but it is asserted that it deprives a large and meritorious class of citizens — the whole of the butchers of the city — of the right to exercise their trade, the business to which they have been trained and on which they depend for the support of themselves and their families, and that the unrestricted exercise of the business of butchering is necessary to the daily subsistence of the population of the city.

But a critical examination of the act hardly justifies these assertions.

* * *

It is not, and cannot be successfully controverted, that it is both the right and the duty of the legislative body — the supreme power of the State or municipality — to prescribe and determine the localities where the business of slaughtering for a great city may be conducted. To do this effectively it is indispensable that all persons who slaughter animals for food shall do it in those places *and nowhere else.*

* * *

The wisdom of the monopoly granted by the legislature may be open to question, but it is difficult to see a justification for the assertion that the butchers are deprived of the right to labor in their occupation, or the people of their daily service in preparing food, or how this statute, with the duties and guards imposed upon the company, can be said to destroy the business of the butcher, or seriously interfere with its pursuit.

The power here exercised by the legislature of Louisiana is, in its essential nature, one which has been, up to the present period in the constitutional history of this country, always conceded to belong to the States, however it may *now* be questioned in some of its details.

"Unwholesome trades, slaughter-houses, operations offensive to the senses, the deposit of powder, the application of steam power to propel cars, the building with combustible materials, and the burial of the dead, may all," says Chancellor Kent, "be interdicted by law, in the midst of dense masses of population, on the general and rational principle, that every person ought so to use his property as not to injure his neighbors; and that private interests must be made subservient to the general interests of the community." . . .

This power is, and must be from its very nature, incapable of any very exact definition or limitation. Upon it depends the security of social order, the life and health of the citizen, the comfort of an existence in a thickly populated community, the enjoyment of private and social life, and the beneficial use of property. . . .

* * *

. . . But it is said that in creating a [private] corporation for this purpose, and conferring upon it exclusive privileges — privileges which it is said constitute a monopoly — the legislature has exceeded its power. If this statute had imposed on the city of New Orleans precisely the same duties, accompanied by the same privileges, which it has on the corporation which it created, it is believed that no question would have been raised as to its constitutionality. In that case the effect on the butchers in pursuit of their occupation and on the public would have been the same as it is now. Why cannot the legislature confer the same powers on another corporation, created for a lawful and useful public object, that it can on the municipal corporation already existing? . . .

* * *

The proposition is, therefore, reduced to these terms: Can any exclusive privileges be granted to any of its citizens, or to a corporation, by the legislature of a State?

The eminent and learned counsel who has twice argued the negative of this question, has displayed a research into the history of monopolies in England, and the European continent, only equaled by the eloquence with which they are denounced.

But it is to be observed, that all such references are to monopolies established by the monarch in derogation of the rights of his subjects, or arise out of transactions in which the people were unrepresented, and their interests uncared for. The great *Case of Monopolies*, reported by Coke, and so fully stated in the brief, was undoubtedly a contest of the commons against the monarch. The decision is based upon the ground that it was against common law, and the argument was aimed at the unlawful assumption of power by the crown. . . .

But we think it may be safely affirmed, that the Parliament of Great Britain, representing the people in their legislative functions, and the legislative bodies of this country, have from time immemorial to the present day, continued to grant to persons and corporations exclusive privileges — privileges denied to other citizens — privileges which come within any just definition of the word monopoly, as much as those now under consideration; and that the power to do this has never been questioned or denied. . . .

It may, therefore, be considered as established, that the authority of the legislature of Louisiana to pass the present statute is ample, unless some restraint in the exercise of that power be found in the constitution of that State or in the amendments to the Constitution of the United States, adopted since the date of the decisions we have already cited.

If any such restraint is supposed to exist in the constitution of the State, the Supreme Court of Louisiana having necessarily passed on that question, it would not be open to review in this court.

The [Butchers' Association] . . . allege[s] that the statute is a violation of the Constitution of the United States in these several particulars:

That it creates an involuntary servitude forbidden by the thirteenth article of amendment;

That it abridges the privileges and immunities of citizens of the United States;

That it denies to the plaintiffs the equal protection of the laws; and,

That it deprives them of their property without due process of law; contrary to the provisions of the first section of the fourteenth article of amendment.

This court is thus called upon for the first time to give construction to these articles.

We do not conceal from ourselves the great responsibility which this duty devolves upon us. No questions so far-reaching and pervading in their consequences, so profoundly interesting to the people of this country, and so important in their bearing upon the relations of the United States, and of the several States to each other and to the citizens of the States and of the United States, have been before this court during the official life of any of its present members. . . .

* * *

The most cursory glance at these articles discloses a unity of purpose, when taken in connection with the history of the times, which cannot fail to have an important bearing on any question of doubt concerning their true meaning. . . .

* * *

In [the Civil War] slavery, as a legalized social relation, perished. . . . The proclamation of President Lincoln expressed an accomplished fact as to a large portion of the insurrectionary districts, when he declared slavery abolished in them all. But the war being over, those who had succeeded in re-establishing the authority of the Federal government were not content to permit this great act of emancipation to rest on the actual results of the contest or the proclamation of the Executive, both of which might have been questioned in after times, and they determined to place this main and most valuable result in the Constitution of the restored Union as one of its fundamental articles. Hence the thirteenth article of amendment of that instrument. . . .

* * *

To withdraw the mind from the contemplation of this grand yet simple declaration of the personal freedom of all the human race within the jurisdiction of this government — a declaration designed to establish the freedom of four millions of slaves — and with a microscopic search endeavor to find in it a reference to servitudes, which may have been attached to property in certain localities, requires an effort, to say the least of it.

* * *

. . . [In] the light of this recapitulation of events, almost too recent to be called history, but which are familiar to us all; and on the most casual examination of the language of these amendments, no one can fail to be impressed with the one pervading purpose found in them all, lying at the foundation of each, and without which none of them would have been even suggested; we mean the freedom of the slave race, the security and firm establishment of that freedom, and the protection of the newly-made freeman and citizen from the oppressions of those who had formerly exercised unlimited dominion over him. . . .

We do not say that no one else but the negro can share in this protection. . . . And so if other rights are assailed by the States which properly and necessarily fall within the protection of these articles, that protection will apply, though the party interested may not be of African descent. But what we do say, and what we wish to be understood is, that in any fair and just construction of any section or phrase of these amendments, it is necessary to look to the purpose which we have said was the pervading spirit of them all, the evil which they were designed to remedy, and the process of continued addition to the Constitution, until that purpose was supposed to be accomplished, as far as constitutional law can accomplish it.

The first section of the fourteenth article, to which our attention is more specially invited, opens with a definition of citizenship — not only citizenship of the United States, but citizenship of the States. . . .

* * *

. . . Not only may a man be a citizen of the United States without being a citizen of a State, but an important element is necessary to convert the former into the latter. He must reside within the State to make him a citizen of it, but it is only necessary that he should be born or naturalized in the United States to be a citizen of the Union.

It is quite clear, then, that there is a citizenship of the United States, and a citizenship of a State, which are distinct from each other, and which depend upon different characteristics or circumstances in the individual.

We think this distinction and its explicit recognition in this amendment of great weight in this argument, because the next paragraph of this same section, which is the one mainly relied on by the [Butchers' Association], speaks only of privileges and immunities of citizens of the United States, and does not speak of those of citizens of the several States. The argument, however, in favor of the [Butchers' Association] rests wholly on the assumption that the citizenship is the same, and the privileges and immunities guaranteed by the clause are the same.

The language is, "No State shall make or enforce any law which shall abridge the privileges or immunities of citizens of *the United States*." It is a little remarkable, if this clause was intended as a protection to the citizen of a State against the legislative power of his own State, that the word citizen of the State should be left out when it is so carefully used, and used in contradistinction to citizens of the United States, in the very sentence which precedes it. It is too clear for argument that the change in phraseology was adopted understandingly and with a purpose.

Of the privileges and immunities of the citizen of the United States, and of the privileges and immunities of the citizen of the State, and what they respectively are, we will presently consider; but we wish to state here that it is only the former which are placed by this clause under the protection of the Federal Constitution, and that the latter, whatever they may be, are not intended to have any additional protection by this paragraph of the amendment.

If, then, there is a difference between the privileges and immunities belonging to a citizen of the United States as such, and those belonging to the citizen of the State as such the latter must rest for their security and protection where they have heretofore rested; for they are not embraced by this paragraph of the amendment.

* * *

In the Constitution of the United States, which superseded the Articles of Confederation, the corresponding provision is found in section two of the fourth article, in the following words: "The citizens of each State shall be entitled to all the privileges and immunities of citizens of the several States."

There can be but little question that the purpose of both these provisions is the same, and that the privileges and immunities intended are the same in each. In the article of the Confederation we have some of these specifically mentioned, and enough perhaps to give some general idea of the class of civil rights meant by the phrase.

Fortunately we are not without judicial construction of this clause of the Constitution. The first and the leading case on the subject is that of *Corfield v. Coryell*, decided by Mr. Justice Washington in the Circuit Court for the District of Pennsylvania in 1823.

"The inquiry," he says, "is, what are the privileges and immunities of citizens of the several States? We feel no hesitation in confining these expressions to those privileges and immunities which are *fundamental*; which belong of right to the citizens of all free governments, and which have at all times been enjoyed by citizens of the several States which compose this Union, from the time of their becoming free, independent, and sovereign. What these fundamental principles are, it would be more tedious than difficult to enumerate. They may all, however, be comprehended under the following general heads: protection by the government, with the right to acquire and possess property of every kind, and to pursue and obtain happiness and safety, subject, nevertheless, to such restraints as the government may prescribe for the general good of the whole."

* * *

The constitutional provision there alluded to did not create those rights, which it called privileges and immunities of citizens of the States. It threw around them in that clause no security for the citizen of the State in which they were claimed or exercised. Nor did it profess to control the power of the State governments over the rights of its own citizens.

Its sole purpose was to declare to the several States, that whatever those rights, as you grant or establish them to your own citizens, or as you limit or qualify, or impose restrictions on their exercise, the same, neither more nor less, shall be the measure of the rights of citizens of other States within your jurisdiction.

It would be the vainest show of learning to attempt to prove by citations of authority, that up to the adoption of the recent amendments, no claim or pretense was set up that those rights depended on the Federal government for their existence or protection, beyond the very few express limitations which the Federal Constitution imposed upon the States — such, for instance, as the prohibition against ex post facto laws, bills of attainder, and laws impairing the obligation of contracts. But with the exception of these and a few other restrictions, the entire domain of the privileges and immunities of citizens of the States, as above defined, lay within the constitutional and legislative power of the States, and without that of the Federal government. Was it the purpose of the fourteenth amendment, by the simple declaration that no State should make or enforce any law which shall abridge the privileges and immunities of *citizens of the United States*, to transfer the security and protection of all the civil rights which we have mentioned, from the States to the Federal government? And where it is declared that Congress shall have the power to enforce that article, was it intended to bring within the power of Congress the entire domain of civil rights heretofore belonging exclusively to the States?

. . . [S]uch a construction followed by the reversal of the judgments of the Supreme Court of Louisiana in these cases, would constitute this court a perpetual censor upon all legislation of the States, on the civil rights of their own citizens, with authority to nullify such as it did not approve as consistent with those rights, as they existed at the time of the adoption of this amendment. . . .

We are convinced that no such results were intended by the Congress which proposed these amendments, nor by the legislatures of the States which ratified them.

Having shown that the privileges and immunities relied on in the argument are those which belong to citizens of the States as such, and that they are left to the State governments for security and protection, and not by this article placed under the special care of the Federal government, we may hold ourselves excused from defining the privileges and immunities of citizens of the United States which no State can abridge, until some case involving those privileges may make it necessary to do so.

But lest it should be said that no such privileges and immunities are to be found if those we have been considering are excluded, we venture to suggest some which owe their existence to the Federal government, its National character, its Constitution, or its laws.

. . . It is said to be the right of the citizen of this great country, protected by implied guarantees of its Constitution, "to come to the seat of government to assert any claim he may have upon that government, to transact any business he may have with it, to seek its protection, to share its offices, to engage in administering its functions. He has the right of free access to its seaports, through which all operations of foreign commerce are conducted, to the subtreasuries, land offices, and courts of justice in the several States." . . .

Another privilege of a citizen of the United States is to demand the care and protection of the Federal government over his life, liberty, and property when on the high seas or within the jurisdiction of a foreign government. Of this there can be no doubt, nor that the right depends upon his character as a citizen of the United States. The right to peaceably assemble and petition for redress of grievances, the privilege of the writ of *habeas corpus*, are rights of the citizen guaranteed by the Federal Constitution. The right to use the navigable waters of the United States, however they may penetrate the territory of the several States, all rights secured to our citizens by treaties with foreign nations, are dependent upon citizenship of the United States, and not citizenship of a State. One of these privileges is conferred by the very article under consideration. It is that a citizen of the United States can, of his own volition, become a citizen of any State of the Union by a *bona fide* residence therein, with the same rights as other citizens of that State. To these may be added the rights secured by the thirteenth and fifteenth articles of amendment, and by the other clause of the fourteenth, next to be considered.

But it is useless to pursue this branch of the inquiry, since we are of opinion that the rights claimed by [the Butchers' Association] if they have any existence, are not privileges and immunities of citizens of the United States within the meaning of the clause of the fourteenth amendment under consideration.

* * *

The argument has not been much pressed in these cases that the defendant's charter deprives the [Butchers' Association] of their property without due process of law, or that it denies to them the equal protection of the law. The first of these paragraphs has been in the Constitution since the adoption of the fifth amendment, as a restraint upon the Federal power. It is also to be found in some form of expression in the constitutions of nearly all the States, as a restraint upon the power of the States. This law then, has practically been the same as it now is during the existence of the government, except so far as the present amendment may place the restraining power over the States in this matter in the hands of the Federal government.

We are not without judicial interpretation, therefore, both State and National, of the meaning of this clause. And it is sufficient to say that under no construction of that provision that we have ever seen, or any that we deem admissible, can the restraint imposed by the State of Louisiana upon the exercise of their trade by the butchers of New Orleans be held to be a deprivation of property within the meaning of that provision.

"Nor shall any State deny to any person within its jurisdiction the equal protection of the laws."

In the light of the history of these amendments, and the pervading purpose of them, which we have already discussed, it is not difficult to give a meaning to this clause. The existence of laws in the States where the newly emancipated negroes resided, which discriminated with gross injustice and hardship against them as a class, was the evil to be remedied by this clause, and by it such laws are forbidden.

* * *

MR. JUSTICE FIELD, dissenting:

* * *

It is contended in justification for the act in question that it was adopted in the interest of the city, to promote its cleanliness and protect its health, and was the legitimate exercise of what is termed the police power of the State. . . .

*　*　*

In the law in question there are only two provisions which can properly be called police regulations — the one which requires the landing and slaughtering of animals below the city of New Orleans, and the other which requires the inspection of the animals before they are slaughtered. When these requirements are complied with, the sanitary purposes of the act are accomplished. In all other particulars the act is a mere grant to a corporation created by it of special and exclusive privileges by which the health of the city is in no way promoted. It is plain that if the corporation can, without endangering the health of the public, carry on the business of landing, keeping, and slaughtering cattle within a district below the city embracing an area of over a thousand square miles, it would not endanger the public health if other persons were also permitted to carry on the same business within the same district under similar conditions as to the inspection of the animals. The health of the city might require the removal from its limits and suburbs of all buildings for keeping and slaughtering cattle, but no such object could possibly justify legislation removing such buildings from a large part of the State for the benefit of a single corporation. The pretense of sanitary regulations for the grant of the exclusive privileges is a shallow one, which merits only this passing notice.

It is also sought to justify the act in question on the same principle that exclusive grants for ferries, bridges, and turnpikes are sanctioned. But it can find no support there. Those grants are of franchises of a public character appertaining to the government. Their use usually requires the exercise of the sovereign right of eminent domain. It is for the government to determine when one of them shall be granted, and the conditions upon which it shall be enjoyed. It is the duty of the government to provide suitable roads, bridges, and ferries for the convenience of the public, and if it chooses to devolve this duty to any extent, or in any locality, upon particular individuals or corporations, it may of course stipulate for such exclusive privileges connected with the franchise as it may deem proper, without encroaching upon the freedom or the just rights of others. The grant, with exclusive privileges, of a right thus appertaining to the government, is a very different thing from a grant, with exclusive privileges, of a right to pursue one of the ordinary trades or callings of life, which is a right appertaining solely to the individual.

Nor is there any analogy between this act of Louisiana and the legislation which confers upon the inventor of a new and useful improvement an exclusive right to make and sell to others his invention. The government in this way only secures to the inventor the temporary enjoyment of that which, without him, would not have existed. It thus only recognizes in the inventor a temporary property in the product of his own brain.

The act of Louisiana presents the naked case, unaccompanied by any public considerations, where a right to pursue a lawful and necessary calling, previously enjoyed by every citizen, and in connection with which a thousand persons were daily employed, is taken away and vested exclusively for twenty-five years, for an extensive district and a large population, in a single corporation, or its exercise is for that period restricted to the establishments of the corporation, and there allowed only upon onerous conditions.

* * *

But if the exclusive privileges conferred upon the Louisiana corporation can be sustained, it is not perceived why exclusive privileges for the construction and keeping of ovens, machines, grindstones, wine-presses, and for all the numerous trades and pursuits for the prosecution of which buildings are required, may not be equally bestowed upon other corporations or private individuals, and for periods of indefinite duration.

. . . The provisions of the fourteenth amendment, . . . cover, in my judgment, the case before us, and inhibit any legislation which confers special and exclusive privileges like these under consideration. The amendment was adopted to obviate objections which had been raised and pressed with great force to the validity of the Civil Rights Act, and to place the common rights of American citizens under the protection of the National government. . . .

The first clause of the fourteenth amendment changes this whole subject, and removes it from the region of discussion and doubt. . . . The fundamental rights, privileges, and immunities which belong to him as a free man and a free citizen, now belong to him as a citizen of the United States, and are not dependent upon his citizenship of any State. The exercise of these rights and privileges, and the degree of enjoyment received from such exercise, are always more or less affected by the condition and the local institutions of the State, or city, or town where he resides. They are thus affected in a State by the wisdom of its laws, the ability of its officers, the efficiency of its magistrates, the education and morals of its people, and by many other considerations. This is a result which follows from the constitution of society, and can never be avoided, but in no other way can they be affected by the action of the State, or by the residence of the citizen therein. They do not derive their existence from its legislation, and cannot be destroyed by its power.

The amendment does not attempt to confer any new privileges or immunities upon citizens, or to enumerate or define those already existing. It assumes that there are such privileges and immunities which belong of right to citizens as such, and ordains that they shall not be abridged by State legislation. If this inhibition has no reference to privileges and immunities of this character, but only refers, as held by the majority of the court in their opinion, to such privileges and immunities as were before its adoption specially designated in the Constitution or necessarily implied as belonging to citizens of the United States, it was a vain and idle enactment, which accomplished nothing, and most unnecessarily excited Congress and the people on its passage. With privileges and immunities thus designated or implied no State could ever have interfered by its laws, and no new constitutional provision was required to inhibit such interference. The supremacy of the Constitution and the laws of the United States always controlled any State legislation of that character. But if the amendment refers to the natural and inalienable rights which belong to all citizens, the inhibition has a profound significance and consequence.

What, then, are the privileges and immunities which are secured against abridgment by State legislation?

In the first section of the Civil Rights Act [of 1866] Congress has given its interpretation to these terms, or at least has stated some of the rights which, in its judgment, these terms include; it has there declared that they include the right "to make and enforce contracts, to sue, be parties and give evidence, to inherit, purchase, lease, sell, hold, and convey real and personal property, and to full and equal benefit of all laws and proceedings for the security of person and property." That act, it is true, was passed before the fourteenth amendment, but the amendment was adopted, as I have already said, to obviate objections to the act, or, speaking more accurately, I should say, to obviate objections to legislation of a similar character, extending the protection of the National government over the common rights of all citizens of the United States. Accordingly, after its ratification, Congress re-enacted the act under the belief that whatever doubts may have previously existed of its validity, they were removed by the amendment.

The terms, privileges and immunities, are not new in the amendment; they were in the Constitution before the amendment was adopted. They are found in the second section of the fourth article, which declares that "the citizens of each State shall be entitled to all privileges and immunities of citizens in the several States," and they have been the subject of frequent consideration in judicial decisions. In *Corfield v. Coryell*, Mr. Justice Washington said he had "no hesitation in confining these expressions to those privileges and immunities which were, in their nature, fundamental; which belong of right to citizens of all free governments, and which have at all times been enjoyed by the citizens of the several States which compose the Union, from the time of their becoming free, independent, and sovereign"; and, in considering what those fundamental privileges were, he said that perhaps it would be more tedious than difficult to enumerate them, but that they might be "all comprehended under the following general heads: protection by the government; the enjoyment of life and liberty, with the right to acquire and possess property of every kind, and to pursue and obtain happiness and safety, subject, nevertheless, to such restraints as the government may justly prescribe for the general good of the whole." This appears to me to be a sound construction of the clause in question. The privileges and immunities designated are those *which of right belong to the citizens of all free governments*. Clearly among these must be placed the right to pursue a lawful employment in a lawful manner, without other restraint than such as equally affects all persons. In the discussions in Congress upon the passage of the Civil Rights Act repeated reference was made to this language of Mr. Justice Washington. It was cited by Senator Trumbull with the observation that it enumerated the very rights belonging to a citizen of the United States set forth in the first section of the act, and with the statement that all persons born in the United States, being declared by the act citizens of the United States, would thenceforth be entitled to the rights of citizens, and that these were the great fundamental rights set forth in the act; and that they were set forth "as appertaining to every freeman."

* * *

. . . The common privileges and immunities which of right belong to all citizens, stand on a very different footing. These the citizens of each State do carry with them into other States and are secured by the clause in question, in their enjoyment upon terms of equality with citizens of the latter States. . . .

* * *

A monopoly is defined "to be an institution or allowance from the sovereign power of the State by grant, commission, or otherwise, to any person or corporation, for the sole buying, selling, making, working, or using of anything, whereby any person or persons, bodies politic or corporate, are sought to be restrained of any freedom or liberty they had before, or hindered in their lawful trade." All such grants relating to any known trade or manufacture have been held by all the judges of England, whenever they have come up for consideration, to be void at common law as destroying the freedom of trade, discouraging labor and industry, restraining persons from getting an honest livelihood, and putting it into the power of the grantees to enhance the price of commodities. The definition embraces, it will be observed, not merely the sole privilege of buying and selling particular articles, or of engaging in their manufacture, but also the sole privilege of using anything by which others may be restrained of the freedom or liberty they previously had in any lawful trade, or hindered in such trade. It thus covers in every particular the possession and use of suitable yards, stables, and buildings for keeping and protecting cattle and other animals, and for their slaughter. Such establishments are essential to the free and successful prosecution by any butcher of the lawful trade of preparing animal food for market. The exclusive privilege of supplying such yards, buildings, and other conveniences for the prosecution of this business in a large district of country, granted by the act of Louisiana to seventeen persons, is as much a monopoly as though the act had granted to the company the exclusive privilege of buying and selling the animals themselves. It equally restrains the butchers in the freedom and liberty they previously had, and hinders them in their lawful trade.

* * *

. . . [T]he fourteenth amendment secures the like protection to all citizens in that State against any abridgment of their common rights, as in other States. That amendment was intended to give practical effect to the declaration of 1776 of inalienable rights, rights which are the gift of the Creator, which the law does not confer, but only recognizes. If the trader in London could plead that he was a free citizen of that city against the enforcement to his injury of monopolies, surely under the fourteenth amendment every citizen of the United States should be able to plead his citizenship of the republic as a protection against any similar invasion of his privileges and immunities.

* * *

. . . The State may prescribe such regulations for every pursuit and calling of life as will promote the public health, secure the good order and advance the general prosperity of society, but when once prescribed, the pursuit or calling must be free to be followed by every citizen who is within the conditions designated, and will conform to the regulations. This is the fundamental idea upon which our institutions rest, and unless adhered to in the legislation of the country our government will be a republic only in name. The fourteenth amendment, in my judgment, makes it essential to the validity of the legislation of every State that this equality of right should be respected. . . .

* * *

MR. JUSTICE BRADLEY, dissenting:

I concur [with] Mr. Justice Field; but desire to add a few observations for the purpose of more fully illustrating my views on the important question decided in these cases, and the special grounds on which they rest.

The fourteenth amendment to the Constitution of the United States, section 1, declares that no State shall make or enforce any law which shall abridge the privileges and immunities of citizens of the United States.

* * *

First. Is it one of the rights and privileges of a citizen of the United States to pursue such civil employment as he may choose to adopt, subject to such reasonable regulations as may be prescribed by law?

Secondly. Is a monopoly, or exclusive right, given to one person to the exclusion of all others, to keep slaughter-houses, in a district of nearly twelve hundred square miles, for the supply of meat for a large city, a reasonable regulation of that employment which the legislature has a right to impose?

The first of these questions is one of vast importance, and lies at the very foundations of our government. The question is now settled by the fourteenth amendment itself, that citizenship of the United States is the primary citizenship in this country; and that State citizenship is secondary and derivative, depending upon citizenship of the United States and the citizen's place of residence. The States have not now, if they ever had, any power to restrict their citizenship to any classes or persons. A citizen of the United States has a perfect constitutional right to go to and reside in any State he chooses, and to claim citizenship therein, and an equality of rights with every other citizen; and the whole power of the nation is pledged to sustain him in that right. . . .

Every citizen, then, being primarily a citizen of the United States, and, secondarily, a citizen of the State where he resides, what, in general, are the privileges and immunities of a citizen of the United States? Is the right, liberty, or privilege of choosing any lawful employment one of them?

If a State legislature should pass a law prohibiting the inhabitants of a particular township, county, or city, from tanning leather or making shoes, would such a law violate any privileges or immunities of those inhabitants as citizens of the United States, or only their privileges and immunities as citizens of that particular State? Or if a State legislature should pass a law of caste, making all trades and professions, or certain enumerated trades and professions, hereditary, so that no one could follow any such trades or professions except that which was pursued by his father, would such a law violate the privileges and immunities of the people of that State as citizens of the United States, or only as citizens of the State? Would they have no redress but to appeal to the courts of that particular State?

This seems to me to be the essential question before us for consideration. And, in my judgment, the right of any citizen to follow whatever lawful employment he chooses to adopt (submitting himself to all lawful regulations) is one of his most valuable rights, and one which the legislature of a State cannot invade, whether restrained by its own constitution or not.

* * *

The privileges and immunities of Englishmen were established and secured by long usage and by various acts of Parliament. But it may be said that the Parliament of England has unlimited authority, and might repeal the laws which have from time to time been enacted. Theoretically this is so, but practically it is not. England has no written constitution, it is true; but it has an unwritten one, resting in the acknowledged, and frequently declared, privileges of Parliament and the people, to violate which in any material respect would produce a revolution in an hour. A violation of one of the fundamental principles of that constitution in the Colonies, namely, the principle that recognizes the property of the people as their own, and which, therefore, regards all taxes for the support of government as gifts of the people through their representatives, and regards taxation without representation as subversive of free government, was the origin of our own revolution.

This, it is true, was the violation of a political right; but personal rights were deemed equally sacred, and were claimed by the very first Congress of the Colonies, assembled in 1774, as the undoubted inheritance of the people of this country; and the Declaration of Independence, which was the first political act of the American people in their independent sovereign capacity, lays the foundation of our National existence upon this broad proposition: "That all men are created equal; that they are endowed by their Creator with certain inalienable rights; that among these are life, liberty, and the pursuit of happiness." Here again we have the great threefold division of the rights of freemen, asserted as the rights of man. Rights to life, liberty, and the pursuit of happiness are equivalent to the rights of life, liberty, and property. These are the fundamental rights which can only be taken away by due process of law, and which can only be interfered with, or the enjoyment of which can only be modified, by lawful regulations necessary or proper for the mutual good of all; and these rights, I contend, belong to the citizens of every free government.

For the preservation, exercise, and enjoyment of these rights the individual citizen, as a necessity, must be left free to adopt such calling, profession, or trade as may seem to him most conducive to that end. Without this right he cannot be a freeman. This right to choose one's calling is an essential part of that liberty which it is the object of government to protect; and a calling, when chosen, is a man's property and right. Liberty and property are not protected where these rights are arbitrarily assailed.

* * *

It is pertinent to observe that both [in Article IV, Section 2] of the Constitution, and Justice Washington in his comment on it, speak of the privileges and immunities of citizens *in* a State; not of citizens *of* a State. It is the privileges and immunities of citizens, that is, of citizens as such, that are to be accorded to citizens of other States when they are found in any State; or, as Justice Washington says, "privileges and immunities which are, in their nature, fundamental; which belong, of right, to the citizens of all free governments."

It is true the courts have usually regarded the clause referred to as securing only an equality of privileges with the citizens of the State in which the parties are found. Equality before the law is undoubtedly one of the privileges and immunities of every citizen. I am not aware that any case has arisen in which it became necessary to vindicate any other fundamental privilege of citizenship; although rights have been claimed which were not deemed fundamental, and have been rejected as not within the protection of this clause. Be this, however, as it may, the language of the clause is as I have stated it, and seems fairly susceptible of a broader interpretation than that which makes it a guarantee of mere equality of privileges with other citizens.

But we are not bound to resort to implication, or to the constitutional history of England, to find an authoritative declaration of some of the most important privileges and immunities of citizens of the United States. It is in the Constitution itself. The Constitution, it is true, as it stood prior to the recent amendments, specifies, in terms, only a few of the personal privileges and immunities of citizens, but they are very comprehensive in their character. The States were merely prohibited from passing bills of attainder, *ex post facto* laws, laws impairing the obligation of contracts, and perhaps one or two more. But others of the greatest consequence were enumerated, although they were only secured, in express terms, from invasion by the Federal government; such as the right of *habeas corpus*, the right of trial by jury, of free exercise of religious worship, the right of free speech and a free press, the right peaceably to assemble for the discussion of public measures, the right to be secure against unreasonable searches and seizures, and above all, and including almost all the rest, the right of *not being deprived of life, liberty, or property, without due process of law*. These, and still others are specified in the original Constitution, or in the early amendments of it, as among the privileges and immunities of citizens of the United States, or, what is still stronger for the force of the argument, the rights of all persons, whether citizens or not.

But even if the Constitution were silent, the fundamental privileges and immunities of citizens, as such, would be no less real and no less inviolable than they now are. . . .

The next question to be determined in this case is: Is a monopoly or exclusive right, given to one person, or corporation, to the exclusion of all others, to keep slaughter-houses in a district of nearly twelve hundred square miles, for the supply of meat for a great city, a reasonable regulation of that employment which the legislature has a right to impose?

* * *

It has been suggested that this was a mere legislative act, and that the British Parliament, as well as our own legislatures, have frequently disregarded it by granting exclusive privileges for erecting ferries, railroads, markets, and other establishments of a public kind. It requires but a slight acquaintance with legal history to know that grants of this kind of franchises are totally different from the monopolies of commodities or of ordinary callings or pursuits. These public franchises can only be exercised under authority from the government, and the government may grant them on such conditions as it sees fit. But even these exclusive privileges are becoming more and more odious, and are getting to be more and more regarded as wrong in principle, and as inimical to the just rights and greatest good of the people. But to cite them as proof of the power of legislatures to create mere monopolies, such as no free and enlightened community any longer endures, appears to me, to say the least, very strange and illogical.

Lastly: Can the Federal courts administer relief to citizens of the United States whose privileges and immunities have been abridged by a State? Of this I entertain no doubt. Prior to the fourteenth amendment this could not be done, except in a few instances, for the want of the requisite authority.

* * *

Admitting, therefore, that formerly the States were not prohibited from infringing any of the fundamental privileges and immunities of citizens of the United States, except in a few specified cases, that cannot be said now, since the adoption of the fourteenth amendment. In my judgment, it was the intention of the people of this country in adopting that amendment to provide National security against violation by the States of the fundamental rights of the citizen.

* * *

The amendment also prohibits any State from depriving any person (citizen or otherwise) of life, liberty, or property, without due process of law.

In my view, a law which prohibits a large class of citizens from adopting a lawful employment, or from following a lawful employment previously adopted, does deprive them of liberty as well as property, without due process of law. Their right of choice is a portion of their liberty; their occupation is their property. Such a law also deprives those citizens of the equal protection of the laws, contrary to the last clause of the section.

The constitutional question is distinctly raised in these cases; the constitutional right is expressly claimed; it was violated by State law, which was sustained by the State court, and we are called upon in a legitimate and proper way to afford redress. Our jurisdiction and our duty are plain and imperative.

* * *

MR. JUSTICE SWAYNE, dissenting:

I concur in the dissent in these cases and in the views expressed by my brethren, Mr. Justice Field and Mr. Justice Bradley. [Additional remarks omitted.]

NOTE: A REPLAY?

The *Slaughter-House* opinion remained highly controverted. More than a decade later, the case was before the Court in another form in *Butchers' Union Slaughter-House and Live-Stock Landing Co. v. Crescent City Live-Stock Landing and Slaughter-House Co.*, 111 U.S. 746 (1884). In 1879, the Louisiana state constitution was amended to outlaw the previously granted monopoly. Crescent City, the holder of the monopoly, went to Court arguing that the amendment was an unconstitutional impairment of contract. The members of the Court were entirely agreed that Louisiana could repeal the previous monopoly, but for very different reasons. Justice Miller, who wrote the first *Slaughter-House* opinion, justified the repeal with the proposition that no sovereign can bargain away the police power, a proposition discussed in Chapter Six. The concurring justices, however, were still smarting from Justice Miller's earlier *Slaughter-House* opinion. Justice Bradley categorically argued that the original grant of monopoly was wrongful, as "all mere monopolies are odious and against common right." *Id.* at 761 (Bradley, J., concurring). To not recognize this would be to abridge the basic privileges or immunities of all citizens, he argued.

NOTES AND QUESTIONS

1. *Slaughter-House* was decided 5-4, but even that does not fully reflect the division on the Court. The case yielded the majority opinion authored by Justice Miller, and three separate dissenting opinions: one written by Justice Stephen Field (joined by Chief Justice Salmon Chase, and Justices Swayne and Bradley), another by Justice Bradley with Justice Swayne, and finally, Justice Swayne writing individually. Legal historian Michael Kent Curtis believes the outcome in *Slaughter-House* reflects a "strange reading of the language of the Fourteenth Amendment" and that "[t]he history of abuses that led to the amendment received superficial and cursory attention at best," while legislative history "received no attention at all." MICHAEL KENT CURTIS, NO STATE SHALL ABRIDGE 175, 173 (1986).

2. The Fourteenth Amendment was intended to re-order the state-federal balance. That this was so can be seen in the fact that the Butcher's Association in *Slaughter-House* was represented by John A. Campbell, a former justice of the Supreme Court who had resigned when his home state of Alabama seceded from the Union prior to the Civil War. Former Justice Campbell's prior actions tend to give even greater credence to his losing argument in favor of a position that would allow the national (if you will, Union) Supreme Court to set aside state action contrary to a nationally defined set of privileges or immunities. Indeed, Campbell, himself, recognized the profound shift from pre-Civil War position, writing:

> The doctrine of the "States-Rights party," led in modern times by Mr. Calhoun, was, that there was no citizenship in the whole United States, except *sub modo* and by the permission of the States. . . . The fourteenth amendment struck at, and forever destroyed, all such doctrines. . . . By it the national principle has received an indefinite enlargement. The tie between the United States and every citizen in every part of its own jurisdiction has been made intimate and familiar.

The Slaughter House Cases, 83 U.S. (16 Wall.) 36, 52-53 (1873) (argument of John A. Campbell on behalf of The Butchers' Benevolent Association of New Orleans). The full argument of former Justice Campbell can be found in the official report of the case, 83 U.S. (16 Wall.) at 44-57.

3. Civil Rights Is More Than Equality. The decimation of the Privileges or Immunities Clause in *Slaughter-House* transformed the modern concept of civil right from a guarantee of inalienable or natural right to a concept almost totally focused on equality. As we discuss in Chapter Eight, equal treatment under law is no small matter, yet, this exclusive focus was not in keeping with the original understanding of the Fourteenth Amendment. As Alfred Avins, a scholar of the post-Civil War era writes, the framers of the Fourteenth Amendment intended "to confer certain civil or natural rights on all persons, white as well as black, and not merely to abolish racial discrimination." THE RECONSTRUCTION AMENDMENTS' DEBATES at vii (Alfred Avins ed., 1967). The original conception of civil right or liberty which the drafters of the Fourteenth Amendment had carried forward, was that of Sir William Blackstone, who defined civil liberty as "no other than natural liberty so far restrained by human laws (and no farther) as is necessary and expedient for the general advantage of the publick." 1 WILLIAM BLACKSTONE, COMMENTARIES *125 (citing JUSTINIAN, INSTITUTES 1.3.1). Similarly,

Senator John Sherman a few years after the drafting of the Privileges or Immunities Clause reflected:

> What are those privileges and immunities? Are they only those defined in the Constitution, the rights secured by the [Bill of Rights]? Not at all. The great fountainhead, the great reservoir of the rights of an American citizen is in the common law. . . .

* * *

> . . . [And such] right must be determined from time to time by the judicial tribunals, and in determining it they will look first at the Constitution of the United States as the primary fountain of authority. If that does not define the right they will look for the unenumerated powers to the Declaration of American Independence, . . . [and] to the common law of England. . . .

CONG. GLOBE, 42d Cong., 2d Sess. 843-44 (1872). Without question, those who crafted the Privileges or Immunities Clause expected that economic liberty would be protected. Representative John A. Bingham, the principal author of the first section of the 14th Amendment, included within its scope "the liberty . . . to work in an honest calling and contribute by your own toil in some sort to the support of yourself, to the support of your fellowmen, and to be secure in the enjoyment of the fruits of your toil." CONG. GLOBE, 42d Cong., 1st Sess. app. 86 (1871). But, of course, even if there is a general right of economic liberty, does that mean that the Court is to second-guess every legislative restriction of that right? Assuming for the sake of argument, *Slaughter-House* to be in error on the content of privilege or immunity does not answer this further question. And the difficulty of giving answer became clear to the Court as it tried to correct the damage done in *Slaughter-House* by bootstrapping freedom of contract into the Due Process Clause. We will thus return to this question after we examine the *Lochner*, *Nebbia*, and *Carolene Products* cases, below.

4. Civil Liberty and Equality Have Common Cause. As an historical matter, it should be recognized that protecting equality and economic liberty were interrelated. Following the Civil War, various southern states and localities effectively tried to negate emancipation by precluding the economic liberty of the freedmen with the so-called "Black Codes." As one report to Congress put it:

> The opposition to the negro's controlling his own labor, carrying on business independently on his own account — in one word, working for his own benefit — showed itself in a variety of ways. Here and there municipal regulations were gotten up heavily taxing or otherwise impeding those trades and employments in which colored people are most likely to engage.

S. EXEC. DOC. NO. 39-2, at 24 (1865), *reprinted in* THE RECONSTRUCTION AMENDMENTS' DEBATES, *supra*, at 90. To counteract these Black Codes, Congress passed the Civil Rights Act of 1866, providing that all citizens shall "have the same right . . . to make and enforce contracts, to sue, be parties, and give evidence, to inherit, purchase, lease, sell, hold, and convey real and personal property, and to full and equal benefit of all laws." Civil Rights Act of 1866, ch. 31, § 1, 14 Stat. 27, 27 (codified as amended at 42 U.S.C. §§ 1981-1982 (1994)). President Andrew Johnson vetoed this legislation. Concerned that Congress lacked authority, Section 2 had been construed only to secure such privileges and immunities as each state chose to give its own citizens and states were merely prohibited from discriminating in favor of its own citizens. Some in Congress argued that Article IV was a broader security of natural right generally, and on this and other grounds, Congress overrode the veto. Nevertheless, the Fourteenth Amendment resulted to erase any doubt about congressional authority. Thus, Senator Jacob Howard would explain that under the original Privileges and Immunities Clause of Article IV, Section 2 and the Bill of Rights, "the States are not restrained from violating the principles embraced in them except by their own local constitutions. [By contrast, the] great object of the [Fourteenth] amendment is . . . to restrain the power of the States and compel them at all times to respect these great fundamental guarantees." CONG. GLOBE, 39th Cong., 1st Sess. 2766 (1866).

5. The Evil of Monopoly. No one wants a slaughter-house in their backyard, so the legislation in the *Slaughter-House Cases* did have some obvious public health merit. However, the record also established that "legislative bribery had greased passage of the law, with its most immediate beneficiaries — the seventeen participants in the corporation it established — adroitly distributing shares of stock and cash." CHARLES A. LOFGREN, THE PLESSY CASE 67 (1987). It was not the inspection and health aspects of the law that deserved scrutiny, but the arguably unnecessary grant of monopoly. The common law of England condemned all monopolies, not merely because of the increase in price and deterioration in quality of goods (although this is often economically undeniable), but as Justice Field recognized, because of the interference with the liberty of citizens to pursue the maintenance of family through any lawful trade or occupation. At common law, regulated monopolies or those that arose from grants of special privilege from the government were especially suspect. Economic monopolies are constrained by market competition; government monopolies are more durable and thus pernicious because of their legal protection. This was a well-established point of common law inherited by the American colonies. Justice Field observed in dissent that:

> The common law of England is the basis of the jurisprudence of the United States. It was brought to this country by the colonists, together with the English statutes, and was established here so far as it was applicable to their condition. That law and the benefit of such of the English statutes as existed at the time of their colonization, and which they had by experience found to be applicable to their circumstances, were claimed by the Congress of the United Colonies in 1774 as a part of their "indubitable rights and liberties." Of the statutes, the benefits of which was thus claimed, the statute of James I against monopolies

was one of the most important. And when the Colonies separated from the mother country no privilege was more fully recognized or more completely incorporated into the fundamental law of the country than that every free subject in the British empire was entitled to pursue his happiness by following any of the known established trades and occupations of the country, subject only to such restraints as equally affected all others. The immortal document which proclaimed the independence of the country declared as self-evident truths that the Creator had endowed all men "with certain unalienable rights, and that among these are life, liberty, and the pursuit of happiness; and that to secure these rights governments are instituted among men."

The Slaughter-House Cases, 83 U.S. (16 Wall.) at 104-05 (Field, J., dissenting) (footnote omitted).

6. Is Louisiana Special? It might be argued that as the only civil law jurisdiction in the United States, common law dislike of monopoly was irrelevant to the outcome in *Slaughter-House*. However, Justice Field pointed out in part of his dissent not reprinted that Louis XVI abolished all trade monopolies in 1776, and that this law prevailed in the French colony at the time of its cession to the United States. *Id.* at 105 (Field, J., dissenting).

7. Slaughtered by *Slaughter-House*. From the time of its decision to the present, *Slaughter-House* has done considerable damage to the cause of economic liberty. Almost immediately, for example, the Court used *Slaughter-House* to uphold an Illinois law that forbade qualified women from practicing law. *Bradwell v. Illinois*, 83 U.S. (16 Wall.) 130 (1872). So too, the majority's reasoning that the Privileges or Immunities Clause referred only to minor features of national citizenship was used to argue that Congress lacked remedial authority to address racial segregation in public accommodations. THE RECONSTRUCTION AMENDMENTS' DEBATES, *supra*, at xxiv. *Slaughter-House* thus prompted the impulse for the Court to distort other provisions of the Constitution in order to reach that which would have been better addressed under the privileges or immunities rubric, with its direct philosophical linkage to the Declaration of Independence and natural law. To address racial discrimination in public accommodations, the Court nourished an ever-expanding view of the commerce power, and with far less judicial warrant, elaborated substantive due process to temporarily ensure economic liberty.

8. Can *Slaughter-House* Be Overruled? Professor Philip Kurland has observed that the Privileges or Immunities Clause "is in repose, it is not yet dead." Philip B. Kurland, *The Privileges or Immunities Clause, "Its Hour Come Round at Last"?*, 1972 WASH. U. L.Q. 405, 413. Similarly, Clint Bolick of the Institute for Justice argues that "we should establish as our ultimate objective the reversal of the *Slaughter-House Cases*, much as the NAACP did when it set as its long-range goal the toppling of *Plessy v. Ferguson* [and the odious doctrine of separate but equal in matters of race]." CLINT BOLICK, UNFINISHED BUSINESS: A CIVIL RIGHTS STRATEGY FOR AMERICA'S THIRD CENTURY 76 (1990).

9. A Supreme Concurrence? Before his appointment to the Supreme Court, Justice Clarence Thomas speculated that:

> While it may be idle to think in terms of overruling the *Slaughter-House Cases*, there is an even more important point to be emphasized here. It goes to the fundamental rights of the American regime — those of life, liberty, and property. These rights are inalienable ones, given to man by his Creator, and did not simply come from a piece of paper.

Clarence Thomas, *The Higher Law Background of the Privileges or Immunities Clause of the Fourteenth Amendment*, 12 HARV. J.L. & PUB. POL'Y 63, 68 (1989) (footnotes omitted). In fact, much of *Slaughter-House* has been overruled — at least that which narrowed the scope of the Equal Protection and Due Process Clauses. Justice Miller's prediction that the Equal Protection Clause would likely never have application outside the area of racial discrimination has proven entirely false, as gender, alienage and legitimacy, for example, have come within its reach. *See* Chapter Eight. Similarly, as discussed in the section immediately below, during the first third of the 20th century, the Due Process Clause was employed by the Court to protect economic liberty. *Compare Lochner v. New York*, 198 U.S. 45 (1905), *with Nebbia v. New York*, 291 U.S. 502 (1933). The modern Court has backed away from this, however, finding the due process-based protection of economic liberty to be judicial activism, and insufficiently attentive to majority or legislative outcome. Oddly, the Court continues the very same substantive due process theory to create contraceptive and abortion rights. *See* Chapter Nine and Joseph D. Grano, *Teaching* Roe *and* Lochner, 42 WAYNE L. REV. 1973 (1996) (demonstrating that *Roe* and *Lochner* are the same cases from a methodological perspective because both single out certain unenumerated liberties for special protection without textual guidance).

The dichotomy between the protection of abortion-related and other personal liberties, and the post-*Lochner* disregard of economic liberty is orchestrated by footnote 4 in *United States v. Carolene Products*, 304 U.S. 144 (1938). Conservative legal theorists resist any efforts to revive or strengthen the judicial protection of economic liberty under either privileges or immunities or due process analysis, thinking, perhaps mistakenly, this to be the only principled position against judicial activism. *But see* Douglas W. Kmiec, *Natural Law Originalism or Why Justice Scalia (Almost) Gets It Right*, 21 HARV. J.L. & PUB. POL'Y 627 (1997). Justice Thomas disagrees.

> The best defense of limited government, of the separation of powers, and of the judicial restraint that flows from the commitment to limited government, is the higher law political philosophy of the Founding Fathers. Contrary to the worst fears of my conservative allies, such a view is far from being a license for unlimited government and a roving judiciary. Rather, natural rights and higher law arguments are the best defense of liberty and of limited government. . . . Rather than being a justification of the worst type of judicial activism, higher law is the only alter-

native to the willfulness of both run-amok majorities and run-amok judges.

Thomas, *supra*, at 64-65.

SAENZ v. ROE
526 U.S. 489 (1999)

JUSTICE STEVENS delivered the opinion of the Court.

In 1992, California enacted a statute limiting the maximum welfare benefits available to newly arrived residents. The scheme limits the amount payable to a family that has resided in the State for less than 12 months to the amount payable by the State of the family's prior residence. The questions presented by this case are whether the 1992 statute was constitutional when it was enacted and, if not, whether an amendment to the Social Security Act enacted by Congress in 1996 affects that determination.

* * *

III

The word "travel" is not found in the text of the Constitution. Yet the "constitutional right to travel from one State to another" is firmly embedded in our jurisprudence. . . . The right is so important that it is "assertable against private interference as well as governmental action . . . a virtually unconditional personal right, guaranteed by the Constitution to us all."

In *Shapiro v. Thompson* (1969), we reviewed the constitutionality of three statutory provisions that denied welfare assistance to residents of Connecticut, the District of Columbia, and Pennsylvania, who had resided within those respective jurisdictions less than one year immediately preceding their applications for assistance. Without pausing to identify the specific source of the right, we began by noting that the Court had long "recognized that the nature of our Federal Union and our constitutional concepts of personal liberty unite to require that all citizens be free to travel throughout the length and breadth of our land uninhibited by statutes, rules, or regulations which unreasonably burden or restrict this movement." We squarely held that it was "constitutionally impermissible" for a State to enact durational residency requirements for the purpose of inhibiting the migration by needy persons into the State. We further held that a classification that had the effect of imposing a penalty on the exercise of the right to travel violated the Equal Protection Clause "unless shown to be necessary to promote a compelling governmental interest," and that no such showing had been made.

In this case California argues that [the state statute] was not enacted for the impermissible purpose of inhibiting migration by needy persons and that, unlike the legislation reviewed in *Shapiro*, it does not penalize the right to travel because new arrivals are not ineligible for benefits during their first year of residence. California submits that, instead of being subjected to the strictest scrutiny, the statute should be upheld if it is supported by a rational basis and that the State's legitimate interest in saving over $10 million a year satisfies that test. Although the United States did not elect to participate in the proceedings in the District Court or the Court of Appeals, it has participated as *amicus curiae* in this Court. It has advanced the novel argument that the enactment of [a federal statute] allows the States to adopt a "specialized choice-of-law-type provision" that "should be subject to an intermediate level of constitutional review," merely requiring that durational residency requirements be "substantially related to an important governmental objective." The debate about the appropriate standard of review, together with the potential relevance of the federal statute, persuades us that it will be useful to focus on the source of the constitutional right on which respondents rely.

IV

The "right to travel" discussed in our cases embraces at least three different components. It protects the right of a citizen of one State to enter and to leave another State, the right to be treated as a welcome visitor rather than an unfriendly alien when temporarily present in the second State, and, for those travelers who elect to become permanent residents, the right to be treated like other citizens of that State.

It was the right to go from one place to another, including the right to cross state borders while en route, that was vindicated in *Edwards v. California* (1941), which invalidated a state law that impeded the free interstate passage of the indigent. . . . Given that [the state law here] imposed no obstacle to respondents' entry into California, we think the State is correct when it argues that the statute does not directly impair the exercise of the right to free interstate movement. For the purposes of this case, therefore, we need not identify the source of that particular right in the text of the Constitution. The right of "free ingress and regress to and from" neighboring States, which was expressly mentioned in the text of the Articles of Confederation, may simply have been "conceived from the beginning to be a necessary concomitant of the stronger Union the Constitution created."

The second component of the right to travel is, however, expressly protected by the text of the Constitution. The first sentence of Article IV, § 2, provides:

> "The Citizens of each State shall be entitled to all Privileges and Immunities of Citizens in the several States."

Thus, by virtue of a person's state citizenship, a citizen of one State who travels in other States, intending to return home at the end of his journey, is entitled to enjoy the "Privileges and Immunities of Citizens in the several States" that he visits.[14] This provision removes "from the citizens of each State

---

14 *Corfield v. Coryell* (1823) (Washington, J., on circuit) ("fundamental" rights protected by the privileges and immunities clause include "the right of a citizen of one state to pass through, or to reside in any other state").

the disabilities of alienage in the other States." . . . Those protections are not "absolute," but the Clause "does bar discrimination against citizens of other States where there is no substantial reason for the discrimination beyond the mere fact that they are citizens of other States." There may be a substantial reason for requiring the nonresident to pay more than the resident for a hunting license, but our cases have not identified any acceptable reason for qualifying the protection afforded by the Clause for "the 'citizen of State A who ventures into State B' to settle there and establish a home." Permissible justifications for discrimination between residents and nonresidents are simply inapplicable to a nonresident's exercise of the right to move into another State and become a resident of that State.

What is at issue in this case, then, is this third aspect of the right to travel — the right of the newly arrived citizen to the same privileges and immunities enjoyed by other citizens of the same State. That right is protected not only by the new arrival's status as a state citizen, but also by her status as a citizen of the United States.[15] That additional source of protection is plainly identified in the opening words of the Fourteenth Amendment:

> "All persons born or naturalized in the United States, and subject to the jurisdiction thereof, are citizens of the United States and of the State wherein they reside. No State shall make or enforce any law which shall abridge the privileges or immunities of citizens of the United States; . . . ."

Despite fundamentally differing views concerning the coverage of the Privileges or Immunities Clause of the Fourteenth Amendment, most notably expressed in the majority and dissenting opinions in the *Slaughter-House Cases* (1872), it has always been common ground that this Clause protects the third component of the right to travel. Writing for the majority in the *Slaughter-House Cases*, Justice Miller explained that one of the privileges conferred by this Clause "is that a citizen of the United States can, of his own volition, become a citizen of any State of the Union by a bona fide residence therein, with the same rights as other citizens of that State." Justice Bradley, in dissent, used even stronger language to make the same point:

> "The states have not now, if they ever had, any power to restrict their citizenship to any classes or persons. A citizen of the United States has a perfect constitutional right to go to and reside in any State he chooses, and to claim citizenship therein, and an equality of rights with every

---

[15] The Framers of the Fourteenth Amendment modeled this Clause upon the "Privileges and Immunities" Clause found in Article IV. Cong. Globe, 39th Cong., 1st Sess., 1033-1034 (1866) (statement of Rep. Bingham). In *Dred Scott v. Sandford*, 19 How. 393, 15 L.Ed. 691 (1856), this Court had limited the protection of Article IV to rights under state law and concluded that free blacks could not claim citizenship. The Fourteenth Amendment overruled this decision. The Amendment's Privileges and Immunities Clause and Citizenship Clause guaranteed the rights of newly freed black citizens by ensuring that they could claim the state citizenship of any State in which they resided and by precluding that State from abridging their rights of national citizenship.

other citizen; and the whole power of the nation is pledged to sustain him in that right. He is not bound to cringe to any superior, or to pray for any act of grace, as a means of enjoying all the rights and privileges enjoyed by other citizens."

That newly arrived citizens "have two political capacities, one state and one federal," adds special force to their claim that they have the same rights as others who share their citizenship. Neither mere rationality nor some intermediate standard of review should be used to judge the constitutionality of a state rule that discriminates against some of its citizens because they have been domiciled in the State for less than a year. The appropriate standard may be more categorical than that articulated in *Shapiro*, but it is surely no less strict.

V

* * *

It is undisputed that respondents and the members of the class that they represent are citizens of California and that their need for welfare benefits is unrelated to the length of time that they have resided in California. We thus have no occasion to consider what weight might be given to a citizen's length of residence if the bona fides of her claim to state citizenship were questioned. Moreover, because whatever benefits they receive will be consumed while they remain in California, there is no danger that recognition of their claim will encourage citizens of other States to establish residency for just long enough to acquire some readily portable benefit, such as a divorce or a college education, that will be enjoyed after they return to their original domicile.

* * *

California must therefore explain not only why it is sound fiscal policy to discriminate against those who have been citizens for less than a year, but also why it is permissible to apply such a variety of rules within that class.

These classifications may not be justified by a purpose to deter welfare applicants from migrating to California for three reasons. First, although it is reasonable to assume that some persons may be motivated to move for the purpose of obtaining higher benefits, the empirical evidence reviewed by the District Judge, which takes into account the high cost of living in California, indicates that the number of such persons is quite small — surely not large enough to justify a burden on those who had no such motive. Second, California has represented to the Court that the legislation was not enacted for any such reason. Third, even if it were, as we squarely held in *Shapiro v. Thompson* (1969), such a purpose would be unequivocally impermissible.

* * *

VI

The question that remains is whether congressional approval of durational residency requirements in the 1996 amendment to the Social Security Act somehow resuscitates the constitutionality of [the state law]. That question is readily answered, for we have consistently held that Congress may not authorize the States to violate the Fourteenth Amendment. Moreover, the protection afforded to the citizen by the Citizenship Clause of that Amendment is a limitation on the powers of the National Government as well as the States.

Article I of the Constitution grants Congress broad power to legislate in certain areas. Those legislative powers are, however, limited not only by the scope of the Framers' affirmative delegation, but also by the principle "that they may not be exercised in a way that violates other specific provisions of the Constitution."

* * *

Citizens of the United States, whether rich or poor, have the right to choose to be citizens "of the State wherein they reside." The States, however, do not have any right to select their citizens.

* * *

The judgment of the Court of Appeals is affirmed.

CHIEF JUSTICE REHNQUIST, with whom JUSTICE THOMAS joins, dissenting.

The Court today breathes new life into the previously dormant Privileges or Immunities Clause of the Fourteenth Amendment. . . . Because I do not think any provision of the Constitution — and surely not a provision relied upon for only the second time since its enactment 130 years ago — requires this result, I dissent.

I

Much of the Court's opinion is unremarkable and sound. The right to travel clearly embraces the right to go from one place to another, and prohibits States from impeding the free interstate passage of citizens.

* * *

I also have no difficulty with aligning the right to travel with the protections afforded by the Privileges and Immunities Clause of Article IV, § 2, to nonresidents who enter other States "intending to return home at the end of [their] journey." Nonresident visitors of other States should not be subject to discrimination solely because they live out of State.

Finally, I agree with the proposition that a "citizen of the United States can, of his own volition, become a citizen of any State of the Union by a bona fide residence therein, with the same rights as other citizens of that State." *Slaughter-House Cases* (1872).

But I cannot see how the right to become a citizen of another State is a necessary "component" of the right to travel, or why the Court tries to marry these separate and distinct rights. A person is no longer "traveling" in any sense of the word when he finishes his journey to a State which he plans to make his home. Indeed, under the Court's logic, the protections of the Privileges or Immunities Clause recognized in this case come into play only when an individual stops traveling with the intent to remain and become a citizen of a new State. The right to travel and the right to become a citizen are distinct, their relationship is not reciprocal, and one is not a "component" of the other. Indeed, the same dicta from the *Slaughter-House Cases* quoted by the Court actually treats the right to become a citizen and the right to travel as separate and distinct rights under the Privileges or Immunities Clause of the Fourteenth Amendment. At most, restrictions on an individual's right to become a citizen indirectly affect his calculus in deciding whether to exercise his right to travel in the first place, but such an attenuated and uncertain relationship is no ground for folding one right into the other.

No doubt the Court has, in the past 30 years, essentially conflated the right to travel with the right to equal state citizenship in striking down durational residence requirements similar to the one challenged here. *See, e.g., Shapiro v. Thompson* (1969) (striking down 1-year residence before receiving any welfare benefit); *Dunn v. Blumstein*, 405 U.S. 330 (1972) (striking down 1-year residence before receiving the right to vote in state elections); [*Memorial Hospital v.*] *Maricopa County*, 415 U.S. at 280-283 (striking down 1-year county residence before receiving entitlement to nonemergency hospitalization or emergency care). These cases marked a sharp departure from the Court's prior right-to-travel cases because in none of them was travel itself prohibited.

Instead, the Court in these cases held that restricting the provision of welfare benefits, votes, or certain medical benefits to new citizens for a limited time impermissibly "penalized" them under the Equal Protection Clause of the Fourteenth Amendment for having exercised their right to travel. . . . In other cases, the Court recognized that laws dividing new and old residents had little to do with the right to travel and merely triggered an inquiry into whether the resulting classification rationally furthered a legitimate government purpose. *See Zobel v. Williams* 457 U.S. 55 (1982); *Hooper v. Bernalillo County Assessor*, 472 U.S. 612 (1985).

* * *

The Court today tries to clear much of the underbrush created by these prior right-to-travel cases, abandoning its effort to define what residence requirements deprive individuals of "important rights and benefits" or "penalize" the right to travel. Under its new analytical framework, a State, outside certain ill-defined circumstances, cannot classify its citizens by the length of their residence in the State without offending the Privileges or Immunities Clause of the Fourteenth Amendment. The Court thus departs from *Shapiro* and its progeny, and, while paying lipservice to the right to travel, the Court does little to explain how the right to travel is involved at all.

* * *

II

In unearthing from its tomb the right to become a state citizen and to be treated equally in the new State of residence, however, the Court ignores a State's need to assure that only persons who establish a bona fide residence receive the benefits provided to current residents of the State.

* * *

. . . [T]he Court has consistently recognized that while new citizens must have the same opportunity to enjoy the privileges of being a citizen of a State, the States retain the ability to use bona fide residence requirements to ferret out those who intend to take the privileges and run. . . . "[R]esidence" requires "both physical presence and an intention to remain" . . . .

While the physical presence element of a bona fide residence is easy to police, the subjective intent element is not. It is simply unworkable and futile to require States to inquire into each new resident's subjective intent to remain. Hence, States employ objective criteria such as durational residence requirements to test a new resident's resolve to remain before these new citizens can enjoy certain in-state benefits. Recognizing the practical appeal of such criteria, this Court has repeatedly sanctioned the State's use of durational residence requirements before new residents receive in-state tuition rates at state universities. *Starns v. Malkerson*, 401 U.S. 985 (1971) (upholding 1-year residence requirement for in-state tuition). . . . The Court has done the same in upholding a 1-year residence requirement for eligibility to obtain a divorce in state courts, *see Sosna v. Iowa*, 419 U.S. 393 (1975), and in upholding political party registration restrictions that amounted to a durational residency requirement for voting in primary elections, *see Rosario v. Rockefeller*, 410 U.S. 752 (1973).

If States can require individuals to reside in-state for a year before exercising the right to educational benefits, the right to terminate a marriage, or the right to vote in primary elections that all other state citizens enjoy, then States may surely do the same for welfare benefits. Indeed, there is no material difference between a 1-year residence requirement applied to the level of welfare benefits given out by a State, and the same requirement applied to the level of tuition subsidies at a state university. The welfare payment here and in-state tuition rates are cash subsidies provided to a limited class of people, and California's standard of living and higher education system make both subsidies quite attractive. Durational residence requirements were upheld when used to regulate the provision of higher education subsidies, and the same deference should be given in the case of welfare payments. . . .

The Court today recognizes that States retain the ability to determine the bona fides of an individual's claim to residence, but then tries to avoid the issue. It asserts that because respondents' need for welfare benefits is unrelated to the length of time they have resided in California, it has "no occasion to consider what weight might be given to a citizen's length of residence if the bona fides of her claim to state citizenship were questioned." But I do not understand how the absence of a link between need and length of residency bears on the State's ability to objectively test respondents' resolve to stay in California. There is no link between the need for an education or for a divorce and the length of residence, and yet States may use length of residence as an objective yardstick to channel their benefits to those whose intent to stay is legitimate.

In one respect, the State has a greater need to require a durational residence for welfare benefits than for college eligibility. The impact of a large number of new residents who immediately seek welfare payments will have a far greater impact on a State's operating budget than the impact of new residents seeking to attend a state university. In the case of the welfare recipients, a modest durational residence requirement to allow for the completion of an annual legislative budget cycle gives the State time to decide how to finance the increased obligations.

The Court tries to distinguish education and divorce benefits by contending that the welfare payment here will be consumed in California, while a college education or a divorce produces benefits that are "portable" and can be enjoyed after individuals return to their original domicile. But this "you can't take it with you" distinction is more apparent than real, and offers little guidance to lower courts who must apply this rationale in the future.

* * *

I therefore believe that the durational residence requirement challenged here is a permissible exercise of the State's power to "assur[e] that services provided for its residents are enjoyed only by residents." The 1-year period established in [the state law here] is the same period this Court approved in *Starns* and *Sosna*. The requirement does not deprive welfare recipients of all benefits; indeed, the limitation has no effect whatsoever on a recipient's ability to enjoy the full 5-year period of welfare eligibility; to enjoy the full range of employment, training, and accompanying supportive services; or to take full advantage of health care benefits under Medicaid. This waiting period does not preclude new residents from all cash payments, but merely limits them to what they received in their prior State of residence. Moreover, as the Court recognizes, any pinch resulting from this limitation during the 1-year period is mitigated by other programs such as homeless assistance and an increase in food stamp allowance. The 1-year period thus permissibly balances the new resident's needs for subsistence with the State's need to ensure the bona fides of their claim to residence.

Finally, Congress' express approval of durational residence requirements for welfare recipients like the one established by California only goes to show the reasonableness of a law like [the state law here]. The National Legislature, where people from Mississippi as well as California are represented, has recognized the need to protect state resources in a time of experimentation and welfare reform. . . .

JUSTICE THOMAS, with whom THE CHIEF JUSTICE joins, dissenting.

I join THE CHIEF JUSTICE's dissent. . . . In my view, the majority attributes a meaning to the Privileges or Immunities Clause that likely was unintended when the Fourteenth Amendment was enacted and ratified.

The Privileges or Immunities Clause of the Fourteenth Amendment provides that "[n]o State shall make or enforce any law which shall abridge the privileges or immunities of citizens of the United States." U.S. Const., Amdt. 14, § 1. Unlike the Equal Protection and Due Process Clauses, which have assumed near-talismanic status in modern constitutional law, the Court all but read the Privileges or Immunities Clause out of the Constitution in the *Slaughter-House Cases* (1872).

* * *

Unlike the majority, I would look to history to ascertain the original meaning of the Clause. At least in American law, the phrase (or its close approximation) appears to stem from the 1606 Charter of Virginia, which provided that "all and every the Persons being our Subjects, which shall dwell and inhabit within every or any of the said several Colonies . . . shall HAVE and enjoy all Liberties, Franchises, and Immunities . . . as if they had been abiding and born, within this our Realme of England." Years later, as tensions between England and the American Colonies increased, the colonists adopted resolutions reasserting their entitlement to the privileges or immunities of English citizenship.[3]

The Constitution, which superceded the Articles of Confederation, similarly guarantees that "[t]he Citizens of each State shall be entitled to all Privileges and Immunities of Citizens in the several States." Art. IV, § 2, cl. 1.

Justice Bushrod Washington's landmark opinion in *Corfield v. Coryell* (1825), reflects this historical understanding.

* * *

Washington rejected the proposition that the Privileges and Immunities Clause guaranteed equal access to all public benefits (such as the right to harvest oysters in public waters) that a State chooses to make available. Instead, he endorsed the colonial-era conception of the terms "privileges" and "immunities," concluding that Article IV encompassed only fundamental rights that belong to all citizens of the United States.

---

[3] *See, e.g., The Massachusetts Resolves, in* PROLOGUE TO REVOLUTION: SOURCES AND DOCUMENTS ON THE STAMP ACT CRISIS 56 (E. Morgan ed. 1959) ("Resolved, That there are certain essential Rights of the British Constitution of Government, which are founded in the Law of God and Nature, and are the common Rights of Mankind — Therefore, . . . Resolved that no Man can justly take the Property of another without his Consent . . . this inherent Right, together with all other essential Rights, Liberties, Privileges and Immunities of the People of Great Britain have been fully confirmed to them by Magna Charta"). . . .

Justice Washington's opinion in *Corfield* indisputably influenced the Members of Congress who enacted the Fourteenth Amendment. When Congress gathered to debate the Fourteenth Amendment, members frequently, if not as a matter of course, appealed to *Corfield*, arguing that the Amendment was necessary to guarantee the fundamental rights that Justice Washington identified in his opinion. . . .

That Members of the 39th Congress appear to have endorsed the wisdom of Justice Washington's opinion does not, standing alone, provide dispositive insight into their understanding of the Fourteenth Amendment's Privileges or Immunities Clause. Nevertheless, their repeated references to the *Corfield* decision, combined with what appears to be the historical understanding of the Clause's operative terms, supports the inference that, at the time the Fourteenth Amendment was adopted, people understood that "privileges or immunities of citizens" were fundamental rights, rather than every public benefit established by positive law. Accordingly, the majority's conclusion — that a State violates the Privileges or Immunities Clause when it "discriminates" against citizens who have been domiciled in the State for less than a year in the distribution of welfare benefit — appears contrary to the original understanding and is dubious at best.

. . . The *Slaughter-House Cases* sapped the Clause of any meaning. Although the majority appears to breathe new life into the Clause today, it fails to address its historical underpinnings or its place in our constitutional jurisprudence. Because I believe that the demise of the Privileges or Immunities Clause has contributed in no small part to the current disarray of our Fourteenth Amendment jurisprudence, I would be open to reevaluating its meaning in an appropriate case. Before invoking the Clause, however, we should endeavor to understand what the framers of the Fourteenth Amendment thought that it meant. We should also consider whether the Clause should displace, rather than augment, portions of our equal protection and substantive due process jurisprudence. The majority's failure to consider these important questions raises the specter that the Privileges or Immunities Clause will become yet another convenient tool for inventing new rights, limited solely by the "predilections of those who happen at the time to be Members of this Court."

I respectfully dissent.

NOTES AND QUESTIONS

1. California's welfare benefits are some of the highest in the nation, and state leaders thought it fiscally prudent to limit the welfare benefits of new residents in order to save over ten million dollars, coordinate other assistance programs, and, frankly, to keep from becoming a "welfare magnet." With these rational legislative thoughts, California may have reasoned it could allocate its own funds, but it was wrong. Why does the Court, including two of the Court's strongest federalism advocates — Justices Scalia and O'Connor — deny California this latitude?

2. Justice Stevens' majority opinion in *Saenz* argues that Justice Miller's meager holding in *Slaughter-House* is enough to secure the Golden State's largesse for the new residents, but was that your impression of *Slaughter-House*? Said Stevens: "[d]espite fundamentally differing views concerning the coverage of the Privileges or Immunities Clause, . . . it has always been common ground that this Clause protects [the right of the newly arrived citizen to the same privileges and immunities enjoyed by other citizens of the same State]." Maybe, except that notwithstanding the claim of "common ground" over the dicta in *Slaughter-House*, the Fourteenth Amendment Privileges or Immunities Clause had never been applied in that categorical way. Indeed, in over 130 years, the Clause had never been used at all, save in a minor tax dispute the Court rather promptly overruled.

3. Remember that the words privileges *and* immunities also appear in Article IV distinct from the Privileges *or* Immunities Clause in the Fourteenth Amendment. Article IV is basically a limited nondiscrimination principle between residents and visitors, and thus, Article IV has no application in *Saenz* dealing with two classes of residents. Moreover, according to the Court, Article IV was intended to "fuse into one Nation, a collection of independent, sovereign States." As interpreted by the modern Supreme Court, such distinctions need only be avoided with regard to a somewhat uncertain category of fundamental liberties, like lawyering in a neighboring state, but not, say, differentially calculated elk hunting fees.

4. So where does the right to travel fit into the Fourteenth Amendment? In *Saenz*, Justice Stevens more or less re-made the Privileges or Immunities Clause of the Fourteenth Amendment into both the right to travel from state to state and the right of new residents to be treated as well as old ones. Chief Justice Rehnquist thought this a ruse. "I cannot see how the right to become a citizen of another State," Rehnquist wrote in dissent, "is a necessary 'component' of the right to travel." The only reason the Court "unearth[ed] from its tomb" the Privileges or Immunities Clause, argued Rehnquist, was to clean up its decidedly messy right to travel cases that "in the past 30 years, essentially conflated the right to travel with the right to equal citizenship." Most of these cases dealt with durational residency requirements, with the Court inquiring whether restricting the provision of welfare benefits, voting, or medical assistance to new residents for a limited time impermissibly penalized them under the Equal Protection Clause. To some degree, the Court's earlier cases turned on a judicial assessment of the importance of a right like voting, but as the Chief Justice observes, in light of *Saenz,* outside a few ill-defined circumstances, states generally can no longer classify their citizens by the length of their residence. And the noted qualification of "a few ill-defined circumstances" is only the majority's assertion in *Saenz* that differences between in-state and out-of-state college tuition levels and state waiting periods for divorce are somehow still okay.

5. The most interesting opinion in *Saenz* may be the dissent of Justice Thomas. Justice Thomas agrees with the Chief Justice that the Fourteenth Amendment Privileges or Immunities Clause has nothing to do with a durational residency requirement for a welfare benefit, but Justice Thomas is far more congenial to exhuming privileges or immunities generally. Writes Justice Thomas: "[b]ecause I believe that the demise of the Privileges or Immunities Clause has contributed in no small part to the current disarray of our Fourteenth Amendment jurisprudence, I would be open to reevaluating its meaning in an appropriate case. Before invoking the Clause, however, we should endeavor to understand what the framers of the Fourteenth Amendment thought that it meant."

Justice Thomas traces the language to 17th century colonial charters, noting that scholars have attributed the specific use of the language in the Fourteenth Amendment to support for the 1866 Civil Rights Act and its protection of contract and property rights that were being denied the freed slaves. In addition, it appears that some drafters of the Fourteenth Amendment thought the Privileges or Immunities Clause would secure from state infringement all of the rights expressed in the first Eight Amendments, as well as those unenumerated fundamental rights anchored in common law tradition, or as it is sometimes formulated, "those rights, common to all men which no man or state may rightfully take away." Natural law formulations like these can be abused by partisans of many stripes, but as the criticism of the *Slaughter-House* majority across the scholarly spectrum discloses, the price for judicially ignoring natural rights is often abdication of them. On the social side of liberty, the protection of the rights to marry, procreate, live in extended families, and direct the upbringing of children have all been discovered in modern times by recurring "to the most specific level at which a relevant tradition protecting, or denying protection to, the asserted right can be identified." *Michael H. v. Gerald D.* (1989). Is there any principled reason not to employ the same type of careful judicial inquiry in the economic realm? What would an historically accurate definition of privileges or immunities be? Justice Field, in dissent in *Slaughter-House,* gave this description: "the right to pursue a lawful employment in a lawful manner, without other restraint than such as equally affects all persons."

Justice Thomas cautioned that without its proper historical grounding, the Clause "will become yet another convenient tool for inventing new rights, limited solely by the 'predilections of those who happen at the time to be Members of this Court.'" Substantive economic due process, which we take up next, is often pointed to as the archetypical example of where personal judicial "predilections" first became part of the Court's opinions.

3. Substantive Economic Due Process

Slaughter-House both undermined the privileges or immunities envisioned by the Fourteenth Amendment, and cursorily dismissed the Butchers' Association's alternative ground for recovery, due process. The Court wrote:

> [U]nder no construction of that provision that we have ever seen, or any that we deem admissible, can the restraint imposed by the State of Louisiana upon the exercise of their trade by the butchers of New Orleans be held to be a deprivation of property within the meaning of that provision.

83 U.S. (16 Wall.) 36, 81 (1873). In essence, the Court was saying due process relates to procedure, and no more. More recently, Justice Scalia has written that he agrees, since the Clause "[b]y its inescapable terms . . . guarantees only process. . . . To say otherwise is to abandon textualism, and to render democratically adopted texts mere springboards for judicial lawmaking." ANTONIN SCALIA, A MATTER OF INTERPRETATION 24-25 (1997). The counter to this argument is that textualism requires context, and specifically, the natural law context of the framers to protect certain fundamental rights. This is what we saw the early Supreme Court do in *Calder v. Bull*, 3 U.S. (3 Dall.) 386 (1798), *Fletcher v. Peck*, 10 U.S. (6 Cranch) 87 (1810), and *Terrett v. Taylor*, 13 U.S. (9 Cranch) 43 (1815), discussed in Chapter Two. When Justice Scalia argues that the first substantive use of due process was to uphold slavery in *Dred Scott v. Sanford*, 60 U.S. (19 How.) 393 (1856) (*see* Chapter Eight), he thus omits this crucial bit of originalism. No one can justify *Dred Scott*, then or now; however, its lack of justification, too, depends upon the recognition that, despite the political compromise of the Fugitive Slave Clause in the original Constitution (Article IV, Section 2, Paragraph 3), providing for the return of escaping slaves, the founders understood slavery to be a disregard of the basic human dignity of all persons recognized by the natural law. *See* THE FEDERALIST NO. 54 (James Madison) (describing slavery as a legal artifice, not part of the natural order).

But does due process guarantee economic liberty? Dissenting Justices Field and Bradley thought so in *Slaughter-House*. Bradley wrote:

> [T]he individual citizen, as a necessity, must be left free to adopt such calling, profession, or trade as may seem to him most conducive to that end. Without this right he cannot be a freeman. This right to choose one's calling is an essential part of that liberty which is the object of government to protect; and a calling, when chosen, is a man's property and right. Liberty and property are not protected where these rights are arbitrarily assailed.

83 U.S. (16 Wall.) at 116 (Bradley, J., dissenting). In other words, the Due Process Clause guaranteed not just procedure, but limited the ability of states to adopt arbitrary laws at all.

The year after *Slaughter-House*, the Court seemed effectively to adopt the Field and Bradley dissenting view and began to articulate economic liberty as a judicially-protectible fundamental interest. In the next case, *Loan Association v. Topeka*, 87 U.S. (20 Wall.) 655 (1874), the Court invalidated a city ordinance that authorized the issuance of bonds "to encourage the establishment of manufactories and such other enterprises." *Id.* at 42 (statement of the case). These bonds would be paid for by public monies raised through taxation, even as the proceeds of the bonds were primarily of benefit to private manufacturing concerns. Justice Miller, who had refused to find economic freedom to be a privilege or immunity of citizenship and who quickly dismissed due process as a basis for such liberty, wrote the majority opinion, in which he found the bonding authority to be beyond the legislative power and an invasion of private right.

LOAN ASSOCIATION v. TOPEKA
87 U.S. (20 Wall.) 655 (1874)

MR. JUSTICE MILLER delivered the opinion of the court.

* * *

[It is argued] that the act authorizes the towns and other municipalities to which it applies, by issuing bonds or loaning their credit, to take the property of the citizen under the guise of taxation to pay these bonds, and use it in aid of the enterprises of others which are not of a public character, thus perverting the right of taxation, which can only be exercised for a public use, to the aid of individual interests and personal purposes of profit and gain.

* * *

[Prior cases upheld the use of public bonds for private railroads.] In all these cases, however, the decision has turned upon the question whether the taxation by which this aid was afforded to the building of railroads was for a public purpose. Those who came to the conclusion that it was, held the laws for that purpose valid. Those who could not reach that conclusion held them void. In all the controversy this has been the turning-point of the judgments of the courts. And it is safe to say that no court has held debts created in aid of railroad companies, by counties or towns, valid on any other ground than that the purpose for which the taxes were levied was a public use, a purpose or object which it was the right and the duty of State governments to assist by money raised from the people by taxation. . . .

* * *

It must be conceded that there are such rights in every free government beyond the control of the State. A government which recognized no such rights, which held the lives, the liberty, and the property of its citizens subject at all times to the absolute disposition and unlimited control of even the most democratic depository of power, is after all but a despotism. It is true it is a despotism of the many, of the majority, if you choose to call it so, but it is none the less a despotism. It may well be doubted if a man is to hold all that he is accustomed to call his own, all in which he has placed his happiness, and the security of which is essential to that happiness, under the unlimited dominion of others, whether it is not wiser that this power should be exercised by one man than by many.

The theory of our governments, State and National, is opposed to the deposit of unlimited power anywhere. The executive, the legislative, and the judicial branches of these governments are all of limited and defined powers.

There are limitations on such power which grow out of the essential nature of all free governments. Implied reservations of individual rights, without which the social compact could not exist, and which are respected by all governments entitled to the name. No court, for instance, would hesitate to declare void a statute which enacted that A. and B. who were husband and wife to each other should be so no longer, but that A. should thereafter be the husband of C., and B. the wife of D. Or which should enact that the homestead now owned by A. should no longer be his, but should henceforth be the property of B.

Of all the powers conferred upon government that of taxation is most liable to abuse. . . .

. . . It was said by Chief Justice Marshall, in the case of *McCulloch v. The State of Maryland,* that the power to tax is the power to destroy. . . . This power can as readily be employed against one class of individuals and in favor of another, so as to ruin the one class and give unlimited wealth and prosperity to the other, if there is no implied limitation of the uses for which the power may be exercised.

To lay with one hand the power of the government on the property of the citizen, and with the other to bestow it upon favored individuals to aid private enterprises and build up private fortunes, is none the less a robbery because it is done under the forms of law and is called taxation. This is not legislation. It is a decree under legislative forms.

Nor is it taxation. A "tax," says Webster's Dictionary, "is a rate or sum of money assessed on the person or property of a citizen by government for the use of the nation or state." "Taxes are burdens or charges imposed by the legislature upon persons or property to raise money for public purposes."

* * *

We have established, we think, beyond cavil that there can be no lawful tax which is not laid for a *public purpose*. It may not be easy to draw the line in all cases so as to decide what is a public purpose in this sense and what is not.

It is undoubtedly the duty of the legislature which imposes or authorizes municipalities to impose a tax to see that it is not to be used for purposes of private interest instead of a public use, and the courts can only be justified in interposing when a violation of this principle is clear and the reason for inter-ference cogent. And in deciding whether, in the given case, the object for which the taxes are assessed falls upon the one side or the other of this line, they must be governed mainly by the course and usage of the government, the objects for which taxes have been customarily and by long course of legislation levied, what objects or purposes have been considered necessary to the support and for the proper use of the government, whether State or municipal. Whatever law-fully pertains to this and is sanctioned by time and the acquiescence of the people may well be held to belong to the public use, and proper for the mainte-nance of good government, though this may not be the only criterion of rightful taxation.

But in the case before us, in which the towns are authorized to contribute aid by way of taxation to any class of manufacturers, there is no difficulty in hold-ing that this is not such a public purpose as we have been considering. If it be said that a benefit results to the local public of a town by establishing manu-factures, the same may be said of any other business or pursuit which employs capital or labor. The merchant, the mechanic, the innkeeper, the banker, the builder, the steamboat owner are equally promoters of the public good, and equally deserving the aid of the citizens by forced contributions. No line can be drawn in favor of the manufacturer which would not open the coffers of the pub-lic treasury to the importunities of two-thirds of the business men of the city or town.

* * *

Mr. Justice Clifford, dissenting:

* * *

Corporations of a municipal character are created by the legislature, and the legislature, as the trustee or guardian of the public interest, has the exclu-sive and unrestrained control over such a franchise, and may enlarge, diminish, alter, change, or abolish the same at pleasure. Where the grantees of a franchise, as well as the grantors, are public bodies and the franchise is created solely for municipal objects, the grant is at all times within the control of the legisla-ture, and consequently the charter is subject to amendment or repeal at the will of the granting power.

* * *

Unwise laws and such as are highly inexpedient and unjust are frequently passed by legislative bodies, but there is no power vested in a Circuit Court nor in this court, to determine that any law passed by a State legislature is void if it is not repugnant to their own constitution nor the Constitution of the United States.

NOTES AND QUESTIONS

1. Does *Loan Association* follow natural law principles? It would seem to insofar as it protects the economic resources of one private party from being expropriated for the benefit of another. From 1874 to 1897, the Court continued this thinking and to hint that the Due Process Clause placed a substantive limit on the activities of government. In *Munn v. Illinois*, 94 U.S. 113 (1877), the Court sustained the regulation of grain warehouses because the business was "affected with the public interest"; however, the Court indicated that absent that interrelationship, the regulation of business would violate due process. *Id.* at 125-26. In a subsequent case, the Court upheld state regulation of railroad rates, but did so with the caveat that "[t]he question of the reasonableness of a rate of charge for transportation by a railroad company . . . is eminently a question for judicial investigation, requiring due process of law for its determination." *Chicago, Milwaukee & St. Paul Ry. Co. v. Minnesota*, 134 U.S. 418, 458 (1890). Similarly, in *Mugler v. Kansas*, 123 U.S. 623 (1887), the Court found no reason to set aside the prohibition of the sale of alcoholic beverages, but noted that if "a statute purporting to have been enacted to protect the public health, the public morals, or the public safety, has no real or substantial relation to those objects, or is a palpable invasion of rights secured by the fundamental law, it is the duty of the courts to so adjudge, and thereby give effect to the Constitution." *Id.* at 661. A year earlier, the Court made it clear that corporations could bring suit under the Fourteenth Amendment because they would be treated as "persons." *Santa Clara County v. Southern Pacific R.R. Co.*, 118 U.S. 394, 396 (1886) (statement of facts) (Chief Justice Waite stated before oral argument that the Court would not hear argument on whether a corporation constitutes a "person" under the Equal Protection Clause, as the Court was "all of the opinion that it does."). Remember that corporations are not "persons" under the Privileges or Immunities Clause, so this difference invited corporate litigation.

2. In 1897, a Louisiana law prohibiting payments on insurance policies issued by non-Louisiana companies that were not licensed to do business in the state was struck down. *Allgeyer v. Louisiana*, 165 U.S. 578 (1897). In *Allgeyer*, the Court made it plain that substantive due process protected economic liberty, writing:

> The "liberty" mentioned in [the Fourteenth Amendment is] deemed to embrace the right of . . . citizen[s] to be free in the enjoyment of all [their] faculties; to be free to use them in all lawful ways; to live and work where [they] will; to earn [their] livelihood by any lawful calling; to pursue any livelihood or avocation; and for that purpose to enter into all contacts which may be proper, necessary, and essential to [their] carrying out to a successful completion the purposes above mentioned.

Id. at 589. This was the formal beginning to an era of judicial intervention in favor of freedom of contract that would not end until the Depression of the 1930s led to political demands for extensive government regulation of the free market, at least during economic emergency. The constitutional doctrine came to be known as "Lochnerism," after the next case.

LOCHNER v. NEW YORK
198 U.S. 45 (1905)

MR. JUSTICE PECKHAM . . . delivered the opinion of the court:

[New York Law provided that "No employee shall be required or permitted to work in a biscuit, bread, or cake bakery or confectionery establishment more than sixty hours in any one week, or more than ten hours in any one day, unless for the purpose of making a shorter work day on the last day of the week; nor more hours in any one week than will make an average of ten hours per day for the number of days during such week in which such employee shall work."]

The indictment, it will be seen, charges that [Lochner] violated . . . the labor law of the State of New York, in that he wrongfully and unlawfully required and permitted an employee working for him to work more than sixty hours in one week. . . . The mandate of the statute, that "no employee shall be required or permitted to work," is the substantial equivalent of an enactment that "no employee shall contract or agree to work," more than ten hours per day, and as there is no provision for special emergencies the statute is mandatory in all cases. It is not an act merely fixing the number of hours which shall constitute a legal day's work, but an absolute prohibition upon the employer, permitting, under any circumstances, more than ten hours work to be done in his establishment. The employee may desire to earn the extra money, which would arise from his working more than the prescribed time, but this statute forbids the employer from permitting the employee to earn it.

The statute necessarily interferes with the right of contract between the employer and employees, concerning the number of hours in which the latter may labor in the bakery of the employer. The general right to make a contract in relation to his business is part of the liberty of the individual protected by the Fourteenth Amendment of the Federal Constitution. *Allgeyer v. Louisiana* (1897). Under that provision no state can deprive any person of life, liberty or property without due process of law. The right to purchase or to sell labor is part of the liberty protected by this amendment, unless there are circumstances which exclude the right. There are, however, certain powers, existing in the sovereignty of each State in the Union, somewhat vaguely termed police powers, the exact description and limitation of which have not been attempted by the courts. Those powers, broadly stated and without, at present, any attempt at a more specific limitation, relate to the safety, health, morals and general welfare of the public. Both property and liberty are held on such reasonable conditions as may be imposed by the governing power of the State in the exercise of those powers, and with such conditions the Fourteenth Amendment was not designed to interfere.

* * *

It must, of course, be conceded that there is a limit to the valid exercise of the police power by the State. There is no dispute concerning this general proposition. Otherwise the Fourteenth Amendment would have no efficacy and the legislatures of the States would have unbounded power, and it would be enough to say that any piece of legislation was enacted to conserve the morals, the health or the safety of the people; such legislation would be valid, no matter how absolutely without foundation the claim might be. . . .

This is not a question of substituting the judgment of the court for that of the legislature. If the act be within the power of the State it is valid, although the judgment of the court might be totally opposed to the enactment of such a law. But the question would still remain: Is it within the police power of the State? and that question must be answered by the court.

The question whether this act is valid as a labor law, pure and simple, may be dismissed in a few words. There is no reasonable ground for interfering with the liberty of person or the right of free contract, by determining the hours of labor, in the occupation of a baker. There is no contention that bakers as a class are not equal in intelligence and capacity to men in other trades or manual occupations, or that they are not able to assert their rights and care for themselves without the protecting arm of the State, interfering with their independence of judgment and of action. They are in no sense wards of the State. Viewed in the light of a purely labor law, with no reference whatever to the question of health, we think that a law like the one before us involves neither the safety, the morals nor the welfare of the public, and that the interest of the public is not in the slightest degree affected by such an act. The law must be upheld, if at all, as a law pertaining to the health of the individual engaged in the occupation of a baker. It does not affect any other portion of the public than those who are engaged in that occupation. Clean and wholesome bread does not depend upon whether the baker works but ten hours per day or only sixty hours a week. The limitation of the hours of labor does not come within the police power on that ground.

It is a question of which of two powers or rights shall prevail — the power of the State to legislate or the right of the individual to liberty of person and freedom of contract. The mere assertion that the subject relates though but in a remote degree to the public health does not necessarily render the enactment valid. The act must have a more direct relation, as a means to an end, and the end itself must be appropriate and legitimate, before an act can be held to be valid which interferes with the general right of an individual to be free in his person and in his power to contract in relation to his own labor.

. . . Although found in what is called a labor law of the state, the court of appeals has upheld the act as one relating to the public health, — in other words, as a health law. One of the judges of the court of appeals, in upholding the law, stated that, in his opinion, the regulation in question could not be sustained unless they were able to say, from common knowledge, that working in a bakery and candy factory was an unhealthy employment. The judge held that, while the evidence was not uniform, it still led him to the conclusion that the occupation of a baker or confectioner was unhealthy and tended to result in diseases of the respiratory organs. Three of the judges dissented from that view, and they thought the occupation of a baker was not to such an extent unhealthy as to warrant the interference of the legislature with the liberty of the individual.

We think the limit of the police power has been reached and passed in this case. There is, in our judgment, no reasonable foundation for holding this to be necessary or appropriate as a health law to safeguard the public health or the health of the individuals who are following the trade of a baker. If this statute be valid, and if, therefore, a proper case is made out in which to deny the right of an individual, *sui juris*, as employer or employee, to make contracts for the labor of the latter under the protection of the provisions of the Federal Constitution, there would seem to be no length to which legislation of this nature might not go. . . .

We think that[, unlike in *Holden v. Hardy* (1898), where we upheld maximum hour restrictions on coal miners,] there can be no fair doubt that the trade of a baker, in and of itself, is not an unhealthy one to that degree which would authorize the legislature to interfere with the right to labor, and with the right of free contract on the part of the individual, either as employer or employee. In looking through statistics regarding all trades and occupations, it may be true that the trade of a baker does not appear to be as healthy as some other trades, and is also vastly more healthy than still others. To the common understanding the trade of a baker has never been regarded as an unhealthy one. . . . There must be more than the mere fact of the possible existence of some small amount of unhealthiness to warrant legislative interference with liberty. It is unfortunately true that labor, even in any department, may possibly carry with it the seeds of unhealthiness. But are we all, on that account, at the mercy of legislative majorities? A printer, a tinsmith, a locksmith, a carpenter, a cabinetmaker, a dry goods clerk, a bank's, a lawyer's or a physician's clerk, or a clerk in almost any kind of business, would all come under the power of the legislature, on this assumption. No trade, no occupation, no mode of earning one's living, could escape this all-pervading power, and the acts of the legislature in limiting the hours of labor in all employments would be valid, although such limitation might seriously cripple the ability of the laborer to support himself and his family. In our large cities there are many buildings into which the sun penetrates for but a short time in each day, and these buildings are occupied by people carrying on the business of bankers, brokers, lawyers, real estate, and many other kinds of business, aided by many clerks, messengers, and other employees. Upon the assumption of the validity of this act under review, it is not possible to say that an act, prohibiting lawyers' or bank clerks, or others, from contracting to labor for their employers more than eight hours a day would be invalid. . . .

. . . The act is not, within any fair meaning of the term, a health law, but is an illegal interference with the rights of individuals, both employers and employees, to make contracts regarding labor upon such terms as they may think best, or which they may agree upon with the other parties to such contracts. Statutes of the nature of that under review, limiting the hours in which grown and intelligent men may labor to earn their living, are mere meddlesome interferences with the rights of the individual, and they are not saved from condemnation by the claim that they are passed in the exercise of the police power and upon the subject of the health of the individual whose rights are interfered with, unless there be some fair ground, reasonable in and of itself, to say that there is material danger to the public health or to the health of the employees, if the hours of labor are not curtailed. If this be not clearly the case the individuals, whose rights are thus made the subject of legislative interference, are under the protection of the Federal Constitution regarding their liberty of contract as well as of person; and the legislature of the State has no power to limit their right as proposed in this statute. All that it could properly do has been done by it with regard to the conduct of bakeries, as provided for in the other sections of the act. These several sections provide for the inspection of the premises where the bakery is carried on, with regard to furnishing proper wash rooms and waterclosets, apart from the bake room, also with regard to providing proper drainage, plumbing and painting; the sections, in addition, provide for the height of the ceiling, the cementing or tiling of floors, where necessary in the opinion of the factory inspector, and for other things of that nature; alterations are also provided for and are to be made where necessary in the opinion of the inspector, in order to comply with the provisions of the statute. These various sections may be wise and valid regulations, and they certainly go to the full extent of providing for the cleanliness and the healthiness, so far as possible, of the quarters in which bakeries are to be conducted. Adding to all these requirements, a prohibition to enter into any contract of labor in a bakery for more than a certain number of hours a week, is, in our judgment, so wholly beside the matter of a proper, reasonable and fair provision, as to run counter to that liberty of person and of free contract provided for in the Federal Constitution.

. . . In our judgment it is not possible in fact to discover the connection between the number of hours a baker may work in the bakery and the healthful quality of the bread made by the workman. The connection, if any exist, is too shadowy and thin to build any argument for the interference of the legislature. If the man works ten hours a day it is all right, but if ten and a half or eleven his health is in danger and his bread may be unhealthy, and, therefore, he shall not be permitted to do it. This, we think, is unreasonable and entirely arbitrary. . . .

* * *

It is impossible for us to shut our eyes to the fact that many of the laws of this character, while passed under what is claimed to be the police power for the purpose of protecting the public health or welfare, are, in reality, passed from other motives. . . .

. . . It seems to us that the real object and purpose were simply to regulate the hours of labor between the master and his employees (all being men, *sui juris*), in a private business, not dangerous in any degree to morals or in any real and substantial degree, to the health of the employees. Under such circumstances the freedom of master and employee to contract with each other in relation to their employment, and in defining the same, cannot be prohibited or interfered with, without violating the Federal Constitution.

* * *

Mr. Justice Harlan, with whom Mr. Justice White and Mr. Justice Day concurred, dissenting.

* * *

Granting then that there is a liberty of contract which cannot be violated even under the sanction of direct legislative enactment, but assuming, as according to settled law we may assume, that such liberty of contract is subject to such regulations as the State may reasonably prescribe for the common good and the well-being of society, what are the conditions under which the judiciary may declare such regulations to be in excess of legislative authority and void? Upon this point there is no room for dispute; for, the rule is universal that a legislative enactment, Federal or state, is never to be disregarded or held invalid unless it be, beyond question, plainly and palpably in excess of legislative power. . . . If there be doubt as to the validity of the statute, that doubt must therefore be resolved in favor of its validity, and the courts must keep their hands off, leaving the legislature to meet the responsibility for unwise legislation. If the end which the legislature seeks to accomplish be one to which its power extends, and if the means employed to that end, although not the wisest or best, are yet not plainly and palpably unauthorized by law, then the court cannot interfere. In other words, when the validity of a statute is questioned, the burden of proof, so to speak, is upon those who assert it to be unconstitutional. *McCulloch v. Maryland*, 4 Wheat. 316, 421.

* * *

. . . Whether or not this be wise legislation it is not the province of the court to inquire. Under our systems of government the courts are not concerned with the wisdom or policy of legislation. So that in determining the question of power to interfere with liberty of contract, the court may inquire whether the means devised by the State are germane to an end which may be lawfully accomplished and have a real or substantial relation to the protection of health, as involved in the daily work of the persons, male and female, engaged in bakery and confectionery establishments. But when this inquiry is entered upon I find it impossible, in view of common experience, to say that there is here no real or substantial relation between the means employed by the State and the end sought to be accomplished by its legislation. . . .

* * *

I take leave to say that the New York statute, in the particulars here involved, cannot be held to be in conflict with the Fourteenth Amendment, without enlarging the scope of the Amendment far beyond its original purpose and without bringing under the supervision of this court matters which have been supposed to belong exclusively to the legislative departments of the several States when exerting their conceded power to guard the health and safety of their citizens by such regulations as they in their wisdom deem best. Health laws of every description constitute, said Chief Justice Marshall, a part of that mass of legislation which "embraces everything within the territory of a state, not surrendered to the General Government; all which can be most advantageously exercised by the States themselves." A decision that the New York statute is void under the Fourteenth Amendment will, in my opinion, involve consequences of a far-reaching and mischievous character; for such a decision would seriously cripple the inherent power of the States to care for the lives, health and well-being of their citizens. Those are matters which can be best controlled by the states. The preservation of the just powers of the States is quite as vital as the preservation of the powers of the General Government.

* * *

MR. JUSTICE HOLMES dissenting.

I regret sincerely that I am unable to agree with the judgment in this case, and that I think it my duty to express my dissent.

This case is decided upon an economic theory which a large part of the country does not entertain. If it were a question whether I agreed with that theory, I should desire to study it further and long before making up my mind. But I do not conceive that to be my duty, because I strongly believe that my agreement or disagreement has nothing to do with the right of a majority to embody their opinions in law. It is settled by various decisions of this court that state constitutions and state laws may regulate life in many ways which we as legislators might think as injudicious or if you like as tyrannical as this, and which equally with this interfere with the liberty to contract. Sunday laws and usury laws are ancient examples. A more modern one is the prohibition of lotteries. The liberty of the citizen to do as he likes so long as he does not interfere with the liberty of others to do the same, which has been a shibboleth for some well-known writers, is interfered with by school laws, by the Post office, by every state or municipal institution which takes his money for purposes thought desirable, whether he likes it or not. The 14th Amendment does not enact Mr. Herbert Spencer's Social Statics. . . .

. . . I think that the word liberty, in the Fourteenth Amendment is perverted when it is held to prevent the natural outcome of a dominant opinion, unless it can be said that a rational and fair man necessarily would admit that the statute proposed would infringe fundamental principles as they have been understood by the traditions of our people and our law. It does not need research to show that no such sweeping condemnation can be passed upon the statute before us. A reasonable man might think it a proper measure on the score of health. Men whom I certainly could not pronounce unreasonable would uphold it as a first instalment of a general regulation of the hours of work. Whether in the latter aspect it would be open to the charge of inequality I think it unnecessary to discuss.

NOTES AND QUESTIONS

1. Because of his famous line that the "14th Amendment does not enact Mr. Herbert Spencer's Social Statics," Holmes is often argued to be "expressly reject[ing] the majority's premise that the Constitution should be used to limit government regulation and protect a laissez-faire economy." ERWIN CHEMERINSKY, CONSTITUTIONAL LAW PRINCIPLES AND POLICIES 482 (1997). But is that entirely true? What does Holmes mean in his dissent when he states that:

> [T]he word liberty, in the Fourteenth Amendment is perverted when it is held to prevent the natural outcome of a dominant opinion, unless it can be said that a rational and fair man necessarily would admit that the statute proposed would infringe fundamental principles as they have been understood by the traditions of our people and our law.

198 U.S. at 76 (Holmes, J., dissenting). Doesn't that statement admit of a natural law limitation on government power, informed by tradition and the common law, even as Holmes in this particular case disagrees with the majority that a regulation of a baker's hours violates that tradition?

2. *Lochner* established or confirmed a number of judicial statements that had been made in dicta prior to it: freedom of contract related to the carrying out of a trade or profession was within the protected liberty of the Fifth and Fourteenth Amendment Due Process Clauses, 198 U.S. at 53; liberty may be limited by government power if the limitation truly relates to health and safety (the "police power"), *id.*; and the Court must carefully inquire as to whether the regulation is within its proper police power scope, *id.* at 56. On the last point, the Court was particularly concerned that government regulation was being too frequently used to redistribute wealth to the politically favored, rather than addressing genuine public purposes. Had the Court learned the lesson of the evils of monopoly that it disregarded in *Slaughter-House*? Or was the Court now overcorrecting and intruding too deeply into matters that, while related remotely to the principle of economic liberty, require the specific policy determination of the legislature? Justice Harlan's dissent in *Lochner* thought the latter, arguing that bakers suffered from serious health problems, including prolonged exposure to flour dust and intense heat.

3. Does the Court undermine its conclusion by attempting to distinguish rather than overrule *Holden v. Hardy*? With respect to concerns about the *public* health (as opposed to the *private* health of individual workers), is a minor who works more than 10 hours a day any more likely to cause harm *to others* than a baker? Does the fact that mining is more inherently dangerous than baking to those engaged in it effect the *public health* calculus in the least? The Court subsequently allowed maximum hour laws for women, but not minimum wage laws. *Compare Muller v. Oregon*, 208 U.S. 412 (1908) (this case gave rise to the expression "Brandeis brief" [not a compliment] in which not yet Supreme Court Justice Louis Brandeis filed a brief of 113 pages supporting the limitation of women's efforts outside domestic work), *with Adkins v. Children's Hospital*, 261 U.S. 525 (1923) (finding women perfectly capable of fending for themselves in the negotiation of wages). Brandeis argued in his brief, and the Court accepted, that maximum hour restrictions on women protected the *public's* interest in insuring that women would be available for child-rearing. Is that more, or less, of a legitimate governmental interest than was claimed by New York in *Lochner*? Would you support using the Due Process Clause to invalidate such a law today?

4. For a while following *Lochner*, the Court upheld the natural right of economic liberty under the auspices of the Due Process Clause. For example, the Court invalidated irrational barriers to entry into trade or business. *New State Ice Co. v. Liebmann*, 285 U.S. 262 (1932) (striking down permitting requirements that tended to create monopoly in the ice business). Tartly, the Court observed that government power cannot be used "to prevent a shoemaker from making or selling shoes because shoemakers already in that occupation can make and sell all the shoes that are needed." *Id.* at 279.

5. Much academic criticism of *Lochner* is not principled, but merely advocacy for an activist government that sets prices and otherwise favors the public or quasi-public delivery of goods, rather than the private market. For scholarly criticism of this position, see RICHARD EPSTEIN, TAKINGS: PRIVATE PROPERTY AND THE POWER OF EMINENT DOMAIN (1985); and BERNARD SIEGAN, ECONOMIC LIBERTIES AND THE CONSTITUTION (1980). Whatever side you are on in such matters, if this is a political argument, should it be dressed in constitutional garb?

6. Today, of course, maximum hour restrictions and a host of other workplace regulations are commonplace; the *Lochner* Court's protection of economic liberty eventually gave way to deference by the Court to the regulatory state. Why did the *Lochner* era end? Professor Laurence Tribe writes:

> In large measure . . . it was the economic realities of the Depression. . . . The legal "freedom" of contract and property came increasingly to be seen as an illusion, subject as it was to impersonal economic forces. Positive government intervention came to be more widely accepted as essential to economic survival, and legal doctrines would henceforth have to operate from that premise.

LAURENCE TRIBE, AMERICAN CONSTITUTIONAL LAW § 8-6, at 578 (2d ed. 1988). In the face of the tens of millions unemployed during the 1930s, Professor Tribe is surely right. However, given the thankfully transient nature of the Depression, should the fundamental right of economic liberty have been abandoned or merely deferred until the passing of a temporary or unusual economic circumstance? The *Nebbia* case reveals how much the initial limitation of "economic "liberty related to the then present economic distress.

NEBBIA v. NEW YORK
291 U.S. 502 (1933)

MR. JUSTICE ROBERTS delivered the opinion of the Court.

The Legislature of New York established a Milk Control Board with power, among other things, to "fix minimum and maximum . . . retail prices to be charged [for milk] by . . . stores to consumers for consumption off the premises where sold." The Board fixed nine cents as the price to be charged by a store for a quart of milk. Nebbia, the proprietor of a grocery store in Rochester, sold two quarts and a 5-cent loaf of bread for 18 cents; and was convicted for violating the Board's order. At his trial he asserted the statute and order contravene the equal protection clause and the due process clause of the Fourteenth Amendment, and renewed the contention in successive appeals to the county court and Court of Appeals. Both overruled his claim and affirmed the conviction.

The question for decision is whether the Federal Constitution prohibits a state from so fixing the selling price of milk. . . .

* * *

Save the conduct of railroads, no business has been so thoroughly regimented and regulated by the State of New York as the milk industry. . . .

Under our form of government the use of property and the making of contracts are normally matters of private and not of public concern. The general rule is that both shall be free of governmental interference. But neither property rights nor contract rights are absolute; for government cannot exist if the citizen may at will use his property to the detriment of his fellows, or exercise his freedom of contract to work them harm. Equally fundamental with the private right is that of the public to regulate it in the common interest. . . .

* * *

. . . These correlative rights, that of the citizen to exercise exclusive dominion over property and freely to contract about his affairs, and that of the state to regulate the use of property and the conduct of business, are always in collision. No exercise of the private right can be imagined which will not in some respect, however slight, affect the public; no exercise of the legislative prerogative to regulate the conduct of the citizen which will not to some extent abridge his liberty or affect his property. But subject only to constitutional restraint the private right must yield to the public need.

The Fifth Amendment, in the field of federal activity, and the Fourteenth, as respects state action, do not prohibit governmental regulation for the public welfare. They merely condition the exertion of the admitted power, by securing that the end shall be accomplished by methods consistent with due process. And the guaranty of due process, as has often been held, demands only that the law shall not be unreasonable, arbitrary or capricious, and that the means selected shall have a real and substantial relation to the object sought to be attained. It results that a regulation valid for one sort of business, or in given circumstances, may be invalid for another sort, or for the same business under other circumstances, because the reasonableness of each regulation depends upon the relevant facts.

* * *

The court has repeatedly sustained curtailment of enjoyment of private property, in the public interest. The owner's rights may be subordinated to the needs of other private owners whose pursuits are vital to the paramount interests of the community. The state may control the use of property in various ways; may prohibit advertising bill boards except of a prescribed size and location, or their use for certain kinds of advertising; may in certain circumstances authorize encroachments by party walls in cities; may fix the height of buildings, the character of materials, and methods of construction, the adjoining area which must be left open, and may exclude from residential sections offensive trades, industries and structures likely injuriously to affect the public health or safety; or may establish zones within which certain types of buildings or businesses are permitted and others excluded. And although the Fourteenth Amendment extends protection to aliens as well as citizens, a state may for adequate reasons of policy exclude aliens altogether from the use and occupancy of land.

Laws passed for the suppression of immorality, in the interest of health, to secure fair trade practices, and to safeguard the interests of depositors in banks, have been found consistent with due process. . . .

* * *

Legislation concerning sales of goods, and incidentally affecting prices, has repeatedly been held valid. In this class fall laws forbidding unfair competition by the charging of lower prices in one locality than those exacted in another, by giving trade inducements to purchasers, and by other forms of price discrimination. The public policy with respect to free competition has engendered state and federal statutes prohibiting monopolies, which have been upheld. On the other hand, where the policy of the state dictated that a monopoly should be granted, statutes having that effect have been held inoffensive to the constitutional guarantees.[34] Moreover, the state or a municipality may itself enter into business in competition with private proprietors, and thus effectively although indirectly control the prices charged by them.

* * *

---

[34] *Slaughter-House Cases.* . . .

. . . The argument runs that the public control of rates or prices is *per se* unreasonable and unconstitutional, save as applied to businesses affected with a public interest; that a business so affected is one in which property is devoted to an enterprise of a sort which the public itself might appropriately undertake, or one whose owner relies on a public grant or franchise for the right to conduct the business, or in which he is bound to serve all who apply; in short, such as is commonly called a public utility; or a business in its nature a monopoly. The milk industry, it is said, possesses none of these characteristics, and, therefore, not being affected with a public interest, its charges may not be controlled by the state. Upon the soundness of this contention the appellant's case against the statute depends.

We may as well say at once that the dairy industry is not, in the accepted sense of the phrase, a public utility. We think the appellant is also right in asserting that there is in this case no suggestion of any monopoly or monopolistic practice. It goes without saying that those engaged in the business are in no way dependent upon public grants or franchises for the privilege of conducting their activities. But if, as must be conceded, the industry is subject to regulation in the public interest, what constitutional principle bars the state from correcting existing maladjustments by legislation touching prices? We think there is no such principle. The due process clause makes no mention of sales or of prices any more than it speaks of business or contracts or buildings or other incidents of property. . . .

* * *

Many other decisions show that the private character of a business does not necessarily remove it from the realm of regulation of charges or prices. The usury laws fix the price which may be exacted for the use of money, although no business more essentially private in character can be imagined than that of loaning one's personal funds. Insurance agents' compensation may be regulated, though their contracts are private, because the business of insurance is considered one properly subject to public control. Statutes prescribing in the public interest the amounts to be charged by attorneys for prosecuting certain claims, a matter ordinarily one of personal and private nature, are not a deprivation of due process. . . .

It is clear that there is no closed class or category of businesses affected with a public interest, and the function of courts in the application of the Fifth and Fourteenth Amendments is to determine in each case whether circumstances vindicate the challenged regulation as a reasonable exertion of governmental authority or condemn it as arbitrary or discriminatory. The phrase "affected with a public interest" can, in the nature of things, mean no more than that an industry, for adequate reason, is subject to control for the public good. In several of the decisions of this court wherein the expressions "affected with a public interest," and "clothed with a public use," have been brought forward as the criteria of the validity of price control, it has been admitted that they are not susceptible of definition and form an unsatisfactory test of the constitutionality of legislation directed at business practices or prices. These decisions must rest, finally, upon the basis that the requirements of due process were not met because the laws were found arbitrary in their operation and effect. But there can be no doubt that upon proper occasion and by appropriate measures the state may regulate a business in any of its aspects, including the prices to be charged for the products or commodities it sells.

So far as the requirement of due process is concerned, and in the absence of other constitutional restriction, a state is free to adopt whatever economic policy may reasonably be deemed to promote public welfare, and to enforce that policy by legislation adapted to its purpose. The courts are without authority either to declare such policy, or, when it is declared by the legislature, to override it. If the laws passed are seen to have a reasonable relation to a proper legislative purpose, and are neither arbitrary nor discriminatory, the requirements of due process are satisfied, and judicial determination to that effect renders a court *functus officio.* "Whether the free operation of the normal laws of competition is a wise and wholesome rule for trade and commerce is an economic question which this court need not consider or determine." . . .

The law-making bodies have in the past endeavored to promote free competition by laws aimed at trusts and monopolies. The consequent interference with private property and freedom of contract has not availed with the courts to set these enactments aside as denying due process. Where the public interest was deemed to require the fixing of minimum prices, that expedient has been sustained. If the law-making body within its sphere of government concludes that the conditions or practices in an industry make unrestricted competition an inadequate safeguard of the consumer's interests, produce waste harmful to the public, threaten ultimately to cut off the supply of a commodity needed by the public, or portend the destruction of the industry itself, appropriate statutes passed in an honest effort to correct the threatened consequences may not be set aside because the regulation adopted fixes prices reasonably deemed by the Legislature to be fair to those engaged in the industry and to the consuming public. And this is especially so where, as here, the economic maladjustment is one of price, which threatens harm to the producer at one end of the series and the consumer at the other. The Constitution does not secure to any one liberty to conduct his business in such fashion as to inflict injury upon the public at large, or upon any substantial group of the people. Price control, like any other form of regulation, is unconstitutional only if arbitrary, discriminatory, or demonstrably irrelevant to the policy the legislature is free to adopt, and hence an unnecessary and unwarranted interference with individual liberty.

Tested by these considerations we find no basis in the due process clause of the Fourteenth Amendment for condemning the provisions of the Agriculture and Markets Law here drawn into question.

The judgment is affirmed.

MR. JUSTICE MCREYNOLDS[, dissenting].

* * *

The Fourteenth Amendment wholly disempowered the several States to "deprive any person of life, liberty, or property, without due process of law." The assurance of each of these things is the same. If now liberty or property may be struck down because of difficult circumstances, we must expect that hereafter every right must yield to the voice of an impatient majority when stirred by distressful exigency. . . .

* * *

. . . "That the right to contract about one's affairs is a part of the liberty of the individual protected by this clause [Fifth Amendment] is settled by the decisions of this court and is no longer open to question." [*Adkins v. Childrens Hospital* (1923)].

Meyer v. Nebraska (1919) held invalid a state enactment, which forbade the teaching in schools of any language other than English. "While this court has not attempted to define with exactness the liberty thus guaranteed, the term has received much consideration and some of the included things have been definitely stated. Without doubt, it denotes not merely freedom from bodily restraint but also the right of the individual to contract, to engage in any of the common occupations of life, to acquire useful knowledge, to marry, establish a home and bring up children, to worship God according to the dictates of his own conscience, and generally to enjoy those privileges long recognized at common law as essential to the orderly pursuit of happiness by free men."

* * *

If validity of the enactment depends upon emergency, then to sustain this conviction we must be able to affirm that an adequate one has been shown by competent evidence of essential facts. The asserted right is federal. Such rights may demand and often have received affirmation and protection here. They do not vanish simply because the power of the State is arrayed against them. Nor are they enjoyed in subjection to mere legislative findings.

If she relied upon the existence of emergency, the burden was upon the State to establish it by competent evidence. None was presented at the trial. If necessary for [Nebbia] to show absence of the asserted conditions, the little grocer was helpless from the beginning — the practical difficulties were too great for the average man.

* * *

Thus we are told the number of dairy cows had been increasing and that favorable prices for milk bring more cows. For two years notwithstanding low prices the per capita consumption had been falling. "The obvious cause is the reduced buying power of consumers." Notwithstanding the low prices, farmers continued to produce a large surplus of wholesome milk for which there was no market. They had yielded to "the human tendency to raise too many heifers" when prices were high and "not until seven or eight years" after 1930 could one reasonably expect a reverse trend. This failure of demand had nothing to do with the quality of the milk — that was excellent. Consumers lacked funds with which to buy. In consequence the farmers became impoverished and their lands depreciated in value. Naturally they became discontented.

The exigency is of the kind which inevitably arises when one set of men continue to produce more than all others can buy. The distressing result to the producer followed his ill-advised but voluntary efforts. Similar situations occur in almost every business. If here we have an emergency sufficient to empower the Legislature to fix sales prices, then whenever there is too much or too little of an essential thing — whether of milk or grain or pork or coal or shoes or clothes — constitutional provisions may be declared inoperative. . . .

* * *

Is the milk business so affected with public interest that the Legislature may prescribe prices for sales by stores? This Court has approved the contrary view; has emphatically declared that a State lacks power to fix prices in similar private businesses.

* * *

Regulation to prevent recognized evils in business has long been upheld as permissible legislative action. But fixation of the price at which "A", engaged in an ordinary business, may sell, in order to enable "B", a producer, to improve his condition, has not been regarded as within legislative power. This is not regulation, but management, control, dictation — it amounts to the deprivation of the fundamental right which one has to conduct his own affairs honestly and along customary lines. The argument advanced here would support general prescription of prices for farm products, groceries, shoes, clothing, all the necessities of modern civilization, as well as labor, when some legislature finds and declares such action advisable and for the public good. This Court has declared that a State may not by legislative fiat convert a private business into a public utility. And if it be now ruled that one dedicates his property to public use whenever he embarks on an enterprise which the Legislature may think it desirable to bring under control, this is but to declare that rights guaranteed by the Constitution exist only so long as supposed public interest does not require their extinction. To adopt such a view, of course, would put an end to liberty under the Constitution.

* * *

Of the assailed statute the Court of Appeals says — "It first declares that milk has been selling too cheaply in the State of New York, and has thus created a temporary emergency; this emergency is remedied by making the sale of milk at a low price a crime; the question of what is a low price is determined by the majority vote of three officials." Also — "With the wisdom of the legislation we have naught to do. It may be vain to hope by laws to oppose the general course of trade." Maybe, because of this conclusion, it said nothing concerning the possibility of obtaining increase of prices to producers — the thing definitely aimed at — through the means adopted.

But plainly, I think, this Court must have regard to the wisdom of the enactment. At least, we must inquire concerning its purpose and decide whether the means proposed have reasonable relation to something within legislative power — whether the end is legitimate, and the means appropriate. If a statute to prevent conflagrations, should require householders to pour oil on their roofs as a means of curbing the spread of fire when discovered in the neighborhood, we could hardly uphold it. Here, we find direct interference with guaranteed rights defended upon the ground that the purpose was to promote the public welfare by increasing milk prices at the farm. Unless we can affirm that the end proposed is proper and the means adopted have reasonable relation to it, this action is unjustifiable.

The court below has not definitely affirmed this necessary relation; it has not attempted to indicate how higher charges at stores to impoverished customers when the output is excessive and sale prices by producers are unrestrained, can possibly increase receipts at the farm. The Legislative Committee pointed out as the obvious cause of decreased consumption, notwithstanding low prices, the consumers' reduced buying power. Higher store prices will not enlarge this power; nor will they decrease production. Low prices will bring less cows only after several years. The prime causes of the difficulties will remain. Nothing indicates early decreased output. Demand at low prices being wholly insufficient, the proposed plan is to raise and fix higher minimum prices at stores and thereby aid the producer whose output and prices remain unrestrained! It is not true as stated that "the State seeks to protect the producer by fixing a minimum price for his milk." She carefully refrained from doing this; but did undertake to fix the price after the milk had passed to other owners. . . .

Not only does the statute interfere arbitrarily with the rights of the little grocer to conduct his business according to standards long accepted — complete destruction may follow; but it takes away the liberty of 12,000,000 consumers to buy a necessity of life in an open market. It imposes direct and arbitrary burdens upon those already seriously impoverished with the alleged immediate design of affording special benefits to others. To him with less than nine cents it says — You cannot procure a quart of milk from the grocer although he is anxious to accept what you can pay and the demands of your household are urgent! A superabundance; but no child can purchase from a willing storekeeper below the figure appointed by three men at headquarters! And this is true although the storekeeper himself may have bought from a willing producer at half that rate and must sell quickly or lose his stock through deterioration. The fanciful scheme is to protect the farmer against undue exactions by prescribing the price at which milk disposed of by him at will may be resold!

The statement by the court below that — "Doubtless the statute before us would be condemned by an earlier generation as a temerarious interference with the rights of property and contract . . . ; with the natural law of supply and demand," is obviously correct. But another, that "statutes aiming to stimulate the production of a vital food product by fixing living standards of prices for the producer, are to be interpreted with that degree of liberality which is essential to the attainment of the end in view," conflicts with views of Constitutional rights accepted since the beginning. An end although apparently desirable cannot justify inhibited means. Moreover the challenged act was not designed to stimulate production — there was too much milk for the demand and no prospect of less for several years; also "standards of prices" at which the producer might sell were not prescribed. The Legislature cannot lawfully destroy guaranteed rights of one man with the prime purpose of enriching another, even if for the moment, this may seem advantageous to the public. And the adoption of any "concept of jurisprudence" which permits facile disregard of the Constitution as long interpreted and respected will inevitably lead to its destruction. Then, all rights will be subject to the caprice of the hour; government by stable laws will pass.

The somewhat misty suggestion below that condemnation of the challenged legislation would amount to holding "that the due process clause has left milk producers unprotected from oppression," I assume, was not intended as a material contribution to the discussion upon the merits of the cause. Grave concern for embarrassed farmers is everywhere; but this should neither obscure the rights of others nor obstruct judicial appraisement of measures proposed for relief. The ultimate welfare of the producer, like that of every other class, requires dominance of the Constitution. And zealously to uphold this in all its parts is the highest duty intrusted to the courts.

The judgment of the court below should be reversed.

MR. JUSTICE VAN DEVANTER, MR. JUSTICE SUTHERLAND, and MR. JUSTICE BUTLER authorize me to say that they concur in this opinion.

NOTES AND QUESTIONS

1. Why does *Nebbia* indulge a level of economic regulation greater than that acknowledged by the Court previously? As noted earlier, in the late 19th and early 20th centuries, the Court relied upon the fact that certain industries were "affected with the public interest" in order to justify regulation. *See Munn v. Illinois*, 94 U.S. 113, 126 (1876). In *Nebbia*, the Court denies the significance of this earlier explanation, writing:

> It is true that the court cited a statement from Lord Hale's *De Portibus Maris*, to the effect that when private property is "affected with a public interest, it ceases to be *juris privati* only"; but the court proceeded at once to define what it understood by the expression, saying: "Property

does become clothed with a public interest when used in a manner to make it of public consequence, and affect the community at large." Thus understood, "affected with a public interest" is the equivalent of "subject to the exercise of the police power"; and it is plain that nothing more was intended by the expression.

291 U.S. at 532-33 (quoting *Munn*, 94 U.S. at 126). Notwithstanding the disclaimer, was the abandonment of the "public interest" limitation on the police power a break with the common law, and the natural law protection of economic liberty? As Justice McReynolds illustrates in his dissent:

> [N]othing [in *Munn*] sustains the notion that the ordinary business of dealing in commodities is charged with a public interest and subject to legislative control. The contrary has been distinctly announced. To undertake now to attribute a repudiated implication to that opinion is to affirm that it means what this Court has declared again and again was not intended. The painstaking effort there to point out that certain businesses like ferries, mills, etc., were subject to legislative control at common law and then to show that warehousing at Chicago occupied like relation to the public would have been pointless if "affected with a public interest" only means that the public has serious concern about the perpetuity and success of the undertaking. That is true of almost all ordinary business affairs. Nothing in the opinion lends support, directly or otherwise, to the notion that in times of peace a legislature may fix the price of ordinary commodities — grain, meat, milk, cotton, etc.

Id. at 555-56 (McReynolds, J., dissenting).

2. *Nebbia* thus signaled the beginning of the end of meaningful review of questions pertaining to economic liberty under the Due Process Clause. A few years later, for example, the Court upheld a minimum wage law for women. *West Coast Hotel Co v. Parrish*, 300 U.S. 379 (1937). Dissenting, Justice Sutherland bemoaned the loss of the presumption in favor of economic freedom. "[F]reedom of contract was the general rule and restraint the exception; and . . . the power to abridge that freedom could only be justified by the existence of exceptional circumstances." *Id.* at 406 (Sutherland, J., dissenting). The modern highly deferential standard of review applied by the Court presumes not economic freedom, but the constitutionality of regulation.

3. The rethinking in *Nebbia* occurred in conjunction with a similar qualification of the application of the constitutional provision forbidding the impairment of contract. *See Home Bldg. & Loan Ass'n v. Blaisdell*, 290 U.S. 398 (1934) (upholding a state mortgage foreclosure moratorium law). Recall, however, from our discussion in Chapter Six that the impairment accepted in *Blaisdell* was viewed as minor and not vitiating the underlying contract. What's more, that impairment was again viewed as necessary to meet an emergency. After the emergency passed, the Court — initially, at least — returned to an undiminished enforcement of the Contract Clause.

4. Lochnerism may have ended less from an abandonment of fundamental principle, than a threatened change in personnel yielding a noticeable change of perspective. We aspire to be a nation under law, but it is undeniable that our imperfect human nature must apply that law. The imperfections of human nature were well on display in Franklin Roosevelt's attempt to pack the Supreme Court with his political partisans. Following his landslide re-election in 1936, Roosevelt proposed that Congress adopt legislation increasing the size of the Court by one new Justice for each over the age of 70 who had served for 10 or more years on any federal court up to a maximum of 15 Justices. Practically, this would have allowed Roosevelt to add six new justices and rid himself of a judiciary that believed federal power ought to be limited to enumerated subjects. Roosevelt claimed in a radio address that his proposal was simply inspired by a desire for "new blood" to carry out the heavy burdens of the judiciary. Chief Justice Charles Evans Hughes responded in a letter to the Senate that no new blood was needed, thank you. The Chief Justice said the Court was fully abreast of its work and more Justices would add, not subtract, from the complexity of the work. The Congress was appalled by the President's action and the Senate Judiciary Committee recommended that Roosevelt's proposal was "a needless, futile, and utterly dangerous abandonment of constitutional principle. . . . It is a measure which should be so emphatically rejected that its parallel will never again be presented to the free representatives of the free people of America." SENATE COMM. ON THE JUDICIARY, REORGANIZATION OF THE FEDERAL JUDICIARY, S. REP. NO. 75-711, at 23 (1937). It was. Nevertheless, the message did not go unheard at the Supreme Court. While Justice Owen Roberts in particular denied being affected by the threatened reorganization plan (*see* Felix Frankfurter, *Mr. Justice Roberts*, 104 U. PA. L. REV. 311 (1955) (arguing that Roberts' later pro-FDR votes began before the Court packing plan was announced)), Justice Roberts became more cordial to governmental efforts to regulate economic matters. His opinion above in *Nebbia* was already primed in that direction. Roosevelt's ill-conceived plan is discussed at length in ROBERT JACKSON, THE STRUGGLE FOR JUDICIAL SUPREMACY (1941). Death and retirement allowed Roosevelt to have his way with the Court in any event. Between the years 1937 and 1941, Roosevelt made eight appointments.

5. The next case illustrates the Court's present disposition to uphold virtually any economic regulation so long as it has some conceivable rational basis, even if it is the Court, and not the legislature, that conceives of it. As Justice Stone writes:

> [T]he existence of facts supporting the legislative judgment is to be presumed, for regulatory legislation affecting ordinary commercial transactions is not to be pronounced unconstitutional unless in the light of the facts made known or generally assumed it is of such a character as to preclude the assumption that it rests upon some rational basis.

United States v. Carolene Products Co., 304 U.S. 144, 152 (1938). The following case also contains a famous footnote (note 4) that is held responsible for creating the present-day anomaly of heightened due process review for personal liberties, like speech, but almost nonexistent review for economic freedom.

UNITED STATES v. CAROLENE PRODUCTS CO.
304 U.S. 144 (1938)

MR. JUSTICE STONE delivered the opinion of the Court.

The question for decision is whether the "Filled Milk Act" of Congress of March 4, 1923, which prohibits the shipment in interstate commerce of skimmed milk compounded with any fat or oil other than milk fat, so as to resemble milk or cream, transcends the power of Congress to regulate interstate commerce or infringes the Fifth Amendment.

* * *

Second. [We find t]he prohibition of shipment of [Carolene's] product in interstate commerce does not infringe the Fifth Amendment. . . .

. . . [W]e might rest decision wholly on the presumption of constitutionality. But affirmative evidence also sustains the statute. In twenty years evidence has steadily accumulated of the danger to the public health from the general consumption of foods which have been stripped of elements essential to the maintenance of health. The Filled Milk Act was adopted by Congress after committee hearings, in the course of which eminent scientists and health experts testified. An extensive investigation was made of the commerce in milk compounds in which vegetable oils have been substituted for natural milk fat, and of the effect upon the public health of the use of such compounds as a food substitute for milk. The conclusions drawn from evidence presented at the hearings were embodied in reports of the House Committee on Agriculture, and the Senate Committee on Agriculture and Forestry. Both committees concluded, as the statute itself declares, that the use of filled milk as a substitute for pure milk is generally injurious to health and facilitates fraud on the public.

* * *

There is nothing in the Constitution which compels a legislature, either national or state, to ignore such evidence, nor need it disregard the other evidence which amply supports the conclusions of the Congressional committees that the danger is greatly enhanced where an inferior product, like [Carolene Products'], is indistinguishable from a valuable food of almost universal use, thus making fraudulent distribution easy and protection of the consumer difficult.

Here the prohibition of the statute is inoperative unless the product is "in imitation or semblance of milk, cream, or skimmed milk, whether or not condensed." Whether in such circumstance the public would be adequately protected by the prohibition of false labels and false branding imposed by the Pure Food and Drugs Act, or whether it was necessary to go farther and prohibit a substitute food product thought to be injurious to health if used as a substitute when the two are not distinguishable, was a matter for the legislative judgment and not that of courts. . . .

* * *

Third. We may assume for present purposes that no pronouncement of a legislature can forestall attack upon the constitutionality of the prohibition which it enacts by applying opprobrious epithets to the prohibited act, and that a statute would deny due process which precluded the disproof in judicial proceedings of all facts which would show or tend to show that a statute depriving the suitor of life, liberty, or property had a rational basis.

But such we think is not the purpose or construction of the statutory characterization of filled milk as injurious to health and as a fraud upon the public. There is no need to consider it here as more than a declaration of the legislative findings deemed to support and justify the action taken as a constitutional exertion of the legislative power, aiding informed judicial review, as do the reports of legislative committees, by revealing the rationale of the legislation. Even in the absence of such aids the existence of facts supporting the legislative judgment is to be presumed, for regulatory legislation affecting ordinary commercial transactions is not to be pronounced unconstitutional unless in the light of the facts made known or generally assumed it is of such a character as to preclude the assumption that it rests upon some rational basis within the knowledge and experience of the legislators.[4] The present statutory findings affect [Carolene Products] no more than the reports of the Congressional committees and since in the absence of the statutory findings they would be presumed, their incorporation in the statute is no more prejudicial than surplusage.

Where the existence of a rational basis for legislation whose constitutionality is attacked depends upon facts beyond the sphere of judicial notice, such facts may properly be made the subject of judicial inquiry, and the constitutionality of a statute predicated upon the existence of a particular state of facts may be challenged by showing to the court that those facts have ceased to exist. Similarly we recognize that the constitutionality of a statute, valid on its face, may be assailed by proof of facts tending to show that the statute as applied to a particular article is without support in reason because the article, although within

---

[4] There may be narrower scope for operation of the presumption of constitutionality when legislation appears on its face to be within a specific prohibition of the Constitution, such as those of the first ten Amendments, which are deemed equally specific when held to be embraced within the Fourteenth.

It is unnecessary to consider now whether legislation which restricts those political processes which can ordinarily be expected to bring about repeal of undesirable legislation, is to be subjected to more exacting judicial scrutiny under the general prohibitions of the Fourteenth Amendment than are most other types of legislation.

Nor need we enquire whether similar considerations enter into the review of statutes directed at particular religious, or national, or racial minorities: whether prejudice against discrete and insular minorities may be a special condition, which tends seriously to curtail the operation of those political processes ordinarily to be relied upon to protect minorities, and which may call for a correspondingly more searching judicial inquiry.

the prohibited class, is so different from others of the class as to be without the reason for the prohibition, though the effect of such proof depends on the relevant circumstances of each case, as for example the administrative difficulty of excluding the article from the regulated class. But by their very nature such inquiries, where the legislative judgment is drawn in question, must be restricted to the issue whether any state of facts either known or which could reasonably be assumed affords support for it. Here [Carolene Products] challenges the validity of the statute on its face and it is evident from all the considerations presented to Congress, and those of which we may take judicial notice, that the question is at least debatable whether commerce in filled milk should be left unregulated, or in some measure restricted, or wholly prohibited. As that decision was for Congress, neither the finding of a court arrived at by weighing the evidence, nor the verdict of a jury can be substituted for it.

* * *

Mr. Justice Black concurs in the result and in all of the opinion except the part marked "Third."

Mr. Justice McReynolds thinks that the judgment should be affirmed.

Mr. Justice Cardozo and Mr. Justice Reed took no part in the consideration or decision of this case.

Mr. Justice Butler[, concurring].

I concur in the result. Prima facie the facts alleged in the indictment are sufficient to constitute a violation of the statute. But they are not sufficient conclusively to establish guilt of the accused. At the trial it may introduce evidence to show that the declaration of the Act that the described product is injurious to public health and that the sale of it is a fraud upon the public are without any substantial foundation. The provisions on which the indictment rests should if possible be construed to avoid the serious question of constitutionality. If construed to exclude from interstate commerce wholesome food products that demonstrably are neither injurious to health nor calculated to deceive, they are repugnant to the Fifth Amendment. The allegation of the indictment that Milnut "is an adulterated article of food, injurious to the public health," tenders an issue of fact to be determined upon evidence.

NOTES AND QUESTIONS

1. Does the dichotomy between personal and economic liberties created in *Carolene Products* and maintained thereafter by the Court make sense? Since 1937, not a single law dealing with an economic question has been found invalid by the Court under substantive due process analysis. In *Williamson v. Lee Optical of Oklahoma*, 348 U.S. 483 (1955), for example, the Court upheld Oklahoma's requirement that only licensed optometrists and ophthalmologists could fit eyeglasses or replicate existing lenses, thus prohibiting opticians from replacing eyeglasses without a prescription and protecting optometrists and oph-thalmologosists from competition. Noted the Court: "The day is gone when this Court uses the Due Process Clause of the Fourteenth Amendment to strike down state laws, regulatory of business and industrial conditions, because they may be unwise, improvident, or out of harmony with a particular school of thought." *But cf. BMW of North America, Inc. v. Gore*, 517 U.S. 559 (1996) (using due process to find a punitive damage award by a jury of $2 million for a scratched automobile to be "grossly excessive" discussed in Chapter Six). Didn't the natural law thinking of the founders understand government's primary purpose to be the preservation of property and the economic liberty or initiative that gives rise to it?

For an assessment of *Carolene Products* calling for its re-examination, see Geoffrey P. Miller, *The True Story of* Carolene Products, 1987 SUP. CT. REV. 397 (1987).

2. *Slaughter-House* was earlier said to disregard natural rights, including the right to economic liberty, arguably intended to be protected by the Privileges or Immunities Clause. Does natural law originalism answer whether legislation like that in *Lochner, Nebbia*, and *Carolene Products* is valid or invalid? Perhaps one can argue that the natural law of the American founding operates on two levels: first, establishing economic liberty, and against unnecessary restraint in matters of trade or calling, as a privilege of citizenship, but second, that save for the exceptional case, such natural law precept is to be applied by the legislature, not the Court. In this way, might natural law be distinguished from noninter-pretivism and the less consistent and uncharted course of the *Lochner* majority? If so, specific claims like the right to be free of particular educational requirements for a given occupational license cannot be said to arise inexorably from immutable aspects of human nature and justice. Burdensome or debateable occupational licensing requirements may be economically unwise, but such arguments are better aimed at the legislature. By contrast, the judiciary might be expected to safeguard the fundamental right of economic liberty, itself, where state imposed monopolies stand as insurmountable. As one writer put it well:

> [Natural law] principles and precepts[, like the injunction to seek the good or the proscription against killing or theft,] are incapable by themselves of governing action, — for different reasons, . . . : in the case of principles, because they specify only the end, and action depends on specification of means; in the case of precepts, because they specify the means only generally and without reference to the contingent circumstances which are always involved in action.

Harold R. McKinnon, *Natural Law and Positive Law*, 23 NOTRE DAME L. REV. 125, 134-35 (1948). It is the contingent circumstances that make rules the usual subject of positive law, and far different from principles and precepts. In this may also lie the difference between a fundamental privilege or immunity and a spuriously substantive due process violation. As Professor Philip Kurland observes: "only the privileges or immunities clause speaks to matters of substance; certainly the language of due process and equal protection does not." Philip B. Kurland, *The Privileges or Immunities Clause, "Its Hour Come Round at Last"?*, 1972 WASH. U. L.Q. 405, 406.

3. The manageability of judicial application of the Privileges or Immunities Clause, and the protection of economic liberty, may also increase over time as articulated by Justice Bradley in his dissent in *Slaughter-House*:

> Like the prohibition against passing a law impairing the obligation of a contract, it would execute itself. The point would be regularly raised, in a suit at law, and settled by final reference to the Federal court. As the privileges and immunities protected are only those fundamental ones which belong to every citizen, they would soon become so far defined as to cause but a slight accumulation of business in the Federal courts. Besides, the recognized existence of the law would prevent its frequent violation.

83 U.S. at 123-24.

4. Can the Court effectively balance a proper posture of judicial restraint with the needed protection of individual right? For one thoughtful suggestion, see Rosalie Berger Levinson, *Protection Against Government Abuse of Power: Has the Court Taken the Substance Out of Substantive Due Process?*, 16 U. DAYTON L. REV. 313 (1991) (discussing concerns that justify a narrow interpretation of substantive due process and proposing a balanced approach that maintains the guarantees of substantive due process while minimizing the impact on democratic policy).

Chapter 8

A GOVERNMENT COMMITMENT TO EQUALITY

The premise of equality is explicit in the Declaration of Independence ("all men are created equal"), and upon this premise the founders debunked the earlier notion that some were Divinely entitled to rule over others. Equality of human creation under God meant plainly that if law was to have binding authority it was to be premised upon the consent of the governed. If no one had an entitlement to rule, then assent to live under that rule would be needed. Of course, the noble premise of equality was besmirched in our national record by the institution of slavery. How the framers who knew slavery to be against natural and common law, as recorded in English cases, could tolerate this vast disregard of the human nature is a story of perhaps necessary political expediency in the forming of a union, but expediency nonetheless.

The original constitutional document is also anomalous by containing no explicit provision providing for equal treatment under law. This would not be added until after the Civil War and the Fourteenth Amendment ("No state shall . . . deny to any person within its jurisdiction the equal protection of the laws.") Even when added, the provision went largely ignored until the mid-20th century. To this day, the Constitution does not explicitly exact a promise of equality from the federal government, though such has been judicially required. *Bolling v. Sharpe*, 347 U.S. 497 (1954) (reading the Equal Protection Clause into the Fifth Amendment due process limitation on the federal government).

What the equal protection inquiry is about is the appropriateness of government classification. Most laws draw distinctions. For example, to obtain a work permit one frequently needs to be 16 or older. Thus, those under the age of 16 are being treated differently than the rest of the population. Similarly, those under the age of majority (18 or 21 in most jurisdictions) may be excused from contracts they enter into. These distinctions or classifications are almost always upheld so long as the government has some rational basis for them — e.g., protecting children from work or economic commitment inconsistent with their age or maturity.

You will see that the equal protection analysis of the modern Court will often proceed in three steps: an identification of the classification, the application of the appropriate level of judicial scrutiny (deferential, intermediate, or strict), and an assessment of whether the government's explanation for the classification meets the applicable level of scrutiny. In this Chapter, we primarily concentrate on classifications that warrant either strict or intermediate scrutiny. For example, classifications based on race need a compelling governmental interest to survive this most careful review. Intermediate scrutiny is applicable to gender distinctions in law. This standard requires a lesser justification, but still an "important" one, and the government bears the burden of proving that its classification substantially advances that important justification. We will also take a look at classifications that affect an exercise of a fundamental right, namely, voting, and discover that the Court has crafted a special concept of numerical equality out of the Equal Protection Clause — namely, the guarantee of one person/one vote.

Most classifications under law not implicating a suspect classification like race or a fundamental right are reviewed under the rational basis standard. This is a highly deferential standard. The Court will uphold a statute or regulation if the Court can conceive of any legitimate governmental purpose served by the statute or regulation. The burden of proof is on those challenging such classification, and only rarely, as in the case of *Romer v. Evans* dealing with a sexual orientation classification, has the Court found it to be wanting. Thus, in *Hodel v. Irving*, 452 U.S. 314 (1981), the Court stated: "[s]ocial and economic legislation . . . that does not employ suspect classifications or impinge in fundamental rights must be upheld against equal protection attack when the legislative means are rationally related to a legitimate government purpose. Moreover, such legislation carries with it a presumption of rationality that can only be overcome by a clear showing of arbitrariness and irrationality." *Id.* at 331-332. In *Federal Communications Commission v. Beach Communications, Inc.*, 508 U.S. 307 (1993), the Court further illustrated its deference at this level by observing that "those attacking the rationality of the legislative classification have the burden to negate every conceivable basis which might support it." *Id.* at 315. Again, this is seldom accomplished, but not impossible, as we will see when we turn to *Bush v. Gore* in section B, and *Romer v. Evans* in Section D below and *Lawrence v. Texas* in Chapter 9. While it is rare for traditional equal protection review — that is, a case not involving either a suspect classification or implicating a fundamental right — to result in invalidation, a much different story exists with regard to the use of race as a class. Sadly, this was not always true. Prior to the Civil War, several provisions of the original Constitution protected the institution of slavery. Article I, section 9 prevented Congress from banning the importation of slaves before 1808. Article IV, section 2 — the so-called fugitive slave clause — required the return of escaping slaves. In *Prigg v. Pennsylvania*, 41 U.S. (16 Pet.) 539 (1842), discussed in the case below, the Court invalidated a state law that prohibited the use of force or violence to return an escaped slave. The next case raised the question of federal limitations on slavery. By the Missouri Compromise, Congress attempted to admit Missouri as a state on condition that slavery be kept out of the new territories north of latitude 36 degrees, 30 minutes. Scott, a slave of the late John Emerson, had been taken north of this line, and by virtue of this, he claimed his freedom. He lost, and so did a Nation unable to come to terms with its natural law principles.

A. Race

1. Slavery

SCOTT v. SANDFORD
60 U.S. (19 How.) 393 (1856)

MR. CHIEF JUSTICE TANEY delivered the opinion of the court.

* * *

There are two leading questions presented by the record:

1. Had the Circuit Court of the United States jurisdiction to hear and determine the case between these parties? And

2. If it had jurisdiction, is the judgment it has given erroneous or not?

The plaintiff in error, who was also the plaintiff in the court below, was, with his wife and children, held as slaves by the defendant, in the State of Missouri; and he brought this action in the Circuit Court of the United States for that district, to assert the title of himself and his family to freedom.

* * *

The question [about jurisdiction turns on whether or not the plaintiff is a citizen of Missouri, and, in effect] is simply this: Can a negro, whose ancestors were imported into this country, and sold as slaves, become a member of the political community formed and brought into existence by the Constitution of the United States, and as such become entitled to all the rights, and privileges, and immunities, guarantied by that instrument to the citizen? . . .

It will be observed, that the plea applies to that class of persons only whose ancestors were negroes of the African race, and imported into this country, and sold and held as slaves. The only matter in issue before the court, therefore, is, whether the descendants of such slaves, when they shall be emancipated, or who are born of parents who had become free before their birth, are citizens of a State, in the sense in which the word citizen is used in the Constitution of the United States. . . .

* * *

The words "people of the United States" and "citizens" are synonymous terms, and mean the same thing. They both describe the political body who, according to our republican institutions, form the sovereignty, and who hold the power and conduct the Government through their representatives. They are what we familiarly call the "sovereign people," and every citizen is one of this people, and a constituent member of this sovereignty. The question before us is, whether the class of persons described in the plea in abatement compose a portion of this people, and are constituent members of this sovereignty? We think they are not, and that they are not included, and were not intended to be included, under the word "citizens" in the Constitution. . . . On the contrary, they were at that time considered as a subordinate and inferior class of beings, who had been subjugated by the dominant race, and, whether emancipated or not, yet remained subject to their authority, and had no rights or privileges but such as those who held the power and the Government might choose to grant them.

It is not the province of the court to decide upon the justice or injustice, the policy or impolicy, of these laws. The decision of that question belonged to the political or law-making power; to those who formed the sovereignty and framed the Constitution. The duty of the court is, to interpret the instrument they have framed, with the best lights we can obtain on the subject, and to administer it as we find it, according to its true intent and meaning when it was adopted.

In discussing this question, we must not confound the rights of citizenship which a State may confer within its own limits, and the rights of citizenship as a member of the Union. It does not by any means follow, because he has all the rights and privileges of a citizen of a State, that he must be a citizen of the United States. . . . For, previous to the adoption of the Constitution of the United States, every State had the undoubted right to confer on whomsoever it pleased the character of citizen, and to endow him with all its rights. But this character of course was confined to the boundaries of the State, and gave him no rights or privileges in other States beyond those secured to him by the laws of nations and the comity of States. Nor have the several States surrendered the power of conferring these rights and privileges by adopting the Constitution of the United States. Each State may still confer them upon an alien, or any one it thinks proper, or upon any class or description of persons; yet he would not be a citizen in the sense in which that word is used in the Constitution of the United States, nor entitled to sue as such in one of its courts, nor to the privileges and immunities of a citizen in the other States. . . . The Constitution has conferred on Congress the right to establish an uniform rule of naturalization, and this right is evidently exclusive, and has always been held by this court to be so. Consequently, no State, since the adoption of the Constitution, can by naturalizing an alien invest him with the rights and privileges secured to a citizen of a State under the Federal Government. . . .

* * *

The question then arises, whether the provisions of the Constitution, in relation to the personal rights and privileges to which the citizen of a State should be entitled, embraced the negro African race, at that time in this country, or who might afterwards be imported, who had then or should afterwards be made free in any State; and to put it in the power of a single State to make him a citizen of the United States, and endue him with the full rights of citizenship in every other State without their consent? Does the Constitution of the United States act upon him whenever he shall be made free under the laws of a State, and raised there to the rank of a citizen, and immediately clothe him with all the privileges of a citizen in every other State, and in its own courts?

The court think the affirmative of these propositions cannot be maintained. And if it cannot, the plaintiff in error could not be a citizen of the State of Missouri, within the meaning of the Constitution of the United States, and, consequently, was not entitled to sue in its courts.

* * *

In the opinion of the court, the legislation and histories of the times, and the language used in the Declaration of Independence, show, that neither the class of persons who had been imported as slaves, nor their descendants, whether they had become free or not, were then acknowledged as a part of the people, nor intended to be included in the general words used in that memorable instrument.

It is difficult at this day to realize the state of public opinion in relation to that unfortunate race, which prevailed in the civilized and enlightened portions of the world at the time of the Declaration of Independence, and when the Constitution of the United States was framed and adopted. But the public history of every European nation displays it in a manner too plain to be mistaken.

They had for more than a century before been regarded as beings of an inferior order, and altogether unfit to associate with the white race, either in social or political relations; and so far inferior, that they had no rights which the white man was bound to respect; and that the negro might justly and lawfully be reduced to slavery for his benefit. He was bought and sold, and treated as an ordinary article of merchandise and traffic, whenever a profit could be made by it. This opinion was at that time fixed and universal in the civilized portion of the white race. . . .

* * *

The language of the Declaration of Independence is equally Conclusive:

It begins by declaring that, "when in the course of human events it becomes necessary for one people to dissolve the political bands which have connected them with another, and to assume among the powers of the earth the separate and equal station to which the laws of nature and nature's God entitle them, a decent respect for the opinions of mankind requires that they should declare the causes which impel them to the separation."

It then proceeds to say: "We hold these truths to be self-evident: that all men are created equal; that they are endowed by their Creator with certain unalienable rights; that among them is life, liberty, and the pursuit of happiness; that to secure these rights, Governments are instituted, deriving their just powers from the consent of the governed."

The general words above quoted would seem to embrace the whole human family, and if they were used in a similar instrument at this day would be so understood. But it is too clear for dispute, that the enslaved African race were not intended to be included, and formed no part of the people who framed and adopted this declaration; for if the language, as understood in that day, would embrace them, the conduct of the distinguished men who framed the Declaration of Independence would have been utterly and flagrantly inconsistent with the principles they asserted; and instead of the sympathy of mankind, to which they so confidently appealed, they would have deserved and received universal rebuke and reprobation.

Yet the men who framed this declaration were great men — high in literary acquirements — high in their sense of honor, and incapable of asserting principles inconsistent with those on which they were acting. They perfectly understood the meaning of the language they used, and how it would be understood by others; and they knew that it would not in any part of the civilized world be supposed to embrace the negro race, which, by common consent, had been excluded from civilized Governments and the family of nations, and doomed to slavery. They spoke and acted according to the then established doctrines and principles, and in the ordinary language of the day, no one misunderstood them. . . .

This state of public opinion had undergone no change when the Constitution was adopted, as is equally evident from its provisions and language.

The brief preamble sets forth by whom it was formed, for what purposes, and for whose benefit and protection. It declares that it is formed by the *people* of the United States; that is to say, by those who were members of the different political communities in the several States; and its great object is declared to be to secure the blessings of liberty to themselves and their posterity. It speaks in general terms of the *people* of the United States, and of *citizens* of the several States, when it is providing for the exercise of the powers granted or the privileges secured to the citizen. It does not define what description of persons are intended to be included under these terms, or who shall be regarded as a citizen and one of the people. . . .

But there are two clauses in the Constitution which point directly and specifically to the negro race as a separate class of persons, and show clearly that they were not regarded as a portion of the people or citizens of the Government then formed.

One of these clauses reserves to each of the thirteen States the right to import slaves until the year 1808, if it thinks proper. And the importation which it thus sanctions was unquestionably of persons of the race of which we are speaking, as the traffic in slaves in the United States had always been confined to them. And by the other provision the States pledge themselves to each other to maintain the right of property of the master, by delivering up to him any slave who may have escaped from his service, and be found within their respective territories. . . . And these two provisions show, conclusively, that neither the description of persons therein referred to, nor their descendants, were embraced in any of the other provisions of the Constitution; for certainly these two clauses were not intended to confer on them or their posterity the blessings of liberty, or any of the personal rights so carefully provided for the citizen.

* * *

And upon a full and careful consideration of the subject, the court is of opinion, that, upon the facts stated in the plea in abatement, Dred Scott was not a citizen of Missouri within the meaning of the Constitution of the United States, and not entitled as such to sue in its courts; and, consequently, that the Circuit Court had no jurisdiction of the case, and that the judgment on the plea in abatement is erroneous.

* * *

[Having disposed of the first issue, that regarding jurisdiction, Justice Taney nevertheless proceeds to address the other question in the case, whether Scott was entitled to his freedom.]

The case, as he himself states it, on the record brought here by his writ of error, is this:

The plaintiff was a negro slave, belonging to Dr. Emerson, who was a surgeon in the army of the United States. In the year 1834, he took the plaintiff from the State of Missouri to the military post at Rock Island, in the State of Illinois, and held him there as a slave until the month of April or May, 1836. At the time last mentioned, said Dr. Emerson removed the plaintiff from said military post at Rock Island to the military post at Fort Snelling, situate on the west bank of the Mississippi river, in the Territory known as Upper Louisiana, acquired by the United States of France, and situate north of the latitude of thirty-six degrees thirty minutes north, and north of the State of Missouri. Said Dr. Emerson held the plaintiff in slavery at said Fort Snelling, from said last-mentioned date until the year 1838.

* * *

In the year 1838, said Dr. Emerson removed the plaintiff and [his family] from said Fort Snelling to the State of Missouri, where they have ever since resided.

Before the commencement of this suit, said Dr. Emerson sold and conveyed the plaintiff . . . to the defendant . . . and the defendant has ever since claimed to hold [him and his family] as slaves.

In considering this part of the controversy, two questions arise: 1. Was he, together with his family, free in Missouri by reason of the stay in the territory of the United States hereinbefore mentioned? And 2. If they were not, is Scott himself free by reason of his removal to Rock Island, in the State of Illinois, as stated in the above admissions?

* * *

. . . [T]he right of property in a slave is distinctly and expressly affirmed in the Constitution. The right to traffic in it, like an ordinary article of merchandise and property, was guarantied to the citizens of the United States, in every State that might desire it, for twenty years. And the Government in express terms is pledged to protect it in all future time, if the slave escapes from his owner. . . . And no word can be found in the Constitution which gives Congress a greater power over slave property, or which entitles property of that kind to less protection than property of any other description. The only power conferred is the power coupled with the duty of guarding and protecting the owner in his rights.

Upon these considerations, it is the opinion of the court that the act of Congress which prohibited a citizen from holding and owning property of this kind in the territory of the United States north of the line therein mentioned, is not warranted by the Constitution, and is therefore void; and that neither Dred Scott himself, nor any of his family, were made free by being carried into this territory; even if they had been carried there by the owner, with the intention of becoming a permanent resident.

We have so far examined the case, as it stands under the Constitution of the United States, and the powers thereby delegated to the Federal Government.

But there is another point in the case which depends on State power and State law. And it is contended, on the part of the plaintiff, that he is made free by being taken to Rock Island, in the State of Illinois, independently of his residence in the territory of the United States; and being so made free, he was not again reduced to a state of slavery by being brought back to Missouri.

Our notice of this part of the case will be very brief; for the principle on which it depends was decided in this court, upon much consideration, in the case of *Strader v. Graham* [(1850)]. In that case, the slaves had been taken from Kentucky to Ohio, with the consent of the owner, and afterwards brought back to Kentucky. And this court held that their *status* or condition, as free or slave, depended upon the laws of Kentucky, when they were brought back into that State, and not of Ohio; and that this court had no jurisdiction to revise the judgment of a State court upon its own laws. . . .

So in this case. As Scott was a slave when taken into the State of Illinois by his owner, and was there held as such, and brought back in that character, his *status*, as free or slave, depended on the laws of Missouri, and not of Illinois.

* * *

Upon the whole, therefore, it is the judgment of this court, that it appears by the record before us that the plaintiff in error is not a citizen of Missouri, in the sense in which that word is used in the Constitution; and that the Circuit Court of the United States, for that reason, had no jurisdiction in the case, and could give no judgment in it. Its judgment for the defendant must, consequently, be reversed, and a mandate issued, directing the suit to be dismissed for want of jurisdiction.

[The concurring opinions of JUSTICES WAYNE, NELSON, GRIER, DANIEL, CAMP-BELL, and CATRON are omitted.]

MR. JUSTICE MCLEAN dissenting.

* * *

There is no averment in this plea which shows or conduces to show an inability in the plaintiff to sue in the Circuit Court. . . .

Being born under our Constitution and laws, no naturalization is required, as one of foreign birth, to make him a citizen. The most general and appropriate definition of the term citizen is "a freeman." Being a freeman, and having his domicil in a State different from that of the defendant, he is a citizen within the act of Congress, and the courts of the Union are open to him.

* * *

In the great and leading case of *Prigg v. The State of Pennsylvania* [(1842)], this court say that, by the general law of nations, no nation is bound to recognize the state of slavery, as found within its territorial dominions, where it is in opposition to its own policy and institutions, in favor of the subjects of other nations where slavery is organized. If it does it, it is as a matter of comity, and not as a matter of international right. The state of slavery is deemed to be a mere municipal regulation, founded upon and limited to the range of the territorial laws. This was fully recognized in *Somersett's case* [(1772)], which was decided before the American Revolution.

* * *

No case in England appears to have been more thoroughly examined than that of *Somersett*. . . .

In giving the opinion of the court, Lord Mansfield said:

> "The state of slavery is of such a nature that it is incapable of being introduced on any reasons, moral or political, but only by positive law, which preserves its force long after the reasons, occasion, and time itself, from whence it was created, is erased from the memory; it is of a nature that nothing can be suffered to support it but positive law."

* * *

. . . The words of Lord Mansfield, in giving the opinion of the court, were such as were fit to be used by a great judge, in a most important case. It is a sufficient answer to all objections to that judgment, that it was pronounced before the Revolution, and that it was considered by this court as the highest authority. For near a century, the decision in *Somersett's case* has remained the law of England. . . .

* * *

In the case of *Rankin v. Lydia* [(Ky. 1820)], Judge Mills, speaking for the Court of Appeals of Kentucky, says: "In deciding the question, [of slavery,] we disclaim the influence of the general principles of liberty, which we all admire, and conceive it ought to be decided by the law as it is, and not as it ought to be. Slavery is sanctioned by the laws of this State, and the right to hold slaves under our municipal regulations is unquestionable. But we view this as a right existing by positive law of a municipal character, without foundation in the law of nature, or the unwritten and common law."

I will now consider the relation which the Federal Government bears to slavery in the States:

Slavery is emphatically a State institution. In the ninth section of the first article of the Constitution, it is provided "that the migration or importation of such persons as any of the States now existing shall think proper to admit, shall not be prohibited by the Congress prior to the year 1808, but a tax or duty may be imposed on such importation, not exceeding ten dollars for each person."

In the Convention, it was proposed by a committee of eleven to limit the importation of slaves to the year 1800, when Mr. Pinckney moved to extend the time to the year 1808. This motion was carried. . . . In opposition to the motion, Mr. Madison said: "Twenty years will produce all the mischief that can be apprehended from the liberty to import slaves; so long a term will be more dishonorable to the American character than to say nothing about it in the Constitution."

The provision in regard to the slave trade shows clearly that Congress considered slavery a State institution, to be continued and regulated by its individual sovereignty; and to conciliate that interest, the slave trade was continued twenty years, not as a general measure, but for the "benefit of such States as shall think proper to encourage it."

* * *

In the formation of the Federal Constitution, care was taken to confer no power on the Federal Government to interfere with this institution in the States. In the provision respecting the slave trade, in fixing the ratio of representation, and providing for the reclamation of fugitives from labor, slaves were referred to as persons, and in no other respect are they considered in the Constitution.

We need not refer to the mercenary spirit which introduced the infamous traffic in slaves, to show the degradation of negro slavery in our country. This system was imposed upon our colonial settlements by the mother country, and it is due to truth to say that the commercial colonies and States were chiefly engaged in the traffic. But we know as a historical fact, that James Madison, that great and good man, a leading member in the Federal Convention, was solicitous to guard the language of that instrument so as not to convey the idea that there could be property in man.

I prefer the lights of Madison, Hamilton, and Jay, as a means of construing the Constitution in all its bearings, rather than to look behind that period, into a traffic which is now declared to be piracy, and punished with death by Christian nations. I do not like to draw the sources of our domestic relations from so dark a ground. Our independence was a great epoch in the history of freedom; and while I admit the Government was not made especially for the colored race, yet many of them were citizens of the New England States, and exercised the rights of suffrage when the Constitution was adopted, and it was not doubted by any intelligent person that its tendencies would greatly ameliorate their condition.

Many of the States, on the adoption of the Constitution, or shortly afterward, took measures to abolish slavery within their respective jurisdictions; and it is a well-known fact that a belief was cherished by the leading men, South as well as North, that the institution of slavery would gradually decline, until it would become extinct. The increased value of slave labor, in the culture of cotton and sugar, prevented the realization of this expectation. Like all other communities and States, the South were influenced by what they considered to be their own interests.

* * *

On the 13th of July, the Ordinance of 1787 was passed, "for the government of the United States territory northwest of the river Ohio," with but one dissenting vote. This instrument provided there should be organized in the territory not less than three nor more than five States, designating their boundaries. It was passed while the Federal Convention was in session, about two months before the Constitution was adopted by the Convention. The members of the Convention must therefore have been well acquainted with the provisions of the Ordinance. It provided for a temporary Government, as initiatory to the formation of State Governments. Slavery was prohibited in the territory.

* * *

If Congress may establish a Territorial Government in the exercise of its discretion, it is a clear principle that a court cannot control that discretion. This being the case, I do not see on what ground the act is held to be void. It did not purport to forfeit property, or take it for public purposes. It only prohibited slavery; in doing which, it followed the ordinance of 1787.

I will now consider . . . "The effect of taking slaves into a State or Territory, and so holding them, where slavery is prohibited."

If the principle laid down in the case of *Prigg v. The State of Pennsylvania* is to be maintained, and it is certainly to be maintained until overruled, as the law of this court, there can be no difficulty on this point. In that case, the court says: "The state of slavery is deemed to be a mere municipal regulation, founded upon and limited to the range of the territorial laws." If this be so, slavery can exist nowhere except under the authority of law, founded on usage having the force of law, or by statutory recognition. And the court further says: "It is manifest, from this consideration, that if the Constitution had not contained the clause requiring the rendition of fugitives from labor, every non-slaveholding State in the Union would have been at liberty to have declared free all runaway slaves coming within its limits, and to have given them entire immunity and protection against the claims of their masters."

Now, if a slave abscond, he may be reclaimed; but if he accompany his master into a State or Territory where slavery is prohibited, such slave cannot be said to have left the service of his master where his services were legalized. And if slavery be limited to the range of the territorial laws, how can the slave be coerced to serve in a State or Territory, not only without the authority of law, but against its express provisions? What gives the master the right to control the will of his slave? The local law, which exists in some form. But where there is no such law, can the master control the will of the slave by force? Where no slavery exists, the presumption, without regard to color, is in favor of freedom. . . .

* * *

When Dred Scott, his wife and children, were removed from Fort Snelling to Missouri, in 1838, they were free, as the law was then settled, and continued for fourteen years afterwards, up to 1852, when the above decision was made. Prior to this, for nearly thirty years, as Chief Justice Gamble declares, the residence of a master with his slave in the State of Illinois, or in the Territory north of Missouri, where slavery was prohibited by the act called the Missouri compromise, would manumit the slave as effectually as if he had executed a deed of emancipation. . . . Such was the settled law of Missouri until the decision of [Dred] Scott [v.] Emerson.

* * *

Under the fifth head, we were to consider whether the status of slavery attached to the plaintiff and wife, on their return to Missouri.

This doctrine is not asserted in the late opinion of the Supreme Court of Missouri, and up to 1852 the contrary doctrine was uniformly maintained by that court.

* * *

In every decision of a slave case prior to that of Dred Scott v. Emerson, the Supreme Court of Missouri considered it as turning upon the Constitution of Illinois, the ordinance of 1787, or the Missouri compromise act of 1820. The court treated these acts as in force, and held itself bound to execute them, by declaring the slave to be free who had acquired a domicil under them with the consent of his master.

The late decision reversed this whole line of adjudication, and held that neither the Constitution and laws of the States, nor acts of Congress in relation to Territories, could be judicially noticed by the Supreme Court of Missouri. This is believed to be in conflict with the decisions of all the courts in the Southern States, with some exceptions of recent cases.

* * *

I now come to inquire, under the sixth and last head, "whether the decisions of the Supreme Court of Missouri, on the question before us, are binding on this court."

While we respect the learning and high intelligence of the State courts, and consider their decisions, with others, as authority, we follow them only where they give a construction to the State statutes. . . .

. . . [As Supreme Court JUSTICE GRIER said in an earlier case,] "When the decisions of the State court are not consistent, we do not feel bound to follow the last, if it is contrary to our own convictions; and much more is this the case where, after a long course of consistent decisions, some new light suddenly springs up, or an excited public opinion has elicited new doctrines subversive of former safe precedent."

These words, it appears to me, have a stronger application to the case before us than they had to the cause in which they were spoken as the opinion of this court; and I regret that they do not seem to be as fresh in the recollection of some of my brethren as in my own. For twenty-eight years, the decisions of the Supreme Court of Missouri were consistent on all the points made in this case. But this consistent course was suddenly terminated, whether by some new light suddenly springing up, or an excited public opinion, or both, it is not necessary to say. In the case of *Scott v. Emerson*, in 1852, they were overturned and repudiated.

This, then, is the very case in which seven of my brethren declared they would not follow the last decision. On this authority I may well repose. I can desire no other or better basis.

* * *

MR. JUSTICE CURTIS dissenting [omitted].

* * *

NOTES AND QUESTIONS

1. You have just read one of the most important constitutional law decisions ever rendered, and the one believed by nearly every constitutional law professor to have been decided egregiously wrongly. Note that Chief Justice Taney's majority opinion has two important foci — (1) the question whether Dred Scott, even if he were not a slave, was a citizen of the United States qualified to bring a lawsuit in a federal court, and (2) the question whether Congress possessed the power to forbid slavery in the territories. Chief Justice Taney addresses a third question, whether Scott's temporary residence in Illinois, a free state, could give him his freedom, but that question turns on the interpretation of Missouri law, and is not as important as the other two questions, which can only be answered by reference to the first principles involved in our constitutional order.

2. Consider the first question — was Dred Scott a "citizen" as that word was employed in the constitutional and statutory provisions which permitted "citizens" of different states to bring suit in federal courts? Taney says, "No," because he finds that even free blacks were not regarded as members of the body which originally made up "the people of the United States." Who has the better of this argument, Taney or the dissent? Note the dissent's evidence on the point — principally that there were several states at the time of the Constitution which permitted blacks to vote, and who accorded them full state citizenship. Does this successfully meet Taney's argument? How does he come to grips with this problem? Why did seven out of the nine Justices apparently agree with Taney? Would you be surprised to learn that in late 1997, no member of *H-Law*, the legal history Internet discussion list, was able to produce a single pre-Civil War decision in which a free black or a woman was permitted to bring suit as a plaintiff? Did this mean that Taney got the "citizenship" question right — at least as a matter of law?

3. Generally speaking, those who have condemned the *Dred Scott* opinion have done so because of what they have found to be the racist attitudes manifested by Chief Justice Taney and his brethren. Was Taney a racist? Do his views on the merits or demerits of members of the African American race influence his opinion? Does he claim that they do? Moreover, does he believe that current attitudes toward blacks should determine the constitutional law questions involved? What then should? Why was it so important that the questions at issue in *Dred Scott* be settled? Perhaps you have learned enough American history to know that during the years 1830 to 1860 the United States was roiled in sectional controversy over many issues relating to slavery, and, in particular, whether slavery ought to be allowed in the Territories, those lands, principally acquired through purchase from foreign governments, that would eventually become states. Indeed, perhaps it is not too much to say that *Scott v. Sanford* is not just about the claims to freedom of a particular former slave, but is about the continued validity of the institution of slavery itself.

4. Is slavery constitutional? At one level this is a fatuous question, since the Constitution very clearly provides both for the counting of unfree persons in determining representation in Congress and also for the return of fugitive slaves ("persons held to service"). Indeed, were it not for these nods in the direction of the legitimacy of Southern slavery, the Constitution would never have been ratified in the Southern states. At another level, however, even the Constitution itself implicitly condemns slavery, as it carries the potential for the eventual restriction of the slave trade. During debate over the Missouri compromise, some members of Congress argued that the Article IV Guarantee

Clause codified the Declaration's mandate of government by consent and therefore barred the spread of slavery beyond the original states where it was protected by the Constitution's compromises. *See* John C. Eastman, *The Declaration of Independence as Viewed from the States, in* SCOTT GERBER, ED., THE DECLARATION OF INDEPENDENCE: ORIGINS AND IMPACT (Congressional Quarterly Press 2002). There were also plenty of Northern abolitionists who argued that slavery violated a higher natural law than the Constitution, and that even the Constitution itself could not justify it. Many of these abolitionists were willing to and did risk injury and death for their views. Their argument, essentially, was that slavery was against natural law and the law of God. Is this a somewhat problematic argument, since the Bible itself references slavery, without denunciation? Of course, perhaps the Bible's references to slavery are simply that whatever one's status, slave or free, it is irrelevant to one's religious duty. The common law, as an embodiment of natural law applied to human circumstance, is far more explicitly condemning of slavery. You will have already noticed the statement quoted from Lord Mansfield's famous opinion in *Somerset v. Stewart*, 98 Eng. Rep. 499, 510 (K.B. 1772):

> The state of slavery is of such a nature, that it is incapable of being introduced on any reasons, moral or political; but only positive law, which preserves its force long after the reasons, occasion, and time itself from whence it was created, is erased from memory: it's so odious, that nothing can be suffered to support it, but positive law.

Lord Mansfield, after uttering these words, freed a black man who had been held as a slave in Virginia and brought to England temporarily by his Virginia master. The gist of Mansfield's holding was that since slavery was not permitted in England, Somerset had to be set free. Mansfield's words and his holding were influential in several American decisions, and his views gave comfort to the enemies of slavery right up to the Civil War. Mansfield's views were declared to be the law of America, as well, in Justice Story's influential treatise, COMMENTARIES ON THE CONFLICT OF LAWS § 96 (Boston, Little, Brown & Co. 4th ed. 1852), and Story clearly believed that slavery was contrary to the law of nations, which he believed to be founded on natural law. *See also* Story's opinion in *United States v. The La Jeune Eugenie*, 26 F. Cas. 832, 846 (C.C.D. Mass. 1822) (No. 15,551).

5. Why, then, if slavery was contrary to the law of nations and the law of nature, does Taney determine that Congress is barred from ensuring that the basic postulate of the law of nature, the equality of all men, whatever their race, is enforced in the territories? What does Taney mean when he says that there is no "law of nations" standing between a slaveholder and his property? Doesn't the law of nations, as part of the common law, have force in America, even as an implicit part of the Constitution? And doesn't this mean that property in slaves might be dealt with on a different footing than other property? In other words, even if the Due Process Clause of the Fifth Amendment might bar Congress from depriving persons of all of their property merely because they chose to live in a territory, might property in slaves still be singled out for different treatment, since such property was condemned by the law of nations and the law of nature? You will have noticed that this is a point made by both of the dissenters in the case. Why isn't it persuasive to Taney? Remember that Taney's philosophy of constitutional interpretation is "original understanding." Is his opinion with regard to the Due Process Clause consistent with this constitutional philosophy? At the end of the 18th century virtually all federal jurists would have said that the common law (with its attendant law of nations and law of nature) was a part of the Constitution. When Taney ignores or seems unaware of this, isn't he betraying his own jurisprudence? Do members of the modern Court who subscribe to original understanding without reference to natural law commit the same error?

6. Whatever the correctness of Taney's views, his opinion served as a bloody shirt for anti-slavery advocates, who saw in it the potential for the establishment of slavery — by the Court — in all the states. Was this a fair reading of the opinion? You may remember Abraham Lincoln's famous statement about how a "house divided" could not stand, and consequently the country could not endure forever half slave and half free — it had to become entirely one or the other. Can you understand why some people believe that *Scott v. Sanford* caused the Civil War? Lincoln not only condemned the *Dred Scott* opinion in his famous debates with Judge Douglas in 1858, but boldly took the position that the Declaration of Independence's words had to be read to apply to blacks as well as whites — a position which you will remember Taney rejected. For these debates, which established Lincoln's reputation and eventually made him a nominee for President, *see, e.g.,* CREATED EQUAL? THE COMPLETE LINCOLN-DOUGLAS DEBATES OF 1858 (Paul M. Angle ed., 1958).

7. Both those who fought for the South in defense of their "peculiar institution" and those who fought for the North against slavery and for Union believed that they had God on their side. The North emerged victorious, and in the debates over the Post-Civil War Amendments, which eventually abolished slavery (the Thirteenth Amendment), and made blacks citizens (the Fourteenth Amendment), their advocates referred often to the natural law of human equality. The Thirteenth Amendment at first foundered in the House of Representatives in 1864, and its opponents, such as Representative C.A. White, argued that an Amendment overruling slavery would be "unconstitutional" because of the Constitution's foundation in the positive law of property (an argument not unlike that of Justice Taney). The Thirteenth Amendment was finally passed by Congress in 1865, and ratified by the requisite three quarters majority of the states, but only after such ratification was, in effect, demanded by President Johnson in the exercise of his powers as commander-in-chief over the still subjugated Southern states. Eventually the Fourteenth Amendment was similarly passed under threats, this time as a condition of readmission to the Union for the Southern states. From that time to this, some Southern partisans and others have argued that the Reconstruction Amendments ought to be of suspect validity, since they were, in effect, "passed at gunpoint." Perhaps their grounding in American common law, and natural law theories of equality have never allowed this "gunpoint" argument to gain much headway. Did the Thirteenth Amendment, the Civil Rights Act of 1866 (which gave the newly freed blacks the property and contract rights of their white fellow Americans), and the Fourteenth Amendment (designed, at least in part, to give a firmer constitutional basis to the 1866 Civil Rights Act) finally win equality for African Americans? The following cases explore this problem.

8. Those wishing to examine further Taney's and the dissenters' constitutional theories should begin with the recent brilliant article by Mark A. Graber, *Desperately Ducking Slavery:* Dred Scott *and Contemporary Constitutional Theory*, 14 Const. Commentary 271 (1997), which builds a dispassionate case for the correctness of Taney's views, but which also suggests the validity of some of the views of the dissenters, and gives a full summary of current constitutional theorists' inability to analyze the case on its own terms.

2. Civil Rights and Non-Discrimination

PLESSY v. FERGUSON
163 U.S. 537 (1896)

Mr. Justice Brown . . . delivered the opinion of the court.

This case turns upon the constitutionality of an act of the General Assembly of the State of Louisiana, passed in 1890, providing for separate railway carriages for the white and colored races.

The first section of the statute enacts "that all railway companies carrying passengers in their coaches in this State, shall provide equal but separate accommodations for the white, and colored races, by providing two or more passenger coaches for each passenger train, or by dividing the passenger coaches by a partition so as to secure separate accommodations: . . . No person or persons, shall be admitted to occupy seats in coaches, other than the ones assigned to them, on account of the race they belong to."

By the second section it was enacted "that the officers of such passenger trains shall have power and are hereby required to assign each passenger to the coach or compartment used for the race to which such passenger belongs; any passenger insisting on going into a coach or compartment to which by race he does not belong, shall be liable to a fine of twenty-five dollars, or in lieu thereof to imprisonment for a period of not more than twenty days in the parish prison, and any officer of any railroad insisting on assigning a passenger to a coach or compartment other than the one set aside for the race to which said passenger belongs, shall be liable to a fine of twenty-five dollars, or in lieu thereof to imprisonment for a period of not more than twenty days in the parish prison; and should any passenger refuse to occupy the coach or compartment to which he or she is assigned by the officer of such railway, said officer shall have power to refuse to carry such passenger on his train, and for such refusal neither he nor the railway company which he represents shall be liable for damages in any of the courts of this State."

The third section . . . [includes] a proviso that "nothing in this act shall be construed as applying to nurses attending children of the other race." . . .

The information filed in the criminal District Court charged in substance that Plessy, being a passenger between two stations within the State of Louisiana, was assigned by officers of the company to the coach used for the race to which he belonged, but he insisted upon going into a coach used by the race to which he did not belong. Neither in the information nor plea was his particular race or color averred.

* * *

The constitutionality of this act is attacked upon the ground that it conflicts both with the Thirteenth Amendment of the Constitution, abolishing slavery, and the Fourteenth Amendment, which prohibits certain restrictive legislation on the part of the States.

1. That it does not conflict with the Thirteenth Amendment, which abolished slavery and involuntary servitude, except as a punishment for crime, is too clear for argument. Slavery implies involuntary servitude — a state of bondage; the ownership of mankind as a chattel, or at least the control of the labor and services of one man for the benefit of another, and the absence of a legal right to the disposal of his own person, property and services. This amendment was said in the *Slaughter-House Cases* [(1872)], to have been intended primarily to abolish slavery, as it had been previously known in this country, and that it equally forbade Mexican peonage or the Chinese coolie trade, when they amounted to slavery or involuntary servitude, and that the use of the word "servitude" was intended to prohibit the use of all forms of involuntary slavery, of whatever class or name. It was intimated, however, in that case that this amendment was regarded by the statesmen of that day as insufficient to protect the colored race from certain laws which had been enacted in the Southern States, imposing upon the colored race onerous disabilities and burdens, and curtailing their rights in the pursuit of life, liberty and property to such an extent that their freedom was of little value; and that the Fourteenth Amendment was devised to meet this exigency.

So, too, in the *Civil Rights Cases* [(1883)], it was said that the act of a mere individual, the owner of an inn, a public conveyance or place of amusement, refusing accommodations to colored people, cannot be justly regarded as imposing any badge of slavery or servitude upon the applicant, but only as involving an ordinary civil injury, properly cognizable by the laws of the State, and presumably subject to redress by those laws until the contrary appears. . . .

A statute which implies merely a legal distinction between the white and colored races — a distinction which is founded in the color of the two races, and which must always exist so long as white men are distinguished from the other race by color — has no tendency to destroy the legal equality of the two races, or re-establish a state of involuntary servitude. . . .

2. By the Fourteenth Amendment, all persons born or naturalized in the United States, and subject to the jurisdiction thereof, are made citizens of the United States and of the State wherein they reside; and the States are forbidden from making or enforcing any law which shall abridge the privileges or immunities of citizens of the United States, or shall deprive any person of life, liberty or property without due process of law, or deny to any person within their jurisdiction the equal protection of the laws.

The proper construction of this amendment was first called to the attention of this court in the *Slaughter-House Cases*, which involved, however, not a question of race, but one of exclusive privileges. The case did not call for any expression of opinion as to the exact rights it was intended to secure to the colored race, but it was said generally that its main purpose was to establish the citizenship of the negro; to give definitions of citizenship of the United States and of the States, and to protect from the hostile legislation of the States the privileges and immunities of citizens of the United States, as distinguished from those of citizens of the States.

The object of the amendment was undoubtedly to enforce the absolute equality of the two races before the law, but in the nature of things it could not have been intended to abolish distinctions based upon color, or to enforce social, as distinguished from political equality, or a commingling of the two races upon terms unsatisfactory to either. Laws permitting, and even requiring, their separation in places where they are liable to be brought into contact do not necessarily imply the inferiority of either race to the other, and have been generally, if not universally, recognized as within the competency of the state legislatures in the exercise of their police power. The most common instance of this is connected with the establishment of separate schools for white and colored children, which has been held to be a valid exercise of the legislative power even by courts of States where the political rights of the colored race have been longest and most earnestly enforced.

One of the earliest of these cases is that of *Roberts v. City of Boston* [(Mass. 1849)], in which the Supreme Judicial Court of Massachusetts held that the general school committee of Boston had power to make provision for the instruction of colored children in separate schools established exclusively for them, and to prohibit their attendance upon the other schools. "The great principle," said Chief Justice Shaw, "advanced by the learned and eloquent advocate for the plaintiff," [Mr. Charles Sumner,] "is, that by the constitution and laws of Massachusetts, all persons without distinction of age or sex, birth or color, origin or condition, are equal before the law. . . . But, when this great principle comes to be applied to the actual and various conditions of persons in society, it will not warrant the assertion, that men and women are legally clothed with the same civil and political powers, and that children and adults are legally to have the same functions and be subject to the same treatment; but only that the rights of all, as they are settled and regulated by law, are equally entitled to the paternal consideration and protection of the law for their maintenance and security." It was held that the powers of the committee extended to the establishment of separate schools for children of different ages, sexes and colors. . . . Similar laws have been enacted by Congress under its general power of legislation over the District of Columbia, as well as by the legislatures of many of the States, and have been generally, if not uniformly, sustained by the courts.

Laws forbidding the intermarriage of the two races may be said in a technical sense to interfere with the freedom of contract, and yet have been universally recognized as within the police power of the State.

The distinction between laws interfering with the political equality of the negro and those requiring the separation of the two races in schools, theatres and railway carriages has been frequently drawn by this court. Thus in *Strauder v. West Virginia* [(1879)], it was held that a law of West Virginia limiting to white male persons, 21 years of age and citizens of the State, the right to sit upon juries, was a discrimination which implied a legal inferiority in civil society, which lessened the security of the right of the colored race, and was a step toward reducing them to a condition of servility. Indeed, the right of a colored man that, in the selection of jurors to pass upon his life, liberty and property, there shall be no exclusion of his race, and no discrimination against them because of color, has been asserted in a number of cases. So, where the laws of a particular locality or the charter of a particular railway corporation has provided that no person shall be excluded from the cars on account of color, we have held that this meant that persons of color should travel in the same car as white ones, and that the enactment was not satisfied by the company's providing cars assigned exclusively to people of color, though they were as good as those which they assigned exclusively to white persons.

Upon the other hand, where a statute of Louisiana required those engaged in the transportation of passengers among the States to give to all persons travelling within that State, upon vessels employed in that business, equal rights and privileges in all parts of the vessel, without distinction on account of race or color, and subjected to an action for damages the owner of such a vessel, who excluded colored passengers on account of their color from the cabin set aside by him for the use of whites, it was held to be so far as it applied to interstate commerce, unconstitutional and void. The court in this case, however, expressly disclaimed that it had anything whatever to do with the statute as a regulation of internal commerce, or affecting anything else than commerce among the States.

In the *Civil Rights Cases*, it was held that an act of Congress, entitling all persons within the jurisdiction of the United States to the full and equal enjoyment of the accommodations, advantages, facilities and privileges of inns, public conveyances, on land or water, theatres and other places of public amusement, and made applicable to citizens of every race and color, regardless of any previous condition of servitude, was unconstitutional and void, upon the ground that the Fourteenth Amendment was prohibitory upon the States only, and the legislation authorized to be adopted by Congress for enforcing it was not direct legislation on matters respecting which the States were prohibited from making or enforcing certain laws, or doing certain acts, but was corrective legislation, such as might be necessary or proper for counteracting and redressing the effect of such laws or acts. In delivering the opinion of the court Mr. Justice Bradley observed that the Fourteenth Amendment "does not invest Congress with power to legislate upon subjects that are within the domain of state legislation; but to provide modes of relief against state legislation, or state action, of the kind referred to. It does not authorize Congress to create a code of municipal law for the regulation of private rights; but to provide modes of redress against the operation of state laws, and the action of state officers, executive or judicial, when these are subversive of the fundamental rights specified in the amendment. Positive rights and privileges are undoubtedly secured by the Fourteenth Amendment; but they are secured by way of prohibition against state laws and state proceedings affecting those rights and privileges, and by power given to Congress to legislate for the purpose of carrying such prohibition into effect; and such legislation must necessarily be predicated upon such supposed state laws or state proceedings, and be directed to the correction of their operation and effect."

Much nearer, and, indeed, almost directly in point, is the case of the *Louisville, New Orleans &c. Railway v. Mississippi* [(1890)], wherein the railway company was indicted for a violation of a statute of Mississippi, enacting that all railroads carrying passengers should provide equal, but separate, accommodations for the white and colored races, by providing two or more passenger cars for each passenger train, or by dividing the passenger cars by a partition, so as to secure separate accommodations. The case was presented in a different aspect from the one under consideration, inasmuch as it was an indictment against the railway company for failing to provide the separate accommodations, but the question considered was the constitutionality of the law. In that case, the Supreme Court of Mississippi had held that the statute applied solely to commerce within the State, and, that being the construction of the state statute by its highest court, was accepted as conclusive. "If it be a matter," said the court, "respecting commerce wholly within a State, and not interfering with commerce between the States, then, obviously, there is no violation of the commerce clause of the Federal Constitution. . . . No question arises under this section, as to the power of the State to separate in different compartments interstate passengers, or affect, in any manner, the privileges and rights of such passengers. All that we can consider is, whether the State has the power to require that railroad trains within her limits shall have separate accommodations for the two races; that affecting only commerce within the State is no invasion of the power given to Congress by the commerce clause."

A like course of reasoning applies to the case under consideration, since the Supreme Court of Louisiana . . . held that the statute in question did not apply to interstate passengers, but was confined in its application to passengers travelling exclusively within the borders of the State. . . . Similar statutes for the separation of the two races upon public conveyances were held to be constitutional [in cases from the state courts of Pennsylvania, Michigan, Illinois, Tennessee, and several other cases from the lower federal courts and from the Interstate Commerce Commission].

* * *

In this connection, it is also suggested by the learned counsel for the plaintiff in error that the same argument that will justify the state legislature in requiring railways to provide separate accommodations for the two races will also authorize them to require separate cars to be provided for people whose hair is of a certain color, or who are aliens, or who belong to certain nationalities, or to enact laws requiring colored people to walk upon one side of the street, and white people upon the other, or requiring white men's houses to be painted white, and colored men's black, or their vehicles or business signs to be of different colors, upon the theory that one side of the street is as good as the other, or that a house or vehicle of one color is as good as one of another color. The reply to all this is that every exercise of the police power must be reasonable, and extend only to such laws as are enacted in good faith for the promotion for the public good, and not for the annoyance or oppression of a particular class. Thus in *Yick Wo v. Hopkins* [(1886)], it was held by this court that a municipal ordinance of the city of San Francisco, to regulate the carrying on the public laundries within the limits of the municipality, violated the provisions of the Constitution of the United States, if it conferred upon the municipal authorities arbitrary power, at their own will, and without regard to discretion, in the legal sense, of the term, to give or withhold consent as to persons or places, without regard to the competency of the persons applying, or the propriety of the places selected for the carrying on the business. It was held to be a covert attempt on the part of the municipality to make an arbitrary and unjust discrimination against the Chinese race. While this was the case of a municipal ordinance, a like principle has been held to apply to acts of a state legislature passed in the exercise of the police power.

So far, then, as a conflict with the Fourteenth Amendment is concerned, the case reduces itself to the question whether the statute of Louisiana is a reasonable regulation, and with respect to this there must necessarily be a large discretion on the part of the legislature. In determining the question of reasonableness it is at liberty to act with reference to the established usages, customs and traditions of the people, and with a view to the promotion of their comfort, and the preservation of the public peace and good order. Gauged by this standard, we cannot say that a law which authorizes or even requires the separation of the two races in public conveyances is unreasonable, or more obnoxious to the Fourteenth Amendment than the acts of Congress requiring separate schools for colored children in the District of Columbia, the constitutionality of which does not seem to have been questioned, or the corresponding acts of state legislatures.

We consider the underlying fallacy of the plaintiff's argument to consist in the assumption that the enforced separation of the two races stamps the colored race with a badge of inferiority. If this be so, it is not by reason of anything found in the act, but solely because the colored race chooses to put that construction upon it. The argument necessarily assumes that if, as has been more than once the case, and is not unlikely to be so again, the colored race should become the dominant power in the state legislature, and should enact a law in precisely similar terms, it would thereby relegate the white race to an inferior position. We imagine that the white race, at least, would not acquiesce in this assumption. The argument also assumes that social prejudices may be overcome by legislation, and that equal rights cannot be secured to the negro except by an enforced commingling of the two races. We cannot accept this proposition. If the two races are to meet upon terms of social equality, it must be the result of natural affinities, a mutual appreciation of each other's merits and a voluntary consent of individuals. As was said by the Court of Appeals of New York in *People v. Gallagher* [(1883)], "this end can neither be accomplished nor promoted by laws which conflict with the general sentiment of the community upon whom they are designed to operate. When the government, therefore, has secured to each of its citizens equal rights before the law and equal opportunities for improvement and progress, it has accomplished the end for which it was organized and performed all of the functions respecting social advantages with which it is endowed." Legislation is powerless to eradicate racial instincts or to abolish distinctions based upon physical differences, and the attempt to do so can only result in accentuating the difficulties of the present situation. If the civil and political rights of both races be equal one cannot be inferior to the other civilly or politically. If one race be inferior to the other socially, the Constitution of the United States cannot put them upon the same plane.

* * *

The judgment of the court below is, therefore,

Affirmed.

MR. JUSTICE HARLAN dissenting.

* * *

In respect of civil rights, common to all citizens, the Constitution of the United States does not, I think, permit any public authority to know the race of those entitled to be protected in the enjoyment of such rights. Every true man has pride of race, and under appropriate circumstances when the rights of others, his equals before the law, are not to be affected, it is his privilege to express such pride and to take such action based upon it as to him seems proper. But I deny that any legislative body or judicial tribunal may have regard to the race of citizens when the civil rights of those citizens are involved. Indeed, such legislation, as that here in question, is inconsistent not only with that equality of rights which pertains to citizenship, National and State, but with the personal liberty enjoyed by every one within the United States.

* * *

It is one thing for railroad carriers to furnish, or to be required by law to furnish, equal accommodations for all whom they are under a legal duty to carry. It is quite another thing for government to forbid citizens of the white and black races from traveling in the same public conveyance, and to punish officers of railroad companies for permitting persons of the two races to occupy the same passenger coach. If a State can prescribe, as a rule of civil conduct, that whites and blacks shall not travel as passengers in the same railroad coach, why may it not so regulate the use of the streets of its cities and towns as to compel white citizens to keep on one side of a street and black citizens to keep on the other? Why may it not, upon like grounds, punish whites and blacks who ride together in street cars or in open vehicles on a public road or street? Why may it not require sheriffs to assign whites to one side of a court-room and blacks to the other? And why may it not also prohibit the commingling of the two races in the galleries of legislative halls or in public assemblages convened for the considerations of the political questions of the day? Further, if this statute of Louisiana is consistent with the personal liberty of citizens, why may not the State require the separation in railroad coaches of native and naturalized citizens of the United States, or of Protestants and Roman Catholics?

The answer given at the argument to these questions was that regulations of the kind they suggest would be unreasonable, and could not, therefore, stand before the law. Is it meant that the determination of questions of legislative power depends upon the inquiry whether the statute whose validity is questioned is, in the judgment of the courts, a reasonable one, taking all the circumstances into consideration? A statute may be unreasonable merely because a sound public policy forbade its enactment. But I do not understand that the courts have anything to do with the policy or expediency of legislation. A statute may be valid, and yet, upon grounds of public policy, may well be characterized as unreasonable. . . . [T]he legislative intention being clearly ascertained, "the courts have no other duty to perform than to execute the legislative will, without any regard to their views as to the wisdom or justice of the particular enactment." There is a dangerous tendency in these latter days to enlarge the functions of the courts, by means of judicial interference with the will of the people as expressed by the legislature. Our institutions have the distinguishing characteristic that the three departments of government are coordinate and separate. Each must keep within the limits defined by the Constitution. And the courts best discharge their duty by executing the will of the law-making power, constitutionally expressed, leaving the results of legislation to be dealt with by the people through their representatives. Statutes must always have a reasonable construction. Sometimes they are to be construed strictly; sometimes, liberally, in order to carry out the legislative will. But however construed, the intent of the legislature is to be respected, if the particular statute in question is valid, although the courts, looking at the public interests, may conceive the statute to be both unreasonable and impolitic. . . .

The white race deems itself to be the dominant race in this country. And so it is, in prestige, in achievements, in education, in wealth and in power. So, I doubt not, it will continue to be for all time, if it remains true to its great heritage and holds fast to the principles of constitutional liberty. But in view of the Constitution, in the eye of the law, there is in this country no superior, dominant, ruling class of citizens. There is no caste here. Our Constitution is color-blind, and neither knows nor tolerates classes among citizens. In respect of civil rights, all citizens are equal before the law. The humblest is the peer of the most powerful. The law regards man as man, and takes no account of his surroundings or of his color when his civil rights as guaranteed by the supreme law of the land are involved. It is, therefore, to be regretted that this high tribunal, the final expositor of the fundamental law of the land, has reached the conclusion that it is competent for a State to regulate the enjoyment by citizens of their civil rights solely upon the basis of race.

In my opinion, the judgment this day rendered will, in time, prove to be quite as pernicious as the decision made by this tribunal in the *Dred Scott* case. . . .

* * *

BROWN v. BOARD OF EDUCATION
347 U.S. 483 (1954)

MR. CHIEF JUSTICE WARREN delivered the opinion of the Court.

These cases come to us from the States of Kansas, South Carolina, Virginia, and Delaware. They are premised on different facts and different local conditions, but a common legal question justifies their consideration together in this consolidated opinion.

In each of the cases, minors of the Negro race, through their legal representatives, seek the aid of the courts in obtaining admission to the public schools of their community on a nonsegregated basis. In each instance, they had been denied admission to schools attended by white children under laws requiring or permitting segregation according to race. This segregation was alleged to deprive the plaintiffs of the equal protection of the laws under the Fourteenth Amendment. In each of the cases other than the Delaware case, a three-judge federal district court denied relief to the plaintiffs on the so-called "separate but equal" doctrine announced by this Court in *Plessy v. Ferguson* [(1896)]. Under that doctrine, equality of treatment is accorded when the races are provided substantially equal facilities, even though these facilities be separate. In the Delaware case, the Supreme Court of Delaware adhered to that doctrine, but ordered that the plaintiffs be admitted to the white schools because of their superiority to the Negro schools.

The plaintiffs contend that segregated public schools are not "equal" and cannot be made "equal," and that hence they are deprived of the equal protection of the laws. . . .

[Pursuant to our request, there was r]eargument [which] was largely devoted to the circumstances surrounding the adoption of the Fourteenth Amendment in 1868. It covered exhaustively consideration of the Amendment in Congress, ratification by the states, then existing practices in racial segregation, and the views of proponents and opponents of the Amendment. This discussion and our own investigation convince us that, although these sources cast some light, it is not enough to resolve the problem with which we are faced. At best, they are inconclusive. The most avid proponents of the post-[Civil] War Amendments undoubtedly intended them to remove all legal distinctions among "all persons born or naturalized in the United States." Their opponents, just as certainly, were antagonistic to both the letter and the spirit of the Amendments and wished them to have the most limited effect. What others in Congress and the state legislatures had in mind cannot be determined with any degree of certainty.

An additional reason for the inconclusive nature of the Amendment's history, with respect to segregated schools, is the status of public education at that time. In the South, the movement toward free common schools, supported by general taxation, had not yet taken hold. Education of white children was largely in the hands of private groups. Education of Negroes was almost nonexistent, and practically all of the race were illiterate. In fact, any education of Negroes was forbidden by law in some states. Today, in contrast, many Negroes have achieved outstanding success in the arts and sciences as well as in the business and professional world. It is true that public school education at the time of the Amendment had advanced further in the North, but the effect of the Amendment on Northern States was generally ignored in the congressional debates. Even in the North, the conditions of public education did not approximate those existing today. The curriculum was usually rudimentary; ungraded schools were common in rural areas; the school term was but three months a year in many states; and compulsory school attendance was virtually unknown. As a consequence, it is not surprising that there should be so little in the history of the Fourteenth Amendment relating to its intended effect on public education.

In the first cases in this Court construing the Fourteenth Amendment, decided shortly after its adoption, the Court interpreted it as proscribing all state-imposed discriminations against the Negro race.[5] The doctrine of "separate

---

[5] *Slaughter-House Cases* (1873); *Strauder v. West Virginia* (1880):

"It ordains that no State shall deprive any person of life, liberty, or property, without due process of law, or deny to any person within its jurisdiction the equal protection of the laws. What is this but declaring that the law in the States shall be the same for the black as for the white; that all persons, whether colored or white, shall stand equal before the laws of the States, and, in regard to the colored race, for whose protection the amendment was primarily designed, that no discrimination shall be made against them by law because of their color? The words of the amendment, it is true, are prohibitory, but they contain a necessary implication of a positive immunity, or right, most valuable to the colored race, —

but equal" did not make its appearance in this Court until 1896 in the case of *Plessy v. Ferguson*, involving not education but transportation. American courts have since labored with the doctrine for over half a century. In this Court, there have been six cases involving the "separate but equal" doctrine in the field of public education. In [two of these cases], the validity of the doctrine itself was not challenged. In more recent cases, all on the graduate school level, inequality was found in that specific benefits enjoyed by white students were denied to Negro students of the same educational qualifications. In none of these cases was it necessary to re-examine the doctrine to grant relief to the Negro plaintiff. And in [one of these cases,] *Sweatt v. Painter* [(1950)], the Court expressly reserved decision on the question whether *Plessy v. Ferguson* should be held inapplicable to public education.

In the instant cases, that question is directly presented. Here, unlike *Sweatt v. Painter*, there are findings below that the Negro and white schools involved have been equalized, or are being equalized, with respect to buildings, curricula, qualifications and salaries of teachers, and other "tangible" factors. Our decision, therefore, cannot turn on merely a comparison of these tangible factors in the Negro and white schools involved in each of the cases. We must look instead to the effect of segregation itself on public education.

In approaching this problem, we cannot turn the clock back to 1868 when the Amendment was adopted, or even to 1896 when *Plessy v. Ferguson* was written. We must consider public education in the light of its full development and its present place in American life throughout the Nation. Only in this way can it be determined if segregation in public schools deprives these plaintiffs of the equal protection of the laws.

Today, education is perhaps the most important function of state and local governments. Compulsory school attendance laws and the great expenditures for education both demonstrate our recognition of the importance of education to our democratic society. It is required in the performance of our most basic public responsibilities, even service in the armed forces. It is the very foundation of good citizenship. Today it is a principal instrument in awakening the child to cultural values, in preparing him for later professional training, and in helping him to adjust normally to his environment. In these days, it is doubtful that any child may reasonably be expected to succeed in life if he is denied the opportunity of an education. Such an opportunity, where the state has undertaken to provide it, is a right which must be made available to all on equal terms.

We come then to the question presented: Does segregation of children in public schools solely on the basis of race, even though the physical facilities and

---

the right to exemption from unfriendly legislation against them distinctively as colored, — exemption from legal discriminations, implying inferiority in civil society, lessening the security of their enjoyment of the rights which others enjoy, and discriminations which are steps towards reducing them to the condition of a subject race."

other "tangible" factors may be equal, deprive the children of the minority group of equal educational opportunities? We believe that it does.

In *Sweatt v. Painter, supra,* in finding that a segregated law school for Negroes could not provide them equal educational opportunities, this Court relied in large part on "those qualities which are incapable of objective measurement but which make for greatness in a law school." In *McLaurin v. Oklahoma State Regents* [(1950)], [another 14th Amendment education case involving a graduate school], the Court, in requiring that a Negro admitted to a white graduate school be treated like all other students, again resorted to intangible considerations: ". . . his ability to study, to engage in discussions and exchange views with other students, and, in general, to learn his profession." Such considerations apply with added force to children in grade and high schools. To separate them from others of similar age and qualifications solely because of their race generates a feeling of inferiority as to their status in the community that may affect their hearts and minds in a way unlikely ever to be undone. The effect of this separation on their educational opportunities was well stated by a finding in the Kansas case by a court which nevertheless felt compelled to rule against the Negro plaintiffs:

> "Segregation of white and colored children in public schools has a detrimental effect upon the colored children. The impact is greater when it has the sanction of the law; for the policy of separating the races is usually interpreted as denoting the inferiority of the negro group. A sense of inferiority affects the motivation of a child to learn. Segregation with the sanction of law, therefore, has a tendency to [retard] the educational and mental development of negro children and to deprive them of some of the benefits they would receive in a racial[ly] integrated school system."

Whatever may have been the extent of psychological knowledge at the time of *Plessy v. Ferguson,* this finding is amply supported by modern authority.[11] Any language in *Plessy v. Ferguson* contrary to this finding is rejected.

We conclude that in the field of public education the doctrine of "separate but equal" has no place. Separate educational facilities are inherently unequal. Therefore, we hold that the plaintiffs and others similarly situated for whom the actions have been brought are, by reason of the segregation complained of, deprived of the equal protection of the laws guaranteed by the Fourteenth Amendment.

---

[11] K.B. CLARK, EFFECT OF PREJUDICE AND DISCRIMINATION ON PERSONALITY DEVELOPMENT (Midcentury White House Conference on Children and Youth, 1950); WITMER AND KOTINSKY, PERSONALITY IN THE MAKING, ch. 6 (1952); Deutscher & Chein, *The Psychological Effects of Enforced Segregation: A Survey of Social Science Opinion,* 26 J. PSYCHOL. 259 (1948); Chein, *What are the Psychological Effects of Segregation Under Conditions of Equal Facilities?,* 3 INT. J. OPINION & ATTITUDE RES. 229 (1949); BRAMELD, EDUCATIONAL COSTS, IN DISCRIMINATION AND NATIONAL WELFARE 44-48 (MacIver ed., 1949); FRAZIER, THE NEGRO IN THE UNITED STATES 674-81 (1949). And see generally MYRDAL, AN AMERICAN DILEMMA (1944).

NOTES AND QUESTIONS

1. There is universal agreement in the American legal academy to the proposition that *Plessy* was wrongly decided and *Brown* was correct. How could a majority have reached the conclusion that it did in *Plessy*? Is it simply that the times were different, as the *Brown* Court all but implicitly concedes? Should different times make for different constitutional law? What do you make of Earl Warren's famous suggestion in *Brown* that one can't "turn the clock back"? 347 U.S. at 492. Can clocks be turned back? Some philosophers, most notably the famous Christian apologist C.S. Lewis, have gone so far as to suggest that turning back the clock may be the only rational strategy when the times have gone badly wrong. Should one ever turn back the clock in constitutional law?

2. What's wrong with the "separate but equal" doctrine enunciated in *Plessy*? Would it surprise you to learn that the owners of the public transportation providers in *Plessy* were hoping for a ruling that would remove the necessity to operate parallel accommodations in transportation? What are the economic aspects of state-supported racial discrimination? Is it efficient or inefficient, and should this be a concern?

3. Note Justice Harlan's eloquent dissent in *Plessy*, and, in particular his assertion that the Constitution is "color-blind." 163 U.S. at 559 (Harlan, J., dissenting). Where does this idea come from, and do you agree? Were the framers of the Constitution "color-blind"? Was the document they produced? Is natural law "color blind"? Do you find any help in deciding whether *Brown* was correctly reasoned in the dissenting opinions in *Dred Scott*? Generally those people who believe that *Dred Scott* was the worst decision ever rendered by the Supreme Court believe that *Brown* was the best. Would you have guessed this? Are the constitutional theories implemented in the majority opinions in the two cases fundamentally at odds, as well as their substantive conclusions?

Are there any explicit references to race in the body of the Constitution? Should the Thirteenth or Fourteenth Amendments be construed as implementing a "color-blind" society, even if the Constitution did not? Clearly the Thirteenth and Fourteenth Amendments were designed to overrule *Dred Scott*. Is *Plessy* consistent with this historical understanding? Why, by the way, did the plaintiffs in *Plessy* believe that they had a case to make under the Thirteenth Amendment, and why did the court reject their claim?

4. Does *Brown* completely overrule *Plessy*? If not, to what extent is *Plessy* still good law after *Brown*? Do you suppose the doctrines in *Plessy* have any remaining force today? Is this because of what *Brown* decided, or for other reasons?

5. *Brown* was a unanimous decision. Can you understand why *Brown* is universally regarded as the most important Supreme Court case of the 20th century? What do you think of the principles of constitutional interpretation that triumph in *Brown*? Are they the same as those that you have observed in other Supreme Court decisions? How, by the way, would Justices Rehnquist, Scalia, and Thomas, to pick the court's currently most conservative members, have decided *Brown*? Would *Plessy* have been overruled by the trio of Justices — O'Connor, Kennedy, and Souter — who refused to overrule *Roe v. Wade* in *Planned Parenthood v. Casey*? See Chapter Nine discussing these abortion decisions. Would their principles of *stare decisis* have required an affirmance of *Plessy* in *Brown*? Ask yourself this question when you read *Casey* in the following Chapter.

6. Consider *Brown*'s famous "footnote 11," one of the most famous in all constitutional law. What is its significance? Can *Brown* be explained without reference to the social psychological data collected in footnote 11? Footnote 11 exists to buttress the conclusion that forced separation of the races harms the black race, at least with regard to elementary school education. Why wasn't such an argument persuasive in *Plessy*?

7. Does *Brown* end state-sponsored racial separation? What is the extent of its reach? In a series of short *per curiam* opinions rendered shortly after *Brown*, the Court struck down segregation at public beaches and bathhouses, *Mayor and City Council of Baltimore v. Dawson* (1955); at municipal golf courses, *Holmes v. City of Atlanta* (1955); and on city buses, *Gayle v. Browder* (1956), merely citing to *Brown* in each instance without further discussion. Do these decisions necessarily follow from the rationale adopted in *Brown*? With them, must *Brown* be viewed as establishing a principled objection to segregation *per se* that was not expressly articulated in the *Brown* opinion itself?

3. Vestiges of Discrimination — The Difficulty of Past Racial Effect

FREEMAN v. PITTS
503 U.S. 467 (1992)

JUSTICE KENNEDY delivered the opinion of the Court.

DeKalb County, Georgia, is a major suburban area of Atlanta. This case involves a court-ordered desegregation decree for the DeKalb County School System (DCSS). DCSS now serves some 73,000 students in kindergarten through high school and is the 32nd largest elementary and secondary school system in the Nation.

DCSS has been subject to the supervision and jurisdiction of the United States District Court for the Northern District of Georgia since 1969, when it was ordered to dismantle its dual school system. In 1986, petitioners filed a motion for final dismissal. The District Court ruled that DCSS had not achieved unitary status in all respects but had done so in student attendance and three other categories. In its order the District Court relinquished remedial control as to those aspects of the system in which unitary status had been achieved, and retained supervisory authority only for those aspects of the school system in which the district was not in full compliance. The Court of Appeals for the Eleventh Circuit reversed, holding that a district court should retain full remedial authority over a school system until it achieves unitary status in six categories at the same time for several years. We now reverse the judgment of the Court of Appeals. . . .

I

A

For decades before our decision in *Brown v. Board of Education* (1954) (*Brown I*) . . . DCSS was segregated by law. DCSS' initial response to the mandate of [a later decision by the Supreme Court in *Brown v. Board of Education*, known as "*Brown II*," which mandated desegregation of the nation's public schools "with all deliberate speed,"] was an all too familiar one. Interpreting "all deliberate speed" as giving latitude to delay steps to desegregate, DCSS took no positive action toward desegregation until the 1966-1967 school year, when it did nothing more than adopt a freedom of choice transfer plan. Some black students chose to attend former *de jure* white schools, but the plan had no significant effect on the former *de jure* black schools.

In 1968, we decided *Green v. School Bd. of New Kent County*. We held that adoption of a freedom of choice plan does not, by itself, satisfy a school district's mandatory responsibility to eliminate all vestiges of a dual system. . . . Concerned by more than a decade of inaction, we stated that "'[t]he time for mere "deliberate speed" has run out.'" We said that the obligation of school districts once segregated by law was to come forward with a plan that "promises realistically to work, and promises realistically to work *now*." . . .

Within two months of our ruling in *Green*, respondents, who are black schoolchildren and their parents, instituted this class action in the United States District Court for the Northern District of Georgia. After the suit was filed, DCSS voluntarily began working with the Department of Health, Education, and Welfare to devise a comprehensive and final plan of desegregation. The District Court, in June 1969, entered a consent order approving the proposed plan, which was to be implemented in the 1969-1970 school year. The order abolished the freedom of choice plan and adopted a neighborhood school attendance plan that had been proposed by DCSS and accepted by the Department of Health, Education, and Welfare subject to a minor modification. Under the plan all of the former *de jure* black schools were closed, and their students were reassigned among the remaining neighborhood schools. The District Court retained jurisdiction.

Between 1969 and 1986, respondents sought only infrequent and limited judicial intervention into the affairs of DCSS. They did not request significant changes in student attendance zones or student assignment policies. In 1976, DCSS was ordered to expand its Majority-to-Minority (M-to-M) student transfer program, allowing students in a school where they are in the majority race to transfer to a school where they are in the minority; to establish a biracial committee to oversee the transfer program and future boundary line changes; and to reassign teachers so that the ratio of black to white teachers in each school would be, in substance, similar to the racial balance in the school population systemwide. From 1977 to 1979, the District Court approved a boundary line change for one elementary school attendance zone and rejected DCSS proposals to restrict the M-to-M transfer program. In 1983, DCSS was ordered to make further adjustments to the M-to-M transfer program.

In 1986, petitioners filed a motion for final dismissal of the litigation. They sought a declaration that DCSS had satisfied its duty to eliminate the dual education system. . . . The District Court approached the question whether DCSS had achieved unitary status by asking whether DCSS was unitary with respect to each of the factors identified in *Green*. The court considered an additional factor that is not named in *Green*: the quality of education being offered to the white and black student populations.

The District Court found DCSS to be "an innovative school system that has travelled the often long road to unitary status almost to its end," noting that "the court has continually been impressed by the successes of the DCSS and its dedication to providing a quality education for all students within that system." It found that DCSS is a unitary system with regard to student assignments, transportation, physical facilities, and extracurricular activities, and ruled that it would order no further relief in those areas. The District Court stopped short of dismissing the case, however, because it found that DCSS was not unitary in every respect. The court said that vestiges of the dual system remain in the areas of teacher and principal assignments, resource allocation, and quality of education. DCSS was ordered to take measures to address the remaining problems.

B

Proper resolution of any desegregation case turns on a careful assessment of its facts. Here, as in most cases where the issue is the degree of compliance with a school desegregation decree, a critical beginning point is the degree of racial imbalance in the school district. . . . This inquiry is fundamental, for under the former *de jure* regimes racial exclusion was both the means and the end of a policy motivated by disparagement of, or hostility towards, the disfavored race. In accord with this principle, the District Court began its analysis with an assessment of the current racial mix in the schools throughout DCSS and the explanation for the racial imbalance it found. Respondents did not contend on appeal that the findings of fact were clearly erroneous, and the Court of Appeals did not find them to be erroneous. The Court of Appeals did disagree with the conclusion reached by the District Court respecting the need for further supervision of racial balance in student assignments.

In the extensive record that comprises this case, one fact predominates: Remarkable changes in the racial composition of the county presented DCSS and the District Court with a student population in 1986 far different from the one they set out to integrate in 1969. Between 1950 and 1985, DeKalb County grew from 70,000 to 450,000 in total population, but most of the gross increase in student enrollment had occurred by 1969, the relevant starting date for our purposes. Although the public school population experienced only modest changes between 1969 and 1986 (remaining in the low 70,000s), a striking change occurred in the racial proportions of the student population. The school system that the District Court ordered desegregated in 1969 had 5.6% black students; by 1986 the percentage of black students was 47%.

To compound the difficulty of working with these radical demographic changes, the northern and southern parts of the county experienced much different growth patterns. The District Court found that "[a]s the result of these demographic shifts, the population of the northern half of DeKalb County is now predominantly white and the southern half of DeKalb County is predominantly black." . . . Most of the growth in the nonwhite population in the southern portion of the county was due to the migration of black persons from the city of Atlanta. . . .

The District Court made findings with respect to the number of nonwhite citizens in the northern and southern parts of the county for the years 1970 and 1980 without making parallel findings with respect to white citizens. Yet a clear picture does emerge. During the relevant period, the black population in the southern portion of the county experienced tremendous growth while the white population did not, and the white population in the northern part of the county experienced tremendous growth while the black population did not.

The demographic changes that occurred during the course of the desegregation order are an essential foundation for the District Court's analysis of the current racial mix of DCSS. As the District Court observed, the demographic shifts have had "an immense effect on the racial compositions of the DeKalb County schools." From 1976 to 1986, enrollment in elementary schools declined overall by 15%, while black enrollment in elementary schools increased by 86%. During the same period, overall high school enrollment declined by 16%, while black enrollment in high schools increased by 119%. These effects were even more pronounced in the southern portion of DeKalb County.

Concerned with racial imbalance in the various schools of the district, respondents presented evidence that during the 1986-1987 school year DCSS had the following features: (1) 47% of the students attending DCSS were black; (2) 50% of the black students attended schools that were over 90% black; (3) 62% of all black students attended schools that had more than 20% more blacks than the system-wide average; (4) 27% of white students attended schools that were more than 90% white; (5) 59% of the white students attended schools that had more than 20% more whites than the system-wide average; (6) of the 22 DCSS high schools, five had student populations that were more than 90% black, while five other schools had student populations that were more than 80% white; and (7) of the 74 elementary schools in DCSS, 18 are over 90% black, while 10 are over 90% white.

Respondents argued in the District Court that this racial imbalance in student assignment was a vestige of the dual system, rather than a product of independent demographic forces. In addition to the statistical evidence that the ratio of black students to white students in individual schools varied to a significant degree from the system-wide average, respondents contended that DCSS had not used all available desegregative tools in order to achieve racial balancing. Respondents pointed to the following alleged shortcomings in DCSS' desegregative efforts: (1) DCSS did not break the county into subdistricts and racially balance each subdistrict; (2) DCSS failed to expend sufficient funds for minority learning opportunities; (3) DCSS did not establish community advisory organizations; (4) DCSS did not make full use of the freedom of choice plan; (5) DCSS did not cluster schools, that is, it did not create schools for separate grade levels which could be used to establish a feeder pattern; (6) DCSS did not institute its magnet school program as early as it might have; and (7) DCSS did not use busing to facilitate urban to suburban exchanges.

According to the District Court, respondents conceded that the 1969 order assigning all students to their neighborhood schools "effectively desegregated the DCSS for a period of time" with respect to student assignment. The District Court noted, however, that despite this concession respondents contended there was an improper imbalance in two schools even in 1969. Respondents made much of the fact that despite the small percentage of blacks in the county in 1969, there were then two schools that contained a majority of black students. . . .

The District Court found the racial imbalance in these schools was not a vestige of the prior *de jure* system. It observed that both the . . . schools were *de jure* white schools before the freedom of choice plan was put in place. It cited expert witness testimony that [one of the schools,] Terry Mill[,] had become a majority black school as a result of demographic shifts unrelated to the actions of petitioners or their predecessors. In 1966, the overwhelming majority of students at Terry Mill were white. By 1967, due to migration of black citizens from Atlanta into DeKalb County — and into the neighborhood surrounding the Terry Mill school in particular — 23% of the students at Terry Mill were black. By 1968, black students constituted 50% of the school population at Terry Mill. By 1969, when the plan was put into effect, the percentage of black students had grown to 76. In accordance with the evidence of demographic shifts, and in the absence of any evidence to suggest that the former dual system contributed in any way to the rapid racial transformation of the Terry Mill student population, the District Court found that the pre-1969 unconstitutional acts of petitioners were not responsible for the high percentage of black students at the Terry Mill school in 1969. Its findings in this respect are illustrative of the problems DCSS and the District Court faced in integrating the whole district.

Although the District Court found that DCSS was desegregated for at least a short period under the court-ordered plan of 1969, it did not base its finding that DCSS had achieved unitary status with respect to student assignment on that circumstance alone. Recognizing that "the achievement of unitary status in the area of student assignment cannot be hedged on the attainment of such status for a brief moment," the District Court examined the interaction between DCSS policy and demographic shifts in DeKalb County.

The District Court noted that DCSS had taken specific steps to combat the effects of demographics on the racial mix of the schools. Under the 1969 order, a biracial committee had reviewed all proposed changes in the boundary lines of school attendance zones. Since the original desegregation order, there had been about 170 such changes. It was found that only three had a partial segregative effect. An expert testified, and the District Court found, that even those changes had no significant effect on the racial mix of the school population, given the tremendous demographic shifts that were taking place at the same time.

The District Court also noted that DCSS, on its own initiative, started an M-to-M program in the 1972 school year. The program was a marked success. Participation increased with each passing year, so that in the 1986-1987 school year, 4,500 of the 72,000 students enrolled in DCSS participated. An expert testified that the impact of an M-to-M program goes beyond the number of students transferred because students at the receiving school also obtain integrated learning experiences. The District Court found that about 19% of the students attending DCSS had an integrated learning experience as a result of the M-to-M program.

In addition, in the 1980's, DCSS instituted a magnet school program in schools located in the middle of the county. The magnet school programs included a performing arts program, two science programs, and a foreign language program. There was testimony in the District Court that DCSS also had plans to operate additional magnet programs in occupational education and gifted and talented education, as well as a preschool program and an open campus. By locating these programs in the middle of the county, DCSS sought to attract black students from the southern part of the county and white students from the northern part.

Further, the District Court found that DCSS operates a number of experience programs integrated by race, including a writing center for fifth and seventh graders, a driving range, summer school programs, and a dialectical speech program. DCSS employs measures to control the racial mix in each of these special areas.

In determining whether DCSS has achieved unitary status with respect to student assignment, the District Court saw its task as one of deciding if petitioners "have accomplished maximum practical desegregation of the DCSS or if the DCSS must still do more to fulfill their affirmative constitutional duty." Petitioners and respondents presented conflicting expert testimony about the potential effects that desegregative techniques not deployed might have had upon the racial mix of the schools. The District Court found that petitioners' experts were more reliable, citing their greater familiarity with DCSS, their experience, and their standing within the expert community. The District Court made these findings:

> "[The actions of DCSS] achieved maximum practical desegregation from 1969 to 1986. The rapid population shifts in DeKalb County were not caused by any action on the part of the DCSS. These demographic shifts were inevitable as the result of suburbanization, that is, work opportunities arising in DeKalb County as well as the City of Atlanta, which attracted blacks to DeKalb; the decline in the number of children born to white families during this period while the number of children born to black families did not decrease; blockbusting of formerly white neighborhoods leading to selling and buying of real estate in the DeKalb area on a highly dynamic basis; and the completion of Interstate 20, which made access from DeKalb County into the City of Atlanta much easier. . . . There is no evidence that the school system's previous unconstitutional conduct may have contributed to this segregation. This court is convinced that any further actions taken by defendants, while the actions might have made marginal adjustments in the population trends, would not have offset the factors that were described above and the same racial segregation would have occurred at approximately the same speed."

The District Court added:

> "[A]bsent massive bussing, which is not considered as a viable option by either the parties or this court, the magnet school program and the M-to-M program, which the defendants voluntarily implemented and to which the defendants obviously are dedicated, are the most effective ways to deal with the effects on student attendance of the residential segregation existing in DeKalb County at this time."

Having found no constitutional violation with respect to student assignment, the District Court next considered the other *Green* factors, beginning with faculty and staff assignments. The District Court first found that DCSS had fulfilled its constitutional obligation with respect to hiring and retaining minority teachers and administrators. DCSS has taken active steps to recruit qualified black applicants and has hired them in significant numbers, employing a greater percentage of black teachers than the statewide average. The District Court also noted that DCSS has an "equally exemplary record" in retention of black teachers and administrators. Nevertheless, the District Court found that DCSS had not achieved or maintained a ratio of black to white teachers and administrators in each school to approximate the ratio of black to white teachers and administrators throughout the system. In other words, a racial imbalance existed in the assignment of minority teachers and administrators. The District Court found that in the 1984-1985 school year, seven schools deviated by more than 10% from the system-wide average of 26.4% minority teachers in elementary schools and 24.9% minority teachers in high schools. The District Court also found that black principals and administrators were over-represented in schools with high percentages of black students and underrepresented in schools with low percentages of black students.

The District Court found the crux of the problem to be that DCSS has relied on the replacement process to attain a racial balance in teachers and other staff and has avoided using mandatory reassignment. DCSS gave as its reason for not using mandatory reassignment that the competition among local school districts is stiff, and that it is difficult to attract and keep qualified teachers if they are required to work far from their homes. In fact, because teachers prefer to work close to their homes, DCSS has a voluntary transfer program in which teachers who have taught at the same school for a period of three years may ask for a transfer. Because most teachers request to be transferred to schools near their homes, this program makes compliance with the objective of racial balance in faculty and staff more difficult.

The District Court stated that it was not "unsympathetic to the difficulties that DCSS faces in this regard," but . . . ordered DCSS to devise a plan to achieve compliance with [prior Supreme Court precedent requiring racial balance in teachers and staff] noting that "[i]t would appear that such compliance will necessitate reassignment of both teachers and principals." With respect to faculty, the District Court noted that [this] would not be difficult, citing petitioners' own estimate that most schools' faculty could conform by moving, at most, two or three teachers.

Addressing the more ineffable category of quality of education, the District Court rejected most of respondents' contentions that there was racial disparity in the provision of certain educational resources (*e.g.*, teachers with advanced degrees, teachers with more experience, library books), contentions made to show that black students were not being given equal educational opportunity. The District Court went further, however, and examined the evidence concerning achievement of black students in DCSS. It cited expert testimony praising the overall educational program in the district, as well as objective evidence of black achievement: Black students at DCSS made greater gains on the Iowa Tests of Basic Skills than white students, and black students at DCSS are more successful than black students nationwide on the Scholastic Aptitude Test. . . .

* * *

Despite its finding that there was no intentional violation, the District Court found that DCSS had not achieved unitary status with respect to quality of education because teachers in schools with disproportionately high percentages of white students tended to be better educated and have more experience than their counterparts in schools with disproportionately high percentages of black students, and because per-pupil expenditures in majority white schools exceeded per-pupil expenditures in majority black schools. From these findings, the District Court ordered DCSS to equalize spending and remedy the other problems.

The final *Green* factors considered by the District Court were: (1) physical facilities, (2) transportation, and (3) extracurricular activities. The District Court noted that although respondents expressed some concerns about the use of portable classrooms in schools in the southern portion of the county, they in effect conceded that DCSS has achieved unitary status with respect to physical facilities.

In accordance with its factfinding, the District Court held that it would order no further relief in the areas of student assignment, transportation, physical facilities, and extracurricular activities. The District Court, however, did order DCSS to establish a system to balance teacher and principal assignments and to equalize per-pupil expenditures throughout DCSS. Having found that blacks were represented on the school board and throughout DCSS administration, the District Court abolished the biracial committee as no longer necessary.

Both parties appealed to the United States Court of Appeals for the Eleventh Circuit. The Court of Appeals affirmed the District Court's ultimate conclusion that DCSS has not yet achieved unitary status, but reversed the District Court's ruling that DCSS has no further duties in the area of student assignment. The Court of Appeals held that the District Court erred by considering the six *Green* factors as separate categories. The Court of Appeals rejected the District Court's incremental approach, . . . and held that a school system achieves unitary status only after it has satisfied all six factors at the same time for several years. Because, under this test, DCSS had not achieved unitary status at any time, the Court of Appeals held that DCSS could "not shirk its constitutional duties by pointing to demographic shifts occurring prior to unitary status." The Court of Appeals held that petitioners bore the responsibility for the racial imbalance, and in order to correct that imbalance would have to take actions that "may be administratively awkward, inconvenient, and even bizarre in some situations," such as pairing and clustering of schools, drastic gerrymandering of school zones, grade reorganization, and busing. . . .

II

Two principal questions are presented. The first is whether a district court may relinquish its supervision and control over those aspects of a school system in which there has been compliance with a desegregation decree if other aspects of the system remain in noncompliance. As we answer this question in the affirmative, the second question is whether the Court of Appeals erred in reversing the District Court's order providing for incremental withdrawal of supervision in all the circumstances of this case.

A

The duty and responsibility of a school district once segregated by law is to take all steps necessary to eliminate the vestiges of the unconstitutional *de jure* system. . . .

The objective of *Brown I* was made more specific by our holding in *Green* that the duty of a former *de jure* district is to "take whatever steps might be necessary to convert to a unitary system in which racial discrimination would be eliminated root and branch." We also identified various parts of the school system which, in addition to student attendance patterns, must be free from racial discrimination before the mandate of *Brown* is met: faculty, staff, transportation, extracurricular activities, and facilities. The *Green* factors are a measure of the racial identifiability of schools in a system that is not in compliance with *Brown*, and we instructed the District Courts to fashion remedies that address all these components of elementary and secondary school systems.

The concept of unitariness has been a helpful one in defining the scope of the district courts' authority, for it conveys the central idea that a school district that was once a dual system must be examined in all of its facets, both when a remedy is ordered and in the later phases of desegregation when the question is whether the district courts' remedial control ought to be modified, lessened, or withdrawn. But, as we explained last Term . . . , the term "unitary" is not a precise concept:

> "[I]t is a mistake to treat words such as 'dual' and 'unitary' as if they were actually found in the Constitution. . . . Courts have used the terms 'dual' to denote a school system which has engaged in intentional segregation of students by race, and 'unitary' to describe a school system which has been brought into compliance with the command of the Constitution. We are not sure how useful it is to define these terms more precisely, or to create subclasses within them."

It follows that we must be cautious not to attribute to the term a utility it does not have. . . .

That the term "unitary" does not have fixed meaning or content is not inconsistent with the principles that control the exercise of equitable power. The essence of a court's equity power lies in its inherent capacity to adjust remedies in a feasible and practical way to eliminate the conditions or redress the injuries caused by unlawful action. Equitable remedies must be flexible if these underlying principles are to be enforced with fairness and precision. . . .

Our application of these guiding principles in *Pasadena Bd. of Education v. Spangler* (1976), is instructive. There we held that a District Court exceeded its remedial authority in requiring annual readjustment of school attendance zones in the Pasadena school district when changes in the racial makeup of the schools were caused by demographic shifts "not attributed to any segregative acts on the part of the [school district]." In so holding we said:

> "It may well be that petitioners have not yet totally achieved the unitary system contemplated by . . . [the earlier desegregation case,] *Swann* [*v. Charlotte-Mecklenburg Bd. of Education* (1970) (which approved of busing as a remedy to achieve racial balance)]. There has been, for example, dispute as to the petitioners' compliance with those portions of the

plan specifying procedures for hiring and promoting teachers and administrators.["] . . .

[Nevertheless, t]oday, [we hold that] . . . [a] federal court in a school desegregation case has the discretion to order an incremental or partial withdrawal of its supervision and control. This discretion derives both from the constitutional authority which justified its intervention in the first instance and its ultimate objectives in formulating the decree. The authority of the court is invoked at the outset to remedy particular constitutional violations. In construing the remedial authority of the district courts, we have been guided by the principles that "judicial powers may be exercised only on the basis of a constitutional violation," and that "the nature of the violation determines the scope of the remedy." A remedy is justifiable only insofar as it advances the ultimate objective of alleviating the initial constitutional violation.

We have said that the court's end purpose must be to remedy the violation and, in addition, to restore state and local authorities to the control of a school system that is operating in compliance with the Constitution. Partial relinquishment of judicial control, where justified by the facts of the case, can be an important and significant step in fulfilling the district court's duty to return the operations and control of schools to local authorities. . . . [F]ederal judicial supervision of local school systems was intended as a "temporary measure." Although this temporary measure has lasted decades, the ultimate objective has not changed — to return school districts to the control of local authorities. A transition phase in which control is relinquished in a gradual way is an appropriate means to this end.

As we have long observed, "local autonomy of school districts is a vital national tradition." Returning schools to the control of local authorities at the earliest practicable date is essential to restore their true accountability in our governmental system. When the school district and all state entities participating with it in operating the schools make decisions in the absence of judicial supervision, they can be held accountable to the citizenry, to the political process, and to the courts in the ordinary course. As we discuss below, one of the prerequisites to relinquishment of control in whole or in part is that a school district has demonstrated its commitment to a course of action that gives full respect to the equal protection guarantees of the Constitution. Yet it must be acknowledged that the potential for discrimination and racial hostility is still present in our country, and its manifestations may emerge in new and subtle forms after the effects of *de jure* segregation have been eliminated. It is the duty of the State and its subdivisions to ensure that such forces do not shape or control the policies of its school systems. . . .

We hold that, in the course of supervising desegregation plans, federal courts have the authority to relinquish supervision and control of school districts in incremental stages, before full compliance has been achieved in every area of school operations. . . . In particular, the district court may determine that it will not order further remedies in the area of student assignments where racial imbalance is not traceable, in a proximate way, to constitutional violations.

A court's discretion to order the incremental withdrawal of its supervision in a school desegregation case must be exercised in a manner consistent with the purposes and objectives of its equitable power. Among the factors which must inform the sound discretion of the court in ordering partial withdrawal are the following: whether there has been full and satisfactory compliance with the decree in those aspects of the system where supervision is to be withdrawn; whether retention of judicial control is necessary or practicable to achieve compliance with the decree in other facets of the school system; and whether the school district has demonstrated, to the public and to the parents and students of the once disfavored race, its good-faith commitment to the whole of the court's decree and to those provisions of the law and the Constitution that were the predicate for judicial intervention in the first instance.

In considering these factors, a court should give particular attention to the school system's record of compliance. . . .

* * *

B

We reach now the question whether the Court of Appeals erred in prohibiting the District Court from returning to DCSS partial control over some of its affairs. . . .

It was an appropriate exercise of its discretion for the District Court to address the elements of a unitary system discussed in *Green*, to inquire whether other elements ought to be identified, and to determine whether minority students were being disadvantaged in ways that required the formulation of new and further remedies to ensure full compliance with the court's decree. Both parties agreed that quality of education was a legitimate inquiry in determining DCSS' compliance with the desegregation decree, and the trial court found it workable to consider the point in connection with its findings on resource allocation. . . . The District Court's approach illustrates that the *Green* factors need not be a rigid framework. It illustrates also the uses of equitable discretion. By withdrawing control over areas where judicial supervision is no longer needed, a district court can concentrate both its own resources and those of the school district on the areas where the effects of *de jure* discrimination have not been eliminated and further action is necessary in order to provide real and tangible relief to minority students.

The Court of Appeals' rejection of the District Court's order rests on related premises: first, that given noncompliance in some discrete categories, there can be no partial withdrawal of judicial control; and second, until there is full compliance, heroic measures must be taken to ensure racial balance in student assignments system wide. Under our analysis and our precedents, neither premise is correct.

The Court of Appeals was mistaken in ruling that our opinion in *Swann* requires "awkward," "inconvenient," and "even bizarre" measures to achieve racial balance in student assignments in the late phases of carrying out a decree, when the imbalance is attributable neither to the prior *de jure* system nor to a later violation by the school district but rather to independent demographic forces. In *Swann* we undertook to discuss the objectives of a comprehensive desegregation plan and the powers and techniques available to a district court in designing it at the outset. We confirmed that racial balance in school assignments was a necessary part of the remedy in the circumstances there presented. In the case before us the District Court designed a comprehensive plan for desegregation of DCSS in 1969, one that included racial balance in student assignments. The desegregation decree was designed to achieve maximum practicable desegregation. Its central remedy was the closing of black schools and the reassignment of pupils to neighborhood schools, with attendance zones that achieved racial balance. The plan accomplished its objective in the first year of operation, before dramatic demographic changes altered residential patterns. For the entire 17-year period respondents raised no substantial objection to the basic student assignment system, as the parties and the District Court concentrated on other mechanisms to eliminate the *de jure* taint.

That there was racial imbalance in student attendance zones was not tantamount to a showing that the school district was in noncompliance with the decree or with its duties under the law. Racial balance is not to be achieved for its own sake. It is to be pursued when racial imbalance has been caused by a constitutional violation. Once the racial imbalance due to the *de jure* violation has been remedied, the school district is under no duty to remedy imbalance that is caused by demographic factors. . . .

The findings of the District Court that the population changes which occurred in DeKalb County were not caused by the policies of the school district, but rather by independent factors, are consistent with the mobility that is a distinct characteristic of our society. In one year (from 1987 to 1988) over 40 million Americans, or 17.6% of the total population, moved households. Over a third of those people moved to a different county, and over six million migrated between States. In such a society it is inevitable that the demographic makeup of school districts, based as they are on political subdivisions such as counties and municipalities, may undergo rapid change.

The effect of changing residential patterns on the racial composition of schools, though not always fortunate, is somewhat predictable. Studies show a high correlation between residential segregation and school segregation. The District Court in this case heard evidence tending to show that racially stable neighborhoods are not likely to emerge because whites prefer a racial mix of 80% white and 20% black, while blacks prefer a 50-50 mix.

Where resegregation is a product not of state action but of private choices, it does not have constitutional implications. It is beyond the authority and beyond the practical ability of the federal courts to try to counteract these kinds of continuous and massive demographic shifts. . . .

In one sense of the term, vestiges of past segregation by state decree do remain in our society and in our schools. Past wrongs to the black race, wrongs committed by the State and in its name, are a stubborn fact of history. And stubborn facts of history linger and persist. But though we cannot escape our history, neither must we overstate its consequences in fixing legal responsibilities. The vestiges of segregation that are the concern of the law in a school case may be subtle and intangible but nonetheless they must be so real that they have a causal link to the *de jure* violation being remedied. It is simply not always the case that demographic forces causing population change bear any real and substantial relation to a *de jure* violation. . . .

As the *de jure* violation becomes more remote in time and these demographic changes intervene, it becomes less likely that a current racial imbalance in a school district is a vestige of the prior *de jure* system. The causal link between current conditions and the prior violation is even more attenuated if the school district has demonstrated its good faith. In light of its finding that the demographic changes in DeKalb County are unrelated to the prior violation, the District Court was correct to entertain the suggestion that DCSS had no duty to achieve system-wide racial balance in the student population. It was appropriate for the District Court to examine the reasons for the racial imbalance before ordering an impractical, and no doubt massive, expenditure of funds to achieve racial balance after 17 years of efforts to implement the comprehensive plan in a district where there were fundamental changes in demographics, changes not attributable to the former *de jure* regime or any later actions by school officials. The District Court's determination to order instead the expenditure of scarce resources in areas such as the quality of education, where full compliance had not yet been achieved, underscores the uses of discretion in framing equitable remedies.

To say, as did the Court of Appeals, that a school district must meet all six *Green* factors before the trial court can declare the system unitary and relinquish its control over school attendance zones, and to hold further that racial balancing by all necessary means is required in the interim, is simply to vindicate a legal phrase. The law is not so formalistic. . . .

We next consider whether retention of judicial control over student attendance is necessary or practicable to achieve compliance in other facets of the school system. Racial balancing in elementary and secondary school student assignments may be a legitimate remedial device to correct other fundamental inequities that were themselves caused by the constitutional violation. We have long recognized that the *Green* factors may be related or interdependent. Two or more *Green* factors may be intertwined or synergistic in their relation, so that a constitutional violation in one area cannot be eliminated unless the judicial remedy addresses other matters as well. We have observed, for example, that student segregation and faculty segregation are often related problems. . . .

There was no showing that racial balancing was an appropriate mechanism to cure other deficiencies in this case. . . .

. . . [T]he good-faith compliance of the district with the court order over a reasonable period of time is a factor to be considered in deciding whether or not jurisdiction could be relinquished. A history of good-faith compliance is evidence that any current racial imbalance is not the product of a new *de jure* violation, and enables the district court to accept the school board's representation that it has accepted the principle of racial equality and will not suffer intentional discrimination in the future.

When a school district has not demonstrated good faith under a comprehensive plan to remedy ongoing violations, we have without hesitation approved comprehensive and continued district court supervision.

* * *

The judgment is reversed, and the case is remanded to the Court of Appeals. . . .

* * *

JUSTICE THOMAS took no part in the consideration or decision of this case.

JUSTICE SCALIA, concurring.

* * *

Almost a quarter century ago, in *Green v. School Bd. of New Kent County* (1968), this Court held that school systems which had been enforcing *de jure* segregation at the time of *Brown* had not merely an obligation to assign students and resources on a race-neutral basis but also an "affirmative duty" to "desegregate," that is, to achieve insofar as practicable racial balance in their schools. This holding has become such a part of our legal fabric that there is a tendency, reflected in the Court of Appeals opinion in this case, to speak as though the Constitution requires such racial balancing. Of course it does not: The Equal Protection Clause reaches only those racial imbalances shown to be intentionally caused by the State. . . .

* * *

Racially imbalanced schools are hence the product of a blend of public and private actions, and any assessment that they would not be segregated, or would not be *as* segregated, in the absence of a particular one of those factors is guesswork. It is similarly guesswork, of course, to say that they *would* be segregated, or would be *as* segregated, in the absence of one of those factors. Only in rare cases such as this one . . . , where the racial imbalance had been temporarily corrected after the abandonment of *de jure* segregation, can it be asserted with any degree of confidence that the past discrimination is no longer playing a proximate role. Thus, allocation of the burden of proof foreordains the result in almost all of the "vestige of past discrimination" cases. If, as is normally the case under our equal protection jurisprudence (and in the law generally), we require the plaintiffs to establish the asserted facts entitling them to relief — that the racial imbalance they wish corrected is at least in part the vestige of an old *de jure* system — the plaintiffs will almost always lose. Conversely, if we alter our normal approach and require the school authorities to establish the negative — that the imbalance is *not* attributable to their past discrimination — the plaintiffs will almost always win.

Since neither of these alternatives is entirely palatable, an observer unfamiliar with the history surrounding this issue might suggest that we avoid the problem by requiring only that the school authorities establish a regime in which parents are free to disregard neighborhood-school assignment, and to send their children (with transportation paid) to whichever school they choose. So long as there is free choice, he would say, there is no reason to require that the schools be made identical. The constitutional right is equal racial access to schools, not access to racially equal schools; whatever racial imbalances such a free-choice system might produce would be the product of private forces. We apparently envisioned no more than this in our initial post-*Brown* cases. It is also the approach we actually adopted in *Bazemore v. Friday* (1986), which concerned remedies for prior *de jure* segregation of state university-operated clubs and services.

But we ultimately charted a different course with respect to public elementary and secondary schools. We concluded in *Green* that a "freedom of choice" plan was not necessarily sufficient, and later applied this conclusion to all jurisdictions with a history of intentional segregation. . . . Thus began judicial recognition of an "affirmative duty" to desegregate, achieved by allocating the burden of negating causality to the defendant. Our post-*Green* cases provide that, once state-enforced school segregation is shown to have existed in a jurisdiction in 1954, there arises a presumption, effectively irrebuttable (because the school district cannot prove the negative), that any current racial imbalance is the product of that violation, at least if the imbalance has continuously existed.

In the context of elementary and secondary education, the presumption was extraordinary in law but not unreasonable in fact. . . . The extent and recency of the prior discrimination, and the improbability that young children (or their parents) would use "freedom of choice" plans to disrupt existing patterns "warrant[ed] a presumption [that] schools that are substantially disproportionate in their racial composition" were remnants of the *de jure* system.

But granting the merits of this approach at the time of *Green*, it is now 25 years later. "From the very first, federal supervision of local school systems was intended as a *temporary* measure to remedy past discrimination." We envisioned it as temporary partly because "[n]o single tradition in public education is more deeply rooted than local control over the operation of schools," and because no one's interest is furthered by subjecting the Nation's educational system to "judicial tutelage for the indefinite future." But we also envisioned it as temporary, I think, because the rational basis for the extraordinary presumption of causation simply must dissipate as the *de jure* system and the school boards who produced it recede further into the past. Since a multitude of private factors has shaped school systems in the years after abandonment of *de jure* segregation — normal migration, population growth (as in this case), "white flight" from the inner cities, increases in the costs of new facilities — the percentage of the current makeup of school systems attributable to the prior, government-enforced discrimination has diminished with each passing year, to the point where it cannot realistically be assumed to be a significant factor.

At some time, we must acknowledge that it has become absurd to assume, without any further proof, that violations of the Constitution dating from the days when Lyndon Johnson was President, or earlier, continue to have an appreciable effect upon current operation of schools. We are close to that time. While we must continue to prohibit, without qualification, all racial discrimination in the operation of public schools, and to afford remedies that eliminate not only the discrimination but its identified consequences, we should consider laying aside the extraordinary, and increasingly counterfactual, presumption of *Green*. We must soon revert to the ordinary principles of our law, of our democratic heritage, and of our educational tradition: that plaintiffs alleging equal protection violations must prove intent and causation and not merely the existence of racial disparity; that public schooling, even in the South, should be controlled by locally elected authorities acting in conjunction with parents; and that it is "desirable" to permit pupils to attend "schools nearest their homes."

JUSTICE SOUTER, concurring. [Omitted.]

JUSTICE BLACKMUN, with whom JUSTICE STEVENS and JUSTICE O'CONNOR join, concurring in the judgment. [Omitted.]

NOTES AND QUESTIONS

1. Reading between the lines of this case you can get some notion of what happened in the almost forty years which elapsed between *Brown* and *Freeman*. There was massive resistance, especially in the South, to the *Brown* case, and in particular to the Supreme Court's effectively making the federal courts the supervisors of the local school systems instead of state and local governments. As the years dragged on, and as many school systems, particularly in the South, remained virtually segregated, the federal courts devised a variety of new strategies for dealing with the problem. You have read, for example in *Freeman*, about the watershed decision in *Green v. County School Board of New Kent County*, 391 U.S. 430 (1968), an opinion by the great liberal Justice William Brennan, in which he held that on the facts before him a so-called "freedom of choice" plan, which allowed school children the option of choosing whether to attend a predominantly-white or a predominately-black school, did not meet the constitutional mandate expressed in *Brown*, because it failed to eradicate the "dual school system" condemned in *Brown*. But *Green*, in many ways, repre-

sented a radically different approach to school desegregation than that taken in *Brown*. *Brown* had only required that the state not dictate by law the schools students were to attend based on their race. Paradoxically, when *Green* required positive steps by the states to end the dual school systems, the states and localities found themselves actually required, once again, to assign pupils to schools based on their races, and the era of school busing, based on the race of students, began. The constitutional imprimatur approving of busing to achieve racial balance was secured in the 1971 decision of *Swann v. Charlotte-Meckenbourg Board of Education*, 402 U.S. 1 (1971), when the Supreme Court approved of a district court's order that school children be taken by buses away from their neighborhood schools, in order to achieve racial balance in a public school system.

2. You can probably discern from the opinions in *Freeman*, and particularly that of Justice Scalia, the results of decisions such as *Green* and *Swann*. For many school districts, they ended the concept of "neighborhood schools," in the interests of racial integration. Was this what *Brown* intended? Does *Freeman* represent a departure from, or a return to the aims of *Brown*? *See* Michael Heise, *Assessing the Efficacy of School Desegregation,* 46 SYRACUSE L. REV. 1093 (1996) ("Too many students particularly those from low-income families attending inner-city public schools, may bear a disproportionate share of desegregation's [economic, educational, and other] costs"); *but see* Bernard James & Julie M. Hoffman, Brown *in State Hands: State Policymaking and Educational Equality after* Freeman v. Pitts, 20 HASTINGS CONST. L.Q. 521 (1993) (arguing that the legacy of *Brown*'s equality principle has been turned over to the states after *Freeman* and that state constitutional notions of equality thus take on greater importance).

3. One of the effects of *Brown* was "white flight," the movement of whites who feared the consequences of racial integration in the pubic schools to the suburbs, which, for a while at least, were not as racially mixed as the inner cities. Is the decline in the quality of urban education, which followed "white flight," a consequence of *Brown*? Should the Court have followed a strategy of insisting that school administrations be expanded so that both suburban and urban areas be administered together, in order to achieve racial balance and defeat the plans of those who fled from the urban schools? *Cf. Milliken v. Bradley,* 418 U.S. 717 (1974) (precluding an inter-district or multi-district remedy where there was no evidence that district boundaries were drawn purposefully on racial lines). Would a better strategy have been to insist on state-wide equality of per pupil expenditures? Such a strategy appears to be gaining in some states, though the proposition has yet to win universal acceptance. Who should be making decisions about how much is spent in local school systems — the federal courts, the federal legislature, the state legislatures, or local governments? What light does *Freeman* cast on the problem? Is race an intractable problem in American law? Consider the next group of cases.

4. Proving Discriminatory Intent

WASHINGTON v. DAVIS
426 U.S. 229 (1976)

MR. JUSTICE WHITE delivered the opinion of the Court.

This case involves the validity of a qualifying test administered to applicants for positions as police officers in the District of Columbia Metropolitan Police Department. . . .

I

This action began on April 10, 1970, when two Negro police officers filed suit against the then Commissioner of the District of Columbia, the Chief of the District's Metropolitan Police Department, and the Commissioners of the United States Civil Service Commission. An amended complaint, filed December 10, alleged that the promotion policies of the Department were racially discriminatory and sought a declaratory judgment and an injunction. The respondents Harley and Sellers were permitted to intervene, their amended complaint asserting that their applications to become officers in the Department had been rejected, and that the Department's recruiting procedures discriminated on the basis of race against black applicants by . . . a written personnel test which excluded a disproportionately high number of Negro applicants. . . . Respondents then filed a motion for partial summary judgment with respect to the recruiting phase of the case, seeking a declaration that the test administered to those applying to become police officers is "unlawfully discriminatory and thereby in violation of the due process clause of the Fifth Amendment." . . . The District of Columbia defendants, petitioners here, and the federal parties also filed motions for summary judgment. . . . The District Court granted petitioners' and denied respondents' motions.

According to the findings and conclusions of the District Court, to be accepted by the Department and to enter an intensive 17-week training program, the police recruit was required to satisfy certain physical and character standards, to be a high school graduate or its equivalent, and to receive a grade of at least 40 out of 80 on "Test 21," which is "an examination that is used generally throughout the federal service," which "was developed by the Civil Service Commission, not the Police Department," and which was "designed to test verbal ability, vocabulary, reading and comprehension."

The validity of Test 21 was the sole issue before the court on the motions for summary judgment. The District Court noted that there was no claim of "an intentional discrimination or purposeful discriminatory acts" but only a claim that Test 21 bore no relationship to job performance and "has a highly discriminatory impact in screening out black candidates." Respondents' evidence, the District Court said, warranted three conclusions: "(a) The number of black police officers, while substantial, is not proportionate to the population mix of the city. (b) A higher percentage of blacks fail the Test than whites. (c) The Test has not been validated to establish its reliability for measuring subsequent job performance." This showing was deemed sufficient to shift the burden of proof to the defendants in the action, petitioners here; but the court nevertheless concluded that on the undisputed facts respondents were not entitled to relief. The District Court relied on several factors. Since August 1969, 44% of new police force recruits had been black; that figure also represented the proportion of blacks on the total force and was roughly equivalent to 20- to 29-year-old blacks in the 50-mile radius in which the recruiting efforts of the Police Department had been concentrated. It was undisputed that the Department had systematically and affirmatively sought to enroll black officers many of whom passed the test but failed to report for duty. The District Court rejected the assertion that Test 21 was culturally slanted to favor whites and was "satisfied that the undisputable facts prove the test to be reasonably and directly related to the requirements of the police recruit training program and that it is neither so designed nor operates [*sic*] to discriminate against otherwise qualified blacks." It was thus not necessary to show that Test 21 was not only a useful indicator of training school performance but had also been validated in terms of job performance — "The lack of job performance validation does not defeat the Test, given its direct relationship to recruiting and the valid part it plays in this process." The District Court ultimately concluded that "[t]he proof is wholly lacking that a police officer qualifies on the color of his skin rather than ability" and that the Department "should not be required on this showing to lower standards or to abandon efforts to achieve excellence."

. . . [R]espondents brought the case to the Court of Appeals claiming that their summary judgment motion, which rested on purely constitutional grounds, should have been granted. The tendered constitutional issue was whether the use of Test 21 invidiously discriminated against Negroes and hence denied them due process of law contrary to the commands of the Fifth Amendment. The Court of Appeals, addressing that issue, announced that it would be guided by *Griggs v. Duke Power Co.* (1971), a case involving the interpretation and application of Title VII of the Civil Rights Act of 1964, and held that the statutory standards elucidated in that case were to govern the due process question tendered in this one. The court went on to declare that lack of discriminatory intent in designing and administering Test 21 was irrelevant; the critical fact was rather that a far greater proportion of blacks — four times as many — failed the test than did whites. This disproportionate impact, standing alone and without regard to whether it indicated a discriminatory purpose, was held sufficient to establish a constitutional violation, absent proof by petitioners that the test was an adequate measure of job performance in addition to being an indicator of probable success in the training program, a burden which the court ruled petitioners had failed to discharge. That the Department had made substantial efforts to recruit blacks was held beside the point and the fact that the racial distribution of recent hirings and of the Department itself might be roughly equivalent to the racial makeup of the surrounding community, broadly conceived, was put aside as a "comparison [not] material to this appeal." . . .

II

Because the Court of Appeals erroneously applied the legal standards applicable to Title VII cases in resolving the constitutional issue before it, we reverse its judgment in respondents' favor. . . .

As the Court of Appeals understood Title VII, employees or applicants proceeding under it need not concern themselves with the employer's possibly discriminatory purpose but instead may focus solely on the racially differential impact of the challenged hiring or promotion practices. This is not the constitutional rule. We have never held that the constitutional standard for adjudicating claims of invidious racial discrimination is identical to the standards applicable under Title VII, and we decline to do so today.

The central purpose of the Equal Protection Clause of the Fourteenth Amendment is the prevention of official conduct discriminating on the basis of race. It is also true that the Due Process Clause of the Fifth Amendment contains an equal protection component prohibiting the United States from invidiously discriminating between individuals or groups. *Bolling v. Sharpe* (1954). But our cases have not embraced the proposition that a law or other official act, without regard to whether it reflects a racially discriminatory purpose, is unconstitutional *solely* because it has a racially disproportionate impact.

Almost 100 years ago, *Strauder v. West Virginia* (1880) established that the exclusion of Negroes from grand and petit juries in criminal proceedings violated the Equal Protection Clause, but the fact that a particular jury or a series of juries does not statistically reflect the racial composition of the community does not in itself make out an invidious discrimination forbidden by the Clause. "A purpose to discriminate must be present which may be proven by systematic exclusion of eligible jurymen of the proscribed race or by unequal application of the law to such an extent as to show intentional discrimination." . . .

The rule is the same in other contexts. *Wright v. Rockefeller* (1964) upheld a New York congressional apportionment statute against claims that district lines had been racially gerrymandered. The challengers did not prevail because they failed to prove that the New York Legislature "was either motivated by racial considerations or in fact drew the districts on racial lines" . . . .

The school desegregation cases have also adhered to the basic equal protection principle that the invidious quality of a law claimed to be racially discriminatory must ultimately be traced to a racially discriminatory purpose. That there are both predominantly black and predominantly white schools in a community is not alone violative of the Equal Protection Clause. The essential element of *de jure* segregation is "a current condition of segregation resulting from intentional state action." . . . The Court has also recently rejected allegations of racial discrimination based solely on the statistically disproportionate racial impact of various provisions of the Social Security Act because "[t]he acceptance of appellants' constitutional theory would render suspect each difference in treatment among the grant classes, however lacking in racial motivation and however otherwise rational the treatment might be."

This is not to say that the necessary discriminatory racial purpose must be express or appear on the face of the statute, or that a law's disproportionate impact is irrelevant in cases involving Constitution-based claims of racial discrimination. . . . It is also clear from the cases dealing with racial discrimination in the selection of juries that the systematic exclusion of Negroes is itself such an "unequal application of the law . . . as to show intentional discrimination." A prima facie case of discriminatory purpose may be proved as well by the absence of Negroes on a particular jury combined with the failure of the jury commissioners to be informed of eligible Negro jurors in a community, or with racially non-neutral selection procedures. With a prima facie case made out, "the burden of proof shifts to the State to rebut the presumption of unconstitutional action by showing that permissible racially neutral selection criteria and procedures have produced the monochromatic result."

Necessarily, an invidious discriminatory purpose may often be inferred from the totality of the relevant facts. . . . It is also not infrequently true that the discriminatory impact — in the jury cases for example, the total or seriously disproportionate exclusion of Negroes from jury venires — may for all practical purposes demonstrate unconstitutionality because in various circumstances the discrimination is very difficult to explain on nonracial grounds. Nevertheless, we have not held that a law, neutral on its face and serving ends otherwise within the power of government to pursue, is invalid under the Equal Protection Clause simply because it may affect a greater proportion of one race than of another. . . .

As an initial matter, we have difficulty understanding how a law establishing a racially neutral qualification for employment is nevertheless racially discriminatory and denies "any person . . . equal protection of the laws" simply because a greater proportion of Negroes fail to qualify than members of other racial or ethnic groups. Had respondents, along with all others who had failed Test 21, whether white or black, brought an action claiming that the test denied each of them equal protection of the laws as compared with those who had passed with high enough scores to qualify them as police recruits, it is most unlikely that their challenge would have been sustained. Test 21, which is administered generally to prospective Government employees, concededly seeks to ascertain whether those who take it have acquired a particular level of verbal skill; and it is untenable that the Constitution prevents the Government from seeking modestly to upgrade the communicative abilities of its employees rather than to be satisfied with some lower level of competence, particularly where the job requires special ability to communicate orally and in writing. Respondents, as Negroes, could no more successfully claim that the test denied them equal protection than could white applicants who also failed. The conclusion would not be different in the face of proof that more Negroes than whites had been disqualified by Test 21. That other Negroes also failed to score well would, alone, not demonstrate that respondents individually were being denied equal protection of the laws by the application of an otherwise valid qualifying test being administered to prospective police recruits.

Nor on the facts of the case before us would the disproportionate impact of Test 21 warrant the conclusion that it is a purposeful device to discriminate against Negroes and hence an infringement of the constitutional rights of respondents as well as other black applicants. As we have said, the test is neutral on its face and rationally may be said to serve a purpose the Government is constitutionally empowered to pursue. Even agreeing with the District Court that the differential racial effect of Test 21 called for further inquiry, we think the District Court correctly held that the affirmative efforts of the Metropolitan Police Department to recruit black officers, the changing racial composition of the recruit classes and of the force in general, and the relationship of the test to the training program negated any inference that the Department discriminated on the basis of race or that "a police officer qualifies on the color of his skin rather than ability."

Under Title VII, Congress provided that when hiring and promotion practices disqualifying substantially disproportionate numbers of blacks are challenged, discriminatory purpose need not be proved, and that it is an insufficient response to demonstrate some rational basis for the challenged practices. It is necessary, in addition, that they be "validated" in terms of job performance in any one of several ways, perhaps by ascertaining the minimum skill, ability, or potential necessary for the position at issue and determining whether the qualifying tests are appropriate for the selection of qualified applicants for the job in question. However this process proceeds, it involves a more probing judicial review of, and less deference to, the seemingly reasonable acts of administrators and executives than is appropriate under the Constitution where special racial impact, without discriminatory purpose, is claimed. We are not disposed to adopt this more rigorous standard for the purposes of applying the Fifth and the Fourteenth Amendments in cases such as this.

A rule that a statute designed to serve neutral ends is nevertheless invalid, absent compelling justification, if in practice it benefits or burdens one race more than another would be far reaching and would raise serious questions about, and perhaps invalidate, a whole range of tax, welfare, public service, regulatory, and licensing statutes that may be more burdensome to the poor and to the average black than to the more affluent white.

Given that rule, such consequences would perhaps be likely to follow. However, in our view, extension of the rule beyond those areas where it is already applicable by reason of statute, such as in the field of public employment, should await legislative prescription.

* * *

III

* * *

The judgment of the Court of Appeals accordingly is reversed.

MR. JUSTICE STEVENS, concurring. [Omitted.]

MR. JUSTICE BRENNAN, with whom MR. JUSTICE MARSHALL joins, dissenting. [Omitted.]

NOTES AND QUESTIONS

1. Under this case, what is the standard required to show unconstitutional racial discrimination? There seems to be a clear finding that a disproportionately high number of African-American applicants failed the written personnel test at issue. The plaintiffs believed that this disproportionate impact was enough to show a violation of the Equal Protection Clause, and the court of appeals apparently agreed. Why did the Supreme Court reject this argument?

2. Note than in its decision of the case the majority departs from the standard under anti-discrimination statutory law (Title VII of the Civil Rights Act of 1964, 42 U.S.C. §§ 2000e to 2000e-17 (1994)), under which the showing of disproportionate impact would be enough to make out a presumption of a violation. The constitutional standard, according to the majority, is stricter, and requires an actual intent to discriminate. While the Court indicates that one must look to the totality of the circumstances, and disproportionate impact is one factor to be examined, given the circumstances of the case at bar, where the test seemed neutral on its face, and where there were efforts made to recruit black officers, the Court determined that there was no intent to discriminate.

3. Why, then, do you suppose a dissenting opinion was filed by Justices Brennan and Marshall? Should intent be the test for a constitutional violation, or should disparate impact be enough? How, by the way, can Congress adopt an impact standard in Title VII if the constitutional standard is based on intent? Can it do so after *City of Boerne v. Flores* (discussed in Chapter 5)?

4. In *Alexander v. Sandoval,* 532 U.S. 275 (2001), the Court used another statutory interpretation case to speculate further about the constitutionality of disparate impact statutes. *Alexander v. Sandoval* involved a class action claim that Alabama's policy of administering driver's license exams only in English violated U.S. Department of Transportation regulations forbidding recipients of federal funds from engaging in practices that have a disproportionate effect on the basis of national origin.

The Court, by a 5-4 majority, per Justice Scalia, concluded that, under Title VI of the Civil Rights Act of 1964, there is no private right of action to claim a disparate impact violation of federal regulations. In reaching this result, the Court largely relied upon established precedent against implying a private cause of action where none is intended by Congress. Justice Scalia noted that Title VI itself has been interpreted by the Court to forbid only intentional discrimination — disparate treatment — but the Department of Transportation regulations at issue went beyond that to ban actions that have only a disproportionate effect.

For reasons of its own, Alabama chose not to raise the constitutionality of reaching disparate impact. Nevertheless, in a footnote, Justice Scalia noted that "[w]e cannot help observing . . . how strange it is to say that disparate-impact regulations" implement Title VI when the statute "permits the very behavior that the regulations forbid."

As *Washington v. Davis* (1976) makes apparent, the Court has treated the difference between disparate treatment (intentional conduct) and disparate impact (unintended consequence) as one of kind, not degree. And the Court has been especially jealous of the Congress expanding or redefining the meaning of constitutional terms. *See, e.g., City of Boerne v. Flores* (1997), where Congress was not allowed to expand the free exercise guarantee. If Congress can't do it, then executive agencies cannot either. This is especially true when executive agencies seek to impose their expansive regulations on the states, who were not forewarned in the acceptance of the federal money, as the Court has required since *Atascadero State Hospital v. Scanlon* (1985).

As these notes explore and the decision in *Arlington Heights* below suggests, however, the difference between intent and impact can be blurred in practice by the assessment of circumstantial evidence, including impact of indirect changes in procedures and the like. Pragmatically, many businesses simply hire by the numbers or settle cases where practices are alleged to have disproportionate impact. Defendants do have the opportunity to rebut disparate impact claims by proving that the challenged practices are justified by some "necessity," but this is often difficult and costly. These defendants are clearly advantaged by the indirect reminder in *Alexander* that intent remains the constitutional standard.

VILLAGE OF ARLINGTON HEIGHTS v. METROPOLITAN HOUSING DEVELOPMENT CORP.
429 U.S. 252 (1977)

MR. JUSTICE POWELL delivered the opinion of the Court.

In 1971 respondent Metropolitan Housing Development Corporation (MHDC) applied to petitioner, the Village of Arlington Heights, Ill., for the rezoning of a 15-acre parcel from single-family to multiple-family classification. Using federal financial assistance, MHDC planned to build 190 clustered townhouse units for low- and moderate-income tenants. The Village denied the rezoning request. MHDC, joined by other plaintiffs who are also respondents here, brought suit in the United States District Court for the Northern District of Illinois. They alleged that the denial was racially discriminatory and that it violated, *inter alia*, the Fourteenth Amendment and the Fair Housing Act of 1968. Following a bench trial, the District Court entered judgment for the Village, and respondents appealed. The Court of Appeals for the Seventh Circuit reversed, finding that the "ultimate effect" of the denial was racially discriminatory, and that the refusal to rezone therefore violated the Fourteenth Amendment. We . . . now reverse.

I

Arlington Heights is a suburb of Chicago, located about 26 miles northwest of the downtown Loop area. Most of the land in Arlington Heights is zoned for detached single-family homes, and this is in fact the prevailing land use. The Village experienced substantial growth during the 1960's, but, like other communities in northwest Cook County, its population of racial minority groups remained quite low. According to the 1970 census, only 27 of the Village's 64,000 residents were black.

The Clerics of St. Viator, a religious order (Order), own an 80-acre parcel just east of the center of Arlington Heights. Part of the site is occupied by the Viatorian high school, and part by the Order's three-story novitiate building, which houses dormitories and a Montessori school. Much of the site, however, remains vacant. Since 1959, when the Village first adopted a zoning ordinance, all the land surrounding the Viatorian property has been zoned R-3, a single family specification with relatively small minimum lot-size requirements. On three sides of the Viatorian land there are single-family homes just across a street; to the east the Viatorian property directly adjoins the backyards of other single-family homes.

The Order decided in 1970 to devote some of its land to low- and moderate-income housing. Investigation revealed that the most expeditious way to build such housing was to work through a nonprofit developer experienced in the use of federal housing subsidies. . . .

MHDC is such a developer. . . .

After some negotiation, MHDC and the Order entered into a 99-year lease and an accompanying agreement of sale covering a 15-acre site in the southeast corner of the Viatorian property. MHDC became the lessee immediately, but the sale agreement was contingent upon MHDC's securing zoning clearances from the Village and . . . housing assistance from the Federal Government. If MHDC proved unsuccessful in securing either, both the lease and the contract of sale would lapse. The agreement established a bargain purchase price of $300,000, low enough to comply with federal limitations governing land-acquisition costs. . . .

MHDC engaged an architect and proceeded with the project, to be known as Lincoln Green. The plans called for 20 two-story buildings with a total of 190 units, each unit having its own private entrance from the outside. One hundred of the units would have a single bedroom, thought likely to attract elderly citizens. The remainder would have two, three, or four bedrooms. A large portion of the site would remain open, with shrubs and trees to screen the homes abutting the property to the east.

The planned development did not conform to the Village's zoning ordinance and could not be built unless Arlington Heights rezoned the parcel to R-5, its multiple-family housing classification. Accordingly, MHDC filed with the Village Plan Commission a petition for rezoning, accompanied by supporting materials describing the development and specifying that it would be subsidized. . . . The materials made clear that one requirement under [federal law] is an affirmative marketing plan designed to assure that a subsidized development is racially integrated. MHDC also submitted studies demonstrating the need for housing of this type and analyzing the probable impact of the development. . . .

During the spring of 1971, the Plan Commission considered the proposal at a series of three public meetings, which drew large crowds. . . . Some of the comments, both from opponents and supporters, addressed what was referred to as the "social issue" — the desirability or undesirability of introducing at this location in Arlington Heights low- and moderate-income housing, housing that would probably be racially integrated.

Many of the opponents, however, focused on the zoning aspects of the petition, stressing two arguments. First, the area always had been zoned single-family, and the neighboring citizens had built or purchased there in reliance on that classification. Rezoning threatened to cause a measurable drop in property value for neighboring sites. Second, the Village's apartment policy, adopted by the Village Board in 1962 and amended in 1970, called for R-5 zoning primarily to serve as a buffer between single-family development and land uses thought incompatible, such as commercial or manufacturing districts. Lincoln Green did not meet this requirement, as it adjoined no commercial or manufacturing district.

At the close of the third meeting, the Plan Commission adopted a motion to recommend to the Village's Board of Trustees that it deny the request. The motion stated: "While the need for low and moderate income housing may exist in Arlington Heights or its environs, the Plan Commission would be derelict in recommending it at the proposed location." Two members voted against the motion and submitted a minority report, stressing that in their view the change to accommodate Lincoln Green represented "good zoning." The Village Board met on September 28, 1971, to consider MHDC's request and the recommendation of the Plan Commission. After a public hearing, the Board denied the rezoning by a 6-1 vote.

The following June MHDC and three Negro individuals filed this lawsuit against the Village, seeking declaratory and injunctive relief. A second nonprofit corporation and an individual of Mexican-American descent intervened as plaintiffs. The trial resulted in a judgment for petitioners. Assuming that MHDC had standing to bring the suit, the District Court held that the petitioners were not motivated by racial discrimination or intent to discriminate against low-income groups when they denied rezoning, but rather by a desire "to protect property values and the integrity of the Village's zoning plan." The District Court concluded also that the denial would not have a racially discriminatory effect.

A divided Court of Appeals reversed. It first approved the District Court's finding that the defendants were motivated by a concern for the integrity of the zoning plan, rather than by racial discrimination. Deciding whether their refusal to rezone would have discriminatory effects was more complex. The court observed that the refusal would have a disproportionate impact on blacks. Based upon family income, blacks constituted 40% of those Chicago area residents who were eligible to become tenants of Lincoln Green, although they composed a far lower percentage of total area population. The court reasoned, however, that under our decision in *James v. Valtierra* (1971), such a disparity in racial impact alone does not call for strict scrutiny of a municipality's decision that prevents the construction of the low-cost housing.

There was another level to the court's analysis of allegedly discriminatory results. Invoking language from *Kennedy Park Homes Assn. v. City of Lackawanna* (2d Cir. 1970), the Court of Appeals ruled that the denial of rezoning must be examined in light of its "historical context and ultimate effect." Northwest Cook County was enjoying rapid growth in employment opportunities and population, but it continued to exhibit a high degree of residential segregation. The court held that Arlington Heights could not simply ignore this problem. Indeed, it found that the Village had been "exploiting" the situation by allowing itself to become a nearly all-white community. The Village had no other current plans for building low- and moderate-income housing, and no other R-5 parcels in the Village were available to MHDC at an economically feasible price.

Against this background, the Court of Appeals ruled that the denial of the Lincoln Green proposal had racially discriminatory effects and could be tolerated only if it served compelling interests. Neither the buffer policy nor the desire to protect property values met this exacting standard. The court therefore concluded that the denial violated the Equal Protection Clause of the Fourteenth Amendment.

II

At the outset, petitioners challenge the respondents' standing to bring the suit. . . .

. . . The essence of the standing question in its constitutional dimension, is "whether the plaintiff has 'alleged such a personal stake in the outcome of the controversy' as to warrant *his* invocation of federal-court jurisdiction and to justify exercise of the court's remedial powers on his behalf." The plaintiff must show that he himself is injured by the challenged action of the defendant. . . .

A

Here there can be little doubt that MHDC meets the constitutional standing requirements. The challenged action of the petitioners stands as an absolute barrier to constructing the housing MHDC had contracted to place on the Viatorian site. If MHDC secures the injunctive relief it seeks, that barrier will be removed. . . .

Petitioners nonetheless appear to argue that MHDC lacks standing because it has suffered no economic injury. MHDC, they point out, is not the owner of the property in question. Its contract of purchase is contingent upon securing rezoning. MHDC owes the owners nothing if rezoning is denied.

We cannot accept petitioners' argument. In the first place, it is inaccurate to say that MHDC suffers no economic injury from a refusal to rezone, despite the contingency provisions in its contract. MHDC has expended thousands of dollars on the plans for Lincoln Green and on the studies submitted to the Village in support of the petition for rezoning. Unless rezoning is granted, many of these plans and studies will be worthless even if MHDC finds another site at an equally attractive price.

Petitioners' argument also misconceives our standing requirements. It has long been clear that economic injury is not the only kind of injury that can support a plaintiff's standing. MHDC is a nonprofit corporation. Its interest in building Lincoln Green stems not from a desire for economic gain, but rather from an interest in making suitable low-cost housing available in areas where such housing is scarce. This is not mere abstract concern about a problem of general interest. The specific project MHDC intends to build, whether or not it will generate profits, provides that "essential dimension of specificity" that informs judicial decisionmaking.

B

Clearly MHDC has met the constitutional requirements, and it therefore has standing to assert its own rights. Foremost among them is MHDC's right to be free of arbitrary or irrational zoning actions. But the heart of this litigation . . . has been the claim that the Village's refusal to rezone discriminates against racial minorities in violation of the Fourteenth Amendment. As a corporation, MHDC has no racial identity and cannot be the direct target of the petitioners' alleged discrimination. In the ordinary case, a party is denied standing to assert the rights of third persons. But we need not decide whether the circumstances of this case would justify departure from that prudential limitation and permit MHDC to assert the constitutional rights of its prospective minority tenants. For we have at least one individual plaintiff who has demonstrated standing to assert these rights as his own.

Respondent Ransom, a Negro, works at the Honeywell factory in Arlington Heights and lives approximately 20 miles away in Evanston in a 5-room house with his mother and his son. The complaint alleged that he seeks and would qualify for the housing MHDC wants to build in Arlington Heights. Ransom testified at trial that if Lincoln Green were built he would probably move there, since it is closer to his job.

The injury Ransom asserts is that his quest for housing nearer his employment has been thwarted by official action that is racially discriminatory. If a court grants the relief he seeks, there is at least a "substantial probability," that the Lincoln Green project will materialize, affording Ransom the housing opportunity he desires in Arlington Heights. His is not a generalized grievance. Instead, . . . it focuses on a particular project and is not dependent on speculation about the possible actions of third parties not before the court. . . . Ransom has adequately averred an "actionable causal relationship" between Arlington Heights' zoning practices and his asserted injury. We therefore proceed to the merits.

III

Our decision last Term in *Washington v. Davis* (1976), made it clear that official action will not be held unconstitutional solely because it results in a racially disproportionate impact. "Disproportionate impact is not irrelevant, but it is not the sole touchstone of an invidious racial discrimination." Proof of racially discriminatory intent or purpose is required to show a violation of the Equal Protection Clause. . . .

Davis does not require a plaintiff to prove that the challenged action rested solely on racially discriminatory purposes. Rarely can it be said that a legislature or administrative body operating under a broad mandate made a decision motivated solely by a single concern, or even that a particular purpose was the "dominant" or "primary" one. In fact, it is because legislators and administrators are properly concerned with balancing numerous competing considerations that courts refrain from reviewing the merits of their decisions, absent a showing of arbitrariness or irrationality. But racial discrimination is not just another competing consideration. When there is a proof that a discriminatory purpose has been a motivating factor in the decision, this judicial deference is no longer justified.

Determining whether invidious discriminatory purpose was a motivating factor demands a sensitive inquiry into such circumstantial and direct evidence of intent as may be available. The impact of the official action — whether it "bears more heavily on one race than another," — may provide an important starting point. Sometimes a clear pattern, unexplainable on grounds other than race, emerges from the effect of the state action even when the governing legislation appears neutral on its face. The evidentiary inquiry is then relatively easy. But such cases are rare. . . .

The historical background of the decision is one evidentiary source, particularly if it reveals a series of official actions taken for invidious purposes. The specific sequence of events leading up to the challenged decision also may shed some light on the decisionmaker's purposes. For example, if the property involved here always had been zoned R-5 but suddenly was changed to R-3 when the town learned of MHDC's plans to erect integrated housing, we would have a far different case. Departures from the normal procedural sequence also might afford evidence that improper purposes are playing a role. Substantive departures too may be relevant, particularly if the factors usually considered important by the decisionmaker strongly favor a decision contrary to the one reached.

The legislative or administrative history may be highly relevant, especially where there are contemporary statements by members of the decisionmaking body, minutes of its meetings, or reports. In some extraordinary instances the members might be called to the stand at trial to testify concerning the purpose of the official action, although even then such testimony frequently will be barred by privilege.

* * *

IV

This case was tried in the District Court and reviewed in the Court of Appeals before our decision in *Washington v. Davis*. The respondents proceeded on the erroneous theory that the Village's refusal to rezone carried a racially discriminatory effect and was, without more, unconstitutional. But both courts below understood that at least part of their function was to examine the purpose underlying the decision. In making its findings on this issue, the District Court noted that some of the opponents of Lincoln Green who spoke at the various hearings might have been motivated by opposition to minority groups. The court held, however, that the evidence "does not warrant the conclusion that this motivated the defendants."

On appeal the Court of Appeals focused primarily on respondents' claim that the Village's buffer policy had not been consistently applied and was being invoked with a strictness here that could only demonstrate some other underlying motive. The court concluded that the buffer policy, though not always applied with perfect consistency, had on several occasions formed the basis for the Board's decision to deny other rezoning proposals. "The evidence does not necessitate a finding that Arlington Heights administered this policy in a discriminatory manner." The Court of Appeals therefore approved the District Court's findings concerning the Village's purposes in denying rezoning to MHDC.

We also have reviewed the evidence. The impact of the Village's decision does arguably bear more heavily on racial minorities. Minorities constitute 18% of the Chicago area population, and 40% of the income groups said to be eligible for Lincoln Green. But there is little about the sequence of events leading up to the decision that would spark suspicion. The area around the Viatorian property has been zoned R-3 since 1959, the year when Arlington Heights first adopted a zoning map. Single-family homes surround the 80-acre site, and the Village is undeniably committed to single-family homes as its dominant residential land use. The rezoning request progressed according to the usual procedures. The Plan Commission even scheduled two additional hearings, at least in part to accommodate MHDC and permit it to supplement its presentation with answers to questions generated at the first hearing.

The statements by the Plan Commission and Village Board members, as reflected in the official minutes, focused almost exclusively on the zoning aspects of the MHDC petition, and the zoning factors on which they relied are not novel criteria in the Village's rezoning decisions. There is no reason to doubt that there has been reliance by some neighboring property owners on the maintenance of single-family zoning in the vicinity. The Village originally adopted its buffer policy long before MHDC entered the picture and has applied the policy too consistently for us to infer discriminatory purpose from its application in this case. Finally, MHDC called one member of the Village Board to the stand at trial. Nothing in her testimony supports an inference of invidious purpose.

In sum, the evidence does not warrant overturning the concurrent findings of both courts below. Respondents simply failed to carry their burden of proving that discriminatory purpose was a motivating factor in the Village's decision. This conclusion ends the constitutional inquiry. The Court of Appeals' further finding that the Village's decision carried a discriminatory "ultimate effect" is without independent constitutional significance.

V

Respondents' complaint also alleged that the refusal to rezone violated the Fair Housing Act, 42 U.S.C. § 3601 *et seq*. They continue to urge here that a zoning decision made by a public body may, and that petitioners' action did, violate § 3604 or § 3617. The Court of Appeals, however, proceeding in a somewhat [unorthodox] fashion, did not decide the statutory question. We remand the case for further consideration of respondents' statutory claims.

Reversed and remanded.

MR. JUSTICE MARSHALL, with whom MR. JUSTICE BRENNAN joins, concurring in part and dissenting in part.

I concur in Parts I-III of the Court's opinion. However, I believe the proper result would be to remand this entire case to the Court of Appeals for further proceedings consistent with *Washington v. Davis* (1976), and today's opinion. The Court of Appeals is better situated than this Court both to reassess the significance of the evidence developed below in light of the standards we have set forth and to determine whether the interests of justice require further District Court proceedings directed toward those standards.

MR. JUSTICE WHITE, dissenting.

The Court reverses the judgment of the Court of Appeals because it finds, after re-examination of the evidence supporting the concurrent findings below, that "[r]espondents . . . failed to carry their burden of proving that discriminatory purpose was a motivating factor in the Village's decision." The Court reaches this result by interpreting our decision in *Washington v. Davis* (1976), and applying it to this case, notwithstanding that the Court of Appeals rendered its decision in this case before *Washington v. Davis* was handed down, and thus did not have the benefit of our decision when it found a Fourteenth Amendment violation.

The Court gives no reason for its failure to follow our usual practice in this situation of vacating the judgment below and remanding in order to permit the lower court to reconsider its ruling in light of our intervening decision. The Court's articulation of a legal standard nowhere mentioned in *Davis* indicates that it feels that the application of *Davis* to these facts calls for substantial analysis. If this is true, we would do better to allow the Court of Appeals to attempt that analysis in the first instance. Given that the Court deems it necessary to re-examine the evidence in the case in light of the legal standard it adopts, a remand is especially appropriate. . . . A further justification for remanding on the constitutional issue is that a remand is required in any event on respondents' Fair Housing Act claim. . . .

Even if I were convinced that it was proper for the Court to reverse the judgment below on the basis of an intervening decision of this Court and after a re-examination of concurrent findings of fact below, I believe it is wholly unnecessary for the Court to embark on a lengthy discussion of the standard for proving the racially discriminatory purpose required by *Davis* for a Fourteenth Amendment violation. The District Court found that the Village was motivated "by a legitimate desire to protect property values and the integrity of the Village's zoning plan." The Court of Appeals accepted this finding as not clearly erroneous, and the Court quite properly refuses to overturn it on review here. There is thus no need for this Court to list various "evidentiary sources" or "subjects of proper inquiry" in determining whether a racially discriminatory purpose existed.

NOTES AND QUESTIONS

1. Once again the issue in the case is the standard for proving racial discrimination which violates the Fourteenth Amendment. We learned from the last case that the issue was the intent of the lawmaker, and, indeed, the Court in *Arlington Heights* follows *Washington v. Davis* in declaring that a racially disproportionate impact is not enough for a constitutional violation.

2. The officers of the village certainly gave no clear indication that their purpose was unconstitutional racial discrimination, but is an express intent to violate the Constitution what is required? What sort of circumstantial evidence would be enough to make out a claim of denial of equal protection? *Arlington Heights* usefully catalogues the ways in which discriminatory purpose may be demonstrated. First, the impact of the law may be so significantly discriminatory that no other explanation is tenable. Second, an unusual history may also demonstrate discrimination. Thus, the Court cites *Griffin v. School Board of*

Prince Edward County, 377 U.S. 218 (1964), in which the closure of public schools following a desegregation order in order to underwrite the attendance of children at private segregated schools manifested the discriminatory purpose. Finally, statements by legislators or administrators may reveal a discriminatory intent.

3. Why did the Court fail to follow the dissenting Justice White's suggestion (in which Justices Marshall and Brennan concurred) of remanding the case for a determination in light of the holding in *Washington v. Davis*?

4. The Court has maintained the requirement of discriminatory intent or purpose in other cases. In *Mobile v. Bolden*, 446 U.S. 55 (1980), the Court refused to invalidate at-large voting in a predominately white town, writing "only if there is purposeful discrimination can there be a violation of the Equal Protection Clause. . . . [T]his principle applies to claims of racial discrimination affecting voting just as it does to other claims of racial discrimination." *Id.* at 67. Similarly, in *McClesky v. Kemp*, 481 U.S. 279 (1987), the Court refused to rely on statistical disparity in the administration of the death penalty to find an equal protection violation.

5. Civil Right or Preference?

We move now to a discussion of the use of racial preference in public decision making. In *City of Richmond v. Croson*, 488 U.S. 469 (1969), the Court, per Justice O'Connor, held that "generalized assertions" of past racial discrimination could not justify a racial set-aside in the award of public contracts. The City Council of Richmond, Virginia, had required that companies doing business with the city subcontract 30 percent of their business to minority business enterprises. While over 50% of the population in Richmond was black, only .67% of the city's prime contracts had been awarded to minority contractors. The City's legal counsel opined that the set-aside would be constitutional since the Supreme Court had previously approved a 10% set-aside in *Fullilove v. Klutznick*, 448 U.S. 448 (1980), in federal contracting. The Supreme Court ruled otherwise when the J.A. Croson Company challenged the program as a "rigid" racial quota. Justice O'Connor's opinion noted that the 30 percent set-aside figure had not been linked with "any injury suffered by anyone." Distinguishing *Fullilove*, the Court noted that Congress had documented widespread discrimination in the construction industry. Moreover, the fact that "Congress may identify and redress the effects of society-wide discrimination does not mean that, *a fortiori*, the States and their political subdivisions are free to decide that such remedies are appropriate." Congress, she noted, has a specific mandate to enforce the Fourteenth Amendment, while the states are constrained by it. At a minimum, the use of a racial preference by a state must be tied to a showing of prior discrimination by the state or its political subdivision and the preference must be narrowly tailored to remedy that prior discrimination, which would necessarily mean employing race-neutral means of greater inclusiveness first. Justice O'Connor left open the possibility that the Constitution would also permit a city to be racially sensitive in its contracting practice to avoid becoming a passive participant in the demonstrable discrimination of others, but here, there simply was no particularized showing of discrimination of any kind. Allowing unrefined claims of past discrimination to serve as the basis for racial quotas would subvert constitutional values. Wrote Justice O'Connor: "The dream of a Nation of equal citizens in a society where race is irrelevant to personal opportunity and achievement would be lost in a mosaic of shifting preferences based on inherently unmeasurable claims of past wrongs."

Justice Marshall, joined by Justices Brennan and Blackmun, dissented, in the following terms:

A

Today, for the first time, a majority of this Court has adopted strict scrutiny as its standard of Equal Protection Clause review of race-conscious remedial measures. . . .

Racial classifications "drawn on the presumption that one race is inferior to another or because they put the weight of government behind racial hatred and separatism" warrant the strictest judicial scrutiny because of the very irrelevance of these rationales. By contrast, racial classifications drawn for the purpose of remedying the effects of discrimination that itself was race based have a highly pertinent basis: the tragic and indelible fact that discrimination against blacks and other racial minorities in this Nation has pervaded our Nation's history and continues to scar our society. As I stated in *Fullilove*: "Because the consideration of race is relevant to remedying the continuing effects of past racial discrimination, and because governmental programs employing racial classifications for remedial purposes can be crafted to avoid stigmatization, . . . such programs should not be subjected to conventional 'strict scrutiny' — scrutiny that is strict in theory, but fatal in fact."

* * *

B

I am also troubled by the majority's assertion that, even if it did not believe generally in strict scrutiny of race-based remedial measures, "the circumstances of this case" require this Court to look upon the Richmond City Council's measure with the strictest scrutiny. The sole such circumstance which the majority cites, however, is the fact that blacks in Richmond are a "dominant racial grou[p]" in the city. In support of this characterization of dominance, the majority observes that "blacks constitute approximately 50% of the population of the city of Richmond" and that "[f]ive of the nine seats on the City Council are held by blacks."

While I agree that the numerical and political supremacy of a given racial group is a factor bearing upon the level of scrutiny to be applied, this Court has never held that numerical inferiority, standing alone, makes a racial group "suspect" and thus entitled to strict scrutiny review. Rather, we have identified *other* "traditional indicia of suspectness": whether a group has been "saddled with such disabilities, or subjected to such a history of purposeful unequal treatment, or relegated to such a position of political powerlessness as to command extraordinary protection from the majoritarian political process."

It cannot seriously be suggested that nonminorities in Richmond have any "history of purposeful unequal treatment." . . .

In my view, the "circumstances of this case," underscore the importance of *not* subjecting to a strict scrutiny straitjacket the increasing number of cities which have recently come under minority leadership and are eager to rectify, or at least prevent the perpetuation of, past racial discrimination. In many cases, these cities will be the ones with the most in the way of prior discrimination to rectify. Richmond's leaders had just witnessed decades of publicly sanctioned racial discrimination in virtually all walks of life — discrimination amply documented in the decisions of the federal judiciary. This history of "purposefully unequal treatment" forced upon minorities, not imposed by them, should raise an inference that minorities in Richmond had much to remedy — and that the 1983 set-aside was undertaken with sincere remedial goals in mind, not "simple racial politics."

* * *

C

Today's decision, finally, is particularly noteworthy for the daunting standard it imposes upon States and localities contemplating the use of race-conscious measures to eradicate the present effects of prior discrimination and prevent its perpetuation. The majority restricts the use of such measures to situations in which a State or locality can put forth "a prima facie case of a constitutional or statutory violation." In so doing, the majority calls into question the validity of the business set-asides which dozens of municipalities across this Nation have adopted on the authority of *Fullilove*.

Notice that Justice O'Connor's majority opinion leaves open the possibility that the Federal government has more freedom than the states to engage in allegedly benign racial discrimination pursuant to Section 5 of the Fourteenth Amendment. This issue was first addressed in *Metro Broadcasting, Inc. v. Federal Communications Commission*, 497 U.S. 547 (1990), in which a badly divided 5-4 Court upheld congressional preferences for minority-owned businesses in broadcast licensing. Writing for the Court, the late Justice Brennan asserted that the federal government somehow was held to a lesser standard of equality than the states in *Richmond v. Croson*. This was an unstable outcome, as the next case reflects.

ADARAND CONSTRUCTORS, INC. v. PENA
515 U.S. 200 (1995)

JUSTICE O'CONNOR announced the judgment of the Court and delivered an opinion with respect to Parts I, II, III-A, III-B, III-D, and IV, which is for the Court except insofar as it might be inconsistent with the views expressed in JUSTICE SCALIA's concurrence, and an opinion with respect to Part III-C in which JUSTICE KENNEDY joins.

Petitioner Adarand Constructors, Inc., claims that the Federal Government's practice of giving general contractors on government projects a financial incentive to hire subcontractors controlled by "socially and economically disadvantaged individuals," and in particular, the Government's use of race-based presumptions in identifying such individuals, violates the equal protection component of the Fifth Amendment's Due Process Clause. . . .

I

In 1989, the Central Federal Lands Highway Division (CFLHD), which is part of the United States Department of Transportation (DOT), awarded the prime contract for a highway construction project in Colorado to Mountain Gravel & Construction Company. Mountain Gravel then solicited bids from subcontractors for the guardrail portion of the contract. Adarand, a Colorado-based highway construction company specializing in guardrail work, submitted the low bid. Gonzales Construction Company also submitted a bid.

The prime contract's terms provide that Mountain Gravel would receive additional compensation if it hired subcontractors certified as small businesses controlled by "socially and economically disadvantaged individuals." Gonzales is certified as such a business; Adarand is not. Mountain Gravel awarded the subcontract to Gonzales, despite Adarand's low bid, and Mountain Gravel's Chief Estimator has submitted an affidavit stating that Mountain Gravel would have accepted Adarand's bid, had it not been for the additional payment it received by hiring Gonzales instead. Federal law requires that a subcontracting clause similar to the one used here must appear in most federal agency contracts, and it also requires the clause to state that "the contractor shall presume that socially and economically disadvantaged individuals include Black Americans, Hispanic Americans, Native Americans, Asian Pacific Americans, and other minorities, or any other individual found to be disadvantaged by the [Small Business] Administration pursuant to section 8(a) of the Small Business Act." Adarand claims that the presumption set forth in that statute discriminates on the basis of race in violation of the Federal Government's Fifth Amendment obligation not to deny anyone equal protection of the laws.

These fairly straightforward facts implicate a complex scheme of federal statutes and regulations, to which we now turn. The Small Business Act declares it to be "the policy of the United States that small business concerns, [and] small business concerns owned and controlled by socially and economically disadvantaged individuals, . . . shall have the maximum practicable opportunity to participate in the performance of contracts let by any Federal agency." The Act defines "socially disadvantaged individuals" as "those who have been subjected to racial or ethnic prejudice or cultural bias because of their identity as a member of a group without regard to their individual qualities," and it defines "economically disadvantaged individuals" as "those socially disadvantaged individuals whose ability to compete in the free enterprise system has been impaired due to diminished capital and credit opportunities as compared to others in the same business area who are not socially disadvantaged."

In furtherance of [its] policy . . . the Act establishes "[t]he Government-wide goal for participation by small business concerns owned and controlled by socially and economically disadvantaged individuals" at "not less than 5 percent of the total value of all prime contract and subcontract awards for each fiscal year." It also requires the head of each Federal agency to set agency-specific goals for participation by businesses controlled by socially and economically disadvantaged individuals.

The Small Business Administration (SBA) has implemented these statutory directives in a variety of ways, two of which are relevant here. One is the "8(a) program," which is available to small businesses controlled by socially and economically disadvantaged individuals as the SBA has defined those terms. The 8(a) program confers a wide range of benefits on participating businesses, one of which is automatic eligibility for subcontractor compensation provisions of the kind at issue in this case. To participate in the 8(a) program, a business must be "small," . . . and it must be 51% owned by individuals who qualify as "socially and economically disadvantaged." The SBA presumes that Black, Hispanic, Asian Pacific, Subcontinent Asian, and Native Americans, as well as "members of other groups designated from time to time by SBA," are "socially disadvantaged." It also allows any individual not a member of a listed group to prove social disadvantage "on the basis of clear and convincing evidence" . . . . Social disadvantage is not enough to establish eligibility, however; SBA also requires each 8(a) program participant to prove "economic disadvantage" . . . .

The other SBA program relevant to this case is the "8(d) subcontracting program," which unlike the 8(a) program is limited to eligibility for subcontracting provisions like the one at issue here. In determining eligibility, the SBA presumes social disadvantage based on membership in certain minority groups, just as in the 8(a) program, and again appears to require an individualized, although "less restrictive," showing of economic disadvantage. A different set of regulations, however, says that members of minority groups wishing to participate in the 8(d) subcontracting program are entitled to a race-based presumption of social *and* economic disadvantage. We are left with some uncertainty as to whether participation in the 8(d) subcontracting program requires an individualized showing of economic disadvantage. In any event, in both the 8(a) and the 8(d) programs, the presumptions of disadvantage are rebuttable if a third party comes forward with evidence suggesting that the participant is not, in fact, either economically or socially disadvantaged.

The contract giving rise to the dispute in this case came about as a result of the Surface Transportation and Uniform Relocation Assistance Act of 1987 ("STURAA"), a DOT appropriations measure. [It] provides that "not less than 10 percent" of the appropriated funds "shall be expended with small business concerns owned and controlled by socially and economically disadvantaged individuals." STURAA adopts the Small Business Act's definition of "socially and economically disadvantaged individual," including the applicable race-based presumptions, and adds that "women shall be presumed to be socially and economically disadvantaged individuals for purposes of this subsection." STURAA also requires the Secretary of Transportation to establish "minimum uniform criteria for State governments to use in certifying whether a concern qualifies for purposes of this subsection." The Secretary has [issued] . . . regulations [which] say that the certifying authority should presume both social and economic disadvantage (i.e., eligibility to participate) if the applicant belongs to certain racial groups, or is a woman. As with the SBA programs, third parties may come forward with evidence in an effort to rebut the presumption of disadvantage for a particular business.

The operative clause in the contract in this case reads as follows:

"*Subcontracting.* This subsection is supplemented to include a Disadvantaged Business Enterprise (DBE) Development and Subcontracting Provision as follows:

"Monetary compensation is offered for awarding subcontracts to small business concerns owned and controlled by socially and economically disadvantaged individuals. . . .

"A small business concern will be considered a DBE after it has been certified as such by the U.S. Small Business Administration or any State Highway Agency. . . . If the Contractor requests payment under this provision, the Contractor shall furnish the engineer with acceptable evidence of the subcontractor(s') DBE certification and shall furnish one certified copy of the executed subcontract(s).

* * *

"The Contractor will be paid an amount computed as follows:

"1. If a subcontract is awarded to one DBE, 10 percent of the final amount of the approved DBE subcontract, not to exceed 1.5 percent of the original contract amount.

"2. If subcontracts are awarded to two or more DBEs, 10 percent of the final amount of the approved DBE subcontracts, not to exceed 2 percent of the original contract amount."

To benefit from this clause, Mountain Gravel had to hire a subcontractor who had been certified as a small disadvantaged business by the SBA, a state highway agency, or some other certifying authority acceptable to the Contracting Officer. . . .

After losing the guardrail subcontract to Gonzales, Adarand filed suit against various federal officials in the United States District Court for the District of Colorado, claiming that the race-based presumptions involved in the use of subcontracting compensation clauses violate Adarand's right to equal protection. The District Court granted the Government's motion for summary judgment. The Court of Appeals for the Tenth Circuit affirmed. It understood our decision in *Fullilove v. Klutznick* (1980), to have adopted "a lenient standard, resembling intermediate scrutiny, in assessing" the constitutionality of federal race-based action. Applying that "lenient standard," as further developed in *Metro Broadcasting, Inc. v. FCC* (1990), the Court of Appeals upheld the use of subcontractor compensation clauses. . . .

* * *

III

[The Government] urge[s] that "[t]he Subcontracting Compensation Clause program is . . . a program based on *disadvantage*, not on race," and thus that it is subject only to "the most relaxed judicial scrutiny." To the extent that the statutes and regulations involved in this case are race neutral, we agree. [The Government] concede[s], however, that "the race-based rebuttable presumption used in some certification determinations under the Subcontracting Compensation Clause" is subject to some heightened level of scrutiny. The parties disagree as to what that level should be. . . .

Adarand's claim arises under the Fifth Amendment to the Constitution, which provides that "No person shall . . . be deprived of life, liberty, or property, without due process of law." Although this Court has always understood that Clause to provide some measure of protection against *arbitrary* treatment by the Federal Government, it is not as explicit a guarantee of *equal* treatment as the Fourteenth Amendment, which provides that "No *State* shall . . . deny to any person within its jurisdiction the equal protection of the laws" (emphasis added). Our cases have accorded varying degrees of significance to the difference in the language of those two Clauses. We think it necessary to revisit the issue here.

A

Through the 1940s, this Court had routinely taken the view in non-race-related cases that, "[u]nlike the Fourteenth Amendment, the Fifth contains no equal protection clause and it provides no guaranty against discriminatory legislation by Congress." When the Court first faced a Fifth Amendment equal protection challenge to a federal racial classification, it adopted a similar approach, with most unfortunate results. In *Hirabayashi v. United States* (1943), the Court considered a curfew applicable only to persons of Japanese ancestry. The Court observed — correctly — that "[d]istinctions between citizens solely because of their ancestry are by their very nature odious to a free people whose institutions are founded upon the doctrine of equality," and that "racial discriminations are in most circumstances irrelevant and therefore prohibited." But it also [held] that the Fifth Amendment "restrains only such discriminatory legislation by Congress as amounts to a denial of due process," and upheld the curfew because "circumstances within the knowledge of those charged with the responsibility for maintaining the national defense afforded a rational basis for the decision which they made."

Eighteen months later, the Court again approved wartime measures directed at persons of Japanese ancestry. *Korematsu v. United States* (1944), concerned an order that completely excluded such persons from particular areas. The Court did not address the view, expressed in cases like *Hirabayashi* . . . that the Federal Government's obligation to provide equal protection differs significantly from that of the States. Instead, it began by noting that "all legal restrictions which curtail the civil rights of a single racial group are immediately suspect . . . [and] courts must subject them to the most rigid scrutiny." . . . But in spite of the "most rigid scrutiny" standard it had just set forth, the Court then inexplicably relied on "the principles we announced in the *Hirabayashi* case," to conclude that, although "exclusion from the area in which one's home is located is a far greater deprivation than constant confinement to the home from 8 p.m. to 6 a.m.," the racially discriminatory order was nonetheless within the Federal Government's power.

In *Bolling v. Sharpe* (1954) [a companion case to *Brown*, forbidding legally-mandated segregation in the District of Columbia's schools], the Court for the first time explicitly questioned the existence of any difference between the obligations of the Federal Government and the States to avoid racial classifications. *Bolling* did note that "[t]he 'equal protection of the laws' is a more explicit safeguard of prohibited unfairness than 'due process of law.'" But *Bolling* then concluded that, "[i]n view of [the] decision that the Constitution prohibits the states from maintaining racially segregated public schools, it would be unthinkable that the same Constitution would impose a lesser duty on the Federal Government."

Bolling's facts concerned school desegregation, but its reasoning was not so limited. . . .

Later cases in contexts other than school desegregation did not distinguish between the duties of the States and the Federal Government to avoid racial classifications. . . .

. . . Thus, in 1975, the Court stated explicitly that "this Court's approach to Fifth Amendment equal protection claims has always been precisely the same as to equal protection claims under the Fourteenth Amendment." We do not understand a few contrary suggestions appearing in cases in which we found special deference to the political branches of the Federal Government to be appropriate to detract from this general rule.

B

. . . In 1978, the Court confronted the question whether race-based governmental action designed to *benefit* such groups [which had previously suffered discrimination] should also be subject to "the most rigid scrutiny." *Regents of Univ. of California v. Bakke* (1978) involved an equal protection challenge to a state-run medical school's practice of reserving a number of spaces in its entering class for minority students. The petitioners argued that "strict scrutiny" should apply only to "classifications that disadvantage 'discrete and insular minorities.'" *Bakke* did not produce an opinion for the Court, but Justice Powell's opinion announcing the Court's judgment rejected the argument. In a passage joined by Justice White, Justice Powell wrote that "[t]he guarantee of equal protection cannot mean one thing when applied to one individual and something else when applied to a person of another color." . . . On the other hand, four Justices in *Bakke* would have applied a less stringent standard of review to racial classifications "designed to further remedial purposes." And four Justices thought the case should be decided on statutory grounds.

Two years after *Bakke*, . . . [i]n *Fullilove v. Klutznick* (1980), the Court upheld Congress' inclusion of a 10% set-aside for minority-owned businesses in the Public Works Employment Act of 1977. As in *Bakke*, there was no opinion for the Court. Chief Justice Burger, in an opinion joined by Justices White and Powell, observed that "[a]ny preference based on racial or ethnic criteria must necessarily receive a most searching examination to make sure that it does not conflict with constitutional guarantees." That opinion, however, "d[id] not adopt, either expressly or implicitly, the formulas of analysis articulated in such cases as [*Bakke*]." It employed instead a two-part test which asked, first, "whether the *objectives* of th[e] legislation are within the power of Congress," and second, "whether the limited use of racial and ethnic criteria, in the context presented, is a constitutionally permissible *means* for achieving the congressional objectives." It then upheld the program under that test, adding at the end of the opinion that the program also "would survive judicial review under either 'test' articulated in the several *Bakke* opinions." Justice Powell wrote separately to express his view that the plurality opinion had essentially applied "strict scrutiny" as described in his *Bakke* opinion. . . . Justice Stewart (joined by then-JUSTICE REHNQUIST) dissented, arguing that the Constitution required the Federal Government to meet the same strict standard as the States when enacting racial classifications, and that the program before the Court failed that standard. JUSTICE STEVENS also dissented, arguing that "[r]acial classifications are simply too pernicious to permit any but the most exact connection between justification and classification," and that the program before the Court could not be characterized "as a 'narrowly tailored' remedial measure." Justice Marshall (joined by Justices Brennan and Blackmun) concurred in the judgment, reiterating the view of four Justices in *Bakke* that any race-based governmental action designed to "remed[y] the present effects of past racial discrimination" should be upheld if it was "substantially related" to the achievement of an "important governmental objective" — *i.e.*, such action should be subjected only to what we now call "intermediate scrutiny."

In *Wygant v. Jackson Board of Ed.* (1986), the Court considered a Fourteenth Amendment challenge to another form of remedial racial classification. The issue in *Wygant* was whether a school board could adopt race-based preferences in determining which teachers to lay off. Justice Powell's plurality opinion observed that "the level of scrutiny does not change merely because the challenged classification operates against a group that historically has not been subject to governmental discrimination," and stated the two-part inquiry as "whether the layoff provision is supported by a compelling state purpose and whether the means chosen to accomplish that purpose are narrowly tailored." In other words, "racial classifications of any sort must be subjected to 'strict scrutiny.'" The plurality then concluded that the school board's interest in "providing minority role models for its minority students, as an attempt to alleviate the effects of societal discrimination," was not a compelling interest that could justify the use of a racial classification. It added that "[s]ocietal discrimination, without more, is too amorphous a basis for imposing a racially classified remedy," and insisted instead that "a public employer . . . must ensure that, before it embarks on an affirmative-action program, it has convincing evidence that remedial action is warranted. That is, it must have sufficient evidence to justify the conclusion that there has been prior discrimination." Justice White concurred only in the judgment, although he agreed that the school board's asserted interests could not, "singly or together, justify this racially discriminatory layoff policy." Four Justices dissented, three of whom again argued for intermediate scrutiny of remedial race-based government action.

The Court's failure to produce a majority opinion in *Bakke*, *Fullilove*, and *Wygant* left unresolved the proper analysis for remedial race-based governmental action. Lower courts found this lack of guidance unsettling.

The Court resolved the issue, at least in part, in . . . *Richmond v. J.A. Croson Co.* (1989) . . . .

With *Croson*, the Court finally agreed that the Fourteenth Amendment requires strict scrutiny of all race-based action by state and local governments. But *Croson* of course had no occasion to declare what standard of review the Fifth Amendment requires for such action taken by the Federal Government. . . .

. . . [T]he Court's cases through *Croson* had established three general propositions with respect to governmental racial classifications. First, skepticism: "'any preference based on racial or ethnic criteria must necessarily receive a most searching examination.'" Second, consistency: "[T]he standard of review under the Equal Protection Clause is not dependent on the race of those burdened or benefitted by a particular classification" . . . . And third, congruence: "Equal protection analysis in the Fifth Amendment area is the same as that under the Fourteenth Amendment." Taken together, these three propositions lead to the conclusion that any person, of whatever race, has the right to demand that any governmental actor subject to the Constitution justify any racial classification subjecting that person to unequal treatment under the strictest judicial scrutiny. . . .

A year later, however, the Court took a surprising turn. *Metro Broadcasting, Inc. v. FCC* [(1990)], involved a Fifth Amendment challenge to two race-based policies of the Federal Communications Commission. In *Metro Broadcasting*, the Court repudiated the long-held notion that "it would be unthinkable that the same Constitution would impose a lesser duty on the Federal Government" than it does on a State to afford equal protection of the laws. It did so by holding that "benign" federal racial classifications need only satisfy intermediate scrutiny, even though *Croson* had recently concluded that such classifications enacted by a State must satisfy strict scrutiny. "[B]enign" federal racial classifications, the Court said, " — even if those measures are not 'remedial' in the sense of being designed to compensate victims of past governmental or societal discrimination — are constitutionally permissible to the extent that they serve *important* governmental objectives within the power of Congress and are *substantially related* to achievement of those objectives." (emphasis added). The Court did not explain how to tell whether a racial classification should be deemed "benign," other than to express "confidence that an 'examination of the legislative scheme and its history' will separate benign measures from other types of racial classifications."

Applying this test, the Court first noted that the FCC policies at issue did not serve as a remedy for past discrimination. Proceeding on the assumption that the policies were nonetheless "benign," it concluded that they served the "important governmental objective" of "enhancing broadcast diversity," and that they were "substantially related" to that objective. It therefore upheld the policies.

By adopting intermediate scrutiny as the standard of review for congressionally mandated "benign" racial classifications, *Metro Broadcasting* departed from prior cases in two significant respects. First, it turned its back on *Croson*'s explanation of why strict scrutiny of all governmental racial classifications is essential:

> "Absent searching judicial inquiry into the justification for such race-based measures, there is simply no way of determining what classifications are 'benign' or 'remedial' and what classifications are in fact motivated by illegitimate notions of racial inferiority or simple racial politics. Indeed, the purpose of strict scrutiny is to 'smoke out' illegitimate uses of race by assuring that the legislative body is pursuing a goal important enough to warrant use of a highly suspect tool. The test also

ensures that the means chosen 'fit' this compelling goal so closely that there is little or no possibility that the motive for the classification was illegitimate racial prejudice or stereotype." (plurality opinion of O'CON-NOR, J.).

We adhere to that view today, despite the surface appeal of holding "benign" racial classifications to a lower standard, because "it may not always be clear that a so-called preference is in fact benign," *Bakke* (opinion of Powell, J.). "[M]ore than good motives should be required when government seeks to allocate its resources by way of an explicit racial classification system."

Second, *Metro Broadcasting* squarely rejected one of the three propositions established by the Court's earlier equal protection cases, namely, congruence between the standards applicable to federal and state racial classifications, and in so doing also undermined the other two — skepticism of all racial classifications and consistency of treatment irrespective of the race of the burdened or benefited group. . . .

The three propositions undermined by *Metro Broadcasting* all derive from the basic principle that the Fifth and Fourteenth Amendments to the Constitution protect *persons*, not *groups*. It follows from that principle that all governmental action based on race — a *group* classification long recognized as "in most circumstances irrelevant and therefore prohibited" — should be subjected to detailed judicial inquiry to ensure that the *personal* right to equal protection of the laws has not been infringed. . . . Accordingly, we hold today that all racial classifications, imposed by whatever federal, state, or local governmental actor, must be analyzed by a reviewing court under strict scrutiny. In other words, such classifications are constitutional only if they are narrowly tailored measures that further compelling governmental interests. To the extent that *Metro Broadcasting* is inconsistent with that holding, it is overruled.

* * *

C

"Although adherence to precedent is not rigidly required in constitutional cases, any departure from the doctrine of *stare decisis* demands special justification." In deciding whether this case presents such justification, we recall Justice Frankfurter's admonition that "*stare decisis* is a principle of policy and not a mechanical formula of adherence to the latest decision, however recent and questionable, when such adherence involves collision with a prior doctrine more embracing in its scope, intrinsically sounder, and verified by experience." Remaining true to an "intrinsically sounder" doctrine established in prior cases better serves the values of *stare decisis* than would following a more recently decided case inconsistent with the decisions that came before it; the latter course would simply compound the recent error and would likely make the unjustified break from previously established doctrine complete. In such a situation, "special justification" exists to depart from the recently decided case.

As we have explained, *Metro Broadcasting* undermined important principles of this Court's equal protection jurisprudence, established in a line of cases stretching back over fifty years. Those principles together stood for an "embracing" and "intrinsically soun[d]" understanding of equal protection "verified by experience," namely, that the Constitution imposes upon federal, state, and local governmental actors the same obligation to respect the personal right to equal protection of the laws. . . .

* * *

It is worth pointing out the difference between the applications of *stare decisis* in this case and in *Planned Parenthood of Southeastern Pa. v. Casey* (1992). *Casey* explained how considerations of *stare decisis* inform the decision whether to overrule a long-established precedent that has become integrated into the fabric of the law. Overruling precedent of that kind naturally may have consequences for "the ideal of the rule of law." In addition, such precedent is likely to have engendered substantial reliance, as was true in *Casey* itself. But in this case, as we have explained, we do not face a precedent of that kind, because *Metro Broadcasting* itself *departed* from our prior cases — and did so quite recently. By refusing to follow *Metro Broadcasting*, then, we do not depart from the fabric of the law; we restore it. . . .

* * *

D

Our action today makes explicit what Justice Powell thought implicit in the *Fullilove* lead opinion: Federal racial classifications, like those of a State, must serve a compelling governmental interest, and must be narrowly tailored to further that interest. Of course, it follows that to the extent (if any) that *Fullilove* held federal racial classifications to be subject to a less rigorous standard, it is no longer controlling. But we need not decide today whether the program upheld in *Fullilove* would survive strict scrutiny as our more recent cases have defined it.

Some have questioned the importance of debating the proper standard of review of race-based legislation. But we agree with JUSTICE STEVENS that, "[b]ecause racial characteristics so seldom provide a relevant basis for disparate treatment, and because classifications based on race are potentially so harmful to the entire body politic, it is especially important that the reasons for any such classification be clearly identified and unquestionably legitimate," and that "[r]acial classifications are simply too pernicious to permit any but the most exact connection between justification and classification." We think that requiring strict scrutiny is the best way to ensure that courts will consistently give racial classifications that kind of detailed examination, both as to ends and as to means. . . .

Finally, we wish to dispel the notion that strict scrutiny is "strict in theory, but fatal in fact." *Fullilove, supra* (Marshall, J., concurring in judgment). The unhappy persistence of both the practice and the lingering effects of racial discrimination against minority groups in this country is an unfortunate reality, and government is not disqualified from acting in response to it. As recently as 1987, for example, every Justice of this Court agreed that the Alabama Department of Public Safety's "pervasive, systematic, and obstinate discriminatory conduct" justified a narrowly tailored race-based remedy. *See United States v. Paradise* (1987). When race-based action is necessary to further a compelling interest, such action is within constitutional constraints if it satisfies the "narrow tailoring" test this Court has set out in previous cases.

IV

Because our decision today alters the playing field in some important respects, we think it best to remand the case to the lower courts for further consideration in light of the principles we have announced. The Court of Appeals, following *Metro Broadcasting* and *Fullilove*, analyzed the case in terms of intermediate scrutiny. It upheld the challenged statutes and regulations because it found them to be "narrowly tailored to achieve [their] *significant governmental purpose* of providing subcontracting opportunities for small disadvantaged business enterprises." (emphasis added). The Court of Appeals did not decide the question whether the interests served by the use of subcontractor compensation clauses are properly described as "compelling." It also did not address the question of narrow tailoring in terms of our strict scrutiny cases, by asking, for example, whether there was "any consideration of the use of race-neutral means to increase minority business participation" in government contracting, *Croson*, or whether the program was appropriately limited such that it "will not last longer than the discriminatory effects it is designed to eliminate," *Fullilove* (Powell, J., concurring).

* * *

Accordingly, the judgment of the Court of Appeals is vacated, and the case is remanded for further proceedings consistent with this opinion.

JUSTICE SCALIA, concurring in part and concurring in the judgment.

I join the opinion of the Court, except Part III-C, and except insofar as it may be inconsistent with the following: In my view, government can never have a "compelling interest" in discriminating on the basis of race in order to "make up" for past racial discrimination in the opposite direction. Individuals who have been wronged by unlawful racial discrimination should be made whole; but under our Constitution there can be no such thing as either a creditor or a debtor race. That concept is alien to the Constitution's focus upon the individual, and its rejection of dispositions based on race, or based on blood, *see* Art. III, § 3 ("[N]o Attainder of Treason shall work Corruption of Blood"); Art. I, § 9, cl. 8 ("No Title of Nobility shall be granted by the United States"). To pursue the concept of racial entitlement — even for the most admirable and benign of purposes — is to reinforce and preserve for future mischief the way of thinking that produced race slavery, race privilege and race hatred. In the eyes of government, we are just one race here. It is American.

* * *

JUSTICE THOMAS, concurring in part and concurring in the judgment.

I agree with the majority's conclusion that strict scrutiny applies to *all* government classifications based on race. I write separately, however, to express my disagreement with the premise underlying JUSTICE STEVENS' and JUSTICE GINSBURG's dissents: that there is a racial paternalism exception to the principle of equal protection. I believe that there is a "moral [and] constitutional equivalence," between laws designed to subjugate a race and those that distribute benefits on the basis of race in order to foster some current notion of equality. Government cannot make us equal; it can only recognize, respect, and protect us as equal before the law.

That these programs may have been motivated, in part, by good intentions cannot provide refuge from the principle that under our Constitution, the government may not make distinctions on the basis of race. As far as the Constitution is concerned, it is irrelevant whether a government's racial classifications are drawn by those who wish to oppress a race or by those who have a sincere desire to help those thought to be disadvantaged. There can be no doubt that the paternalism that appears to lie at the heart of this program is at war with the principle of inherent equality that underlies and infuses our Constitution. *See* Declaration of Independence ("We hold these truths to be self-evident, that all men are created equal, that they are endowed by their Creator with certain unalienable Rights, that among these are Life, Liberty, and the pursuit of Happiness").

These programs not only raise grave constitutional questions, they also undermine the moral basis of the equal protection principle. Purchased at the price of immeasurable human suffering, the equal protection principle reflects our Nation's understanding that such classifications ultimately have a destructive impact on the individual and our society. Unquestionably, "[i]nvidious [racial] discrimination is an engine of oppression." It is also true that "[r]emedial" racial preferences may reflect "a desire to foster equality in society." But there can be no doubt that racial paternalism and its unintended consequences can be as poisonous and pernicious as any other form of discrimination. So-called "benign" discrimination teaches many that because of chronic and apparently immutable handicaps, minorities cannot compete with them without their patronizing indulgence. Inevitably, such programs engender attitudes of superiority or, alternatively, provoke resentment among those who believe that they have been wronged by the government's use of race. These programs stamp minorities with a badge of inferiority and may cause them to develop dependencies or to adopt an attitude that they are "entitled" to preferences. . . .

In my mind, government-sponsored racial discrimination based on benign prejudice is just as noxious as discrimination inspired by malicious prejudice. In each instance, it is racial discrimination, plain and simple.

JUSTICE STEVENS, with whom JUSTICE GINSBURG joins, dissenting.

Instead of deciding this case in accordance with controlling precedent, the Court today delivers a disconcerting lecture about the evils of governmental racial classifications. . . .

* * *

The Court's concept of "consistency" assumes that there is no significant difference between a decision by the majority to impose a special burden on the members of a minority race and a decision by the majority to provide a benefit to certain members of that minority notwithstanding its incidental burden on some members of the majority. In my opinion that assumption is untenable. There is no moral or constitutional equivalence between a policy that is designed to perpetuate a caste system and one that seeks to eradicate racial subordination. Invidious discrimination is an engine of oppression, subjugating a disfavored group to enhance or maintain the power of the majority. Remedial race-based preferences reflect the opposite impulse: a desire to foster equality in society. . . .

* * *

The consistency that the Court espouses would disregard the difference between a "No Trespassing" sign and a welcome mat. It would treat a Dixiecrat Senator's decision to vote against Thurgood Marshall's confirmation in order to keep African Americans off the Supreme Court as on a par with President Johnson's evaluation of his nominee's race as a positive factor. It would equate a law that made black citizens ineligible for military service with a program aimed at recruiting black soldiers. An attempt by the majority to exclude members of a minority race from a regulated market is fundamentally different from a subsidy that enables a relatively small group of newcomers to enter that market. An interest in "consistency" does not justify treating differences as though they were similarities.

The Court's explanation for treating dissimilar race-based decisions as though they were equally objectionable is a supposed inability to differentiate between "invidious" and "benign" discrimination. But the term "affirmative action" is common and well understood. Its presence in everyday parlance shows that people understand the difference between good intentions and bad. . . .

Indeed, our jurisprudence has made the standard to be applied in cases of invidious discrimination turn on whether the discrimination is "intentional," or whether, by contrast, it merely has a discriminatory "effect." *Washington v. Davis* (1976). Surely this distinction is at least as subtle, and at least as difficult to apply, as the usually obvious distinction between a measure intended to benefit members of a particular minority race and a measure intended to burden a minority race. . . .

* * *

Second, *Metro Broadcasting*'s holding rested on more than its application of "intermediate scrutiny." Indeed, I have always believed that, labels notwithstanding, the FCC program we upheld in that case would have satisfied any of our various standards in affirmative-action cases — including the one the majority fashions today. What truly distinguishes *Metro Broadcasting* from our other affirmative-action precedents is the distinctive goal of the federal program in that case. Instead of merely seeking to remedy past discrimination, the FCC program was intended to achieve future benefits in the form of broadcast diversity. Reliance on race as a legitimate means of achieving diversity was first endorsed by Justice Powell in *Regents of Univ. of California v. Bakke* (1978). Later, in *Wygant v. Jackson Board of Ed.* (1986), I also argued that race is not always irrelevant to governmental decisionmaking; in response, JUSTICE O'CONNOR correctly noted that, although the School Board had relied on an interest in providing black teachers to serve as role models for black students, that interest "should not be confused with the very different goal of promoting racial diversity among the faculty." She then added that, because the school board had not relied on an interest in diversity, it was not "necessary to discuss the magnitude of that interest or its applicability in this case."

Thus, prior to *Metro Broadcasting*, the interest in diversity had been mentioned in a few opinions, but it is perfectly clear that the Court had not yet decided whether that interest had sufficient magnitude to justify a racial classification. *Metro Broadcasting*, of course, answered that question in the affirmative. The majority today overrules *Metro Broadcasting* only insofar as it is "inconsistent with [the] holding" that strict scrutiny applies to "benign" racial classifications promulgated by the Federal Government. The proposition that fostering diversity may provide a sufficient interest to justify such a program is *not* inconsistent with the Court's holding today — indeed, the question is not remotely presented in this case — and I do not take the Court's opinion to diminish that aspect of our decision in *Metro Broadcasting*.

* * *

JUSTICE SOUTER, with whom JUSTICE GINSBURG and JUSTICE BREYER join, dissenting.

* * *

As the Court's opinion explains in detail, the scheme in question provides financial incentives to general contractors to hire subcontractors who have been certified as disadvantaged business enterprises on the basis of certain race-based presumptions. These statutes (or the originals, of which the current ones are reenactments) have previously been justified as providing remedies for the continuing effects of past discrimination, *see, e.g., Fullilove,* and the

Government has so defended them in this case. Since petitioner has not claimed the obsolescence of any particular fact on which the *Fullilove* Court upheld the statute, no issue has come up to us that might be resolved in a way that would render *Fullilove* inapposite.

In these circumstances, I agree with JUSTICE STEVENS's conclusion that *stare decisis* compels the application of *Fullilove*. Although *Fullilove* did not reflect doctrinal consistency, its several opinions produced a result on shared grounds that petitioner does not attack: that discrimination in the construction industry had been subject to government acquiescence, with effects that remain and that may be addressed by some preferential treatment falling within the congressional power under § 5 of the Fourteenth Amendment. Once *Fullilove* is applied, as JUSTICE STEVENS points out, it follows that the statutes in question here (which are substantially better tailored to the harm being remedied than the statute endorsed in *Fullilove*) pass muster under Fifth Amendment due process and Fourteenth Amendment equal protection.

* * *

JUSTICE GINSBURG, with whom JUSTICE BREYER joins, dissenting [omitted].

NOTES AND QUESTIONS

1. *Adarand*, if possible, created even more of a stir than did *Richmond v. Croson*. You will remember that *Richmond* suggested, and *Metro Broadcasting* held, that the federal government had more freedom to engage in "benign" racial classifications than did the state governments. Suddenly, in 1995, that was no longer the case, and even very recent federal court precedents were no longer good law. Why? What, if anything, had changed? Was it that the Court in 1995 came to see the validity of Justice O'Connor's reasoning in dissent in *Metro Broadcasting* that "[m]odern equal protection doctrine has recognized only one [sufficient] interest [for employing a racial classification]: remedying the effects of racial discrimination. The interest in increasing diversity of broadcast viewpoints is clearly not a compelling interest." 497 U.S. at 612 (O'Connor, J., dissenting).

Does Justice O'Connor's view now prevail? Has diversity as a rationale, say for racial preference in an educational setting, been ruled off-limits? A decade prior to *Adarand*, a plurality of the Court articulated in *Wygant v. Jackson Bd. of Ed.*, 476 U.S. 267 (1986) (holding that a school board could not use race-based preferences to determine teacher layoffs), that a compelling governmental interest only exists when it seeks to remedy prior discrimination. As Justice Powell wrote for the Court's plurality: "[A] public employer . . . must ensure that, before it embarks on an affirmative-action program, it has convincing evidence that remedial action is warranted. That is, it must have sufficient evidence to justify the conclusion that there has been prior discrimination." *Id.* at 277.

Again, does this mean that racial preference is now off-limits for non-remedial purposes?

In *Adarand*, the Court properly reminds us that because our Nation is still beset by "both the practice and the lingering effects of racial discrimination against minority groups," strict scrutiny is not "'strict in theory, but fatal in fact.'" 515 U.S. at 237 (quoting *Fullilove v. Klutznick*, 448 U.S. 448, 519 (1980) (Marshall, J., concurring in the judgment) (*Fullilove* upheld a federal government set-aside for minority businesses, but its plurality opinion failed to supply a coherent rationale.)). However, does the general recognition of these "lingering effects" allow the transforming of the very constitutional standard of remedying prior discrimination clarified in *Wygant*, *Croson*, and *Adarand*, into a broad undifferentiated claim of advancing diversity?

Answering the question is somewhat complicated, in part, because there remains disagreement among members of the Court on the manner in which prior discrimination is to be proven. Justice Scalia, for example, argues that "government can never have a 'compelling interest' in discriminating on the basis of race in order to 'make up' for past racial discrimination in the opposite direction." 515 U.S. at 239 (Scalia, J., concurring in part and concurring in the judgment). Similarly, Justice Thomas characterizes racial preferences by the government as a type of "paternalism" that is "at war with the principle of inherent equality that underlies and infuses our Constitution." *Id.* at 240 (Thomas, J., concurring in part and concurring in the judgment) (referencing The Declaration of Independence para. 1 (U.S. 1776)). By comparison, Justice O'Connor speculated in *Croson* that a state may act to prevent itself from being used as a "passive participant" in private discrimination. 488 U.S. at 491-92 (plurality opinion of O'Connor, J.).

2. Note Justice Scalia's consistent position that no racial classifications are supportable under the Fourteenth Amendment. Note also the strong opinion by Justice Thomas, the Court's only African-American Justice. What disturbs him about the racial classification at issue, given that the classification was made in order to help African Americans? Justice Thomas was the subject of powerful criticism for his affirmative action constitutional opinions, given that he was supposedly himself the beneficiary of affirmative action. Or was he? Before Thomas assumed the bench, he was one of the most vocal proponents of the notion that natural law ought to be a part of constitutional jurisprudence. Do you see any signs of that in his opinion in this case?

3. What about societal discrimination? Whatever differences remain on the Court concerning the demonstration of prior discrimination (see Note 1 above), a clear majority of the Court subscribes to the belief articulated by the plurality in *Wygant* that "[i]n the absence of particularized findings [of prior discrimination], a court could uphold remedies that are ageless in their reach into the past, and timeless in their ability to affect the future." 476 U.S. at 276 (plurality opinion). Likewise, Justice O'Connor writes: "I agree with the plurality that a governmental agency's interest in remedying 'societal' discrimination, that is, discrimination not traceable to its own actions, cannot be deemed sufficiently compelling to pass constitutional muster under strict scrutiny." *Id.* at 288 (O'Connor, J., concurring in part and concurring in the judgment).

4. So what about racial diversity, then, in say, an educational setting? In *Regents of the University of California v. Bakke*, 438 U.S. 265 (1978), the Court could reach no majority opinion in a case dealing with the reservation of 16 slots in the UC Davis medical school for minority students. Four Justices assumed that racial affirmative action might be reviewed under intermediate scrutiny, a proposition since rejected by the Court, and Justice Powell opined that while the reservation of places was unconstitutional, race could be used by admissions committees as a "factor" to enhance diversity. There is considerable question whether Justice Powell's suggestion remains good law. Justice O'Connor made glancing reference to the Powell's view in *Wygant*, but as one appellate court determined in rejecting the race-based admission policy of the University of Texas law school: "The . . . argument is not persuasive. Justice O'Connor's statement is purely descriptive and [does] not purport to express her approval or disapproval of diversity as a compelling interest." *Hopwood v. Texas*, 78 F.3d 932, 845 n.27, *cert. denied,* 116 S. Ct. 2581 (1996). Duke law professor Walter Dellinger, while serving President Clinton in the Department of Justice, records that the Court has *never* accepted diversity as a constitutionally sufficient justification for racial preference. Office of Legal Counsel Memorandum to General Counsels, Re: *Adarand* at 12 (available on Westlaw at 1995 DLR 125 d33 (June 29, 1995).

5. But can't racial diversity be justified on the same basis as school desegregation? This, too, seems difficult. The discretion federal courts have to integrate student bodies is necessarily linked in *Swann v. Charlotte-Mecklenburg Bd. of Educ.*, 402 U.S. 1 (1971), and other similar cases to a finding of past discrimination or publicly imposed segregation (i.e., a "dual school system"). *See, e.g., Keyes v. School District No. 1, Denver, Colorado*, 413 U.S. 189 (1973) (specifically adhering to the distinction between de jure and de facto discrimination, which mirrors the distinction later drawn by the Court between discrimination by the governmental entity, itself, and societal discrimination). It was only if school authorities failed in their affirmative obligation to eliminate the official and egregious segregation condemned in *Brown v. Board of Education*, 347 U.S. 483 (1954), and following cases, that the equitable authority of district courts could be invoked. 402 U.S. at 15. Even in the face of clearly demonstrated past discrimination, the Court was careful to note in *Swann* that "the constitutional command to desegregate schools does not mean that every school in every community must always reflect the racial composition of the school system as a whole." *Id.* at 24. Undifferentiated claims for the non-remedial use of race in public decisions have unfortunately marred the otherwise admirable effort of federal judges to address the real harms of past discrimination in the school context. *See, e.g., Missouri v. Jenkins*, 515 U.S. 70 (1995) (finding the order of teacher salary increases and similar measures to enhance the "desegregative attractiveness" of the schools to far exceed the scope of the constitutional violation and thus the district court's equitable discretion) ("[W]ithout an interdistrict violation and interdistrict effect, there is no constitutional wrong calling for an interdistrict remedy." 515 U.S. at 87). One writer puts the problem of justifying a diversity claim this way:

> [T]he diversity rationale neatly disposes of pesky questions about when affirmative action will end. Compensatory affirmative action was always advertised as temporary, and the passage of time has created . . . legal . . . problems. The legal problem is that those affirmative action programs that the Court approved as having an adequate factual predicate must also, in order to gain approval, have a self-destruct mechanism. And as the most egregious forms of discrimination are reined in, the likelihood of new court-ordered affirmative action remedies drops precipitously. . . . Since diversity is unrelated to historical wrongs, its rationale . . . applies in *perpetuity*. . . .

RICHARD D. KAHLENBERG, THE REMEDY: CLASS, RACE, AND AFFIRMATIVE ACTION 39-40 (1996) (emphasis added). Justice O'Connor recognized the inherent problem with diversity claims when she wrote in *Croson* for the plurality that "[t]he dissent's watered down version of equal protection review effectively assures that race will always be relevant in American life, and that the 'ultimate goal' of 'eliminat[ing] entirely from government decisionmaking such irrelevant factors as a human being's race' . . . will never be achieved." 488 U.S. at 495 (plurality opinion of O'Connor, J.) (quoting *Wygant*, 476 U.S. at 320 (Stevens, J., dissenting)).

6. Isn't diversity a good way to secure necessary services to underserved areas or populations? This certainly has surface plausibility. However, as Justice Powell found in *Bakke*, there was "virtually no evidence" the preference for minority applicants was "either needed or geared to promote that goal " 438 U.S. at 310. The simple fact is: race as proxy is racial stereotype. "[T]he use of a racial characteristic to establish a presumption that the individual also possesses other, and socially relevant, characteristics, exemplifies, encourages and legitimizes the mode of thought and behavior that underlies most prejudice and bigotry in modern America." Richard A. Posner, *The* DeFunis *Case and the Constitutionality of Preferential Treatment of Racial Minorities,* 1974 SUP. CT. REV. 12 (1974). Are race-neutral and more narrowly tailored programs more effective means of facilitating such objectives? *See* Eugene Volokh, *Race as Proxy, and Religion as Proxy,* 43 UCLA L. REV. 2059, 2064-70 (1996) (arguing that there are better ways). "Social scientists may debate how peoples' thoughts and behavior reflect their background, but the Constitution provides that the government may not allocate benefits or burdens among individuals based on the assumption that race or ethnicity determines how they act or think." *Metro Broadcasting v. Federal Communications Commission,* 497 U.S. at 602 (O'Connor, J., dissenting).

7. Could it be that diversity claims are simply not well addressed by clumsy or anonymous set-aside mechanisms that large public bureaucracies employ, and that diversity would be better pursued voluntarily by private actors in contexts where the effect of race on individual life can be meaningfully considered without subverting the principle of equal justice under law? *See* Douglas W. Kmiec, *The Abolition of Public Racial Preference — An Invitation to Private Racial Sensitivity*, 11 NOTRE DAME J.L. ETHICS & PUB. POL'Y 1 (1997). Diversity can enrich debate and discussion, but it can also aggravate racial division. Professor Robert Alt writes:

> The inevitable conclusion to which this system leads is that if you are not my color, you are not qualified to police me, to represent me, or to judge me; you do not know my experiences, and therefore you lack legitimacy. . . . [I]t is [just] this sort of racial classification and segregation that the Equal Protection Clause and Civil Rights Act [were] intended to prevent, not to foster.

Robert D. Alt, *Toward Equal Protection*, 36 WASHBURN L.J. 179, 189 (1997). Diversity as an abstract concept remains high-sounding, but it may have more troubling implications than first thought. Perhaps the most troubling is that some see diversity as "discarding the aspiration of color blindness in the long run. . . . [T]he . . . advocates of diversity argue that the color-blind ideal was wrong all along. Race does matter, and it always will . . . ." KAHLENBERG, *supra*, at 28. Would the elder Justice Harlan see diversity thus conceived as antithetical to the Constitution? The Court took up the question in the following twin cases involving the University of Michigan's undergraduate and law school admissions programs.

GRUTTER v. BOLLINGER
539 U.S. 306 (2003)

JUSTICE O'CONNOR delivered the opinion of the Court.

This case requires us to decide whether the use of race as a factor in student admissions by the University of Michigan Law School (Law School) is unlawful.

I

A

The Law School ranks among the Nation's top law schools. . . . The Law School sought to ensure that its efforts to achieve student body diversity complied with this Court's most recent ruling on the use of race in university admissions. *See Regents of Univ. of Cal. v. Bakke* (1978). . . .

The hallmark of that policy is its focus on academic ability coupled with a flexible assessment of applicants' talents, experiences, and potential "to contribute to the learning of those around them." The policy requires admissions officials to evaluate each applicant based on all the information available in the file, including a personal statement, letters of recommendation, and an essay describing the ways in which the applicant will contribute to the life and diversity of the Law School. In reviewing an applicant's file, admissions officials must consider the applicant's undergraduate grade point average (GPA) and Law School Admissions Test (LSAT) score because they are important (if imperfect) predictors of academic success in law school. The policy stresses that "no applicant should be admitted unless we expect that applicant to do well enough to graduate with no serious academic problems."

. . . The policy requires admissions officials to look beyond grades and test scores to other criteria that are important to the Law School's educational objectives. So-called "'soft' variables" such as "the enthusiasm of recommenders, the quality of the undergraduate institution, the quality of the applicant's essay, and the areas and difficulty of undergraduate course selection" are all brought to bear in assessing an "applicant's likely contributions to the intellectual and social life of the institution."

. . . The policy does not restrict the types of diversity contributions eligible for "substantial weight" in the admissions process, but instead recognizes "many possible bases for diversity admissions." The policy does, however, reaffirm the Law School's longstanding commitment to "one particular type of diversity," that is, "racial and ethnic diversity with special reference to the inclusion of students from groups which have been historically discriminated against, like African-Americans, Hispanics and Native Americans, who without this commitment might not be represented in our student body in meaningful numbers." By enrolling a "'critical mass' of [underrepresented] minority students," the Law School seeks to "ensur[e] their ability to make unique contributions to the character of the Law School."

The policy does not define diversity "solely in terms of racial and ethnic status." Nor is the policy "insensitive to the competition among all students for admission to the [L]aw [S]chool." Rather, the policy seeks to guide admissions officers in "producing classes both diverse and academically outstanding, classes made up of students who promise to continue the tradition of outstanding contribution by Michigan Graduates to the legal profession."

B

Petitioner Barbara Grutter is a white Michigan resident who applied to the Law School in 1996 with a 3.8 grade point average and 161 LSAT score. The Law School initially placed petitioner on a waiting list, but subsequently rejected her application. . . . .

Petitioner further alleged that her application was rejected because the Law School uses race as a "predominant" factor, giving applicants who belong to certain minority groups "a significantly greater chance of admission than students with similar credentials from disfavored racial groups." Petitioner also alleged that respondents "had no compelling interest to justify their use of race in the admissions process." Petitioner requested compensatory and punitive damages, an order requiring the Law School to offer her admission, and an injunction prohibiting the Law School from continuing to discriminate on the basis of race.

* * *

During the 15-day bench trial, the parties introduced extensive evidence concerning the Law School's use of race in the admissions process. Dennis Shields, Director of Admissions when petitioner applied to the Law School, testified that he did not direct his staff to admit a particular percentage or number of minority students, but rather to consider an applicant's race along with all other factors.

* * *

[Petitioner's expert, Dr. Kinley Larntz] concluded that membership in certain minority groups "'is an extremely strong factor in the decision for acceptance,'" and that applicants from these minority groups "'are given an extremely large allowance for admission'" as compared to applicants who are members of non-favored groups. Dr. Larntz conceded, however, that race is not the predominant factor in the Law School's admissions calculus.

* * *

In the end, the District Court concluded that the Law School's use of race as a factor in admissions decisions was unlawful. Applying strict scrutiny, the District Court determined that the Law School's asserted interest in assembling a diverse student body was not compelling because "the attainment of a racially diverse class . . . was not recognized as such by *Bakke* and is not a remedy for past discrimination." . . .

Sitting en banc, the Court of Appeals reversed. . . . Four dissenting judges would have held the Law School's use of race unconstitutional. . . .

* * *

II

A

Since this Court's splintered decision in *Bakke,* Justice Powell's opinion announcing the judgment of the Court has served as the touchstone for constitutional analysis of race-conscious admissions policies. . . .

Justice Powell began by stating that "[t]he guarantee of equal protection cannot mean one thing when applied to one individual and something else when applied to a person of another color. . . ." First, Justice Powell rejected an interest in "'reducing the historic deficit of traditionally disfavored minorities in medical schools and in the medical profession'" as an unlawful interest in racial balancing. Second, Justice Powell rejected an interest in remedying societal discrimination because such measures would risk placing unnecessary burdens on innocent third parties "who bear no responsibility for whatever harm the beneficiaries of the special admissions program are thought to have suffered." Third, Justice Powell rejected an interest in "increasing the number of physicians who will practice in communities currently underserved," concluding that even if such an interest could be compelling in some circumstances the program under review was not "geared to promote that goal."

Justice Powell approved the university's use of race to further only one interest: "the attainment of a diverse student body." With the important proviso that "constitutional limitations protecting individual rights may not be disregarded," Justice Powell grounded his analysis in the academic freedom that "long has been viewed as a special concern of the First Amendment." . . .

Justice Powell was, however, careful to emphasize that in his view race "is only one element in a range of factors a university properly may consider in attaining the goal of a heterogeneous student body." For Justice Powell, "[i]t is not an interest in simple ethnic diversity, in which a specified percentage of the student body is in effect guaranteed to be members of selected ethnic groups," that can justify the use of race. Rather, "[t]he diversity that furthers a compelling state interest encompasses a far broader array of qualifications and characteristics of which racial or ethnic origin is but a single though important element."

* * *

For the reasons set out below, today we endorse Justice Powell's view that student body diversity is a compelling state interest that can justify the use of race in university admissions.

B

The Equal Protection Clause provides that no State shall "deny to any person within its jurisdiction the equal protection of the laws." U.S. Const., Amdt. 14, § 2. Because the Fourteenth Amendment "protect[s] *persons,* not *groups,*" all "governmental action based on race — a *group* classification long recognized as in most circumstances irrelevant and therefore prohibited — should be subjected to detailed judicial inquiry to ensure that the *personal* right to equal protection of the laws has not been infringed." . . .

We have held that all racial classifications imposed by government "must be analyzed by a reviewing court under strict scrutiny." This means that such classifications are constitutional only if they are narrowly tailored to further compelling governmental interests. "Absent searching judicial inquiry into the justification for such race-based measures," we have no way to determine what "classifications are 'benign' or 'remedial' and what classifications are in fact motivated by illegitimate notions of racial inferiority or simple racial politics." . . .

Strict scrutiny is not "strict in theory, but fatal in fact." Although all governmental uses of race are subject to strict scrutiny, not all are invalidated by it. . . .

Context matters when reviewing race-based governmental action under the Equal Protection Clause. . . .

III

A

With these principles in mind, we turn to the question whether the Law School's use of race is justified by a compelling state interest. Before this Court, as they have throughout this litigation, respondents assert only one justification for their use of race in the admissions process: obtaining "the educational benefits that flow from a diverse student body." . . .

* * *

The Law School's educational judgment that such diversity is essential to its educational mission is one to which we defer. . . .

We have long recognized that, given the important purpose of public education and the expansive freedoms of speech and thought associated with the university environment, universities occupy a special niche in our constitutional tradition. . . .

As part of its goal of "assembling a class that is both exceptionally academically qualified and broadly diverse," the Law School seeks to "enroll a 'critical mass' of minority students." The Law School's interest is not simply "to assure within its student body some specified percentage of a particular group merely because of its race or ethnic origin." That would amount to outright racial balancing, which is patently unconstitutional. *Freeman v. Pitts* (1992) ("Racial balance is not to be achieved for its own sake"). Rather, the Law School's concept of critical mass is defined by reference to the educational benefits that diversity is designed to produce.

These benefits are substantial. As the District Court emphasized, the Law School's admissions policy promotes "cross-racial understanding," helps to break down racial stereotypes, and "enables [students] to better understand persons of different races." These benefits are "important and laudable," because "classroom discussion is livelier, more spirited, and simply more enlightening and interesting" when the students have "the greatest possible variety of backgrounds."

The Law School's claim of a compelling interest is further bolstered by its *amici*, who point to the educational benefits that flow from student body diversity. In addition to the expert studies and reports entered into evidence at trial, numerous studies show that student body diversity promotes learning outcomes, and "better prepares students for an increasingly diverse workforce and society, and better prepares them as professionals." . . .

These benefits are not theoretical but real, as major American businesses have made clear that the skills needed in today's increasingly global marketplace can only be developed through exposure to widely diverse people, cultures, ideas, and viewpoints. . . . To fulfill its mission, the military "must be selective in admissions for training and education for the officer corps, *and* it must train and educate a highly qualified, racially diverse officer corps in a racially diverse setting." We agree that "[i]t requires only a small step from this analysis to conclude that our country's other most selective institutions must remain both diverse and selective."

* * *

Moreover, universities, and in particular, law schools, represent the training ground for a large number of our Nation's leaders. . . . A handful of these schools accounts for 25 of the 100 United States Senators, 74 United States Courts of Appeals judges, and nearly 200 of the more than 600 United States District Court judges.

* * *

The Law School does not premise its need for critical mass on "any belief that minority students always (or even consistently) express some characteristic minority viewpoint on any issue." To the contrary, diminishing the force of such stereotypes is both a crucial part of the Law School's mission, and one that it cannot accomplish with only token numbers of minority students. Just as growing up in a particular region or having particular professional experiences is likely to affect an individual's views, so too is one's own, unique experience of being a racial minority in a society, like our own, in which race unfortunately still matters. The Law School has determined, based on its experience and expertise, that a "critical mass" of underrepresented minorities is necessary to further its compelling interest in securing the educational benefits of a diverse student body.

B

Even in the limited circumstance when drawing racial distinctions is permissible to further a compelling state interest, government is still "constrained in how it may pursue that end: [T]he means chosen to accomplish the [government's] asserted purpose must be specifically and narrowly framed to accomplish that purpose."

* * *

To be narrowly tailored, a race-conscious admissions program cannot use a quota system — it cannot "insulat[e] each category of applicants with certain desired qualifications from competition with all other applicants." Instead, a university may consider race or ethnicity only as a "'plus' in a particular applicant's file," without "insulat[ing] the individual from comparison with all other candidates for the available seats." In other words, an admissions program must be "flexible enough to consider all pertinent elements of diversity in light of the particular qualifications of each applicant, and to place them on the same footing for consideration, although not necessarily according them the same weight."

. . . It follows from this mandate that universities cannot establish quotas for members of certain racial groups or put members of those groups on separate admissions tracks. Nor can universities insulate applicants who belong to certain racial or ethnic groups from the competition for admission. Universities can, however, consider race or ethnicity more flexibly as a "plus" factor in the context of individualized consideration of each and every applicant.

* * *

THE CHIEF JUSTICE believes that the Law School's policy conceals an attempt to achieve racial balancing, and cites admissions data to contend that the Law School discriminates among different groups within the critical mass. (dissenting opinion).

* * *

Here, the Law School engages in a highly individualized, holistic review of each applicant's file, giving serious consideration to all the ways an applicant might contribute to a diverse educational environment. The Law School affords this individualized consideration to applicants of all races. There is no policy, either *de jure* or *de facto,* of automatic acceptance or rejection based on any single "soft" variable. Unlike the program at issue in *Gratz v. Bollinger,* the Law School awards no mechanical, predetermined diversity "bonuses" based on race or ethnicity. . . .

We also find that, like the Harvard plan Justice Powell referenced in *Bakke,* the Law School's race-conscious admissions program adequately ensures that all factors that may contribute to student body diversity are meaningfully considered alongside race in admissions decisions. With respect to the use of race itself, all underrepresented minority students admitted by the Law School have been deemed qualified. . . .

The Law School does not, however, limit in any way the broad range of qualities and experiences that may be considered valuable contributions to student body diversity. To the contrary, the 1992 policy makes clear "[t]here are many possible bases for diversity admissions," and provides examples of admittees who have lived or traveled widely abroad, are fluent in several languages, have overcome personal adversity and family hardship, have exceptional records of extensive community service, and have had successful careers in other fields. The Law School seriously considers each "applicant's promise of making a notable contribution to the class by way of a particular strength, attainment, or characteristic — *e.g.,* an unusual intellectual achievement, employment experience, nonacademic performance, or personal background." All applicants have the opportunity to highlight their own potential diversity contributions through the submission of a personal statement, letters of recommendation, and an essay describing the ways in which the applicant will contribute to the life and diversity of the Law School.

What is more, the Law School actually gives substantial weight to diversity factors besides race. The Law School frequently accepts nonminority applicants with grades and test scores lower than underrepresented minority applicants (and other nonminority applicants) who are rejected. This shows that the Law

School seriously weighs many other diversity factors besides race that can make a real and dispositive difference for nonminority applicants as well. By this flexible approach, the Law School sufficiently takes into account, in practice as well as in theory, a wide variety of characteristics besides race and ethnicity that contribute to a diverse student body. JUSTICE KENNEDY speculates that "race is likely outcome determinative for many members of minority groups" who do not fall within the upper range of LSAT scores and grades. (dissenting opinion). But the same could be said of the Harvard plan discussed approvingly by Justice Powell in *Bakke,* and indeed of any plan that uses race as one of many factors.

Petitioner and the United States argue that the Law School's plan is not narrowly tailored because race-neutral means exist to obtain the educational benefits of student body diversity that the Law School seeks. We disagree. Narrow tailoring does not require exhaustion of every conceivable race-neutral alternative. Nor does it require a university to choose between maintaining a reputation for excellence or fulfilling a commitment to provide educational opportunities to members of all racial groups. . . . Narrow tailoring does, however, require serious, good faith consideration of workable race-neutral alternatives that will achieve the diversity the university seeks.

We agree with the Court of Appeals that the Law School sufficiently considered workable race-neutral alternatives. The District Court took the Law School to task for failing to consider race-neutral alternatives such as "using a lottery system" or "decreasing the emphasis for all applicants on undergraduate GPA and LSAT scores." But these alternatives would require a dramatic sacrifice of diversity, the academic quality of all admitted students, or both.

The Law School's current admissions program considers race as one factor among many, in an effort to assemble a student body that is diverse in ways broader than race. Because a lottery would make that kind of nuanced judgment impossible, it would effectively sacrifice all other educational values, not to mention every other kind of diversity. So too with the suggestion that the Law School simply lower admissions standards for all students, a drastic remedy that would require the Law School to become a much different institution and sacrifice a vital component of its educational mission. The United States advocates "percentage plans," recently adopted by public undergraduate institutions in Texas, Florida, and California to guarantee admission to all students above a certain class rank threshold in every high school in the State. The United States does not, however, explain how such plans could work for graduate and professional schools. Moreover, even assuming such plans are race-neutral, they may preclude the university from conducting the individualized assessments necessary to assemble a student body that is not just racially diverse, but diverse along all the qualities valued by the university. We are satisfied that the Law School adequately considered race-neutral alternatives currently capable of producing a critical mass without forcing the Law School to abandon the academic selectivity that is the cornerstone of its educational mission.

We acknowledge that "there are serious problems of justice connected with the idea of preference itself." Narrow tailoring, therefore, requires that a race-conscious admissions program not unduly harm members of any racial group. Even remedial race-based governmental action generally "remains subject to continuing oversight to assure that it will work the least harm possible to other innocent persons competing for the benefit." To be narrowly tailored, a race-conscious admissions program must not "unduly burden individuals who are not members of the favored racial and ethnic groups."

We are satisfied that the Law School's admissions program does not. Because the Law School considers "all pertinent elements of diversity," it can (and does) select nonminority applicants who have greater potential to enhance student body diversity over underrepresented minority applicants.

* * *

We are mindful, however, that "[a] core purpose of the Fourteenth Amendment was to do away with all governmentally imposed discrimination based on race." Accordingly, race-conscious admissions policies must be limited in time. This requirement reflects that racial classifications, however compelling their goals, are potentially so dangerous that they may be employed no more broadly than the interest demands. Enshrining a permanent justification for racial preferences would offend this fundamental equal protection principle. We see no reason to exempt race-conscious admissions programs from the requirement that all governmental use of race must have a logical end point. The Law School, too, concedes that all "race-conscious programs must have reasonable durational limits."

In the context of higher education, the durational requirement can be met by sunset provisions in race-conscious admissions policies and periodic reviews to determine whether racial preferences are still necessary to achieve student body diversity. Universities in California, Florida, and Washington State, where racial preferences in admissions are prohibited by state law, are currently engaged in experimenting with a wide variety of alternative approaches. . . .

* * *

It has been 25 years since Justice Powell first approved the use of race to further an interest in student body diversity in the context of public higher education. Since that time, the number of minority applicants with high grades and test scores has indeed increased. We expect that 25 years from now, the use of racial preferences will no longer be necessary to further the interest approved today.

IV

In summary, the Equal Protection Clause does not prohibit the Law School's narrowly tailored use of race in admissions decisions to further a compelling interest in obtaining the educational benefits that flow from a diverse student body. . . .

It is so ordered.

JUSTICE GINSBURG, with whom JUSTICE BREYER joins, concurring.

* * *

However strong the public's desire for improved education systems may be, it remains the current reality that many minority students encounter markedly inadequate and unequal educational opportunities. Despite these inequalities, some minority students are able to meet the high threshold requirements set for admission to the country's finest undergraduate and graduate educational institutions. As lower school education in minority communities improves, an increase in the number of such students may be anticipated. From today's vantage point, one may hope, but not firmly forecast, that over the next generation's span, progress toward nondiscrimination and genuinely equal opportunity will make it safe to sunset affirmative action.

* * *

CHIEF JUSTICE REHNQUIST, with whom JUSTICE SCALIA, JUSTICE KENNEDY, and JUSTICE THOMAS join, dissenting.

. . . I do not believe that the University of Michigan Law School's (Law School) means are narrowly tailored to the interest it asserts. The Law School claims it must take the steps it does to achieve a "'critical mass'" of underrepresented minority students. But its actual program bears no relation to this asserted goal. Stripped of its "critical mass" veil, the Law School's program is revealed as a naked effort to achieve racial balancing.

* * *

Before the Court's decision today, we consistently applied the same strict scrutiny analysis regardless of the government's purported reason for using race and regardless of the setting in which race was being used. We rejected calls to use more lenient review in the face of claims that race was being used in "good faith" because "'[m]ore than good motives should be required when government seeks to allocate its resources by way of an explicit racial classification system.'" . . .

Although the Court recites the language of our strict scrutiny analysis, its application of that review is unprecedented in its deference.

* * *

In practice, the Law School's program bears little or no relation to its asserted goal of achieving "critical mass." Respondents explain that the Law School seeks to accumulate a "critical mass" of *each* underrepresented minority group.

But the record demonstrates that the Law School's admissions practices with respect to these groups differ dramatically and cannot be defended under any consistent use of the term "critical mass."

From 1995 through 2000, the Law School admitted between 1,130 and 1,310 students. Of those, between 13 and 19 were Native American, between 91 and 108 were African Americans, and between 47 and 56 were Hispanic. If the Law School is admitting between 91 and 108 African Americans in order to achieve "critical mass," thereby preventing African American students from feeling "isolated or like spokespersons for their race," one would think that a number of the same order of magnitude would be necessary to accomplish the same purpose for Hispanics and Native Americans. Similarly, even if all of the Native American applicants admitted in a given year matriculate, which the record demonstrates is not at all the case, how can this possibly constitute a "critical mass" of Native Americans in a class of over 350 students? In order for this pattern of admission to be consistent with the Law School's explanation of "critical mass," one would have to believe that the objectives of "critical mass" offered by respondents are achieved with only half the number of Hispanics and one sixth the number of Native Americans as compared to African Americans. But respondents offer no race specific reasons for such disparities. Instead, they simply emphasize the importance of achieving "critical mass," without any explanation of why that concept is applied differently among the three underrepresented minority groups.

These different numbers, moreover, come only as a result of substantially different treatment among the three underrepresented minority groups, as is apparent in an example offered by the Law School and highlighted by the Court: The school asserts that it "frequently accepts nonminority applicants with grades and test scores lower than underrepresented minority applicants (and other nonminority applicants) who are rejected." Specifically, the Law School states that "[s]ixty-nine minority applicants were rejected between 1995 and 2000 with at least a 3.5 [Grade Point Average (GPA)] and a [score of] 159 or higher on the [Law School Admissions Test (LSAT)]" while a number of Caucasian and Asian American applicants with similar or lower scores were admitted.

Review of the record reveals only 67 such individuals. Of these 67 individuals, *56* were Hispanic, while only 6 were African American, and only 5 were Native American. This discrepancy reflects a consistent practice. For example, in 2000, 12 Hispanics who scored between a 159-160 on the LSAT and earned a GPA of 3.00 or higher applied for admission and only 2 were admitted. Meanwhile, 12 African Americans in the same range of qualifications applied for admission and all 12 were admitted. Likewise, that same year, 16 Hispanics who scored between a 151-153 on the LSAT and earned a 3.00 or higher applied for admission and only 1 of those applicants was admitted. Twenty-three similarly qualified African Americans applied for admission and 14 were admitted.

These statistics have a significant bearing on petitioner's case. Respondents have *never* offered any race specific arguments explaining why significantly more individuals from one underrepresented minority group are needed in order to achieve "critical mass" or further student body diversity. They certainly have not explained why Hispanics, who they have said are among "the groups most isolated by racial barriers in our country," should have their admission capped out in this manner. The Law School's disparate admissions practices with respect to these minority groups demonstrate that its alleged goal of "critical mass" is simply a sham. . . . Surely strict scrutiny cannot permit these sort of disparities without at least some explanation.

Only when the "critical mass" label is discarded does a likely explanation for these numbers emerge. The Court states that the Law School's goal of attaining a "critical mass" of underrepresented minority students is not an interest in merely "'assur[ing] within its student body some specified percentage of a particular group merely because of its race or ethnic origin.'" The Court recognizes that such an interest "would amount to outright racial balancing, which is patently unconstitutional." . . .

But the correlation between the percentage of the Law School's pool of applicants who are members of the three minority groups and the percentage of the admitted applicants who are members of these same groups is far too precise to be dismissed as merely the result of the school paying "some attention to [the] numbers."

* * *

For example, in 1995, when 9.7% of the applicant pool was African American, 9.4% of the admitted class was African American. By 2000, only 7.5% of the applicant pool was African American, and 7.3% of the admitted class was African American. This correlation is striking. . . . The tight correlation between the percentage of applicants and admittees of a given race, therefore, must result from careful race based planning by the Law School. It suggests a formula for admission based on the aspirational assumption that all applicants are equally qualified academically, and therefore that the proportion of each group admitted should be the same as the proportion of that group in the applicant pool.

Not only do respondents fail to explain this phenomenon, they attempt to obscure it. ("The Law School's minority enrollment percentages . . . diverged from the percentages in the applicant pool by as much as 17.7% from 1995-2000"). But the divergence between the percentages of underrepresented minorities in the applicant pool and in the *enrolled* classes is not the only relevant comparison. In fact, it may not be the most relevant comparison. The Law School cannot precisely control which of its admitted applicants decide to attend the university. But it can and, as the numbers demonstrate, clearly does employ racial preferences in extending offers of admission. Indeed, the ostensibly flexible nature of the Law School's admissions program that the Court finds appealing, appears to be, in practice, a carefully managed program designed to ensure proportionate representation of applicants from selected minority groups.

I do not believe that the Constitution gives the Law School such free rein in the use of race. The Law School has offered no explanation for its actual admissions practices and, unexplained, we are bound to conclude that the Law School has managed its admissions program, not to achieve a "critical mass," but to extend offers of admission to members of selected minority groups in proportion to their statistical representation in the applicant pool. But this is precisely the type of racial balancing that the Court itself calls "patently unconstitutional."

Finally, I believe that the Law School's program fails strict scrutiny because it is devoid of any reasonably precise time limit on the Law School's use of race in admissions. . . . The Court suggests a possible 25-year limitation on the Law School's current program. . . . The Court, in an unprecedented display of deference under our strict scrutiny analysis, upholds the Law School's program despite its obvious flaws. We have said that when it comes to the use of race, the connection between the ends and the means used to attain them must be precise. But here the flaw is deeper than that; it is not merely a question of "fit" between ends and means. Here the means actually used are forbidden by the Equal Protection Clause of the Constitution.

JUSTICE KENNEDY, dissenting [omitted].

JUSTICE SCALIA, with whom JUSTICE THOMAS joins, concurring in part and dissenting in part.

I join the opinion of THE CHIEF JUSTICE. As he demonstrates, the University of Michigan Law School's mystical "critical mass" justification for its discrimination by race challenges even the most gullible mind. The admissions statistics show it to be a sham to cover a scheme of racially proportionate admissions.

I also join Parts I through VII of JUSTICE THOMAS's opinion. I find particularly unanswerable his central point: that the allegedly "compelling state interest" at issue here is not the incremental "educational benefit" that emanates from the fabled "critical mass" of minority students, but rather Michigan's interest in maintaining a "prestige" law school whose normal admissions standards disproportionately exclude blacks and other minorities. If that is a compelling state interest, everything is.

I add the following: The "educational benefit" that the University of Michigan seeks to achieve by racial discrimination consists, according to the Court, of "'cross-racial understanding,'" and "'better prepar[ation of] students for an increasingly diverse workforce and society,'" all of which is necessary not only for work, but also for good "citizenship." This is not, of course, an "educational benefit" on which students will be graded on their Law School transcript (Works and Plays Well with Others: B+) or tested by the bar examiners (Q: Describe in 500 words or less your cross-racial understanding). For it is a lesson of life rather than law — essentially the same lesson taught to (or rather learned by, for it cannot be "taught" in the usual sense) people three feet shorter and twenty years younger than the full-grown adults at the University of Michigan Law School, in institutions ranging from Boy Scout troops to public-school kindergartens. If properly considered an "educational benefit" at all, it is surely not one that is either uniquely relevant to law school or uniquely "teachable" in a formal educational setting. *And therefore:* If it is appropriate for the University of Michigan Law School to use racial discrimination for the purpose of putting together a "critical mass" that will convey generic lessons in socialization and good citizenship, surely it is no less appropriate — indeed, *particularly* appropriate — for the civil service system of the State of Michigan to do so. There, also, those exposed to "critical masses" of certain races will presumably become better Americans, better Michiganders, better civil servants. And surely private employers cannot be criticized — indeed, should be praised — if they also "teach" good citizenship to their adult employees through a patriotic, all-American system of racial discrimination in hiring. The nonminority individuals who are deprived of a legal education, a civil service job, or any job at all by reason of their skin color will surely understand.

Unlike a clear constitutional holding that racial preferences in state educational institutions are impermissible, or even a clear anticonstitutional holding that racial preferences in state educational institutions are OK, today's *Grutter-Gratz* split double header seems perversely designed to prolong the controversy and the litigation. [*Gratz v. Bollinger*, 539 U.S. 244 (2003), decided the same day as *Grutter*, was a parallel case involving the University of Michigan's undergraduate affirmative action program, under which applications were rated on a point scale, with 150 points being the maximum. Minority students were given a 20-point bonus. The Court ruled the program unconstitutional. *Gratz* is explored in the Notes following this case. — Eds.] Some future lawsuits will presumably focus on whether the discriminatory scheme in question contains enough evaluation of the applicant "as an individual," and sufficiently avoids "separate admissions tracks" to fall under *Grutter* rather than *Gratz*. Some will focus on whether a university has gone beyond the bounds of a "'good faith effort'" and has so zealously pursued its "critical mass" as to make it an unconstitutional *de facto* quota system, rather than merely "'a permissible goal.'" Other lawsuits may focus on whether, in the particular setting at issue, any educational benefits flow from racial diversity. (That issue was not contested in *Grutter;* and while the opinion accords "a degree of deference to a university's academic decisions," "deference does not imply abandonment or abdication of judicial review.") Still other suits may challenge the bona fides of the institution's expressed commitment to the educational benefits of diversity that immunize the discriminatory scheme in *Grutter.* (Tempting targets, one would suppose, will be those universities that talk the talk of multiculturalism and racial diversity in the courts but walk the walk of tribalism and racial segregation on their campuses — through minority only student organizations, separate minority housing opportunities, separate minority student centers, even separate minority only graduation ceremonies.) And still other suits may claim that the institution's racial preferences have gone below or above the mystical *Grutter*-approved "critical mass." Finally, litigation can be expected on behalf of minority groups intentionally short changed in the institution's composition of its generic minority "critical mass." I do not look forward to any of these cases. The Constitution proscribes government discrimination on the basis of race, and state-provided education is no exception.

JUSTICE THOMAS, with whom JUSTICE SCALIA joins as to Parts I-VII, concurring in part and dissenting in part.

Frederick Douglass, speaking to a group of abolitionists almost 140 years ago, delivered a message lost on today's majority:

> "[I]n regard to the colored people, there is always more that is benevolent, I perceive, than just, manifested towards us. What I ask for the negro is not benevolence, not pity, not sympathy, but simply *justice*. The American people have always been anxious to know what they shall do with us . . . . I have had but one answer from the beginning. Do nothing with us! Your doing with us has already played the mischief with us. Do nothing with us! If the apples will not remain on the tree of their own strength, if they are worm-eaten at the core, if they are early ripe and disposed to fall, let them fall! . . . And if the negro cannot stand on his own legs, let him fall also. All I ask is, give him a chance to stand on his own legs! Let him alone! . . . [Y]our interference is doing him positive injury." What the Black Man Wants: An Address Delivered in Boston, Massachusetts, on 26 January 1865.

Like Douglass, I believe blacks can achieve in every avenue of American life without the meddling of university administrators. Because I wish to see all students succeed whatever their color, I share, in some respect, the sympathies of those who sponsor the type of discrimination advanced by the University of Michigan Law School (Law School). The Constitution does not, however, tolerate institutional devotion to the status quo in admissions policies when such devotion ripens into racial discrimination. Nor does the Constitution countenance the unprecedented deference the Court gives to the Law School, an approach inconsistent with the very concept of "strict scrutiny."

No one would argue that a university could set up a lower general admission standard and then impose heightened requirements only on black applicants. Similarly, a university may not maintain a high admission standard and grant exemptions to favored races. The Law School, of its own choosing, and for its own purposes, maintains an exclusionary admissions system that it knows produces racially disproportionate results. Racial discrimination is not a permissible solution to the self-inflicted wounds of this elitist admissions policy.

The majority upholds the Law School's racial discrimination not by interpreting the people's Constitution, but by responding to a faddish slogan of the cognoscenti. Nevertheless, I concur in part in the Court's opinion. First, I agree with the Court insofar as its decision, which approves of only one racial classification, confirms that further use of race in admissions remains unlawful. Second, I agree with the Court's holding that racial discrimination in higher education admissions will be illegal in 25 years. (stating that racial discrimination will no longer be narrowly tailored, or "necessary to further" a compelling state interest, in 25 years). I respectfully dissent from the remainder of the Court's opinion and the judgment, however, because I believe that the Law School's current use of race violates the Equal Protection Clause and that the Constitution means the same thing today as it will in 300 months.

* * *

IV

The interest in remaining elite and exclusive that the majority thinks so obviously critical requires the use of admissions "standards" that, in turn, create the Law School's "need" to discriminate on the basis of race. The Court validates these admissions standards by concluding that alternatives that would require "a dramatic sacrifice of . . . the academic quality of all admitted students," need not be considered before racial discrimination can be employed. In the majority's view, such methods are not required by the "narrow tailoring" prong of strict scrutiny because that inquiry demands, in this context, that any race-neutral alternative work "'about as well.'" The majority errs, however, because race-neutral alternatives must only be "workable," and do "about as well" *in vindicating the compelling state interest.* The Court never explicitly holds that the Law School's desire to retain the status quo in "academic selectivity" is itself a compelling state interest, and, as I have demonstrated, it is not. Therefore, the Law School should be forced to choose between its classroom aesthetic and its exclusionary admissions system — it cannot have it both ways.

With the adoption of different admissions methods, such as accepting all students who meet minimum qualifications, the Law School could achieve its vision of the racially aesthetic student body without the use of racial discrimination. The Law School concedes this, but the Court holds, implicitly and under the guise of narrow tailoring, that the Law School has a compelling state interest in doing what it wants to do. I cannot agree. First, under strict scrutiny, the Law School's assessment of the benefits of racial discrimination and devotion to the admissions status quo are not entitled to any sort of deference, grounded in the First Amendment or anywhere else. Second, even if its "academic selectivity" must be maintained at all costs along with racial discrimination, the Court ignores the fact that other top law schools have succeeded in meeting their aesthetic demands without racial discrimination.

A

The Court bases its unprecedented deference to the Law School — deference antithetical to strict scrutiny — on an idea of "educational autonomy" grounded in the First Amendment. In my view, there is no basis for a right of public universities to do what would otherwise violate the Equal Protection Clause.

* * *

B

1

The Court's deference to the Law School's conclusion that its racial experimentation leads to educational benefits will, if adhered to, have serious collateral consequences. The Court relies heavily on social science evidence to justify its deference. The Court never acknowledges, however, the growing evidence that racial (and other sorts) of heterogeneity actually impairs learning among black students. *See, e.g.,* Flowers & Pascarella, *Cognitive Effects of College Racial Composition on African American Students After 3 Years of College*, 40 J. OF COLLEGE STUDENT DEVELOPMENT 669, 674 (1999) (concluding that black students experience superior cognitive development at Historically Black Colleges (HBCs) and that, even among blacks, "a substantial diversity moderates the cognitive effects of attending an HBC"); Allen, *The Color of Success: African American College Student Outcomes at Predominantly White and Historically Black Public Colleges and Universities*, 62 HARV. EDUC. REV. 26, 35 (1992) (finding that black students attending HBCs report higher academic achievement than those attending predominantly white colleges).

* * *

The sky has not fallen at Boalt Hall at the University of California, Berkeley, for example. Prior to Proposition 209's adoption of Cal. Const., Art. 1, § 31(a), which bars the State from "grant[ing] preferential treatment . . . on the basis of race . . . in the operation of . . . public education," Boalt Hall enrolled 20 blacks and 28 Hispanics in its first year class for 1996. In 2002, without deploying express racial discrimination in admissions, Boalt's entering class enrolled 14 blacks and 36 Hispanics. Total underrepresented minority student enrollment at Boalt Hall now exceeds 1996 levels. Apparently the Law School cannot be counted on to be as resourceful. The Court is willfully blind to the very real experience in California and elsewhere, which raises the inference that institutions with "reputation[s] for excellence," rivaling the Law School's have satisfied their sense of mission without resorting to prohibited racial discrimination.

V

Putting aside the absence of any legal support for the majority's reflexive deference, there is much to be said for the view that the use of tests and other measures to "predict" academic performance is a poor substitute for a system that gives every applicant a chance to prove he can succeed in the study of law. The rallying cry that in the absence of racial discrimination in admissions there would be a true meritocracy ignores the fact that the entire process is poisoned by numerous exceptions to "merit." For example, in the national debate on racial discrimination in higher education admissions, much has been made of the fact that elite institutions utilize a so-called "legacy" preference to give the children of alumni an advantage in admissions. This, and other, exceptions to a "true" meritocracy give the lie to protestations that merit admissions are in fact the order of the day at the Nation's universities. The Equal Protection

Clause does not, however, prohibit the use of unseemly legacy preferences or many other kinds of arbitrary admissions procedures. What the Equal Protection Clause does prohibit are classifications made on the basis of race. So while legacy preferences can stand under the Constitution, racial discrimination cannot. I will not twist the Constitution to invalidate legacy preferences or otherwise impose my vision of higher education admissions on the Nation. The majority should similarly stay its impulse to validate faddish racial discrimination the Constitution clearly forbids.

* * *

Putting aside what I take to be the Court's implicit rejection of *Adarand*'s holding that beneficial and burdensome racial classifications are equally invalid, I must contest the notion that the Law School's discrimination benefits those admitted as a result of it. The Court spends considerable time discussing the impressive display of *amicus* support for the Law School in this case from all corners of society. But nowhere in any of the filings in this Court is any evidence that the purported "beneficiaries" of this racial discrimination prove themselves by performing at (or even near) the same level as those students who receive no preferences. *Cf.* Thernstrom & Thernstrom, *Reflections on the Shape of the River*, 46 UCLA L. REV. 1583, 1605-1608 (1999) (discussing the failure of defenders of racial discrimination in admissions to consider the fact that its "beneficiaries" are underperforming in the classroom).

The silence in this case is deafening to those of us who view higher education's purpose as imparting knowledge and skills to students, rather than a communal, rubber-stamp, credentialing process. The Law School is not looking for those students who, despite a lower LSAT score or undergraduate grade point average, will succeed in the study of law. The Law School seeks only a façade — it is sufficient that the class looks right, even if it does not perform right.

The Law School tantalizes unprepared students with the promise of a University of Michigan degree and all of the opportunities that it offers. These overmatched students take the bait, only to find that they cannot succeed in the cauldron of competition. And this mismatch crisis is not restricted to elite institutions. *See* T. SOWELL, RACE AND CULTURE 176-177 (1994) ("Even if most minority students are able to meet the normal standards at the 'average' range of colleges and universities, the systematic mismatching of minority students begun at the top can mean that such students are generally overmatched throughout all levels of higher education"). Indeed, to cover the tracks of the aestheticists, this cruel farce of racial discrimination must continue — in selection for the Michigan Law Review, *see* University of Michigan Law School Student Handbook 2002-2003, (noting the presence of a "diversity plan" for admission to the review), and in hiring at law firms and for judicial clerkships until the "beneficiaries" are no longer tolerated. While these students may graduate with law degrees, there is no evidence that they have received a qualitatively better legal education (or become better lawyers) than if they had gone to a less "elite" law school for which they were better prepared. And the aestheticists will never address the real problems facing "underrepresented minorities," instead continuing their social experiments on other people's children.

Beyond the harm the Law School's racial discrimination visits upon its test subjects, no social science has disproved the notion that this discrimination "engender[s] attitudes of superiority or, alternatively, provoke[s] resentment among those who believe that they have been wronged by the government's use of race." "These programs stamp minorities with a badge of inferiority and may cause them to develop dependencies or to adopt an attitude that they are 'entitled' to preferences."

It is uncontested that each year, the Law School admits a handful of blacks who would be admitted in the absence of racial discrimination. Who can differentiate between those who belong and those who do not? The majority of blacks are admitted to the Law School because of discrimination, and because of this policy all are tarred as undeserving. This problem of stigma does not depend on determinacy as to whether those stigmatized are actually the "beneficiaries" of racial discrimination. When blacks take positions in the highest places of government, industry, or academia, it is an open question today whether their skin color played a part in their advancement. The question itself is the stigma — because either racial discrimination did play a role, in which case the person may be deemed "otherwise unqualified," or it did not, in which case asking the question itself unfairly marks those blacks who would succeed without discrimination. Is this what the Court means by "visibly open"?

* * *

VII

As the foregoing makes clear, I believe the Court's opinion to be, in most respects, erroneous. I do, however, find two points on which I agree.

A

First, I note that the issue of unconstitutional racial discrimination among the groups the Law School prefers is not presented in this case, because petitioner has never argued that the Law School engages in such a practice, and the Law School maintains that it does not. I join the Court's opinion insofar as it confirms that this type of racial discrimination remains unlawful. Under today's decision, it is still the case that racial discrimination that does not help a university to enroll an unspecified number, or "critical mass," of underrepresented minority students is unconstitutional. Thus, the Law School may not discriminate in admissions between similarly situated blacks and Hispanics, or between whites and Asians. This is so because preferring black to Hispanic applicants, for instance, does nothing to further the interest recognized by the majority today. Indeed, the majority describes such racial balancing as "patently unconstitutional." Like the Court, I express no opinion as to whether the Law School's current admissions program runs afoul of this prohibition.

B

The Court also holds that racial discrimination in admissions should be given another 25 years before it is deemed no longer narrowly tailored to the Law School's fabricated compelling state interest. While I agree that in 25 years the practices of the Law School will be illegal, they are, for the reasons I have given, illegal now. The majority does not and cannot rest its time limitation on any evidence that the gap in credentials between black and white students is shrinking or will be gone in that timeframe. In recent years there has been virtually no change, for example, in the proportion of law school applicants with LSAT scores of 165 and higher who are black. In 1993 blacks constituted 1.1% of law school applicants in that score range, though they represented 11.1% of all applicants. In 2000 the comparable numbers were 1.0% and 11.3%. No one can seriously contend, and the Court does not, that the racial gap in academic credentials will disappear in 25 years. Nor is the Court's holding that racial discrimination will be unconstitutional in 25 years made contingent on the gap closing in that time.

Indeed, the very existence of racial discrimination of the type practiced by the Law School may impede the narrowing of the LSAT testing gap. An applicant's LSAT score can improve dramatically with preparation, but such preparation is a cost, and there must be sufficient benefits attached to an improved score to justify additional study. Whites scoring between 163 and 167 on the LSAT are routinely rejected by the Law School, and thus whites aspiring to admission at the Law School have every incentive to improve their score to levels above that range. (showing that in 2000, 209 out of 422 white applicants were rejected in this scoring range). Blacks, on the other hand, are nearly guaranteed admission if they score above 155. (showing that 63 out of 77 black applicants are accepted with LSAT scores above 155). As admission prospects approach certainty, there is no incentive for the black applicant to continue to prepare for the LSAT once he is reasonably assured of achieving the requisite score. It is far from certain that the LSAT test-taker's behavior is responsive to the Law School's admissions policies. Nevertheless, the possibility remains that this racial discrimination will help fulfill the bigot's prophecy about black underperformance — just as it confirms the conspiracy theorist's belief that "institutional racism" is at fault for every racial disparity in our society.

* * *

For the immediate future, however, the majority has placed its *imprimatur* on a practice that can only weaken the principle of equality embodied in the Declaration of Independence and the Equal Protection Clause. "Our Constitution is color-blind, and neither knows nor tolerates classes among citizens." *Plessy v. Ferguson* (1896) (Harlan, J., dissenting). It has been nearly 140 years since Frederick Douglass asked the intellectual ancestors of the Law School to "[d]o nothing with us!" and the Nation adopted the Fourteenth Amendment. Now we must wait another 25 years to see this principle of equality vindicated. I therefore respectfully dissent from the remainder of the Court's opinion and the judgment.

NOTES AND QUESTIONS

1. How deferential was the Court to the University in *Grutter*? And was this deference consistent with prior equal protection precedent and strict scrutiny? Is there some other constitutional basis to giving deference to universities especially? Arguably, academic freedom has a constitutional root. Justice Thomas in his dissent in *Grutter* noted that "the constitutionalization of 'academic freedom' began with the concurring opinion of Justice Frankfurter in *Sweezy v. New Hampshire,* 354 U.S. 234 (1957). Sweezy, a Marxist economist, was investigated by the Attorney General of New Hampshire on suspicion of being a subversive. The prosecution sought, *inter alia,* the contents of a lecture Sweezy had given at the University of New Hampshire. The Court held that the investigation violated due process." But what does this have to do with race conscious admissions? Justice Thomas thought not much, do you agree?

2. In a parallel case involving the University of Michigan's undergraduate admission's affirmative action program, *Gratz v. Bollinger,* 539 U.S. 244 (2003), Justice O'Connor, who authored the principal opinion in *Grutter*, joined an opinion by Chief Justice Rehnquist and the other *Grutter* dissenters holding that the undergraduate program was unconstitutional. The University employed a "selection index," on which an applicant could score a maximum of 150 points. Applicants with a score of 100 or more were automatically admitted; applicants with scores of 90-99 were usually admitted after an individualized review; applicants with scores between 75 and 89 were usually denied, but could be admitted after an individualized review; and applicants with scores of 74 and below were almost always denied admission, although individualized review was also possible for some in this range as well. Points were award for high school GPA, standardized test scores, strength of high school, in-state residency, alumni relationship, personal essay, and personal achievement. "Underrepresented minorities" were awarded to 20 points based solely on membership in the racial or ethnic minority group. The Court, by a 5-4 vote, found that this point system had "the effect of making 'the factor of race . . . decisive' for virtually every minimally qualified underrepresented minority applicant," and therefore unconstitutional even under the Court's holding in *Grutter*.

3. In *Gratz*, Justice Ginsburg dissented, arguing that "[o]ne can reasonably anticipate . . . that colleges and universities will seek to maintain their minority enrollment . . . whether or not they can do so in full candor through adoption of affirmative action plans of the kind here at issue." Does this suggest that Justice Ginsburg believes the University of Michigan and other public institutions would have pursued race conscious admissions policies, whether or not the Court accepted them? That would seem to be the case, since Justice Ginsburg goes on to say that "[i]f honesty is the best policy, surely Michigan's accurately described, fully disclosed College affirmative action program is preferable to achieving similar numbers through winks, nods, and disguises." Chief Justice Rehnquist thought these comments "remarkable" since they hardly support giving deference to the University "whose academic judgment we are told in *Grutter v. Bollinger*," was worthy of deference." Since when, the Chief Justice wondered, do we change the Constitution so that "it conforms to the conduct of the universities"?

4. Can private universities now also use race to achieve diversity in admissions? In previous cases, the Court has explained that actions that would violate the Equal Protection Clause of the Fourteenth Amendment if committed by a private institution accepting federal funds would also violate Title VI. *See Alexander v. Sandoval* (2001). But is the converse true? That is, just because a public university has been given latitude to use race if it chooses under the Equal Protection Clause, does that necessarily tell us that a statutory prohibition against race-based decisions now permits this as well? Isn't it the intent of the Congress at the time the particular statute was enacted that governs? After all, with respect to 42 U.S.C. § 1981 as well, which applies to private and public parties, the Court has explained that the provision was "meant, by its broad terms, to proscribe discrimination in the making or enforcement of contracts against, or in favor of, any race." *McDonald v. Santa Fe Trail Transp. Co.* (1976). The court has even held that a contract for educational services is a "contract" for purposes of § 1981. *See Runyon v. McCrary* (1976). And it is well-settled that purposeful discrimination that violates the Equal Protection Clause of the Fourteenth Amendment will also violate § 1981. *See General Building Contractors Assn., Inc. v. Pennsylvania* (1982). At the end of her opinion in *Grutter*, Justice O'Connor declares (without elaboration) that a public university law school, Michigan, has no statutory liability since Title VI and 1981 have been construed "co-extensively" with the Equal Protection Clause. Assuming that to be so, does *Grutter* preclude the Congress from amending these laws to expressly prohibit that which the Court has permitted? To prohibit private and public institutions, or just private? It is clear that states retain the authority to deny what the federal Constitution has been construed to permit, as California has expressly prohibited preferential treatment on the basis of race, sex, color, ethnicity or national origin in its State Constitution, Cal. Const. Art I, § 31(a).

5. Given that race-based decision making is so odious in our history, why do you think the Court did not tell Michigan Law just to employ an admissions test other than the LSAT upon which minority students, on average, do not perform well? In this regard, Justice Thomas noted that "there is nothing ancient, honorable, or constitutionally protected about 'selective' admissions. The University of Michigan should be well aware that alternative methods have historically been used for the admission of students, for it brought to this country the German certificate system in the late 19th century. *See* H. WECHSLER, THE QUALIFIED STUDENT 16-39 (1977) (hereinafter QUALIFIED STUDENT). Under this system, a secondary school was certified by a university so that any graduate who completed the course offered by the school was offered admission to the university.

The certification regime supplemented, and later virtually replaced (at least in the Midwest), the prior regime of rigorous subject matter entrance examinations. The facially race-neutral 'percent plans' now used in Texas, California, and Florida are in many ways the descendents of the certificate system."

So what prompts universities to use highly selective examinations? Justice Thomas continues: "certification was replaced by selective admissions in the beginning of the 20th century, as universities sought to exercise more control over the composition of their student bodies. Since its inception, selective admissions has been the vehicle for racial, ethnic, and religious tinkering and experimentation by university administrators. The initial driving force for the relocation of the selective function from the high school to the universities was the same desire to select racial winners and losers that the Law School exhibits today. Columbia, Harvard, and others infamously determined that they had 'too many' Jews, just as today the Law School argues it would have 'too many' whites or Asian-Americans if it could not discriminate in its admissions process. *See* QUALIFIED STUDENT 155-168 (Columbia); H. BROUN & G. BRITT, CHRISTIANS ONLY: A STUDY IN PREJUDICE 53-54 (1931) (Harvard)."

"Columbia employed intelligence tests precisely because Jewish applicants, who were predominantly immigrants, scored worse on such tests. Thus, Columbia could claim (falsely) that "'[w]e have not eliminated boys because they were Jews and do not propose to do so. We have honestly attempted to eliminate the lowest grade of applicant [through the use of intelligence testing] and it turns out that a good many of the low grade men are New York City Jews.'" Letter from Herbert E. Hawkes, dean of Columbia College, to E.B. Wilson, June 16, 1922 (reprinted in QUALIFIED STUDENT 160-161). In other words, the tests were adopted with full knowledge of their disparate impact. *Cf. DeFunis v. Odegaard,* 416 U.S. 312, 335 (1974) (*per curiam*) (Douglas, J., dissenting)." If all this is true, why isn't use of a testing regimen with full knowledge of its disparate impact, an equal protection violation?

6. If you think the LSAT a reasonable measure of likely success in law school (and later the bar exam — and there is some positive correlation), is Michigan or another public university authorized to employ race if it means sacrificing these "learning outcomes," as Justice O'Connor described them? Could it be that the legal permission to take the extraordinary step of employing race is necessarily hinged on the institution being fully capable of carrying out its educational mission *and* achieving diversity?

There is much in Justice O'Connor's opinion to suggest that only the most elite educational institutions will be able to accomplish both goals and that therefore, public (and vicariously) private institutions that cannot do so are *not* permitted by the Constitution to shape their decisions by race. Justice O'Connor specifically links approval of the Michigan law school pursuit of a "critical mass" of minority students to the fact that the law school "ranks among the Nation's top law schools" and that admission to such a selective institution is a prelude to power and essential to creating leaders for private and public contexts, whether politics, the military, or business.

Arguably, that highly selective institutions satisfy these educational outcomes is what allows them to satisfy strict scrutiny and demonstrate a compelling governmental interest. It is also what allows Justice O'Connor to remain faithful to the Court's precedents, many of which she authored, that demand nothing less. To be sure, this is obscured somewhat by the presumption of good faith that the majority gives the Michigan law school. As the dissenters point out, the presumption seems incongruous given how the factual record illustrates that minority students were admitted to Michigan with significantly lower credentials than their white and Asian counterparts. These facts lead Justice Kennedy — who states explicitly that he shares the view articulated by the late Justice Powell that race can be used in admissions as a nonpredominant factor — to believe that the majority had "abandoned or manipulated [or] distort[ed] [the] real and accepted meaning" of strict scrutiny.

While that is possible, of course, it should not be assumed that Justice O'Connor intended to overturn decades of precedent establishing that there is only one Equal Protection Clause, and that it applies to black and white alike, regardless of whether the government's desired classification is said to help or hurt the particular group. There is nothing in the majority opinion to suggest that Justice O'Connor formally abandons "searching judicial inquiry for race-based measures" or the proposition that there is no way to determine whether classifications are "benign" or "remedial." She cites both with approval. Instead, Justice O'Connor writes: "context matters," and the context that matters most are the words with which she begins her opinion: in the case under review the sought-after diversity occurs within one of the Nation's top schools.

When Justice Thomas in dissent argues that Michigan ought to be made to choose between its elite status and the diversity that it seeks, Justice O'Connor rejects that notion. She calls the prospect of lowering admissions standards, "a drastic remedy that would require the Law School to become a much different institution and sacrifice a vital component of its educational mission." It is for this same reason that Justice O'Connor finds that the Michigan law school has acted in a "narrowly tailored" manner without having exhausted all race-neutral means to achieve diversity, as the Bush administration had urged the Court. Percentage plans and lotteries do have greater racial fairness, but the law school does not need to consider them since that would force the school "to abandon the academic selectivity that is the cornerstone of its educational mission."

But which schools would qualify as elite? Certainly, it is open to debate at any given time how many universities or law schools see themselves as elite or selective, and therefore, as qualifying for this rare constitutional dispensation. Each school has unique features that make it attractive, but the reality is that applicants with high grades and test scores rationally seek out places, on average, that have large endowments and the traditions and faculties which give rise to them. All sides in the affirmative action debate also concede that for reasons that remain perplexing and intractable (and that cry out to be addressed in non-cosmetic ways), far too few minority students fall within the upper ranges of the entrance exam. Of the 4,461 applicants to law school who had scores in roughly the 93rd percentile in 2002, 29 were black. About 25-30 law schools consistently and exclusively take their nonminority students from this range. Is that the contextual universe Justice O'Connor was writing about? If so, the opinion is far less of a blockbuster, but then, it would also keep the use of race to the extraordinary.

7. Didn't the Court previously reject the diversity model in *Wygant* when it refused to accept a minority role model argument? Is *Wygant* still good law? If the Court defers to the law school's judgment that a racially mixed student body confers educational benefits to all, then why would the *Wygant* Court not defer to the school board's judgment with respect to the benefits a racially mixed faculty confers?

8. In your own law school environment, do you see the benefits of diversity of viewpoint and experience regularly in classroom discussion? Justice Thomas thought that unlikely. He writes: "'[D]iversity,' for all of its devotees, is more a fashionable catchphrase than it is a useful term, especially when something as serious as racial discrimination is at issue. Because the Equal Protection Clause renders the color of one's skin constitutionally irrelevant to the law school's mission, he referred to the Michigan law school's interest as an "aesthetic." That is, the Law School wants to have a certain appearance, from the shape of the desks and tables in its classrooms to the color of the students sitting at them.

The aesthetic label was also intended to suggest that affirmative action does little for the least advantaged poor. Justice Thomas again writes: "It must be remembered that the Law School's racial discrimination does nothing for those too poor or uneducated to participate in elite higher education and therefore presents only an illusory solution to the challenges facing our Nation." Do you agree? Or does the inclusion of diversity "trickle down" somehow to encourage all?

9. Does affirmative action skirt the real issue? As an *amicus* for the Center for New Black Leadership authored by the Institute for Justice observes: "the real cause of racial disparities in post-secondary education [is] a severe racial gap in academic achievement in the K-12 years, owing significantly to the concentration of economically disadvantaged black and Hispanic students in defective inner-city public schools." The 2000 National Assessment of Educational Progress (NAEP) found that 63 percent of black and 56 percent of Hispanic fourth-graders are below the most basic levels of proficiency in reading. The average black 17-year-old is three to five years behind in reading and science and math. All of this shows up of course on college and law school entrance exams. And racial preferences do nothing to close this gap. *See generally* THERNSTROM AND THERNSTROM, AMERICA IN BLACK AND WHITE (1997). Arguably, preferences make the situation worse by creating the illusion of improvement when the underlying reality is left unaddressed. The absence of racial preference, of course, would shatter the illusion. But as the *New York Times* concluded: "ending affirmative action [in California and elsewhere] has had one unpublicized and profoundly desirable consequence: it has forced the universit[ies] to try to expand the pool of eligible minority students." James Traub, *The Class of Prop. 209*, NEW YORK TIMES at 44 (May 2, 1999).

10. Is there a better way? Some public and private universities have begun to realize that action is needed years before students apply. On the private side, the University of Southern California was recently named Time Magazine's "University of the Year" for an elaborate and well-conceived effort enlisting college students and professors to help educationally disadvantaged students build their skills for college admission. Most recently, it has added a web-site directed at middle and high school students (and their parents and counselors) to help them prepare for college with detailed planning tools extending into 8th grade. Similar efforts are now underway in public education at Berkeley, the University of Washington, and Wisconsin. Of course, increased opportunities for parents to choose among available primary and secondary school options to escape failing schools or school systems are thought helpful as well. *See Zelman v. Simmons-Harris*, 122 S. Ct. 2460 (2002) (upholding the Cleveland school voucher program for low and moderate income students).

11. Obviously, affirmative action gives us much to think about. Even if *Grutter* applies outside elite institutions, it is important to remember that it did come with some explicit limits. In endorsing Justice Powell's views in *Bakke*, the Court accepted many qualifications for the use of race in university admissions: applicant review must be on an individual basis; the process must not be a disguised attempt to achieve racial balance; and one minority racial group cannot be preferred or played off against another. A faculty cannot spuriously conclude that it wants more African Americans, say, than Hispanics. That's not an overall critical mass of minority students but racial balancing, said the majority, which would be "patently unconstitu-tional." On the last point, Justices Scalia and Thomas joined the majority in partial concurrence.

12. Is the use of race acceptable in the drawing of voting districts? Some argue that it is since such districts have a long history of being gerrymandered in numerous ways reflecting such things as politics, ethnicity and urban vs. suburban proclivities. Why, it is claimed, should race be any different? The Court tries to answer in the next case.

MILLER v. JOHNSON
515 U.S. 900 (1995)

JUSTICE KENNEDY delivered the opinion of the Court.

The constitutionality of Georgia's congressional redistricting plan is at issue here. In *Shaw v. Reno* (1993), we held that a plaintiff states a claim under the Equal Protection Clause by alleging that a state redistricting plan, on its face, has no rational explanation save as an effort to separate voters on the basis of race. The question we now decide is whether Georgia's new Eleventh District gives rise to a valid equal protection claim under the principles announced in *Shaw*, and, if so, whether it can be sustained nonetheless as narrowly tailored to serve a compelling governmental interest.

I

A

The Equal Protection Clause of the Fourteenth Amendment provides that no State shall "deny to any person within its jurisdiction the equal protection of the laws." Its central mandate is racial neutrality in governmental decisionmaking. Though application of this imperative raises difficult questions, the basic principle is straightforward: "Racial and ethnic distinctions of any sort are inherently suspect and thus call for the most exacting judicial examination. . . . This perception of racial and ethnic distinctions is rooted in our Nation's constitutional and demographic history." *Regents of Univ. of California v. Bakke* (1978) (opinion of Powell, J.). This rule obtains with equal force regardless of "the race of those burdened or benefited by a particular classification." *Richmond v. J.A. Croson Co.* (1989) (SCALIA, J., concurring in judgment); *see also Adarand Constructors, Inc. v. Pena* [(1995)]. Laws classifying citizens on the basis of race cannot be upheld unless they are narrowly tailored to achieving a compelling state interest.

. . . Applying this basic Equal Protection analysis in the voting rights context, we held that "redistricting legislation that is so bizarre on its face that it is 'unexplainable on grounds other than race,' . . . demands the same close scrutiny that we give other state laws that classify citizens by race."

This case requires us to apply the principles articulated in *Shaw* to the most recent congressional redistricting plan enacted by the State of Georgia.

B

In 1965, the Attorney General designated Georgia a covered jurisdiction under § 4(b) of the Voting Rights Act (Act). In consequence, § 5 of the Act requires Georgia to obtain either administrative preclearance by the Attorney General or approval by the United States District Court for the District of Columbia of any change in a "standard, practice, or procedure with respect to voting" made after November 1, 1964. The preclearance mechanism applies to congressional redistricting plans, and requires that the proposed change "not have the purpose and will not have the effect of denying or abridging the right to vote on account of race or color." . . .

Between 1980 and 1990, one of Georgia's 10 congressional districts was a majority-black district, that is, a majority of the district's voters were black. The 1990 Decennial Census indicated that Georgia's population of 6,478,216 persons, 27% of whom are black, entitled it to an additional eleventh congressional seat, prompting Georgia's General Assembly to redraw the State's congressional districts. Both the House and the Senate adopted redistricting guidelines which, among other things, required single-member districts of equal population, contiguous geography, nondilution of minority voting strength, fidelity to precinct lines where possible, and compliance with §§ 2 and 5 of the Act. Only after these requirements were met did the guidelines permit drafters to consider other ends, such as maintaining the integrity of political subdivisions, preserving the core of existing districts, and avoiding contests between incumbents.

A special session opened in August 1991, and the General Assembly submitted a congressional redistricting plan to the Attorney General for preclearance on October 1, 1991. The legislature's plan contained two majority-minority districts, the Fifth and Eleventh, and an additional district, the Second, in which blacks comprised just over 35% of the voting age population. Despite the plan's increase in the number of majority-black districts from one to two and the absence of any evidence of an intent to discriminate against minority voters, the Department of Justice refused preclearance on January 21, 1992. The Department's objection letter noted a concern that Georgia had created only two majority-minority districts, and that the proposed plan did not "recognize" certain minority populations by placing them in a majority-black district.

. . . A new plan was enacted and submitted for preclearance. This second attempt assigned the black population in Central Georgia's Baldwin County to the Eleventh District and increased the black populations in the Eleventh, Fifth and Second Districts. The Justice Department refused preclearance again, relying on alternative plans proposing three majority-minority districts. One of the alternative schemes relied on by the Department was the so-called "max-black" plan, drafted by the American Civil Liberties Union (ACLU) for the General Assembly's black caucus. The key to the ACLU's plan was the "Macon/Savannah trade." The dense black population in the Macon region would be transferred from the Eleventh District to the Second, converting the Second into a majority-black district, and the Eleventh District's loss in black population would be offset by extending the Eleventh to include the black populations in Savannah. Pointing to the General Assembly's refusal to enact the Macon/Savannah swap into law, the Justice Department concluded that Georgia had "failed to explain adequately" its failure to create a third majority-minority district. . . .

Twice spurned, the General Assembly set out to create three majority-minority districts to gain preclearance. Using the ACLU's "max-black" plan as its benchmark, the General Assembly enacted a plan that

"bore all the signs of [the Justice Department's] involvement: The black population of Meriwether County was gouged out of the Third District and attached to the Second District by the narrowest of land bridges; Effingham and Chatham Counties were split to make way for the Savannah extension, which itself split the City of Savannah; and the plan as a whole split 26 counties, 23 more than the existing congressional districts."

The new plan also enacted the Macon/Savannah swap necessary to create a third majority-black district. The Eleventh District lost the black population of Macon, but picked up Savannah, thereby connecting the black neighborhoods of metropolitan Atlanta and the poor black populace of coastal Chatham County, though 260 miles apart in distance and worlds apart in culture. In short, the social, political and economic makeup of the Eleventh District tells a tale of disparity, not community. . . . The Almanac of American Politics has this to say about the Eleventh District: "Geographically, it is a monstrosity, stretching from Atlanta to Savannah. Its core is the plantation country in the center of the state, lightly populated, but heavily black. It links by narrow corridors the black neighborhoods in Augusta, Savannah and southern DeKalb County." Georgia's plan included three majority-black districts, though, and received Justice Department preclearance on April 2, 1992.

Elections were held under the new congressional redistricting plan on November 4, 1992, and black candidates were elected to Congress from all three majority-black districts. On January 13, 1994, appellees, five white voters from the Eleventh District, filed this action. . . . As residents of the challenged Eleventh District, . . . [t]heir suit alleged that Georgia's Eleventh District was a racial gerrymander and so a violation of the Equal Protection Clause as interpreted in *Shaw v. Reno*. A three-judge court was convened . . . , and the United States and a number of Georgia residents intervened in support of the defendant-state officials.

A majority of the District Court panel agreed that the Eleventh District was invalid under *Shaw*, with one judge dissenting. After sharp criticism of the Justice Department for its use of partisan advocates in its dealings with state officials and for its close cooperation with the ACLU's vigorous advocacy of minority district maximization, the majority turned to a careful interpretation of our opinion in *Shaw*. It read *Shaw* to require strict scrutiny whenever race is the "overriding, predominant force" in the redistricting process. Citing much evidence of the legislature's purpose and intent in creating the final plan, as well as the irregular shape of the district . . . , the court found that race was the overriding and predominant force in the districting determination. The court proceeded to apply strict scrutiny. Though rejecting proportional representation as a compelling interest, it was willing to assume that compliance with the Voting Rights Act would be a compelling interest. As to the latter, however, the court found that the Act did not require three majority-black districts, and that Georgia's plan for that reason was not narrowly tailored to the goal of complying with the Act.

* * *

II

A

Finding that the "evidence of the General Assembly's intent to racially ger-rymander the Eleventh District is overwhelming, and practically stipulated by the parties involved," the District Court held that race was the predominant, overriding factor in drawing the Eleventh District. Appellants do not take issue with the court's factual finding of this racial motivation. Rather, they contend that evidence of a legislature's deliberate classification of voters on the basis of race cannot alone suffice to state a claim under *Shaw*. They argue that, regard-less of the legislature's purposes, a plaintiff must demonstrate that a district's shape is so bizarre that it is unexplainable other than on the basis of race, and that appellees failed to make that showing here. Appellants' conception of the constitutional violation misapprehends our holding in *Shaw* and the Equal Protection precedent upon which *Shaw* relied.

Shaw recognized a claim "analytically distinct" from a vote dilution claim. Whereas a vote dilution claim alleges that the State has enacted a particular voting scheme as a purposeful device "to minimize or cancel out the voting potential of racial or ethnic minorities," an action disadvantaging voters of a par-ticular race, the essence of the equal protection claim recognized in *Shaw* is that the State has used race as a basis for separating voters into districts. Just as the State may not, absent extraordinary justification, segregate citizens on the basis of race in its public parks, buses, golf courses, beaches, and schools, so did we recognize in *Shaw* that it may not separate its citizens into different voting districts on the basis of race. The idea is a simple one: "At the heart of the Con-stitution's guarantee of equal protection lies the simple command that the Gov-ernment must treat citizens 'as individuals, not "as simply components of a racial, religious, sexual or national class."'" *Metro Broadcasting, Inc. v. FCC* (1990). When the State assigns voters on the basis of race, it engages in the offensive and demeaning assumption that voters of a particular race, because of their race, "think alike, share the same political interests, and will prefer the same candidates at the polls." Race-based assignments "embody stereotypes that treat individuals as the product of their race, evaluating their thoughts and efforts — their very worth as citizens — according to a criterion barred to the Government by history and the Constitution." . . . As we concluded in *Shaw*:

> "Racial classifications with respect to voting carry particular dangers. Racial gerrymandering, even for remedial purposes, may balkanize us into competing racial factions; it threatens to carry us further from the goal of a political system in which race no longer matters — a goal that the Fourteenth and Fifteenth Amendments embody, and to which the Nation continues to aspire.["] . . .

Our observation in *Shaw* of the consequences of racial stereotyping was not meant to suggest that a district must be bizarre on its face before there is a con-stitutional violation. . . . Our circumspect approach and narrow holding in

Shaw did not erect an artificial rule barring accepted equal protection analysis in other redistricting cases. Shape is relevant not because bizarreness is a necessary element of the constitutional wrong or a threshold requirement of proof, but because it may be persuasive circumstantial evidence that race for its own sake, and not other districting principles, was the legislature's dominant and controlling rationale in drawing its district lines. The logical implication, as courts applying *Shaw* have recognized, is that parties may rely on evidence other than bizarreness to establish race-based districting.

. . . We recognized in *Shaw* that, outside the districting context, statutes are subject to strict scrutiny under the Equal Protection Clause not just when they contain express racial classifications, but also when, though race neutral on their face, they are motivated by a racial purpose or object. In the rare case, where the effect of government action is a pattern "'unexplainable on grounds other than race,'" "[t]he evidentiary inquiry is . . . relatively easy." As early as *Yick Wo v. Hopkins* (1886), the Court recognized that a laundry permit ordinance was administered in a deliberate way to exclude all Chinese from the laundry business; and in *Gomillion v. Lightfoot* (1960), the Court concluded that the redrawing of Tuskegee, Alabama's municipal boundaries left no doubt that the plan was designed to exclude blacks. Even in those cases, however, it was the presumed racial purpose of state action, not its stark manifestation, that was the constitutional violation. . . . In the absence of a pattern as stark as those in *Yick Wo* or *Gomillion*, "impact alone is not determinative, and the Court must look to other evidence" of race-based decisionmaking.

* * *

B

Federal-court review of districting legislation represents a serious intrusion on the most vital of local functions. It is well settled that "reapportionment is primarily the duty and responsibility of the State." Electoral districting is a most difficult subject for legislatures, and so the States must have discretion to exercise the political judgment necessary to balance competing interests. Although race-based decisionmaking is inherently suspect, until a claimant makes a showing sufficient to support that allegation the good faith of a state legislature must be presumed. The courts, in assessing the sufficiency of a challenge to a districting plan, must be sensitive to the complex interplay of forces that enter a legislature's redistricting calculus. Redistricting legislatures will, for example, almost always be aware of racial demographics; but it does not follow that race predominates in the redistricting process. The distinction between being aware of racial considerations and being motivated by them may be difficult to make. This evidentiary difficulty, together with the sensitive nature of redistricting and the presumption of good faith that must be accorded legislative enactments, requires courts to exercise extraordinary caution in adjudicating claims that a state has drawn district lines on the basis of race. The plaintiff's burden is to show, either through circumstantial evidence of a district's shape and demographics or more direct evidence going to legislative purpose, that race was the predominant factor motivating the legislature's decision to place a significant number of voters within or without a particular district. To make this showing, a plaintiff must prove that the legislature subordinated traditional race-neutral districting principles, including but not limited to compactness, contiguity, respect for political subdivisions or communities defined by actual shared interests, to racial considerations. Where these or other race-neutral considerations are the basis for redistricting legislation, and are not subordinated to race, a state can "defeat a claim that a district has been gerrymandered on racial lines." . . .

In our view, the District Court applied the correct analysis, and its finding that race was the predominant factor motivating the drawing of the Eleventh District was not clearly erroneous. The court found it was "exceedingly obvious" from the shape of the Eleventh District, together with the relevant racial demographics, that the drawing of narrow land bridges to incorporate within the District outlying appendages containing nearly 80% of the district's total black population was a deliberate attempt to bring black populations into the district. Although by comparison with other districts the geometric shape of the Eleventh District may not seem bizarre on its face, when its shape is considered in conjunction with its racial and population densities, the story of racial gerrymandering seen by the District Court becomes much clearer. . . . The District Court had before it considerable additional evidence showing that the General Assembly was motivated by a predominant, overriding desire to assign black populations to the Eleventh District and thereby permit the creation of a third majority-black district in the Second.

The court found that "it became obvious," both from the Justice Department's objection letters and the three preclearance rounds in general, "that [the Justice Department] would accept nothing less than abject surrender to its maximization agenda." . . . The State admitted that it "'would not have added those portions of Effingham and Chatham Counties that are now in the [far southeastern extension of the] present Eleventh Congressional District but for the need to include additional black population in that district to offset the loss of black population caused by the shift of predominantly black portions of Bibb County in the Second Congressional District which occurred in response to the Department of Justice's March 20th, 1992, objection letter.'" It conceded further that "[t]o the extent that precincts in the Eleventh Congressional District are split, a substantial reason for their being split was the objective of increasing the black population of that district." And in its brief to this Court, the State concedes that "[i]t is undisputed that Georgia's eleventh is the product of a desire by the General Assembly to create a majority black district." . . . On this record, we fail to see how the District Court could have reached any conclusion other than that race was the predominant factor in drawing Georgia's Eleventh District. . . .

* * *

. . . As a result, Georgia's congressional redistricting plan cannot be upheld unless it satisfies strict scrutiny, our most rigorous and exacting standard of constitutional review.

III

To satisfy strict scrutiny, the State must demonstrate that its districting legislation is narrowly tailored to achieve a compelling interest. There is a "significant state interest in eradicating the effects of past racial discrimination." The State does not argue, however, that it created the Eleventh District to remedy past discrimination, and with good reason: There is little doubt that the State's true interest in designing the Eleventh District was creating a third majority-black district to satisfy the Justice Department's preclearance demands. Whether or not in some cases compliance with the Voting Rights Act, standing alone, can provide a compelling interest independent of any interest in remedying past discrimination, it cannot do so here. As we suggested in *Shaw*, compliance with federal antidiscrimination laws cannot justify race-based districting where the challenged district was not reasonably necessary under a constitutional reading and application of those laws. The congressional plan challenged here was not required by the Voting Rights Act under a correct reading of the statute. . . .

We do not accept the contention that the State has a compelling interest in complying with whatever preclearance mandates the Justice Department issues. When a state governmental entity seeks to justify race-based remedies to cure the effects of past discrimination, we do not accept the government's mere assertion that the remedial action is required. Rather, we insist on a strong basis in evidence of the harm being remedied. "The history of racial classifications in this country suggests that blind judicial deference to legislative or executive pronouncements of necessity has no place in equal protection analysis." Our presumptive skepticism of all racial classifications prohibits us as well from accepting on its face the Justice Department's conclusion that racial districting is necessary under the Voting Rights Act. Where a State relies on the Department's determination that race-based districting is necessary to comply with the Voting Rights Act, the judiciary retains an independent obligation in adjudicating consequent equal protection challenges to ensure that the State's actions are narrowly tailored to achieve a compelling interest. Were we to accept the Justice Department's objection itself as a compelling interest adequate to insulate racial districting from constitutional review, we would be surrendering to the Executive Branch our role in enforcing the constitutional limits on race-based official action. We may not do so.

For the same reasons, we think it inappropriate for a court engaged in constitutional scrutiny to accord deference to the Justice Department's interpretation of the Act. Although we have deferred to the Department's interpretation in certain statutory cases, we have rejected agency interpretations to which we would otherwise defer where they raise serious constitutional questions. When the Justice Department's interpretation of the Act compels race-based districting, it by definition raises a serious constitutional question, and should not receive deference.

Georgia's drawing of the Eleventh District was not required under the Act because there was no reasonable basis to believe that Georgia's earlier enacted plans violated § 5. Wherever a plan is "ameliorative," a term we have used to describe plans increasing the number of majority-minority districts, it "cannot violate § 5 unless the new apportionment itself so discriminates on the basis of race or color as to violate the Constitution." Georgia's first and second proposed plans increased the number of majority-black districts from 1 out of 10 (10%) to 2 out of 11 (18.18%). These plans were "ameliorative" and could not have violated § 5's non-retrogression principle. Acknowledging as much, the United States now relies on the fact that the Justice Department may object to a state proposal either on the ground that it has a prohibited purpose or a prohibited effect. The Government justifies its preclearance objections on the ground that the submitted plans violated § 5's purpose element. The key to the Government's position . . . is and always has been that Georgia failed to proffer a nondiscriminatory purpose for its refusal in the first two submissions to take the steps necessary to create a third majority-minority district.

The Government's position is insupportable. "[A]meliorative changes, even if they fall short of what might be accomplished in terms of increasing minority representation, cannot be found to violate section 5 unless they so discriminate on the basis of race or color as to violate the Constitution." Although it is true we have held that the State has the burden to prove a nondiscriminatory purpose under § 5, Georgia's Attorney General provided a detailed explanation for the State's initial decision not to enact the max-black plan. The District Court accepted this explanation, and found an absence of any discriminatory intent. The State's policy of adhering to other districting principles instead of creating as many majority-minority districts as possible does not support an inference that the plan "so discriminates on the basis of race or color as to violate the Constitution," and thus cannot provide any basis under § 5 for the Justice Department's objection.

Instead of grounding its objections on evidence of a discriminatory purpose, it would appear the Government was driven by its policy of maximizing majority-black districts. In utilizing § 5 to require States to create majority-minority districts wherever possible, the Department of Justice expanded its authority under the statute beyond what Congress intended and we have upheld.

* * *

IV

The Voting Rights Act, and its grant of authority to the federal courts to uncover official efforts to abridge minorities' right to vote, has been of vital importance in eradicating invidious discrimination from the electoral process and enhancing the legitimacy of our political institutions. Only if our political system and our society cleanse themselves of that discrimination will all members of the polity share an equal opportunity to gain public office regardless of race. As a Nation we share both the obligation and the aspiration of working toward this end. The end is neither assured nor well served, however, by carving electorates into racial blocs. "If our society is to continue to progress as a multiracial democracy, it must recognize that the automatic invocation of race stereotypes retards that progress and causes continued hurt and injury." It takes a shortsighted and unauthorized view of the Voting Rights Act to invoke that statute, which has played a decisive role in redressing some of our worst forms of discrimination, to demand the very racial stereotyping the Fourteenth Amendment forbids.

* * *

JUSTICE O'CONNOR, concurring. [Omitted.]

JUSTICE STEVENS, dissenting.

* * *

In *Shaw v. Reno* (1993), the Court crafted a new cause of action with two novel, troubling features. First, the Court misapplied the term "gerrymander," previously used to describe grotesque line-drawing by a dominant group to maintain or enhance its political power at a minority's expense, to condemn the efforts of a majority (whites) to share its power with a minority (African Americans). Second, the Court dispensed with its previous insistence in vote dilution cases on a showing of injury to an identifiable group of voters, but it failed to explain adequately what showing a plaintiff must make to establish standing to litigate the newly minted *Shaw* claim. Neither in *Shaw* itself nor in the cases decided today has the Court coherently articulated what injury this cause of action is designed to redress. Because respondents have alleged no legally cognizable injury, they lack standing, and these cases should be dismissed.

Even assuming the validity of *Shaw*, I cannot see how respondents in these cases could assert the injury the Court attributes to them. Respondents, plaintiffs below, are white voters in Georgia's Eleventh Congressional District. The Court's conclusion that they have standing to maintain a *Shaw* claim appears to rest on a theory that their placement in the Eleventh District caused them "'representational harms.'" The *Shaw* Court explained the concept of "representational harms" as follows: "When a district obviously is created solely to effectuate the perceived common interests of one racial group, elected officials are more likely to believe that their primary obligation is to represent only the members of that group, rather than their constituency as a whole." Although the *Shaw* Court attributed representational harms solely to a message sent by the legislature's action, those harms can only come about if the message is received — that is, first, if all or most black voters support the same candidate, and, second, if the successful candidate ignores the interests of her white constituents. Respondents' standing, in other words, ultimately depends on the very premise the Court purports to abhor: that voters of a particular race "'think alike, share the same political interests, and will prefer the same candidates at the polls.'" This generalization, as the Court recognizes, is "offensive and demeaning."

* * *

The Court attempts an explanation in these cases by equating the injury it imagines respondents have suffered with the injuries African Americans suffered under segregation. The heart of respondents' claim, by the Court's account, is that "a State's assignment of voters on the basis of race," violates the Equal Protection Clause for the same reason a State may not "segregate citizens on the basis of race in its public parks, buses, golf courses, beaches, and schools." This equation, however, fails to elucidate the elusive *Shaw* injury. Our desegregation cases redressed the *exclusion* of black citizens from public facilities reserved for whites. In this case, in contrast, any voter, black or white, may live in the Eleventh District. What respondents contest is the *inclusion* of too many black voters in the District as drawn. In my view, if respondents allege no vote dilution, that inclusion can cause them no conceivable injury.

The Court's equation of *Shaw* claims with our desegregation decisions is inappropriate for another reason. In each of those cases, legal segregation frustrated the public interest in diversity and tolerance by barring African Americans from joining whites in the activities at issue. The districting plan here, in contrast, serves the interest in diversity and tolerance by increasing the likelihood that a meaningful number of black representatives will add their voices to legislative debates. "There is no moral or constitutional equivalence between a policy that is designed to perpetuate a caste system and one that seeks to eradicate racial subordination." . . .

Equally distressing is the Court's equation of traditional gerrymanders, designed to maintain or enhance a dominant group's power, with a dominant group's decision to share its power with a previously underrepresented group. In my view, districting plans violate the Equal Protection Clause when they "serve no purpose other than to favor one segment — whether racial, ethnic, religious, economic, or political — that may occupy a position of strength at a particular point in time, or to disadvantage a politically weak segment of the community." In contrast, I do not see how a districting plan that favors a politically weak group can violate equal protection. The Constitution does not mandate any form of proportional representation, but it certainly permits a State to adopt a policy that promotes fair representation of different groups. . . .

The Court's refusal to distinguish an enactment that helps a minority group from enactments that cause it harm is especially unfortunate at the intersection of race and voting, given that African Americans and other disadvantaged groups have struggled so long and so hard for inclusion in that most central exercise of our democracy. I have long believed that treating racial groups differently from other identifiable groups of voters, as the Court does today, is itself an invidious racial classification. Racial minorities should receive neither more nor less protection than other groups against gerrymanders. *A fortiori,* racial minorities should not be less eligible than other groups to benefit from districting plans the majority designs to aid them.

* * *

JUSTICE GINSBURG, with whom JUSTICE STEVENS and JUSTICE BREYER join, and with whom JUSTICE SOUTER joins except as to Part III-B, dissenting.

Two Terms ago, in *Shaw v. Reno* (1993), this Court took up a claim "analytically distinct" from a vote dilution claim. *Shaw* authorized judicial intervention in "extremely irregular" apportionments, in which the legislature cast aside traditional districting practices to consider race alone. . . .

Today the Court expands the judicial role, announcing that federal courts are to undertake searching review of any district with contours "predominant[ly] motivat[ed]" by race: "[S]trict scrutiny" will be triggered not only when traditional districting practices are abandoned, but also when those practices are "subordinated to" — given less weight than — race. Applying this new "race-as-predominant-factor" standard, the Court invalidates Georgia's districting plan even though Georgia's Eleventh District, the focus of today's dispute, bears the imprint of familiar districting practices. . . .

I

At the outset, it may be useful to note points on which the Court does not divide. First, we agree that federalism and the slim judicial competence to draw district lines weigh heavily against judicial intervention in apportionment decisions; as a rule, the task should remain within the domain of state legislatures. Second, for most of our Nation's history, the franchise has not been enjoyed equally by black citizens and white voters. To redress past wrongs and to avert any recurrence of exclusion of blacks from political processes, federal courts now respond to Equal Protection Clause and Voting Rights Act complaints of state action that dilutes minority voting strength. Third, to meet statutory requirements, state legislatures must sometimes consider race as a factor highly relevant to the drawing of district lines. Finally, state legislatures may recognize communities that have a particular racial or ethnic makeup, even in the absence of any compulsion to do so, in order to account for interests common to or shared by the persons grouped together. *See Shaw* ("[W]hen members of a racial group live together in one community, a reapportionment plan that concentrates members of the group in one district and excludes them from others may reflect wholly legitimate purposes.").

Therefore, the fact that the Georgia General Assembly took account of race in drawing district lines — a fact not in dispute — does not render the State's plan invalid. . . .

* * *

II

A

Before *Shaw v. Reno* (1993), this Court invoked the Equal Protection Clause to justify intervention in the quintessentially political task of legislative districting in two circumstances: to enforce the one-person-one-vote requirement, *see Reynolds v. Sims* (1964); and to prevent dilution of a minority group's voting strength.

In *Shaw*, the Court recognized a third basis for an equal protection challenge to a State's apportionment plan. The Court wrote cautiously, emphasizing that judicial intervention is exceptional: Strict judicial scrutiny is in order, the Court declared, if a district is "so extremely irregular on its face that it rationally can be viewed only as an effort to segregate the races for purposes of voting."

. . . The problem in *Shaw* was not the plan architects' consideration of race as relevant in redistricting. Rather, in the Court's estimation, it was the virtual exclusion of other factors from the calculus. Traditional districting practices were cast aside, the Court concluded, with race alone steering placement of district lines.

B

The record before us does not show that race similarly overwhelmed traditional districting practices in Georgia. Although the Georgia General Assembly prominently considered race in shaping the Eleventh District, race did not crowd out all other factors, as the Court found it did in North Carolina's delineation of the *Shaw* district.

In contrast to the snake-like North Carolina district inspected in *Shaw*, Georgia's Eleventh District is hardly "bizarre," "extremely irregular," or "irrational on its face." Instead, the Eleventh District's design reflects significant consideration of "traditional districting factors (such as keeping political subdivisions intact) and the usual political process of compromise and trades for a variety of nonracial reasons." The District covers a core area in central and eastern Georgia, and its total land area of 6,780 square miles is about average for the State. The border of the Eleventh District runs 1,184 miles, in line with Georgia's Second District, which has a 1,243-mile border, and the State's Eighth District, with a border running 1,155 miles.

Nor does the Eleventh District disrespect the boundaries of political subdivisions. Of the 22 counties in the District, 14 are intact and 8 are divided. That puts the Eleventh District at about the state average in divided counties. By contrast, of the Sixth District's 5 counties, none are intact, and of the Fourth District's four counties, just one is intact. Seventy-one percent of the Eleventh District's boundaries track the borders of political subdivisions. Of the State's 11 districts, 5 score worse than the Eleventh District on this criterion, and 5 score better. Eighty-three percent of the Eleventh District's geographic area is composed of intact counties, above average for the State's congressional districts. And notably, the Eleventh District's boundaries largely follow precinct lines.

Evidence at trial similarly shows that considerations other than race went into determining the Eleventh District's boundaries. For a "political reason" — to accommodate the request of an incumbent State Senator regarding the placement of the precinct in which his son lived — the DeKalb County portion of the Eleventh District was drawn to include a particular (largely white) precinct. The corridor through Effingham County was substantially narrowed at the request of a (white) State Representative. In Chatham County, the District was trimmed to exclude a heavily black community in Garden City because a State Representative wanted to keep the city intact inside the neighboring First District. The Savannah extension was configured by "the narrowest means possible" to avoid splitting the city of Port Wentworth.

Georgia's Eleventh District, in sum, is not an outlier district shaped without reference to familiar districting techniques. Tellingly, the District that the Court's decision today unsettles is not among those on a statistically calculated list of the 28 most bizarre districts in the United States, a study prepared in the wake of our decision in *Shaw*.

C

The Court suggests that it was not Georgia's legislature, but the U.S. Department of Justice, that effectively drew the lines, and that Department officers did so with nothing but race in mind. Yet the "Max-Black" plan advanced by the Attorney General was not the plan passed by the Georgia General Assembly. [As the dissenting District Judge below stated,] "The Max-Black plan did influence to some degree the shape of the ultimate Eleventh District. . . . [But] the actual Eleventh is *not* identical to the Max-Black plan. The Eleventh, to my eye, is significantly different in shape in many ways. These differences show . . . consideration of other matters beyond race. . . ."

And although the Attorney General refused preclearance to the first two plans approved by Georgia's legislature, the State was not thereby disarmed; Georgia could have demanded relief from the Department's objections by instituting a civil action in the United States District Court for the District of Columbia, with ultimate review in this Court. Instead of pursuing that avenue, the State chose to adopt the plan here in controversy — a plan the State forcefully defends before us. We should respect Georgia's choice by taking its position on brief as genuine.

D

Along with attention to size, shape, and political subdivisions, the Court recognizes as an appropriate districting principle, "respect for . . . communities defined by actual shared interests." The Court finds no community here, however, because a report in the record showed "fractured political, social, and economic interests within the Eleventh District's black population."

But ethnicity itself can tie people together, as volumes of social science literature have documented — even people with divergent economic interests. For this reason, ethnicity is a significant force in political life. . . .

To accommodate the reality of ethnic bonds, legislatures have long drawn voting districts along ethnic lines. Our Nation's cities are full of districts identified by their ethnic character — Chinese, Irish, Italian, Jewish, Polish, Russian, for example. The creation of ethnic districts reflecting felt identity is not ordinarily viewed as offensive or demeaning to those included in the delineation.

III

To separate permissible and impermissible use of race in legislative apportionment, the Court orders strict scrutiny for districting plans "predominantly motivated" by race. No longer can a State avoid judicial oversight by giving — as in this case — genuine and measurable consideration to traditional districting practices. Instead, a federal case can be mounted whenever plaintiffs plausibly allege that other factors carried less weight than race. This invitation to litigate against the State seems to me neither necessary nor proper.

A

The Court derives its test from diverse opinions on the relevance of race in contexts distinctly unlike apportionment. The controlling idea, the Court says, is "'the simple command [at the heart of the Constitution's guarantee of equal protection] that the Government must treat citizens as individuals, not as simply components of a racial, religious, sexual or national class.'"

In adopting districting plans, however, States do not treat people as individuals. Apportionment schemes, by their very nature, assemble people in groups. States do not assign voters to districts based on merit or achievement, standards States might use in hiring employees or engaging contractors. Rather, legislators classify voters in groups — by economic, geographical, political, or social characteristics — and then "reconcile the competing claims of [these] groups."

That ethnicity defines some of these groups is a political reality. Until now, no constitutional infirmity has been seen in districting Irish or Italian voters together, for example, so long as the delineation does not abandon familiar apportionment practices. If Chinese-Americans and Russian-Americans may seek and secure group recognition in the delineation of voting districts, then African-Americans should not be dissimilarly treated. Otherwise, in the name of equal protection, we would shut out "the very minority group whose history in the United States gave birth to the Equal Protection Clause."

B

Under the Court's approach, judicial review of the same intensity, *i.e.*, strict scrutiny, is in order once it is determined that an apportionment is predominantly motivated by race. It matters not at all, in this new regime, whether the apportionment dilutes or enhances minority voting strength. As very recently observed, however, "[t]here is no moral or constitutional equivalence between a policy that is designed to perpetuate a caste system and one that seeks to eradicate racial subordination." *Adarand Constructors, Inc. v. Pena* (STEVENS, J., dissenting).

Special circumstances justify vigilant judicial inspection to protect minority voters — circumstances that do not apply to majority voters. A history of exclusion from state politics left racial minorities without clout to extract provisions for fair representation in the lawmaking forum. The equal protection rights of minority voters thus could have remained unrealized absent the Judiciary's close surveillance. The majority, by definition, encounters no such blockage. White voters in Georgia do not lack means to exert strong pressure on their state legislators. The force of their numbers is itself a powerful determiner of what the legislature will do that does not coincide with perceived majority interests.

State legislatures like Georgia's today operate under federal constraints imposed by the Voting Rights Act — constraints justified by history and designed by Congress to make once-subordinated people free and equal citizens. But these federal constraints do not leave majority voters in need of extraordinary judicial solicitude. The Attorney General, who administers the Voting Rights Act's preclearance requirements, is herself a political actor. She has a duty to enforce the law Congress passed, and she is no doubt aware of the political cost of venturing too far to the detriment of majority voters. Majority voters, furthermore, can press the State to seek judicial review if the Attorney General refuses to preclear a plan that the voters favor. Finally, the Act is itself a political measure, subject to modification in the political process.

C

The Court's disposition renders redistricting perilous work for state legislatures. Statutory mandates and political realities may require States to consider race when drawing district lines. But today's decision is a counterforce; it opens the way for federal litigation if "traditional . . . districting principles" arguably were accorded less weight than race. Genuine attention to traditional districting practices and avoidance of bizarre configurations seemed, under *Shaw*, to provide a safe harbor. In view of today's decision, that is no longer the case.

NOTES AND QUESTIONS

1. You will have been able to discern that this case, like *Shaw v. Reno,* came about because of vigorous Justice Department efforts to secure more African-American and other minority representatives in Congress. Is that a worthy goal? Or is there something unsavory in the notion that representatives should be selected on the basis that they are of a particular race or ethnic group? The majority in the case seems to believe that racial re-districting is, in a sense, a betrayal of American notions of equality, notions presumably based not only in the Equal Protection Clause of the Fourteenth Amendment, but also in the Declaration of Independence and in natural law. Do you agree?

2. The dissenters argue that the Supreme Court has gone even further in this case than it did in *Shaw v. Reno* to interfere with the "political process," and that such interference with a state's attempt to draw its own representational boundaries (albeit with a thumb on the scale provided by the Justice Department) is unwarranted. Do you agree? Do you discern a trend in the Supreme Court's decisions that seems to be moving in a different direction from the cases that followed the landmark decisions in *Brown*, *Green*, and *Swann*? Race, as indicated already, continues to be one of the most intractable problems in American society. What should be the role of the courts in ameliorating that problem, or do they have much of a role to play?

3. *Miller* establishes that race cannot be a predominant factor in the drawing of district lines. After *Miller*, a plurality of the Court led by Justice O'Connor indicated that predominance meant more than race consciousness, it meant that legitimate districting principles were subordinated to race. *Bush v. Vera*, 517 U.S. 952, 962 (1996). And in *Hunt v. Cromartie*, 526 U.S. 541 (1999), the Court held that it was inappropriate to determine whether race predominates as a matter of summary judgment where the state contends that it was not attempting to employ race, but party affiliation, in the redrawing of the same district (District 12, North Carolina) that was at issue in *Shaw v. Reno* (1993). Applying the normal presumptions, the Court said summary judgment was only appropriate where there is no genuine issue of material fact and the moving party is entitled to judgment as a matter of law. Those challenging District 12 had, however, offered only circumstantial evidence of racial predominance (bizarre shape; lack of compactness; disregard for political subdivision [the only district in the State containing no undivided county]), and the state did contest the alleged racial motivation, arguing that it was attempting to "protect incumbents, to adhere to traditional districting criteria, and to preserve the existing partisan balance in the State's congressional delegation . . . ." In addition, factual evidence tended to show that there was a high correlation between race and party in North Carolina. Given that the District court was obliged to assume the state's explanations as true for purposes of evaluating the summary judgment claim (the nonmoving party's evidence is to be believed and all justifiable inferences are to be drawn in that party's favor), the challengers were not entitled to judgment as a matter of law. "Our prior decisions have made clear that a jurisdiction may engage in constitutional political gerrymandering, even if it so happens that the most loyal Democrats happen to be black Democrats and even if the State were conscious of that fact."

In response to the Court's remand, the District Court conducted a 3 day trial and once again found that the congressional district was premised upon race. 5-4, the Supreme Court overturned the District Court as "clearly erroneous." *Easley v. Cromartie*, 532 U.S. 234 (2001). Writing for the Court, Justice Breyer articulated the view that those challenging a district as motivated predominantly by race have a heavy burden. Race must not just be a factor, but the predominant one; that is, one unexplainable on grounds other than race. This considerable burden reflects that districting is a legislative decision. Said Justice Breyer: "Caution is especially appropriate in this case, where the State has articulated a legitimate political explanation for its districting decision, and the voting population is one in which race and political affiliation are highly correlated." Justice Thomas wrote for the dissent, arguing that the Court had engaged in its own factfinding and improperly set aside the trial court. The dissent noted that the District Court used objective measures to find the legislative district "could not have been explained by political [that is, nonracial] motives."

4. Elaborating on its recognition in *Cromartie* that redistricting is fundamentally a legislative decision, the Supreme Court in *Georgia v. Ashcroft*, 539 U.S. 461 (2003), held that it was permissible for a legislature to choose to create "black influence districts" rather than a few districts in which blacks were a large enough majority of the voting age population to ensure the election of a candidate of their choice, and therefore remanded the case to the district court to consider whether pre-clearance was required once the entire effect of the redistricting plan was considered. "Section 5 gives States the flexibility to implement the type of plan that Georgia has submitted for preclearance — a plan that increases the number of districts with a majority-black voting age population, even if it means that in some of those districts, minority voters will face a somewhat reduced opportunity to elect a candidate of their choice." Thus, Justice O'Connor (writing for the five-member majority) held, because "the Voting Rights Act, as properly interpreted, should encourage the transition to a society where race no longer matters: a society where integration and color-blindness are not just qualities to be proud of, but are simple facts of life." *But see Grutter v. Bollinger, supra.*

5. What justifications remain for using race at all in districting? Here, the Court is divided. Justices Thomas and Scalia believe that strict scrutiny is appropriate whenever race is intentionally used in districting, whether or not it predominates. The dissenters in these cases (Justices Stevens, Souter, Ginsburg, and Breyer) would rather freely allow the use of race to create so-called majority-minority districts. In *Shaw v. Hunt*, 517 U.S. 899 (1996), the Court expressly held that compliance with the views of the Justice Department, especially as it applied section 5 of the Voting Rights Act, could not be used to justify the use of race. Section 5 requires pre-clearance by the Department of changes by states with a history of racial discrimination in voting matters. An unanswered question is whether compliance with section 2 of that Act, which prohibits changes in election systems with discriminatory effect (as opposed to intent), could justify a policy of maximizing minority districts. The Court implies a negative answer since the refusal to use race, itself, to maximize minority districts has not been viewed by the Court as an action with a prohibited discriminatory impact.

6. The Voting Rights Act, like Title VII of the Civil Rights Act, has provisions precluding not just racial intent, but racial impact. Given that the standard for an equal protection violation is purposeful or intentional discrimination, by what authority has Congress passed such legislation? If your thought is section 5 of the Fourteenth Amendment, the answer may not be sufficient. While the Voting Rights Act or Title VII may employ more lenient evidentiary means to identify constitutional violations, such means do not permit a public decision maker to make use of race in ways not permitted by the Constitution. According to the Court, race cannot be used for non-remedial purposes in employment and it must not be a predominant factor in the drawing of district lines. When Congress penalizes the racial impact of a neutral practice either in employment or voting, is Congress seeking to contradict the Court's fundamental requirement of racial intent for an equal protection violation? In *City of Boerne v. Flores*, 521 U.S. 507 (1997) (considered in Chapter Five), the Court invalidated the Religious Freedom Restoration Act (RFRA) by which Congress sought to explicitly displace the Court's interpretation of the Free Exercise Clause with a standard of its own choosing. Is Congress displacing the Court's view of equal protection in the Voting Rights Act or Title VII? As important as Congress' Fourteenth Amendment enforcement power is, does it include substantively rewriting constitutional text? In this regard, the Court held in *Boerne* that "Congress does not enforce a constitutional right by changing what the right is. It has been given the power 'to enforce,' not the power to determine what constitutes a constitutional violation. Were it not so, what Congress would be enforcing would no longer be, in any meaningful sense, the 'provisions of [the Constitution].'" 521 U.S. 519 (1997). "If Congress could define its own powers by altering the Fourteenth Amendment's meaning, no longer would the Constitution be 'superior paramount law, unchangeable by ordinary means.' It would be 'on a level with ordinary legislative acts, and, like other acts, . . . alterable when the legislature shall please to alter it.'" *Id.* at 529 (citing *Marbury v. Madison*, 5 U.S. (1 Cranch) 137, 177 (1803)).

7. Before moving on to consider gender and other bases of classification, mention of the topic of voting allows us to see another implication of the concept of equal protection.

B. Numerical Equality — One Person/One Vote

Equal protection has also been applied in the context of malapportionment — that is, the failure to keep voting districts of reasonably equal population. Applying equal protection to this issue was controversial since it was initially thought that voting was a political right to be determined by the political branches, most notably the state legislatures, of the several states. In *Baker v. Carr,* 369 U.S. 186 (1962), the Court concluded that a constitutional equal protection challenge was not solely a political question, and the issue was brought — over vigorous dissent — before the Supreme Court. The first case to articulate the one person/one vote standard was *Gray v. Sanders*, 372 U.S. 368 (1963), involving a challenge to the method of electing members to the Georgia House of Representatives. The Court asserted that "[t]he conception of political equality from the Declaration of Independence, to Lincoln's Gettysburg Address, to the Fifteenth, Seventeenth, and Nineteenth Amendments can mean only one thing — one person, one vote." *Id.* at 381. The Court subsequently applied this principle to districts for the U.S. House of Representatives in *Wesberry v. Sanders*, 376 U.S. 1 (1964). Perhaps all this seems obvious to us today. However, a moment's reflection reveals that the national legislature — the Congress — does not fully follow this principle. The Senate of the United States is made up of two representatives from each state regardless of population. This was part of the so-called great compromise at the 1787 constitutional convention, whereby regional, and to some extent slavery-determined, differences were assuaged by having a bicameral legislature made up of both population- and non-population-based interests in its composition. Why shouldn't the same political latitude be allowed within the states? Might not an individual state that is mostly rural and concerned with agricultural matters not want to counterbalance the urban interests of a singularly large city within the boundaries of the state? Of course, then the urban interests might be offended. As the mayor of Nashville complained about the situation in Tennessee litigated in *Baker*, the state was governed "by the hog lot and the cow pasture." ED CRAY, CHIEF JUSTICE: A BIOGRAPHY OF EARL WARREN 379 (1997).

One real problem confronted by the Court in *Baker* was the Supreme Court's prior opinion in *Colegrove v. Green*, 328 U.S. 549 (1946), written by Justice Frankfurter, which refused to interfere with the apportionment of Illinois congressional districts, even though population disparities in them ran as high as nine to one. Justice Frankfurter passionately dissented in *Baker*. He accused the majority, among other things, of imperiling the Court's high standing in American society and of producing an "umbrageous disposition." 369 U.S. at 267 (Frankfurter, J., dissenting). Why was there such obvious ire behind his opinion? Felix Frankfurter was undoubtedly one of the most talented men ever to sit on the Supreme Court. He was a professor at Harvard when he was nominated by President Franklin D. Roosevelt, and he was very much sympathetic to the New Deal. He was, then, very much a liberal in politics. Once on the Court, however, he became a champion for "judicial restraint" — that is, for articulating the view that the Court weakened its legitimacy when it took on social issues that, in Frankfurter's opinion, more properly belonged to other branches of government, or perhaps to the states rather than the federal government. When Frankfurter realized that a majority of the Court in *Baker* was going to repudiate his conclusion in *Colegrove* that apportionment was a "political question" that the Supreme Court should not touch, Frankfurter declared to his clerks that "[t]his is the darkest day in the history of the Court." CRAY, *supra*, at 382. Was he right? Whether or not it was the darkest day in the history of the Court, it was certainly a dark day for Frankfurter. Ten days after Brennan's opinion for the Court was announced in *Baker*, Frankfurter suffered a "massive stroke that left his left side paralyzed." *Id.* at 385. It is quite likely that the redistricting decision contributed to the tension and exertion that resulted in this crippling affliction. It was, Earl Warren's biographer notes, "the last and greatest blow" to Frankfurter, whose philosophy had been abandoned by his brethren. *Id.* The term in which *Baker* was decided was Frankfurter's last. Six months after the decision, realizing that he no longer had the physical capacity to participate fully in the work of the Court, Frankfurter submitted his resignation to the President. This marked "the end of an era." *Id.* When Frankfurter left the Court it was left to Justice Harlan to carry on Frankfurter's role as a champion of judicial restraint. You will be able to evaluate how well Harlan performed his task by considering his dissent in the case that follows — one made inevitable by *Baker*. The essence of Harlan's problem with what the majority decided *sub silentio* in *Baker* was that he could find no Fourteenth Amendment declaration that each person's vote ought to be counted equally. What was implicit in *Baker* became explicit in *Reynolds v. Sims.*

REYNOLDS v. SIMS
377 U.S. 533 (1964)

MR. CHIEF JUSTICE WARREN delivered the opinion of the Court.

* * *

I.

On August 26, 1961, the original plaintiffs . . . , residents, taxpayers and voters of Jefferson County, Alabama, filed a complaint in the United States District Court for the Middle District of Alabama, in their own behalf and on behalf of all similarly situated Alabama voters, challenging the apportionment of the Alabama Legislature. . . . The complaint alleged a deprivation of rights under the Alabama Constitution and under the Equal Protection Clause of the Fourteenth Amendment. . . .

* * *

Plaintiffs below alleged that the last apportionment of the Alabama Legislature was based on the 1900 federal census, despite the requirement of the State Constitution that the legislature be reapportioned decennially. They asserted that, since the population growth in the State from 1900 to 1960 had been uneven, Jefferson and other counties were now victims of serious discrimination with respect to the allocation of legislative representation. As a result of the failure of the legislature to reapportion itself, plaintiffs asserted, they were denied "equal suffrage in free and equal elections . . . and the equal protection of the laws" in violation of the Alabama Constitution and the Fourteenth Amendment to the Federal Constitution . . . and that, while the Alabama Supreme Court had found that the legislature had not complied with the State Constitution in failing to reapportion according to population decennially, that court had nevertheless indicated that it would not interfere with matters of legislative reapportionment.

* * *

On April 14, 1962, the District Court . . . [r]elying on our decision in *Baker v. Carr* . . . found jurisdiction, justiciability and standing. . . . [T]he Court stated that if the legislature complied with the Alabama constitutional provision requiring legislative representation to be based on population there could be no objection on federal constitutional grounds to such an apportionment. The Court further indicated that, if the legislature failed to act, or if its actions did not meet constitutional standards, it would be under a "clear duty" to take some action on the matter prior to the November 1962 general election. . . . Subsequently, plaintiffs were permitted to amend their complaint by adding a further prayer for relief, which asked the District Court to reapportion the Alabama Legislature provisionally so that the rural strangle hold would be relaxed enough to permit it to reapportion itself.

On July 12, 1962, an extraordinary session of the Alabama Legislature adopted two reapportionment plans to take effect for the 1966 elections. One was a proposed constitutional amendment, referred to as the "67-Senator Amendment." It provided for a House of Representatives consisting of 106 members, apportioned by giving one seat to each of Alabama's 67 counties and distributing the others according to population by the "equal proportions" method. Using this formula, the constitutional amendment specified the number of representatives allotted to each county until a new apportionment could be made on the basis of the 1970 census. The Senate was to be composed of 67 members, one from each county. The legislation provided that the proposed amendment should be submitted to the voters for ratification at the November 1962 general election.

The other reapportionment plan was embodied in a statutory measure adopted by the legislature and signed into law by the Alabama Governor, and was referred to as the "Crawford-Webb Act." It was enacted as standby legislation to take effect in 1966 if the proposed constitutional amendment should fail of passage by a majority of the State's voters, or should the federal courts refuse to accept the proposed amendment. . . . The act provided for a Senate consisting of 35 members, representing 35 senatorial districts established along county lines, and altered only a few of the former districts. In apportioning the 106 seats in the Alabama House of Representatives, the statutory measure gave each county one seat, and apportioned the remaining 39 on a rough population basis, under a formula requiring increasingly more population for a county to be accorded additional seats. . . .

* * *

On July 21, 1962, the District Court held that the inequality of the existing representation in the Alabama Legislature violated the Equal Protection Clause of the Fourteenth Amendment, a finding which the Court noted had been "generally conceded" by the parties to the litigation, since population growth and shifts had converted the 1901 scheme, as perpetuated some 60 years later, into an invidiously discriminatory plan completely lacking in rationality. . . . Population-variance ratios of up to about 41-to-1 existed in the Senate, and up to about 16-to-1 in the House. . . .

* * *

II.

Undeniably the Constitution of the United States protects the right of all qualified citizens to vote, in state as well as in federal elections. A consistent line of decisions by this Court in cases involving attempts to deny or restrict the right of suffrage has made this indelibly clear. . . . The right to vote freely for the candidate of one's choice is of the essence of a democratic society, and any restrictions on that right strike at the heart of representative government. And the right of suffrage can be denied by a debasement or dilution of the weight of a citizen's vote just as effectively as by wholly prohibiting the free exercise of the franchise.

In *Baker v. Carr* (1962) we held that a claim asserted under the Equal Protection Clause challenging the constitutionality of a State's apportionment of seats in its legislature, on the ground that the right to vote of certain citizens was effectively impaired since debased and diluted, in effect presented a justiciable controversy subject to adjudication by federal courts. The spate of similar cases filed and decided by lower courts since our decision in *Baker* amply shows that the problem of state legislative malapportionment is one that is perceived to exist in a large number of the States. In *Baker*, a suit involving an attack on the apportionment of seats in the Tennessee Legislature, we remanded to the District Court, which had dismissed the action, for consideration on the merits. We intimated no view as to the proper constitutional standards for evaluating the validity of a state legislative apportionment scheme. Nor did we give any consideration to the question of appropriate remedies. . . .

In *Gray v. Sanders* (1963) we held that the Georgia county unit system, applicable in statewide primary elections, was unconstitutional since it resulted in a dilution of the weight of the votes of certain Georgia voters merely because of where they resided. After indicating that the Fifteenth and Nineteenth Amendments prohibit a State from overweighting or diluting votes on the basis of race or sex, we stated . . . that "there is no indication in the Constitution that homesite or occupation affords a permissible basis for distinguishing between qualified voters within the State." And, finally, we concluded: "The conception of political equality from the Declaration of Independence, to Lincoln's Gettysburg Address, to the Fifteenth, Seventeenth, and Nineteenth Amendments can mean only one thing — one person, one vote."

We stated in *Gray*, however, that that case,

"unlike *Baker v. Carr*, . . . does not involve a question of the degree to which the Equal Protection Clause of the Fourteenth Amendment limits the authority of a State Legislature in designing the geographical districts from which representatives are chosen either for the State

Legislature or for the Federal House of Representatives. . . . Nor does it present the question, inherent in the bicameral form of our Federal Government, whether a State may have one house chosen without regard to population."

Of course, in these cases we are faced with the problem not presented in *Gray* — that of determining the basic standards and stating the applicable guidelines for implementing our decision in *Baker v. Carr*.

In *Wesberry v. Sanders* (1964), decided earlier this Term, we held that attacks on the constitutionality of congressional districting plans enacted by state legislatures do not present nonjusticiable questions and should not be dismissed generally for "want of equity." We determined that the constitutional test for the validity of congressional districting schemes was one of substantial equality of population among the various districts established by a state legislature for the election of members of the Federal House of Representatives.

In that case we decided that an apportionment of congressional seats which "contracts the value of some votes and expands that of others" is unconstitutional, since "the Federal Constitution intends that when qualified voters elect members of Congress each vote be given as much weight as any other vote . . . ." We concluded that the constitutional prescription for election of members of the House of Representatives "by the People," construed in its historical context, "means that as nearly as is practicable one man's vote in a congressional election is to be worth as much as another's." . . . We found further, in *Wesberry*, that "our Constitution's plain objective" was that "of making equal representation for equal numbers of people the fundamental goal." . . .

* * *

III.

A predominant consideration in determining whether a State's legislative apportionment scheme constitutes an invidious discrimination violative of rights asserted under the Equal Protection Clause is that the rights allegedly impaired are individual and personal in nature. . . .

Legislators represent people, not trees or acres. Legislators are elected by voters, not farms or cities or economic interests. As long as ours is a representative form of government, and our legislatures are those instruments of government elected directly by and directly representative of the people, the right to elect legislators in a free and unimpaired fashion is a bedrock of our political system. It could hardly be gainsaid that a constitutional claim had been asserted by an allegation that certain otherwise qualified voters had been entirely prohibited from voting for members of their state legislature. And, if a State should provide that the votes of citizens in one part of the State should be given two times, or five times, or 10 times the weight of votes of citizens in another part of the State, it could hardly be contended that the right to vote of those residing in the disfavored areas had not been effectively diluted. . . . Of course, the effect of state legislative districting schemes which give the same number of representatives to unequal numbers of constituents is identical. Overweighting and overvaluation of the votes of those living here has the certain effect of dilution and undervaluation of the votes of those living there. The resulting discrimination against those individual voters living in disfavored areas is easily demonstrable mathematically. Their right to vote is simply not the same right to vote as that of those living in a favored part of the State. . . . Weighting the votes of citizens differently, by any method or means, merely because of where they happen to reside, hardly seems justifiable. . . .

* * *

We are told that the matter of apportioning representation in a state legislature is a complex and many-faceted one. We are advised that States can rationally consider factors other than population in apportioning legislative representation. We are admonished not to restrict the power of the States to impose differing views as to political philosophy on their citizens. We are cautioned about the dangers of entering into political thickets and mathematical quagmires. Our answer is this: a denial of constitutionally protected rights demands judicial protection; our oath and our office require no less of us. . . . To the extent that a citizen's right to vote is debased, he is that much less a citizen. The fact that an individual lives here or there is not a legitimate reason for overweighting or diluting the efficacy of his vote. . . . [T]he basic principle of representative government remains, and must remain, unchanged — the weight of a citizen's vote cannot be made to depend on where he lives. . . . This is the clear and strong command of our Constitution's Equal Protection Clause. This is an essential part of the concept of a government of laws and not men. This is at the heart of Lincoln's vision of "government of the people, by the people, [and] for the people." The Equal Protection Clause demands no less than substantially equal state legislative representation for all citizens, of all places as well as of all races.

IV.

We hold that, as a basic constitutional standard, the Equal Protection Clause requires that the seats in both houses of a bicameral state legislature must be apportioned on a population basis. Simply stated, an individual's right to vote for state legislators is unconstitutionally impaired when its weight is in a substantial fashion diluted when compared with votes of citizens living in other parts of the State. Since, under neither the existing apportionment provisions nor either of the proposed plans was either of the houses of the Alabama Legislature apportioned on a population basis, the District Court correctly held that all three of these schemes were constitutionally invalid. Furthermore, the existing apportionment, and also to a lesser extent the apportionment under the Crawford-Webb Act, presented little more than crazy quilts, completely lacking in rationality, and could be found invalid on that basis alone. Although the District Court presumably found the apportionment of the Alabama House of Representatives under the 67-Senator Amendment to be acceptable, we conclude that the deviations from a strict population basis are too egregious to permit us to find that that body, under this proposed plan, was apportioned sufficiently on a population basis so as to permit the arrangement to be constitutionally sustained. . . .

Legislative apportionment in Alabama is signally illustrative and symptomatic of the seriousness of this problem in a number of the States. At the time this litigation was commenced, there had been no reapportionment of seats in the Alabama Legislature for over 60 years. Legislative inaction, coupled with the unavailability of any political or judicial remedy, had resulted, with the passage of years, in the perpetuated scheme becoming little more than an irrational anachronism. . . .

V.

Since neither of the houses of the Alabama Legislature, under any of the three plans considered by the District Court, was apportioned on a population basis, we would be justified in proceeding no further. However, one of the proposed plans, that contained in the so-called 67-Senator Amendment, at least superficially resembles the scheme of legislative representation followed in the Federal Congress. Under this plan, each of Alabama's 67 counties is allotted one senator, and no counties are given more than one Senate seat. Arguably, this is analogous to the allocation of two Senate seats, in the Federal Congress, to each of the 50 States, regardless of population. Seats in the Alabama House, under the proposed constitutional amendment, are distributed by giving each of the 67 counties at least one, with the remaining 39 seats being allotted among the more populous counties on a population basis. This scheme, at least at first glance, appears to resemble that prescribed for the Federal House of Representatives, where the 435 seats are distributed among the States on a population basis, although each State, regardless of its population, is given at least one Congressman. . . .

Much has been written since our decision in *Baker v. Carr* about the applicability of the so-called federal analogy to state legislative apportionment arrangements. After considering the matter, the court below concluded that no conceivable analogy could be drawn between the federal scheme and the apportionment of seats in the Alabama Legislature under the proposed constitutional amendment. We agree with the District Court, and find the federal analogy inapposite and irrelevant to state legislative districting schemes. . . . [T]he Founding Fathers clearly had no intention of establishing a pattern or model for the apportionment of seats in state legislatures when the system of representation in the Federal Congress was adopted. Demonstrative of this is the fact that the Northwest Ordinance, adopted in the same year, 1787, as the Federal Constitution, provided for the apportionment of seats in territorial legislatures solely on the basis of population.

The system of representation in the two Houses of the Federal Congress is one ingrained in our Constitution, as part of the law of the land. It is one conceived out of compromise and concession indispensable to the establishment of our federal republic. Arising from unique historical circumstances, it is based on the consideration that in establishing our type of federalism a group of formerly independent States bound themselves together under one national government. . . .

Political subdivisions of States — counties, cities, or whatever — never were and never have been considered as sovereign entities. Rather, they have been traditionally regarded as subordinate governmental instrumentalities created by the State to assist in the carrying out of state governmental functions. . . .

Thus, we conclude that the plan contained in the 67-Senator Amendment for apportioning seats in the Alabama Legislature cannot be sustained by recourse to the so-called federal analogy. Nor can any other inequitable state legislative apportionment scheme be justified on such an asserted basis. This does not necessarily mean that such a plan is irrational or involves something other than a "republican form of government." We conclude simply that such a plan is impermissible for the States under the Equal Protection Clause, since perforce resulting, in virtually every case, in submergence of the equal population principle in at least one house of a state legislature.

Since we find the so-called federal analogy inapposite to a consideration of the constitutional validity of state legislative apportionment schemes, we necessarily hold that the Equal Protection Clause requires both houses of a state legislature to be apportioned on a population basis. . . .

* * *

VI.

By holding that as a federal constitutional requisite both houses of a state legislature must be apportioned on a population basis, we mean that the Equal Protection Clause requires that a State make an honest and good faith effort to construct districts, in both houses of its legislature, as nearly of equal population as is practicable. We realize that it is a practical impossibility to arrange legislative districts so that each one has an identical number of residents, or citizens, or voters. Mathematical exactness or precision is hardly a workable constitutional requirement.

* * *

A State may legitimately desire to maintain the integrity of various political subdivisions, insofar as possible, and provide for compact districts of contiguous territory in designing a legislative apportionment scheme. Valid considerations may underlie such aims. Indiscriminate districting, without any regard for political subdivision or natural or historical boundary lines, may be little more than an open invitation to partisan gerrymandering. Single-member districts may be the rule in one State, while another State might desire to achieve some flexibility by creating multimember or floterial districts. Whatever the means of accomplishment, the overriding objective must be substantial equality of population among the various districts, so that the vote of any citizen is approximately equal in weight to that of any other citizen in the State.

History indicates, however, that many States have deviated, to a greater or lesser degree, from the equal-population principle in the apportionment of seats in at least one house of their legislatures. So long as the divergences from a strict population standard are based on legitimate considerations incident to the effectuation of a rational state policy, some deviations from the equal-population principle are constitutionally permissible with respect to the apportionment of seats in either or both of the two houses of a bicameral state legislature. But neither history alone, nor economic or other sorts of group interests, are permissible factors in attempting to justify disparities from population-based representation. Citizens, not history or economic interests, cast votes. Considerations of area alone provide an insufficient justification for deviations from the equal-population principle. Again, people, not land or trees or pastures, vote. Modern developments and improvements in transportation and communications make rather hollow, in the mid-1960's, most claims that deviations from population-based representation can validly be based solely on geographical considerations. Arguments for allowing such deviations in order to insure effective representation for sparsely settled areas and to prevent legislative districts from becoming so large that the availability of access of citizens to their representatives is impaired are today, for the most part, unconvincing.

A consideration that appears to be of more substance in justifying some deviations from population-based representation in state legislatures is that of insuring some voice to political subdivisions, as political subdivisions. Several factors make more than insubstantial claims that a State can rationally consider according political subdivisions some independent representation in at least one body of the state legislature, as long as the basic standard of equality of population among districts is maintained. Local governmental entities are frequently charged with various responsibilities incident to the operation of state government. In many States much of the legislature's activity involves the enactment of so-called local legislation, directed only to the concerns of particular political subdivisions. And a State may legitimately desire to construct districts along political subdivision lines to deter the possibilities of gerrymandering. However, permitting deviations from population-based representation does not mean that each local governmental unit or political subdivision can be given separate representation, regardless of population. Carried too far, a scheme of giving at least one seat in one house to each political subdivision (for example, to each county) could easily result, in many States, in a total subversion of the equal-population principle in that legislative body. . . .

VII.

One of the arguments frequently offered as a basis for upholding a State's legislative apportionment arrangement, despite substantial disparities from a population basis in either or both houses, is grounded on congressional approval, incident to admitting States into the Union, of state apportionment plans containing deviations from the equal-population principle. Proponents of this argument contend that congressional approval of such schemes, despite their disparities from population-based representation, indicates that such arrangements are plainly sufficient as establishing a "republican form of government." As we stated in *Baker v. Carr*, some questions raised under the Guaranty Clause are nonjusticiable, where "political" in nature and where there is a clear absence of judicially manageable standards. Nevertheless, it is not inconsistent with this view to hold that, despite congressional approval of state legislative apportionment plans at the time of admission into the Union, even though deviating from the equal-population principle here enunciated, the Equal Protection Clause can and does require more. And an apportionment scheme in which both houses are based on population can hardly be considered as failing to satisfy the Guaranty Clause requirement. Congress presumably does not assume, in admitting States into the Union, to pass on all constitutional questions relating to the character of state governmental organization. In any event, congressional approval, however well-considered, could hardly validate an unconstitutional state legislative apportionment. . . .

VIII.

That the Equal Protection Clause requires that both houses of a state legislature be apportioned on a population basis does not mean that States cannot adopt some reasonable plan for periodic revision of their apportionment schemes. Decennial reapportionment appears to be a rational approach to readjustment of legislative representation in order to take into account population shifts and growth. . . . While we do not intend to indicate that decennial reapportionment is a constitutional requisite, compliance with such an approach would clearly meet the minimal requirements for maintaining a reasonably current scheme of legislative representation. And we do not mean to intimate that more frequent reapportionment would not be constitutionally permissible or practicably desirable. But if reapportionment were accomplished with less frequency, it would assuredly be constitutionally suspect.

* * *

X.

We do not consider here the difficult question of the proper remedial devices which federal courts should utilize in state legislative apportionment cases. Remedial techniques in this new and developing area of the law will probably often differ with the circumstances of the challenged apportionment and a variety of local conditions. It is enough to say now that, once a State's legislative apportionment scheme has been found to be unconstitutional, it would be the unusual case in which a court would be justified in not taking appropriate action to insure that no further elections are conducted under the invalid plan. . . .

We feel that the District Court in this case acted in a most proper and commendable manner. It initially acted wisely in declining to stay the impending primary election in Alabama, and properly refrained from acting further until the Alabama Legislature had been given an opportunity to remedy the admitted discrepancies in the State's legislative apportionment scheme, while initially stating some of its views to provide guidelines for legislative action. And it correctly recognized that legislative reapportionment is primarily a matter for legislative consideration and determination, and that judicial relief becomes appropriate only when a legislature fails to reapportion according to federal constitutional requisites in a timely fashion after having had an adequate opportunity to do so. Additionally, the court below acted with proper judicial restraint, after the Alabama Legislature had failed to act effectively in remedying the constitutional deficiencies in the State's legislative apportionment scheme, in ordering its own temporary reapportionment plan into effect, at a time sufficiently early to permit the holding of elections pursuant to that plan without great difficulty, and in prescribing a plan admittedly provisional in purpose so as not to usurp the primary responsibility for reapportionment which rests with the legislature.

We find, therefore, that the action taken by the District Court in this case, in ordering into effect a reapportionment of both houses of the Alabama Legislature for purposes of the 1962 primary and general elections, by using the best parts of the two proposed plans which it had found, as a whole, to be invalid, was an appropriate and well-considered exercise of judicial power. . . . In retaining jurisdiction while deferring a hearing on the issuance of a final injunction in order to give the provisionally reapportioned legislature an opportunity to act effectively, the court below proceeded in a proper fashion. Since the District Court evinced its realization that its ordered reapportionment could not be sustained as the basis for conducting the 1966 election of Alabama legislators, and avowedly intends to take some further action should the reapportioned Alabama Legislature fail to enact a constitutionally valid, permanent apportionment scheme in the interim, we affirm the judgment below and remand the cases for further proceedings consistent with the views stated in this opinion.

It is so ordered.

MR. JUSTICE CLARK, concurring in the affirmance.

The Court goes much beyond the necessities of this case in laying down a new "equal population" principle for state legislative apportionment. . . .

It seems to me that all that the Court need say in this case is that each plan considered by the trial court is "a crazy quilt," clearly revealing invidious discrimination in each house of the Legislature and therefore violative of the Equal Protection Clause. . . .

I, therefore, do not reach the question of the so-called "federal analogy." But in my view, if one house of the State Legislature meets the population standard, representation in the other house might include some departure from it so as to take into account, on a rational basis, other factors in order to afford some representation to the various elements of the State. . . .

Mr. Justice Stewart. [Omitted.]

Mr. Justice Harlan, dissenting.

In these cases the Court holds that seats in the legislatures . . . are apportioned in ways that violate the Federal Constitution. Under the Court's ruling it is bound to follow that the legislatures in all but a few of the other . . . States will meet the same fate. These decisions, with *Wesberry v. Sanders* (1964) involving congressional districting by the States, and *Gray v. Sanders* (1963) relating to elections for statewide office, have the effect of placing basic aspects of state political systems under the pervasive overlordship of the federal judiciary. Once again, I must register my protest.

Preliminary Statement.

Today's holding is that the Equal Protection Clause of the Fourteenth Amendment requires every State to structure its legislature so that all the members of each house represent substantially the same number of people; other factors may be given play only to the extent that they do not significantly encroach on this basic "population" principle. Whatever may be thought of this holding as a piece of political ideology — and even on that score the political history and practices of this country from its earliest beginnings leave wide room for debate — I think it demonstrable that the Fourteenth Amendment does not impose this political tenet on the States or authorize this Court to do so.

The Court's constitutional discussion . . . is remarkable . . . for its failure to address itself at all to the Fourteenth Amendment as a whole or to the legislative history of the Amendment pertinent to the matter at hand. Stripped of aphorisms, the Court's argument boils down to the assertion that appellees' right to vote has been invidiously "debased" or "diluted" by systems of apportionment which entitle them to vote for fewer legislators than other voters, an assertion which is tied to the Equal Protection Clause only by the constitutionally frail tautology that "equal" means "equal."

Had the Court paused to probe more deeply into the matter, it would have found that the Equal Protection Clause was never intended to inhibit the States in choosing any democratic method they pleased for the apportionment of their legislatures. This is shown by the language of the Fourteenth Amendment taken as a whole, by the understanding of those who proposed and ratified it, and by the political practices of the States at the time the Amendment was adopted. It is confirmed by numerous state and congressional actions since the adoption of the Fourteenth Amendment, and by the common understanding of the Amendment as evidenced by subsequent constitutional amendments and decisions of this Court before *Baker v. Carr* made an abrupt break with the past in 1962.

The failure of the Court to consider any of these matters cannot be excused or explained by any concept of "developing" constitutionalism. It is meaningless to speak of constitutional "development" when both the language and history of the controlling provisions of the Constitution are wholly ignored. Since it can, I think, be shown beyond doubt that state legislative apportionments, as such, are wholly free of constitutional limitations, save such as may be imposed by the Republican Form of Government Clause (Const., Art. IV, § 4), the Court's action now bringing them within the purview of the Fourteenth Amendment amounts to nothing less than an exercise of the amending power by this Court.

So far as the Federal Constitution is concerned, the complaints in these cases should all have been dismissed below for failure to state a cause of action, because what has been alleged or proved shows no violation of any constitutional right.

* * *

I.

* * *

. . . In my judgment, today's decisions are refuted by the language of the Amendment which they construe and by the inference fairly to be drawn from subsequently enacted Amendments. They are unequivocally refuted by history and by consistent theory and practice from the time of the adoption of the Fourteenth Amendment until today.

II.

The Court's elaboration of its new "constitutional" doctrine indicates how far — and how unwisely — it has strayed from the appropriate bounds of its authority. The consequence of today's decision is that in all but the handful of States which may already satisfy the new requirements, the local District Court or, it may be, the state courts, are given blanket authority and the constitutional duty to supervise apportionment of the State Legislatures. It is difficult to imagine a more intolerable and inappropriate interference by the judiciary with the independent legislatures of the States.

* * *

. . . [T]hese cases do not mark the end of reapportionment problems in the courts. Predictions once made that the courts would never have to face the problem of actually working out an apportionment have proved false. This Court, however, continues to avoid the consequences of its decisions, simply assuring us that the lower courts "can and . . . will work out more concrete and specific standards." Deeming it "expedient" not to spell out "precise constitutional tests," the Court contents itself with stating "only a few rather general considerations."

Generalities cannot obscure the cold truth that cases of this type are not amenable to the development of judicial standards. No set of standards can guide a court which has to decide how many legislative districts a State shall have, or what the shape of the districts shall be, or where to draw a particular district line. No judicially manageable standard can determine whether a State should have single-member districts or multimember districts or some combination of both. No such standard can control the balance between keeping up with population shifts and having stable districts. In all these respects, the courts will be called upon to make particular decisions with respect to which a principle of equally populated districts will be of no assistance whatsoever. Quite obviously, there are limitless possibilities for districting consistent with such a principle. Nor can these problems be avoided by judicial reliance on legislative judgments so far as possible. Reshaping or combining one or two districts, or modifying just a few district lines, is no less a matter of choosing among many possible solutions, with varying political consequences, than reapportionment broadside.[82]

The Court ignores all this, saying only that "what is marginally permissible in one State may be unsatisfactory in another, depending on the particular circumstances of the case." It is well to remember that the product of today's decisions will not be readjustment of a few districts in a few States which most glaringly depart from the principle of equally populated districts. It will be a redetermination, extensive in many cases, of legislative districts in all but a few States.

Although the Court — necessarily, as I believe — provides only generalities in elaboration of its main thesis, its opinion nevertheless fully demonstrates how far removed these problems are from fields of judicial competence. Recognizing that "indiscriminate districting" is an invitation to "partisan gerrymandering," the Court nevertheless excludes virtually every basis for the formation of electoral districts other than "indiscriminate districting." In one or another of today's opinions, the Court declares it unconstitutional for a State to give effective consideration to any of the following in establishing legislative districts:

(1) history;

(2) "economic or other sorts of group interests";

(3) area;

(4) geographical considerations;

(5) a desire "to insure effective representation for sparsely settled areas";

(6) "availability of access of citizens to their representatives";

(7) theories of bicameralism (except those approved by the Court);

(8) occupation;

(9) "an attempt to balance urban and rural power";

(10) the preference of a majority of voters in the State.

---

[82] It is not mere fancy to suppose that in order to avoid problems of this sort, the Court may one day be tempted to hold that all state legislators must be elected in statewide elections.

So far as presently appears, the *only* factor which a State may consider, apart from numbers, is political subdivisions. But even "a clearly rational state policy" recognizing this factor is unconstitutional if "population is submerged as the controlling consideration. . . ."

I know of no principle of logic or practical or theoretical politics, still less any constitutional principle, which establishes all or any of these exclusions. Certain it is that the Court's opinion does not establish them. So far as the Court says anything at all on this score, it says only that "legislators represent people, not trees or acres"; that "citizens, not history or economic interests, cast votes"; that "people, not land or trees or pastures, vote." All this may be conceded. But it is surely equally obvious, and, in the context of elections, more meaningful to note that people are not ciphers and that legislators can represent their electors only by speaking for their interests — economic, social, political — many of which do reflect the place where the electors live. The Court does not establish, or indeed even attempt to make a case for the proposition that conflicting interests within a State can only be adjusted by disregarding them when voters are grouped for purposes of representation.

Conclusion.

. . . What is done today deepens my conviction that judicial entry into this realm is profoundly ill-advised and constitutionally impermissible. As I have said before, I believe that the vitality of our political system, on which in the last analysis all else depends, is weakened by reliance on the judiciary for political reform; in time a complacent body politic may result.

These decisions also cut deeply into the fabric of our federalism. What must follow from them may eventually appear to be the product of state legislatures. Nevertheless, no thinking person can fail to recognize that the aftermath of these cases, however desirable it may be thought in itself, will have been achieved at the cost of a radical alteration in the relationship between the States and the Federal Government, more particularly the Federal Judiciary. Only one who has an overbearing impatience with the federal system and its political processes will believe that that cost was not too high or was inevitable.

Finally, these decisions give support to a current mistaken view of the Constitution and the constitutional function of this Court. This view, in a nutshell, is that every major social ill in this country can find its cure in some constitutional "principle," and that this Court should "take the lead" in promoting reform when other branches of government fail to act. The Constitution is not a panacea for every blot upon the public welfare, nor should this Court, ordained as a judicial body, be thought of as a general haven for reform movements. The Constitution is an instrument of government, fundamental to which is the premise that in a diffusion of governmental authority lies the greatest promise that this Nation will realize liberty for all its citizens. This Court, limited in function in accordance with that premise, does not serve its high purpose when it exceeds its authority, even to satisfy justified impatience with the slow workings of the political process. For when, in the name of constitutional interpretation, the Court *adds* something to the Constitution that was deliberately excluded from it, the Court in reality substitutes its view of what should be so for the amending process.

* * *

NOTES AND QUESTIONS

1. Warren's biographer calls the case you have just read "the most influential of the 170 majority opinions he would write, more important than *Brown*, more important than the communist cases that so angered his critics, more important than the criminal law decisions that purportedly had loosed a crime wave upon the nation." ED CRAY, CHIEF JUSTICE: A BIOGRAPHY OF EARL WARREN 432 (1997). Why do you suppose *Reynolds* is regarded as so important? Earl Warren appears to have been passionate about the case because he thought his Court was correcting an evil which had resulted in the exclusion of Southern African Americans from state legislatures, and, indeed, a generation after *Reynolds*, 3,000 black men and women held elective office in the United States, whereas before *Reynolds*, almost none did. *Id.* at 437. Another effect of *Reynolds*, perhaps unintended by Warren, was that after decades of domination of Southern legislatures by the Democratic party, "the two-party system had returned." *Id.* These ends seem worthy, but did they justify the means used?

2. There can be no doubt that the Alabama constitutional mandate for reapportionment was ignored by the Alabama legislature. It does not seem too difficult to conclude that the rights of Alabamans were violated (and this, and this alone may be why Justice Stewart concurred in the result in the case), but should there be a federal judicial remedy for such a violation of a state constitution? Does *Baker v. Carr* answer that question?

3. What of the particular selection scheme for the bicameral legislature which the Alabama Constitution mandates? If the Court bases its grant of relief in part on the Alabama Constitution's requirement of decennial updates, why does it depart from the Alabama Constitution, and declare that one House of the Alabama Legislature may not represent counties, while the other represents the population? What's wrong with the so-called "federal analogy" (on which the "67-Senator Amendment" was based)? The analogy is based on the federal scheme whereby the Senate represents the states and the House of Representatives represents the people. Why is it a violation of the Fourteenth Amendment when a state seeks to emulate the governmental model of the Federal Government? If it is unconstitutional for a state to do that, why is it still constitutional at the federal level? The Fourteenth Amendment forbids only state action, of course, but aren't there principles of due process, equity, or perhaps natural law that would also impose equal protection obligations on the federal government? Justice Warren calls the Alabama plans clearly "discriminatory, arbitrary and irrational," 377 U.S. at 547, but if they are simply an attempt to replicate the federal system is this characterization valid?

4. But moving back to the problem of what the state legislatures can and cannot do with regard to apportionment, is it necessarily correct that just as the Fifteenth and Nineteenth Amendments prohibit a state from overweighting or diluting votes on the basis of race or sex, votes may not be "diluted" on the basis of where a person resides? The Chief Justice's pronouncement that "[t]he Equal Protection Clause demands no less than substantially equal state legislative representation for all citizens, of all places as well as of all races," 377 U.S. at 568, has a fine ring to it, and even rhymes, but is it a *non sequitur*? Might it well be a non-arbitrary and quite rational, albeit discriminatory, decision to make sure that urban voters do not always have their way against rural voters? Is it made less arbitrary and less irrational by the fact that throughout most of our history America has been an agricultural and pastoral place, even though the majority of our population is not now so situated? Is it true, as the Court declared in *Gray v. Sanders*, that "[t]he conception of political equality from the Declaration of Independence, to Lincoln's Gettysburg Address, to the Fifteenth, Seventeenth, and Nineteenth Amendments can mean only one thing — one person, one vote"? *Gray v. Sanders*, 372 U.S. 368, 381 (1963). How do each of these Amendments (to say nothing of the Gettysburg Address and the Declaration) lead to that conclusion? Would the framers have agreed with this interpretation of the political tradition they were founding?

5. "One person, one vote," which comes from *Gray v. Sanders* (why, by the way, is that case which invalidated malapportionment in the Georgia House not dispositive of *Reynolds*? Is it that *Reynolds* requires *both* houses of a state legislature to be apportioned by population?), is some of the most famous language used in *Reynolds*, and *Reynolds* is often taken to stand for that proposition. More pungent, perhaps, is the language of Chief Justice Warren making a correlate point: "Legislators represent people, not trees or acres. Legislators are elected by voters, not farms or cities or economic interests." *Reynolds*, 377 U.S. at 562. Is he right? Do legislators represent only the people, or is something more at stake? The one person/one vote standard was applied to districts for the U.S. House of Representatives in *Wesberry v. Sanders*, 376 U.S. 1 (1964). Local governments were covered in *Avery v. Midland County*, 390 U.S. 474 (1968). Even limited governing bodies, like school districts, are now within the rule. *Hadley v. Junior College District*, 397 U.S. 50 (1970). The rule of one person/one vote does not require mathematical exactness, but it is more demanding for the U.S. House than for state and local offices.

6. The only dissent is that of Justice Harlan, who relies on "detailed analysis of the history, drafting, language and ratification of the Fourteenth Amendment." Gordon E. Baker, Reynolds v. Sims, *in* THE OXFORD COMPANION TO THE SUPREME COURT OF THE UNITED STATES 732, 733 (Kermit L. Hall et al. eds., 1992). Which part of his analysis is most convincing? Chief Justice Warren also purports to rely on history. Who does the better job? Why do you suppose that

Harlan was unable to gather any other votes in support of his position? At issue in *Reynolds* and its accompanying cases were redistricting decisions for six state legislatures, and one week later the Court handed down similar rulings, without accompanying opinions, invalidating apportionment in ten other states. Indeed, it appears that *Reynolds* declared the invalidity of "at least one house in nearly all state legislatures . . . and both houses in most." Baker, *supra*, at 732. Which is more likely, that fifty state legislatures got it wrong, or that eight men on the Supreme Court did? Can you understand why shortly after *Reynolds* (and several other Warren Court decisions involving criminal law and racial integration) billboards even began to appear in some rural areas with the legend "Impeach Earl Warren"? He was never impeached, of course, but he was subjected to more vilification than any other Chief Justice before or since, with the possible exception of Chief Justice Taney. Did he deserve the calumny?

7. Justice Harlan is concerned that the majority is dangerously undercutting federalism, and he is similarly disturbed by the Court's "judicial activism to cure perceived social ills." Baker, *supra*, at 733. Do you agree with Harlan's basic point, that "[t]he Constitution is not a panacea for every blot upon the public welfare, nor should th[e] Court, ordained as a judicial body, be thought of as a general haven for reform movements"? *Reynolds*, 377 U.S. at 624-25 (Harlan, J., dissenting). Why would he believe in such a limited role for the Supreme Court? Would Frankfurter have agreed? Who, if anyone, today maintains this Harlan/Frankfurter legacy? Would you?

8. An issue related to the proportionality of voting districts is the enumeration of the general population for the purpose of apportioning congressional representation among the states. Article I, section 2, clause 3 of the Constitution provides: "The actual Enumeration shall be made within . . . every subsequent Term of ten Years, in such Manner as they [the Congress] shall by Law direct." Section 2 of the Fourteenth Amendment provides that "Representatives shall be apportioned among the several States according to their respective numbers . . . ." Dictionaries contemporaneous with the founding define "enumeration" as actual counting, not estimation. The Congressional Census Acts have similarly so required; indeed, the Acts of 1810 through 1950 required census enumerators to visit each home in person. Thus, it came as a significant departure from tradition when the Clinton administration proposed to use statistical sampling methods (methods of estimation) to arrive at part of the Census for the Year 2000. The plan was challenged by private citizens who would suffer a loss of representation under the estimated methods or who would be adversely affected by intrastate redistricting. To meet the *Reynolds* standard, many states use population numbers generated by the Census. Members of Congress also filed suit alleging a congressional interest in the composition of the House. In *Department of Commerce v. United States House of Representatives*, 525 U.S. 316 (1999), the Court held that the private parties had standing and that the Census Act requires actual enumeration (counting) not estimation or sampling for apportionment purposes.

9. The next case is well-known, and while not everyone was satisfied with either the effective political outcome or its remedial considerations, it was apparent to seven Justices that the case presented a basic equal protection problem that could not survive even the most lenient standard of judicial examination. The majority of the Court and Justices Souter and Breyer in dissent were in common agreement that disparate standards could not be applied in different electoral jurisdictions to otherwise identical facts. As Justices Souter and Breyer explained: "It is true that the Equal Protection Clause does not forbid the use of a variety of voting mechanisms within a jurisdiction, even though different mechanisms will have different levels of effectiveness in recording voters' intentions; local variety can be justified by concerns about cost, the potential value of innovation, and so on. But evidence in the record here suggests that a different order of disparity obtains under rules for determining a voter's intent that have been applied (and could continue to be applied) to identical types of ballots used in identical brands of machines and exhibiting identical physical characteristics (such as 'hanging' or 'dimpled' chads). . . . [We] can conceive of no legitimate state interest served by these differing treatments of the expressions of voters' fundamental rights. The differences appear wholly arbitrary." (Souter and Breyer, JJ., dissenting). To be wholly arbitrary in classification in reference to voting was not constitutionally permissible.

BUSH v. GORE
531 U.S. 98 (2000)

PER CURIAM

On December 8, 2000, the Supreme Court of Florida ordered that the Circuit Court of Leon County tabulate by hand 9,000 ballots in Miami-Dade County. It also ordered the inclusion in the certified vote totals of 215 votes identified in Palm Beach County and 168 votes identified in Miami-Dade County for Vice President Albert Gore, Jr., and Senator Joseph Lieberman, Democratic Candidates for President and Vice President. The court further held that relief would require manual recounts in all Florida counties where so-called "undervotes" had not been subject to manual tabulation. The court ordered all manual recounts to begin at once. Governor Bush and Richard Cheney, Republican Candidates for the Presidency and Vice Presidency, filed an emergency application for a stay of this mandate. On December 9, we granted the application, treated the application as a petition for a writ of certiorari, and granted certiorari.

On November 8, 2000, the day following the Presidential election, the Florida Division of Elections reported that petitioner, Governor Bush, had received 2,909,135 votes, and respondent, Vice President Gore, had received 2,907,351 votes, a margin of 1,784 for Governor Bush. Because Governor Bush's margin of victory was less than "one-half of a percent of the votes cast," an automatic machine recount was conducted under . . . the election code, the results of which showed Governor Bush still winning the race but by a diminished margin. Vice

President Gore then sought manual recounts in Volusia, Palm Beach, Broward, and Miami-Dade Counties, pursuant to Florida's election protest provisions. . . . A dispute arose concerning the deadline for local county canvassing boards to submit their returns to the Secretary of State (Secretary). The Secretary declined to waive the November 14 deadline imposed by statute. The Florida Supreme Court, however, set the deadline at November 26. We granted certiorari and vacated the Florida Supreme Court's decision, finding considerable uncertainty as to the grounds on which it was based. On December 11, the Florida Supreme Court issued a decision on remand reinstating that date.

On November 26, the Florida Elections Canvassing Commission certified the results of the election and declared Governor Bush the winner of Florida's 25 electoral votes. On November 27, Vice President Gore, pursuant to Florida's contest provisions, filed a complaint in Leon County Circuit Court contesting the certification. He sought relief pursuant to [Florida law] which provides that "[r]eceipt of a number of illegal votes or rejection of a number of legal votes sufficient to change or place in doubt the result of the election" shall be grounds for a contest. The Circuit Court denied relief, stating that Vice President Gore failed to meet his burden of proof. He appealed to the First District Court of Appeal, which certified the matter to the Florida Supreme Court.

* * *

The [Florida] Supreme Court held that Vice President Gore had satisfied his burden of proof with respect to his challenge to Miami-Dade County's failure to tabulate, by manual count, 9,000 ballots on which the machines had failed to detect a vote for President ("undervotes"). Noting the closeness of the election, the Court explained that "[o]n this record, there can be no question that there are legal votes within the 9,000 uncounted votes sufficient to place the results of this election in doubt." A "legal vote," as determined by the Supreme Court, is "one in which there is a 'clear indication of the intent of the voter.'" The court therefore ordered a hand recount of the 9,000 ballots in Miami-Dade County. Observing that the contest provisions vest broad discretion in the circuit judge to "provide any relief appropriate under such circumstances," the Supreme Court further held that the Circuit Court could order "the Supervisor of Elections and the Canvassing Boards, as well as the necessary public officials, in all counties that have not conducted a manual recount or tabulation of the undervotes to do so forthwith, said tabulation to take place in the individual counties where the ballots are located."

The Supreme Court also determined that both Palm Beach County and Miami-Dade County, in their earlier manual recounts had identified a net gain of 215 and 168 legal votes for Vice President Gore. Rejecting the Circuit Court's conclusion that Palm Beach County lacked the authority to include the 215 net votes submitted past the November 26 deadline, the Supreme Court explained that the deadline was not intended to exclude votes identified after that date through ongoing manual recounts. As to Miami-Dade County, the Court concluded that although the 168 votes identified were the result of a partial recount, they were "legal votes [that] could change the outcome of the election." The Supreme Court therefore directed the Circuit Court to include those totals in the certified results, subject to resolution of the actual vote total from the Miami-Dade partial recount.

The petition presents the following questions: whether the Florida Supreme Court established new standards for resolving Presidential election contests, thereby violating Art. II, § 1, cl. 2, of the United States Constitution and failing to comply with 3 U.S.C. § 5, and whether the use of standardless manual recounts violates the Equal Protection and Due Process Clauses. With respect to the equal protection question, we find a violation of the Equal Protection Clause.

II

A

The closeness of this election, and the multitude of legal challenges which have followed in its wake, have brought into sharp focus a common, if heretofore unnoticed, phenomenon. Nationwide statistics reveal that an estimated 2% of ballots cast do not register a vote for President for whatever reason, including deliberately choosing no candidate at all or some voter error, such as voting for two candidates or insufficiently marking a ballot. . . . In certifying election results, the votes eligible for inclusion in the certification are the votes meeting the properly established legal requirements.

This case has shown that punch card balloting machines can produce an unfortunate number of ballots which are not punched in a clean, complete way by the voter. After the current counting, it is likely legislative bodies nationwide will examine ways to improve the mechanisms and machinery for voting.

B

The individual citizen has no federal constitutional right to vote for electors for the President of the United States unless and until the state legislature chooses a statewide election as the means to implement its power to appoint members of the Electoral College. U.S. Const., Art. II, § 1. This is the source for the statement in *McPherson v. Blacker,* 146 U.S. 1, 35 (1892), that the State legislature's power to select the manner for appointing electors is plenary; it may, if it so chooses, select the electors itself, which indeed was the manner used by State legislatures in several States for many years after the Framing of our Constitution. History has now favored the voter, and in each of the several States the citizens themselves vote for Presidential electors. When the state legislature vests the right to vote for President in its people, the right to vote as the legislature has prescribed is fundamental; and one source of its fundamental nature lies in the equal weight accorded to each vote and the equal dignity owed to each voter. The State, of course, after granting the franchise in the special context of Article II, can take back the power to appoint electors. ("[T]here is no doubt of the right of the legislature to resume the power at any time, for it can neither be taken away nor abdicated").

The right to vote is protected in more than the initial allocation of the franchise. Equal protection applies as well to the manner of its exercise. Having once granted the right to vote on equal terms, the State may not, by later arbitrary and disparate treatment, value one person's vote over that of another. It must be remembered that "the right of suffrage can be denied by a debasement or dilution of the weight of a citizen's vote just as effectively as by wholly prohibiting the free exercise of the franchise." *Reynolds v. Sims,* 377 U.S. 533, 555 (1964).

There is no difference between the two sides of the present controversy on these basic propositions. Respondents say that the very purpose of vindicating the right to vote justifies the recount procedures now at issue. The question before us, however, is whether the recount procedures the Florida Supreme Court has adopted are consistent with its obligation to avoid arbitrary and disparate treatment of the members of its electorate.

Much of the controversy seems to revolve around ballot cards designed to be perforated by a stylus but which, either through error or deliberate omission, have not been perforated with sufficient precision for a machine to count them. In some cases a piece of the card — a chad — is hanging, say by two corners. In other cases there is no separation at all, just an indentation.

The Florida Supreme Court has ordered that the intent of the voter be discerned from such ballots. For purposes of resolving the equal protection challenge, it is not necessary to decide whether the Florida Supreme Court had the authority under the legislative scheme for resolving election disputes to define what a legal vote is and to mandate a manual recount implementing that definition. The recount mechanisms implemented in response to the decisions of the Florida Supreme Court do not satisfy the minimum requirement for non-arbitrary treatment of voters necessary to secure the fundamental right. Florida's basic command for the count of legally cast votes is to consider the "intent of the voter" . . . . This is unobjectionable as an abstract proposition and a starting principle. The problem inheres in the absence of specific standards to ensure its equal application. The formulation of uniform rules to determine intent based on these recurring circumstances is practicable and, we conclude, necessary.

The law does not refrain from searching for the intent of the actor in a multitude of circumstances; and in some cases the general command to ascertain intent is not susceptible to much further refinement. In this instance, however, the question is not whether to believe a witness but how to interpret the marks or holes or scratches on an inanimate object, a piece of cardboard or paper which, it is said, might not have registered as a vote during the machine count. The factfinder confronts a thing, not a person. The search for intent can be confined by specific rules designed to ensure uniform treatment.

The want of those rules here has led to unequal evaluation of ballots in various respects. . . . As seems to have been acknowledged at oral argument, the standards for accepting or rejecting contested ballots might vary not only from county to county but indeed within a single county from one recount team to another.

The record provides some examples. A monitor in Miami-Dade County testified at trial that he observed that three members of the county canvassing board applied different standards in defining a legal vote. And testimony at trial also revealed that at least one county changed its evaluative standards during the counting process. Palm Beach County, for example, began the process with a 1990 guideline which precluded counting completely attached chads, switched to a rule that considered a vote to be legal if any light could be seen through a chad, changed back to the 1990 rule, and then abandoned any pretense of a *per se* rule, only to have a court order that the county consider dimpled chads legal. This is not a process with sufficient guarantees of equal treatment.

An early case in our one person, one vote jurisprudence arose when a State accorded arbitrary and disparate treatment to voters in its different counties. *Gray v. Sanders* (1963). The Court found a constitutional violation. We relied on these principles in the context of the Presidential selection process in *Moore v. Ogilvie,* 394 U.S. 814 (1969), where we invalidated a county-based procedure that diluted the influence of citizens in larger counties in the nominating process. There we observed that "[t]he idea that one group can be granted greater voting strength than another is hostile to the one man, one vote basis of our representative government."

The State Supreme Court ratified this uneven treatment. It mandated that the recount totals from two counties, Miami-Dade and Palm Beach, be included in the certified total. The court also appeared to hold *sub silentio* that the recount totals from Broward County, which were not completed until after the original November 14 certification by the Secretary of State, were to be considered part of the new certified vote totals even though the county certification was not contested by Vice President Gore. Yet each of the counties used varying standards to determine what was a legal vote. Broward County used a more forgiving standard than Palm Beach County, and uncovered almost three times as many new votes, a result markedly disproportionate to the difference in population between the counties.

In addition, the recounts in these three counties were not limited to so-called undervotes but extended to all of the ballots. The distinction has real consequences. A manual recount of all ballots identifies not only those ballots which show no vote but also those which contain more than one, the so-called overvotes. Neither category will be counted by the machine. This is not a trivial concern. At oral argument, respondents estimated there are as many as 110,000 overvotes statewide. As a result, the citizen whose ballot was not read by a machine because he failed to vote for a candidate in a way readable by a machine may still have his vote counted in a manual recount; on the other hand, the citizen who marks two candidates in a way discernable by the machine will not have the same opportunity to have his vote count, even if a manual examination of the ballot would reveal the requisite indicia of intent. Furthermore, the citizen who marks two candidates, only one of which is discernable by the machine, will have his vote counted even though it should have been read as an invalid ballot. The State Supreme Court's inclusion of vote counts based on these variant standards exemplifies concerns with the remedial processes that were under way.

That brings the analysis to yet a further equal protection problem. The votes certified by the court included a partial total from one county, Miami-Dade. The Florida Supreme Court's decision thus gives no assurance that the recounts included in a final certification must be complete. Indeed, it is respondent's submission that it would be consistent with the rules of the recount procedures to include whatever partial counts are done by the time of final certification, and we interpret the Florida Supreme Court's decision to permit this. This accommodation no doubt results from the truncated contest period established by the Florida Supreme Court in *Bush I* [*Bush v. Palm Beach County Canvassing Board*], at respondents' own urging. The press of time does not diminish the constitutional concern. A desire for speed is not a general excuse for ignoring equal protection guarantees.

In addition to these difficulties the actual process by which the votes were to be counted under the Florida Supreme Court's decision raises further concerns. That order did not specify who would recount the ballots. The county canvassing boards were forced to pull together ad hoc teams comprised of judges from various Circuits who had no previous training in handling and interpreting ballots. Furthermore, while others were permitted to observe, they were prohibited from objecting during the recount.

The recount process, in its features here described, is inconsistent with the minimum procedures necessary to protect the fundamental right of each voter in the special instance of a statewide recount under the authority of a single state judicial officer. Our consideration is limited to the present circumstances, for the problem of equal protection in election processes generally presents many complexities.

. . . The question before the Court is not whether local entities, in the exercise of their expertise, may develop different systems for implementing elections. Instead, we are presented with a situation where a state court with the power to assure uniformity has ordered a statewide recount with minimal procedural safeguards. When a court orders a statewide remedy, there must be at least some assurance that the rudimentary requirements of equal treatment and fundamental fairness are satisfied.

Given the Court's assessment that the recount process underway was probably being conducted in an unconstitutional manner, the Court stayed the order directing the recount so it could hear this case and render an expedited decision. The contest provision, as it was mandated by the State Supreme Court, is not well calculated to sustain the confidence that all citizens must have in the outcome of elections. The State has not shown that its procedures include the necessary safeguards. The problem, for instance, of the estimated 110,000 overvotes has not been addressed, although Chief Justice Wells called attention to the concern in his dissenting opinion.

Upon due consideration of the difficulties identified to this point, it is obvious that the recount cannot be conducted in compliance with the requirements of equal protection and due process without substantial additional work. It would require not only the adoption (after opportunity for argument) of adequate statewide standards for determining what is a legal vote, and practicable procedures to implement them, but also orderly judicial review of any disputed matters that might arise. In addition, the Secretary of State has advised that the recount of only a portion of the ballots requires that the vote tabulation equipment be used to screen out undervotes, a function for which the machines were not designed. If a recount of overvotes were also required, perhaps even a second screening would be necessary. Use of the equipment for this purpose, and any new software developed for it, would have to be evaluated for accuracy by the Secretary of State, as required by [Florida law].

The Supreme Court of Florida has said that the legislature intended the State's electors to "participat[e] fully in the federal electoral process," as provided in 3 U.S.C. § 5. That statute, in turn, requires that any controversy or contest that is designed to lead to a conclusive selection of electors be completed by December 12. That date is upon us, and there is no recount procedure in place under the State Supreme Court's order that comports with minimal constitutional standards. Because it is evident that any recount seeking to meet the December 12 date will be unconstitutional for the reasons we have discussed, we reverse the judgment of the Supreme Court of Florida ordering a recount to proceed.

Seven Justices of the Court agree that there are constitutional problems with the recount ordered by the Florida Supreme Court that demand a remedy. *See* (SOUTER, J., dissenting); (BREYER, J., dissenting). The only disagreement is as to the remedy. Because the Florida Supreme Court has said that the Florida Legislature intended to obtain the safe-harbor benefits of 3 U.S.C. § 5, JUSTICE BREYER's proposed remedy — remanding to the Florida Supreme Court for its ordering of a constitutionally proper contest until December 18 — contemplates action in violation of the Florida election code, and hence could not be part of an "appropriate" order authorized by [Florida Statute].

* * *

None are more conscious of the vital limits on judicial authority than are the members of this Court, and none stand more in admiration of the Constitution's design to leave the selection of the President to the people, through their legislatures, and to the political sphere. When contending parties invoke the process of the courts, however, it becomes our unsought responsibility to resolve the federal and constitutional issues the judicial system has been forced to confront.

The judgment of the Supreme Court of Florida is reversed, and the case is remanded for further proceedings not inconsistent with this opinion.

It is so ordered.

CHIEF JUSTICE REHNQUIST, with whom JUSTICE SCALIA and JUSTICE THOMAS join, concurring.

We join the *per curiam* opinion. We write separately because we believe there are additional grounds that require us to reverse the Florida Supreme Court's decision.

I

We deal here not with an ordinary election, but with an election for the President of the United States.

* * *

In most cases, comity and respect for federalism compel us to defer to the decisions of state courts on issues of state law. That practice reflects our understanding that the decisions of state courts are definitive pronouncements of the will of the States as sovereigns. *Cf. Erie R. Co. v. Tompkins* (1938). Of course, in ordinary cases, the distribution of powers among the branches of a State's government raises no questions of federal constitutional law, subject to the requirement that the government be republican in character. *See* U.S. Const., Art. IV, § 4. But there are a few exceptional cases in which the Constitution imposes a duty or confers a power on a particular branch of a State's government. This is one of them. Article II, § 1, cl. 2, provides that "[e]ach State shall appoint, in such Manner as the *Legislature* thereof may direct," electors for President and Vice President. (Emphasis added.) Thus, the text of the election law itself, and not just its interpretation by the courts of the States, takes on independent significance.

In *McPherson v. Blacker,* 146 U.S. 1 (1892), we explained that Art. II, § 1, cl. 2, "convey[s] the broadest power of determination" and "leaves it to the legislature exclusively to define the method" of appointment. *Id.* at 27. A significant departure from the legislative scheme for appointing Presidential electors presents a federal constitutional question.

3 U.S.C. § 5 informs our application of Art. II, § 1, cl. 2, to the Florida statutory scheme, which, as the Florida Supreme Court acknowledged, took that statute into account. Section 5 provides that the State's selection of electors "shall be conclusive, and shall govern in the counting of the electoral votes" if the electors are chosen under laws enacted prior to election day, and if the selection process is completed six days prior to the meeting of the electoral college. As we noted in *Bush v. Palm Beach County Canvassing Bd.*:

"Since § 5 contains a principle of federal law that would assure finality of the State's determination if made pursuant to a state law in effect before the election, a legislative wish to take advantage of the 'safe harbor' would counsel against any construction of the Election Code that Congress might deem to be a change in the law."

If we are to respect the legislature's Article II powers, therefore, we must ensure that postelection state-court actions do not frustrate the legislative desire to attain the "safe harbor" provided by § 5.

In Florida, the legislature has chosen to hold statewide elections to appoint the State's 25 electors. Importantly, the legislature has delegated the authority to run the elections and to oversee election disputes to the Secretary of State (Secretary) . . . . Isolated sections of the code may well admit of more than one interpretation, but the general coherence of the legislative scheme may not be altered by judicial interpretation so as to wholly change the statutorily provided apportionment of responsibility among these various bodies. In any election but a Presidential election, the Florida Supreme Court can give as little or as much deference to Florida's executives as it chooses, so far as Article II is concerned, and this Court will have no cause to question the court's actions. But, with respect to a Presidential election, the court must be both mindful of the legislature's role under Article II in choosing the manner of appointing electors and deferential to those bodies expressly . . . empowered by the legislature to carry out its constitutional mandate.

In order to determine whether a state court has infringed upon the legislature's authority, we necessarily must examine the law of the State as it existed prior to the action of the court. Though we generally defer to state courts on the interpretation of state law . . . there are of course areas in which the Constitution requires this Court to undertake an independent, if still deferential, analysis of state law.

What we would do in the present case is precisely parallel: Hold that the Florida Supreme Court's interpretation of the Florida election laws impermissibly distorted them beyond what a fair reading required, in violation of Article II.[1]

This inquiry does not imply a disrespect for state *courts* but rather a respect for the constitutionally prescribed role of state *legislatures*. To attach definitive weight to the pronouncement of a state court, when the very question at issue is whether the court has actually departed from the statutory meaning, would be to abdicate our responsibility to enforce the explicit requirements of Article II.

---

[1] Similarly, our jurisprudence requires us to analyze the "background principles" of state property law to determine whether there has been a taking of property in violation of the Takings Clause. That constitutional guarantee would, of course, afford no protection against state power if our inquiry could be concluded by a state supreme court holding that state property law accorded the plaintiff no rights. *See Lucas v. South Carolina Coastal Council* (1992).

II

Acting pursuant to its constitutional grant of authority, the Florida Legislature has created a detailed, if not perfectly crafted, statutory scheme that provides for appointment of Presidential electors by direct election. Under the statute, "[v]otes cast for the actual candidates for President and Vice President shall be counted as votes cast for the presidential electors supporting such candidates." The legislature has designated the Secretary of State as the "chief election officer," with the responsibility to "[o]btain and maintain uniformity in the application, operation, and interpretation of the election laws." The state legislature has delegated to county canvassing boards the duties of administering elections. Those boards are responsible for providing results to the state Elections Canvassing Commission, comprising the Governor, the Secretary of State, and the Director of the Division of Elections.

* * *

In its first decision, *Palm Beach Canvassing Bd. v. Harris* the Florida Supreme Court extended the 7-day statutory certification deadline established by the legislature.[2] This modification of the code, by lengthening the protest period, necessarily shortened the contest period for Presidential elections. Underlying the extension of the certification deadline and the shortchanging of the contest period was, presumably, the clear . . . implication that certification was a matter of significance: The certified winner would enjoy presumptive validity, making a contest proceeding by the losing candidate an uphill battle. In its latest opinion, however, the court empties certification of virtually all legal consequence during the contest, and in doing so departs from the provisions enacted by the Florida Legislature.

The court determined that canvassing boards' decisions regarding whether to recount ballots past the certification deadline (even the certification deadline [judicially established] . . .) are to be reviewed *de novo,* although the election code clearly vests discretion whether to recount in the boards, and sets strict deadlines subject to the Secretary's rejection of late tallies and monetary fines for tardiness. Moreover, the Florida court held that all late vote tallies arriving during the contest period should be automatically included in the certification regardless of the certification deadline (even the certification deadline established by *Harris I* [judicially extended], thus virtually eliminating both the deadline and the Secretary's discretion to disregard recounts that violate it. . . .

Moreover, the court's interpretation of "legal vote," and hence its decision to order a contest-period recount, plainly departed from the legislative scheme. Florida statutory law cannot reasonably be thought to *require* the counting of improperly marked ballots. Each Florida precinct before election day provides instructions on how properly to cast a vote, each polling place on election day

---

[2] We vacated that decision [in *Bush I*] and remanded that case; the Florida Supreme Court reissued the same judgment with a new opinion on December 11, 2000. . . .

contains a working model of the voting machine it uses and each voting booth contains a sample ballot. In precincts using punch-card ballots, voters are instructed to punch out the ballot cleanly:

> AFTER VOTING, CHECK YOUR BALLOT CARD TO BE SURE YOUR VOTING SELECTIONS ARE CLEARLY AND CLEANLY PUNCHED AND THERE ARE NO CHIPS LEFT HANGING ON THE BACK OF THE CARD.

No reasonable person would call it "an error in the vote tabulation," or a "rejection of legal votes," when electronic or electromechanical equipment performs precisely in the manner designed, and fails to count those ballots that are not marked in the manner that these voting instructions explicitly and prominently specify. The scheme that the Florida Supreme Court's opinion attributes to the legislature is one in which machines are *required* to be "capable of correctly counting votes," but which nonetheless regularly produces elections in which legal votes are predictably *not* tabulated, so that in close elections manual recounts are regularly required. This is of course absurd. The Secretary of State, who is authorized by law to issue binding interpretations of the election code, rejected this peculiar reading of the statutes. . . . The Florida Supreme Court, although it must defer to the Secretary's interpretations rejected her reasonable interpretation and embraced the peculiar one.

But as we indicated in our remand of the earlier case, in a Presidential election the clearly expressed intent of the legislature must prevail. And there is no basis for reading the Florida statutes as requiring the counting of improperly marked ballots, as an examination of the Florida Supreme Court's textual analysis shows. The State's Attorney General (who was supporting the Gore challenge) confirmed in oral argument here that never before the present election had a manual recount been conducted on the basis of the contention that "undervotes" should have been examined to determine voter intent. For the court to step away from this established practice, prescribed by the Secretary of State, the state official charged by the legislature with "responsibility to [o]btain and maintain uniformity in the application, operation, and interpretation of the election laws," was to depart from the legislative scheme.

III

The scope and nature of the remedy ordered by the Florida Supreme Court jeopardizes the "legislative wish" to take advantage of the safe harbor provided by 3 U.S.C. § 5 is the last date for a final determination of the Florida electors that will satisfy § 5. Yet in the late afternoon of December 8th — four days before this deadline — the Supreme Court of Florida ordered recounts of tens of thousands of so-called "undervotes" spread through 64 of the State's 67 counties. This was done in a search for elusive — perhaps delusive — certainty as to the exact count of 6 million votes. But no one claims that these ballots have not previously been tabulated; they were initially read by voting machines at the time of the election, and thereafter reread by virtue of Florida's automatic recount provision. No one claims there was any fraud in the election. The Supreme Court of Florida ordered this additional recount under the provision of the election code giving the circuit judge the authority to provide relief that is "appropriate under such circumstances."

Surely when the Florida Legislature empowered the courts of the State to grant "appropriate" relief, it must have meant relief that would have become final by the cut-off date of 3 U.S.C. § 5. In light of the inevitable legal challenges and ensuing appeals to the Supreme Court of Florida and petitions for certiorari to this Court, the entire recounting process could not possibly be completed by that date.

* * *

Given all these factors, and in light of the legislative intent identified by the Florida Supreme Court to bring Florida within the "safe harbor" provision of 3 U.S.C. § 5, the remedy prescribed by the Supreme Court of Florida cannot be deemed an "appropriate" one as of December 8. It significantly departed from the statutory framework in place on November 7, and authorized open-ended further proceedings which could not be completed by December 12, thereby preventing a final determination by that date.

For these reasons, in addition to those given in the *per curiam,* we would reverse.

JUSTICE STEVENS, with whom JUSTICE GINSBURG and JUSTICE BREYER join, dissenting.

* * *

The federal questions that ultimately emerged in this case are not substantial. Article II provides that "[e]ach *State* shall appoint, in such Manner as the Legislature *thereof* may direct, a Number of Electors." *Ibid.* (emphasis added). It does not create state legislatures out of whole cloth, but rather takes them as they come — as creatures born of, and constrained by, their state constitutions. Lest there be any doubt, we stated over 100 years ago in *McPherson v. Blacker* (1892), that "[w]hat is forbidden or required to be done by a State" in the Article II context "is forbidden or required of the legislative power under state constitutions as they exist." In the same vein, we also observed that "[t]he [State's] legislative power is the supreme authority except as limited by the constitution of the State." The legislative power in Florida is subject to judicial review pursuant to Article V of the Florida Constitution, and nothing in Article II of the Federal Constitution frees the state legislature from the constraints in the state constitution that created it. Moreover, the Florida Legislature's own decision to employ a unitary code for all elections indicates that it intended the Florida Supreme Court to play the same role in Presidential elections that it has historically played in resolving electoral disputes. The Florida Supreme Court's exercise of appellate jurisdiction therefore was wholly consistent with, and indeed contemplated by, the grant of authority in Article II.

* * *

Nor are petitioners correct in asserting that the failure of the Florida Supreme Court to specify in detail the precise manner in which the "intent of the voter" is to be determined rises to the level of a constitutional violation.[2] We found such a violation when individual votes within the same State were weighted unequally, see, *e.g., Reynolds v. Sims* (1964), but we have never before called into question the substantive standard by which a State determines that a vote has been legally cast. And there is no reason to think that the guidance provided to the factfinders, specifically the various canvassing boards, by the "intent of the voter" standard is any less sufficient — or will lead to results any less uniform — than, for example, the "beyond a reasonable doubt" standard employed every-day by ordinary citizens in courtrooms across this country.

Admittedly, the use of differing substandards for determining voter intent in different counties employing similar voting systems may raise serious concerns. Those concerns are alleviated — if not eliminated — by the fact that a single impartial magistrate will ultimately adjudicate all objections arising from the recount process. Of course, as a general matter, "[t]he interpretation of consti-tutional principles must not be too literal. We must remember that the machin-ery of government would not work if it were not allowed a little play in its joints." If it were otherwise, Florida's decision to leave to each county the deter-mination of what balloting system to employ — despite enormous differences in accuracy[4] — might run afoul of equal protection. So, too, might the similar decisions of the vast majority of state legislatures to delegate to local authori-ties certain decisions with respect to voting systems and ballot design.

Even assuming that aspects of the remedial scheme might ultimately be found to violate the Equal Protection Clause, I could not subscribe to the major-ity's disposition of the case. As the majority explicitly holds, once a state legis-lature determines to select electors through a popular vote, the right to have one's vote counted is of constitutional stature. As the majority further acknowl-edges, Florida law holds that all ballots that reveal the intent of the voter con-stitute valid votes. Recognizing these principles, the majority nonetheless orders the termination of the contest proceeding before all such votes have been tab-ulated. Under their own reasoning, the appropriate course of action would be to remand to allow more specific procedures for implementing the legislature's uniform general standard to be established.

* * *

---

[2] The Florida statutory standard is consistent with the practice of the majority of States, which apply either an "intent of the voter" standard or an "impossible to determine the elector's choice" standard in ballot recounts. (cita-tions omitted).

[4] The percentage of nonvotes in this election in counties using a punch-card system was 3.92%; in contrast, the rate of error under the more modern optical-scan systems was only 1.43%. . . . Put in other terms, for every 10,000 votes cast, punch-card systems result in 250 more nonvotes than optical-scan systems. A total of 3,718,305 votes were cast under punch-card systems, and 2,353,811 votes were cast under optical-scan systems. . . .

Finally, neither in this case, nor in its earlier opinion, did the Florida Supreme Court make any substantive change in Florida electoral law. Its decisions were rooted in long-established precedent and were consistent with the relevant statutory provisions, taken as a whole. It did what courts do — it decided the case before it in light of the legislature's intent to leave no legally cast vote uncounted. In so doing, it relied on the sufficiency of the general "intent of the voter" standard articulated by the state legislature, coupled with a procedure for ultimate review by an impartial judge, to resolve the concern about disparate evaluations of contested ballots. If we assume — as I do — that the members of that court and the judges who would have carried out its mandate are impartial, its decision does not even raise a colorable federal question.

* * *

I respectfully dissent.

JUSTICE SOUTER, with whom JUSTICE BREYER joins and with whom JUSTICE STEVENS and JUSTICE GINSBURG join with regard to all but Part C, dissenting.

The Court should not have reviewed either *Bush v. Palm Beach County Canvassing Bd.* [*Bush I*] or this case, and should not have stopped Florida's attempt to recount all undervote ballots, by issuing a stay of the Florida Supreme Court's orders during the period of this review. If this Court had allowed the State to follow the course indicated by the opinions of its own Supreme Court, it is entirely possible that there would ultimately have been no issue requiring our review, and political tension could have worked itself out in the Congress following the procedure provided in 3 U.S.C. § 15. The case being before us, however, its resolution by the majority is another erroneous decision.

* * *

B

The issue is whether the judgment of the state supreme court has displaced the state legislature's provisions for election contests: is the law as declared by the court different from the provisions made by the legislature, to which the national Constitution commits responsibility for determining how each State's Presidential electors are chosen? *See* U.S. Const., Art. II, § 1, cl. 2. Bush does not, of course, claim that any judicial act interpreting a statute of uncertain meaning is enough to displace the legislative provision and violate Article II; statutes require interpretation, which does not without more affect the legislative character of a statute within the meaning of the Constitution. What Bush does argue, as I understand the contention, is that the interpretation was so unreasonable as to transcend the accepted bounds of statutory interpretation, to the point of being a nonjudicial act and producing new law untethered to the legislative act in question.

* * *

The majority view is in each instance within the bounds of reasonable interpretation, and the law as declared is consistent with Article II.

The statute does not define a "legal vote," the rejection of which may affect the election. The State Supreme Court was therefore required to define it, and in doing that the court looked to another election statute, dealing with damaged or defective ballots, which contains a provision that no vote shall be disregarded "if there is a clear indication of the intent of the voter as determined by a canvassing board." The court read that objective of looking to the voter's intent as indicating that the legislature probably meant "legal vote" to mean a vote recorded on a ballot indicating what the voter intended. It is perfectly true that the majority might have chosen a different reading. *E.g.,* (defining "legal votes" as "votes properly executed in accordance with the instructions provided to all registered voters in advance of the election and in the polling places"). But even so, there is no constitutional violation in following the majority view; Article II is unconcerned with mere disagreements about interpretive merits.

* * *

C

* * *

Petitioners have raised an equal protection claim (or, alternatively, a due process claim, see generally *Logan v. Zimmerman Brush Co.* (1982)), in the charge that unjustifiably disparate standards are applied in different electoral jurisdictions to otherwise identical facts. It is true that the Equal Protection Clause does not forbid the use of a variety of voting mechanisms within a jurisdiction, even though different mechanisms will have different levels of effectiveness in recording voters' intentions; local variety can be justified by concerns about cost, the potential value of innovation, and so on. But evidence in the record here suggests that a different order of disparity obtains under rules for determining a voter's intent that have been applied (and could continue to be applied) to identical types of ballots used in identical brands of machines and exhibiting identical physical characteristics (such as "hanging" or "dimpled" chads). I can conceive of no legitimate state interest served by these differing treatments of the expressions of voters' fundamental rights. The differences appear wholly arbitrary.

In deciding what to do about this, we should take account of the fact that electoral votes are due to be cast in six days. I would therefore remand the case to the courts of Florida with instructions to establish uniform standards for evaluating the several types of ballots that have prompted differing treatments, to be applied within and among counties when passing on such identical ballots in any further recounting (or successive recounting) that the courts might order.

* * *

I respectfully dissent.

JUSTICE GINSBURG with whom JUSTICE STEVENS joins, and with whom JUSTICE SOUTER and JUSTICE BREYER join as to Part I, dissenting.

I

THE CHIEF JUSTICE acknowledges that provisions of Florida's Election Code "may well admit of more than one interpretation." But instead of respecting the state high court's province to say what the State's Election Code means, THE CHIEF JUSTICE maintains that Florida's Supreme Court has veered so far from the ordinary practice of judicial review that what it did cannot properly be called judging. I might join THE CHIEF JUSTICE were it my commission to interpret Florida law. But disagreement with the Florida court's interpretation of its own State's law does not warrant the conclusion that the justices of that court have legislated. There is no cause here to believe that the members of Florida's high court have done less than "their mortal best to discharge their oath of office," and no cause to upset their reasoned interpretation of Florida law.

* * *

THE CHIEF JUSTICE says that Article II, by providing that state legislatures shall direct the manner of appointing electors, authorizes federal superintendence over the relationship between state courts and state legislatures, and licenses a departure from the usual deference we give to state court interpretations of state law. The Framers of our Constitution, however, understood that in a republican government, the judiciary would construe the legislature's enactments.[2]

* * *

Article II does not call for the scrutiny undertaken by this Court.

* * *

II

I agree with JUSTICE STEVENS that petitioners have not presented a substantial equal protection claim. Ideally, perfection would be the appropriate standard for judging the recount. But we live in an imperfect world, one in which thousands of votes have not been counted. I cannot agree that the recount adopted by the Florida court, flawed as it may be, would yield a result any less fair or precise than the certification that preceded that recount.

* * *

Equally important, as JUSTICE BREYER explains, the December 12 "deadline" for bringing Florida's electoral votes into 3 U.S.C. § 5's safe harbor lacks the significance the Court assigns it. Were that date to pass, Florida would still be enti-

---

[2] Even in the rare case in which a State's "manner" of making and construing laws might implicate a structural constraint, Congress, not this Court, is likely the proper governmental entity to enforce that constraint. *See* U.S. Const., amend. XII; 3 U.S.C. §§ 1-15.

tled to deliver electoral votes Congress *must* count unless both Houses find that the votes "ha [d] not been regularly given." 3 U.S.C. § 15. The statute identifies other significant dates. *See, e.g.,* § 7 (specifying December 18 as the date electors "shall meet and give their votes"); § 12 (specifying "the fourth Wednesday in December" — this year, December 27 — as the date on which Congress, if it has not received a State's electoral votes, shall request the state secretary of state to send a certified return immediately). But none of these dates has ultimate significance in light of Congress' detailed provisions for determining, on "the sixth day of January," the validity of electoral votes. § 15.

The Court assumes that time will not permit "orderly judicial review of any disputed matters that might arise." But no one has doubted the good faith and diligence with which Florida election officials, attorneys for all sides of this controversy, and the courts of law have performed their duties. Notably, the Florida Supreme Court has produced two substantial opinions within 29 hours of oral argument. In sum, the Court's conclusion that a constitutionally adequate recount is impractical is a prophecy the Court's own judgment will not allow to be tested. Such an untested prophecy should not decide the Presidency of the United States.

I dissent.

JUSTICE BREYER, with whom JUSTICE STEVENS and JUSTICE GINSBURG join except as to Part I-A-1, and with whom JUSTICE SOUTER joins as to Part I, dissenting.

The Court was wrong to take this case. It was wrong to grant a stay. It should . . . now vacate that stay and permit the Florida Supreme Court to decide whether the recount should resume.

I

The political implications of this case for the country are momentous. But the federal legal questions presented, with one exception, are insubstantial.

A

1

The majority raises three Equal Protection problems with the Florida Supreme Court's recount order: first, the failure to include overvotes in the manual recount; second, the fact that *all* ballots, rather than simply the undervotes, were recounted in some, but not all, counties; and third, the absence of a uniform, specific standard to guide the recounts. As far as the first issue is concerned, petitioners presented no evidence, to this Court or to any Florida court, that a manual recount of overvotes would identify additional legal votes. The same is true of the second, and, in addition, the majority's reasoning would seem to invalidate any state provision for a manual recount of individual counties in a statewide election.

The majority's third concern does implicate principles of fundamental fairness. The majority concludes that the Equal Protection Clause requires that a manual recount be governed not only by the uniform general standard of the "clear intent of the voter," but also by uniform subsidiary standards (for example, a uniform determination whether indented, but not perforated, "undervotes" should count). The opinion points out that the Florida Supreme Court ordered the inclusion of Broward County's undercounted "legal votes" even though those votes included ballots that were not perforated but simply "dimpled," while newly recounted ballots from other counties will likely include only votes determined to be "legal" on the basis of a stricter standard. In light of our previous remand, the Florida Supreme Court may have been reluctant to adopt a more specific standard than that provided for by the legislature for fear of exceeding its authority under Article II. However, since the use of different standards could favor one or the other of the candidates, since time was, and is, too short to permit the lower courts to iron out significant differences through ordinary judicial review, and since the relevant distinction was embodied in the order of the State's highest court, I agree that, in these very special circumstances, basic principles of fairness may well have counseled the adoption of a uniform standard to address the problem. In light of the majority's disposition, I need not decide whether, or the extent to which, as a remedial matter, the Constitution would place limits upon the content of the uniform standard.

2

Nonetheless, there is no justification for the majority's remedy, which is simply to reverse the lower court and halt the recount entirely. An appropriate remedy would be, instead, to remand this case with instructions that, even at this late date, would permit the Florida Supreme Court to require recounting *all* undercounted votes in Florida, including those from Broward, Volusia, Palm Beach, and Miami-Dade Counties, whether or not previously recounted prior to the end of the protest period, and to do so in accordance with a single-uniform substandard.

. . . The majority finds facts outside of the record on matters that state courts are in a far . . . better position to address. Of course, it is too late for any such recount to take place by December 12, the date by which election disputes must be decided if a State is to take advantage of the safe harbor provisions of 3 U.S.C. § 5. Whether there is time to conduct a recount prior to December 18, when the electors are scheduled to meet, is a matter for the state courts to determine. And whether, under Florida law, Florida could or could not take further action is obviously a matter for Florida courts, not this Court, to decide.

B

* * *

[T]he concurrence says that "the Florida Supreme Court's interpretation of the Florida election laws impermissibly distorted them beyond what a fair reading required, in violation of Article II." But what precisely is the distortion?

Apparently, it has three elements. First, the Florida court, in its earlier opinion, changed the election certification date from November 14 to November 26. Second, the Florida court ordered a manual recount of "undercounted" ballots that could not have been fully completed by the December 12 "safe harbor" deadline. Third, the Florida court, in the opinion now under review, failed to give adequate deference to the determinations of canvassing boards and the Secretary.

To characterize the first element as a "distortion," however, requires the concurrence to second-guess the way in which the state court resolved a plain conflict in the language of different statutes.

To characterize the second element as a "distortion" requires the concurrence to overlook the fact that the inability of the Florida courts to conduct the recount on time is, in significant part, a problem of the Court's own making. The Florida Supreme Court thought that the recount could be completed on time, and, within hours, the Florida Circuit Court was moving in an orderly fashion to meet the deadline. This Court improvidently entered a stay. As a result, we will never know whether the recount could have been completed.

Nor can one characterize the third element as "impermissibl[e] distort[ing]" once one understands that there are two sides to the opinion's argument that the Florida Supreme Court "virtually eliminated the Secretary's discretion" . . . . And the parties have argued about the proper meaning of the statute's term "legal vote." . . . The Secretary has claimed that a "legal vote" is a vote "properly executed in accordance with the instructions provided to all registered voters" . . . . On that interpretation, punchcard ballots for which the machines cannot register a vote are not "legal" votes. The Florida Supreme Court did not accept her definition. But it had a reason. Its reason was that a different provision of Florida election laws (a provision that addresses damaged or defective ballots) says that no vote shall be disregarded "if there is a clear indication of the intent of the voter as determined by the canvassing board" (adding that ballots should not be counted "if it is impossible to determine the elector's choice").

* * *

II

Petitioners invoke fundamental fairness, namely, the need for procedural fairness, including finality. But with the one "equal protection" exception, they rely upon law that focuses, not upon that basic need, but upon the constitutional allocation of power. Respondents invoke a competing fundamental consideration — the need to determine the voter's true intent. Neither side claims electoral fraud, dishonesty, or the like. And the more fundamental equal protection claim might have been left to the state court to resolve if and when it was discovered to have mattered. It could still be resolved through a remand conditioned upon issuance of a uniform standard; it does not require reversing the Florida Supreme Court.

Of course, the selection of the President is of fundamental national importance. But that importance is political, not legal. And this Court should resist the temptation unnecessarily to resolve tangential legal disputes, where doing so threatens to determine the outcome of the election.

* * *

[T]he Twelfth Amendment commits to Congress the authority and responsibility to count electoral votes. A federal statute, the Electoral Count Act, enacted after the close 1876 Hayes-Tilden Presidential election, specifies that, after States have tried to resolve disputes (through "judicial" or other means), Congress is the body primarily authorized to resolve remaining disputes. *See* Electoral Count Act of 1887, 3 U.S.C. §§ 5, 6, and 15.

The legislative history of the Act makes clear its intent to commit the power to resolve such disputes to Congress, rather than the courts:

> "The two Houses are, by the Constitution, authorized to make the count of electoral votes. They can only count legal votes, and in doing so must determine, from the best evidence to be had, what are legal votes. The power to determine rests with the two Houses, and there is no other constitutional tribunal."

The Member of Congress who introduced the Act added:

> "The power to judge of the legality of the votes is a necessary consequent of the power to count. The existence of this power is of absolute necessity to the preservation of the Government. The interests of all the States in their relations to each other in the Federal Union demand that the ultimate tribunal to decide upon the election of President should be a constituent body, in which the States in their federal relationships and the people in their sovereign capacity should be represented." 18 Cong. Rec. 30 (1886).

> "Under the Constitution who else could decide? Who is nearer to the State in determining a question of vital importance to the whole union of States than the constituent body upon whom the Constitution has devolved the duty to count the vote?" *Id.* at 31.

The decision by both the Constitution's Framers and the 1886 Congress to minimize this Court's role in resolving close federal presidential elections is as wise as it is clear. However awkward or difficult it may be for Congress to resolve difficult electoral disputes, Congress, being a political body, expresses the people's will far more accurately than does an unelected Court. And the people's will is what elections are about.

This history may help to explain why I think it not only legally wrong, but also most unfortunate, for the Court simply to have terminated the Florida recount. Those who caution judicial restraint in resolving political disputes have described the quintessential case for that restraint as a case marked, among other things, by the "strangeness of the issue," its "intractability to principled resolution," its "sheer momentousness, which tends to unbalance judicial judgment," and "the inner vulnerability, the self-doubt of an institution which is electorally irresponsible and has no earth to draw strength from." Those characteristics mark this case.

At the same time, as I have said, the Court is not acting to vindicate a fundamental constitutional principle, such as the need to protect a basic human liberty. No other strong reason to act is present. Congressional statutes tend to obviate the need. And, above all, in this highly politicized matter, the appearance of a split decision runs the risk of undermining the public's confidence in the Court itself. That confidence is a public treasure. It has been built slowly over many years, some of which were marked by a Civil War and the tragedy of segregation. It is a vitally necessary ingredient of any successful effort to protect basic liberty and, indeed, the rule of law itself. We run no risk of returning to the days when a President (responding to this Court's efforts to protect the Cherokee Indians) might have said, "John Marshall has made his decision; now let him enforce it!" But we do risk a self-inflicted wound — a wound that may harm not just the Court, but the Nation.

I fear that in order to bring this agonizingly long election process to a definitive conclusion, we have not adequately attended to that necessary "check upon our own exercise of power," "our own sense of self-restraint." Justice Brandeis once said of the Court, "The most important thing we do is not doing." What it does today, the Court should have left undone. I would repair the damage done as best we now can, by permitting the Florida recount to continue under uniform standards.

I respectfully dissent.

NOTES AND QUESTIONS

1. Did the U.S. Supreme Court have to get involved? Wasn't this just an issue of state law or a nonjusticiable political dispute? Seven Justices apparently thought not since, according to the per curiam opinion, basic principles of equal protection require that once a state has granted the people the right to vote for presidential electors, "the State may not, by later arbitrary and disparate treatment, value one person's vote over that of another." True, at an earlier point in our history, the Court might have been inclined to treat this matter as a nonjusticiable political question, but modernly, such judicial reticence in the voting context cannot be reconciled with decisions like *Baker v. Carr* and *Reynolds v. Sims* (1964). Remember that in *Baker* and *Reynolds*, the Court applied equal protection principles to establish the one person/one vote maxim in the context of voting districts that were malapportioned in terms of population. A vote is diluted when 10,000 voters in one district have the same number of political representatives in the legislative assembly as 100,000 voters in another. By parity of reasoning, inequality results in a statewide race for presidential electors when an incomplete or ambiguously completed ballot in one county is counted and in another is discarded. The inequality is magnified when the same types of ballots are differently treated even within the same county, which counsel for Vice President Gore conceded was occurring at oral argument. In other words, it was a bit of a free for all. Count first; figure out the standards later. How would you feel if your professor graded each final exam in this class by a different standard, and if asked what standard she applied, proclaimed that it varied from bluebook to bluebook?

2. But what about the differences in voting machine technology? As the Court discovered, punch card machines are less reliable than optical scanners. Does the failure to supply the best or most fool-proof equipment to all counties violate equal protection? The Court doesn't say, and it is highly unlikely. First, the Court emphasizes that its ruling pertains to the unique risks and circumstances before it — namely, a *judicially* mandated *recount* of real, *inanimate objects* (the ballots). In the Court's words, "[o]ur consideration is limited to the present circumstances, for the problem of equal protection in election processes generally presents many complexities." For example, the case does not answer whether it is unconstitutional to allow local decision-makers to employ different types of machines in the future; in other words, to have the discretion to update voting equipment in a non-discriminatory, rational way as scarce equipment budgets permit. This would seem minimally rational, even if not ideal. Second, the recount process is especially susceptible to abuse because it occurs after the fact, in essence allowing the contesting candidate an opportunity to manipulate the recount in light of his initial losing margin. Third, when the judiciary inserts itself into election recounts, it must at least anticipate basic due process questions like who will count the votes and how objections can be made and disposed.

3. Was the decision in *Bush* politically motivated? There was a good deal of unfortunate public commentary, even from members of the legal academy, that more than suggested this possibility in intemperate language. The Court civilly and concisely anticipated this criticism in its opinion, characterizing the matter before it as an "unsought responsibility to resolve . . . federal and constitutional issues." Indeed, in fairness to the Court, it went out of its way to avoid ruling on federal grounds. The first time the dispute was presented to the Court in *Bush v. Palm Beach County Canvassing Board*, 531 U.S. 70 (2000), *vacating* and *remanding* 772 So. 2d 1220 (Fla. 2000) (*Bush I*), the Court unanimously returned the matter to the state for clarification. In *Bush I,* the central issue was not equal protection — because the absence of a recount standard had yet to fully manifest itself — but whether the Florida Supreme Court had faithfully followed the state election code. Normally, the Court defers to a state court's interpretation of a state statute, but Article II, section 1, clause 2 posed the unique circumstance in which the state legislature was acting pursuant not to its own reserved power, but power delegated by the federal Constitution. In that circumstance, it was unresolved whether a state court, even a state supreme court acting under the state constitution, could substantially vary the legislative will. In *Bush I*, a unanimous Court reasoned that: "It is fundamental that state courts be left free and unfettered by us in interpreting their state constitutions. But it is equally important that ambiguous or obscure adjudications by state courts do not stand as barriers to a determination by this Court of the validity under the federal constitution of state action." Nevertheless, the Court did not immediately decide the issue, but remanded asking the Florida Supreme Court whether it saw the Florida Constitution as circumscribing the legislature's authority under Article II, section 1, clause 2.

4. Why didn't the fracas end there? That is, why didn't the Florida Supreme Court rule that it was merely interpreting the state election code, and not judicially altering it pursuant to equitable or state constitutional power? Well, here the compressed sequence of events took over. The state court would ultimately get around to saying just that, but not until December 11, 2000. *Palm Beach County Canvassing Bd. v. Harris*, 772 So. 2d 1273 (Fla. 2000). The U.S. Supreme Court had asked for clarification on December 4, and while a week is normally quite expeditious, it was an eternity in the context of this closely fought presidential election. Following the state high court's first opinion, Governor Bush had been certified the winner by state election officials. This triggered a contest by Vice President Gore, which he lost at trial and appealed to the Florida Supreme Court on December 7. At this point, the Florida Supreme Court could have insulated its ultimate determination from further U.S. Supreme Court review by doing two things: affirming the state trial court ruling denying the Gore contest or reversing it (with a full statewide recount of all ballots pursuant to a uniform standard) and briefly answering the Court's query from *Bush I* that it had not used the state constitution to undermine the legislative will. In allocating its work load, however, the state high court chose to answer the appeal first on December 8 and wait until December 11 to answer the U.S. Supreme Court. As it turned out, this only highlighted the equal protection concerns, since by a vote of 4-3 in *Gore v. Harris*, 772 So. 2d 1243 (Fla. 2000), the state high court authorized a qualified statewide recount that had already been comprised with ballots that had only been counted pursuant to its previous opinion which had been unanimously vacated in *Bush I* and had yet to be satisfactorily justified and re-issued.

5. Was the Vice President entitled to further recounts? As noted above, this closely divided the state supreme court, and had it not raised basic equal protection concerns, might have been resolved entirely without further U.S. Supreme Court review. The essential issue under the Florida code was whether Mr. Gore had demonstrated sufficient evidence to "change or place in doubt the result of the election." The four justice majority thought the Vice President had done so merely by showing the existence of a number of so-called "undervotes" in selective — that is, heavily Democratic — counties. The dissent thought the Vice President's county-based evidence wholly wanting since he needed to show not just that the result would be different in a single county or set of favored counties, but statewide. As dissenting Justice Major Harding reasoned: "the selective recounting requested by [Vice President Gore] is not available under the election contest provisions of [the Florida code]. Such an application does not provide for a more accurate reflection of the will of the voters but, rather, allows for an unfair distortion of the statewide vote. It is patently unlawful to permit the recount of [undervotes] in a single county to determine the outcome of the November 7, 2000 election for the next President of the United States. We are a nation of laws, and we have survived and prospered as a free nation because we have adhered to the rule of law. Fairness is achieved by following the rules." The dissent's point went unanswered by the state high court majority triggering the principal case.

6. But wait a minute, isn't it unprecedented for the U.S. Supreme Court to rule that a state court interpretation of state law violates the federal Constitution? Unprecedented, no; rare, yes. In *Fairfax's Devisee v. Hunter's Lessee,* 7 Cranch 603 (1813), the Supreme Court early in our history disagreed with the Supreme Court of Appeals of Virginia that a 1782 state law had extinguished the property interests of one Denny Fairfax, so that a 1789 ejectment order against Fairfax supported by a 1785 state law did not constitute a future confiscation under the 1783 peace treaty with Great Britain. Other more contemporary, but not numerous, examples can be found from the protection of civil rights. In *NAACP v. Alabama ex rel. Patterson,* 357 U.S. 449 (1958), it was argued that the Court was without jurisdiction because the petitioner had not pursued the correct appellate remedy in Alabama's state courts. Petitioners had sought a state-law writ of certiorari in the Alabama Supreme Court when a writ of mandamus, according to that court, was proper. The Court found this state-law ground inadequate to defeat its jurisdiction because it was "unable to reconcile the procedural holding of the Alabama Supreme Court" with prior Alabama precedent. *Id.* at 456. The purported state-law ground was so novel, in the Court's independent estimation, that "petitioner could not fairly be deemed to have been apprised of its existence." *Id.* at 457. Similarly, six years later in *Bouie v. City of Columbia,* 378 U.S. 347 (1964), the state court had held, contrary to precedent, that the state trespass law applied to black sit-in demonstrators who had consent to enter private property but were then asked to leave. Relying upon *NAACP,* the Court concluded that the South Carolina Supreme Court's interpretation of a state penal statute had impermissibly broadened the scope of that statute beyond what a fair reading provided, in violation of due process.

7. Wouldn't it have been more prudent to simply reverse and remand and allow Florida to figure out whether it could get the counting done in time in accordance with federal constitutional principle? While this is much obscured in public commentary and even confused a bit by the Court's own dicta, that is technically what the Court did. The Supreme Court reversed and remanded, it did not dismiss. But, of course, it was by then December 12, and this date was clearly thought by at least five of the seven Justices who raised the equal protection concern to be pivotal. The date was not significant because of federal statute alone — the so-called, "safe harbor" provision in 3 U.S.C. § 5 — but because the Florida Supreme Court had held that the Florida legislature had wanted to take advantage of that date. Said the Court in its Per Curiam, "[t]he Supreme Court of Florida has said that the legislature intended the State's electors to 'participat[e] fully in the federal electoral process,' as provided in 3 U.S.C. § 5. . . . That statute, in turn, requires that any controversy or contest that is designed to lead to a conclusive selection of electors be completed by December 12. That date is upon us, and there is no recount procedure in place under the State Supreme Court's order that comports with minimal constitutional standards."

The absence of time to do a constitutionally sufficient recount had also been noted in dissent by Chief Justice Wells of the Florida Supreme Court, who observed that: in the four days remaining, "all questionable ballots must be reviewed by the judicial officer appointed to discern the intent of the voter in a process open to the public. Fairness dictates that a provision be made for either party to object to how a particular ballot is counted. Additionally, this short time period must allow for judicial review. I respectfully submit this cannot be completed without taking Florida's presidential electors outside the safe harbor provision, creating the very real possibility of disenfranchising those nearly 6 million voters who are able to correctly cast their ballots on election day." (Wells, C.J., dissenting.)

8. It is not entirely true that Florida would have been disenfranchised if it missed the December 12th date. The actual casting of the vote by presidential electors was not required to take place until December 18th and the votes would not be opened and counted until January 6, 2001. This prompted Justice Stevens to write in dissent in the principal case that the majority acted "on the basis of the deadlines set forth in Title 3 of the United States Code. But . . . those provisions merely provide rules of decision for Congress to follow when selecting among conflicting slates of electors. They do not prohibit a State from counting what the majority concedes to be legal votes until a bona fide winner is determined. Indeed, in 1960, Hawaii appointed two slates of electors and Congress chose to count the one appointed on January 4, 1961, well after the Title 3 deadlines. *See* Josephson & Ross, *Repairing the Electoral College*, 22 J. LEGIS. 145, 166, n. 154 (1996)." Would this have been a better course? Before you answer, remember that the Florida legislature was in session and preparing — if the U.S. Supreme Court decided against Governor Bush, who had been certified the winner, to substitute its hand-chosen set of Bush electors.

The possibility of competing slates did not trouble Justice Breyer, who thought this had been well provided for by the political process in the Electoral Count Act in Title 3. As he observed, that Act sets out rules for the congressional determination of disputes. Justice Breyer reasoned: "If, for example, a state submits a single slate of electors, Congress must count those votes unless both Houses agree that the votes 'have not been . . . regularly given.' 3 U.S.C. § 15. If, as occurred in 1876, one or more states submits two sets of electors, then Congress must determine whether a slate has entered the safe harbor of § 5, in which case its votes will have 'conclusive' effect. If, as also occurred in 1876, there is controversy about 'which of two or more of such State authorities is the lawful tribunal' authorized to appoint electors, then each House shall determine separately which votes are 'supported by the decision of such State so authorized by its law.' If the two Houses of Congress agree, the votes they have approved will be counted. If they disagree, then 'the votes of the electors whose appointment shall have been certified by the executive of the State, under the seal thereof, shall be counted.'" *Ibid.*

It was this "detailed, comprehensive scheme for counting electoral votes," that suggested to Justice Breyer that there was "no reason to believe that federal law either foresees or requires resolution of such a political issue by this Court."

9. Historical perspective. Just after the 1876 Presidential election, Florida, South Carolina, and Louisiana each sent two slates of electors to Washington. Without these states, Tilden, the Democrat, had 184 electoral votes, one short of the number required to win the Presidency. With those States, Hayes, his Republican opponent, would have had 185. In order to choose between the two slates of electors, Congress decided to appoint an electoral commission composed of five Senators, five Representatives, and five Supreme Court Justices. Initially the Commission was to be evenly divided between Republicans and Democrats, with Justice David Davis, an Independent, to possess the decisive vote. However, when at the last minute the Illinois Legislature elected Justice Davis to the United States Senate, the final position on the Commission was filled by Supreme Court Justice Joseph P. Bradley. When the Commission divided along partisan lines, the deciding vote fell to Justice Bradley. He decided to accept the votes by the Republican electors, and thereby awarded the Presidency to Hayes.

Justice Breyer remarks that Justice Bradley immediately became the subject of vociferous attacks. "Bradley was accused of accepting bribes, of being captured by railroad interests, and of an eleventh-hour change in position after a night in which his house 'was surrounded by the carriages' of Republican partisans and railroad officials. C. Woodward, *Reunion and Reaction* 159-160 (1966)." For Justice Breyer the history lesson is that Bradley's participation did not lend legitimacy to the Court and the "Congress that later enacted the Electoral Count Act knew it."

10. Was the Court's legitimacy enhanced or prejudiced by its ruling in the principal case? The opinions continue to run strongly in both directions. Harvard's Professor Dershowitz has penned a book summarizing and advocating the complaints against the Court's resolution. ALAN DERSHOWITZ, SUPREME INJUSTICE (2001). Dean Kmiec, your co-author, is more accepting of the Court's ruling, writing in popular commentary immediately following the decision that "[t]he ruling of the U.S. Supreme Court was not along partisan or ideological lines. As the justices pointedly observed in the opinion, 'seven justices of the court agree that there are constitutional problems with the recount ordered by the Florida Supreme Court that demand a remedy.'" Kmiec, *The Court's Decision is Law, Not Politics*, L.A. TIMES B11 (December 14, 2000).

Justice Breyer's historical reference is interesting, but not entirely parallel to *Bush v. Gore* where the Justices participated because an aggrieved litigant brought the case to them, not in an extra-judicial capacity like the isolated Justice Bradley in the 1876 election. In this regard, Yale's Professor Paul Kahn commented that: "The rule of law is our national myth. We must believe the myth if we are to overcome our political disagreements. We need a point of reconciliation beyond our political disputes. That point is our faith in law, and the institutional locus of that faith is the U.S. Supreme Court. To be sure, we can always find the politician behind the robes of the justice, but . . . . It is the U.S. Supreme Court's role to preserve [the rule of law]. When the court speaks, it speaks in the name of the sovereign people. When it presents to us the Constitution, it purports only to hold up a mirror to the people. Its legitimacy comes not from its knowledge of legal science nor from the justices' political appointments, but from the capacity to persuade us that the rule of law is the rule of the people. At that moment, we overcome the divide between law and politics." Paul W. Kahn, *The Call to Law Is a Call to a Faith in Higher Politics*, L.A. TIMES, B7 (November 24, 2000).

11. We now move from racial discrimination and the "numerical" concept of equal protection as it applies to voting, to tackle another problematic area for the courts, that of gender discrimination. As you read these cases, ask yourself whether the Court's opinions in this area have been more consistent or clear than those regarding racial classifications.

C. Gender

MINOR v. HAPPERSETT
88 U.S. (21 Wall.) 162 (1874)

The CHIEF JUSTICE [WAITE] delivered the opinion of the court.

* * *

If the right of suffrage is one of the necessary privileges of a citizen of the United States, then the constitution and laws of Missouri confining it to men are in violation of the Constitution of the United States, as amended, and consequently void. The direct question is, therefore, presented whether all citizens are necessarily voters.

* * *

The [Fourteenth] amendment did not add to the privileges and immunities of a citizen. It simply furnished an additional guaranty for the protection of such as he already had. No new voters were necessarily made by it. Indirectly it may have had that effect, because it may have increased the number of citizens entitled to suffrage under the constitution and laws of the States, but it operates for this purpose, if at all, through the States and the State laws, and not directly upon the citizen.

It is clear, therefore, we think, that the Constitution has not added the right of suffrage to the privileges and immunities of citizenship as they existed at the time it was adopted. This makes it proper to inquire whether suffrage was coextensive with the citizenship of the States at the time of its adoption. If it was, then it may with force be argued that suffrage was one of the rights which belonged to citizenship, and in the enjoyment of which every citizen must be protected. But if it was not, the contrary may with propriety be assumed.

When the Federal Constitution was adopted, all the States, with the exception of Rhode Island and Connecticut, had constitutions of their own. These two continued to act under their charters from the Crown. Upon an examination of those constitutions we find that in no State were all citizens permitted to vote. Each State determined for itself who should have that power. Thus, in New Hampshire, "every male inhabitant of each town and parish with town privileges, and places unincorporated in the State, of twenty-one years of age and upwards, excepting paupers and persons excused from paying taxes at their own request," were its voters; in Massachusetts "every male inhabitant of twenty-one years of age and upwards, having a freehold estate within the commonwealth of the annual income of three pounds, or any estate of the value of sixty pounds;" in Rhode Island "such as are admitted free of the company and society" of the colony; in Connecticut such persons as had "maturity in years, quiet and peaceable behavior, a civil conversation, and forty shillings freehold or forty pounds personal estate," if so certified by the selectmen; in New York "every male inhabitant of full age who shall have personally resided within one of the counties of the State for six months immediately preceding the day of election . . . if during the time aforesaid he shall have been a freeholder, possessing a freehold of the value of twenty pounds within the county, or have rented a tenement therein of the yearly value of forty shillings, and been rated and actually paid taxes to the State;" in New Jersey "all inhabitants . . . of full age who are worth fifty pounds, proclamation-money, clear estate in the same, and have resided in the county in which they claim a vote for twelve months immediately preceding the election;" in Pennsylvania "every freeman of the age of twenty-one years, having resided in the State two years next before the election, and within that time paid a State or county tax which shall have been assessed at least six months before the election;" . . . .

In this condition of the law in respect to suffrage in the several States it cannot for a moment be doubted that if it had been intended to make all citizens of the United States voters, the framers of the Constitution would not have left it to implication. . . .

But if further proof is necessary to show that no such change was intended, it can easily be found both in and out of the Constitution. By Article 4, section 2, it is provided that "the citizens of each State shall be entitled to all the privileges and immunities of citizens in the several States." If suffrage is necessarily a part of citizenship, then the citizens of each State must be entitled to vote in the several States precisely as their citizens are. . . .

And still again, after the adoption of the fourteenth amendment, it was deemed necessary to adopt a fifteenth, as follows: "The right of citizens of the United States to vote shall not be denied or abridged by the United States, or by any State, on account of race, color, or previous condition of servitude." The fourteenth amendment had already provided that no State should make or enforce any law which should abridge the privileges or immunities of citizens of the United States. If suffrage was one of these privileges or immunities, why amend the Constitution to prevent its being denied on account of race, &c.? . . .

It is true that the United States guarantees to every State a republican form of government. It is also true that no State can pass a bill of attainder, and that no person can be deprived of life, liberty, or property without due process of law. All these several provisions of the Constitution must be construed in connection with the other parts of the instrument, and in the light of the surrounding circumstances.

The guaranty is of a republican form of government. No particular government is designated as republican, neither is the exact form to be guaranteed, in any manner especially designated. Here, as in other parts of the instrument, we are compelled to resort elsewhere to ascertain what was intended.

The guaranty necessarily implies a duty on the part of the States themselves to provide such a government. All the States had governments when the Constitution was adopted. In all the people participated to some extent, through their representatives elected in the manner specially provided. These governments the Constitution did not change. They were accepted precisely as they were, and it is, therefore, to be presumed that they were such as it was the duty of the States to provide. Thus we have unmistakable evidence of what was republican in form, within the meaning of that term as employed in the Constitution.

As has been seen, all the citizens of the States were not invested with the right of suffrage. In all, save perhaps New Jersey, this right was only bestowed upon men and not upon all of them. Under these circumstances it is certainly now too late to contend that a government is not republican, within the meaning of this guaranty in the Constitution, because women are not made voters.

The same may be said of the other provisions just quoted. Women were excluded from suffrage in nearly all the States by the express provision of their constitutions and laws. If that had been equivalent to a bill of attainder, certainly its abrogation would not have been left to implication. Nothing less than express language would have been employed to effect so radical a change. So also of the amendment which declares that no person shall be deprived of life, liberty, or property without due process of law, adopted as it was as early as 1791. If suffrage was intended to be included within its obligations, language better adapted to express that intent would most certainly have been employed. The right of suffrage, when granted, will be protected. He who has it can only be deprived of it by due process of law, but in order to claim protection he must first show that he has the right.

But we have already sufficiently considered the proof found upon the inside of the Constitution. That upon the outside is equally effective.

The Constitution was submitted to the States for adoption in 1787, and was ratified by nine States in 1788, and finally by the thirteen original States in 1790. Vermont was the first new State admitted to the Union, and it came in under a constitution which conferred the right of suffrage only upon men of the full age of twenty-one years, having resided in the State for the space of one whole year next before the election, and who were of quiet and peaceable behavior. This was in 1791. . . . No new State has ever been admitted to the Union which has conferred the right of suffrage upon women, and this has never been considered a valid objection to her admission. On the contrary, as is claimed in the argument, the right of suffrage was withdrawn from women as early as 1807 in the State of New Jersey, without any attempt to obtain the interference of the United States to prevent it. Since then the governments of the insurgent States have been reorganized under a requirement that before their representatives could be admitted to seats in Congress they must have adopted new constitutions, republican in form. In no one of these constitutions was suffrage conferred upon women, and yet the States have all been restored to their original position as States in the Union.

Besides this, citizenship has not in all cases been made a condition precedent to the enjoyment of the right of suffrage. Thus, in Missouri, persons of foreign birth, who have declared their intention to become citizens of the United States, may under certain circumstances vote. The same provision is to be found in the constitutions of Alabama, Arkansas, Florida, Georgia, Indiana, Kansas, Minnesota, and Texas.

Certainly, if the courts can consider any question settled, this is one. . . . Our province is to decide what the law is, not to declare what it should be.

We have given this case the careful consideration its importance demands. If the law is wrong, it ought to be changed; but the power for that is not with us. . . .

NOTES AND QUESTIONS

1. Why don't the reconstruction amendments, particularly the Fourteenth Amendment's guarantee of equal protection, guarantee a woman's right to vote? By the way, was the argument supporting the right of women to vote grounded in the Equal Protection Clause? If not, why not? Does it surprise you that the Court was unanimous in its decision in the case? It would not be until 1920 that this case would be overruled by amendment. More on that after the next case.

2. Note that the Court holds that the reconstruction amendments' guarantees of citizenship do not necessarily guarantee the franchise. Did this understanding of these amendments last throughout the twentieth century? This case, as well as *United States v. Anthony*, 24 F. Cas. 829 (N.D.N.Y. 1873) (No. 14,459), which follows, were closely contemporary with the Fourteenth and Fifteenth Amendments. Do they help us discern the original understanding of their text? Have the courts been faithful to that original understanding?

UNITED STATES v. ANTHONY
24 F. Cas. 829 (N.D.N.Y. 1873) (No. 14,459)

HUNT, Circuit Justice . . . ruled as follows:

The defendant is indicted under the act of congress of May 31st, 1870, for having voted for a representative in congress, in November, 1872. Among other things, that act makes it an offence for any person knowingly to vote for such representative without having a lawful right to vote. It is charged that the defendant thus voted, she not having a right to vote, because she is a woman. The defendant insists that she has a right to vote; and that the provision of the constitution of this state, limiting the right to vote to persons of the male sex, is in violation of the fourteenth amendment of the constitution of the United States, and is void.

The thirteenth, fourteenth and fifteenth amendments were designed mainly for the protection of the newly emancipated negroes, but full effect must, nevertheless, be given to the language employed. . . .

The fourteenth amendment creates and defines citizenship of the United States. It had long been contended, and had been held by many learned authorities, and had never been judicially decided to the contrary, that there was no such thing as a citizen of the United States, except as that condition arose from citizenship of some state. No mode existed, it was said, of obtaining a citizenship of the United States, except by first becoming a citizen of some state. This question is now at rest. The fourteenth amendment defines and declares who shall be citizens of the United States, to wit, "all persons born or naturalized in the United States, and subject to the jurisdiction thereof." The latter qualification was intended to exclude the children of foreign representatives and the like. With this qualification, every person born in the United States or naturalized is declared to be a citizen of the United States and of the state wherein he resides.

After creating and defining citizenship of the United States, the fourteenth amendment provides, that "no state shall make or enforce any law which shall abridge the privileges or immunities of citizens of the United States." This clause is intended to be a protection, not to all our rights, but to our rights as citizens of the United States only; that is, to rights existing or belonging to that condition or capacity. The expression, citizen of a state, used in the previous paragraph, is carefully omitted here. In article 4, § 2, subd. 1, of the constitution of the United States, it had been already provided, that "the citizens of each state shall be entitled to all privileges and immunities of citizens in the several states." The rights of citizens of the states and of citizens of the United States are each guarded by these different provisions. That these rights are separate and distinct, was held in the *Slaughter-House Cases*, recently decided by the supreme court. . . .

* * *

HUNT, Circuit Justice, in denying the motion, said, in substance:

The whole law of the case has been reargued, and I have given the best consideration in my power to the arguments presented. But for the evident earnestness of the learned counsel for the defendant, for whose ability and integrity I have the highest respect, I should have no hesitation. . . .

The learned counsel insists, however, that an error was committed in directing the jury to render a verdict of guilty. This direction, he argues, makes the verdict that of the court and not of the jury, and it is contended that the provisions of the constitution looking to and securing a trial by jury in criminal cases have been violated.

The right of trial by jury in civil as well as in criminal cases is a constitutional right. The second section of the first article of the constitution of the state of New York provides, that "the trial by jury, in all cases in which it has been heretofore used, shall remain inviolate forever." Articles six and seven of the amendments to the constitution of the United States contain a similar provision. Yet, in cases where the facts are all conceded, or where they are proved and uncontradicted by evidence, it has always been the practice of the courts to take the case from the jury and decide it as a question of law. No counsel has ever disputed the right of the court to do so. No respectable counsel will venture to doubt the correctness of such practice. . . . The right of a trial by jury in a criminal case is not more distinctly secured than it is in a civil case. In each class of cases this right exists only in respect of a disputed fact. To questions of fact the jury respond. Upon questions of law, the decision of the court is conclusive, and the jury are bound to receive the law as declared by the court. Such is the established practice in criminal as well as in civil cases, and this practice is recognized by the highest authorities. It has been so held by the former supreme court of this state, and by the present court of appeals of this state.

At a circuit court of the United States, held by Judges Woodruff and Blatchford, upon deliberation and consultation, it was decided, that, in a criminal case, the court was not bound to submit the case to the jury, there being no sufficient evidence to justify a conviction, and the court accordingly instructed the jury to find a verdict of not guilty. The district attorney now states, that, on several occasions, since he has been in office, Judge Hall, being of opinion that the evidence did not warrant a conviction, has directed the jury to find a verdict of not guilty.

In the case of *People v. Bennett* (N.Y. 1872), the court of appeals of the state of New York, through its chief justice, uses the following language:

"Contrary to an opinion formerly prevailing, it has been settled that the juries are not judges of the law, as well as the facts, in criminal cases, but that they must take the law from the court. All questions of law during the trial are to be determined by the court, and it is the duty of the jury to regard and abide by such determination. . . . I can see no reason, therefore, why the court may not, in a case presenting a question of law only, instruct the jury to acquit the prisoner, or to direct an acquittal, and enforce the direction, nor why it is not the duty of the court to do so. This results from the rule, that the jury must take the law as adjudged by the court, and I think it is a necessary result."

In these cases the question, in each instance, was, whether the court had power to direct a verdict of not guilty to be rendered. But the counsel for defendant expressly admits that the authority which justifies a direction to acquit will, in a proper case, justify a direction to convict; that it is a question of power; and that, if the power may be exercised in favor of the defendant, it may be exercised against him. . . . The duty of the jury to take the law from the court is the same, whether it is favorable to the defendant, or unfavorable to him. . . .

In the present case, the court had decided, as matter of law, that Miss Anthony was not a legal voter. It had also decided, as matter of law, that, knowing every fact in the case, and intending to do just what she did, she had knowingly voted, not having a right to vote, and that her belief did not affect the question. Every fact in the case was undisputed. There was no inference to be drawn or point made on the facts, that could, by possibility, alter the result. It was, therefore, not only the right, but it seems to me, upon the authorities, the plain duty of the judge to direct a verdict of guilty. The motion for a new trial is denied.

The defendant was thereupon sentenced to pay a fine of $100 and the costs of the prosecution.

NOTES AND QUESTIONS

1. Susan Anthony was one of the great champions of female suffrage, and was willing to suffer the consequences of the criminal justice system to make her views known. Does she get a fair trial in this case? What do you make of the directed verdict of guilty? Have you ever encountered that before? Is Judge Hunt convincing in his argument for such a procedural move?

2. Ms. Anthony and her fellow suffragettes had been arguing since even before the time of the Civil War that to deprive women of the vote, and, indeed to relegate them to the second-class citizenship to which they were subject under the common law, was a violation of the law of nature and nature's God.

Such was the point of the famous "Seneca Falls Resolutions" in 1848, a set of propositions that resulted from the first women's rights convention, held in Seneca Falls, New York.

3. Not until the Constitution was amended to provide, in Amendment Nineteen (ratified in 1920), that "the right of citizens of the United States to vote shall not be denied or abridged by the United States or by any state on account of sex," U.S. Const., amend. XIX, did Susan Anthony's views become part of the Constitution. For many years the text that was to become the Nineteenth Amendment was known as the "Anthony Amendment," in fitting tribute. A woman's suffrage amendment was first introduced into Congress in 1868. Why did it take more than fifty years to secure its passage?

4. In the 19th century, women were legally precluded from entering various professions. For example, in *Bradwell v. Illinois*, 16 U.S. (Wall.) 130 (1872), the Court upheld an Illinois law that denied women a license to practice law. One member of the Court reasoned: "The paramount destiny and mission of women are to fulfill the noble and benign offices of wife and mother. This is the law of the [C]reator. And the rules of civil society must be adapted in the general constitution of things, and cannot be based on exceptional cases." *Id.* at 141 (Bradley, J. concurring). Is this a misstatement, or at least misapplication of natural law? Is it one thing to recognize the undeniable importance of women in the nurturing and stability of family life and another to require under law that *all* women see this as their "paramount destiny and mission"? In modern gender analysis, is it possible to rid the law of this inflexibility without denigrating the significance of the choice many modern women still make, either with or without a market career, to dedicate extraordinary time to the well-being of families?

In *Goesart v. Cleary*, 335 U.S. 464 (1948), the Court upheld a Michigan law preventing the licensing of women as bartenders unless the bar was owned by her husband or father. Justice Frankfurter, a well-known liberal appointed to the bench by FDR from the Harvard Law School, stated: "Michigan could, beyond question, forbid all women from working behind a bar." *Id.* at 465. Again, even assuming such moral judgments are defensible as a matter of philosophy, isn't this an example of a disregard of the natural law precept articulated by Thomas Aquinas that every vice ought not be prohibited under law? In the 1970s, the Court began to eliminate these distinctions and the legal issue turned to the level of judicial scrutiny to be applied to gender classifications. Ultimately, the Court settled on intermediate scrutiny in *Craig v. Boren*, 429 U.S. 190 (1976) (invalidating a state law that allowed women to drink some alcohol at 18; while men were precluded until 21). Similarly, in *Mississippi University for Women v. Hogan*, 458 U.S. 718 (1982), the Court used intermediate scrutiny to declare unconstitutional the practice of limiting a state nursing school to women. We saw in our review of the cases regarding racial discrimination movement since, at least in recent years, toward a "color blind Constitution." Is the current attitude toward gender discrimination in support of a "gender blind Constitution"? Consider the important case which follows.

UNITED STATES v. VIRGINIA
518 U.S. 515 (1996)

JUSTICE GINSBURG delivered the opinion of the Court.

Virginia's public institutions of higher learning include an incomparable military college, Virginia Military Institute (VMI). The United States maintains that the Constitution's equal protection guarantee precludes Virginia from reserving exclusively to men the unique educational opportunities VMI affords. We agree.

I

Founded in 1839, VMI is today the sole single-sex school among Virginia's 15 public institutions of higher learning. VMI's distinctive mission is to produce "citizen-soldiers," men prepared for leadership in civilian life and in military service. VMI pursues this mission through pervasive training of a kind not available anywhere else in Virginia. Assigning prime place to character development, VMI uses an "adversative method" modeled on English public schools and once characteristic of military instruction. VMI constantly endeavors to instill physical and mental discipline in its cadets and impart to them a strong moral code. The school's graduates leave VMI with heightened comprehension of their capacity to deal with duress and stress, and a large sense of accomplishment for completing the hazardous course.

VMI has notably succeeded in its mission to produce leaders; among its alumni are military generals, Members of Congress, and business executives. The school's alumni overwhelmingly perceive that their VMI training helped them to realize their personal goals. VMI's endowment reflects the loyalty of its graduates; VMI has the largest per-student endowment of all public undergraduate institutions in the Nation.

* * *

II

A

* * *

VMI cadets live in spartan barracks where surveillance is constant and privacy nonexistent; they wear uniforms, eat together in the mess hall, and regularly participate in drills. Entering students are incessantly exposed to the rat line, "an extreme form of the adversative model," comparable in intensity to Marine Corps boot camp. Tormenting and punishing, the rat line bonds new cadets to their fellow sufferers and, when they have completed the 7-month experience, to their former tormentors.

VMI's "adversative model" is further characterized by a hierarchical "class system" of privileges and responsibilities, a "dyke system" for assigning a senior class mentor to each entering class "rat," and a stringently enforced "honor code," which prescribes that a cadet "'does not lie, cheat, steal nor tolerate those who do.'"

VMI attracts some applicants because of its reputation as an extraordinarily challenging military school, and "because its alumni are exceptionally close to the school." "[W]omen have no opportunity anywhere to gain the benefits of [the system of education at VMI]."

B

In 1990, prompted by a complaint filed with the Attorney General by a female high-school student seeking admission to VMI, the United States sued the Commonwealth of Virginia and VMI, alleging that VMI's exclusively male admission policy violated the Equal Protection Clause of the Fourteenth Amendment. . . .

* * *

The District Court ruled in favor of VMI, however, and rejected the equal protection challenge pressed by the United States. That court correctly recognized that *Mississippi Univ. for Women v. Hogan* (1982), was the closest guide. There, this Court underscored that a party seeking to uphold government action based on sex must establish an "exceedingly persuasive justification" for the classification. To succeed, the defender of the challenged action must show "at least that the classification serves important governmental objectives and that the discriminatory means employed are substantially related to the achievement of those objectives."

The District Court reasoned that education in "a single-gender environment, be it male or female," yields substantial benefits. VMI's school for men brought diversity to an otherwise coeducational Virginia system, and that diversity was "enhanced by VMI's unique method of instruction." If single-gender education for males ranks as an important governmental objective, it becomes obvious, the District Court concluded, that the *only* means of achieving the objective "is to exclude women from the all-male institution — VMI."

"Women are [indeed] denied a unique educational opportunity that is available only at VMI," the District Court acknowledged. But "[VMI's] single-sex status would be lost, and some aspects of the [school's] distinctive method would be altered" if women were admitted: "Allowance for personal privacy would have to be made," "[p]hysical education requirements would have to be altered, at least for the women," the adversative environment could not survive unmodified. Thus, "sufficient constitutional justification" had been shown, the District Court held, "for continuing [VMI's] single-sex policy."

The Court of Appeals for the Fourth Circuit disagreed and vacated the District Court's judgment. The appellate court held: "The Commonwealth of Virginia has not . . . advanced any state policy by which it can justify its determination, under an announced policy of diversity, to afford VMI's unique type of program to men and not to women."

* * *

The parties agreed that "some women can meet the physical standards now imposed on men," and the court was satisfied that "neither the goal of producing citizen soldiers nor VMI's implementing methodology is inherently unsuitable to women." The Court of Appeals, however, accepted the District Court's finding that "at least these three aspects of VMI's program — physical training, the absence of privacy, and the adversative approach — would be materially affected by coeducation." Remanding the case, the appeals court assigned to Virginia, in the first instance, responsibility for selecting a remedial course. The court suggested these options for the State: Admit women to VMI; establish parallel institutions or programs; or abandon state support, leaving VMI free to pursue its policies as a private institution. In May 1993, this Court denied certiorari.

C

In response to the Fourth Circuit's ruling, Virginia proposed a parallel program for women: Virginia Women's Institute for Leadership (VWIL). The 4-year, state-sponsored undergraduate program would be located at Mary Baldwin College, a private liberal arts school for women, and would be open, initially, to about 25 to 30 students. Although VWIL would share VMI's mission — to produce "citizen-soldiers" — the VWIL program would differ, as does Mary Baldwin College, from VMI in academic offerings, methods of education, and financial resources.

The average combined SAT score of entrants at Mary Baldwin is about 100 points lower than the score for VMI freshmen. Mary Baldwin's faculty holds "significantly fewer Ph.D.'s than the faculty at VMI," and receives significantly lower salaries. While VMI offers degrees in liberal arts, the sciences, and engineering, Mary Baldwin, at the time of trial, offered only bachelor of arts degrees. A VWIL student seeking to earn an engineering degree could gain one, without public support, by attending Washington University in St. Louis, Missouri, for two years, paying the required private tuition.

Experts in educating women at the college level composed the Task Force charged with designing the VWIL program; Task Force members were drawn from Mary Baldwin's own faculty and staff. Training its attention on methods of instruction appropriate for "most women," the Task Force determined that a military model would be "wholly inappropriate" for VWIL.

VWIL students would participate in ROTC programs and a newly established, "largely ceremonial" Virginia Corps of Cadets, but the VWIL House would not have a military format, and VWIL would not require its students to eat meals together or to wear uniforms during the school day. In lieu of VMI's adversative method, the VWIL Task Force favored "a cooperative method which reinforces self-esteem." In addition to the standard bachelor of arts program offered at Mary Baldwin, VWIL students would take courses in leadership, complete an off-campus leadership externship, participate in community service projects, and assist in arranging a speaker series.

Virginia represented that it will provide equal financial support for in-state VWIL students and VMI cadets and the VMI Foundation agreed to supply a $5.4625 million endowment for the VWIL program. Mary Baldwin's own endowment is about $19 million; VMI's is $131 million. Mary Baldwin will add $35 million to its endowment based on future commitments; VMI will add $220 million. The VMI Alumni Association has developed a network of employers interested in hiring VMI graduates. The Association has agreed to open its network to VWIL graduates, but those graduates will not have the advantage afforded by a VMI degree.

D

Virginia returned to the District Court seeking approval of its proposed remedial plan, and the court decided the plan met the requirements of the Equal Protection Clause. The District Court again acknowledged evidentiary support for these determinations: "[T]he VMI methodology could be used to educate women and, in fact, some women . . . may prefer the VMI methodology to the VWIL methodology." But the "controlling legal principles," the District Court decided, "do not require the Commonwealth to provide a mirror image VMI for women." The court anticipated that the two schools would "achieve substantially similar outcomes." It concluded: "If VMI marches to the beat of a drum, then Mary Baldwin marches to the melody of a fife and when the march is over, both will have arrived at the same destination."

A divided Court of Appeals affirmed the District Court's judgment. . . .

"[P]roviding the option of a single-gender college education may be considered a legitimate and important aspect of a public system of higher education," the appeals court observed; that objective, the court added, is "not pernicious." Moreover, the court continued, the adversative method vital to a VMI education "has never been tolerated in a sexually heterogeneous environment." The method itself "was not designed to exclude women," the court noted, but women could not be accommodated in the VMI program, the court believed, for female participation in VMI's adversative training "would destroy . . . any sense of decency that still permeates the relationship between the sexes."

* * *

The Fourth Circuit denied rehearing en banc. . . .

III

The cross-petitions in this case present two ultimate issues. First, does Virginia's exclusion of women from the educational opportunities provided by VMI — extraordinary opportunities for military training and civilian leadership development — deny to women "capable of all of the individual activities required of VMI cadets," the equal protection of the laws guaranteed by the Fourteenth Amendment? Second, if VMI's "unique" situation — as Virginia's sole single-sex public institution of higher education — offends the Constitution's equal protection principle, what is the remedial requirement?

IV

We note, once again, the core instruction of this Court's pathmarking decisions in *J.E.B. v. Alabama ex rel. T.B.* (1994), and *Mississippi Univ. for Women*: Parties who seek to defend gender-based government action must demonstrate an "exceedingly persuasive justification" for that action.

Today's skeptical scrutiny of official action denying rights or opportunities based on sex responds to volumes of history. As a plurality of this Court acknowledged a generation ago, "our Nation has had a long and unfortunate history of sex discrimination." *Frontiero v. Richardson* (1973). Through a century plus three decades and more of that history, women did not count among voters composing "We the People"; not until 1920 did women gain a constitutional right to the franchise. And for a half century thereafter, it remained the prevailing doctrine that government, both federal and state, could withhold from women opportunities accorded men so long as any "basis in reason" could be conceived for the discrimination.

In 1971, for the first time in our Nation's history, this Court ruled in favor of a woman who complained that her State had denied her the equal protection of its laws. *Reed v. Reed* (1971) (holding unconstitutional Idaho Code prescription that, among "'several persons claiming and equally entitled to administer [a decedent's estate], males must be preferred to females'"). Since *Reed*, the Court has repeatedly recognized that neither federal nor state government acts compatibly with the equal protection principle when a law or official policy denies to women, simply because they are women, full citizenship stature — equal opportunity to aspire, achieve, participate in and contribute to society based on their individual talents and capacities.

. . . To summarize the Court's current directions for cases of official classification based on gender: Focusing on the differential treatment or denial of opportunity for which relief is sought, the reviewing court must determine whether the proffered justification is "exceedingly persuasive." The burden of justification is demanding and it rests entirely on the State. The State must show "at least that the [challenged] classification serves 'important governmental objectives and that the discriminatory means employed' are 'substantially related to the achievement of those objectives.'" . . .

The heightened review standard our precedent establishes does not make sex a proscribed classification. Supposed "inherent differences" are no longer accepted as a ground for race or national origin classifications. *See Loving v. Virginia* (1967). Physical differences between men and women, however, are enduring: "[T]he two sexes are not fungible; a community made up exclusively of one [sex] is different from a community composed of both."

"Inherent differences" between men and women, we have come to appreciate, remain cause for celebration, but not for denigration of the members of either sex or for artificial constraints on an individual's opportunity. Sex classifications may be used to compensate women "for particular economic disabilities [they have] suffered," to "promote equal employment opportunity," to advance full development of the talent and capacities of our Nation's people. But such classifications may not be used, as they once were to create or perpetuate the legal, social, and economic inferiority of women.

Measuring the record in this case against the review standard just described, we conclude that Virginia has shown no "exceedingly persuasive justification" for excluding all women from the citizen-soldier training afforded by VMI. . . . Because the remedy proffered by Virginia — the Mary Baldwin VWIL program — does not cure the constitutional violation, i.e., it does not provide equal opportunity, we reverse the Fourth Circuit's final judgment in this case.

V

. . . Virginia . . . asserts two justifications in defense of VMI's exclusion of women. First, the Commonwealth contends, "single-sex education provides important educational benefits" and the option of single-sex education contributes to "diversity in educational approaches." Second, the Commonwealth argues, "the unique VMI method of character development and leadership training," the school's adversative approach, would have to be modified were VMI to admit women. . . .

A

. . . Virginia has not shown that VMI was established, or has been maintained, with a view to diversifying, by its categorical exclusion of women, educational opportunities within the State. In cases of this genre, our precedent instructs that "benign" justifications proffered in defense of categorical exclusions will not be accepted automatically; a tenable justification must describe actual state purposes, not rationalizations for actions in fact differently grounded.

Mississippi Univ. for Women is immediately in point. There the State asserted, in justification of its exclusion of men from a nursing school, that it was engaging in "educational affirmative action" by "compensat[ing] for discrimination against women." Undertaking a "searching analysis," the Court found no close resemblance between "the alleged objective" and "the actual purpose underlying the discriminatory classification[.]" Pursuing a similar inquiry here, we reach the same conclusion.

Neither recent nor distant history bears out Virginia's alleged pursuit of diversity through single-sex educational options. In 1839, when the State established VMI, a range of educational opportunities for men and women was scarcely contemplated. Higher education at the time was considered dangerous for women;[9] reflecting widely held views about women's proper place, the Nation's first universities and colleges — for example, Harvard in Massachusetts, William and Mary in Virginia — admitted only men. VMI was not at all novel in this respect: In admitting no women, VMI followed the lead of the State's flagship school, the University of Virginia, founded in 1819.

"[N]o struggle for the admission of women to a state university," a historian has recounted, "was longer drawn out, or developed more bitterness, than that at the University of Virginia." In 1879, the State Senate resolved to look into the possibility of higher education for women, recognizing that Virginia "'has never, at any period of her history,'" provided for the higher education of her daughters, though she "'has liberally provided for the higher education of her sons.'" Despite this recognition, no new opportunities were instantly open to women.

Virginia eventually provided for several women's seminaries and colleges. Farmville Female Seminary became a public institution in 1884. Two women's schools, Mary Washington College and James Madison University, were founded in 1908; another, Radford University, was founded in 1910. By the mid-1970's, all four schools had become coeducational.

* * *

. . . [W]e find no persuasive evidence in this record that VMI's male-only admission policy "is in furtherance of a state policy of 'diversity.'" . . . A purpose genuinely to advance an array of educational options, as the Court of Appeals recognized, is not served by VMI's historic and constant plan — a plan to "affor[d] a unique educational benefit only to males." However "liberally" this plan serves the State's sons, it makes no provision whatever for her daughters. That is not *equal* protection.

B

Virginia next argues that VMI's adversative method of training provides educational benefits that cannot be made available, unmodified, to women. Alterations to accommodate women would necessarily be "radical," so "drastic," Virginia asserts, as to transform, indeed "destroy," VMI's program. Neither sex would be favored by the transformation, Virginia maintains: Men would be

---

9 Dr. Edward H. Clarke of Harvard Medical School, whose influential book, Sex in Education, went through 17 editions, was perhaps the most well-known speaker from the medical community opposing higher education for women. He maintained that the physiological effects of hard study and academic competition with boys would interfere with the development of girls' reproductive organs. See E. CLARKE, SEX IN EDUCATION 38-39, 62-63 (1873); *id.*, at 127 ("identical education of the two sexes is a crime before God and humanity, that physiology protests against, and that experience weeps over"); see also H. MAUDSLEY, SEX IN MIND AND IN EDUCATION 17 (1874) ("It is not that girls have not ambition, nor that they fail generally to run the intellectual race [in coeducational settings], but it is asserted that they do it at a cost to their strength and health which entails life-long suffering, and even incapacitates them for the adequate performance of the natural functions of their sex."); C. MEIGS, FEMALES AND THEIR DISEASES 350 (1848) (after five or six weeks of "mental and educational discipline," a healthy woman would "lose . . . the habit of menstruation" and suffer numerous ills as a result of depriving her body for the sake of her mind).

deprived of the unique opportunity currently available to them; women would not gain that opportunity because their participation would "eliminat[e] the very aspects of [the] program that distinguish [VMI] from . . . other institutions of higher education in Virginia."

* * *

In support of its initial judgment for Virginia, a judgment rejecting all equal protection objections presented by the United States, the District Court made "findings" on "gender-based developmental differences." These "findings" restate the opinions of Virginia's expert witnesses, opinions about typically male or typically female "tendencies." For example, "[m]ales tend to need an atmosphere of adversativeness," while "[f]emales tend to thrive in a cooperative atmosphere." "I'm not saying that some women don't do well under [the] adversative model," VMI's expert on educational institutions testified, "undoubtedly there are some [women] who do"; but educational experiences must be designed "around the rule," this expert maintained, and not "around the exception."

The United States does not challenge any expert witness estimation on average capacities or preferences of men and women. Instead, the United States emphasizes that time and again since this Court's turning point decision in *Reed v. Reed* (1971), we have cautioned reviewing courts to take a "hard look" at generalizations or "tendencies" of the kind pressed by Virginia, and relied upon by the District Court. State actors controlling gates to opportunity, we have instructed, may not exclude qualified individuals based on "fixed notions concerning the roles and abilities of males and females."

It may be assumed, for purposes of this decision, that most women would not choose VMI's adversative method. As Fourth Circuit Judge Motz observed, however, in her dissent from the Court of Appeals' denial of rehearing en banc, it is also probable that "many men would not want to be educated in such an environment." Education, to be sure, is not a "one size fits all" business. The issue, however, is not whether "women — or men — should be forced to attend VMI"; rather, the question is whether the State can constitutionally deny to women who have the will and capacity, the training and attendant opportunities that VMI uniquely affords.

* * *

VI

In the second phase of the litigation, Virginia presented its remedial plan — maintain VMI as a male-only college and create VWIL as a separate program for women. The plan met District Court approval. The Fourth Circuit, in turn, deferentially reviewed the State's proposal and decided that the two single-sex programs directly served Virginia's reasserted purposes: single-gender education, and "achieving the results of an adversative method in a military environment." Inspecting the VMI and VWIL educational programs to determine whether they "afford[ed] to both genders benefits comparable in substance, [if] not in form and detail," the Court of Appeals concluded that Virginia had arranged for men and women opportunities "sufficiently comparable" to survive equal protection evaluation. The United States challenges this "remedial" ruling as pervasively misguided.

A

A remedial decree, this Court has said, must closely fit the constitutional violation; it must be shaped to place persons unconstitutionally denied an opportunity or advantage in "the position they would have occupied in the absence of [discrimination]." The constitutional violation in this case is the categorical exclusion of women from an extraordinary educational opportunity afforded men. A proper remedy for an unconstitutional exclusion, we have explained, aims to "eliminate [so far as possible] the discriminatory effects of the past" and to "bar like discrimination in the future."

Virginia chose not to eliminate, but to leave untouched, VMI's exclusionary policy. For women only, however, Virginia proposed a separate program, different in kind from VMI and unequal in tangible and intangible facilities. Having violated the Constitution's equal protection requirement, Virginia was obliged to show that its remedial proposal "directly address[ed] and relate[d] to" the violation, the equal protection denied to women ready, willing, and able to benefit from educational opportunities of the kind VMI offers. Virginia described VWIL as a "parallel program," and asserted that VWIL shares VMI's mission of producing "citizen-soldiers" and VMI's goals of providing "education, military training, mental and physical discipline, character . . . and leadership development." If the VWIL program could not "eliminate the discriminatory effects of the past," could it at least "bar like discrimination in the future"? A comparison of the programs said to be "parallel" informs our answer. . . .

VWIL affords women no opportunity to experience the rigorous military training for which VMI is famed. Instead, the VWIL program "deemphasize[s]" military education, and uses a "cooperative method" of education "which reinforces self-esteem[.]"

VWIL students participate in ROTC and a "largely ceremonial" Virginia Corps of Cadets, but Virginia deliberately did not make VWIL a military institute. The VWIL House is not a military-style residence and VWIL students need not live together throughout the 4-year program, eat meals together, or wear uniforms during the school day. VWIL students thus do not experience the "barracks" life "crucial to the VMI experience," the spartan living arrangements designed to foster an "egalitarian ethic." . . .

VWIL students receive their "leadership training" in seminars, externships, and speaker series, episodes and encounters lacking the "[p]hysical rigor, mental stress, . . . minute regulation of behavior, and indoctrination in desirable values" made hallmarks of VMI's citizen-soldier training. . . .

Virginia maintains that these methodological differences are "justified pedagogically," based on "important differences between men and women in learning and developmental needs," "psychological and sociological differences" Virginia describes as "real" and "not stereotypes." The Task Force charged with developing the leadership program for women, drawn from the staff and faculty at Mary Baldwin College, "determined that a military model and, especially VMI's adversative method, would be wholly inappropriate for educating and training *most women*." . . .

As earlier stated, generalizations about "the way women are," estimates of what is appropriate for *most women*, no longer justify denying opportunity to women whose talent and capacity place them outside the average description. Notably, Virginia never asserted that VMI's method of education suits *most men*. It is also revealing that Virginia accounted for its failure to make the VWIL experience "the entirely militaristic experience of VMI" on the ground that VWIL "is planned for women who do not necessarily expect to pursue military careers." By that reasoning, VMI's "entirely militaristic" program would be inappropriate for men in general or as a group, for "[o]nly about 15% of VMI cadets enter career military service."

In contrast to the generalizations about women on which Virginia rests, we note again these dispositive realties: VMI's "implementing methodology" is not "inherently unsuitable to women," "some women . . . do well under [the] adversative model," "some women, at least, would want to attend [VMI] if they had the opportunity," "some women are capable of all of the individual activities required of VMI cadets," and "can meet the physical standards [VMI] now impose[s] on men[.]" It is on behalf of these women that the United States has instituted this suit, and it is for them that a remedy must be crafted,[19] a remedy that will end their exclusion from a state-supplied educational opportunity for which they are fit, a decree that will "bar like discrimination in the future."

B

In myriad respects other than military training, VWIL does not qualify as VMI's equal. VWIL's student body, faculty, course offerings, and facilities hardly match VMI's. Nor can the VWIL graduate anticipate the benefits associated with VMI's 157-year history, the school's prestige, and its influential alumni network.

---

[19] Admitting women to VMI would undoubtedly require alterations necessary to afford members of each sex privacy from the other sex in living arrangements, and to adjust aspects of the physical training programs. *See* Brief for Petitioner 27-29; *cf.* note following 10 U.S.C. § 4342 (academic and other standards for women admitted to the Military, Naval, and Air Force Academies "shall be the same as those required for male individuals, except for those minimum essential adjustments in such standards required because of physiological differences between male and female individuals"). Experience shows such adjustments are manageable. *See* U.S. MILITARY ACADEMY, A. VITTERS, N. KINZER, & J. ADAMS, REPORT OF ADMISSION OF WOMEN (Project Athena I-IV) (1977-1980) (4-year longitudinal study of the admission of women to West Point); DEFENSE ADVISORY COMMITTEE ON WOMEN IN THE SERVICES, REPORT ON THE INTEGRATION AND PERFORMANCE OF WOMEN AT WEST POINT 17-18 (1992).

* * *

Virginia, in sum, while maintaining VMI for men only, has failed to provide any "comparable single-gender women's institution." Instead, the Commonwealth has created a VWIL program fairly appraised as a "pale shadow" of VMI in terms of the range of curricular choices and faculty stature, funding, prestige, alumni support and influence.

Virginia's VWIL solution is reminiscent of the remedy Texas proposed 50 years ago, in response to a state trial court's 1946 ruling that, given the equal protection guarantee, African Americans could not be denied a legal education at a state facility. *Sweatt v. Painter* (1950). Reluctant to admit African Americans to its flagship University of Texas Law School, the State set up a separate school for Heman Sweatt and other black law students. As originally opened, the new school had no independent faculty or library, and it lacked accreditation. Nevertheless, the state trial and appellate courts were satisfied that the new school offered Sweatt opportunities for the study of law "substantially equivalent to those offered by the State to white students at the University of Texas."

Before this Court considered the case, the new school had gained "a faculty of five full-time professors; a student body of 23; a library of some 16,500 volumes serviced by a full-time staff; a practice court and legal aid association; and one alumnus who had become a member of the Texas Bar." This Court contrasted resources at the new school with those at the school from which Sweatt had been excluded. The University of Texas Law School had a full-time faculty of 16, a student body of 850, a library containing over 65,000 volumes, scholarship funds, a law review, and moot court facilities.

More important than the tangible features, the Court emphasized, are "those qualities which are incapable of objective measurement but which make for greatness" in a school, including "reputation of the faculty, experience of the administration, position and influence of the alumni, standing in the community, traditions and prestige." Facing the marked differences reported in the *Sweatt* opinion, the Court unanimously ruled that Texas had not shown "substantial equality in the [separate] educational opportunities" the State offered. Accordingly, the Court held, the Equal Protection Clause required Texas to admit African Americans to the University of Texas Law School. In line with *Sweatt*, we rule here that Virginia has not shown substantial equality in the separate educational opportunities the State supports at VWIL and VMI.

C

When Virginia tendered its VWIL plan, the Fourth Circuit did not inquire whether the proposed remedy, approved by the District Court, placed women denied the VMI advantage in "the position they would have occupied in the absence of [discrimination]." Instead, the Court of Appeals considered whether the State could provide, with fidelity to the equal protection principle, separate and unequal educational programs for men and women.

... [T]he appeals court declared the substantially different and significantly unequal VWIL program satisfactory. The court reached that result by revising the applicable standard of review. The Fourth Circuit displaced the standard developed in our precedent and substituted a standard of its own invention.

We have earlier described the deferential review in which the Court of Appeals engaged, a brand of review inconsistent with the more exacting standard our precedent requires. ... [T]he Court of Appeals candidly described its own analysis as one capable of checking a legislative purpose ranked as "pernicious," but generally according "deference to [the] legislative will." Recognizing that it had extracted from our decisions a test yielding "little or no scrutiny of the effect of a classification directed at [single-gender education]," the Court of Appeals devised another test, a "substantive comparability" inquiry and proceeded to find that new test satisfied.

The Fourth Circuit plainly erred in exposing Virginia's VWIL plan to a deferential analysis, for "all gender-based classifications today" warrant "heightened scrutiny." Valuable as VWIL may prove for students who seek the program offered, Virginia's remedy affords no cure at all for the opportunities and advantages withheld from women who want a VMI education and can make the grade. In sum, Virginia's remedy does not match the constitutional violation; the State has shown no "exceedingly persuasive justification" for withholding from women qualified for the experience premier training of the kind VMI affords.

VII

A generation ago, "the authorities controlling Virginia higher education," despite long established tradition, agreed "to innovate and favorably entertain[ed] the [then] relatively new idea that there must be no discrimination by sex in offering educational opportunity." Commencing in 1970, Virginia opened to women "educational opportunities at the Charlottesville campus that [were] not afforded in other [State-operated] institutions." ...

VMI, too, offers an educational opportunity no other Virginia institution provides, and the school's "prestige" — associated with its success in developing "citizen-soldiers" — is unequaled. Virginia has closed this facility to its daughters and, instead, has devised for them a "parallel program," with a faculty less impressively credentialed and less well paid, more limited course offerings, fewer opportunities for military training and for scientific specialization. VMI, beyond question, "possesses to a far greater degree" than the VWIL program "those qualities which are incapable of objective measurement but which make for greatness in a ... school," including "position and influence of the alumni, standing in the community, traditions and prestige." Women seeking and fit for a VMI-quality education cannot be offered anything less, under the State's obligation to afford them genuinely equal protection.

A prime part of the history of our Constitution, historian Richard Morris recounted, is the story of the extension of constitutional rights and protections to people once ignored or excluded. VMI's story continued as our comprehension of "We the People" expanded. There is no reason to believe that the admission of women capable of all the activities required of VMI cadets would destroy the Institute rather than enhance its capacity to serve the "more perfect Union."

* * *

. . . [T]he case is remanded for further proceedings consistent with this opinion.

It is so ordered.

JUSTICE THOMAS took no part in the consideration or decision of this case.

CHIEF JUSTICE REHNQUIST, concurring in judgment. [omitted]

JUSTICE SCALIA, dissenting.

Today the Court shuts down an institution that has served the people of the Commonwealth of Virginia with pride and distinction for over a century and a half. To achieve that desired result, it rejects (contrary to our established practice) the factual findings of two courts below, sweeps aside the precedents of this Court, and ignores the history of our people. As to facts: it explicitly rejects the finding that there exist "gender-based developmental differences" supporting Virginia's restriction of the "adversative" method to only a men's institution, and the finding that the all-male composition of the Virginia Military Institute (VMI) is essential to that institution's character. As to precedent: it drastically revises our established standards for reviewing sex-based classifications. And as to history: it counts for nothing the long tradition, enduring down to the present, of men's military colleges supported by both States and the Federal Government.

Much of the Court's opinion is devoted to deprecating the closed-mindedness of our forebears with regard to women's education, and even with regard to the treatment of women in areas that have nothing to do with education. Closed-minded they were — as every age is, including our own, with regard to matters it cannot guess, because it simply does not consider them debatable. The virtue of a democratic system with a First Amendment is that it readily enables the people, over time, to be persuaded that what they took for granted is not so, and to change their laws accordingly. That system is destroyed if the smug assurances of each age are removed from the democratic process and written into the Constitution. So to counterbalance the Court's criticism of our ancestors, let me say a word in their praise: they left us free to change. The same cannot be said of this most illiberal Court, which has embarked on a course of inscribing one after another of the current preferences of the society (and in some cases only the counter-majoritarian preferences of the society's law-trained elite) into our Basic Law. Today it enshrines the notion that no substantial educational value is to be served by an all-men's military academy — so that the decision by the people of Virginia to maintain such an institution denies equal protection to women who cannot attend that institution but can attend others. Since it is entirely clear that the Constitution of the United States — the old one — takes no sides in this educational debate, I dissent.

* * *

IV

* * *

A

Under the constitutional principles announced and applied today, single-sex public education is unconstitutional. By going through the motions of applying a balancing test — asking whether the State has adduced an "exceedingly persuasive justification" for its sex-based classification — the Court creates the illusion that government officials in some future case will have a clear shot at justifying some sort of single-sex public education. Indeed, the Court seeks to create even a greater illusion than that: It purports to have said nothing of relevance to *other* public schools at all. "We address specifically and only an educational opportunity recognized . . . as 'unique' . . . ."

The Supreme Court of the United States does not sit to announce "unique" dispositions. Its principal function is to establish *precedent* — that is, to set forth principles of law that every court in America must follow. . . .

And the rationale of today's decision is sweeping: for sex-based classifications, a redefinition of intermediate scrutiny that makes it indistinguishable from strict scrutiny. Indeed, the Court indicates that if any program restricted to one sex is "uniqu[e]," it must be opened to members of the opposite sex "who have the will and capacity" to participate in it. I suggest that the single-sex program that will not be capable of being characterized as "unique" is not only unique but nonexistent.

In any event, regardless of whether the Court's rationale leaves some small amount of room for lawyers to argue, it ensures that single-sex public education is functionally dead. The costs of litigating the constitutionality of a single-sex education program, and the risks of ultimately losing that litigation, are simply too high to be embraced by public officials. Any person with standing to challenge any sex-based classification can haul the State into federal court and compel it to establish by evidence (presumably in the form of expert testimony) that there is an "exceedingly persuasive justification" for the classification. Should the courts happen to interpret that vacuous phrase as establishing a standard that is not utterly impossible of achievement, there is considerable risk that whether the standard has been met will not be determined on the basis of the record evidence — indeed, that will necessarily be the approach of any court that seeks to walk the path the Court has trod today. No state official in his right mind will buy such a high-cost, high-risk lawsuit by commencing a single-sex program. The enemies of single-sex education have won. . . .

This is especially regrettable because, as the District Court here determined, educational experts in recent years have increasingly come to "suppor[t] [the] view that substantial educational benefits flow from a single-gender environment, be it male or female, *that cannot be replicated in a coeducational setting*."

. . . Until quite recently, some public officials have attempted to institute new single-sex programs, at least as experiments. In 1991, for example, the Detroit Board of Education announced a program to establish three boys-only schools for inner-city youth; it was met with a lawsuit, a preliminary injunction was swiftly entered by a District Court that purported to rely on *Hogan*, and the Detroit Board of Education voted to abandon the litigation and thus abandon the plan[.] Today's opinion assures that no such experiment will be tried again.

B

There are few extant single-sex public educational programs. The potential of today's decision for widespread disruption of existing institutions lies in its application to *private* single-sex education. Government support is immensely important to private educational institutions. Mary Baldwin College — which designed and runs VWIL — notes that private institutions of higher education in the 1990-1991 school year derived approximately 19 percent of their budgets from federal, state, and local government funds, *not including financial aid to students*. Charitable status under the tax laws is also highly significant for private educational institutions, and it is certainly not beyond the Court that rendered today's decision to hold that a donation to a single-sex college should be deemed contrary to public policy and therefore not deductible if the college discriminates on the basis of sex.

* * *

The only hope for state-assisted single-sex private schools is that the Court will not apply in the future the principles of law it has applied today. That is a substantial hope, I am happy and ashamed to say. After all, did not the Court today abandon the principles of law it has applied in our earlier sex-classification cases? And does not the Court positively invite private colleges to rely upon our ad-hocery by assuring them this case is "unique"? I would not advise the foundation of any new single-sex college (especially an all-male one) with the expectation of being allowed to receive any government support; but it is too soon to abandon in despair those single-sex colleges already in existence. It will certainly be possible for this Court to write a future opinion that ignores the broad principles of law set forth today, and that characterizes as utterly dispositive the opinion's perceptions that VMI was a uniquely prestigious all-male institution, conceived in chauvinism, etc., etc. I will not join that opinion.

* * *

Justice Brandeis said it is "one of the happy incidents of the federal system that a single courageous State may, if its citizens choose, serve as a laboratory; and try novel social and economic experiments without risk to the rest of the country." *New State Ice Co. v. Liebmann* (1932) (dissenting opinion). But it is one of the unhappy incidents of the federal system that a self-righteous Supreme Court, acting on its Members' personal view of what would make a "more perfect Union," (a criterion only slightly more restrictive than a "more perfect world"), can impose its own favored social and economic dispositions nationwide.

As today's disposition, and others this single Term, show, this places it beyond the power of a "single courageous State," not only to introduce novel dispositions that the Court frowns upon, but to reintroduce, or indeed even adhere to, disfavored dispositions that are centuries old. The sphere of self-government reserved to the people of the Republic is progressively narrowed.

* * *

In an odd sort of way, it is precisely VMI's attachment to such old-fashioned concepts as manly "honor" that has made it, and the system it represents, the target of those who today succeed in abolishing public single-sex education. The record contains a booklet that all first-year VMI students (the so-called "rats") were required to keep in their possession at all times. Near the end there appears the following period-piece, entitled "The Code of a Gentleman":

> "Without a strict observance of the fundamental Code of Honor, no man, no matter how 'polished,' can be considered a gentleman. The honor of a gentleman demands the inviolability of his word, and the incorruptibility of his principles. He is the descendant of the knight, the crusader; he is the defender of the defenseless and the champion of justice . . . or he is not a Gentleman.
>
> "A Gentleman . . .
>
> "Does not discuss his family affairs in public or with acquaintances.
>
> "Does not speak more than casually about his girl friend.
>
> "Does not go to a lady's house if he is affected by alcohol. He is temperate in the use of alcohol.
>
> "Does not lose his temper; nor exhibit anger, fear, hate, embarrassment, ardor or hilarity in public.
>
> "Does not hail a lady from a club window.
>
> "A gentleman never discusses the merits or demerits of a lady.
>
> "Does not mention names exactly as he avoids the mention of what things cost.
>
> "Does not borrow money from a friend, except in dire need. Money borrowed is a debt of honor, and must be repaid as promptly as possible. Debts incurred by a deceased parent, brother, sister or grown child are assumed by honorable men as a debt of honor.
>
> "Does not display his wealth, money or possessions.
>
> "Does not put his manners on and off, whether in the club or in a ballroom. He treats people with courtesy, no matter what their social position may be.

"Does not slap strangers on the back nor so much as lay a finger on a lady.

"Does not 'lick the boots of those above' nor 'kick the face of those below him on the social ladder.'

"Does not take advantage of another's helplessness or ignorance and assumes that no gentleman will take advantage of him."

* * *

I do not know whether the men of VMI lived by this Code; perhaps not. But it is powerfully impressive that a public institution of higher education still in existence sought to have them do so. I do not think any of us, women included, will be better off for its destruction.

NOTES AND QUESTIONS

1. What is the argument for invoking the Fourteenth Amendment as a prohibition on gender discrimination? For example, if Susan B. Anthony was unsuccessful in arguing that the Fourteenth Amendment gave her the right to vote, why should it give young Virginia women the right to enter VMI? Why doesn't "separate but equal" work in this case, or does it? Was the VMI program really premised upon gender stereotypes or is it simply that single-gender education can, for some people, be particularly effective? Does it matter that empirical studies tend to suggest that teenage girls in secondary school do particularly well in a single-sex environment? *See* Rodney K. Smith, *When Ignorance Is Not Bliss: In Search of Racial and Gender Equality in Intercollegiate Athletics,* 61 Mo. L. Rev. 329 (1996) (discussing gender and racial inequities that permeate college athletics and arguing that an academically prejudicial reluctance on the part of scholars to study the subject is perpetuating the problem).

2. Why is "intermediate scrutiny" the appropriate test for gender discrimination? Why not "rational basis" or "strict scrutiny"? Is gender, unlike race, a sometimes acceptable criteria for public decision making? What are those times? Is Justice Scalia correct that the majority actually uses a "strict scrutiny" test? Why the need for a middle or a middle and a half tier? Is he correct that publically-funded single-sex education is now unconstitutional? Justice Scalia's opinion boils down to the simple contention that the Court is legislating its value preferences into constitutional law. Why does he believe this, and do you agree?

3. Not all gender classifications have been struck down. In *Michael M. v. Superior Court,* 450 U.S. 464 (1981), the Court upheld a statutory rape law that punishes men for having sexual intercourse with a women under 18, but not vice versa, and in *Rostker v. Goldberg,* 453 U.S. 57 (1981), the Court sustained the federal law that requires only men to register for the military draft. Are these gender distinctions in doubt in light of *VMI*? Are gender distinctions ever acceptable on the theory of anatomical or biological difference? In *Dothard* *v. Rawlinson*, 433 U.S. 321 (1977), the Court upheld the exclusion of women from so-called "contact positions" in an all-male prison. *Michael M.* was premised on the belief that the consequences of teenage pregnancy are naturally harder for a female who must bear the pregnancy, and hence, the law could rationally distinguish between male and female penalties under the rape statute. Do you agree? If so, do these biological differences also justify the exemption from the draft?

4. Are classifications that benefit women contrary to equal protection? Sometimes. For example, in *Orr v. Orr*, 440 U.S. 268 (1979), the Court struck an Alabama law that allowed alimony to women, but not men. Similarly, in *Califano v. Goldfarb*, 430 U.S. 199 (1977), a provision of the federal law providing benefits to a surviving spouse was invalidated because it gave preference to a surviving wife, but required a surviving husband to prove that he received half of his support from his wife. Given that, statistically, there are still more dependent women than men, why is it wrong for legislatures to take cognizance of this fact? Should the law be used as a form of social engineering to undo, or create incentives to undo, choices made by spouses in their individual lives? Not all legal preferences for women have been invalidated, either. For example, in *Califano v. Webster*, 430 U.S. 313 (1977), the Court upheld more favorable benefits calaculation for women under the Social Security Act than men. Similarly, in *Schlesinger v. Ballard*, 419 U.S. 498 (1975), a Navy regulation that allowed women four additional years to obtain promotion in rank than men before involuntary discharge was accepted. Are some benefits under law for women based on stereotype and others designed to redress past discrimination? Does Justice Ginsburg in *VMI* rule out a state-run single-sex institution for women?

5. While thus far our study of equal protection has been of race and gender classifications, others sometimes exist under law. Do any others require heightened scrutiny? Yes, with regard to aliens and illegitimate children, but it's a bit complicated. Because the text of the equal protection clause extends to "persons," and not merely citizens, aliens may not be discriminated against, except in particular cases mentioned below. *See Graham v. Richardson*, 403 U.S. 365 (1971) (invalidating a Pennsylvania law that excluded aliens from state public assistance). The Court in *Graham* applied strict scrutiny, reasoning that aliens were a particularly disabled class since they are unable to vote and may often be the target of economic protectionism or bias. However, strict scrutiny does not apply to the exclusion of aliens from the right to vote, itself, or public office or service on a jury. These matters of basic citizenship or self-government can be reserved to citizens, and the government needs only a rational basis to do so. *See, e.g., Foley v. Connelie*, 435 U.S. 291 (1978) (upholding a state law requiring citizenship to be a police officer). *Accord Ambach v. Norwich*, 441 U.S. 68 (1979) (citizenship required for public school teacher). Aliens may also be excluded because of Congress' plenary authority over immigration. Thus, in *Matthews v. Diaz*, 426 U.S. 67 (1976), the Court upheld the federal exclusion of those aliens who had not been admitted for permanent residence and resided in America for at least five years from Medicaid benefits. Thus, unlike state and

local governments who are bound by the Court's decision in *Graham, supra,*
Congress and the President in the implementation of foreign policy, of which
immigration is a part, may discriminate against aliens for rational reasons.
Cf. Hampton v. Wong, 426 U.S. 88 (1976) (the deference does not extend to federal decisions made by subordinate agencies unless they are directly implementing immigration or foreign policy). In a decision of some controversy, the
Supreme Court held in *Plyler v. Doe,* 457 U.S. 202 (1982), that it was irrational
for a state to exclude the children of illegal aliens from public schools unless they
reimbursed the school system. The Court, as a matter of social compassion,
saw the children as "blameless," and that in any event, creating an illiterate sub-
class would simply aggravate crime and other social problems. Chief Justice
Burger in dissent thought the matter better handled by the legislature since neither a fundamental right nor suspect class was implicated. California responded
to *Plyler* by passing Proposition 187 denying undocumented aliens a public
education. A lower court has invalidated the measure as preempted by Congress'
immigration authority. *League of United American Citizens v. Wilson,* 908 F.
Supp. 755 (C.D. Cal. 1995).

Illegitimate children are accorded intermediate scrutiny in the Court's cases.
For example, in *Trimble v. Gordon,* 430 U.S. 762 (1977), the Court struck an Illinois law that prevented illegitimate children from inheriting from a father who
died without a will. *Cf. Labine v. Vincent,* 401 U.S. 532 (1971), a state law denying inheritance from the father of an illegitimate child unless the child has
been formally acknowledged during the father's lifetime is constitutional. The
Court thus appears unwilling to deny all benefits or privileges to illegitimate
children, but willing to accept reasonable distinctions within the class of illegitimate children.

6. Other classifications — those premised upon age, wealth, and disability, for
example — are subject to rational basis review. In *Massachusetts Board of
Retirement v. Murgia,* 427 U.S. 307 (1976), the Court sustained a Massachusetts
law requiring police officers to retire at age 50. Unlike race or gender, age is a
stage that all reach, it is not an immutable characteristic and states must have
reasonable discretion to make policy judgments about its effect on given responsibilities. Nor has the Court applied heightened scrutiny to wealth. For example, in *Dandridge v. Williams,* 397 U.S. 471 (1970), the Court sustained a welfare
cap on families regardless of the size of the family. Different laws affect income
groups differently, and again, the Court was unwilling to second-guess the legislature in matters of policy. In any event, one's relative wealth is also not
immutable and therefore less likely to be the basis of invidious distinction.
Finally, with respect to disability, the Court, too, has applied a rational basis
standard, though occasionally one with a "bite." In *City of Cleburne v. Cleburne
Living Center, Inc.,* 473 U.S. 432 (1985), the Court invalidated a special permit
requirement for a group home for the mentally disabled, even though its general
deference in economic and land use matters would have led to the opposite
result. Since the local ordinance allowed for other congregate uses in the same
place, like boarding houses and fraternities, the Court could discern no rational

basis — other than bias — for the permit requirement's application to the mentally disabled.

7. In recent years, the issue of gay rights has presented the Court with some opportunity to evaluate whether sexual orientation is a legitimate basis for legal characterization. The issue is complicated because much religious and moral teaching finds homosexual practice to be spiritually or culturally disordered. *See, e.g.,* John M. Finnis, *Law, Morality and "Sexual Orientation"*, 69 NOTRE DAME L. REV. 1049, 1070-76 (1994) (arguing that homosexual activity may be banned because it is against the common good and different than heterosexual activity that is an authentic union and open to the possibility, though not the certainty, of childbirth); Robert P. George & Gerard V. Bradley, *Marriage and the Liberal Imagination*, 84 GEO. L.J. 301, 318-20 (1995) (arguing that homosexual activity is intrinsically immoral and that "the state ought not to institutionalize . . . same sex [marriage]"); *but see also* Michael J. Perry, *The Morality of Homosexual Conduct: A Response to John Finnis*, 9 NOTRE DAME J.L. ETHICS & PUB. POL'Y 41, 47-49 (1995) (questioning Finnis' premise that only the sexual union of a married couple can be a "single reality"). The issue is further complicated by the fact that sexual orientation classifications arguably implicate both status and conduct. Because of the former, there are political calls to treat sexual orientation classifications as the equivalent of race or gender classifications, and thus entitled to heightened scrutiny. Thus far, the Court has not reached that result — at least, not explicitly. The classification side of the sexual orientation debate is taken up in *Romer v. Evans*, below.

The conduct aspect of the sexual orientation debate, on the other hand, invokes notions of liberty and hence of the potential for heightened scrutiny under the "fundamental rights" aspect of equal protection analysis. That aspect of the debate, and the Court's contribution to it, is taken up in Chapter 9.

D. Sexual Orientation

ROMER v. EVANS
517 U.S. 620 (1996)

JUSTICE KENNEDY delivered the opinion of the Court.

One century ago, the first Justice Harlan admonished this Court that the Constitution "neither knows nor tolerates classes among citizens." *Plessy v. Ferguson* (1896) (dissenting opinion). Unheeded then, those words now are understood to state a commitment to the law's neutrality where the rights of persons are at stake. The Equal Protection Clause enforces this principle and today requires us to hold invalid a provision of Colorado's Constitution.

I

The enactment challenged in this case is an amendment to the Constitution of the State of Colorado, adopted in a 1992 statewide referendum. The parties and the state courts refer to it as "Amendment 2," its designation when submitted to the voters. The impetus for the amendment and the contentious campaign that preceded its adoption came in large part from ordinances that had been passed in various Colorado municipalities. For example, the cities of Aspen and Boulder and the City and County of Denver each had enacted ordinances which banned discrimination in many transactions and activities, including housing, employment, education, public accommodations, and health and welfare services. What gave rise to the statewide controversy was the protection the ordinances afforded to persons discriminated against by reason of their sexual orientation. Amendment 2 repeals these ordinances to the extent they prohibit discrimination on the basis of "homosexual, lesbian or bisexual orientation, conduct, practices or relationships."

Yet Amendment 2, in explicit terms, does more than repeal or rescind these provisions. It prohibits all legislative, executive or judicial action at any level of state or local government designed to protect the named class, a class we shall refer to as homosexual persons or gays and lesbians. . . .

Soon after Amendment 2 was adopted, this litigation to declare its invalidity and enjoin its enforcement was commenced in the District Court for the City and County of Denver. Among the plaintiffs (respondents here) were homosexual persons, some of them government employees. They alleged that enforcement of Amendment 2 would subject them to immediate and substantial risk of discrimination on the basis of their sexual orientation. . . .

The trial court granted a preliminary injunction to stay enforcement of Amendment 2, and an appeal was taken to the Supreme Court of Colorado. Sustaining the interim injunction and remanding the case for further proceedings, the State Supreme Court held that Amendment 2 was subject to strict scrutiny under the Fourteenth Amendment because it infringed the fundamental right of gays and lesbians to participate in the political process. To reach this conclusion, the state court relied on our voting rights cases, and on our precedents involving discriminatory restructuring of governmental decisionmaking. On remand, the State advanced various arguments in an effort to show that Amendment 2 was narrowly tailored to serve compelling interests, but the trial court found none sufficient. It enjoined enforcement of Amendment 2, and the Supreme Court of Colorado, in a second opinion, affirmed the ruling. We granted certiorari and now affirm the judgment, but on a rationale different from that adopted by the State Supreme Court.

II

The State's principal argument in defense of Amendment 2 is that it puts gays and lesbians in the same position as all other persons. So, the State says, the measure does no more than deny homosexuals special rights. This reading of the amendment's language is implausible. We rely not upon our own interpretation of the amendment but upon the authoritative construction of Colorado's Supreme Court. The state court, deeming it unnecessary to determine the full extent of the amendment's reach, found it invalid even on a modest reading of its implications. The critical discussion of the amendment . . . is as follows:

> "The immediate objective of Amendment 2 is, at a minimum, to repeal existing statutes, regulations, ordinances, and policies of state and local entities that barred discrimination based on sexual orientation.

> "The 'ultimate effect' of Amendment 2 is to prohibit any governmental entity from adopting similar, or more protective statutes, regulations, ordinances, or policies in the future unless the state constitution is first amended to permit such measures."

Sweeping and comprehensive is the change in legal status effected by this law. So much is evident from the ordinances that the Colorado Supreme Court declared would be void by operation of Amendment 2. Homosexuals, by state decree, are put in a solitary class with respect to transactions and relations in both the private and governmental spheres. The amendment withdraws from homosexuals, but no others, specific legal protection from the injuries caused by discrimination, and it forbids reinstatement of these laws and policies.

The change that Amendment 2 works in the legal status of gays and lesbians in the private sphere is far-reaching, both on its own terms and when considered in light of the structure and operation of modern anti-discrimination laws. That structure is well illustrated by contemporary statutes and ordinances prohibiting discrimination by providers of public accommodations. "At common law, innkeepers, smiths, and others who 'made profession of a public employment,' were prohibited from refusing, without good reason, to serve a customer." The duty was a general one and did not specify protection for particular groups. The common law rules, however, proved insufficient in many instances, and it was settled early that the Fourteenth Amendment did not give Congress a general power to prohibit discrimination in public accommodations, *Civil Rights Cases* (1883). In consequence, most States have chosen to counter discrimination by enacting detailed statutory schemes.

Colorado's state and municipal laws typify this emerging tradition of statutory protection and follow a consistent pattern. . . .

These statutes and ordinances also depart from the common law by enumerating the groups or persons within their ambit of protection. Enumeration is the essential device used to make the duty not to discriminate concrete and to provide guidance for those who must comply. In following this approach, Colorado's state and local governments have not limited anti-discrimination laws to groups that have so far been given the protection of heightened equal protection scrutiny under our cases. [sex, illegitimacy, race, ancestry] Rather, they set forth an extensive catalogue of traits which cannot be the basis for discrimination, including age, military status, marital status, pregnancy, parenthood, custody of a minor child, political affiliation, physical or mental disability of an individual or of his or her associates — and, in recent times, sexual orientation.

Amendment 2 bars homosexuals from securing protection against the injuries that these public-accommodations laws address. That in itself is a severe consequence, but there is more. Amendment 2, in addition, nullifies specific legal protections for this targeted class in all transactions in housing, sale of real estate, insurance, health and welfare services, private education, and employment.

Not confined to the private sphere, Amendment 2 also operates to repeal and forbid all laws or policies providing specific protection for gays or lesbians from discrimination by every level of Colorado government. The State Supreme Court cited two examples of protections in the governmental sphere that are now rescinded and may not be reintroduced. The first is Colorado Executive Order D0035 (1990), which forbids employment discrimination against "'all state employees, classified and exempt' on the basis of sexual orientation." Also repealed, and now forbidden, are "various provisions prohibiting discrimination based on sexual orientation at state colleges." The repeal of these measures and the prohibition against their future reenactment demonstrates that Amendment 2 has the same force and effect in Colorado's governmental sector as it does elsewhere and that it applies to policies as well as ordinary legislation.

Amendment 2's reach may not be limited to specific laws passed for the benefit of gays and lesbians. It is a fair, if not necessary, inference from the broad language of the amendment that it deprives gays and lesbians even of the protection of general laws and policies that prohibit arbitrary discrimination in governmental and private settings. At some point in the systematic administration of these laws, an official must determine whether homosexuality is an arbitrary and thus forbidden basis for decision. Yet a decision to that effect would itself amount to a policy prohibiting discrimination on the basis of homosexuality, and so would appear to be no more valid under Amendment 2 than the specific prohibitions against discrimination the state court held invalid.

If this consequence follows from Amendment 2, as its broad language suggests, it would compound the constitutional difficulties the law creates. The state court did not decide whether the amendment has this effect, however, and neither need we. In the course of rejecting the argument that Amendment 2 is intended to conserve resources to fight discrimination against suspect classes, the Colorado Supreme Court made the limited observation that the amendment is not intended to affect many anti-discrimination laws protecting non-suspect classes. . . .

III

The Fourteenth Amendment's promise that no person shall be denied the equal protection of the laws must co-exist with the practical necessity that most legislation classifies for one purpose or another, with resulting disadvantage to various groups or persons. We have attempted to reconcile the principle with the reality by stating that, if a law neither burdens a fundamental right nor targets a suspect class, we will uphold the legislative classification so long as it bears a rational relation to some legitimate end.

Amendment 2 fails, indeed defies, even this conventional inquiry. First, the amendment has the peculiar property of imposing a broad and undifferentiated disability on a single named group, an exceptional and, as we shall explain, invalid form of legislation. Second, its sheer breadth is so discontinuous with the reasons offered for it that the amendment seems inexplicable by anything but animus toward the class that it affects; it lacks a rational relationship to legitimate state interests.

Taking the first point, even in the ordinary equal protection case calling for the most deferential of standards, we insist on knowing the relation between the classification adopted and the object to be attained. . . . In the ordinary case, a law will be sustained if it can be said to advance a legitimate government interest, even if the law seems unwise or works to the disadvantage of a particular group, or if the rationale for it seems tenuous. . . . By requiring that the classification bear a rational relationship to an independent and legitimate legislative end, we ensure that classifications are not drawn for the purpose of disadvantaging the group burdened by the law.

Amendment 2 confounds this normal process of judicial review. It is at once too narrow and too broad. It identifies persons by a single trait and then denies them protection across the board. The resulting disqualification of a class of persons from the right to seek specific protection from the law is unprecedented in our jurisprudence. The absence of precedent for Amendment 2 is itself instructive; "[d]iscriminations of an unusual character especially suggest careful consideration to determine whether they are obnoxious to the constitutional provision."

It is not within our constitutional tradition to enact laws of this sort. Central both to the idea of the rule of law and to our own Constitution's guarantee of equal protection is the principle that government and each of its parts remain open on impartial terms to all who seek its assistance. "Equal protection of the laws is not achieved through indiscriminate imposition of inequalities." Respect for this principle explains why laws singling out a certain class of citizens for disfavored legal status or general hardships are rare. A law declaring that in general it shall be more difficult for one group of citizens than for all others to seek aid from the government is itself a denial of equal protection of the laws in the most literal sense. "The guaranty of 'equal protection of the laws is a pledge of the protection of equal laws.'"

Davis v. Beason (1890), not cited by the parties but relied upon by the dissent, is not evidence that Amendment 2 is within our constitutional tradition, and any reliance upon it as authority for sustaining the amendment is misplaced. In *Davis*, the Court approved an Idaho territorial statute denying Mormons, polygamists, and advocates of polygamy the right to vote and to hold office because, as the Court construed the statute, it "simply excludes from the privilege of voting, or of holding any office of honor, trust or profit, those who have been convicted of certain offences, and those who advocate a practical resistance to the laws of the Territory and justify and approve the commission of crimes forbidden by it." To the extent *Davis* held that persons advocating a certain practice may be denied the right to vote, it is no longer good law. *Brandenburg v. Ohio* (1969) (per curiam). To the extent it held that the groups designated in the statute may be deprived of the right to vote because of their status, its ruling could not stand without surviving strict scrutiny, a most doubtful outcome. To the extent *Davis* held that a convicted felon may be denied the right to vote, its holding is not implicated by our decision and is unexceptionable.

A second and related point is that laws of the kind now before us raise the inevitable inference that the disadvantage imposed is born of animosity toward the class of persons affected. "[I]f the constitutional conception of 'equal protection of the laws' means anything, it must at the very least mean that a bare . . . desire to harm a politically unpopular group cannot constitute a legitimate governmental interest." Even laws enacted for broad and ambitious purposes often can be explained by reference to legitimate public policies which justify the incidental disadvantages they impose on certain persons. Amendment 2, however, in making a general announcement that gays and lesbians shall not have any particular protections from the law, inflicts on them immediate, continuing, and real injuries that outrun and belie any legitimate justifications that may be claimed for it. We conclude that, in addition to the far-reaching deficiencies of Amendment 2 that we have noted, the principles it offends, in another sense, are conventional and venerable; a law must bear a rational relationship to a legitimate governmental purpose, and Amendment 2 does not.

The primary rationale the State offers for Amendment 2 is respect for other citizens' freedom of association, and in particular the liberties of landlords or employers who have personal or religious objections to homosexuality. Colorado also cites its interest in conserving resources to fight discrimination against other groups. The breadth of the Amendment is so far removed from these particular justifications that we find it impossible to credit them. We cannot say that Amendment 2 is directed to any identifiable legitimate purpose or discrete objective. It is a status-based enactment divorced from any factual context from which we could discern a relationship to legitimate state interests; it is a classification of persons undertaken for its own sake, something the Equal Protection Clause does not permit. "[C]lass legislation . . . [is] obnoxious to the prohibitions of the Fourteenth Amendment. . . ."

We must conclude that Amendment 2 classifies homosexuals not to further a proper legislative end but to make them unequal to everyone else. This Colorado cannot do. A State cannot so deem a class of persons a stranger to its laws. . . .

JUSTICE SCALIA, with whom THE CHIEF JUSTICE and JUSTICE THOMAS join, dissenting.

The Court has mistaken a Kulturkampf for a fit of spite. The constitutional amendment before us here is not the manifestation of a "'bare . . . desire to harm'" homosexuals, but is rather a modest attempt by seemingly tolerant Coloradans to preserve traditional sexual mores against the efforts of a politically powerful minority to revise those mores through use of the laws. That objective, and the means chosen to achieve it, are not only unimpeachable under any constitutional doctrine hitherto pronounced (hence the opinion's heavy reliance upon principles of righteousness rather than judicial holdings); they have been specifically approved by the Congress of the United States and by this Court.

In holding that homosexuality cannot be singled out for disfavorable treatment, the Court contradicts a decision, unchallenged here, pronounced only 10 years ago, *see Bowers v. Hardwick* (1986), and places the prestige of this institution behind the proposition that opposition to homosexuality is as reprehensible as racial or religious bias. Whether it is or not is *precisely* the cultural debate that gave rise to the Colorado constitutional amendment (and to the preferential laws against which the amendment was directed). Since the Constitution of the United States says nothing about this subject, it is left to be resolved by normal democratic means, including the democratic adoption of provisions in state constitutions. This Court has no business imposing upon all Americans the resolution favored by the elite class from which the Members of this institution are selected, pronouncing that "animosity" toward homosexuality is evil. I vigorously dissent.

* * *

Today's opinion has no foundation in American constitutional law, and barely pretends to. The people of Colorado have adopted an entirely reasonable provision which does not even disfavor homosexuals in any substantive sense, but merely denies them preferential treatment. Amendment 2 is designed to prevent piecemeal deterioration of the sexual morality favored by a majority of Coloradans, and is not only an appropriate means to that legitimate end, but a means that Americans have employed before. Striking it down is an act, not of judicial judgment, but of political will. I dissent.

NOTES AND QUESTIONS

1. What does Justice Scalia mean when he says, dissenting, that "[t]he Court has mistaken a Kulturkampf for a fit of spite." *Romer*, 517 U.S. at 636 (Scalia, J., dissenting). What does that have to do with constitutional law? It was often said in the late twentieth century that the United States was engaged in a cultural civil war. Does Scalia's opinion operate on this basis? Which side do you favor in the "culture war"? How should constitutional law take sides in the war? Professor Richard Duncan argues that that the special treatment of sexual orientation "stigmatizes, marginalizes and silences religious and moral traditionalists" and denies them "authentic participation in the economic and social life of the community." Richard F. Duncan, *Wigstock and the Kulturkampf: Supreme Court Storytelling, the Culture War, and* Romer v. Evans, 72 NOTRE DAME L. REV. 345, 370 (1997). Do you agree? Is the primary difficulty, then, with recognizing sexual orientation as a protected class that it denies the free exercise of religion — say, by requiring that a Christian high school not discriminate against a homosexual man applying for the position of, say, football coach? Or is it more broadly that making sexual orientation a protected class weakens or even threatens longstanding religious teaching acknowledging the centrality of heterosexual marriage and its importance to culture and family?

2. *Romer* is to some degree an example of the occasional inconsistent application of the deferential rational basis standard. There have been a few other examples. As mentioned earlier in this Chapter, in *City of Cleburne v. Cleburne Living Center*, 473 U.S. 432 (1985), the Court ostensibly used rational basis review to invalidate a zoning ordinance that irrationally (but no more so than many land use requirements) excluded a home for the mentally disabled from a residential district. Today, such practices would violate the federal Fair Housing Act, as amended, but *Cleburne* pre-dated that amendment. Also, *Metropolitan Life Insurance Company v. Ward,* 470 U.S. 869 (1985), invalidated an Alabama law that taxed in-state insurers much less than out-of-state companies.

3. In *Equality Foundation of Greater Cincinnati, Inc. v. City of Cincinnati*, 54 F.3d 261 (6th Cir. 1995), the appellate court held that sexual orientation was not a suspect classification. The court thus approved a city charter amendment providing that the "City of Cincinnati and its various Boards and Commissions may not enact, adopt, enforce or administer any ordinance, regulation, rule or policy which provides that homosexual, lesbian, or bisexual orientation, status, conduct, or relationship constitutes, entitles, or otherwise provides a person with the basis to have any claim of minority or protected status, quota preference or other preferential treatment." The appellate court found sexual orientation not to be a suspect class with the following reasoning:

> Assuming *arguendo* the truth of the scientific theory that sexual orientation is a "characteristic beyond the control of the individual" as found by the trial court, the reality remains that no law can successfully be drafted that is calculated to burden or penalize, or to benefit or protect, an unidentifiable group or class of individuals whose identity is defined by subjective and unapparent characteristics such as innate desires, drives, and thoughts. Those persons having a homosexual "orientation" simply do not, as such, comprise an identifiable class. Many homosexuals successfully conceal their orientation. Because homosexuals generally are not identifiable "on sight" unless they elect to be so identifiable by conduct (such as public displays of homosexual affection or self-proclamation of homosexual tendencies), they cannot constitute a suspect class or a quasi-suspect class because "they do not

[necessarily] exhibit obvious, immutable, or distinguishing character-istics that define them as a discrete group[.]"

Therefore, *Bowers v. Hardwick* and its progeny command that, as a matter of law, gays, lesbians, and bisexuals cannot constitute either a "suspect class" or a "quasi-suspect class," and, accordingly, the district court's application of the intermediate heightened scrutiny standard to the constitutional analysis of the Amendment was erroneous.

Bowers v. Hardwick (1986) held that homosexual sodomy was not a protected liberty under the Due Process Clause of the Fourteenth Amendment, and as dis-cussed in the next Chapter, has since been overruled in *Lawrence v. Texas* (2003), which found a privacy protection for intimate sexual activity in one's home under a due process analysis. Does the overruling of *Bowers* affect the determination of whether or not sexual orientation is a suspect class? The Sixth Circuit's decision in *Equality Foundation*, itself, was vacated and remanded for further consideration in light of the Court's decision in *Romer*. Justices Scalia and Thomas and the Chief Justice dissented from that remand.

4. The issues surrounding sexual orientation are not easy questions and the moral and cultural issues at stake go to the heart of the Republic. What would the natural law thinkers that influenced the Nation's founding have to say on this subject? In the next Chapter — devoted to issues of family and even life, itself — we conclude these materials exploring constitutional theory and appli-cation in light of the Nation's natural law premises and related history.

Chapter 9

A GOVERNMENT OF IMPERFECT KNOWLEDGE — OF INKBLOTS, LIBERTY AND LIFE ITSELF

We asked at the beginning of our exploration into the history and nature of the Constitution whether this founding document was an end in itself or a means to some larger end, such as the pursuit of happiness, or more simply, a good life. As the original meaning we have recovered reveals, the structural provisions of the Constitution divide and limit government power, so that individual liberty might be preserved. This liberty or personal freedom is further secured by express subject matter restraints on the power of government primarily in the Bill of Rights and the Fourteenth Amendment. In this way, the Constitution is not the source of our liberty, but its guarantor. The Constitution constrains governments, federal and state, from interfering *unnecessarily* with particularly vital freedoms, such as speech, religion, and the ownership of property.

Does the Constitution then facilitate the larger end of a good life? Yes, but it is primarily up to each citizen to pursue that end through the prudent exercise of liberty. It was Madison who opined that only a virtuous citizen could be free. That is because any freedom can be abused. Free speech permits the search for truth and wisdom, but it also allows libel and perjury and forms of entertainment that degrade. The free exercise of religion for a great many will be an indispensable opening to an understanding of God, but for a few it invites or shields counter-cultural practices or rituals that threaten the civic order. Property can provide a level of economic security for individual and family and human flourishing through work within a larger civilized community, or it can be abused to magnify environmental harms or to deny a just wage to an employee.

As a general matter, most people would agree that it is not the job of the government to instruct in matters of virtue. Especially to the extent that virtue is derived from religion, the Constitution makes it abundantly clear that the federal government is not to prescribe (establish) or proscribe (as in prohibiting free exercise) the particular ways individuals come to know God. Yet, in the past fifty years especially, the federal government has undertaken to be our moral instructor. The expansion of the commerce power has allowed Congress to speak its mind on everything from lottery tickets to civil rights. So too, in giving meaning to words like "liberty" and "equal protection," the Court necessarily supplies at least a minimalist conception of what is, and is not, an accepted exercise of liberty. For example, in *Board of Regents v. Roth*, 408 U.S. 564 (1972), the Court said:

"While this Court has not attempted to define with exactness the liberty
. . . guaranteed [by the Fifth and Fourteenth Amendments], the term
. . . denotes not merely freedom from bodily restraint but also the right
of the individual to contract, to engage in any of the common occupations
of life, to acquire useful knowledge, to marry, establish a home and
bring up children, to worship God according to the dictates of his own
conscience, and generally to enjoy those privileges long recognized . . .
as essential to the orderly pursuit of happiness by free men." In a Constitution for a free people, there can be no doubt that the meaning of "liberty" must be broad indeed.

Id. at 572 (quoting *Meyer v. Nebraska*, 262 U.S. 390, 399 (1923) (discussed
below)). Notice that the Court's definition includes both enumerated or textual
rights, like the free exercise of religion, but also other non-textual rights, such
as the right to marry and to bring up children. Part of the task of this Chapter
is to explore why the Court has found some non-textual rights, but denied others.

The federal government, pursuant to its enumerated powers, or the states by
their reserved powers, may restrain liberty. To give an obvious example, Congress has the enumerated power to "coin Money [and] regulate the Value
thereof," and therefore, federal laws limiting counterfeiting are a fully justifiable
limitation upon the liberty one might otherwise have to print currency. U.S.
Const., art. I, § 8, cl. 5. So too, under the Tenth Amendment, the "police powers,"
that by tradition are described as the maintenance of the health, safety, morals,
and general welfare of the community, are reserved to the states so that life and
property can be protected with laws punishing murder and theft. U.S. Const.,
amend. X. There is general agreement that neither the fraud of the counterfeiter,
the violence of the murderer, nor the intrusion of the thief are exercises of liberty that need be tolerated. But what of other practices? In this Chapter, we will
explore claims that constitutionally-protected liberty includes the right to marry,
to engage in homosexual sodomy, and to have access to contraceptives, abortion,
and assisted suicide. None of these matters are dealt with expressly in the text
of the Constitution, and yet, we modernly turn to the Supreme Court to evaluate whether such claimed liberties exist or are legitimate. Where these libertarian claims have succeeded, ask yourself as you read the cases if the Court is
drawing upon any discernible moral principle, such as the natural law, in reaching its decisions. As a formal matter, the legal theory involved in most of them
is the rather stark proposition that the Due Process Clause substantively limits government infringements of these liberties. In a few cases, mention will be
made of the Ninth Amendment, providing that the "enumeration in the Constitution, of certain rights, shall not be construed to deny or disparage others
retained by the people."

To what rights (liberties) is the Ninth Amendment referring? In the context
of hearings on his nomination to the Supreme Court, federal Judge Robert
Bork remarked that he did not know, analogizing the provision to an indeci-
pherable inkblot. Judge Bork stated:

> I do not think you can use the Ninth Amendment unless you know something of what it means. For example, if you had an amendment that says "Congress shall make no" and then there is an inkblot, and you cannot read the rest of it, and that is the only copy you have, I do not think the court can make up what might be under the inkblot.

The Bork Disinformers, WALL ST. J., Oct. 5, 1987, at 22. For a scholarly elaboration of the Bork view, *see* Thomas B. McAffee, *A Critical Guide to the Ninth Amendment*, 69 TEMP. L. REV. 61 (1996) (explaining the *Griswold v. Connecticut* debate and concluding that a "rights-foundationalist theory of the Constitution . . . carries the potential to privilege judicial views of the 'natural law,' or political morality, over the views of the people who are the source of their office"). Since no part of the Constitution ought to be assumed meaningless or superfluous, the Amendment must have more significance than an inkblot, but what?

At a minimum, the Amendment on its face appears to be a rule of construction. It states, after all, that the enumeration of the Bill of Rights "shall not be *construed* to deny or disparage others retained by the people." U.S. Const., amend. IX (emphasis added). Ninth Amendment scholar Professor Randy E. Barnett thus observes: "the Ninth Amendment stands ready to respond to a crabbed construction that limits the scope of this protection to the enumerated rights." Randy E. Barnett, *Reconceiving the Ninth Amendment*, 74 CORNELL L. REV. 1, 42 (1988). However, broader claims are made for the Ninth Amendment. Professor Laurence Tribe understands the Ninth Amendment as "a uniquely central text in any attempt to take seriously the process of *construing* the Constitution." Laurence H. Tribe, *Contrasting Constitutional Visions: Of Real and Unreal Differences*, 22 HARV. C.R.-C.L. L. REV. 95, 100 (1987). For him, both textual and nontextual rights and liberties rely upon the Ninth Amendment as their supporting ground. Others suggest that the Ninth Amendment is a denial of government power. Harvard historian Raoul Berger sees the Ninth Amendment as an "'affirmation that rights exist independently of government, that they constitute an area of no-power.'" Raoul Berger, *The Ninth Amendment*, 66 CORNELL L. REV. 1, 9 (1980) (quoting Leslie W. Dunbar, *James Madison and the Ninth Amendment*, 42 VA. L. REV. 627, 641 (1956)).

All well and good, but don't we still need to know just what rights are retained by the people? This raises the problem of imperfect knowledge alluded to in the title to this Chapter. Upon further reflection after his confirmation failed, Judge Bork posited that the retained rights refer to those that are guaranteed outside the federal constitution in "state constitutions, statutes and common law." ROBERT BORK, THE TEMPTING OF AMERICA 184 (1990) (citing Russell Caplan, *The History and Meaning of the Ninth Amendment*, 69 VA. L. REV. 223 (1983)). The reference to the common law is an especially apt one because it reminds us that the founders' conception of retained rights was much shaped by the common or natural law idea that rights are derived from reasoned reflection upon human nature over time, and not located, as Alexander Hamilton observed, in musty parchments. But what can we know from a reasoned reflection upon human nature?

Philosophy of any type asks what we can know about ourselves and our world, and this in turn, raises the age-old problem of whether anything can be known by reason at all. Skeptics, like Montaigne for example, denied the accessibility of such knowledge by unaided reason. Montaigne writes:

> [T]here cannot be first principles for men, unless the Divinity has revealed them; all the rest — beginning, middle, and end — is nothing but dreams and smoke. . . . [E]very human presupposition and every enunciation has as much authority as another. . . . The impression of certainty is a certain token of folly and extreme uncertainty.

Michel de Montaigne, *Apology for Raymond Sebond, in* THE ESSAYS (1588), *reprinted in* 23 GREAT BOOKS OF THE WESTERN WORLD 248, 301 (Mortimer J. Adler ed. & Donald M. Frame trans., 2d ed., Encyclopaedia Britannica 1990). Modernly, this may be the credo of much of the legal academy, but none of the framers assumed this extreme position, and thus what we might call "natural law originalism" does not either. Jefferson, after all, premised the independence of the American republic upon "truths," not only known, but held to be "self-evident."

But is such knowledge merely assertion on Jefferson's part? Long before Jefferson, in the *Metaphysics*, Aristotle confronted the extreme skepticism of those who would assert that all propositions are either true, or the converse, that all are false. Again, this is to claim that nothing can be truly known, a proposition that violates Jefferson's practical assertion of self-evidence, and more subtly, the philosophical principle of noncontradiction that something cannot both be and not be at the same time. (Thus, Thomas Aquinas writes: "the first indemonstrable principle is that *the same thing cannot be affirmed and denied at the same time*, which is based on the notion of *being* and *not-being*; and on this principle all others are based, as is stated in [the] *Metaphysics*." 1 THOMAS AQUINAS, SUMMA THEOLOGICA I-II, Q. 94, art. 2, at 1009 (Fathers of the English Dominican Province trans., Benziger Brothers 1947) (citing ARISTOTLE, METAPHYSICS bk. 4, ch. 3). Any skeptic who maintains otherwise would necessarily contradict himself. As the modern expositor of the great book tradition, Mortimer Adler writes, "if all propositions are true, then the proposition 'Some propositions are false' is also true; if all propositions are false, the proposition 'All propositions are false' is also false." 1 THE SYNTOPICON: AN INDEX TO THE GREAT IDEAS 686 (Mortimer J. Adler ed., 2d ed. 1990).

Now the principle of noncontradiction may seem far removed from constitutional interpretation, but it is not. While Montaigne declared there were no "first principles" knowable to reason alone to guide us, the cases in this Chapter illustrate the Court's search for these first principles. You will need to make up your own mind if the Court has been faithful to Jefferson's idea that human natural right flows from the self-evident premise that we exist, from the fact of being, itself (in Jefferson's terminology, that "[we] are endowed by [our] Creator with certain unalienable Rights." THE DECLARATION OF INDEPENDENCE para. 2 (U.S. 1776)). The most controversial and sensitive topics of constitutional discourse interrelate with the Court's performance here. As Professor Michael Zuckert has written in his superb book explicating the natural rights foundation of the American republic, "[t]he truths about the institution of government . . . follow from the truths about prepolitical society as the truths about the post-political situation follow from the truths about the institution of government." MICHAEL P. ZUCKERT, THE NATURAL RIGHTS REPUBLIC 48 (1996). As Zuckert explains, the pre-political recognition of the self-evident truth that all human beings are "created equal" and endowed with unalienable rights leads directly to the subsidiary truth that no human being has a natural right to govern another. Thus, just power comes from the consent of the governed and governments are instituted to secure the pre-political, unalienable rights. Governments that fail this purpose may be, post-politically, "alter[ed] or abolish[ed]." *Id.* at 47 (quoting THE DECLARATION OF INDEPENDENCE para. 2 (U.S. 1776)).

Assuming natural rights are knowable in the manner suggested, and that these rights give meaning to the constitutional concept of liberty, there is the further question of whether such rights are instructive to legislative bodies only or whether they are to be judicially enforced. Madison arguably thought the judiciary had a role, and that it was not a role wholly limited to constitutional text. First, in introducing the Bill of Rights in Congress, Madison reflected on the purpose of what would become the Ninth Amendment, stating:

> It has been objected . . . against a bill of rights, that, by enumerating particular exceptions to the grant of power, it would disparage those rights which were not placed in that enumeration; and it might follow by implication, that those rights which were not singled out, were intended to be assigned into the hands of the General Government, and were consequently insecure. This is one of the most plausible arguments I have ever heard urged against the admission of a bill of rights into this system; but, I conceive, that may be guarded against. I have attempted it, as gentlemen may see by turning to [what would become the Ninth Amendment].

1 ANNALS OF CONG. 439 (Joseph Gales ed., 1789) (a more complete version of this speech is reproduced in Chapter Two). But Madison's method for guarding against the encroachment of unenumerated rights was thought too indeterminate. Governor Randolph of Virginia argued that "there was no criterion by which it could be determined whether any other particular right was retained or not." Letter from Hardin Burnley to James Madison (Nov. 28, 1789), *in* 12 THE PAPERS OF JAMES MADISON 455, 456 (Charles F. Hobson et al. eds., 1979) (stating Randolph's objections). Madison denied the problem, but he also tried to answer it, positing that "if [the amendments] are incorporated into the constitution, independent tribunals of justice will consider themselves in a peculiar manner the guardians of those rights; they will be an impenetrable bulwark against every assumption of power in the legislative or executive." 1 ANNALS OF CONG. 439 (Joseph Gales ed., 1789).

Before exploring more attenuated claims of liberty, it should be noted that the Court has always assumed that liberty in the Fifth and Fourteenth Amendments means "freedom from bodily restraint." *Board of Regents v. Roth*, 408 U.S. 564, 572 (1972). Much of your course work in criminal law and procedure concerns this aspect of liberty, and it will not be repeated here. Numerous provisions of the Bill of Rights concern procedures that the government must follow before restraining the physical liberty of a person. For example, the Eighth Amendment prohibits excessive bail and the Sixth Amendment includes the right to a "speedy and public trial, by an impartial jury" and the right "to be informed of the nature and cause of the accusation [of a crime]" and "to be confronted [by] witnesses." U.S. Const., amend. VI. Similarly, some of the colloquial aspects of American criminal justice are judicial glosses on these provisions, such as the presumption of innocence, *Taylor v. Kentucky*, 436 U.S. 478 (1978), and the requirement of proof beyond a reasonable doubt, *In re Winship*, 397 U.S. 358 (1970).

Due process must also be afforded a person whose liberty is sought to be deprived in a civil proceeding. *Addington v. Texas*, 441 U.S. 418, 425 (1979). In *Kansas v. Hendricks*, 521 U.S. 346 (1997), the Court upheld a state statute that provides for the involuntary and indeterminate commitment in a mental hospital of a person charged with a sexually violent act, like rape or sexual exploitation of a child, and who has been proven beyond a reasonable doubt to have a mental abnormality that leaves him unable to control his sexual conduct. Sexually Violent Predators Act, Kan. Stat. Ann. §§ 59-29a01 to -29a15 (1994). Due process was satisfied, said the Court, because Hendricks' continued confinement was premised upon a showing of his dangerousness and mental incapacity. 521 U.S. at 360. The Court also found that such commitment does not count as criminal incarceration for purposes of the Double Jeopardy Clause, amend. V, cl. 2, or the Ex Post Facto Clause, Article I, § 9, cl. 3. 521 U.S. at 361-68.

Moving beyond mere freedom from physical restraint, let's examine what else the Court has found essential to "ordered liberty."

A. Natural Law Echoes — Parental and Family Rights

1. Directing the Upbringing of Children

The next two cases are viewed as the foundation of the substantive due process right to direct the upbringing of children. In *Meyer v. Nebraska*, 262 U.S. 390 (1923), the Court invalidates a state law prohibiting the teaching in languages other than English in public schools. *Pierce v. Society of Sisters of the Holy Names of Jesus and Mary*, 268 U.S. 510 (1925), strikes down an Oregon law requiring all children to attend public schools. The third case, *Troxel v. Granville*, 530 U.S. 57 (2000), is a recent application of the same principle.

MEYER v. NEBRASKA
262 U.S. 390 (1923)

MR. JUSTICE MCREYNOLDS delivered the opinion of the Court.

Plaintiff in error was tried and convicted in the District Court for Hamilton County, Nebraska, under an information which charged that on May 25, 1920, while an instructor in Zion Parochial School, he unlawfully taught the subject of reading in the German language. . . .

The Supreme Court of the State affirmed the judgment of conviction [writing:]

> "The salutary purpose of the statute is clear. The Legislature had seen the baneful effects of permitting foreigners, who had taken residence in this country, to rear and educate their children in the language of their native land. The result of that condition was found to be inimical to our own safety. . . . The obvious purpose of this statute was that the English language should be and become the mother tongue of all children reared in this state. The enactment of such a statute comes reasonably within the police power of the state.

* * *

The problem for our determination is whether the statute as construed and applied unreasonably infringes the liberty guaranteed to the plaintiff in error by the Fourteenth Amendment:

> "No state shall . . . deprive any person of life, liberty, or property, without due process of law."

While this court has not attempted to define with exactness the liberty thus guaranteed, the term has received much consideration and some of the included things have been definitely stated. Without doubt, it denotes not merely freedom from bodily restraint but also the right of the individual to contract, to engage in any of the common occupations of life, to acquire useful knowledge, to marry, establish a home and bring up children, to worship God according to the dictates of his own conscience, and generally to enjoy those privileges long recognized at common law as essential to the orderly pursuit of happiness by free men. *Slaughter-House Cases*. The established doctrine is that this liberty may not be interfered with, under the guise of protecting the public interest, by legislative action which is arbitrary or without reasonable relation to some purpose within the competency of the State to effect. Determination by the Legislature of what constitutes proper exercise of police power is not final or conclusive but is subject to supervision by the courts.

* * *

Practically, education of the young is only possible in schools conducted by especially qualified persons who devote themselves thereto. The calling always has been regarded as useful and honorable, essential, indeed, to the public welfare. Mere knowledge of the German language cannot reasonably be regarded as harmful. Heretofore it has been commonly looked upon as helpful and desirable. Plaintiff in error taught this language in school as part of his occupation. His right thus to teach and the right of parents to engage him so to instruct their children, we think, are within the liberty of the Amendment.

The challenged statute forbids the teaching in school of any subject except in English; also the teaching of any other language until the pupil has attained and successfully passed the eighth grade, which is not usually accomplished before the age of twelve. The Supreme Court of the State has held that "the so-called ancient or dead languages" are not "within the spirit or the purpose of the act." *Neb. Dist. of Evangelical Lutheran Synod v. McKelvie*, (Neb. 1922). Latin, Greek, Hebrew are not proscribed; but German, French, Spanish, Italian, and every other alien speech are within the ban. Evidently the Legislature has attempted materially to interfere with the calling of modern language teachers, with the opportunities of pupils to acquire knowledge, and with the power of parents to control the education of their own.

* * *

That the State may do much, go very far, indeed, in order to improve the quality of its citizens, physically, mentally and morally, is clear; but the individual has certain fundamental rights which must be respected. The protection of the Constitution extends to all, to those who speak other languages as well as to those born with English on the tongue. Perhaps it would be highly advantageous if all had ready understanding of our ordinary speech, but this cannot be coerced by methods which conflict with the Constitution — a desirable end cannot be promoted by prohibited means.

For the welfare of his Ideal Commonwealth, Plato suggested a law which should provide: "That the wives of our guardians are to be common, and their children are to be common, and no parent is to know his own child, nor any child his parent. . . . The proper officers will take the offspring of the good parents to the pen or fold, and there they will deposit them with certain nurses who dwell in a separate quarter; but the offspring of the inferior, or of the better when they chance to be deformed, will be put away in some mysterious, unknown place, as they should be." In order to submerge the individual and develop ideal citizens, Sparta assembled the males at seven into barracks and intrusted their subsequent education and training to official guardians. Although such measures have been deliberately approved by men of great genius, their ideas touching the relation between individual and State were wholly different from those upon which our institutions rest; and it hardly will be affirmed that any Legislature could impose such restrictions upon the people of a State without doing violence to both letter and spirit of the Constitution.

The desire of the legislature to foster a homogeneous people with American ideals prepared readily to understand current discussions of civic matters is easy to appreciate. Unfortunate experiences during the late war and aversion toward every character of truculent adversaries were certainly enough to quicken that aspiration. But the means adopted, we think, exceed the limitations upon the power of the State and conflict with rights assured to plaintiff in error. The interference is plain enough and no adequate reason therefor in time of peace and domestic tranquility has been shown.

The power of the State to compel attendance at some school and to make reasonable regulations for all schools, including a requirement that they shall give instructions in English, is not questioned. Nor has challenge been made of the State's power to prescribe a curriculum for institutions which it supports. Those matters are not within the present controversy. Our concern is with the prohibition approved by the [Nebraska] Supreme Court. . . . We are constrained to conclude that the statute as applied is arbitrary and without reasonable relation to any end within the competency of the State.

* * *

Reversed.

MR. JUSTICE HOLMES and MR. JUSTICE SUTHERLAND, dissent. [Omitted.]

PIERCE v. SOCIETY OF THE SISTERS OF THE HOLY NAMES OF JESUS AND MARY
268 U.S. 510 (1925)

MR. JUSTICE MCREYNOLDS delivered the opinion of the Court.

* * *

The challenged act, effective September 1, 1926, requires every parent, guardian, or other person having control or charge or custody of a child between eight and sixteen years to send him "to a public school for the period of time a public school shall be held during the current year" in the district where the child resides; and failure so to do is declared a misdemeanor. . . . The manifest purpose is to compel general attendance at public schools by normal children, between eight and sixteen, who have not completed the eighth grade. And without doubt enforcement of the statute would seriously impair, perhaps destroy, the profitable features of appellees' business and greatly diminish the value of their property.

Appellee, the Society of Sisters, is an Oregon corporation, organized in 1880, with power to care for orphans, educate and instruct the youth, establish and maintain academies or schools, and acquire necessary real and personal property. It has long devoted its property and effort to the secular and religious education and care of children, and has acquired the valuable good will of many parents and guardians. It conducts interdependent primary and high schools and junior colleges, and maintains orphanages for the custody and control of children between eight and sixteen. In its primary schools many children between those ages are taught the subjects usually pursued in Oregon public schools during the first eight years. Systematic religious instruction and moral training according to the tenets of the Roman Catholic Church are also regularly provided. . . . The Compulsory Education Act of 1922 has already caused the withdrawal from its schools of children who would otherwise continue, and their income has steadily declined. The appellants, public officers, have proclaimed their purpose strictly to enforce the statute.

After setting out the above facts, the Society's bill alleges that the enactment conflicts with the right of parents to choose schools where their children will receive appropriate mental and religious training, the right of the child to influence the parents' choice of a school, the right of schools and teachers therein to engage in a useful business or profession, and is accordingly repugnant to the Constitution and void. And, further, that unless enforcement of the measure is enjoined the corporation's business and property will suffer irreparable injury.

* * *

No question is raised concerning the power of the State reasonably to regulate all schools, to inspect, supervise and examine them, their teachers and pupils; to require that all children of proper age attend some school, that teachers shall be of good moral character and patriotic disposition, that certain studies plainly essential to good citizenship must be taught, and that nothing be taught which is manifestly inimical to the public welfare.

The inevitable practical result of enforcing the Act under consideration would be destruction of appellees' primary schools, and perhaps all other private primary schools for normal children within the State of Oregon. These parties are engaged in a kind of undertaking not inherently harmful, but long regarded as useful and meritorious. Certainly there is nothing in the present records to indicate that they have failed to discharge their obligations to patrons, students or the State. And there are no peculiar circumstances or present emergencies which demand extraordinary measures relative to primary education.

Under the doctrine of *Meyer v. Nebraska*, we think it entirely plain that the Act of 1922 unreasonably interferes with the liberty of parents and guardians to direct the upbringing and education of children under their control. As often heretofore pointed out, rights guaranteed by the Constitution may not be abridged by legislation which has no reasonable relation to some purpose within the competency of the State. The fundamental theory of liberty upon which all governments in this Union repose excludes any general power of the State to standardize its children by forcing them to accept instruction from public teachers only. The child is not the mere creature of the State; those who nurture him and direct his destiny have the right, coupled with the high duty, to recognize and prepare him for additional obligations.

Appellees are corporations, and therefore, it is said, they cannot claim for themselves the liberty which the Fourteenth Amendment guarantees. Accepted in the proper sense, this is true. But they have business and property for which they claim protection. These are threatened with destruction through the unwarranted compulsion which appellants are exercising over present and prospective patrons of their schools. And this court has gone very far to protect against loss threatened by such action. *Truax v. Raich* [(1915)]; *Truax v. Corrigan* [(1921)]; *Terrace v. Thompson* [(1923)].

* * *

Generally it is entirely true, as urged by counsel, that no person in any business has such an interest in possible customers as to enable him to restrain exercise of proper power of the State upon the ground that he will be deprived of patronage. But the injunctions here sought are not against the exercise of any *proper* power. Appellees asked protection against arbitrary, unreasonable and unlawful interference with their patrons and the consequent destruction of their business and property. Their interest is clear and immediate, within the rule approved in *Truax v. Raich*, *Truax v. Corrigan*, and *Terrace v. Thompson*, *supra*, and many other cases where injunctions have issued to protect business enterprises against interference with the freedom of patrons or customers.

* * *

The decrees below [grant of injunctive relief] are affirmed.

TROXEL v. GRANVILLE
530 U.S. 57 (2000)

JUSTICE O'CONNOR announced the judgment of the Court and delivered an opinion, in which THE CHIEF JUSTICE, JUSTICE GINSBURG, and JUSTICE BREYER join.

Section 26.10.160(3) of the Revised Code of Washington permits "[a]ny person" to petition a superior court for visitation rights "at any time," and authorizes that court to grant such visitation rights whenever "visitation may serve the best interest of the child." Petitioners Jenifer and Gary Troxel petitioned a Washington Superior Court for the right to visit their grandchildren, Isabelle and Natalie Troxel. Respondent Tommie Granville, the mother of Isabelle and Natalie, opposed the petition. The case ultimately reached the Washington Supreme Court, which held that § 26.10.160(3) unconstitutionally interferes with the fundamental right of parents to rear their children.

I

Tommie Granville and Brad Troxel shared a relationship that ended in June 1991. The two never married, but they had two daughters, Isabelle and Natalie. Jenifer and Gary Troxel are Brad's parents, and thus the paternal grandparents of Isabelle and Natalie. After Tommie and Brad separated in 1991, Brad lived with his parents and regularly brought his daughters to his parents' home for weekend visitation. Brad committed suicide in May 1993. Although the Troxels at first continued to see Isabelle and Natalie on a regular basis after their son's death, Tommie Granville informed the Troxels in October 1993 that she wished to limit their visitation with her daughters to one short visit per month.

. . . At trial, the Troxels requested two weekends of overnight visitation per month and two weeks of visitation each summer. Granville did not oppose visitation altogether, but instead asked the court to order one day of visitation per month with no overnight stay. . . .

* * *

The Washington Court of Appeals reversed the lower court's visitation order and dismissed the Troxels' petition for visitation, holding that nonparents lack standing to seek visitation under §§ 26.10.160(3) unless a custody action is pending. In the Court of Appeals' view, that limitation on nonparental visitation actions was "consistent with the constitutional restrictions on state interference with parents' fundamental liberty interest in the care, custody, and management of their children." . . .

The Washington Supreme Court granted the Troxels' petition for review and, after consolidating their case with two other visitation cases, affirmed. The court disagreed with the Court of Appeals' decision on the statutory issue and found that the plain language of § 26.10.160(3) gave the Troxels standing to seek visitation, irrespective of whether a custody action was pending. The Washington Supreme Court nevertheless agreed with the Court of Appeals' ultimate conclusion that the Troxels could not obtain visitation of Isabelle and Natalie pursuant to § 26.10.160(3). The court rested its decision on the Federal Constitution, holding that § 26.10.160(3) unconstitutionally infringes on the fundamental right of parents to rear their children. In the court's view, there were at least two problems with the nonparental visitation statute. First, according to the Washington Supreme Court, the Constitution permits a State to interfere with the right of parents to rear their children only to prevent harm or potential harm to a child. Section 26.10.160(3) fails that standard because it requires no threshold showing of harm. Second, by allowing "'any person' to petition for forced visitation of a child at 'any time' with the only requirement being that the visitation serve the best interest of the child," the Washington visitation statute sweeps too broadly. "It is not within the province of the state to make significant decisions concerning the custody of children merely because it could make a 'better' decision." The Washington Supreme Court held that "[p]arents have a right to limit visitation of their children with third persons," and that between parents and judges, "the parents should be the ones to choose whether to expose their children to certain people or ideas."

II

The demographic changes of the past century make it difficult to speak of an average American family. The composition of families varies greatly from household to household. While many children may have two married parents and grandparents who visit regularly, many other children are raised in single-parent households. In 1996, children living with only one parent accounted for 28 percent of all children under age 18 in the United States. Understandably, in these single-parent households, persons outside the nuclear family are called upon with increasing frequency to assist in the everyday tasks of child rearing. In many cases, grandparents play an important role. For example, in 1998, approximately 4 million children — or 5.6 percent of all children under age 18 — lived in the household of their grandparents.

The Fourteenth Amendment provides that no State shall "deprive any person of life, liberty, or property, without due process of law." We have long recognized that the Amendment's Due Process Clause, like its Fifth Amendment counterpart, "guarantees more than fair process." The Clause also includes a substantive component that "provides heightened protection against government interference with certain fundamental rights and liberty interests."

The liberty interest at issue in this case — the interest of parents in the care, custody, and control of their children — is perhaps the oldest of the fundamental liberty interests recognized by this Court. More than 75 years ago, in *Meyer v. Nebraska* (1923), we held that the "liberty" protected by the Due Process Clause includes the right of parents to "establish a home and bring up children" and "to control the education of their own." Two years later, in *Pierce v. Society of Sisters* (1925), we again held that the "liberty of parents and guardians" includes the right "to direct the upbringing and education of children under their control." We explained in *Pierce* that "[t]he child is not the mere creature of the State; those who nurture him and direct his destiny have the right, coupled with the high duty, to recognize and prepare him for additional obligations." We returned to the subject in *Prince v. Massachusetts* (1944), and again confirmed that there is a constitutional dimension to the right of parents to direct the upbringing of their children. "It is cardinal with us that the custody, care and nurture of the child reside first in the parents, whose primary function and freedom include preparation for obligations the state can neither supply nor hinder."

In subsequent cases also, we have recognized the fundamental right of parents to make decisions concerning the care, custody, and control of their children. (citing cases) In light of this extensive precedent, it cannot now be doubted that the Due Process Clause of the Fourteenth Amendment protects the fundamental right of parents to make decisions concerning the care, custody, and control of their children.

Section 26.10.160(3), as applied to Granville and her family in this case, unconstitutionally infringes on that fundamental parental right. The Washington nonparental visitation statute is breathtakingly broad. According to the statute's text, "*any person* may petition the court for visitation rights *at any time*," and the court may grant such visitation rights whenever "visitation may serve *the best interest of the child*." § 26.10.160(3) (emphases added). That language effectively permits any third party seeking visitation to subject any decision by a parent concerning visitation of the parent's children to state-court review.

. . . The Troxels did not allege, and no court has found, that Granville was an unfit parent. That aspect of the case is important, for there is a presumption that fit parents act in the best interests of their children.

The problem here is not that the Washington Superior Court intervened, but that when it did so, it gave no special weight at all to Granville's determination of her daughters' best interests. More importantly, it appears that the Superior Court applied exactly the opposite presumption.

The judge's comments suggest that he presumed the grandparents' request should be granted unless the children would be "impact[ed] adversely." In effect, the judge placed on Granville, the fit custodial parent, the burden of disproving that visitation would be in the best interest of her daughters.

The decisional framework employed by the Superior Court directly contravened the traditional presumption that a fit parent will act in the best interest of his or her child. In an ideal world, parents might always seek to cultivate the bonds between grandparents and their grandchildren. Needless to say, however, our world is far from perfect, and in it the decision whether such an intergenerational relationship would be beneficial in any specific case is for the parent to make in the first instance. And, if a fit parent's decision of the kind at issue here becomes subject to judicial review, the court must accord at least some special weight to the parent's own determination.

Finally, we note that there is no allegation that Granville ever sought to cut off visitation entirely. Rather, the present dispute originated when Granville informed the Troxels that she would prefer to restrict their visitation with Isabelle and Natalie to one short visit per month and special holidays.

Considered together with the Superior Court's reasons for awarding visitation to the Troxels, the combination of these factors demonstrates that the visitation order in this case was an unconstitutional infringement on Granville's fundamental right to make decisions concerning the care, custody, and control of her two daughters.

Because we rest our decision on the sweeping breadth of § 26.10.160(3) and the application of that broad, unlimited power in this case, we do not consider the primary constitutional question passed on by the Washington Supreme Court — whether the Due Process Clause requires all nonparental visitation statutes to include a showing of harm or potential harm to the child as a condition precedent to granting visitation. We do not, and need not, define today the visitation context. In this respect, we agree with JUSTICE KENNEDY that the constitutionality of any standard for awarding visitation turns on the specific manner in which that standard is applied and that the constitutional protections in this area are best "elaborated with care." (dissenting opinion). Because much state-court adjudication in this context occurs on a case-by-case basis, we would be hesitant to hold that specific nonparental visitation statutes violate the Due Process Clause as a per se matter.

Accordingly, the judgment of the Washington Supreme Court is affirmed.

JUSTICE SOUTER, concurring in the judgment. (omitted)

JUSTICE THOMAS, concurring in the judgment.

I write separately to note that neither party has argued that our substantive due process cases were wrongly decided and that the original understanding of the Due Process Clause precludes judicial enforcement of unenumerated rights under that constitutional provision. As a result, I express no view on the merits of this matter, and I understand the plurality as well to leave the resolution of that issue for another day.*

Consequently, I agree with the plurality that this Court's recognition of a fundamental right of parents to direct the upbringing of their children resolves this case. Our decision in *Pierce v. Society of Sisters* (1925), holds that parents have a fundamental constitutional right to rear their children, including the right to determine who shall educate and socialize them. The opinions of the plurality, JUSTICE KENNEDY, and JUSTICE SOUTER recognize such a right, but curiously none of them articulates the appropriate standard of review. I would apply strict scrutiny to infringements of fundamental rights. Here, the State of Washington lacks even a legitimate governmental interest — to say nothing of a compelling one — in second-guessing a fit parent's decision regarding visitation with third parties. On this basis, I would affirm the judgment below.

JUSTICE STEVENS, dissenting [omitted].

JUSTICE SCALIA, dissenting.

In my view, a right of parents to direct the upbringing of their children is among the "unalienable Rights" with which the Declaration of Independence proclaims "all Men . . . are endowed by their Creator." And in my view that right is also among the "othe[r] [rights] retained by the people" which the Ninth Amendment says the Constitution's enumeration of rights "shall not be construed to deny or disparage." The Declaration of Independence, however, is not a legal prescription conferring powers upon the courts; and the Constitution's refusal to "deny or disparage" other rights is far removed from affirming any one of them, and even farther removed from authorizing judges to identify what they might be, and to enforce the judges' list against laws duly enacted by the people. Consequently, while I would think it entirely compatible with the commitment to representative democracy set forth in the founding documents to argue, in legislative chambers or in electoral campaigns, that the state has no power to interfere with parents' authority over the rearing of their children, I do not believe that the power which the Constitution confers upon me as a judge entitles me to deny legal effect to laws that (in my view) infringe upon what is (in my view) that unenumerated right.

---

* This case also does not involve a challenge based upon the Privileges and Immunities Clause and thus does not present an opportunity to reevaluate the meaning of that Clause. *See Saenz v. Roe* (1999) (THOMAS, J., dissenting).

Only three holdings of this Court rest in whole or in part upon a substantive constitutional right of parents to direct the upbringing of their children — two of them from an era rich in substantive due process holdings that have since been repudiated. *See Meyer v. Nebraska* (1923); *Pierce v. Society of Sisters* (1925); *Wisconsin v. Yoder* (1972). The sheer diversity of today's opinions persuades me that the theory of unenumerated parental rights underlying these three cases has small claim to stare decisis protection. A legal principle that can be thought to produce such diverse outcomes in the relatively simple case before us here is not a legal principle that has induced substantial reliance. While I would not now overrule those earlier cases (that has not been urged), neither would I extend the theory upon which they rested to this new context.

Judicial vindication of "parental rights" under a Constitution that does not even mention them requires (as JUSTICE KENNEDY's opinion rightly points out) not only a judicially crafted definition of parents, but also — unless, as no one believes, the parental rights are to be absolute — judicially approved assessments of "harm to the child" and judicially defined gradations of other persons (grandparents, extended family, adoptive family in an adoption later found to be invalid, long-term guardians, etc.) who may have some claim against the wishes of the parents. If we embrace this unenumerated right, I think it obvious — whether we affirm or reverse the judgment here, or remand as JUSTICE STEVENS or JUSTICE KENNEDY would do — that we will be ushering in a new regime of judicially prescribed, and federally prescribed, family law. I have no reason to believe that federal judges will be better at this than state legislatures; and state legislatures have the great advantages of doing harm in a more circumscribed area, of being able to correct their mistakes in a flash, and of being removable by the people.[2]

For these reasons, I would reverse the judgment below.

JUSTICE KENNEDY, dissenting.

Turning to the question whether harm to the child must be the controlling standard in every visitation proceeding, there is a beginning point that commands general, perhaps unanimous, agreement in our separate opinions: As our case law has developed, the custodial parent has a constitutional right to determine, without undue interference by the state, how best to raise, nurture, and educate the child. The parental right stems from the liberty protected by the Due Process Clause of the Fourteenth Amendment. *Pierce* and *Meyer*, had they been decided in recent times, may well have been grounded upon First Amendment principles protecting freedom of speech, belief, and religion. Their formulation and subsequent interpretation have been quite different, of course; and they long have been interpreted to have found in Fourteenth Amendment concepts of lib-

---

[2] I note that respondent is asserting only, on her own behalf, a substantive due process right to direct the upbringing of her own children, and is not asserting, on behalf of her children, their First Amendment rights of association or free exercise. I therefore do not have occasion to consider whether, and under what circumstances, the parent could assert the latter enumerated rights.

erty an independent right of the parent in the "custody, care and nurture of the child," free from state intervention. The principle exists, then, in broad formulation; yet courts must use considerable restraint, including careful adherence to the incremental instruction given by the precise facts of particular cases, as they seek to give further and more precise definition to the right.

On the question whether one standard must always take precedence over the other in order to protect the right of the parent or parents, "[o]ur Nation's history, legal traditions, and practices" do not give us clear or definitive answers. The consensus among courts and commentators is that at least through the 19th century there was no legal right of visitation; court-ordered visitation appears to be a 20th-century phenomenon.

To say that third parties have had no historical right to petition for visitation does not necessarily imply, as the Supreme Court of Washington concluded, that a parent has a constitutional right to prevent visitation in all cases not involving harm.

Indeed, contemporary practice should give us some pause before rejecting the best interests of the child standard in all third-party visitation cases, as the Washington court has done. The standard has been recognized for many years as a basic tool of domestic relations law in visitation proceedings. Since 1965 all 50 States have enacted a third-party visitation statute of some sort.

In light of the inconclusive historical record and case law, as well as the almost universal adoption of the best interests standard for visitation disputes, I would be hard pressed to conclude the right to be free of such review in all cases is itself "'implicit in the concept of ordered liberty.'" In my view, it would be more appropriate to conclude that the constitutionality of the application of the best interests standard depends on more specific factors. In short, a fit parent's right vis-a-vis a complete stranger is one thing; her right vis-a-vis another parent or a de facto parent may be another. The protection the Constitution requires, then, must be elaborated with care, using the discipline and instruction of the case law system. We must keep in mind that family courts in the 50 States confront these factual variations each day, and are best situated to consider the unpredictable, yet inevitable, issues that arise.

NOTES AND QUESTIONS

1. Is the liberty recognized in *Meyer*, *Pierce* and *Troxel* a fundamental right demanding strict scrutiny or some lesser standard of review? Prior to *Troxel*, modern Supreme Court dicta supported the proposition that the right to educate one's children is deserving of strict scrutiny, and both the plurality and Justice Thomas seem inclined in this direction in *Troxel*, itself. *See, e.g., Employment Div. v. Smith*, 494 U.S. 872, 881 (1990) (equating the "right of parents . . . to direct the education of their children" with "freedom of speech and of the press"); *Griswold v. Connecticut*, 381 U.S. 479, 482 (1965) (referring to the right to direct the education of one's children as if it were fundamental); *id.* at 498 (Goldberg, J., concurring) (noting that the rights recognized in *Pierce* and *Meyer* are fundamental). Not surprisingly, some state authorities, like the Washington Supreme Court in *Troxel*, also have concluded that the right of parents to direct the education of their children is fundamental. *See, e.g., Michigan Dep't of Soc. Services v. Emmanuel Baptist Preschool*, 455 N.W.2d 1, 16 (Mich. 1990) (Cavanagh, J., concurring); *Sheridan Rd. Baptist Church v. Department of Educ.*, 396 N.W.2d 373, 407-09 (Mich. 1986) (Riley, J., dissenting) (finding the right to direct the education of one's children to be a fundamental right); *Ohio v. Whisner*, 351 N.E.2d 750, 769 (Ohio 1976) ("it has long been recognized that the right of a parent to guide the education, including the religious education, of his or her children is indeed a 'fundamental right' guaranteed by the due process clause of the Fourteenth Amendment.").

So does *Troxel* clarify the status of this right or not? The answer is unfortunately not. The plurality is content to rest its opinion on the sweep of the Washington visitation statute. Justice Thomas refrains from answering the question as well, and Justice Scalia admits that the natural rights of parents exist, but refuses to defend them judicially. Indeed, Justice Scalia's opinion may be the most perplexing insofar as he proclaims "the theory of unenumerated parental rights underlying these three cases has small claim to stare decisis protection." Do you agree? What support does Justice Scalia give for disregarding what even he concedes was one of the natural rights for which the Constitution was framed? Because Justice Scalia is an opponent of the unenumerated right claim to terminate a pregnancy (abortion), is he driven to this conclusion by symmetry — *i.e.,* a belief that he must neither be pro- nor anti-parent? Is this a correct understanding of natural law? Judicial restraint? Justice Scalia's view seems to be grounded in his textualism: parental rights are not mentioned in the Constitution, so he has no authority to vindicate them against state legislation. But is it so clear that parental rights are not protected by the text of the Constitution? Are they not a "privilege or immunity" of citizenship protected both by Article IV and the Fourteenth Amendment? *See Corfield v. Coryell, supra,* Chapter 2. Why do you think Justice Scalia is unwilling to give effect to this constitutional text?

The casual willingness of the Court to leave the issue ambiguous belies the general importance of the parental right to the average citizen. In this regard, the right has taken on increased relevance because of the interest and success of home schooling. *See, e.g., Michigan v. DeJonge*, 501 N.W.2d 127 (Mich. 1993) (Michigan's teacher certification requirement violated the Free Exercise Clause and parents' right to direct the upbringing of their children, as the state failed to demonstrate that the requirement achieved its interest by the least restrictive means); *but see Michigan v. Bennett*, 501 N.W.2d 106 (Mich. 1993) (upholding the certification requirement as applied to home school parents who raised the parental right apart from a claim of religious freedom. The *Bennett* court also characterized the parental right as not fundamental, seemingly putting the Michigan court at odds with the contrary dicta in *DeJonge*).

As a matter of policy, many states have rejected the archaic notion that certified instruction is necessary for home schools. Within the last decade, over twenty states have repealed teacher certification requirements for home schools. Neal Devins, *Fundamentalist Christian Educators v. State: An Inevitable Compromise*, 60 GEO. WASH. L. REV. 818, 819 (1992). Besides Michigan, only two states, California and Alabama, appear to mandate teacher certification in home schools. Cal. Educ. Code § 48224 (1993); Ala. Code § 16-28-5 (1995). Alabama, however, exempts "church schools" from the teacher certification requirement, Ala. Code § 16-28-1(2) (1995). Although Kansas bars the usual home school, *In re Sawyer*, 672 P.2d 1093 (Kan. 1983), it permits private, denominational, and parochial instruction by "competent" instructors. Kan. Stat. Ann. § 72-1111 (1992), *as amended by* Juvenile Justice Reform Act of 1996, ch. 229, § 121, 1996 Kan. Sess. Laws 1274, 1404.

2. Apart from the issue of home schooling, the Supreme Court has held that the right to direct the upbringing of one's children is not absolute. This is not dispositive of the fundamental/non-fundamental debate, however, because no fundamental right is absolute, that is, free of limitation. Thus, in *Prince v. Massachusetts*, 321 U.S. 158 (1944), the Court sustained the application of child labor laws to prevent parents from engaging a nine-year-old girl in the solicitation practices of Jehovah's Witnesses parents.

Prince is somewhat unusual because where parental rights are motivated by religious belief, it is normally a formidable constitutional combination. Judicial deference to parents here coincides with the teaching of many, if not all, faiths that parents have the primary responsibility for the education of their children. This education, it is supposed, will include not just the tenets of the family's faith tradition, but also the common virtues necessary to lead a responsible life, such as prudence (making informed decisions), temperance (avoiding excess — a virtue spoken of extensively by Aristotle), courage (the ability to see a task to its completion), and justice (being honorable in our dealings with others; fulfilling the obligation of what we owe). For a practical, readable account of the role of family in the pursuit of virtue for children, see DOUGLAS W. KMIEC, CEASE-FIRE ON THE FAMILY (1995). Contrasted with Professor Kmiec's view should be that of Professor Barbara Woodhouse who argues that the state should assume a larger role in the governance of children in order to break down the "attachment to the patriarchal family." Barbara Bennett Woodhouse, *Who Owns the Child?* Meyer *and* Pierce *and the Child as Property*, 33 WM. & MARY L. REV. 995, 997 (1992). Professor Woodhouse's vision of the child is "as public resource and public ward, entitled both to make claims upon the community and to be claimed by the community." *Id.* at 1091. But is this "vision" sufficient to accomplish the role played throughout recorded western civilization? As Dean Bruce Hafen of the Brigham Young Law School notes:

> [T]he cultural patterns of American family life have contributed enormously to the ultimate purposes of a democratic society by providing the

stability and the structure that are essential to sustaining individual liberty over the long term.

* * *

. . . Only in the master-apprentice relationship of parent and child, committed to one another by the bonds of kinship, can the skills, normative standards, and virtues that maintain our cultural bedrock be transmitted.

Bruce C. Hafen, *The Constitutional Status of Marriage, Kinship, and Sexual Privacy — Balancing the Individual and Social Interests*, 81 MICH. L. REV. 463, 473, 478 (1983) (footnote omitted).

3. The decision in *Prince* should be contrasted with that of *Wisconsin v. Yoder*, 406 U.S. 205 (1972), discussed in Chapter Two. In *Yoder* it will be recalled, the Court allowed Amish parents to educate their children at home after the eighth grade, notwithstanding compulsory school requirements. The Court observed that:

> [A] State's interest in universal education, however highly we rank it, is not totally free from a balancing process when it impinges on fundamental rights and interests, such as those specifically protected by the Free Exercise Clause of the First Amendment, and the traditional interest of parents with respect to the religious upbringing of their children.

Id. at 214.

Alfonso v. Fernandez, 606 N.Y.S.2d 259 (N.Y. App. Div. 1993), reveals a frequent source of conflict between parental and school direction. In this case, parents brought suit against New York city public high schools, claiming that the schools' condom distribution program violated their due process and free exercise rights because the program did not contain a parental consent or opt-out provision. The New York Supreme Court, Appellate Division, held that such a program violated the parents' due process rights to "direct the upbringing of their children." *Id.* at 261. The parents, said the New York court, "enjoy a well-recognized liberty interest in rearing and educating their children in accord with their own views." *Id.* at 265. Thus, the court said that a parental consent or opt-out provision is required under the Due Process Clause. Contrast *Alfonso* with *Curtis v. School Committee*, 652 N.E.2d 580 (Mass. 1995). In *Curtis*, the Massachusetts Supreme Judicial Court upheld the constitutionality of a school condom distribution program against a due process and free exercise challenge by some of the students' parents. The Massachusetts court, critical of the *Alfonso* court, found that because the parents' children were not forced to participate in the program, their parental liberties were not violated, and an opt-out provision or parental consent was unnecessary to preserve the program's constitutionality. *Id.* at 586-87.

2. Family-Related Rights Beyond Parenting

a. Marriage

LOVING v. VIRGINIA
388 U.S. 1 (1967)

MR. CHIEF JUSTICE WARREN delivered the opinion of the Court.

This case presents a constitutional question never addressed by this Court: whether a statutory scheme adopted by the State of Virginia to prevent marriages between persons solely on the basis of racial classifications violates the Equal Protection and Due Process Clauses of the Fourteenth Amendment. For reasons which seem to us to reflect the central meaning of those constitutional commands, we conclude that these statutes cannot stand consistently with the Fourteenth Amendment.

In June 1958, two residents of Virginia, Mildred Jeter, a Negro woman, and Richard Loving, a white man, were married in the District of Columbia pursuant to its laws. Shortly after their marriage, the Lovings returned to Virginia and established their marital abode in Caroline County. At the October Term, 1958, of the Circuit Court of Caroline County, a grand jury issued an indictment charging the Lovings with violating Virginia's ban on interracial marriages. On January 6, 1959, the Lovings pleaded guilty to the charge and were sentenced to one year in jail; however, the trial judge suspended the sentence for a period of 25 years on the condition that the Lovings leave the State and not return to Virginia together for 25 years. . . .

* * *

The Supreme Court of Appeals upheld the constitutionality of the antimiscegenation statutes and, after modifying the sentence, affirmed the convictions. The Lovings appealed this decision, and we noted probable jurisdiction. . . .

The two statutes under which appellants were convicted and sentenced are part of a comprehensive statutory scheme aimed at prohibiting and punishing interracial marriages. The Lovings were convicted of violating § 20-58 of the Virginia Code:

> "*Leaving State to evade law.* — If any white person and colored person shall go out of this State, for the purpose of being married, and with the intention of returning, and be married out of it, and afterwards return to and reside in it, cohabiting as man and wife, they shall be punished as provided in § 20-59, and the marriage shall be governed by the same law as if it had been solemnized in this State. The fact of their cohabitation here as man and wife shall be evidence of their marriage."

Section 20-59, which defines the penalty for miscegenation, provides:

"Punishment for marriage. — If any white person intermarry with a colored person, or any colored person intermarry with a white person, he shall be guilty of a felony and shall be punished by confinement in the penitentiary for not less than one nor more than five years." . . .

* * *

Virginia is now one of 16 States which prohibit and punish marriages on the basis of racial classifications.[5] Penalties for miscegenation arose as an incident to slavery and have been common in Virginia since the colonial period. The present statutory scheme dates from the adoption of the Racial Integrity Act of 1924, passed during the period of extreme nativism which followed the end of the First World War. The central features of this Act, and current Virginia law, are the absolute prohibition of a "white person" marrying other than another "white person," a prohibition against issuing marriage licenses until the issuing official is satisfied that the applicants' statements as to their race are correct, certificates of "racial composition" to be kept by both local and state registrars, and the carrying forward of earlier prohibitions against racial intermarriage.

I.

* * *

While the state court is no doubt correct in asserting that marriage is a social relation subject to the State's police power, the State does not contend in its argument before this Court that its powers to regulate marriage are unlimited notwithstanding the commands of the Fourteenth Amendment. Nor could it do so in light of *Meyer v. Nebraska* (1923), and *Skinner v. Oklahoma* (1942). Instead, the State argues that the meaning of the Equal Protection Clause, as illuminated by the statements of the Framers, is only that state penal laws containing an interracial element as part of the definition of the offense must apply equally to whites and Negroes in the sense that members of each race are punished to the same degree. Thus, the State contends that, because its miscegenation statutes punish equally both the white and the Negro participants

---

5 After the initiation of this litigation, Maryland repealed its prohibitions against interracial marriage, Md. Laws 1967, c. 6, leaving Virginia and 15 other States with statutes outlawing interracial marriage: Alabama, Ala. Const., Art. 4, § 102, Ala. Code, Tit. 14, § 360 (1958); Arkansas, Ark. Stat. Ann. § 55-104 (1947); Delaware, Del. Code Ann., Tit. 13, § 101 (1953); Florida, Fla. Const., Art. 16, § 24, Fla. Stat. § 741.11 (1965); Georgia, Ga. Code Ann. § 53-106 (1961); Kentucky, Ky. Rev. Stat. Ann. § 402.020 (Supp. 1966); Louisiana, La. Rev. Stat. § 14:79 (1950); Mississippi, Miss. Const., Art. 14, § 263, Miss. Code Ann. § 459 (1956); Missouri, Mo. Rev. Stat. § 451.020 (Supp. 1966); North Carolina, N. C. Const., Art. XIV, § 8, N. C. Gen. Stat. § 14-181 (1953); Oklahoma, Okla. Stat., Tit 43, § 12 (Supp. 1965); South Carolina, S. C. Const., Art. 3, § 33, S. C. Code Ann. § 20-7 (1962); Tennessee, Tenn. Const., Art. 11, § 14, Tenn. Code Ann. § 36-402 (1955); Texas, Tex. Pen. Code, Art. 492 (1952); West Virginia, W. Va. Code Ann. § 4697 (1961).

Over the past 15 years, 14 States have repealed laws outlawing interracial marriages: Arizona, California, Colorado, Idaho, Indiana, Maryland, Montana, Nebraska, Nevada, North Dakota, Oregon, South Dakota, Utah, and Wyoming.

The first state court to recognize that miscegenation statutes violate the Equal Protection Clause was the Supreme Court of California. *Perez v. Sharp*, 198 P.2d 17 (Cal. 1948).

in an interracial marriage, these statutes, despite their reliance on racial classifications, do not constitute an invidious discrimination based upon race. . . .

* * *.

. . . We have rejected the proposition that the debates in the Thirty-ninth Congress or in the state legislatures which ratified the Fourteenth Amendment supported the theory advanced by the State, that the requirement of equal protection of the laws is satisfied by penal laws defining offenses based on racial classifications so long as white and Negro participants in the offense were similarly punished.

. . . As we [have previously] demonstrated, the Equal Protection Clause requires the consideration of whether the classifications drawn by any statute constitute an arbitrary and invidious discrimination. The clear and central purpose of the Fourteenth Amendment was to eliminate all official state sources of invidious racial discrimination in the States. *Slaughter-House Cases.*

There can be no question but that Virginia's miscegenation statutes rest solely upon distinctions drawn according to race. The statutes proscribe generally accepted conduct if engaged in by members of different races. Over the years, this Court has consistently repudiated "[d]istinctions between citizens solely because of their ancestry" as being "odious to a free people whose institutions are founded upon the doctrine of equality." At the very least, the Equal Protection Clause demands that racial classifications, especially suspect in criminal statutes, be subjected to the "most rigid scrutiny," and, if they are ever to be upheld, they must be shown to be necessary to the accomplishment of some permissible state objective, independent of the racial discrimination which it was the object of the Fourteenth Amendment to eliminate. Indeed, two members of this Court have already stated that they "cannot conceive of a valid legislative purpose . . . which makes the color of a person's skin the test of whether his conduct is a criminal offense." *McLaughlin v. Florida* (1964) (STEWART, J., joined by DOUGLAS, J., concurring).

There is patently no legitimate overriding purpose independent of invidious racial discrimination which justifies this classification. . . .

II.

These statutes also deprive the Lovings of liberty without due process of law in violation of the Due Process Clause of the Fourteenth Amendment. The freedom to marry has long been recognized as one of the vital personal rights essential to the orderly pursuit of happiness by free men.

Marriage is one of the "basic civil rights of man," fundamental to our very existence and survival. *Skinner v. Oklahoma* (1942). To deny this fundamental freedom on so unsupportable a basis as the racial classifications embodied in these statutes, classifications so directly subversive of the principle of equality at the heart of the Fourteenth Amendment, is surely to deprive all the State's citizens of liberty without due process of law. The Fourteenth Amendment requires that the freedom of choice to marry not be restricted by invidious racial discriminations. Under our Constitution, the freedom to marry, or not marry, a person of another race resides with the individual and cannot be infringed by the State.

These convictions must be reversed. It is so ordered.

MR. JUSTICE STEWART, concurring. [Omitted.]

NOTES AND QUESTIONS

1. Marriage is said to have deep roots in history and tradition, and therefore, it must be recognized as a nontextual constitutional right. Why is marriage so important? Does the stability of marriage and family have much to do with the level of civility and achievement in the larger culture? Tocqueville wrote: "Certainly of all Countries in the world America is the one in which the marriage tie is most respected and where the highest and truest conception of conjugal happiness has been conceived." ALEXIS DE TOCQUEVILLE, DEMOCRACY IN AMERICA 291 (J.P. Mayer ed. & George Lawrence trans., Doubleday 1969) (1850). The marriage root is far deeper than the American experience, of course. Biblically, marriage is represented in the following way:

> Have ye not read, that he who made man from the beginning, Made them male and female? And he [Christ] said: For this cause shall a man leave father and mother, and shall cleave to his wife, and they two shall be in one flesh. Therefore now they are not two, but one flesh. What, therefore, God hath joined together, let no man put asunder.

Matthew 19:4-6.

2. Unlike some religious conceptions of marriage, the constitutional right to marry includes the right to divorce. *Boddie v. Connecticut*, 401 U.S. 371 (1971). In *Boddie*, the Court invalidated a state law as it applied to an indigent that required the payment of filing fees and costs in a divorce proceeding. The theory: preventing someone from divorcing also prevents them from marrying someone else. Given the often negative consequences of divorce on the individuals involved, their children, and the larger community, *see* BARBARA DAFOE WHITEHEAD, THE DIVORCE CULTURE (1997), is the Court really protecting the natural right of marriage by facilitating its termination? Or is the Court's conception of marriage merely that of individual, personal autonomy, as opposed to a lifetime promise and assumption of duty to others — most notably, spouse and children? At one time, a Wisconsin law prevented an individual from marrying if he or she had a minor child not in his or her custody and the individual was in arrears on child support. The Court invalidated the law in *Zablocki v. Redhail*, 434 U.S. 374 (1978), under the Equal Protection Clause. Again, the Court waxed eloquent about the decision to marry being "on the same level of importance as decisions relating to procreation, childbirth, child rearing, and family relationships." *Id.* at 386. Admitting that the state had a substantial interest in seeing to the prompt payment of child support, the Court thought the state had better alternatives to further its interest, such as wage garnishment or civil or criminal penalties for default. *Id.* at 388-91.

b. Procreation

SKINNER v. OKLAHOMA
316 U.S. 535 (1942)

MR. JUSTICE DOUGLAS delivered the opinion of the Court.

This case touches a sensitive and important area of human rights. Oklahoma deprives certain individuals of a right which is basic to the perpetuation of a race — the right to have offspring. Oklahoma has decreed the enforcement of its law against petitioner, overruling his claim that it violated the Fourteenth Amendment. Because that decision raised grave and substantial constitutional questions, we granted the petition for certiorari.

The statute involved is Oklahoma's Habitual Criminal Sterilization Act. That Act defines an "habitual criminal" as a person who, having been convicted two or more times for crimes "amounting to felonies involving moral turpitude," either in an Oklahoma court or in a court of any other State, is thereafter convicted of such a felony in Oklahoma and is sentenced to a term of imprisonment in an Oklahoma penal institution. Machinery is provided for the institution by the Attorney General of a proceeding against such a person in the Oklahoma courts for a judgment that such person shall be rendered sexually sterile. Notice, an opportunity to be heard, and the right to a jury trial are provided. The issues triable in such a proceeding are narrow and confined. If the court or jury finds that the defendant is an "habitual criminal" and that he "may be rendered sexually sterile without detriment to his or her general health," then the court "shall render judgment to the effect that said defendant be rendered sexually sterile" by the operation of vasectomy in case of a male, and of salpingectomy in case of a female. Only one other provision of the Act is material here, . . . which provides that "offenses arising out of the violation of the prohibitory laws, revenue acts, embezzlement, or political offenses, shall not come or be considered within the terms of this Act."

Petitioner was convicted in 1926 of the crime of stealing chickens, and was sentenced to the Oklahoma State Reformatory. In 1929 he was convicted of the crime of robbery with firearms, and was sentenced to the reformatory. In 1934 he was convicted again of robbery with firearms, and was sentenced to the penitentiary. He was confined there in 1935 when the Act was passed. In 1936 the Attorney General instituted proceedings against him. Petitioner in his answer challenged the Act as unconstitutional by reason of the Fourteenth Amendment. A jury trial was had. The court instructed the jury that the crimes of which petitioner had been convicted were felonies involving moral turpitude, and that the only question for the jury was whether the operation of vasectomy could be performed on petitioner without detriment to his general health. The jury found that it could be. A judgment directing that the operation of vasectomy be performed on petitioner was affirmed by the Supreme Court of Oklahoma by a five to four decision.

Several objections to the constitutionality of the Act have been pressed upon us. . . . We pass those points without intimating an opinion on them, for there is a feature of the Act which clearly condemns it. That is, its failure to meet the requirements of the equal protection clause of the Fourteenth Amendment.

We do not stop to point out all of the inequalities in this Act. A few examples will suffice. In Oklahoma, grand larceny is a felony. Larceny is grand larceny when the property taken exceeds $20 in value. Embezzlement is punishable "in the manner prescribed for feloniously stealing property of the value of that embezzled." Hence, he who embezzles property worth more than $20 is guilty of a felony. A clerk who appropriates over $20 from his employer's till and a stranger who steals the same amount are thus both guilty of felonies. If the latter repeats his act and is convicted three times, he may be sterilized. But the clerk is not subject to the pains and penalties of the Act no matter how large his embezzlements nor how frequent his convictions. A person who enters a chicken coop and steals chickens commits a felony; and he may be sterilized if he is thrice convicted. If, however, he is a bailee of the property and fraudulently appropriates it, he is an embezzler. Hence, no matter how habitual his proclivities for embezzlement are and no matter how often his conviction, he may not be sterilized. . . .

It was stated in *Buck v. Bell* [(1927)] that the claim that state legislation violates the equal protection clause of the Fourteenth Amendment is "the usual last resort of constitutional arguments." Under our constitutional system the States in determining the reach and scope of particular legislation need not provide "abstract symmetry." They may mark and set apart the classes and types of problems according to the needs and as dictated or suggested by experience. . . .

But the instant legislation runs afoul of the equal protection clause, though we give Oklahoma that large deference which the rule of the foregoing cases requires. We are dealing here with legislation which involves one of the basic civil rights of man. Marriage and procreation are fundamental to the very existence and survival of the race. The power to sterilize, if exercised, may have subtle, far reaching and devastating effects. In evil or reckless hands it can cause races or types which are inimical to the dominant group to wither and disappear. There is no redemption for the individual whom the law touches. Any experiment which the State conducts is to his irreparable injury. He is forever deprived of a basic liberty. We mention these matters not to reexamine the scope of the police power of the States. We advert to them merely in emphasis of our view that strict scrutiny of the classification which a State makes in a sterilization law is essential, lest unwittingly, or otherwise, invidious discriminations are made against groups or types of individuals in violation of the constitutional guaranty of just and equal laws. The guaranty of "equal protection of the laws is a pledge of the protection of equal laws." When the law lays an unequal hand on those who have committed intrinsically the same quality of offense and sterilizes one and not the other, it has made as invidious a discrimination as if it had selected a particular race or nationality for oppressive treatment. Sterilization of those who have thrice committed grand larceny, with immunity for those who are embezzlers, is a clear, pointed, unmistakable discrimination. Oklahoma makes no attempt to say that he who commits larceny by trespass or trick or fraud has biologically inheritable traits which he who commits embezzlement lacks. . . . In terms of fines and imprisonment the crimes of larceny and embezzlement rate the same under the Oklahoma code. Only when it comes to sterilization are the pains and penalties of the law different. The equal protection clause would indeed be a formula of empty words if such conspicuously artificial lines could be drawn. . . .

* * *

Reversed.

MR. CHIEF JUSTICE STONE, concurring.

I concur in the result, but I am not persuaded that we are aided in reaching it by recourse to the equal protection clause.

If Oklahoma may resort generally to the sterilization of criminals on the assumption that their propensities are transmissible to future generations by inheritance, I seriously doubt that the equal protection clause requires it to apply the measure to all criminals in the first instance, or to none.

Moreover, if we must presume that the legislature knows — what science has been unable to ascertain — that the criminal tendencies of any class of habitual offenders are transmissible regardless of the varying mental characteristics of its individuals, I should suppose that we must likewise presume that the legislature, in its wisdom, knows that the criminal tendencies of some classes of offenders are more likely to be transmitted than those of others. And so I think the real question we have to consider is not one of equal protection, but whether the wholesale condemnation of a class to such an invasion of personal liberty, without opportunity to any individual to show that his is not the type of case which would justify resort to it, satisfies the demands of due process.

There are limits to the extent to which the presumption of constitutionality can be pressed, especially where the liberty of the person is concerned (*see United States v. Carolene Products Co.*, 304 U.S. 144, 152, n. 4) and where the presumption is resorted to only to dispense with a procedure which the ordinary dictates of prudence would seem to demand for the protection of the individual from arbitrary action. Although petitioner here was given a hearing to ascertain whether sterilization would be detrimental to his health, he was given none to discover whether his criminal tendencies are of an inheritable type. Undoubtedly a state may, after appropriate inquiry, constitutionally interfere with the personal liberty of the individual to prevent the transmission by inheritance of his socially injurious tendencies. *Buck v. Bell.* But until now we have not been called upon to say that it may do so without giving him a hearing and opportunity to challenge the existence as to him of the only facts which could justify so drastic a measure.

Science has found and the law has recognized that there are certain types of mental deficiency associated with delinquency which are inheritable. But the State does not contend — nor can there be any pretense — that either common knowledge or experience, or scientific investigation, has given assurance that the criminal tendencies of any class of habitual offenders are universally or even generally inheritable. In such circumstances, inquiry whether such is the fact in the case of any particular individual cannot rightly be dispensed with. Whether the procedure by which a statute carries its mandate into execution satisfies due process is a matter of judicial cognizance. A law which condemns, without hearing, all the individuals of a class to so harsh a measure as the present because some or even many merit condemnation, is lacking in the first principles of due process. And so, while the state may protect itself from the demonstrably inheritable tendencies of the individual which are injurious to society, the most elementary notions of due process would seem to require it to take appropriate steps to safeguard the liberty of the individual by affording him, before he is condemned to an irreparable injury in his person, some opportunity to show that he is without such inheritable tendencies. The state is called on to sacrifice no permissible end when it is required to reach its objective by a reasonable and just procedure adequate to safeguard rights of the individual which concededly the Constitution protects.

MR. JUSTICE JACKSON concurring.

I join the CHIEF JUSTICE in holding that the hearings provided are too limited in the context of the present Act to afford due process of law. I also agree with the opinion of MR. JUSTICE DOUGLAS that the scheme of classification set forth in the Act denies equal protection of the law. I disagree with the opinion of each in so far as it rejects or minimizes the grounds taken by the other.

* * *

I also think the present plan to sterilize the individual in pursuit of a eugenic plan to eliminate from the race characteristics that are only vaguely identified and which in our present state of knowledge are uncertain as to transmissibility presents other constitutional questions of gravity. This Court has sustained such an experiment with respect to an imbecile, a person with definite and observable characteristics, where the condition had persisted through three generations and afforded grounds for the belief that it was transmissible and would continue to manifest itself in generations to come. *Buck v. Bell.*

There are limits to the extent to which a legislatively represented majority may conduct biological experiments at the expense of the dignity and personality and natural powers of a minority — even those who have been guilty of what the majority define as crimes. But this Act falls down before reaching this problem, which I mention only to avoid the implication that such a question may not exist because not discussed. On it I would also reserve judgment.

NOTES AND QUESTIONS

1. Is it extraordinary to think of government-imposed sterilization? Prior to *Skinner*, the Court upheld the power of the government to impose involuntary sterilization. In *Buck v. Bell*, 274 U.S. 200 (1927), the Court ruled that it was constitutional for Virginia to involuntarily sterilize the mentally retarded. The Court's opinion in *Buck* was written by Oliver Wendell Holmes, an antagonist of the American natural law tradition. Holmes explained his opposition by writing: "[t]he jurists who believe in natural law seem to me to be in that naive state of mind that accepts what has been familiar and accepted by them and their neighbors as something that must be accepted by all men everywhere." Oliver Wendell Holmes, *Natural Law*, 32 HARV. L. REV. 40, 41 (1918). What Carrie Bell, the 18-year-old woman in *Buck* asked to have accepted were the fundamental elements of her human personhood. However, Justice Holmes responded cooly: "It is better for all the world, if instead of waiting to execute degenerate offspring for crime, or to let them starve for their imbecility, society can prevent those who are manifestly unfit from continuing their kind. . . . Three generations of imbeciles are enough." 274 U.S. at 207. The reasoning in *Skinner* disavows this stark proposition, even as it does not formally overrule *Buck*.

Justice Holmes' coarse language drew rebuke from many, but especially from law faculties of religious schools. For example, the late Professor Edward Barrett of Notre Dame reminded his students of the decision in *Buck* to urge them never to remain complacent when the integrity of the human person was at stake. How many law school graduates, Professor Barrett wondered, were prepared to

> cut through at once to the fallacious "inarticulate premise" of Justice Holmes' defense of compulsory sterilization (less than ten years before Hitler): "the principle that sustains compulsory vaccination is broad enough to cover the cutting of the Fallopian tubes?" How many [students educated in the tradition of natural law originalism] were content, like Justice Butler, to "dissent without opinion?" How many more, charmed by the word-witchery of Holmes, silently acquiesced? All teaching is an act of faith.

Edward Barrett, *The "Catholic" Law School and the Natural Law — The Notre Dame Experiment*, 56 HOMILETIC & PASTORAL REV. 904, 905-06 (1956) (quoting *Buck*, 274 U.S. at 207). What is the "fallacious logic" Barrett assails? On what principle can anyone distinguish state-required immunization from state-required sterilization? From what source does that principle derive?

2. As a precise matter of constitutional adjudication, *Skinner* is mostly an equal protection case. As explained by Justice Douglas, the law discriminates among similarly situated people, the larcenist and the embezzler for example, in respect to the exercise of what the Court describes as "one of the basic civil rights of man." 316 U.S. at 541. We discussed equal protection at length in Chapter Eight; there, we saw that it was generally inappropriate for government to draw distinctions among individuals on the basis of suspect (race, national origin, and sometimes alienage) or quasi-suspect (gender, illegitimacy) classifications. If these classifications are employed, the government needs a compelling or important governmental purpose, respectively. *Skinner* illustrates another aspect of equal protection review. Where a fundamental right is at issue, government distinctions among individuals with respect to that right are all suspect. Other fundamental rights triggering this analysis include voting, *see, e.g., Harper v. Virginia Bd. of Elections*, 383 U.S. 663 (1966) (holding that the Equal Protection Clause forbids states from conditioning the right to vote on the affluence of the voter or on the payment of a fee); *Reynolds v. Sims*, 377 U.S. 533 (1964) (finding that the Constitution requires a standard of one person/one vote), access to the court system, *see, e.g., Douglas v. California*, 372 U.S. 353 (1963) (right to counsel for indigents); *Griffin v. Illinois*, 351 U.S. 12 (1956) (free transcripts for indigents in a criminal proceeding); *M.L.B. v. S.L.J.*, 519 U.S. 102 (1996) (right to free transcript in civil custody proceeding because of the fundamental parent-child relationship), and interstate travel, *Shapiro v. Thompson*, 394 U.S. 618 (1969) (one-year residency requirement to receive welfare was an unconstitutional infringement of the travel right. Right to travel cases may also be handled as a privilege or immunity of citizenship, *see* Chapter Seven). It is possible for equal protection analysis to apply as well with respect to any of the textual Bill of Rights, although violations of free speech and religion, for example, are frequently dealt with directly within the terms of their separate history and case authority.

c. Family Living Arrangements

The importance of the family to the well-being of the nation cannot be understated. Professor Sylvia Law writes that to the founders: "The family was the central economic unit of society, both producing and consuming almost all goods and services. . . . Custom and law strongly encouraged family formation and virtually everyone lived in a family." Sylvia A. Law, *The Founders on Families*, 39 U. FLA. L. REV. 583, 591-92 (1987). The family, of course, pre-dates the State and has long been recognized as its own sovereignty. As one 17th century writer observed:

> A family is a little church, and a little commonwealth, at least a lively representation thereof, whereby trial may be made of such as are fit for any place of authority, or of subjection, in church or commonwealth. Or rather, it is as a school wherein the first principles and grounds of

government are learned; whereby men are fitted to greater matters in church and commonwealth.

WILLIAM GOUGE, OF DOMESTICALL DUTIES (1622), *quoted in* John Demos, *Images of the American Family, Then and Now*, *in* CHANGING IMAGES OF THE FAMILY 43, 46 (Virginia Tufte & Barbara Myerhoff eds., 1979).

In *Moore v. City of East Cleveland*, 431 U.S. 494 (1977), the Court manifested respect for the extended family as well — that is, family based on kinship (blood, marriage or adoption) relationships. In *Moore*, the Court invalidated a municipal ordinance that so narrowly defined family that it precluded a grandmother from living with her two grandsons, who were cousins, rather than brothers. (The city was by this awkward means attempting to keep public school enrollments in balance.) *Moore*'s respect for the extended family is consistent with original understanding. In the words of one commentator:

> From our colonial beginnings, and throughout most of the republican experience, American legal and cultural systems gave broad and deep support to large families and to family-based economic enterprise. To get intact families started in the new world, colonial charters offered free inheritable land and protection against taxes. To encourage the creation of large families, special incentives were offered such as additional land or longer tax exemptions for each newborn child.

Robert Kimball Shinkoskey, *Without Law*, FAM. AMERICA (Rockford Inst. Ctr. on the Family in Am., Rockford, Il.), Jan. 1993, at 1, 3.

Moore's solicitude for the family does not extend to unrelated individuals. In *Village of Belle Terre v. Boraas*, 416 U.S. 1 (1974), the Court upheld a zoning ordinance limiting the number of individuals not related by "blood, marriage, or adoption" who could live together. A group of college students were thereby precluded from sharing a rented house. The Court held that the ordinance infringed no fundamental right and thus the applicable standard was whether the statute bore a rational relationship to a permissible state objective. *Id.* at 8-9. The Court concluded that Belle Terre met this standard because the state's objective, "[a] quiet place where yards are wide, people few, and motor vehicles restricted [provided] legitimate guidelines in a land-use project addressed to family needs." *Id.* at 9. A similar distinction between related and unrelated individuals was drawn in *Smith v. Organization of Foster Families for Equality and Reform*, 431 U.S. 816 (1977) (upholding a pre-removal hearing for foster parents only where the foster child had been in the home for 18 months or more). Unlike biological parents, the state, said the Court, "has been a partner from the outset" in the foster child context. *Id.* at 845.

Indirect economic pressures arising from the structure of government benefit programs that may cause related family members to live apart do not fall within the *Moore* holding. For example, in *Lyng v. Castillo*, 477 U.S. 635 (1986), the Court sustained the federal provision of food stamps to household units, consisting of parents, children and siblings who live together. Effectively, this meant that families or households received less food assistance if they lived together than if they lived apart. Because the law did not "order" relatives to live separately, but only created an economic incentive to do so, it did not transgress the fundamental right articulated in *Moore. Id.* at 638-39. The Court is more deferential generally when a government benefit, rather than a prohibition, is said to have a negative impact on the family. Thus, in *Bowen v. Gilliard*, 483 U.S. 587 (1987), the Court allowed Aid to Families with Dependent Children to be calculated in relation to the income of parents and siblings living together, even if again, that meant they received less than if they lived apart. This may be unwise social policy, but the Court held that Congress' power is plenary when it defines "'the scope and the duration of the entitlement to . . . benefits, and to increase, to decrease, or to terminate those benefits.'" *Id.* at 598 (quoting *Atkins v. Parker*, 472 U.S. 115, 129 (1985)).

MICHAEL H. v. GERALD D.
491 U.S. 110 (1989)

JUSTICE SCALIA announced the judgment of the Court and delivered an opinion, in which THE CHIEF JUSTICE joins, and in all but footnote 6 of which JUSTICE O'CONNOR and JUSTICE KENNEDY join.

Under California law, a child born to a married woman living with her husband is presumed to be a child of the marriage. Cal. Evid. Code Ann. § 621 (Supp. 1989). The presumption of legitimacy may be rebutted only by the husband or wife, and then only in limited circumstances. The instant appeal presents the claim that this presumption infringes upon the due process rights of a man who wishes to establish his paternity of a child born to the wife of another man, and the claim that it infringes upon the constitutional right of the child to maintain a relationship with her natural father.

I

The facts of this case are, we must hope, extraordinary. On May 9, 1976, in Las Vegas, Nevada, Carole D., an international model, and Gerald D., a top executive in a French oil company, were married. The couple established a home in Playa del Rey, California, in which they resided as husband and wife when one or the other was not out of the country on business. In the summer of 1978, Carole became involved in an adulterous affair with a neighbor, Michael H. In September 1980, she conceived a child, Victoria D., who was born on May 11, 1981. Gerald was listed as father on the birth certificate and has always held Victoria out to the world as his daughter. Soon after delivery of the child, however, Carole informed Michael that she believed he might be the father.

In the first three years of her life, Victoria remained always with Carole, but found herself within a variety of quasi-family units. In October 1981, Gerald moved to New York City to pursue his business interests, but Carole chose to remain in California. At the end of that month, Carole and Michael had blood tests of themselves and Victoria, which showed a 98.07% probability that Michael was Victoria's father. In January 1982, Carole visited Michael in St. Thomas, where his primary business interests were based. There Michael held Victoria out as his child. In March, however, Carole left Michael and returned to California, where she took up residence with yet another man, Scott K. Later that spring, and again in the summer, Carole and Victoria spent time with Gerald in New York City, as well as on vacation in Europe. In the fall, they returned to Scott in California.

In November 1982, rebuffed in his attempts to visit Victoria, Michael filed a filiation action in California Superior Court to establish his paternity and right to visitation. In March 1983, the court appointed an attorney and guardian ad litem to represent Victoria's interests. Victoria then filed a cross-complaint asserting that if she had more than one psychological or *de facto* father, she was entitled to maintain her filial relationship, with all of the attendant rights, duties, and obligations, with both. In May 1983, Carole filed a motion for summary judgment. During this period, from March through July 1983, Carole was again living with Gerald in New York. In August, however, she returned to California, became involved once again with Michael, and instructed her attorneys to remove the summary judgment motion from the calendar.

For the ensuing eight months, when Michael was not in St. Thomas he lived with Carole and Victoria in Carole's apartment in Los Angeles and held Victoria out as his daughter. In April 1984, Carole and Michael signed a stipulation that Michael was Victoria's natural father. Carole left Michael the next month, however, and instructed her attorneys not to file the stipulation. In June 1984, Carole reconciled with Gerald and joined him in New York, where they now live with Victoria and two other children since born into the marriage.

In May 1984, Michael and Victoria, through her guardian ad litem, sought visitation rights for Michael *pendente lite*. To assist in determining whether visitation would be in Victoria's best interests, the Superior Court appointed a psychologist to evaluate Victoria, Gerald, Michael, and Carole. The psychologist recommended that Carole retain sole custody, but that Michael be allowed continued contact with Victoria pursuant to a restricted visitation schedule. The court concurred and ordered that Michael be provided with limited visitation privileges *pendente lite*.

On October 19, 1984, Gerald, who had intervened in the action, moved for summary judgment on the ground that under Cal. Evid. Code § 621 there were no triable issues of fact as to Victoria's paternity. This law provides that "the issue of a wife cohabiting with her husband, who is not impotent or sterile, is conclusively presumed to be a child of the marriage." Cal. Evid. Code Ann. § 621(a) (Supp. 1989). The presumption may be rebutted by blood tests, but only if a motion for such tests is made, within two years from the date of the child's birth, either by the husband or, if the natural father has filed an affidavit acknowledging paternity, by the wife. §§ 621(c) and (d).

On January 28, 1985, having found that affidavits submitted by Carole and Gerald sufficed to demonstrate that the two were cohabiting at conception and birth and that Gerald was neither sterile nor impotent, the Superior Court granted Gerald's motion for summary judgment, rejecting Michael's and Victoria's challenges to the constitutionality of § 621. The court also denied their motions for continued visitation pending the appeal under Cal. Civ. Code § 4601, which provides that a court may, in its discretion, grant "reasonable visitation rights . . . to any . . . person having an interest in the welfare of the child." Cal. Civ. Code Ann. § 4601 (Supp. 1989). It found that allowing such visitation would "violat[e] the intention of the Legislature by impugning the integrity of the family unit."

* * *

III

* * *

Michael contends as a matter of substantive due process that, because he has established a parental relationship with Victoria, protection of Gerald's and Carole's marital union is an insufficient state interest to support termination of that relationship. This argument is, of course, predicated on the assertion that Michael has a constitutionally protected liberty interest in his relationship with Victoria.

It is an established part of our constitutional jurisprudence that the term "liberty" in the Due Process Clause extends beyond freedom from physical restraint. *See, e.g., Pierce v. Society of Sisters* (1925); *Meyer v. Nebraska* (1923). Without that core textual meaning as a limitation, defining the scope of the Due Process Clause "has at times been a treacherous field for this Court," giving "reason for concern lest the only limits to . . . judicial intervention become the predilections of those who happen at the time to be Members of this Court." *Moore v. East Cleveland* (1977). . . . In an attempt to limit and guide interpretation of the Clause, we have insisted not merely that the interest denominated as a "liberty" be "fundamental" (a concept that, in isolation, is hard to objectify), but also that it be an interest traditionally protected by our society.[2] As we have put it, the Due Process Clause affords only those protections "so rooted in the traditions and conscience of our people as to be ranked as fundamental." *Snyder v. Massachusetts* (1934) (Cardozo, J.). Our cases reflect "continual insistence upon respect for the teachings of history [and] solid recognition of the basic values that underlie our society . . . ." *Griswold v. Connecticut* (1965) (Harlan, J., concurring in judgment).

---

[2] We do not understand what JUSTICE BRENNAN has in mind by an interest "that society traditionally has thought important . . . without protecting it." The protection need not take the form of an explicit constitutional provision or statutory guarantee, but it must at least exclude (all that is necessary to decide the present case) a societal tradition of enacting laws *denying* the interest. Nor do we understand why our practice of limiting the Due Process Clause to traditionally protected interests turns the Clause "into a redundancy." Its purpose is to prevent future generations from lightly casting aside important traditional values — not to enable this Court to invent new ones.

This insistence that the asserted liberty interest be rooted in history and tradition is evident, as elsewhere, in our cases according constitutional protection to certain parental rights. . . . [These cases] rest not upon such isolated factors but upon the historic respect — indeed, sanctity would not be too strong a term — traditionally accorded to the relationships that develop within the unitary family.[3] . . .

Thus, the legal issue in the present case reduces to whether the relationship between persons in the situation of Michael and Victoria has been treated as a protected family unit under the historic practices of our society, or whether on any other basis it has been accorded special protection. We think it impossible to find that it has. In fact, quite to the contrary, our traditions have protected the marital family (Gerald, Carole, and the child they acknowledge to be theirs) against the sort of claim Michael asserts.

The presumption of legitimacy was a fundamental principle of the common law. Traditionally, that presumption could be rebutted only by proof that a husband was incapable of procreation or had had no access to his wife during the relevant period. H. NICHOLAS, ADULTURINE BASTARDY 9-10 (1836) (citing BRACTON, DE LEGIBUS ET CONSUETUDINIBUS ANGLIAE, bk. i, ch. 9, at 6; bk. ii, ch. 29, at 63, ch. 32, at 70 (1569)). As explained by Blackstone, nonaccess could only be proved "if the husband be out of the kingdom of England (or, as the law somewhat loosely phrases it, *extra quatuor maria* [beyond the four seas]) for above nine months . . . ." 1 BLACKSTONE'S COMMENTARIES 456 (J. Chitty ed., 1826). And, under the common law both in England and here, "neither husband nor wife [could] be a witness to prove access or nonaccess." J. SCHOULER, LAW OF THE DOMESTIC RELATIONS § 225, at 306 (3d ed. 1882). The primary policy rationale underlying the common law's severe restrictions on rebuttal of the presumption appears to have been an aversion to declaring children illegitimate, thereby depriving them of rights of inheritance and succession, and likely making them wards of the state. A secondary policy concern was the interest in promoting the "peace and tranquillity of States and families," a goal that is obviously impaired by facilitating suits against husband and wife asserting that their children are illegitimate. . . .

We have found nothing in the older sources, nor in the older cases, addressing specifically the power of the natural father to assert parental rights over a child born into a woman's existing marriage with another man. Since it is Michael's burden to establish that such a power (at least where the natural

---

3 JUSTICE BRENNAN asserts that only a "pinched conception of 'the family'" would exclude Michael, Carole, and Victoria from protection. We disagree. The family unit accorded traditional respect in our society, which we have referred to as the "unitary family," is typified, of course, by the marital family, but also includes the household of unmarried parents and their children. Perhaps the concept can be expanded even beyond this, but it will bear no resemblance to traditionally respected relationships — and will thus cease to have any constitutional significance — if it is stretched so far as to include the relationship established between a married woman, her lover, and their child, during a 3-month sojourn in St. Thomas, or during a subsequent 8-month period when, if he happened to be in Los Angeles, he stayed with her and the child.

father has established a relationship with the child) is so deeply embedded within our traditions as to be a fundamental right, the lack of evidence alone might defeat his case. But the evidence shows that even in modern times — when, as we have noted, the rigid protection of the marital family has in other respects been relaxed — the ability of a person in Michael's position to claim paternity has not been generally acknowledged. . . .

Moreover, even if it were clear that one in Michael's position generally possesses, and has generally always possessed, standing to challenge the marital child's legitimacy, that would still not establish Michael's case. . . . What counts is whether the States in fact award substantive parental rights to the natural father of a child conceived within, and born into, an extant marital union that wishes to embrace the child. We are not aware of a single case, old or new, that has done so. This is not the stuff of which fundamental rights qualifying as liberty interests are made.[6]

---

[6] JUSTICE BRENNAN criticizes our methodology in using historical traditions specifically relating to the rights of an adulterous natural father, rather than inquiring more generally "whether parenthood is an interest that historically has received our attention and protection." There seems to us no basis for the contention that this methodology is "nove[l]." For example, in *Bowers v. Hardwick*, 478 U.S. 186 (1986), we noted that at the time the Fourteenth Amendment was ratified all but 5 of the 37 States had criminal sodomy laws, that all 50 of the States had such laws prior to 1961, and that 24 States and the District of Columbia continued to have them; and we concluded from that record, regarding that very specific aspect of sexual conduct, that "to claim that a right to engage in such conduct is 'deeply rooted in this Nation's history and tradition' or 'implicit in the concept of ordered liberty' is, at best, facetious." In *Roe v. Wade*, 410 U.S. 113 (1973), we spent about a fifth of our opinion negating the proposition that there was a longstanding tradition of laws proscribing abortion.

We do not understand why, having rejected our focus upon the societal tradition regarding the natural father's rights vis-a-vis a child whose mother is married to another man, JUSTICE BRENNAN would choose to focus instead upon "parenthood." Why should the relevant category not be even more general — perhaps "family relationships"; or "personal relationships"; or even "emotional attachments in general"? Though the dissent has no basis for the level of generality it would select, we do: We refer to the most specific level at which a relevant tradition protecting, or denying protection to, the asserted right can be identified. If, for example, there were no societal tradition, either way, regarding the rights of the natural father of a child adulterously conceived, we would have to consult, and (if possible) reason from, the traditions regarding natural fathers in general. But there is such a more specific tradition, and it unqualifiedly denies protection to such a parent.

One would think that JUSTICE BRENNAN would appreciate the value of consulting the most specific tradition available, since he acknowledges that "[e]ven if we can agree . . . that 'family' and 'parenthood' are part of the good life, it is absurd to assume that we can agree on the content of those terms and destructive to pretend that we do." Because such general traditions provide such imprecise guidance, they permit judges to dictate rather than discern the society's views. The need, if arbitrary decisionmaking is to be avoided, to adopt the most specific tradition as the point of reference — or at least to announce, as JUSTICE BRENNAN declines to do, some other criterion for selecting among the innumerable relevant traditions that could be consulted — is well enough exemplified by the fact that in the present case JUSTICE BRENNAN's opinion and JUSTICE O'CONNOR's opinion, which disapproves this footnote, *both* appeal to tradition, but on the basis of the tradition they select reach opposite results. Although assuredly having the virtue (if it be that) of leaving judges free to decide as they think best when the unanticipated occurs, a rule of law that binds neither by text nor by any particular, identifiable tradition is no rule of law at all.

Finally, we may note that this analysis is not inconsistent with the result in cases such as *Griswold v. Connecticut*, or *Eisenstadt v. Baird*, 405 U.S. 438 (1972). None of those cases acknowledged a longstanding and still extant societal tradition withholding the very right pronounced to be the subject of a liberty interest and then rejected it. JUSTICE BRENNAN must do so here. In this case, the existence of such a tradition, continuing to the present day, refutes any possible contention that the alleged right is "so rooted in the traditions and conscience of our people as to be ranked as fundamental," or "implicit in the concept of ordered liberty."

. . . It is a question of legislative policy and not constitutional law whether California will allow the presumed parenthood of a couple desiring to retain a child conceived within and born into their marriage to be rebutted.

We do not accept JUSTICE BRENNAN's criticism that this result "squashes" the liberty that consists of "the freedom not to conform." It seems to us that reflects the erroneous view that there is only one side to this controversy — that one disposition can expand a "liberty" of sorts without contracting an equivalent "liberty" on the other side. Such a happy choice is rarely available. Here, to *provide* protection to an adulterous natural father is to *deny* protection to a marital father, and vice versa. If Michael has a "freedom not to conform" (whatever that means), Gerald must equivalently have a "freedom to conform." One of them will pay a price for asserting that "freedom" — Michael by being unable to act as father of the child he has adulterously begotten, or Gerald by being unable to preserve the integrity of the traditional family unit he and Victoria have established. Our disposition does not choose between these two "freedoms," but leaves that to the people of California. JUSTICE BRENNAN's approach chooses one of them as the constitutional imperative, on no apparent basis except that the unconventional is to be preferred.

IV

* * *

The judgment of the California Court of Appeal is

Affirmed.

JUSTICE O'CONNOR, with whom JUSTICE KENNEDY joins, concurring in part.

I concur in all but footnote 6 of JUSTICE SCALIA's opinion. This footnote sketches a mode of historical analysis to be used when identifying liberty interests protected by the Due Process Clause of the Fourteenth Amendment that may be somewhat inconsistent with our past decisions in this area. *See Griswold v. Connecticut; Eisenstadt v. Baird.* On occasion the Court has characterized relevant traditions protecting asserted rights at levels of generality that might not be "the most specific level" available. *See Loving v. Virginia,* 388 U.S. 1 (1967). I would not foreclose the unanticipated by the prior imposition of a single mode of historical analysis.

JUSTICE STEVENS, concurring in the judgment. [Omitted.]

JUSTICE BRENNAN, with whom JUSTICE MARSHALL and JUSTICE BLACKMUN join, dissenting.

* * *

I

Once we recognized that the "liberty" protected by the Due Process Clause of the Fourteenth Amendment encompasses more than freedom from bodily restraint, today's plurality opinion emphasizes, the concept was cut loose from one natural limitation on its meaning. This innovation paved the way, so the plurality hints, for judges to substitute their own preferences for those of elected officials. Dissatisfied with this supposedly unbridled and uncertain state of affairs, the plurality casts about for another limitation on the concept of liberty.

It finds this limitation in "tradition." Apparently oblivious to the fact that this concept can be as malleable and as elusive as "liberty" itself, the plurality pretends that tradition places a discernible border around the Constitution. The pretense is seductive; it would be comforting to believe that a search for "tradition" involves nothing more idiosyncratic or complicated than poring through dusty volumes on American history. Yet, . . . the plurality has not found the objective boundary that it seeks.

* * *

Today's plurality, however, does not ask whether parenthood is an interest that historically has received our attention and protection; the answer to that question is too clear for dispute. Instead, the plurality asks whether the specific variety of parenthood under consideration — a natural father's relationship with a child whose mother is married to another man — has enjoyed such protection.

* * *

In construing the Fourteenth Amendment to offer shelter only to those interests specifically protected by historical practice, moreover, the plurality ignores the kind of society in which our Constitution exists. We are not an assimilative, homogeneous society, but a facilitative, pluralistic one, in which we must be willing to abide someone else's unfamiliar or even repellent practice because the same tolerant impulse protects our own idiosyncracies. Even if we can agree, therefore, that "family" and "parenthood" are part of the good life, it is absurd to assume that we can agree on the content of those terms and destructive to pretend that we do. In a community such as ours, "liberty" must include the freedom not to conform. The plurality today squashes this freedom by requiring specific approval from history before protecting anything in the name of liberty.

The document that the plurality construes today is unfamiliar to me. It is not the living charter that I have taken to be our Constitution; it is instead a stagnant, archaic, hidebound document steeped in the prejudices and superstitions of a time long past. *This* Constitution does not recognize that times change, does not see that sometimes a practice or rule outlives its foundations. I cannot accept an interpretive method that does such violence to the charter that I am bound by oath to uphold.

II

* * *

Thus, to describe the issue in this case as whether the relationship existing between Michael and Victoria "has been treated as a protected family unit under the historic practices of our society, or whether on any other basis it has been accorded special protection," is to reinvent the wheel. The better approach — indeed, the one commanded by our prior cases and by common sense — is to ask whether the specific parent-child relationship under consideration is close enough to the interests that we already have protected to be deemed an aspect of "liberty" as well. On the facts before us, therefore, the question is not what "level of generality" should be used to describe the relationship between Michael and Victoria, but whether the relationship under consideration is sufficiently substantial to qualify as a liberty interest under our prior cases.

* * *

JUSTICE WHITE, with whom JUSTICE BRENNAN joins, dissenting [omitted].

NOTES AND QUESTIONS

1. *Michael H.* raises the issue of the interest of unmarried fathers. As you might guess, and as *Michael H.* illustrates, they are treated with far less judicial deference than those of married fathers, or for that matter, married parents. For example, in *Santosky v. Kramer*, 455 U.S. 745 (1982), the Court held that a parent's custodial right can be terminated only upon a showing of clear and convincing evidence. "The fundamental liberty interest of natural parents in the care, custody, and management of their child" is protected by the Fourteenth Amendment. *Id.* at 753. By contrast, in *Lehr v. Robertson*, 463 U.S. 248 (1983), the Court allowed an unmarried father's interest in his progeny to be terminated without notice or hearing. The Court made special note of the fact that the father had shown no interest in the child in terms of either support or paternity. *Id.* at 251-52.

Nevertheless, unmarried parents do have a constitutionally-protected interest where they have demonstrated "a full commitment to the responsibilities of parenthood by 'coming forward to participate in the rearing of [their] child[ren].'" *Lehr*, 463 U.S. at 261 (quoting *Caban v. Mohammed*, 441 U.S. 380, 392 (1979)). Thus, in the earlier case of *Stanley v. Illinois*, 405 U.S. 645 (1972), it was a due process and equal protection violation for Illinois to terminate an unmarried father's interest in custody when the father had lived for eighteen years with the children and their mother until her death.

2. *Michael H.* is most often cited because of Justice Scalia's instruction of how the Court should articulate non-textual fundamental rights. How convincing do you find his argument? Here, Justice Scalia wrote only for himself and Chief Justice Rehnquist, yet, the methodology is of considerable importance and the subject of much debate. In directing the Court to protect nontextual rights under the Due Process Clause at their most specific level of abstraction, Justice Scalia was providing a mechanism for constitutional flexibility over time as well as judicial restraint. The Court's most activist member in modern time, the late William Brennan, strongly objected to the Court's, and in particular, Scalia's defense of the liberty of the traditional family, but not others. Justice Brennan argued for accepting "someone else's unfamiliar or even repellent practice[s]," *id.* at 141 (Brennan, J., dissenting), including those of an individual engaging in adultery who wished to insert himself unwelcomely into the rearing of a child being raised by the married spouse who bore the pain of his spouse's infidelity. Notwithstanding Justice Brennan's severe dissent, the Court has relied upon Justice Scalia's approach several times since. For example, in *Reno v. Flores*, 507 U.S. 292 (1993), the Justices described as "mere novelty" the claim that the government as custodial guardian of immigrant children was constitutionally required to provide the best schooling and health care at the highest possible funding level. *Id.* at 303. The claim was "novel," said the Court, because it could not in any way be considered "rooted in the traditions and conscience of our people." *Id.* (quoting *Snyder v. Massachusetts*, 291 U.S. 97, 105 (1934)). Similarly, as we will see below, the Court employed the *Michael H.* approach to reject the claimed assisted suicide right.

3. When Justice Scalia's approach is not followed the Court tends to go off in far less precise directions in the discovery of implied fundamental rights. For a scholarly appraisal of the methods employed, see David Crump, *How Do the Courts Really Discover Unenumerated Fundamental Rights? Cataloguing the Methods of Judicial Alchemy*, 19 HARV. J.L. & PUB. POL'Y 795 (1996) (demonstrating how current judicial practice uses multiple and complex legal formulae to create fundamental rights perhaps often derived from personal inclination or experience).

B. The Ninth Amendment — A Right of Privacy?

1. Contraception

GRISWOLD v. CONNECTICUT
381 U.S. 479 (1965)

MR. JUSTICE DOUGLAS delivered the opinion of the Court.

Appellant Griswold is Executive Director of the Planned Parenthood League of Connecticut. Appellant Buxton is a licensed physician and a professor at the Yale Medical School who served as Medical Director for the League at its Center in New Haven — a center open and operating from November 1 to November 10, 1961, when appellants were arrested.

They gave information, instruction, and medical advice to *married persons* as to the means of preventing conception. . . .

The statutes whose constitutionality is involved in this appeal are §§ 53-32 and 54-196 of the General Statutes of Connecticut (1958 rev.). The former provides:

"Any person who uses any drug, medicinal article or instrument for the purpose of preventing conception shall be fined not less than fifty dollars or imprisoned not less than sixty days nor more than one year or be both fined and imprisoned."

Section 54-196 provides:

"Any person who assists, abets, counsels, causes, hires or commands another to commit any offense may be prosecuted and punished as if he were the principal offender."

The appellants were found guilty as accessories and fined $100 each, against the claim that the accessory statute as so applied violated the Fourteenth Amendment. . . .

We think that appellants have standing to raise the constitutional rights of the married people with whom they had a professional relationship. . . .

* * *

Coming to the merits, we are met with a wide range of questions that implicate the Due Process Clause of the Fourteenth Amendment. Overtones of some arguments suggest that *Lochner v. New York* [(1905)] should be our guide. But we decline that invitation. . . . We do not sit as a super-legislature to determine the wisdom, need, and propriety of laws that touch economic problems, business affairs, or social conditions. This law, however, operates directly on an intimate relation of husband and wife and their physician's role in one aspect of that relation.

The association of people is not mentioned in the Constitution nor in the Bill of Rights. The right to educate a child in a school of the parents' choice — whether public or private or parochial — is also not mentioned. Nor is the right to study any particular subject or any foreign language. Yet the First Amendment has been construed to include certain of those rights.

By *Pierce v. Society of Sisters*, the right to educate one's children as one chooses is made applicable to the States by the force of the First and Fourteenth Amendments. By *Meyer v. Nebraska*, the same dignity is given the right to study the German language in a private school. In other words, the State may not, consistently with the spirit of the First Amendment, contract the spectrum of available knowledge. The right of freedom of speech and press includes not only the right to utter or to print, but the right to distribute, the right to receive, the right to read and freedom of inquiry, freedom of thought, and freedom to teach — indeed the freedom of the entire university community. Without those peripheral rights the specific rights would be less secure. And so we reaffirm the principle of the *Pierce* and the *Meyer* cases.

In *NAACP v. Alabama* [(1958)] we protected the "freedom to associate and privacy in one's associations," noting that freedom of association was a peripheral First Amendment right. Disclosure of membership lists of a constitutionally valid association, we held, was invalid "as entailing the likelihood of a substantial restraint upon the exercise by petitioner's members of their right to freedom of association." In other words, the First Amendment has a penumbra where privacy is protected from governmental intrusion. . . .

Those cases involved more than the "right of assembly" — a right that extends to all irrespective of their race or ideology. The right of "association," like the right of belief, is more than the right to attend a meeting; it includes the right to express one's attitudes or philosophies by membership in a group or by affiliation with it or by other lawful means. Association in that context is a form of expression of opinion; and while it is not expressly included in the First Amendment its existence is necessary in making the express guarantees fully meaningful.

The foregoing cases suggest that specific guarantees in the Bill of Rights have penumbras, formed by emanations from those guarantees that help give them life and substance. Various guarantees create zones of privacy. The right of association contained in the penumbra of the First Amendment is one, as we have seen. The Third Amendment in its prohibition against the quartering of soldiers "in any house" in time of peace without the consent of the owner is another facet of that privacy. The Fourth Amendment explicitly affirms the "right of the people to be secure in their persons, houses, papers, and effects, against unreasonable searches and seizures." The Fifth Amendment in its Self-Incrimination Clause enables the citizen to create a zone of privacy which government may not force him to surrender to his detriment. The Ninth Amendment provides: "The enumeration in the Constitution, of certain rights, shall not be construed to deny or disparage others retained by the people."

* * *

We have had many controversies over these penumbral rights of "privacy and repose." These cases bear witness that the right of privacy which presses for recognition here is a legitimate one.

The present case, then, concerns a relationship lying within the zone of privacy created by several fundamental constitutional guarantees. And it concerns a law which, in forbidding the *use* of contraceptives rather than regulating their manufacture or sale, seeks to achieve its goals by means having a maximum destructive impact upon that relationship. Such a law cannot stand in light of the familiar principle, so often applied by this Court, that a "governmental purpose to control or prevent activities constitutionally subject to state regulation may not be achieved by means which sweep unnecessarily broadly and thereby invade the area of protected freedoms." Would we allow the police to search the sacred precincts of marital bedrooms for telltale signs of the use of contraceptives? The very idea is repulsive to the notions of privacy surrounding the marriage relationship.

We deal with a right of privacy older than the Bill of Rights — older than our political parties, older than our school system. Marriage is a coming together for better or for worse, hopefully enduring, and intimate to the degree of being sacred. It is an association that promotes a way of life, not causes; a harmony in living, not political faiths; a bilateral loyalty, not commercial or social projects. Yet it is an association for as noble a purpose as any involved in our prior decisions.

Reversed.

MR. JUSTICE GOLDBERG, whom THE CHIEF JUSTICE and MR. JUSTICE BRENNAN join, concurring.

I agree with the Court that Connecticut's birth-control law unconstitutionally intrudes upon the right of marital privacy, and I join in its opinion and judgment. Although I have not accepted the view that "due process" as used in the Fourteenth Amendment includes all of the first eight Amendments, I do agree that the concept of liberty protects those personal rights that are fundamental, and is not confined to the specific terms of the Bill of Rights. My conclusion that the concept of liberty is not so restricted and that it embraces the right of marital privacy though that right is not mentioned explicitly in the Constitution is supported both by numerous decisions of this Court, referred to in the Court's opinion, and by the language and history of the Ninth Amendment. In reaching the conclusion that the right of marital privacy is protected, as being within the protected penumbra of specific guarantees of the Bill of Rights, the Court refers to the Ninth Amendment. I add these words to emphasize the relevance of that Amendment to the Court's holding.

* * *

This Court, in a series of decisions, has held that the Fourteenth Amendment absorbs and applies to the States those specifics of the first eight amendments which express fundamental personal rights. The language and history of the Ninth Amendment reveal that the Framers of the Constitution believed that there are additional fundamental rights, protected from governmental infringement, which exist alongside those fundamental rights specifically mentioned in the first eight constitutional amendments.

The Ninth Amendment reads, "The enumeration in the Constitution, of certain rights, shall not be construed to deny or disparage others retained by the people." The Amendment is almost entirely the work of James Madison. It was introduced in Congress by him and passed the House and Senate with little or no debate and virtually no change in language. It was proffered to quiet expressed fears that a bill of specifically enumerated rights[3] could not be sufficiently broad to cover all essential rights and that the specific mention of certain rights would be interpreted as a denial that others were protected.[4]

---

[3] Madison himself had previously pointed out the dangers of inaccuracy resulting from the fact that "no language is so copious as to supply words and phrases for every complex idea." THE FEDERALIST No. 37, at 236 (James Madison) (Cooke ed., 1961).

[4] Alexander Hamilton was opposed to a bill of rights on the ground that it was unnecessary because the Federal Government was a government of delegated powers and it was not granted the power to intrude upon funda-

In presenting the proposed Amendment, Madison said:

> "It has been objected also against a bill of rights, that, by enumerating particular exceptions to the grant of power, it would disparage those rights which were not placed in that enumeration; and it might follow by implication, that those rights which were not singled out, were intended to be assigned into the hands of the General Government, and were consequently insecure. This is one of the most plausible arguments I have ever heard urged against the admission of a bill of rights into this system; but, I conceive, that it may be guarded against. I have attempted it, as gentlemen may see by turning to the last clause of the fourth resolution [the Ninth Amendment]." 1 ANNALS OF CONG. 439 (Gales and Seaton eds., 1834).

Mr. Justice Story wrote of this argument against a bill of rights and the meaning of the Ninth Amendment:

> "In regard to . . . [a] suggestion, that the affirmance of certain rights might disparage others, or might lead to argumentative implications in favor of other powers, it might be sufficient to say that such a course of reasoning could never be sustained upon any solid basis. . . . But a conclusive answer is, that such an attempt may be interdicted (as it has been) by a positive declaration in such a bill of rights that the enumeration of certain rights shall not be construed to deny or disparage others retained by the people." 2 JOSEPH STORY, COMMENTARIES ON THE CONSTITUTION OF THE UNITED STATES 626-27 (5th ed. 1891).

He further stated, referring to the Ninth Amendment:

> "This clause was manifestly introduced to prevent any perverse or ingenious misapplication of the well known maxim, that an affirmation in particular cases implies a negation in all others; and, *e converso*, that a negation in particular cases implies an affirmation in all others." *Id.* at 651.

---

mental personal rights. THE FEDERALIST No. 84, at 578-79 (Alexander Hamilton) (Cooke ed., 1961). He also argued,

> "I go further, and affirm that bills of rights, in the sense and in the extent in which they are contended for, are not only unnecessary in the proposed constitution, but would even be dangerous. They would contain various exceptions to powers which are not granted; and on this very account, would afford a colourable pretext to claim more than were granted. For why declare that things shall not be done which there is no power to do? Why for instance, should it be said, that the liberty of the press shall not be restrained, when no power is given by which restrictions may be imposed? I will not contend that such a provision would confer a regulating power; but it is evident that it would furnish, to men disposed to usurp, a plausible pretence for claiming that power." *Id.* at 579.

The Ninth Amendment and the Tenth Amendment, which provides, "The powers not delegated to the United States by the Constitution, nor prohibited by it to the States, are reserved to the States respectively, or to the people," were apparently also designed in part to meet the above-quoted argument of Hamilton.

These statements of Madison and Story make clear that the Framers did not intend that the first eight amendments be construed to exhaust the basic and fundamental rights which the Constitution guaranteed to the people.[5]

While this Court has had little occasion to interpret the Ninth Amendment, "[i]t cannot be presumed that any clause in the constitution is intended to be without effect." *Marbury v. Madison* [(1803)]. In interpreting the Constitution, "real effect should be given to all the words it uses." *Myers v. United States* [(1926)]. The Ninth Amendment to the Constitution may be regarded by some as a recent discovery and may be forgotten by others, but since 1791 it has been a basic part of the Constitution which we are sworn to uphold. To hold that a right so basic and fundamental and so deep-rooted in our society as the right of privacy in marriage may be infringed because that right is not guaranteed in so many words by the first eight amendments to the Constitution is to ignore the Ninth Amendment and to give it no effect whatsoever. Moreover, a judicial construction that this fundamental right is not protected by the Constitution because it is not mentioned in explicit terms by one of the first eight amendments or elsewhere in the Constitution would violate the Ninth Amendment, which specifically states that "[t]he enumeration in the Constitution, of certain rights, shall not be *construed* to deny or disparage others retained by the people." (Emphasis added.)

A dissenting opinion suggests that my interpretation of the Ninth Amendment somehow "broaden[s] the powers of this Court." With all due respect, I believe that it misses the import of what I am saying. I do not take the position of my Brother BLACK in his dissent in *Adamson v. California*, 332 U.S. 46, 68, that the entire Bill of Rights is incorporated in the Fourteenth Amendment, and I do not mean to imply that the Ninth Amendment is applied against the States by the Fourteenth. Nor do I mean to state that the Ninth Amendment constitutes an independent source of rights protected from infringement by either the States or the Federal Government. Rather, the Ninth Amendment shows a belief of the Constitution's authors that fundamental rights exist that are not expressly enumerated in the first eight amendments and an intent that the list of rights included there not be deemed exhaustive. As any student of this Court's opinions knows, this Court has held, often unanimously, that the Fifth and Fourteenth Amendments protect certain fundamental personal liberties from abridgment by the Federal Government or the States. The Ninth Amendment simply shows the intent of the Constitution's authors that other fundamental personal rights should not be denied such protection or disparaged in any other way simply because they are not specifically listed in the first eight constitutional amendments. I do not see how this broadens the authority of the Court; rather it serves to support what this Court has been doing in protecting fundamental rights.

---

[5] The Tenth Amendment similarly made clear that the States and the people retained all those powers not expressly delegated to the Federal Government.

Nor am I turning somersaults with history in arguing that the Ninth Amendment is relevant in a case dealing with a *State's* infringement of a fundamental right. While the Ninth Amendment — and indeed the entire Bill of Rights — originally concerned restrictions upon *federal* power, the subsequently enacted Fourteenth Amendment prohibits the States as well from abridging fundamental personal liberties. And, the Ninth Amendment, in indicating that not all such liberties are specifically mentioned in the first eight amendments, is surely relevant in showing the existence of other fundamental personal rights, now protected from state, as well as federal, infringement. In sum, the Ninth Amendment simply lends strong support to the view that the "liberty" protected by the Fifth and Fourteenth Amendments from infringement by the Federal Government or the States is not restricted to rights specifically mentioned in the first eight amendments.

In determining which rights are fundamental, judges are not left at large to decide cases in light of their personal and private notions. Rather, they must look to the "traditions and [collective] conscience of our people" to determine whether a principle is "so rooted [there] . . . as to be ranked as fundamental." The inquiry is whether a right involved "is of such a character that it cannot be denied without violating those 'fundamental principles of liberty and justice which lie at the base of all our civil and political institutions' . . . ." "Liberty" also "gains content from the emanations of . . . specific [constitutional] guarantees" and "from experience with the requirements of a free society."

I agree fully with the Court that, applying these tests, the right of privacy is a fundamental personal right, emanating "from the totality of the constitutional scheme under which we live." Mr. Justice Brandeis, dissenting in *Olmstead v. United States* [(1928)], comprehensively summarized the principles underlying the Constitution's guarantees of privacy:

> "The protection guaranteed by the [Fourth and Fifth] amendments is much broader in scope. The makers of our Constitution undertook to secure conditions favorable to the pursuit of happiness. They recognized the significance of man's spiritual nature, of his feelings and of his intellect. They knew that only a part of the pain, pleasure and satisfactions of life are to be found in material things. They sought to protect Americans in their beliefs, their thoughts, their emotions and their sensations. They conferred, as against the Government, the right to be let alone — the most comprehensive of rights and the right most valued by civilized men."

The Connecticut statutes here involved deal with a particularly important and sensitive area of privacy — that of the marital relation and the marital home. This Court recognized in *Meyer v. Nebraska*, that the right "to marry, establish a home and bring up children" was an essential part of the liberty guaranteed by the Fourteenth Amendment. In *Pierce v. Society of Sisters*, the Court held unconstitutional an Oregon Act which forbade parents from sending their children to private schools because such an act "unreasonably interferes with the liberty of parents and guardians to direct the upbringing and education of children under their control." As this Court said in *Prince v. Massachusetts* [(1944)], the *Meyer* and *Pierce* decisions "have respected the private realm of family life which the state cannot enter."

I agree with MR. JUSTICE HARLAN's statement in his dissenting opinion in *Poe v. Ullman* [(1961)]: "Certainly the safeguarding of the home does not follow merely from the sanctity of property rights. The home derives its pre-eminence as the seat of family life. And the integrity of that life is something so fundamental that it has been found to draw to its protection the principles of more than one explicitly granted Constitutional right. . . . Of this whole 'private realm of family life' it is difficult to imagine what is more private or more intimate than a husband and wife's marital relations."

The entire fabric of the Constitution and the purposes that clearly underlie its specific guarantees demonstrate that the rights to marital privacy and to marry and raise a family are of similar order and magnitude as the fundamental rights specifically protected.

Although the Constitution does not speak in so many words of the right of privacy in marriage, I cannot believe that it offers these fundamental rights no protection. The fact that no particular provision of the Constitution explicitly forbids the State from disrupting the traditional relation of the family — a relation as old and as fundamental as our entire civilization — surely does not show that the Government was meant to have the power to do so. Rather, as the Ninth Amendment expressly recognizes, there are fundamental personal rights such as this one, which are protected from abridgment by the Government though not specifically mentioned in the Constitution.

My Brother STEWART, while characterizing the Connecticut birth control law as "an uncommonly silly law," would nevertheless let it stand on the ground that it is not for the courts to "'substitute their social and economic beliefs for the judgment of legislative bodies, who are elected to pass laws.'" Elsewhere, I have stated that "[w]hile I quite agree with Mr. Justice Brandeis that . . . 'a . . . State may . . . serve as a laboratory; and try novel social and economic experiments,' I do not believe that this includes the power to experiment with the fundamental liberties of citizens. . . ." The vice of the dissenters' views is that it would permit such experimentation by the States in the area of the fundamental personal rights of its citizens. I cannot agree that the Constitution grants such power either to the States or to the Federal Government.

The logic of the dissents would sanction federal or state legislation that seems to me even more plainly unconstitutional than the statute before us. Surely the Government, absent a showing of a compelling subordinating state interest, could not decree that all husbands and wives must be sterilized after two children have been born to them. Yet by their reasoning such an invasion of marital privacy would not be subject to constitutional challenge because, while it might be "silly," no provision of the Constitution specifically prevents the

Government from curtailing the marital right to bear children and raise a family. While it may shock some of my Brethren that the Court today holds that the Constitution protects the right of marital privacy, in my view it is far more shocking to believe that the personal liberty guaranteed by the Constitution does not include protection against such totalitarian limitation of family size, which is at complete variance with our constitutional concepts. Yet, if upon a showing of a slender basis of rationality, a law outlawing voluntary birth control by married persons is valid, then, by the same reasoning, a law requiring compulsory birth control also would seem to be valid. In my view, however, both types of law would unjustifiably intrude upon rights of marital privacy which are constitutionally protected.

In a long series of cases this Court has held that where fundamental personal liberties are involved, they may not be abridged by the States simply on a showing that a regulatory statute has some rational relationship to the effectuation of a proper state purpose. "Where there is a significant encroachment upon personal liberty, the State may prevail only upon showing a subordinating interest which is compelling." . . .

Although the Connecticut birth-control law obviously encroaches upon a fundamental personal liberty, the State does not show that the law serves any "subordinating [state] interest which is compelling" or that it is "necessary . . . to the accomplishment of a permissible state policy." The State, at most, argues that there is some rational relation between this statute and what is admittedly a legitimate subject of state concern — the discouraging of extra-marital relations. It says that preventing the use of birth-control devices by married persons helps prevent the indulgence by some in such extra-marital relations. The rationality of this justification is dubious, particularly in light of the admitted widespread availability to all persons in the State of Connecticut, unmarried as well as married, of birth-control devices for the prevention of disease, as distinguished from the prevention of conception. But, in any event, it is clear that the state interest in safeguarding marital fidelity can be served by a more discriminately tailored statute, which does not, like the present one, sweep unnecessarily broadly, reaching far beyond the evil sought to be dealt with and intruding upon the privacy of all married couples. Here, as elsewhere, "[p]recision of regulation must be the touchstone in an area so closely touching our most precious freedoms." The State of Connecticut does have statutes, the constitutionality of which is beyond doubt, which prohibit adultery and fornication. These statutes demonstrate that means for achieving the same basic purpose of protecting marital fidelity are available to Connecticut without the need to "invade the area of protected freedoms."

Finally, it should be said of the Court's holding today that it in no way interferes with a State's proper regulation of sexual promiscuity or misconduct. As my Brother HARLAN so well stated in his dissenting opinion in *Poe v. Ullman* [(1961)]:

> "Adultery, homosexuality and the like are sexual intimacies which the State forbids . . . but the intimacy of husband and wife is necessarily an essential and accepted feature of the institution of marriage, an institution which the State not only must allow, but which always and in every age it has fostered and protected. It is one thing when the State exerts its power either to forbid extra-marital sexuality . . . or to say who may marry, but it is quite another when, having acknowledged a marriage and the intimacies inherent in it, it undertakes to regulate by means of the criminal law the details of that intimacy."

In sum, I believe that the right of privacy in the marital relation is fundamental and basic — a personal right "retained by the people" within the meaning of the Ninth Amendment. Connecticut cannot constitutionally abridge this fundamental right, which is protected by the Fourteenth Amendment from infringement by the States. I agree with the Court that petitioners' convictions must therefore be reversed.

MR. JUSTICE HARLAN, concurring in the judgment.

I fully agree with the judgment of reversal, but find myself unable to join the Court's opinion. The reason is that it seems to me to evince an approach to this case very much like that taken by my Brothers BLACK and STEWART in dissent, namely: the Due Process Clause of the Fourteenth Amendment does not touch this Connecticut statute unless the enactment is found to violate some right assured by the letter or penumbra of the Bill of Rights.

In other words, what I find implicit in the Court's opinion is that the "incorporation" doctrine may be used to *restrict* the reach of Fourteenth Amendment Due Process. For me this is just as unacceptable constitutional doctrine as is the use of the "incorporation" approach to *impose* upon the States all the requirements of the Bill of Rights as found in the provisions of the first eight amendments and in the decisions of this Court interpreting them.

In my view, the proper constitutional inquiry in this case is whether this Connecticut statute infringes the Due Process Clause of the Fourteenth Amendment because the enactment violates basic values "implicit in the concept of ordered liberty," *Palko v. Connecticut* [(1937)]. For reasons stated at length in my dissenting opinion in *Poe v. Ullman*, I believe that it does. While the relevant inquiry may be aided by resort to one or more of the provisions of the Bill of Rights, it is not dependent on them or any of their radiations. The Due Process Clause of the Fourteenth Amendment stands, in my opinion, on its own bottom.

A further observation seems in order respecting the justification of my Brothers BLACK and STEWART for their "incorporation" approach to this case. Their approach does not rest on historical reasons, . . . but on the thesis that by limiting the content of the Due Process Clause of the Fourteenth Amendment to the protection of rights which can be found elsewhere in the Constitution, in this instance in the Bill of Rights, judges will thus be confined to "interpretation" of specific constitutional provisions, and will thereby be restrained from introducing their own notions of constitutional right and wrong into the "vague contours of the Due Process Clause."

While I could not more heartily agree that judicial "self restraint" is an indispensable ingredient of sound constitutional adjudication, I do submit that the formula suggested for achieving it is more hollow than real. "Specific" provisions of the Constitution, no less than "due process," lend themselves as readily to "personal" interpretations by judges whose constitutional outlook is simply to keep the Constitution in supposed "tune with the times." . . .

Judicial self-restraint will not, I suggest, be brought about in the "due process" area by the historically unfounded incorporation formula long advanced by my Brother BLACK, and now in part espoused by my Brother STEWART. It will be achieved in this area, as in other constitutional areas, only by continual insistence upon respect for the teachings of history, solid recognition of the basic values that underlie our society, and wise appreciation of the great roles that the doctrines of federalism and separation of powers have played in establishing and preserving American freedoms. . . .

MR. JUSTICE WHITE, concurring in the judgment.

In my view this Connecticut law as applied to married couples deprives them of "liberty" without due process of law, as that concept is used in the Fourteenth Amendment. I therefore concur in the judgment of the Court reversing these convictions under Connecticut's aiding and abetting statute.

* * *

. . . There is no serious contention that Connecticut thinks the use of artificial or external methods of contraception immoral or unwise in itself, or that the anti-use statute is founded upon any policy of promoting population expansion. Rather, the statute is said to serve the State's policy against all forms of promiscuous or illicit sexual relationships, be they premarital or extramarital, concededly a permissible and legitimate legislative goal.

Without taking issue with the premise that the fear of conception operates as a deterrent to such relationships in addition to the criminal proscriptions Connecticut has against such conduct, I wholly fail to see how the ban on the use of contraceptives by married couples in any way reinforces the State's ban on illicit sexual relationships. Connecticut does not bar the importation or possession of contraceptive devices; they are not considered contraband material under state law, and their availability in that State is not seriously disputed. The only way Connecticut seeks to limit or control the availability of such devices is through its general aiding and abetting statute whose operation in this context has been quite obviously ineffective and whose most serious use has been against birth-control clinics rendering advice to married, rather than unmarried, persons. . . .

In these circumstances one is rather hard pressed to explain how the ban on use by married persons in any way prevents use of such devices by persons engaging in illicit sexual relations and thereby contributes to the State's policy against such relationships. Neither the state courts nor the State before the bar of this Court has tendered such an explanation. It is purely fanciful to believe that the broad proscription on use facilitates discovery of use by persons engaging in a prohibited relationship or for some other reason makes such use more unlikely and thus can be supported by any sort of administrative consideration. Perhaps the theory is that the flat ban on use prevents married people from possessing contraceptives and without the ready availability of such devices for use in the marital relationship, there will be no or less temptation to use them in extramarital ones. This reasoning rests on the premise that married people will comply with the ban in regard to their marital relationship, notwithstanding total nonenforcement in this context and apparent nonenforcibility, but will not comply with criminal statutes prohibiting extramarital affairs and the anti-use statute in respect to illicit sexual relationships, a premise whose validity has not been demonstrated and whose intrinsic validity is not very evident. At most the broad ban is of marginal utility to the declared objective. A statute limiting its prohibition on use to persons engaging in the prohibited relationship would serve the end posited by Connecticut in the same way, and with the same effectiveness, or ineffectiveness, as the broad anti-use statute under attack in this case. I find nothing in this record justifying the sweeping scope of this statute, with its telling effect on the freedoms of married persons, and therefore conclude that it deprives such persons of liberty without due process of law.

MR. JUSTICE BLACK, with whom MR. JUSTICE STEWART joins, dissenting.

* * *

The Court talks about a constitutional "right of privacy" as though there is some constitutional provision or provisions forbidding any law ever to be passed which might abridge the "privacy" of individuals. But there is not. There are, of course, guarantees in certain specific constitutional provisions which are designed in part to protect privacy at certain times and places with respect to certain activities. . . .

One of the most effective ways of diluting or expanding a constitutionally guaranteed right is to substitute for the crucial word or words of a constitutional guarantee another word or words, more or less flexible and more or less restricted in meaning. This fact is well illustrated by the use of the term "right of privacy" as a comprehensive substitute for the Fourth Amendment's guarantee against "unreasonable searches and seizures." "Privacy" is a broad, abstract and ambiguous concept which can easily be shrunken in meaning but which can also, on the other hand, easily be interpreted as a constitutional ban against many things other than searches and seizures. . . . I like my privacy as well as the next one, but I am nevertheless compelled to admit that government has a right to invade it unless prohibited by some specific constitutional provision. For these reasons I cannot agree with the Court's judgment and the reasons it gives for holding this Connecticut law unconstitutional.

. . . I think that if properly construed neither the Due Process Clause nor the Ninth Amendment, nor both together, could under any circumstances be a proper basis for invalidating the Connecticut law. I discuss the due process and Ninth Amendment arguments together because on analysis they turn out to be the same thing — merely using different words to claim for this Court and the federal judiciary power to invalidate any legislative act which the judges find irrational, unreasonable or offensive.

The due process argument which my Brothers HARLAN and WHITE adopt here is based, as their opinions indicate, on the premise that this Court is vested with power to invalidate all state laws that it considers to be arbitrary, capricious, unreasonable, or oppressive, or this Court's belief that a particular state law under scrutiny has no "rational or justifying" purpose, or is offensive to a "sense of fairness and justice." If these formulas based on "natural justice," or others which mean the same thing, are to prevail, they require judges to determine what is or is not constitutional on the basis of their own appraisal of what laws are unwise or unnecessary. The power to make such decisions is of course that of a legislative body. Surely it has to be admitted that no provision of the Constitution specifically gives such blanket power to courts to exercise such a supervisory veto over the wisdom and value of legislative policies and to hold unconstitutional those laws which they believe unwise or dangerous. I readily admit that no legislative body, state or national, should pass laws that can justly be given any of the invidious labels invoked as constitutional excuses to strike down state laws. But perhaps it is not too much to say that no legislative body ever does pass laws without believing that they will accomplish a sane, rational, wise and justifiable purpose. While I completely subscribe to the holding of *Marbury v. Madison*, and subsequent cases, that our Court has constitutional power to strike down statutes, state or federal, that violate commands of the Federal Constitution, I do not believe that we are granted power by the Due Process Clause or any other constitutional provision or provisions to measure constitutionality by our belief that legislation is arbitrary, capricious or unreasonable, or accomplishes no justifiable purpose, or is offensive to our own notions of "civilized standards of conduct." Such an appraisal of the wisdom of legislation is an attribute of the power to make laws, not of the power to interpret them. . . .

. . . I merely point out that the reasoning stated in *Meyer* and *Pierce* was the same natural law due process philosophy which many later opinions repudiated, and which I cannot accept. . . .

My Brother GOLDBERG has adopted the recent discovery[12] that the Ninth Amendment as well as the Due Process Clause can be used by this Court as

---

12 See PATTERSON, THE FORGOTTEN NINTH AMENDMENT (1955). Mr. Patterson urges that the Ninth Amendment be used to protect unspecified "natural and inalienable rights." *Id*. at 4. The Introduction by Roscoe Pound states that "there is a marked revival of natural law ideas throughout the world. Interest in the Ninth Amendment is a symptom of that revival." *Id*. at iii.

authority to strike down all state legislation which this Court thinks violates "fundamental principles of liberty and justice," or is contrary to the "traditions and [collective] conscience of our people." . . . That Amendment was passed, not to broaden the powers of this Court or any other department of "the General Government," but, as every student of history knows, to assure the people that the Constitution in all its provisions was intended to limit the Federal Government to the powers granted expressly or by necessary implication. If any broad, unlimited power to hold laws unconstitutional because they offend what this Court conceives to be the "[collective] conscience of our people" is vested in this Court by the Ninth Amendment, the Fourteenth Amendment, or any other provision of the Constitution, it was not given by the Framers, but rather has been bestowed on the Court by the Court. . . .

I repeat so as not to be misunderstood that this Court does have power, which it should exercise, to hold laws unconstitutional where they are forbidden by the Federal Constitution. My point is that there is no provision of the Constitution which either expressly or impliedly vests power in this Court to sit as a supervisory agency over acts of duly constituted legislative bodies and set aside their laws because of the Court's belief that the legislative policies adopted are unreasonable, unwise, arbitrary, capricious or irrational. . . .

* * *

MR. JUSTICE STEWART, whom MR. JUSTICE BLACK joins, dissenting. [Omitted.]

NOTES AND QUESTIONS

1. Note that Justice Douglas expressly declines to locate the contraceptive right in the Due Process Clause of the Fourteenth Amendment, writing "[o]vertones of some arguments suggest that *Lochner v. New York* should be our guide. But we decline that invitation." 381 U.S. at 481-82. Did the Court really avoid *Lochner*, or was Justice Douglas' recital of reliance upon the penumbras of the First, Third, Fourth, and Fifth Amendments merely a smokescreen? Could *Lochner* and *Griswold* have been distinguished simply by noting that in the former the Court's action was prompted largely by disagreement with the adopted economic policy even though the maximum hour law could have been easily enforced, while in *Griswold* the Connecticut law was largely unenforceable, except in the rarest of circumstances or with a severe invasion of marital privacy? In this regard, unlike the abortion cases that would build on *Griswold*, this case did not establish any undifferentiated right of reproductive autonomy, but concentrated on avoiding intrusion into the marital bedroom.

2. Do you think that Justice White is correct in his concurring opinion that the Connecticut law fails even the rational basis standard? White failed to see "how the ban on the use of contraceptives by married couples in any way reinforce[d] the State's ban on illicit sexual relationships." *Id.* at 505 (White, J., concurring in the judgment). But is that really so far-fetched? Later, the Supreme

Court will argue that abortion is necessary to facilitate the participation of women in the "economic and social life of the nation." *Casey v. Planned Parenthood*, 505 U.S. 833, 835 (1992). If some women are willing to undergo a more costly and physically intrusive abortion procedure to not have their lives fettered with obligations to children, might they not also more willingly engage in sexual relationships, licit or illicit, if contraception also avoids the consequences of pregnancy and childbirth?

3. Contraception as a moral matter remains highly controversial, especially in the Christian (most notably Catholic) tradition. One writer states, for example:

> By its very nature, contraceptive behavior seeks to take apart what God in His wisdom has put together — the procreative and the affective aspects of sexual relations. Natural Family Planning, on the other hand, respects God's order of creation; it respects the alternating periods of fertility and infertility that God has established and the integrity of the sexual act as God intends it.

JOHN F. KIPPLEY, BIRTH CONTROL AND CHRISTIAN DISCIPLESHIP 16 (1985). Artificial contraception has also been described as a grave evil that can lead to the degradation of women and a distortion of the meaning and purpose of human sexuality, as both an unconditional gift of self and, should the union produce children, a responsible willingness to assume the duties of parenting. The Catholic position is summarized:

> Within [the cultural climate in which the sense of God and of man is eclipsed], the *body* is no longer perceived as a properly personal reality, a sign and place of relations with others, with God and with the world. It is reduced to pure materiality: it is simply a complex of organs, functions and energies to be used according to the sole criteria of pleasure and efficiency. Consequently, *sexuality* too is depersonalized and exploited: from being the sign, place and language of love, that is, of the gift of self and acceptance of another, in all the other's richness as a person, it increasingly becomes the occasion and instrument for self-assertion and the selfish satisfaction of personal desires and instincts. Thus the original import of human sexuality is distorted and falsified, and the two meanings, unitive and procreative, inherent in the very nature of the conjugal act, are artificially separated: in this way the marriage union is betrayed and its fruitfulness is subjected to the caprice of the couple. *Procreation* then becomes the "enemy" to be avoided in sexual activity: if it is welcomed, this is only because it expresses a desire, or indeed the intention, to have a child "at all costs", and not because it signifies the complete acceptance of the other and therefore an openness to the richness of life which the child represents.

POPE JOHN PAUL II, THE GOSPEL OF LIFE [EVANGELIUM VITAE] No. 23, at 42-43 (1995).

Despite the moral difficulty with contraception, eminent Catholic theologians have argued against incorporating any distinctively religious view into law. For example, in a memorandum to Cardinal Richard Cushing in the mid-1960s, Father John Courtney Murray, S.J., a renown scholar of Catholic theology, noted that "[i]t is not the function of civil law to prescribe everything that is morally right and to forbid everything that is morally wrong." JOHN COURT-NEY MURRAY, S.J., *Memo. to Cardinal Cushing on Contraception Legislation, in* BRIDGING THE SACRED AND THE SECULAR 81, 82 (J. Leon Hooper, S.J. ed., 1994). A matter of public morality only arises, wrote Murray, when "a practice seriously undermines the foundations of society or gravely damages the moral life of the community as such." *Id.* Father Murray was especially mindful of the fact that there "must be a reasonable correspondence between the moral standards generally recognized by the conscience of the community and the legal statutes concerning public morality. Otherwise laws will be unenforceable and ineffective and they will be resented as undue restrictions on civil or personal freedom." *Id.* at 83. In this regard, Murray noted that the practice of contraception had become widespread, and as a matter of "responsible parenthood," had received some religious sanction among other denominations. *Id.* Thus, he thought individuals also had the right to make up their own mind about the practice as a matter of religious freedom. Father Murray urged the Cardinal to instruct Catholics to be open about stating their moral objection to contraception, but not to use law "to enforce upon the whole community moral standards that the community itself does not accept." *Id.* at 85-86. Religious believers, he said, must "lift the standards of public morality in all its dimensions, not by appealing to law and police action, but by the integrity of their Christian lives." *Id.* at 86. Does the same analysis apply to abortion or assisted suicide? Or are these latter matters the type that must be matters of public morality because of their external consequences to others and the community as a whole?

EISENSTADT v. BAIRD
405 U.S. 438 (1972)

MR. JUSTICE BRENNAN delivered the opinion of the Court.

Appellee William Baird was convicted at a bench trial in the Massachusetts Superior Court under Massachusetts General Laws Ann., c. 272, § 21, first, for exhibiting contraceptive articles in the course of delivering a lecture on contraception to a group of students at Boston University and, second, for giving a young woman a package of Emko vaginal foam at the close of his address.[1] The Massachusetts Supreme Judicial Court unanimously set aside the conviction for exhibiting contraceptives on the ground that it violated Baird's First Amendment rights, but by a four-to-three vote sustained the conviction for giving away the foam. *Massachusetts v. Baird* (Mass. 1969). Baird subsequently

---

[1] ... The Court of Appeals below described the recipient of the foam as "an unmarried adult woman." 429 F.2d 1398, 1399 (1970). . . .

filed a petition for a federal writ of habeas corpus, which the District Court dismissed. On appeal, however, the Court of Appeals for the First Circuit vacated the dismissal and remanded the action with directions to grant the writ discharging Baird. This appeal by the Sheriff of Suffolk County, Massachusetts, followed. . . . We affirm.

Massachusetts General Laws Ann., c. 272, § 21, under which Baird was convicted, provides a maximum five-year term of imprisonment for "whoever . . . gives away . . . any drug, medicine, instrument or article whatever for the prevention of conception," except as authorized in § 21A. Under § 21A, "[a] registered physician may administer to or prescribe for any married person drugs or articles intended for the prevention of pregnancy or conception . . . ." As interpreted by the State Supreme Judicial Court, these provisions make it a felony for anyone, other than a registered physician or pharmacist acting in accordance with the terms of § 21A, to dispense any article with the intention that it be used for the prevention of conception. The statutory scheme distinguishes among three distinct classes of distributees — *first*, married persons may obtain contraceptives to prevent pregnancy, but only from doctors or druggists on prescription; *second*, single persons may not obtain contraceptives from anyone to prevent pregnancy; and, *third*, married or single persons may obtain contraceptives from anyone to prevent, not pregnancy, but the spread of disease. . . .

The legislative purposes that the statute is meant to serve are not altogether clear. . . .[3]

* * *

II

The basic principles governing application of the Equal Protection Clause of the Fourteenth Amendment are familiar. As THE CHIEF JUSTICE only recently explained in *Reed v. Reed* (1971):

> "In applying that clause, this Court has consistently recognized that the Fourteenth Amendment does not deny to States the power to treat different classes of persons in different ways. The Equal Protection Clause of that amendment does, however, deny to States the power to legislate that different treatment be accorded to persons placed by a statute into different classes on the basis of criteria wholly unrelated to the objective of that statute. A classification 'must be reasonable, not arbitrary, and must rest upon some ground of difference having a fair and substantial relation to the object of the legislation, so that all persons similarly circumstanced shall be treated alike.'"

---

[3] Appellant suggests that the purpose of the Massachusetts statute is to promote marital fidelity as well as to discourage premarital sex. Under § 21A, however, contraceptives may be made available to married persons without regard to whether they are living with their spouses or the uses to which the contraceptives are to be put. Plainly the legislation has no deterrent effect on extramarital sexual relations.

The question for our determination in this case is whether there is some ground of difference that rationally explains the different treatment accorded married and unmarried persons under Massachusetts General Laws Ann., c. 272, §§ 21 and 21A.[7] For the reasons that follow, we conclude that no such ground exists.

First. Section 21 stems from Mass. Stat. 1879, c. 159, § 1, which prohibited, without exception, distribution of articles intended to be used as contraceptives. In *Massachusetts v. Allison* (Mass. 1917), the Massachusetts Supreme Judicial Court explained that the law's "plain purpose is to protect purity, to preserve chastity, to encourage continence and self restraint, to defend the sancity of the home, and thus to engender in the State and nation a virile and virtuous race of men and women." Although the State clearly abandoned that purpose with the enactment of § 21A, at least insofar as the illicit sexual activities of married persons are concerned, *see* n. 3, *supra*, the court reiterated in *Sturgis v. Attorney General* [(Mass. 1970)] that the object of the legislation is to discourage premarital sexual intercourse. Conceding that the State could, consistently with the Equal Protection Clause, regard the problems of extramarital and premarital sexual relations as "[e]vils . . . of different dimensions and proportions, requiring different remedies," we cannot agree that the deterrence of premarital sex may reasonably be regarded as the purpose of the Massachusetts law.

It would be plainly unreasonable to assume that Massachusetts has prescribed pregnancy and the birth of an unwanted child as punishment for fornication, which is a misdemeanor under Massachusetts General Laws Ann., c. 272, § 18. Aside from the scheme of values that assumption would attribute to the State, it is abundantly clear that the effect of the ban on distribution of contraceptives to unmarried persons has at best a marginal relation to the proffered objective. . . . Nor, in making contraceptives available to married persons without regard to their intended use, does Massachusetts attempt to deter married persons from engaging in illicit sexual relations with unmarried persons. Even on the assumption that the fear of pregnancy operates as a deterrent to fornication, the Massachusetts statute is thus so riddled with exceptions that deterrence of premarital sex cannot reasonably be regarded as its aim.

Moreover, §§ 21 and 21A on their face have a dubious relation to the State's criminal prohibition on fornication. As the Court of Appeals explained, "Fornication is a misdemeanor [in Massachusetts], entailing a thirty dollar fine, or three months in jail. Violation of the present statute is a felony, punishable by five years in prison. We find it hard to believe that the legislature adopted a statute carrying a five-year penalty for its possible, obviously by no means fully effective, deterrence of the commission of a ninety-day misdemeanor." Even

---

[7] Of course, if we were to conclude that the Massachusetts statute impinges upon fundamental freedoms under *Griswold*, the statutory classification would have to be not merely *rationally related* to a valid public purpose but *necessary* to the achievement of a *compelling* state interest. . . . [W]e do not have to address the statute's validity under that test because the law fails to satisfy even the more lenient equal protection standard.

conceding the legislature a full measure of discretion in fashioning means to prevent fornication, and recognizing that the State may seek to deter prohibited conduct by punishing more severely those who facilitate than those who actually engage in its commission, we, like the Court of Appeals, cannot believe that in this instance Massachusetts has chosen to expose the aider and abetter who simply *gives away* a contraceptive to *20* times the *90-day* sentence of the offender himself. The very terms of the State's criminal statutes, coupled with the *de minimis* effect of §§ 21 and 21A in deterring fornication, thus compel the conclusion that such deterrence cannot reasonably be taken as the purpose of the ban on distribution of contraceptives to unmarried persons.

     Second. . . .

     . . . "If there is need to have a physician prescribe (and a pharmacist dispense) contraceptives, that need is as great for unmarried persons as for married persons." . . .[8] Furthermore, we must join the Court of Appeals in noting that not all contraceptives are potentially dangerous. As a result, if the Massachusetts statute were a health measure, it would not only invidiously discriminate against the unmarried, but also be overbroad with respect to the married. . . . "In this posture," as the Court of Appeals concluded, "it is impossible to think of the statute as intended as a health measure for the unmarried, and it is almost as difficult to think of it as so intended even as to the married."

* * *

     Third. If the Massachusetts statute cannot be upheld as a deterrent to fornication or as a health measure, may it, nevertheless, be sustained simply as a prohibition on contraception? The Court of Appeals analysis "led inevitably to the conclusion that, so far as morals are concerned, it is contraceptives per se that are considered immoral — to the extent that *Griswold* will permit such a declaration." The Court of Appeals went on to hold:

> "To say that contraceptives are immoral as such, and are to be forbidden to unmarried persons who will nevertheless persist in having intercourse, means that such persons must risk for themselves an unwanted pregnancy, for the child, illegitimacy, and for society, a possible obligation of support. Such a view of morality is not only the very mirror image of sensible legislation; we consider that it conflicts with fundamental human rights. In the absence of demonstrated harm, we hold it is beyond the competency of the state."

---

     8 Appellant insists that the unmarried have no right to engage in sexual intercourse and hence no health interest in contraception that needs to be served. The short answer to this contention is that the same devices the distribution of which the State purports to regulate when their asserted purpose is to forestall pregnancy are available without any controls whatsoever so long as their asserted purpose is to prevent the spread of disease. It is inconceivable that the need for health controls varies with the purpose for which the contraceptive is to be used when the physical act in all cases is one and the same.

We need not and do not, however, decide that important question in this case because, whatever the rights of the individual to access to contraceptives may be, the rights must be the same for the unmarried and the married alike.

If under *Griswold* the distribution of contraceptives to married persons cannot be prohibited, a ban on distribution to unmarried persons would be equally impermissible. It is true that in *Griswold* the right of privacy in question inhered in the marital relationship. Yet the marital couple is not an independent entity with a mind and heart of its own, but an association of two individuals each with a separate intellectual and emotional makeup. If the right of privacy means anything, it is the right of the *individual*, married or single, to be free from unwarranted governmental intrusion into matters so fundamentally affecting a person as the decision whether to bear or beget a child.

On the other hand, if *Griswold* is no bar to a prohibition on the distribution of contraceptives, the State could not, consistently with the Equal Protection Clause, outlaw distribution to unmarried but not to married persons. In each case the evil, as perceived by the State, would be identical, and the underinclusion would be invidious. . . . We hold that by providing dissimilar treatment for married and unmarried persons who are similarly situated, Massachusetts General Laws Ann., c. 272, §§ 21 and 21A, violate the Equal Protection Clause. The judgment of the Court of Appeals is

Affirmed.

MR. JUSTICE POWELL and MR. JUSTICE REHNQUIST took no part in the consideration or decision of this case.

MR. JUSTICE DOUGLAS, concurring. [Omitted.]

MR. JUSTICE WHITE, with whom MR. JUSTICE BLACKMUN joins, concurring in the result [omitted].

MR. CHIEF JUSTICE BURGER, dissenting.

* * *

It is revealing, I think, that those portions of the majority and concurring opinions rejecting the statutory limitation on distributors rely on no particular provision of the Constitution. I see nothing in the Fourteenth Amendment or any other part of the Constitution that even vaguely suggests that these medicinal forms of contraceptives must be available in the open market. I do not challenge *Griswold v. Connecticut, supra,* despite its tenuous moorings to the text of the Constitution, but I cannot view it as controlling authority for this case. The Court was there confronted with a statute flatly prohibiting the use of contraceptives, not one regulating their distribution. I simply cannot believe that the limitation on the class of lawful distributors has significantly impaired the right to use contraceptives in Massachusetts. By relying in *Griswold* in the present context, the Court has passed beyond the penumbras of the specific guarantees into the uncircumscribed area of personal predilections.

NOTES AND QUESTIONS

1. In *Eisenstadt*, the Court concludes: "[W]hatever the rights of the individual to access to contraceptives may be, the rights must be the same for the unmarried and the married alike." 405 U.S. at 453. However, wasn't the right to use contraceptives premised on marital privacy in *Griswold*? If so, why did the Court in *Eisenstadt* feel compelled to expand the right to unmarried individuals? The answer may lie in the fact that the *Eisenstadt* Court lost sight of the fact that the fundamental right offended in *Griswold* was marriage, and *its* associated right of privacy, and not an undifferentiated right of privacy. Note, too, that the *Eisenstadt* Court interchanges a prohibition on contraceptive use and a prohibition on distribution, even as the latter has far fewer, if any, privacy implications. Nevertheless, the Court in *Eisenstadt* writes:

> If under *Griswold* the distribution of contraceptives to married persons cannot be prohibited, a ban on distribution to unmarried persons would be equally impermissible. It is true that in *Griswold* the right of privacy in question inhered in the marital relationship. Yet the marital couple is not an independent entity with a mind and heart of its own, but an association of two individuals each with a separate intellectual and emotional makeup. If the right of privacy means anything, it is the right of the *individual*, married or single, to be free from unwarranted governmental intrusion into matters so fundamentally affecting a person as the decision whether to bear or beget a child.

> On the other hand, if *Griswold* is no bar to a prohibition on the distribution of contraceptives, the State could not, consistently with the Equal Protection Clause, outlaw distribution to unmarried but not to married persons. In each case the evil, as perceived by the State, would be identical, and the underinclusion would be invidious.

Id. at 453-54.

2. Justice Brennan argues that "[i]t would be plainly unreasonable to assume that Massachusetts has prescribed pregnancy and the birth of an unwanted child as punishment for fornication." 405 U.S. at 448. Yet later in *Michael M. v. Superior Court*, 450 U.S. 464 (1981), California's statutory rape law would be upheld against an equal protection challenge, even though men alone could be held criminally liable for the act of sexual intercourse with a female under the age of 18 not one's wife. In *Michael M.,* Justice Rehnquist writing for a plurality of the Court reasoned:

> Because virtually all of the significant harmful and inescapably identifiable consequences of teenage pregnancy fall on the young female, a legislature acts well within its authority when it elects to punish only the participant who, by nature, suffers few of the consequences of his conduct. . . . Moreover, the risk of pregnancy itself constitutes a substantial deterrence to young females.

Id. at 473. True, Justice Brennan dissented in *Michael M.*, but whose argument is more in line with human nature? Aren't the consequences and difficulties of giving birth outside the stability and structure of marriage some disincentive to sexual intercourse by unmarried individuals?

3. Given that some contraceptives do have sometimes profound health effects, why wasn't Chief Justice Burger correct that the state could rightly limit the distribution of contraceptives to those under the supervision of a licensed pharmacist? *See, e.g.,* E. Daly et al., *Risk of Venous Thromboembolism in Users of Hormone Replacement Therapy*, 348 LANCET 977 (1996) (finding an increased risk of deep vein thrombosis in users of oral contraceptives); D.B. Thomas & R.M. Ray, *Oral Contraceptives and Invasive Adenocarcinomas and Adenosquamous Carcinomas of the Uterine Cervix, The World Health Organization Collaborative Study of Neoplasia and Steroid Contraceptives*, 144 AM. J. EPIDEMIOLOGY 281 (1996) (finding an increased risk of cervical cancer in users of oral contraceptives); F. Levi et al., *Oral Contraceptives, Menopausal Hormone Replacement Treatment and Breast Cancer Risk*, 5 EUR. J. CANCER PREVENTION 259 (1996) (confirming that breast cancer is related to oral contraceptive use and concluding that such findings ought to be considered in any risk/health assessment and public health evaluation).

4. After *Eisenstadt*, the Court leaped from clearing legal hurdles in the way of unmarried access to contraceptives to doing the same with respect to minors. In the meantime, the Court had decided *Roe v. Wade*, 410 U.S. 113 (1973), finding a right of reproductive autonomy protected under Fourteenth Amendment "liberty," and thus, it was relatively easy for the Court to invalidate a New York law that made it a crime to sell or distribute contraceptives to minors under the age of 16. *Carey v. Population Services Int'l*, 431 U.S. 678 (1977). Again, Justice Brennan wrote for the Court, stating: "[s]ince the State may not impose a blanket prohibition, or even a blanket requirement of parental consent, on the choice of a minor to terminate her pregnancy, the constitutionality of a blanket prohibition of the distribution of contraceptives to minors is *a fortiori* foreclosed." *Id.* at 694.

5. The imprecision in the identification of the fundamental right has been identified by the Justices, themselves, as a serious or at least problematic source of judicial error. Interestingly, while their methodologies differ, both Justice Scalia in *Michael H.*, and as we will shortly see, Justice Souter in the context of assisted suicide, bemoan the failure of the Court to speak at the proper level of "generality" (Scalia), 491 U.S. at 127 n.6, or "exactitude" (Souter), *Washington v. Glucksberg*, 521 U.S. 702, 772 (1997) (Souter, J., concurring).

2. Abortion

There is no more controversial subject in American constitutional law than that of abortion. In 1973 when *Roe* was decided, thirty-one states had laws prohibiting abortion except to save the life of the mother. Clark D. Forsythe, *The*

Effective Enforcement of Abortion Law Before Roe v. Wade, *in* THE SILENT SUB-JECT 179, 194 (Brad Stetson ed., 1996). Just before *Roe v. Wade*, 410 U.S. 113 (1973), Michigan and North Dakota voters overwhelmingly rejected liberalization of their state abortion restrictions. *Id.* If nontextual fundamental rights originate in the history and tradition of the nation, abortion presents the stark anomaly of the crime made into fundamental right.

ROE v. WADE
410 U.S. 113 (1973)

MR. JUSTICE BLACKMUN delivered the opinion of the Court.

This Texas federal appeal and its Georgia companion, *Doe v. Bolton*, present constitutional challenges to state criminal abortion legislation. The Texas statutes under attack here are typical of those that have been in effect in many States for approximately a century. The Georgia statutes, in contrast, have a modern cast and are a legislative product that, to an extent at least, obviously reflects the influences of recent attitudinal change, of advancing medical knowledge and techniques, and of new thinking about an old issue.

We forthwith acknowledge our awareness of the sensitive and emotional nature of the abortion controversy, of the vigorous opposing views, even among physicians, and of the deep and seemingly absolute convictions that the subject inspires. One's philosophy, one's experiences, one's exposure to the raw edges of human existence, one's religious training, one's attitudes toward life and family and their values, and the moral standards one establishes and seeks to observe, are all likely to influence and to color one's thinking and conclusions about abortion.

* * *

Our task, of course, is to resolve the issue by constitutional measurement, free of emotion and of predilection. We seek earnestly to do this, and, because we do, we . . . place some emphasis upon, medical and medical-legal history and what that history reveals about man's attitudes toward the abortion procedure over the centuries. We bear in mind, too, Mr. Justice Holmes' admonition in his now-vindicated dissent in *Lochner v. New York* (1905*)*:

> "[The Constitution] is made for people of fundamentally differing views, and the accident of our finding certain opinions natural and familiar, or novel, and even shocking, ought not to conclude our judgment upon the question whether statutes embodying them conflict with the Constitution of the United States."

I

The Texas statutes that concern us here . . . make it a crime to "procure an abortion," . . . except with respect to "an abortion procured or attempted by medical advice for the purpose of saving the life of the mother." . . .

Texas first enacted a criminal abortion statute in 1854. . . .

II

Jane Roe, a single woman who was residing in Dallas County, Texas, instituted this federal action in March 1970 against the District Attorney of the county. She sought a declaratory judgment that the Texas criminal abortion statutes were unconstitutional on their face, and an injunction restraining the defendant from enforcing the statutes.

Roe alleged that she was unmarried and pregnant; that she wished to terminate her pregnancy by an abortion "performed by a competent, licensed physician, under safe, clinical conditions"; that she was unable to get a "legal" abortion in Texas because her life did not appear to be threatened by the continuation of her pregnancy; and that she could not afford to travel to another jurisdiction in order to secure a legal abortion under safe conditions. She claimed that the Texas statutes were unconstitutionally vague and that they abridged her right of personal privacy, protected by the First, Fourth, Fifth, Ninth, and Fourteenth Amendments. By an amendment to her complaint Roe purported to sue "on behalf of herself and all other women" similarly situated.

* * *

IV

We are next confronted with issues of justiciability, standing, and abstention. . . .

* * *

Viewing Roe's case as of the time of its filing and thereafter until as late as May, there can be little dispute that it then presented a case or controversy and that, wholly apart from the class aspects, she, as a pregnant single woman thwarted by the Texas criminal abortion laws, had standing to challenge those statutes. . . .

The appellee notes, however, that the record does not disclose that Roe was pregnant at the time of the District Court hearing on May 22, 1970, or on the following June 17 when the court's opinion and judgment were filed. And he suggests that Roe's case must now be moot because she and all other members of her class are no longer subject to any 1970 pregnancy.

The usual rule in federal cases is that an actual controversy must exist at stages of appellate or certiorari review, and not simply at the date the action is initiated. But when, as here, pregnancy is a significant fact in the litigation, the normal 266-day human gestation period is so short that the pregnancy will come to term before the usual appellate process is complete. If that termination makes a case moot, pregnancy litigation seldom will survive much beyond the trial stage, and appellate review will be effectively denied. Our law should not be that rigid. Pregnancy often comes more than once to the same woman, and in the general population, if man is to survive, it will always be with us. Pregnancy provides a classic justification for a conclusion of nonmootness. It truly could be "capable of repetition, yet evading review."

We, therefore, agree with the District Court that Jane Roe had standing to undertake this litigation, that she presented a justiciable controversy, and that the termination of her 1970 pregnancy has not rendered her case moot.

* * *

V

The principal thrust of appellant's attack on the Texas statutes is that they improperly invade a right, said to be possessed by the pregnant woman, to choose to terminate her pregnancy. Appellant would discover this right in the concept of personal "liberty" embodied in the Fourteenth Amendment's Due Process Clause; or in personal marital, familial, and sexual privacy said to be protected by the Bill of Rights or its penumbras, *see Griswold v. Connecticut* (1965); *Eisenstadt v. Baird* (1972), or among those rights reserved to the people by the Ninth Amendment, *Griswold* (Goldberg, J., concurring). Before addressing this claim, we feel it desirable briefly to survey, in several aspects, the history of abortion, for such insight as that history may afford us, and then to examine the state purposes and interests behind the criminal abortion laws.

VI

It perhaps is not generally appreciated that the restrictive criminal abortion laws in effect in a majority of States today are of relatively recent vintage. Those laws, generally proscribing abortion or its attempt at any time during pregnancy except when necessary to preserve the pregnant woman's life, are not of ancient or even of common-law origin. Instead, they derive from statutory changes effected, for the most part, in the latter half of the 19th century.

1. Ancient attitudes. . . . Greek and Roman law afforded little protection to the unborn. If abortion was prosecuted in some places, it seems to have been based on a concept of a violation of the father's right to his offspring. Ancient religion did not bar abortion.

2. The Hippocratic Oath. What then of the famous Oath that has stood so long as the ethical guide of the medical profession . . . ? The Oath varies somewhat according to the particular translation, but in any translation the content is clear: "I will give no deadly medicine to anyone if asked . . . . Similarly, I will not give to a woman an abortive remedy."

. . . The Oath was not uncontested even in Hippocrates' day; only the Pythagorean school of philosophers frowned upon the related act of suicide. Most Greek thinkers, on the other hand, commended abortion, at least prior to viability. *See* PLATO, REPUBLIC, V, 461; ARISTOTLE, POLITICS, VII, 1335b 25. For the Pythagoreans, however, it was a matter of dogma. For them the embryo was animate from the moment of conception, and abortion meant destruction of a living being. The abortion clause of the Oath, therefore, "echoes Pythagorean doctrines," and "[i]n no other stratum of Greek opinion were such views held or proposed in the same spirit of uncompromising austerity."

. . . But with the end of antiquity a decided change took place. Resistance against suicide and against abortion became common. The Oath came to be popular. The emerging teachings of Christianity were in agreement with the Pythagorean ethic. The Oath "became the nucleus of all medical ethics" and "was applauded as the embodiment of truth." . . .

3. The common law. It is undisputed that at common law, abortion performed before "quickening" — the first recognizable movement of the fetus in utero, appearing usually from the 16th to the 18th week of pregnancy — was not an indictable offense. The absence of a common-law crime for pre-quickening abortion appears to have developed from a confluence of earlier philosophical, theological, and civil and canon law concepts of when life begins. These disciplines variously approached the question in terms of the point at which the embryo or fetus became "formed" or recognizably human, or in terms of when a "person" came into being, that is, infused with a "soul" or "animated." A loose consensus evolved in early English law that these events occurred at some point between conception and live birth. This was "mediate animation." Although Christian theology and the canon law came to fix the point of animation at 40 days for a male and 80 days for a female, a view that persisted until the 19th century, there was otherwise little agreement about the precise time of formation or animation. There was agreement, however, that prior to this point the fetus was to be regarded as part of the mother, and its destruction, therefore, was not homicide. Due to continued uncertainty about the precise time when animation occurred, to the lack of any empirical basis for the 40-80-day view, and perhaps to Aquinas' definition of movement as one of the two first principles of life, Bracton focused upon quickening as the critical point. The significance of quickening was echoed by later common-law scholars and found its way into the received common law in this country.

Whether abortion of a quick fetus was a felony at common law, or even a lesser crime, is still disputed. Bracton, writing early in the 13th century, thought it homicide. But the later and predominant view, following the great common-law scholars, has been that it was, at most, a lesser offense. In a frequently cited passage, Coke took the position that abortion of a woman "quick with childe" is "a great misprision, and no murder." Blackstone followed, saying that while abortion after quickening had once been considered manslaughter (though not murder), "modern law" took a less severe view. A recent review of the common-law precedents argues, however, that those precedents contradict Coke and that even post-quickening abortion was never established as a common-law crime. This is of some importance because while most American courts ruled, in holding or dictum, that abortion of an unquickened fetus was not criminal under their received common law, others followed Coke in stating that abortion of a quick fetus was a "misprision," a term they translated to mean "misdemeanor." That their reliance on Coke on this aspect of the law was uncritical and, apparently in all the reported cases, dictum (due probably to the paucity of common-law prosecutions for post-quickening abortion), makes it now appear doubtful that abortion was ever firmly established as a common-law crime even with respect to the destruction of a quick fetus.

4. The English statutory law. England's first criminal abortion statute . . . came in 1803. It made abortion of a quick fetus a capital crime, but it provided lesser penalties for the felony of abortion before quickening, and thus preserved the "quickening" distinction. . . .

5. The American law. In this country, the law in effect in all but a few States until mid-19th century was the pre-existing English common law. Connecticut, the first State to enact abortion legislation, adopted in 1821 that part of Lord Ellenborough's Act that related to a woman "quick with child." The death penalty was not imposed. Abortion before quickening was made a crime in that State only in 1860. In 1828, New York enacted legislation that, in two respects, was to serve as a model for early anti-abortion statutes. First, while barring destruction of an unquickend fetus as well as a quick fetus, it made the former only a misdemeanor, but the latter second-degree manslaughter. Second, it incorporated a concept of therapeutic abortion by providing that an abortion was excused if it "shall have been necessary to preserve the life of such mother, or shall have been advised by two physicians to be necessary for such purpose." By 1840, when Texas had received the common law, only eight American States had statutes dealing with abortion. It was not until after the War Between the States that legislation began generally to replace the common law. Most of these initial statutes dealt severely with abortion after quickening but were lenient with it before quickening. . . .

Gradually, in the middle and late 19th century the quickening distinction disappeared from the statutory law of most States and the degree of the offense and the penalties were increased. By the end of the 1950's a large majority of the jurisdictions banned abortion, however and whenever performed, unless done to save or preserve the life of the mother. . . . In the past several years, however, a trend toward liberalization of abortion statutes has resulted in adoption, by about one-third of the States, of less stringent laws . . . .

It is thus apparent that at common law, at the time of the adoption of our Constitution, and throughout the major portion of the 19th century, abortion was viewed with less disfavor than under most American statutes currently in effect. Phrasing it another way, a woman enjoyed a substantially broader right to terminate a pregnancy than she does in most States today. At least with respect to the early stage of pregnancy, and very possibly without such a limitation, the opportunity to make this choice was present in this country well into the 19th century. Even later, the law continued for some time to treat less punitively an abortion procured in early pregnancy.

6. The position of the American Medical Association. The anti-abortion mood prevalent in this country in the late 19th century was shared by the medical pro-

fession. Indeed, the attitude of the profession may have played a significant role in the enactment of stringent criminal abortion legislation during that period.

An AMA Committee on Criminal Abortion was appointed in May 1857. It presented its report to the Twelfth Annual Meeting. That report observed that the Committee had been appointed to investigate criminal abortion "with a view to its general suppression." It deplored abortion and its frequency and it listed three causes of "this general demoralization":

> "The first of these causes is a wide-spread popular ignorance of the true character of the crime — a belief, even among mothers themselves, that the foetus is not alive till after the period of quickening.

> "The second of the agents alluded to is the fact that the profession themselves are frequently supposed careless of foetal life. . . .

> "The third reason of the frightful extent of this crime is found in the grave defects of our laws, both common and statute, as regards the independent and actual existence of the child before birth, as a living being. These errors, which are sufficient in most instances to prevent conviction, are based, and only based, upon mistaken and exploded medical dogmas. With strange inconsistency, the law fully acknowledges the foetus in utero and its inherent rights, for civil purposes; while personally and as criminally affected, it fails to recognize it, and to its life as yet denies all protection."

The Committee then offered, and the Association adopted, resolutions protesting "against such unwarrantable destruction of human life," calling upon state legislatures to revise their abortion laws, and requesting the cooperation of state medical societies "in pressing the subject."

Except for periodic condemnation of the criminal abortionist, no further formal AMA action took place until 1967. In that year, the Committee on Human Reproduction urged the adoption of a stated policy of opposition to induced abortion, except when there is "documented medical evidence" of a threat to the health or life of the mother, or that the child "may be born with incapacitating physical deformity or mental deficiency," or that a pregnancy "resulting from legally established statutory or forcible rape or incest may constitute a threat to the mental or physical health of the patient" . . . .

In 1970, . . . the House of Delegates adopted . . . resolutions[, which] emphasized "the best interests of the patient," "sound clinical judgment," and "informed patient consent," in contrast to "mere acquiescence to the patient's demand." The resolutions asserted that abortion is a medical procedure that should be performed by a licensed physician in an accredited hospital only after consultation with two other physicians and in conformity with state law, and that no party to the procedure should be required to violate personally held moral principles. . . .

* * *

VII

Three reasons have been advanced to explain historically the enactment of criminal abortion laws in the 19th century and to justify their continued existence.

It has been argued occasionally that these laws were the product of a Victorian social concern to discourage illicit sexual conduct. Texas, however, does not advance this justification in the present case, and it appears that no court or commentator has taken the argument seriously. The appellants and *amici* contend, moreover, that this is not a proper state purpose at all and suggest that, if it were, the Texas statutes are overbroad in protecting it since the law fails to distinguish between married and unwed mothers.

A second reason is concerned with abortion as a medical procedure. When most criminal abortion laws were first enacted, the procedure was a hazardous one for the woman. . . . Abortion mortality was high. Even after 1900, and perhaps until as late as the development of antibiotics in the 1940's, standard modern techniques such as dilation and curettage were not nearly so safe as they are today. Thus, it has been argued that a State's real concern in enacting a criminal abortion law was to protect the pregnant woman, that is, to restrain her from submitting to a procedure that placed her life in serious jeopardy.

Modern medical techniques have altered this situation. Appellants and various *amici* refer to medical data indicating that abortion in early pregnancy, that is, prior to the end of the first trimester, although not without its risk, is now relatively safe. Mortality rates for women undergoing early abortions, where the procedure is legal, appear to be as low as or lower than the rates for normal childbirth. Consequently, any interest of the State in protecting the woman from an inherently hazardous procedure, except when it would be equally dangerous for her to forgo it, has largely disappeared. Of course, important state interests in the areas of health and medical standards do remain. The State has a legitimate interest in seeing to it that abortion, like any other medical procedure, is performed under circumstances that insure maximum safety for the patient. . . . Moreover, the risk to the woman increases as her pregnancy continues. Thus, the State retains a definite interest in protecting the woman's own health and safety when an abortion is proposed at a late stage of pregnancy.

The third reason is the State's interest — some phrase it in terms of duty — in protecting prenatal life. Some of the argument for this justification rests on the theory that a new human life is present from the moment of conception. The State's interest and general obligation to protect life then extends, it is argued, to prenatal life. Only when the life of the pregnant mother herself is at stake, balanced against the life she carries within her, should the interest of the embryo or fetus not prevail. Logically, of course, a legitimate state interest in this area need not stand or fall on acceptance of the belief that life begins at conception or at some other point prior to live birth. In assessing the State's interest, recognition may be given to the less rigid claim that as long as at least potential life is involved, the State may assert interests beyond the protection of the pregnant woman alone.

It is with these interests, and the weight to be attached to them, that this case is concerned.

VIII

The Constitution does not explicitly mention any right of privacy. In a line of decisions, however, . . . the Court has recognized that a right of personal privacy, or a guarantee of certain areas or zones of privacy, does exist under the Constitution. In varying contexts, the Court or individual Justices have, indeed, found at least the roots of that right in the First Amendment, *Stanley v. Georgia* (1969); in the Fourth and Fifth Amendments, *Terry v. Ohio* (1968); in the penumbras of the Bill of Rights, *Griswold v. Connecticut* (1969); in the Ninth Amendment, *id.* (Goldberg, J., concurring); or in the concept of liberty guaranteed by the first section of the Fourteenth Amendment, *see Meyer v. Nebraska* (1923). These decisions make it clear that only personal rights that can be deemed "fundamental" or "implicit in the concept of ordered liberty," *Palko v. Connecticut* (1937), are included in this guarantee of personal privacy. They also make it clear that the right has some extension to activities relating to marriage, *Loving v. Virginia* (1967); procreation, *Skinner v. Oklahoma* (1942); contraception, *Eisenstadt v. Baird*; family relationships, *Prince v. Massachusetts* (1944); and child rearing and education, *Pierce v. Society of Sisters* (1925), *Meyer v. Nebraska, supra.*

This right of privacy, whether it be founded in the Fourteenth Amendment's concept of personal liberty and restrictions upon state action, as we feel it is, or, as the District Court determined, in the Ninth Amendment's reservation of rights to the people, is broad enough to encompass a woman's decision whether or not to terminate her pregnancy. The detriment that the State would impose upon the pregnant woman by denying this choice altogether is apparent. Specific and direct harm medically diagnosable even in early pregnancy may be involved. Maternity, or additional offspring, may force upon the woman a distressful life and future. Psychological harm may be imminent. Mental and physical health may be taxed by child care. There is also the distress, for all concerned, associated with the unwanted child, and there is the problem of bringing a child into a family already unable, psychologically and otherwise, to care for it. In other cases, as in this one, the additional difficulties and continuing stigma of unwed motherhood may be involved. All these are factors the woman and her responsible physician necessarily will consider in consultation.

On the basis of elements such as these, appellant and some *amici* argue that the woman's right is absolute and that she is entitled to terminate her pregnancy at whatever time, in whatever way, and for whatever reason she alone chooses. With this we do not agree. Appellant's arguments that Texas either has no valid interest at all in regulating the abortion decision, or no interest strong enough to support any limitation upon the woman's sole determination, are unpersuasive. The Court's decisions recognizing a right of privacy also acknowledge that some state regulation in areas protected by that right is appropriate. As noted above, a State may properly assert important interests in safeguarding health, in maintaining medical standards, and in protecting potential life. At some point in pregnancy, these respective interests become sufficiently compelling to sustain regulation of the factors that govern the abortion decision. The privacy right involved, therefore, cannot be said to be absolute. In fact, it is not clear to us that the claim asserted by some *amici* that one has an unlimited right to do with one's body as one pleases bears a close relationship to the right of privacy previously articulated in the Court's decisions. The Court has refused to recognize an unlimited right of this kind in the past. *Jacobson v. Massachusetts* (1905) (vaccination); *Buck v. Bell* (1927) (sterilization).

We, therefore, conclude that the right of personal privacy includes the abortion decision, but that this right is not unqualified and must be considered against important state interests in regulation.

* * *

Where certain "fundamental rights" are involved, the Court has held that regulation limiting these rights may be justified only by a "compelling state interest," and that legislative enactments must be narrowly drawn to express only the legitimate state interests at stake.

* * *

IX

* * *

A. The appellee and certain *amici* argue that the fetus is a "person" within the language and meaning of the Fourteenth Amendment. In support of this, they outline at length and in detail the well-known facts of fetal development. If this suggestion of personhood is established, the appellant's case, of course, collapses, for the fetus' right to life would then be guaranteed specifically by the Amendment. The appellant conceded as much on reargument. On the other hand, the appellee conceded on reargument that no case could be cited that holds that a fetus is a person within the meaning of the Fourteenth Amendment.

The Constitution does not define "person" in so many words. Section 1 of the Fourteenth Amendment contains three references to "person." The first, in defining "citizens," speaks of "persons born or naturalized in the United States." The word also appears both in the Due Process Clause and in the Equal Protection Clause. "Person" is used in other places in the Constitution . . . . But in nearly all these instances, the use of the word is such that it has application only postnatally. None indicates, with any assurance, that it has any possible prenatal application.

All this, together with our observation, *supra*, that throughout the major portion of the 19th century prevailing legal abortion practices were far freer than they are today, persuades us that the word "person," as used in the Fourteenth Amendment, does not include the unborn. . . .

This conclusion, however, does not of itself fully answer the contentions raised by Texas, and we pass on to other considerations.

B. The pregnant woman cannot be isolated in her privacy. She carries an embryo and, later, a fetus, if one accepts the medical definitions of the developing young in the human uterus. The situation therefore is inherently different from marital intimacy, or bedroom possession of obscene material, or marriage, or procreation, or education, with which *Eisenstadt* and *Griswold, Stanley, Loving, Skinner* and *Pierce* and *Meyer* were respectively concerned. As we have intimated above, it is reasonable and appropriate for a State to decide that at some point in time another interest, that of health of the mother or that of potential human life, becomes significantly involved. The woman's privacy is no longer sole and any right of privacy she possesses must be measured accordingly.

Texas urges that, apart from the Fourteenth Amendment, life begins at conception and is present throughout pregnancy, and that, therefore, the State has a compelling interest in protecting that life from and after conception. We need not resolve the difficult question of when life begins. When those trained in the respective disciplines of medicine, philosophy, and theology are unable to arrive at any consensus, the judiciary, at this point in the development of man's knowledge, is not in a position to speculate as to the answer.

It should be sufficient to note briefly the wide divergence of thinking on this most sensitive and difficult question. There has always been strong support for the view that life does not begin until live birth. This was the belief of the Stoics. It appears to be the predominant, though not the unanimous, attitude of the Jewish faith. It may be taken to represent also the position of a large segment of the Protestant community, insofar as that can be ascertained; organized groups that have taken a formal position on the abortion issue have generally regarded abortion as a matter for the conscience of the individual and her family. As we have noted, the common law found greater significance in quickening. Physicians and their scientific colleagues have regarded that event with less interest and have tended to focus either upon conception, upon live birth, or upon the interim point at which the fetus becomes "viable," that is, potentially able to live outside the mother's womb, albeit with artificial aid. Viability is usually placed at about seven months (28 weeks) but may occur earlier, even at 24 weeks. The Aristotelian theory of "mediate animation," that held sway throughout the Middle Ages and the Renaissance in Europe, continued to be official Roman Catholic dogma until the 19th century, despite opposition to this "ensoulment" theory from those in the Church who would recognize the existence of life from the moment of conception. The latter is now, of course, the official belief of the Catholic Church. As one *amicus* brief discloses, this is a view strongly held by many non-Catholics as well, and by many physicians. Substantial problems for precise definition of this view are posed, however, by new embryological data that purport to indicate that conception is a "process" over time, rather than an event, and by new medical techniques such as menstrual extraction, the "morning-after" pill, implantation of embryos, artificial insemination, and even artificial wombs.

In areas other than criminal abortion, the law has been reluctant to endorse any theory that life, as we recognize it, begins before life birth or to accord legal rights to the unborn except in narrowly defined situations and except when the rights are contingent upon live birth. For example, the traditional rule of tort law denied recovery for prenatal injuries even though the child was born alive. That rule has been changed in almost every jurisdiction. In most States, recovery is said to be permitted only if the fetus was viable, or at least quick, when the injuries were sustained, though few courts have squarely so held. In a recent development, generally opposed by the commentators, some States permit the parents of a stillborn child to maintain an action for wrongful death because of prenatal injuries. Such an action, however, would appear to be one to vindicate the parents' interest and is thus consistent with the view that the fetus, at most, represents only the potentiality of life. Similarly, unborn children have been recognized as acquiring rights or interests by way of inheritance or other devolution of property, and have been represented by guardians ad litem. Perfection of the interests involved, again, has generally been contingent upon live birth. In short, the unborn have never been recognized in the law as persons in the whole sense.

X

In view of all this, we do not agree that, by adopting one theory of life, Texas may override the rights of the pregnant woman that are at stake. We repeat, however, that the State does have an important and legitimate interest in preserving and protecting the health of the pregnant woman, whether she be a resident of the State or a non-resident who seeks medical consultation and treatment there, and that it has still another important and legitimate interest in protecting the potentiality of human life. These interests are separate and distinct. Each grows in substantiality as the woman approaches term and, at a point during pregnancy, each becomes "compelling."

With respect to the State's important and legitimate interest in the health of the mother, the "compelling" point, in the light of present medical knowledge, is at approximately the end of the first trimester. This is so because of the now-established medical fact, referred to above, that until the end of the first trimester mortality in abortion may be less than mortality in normal childbirth. It follows that, from and after this point, a State may regulate the abortion procedure to the extent that the regulation reasonably relates to the preservation and protection of maternal health. Examples of permissible state regulation in this area are requirements as to the qualifications of the person who is to perform the abortion; as to the licensure of that person; as to the facility in which the procedure is to be performed, that is, whether it must be a hospital or may be a clinic or some other place of less-than-hospital status; as to the licensing of the facility; and the like.

This means, on the other hand, that, for the period of pregnancy prior to this "compelling" point, the attending physician, in consultation with his patient, is free to determine, without regulation by the State, that, in his medical judgment, the patient's pregnancy should be terminated. If that decision is reached, the judgment may be effectuated by an abortion free of interference by the State.

With respect to the State's important and legitimate interest in potential life, the "compelling" point is at viability. This is so because the fetus then presumably has the capability of meaningful life outside the mother's womb. State regulation protective of fetal life after viability thus has both logical and biological justifications. If the State is interested in protecting fetal life after viability, it may go so far as to proscribe abortion during that period, except when it is necessary to preserve the life or health of the mother.

Measured against these standards, Art. 1196 of the Texas Penal Code, in restricting legal abortions to those "procured or attempted by medical advice for the purpose of saving the life of the mother," sweeps too broadly. The statute makes no distinction between abortions performed early in pregnancy and those performed later, and it limits to a single reason, "saving" the mother's life, the legal justification for the procedure. The statute, therefore, cannot survive the constitutional attack made upon it here.

* * *

XI

To summarize and to repeat:

1. A state criminal abortion statute of the current Texas type, that excepts from criminality only a life-saving procedure on behalf of the mother, without regard to pregnancy stage and without recognition of the other interests involved, is violative of the Due Process Clause of the Fourteenth Amendment.

(a) For the stage prior to approximately the end of the first trimester, the abortion decision and its effectuation must be left to the medical judgment of the pregnant woman's attending physician.

(b) For the stage subsequent to approximately the end of the first trimester, the State, in promoting its interest in the health of the mother, may, if it chooses, regulate the abortion procedure in ways that are reasonably related to maternal health.

(c) For the stage subsequent to viability, the State in promoting its interest in the potentiality of human life may, if it chooses, regulate, and even proscribe, abortion except where it is necessary, in appropriate medical judgment, for the preservation of the life or health of the mother.

2. The State may define the term "physician," as it has been employed in the preceding paragraphs of this Part XI of this opinion, to mean only a physician currently licensed by the State, and may proscribe any abortion by a person who is not a physician as so defined.

* * *

This holding, we feel, is consistent with the relative weights of the respective interests involved, with the lessons and examples of medical and legal history, with the lenity of the common law, and with the demands of the profound problems of the present day. The decision leaves the State free to place increasing restrictions on abortion as the period of pregnancy lengthens, so long as those restrictions are tailored to the recognized state interests. The decision vindicates the right of the physician to administer medical treatment according to his professional judgment up to the points where important state interests provide compelling justifications for intervention. Up to those points, the abortion decision in all its aspects is inherently, and primarily, a medical decision, and basic responsibility for it must rest with the physician. If an individual practitioner abuses the privilege of exercising proper medical judgment, the usual remedies, judicial and intra-professional, are available.

XII

* * *

We find it unnecessary to decide whether the District Court erred in withholding injunctive relief, for we assume the Texas prosecutorial authorities will give full credence to this decision that the present criminal abortion statutes of that State are unconstitutional.

Affirmed in part and reversed in part.

MR. JUSTICE STEWART, concurring.

In 1963, this Court purported to sound the death knell for the doctrine of substantive due process, a doctrine under which many state laws had in the past been held to violate the Fourteenth Amendment. As Mr. Justice Black's opinion for the Court in [*Ferguson v.*] *Skrupa* put it: "We have returned to the original constitutional proposition that courts do not substitute their social and economic beliefs for the judgment of legislative bodies, who are elected to pass laws."

Barely tho years later, in *Griswold*, the Court held a Connecticut birth control law unconstitutional. In view of what had been so recently said in *Skrupa*, the Court's opinion in *Griswold* understandably did its best to avoid reliance on the Due Process Clause of the Fourteenth Amendment as the ground for decision. Yet, the Connecticut law did not violate any provision of the Bill of Rights, nor any other specific provision of the Constitution. So it was clear to me then, and it is equally clear to me now, that the *Griswold* decision can be rationally understood only as a holding that the Connecticut statute substantively invaded the "liberty" that is protected by the Due Process Clause of the Fourteenth

Amendment. As so understood, *Griswold* stands as one in a long line of pre-*Skrupa* cases decided under the doctrine of substantive due process, and I now accept it as such.

* * *

As Mr. Justice Harlan once wrote: "[T]he full scope of the liberty guaranteed by the Due Process Clause cannot be found in or limited by the precise terms of the specific guarantees elsewhere provided in the Constitution. This 'liberty' is not a series of isolated points priced out in terms of the taking of property; the freedom of speech, press, and religion; the right to keep and bear arms; the freedom from unreasonable searches and seizures; and so on. It is a rational continuum which, broadly speaking, includes a freedom from all substantial arbitrary impositions and purposeless restraints . . . and which also recognizes, what a reasonable and sensitive judgment must, that certain interests require particularly careful scrutiny of the state needs asserted to justify their abridgment." In the words of Mr. Justice Frankfurter, "Great concepts like . . . 'liberty' . . . were purposely left to gather meaning from experience. For they relate to the whole domain of social and economic fact, and the statesmen who founded this Nation knew too well that only a stagnant society remains unchanged."

Several decisions of this Court make clear that freedom of personal choice in matters of marriage and family life is one of the liberties protected by the Due Process Clause of the Fourteenth Amendment. *Loving v. Virginia, Griswold v. Connecticut, Pierce v. Society of Sisters, Meyer v. Nebraska.* As recently as last Term, in *Eisenstadt*, we recognized "the right of the individual, married or single, to be free from unwarranted governmental intrusion into matters so fundamentally affecting a person as the decision whether to bear or beget a child." That right necessarily includes the right of a woman to decide whether or not to terminate her pregnancy. "Certainly the interests of a woman in giving of her physical and emotional self during pregnancy and the interests that will be affected throughout her life by the birth and raising of a child are of a far greater degree of significance and personal intimacy than the right to send a child to private school protected in *Pierce*, or the right to teach a foreign language protected in *Meyer*.

Clearly, therefore, the Court today is correct in holding that the right asserted by Jane Roe is embraced within the personal liberty protected by the Due Process Clause of the Fourteenth Amendment.

It is evident that the Texas abortion statute infringes that right directly. Indeed, it is difficult to imagine a more complete abridgment of a constitutional freedom than that worked by the inflexible criminal statute now in force in Texas. The question then becomes whether the state interests advanced to justify this abridgment can survive the "particularly careful scrutiny" that the Fourteenth Amendment here requires.

The asserted state interests are protection of the health and safety of the pregnant woman, and protection of the potential future human life within her.

These are legitimate objectives, amply sufficient to permit a State to regulate abortions as it does other surgical procedures, and perhaps sufficient to permit a State to regulate abortions more stringently or even to prohibit them in the late stages of pregnancy. But such legislation is not before us, and I think the Court today has thoroughly demonstrated that these state interests cannot constitutionally support the broad abridgment of personal liberty worked by the existing Texas law. Accordingly, I join the Court's opinion holding that that law is invalid under the Due Process Clause of the Fourteenth Amendment.

MR. JUSTICE REHNQUIST, dissenting.

* * *

While the Court's opinion quotes from the dissent of Mr. Justice Holmes in *Lochner v. New York* (1905), the result it reaches is more closely attuned to the majority opinion of Mr. Justice Peckham in that case. As in *Lochner* and similar cases applying substantive due process standards to economic and social welfare legislation, the adoption of the compelling state interest standard will inevitably require this Court to examine the legislative policies and pass on the wisdom of these policies in the very process of deciding whether a particular state interest put forward may or may not be "compelling." The decision here to break pregnancy into three distinct terms and to outline the permissible restrictions the State may impose in each one, for example, partakes more of judicial legislation than it does of a determination of the intent of the drafters of the Fourteenth Amendment.

The fact that a majority of the States reflecting, after all, the majority sentiment in those States, have had restrictions on abortions for at least a century is a strong indication, it seems to me, that the asserted right to an abortion is not "so rooted in the traditions and conscience of our people as to be ranked as fundamental." Even today, when society's views on abortion are changing, the very existence of the debate is evidence that the "right" to an abortion is not so universally accepted as the appellant would have us believe.

To reach its result, the Court necessarily has had to find within the scope of the Fourteenth Amendment a right that was apparently completely unknown to the drafters of the Amendment. As early as 1821, the first state law dealing directly with abortion was enacted by the Connecticut Legislature. By the time of the adoption of the Fourteenth Amendment in 1868, there were at least 36 laws enacted by state or territorial legislatures limiting abortion. While many States have amended or updated their laws, 21 of the laws on the books in 1868 remain in effect today. Indeed, the Texas statute struck down today was, as the majority notes, first enacted in 1857 and "has remained substantially unchanged to the present time."

There apparently was no question concerning the validity of this provision or of any of the other state statutes when the Fourteenth Amendment was adopted. The only conclusion possible from this history is that the drafters did not intend to have the Fourteenth Amendment withdraw from the States the power to legislate with respect to this matter.

III

Even if one were to agree that the case that the Court decides were here, and that the enunciation of the substantive constitutional law in the Court's opinion were proper, the actual disposition of the case by the Court is still difficult to justify. The Texas statute is struck down in toto, even though the Court apparently concedes that at later periods of pregnancy Texas might impose these selfsame statutory limitations on abortion. My understanding of past practice is that a statute found to be invalid as applied to a particular plaintiff, but not unconstitutional as a whole, is not simply "struck down" but is, instead, declared unconstitutional as applied to the fact situation before the Court.

For all of the foregoing reasons, I respectfully dissent.

NOTES AND QUESTIONS

1. Recent scholarship questions Justice Blackmun's history. As Clark D. Forsythe, president of Americans United for Life, writes:

> [T]he Court relied almost entirely on the work of one law professor, Cyril Means, who happened to be chief counsel for [the National Abortion Rights Action League]. . . . [T]here can be no question, if the historical facts are considered, that abortion was considered a crime of some degree by the common law at *every* stage of gestation and was *never* protected as a right.

Clark D. Forsythe, *The Effective Enforcement of Abortion Law Before* Roe v. Wade, *in* THE SILENT SUBJECT 183 (Brad Stetson ed., 1996). Regardless of one's view of the issue, there is indeed evidence that abortion prohibitions date back at least to the 13th century, and an excellent catalogue of the common law cases prohibiting the practice can be found in Brief for the American Academy of Medical Ethics at 13 n.18, *Hope v. Perales*, 634 N.E.2d 183 (N.Y. 1994) (No. 23); *see also*, Joseph W. Dellapenna, *The Historical Case Against Abortion*, 13 CONTINUITY 59 (1989). Feminist historians have documented several 17th century cases in colonial America of the crime of abortion. *See* JULIA CHERRY SPRUILL, WOMEN'S LIFE AND WORK IN THE SOUTHERN COLONIES 325-26 (1972).

The most obvious explanation for some of these historical differences of opinion was the difficulty of determining the existence of an early pregnancy until well into the 20th century. Pregnancy tests as late as the 1960s were unreliable. CLINICAL OBSTETRICS 110-14 (Carl J. Pauerstein ed., 1987). The common law therefore focused on quickening, the first physical movement of the child felt by the mother, but this often does not occur until 16-18 weeks in the pregnancy. It was impossible to treat abortion and homicide as one, not by reason of moral approval, but because of evidentiary difficulty. As a mid-19th century treatise explained: "[t]he signs of abortion, as obtained by an *examination of the female*, are not very certain in their character. . . . When abortion occurs in the early months, it leaves but slight and evanescent traces behind it." 3 FRANCIS WHAR- TON & MORETON STILLE, A TREATISE ON MEDICAL JURISPRUDENCE § 107, at 77 (Philadelphia, Kay & Brother, 4th ed. 1884).

2. Does *Roe* forsake the principle of the sanctity of human life? Is this depar- ture from natural law principle required or contemplated by constitutional text? Without any firm grounding in history, and even less in text, Justice Blackmun argues:

> This right of privacy, whether it be founded in the Fourteenth Amend- ment's conception of personal liberty and restrictions upon state action, as we feel it is, or, . . . in the Ninth Amendment's reservation of rights to the people, is broad enough to encompass a woman's decision whether or not to terminate her pregnancy.

410 U.S. at 153. Categorizing abortion as a fundamental, but not absolute, right, the Court held that any state restriction must be in pursuit of a compelling interest and "narrowly drawn to express only the legitimate state interests at stake." *Id.* at 155.

Because the word "persons" is employed in the text of the Constitution and these persons are guaranteed due process as well as equal protection, the *Roe* Court needed to exclude unborn children from legal "personhood" and thus, the protection of the law. *Cf.*, Raymond B. Marcin, *"Posterity" in the Preamble and a Positivist Pro-Life Position*, 38 AM. J. JURIS. 273 (1993) ("the Constitution can and perhaps should be interpreted [from a positivist perspective] as [pro- tecting] the right to life of fetuses or unborn children"). Yet, the Court states:

> The Constitution does not define "person" in so many words. Section 1 of the Fourteenth Amendment contains three references to "person." The first, in defining "citizens," speaks of "persons born or naturalized in the United States." The word also appears both in the Due Process Clause and the Equal Protection Clause. . . . But in nearly all these instances, the use of the word is such that it has application only postnatally. None indicates, with any assurance, that it has any possible prenatal application.

Id. at 157 (footnote omitted). Do you find the Court's reasoning persuasive?

3. The decision in *Roe* incorporated what became known as a trimester analy- sis. During the first three months of pregnancy, states were allowed only to pro- tect maternal health and regulate abortion as they would medical procedures generally — effectively, this meant no specialized abortion regulation; in the sec- ond trimester, the government "may, if it chooses, regulate the abortion proce- dure in ways that are reasonably related to maternal health," *id.* at 164, and in the last trimester — after viability — the government may prohibit abortions except if necessary to preserve the life or health of the mother. Presumably, the state's interest in prenatal life was recognized in these last months, but the health exception was open-ended. In particular, the "health" of the mother exception was given an expansive definition in the companion case of *Doe v. Bolton*, 410 U.S. 179 (1973). Justice Blackmun wrote that an abortion may be directed by the exercise of professional judgment "in the light of all factors — physical, emotional, psychological, familial, and the woman's age — relevant to the well-being of the patient." *Id.* at 192.

Justices White and Rehnquist dissented in *Roe*. White called the opinion "an exercise of raw judicial power" that in his view was "improvident." 410 U.S. at 222 (White, J., dissenting). Both of the dissenting justices would have left the matter to state legislatures.

4. *Roe* triggered great controversy. John Hart Ely wrote that:

> The problem with *Roe* is not so much that it bungles the question it sets itself, but rather that it sets itself a question the Constitution has not made the Court's business.

* * *

> . . . [*Roe* is] a very bad decision. . . . It is bad because it is bad constitutional law, or rather because it is *not* constitutional law and gives almost no sense of an obligation to try to be.

John Hart Ely, *The Wages of Crying Wolf: A Comment on* Roe v. Wade, 82 YALE L.J. 920, 943, 947 (1973). But can *Roe* really be singled out in this way, given the Court's earlier decision in say, *Eisenstadt*? What distinguishes *Roe* from the non-textual recognition of the right to marry or to direct the upbringing of children? If your answer is that marriage and parenting are consistent with human life and its development, while abortion is the opposite, is this a natural law argument, and is it the kind of argument that can be made to the Supreme Court? Of course, if the criticism of *Roe* is that it devalues human life, isn't the very premise of that assessment a natural law one in the sense that it depends upon a belief that what counts as life is a natural fact to be discovered. However, Frances Olsen argues, "[t]he value of life is not a simple attribute of any particular life form, something that can be discovered. Culturally created, the value of life rests on social meanings, and, importantly, on sexual politics." Frances Olsen, *Unraveling Compromise*, 103 HARV. L. REV. 105, 127-28 (1989). If you think Ms. Olsen is on to something, was it also true that the value of slave life was the product of "social meanings" and racial politics?

5. By 1989, the Court, with some new members appointed by President Reagan, seemed ready to overrule *Roe*. Five times, President Reagan had his Solicitor General ask the Supreme Court to re-consider *Roe*, but each time the Court refused. In the next case, the Court again reaffirms *Roe*, but with modifications or qualifications that continue to be the source of litigation and dispute.

PLANNED PARENTHOOD OF SOUTHEASTERN PENN-SYLVANIA v. CASEY
505 U.S. 833 (1992)

JUSTICE O'CONNOR, JUSTICE KENNEDY, and JUSTICE SOUTER announced the judgment of the Court and delivered the opinion of the Court with respect to Parts I, II, III, V-A, V-C, and VI, an opinion with respect to Part V-E, in which JUSTICE STEVENS joins, and an opinion with respect to Parts IV, V-B, and V-D.

I

Liberty finds no refuge in a jurisprudence of doubt. Yet 19 years after our holding that the Constitution protects a woman's right to terminate her pregnancy in its early stages, *Roe v. Wade* (1973), that definition of liberty is still questioned. Joining the respondents as *amicus curiae*, the United States, as it has done in five other cases in the last decade, again asks us to overrule *Roe*.

At issue in these cases are five provisions of the Pennsylvania Abortion Control Act of 1982, as amended in 1988 and 1989. 18 Pa. Cons. Stat. §§ 3203-3220 (1990). The Act requires that a woman seeking an abortion give her informed consent prior to the abortion procedure, and specifies that she be provided with certain information at least 24 hours before the abortion is performed. § 3205. For a minor to obtain an abortion, the Act requires the informed consent of one of her parents, but provides for a judicial bypass option if the minor does not wish to or cannot obtain a parent's consent. § 3206. Another provision of the Act requires that, unless certain exceptions apply, a married woman seeking an abortion must sign a statement indicating that she has notified her husband of her intended abortion. § 3209. The Act exempts compliance with these three requirements in the event of a "medical emergency," which is defined in § 3203 of the Act. In addition to the above provisions regulating the performance of abortions, the Act imposes certain reporting requirements on facilities that provide abortion services. §§ 3207(b), 3214(a), 3214(f).

* * *

After considering the fundamental constitutional questions resolved by *Roe*, principles of institutional integrity, and the rule of *stare decisis*, we are led to conclude this: the essential holding of *Roe v. Wade* should be retained and once again reaffirmed.

It must be stated at the outset and with clarity that *Roe*'s essential holding, the holding we reaffirm, has three parts. First is a recognition of the right of the woman to choose to have an abortion before viability and to obtain it without undue interference from the State. Before viability, the State's interests are not strong enough to support a prohibition of abortion or the imposition of a substantial obstacle to the woman's effective right to elect the procedure. Second is a confirmation of the State's power to restrict abortions after fetal viability, if the law contains exceptions for pregnancies which endanger the woman's life or health. And third is the principle that the State has legitimate interests from the outset of the pregnancy in protecting the health of the woman and the life of the fetus that may become a child. These principles do not contradict one another; and we adhere to each.

II

Constitutional protection of the woman's decision to terminate her pregnancy derives from the Due Process Clause of the Fourteenth Amendment. It declares that no State shall "deprive any person of life, liberty, or property, without due process of law." . . .

The most familiar of the substantive liberties protected by the Fourteenth Amendment are those recognized by the Bill of Rights. We have held that the Due Process Clause of the Fourteenth Amendment incorporates most of the Bill of Rights against the States. *See, e.g., Duncan v. Louisiana* (1968). It is tempting, as a means of curbing the discretion of federal judges, to suppose that liberty encompasses no more than those rights already guaranteed to the individual against federal interference by the express provisions of the first eight Amendments to the Constitution. But of course this Court has never accepted that view.

* * *

Neither the Bill of Rights nor the specific practices of States at the time of the adoption of the Fourteenth Amendment marks the outer limits of the substantive sphere of liberty which the Fourteenth Amendment protects. *See* U.S. Const., Amdt. 9. . . .

The inescapable fact is that adjudication of substantive due process claims may call upon the Court in interpreting the Constitution to exercise that same capacity which by tradition courts always have exercised: reasoned judgment. Its boundaries are not susceptible of expression as a simple rule. That does not mean we are free to invalidate state policy choices with which we disagree; yet neither does it permit us to shrink from the duties of our office. . . .

* * *

Our law affords constitutional protection to personal decisions relating to marriage, procreation, contraception, family relationships, child rearing, and education. . . . These matters, involving the most intimate and personal choices a person may make in a lifetime, choices central to personal dignity and autonomy, are central to the liberty protected by the Fourteenth Amendment. At the heart of liberty is the right to define one's own concept of existence, of meaning, of the universe, and of the mystery of human life. . . .

* * *

III

A

The obligation to follow precedent begins with necessity, and a contrary necessity marks its outer limit. . . .

Even when the decision to overrule a prior case is not, as in the rare, latter instance, virtually foreordained, it is common wisdom that the rule of *stare decisis* is not an "inexorable command," and certainly it is not such in every constitutional case. Rather, when this Court reexamines a prior holding, its judgment is customarily informed by a series of prudential and pragmatic considerations designed to test the consistency of overruling a prior decision with the ideal of the rule of law, and to gauge the respective costs of reaffirming and overruling a prior case. . . .

So in this case we may enquire whether *Roe*'s central rule has been found unworkable; whether the rule's limitation on state power could be removed without serious inequity to those who have relied upon it or significant damage to the stability of the society governed by it; whether the law's growth in the intervening years has left *Roe*'s central rule a doctrinal anachronism discounted by society; and whether *Roe*'s premises of fact have so far changed in the ensuing two decades as to render its central holding somehow irrelevant or unjustifiable in dealing with the issue it addressed.

1

Although *Roe* has engendered opposition, it has in no sense proven "unworkable" . . . . While *Roe* has, of course, required judicial assessment of state laws affecting the exercise of the choice guaranteed against government infringement, and although the need for such review will remain as a consequence of today's decision, the required determinations fall within judicial competence.

2

The inquiry into reliance counts the cost of a rule's repudiation as it would fall on those who have relied reasonably on the rule's continued application. . . .

. . . Abortion is customarily chosen as an unplanned response to the consequence of unplanned activity or to the failure of conventional birth control, and except on the assumption that no intercourse would have occurred but for *Roe*'s holding, such behavior may appear to justify no reliance claim. Even if reliance could be claimed on that unrealistic assumption, the argument might run, any reliance interest would be *de minimis*. This argument would be premised on the hypothesis that reproductive planning could take virtually immediate account of any sudden restoration of state authority to ban abortions.

To eliminate the issue of reliance that easily, however, one would need to limit cognizable reliance to specific instances of sexual activity. But to do this would be simply to refuse to face the fact that for two decades of economic and social developments, people have organized intimate relationships and made choices that define their views of themselves and their places in society, in reliance on the availability of abortion in the event that contraception should fail. The ability of women to participate equally in the economic and social life of the Nation has been facilitated by their ability to control their reproductive lives. . . .

3

No evolution of legal principle has left *Roe*'s doctrinal footings weaker than they were in 1973. No development of constitutional law since the case was decided has implicitly or explicitly left *Roe* behind as a mere survivor of obsolete constitutional thinking.

It will be recognized, of course, that *Roe* stands at an intersection of two lines of decisions, but in whichever doctrinal category one reads the case, the result for present purposes will be the same. The *Roe* Court itself placed its holding in the succession of cases most prominently exemplified by *Griswold v. Connecticut*. When it is so seen, *Roe* is clearly in no jeopardy, since subsequent constitutional developments have neither disturbed, nor do they threaten to diminish, the scope of recognized protection accorded to the liberty relating to intimate relationships, the family, and decisions about whether or not to beget or bear a child.

* * *

Nor will courts building upon *Roe* be likely to hand down erroneous decisions as a consequence. Even on the assumption that the central holding of *Roe* was in error, that error would go only to the strength of the state interest in fetal protection, not to the recognition afforded by the Constitution to the woman's liberty. . . .

4

We have seen how time has overtaken some of *Roe*'s factual assumptions: advances in maternal health care allow for abortions safe to the mother later in pregnancy than was true in 1973, and advances in neonatal care have advanced viability to a point somewhat earlier. But these facts go only to the scheme of time limits on the realization of competing interests, and the divergences from the factual premises of 1973 have no bearing on the validity of *Roe*'s central holding, that viability marks the earliest point at which the State's interest in fetal life is constitutionally adequate to justify a legislative ban on nontherapeutic abortions. The soundness or unsoundness of that constitutional judgment in no sense turns on whether viability occurs at approximately 28 weeks, as was usual at the time of *Roe*, at 23 to 24 weeks, as it sometimes does today, or at some moment even slightly earlier in pregnancy, as it may if fetal respiratory capacity can somehow be enhanced in the future. Whenever it may occur, the attainment of viability may continue to serve as the critical fact, just as it has done since *Roe* was decided; which is to say that no change in *Roe*'s factual underpinning has left its central holding obsolete, and none supports an argument for overruling it.

* * *

B

In a less significant case, *stare decisis* analysis could, and would, stop at the point we have reached. But the sustained and widespread debate *Roe* has provoked calls for some comparison between that case and others of comparable dimension that have responded to national controversies and taken on the impress of the controversies addressed. Only two such decisional lines from the past century present themselves for examination, and in each instance the result reached by the Court accorded with the principles we apply today.

The first example is that line of cases identified with *Lochner v. New York* (1905), which imposed substantive limitations on legislation limiting economic autonomy in favor of health and welfare regulation, adopting, in Justice Holmes's view, the theory of laissez-faire. (dissenting opinion). . . . [Thirty-two] years later, *West Coast Hotel Co. v. Parrish* (1937), signaled the demise of *Lochner.* . . . In the meantime, the Depression had come and, with it, the lesson that seemed unmistakable to most people by 1937, that the interpretation of contractual freedom . . . rested on fundamentally false factual assumptions about the capacity of a relatively unregulated market to satisfy minimal levels of human welfare. As Justice Jackson wrote of the constitutional crisis of 1937 shortly before he came on the bench: "The older world of *laissez-faire* was recognized everywhere outside the Court to be dead." The facts upon which the earlier case had premised a constitutional resolution of social controversy had proven to be untrue, and history's demonstration of their untruth not only justified but required the new choice of constitutional principle that *West Coast Hotel* announced. Of course, it was true that the Court lost something by its misperception, or its lack of prescience, and the Court-packing crisis only magnified the loss; but the clear demonstration that the facts of economic life were different from those previously assumed warranted the repudiation of the old law.

The second comparison that 20th century history invites is with the cases employing the separate-but-equal rule for applying the Fourteenth Amendment's equal protection guarantee. They began with *Plessy v. Ferguson* (1896), holding that legislatively mandated racial segregation in public transportation works no denial of equal protection, rejecting the argument that racial separation enforced by the legal machinery of American society treats the black race as inferior. The *Plessy* Court considered "the underlying fallacy of the plaintiff's argument to consist in the assumption that the enforced separation of the two races stamps the colored race with a badge of inferiority. If this be so, it is not by reason of anything found in the act, but solely because the colored race chooses to put that construction upon it." Whether, as a matter of historical fact, the Justices in the *Plessy* majority believed this or not, this understanding of the implication of segregation was the stated justification for the Court's opinion.

But this understanding of the facts and the rule it was stated to justify were repudiated in *Brown v. Board of Education* (1954). As one commentator observed, the question before the Court in *Brown* was "whether discrimination inheres in that segregation which is imposed by law in the twentieth century in certain specific states in the American Union. And that question has meaning and can find an answer only on the ground of history and of common knowledge about the facts of life in the times and places aforesaid." Charles L. Black, Jr., *The Lawfulness of the Segregation Decisions*, 69 YALE L.J. 421, 427 (1960).

. . . While we think *Plessy* was wrong the day it was decided, we must also recognize that the *Plessy* Court's explanation for its decision was so clearly at odds with the facts apparent to the Court in 1954 that the decision to reexamine *Plessy* was on this ground alone not only justified but required.

West Coast Hotel and *Brown* each rested on facts, or an understanding of facts, changed from those which furnished the claimed justifications for the earlier constitutional resolutions. Each case was comprehensible as the Court's response to facts that the country could understand, or had come to understand already, but which the Court of an earlier day, as its own declarations disclosed, had not been able to perceive. . . .

. . . Because neither the factual underpinnings of *Roe*'s central holding nor our understanding of it has changed (and because no other indication of weakened precedent has been shown), the Court could not pretend to be reexamining the prior law with any justification beyond a present doctrinal disposition to come out differently from the Court of 1973. . . .

C

. . . Our analysis would not be complete, however, without explaining why overruling *Roe*'s central holding would not only reach an unjustifiable result under principles of *stare decisis*, but would seriously weaken the Court's capacity to exercise the judicial power and to function as the Supreme Court of a Nation dedicated to the rule of law. To understand why this would be so it is necessary to understand the source of this Court's authority, the conditions necessary for its preservation, and its relationship to the country's understanding of itself as a constitutional Republic.

The root of American governmental power is revealed most clearly in the instance of the power conferred by the Constitution upon the Judiciary of the United States and specifically upon this Court. As Americans of each succeeding generation are rightly told, the Court cannot buy support for its decisions by spending money and, except to a minor degree, it cannot independently coerce obedience to its decrees. The Court's power lies, rather, in its legitimacy, a product of substance and perception that shows itself in the people's acceptance of the Judiciary as fit to determine what the Nation's law means and to declare what it demands.

The underlying substance of this legitimacy is of course the warrant for the Court's decisions in the Constitution and the lesser sources of legal principle on which the Court draws. . . . Thus, the Court's legitimacy depends on making legally principled decisions under circumstances in which their principled character is sufficiently plausible to be accepted by the Nation.

The need for principled action to be perceived as such is implicated to some degree whenever this, or any other appellate court, overrules a prior case. This is not to say, of course, that this Court cannot give a perfectly satisfactory explanation in most cases. . . .

In two circumstances, however, the Court would almost certainly fail to receive the benefit of the doubt in overruling prior cases. There is, first, a point beyond which frequent overruling would overtax the country's belief in the Court's good faith. Despite the variety of reasons that may inform and justify a decision to overrule, we cannot forget that such a decision is usually perceived (and perceived correctly) as, at the least, a statement that a prior decision was wrong. . . .

. . . Where, in the performance of its judicial duties, the Court decides a case in such a way as to resolve the sort of intensely divisive controversy reflected in *Roe* and those rare, comparable cases, its decision has a dimension that the resolution of the normal case does not carry. It is the dimension present whenever the Court's interpretation of the Constitution calls the contending sides of a national controversy to end their national division by accepting a common mandate rooted in the Constitution.

The Court is not asked to do this very often, having thus addressed the Nation only twice in our lifetime, in the decisions of *Brown* and *Roe*. But when the Court does act in this way, its decision requires an equally rare precedential force to counter the inevitable efforts to overturn it and to thwart its implementation. Some of those efforts may be mere unprincipled emotional reactions; others may proceed from principles worthy of profound respect. But whatever the premises of opposition may be, only the most convincing justification under accepted standards of precedent could suffice to demonstrate that a later decision overruling the first was anything but a surrender to political pressure, and an unjustified repudiation of the principle on which the Court staked its authority in the first instance. So to overrule under fire in the absence of the most compelling reason to reexamine a watershed decision would subvert the Court's legitimacy beyond any serious question.

* * *

The Court's duty in the present cases is clear. In 1973, it confronted the already-divisive issue of governmental power to limit personal choice to undergo abortion, for which it provided a new resolution based on the due process guaranteed by the Fourteenth Amendment. Whether or not a new social consensus is developing on that issue, its divisiveness is no less today than in 1973, and pressure to overrule the decision, like pressure to retain it, has grown only more intense. A decision to overrule *Roe*'s essential holding under the existing circumstances would address error, if error there was, at the cost of both profound and unnecessary damage to the Court's legitimacy, and to the Nation's commitment to the rule of law. It is therefore imperative to adhere to the essence of *Roe*'s original decision, and we do so today.

IV

* * *

Roe established a trimester framework to govern abortion regulations. Under this elaborate but rigid construct, almost no regulation at all is permitted during the first trimester of pregnancy; regulations designed to protect the woman's health, but not to further the State's interest in potential life, are permitted during the second trimester; and during the third trimester, when the fetus is viable, prohibitions are permitted provided the life or health of the mother is not at stake. . . .

The trimester framework no doubt was erected to ensure that the woman's right to choose not become so subordinate to the State's interest in promoting fetal life that her choice exists in theory but not in fact. We do not agree, however, that the trimester approach is necessary to accomplish this objective. A framework of this rigidity was unnecessary and in its later interpretation sometimes contradicted the State's permissible exercise of its powers.

Though the woman has a right to choose to terminate or continue her pregnancy before viability, it does not at all follow that the State is prohibited from taking steps to ensure that this choice is thoughtful and informed. Even in the earliest stages of pregnancy, the State may enact rules and regulations designed to encourage her to know that there are philosophic and social arguments of great weight that can be brought to bear in favor of continuing the pregnancy to full term and that there are procedures and institutions to allow adoption of unwanted children as well as a certain degree of state assistance if the mother chooses to raise the child herself. "'[T]he Constitution does not forbid a State or city, pursuant to democratic processes, from expressing a preference for normal childbirth.'" It follows that States are free to enact laws to provide a reasonable framework for a woman to make a decision that has such profound and lasting meaning. This, too, we find consistent with *Roe*'s central premises, and indeed the inevitable consequence of our holding that the State has an interest in protecting the life of the unborn.

We reject the trimester framework, which we do not consider to be part of the essential holding of *Roe*. . . . A logical reading of the central holding in *Roe* itself, and a necessary reconciliation of the liberty of the woman and the interest of the State in promoting prenatal life, require, in our view, that we abandon the trimester framework as a rigid prohibition on all previability regulation aimed at the protection of fetal life. The trimester framework suffers from these basic flaws: in its formulation it misconceives the nature of the pregnant woman's interest; and in practice it undervalues the State's interest in potential life, as recognized in *Roe*.

* * *

These considerations of the nature of the abortion right illustrate that it is an overstatement to describe it as a right to decide whether to have an abortion "without interference from the State." All abortion regulations interfere to some degree with a woman's ability to decide whether to terminate her pregnancy. It is, as a consequence, not surprising that despite the protestations contained in the original *Roe* opinion to the effect that the Court was not recognizing an absolute right, the Court's experience applying the trimester framework has led to the striking down of some abortion regulations which in no real sense deprived women of the ultimate decision. Those decisions went too far because the right recognized by *Roe* is a right "to be free from unwarranted governmental intrusion into matters so fundamentally affecting a person as the decision whether to bear or beget a child." Not all governmental intrusion is of necessity unwarranted; and that brings us to the other basic flaw in the trimester framework: even in *Roe*'s terms, in practice it undervalues the State's interest in the potential life within the woman.

Roe v. Wade was express in its recognition of the State's "important and legitimate interest[s] in preserving and protecting the health of the pregnant woman [and] in protecting the potentiality of human life." The trimester framework, however, does not fulfill *Roe*'s own promise that the State has an interest in protecting fetal life or potential life. *Roe* began the contradiction by using the trimester framework to forbid any regulation of abortion designed to advance that interest before viability. Before viability, *Roe* and subsequent cases treat all governmental attempts to influence a woman's decision on behalf of the potential life within her as unwarranted. This treatment is, in our judgment, incompatible with the recognition that there is a substantial state interest in potential life throughout pregnancy.

The very notion that the State has a substantial interest in potential life leads to the conclusion that not all regulations must be deemed unwarranted. Not all burdens on the right to decide whether to terminate a pregnancy will be undue. In our view, the undue burden standard is the appropriate means of reconciling the State's interest with the woman's constitutionally protected liberty.

The concept of an undue burden has been utilized by the Court as well as individual Members of the Court, including two of us, in ways that could be considered inconsistent. Because we set forth a standard of general application to which we intend to adhere, it is important to clarify what is meant by an undue burden.

A finding of an undue burden is a shorthand for the conclusion that a state regulation has the purpose or effect of placing a substantial obstacle in the path of a woman seeking an abortion of a nonviable fetus. A statute with this purpose is invalid because the means chosen by the State to further the interest in potential life must be calculated to inform the woman's free choice, not hinder it. And a statute which, while furthering the interest in potential life or some other valid state interest, has the effect of placing a substantial obstacle in the path of a woman's choice cannot be considered a permissible means of serving its legitimate ends. To the extent that the opinions of the Court or of individual Justices use the undue burden standard in a manner that is inconsistent with this analysis, we set out what in our view should be the controlling standard. . . .

Some guiding principles should emerge. What is at stake is the woman's right to make the ultimate decision, not a right to be insulated from all others in doing so. Regulations which do no more than create a structural mechanism by which the State, or the parent or guardian of a minor, may express profound respect for the life of the unborn are permitted, if they are not a substantial obstacle to the woman's exercise of the right to choose. Unless it has that effect on her right of choice, a state measure designed to persuade her to choose childbirth over abortion will be upheld if reasonably related to that goal. Regulations designed to foster the health of a woman seeking an abortion are valid if they do not constitute an undue burden.

. . . We give this summary:

(a) To protect the central right recognized by *Roe v. Wade* while at the same time accommodating the State's profound interest in potential life, we will employ the undue burden analysis as explained in this opinion. An undue burden exists, and therefore a provision of law is invalid, if its purpose or effect is to place a substantial obstacle in the path of a woman seeking an abortion before the fetus attains viability.

(b) We reject the rigid trimester framework of *Roe v. Wade*. To promote the State's profound interest in potential life, throughout pregnancy the State may take measures to ensure that the woman's choice is informed, and measures designed to advance this interest will not be invalidated as long as their purpose is to persuade the woman to choose childbirth over abortion. These measures must not be an undue burden on the right.

(c) As with any medical procedure, the State may enact regulations to further the health or safety of a woman seeking an abortion. Unnecessary health regulations that have the purpose or effect of presenting a substantial obstacle to a woman seeking an abortion impose an undue burden on the right.

(d) Our adoption of the undue burden analysis does not disturb the central holding of *Roe v. Wade*, and we reaffirm that holding. Regardless of whether exceptions are made for particular circumstances, a State may not prohibit any woman from making the ultimate decision to terminate her pregnancy before viability.

(e) We also reaffirm *Roe*'s holding that "subsequent to viability, the State in promoting its interest in the potentiality of human life may, if it chooses, regulate, and even proscribe, abortion except where it is necessary, in appropriate medical judgment, for the preservation of the life or health of the mother."

These principles control our assessment of the Pennsylvania statute, and we now turn to the issue of the validity of its challenged provisions.

V

The Court of Appeals applied what it believed to be the undue burden standard and upheld each of the provisions except for the husband notification requirement. We agree generally with this conclusion. . . .

A

Because it is central to the operation of various other requirements, we begin with the statute's definition of medical emergency. Under the statute, a medical emergency is

> "[t]hat condition which, on the basis of the physician's good faith clinical judgment, so complicates the medical condition of a pregnant woman as to necessitate the immediate abortion of her pregnancy to avert her death or for which a delay will create serious risk of substantial and irreversible impairment of a major bodily function." 18 Pa. Cons. Stat. § 3203 (1990).

Petitioners argue that the definition is too narrow, contending that it forecloses the possibility of an immediate abortion despite some significant health risks. . . .

. . . While the definition could be interpreted in an unconstitutional manner, the Court of Appeals construed the phrase "serious risk" to include those circumstances. . . . We . . . conclude that, as construed by the Court of Appeals, the medical emergency definition imposes no undue burden on a woman's abortion right.

B

We next consider the informed consent requirement. 18 Pa. Cons. Stat. § 3205 (1990). Except in a medical emergency, the statute requires that at least 24 hours before performing an abortion a physician inform the woman of the nature of the procedure, the health risks of the abortion and of childbirth, and the "probable gestational age of the unborn child." The physician or a qualified nonphysician must inform the woman of the availability of printed materials published by the State describing the fetus and providing information about medical assistance for childbirth, information about child support from the father, and a list of agencies which provide adoption and other services as alternatives to abortion. An abortion may not be performed unless the woman certifies in writing that she has been informed of the availability of these printed materials and has been provided them if she chooses to view them.

Our prior decisions establish that as with any medical procedure, the State may require a woman to give her written informed consent to an abortion. . . .

In *Akron* [*v. Akron Center for Reproductive Health*] (1983), we invalidated an ordinance which required that a woman seeking an abortion be provided by her physician with specific information "designed to influence the woman's informed choice between abortion or childbirth." As we later described the *Akron* holding in *Thornburgh v. American College of Obstetricians and Gynecologists* [(1986)], there were two purported flaws in the Akron ordinance: the information was designed to dissuade the woman from having an abortion and the ordinance imposed "a rigid requirement that a specific body of information be given in all cases, irrespective of the particular needs of the patient. . . ."

To the extent *Akron* and *Thornburgh* find a constitutional violation when the government requires, as it does here, the giving of truthful, nonmisleading information about the nature of the procedure, the attendant health risks and those of childbirth, and the "probable gestational age" of the fetus, those cases go too far, are inconsistent with *Roe*'s acknowledgment of an important interest in potential life, and are overruled. . . .

We also see no reason why the State may not require doctors to inform a woman seeking an abortion of the availability of materials relating to the consequences to the fetus, even when those consequences have no direct relation to her health. . . .

* * *

The Pennsylvania statute also requires us to reconsider the holding in *Akron* that the State may not require that a physician, as opposed to a qualified assistant, provide information relevant to a woman's informed consent. Since there is no evidence on this record that requiring a doctor to give the information as provided by the statute would amount in practical terms to a substantial obstacle to a woman seeking an abortion, we conclude that it is not an undue burden. . . .

Our analysis of Pennsylvania's 24-hour waiting period between the provision of the information deemed necessary to informed consent and the performance of an abortion under the undue burden standard requires us to reconsider the premise behind the decision in *Akron* invalidating a parallel requirement. In *Akron* we said: "Nor are we convinced that the State's legitimate concern that the woman's decision be informed is reasonably served by requiring a 24-hour delay as a matter of course." We consider that conclusion to be wrong. The idea that important decisions will be more informed and deliberate if they follow some period of reflection does not strike us as unreasonable, particularly where the statute directs that important information become part of the background of the decision. The statute, as construed by the Court of Appeals, permits avoidance of the waiting period in the event of a medical emergency and the record evidence shows that in the vast majority of cases, a 24-hour delay does not create any appreciable health risk. In theory, at least, the waiting period is a reasonable measure to implement the State's interest in protecting the life of the unborn, a measure that does not amount to an undue burden.

* * *

We are left with the argument that the various aspects of the informed consent requirement are unconstitutional because they place barriers in the way of abortion on demand. Even the broadest reading of *Roe*, however, has not suggested that there is a constitutional right to abortion on demand. Rather, the right protected by *Roe* is a right to decide to terminate a pregnancy free of undue interference by the State. Because the informed consent requirement facilitates the wise exercise of that right, it cannot be classified as an interference with the right *Roe* protects. The informed consent requirement is not an undue burden on that right.

C

Section 3209 of Pennsylvania's abortion law provides, except in cases of medical emergency, that no physician shall perform an abortion on a married woman without receiving a signed statement from the woman that she has notified her spouse that she is about to undergo an abortion. The woman has the option of providing an alternative signed statement certifying that her husband is not the man who impregnated her; that her husband could not be located; that the pregnancy is the result of spousal sexual assault which she has reported; or that the woman believes that notifying her husband will cause him or someone else to inflict bodily injury upon her. A physician who performs an abortion on a married woman without receiving the appropriate signed statement will have his or her license revoked, and is liable to the husband for damages.

The District Court heard the testimony of numerous expert witnesses, and made detailed findings of fact regarding the effect of this statute. These included:

> "273. The vast majority of women consult their husbands prior to deciding to terminate their pregnancy. . . .

* * *

> "279. The 'bodily injury' exception could not be invoked by a married woman whose husband, if notified, would, in her reasonable belief, threaten to (a) publicize her intent to have an abortion to family, friends or acquaintances; (b) retaliate against her in future child custody or divorce proceedings; (c) inflict psychological intimidation or emotional harm upon her, her children or other persons; (d) inflict bodily harm on other persons such as children, family members or other loved ones; or (e) use his control over finances to deprive of necessary monies for herself or her children. . . ."

* * *

. . . The American Medical Association (AMA) has published a summary of the recent research in this field, which indicates that in an average 12-month period in this country, approximately two million women are the victims of severe assaults by their male partners. . . .

Other studies fill in the rest of this troubling picture. Physical violence is only the most visible form of abuse. Psychological abuse, particularly forced social and economic isolation of women, is also common. . . .

The limited research that has been conducted with respect to notifying one's husband about an abortion, although involving samples too small to be representative, also supports the District Court's findings of fact. The vast majority of women notify their male partners of their decision to obtain an abortion. In many cases in which married women do not notify their husbands, the pregnancy is the result of an extramarital affair. Where the husband is the father, the primary reason women do not notify their husbands is that the husband and wife are experiencing marital difficulties, often accompanied by incidents of violence.

This information and the District Court's findings reinforce what common sense would suggest. In well-functioning marriages, spouses discuss important intimate decisions such as whether to bear a child. But there are millions of women in this country who are the victims of regular physical and psychological abuse at the hands of their husbands. Should these women become pregnant, they may have very good reasons for not wishing to inform their husbands of their decision to obtain an abortion. Many may have justifiable fears of physical abuse, but may be no less fearful of the consequences of reporting prior abuse to the Commonwealth of Pennsylvania. Many may have a reasonable fear that notifying their husbands will provoke further instances of child abuse; these women are not exempt from § 3209's notification requirement. Many may fear devastating forms of psychological abuse from their husbands, including verbal harassment, threats of future violence, the destruction of possessions, physical confinement to the home, the withdrawal of financial support, or the disclosure of the abortion to family and friends. These methods of psychological abuse may act as even more of a deterrent to notification than the possibility of physical violence, but women who are the victims of the abuse are not exempt from § 3209's notification requirement. And many women who are pregnant as a result of sexual assaults by their husbands will be unable to avail themselves of the exception for spousal sexual assault, § 3209(b)(3), because the exception requires that the woman have notified law enforcement authorities within 90 days of the assault, and her husband will be notified of her report once an investigation begins, § 3128(c). If anything in this field is certain, it is that victims of spousal sexual assault are extremely reluctant to report the abuse to the government; hence, a great many spousal rape victims will not be exempt from the notification requirement imposed by § 3209.

The spousal notification requirement is thus likely to prevent a significant number of women from obtaining an abortion. . . .

Respondents attempt to avoid the conclusion that § 3209 is invalid by pointing out that it imposes almost no burden at all for the vast majority of women seeking abortions. They begin by noting that only about 20 percent of the women who obtain abortions are married. They then note that of these women about 95 percent notify their husbands of their own volition. Thus, respondents argue, the effects of § 3209 are felt by only one percent of the women who obtain abortions. Respondents argue that since some of these women will be able to notify their husbands without adverse consequences or will qualify for one of the exceptions, the statute affects fewer than one percent of women seeking abortions. For this reason, it is asserted, the statute cannot be invalid on its face. We disagree with respondents' basic method of analysis.

The analysis does not end with the one percent of women upon whom the statute operates; it begins there. Legislation is measured for consistency with the Constitution by its impact on those whose conduct it affects. . . .

* * *

This conclusion is in no way inconsistent with our decisions upholding parental notification or consent requirements. Those enactments, and our judgment that they are constitutional, are based on the quite reasonable assumption that minors will benefit from consultation with their parents and that children will often not realize that their parents have their best interests at heart. We cannot adopt a parallel assumption about adult women.

We recognize that a husband has a "deep and proper concern and interest . . . in his wife's pregnancy and in the growth and development of the fetus she is carrying." With regard to the children he has fathered and raised, the Court has recognized his "cognizable and substantial" interest in their custody. If these cases concerned a State's ability to require the mother to notify the father before taking some action with respect to a living child raised by both, therefore, it would be reasonable to conclude as a general matter that the father's interest in the welfare of the child and the mother's interest are equal.

Before birth, however, the issue takes on a very different cast. It is an inescapable biological fact that state regulation with respect to the child a woman is carrying will have a far greater impact on the mother's liberty than on the father's. . . . ["]Inasmuch as it is the woman who physically bears the child and who is the more directly and immediately affected by the pregnancy, as between the two, the balance weighs in her favor." This conclusion rests upon the basic nature of marriage and the nature of our Constitution: "[T]he marital couple is not an independent entity with a mind and heart of its own, but an association of two individuals each with a separate intellectual and emotional makeup. If the right of privacy means anything, it is the right of the *individual*, married or single, to be free from unwarranted governmental intrusion into matters so fundamentally affecting a person as the decision whether to bear or beget a child." *Eisenstadt v. Baird*. . . .

There was a time, not so long ago, when a different understanding of the family and of the Constitution prevailed. . . . Only one generation has passed since this Court observed that "woman is still regarded as the center of home and family life," with attendant "special responsibilities" that precluded full and independent legal status under the Constitution. These views, of course, are no longer consistent with our understanding of the family, the individual, or the Constitution.

In keeping with our rejection of the common-law understanding of a woman's role within the family, the Court held in [*Planned Parenthood of Central Missouri v.*] *Danforth* [(1976)] that the Constitution does not permit a State to require a married woman to obtain her husband's consent before undergoing an abortion. The principles that guided the Court in *Danforth* should be our guides today. For the great many women who are victims of abuse inflicted by their husbands, or whose children are the victims of such abuse, a spousal notice requirement enables the husband to wield an effective veto over his wife's decision. Whether the prospect of notification itself deters such women from seeking abortions, or whether the husband, through physical force or psychological pressure or economic coercion, prevents his wife from obtaining an abortion until it is too late, the notice requirement will often be tantamount to the veto found unconstitutional in *Danforth*. The women most affected by this law — those who most reasonably fear the consequences of notifying their husbands that they are pregnant — are in the gravest danger.

* * *

Section 3209 embodies a view of marriage consonant with the common-law status of married women but repugnant to our present understanding of marriage and of the nature of the rights secured by the Constitution. Women do not lose their constitutionally protected liberty when they marry. The Constitution protects all individuals, male or female, married or unmarried, from the abuse of governmental power, even where that power is employed for the supposed benefit of a member of the individual's family. These considerations confirm our conclusion that § 3209 is invalid.

D

We next consider the parental consent provision. Except in a medical emergency, an unemancipated young woman under 18 may not obtain an abortion unless she and one of her parents (or guardian) provides informed consent as defined above. If neither a parent nor a guardian provides consent, a court may authorize the performance of an abortion upon a determination that the young woman is mature and capable of giving informed consent and has in fact given her informed consent, or that an abortion would be in her best interests.

We have been over most of this ground before. Our cases establish, and we reaffirm today, that a State may require a minor seeking an abortion to obtain the consent of a parent or guardian, provided that there is an adequate judicial bypass procedure. Under these precedents, in our view, the one-parent consent requirement and judicial bypass procedure are constitutional.

* * *

E

Under the recordkeeping and reporting requirements of the statute, every facility which performs abortions is required to file a report stating its name and address as well as the name and address of any related entity, such as a controlling or subsidiary organization. In the case of state-funded institutions, the information becomes public.

For each abortion performed, a report must be filed identifying: the physician (and the second physician where required); the facility; the referring physician or agency; the woman's age; the number of prior pregnancies and prior abortions she has had; gestational age; the type of abortion procedure; the date of the abortion; whether there were any pre-existing medical conditions which would complicate pregnancy; medical complications with the abortion; where applicable, the basis for the determination that the abortion was medically necessary; the weight of the aborted fetus; and whether the woman was married, and if so, whether notice was provided or the basis for the failure to give notice. Every abortion facility must also file quarterly reports showing the number of abortions performed broken down by trimester. *See* 18 Pa. Cons. Stat. §§ 3207, 3214 (1990). In all events, the identity of each woman who has had an abortion remains confidential.

In *Danforth* we held that recordkeeping and reporting provisions "that are reasonably directed to the preservation of maternal health and that properly respect a patient's confidentiality and privacy are permissible." We think that under this standard, all the provisions at issue here, except that relating to spousal notice, are constitutional. . . .

* * *

The judgment . . . is affirmed in part and reversed in part. . . .

It is so ordered.

Justice Stevens, concurring in part and dissenting in part [omitted].

Justice Blackmun, concurring in part, concurring in the judgment in part, and dissenting in part.

I join Parts I, II, III, V-A, V-C, and VI of the joint opinion of Justices O'Connor, Kennedy, and Souter.

Three years ago, in *Webster v. Reproductive Health Services* (1989), four Members of this Court appeared poised to "cas[t] into darkness the hopes and visions of every woman in this country" who had come to believe that the Constitution guaranteed her the right to reproductive choice. All that remained between the promise of *Roe* and the darkness of the plurality was a single, flickering flame. Decisions since *Webster* gave little reason to hope that this flame would cast much light. But now, just when so many expected the darkness to fall, the flame has grown bright.

I do not underestimate the significance of today's joint opinion. Yet I remain steadfast in my belief that the right to reproductive choice is entitled to the full protection afforded by this Court before *Webster*. And I fear for the darkness as four Justices anxiously await the single vote necessary to extinguish the light.

I

* * *

II

Today, no less than yesterday, the Constitution and decisions of this Court require that a State's abortion restrictions be subjected to the strictest of judicial scrutiny. Our precedents and the joint opinion's principles require us to subject all non-*de-minimis* abortion regulations to strict scrutiny. Under this standard, the Pennsylvania statute's provisions requiring content-based counseling, a 24-hour delay, informed parental consent, and reporting of abortion-related information must be invalidated.

A

* * *

A State's restrictions on a woman's right to terminate her pregnancy also implicate constitutional guarantees of gender equality. State restrictions on abortion compel women to continue pregnancies they otherwise might terminate. By restricting the right to terminate pregnancies, the State conscripts women's bodies into its service, forcing women to continue their pregnancies, suffer the pains of childbirth, and in most instances, provide years of maternal care. The State does not compensate women for their services; instead, it assumes that they owe this duty as a matter of course. This assumption — that women can simply be forced to accept the "natural" status and incidents of motherhood — appears to rest upon a conception of women's role that has triggered the protection of the Equal Protection Clause. . . .

B

* * *

In my view, application of [the timetable] analytical framework is no less warranted than when it was approved by seven Members of this Court in *Roe*. Strict scrutiny of state limitations on reproductive choice still offers the most secure protection of the woman's right to make her own reproductive decisions, free from state coercion. No majority of this Court has ever agreed upon an alternative approach. The factual premises of the trimester framework have not been undermined, and the *Roe* framework is far more administrable, and far less manipulable, than the "undue burden" standard adopted by the joint opinion.

* * *

C

Application of the strict scrutiny standard results in the invalidation of all the challenged provisions. . . .

* * *

IV

In one sense, the Court's approach is worlds apart from that of THE CHIEF JUSTICE[,] JUSTICE SCALIA [and JUSTICES WHITE and THOMAS]. And yet, in another sense, the distance between the two approaches is short — the distance is but a single vote.

I am 83 years old. I cannot remain on this Court forever, and when I do step down, the confirmation process for my successor well may focus on the issue before us today. That, I regret, may be exactly where the choice between the two worlds will be made.

CHIEF JUSTICE REHNQUIST, with whom JUSTICE WHITE, JUSTICE SCALIA, and JUSTICE THOMAS join, concurring in the judgment in part and dissenting in part.

The joint opinion, following its newly minted variation on *stare decisis*, retains the outer shell of *Roe v. Wade* (1973), but beats a wholesale retreat from the substance of that case. We believe that *Roe* was wrongly decided, and that it can and should be overruled consistently with our traditional approach to *stare decisis* in constitutional cases. We would . . . uphold the challenged provisions of the Pennsylvania statute in their entirety.

I

* * *

. . . Although they reject the trimester framework that formed the underpinning of *Roe*, JUSTICES O'CONNOR, KENNEDY, and SOUTER adopt a revised undue burden standard to analyze the challenged regulations. We conclude, however, that such an outcome is an unjustified constitutional compromise, one which leaves the Court in a position to closely scrutinize all types of abortion regulations despite the fact that it lacks the power to do so under the Constitution.

* * *

We have held that a liberty interest protected under the Due Process Clause of the Fourteenth Amendment will be deemed fundamental if it is "implicit in the concept of ordered liberty." . . .

In construing the phrase "liberty" incorporated in the Due Process Clause of the Fourteenth Amendment, we have recognized that its meaning extends beyond freedom from physical restraint. In *Pierce v. Society of Sisters* (1925), we held that it included a parent's right to send a child to private school; in *Meyer v. Nebraska* (1923), we held that it included a right to teach a foreign language in a parochial school. Building on these cases, we have held that the term "liberty" includes a right to marry, *Loving v. Virginia* (1967); a right to procreate, *Skinner v. Oklahoma ex rel Williamson* (1942); and a right to use contraceptives, *Griswold v. Connecticut* (1965); *Eisenstadt v. Baird* (1972). But a reading of these opinions makes clear that they do not endorse any all-encompassing "right of privacy."

. . . We are now of the view that, in terming this right fundamental, the Court in *Roe* read the earlier opinions upon which it based its decision much too broadly. Unlike marriage, procreation, and contraception, abortion "involves the purposeful termination of a potential life." *Harris v. McRae*, 448 U.S. 297, 325 (1980). The abortion decision must therefore "be recognized as *sui generis*, different in kind from the others that the Court has protected under the rubric of personal or family privacy and autonomy." One cannot ignore the fact that a woman is not isolated in her pregnancy, and that the decision to abort necessarily involves the destruction of a fetus.

Nor do the historical traditions of the American people support the view that the right to terminate one's pregnancy is "fundamental." The common law which we inherited from England made abortion after "quickening" an offense. At the time of the adoption of the Fourteenth Amendment, statutory prohibitions or restrictions on abortion were commonplace; in 1868, at least 28 of the then-37 States and 8 Territories had statutes banning or limiting abortion. J. Mohr, Abortion in America 200 (1978). By the turn of the century virtually every State had a law prohibiting or restricting abortion on its books. By the middle of the present century, a liberalization trend had set in. But 21 of the restrictive abortion laws in effect in 1868 were still in effect in 1973 when *Roe* was decided, and an overwhelming majority of the States prohibited abortion unless necessary to preserve the life or health of the mother. On this record, it can scarcely be said that any deeply rooted tradition of relatively unrestricted abortion in our history supported the classification of the right to abortion as "fundamental" under the Due Process Clause of the Fourteenth Amendment.

We think, therefore, both in view of this history and of our decided cases dealing with substantive liberty under the Due Process Clause, that the Court was mistaken in *Roe* when it classified a woman's decision to terminate her pregnancy as a "fundamental right" that could be abridged only in a manner which withstood "strict scrutiny." . . .

. . . The Court in *Roe* reached too far when it analogized the right to abort a fetus to the rights involved in *Pierce*, *Meyer*, *Loving*, and *Griswold*, and thereby deemed the right to abortion fundamental.

II

The joint opinion of Justices O'Connor, Kennedy, and Souter cannot bring itself to say that *Roe* was correct as an original matter, but the authors are of the view that "the immediate question is not the soundness of *Roe*'s resolution of the issue, but the precedential force that must be accorded to its holding." . . . Th[e] discussion of the principle of *stare decisis* appears to be almost entirely dicta, because the joint opinion does not apply that principle in dealing with *Roe*. *Roe* decided that a woman had a fundamental right to an abortion. The joint opinion rejects that view. *Roe* decided that abortion regulations were to be subjected to "strict scrutiny" and could be justified only in the light of "compelling state interests." The joint opinion rejects that view. *Roe* analyzed abortion regulation under a rigid trimester framework, a framework which has guided this Court's decisionmaking for 19 years. The joint opinion rejects that framework.

. . . While purporting to adhere to precedent, the joint opinion instead revises it. *Roe* continues to exist, but only in the way a storefront on a western movie set exists: a mere facade to give the illusion of reality. Decisions following *Roe*, such as *Akron v. Akron Center for Reproductive Health, Inc.* (1983), and *Thornburgh v. American College of Obstetricians and Gynecologists* (1986), are frankly overruled in part under the "undue burden" standard expounded in the joint opinion.

In our view, authentic principles of *stare decisis* do not require that any portion of the reasoning in *Roe* be kept intact. . . .

* * *

The joint opinion thus turns to what can only be described as an unconventional — and unconvincing — notion of reliance, a view based on the surmise that the availability of abortion since *Roe* has led to "two decades of economic and social developments" that would be undercut if the error of *Roe* were recognized. The joint opinion's assertion of this fact is undeveloped and totally conclusory. In fact, one cannot be sure to what economic and social developments the opinion is referring. Surely it is dubious to suggest that women have reached their "places in society" in reliance upon *Roe*, rather than as a result of their determination to obtain higher education and compete with men in the job market, and of society's increasing recognition of their ability to fill positions that were previously thought to be reserved only for men.

* * *

Apparently realizing that conventional *stare decisis* principles do not support its position, the joint opinion advances a belief that retaining a portion of *Roe* is necessary to protect the "legitimacy" of this Court. . . .

But the joint opinion goes on to state that when the Court "resolve[s] the sort of intensely divisive controversy reflected in *Roe* and those rare, comparable cases," its decision is exempt from reconsideration under established principles of *stare decisis* in constitutional cases. . . . This is a truly novel principle, one which is contrary to both the Court's historical practice and to the Court's traditional willingness to tolerate criticism of its opinions. Under this principle, when the Court has ruled on a divisive issue, it is apparently prevented from overruling that decision for the sole reason that it was incorrect, *unless opposition to the original decision has died away.*

* * *

. . . A woman's interest in having an abortion is a form of liberty protected by the Due Process Clause, but States may regulate abortion procedures in ways rationally related to a legitimate state interest. . . .

III

A

[After indicating that he would uphold the informed consent, disclosure of abortion alternatives, waiting period, and parental consent provisions, as the joint opinion also did, the Chief Justice turned to spousal notice.]

* * *

C

* * *

The question before us is therefore whether the spousal notification requirement rationally furthers any legitimate state interests. We conclude that it does. First, a husband's interests in procreation within marriage and in the potential life of his unborn child are certainly substantial ones. The State itself has legitimate interests both in protecting these interests of the father and in protecting the potential life of the fetus, and the spousal notification requirement is reasonably related to advancing those state interests. By providing that a husband will usually know of his spouse's intent to have an abortion, the provision makes it more likely that the husband will participate in deciding the fate of his unborn child, a possibility that might otherwise have been denied him. . . .

The State also has a legitimate interest in promoting "the integrity of the marital relationship." This Court has previously recognized "the importance of the marital relationship in our society." In our view, the spousal notice requirement is a rational attempt by the State to improve truthful communication between spouses and encourage collaborative decisionmaking, and thereby fosters marital integrity. . . . The Pennsylvania Legislature was in a position to weigh the likely benefits of the provision against its likely adverse effects, and presumably concluded, on balance, that the provision would be beneficial. Whether this was a wise decision or not, we cannot say that it was irrational. We therefore conclude that the spousal notice provision comports with the Constitution.

* * *

IV

For the reasons stated, we therefore would hold that each of the challenged provisions of the Pennsylvania statute is consistent with the Constitution. . . .

JUSTICE SCALIA, with whom THE CHIEF JUSTICE, JUSTICE WHITE, and JUSTICE THOMAS join, concurring in the judgment in part and dissenting in part.

. . . The States may, if they wish, permit abortion on demand, but the Constitution does not *require* them to do so. The permissibility of abortion, and the limitations upon it, are to be resolved like most important questions in our democracy: by citizens trying to persuade one another and then voting. As the Court acknowledges, "where reasonable people disagree the government can adopt one position or the other." . . . A State's choice between two positions on which reasonable people can disagree is constitutional even when (as is often the case) it intrudes upon a "liberty" in the absolute sense. Laws against bigamy, for example — with which entire societies of reasonable people disagree — intrude upon men and women's liberty to marry and live with one another. But bigamy happens not to be a liberty specially "protected" by the Constitution.

That is, quite simply, the issue in these cases: not whether the power of a woman to abort her unborn child is a "liberty" in the absolute sense; or even whether it is a liberty of great importance to many women. Of course it is both. The issue is whether it is a liberty protected by the Constitution of the United States. I am sure it is not. I reach that conclusion not because of anything so exalted as my views concerning the "concept of existence, of meaning, of the universe, and of the mystery of human life." Rather, I reach it for the same reason I reach the conclusion that bigamy is not constitutionally protected — because of two simple facts: (1) the Constitution says absolutely nothing about it, and (2) the longstanding traditions of American society have permitted it to be legally proscribed.[1]

* * *

Beyond that brief summary of the essence of my position, I will not swell the United States Reports with repetition of what I have said before; and applying the rational basis test, I would uphold the Pennsylvania statute in its entirety. I must, however, respond to a few of the more outrageous arguments in today's opinion, which it is beyond human nature to leave unanswered. I shall discuss each of them under a quotation from the Court's opinion to which they pertain.

---

[1] The Court's suggestion that adherence to tradition would require us to uphold laws against interracial marriage is entirely wrong. Any tradition in that case was contradicted *by a text* — an Equal Protection Clause that explicitly establishes racial equality as a constitutional value. *See Loving v. Virginia* (1967). The enterprise launched in *Roe v. Wade* (1973), by contrast, sought to *establish* "in the teeth of a clear, contrary tradition" a value found nowhere in the constitutional text.

There is, of course, no comparable tradition barring recognition of a "liberty interest" in carrying one's child to term free from state efforts to kill it. For that reason, it does not follow that the Constitution does not protect childbirth simply because it does not protect abortion. The Court's contention that the only way to protect childbirth is to protect abortion shows the utter bankruptcy of constitutional analysis deprived of tradition as a validating factor. It drives one to say that the only way to protect the right to eat is to acknowledge the constitutional right to starve oneself to death.

"The inescapable fact is that adjudication of substantive due process claims may call upon the Court in interpreting the Constitution to exercise that same capacity which by tradition courts always have exercised: reasoned judgment."

Assuming that the question before us is to be resolved at such a level of philosophical abstraction, in such isolation from the traditions of American society, as by simply applying "reasoned judgment," I do not see how that could possibly have produced the answer the Court arrived at in *Roe v. Wade*. Today's opinion describes the methodology of *Roe*, quite accurately, as weighing against the woman's interest the State's "'important and legitimate interest in protecting the potentiality of human life.'" But "reasoned judgment" does not begin by begging the question, as *Roe* and subsequent cases unquestionably did by assuming that what the State is protecting is the mere "potentiality of human life." The whole argument of abortion opponents is that what the Court calls the fetus and what others call the unborn child *is a human life*. Thus, whatever answer *Roe* came up with after conducting its "balancing" is bound to be wrong, unless it is correct that the human fetus is in some critical sense merely potentially human. There is of course no way to determine that as a legal matter; it is in fact a value judgment. Some societies have considered newborn children not yet human, or the incompetent elderly no longer so.

The authors of the joint opinion, of course, do not squarely contend that *Roe v. Wade* was a *correct* application of "reasoned judgment;" merely that it must be followed, because of *stare decisis*. But in their exhaustive discussion of all the factors that go into the determination of when *stare decisis* should be observed and when disregarded, they never mention "how wrong was the decision on its face?" Surely, if "[t]he Court's power lies . . . in its legitimacy, a product of substance and perception," the "substance" part of the equation demands that plain error be acknowledged and eliminated. *Roe* was plainly wrong — even on the Court's methodology of "reasoned judgment," and even more so (of course) if the proper criteria of text and tradition are applied.

The emptiness of the "reasoned judgment" that produced *Roe* is displayed in plain view by the fact that, after more than 19 years of effort by some of the brightest (and most determined) legal minds in the country, after more than 10 cases upholding abortion rights in this Court, and after dozens upon dozens of *amicus* briefs submitted in these and other cases, the best the Court can do to explain how it is that the word "liberty" *must* be thought to include the right to destroy human fetuses is to rattle off a collection of adjectives that simply decorate a value judgment and conceal a political choice. The right to abort, we are told, inheres in "liberty" because it is among "a person's most basic decisions;" it involves a "most intimate and personal choic[e];" it is "central to personal dignity and autonomy;" it "originate[s] within the zone of conscience and belief;" it is "too intimate and personal" for state interference; it reflects "intimate views" of a "deep, personal character;" it involves "intimate relationships" and notions of "personal autonomy and bodily integrity;" and it concerns a particularly "'important decisio[n].'" But it is obvious to anyone applying "reasoned judgment" that the same adjectives can be applied to many forms of conduct that this Court (including one of the Justices in today's majority, *see Bowers v. Hardwick* (1986)) has held are *not* entitled to constitutional protection — because, like abortion, they are forms of conduct that have long been criminalized in American society. Those adjectives might be applied, for example, to homosexual sodomy, polygamy, adult incest, and suicide, all of which are equally "intimate" and "deep[ly] personal" decisions involving "personal autonomy and bodily integrity," and all of which can constitutionally be proscribed because it is our unquestionable constitutional tradition that they are proscribable. It is not reasoned judgment that supports the Court's decision; only personal predilection. Justice Curtis's warning is as timely today as it was 135 years ago:

> "[W]hen a strict interpretation of the Constitution, according to the fixed rules which govern the interpretation of laws, is abandoned, and the theoretical opinions of individuals are allowed to control its meaning, we have no longer a Constitution; we are under the government of individual men, who for the time being have power to declare what the Constitution is, according to their own views of what it ought to mean." *Dred Scott v. Sandford* (1857) (dissenting opinion).

"Liberty finds no refuge in a jurisprudence of doubt."

One might have feared to encounter this august and sonorous phrase in an opinion defending the real *Roe v. Wade*, rather than the revised version fabricated today by the authors of the joint opinion. The shortcomings of *Roe* did not include lack of clarity: Virtually all regulation of abortion before the third trimester was invalid. But to come across this phrase in the joint opinion — which calls upon federal district judges to apply an "undue burden" standard as doubtful in application as it is unprincipled in origin — is really more than one should have to bear.

* * *

To the extent I can discern *any* meaningful content in the "undue burden" standard as applied in the joint opinion, it appears to be that a State may not regulate abortion in such a way as to reduce significantly its incidence. The joint opinion repeatedly emphasizes that an important factor in the "undue burden" analysis is whether the regulation "prevent[s] a significant number of women from obtaining an abortion;" whether a "significant number of women . . . are likely to be deterred from procuring an abortion;" and whether the regulation often "deters" women from seeking abortions. We are not told, however, what forms of "deterrence" are impermissible or what degree of success in deterrence is too much to be tolerated. If, for example, a State required a woman to read a pamphlet describing, with illustrations, the facts of fetal development before she could obtain an abortion, the effect of such legislation might be to "deter" a "significant number of women" from procuring abortions, thereby seemingly allowing a district judge to invalidate it as an undue burden. Thus, despite flowery rhetoric about the State's "substantial" and "profound" interest in "potential human life," and criticism of *Roe* for undervaluing that interest, the joint opinion permits the State to pursue that interest only so long as it is not too successful. . . .

> **"While we appreciate the weight of the arguments . . . that *Roe* should be overruled, the reservations any of us may have in reaffirming the central holding of *Roe* are outweighed by the explication of individual liberty we have given combined with the force of *stare decisis*."**

The Court's reliance upon *stare decisis* can best be described as contrived. It insists upon the necessity of adhering not to all of *Roe*, but only to what it calls the "central holding." It seems to me that *stare decisis* ought to be applied even to the doctrine of *stare decisis*, and I confess never to have heard of this new, keep-what-you-want-and-throw-away-the-rest version. . . .

I am certainly not in a good position to dispute that the Court *has saved* the "central holding" of *Roe*, since to do that effectively I would have to know what the Court has saved, which in turn would require me to understand (as I do not) what the "undue burden" test means. I must confess, however, that I have always thought, and I think a lot of other people have always thought, that the arbitrary trimester framework, which the Court today discards, was quite as central to *Roe* as the arbitrary viability test, which the Court today retains. It seems particularly ungrateful to carve the trimester framework out of the core of *Roe*, since its very rigidity (in sharp contrast to the utter indeterminability of the "undue burden" test) is probably the only reason the Court is able to say, in urging *stare decisis*, that *Roe* "has in no sense proven 'unworkable.'" I suppose the Court is entitled to call a "central holding" whatever it wants to call a "central holding" — which is, come to think of it, perhaps one of the difficulties with this modified version of *stare decisis*. I thought I might note, however, that the following portions of *Roe* have not been saved:

Under *Roe*, requiring that a woman seeking an abortion be provided truthful information about abortion before giving informed written consent is unconstitutional, if the information is designed to influence her choice. Under the joint opinion's "undue burden" regime (as applied today, at least) such a requirement is constitutional.

Under *Roe*, requiring that information be provided by a doctor, rather than by nonphysician counselors, is unconstitutional. Under the "undue burden" regime (as applied today, at least) it is not.

Under *Roe*, requiring a 24-hour waiting period between the time the woman gives her informed consent and the time of the abortion is unconstitutional. Under the "undue burden" regime (as applied today, at least) it is not.

Under *Roe*, requiring detailed reports that include demographic data about each woman who seeks an abortion and various information about each abortion is unconstitutional. Under the "undue burden" regime (as applied today, at least) it generally is not.

> **"Where, in the performance of its judicial duties, the Court decides a case in such a way as to resolve the sort of intensely divisive controversy reflected in *Roe* . . ., its decision has a dimension that the resolution of the normal case does not carry. It is the dimension present whenever the Court's interpretation of the Constitution calls the contending sides of a national controversy to end their national division by accepting a common mandate rooted in the Constitution."**

The Court's description of the place of *Roe* in the social history of the United States is unrecognizable. Not only did *Roe* not, as the Court suggests, *resolve* the deeply divisive issue of abortion; it did more than anything else to nourish it, by elevating it to the national level where it is infinitely more difficult to resolve. National politics were not plagued by abortion protests, national abortion lobbying, or abortion marches on Congress before *Roe v. Wade* was decided. Profound disagreement existed among our citizens over the issue — as it does over other issues, such as the death penalty — but that disagreement was being worked out at the state level. As with many other issues, the division of sentiment within each State was not as closely balanced as it was among the population of the Nation as a whole, meaning not only that more people would be satisfied with the results of state-by-state resolution, but also that those results would be more stable. Pre-*Roe*, moreover, political compromise was possible.

Roe's mandate for abortion on demand destroyed the compromises of the past, rendered compromise impossible for the future, and required the entire issue to be resolved uniformly, at the national level. At the same time, *Roe* created a vast new class of abortion consumers and abortion proponents by eliminating the moral opprobrium that had attached to the act. ("If the Constitution *guarantees* abortion, how can it be bad?" — not an accurate line of thought, but a natural one.) Many favor all of those developments, and it is not for me to say that they are wrong. But to portray *Roe* as the statesmanlike "settlement" of a divisive issue, a jurisprudential Peace of Westphalia that is worth preserving, is nothing less than Orwellian. *Roe* fanned into life an issue that has inflamed our national politics in general, and has obscured with its smoke the selection of Justices to this Court in particular, ever since. And by keeping us in the abortion-umpiring business, it is the perpetuation of that disruption, rather than of any *Pax Roeana*, that the Court's new majority decrees.

> **"[T]o overrule under fire . . . would subvert the Court's legitimacy. . . .**
>
> **". . . To all those who will be . . . tested by following, the Court implicitly undertakes to remain steadfast. . . . The promise of constancy, once given, binds its maker for as long as the power**

to stand by the decision survives and . . . the commitment [is not] obsolete. . . .

"[The American people's] belief in themselves as . . . a people [who aspire to live according to the rule of law] is not readily separable from their understanding of the Court invested with the authority to decide their constitutional cases and speak before all others for their constitutional ideals. If the Court's legitimacy should be undermined, then, so would the country be in its very ability to see itself through its constitutional ideals."

The Imperial Judiciary lives. It is instructive to compare this Nietzschean vision of us unelected, life-tenured judges — leading a Volk who will be "tested by following," and whose very "belief in themselves" is mystically bound up in their "understanding" of a Court that "speak[s] before all others for their constitutional ideals" — with the somewhat more modest role envisioned for these lawyers by the Founders.

"The judiciary . . . has . . . no direction either of the strength or of the wealth of the society, and can take no active resolution whatever. It may truly be said to have neither Force nor Will, but merely judgment. . . ." THE FEDERALIST NO. 78.

Or, again, to compare this ecstasy of a Supreme Court in which there is, especially on controversial matters, no shadow of change or hint of alteration ("There is a limit to the amount of error that can plausibly be imputed to prior Courts"), with the more democratic views of a more humble man:

"[T]he candid citizen must confess that if the policy of the Government upon vital questions affecting the whole people is to be irrevocably fixed by decisions of the Supreme Court, . . . the people will have ceased to be their own rulers, having to that extent practically resigned their Government into the hands of that eminent tribunal." A. Lincoln, First Inaugural Address (Mar. 4, 1861).

It is particularly difficult, in the circumstances of the present decision, to sit still for the Court's lengthy lecture upon the virtues of "constancy," of "remain[ing] steadfast," and adhering to "principle." Among the five Justices who purportedly adhere to *Roe*, at most three agree upon the *principle* that constitutes adherence (the joint opinion's "undue burden" standard) — and that principle is inconsistent with *Roe*. To make matters worse, two of the three, in order thus to remain steadfast, had to abandon previously stated positions. It is beyond me how the Court expects these accommodations to be accepted "as grounded truly in principle, not as compromises with social and political pressures having, as such, no bearing on the principled choices that the Court is obliged to make." The only principle the Court "adheres" to, it seems to me, is the principle that the Court must be seen as standing by *Roe*. That is not a principle of law (which is what I thought the Court was talking about), but a principle of *Realpolitik* — and a wrong one at that.

I cannot agree with, indeed I am appalled by, the Court's suggestion that the decision whether to stand by an erroneous constitutional decision must be strongly influenced — *against* overruling, no less — by the substantial and continuing public opposition the decision has generated. The Court's judgment that any other course would "subvert the Court's legitimacy" must be another consequence of reading the error-filled history book that described the deeply divided country brought together by *Roe*. In my history-book, the Court was covered with dishonor and deprived of legitimacy by *Dred Scott v. Sandford* (1857), an erroneous (and widely opposed) opinion that it did not abandon, rather than by *West Coast Hotel Co. v. Parrish* (1937), which produced the famous "switch in time" from the Court's erroneous (and widely opposed) constitutional opposition to the social measures of the New Deal. . . .

But whether it would "subvert the Court's legitimacy" or not, the notion that we would decide a case differently from the way we otherwise would have in order to show that we can stand firm against public disapproval is frightening. It is a bad enough idea, even in the head of someone like me, who believes that the text of the Constitution, and our traditions, say what they say and there is no fiddling with them. But when it is in the mind of a Court that believes the Constitution has an evolving meaning; that the Ninth Amendment's reference to "othe[r]" rights is not a disclaimer, but a charter for action; and that the function of this Court is to "speak before all others for [the people's] constitutional ideals" unrestrained by meaningful text or tradition — then the notion that the Court must adhere to a decision for as long as the decision faces "great opposition" and the Court is "under fire" acquires a character of almost czarist arrogance. We are offended by these marchers who descend upon us, every year on the anniversary of *Roe*, to protest our saying that the Constitution requires what our society has never thought the Constitution requires. These people who refuse to be "tested by following" must be taught a lesson. We have no Cossacks, but at least we can stubbornly refuse to abandon an erroneous opinion that we might otherwise change — to show how little they intimidate us.

Of course, as THE CHIEF JUSTICE points out, we have been subjected to what the Court calls "'political pressure'" by *both* sides of this issue. Maybe today's decision *not* to overrule *Roe* will be seen as buckling to pressure from *that* direction. Instead of engaging in the hopeless task of predicting public perception — a job not for lawyers but for political campaign managers — the Justices should do what is *legally* right by asking two questions: (1) Was *Roe* correctly decided? (2) Has *Roe* succeeded in producing a settled body of law? If the answer to both questions is no, *Roe* should undoubtedly be overruled.

. . . How upsetting it is, that so many of our citizens (good people, not lawless ones, on both sides of this abortion issue, and on various sides of other issues as well) think that we Justices should properly take into account their views, as though we were engaged not in ascertaining an objective law but in determining some kind of social consensus. The Court would profit, I think, from giving less attention to the *fact* of this distressing phenomenon, and more attention to the *cause* of it. That cause permeates today's opinion: a new mode of constitutional adjudication that relies not upon text and traditional practice to determine the law, but upon what the Court calls "reasoned judgment," which turns out to be nothing but philosophical predilection and moral intuition. All manner of "liberties," the Court tells us, inhere in the Constitution and are enforceable by this Court — not just those mentioned in the text or established in the traditions of our society. Why even the Ninth Amendment — which says only that "[t]he enumeration in the Constitution, of certain rights, shall not be construed to deny or disparage others retained by the people" — is, despite our contrary understanding for almost 200 years, a literally boundless source of additional, unnamed, unhinted-at "rights," definable and enforceable by us, through "reasoned judgment."

What makes all this relevant to the bothersome application of "political pressure" against the Court are the twin facts that the American people love democracy and the American people are not fools. As long as this Court thought (and the people thought) that we Justices were doing essentially lawyers' work up here — reading text and discerning our society's traditional understanding of that text — the public pretty much left us alone. Texts and traditions are facts to study, not convictions to demonstrate about. But if in reality our process of constitutional adjudication consists primarily of making *value judgments*; if we can ignore a long and clear tradition clarifying an ambiguous text, as we did, for example, five days ago in declaring unconstitutional invocations and benedictions at public high school graduation ceremonies, *Lee v. Weisman* (1992); if, as I say, our pronouncement of constitutional law rests primarily on value judgments, then a free and intelligent people's attitude towards us can be expected to be (*ought* to be) quite different. The people know that their value judgments are quite as good as those taught in any law school — maybe better. If, indeed, the "liberties" protected by the Constitution are, as the Court says, undefined and unbounded, then the people *should* demonstrate, to protest that we do not implement *their* values instead of *ours*. Not only that, but confirmation hearings for new Justices *should* deteriorate into question-and-answer sessions in which Senators go through a list of their constituents' most favored and most disfavored alleged constitutional rights, and seek the nominee's commitment to support or oppose them. Value judgments, after all, should be voted on, not dictated; and if our Constitution has somehow accidently committed them to the Supreme Court, at least we can have a sort of plebiscite each time a new nominee to that body is put forward. JUSTICE BLACKMUN not only regards this prospect with equanimity, he solicits it.

* * *

There is a poignant aspect to today's opinion. Its length, and what might be called its epic tone, suggest that its authors believe they are bringing to an end a troublesome era in the history of our Nation and of our Court. "It is the dimension" of authority, they say, to "cal[l] the contending sides of national controversy to end their national division by accepting a common mandate rooted in the Constitution."

There comes vividly to mind a portrait by Emanuel Leutze that hangs in the Harvard Law School: Roger Brooke Taney, painted in 1859, the 82d year of his life, the 24th of his Chief Justiceship, the second after his opinion in *Dred Scott*. He is all in black, sitting in a shadowed red armchair, left hand resting upon a pad of paper in his lap, right hand hanging limply, almost lifelessly, beside the inner arm of the chair. He sits facing the viewer and staring straight out. There seems to be on his face, and in his deep-set eyes, an expression of profound sadness and disillusionment. Perhaps he always looked that way, even when dwelling upon the happiest of thoughts. But those of us who know how the lustre of his great Chief Justiceship came to be eclipsed by *Dred Scott* cannot help believing that he had that case — its already apparent consequences for the Court and its soon-to-be-played-out consequences for the Nation — burning on his mind. I expect that two years earlier he, too, had thought himself "call[ing] the contending sides of national controversy to end their national division by accepting a common mandate rooted in the Constitution."

It is no more realistic for us in this litigation, than it was for him in that, to think that an issue of the sort they both involved — an issue involving life and death, freedom and subjugation — can be "speedily and finally settled" by the Supreme Court, as President James Buchanan in his inaugural address said the issue of slavery in the territories would be. *See* Inaugural Addresses of the Presidents of the United States, S. Doc. No. 101-10, p. 126 (1989). Quite to the contrary, by foreclosing all democratic outlet for the deep passions this issue arouses, by banishing the issue from the political forum that gives all participants, even the losers, the satisfaction of a fair hearing and an honest fight, by continuing the imposition of a rigid national rule instead of allowing for regional differences, the Court merely prolongs and intensifies the anguish.

We should get out of this area, where we have no right to be, and where we do neither ourselves nor the country any good by remaining.

NOTES AND QUESTIONS

1. *Roe* was criticized for its reliance upon the Due Process, rather than Equal Protection, Clause. *See, e.g.*, Ruth Bader Ginsburg, *Some Thoughts on Autonomy and Equality in Relation to* Roe v. Wade, 63 N.C. L. REV. 375, 383 (1985). Does the Court in *Casey* address that criticism by its allusion to the importance of abortion to a woman's participation in the "economic and social life of the nation"? 505 U.S. at 835. If women must have the option of terminating pregnancies to be equal participants in our national economic life, is there something amiss in our economic system? In any event, since gender is a quasi-suspect class that can be employed to further an important governmental interest, wouldn't the interest in potential life — which the *Casey* Court says exists throughout the pregnancy — justify most abortion regulations?

2. Justice Blackmun wrote in *Roe v. Wade* that "[w]e need not resolve the difficult question of when life begins. When those trained in . . . medicine . . . are unable to arrive at any consensus, the judiciary, at this point in the development of man's knowledge, is not in a position to speculate as to the answer." 410 U.S. at 159. Doesn't the Court's focus on viability in *Roe*, and again in *Casey*, effectively decide this question?

3. In rendering its reaffirmation of abortion in *Casey v. Planned Parenthood*, the Court concluded that the "factual underpinnings of *Roe*'s central holding" have not changed. 505 U.S. at 864. Yet, in its very lengthy opinion, the Court nowhere discusses modern science. The late Dr. Jerome LeJeune, M.D., Ph.D., the world-famous geneticist from the University of Paris who is credited with discovering the first chromosomal abnormality in man, Down's Syndrome, however, stated well before *Casey* that there is a specific and unique human being present from the moment of conception. According to LeJeune this is not inference, but a deduction. It is just plain observation. Moreover, in Dr. LeJeune's view this is the consensus of scientists everywhere. In LeJeune's words, "[t]o accept the fact that after fertilization has taken place a new human has come into being is no longer a matter of taste or opinion. The human nature of the human being from conception to old age is not a metaphysical contention, it is plain experimental evidence." *The Human Life Bill: Hearings on S. 158 Before the Subcomm. on Separation of Powers of the Senate Comm. on the Judiciary*, 97th Cong. 10 (1982) (statement of Dr. Jerome LeJeune).

Scientists today can make direct observation of the chromosomal and molecular structure of the first cell of life because of a method developed by Dr. Alec Jeffreys of Leicester University (U.K.) for extracting molecules of DNA (deoxyribonucleic acid), the so-called building block of life. With Dr. Jeffreys' methodology, scientists are able to demonstrate that each person — from the moment of the first fertilized cell — is unique. In essence, there is a "bar code" for a person, much like the codes on products in the supermarket, with one very important difference: no two persons in the world have exactly the same code. If John and Mary Doe decide to have a child, Baby Doe is a unique individual like none other to recur in the universe. Should the scientifically-provable uniqueness of the unborn child determine personhood? Does it matter that only a small amount of genetic information is fully expressed in a fertilized egg? Or is genetic expression less important than the fact that *all* of the genetic information that a person will ever have is contained in the first cell, whether it is expressed or not? After all, genetic expression does not end at birth, but continues throughout life. Surely, no one would seriously argue that a six month old infant could be denied nutrition because of insufficient genetic expression, would they?

4. Maybe the distinction between born and unborn can be found in the fact that there is an absence of differentiated neurons or a functioning brain stem in the fertilized cell. Since those without such functions are said to be "brain dead" at the other end of life, perhaps that is why the unborn child is claimed to be not yet "alive." This, however, ignores that withdrawing life support from a person in a vegetative state does nothing to revive the brain stem; whereas, it is the violent intervention of abortion that stops the development of the brain stem and nervous system in the unborn child. In *Vacco v. Quill*, 521 U.S. 793 (1997), dealing with assisted suicide, we will see the Court reject an analogy between withdrawing life support and affirmatively assisting in the killing of patient.

5. When Texas defended its criminal prohibition of abortion in *Roe*, the nature of fetal development was premised upon inference. Anyone who has ever listened to the audio tape of the oral argument knows that the Court and the advocates had only a rudimentary understanding of science at the time *Roe* was decided. Yet, the science of the unborn was far fuller at the time of *Casey*. In *Roe*, Justice Blackmun wrote: "[i]f this suggestion of personhood is established, the [pro-abortion] case, of course, collapses," 410 U.S. at 156; did he forget? Or can the law declare personhood to be one thing, when scientific fact affirms another? What would the founders say in the tradition of natural law originalism? Justice James Wilson, who both signed the Declaration of Independence and the Constitution, sagely counseled that "law can never attain either the extent or the elevation of a science, unless it be raised upon the science of man." 1 JAMES WILSON, THE WORKS OF JAMES WILSON 197 (Robert Green McCloskey ed., Belknap Press 1967) (1804).

6. After *Casey*, the constitutionality of regulation of abortion practice depends upon whether the regulation, at least prior to viability, constitutes an undue burden. But what exactly is an undue burden? The joint opinion of Justices Kennedy, O'Connor and Souter define it as a law with the "purpose or effect [of placing] a substantial obstacle in the path of a woman seeking an abortion" 505 U.S. at 878. By the same token, the *Casey* opinion articulates that the state has a profound interest in unborn life throughout the pregnancy and "may take measures to ensure that the woman's choice is informed, and measures designed to advance this interest will not be invalidated as long as their purpose is to persuade the woman to choose childbirth over abortion." *Id.* But aren't measures designed to favor childbirth, obstacles? If the answer is yes, then why are they tolerated? Presumably, it is because they are not undue burdens or undue obstacles. Caught in this circular thought pattern, the most one can say is — states are permitted to encourage life (and thereby discourage abortion), but not too much.

Post-*Casey*, the following types of abortion restrictions, all considered in *Casey*, are likely constitutional: a 24 hour waiting period, 505 U.S. at 885-886; an informed consent requirement calling for the provision of truthful, nonmisleading information about the nature of the abortion procedure, associated health risks, as well as information about the development of the unborn child, *id.* at 838; and medical recordkeeping and reporting requirements specifying the name of the abortionist, marital status of the woman, prior pregnancies, and fetal condition, *id.* at 900. Recordkeeping laws that do not preserve the confidentiality of the woman choosing to take the life of her unborn child may, under pre-*Casey* decision, be open to constitutional doubt. *See, e.g., Thornburgh v. American College of Obstetricians and Gynecologists*, 476 U.S. at 766 (characterizing the record requirements there as "extreme" with identification of the patient being their only "obvious" purpose). In addition, in an earlier decision, *Webster v. Reproductive Health Services*, a plurality of the Court and a separate concurring opinion by Justice O'Connor accepted responsible testing of the unborn child to determine viability. As Justice O'Connor wrote, "[i]t is clear to me that requiring the performance of examinations and tests useful to determining whether a fetus is viable, when viability is possible, and when it would not be medically imprudent to do so, does not impose an undue burden on a woman's abortion decision." 492 U.S. at 530.

While pre-*Casey* decisions invalidated most abortion method restrictions, *Casey* more forthrightly acknowledges the state's interest in unborn life throughout the pregnancy, so it is possible that requirements that abortions be performed in a hospital setting (today, most are not, rather they are performed in "clinics" very loosely defined) might be sustained. In the earlier decision of *Planned Parenthood of Kansas City, Mo. v. Ashcroft*, a state law requiring a second physician where an abortion is performed after viability was sustained. 462 U.S. at 486.

Parental notice or consent requirements applicable to unmarried minors are constitutional, subject to the availability of an alternative judicial procedure that would allow authorization of the abortion where a court finds that the minor is sufficiently mature to make her own decision or where the court independently finds the abortion to be in her best interests. *Bellotti v. Baird,* 443 U.S. 622 (1979) (invalidating a two parent consent requirement because it did not provide for a sufficiently porous judicial by-pass). See also *Hodgson v. Minnesota,* 497 U.S. 417 (1990), upholding a two parent notification requirement applicable to minors, so long as a judicial by-pass mechanism was available. Given that parents have the right — perhaps a fundamental right — to direct the upbringing of their children, why is it that the state can preempt parental direction in this morally sensitive context? Generally, parental consent is required whenever a medical procedure is performed on a minor child. Given that *Casey* more completely recognizes the interest of the state in discouraging abortion based upon its generalized interest in the preservation of human life, why isn't the specific, familial interest of a grandparent in the life of an unborn grandchild equally weighty?

Another anomaly is the Court's refusal to acknowledge a spouse's interest in being informed of an abortion decision. *Casey*, of course, invalidates even a highly qualified spousal notification. 505 U.S. at 887-98. In so doing, the joint opinion without record evidence tends to assume widespread spousal abuse and thereby makes dysfunctional marriages the norm. Apart from the dubious sociology, the invalidation of the notice requirement is seemingly a misapplication of the undue burden standard. As the Chief Justice points out in dissent, "[i]n most instances the notification requirement operates without difficulty." *See* footnote 2 of the Chief Justice's dissenting opinion (not included above). Admitting that some marriages are troubled by abuse, the Pennsylvania statute did not require spousal notice where the woman could reasonably believe that it would result in her bodily harm. A husband's interest in procreation within marriage is substantial — and again, more personal than the state's generalized interest in the preservation of life — and yet, the Court fails to explain persuasively why this substantial interest cannot be credited.

Apart from restrictions on abortion, the government is under no constitutional obligation to subsidize the practice. In other words, the existence of a constitutional right, perhaps especially a highly controverted one like abortion, implies no obligation on the part of the government to facilitate its exercise. In *Maher v. Roe*, the Court wrote that the judicial discovery of an abortion right "implies no limitation on the authority of a State to make a value judgment favoring childbirth over abortion, and to implement that judgment by the allocation of public funds." 432 U.S. at 474. Thus, the state prohibition of the use of Medicaid funds for abortions in *Maher* "place[d] no obstacles — absolute or otherwise — in the pregnant woman's path to an abortion. An indigent woman who desires an abortion suffers no disadvantage as a consequence of Connecticut's decision to fund childbirth." *Id.* The Court has also sustained express federal restrictions on the use of public funds for abortion. *Harris v. McRae,* 448 U.S. 297, 302 (1980) (sustaining the Hyde amendment prohibiting federal funding of abortion, except in limited cases). In *Rust v. Sullivan*, 500 U.S. 173 (1991), the Court upheld the ability of government to fund only speech that promotes its interest in childbirth. "[The] Government can, without violating the Constitution, selectively fund a program to encourage certain activities it believes to be in the public interest, without at the same time funding an alternate program which seeks to deal with the problem another way. In so doing, the Government has not discriminated on the basis of viewpoint; it has merely chosen to fund one activity to the exclusion of another." *Id.* at 193.

7. Previously we mentioned the troubling imprecision in the Court's identification of nontextual fundamental rights. From a natural law respect for family, marriage, and procreation, the Court moved — without explicit justification — to an unrefined concept of privacy, and then, liberty, that included largely unfettered access to contraception and abortion by married and unmarried alike. As suggested in *Casey*, the Court had already allowed the sweep of these privacy rights to remove reasonable distinctions between an adult and a minor child. *See, e.g., Carey v. Population Services Int'l*, 431 U.S. 678 (1977), where a plurality of the Court extended the abortion right of privacy to minors, asserting "the right to privacy in connection with decisions affecting procreation extends to minors as well as to adults." *Id.* at 693. Some might argue that discovering implied rights in "natural law" is no more precise than loose formulations of "implicit in ordered liberty" and other similar terminology that the Court has employed from time to time; however, as you surely recognize by now, the natural law tradition is a longstanding jurisprudential effort (much of which was introduced in Chapters One and Two) to discern human good from human nature, itself. In addition, the Framers expressly adopted this natural law system in premising the claim of constitutional liberty and inalienable right upon the "laws of nature and nature's God." Do you believe, like the Framers did, that human nature is knowable? Does the very make-up of your-self instruct you in the basics of how to live? If it is fair to say that by reasoned reflection, you can determine what foods are compatible with your body, what clothing is appropriate for the external climate, and what knowledge brings happiness and fulfillment, might it not also be true that by the same course of deductive reasoning some exercises of liberty will be more readily seen to promote human good? Are the vaguer formulations of "ordered liberty" or "fundamental notions of fair play" less helpful because they do not specifically avert to the philosophical system identified by the framers and declared to be the basis of our independence? Do overly broad and untethered ideas of autonomy tend to dissolve into constitutional right claims that not only do not further human nature, but also disregard (slavery) or destroy (abortion) it? *Cf.* David Crump, *How Do the Courts Really Discover Unenumerated Fundamental Rights? Cataloguing the Methods of Judicial Alchemy,* 19 HARV. J.L. & PUB. POL'Y 795 (1996) (demonstrating how current judicial practice uses convulted legal formulae to create fundamental rights from personal inclinations).

8. The Supreme Court proclaims in *Casey* that every person has "the right to define [their] own concept of existence, of meaning, of the universe, and of the mystery of human life," 505 U.S. at 852, but natural law originalism, as restated by John Locke, gave God the benefit of the doubt in such matters. As Locke's thinking is summarized:

> [H]uman beings are the creation or "workmanship" of God; they there-fore belong to God, are his property. From this fact derives a set of pre-scriptions under the natural law; these mainly have the form of limitations on what human beings may do: they may not use force, i.e., directly harm each other, for they belong to God, not to each other; they may not harm themselves, e.g., they may not commit suicide, for the same reason; and they may not indirectly harm each other through taking more than their fair share of the goods of the external world.

Michael P. Zuckert, *Do Natural Rights Derive from Natural Law?,* 21 HARV. J.L. & PUB. POL'Y 695 (1997) (referencing JOHN LOCKE, QUESTIONS CONCERNING THE LAW OF NATURE (Robert Horwitz et al. trans., 1990)). And it is our equality vis-a-vis a transcendent God that supplies the necessary insight for democratic rule. When all are created equal, no one has a superior right to govern. *See* HARRY V. JAFFA, ORIGINAL INTENT AND THE FRAMERS OF THE CONSTITUTION 62-63 (1994) (indicating that the legitimacy of the consent of the governed is a recip-rocal of natural human equality). The passage from *Casey* mentioned above is sometimes denigratingly referred to as the Court's "mystery passage." It was this mystery passage that led lower courts to find an assisted suicide right.

See Compassion in Dying v. Washington, 79 F.3d 790, 813 (9th Cir. 1996), *rev'd sub nom. Washington v. Glucksberg*, 521 U.S. 702 (1997); *Quill v. Vacco*, 80 F.2d 716, 730 (2d Cir. 1996), *rev'd*, 521 U.S. 793 (1997). When you read the Supreme Court's ruling in the assisted suicide cases below consider whether the Court has retrenched from the mystery passage. In particular, does the Court indicate that its decision about what aspects of personal autonomy are to receive constitutional protection must be more than a "philosophical exercise"? "That many of the rights and liberties protected by the Due Process Clause sound in personal autonomy," said the Court, "does not warrant the sweeping conclusion that any and all important, intimate, and personal decisions are so protected." 521 U.S. at 727. For a claim of personal autonomy to be protected, the claim must be "deeply rooted in our history and traditions, or so fundamental to our concept of constitutionally ordered liberty, that they are protected by the Fourteenth Amendment." *Id.*

9. Are contraception and abortion related? Consider the following:

> But despite their differences of nature and moral gravity, contraception and abortion are often closely connected, as fruits of the same tree. It is true that in many cases contraception and even abortion are practised under the pressure of real life difficulties, which nonetheless can never exonerate from striving to observe God's law fully. Still, in very many other instances such practices are rooted in a hedonistic mentality unwilling to accept responsibility in matters of sexuality, and they imply a self-centered concept of freedom, which regards procreation as an obstacle to personal fulfillment. The life which could result from a sexual encounter thus becomes an enemy to be avoided at all costs, and abortion becomes the only possible decisive response to failed contraception.

> The close connection which exists, in mentality, between the practice of contraception and that of abortion is becoming increasingly obvious. It is being demonstrating in an alarming way by the development of chemical products, intrauterine devices and vaccines which, distributed with the same ease as contraceptives, really act as abortifacients in the very early stages of the development of the life of the new human being.

POPE JOHN PAUL II, THE GOSPEL OF LIFE [EVANGELIUM VITAE] No. 13, at 28-29 (1995).

10. There is another aspect to the abortion debate that warrants mention. Several studies have indicated that there may be a correlation between abortion and increased risk of breast cancer. Another recent study has shown a strong correlation between legalized abortion and sexually transmitted diseases:

> Our regression results show that abortion legalization led to an increase of sexually transmitted diseases; this result is robust to a wide range of time periods and covariates and is constant across the sexes. The point

> estimates indicate that legalization caused an increase in the gonorrhea and syphilis rates potentially as large as 25 percent. . . . If a similar abortion effect exists for other STDs, which we could not examine because of data limitations, additional treatment expenditures might amount to more than $4 billion annually.

Klick and Stratmann, 32 J. LEGAL STUDIES 407 (June 2003). What effect, if any, should this kind of evidence have on the states' ability to regulate or restrict abortion as a means of protecting maternal health?

11. Slavery spawned a civil war. Does abortion pose the same threat to the body politic? *See* David M. Smolin, *The Religious Root and Branch of Anti-Abortion Lawlessness,* 47 BAYLOR L. REV. 960 (1995) (asserting that the roots of anti-abortion lawlessness stem first from the perceived lawlessness of the Supreme Court and other political institutions and second from the "sense of displacement felt by traditionalist Christians in contemporary America"). *But see,* Ruth Colker, *Abortion and Violence,* 1 WM. & MARY J. WOMEN & L. 93 (1994) (arguing that the consequences of anti-abortion violence are worse). Consider the following case:

STENBERG v. CARHART
530 U.S. 914 (2000)

JUSTICE BREYER delivered the opinion of the Court.

* * *

Three established principles determine the issue before us. We shall set them forth in the language of the joint opinion in *Casey*. First, before "viability . . . the woman has a right to choose to terminate her pregnancy." (joint opinion of O'CONNOR, KENNEDY, and SOUTER, JJ.).

Second, "a law designed to further the State's interest in fetal life which imposes an undue burden on the woman's decision before fetal viability" is unconstitutional. An "undue burden is . . . shorthand for the conclusion that a state regulation has the purpose or effect of placing a substantial obstacle in the path of a woman seeking an abortion of a nonviable fetus."

Third, "'subsequent to viability, the State in promoting its interest in the potentiality of human life may, if it chooses, regulate, and even proscribe, abortion except where it is necessary, in appropriate medical judgment, for the preservation of the life or health of the mother.'"

We apply these principles to a Nebraska law banning "partial birth abortion." The statute reads as follows:

> "No partial birth abortion shall be performed in this state, unless such procedure is necessary to save the life of the mother whose life is endangered by a physical disorder, physical illness, or physical injury, includ-

ing a life-endangering physical condition caused by or arising from the pregnancy itself."

The statute defines "partial birth abortion" as:

"an abortion procedure in which the person performing the abortion partially delivers vaginally a living unborn child before killing the unborn child and completing the delivery."

It further defines "partially delivers vaginally a living unborn child before killing the unborn child" to mean

"deliberately and intentionally delivering into the vagina a living unborn child, or a substantial portion thereof, for the purpose of performing a procedure that the person performing such procedure knows will kill the unborn child and does kill the unborn child."

The law classifies violation of the statute as a "Class III felony" carrying a prison term of up to 20 years, and a fine of up to $25,000. It also provides for the automatic revocation of a doctor's license to practice medicine in Nebraska.

We hold that this statute violates the Constitution.

I

A

Dr. Leroy Carhart is a Nebraska physician who performs abortions in a clinical setting.

B

Because Nebraska law seeks to ban one method of aborting a pregnancy, we must describe and then discuss several different abortion procedures.

The evidence before the trial court, as supported or supplemented in the literature, indicates the following:

1. About 90% of all abortions performed in the United States take place during the first trimester of pregnancy, before 12 weeks of gestational age. During the first trimester, the predominant abortion method is "vacuum aspiration," which involves insertion of a vacuum tube (cannula) into the uterus to evacuate the contents. Such an abortion is typically performed on an outpatient basis under local anesthesia.

2. Approximately 10% of all abortions are performed during the second trimester of pregnancy (12 to 24 weeks). The most commonly used procedure is called "dilation and evacuation" (D & E). That procedure (together with a modified form of vacuum aspiration used in the early second trimester) accounts for about 95% of all abortions performed from 12 to 20 weeks of gestational age.

3. D & E "refers generically to transcervical procedures performed at 13 weeks gestation or later."

After 15 weeks:

"Because the fetus is larger at this stage of gestation (particularly the head), and because bones are more rigid, dismemberment or other destructive procedures are more likely to be required than at earlier gestational ages to remove fetal and placental tissue."

* * *

5. The D & E procedure carries certain risks. The use of instruments within the uterus creates a danger of accidental perforation and damage to neighboring organs. Sharp fetal bone fragments create similar dangers. And fetal tissue accidentally left behind can cause infection and various other complications.

* **

8. The American College of Obstetricians and Gynecologists describes the D & X ["dilation and extraction"] procedure in a manner corresponding to a breech-conversion intact D & E, including the following steps:

"1. deliberate dilatation of the cervix, usually over a sequence of days;

"2. instrumental conversion of the fetus to a footling breech;

"3. breech extraction of the body excepting the head; and

"4. partial evacuation of the intracranial contents of a living fetus to effect vaginal delivery of a dead but otherwise intact fetus."

Despite the technical differences we have just described, intact D & E and D & X are sufficiently similar for us to use the terms interchangeably.

* * *

II

The question before us is whether Nebraska's statute, making criminal the performance of a "partial birth abortion," violates the Federal Constitution, as interpreted in *Planned Parenthood of Southeastern Pa. v. Casey* (1992), and *Roe v. Wade* (1973). We conclude that it does for at least two independent reasons. First, the law lacks any exception "'for the preservation of the . . . health of the mother.'" Second, it "imposes an undue burden on a woman's ability" to choose a D & E abortion, thereby unduly burdening the right to choose abortion itself. We shall discuss each of these reasons in turn.

A

The *Casey* joint opinion reiterated what the Court held in *Roe*; that "'subsequent to viability, the State in promoting its interest in the potentiality of human life may, if it chooses, regulate, and even proscribe, abortion except where it is necessary, in appropriate medical judgment, for the preservation of the life or health of the mother.'"

* * *

1

Nebraska responds that the law does not require a health exception unless there is a need for such an exception. And here there is no such need, it says. It argues that "safe alternatives remain available" and "a ban on partial-birth abortion/D & X would create no risk to the health of women." The problem for Nebraska is that the parties strongly contested this factual question in the trial court below; and the findings and evidence support Dr. Carhart. The State fails to demonstrate that banning D & X without a health exception may not create significant health risks for women, because the record shows that significant medical authority supports the proposition that in some circumstances, D & X would be the safest procedure.

* * *

B

* * *

. . . Evidence before the trial court makes clear that D & E will often involve a physician pulling a "substantial portion" of a still living fetus, say, an arm or leg, into the vagina prior to the death of the fetus. Indeed D & E involves dismemberment that commonly occurs only when the fetus meets resistance that restricts the motion of the fetus: "The dismemberment occurs between the traction of . . . [the] instrument and the counter-traction of the internal os of the cervix." And these events often do not occur until after a portion of a living fetus has been pulled into the vagina.

Even if the statute's basic aim is to ban D & X, its language makes clear that it also covers a much broader category of procedures. The language does not track the medical differences between D & E and D & X — though it would have been a simple matter, for example, to provide an exception for the performance of D & E and other abortion procedures. E.g., Kan. Stat. Ann. § 65- 6721(b)(1) (Supp.1999). Nor does the statute anywhere suggest that its application turns on whether a portion of the fetus' body is drawn into the vagina as part of a process to extract an intact fetus after collapsing the head as opposed to a process that would dismember the fetus. Thus, the dissenters' argument that the law was generally intended to bar D & X can be both correct and irrelevant. The relevant question is not whether the legislature wanted to ban D & X; it is whether the law was intended to apply only to D & X. The plain language covers both procedures.

The Nebraska State Attorney General argues that the statute does differentiate between the two procedures. He says that the statutory words "substantial portion" mean "the child up to the head." He consequently denies the statute's application where the physician introduces into the birth canal a fetal arm or leg or anything less than the entire fetal body. He argues further that we must defer to his views about the meaning of the state statute.

We cannot accept the Attorney General's narrowing interpretation of the Nebraska statute. This Court's case law makes clear that we are not to give the Attorney General's interpretative views controlling weight.

* * *

Regardless, even were we to grant the Attorney General's views "substantial weight," we still have to reject his interpretation, for it conflicts with the statutory language. The Attorney General, echoed by the dissents, tries to overcome that language by relying on other language in the statute; in particular, the words "partial birth abortion," a term ordinarily associated with the D & X procedure, and the words "partially delivers vaginally a living unborn child." But these words cannot help the Attorney General. They are subject to the statute's further explicit statutory definition, specifying that both terms include "delivering into the vagina a living unborn child, or a substantial portion thereof."

* * *

We are aware that adopting the Attorney General's interpretation might avoid the constitutional problem discussed in this section. But we are "without power to adopt a narrowing construction of a state statute unless such a construction is reasonable and readily apparent."

Finally, the law does not require us to certify the state law question to the Nebraska Supreme Court. Of course, we lack any authoritative state-court construction. But "we have never held that a federal litigant must await a state-court construction or the development of an established practice before bringing the federal suit."

* * *

The result is an undue burden upon a woman's right to make an abortion decision. We must consequently find the statute unconstitutional.

JUSTICE STEVENS, with whom JUSTICE GINSBURG joins, concurring.

Although much ink is spilled today describing the gruesome nature of late-term abortion procedures, that rhetoric does not provide me a reason to believe that the procedure Nebraska here claims it seeks to ban is more brutal, more gruesome, or less respectful of "potential life" than the equally gruesome procedure Nebraska claims it still allows. That the word "liberty" in the Fourteenth Amendment includes a woman's right to make this difficult and extremely personal decision — makes it impossible for me to understand how a State has any legitimate interest in requiring a doctor to follow any procedure other than the one that he or she reasonably believes will best protect the woman in her exercise of this constitutional liberty. But one need not even approach this view today to conclude that Nebraska's law must fall. For the notion that either of these two equally gruesome procedures performed at this late stage of gestation is more akin to infanticide than the other, or that the State furthers any legitimate interest by banning one but not the other, is simply irrational.

JUSTICE O'CONNOR, concurring.

First, the Nebraska statute is inconsistent with *Casey* because it lacks an exception for those instances when the banned procedure is necessary to preserve the health of the mother.

* * *

Second, Nebraska's statute is unconstitutional on the alternative and independent ground that it imposes an undue burden on a woman's right to choose to terminate her pregnancy before viability. Nebraska's ban covers not just the dilation and extraction (D & X) procedure, but also the dilation and evacuation (D & E) procedure, "the most commonly used method for performing previability second trimester abortions."

It is important to note that, unlike Nebraska, some other States have enacted statutes more narrowly tailored to proscribing the D & X procedure alone. Some of those statutes have done so by specifically excluding from their coverage the most common methods of abortion, such as the D & E and vacuum aspiration procedures. For example, the Kansas statute states that its ban does not apply to the "(A) [s]uction curettage abortion procedure; (B) suction aspiration abortion procedure; or (C) dilation and evacuation abortion procedure involving dismemberment of the fetus prior to removal from the body of the pregnant woman." The Utah statute similarly provides that its prohibition "does not include the dilation and evacuation procedure involving dismemberment prior to removal, the suction curettage procedure, or the suction aspiration procedure for abortion." Likewise, the Montana statute. By restricting their prohibitions to the D & X procedure exclusively, the Kansas, Utah, and Montana statutes avoid a principal defect of the Nebraska law.

If Nebraska's statute limited its application to the D & X procedure and included an exception for the life and health of the mother, the question presented would be quite different than the one we face today. As we held in *Casey*, an abortion regulation constitutes an undue burden if it "has the purpose or effect of placing a substantial obstacle in the path of a woman seeking an abortion of a nonviable fetus." If there were adequate alternative methods for a woman safely to obtain an abortion before viability, it is unlikely that prohibiting the D & X procedure alone would "amount in practical terms to a substantial obstacle to a woman seeking an abortion." Thus, a ban on partial-birth abortion that only proscribed the D & X method of abortion and that included an exception to preserve the life and health of the mother would be constitutional in my view.

Nebraska's statute, however, does not meet these criteria. For these reasons, I agree with the Court that Nebraska's law is unconstitutional.

JUSTICE GINSBURG, with whom JUSTICE STEVENS joins, concurring.

A state regulation that "has the purpose or effect of placing a substantial obstacle in the path of a woman seeking an abortion of a nonviable fetus" violates the Constitution. Such an obstacle exists if the State stops a woman from choosing the procedure her doctor "reasonably believes will best protect the woman in [the] exercise of [her] constitutional liberty."

CHIEF JUSTICE REHNQUIST, dissenting.

I did not join the joint opinion in *Planned Parenthood of Southeastern Pa. v. Casey* (1992), and continue to believe that case is wrongly decided. Despite my disagreement with the opinion, the *Casey* joint opinion represents the holding of the Court in that case. I believe JUSTICE KENNEDY and JUSTICE THOMAS have correctly applied *Casey*'s principles and join their dissenting opinions.

JUSTICE SCALIA, dissenting.

I am optimistic enough to believe that, one day, *Stenberg v. Carhart* will be assigned its rightful place in the history of this Court's jurisprudence beside *Korematsu* and *Dred Scott*. The method of killing a human child — one cannot even accurately say an entirely unborn human child — proscribed by this statute is so horrible that the most clinical description of it evokes a shudder of revulsion. The notion that the Constitution of the United States, designed, among other things, "to establish Justice, insure domestic Tranquility, . . . and secure the Blessings of Liberty to ourselves and our Posterity," prohibits the States from simply banning this visibly brutal means of eliminating our half-born posterity is quite simply absurd.

* * *

The two lengthy dissents in this case have, appropriately enough, set out to establish that today's result does not follow from this Court's most recent pronouncement on the matter of abortion, *Planned Parenthood of Southeastern Pa. v. Casey* (1992). It would be unfortunate, however, if those who disagree with the result were induced to regard it as merely a regrettable misapplication of *Casey*. It is not that, but is *Casey*'s logical and entirely predictable consequence. To be sure, the Court's construction of this statute so as to make it include procedures other than live-birth abortion involves not only a disregard of fair meaning, but an abandonment of the principle that even ambiguous statutes should be interpreted in such fashion as to render them valid rather than void. *Casey* does not permit that jurisprudential novelty — which must be chalked up to the Court's inclination to bend the rules when any effort to limit abortion, or even to speak in opposition to abortion, is at issue. It is of a piece, in other words, with *Hill v. Colorado,* also decided today.

But the Court gives a second and independent reason for invalidating this humane (not to say anti-barbarian) law: That it fails to allow an exception for the situation in which the abortionist believes that this live-birth method of destroying the child might be safer for the woman. (As pointed out by JUSTICE THOMAS, and elaborated upon by JUSTICE KENNEDY, there is no good reason to believe this is ever the case, but — who knows? — it sometime might be.)

I have joined JUSTICE THOMAS's dissent because I agree that today's decision is an "unprecedented expansio[n]" of our prior cases, "is not mandated" by *Casey*'s "undue burden" test. But I never put much stock in *Casey*'s explication of the inexplicable. In the last analysis, my judgment that *Casey* does not support today's tragic result can be traced to the fact that what I consider to be an "undue burden" is different from what the majority considers to be an "undue burden" — a conclusion that can not be demonstrated true or false by factual inquiry or legal reasoning. It is a value judgment, dependent upon how much one respects (or believes society ought to respect) the life of a partially delivered fetus, and how much one respects (or believes society ought to respect) the freedom of the woman who gave it life to kill it. Evidently, the five Justices in today's majority value the former less, or the latter more (or both), than the four of us in dissent. Case closed. There is no cause for anyone who believes in *Casey* to feel betrayed by this outcome. It has been arrived at by precisely the process *Casey* promised — a democratic vote by nine lawyers, not on the question whether the text of the Constitution has anything to say about this subject (it obviously does not); nor even on the question (also appropriate for lawyers) whether the legal traditions of the American people would have sustained such a limitation upon abortion (they obviously would); but upon the pure policy question whether this limitation upon abortion is "undue" — i.e., goes too far.

* * *

Today's decision, that the Constitution of the United States prevents the prohibition of a horrible mode of abortion, will be greeted by a firestorm of criticism — as well it should. If only for the sake of its own preservation, the Court should return this matter to the people — where the Constitution, by its silence on the subject, left it — and let them decide, State by State, whether this practice should be allowed. *Casey* must be overruled.

JUSTICE KENNEDY, with whom THE CHIEF JUSTICE joins, dissenting.

For close to two decades after *Roe v. Wade* (1973), the Court gave but slight weight to the interests of the separate States when their legislatures sought to address persisting concerns raised by the existence of a woman's right to elect an abortion in defined circumstances. When the Court reaffirmed the essential holding of *Roe*, a central premise was that the States retain a critical and legitimate role in legislating on the subject of abortion, as limited by the woman's right the Court restated and again guaranteed. *Planned Parenthood of Southeastern Pa. v. Casey* (1992). The political processes of the State are not to be foreclosed from enacting laws to promote the life of the unborn and to ensure respect for all human life and its potential. The State's constitutional authority is a vital means for citizens to address these grave and serious issues, as they must if we are to progress in knowledge and understanding and in the attainment of some degree of consensus.

The Court's decision today, in my submission, repudiates this understanding by invalidating a statute advancing critical state interests, even though the law denies no woman the right to choose an abortion and places no undue burden upon the right. The legislation is well within the State's competence to enact. Having concluded Nebraska's law survives the scrutiny dictated by a proper understanding of *Casey*, I dissent from the judgment invalidating it.

I

The Court's failure to accord any weight to Nebraska's interest in prohibiting partial-birth abortion is erroneous and undermines its discussion and holding.

* * *

As described by Dr. Carhart, the D & E procedure requires the abortionist to use instruments to grasp a portion (such as a foot or hand) of a developed and living fetus and drag the grasped portion out of the uterus into the vagina. The fetus, in many cases, dies just as a human adult or child would: It bleeds to death as it is torn from limb from limb. The fetus can be alive at the beginning of the dismemberment process and can survive for a time while its limbs are being torn off. Dr. Carhart agreed that "[w]hen you pull out a piece of the fetus, let's say, an arm or a leg and remove that, at the time just prior to removal of the portion of the fetus, . . . the fetus [is] alive." Dr. Carhart has observed fetal heartbeat via ultrasound with "extensive parts of the fetus removed," and testified that mere dismemberment of a limb does not always cause death because he knows of a physician who removed the arm of a fetus only to have the fetus go on to be born "as a living child with one arm." At the conclusion of a D & E abortion no intact fetus remains. In Dr. Carhart's words, the abortionist is left with "a tray full of pieces."

In the D & X, the abortionist initiates the woman's natural delivery process by causing the cervix of the woman to be dilated, sometimes over a sequence of days. The fetus' arms and legs are delivered outside the uterus while the fetus is alive; witnesses to the procedure report seeing the body of the fetus moving outside the woman's body. At this point, the abortion procedure has the appearance of a live birth. As stated by one group of physicians, "[a]s the physician manually performs breech extraction of the body of a live fetus, excepting the head, she continues in the apparent role of an obstetrician delivering a child." With only the head of the fetus remaining in utero, the abortionist tears open the skull. According to Dr. Martin Haskell, a leading proponent of the procedure, the appropriate instrument to be used at this stage of the abortion is a pair of scissors. Witnesses report observing the portion of the fetus outside the woman react to the skull penetration. The abortionist then inserts a suction tube and vacuums out the developing brain and other matter found within the skull. Brain death does not occur until after the skull invasion, and, according to Dr. Carhart, the heart of the fetus may continue to beat for minutes after the contents of the skull are vacuumed out. The abortionist next completes the delivery of a dead fetus, intact except for the damage to the head and the missing contents of the skull.

Of the two described procedures, Nebraska seeks only to ban the D & X. In light of the description of the D & X procedure, it should go without saying that Nebraska's ban on partial-birth abortion furthers purposes States are entitled to pursue. Dr. Carhart nevertheless maintains the State has no legitimate interest in forbidding the D & X. As he interprets the controlling cases in this Court, the only two interests the State may advance through regulation of abortion are in the health of the woman who is considering the procedure and in the life of the fetus she carries. The Court, as I read its opinion, accedes to his views, misunderstanding *Casey* and the authorities it confirmed.

* * *

States may take sides in the abortion debate and come down on the side of life, even life in the unborn:

> "Even in the earliest stages of pregnancy, the State may enact rules and regulations designed to encourage [a woman] to know that there are philosophic and social arguments of great weight that can be brought to bear in favor of continuing the pregnancy to full term and that there are procedures and institutions to allow adoption of unwanted children as well as a certain degree of state assistance if the mother chooses to raise the child herself." (joint opinion of O'CONNOR, KENNEDY, and SOUTER, JJ.).

States also have an interest in forbidding medical procedures which, in the State's reasonable determination, might cause the medical profession or society as a whole to become insensitive, even disdainful, to life, including life in the human fetus. Abortion, *Casey* held, has consequences beyond the woman and her fetus. The States' interests in regulating are of concomitant extension. *Casey* recognized that abortion is, "fraught with consequences for . . . the persons who perform and assist in the procedure [and for] society which must confront the knowledge that these procedures exist, procedures some deem nothing short of an act of violence against innocent human life."

A State may take measures to ensure the medical profession and its members are viewed as healers, sustained by a compassionate and rigorous ethic and cognizant of the dignity and value of human life, even life which cannot survive without the assistance of others. *Washington v. Glucksberg.*

Casey demonstrates that the interests asserted by the State are legitimate and recognized by law. It is argued, however, that a ban on the D & X does not further these interests. This is because, the reasoning continues, the D & E method, which Nebraska claims to be beyond its intent to regulate, can still be used to abort a fetus and is no less dehumanizing than the D & X method. While not adopting the argument in express terms, the Court indicates tacit approval of it by refusing to reject it in a forthright manner. Rendering express what is only implicit in the majority opinion, JUSTICE STEVENS and JUSTICE GINSBURG are forthright in declaring that the two procedures are indistinguishable and that Nebraska has acted both irrationally and without a proper purpose in enacting the law. The issue is not whether members of the judiciary can see a difference between the two procedures. It is whether Nebraska can. The Court's refusal to recognize Nebraska's right to declare a moral difference between the procedures is a dispiriting disclosure of the illogic and illegitimacy of the Court's approach to the entire case.

Nebraska was entitled to find the existence of a consequential moral difference between the procedures. We are referred to substantial medical authority that D & X perverts the natural birth process to a greater degree than D & E, commandeering the live birth process until the skull is pierced. American Medical Association (AMA) publications describe the D & X abortion method as "ethically wrong." The D & X differs from the D & E because in the D & X the fetus is "killed outside of the womb" where the fetus has "an autonomy which separates it from the right of the woman to choose treatments for her own body." D & X's stronger resemblance to infanticide means Nebraska could conclude the procedure presents a greater risk of disrespect for life and a consequent greater risk to the profession and society, which depend for their sustenance upon reciprocal recognition of dignity and respect. The Court is without authority to second-guess this conclusion.

Those who oppose abortion would agree, indeed would insist, that both procedures are subject to the most severe moral condemnation, condemnation reserved for the most repulsive human conduct. This is not inconsistent, however, with the further proposition that as an ethical and moral matter D & X is distinct from D & E and is a more serious concern for medical ethics and the morality of the larger society the medical profession must serve. Nebraska must obey the legal regime which has declared the right of the woman to have an abortion before viability. Yet it retains its power to adopt regulations which do not impose an undue burden on the woman's right. By its regulation, Nebraska instructs all participants in the abortion process, including the mother, of its moral judgment that all life, including the life of the unborn, is to be respected. The participants, Nebraska has determined, cannot be indifferent to the procedure used and must refrain from using the natural delivery process to kill the fetus. The differentiation between the procedures is itself a moral statement, serving to promote respect for human life; and if the woman and her physician in contemplating the moral consequences of the prohibited procedure conclude that grave moral consequences pertain to the permitted abortion process as well, the choice to elect or not to elect abortion is more informed; and the policy of promoting respect for life is advanced.

It ill-serves the Court, its institutional position, and the constitutional sources it seeks to invoke to refuse to issue a forthright affirmation of Nebraska's right to declare that critical moral differences exist between the two procedures. The natural birth process has been appropriated; yet the Court refuses to hear the State's voice in defining its interests in its law. The Court's holding contradicts *Casey*'s assurance that the State's constitutional position in the realm of promoting respect for life is more than marginal.

II

Demonstrating a further and basic misunderstanding of *Casey*, the Court holds the ban on the D & X procedure fails because it does not include an exception permitting an abortionist to perform a D & X whenever he believes it will best preserve the health of the woman. Casting aside the views of distinguished physicians and the statements of leading medical organizations, the Court awards each physician a veto power over the State's judgment that the procedures should not be performed. Dr. Carhart has made the medical judgment to use the D & X procedure in every case, regardless of indications, after 15 weeks gestation. Requiring Nebraska to defer to Dr. Carhart's judgment is no different than forbidding Nebraska from enacting a ban at all; for it is now Dr. Leroy Carhart who sets abortion policy for the State of Nebraska, not the legislature or the people. *Casey* does not give precedence to the views of a single physician or a group of physicians regarding the relative safety of a particular procedure.

* * *

The holding of *Casey,* allowing a woman to elect abortion in defined circumstances, is not in question here. Nebraska, however, was entitled to conclude that its ban, while advancing important interests regarding the sanctity of life, deprived no woman of a safe abortion and therefore did not impose a substantial obstacle on the rights of any woman. The American College of Obstetricians and Gynecologists (ACOG) "could identify no circumstances under which [D & X] would be the only option to save the life or preserve the health of the woman." The American Medical Association agrees, stating the "AMA's expert panel, which included an ACOG representative, could not find 'any' identified circumstance where it was 'the only appropriate alternative.'"

* * *

JUSTICE O'CONNOR assures the people of Nebraska they are free to redraft the law to include an exception permitting the D & X to be performed when "the procedure, in appropriate medical judgment, is necessary to preserve the health of the mother." The assurance is meaningless. She has joined an opinion which accepts that Dr. Carhart exercises "appropriate medical judgment" in using the D & X for every patient in every procedure, regardless of indications, after 15 weeks' gestation. (requiring any health exception to "tolerate responsible differences of medical opinion" which "are present here."). A ban which depends on the "appropriate medical judgment" of Dr. Carhart is no ban at all. He will be unaffected by any new legislation. This, of course, is the vice of a health exception resting in the physician's discretion.

In light of divided medical opinion on the propricty of the partial-birth abortion technique (both in terms of physical safety and ethical practice) and the vital interests asserted by Nebraska in its law, one is left to ask what the first Justice Harlan asked: "Upon what sound principles as to the relations existing between the different departments of government can the court review this action of the legislature?" The answer is none.

III

* * *

The United States District Court in this case leaped to prevent the law from being enforced, granting an injunction before it was applied or interpreted by Nebraska. In so doing, the court excluded from the abortion debate not just the Nebraska legislative branch but the State's executive and judiciary as well. The law was enjoined before the chief law enforcement officer of the State, its Attorney General, had any opportunity to interpret it. The federal court then ignored the representations made by that officer during this litigation. In like manner, Nebraska's courts will be given no opportunity to define the contours of the law, although by all indications those courts would give the statute a more narrow construction than the one so eagerly adopted by the Court today. Thus the court denied each branch of Nebraska's government any role in the interpretation or enforcement of the statute. This cannot be what *Casey* meant when it said we would be more solicitous of state attempts to vindicate interests related to abortion. *Casey* did not assume this state of affairs.

IV

Ignoring substantial medical and ethical opinion, the Court substitutes its own judgment for the judgment of Nebraska and some 30 other States and sweeps the law away. The Court's holding stems from misunderstanding the record, misinterpretation of *Casey*, outright refusal to respect the law of a State, and statutory construction in conflict with settled rules. The decision nullifies a law expressing the will of the people of Nebraska that medical procedures must be governed by moral principles having their foundation in the intrinsic value of human life, including life of the unborn. Through their law the people of Nebraska were forthright in confronting an issue of immense moral consequence. The State chose to forbid a procedure many decent and civilized people find so abhorrent as to be among the most serious of crimes against human life, while the State still protected the woman's autonomous right of choice as reaffirmed in *Casey*. The Court closes its eyes to these profound concerns.

From the decision, the reasoning, and the judgment, I dissent.

JUSTICE THOMAS, with whom THE CHIEF JUSTICE and JUSTICE SCALIA join, dissenting.

In 1973, this Court struck down an Act of the Texas Legislature that had been in effect since 1857, thereby rendering unconstitutional abortion statutes in dozens of States. *Roe v. Wade*. As some of my colleagues on the Court, past and present, ably demonstrated, that decision was grievously wrong.

In the years following *Roe*, this Court applied, and, worse, extended, that decision to strike down numerous state statutes that purportedly threatened a woman's ability to obtain an abortion.

It appeared that this era of Court-mandated abortion on demand had come to an end, first with our decision in *Webster v. Reproductive Health Services*, and then finally (or so we were told) in our decision in *Planned Parenthood of Southeastern Pa. v. Casey* (1992). Although in *Casey* the separate opinions of THE CHIEF JUSTICE and JUSTICE SCALIA urging the Court to overrule *Roe* did not command a majority, seven Members of that Court, including six Members sitting today, acknowledged that States have a legitimate role in regulating abortion and recognized the States' interest in respecting fetal life at all stages of development.

Even assuming, however, as I will for the remainder of this dissent, that *Casey*'s fabricated undue-burden standard merits adherence (which it does not), today's decision is extraordinary. Today, the Court inexplicably holds that the States cannot constitutionally prohibit a method of abortion that millions find hard to distinguish from infanticide and that the Court hesitates even to describe. This holding cannot be reconciled with *Casey*'s undue-burden standard, as that standard was explained to us by the authors of the joint opinion, and the majority hardly pretends otherwise. In striking down this statute — which expresses a profound and legitimate respect for fetal life and which leaves unimpeded several other safe forms of abortion — the majority opinion gives the lie to the promise of *Casey* that regulations that do no more than "express profound respect for the life of the unborn are permitted, if they are not a substantial obstacle to the woman's exercise of the right to choose" whether or not to have an abortion. Today's decision is so obviously irreconcilable with *Casey*'s explication of what its undue-burden standard requires, let alone the Constitution, that it should be seen for what it is, a reinstitution of the pre-*Webster* abortion-on-demand era in which the mere invocation of "abortion rights" trumps any contrary societal interest. If this statute is unconstitutional under *Casey*, then *Casey* meant nothing at all, and the Court should candidly admit it.

* * *

I respectfully dissent.

NOTES AND QUESTIONS

1. Is the dissent right that the deal struck in *Casey* to both avoid undue burdening of the abortion right claim and to preserve state authority in behalf of human life throughout the pregnancy has been abrogated by the decision in *Stenberg*? Was Justice Kennedy simply mistaken as to the meaning of the joint opinion? Or is Justice Scalia correct that *Casey* involves an unworkable standard discernible only to the members of the Court?

2. Do you think the opponents of partial-birth abortion have any reason to reform existing prohibitions to conform to the "health exception" required by Justice O'Connor? Doesn't the health exception she envisions make any state's regulation subject to the unilateral waiver of any and every individual abortion provider?

3. Do you think it irrational for states to prohibit an abortion practice that kills a child during delivery, while doing nothing to limit or prohibit abortion practices involving dismemberment?

4. Some years ago, Professor Laurence Tribe wrote a thought-provoking volume entitled ABORTION: A CLASH OF ABSOLUTES (1992). The title implies why the debate over abortion is so often acrimonious and unresolvable. As Professor Tribe suggested, those advocating abortion rights frequently elide past difficult questions surrounding the moral obligations of pregnancy while those in favor of unborn life view those questions and obligations as a wholly dispositive premise. There were substantial public and legislative majorities against partial birth abortion (Nebraska, for example, passed its ban with only one dissenting vote). Why didn't the Court apply its usual rules of construction in favor of Nebraska's statute to avoid re-inserting the Court into a question that so divides the Nation? Wasn't this singular practice that all admit borders on infanticide likely to be one of the few places of common ground? Why does Justice Scalia say that this case deserves to be ranked with *Dred Scott* and *Korematsu*? Do you agree?

3. Assisted Suicide

WASHINGTON v. GLUCKSBERG
521 U.S. 702 (1997)

CHIEF JUSTICE REHNQUIST delivered the opinion of the Court.

The question presented in this case is whether Washington's prohibition against "caus[ing]" or "aid[ing]" a suicide offends the Fourteenth Amendment to the United States Constitution. We hold that it does not.

. . . Today, Washington law provides: "a person is guilty of promoting a suicide attempt when he knowingly causes or aids another person to attempt suicide." "Promoting a suicide attempt" is a felony, punishable by up to five years' imprisonment and up to a $10,000 fine. At the same time, Washington's Natural Death Act, enacted in 1979, states that the "withholding or withdrawal of life-sustaining treatment" at a patient's direction "shall not, for any purpose, constitute a suicide."

. . . In January 1994, [four physicians who practice in Washington], along with three gravely ill, pseudonymous plaintiffs who have since died and Compassion in Dying, a nonprofit organization that counsels people considering physician-assisted suicide, sued in the United States District Court, seeking a declaration that [the prohibition against assisted suicide] is, on its face, unconstitutional.

The plaintiffs asserted "the existence of a liberty interest protected by the Fourteenth Amendment which extends to a personal choice by a mentally competent, terminally ill adult to commit physician-assisted suicide." Relying primarily on *Planned Parenthood v. Casey* and *Cruzan v. Director, Missouri Dept. of Health*, the District Court agreed, and concluded that Washington's assisted-suicide ban is unconstitutional because it "places an undue burden on the exercise of [that] constitutionally protected liberty interest." The District Court also decided that the Washington statute violated the Equal Protection Clause's requirement that "'all persons similarly situated . . . be treated alike.'"

A panel of the Court of Appeals for the Ninth Circuit reversed, emphasizing that "[i]n the two hundred and five years of our existence no constitutional right to aid in killing oneself has ever been asserted and upheld by a court of final jurisdiction." The Ninth Circuit reheard the case en banc, reversed the panel's decision, and affirmed the District Court. . . .

I

We begin, as we do in all due-process cases, by examining our Nation's history, legal traditions, and practices. In almost every State — indeed, in almost every western democracy — it is a crime to assist a suicide. The States' assisted-suicide bans are not innovations. Rather, they are longstanding expressions of the States' commitment to the protection and preservation of all human life. . . .

More specifically, for over 700 years, the Anglo-American common-law tradition has punished or otherwise disapproved of both suicide and assisting suicide. In the 13th century, Henry de Bracton, one of the first legal-treatise writers, observed that "[j]ust as a man may commit felony by slaying another so may he do so by slaying himself." 2 BRACTON ON LAWS AND CUSTOMS OF ENGLAND 423 (§150) (G. Woodbine ed., S. Thorne trans., 1968). The real and personal property of one who killed himself to avoid conviction and punishment for a crime were forfeit to the king. . . . Centuries later, Sir William Blackstone, whose Commentaries on the Laws of England not only provided a definitive summary of the common law but was also a primary legal authority for 18th and 19th century American lawyers, referred to suicide as "self-murder" and "the pretended heroism, but real cowardice, of the Stoic philosophers, who destroyed themselves to avoid those ills which they had not the fortitude to endure. . . ." 4 W. BLACKSTONE, COMMENTARIES *189. . . .

For the most part, the early American colonies adopted the common-law approach. . . .

Over time, however, the American colonies abolished the[] harsh common-law penalties [associated with suicide]. . . . [T]he movement away from the common law's harsh sanctions did not represent an acceptance of suicide; rather, . . . this change reflected the growing consensus that it was unfair to punish the suicide's family for his wrongdoing. . . .

That suicide remained a grievous, though nonfelonious, wrong is confirmed by the fact that colonial and early state legislatures and courts did not retreat from prohibiting assisting suicide. Swift, in his early 19th century treatise on the laws of Connecticut, stated that "[i]f one counsels another to commit suicide, and the other by reason of the advice kills himself, the advisor is guilty of murder as principal." 2 Z. SWIFT, A DIGEST OF THE LAWS OF THE STATE OF CONNECTICUT 270 (1823). This was the well established common-law view. . . . And the prohibitions against assisting suicide never contained exceptions for those who were near death. Rather, "[t]he life of those to whom life ha[d] become a burden — of those who [were] hopelessly diseased or fatally wounded — nay, even the lives of criminals condemned to death, [were] under the protection of law, equally as the lives of those who [were] in the full tide of life's enjoyment, and anxious to continue to live." *Blackburn v. State* (1872).

The earliest American statute explicitly to outlaw assisting suicide was enacted in New York in 1828. . . . By the time the Fourteenth Amendment was ratified, it was a crime in most States to assist a suicide. . . .

Though deeply rooted, the States' assisted-suicide bans have in recent years been reexamined and, generally, reaffirmed. Because of advances in medicine and technology, Americans today are increasingly likely to die in institutions, from chronic illnesses. Public concern and democratic action are therefore sharply focused on how best to protect dignity and independence at the end of life, with the result that there have been many significant changes in state laws and in the attitudes these laws reflect. Many States, for example, now permit "living wills," surrogate health-care decisionmaking, and the withdrawal or refusal of life-sustaining medical treatment. At the same time, however, voters and legislators continue for the most part to reaffirm their States' prohibitions on assisting suicide.

The Washington statute at issue in this case was enacted in 1975 as part of a revision of that State's criminal code. . . . In 1991, Washington voters rejected a ballot initiative which, had it passed, would have permitted a form of physician-assisted suicide. Washington then added a provision to the Natural Death Act expressly excluding physician-assisted suicide.

California voters rejected an assisted-suicide initiative similar to Washington's in 1993. On the other hand, in 1994, voters in Oregon enacted, also through ballot initiative, that State's "Death With Dignity Act," which legalized physician-assisted suicide for competent, terminally ill adults.[14] Since the Oregon

---

14 Ore. Rev. Stat. §§ 127.800 *et seq.* (1996); *Lee v. Oregon*, 891 F. Supp. 1429 (Ore. 1995) (Oregon Act does not provide sufficient safeguards for terminally ill persons and therefore violates the Equal Protection Clause), *vacated*, 107 F.3d 1382 (9th Cir. 1997)[, *cert. denied. sub nom. Lee v. Harcleroad*, 118 S. Ct. 328 (1997)].

vote, many proposals to legalize assisted-suicide have been and continue to be introduced in the States' legislatures, but none has been enacted. And just last year, Iowa and Rhode Island joined the overwhelming majority of States explicitly prohibiting assisted suicide. Also, on April 30, 1997, President Clinton signed the Federal Assisted Suicide Funding Restriction Act of 1997, which prohibits the use of federal funds in support of physician-assisted suicide.

* * *

Attitudes toward suicide itself have changed since Bracton, but our laws have consistently condemned, and continue to prohibit, assisting suicide. Despite changes in medical technology and notwithstanding an increased emphasis on the importance of end-of-life decisionmaking, we have not retreated from this prohibition. Against this backdrop of history, tradition, and practice, we now turn to respondents' constitutional claim.

II

The Due Process Clause guarantees more than fair process, and the "liberty" it protects includes more than the absence of physical restraint. The Clause also provides heightened protection against government interference with certain fundamental rights and liberty interests. In a long line of cases, we have held that, in addition to the specific freedoms protected by the Bill of Rights, the "liberty" specially protected by the Due Process Clause includes the rights to marry, *Loving v. Virginia* (1967); to have children, *Skinner v. Oklahoma ex rel. Williamson* (1942); to direct the education and upbringing of one's children, *Meyer v. Nebraska* (1923); *Pierce v. Society of Sisters* (1925); to marital privacy, *Griswold v. Connecticut* (1965); to use contraception, *ibid*; *Eisenstadt v. Baird* (1972); to bodily integrity, *Rochin v. California* (1952), and to abortion, *Casey, supra*. We have also assumed, and strongly suggested, that the Due Process Clause protects the traditional right to refuse unwanted lifesaving medical treatment. *Cruzan.*

But we "ha[ve] always been reluctant to expand the concept of substantive due process because guideposts for responsible decisionmaking in this unchartered area are scarce and open-ended." By extending constitutional protection to an asserted right or liberty interest, we, to a great extent, place the matter outside the arena of public debate and legislative action. We must therefore "exercise the utmost care whenever we are asked to break new ground in this field," lest the liberty protected by the Due Process Clause be subtly transformed into the policy preferences of the members of this Court.

Our established method of substantive-due-process analysis has two primary features: First, we have regularly observed that the Due Process Clause specially protects those fundamental rights and liberties which are, objectively, "deeply rooted in this Nation's history and tradition," and "implicit in the concept of ordered liberty," such that "neither liberty nor justice would exist if they were sacrificed." Second, we have required in substantive-due-process cases a "careful description" of the asserted fundamental liberty interest. Our Nation's history, legal traditions, and practices thus provide the crucial "guideposts for responsible decisionmaking," that direct and restrain our exposition of the Due Process Clause. . . .

JUSTICE SOUTER, relying on Justice Harlan's dissenting opinion in *Poe v. Ullman*, would largely abandon this restrained methodology, and instead ask "whether [Washington's] statute sets up one of those 'arbitrary impositions' or 'purposeless restraints' at odds with the Due Process Clause of the Fourteenth Amendment" (quoting *Poe* (1961) (Harlan, J., dissenting)).[17] In our view, however, the development of this Court's substantive-due-process jurisprudence, described briefly above, has been a process whereby the outlines of the "liberty" specially protected by the Fourteenth Amendment — never fully clarified, to be sure, and perhaps not capable of being fully clarified — have at least been carefully refined by concrete examples involving fundamental rights found to be deeply rooted in our legal tradition. This approach tends to rein in the subjective elements that are necessarily present in due-process judicial review. In addition, by establishing a threshold requirement — that a challenged state action implicate a fundamental right — before requiring more than a reasonable relation to a legitimate state interest to justify the action, it avoids the need for complex balancing of competing interests in every case.

Turning to the claim at issue here, . . . the question before us is whether the "liberty" specially protected by the Due Process Clause includes a right to commit suicide which itself includes a right to assistance in doing so.

We now inquire whether this asserted right has any place in our Nation's traditions. Here, as discussed above, we are confronted with a consistent and almost universal tradition that has long rejected the asserted right, and continues explicitly to reject it today, even for terminally ill, mentally competent adults. To hold for respondents, we would have to reverse centuries of legal doctrine and practice, and strike down the considered policy choice of almost every State.

Respondents contend, however, that the liberty interest they assert *is* consistent with this Court's substantive-due-process line of cases, if not with this Nation's history and practice. Pointing to *Casey* and *Cruzan*, respondents read our jurisprudence in this area as reflecting a general tradition of "self-sover-

---

[17] In JUSTICE SOUTER's opinion, Justice Harlan's *Poe* dissent supplies the "modern justification" for substantive-due-process review. (SOUTER, J., concurring in judgment). But although Justice Harlan's opinion has often been cited in due-process cases, we have never abandoned our fundamental-rights-based analytical method. Just four Terms ago, six of the Justices now sitting joined the Court's opinion in *Reno v. Flores*, 507 U.S. 292, 301-305 (1993); *Poe* was not even cited. And in *Cruzan*, neither the Court's nor the concurring opinions relied on *Poe*; rather, we concluded that the right to refuse unwanted medical treatment was so rooted in our history, tradition, and practice as to require special protection under the Fourteenth Amendment. True, the Court relied on Justice Harlan's dissent in *Casey*, but, as *Flores* demonstrates, we did not in so doing jettison our established approach. Indeed, to read such a radical move into the Court's opinion in *Casey* would seem to fly in the face of that opinion's emphasis on *stare decisis*.

eignty," and as teaching that the "liberty" protected by the Due Process Clause includes "basic and intimate exercises of personal autonomy" . . . .

In *Cruzan*, we considered whether Nancy Beth Cruzan, who had been severely injured in an automobile accident and was in a persistive vegetative state, "ha[d] a right under the United States Constitution which would require the hospital to withdraw life-sustaining treatment" at her parents' request. . . . "[F]or purposes of [that] case, we assume[d] that the United States Constitution would grant a competent person a constitutionally protected right to refuse lifesaving hydration and nutrition." We concluded that, notwithstanding this right, the Constitution permitted Missouri to require clear and convincing evidence of an incompetent patient's wishes concerning the withdrawal of life-sustaining treatment.

* * *

The right assumed in *Cruzan*, however, was not simply deduced from abstract concepts of personal autonomy. Given the common-law rule that forced medication was a battery, and the long legal tradition protecting the decision to refuse unwanted medical treatment, our assumption was entirely consistent with this Nation's history and constitutional traditions. The decision to commit suicide with the assistance of another may be just as personal and profound as the decision to refuse unwanted medical treatment, but it has never enjoyed similar legal protection. Indeed, the two acts are widely and reasonably regarded as quite distinct. *See Vacco v. Quill* [the companion case below]. . . .

[R]espondents also rely on *Casey*. . . .

. . . Respondents emphasize the statement in *Casey* that:

> "At the heart of liberty is the right to define one's own concept of existence, of meaning, of the universe, and of the mystery of human life. Beliefs about these matters could not define the attributes of personhood were they formed under compulsion of the State."

By choosing this language, the Court's opinion in *Casey* described, in a general way and in light of our prior cases, those personal activities and decisions that this Court has identified as so deeply rooted in our history and traditions, or so fundamental to our concept of constitutionally ordered liberty, that they are protected by the Fourteenth Amendment. The opinion moved from the recognition that liberty necessarily includes freedom of conscience and belief about ultimate considerations to the observation that "though the abortion decision may originate within the zone of conscience and belief, it is *more than a philosophic exercise*." That many of the rights and liberties protected by the Due Process Clause sound in personal autonomy does not warrant the sweeping conclusion that any and all important, intimate, and personal decisions are so protected, *San Antonio Independent School Dist. v. Rodriguez* (1973), and *Casey* did not suggest otherwise.

The history of the law's treatment of assisted suicide in this country has been and continues to be one of the rejection of nearly all efforts to permit it. That being the case, our decisions lead us to conclude that the asserted "right" to assistance in committing suicide is not a fundamental liberty interest protected by the Due Process Clause. The Constitution also requires, however, that Washington's assisted-suicide ban be rationally related to legitimate government interests. . . . Washington's assisted-suicide ban implicates a number of state interests.

First, Washington has an "unqualified interest in the preservation of human life." The State's prohibition on assisted suicide, like all homicide laws, both reflects and advances its commitment to this interest. . . .

Respondents admit that "[t]he State has a real interest in preserving the lives of those who can still contribute to society and enjoy life." . . . Washington, however, has rejected this sliding-scale approach and, through its assisted-suicide ban, insists that all persons' lives, from beginning to end, regardless of physical or mental condition, are under the full protection of the law. As we have previously affirmed, the States "may properly decline to make judgments about the 'quality' of life that a particular individual may enjoy," *Cruzan*. This remains true, as *Cruzan* makes clear, even for those who are near death.

Relatedly, all admit that suicide is a serious public-health problem, especially among persons in otherwise vulnerable groups. . . .

Those who attempt suicide — terminally ill or not — often suffer from depression or other mental disorders. [The] New York [State] Task Force [on Life and the Law found that] more than 95% of those who commit suicide had a major psychiatric illness at the time of death; among the terminally ill, uncontrolled pain is a "risk factor" because it contributes to depression. . . . The New York Task Force, however, expressed its concern that, because depression is difficult to diagnose, physicians and medical professionals often fail to respond adequately to seriously ill patients' needs. Thus, legal physician-assisted suicide could make it more difficult for the State to protect depressed or mentally ill persons, or those who are suffering from untreated pain, from suicidal impulses.

The State also has an interest in protecting the integrity and ethics of the medical profession. In contrast to the Court of Appeals' conclusion that "the integrity of the medical profession would [not] be threatened in any way by [physician-assisted suicide]," the American Medical Association, like many other medical and physicians' groups, has concluded that "[p]hysician-assisted suicide is fundamentally incompatible with the physician's role as healer." American Medical Association, Code of Ethics § 2.211 (1994). . . . And physician-assisted suicide could, it is argued, undermine the trust that is essential to the doctor-patient relationship by blurring the time-honored line between healing and harming.

Next, the State has an interest in protecting vulnerable groups — including the poor, the elderly, and disabled persons — from abuse, neglect, and mistakes. . . . If physician-assisted suicide were permitted, many might resort to it to spare their families the substantial financial burden of end-of-life health-care costs.

The State's interest here goes beyond protecting the vulnerable from coercion; it extends to protecting disabled and terminally ill people from prejudice, negative and inaccurate stereotypes, and "societal indifference." . . .

Finally, the State may fear that permitting assisted suicide will start it down the path to voluntary and perhaps even involuntary euthanasia. The Court of Appeals struck down Washington's assisted-suicide ban only "as applied to competent, terminally ill adults who wish to hasten their deaths by obtaining medication prescribed by their doctors." Washington insists, however, that the impact of the court's decision will not and cannot be so limited. If suicide is protected as a matter of constitutional right, it is argued, "every man and woman in the United States must enjoy it." The Court of Appeals' decision, and its expansive reasoning, provide ample support for the State's concerns. . . .

This concern is further supported by evidence about the practice of euthanasia in the Netherlands. The Dutch government's own study revealed that in 1990, there were 2,300 cases of voluntary euthanasia (defined as "the deliberate termination of another's life at his request"), 400 cases of assisted suicide, and more than 1,000 cases of euthanasia without an explicit request. In addition to these latter 1,000 cases, the study found an additional 4,941 cases where physicians administered lethal morphine overdoses without the patients' explicit consent. Physician-Assisted Suicide and Euthanasia in the Netherlands: A Report of Chairman Charles T. Canady, at 12-13 (citing Dutch study). This study suggests that, despite the existence of various reporting procedures, euthanasia in the Netherlands has not been limited to competent, terminally ill adults who are enduring physical suffering, and that regulation of the practice may not have prevented abuses in cases involving vulnerable persons, including severely disabled neonates and elderly persons suffering from dementia. . . .

We need not weigh exactly the relative strengths of these various interests. They are unquestionably important and legitimate, and Washington's ban on assisted suicide is at least reasonably related to their promotion and protection. We therefore hold that [the Washington assisted suicide ban] does not violate the Fourteenth Amendment, either on its face or "as applied to competent, terminally ill adults who wish to hasten their deaths by obtaining medication prescribed by their doctors."

* * *

Throughout the Nation, Americans are engaged in an earnest and profound debate about the morality, legality, and practicality of physician-assisted suicide. Our holding permits this debate to continue, as it should in a democratic society. The decision of the en banc Court of Appeals is reversed, and the case is remanded for further proceedings consistent with this opinion.

JUSTICE O'CONNOR, concurring [in both *Glucksberg*, and in *Vacco v. Quill*, a companion case to *Glucksberg*, which follows].

* * *

. . . I join the Court's opinions because I agree that there is no generalized right to "commit suicide." But respondents urge us to address the narrower question whether a mentally competent person who is experiencing great suffering has a constitutionally cognizable interest in controlling the circumstances of his or her imminent death. I see no need to reach that question in the context of the facial challenges to the New York and Washington laws at issue here. The parties and *amici* agree that in these States a patient who is suffering from a terminal illness and who is experiencing great pain has no legal barriers to obtaining medication, from qualified physicians, to alleviate that suffering, even to the point of causing unconsciousness and hastening death. . . .

* * *

In sum, there is no need to address the question whether suffering patients have a constitutionally cognizable interest in obtaining relief from the suffering that they may experience in the last days of their lives. There is no dispute that dying patients in Washington and New York can obtain palliative care, even when doing so would hasten their deaths. The difficulty in defining terminal illness and the risk that a dying patient's request for assistance in ending his or her life might not be truly voluntary justifies the prohibitions on assisted suicide we uphold here.

JUSTICE STEVENS, concurring in the judgments [of both *Glucksberg* and *Vacco*].

* * *

I

* * *

Today, the Court decides that Washington's statute prohibiting assisted suicide is not invalid "on its face," that is to say, in all or most cases in which it might be applied. That holding, however, does not foreclose the possibility that some applications of the statute might well be invalid.

* * *

III

The state interests supporting a general rule banning the practice of physician-assisted suicide do not have the same force in all cases. . . .

Many terminally ill people find their lives meaningful even if filled with pain or dependence on others. Some find value in living through suffering; some have an abiding desire to witness particular events in their families' lives; many believe it a sin to hasten death. Individuals of different religious faiths make different judgments and choices about whether to live on under such circumstances. There are those who will want to continue aggressive treatment; those who would prefer terminal sedation; and those who will seek withdrawal from life-support systems and death by gradual starvation and dehydration. Although as a general matter the State's interest in the contributions each person may make to society outweighs the person's interest in ending her life, this interest does not have the same force for a terminally ill patient faced not with the choice of whether to live, only of how to die. Allowing the individual, rather than the State, to make judgments "'about the "quality" of life that a particular individual may enjoy,'" does not mean that the lives of terminally-ill, disabled people have less value than the lives of those who are healthy. Rather, it gives proper recognition to the individual's interest in choosing a final chapter that accords with her life story, rather than one that demeans her values and poisons memories of her. . . .

. . . I agree that the State has a compelling interest in preventing persons from committing suicide because of depression, or coercion by third parties. But the State's legitimate interest in preventing abuse does not apply to an individual who is not victimized by abuse, who is not suffering from depression, and who makes a rational and voluntary decision to seek assistance in dying. . . .

Relatedly, the State and *amici* express the concern that patients whose physical pain is inadequately treated will be more likely to request assisted suicide. Encouraging the development and ensuring the availability of adequate pain treatment is of utmost importance; palliative care, however, cannot alleviate all pain and suffering. . . .

The final major interest asserted by the State is its interest in preserving the traditional integrity of the medical profession. The fear is that a rule permitting physicians to assist in suicide is inconsistent with the perception that they serve their patients solely as healers. But for some patients, it would be a physician's refusal to dispense medication to ease their suffering and make their death tolerable and dignified that would be inconsistent with the healing role. . . .

As the New York State Task Force on Life and the Law recognized, a State's prohibition of assisted suicide is justified by the fact that the "'ideal'" case in which "patients would be screened for depression and offered treatment, effective pain medication would be available, and all patients would have a supportive committed family and doctor" is not the usual case. Although, as the Court concludes today, these *potential* harms are sufficient to support the State's general public policy against assisted suicide, they will not always outweigh the individual liberty interest of a particular patient. Unlike the Court of Appeals, I would not say as a categorical matter that these state interests are invalid as to the entire class of terminally ill, mentally competent patients. I do not, however, foreclose the possibility that an individual plaintiff seeking to hasten her death, or a doctor whose assistance was sought, could prevail in a more particularized challenge. Future cases will determine whether such a challenge may succeed.

* * *

Justice Souter, concurring in the judgment.

* * *

II

* * *

Before the ratification of the Fourteenth Amendment, substantive constitutional review resting on a theory of unenumerated rights occurred largely in the state courts applying state constitutions that commonly contained either due process clauses like that of the Fifth Amendment (and later the Fourteenth) or the textual antecedents of such clauses, repeating Magna Carta's guarantee of "the law of the land." On the basis of such clauses, or of general principles untethered to specific constitutional language, state courts evaluated the constitutionality of a wide range of statutes.

* * *

Even in this early period, however, this Court anticipated the developments that would presage both the Civil War and the ratification of the Fourteenth Amendment, by making it clear on several occasions that it too had no doubt of the judiciary's power to strike down legislation that conflicted with important but unenumerated principles of American government. In most such instances, after declaring its power to invalidate what it might find inconsistent with rights of liberty and property, the Court nevertheless went on to uphold the legislative acts under review. *See, e.g., Wilkinson v. Leland* (1829); *Calder v. Bull* (1798) (opinion of Chase, J.); *see also Corfield v. Coryell*, 6 F. Cas. (1823). But in *Fletcher v. Peck* (1810), the Court went further. It struck down an act of the Georgia legislature that purported to rescind a sale of public land *ab initio* and reclaim title for the State, and so deprive subsequent, good-faith purchasers of property conveyed by the original grantees. The Court rested the invalidation on alternative sources of authority: the specific prohibitions against bills of attainder, *ex post facto* laws, laws impairing contracts in Article I, § 10 of the Constitution; and "general principles which are common to our free institutions," by which Chief Justice Marshall meant that a simple deprivation of property by the State could not be an authentically "legislative" act.

Fletcher was not, though, the most telling early example of such review. For its most salient instance in this Court before the adoption of the Fourteenth Amendment was, of course, the case that the Amendment would in due course overturn, *Dred Scott v. Sandford* (1857). Unlike *Fletcher*, *Dred Scott* was textually based on a due process clause (in the Fifth Amendment, applicable to the national government), and it was in reliance on that clause's protection of property that the Court invalidated the Missouri Compromise. This substantive protection of an owner's property in a slave taken to the territories was traced to the absence of any enumerated power to affect that property granted to the Congress by Article I of the Constitution, *id.*, the implication being that the government had no legitimate interest that could support the earlier congressional compromise. The ensuing judgment of history needs no recounting here.

After the ratification of the Fourteenth Amendment, with its guarantee of due process protection against the States, interpretation of the words "liberty" and "property" as used in due process clauses became a sustained enterprise, with the Court generally describing the due process criterion in converse terms of reasonableness or arbitrariness. That standard is fairly traceable to Justice Bradley's dissent in the *Slaughter-House Cases*, in which he said that a person's right to choose a calling was an element of liberty (as the calling, once chosen, was an aspect of property) and declared that the liberty and property protected by due process are not truly recognized if such rights may be "arbitrarily assailed."[6] After that, opinions comparable to those that preceded *Dred Scott* expressed willingness to review legislative action for consistency with the Due Process Clause even as they upheld the laws in question.

The theory became serious, however, beginning with *Allgeyer v. Louisiana* (1897), where the Court invalidated a Louisiana statute for excessive interference with Fourteenth Amendment liberty to contract, and offered a substantive interpretation of "liberty," that in the aftermath of the so-called Lochner Era has been scaled back in some respects, but expanded in others, and never repudiated in principle. The Court said that Fourteenth Amendment liberty includes "the right of the citizen to be free in the enjoyment of all his faculties; to be free to use them in all lawful ways; to live and work where he will; to earn his livelihood by any lawful calling; to pursue any livelihood or avocation; and for that purpose to enter into all contracts which may be proper, necessary and essential to his carrying out to a successful conclusion the purposes above mentioned." *Id.* "[W]e do not intend to hold that in no such case can the State exercise its police power," the Court added, but "[w]hen and how far such power may be legitimately exercised with regard to these subjects must be left for determination to each case as it arises."

Although this principle was unobjectionable, what followed for a season was, in the realm of economic legislation, the echo of *Dred Scott. Allgeyer* was succeeded within a decade by *Lochner v. New York* (1905), and the era to which that case gave its name, famous now for striking down as arbitrary various sorts of economic regulations that post-New Deal courts have uniformly thought con-

---

[6] The *Slaughter-House Cases* are important, of course, for their holding that the Privileges or Immunities Clause was no source of any but a specific handful of substantive rights. *Slaughter-House Cases*, 16 Wall., at 74-80. To a degree, then, that decision may have led the Court to look to the Due Process Clause as a source of substantive rights. In *Twining v. New Jersey*, 211 U.S. 78, 95-97 (1908), for example, the Court of the Lochner Era acknowledged the strength of the case against *Slaughter-House*'s interpretation of the Privileges or Immunities Clause but reaffirmed that interpretation without questioning its own frequent reliance on the Due Process Clause as authorization for substantive judicial review. *See also* J. ELY, DEMOCRACY AND DISTRUST 14-30 (1980) (arguing that the Privileges or Immunities Clause and not the Due Process Clause is the proper warrant for courts' substantive oversight of state legislation). But the courts' use of due process clauses for that purpose antedated the 1873 decision, as we have seen, and would in time be supported in the *Poe* dissent, as we shall see.

stitutionally sound. *Compare, e.g., id.* (finding New York's maximum-hours law for bakers "unreasonable and entirely arbitrary"), *and Adkins v. Children's Hospital of D.C.* (1923) (holding a minimum wage law "so clearly the product of a naked, arbitrary exercise of power that it cannot be allowed to stand under the Constitution of the United States"), *with West Coast Hotel Co. v. Parrish* (1937) (overruling *Adkins* and approving a minimum-wage law on the principle that "regulation which is reasonable in relation to its subject and is adopted in the interests of the community is due process"). As the parentheticals here suggest, while the cases in the *Lochner* line routinely invoked a correct standard of constitutional arbitrariness review, they harbored the spirit of *Dred Scott* in their absolutist implementation of the standard they espoused.

Even before the deviant economic due process cases had been repudiated, however, the more durable precursors of modern substantive due process were reaffirming this Court's obligation to conduct arbitrariness review, beginning with *Meyer v. Nebraska* (1923). Without referring to any specific guarantee of the Bill of Rights, the Court invoked precedents from the *Slaughter-House Cases* through *Adkins* to declare that the Fourteenth Amendment protected "the right of the individual to contract, to engage in any of the common occupations of life, to acquire useful knowledge, to marry, establish a home and bring up children, to worship God according to the dictates of his own conscience, and generally to enjoy those privileges long recognized at common law as essential to the orderly pursuit of happiness by free men." The Court then held that the same Fourteenth Amendment liberty included a teacher's right to teach and the rights of parents to direct their children's education without unreasonable interference by the States, with the result that Nebraska's prohibition on the teaching of foreign languages in the lower grades was, "arbitrary and without reasonable relation to any end within the competency of the State." *See also Pierce v. Society of Sisters* (1925) (finding that a statute that all but outlawed private schools lacked any "reasonable relation to some purpose within the competency of the State"); *Palko v. Connecticut* (1937) ("even in the field of substantive rights and duties the legislative judgment, if oppressive and arbitrary, may be overridden by the courts"; "Is that [injury] to which the statute has subjected [the appellant] a hardship so acute and shocking that our polity will not endure it? Does it violate those fundamental principles of liberty and justice which lie at the base of all our civil and political institutions?") (citation and internal quotation marks omitted).

After *Meyer* and *Pierce*, two further opinions took the major steps that lead to the modern law. The first was not even in a due process case but one about equal protection, *Skinner v. Oklahoma ex rel. Williamson* (1942), where the Court emphasized the "fundamental" nature of individual choice about procreation and so foreshadowed not only the later prominence of procreation as a subject of liberty protection, but the corresponding standard of "strict scrutiny," in this Court's Fourteenth Amendment law. *Skinner*, that is, added decisions regarding procreation to the list of liberties recognized in *Meyer* and *Pierce* and loosely suggested, as a gloss on their standard of arbitrariness, a judicial obligation to scrutinize any impingement on such an important interest with heightened care. In so doing, it suggested a point that Justice Harlan would develop, that the kind and degree of justification that a sensitive judge would demand of a State would depend on the importance of the interest being asserted by the individual.

The second major opinion leading to the modern doctrine was Justice Harlan's *Poe* dissent just cited, the conclusion of which was adopted in *Griswold v. Connecticut* (1965), and the authority of which was acknowledged in *Planned Parenthood of Southeastern Pa. v. Casey* (1992). The dissent is important for three things that point to our responsibilities today. The first is Justice Harlan's respect for the tradition of substantive due process review itself, and his acknowledgement of the Judiciary's obligation to carry it on. For two centuries American courts, and for much of that time this Court, have thought it necessary to provide some degree of review over the substantive content of legislation under constitutional standards of textual breadth. The obligation was understood before *Dred Scott* and has continued after the repudiation of *Lochner*'s progeny, most notably on the subjects of segregation in public education, *Bolling v. Sharpe* (1954), interracial marriage, *Loving v. Virginia* (1967), marital privacy and contraception, *Carey v. Population Services Int'l* (1977), *Griswold v. Connecticut, supra,* abortion, *Planned Parenthood of Southeastern Pa. v. Casey* (1992) (joint opinion of O'CONNOR, KENNEDY, and SOUTER, JJ.), *Roe v. Wade* (1973), personal control of medical treatment, *Cruzan v. Director, Mo. Dept. of Health* (1990) (O'CONNOR, J., concurring); *id.* (BRENNAN, J., dissenting); *id.* (STEVENS, J., dissenting); *see also id.* (majority opinion), and physical confinement, *Foucha v. Louisiana* (1992). This enduring tradition of American constitutional practice is, in Justice Harlan's view, nothing more than what is required by the judicial authority and obligation to construe constitutional text and review legislation for conformity to that text. *See Marbury v. Madison* (1803). Like many judges who preceded him and many who followed, he found it impossible to construe the text of due process without recognizing substantive, and not merely procedural, limitations. "Were due process merely a procedural safeguard it would fail to reach those situations where the deprivation of life, liberty or property was accomplished by legislation which by operating in the future could, given even the fairest possible procedure in application to individuals, nevertheless destroy the enjoyment of all three." The text of the Due Process Clause thus imposes nothing less than an obligation to give substantive content to the words "liberty" and "due process of law."

* * *

JUSTICE GINSBURG, concurring in the judgments [of both *Glucksberg* and *Vacco*].

I concur in the Court's judgments in these cases substantially for the reasons stated by JUSTICE O'CONNOR in her concurring opinion.

JUSTICE BREYER, concurring in the judgments [of both *Glucksberg* and *Vacco*].

I believe that JUSTICE O'CONNOR's views, which I share, have greater legal significance than the Court's opinion suggests. I join her separate opinion, except insofar as it joins the majority. And I concur in the judgments. I shall briefly explain how I differ from the Court.

. . . I do not agree . . . with the Court's formulation of that claimed "liberty" interest. The Court describes it as a "right to commit suicide with another's assistance." But I would not reject the respondents' claim without considering a different formulation, for which our legal tradition may provide greater support. That formulation would use words roughly like a "right to die with dignity." But irrespective of the exact words used, at its core would lie personal control over the manner of death, professional medical assistance, and the avoidance of unnecessary and severe physical suffering — combined.

* * *

I do not believe, however, that this Court need or now should decide whether or a not such a right is "fundamental." That is because, in my view, the avoidance of severe physical pain (connected with death) would have to comprise an essential part of any successful claim and because, as JUSTICE O'CONNOR points out, the laws before us do not *force* a dying person to undergo that kind of pain. . . .

Medical technology, we are repeatedly told, makes the administration of pain-relieving drugs sufficient, except for a very few individuals for whom the ineffectiveness of pain control medicines can mean, not pain, but the need for sedation which can end in a coma. . . .

This legal circumstance means that the state laws before us do not infringe directly upon the (assumed) central interest (what I have called the core of the interest in dying with dignity) as, by way of contrast, the state anticontraceptive laws at issue in *Poe* did interfere with the central interest there at stake — by bringing the State's police powers to bear upon the marital bedroom.

Were the legal circumstances different — for example, were state law to prevent the provision of palliative care, including the administration of drugs as needed to avoid pain at the end of life — then the law's impact upon serious and otherwise unavoidable physical pain (accompanying death) would be more directly at issue. And as JUSTICE O'CONNOR suggests, the Court might have to revisit its conclusions in these cases.

VACCO v. QUILL
521 U.S. 793 (1997)

CHIEF JUSTICE REHNQUIST delivered the opinion of the Court.

In New York, as in most States, it is a crime to aid another to commit or attempt suicide, but patients may refuse even lifesaving medical treatment. The question presented by this case is whether New York's prohibition on assisting suicide therefore violates the Equal Protection Clause of the Fourteenth Amendment. We hold that it does not.

* * *

The Equal Protection Clause commands that no State shall "deny to any person within its jurisdiction the equal protection of the laws." This provision creates no substantive rights. . . .

New York's statutes outlawing assisting suicide affect and address matters of profound significance to all New Yorkers alike. They neither infringe fundamental rights nor involve suspect classifications. *Washington v. Glucksberg*. . . .

On their faces, neither New York's ban on assisting suicide nor its statutes permitting patients to refuse medical treatment treat anyone differently than anyone else or draw any distinctions between persons. *Everyone*, regardless of physical condition, is entitled, if competent, to refuse unwanted lifesaving medical treatment; *no one* is permitted to assist a suicide. Generally speaking, laws that apply evenhandedly to all "unquestionably comply" with the Equal Protection Clause. . . .

. . . Unlike the Court of Appeals, we think the distinction between assisting suicide and withdrawing life-sustaining treatment, a distinction widely recognized and endorsed in the medical profession[6] and in our legal traditions, is both important and logical; it is certainly rational.

The distinction comports with fundamental legal principles of causation and intent. First, when a patient refuses life-sustaining medical treatment, he dies from an underlying fatal disease or pathology; but if a patient ingests lethal medication prescribed by a physician, he is killed by that medication.

---

6 The American Medical Association emphasizes the "fundamental difference between refusing life-sustaining treatment and demanding a life-ending treatment." American Medical Association, Council on Ethical and Judicial Affairs, *Physician-Assisted Suicide*, 10 ISSUES IN LAW & MEDICINE 91, 93 (1994); *see also* American Medical Association, Council on Ethical and Judicial Affairs, *Decisions Near the End of Life*, 267 JAMA 2229, 2230-2231, 2233 (1992) ("The withdrawing or withholding of life-sustaining treatment is not inherently contrary to the principles of beneficence and nonmaleficence," but assisted suicide "is contrary to the prohibition against using the tools of medicine to cause a patient's death"); NEW YORK STATE TASK FORCE ON LIFE AND THE LAW, WHEN DEATH IS SOUGHT: ASSISTED SUICIDE AND EUTHANASIA IN THE MEDICAL CONTEXT 108 (1994) ("[Professional organizations] consistently distinguish assisted suicide and euthanasia from the withdrawing or withholding of treatment, and from the provision of palliative treatments or other medical care that risk fatal side effects"). . . .

Furthermore, a physician who withdraws, or honors a patient's refusal to begin, life-sustaining medical treatment purposefully intends, or may so intend, only to respect his patient's wishes and "to cease doing useless and futile or degrading things to the patient when [the patient] no longer stands to benefit from them." The same is true when a doctor provides aggressive palliative care; in some cases, painkilling drugs may hasten a patient's death, but the physician's purpose and intent is, or may be, only to ease his patient's pain. A doctor who assists a suicide, however, "must, necessarily and indubitably, intend primarily that the patient be made dead." . . .

* * *

This Court has also recognized, at least implicitly, the distinction between letting a patient die and making that patient die. In *Cruzan v. Director, Mo. Dept. of Health* (1990), we concluded that "[t]he principle that a competent person has a constitutionally protected liberty interest in refusing unwanted medical treatment may be inferred from our prior decisions," and we assumed the existence of such a right for purposes of that case. But our assumption of a right to refuse treatment was grounded not, as the Court of Appeals supposed, on the proposition that patients have a general and abstract "right to hasten death," but on well established, traditional rights to bodily integrity and freedom from unwanted touching. . . .

For all these reasons, we disagree with respondents' claim that the distinction between refusing lifesaving medical treatment and assisted suicide is "arbitrary" and "irrational." . . .

* * *

The judgment of the Court of Appeals is reversed.

JUSTICE O'CONNOR, concurring [in both *Vacco* and *Glucksberg*. *See* JUSTICE O'CONNOR's concurring opinion in *Glucksberg*].

JUSTICE STEVENS, concurring in the judgments [of both *Vacco* and *Glucksberg*].

* * *

IV

In New York, a doctor must respect a competent person's decision to refuse or to discontinue medical treatment even though death will thereby ensue, but the same doctor would be guilty of a felony if she provided her patient assistance in committing suicide. Today we hold that the Equal Protection Clause is not violated by the resulting disparate treatment of two classes of terminally ill people who may have the same interest in hastening death. I agree that the distinction between permitting death to ensue from an underlying fatal disease and causing it to occur by the administration of medication or other means provides a constitutionally sufficient basis for the State's classification. Unlike the Court, however, I am not persuaded that in all cases there will in fact be a significant difference between the intent of the physicians, the patients or the families in the two situations.

There may be little distinction between the intent of a terminally-ill patient who decides to remove her life-support and one who seeks the assistance of a doctor in ending her life; in both situations, the patient is seeking to hasten a certain, impending death. The doctor's intent might also be the same in prescribing lethal medication as it is in terminating life support. A doctor who fails to administer medical treatment to one who is dying from a disease could be doing so with an intent to harm or kill that patient. Conversely, a doctor who prescribes lethal medication does not necessarily intend the patient's death — rather that doctor may seek simply to ease the patient's suffering and to comply with her wishes. The illusory character of any differences in intent or causation is confirmed by the fact that the American Medical Association unequivocally endorses the practice of terminal sedation — the administration of sufficient dosages of pain-killing medication to terminally ill patients to protect them from excruciating pain even when it is clear that the time of death will be advanced. The purpose of terminal sedation is to ease the suffering of the patient and comply with her wishes, and the actual cause of death is the administration of heavy doses of lethal sedatives. This same intent and causation may exist when a doctor complies with a patient's request for lethal medication to hasten her death.

Thus, although the differences the majority notes in causation and intent between terminating life-support and assisting in suicide support the Court's rejection of the respondents' facial challenge, these distinctions may be inapplicable to particular terminally ill patients and their doctors. Our holding today in *Vacco v. Quill* that the Equal Protection Clause is not violated by New York's classification, just like our holding in *Washington v. Glucksberg* that the Washington statute is not invalid on its face, does not foreclose the possibility that some applications of the New York statute may impose an intolerable intrusion on the patient's freedom.

* * *

JUSTICE SOUTER, concurring in the judgment.

Even though I do not conclude that assisted suicide is a fundamental right entitled to recognition at this time, I accord the claims raised by the patients and physicians in this case and *Washington v. Glucksberg* a high degree of importance, requiring a commensurate justification. The reasons that lead me to conclude in *Glucksberg* that the prohibition on assisted suicide is not arbitrary under the due process standard also support the distinction between assistance to suicide, which is banned, and practices such as termination of artificial life support and death-hastening pain medication, which are permitted. I accordingly concur in the judgment of the Court.

JUSTICE GINSBURG, concurring in the judgments [of both *Vacco* and *Glucksberg*].

I concur in the Court's judgments in these cases substantially for the reasons stated by JUSTICE O'CONNOR in her concurring opinion.

JUSTICE BREYER, concurring in the judgments [of both *Vacco* and *Glucksberg*]. [Omitted.]

NOTES AND QUESTIONS

1. How does the Court disavow a right to assisted suicide, after it has declared an abortion right? Aren't they both exercises of personal autonomy? Chief Justice Rehnquist writes that even as "many of the rights and liberties protected by the Due Process Clause sound in personal autonomy does not warrant the sweeping conclusion that any and all important, intimate, and personal decisions are so protected . . . ." But, why not? Presumably, the Chief Justice's answer is that the constitutional protection of personal liberty has a boundary, but where can it be found? His answer: in the "deeply rooted" traditions of our nation, as reflected in our history. Alternatively stated, only those personal activities that are "so fundamental to our concept of constitutionally ordered liberty" are protected. Assisted suicide does not fall within this category because of its common law condemnation going back 700 years before the nation itself. *See* Robert A. Destro, *The Scope of the Fourteenth Amendment Liberty Interest: Does the Constitution Encompass a Right to Define Oneself Out of Existence? An Exchange of Views with John A. Powell, Legal Director, American Civil Liberties Union,* 10 ISSUES L. & MED. 183 (1994) (asserting that arguments in favor of a "right to suicide fail because they assume . . . that the right to be a homicide victim — by one's own hand or that of another — is (or should be) one of the liberties protected by the Bill of Rights").

2. How significantly does Justice Souter's due process methodology based upon Justice Harlan's earlier dissenting opinion in *Poe v. Ullman* differ from that of the Court? Chief Justice Rehnquist suggests that the Souter/Harlan view is prone to subjectivity, and therefore, judicial misuse. Do you agree? Justice Souter proclaims that substantive due process is important and is a proper function of the Court, but that it cannot depend then on "extratextual absolutes." By this is Justice Souter disavowing his allegiance to the natural law principles — the self-evident truths — that underlie the Constitution? If Justice Souter does not wish to depend on first principle, isn't he inevitably led merely to impose his own view of what *he* thinks is reasonable? Justice Souter tries to soften this conclusion by writing that he sees his function as merely a benign supervisor of clashing principles, substituting his view "only when [the government has reached an outcome that] falls outside the realm of the reasonable." Reasonable to whom, and by what standard? Similarly, Justice Souter talks about judicial protection of only fundamental rights or those "truly deserving constitutional stature." He then identifies these, however, in relation to either "in constitutional text, or those exemplified by 'traditions from which [the

Nation] developed,' or revealed by contrast with 'the traditions from which it broke.'"

3. Justice Souter pointedly attempts to distinguish his approach from that which invalidated the Missouri Compromise and kept Dred Scott a slave, but is the attempt comprehensible once he separates himself from the natural law? It is surely understandable to interpret the word "person" in the Constitution as including all human beings in light of their "created" natures and accompanying unalienable rights, but once these "absolutist failings," as Justice Souter disparages them, are disavowed, why wasn't Chief Justice Taney correct that the Court was duty-bound to protect whatever the positive law declares to be property? The significance of recognizing the created or transcendent origin of personhood, as our founding Declaration does, cannot be understated in this regard. Indeed, religious leaders frequently make this point. For example, John Cardinal O'Connor writes:

> I am not sure that even a sense of humanity, even a recognition that the unborn, the cancer-ridden, the vulnerable are persons will change anything. What will change it? I am not sure that anything will change it except a recognition of the sacredness of the human person, not simply the humanity, but that human beings belong to God. As St. Paul says, "You are not your own. You have been purchased, and at what a price! So glorify God in your body." No, human beings will not be safe unless we recognize they are sacred persons.

John Cardinal O'Connor, *"You Are Not Your Own" A Teaching From St. Paul Has Everything To Do With* Roe v. Wade, 37 CATH. LAW. 261, 266 (1997) (quoting 1 *Corinthians* 6:19-20).

4. In description, the Souter method seems tame or restrained. "Only," he says, "when the legislation's justifying principle, critically valued, is so far from being commensurate with the individual interest as to be arbitrarily or pointlessly applied that the statute must give way." Unfortunately, since Justice Souter is one of the principle architects of the reformed reaffirmation of the abortion right, the description does not seem to match application. After all, can it really be said that the state's desire to preserve unborn life is arbitrary and pointless? Similarly, Justice Souter goes to great length to insist that his weighing of "clashing principles" notion only properly works if the principles are described at the right level of detail or generality. In making his argument, Justice Souter highlights how the prohibition against the use of contraceptives foundered because the regulation invaded the *marital* bedroom. A broader claim for constitutional protection for sexual relations outside marriage, he states, would "be shot-through by exception." Since the Justice implies that the state might legitimately enforce such limits outside the marital relationship, one wonders why his voice was not heard in *Romer v. Evans*, discussed in Chapter Eight.

5. Outside of Justice Souter's attempt to re-center constitutional due process analysis upon "nuanced" judicial balancing, the common theme among the concurrences is to reserve the right to revisit the issue if state laws against assisting suicide as applied prevent the provision of palliative care. Only Justice Stevens explains the origin of this reserved authority. Curiously, he describes the interest in "hastening death," as he calls it, as a pre-societal liberty traceable to the fact that "it [is] self-evident that all men were endowed by their Creator with liberty as one of the cardinal unalienable rights." Unfortunately, Justice Stevens fails to then explain how an *un*alienable right (that is, one incapable of sale or forfeiture even by the person holding the right) produces a liberty interest that includes unnatural or premature alienation.

6. The Court's opinion in *Vacco* rejecting the equal protection challenge is in some ways a better reflection of natural law than *Glucksberg*'s refusal to find a due process violation. In *Glucksberg*, the Court supplies less an affirmation of the unalienability of human life, except by reference to the common law sources that contain that affirmation, than a refusal to impose a judicial outcome that would have preempted the debate about the "morality, legality, and practicality of physician-assited suicide." The Court in *Glucksberg* proclaims that its "holding permits this debate to continue, as it should in a democratic society." By contrast, the *Vacco* opinion suggests that even democratic debate cannot lead to immoral end, at least not given "fundamental legal principles of causation and intent" that the Court claims aptly distinguish a refusal of continued care, including a withdrawal of treatment, from the affirmative aiding of the taking of life.

7. In 1994, Oregon voters approved a so-called "Death With Dignity Act," by a narrow margin permitting doctors to prescribe lethal medications at a dying patient's request. Initially, the Act was enjoined in the view that the law treated terminal patients unequally under the law. *Lee v. Oregon*, 891 F. Supp. 1429 (D. Or. 1995). Applying deferential rational basis, the district judge found that the terminally ill were being singled out irrationally and denied protections that otherwise applied to medical patients. Specifically, the court found that the duty of reasonable care to which all other patients were entitled was suspended with regard to the terminally ill and replaced with a subjective good faith standard. *Id.* at 1437. The Ninth Circuit reversed and vacated the lower court judgment finding that even if the unequal standard existed there was no adversely affected plaintiff with standing before the court. 107 F.3d 1382 (9th Cir. 1997), *cert. denied sub nom. Lee v. Harcleroad*, 118 S. Ct. 328 (1997).

For a while it looked as if Oregon might repeal the Act. However, in November 1997, Oregon voters defeated a repeal measure, and thus, Oregon law presently provides that a doctor may prescribe on request a lethal dosage of oral mediation to a terminally ill person who is deemed to have less than six months to live. The person receiving the drugs must wait 15 days before self-administering them.

While many religions have spoken out strongly against assisted suicide, as the Court's decisions make plain there are non-religious reasons for concern as well. For a superb appraisal of these considerations by an eminent scholar well before the controversy made its way to the Court, see Yale Kamisar, *Some Non-Religious Views Against Proposed "Mercy-Killing" Legislation*, 42 MINN. L. REV. 969 (1958), and later views in Yale Kamisar, *The "Right to Die": On Drawing (and Erasing) Lines*, 35 DUQ. L. REV. 481 (1996) (arguing that *Quill* and *Compassion in Dying* imprudently erased the line between foregoing life-sustaining medical treatment and actively intervening to bring about death). For articles advising the Court to be hesitant about resolving the issue prematurely, see Thomas W. Mayo, *Constitutionalizing the "Right to Die"*, 49 MD. L. REV. 103 (1990); *see also,* Victor G. Rosenblum & Clarke D. Forsythe, *The Right to Assisted Suicide: Protection of Autonomy or an Open Door to Social Killing?*, 6 ISSUES L. & MED. 3 (1990) (discussing the legalization of assisted suicide in light of a clear historical understanding of the nation's legal and medical foundations, and calling on the medical profession to resist the transformation from "healers" to "killers"); and see Richard S. Meyers, *An Analysis of the Constitutionality of Laws Banning Assisted Suicide from the Perspective of Catholic Moral Teaching,* 72 U. DET. MERCY L. REV. 771 (1996) (examining two approaches to the constitutionality of laws banning assisted suicide: the "liberal" position hinged on personal "choice" and autonomy" and the "conservative" position based on objective moral standards from history and tradition).

4. Homosexual Conduct

In *Bowers v. Hardwick*, 478 U.S. 186 (1986), the Court, 5-4, held that homosexual sodomy was not a protected liberty interest, and therefore, Georgia could make it unlawful. Justice White wrote for the majority:

> [W]e think it evident that none of the rights announced in those cases bears any resemblance to the claimed constitutional right of homosexuals to engage in acts of sodomy that is asserted in this case. No connection between family, marriage, or procreation on the one hand and homosexual activity on the other has been demonstrated, either by the Court of Appeals or by respondent. Moreover, any claim that these cases nevertheless stand for the proposition that any kind of private sexual conduct between consenting adults is constitutionally insulated from state proscription is unsupportable. Indeed, the Court's opinion in *Carey* [*v. Population Services International* (1977)] twice asserted that the privacy right, which the *Griswold* [*v. Connecticut* (1965)] line of cases found to be one of the protections provided by the Due Process Clause, did not reach so far.

> Precedent aside, however, respondent would have us announce, as the Court of Appeals did, a fundamental right to engage in homosexual sodomy. This we are quite unwilling to do. It is true that despite the lan-

guage of the Due Process Clauses of the Fifth and Fourteenth Amendments, which appears to focus only on the processes by which life, liberty, or property is taken, the cases are legion in which those Clauses have been interpreted to have substantive content, subsuming rights that to a great extent are immune from federal or state regulation or proscription. Among such cases are those recognizing rights that have little or no textual support in the constitutional language. . . .

Striving to assure itself and the public that announcing rights not readily identifiable in the Constitution's text involves much more than the imposition of the Justices' own choice of values on the States and the Federal Government, the Court has sought to identify the nature of the rights qualifying for heightened judicial protection. In *Palko v. Connecticut* (1937), it was said that this category includes those fundamental liberties that are "implicit in the concept of ordered liberty," such that "neither liberty nor justice would exist if [they] were sacrificed." A different description of fundamental liberties appeared in *Moore v. East Cleveland* (1977) (opinion of POWELL, J.), where they are characterized as those liberties that are "deeply rooted in this Nation's history and tradition."

It is obvious to us that neither of these formulations would extend a fundamental right to homosexuals to engage in acts of consensual sodomy. Proscriptions against that conduct have ancient roots. Sodomy was a criminal offense at common law and was forbidden by the laws of the original 13 States when they ratified the Bill of Rights. In 1868, when the Fourteenth Amendment was ratified, all but 5 of the 37 States in the Union had criminal sodomy laws. In fact, until 1961, all 50 States outlawed sodomy, and today, 24 States and the District of Columbia continue to provide criminal penalties for sodomy performed in private and between consenting adults. Against this background, to claim that a right to engage in such conduct is "deeply rooted in this Nation's history and tradition" or "implicit in the concept of ordered liberty" is, at best, facetious.

* * *

Even if the conduct at issue here is not a fundamental right, respondent asserts that there must be a rational basis for the law and that there is none in this case other than the presumed belief of a majority of the electorate in Georgia that homosexual sodomy is immoral and unacceptable. This is said to be an inadequate rationale to support the law. The law, however, is constantly based on notions of morality, and if all laws representing essentially moral choices are to be invalidated under the Due Process Clause, the courts will be very busy indeed. Even respondent makes no such claim, but insists that majority sentiments about the morality of homosexuality should be declared inadequate. We do not agree, and are unpersuaded that the sodomy laws of some 25 States should be invalidated on this basis.

Justice Blackmun, the author of *Roe v. Wade*, filed a vigorous dissent in *Bowers*. Blackmun claimed that the case was not about a "fundamental right to engage in homosexual sodomy," but rather was about "the most comprehensive of rights and the right most valued by civilized men . . . the right to be let alone." Was he right about that? Where does this right come from? The Constitution is about forming a "more perfect union" — a community — not about being left alone, right? Is that why the majority rejected Blackmun's claim, or was the majority merely reflecting the historical disapproval of homosexual practice? Can a state, then, decide to express that disapproval in law? Consider the next case.

LAWRENCE v. TEXAS
539 U.S. 558 (2003)

Justice Kennedy delivered the opinion of the Court.

Liberty protects the person from unwarranted government intrusions into a dwelling or other private places. In our tradition the State is not omnipresent in the home. And there are other spheres of our lives and existence, outside the home, where the State should not be a dominant presence. Freedom extends beyond spatial bounds. Liberty presumes an autonomy of self that includes freedom of thought, belief, expression, and certain intimate conduct. The instant case involves liberty of the person both in its spatial and more transcendent dimensions.

I

The question before the Court is the validity of a Texas statute making it a crime for two persons of the same sex to engage in certain intimate sexual conduct.

In Houston, Texas, officers of the Harris County Police Department were dispatched to a private residence in response to a reported weapons disturbance. They entered an apartment where one of the petitioners, John Geddes Lawrence, resided. The right of the police to enter does not seem to have been questioned. The officers observed Lawrence and another man, Tyron Garner, engaging in a sexual act. The two petitioners were arrested, held in custody over night, and charged and convicted before a Justice of the Peace.

The complaints described their crime as "deviate sexual intercourse, namely anal sex, with a member of the same sex (man)." . . . The statute defines "[d]eviate sexual intercourse" as follows:

"(A) any contact between any part of the genitals of one person and the mouth or anus of another person; or

"(B) the penetration of the genitals or the anus of another person with an object."

* * *

The Court of Appeals for the Texas Fourteenth District considered the petitioners' federal constitutional arguments under both the Equal Protection and Due Process Clauses of the Fourteenth Amendment. After hearing the case en banc the court, in a divided opinion, rejected the constitutional arguments and affirmed the convictions. The majority opinion indicates that the Court of Appeals considered our decision in *Bowers v. Hardwick,* (1986), to be controlling on the federal due process aspect of the case. *Bowers* then being authoritative, this was proper.

* **

The petitioners were adults at the time of the alleged offense. Their conduct was in private and consensual.

II

We conclude the case should be resolved by determining whether the petitioners were free as adults to engage in the private conduct in the exercise of their liberty under the Due Process Clause of the Fourteenth Amendment to the Constitution. For this inquiry we deem it necessary to reconsider the Court's holding in *Bowers.*

* * *

The Court began its substantive discussion in *Bowers* as follows: "The issue presented is whether the Federal Constitution confers a fundamental right upon homosexuals to engage in sodomy and hence invalidates the laws of the many States that still make such conduct illegal and have done so for a very long time." That statement, we now conclude, discloses the Court's own failure to appreciate the extent of the liberty at stake. To say that the issue in *Bowers* was simply the right to engage in certain sexual conduct demeans the claim the individual put forward, just as it would demean a married couple were it to be said marriage is simply about the right to have sexual intercourse. . . . When sexuality finds overt expression in intimate conduct with another person, the conduct can be but one element in a personal bond that is more enduring. The liberty protected by the Constitution allows homosexual persons the right to make this choice.

Having misapprehended the claim of liberty there presented to it, and thus stating the claim to be whether there is a fundamental right to engage in consensual sodomy, the *Bowers* Court said: "Proscriptions against that conduct have ancient roots." In academic writings, and in many of the scholarly *amicus* briefs filed to assist the Court in this case, there are fundamental criticisms of the historical premises relied upon by the majority and concurring opinions in *Bowers.* We need not enter this debate in the attempt to reach a definitive historical judgment, but the following considerations counsel against adopting the definitive conclusions upon which *Bowers* placed such reliance.

At the outset it should be noted that there is no longstanding history in this country of laws directed at homosexual conduct as a distinct matter. Beginning in colonial times there were prohibitions of sodomy derived from the English criminal laws passed in the first instance by the Reformation Parliament of 1533.

. . . The early American sodomy laws were not directed at homosexuals as such but instead sought to prohibit nonprocreative sexual activity more generally. This does not suggest approval of homosexual conduct. It does tend to show that this particular form of conduct was not thought of as a separate category from like conduct between heterosexual persons.

* * *

To the extent that there were any prosecutions for the acts in question, 19th-century evidence rules imposed a burden that would make a conviction more difficult to obtain even taking into account the problems always inherent in prosecuting consensual acts committed in private. Under then-prevailing standards, a man could not be convicted of sodomy based upon testimony of a consenting partner, because the partner was considered an accomplice. A partner's testimony, however, was admissible if he or she had not consented to the act or was a minor, and therefore incapable of consent. . . . In all events that infrequency makes it difficult to say that society approved of a rigorous and systematic punishment of the consensual acts committed in private and by adults. The longstanding criminal prohibition of homosexual sodomy upon which the *Bowers* decision placed such reliance is as consistent with a general condemnation of nonprocreative sex as it is with an established tradition of prosecuting acts because of their homosexual character.

* * *

American laws targeting same-sex couples did not develop until the last third of the 20th century. The reported decisions concerning the prosecution of consensual, homosexual sodomy between adults for the years 1880-1995 are not always clear in the details, but a significant number involved conduct in a public place.

* * *

In summary, the historical grounds relied upon in *Bowers* are more complex than the majority opinion and the concurring opinion by Chief Justice Burger indicate. Their historical premises are not without doubt and, at the very least, are overstated.

It must be acknowledged, of course, that the Court in *Bowers* was making the broader point that for centuries there have been powerful voices to condemn homosexual conduct as immoral. The condemnation has been shaped by religious beliefs, conceptions of right and acceptable behavior, and respect for the traditional family. For many persons these are not trivial concerns but profound and deep convictions accepted as ethical and moral principles to which they aspire and which thus determine the course of their lives. These considerations do not answer the question before us, however. The issue is whether the majority may use the power of the State to enforce these views on the whole society through operation of the criminal law. "Our obligation is to define the liberty of all, not to mandate our own moral code." *Planned Parenthood of Southeastern Pa. v. Casey.*

Chief Justice Burger joined the opinion for the Court in *Bowers* and further explained his views as follows: "Decisions of individuals relating to homosexual conduct have been subject to state intervention throughout the history of Western civilization. Condemnation of those practices is firmly rooted in Judeao-Christian moral and ethical standards." . . . We think that our laws and traditions in the past half century are of most relevance here. These references show an emerging awareness that liberty gives substantial protection to adult persons in deciding how to conduct their private lives in matters pertaining to sex." . . .

This emerging recognition should have been apparent when *Bowers* was decided. In 1955 the American Law Institute promulgated the Model Penal Code and made clear that it did not recommend or provide for "criminal penalties for consensual sexual relations conducted in private." ALI, Model Penal Code § 213.2, Comment 2, p. 372 (1980). It justified its decision on three grounds: (1) The prohibitions undermined respect for the law by penalizing conduct many people engaged in; (2) the statutes regulated private conduct not harmful to others; and (3) the laws were arbitrarily enforced and thus invited the danger of blackmail. . . .

In *Bowers* the Court referred to the fact that before 1961 all 50 States had outlawed sodomy, and that at the time of the Court's decision 24 States and the District of Columbia had sodomy laws. . . .

The sweeping references by Chief Justice Burger to the history of Western civilization and to Judeo-Christian moral and ethical standards did not take account of other authorities pointing in an opposite direction. A committee advising the British Parliament recommended in 1957 repeal of laws punishing homosexual conduct. . . .

Of even more importance, almost five years before *Bowers* was decided the European Court of Human Rights considered a case with parallels to *Bowers* and to today's case. An adult male resident in Northern Ireland alleged he was a practicing homosexual who desired to engage in consensual homosexual conduct. The laws of Northern Ireland forbade him that right. He alleged that he had been questioned, his home had been searched, and he feared criminal prosecution. The court held that the laws proscribing the conduct were invalid under the European Convention on Human Rights. *Dudgeon v. United Kingdom,*

45 Eur. Ct. H.R. (1981) & ¶ 52. Authoritative in all countries that are members of the Council of Europe (21 nations then, 45 nations now), the decision is at odds with the premise in *Bowers* that the claim put forward was insubstantial in our Western civilization.

In our own constitutional system the deficiencies in *Bowers* became even more apparent in the years following its announcement. The 25 States with laws prohibiting the relevant conduct referenced in the *Bowers* decision are reduced now to 13, of which 4 enforce their laws only against homosexual conduct. In those States where sodomy is still proscribed, whether for same-sex or heterosexual conduct, there is a pattern of nonenforcement with respect to consenting adults acting in private. The State of Texas admitted in 1994 that as of that date it had not prosecuted anyone under those circumstances.

Two principal cases decided after *Bowers* cast its holding into even more doubt. In *Planned Parenthood of Southeastern Pa. v. Casey* (1992), the Court reaffirmed the substantive force of the liberty protected by the Due Process Clause. The *Casey* decision again confirmed that our laws and tradition afford constitutional protection to personal decisions relating to marriage, procreation, contraception, family relationships, child rearing, and education. In explaining the respect the Constitution demands for the autonomy of the person in making these choices, we stated as follows:

> "These matters, involving the most intimate and personal choices a person may make in a lifetime, choices central to personal dignity and autonomy, are central to the liberty protected by the Fourteenth Amendment. At the heart of liberty is the right to define one's own concept of existence, of meaning, of the universe, and of the mystery of human life. Beliefs about these matters could not define the attributes of personhood were they formed under compulsion of the State."

Persons in a homosexual relationship may seek autonomy for these purposes, just as heterosexual persons do. The decision in *Bowers* would deny them this right.

The second post-*Bowers* case of principal relevance is *Romer v. Evans* (1996).

. . .

As an alternative argument in this case, counsel for the petitioners and some *amici* contend that *Romer* provides the basis for declaring the Texas statute invalid under the Equal Protection Clause. That is a tenable argument, but we conclude the instant case requires us to address whether *Bowers* itself has continuing validity. Were we to hold the statute invalid under the Equal Protection Clause some might question whether a prohibition would be valid if drawn differently, say, to prohibit the conduct both between same-sex and different-sex participants.

Equality of treatment and the due process right to demand respect for conduct protected by the substantive guarantee of liberty are linked in important respects, and a decision on the latter point advances both interests. . . . The central holding of *Bowers* has been brought in question by this case, and it should be addressed. Its continuance as precedent demeans the lives of homosexual persons.

* * *

The doctrine of *stare decisis* is essential to the respect accorded to the judgments of the Court and to the stability of the law. It is not, however, an inexorable command.

* * *

Bowers was not correct when it was decided, and it is not correct today. It ought not to remain binding precedent. *Bowers v. Hardwick* should be and now is overruled.

The present case does not involve minors. It does not involve persons who might be injured or coerced or who are situated in relationships where consent might not easily be refused. It does not involve public conduct or prostitution. It does not involve whether the government must give formal recognition to any relationship that homosexual persons seek to enter. The case does involve two adults who, with full and mutual consent from each other, engaged in sexual practices common to a homosexual lifestyle. The petitioners are entitled to respect for their private lives. The State cannot demean their existence or control their destiny by making their private sexual conduct a crime. Their right to liberty under the Due Process Clause gives them the full right to engage in their conduct without intervention of the government. "It is a promise of the Constitution that there is a realm of personal liberty which the government may not enter." The Texas statute furthers no legitimate state interest which can justify its intrusion into the personal and private life of the individual.

Had those who drew and ratified the Due Process Clauses of the Fifth Amendment or the Fourteenth Amendment known the components of liberty in its manifold possibilities, they might have been more specific. They did not presume to have this insight. They knew times can blind us to certain truths and later generations can see that laws once thought necessary and proper in fact serve only to oppress. As the Constitution endures, persons in every generation can invoke its principles in their own search for greater freedom.

The judgment of the Court of Appeals for the Texas Fourteenth District is reversed, and the case is remanded for further proceedings not inconsistent with this opinion.

It is so ordered.

JUSTICE O'CONNOR, concurring in the judgment.

The Court today overrules *Bowers v. Hardwick* (1986). I joined *Bowers,* and do not join the Court in overruling it. Nevertheless, I agree with the Court that Texas' statute banning same-sex sodomy is unconstitutional. Rather than relying on the substantive component of the Fourteenth Amendment's Due Process

Clause, as the Court does, I base my conclusion on the Fourteenth Amendment's Equal Protection Clause.

The Equal Protection Clause of the Fourteenth Amendment "is essentially a direction that all persons similarly situated should be treated alike." *Cleburne v. Cleburne Living Center, Inc.* (1982). Under our rational basis standard of review, "legislation is presumed to be valid and will be sustained if the classification drawn by the statute is rationally related to a legitimate state interest."

Laws such as economic or tax legislation that are scrutinized under rational basis review normally pass constitutional muster, since "the Constitution presumes that even improvident decisions will eventually be rectified by the democratic processes." We have consistently held, however, that some objectives, such as "a bare . . . desire to harm a politically unpopular group," are not legitimate state interests. When a law exhibits such a desire to harm a politically unpopular group, we have applied a more searching form of rational basis review to strike down such laws under the Equal Protection Clause.

We have been most likely to apply rational basis review to hold a law unconstitutional under the Equal Protection Clause where, as here, the challenged legislation inhibits personal relationships. In *Department of Agriculture v. Moreno,* for example, we held that a law preventing those households containing an individual unrelated to any other member of the household from receiving food stamps violated equal protection because the purpose of the law was to "'discriminate against hippies.'" The asserted governmental interest in preventing food stamp fraud was not deemed sufficient to satisfy rational basis review. In *Eisenstadt v. Baird* (1972), we refused to sanction a law that discriminated between married and unmarried persons by prohibiting the distribution of contraceptives to single persons. Likewise, in *Cleburne v. Cleburne Living Center, supra,* we held that it was irrational for a State to require a home for the mentally disabled to obtain a special use permit when other residences — like fraternity houses and apartment buildings — did not have to obtain such a permit. And in *Romer v. Evans,* we disallowed a state statute that "impos[ed] a broad and undifferentiated disability on a single named group" — specifically, homosexuals. The dissent apparently agrees that if these cases have *stare decisis* effect, Texas' sodomy law would not pass scrutiny under the Equal Protection Clause, regardless of the type of rational basis review that we apply.

The statute at issue here makes sodomy a crime only if a person "engages in deviate sexual intercourse with another individual of the same sex." Sodomy between opposite-sex partners, however, is not a crime in Texas. . . .

* * *

Texas attempts to justify its law, and the effects of the law, by arguing that the statute satisfies rational basis review because it furthers the legitimate governmental interest of the promotion of morality. In *Bowers,* we held that a state law criminalizing sodomy as applied to homosexual couples did not violate substantive due process. We rejected the argument that no rational basis existed to justify the law, pointing to the government's interest in promoting morality. The only question in front of the Court in *Bowers* was whether the substantive component of the Due Process Clause protected a right to engage in homosexual sodomy. *Bowers* did not hold that moral disapproval of a group is a rational basis under the Equal Protection Clause to criminalize homosexual sodomy when heterosexual sodomy is not punished.

This case raises a different issue than *Bowers:* whether, under the Equal Protection Clause, moral disapproval is a legitimate state interest to justify by itself a statute that bans homosexual sodomy, but not heterosexual sodomy. It is not. Moral disapproval of this group, like a bare desire to harm the group, is an interest that is insufficient to satisfy rational basis review under the Equal Protection Clause. . . .

* * *

Texas argues, however, that the sodomy law does not discriminate against homosexual persons. Instead, the State maintains that the law discriminates only against homosexual conduct. While it is true that the law applies only to conduct, the conduct targeted by this law is conduct that is closely correlated with being homosexual. . . .

* * *

Whether a sodomy law that is neutral both in effect and application, would violate the substantive component of the Due Process Clause is an issue that need not be decided today. I am confident, however, that so long as the Equal Protection Clause requires a sodomy law to apply equally to the private consensual conduct of homosexuals and heterosexuals alike, such a law would not long stand in our democratic society. In the words of Justice Jackson:

> "The framers of the Constitution knew, and we should not forget today, that there is no more effective practical guaranty against arbitrary and unreasonable government than to require that the principles of law which officials would impose upon a minority be imposed generally. Conversely, nothing opens the door to arbitrary action so effectively as to allow those officials to pick and choose only a few to whom they will apply legislation and thus to escape the political retribution that might be visited upon them if larger numbers were affected."

That this law as applied to private, consensual conduct is unconstitutional under the Equal Protection Clause does not mean that other laws distinguishing between heterosexuals and homosexuals would similarly fail under rational basis review. Texas cannot assert any legitimate state interest here, such as national security or preserving the traditional institution of marriage. Unlike the moral disapproval of same-sex relations — the asserted state interest in this case — other reasons exist to promote the institution of marriage beyond mere moral disapproval of an excluded group.

A law branding one class of persons as criminal solely based on the State's moral disapproval of that class and the conduct associated with that class runs contrary to the values of the Constitution and the Equal Protection Clause, under any standard of review. I therefore concur in the Court's judgment that Texas' sodomy law banning "deviate sexual intercourse" between consenting adults of the same sex, but not between consenting adults of different sexes, is unconstitutional.

JUSTICE SCALIA, with whom THE CHIEF JUSTICE and JUSTICE THOMAS join, dissenting.

* * *

Most of today's opinion has no relevance to its actual holding — that the Texas statute "furthers no legitimate state interest which can justify" its application to petitioners under rational-basis review. (overruling *Bowers* to the extent it sustained Georgia's anti-sodomy statute under the rational-basis test). Though there is discussion of "fundamental proposition[s]," and "fundamental decisions," nowhere does the Court's opinion declare that homosexual sodomy is a "fundamental right" under the Due Process Clause; nor does it subject the Texas law to the standard of review that would be appropriate (strict scrutiny) if homosexual sodomy *were* a "fundamental right." Thus, while overruling the *outcome* of *Bowers,* the Court leaves strangely untouched its central legal conclusion: "[R]espondent would have us announce . . . a fundamental right to engage in homosexual sodomy. This we are quite unwilling to do." Instead the Court simply describes petitioners' conduct as "an exercise of their liberty" — which it undoubtedly is — and proceeds to apply an unheard-of form of rational-basis review that will have far-reaching implications beyond this case.

I

I begin with the Court's surprising readiness to reconsider a decision rendered a mere 17 years ago in *Bowers v. Hardwick.* I do not myself believe in rigid adherence to *stare decisis* in constitutional cases; but I do believe that we should be consistent rather than manipulative in invoking the doctrine. Today's opinions in support of reversal do not bother to distinguish — or indeed, even bother to mention — the paean to *stare decisis* coauthored by three Members of today's majority in *Planned Parenthood v. Casey.* There, when *stare decisis* meant preservation of judicially invented abortion rights, the widespread criticism of *Roe* was strong reason to *reaffirm* it:

> "Where, in the performance of its judicial duties, the Court decides a case in such a way as to resolve the sort of intensely divisive controversy reflected in *Roe*[,] . . . its decision has a dimension that the resolution of the normal case does not carry . . . . [T]o overrule under fire in the absence of the most compelling reason . . . would subvert the Court's legitimacy beyond any serious question."

Today, however, the widespread opposition to *Bowers,* a decision resolving an issue as "intensely divisive" as the issue in *Roe,* is offered as a reason in favor of *overruling* it. Gone, too, is any "enquiry" (of the sort conducted in *Casey*) into whether the decision sought to be overruled has "proven 'unworkable.'"

Today's approach to *stare decisis* invites us to overrule an erroneously decided precedent (including an "intensely divisive" decision) *if:* (1) its foundations have been "eroded" by subsequent decisions, (2) it has been subject to "substantial and continuing" criticism; and (3) it has not induced "individual or societal reliance" that counsels against overturning. The problem is that *Roe* itself — which today's majority surely has no disposition to overrule — satisfies these conditions to at least the same degree as *Bowers.*

* * *

"[T]here has been," the Court says, "no individual or societal reliance on *Bowers* of the sort that could counsel against overturning its holding . . . ." It seems to me that the "societal reliance" on the principles confirmed in *Bowers* and discarded today has been overwhelming. Countless judicial decisions and legislative enactments have relied on the ancient proposition that a governing majority's belief that certain sexual behavior is "immoral and unacceptable" constitutes a rational basis for regulation. *See, e.g., Williams v. Pryor* (C.A.11 2001) (citing *Bowers* in upholding Alabama's prohibition on the sale of sex toys on the ground that "[t]he crafting and safeguarding of public morality . . . indisputably is a legitimate government interest under rational basis scrutiny"); *Milner v. Apfel* (C.A.7 1998) (citing *Bowers* for the proposition that "[l]egislatures are permitted to legislate with regard to morality . . . rather than confined to preventing demonstrable harms"); *Holmes v. California Army National Guard* (C.A.9 1997) (relying on *Bowers* in upholding the federal statute and regulations banning from military service those who engage in homosexual conduct); *Owens v. State* (1999) (relying on *Bowers* in holding that "a person has no constitutional right to engage in sexual intercourse, at least outside of marriage"); *Sherman v. Henry* (Tex.1996) (relying on *Bowers* in rejecting a claimed constitutional right to commit adultery). We ourselves relied extensively on *Bowers* when we concluded, in *Barnes v. Glen Theatre, Inc.* (1991), that Indiana's public indecency statute furthered "a substantial government interest in protecting order and morality," (plurality opinion). State laws against bigamy, same-sex marriage, adult incest, prostitution, masturbation, adultery, fornication, bestiality, and obscenity are likewise sustainable only in light of *Bowers'* validation of laws based on moral choices. Every single one of these laws is called into question by today's decision; the Court makes no effort to cabin the scope of its decision to exclude them from its holding (noting "an emerging awareness that liberty gives substantial protection to adult persons in deciding how to conduct their private lives *in matters pertaining to sex*" (emphasis added)). The impossibility of distinguishing homosexuality from other traditional "morals" offenses is precisely why *Bowers* rejected the rational-basis challenge. "The law," it said, "is constantly based on notions of morality, and if all laws representing essentially moral choices are to be invalidated under the Due Process Clause, the courts will be very busy indeed."

* * *

What a massive disruption of the current social order, therefore, the overruling of *Bowers* entails. Not so the overruling of *Roe,* which would simply have restored the regime that existed for centuries before 1973, in which the permissibility of and restrictions upon abortion were determined legislatively State-by-State. *Casey,* however, chose to base its *stare decisis* determination on a different "sort" of reliance. "[P]eople," it said, "have organized intimate relationships and made choices that define their views of themselves and their places in society, in reliance on the availability of abortion in the event that contraception should fail." This falsely assumes that the consequence of overruling *Roe* would have been to make abortion unlawful. It would not; it would merely have *permitted* the States to do so. Many States would unquestionably have declined to prohibit abortion, and others would not have prohibited it within six months (after which the most significant reliance interests would have expired). Even for persons in States other than these, the choice would not have been between abortion and childbirth, but between abortion nearby and abortion in a neighboring State.

To tell the truth, it does not surprise me, and should surprise no one, that the Court has chosen today to revise the standards of *stare decisis* set forth in *Casey.* It has thereby exposed *Casey*'s extraordinary deference to precedent for the result-oriented expedient that it is.

II

* * *

The Texas law undoubtedly imposes constraints on liberty. So do laws prohibiting prostitution, recreational use of heroin, and, for that matter, working more than 60 hours per week in a bakery. But there is no right to "liberty" under the Due Process Clause, though today's opinion repeatedly makes that claim. . . . The Fourteenth Amendment *expressly allows* States to deprive their citizens of "liberty," *so long as "due process of law" is provided:*

> "No state shall . . . deprive any person of life, liberty, or property, *without due process of law.*" Amdt. 14 (emphasis added).

Our opinions applying the doctrine known as "substantive due process" hold that the Due Process Clause prohibits States from infringing *fundamental* liberty interests, unless the infringement is narrowly tailored to serve a compelling state interest. *Washington v. Glucksberg.*

* * *

Bowers held, first, that criminal prohibitions of homosexual sodomy are not subject to heightened scrutiny because they do not implicate a "fundamental right" under the Due Process Clause. Noting that "[p]roscriptions against that conduct have ancient roots," that "[s]odomy was a criminal offense at common law and was forbidden by the laws of the original 13 States when they ratified the Bill of Rights," *ibid.,* and that many States had retained their bans on sodomy, *Bowers* concluded that a right to engage in homosexual sodomy was not "'deeply rooted in this Nation's history and tradition.'"

The Court today does not overrule this holding. Not once does it describe homosexual sodomy as a "fundamental right" or a "fundamental liberty interest," nor does it subject the Texas statute to strict scrutiny. Instead, having failed to establish that the right to homosexual sodomy is "'deeply rooted in this Nation's history and tradition,'" the Court concludes that the application of Texas's statute to petitioners' conduct fails the rational-basis test, and overrules *Bowers'* holding to the contrary. "The Texas statute furthers no legitimate state interest which can justify its intrusion into the personal and private life of the individual."

* * *

III

The Court's description of "the state of the law" at the time of *Bowers* only confirms that *Bowers* was right. The Court points to *Griswold v. Connecticut* (1965). But that case *expressly disclaimed* any reliance on the doctrine of "substantive due process," and grounded the so-called "right to privacy" in penumbras of constitutional provisions *other than* the Due Process Clause. *Eisenstadt v. Baird* (1972), likewise had nothing to do with "substantive due process"; it invalidated a Massachusetts law prohibiting the distribution of contraceptives to unmarried persons solely on the basis of the Equal Protection Clause. Of course *Eisenstadt* contains well known dictum relating to the "right to privacy," but this referred to the right recognized in *Griswold* — a right penumbral to the *specific* guarantees in the Bill of Rights, and not a "substantive due process" right.

Roe v. Wade recognized that the right to abort an unborn child was a "fundamental right" protected by the Due Process Clause. The *Roe* Court, however, made no attempt to establish that this right was "'deeply rooted in this Nation's history and tradition'"; instead, it based its conclusion that "the Fourteenth Amendment's concept of personal liberty . . . is broad enough to encompass a woman's decision whether or not to terminate her pregnancy" on its own normative judgment that anti-abortion laws were undesirable. We have since rejected *Roe*'s holding that regulations of abortion must be narrowly tailored to serve a compelling state interest, *see Planned Parenthood v. Casey* (joint opinion of O'CONNOR, KENNEDY, and SOUTER, JJ.); (REHNQUIST, C.J., concurring in judgment in part and dissenting in part) — and thus, by logical implication, *Roe*'s holding that the right to abort an unborn child is a "fundamental right." . . .

* * *

It is (as *Bowers* recognized) entirely irrelevant whether the laws in our long national tradition criminalizing homosexual sodomy were "directed at homosexual conduct as a distinct matter." Whether homosexual sodomy was prohibited by a law targeted at same-sex sexual relations or by a more general law prohibiting both homosexual and heterosexual sodomy, the only relevant point is that it *was* criminalized — which suffices to establish that homosexual sodomy is not a right "deeply rooted in our Nation's history and tradition." The Court today agrees that homosexual sodomy was criminalized and thus does not dispute the facts on which Bowers *actually* relied.

* * *

Realizing that fact, the Court instead says: "[W]e think that our laws and traditions in the past half century are of most relevance here. These references show *an emerging awareness* that liberty gives substantial protection to adult persons in deciding how to conduct their private lives *in matters pertaining to sex*." Apart from the fact that such an "emerging awareness" does not establish a "fundamental right," the statement is factually false. States continue to prosecute all sorts of crimes by adults "in matters pertaining to sex": prostitution, adult incest, adultery, obscenity, and child pornography. Sodomy laws, too, have been enforced "in the past half century," in which there have been 134 reported cases involving prosecutions for consensual, adult, homosexual sodomy. . . .

In any event, an "emerging awareness" is by definition not "deeply rooted in this Nation's history and tradition[s]," as we have said "fundamental right" status requires. Constitutional entitlements do not spring into existence because some States choose to lessen or eliminate criminal sanctions on certain behavior. Much less do they spring into existence, as the Court seems to believe, because *foreign nations* decriminalize conduct. . . .

IV

I turn now to the ground on which the Court squarely rests its holding: the contention that there is no rational basis for the law here under attack. This proposition is so out of accord with our jurisprudence — indeed, with the jurisprudence of *any* society we know — that it requires little discussion.

The Texas statute undeniably seeks to further the belief of its citizens that certain forms of sexual behavior are "immoral and unacceptable," — the same interest furthered by criminal laws against fornication, bigamy, adultery, adult incest, bestiality, and obscenity. *Bowers* held that this *was* a legitimate state interest. The Court today reaches the opposite conclusion. The Texas statute, it says, "furthers *no legitimate state interest* which can justify its intrusion into the personal and private life of the individual." The Court embraces instead JUSTICE STEVENS' declaration in his *Bowers* dissent, that "the fact that the governing majority in a State has traditionally viewed a particular practice as immoral is not a sufficient reason for upholding a law prohibiting the practice." This effectively decrees the end of all morals legislation. If, as the Court asserts, the promotion of majoritarian sexual morality is not even a *legitimate* state interest, none of the above-mentioned laws can survive rational-basis review.

V

Finally, I turn to petitioners' equal-protection challenge, which no Member of the Court save JUSTICE O'CONNOR embraces: On its face the law applies equally to all persons. Men and women, heterosexuals and homosexuals, are all subject to its prohibition of deviate sexual intercourse with someone of the same sex. To be sure, the law does distinguish between the sexes insofar as concerns the partner with whom the sexual acts are performed: men can violate the law only with other men, and women only with other women. But this cannot itself be a denial of equal protection, since it is precisely the same distinction regarding partner that is drawn in state laws prohibiting marriage with someone of the same sex while permitting marriage with someone of the opposite sex.

The objection is made, however, that the antimiscegenation laws invalidated in *Loving v. Virginia* (1967), similarly were applicable to whites and blacks alike, and only distinguished between the races insofar as the *partner* was concerned. In *Loving,* however, we correctly applied heightened scrutiny, rather than the usual rational-basis review, because the Virginia statute was "designed to maintain White Supremacy." A racially discriminatory purpose is always sufficient to subject a law to strict scrutiny, even a facially neutral law that makes no mention of race.

JUSTICE O'CONNOR argues that the discrimination in this law which must be justified is not its discrimination with regard to the sex of the partner but its discrimination with regard to the sexual proclivity of the principal actor.

* * *

Of course the same could be said of any law. A law against public nudity targets "the conduct that is closely correlated with being a nudist," and hence "is targeted at more than conduct"; it is "directed toward nudists as a class." But be that as it may. Even if the Texas law *does* deny equal protection to "homosexuals as a class," that denial *still* does not need to be justified by anything more than a rational basis, which our cases show is satisfied by the enforcement of traditional notions of sexual morality.

JUSTICE O'CONNOR simply decrees application of "a more searching form of rational basis review" to the Texas statute. The cases she cites do not recognize such a standard, and reach their conclusions only after finding, as required by conventional rational-basis analysis, that no conceivable legitimate state interest supports the classification at issue. *See Romer v. Evans* (1973). Nor does JUSTICE O'CONNOR explain precisely what her "more searching form" of rational-basis review consists of. It must at least mean, however, that laws exhibiting "'a . . . desire to harm a politically unpopular group,'" are invalid *even though* there may be a conceivable rational basis to support them.

This reasoning leaves on pretty shaky grounds state laws limiting marriage to opposite-sex couples. JUSTICE O'CONNOR seeks to preserve them by the conclusory statement that "preserving the traditional institution of marriage" is a legitimate state interest. But "preserving the traditional institution of marriage" is just a kinder way of describing the State's *moral disapproval* of same-sex couples. Texas's interest could be recast in similarly euphemistic terms: "preserving the traditional sexual mores of our society." In the jurisprudence JUSTICE O'CONNOR has seemingly created, judges can validate laws by characterizing them as "preserving the traditions of society" (good); or invalidate them by characterizing them as "expressing moral disapproval" (bad).

* * *

Today's opinion is the product of a Court, which is the product of a law-profession culture, that has largely signed on to the so-called homosexual agenda, by which I mean the agenda promoted by some homosexual activists directed at eliminating the moral opprobrium that has traditionally attached to homosexual conduct. I noted in an earlier opinion the fact that the American Association of Law Schools (to which any reputable law school *must* seek to belong) excludes from membership any school that refuses to ban from its job-interview facilities a law firm (no matter how small) that does not wish to hire as a prospective partner a person who openly engages in homosexual conduct.

* * *

Let me be clear that I have nothing against homosexuals, or any other group, promoting their agenda through normal democratic means. Social perceptions of sexual and other morality change over time, and every group has the right to persuade its fellow citizens that its view of such matters is the best. That homosexuals have achieved some success in that enterprise is attested to by the fact that Texas is one of the few remaining States that criminalize private, consensual homosexual acts. But persuading one's fellow citizens is one thing, and imposing one's views in absence of democratic majority will is something else. I would no more *require* a State to criminalize homosexual acts — or, for that matter, display *any* moral disapprobation of them — than I would *forbid* it to do so. What Texas has chosen to do is well within the range of traditional democratic action, and its hand should not be stayed through the invention of a brand-new "constitutional right" by a Court that is impatient of democratic change. It is indeed true that "later generations can see that laws once thought necessary and proper in fact serve only to oppress," and when that happens, later generations can repeal those laws. But it is the premise of our system that those judgments are to be made by the people, and not imposed by a governing caste that knows best.

One of the benefits of leaving regulation of this matter to the people rather than to the courts is that the people, unlike judges, need not carry things to their logical conclusion. The people may feel that their disapprobation of homosexual conduct is strong enough to disallow homosexual marriage, but not strong enough to criminalize private homosexual acts — and may legislate accordingly. The Court today pretends that it possesses a similar freedom of action, so that that we need not fear judicial imposition of homosexual marriage, as has recently occurred in Canada (in a decision that the Canadian Government has chosen not to appeal). At the end of its opinion — after having laid waste the foundations of our rational-basis jurisprudence — the Court says that the present case "does not involve whether the government must give formal recognition to any relationship that homosexual persons seek to enter." Do not believe it. More illuminating than this bald, unreasoned disclaimer is the progression of thought displayed by an earlier passage in the Court's opinion, which notes the constitutional protections afforded to "personal decisions relating to *marriage,* procreation, contraception, family relationships, child rearing, and education," and then declares that "[p]ersons in a homosexual relationship may seek autonomy for these purposes, just as heterosexual persons do." Today's opinion dismantles the structure of constitutional law that has permitted a distinction to be made between heterosexual and homosexual unions, insofar as formal recognition in marriage is concerned. If moral disapprobation of homosexual conduct is "no legitimate state interest" for purposes of proscribing that conduct, and if, as the Court coos (casting aside all pretense of neutrality), "[w]hen sexuality finds overt expression in intimate conduct with another person, the conduct can be but one element in a personal bond that is more enduring;" what justification could there possibly be for denying the benefits of marriage to homosexual couples exercising "[t]he liberty protected by the Constitution"? Surely not the encouragement of procreation, since the sterile and the elderly are allowed to marry. This case "does not involve" the issue of homosexual marriage only if one entertains the belief that principle and logic have nothing to do with the decisions of this Court. Many will hope that, as the Court comfortingly assures us, this is so.

The matters appropriate for this Court's resolution are only three: Texas's prohibition of sodomy neither infringes a "fundamental right" (which the Court does not dispute), nor is unsupported by a rational relation to what the Constitution considers a legitimate state interest, nor denies the equal protection of the laws. I dissent.

Justice Thomas, dissenting.

I join Justice Scalia's dissenting opinion. I write separately to note that the law before the Court today "is . . . uncommonly silly." If I were a member of the Texas Legislature, I would vote to repeal it. Punishing someone for expressing his sexual preference through noncommercial consensual conduct with another adult does not appear to be a worthy way to expend valuable law enforcement resources.

Notwithstanding this, I recognize that as a member of this Court I am not empowered to help petitioners and others similarly situated. My duty, rather, is to "decide cases 'agreeably to the Constitution and laws of the United States.'" And, just like Justice Stewart in *Griswold*, I "can find [neither in the Bill of

Rights nor any other part of the Constitution a] general right of privacy," or as the Court terms it today, the "liberty of the person both in its spatial and more transcendent dimensions."

NOTES AND QUESTIONS

1. Is this case faithful to any of the methods the Court has historically used to discover unenumerated fundamental rights? The Court is quite right that "history and tradition are the starting point but not in all cases the ending point of the substantive due process inquiry." An asserted "fundamental liberty interest" must not only be "deeply rooted in this Nation's history and tradition," *Washington v. Glucksberg,* 521 U.S. 702, 721 (1997), but it must *also* be "implicit in the concept of ordered liberty," so that "neither liberty nor justice would exist if [it] were sacrificed." Do you think the right of intimate privacy is so "deeply rooted"? After all, no one in this case disputes that sodomy generally was a *criminal* act throughout our history, not a matter of right, do they? Is it enough to say that a claim unsupported by history and tradition, and thus not deserving of "heightened scrutiny," should still be protected? Was the problem here simply that laws that cannot be meaningfully enforced are inherently irrational and arbitrary? Wouldn't that have been a far narrower, perhaps better holding, reflecting what philosophers for millennia, including Thomas Aquinas, knew well: that one cannot enact every virtue or prohibit every vice in law? Everyone conceded that sodomy statutes, down through the ages, had never been applied, and that it was applied here largely by the accident of the false report of gun activity. If that is the case, why did the Court reach out to decide this dispute or decide it on the sweeping grounds that it did?

Justice Scalia thinks the Court took the case in order to take "sides in the culture war, departing from its role of assuring, as neutral observer, that the democratic rules of engagement are observed." First, is there such a war or is this merely the natural tendency to ask questions even about what appears to be even well-settled matters like marriage and family? Justice Scalia may be right that "many Americans do not want persons who openly engage in homosexual conduct as partners in their business, as scoutmasters for their children, as teachers in their children's schools, or as boarders in their home," but if that is the case shouldn't we as a people, in order to insure that we are not acting out of hate or stereotype, be asked to give a clear answer as to why sexual relations within marriage are culturally important and why they are reserved to a man and woman? Did Texas make adequate defense? But, absent the presence of either suspect class or fundamental right, is it the place of the Court to even ask or opine? The dissent writes: "in most States what the Court calls 'discrimination' against those who engage in homosexual acts is perfectly legal; that proposals to ban such 'discrimination' under Title VII have repeatedly been rejected by Congress, *see* Employment Non-Discrimination Act of 1994, S. 2238, 103d Cong., 2d Sess. (1994); Civil Rights Amendments, H.R. 5452, 94th Cong., 1st

Sess. (1975); that in some cases such 'discrimination' is *mandated* by federal statute, *see* 10 U.S.C. § 654(b)(1) (mandating discharge from the armed forces of any service member who engages in or intends to engage in homosexual acts); and that in some cases such 'discrimination' is a constitutional right, *see* *Boy Scouts of America v. Dale* (2000)."

2. A political firestorm, of sorts, erupted after an Associated Press interview with Pennsylvania's Republican Senator Rick Santorum, on April 7, 2003, where he was commenting on the fact that the Texas sodomy legislation was before the Court, and he stated that:

> We have laws in states, like the one at the Supreme Court right now, that has sodomy laws and they were there for a purpose. Because, again, I would argue, they undermine the basic tenets of our society and the family. And if the Supreme Court says that you have the right to consensual sex within your home, then you have the right to bigamy, you have the right to polygamy, you have the right to incest, you have the right to adultery. You have the right to anything. Does that undermine the fabric of our society? I would argue yes, it does. It all comes from, I would argue, this right to privacy that doesn't exist in my opinion in the United States Constitution . . . .

Now that six Justices of the United States Supreme Court have declared that Texas may not punish homosexual acts between willing adults, does this mean that Senator Santorum was correct? Is there a way in which the Supreme Court's reading of the "right to privacy" can be limited so that polygamy, incest, adultery, or any other sexual acts between willing adults do not necessarily receive constitutional protection?

3. Carried to its logical extreme, Justice Antonin Scalia in his dissent opined that the ruling seriously hobbles state morals legislation. Indeed, promoting morality through law is all but declared irrational. Yet, perhaps the case should not be over-read. Justice Anthony Kennedy disclaimed any purpose other than securing basic privacy. His ruling, he said, does not involve the government giving formal recognition to any relationship (which presumably means he is not endorsing gay marriage) and does not involve minors, coercion, or public activity such as disqualification from the military for overt conduct.

The analytical problem is why these matters should remain undisturbed — other than that the Court controls its own docket.

4. What does this case mean for "gay marriage"? Vermont already recognizes gay relationships in all but name, calling them "civil unions" with most of the attendant secular or civil benefits, like rights of inheritance, health care proxy authorization, adoption, etc. and in *Goodridge v. Department of Public Health*, 440 Mass. 309, 798 N.E.2d 941 (2003), the Massachusetts Supreme Judicial Court held that its state law must be interpreted to allow qualified same-sex couples to marry. If an American same-sex couple obtains a marriage in Massachusetts, are other states required to give it effect? Congress passed the

Defense of Marriage Act, P.L. 104-199, which provides that "no State, territory, or possession of the United States, or Indian tribe, shall be *required* to give effect to any public act, record, or judicial proceeding of any other State, territory, possession, or tribe respecting a relationship between persons of the same sex that is treated as a marriage under the laws of such other State, territory, possession, or tribe, or a right or claim arising from such relationship." By what authority did Congress pass such statute and President Clinton sign it into law? Article IV, section 1 provides for the "full faith and credit" to be given in every State to the "public Acts, Records, and judicial Proceedings of every other State." Congress is given express power in Article IV to pass "general laws prescribing the *manner*" in which such acts may be proved, and "the *Effect* thereof" (emphasis supplied). Is this sufficient or likely subject to serious challenge? Does the fact that President Bush has called for a federal marriage amendment limiting marriage to a man and a woman mean he questions the constitutionality of the Defense of Marriage Act?

Table of Cases

(Principal cases are in italics; references are to pages.)

N

T

TABLE OF ARTICLES

INDEX

[References are to pages.]

A

ABORTION (See UNENUMERATED RIGHTS)

AFFIRMATIVE ACTION (See EQUAL PROTECTION)

APPORTIONMENT (See EQUAL PROTECTION)

ASSISTED SUICIDE (See UNENUMERATED RIGHTS)

C

COMMERCE CLAUSE
"Commerce" defined . . . 542
"Interstate" defined . . . 574
Police powers and commerce distinguished . . . 556

CONTRACEPTION (See UNENUMERATED RIGHTS)

CONTRACT RIGHTS
Police power . . . 841
Prospective laws, non-prohibition of . . 797
Protection from state impairment . . . 791
Public contracts, extension to . . . 802
Retrospective laws, prohibition of . . . 797
State impairment, protection against . . 791
Weakening of contract protection . . . 841

D

DECLARATION OF INDEPENDENCE
Bill of Rights and . . . 114
Constitution's non-displacement of . . . 107
Constitutional formation and . . . 101
Constitutional interpretation, relationship to . . . 93
Constitutional ratification, influence upon . . . 117
Natural law, expression as . . . 93
Preamble . . . 100
Supreme Court references . . . 127
Text of . . . xxix

DOMINANT COMMERCE POWER (See also FEDERALISM; PRIVILEGES AND IMMUNITIES)
Cooley Doctrine (nonexclusivity of federal authority) . . . 609

DRAFT CARD BURNING
Freedom of speech . . . 1026

DUE PROCESS (See SUBSTANTIVE DUE PROCESS)

E

ECONOMIC LIBERTY (See also SUBSTANTIVE DUE PROCESS)
Generally . . . 1144, 1157
Judicial (rational basis) deference . . . 1193
Liberty of contract before 1930 . . . 1193
New Deal retrenchment . . . 1193
Personal liberty, dichotomy with . . . 1193

ELEVENTH AMENDMENT (See FEDERALISM)

EQUAL PROTECTION
Affirmative action . . . 1286
Age, classification based on . . . 1416
Alienage, classification based on . . . 1416
Apportionment (one person/one vote) 1347
Disability, classification based on . . . 1416
Discriminatory intent requirement . . 1268
Gender discrimination . . . 1392
Gender preference . . . 1392
Legitimacy, classification based on . . 1416
Non-suspect classification . . . 1221
Race and slavery . . . 1223
Racial preference . . . 1286
Racial redistricting . . . 1286
School desegregation . . . 1250
Sexual orientation . . . 1420
Vestiges of discrimination, correction of . . . 1250
Wealth, classification based on . . . 1416

ESTABLISHMENT CLAUSE
The equal protection concept . . . 201
The exclusionary view . . . 169
The no-endorsement speculation . . . 192
The non-coercion view . . . 176
Even-handed funding of religion and non-religion . . . 201
Funding of religious schools . . . 229
Religious displays . . . 192
School prayer . . . 262

EXECUTIVE POWER
Administrative agencies . . . 387
Beauracracy and the president . . . 435
Commander-in-Chief . . . 503
Domestic authority . . . 413
Executive privilege . . . 468
Foreign affairs authority . . . 503
Government-attorney client privilege . . 464

I–1

[References are to pages.]

[References are to pages.]

[References are to pages.]

[References are to pages.]

U

V